by Thomas Rowlandson

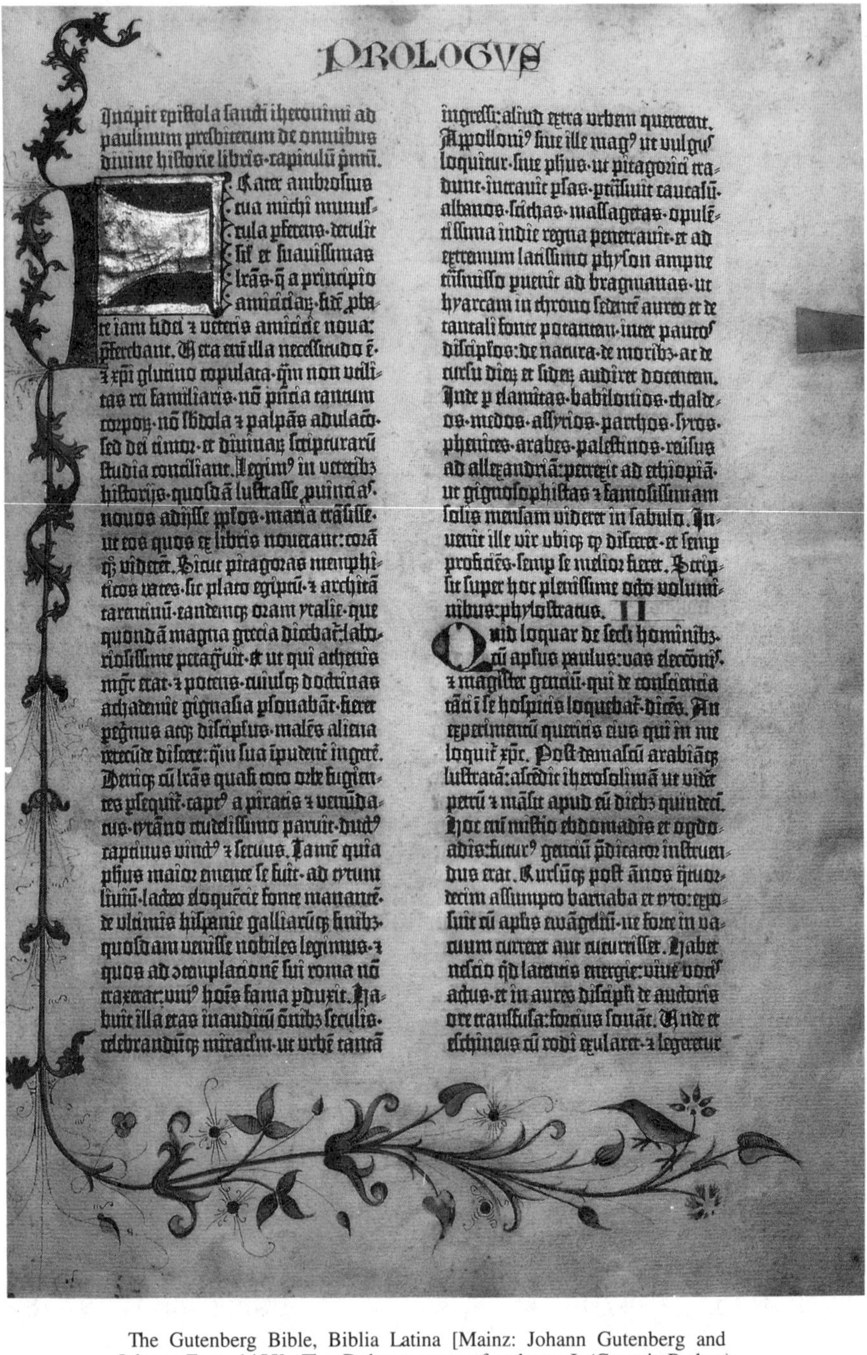
PROLOGVS

The Gutenberg Bible, Biblia Latina [Mainz: Johann Gutenberg and Johann Fust, 1455]. The Doheny copy of volume I (Genesis-Psalms). Sold at Christie's New York on October 22, 1987 for $4,900,000. A world record price for a printed book.

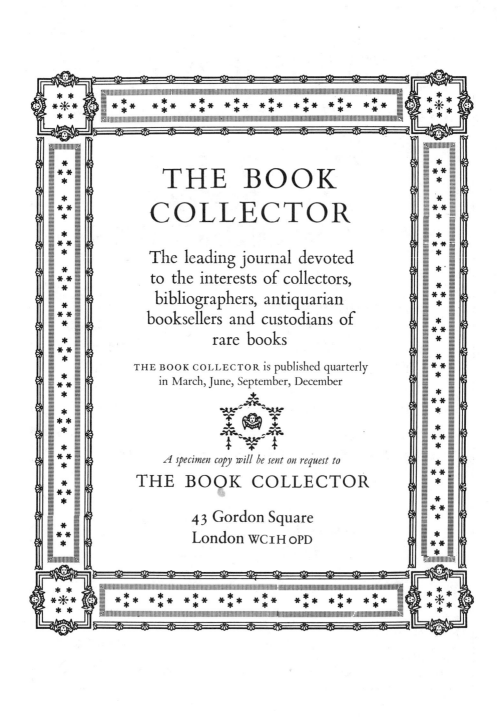

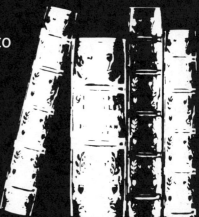

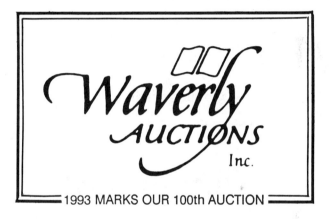

AMERICAN
BOOK PRICES
CURRENT
VOLUME 98

1991-1992

AMERICAN

BOOK PRICES CURRENT 1992

VOLUME 98

The Auction Season September 1991 – August 1992

BOOK PRICES CURRENT

BANCROFT-PARKMAN, INC.

1993

EDITORS

KATHARINE KYES LEAB
DANIEL J. LEAB
MARIE-LUISE FRINGS
JANE MALLISON

Please send all inquiries and suggestions to:

American Book Prices Current
P.O. Box 1236
Washington, CT 06793
TEL: (212) RE 7-2715
TEL: (203) 868-7408
FAX: (203) 868-0080

ISBN: 0-914022-27-X
ISSN: 0091-9357
Library of Congress Card No. 3-14557
Printed in the United States of America

CONTENTS

ABBREVIATIONS

ad, ads Advertisement(s)
ACs Autograph Card, signed
ADs Autograph Document, signed
ALs Autograph Letter, signed
A Ls s Autograph Letters, signed
Amst. Amsterdam
anr Another
Anon Anonymous
ANs Autograph Note, signed
armorial bdg Binding with coat of arms on cover
Balt. Baltimore
bdg Binding
bds Boards
Birm. Birmingham
Bost. Boston
c. Circa
Cambr. Cambridge
cat Catalogue
cent Century
contemp Contemporary
def Defective
Ds Document, signed
d/j Dust-jacket
Ed Edition; Edited; Editor
Edin. Edinburgh
extra bdg Elaborate binding
f, ff Folio(s)
frontis Frontispiece
H of R House of Representatives
illus, illusts Illustrate(d); Illustrations
imperf Imperfect
inscr Inscribed; Inscription
intro Introduction
L London
lea Leather
lev Levant
litho Lithograph
L.p. Large paper
Ls Letter, signed
Ls s Letters, signed
Ltd Limited
mor Morocco
Ms, Mss Manuscript; Manuscripts
mtd Mounted
n.d. No date
n.p. No place
n.y. No year
NY New York
no, nos Number; Numbers
orig Original
pbd, pbr Published; Publisher
Phila. Philadelphia
port Portrait
pp Pages
prelim Preliminary
pseud. Pseudonym
ptd, ptg, ptr Printed; Printing; Printer
pvtly Privately
Sen. Senate
sgd Signed
syn Synthetic
tp Title-page
trans Translated; Translation; translator
vol, vols Volume; volumes
w.a.f. With all faults
Wash. Washington
wrap, wraps Wrapper; Wrappers

Book sizes are listed as:

folio	**12 mo**
4to	**16 mo**
8vo	**etc.**

INTRODUCTION

Volume 98 of *American Book Prices Current* has been prepared by a team of editors highly experienced in the field of rare books and manuscripts. As its users know, ABPC is not just a transcribed record of titles and prices, copied unquestioningly from the season's auction catalogues. It is, on the contrary, the only work in English in which every listing of printed material has been checked as to title, format, date of publication, edition, and limitation. Bindings are described, with condition when relevant, and whenever possible maps and plates in books are verified. Moreover, sales of autographs and manuscripts are reported. Because of this, ABPC is an essential tool for buying, selling and evaluating books, serials, autographs, manuscripts, broadsides, and maps, based on actual figures realized at auction. In the words of a reviewer in *The Times Literary Supplement,* it is "an accurate, indispensable tool for the antiquarian bookseller and collector." And, in addition to meeting the need for a dependable guide in determining the value of old and out-of-print books, ABPC serves as a reference work and as an aid to scholars in locating printed works and manuscripts of all centuries, from the earliest years to the present.

American Book Prices Current is composed of two parts. Part I, Autographs & Manuscripts, includes original illustrations for printed books, documents, letters, typescripts, corrected proofs, signed photographs, and signatures, as well as manuscripts. Part II, Books, includes broadsides, single-sheet printings, maps, and charts and uncorrected proof copies of books.

Entries are listed alphabetically by author whenever possible, by title when the author's name is unknown, or by Private Press and Club, printer, or publisher headings if such are the associations which attract the collector. In general, illustrated books are listed under the author of the text. Subject headings such as England, Maps & Charts, Hebrew Books and Miniature Books or those for individual U.S. states or cities have also been used. Individual works are in turn listed alphabetically under each heading and include: Title; place & date of publication; edition designation; number of volumes when more than one; size; binding; condition of binding; descriptive material; limitation notes, and the sale record—auction houses (in code), date or number of sale, lot number, price and purchaser (buyers' names are given when and as listed in price lists.) There are cross-references to Club or Press books, to books bound together, and to books by more than one author.

Volume 98 lists only those books and manuscripts which sold for at least $50 or its equivalent in another currency. In keeping with previous editorial policy, auction lots consisting of groupings of miscellaneous volumes are not listed, for the prices realized by such lots can give no accurate indication of the value of individual items. Similarly, listings of badly broken runs or seriously incomplete sets of printed books do not appear. Listings of books in non-Western languages realizing less than $100 have been selectively excluded, as have peripheral works as printings of musical scores, collections of plates, and panoramas. We are selective in approaching German and Dutch sales, for our aim here is to include some items of particular interest to our readers.

Listings of 20th century books frequently appear without format or binding information. In such instances it may be assumed that these books are octavo or doudecimo and bound in cloth or boards. Items which are sold by auction house as "a collection of plates" or which are deemed to be bound prints rather than books, are excluded from these pages. Considerable effort has been made to secure price lists for all of the relevant sales held by the auction houses listed herein. We make great efforts to be comprehensive, but not all auction houses are equally diligent in sending us price lists, or equally responsive to our inquiries.

Buyer's Surcharges

The following buyer's surcharges should be noted: in England 10%; in the Netherlands, 14%; in Monaco, 11%; in Germany, 15% in Italy, 13%; in the United States, 10%.

AUCTION HOUSES

The sales recorded in this volume are from the auction houses listed below and are designated by code letters. On the following pages are a list of the season's sales from each house and a record of the named consignors of merchandise.

B	**J. L. Beijers** **Achter Sint Pieter 140, Utrecht, The Netherlands**
b	**W & FC Bonham & Sons Ltd.** **Montpelier Street, London SW7 1HH England**
b&b	**Butterfield & Butterfield** **220 San Bruno Avenue, San Francisco, CA 94103**
bba	**Bloomsbury Book Auctions** **3 & 4 Hardwick Street, London EC1 England**
bbc	**Baltimore Book Company** **2112 N. Charles Street, Baltimore, MD 21218**
br	**Bradford Galleries** **Route 7, Sheffield, MA 01257**
C	**Christie, Manson & Woods** **8 King Street, St. James's, London SW1Y 6QT England**
cb	**California Book Auction Galleries** **(Out of business; successor firm of same name** **will be listed in our next volume)**
CG	**Christie's Scotland** **164-166 Bath Street, Glasgow G2 4TG Scotland**
CGen	**Christie's International S.A.** **8 place de la Taconnerie, 1204 Geneva, Switzerland**
Ck	**Christie's South Kensington** **85 Old Brompton Road, London SW7 3JS England**
CNY	**Christie, Manson & Woods International, Inc.** **502 Park Avenue, New York, NY 10022**
Dar	**Herman Darvick Autograph Auctions** **P. O. Box 467, Rockville Centre, NY 11571-0467**
DW	**Dominic Winter** **The Old School, Maxwell Street, Swindon,** **Wiltshire SN1 5DR England**
F	**Freeman/Fine Arts** **1808 Chestnut Street, Philadelphia, PA 19103**

AUCTION HOUSES

FD	**F. Doerling** **Neuer Wall 40-42, 2000 Hamburg 36 Germany**
HH	**Hartung und Hartung** **Karolinenplatz 5a, D 8000 Munich 2 Germany**
hen	**Henner Wachholtz** **Mittleweg 43, D 2000 Hamburg 13 Germany**
HN	**Hauswedell und Nolte** **Poseldorfer Weg 1, D 2000 Hamburg 13 Germany**
JG	**Jochen Granier** **4800 Bielefeld 1 Welle 9 Germany**
K	**Kane Antiquarian Auction** **1525 Shenkel Road, Pottstown PA 19464**
kh	**Kenneth Hince** **485 High Street, Prahan, Victoria 3181 Australia**
L	**Lawrence Fine Art** **South Street, Crewkerne, Somerset TA18 8AB England**
LH	**Leslie Hindman Auctioneers** **215 W. Ohio Street, Chicago, IL 60610**
Met	**Metropolitan Art & Antiques Pavilion** **110 West 19th Street, New York, NY 10011**
NH	**New Hampshire Book Auction** **Woodcurry Road, Weare, NH 03281**
O	**Richard E. Oinonen Book Auctions** **Box 470, Sunderland, MA 01375**
P	**Sotheby Parke Bernet, Inc.** **1334 York Avenue, New York NY 10021**
pba	**Pacific Book Auction Galleries** **1924 Leavenworth, San Francisco CA 94133**
pn	**Phillips, Son & Neale** **101 New Bond Street, London W1Y OAS England**
pnE	**Phillips in Scotland** **65 George Street, Edinburgh EH2 2JL Scotland**
pnL	**Phillips in Leeds** **Hepper House, 17a East Parade, Leeds, West Yorkshire LS12BU England**

AUCTION HOUSES

R	**Riba Auctions** **P.O. Box 53, Main Street, South Glastonbury, CT 06073**
rs	**Skinner, Inc.** **357 Main Street, Bolton, MA 01740**
S	**Sotheby Parke Bernet & Co.** **34-35 New BOnd Street, London W1A 2AA England**
SI	**Sotheby's Italia** **Via Pietro Mascagni, 20122 Milan, Italy**
sg	**Swann Galleries** **104 East 25th Street, New York, NY 10010**
SM	**Sotheby Parke Bernet Monaco** **Le Sporting d'Hiver, Place du Casino, Monaco 98001**
star	**J. A. Stargardt** **Rade-Strasse 10, D-3550 Marburg, Germany**
sp	**The Scribe's Perch** **316 Broadway, Box 3295, Newport, RI 02840**
sup	**Superior Galleries** **9478 W. Olympic Blvd., Beverly Hills, CA 90212**
vgr	**Villa Grisebach Auktionen** **Fasanenstrasse 25, D-1000 Berlin 15, Germany**
W	**Wooley & Wallis** **Castle Street, Salisbury, Wiltshire, England**
wa	**Waverly Auctions** **4931 Cordell Avenue, Suite AA, Bethesda, MD 10814**
wd	**William Doyle Galleries** **175 East 87th Street, New York, NY 10128**
Z	**Zubal Auction Company** **2969 West 25th Street, Cleveland, OH 44113**

NAMED CONSIGNORS

Abromson Collection	sg June 11
Adams, Joseph Quincy	S June 16
Arnhold, Kurt	S June 23
Barbaria, Francis J.	LH Dec 11
Beecham, Sir Thomas	pn Apr 23
Blass, Dr. Robert	Ck May 8
Blaustein, Norman	CNY Dec 5
Born, Byron & Elaine	sg Sept 5
Bristed, Charles Astor	br May 29
Bristol Baptist College	S Dec 17
Camoys, The Dowager Lady	C Nov 12
Campion Hall, Oxford	S June 23
Cordy, Ray	DW Jan 15
Cromme Estate	C Oct 30
Davis, Chester L.	CNY Dec 5 CNY June 9
Delafield, Maj. Gen R.	CNY June 9
Donner, Edward	b June 22
Dunchock, David H.	cb Dec 12
duPont, Pierre S. III	CNY Oct 8 CNY Dec 5
Clarendon, The Earl of	C June 24
Epstein Family	sg Apr 29-30 sg June 11
Esher, The Viscount	S June 30 S July 1, 9
Evans, Guy	S June 30 S July 1, 9
Evans, Mrs. Owen Caradoc	DW Nov 20
Felver, Charles S.	cb Sept 26 cb Jan 9
Fishberg, Arthur	wd June 12
Frear, Corinne R.	wd Dec 12
Frick Library	CNY Dec 5
Fyfe, Jean	pnE Oct 1,2
George, H.H.	S June 23
Glover, Maj. Michael	pn Nov 14
Gorlin, Jack	sg Mar 26
Gottshalk Collection	C Dec 16
Graff, Elizabeth	CNY June 9
Green, Herbert	wd Dec 12
Grey, Rex	S Apr 28, 29 S May 13, 14
Hartz, R. & E.	P Dec 12
Horblit, Harrison D.	S June 16
Hubbard, Donald E.	wd Dec 12
Ingilby, Sir Thomas	pn Nov 14
Institute of Metals	S Dec 17
Jennings, Dorothy Lee	LH Dec 11
Jensen, Harold W.	cb Nov 7
Karu, Stuart E.	P June 16
Klee, Anne Baxter	CNY June 9
Kochno, Boris	SM Oct 11, 12
Koffman, Pierre	Ck Oct 18
Kollek, Teddy	S June 30 S July 1, 9
Koopman, Richard	O Oct 29
Landowski, Rose	wd June 12
Larkin, Colin	b Oct 15
Lawrence, Dr. John R.	LH Dec 11

NAMED CONSIGNORS

Lesieur, Fleur & Henri	wd Dec 12
McCarty-Cooper, William A.	CNY Jan 25
McDonald, Dr. McLean	C Oct 30
MacGregor, Mrs. S. B.	C Nov 27
McLean, John	S June 16
Manhattan College	Ck Nov 29 C June 24
Manney, Richard	P Oct 11
Marine Archeological Recovery	C May 28
Martin, George W.	C June 24
Maxwell, Augustus	CNY Dec 5
Merron, Jules L.	CNY June 9
Milne, George	CNY Dec 5 Ck June 12
Moffett, George H.	CNY June 9
Moskowitz, Saul	Ck June 18
Myer, Bertie F.	wd Dec 12
National Audubon Society	CNY Dec 5
Newell, Winston B.	CNY June 9
Northbrook Hist. Society	LH Dec 11
Nourse, Margaret S.	wd Dec 12
O'Driscoll, Col. Sean	S June 30 S July 1, 9
Perlin, Paul	P Dec 12
Pforzheimer Foundation	P June 16
Platten, Donald C.	P June 16
Pullman, Madeleine Childs	LH May 17-19
Quanjer, J.	B Nov 5
Rabaiotti, Renato	C June 24

Redwood Library	CNY Apr 24
Richard, Frank & Lee	wa Dec 19
Robinson, Philip	S June 23
Rootes, Lord	C June 24
Rose, Elaine W.	wd June 12
Rowland, Benjamin A.	C June 24
Rowland, B. Allen	C June 24
Salloch, W. & M.	Ck Oct 31 Ck Nov 1
Salt, Dr. George	S Dec 17
Scharf, Dr. Alfred	S Feb 11 S Feb 25, 26
Schimek Family	sg Dec 12
Schimmel, Herbert D.	CNY Dec 5
Schlosser, Leonard B.	P June 17,18
Schoyen Collection	P Dec 12
Searles, Edward F.	C June 24
Sgourdeos, Alexander	S June 30 S July 1, 9
Smith, Malcolm	wd Dec 12
Spark, Victor D.	Ck Feb 14
Spiro, Harry & Bridget	CNY May 14 CNY June 9
Spurgeon's College	S June 23
Sutton, Denys	bba Feb 13 bba Mar 26
Trace, Timothy	O Sept 24
Turner, Dawson	pn Nov 14
Tweney, George H.	cg Apr 23
University of Edinburgh	CNY Apr 24

NAMED CONSIGNORS

University of Tennessee	CNY Dec 5	Whitlock, Marion Elise	wd June 12
Veitch, G. Seton	C May 20	Witten, Laurence	sg Oct 31

SEASON'S SALES

(arranged alphabetically by code letters)

Please note that September-December are 1991; January-August are 1992

	J. L. BEIJERS
B Nov 5	Railroadiana
B Nov 5-6	Rara Rariora Rarissima
B May 12,13	Printed Books
	W. & F.C. BONHAM
b Oct 15	The Pan Archive
b Nov 18	Printed Books, Manuscripts
b Mar 11	Printed Books & Maps
b June 22	Printed Books & Manuscripts
	BUTTERFIELD & BUTTERFIELD
b&b Feb 19	Books & Autographs
	BLOOMSBURY BOOK AUCTIONS
bba Sept 5	Natural History, Science
bba Sept 19	Travel & Topography
bba Oct 10	Children's, Illustrated Books
bba Oct 24	Printed Books
bba Nov 7	Decorative & Topographical Prints
bba Nov 28	Printed Books
bba Dec 19	Printed Books
bba Jan 16	Printed Books
bba Jan 30	Printed Books & Manuscripts
bba Feb 13	Denys Sutton Art Reference I
bba Feb 27	Printed Books
bba Mar 26	Denys Sutton Art Reference II
bba Apr 9	Printed Books
bba Apr 30	Printed Books
bba May 14	Printed Books
bba May 28	Printed Books & Manuscripts
bba June 11	Printed Books
bba June 25	Manuscripts & Printed Books
bba July 9	Printed Books
bba July 23	Children's Books
bba Aug 13	Printed Books
	BALTIMORE BOOK COMPANY
bbc Sept 23	Books, Autographs
bbc Dec 9	Books, Autographs
bbc Feb 17	The Civil War
bbc Apr 27	Books, Autographs
bbc June 29	Lincoln, Baltimore

SEASON'S SALES

	BRADFORD GALLERIES
br May 29	C. A. Bristed Library
	CHRISTIE, MANSON & WOODS
C Oct 30	Travel & Natural History
C Nov 11	Japanese Works of Art
C Nov 27	Early Printed Books & Illuminated Manuscripts
C Dec 16	Literature; Gottschallk Collection of Heine
C May 20	Travel & Natural History
C May 20	The Camerarius Florilegium
C May 28	Spanish Art I
C June 24	Musical Manuscripts
C June 24	Manuscripts & Books
	CALIFORNIA BOOK AUCTION
cb Sept 5	Autumn Miscellany
cb Sept 12	Western Americana
cb Sept 19	Modern Literature & Detective Fiction
cb Sept 26	C. S. Felver Victorial Literature
cb Oct 10	Cartography
cb Oct 17,18	Books about Books
cb Oct 25	Book Fair Miscellany
cb Oct 31	Limited Editions Club
cb Nov 7	H. W. Jenson Aviation Collection
cb Nov 14	Fine Western Americana
cb Nov 21	Thanksgiving Miscellany
cb Dec 5	The Four Hundredth Catalogue
cb Dec 12	Modern Literature; Science Fiction
cb Dec 19	Christmas Miscellany
cb Jan 9	C. S. Felver Victorian Literature II
cb Jan 16	January Miscellany
cb Jan 30	Cartography
cb Feb 12	Western Americana
cb Feb 12	Book Fair Miscellany
cb Feb 13	Railroadiana
cb Feb 27	Miscellany - Horology
cb Mar 5	Modern Literature
cb Mar 12	Western Americana
cb Mar 26	Sprint Miscellany
cb Apr 9	Travel & Exploration
cb Apr 23	Arctic, Antarctic, Alaska
cb Apr 24	Book Fair Miscellany
	CHRISTIE'S SCOTLAND
CG Oct 7, 8	Castletown House
	CHRISTIE'S GENEVA
CGen Nov 18	Modern Illustrated Books

SEASON'S SALES

	CHRISTIE'S SOUTH KENSINGTON
Ck Sept 6	Printed Books
Ck Oct 18	Printed Books
Ck Oct 31, Nov 1	Salloch Collection
Ck Nov 15	Autograph Letters
Ck Nov 29	Manhattan College Rare Books
Ck Dec 11	Printed Books & Illustrations
Ck Feb 14	V. D. Spark Art Reference
Ck Mar 6	Manhattan College Part II
Ck Apr 3	Autograph Letters
Ck May 8	R. Bass Chess Library
Ck May 15	Printed Books
Ck June 12	G. Milne Collection
Ck June 18	Science- Moskowitz Collection
Ck July 10	Printed Books & Illustrations
	CHRISTIE'S NEW YORK
CNY Oct 8	P. S. duPont III Collection
CNY Dec 5	Printed Books & Manuscripts
CNY Jan 25	W. A. McCarty-Cooper Collection
CNY Apr 24	Audubon Birds of America
CNY May 14	H. & B. Spiro Collection
CNY June 9	Printed Books & Manuscripts
	HERMAN DARVICK AUTOGRAPH AUCTIONS
Dar Oct 10	Autographs
Dar Dec 26	Autographs
Dar Feb 13	Autographs
Dar Apr 9	Autographs
Dar June 11	Autographs
Dar Aug 6	Autographs
	DOMINIC WINTER
DW Oct 2	Printed Books & Maps
DW Oct 9	Fine Art Sale
DW Nov 6	Printed Books
DW Nov 20	Antique Maps, Prints & Books
DW Dec 10	Printed Books
DW Jan 15	The Ray Cordy Collection
DW Jan 29	Printed Books
DW Mar 4	Printed Books
DW Mar 11	Fine Art Sale
DW Apr 8	Printed Books
DW Apr 15	Cricket Books
DW May 13	Printed Books & Maps
	FREEMAN /FINE ARTS
F Sept 26	Books, Photos
F Dec 19	Books

F Mar 26	Books & Graphics
F June 25	Books & Graphics
	F. DOERLING
FD Dec 2,3	Wertvolle Buecher
FD June 1,2	Wertvolle Buecher
	HENNER WACHHOLTZ
hen Nov 11	Geografie, Reisen
hen Nov 12	Literatur & Kunst
	HARTUNG & HARTUNG
HH Nov 5-7	Wertvolle Buecher
HH Nov 5	Alte Medizin
HH May 12-14	Wertvolle Buecher
HH May 14	Graphik
	HAUSWEDELL & NOLTE
HN Nov 27,28	Wertvolle Buecher
	JOCHEN GRANIER
JG Mar 27	Wertvolle Buecher
	KANE ANTIQUARIAN AUCTION
K Sept 29	Printed Books
K Dec 1	Printed Books
K Mar 22	Printed Books
K July 12	Printed Books
	KENNETH HINCE
kh Nov 11	Books, Maps
	LAWRENCE FINE ART
L Nov 14	Printed Books, Manuscripts
L Jan 30	Paintings...Books
L Feb 13,27	Paintings...Books
	LESLIE HINDMAN AUCTIONEERS
LH Dec 11	Books, Manuscripts
LH May 17-19	Books, Manuscripts
	METROPOLITAN ARTS & ANTIQUES PAVILION
Met Apr 27-28	Fine Books

SEASON'S SALES

NEW HAMPSHIRE BOOK AUCTIONS

NH Oct 6	Printed Books
NH May 30	Printed Books
NH Aug 23	Early Printed Books

RICHARD E. OINONEN BOOK AUCTIONS

O Sept 24	T. Trace Bibliographical Library
O Oct 29	R. Koopman Angling Library
O Nov 26	Rare Books, Manuscripts
O Dec 17	Bibliography & Reference
O Jan 14	Winter Miscellany
O Feb 25	Leather Bindings, Travel
O Mar 31	Americana, Bibliography
O Apr 28	P. Ledlie Natural History Stock
O May 26	Rare Books, Manuscripts
O July 14	Early Printing
O Aug 25	Americana, Early Printing

SOTHEBY - NEW YORK

P Oct 11	R. Manney Library
P Dec 12	Schoyen Incunables
P Dec 12	Fine Books & Manuscripts
P Dec 17	Rock 'n' Roll
P June 16	Printed & Manuscript Americana
P June 17, 18	Fine Books - L. B. Schlosser Collection

PACIFIC BOOK AUCTION GALLERIES

pba July 9	Modern Literature
pba July 23	Fine Printing; Book Arts
pba Aug 20	August Assortment

PHILLIPS, SON & NEALE

pn Sept 12	Printed Books, Atlases
pn Oct 24	Music
pn Nov 14	Autograph Letter, Manuscripts
pn Dec 12	Printed Books
pn Mar 19	Autograph Letters, Manuscripts
pn Apr 23	Printed Books
pn May 14	Printed Books
pn June 11	Autograph Letters, Manuscripts
pn July 16	Printed Books

PHILLIPS IN SCOTLAND

pnE Oct 1,2	Meldonfoot Collection
pnE Oct 2	Printed Books
pnE Dec 4	Printed Books
pnE Mar 11	Printed Books
pnE May 13	Printed Books
pnE Aug 12	Printed Books

SEASON'S SALES

	PHILLIPS IN LEEDS
pnL Nov 20	Printed Books
	RIBA AUCTIONS
R Nov 9	American History
R Mar 7	American History
R June 13	American History
	RICHARD C. FRAJOLA
rf Sept 21	United States Postal History
	SKINNER
rs Oct 17,18	Discovery Auction
	SOTHEBY'S
S Oct 10,11	Islamic & Indian Art
S Nov 14,15	Books & Maps
S Nov 21	Atlases, Travel
S Dec 5	Continental Books & Manuscripts
S Dec 6	Music, including Mannheim Collection
S Dec 12	English Literature, History
S Dec 17	Western Manuscripts & Miniatures
S Feb 11,25,26	Books & Maps
S Apr 29,30	Islamic & Indian Art
S Apr 28,29	Books & Maps
S May 13,14	Books & Maps
S May 28,29	Continental Books & Manuscripts
S June 23	Western Manuscripts
S June 25	Longueville Collection
S June 25, 26	Atlases, Travel
S June 30	Greece, Cyprus, Turkey
S July 1,9	Greece, Cyprus, Turkey
S July 21,22	English Literature, History
	SWANN GALLERIES
sg Sept 5	Art & Architecture
sg Sept 12	Autographs
sg Sept 19	Maps & Atlases
sg Sept 26	Modern Press & Illustrated Books
sg Oct 8	Photographica
sg Oct 17	Performing Arts
sg Oct 24	Early Printed Books
sg Oct 31	Bibliography - L. Witten
sg Nov 7	Rare Books
sg Nov 14	Medicine & Natural History
sg Dec 5	Americana
sg Dec 12	Modern Literature
sg Dec 19	Hebraica & Judaica
sg Jan 9	Travel, Topography

sg Jan 30	Modern Press & Illustrated Books
sg Feb 6	Art & Architecture
sg Feb 13	Maps & Atlases
sg Feb 27	Autographs
sg Mar 5	Sets & Bindings
sg Mar 12	Early Printed Books
sg Mar 26	J. Gorlin Fencing Book
sg Apr 2	Art & Architecture
sg Apr 13	Photographica
sg Apr 29,30	Epstein Family Collection
sg May 7	Rare Books
sg May 14	Medicine, Natural History
sg May 21	Travel & Sporting Books
sg June 11	Modern Literature
sg June 18	Americana
sg June 25	Hebraica & Judaica
	SOTHEBY'S ITALIA
SI Dec 5	Libri Antichi
SI June 9, 10	Libri Antichi e Moderni
	SOTHEBY'S MONACO
SM Oct 11,12	Collection Boris Kochno
	SCRIBE'S PERCH
sp Sept 22	Printed Books
sp Nov 24	Printed Books
sp Feb 6	Printed Books
sp Apr 16	Printed Books
sp June 18	Printed Books
	SUPERIOR GALLERIES
sup Oct 15	Manuscript Auction
sup May 9	Autographs, Manuscripts
sup July 8-10	Sports
	J. A. STARGARDT
star Mar 26-27	Autographen
	VILLA GRISEBACH AUKTIONEN
vgr May 30	Arts
	WOOLEY & WALLIS
W Mar 6	Selected Books & Prints
W July 8	Selected Books & Prints

SEASON'S SALES

WAVERLY AUCTIONS

wa Sept 26	Book Fair Miscellany
wa Oct 19	Autographs & Manuscripts
wa Nov 21	Printed Books
wa Dec 19	Fine Books- Richard Orchid Library
wa Feb 20	February Miscellany
wa Mar 5	Fine Books, Autographs
wa Apr 9	Works on Paper & Canvas
wa June 25	Works on Paper & Canvas

WILLIAM DOYLE GALLERIES

wd Dec 12	Books & Autographs
wd June 12	Books & Autographs

ZUBAL AUCTION COMPANY

Z Oct 26	Antiquarian & Rare Books
Z Nov 23	Antiquarian & Rare Books
Z Apr 18	Antiquarian & Rare Books

Exchange Rates in Terms of Dollars

Currency	Aug 31/92	Jul 31/92	Jun 30/92	May 31/92	Apr 30/92	Mar 31/92
Swiss Franc	1.2480	1.3186	1.3750	1.4565	1.5120	1.4995
Deutsche Mark	1.4020	1.4748	1.5243	1.6075	1.6490	1.6435
Pound Sterling*	1.9885	1.9265	1.9010	1.8295	1.7764	1.7360
ECU	1.4415	1.3823	1.3495	1.2787	1.2441	1.2430
Dutch Guilder	1.5806	1.6628	1.7215	1.8103	1.8550	1.8595
Australian $	1.3976	1.3437	1.3396	1.3207	1.3205	1.2987
French Franc	4.7775	4.9800	5.1265	5.3930	5.5630	5.5730
Gold	341.00	353.76	343.40	337.50	337.50	340.00

Currency	Feb 29/92	Jan 31/92	Dec 31/91	Nov 30/91	Oct31/91	Sep 30/91
Swiss Franc	1.4880	1.4350	1.3612	1.4340	1.4713	1.4499
Deutsche Mark	1.4020	1.4748	1.5243	1.6075	1.6490	1.6435
Pound Sterling*	1.7555	1.7860	1.8670	1.7678	1.7372	1.7510
ECU	1.2484	1.2675	1.3413	1.2495	1.2235	1.2146
Dutch Guilder	1.8443	1.8150	1.7285	1.8310	1.8873	1.8751
Australian $	1.3268	1.3324	1.3158	1.2747	1.2862	1.2516
French Franc	5.5750	5.4950	5.1835	5.5445	5.7270	5.6689
Gold	353.00	354.10	354.10	367.50	358.03	348.45

*The Pound Sterling is expressed in terms of dollars to the pound.

PART I

Autographs & Manuscripts

A

Abbe, Cleveland, 1838-1916

ALs, 7 Jan 1877. 2 pp, 8vo. To Hugo Gylden. Thanking for reports from his observatory. star Mar 26 (542) DM260

Abbot, Bud, 1895-1974

Photograph, sgd & inscr, [c.1948]. 8 by 10 inches. Inscr to Frank. Also sgd by Lou Costello. Dar Apr 9 (1) $450

Acton, Sir John, Baron, 1834-1902

Series of 4 A Ls s, 23 Oct [1890] to 8 Dec 1896. 6 pp, 8vo. To Thomas Hodgkin. About the Cambridge Modern History & other matters. bba May 28 (157) £160 [Kunkler]

Adams, Abigail Amelia, 1765-1813. See: Smith, Abigail Adams

Adams, Abigail Smith, 1744-1818

ALs, 15 May 1805. 1 p, 4to. To Ann. Expressing good wishes for her wedding & reflecting on matrimony. Illus in cat. sup May 9 (312) $2,500

Adams, Charles Francis, 1835-1915

Ls, 12 Jan 1903. 2 pp, 4to. To Addison Allen. Giving his religious views. sg Feb 27 (4) $70

Adams, John, 1735-1826

ALs, 9 Aug 1770. 3 pp, 4to. To Catharine Macaulay. Praising her History of England & offering to enter into regular correspondence. pn June 11 (1) £18,000

— 19 Apr 1773. 3 pp, folio. To Catharine Macaulay. Describing the battle between Gov. Hutchinson & the Massachusetts legislature & denying the sovereignty of Parliament over the colonies. With retained draft of Macaulay's reply, 2 pp, folio. pn June 11 (2) £21,000

— 28 June 1773. 3 pp, 4to. To Catharine Macaulay. About the deteriorating relations between Great Britain & the American colonies. pn June 11 (3) £20,000

— 11 Dec 1773. 1 p, folio. To Catharine Macaulay. Expecting "determined Resistance" to the "last ministerial Maneuvre" & predicting the breach between the colonies & Great Britain. pn June 11 (4) £27,000

— 28 Dec 1774. 4 pp, 4to. To Catharine Macaulay. Analyzing British policy towards the colonies & prophesying the American Revolution. pn June 11 (5) £80,000

— 3 Oct 1775. 1 p, 4to. To Joseph Palmer. Sending a newspaper & introducing B. Franklin, Th. Lynch & B. Harrison. Framed. P June 16 (184) $24,000

— 2 June 1785. 8 pp, 4to. To Sec of State John Jay. Duplicate, describing his 1st audience with George III. Illus in cat. Sang & Spiro collections. CNY May 14 (28) $190,000

— 24 Jan 1801. 2 pp, 4to. To George Churchman & Jacob Lindley. Giving his views on the abolition of slavery. Imperf. CNY Dec 5 (2) $30,000

— 1 Aug 1817. 2 pp, 4to. To Henry Channing. Thanking for some newspapers, & recalling J. A. Bayard & negotiations at Ghent. CNY May 14 (1) $12,000

— 26 Sept 1818. 1 p, 4to. To Caesar A. Rodney. Asking for copies of letters by James Otis & commenting on the revolutions in South America. CNY Dec 5 (3) $18,000

— 24 May 1821. 1 p, 4to. To Matthew Carey. Complaining that the present "Policy of this Country is erroneous in several particulars." Illus in cat. P June 16 (185) $8,500

Ds, 2 Aug 1799. 1 p, folio. Ship's paper in 4 languages for the schooner Jason. Countersgd by Pickering. Illus in cat. sup May 9 (168) $1,000

— 27 Feb 1800. 1 p, folio. Military land grant in the Ohio Territory. CNY Dec 5 (1)

$2,200

Cut signature, [n.d.]. Mtd; overall size 2.75 by 7.8 inches. Including subscription. R Nov 9 (1) $1,000

Adams, John Quincy, 1767-1848

Series of 10 A Ls s & AL, 17 Nov 1787 to 23 June 1802. 39 pp, various sizes. To James Bridge. Discussing a wide range of private & public matters. 1 fragment. Tipped into 19th-cent notebook also containing other letters to Bridge. P Dec 12 (96) $22,000

ALs, 2 Dec 1794. 1 p, 4to. To Sylvanus Bourne. Informing him of the signing of Jay's Treaty. Spiro collection. CNY May 14 (29) $3,000

— 4 Aug 1812. 4 pp, 4to. To George Joy. Reflecting on the state of British-American relations after the Chesapeake incident. Spiro collection. CNY May 14 (30) $9,500

— 6 May 1824. 2 pp, 4to. To John McLean. Discussing the government's responsibility for internal improvements. With copy of his 1807 Senate resolution on integral blank in a secretarial hand. Framed. P June 16 (186) $9,500

— 23 Mar 1839. 1 p, 4to. To Joseph Blunt. Agreeing to speak to the Historical Society if his health permits it. Illus in cat. R June 13 (172) $1,100

— 10 Feb 1845. 1 p, 4to. To John Angier. Expressing condolences on the death of his wife. CNY Dec 5 (4) $1,200

— 10 Feb 1845. 1 p, 4to. To John Angier. Expressing condolences on the death of his wife. Illus in cat. Dar Apr 9 (18) $1,800

Ls, 26 July 1823. 1 p, 4to. To the Governor of Alabama. Conveying Congressional documents. Framed. wa Mar 5 (268) $500

— 30 June 1824. 1 p, 8vo. To the Governor of Connecticut. Ptd circular, sending copies of William Stone's facsimile of the Declaration of Independence. With related congressional resolution ptd on integral leaf. Framed. Illus in cat. P June 16 (187) $12,000

Ds, 1 Apr 1825. 1 p, folio. Land grant to Richard Peirce. Dar Aug 6 (43) $450

— 4 Apr 1825. 1 p, folio. Land grant to Jonathan Inman. Framed. wa Oct 19 (259) $300

— 1 Sept 1825. 1 p, folio. Grant of land at Detroit. R Nov 9 (2) $550

— 18 Feb 1826. 1 p, folio. Land grant to Bingham Simons. cb Feb 12 (2) $225

Check, accomplished & sgd, 8 Dec 1830. Payable to himself. Also sgd by Josiah Quincy. Illus in cat. sup Oct 15 (1758) $1,200

— Anr, accomplished & sgd, 18 Jan 1843. Payable to his daughter-in-law Mary C. Adams. Illus in cat. Dar Apr 9 (19) $1,100

Cut signature, 17 Jan 1828. 10 by 5 inches. Lower portion of document countersgd by Henry Clay. Dar Dec 26 (9) $400

Franking signature, [2 Jan 1824]. On integral address leaf of ALs of Richard Forest to Samuel Myers, 1 p, 4to. Dar June 11 (6) $275

Adams, John Quincy, 1767-1848 —& Lafayette, Gilbert du Motier, Marquis de, 1757-1834

[An album, sgd & with lengthy inscr to a young lady on 1st page each by Adams, Lafayette & William White, 23 Feb to 23 Mar 1825, sold at R on 13 June 1992, lot 172A, for $3,500.]

Adams, Louisa Catherine Johnson, 1775-1852

Autograph Ms, poem, beginning "At sweet sixteen, when life is new...", 24 July 1842. 1 p, 4to. 3 five-line stanzas, sgd & inscr to Eliza Triplett. Dar Feb 13 (3) $1,200

ALs, [n.d.]. 3 pp, 12mo. To [Mrs. Thomas Sidney Jesup]. Thanking for chandeliers borrowed for a party in honor of Henry Clay. wa Oct 19 (260) $1,200

Adams, Samuel, Signer from Massachusetts

Ls, 17 Dec 1785. 1 p, 4to. To Elbridge Gerry. Referring to Gerry's forthcoming marriage & reminding him of Capt. Landars's request. Spiro collection. CNY May 14 (31) $2,400

Ds, 16 Aug 1753. 1 p, 4to. Promissory note to Joshua Blanchard; also sgd by 4 others. Matted with engraved port. Dar June 11 (7) $800

— 20 Mar 1797. 1 p, folio. Appointment of William Hunt as Justice of the Peace. Imperf. R June 13 (153) $850

Addison, Joseph, 1672-1719

ALs, 21 July 1711. 1 p, 4to. Recipient unnamed. Sending a copy of the Spectator & contemplating recent financial losses. CNY Dec 5 (151) $750

Adelaide, Princesse d'Orleans, 1777-1847

AL, 3/4 Aug 1815. 8 pp, 4to. To her brother [the future] King Louis Philippe of France. About Napoleon's departure for Elba & the political situation. star Mar 27 (1358) DM260

Adenauer, Konrad, 1876-1967

Autograph Ms, draft of a speech on federalism, the political future of the Saar, & the defense of Germany, [June 1951]. 16 pp, 8vo. In pencil; incomplete. Illus in cat. star Mar 27 (1233) DM8,000

Transcript, quotation referring to his political aims, [19]54. 1 p, 12mo (card). Sgd. Dar Dec 26 (10) $110

Ls s (2), 26 Apr 1950 & 7 Feb 1964. 2 pp, folio. To Hermann Jung. Thanking for books. star Mar 27 (1234) DM350

Ls, 11 Nov 1955. 1 p, 4to. To Bertha Hofer. About a recently restored painting. HH May 13 (1889) DM200

Adolph, Grand Duc de Luxembourg, 1817-1905

Ds, 3 Sept 1842. 1 p, 4to. As Duke of Nassau; contents not stated. Illus in cat. Dar Feb 13 (4) $110

Aegidius Romanus, d.1316

Ms, Liber de regimine principum. [England, c.1420]. 262 leaves (c.10 lacking), vellum, 200mm by 140mm. Contemp sheepskin over wooden bds. In a neat English secretary bookhand. With numerous decorated initials. C Nov 27 (3) £7,500 [Quaritch]

Aeneas Sylvius Piccolomini, (Pope Pius II), 1405-64

Document, [11 Jan] 1459. 1 p, 385mm by 575mm. Bull regarding the church at Arneburg near Halberstadt. Illus in cat. FD June 2 (1284) DM1,680

— [30 Mar] 1463. 1 p, vellum, folio. Bull granting an indulgence to penitents supporting Hans Siebenhirter's chapel at Wiener Neustadt. Including seal; repaired. star Mar 27 (1543) DM1,400

Agassiz, Louis, 1807-73

ALs, 22 Apr 1844. 2 pp, 4to. To David Thomas Ansted. Giving permission to reprint parts of his Recherches sur les poissons fossiles. star Mar 26 (543) DM320

— 16 Oct 1873. 1 p, 8vo. To Mr. Garrigue. Expressing his willingness to acquire a collection at a reduced price. hen Nov 12 (2514) DM270

Agnon, Shmuel Yosef, Pseud. of Samuel Josef Czaczkas, 1888-1970

ALs, [2 Apr] 1936. 1 p, folio. To Judah Bergmann. Regarding an article for a Festschrift for Chief Rabbi Judah Loeb Landau. sg Dec 19 (3) $50

Agoult, Marie, Comtesse d', 1805-76

ALs, [n.d.]. 1 p, 8vo. To an unnamed baron. Discussing the founding of a charitable society. star Mar 26 (1) DM250

Aiken, Conrad, 1889-1973

Ls, 25 June 1970. 1 p, 8vo. To Jay Dillon. Responding to an inquiry about his works. CNY June 9 (1) $160

Albers, Hans, 1891-1960

Group photograph, 17 Feb 1951. 30cm by 25cm. By Hanns Hubmann. With Cecile Aubry, sgd by both. star Mar 27 (1209) DM260

Albert, Prince Consort of Victoria of England, 1819-61

ALs, 1 Dec 1851. 2 pp, 8vo. To Col. Grey. Expressing congratulations on the birth of a son. In pencil. sg Sept 12 (2) $175

Albert, Eugen d', 1864-1932

Autograph music, draft for Jzeyl, Act 2, Scene 3; [1909 or earlier]. 1 leaf, 4to. Sgd. HH May 13 (1890) DM220

Collection of 2 A Ls s & ANs, 18 & 23 Feb 1891 & [n.d.]. 3 pp, 8vo. To his agent in Kiel. Discussing the program for a projected concert, & announcing his arrival. HN June 26 (886) DM500

ALs, 30 Mar 1911. 1 p, 4to. To [Arthur Schnitzler]. Regretting he did not see him in Vienna. star Mar 27 (967) DM650

Albrecht von Brandenburg, Kurfuerst von Mainz, 1490-1545

Ls, [29 Nov] 1516. 1 p, 8vo. To an unnamed tax official. Informing him that Heinrich von Hoym at Halberstadt has paid the taxes required. star Mar 27 (1287) DM1,300

Alchemical Manuscripts

Ms, compilation of mainly anonymous alchemical recipes & treatises. [Southern Germany, 1531]. 254 leaves, 4to, in modern vellum bdg. In Latin & German in a German gothic cursive hand by 2 different scribes. Sgd by Johannes Kempach. C June 24 (81) £3,200 [Finch]

— Ms, miscellany, Libro de Raymundo Lulio y otros Filosofos. [Spain, late 17th cent]. 544 pp, 4to, in modern vellum-backed cloth. In a cursive bookhand by c.6 different scribes. C June 24 (83) £1,100 [Mediolanum]

— Ms, Question Proemial utrum seu possible el hacer oro o plata de los otros metales por el arte Philichimica? [Spain, early 18th cent]. 332 pp, 4to, in contemp blind-tooled lea over pastebds. In a cursive bookhand. With 7 ink drawings of alchemical implements pasted in. C June 24 (84) £2,000 [Mediolanum]

— Ms, treatise relating chemical science & experiments to the human body & soul. [England, 1702; copied from a Ms dated 1677]. 663 leaves & blanks, 4to. Contemp reversed calf. In a cursive bookhand, with some later additions. Lacking tp. C June 24 (85) £700 [Edwards]

Aldrin, Edwin E.

Photograph, sgd, [n.d.]. 8 by 10 inches. Dar Feb 13 (27) $200

Aleichem, Sholem, 1859-1916. See: Rabinowitz, Shalom ("Sholem Aleichem")

Alexander, Grover Cleveland, 1887-1950

Cut signature, [n.d.]. 4.25 by 0.5 inches. Dar Apr 9 (99) $160

Signature, [n.d.]. 16mo (card). Dar Dec 26 (72) $700

Alexander I, Emperor of Russia, 1777-1825

Ds, 31 Jan 1805. 1 p, size not stated. Military promotion for Philip Kuzoulev. Ck Apr 3 (95) £220

Alexander II, Emperor of Russia, 1818-81

Ds, 21 Sept 1869. 2 pp, folio. Conferral of a decoration on Julius Tengoborski. star Mar 27 (1687) DM750

Alexander III, Emperor of Russia, 1845-94

ALs, 9/21 Apr 1875. 4 pp, 8vo. To [Prince] Nikolai Alekseyevich. Thanking for congratulations on the birth of his daughter. Illus in cat. sg Feb 27 (6) $1,000

Alexandra, Queen of Edward VII of England, 1844-1925

ALs, 12 July 1883. 3 pp, size not stated. To Mrs. Gladstone. Discussing arrangements for a meeting. wd Dec 12 (300) $200

Alexis, Willibald, 1798-1871

Autograph Ms, novel, Der Roland von Berlin, parts of vol 1 & vol 3, [1840]. 258 pp, 4to. Working Ms. star Mar 26 (8) DM2,400

ALs, 10 Oct 1852. 2 pp, 8vo. To Herr Pabst. About his plans to move to Arnstadt. star Mar 26 (9) DM320

Allen, Thomas, 1608-73

Ms, 2 sermons, 1667. 81 pp, 8vo, in 19th-cent half roan. Phillipps Ms 22324. bba May 28 (201) £120 [Edwards]

Allenby, Edmund Henry Hynman, Viscount Allenby of Megiddo, 1861-1936

ALs, 3 Jan 1920. 1 p, 8vo. To L. Portalis. Thanking for a communication. Dar June 11 (253) $200

Photograph, sgd, [n.d.]. 3.5 by 5.5 inches. Dar Apr 9 (250) $130

Allingham, William, 1824-89

Collection of ALs & autograph Ms, 23 Nov 1866. 2 pp, 8vo. To Miss Simeon. Sending her a poem (included, beginning "In a lonely hut on the moor"; 16 lines). bba Jan 30 (264) £220

Almosnino, Moses ben Baruch, c.1516-80. See: Hebrew Manuscripts

Altenberg, Peter, 1859-1919

Autograph Ms, literary text referring to overwhelming tears, [n.d.]. 2 pp, 8vo. On hotel letterhead. HH May 13 (1891) DM420

— Autograph Ms, Maien-Sommer-Abend, 15 May 1911. 3 pp, 4to. Sgd. HH May 13 (1892) DM450

ALs, 4 Oct 1905. 2 pp, folio. To the Schiller Foundation at Weimar. Asking for financial help. star Mar 26 (10) DM620

Alter, Abraham Mordecai, 1866-1948

Autograph postcard, sgd, [n.d.]. Recipient unnamed. Regarding a prospective visit to a follower. sg Dec 19 (5) $400

American Revolution

Ms, contemp letterbook of the correspondence between Lieut. Gen. Clinton & Commodore Sir Peter Parker relating to their expedition against Charleston & the reduction of Rhode Island, 30 May 1776 to 4 Jan 1777. 45 pp, folio; stitched. S July 21 (310) £1,000 [Felone]

Single sheet ptg, Resolution in the Provincial Congress at Watertown, Massachusetts, "that thirteen thousand coats be provided", 29 June 1775. 1 p, 20 by 7.5 inches. With Ms addition on verso listing coats. Illus in cat. R June 13 (136) $3,000

— Boston Massacre. - Ms, official memorandum in the hand of William Cooper, with letter of transmittal to Catharine Macaulay, sgd by James Bowdoin, Samuel Pemberton & Joseph Warren, & related ALs by William Cooper, 22 & 23 Mar 1770 & 8 Dec 1772, 5 pp, folio & 4to. Giving information about the "late horrid Massacre in Boston" & subsequent town meetings. pn June 11 (6) £12,000

— Cone, Joshua, Minuteman. - Ds, 1783. Size not stated. Pay order, sgd on verso in receipt. sup Oct 15 (1396) $90

— Dixon, John, Minuteman. - Ds, 1777. Size not stated. Pay order, sgd on verso in receipt. sup Oct 15 (1397) $90

— Gray, Samuel. - ALs, 30 July 1778. Length not stated. To Capt. Asa Waterman. Requesting writing paper, & mentioning movements of the French fleet & Washington's army. R Nov 9 (131) $450

— Lincoln, Massachusetts. - Letter, Feb 1773. 1 p, 4to. To the inhabitants of Boston. Retained copy, responding to a communication about the "state of our Rights, together with a List of the Infringements & violations of them". Dar Dec 26 (12) $550

— Massachusetts. - Document, 30 June 1781. 3 pp, folio. Ptd resolution of the House of Representatives for the raising of men for the Continental Army. Endorsed & sgd by John Avery. R Nov 9 (143) $950

— Massachusetts. - 3 Mss, 1788. Length not stated. Diaries kept by a selectman from Belchertown on his way to & at the Convention in Boston. R June 13 (133) $5,500

— Massachusetts. - Document, 1776. 1 p,

legal size. Ptd confirmation that the subscribers believe that the war against Great Britain "is just and necessary." Sgd by 24 men. Illus in cat. R June 13 (138) $4,200

— PITKIN, GEORGE, MINUTEMAN. - Ds, 1777. Size not stated. Pay order. sup Oct 15 (1398) $90

— RHEA, COL. JONATHAN. - Ds, [n.d.]. Size not stated. Paterson lottery ticket. Mtd. R June 13 (167) $140

— RHODE ISLAND. - Letter, probably in the hand of Gov. William Greene, 5 Feb 1782. 2 pp, 4to. To Benjamin Lincoln. Sending a resolution by the Legislature (included) & warning of a possible British attack on Newport. Dar Aug 6 (47) $160

— SCOTT, CHARLES. - ADs, 2 Feb 1778. 1 p, 8vo. As Brigadier Gen. at Valley Forge, certificate for John Rosson. Dar Dec 26 (13) $1,100

Amherst, William Pitt, Earl Amherst of Arracan, 1773-1857

Series of 41 A Ls s, 16 Feb 1816 to 22 July 1817. 182 pp, 4to. To his wife. Reporting from his voyages on a diplomatic mission to the Emperor of China. With related material. C June 24 (357) £2,800 [Browning]

Ampere, Andre M., 1775-1836

ALs, 28 Oct 1809. 3 pp, 4to. To M. Ruffy. Requesting that recipient recommend 2 young people at schools in Paris. Illus in cat. sup Oct 15 (1004) $1,000

Amundsen, Roald, 1872-1928

[An album of 101 photographs of his stay in Alaska, 1906, mostly 196mm by 247mm, with related material including a photograph, sgd, sold at CNY on 5 Dec 1991, lot 7, for $3,800.]

Ancillon, Jean Pierre Friedrich, 1767-1837

ALs, 29 Aug 1832. 3 pp, 4to. To [Duke Karl von Mecklenburg-Strelitz?]. Suggesting improvements to the organization of the Prussian State Archives. star Mar 27 (1237) DM400

Andersen, Hans Christian, 1805-75

ALs, 16 May 1850. 3 pp, 8vo. To J. A. Josephson. Sending 2 fairy tales, & discussing a libretto. Illus in cat. P June 17 (1) $3,000

Autograph sentiment, sgd, [n.d.]. Size not stated. Framed with a port. sg Feb 27 (10) $650

Anderson, Robert, 1805-71

Photograph, sgd, [n.d.]. Carte size. In uniform. By Anthony, from a Brady negative. Illus in cat. R June 13 (102) $450

Andrae, Louis

Ms, Weberei in Schriftmuster, Trittmuster ... Jacquard-Muster; [n.d.]. 118 leaves, folio, in contemp lea bdg. Detailed description of weaving patterns, etc. Including numerous illusts & c.110 mtd samples of material. JG Mar 27 (204) DM2,400

Andreas-Salome, Lou, 1861-1937

ALs, 3 May 1895. 2 pp, 8vo. To an unnamed lady. About a visit. star Mar 26 (11) DM360

Angelo, Valenti

Original drawing, watercolor map of North America, to illus the tp of the Grabhorn Press Ed of The Letter of Amerigo Vespucci, [c.1926]. 6 by 7.75 inches; framed. Sgd. cb Feb 12 (5) $425

Anouilh, Jean, 1910-87

ALs, [n.d.]. 1 p, 8vo. To Matei Roussou. Suggesting that he ask for an interview with Claude Sainval & Roland Pietri. star Mar 26 (15) DM220

Anson, Adrian Constantine ("Cap"), 1852-1922

Signature, [n.d.]. 4.25 by 1 inches. Dar Aug 6 (90) $850

Antarctica

Group photograph, 6 members of the international Trans-Antarctica Expedition Team, [1989/90], 4to. Sgd by all 6 & a 7th member. Framed. wa Oct 19 (114) $100

— ORDE-LEES, T. - Autograph Ms, journal of Shackleton's expedition, 24 Mar 1915 to 16 Apr 1916. In all c.370 pp, folio, in dark green cloth. Reporting the loss of the Endurance, etc. Including numerous drawings & typewritten continuation concerning the period on Elephant Island. In ink & pencil; sgd. Revised for possible publication. P Oct 11 (203) $12,000

— VINCENDON-DUMOULIN, ADRIEN. - Autograph Ms, Voyage des corvettes de l'etat L'Astrolabe et La Zelee au pole australe et autour du monde, 1837-1840. 225 leaves & blanks in 2 vols, folio. Orig half cloth & marbled bds; 2d vol def. Kept during the Dumont d'Urville expedition to the South Pole. C Oct 30 (26) £5,000 [Nolen]

Anthology

Ms, compilation of Renaissance Latin verse, including Hermaphroditus by Antonio Beccadelli, Triumphus amoris by Gregorio Tifernas, & works by Pompeius of Bologna, Basinius of Parma, Sigismund Paldulfus, & others; [Italy, 15th cent]. About 250 pp, 4to, in vellum wraps. In a single neat Italic hand. S May 28 (33) £5,800 [Maggs]

Anthony, Susan B., 1820-1906

A Ls s (2), 30 June 1886 & [n.d.]. 5 pp, 8vo. To [John Weinheimer]. Inquiring about the index for "the last vol of Woman Suffrage History". sg Sept 12 (7) $750

ALs, 9 July 1886. 3 pp, 8vo. To [John] Weinheimer. Inquiring about the index for her History of Women. R Nov 9 (47) $480

— 25 Apr 1898. 2 pp, 8vo. To Alexander Hill. Thanking for an autograph of B. Gratz Brown. Dar June 11 (17) $700

— 11 Apr 1900. 2 pp, 4to. To an unnamed lady. About literature on woman suffrage for a projected debate. Spiro collection. CNY May 14 (34) $950

Autograph quotation, sgd, 25 Sept [18]81. 4 by 2.5 inches (card). About the importance of the right to vote. Dar June 11 (16) $650

— Anr, sgd, 23 June [18]87. 2.5 by 4 inches. Referring to equality of rights for women. Mtd. sg Feb 27 (11) $375

Antiphoner

Ms, Antiphonal. [Germany, 16th cent?]. 190 leaves, vellum, 475mm by 300mm. Contemp lea over wooden bds. With music on a 5-line red stave, numerous calligraphic & some decorated initials. Dampstained. Ck Mar 6 (152) £1,700

— Ms, Antiphonal. [Spain, 16th or 17th cent] 88 leaves, 520mm by 375mm, in old blind-tooled sheep over wooden bds with brass fittings. Written in a gothic hand in red & black ink beneath 5-line staves in red with music notation in black. With large heraldic headpiece painted in colors & gold on vellum mtd on 1st leaf verso; initials in blue & red with penwork decoration. sg May 7 (6) $4,000

— Ms, Antiphoner, comprising Temporal from Maundy Thursday until the 1st Saturday in Sept. [Beira, Portugal, 1531]. Of Franciscan use. 180 leaves (8 lacking), vellum, 452mm by 317mm. Old tanned lea over massive wooden bds. With 5 lines each of text in a rounded gothic hand & of music on a 5-line red stave. With painted initials throughout in red or blue. Worn; repaired. S June 23 (81) £1,000 [Feldman]

— Ms, Antiphoner. [Germany, c.1465]. 2 leaves only, vellum, 492mm by 368mm. With 8 lines each of text in a gothic textura & of music on a 4-line black stave. With large illuminated initial. Illus in cat. HH May 12 (30) DM4,200

— Ms, [Bologna, early 14th cent]. Single leaf, vellum, 509mm by 368mm. With 6 lines each of text in a rounded gothic hand & of music on a 4-line red stave. With large historiated initial with illuminated 3-quarter border. Mtd. S Dec 17 (26) £1,600 [Schuster]

— Ms, [Bologna or Ferrara, c.1450]. Single leaf, vellum, 568mm by 419mm. In a rounded gothic hand, with music on a 4-line red stave. With large historiated initial on burnished gold panel ground supporting a 2-sided foliate border. Illus in cat. S June 23 (16) £5,500 [Fogg]

— Ms, [Regensburg, c.1310]. Single leaf, vellum, 378mm by 296mm. With 9 lines each of text in a gothic liturgical hand & of music on a 4-line red stave. With large historiated initial in full colors on a thickly raised burnished gold ground. Illus in cat. S June 23 (10) £12,500 [Gunther]

Anton Ulrich, Herzog von Braunschweig-Wolfenbuettel, 1633-1714

Ls, 17 Oct 1709. 2 pp, folio. To Landgraf Karl von Hessen-Kassel. Responding to an inquiry regarding the resumption of the Polish Crown by Elector August of Saxony. star Mar 27 (1292) DM560

Arabic Manuscripts

Ms, philosophical essay about the creation of the world, by a Maronite priest. [Syria or Lebanon, 17th cent]. 176 leaves, 158mm by 116mm. Contemp blindstamped lea. In naskhi script in 2 hands. With 2 ornamental headpieces. HH Nov 5 (884) DM3,000

— AL-IMAM MALIK IBN ANAS. - Muwatta. [Andalusia or North Africa, A.H.754/A.D.1353]. 112 leaves (some lacking), 230mm by 175mm. Def brown mor bdg tooled in blind. In maghribi script in the Andalusian tradition by Muhammad Abd al-Rahman al-Ansari. With extensive glosses in margins. S Apr 30 (349) £6,000

— AL-JAZULI. - Dala'il al-Khayrat. [Ayub, Turkey, A.H.1160/A.D.1747-48]. 47 leaves, 158mm by 110mm. Def black lea gilt. In naskhi script by al-Sayyid 'Abd al-Karim al-Alataghi. With illuminated headpieces & 2 miniatures of Mecca & Medina. sg Nov 7 (4) $275

— MAALOULI, DIMITRI. - Ms, Maronite prayer book, 6 Feb 1847. 172 leaves, 116mm by 75mm. Contemp blindstamped lea. In naskhi script. HH Nov 5 (882) DM2,200

Aristotle, 384-322 B.C.

Ms, Meteora, with the commentary of Albertus Magnus; & Avicenna, De Mineralibus. [England, c.1275]. 96 leaves & 2 flyleaves, vellum, 313mm by 208mm. Medieval bdg of wooden bds, partly covered with red lea. In 2 sizes of a small scholastic bookhand, with 2 scientific diagrams. Illus in cat. S Dec 17 (48) £22,000 [Kraus]

— ANON. - Ms, Disputationes in octo libros Aristotelis de physica, in duodecim libros metaphysicae et in tre libros de anima. [Italy, c. 1600]. 260 leaves, 190mm by

130mm. Limp vellum bdg incorporating 15th-cent liturgical Ms. HH May 12 (2) DM900

Armenian Manuscripts

Ms, Four Gospels. [Jors Asota (Ayrarat), 1478]. 296 leaves, 225mm by 176mm. Contemp calf over wooden bds. In black ink in a regular bolorgir hand by the scribe Zak'aria for the priest Ter Khachatur. With 10 pp of decoration & 4 full-page miniatures. S June 23 (56) £5,500 [Fogg]

— Ms, Four Gospels. [Sep'i, Armenia, 1581]. 292 leaves, vellum & paper, 270mm by 200mm. Contemp calf over wooden bds. In black ink in a regular bolorgir hand by the scribe T'oros for Ter Melk'eset. With 10 pp of decoration & 12 full-page miniatures. Including four 12th-cent flyleaves with text attributed to Philo of Alexandria. S June 23 (57) £15,000 [Tyler]

— Ms, Saraknoc; hymnal. [Constantinople or Eastern Turkey, 1417]. 387 leaves (some lacking) & 2 vellum flyleaves, 138mm by 88mm. Modern lea-covered pastebds incorporating remains of contemp bdg. In a regular bolorgir hand, with neumes often marked above text. With 5 illuminated headpieces in interlocking designs in colors on liquid gold grounds. Worn. S Dec 17 (44) £1,600 [Azezian]

Armstrong, Louis, 1900-71

[3 photographs, sgd & inscr to Chris Clufetos (Clifton), [c.1955 to 1965], 142mm by 91mm & 256mm by 204mm, sold at CNY on 9 June 1992, lot 5, for $1,100.]

Collection of ALs & photograph, sgd & inscr, 24 Jan 1969 & [1953]. 2 pp, 4to, & 202mm by 250mm. To Chris Clufetos. About his health problems. On verso of ptd sheets bearing his 9-day diet. CNY June 9 (3) $3,000

— Collection of ALs & photograph, sgd & inscr, 16 June 1970 & [n.d.]. 3 pp, 4to, & 253mm by 207mm. To Chris Clufetos. Reminiscing about the 1920s & encouraging him to keep playing the trumpet. CNY June 9 (4) $1,900

Collection of Ls & photograph, sgd & inscr, 6 Feb 1954 & [n.d.]. 2 pp, 4to, & 257mm by 205mm. To Chris Clufetos. Expressing enthusiasm for "the greatest music on this man's earth, - DIXIELAND". CNY June 9 (2) $3,200

Armstrong, Neil

Autograph sentiment, sgd, [n.d.]. On postcard photograph of Buzz Aldrin on the Moon; inscr to the Hall family. Dar Feb 13 (29) $190

Photograph, sgd, [n.d.]. 8 by 10 inches. In space suit. wa Oct 19 (33) $180

Photograph, sgd & inscr, [n.d.]. 8 by 10 inches. In space suit. wa Oct 19 (185) $170

Signature, [16 June 1969]. On philatelic envelope. Dar Dec 26 (46) $275

— Anr, [n.d.]. On ptd reproduction of a photograph of the moon, 8.5 by 11 inches. Dar Feb 13 (28) $160

Armstrong, Neil —& Others

[The signatures of Armstrong, B. Aldrin & M. Collins of Apollo 11, & of B. Abruzzo, M. Anderson & L. Newman of the balloon Double Eagle II, [n.d.], on a $1.00 bill, sold at Dar on 11 June 1992, lot 70, for 550.]

Armstrong, Sir Thomas, 1624?-84

— ARMSTRONG, LADY KATHARINE. - Ms, A copy of the paper delivered to the Keeper and my Lord Chief Justice and Mr Attorney General by me on behalf of my husband Sir Thomas Armstrong, 1684. 1 p, folio, on verso of related ptd broadside. Imperf. bba Sept 19 (426) £55 [Lynch]

Arndt, Ernst Moritz, 1769-1860

Autograph transcript, poem, Lied der Freien, beginning "Der Gott, der Eisen wachsen liess...", [n.d.]. 2 pp, 4to. 6 stanzas. star Mar 26 (16) DM9,000

ALs, 19 Sept 1815. 4 pp, 8vo. To an unnamed pbr. Commenting on the results of the Congress of Vienna. star Mar 26 (17) DM1,050

— [n.d.]. 1 p, 8vo. To Capt. von Siebold. Regretting he cannot accept an invitation. star Mar 26 (18) DM400

Arnim, Bettina von, 1785-1859

ALs, [June 1806]. 2 pp, 4to. To Friedrich Karl von Savigny. Chatting about Gall's lectures on phrenology, various friends, etc. star Mar 26 (19) DM8,500

— 27 Aug [1844]. 1 p, 4to. To Henriette Sontag, Countess Rossi. Enlisting her help for Max Erlanger. star Mar 26 (20) DM1,150

— [after 1852]. 1 p, 8vo. To Maximilian Moltke. Concerning publishing matters. star Mar 26 (21) DM750

— [n.d.]. Size not stated. To Sophie Reichardt. Expressing happiness about their friendship, & sending a present. HH May 13 (1893) DM900

Arnold, Benedict, 1741-1801

ALs, 8 July 1780. 1 p, folio. To Titus Hosmer. About the settlement of his accounts, & informing him that he will accept the Westpoint command. Illus in cat. Spiro collection. CNY May 14 (35) $11,000

— 28 Oct 1794. 2 pp, 4to. To Col. Fisher. Discussing a sale of oxen to the British at St. Lucia. sup May 9 (361) $3,200

ADs, 15 Oct 1794. 1 p, 4to. Reward notice for the apprehension of his clerk John Parker. Spiro collection. CNY May 14 (36) $4,200

Arnold, Henry Harley, 1886-1950

Ls, 16 Oct 1947. 1 p, 4to. To Joseph Kraiewsky. Encouraging letter to a handicapped correspondent. Dar Dec 26 (21) $200

Photograph, sgd & inscr, [16 Oct 1947]. 8 by 10 inches. Inscr to Joseph Kraiewsky. Dar Dec 26 (22) $170

— Anr, [n.d.]. 8 by 10 inches. Inscr to Frank Ruppenthal. Dar Oct 10 (28) $120

Arnold, Matthew, 1822-88

ALs, [n.d.], "Friday". 1 p, 8vo. To [A. C.] Sellar. Declining an invitation. Ingilby collection. pn Nov 14 (50) £80 [Dupre]

Arrhenius, Svante, 1859-1927

ALs, 23 Dec 1911. 2 pp, 8vo. To Gustav Hagemann. About a new scientific society at Copenhagen. Dar Apr 9 (35) $150

Arthur, Chester A., 1830-86

ALs, 22 July 1871. 1 p, 8vo. Recipient unnamed. About an appointment for Mr. Box. Illus in cat. R June 13 (173) $450

— 29 June [1880]. 1 p, 8vo. To George Jones. Regarding arrangements for their departure. Dar June 11 (20) $700

— 25 Aug 1881. 1 p, 8vo. To Mrs. Maury. Thanking for her kind letter. Illus in cat. R Mar 7 (109) $1,300

— 25 Aug 1881. 1 p, 8vo. To Mrs. Lewis Manny. Thanking for her letter. sup Oct 15 (1562) $700

Ls, 18 Nov 1862. 1 p, 4to. To Gen. Thomas Hillhouse. Returning some memoranda. Framed with a port. Dar June 11 (18) $700

— 24 Apr 1876. 1 p, 8vo. To US Consuls. Letter of recommendation for William Arenfred. Dar Apr 9 (36) $550

— 3 July 1880. 1 p, 8vo. Recipient unnamed. Thanking for congratulations. wa Oct 19 (261) $250

— 12 Dec 1881. 1 p, 8vo. To Thurlow Weed Barnes. Thanking for a letter. Illus in cat. Dar Feb 13 (15) $800

Ds, [late 1862]. 1 p, 4to. Military Pass for NY State Volunteers, no 1338; unaccomplished. Dar Oct 10 (29) $225

— [1862]. 1 p, 4to. Military Pass no 1338; unaccomplished. Dar June 11 (19) $275

— 20 July 1883. 1 p, folio. Appointment of Anna Gangewer as Visitor to the Hospital for the Insane. sg Sept 12 (9) $200

— 26 Dec 1883. 1 p, folio. Commission of David Hall as 1st Lieutenant in the Revenue Service. sg Sept 12 (8) $375

Check, accomplished & sgd, 8 Aug 1864. Payable to Thomas G. Davis. Dar June 11 (21) $600

— Anr, accomplished & sgd, 18 June 1879. Payable to D. Schrieffer. Repaired. Illus in cat. Dar Apr 9 (37) $850

Cut signature, 4 July 1884. 18.25 by 7.25 inches. Fragment of a patent document. Dar Feb 13 (16) $300

Executive Mansion card, sgd, [n.d.]. wa Oct 19 (262) $280

Photograph, sgd, [n.d.]. 4.25 by 6.5 inches. By W. Kurtz. Illus in cat. Dar Feb 13 (17) $3,250

Ashby, Turner, 1828-62

Signature, [n.d.]. Inside a diary cover, 5.5 by 9 inches. Dar June 11 (22) $170

Astaire, Fred, 1899-1987

Group photograph, [n.d.]. 8 by 10 inches. With Virginia Dale; sgd by Astaire. LH Dec 11 (314) $70

Astaire, Fred, 1899-1987 —& Rogers, Ginger

Group photograph, [1930s]. 8 by 10 inches. Sgd & inscr by both. Dar Dec 26 (37) $250

— Anr, [n.d.]. 10 by 8 inches. Sgd by both. Dar Apr 9 (51) $140

— Anr, [n.d.]. 11 by 14 inches. Sgd by both; inscr to Michelle by Rogers. Dar Apr 9 (52) $140

Ptd photograph, on cover of orig sheet music for The Way You Look To-Night, NY 1936. 6 pp, 4to. Sgd by both. Dar Dec 26 (38) $400

Astrid, Queen of Leopold III, King of the Belgians, 1905-35

ANs, [1920s]. 1 p, on verso of port postcard. To "Nanna". Chatting about family activities. Dar Apr 9 (53) $110

Astronauts

[The signatures of S. D. Griggs, E. Rainey & T. Mendenhall, [n.d.], on a photograph of NASA's Shuttle Training Aircraft, 10 by 8 inches, sold at Dar on 9 Apr 1992, lot 59, for $100.]

— APOLLO 11. - The signatures of Neil Armstrong, Buzz Aldrin & Richard Nixon, [n.d.], on a photograph of the plaque Armstrong & Aldrin left on the Moon, 8 by 10 inches, sold at Dar on 9 Apr 1992, lot 57, for $600.

— APOLLO 12. - Group photograph of crew, [n.d.]. 8 by 10 inches. Sgd by D. Gordon, C. Conrad & A. L. Bean. Dar Apr 9 (58) $250

— APOLLO 17. - Photograph of the curvature of the Moon taken during the Apollo 17 mission. 102 by 9.5 inches, rolled. Sgd by G. Cernan, R. Evans & H. H. Schmitt. Dar June 11 (53) $350

— CHALLENGER 41-B. - Group photograph of

the crew, 1984. 8 by 10 inches. Sgd by Ron McNair, Bob Stewart, Bruce McCandless, Vance Brand & Robert L. Gibson. Dar Dec 26 (42) $130

— DISCOVERY. - Group photograph of crew, [n.d.]. 10 by 8 inches. Sgd by J. Resnik, C. Walker, M. Mullane, S. A. Hawley, H. Hartsfield & M. L. Coates. Dar Aug 6 (55) $200

— PROJECT MERCURY. - Group photograph, [n.d.]. 10 by 8 inches. Sgd by all 7 orig Project Mercury astronauts. Dar Oct 10 (32) $400

Astronomical Manuscripts

Ms, Introduction to Astronomy. [England, c.1812?]. 22 leaves, 282mm by 425mm, in orig bds. With 24 superb pen-&-watercolor celestial maps & other maps & diagrams, including 4 with working volvelles. With 2 separate leaves of volvelles of considerable complexity. sg Nov 7 (11) $2,600

— LA BROSSE, LOUIS-PHILIPPE. - Ms, Traite de Sphere ou L'on explique le mouvement des astres... [Lorraine, 1724]. 54 leaves (2 blank), folio. Brown calf bdg. With 22 pen-&-ink diagrams. Possibly unpbd. FD Dec 2 (3) DM6,000

Atwill, Lionel, 1885-1946

Ds, 16 Oct 1942. 2 pp, folio. Contract with Universal Pictures; carbon copy. Dar Dec 26 (51) $450

Auden, Wystan Hugh, 1907-73

Autograph Ms, clerihew, beginning "Good Queen Victoria...", [n.d.]. 1 p, folio. Sgd. star Mar 26 (22) DM340

Audubon, John James, 1785-1851

ALs, 12 Sept 1836. 3 pp, 4to. To Thomas McCulloch. Asking for specimens of birds (list included). Sgd twice. CNY Dec 5 (8) $4,000

Auerbach, Berthold, 1812-82

[The galley proofs & page proofs of the 2d Ed of his biography of Spinoza in Spinoza's saemmtliche Werke, vol 1, pp I - LXIV, [1871], with numerous autograph corrections, sold at HH on 13 May 1992, lot 1893a, for DM850.]

ALs, 5 Jan 1863. 2 pp, 8vo. To Franz von Dingelstedt. About Otto Ludwig's illness. star Mar 26 (24) DM340

Augereau, Pierre Francois Charles, Duc de Castiglione, 1757-1816

Ls, 5 Nov 1805. 1 p, 4to. To Gen. St. Suzanne. Introducing a young sergeant. sg Feb 27 (12) $150

August, Kurfuerst von Sachsen, 1526-86

Ls, 13 Mar 1574. 1 p, folio. To Hans Kitzscher & Ludwig Kinast. Giving instructions concerning use of a grist mill. star Mar 27 (1692) DM600

Augustine, Saint, 354-430

Ms, The Rule of St. Augustine, in Latin & Spanish. [Spain, late 16th cent]. 30 leaves (1 lacking), vellum, 230mm by 170mm. Contemp lea over wooden bds, with flyleaves from a 14th-cent Italian canon law Ms. In a large rounded roman hand in imitation of ptd type. With 16 very large decorated or historiated initials. S Dec 17 (62) £800 [Schwartz]

Augustus II, King of Poland, 1670-1733

Ls, 20 Jan 1700. 1 p, folio. To Cardinal Colloredo. Thanking for Christmas wishes. star Mar 27 (1694) DM600

— 31 May 1728. 1 p, 4to. To Cardinal Collicola. Expressing congratulations. In Italian. Imperf. hen Nov 12 (2471) DM370

Auric, Georges, 1899-1983

Collection of 11 A Ls s & 2 Ls s, 1925 to 1960. Length not stated, various sizes. To Boris Kochno & Christian Berard. About the ballet Les Matelots & other matters; including musical quotation. With related material. Boris Kochno collection. SM Oct 12 (347) FF7,000

Austen, Jane, 1775-1815

Autograph Ms, poem, beginning "I've a pain in my head", [n.d.]. 1 p, 125mm by 102mm, cut from larger sheet. 4 four-line stanzas, sgd. Including fragment of autograph poem by Cassandra Austen on verso. With related correspondence. C Dec 16 (275) £10,000 [Ross]

ALs, [8 -] 11 Apr 1805. 4 pp, 4to. To her sister Cassandra. Recording her activities in Bath. Sgd J A. Seal tear. Illus in cat. P June 17 (102) $12,000

Austin, Moses, 1761-1821 —& Others

Ls, 16 Mar 1805. 1 p, 4to. To William H. Harrison. Recommending Nathaniel Cook as Justice of the Peace. Also sgd by 5 others. With ANs by Harrison below; sgd W.H.H. sg Sept 12 (107) $700

Austin, Stephen F., 1793-1836

Ds, 11 Jan 1836. 1 p, 4to. Texan Loan Certificate No 371 issued to Thomas D. Carneal. Also sgd by others. Dar Dec 26 (52) $1,100

Austin, Stephen F., 1793-1836 —& Others

Ds, 11 Jan 1836. 1 p, 4to. Texas loan certificate no 154 for $32, issued to Robert Triplett; also sgd by B. T. Archer & W. H. Wharton. Illus in cat. sup Oct 15 (1826) $1,350

— 11 Jan 1836. 2 p, 4to. Texian Loan Certificate no 158 issued to Robert Triplett. Also sgd by B. T. Archer & W. H. Wharton. Illus in cat. sup May 9 (362) $1,800

Australia

Transcript, contemp copy of the contract with George Whitlock to convey convicts to New South Wales on the ships Neptune, Surprize, & Scarborough, 27 Aug 1789. 7 pp, folio, in modern mor-backed bdg. Longueville collection. S June 25 (115) £6,500 [Quaritch/Hordern]

— BAUDIN, NICOLAS. - ALs, [19 July 1802]. 1 p, 4to. To Citizen Davout. At Port Jackson, asking him to set up a commission of inquiry into thefts of property from the ship Geographe. Longueville collection. S June 25 (196) £1,700 [Renard]

— DAWES, LIEUT. WILLIAM. - Ds, 30 Sept 1788. 2 pp, folio. Bill of exchange in favor of George B. Worgan, issued in New South Wales & addressed to Charles Cox in London. Endorsed in several hands. Illus in cat. Longueville collection. S June 25 (105) £2,200 [Renard]

— FADDY, LIEUT. WILLIAM. - ADs, 28 Sept 1788. 2 pp, folio. Bill of exchange in favor of Jens Jansson, issued in Port Jackson, New Holland & addressed to Charles Cox in London. Endorsed in several hands. Illus in cat. Longueville collection. S June 25 (106) £2,000 [ANZ Bank]

— FADDY, LIEUT. WILLIAM. - ADs, 28 Sept 1788. 2 pp, folio. Bill of exchange no 2 in favor of Jens Jansson, issued in Port Jackson, New Holland & addressed to Charles Cox in London. Endorsed in several hands. Longueville collection. S June 25 (107) £1,800 [Stokes]

— REDFERN, WILLIAM. - ALs, 18 Feb 1815. 1 p, 4to. To D'Arcy Wentworth. Asking him to convey his resignation as Assistant Surgeon at Sydney Hospital to Gov. Macquarie. Longueville collection. S June 25 (180) £1,300 [Quaritch/Hordern]

Aviation

Menu, The Progress Club, NY, 27 June 1930. 4 pp, 8vo. Sgd on cover by C. Kingsford-Smith, E. Van Dyke, J. S. W. Stannage, & J. P. Saul (the crew of the Southern Cross), & by Anthony Fokker. Dar Apr 9 (67) $225

Avison, Charles, 1710?-70

— CALLANDER, J. - Ls, 6 July 1781. 4 pp, folio. Recipient unnamed. Giving a detailed account of Avison's character, his career as a composer & thinker on music, etc. Including autograph postscript. S Dec 6 (28) £500 [Macnutt]

B

Bach, Johann Christian, 1743-1814 —& Clementi, Muzio, 1752-1832

[A musical Ms, comprising an apparently undocumented sonata, 2 autograph cadenzas, & a partly autograph piano concerto by Bach, with autograph music by Clementi, including a transcription of a Bach sonata, England, early 1770s, 59 pp, in contemp blue bds, sold at S on 29 May, lot 463, for £24,000 to Haas.]

Bach, Johann Sebastian, 1685-1750

Ms, "Clavier Sonate", suite for lute & piano BWZ 997, piano score; [2d half of 18th cent]. 11 pp, 335mm by 215mm. In a scribal hand. star Mar 27 (969) DM3,200

— Ms, Passacaglia in C minor, BWV 583, for organ; [1st half of 18th cent]. 9 pp, folio. In a scribal hand on up to seven systems per page. Inscr to Moscheles in anr hand. Illus in cat. S May 29 (468) £2,500 [Haas]

A Ds s (2), 26 Oct 1743 & 1745. 2 pp, 9cm by 7 cm. Receipts for payments for an annual memorial service. Mtd. Illus in cat. Mannheim collection. S Dec 6 (1) £12,000 [Schneider]

Bachem, Bele, Pseud. of Renate Gabriele Boehmer

ALs, 3 Jan 1981. 1 p, folio. Recipient unnamed. Sending a sketch (included). star Mar 27 (866) DM220

Bacher, Theobald Jacques Justin, Baron de, 1748-1813

Ls, [24 June 1794]. 2 pp, folio. To Gen. Michaud. About an exchange of hostages. star Mar 27 (1380) DM300

Bacon, Sir Francis, 1561-1626

Transcript, poem, The World's a Bubble; [c.1620s-1630s]. 1 leaf, folio. 4-stanza version; including other poems. Transcribed by Thomas Everard. S July 21 (9) £500 [Quaritch]

Baden-Powell of Gilwell, Robert S. S. Baden-Powell, 1st Baron, 1857-1941

ALs, 27 Jan 1908. 1 p, 8vo. Recipient unnamed. Declining an invitation. sup Oct 15 (1010) $200

Autograph postcard, sgd, 1 May [19]09. To J. M. Mullaley. Informing him that he reached home safely after a visit to Buenos Aires. Ck Nov 15 (36) £150

Badfinger

[The signatures of all 4 members of the band on an album cover, [n.d.], framed, overall size 25 by 13 inches, sold at P on 17 Dec 1991, lot 355, for $500.]

Baedecker, Gottschalk Diederich, 1778-1841

ALs, 16 Sept 1816. 1 p, 8vo. To Carl Schulz. Asking him to accompany his daughter Amalie to Essen. HN June 26 (887a) DM270

Baer, Max, 1909-59

Autograph sentiment, sgd, 7 July [19]34. 5.25 by 4.5 inches. Inscr to Izzy. Dar Feb 13 (119) $130

Photograph, sgd & inscr, 10 Jan [19]34. Framed, overall size 14 by 18 inches. Inscr to Billy House. Illus in cat. sup July 8 (229) $440

Baeumer, Gertrud, 1873-1954

Collection of 9 A Ls s & autograph postcard, sgd; 27 July 1948 to 15 May 1950 & [n.d.]. 18 pp, folio & 8vo. To Bernhard Martin. Concerning contributions to the journal Die neue Schau. star Mar 26 (33) DM550

Bahr, Hermann, 1863-1934

Autograph Ms, essay, Konrad Burdach zum siebzigsten Geburtstag, [1929]. 10 pp, 8vo. Sgd at head. star Mar 26 (27) DM220

Baker, John Franklin, 1886-1963

Cut signature, [n.d.]. Mtd on card, 5 by 3 inches. Cut from a bank check. Dar Aug 6 (91) $250

Photograph, sgd, [8 Sept 1951]. 10 by 8 inches. Being carried off the field on a stretcher. Illus in cat. sup July 10 (969) $300

Baker, Josephine, 1906-75

ALs, 9 Apr 1964. 6 pp, 8vo. To Mme Bruning. About children, arrangements, etc. sup Oct 15 (1011) $350

Baker, Sir Samuel White, 1821-93

ALs, 6 Sept 1893. 2 pp, 8vo. To Mr. Watts. Thanking for a present of grouse. bba Sept 19 (348) £110 [Freddie]

Bakunin, Mikhail Aleksandrovich, 1814-76

ALs, 25 Nov 1861. 1 p, 8vo. Recipient unnamed. Urging him to meet him in Boston. In French. star Mar 27 (1244) DM1,000

Balakirev, Mily Alekseyevich, 1837-1910

ALs, 12 May 1888. 2 pp, 8vo. To Cesar Cui. Giving an assessment of Cui's Suite for piano duet. Illus in cat. S Dec 6 (29) £1,600 [Diamond]

Balanchine, George, 1904-83

Collection of 14 A Ls s, Ls s & postcards, sgd, 1920s & 1930s. 33 pp, various sizes. To Boris Kochno. Gossipy letters about a variety of professional matters. With related material. SM Oct 12 (349) FF30,000

Baldwin, Roger

Ls, 9 Sept 1938. 2 pp, 4to. To Jesse Gorkin. Describing early victories of the American Civil Liberties Union. sup Oct 15 (1012) $420

Balfour, Arthur James, 1st Earl, 1848-1930

Ls, 8 Apr 1897. 7 pp, 8vo. To Charles Waldstein. Discussing Greek politics. pn Mar 19 (93) £80

Ball, Crispin Alfred, 1883-1914

Series of 40 A Ls s, 1906 to 1914. 180 pp, 4to & 8vo. To Mrs. Eden. Describing his life & work in the Sudan. In an album with related material. pn June 11 (55) £280

Ball, Hugo, 1886-1927

Ls, 9 Nov 1924. 2 pp, 8vo. To Franz Blei. Responding to a request for a contribution to a journal. With related material. star Mar 26 (28) DM550

Ball, Lucille, 1910-89

Photograph, sgd & inscr, 15 Oct 1940. 7.5 by 9.5 inches. Inscr to Edna. Dar Aug 6 (8) $250

Ballin, Albert, 1857-1918

ALs, 25 Dec 1912. 4 pp, 8vo. To Alice Warburg. About a projected visit. star Mar 27 (1245) DM440

Bamberger, Seckel, 1863-1934

A Ls s (2), 1922 & 1923. 4 pp, 8vo. Recipient unnamed. Requesting financial sponsorship to publish his father's writings, & offering to exchange publications. sg Dec 19 (22) $175

Banks, Sir Joseph, 1743-1820

ALs, 7 May 1792. 2 pp, 4to. Recipient unnamed. Discussing extra-terrestrial life. Ingilby collection. pn Nov 14 (52) £240

— 23 Sept 1799. 4 pp, 4to. Recipient unnamed. Referring to "the situation of our new Colony", the fitting out of a vessel, etc. Longueville collection. S June 25 (69) £1,600 [Quaritch/Hordern]

Banks, Nathaniel P., 1816-94

Photograph, sgd, [n.d.]. Carte size. Full length, in dress uniform. By Anthony, from a Brady negative. Illus in cat. R June 13 (97) $450

Banting, Frederick Grant, 1891-1941

Signature, [n.d.]. 8.5 by 4.75 inches. Dar Apr 9 (74) $275

Bantock, Granville, 1868-1946

Autograph music, Five Ghazals of Hafiz, 30 July 1937. 164 pp, folio, in bds. Orchestral score, notated on up to 29 staves per page. Sgd. S May 29 (471) £500 [Quaritch]

Barbusse, Henri, 1874-1935

[A group of 21 typescripts (20 sgd), 1922 to 1925, c.100 pp, 4to, articles written for the newspaper La Razon, sold at S on 5 Dec 1991, lot 468, for £600 to Lionheart.]

Barlach, Ernst, 1870-1938

Autograph Ms, 2 poems, Sorgen (8 lines), & Juengstes Gericht (20 lines), [n.d.]. 1 p, 4to, on a leaf from an exercise book. Illus in cat. star Mar 27 (868) DM1,300

ALs, 23 Mar 1892. 9 pp, 8vo. To Friedrich Duesel. About his professional prospects, Social Democrats, & other matters. star Mar 27 (870) DM2,800

— 21 Aug 1937. 2 pp, folio. To Waltraud Adler. Sending some prints, & commenting on his political problems & persecution. star Mar 27 (871) DM3,600

Autograph postcard, sgd, 4 Feb 189[1]. To Friedrich Duesel. Sending good wishes for his examination. star Mar 27 (869) DM520

Barlow, Joel, 1754-1812

ADs, 8 Mar 1790. 2 pp, size not stated. Sale of 3 million acres of land in the Northwest Territory to William Playfair; sgd & initialled by both. Dar Oct 10 (62) $500

Barnave, Antoine, 1761-97

Autograph Ms (2), deliberations on the chances of a counterrevolutionary movement & on political groups in France, [n.d.]. 4 pp, 4to. star Mar 27 (1381) DM650

Barnum, Phineas Taylor, 1810-91

ALs, 22 Feb 1866. 1 p, 4to. To Mr. Layard. Soliciting exhibits for his zoo. On ptd letterhead, with vignette. R Nov 9 (50) $1,700

Autograph sentiment, sgd, Apr 1881. 4 by 3 inches. sup Oct 15 (1013) $90

Barres, Maurice, 1862-1923

Ms, Lettre a Pierre Loti..., [n.d.]. 28 pp, 4to, in half cloth bdg. Sgd. Partly autograph, & with autograph revisions throughout. star Mar 26 (30) DM240

Barrie, Sir James Matthew, 1860-1937

Autograph Ms, dialogue cards for subtitles to be used for a proposed movie of Peter Pan, [1921]. 3 pp, 8vo. Illus in cat. CNY June 9 (7) $4,000

A Ls s (2), 13 June & 6 July 1921. 2 pp, 8vo. To Josephine Lovett Robertson. Making plans for a movie version of Peter Pan. Illus in cat. CNY June 9 (6) $1,100

— ROBERTSON, JOSEPHINE LOVETT. - Typescript, scenario for a movie version of Peter Pan, [1921]. 108 pp, folio, on rectos only. Including additions & revisions on Barrie's hand on c.40 pp. CNY June 9 (8) $20,000

Barrow, Sir John, 1764-1848

Ds, 15 Dec 1840. 1 p, 13 by 11 inches. Naval appointment, also sgd by 2 others. Dar June 11 (71) $160

Barrymore, John, 1882-1942

ALs, [c.1924]. 1 p, 8vo. To Whitford [Kane]. Apologizing for forgetting "my bally lines last night". Framed with related material. Illus in cat. wd Dec 12 (301) $175

Ds, 16 June 1941. 32 pp, folio. Contract with RKO Radio Pictures for the film Playmates; carbon copy. Sgd twice. sg Feb 27 (21) $300

Barrymore, Lionel, 1878-1954

Ls, 5 Jan 1939. 1 p, 8vo. To the Rev. Walter W. Reid. Saying that "the broadcasting of 'Scrooge" has become the 'happy" part of my Christmas Day". Dar Feb 13 (45) $140

— [n.d.]. 1 p, 4to. To Rabbi Edgar F. Magnin. Expressing congratulations on the anniversary of a temple's founding. Dar Dec 26 (225) $110

Bartholdi, Frederic A., 1834-1904

Series of 14 A Ls s, 23 Dec 1874 to 21 Feb 1884. 36 pp, various sizes. To Adolphe Salmon. About the fund-raising campaign for the Statue of Liberty. With related material. P June 17 (106) $13,000

ALs, 17 May 1893. 2 pp, 8vo. To Mr. Botta. Letter of introduction for Professor Haller. Spiro collection. CNY May 14 (37) $150

Bartlett, Josiah, Signer from New Hampshire

Autograph Ms, reward notice for his runaway slave Peter, 20 Sept 1781. 1 p, 7.5 by 8 inches. Sgd. Trimmed. Dar June 11 (72) $700

ADs, 10 Sept 1783. 1 p, 13 by 8 inches. Deed conveying 2 acres in Kingston, New Hampshire, from Mary Gilman to Bartlett. Sgd 7 times; also sgd by others. R Mar 7 (185) $280

Bartok, Bela, 1881-1945

Autograph quotation, Allegro barbaro, [n.d.]. 12cm by 17cm. 13 bars, sgd. Illus in cat. S May 29 (473) £1,900 [Harrison]

Bartram, John, 1699-1777. See: Franklin, Benjamin & Bartram

Baruch, Bernard M., 1870-1965

Ls, 31 Dec 1953. 2 pp, 4to. To Harold A. Friedman. On relations with Israel. Illus in cat. sg Feb 27 (22) $1,300

Baseball

[The signatures of Joe Cronin, Bill Dickey, Joe DiMaggio, Charles Gehringer & Hank Greenberg on a ptd group photograph, [1937], 6.25 by 4.5 inches, sold at Dar on 9 Apr 1992, lot 111, for $100.]

[The signatures of Travis Jackson, Eddie Mathews, Ed Roush, Buck Leonard, Cool Papa Bell & Burleigh Grimes on a card, [n.d.], 3 by 4.5 inches, sold at wa on 19 Oct 1991, lot 77, for $80.]

[The signatures of Willie Mays, Mickey Mantle & Duke Snyder, [n.d.], on a photo after a painted composite group port, 4to, sold at wa on 19 Oct 1991, lot 84, for $120.]

[A sheet sgd by 11 baseball players who have hit at least 500 career home runs, [n.d.], folio, framed with signatures of Mel Ott, Babe Ruth & Jimmy Foxx, sold at Dar on 13 Feb 1992, lot 54, for $800.]

[The signatures of Connie Mack, Pinky Higgins, Wally Moses & Dusty Rhodes, [n.d.], on a "Wine List" for the NY Central System, 4 pp, 8vo, sold at Dar on 9 Apr 1992, lot 77, for $100.]

— Hall of Fame. - Group photograph, 21 July 1991. 14 by 11 inches. 36 Hall of Famers & baseball officials; sgd by 35, with anr signature of a person not pictured. Dar Feb 13 (68) $1,000

— NY Giants & Brooklyn Dodgers. - Photograph, 3 Oct 1951, 10 by 8 inches, of Bobby Thomson; sgd by Thomson & 17 other members of both teams. Dar Aug 6 (84) $200

— NY Yankees. - Group photograph, 1956. 10 by 8 inches. Sgd by 27 team members. Dar Dec 26 (68) $600

— NY Yankees. - Group photograph, 1952. 10 by 8 inches. Sgd by 26 members of the team. Dar Feb 13 (62) $350

— NY Yankees. - Group photograph, 1954. 10 by 8 inches. Sgd by 28 members of the team. Dar Feb 13 (63) $450

— NY Yankees. - Group photograph, 1955. 10 by 8 inches. Sgd by 27 members of the team. Dar Feb 13 (64) $300

— NY Yankees. - Group photograph, 1957. 10 by 8 inches. Sgd by 26 members of the team. Dar Feb 13 (66) $500

— NY Yankees. - Group photograph of 7 players, [n.d.]. 7 by 10 inches. Sgd by J.McCarthy, L. Gehrig, R. Ruffing, L. Gomez, J. DiMaggio, B. Dickey & R. Rolfe. Illus in cat. Shaw collection. sup July 10 (857) $3,000

— Utica BBC. - Group photograph of 13 players, 1886. 15.5 by 20.25 inches. By Mundy. R Nov 9 (216) $650

Basinio da Parma, 1425-57

Ms, Astronomicon, dedicated to Malatesta Novello. [Romagna, Rimini?, c.1455-60]. 39 leaves, vellum, 235mm by 165mm. Def 18th-cent English calf over pastebds. In a well-spaced upright rounded humanistic minuscule. With burnished gold initials throughout, 2 large whitevine initials in gold outlined in black, 3 astronomical diagrams, & 35 large miniatures. S June 23 (72) £105,000 [Pelluccioni]

Bassermann, Friedrich Daniel, 1811-55

ALs, 10 May 1848. 2 pp, 8vo. To an unnamed politician. Supporting the election of Herr Helmreich to the Frankfurt Assembly. With engraved port. star Mar 27 (1335) DM850

Bates, Edward, 1793-1869

Ls, 8 Mar 1860. 4 pp, 4to. To Joseph H. Barrett. Explaining his views on slavery in the territories, the Dred Scott decision, the admission of Kansas, etc. Sang & Spiro collections. CNY May 14 (107) $1,500

Bates, Katherine Lee, 1859-1929

Ls, 14 Jan 1924. 4 pp, 8vo. To Viola C. White. About a lecture in NY. Illus in cat. sup Oct 15 (1014) $700

Signature, [n.d.]. On ptd reproduction of her poem America the Beautiful, 3.5 by 5.5 inches. Inscr to William Charles. Framed. Dar Feb 13 (95) $400

Baudelaire, Charles, 1821-67

Autograph Ms, poem, Le vin de l'assassin, [n.d.]. 4 pp, 8vo. Working draft, sgd. P June 17 (107) $16,000

ALs, 18 Jan 1855. 1 p, 4to. To [Josephine-Elise Huriez]. Asking for news about her brother Jules Champfleury. star Mar 26 (31) DM3,100

Baudin, Nicolas, 1754-1803. See: Australia

Baudouin, King of the Belgians

Christmas card, sgd, [n.d.]. Size not stated. Also sgd by Queen Fabiola. Dar Aug 6 (111) $120

Baum, Lyman Frank, 1856-1919

ALs, 15 May 1901. 3 pp, 8vo. To the Kendall family. Thanking for flowers. sg Sept 12 (24) $1,200

Beach, Amy Marcy Cheney, 1867-1944

Autograph quotation, 3 bars "From French Suite", 2 July 1919. 5.75 by 3.75 inches. With musical quotation, sgd, by Arthur Foote on verso. Dar Feb 13 (96) $110

Bean, Roy, 1825?-1904

ALs, 25 Feb 1895. 1 p, 8vo. To G. W. Brown. Regarding papers relating to his [liquor?] license. In pencil. R Nov 9 (149) $3,500

Ds, 3 Oct 1853. 4 pp, folio. Affidavit in the Los Angeles County Court regarding his indictment for assault. sup May 9 (431) $4,600

Beatles, The

[The signatures of all 4 on their 1963 tourbook, 9 by 11 inches, sold at P on 17 Dec 1991, lot 310, for $1,600.]

[Their signatures, [c.1964], on a single piece of paper, framed with a group port, overall size 20 by 24 inches, sold at P on 17 Dec 1991, lot 322, for $1,000.]

[The signatures of all 4 on an album cover, [c.1964], sold at sup on 9 May 1992, lot 5, for $5,500.]

[Their signatures on an album cover, [n.d.], framed, 29 by 17 inches, sold at P on 17 Dec 1991, lot 344, for $1,500.]

Ds, 11 Feb 1964. 8 by 10 inches. Contract, sgd by all 4. P Dec 17 (335) $2,500

Group photograph, [n.d.]. Framed, overall size 24 by 20 inches. Sgd by all 4. Illus in cat. P Dec 17 (326) $1,400

Beaton, Cecil, 1904-80

Collection of 29 A Ls s, Ls s, & cards, sgd, 1937 to 1967. 65 pp, 4to & 8vo. To Boris Kochno & Christian Berard. About a variety of professional & personal matters. With related material. SM Oct 12 (350) FF13,000

Series of 6 A Ls s, [n.d.]. 6 pp, 4to. To Arnold Weissberger. About a variety of matters. Dar Aug 6 (9) $110

Ds, 18 Aug 1958. 2 pp, size not stated. Permission for Robert W. Lerner to use his costume designs for My Fair Lady. Also sgd by Lerner. Dar Aug 6 (41) $110

Beatty, Warren

Ds, 13 May 1974. 1 p, 4to. Contract with Michelle Phillips for the film Shampoo; also sgd by Phillips. Dar Feb 13 (97) $250

Beauharnais, Eugene de, 1781-1824

Ls, 15 May 1812. 1 p, 4to. To an unnamed prince. Requesting information about the Russian troops. star Mar 27 (1512) DM220

Beauregard, Pierre G. T., 1818-93

ALs, 3 June 1864. 2 pp, folio. To Gen. Braxton Bragg. Advising against the withdrawal of further troops from the Petersburg area. CNY Dec 5 (9) $3,800

— 31 Mar 1873. 1 p, 8vo. To Gen. W. S. Walker. Concerning recommendations for 2 officers going to Texas. Matted with ptd port. Dar June 11 (99) $550

Beauvoir, Simone de, 1908-86

Autograph Ms, Le concept chez Leibniz, initial section of an essay for the diplome d'etudes superieures en philosophie; [c.1928-29]. 20 pp, folio. Cover detached. S May 28 (195) £750 [Leinweber]

Bebel, August, 1840-1913

ALs, 8 Dec 1902. 2 pp, 8vo. Recipient unnamed. Responding to a request for help in a legal matter. star Mar 27 (1270) DM750

Bechstein, Ludwig, 1801-60

Autograph Ms (2), stories, Die Bauern von Lappenhausen, 4 chapters; & Das Pferdefleisch-Mahl; [n.d.]. 11 pp, folio & 4to. 1 sgd L.B. at head. With anr, fragment. star Mar 26 (34) DM370

Beck, Ludwig, 1880-1944

Collection of ALs & photograph, 6 May 1939. 1 p, folio, & size not stated. To [H. E.] Friedrich. Suggesting a date for his visit. star Mar 27 (1751) DM660

Beckett, Samuel, 1906-89

Collection of 2 A Ls s & 14 autograph postcards, sgd, 22 June 1964 to 27 June 1989. 16 pp, 8vo. To Sean (1) & Eileen O'Casey. Referring to his activities, his health, O'Casey's plays, etc. C Dec 16 (277) £1,500 [Doran]

Corrected proof, Collected Shorter Prose 1945-1980; [1984]. 111 large double-page sheets of photocopies. Including several hundred autograph corrections. With 7 pp of queries by the copy-editor with autograph answers & further related material. S July 21 (89) £3,000 [Horowitz]

— Anr, Collected Poems 1930-1978; [1984]. 95 double-page sheets of photocopies. Including autograph corrections on c.60 pp. With related ANs. S July 21 (90) £3,000 [Horowitz]

Beckley, Jacob P., 1867-1918

Signature, [n.d.]. Matted with Hall of Fame card, overall size 8 by 10 inches. Dar Feb 13 (70) $450

Beckwith, James Carroll, 1852-1917

Autograph Ms, diary, [n.d.]. 60 pp, 12mo, in limp cloth bdg. Mostly about his travels from Paris to Switzerland; sgd. wa Oct 19 (16) $130

Bee, Barnard Elliott, 1791?-1855

ALs, 2 Aug 1839. 3 pp, size not stated. To the US Consul at Vera Cruz. Mentioning Santa Anna & the growth of the Texas Navy. rf Sept 21 (3) $325

Bee, Barnard Elliott, 1824-61

Photograph, sgd, [n.d.]. Carte size. Sgd on mount. R Nov 9 (78) $750

Beerbohm, Max, 1872-1956

Autograph Ms, introduction to John Rothenstein's The Portrait Drawings of William Rothenstein, sgd & dated 19 Aug 1925. 9 pp, folio, on rectos only. CNY Dec 5 (162) $5,000

Original drawing, caricature of "Archbishop of Benson giving Mr Henry James the idea for The Turn of The Screw", 1920. 10 by 13.5 inches. In pencil & wash. Sgd Max & inscr to E[dmund] G[osse]. S July 21 (96) £1,200 [Piccadilly Gallery]

ALs, 23 Feb 1909. 3 pp, 8vo. To Frederick Whelen. Asking for the script of a play by Henry James. pn June 11 (69) £220

— 6 May 1947. 1 p, size not stated. To Mr. Carson. Declining to write a preface for James Agate's work. Ck Apr 3 (2) £60

Beethoven, Ludwig van, 1770-1827

Autograph music, 2 canons, Schwenke dich, ohne Schwaenke; & Hoffmann, sei ja kein Hofmann; [1820s]. 1 p, 4to. On six staves; including some corrections. Illus in cat. Mannheim collection. S Dec 6 (3) £19,000 [Wilson]

— Autograph music, Piano Sonata in E minor Op. 90, 16 Aug 1814 & later. 28 pp & blanks, folio, in 19th-cent half calf bdg. Working Ms of the complete sonata, sgd. Notated on up to 12 staves per page. Including later ownership inscr. Illus in cat. S Dec 6 (32) £1,000,000 [Haas]

— Autograph music, sketches for Die Weihe des Hauses, Op. 124; [Sept 1822]. 4 pp, 4to, in later yellow mor bdg. 32 bars on 2 systems of 8 staves per page. In black ink & pencil. Including material relating to provenance. Illus in cat. Searles-Rowland collection. C June 24 (3) £30,000 [Zia]

Autograph transcript, Chorus "And with his Stripes", from Handel's Messiah; [c.1821]. 5 pp & 3 blanks, folio. Vocal parts only, without continuo; 91 bars notated on up to 4 systems per page, 4 staves each. Including some sketches, possibly for the Missa Solemnis. Illus in cat. S Dec 6 (33) £45,000 [Sawyer]

Ms, part of his household account book, also used as conversation book, 7 July to 1 Aug [1823]. 8 pp, folio. In the hand of a servant, extensively annotated by Beethoven; recording purchases, menus, & conversations. Illus in cat. S Dec 6 (35) £17,000 [Bagnasco]

ALs, [Summer 1811]. 1 p, 8vo. To Friedrich von Drieberg. Agreeing to review recipient's compositions. Illus in cat. star Mar 27 (970) DM32,000

— 23 Aug [1823]. 1 p, 4to. To K. F. Mueller. Expressing his willingness to be of assistance. Illus in cat. Mannheim collection. S Dec 6 (2) £10,500 [Haas]

Behan, Brendan, 1923-64

Autograph postcard, sgd, [26 Nov 1960]. To Louis Sobel. Reporting about a musical. Dar Apr 9 (118) $160

Behrens, Peter, 1868-1940

ALs, 24 Mar 1901. 1 p, 4to. To Otto Harnack. Sending 2 essays. star Mar 27 (873) DM280

Beiderbecke, Leon B. ("Bix"), 1903-31

Cut signature, [n.d.]. 3.12 by 1 inches. Illus in cat. Dar Apr 9 (119) $400

Signature, [n.d.]. Size not stated. Framed with a photograph. Dar Oct 10 (88) $1,800

Beireis, Gottfried Christoph, 1730-1809

ALs, 30 Oct 1789. 1 p, 4to. To [Friederike Lohmann?]. Sending some medication. star Mar 26 (548) DM700

Belais, Abraham, 1773-1853

Ms, acrostic poems in honor of Augustus Frederick, Duke of Sussex, in Hebrew. [London, 1824]. 13 pp, 187mm by 140mm. Contemp red mor gilt. Probably autograph. Phillipps Ms 14068. S June 23 (53) £650 [Landau]

Belasco, David, 1853-1931

Photograph, sgd & inscr, 9 May 1921. 6.5 by 9 inches. Inscr to Marguerite St. Clair. Dar Feb 13 (98) $170

Belknap, William Worth, 1829-90

ALs, 3 Sept 1870. 1 p, 8vo. To the committee of the "Schuetzen Verein Germania". Declining an invitation. Framed. Illus in cat. Armstrong collection. sup Oct 15 (1110) $140

Cut signature, 16 May [n.y.]. 5 by 1.75 inches. Framed. Armstrong collection. sup Oct 15 (1111) $100

Bell, Alexander Graham, 1847-1922

ALs, 6 Jan 1889. 1 p, 8vo. To Alonzo Bell. Forwarding a check. sup Oct 15 (1017) $900

— 10 June 1891. 4 pp, 4to. To Daisy M. Way. About the teaching of speech to the deaf &

the Whipple Natural Alphabet. With related material. Illus in cat. sup Oct 15 (1015) $1,900

— [n.d.]. 1 p, 8vo. To President Gilman of Johns Hopkins University. Arranging a meeting with Simon Newcomb. wa Oct 19 (85) $950

Ls, 15 Feb 1897. 1 p, 8vo. To Daisy Way. Responding to her offer to come & help in a school matter. Illus in cat. sup Oct 15 (1018) $1,250

— 12 Mar 1912. 1 p, 4to. To Howard T. Myers. Sending his autograph. sup Oct 15 (1019) $850

— 6 June 1912. 1 p, 4to. To Daisy Way. Offering his help if she is seeking new employment. Illus in cat. sup Oct 15 (1016) $900

— 15 Aug 1919. 1 p, 8vo. To Sec of the Interior Franklin K. Lane. Thanking for a copy of recipient's address relating to the ratification of the treaty of peace. Framed with a photograph. Dar June 11 (100) $950

— 10 Mar 1922. 1 p, 8vo. Recipient unnamed. Sending his autograph. Illus in cat. Dar Feb 13 (99) $500

Bellini, Vincenzo, 1801-35

Autograph music, beginning of the chorus Guerra, Guerra le Galliche selve, from his opera Norma, [c.Oct 1831]. 4 pp, folio. 46 bars in full score, including revisions. Partly differing from pbd score. Illus in cat. S Dec 6 (37) £42,000 [Franks]

— Autograph music, drafts of melodies for his operas Norma, Beatrice di Tenda, & I Puritani, [c.Sept 1831]. 2 pp, folio. 140 bars in 16 separate sketches, notated on 15 staves. Illus in cat. S Dec 6 (38) £34,000 [Franks]

— Autograph music, sketches for Act 2, scene 1 of his opera La Sonnambula, [c.15 Feb 1831]. 2 pp, folio. About 140 bars, notated on 5 systems of up to 3 staves each. Illus in cat. S Dec 6 (36) £8,000 [Franks]

ALs, 23 Sept [1834]. 3 pp, 8vo. To Giovanni Ricordi. Complaining that Ricordi has sold copies of his opera Norma without telling him, & reporting about progress on I Puritani. Illus in cat. S Dec 6 (39) £19,000 [Franks]

— 1 July [18]35. 3 pp, 8vo. To Paul Barroilhet. Describing the weaknesses of the libretto for I Puritani, & making suggestions for a forthcoming performance at Palermo. Illus in cat. S May 29 (483) £12,500 [Franks]

— Bishop, Sir Henry R. - Autograph Ms, orchestration of Bellini's La Sonnambula for a performance in London, 1833. 460 pp, folio, in 2 vols. Working Ms. S May 29 (484) £2,400 [Verzi]

— Pacini, Giovanni. - Ls, 24 Apr 1855. 2 pp, 4to. To Filippo Cicconetti. Recounting how he consoled Bellini after the failure of Norma in Milan. S May 29 (485) £2,000 [Verzi]

Bellow, Saul

Ls, 15 Oct 1953. 1 p, 4to. To Ted [Hubler?]. Reacting to reviews of his novel The Adventures of Augie March. CNY June 9 (14) $380

Beloe, Edward Milligan

Series of c.295 A Ls s, 13 May 1879 to 24 May 1892. About 700 pp, 4to & 8vo. To his son Edward. Referring to family matters, his professional & literary work, etc. With numerous pen-&-ink sketches. bba Sept 19 (347) £400 [Quaritch]

Benda, Georg, 1722-95

ADs, 7 Jan 1751. 1 p, 4to. Receipt to the treasury of Sachsen-Gotha for paper & writing material for the orchestra. star Mar 27 (972) DM850

Bender, Charles Albert ("Chief"), 1883-1954

Photograph, sgd, 1953. 7 by 10 inches. Dar Dec 26 (73) $600

Signature, [n.d.]. 16mo (card). Dar Dec 26 (74) $300

Ben-Gurion, David, 1886-1973

ALs, 6 May 1954. 1 p, 8vo. To Moshe Sharett. Expressing frustration with the United Nations & Egytian violations of the freedom of passage through the Suez Canal. Dar Oct 10 (226) $1,500

— 13 Oct [19]54. 1 p, 8vo. To Henry Isaac. Commenting on "the best way ... to contribute to a world of better understanding". sg Sept 12 (26) $550

— 28 Mar 1955. 1 p, 8vo. To Rabbi Zalman Kahana. Insisting that Israel cannot be ruled on a purely religious basis but must be established as a democracy. Illus in cat. Dar Aug 6 (187) $1,200

— 4 July 1955. 3 pp, 8vo. To Moshe Sharett. Deciding that the Foreign Ministry has no authority concerning cease-fire instructions. Illus in cat. sup May 9 (458) $1,000

— 15 Mar 1966. 1 p, 8vo. To Yariv Shapira. Looking forward to meeting the son of a friend of his youth. Dar June 11 (255) $750

— 21 Jan 1967. 1 p, 8vo. To Ida M. Silverman. Protesting that he "never heard that [his] records and memoirs are or will be at Brandeis University." Dar Oct 10 (227) $550

— 6 July 1967. 1 p, 8vo. To Justin Turner. Asking for an old photograph & referring to the Six Day War. Illus in cat. sup Oct 15 (1021) $1,300

Ls, 26 Aug 1951. 1 p, 4to. To Rabbi Isadore

Breslau. Thanking for help in the USA. wa Mar 5 (273) $550

— 14 May 1955. 1 p, 8vo. To Seif el Din Zoubi. Commenting on the Egyptian revolution. Dar Dec 26 (227) $1,100

— 16 Oct 1955. 1 p, 8vo. To Moshe Dayan. Carbon copy addressed to Moshe Sharett, insisting on the importance of air power for Israel's defense against Egypt. Dar Oct 10 (229) $1,800

— [1955]. 1 p, 8vo. To Yakov Riftin. Carbon copy addressed to Moshe Sharett, referring to the banning of Zionist movements in communist countries. Dar Oct 10 (228) $1,200

— 20 Feb 1956. 1 p, 8vo. To Zerah Warhaftig. Stating that Israelis will "read literature of all nations and ... will seek wisdom wherever we can find it". Dar Aug 6 (188) $1,500

Autograph postcard, sgd, 30 June 1921. To his father Wiktor Gruen. About sightseeing in Rome, Michelangelo's Moses & the Vatican Museums. Dar June 11 (254) $1,200

Group photograph, [1957]. 9 by 7 inches. With 3 others; sgd by Ben-Gurion. Dar Oct 10 (230) $400

Photograph, sgd & inscr, [n.d.]. 8 by 10 inches. By Shelburne Studios. sg Sept 12 (25) $275

Benjamin, Judah P., 1811-84

ALs, 7 Oct 1861. 1 p, 4to. To Major Gen. Gustavus Woodson Smith. Responding to a memorandum addressed to President Davis regarding 2 officers. Illus in cat. Spiro collection. CNY May 14 (38) $5,500

ADs, 20 May 1835. 1 p, 4to. As attorney in the case of James Watt v. John P. Phillips, consent to take the testimony of a witness. Dar Dec 26 (226) $400

Benjamin, Walter, 1892-1940

ALs, 16 May 1939. 1 p, 8vo. To Bernard von Brentano. Reporting about his stay at Pontigny. star Mar 26 (38) DM2,800

Ls, 23 Oct 1930. 1 p, 4to. To Bernard von Brentano. About several literary projects. star Mar 26 (37) DM1,800

Benn, Gottfried, 1886-1956

Collection of ALs & ANs, 30 Dec 1940 & 24 Dec 1941. 3 pp, 12mo. To Alexander Amersdorffer. Contents not stated. star Mar 26 (40) DM800

ALs, 13 Mar 1914. 1 p, 8vo. To Paul Zech. Denying that others have persuaded him not to publish in Zech's journal. star Mar 26 (39) DM1,600

— 30 June 1924. 2 pp, 8vo. To Dr. Sinsheimer. Expressing doubts that he will be able to contribute to the journal Simplizissimus. HH Nov 6 (2024) DM900

Bennett, William Sterndale, 1816-75

Autograph music, 2 piano works, Etudes in G minor & E flat major, Jan 1841. 8 pp, folio, in modern bds. Working Mss, sgd. Marked by the ptr. S May 29 (486) £850 [Macnutt]

Benny, Jack, 1894-1974

Series of 3 Ls s, 1968 & 1969. 3 pp, 4to. Recipient unnamed. Regarding a book & a TV tribute to Eleanor Roosevelt. Dar June 11 (101) $225

Benson, Edward Frederic, 1867-1940

Series of 7 A Ls s, March 1932 to March 1936. Length not stated. To Mr. Riggs. Discussing literature & advising him on style. Ck Apr 3 (3) £170

Bentham, Jeremy, 1748-1832

ALs, 25 Feb 1801. 2 pp, 4to. To J. H. Pye. Discussing a financial pamphlet by Boyd. Def. Dawson Turner collection. pn Nov 14 (116) £130 [Browning]

— 17 June 1803. 2 pp, 8vo. To Sir Charles Bunbury. Complaining about Lord Pelham's reaction to a proposal put forward by Bentham. Dawson Turner collection. pn Nov 14 (117) £340 [Wilson]

Ben-Yehuda, Eliezer, 1858-1922

Autograph Ms, notes concerning the origins of the Hebrew word for "inferior". 1 p, 8vo. Frayed. With a photograph. Dar June 11 (256) $400

ALs, [n.d.]. 3 pp, 8vo. To Chief Rabbi Abraham Isaac Kook. Requesting assistance in a trans problem. sg Dec 19 (23) $350

Berard, Christian, 1902-49

[An archive of letters & papers of Berard, including letters by Boris Kochno (c.50) & numerous artists, authors, etc., c.1930 to 1949, c.150 pp, various sizes, sold at SM on 12 Oct 1991, lot 353, for FF22,000.]

Original drawings, to illus Colette's Gigi, 1950. Number not stated; various sizes. In gouache & pastel. With copy of the book. Boris Kochno collection. SM Oct 11 (134) FF92,000

— Original drawings, to illus J. Gaultier-Boissiere's La Bonne Vie, 1944. Number not stated; various sizes. In gouache, colored crayons & pastel. With copy of the book. Boris Kochno collection. SM Oct 11 (132) FF120,000

— Original drawings, to illus Jean Giradoux's Sodome et Gomorrhe, 1943. Number not stated; various sizes. Mainly in gouache. Boris Kochno collection. SM Oct 11 (133) FF13,000

Berg, Alban, 1885-1935

AL, 20/21 Mar [1932]. 4 pp, 8vo. To [Anny A.]. Love letter, reminiscing about their meeting. star Mar 27 (973a) DM3,200

— [Spring 1932]. 2 p, 8vo. To [Anny A.]. Love letter, about their separation. Fragment. star Mar 27 (973b) DM1,100

Bergengruen, Werner, 1892-1964

Ls s (2), 19 June 1936 & 19 Jan 1937. 5 pp, folio. To Bruno Schneider. Interpreting his novel Der Grosstyrann und das Gericht, & mentioning work on his new novel. With related material. star Mar 26 (41) DM850

Bergman, Ingrid, 1915-82

ALs, 3 Sept 1949. 5 pp, 4to. Recipient unnamed. Discussing her marriage & her love affair with Rosselini. With related material. wd Dec 12 (302) $1,200

Ds, 22 Jan 1947. 1 p, 4to. Contract for a "radio version of the play Still Life". Dar June 11 (102) $120

Group photograph, 1944. 7.5 by 9.75 inches. With Joseph Cotten; sgd by Bergman. Dar Feb 13 (100) $275

Photograph, sgd, [n.d.]. 8 by 10 inches. Half length. Dar Dec 26 (122) $170

Bergmann, Ernst von, 1836-1907

A Ls s (2), 30 Nov & 19 Dec 1902. 6 pp, 8vo. To an unnamed colleague. Regarding recipient's contribution to his Handbuch der speziellen Chirurgie. star Mar 26 (549) DM480

Berkeley, Busby, 1895-1976

ALs, 14 Aug 1964. 1 p, 4to. To Mary Garvin. Mentioning pictures made for a television series. Dar Oct 10 (89) $130

Berkeley, George Cranfield, 17th Baron Berkeley, 1753-1818

ALs, 24 June 1811. 3 pp, 4to. To Francis Freeling. Putting forward a plan for the improvement of postal services in the Mediterranean & at Cadiz. With anr. pn Nov 14 (138) £200

Berlin, Irving, 1888-1989

Typescript, lyrics for his song Easter Parade, [n.d.]. Size not stated. Sgd. Illus in cat. sup Oct 15 (1023) $1,500

Ls, 9 Nov 1927. 1 p, 8vo. To Nat Shilkret. About a projected show at the Strand Theatre. Framed with a telegram. Dar Apr 9 (121) $350

— 15 Feb 1963. 1 p, 4to. To Harry Ruby. About a forthcoming dinner in his honor. Dar Oct 10 (90) $300

— 10 Feb 1971. 1 p, 4to. To Harry Ruby. Complimenting him on a show & mentioning Groucho Marx. Dar Oct 10 (91) $400

— 1 June 1973. 1 p, 4to. To Sol C. Siegel. Thanking for congratulations on his birthday. sup Oct 15 (1024) $450

Photograph, sgd, [1930s]. 7 by 9 inches. Framed. Dar Apr 9 (122) $300

Berlioz, Hector, 1803-69

ALs, 6 Mar [1834]. 2 pp, 8vo. To Antoni Deschamps. Thanking for his verses in praise of his overture King Lear. S May 29 (488) £1,000 [Gorsen]

— 29 Dec 1838. 1 p, 8vo. To M. Barbier. Sending 6 copies of his mass composed for the funeral service of Gen. Danremont. Framed with a port. P June 17 (2) $1,300

— [1853]. 1 p, 4to. To Louis Pierre Deffes. Inquiring about a missing score. star Mar 27 (975) DM1,000

— 2 Feb [n.y.]. 1 p, 8vo. To the prefect of the Departement de la Seine. Asking for an interview. star Mar 27 (977) DM1,000

— [n.d.], "Monday". 3 pp, 12mo. To Ferdinand David. About changes to the German Ed of a score. Including 4 musical quotations. star Mar 27 (976) DM3,000

Autograph quotation, 13 bars from Romeo et Juliette, 12 Feb 1846. 1 p, 21cm by 28.5cm. Sgd. S Dec 6 (41) £2,500 [Benjamin]

— Anr, Theme de la Sicilienne de Beatrice et Benedict, 4 Apr 1863. 1 p, 8vo. 8 bars, sgd. Illus in cat. star Mar 27 (974) DM4,800

Berman, Eugene

Series of 15 A Ls s, 1936 to [1960]. 39 pp, 4to. To Boris Kochno. About ballets, his naturalization as American citizen, etc. SM Oct 12 (352) FF10,000

Bernadotte, Jean Baptiste, 1763-1844. See: Charles XIV John, 1763-1844

Bernard, Saint (Bernardus Claravallensis, 1091-1153

Ms, Meditationes de Cognitione Humanae Conditionis. [Germany, c.1450]. 12 pp, 278mm by 195mm. 19th-cent vellum bdg. In a gothic bookhand. S Dec 17 (51) £550 [Derry]

Berners, Gerald, Lord, 1883-1950. See: Tyrwhitt-Wilson, Gerald Hugh

Bernhard, Herzog von Sachsen-Weimar, 1604-39

ALs, 5 Apr [n.y.]. 1 p, folio. To an unnamed prince. Responding to recipient's letter & requesting more time. Illus in cat. HN Nov 28 (1639) DM4,800

Ls, 23 Nov 1632. 1 p, folio. To Landgraf Wilhelm V von Hessen-Kassel. Urging him to come to his camp to discuss some important matters. star Mar 27 (1704) DM1,000

Bernhardt, Sarah, .1923

ALs, 1869. 1 p, 8vo. Recipient unnamed. Announcing her visit. sup Oct 15 (1025) $400

Bernstein, Eduard, 1850-1932

Autograph postcard, sgd, 28 Oct 1902. To E. A. Marescotti. Reflecting on the prospects of socialism as a political idea. In French. star Mar 27 (1275) DM320

Bernstein, Leonard, 1918-90 —& Hellman, Lilian, 1905-84

Ds, 14 Jan 1955. 15 pp, 4to. Production contract for Candide. Also initialled by both on 8 pages. Dar Apr 9 (224) $425

Berthier, Alexandre, Prince de Wagram, 1753-1815

Ls, [Nov 1805]. 1 p, folio. To Moreau de St. Mercy at Parma. Instructing him to report about Italian affairs. star Mar 27 (1366) DM280

Berzelius, Jons Jacob von, 1779-1848

ALs, 24 Apr 1832. 3 pp, 4to. To Pierre Louis Dulong. Worrying about recipient's health & reporting about his recent experiments. star Mar 26 (550) DM1,400

Bessieres, Jean Baptiste, Duc d'Istrie, 1768-1813

Ls, 3 Sept 1808. 1 p, 4to. To the Paymaster General. Asking him to order the corps paymaster to report to headquarters. sg Feb 27 (24) $250

Bewick, Thomas, 1753-1828

ALs, 21 Nov 1804. 1 p, size not stated. Recipient unnamed. Discussing the work on a new Ed of his 2 vols on birds. Ck Apr 3 (79) £800

Bialik, Hayyim Nahman, 1873-1934

Autograph postcard, sgd, [n.d.]. To Hadassa Segalowitsch. Sending greetings from Carlsbad. Addressed in anr hand; also inscr by others. Dar Oct 10 (232) $150

Photograph, sgd, [n.d.]. Postcard size. Sgd on verso. Dar Oct 10 (231) $300

Bible Manuscripts, Latin

— [Northern Italy, c.1075]. Single leaf, vellum, 456mm by 324mm. In black ink in late Caroline minuscules by more than one hand. With large decorated initial. Recovered from a bdg. pn Nov 14 (236) £2,600 [Finch]

— [Paris, c.1250-75]. 463 leaves, vellum, 148mm by 102mm. 18th-cent red mor gilt. With Prologues & Interpretation of Hebrew Names. In a very small gothic bookhand by more than 1 scribe. With c.80 large painted initials often incorporating dragons & animals, & very large historiated initial. S June 23 (58) £12,000 [Enlumineures]

— [Central Italy, Bologna?, c.1285]. Single leaf, end of Leviticus & opening of Book of Numbers, vellum, 197mm by 225mm. In brown ink in a small round gothic bookhand. With 3-line painted initial with full-length penwork extension & historiated initial in grey, pink & orange on blue ground. C Dec 16 (1) £800 [Gibbs]

— [Northern France, c.1330]. Single leaf, opening of the Book of Wisdom, vellum, 400mm by 265mm. In brown ink in a gothic bookhand. With 4 illuminated initials extending into bar borders & large historiated initial. C Dec 16 (2) £1,600 [Fogg]

— [Bologna, 1471]. The Bible of the Fishmongers' Guild of Bologna. 448 leaves, vellum, 303mm by 204mm. 19th-cent blindstamped calf bdg by Tartagli. In a small semi-gothic notarial hand by Nicolaus of Scardona. With 3-line chapter initials throughout in burnished gold on panel grounds, c.175 very large illuminated initials in leafy & floral designs in colors on highly burnished gold panel grounds with marginal sprays of gold bezants within penwork, & coat of arms within gold wreath. 2 miniatures cut out. S Dec 17 (53) £18,000 [Fogg]

Ms, Books of Solomon; glossed. [Paris?, c.1200-20]. 229 leaves, vellum, 260mm by 190mm. Late 19th-cent English tan mor gilt. In 2 sizes of very early gothic hands by 3 scribes. With 8 very large initials in colors in 2 different styles & contemp sidenotes throughout with many small drawings as cartouches around notes including animals & faces. Illus in cat. S June 23 (59) £23,000 [Fogg]

— Ms, New Testament, with concordances & prologues. [Germany, c.1450]. 264 leaves (11 lacking), 316mm by 217mm. Contemp blindstamped tanned lea over wooden bds with metal corner-pieces. In a gothic cursive bookhand. With large & small decorated initials throughout. S June 23 (62) £5,000 [Fogg]

Bienek, Horst

Autograph transcript, poem, Angeklagt, Feb 1979. 1 p, 8vo. 11 lines, sgd. star Mar 26 (43) DM450

Billroth, Theodor, 1829-94

ALs, 21 May 1881. 8 pp, 8vo. Recipient unnamed. Giving advice about a patient, discussing weakness & frailty as a hereditary problem, etc. star Mar 26 (551) DM3,600

— 24 Aug 1891. 2 pp, 8vo (lettercard). To Anton von Eiselsberg. Giving instructions about a knee bandage for a patient. star Mar 26 (552) DM580

Bishop, Henry R., Sir, 1786-1855. See: Bellini, Vincenzo

Bismarck, Herbert von, 1849-1904

Series of 3 A Ls s, 9 June 1901 to 24 June 1904. 12 pp, 8vo. To "Uncle Janos". About family matters. star Mar 27 (1280) DM230

Bismarck, Otto von, 1815-98

Autograph Ms, school essay, De expeditione Athenensium in Siciliam insulam suscepta, [1831]. 3 pp, 4to. Sgd at head. star Mar 27 (1276) DM3,000

ALs, 19 Jan 1832. 1 p, 4to. To Gustav von Kessel. Humorous letter inquiring about a wish voiced by his brother. star Mar 27 (1277) DM2,800

— 26 May 1875. 2 pp, 4to. To Chlodwig Fuerst von Hohenlohe-Schillingsfuerst. About relations with France & the German embassy in Paris. Illus in cat. HH May 13 (1898) DM1,400

— 5 Apr 1892. 1 p, 21cm by 14cm. Recipient & contents not stated. Mtd with a port. JG Sept 27 (312) DM360

Ls, 18 Jan 1869. 1 p, 4to. To Graf von Stillfried. Inquiring about the program for a festivity. HN Nov 28 (1642) DM220

— 21 Apr 1878. 2 pp, 4to. To Crown Prince Friedrich Wilhelm. Hoping that his health will allow him to return to Berlin soon. Repaired. star Mar 27 (1278) DM650

Bizet, Georges, 1838-75

ALs, [Dec 1872]. 2 pp, 16mo & 8vo. To [the singer Daram?]. Explaining that he has been absorbed in rehearsals for Gounod's Romeo et Juliette. S May 29 (492) £1,300 [Franks]

— [c.1872]. 1 p, 4to. Recipient unnamed. Thanking for a review of his opera Djamileh. S May 29 (493) £750 [Franks]

Bjoernson, Bjoernstjerne, 1832-1910

ALs, 7 Apr 1901. 1 p, 4to. To his daughter Dagny & her husband Albert Langen. About his recovery after a long bout with influenza. Sgd B.B. star Mar 26 (46) DM230

Black, Shirley Temple. See: Temple, Shirley

Blaine, James G., 1830-93

Series of 4 Ls s, 1889 & 1890. 13 pp, size not stated. To Felix C. C. Zegarra. Regarding matters pertaining to relations with Peru. Dar Aug 6 (122) $100

Blair, Ida Muriel, 1875-1943. See: Orwell, George & Blair

Blanc, Mel, 1908-89

ALs, 30 Apr 1973. 1 p, 8vo. To R. D. Stating that he does "about 97% of all the voices in Warner Bros Cartoons". Dar Dec 26 (124) $250

Photograph, sgd & inscr, 17 Sept [19]84. 8 by 10 inches. With cartoon characters; inscr to Andrew. Dar Apr 9 (124) $120

Bland, Theodorick, 1742-90

ALs, [22 Apr 1777]. 2 pp, 4to. To an unnamed general. About problems with his regiment. Dar Apr 9 (125) $120

Blane, Ralph. See: Martin, Hugh & Blane

Bligh, William, 1754-1817

ALs, 25 June 1817. 1 p, 4to. Recipient unnamed. Sending an account of his family. Longueville collection. S June 25 (174) £2,500 [Maddalena]

Bloch, Ernst, 1885-1977

ALs, [24 Jan 1966]. 2 pp, 8vo. To Erwin von Bendemann. Regretting that he was not able to attend a friend's funeral. star Mar 26 (553) DM650

Bloch, Felix, 1905-83

Ls, 11 Mar 1975. 1 p, folio. Recipient unnamed. Insisting that there is nothing comparable to the hippocratic oath in science. star Mar 26 (554) DM300

Blomberg, Werner von, 1878-1946

Ls, 25 Oct 1933. 1 p, 4to. To Heinrich Himmler. Regarding an interrogation to be reported to President Hindenburg. Initialled by Himmler. Dar Apr 9 (126) $225

Blount, William, 1749-1800

Ds, 16 May 1795. 1 p, folio. As Governor, pay order in favor of William Rickard. sg Sept 12 (27) $550

— 14 July 1795. 1 p, 4to. To David Henley. Pay order in favor of William Rickard. sup Oct 15 (1027) $500

Bluecher von Wahlstatt, Gebhard Leberecht, Fuerst, 1742-1819

ALs, 21 May 1797. 1 p, 4to. To A. W. von Pletz. Sending a list of emigrants intending to return to their native country. star Mar 27 (1281) DM1,800

— [1810]. 1 p, 4to. To some army officials. Inquiring about a reduction in his salary. star Mar 27 (1282) DM1,100

— 7 Oct 1813. 2 pp, 4to. To his wife. Worrying about their son's wounds, & suggesting that she stay in Breslau. Illus in cat. star Mar 27 (1284) DM2,600

— 3 June 1814. 4 pp, 4to. To his wife. About honors received in Paris & his projected stay in England, & promising not to leave her again after this campaign. star Mar 27 (1285) DM8,500

Ls, 31 Mar 1813. 1 p, folio. To Prince August of Prussia. Suggesting that guns be provided for Major von Luetzow's company. Endorsed by recipient on verso. star Mar 27 (1283) DM900

Blumenbach, Johann Friedrich, 1752-1840

ALs, 20 Oct 1814. 3 pp, 8vo. To Friedrich von Matthisson. About his Handbuch der Naturgeschichte, & reminiscing about their meeting 20 years ago. star Mar 26 (555) DM320

Blunden, Edmund Charles, 1896-1974

Autograph Ms, essay, A Appreciation [of Coleridge's The Ancient Mariner], n.d. 11 pp, size not stated. Including some corrections; sgd. Ck Apr 3 (43) £380

Collection of 22 A Ls s & 2 Mss, 12 Mar 1922 to 1924. Length not stated. To Henry Major Tomlinson. On a variety of matters, & 2 book reviews. Ck Apr 3 (42) £1,300

Bly, Nellie, 1867-1922. See: Seaman, Elizabeth Cochrane ("Nellie Bly")

Boccherini, Luigi, 1743-1805

Ds, 18 Aug 1797. 1 p, 12cm by 18cm. Receipt to the pbr Pleyel for payment for "douze Arietes". S Dec 6 (44) £2,200 [Haas]

Boehm, Karl, 1894-1981

ADs, 29 May 1952. 1 p, folio. Testimonial for Marcel Cuvelier. HN Nov 28 (1644) DM200

Boell, Heinrich, 1917-85

ALs, 31 Mar 1960. 1 p, 8vo. Recipient unnamed. Responding to a request for his autograph. star Mar 26 (50) DM260

Boetticher, Hans, 1883-1934. See: Ringelnatz, Joachim

Bogart, Humphrey, 1899-1957

Ds, 22 Sept 1953. 1 p, 4to. Release from his contract with Warner Brothers. Dar Dec 26 (126) $900

Photograph, sgd & inscr, [n.d.]. 8 by 10 inches. Inscr to Elaine. Dar Dec 26 (125) $1,300

Signature, [26 Sept 1936]. Framed with a photograph, overall size 18 by 29 inches. sup Oct 15 (1028) $320

Bohemia

[A vol of contemp official certified copies of the agreements preceeding the Letter of Majesty, 19 Mar to 3 July 1690, 78 pp, folio, in contemp vellum wraps, sold at S on 5 Dec 1991, lot 470, for £5,000 to Mandl.]

Bohr, Niels, 1885-1962

Ptd photograph, sgd, [n.d.]. 3 by 2.5 inches. With Irene Joliot-Curie & J. H. Bhsaghn. Mtd. Dar Apr 9 (127) $150

Boie, Heinrich Christian, 1744-1806

ALs, 4 Oct 1780. 1 p, 8vo. To Christian Julius Ludwig Steltzer. Hoping that he will soon be able to publish the German trans of the Odyssey by J. H. Voss. 4 lines deleted. star Mar 26 (49) DM1,900

Bolingbroke, Henry St. John, Viscount, 1678-1751

— PALMER?, SECRETARY TO BOLINGBROKE. - Ms, Bacchanalian Triumphs, [early 18th cent]. 77 leaves & blanks, 4to, in 18th-cent black mor. Elaborate mock-scholarly essay, written on the occasion of a gift of a hogshed of wine from Bolingbroke. In a calligraphic hand, with 2 pen-&-ink headpieces & historiated initials. bba June 25 (144) £950 [Maggs]

Bolivar, Simon, 1783-1830

Ls, 22 Jan 1830. 2 pp, 4to. To Jose Rafael Arboleda. Informing him about changes in the ministry. CNY Dec 5 (11) $4,000

— 27 Feb 1830. 2 pp, 4to. To Jose Rafael Arboleda. Informing him about a commission sent to Venezuela. CNY Dec 5 (12) $1,500

— 5 Nov 1830. 2 pp, 4to. To Gen. Mariano Montilla. Worrying about the military situation. CNY Dec 5 (13) $1,800

— 18 Nov 1830. 3 pp, 4to. To Gen. Mariano Montilla. Commenting on regional strife & the necessity of ending disaccord. Including autograph postscript. CNY Dec 5 (14) $2,800

— 7 Dec 1830. 4 pp, 4to. To Gen. Rafael Urdaneta. Urging him to reconcile his differences with Gen. Briceno. With autograph postscript. CNY Dec 5 (15) $2,800

Ds, 26 Feb 1819. 2 pp, 4to. Order to deliver cattle for the army. Illus in cat. sup May 9 (459) $2,100

— 7 Sept 1819. 1 p, folio. Military promotion for Lieut. Rafael Villalobos. S May 28 (163) £600 [Saggiori]

Bonaparte, Jerome, 1784-1860

Ls, 3 Jan 1814. 1 p, 4to. To Gen. Clarke. Letter of recommendation for Gen. Chabert. star Mar 27 (1511) DM420

Ds, 19 Aug 1808. 35 pp, folio. Code de Procedure criminelle for the Kingdom of Westfalia; also sgd by others. star Mar 27 (1510) DM2,400

Bonaparte, Joseph, 1768-1844

ALs, 15 Mar 1822. 1 p, 4to. To Mr. Nancrede. In 3d person, transmitting a payment. sg Feb 27 (26) $90

Boone, Daniel, 1734-1820

ALs, 6 May 1803. 1 p, 8vo. To the Court of the Distict of St. Charles. Concerning payment of a bill. Illus in cat. sup May 9 (363) $11,000

Ds, 12 Mar 1783. 1 p, 7.75 by 2.6 inches. Certification of an appraisal of a horse lost in the battle at Blue Licks, 1782. Illus in cat. sup May 9 (364) $5,000

— 24 Oct 1787. 3 by 9.25 inches. Receipt for £101 for provisions for Indian prisoners. Illus in cat. sup Oct 15 (1030) $7,500

— 15 June 1795. 1 p, folio. Deposition in behalf of Richard Allen in a case of disputed title to land in Kentucky. CNY Dec 5 (16) $6,500

Booth, Edwin, 1833-93

ALs, 2 May 1890. 3 pp, 12mo. To Mr. Lampheimer. Responding to a request for a contribution 'For our friend, Levin". Dar Feb 13 (102) $150

Engraving, bust port, Dec 1881. 4 by 4 inches, mtd on card. Sgd & inscr to J. H. Ammon. Imperf. Dar Aug 6 (10) $110

Booth, John Wilkes, 1838-65

Photograph, sgd & inscr, [n.d.]. Carte size. Signature imperf. R Nov 9 (95) $2,800

Photograph, [n.d.]. Carte size. By D. K. Wilkes. With related material. Dar Oct 10 (96) $200

Booth, Junius Brutus, 1796-1852

ALs, [n.d.]. 2 pp, 8vo. To [his father] R[ichard] Booth. Mentioning his performance of Richard III in Washington. wd June 12 (306) $100

Bormann, Martin

Ls, 24 July 1934. 1 p, 4to. To Heinrich Himmler. Discussing the request of Nazi party member Hinkel to be readmitted to the SS. Illus in cat. Dar Apr 9 (128) $950

Boston

Document, 1 Jan 1881. Size not stated. Certificate that T. Emerson Hibbard has served in the Boston Fire Department for 7 years; sgd by Mayor Frederick O. Prince & others. Framed. R Mar 7 (269) $250

Boswell, James, 1740-95

Autograph Ms, dream of Samuel Johnson, draft of a letter, birth dates, etc., [c.1785]. 17 pp, various sizes, in a fragment of a notebook; partly laid in. CNY Dec 5 (170) $15,000

— Autograph Ms, memorandum submitted to David Garrick with a bibliography of Samuel Johnson's works in anr hand, Sept 1772. 2 pp, folio. Bibliography annotated by Boswell & Garrick. Illus in cat. pn Mar 19 (34) £13,000

ALs, 1 Feb 1768. 2 pp, 4to. To Catharine Macaulay. Informing her that he has forwarded her pamphlet on Hobbes to Paoli. Def at head. pn June 11 (7) £2,100 [Burgess]

— 5 Dec 1792. 1 p, folio. To Andrew Gibb. Giving instructions regarding his estate. CNY Dec 5 (171) $1,700

Botanical Manuscripts

Ms, Differentes fleurs du pais colorees. [France, 1st half of 18th cent]. 63 pp, 205mm by 160mm. Contemp lea bdg. Watercolors of flowers. Including ownership inscr of "elizabhet de clamerey". HH May 12 (3) DM3,800

Bottomley, Jim, 1900-59

Signature, [9 June 1952]. 5 by 3 inches, on verso of trimmed postcard. Dar Dec 26 (75) $450

Boudinot, Elias, 1740-1821

ALs, 26 Feb 1787. 2 pp, folio. To James Parker. Discussing a legal matter. Illus in cat. sup Oct 15 (1037) $525

Bow, Clara, 1905-65

Autograph sentiment, 28 Mar 1929. 1 p, 12mo. Expressing good wishes. Dar June 11 (108) $180

Boyle, Robert, 1627-91

Ls, 8 Aug 1668. 2 pp, 4to. To Samuel [Clarke]. About problems in setting aside an unsatisfactory text by an unnamed author, & about the publication of "the Pneumatical Exp[erimen]ts." Illus in cat. C June 24 (358) £900 [Wilson]

Brackett, Rufus

Autograph Ms, mathematical exercise work book, 16 Feb 1816. 96 pp, size not stated; disbound. Including watercolor drawing. R Nov 9 (266) $650

Bradbury, Ray

Typescript, Long after Midnight a short novel in 3 parts (early draft of Fahrenheit 451); [1952-53]. 99 pp, 4to. With numerous autograph emendations. In red mor gilt with typescript of portions of The Illustrated Man, & of The Exiles. With inscr copies of ptd works. P Oct 11 (21) $6,500

Braddock, James J., 1905-74

ALs, 6 June 1935. 1 p, 8vo. To Miss Spencer. Sending his autograph & referring to his upcoming fight with Max Baer. Dar Aug 6 (123) $180

Photograph, sgd, [n.d.]. Size not stated. Framed with check, accomplished & sgd. sg Sept 12 (29) $200

Bradford, William, 1755-95

ADs, 13 Dec 1787. 1 p, 8vo. Writ in the case of Pratt v. Newman. sup Oct 15 (1039) $100

Bragg, Braxton, 1817-76

ALs, 22 July [1862]. 4 pp, 8vo. To Gen. [P. G. T. Beauregard?]. Explaining his plans for the invasion of Kentucky. CNY Dec 5 (18) $3,800

Bragg, Braxton, 1817-76 —&
Hunt, Henry Jackson, 1819-89

[An exchange of A Ls s from Bragg to Hunt, [21 Apr 1861] & from Hunt to Bragg, 23 Apr 1861, 6 pp, 4to, explaining sectional differences & regretting "that we are in hectic array against each other", sold at CNY on 5 Dec 1991, lot 17, for $11,000.]

Brahms, Johannes, 1833-97

Autograph music, 2 partsongs, Sehnsucht, & Naechtens, Op. 112 nos 1 & 2, [c.1888]. 8 pp, folio. Working Ms, scored for 4 voices & piano. Sgd & inscr to Antonia Speyer-Kufferath, spring 1891. Illus in cat. Mannheim collection. S Dec 6 (4) £24,000 [Biba]

Ms, 2 Rhapsodies, Op. 79, [c.1879]. 13 pp, 4to. Copyist's Ms, with numerous autograph corrections & autograph dedication to Elisabeth von Herzogenberg. C June 24 (18) £9,000 [Schneider]

Series of 26 A Ls s, 1884 & 1885. 26 pp, 8vo. To Fritz Simrock. About the publication of his works & a variety of other matters. S Dec 6 (49) £12,000 [Biba]

ALs, [9 July 1885]. 4 pp, 8vo. To Max Kalbeck. Chatting about the summer heat, plans to visit Berchtesgaden, a recent earthquake, etc. Dar Dec 26 (130) $4,750

— 29 Mar 1887. 4 pp, 8vo. To Fritz Simrock. Planning a tour of Italy. star Mar 27 (979) DM5,000

— [8 June 1894]. 4 pp, 8vo. To Fritz Simrock. Discussing his collection of German folk songs. star Mar 27 (980) DM4,000

— [11 Nov 1895]. 3 pp, 4to. To Fritz Simrock. Sympathizing with recipient's problems & mentioning projected trips to Berlin & Leipzig. S May 29 (498) £1,300 [Saggiori]

— [13 May 1896]. 3 pp, 8vo. To Fritz Schnack. Reporting about family matters. Mtd. JG Sept 27 (314) DM4,000

— [n.d.]. 3 pp, 8vo. Recipient unnamed. Inquiring about Max Bruch's proposed trip to America. S Dec 6 (48) £1,100 [Biba]

— [n.d.]. 2 pp, 8vo. To an unnamed pbr. Expressing apologies & hoping for a meeting. star Mar 27 (981) DM3,400

Series of 24 autograph postcards, sgd, 1890 & 1891. To Fritz Simrock. About the publication of his own compositions, other composers & musicians, etc. S May 29 (494) £10,000 [Macnutt]

— Series of 26 autograph postcards, sgd, 1895 & 1896. To Fritz Simrock. About the publication of his compositions & other musical matters. S May 29 (497) £10,500 [Macnutt]

Autograph postcard, sgd, 2 Aug [18]75. To Fritz Simrock. Giving instructions regarding the publication of his Neue Liebeslieder Walzer, Op. 65. Illus in cat. S Dec 6 (51) £1,000 [Haas]

— [15 Dec 1883]. To Eusebius Mandyczewski. Inquiring about scores sent by Haertel. star Mar 27 (978) DM1,700

— [18 Feb 1888]. To Fritz Simrock. Thanking for 2 vols of Dvorak's Slavonic Dances & asking for the rest. S May 29 (496) £800 [Gorsen]

— [4 Feb 1896]. To Fritz Simrock. Inquiring about the full scores of 2 operas by Bizet. S May 29 (499) £750 [Mazzucchetti]

— [27 Feb 1896]. To Fritz Simrock. Reporting on the successful premiere of Dvorak's 9th Symphony in Vienna. Illus in cat. S May 29 (495) £2,000 [Harrison]

— 4 Mar [18]97. To Fritz Simrock. Referring to a missing Cello Concerto. S Dec 6 (53) £1,300 [Giesen]

AN, [n.d.]. 1 p, 16mo, on verso of visiting card. Recipient unnamed. Postponing a meeting. Illus in cat. star Mar 27 (982) DM700

— [n.d.]. 1 p, 16mo, on verso of visiting card. Recipient unnamed. Declining an invitation. Def. star Mar 27 (983) DM330

Autograph quotation, opening of the Hungarian Dance in D flat major (here in C), [n.d.]. 27cm by 25cm. Sgd & inscr. Framed. Illus in cat. S Dec 6 (47) £2,200 [L'Autographe]

Braithwaite, William S., 1878-1962

ALs, [n.d.]. 1 p, 8vo. To Maynard. About the sale of some poems. With ptd photograph. Dar June 11 (111) $100

Brandeis, Louis D., 1856-1941

Series of 6 A Ls s, 1940 & 1941. 6 pp, 8vo. To Rabbi Isadore Breslau. About a variety of matters. wa Mar 5 (278) $700

A Ls s (2), 14 Mar 1937 & 3 July 1938. 2 pp, 8vo. To Rabbi Isadore Breslau. Expressing thanks. wa Mar 5 (277) $500

— A Ls s (2), 29 Sept & 13 Oct 1937. 2 pp, 8vo. To [Edmund] Kaufmann. Expressing thanks. wa Mar 5 (276) $500

ALs, 5 May 1937. 1 p, 4to. To Edmund Kaufmann. Advising that J. H. Rosenberg's telegram be sent to the Sec of State, wa Mar 5 (280) $350

— 8 July 1938. 1 p, 8vo. To Edmund Kaufmann. About fund raising for Jewish causes. wa Mar 5 (279) $500

Brando, Marlon

Ds, 16 July 1964. 1 p, 4to. Waiver of notice & consent to a meeting of the Board of Directors of Colony Productions. sup Oct 15 (1041) $210

— 17 Sept 1965. 1 p, 4to. Lease on land in Colorado. Dar June 11 (112) $325

Brandt, Willy

Autograph Ms, fragment from a speech given at Vienna on developments in Eastern Europe, 30 Sept 1990. 1 p, 4to. With photograph, sgd. HH Nov 6 (2025) DM300

Ls, 20 July 1966. 1 p, 4to. To Ferdinand Friedensburg. Thanking for a message. HH May 13 (1900) DM260

Bratby, John

Collection of 270 A Ls s, cards, sgd, telegrams, etc., 1971 to 1974. About 500 pp, various sizes. To Diane Hills. Discussing his work & referring to a variety of contemp figures. Including some sketches. S July 21 (331) £3,200 [West]

Braun, Wernher von, 1912-77

ALs, 6 June 1969. 2 pp, 4to. To the publishing house Burda. Sending corrected proofs. star Mar 26 (557) DM320

AL, [c.1959]. 3 pp, folio. To Gen. Bergeron. Draft, regarding research papers by Professor Allais. In German. Illus in cat. HH May 13 (1901) DM1,050

Ls, 20 Sept 1968. 2 pp, 4to. To Thomas Sarnoff. Inviting him to the launching of the 1st manned Apollo/Saturn space vehicle. sup Oct 15 (1845) $350

Braxton, Carter, Signer from Virginia

ALs, 22 June 1780. 1 p, 8vo. To John Taylor. Regarding business matters. Waterstained. sup Oct 15 (1195) $170

Brecht, Bertolt, 1898-1956

[A typescript, Die Legende vom toten Soldaten, & 4 Mss, early copies of poems, [n.d.]., 10 pp, various sizes, sold at star on 26 Mar 1992, lot 55, for DM12,000.]

Autograph Ms, poem, beginning "Seine Musse zu geniessen...", [1920-23]. 1 p, folio. 7 four-line stanzas. star Mar 26 (53) DM8,000

— Autograph Ms, poem, Die Maenner der See, 1916. 2 pp, 4to. 4 five-line stanzas, sgd. Possibly unpbd. star Mar 26 (51) DM12,000

— Autograph Ms, poem, Psalm II, [c.1918]. 2 pp, folio. 24 lines, sgd. Possibly unpbd. star Mar 26 (52) DM8,500

A Ls s (2), [1921]. 2 pp, folio & 8vo. To [Efraim Frisch]. Regarding contributions to a literary journal. star Mar 26 (56) DM4,000

ALs, [n.d.]. 1 p, 8vo. To [Ruth Berlau?]. Looking forward to seeing her, & making travel plans. star Mar 26 (60) DM1,700

Ls, 7 Mar 1927. 2 pp, 4to. To Dr. Sinsheimer. Regretting being unable to send a contribution for the journal Simplizissimus. With related material. HH Nov 6 (2026) DM3,000

— 13 Apr 1939. 1 p, 4to. To [Dorothy] Thompson. Regretting that he cannot attend a P.E.N. conference. sg Sept 12 (30) $225

— [July 1943]. 1 p, 4to. To Ruth Berlau. Concerning a trans of his play Schweyk im Zweiten Weltkrieg. Sgd b. star Mar 26 (58) DM1,600

ANs, 18 Dec 1952. 1 p, 8vo. To the publishing house Suhrkamp. About a request for copies of his work Theaterarbeit. star Mar 26 (59) DM1,300

Brecht, Bertolt, 1898-1956 —& Eisler, Hanns, 1898-1962

[A group of letters comprising a letter sgd by both, a letter by Brecht, & 2 Ls s by Eisler, Sept to Nov 1935, to the Theatre Union in NY, protesting about the inadequate staging of the play Die Mutter, sold at star on 26 Mar 1992, lot 57, for DM3,200.]

Brehm, Alfred, 1829-84

ALs, 28 Dec 1869. 2 pp, 8vo. To F. Graessner. Discussing bird cages. star Mar 26 (558) DM440

Collection of Ls & autograph postcard, sgd, 14 & [22] Oct 1875. 2 pp, 8vo, & card. To the bookseller Waldmann. About a projected lecture. star Mar 26 (559) DM280

Breitkopf, Johann Gottlob Immanuel, 1719-94

ALs, 5 Nov 1783. 1 p, 4to. To the Rev. Sievers at Magdeburg Cathedral. Letter of recommendation. Illus in cat. star Mar 27 (984) DM1,700

Bresgen, Cesar, 1913-88

Autograph music, fragment from an unidentified composition for piano & several voices, [n.d.]. 2 pp, size not stated. star Mar 27 (985) DM280

Bresnahan, Roger P., 1879-1944

Ds, 26 Apr 1919. 1 p, 4to. Transfer of Neal J. Brady from the NY Yankees to the Toledo Base Ball Co.; also sgd by Jacob Ruppert. Dar Dec 26 (76) $1,100

Cut signature, [n.d.]. Size not stated. With Hall of Fame card. Dar June 11 (84) $250

Breteuil, Louis Auguste Le Tonnelier, Baron de, 1730-1807

Ls s (2), 15 Mar & 31 May 1792. 10 pp, folio. To Marshal de Castries. Discussing European courts & the prospects of the monarchist forces. sg Sept 12 (31) $650

Breviarium -- Latin Manuscripts

— [Paris, c.1415]. Use of Paris. 361 leaves, vellum, 88mm by 65mm. 17th-cent calf gilt. In 2 sizes of a very small & skilful gothic liturgical hand. With small initials throughout in burnished gold, larger initials thoughout in floral designs on burnished gold grounds with partial borders of colored flowers & burnished gold leaves on hairline stems, large miniature within full border, & 11 leaves pasted in later with large miniatures probably by Antoine de Lonhy, c.1470. S Dec 17 (70) £26,000 [Mirandola]

— [Italy, c.1450]. Of Dominican Use. 210 leaves, vellum, 245mm by 165mm. Repaired contemp Italian blindtooled calf. In a gothic liturgical hand; some pages with music of square black neums on a 3-line red stave. With several hundred 2- to 5-line initials in red & blue with penwork decoration. bba June 25 (116) £3,600 [Braunschweig]

— [Italy, 15th cent]. 32 leaves, vellum, 156mm by 113mm. Contemp blindstamped calf over wooden bds. From Sunday in the octave of Epiphany to the 3d Sunday in Lent. With 3 armorial shields & historiated initial. pn Nov 14 (239) £420 [Schuster]

— [French Flanders, Priory of Beaurepaire?, c.1450]. Of monastic use. 314 leaves (2 lacking), vellum, 142mm by 100mm. Modern vellum bdg. In a very small gothic hand. With 31 large illuminated initials with 3-quarter or full illuminated borders. S June 23 (78) £2,900 [Day]

— [Senlis, c.1750]. For the use of the Bishop of Senlis. 60 leaves, vellum, 433mm by 303mm. Rebacked contemp armorial red mor gilt bdg. In a fine rounded roman hand in imitation of ptd type, probably with a stencil. With c.40 large illuminated initials, c.37 large historiated initials on panels of camaieu d'or designs, & 13 large floral or other headpieces & tailpieces, sometimes formed of miniatures. S June 23 (83) £8,000 [Ladriere]

Brezhnev, Leonid Ilich, 1906-82

Signature, on philatelic envelope, [28 Oct 1974]. wa Oct 19 (205) $140

Brice, Fanny, 1891-1951

Ds, 6 Sept 1949. 2 pp, 4to. Resignation as trustee of the Union Bank & Trust Co. Dar Apr 9 (133) $110

Bright, John, 1822-89

ALs, [28 May 1840]. 3 pp, 4to. To Thomas Bates. Denouncing the Corn Laws. pn June 11 (30) £260

Brisbin, James S., 1838-92

Series of 6 A Ls s, 20 July 1861 to 22 Sept 1864. 12 pp, 4to & 8vo. To his wife. Reporting from the Battle at Bull Run & other Civil War scenes. sup May 9 (114) $1,200

Briton, George Andrew. See: Torrington, Alfred & Briton

Britten, Benjamin, 1913-76

ALs, 27 Aug 1952. 2 pp, 8vo. Recipient unnamed. Responding to a young admirer's request for an autograph. wa Oct 19 (155) $200

Broch, Hermann, 1886-1951

Ls, 28 Nov 1948. 1 p, folio. To Emmi Friedlaender. Interpreting his work Vergil. star Mar 26 (61) DM520

Brod, Max, 1884-1968

ALs, 8 Nov 1912. 2 pp, 8vo. To an unnamed literary critic. Announcing his book Die Hoehe des Gefuehls. star Mar 26 (62) DM420

Broglie, Louis Victor, Prince de, 1892-1987

Autograph Ms, preface to an unspecified work, fragment; [n.d.]. 2 pp, folio. star Mar 26 (560) DM320

Bromfield, Louis, 1896-1956

Collection of 2 A Ls s, AL, 2 Ls s & letter, 1917 to 1919. 20 pp, 8vo & 4to. To Edith Braun. About personal matters & events at the front. Mostly incomplete. sg June 11 (30) $150

Brooke, Sir Arthur de Capell, 1791-1858

ALs, 1823. 3 pp, 4to. To Mr. Martin. Giving instructions regarding the ptg of his Travels through Sweden, Norway and Finland. Dawson Turner collection. pn Nov 14 (118) £160

Brouthers, Dan, 1858-1932

Autograph sentiment, sgd, 1909. 4 by 3 inches (card). Expressing best wishes. Dar Feb 13 (71) $800

Brown, James

Ds, 9 Aug 1965. 1 p, 4to. Television contract. Dar Apr 9 (135) $160

Concert program, sgd & inscr, [summer 1967]. 14 pp, 4to. Also sgd & inscr by 4 others. wa Oct 19 (146) $130

Brown, John, of Osawatomie, 1800-59

ALs, 3 June 1839. 1 p, 4to. To Oliver O. Brown & William H. Munroe. Informing them that he will send an agent to examine his lands in Ohio. Spiro collection. CNY May 14 (39) $2,200

— 17 Mar 1848. 2 pp, 4to. To Simon Perkins. Providing information about their wool-

trading business. CNY Dec 5 (21) $1,900
— 13 Mar 1856. 1 p, 4to. To his family. Hoping for political developments "that would set Kansas matters right". CNY Dec 5 (22) $5,000
— 24 Apr 1856. 2 pp, 4to. To his wife. Discussing family matters, financial affairs & the situation in Kansas. CNY Dec 5 (23) $5,000

Brown, Mordecai, 1876-1948

Signature, [8 May 1946]. 5 by 3 inches, on verso of trimmed postcard. Dar Dec 26 (77) $550

Browning, Elizabeth Barrett, 1806-61

ALs, [n.d.], "Monday". 1 p, 12mo. To Mrs. Stowe. Hoping to see her. Illus in cat. Dar Feb 13 (122) $900
— "Friday" [c.1854]. 2 pp, 12mo. To Mr. Crawford. Regretting they have not met during the past few months. CNY Dec 5 (173) $1,600

Browning, Robert, 1812-89

Autograph Ms, Song from Pippa Passes, beginning "Give her but a least excuse to love me!", 8 Nov 1887. 1 p, 8vo. 18 lines, sgd. Framed with a port. P June 17 (5) $2,750

ALs, 20 Dec 1867. 3 pp, 8vo. To Robinson Ellis. Thanking for his recent book & asking that his son be allowed to read with him. pn Nov 14 (219) £500 [Wilson]
— 24 Mar 1874. 2 pp, 8vo. To Mrs. Joachim. Hoping to be able to accept an invitation. bba May 28 (202) £320 [Wise]
— 27 June 1882. 1 p, 8vo. To Mrs. [W. H.] Flower. Looking forward to an evening of Schumann's music. Ingilby collection. pn Nov 14 (54) £500 [Wilson]
— 15 Feb 1886. 1 p, 8vo. To Mr. Raffalovich. Declining an invitation. sup Oct 15 (1044) $600
— 16 Nov 1886. 1 p, 8vo. To Mrs. Ward. Declining an invitation. bba Jan 30 (266) £230 [Holleyman & Treacher]
— 25 Jan 1887. 1 p, 12mo. Recipient unnamed. Declining to give a lecture. Framed with engraved port. Dar Apr 9 (136) $800
— 15 Dec 1887. 1 p, 8vo. To [Mrs. Rawlinson Ford]. Referring her to his pbr for permission to use his poems. pn June 11 (70) £380 [Wilson]
— 20 Feb 1889. 1 p, 8vo. Recipient unnamed. Discussing an autographed book that he has sent. Framed with engraved port. wd June 12 (307) $275
— 27 Apr 1889. 1 p, 8vo. To Mrs. Ward. Declining an invitation. bba Jan 30 (267) £230 [Holleyman & Treacher]
— [n.d.]. 1 p, 12mo, cut from larger sheet. Recipient unnamed. Fragment, concluding 5 lines, citing Massinger's use of the word "plush". Ingilby collection. pn Nov 14 (55) £95 [Wilson]

Bruce, James, 1730-94

ALs, [n.d.], "Thursday". 1 p, 4to. To Jenny Graham. Announcing publication of anr installment of his Travels. pn Mar 19 (104) £140 [Dupre]

Bruce, Lenny, 1926-66

Ds, 28 June 1958. 1 p, 8vo. Charge receipt for gasoline & tires. Matted with a photograph. sup Oct 15 (1045) $160

Check, accomplished & sgd, 7 Dec 1962. Dar Oct 10 (100) $300
— Anr, accomplished & sgd, 15 Feb 1965. Payable to John Judnich. Matted with a photograph. Illus in cat. sup Oct 15 (1046) $220

Bruch, Max, 1838-1920

Collection of 10 A Ls s & autograph postcard, sgd, 27 Nov 1914 to 23 Feb 1919. 37 pp, 8vo. To Herr Hoepffner. About his son & the political situation in Germany. star Mar 27 (987) DM2,600

ALs, 11 June 1858. 3 pp, 8vo. Recipient unnamed. About his plans to write a cantata, his search for a good libretto for an opera, etc. S May 29 (505) £450 [Haas]
— 20 Jan [18]93. 4 pp, 8vo. To Oscar Straus. Offering advice & criticism of his opera. S Dec 6 (56) £450 [Haas]

Bruckner, Anton, 1824-96

Autograph music, 2 sketches for the final part of his 7th Symphony, [n.d.]. 4 pp, 258mm by 328mm. Illus in cat. star Mar 27 (988) DM14,000

ALs, 15 Jan 1885. 1 p, 8vo. To Alfred Stross. Explaining that he has not been able to find a pbr for him. Framed with a port. P June 17 (6) $2,500

ANs, [c.1888]. 1 p, 8vo. To [Ferry B]eraton. Asking for some changes in a port. star Mar 27 (989) DM4,200

Bruecke, Ernst Wilhelm von, 1819-92

ALs, [n.d.]. 4 pp, 8vo. To an unnamed colleague. Congratulating him on his book & refuting theories advocated by Hyrtl. star Mar 26 (561) DM600

Bruehl, Heinrich, Graf von, 1700-63

Ls, 12 Sept 1746. 2 pp, folio. To the magistrate Schoenberger at Tauttenburg. Giving instructions regarding the pastorate at Pfuhlsborn. star Mar 27 (1695) DM240

Brugsch, Heinrich Karl, 1827-94

Autograph Ms, Erinnerungen an Prinz Friedrich Karl von Preussen, [1894]. 9 pp, folio. star Mar 26 (562) DM1,200

ALs, 11 Aug 1884. 3 pp, 8vo. To an unnamed official in the German Foreign Office. Informing him that he has sent a telegram to Bismarck accepting a foreign assignment. star Mar 26 (563) DM280

Brunel, Isambard Kingdom, 1806-59

ALs, 12 Jan 1839. 1 p, 8vo. Recipient unnamed. Asking him to furnish Mr. Banks with tickets to see the works. pn Nov 14 (185) £90 [Wilson]

Bryan, William Jennings, 1860-1925

Collection of AL & autograph telegram, sgd, 18 May 1914. 7 pp, 8vo. To Mr. Gonzales at the American Legation at Havana, Cuba. Strongly advising against a projected Cuban marriage & divorce law. Dar Dec 26 (133) $700

Series of 3 Ls s, 1913 to 1915. 6 pp, 4to. To Federico Alfonso Pezet. Communications to the Minister of Peru. Dar Aug 6 (125) $550

Ls, 20 Dec 1922. 1 p, 4to. Recipient unnamed. Commenting on the League of Nations. Dar Feb 13 (123) $400

ANs, [n.d.]. 1 p, 8vo. Recipient unnamed. Statement recommending a book. Dar Dec 26 (134) $120

Bryant, William Cullen, 1794-1878

Autograph Ms, poem, The Death of Slavery, 5 June 1866. 5 pp, 8vo, on rectos only. In purple levant mor gilt bdg with related ALs, 2 engraved portraits, & ptd poem. Illus in cat. Sang & Spiro collections. CNY May 14 (40) $7,500

ALs, 23 May 1871. 1 p, 8vo. To Mary Wilson. Responding to an inquiry about his use of the word "brood". bbc Dec 9 (159) $150

Buch, Leopold von, 1774-1853

ALs, 12 Dec 1830. 1 p, 8vo. To Herr Hehl. Thanking for 2 ammonites & discussing K. H. F. Zieten's work about fossils in Wuerttemberg. Illus in cat. hen Nov 12 (2519) DM420

Buchanan, James, 1791-1868

ALs, 7 Jan 1835. 1 p, 4to. To G. M. Dallas & others. Declining an invitation to attend celebrations on the anniversay of the victory at New Orleans. Def. sg Sept 12 (33) $225

— 10 Feb 1838. 1 p, 4to. To Mahlon Dickerson. Recommending "young Judson" for an appointment in the Navy. Illus in cat. R Mar 7 (110) $450

— 27 Feb 1838. 1 p, 4to. To Joel R. Poinsett. Letter of recommendation for Joseph B. Harris. sup Oct 15 (1521) $210

— 7 June 1843. 1 p, 4to. To H. L. Harvey. Regretting he will not be able to visit him. Framed with a port. Illus in cat. sup Oct 15 (1522) $850

— 11 May 1846. 2 pp, 4to. To Col. Reah Frazer. Explaining War Department regulations for appointments of cadets at West Point. Spiro collection. CNY May 14 (41) $1,200

— 31 Mar 1851. 1 p, 4to. To W. W. H. Davis. Acknowledging newspaper articles on the tariff. R Nov 9 (3) $550

— 3 May 1853. 1 p, 4to. To Eliza Watterston. Promising to visit her in Washington. Spiro collection. CNY May 14 (42) $4,200

— 30 Apr 1857. 1 p, 8vo. To Henry M. Phillips. Regarding an appointment at the Philadelphia Navy Yard. Dar Dec 26 (135) $850

— 24 June 1859. 1 p, 8vo. To Mrs. Pringle. Sending a letter of introduction (not included). Dar Dec 26 (136) $700

— 24 June [18]59. 1 p, 8vo. To Mrs. Pringle. Sending a letter of introduction (not included). sg Sept 12 (35) $350

— 13 Feb 1863. 1 p, 4to. To O. Vincent Coffin. Declining to speak "on the affairs of our weary & war worn country". CNY Dec 5 (24) $1,100

— [n.d.]. 2 pp, 8vo. To Rev. Henry Slicer. Congratulating him on his appointment as Chaplain to the Senate. sup Oct 15 (1520) $400

Ls, 13 Apr 1846. 1 p, folio. To Charles Ward. Sending his commission as Consul for Zanzibar (not included). Framed. wa Mar 5 (281) $300

— 26 Jan 1858. 1 p, 4to. To King Ferdinand of the Two Sicilies. Expressing condolences on the death of his sister. Dar Apr 9 (137) $1,100

Ds s (2)14 July 1858 & 11 Aug 1859. 2 pp, 8vo. Appointments of auditors. sup Oct 15 (1525) $725

Ds, 3 Apr 1858. 1 p, folio. Appointment of Francis Ramsay as Lieut. in the Navy. Framed with engraved port. Illus in cat. sup Oct 15 (1523) $850

— 18 Aug 1858. 1 p, 8vo. Order to affix the US Seal to a letter addressed to the President of Bolivia. Framed with engraved port. Dar Apr 9 (138) $550

— 18 Aug 1858. 1 p, 4to. Order to affix the US Seal to a letter to the President of Bolivia. sup Oct 15 (1524) $450

Autograph check, sgd, 24 Apr [18]68. 6 by 3 inches. Payable to George H. Eula. Dar Apr 9 (139) $1,300

Franking signature, [1861]. On autograph envelope addressed to Edwin M. Stanton. Dar

June 11 (113) $200

— Anr, [19 Feb n.y.]. On autograph address leaf to John R. Thomson; 4to. Dar June 11 (114) $140

Buchanan, James, 1791-1868 —& Others

ADs, 29 Feb 1836. 1 p, 4to. Testimonial to A. Boyd Hamilton, also sgd by 17 others. sg Sept 12 (34) $225

Buchanan, James, 1791-1868. See: Polk, James K.

Buck, Pearl S., 1892-1973

Ls, 19 Feb 1951. 1 p, 4to. To Mark E. Brown. Referring to the "Cardozo High School affair in Washington". sup Oct 15 (1047) $105

Buechmann, Georg, 1822-84

ALs, 2 Jan 1873. 1 p, 8vo. Recipient unnamed. Thanking for an addition to his Gefluegelte Worte. star Mar 26 (564) DM200

Buechner, Ludwig, 1824-99

Series of 4 A Ls s, 13 May 1888 to 7 June 1889. 10 pp, 8vo. Recipient unnamed. About affairs of the Deutscher Freidenkerbund. star Mar 26 (565) DM380

Buelow, Hans von, 1830-94

Autograph music, 6 songs to texts by Heine, & 3 songs from Goethe & Uhland, scored for voice & piano; 13 June 1848. 15 pp, folio. Sgd & inscr to Livia Frege. Gottschalk collection. C Dec 16 (422) £1,200 [Rosenthal]

ALs, 15 Nov 1874. 2 pp, 8vo. To [Eduard Lassen?]. Chatting about a recent concert in London, a performance of Tristan, etc. star Mar 27 (990) DM650

— BUELOW, MARIE VON. - ALs, 21 July 1890. 2 pp, 8vo. Recipient unnamed. Informing him that her husband is ailing & has not made any plans for the coming winter yet. HN June 26 (891) DM220

Buelow von Dennewitz, Friedrich Wilhelm, Graf, 1755-1816

ALs, 13 Mar 1810. 1 p, 4to. Recipient unnamed. Witty dinner invitation. star Mar 27 (1295) DM340

Buerger, Gottfried August, 1747-94

ADs, 23 Feb 1773. 1 p, 4to. Receipt for several judicial files. star Mar 26 (65) DM320

Ds, 30 June 1773. 2 pp, folio. Sentence in a case against Nicolaus Casper. star Mar 26 (66) DM350

Bulkeley, Morgan Gardner, 1837-1922

Cut signature, [n.d.]. 4.5 by 0.75 inches. Dar Dec 26 (78) $700

Bullen, Frank Thomas, 1857-1915

Autograph Ms, novel, A Bounty Boy: Being some adventures of a Christian Barbarian on an unpremeditated trip round the World; sgd, inscr & dated Oct 1907. 306 pp, 4to, on rectos only. Dark blue calf bdg. CNY Oct 8 (28) $3,000

— Autograph Ms, novel, Beyond; [ptd 1909]. 324 pp, 4to, on rectos only. Def black half mor bdg. Including cut signature & photograph pasted in. CNY Oct 8 (29) $2,400

Bunche, Ralph J., 1904-71

Ls, 16 June 1953. 1 p, 4to. To Paul Walker. Commenting on a statement by Adam Powell. With a photograph. wa Oct 19 (212) $110

Bunker, Chang & Eng, 1811-74. See: Chang & Eng

Bunsen, Robert Wilhelm, 1811-99

ALs, 24 Oct 1862. 4 pp, 8vo. To Jean Servais Stas. About travels in Scotland, scientific experiments, etc. star Mar 26 (567) DM2,800

— 19 Feb 1868. 2 pp, 4to. To Robert Du Bois Reymond. Concerning recipient's university schedule. hen Nov 12 (2521) DM400

— 5 Oct 1873. 2 pp, 8vo. Recipient unnamed. About an opportunity to work in his laboratory. star Mar 26 (568) DM480

Burbank, Luther, 1849-1926

Ls, 5 Dec 1921. 1 p, 8vo. To Ida Porter-Boyer. Agreeing to test seeds taken from Cliff Dweller's ruins. sg Sept 12 (36) $150

Burdach, Konrad, 1859-1936

Collection of 3 A Ls s & autograph postcard, sgd, 29 Jan 1931 to 27 Nov 1933. 9 pp, 8vo, & card. To Heinrich Spiero. About financial help for a needy actor, the sale of his library, a publication project, etc. star Mar 26 (569) DM240

Burke, Edmund, 1729-97

A Ls s (2), 4 & 5 Nov 1794. 4 pp, 4to. To Henry Dundas, Vicount Melville. Offering his help to conciliate dissenting factions in the government. CNY Dec 5 (176) $1,400

ALs, [c.1787-1788]. 2 pp, 4to. To E. Malone. Concerning efforts to obtain a ticket for the impeachment trial of Warren Hastings. CNY Dec 5 (175) $1,100

Burkett, Jesse C., 1868-1953

Signature, [n.d.]. Matted with Hall of Fame card, overall size 8 by 10 inches. Dar Feb 13 (72) $200

Burma. See: Siam

Burmese Manuscripts

Ms, Buddhist text. [Burma, Shan State, 19th cent]. 140 leaves in concertina form, 200mm by 408mm. Black lacquered covers. With stylized cloud decoration at beginning. S Apr 30 (361) £300

Burnet, David Gouverneur, 1788-1870

Series of 3 A Ls s, 10 Jan to 19 Nov 1845. 7 pp, 4to & folio. To Col. Thomas Ward. About Texas politics. CNY June 9 (275) $5,000

Ls, 15 Aug 1836. 1 p, 4to. To H. C. Hudson. Directing him to take charge of the Texas archives. Illus in cat. sg Feb 27 (203) $1,300

Burney, Charles, 1726-1814

ALs, 11 Jan 1800. 2 pp, 4to. To Longman, Clementi & Co. In 3d person, discussing efforts to find English subscribers for Haydn's oratorio The Creation. S Dec 6 (57) £2,700 [Cox]

Burns, Robert, 1759-96

Autograph Ms, poem, Countrie Lassie; [n.d.]. 2 pp, folio. 5 eight-line stanzas. C Dec 16 (279) £1,800 [Silverman]

Ms, music for The German Lairdie; [n.d.]. 1 p, 8vo, cut from larger sheet. Title in Burns's hand. pn June 11 (71) £150 [Wilson]

Burns, Tommy, 1881-1955

Photograph, sgd & inscr, 2 July [19]49. 3 by 5 inches. Inscr to John Smith on verso. Dar Feb 13 (112) $450

Signature, [n.d.]. On ptd card, 3.75 by 2.12 inches. With ptd religious statement on verso. Illus in cat. Dar Feb 13 (113) $350

Burnside, Ambrose E., 1824-81

Photograph, sgd, [n.d.]. Carte size. In uniform. By J. W. Black. Illus in cat. R June 13 (107) $500

Burr, Aaron, 1756-1836

ALs, 20 Sept 1786. 1 p, 4to. To James Duane. Sending a list of cases for trial (at head). Illus in cat. sup Oct 15 (1487) $575

— 8 June 1790. 1 p, size not stated. To Gerard Banckes. Concerning mortgages in the estate of Mary Walton. On verso of legal document. wd Dec 12 (303) $425

— 29 June 1793. 1 p, 4to. To John Henry. Declining to buy land in the Catskills. Illus in cat. R June 13 (155) $650

— 18 July 1796. 1 p, 4to. To Clement Biddle. Inquiring about an unpaid bill. Illus in cat. sup Oct 15 (1488) $500

— 3 Mar 1797. 1 p, 4to. Recipient unnamed. Promising to pay a sight draft. sup Oct 15 (1489) $500

— 16 Feb [1804]. 1 p, folio. To David Gelston. Concerning a real estate deal with John Jacob Astor. Sgd AB. Spiro collection. CNY May 14 (43) $3,500

— [c.7 Feb 1807]. 2 pp, 4to. To Gov. Williams. Stating conditions for his return into custody. Endorsed by C. A. Rodney on verso. Illus in cat. sup May 9 (368) $13,000

— 25 July 1807. 2 pp, 4to. To Jonathan Rhea. Inquiring about witnesses who might testify against Col. Morgan & his sons on his behalf. Spiro collection. CNY May 14 (44) $2,200

— 30 Oct [n.y.]. 1 p, 4to. To Col. Henry Rogers. Regarding arrangements for some titles to be exhibited. Framed with a port. P June 16 (201) $900

Cut signature, [n.d.]. 3 by 0.9 inches. Dar Dec 26 (137) $150

— Anr, [n.d.]. 2.75 by 1.5 inches. Dar Apr 9 (140) $140

Burritt, Elihu, 1810-79

ALs, 30 June [n.y.]. 1 p, 8vo. To "Friend Burdekin". About affairs of the League of Universal Brotherhood. bba May 28 (164) £75 [Weinstein]

Burroughs, Edgar Rice, 1875-1950

Ls, 28 Dec 1922. 1 p, 4to. To D. Pierson Ricks. Responding to an inquiry whether he believes that Mars is inhabited. Dar Feb 13 (125) $325

Autograph sentiment, sgd, 15 June 1923. 1 p, 12mo. Explaining that the League of Nations, "like Socialism, ... is a lovely theory." Dar Aug 6 (126) $325

Burton, Richard, 1925-84

Ds, Oct 1977. 2 pp, 4to. Lending Agreement relating to the film Equus. Dar Apr 9 (141) $160

Burton, Sir Richard Francis, 1821-90

Autograph Ms, notes, "Records of the Past", [n.d.]. 2 pp, 16mo. With signature in English & Arabic, 4 by 4.75 inches. sg Sept 12 (37) $550

Busch, Wilhelm, 1832-1908

ALs, [1 May 1897]. 1 p, 8vo. To Hermann Noeldeke. Announcing his visit. Including letter of transferral by Noeldeke on verso. star Mar 26 (67) DM520

— 31 Dec 1900. 1 p, 8vo. To Alwine Busch. Sending New Year's greetings. star Mar 26 (68) DM540

Autograph postcard, sgd, [15 Dec 1896]. To the Rev [Otto] Noeldeke. Announcing his visit. Sgd W. B. hen Nov 12 (2473) DM650

Bush, Barbara. See: Bush, George & Bush

Bush, George

[2 typescripts, sgd, 5 Jan & 2 Oct 1990, 2 pp, 4to, 1 addressed to the people of Kansas, paying tribute to Dwight Eisenhower, sold at sup on 15 Oct 1991, lot 1746, for $2,500.]

Ls, 2 Apr 1986. 1 p, 8vo. To Ross E. Rowland. Thanking for some tapes. Dar Apr 9 (144) $160

— 4 May 1989. 1 p, 4to. To Harold Russell. Thanking him for 42 years of service on The President's Committee on Unemployment of People with Disabilities. Dar Aug 6 (127) $950

ANs, [n.d.]. Size not stated (card). To Mr. & Mrs. Britton. Saying he "can't make the dinner". Illus in cat. Dar Apr 9 (142) $275

Photograph, sgd & inscr, 6 May 1983. 8 by 10 inches. Inscr to Jane Mendoza. Dar Apr 9 (143) $150

— Anr, [n.d.]. 8 by 10 inches. Inscr to Lisa Waldner. Dar Dec 26 (139) $300

Bush, George —&
Bush, Barbara

Christmas card, 1990. Size not stated. Sgd by both. Illus in cat. sup Oct 15 (1748) $1,200

Bushnell, David, c.1742-1824

ADs, 11 Feb 1783. 1 p, 8vo. Certification that Jonathan Russ is serving in the Corps of Sappers & Miners. With ADs by Russ at foot & related material. Dar Oct 10 (102) $800

Busoni, Ferruccio, 1866-1924

Photograph, sgd & inscr, 1915. 5 by 7 inches. Inscr to Harriet Lanier. wd Dec 12 (304) $50

Bussy-Rabutin, Roger, Comte de, 1618-93

Ls, 8 Jan 1662. 2 pp, 4to. To [Colbert]. Asking for payment of at least part of the sum due him. star Mar 27 (1350) DM400

Butenandt, Adolf

Photograph, sgd, 6 Aug 1968. 29cm by 21cm. By Hanns Hubmann. star Mar 26 (570) DM320

Butler, Benjamin F., 1795-1858

ALs, 11 July 1840. 4 pp, 4to. To H. D. Gilpin. Referring to assaults made upon his personal character. sup Oct 15 (1048) $210

Butler, Benjamin F., 1818-93

Photograph, sgd, [n.d.]. Carte size. Seated, in uniform. By Anthony, from a Brady negative. Illus in cat. R June 13 (103) $500

Byrd, Richard E., 1888-1957

Signature, on ptd program for the 66th Annual Commencement of Pennsylvania Military College, 20 June 1928. 10 by 6.5 inches. sup Oct 15 (1049) $105

Byrd, Richard E., 1888-1957 —& Others

Group photograph, crew of the tri-motor plane America, [n.d.]. 3.25 by 5.5 inches. Sgd by Byrd, G. O. Noville, & Bernt Balchen. Dar Apr 9 (66) $275

Byron, George Gordon Noel, Lord, 1788-1824

ALs, 18 Sept 1820. 1 p, 4to. To Jean Antoine Galignani. Complaining of irregularities in the delivery of his paper. P June 17 (142) $9,000

— 15 June 1822. 2 pp, 8vo. To George W. Bruen. Paying tribute to Patrick Henry. S July 21 (43) £3,200 [Edwards]

— 26 Mar 1823. 2 pp, 4to. To Jean Antoine Galignani. About his subscription to recipient's Literary Messenger, & ordering books. CNY Dec 5 (178) $7,000

— 27 May 1823. 3 pp, 8vo. To Jean Antoine Galignani. Correcting a book order, discussing the Italian trans of Don Juan, etc. CNY Dec 5 (179) $5,000

— [n.d.]. 1 p, 8vo. Recipient unnamed. Concerning a prescription for medicine. Framed with engraved port. Illus in cat. wd Dec 12 (305) $1,900

Autograph check, sgd, 25 Oct 1811. 3 by 9 inches. Payable to Mr. Hawke. Illus in cat. sup Oct 15 (1050) $2,500

C

Cadell, Robert, 1788-1849

ALs, 31 July 1824. 1 p, 4to. To J. Robinson. Sending "three bills to Sir W. Scott". bba Sept 19 (351) £120 [Quaritch]

Cadman, Charles Wakefield, 1881-1946

ALs, [n.d.]. 2 pp, 8vo. To Mr. Briggs. Urging him to confirm "what dates you have positively for me for this fall" & stating his fee. Dar Feb 13 (126) $300

Cagney, James, 1899-1986

Ls s (2), 27 July [19]74 & 29 Nov [19]75. 3 pp, 8vo & 4to. To Joseph Shipley. About mistakes in a biographical entry, & commenting on staying active in old age. sg Feb 27 (30) $250

Ds, 24 Mar 1958. 3 pp, size not stated. Carbon copy, amendment to contracts for 3 films. Dar Dec 26 (140) $200

Signature, [n.d.]. On tp of You're A Grand Old Flag, by George M. Cohan; 6 pp, 4to. wa Oct 19 (3) $80

Calder, Alexander, 1898-1976

Autograph postcard, sgd, [23 Feb 1963]. To Katherine Dudley. Reporting about his travels. On verso of group photograph with 5 others next to a stabile at Spoleto. Dar June 11 (115) $130

Calhoun, James C., d.1876

Autograph Ms, short story about a man named Tennessee, [n.d.]. 7 pp, 4to. Sgd. Framed. Armstrong collection. sup Oct 15 (1113) $650

Calhoun, John C., 1782-1850

Ds s (2)27 Feb & 30 June 1923. Size not stated. Appointments of John Child as cadet at West Point. rs Oct 17 (25C) $300

Franking signature, [15 Aug n.y.]. On autograph envelope. wa Oct 19 (215) $120

California

— GOLD RUSH. - 3 A Ls s, 1849 & 1850, 7 pp, 4to, of Ellis Barnes to his brother William. Reporting about his intention to leave for California, about the voyage, & from San Francisco. sg June 18 (75) $600

— GOLD RUSH. - 3 A Ls s, 1852, 8 pp, 4to, of Charles H. Jones to his sister. About the voyage to California & his activities at Placerville. sg June 18 (76) $475

— GOLD RUSH. - ALs, 25 Sept 1849, 2 pp, 4to, of Leonard House to his mother & sister. Announcing his intention of going to California for gold prospecting. sg June 18 (73) $350

— GOLD RUSH. - ALs, 24 Feb 1850, 4 pp, 4to, of A. Montgomery Schell to his sister. Mentioning prices in Califormia, friends, his homesickness, etc. sg June 18 (74) $250

— LOS ANGELES. - 2 documents, 1836 & 1838, 12 pp, size not stated. Banns of matrimony for marriages of Francisco Araujo & Jose Contreras, sgd by Judge Narcisco Duran & others at the Mission de San Gabriel. rf Sept 21 (13) $200

— PACIFIC EXPRESS COMPANY. - Document, 11 Feb 1857. Length not stated. Receipt for merchandise; partly ptd. rf Sept 21 (17) $65

— SHUBRICK, WILLIAM BRANFORD. - Ls, 29 Aug 1847. 1 p, folio. To a USN store keeper on the Sandwich Islands. Advising him that a naval depot will be transferred to California. rf Sept 21 (21) $200

Callas, Maria, 1923-77

Ptd photograph, sgd, [19 Mar 1969]. 8vo; mtd. HH May 13 (1906) DM220

Calligraphy

Ms, Elegy written in a Country Churchyard, by Thomas Gray, [n.d.]. 7 leaves, vellum, 190mm by 280mm, in dark blue mor gilt. In an upright roman script. In the style of Alberto Sangorski, with illuminated tp, full-page frontis, small miniature, & 37 gold initials with fine penwork tracery. CNY Dec 5 (436) $1,700

— PARELON, PAUL. - Ms, Episode du Siege de Paris en 1870. Chansons Orleanistes Chantees aux Grand'Gardes devant le Fort de Nogent-s-M. [Paris, 1876]. 18 leaves, 8vo, in full gilt blue bdg by Chambolle-Duru. With initials in red, gold or blue. O May 26 (30) $425

— PORTEUS, BEILBY. - Ms, The Gospel Narrative... Illus with photographs from modern & ancient masters, 12 June 1861 to 14 Dec 1869. 150 leaves, 244mm by 216mm, in elaborately tooled orig brown mor over bevelled wooden bds by Ackermann. With calligraphic text in various styles frequently highlighted by illumination, & illusts with full-page polychromatic borders incorporating insects, grotesques & plants. C June 24 (69) £1,900 [Smith]

— ROBERT, JEAN. - Ms, Cahier curieux d'arithmetique et d'autres choses. [Barsac, France, 1804-07]. 50 leaves, 305mm by 200mm, in old vellum wraps. In a variety of scripts. Profusely illus with pen-&-ink drawings. FD June 1 (25) DM7,000

— SANGORSKI & SUTCLIFFE. - Ms, The Raven, by Edgar Allan Poe; [n.d.]. 11 leaves & 5 flyleaves, vellum, 4to, in extra jewelled bdg by Sangorski & Sutcliffe. In a semi-gothic hand. With initials in red, blue or burnished gold, 2 ornamental initials & large historiated initial with 3-quarter or full borders, & watercolor vignette. CNY June 9 (175) $8,500

— SANGORSKI & SUTCLIFFE. - Ms, Adieux a Marie Stuart, by Algernon Charles Swinburne; [c.1916]. 11 leaves & 5 flyleaves, vellum, 4to, in mor extra floral, armorial bdg by Riviere. In a semi-gothic hand. With 1 full-page miniature, sgd by Sangorski with his AS cipher & dated 1916; 10 illuminated initials, 4 of them incorporating elaborate borders with penwork tracery; other verse-opening initials in alternating red, blue, or gold, some with penwork tracery; full-page & smaller borders in many colors, all in stylized floral & foliate design & heightened with gold. sg May 7 (200) $10,000

— SANGORSKI, ALBERTO. - Ms, Paradise and the Peri, by Thomas Moore; 1909. 16 leaves & 4 flyleaves, vellum, 269mm by 210mm, in extra jewelled blue levant mor by Sangorski & Sutcliffe. In an upright roman script.

With 19 gold initials with borders of various colors, full-page frontis, historiated initial & 7 vignettes & large borders. CNY Dec 5 (435) $15,000

— SANGORSKI, ALBERTO. - Ms, Love among the Ruins, by Robert Browning; 1918. 12 leaves, 235mm by 169mm, in extra jewelled salmon-pink mor bdg [by Riviere & Son?]. Richly illuminated throughout; including 5 miniatures (2 full-page). Executed for Messrs John & Edward Bumpus. P June 17 (127) $8,000

— SANGORSKI, ALBERTO. - Ms, The Volunteer and other Poems, by Herbert Asquith; 1917. 26 leaves, 8vo, in dark blue mor by Riviere. With 9 illuminated initials & 7 miniatures (1 full-page). S Dec 12 (198) £1,700 [Bechtel]
See also: Merard de Saint Just, Simon Pierre

Calvert, Charles, 3d Baron Baltimore, 1637-1715

Ds, 1665. 1 p, folio. Land deed for a tract in Talbot County. bbc Sept 23 (24) $300

Camerarius, Joachim, 1534-98

Ms, The Camerarius Florilegium, flower book. [Nuremberg, c.1589]. 194 leaves, c.365mm by 245mm, mtd on early 18th-cent sheets, 435mm by 280mm. 18th-cent mottled calf. Containing 473 drawings of ornamental plants in watercolor, with plant names in Latin (some in German & Italian). C May 20 (151) £580,000 [Rosenthal]

Campanella, Roy

Signature, [n.d.]. 16mo (card). Dar Dec 26 (79) $190

— Anr, [n.d.]. On card reproducing Hall of Fame plaque. Dar Aug 6 (92) $375

Campbell, James, 1812-93

Autograph sentiment, sgd, 22 Nov 1867. 1 p, 9 by 2 inches. "This is a Republic, in which the will of the People, is the law of the land." sup Oct 15 (1058) $100

Campe, Friedrich, 1777-1846

ALs, 24 Apr 1810. 4 pp, 4to. To Franz Haas. About his publication business. star Mar 26 (70) DM600

Campe, Joachim Heinrich, 1746-1818

ALs, 14 Nov 1777. 6 pp, 4to. To Alexander Georg von Humboldt. Justifying his decision to leave the Philanthropin at Dessau. star Mar 26 (571) DM2,200

Campe, Julius, 1792-1867. See: Heine, Heinrich

Campra, Andre, 1660-1744

Ms, vocal & instrumental parts for the opera Hesione & the ballet Arethuse, 1703. 6 vols, 4to, in armorial calf bdg. Copied for the Comte de Toulouse by a scribe from the circle of Philidor l'aine. S Dec 6 (58) £1,500 [Bibliotheque Nationale]

Canetti, Elias

Autograph Ms, working draft for his Die Leute von Marrakesch, [c.1965]. 70 pp, 4to, in limp cloth bdg. HN Nov 28 (1649) DM41,000

Canova, Antonio, 1757-1822

Collection of 8 A Ls s & 3 Ls s, 12 Sept 1801 to 27 Sept 1812. 16 pp, 4to. To Giuseppe Bossi. About his statues of Napoleon, Perseus, & other works. S May 28 (164) £4,200 [Ars Libri]

Capone, Alphonse ("Al"), 1899-1947

Ds, [18 May 1926]. 1 p, 8.75 by 3 inches. Interest note for Loan No 6223 at the Lawndale National Bank; also sgd by Theresa & Mae Capone. Endorsed by all 3 on verso. Torn. Dar Dec 26 (161) $3,250

— 18 Nov 1926. 1 p, 9 by 3 inches. Interest note for Loan No 6223 at the Lawndale National Bank; also sgd by Theresa & Mae Capone. Endorsed by all 3 on verso. Dar Oct 10 (104) $4,000

— 18 Nov 1926. 1 p, 8.75 by 3 inches. Interest note, also sgd by Theresa & Mae Capone; also sgd by all 3 on verso. Dar June 11 (117) $5,500

Capote, Truman, 1924-84

Autograph Ms, Mr. Jones, Mar 1979. 16 pp, 8vo, on rectos only. Including corrections; sgd. sg June 11 (56) $3,600

Ds, 17 Mar 1975. 2 pp, size not stated. Contract with John M. O'Shea; sgd by both. Dar Apr 9 (145) $130

Capote, Truman, 1924-84 —& Warhol, Andy, d.1987

[Their signatures on the cover of Warhol's "Interview" newspaper, 1979, 16.5 by 11 inches, sold at Dar on 10 Oct 1991, lot 105, for $120.]

[Their signatures on the front cover of a copy of Interview Magazine, vol IX, no 6, containing Conversations with Capote, framed, sold at wd on 12 June 1992, lot 308, for $150.]

Capra, Frank, 1897-1991

Ds, 25 Nov 1935. 1 p, 4to. Contract with Columbia Pictures; also sgd by Harry Cohn. Dar Oct 10 (106) $500

Caradoc, John Francis, Sir, 1759-1839. See: South Africa

Cardozo, Benjamin N., 1870-1938

ALs, 21 Aug 1930. 2 pp, 4to. To Henry Hurwitz. Thanking for a book. Illus in cat. sup Oct 15 (1059) $750

Carlota, Empress of Mexico, 1840-1927

ALs, 27 Mar 1867. 1 p, 8vo. To Manuela Gutierrez del Barrio. Expressing pleasure about receiving a letter in Spanish. star Mar 27 (1487) DM1,200

Carlyle, Thomas, 1795-1881

Collection of 2 A Ls s & card, sgd, 25 Feb 1865 & [n.y.]. 6 pp, 12mo & 16mo. To his sister Mrs. Aitken. About his wife's illness, his own ailments, etc. C Dec 16 (281) £360 [Quaritch]

ALs, 27 Mar 1837. 1 p, 8vo. Recipient unnamed. Informing him that his wife is unable to meet him. wa Oct 19 (47) $140

— 26 Feb 1847. 2 pp, 8vo. To Thomas Erskine. Arranging a meeting & giving his views on Prince Albert's candidature as Chancellor of Cambridge. Ingilby collection. pn Nov 14 (58) £240 [Quaritch]

— 27 Oct 1858. 4 pp, 8vo. To [John?] Fergus. Thanking for a case of Scotch whisky & mentioning his recent visit to Germany. Ingilby collection. pn Nov 14 (59) £340 [Quaritch]

Carmer, Johann Heinrich Casimir, Graf von, 1721-1801

ALs, 16 June 1750. 3 pp, 4to. To a court official in Berlin. Conveying orders & information from an inspection tour of courts in Silesia. star Mar 27 (1296) DM600

Carnegie, Andrew, 1835-1919

Signature, on poster for a dinner at the Lotus Club, NY, 17 Mar 1909. 18.5 by 12 inches. Illus in cat. R June 13 (199) $300

Carnera, Primo, 1906-67

Signature, 1933. 4 by 2.25 inches (card). Dar Apr 9 (131) $250

— Anr, [n.d.]. 5 by 3 inches (card). Dar Feb 13 (118) $225

Carnot, Lazare, Comte, 1753-1823

Ls, 9 May 1815. 1 p, folio. To Marshal Davout. Informing him of decorations awarded by Napoleon. star Mar 27 (1367) DM280

Caro, Annibale, 1507-66. See: Guidiccioni, Giovanni & Caro

Carol I, King of Romania, 1839-1914

Ds, 28 Mar 1911. 1 p, 4to. Contents not stated. Dar June 11 (118) $225

Carossa, Hans, 1878-1956

Autograph Ms, essay, Stunden in Verona, [n.d.]. 15 pp, 4to, on rectos only. Fair copy, including some corrections. Sgd on tp. star Mar 26 (71) DM2,000

Collection of 14 A Ls s & autograph postcard, sgd, 11 Aug 1947 to 9 Jan 1955. 32 pp, various sizes. To Ivar Ljungerud. Interesting correspondence about various aspects of his work. star Mar 26 (74) DM3,400

ALs, 5 Nov 1937. 2 pp, 8vo. To Kurt Fried. Discussing some medication. star Mar 26 (72) DM500

— [5 June] 1938. 2 pp, folio. To Franz Burri. Declining an invitation to lecture in Austria. star Mar 26 (73) DM230

Carradine, John, 1906-88

Ds, 30 Mar 1936. 1 p, 4to. Agreement with 20th Century-Fox. Dar Apr 9 (146) $150

— 21 Nov 1949. 2 pp, 4to. Contract with The Theatre Guild Radio Division; carbon copy. Dar Feb 13 (127) $100

Carroll, Charles, Signer from Maryland

ALs, 24 Feb 1825. 1 p, 4to. To an unnamed legislator. Referring to "the resolution respecting the suit instituted by Mr. Browning against me." bbc Dec 9 (160) $285

— 19 Apr 1825. 1 p, 4to. To Robert Barry. Thanking for a box of chocolate & sending payment. With engraved port. Illus in cat. sup Oct 15 (1196) $360

— 11 Feb 1828. 1 p, 8vo. To Roswell L. Colt. About interest on a bond. With clipped address. Mtd. wd Dec 12 (306) $325

Carte, Richard D'Oyly, 1844-1901

Ls, 18 Sept 1879. 1 p, 8vo. To W. Rossiter. Apologizing for "any inconvenience at my theatre". Imperf. Dar Apr 9 (147) $160

Carter, James Earl ("Jimmy")

Transcript, excerpts from his interview with Playboy magazine, 1976; sgd. 2 sheets, 12mo. Framed with related material. Dar Dec 26 (141) $650

Typescript, excerpts from his interview with Playboy, 1976. 2 pp, 8vo. Sgd. Framed with a group photograph with Cheryl Prewitt. Dar June 11 (119) $200

Ls, 1 Sept 1977. 1 p, 4to. To Walter Sanders. Concerning the designation of a regional solar energy center. Including autograph postscript, sgd J.C. Illus in cat. sup May 9 (294) $1,800

— 14 Mar 1985. 1 p, 8vo. To Leslie Lynch King. Thanking for a 1924 Ed of the National Geographic Magazine. Dar Feb

13 (128) $100

ANs, [Sept 1976]. On cover of ptd campaign brochure. To Edith Greene. Hoping for advice & support. Dar Oct 10 (107) $275

Signature, [n.d.]. 1 p, 8vo. On typescript of Presidential Oath of Office. Matted with a photograph. Dar Oct 10 (108) $200

Carter, James Earl ("Jimmy") —& Ford, Gerald R.

[Their signatures on a card with affixed White House vignette, [n.d.], 12mo, matted with a photograph, sold at Dar on 10 Oct 1991, lot 279, for $110.]

Carter, Sonny, 1955-91

Photograph, sgd & inscr, [n.d.]. 8 by 10 inches. Inscr to Albert. Dar Dec 26 (47) $110

Caruso, Enrico, 1873-1921

Original drawing, full-length caricature, 1908. 5 by 8.5 inches. In pencil; sgd. Dar Apr 9 (152) $300

— Original drawing, self-port, 1904. 8vo. In pen-&-ink; sgd. star Mar 27 (993) DM1,700

ALs, 13 Feb 1912. 1 p, 4to. To Mr. Bagby. Suggesting that he engage Mr. Schonberger to accompany him in a concert. cb Feb 12 (154) $250

— 6 Nov 1914. 1 p, 4to. To Gaetano Capone. Expressing thanks. sg Sept 12 (40) $300

— 28 Feb 1919. 4 pp, 8vo. To Dr. Luigi Pane. Thanking for a gift. Framed with a port. P June 17 (9) $700

Autograph postcard, sgd, 16 May 1905. To Blanche Alexander. Expressing thanks. Framed with a port. sg Sept 12 (39) $225

— [2 Apr 1907]. Recipient unnamed. Sending greetings from Boston. wa Oct 19 (156) $250

Autograph sentiment, sgd, 9 words. 12mo; on postcard reproducing self-caricature. Inscr to D. Alfiero. Dar Dec 26 (144) $300

Caricature, profile bust pose of a lady wearing large hat, 7 Sept 1905. 5 by 7.5 inches. Sgd. sg Feb 27 (32) $550

Christmas card, sgd, [24 Dec 1915]. 12mo (postcard). To Maria del Pezzo. Dar Dec 26 (142) $225

— Anr, sgd, [24 Dec 1915]. 12mo (postcard). To Jessie Petti. Dar Dec 26 (143) $180

Group photograph, sgd & inscr, [n.d.]. 5.5 by 3.5 inches. With others at a luncheon table. Illus in cat. Dar Apr 9 (154) $150

Photograph, sgd, [c.1910]. Postcard. HH May 13 (1912) DM470

— Anr, 1911. Postcard. Six-fold photograph, sitting around a table. pn Mar 19 (116) £280 [Macnutt]

— Anr, [n.d.]. 9.5 by 5 inches. By Langfier. Framed. Illus in cat. R June 13 (225A) $500

Photograph, sgd & inscr, 1901. 140mm by 95mm. Inscr to Bruno Cittadini. By Sciutto. C June 24 (23) £450 [L'Autographe]

— Anr, [c.1915]. 3.5 by 5.5 inches. With anr, unsgd. sg Sept 12 (41) $450

— Anr, [n.d.]. 5.5 by 3.5 inches. Dar Apr 9 (153) $250

— Anr, [n.d.]. 5.4 by 7.4 inches. Inscr to Edith P. Kendall. sg Feb 27 (31) $325

Self-caricature, 1906. 8vo. Sgd. Illus in cat. sup Oct 15 (1060) $900

— Anr, [18 Aug] 1909. 46cm by 36cm. Singing at a concert; in brown pen & ink wash. Sgd. Illus in cat. S Dec 6 (64) £1,700 [Dr. Laren]

— Anr, [n.d.]. 32cm by 21.5cm. In stage costume; sgd. Illus in cat. S May 29 (509) £1,150 [Billington]

Carver, George Washington, 1864-1943

Signature, 14 Feb 1938. On unaddressed philatelic envelope. Dar June 11 (121) $325

Casas, Bartolome de las, 1474-1566

Ms, Laz conclusiones y paraceres q[ue] dio fray bar[tolo]me de las casas en la congregation g[enera]l sobre el R[ein]o de las Indias, [c.1542]. 16 pp, folio. In a single Italic scribal hand. Summary of his 40 proposals for reform of the colonial system. S June 25 (452) £58,000 [De Jonge]

Cassidy, Ted, 1932-79

Photograph, sgd, [n.d.]. 7 by 9 inches. Dar Apr 9 (155) $225

Cather, Willa S., 1873-1947

ALs, [18 Mar 1922]. 2 pp, size not stated (card). To Lawrence Rising. Thanking for a present. wd June 12 (310) $250

Catherine II, Empress of Russia, 1729-96

Ls, 24 June 1782. 1 p, 4to. To Prince Ferdinand. Sending congratulations on the birth of his daughter. Framed with a port. P June 17 (10) $1,300

Catlin, George, 1796-1872

Original drawing, sketch of 2 chickens, sgd; [n.d.]. 4.75 by 6.5 inches. In pencil. sup Oct 15 (1065) $400

Celine, Louis Ferdinand Destouches, 1894-1961

Autograph Ms, draft of chapter 5 of D'un chateau l'autre; [c.1955-56]. 28 pp, folio. Sgd at end. S May 28 (197) £2,000 [Rota]

Typescript, scenario for a ballet, La Naissance d'une Fee, [1936]. 19 pp, folio. Comprising 8 tableaux; sgd. With covering ALs. Boris Kochno collection. SM Oct 12 (355) FF8,000

ALs, 4 June [1947]. 4 pp, folio. To Theo. About his exile in Denmark. star Mar 26 (75) DM650

Centurione, Alessandro

Ms, Versione di Alcuni Salmi di David ..., 1697. 130 leaves, 4to, in contemp sheep. With Latin & Italian texts on facing pages. Ck Mar 6 (174) £50

Cernan, Gene

Photograph, sgd & inscr, [n.d.]. Size not stated. On moon's surface; sgd twice & inscr to Brooke Allen. Framed. wa Oct 19 (186) $170

Certificates

— BAKER'S CERTIFICATE. - Document, 14 Sept 1846 & 2 Nov 1848. 1 p, folio. Journeyman's certificate for Jakob Friedrich Klumpp, issued at Freudenstadt. Duplicate. HN Nov 28 (1703) DM580

— FIREMAN'S CERTIFICATE. - Document, 6 Apr 1830. 1 p, 16 by 12 inches. Certifying C. F. V. Reevie a member of the Charleston Fire Company, sgd by J. F. Schirmer & J. English. R Nov 9 (299) $100

— GARDENER'S CERTIFICATE. - Document, 18 Feb 1732. 1 p, 330mmm by 578mm. Journeyman's certificate for Johann Conrad Sipp, sgd by C. G. Seyler. With coat-of-arms of Ferdinand Maximilian Graf zu Ysenburg-Buedingen. HH May 12 (59) DM420

— HUNTSMAN'S CERTIFICATE. - Document, 7 Apr 1795. 1 p, 355mm by 525mm. Certificate for Franz Christian Vogt after completing an apprenticeship in hunting, sgd by Friedrich Adolph Krueger, huntsman at the court of the Prince of Lippe. Including 2 drawings of hunting scenes. JG Mar 27 (189) DM350

— NAIL SMITH'S CERTIFICATE. - Document, 25 June 1855. 1 p, folio. Journeyman's certificate for August Pulvermueller, issued at Freudenstadt. Including engraving of the arms of Wuerttemberg. HN Nov 28 (1705) DM370

— SHOEMAKER'S CERTIFICATE. - Document, 13 Apr 1826. 1 p, folio. Attestation that Johan Henzl completed his apprenticeship as shoemaker at Unterkanitz; sgd by the Mayor & several others. Including large woodcut illus of Bruenn. HN Nov 28 (1706) DM340

Cessolis, Jacobus de

Ms, De Ludo Scachorum. [Italy, c.1400] 120 leaves, 302mm by 225mm, in 18th-cent vellu-backed pastebd bdg. In brown ink, in 3 book scripts with notarial & batarde characteristics; index to Cessolis in cursive notarial script. With other medieval texts. Illus in catalogue. Blass Ms Ck May 8 (3) £7,000

— Ms, De Ludo Scachorum Libri I-III. [France, 2d quarter of 15th cent] 37 leaves, vellum, 170mm by 128mm, in 19th-cent bds. In school script, 30-33 lines. Blass Ms Ck May 8 (4) £3,000

— Ms, De Ludo Scachorum. [France, c.1480] 62 (of 68) leaves, vellum, 205mm by 140mm, in 18th-cent sheep. In batarde scripts in brown ink, with red for the headings, 24-30 lines. Illuminated coat-of-arms on 1r; gold initials on red ground; paragraph marks line-fillers in red or blue. Blass Ms Ck May 8 (5) £6,000

— Ms, De Ludo Scachorum, in French. [Northern France, c.1500] Trans by Jean de Vignay. 65 (of 68) leaves, 262mm by 198mm, in contemp flind-tooled calf over pastebd. In batarde script in brown ink, rubricated in red. Blass Ms Ck May 8 (7) £4,000

Chadwick, Henry, 1824-1908

ALs, [n.d.]. 1 p, 12mo. To John P. Green. Asking for a ticket to a baseball game. With recipient's answer on verso. Trimmed. Dar Dec 26 (80) $5,500

Cut signature, [n.d.]. 3 by 0.4 inches. Cut from a document. Illus in cat. Dar Feb 13 (73) $500

Chaffee, Roger B., 1935-67

Ns, [1 Aug 1961]. 3.25 by 7 inches (card). To his father Don L. Chaffee. Birthday card. Dar Dec 26 (48) $400

Chagall, Marc, 1887-1985

ALs, 23 Feb 1947. 1 p, 4to. To Fennenbaum. Thanking for a book. sup Oct 15 (1063) $420

Ls, 27 Aug 1954. 1 p, 4to. To Mrs. Sothmann. Suggesting that she contact his daughter regarding an exhibition of his works. With related material. HN June 26 (893) DM320

Photograph, sgd, [Aug 1934]. 8.25 by 8.5 inches. Painting a port of his wife. Dar Feb 13 (132) $150

Ptd photograph, sgd, [n.d.]. 9.5 by 12 inches. Cut from an art book. Dar Feb 13 (133) $150

Signature, [n.d.]. On ptd photograph of mural in the Paris Theatre National de l'Opera, 19 by 13 inches. Dar Oct 10 (115) $200

— Anr, [n.d.]. On ptd reproduction of 1st sketch for his mural in the Paris Theatre National de l'Opera, 19 by 13 inches. Dar Oct 10 (117) $130

— Anr, [n.d.]. 10.5 by 14 inches. On art photograph removed from a book on his works. Dar Aug 6 (128) $120

— Anr, [n.d.]. On record cover reproducing a Chagall lithograph. Dar Aug 6 (129) $130

Chamberlain, Neville, 1869-1940

Autograph sentiment, sgd, Apr 1940. Presenting a book to the Red Cross Society. On front free endpaper of W. H. Husdon's Far away and Long Ago. L, 1931. With secretarial letter of transferral. wa Oct 19 (92) $220

Chaminade, Cecile, 1857-1944

Autograph quotation, Pastorale, 1 bar of music, sgd; May 1907. Size not stated. Matted with a photograph. wa Oct 19 (157) $95

Chamisso, Adelbert von, 1781-1838

Autograph Ms, poem, Frauen-Liebe und Leben, [n.d.]. 8 pp, 8vo. 42 stanzas, sgd. star Mar 26 (76) DM15,000

AL, [1812]. 2 pp, 8vo. To [Julius Eduard Hitzig]. Reporting about his visit with Mme de Stael at Coppet. Incomplete. star Mar 26 (77) DM1,300

ANs, [n.d.]. 1 p, 8vo. To [Franz Kugler]. Inviting him. star Mar 26 (79) DM270

Chaney, Lon, 1907-73

Photograph, sgd & inscr, [n.d.]. 7 by 5 inches. R June 13 (201) $130

Signature, [n.d.]. 4.5 by 3 inches. In extra frame. Dar Aug 6 (11) $900

Chang, 1811-74 —&
Eng, 1811-74

[Their signatures on a Baltimore Museum admission ticket, [n.d.], 4 by 2.25 inches, framed with 2 photographs & further related material, sold at Dar on 6 Aug 1992, lot 131, for $1,100.]

Chapelain, Jean, 1595-1674

ALs, [n.d.]. 3 pp, 8vo. To Madeleine de Scudery. Requesting her intercession with the Bishop of Le Mans to obtain a living. star Mar 26 (80) DM400

Chapin, Harry, 1942-81

Photograph, sgd, [n.d.]. 5 by 7 inches. Dar Apr 9 (156) $200

Photograph, sgd & inscr, [n.d.]. 8 by 10 inches. Inscr to Gina. wa Oct 19 (158) $80

Chaplin, Charles, 1889-1977

Autograph sentiment, sgd, [n.d.]. Expressing good wishes. Framed with a photograph, overall size 16 by 14 inches. Dar Apr 9 (157) $200

Group photograph, sgd, [n.d.]. 7 by 9 inches. With Jackie Coogan. With signature on philatelic envelope, 1975. Dar June 11 (127) $225

— Anr, sgd, [n.d.]. 8 by 10 inches. With well-wishers & reporters. Including small self-caricature as The Little Tramp below signature. Illus in cat. sup Oct 15 (1068) $820

— Anr, [n.d]. 4to. With Paulette Goddard; sgd by Chaplin. wa Oct 19 (4) $325

Photograph, sgd, [n.d.]. 5 by 7 inches. Half length. b&b Feb 19 (155) $350

— Anr, [n.d.]. 8 by 10 inches. Dar Dec 26 (151) $350

Photograph, sgd & inscr, [c.1915]. 4.5 by 6.5 inches. Dar Oct 10 (118) $225

Signature, [1920s]. 3 by 1.5 inches (card). Illus in cat. Dar Feb 13 (137) $160

— Anr, [n.d.]. On a sheet of Olympic stamps. Including subscription. Dar June 11 (126) $200

— Anr, [n.d.]. On a card. Matted with a photograph, overall size 7 by 16 inches. Illus in cat. sup Oct 15 (1069) $450

Charles, Prince of Wales

Christmas card, sgd, [n.d.]. 8vo. To Jim [Perowne]. Including photograph with his grandmother. wa Oct 19 (171) $500

Charles Albert, King of Sardinia-Piedmont, 1798-1849

Ds, 24 Mar 1838. 2 pp, 4to. Military commission for Conte Carlo Rossi. star Mar 27 (1451) DM280

Charles I, King of England, 1600-49

Ls, 25 Oct 1639. 1 p, folio. To Landgraefin Amalie Elisabeth von Hessen-Kassel. Letter of credence for his envoy Wilhelm Curtius. In Latin. Illus in cat. star Mar 27 (1426) DM2,700

— 23 Jan 1641/42. 1 p, folio. To Friedrich Wilhelm, Elector of Brandenburg. Introducing his legate Joseph Avery. In the hand of Georg Weckherlin. Illus in cat. pn June 11 (47) £520 [Quaritch]

Ds, 17 May 1634. 1 p, folio. Warrant addressed to Sir William Kendall, appointing Thomas Floyd a trumpeter. pn Nov 14 (178) £520 [Wilson]

Document, 9 July 1629. 1 p, vellum, 23 by 32 inches. Letters patent addressed to Henry Hastings, Earl of Huntingdon, confirming letters patent of Henry VIII of 8 Dec 1529. Magnificently illuminated, & with finely executed initial letter port on separate vellum sheet. Framed. Illus in cat. P June 17 (152) $26,000

Charles II, King of England, 1630-85

Ds, 6 Dec 1671. 1 p, folio. Order that Robert Overton be delivered to Capt. Gardiner. S July 21 (198) £900 [Overton]

— 9 July 1672. 2 pp, folio. Pardon to 20 Quakers & other non-conformists. pn Nov 14 (179) £550 [Sawyer]

— 29 Sept 1674. 1 p, 4to. Authorization for Anthony D'Euerall to select a deputy for his absence. Countersgd by Samuel Pepys. Framed with a port of both. P June 17 (12) $1,100

Document, 1 Apr 1674. 1 p, vellum, 23.25 by 30.5 inches. Letters Patent creating Susan Belasyse a Baroness in her own right. Including initial letter port. S Dec 12 (250) £2,200 [Quaritch]

— PRIVY COUNCIL. - Letter, 24 Jan 1679. 2 pp, folio. Recipient unnamed. Ordering a stiffening of action against Catholics. Sgd by several members of the Council. bba May 28 (212) £280 [Byrne]

— TRIPOLI. - Ms, A copie of the Articles of Peace made by Sir John Narbrough in the behalf of His Majesty with the City of Tripoly in Barbary, [c.1675]. 4 leaves, folio; stitched. bba Sept 19 (427) £55 [Hobbes]

Charles IV, King of Spain, 1748-1819

Ds, 13 Dec 1799. 1 p, 4to. Order to the Viceroy of New Spain to execute the appointment of Ramon Benavides as lieutenant. sup Oct 15 (1064) $300

Charles IX, King of Sweden, 1550-1611

Ls, 10 Nov 1598. 4 pp, folio. To [Landgraf Moritz von Hessen-Kassel?]. About his recent victory over King Sigsmund's army at Stangebro. star Mar 27 (1712) DM550

Charles IX, King of France, 1550-74

Ds, 28 Jan 1563. 1 p, vellum, 11 by 14.25 inches. On financial matters. Def. sg Feb 27 (33) $250

Charles of Lorraine, Governor of the Netherlands, 1712-80

Ls, 11 Apr 1760. 2 pp, folio. To Graf von Harrach. About several administrative matters. HN Nov 28 (1742) DM300

— 16 July 1760. 3 pp, folio. To Count Harsch. About a corps of engineers. star Mar 27 (1665) DM260

Charles, Ray

Ds, 9 Feb 1979. 2 pp, 4to. Contract for a televison show. Dar Apr 9 (158) $180

Charles V, Emperor, 1500-58

Ms, Edictum contra Martinum Lutherum. [Italy, 16th cent]. 40 pp, 4to, in modern mor gilt. Copy in an Italic hand; sgd Beatus Arnoldus. S Feb 11 (491) £360 [De Lorenzo]

Ls, 23 Aug 1523. 2 pp, folio. To A. Adorno. Approving of military preparations in Italy. star Mar 27 (1639) DM2,000

— 7 Mar 1530. 1 p, folio. To the Duke of Sessa. Emphasizing the need to unite against the Turkish menace, mentioning his coronation as Emperor, & announcing his departure for Germany. Illus in cat, S Dec 5 (477) £2,200 [Wilson]

Ds, 13 Oct 1525. 1 p, folio. Request addressed to the Inquisitor to take part in a case against a clergyman accused of homicide. Def. sg Feb 27 (186) $1,900

Document, 3 July 1553. 1 p, folio. Order addressed to the Governor at Tournay regarding the organization of the cavalry. star Mar 27 (1640) DM310

Charles VI, Emperor, 1685-1740

Ls, 3 Dec 1711. 1 p, folio. To his mother. Sending an envoy to report about current affairs. star Mar 27 (1652) DM420

Ds, 4 July 1731. 20 pp, 4to, in red velvet bdg. Patent of nobility for Johann Ernst Wenzel von der Goltz. Including full-page painting of the arms in gold & colors. star Mar 27 (1653) DM1,050

Charles VII, Emperor, 1697-1745

Ls, 29 Mar 1727. 3 pp, folio. To Christoph Franz von Hutten-Stolzenberg, Bishop of Wuerzburg. Announcing the birth of his son. star Mar 27 (1252) DM370

Ds, 23 Feb 1728. 1 p, folio. Grant of land to Baron von Preysing. star Mar 27 (1253) DM220

Charles XII, King of Sweden, 1682-1718

ALs, 17 Feb [1716]. 1 p, 4to. To Friedrich von Hessel-Kassel [the future King of Sweden]. Informing him about money put at his disposal for the preparation of the campaign against Norway. star Mar 27 (1714) DM2,200

Charles XIV John, King of Sweden, 1763-1844

Ls, [25 Feb 1805]. 1 p, folio. To the paymaster-in-chief. Concerning funds for expenses of the artillery. sg Feb 27 (23) $275

— [2 May 1805]. 1 p, 4to. To the Ordonnateur en Chef. Authorizing payments. pn June 11 (29) £75

Ds, 5 Oct 1824. 3 pp, 4to. Concerning mining privileges & taxes for Conrad Theodor von Schulzenheim. Dar Feb 13 (268) $160

Charles XV, King of Sweden, 1826-72

ALs, 22 Mar [1871]. 4 pp, 8vo. Recipient unnamed. Expressing dismay about the recent peace treaty of Versailles. star Mar 27 (1716) DM360

Charleston, Oscar, 1896-1954

Signature, [n.d.]. 3.25 by 1.5 inches (card). Dar Aug 6 (93) $275

Charlotte Sophia, Queen of George III of England, 1744-1818

A Ls s (2), 2 Jan 1788 & 31 Jan 1789. 4 pp, size not stated. To Lord Thurlow. Complaining about her husband's physicians, & thanking for the draft of a letter to the Prince of Wales. b June 22 (129) £190

Chase, Salmon P., 1808-73

ALs, 13 Apr 1854. 3 pp, 8vo. To Alexander Lankey Latty. Regarding the anti-slavery movement in Ohio. Illus in cat. sup Oct 15 (1070) $1,050

— 6 Dec 1859. 1 p, 4to. To O. C. Hays. As Governor of Ohio, offering him a position on the Board of Equalization. Dar Feb 13 (138) $110

Cherry-Garrard, Apsley, 1886-1959

ALs, 5 Dec 1922. 1 p, size not stated. To Henry Major Tomlinson. Thanking for a favorable review. Ck Apr 3 (50) £220

Cherubini, Luigi, 1760-1842

ALs, 19 May 1817. 2 pp, 4to. To Salieri. Letter of introduction for Auguste Panseron. S Dec 6 (66) £950 [Macnutt]

Chesbro, Jack, 1874-1931

Check, accomplished & sgd, 10 Dec 1907. 6.75 by 2.75 inches. Payable to James D. Avery. Dar Dec 26 (81) $2,000

Chesterfield, Philip Dormer Stanhope, 4th Earl of, 1694-1773

ALs, 3 Sept 1739. 2 pp, 4to. To [James Hamilton, Viscount Limerick]. Discussing philosophical & political matters. sg Sept 12 (45) $600

Chesterton, Gilbert Keith, 1874-1936

Ls, 3 Oct 1935. 2 pp, 4to. To Antonio Aita. Thanking for an invitation to a PEN conference. star Mar 26 (81) DM560

Chezy, Helmina von, 1783-1856

Autograph Ms, poem, Apolog aus dem Persischen, [n.d.]. 4 pp, 8vo. 59 lines, sgd. star Mar 26 (82) DM400

Chiang Kai-shek, 1887-1975

Photograph, sgd, [n.d.]. 2.75 by 5.75 inches. Dar Apr 9 (160) $110

Chile

Ms, Libro Mayor de la Tresoreria General de Exercito y Real Hacienda de Santiago de Chile, 1806. 143 leaves & blanks, folio. Government & army accounts. bba Sept 19 (399) £190 [Hobbes]

Chodowiecki, Daniel, 1726-1801

[A group of 12 engravings, proof sheets of his illusts to Salomon Gessner's Idyllen, with drafts of captions in Chodowiecki's hand & the signatures of 4 members of the Berlin Academy, 9 Jan 1771, 22cm by 36.5cm, sold at star on 27 Mar 1992, lot 880, for DM4,500.]

ALs, [summer 1894]. 4 pp, 8vo. To [Wilhelm Gottlieb Becker]. Concerning illusts for recipient's publications. star Mar 27 (881) DM620

Chopin, Frederic, 1810-49

Autograph music, Grande Valse Brillante, Op. 18 in E flat major, 10 July 1833. 4 pp, 8vo. 107 bars, sgd & inscr to Laura Horsford. Illus in cat. Searles-Rowland collection. C June 24 (8) £55,000 [Haas]

— Autograph music, song, Wiosna, Op. 74 no 2, to a text by S. Witwicki; [n.d.]. 2 pp, 8vo. Scored for piano. Fair copy, sgd & inscr to Mme Kiere. Illus in cat. Mannheim collection. S Dec 6 (8) £24,000 [Baron]

— Autograph music, Valse, Op. 70 no 1 in G flat major, 8 Aug 1832. 1 p, 8vo. 42 bars, sgd. Illus in cat. Searles-Rowland collection. C June 24 (7) £35,000 [Dreesmann]

— Autograph music, variations on Mozart's La ci darem la mano from Don Giovanni, Op. 2; [1828/29]. 2 pp, 258mm by 348mm. End of variation III, & beginning of variation V. Illus in cat. Pleyel collection. star Mar 27 (996) DM135,000

ALs, [c.1833]. 1 p, 12mo. To Camille Pleyel. Asking him to provide a grand piano for the following evening. Mannheim collection. S Dec 6 (6) £9,000 [Polish Chopin Society]

ANs, [n.d.], "Saturday". 1 p, 16mo. To Jozef Nowakowski. Inviting him to call on him the next day. Mannheim collection. S Dec 6 (7) £5,200 [Baron]

Ds s (2) June 1845. 1 p, folio. Assigning the English copyright of 5 works to Wessel & Co., & receipt for payment. Illus in cat. S May 29 (511) £6,000 [Tamura]

Ds, 31 Oct 1839. 1 p, 8vo. Assigning the English copyright of 4 works to Wessel & Co. & acknowledging payment. Illus in cat. S May 29 (512) £4,000 [Wilson]

— May 1840. 1 p, folio. Contract with the pbr Wessel of London for the publication of his Op. 35, 36 & 37. Sgd twice. Illus in cat. S Dec 6 (70) £4,500 [Wilson]

— HUMMEL, JOHANN NEPOMUK. - ALs, 3 Dec 1833. 3 pp, 4to. To Christian Rudolf Wessel. Explaining that he cannot agree to the same terms as Chopin for the publication of his Rondo. S May 29 (514) £4,000 [Tamura]

Chou En-lai, 1898-1976

Ls, 18 Aug 1946. 1 p, 4to. To Franklin Ray. Relaying a report from the Central China branch of the Communist Areas Relief Committee. Framed. P June 17 (13) $1,900

Christian Ernst, Markgraf von Brandenburg-Bayreuth, 1644-1712

Ls, 26 Feb 1703. 2 pp, folio. To Friedrich Koehler. Regarding property in Nuernberg belonging to Johann Septimus von Stark. HH May 13 (1914) DM420

Christian I, Fuerst von Anhalt-Bernburg, 1568-1630

Ls, 11 Aug 1617. 1 p, folio. To Markgraf Joachim Ernst von Brandenburg-Ansbach. Notifying him of the birth of a daughter. With engraved port. star Mar 27 (1238) DM350

Christian VIII, King of Denmark, 1786-1848

ALs, 22 Oct 1844. 2 pp, 4to. To an unnamed prince. Inviting him for an excursion. HN Nov 28 (1651) DM200

Christina, Queen of Sweden, 1626-89

ANs, [n.d.]. 1 p, 7 by 4 inches. Recipient & contents not stated. Dar Apr 9 (161) $225

Ds, Feb 1650. 1 p, folio. Confirmation of a transaction by Johan [Gran?]. S Dec 5 (478) £550 [Quaritch]

Christophe, Henri, 1767-1820

Autograph endorsement, sgd, 24 Apr 1798. 1 p, 4to. At bottom of a requisition for weapons by Rameau Gajolle; note of approval. Framed with a port. P June 17 (14) $1,500

Christopher III, King of Sweden, 1418-48

Ms, Landslag, laws promulgated in 1442. [Sweden, 1st half of 16th cent]. 136 leaves, 282mm by 196mm. In calf, with sides of contemp blindstamped bdg. In a calligraphic Swedish cursive script with calligraphic flourishes, with headings in a gothic batarde. With decorated initials throughout sometimes including dragons & faces. S June 23 (65) £5,500 [Gunther]

— Ms, Svergislag; Uppland Laws & law codes. [Sweden, 1546]. 152 leaves (1 lacking), 270mm by 180mm. 18th-cent mottled calf. In a calligraphic Swedish cursive script. With headings throughout in red; some later additions. S June 23 (66) £5,000 [Gunther]

Christy, Howard Chandler, 1873-1952

ALs, 19 Jan 1936. 1 p, 4to. To Mrs. Timmons. Expressing enthusiasm for a project. Dar Apr 9 (162) $120

Chronicles

Ms, Les Lignees des Roys de France. [Northern France or Southern Flanders, c.1470]. Scroll of 10 membranes of vellum, 333mm by 6970mm. In a lettre batarde. With c. 80 small & 2 very large illuminated initials, names of kings in colored cartouches, a large town view, & 54 circular vignettes of cities, castles or monasteries. A few later additions. S Dec 17 (56) £23,000 [Fogg]

Churchill, Maria M.

Autograph Ms, diary, July 1845 to May 1848. About 220 leaves in 3 vols, 8vo; in bds. Diary of a New England mother working as a professional seamstress. sg Dec 5 (88) $425

Churchill, Randolph Henry Spencer, Lord, 1849-94

ALs, 3 Apr 1889. 3 pp, 8vo. To Mr. Rockfort. Referring to his recent resignation as Chancellor of the Exchequer. Ingilby collection. pn Nov 14 (60) £100

Churchill, Randolph Spencer, 1911-68

Collection of 13 A Ls s, 8 Ls s, & 11 A Ns s, [n.d.]. Length not stated. To Claire Luce. Love letters. With related material. R Nov 9 (75) $2,800

Churchill, Sir Winston L. S., 1874-1965

[3 large albums of "Official War Office Photographs" of Churchill, presented to him by the War Cabinet, comprising over 470 photographs covering his tours at home & abroad, July 1940 to July 1945, 12.25 by 16.25 inches, sold at P on 12 Dec 1991, lot 287, for £18,000 to Fine Arts Society.]

Typescript, speech at his 2d installation as Lord Warden of the Cinque Ports, 14 Aug 1946. 14 pp, 8vo. Including autograph revisions. With material relating to the ceremony. Illus in cat. S July 21 (247) £6,200 [Wilson]

Collection of ALs & 4 Ls s, 8 June 1909 to 21 Mar 1919. 5 pp, 8vo. To Lord St. Davids. Congratulating him on an appointment, sending a letter to Lloyd George, & referring to various political matters. S July 21 (242) £1,700 [Cunningham]

ALs, 29 Dec 1900. 1 p, 8vo. To Major Pond. Requesting him to visit. Illus in cat. sup May 9 (461) $1,900

— 10 Sept 1901. 2 pp, 8vo. To E. H. Caldbeck. Welcoming him home. star Mar 27 (1297) DM2,200

Collection of Ls & 4 photographs, 4 Aug 1951. 1 p, 4to, & size not stated. To A. H. Frost. Expressing thanks. S July 21 (250) £650 [Cunningham]

— Collection of Ls, telegram, & 17 photographs, 31 Oct & 20 Nov 1951. 1 p, 4to, & size not stated. To A. H. Frost. Thanking for help in the election campain, & congratulatory telegram to his constituency. S July 21 (251) £600 [Cunningham]

— Collection of Ls & 4 photographs, 18 June 1955. 1 p, 4to, & size not stated. To A. H. Frost. Thanking for help during the election. S July 21 (246) £900 [Cunningham]

Series of 3 Ls s, 8 Apr 1932 to 17 May 1935. 3 pp, 4to. To Oliver Locker-Lampson. Regarding publication matters. 2 sgd W. With carbon copies of recipient's letters. S July

21 (243) £1,100 [Cunningham]

Ls s (2), 26 Sept & 8 Oct 1936. 3 pp, 4to. To Lionel [Curtis]. Concerning his speech at the unveiling of a memorial to Lawrence of Arabia. With related material. bba June 25 (126) £1,300 [Blakeney]

Ls, 13 Aug 1909. 4 pp, 4to. To David Lloyd George. Discussing the option for landowners of paying death duties in land. Marked Private. Framed with a port. Illus in cat. P June 17 (15) $15,000

— 28 Mar 1911. 3 pp, 8vo. To Lord St. Aldwyn. Responding to recipient's objections to proposed government loans. S July 21 (252) £600 [Cunningham]

— 11 Sept 1924. 1 p, 4to. To W. F. Louden. Declining the invitation to stand for election at Dumfermline. C Dec 16 (282) £500 [Woodford]

— 15 Jan 1927. 2 pp, 4to. To an unnamed general. Discussing his work on The World Crisis. star Mar 27 (1298) DM3,800

— 16 May 1927. 1 p, 4to. To James Agg-Gardner. Suggesting that he proceed with the publication of his book. S July 21 (253) £600 [Cunningham]

— 1 Feb 1929. 1 p, 4to. To Col. Minnigerode. Giving draft of a telegram to be sent regarding some newspaper articles. Mtd. sg Feb 27 (34) $1,500

— 23 June 1956. 1 p, 4to. To Elaine [Hunter]. Expressing thanks. Including autograph addition. Illus in cat. sup May 9 (463) $950

— 2 Dec 1956. 1 p, 8vo. To Andre de Staercke. Thanking for a gift. sg Feb 27 (36) $950

— 5 Dec 1956. 1 p, 8vo. To Edward Dodd. Looking forward to reading some reviews. Dar Oct 10 (119) $1,200

— May 1964. 1 p, 4to. To the Industrial Life Offices. Sending best wishes on the occasion of their annual luncheon. pn Nov 14 (186) £700

Letter, 13 Nov 1905. 2 pp, size not stated. To Mr. Symonds. Secretarial letter; offering to write a letter of support for a National Reform Union meeting. Ck Nov 15 (68) £500

ANs, 10 Oct 1902. 1 p, 8vo. To Elaine [Hunter]. Praising a speech. Illus in cat. sup May 9 (462) $1,650

Ns, 5 May 1952. 1 p, 12mo. Recipient & contents not stated. With a port. F Mar 26 (809) $775

Group photograph, with his wife Clementine, [n.d.]. 8 by 10 inches. Sgd by both & inscr by Winston Churchill. Framed. Illus in cat. Ck Nov 15 (75) £950

Photograph, sgd, [c.1900]. 8 by 5 inches. By Ernest Mills. Ck Nov 15 (76) £1,600

— Anr, 1941. 9 by 8 inches. Imperf. Ck Nov 15 (78) £420

— Anr, [Aug 1943]. 4 by 3.25 inches. With covering letter. Ck Nov 15 (77) £500

— Anr, 1946. 5 by 4 inches (image). Half length; sgd on mount. S July 21 (255) £700 [Woodford]

— Anr, Jan 1948. 128mm by 178mm. By Bertrand. star Mar 27 (1299) DM2,000

— Anr, [c.May 1948]. 6.5 by 8.5 inches (image). Profile view with cigar. With related Ls by the Marchioness of Reading. Illus in cat. sg Feb 27 (35) $3,000

— Anr, [c.1950s]. 9.25 by 7.25 inches. Seated. Ck Nov 15 (72) £950

— Anr, [c.1950s]. 9.25 by 7.25 inches. With a sprig of heather in his button hole. Ck Nov 15 (73) £850

— Anr, [c.1950s]. 10 by 8 inches. Wearing spotted bowtie & carnation. Framed. Ck Nov 15 (74) £800

— Anr, [1950s]. 6 by 4 inches. Sgd on mount. Ck Apr 3 (115) £320

— Anr, [1950s]. 9.5 by 7.5 inches. Sgd on mount. Framed. Illus in cat. Ck Apr 3 (117) £1,200

— Anr, [c.1960]. 10 by 8 inches. Seated in a car. Framed. Ck Apr 3 (118) £900

— Anr, [n.d.]. 76mm by 123mm. By Thomas. Framed. P June 17 (16) $1,400

Signature, 1955. In the margin of a photograph of Oswald Birley's port, 15.5 by 12.5 inches. Framed. pn Mar 19 (95) £950 [Wilson]

Churchill, Sir Winston L. S., 1874-1965 —& Others

Group photograph, [c.1950s]. 9.5 by 7.5 inches. With Clementine Churchill & Bernard M. Baruch; sgd by W. Churchilll & by Baruch. Framed. Ck Apr 3 (119) £700

Ciano, Galeazzo, Count, 1903-44

Photograph, sgd, June 1936. 7 by 9.25 inches. In white uniform. sg Sept 12 (46) $250

Civil War, American

Ms, list of slaves used as labor for fortifications near Richmond, Virginia, 24 Feb 1864. 3 pp, 4to. Listing name, owner, age & value of slave. R Mar 7 (220) $600

Letter, 27 Dec 1863. 1 p, 4to. Writer & recipient not stated. Reporting from Natchez. sup Oct 15 (1076) $105

Document, 25 Aug 1865. 1 p, 3.5 by 10 inches. Naval discharge from USS Constellation for Thomas Bush. R Nov 9 (91) $160

— Amsden, Ed. - Series of c.25 A Ls s, 1862 to 1865. Length not stated. To Lillias Williams. Reporting from Tennessee & Kentucky. With related material. R Nov 9 (87) $1,000

— Cassitt, Capt. Charles E. - ALs, 14 June 1861. 4 pp, 8vo. To Gen. Gideon J. Pillow. Requesting that his company be detached from the 2d Regiment stationed at Fort Wright. Dar Oct 10 (125) $750

— CUMPSTEN, CORPORAL J. J. - A group of 4 documents relating to his service in the Confederate Army, 10 Apr 1865 to 1899, including contemp copy [in Cumpsten's hand?] of R. E. Lee's General Order no 9. CNY Dec 5 (27) $1,400

— CUTTER, GEORGE H. - 5 Mss, diaries kept as a soldier in the 2d Wisconsin Regiment, Jan 1861 to Feb 1866. Length not stated, 6 by 2.75 inches, in orig sheep. First-hand views of the war, including an account of the Battle of Gettysburg. cb Feb 12 (23) $1,700

— LEE, EDWIN G. - Ds, 14 Jan 1863. 1 p, 4to. Oath of allegiance to the Confederate States; partly ptd. CNY Dec 5 (73) $2,900

— MARSHALL, WILLIAM EDGAR. - Orig drawing, council of war at Gettysburg. Size not stated. In pen-&-ink; sgd in pencil. R Nov 9 (92) $1,400

— MCKIBBIN, CAPT. DANIEL BELL. - Ms, account book detailing various army-related transactions & personal expenses, July 1861 to 31 Mar 1863. About 30 pp & blanks, 8vo, in orig burnt-orange diced sheep. wa Apr 9 (286) $130

— STRONG, MAJOR GEN. GEORGE CROCKETT. - ADs, 14 May 1862. 1 p, 4to. Requisition for supplies to be used at Fort St. Philip. Also sgd by Gen. E. F. Jones. sup Oct 15 (1822) $280

— WARD, DUDLEY H. - 31 A Ls s, 25 Jan 1863 to 14 Sept 1864. About 115 pp, various sizes. To his father Thomas William Ward & his brother James W. Ward (1). Reporting from camps near Vicksburg & in Texas. With parole certificate & further related material. CNY June 9 (276) $5,500

— WRIGHT, SERENO A. - 34 A Ls s, 1862 & 1863. 175 pp, 8vo & 4to. To his family. Letters from the front by a Private in the 24th Regiment of Infantry, Connecticut Volunteers. sg June 18 (175) $1,000

Clark, George Rogers, 1752-1818

Ds, 10 Sept 1781. 1 p, 8vo. Receipt for coffee & sugar "for the sick in Capt. Cheneys company". Imperf. Illus in cat. sup Oct 15 (1078) $1,550

Clarkson, John Gibson, 1861-1909

Signature, [n.d.]. Matted with related material, 8 by 10 inches. Dar Dec 26 (82) $850

Claudius, Matthias, 1740-1815

ALs, 19 Jan 1778. 1 p, 8vo. To [Christian Julius Ludwig Steltzer?]. Thanking for procuring subscriptions, & mentioning Lavater. star Mar 26 (83) DM1,400

— 14 Aug 1799. 3 pp, 8vo. To Herr von Ruoesch. Apologizing for not writing, & sending family news. star Mar 26 (84) DM1,900

Autograph sentiment, sgd, 15 Jan 1813. 1 p, 8vo. Inscr addressed to his grandson Matthias Perthes. Stained. HH Nov 6 (2032) DM650

Clausewitz, Karl von, 1780-1831

ALs, 21 Mar [1821]. Length not stated. To Gneisenau. Informing him about the military situation. star Mar 27 (1300) DM2,400

Clay, Henry, 1777-1852

ALs, 28 Jan 1833. 1 p, 8vo. To Nicholas Biddle. Requesting that a check be honored. With engraved port. sg Sept 12 (48) $275

— [22 May 1834]. 1 p, 16mo, cut from larger sheet. To [Davy] Crockett. In 3d person, returning a speech. Dar Oct 10 (121) $275

— Nov 1843. 1 p, 4to. Letter of recommendation for William E. Robinson. Dar Oct 10 (122) $250

— 19 June 1849. 1 p, 4to. To Thompson Reynolds. About recipient's opposition to his nomination as a candidate for the Presidency. Sang & Spiro collections. CNY May 14 (47) $4,500

Ls, 27 Mar 1828. 4 pp, 4to. To Daniel Huquin. Discussing trade with Canada. sg Sept 12 (47) $600

ADs, [c.1804]. 2 pp, 4to. Legal writ in a land case, sgd as attorney. Dar Aug 6 (134) $200

Clem, John Lincoln

ALs, 7 Nov 1932. 1 p, 4to. Recipient unnamed. Sending his autograph. wa Oct 19 (218) $130

Clemenceau, Georges, 1841-1929

ALs, 30 Dec 1870. 3 pp, 4to. To an unnamed government official. Regarding payments for military expenses. star Mar 27 (1392) DM320

Clemens, Samuel Langhorne, 1835-1910

[A ptd questionnaire with autograph insertions, 1889, 1 p, 8vo, sgd as Twain, responding to an inquiry about his success as an author, sold at CNY on 9 June 1992, lot 32, for $5,200.]

Autograph Ms, An Incident, 11 Sept 1887. 7 pp, 8vo, on rectos only, Recounting "the largest & gratefulest compliment that was ever paid me." Doheny collection. P June 17 (158) $6,500

— Autograph Ms, article, A Word of Explanation, 24 July [1881]. 5 pp, 8vo. Asserting that an imposter has been travelling under his name in Australia. Sgd as Twain. With covering ALs, 3 pp, 4to. CNY Dec 5 (203) $8,500

— Autograph Ms, speech attacking the teaching of religion at Girard College, [1889?]. 11 pp, 8vo, mostly on rectos. In pencil.

Doheny collection. P June 17 (159) $9,500

— Autograph Ms, The Gilded Age, part of pages 58 & 59 of 1st Ed, [1873]. 1 p, 8vo. sup Oct 15 (1833) $2,273

— Autograph Ms, The Steamboat Explosion; chapter 4 from The Gilded Age; [c.1873]. 39 pp, 8vo, on rectos only, in fitted box. With numerous revisions. CNY Dec 5 (202) $24,000

Collection of 2 A Ls s & AL, [Oct 1881?] to 5 Oct 1893. 3 pp, 8vo. To his wife. About a variety of matters. AL fragment; including newspaper clipping. Chester L. Davis collection. CNY Dec 5 (200) $3,500

— Collection of 3 A Ls s & Ls, 20 May 1901 to 14 June [1906]. 5 pp, 12mo & 8vo. To Barbara Mullen. Responding to an invitation to speak at the high school in Hannibal, thanking for a program, etc. CNY June 9 (46) $4,200

Series of 3 A Ls s, [7 Dec 1881? to 20 Sept 1891]. 3 pp, 8vo. To his wife. Reporting from his travels. 1 incomplete. Davis collection. CNY June 9 (38) $2,500

A Ls s (2), 12 Mar 1893 & [28 Aug 1905]. 4 pp, 8vo. To his daughter Clara. Family news. Davis collection. CNY June 9 (39) $2,000

ALs, 12 Dec [1868]. 3 pp, 8vo. To the Rev. Joseph Hopkins Twichell. Praising Olivia Langdon & expressing his love for her. Davis collection. CNY June 9 (34) $3,000

— 5 Feb 1869. 3 pp, 8vo. To his mother & family. Announcing his engagement to Olivia Langdon. Illus in cat. Davis collection. CNY June 9 (35) $9,500

— 20 Dec [1870]. 4 pp, 8vo. To [Elisha] Bliss. Discussing plans to send [J. H.] Riley to Africa to do research on a book. CNY Dec 5 (201) $3,000

— 20 [Aug 1872]. 2 pp, 8vo. To his wife. Informing her that he will board the ship the next day to go to Liverpool. Chester L. Davis collection. CNY Dec 5 (187) $1,800

— 15 Sept [1872]. 3 pp, 8vo. To his wife. About his stay in London, & complaining about having no time to spare. Chester L. Davis collection. CNY Dec 5 (188) $2,200

— "Friday" [1874]. 4 pp, 8vo. To his wife. Describing work on their new house. Chester L. Davis collection. CNY Dec 5 (189) $4,200

— [25 Dec 1875?]. 9 pp, 8vo. To his daughter Susy. Responding to a letter listing Christmas wishes; sgd Santa Claus. Chester L. Davis collection. CNY Dec 5 (190) $30,000

— 4 Sept 1876. 16 pp, 12mo; stitched. To Dr. John Brown. Describing the writing of Tom Sawyer & his farm & studio near Elmira. Including autograph postscript, sgd S.L.C. & note in the hand of his wife at end. CNY June 9 (43) $10,000

— [5 Aug 1878]. 6 pp, 8vo. To his wife. Reporting about his travels in southern Germany. Chester L. Davis collection. CNY Dec 5 (191) $3,000

— 26 [Aug 1878]. 4 pp, 12mo. To his wife. Reporting from his European tour. In pencil. Davis collection. CNY June 9 (36) $1,600

— 11 Nov [1879]. 2 pp, 8vo. To his wife. Reporting about his trip to Chicago. Chester L. Davis collection. CNY Dec 5 (192) $1,800

— [11 May 1886]. 2 pp, 12mo. To his wife. About difficulties in writing a play with [William Dean] Howells. Chester L. Davis collection. CNY Dec 5 (193) $1,300

— 7 Aug 1886. 2 pp, 8vo. To William Dean Howells. About a publication project. CNY June 9 (44) $1,200

— 30 May 1887. 1 p, 8vo. To an unnamed lady. Refusing to approve of an unspecified matter. CNY June 9 (45) $1,400

— 17 Mar 1890. 1 p, 8vo. To Mr. Gilbert. Expressing thanks. Illus in cat. R June 13 (202) $1,600

— 7 Feb 1891. 2 pp, 8vo. To his wife. Chatting about family matters. Chester L. Davis collection. CNY Dec 5 (194) $1,500

— 15 Sept 1891. 1 p, 8vo. To Charles Waldstein. Agreeing with him as to the McClure Syndicate. pn Mar 19 (134) £800 [Wilson]

— 28 Sept [1891]. 4 pp, 8vo. To his wife. Giving a vivid description of dawn & sunrise in southern France. Chester L. Davis collection. CNY Dec 5 (195) $3,500

— [18 Mar 1894]. 1 p, 8vo. To Mrs. [Poultney] Bigelow. Reminding her of a luncheon date. With ALs by P. Bigelow on integral leaf. sg Feb 27 (234) $1,500

— 13 [Apr 1894]. 2 pp, 8vo. To his wife. Describing activities aboard ship. With related material. Chester L. Davis collection. CNY Dec 5 (197) $2,600

— [25 Apr 1894]. 4 pp, 8vo. To his wife. About his bankruptcy proceedings. Davis collection. CNY June 9 (40) $6,500

— [9 Nov 1894?]. 2 pp, 8vo. To his wife. Informing her that he has "got that engraving invention fixed". Chester L. Davis collection. CNY Dec 5 (198) $1,600

— 17 Sept 1900. 4 pp, 8vo. To Mr. Hall. About a visit to an English country home, German words in English, etc. Including postscript in his wife's hand. Illus in cat. S July 21 (47) £1,100 [Cunningham]

— 2 July 1903. 4 pp, 8vo. To his daughter Clara. Giving news about his wife. Chester L. Davis collection. CNY Dec 5 (199) $1,800

— [1907]. 1 p, 16mo. To [Melville E.] Stone.

Supplying a correction to a work about publishers. sg Feb 27 (235) $550

— 14 May [n.y.]. To James Redpath. About attempts to design a circular. sg Feb 27 (233) $850

— [n.d.]. 2 pp, 8vo. To his daughter Jean. Chatting about a variety of matters. Davis collection. CNY June 9 (42) $1,200

— [n.d.]. 1 p, 8vo. To Melville E. Stone. Wittily insisting that he agrees with President Arthur's administration. Illus in cat. sg Feb 27 (237) $3,200

ANs, [c.1890s]. 2 pp, 8vo. To an unnamed theater manager. Requesting tickets for 2 performances. Sgd as Twain. sg Sept 12 (265) $1,100

— [1 Jan] 1907. 1 p, 63mm by 117mm. To his daughter Jean. New Year's wishes. Sgd Father. With related material. Illus in cat. P Dec 12 (25) $2,250

Autograph quotation, sgd, Apr 1883. 1 p, 8vo. Suggesting that it "is easier ... to tell seven lies than make one explanation". Framed with a port. P June 17 (17) $2,250

Autograph sentiment, sgd, [n.d.]. On verso of picture postcard of his house. Advising "never to do wrong when people are looking." Illus in cat. sup Oct 15 (1832) $2,000

Photograph, sgd, [c.1900]. 7.75 by 5.5 inches (image). By Ernest Mills. Framed. pn Nov 14 (220) £850 [Wilson]

Signature, [n.d.]. 2.25 by 4 inches (card). Including subscription. sg Feb 27 (236) $475

Clemens, Samuel Langhorne, 1835-1910 —& Raymond, John T., 1836-87

Group photograph, [c.1875]. Cabinet size. Shaking hands. R Nov 9 (201) $350

Clemens Wenzeslaus von Sachsen, Kurfuerst und Erzbischof von Trier, 1739-1812

Ds, 3 Aug 1771. 1 p, folio, on verso of a petition submitted to him. List of claims to be paid to the heirs of Count Leinigen-Heidesheim. Also sgd by others. star Mar 27 (1413) DM370

Clement XII, Pope, 1652-1740

Ls, 2 Dec 1713. 1 p, 4to. To Gaetano Galletto. Concerning money sent by the Marchese Feroni. star Mar 27 (1545) DM1,600

Document, 15 Jan 1736. 1 leaf, vellum, 425mm by 565mm. Bull accepting a canon's resignation. HH Nov 5 (848) DM360

Clement XIII, Pope, 1693-1769

Document, 3 Feb 1766. 1 p, folio. Bull granting a prebend in the diocese of Como to Philipp Sentini. star Mar 27 (1546) DM480

Clemente, Roberto, 1934-72

Photograph, sgd & inscr, [n.d.]. 8 by 6.5 inches. Inscr to John. Dar Dec 26 (83) $300

Clementi, Muzio, 1752-1832. See: Bach, Johann Christian & Clementi

Clerk-Maxwell, James, 1831-79

ALs, 6 Sept 1876. 1 p, 8vo. Recipient unnamed. About a German trans of his work Theory of Heat. star Mar 26 (729) DM1,600

Cleveland, Frances Folsom, 1864-1947

ALs, 29 May 1893. 9 pp, 8vo. To her sister N. B. Bacon. About her pregnancy. Illus in cat. sup Oct 15 (1570) $675
See also: Cleveland, Grover & Cleveland

Cleveland, Grover, 1837-1908

Collection of ALs & Executive Mansion card, sgd, 24 May 1898 & [n.d.]. 1 p, 8vo, & card. To Dr. Griffiths. Responding to a request for his autograph. sg Sept 12 (49) $300

ALs, 29 Nov 1876. 1 p, 4to. To Emma Folsom. Returning a check (included). R Mar 7 (112) $320

— 18 Mar 1885. 1 p, 12mo. To William E. Wilson. Thanking for a photograph of his inauguration. Dar Dec 26 (153) $350

— 14 June 1891. 2 pp, 8vo. To F. W. Ginn & Co. On behalf of his wife, declining to allow her name to be used in advertisements. wa Oct 19 (273) $260

— 13 Mar 1893. 1 p, 8vo. To Attorney Gen. Richard Olney. Inviting him to a cabinet meeting. Illus in cat. sup Oct 15 (1566) $900

— 3 Sept 1895. 2 pp, 8vo. To A. A. Adee. Responding to a request for approval of recipient's actions. Illus in cat. sup Oct 15 (1568) $600

— 16 Oct 1896. 2 pp, 8vo. To Frieda. Thanking for a "palatable present". Illus in cat. sup May 9 (223) $525

— 24 May 1898. 1 p, 8vo. To W. Patton Griffiths. Sending his autograph. Dar June 11 (133) $250

— 23 Mar 1901. 1 p, 8vo. To Robert Mackay. Declining to contribute an article to a journal. Dar Feb 13 (140) $160

— 19 Mar 1906. 4 pp, 8vo. To Marion Cleveland. Family letter. Illus in cat. R Mar 7 (113) $250

— 24 Mar 1906. 2 pp, 8vo. To the Rev. M. V. Bartlett. Thanking for a birthday letter. R Mar 7 (115) $250

— 30 May 1906. 1 p, 8vo. To J. Nassamer. About a motto for recipient's son. R Mar 7 (114) $300

— 23 June 1906. 2 pp, 8vo. To Edward Bok. Sending an article. Framed with a port. sg Sept 12 (50) $175

Ls, 31 July 1885. 2 pp, 4to. To Oliver Hoyt.

Designating him a pallbearer at Gen. Grant's funeral. Illus in cat. sup May 9 (224) $4,250

— 7 Sept 1887. 1 p, 4to. To Mayor S. R. Marshall. Regretting being unable to visit Nickerson, Kansas. sup Oct 15 (1564) $290

Ds, 25 Aug 1886. 1 p, folio. Appointment of William H. Merritt as postmaster. Dar June 11 (134) $275

— 23 Jan 1888. 1 p, folio. Appointment of James T. Dean as 2d Lieutenant of Infantry. Dar Aug 6 (135) $300

— 23 July 1888. 1 p, 4to. Order to affix the US Seal to a letter to the Emperor of Austria. sup Oct 15 (1565) $340

— 22 Aug 1894. 1 p, folio. Appointment of Martin M. Ramsay as Assistant Paymaster in the Navy. sup Oct 15 (1567) $280

— 23 Aug 1894. 1 p, folio. Appointment of James T. Dean as 1st Lieutenant of Infantry. Dar Aug 6 (136) $325

— 5 Feb 1897. 1 p, folio. Naval appointment for M. Ramsay. Illus in cat. sup Oct 15 (1569) $550

Cut signature, 28 July 1883. 10.5 by 4.5 inches. Framed with ptd port. Dar June 11 (136) $110

Executive Mansion card, sgd, 23 Nov 1888. 4.5 by 2.75 inches. Dar Aug 6 (137) $180

— Anr, sgd, Dec 1894. 4.5 by 2.75 inches. Dar Aug 6 (138) $180

Signature, 18 May 1891. Matted with engraved port, overall size 9 by 12 inches. Dar June 11 (135) $110

— Anr, 30 Nov 1907. 16mo (card). wa Oct 19 (274) $70

Cleveland, Grover, 1837-1908 —&
Cleveland, Frances Folsom, 1864-1947

[Their signatures, 20 May 1887, on one 8vo sheet, framed, sold at wa on 19 Oct 1991, lot 272, for $170.]

Clift, Montgomery, 1920-66

ALs, 29 Mar 1941. 2 pp, 4to. To Ned [W. Smith]. Saying that Hollywood "is a horrible place." Including postscript in anr hand. Framed with a photograph. Illus in cat. wd Dec 12 (307) $550

Ds, 31 Jan 1961. 2 pp, 4to. Agreement regarding compensation for taxes to be paid under the terms of an emploment contract. Dar Apr 9 (164) $350

Clinton, Bill

Ls, 27 Apr 1989. 1 p, 4to. To Harold Russell. Praising his "outstanding service to our nation promoting expanded employment opportunities for people with disabilities." Dar Aug 6 (139) $275

Ds, 26 Dec 1991. 1 p, 4to. Setting the date for the execution of R. R. Rector for murder. Also sgd by B. McCuen & R. R. Rector. Framed with related material. Dar Aug 6 (140) $1,500

Clinton, DeWitt, 1769-1828

Ds, 21 June 1813. 1 p, 7 by 4.5 inches. As Mayor of NY, pay order addressed to the Treasurer. Dar Aug 6 (141) $100

Clinton, George, 1739-1812

Ls, 12 July 1779. 1 p, 8vo. To Thomas Storm. Certifying that "Col. Brown had [his] permission ... to export out of this State five hundred Barrels of Flour". Illus in cat. Dar Feb 13 (141) $225

Ds, 16 Aug 1810. 1 p, folio. Power of attorney. sup Oct 15 (1080) $125

Clive, Caroline, 1801-73

ALs, 8 Sept [1856]. 3 pp, 8vo. To Mrs. Gaskell. Requesting advice & extending an invitation. Ingilby collection. pn Nov 14 (61) £160 [Quaritch]

Cloots, Jean Baptiste ("Anacharsis"), Baron de, 1755-94

ALs, 4 Apr 1789. 4 pp, 4to. To the Marquis de Montesquiou. Analyzing the political situation in France. star Mar 27 (1383) DM2,400

Clymer, George, Signer from Pennsylvania

Ds, [1791-1794]. 1 p, 8.5 by 4.5 inches. As Supervisor of the Revenue, certification that duties on rum have been collected. Dar Oct 10 (124) $275

Cobb, Ty, 1886-1961

ALs, 4 May 1922. 1 p, 8vo. To D. Pierson Ricks. Sending his autograph. Sgd 3 times. Illus in cat. Dar Feb 13 (74) $850

Ls, 29 May 1923. 1 p, 8 by 8 inches. To D. Pierson Ricks. Responding to an inquiry about his opinion on the League of Nations. Dar Feb 13 (75) $1,200

— 19 Jan 1926. 1 p, 4to. To Thomas R. R. Cobb. Referring to proceedings regarding his betting on his team, & expecting vindication. With carbon copy of recipient's letter. Dar Aug 6 (94) $3,250

Cobb, Ty, 1886-1961 —&
Speaker, Tris E., 1888-1958

Group photograph, [1928]. 9.5 by 7.5 inches. With Eddie Collins; sgd by Cobb & Speaker. Imperf. Dar Oct 10 (77) $800

Cobbett, William, 1763-1835

ALs, 6 Aug 1829. 1 p, 8vo. To Sir William Ingilby. Referring to "the 'tranquillized' state of Ireland". Ingilby collection. pn Nov 14 (62) £150

— 1 Apr 1832. 1 p, 4to. To Sir William Ingilby. About the Reform Bill. Ingilby collection. pn Nov 14 (63) £300

— 13 Sept 1832. 1 p, 4to. Recipient unnamed. About his speaking tour in the north of England. bba Sept 19 (333) £70 [Jarndyce]

Cobham, Sir Henry, 1538-1605

Ls, 2 May 1600. 1 p, folio. To Sir Thomas Walsingham & others. Complaining of robberies at Shooter's Hill. pn Nov 14 (16) £110

Cochon de Lapparent, Charles, Comte, 1750-1825

Series of 16 Ls s, 1796 & 1797. 27 pp, 4to. To provincial & municipal officials. As Minister of Police, about police matters & the right of Jews to worship. Thorek collection. sg Sept 12 (129) $800

Cocteau, Jean, 1889-1963

Autograph Ms, notes on his life, his work as an author, homosexuality, etc., including 8 sketches; [c.1929-30]. 43 pp, 4to. Blue cloth & paper bdg decorated by Cocteau with orig drawings in india ink. CGen Nov 18 (327) SF150,000

Collection of ALs & autograph Ms, 20 Mar 1962 & [n.d.]. 2 pp, 4to. To Jean Voulruzan. Responding to an invitation to lecture about his films in Austria. Ms interpreting his film Le testament d'Orphee. star Mar 26 (87) DM550

Series of 11 A Ls s, 1927 to 1944 & [n.d.]. 15 pp, mostly folio. To Boris Kochno. About his row with Vladimir Dukelsky & other professional & personal matters. SM Oct 12 (354) FF65,000

ALs, 9 Aug 1923. 1 p, 4to. To M. Delamain at the Librairie Stock. About some literary matters. star Mar 26 (85) DM500

— Aug 1924. 2 pp, 4to. To Francois. About his friendship for the deceased Raymond Radiguet. Illus in cat. CGen Nov 18 (328) SF20,000

— 27 May 1925. 2 pp, 4to. To Francois. About his opium addiction. Illus in cat. CGen Nov 18 (329) SF9,500

— [9 Feb 1961]. 2 pp, 4to. To the journal Magnum. Fragment, analyzing the art scene in the 20th cent. star Mar 26 (86) DM340

Cody, William F. ("Buffalo Bill"), 1846-1917

ALs, 27 June 1891. To F. J. Griffen. Giving the address of a pbr. Matted with a port. Illus in cat. sup May 9 (432) $1,050

— 3 Aug 1903. 2 pp, 4to. To his cousin Frank. Discussing offers for various projects & financial matters. Illus in cat. sup May 9 (433) $900

— 14 July [1913?]. 1 p, 4to. To "Cousin Frank". About hopes of finding investors for his mines. On letterhead with ptd photograph. Illus in cat. sup Oct 15 (1081) $1,250

— 26 Sept 1913. 1 p, 4to. To his cousin Frank. Informing him that he is leaving on a hunting trip. Illus in cat. sup May 9 (435) $1,000

— 21 Feb 1915. 2 pp, 4to. To Frank & Nellie. Regretting that he is unable to obtain a loan, & hoping to sell his mines. Illus in cat. sup May 9 (437) $950

Ls, 11 Oct 1902. 1 p, 4to. To J. T. McCaddon. Protesting against "dishonorable" financial transactions with traders at Pine Ridge. Illus in cat. R Mar 7 (231) $1,200

Autograph quotation, "True to friend & foe", 1886. 1 p, 2.5 by 4 inches (card). Sgd. Illus in cat. sg Feb 27 (40) $800

Cut signature, [n.d.]. Matted with a photograph, overall size 9 by 14 inches. Illus in cat. Dar June 11 (138) $600

Photograph, sgd & inscr, 13 May 1911. 7.5 by 9.5 (image). Inscr to R. J. Walker. sg Sept 12 (51) $1,000

Photograph, [n.d.]. Cabinet size. Full length; by Stacy. Illus in cat. R June 13 (284) $250

See also: Sitting Bull & Cody

Cohan, George M., 1878-1942

ALs, [1924]. 4 pp, 8vo. To Eddie. Reporting about his dispute with Actors' Equity. Sealed in plastic. Illus in cat. Dar June 11 (139) $1,100

Coleridge, Samuel Taylor, 1772-1834

Autograph Ms (2), fragment of a poem beginning "But now you call...", & fragment of an essay discussing order in the universe; [c.1805]. 4 pp, folio & 4to. With a port drawing, c.1804. C Dec 16 (283) £750 [Waxman]

Autograph Ms, Epitaph on the learned Robert Whitmore, & notes about philosophy, [1810]. 2 pp, folio. With related material. S July 21 (48) £1,000 [Edwards]

— Autograph Ms, poem, [Sancti Dominici Pallium, here entitled:] Poet and Friend, [1826-1827?]. 4 pp, 4to. Sgd. Including prose attack on the Catholic Church at bottom. CNY Dec 5 (205) $3,500

ALs, Oct 1809. 2 pp, folio. To Thomas De Quincey. Discouraging recipient from travelling to Spain. CNY Dec 5 (206) $1,900

— [14 June 1817]. 2 pp, 4to. To [Thomas Boosey]. Ordering books & reporting about a meeting with Ludwig Tieck. CNY Dec 5 (207) $1,100

Colette, Sidonie Gabrielle, 1873-1954

ALs, [n.d.]. 1 p, 4to. Recipient unnamed. Thanking for a letter. star Mar 26 (88) DM240

Collins, Wilkie, 1824-89

Autograph Ms, A Little Fable; [n.d.]. 1 p, 4to. Sgd. With a photograph. CNY Dec 5 (209) $2,000

ALs, 20 May 1861. 1 p, 8vo. To Mr. Watkins. Agreeing to have his photograph taken. wa Oct 19 (48) $210

— 28 Jan 1885. 4 pp, 8vo. To Paul Hamilton Hayne. Asserting that "the spiritual part of [Hayne]... crossed the Atlantic not long since". With a photograph. CNY Dec 5 (210) $650

Colonna, Egidio Roman, Archbishop of Bourges. See: Aegidius Romanus

Columbo, Russ, 1908-34

Photograph, sgd & inscr, [n.d.]. 4.5 by 6.5 inches. Dar Apr 9 (166) $200

Colville, Samuel, fl.1640-80

[2 contemp Mss of The Whigg's Supplication, Part II, [late 17th cent], 2 vols, each over 70 pp, in contemp calf gilt, sold at S on 11 Feb 1992, lot 380, for £150 to Grant.]

Comiskey, Charles A., 1859-1931

Ls, 10 Oct 1924. 1 p, 4to. To Roy Elsh. Sending a check for his salary. Dar Dec 26 (84) $850

Congreve, Sir William, 1772-1828

A Ls s (2), [1803] & 10 Nov 1807. 8 pp, 4to. To George Parker. Discussing the success of his rocket invention, & giving his reasons for publishing the Royal Standard. S July 21 (284) £400 [Scheeres]

Connecticut

— Hartford. - Document, 11 June 1836. 1 p, 13 by 17 inches. Certificate that Benjamin Worthington was admitted a member of the Firemen's Benevolent Society. Corner def. R Mar 7 (270) $70

Connolly, Thomas H., 1870-1961

Cut signature, [n.d.]. 4.5 by 1.25 inches. Cut from typed letter. Dar Feb 13 (76) $200

Connor, Roger, 1857-1931

Signature, [n.d.]. Matted with Hall of Fame card, overall size 8 by 10 inches. Dar Feb 13 (77) $500

Conrad, Joseph, 1857-1924

A Ls s (2), 20 Mar [19]19 & [n.d.]. 2 pp, size not stated. To Henry Major Tomlinson. Thanking for his book, & contents not stated. Ck Apr 3 (45) £900

ALs, 9 May 1922. 2 pp, 4to. To [C. F. Tobbutt]. Interpreting his novel The Arrow of Gold. CNY June 9 (53) $4,000

— 1 Dec [19]22. 2 pp, size not stated. To Henry Major Tomlinson. Thanking for some sympathetic remarks. Illus in cat. Ck Apr 3 (47) £650

Ls, 12 Nov 1919. 1 p, size not stated. To Henry Major Tomlinson. Refusing to review for The Nation. Ck Apr 3 (46) £550

Conradi, Hermann, 1862-90

Autograph Ms, essay, Friedrich Hebbel in seinen Tagebuechern, [c.1887]. 21 pp, 8vo, on rectos only. Some revisions; sgd. With copy of the ptd work. HN Nov 28 (1657) DM620

Constitution of the United States

— Ratification. - ALs by Daniel Davis, 31 Dec 1787. 3 pp, 4to. To Daniel Adams. As Town Clerk of Townshend, Mass., instructing him to vote against ratification of the Constitution & giving reasons. Dar Oct 10 (126) $2,250

Cookery Manuscripts

Ms, cookbook of Maria Rohrweckin. [Southern Germany, 1789]. 60 leaves, 245mm by 193mm. Red half lea bdg. HH May 12 (16) DM320

— Ms, culinary & household recipes. [England, c.1650]. 192 pp, 8vo; stitched. In 2 hands. Ck Mar 6 (68) £200

— Ms, culinary & medical recipes. [England, c.1670 to 1730]. 325 pp, 4to. Contemp vellum bdg. In several hands. Ownership inscr of Elizabeth Stringer, 1693, & Elizabeth Simpson, 1705. Ck Sept 6 (64) £240

— Ms, recipe book of Veronika Manz. [Ulm, Germany, 1857-62]. 62 leaves & blanks, 210mm by 170mm, in bds. Over 200 recipes, suggestions for menus, etc. Some additions in anr hand. HH Nov 5 (809a) DM450

— Ms, recipe book of Theresia Furthner. [Southern Germany or Austria, c.1800]. 164 pp, 202mm by 162mm, in half lea bdg. 232 recipes. HH Nov 5 (809) DM650

— Ms, recipes compiled by Caroline Peirce, 1848 to 1874. 217 pp, 4to. Contemp red mor. Including some general domestic hints. b June 22 (117) £130

Cookson, William, 1754-1820

[A collection of correspondence with his fiancee Dorothy Cowper, including 32 A Ls s by Cookson & 24 A Ls s by Dorothy Cowper, 23 Nov 1780 to 1793, with 3 related A Ls s by William Wilberforce, sold at C on 16 Dec 1991, lot 285, for £1,900.]

Coolidge, Calvin, 1872-1933

ALs, 1 May 1902. 1 p, 4to. To Mr. Haskell. Informing him that he has not received the expected declaration yet. Dar Apr 9 (168) $700

Ls s (2), 2 June 1924 & 31 May 1928. 2 pp, 4to. To Melville E. Stone. Referring to recipient's work as a journalist, & thanking for approval. sg Feb 27 (43) $475

Ls, 15 June 1920. 1 p, 4to. To Joseph L. Otis. Thanking for congratulations. Framed with a port. Dar June 11 (141) $120

— 16 Nov 1920. 1 p, 4to. To Henry J. Ryan. Hoping he will be able to establish a Society for American Education in Massachusetts. sup Oct 15 (1614) $400

— 3 July 1922. 1 p, 8vo. To John Barrett. Expressing doubts that he will be able to visit Grafton in September. Dar Oct 10 (128) $150

— 26 Dec 1924. 1 p, 4to. To Clayton F. Moore. Sending holiday greetings. sg Feb 27 (44) $225

— 16 Jan 1926. 1 p, 8vo. To Myron T. Herrick. Acknowledging a letter. Dar Oct 10 (130) $300

— 8 Apr 1927. 1 p, 4to. To Newton Gilbert. Thanking for a message of approval of his position on the Philippine question. Illus in cat. sg Feb 27 (45) $650

— 14 Apr 1932. 1 p, 4to. To H. V. Woods. Concerning "the installation of the electric plant." Dar Apr 9 (167) $120

— [n.d.]. 1 p, 4to. To Mr. Lane. Concerning an upcoming election in Massachusetts. wa Oct 19 (275) $120

Ds, 25 July 1925. 1 p, folio. Appointment of Nena Miller as Notary Public. sup Oct 15 (1616) $360

— 25 June 1926. 1 p, folio. Postmaster's appointment. R June 13 (174) $140

— 30 June 1927. 1 p, folio. Foreign Service appointment; countersgd by F. B. Kellogg. Matted with a port. Dar June 11 (142) $275

— 4 Nov [n.y.]. 1 p, 8vo. Union Club receipt for breakfast. R Mar 7 (117) $170

Check, sgd, 1 Mar 1929. Payable to Chestnut Farms Dairy. Dar Apr 9 (169) $250

— Anr, sgd, 3 Apr 1929. Payable to Foster-Farrar Company. Illus in cat. sup Oct 15 (1774) $460

— Anr, sgd, 29 Apr 1932. 8.25 by 3 inches. Payable to Alice Reckahn. Dar Oct 10 (131) $110

Photograph, sgd, [11 Sept 1924]. 3.5 by 5.5 inches. Full length. Dar June 11 (143) $130

Photograph, sgd & inscr, 1923. 11.5 by 16 inches. Inscr to Phi Gamma Delta. Dar Oct 10 (129) $500

— Anr, [n.d.]. 6.75 by 9 inches. Inscr to Frank B. Pauly. Dar Feb 13 (150) $150

— Anr, [n.d.]. 9 by 11.5 inches. Inscr to the American Legion. Dar Aug 6 (144) $160

— Anr, [n.d.]. 8 by 10 inches. R Nov 9 (4) $400

White House card, sgd, [n.d.]. Dar Oct 10 (127) $170

Coolidge, Calvin, 1872-1933 —& Others

Group photograph, [n.d.]. 12 by 17 inches. With his cabinet behind the White House. Sgd by Coolidge, Hoover & 9 other cabinet members. Illus in cat. sup Oct 15 (1617) $2,100

— Anr, [n.d.]. Size not stated. With Floyd Bennett; sgd by Coolidge, Bennett & R. E. Byrd. Illus in cat. sup Oct 15 (1618) $1,000

Cooper, Gary, 1901-61

Original drawing, head of a man with cowboy hat, [n.d.]. 4 by 5 inches. Sgd & inscr to John Gary Cooper. Including ptd photograph affixed. sup Oct 15 (1083) $175

Ds, 18 Jan 1951. 1 p, 4to. Contract for a radio play. Dar June 11 (144) $170

Photograph, sgd, [early 1930s]. 3.75 by 5.25 inches. Dar Oct 10 (134) $120

Photograph, sgd & inscr, [c.1939]. 7.75 by 10 inches. Dar Aug 6 (12) $250

— Anr, [n.d.]. 7 by 9 inches. Dar Dec 26 (158) $200

Cooper, James Fenimore, 1789-1851

ALs, 4 Feb 1845. 1 p, 4to. To Joseph Reed Ingersoll. About literary matters. sg Sept 12 (56) $1,100

— 17 May 1847. 2 pp, 4to. To Alexander B. Grant. Responding to an inquiry about Robert Ferguson, & reflecting about his popularity as a writer. CNY Dec 5 (213) $2,500

Check, accomplished & sgd, 7 Oct 1840. Payable to William McClellan. Framed with a port. Dar June 11 (145) $120

— Anr, accomplished & sgd, 13 Apr 1846. Payable to E. & H. Cory. sg Feb 27 (48) $80

Copland, Aaron, 1900-90

Ls, 8 Dec 1971. 1 p, 8vo. To Robert Brawley. Proposing a meeting in NY. wa Oct 19 (159) $80

Autograph quotation, sgd, 3 bars from an unidentified work, 16 Feb 1935. 1 p, 8vo. Sgd by Roger Sessions below. Illus in cat. sg Feb 27 (49) $550

Photograph, sgd, 1982. 14 by 11 inches. Dar Feb 13 (151) $120

Corbett, James John, 1866-1933

Ls, 14 Nov 1924. 1 p, 4to. To Raymond Fellows. Referring to his story The Roar of the Crowd. Dar Feb 13 (108) $500

Cut signature, [n.d.]. Size not stated. Framed with a photograph. Illus in cat. sup July 8 (228) $480

Signature, 19 Sept [18]92. 3.5 by 2 inches (card). Including subscription. Dar Feb 13 (107) $275

Corinth, Lovis, 1858-1925

ALs, 13 July 1918. 1 p, 8vo. To Arthur Lewin-Funcke. Agreeing to serve on a board. HN Nov 28 (1658) DM320

— 7 Apr 1921. 3 pp, 8vo. To Carl Steinbart. Referring to a recent dispute about a painting. With related material. HN June 26 (897) DM500

Autograph postcard, sgd, [7 Feb 1903]. To Mrs. Mainzer. Announcing that he is shipping a painting. HN June 26 (896) DM320

— CORINTH, CHARLOTTE. - Autograph postcard, [c.1920]. On verso of group photograph of the Corinth family. To Rudolf Sieger & his family. Referring to the photograph. Sgd in the name of the family. HN Nov 28 (1659) DM260

Corrigan, Douglas ("Wrong Way")

Collection of ALs & photograph, sgd & inscr, 7 Nov 1938. 1 p, 8vo, & 4 by 3 inches. To Charles Lieb. Referring to a snapshot. Photograph in a cockpit. sup Oct 15 (1084) $140

Cortes, Hernando, 1485-1547

Ds, 20 Aug 1527. 2 pp, 8vo. Pay order in favor of Martin Geronimo. Illus in cat. sup May 9 (131) $15,500

— 31 Dec 1527. 1 p, 8vo. Pay order in favor of Diego de Medina. With receipt by Medina on verso. Illus in cat. sup Oct 15 (1085) $21,000

Cosel, Anna Konstanze, Graefin von, 1680-1765

ALs, 3 Apr 1718. 3 pp, 4to. Recipient unnamed. Informing him of "the jew" Perlheffer's journey to Berlin to look after her financial affairs. star Mar 27 (1696) DM550

Costello, Lou, 1906-59

Photograph, sgd & inscr, [n.d.]. 10 by 8 inches. Inscr to Jackie. R June 13 (204) $110
See also: Abbot, Bud

Cothenius, Christian Andreas von, 1708-89

ALs, 27 Feb 1763. 1 p, 4to. To Christian Friedrich Buchner. Thanking for congratulations on his birthday. star Mar 26 (574) DM560

Coudray, Clemens Wenzel, 1775-1845. See: Goethe, Johann Wolfgang von

Courthope, Frances Elizabeth

Autograph Ms, journal, A Six Weeks Scramble in Switzerland and Savoy, 18 May to 30 June 1852. 153 pp of text illus with 118 drawings & engravings, 4to. Red mor gilt. C Oct 30 (22) £2,000 [Fletcher]

Coward, Noel, 1899-1973

Series of 3 Ls s, 12 Dec 1966 to 9 Oct 1968. 3 pp, 8vo. To Jan. About adapting his stories for television, & discussing ideas for producing some of his plays in Paris. bba Sept 19 (354) £110 [Sutherland]

Photograph, sgd & inscr, [n.d.]. 13.5 by 11 inches. Inscr to Arnold [Weissberger]. Dar Dec 26 (159) $160

Crackanthorpe, William, 1790-1888

[An archive referring to his education & his travels in Europe, 1802 to 1815, comprising 50 A Ls s & 3 autograph journals by Crackanthorpe, 50 letters & notes addressed to him by acquaintances, & 22 letters by members of his family, c.650 pp, 8vo & 4to, sold at C on 24 June 1992, lot 360, for £3,500 to Quaritch.]

Crane, Hart, 1899-1932

Ls, 20 Apr [1932]. 1 p, 4to. To Sam Loveman. Informing him that his income from his father's estate "is cut off indefinitely". CNY June 9 (54) $1,600

Crane, William D.

Autograph Ms, 3 diaries kept on a sporting trip to Scotland & during his service in France in World War I, 1916. Length not stated. Including photographs. wd Dec 12 (309) $125

Crawford, Joan, 1908-77

Collection of 4 Ls s & signature, 1951 to 1961. 5 pp, size not stated. To Leslie Powell. About a variety of matters. Dar Aug 6 (13) $160

Series of 24 Ls s, 5 Nov 1963 to 11 Apr 1973. 26 pp, 8vo. To Ruth Hancock Wilson. Chatting about her films & shows. With related material. Dar Dec 26 (160) $800

Photograph, sgd & inscr, [n.d.]. Size not stated. Inscr to Frances [Spingold]. With 8 other photographs. wd Dec 12 (310) $75

Crawford, John Wallace ("Captain Jack"), 1847-1917

Photograph, sgd & inscr, [n.d.]. Cabinet size. By Eisenmann. R Nov 9 (151) $320

Crawford, William H., 1772-1834

ALs, 12 Nov 1820. 3 pp, 4to. To Caesar Rodney. Regarding relations with Spain & France. Including franking signature. wa Oct 19 (213) $130

Ls, 13 July 1818. 1 p, 4to. To the President of the Office of Discount & Deposit, Savannah, Georgia. As Sec of the Treasury, remitting money. Including franking signature. wa Oct 19 (214) $65

Creuzer, Friedrich, 1771-1858

ALs, 6 Sept 1825. 4 pp, 8vo. To [K. G. Th. Winkler?]. Sending material for print, & mentioning Sulpiz Boisseree. star Mar 26 (575) DM700

Croce, Benedetto, 1866-1952

ALs, [n.d.]. 1 p, 8vo. To Tagliaro. Requesting an answer to an earlier letter. HH May 13 (1917) DM220

Crockett, David, 1786-1836

ALs, 4 Apr 1834. 4 pp, 4to. To John Drurey. Bitterly attacking President Jackson's withdrawal of government funds from the Bank of the US. CNY Dec 5 (28) $24,000

Crofts, Freeman Wills, 1879-1957

[A Ms album of "Subscribers to the Presentation to Mr. ... Crofts, on the occasion of his retirement from the service of the London, Midland and Scottish Railway ...", 31 Dec 1929, 4to, in dark red mor gilt, sold at S on 11 Feb 1992, lot 381, for £150 to A. G. Taylor.]

Croisset, Francis de, 1877-1937

Collection of c.180 A Ls s & 20 Ls s, c.1916 to 1939. About 400 pp, various sizes. To Louis Robin. About his play Cherubin, financial difficulties, other writers, etc. S Dec 5 (485) £500 [Dixon]

Cromwell, Oliver, 1599-1658

Ds, 21 Feb 1656. 1 p, folio. Land deed. Framed with a port. P June 17 (18) $2,250

Cronyn, Hume. See: Tandy, Jessica & Cronyn

Crosby, Bing, 1904-77

Ls, 25 Apr 1965. 1 p, 4to. To Maurie Luxford. Declining to attend a function honoring Bob Hope. With a photograph. wa Oct 19 (5) $65

Cruikshank, George, 1792-1878

Original drawing, long-necked bird, sgd; 10 Oct 1841. 1 p, 8vo. In ink. With franking signature. sg Sept 12 (57) $200

Signature, [n.d.]. Size not stated. Framed with ptd caricature. wd Dec 12 (311) $125

Cruz, Luis de la, 1768-1828

A Ls s (2), 22 Jan & 17 Oct 1818. 5 pp, folio. To Jose Ignacio Zenteno. Discussing naval equipment. Including endorsement, sgd, by Bernardo O'Higgins. HN Nov 28 (1660) DM660

Crystal, Billy

Ds, 5 Feb 1987. 1 p, 4to. Contract to be the host of the 1987 Grammy Awards. Dar Apr 9 (173) $150

Cui, Cesar, 1835-1918

A Ls s (2), 13 May & 3 June 1891. 7 pp, 8vo. To F. Due & his wife. Concerning the possibility of a performance of Le Filibustier at Paris. star Mar 27 (997) DM360

Cukor, George, 1899-1983

Ds, 31 Mar 1939. 3 pp, 4to. Contract with MGM; carbon copy. Dar Oct 10 (135) $200

Cullen, Countee, 1903-46

Ls, 5 Oct 1925. 1 p, 4to. To Robert E. Crosby. Reporting from Harvard. wa Dec 19 (243) $325

Cumberland, Richard, 1732-1811

Ms, play, The Widow of Delphi or The Descent of the Deities, [1780]. 112 pp, in detached half mor bdg. In several professional hands, with some autograph revisions & additions. Used at Covent Garden. S July 21 (280) £600 [Quaritch]

Cummings, Edward Estlin, 1894-1962

AL, [n.d.]. 1 p, 4to. To an unnamed lady. Thanking for a country weekend. In pencil. sg Sept 12 (58) $275

Curie, Marie, 1867-1934

Autograph Ms, laboratory notes, [c.1925]. 1 p, 4to. With ANs by Frederic Joliot-Curie, 16 Dec 1946; note of authenticity. Illus in cat. sup Oct 15 (1088) $2,100

Ds, 8 Nov 1928. 1 p, 8vo. Attestation that M. Montet has taken a course in radioactivity. star Mar 26 (576) DM1,700

Curie, Pierre, 1859-1906

Autograph Ms, lecture notes, [c.1900]. 1 p, 4to. With ANs by Frederic Joliot-Curie, 16 Dec 1946; note of authenticity. Illus in cat. sup Oct 15 (1089) $2,100

Curtius, Ernst, 1814-96

ALs, 23 June 1849. 1 p, 8vo. To Otto Beneke. Thanking for songs & reminiscing about Hamburg. star Mar 26 (577) DM230

Cushing, Frank Hamilton, 1857-1900

ALs, 5 Feb 1889. 4 pp, size not stated. Recipient unnamed. Requesting a copy of a Zuni work he wrote. Illus in cat. R Mar 7 (229) $50

Cushing, Harvey Williams, 1869-1939

ALs, [n.d.]. 2 pp, 12mo (card). To Mrs. Randall. Declining an invitation. wa Oct 19 (136) $400

Custer, Elizabeth Bacon, 1842-1933

ALs, 7 Dec 1876. 4 pp, 8vo. To Mrs. Shelden. Responding to a letter of sympathy. Illus in cat. R June 13 (205) $1,200

— [c.1877]. 3 pp, 8vo. To Mrs. Stoughton. Farewell letter prior to recipient's departure for Russia. Framed. Illus in cat. Armstrong collection. sup Oct 15 (1103) $625

— [n.d.]. 3 pp, 4to. To Mr. Reimers. Informing him that the government has been issuing papers to the Scouts that served under her husband. Framed. Illus in cat. Armstrong collection. sup Oct 15 (1104) $1,000

Custer, George Armstrong, 1839-76

[His wife's name in Custer's hand, June [18]70, cut from the paper cover of a publication, 4.5 by 2 inches, sold at sup on 15 Oct 1991, lot 1100, for $400.]

Collection of ALs & photograph, 9 Dec 1864 & [n.d.]. 2 pp, 4to & carte size. To Gov. Austin Blair. Recommending that [S. H.] Hastings be assigned command of the 5th Michigan Cavalry. CNY Dec 5 (30) $8,500

ALs, [18 Sept 1862]. 2 pp, 12mo. To Col. Colburn. Battlefield note, informing him of the capture of a 3-inch gun on his way to Sharpsburg. In pencil. CNY Dec 5 (29) $6,000

— 4 Jan 1864. 2 pp, 4to. To J. M. Howard. Asking for assistance in his promotion. With a photograph. Illus in cat. Armstrong collection. sup Oct 15 (1090) $12,000

— 5 Jan 1865. 1 p, 4to. To Messrs. Liffey & Co. Ordering a regimental badge for Col. Hastings. With a photograph. Illus in cat. CNY June 9 (225) $5,500

Ls, 7 Jan 1867. 1 p, 4to. To Major H. E. Noyes. Requesting that buildings at Fort Riley be turned over to the Post Quartermaster. Framed. Illus in cat. Armstrong collection. sup Oct 15 (1093) $6,250

Ds, Nov 1865. 2 pp, folio. Certification on a "Statement of Forage". Framed. Illus in cat. Armstrong collection. sup Oct 15 (1092) $4,545

— 13 Sept 1875. 1 p, folio. Certification that telegrams sent were on public service. CNY June 9 (226) $3,200

Photograph, sgd, 15 Feb 1864. Carte size. By Brady. Illus in cat. Armstrong collection. sup Oct 15 (1096) $12,500

Photograph, [c.24 Jan 1872]. Carte size. Copy by Lockhart of an orig by James A. Scholten. Framed. Illus in cat. Armstrong collection. sup Oct 15 (1097) $290

— RYAN, CAPT. JOHN. - Ls, 6 Nov 1922. 1 p, 4to. To Anthony L. Baron. Responding to an inquiry about the Battle of Little Big Horn. Illus in cat. sup May 9 (115) $1,000

Custer, George Armstrong, 1839-76 —& Others

ANs, sgd, 7 May 1865. 2 pp, 4to. Recommending J. G. Birney for a commission as Captain in the cavalry. Including similar notes by Philip H. Sheridan, Wesley Merritt & Thomas C. Devin on same sheet. Framed. Illus in cat. Armstrong collection. sup Oct 15 (1091) $8,500

Custer, Thomas Ward, d.1876

Cut signature, [n.d.]. 3.5 by 1.75 inches. Cut from a document. Framed. Illus in cat. Armstrong collection. sup Oct 15 (1109) $1,200

Cuvier, Georges L. C., Baron, 1769-1832

Autograph Ms, Notice sur quelques fragmens d'un Elephant..., [n.d.]. 7 pp, 4to. Incomplete. star Mar 26 (579) DM600

Czerny, Carl, 1791-1857

ALs, 21 June 1833. 1 p, 4to. To the pbr Karl Friedrich Kistner. Returning proofs of 2 works. star Mar 27 (998) DM750

Czerny, Vinzenz, 1842-1916

ALs, 21 Sept 1866. 1 p, 8vo. Recipient unnamed. Asking for a book. star Mar 26 (581) DM520

D

Dahlgren, John Adolphus Bernard, 1809-70

Ls, 1 Aug 1863. 2 pp, 4to. To Capt. Noble. Declining an invitation to a meeting. bba May 28 (168) £70 [Sakmyster]

Dalberg, Karl, Reichsfreiherr von, Kurfuerst von Mainz, 1744-1817

Autograph Ms, scientific query, addressed to J. B. Trommsdorff (for his Journal de Pharmacie?), [c.1797]. 1 p, 4to. Sgd. star Mar 27 (1414) DM800

D'Albert, Eugen, 1864-1932. See: Albert, Eugen d'

Dali, Salvador, 1904-89

Autograph Ms, scenario, entitled "admosferic - animals - Tragedie. Espectacle surrealiste"; [c.1933]. 12 pp, 4to & folio. Including 2 drawings. Sgd twice. Boris Kochno collection. SM Oct 12 (356) FF200,000

Series of 7 A Ls s, [c.1933 to 1938]. 7 pp, various sizes. To Boris Kochno. Discussing various theatrical matters. With 2 related pen-&-ink sketches. SM Oct 12 (357) FF28,000

Photograph, sgd, [n.d.]. 8 by 10 inches. Seated in front of a painting. Dar June 11 (147) $160

Ptd photograph, sgd, [n.d.]. 10 by 8 inches. Dar Oct 10 (137) $200

Signature, [1966]. On philatelic cover. Dar Apr 9 (175) $110

Dancing

— D'OLEIRE, E. F. - Ms, instructions for various types of dance. [Germany, 18th cent]. 34 leaves, 8vo, in orig calf. Comprising music & pen-&-ink sketches of dance formations. bba Jan 30 (261) £1,300 [Marlborough]

D'Annunzio, Gabriele, 1863-1938

Series of 5 A Ls s, 24 Mar 1879 to 9 Mar 1880. 18 pp, 8vo. To Annibale. About his literary endeavors. star Mar 26 (13) DM1,700

Dante Alighieri, 1265-1321

Ms, L'Inferno, canto XXV, portions of lines 116 to 126 & 145 to 141. [Italy, 14th cent]. Single leaf, vellum, 137mm by 94mm. Palimpsest; re-used as part of a Breviary, c.1500. S Dec 17 (6) £1,500 [Quaritch]

Danton, Georges Jacques, 1759-94

Ds, Oct 1789. 1 p, folio. Report about a meeting of the club of the Cordeliers. star Mar 27 (1384) DM1,900

Darrow, Clarence, 1857-1938

Photograph, sgd & inscr, 24 Mar 1924. 4.5 by 6.5 inches. Inscr to Helena Normanton. Illus in cat. sup Oct 15 (1184) $575

Darwin, Charles, 1809-82

Autograph Ms, fragment from The Descent of Man, part 1, chapter 2, p 46 of 1st Ed; [ptd 1871]. 1 p, folio, on blue paper. Including autograph revisions. Ingilby collection. pn Nov 14 (64) £3,400 [Quaritch]

ALs, 24 Feb [1849]. 2 pp, 8vo. To James Scott Bowerbank. Thanking for some sculpellum fragments. Ingilby collection. pn Nov 14 (65) £1,100 [Wilson]

— 15 Jan [1860]. 4 pp, 8vo. To Mr. Cresy. Inviting him for dinner & requesting his advice on his son's education. S July 21 (286) £1,300 [Cunningham]

— 15 Jan [1860?]. 3 pp, 8vo. To Mr. Cresy. Inquiring about a French trans of his On The Origin of Species. S July 21 (287) £1,700 [Cunningham]

— 21 Feb 1881. 1 p, 8vo. To Henry Edwards. Expressing thanks for his election as honorary member of the Entomological Club of NY. With engraved port. CNY Dec 5 (32) $1,300

— 25 Aug 1881. 1 p, 8vo. To an unnamed Ed. Explaining that he has "made it a rule ... never to write in Periodicals". pn June 11 (60) £580 [Wilson]

— 4 May [n.y.]. 1 p, 8vo. Recipient unnamed. Explaining that a projected book has been announced prematurely. Framed with a port. P June 17 (20) $2,250

— 15 May [n.y.]. 4 pp, 8vo. To [Mr. Cresy?]. Saying that he has given up the "siphon-plan" in favor of an ordinary tank. S July 21 (288) £1,000 [Sakmyster]

Ls, 18 Jan [1865]. 1 p, 12mo. Recipient unnamed. Informing him that he has sent a paper for the Society. Framed with a photograph. Illus in cat. sg Nov 7 (52) $1,600

— 15 Mar [1865]. 2 pp, 8vo. To [Dr. Heine?]. Responding to recipient's theory of a "law of inheritance". Including draft of a letter in recipient's hand. star Mar 26 (582) DM2,200

— 26 Aug 1867. 4 pp, 8vo. To W. Boyd Dawkins. Thanking for papers & expressing interest in recipient's research. In the hand of Emma Darwin. CNY Dec 5 (31) $2,600

— 26 May 1868. 3 pp, 8vo. Recipient unnamed. Thanking for a table about sheep. S July 21 (285) £800 [Sakmyster]

— 12 Oct 1874. 4 pp, 8vo. To an unnamed German scientist. About his study of insectivorous plants. S Dec 12 (318) £1,300 [Quaritch]

— 30 Aug 1877. 4 pp, 8vo. To an unnamed German scholar. Discussing recipient's "observation on the dorsal eyes of Onchidium". hen Nov 12 (2524) DM1,800

ANs, 28 Jan 1875. 1 p, 8vo. Recipient unnamed. In 3d person, sending compliments. Also sgd at head. Illus in cat. Dar Apr 9 (176) $700

— DARWIN, FRANCIS. - 5 A Ls s, 14 Aug 1882 to 2 Jan 1883. 6 pp, 8vo. To Ferdinand Cohn. Asking for his father's letters for a projected Ed of his correspondence. star Mar 26 (583) DM230

Daun, Leopold, Graf von, 1705-66

Ms, list of regiments of infantry encamped "bey der Neyss", 25 May 1741. 2 pp, folio. Sgd. HN Nov 28 (1663) DM320

Ls, 5 Jan 1763. 1 p, folio. To Ferdinand Philipp von Harrsch. Concerning a military promotion. star Mar 27 (1301) DM260

Dauthendey, Max, 1867-1918

Autograph Ms, poem, beginning "Auf Deinem Haupt schmolz eine goldenrothe Krone...", July 1895. 1 p, 4to. 5 lines, sgd Max. Repaired. star Mar 26 (90) DM950

ALs, 30 Nov 1912. 4 pp, 4to. To an unnamed baron. Asking for help in obtaining financial aid from the Schiller Foundation. star Mar 26 (91) DM400

David, Ferdinand, 1810-73

Autograph music, song in B-flat major for violin & piano, 26 Apr 1850. 2 pp, 4to. 46 bars, sgd. star Mar 27 (1000) DM360

David, Jacques Louis, 1748-1825

ALs, 14 Apr 1810. 1 p, folio. To the controller of the Imperial household. Asking for his support in his request to be made a member of the household as Premier Peintre. S Dec 5 (488) £600 [Fox Glove]

— 13 Aug 1810. 1 p, 4to. Recipient unnamed. Expressing pride at the choice of 2 paintings to be put on public display. Illus in cat. S Dec 5 (486) £850 [Dreesman]

Davis, David, 1815-86

Signature, [n.d.]. 2 by 3.5 inches (card). With a photograph. sup Oct 15 (1186) $55

Davis, Jefferson, 1808-89

ALs, 12 June 1846. 1 p, 4to. To President James K. Polk. Recommending W. H. Emory for an appointment as paymaster. Illus in cat. sup May 9 (116) $1,650

— 25 Feb 186[1]. 1 p, 4to. To Howell Cobb. Submitting nominations to his cabinet. R Nov 9 (79) $20,000

— 25 Oct 1867. 2 pp, 12mo. To James Robb. Requesting help to sell land in Arkansas. Matted with a ptd port drawing. Dar June 11 (148) $1,400

— 2 Dec 1872. 2 pp, 8vo. To J. H. Bowmar. Regarding a claim resulting from his brother's legal practice in 1823. sup May 9 (117) $900

— 8 May 1876. 3 pp, 8vo. To Mr. Mikell. Responding to an inquiry about the fate & address of Confederate officers. Illus in cat. Spiro collection. CNY May 14 (52) $4,500

— 2 May 1888. 2 pp, 4to. To Robert Lowry. Asking that the widow of Gen. W. W. Adams succeed her husband as postmaster. sup Oct 15 (1188) $1,000

— 3 Oct 1889. 1 p, 8vo. To Mrs. J. A. Brazell. Regretting his inability to assist in a search. sg Feb 27 (53) $600

Ls, 23 Sept 1861. 1 p, folio. To Queen Victoria of England. Letters of credence for James M. Mason. Illus in cat. Sang & Spiro collections. CNY May 14 (49) $21,000

ANs, 11 Sept 1862. 1 p, size not stated. To L. T. Wigfall. Asking to see him. Matted with a port. bbc Dec 9 (163) $1,400

Ds, 1 Mar 1862. 2 pp, folio. Proclamation of martial law & the suspension of Habeas Corpus in Richmond. Text in the hand of Judah P. Benjamin. Illus in cat. Spiro collection. CNY May 14 (50) $19,000

— 23 Feb 1865. 1 p, folio. Receipt for the last installment of his salary as President of the Confederacy. Illus in cat. Sang & Spiro collections. CNY May 14 (51) $32,000

— 30 Apr 1865. 1 p, folio. Act amending the orig Confederate declaration of war; also sgd by Alexander H. Stephens & Th. S. Bocock. P Dec 12 (100) $15,000

Check, sgd, 3 Aug 1871. Drawn on The Savings Bank of Memphis for $500. Repaired. Illus in cat. Dar June 11 (149) $700

Franking signature, [c.1857-61]. 3.5 by 8.5 inches. On envelope addressed to J. F. Callan. sg Sept 12 (59) $350

— JOHNSTON, R. C. - ALs, 28 June 1861. 1 p, 8vo. To Jefferson Davis. Sending a resolution by the Virginia legislature (included) inquiring about Confederate military strength. bbc Dec 9 (161) $450

Davis, Jim

Original drawing, half-length image of Garfield, [n.d.]. 11 by 14 inches. Sgd & inscr to Chris. Dar Apr 9 (149) $120

Davis, Varina Howell, 1826-1906

ALs, [n.d.]. 2 pp, 12mo. To Mr. Glenn. Conveying a message from her husband. wa Oct 19 (225) $120

Davy, Humphry, 1778-1829

ALs, 30 Oct [1815]. 3 pp, 4to. To Dr. [Robert] Gray. Announcing his discovery of the safety lamp & sending a sketch (not included). pn June 11 (56) £2,100

— 4 Dec 1815. 4 pp, 4to. To Dr. [Robert] Gray. Explaining the principles on which his safety lamp works. pn June 11 (57) £950

— 13 Dec 1815. 4 pp, 4to. To Dr. [Robert] Gray. Defending the originality of his safety lamp as an invention. pn June 11 (58) £400

— 15 Jan 1816. 4 pp, 4to. To Dr. [Robert] Gray. Describing improvements made to his safety lamp. pn June 11 (59) £550 [Browning]

Dawes, William, 1762-1830. See: Australia

Dayan, Moshe, 1915-81

Autograph postcard, sgd, 7 June 1959. To Itzhchak Gurion. Informing him that he is attending a session of the Zionist Actions Committee in Jerusalem. Dar Oct 10 (235) $225

Dayton, Jonathan, 1760-1824

ADs, 14 July 1794. 1 p, 4to. Authorization for Joseph Howell to receive interest due from stocks. Also sgd by others. sup Oct 15 (1190) $300

De Gaulle, Charles, 1890-1970

[A group of 8 autograph drafts of broadcast speeches & of a poem about the war, 8 Dec 1940 to 11 June 1942, with typed transcriptions, together 50 pp, sold at P on 17 June 1992, lot 175, for $65,000.]

Transcript, quotation from his book The Call to Honor, 1955. 12mo (card). Sgd. Dar Dec 26 (169) $325

ALs, 15 Sept 1954. 2 pp, 8vo. To an unnamed

pbr. Discussing the possibility of an Argentinean issue of his Memoires de Guerre. star Mar 27 (1410) DM1,200

De Rudio, Charles C., 1832-1910

Ds, Oct 1879. 2 pp, size not stated. Tobacco Return for the 7th Regiment of Cavalry. Framed. Illus in cat. Armstrong collection. sup Oct 15 (1114) $200

Dean, James, 1931-55

Autograph sentiment, sgd, [n.d.]. 8vo. Inscr to Lucas, written diagonally. Framed with a port. P June 17 (21) $1,800

Deane, Silas, 1737-89

ALs, 22 June 1779. 2 pp, 4to. To his brother. Giving war news. Illus in cat. CNY June 9 (228) $2,300

Dearborn, Henry, 1751-1829

ALs, 21 May 1806. 1 p, 4to. To Stephen Moylan. Asking for information requested by the House of Representatives. Dar June 11 (150) $100

— 18 May 1808. 3 pp, 4to. To his daughter Julia Wingate. Reporting about his life in Washington. Dampstained. Dar June 11 (151) $160

Debussy, Claude, 1862-1918

Autograph music, song, Fantoches, to a text by Verlaine, 8 Jan [18]82. 5 pp, folio, in lea gilt. Working Ms, scored for voice & piano; sgd twice. Illus in cat. S Dec 6 (76) £8,500 [Haas]

ALs, 24 Jan 1904. 1 p, 12mo. To Pierre Louys. Complaining about a negative portrayal in an article. Framed with a port. P June 17 (22) $2,200

— 17 Nov [19]13. 1 p, 8vo. To M. Bertault. Reporting his dealings with "Madame C." S May 29 (519) £550 [Sell]

— [n.d.], "Wednesday". 1 p, 4to. To Rene Peter. About the date of a meeting. star Mar 27 (1001) DM1,000

— [n.d.]. 1 p, 16mo. Recipient unnamed. Expressing uneasiness about being made to agree to more engagements than he can fulfill. S Dec 6 (75) £500 [Giesen]

Proof copy, Pelleas et Melisande, Act 2, vocal score; [1902]. In modern bds. Including many autograph annotations. S May 29 (517) £2,800 [Crawford]

Debye, Peter, 1884-1966

Autograph Ms, essay, Paul Scherrer und die Streuung von Roentgenstrahlen, 16 Aug 1959. 8 pp, 4to, on rectos only. Contribution to the festschrift for Paul Scherrer; sgd at head. star Mar 26 (584) DM3,600

DeCarlo, Dan

Original drawings, (5), complete comic book story entitled "Cool It", from Betty & Me, Sept [n.y.]. 5 pp, 10.5 by 15.5 inches. In black ink; 1 sgd. Dar Oct 10 (113) $225

Decatur, Stephen, 1779-1820

Autograph Ms, letter book containing 12 letters to Sec of the Navy B. W. Crowninshield, 18 Jan to 5 May 1815. 58 pp, 8vo, in contemp quarter sheep & marbled bds. Regarding the defeat & capture of USS President. CNY June 9 (229) $17,000

Degas, Edgar, 1834-1917

ALs, 5 Dec [1872]. 4 pp, 4to. To Henri Rouart. Giving his impressions of New Orleans. C Dec 16 (286) £3,200 [Burgess Browning]

— 10 Apr 1910. 1 p, 8vo. To M. de Koustodier. Regarding Herman Melville's works. JG Sept 27 (324) DM700

AL, [n.d.]. 2 pp, 8vo. To an unnamed actress. Stating that "Apollon le dieu du soleil, ne vous a guere bien traitee." star Mar 27 (883) DM1,250

Dehmel, Richard, 1863-1920

Autograph postcard, sgd, 4 Apr 1912. To Eduard Rudowsky. Regarding a biography of Detlev von Liliencron. With related material. star Mar 26 (92) DM320

Delacroix, Eugene, 1798-1863

ALs, [n.d.]. 1 p, 8vo. Recipient unnamed. Requesting his visit. Mtd. star Mar 27 (884) DM850

Delbrueck, Max, 1906-81

Autograph Ms, leaves from his diary, [9 to 13 Sept 1974]. 4 pp, 8vo. Notes taken during a holiday; sgd later & dated 2 May 1980. star Mar 26 (586) DM220

Delhanty, Ed J., 1867-1903

Signature, [n.d.]. Matted with Hall of Fame card, overall size 8 by 10 inches. Dar Feb 13 (78) $650

Dempsey, Jack, 1895-1983

[A Ms sentiment inscr to Dempsey on the occasion of his fight with Tunney, 22 Sept 1927, sgd by 65 friends, 1 p, size not stated, sold at sup on 8 July 1992, lot 204, for $900.]

[A script, This is Your Life, [n.d.], 47 pp, 9 by 12 inches, in red lea bdg, honoring his lifetime achievements & including contributions by Gene Tunney, Fred Fulton, & others, sold at sup on 8 July 1992, lot 205, for $780.]

Photograph, sgd & inscr, 19 Aug [19]33. 8 by 10 inches. Inscr to Jesse Wilson. sup July 10 (986) $275

— Anr, [late 1930s]. 8.5 by 10.5 inches. Inscr to

Charley Roeder. Framed. Dar Feb 13 (116) $110

Denver, James William, 1817-92

Franking signature, [27 July 1857]. On cover addressed to his wife. rf Sept 21 (29) $90

Derain, Andre, 1880-1954

Series of 6 A Ls s, 1932 to 1946 & [n.d.]. 11 pp, folio & 8vo. To Boris Kochno. Discussing ballets. SM Oct 12 (358) FF13,000

Dering, Sir Edward, 1625-84

Autograph Ms, gardening journal, Dec 1671 to Mar 1675. 50 pp, 8vo, in calf gilt. Discussing plants & trees in his orchards at Surrenden. S July 21 (209) £3,000 [Maggs]

— Autograph Ms, journal, Oct 1675 to Feb 1679. Over 150 pp, 8vo. Vellum gilt bdg. Recording business matters, political & social activities, public events, etc. With related family material. S July 21 (208) £2,800 [Maggs]

Desaix, Louis Charles Antoine, 1768-1800

ALs, [15 Feb 1794]. 2 pp, 4to. To Gen. Michaud. About difficulties in obtaining precise information about enemy movements. Illus in cat. star Mar 27 (1368) DM1,100

Desbordes-Valmore, Marceline, 1786-1859

ALs, 24 Nov 1855. 3 pp, 8vo. To Laure Damoreau-Cinti. About her teaching schedule. star Mar 26 (94) DM220

Detmold, Edward Julius, 1883-1957

Original drawing, The Praying Mantis, to illus J. H. C. Fabre's Book of Insects, 1925. 9.75 by 8.5 inches. In watercolor. Sgd with monogram. Illus in cat. Ck Dec 11 (70) £

Deutsch, Eliezer Hayyim ben Abraham, 1850-1916

ALs, 1906. 1 p, 8vo. Recipient unnamed. Concerning halakhic matter. Illus in cat. sg Dec 19 (65) $175

Devrient, Ludwig, 1784-1832

ALs, 5 Feb 1827. 1 p, 4to. To [August Wilhelm Francke]. Recommending a young actor. star Mar 27 (1212) DM950

Dewey, George, 1837-1917

ALs, 15 Aug 1901. 3 pp, 8vo. To Rear Admiral Charles Sigsbee. Returning "the translation of the defense of Admiral Montojo". sg Sept 12 (229) $425

Diaghilev, Sergei Pavlovich, 1872-1929

[An important archive of letters, drafts, lists, telegrams & notes relating to the Ballets Russes, c.1916 to 1930, c.550 pp, various sizes, some also in the hands of Boris Kochno, Sergei Grigoriev, & others, sold at SM on 12 Oct 1991, lot 360, for FF180,000.]

Collection of 12 A Ls s & A Ns s, & c.80 telegrams, 1920s. Length not stated. To Boris Kochno. About the Ballets Russes & other matters. Including some drawings. SM Oct 12 (359) FF15,000

A Ls s (2), 22 Sept 1922 & 14 July 1926. 2 pp, 8vo & ptd visiting card. To Eric Wollheim. Requesting that money be paid to Boris Kochno. Boris Kochno collection. SM Oct 12 (361) FF8,500

Check, 31 May 1929. Payable to Igor Stravinsky. Def. Ck Nov 15 (33) £420

Diaghilev, Sergei Pavlovich, 1872-1929 —& Others

Document, 26 Apr 1929. 4 pp, 8vo. Group train ticket for the Ballets Russes, sgd by numerous members of the troupe. Diaghilev's & Kochno's names sgd in anr hand. Boris Kochno collection. SM Oct 12 (363) FF4,200

Diaghilev, Sergei Pavlovich, 1872-1929 —& Kochno, Boris

[A collection of c.100 letters from Kochno to Diaghilev, with Kochno's French transcriptions of Diaghilev's replies, 1921 to Aug 1929, c.450 pp, various sizes, discussing productions at the Ballets Russes & personal matters, sold at SM on 12 Oct 1991, lot 362, for FF100,000.]

[2 autograph drafts of a letter from Kochno to Jean Cocteau, presumably dictated by Diaghilev & heavily revised by him, June 1927, 6 pp, size not stated, about Cocteau's row with Dukelsky, sold at SM on 12 Oct 1991, lot 364, for FF13,000.]

Autograph Ms, listing costumes & performers for Aurora's Wedding, [1922]. 5 pp, 8vo. In the hand of Kochno; annotated by Diaghilev. SM Oct 12 (366) FF13,000

Diaries

— Carr, Ariel. - Autograph Ms, diary, 1836 to 1843. 69 pp, 8vo, in orig marbled bds. Describing his early life in Pennsylvania, his apprenticeship as a tanner, work as school teacher, etc. wa Oct 19 (227) $130

Diaz, Porfirio, 1830-1915

Ls, 1894. 1 p, 4to. To Rosa Peres V. de Caloca. Contents not stated. R Mar 7 (238) $70

— 18 Mar 1898. 1 p, 4to. To Melville E. Stone. Agreeing to receive Mrs. Scott. sg Feb 27 (127) $150

— 3 Mar 1900. 1 p, 4to. To the Governor of Missouri. Referring to Mr. Stilwett's mission to Mexico. With related material. wa Oct 19 (204) $75

Ds, 26 Jan 1903. 2 pp, folio. Recipient & contents not stated. sup Oct 15 (1373) $80

Dickens, Charles, 1812-70

Autograph Ms, In Memoriam. Obituary of William Makepeace Thackeray for Cornhill Magazine. With autograph revisions. 5 pp, 8vo, on rectos only; cut into 12 pieces by the ptr. With ALs, 15 Jan 1864, 1 p, 8vo, to George Smith; covering letter for corrected proofs. Illus in cat. P Oct 11 (102) $21,000

— Autograph Ms, story, The Haunted Man and the Ghost's Bargain, [1846-48]. 64 leaves, mostly 4to. Complete draft. In red mor bdg with ALs, 13 Feb 1850, 2 pp, 8vo; letter of transferral to Angela B. Coutts. P Oct 11 (93) $280,000

Collection of ALs & photograph, [n.d.]. Size not stated, & 2.5 by 4 inches. To Edmund. Fragment; cut up & glued around mat of photograph. Illus in cat. Dar Apr 9 (178) $400

ALs, 16 Aug 1841. 2 pp, 8vo. To Daniel Maclise. Inviting him to enjoy "conveniences of all kinds at Margate". Framed with a port. Illus in cat. P June 17 (23) $12,000

— 4 Oct 1845. 3 pp, 8vo. To P. Henry Hatch. Declining to accept the chair at a Crosby Hall gathering. pn June 11 (72) £340

— 15 Aug 1851. 1 p, 12mo. Recipient unknown (name removed). Suggesting they go out to dine. Mtd. Dar Dec 26 (170) $475

— 19 Apr 1853. 2 pp, 8vo. To J. C. d'Arnaud Gerkens. Discussing recipient's illusts to David Copperfield. pn June 11 (73) £720

— 19 Apr 1858. 2 pp, 8vo. To Charles Dance. Concerning an honorary dinner. Ingilby collection. pn Nov 14 (66) £440

— Dec 1860. 2 pp, 12mo. To Edward J. Fraser. As Ed of the magazine All the Year Round, discussing an advertisement. star Mar 26 (119) DM1,500

— 19 Apr 1869. 2 pp, 8vo. To James Freeman. Refusing a seat in the House of Commons. pn Nov 14 (222) £800

— 25 Apr 1869. 2 pp, 8vo. To Frederic Ouvry. Specifying the terms of his new will. CNY Dec 5 (224) $10,000

— [n.d.]. 2 pp, 8vo. To his son Sydney Smith Dickens. Making arrangements for him to come home to recover if his doctor approves. S July 21 (50) £650 [Stodolski]

ANs, [n.d.]. Size not stated. Recipient unnamed. Fragment, referring to George Cruikshank's address. Ck Apr 3 (11) £150

Check, accomplished & sgd, 30 Oct 1860. Drawn on Messrs. Coutts & Co. for£14 10s. With sgd envelope. Illus in cat. Ck Nov 15 (7) £280

— Anr, accomplished & sgd, 16 Jan 1864. Payable to Messrs. Farrer. Framed with engraved port. Illus in cat. wd Dec 12 (312) $850

— Anr, sgd, 6 Apr 1864. Size not stated. Payable to himself. Ck Apr 3 (10) £260

Signature, 31 Jan 1855. 1 p, 8vo. Including subscription. pn Nov 14 (221) £180

Single sheet ptg, The Great International Walking-Match Of February 29, 1868. 530mm by 583mm. Sgd by Dickens & 4 others. Framed; with related material pasted to back of frame. Illus in cat. CNY June 9 (57) $13,000

Dickinson, Emily, 1830-86

Autograph Ms, brief note expressing anguish over the death of her nephew, [1883]. 1 p, 12mo. Framed with a port. Illus in cat. P June 17 (24) $5,500

Dickinson, John, 1732-1808

A Ls s (2), 31 Oct & 17 Dec 1770. 7 pp, 4to. To Catharine Macaulay. Complaining of "the sliding Patriotism of Merchants" & sending an example of American silk. With retained draft of an answer in Macaulay's hand. pn June 11 (8) £4,200

Diebitsch, Hans Karl von, Count, 1785-1831

Ls, 27 Aug 181[3]. 2 pp, 4to. To Gen. d'Auvray. Discussing the military situation [a few days before the battle of Nollendorf]. star Mar 27 (1685) DM360

Diederichs, Eugen, 1867-1930

Collection of 34 A Ls s, 89 Ls s (carbon copies), 7 Ls (carbon copies), & 87 postcards, sgd (82 autograph), 1913 to 1929. 4to & 8vo. To his son Juergen. Covering a wide range of personal & professional matters. With related material. JG Mar 27 (184) DM2,600

Diesel, Rudolf, 1858-1913

Autograph sentiment, suggesting that an inventor's life is martyrdom, 9 June 1907. 1 p, 8vo. Sgd & inscr to a young lady. star Mar 26 (587) DM4,800

Dietrich, Marlene, 1901-92

Group photograph, [n.d.]. 8 by 10 inches. With James Stewart; sgd by both. wd Dec 12 (313) $300

Photograph, sgd & inscr, [n.d.]. 11 by 14 inches. Inscr to Joy [Neumeyer]. wd Dec 12 (314) $200

DiMaggio, Joseph Paul ("Joe")

Photograph, sgd & inscr, [n.d.]. Size not stated. Inscr to Tony & Judy Story. wd Dec 12 (315) $100
See also: Williams, Theodore Samuel ("Ted") & DiMaggio

Dingelstedt, Franz von, 1814-81. See: Heine, Heinrich

Dirksen, Heinrich Eduard, 1790-1868

ALs, 6 May 1838. 3 pp, 4to. To Julius Friedrich Abegg. Discussing recent pamphlets by Albrecht, Dahlmann & Grimm justifying their conduct at Goettingen. star Mar 26 (588) DM340

Disney Studios, Walt

— DISNEY, ROY O. - Ds, 7 Aug 1952. 3 pp, 4to. Assignment of the film Donald's Diary to the Bank of America as security for loans. Dar June 11 (154) $250

Disney, Walter Elias, 1901-66

Ls, 4 Mar 1940. 1 p, 8vo. Letter of recommendation for Robert Neuschotz. Illus in cat. sup Oct 15 (1227) $1,900

— 15 Feb 1941. 2 pp, 4to. To Daisy Beck. Chatting about the gala premiere of Fantasia in NY & other activities & plans. Illus in cat. sup May 9 (13) $3,800

— 31 Dec 1953. 1 p, 8vo. To Josh Meador. Thanking for a painting. Framed with a photograph. Dar Feb 13 (160) $750

— 16 June 1961. 1 p, 4to. Recipient unnamed. Inviting possible sponsors to a presentation of his Hall of Presidents. sup Oct 15 (1228) $2,250

Photograph, sgd, [18 Dec 1952]. 8 by 10 inches. Dar June 11 (155) $2,000

Photograph, sgd & inscr, [n.d.]. 10 by 8 inches. With 2 tigers on his desk; inscr to Alex. Framed. Dar Dec 26 (172) $1,200

Signature, [1960]. 12mo. Framed with a photograph. With related material. Dar Feb 13 (159) $800

— Anr, [n.d.]. 12mo. Framed with related material. Dar Dec 26 (171) $1,300

— Anr, [n.d.]. 4to. Framed with a photograph. Dar June 11 (156) $650

Disney, Walter Elias, 1901-66 —& Others

[A ptd program for the Motion Picture Polo Game, 29 July [n.y.], 1 p, 9 by 14 inches, sgd by Disney & 14 other Hollywood celebrities including Cary Grant, Spencer Tracy, Bette Davis, etc., sold at sup on 15 Oct 1991, lot 1316, for $1,400.]

Disraeli, Benjamin, 1st Earl of Beaconsfield, 1804-81

ALs, 4 May [1849]. 4 pp, 8vo. To H. Drummond. Thanking for a manifesto submitted to the Morning Post, & mocking Utopian politics. Sgd D. pn Nov 14 (192) £400 [Dupre]

— 31 Aug 1869. 3 pp, 8vo. To W. B. Ferrand. Thanking for a present. Ingilby collection. pn Nov 14 (67) £260 [Dupre]

— 4 Nov 1870. 1 p, 8vo. To Lady Marian [Alford]. Announcing his visit. wa Oct 19 (95) $300

— 1 Mar 1872. 3 pp, 8vo. To Lady Marian [Alford]. Asking that an acquaintance "should put his suggestions into the form of a memorandum". Sgd D. wa Oct 19 (94) $240

Ditzen, Rudolf, 1893-1947. See: Fallada, Hans

Dix, Dorothea L., 1802-87

ALs, 24 Feb 1852. 1 p, 4to. To [the state legislators at Annapolis]. Political appeal. Dar Oct 10 (140) $100

Dix, John A., 1798-1879

Photograph, sgd, [n.d.]. Carte size. Sgd recto & verso. In uniform. By Anthony, from a Brady negative. Illus in cat. R June 13 (110) $400

Dix, Otto, 1891-1969

Series of 3 A Ls s, 28 June & 9 Aug 1952 & [n.d.]. 4 pp, 4to. Recipient unnamed. Planning an exhibition at Goslar. star Mar 27 (885) DM1,100

ALs, 29 Aug 1958. 1 p, folio. To Christoph Czwiklitzer. About a projected speech. star Mar 27 (886) DM320

Dizengoff, Meir, 1861-1937

Check, accomplished & sgd, 27 Mar 1906. Payable to Liba Ginzburg. Dar June 11 (257) $100

Doderer, Heimito von, 1896-1966

ALs, 5 Jan 1941. 2 pp, 8vo. To [his future wife] Maria Thoma. Planning a reunion in Vienna. HH May 13 (1924) DM700

— 3 Mar [1941]. 1 p, 4to. To [his future wife] Maria Thoma. Love letter. HH May 13 (1925) DM600

— 5 Mar [1941]. 2 pp, 8vo. To [his future wife] Maria Thoma. About his duties with the army in France. HH May 13 (1926) DM520

— 23 Apr 1941. 2 pp, 4to. To [his future wife] Maria Thoma. Love letter, & planning a reunion. HH May 13 (1927) DM550

— 20 May [1941]. 2 pp, 4to. To [his future wife] Maria Thoma. Asking for photographs. HH May 13 (1928) DM700

— 18 July [1941]. 1 p, 4to. To [his future wife] Maria Thoma. Love letter. HH May 13 (1929) DM500

— 28 Nov [1941]. 1 p, 4to. To [his future wife] Maria Thoma. Love letter, & referring to his current work. HH May 13 (1930) DM600

— 16 July 1949. 1 p, 8vo. To [his future wife] Maria Thoma. Planning a reunion. In red & blue ink; including several small sketches. Illus in cat. HH May 13 (1931) DM600

— 21 Jan 1957. 1 p, folio. Recipients unnamed. Thanking for their hospitality. star Mar 26 (120) DM480

Dodgson, Charles Lutwidge, 1832-98

ALs, 1 Feb 1873. 1 p, 8vo. To Mr. Dubourg. Concerning the project of "a dramatized 'Alice'". sup Oct 15 (1230) $1,050

— 5 Dec 1873. 3 pp, 8vo. To [Caroline] Erskine. Giving advice on books for children. Ingilby collection. pn Nov 14 (68) £1,600 [Browning]

— 11 May 1876. 1 p, 12mo. Recipient unnamed. Declining to write for a journal. Margin torn. Dar Feb 13 (161) $200

— 12 Sept 1883. 1 p, 16mo. To [R. H. M.] Bosanquet. Inquiring about rules for reading time by the stars. Ingilby collection. pn Nov 14 (69) £680 [Maggs]

Doeblin, Alfred, 1878-1957

ALs, 7 Jan [19]28. 3 pp, 4to. To Hans Much. Requesting further information about a projected journey to Hungary. FD Dec 3 (1417) DM680

— [Dec 1940]. 2 pp, 8vo. To his friends Rosin. Postscript to a letter, inquiring about a vol sent to them, & reporting about his current work. HH May 13 (1932) DM340

— 9 Jan 1941. 1 p, 4to. To his friends Rosin. Postscript to a letter by his wife Erna, rejoicing about Mussolini's problems in Africa. HH May 13 (1933) DM500

— 30 Apr 1941. 1 p, 4to. To his friends Rosin. On verso of a letter by his wife Erna, commenting about Hollywood & efforts to find a pbr for a new book. HH May 13 (1934) DM440

— [1942?]. 4 pp, 8vo. To his friends Rosin. About his son, immigration to America, & the probability of Hitler's defeat. HH May 13 (1935) DM900

Autograph quotation, 2 lines, sgd; 8 Dec [19]29. 12cm by 15cm. Mtd with a port. JG Sept 27 (329) DM240

Doenitz, Karl, 1891-1980

Typescript, instrument designating officials empowered to sign the ratification of the unconditional German surrender, 7 May 1945. 1 p, 4to. Souvenir copy, sgd & dated 22 Apr [19]78. sg Feb 27 (255) $350

Dohnanyi, Ernst von, 1877-1960

Photograph, sgd & inscr, 1926. 232mm by 171mm (image). By Vajda. star Mar 27 (1003) DM440

Dohrn, Anton, 1840-1909

A Ls s (2), 30 Dec 1879 & 13 June 1896. 4 pp, 8vo. To Joseph Joachim. About Joachim's concerts in Italy. With related material. star Mar 26 (589) DM420

Dolly, Jenny, 1893-1941 —&
Dolly, Rosie, 1893-1970

[Their signatures, 4 Mar 1916, 1 p, 12mo, with ptd photographs, sold at Dar on 10 Oct 1991, lot 141, for $100.]

Dolly, Rosie, 1893-1970. See: Dolly, Jenny & Dolly

Donizetti, Gaetano, 1797-1848

Autograph Ms, tp for his Miserere, 1843. 1 p, 8vo. Sgd. S Dec 6 (78) £700 [Macnutt]

Ms, duet for Cardenio & Kaidama from his opera Il furioso all'isola di San Domingo, Sept 1833. 43 pp, 4to, in modern half vellum. In a scribal hand, with autograph annotations & corrections. S May 29 (525) £1,200 [Mazzucchetti]

ALs, 26 July 1831. 1 p, 8vo. To Giovanni Ricordi. Regarding the publication of the piano-vocal score of his opera Anna Bolena. S Dec 6 (79) £1,200 [Franks]

Doolittle, James Harold, 1896-1990

Ls, 1966. 1 p, 4to. Recipient unnamed. Paying tribute to Gen. Billy Mitchell. sup Oct 15 (1233) $260

Doors, The

[The signatures of all 4 band members on the ptd music for Light My Fire, [n.d.], framed, 20 by 16 inches, sold at P on 17 Dec 1991, lot 418, for $2,500.]

Dorati, Antal, 1906-89

Autograph music, sketches for his opera Der Kuender, 1983. 2 pp, size not stated. Sgd & inscr. star Mar 27 (1004) DM240

Dore, Gustave, 1832-83

ALs, 15 Mar 1873. 2 pp, 8vo. To Dr. Camuset. Inviting him for dinner. star Mar 27 (887) DM220

Dos Passos, John, 1896-1970

Collection of 2 Ls s & typescript, sgd, 22 May & 19/20 July 1962. 11 pp, 4to. To Antonio Aita. Thanking for an invitation to a PEN conference & sending the typescript of his address to the meeting (included). star Mar 26 (122) DM500

Doubleday, Abner, 1819-93

ALs, 4 May 1866. 1 p, 8vo. To J. H. Ford. Sending a letter for Mr. Gregor. Illus in cat. R Mar 7 (79) $850

— 15 May 1887. 2 pp, 8vo. To Alice N. Burt. Suggesting that illiteracy in the South "had much to do with bringing on the great civil war". sup May 9 (118) $2,500

Signature, [n.d.]. 16mo (card). As Major General. Dar Dec 26 (60) $400

— KELLY. - Orig drawing, pencil port of Doubleday, 6 Nov 1879. 8vo. Sgd by both.

CNY Dec 5 (36) $400

— KELLY. - Orig drawing, bust port of Doubleday, 6 Nov 1879. 4 by 7 inches. In pencil, heightened in white. Sgd by Kelly & Doubleday. Dar June 11 (157) $600

Douglas, Lady Elizabeth K.

Original drawings, (16), to illus The Rise and Fall of Jack; [n.d.]. 9.25 by 13.25 inches & smaller. In watercolor. Ck Dec 11 (19) £

Douglas, Stephen A., 1813-61

Franking signature, [n.d.]. On autograph envelope addressed to Jacob Thompson. Dar Apr 9 (183) $200

Douglas, William O., 1898-1980

Ls, 30 June 1975. 1 p, 4to. To H. Keith Thompson. Expressing his conviction that the Nuremberg trials were based on ex post facto law. Dar June 11 (158) $950

Douglass, Frederick, 1817-95

ALs, 7 Mar 1879. 1 p, 8vo. To Charles L. Brace. Thanking for a copy of a recent address. Dar Aug 6 (114) $700

Ds, 9 May 1884. 1 p, 3.5 by 8.5 inches. As Recorder of the District of Columbia; deed. Dar Feb 13 (162) $170

— [n.d.]. 2 pp, folio. As Recorder of Deeds, bill of sale transferring a bar & store from James Breen & F. P. Cox to George N. Cox. With list of property attached. sup Oct 15 (1234) $210

Autograph quotation, referring to the duty of governments to protect the human rights of the humblest citizens, 22 Aug 1879. 1 p, 12mo. Sgd. Imperf. wa Dec 19 (244) $400

— Anr, sgd, 1880. 1 p, 2.5 by 5 inches. "There can be no true peace..." sg Sept 12 (60) $750

Doyle, Sir Arthur Conan, 1859-1930

Autograph Ms, introduction to The Undiscovered Country, Ed by Harold Bayley; [1918]. 2 pp, folio. Sgd. With a copy of the book. C Dec 16 (284) £880 [Maggs]

— Autograph Ms, The Adventure of the Mazarin Stone, [pbd Oct 1921]. 19 pp, 4to; on rectos only. Some revisions; lacking an insert of 106 words of ptd version. In crushed burgundy mor bdg with small rough diamond inset. P Oct 11 (122) $75,000

— Autograph Ms, The Adventure of the Three Garridebs, 1924. 22 pp, 4to, in white cloth bdg. Sgd twice. Complete Ms; inscr by the ptr on final page. sup May 9 (16) $75,000

ALs, 6 Dec 1916. 2 pp, 8vo. Recipient unnamed. Requesting information about a battle. star Mar 26 (123) DM1,100

— [1929]. 1 p, 5 by 3.5 inches. Recipient unnamed. Refusing to sign photographs without prior purchase of books from the Psychic Bookshop. Imperf. Dar Aug 6 (147) $130

Dreiser, Theodore, 1871-1945

ALs, 3 Oct 1923. 1 p, 8vo. To Mr. Gaines. Suggesting that he paste this letter in his copy of The Genius. Dar Apr 9 (184) $100

Ls, 2 Nov 1920. 1 p, 8vo. To Olga Woolf. Responding to an invitation to lecture. wa Dec 19 (246) $120

Droste-Huelshoff, Annette von, 1797-1848

Autograph Ms, poem, Die Mutter am Grabe, [1840]. 2 pp, 8vo. 6 eight-line stanzas. Including authentication by Hildegard v. Lassberg at bottom. star Mar 26 (125) DM20,000

Drouet, Jean Baptiste, Comte d'Erlon, 1765-1844

Ds, [18 July 1798]. 1 p, 8vo. Receipt to Citizen Richards for a letter from the US Minister. sg Feb 27 (114) $90

Drummond, James, 4th Earl of Perth, 1648-1716

Ds, 5 Nov 1674. 5 pp, folio. Inventory of c.170 household effects belonging to his wife Lilias at the time of their marriage. Also sgd by others. Silked. S July 21 (263) £500 [Maggs]

Du Bois-Reymond, Emil, 1818-96

ALs, 26 June 1855. 2 pp, 8vo. To an unnamed colleague. Saying he is so highly specialized that he must rely on infornmation given by others when teaching physiology as a field. star Mar 26 (593) DM650

— 19 July 1875. 3 pp, 8vo. To an unnamed colleague. Concerning statues of Alexander & Wilhelm von Humboldt to be erected at the university in Berlin. star Mar 26 (594) DM750

Dubnow, Simon, 1860-1941

Autograph postcard, sgd, 19 Mar 1927. To Dr. S. Eisenstadt. Referring to his workload, & declining to cooperate in a publishing venture. Dar Feb 13 (232) $450

Duer, William, 1747-99

Ls, 3 Nov 1790. 3 pp, 4to. To Benjamin Walker. Concerning Joel Barlow & contracts between the Scioto Company & some Frenchmen. Framed. R Mar 7 (186) $3,000

Duffy, Hugh, 1866-1954

Signature, [19 June 1952]. 5 by 3 inches, on verso of trimmed postcard. Dar Dec 26 (86) $300

Dufy, Raoul, 1877-1953

Original drawings, (2), sketches of designs for a ballet (La Lanterne magique), [n.d.]. 15cm by 19cm & 8cm by 21cm. Attached to typescript scenario by Rene Kerdyk. Boris Kochno collection. SM Oct 12 (367) FF6,500

Duke, Vernon, 1903-69

Collection of 30 A Ls s, Ls s & postcards, sgd, [c.1925 to 1946]. 70 pp, various sizes. To Boris Kochno. About his work on a ballet, his other works, his breach with Diaghilev, emigration to the US, etc. SM Oct 12 (368) FF9,000

Dukelsky, Vladimir Alexandrovich, 1903-69. See: Duke, Vernon

Dumas, Alexander, 1802-70

Autograph Ms, article about the Italian fight for independence; [n.d.]. 2 pp, 4to. Sgd. With English trans. sup Oct 15 (1239) $600

ANs, [n.d.]. 1 p, 4to. Recipient unnamed. Requesting that Mr. Blaigue be interviewed about a small portion of land. Framed with a trans. Illus in cat. sup Oct 15 (1240) $800

Dumas, Alexander, 1824-95

ALs, [n.d.]. 7 pp, 8vo. Recipient unnamed. Criticizing recipient's libretto adapted from one of his works. sup Oct 15 (1238) $480

Dunant, Henri, 1828-1910

Ptd photograph, Feb 1902. 4to. Sgd & inscr. Was mtd. Illus in cat. star Mar 27 (1321) DM3,000

Duncan, Isadora, 1878-1927

Collection of ALs & 2 photographs, [n.d.]. 1 p, 8vo, & 2 postcards. To Frau Lang. Informing her about her return from Greece. star Mar 27 (1213) DM700

Duse, Eleonora, 1858-1924

Photograph, sgd & inscr, [n.d.]. 4 by 6.5 inches. Inscr to Mme Saulmann. Repaired. Dar Aug 6 (14) $100

Dvorak, Antonin, 1841-1904

ALs, 4 Nov 1890. 2 pp, 12mo. Recipient unnamed. Regarding the copyright of 2 compositions. In English. Framed with a port. P June 17 (25) $2,250

Autograph postcard, sgd, [23 Jan 1881]. To Max Schuetz. Expressing delight that the Zigeunerlieder have pleased him, & offering to send other works. Illus in cat. S Dec 6 (82) £1,300 [Ragan]

— [10 Oct 1887]. To E. M. Engelmann. Asking for a book to be sent to him. C June 24 (19) £650 [L'Autographe]

Dylan, Bob

Autograph Ms, lyrics for several songs, [1961]. 2 pp, 4to. Illus in cat. P Dec 17 (410) $1,500

— Autograph Ms, lyrics for the song Talking New York, [1961]. 2 pp, 8vo. 10 verses, with revisions. Illus in cat. P Dec 17 (403) $7,500

— Autograph Ms, lyrics for the song Talkin Bear Mountain Blues, [1961]. 1 p, 4to. 10 verses, with revisions. With 6 verses for the song I'll get where I'm Going Someday, on verso. Illus in cat. P Dec 17 (404) $5,500

— Autograph Ms, lyrics for the song California Brown-Eyed Baby, [1961]. 1 p, 4to. 4 verses, with revisions. With lyrics for the song Over the Road, on verso. Illus in cat. P Dec 17 (405) $4,000

— Autograph Ms, lyrics for the song Colorado Blues, unfinished; [1961]. 1 p, 4to. 4 verses, with revisions. With ANs on verso. Illus in cat. P Dec 17 (406) $1,300

— Autograph Ms, lyrics for the song Dope Fiend Robber, [1961]. 1 p, 4to. 18 verses, with revisions. With draft for the song This Train Ain't Bound for Glory, on verso. Illus in cat. P Dec 17 (407) $2,000

— Autograph Ms, lyrics for the song Rocking Chair, [1961]. 1 p, 4to. 5 verses, with revisions. With 1 verse for the song Rocky Mountain Belle No 2, on verso. P Dec 17 (408) $1,800

— Autograph Ms, lyrics for the song V. D. Seaman's Last Letter, [1961]. 1 p, size not stated. 7 verses, with revisions. Illus in cat. P Dec 17 (411) $3,250

— Autograph Ms, lyrics of 5 traditional songs, [1961]. On fragment of album sleeve, 6 by 12 inches. Illus in cat. P Dec 17 (412) $1,500

Original drawings, sketches & doodles, [1961]. 1 leaf, 9 by 12 inches. Illus in cat. P Dec 17 (413) $1,000

Photograph, sgd, 1973. 8 by 10 inches. Movie scene. Dar Dec 26 (173) $170

Signature, [n.d.]. On poster for video release of the film Don't Look Back. Framed, 22 by 30 inches. Illus in cat. P Dec 17 (402) $1,000

E

Earhart, Amelia, 1897-1937

ALs, 7 Apr 1933. 1 p, 4to. To Mrs. Moffet. Expressing condolences on the death of her husband. Illus in cat. CNY June 9 (230) $5,800

Ls, [Jan 1932]. 1 p, 4to. To Roy Chapman Andrews. Protesting against his pbd statement ruling out women explorers. With carbon copy of recipient's answer. Spiro collection. CNY May 14 (54) $5,000

— 8 June 1935. 1 p, 4to. To Dorothy Walworth Crowell. Congratulating her on winning a newspaper contest. With photograph attached. Illus in cat. sup Oct 15 (1241) $1,000

ANs, [n.d.]. 1 p, 8vo. Recipient unnamed. Returning some "attractive neckware". On hotel letterhead. Illus in cat. Dar Aug 6 (148) $900

Ds, 1936. 1 p, folio. Airport landing register; also sgd by 10 other pilots. sup Oct 15 (1242) $625

Photograph, sgd, [n.d.]. 3.75 by 4.5 inches. In airplane cockpit. b&b Feb 19 (152) $650

Early, Jubal Anderson, 1816-94

ALs, 4 Jan 1869. 2 pp, 8vo. To J. K. Finlay. Recalling his attack on Winchester in 1863. Matted with ptd port drawing. Dar June 11 (159) $1,300

Earp, Nicholas Porter, 1813-1907

[A group of 11 legal documents (2 autograph) relating to the case of Emily Smith v. Peter Smith, 1886, sgd 14 times as Justice of the Peace of Colton, 2 also sgd by his son Virgil as Constable, sold at sup on 9 May 1992, lot 444, for $8,500.]

Earp, Virgil

Ds, 14 Oct 1881. 1 p, 8vo. Auditor's receipt, sgd as tax collector. Illus in cat. sup May 9 (445) $3,500

East India Company

— CHAMIER [CHAMEIR?], JOHN. - 4 A Ls s, 27 Jan 1802 to 6 May 1803. 17 pp, 4to. To David Scott. Reporting from Madras & criticizing Lords Clive & Wellesley. bba Jan 30 (275) £190 [Maggs]

Eastman, George, 1854-1932

Ls, 26 Sept 1929. 1 p, 8vo. To Dr. S. W. Stratton. Referring to efforts at calendar simplification. Dar Feb 13 (163) $275

Eastman, Max, 1883-1969

Collection of 2 A Ls s & 3 Ls s, 1941. 8 pp, various sizes. To Mr. Shipley. About the Communist party & other matters. Dar June 11 (160) $190

Collection of 3 Ls s & 2 A Ns s, 5 Aug [19]41 to 31 Jan [19]43. Length not stated. To Joseph Shipley, Jr. Concerning contributions to the Philosophical Library. sg Feb 27 (55) $100

Eastwood, Clint

Ds, 31 Mar 1955. 7 pp, size not stated. Carbon copy, contract with Universal Pictures. Dar Dec 26 (174) $250

Eberhard IV Ludwig, Herzog von Wuerttemberg, 1676-1733

Ls, 19 Apr 1712. 3 pp, folio. To an unnamed general. Informing him about a complaint. HN June 26 (903) DM260

Ebert, Friedrich, 1871-1925

Ds, 28 Jan 1919. 1 p, folio. Administrative appointment for Georg Flatow. Also sgd by Philip Scheidemann. star Mar 27 (1322) DM680

Eckermann, Johann Peter, 1792-1854

Autograph Ms, poem, Bande; [n.d.]. 2 pp, 8vo. 33 lines; sgd. HH May 13 (1952) DM600

Eden, Avraham ("Bren")

Photograph, sgd, [10 Mar 1949]. 9.5 by 12 inches. Raising the Israeli flag in Um-Rashrah. Dar June 11 (258) $120

Edison, Thomas A., 1847-1931

[An archive of documents concerning Edison's purchase of a Spodumene mine near Keystone, South Dakota, 1919 to 1931, sold at sup on 15 Oct 1991, lot 1245, for $5,400.]

ALs, 5 Dec 1898. 1 p, 4to. To his wife. Regarding personal matters. Sgd TAE. sg Sept 12 (62) $750

— 19 Apr [1910?]. 6 pp, 8vo. To R. H. Beach. Discussing the reduction of battery weight for the electric-powered car. Sgd E. CNY Dec 5 (38) $1,600

— 2 Apr [n.y.]. 1 p, 4to. To his wife. About progress at the brick manufacturing plant. Illus in cat. sg Feb 27 (58) $650

— 2 Dec [n.y.]. 2 pp, 4to. To his wife. Giving instructions for handling bonds. Sgd TAE. In pencil. sg Sept 12 (64) $1,100

— [n.d.], "Tuesday". 4 pp, 8vo. To his wife. Love letter. Illus in cat. sup Oct 15 (1244) $1,800

— [n.d.]. 2 pp, 4to. To his wife. Concerning travel arrangements. sg Feb 27 (56) $700

— [n.d.]. 2 pp, 4to. To his wife. About the weather & the work at the laboratory. sg Feb 27 (57) $600

— [n.d.]. 3 pp, 4to. To his wife. Regarding the dust problem at the brick manufacturing plant. sg Feb 27 (59) $1,100

— [n.d.]. 4 pp, 8vo. To his wife. Reporting on progress on X-rays, the kinetoscope, & the phonograph. sg Feb 27 (61) $2,200

— [n.d.]. 3 pp, 8vo. To his wife. About his brick manufacturing plant. Sgd TAE. In pencil. sg Sept 12 (63) $950

— [n.d.]. 3 pp, 4to. To his wife. Discussing family matters. Sgd TAE. In pencil. sg Sept 12 (65) $750

Ls, 27 Jan 1916. 1 p, 8vo. To Elmer A. Sperry. Discussing options for "the location of the Naval Laboratory." Framed with a photograph. Dar Apr 9 (186) $950

— 8 July 1921. 1 p, 4to. To Osborn Curtis. Stating that he will not be able "to take any active part in the campaign" for visual education. Illus in cat. sup Oct 15 (1246) $1,300

— 18 July 1923. 1 p, 4to. To Richard A. Patton. Thanking for a port drawing. Dar June 11 (162) $650

ANs, [c.1914]. 2 pp, 8vo. To an unnamed collaborator. About phonograph records. In pencil. bba May 28 (204) £320 [Lion Heart]

Ds, lithographic plan of electrical circuitry for the incandescent electric light, to accompany his patent application for Bolivia, [7 June 1881]. 1 p, 405mm by 560mm. Also sgd by 2 others. CNY Dec 5 (37) $6,500

— 13 Oct 1926. 2 pp, 4to. Minutes of a meeting of the Board of Directors of the Edison Storage Battery Company; also sgd by 8 others. Dar Apr 9 (185) $450

Check, sgd, 4 Aug 1928. Payable to Falls Clutch & Machinery Co. Cancellation touching signature. Dar Dec 26 (175) $600

— Anr, sgd, 10 Aug 1929. Payable to the "Seminole Lumber & Mfg Co." Dar June 11 (163) $400

Photograph, sgd & inscr, [n.d.]. 8.5 by 6.5 inches (image). Inscr to M. C. Candioti. S Feb 11 (592) £420 [Weber]

Signature, [5 June 1929]. On philatelic envelope. Dar June 11 (161) $450

— Anr, [n.d.]. 2.75 by 2 inches (card). Dar Feb 13 (164) $300

— Anr, [n.d.]. On photograph of an oil port, 8 by 10 inches. Inscr to Joseph Robinson. R Nov 9 (52) $900

Edward I, King of England, 1239-1307

Document, 6 Dec 1293. 1 p, vellum, 121mm by 232mm. License to crenellate Halesowen Abbey. Illus in cat. S June 23 (44) £4,500 [Miller]

Edward VII, King of England, 1841-1910

A Ls s (2), 14 & 18 Aug 1897. 6 pp, 8vo. To Sir Edward Monson. About a visit by the Duc de Chartres to the British Embassy at Paris & his own stay at Bayreuth. bba June 25 (127) £200 [Kunkler]

ALs, 15 Dec 1861. 3 pp, 8vo. To an unnamed Duchess. About the death of his father. pn Nov 14 (181) £220 [Browning]

— 18 June 1873. 3 pp, size not stated. To "cher Wladimir". Thanking for a cigarette case. Ck Apr 3 (94) £80

Edward VIII, King of England, 1894-1972. See: Windsor, Edward
See also: Windsor, Edward & Windsor

Edwards, George, 1694-1773

ALs, 7 May 1763. 1 p, folio. To Lord Cardross. Referring to the publication of the 3d part of his Gleanings of Natural History & the sale of his drawings to the Earl of Bute. C Oct 30 (187) £500 [Royal Coll. of Physicians]

Effingham, Henry Alexander Gordon Howard, 4th Earl of, 1866-1927

Autograph Ms, Half Hours in Remarkable Places, 1910 to 1912. 975 pp in 5 green mor vols gilt. Essays, illus with c.650 photographs, postcards, engravings, etc. bba Sept 19 (431) £1,400 [Fiske]

Egidio Romano, d.1316. See: Aegidius Romanus

Ehrenberg, Christian Gottfried, 1795-1876

ALs, 29 Jan 1846. 3 pp, 8vo. To [Chr. F. Schwaegrichen?]. Sending some moss specimens for identification. Illus in cat. hen Nov 12 (2526) DM200

Ehrlich, Paul, 1854-1915

ALs, [n.d.]. 1 p, 4to. To an unnamed colleague. Requesting information concerning a projected new institute for anatomy. star Mar 26 (598) DM1,300

— [n.d.]. 1 p, 4to. To Frau Morgenroth. Expressing condolences on the death of her husband. star Mar 26 (599) DM950

Eichendorff, Joseph von, 1788-1857

Autograph Ms, 3 poems, Aussicht, Klagen, & Variazion, [1808]. 2 pp, 4to. Working drafts. star Mar 26 (131) DM23,000

— Autograph Ms, Der Ehezwist, free trans of Calderon's El pleito matrimonial, [n.d.]. 2 pp, folio. 111 lines; draft. star Mar 26 (132) DM4,500

Eigen, Manfred

Autograph Ms, 1st part of a scientific paper, [n.d.]. 6 pp, folio. Sgd later & dated 15 July 1983. star Mar 26 (601) DM420

Einstein, Albert, 1879-1955

[Autograph notations in pencil on a carbon typescript of Leo Mattersdorf's Behold the Heavens [pbd as Insight into Astronomy], 139 pp, 4to, with Ls, 18 Mar 1948, conveying his thoughts about the book, & a copy of ptd version of the book, sold at P on 17 June 1992, lot 190, for $5,000.]

Autograph Ms, appeal in favor of the poor, [1929]. 1 p, 8vo. star Mar 26 (602) DM1,850

— Autograph Ms, lecture on The Origins of the General Theory of Relativity, delivered at Glasgow, 1933. 8 pp, 4to. In German; sgd. P Dec 12 (34) $110,000

ALs, 13 June 1933. 2 pp, 4to. To [Walther] Mayer. About his impending arrival at Princeton & their collaborative work. Sgd A.E. Illus in cat. sg Feb 27 (63) $5,000

— [14 Apr 1950?]. 1 p, 4to. Recipient unnamed. Abour recipient's efforts to find a place in an old people's home. star Mar 26 (609) DM4,400

Ls s (2), 3 June 1946. Length not stated. To Hugo Simon. Promising to help him rectify the problem of his assumed identity, & certifying that recipient's real name is Hugo Simon. Ck Apr 3 (12) £2,300

— Ls s (2), 17 Jan 1953. 2 pp, 4to. To a group of schoolchildren & their teacher Robert G. Stillwell. Responding to their question: "What is an animal?" Including letter of transmittal. Illus in cat. sup Oct 15 (1255) $4,000

Ls, 12 Apr 1929. 2 pp, 4to. To Philipp Frank. Hoping that Russian scientists in emigration may soon be able to return home. star Mar 26 (603) DM3,600

— 28 Nov 1929. 1 p, 4to. To Wilhelm Stollmann. Informing him that he has written a letter in his behalf. Including autograph postscript, sgd, suggesting he sell this letter to obtain the money for his trip to Holland. Illus in cat. sup May 9 (405) $1,700

— 1 Aug 19[31]. 1 p, folio. To Ascher Ehlich. About a piece of scientific equipment invented by Ehlich. Silked. S May 28 (201) £750 [Saggiori]

— 15 Aug 1931. 1 p, 4to. To Mario Palmieri. Doubting that recipient's tract on the Unified Field Theory will be understandable to a lay person. Illus in cat. sup Oct 15 (1252) $4,200

— 6 Oct 1932. 2 pp, 4to. To Richard Eder. Expressing scepticism about the success of recipient's efforts to spread pacifist ideas. With related material. star Mar 26 (604) DM8,000

— 28 Mar 1936. 2 pp, 4to. To Dr. H. Beckhardt. Requesting his help in procuring a pro-forma hiring certificate for a medical doctor from Germany. CNY Dec 5 (40) $1,800

— [c.March 1936]. 2 pp, 4to. To Richard Huelsenbeck. Responding to an inquiry about teaching opportunities. star Mar 26 (607) DM2,000

— 2 Dec 1938. 1 p, 4to. To Phineas Wittenberg. Hoping that "Alfred Wittenberg will be spared the terrible fate of most Jews in Germany." Illus in cat. sup Oct 15 (1256) $2,150

— 25 Mar 1939. 1 p, 4to. To Cyril Clemens. Regretting he will not be able to attend the naming of a street in his honor. In German. Illus in cat. sup Oct 15 (1250) $1,500

— 2 June 1939. 1 p, 4to. To A. W. Lissauer. Recommending Paul Gunzburg. sg Sept 12 (67) $1,100

— 10 June 1939. 1 p, 4to. To Morris Whinston. Praising his work "on behalf of the refugees during Dedication Week." Trimmed. Illus in cat. sup Oct 15 (1249) $4,000

— 10 June 1939. 1 p, 4to. To Dr. B. P. Stivelman. Copy, concerning his work on behalf of Jewish refugees. wd June 12 (312) $900

— 2 Feb 1940. 1 p, 4to. To David Hames. Informing him that the work of Mr. Gavarni is not known to him. Illus in cat. sup Oct 15 (1253) $2,000

— 6 Mar 1940. 1 p, 8vo. To Emma Darmstadt-Stern. Agreeing to see her & her husband. Matted with ptd photograph. Dar June 11 (165) $700

— 17 May 1943. 1 p, 8vo. To Samuel Patterson. Agreeing to join a library committee. sg Sept 12 (68) $1,100

— 22 Oct 1943. 2 pp, folio. To Mr. Rogosin. Discussing ways in which Jews might improve their situation. S May 28 (202) £3,000 [Browning]

— 5 Mar 1947. 1 p, 4to. Recipient unnamed. Regarding a contribution to the Emergency Committee of Atomic Scientists. P Dec 12 (35) $3,000

— 18 Jan 1948. 1 p, 4to. To Clara Urquhart. About a contribution for her book. Framed with a port. Illus in cat. R June 13 (206) $1,500

— 23 Feb 1948. 1 p, 4to. To Ludwig Schiff. Letter of recommendation for Dr. Gabriel Segall. Framed with a photograph. CNY Dec 5 (41) $1,700

— 23 Oct 1948. 1 p, 8vo. To W. Foges. Expressing dismay over the possibility of Chanticleer Press altering a book by a German writer. Framed with a port. P June 17 (26) $1,800

— 15 Nov 1949. 1 p, 4to. To Richard de Rochemont. Informing him that he does "not possess the gift of prophecy". Illus in cat. sup Oct 15 (1251) $2,400

— 14 June 1950. 1 p, 4to. To Bernard Weinstein. Insisting "that support of Israel's scientific and cultural institutions must go hand-in-hand with providing for Israel's material well-being". Illus in cat. sup May 9 (406) $4,400

— 2 Jan 1951. 1 p, 4to. To Dr. F. G. Back. Thanking for a book about Korea. R Mar 7 (167) $1,600

— 14 June 1954. 1 p, 8vo. To Leo Stone. Commenting on the special properties of seawater. sg Sept 12 (69) $1,100

ANs, 11 Nov 1924. 1 p, 8vo. To Herr Wassermann. Expressing condolences. CNY June 9 (59) $1,100

— 29 Dec 1930. To Mme Antonina. On postcard written & sgd by his wife; sending greetings. Ck Apr 3 (13) £400

Autograph endorsement, sgd, [12 Dec 1930]. 1 p, 4to. On sheet containing brief non-scholarly definition of the theory of relativity in anr hand; attesting to the truth of the statement. bbc Sept 23 (19) $1,400

Autograph sentiment, 2 lines, sgd; [n.d.]. 12cm by 15cm. Mtd with a port. JG Sept 27 (335) DM1,400

Endorsement, sgd, on verso of check sgd by Florence C. McCarthy, 12 Apr 1950, payable to Einstein. Matted with 3 ptd photographs. Dar June 11 (168) $1,200

Engraving, sgd, 1925. 8 by 10 inches. With a photograph. wd Dec 12 (317) $900

Photograph, sgd, 1953. 10 by 8 inches. rs Oct 17 (9) $1,100

Photograph, sgd & inscr, [19]53. 9.5 by 10 inches. Inscr with 2 lines of poetry in German. Illus in cat. sg Feb 27 (62) $3,400

Signature, 1921. 3.5 by 2.25 inches (card). Illus in cat. Dar June 11 (167) $850

— Anr, [n.d.]. Size not stated. Illus in cat. Dar June 11 (169) $650

— MUELLER, J. J. - Engraving, port of Einstein, [c.1930]. 5.75 by 8 inches. Sgd by both. Framed. Dar Feb 13 (166) $1,500

— STRUCK, HERMANN. - Engraving, port of Einstein, July 1927. 8 by 10 inches. Sgd by both. Framed. Dar June 11 (166) $2,250

Eisenhower, Dwight D., 1890-1969

Typescript, 1st Inaugural Address, [20 Jan 1953]. 9 pp, 4to, on rectos only. Sgd at head. Middendorf & Spiro collections. CNY May 14 (55) $3,500

— Typescript, 24-line copy of his D-Day speech to the Allied Expeditionary Force, [n.d.]. 1 p, 4to. Sgd. wa Oct 19 (283) $310

— Typescript, 24-line quotation, [n.d.]. 1 p, 4to. Sgd. wa Oct 19 (284) $230

ALs, 22 Jan [1943]. 2 pp, 4to. To his wife. Love letter, chatting about a luncheon, a letter to his son, etc. Illus in cat. sup May 9 (268) $2,950

— [15 Sept 1944]. 2 pp, 4to. To his wife. Reflecting on "the sanctity of personal mail". Illus in cat. sup May 9 (269) $1,500

— 18 Jan [1945]. 2 pp, 4to. To his wife. Hoping that the Russian offensive will succeed. Illus in cat. sup Oct 15 (1668) $4,250

Ls, 4 May 1844. 1 p, 4to. To Maurice Prince. Sending an appeal on behalf of the "Salute the Soldier" week. With a photograph, sgd. S Dec 12 (310) £650 [Sakmyster]

— 29 June 1944. 1 p, 8vo. To an unnamed Senator. Responding to a request for photographs. Trimmed. Dar June 11 (171) $250

— 5 Oct 1945. 1 p, 8vo. To Lieutenants Leona Miles, Lila Seals & Dorothy Miles. Contents not stated. F Sept 26 (587) $200

— 18 Dec 1948. 2 pp, 4to. To Philip Sporn. Robotyped inquiry, seeking data about manpower failures. sg Sept 12 (71) $

— 8 Mar 1952. 3 pp, 4to. To Clifford R. Hope. Responding to a letter urging him to run for President. Illus in cat. sup May 9 (270) $2,500

— 23 Sept 1952. 1 p, 4to. To Benjamin F. Caffey. Referring to Richard Nixon's nomination for the Vice Presidency. Dar Apr 9 (189) $1,600

— 14 Oct 1953. 1 p, 4to. To Charles Kohen. Thanking for a coin sent for his birthday. Illus in cat. sup Oct 15 (1673) $400

— 9 Mar 1955. 1 p, 4to. To Lowell Thomas. About film productions of the US Information Agency shown abroad. Matted with philatelic envelope. Dar June 11 (170) $475

— 29 June 1955. 1 p, 4to. To Ruth P. Hirschland. Inviting her to a luncheon of representatives of the sports world. Illus in cat. sup Oct 15 (1674) $1,200

— 5 July 1955. 1 p, 8vo. To Robert C. Preble. Thanking for a dictionary. Mtd. R Mar 7 (118) $280

— 2 July 1956. 1 p, 4to. Recipient unnamed. Expressing thanks after a stay in hospital. star Mar 27 (1323) DM550

— 16 Oct 1956. 1 p, 4to. To Arthur & Louise Eisenhower. Thanking for birthday cards. Sgd D. E. wa Oct 19 (279) $160

— 23 Nov 1956. 1 p, 4to. To Frank D. Parent. Thanking for congratulations on his re-election. Spiro collection. CNY May 14 (56) $700

— 6 Oct 1958. 1 p, 8vo. To Benjamin Fairless. Commenting on Republican objectives & American economics. sg Sept 12 (72) $550

— 20 July 1960. 1 p, 4to. To Lynn U. Stambaugh. Expressing appreciation for recipient's role in financing international trade. Framed. wa Oct 19 (280) $180

— 21 Dec 1963. 1 p, 4to. To Walter Winchell. Thanking for a note, & talking about a book. sup Oct 15 (1678) $210

— 28 May 1965. 1 p, 4to. To Mollie Cullum. Thanking for a telegram received during a golf tournament. Sgd D.E. Dar Apr 9 (191) $400

— 16 Feb 1966. 2 p, 4to. To Gene Schoor. Regretting that most of his "memorabilia of [his] cadet days were lost." With related material. Dar Oct 10 (142) $375

— 25 Aug 1967. 1 p, 4to. To Harold Russell. Expressing appreciation for the work of the Committee on Employment of the Handicapped. With group photograph. Dar Aug 6 (150) $275

— 12 Oct 1967. 1 p, 4to. To Mrs. Benjamin Caffee. Regretting that he did not see her in Washington. Dar Apr 9 (190) $120

— 31 Jan 1969. 1 p, 4to. To Mr. & Mrs. Harry Cubbage. Thanking for some presents. Dar Dec 26 (177) $160

Ds, 2 May 1925. 1 p, 4to. Notification to commanding officer, introducing a soldier reenlisting at Fort Bliss. R Nov 9 (5) $180

— 23 Jan 1953. 1 p, folio. Appointment of Henry Cabot Lodge as Ambassador to the United Nations. Countersgd by J. F. Dulles. Illus in cat. sup Oct 15 (1672) $4,200

— 2 Feb 1954. 1 p, folio. Appointment of G. A. Blowers to the Board of Directors of the Export-Import Bank. Countersgd by J. F. Dulles. Framed. wa Oct 19 (278) $270

— 25 Apr 1959. 1 p, folio. Appointment of Walt Disney as a member of the Advisory Committee on the Arts. Framed. Illus in cat. sup May 9 (263) $4,000

Group photograph, sgd, [31 July 1965]. 11 by 14 inches. With anr man on a park bench; inscr to Howard Young. Dar Oct 10 (144) $150

Photograph, sgd, [n.d.]. Framed, overall size 16 by 20 inches. By Bachrach. sup Oct 15 (1669) $500

Photograph, sgd & inscr, [14 July 1948]. 7.25 by 9.25 inches. Inscr to Walter Domrisch. Dar Oct 10 (143) $300

— Anr, [c.1956-60]. 8 by 10 inches. By J. A. Wills. sg Sept 12 (73) $275

— Anr, [n.d.]. 8 by 10 inches. Inscr to Mrs. Lockwood. Matted with campaign souvenirs. Dar June 11 (172) $400

— Anr, [n.d.]. 8 by 10 inches. Inscr to Howard Potter. R June 13 (175) $300

— Anr, [n.d.]. Folio. Inscr to W. F. Boone. wa Oct 19 (282) $180

Signature, on mount for reproduced color painting by him, [n.d.]. Folio. Framed. wa Oct 19 (281) $65

Eisenhower, Mamie Doud, 1896-1975

Series of 10 Ls s, 20 Jan 1953 to 20 Jan 1961. 4to. To Emma Mulvihill. Expressing thanks & sending family news. Illus in cat. sup Oct 15 (1679) $270

Eisenstadter, Meir ben Judah Leib, d.1852

ALs, [n.d.]. 1 p, 4to. To Rabbi Hayyim Bezalel Panat. Contents not stated. Illus in cat. sg Dec 19 (67) $500

Eisler, Hanns, 1898-1962. See: Brecht, Bertolt & Eisler

Eisner, Kurt, 1867-1919

ALs, 26 Feb 1918. 5 pp, folio. To Herr Kampffmeyer. Sending comments (included) on a recent article to be ptd in the Muenchner Post. star Mar 27 (1325) DM950

Ds, [1919]. 1 p, 8vo. Identification for a member of a reconnaissance detachment; unaccomplished. HH May 13 (1939) DM360

Eleonore, Empress of Leopold I, 1655-1720

Ls, 19 Apr 1711. 4 pp, 4to. To one of the Austrian dominions. Notification of her assumption of power as regent for her son [the future Emperor] Karl. Illus in cat. HN Nov 28 (1767) DM2,000

Elgar, Sir Edward, 1857-1934

Autograph music, draft of the 1st 22 bars of the introduction to scene III of his Cantata Caractacus, Op. 35, [1898]. 2 pp, folio. Scored for piano. In ink, with some additions in pencil. Illus in cat. bba June 25 (124) £3,000 [Macnutt]

— Autograph music, fragment from the full orchestral score of his symphonic study Falstaff, Op. 68; [1913]. 1 p, folio. 5 bars on 30 staves. Marked by the ptr. Framed. Illus in cat. S May 29 (528) £1,600 [Macnutt]

Series of 4 A Ls s, 3 Feb & 1 Mar 1933 & [n.d.]. 4 pp, 4to & 8vo. To Messrs. Gooodwin & Tabb. Ordering music supplies. pn June 11 (63) £440

ALs, 30 May 1906. 4 pp, 4to. To Lord Knollys. Expressing thanks for the King's interest in his work. bba Sept 19 (375) £700 [Kunkler]

— 9 Oct 1930. 1 p, 4to. To John Parker. Declining an invitation. pn June 11 (62) £110 [Macnutt]

— 16 Jan 1933. 2 pp, 8vo. To Sir Adrian Boult. Hoping that Alexander Mackenzie's violin concerto "will bear revival". C June 24 (21) £480 [Macnutt]

Autograph quotation, 3 bars of the prologue to The Apostles, 4 Oct [19]03. Size not stated. Sgd & inscr to A. T. G. Ck Nov 15 (30) £460

Eliot, Thomas Stearns, 1888-1965

Ls, 15 Sept 1949. 1 p, 4to. To Dale Edward Fern. Commenting on recipient's essay on Emily Dickinson & himself. CNY June 9 (61) $500

— 16 June 1952. 1 p, 8vo. To Lucius Shepard. Recommending his poems Practical Cats to a young admirer. wa Oct 19 (49) $425

Signature, [n.d.]. On ptd greeting card, 3.5 by 3.5 inches. Framed with related material. Dar June 11 (173) $200

Elisabeth, Herzogin von Braunschweig-Wolfenbuettel, 1510-58

Ls, [20 July] 1545. 2 pp, folio. Recipient unnamed. Asking that he assist her son during his travels. HN Nov 28 (1668) DM660

Elisabeth, Princess of Braunschweig-Wolfenbuettel, 1746-1840

ALs, 26 Dec 1795. 1 p, 4to. To Herr Roemer. About the handling of an inheritance claim. star Mar 27 (1609) DM450

Elisabeth, Empress of Franz Joseph I of Austria, 1837-98

AL, [n.d.]. 1 p, 8vo. To the Emperor. In 3d person, asking permission to meet Marie in Traunstein. S Dec 5 (489) £850 [Dixon]

Elisabeth, Queen of Carol I of Romania, 1843-1916. See: Sylva, Carmen

Elisabeth Charlotte d'Orleans, Duchesse de Lorraine, 1676-1744

Ls, 8 Aug 1737. 1 p, 8vo. To Wilhelm Reinhard von Neipperg. Expressing thanks for his efforts in behalf of her son. HN Nov 28 (1670) DM520

Elisabeth Christine, Queen of Friedrich II of Prussia, 1715-97

Ls s (2), 9 Jan 1751 & 15 Jan 1763. 2 pp, folio. To the government at Halberstadt. Acknowledging New Year's wishes. star Mar 27 (1603) DM300

Elizabeth, Queen of Bohemia, 1596-1662

ALs, 27 Oct [1653]. 3 pp, 4to. To William, 1st Earl of Craven. Mentioning the Elector of Brandenburg & a rebellion in Stirlingshire. HN Nov 28 (1669) DM5,200

Elizabeth I, Queen of England, 1533-1603

— PRIVY COUNCIL. - Letter, 19 Apr 1575. 1 p, folio. To the Justices of the Peace of the County of Cambridge. Requiring them to enforce the Queen's orders regarding the practice of archery. Sgd by Leicester, Burghley, Walsingham, & others. Annotated in the hand of Sir John Fenn on address leaf. Illus in cat. pn June 11 (42) £600 [Wilson]

— PRIVY COUNCIL. - Document, 5 Oct 1602. 1 p, folio. Pay order in favor of Thomas Lake, addressed to Treasurer Buckhurst. Sgd by 7 members of the Council. Illus in cat. sup May 9 (465) $640

Elizabeth II, Queen of England

Ds, 14 June 1967. 1 p, folio. Pardon for H. I. Smith. sup Oct 15 (1261) $460

— 12 June 1971. 1 p, folio. Award of the Order of the British Empire to Rudolf Bing. Countersgd by Prince Philip. sg Sept 12 (74) $1,500

Elizabeth II, Queen of England —& Philip, Prince, Duke of Edinburgh

Ds, 13 June 1964. 1 p, folio. Conferral of a decoration. Dar Dec 26 (178) $650

Ellery, William, Signer from Rhode Island

Ds, 26 Dec 1761. 1 p, 12mo. Receipt to Joshua Pice. sup Oct 15 (1197) $380

— 29 Aug 1796. 2 pp, 4to. As Port Collector, list of cargo on board the sloop Clemintina. Including autograph list of additional cargo shipped by Alexander Eddy. Dar June 11 (174) $250

Ellicott, Andrew, 1754-1820

ALs, 25 Dec 1815. 1 p, 4to. To William Simmons. Discussing procedures at West Point. bbc Dec 9 (165) $250

Ellington, Duke, 1899-1974

Autograph Ms, report about festivities following the Triennial Music Festival in Leeds, [n.d.]. Length not stated. Sgd in text several times. On hotel letterhead. Illus in cat. sup Oct 15 (1257) $450

— Autograph Ms, thoughts about being a musician & about his friend Mercer, [n.d.]. On a roll of paper towels; length not stated. Initialled in text. sup Oct 15 (1258) $105

Ptd photograph, [n.d.]. 5 by 7 inches. Sgd & inscr to Mrs. Marcus Risley. sup Oct 15 (1260) $200

Signature, [11 Dec 1931]. On invitation to University of Illinois, Champaign, Annual Junior Prom. Dar Aug 6 (115) $200

Ellis, Havelock, 1859-1939

Typescript, Crime and its Remedies, [c.1930]. 6 pp, 4to. Some autograph corrections. Sgd at end. bba Jan 30 (271) £75 [Drury]

Ellsworth, Elmer Ephraim, 1837-61

Autograph Ms, list of 23 names [of Chicago Zouaves], [Apr 1861]. 1 p, 8vo. With related material. Dar June 11 (129) $400

Ellsworth, Oliver, 1745-1807

ADs, 28 Oct 1776. 1 p, 8vo. Pay order. Dar Oct 10 (146) $275

Elyashar, Jacob Saul ben Eliezer Jeroham, 1817-1906

ALs, 1873. 1 p, 8vo. To Rabbi David Chai. About a financial matter. Also sgd by Shalom Moses Gagin. sg Dec 19 (68) $175

Emerson, Ralph Waldo, 1803-82

Autograph Ms, poem, beginning "The men are ripe of Saxon kind"; [n.d.]. 1 p, 8vo. 3 four-line stanzas, sgd. Tipped to larger card. Illus in cat. sup Oct 15 (1263) $2,000

ALs, 20 Aug 1861. 4 pp, 8vo. To Mr. Laighton. Reflecting on Theodore Parker & the Civil War. Spiro collection. CNY May 14 (57) $2,800

Check, accomplished & sgd, 6 July 1871. Payable to J. C. Sanborn. sg Feb 27 (67) $130

Emma, Queen of The Netherlands, 1858-1934
ALs, 15 Apr 1900. 8 pp, 4to. To [Princess Marie zu Wied?]. About her daughter Wilhelmina & the Boer War. star Mar 27 (1524) DM900

Eng, 1811-74. See: Chang & Eng

Englaender, Richard, 1859-1919. See: Altenberg, Peter

England

[A large collection of estate papers relating to the Trumbull family of Easthampstead Park, 1633 to 1872, thousands of pages in 24 vols, sold at S on 21 July 1992, lot 257, for £5,800 to Irvine.]

[A collection of 48 letters, receipts & intelligence reports relating to the maintenance of Lord North's ministry & the French & American stance in the American War of Independence, mostly 1773 to 1783, bound in a 19th-cent mor album, sold at Ck on 3 Apr 1992, lot 99, for £3,800.]

Ms, A Luminary Demonstration ... Of England ... The customarie annual Receipts of the Kingdonm of England, Jan 1612. 21 pp & blanks, 4to. Contemp limp vellum. Listing sources of income & receipts & payments. bba June 25 (138) £520 [Bernard]

— Ms, The iiiith and last part of the great English Chronology, [c.1600]. 266 leaves, folio, in rebacked contemp calf. In several hands. b Nov 18 (265) £200

— Bedford, Thomas. - Document, 19 Jan 1637. 2 pp, vellum, 4to. Indenture conveying land to William Cotton. sg Sept 12 (44) $110

— Brixton Dewell, Wiltshire. - Document, 8 Sept 1609. 1 p, folio. Instructions addressed to Richard Tynes by William Wilkinson regarding the public penance of Richard Humpfry for adultery. bba Sept 19 (424) £60 [Hatchwell]

— Commonwealth. - Document, 2 Nov 1650. 1 p, 4to. Certification, sgd by 2 Justices of the Peace for Middlesex County, that William Barker has taken the engagement to be faithful to the Commonwealth in the form prescribed by Parliament (ptd at head). Trimmed. pn June 11 (33) £190

— Denby. - Ms, notebook recording historical events & notes on the action against the Duke of Monmouth in 1685 & the wars of William of Orange; 1685-1727. 30 pp & blanks, 8vo, in 18th-cent calf. bba May 28 (234) £200 [National Army Museum]

— Essex. - Document, minutes of proceedings of Inspectors appointed to supervise the watch & public lighting at Chipping Ongar, 1836-56. 156 pp, 4to, in calf-backed bds. bba Jan 30 (300) £50 [Essex Record Office]

— Essex. - Ms, Exemplification of the record in Battell v. Cooke, 23 Jan 1531. 1 p, vellum, folio. bba Sept 19 (406) £240 [Essex Record Office]

— Essex. - Ms, extracts from the Pipe Roll for Essex, confirming the accounts of Robert Warwick, 2d Earl of Essex, for duties in that county; [c.1625]. 10 membranes of vellum sewn together, c.670cm by 23cm. bba Jan 30 (299) £100 [Essex Record Office]

— Great Plague. - Ms, Church Wardens' accounts for St. Margaret's Westminster, 9 Apr to 5 Nov 1666. 12 pp, folio. Kept by John Lennard. Worn. pn June 11 (26) £460

— Hereford & Shropshire. - Ms, account book relating to property in Hereford & Shropshire, 1673 to 1696. 115 pp & blanks, folio, in orig limp vellum. With related documents loosely inserted. bba Sept 19 (408) £260 [Knowles]

— Hitchin, Hertfordshire. - The suppression documents of the Carmelite Priory of Hitchin, including royal instructions by Henry VIII, sgd by Thomas Cromwell, 15 Oct 1538, & the surrender document, sgd by the Prior & convent members. S June 23 (50) £1,900 [Quaritch]

— House of Lords. - Ms, Proceedings upon Impeachments from the year 1666 to the year 1681; [18th cent]. 194 pp, folio, in repaired contemp calf. bba May 28 (236) £180 [Lowbook Exchange]

— Lincoln. - Letter, sgd by the scribe Jacobi de Meuania, [13th cent], 1 p, vellum, 194mm by 260mm. To Urbanus, Bishop of Lincoln. Instructing him to combat various ecclesiastical abuses. pn Nov 14 (237) £160

— Little Wrathing, Suffolk. - Document, 1270. 1 p, vellum, 75mm by 185mm. Conveyance of land in Little Wrathing by Thomas Le Bret, Lord of Little Chesterfield in Essex. b June 22 (135) £150

— London. - Ms, estate book of Earls Court Park Estate, [after 1867]. About 120 pp & blanks, size not stated, in red mor bdg. Comprising c.120 ground plans of properties; in colored inks. pn June 11 (27) £220

— Marlborough, Devon. - Ms, A survey taken of all the land belonging to Wm Dyer Esqr of Yarde in the Parish of Marlborough, 1 May 16[9]3. 94 pp & blanks, 4to, in orig limp vellum. Some additions, 1727. bba Sept 19 (405) £300 [Claridge]

— Mayfair. - Document, 24 Feb 1701. 1 p, vellum, 580mm by 650mm. Conveyance of land in Albemarle Street from Sir Henry Bond & others to Robert & Richard Ffryth. Including royal arms within initial letter. C Dec 16 (308) £400 [Marlborough]

— Middlesex. - Ms, Court Rolls of the Manor of Downbarns in Middlesex, 1739 to 1804. 158 pp, folio, in green vellum. bba Sept 19 (413) £110 [Claridge]

— NORFOLK. - 15 documents, 1459 to 1657. Various sizes. Relating to property at Wymondham held by the Abbey. bba Jan 30 (302) £260 [Bernard]

— NORFOLK. - Ms, Lynn Inquisition of Crown Rents for Norfolk, 1403. 58 leaves, folio, in modern cloth bdg. bba Sept 19 (415) £130 [Quaritch]

— PADMAN, ISAAC. - Autograph Ms, A few Observations made upon Journies taken Subsequent to the Deliverance from The House of Bondage ..., vol 2, 1812 to 1816. 99 pp, 4to, in contemp calf. Describing journeys to Cheltenham, Cambridge, Northamptonshire, etc. pn June 11 (22) £170 [White]

— SALISBURY. - Document, 25 Oct 1616. 1 p, 8vo. Order addressed by Thomas Chafin to the Keeper of the goal at Fisherton Anger to receive Alice Luxmore into custody. bba Sept 19 (420) £55 [Kunkler]

— SALISBURY. - Ms, Bishops Court of Frank Pledge or Court Baron. Proceedings; 1731 to 1737. 37 leaves, 4to, in orig vellum. bba Sept 19 (421) £100 [Claridge]

— WAXHAM, NORFOLK. - Document, Michaelmas harvest account made at Waxham, 1392/3. 1 p, vellum, 290mm by 130mm. b June 22 (122) £300

— WOTTON, SURREY. - Document, [c.1240]. 1 p, vellum, 160mm by 230mm. Grant by William de Harteshurst of a rent from lands for the maintenance of a light in the church at Wotton. b June 22 (140) £400

— YORK. - Ms, contemp copy of a petition by the citizens of York for the establishment of a university, addressed to Parliament; [mid-17th cent]. 1 p, double folio. S Dec 12 (301) £1,500 [Quaritch]

— YORKSHIRE. - Ms, account of money expended on the highways of the Parish of Shelley, 1847 to 1872. 155 pp & blanks, 4to, in half calf. bba Jan 30 (305) £110 [Frost]

Epistles

Ms, Epistles of St. Paul; glossed. [Eastern? France, 2d half of 15th cent]. 148 leaves (some lacking), 295mm by 210mm; stitched. In a gothic bookhand. With initials throughout in red. S June 23 (60) £2,800 [Smith]

Equestrianism

Ms, compilation of c.250 drawings of bits in actual size, each with captions explaining the type of horse for which they are intended, in German; [c.1580-1600]. 258 pp, 39cm by 31cm, in contemp vellum bds. With 2 copies of a 19th-cent French trans loosely inserted, 55 pp, folio. S May 28 (44) £9,000 [Horsemans]

Ericsson, John, 1803-89

ALs, 25 Sept 1858. 2 pp, 8 by 7 inches. Recipient unnamed. Referring to an order for nuts & bolts & insisting that an Ericsson's Caloric Engine name plate must be put on an engine. Sgd & initialled. Dar Aug 6 (152) $650

— 12 Nov 1862. 1 p, 8vo. Recipient unnamed. Returning an article "on the subject of my battery". Matted with related material. Dar June 11 (175) $600

Ernst von Bayern, Kurfuerst & Erzbischof von Koeln, 1583-1612

[An album containing the coats of arms of those who supported his attempt to become Archbishop-Elector of Cologne, 1581 to 1597, 30 pp, folio, in later vellum bds, some sgd, some later inscr by Ernst, sold at S on 5 Dec 1991, lot 482, for £16,000 to the Stadtmuseum Muenster.]

Eschenburg, Johann Joachim, 1743-1820

ALs, 22 Aug 1805. 2 pp, 8vo. To Friedrich Matthisson. Concerning contributions to an anthology. star Mar 26 (611) DM270

Eshkol, Levi, 1895-1969

Ls, 14 Mar 1956. 2 pp, size not stated. To Bank Leumi of Israel, Inc. Confirming financial arrangements regarding Israeli exports to Switzerland. Dar Dec 26 (228) $225

Esmarch, Friedrich von, 1823-1908

A Ls s (2), 26 Mar 1874 & 17 Mar 1882. 3 pp, 8vo. To an unnamed lady. Regretting that Wittmaack will stop working for him, & looking forward to a rest. star Mar 26 (612) DM850

Esquirol, Jean Etienne Dominique, 1772-1840

ALs, 14 Dec 1820. 1 p, 8vo. To [Michel] Friedlaender. Sending some statistics. star Mar 26 (614) DM750

Este, Ippolito d', Cardinal, 1509-72. See: Strozzi, Pietro & Este

Ethiopic Manuscripts

Ms, Epistles of St. Paul, with introductions. [Ethiopia, 18th or 19th cent]. 113 leaves (4 blank), vellum, 155mm by 130mm, in contemp wooden bds. In dark brown ink with headings in red. With ornamental headpiece & full-page miniature. FD Dec 2 (5) DM1,700

— Ms, prayer book. [Ethiopia, 19th cent]. 126 leaves (5 blank), vellum, 150mm by 108mm. Contemp wooden bds. With several ornamental vignettes in red & black. HH Nov 5 (859) DM900

Eucken, Rudolf, 1846-1926

ALs, 16 July [n.y.]. 4 pp, 8vo. To [Otto Harnack]. Assuring him that Julius Goldstein is a highly reputable teacher. star Mar 26 (615) DM360

Eugene of Savoy, Prince, 1663-1736

Ls, 6 Aug 1710. 1 p, folio. To the Marchese di Borgomaineo. Discussing several military appointments. star Mar 27 (1328) DM700

— 16 Oct 1719. 4 pp, 4to. To Prince Friedrich von Hessen-Kassel. Discussing the projected Swedish peace treaties & the military situation in Scandinavia. star Mar 27 (1329) DM2,300

— 26 July 1727. 1 p, folio. To Baron Portocarrero. Expressing thanks. With engraved port. star Mar 27 (1330) DM550

— 22 Mar 1732. 1 p, folio. To Count Wachten. Inquiring about recipient's visit to Berlin. HN Nov 28 (1671) DM760

Eulenberg, Herbert, 1876-1949

Autograph Ms, Ikarus und Daedalus. Ein Oratorium; [ptd 1912]. 64 pp, 4to, in dark red mor bdg by Huebel & Denk. Some corrections. FD June 2 (1249) DM1,200

Evans, Sir Arthur John, 1851-1941

A Ls s (2), 8 Sept 1884 & 13 Aug [n.y.]. To Thomas Hodgkin. Referring to his work at Hadrian's Wall, etc. bba May 28 (171) £95 [Silverman]

Everett, Fanny Ethel

Original drawings, (2), to illus Charles Kingley's The Water Babies, 1910. 7.25 by 10.75 inches. In pencil & watercolor; 1 varnished. Sgd. Ck Dec 11 (39) £

Ey, Johanna, 1864-1947

ALs, 15 Jan 1926. 2 pp, folio. To M. Bastian. Referring to various art exhibitions. star Mar 27 (888) DM560

F

Falla, Manuel de, 1876-1946

ALs, 25 Nov 1938. 4 pp, 8vo. To Francis de Miomandre. About the dedication of recipient's novel. star Mar 27 (1005) DM650

Fallada, Hans, Pseud. of Rudolf Ditzen, 1893-1947

Signature, Jan [19]34. 10cm by 14cm. With subscription. Mtd with a port. JG Sept 27 (341) DM300

Faraday, Michael, 1791-1867

ALs, 27 Nov 1835. 2 pp, 8vo. To Mr. [Thomson]. Thanking for the final vols of recipient's work. star Mar 26 (616) DM500

— 18 Apr 1861. 1 p, 12mo. To Edward Walford. Returning a Ms. Dar June 11 (177) $250

Fargo, William George, 1818-81

Ds, 26 Dec 1868. 1 p, 4to. As President of the American Merchants Union Express Company, stock certificate for 15 shares issued to J. W. Cronkhite. Framed with a port. Dar June 11 (178) $400
See also: Wells, Henry & Fargo

Farragut, David G., 1801-70

Autograph Ms, battle plan & register of ships for the Battle of New Orleans; [c.20 &] 21 Apr [1862]. 2 pp, folio. Illus in cat. Sonneborn & Spiro collections. CNY May 14 (59) $40,000

Faure, Gabriel, 1845-1924

ALs, [1918?]. 2 pp, 4to. Recipient unnamed. Regarding his health & recipient's scheduled performances. Repaired. Framed with a port. P June 17 (27) $400

Fawkes, Guy, 1570-1606

Ds, 14 Oct 1591. 1 p, vellum, 8.5 by 16.5 inches. Indenture leasing his lands at Gilligate & Clifton to Christopher Lomleye. Illus in cat. S July 21 (210) £4,200 [West]

Featherston, Winfield Scott, 1819-91

Ds, 17 May 1861. 1 p, 4to. Receipt for supplies. Dar June 11 (130) $250

Feininger, Lyonel, 1871-1956

ALs, 21 June 1935. 2 pp, 8vo. To W. Rahaus. Regarding a projected exhibition at Jena. star Mar 27 (889) DM850

Ferdinand I, Emperor, 1503-64

Ls, 7 Apr 1552. 1 p, folio. To the mayor & magistrate of Sprottau in Silesia. Informing them that his councillors in Prague will decide their differences with a convent. HN June 26 (906) DM420

Ferdinand II, Emperor, 1578-1637

ALs, 12 Feb 1618. 1 p, folio. To Melchior Khlesl. As King of Bohemia, announcing that he will come to Vienna as requested by the Emperor. HN Nov 28 (1673) DM7,000

Ls, 14 Aug 1618. 1 p, folio. To Balthasar de Maragas. Giving instructions regarding a military discharge. HH Nov 6 (2037) DM600

Document, [c.1625]. 6 leaves, vellum, 327mm by 275mm. Grant of arms for Gerhard v.Luchsenstein & his brothers. With painting of the arms in gold & colors. Incomplete. HH Nov 5 (842) DM300
See also: Stadion, Johann Kaspar von
See also: Werdenberg, Johann Baptist von

Ferdinand III, Emperor, 1608-57

Ds, 1639. 1 p, vellum, 535mm by 698mm. Grant of arms for Stephan Taxoni. Including painting of the arms in gold & colors. HH May 12 (46) DM300

Ferdinand IV, Grand Duke of Tuscany, 1835-1908

ALs, 22 Nov 1861. 2 pp, 4to. To Luigi Bargagli. About the usurpation of power in Tuscany by the new Italian government. HN Nov 28 (1848) DM320

Ferdinand V, King of Spain, 1452-1516

Ds, 7 July 1509. Size not stated. Commission for Julio Lopez da Ponte to receive payments for the Order of Santiago. sg Feb 27 (185) $2,200

— 27 June 1513. 1 p, folio. Grant to Alonso Sanz de Berrozpe of the right to collect taxes from the Jews in Tudela. S Dec 5 (493) £1,850 [Wilson]

Ferdinand V, King of Spain, 1452-1516 —& Isabella I, Queen of Spain, 1451-1504

Ls, 4 Aug 1475. 1 p, 8vo. Recipient unnamed. Announcing their intention to reward the services of Francisco del Aguila. S Dec 5 (490) £2,200 [Ragone]

— 17 Aug 1500. 1 p, 4to. To Don Luis Ponce. Informing him that they are sending money for charity. CNY Dec 5 (43) $4,200

Ds, 12 Mar 1486. 1 p, 143mm by 198mm. Order addressed to Juan de Ribera to bring Garcia Peres de Alfaro to them safely. Framed with a port of both. P June 17 (28) $3,000

Ferdinand VII, King of Spain, 1784-1833

Ls, 2 Sept 1824. 1 p, 4to. To the King of the Two Sicilies. Thanking for congratulations on the birth of a daughter. sg Feb 27 (192) $350

Fesch, Joseph, Cardinal, 1763-1839

ALs, [28 Mar 1797]. 2 pp, 4to. To Jakob Christoph Oser. Informing him about his activities as commissioner in Napoleon's army. star Mar 27 (1516) DM360

Fichte, Johann Gottlieb, 1762-1814

Autograph Ms, poem, beginning "Wenn wilde Thiere, deren Brust zum Hassen...", [ptd 1810]. 4 pp, 4to. The story of Inez de Castro, 8 stanzas; adapted from Luis de Camoes, The Lusiad. star Mar 26 (617) DM7,000

Field, Eugene, 1850-95

Autograph transcript, poem, Little Boy Blue, Apr 1888. 1 p, 4to. 3 stanzas, sgd & inscr to his wife. Illus with 2 small drawings. Illus in cat. sup May 9 (19) $3,300

ALs, 28 Sept 1889. 1 p, 4to. To Mr. Stedman. Promising to bring books or proof sheets to New York. sup Oct 15 (1267) $200

Field, Thomas Y.

[A group of c.70 items relating to his military career, [1840s - early 1900s], including commissions by Presidents Polk & Pierce, sold at sg on 12 Sept 1991, lot 79, for $1,700.]

Fielding, Henry, 1707-54

Autograph Ms, discussion of legal aspects of felony, [c.1745?]. 1 p, 8vo. Including note of authenticity by his grandson at bottom. CNY Dec 5 (234) $4,500

Letter, 15 Oct 1748. 2 pp, 4to. To Samuel Richardson. Contemp copy, praising Richardson's novel Clarissa & pondering literary fame. CNY Dec 5 (235) $2,400

Fields, W. C., 1880-1946

Ms, vaudeville sketch, One of the six best cellars; [n.d.]. 14 pp, 6 by 8 inches. Including autograph tp, sgd. Illus in cat. sup Oct 15 (1269) $3,000

ALs, [14 May 1939]. 1 p, 4to. To G. V. Weickert. Forwarding a telegram. Illus in cat. Dar Feb 13 (169) $600

Ls, 12 July 1937. 1 p, 4to. To Mr. Mendelsohn. Thanking for a clipping. Dar Oct 10 (150) $425

— 16 Dec 1939. 1 p, 4to. To G. V. Weickert. Concerning Miss Monti's suit against a lawyer. Dar Feb 13 (170) $325

— 30 Dec 1939. 1 p, 4to. To G. V. Weickert. Informing him that he has forwarded his letter to Miss Monti. Dar Feb 13 (171) $425

— 27 Mar 1941. 2 pp, 4to. To G. V. Weickert. Declining responsibility for Miss Monti's actions. Dar Feb 13 (172) $550

Photograph, sgd, [n.d.]. In extra frame, overall size 19 by 32 inches. Dar Aug 6 (15) $1,400

Photograph, sgd & inscr, [n.d.]. 8 by 10 inches. Full length. b&b Feb 19 (154) $650

— Anr, [n.d.]. Framed; overall size 16 by 20 inches. Inscr to Cinelandia. Illus in cat. sup Oct 15 (1270) $750

Fillmore, Millard, 1800-74

ALs, 3 July 1842. 1 p, 8vo. To M. C. Powers. Asking him to accompany his wife & daughter on their way home. Matted with philatelic envelope. Dar June 11 (179) $350

— 12 Sept 1849. 1 p, 8vo. To Hamilton Fish. Thanking for 2 publications. Illus in cat. sup May 9 (190) $900

— 14 Apr 1865. 5 pp, 4to. To Reverdy Johnson. Giving his views on the emancipation of slaves & worrying about the future of race relations in the US. CNY June 9 (232) $55,000

Ls, 21 Feb 1842. 1 p, 4to. To A. P. Upshur. Recommending Porter Tuffes as midshipman. sup Oct 15 (1515) $240

— 24 June 1850. 1 p, 4to. To Gov. Hamilton Fish. Sending "Mr. Clay's Compromise Bill." Spiro collection. CNY May 14 (61) $1,800

— 26 Apr 1852. 1 p, 4to. To William L. Hodge. Authorizing him to perform the duties of the Sec of the Treasury during Thomas Corwin's illness. Framed with engraved port. sup Oct 15 (1516) $750

ANs, 31 Aug 1857. 1 p, 12mo. To Edward Goodridge. Sending his autograph. sup Oct 15 (1517) $320

Cut signature, [n.d.]. 5 by 2.5 inches. With subscription. Matted with engraved port. Dar Feb 13 (173) $160

Photograph, sgd, 22 Mar 1862. Carte size. Seated. By Anthony, from a Brady negative. Illus in cat. R June 13 (92) $6,500

Finck von Finckenstein, Karl Wilhelm, Graf, 1714-1800

Ls, 1 June 1776. 2 pp, 4to. To the Prince-Abbot of Corvey. Interceding in favor of a soldier from recipient's territory. star Mar 27 (1333) DM200

Firestone, Harvey Samuel, 1868-1938

Autograph telegram, sgd, 10 Dec [19]16. 1 p, 4to, on verso of ptd letter to stockholders. To Henry Ford. Draft, inviting him to an annual dinner with Th. A. Edison & Wm. H. Taft. Dar Dec 26 (179) $1,300

First Ladies of the United States

[The signatures of Eleanor Roosevelt, Lady Bird Johnson, Betty Ford, Rosalynn Carter, Nancy Reagan & Barbara Bush, on a 12mo sheet, sold at Dar on 13 Feb 1992, lot 174, for $300.]

[The signatures of Bess Truman, Mamie Eisenhower, Jacqueline Kennedy, Lady Bird Johnson, Pat Nixon, Betty Ford & Rosalynn Carter on a card with engraved view of the White House, 8 by 6 inches, sold at Dar on 6 Aug 1992, lot 153, for $425.]

Fischer, Edwin, 1886-1960

ALs, [1934]. 2 pp, 4to. To Mrs. Friedlaender. Expressing condolences on the death of her husband. star Mar 27 (1007) DM220

Photograph, sgd & inscr, 31 May 1927. 248mm by 176mm (image). By Ruth Asch. star Mar 27 (1006) DM550

Fisher, Hammmond Edward, 1901?-55

Original drawing, sketch of Joe Palooka, [n.d.]. 10.5 by 7.25 inches. Sgd & inscr to Bob Lasko. Illus in cat. R Mar 7 (264) $100

Fisk, James, 1834-1972 —& Others

Group photograph, [n.d.]. 20.75 by 17.25 inches. With Thomas Lafayette Rosser & anr; by [Alexander Gardner]. Illus in cat. R June 13 (275) $380

Fitzgerald, Barry, 1888-1961

Photograph, sgd & inscr, [n.d.]. 4.25 by 6.25 inches. Dar Apr 9 (195) $120

FitzGerald, Edward, 1809-83

ALs, [n.d.], "Tuesday". 4 pp, 8vo. To Joseph Fletcher. About an excursion on his yacht. S July 21 (55) £600 [Fletcher]

Fitzsimmons, Robert, 1862-1917

Signature, [n.d.]. 4.5 by 2 inches. In pencil. Dar June 11 (109) $425

Signature, [27 Nov 1897]. 4 by 2.25 inches (card). Illus in cat. Dar Feb 13 (109) $900

Fitzsimmons, Thomas, 1741-1811

ALs, 5 Mar 1804. 1 p, 8vo. To James Gibson. Regarding appointments. R Mar 7 (187) $280

Flaubert, Gustave, 1821-80

ALs, [25 June 1853]. 4 pp, 4to. To Louise Colet. Discussing Madame Bovary, & setting out his literary credo. Mannheim collection. S Dec 5 (453) £2,500 [Fox Glove]

— [7 Apr 1854]. 4 pp, 4to. To Louise Colet. Describing his painstaking efforts with the 1st section of Madame Bovary. Mannheim collection. S Dec 5 (452) £2,500 [Fox Glove]

— [n.d.]. 1 p, 8vo. Recipient unnamed. Acknowledging receipt of 2 books. star Mar 26 (138) DM650

Fleming, Victor, 1883-1949

ALs, [n.d.], "Monday". 4 pp, 8vo. To an unnamed lady. Informing her that he is going to Long Island the next morning. Framed with a photograph. sup Oct 15 (1272) $300

Flick, Elmer Harrison, 1876-1971

ALs, 4 Dec 1959. 1 p, 8vo. To Bill Johnson. Referring to his health problems. Dar Dec 26 (87) $160

Flinders, Matthew, 1774-1814

ALs, 19 Oct 1808. 1 p, 4to. To Col. Monistrol. Draft, complaining about his continued detention by the French on Mauritius. In modern quarter mor bdg with a lithographed port & other related material. Illus in cat. Longueville collection. S June 25 (200) £8,000 [Stokes]

Flotow, Friedrich von, 1812-83

ALs, [1868 or later]. 2 pp, 8vo. To [Alfred von Wolzogen?]. Asking for a copy of the score of his opera Indra. star Mar 27 (1008) DM1,050

Floyd, John Buchanan, 1806-63

ALs, 6 Sept 1856. 3 pp, 8vo. To J. S. Cunningham. Giving his opinion of John C. Fremont. Dar June 11 (182) $200

Flynn, Errol, 1909-59

Ls, 5 Mar 1959. 1 p, 4to. To Earl Conrad. About work on his autobiography & financial matters. sg Sept 12 (80) $425

Photograph, sgd & inscr, [c.1940]. 8 by 10 inches. Imperf. Dar Dec 26 (183) $374

Foerster-Nietzsche, Elisabeth, 1846-1935. See: Nietzsche, Friedrich

Fontane, Theodor, 1819-98

Autograph transcript, poem, beginning "An einem Sommermorgen...", 11 Jan 1869. 1 p, 8vo. 4 four-line stanzas, sgd. star Mar 26 (141) DM6,500

Collection of ALs & autograph Ms, [1863]. 7 pp, 8vo. To Bernhard von Lepel. Reporting about his Wanderungen durch die Mark Brandenburg. Draft of a verse dialogue, probably for the literary society Tunnel ueber der Spree. With related material. Illus in cat. HH May 13 (1940) DM15,500

Series of 3 A Ls s, 3 Apr 1895 to 31 July 1896. 5 pp, 8vo. To Max Friedlaender. Thanking for a book & a song, & discussing a financial matter. star Mar 26 (144) DM7,500

ALs, 3 May [1862]. 4 pp, 8vo. To his wife. Reporting about people & places in Brandenburg. HN Nov 28 (1675) DM7,600

— 20 May 1862. 4 pp, 8vo. To his wife. Personal news. star Mar 26 (139) DM5,000

— 24 Dec 1863. 1 p, 8vo. To an unnamed lady. In verse, sending flowers. star Mar 26 (140) DM3,600

— 14 Apr 1879. 3 pp, 8vo. To Friedrich Spielhagen. Sending a contribution for Westermanns Monatshefte & giving instructions for the publication. Illus in cat. HN Nov 28 (1676) DM5,000

— 23 Dec 1884. 4 pp, 8vo. To his son Friedrich. Sending family news. star Mar 26 (142) DM4,200

— 28 Jan 1885. 4 pp, 8vo. To his son Friedel. Giving advice about his search for new employment. HN Nov 28 (1677) DM7,400

— 23 July 1888. 2 pp, 8vo. To his son Friedel. Family news, & commenting on a poem by Liliencron. HN Nov 28 (1678) DM5,600

— 18 Feb 1890. 4 pp, 8vo. To his son Friedel. Discussing the contract for the further publication of his works. HN Nov 28 (1679) DM7,800

Fontane, Theodor, 1819-98 —& Others

Ls, [c.1894]. 3 pp, 8vo. Recipient unnamed. Appealing for financial aid for Johannes Schlaf. Also sgd by Gerhart Hauptmann, Max Liebermann & others. star Mar 26 (143) DM1,700

Fontanne, Lynn, 1887-1983. See: Lunt, Alfred & Fontanne

Foot, Solomon, 1802-66

ALs, 24 May 1861. 1 p, 4to. To J. B. Wallis. Complaining about corruption in the Department of War. R June 13 (207) $120

Ford, Gerald R.

[A 4to sheet with Ford's signature in 4 different styles, [n.d.], sold at Dar on 6 Aug 1992, lot 156, for $350.]

Transcript, part of his proclamation of 8 Sept 1974, granting pardon to Richard Nixon. 1 p, 5 by 5 inches. Sgd. Framed with a photograph. Illus in cat. sup Oct 15 (1734) $1,000

— Transcript, proclamation of 8 Sept 1974, granting pardon to Richard Nixon. 2 pp, 4to. Sgd. Illus in cat. sup Oct 15 (1733) $2,100

Typescript, tribute to Dwight Eisenhower, [n.d.]. 1 p, 8vo. Sgd. With a group photograph. Illus in cat. sup Oct 15 (1736) $700

Ls, 4 Feb 1965. 1 p, 4to. Recipient unnamed. Responding to an inquiry about financial obligations to the United Nations. Dar Dec 26 (188) $350

— 15 June 1970. 1 p, 4to. To Elizabeth Wenger. Commenting on pacifism. Dar Aug 6 (159) $600

— 26 Sept 1975. 1 p, 8vo. To his half-brother Richard. Sending a theater ticket. With autograph postscript. Dar Oct 10 (175) $1,100

— 21 Apr 1989. 1 p, 8vo. To Harold Russell. Thanking him for 42 years of service on the Committee on Employment of People with Disabilities. Dar Aug 6 (158) $190

ANs, [June 1962]. 16mo. On card honoring University of Michigan athletes, stating his "most thrilling experience" on the university's football team. Dar Dec 26 (187) $225

Check, sgd, 17 Dec 1974. Payable to Laurie Ford. Uncancelled. wa Oct 19 (291) $3,000

Franking signature, [16 Dec 1976]. On White House envelope addressed to Charles D. Carroll. Illus in cat. Dar Aug 6 (157) $650

Photograph, sgd, [after Jan 1977]. 4to. Mtd. wa Dec 19 (249) $70

Signature, [18 Jan 1973]. On engraved invitation for an inaugural reception for Vice President Agnew; 8vo. Dar Apr 9 (196) $100

— Anr, [n.d.]. On ptd presentation copy of a photograph, his Oath of Office, & his remarks during the swearing in ceremony, 9 Aug 1974. 1 p, folio. Framed. Illus in cat. sup Oct 15 (1735) $420

— Anr, [n.d.]. 1 p, size not stated. On souvenir typescript of his oath of office. Matted with a photograph. wa Dec 19 (250) $130

See also: Carter, James Earl ("Jimmy") & Ford

Ford, Henry, 1863-1947

Ls, 23 July 1927. 2 pp, 4to. To Herman Bernstein. Reiterating his apology for anti-Jewish articles pbd in the Dearborn Independent. Illus in cat. sup Oct 15 (1273) $9,500

Ford, John Thomson, 1829-94

ALs, 12 June 1859. 2 pp, 4to. Recipient unnamed. Discussing plays for production. Dar June 11 (269) $250

Forrest, Nathan B., 1821-77

Ls, 21 Nov 1864. 2 pp, 8vo. To Col. A. P. Mason. Reporting about the shelling of Columbia, Tennessee, & an interview with Gen. Hatch. CNY Dec 5 (45) $5,000

Letter, 13 July 1862. 1 p, 8vo. To Lieut. Col. John G. Parkhurst. At Murfreesboro, demand for unconditional surrender. In the hand of Major J. P. Strange. CNY May 14 (4) $7,000

Forster, Edward Morgan, 1879-1970

Collection of 9 A Ls s & cards, sgd, 1951 to 1962. 11 pp, 4to & 8vo. To K. W. Gransden. About recipient's verse & other literary matters. S July 21 (113) £450 [Finch]

Forster, Georg, 1754-94

ALs, 18 June 1780. 3 pp, 4to. To Gottfried Grosse. Discussing plans to publish recipient's trans of Pliny. star Mar 26 (620) DM4,200

Forster, Johann Reinhold, 1729-98

ADs, 15 July 1786. 1 p, 4to. Certificate for Heinrich Immanuel Fueller. star Mar 26 (621) DM550

Fortner, Wolfgang, 1907-87

Autograph music, sketches for his opera In seinem Garten liebt Don Perlimplin Belisa, [n.d.]. 4 pp, 34cm by 27cm. Sgd later. With covering letter, 1962 & photograph, sgd & inscr. star Mar 27 (1009) DM420

Fosse, Bob

Photograph, sgd & inscr, [n.d.]. 4to. Profile view. wa Oct 19 (99) $50

Fouche, Joseph, Duc d'Otrante, 1759-1820

Ls, [9 Mar 1801]. 3 pp, 4to. To the Prefect of the Departement Seine-Inferieure. Concerning a suit for defamation of the First Consul. star Mar 27 (1395) DM500

— [13 Apr 1802]. 2 pp, 4to. To the Prefect of the Departement Aveyron. Requesting a report on Pierre Granier. star Mar 27 (1396) DM350

Fouque, Friedrich de la Motte, 1777-1843

ALs, 21 Mar 1822. 2 pp, 4to. Recipient unnamed. Thanking for condolences on the death of his father-in-law & mentioning a projected publication. star Mar 26 (146) DM320

— 5 Feb 1825. 1 p, 4to. To Adolf Baeuerle. Inquiring about an outstanding fee. star Mar 26 (147) DM250

Fox, Charles James, 1749-1806

ALs, [n.d.], "Wednesday". 1 p, 4to. To Mr. A'Court. Urging him to come to vote for an important bill. bba Jan 30 (272) £230 [Goddard]

Foxx, Jimmie, 1907-67

Signature, [n.d.]. 16mo (card). Dar Dec 26 (88) $300

— Anr, [n.d.]. Size not stated. Dar Feb 13 (80) $120

France

Document, 22 Jan 1373. 2 pp, 3.75 by 10.75 inches. Record of several land transactions. Dar Dec 26 (223) $200

— Odile da Venes. - Document, Aug 1321. 1 p, vellum, 250mm by 483mm. Last will & testament; executed at Tournai. S June 23 (46) £450 [Howell]

— Revolution. - Ms, memorandum discussing strategic aspects of French ports between Dunkirk & Bayonne; 16 Feb 1793. 28 pp, folio; stitched. Including annotations in the hand of Marshal de Castries. sg Sept 12 (83) $650

— Toussaints Abbey, Angers. - Ms, record of professions of the Augustinian canons of the abbey, 1415 to 1777. 55 leaves & 4 flyleaves, vellum, 318mm by 222mm. Modern vellum bdg. With many entries on each page in a variety of scripts. S Dec 17 (52) £6,500 [Quaritch]

Francis I, Emperor, 1708-65

ALs, 15 Apr 1741. 2 pp, 4to. To [Count Neipperg?]. About negotiations for an alliance with Saxony & projected troop mouvements. star Mar 27 (1654) DM1,700

— 13 Aug 1741. 4 pp, 4to. Recipient unnamed. Giving instructions concerning affairs with Prussia, & discussing the political & military situation. In French. Illus in cat. HN

Nov 28 (1680) DM650
— [c.1741]. 3 pp, 4to. Recipient unnamed. Requesting that he promote good relations between the Duke of Arenberg & "Milord Steve". In French. HN Nov 28 (1681) DM600
— 22 Nov 1742. 3 pp, 4to. To [Count Neipperg?]. Making plans for the conquest of Bavaria. Illus in cat. star Mar 27 (1655) DM3,200

Franck, Cesar, 1822-90

Autograph music, opening of the 5th no of Les Beatitudes, [n.d.]. 2 pp, folio. Vocal score, notated for "Voix du Christ" & accompaniment. S May 29 (532) £2,000 [Mandl]

Francke, August Hermann, 1663-1727

ALs, 27 July 1715. 1 p, 4to. To the Rev. Werdenhagen. About the illness of recipient's wife. star Mar 26 (622) DM1,200

Frank, Johann Peter, 1745-1821

ALs, 18 June 1788. 2 pp, 4to. To [Francesco Aglietti]. Making plans to travel in Italy. star Mar 26 (623) DM650

Frankfurter, Felix, 1882-1965

ALs, 27 Oct [1915]. 2 pp, 8vo. To Charlotte Rudyard. Personal letter, wishing her good luck. Sgd F. F. Dar Oct 10 (180) $350
— 18 Nov 1945. 2 pp, 12mo. To Gustav Wertheimer. Referring to "the merciful salvation" of recipient's brother. Dar Oct 10 (179) $600
— 22 Oct [19]60. Card, 8vo. To Professor Fein. About Aaron Aronsohn. wa Mar 5 (303) $230

Ls, 19 Nov 1940. 1 p, 8vo. To Gustav Wertheimer. Thanking for good wishes. Dar Oct 10 (178) $350

Signature, 30 Nov [19]59. 5.5 by 3.5 inches. On card with typed quotation. Dar June 11 (186) $350

Franklin, Benjamin, 1706-90

Autograph Ms, Loose Thoughts on a universal Fluid [ptd as Conjectures on the Nature of Fire], 25 June 1784. 7 pp, folio. Repaired. P June 16 (178) $24,000

ALs, 3 May 1753. 3 pp, folio. To William Smith. Commenting on Smith's A General Idea of the College of Mirania. Repaired. P June 16 (176) $15,000
— 18 Apr 1754. 1 p, folio. To William Smith. Lamenting the loss of recipient's letters to him. P June 16 (177) $8,500
— 13 Jan [17]58. 1 p, 8vo. To Mr. Nourse. Ordering a book. Matted with engraving. sg Sept 12 (81) $6,000
— Aug 1767. 1 p, 4to. To the Rev. Mr. Price. Discussing applications for doctorates to be conferred by the University of Ediburgh. Illus in cat. sup Oct 15 (1198) $14,500
— 4 July 1775. 1 p, folio. To [Jonathan Williams]. Expressing concern about the situation in Boston. With letter of transferral, 1829. Illus in cat. bba Sept 19 (334) £10,000 [Maggs]
— 4 July 1775. 1 p, 4to. To Jonathan Williams. Responding to the news of recipient's eviction from Boston & hoping for "deliverance from ... Oppressors". Tipped to letter of transmittal by Samuel Bradford, 1829. P June 16 (171) $42,500
— 2 May 1783. 2 pp, 4to. To his grandson Benjamin Franklin Bache. Informing him that he cannot afford to give him a gold watch. Illus in cat. Spiro collection. CNY May 14 (62) $40,000
— 4 Nov 1787. 2 pp, 4to. To Jane Mecom. Reviewing his feelings about his life in public service. Framed with engraved port. P June 16 (172) $30,000

Ds, 7 Aug 1782. 2 pp, folio. Certification that a commission as Captain in the Navy was issued to Gustavus Conyngham in 1777. Illus in cat. sup Oct 15 (1199) $16,000
— 15 Feb 1784. 1 p, 15 by 11.5 inches. Military land grant to Jonathan Adams. b&b Feb 19 (157A) $3,250
— 6 Dec 1785. 1 p, folio. Land grant to John Atchison. Illus in cat. P Dec 12 (102) $4,500
— 12 May 1786. 1 p, 8vo. Pay order in favor of Benjamin Brink. P Dec 12 (103) $4,500
— 20 June 1786. 1 p, folio. Land grant. CNY June 9 (233) $6,000
— 30 Sept 1787. 1 p, folio. As President of the Supreme Executive Council of Pennsylvania; land grant to John Harper. Framed with engraved port. P June 16 (173) $6,000

Cut signature, [n.d.]. Size not stated. R Nov 9 (112) $3,800

Franklin, Benjamin, 1706-90 —& Bartram, John, 1699-1777

Ds, 1 Sept 1753. 1 p, 322mm by 651mm. Grant of a tract of land by John Bartram & his wife to their son James; sgd by both & by Franklin as Justice of the County of Philadelphia (twice). Also sgd by others. P June 16 (58) $7,000

Franklin, Sir John, 1786-1847

ALs, 2 Aug 1824. 3 pp, 4to. To Commodore Barrie. Requesting assistance in providing supplies for his projected expedition. Ingilby collection. pn Nov 14 (72) £850 [Sawyer]

Franz Ferdinand, Archduke, 1863-1914

ALs, 27 July 1908. 7 pp, 8vo. To [the future Emperor] Karl. Giving advice concerning his financial affairs. Illus in cat. star Mar 27 (1536) DM1,700

Franz I, Emperor of Austria, 1768-1835

Ls, 31 Jan 1830. 1 p, folio. To an unnamed monarch. Notifying him of the death of Archduchess Henriette. star Mar 27 (1529) DM220

Ds, 18 Sept 1792. 13 pp, folio, in red velvet bdg. Patent of nobility & grant of arms for Johann Philipp Roth & his brother Karl August. Including full-page painting of the arms in gold & colors. star Mar 27 (1670) DM1,300

Franz Joseph I, Emperor of Austria, 1830-1916

[His audience book, sgd by c.1000 visitors including members of European nobility, diplomats, statesmen, etc., 1881 to 1894, 109 pp, 4to, in lea bdg, sold at star on 27 Mar 1992, lot 1534, for DM3,000.]

ALs, 14 May 1898. 4 pp, 8vo. To Katharina Schratt. About his current activities. Illus in cat. star Mar 27 (1532) DM3,600

Ls, 28 Oct 1862. 1 p, folio. To Kurfuerst [Friedrich Wilhelm I von Hessen-Kassel]. Announcing the marriage of his brother. HN Nov 28 (1682) DM750

— 9 Nov 1864. 1 p, 4to. To Leopold von Kloyber. Giving permission to exhibit items from his private library. star Mar 27 (1531) DM290

— 20 Dec 1912. 1 p, 4to. To [the future Emperor] Karl. Giving permission to assume command of his batallion in January. Partly autograph. star Mar 27 (1533) DM550

Frazer, Sir James George, 1854-1941

ALs, 28 Feb 1894. 3 pp, 8vo. Thanking for archaeological information. pn Mar 19 (113) £50 [Wilson]

Frederick I, King of Sweden, 1676-1751

ALs, 2 Jan 1714. 2 pp, 4to. To his father Karl von Hessen-Kassel. Reporting about his diplomatic mission to Berlin. star Mar 27 (1715) DM700

Ds, 8 Aug 1723. 2 pp, 4to. Contents not stated. Repaired. Dar Apr 9 (198) $120

Frederik IX, King of Denmark, 1899-1972

Ls, 15 Jan 1959. 2 pp, 4to. To the President of Portugal. Congratulating him on his election. Countersgd by Prime Minister J. O. Krag. Dar Apr 9 (199) $150

Frederik VI, King of Denmark, 1768-1839

Ds, 8 Mar 1837. 2 pp, 4to. Military appointment. Dar Dec 26 (190) $130

Freiligrath, Ferdinand, 1810-76

ALs, 7 Nov 1868. 1 p, 8vo. Recipient unnamed. Responding to a request for photographs. star Mar 26 (155) DM320

Signature, [c.1884]. On photograph of his port by E. Hader, 142mm by 96mm. HH May 13 (1941) DM200

Fremont, Jay C.

ALs, 20 June 1908. 2 pp, 8vo. To Guy L. Abbott. Sending a hand bill for a 4th of July address (included, 1 p, 4to). Dar June 11 (106) $475

French & Indian War

Ms, account of the fall of Quebec & the Minden campaign in Germany by a member of the Regiment des Grenadiers royaux de Modene, 1759 & 1760. 250 pp, 8vo, in def contemp calf bdg. S Dec 5 (475) £1,900 [Maggs]

— Ms, journal & account book kept by a sutler named Foot during the Lake George campaign, 1758 to 1760, with later entries in other hands. 106 pp, 8vo, in def orig sheep bdg. Recording lists of soldiers, sales, etc. CNY Dec 5 (48) $3,800

— Barnard, Major Salah. - Autograph Ms, journal kept during the Lake George campaign, with later entries relating to financial transactions, 26 June 1758 to 1793. 191 pp, 8vo, in contemp vellum bdg. Including related memorandum in anr hand, c.1795. CNY Dec 5 (47) $16,000

— Fuller, Nathanael. - Autograph Ms, journal kept during an expedition to Fort Niagara, 13 Mar to 28 Oct 1760. 73 pp & blanks, 8vo, in orig paper bds. Daily entries by a member of a company of carpenters sent to strengthen Fort Niagara. CNY Dec 5 (46) $8,000

Frerichs, Friedrich Theodor von, 1819-85

AL, 23 July 1881. 2 pp, 8vo. To the Rev. Hoppe. Giving medical advice & sending a prescription (included). On engraved letterhead. star Mar 26 (625) DM1,400

Freud, Anna, 1895-1982

ALs, 21 Nov 1945. 2 pp, 8vo. To Jan H. van der Hoop. Regarding the inability of a patient to pay for necessary psychoanalysis. star Mar 26 (630) DM420

Freud, Sigmund, 1856-1939

Collection of 23 A Ls s, 18 Ls s & 7 autograph postcards, sgd, Sept 1919 to May 1931. 79 pp, 8vo & 4to. To Edward L. Bernays. Concerning the publication of Freud's works in America, recipient's efforts to promote psychoanalysis in the USA, & private matters. CNY Dec 5 (49) $90,000

ALs, 23 May 1911. 1 p, 8vo. To Emil Freund. Seeking payment for a consultation from Gustav Mahler's executor. Framed with a port of both. Illus in cat. P June 17 (29) $11,000

— 5 July 1923. 1 p, 8vo. Recipient unnamed. Responding to an invitation. star Mar 26 (627) DM3,400

— 8 Nov 1926. 1 p, 8vo. To [Heinrich Meng?]. Discussing the agenda for a meeting. star Mar 26 (628) DM3,600

— 13 Feb 1930. 2 pp, 8vo. To the banker Kuekelhahn. Giving advice about possible treatment of recipient's son. With related material. star Mar 26 (629) DM6,500

— 14 June 1932. 1 p, 4to. Recipient unnamed. About a present of cigars. Illus in cat. sup Oct 15 (1277) $4,600

— 14 June 1932. 1 p, 4to. Recipient unnamed. About a present of cigars. Illus in cat. sup May 9 (409) $3,000

— 10 July 1932. 2 pp, 8vo. To an unnamed lady. Regretting that he will not be able to rent her house in the summer. C June 24 (366) £1,400 [Wilson]

Ls, 25 May 1924. 1 p, 8vo. To L. Arnold Weissberger. Referring to recipient's interest in psychoanalysis. Framed. Dar Dec 26 (191) $1,100

AN, 8 Jan [19]08. 1 p, on verso of visiting card. Recipient unnamed. Diagnosis for a patient. star Mar 26 (626) DM2,400

Ns, [30] May 1936. 1 p, size not stated. To Franz Kormendi. Ptd message of thanks for congratulations on his birthday. Ck Nov 15 (8) £650

Freytag, Gustav, 1816-95

ALs, 13 Dec 1882. 1 p, 8vo. Recipient unnamed. Sending a book. star Mar 26 (157) DM240

Ls, 6 Jan 1854. 2 pp, 4to. Recipient unnamed. About several publishing matters. star Mar 26 (156) DM270

Friederike, Queen of Ernst August II of Hannover, 1778-1841

ALs, [n.d.]. 1 p, 8vo. Recipient unnamed. Thanking for a publication. star Mar 27 (1616) DM220

Friedrich August I, King of Saxony, 1750-1827

Series of 3 Ls s, 12 Jan 1796 to 6 Mar 1807. 6 pp, folio. To the commander of his corps of engineers. Concerning promotions. star Mar 27 (1697) DM240

Friedrich August III, King of Saxony, 1865-1932

ALs, 3 Jan 1920. 2 pp, 8vo. To Gen. von Mueller. Thanking for New Year's wishes. star Mar 27 (1702) DM420

Friedrich, Caspar David, 1774-1840

ALs, 1 Oct 1812. 2 pp, 8vo. To Elisabeth Westphal. Welcoming her into the family on her marriage to his brother. S Dec 5 (510) £900 [Dreesman]

Friedrich I, King of Prussia, 1657-1713

ALs, 22 Jan 1703. 2 pp, 4to. To Markgraf Christian Ernst von Brandenburg-Bayreuth. Agreeing to recipient's marriage to his sister, the Duchess of Kurland. Illus in cat. star Mar 27 (1578) DM4,800

Ls, 21 Nov 1684. 2 pp, folio. To the magistracy at Halberstadt. Giving orders concerning the manufacture of saltpeter. star Mar 27 (1290) DM270

Ds, 6 Dec 1701. 4 pp, 4to. Decision in a case regarding property at Haferungen in Saxony. HN Nov 28 (1685) DM340

Friedrich II, Landgraf von Hessen-Kassel, 1720-85

Ls, 18 Jan 1772. 2 pp, folio. To Wilhelm Reinhard von Neipperg. Informing him of the death of his wife. HN Nov 28 (1687) DM260

Friedrich II, Kurfuerst von der Pfalz, 1482-1556

Ds, 22 Apr 1529. 1 p, folio. Ptd decree issued by Emperor Charles V regarding taxes for defense against the Turks; addressed to Count Philipp zu Hanau und Lichtenberg & sgd as Imperial Governor. star Mar 27 (1560) DM950

Friedrich II, King of Prussia, 1712-86

Autograph Ms, "verse will" composed prior to the battle of Rossbach, 1757. 2 pp, 4to. With wrap in Voltaire's hand. Illus in cat. S Dec 5 (497) £5,100 [Lionheart]

ALs, 26 Aug 1736. 3 pp, 4to. To his father. About money to recruit some soldiers & his father's projected visit. star Mar 27 (1587) DM11,000

— 21 Dec 1738. 1 p, 4to. To Tilio de Camas. Congratulating him on an appointment, & reporting about his relationship with his father. Illus in cat. star Mar 27 (1589a) DM8,000

— 10 Jan 1739. 2 pp, 4to. To Tilio de Camas. Expressing disappointment & resignation about his relationship with his father. star Mar 27 (1589b) DM10,500

— 27 July 1739. 2 pp, 4to. To Voltaire. Describing the historical & geographical situation of Lithuania & praising his father's work in restoring it to prosperity. Illus in cat. S Dec 5 (495) £3,200 [Fox Glove]

— 3 Feb 1740. 3 pp, 4to. To Voltaire. Reporting the completion of his Antimachiavel, insisting that it be pbd anonymously, & including 13 lines of verse. Illus in cat. HN June 26 (910) DM17,000

— 10 Oct 1745. 1 p, 4to. To Maupertuis. Insisting that he loves peace & only fights wars out of necessity. star Mar 27 (1592) DM6,500

— 8 Nov 1751. 1 p, 4to. To his wife Elisabeth

Christine. Expressing congratulations on her birthday. star Mar 27 (1594a) DM2,800

— 12 [Feb 1756]. 1 p, 4to. To [the Duc de Nivernois]. Welcoming pledges of goodwill from the King of France. Illus in cat. HN June 26 (911) DM18,000

— 14 Aug 1758. 1 p, 4to. To his sister Sophie. Stressing his determination to win the next battle against the Russians. star Mar 27 (1595) DM7,500

— 24 Apr 1759. 1 p, 4to. To Capt. von Legradi. Vaguely confirming rumors about some military matter. star Mar 27 (1596) DM3,000

— 14 [July 1762]. 2 pp, 4to. To [Henri de Catt]. Complaining about the slow progress of the war & including 20 lines of orig verse. Illus in cat. HN Nov 28 (1690) DM20,000

— 10 June 1763. 1 p, 4to. To his wife Elisabeth Christine. Thanking for a present. star Mar 27 (1597) DM3,000

— 24 [Jan 1765]. 1 p, 4to. To his sister Amalie. Announcing his visit the next day. Illus in cat. HN Nov 28 (1691) DM5,800

— 14 Sept 1780. 1 p, 4to. To his wife Elisabeth. Looking forward to his sister's visit. HN June 26 (912) DM6,500

Series of 4 Ls s, 15 Apr 1737 to 4 July 1738 & [n.d.]. 4 pp, 4to. To M. Thieriot. Requesting books. star Mar 27 (1588) DM2,200

Ls s (2), 5 May 1750 & 15 Nov 1755. 2 pp, 4to. To Francesco Algarotti. Thanking for publications. star Mar 27 (1593) DM1,200

Ls, 22 Jan 1739. 1 p, 4to. Recipient unnamed. Regarding payment to Commissioner Loeb. Framed with a port. P June 17 (30) $800

— 8 Nov 1755. 1 p, 4to. To Kammerdirektor Groschopp. Giving orders for the collection of taxes. HH May 13 (1941a) DM650

— 10 Mar 1757. 1 p, 4to. To administrative officials at Halberstadt. Requesting a report on a case of felony. star Mar 27 (1594b) DM750

— 18 Sept 1773. 1 p, 4to. To Col. von Cocceji. Instructing him concerning an audience for some foreign visitors. star Mar 27 (1598) DM640

— 6 Apr 1776. 1 p, 8vo. To Frau von Schnopp. Informing her that her inquiry has been submitted to the proper department. JG Sept 27 (346) DM800

— 11 May 1776. 2 p, 4to. To Minister von Goerne. Giving instructions in the case of the merchants Grebin & Koepke. HH May 13 (1941b) DM650

— 15 Aug 1777. 1 p, 4to. To his Department of the Treasury. Giving orders to prohibit the importation of vitriol. HH May 13 (1941c) DM550

— 10 Oct 1783. 1 p, 8vo. To Lieut. Gen. W. J. H. von Moellendorff. Thanking for a report about a conflagration. hen Nov 12 (2482) DM550

— 4 Apr 1784. 1 p, 4to. To von Danckelmann. Giving instructions regarding a claim by Lieut. von Hahn. R Nov 9 (53) $320

— 23 Apr 1786. 1 p, 4to. To de la Haye de Launay. Informing him that the Department of Justice will investigate a court case at Schwerin. star Mar 27 (1602) DM600

Ds, 16 May 1744. 14 pp, folio, in red velvet bdg. Patent of nobility & grant of arms for Justus Rudolf Seelhorst. With illuminated coat-of-arms. Seal repaired. star Mar 27 (1591) DM2,000

— 10 Feb 1784. 6 leaves, folio. Administrative appointment. HH May 12 (52) DM1,000

Autograph endorsement, sgd, on a report submitted by Samuel von Marshall, 13 Oct 1740, 1 p, folio, regarding the inability of one von Bodelschwingh to come to Prussia; insisting that he come. star Mar 27 (1590) DM1,900

— Anr, sgd, on a report by Counts Finck von Finckenstein & von Hertzberg, 3 Oct 1779, 1 p, folio, regarding an honorary appointment for an archivist; expressing disapproval. star Mar 27 (1601) DM1,100

Menu, 26 Mar 1775. 1 p, 4to. List of 9 dishes suggested for his dinner, with 2 autograph revisions. star Mar 27 (1600) DM2,100

Friedrich II, Grossherzog von Baden, 1857-1928

ALs, 1 Oct 1888. 4 pp, 8vo. To an unnamed aunt. Responding to condolences on the death of his brother. star Mar 27 (1242) DM370

Friedrich III, Deutscher Kaiser, 1831-88

ALs, 28 Nov 1857. 3 pp, 8vo. To Prince Frederick of Orange. Making plans for a visit at The Hague. star Mar 27 (1624) DM320

— 20 Nov 1865. 8 pp, 8vo. To Ernst Curtius. Sharply criticizing Bismarck's politics. star Mar 27 (1625) DM1,500

— 23 Oct 1870. 2 pp, 8vo. To his aunt, Princess Carl of Prussia. Sending excerpts from his diary kept in the Near East. HH May 13 (1942) DM400

Ls, 7 June 1882. 1 p, 4to. To Emil von Friedberg. Thanking for a book. star Mar 27 (1308) DM260

Photograph, sgd, [n.d.]. 325mm by 185mm. By Scheurich. star Mar 27 (1626) DM360

— Hinkeldey, Karl Ludwig Friedrich von. - ALs, 5 Mar 1856. 2 pp, 4to. To [the future Emperor] Friedrich III. Apologizing for being unable to attend an audience. Including autograph endorsement by recipient. star Mar 27 (1629) DM380

Friedrich Karl, Prince of Prussia, 1828-85

ALs, 19 Dec 1854. 4 pp, 4to. To [Franz Karl] von Werder. Acknowledging congratulations on his marriage, & remembering his travels in Lithuania. star Mar 27 (1627) DM220

Ls, 2 Feb 1871. 1 p, folio. To Gen. von Manstein. Instructing him that Col. von Buelow should be reprimanded for delaying the execution of a military order. star Mar 27 (1628) DM230

Friedrich V, Kurfuerst von der Pfalz, 1596-1632

Ls, 18 Jan 1614. 3 pp, folio. To the knights in Franconia. Notifying them of the birth of his son Heinrich Friedrich. Kuenzel collection. star Mar 27 (1561) DM5,500

Friedrich Wilhelm, Kurfuerst von Brandenburg ("The Great Elector"), 1620-88

Ls, 22 Feb 1668. 2 pp, folio. To his chancellery. Giving instructions that Judge Johann Wilhelm von Mudersbach must be properly addressed. FD June 2 (1251) DM270

— 15 Nov 1673. 3 pp, 4to. Recipient unnamed. Giving instructions "for the better accomodation" of his sons. hen Nov 12 (2483) DM520

Endorsement, sgd, July 1643. 1 p, folio, on detached address leaf of a letter addressed to him. Decision regarding feudal duties. star Mar 27 (1289) DM420

Friedrich Wilhelm I, King of Prussia, 1688-1740

ALs, 12 Dec 1705. 3 pp, 4to. To his aunt Elisabeth, Markgraefin von Brandenburg-Bayreuth. Asking her to obtain her husband's permission for an exchange of officers. Illus in cat. star Mar 27 (1579) DM1,500

Ls, 9 Aug 1714. 1 p, 4to. To administrative officials at Halberstadt. Regarding the salary of the recorders Meyer & Kuhnen. hen Nov 12 (2484) DM270

— 12 Mar 1727. 1 p, folio. To some court officials. Notifying them of a councilor's mission to Poland. star Mar 27 (1581) DM240

— 14 Feb 1737. 1 p, folio. To Charles IV of Naples & Sicily. Requesting permission for Lieut. von Franovich to recruit tall soldiers in his territories. star Mar 27 (1583) DM600

Ds, 17 Sept 1738. 2 pp, folio. To the administration of crown lands in Pomerania. Order to provide wood for the Rehbein family to rebuild their burned down houses. star Mar 27 (1584) DM310

Autograph endorsement, sgd, on a report addressed to him by the 4th administrative department, 7 Mar 1732, 1 p, folio, recommending the building of a house at Muenchelohra; ordering that a cheaper building be erected. star Mar 27 (1582) DM680

Friedrich Wilhelm II, King of Prussia, 1744-97

Ls, 27 Aug 1786. 1 p, 4to. To Abbot Raphael at Kamenz. Acknowledging congratulations on his accession to the throne. star Mar 27 (1605) DM220

— 21 Mar 1788. 1 p, 4to. To the Deacon Zoellner. Requesting information about a former tax official. HN Nov 28 (1695) DM300

— 26 Sept 1795. 1 p, folio. To Konstantin zu Salm-Salm. Notifying him of the birth of a grandson. Including draft of recipient's reply at bottom. star Mar 27 (1607) DM340

— 14 Jan 1797. 1 p, folio. To Philippine Charlotte von Braunschweig. Notifying her of the death of Queen Elisabeth Christine. star Mar 27 (1608) DM380

Friedrich Wilhelm II, King of Prussia, 1770-1840

Ls, 9 Apr 1810. 1 p, 4to. To Major Gen. von Buelow. Informing him of a military appointment. star Mar 27 (1612) DM220

— 23 July 1821. 1 p, 4to. To the commanding officers of an army corps. Confirming the sentence of a court martial (included). star Mar 27 (1613) DM210

Friedrich Wilhelm IV, King of Prussia, 1795-1861

ALs, 15 June 1819. 1 1p, 4to. To King Wilhelm I of Wuerttemberg. Arranging for a brief meeting on his way to Oppeln. Illus in cat. star Mar 27 (1617) DM480

— 12 Apr 1845. 1 p, 8vo. To an unnamed aunt. Returning letters from India. star Mar 27 (1618) DM300

— 9 Apr 1850. 2 pp, 8vo. To Alexander von Schleinitz. About a meeting of the German states at Erfurt, & hoping for improved relations with the Kingdom of Hannover. star Mar 27 (1619) DM800

Ds, 8 May 1852. 1 p, 9 by 14.5 inches. Contents not stated. Dar Apr 9 (200) $200

— 1857. 1 p, folio. Award of the Order of the Red Eagle to Adolph Ludwig von Brockhausen. k Sept 29 (172) $85

Friml, Rudolf, 1879-1972

Ds, 1936. 2 pp, folio. MGM contract for motion picture rights to the operetta Katinka; carbon copy. wa Oct 19 (160) $100

Frisch, Max, 1911-91

ALs, 5 Nov 1974. 1 p, folio. Recipient unnamed. Regarding economic hardships experienced by numerous authors. star Mar 26 (158) DM440

Fronius, Hans, 1903-88

Series of 9 A Ls s, 7 Jan 1970 to 16 Oct 1983. 26 pp, mostly folio. Recipient unnamed. About his illusts, mentioning some books, etc. star Mar 27 (891) DM520

Frost, Robert, 1874-1963

Autograph transcript, poem, Going In, [n.d.]. 1 p, 8vo, on flyleaf of his Collected Poems. NY, 1939. 20 lines, sgd & inscr to Julia Johnson Davis. Dar Aug 6 (162) $1,400

ALs, [n.d.]. 1 p, 8vo. To Mr. Vance. Complying with a request [for his autograph]. Illus in cat. Dar Feb 13 (179) $500

Autograph quotation, sgd, [c.1933]. 1 p, 5 by 5.5 inches, on detached tp of his Collected Poems. "Something there is that doesn't love a wall." sg Sept 12 (84) $400

Photograph, sgd, [n.d.]. 4 by 6.5 inches. wd Dec 12 (318) $300

Fugger, Anton, Graf, 1493-1560

Ls, 5 Dec 1539. 1 p, folio. To Jakob Truchsess von Reinfelden. Requesting venison to be delivered to Augsburg. Including autograph postscript. star Mar 27 (1400) DM1,100

Fulton, Robert, 1765-1815

ALs, 27 Dec 1807. 1 p, 4to. To Dr. [William] Thornton. Inquiring about the cotton gin. Illus in cat. Spiro collection. CNY May 14 (63) $10,000

Signature, [n.d.]. 3 by 1.25 inches. Inlaid with engraving. Illus in cat. Dar June 11 (187) $500

Furtwaengler, Wilhelm, 1886-1954

Collection of 14 A Ls s & 4 Ls s, 1 Apr 1933 to 5 Mar 1950 & [n.d.]. 18 pp, various sizes. To Lydia Panisch. About his concert tours, his situation after the war, his conception of music, etc. With related material. star Mar 27 (1013) DM5,500

Ls, 9 Jan 1949. 1 p, folio. To Erno Balogh. Complaining about the cancellation of a contract at Chicago. With autograph postscript. sg Sept 12 (85) $425

G

Gable, Clark, 1901-60

Check, sgd, 11 June 1945. Payable to Adelson Bros. Matted with a group photograph. Illus in cat. sup Oct 15 (1281) $290

Photograph, sgd & inscr, [n.d.]. Framed; overall size 17 by 20 inches. Inscr to Lola. Illus in cat. sup Oct 15 (1280) $440

Signature, [n.d.]. On taxi cab log. Matted with a photograph; overall size 20 by 16 inches. sup Oct 15 (1282) $90

Gage, Thomas, 1721-87

Ls, 23 Feb 1767. 1 p, folio. To Grey Cooper. Concerning the account for the support of the British forces in North America. Spiro collection. CNY May 14 (64) $300

Gal, Hans, 1890-1987

Autograph music, song, Auch ich war ein Juengling..., [1940]. 2 pp, size not stated. 34 bars in D major, scored for voice & piccolo. Including revisions. With covering letter, 1986. Illus in cat. star Mar 27 (1014) DM850

Gall, Franz Joseph, 1758-1828

Autograph Ms, analyzing the 5 senses, [1830]. 1 p, 8vo. With authentication by J. Ch. Spurzheim on verso. star Mar 26 (631) DM950

Gallatin, Albert, 1761-1849

Autograph endorsement, sgd, on statement sgd by David Gelston, 7 Dec 1802, 1 p, size not stated, recommending that a beacon be erected as requested in a petition by 10 ship pilots (28 Oct 1802, on verso); expressing approval. wa Oct 19 (232) $130

Galli, Angelo, c.1385-c.1460

Ms, Operetta in Laude della Belleza e Detestatione dela Crudeltade dela sua Cara Amorosa del Signor Duca Fernando. [Mantua, 1453]. 87 leaves, 219mm by 144mm. Old limp vellum bdg. In a humanistic cursive, with many textual corrections & emendations probably in the author's hand. Dedicated to Federico da Montefeltro. S Dec 17 (58) £8,000 [Kraus]

Galvin, James F. ("Pud"), 1856-1902

Signature, [n.d.]. Matted with related material, 8 by 10 inches. Dar Dec 26 (89) $650

Gamon, Hannibal, fl.1642

Ms, Oration contra Gentes, [c.1607-19]. 38 leaves, 4to, in orig limp vellum. Lecture at Broadgates Hall, Oxford. With autograph preface & dedication, sgd, to Lord North. bba June 25 (141) £550 [Gammon]

Gandhi, Mohandas K., 1869-1948

Collection of 14 A Ls s, 3 Ls s, & 10 autograph postcards, sgd, 1928 to 1945. 27 pp, 8vo. To Lady Premilla Thakersey. Revealing his preoccupations in prison & while fasting. With related material. C Dec 16 (292) £3,200 [Sawyer]

— Collection of 3 A Ls s, 4 Ls s, 4 cards, sgd (3 autograph), & ANs, 17 Oct 1934 to 8 Oct 1937 & [n.d.]. 16 pp, mostly 4to & 8vo. To Shrimati Janammal. Letters to a disciple. S Dec 12 (288) £1,500 [Maggs]

ALs, 9 Nov 1917. 2 pp, 8vo. To Mrs. Besant. Inquiring about her meeting with the

Viceroy. pn Nov 14 (165) £850 [Sawyer]

Ganghofer, Ludwig, 1855-1920

ALs, 2 Sept 1881. 1 p, 8vo. To Therese Prantl. 16-line poem, assuring her of his affection. Inscr in other hands on verso. star Mar 26 (159) DM600

— 14 Dec 1919. 8 pp, 4to. To Leo Slezak. Commenting on the times. star Mar 26 (160) DM320

Gans, Eduard, 1798-1839

ALs, 27 Oct 1834. 1 p, 4to. Recipient unnamed. Declining an invitation because of the death of an acquaintance. star Mar 26 (633) DM480

Ds, 12 June 1832. 1 p, folio. Certificate of studies issued to K. H. Bitter. With related material. star Mar 26 (632) DM380

Garbo, Greta, 1905-90

Ds, 4 Sept 1941. 1 p, 4to. Addendum to a contract with MGM for Two Faced Woman; carbon copy. Dar Aug 6 (16) $4,000

— [22 Jan 1944]. 3 by 5 inches. Bank card, sgd Greta Garbo [in trust for] Sven Gustafson. Also sgd on verso. Illus in cat. P Dec 17 (283) $1,300

— [n.d.]. 5 by 2.25 inches. Bank deposit card, sgd on verso Greta Garbo trust for Sven Gustafson. Illus in cat. P Dec 17 (284) $1,300

Group photograph, [n.d.]. 3.5 by 5.5 inches. With John Gilbert; sgd by Garbo. Dar Oct 10 (181) $2,000

Menu, sgd & inscr, 5 Sept 1949. Size not stated. Aboard S.S. Ile de France. sg Sept 12 (86) $950

Photograph, sgd, [c.Mar 1965]. 8 by 10 inches. Overlooking the sea. With letter of transferral in anr hand. Illus in cat. sg Feb 27 (74) $3,600

Gardner, Erle Stanley, 1889-1970

Ls, 26 June 1942. 1 p, 4to. To Ken White. Planning anr mystery story. Dar Apr 9 (202) $170

Garfield, James A., 1831-81

ALs, 23 Mar 1867. 2 pp, 4to. To John Sherman. Protesting against the appointment of a postmaster in Ohio. Illus in cat. sup May 9 (217) $1,900

— 23 Apr 1877. 1 p, 8vo. To H. Hubbard. About an appointment. Illus in cat. R Mar 7 (119) $400

— 3 July 1880. 1 p, 4to. To James M. Dalzell. Referring to his recent nomination for the Presidency & thanking for support. Illus in cat. sup May 9 (218) $1,300

— 15 July 1880. 1 p, 12mo. To Charles A. Jones. Sending his autograph. Framed with engraved port. Dar June 11 (188) $400

Ls, 25 Sept 1880. 1 p, 4to. To A. W. Tourgee. Hoping that he will speak in Ohio. sup Oct 15 (1556) $280

— 10 Nov 1880. 1 p, 8vo. To Harry M. Smith. Thanking for congratulations. Illus in cat. sup Oct 15 (1557) $280

— 11 Nov 1880. 1 p, 8vo. To Rev. E. B. Parsons. Thanking for congratulations. With engraved port. Dar Apr 9 (203) $500

Series of Ds s, 3 Ds s, 18 Apr to 1 Aug 1863. 3 pp, 4to. Vouchers for pay, clothing & subsistence for himself & 3 servants. CNY June 9 (234) $2,700

Ds, [Oct 1870]. 1 p, 8vo. Docket page of a court case, Ohio v. Celestin Cappon; sgd as attorney for the defendant. R Mar 7 (120) $220

— 5 May 1881. 1 p, 4to. Order to affix the US Seal to a letter to the King of Romania. Illus in cat. sup Oct 15 (1559) $8,000

Autograph telegram, [1871]. 1 p, 8vo. To J. D. Defries. Inquiring about ptg costs for a speech. In pencil; sgd. R Nov 9 (6) $250

Check, sgd, 13 June 1866. Drawn on the Sergeant-at-Arms, House of Representatives. wa Oct 19 (294) $700

— Anr, sgd, 16 Dec 1869. 8vo. Payable to Bright & Humphrey. sg Sept 12 (87) $300

— Anr, accomplished & sgd, 2 July 1879. Payable to himself. Illus in cat. sup Oct 15 (1767) $750

Cut signature, [n.d.]. 5.5 by 2 inches. Including subscription. Matted with engraved port. Dar Feb 13 (180) $130

Franking signature, [12 Aug n.y.]. On envelope addressed in anr hand. Dar Apr 9 (204) $150

— Anr, [n.d.]. On envelope addressed in anr hand. Dar June 11 (189) $160

— Anr, [n.d.]. Size not stated, cut from an envelope. With a photograph. Dar June 11 (190) $170

Photograph, sgd, [c.1880]. 4 by 6.5 inches. Mtd. Dar Oct 10 (182) $1,100

Signature, 12 Apr 1881. 1 p, 4to. CNY Dec 5 (50) $2,200

— Anr, [n.d.]. On card. Framed. wa Oct 19 (293) $150

— Anr, [n.d.]. 2 by 3.5 inches. Including subscription, inscr to John C. White. wa Oct 19 (295) $140

— GUITEAU, CHARLES. - Signature, 16 Feb 1882. 16mo (card). Mtd with related material. Dar Dec 26 (201) $140

— GUITEAU, CHARLES J. - A partly engraved invitation to his execution on 30 June 1882, sgd by John S. Crocker, 3 by 4.8 inches (card). R Nov 9 (7) $800

— PORTER, JOHN K. - Ds, 8 Nov 1881. 2 pp,

folio. Oath to conduct the prosecution in the case against Charles J. Guiteau. Illus in cat. sup May 9 (220) $2,500

Garfield, Lucretia R., 1832-1918

ALs, 14 July 1881. 2 pp, 8vo. To J. H. Rhodes. Thanking for a message of sympathy. Dar Dec 26 (192) $1,100

Franking signature, [1898]. rf Sept 21 (30) $50

Garibaldi, Giuseppe, 1807-82

ALs, 7 Aug 1867. 1 p, 4to. To Mrs. Schwabe. About his son's efforts to obtain money in England for his fight against the Papal States. star Mar 27 (1408) DM850

Series of 4 Ls s, 18 May to 5 July 1875. 4 pp, 4to & 8vo. To the Mayor & inhabitants of Velletri. Thanking for invitations & addresses. star Mar 27 (1409) DM1,300

Signature, [n.d.]. Matted with a port, overall size 9.5 by 13.5 inches. Dar Feb 13 (181) $100

Garland, Judy, 1922-69

Ds, 8 Feb 1961. 1 p, 4to. Agreement regarding her fee for the film Judgment at Nuremberg. Dar Apr 9 (205) $400

Garner, John Nance, 1868-1967. See: Roosevelt, Franklin D. & Garner

Garrett, Patrick Floyd, 1850-1908

ALs, 19 July 1892. 1 p, 4to. To his wife. Hoping he will have the house arranged in time for her arrival. CNY June 9 (235) $1,400

Ds, 12 May 1893. 1 p, 4to. Benefit certificate from the Knights of Honor. sg Feb 27 (76) $850

— 28 Dec 1899. 1 p, folio. Deed for a mining claim in the County of Dona Ana; sgd twice. sg Feb 27 (75) $900

— 15 Mar 1900. 1 p, folio. Mining Location Notice for a claim in Dona Ana County; partly ptd. sg Sept 12 (89) $1,000

— 15 Sept 1900. 1 p, 7.5 by 3.5 inches. Promissory note, payable to George D. Bowman. sup Oct 15 (1286) $900

— 11 Dec 1906. 2 pp, 4to. Contract with the Englewood Gold Mining Company. sg Sept 12 (90) $850

Garrick, David, 1717-79

[A collection of papers relating to Garrick's acting career & his management of the Drury Lane Theatre, 1741 to 1776, 41 pp, various sizes, sold at pn on 19 Mar 1992, lot 1, for £4,600.]

[A group of 3 autograph & scribal Mss for the epilogue delivered at the end of the season of 1768/69, 8 pp, mostly 4to, sold at pn on 19 Mar 1992, lot 21, for £2,200.]

[A group of 4 Mss (1 autograph) for his eulogy on Henry Fielding, [1778], 11 pp, mostly 4to, sold at pn on 19 Mar 1992, lot 64, for £2,800.]

[His ptd acting copy of The Rehearsal, L, 1687, marked up for the part of Bayes in anr hand & with some additions by Garrick himself, imperf, sold at pn on 19 Mar 1992, lot 2, for £3,000.]

Autograph Ms, 12 lines of verse dealing with critics, [n.d.]. 1 p, 4to. Fragment; with AN below. pn Mar 19 (54) £500

— Autograph Ms, 4 poems on Oliver Goldsmith, [c.1773/74]. 3 pp, 8vo. pn Mar 19 (37) £8,500

— Autograph Ms, draft of his Epilogue to be spoken by Miss Younge at her Benefit, 30 Mar 1778. 1 p, 4to, on verso of a letter by Mrs. Sheridan to Mrs. Garrick. 16 lines. pn Mar 19 (61) £800

— Autograph Ms, "Duett" to be sung by Floridor & Negromant, [n.d.]. 1 p, 4to. 17 lines, including revisions. pn Mar 19 (56) £450

— Autograph Ms, epitaph for Gen. Wolfe, [c.1772?]. 2 pp, size not stated. 2 versions of 4 lines each. pn Mar 19 (33) £800

— Autograph Ms, epitaph for Hogarth, [Dec 1771]. 3 pp, 4to. 2 versions of 3 four-line stanzas each; including revisions. pn Mar 19 (30) £5,000

— Autograph Ms, epitaph for William Gibson, [Sept 1771]. 1 p, 4to, cut from larger sheet. 6 lines. pn Mar 19 (29) £1,200

— Autograph Ms, epitaph upon himself upon his burial in the grotto at Stourhead, 7 Aug 1776. 1 p, folio. 14 lines, sgd D.G. Illus in cat. pn Mar 19 (44) £1,700

— Autograph Ms, Ode to Count H- the Minister from Bavaria; [c.1764]. 4 pp, 4to. Draft of 8 six-line stanzas; heavily revised. pn Mar 19 (10) £1,400

— Autograph Ms, Ode to Musick, [1778]. 1 p, 4to. 4 four-line stanzas, with revisions. pn Mar 19 (63) £900

— Autograph Ms, part of the Prologue for William O'Brien's The Duel, [1772]. 1 p, 4to. 16 lines. With scribal Ms of the complete Prologue. pn Mar 19 (31) £700

— Autograph Ms, poem about his port, 1773. 1 p, 8vo. 10 lines, sgd D.G. & inscr to Thomas Mills. Inscr in anr hand on verso. pn Mar 19 (35) £1,400

— Autograph Ms, poem, beginning "To Windham's Guardians Woodhouse late apply'd..."; [c.1761]. 1 p, 4to. 12 lines; including revisions. pn Mar 19 (6) £500

— Autograph Ms, poem, beginning "Ye Weather-Wise folks who foretell sun & showers...", [n.d.]. 1 p, 4to. 6 lines. pn Mar 19 (55) £900

— Autograph Ms, poem, Extempore On seeing Lady Bathurst with her youngest Son on

Fairy-Hill, 1777. 1 p, 4to. 2 four-line stanzas, initialled. pn Mar 19 (50) £550

— Autograph Ms, poem, Old Painter's Soliloquy upon Seeing Mr Bunbury's drawings, 5 July 1776. 2 pp, 4to. 4 four-line stanzas, sgd DG. Including scribal copy of earlier version with autograph revisions. pn Mar 19 (43) £1,500

— Autograph Ms, poem, On Col. Hale's promotion, [n.d.]. 1 p, folio. Draft of 13 lines, initialled. pn Mar 19 (58) £550

— Autograph Ms, poem, The Bankrupt Beauty, [Dec 1777]. 3 pp, 4to. 35 lines, with extensive revisions. Initialled. Illus in cat. pn Mar 19 (51) £950

— Autograph Ms, poem, The Chatsworth Sportsmen, 6 Sept 1776. 1 p, 4to. 14 lines, with revisions; initialled. pn Mar 19 (46) £800

— Autograph Ms, poem, To Lady Glyn upon her laughing at Lear, [n.d.]. 2 pp, 4to. Draft of 2 six-line stanzas; initialled. pn Mar 19 (42) £1,400

— Autograph Ms, poem, Upon a Certain Person's remarks ... upon [Samuel] Foote's manner of living; [n.d.]. 1 p, 4to. 8 lines, including revisions. pn Mar 19 (49) £2,600

— Autograph Ms, poem, Upon Lord Mansfield's desiring my Picture, [n.d.]. 2 pp, 4to. Draft of 22 lines, with 2 allusions to Hamlet in margin. pn Mar 19 (59) £1,400

— Autograph Ms, poem, Upon Miss Arab More desiring my handwriting for a book..., [Nov 1778]. 1 p, 8vo. Draft of 3 four-line stanzas; sgd. pn Mar 19 (65) £1,300

— Autograph Ms, poem, Upon Mrs Hale calling Hampton Paradise, [c.1771?]. 1 p, 8vo, cut from leaf addressed to him by William Burke. 6 lines, including revisions. Initialled. pn Mar 19 (36) £550

— Autograph Ms, Prologue to introduce [Willoughby] Lacy in the character of Alexander, [Oct 1774]. 2 pp, 4to. 40 lines, including numerous revisions. pn Mar 19 (38) £650

— Autograph Ms, Prologue; written for William O'Brien's 1st appearance on the stage in Dublin, [July 1763]. 1 p, 4to. 18 lines; incomplete. pn Mar 19 (9) £400

— Autograph Ms, To Dr-; 10 lines of insulting verses; [c.1765]. 1 p, 4to. With list of plays in a scribal hand on verso. pn Mar 19 (11) £500

— Autograph Ms, verse invitation, Bayes at Hampton to Col. Hale at London..., [n.d.]. 4 pp, size not stated. 10 five-line stanzas, heavily revised. pn Mar 19 (57) £600

— Autograph Ms, verses on the Duchess of Devonshire's sleeping habits, 1776. 1 p, 4to. Draft of 3 four-line stanzas, including revisions. pn Mar 19 (48) £850

Ms, draft for the re-enactment of the Stratford Jubilee at Drury Lane, [c.Oct 1769]. 9 pp, 4to. 2d half of script; including extensive revisions in Garrick's hand. pn Mar 19 (22) £4,500

— Ms, Shakespeare Jubilee, as revived at Drury Lane, 1775. 40 pp, 4to, on rectos only; stitched. In a scribal hand. pn Mar 19 (40) £1,900

— Ms, sketch, Ragandjaw, a parody of Julius Caesar, 10 July 1746. 8 pp, folio, on rectos only. Dedicated to William Windham. pn Mar 19 (3) £750

— Ms, table of the "Pageant in the Jubilee", as performed at Drury Lane, [1775/76?]. 2 sheets pasted together, 16 by 22 inches. Glue-stained on verso. pn Mar 19 (41) £2,000

AL, 24 Nov 1776. 2 pp, 4to. To [the Committee of the Theatrical Fund]. Draft, complaining about Thomas King's behavior. pn Mar 19 (47) £750

Ds, 31 Aug 1776. 4 pp, folio. Memorandum of agreement letting a property at Hampton to P. W. Mills. pn Mar 19 (45) £400

— Garrick, Eva Maria. - Autograph Ms, journal recording daily activities of herself & her husband, 31 July to 17 Dec 1768. 40 pp, 8vo, in marbled wraps. pn Mar 19 (17) £1,300

— Garrick, Eva Maria. - Autograph Ms, journal kept 13 Sept 1778 to 13 Nov 1779. 90 pp, 8vo, in blue wraps. Recording activities & social events, & recording her husband's last illness & death. pn Mar 19 (67) £3,000

— Griffin, William. - Ds, bill for binding over 1,000 plays for Garrick's library, 3 Dec 1768. 2 pp, folio. Illus in cat. pn Mar 19 (19) £450

See also: Boswell, James
See also: Garrick, David
See also: Johnson, Samuel
See also: Piozzi, Hester Lynch Thrale

Gaskell, Elizabeth Cleghorn, 1810-65

ALs, [n.d.], "Tuesday". 4 pp, 8vo. To Charles Bosanquet. Discussing travel arrangements. Ingilby collection. pn Nov 14 (73) £220 [Quaritch]

Gauguin, Paul, 1848-1903

ALs, [1884]. 4 pp, 12mo. To Camille Pissarro. Commenting on his own painting & the work of Manet. Framed with a port. Illus in cat. P June 17 (31) $12,000

— 25 Aug 1887. 2 pp, folio. To Emile Schuffenecker. Begging him to raise money for his passage back to France from Martinique. Mannheim collection. S Dec 5 (455) £3,500 [Fox Glove]

— [1888]. 6 pp, 8vo. To Emile Bernard.

Discussing the question of shadow in paintings, Van Gogh & the school of Pont-Aven, etc. Mannheim collection. S Dec 5 (454) £4,200 [Burgess Browning]

— [c.1889/90]. 2 pp, 8vo. To Emile Schuffeneker. Reporting that one of his children has sufffered a bad fall, & complaining that none of his works are selling. Illus in cat. Mannheim collection. S Dec 5 (456) £1,050 [Dr. Sam]

— Dec 1900. 2 pp, 4to. To Ambroise Vollard. Reminding him of outstanding payments. Illus in cat. star Mar 27 (892) DM6,000

Gauss, Karl Friedrich, 1777-1855

ALs, [Dec 1846]. 3 pp, 8vo. To Adolf Cornelius Petersen. Thanking for reports about observations of Neptune & sending his own data. Def. star Mar 26 (636) DM1,100

ADs, 15 May 1815. 1 p, 8vo. Bill of exchange for 480 guilders in payment of an astronomical instrument delivered to the observatory at Goettingen. hen Nov 12 (2529) DM550

Autograph endorsement, sgd, on a letter addressed to the Senate of the university at Goettingen by J. W. H. Conradi, 28 Aug 1829, 1 p, folio, regarding the suspension of a student; questioning the location of the student's home town. star Mar 26 (634) DM550

— Anr, sgd, on ANs by J. F. Blumenbach, 28 Mar 1837, sending an enclosure; suggesting that enclosure be filed. Also endorsed by Wilhelm Weber. star Mar 26 (635) DM490

Gehrig, Henry Louis ("Lou"), 1903-41

Check, accomplished & sgd, [10 July 1933]. Payable to Fred Logan. Illus in cat. Dar Feb 13 (82) $3,250

Ptd photograph, [1930s]. 3.5 by 4 inches. Sgd in pencil & in ink. Illus in cat. Shaw collection. sup July 10 (846) $1,350

Signature, [n.d.]. 3.75 by 2 inches (card). Dar Oct 10 (79) $600

Gehringer, Charles —&
Rice, Sam, 1890-1974

Group photograph, 26 July 1965. 5.5 by 3.5 inches. Sgd by both. Dar Dec 26 (120) $110

Gehrts, Carl, 1853-98

Collection of 36 A Ls s & 7 autograph cards, sgd, 1876 to 1898. 124 pp, 8vo, in lea bdg. To an unnamed doctor. Private correspondence, illus with numerous pen-&-ink drawings. FD Dec 3 (1426) DM1,800

Geibel, Emanuel, 1815-84

Autograph Ms, humorous poem, beginning "Hoert ihr Herrn u[nd] l[asst] e[uch] sagen...", [31 Dec 1839]. 2 pp, folio. star Mar 26 (161) DM340

— Autograph Ms, poem, Schulgeschichten, [n.d.]. 3 pp, 8vo. 64 lines, sgd. star Mar 26 (162) DM380

ALs, 26 Mar 1868. 4 pp, 8vo. To an unnamed cousin. Expressing his opinion that Bavaria must cooperate with Prussia for the good of all Germany. star Mar 26 (163) DM520

Gellert, Christian Fuerchtegott, 1715-69

A Ls s (2), 8 Jan 1768 & 15 Apr 1769. 2 pp, 4to. To Friedrike Haebler-Lohmann. Recommending that she read Racine in preference to Voltaire, & commenting on female virtues. star Mar 26 (165) DM1,500

Genet, Edmond Charles, 1763-1834

ALs, 12 May 1826. 1 p, 8vo. To Dr. Romeyn Beck. In 3d person, acknowledging a message from Dr. Pascale. Dar Aug 6 (163) $100

Genet, Jean, 1910-86

Autograph Ms (2), poems, Marche funebre, & La Galere, 1943 & [n.d.]. 23 pp, 8vo & folio. Including revisions. With carbon typescript copies, later typescript, & related letters. Boris Kochno collection. SM Oct 12 (369) FF30,000

Typescript carbon copy, play, Les Bonnes, [c.1946/47]. 47 pp, 4to. Including autograph revisions & sketch of the set; 2 pp entirely autograph. Inscr to [Christian Berard]. Differing from standard version. Boris Kochno collection. SM Oct 12 (370) FF20,000

ALs, [n.d.]. 2 pp, 8vo. To an unnamed lady. Informing her about a trans. sg Feb 27 (77) $150

Gentz, Friedrich von, 1764-1832

ALs, 14 July [c.1830]. 4 pp, 8vo. To [the Countess Fuchs?]. About his relationship with Fanny Elssler. star Mar 27 (1417) DM1,500

ANs, [n.d.]. 1 p, 4to. Recipient unnamed. Responding to an inquiry about journals. star Mar 27 (1418) DM320

Georg Wilhelm, Kurfuerst von Brandenburg, 1595-1640

Ls, 6 Apr 1637. 2 pp, folio. To Ferdinand of Bavaria, Archbishop & Elector of Cologne. Asking him to support his claims on Pommerania. star Mar 27 (1288) DM1,300

George I, King of England, 1660-1727

Ls, 31 Aug 1714. 2 pp, folio. To Landgraf Karl von Hessen-Kassel. Acknowledging congratulations on his accession to the throne of Great Britain conveyed by recipient's envoy von Goertz. star Mar 27 (1428) DM1,050

George II, King of England, 1683-1760

Ls, 19 June 1741. 3 pp, folio. To King Frederick I of Sweden. Acknowledging the mission of recipient's envoy Friedrich Bodo von Adelebsen. star Mar 27 (1429) DM660

George III, King of England, 1738-1820

ALs, 4 Feb 1783. 1 p, 4to. To Admiral Richard Howe. Authorizing him to attend to "the just representation of the Irish Volunteers" at Portsmouth. Spiro collection. CNY May 14 (66) $1,400

— 20 Jan 1795. 1 p, 4to. To his son Frederick Augustus, Duke of York. Requesting information about a projected visit by the Prince of Orange. CNY Dec 5 (51) $500

Series of 17 Ls s, c.1778 to 1792. Length not stated. To Lord Thurlow. About a variety of political matters. b June 22 (107) £1,800

Ls, 17 Jan 1764. 1 p, 4to. To Landgraefin Marie von Hessen-Kassel. Announcing the marriage of his sister Auguste with Karl Wilhelm Ferdinand von Braunschweig-Wolfenbuettel. star Mar 27 (1430) DM520

Ds, 25 May 1772. 1 p, 4to. Appointment of Henry Clinton as Major General. Illus in cat. Sang & Spiro collections. CNY May 14 (65) $4,000

— 1 Sept 1775. 1 p, 4to. Appointment of Henry Clinton as Lieut. General "in America only". Countersgd by George Germain. Illus in cat. CNY June 9 (236) $5,500

— 28 Mar 1783. 2 pp, folio. Order addressed to Major Henry Walter to disband the infantry corps. Def. Illus in cat. sup May 9 (468) $1,050

— 19 Dec 1800. 5 pp, folio. As Elector of Hannover, commission for a customs officer. star Mar 27 (1431) DM200

— 20 Dec 1803. 1 p, folio. Commission for Robert Henry Dick as Lieutenant. sup Oct 15 (1287) $230

Document, 6 Dec 1793. 1 p, 28.5 by 25 inches. Letters Patent creating John Fitzgibbon a Viscount. Including initial letter port & coats-of-arms in margins. S Dec 12 (255) £500 [Heraldry Today]

— 12 June 1795. 1 p, 28.5 by 25 inches. Letters Patent elevating John Viscount Fitzgibbon to the degree of Earl of Clare. Including initial letter port & coats-of-arms in margins. S Dec 12 (257) £550 [Quaritch]

Cut signature, [n.d.]. 4 by 2 inches. Mtd. Dar Dec 26 (193) $140

— Anr, [n.d.]. 2.5 by 1.5 inches. Matted with a family port. Dar June 11 (191) $180

— PHILEMON, I. G. - Ms, History of the reign of George III. [England, 19th cent]. 60 pp & blanks, 4to, in orig vellum. Heavily corrected. bba Jan 30 (292A) £60 [Edwards]

George IV, King of England, 1762-1830

Ds, 22 Apr 1824. 2 pp, 4to. Order that convicts be transferred to the ship Dolphin. Dar Feb 13 (182) $300

George, Stefan, 1868-1933

AN, [1897]. On verso of visiting card. To Theodor Dienstbach. Forwarding some books. star Mar 26 (166) DM1,100

George V, King of England, 1865-1936

Ds, 2 July 1925. 2 pp, 4to. Appointment of Thomas Travers as member of the Order of the British Empire. Also sgd by his son Edward [the future King & Duke of Windsor]. Dar Apr 9 (206) $300

— [n.d.]. 2 pp, 4to. Appointing Frances M. H. Hardman an officer of the Order of the British Empire. sup Oct 15 (1288) $300

George VI, King of England, 1895-1952

Ds, 20 June 1942. 1 p, folio. Pardon for Charles E. Warwick. sup Oct 15 (1289) $150

Photograph, sgd, March 1911. 6 by 4 inches. In cadet's uniform. Ck Apr 3 (112) £110

Georgia

— WRIGHT, JOHN. - ALs, 7 Jan 1742. 2 pp, 4to. To John Tomlinson. Describing life in Georgia. R Nov 9 (132) $450

Germany

Document, 4 July 1551. 12 leaves, 322mm by 225mm. Agreement between Moritz von Hutten, Bishop of Eichstaett, & Georg Friedrich, Markgraf von Brandenburg-Ansbach & Bayreuth regarding administrative matters at Nuernberg. Sgd by Moritz von Hutten & 5 others. HH May 12 (50) DM2,400

— ANNABERG-BUCHHOLZ. - Document, list of feudal dues to be paid at Buchholz, Mar to May 1540. 12 leaves (3 blank), 210mm by 163mm. In the hand of Leonhard Bieger. HH May 12 (24) DM680

— BLANKENBURG, COUNT HEINRICH OF. - Document, [Mar] 1320. 1 p, vellum, 140mm by 185mm. Cession of land at Dingstorf to the Church of St. Nicolas at Dingstorf. Including seal. HH Nov 5 (838) DM1,700

— DENAZIFICATION. - Document, 12 Apr 1946. 102 pp, 4to. Carbon copy of the Law for Liberation from National Socialism & Militarism, sgd by Wilhelm Hoegner, Karl Geiler & Reinhold Maier. Presented to Robert Murphy by Hoegner. Dar June 11 (197) $1,000

— FRANKFURT NATIONAL ASSEMBLY. - 4 documents, 1848 & 1849. 4 pp, folio & 4to. Motions concerning various issues; sgd by 65 representatives. star Mar 27 (1334) DM1,550

— NAZI PARTY. - Document, party member's

book of Helmuth Luecke, 1927 to 1934. 40 pp, 12mo. Sgd by Luecke & Franz Xaver Schwarz as Treasurer. Dar June 11 (194) $160

— NIKOLAUS I, BISHOP OF MEISSEN. - Ds, [21 Oct] 1387. 1 p, vellum, 330mm by 49mm. Confirmation of rents due to the altar of St. Barbara at St. James's church at Doebeln. Illus in cat. HH May 12 (60) DM1,300

— ROTHENKIRCHEN, UPPER FRANCONIA. - Ms, court records, 1523 to 1604. 514 leaves in 2 vols, 205mm by 160mm. In limp vellum; 1 vol disbound. In various hands. HH Nov 5 (817) DM2,000

— SERFDOM. - Document, 17 June 1799. 1 p, folio. Manumission for Anna Bek of Grimmelshofen, issued at Weingarten. HN June 26 (934) DM300

— SERFDOM. - Document, 6 May 1803. 1 p, folio. Manumission for Johann Schley of Oberschwarzach, issued at Wolfegg. Partly ptd. HN June 26 (935) DM260

— SERFDOM. - Document, 13 Nov 1786. 1 p, folio. Manumission for Severin Goeser, issued at Kisslegg. HN June 26 (936) DM300

— SERFDOM. - Document, 29 Feb 1804. 1 p, folio. Manumission for Anna Marie Ilmhten, issued at Donaueschingen. Partly ptd. HN June 26 (937) DM260

— SERFDOM. - Document, 22 Nov 1805. 1 p, folio. Manumission for Anna Mueller, issued at Donaueschingen. Partly ptd. HN June 26 (938) DM300

— SERFDOM. - Document, 14 Jan 1803. 1 p, folio. Manumission for Franz Xaver Precht, issued at Kempten. Partly ptd. HN June 26 (939) DM320

— TRIER. - Ms, commentary on the laws of the Archbishopric of Trier, [c.1770]. 345 leaves, 201mm by 173mm, in contemp half lea bdg. By 3 different scribes. HH May 12 (63a) DM550

— ZITTAU. - Ms, Chronicon Zittaviense..., 1600 to 1658. About 250 leaves, 305mm by 200mm. Contemp green vellum bdg. Recording events & magistrates at Zittau, beginning in 1132. HH May 12 (25) DM400

Geronimo, 1829-1909

Signature, [21 Feb 1896]. Mtd; overall size 6.5 by 4 inches. Inscr in anr hand at head. Illus in cat. sup May 9 (446) $3,600

Gerry, Ann Thompson, c.1765-1849

ALs, 9 Nov 1818. 1 p, folio. To James Monroe. Enlisting his help in obtaining a naval promotion for her son. bbc Sept 23 (20) $220

Gerry, Elbridge, Signer from Massachusetts

Autograph transcript, copy of a Massachusetts General Assembly Committee report, Sept 1780. 2 pp, folio. Regarding Gerry's attempt to reduce the Massachusetts quota for supplies to the Continental Army. bbc Sept 23 (22) $500

ALs, 16 Jan 1813. 1 p, folio. To James Madison. Informing him that he intends to take the oath of office before a district judge. Retained copy, on verso of address leaf of a letter from Madison to Gerry; including Madison's franking signature. Imperf. R Mar 7 (132) $2,500

Cut signature, [n.d.]. Mtd; worn. Dar Oct 10 (183) $100

Gershwin, George, 1898-1937

ALs, 8 Nov 1932. 1 p, 4to. To Miss Olzanova. Responding to a letter by a handwriting analyst. Illus in cat. sup May 9 (31) $2,100

Ls, 11 June 1931. 2 pp, 4to. To George Pallay. Sending news of recent shows, & suggesting "the abstract title 'Second Rhapsody'" for his new work. CNY June 9 (74) $2,500

— 30 July 1931. 2 pp, 4to. To George Pallay. Chatting about musical productions, plans, travels, etc. Sgd twice. CNY Dec 5 (52) $3,000

— 16 July 1935. 1 p, 4to. To Mel Morris. Concerning recipient's search for a job. P June 17 (215) $1,500

Check, accomplished & sgd, 12 Feb 1934. Payable to Paul Muller. With related material. Illus in cat. Dar Apr 9 (208) $900

Group photograph, Jan 1936. Framed, 16 by 14 inches. With DuBose Heyward & Ira Gershwin; sgd by George Gershwin & inscr to Ann Brown with a musical quotation. Dar Dec 26 (194) $9,500

Photograph, sgd, 22 Apr 1935. 9.75 by 7.75 inches. R Nov 9 (54) $3,000

Photograph, sgd & inscr, Jan 1927. 7 by 9 inches. Inscr to Jerry Vogel. Framed. Dar Apr 9 (207) $2,750

— Anr, [16] Jan 1932. Mtd on card, 3.25 by 5 inches. Inscr to Barbara Morey. sg Feb 27 (79) $500

Signature, [n.d.]. 4.25 by 5 inches. sg Feb 27 (78) $600

Gershwin, George, 1898-1937 —& Gershwin, Ira, 1896-1983

Ds, 24 May 1937. 1 p, 4to. Contract with RKO Radio Pictures. Dar Oct 10 (184) $2,750

Gershwin, Ira, 1896-1983. See: Gershwin, George & Gershwin

Gerstaecker, Friedrich, 1816-72

Autograph Ms, poem, Schwere Rache, [n.d.]. 1 p, 8vo. 6 five-line stanzas. star Mar 26 (167) DM460

Series of 7 A Ls s, 18 Aug to 20 Dec 1864. 14 pp, 8vo. To the pbr August Klasing. Concerning recipient's journal Daheim. star Mar 26 (168) DM2,400

ALs, 17 May 1859. 2 pp, 8vo. To Joseph Strauss. Ordering books. HN Nov 28 (1702) DM380

Gerstenberg, Heinrich Wilhelm von, 1737-1823

Series of 7 A Ls s, 15 Apr 1777 to 10 Oct 1780. 21 pp, 8vo. To Dr. Stein. Mentioning friends, other authors, etc. star Mar 26 (169) DM1,600

Gibson, Josh, 1911-47

Signature, [n.d.]. 6 by 1.75 inches. In pencil. Dar Aug 6 (95) $900

Gide, Andre, 1869-1951

Autograph Ms, review of The Post Office, by R. Tagore; [n.d.]. 1 p, 4to. Sgd. sup Oct 15 (1293) $320

— Autograph Ms, trans of 8 poems by Walt Whitman, [n.d.]. 13 pp, folio, in blue half mor bdg. Drafts; partly heavily revised. S May 28 (335) £1,700 [Beres]

ALs, [n.d.]. 3 pp, 8vo. To "chere Royere". Regarding a subscription for a monument to Charles van Lerberghe. star Mar 26 (170) DM320

— [n.d.]. 1 p, 8vo. Recipient unnamed. Announcing his visit. star Mar 26 (171) DM270

Gilbert, John, 1897-1936. See: Mayer, Louis B. & Gilbert

Gilbert, William Schwenck, 1836-1911

ALs, 12 Aug 1876. 2 pp, 8vo. To Messrs. Dalziel. Requesting blocks for illusts for Madam Fortunino. pn Nov 14 (224) £150

Gill, Eric, 1882-1940

Collection of 4 A Ls s, 25 Ls s, & 4 cards, sgd (1 autograph), 10 Oct 1933 to 3 Feb 1940. 4to & 8vo. To J. M. Dent & Sons. Concerning publication projects. With related material. S Dec 12 (209) £450

Ginsberg, Allen

Collection of 4 A Ls s, 3 Ls s, letter, & 16 postcards (14 autograph, 15 sgd), 15 Sept [1950s] to 11 Nov 1977. 27 pp, 4to & 12mo. To Carolyn Cassady; 3 to members of her family. About Jack Kerouac's funeral, various authors, her book & his own writings. Including typescript carbon copy of a poem, Los Gatos. CNY June 9 (76) $5,000

Giovanni da Bologna, d.1314

Ms, De Orthographia. [Bologna?, c.1375]. 14 leaves & flyleaf, vellum, 280mm by 208mm. Medieval blindstamped red-brown goatskin over wooden bds. In a gothic bookhand. With large painted initial. Incomplete. S Dec 17 (55) £7,000 [The Librarian]

Girard, Stephen, 1750-1831

Ls, 5 Aug 1811. 1 p, 4to. To William Adgate. Duplicate; giving instructions for purchases in England. Dar Feb 13 (185) $275

— 13 Jan 1813. 1 p, 4to. To William Adgate. About the ship Good Friends & a shipment of arms. R Mar 7 (188) $280

Giraudoux, Jean, 1882-1944

Autograph Ms (2), part of his novel Simon le pathetique, [1918]; & article, Paris sportit, sgd, 1927. 121 pp, mostly folio. Ptr's copy of the 1st version of the novel. S May 28 (345) £2,400 [Beres]

Typescript, novel, Bella; 1925. 170 pp, folio, in 8 paper wraps. 1 chapter incomplete. Ptr's copy for the 1st publication in the Nouvelle Revue Francaise. S May 28 (343) £900 [Beres]

Gladstone, William E., 1809-98

ALs, [24 Dec 18]45. 3 pp, 4to. To the Rev. E. Coleridge. Asking whether he can recommend a private secretary. Ingilby collection. pn Nov 14 (70) £170

— 9 Mar 1851. 1 p, 12mo. To the Rev. W. K. Hamilton. Arranging a meeting. Dar Feb 13 (186) $350

Glassbrenner, Adolf, 1810-76

ALs, 1 Dec 1838. 4 pp, 4to. To Heinrich Laube. About current literary & political movements. star Mar 26 (172) DM800

Gleim, Johann Wilhelm Ludwig, 1719-1803

Autograph Ms, poem, Auf Kleists Grabe, [n.d.]. 4 pp, 8vo. 13 four-line stanzas. star Mar 26 (173) DM1,300

ALs, 3 Sept 1785. 4 pp, 8vo. To Dr. Stein. About his journey to meet Klopstock in Hamburg. star Mar 26 (174) DM1,200

Glenn, John

Signature, [20 Feb 1962]. On philatelic cover. wa Oct 19 (34) $80

Glinka, Mikhail Ivanovich, 1804-57

ALs, 7 May 1845. 4 pp, 8vo. To Cirilla. Explaining circumstances behind his move to Paris, mentioning recent concerts, Berlioz's article on him, etc. In French. Illus in cat. S Dec 6 (93) £5,000 [Haas]

Gluck, Christoph Willibald, 1714-87

ALs, 30 May 1780. 1 p, 4to. To [Franz Kruthoffer]. Discussing the publication of his opera Echo et Narcisse & complaining about the French taste in music. Illus in cat. S May 29 (534) £8,500 [Haas]

Gneisenau, August, Graf Neithardt von, 1760-1831

ALs, 14 Nov 1808. 1 p, folio. To Ferdinand von Schill. Urging him to be patient & wait for further developments. Sgd with paraph. star Mar 27 (1420) DM1,500

— 7 May 1809. 1 p, 4to. Recipient unnamed. Agreeing with measures taken for the reorganization of troops. star Mar 27 (1421) DM720

— 23 Nov 1814. 6 pp, 4to; stitched. To an unnamed general. Analyzing the deliberations of the Vienna Congress, the situation of the Netherlands, & the Peace of Paris. In French. Illus in cat. star Mar 27 (1422) DM2,200

Godfrey, Edward Settle, 1843-1932

Ds, May 1878. 2 pp, folio. Certification "that the articles above specified are the actual savings of my Company..." Framed. Illus in cat. Armstrong collection. sup Oct 15 (1115) $210

Goebbels, Joseph, 1897-1945

Autograph postcard, sgd, 12 Feb [19]21. To Miss Elow. About her sister's visit to Heidelberg. Also sgd & inscr by others. Illus in cat. Dar Apr 9 (210) $750

Photograph, sgd, [3 Feb 1936]. Postcard. With secretarial letter of transmittal. HH May 13 (1945) DM550

Goering, Hermann, 1893-1946

Photograph, sgd, [8 Mar 1934]. Postcard. With secretarial letter of transmittal. HH May 13 (1946) DM500

Goeschen, Georg Joachim, 1752-1828

Series of 3 A Ls s, 24 Nov 1795 to 28 Mar 1798. 7 pp, 4to. To Adolf Martin Schlesinger. Regarding publishing matters. FD Dec 3 (1427) DM750

ALs, 28 Aug 1790. 1 p, 4to. To a clerk in his publishing house. Giving instructions. HH May 13 (1947) DM300

Goethe, Johann Wolfgang von, 1749-1832

Autograph Ms, comments about a lithograph by Karl Jakob Theodor Leybold, [1826]. 2 pp, 4to. Draft, sgd G. Including draft of a letter in Riemer's hand with corrections by Goethe on recto. star Mar 26 (176) DM13,000

— Autograph Ms, dedicatory verses to Graf Carl Harrach, 25 Sept 1819. 1 p, 4to. 6 lines, sgd. Framed. Illus in cat. S Dec 5 (515) £2,000 [Rosenthal]

Autograph transcript, poem, Der Park; [n.d.]. 1 p, 8vo. 6 lines. HN Nov 28 (1707) DM22,000

ALs, 27 July 1813. 1 p, 4to. To Constanze von Fritsch. Thanking for news from Prague. star Mar 26 (182) DM10,000

— 2 May 1817. 1 p, 4to. To Christian Gottlob von Voigt. Worrying about recipient's health. S May 28 (176) £1,200 [Saggiori]

— 9 Mar 1819. 1 p, 4to. To Sophie Caroline von Hopfgarten. About a date for a visit. star Mar 26 (184) DM3,200

Ls, 25 July 1780. 2 pp, folio. To an unidentified administration. Recommending a military officer for a vacant position at Eisenach. star Mar 26 (177) DM2,200

— 21 Dec 1797. 1 p, folio. To the Treasury at Weimar. Regarding taxes paid at Ilmenau. Also sgd by Ch. G. von Voigt. star Mar 26 (178) DM3,200

— 10 Jan 1811. 1 p, 8vo. To Eichstaedt. Sending a "program" for publication. star Mar 26 (180) DM3,400

— 10 May 1813. 1 p, 4to. To Johann Anton Stolz. Announcing his visit at Aussig. star Mar 26 (181) DM4,600

— 9 Apr 1815. 2 pp, 4to. To Karl Duncker. Concerning the ptg & the performance of Des Epimenides Erwachen. star Mar 26 (183) DM3,600

— 9 July 1820. 1 p, 8vo. To Professor Doebereiner. About an excursion to conduct some smelting experiments. S Dec 5 (513) £650 [Dr. Sam]

— 8 Oct 1829. 1 p, folio. To the building authorities at Weimar. Transmitting an order regarding a projected school. star Mar 26 (185) DM3,200

— [June 1830?]. 2 pp, 4to. To [Mr. Parish?]. Asking him to send a box of books to Thomas Carlyle. C Dec 16 (433) £1,100 [L'Autographe]

ANs, 20 Nov 1811. 1 p, 8vo. To Carl Bertuch. About the ptg of a request for autographs. Mtd with a port. Illus in cat. P June 17 (32) $6,000

ADs, 21 Apr 1801. 1 p, 8vo. Permission for the architect Rabe to use the library at Weimar. star Mar 26 (179) DM3,400

Ds, 1 June 1819. 1 p, folio. Authorization for D. Weller to transfer books from the castle library to the academy. Ingilby collection. pn Nov 14 (74) £1,200 [Maggs]

Autograph quotation, 2 lines from his poem Keins von Allen, sgd; 28 Dec 1813. 1 p, 115mm by 186mm. Mtd. HH Nov 6 (2040a) DM9,000

Autograph sentiment, quatrain, beginning "Aus des Regens duestrer Truebe...", 21 Aug 1827. 1 p, 8vo. Sgd. Illus in cat. Mannheim collection. S Dec 5 (457) £4,000

Cut signature, [n.d.]. 3.25 by 1.5 inches. Mtd. Illus in cat. Dar Apr 9 (211) $1,000

— Anr, [n.d.]. 2 by 7 inches. sg Sept 12 (92) $450

— BARDELEBEN, HEINRICH K. L. VON. - 2 A Ls s, 12 Feb & 15 Sept 1832. 5 pp, 4to. To his sister. Discussing Goethe's Faust. HH May 13 (1950) DM360

— COUDRAY, CLEMENS WENZEL. - Ms, Goethe's letzte Lebenstage und Tod, 22 Mar 1832. 14 pp, folio. Contemp copy. star Mar 26 (188) DM850

Goldberg, Reuben Lucius ("Rube"), 1883-1970

Original drawing, Boob McNutt cartoon, May 1923. 3.25 by 2.25 inches (card). In ink; sgd & inscr to D. Pierson Ricks. Illus in cat. Dar Feb 13 (187) $130

Goll, Ivan, 1891-1950

ALs, 2 Nov [19]24. 1 p, 4to. To Hans Havemann. About various literary matters. JG Mar 27 (185) DM400

Goodman, Benny, 1909-86

Photograph, sgd & inscr, [n.d.]. Size not stated. Inscr to Bill. Dar Apr 9 (212) $100

Gorbachev, Mikhail Sergeyevich

Group photograph, 13 June 1989. 24cm by 18cm. With Rita Suessmuth; sgd by Gorbachev. star Mar 27 (1425) DM1,000

Photograph, sgd, [n.d.]. 11 by 14 inches. Leaving a voting booth. Dar June 11 (199) $700

Signature, [n.d.]. Size not stated. Framed with a ptd photograph. wa Oct 19 (206) $750

Gorbachev, Mikhail Sergeyevich —& Reagan, Ronald

Group photograph, [n.d.]. 14 by 11 inches. At Reagan's ranch. Sgd by both. Illus in cat. Dar June 11 (200) $1,500

Gordon, Charles George, 1833-85

Original drawings, (8), Plans, sections and drawings explaining Ancient Jerusalem...; [1883]. 8 pp, folio. In pen, ink, watercolor & pencil. Including autograph annotations. In an album with typewritten descriptions by C. M. Clode & further related material. C Dec 16 (295) £1,500 [Wilson]

Series of 18 A Ls s, 1881 to 1883. Length not stated. To Mr. Button. About his travels & a variety of topics. Ck Apr 3 (86) £2,200

ALs, 16 Sept 1875. 16 pp, 8vo. To Sir Samuel White Baker. Reporting about his expedition up the Nile, the colonial administration, local politics, etc. CNY Dec 5 (53) $2,800

— 5 Jan 1878. 4 pp, 8vo. To [Louisa Alice] Vivian. Inquiring about his dog. C Dec 16 (293) £400 [Hoopers]

— 28 Jan 1880. 8 pp, 8vo. To Sir Hussey Crespigny Vivian. Denouncing the behavior of British officials over khedival finances. C Dec 16 (294) £450 [Wilson]

Gordon, William, 1728-1807

ALs, 25 Mar 1777. 1 p, folio. To Catharine Macaulay. Seeking her help with his history of the American Revolution. With related ALs by J. Bowdoin, 25 Mar 1777, 3 pp, folio; covering letter. pn June 11 (9) £3,000

Gorki, Maxim, 1868-1936

Photograph, sgd, [1900]. 6.5 by 8.25 inches (image). Sgd on mount. Half-length; seated. Illus in cat. sg Feb 27 (82) $1,600

Gospel Manuscripts

Ms, Gospels of SS. Luke & John; glossed. [Paris, c.1220-30]. 154 leaves (2 lacking), vellum, 360mm by 244mm. Modern dark red mor gilt. In 2 sizes of a very early gothic hand. With red & blue capitals with contrasting penwork throughout, 3 very large initials with penwork in both colors, & many contemp sidenotes. S June 23 (61) £10,000 [Fogg]
See also: Armenian Manuscripts

Gottsched, Johann Christoph, 1700-66

ALs, 22 July 1765. 4 pp, 4to. To his fiancee Ernestine Susanne Katharine Neueness. Discussing the choice of material for her wedding dress. star Mar 26 (197) DM2,200

Goudy, Frederic William, 1865-1947

ALs, 6 Sept [19]36. 2 pp, 4to. Recipient unnamed. About his life & work. sg Sept 12 (93) $90

Gould, John, 1804-81

ALs, 12 Jan 1837. 1 p, 8vo. To George Gray. Criticizing Smith's use of the word "Erythropyiae" for a group of birds. Ingilby collection. pn Nov 14 (75) £150

Gounod, Charles, 1818-93

Autograph music, Invocation a Vesta, for voice & piano, 12 June 1871. 18cm by 27cm, cut from larger sheet. 39 bars in F major, with text; sgd. S Dec 6 (91) £700 [Dreesman]

— Autograph music, L'hotellerie de la Reine. Introduction. (Choeur et Couplets.); [n.d.]. 4 pp, 31cm by 23cm. Scored for bass. star Mar 27 (1018) DM950

Collection of 9 A Ls s & ANs, 31 Dec 1872 to 23 July 1881. 24 pp, 8vo. To Charles Tardieu (1) & his wife [Malvine]. Referring to family & friends. Including postscript by Georgina Weldon. C Dec 16 (332) £400 [Macnutt]

ALs, 18 Apr 1861. 3 pp, 8vo. To an unnamed lady. Regarding efforts to arrange a concert by Sarasate at Baden-Baden. bba May 28 (206) £120 [Mandl]

— 16 Aug 1867. 3 pp, 8vo. To Friedrich Due. Informing him that he will not be able to finish the full score of his opera Romeo et Juliette before the end of the year. star Mar 27 (1019) DM280

— 6 Jan [18]89. 3 pp, 8vo. To Adelina [Patti]. Contents not stated. cb Feb 12 (156) $140

ANs, [n.d.]. On personal card. To Mme [Porcher?]. Introducing Mme Palicot. wa Oct 19 (161) $110

Autograph quotation, 6 bars from a Kyrie eleison, 6 Nov 1879. 175mm by 220mm. Sgd & inscr to Jules Massenet. With a photograph. S May 29 (543) £700 [Macnutt]

Grabbe, Christian Dietrich, 1801-36

ALs, 12 Jan 1829. 1 p, 4to. To [his future wife?]. Sending an enclosure (not present). Kuenzel collection. star Mar 26 (198) DM2,200

Grace, Princesse de Monaco, 1929-82

Ds, 2 Aug 1950. 2 pp, 8.5 by 3.5 inches. Report of Tax Withheld, California Income Tax Division. Sgd twice. Dar Apr 9 (253) $400

Photograph, sgd, [n.d.]. 5.25 by 7.75 inches. Dar Dec 26 (237) $120

Grace, William Gilbert, 1848-1915

Autograph postcard, sgd, 7 July 1900. To H. J. Moffat. Offering to engage professional cricketers for recipient. pn Nov 14 (199) £70 [Maggs]

Gradual

— [Southern Italy, Abruzzi?, c.1200]. Fragment, vellum, 198mm by 53mm. With part of 4 lines each of script in a fine Beneventan minuscule & of music of Beneventan neumes around a single red stave. Recovered from a bdg. S Dec 17 (3) £1,600 [Questor]

— [Venice, c.1420]. Single leaf, vellum, 471mm by 342mm. With 7 lines each of text in a gothic bookhand & of music on a 4-line red stave. With 2 penwork initials & large historiated inital extending into a border of acanthus leaves & including a fantastic bird, by Cristoforo Cortese. C Dec 16 (9) £9,500 [Mirandola]

— [Verona?, c.1460]. Single leaf, vellum, 490mm by 395mm. With 5 & 6 lines each of text in a calligraphic gothic script & of music on a 4-line red stave. With large decorated initial & historiated initial with marginal decoration. bba June 25 (112) £2,500 [Maggs]

— [Austria, c.1485]. 2 leaves only, vellum, 546mm by 355mm. With 6 lines each of text in a rounded italianate liturgical script & of music on a 4-line red stave. With 2 large historiated initials. Illus in cat. S June 23 (18) £5,500 [Rose]

Graefe, Albrecht von, 1828-70

ALs, [1866?]. 3 pp, 8vo. Recipient unnamed. Announcing the birth of a daughter & commenting on the times. star Mar 26 (644) DM1,000

Ls, 21 Feb 1859. 2 pp, 8vo. To an unnamed colleague. Discussing a patient. star Mar 26 (643) DM820

Graham, Martha, 1894-1990

ALs, 19 Feb 1945. 1 p, 4to. To Kit. Expressing her happiness that recipient is back. Framed with a photograph. sup Oct 15 (1297) $105

Gramont, Antoine, Duc de, 1604-78

ALs, 23 Nov 1641. 2 pp, 4to. To de Chavigny. Letter of recommendation. star Mar 27 (1346) DM235

Grant, James Augustus, 1827-92

ALs, 18 July 1865. 3 pp, 8vo. To Sir Joseph Hooker. Asking for flowers from Kew Gardens for his bride. Ingilby collection. pn Nov 14 (76) £80

Grant, Ulysses S., 1822-85

ALs, 9 Mar 1863. 3 pp, 4to. To Major Gen. A. Hurlbut. Planning a cavalry raid into central Mississippi. Illus in cat. Sang & Spiro collections. CNY May 14 (67) $22,000

— 26 May 1864. 5 pp, 4to. To Major Gen. Henry Halleck. Explaining his strategy & expressing confidence that "Lee's Army is really whipped." Including postscript, sgd U.S.G. CNY Dec 5 (54) $32,000

— 24 Jan 1865. 1 p, 4to. To Sec of the Navy G. V. Fox. Arranging to visit Fort Fisher. Sang & Spiro collections. CNY May 14 (68) $3,000

— 9 Mar 1865. 2 pp, 4to. To Major Gen. Canby. Angrily ordering him not to build a railroad but to "take Mobile and hold it". Marked "Cipher" at head. Illus in cat. Sang & Spiro collections. CNY May 14 (70) $30,000

— 6 Apr 1865. 1 p, size not stated. To Gen. Sherman. Informing him about the pursuit of Lee's army. With letter of transferral, 1885. b&b Feb 19 (158A) $29,000

— 13 Apr 1866. 1 p, 8vo. Recipient unnamed. Letter of recommendation for Col. Locke. Illus in cat. sup Oct 15 (1548) $1,800

— 16 Feb 1867. 2 pp, 8vo. To A. D. Russel. Thanking for the gift of a pipe. CNY Dec 5 (55) $600

— 16 Feb 1867. 2 pp, 8vo. To A. D. Russel. Thanking for a pipe & tobacco. Dar June 11 (203) $800

— 28 June 1867. 2 pp, 8vo. To Admiral D. D. Porter. Letter of introduction for Charles Roberts. CNY Dec 5 (56) $1,500

— 28 June 1867. 2 pp, 8vo. To Admiral D. D. Porter. Letter of introduction for Charles Roberts. Dar Apr 9 (214) $1,700

— 5 Feb 1873. 2 pp, 8vo. To Mr. Hoey. Discussing the possibility of a visit to the South. Spiro collection. CNY May 14 (71) $3,000

— 27 Apr 1880. 2 pp, 8vo. To Phillip F. Brennan. Responding to an invitation to a veteran's meeting. Dar June 11 (205) $950

— 17 May 1880. 3 pp, 8vo. To Gen. Hamilton. Making plans for a visit. Dar June 11 (204) $850

— 19 Sept 1880. 2 pp, 8vo. To John Ramsay. Referring to the upcoming Presidential election. Illus in cat. sup Oct 15 (1552) $1,550

— 14 Dec 1882. 2 pp, 8vo. To Mrs. Newman. Inviting her for dinner. With engraved port. R Nov 9 (9) $650

Ls, 11 Dec 1872. 2 pp, folio. To Tomas Guardia, President of Costa Rica. Acknowledging recipient's letter & hoping for friendly commercial relations. sup Oct 15 (1551) $525

ADs, [c.1866]. 4 pp, 4to. List of new geographical divisions & commands of the army. Mtd with a photograph. rs Oct 17 (25B) $5,500

Ds, 6 Dec 1865. 1 p, 4to. Order to affix the US Seal to a pardon warrant. Framed with a port. sg Sept 12 (94) $550

— 12 Jan 1870. 1 p, folio. Appointment of N. R. Marcy as Assistant Paymaster in the Navy. Matted with a port. Dar June 11 (206) $600

— 12 July 1870. 1 p, folio. Appointment of Elliott Arthur as Ensign in the Navy. sup Oct 15 (1549) $420

— 25 Mar 1871. 1 p, folio. Appointment of William R. Smith as Receiver at Sioux City. Framed with a port. Dar June 11 (201) $900

— 17 Apr 1871. 1 p, folio. Appointment of Benjamin R. Cowen as Assistant Sec of the Interior. Framed. Illus in cat. sup Oct 15 (1550) $650

— 13 Dec 1871. 1 p, folio. Ship's papers in 4 languages for the whaling ship Europa. R Nov 9 (8) $1,000

— 15 Oct 1873. 1 p, 4to. Order to affix the US Seal to a pardon warrant. Dar Feb 13 (191) $600

— 10 Dec 1873. 1 p, 8vo. Pardon for Joseph Gilbert. Framed with related material. LH Dec 11 (9) $400

— 15 Dec 1875. 1 p, folio. Appointment of Thomas W. Leach as medical inspector in the Navy. rs Oct 17 (25A) $400

— 2 Nov 1876. 1 p, 8vo. Rent receipt to Mrs. Nemegyei. wd June 12 (313) $400

— 1 Oct 1880. 1 p, 4to. Appointment to The Army of Boys in Blue, sgd as Commander-in-Chief of the veterans' organization; unaccomplished. sg Sept 12 (95) $550

Autograph endorsement, sgd, 7 Feb 1865. 1 p, 4to. On verso of ALs from Major Gen. Robert Scott to Major Gen. H. W. Halleck, describing Gen. Meagher's drunkenness while on duty; recommending that Gen. Meagher be discharged. Spiro collection. CNY May 14 (69) $6,500

Check, accomplished & sgd, 1 Feb 1866. Payable to Georgetown Gas Light Co. Illus in cat. Dar Apr 9 (215) $1,100

— Anr, sgd, 20 Sept 1880. Payable to himself. Illus in cat. sup Oct 15 (1765) $1,135

Franking signature, [n.d.]. As President, on front panel of an envelope. Dar Apr 9 (216) $600

— Anr, [n.d.]. On autograph envelope addressed to A. E. Borie. Ilus in cat. Dar June 11 (202) $800

Photograph, sgd & inscr, 25 May 1885. Cabinet size. Inscr to John Mason Brown on verso. P June 16 (218) $1,300

Signature, [n.d.]. 3.5 by 1 inches. Framed with engraved port. Dar Feb 13 (192) $300

— KELLY. - Orig drawing, pencil port of Grant, 24 Nov 1880. 8vo. Sgd by both. CNY Dec 5 (57) $2,000

Grant, Ulysses S., 1822-85 —& Sheridan, Philip Henry, 1831-88

Menu, Willard's Hotel, 10 May 1865. 4 pp, 8vo. Sgd by both. Illus in cat. sup Oct 15 (1547) $2,200

Grass, Guenter

Typescript, part of Ms (p 100) of his Das Treffen in Telgte. 1 p, folio. Sgd later. star Mar 26 (199) DM480

Graves, Robert, 1895-1985

Autograph Ms, poem, A Violinist, 1918. 1 p, 32mo (card). 6 lines. With part of Graves's ptd visiting card pasted below. pn June 11 (79) £120

Typescript, additions & amendments to the 3d English Ed of The White Goddess, 1960. 27 pp, 4to. Including autograph revisions. S July 21 (119) £1,000 [Sarner]

Gray, Thomas, 1716-71

Autograph Ms, paragraphs 35 - 41 of a work dealing with English churches, [n.d.]. 1 p, 4to. Imperf. sg Sept 12 (97) $450

ALs, 25 Oct 1760. 1 p, 4to. To the Rev. James Browne. Informing him of the death of the King. CNY Dec 5 (243) $1,700

Greek Manuscripts

Letter, [Egypt, c.800]. 1 p, 220mm by 127mm, between sheets of glass. From Kalouta to his "lady sister Syria", mentioning her husband & one Michael. 20 lines & portions of 3 further lines in a slightly sloping Greek literary hand, with address panel on verso. Def. S Dec 17 (43) £850 [Quaritch]

Greeley, Horace, 1811-72

ALs, [c.1848]. 1 p, 7.5 by 7 inches, cut from larger sheet. To [William E.] Robinson. Referring to publishing matters. Dar Oct 10 (190) $100

— 20 Nov 1861. 4 pp, 8vo. To T. S. Randall. Comparing the merits of Jefferson, Hamilton & the Adamses. CNY Dec 5 (58) $1,500

Greely, Adolphus W., 1844-1935

ALs, 28 Sept 1912. 2 pp, 8vo. To Lebbeur H. Rogers. Providing information about his publications. Dar June 11 (207) $100

Green, Hetty Howland Robinson, 1834-1916

Cut signature, [n.d.]. Pasted on 8vo sheet above her son's signature. Dar Apr 9 (194) $180

Greenaway, Kate, 1846-1901

Original drawing, The Little Gatherers at Dawn, to illus a vol of her Almanack. 5 by 3.75 inches. In pencil & watercolor. Sgd & inscr to C. Ryman, 1891. Ck Dec 11 (77) £

ALs, 14 Jan 1894. 2 pp, 16mo. To Mr. Brown[e] of the Fine Arts Society. Sending drawings. pn Nov 14 (212) £120 [Maggs]

Greene, Graham, 1904-91

Collection of 20 A Ls s & Ls s, 20 Jan 1975 to 6 June 1990 & [n.d.]. 25 pp, 8vo. To T. F. Burns. Discussing matters pertaining to the journal The Tablet, mentioning his works, criticizing the Pope, etc. Including 2 poems. S July 21 (124) £1,000 [Rota]

Greene, Nathanael, 1742-86

ALs, 26 May 1779. 2 pp, folio. To Gen. Jacob Weiss. Instructing him to supply tents & other stores to troops from Pennsylvania. Spiro collection. CNY May 14 (72) $3,500

— 26 June 1781. 1 p, folio. To Capt. William Thompson. Expressing thanks, & giving permission to leave the army. Spiro collection. CNY May 14 (73) $2,300

Gregoire, Henri Baptiste, 1750-1831

ALs, 8 Aug 1808. 1 p, 4to. To Dr. Usteri. Inquiring about a trans. star Mar 26 (645) DM360

Gregory I, Saint, Pope, 540-604

Ms, Homiliae super Ezechielem. [Italy, 13th cent]. 219 leaves (some missing), vellum, 145mm by 103mm. Modern vellum bdg. In a small gothic hand with cursive features by several scribes. S Dec 17 (49) £1,800 [Bleeker]

Gregory IX, Pope, d.1241

Ms, Decretales. Single leaf, vellum, 9 by 12 inches. In a lettre batarde. Dar Feb 13 (304) $200

Gregory of Nazianzum, Saint, 329-389

Ms, Homilies. [Constantinople?, c.1075]. 68 leaves only, vellum, 180mm by 142mm; disbound. In a small regular Greek minuscule. With small illuminated initials throughout & 5 large illuminated headpieces. Incomplete; very worn. S June 23 (55) £9,500 [Fogg]

Gregory XVI, Pope, 1765-1846

ALs, 2 Feb 1828. 1 p, 4to. To Ambrogio Bianchi. Asking him to forward a letter. star Mar 27 (1548) DM460

Greiner, Otto, 1869-1916

ALs, 25 Aug 1904. 4 pp, 8vo. To Paul Hartwig. Discussing Degas as a painter. HH May 13 (1959) DM320

Grenville, William Wyndham, Baron, 1759-1834

Collection of 90 A Ls s & 2 Ls s, 18 May 1796 to 15 Jan 1828. About 330 pp, 8vo & 4to. To Richard Wellesley. About the political situation in England, military campaigns, literature, etc. C Dec 16 (297) £4,500 [Quaritch]

Grey, Zane, 1875-1939

Autograph Ms, fragment from the draft of his novel The Heritage of the Desert; [n.d.]. 1 p, legal size. Framed with related material. sup Oct 15 (1300) $480

Grieg, Edvard, 1843-1907

ALs, 15 Jan 1889. 2 pp, 8vo. To Hans von Buelow. Suggesting a change in a concert program. star Mar 27 (1021) DM1,800

— [25 Apr 1894]. 1 p, 8vo. To Friedrich Due. About the date of a meeting. star Mar 27 (1022) DM700

— 26 Dec [18]96. 3 pp, 8vo. To Anton Sistermans. Discussing the program for a forthcoming concert. In German. S May 29 (545) £900 [Royal Norwegian Embassy]

Autograph postcard, sgd, 2 Sept 1899. To August Marten. Declining an invitation. HN June 26 (917) DM570

Autograph quotation, 3 bars from his Lyric Suite, Op. 71, no 1, sgd; 26 July 1903. 1 p, 12mo. Framed with a photograph, inscr to Edith Hawkins. P June 17 (33) $2,750

Concert program, for a concert at Queen's Hall, London, 24 May 1906. 5.5 by 8.5 inches. Sgd on front cover with ptd photograph. sup Oct 15 (1301) $600

Grieshaber, Helmut Andreas Paul, 1909-81

ALs, 4 Aug 1964. 2 pp, 4to. To Joachim Specht. About a joint project, & mentioning Boell & Benn. Including pen-&-ink sketch. star Mar 27 (894) DM650

Griffith, Clark Calvin, 1869-1955. See: Yawkey, Thomas Austin & Griffith

Griffith, John, 1713-76

Autograph Ms, diary, 1747 to 1750. 110 pp, 8vo, in contemp limp vellum wraps. Detailing his voyages to & from America, his capture by a French privateer, his Quaker ministry in Britain, etc. C June 24 (368) £900 [Quaritch]

Griggs, S. David, 1939-89

Photograph, sgd & inscr, [n.d.]. 8 by 10 inches. Dar Feb 13 (30) $100

Grillparzer, Franz, 1791-1872

ALs, [n.d.]. 1 p, 4to. To [the director of the Vienna Burgtheater?]. About a performance of his play Esther. star Mar 26 (200) DM1,700

Grimaldi, Joseph, 1779-1837

ALs, 26 Jan 1824. 1 p, 8vo. To F. Jones. Asking him to call on him. Dar Apr 9 (163) $450

Grimm, Hermann, 1828-1901

Collection of 6 A Ls s & autograph postcard, sgd, 1890 to 1897. 8 pp, 8vo, & card. To Max Friedlaender. About folk songs & other matters. star Mar 26 (646) DM1,500

Grimm, Jacob, 1785-1863

ALs, 25 July 1845. 1 p, 4to. To Hermann Brockhaus. Discussing the Finnish Kalevala & the possibility of a German trans. star Mar 26 (647) DM4,500

Grosz, George, 1893-1959

Autograph postcard, sgd, [27 Jan 1928]. To John Heartfield. Suggesting a meeting. Including caricature of a painter with a cat. HN June 26 (918) DM1,200

Groth, Klaus, 1819-99

Autograph Ms (2), poems, Dat Glueck, & Slecht un Recht, 15 Jan 1885 & 23 Jan 1893. 3 pp, 8vo. Both sgd. star Mar 26 (203) DM520

ALs, 15 June 1869. 1 p, 4to. To the Schiller Foundation. Expressing thanks for financial help. star Mar 26 (204) DM560

Gruen, Anastasius, Pseud. of Anton Alexander von Auersperg, 1806-76

Autograph Ms, poem, Ein Dichterhaus, [n.d.]. 4 pp, 8vo. 18 four-line stanzas, sgd. star Mar 26 (205) DM850

Guarino Veronese, 1370-1460

Ms, De Diphthongis libellus. [Italy, late 15th cent]. 9 leaves, 208mm by 147mm. Modern vellum bds. In a humanistic bookhand. C June 24 (75) £2,600 [Rosenthal]

Guidiccioni, Giovanni, 1500-41 —& Caro, Annibale, 1507-66

Ms, Rime; an exchange of verse, in Italian. [Rome?, c.1540]. 40 leaves (1 blank), vellum, 160mm by 107mm. 18th-cent red mor gilt bdg. In an elegant sloping italic hand. S Dec 17 (61) £6,500 [Giorgio]

Guise, Martin George, 1774-1835

ALs, 8 Oct 1821. 2 pp, folio. To Bernardo O'Higgins. Expressing satisfaction at being able to promote the "great Cause of South American freedom". HN Nov 28 (1710) DM300

Guiteau, Charles, c.1840-82. See: Garfield, James A.

Gulbransson, Olaf, 1873-1958

A Ls s (2), [1932]. 3 pp, 4to. To Max von Schilling. Regarding plans for an exhibition. Including 3 drawings. Illus in cat. star Mar 27 (896) DM1,500

ALs, [n.d.]. 3 pp, 4to & 8vo. To an unnamed official. Humorous letter requesting that his study be returned to him. Including 7 small drawings. HH May 13 (1960) DM900

AL, [n.d.]. 1 p, 4to. To Hans Leip. Agreeing to a suggestion regarding a fee. Including pencil sketch at head; sgd with anr sketch. FD Dec 3 (1428) DM380

Gunn, Thomas Butler, 1826-1904

[An archive containing his unpublished Ms, What I Saw of the American Civil War, [c.1895], c.700 pp, with 2 vols of his orig diaries & a quantity of associated material sold at b on 22 June 1992, lot 138, for £6,000.]

Gustav II Adolf, King of Sweden, 1594-1632

Ds, 31 Dec 1631. 1 p, folio. Safe-conduct for 3 envoys from Magdeburg. With related ALs by Jacob Fabricius attached. Illus in cat. star Mar 27 (1713) DM2,000

Gustav IV Adolf, King of Sweden, 1778-1837

ALs, 10 Nov 1814. 3 pp, 8vo. To M. Ebrey. Deliberating about a possible move to Neuchatel. HN Nov 28 (1710a) DM340

Gustav V, King of Sweden, 1858-1950

Ds, 14 Jan 1921. 1 p, folio. Appointment of Gustav F. Nils von Dardel as minister to Belgium. Dar Feb 13 (194) $100

Gutzkow, Karl Ferdinand, 1811-78

ALs, 30 May 1877. 1 p, 8vo. Recipient unnamed. Encouraging him to remain true to his first judgment. HN June 26 (919) DM400

ADs, 12 Mar 1862. 1 p, folio. As Secretary General of the Schiller Foundation, decision concerning several petitions for financial help. star Mar 26 (209) DM520

H

Haering, Wilhelm, 1798-1871. See: Alexis, Willibald

Hahn, Otto, 1879-1968

Collection of ALs & autograph quotation, 21 Sept 1961. 2 pp, folio & 8vo. To an unnamed lady. Referring to the danger of atomic weapons & Lord Russell's warnings. Limerick, warning of the destructive force of atoms; sgd. star Mar 26 (653) DM1,900

Autograph postcard, sgd, 13 July 1944. To Dr. P. Rosbaud. About his son's war injuries. star Mar 26 (652) DM380

Hahnemann, Samuel, 1755-1843

ALs, 10 Sept 1829. 1 p, 8vo. To Jenny von Pappenheim. Thanking for congratulations & requesting information about her state of health. star Mar 26 (655) DM3,200

Haile Selassie, Emperor of Ethiopia, 1892-1975

Photograph, sgd, Sept 1942. 9 by 7 inches. With secretarial letter of transmittal. sg Sept 12 (99) $500

— Anr, 1967. 7.25 by 8 inches. Speaking at the United Nations, 1963; sgd later. sup Oct 15 (1809) $400

Halberstam, Shalom Eliezer

Ls, [n.d.]. 1 p, 8vo. To Solomon Joseph Sher. Approbation for a book of Hasidic homilies on the Pentateuch. sg Dec 19 (103) $700

Hale, Sarah Josepha, 1788-1879

ALs, 24 Aug 1855. 1 p, 8vo. To Col. Fuller. Introducing her son Horatio Hale. Dar Dec 26 (202) $110

— 13 Feb 1864. 1 p, 4 by 6.25 inches. To Mrs. N. Scholl. Sending her autograph. sup Oct 15 (1303) $200

Haley, Bill, 1927-81

Ds, 8 Apr 1952. 2 pp, size not stated. Contract with the Palda Record Co. Also sgd by others. Illus in cat. P Dec 17 (420) $3,000

Haley, Bill, 1927-81 —& His Comets

Group photograph, [n.d.]. 3 by 5 inches. Sgd by Haley & the 5 Comets. Illus in cat. sup Oct 15 (1304) $350

Hall, Charles Francis, 1821-71

ALs, 19 Feb 1870. 4 pp, 12mo. To Henry Grinnell. Regarding his projected expedition. sg May 21 (42) $1,000

Haller, Albrecht von, 1708-77

ALs, 26 May 1751. 1 p, 4to. To Tobias Roenicke. Promising to review recipient's Ed of Latin poets in the Goettingische Gelehrte Anzeigen. star Mar 26 (660) DM750

ANs, [c.1740]. 1 p, folio. To his colleagues at Goettingen University. Requesting a decision regarding a student accused of duelling. Endorsed by 5 others. star Mar 26 (659) DM500

Halsey, William Frederick, 1882-1959

Ls, 12 Aug 1952. 2 pp, 4to. To Norman Landon. Concerning an invention Landon hopes to patent. wa Oct 19 (239) $110

Hamilton, Alexander, 1757?-1804

ALs, 1 Feb 1782. 1 p, 8vo. To Col. Wadsworth. Requesting a loan. sg Feb 27 (83) $2,500

Ls, 12 July 1791. 2 pp, 4to. To an unnamed port collector. Replying to inquiries about the handling of tea imports. sg Feb 27 (84) $1,900

— 26 Aug 1791. 2 pp, 4to. To John Brown. Correcting a misunderstanding regarding negotiations with Messrs. Elliot & Williams. P June 16 (220) $6,000

— 27 Sept 1791. 2 pp, 4to. To Nathaniel Appleton. Giving instructions regarding the sale & payment of Federal loan obligations. Spiro collection. CNY May 14 (74) $6,500

ADs, 9 Sept 1780. 1 p, 8vo. Receipt to E. Backus for articles for the use of the army. Imperf. b&b Feb 19 (157) $650

Ds, 20 Mar 1792. 1 p, folio. Document for registering & clearing of vessels; partly ptd. R Nov 9 (113) $3,800

— MORRIS, GOUVERNEUR, & OTHERS. - Ds, 29 Nov 1804. 1 p, 8vo. Ptd certificate to Cornelius Ray for a share in the estate of Alexander Hamilton; also sgd by Rufus King, Oliver Wolcott, & others as trustees. Illus in cat. sup May 9 (390) $2,300

Hamilton, Andrew, d.1741

ALs, 29 May 1738. 1 p, folio. To Jeremiah Langhorne. Requesting that a writ be issued against James Robinson. Including draft of writ. Spiro collection. CNY May 14 (75) $1,400

Hamilton, Billy, 1866-1940

Cut signature, [n.d.]. 2.25 by 0.4 inches. Mtd. Illus in cat. Dar Feb 13 (83) $300

Hamilton, Lady Emma, 1761?-1815

ALs, [n.d.], "Monday". 4 pp, 4to. To Lady Plymouth. Sending news from the court of the Queen of Naples. pn June 11 (50) £320

Hamilton, Margaret

Photograph, sgd, [n.d.]. 8 by 10 inches. LH Dec 11 (410) $80

Hamilton, Paul, 1762-1816. See: War of 1812

Hammarskjold, Dag, 1905-61

Transcript, excerpts from comments on the necessity of a world organization, sgd; [n.d.]. 12mo (card). Dar Dec 26 (203) $275

Hammerstein, Oscar, 1847?-1919

ALs, 20 Mar 1911. 1 p, 4to. To Mrs. Josephson. Expressing sympathy over her illness. Framed. wa Oct 19 (162) $160

Hammerstein, Oscar, 1895-1960

Ls, 6 Aug 1959. 1 p, 4to. To Frank Goodman. Insisting that all new songs [from The Sound of Music] "should be new and fresh to the first night public". Dar Oct 10 (196) $400

Hammett, Dashiell, 1894-1961

Collection of 2 A Ls s & 2 Ls s, 20 July 1944 to 15 Jan 1945. 6 pp, 4to. To Prudence Whitfield. Flirtatious letters written while stationed in the Aleutians. With photocopies of 8 further letters. CNY June 9 (81) $1,800

— Peplow, Peggy. - Orig drawing, pencil port of Hammett, 1937. 19 by 14 inches. Sgd by both. F Mar 26 (809B) $310

Hancock, Ebenezer. See: Hancock, John & Hancock

Hancock, John, 1737-93

Autograph Ms, address to the Massachusetts Legislature following the ratification of the Constitution, [1788]. 4 pp, 4to. Draft. Silked. Illus in cat. Sang & Spiro collections. CNY May 14 (80) $36,000

— Autograph Ms, draft of 2 messages to the General Court regarding a bill for an excise tax, 14 Nov 1782. 2 pp, 4to. Sgd J. H., 3 times. Illus in cat. sup Oct 15 (1204) $2,600

— Autograph Ms, Message to the General Court of Massachusetts regarding costs of housing French officers, 10 Feb 1783. 1 p, 4to. Retained draft; initialled & docketed. Spiro collection. CNY May 14 (79) $2,500

ALs, 12 Apr 1760. 1 p, 8vo. To William Ebenezer Hancock. Announcing a shipment of bottles & corks. Illus in cat. sup May 9 (374) $1,700

— 25 Feb 1761. 1 p, 4to. To his brother Ebenezer. Giving news from London. Illus in cat. Spiro collection. CNY May 14 (76) $9,500

— 4 Mar 1777. 1 p, 4to. To his wife. Giving a detailed report about his travels in Pennsylvania. Framed. P June 16 (221) $20,000

— 30 Sept 1779. 3 pp, 4to. To Jeremiah Smith. Complaining about lies that he has not paid for wood delivered to him. Illus in cat. Spiro collection. CNY May 14 (78) $12,000

Ls, 14 Nov 1776. 1 p, folio. To the Maryland Convention. Transmitting a letter warning of a possible attack by the British. Illus in cat. sup Oct 15 (1202) $25,500

ADs, 6 July 1767. 1 p, 8vo. Bill & receipt for slaves; also sgd by Henry Hodge. Framed with engraved port. Illus in cat. sup Oct 15 (1201) $1,900

— 25 Aug 1768. 1 p, 8vo. Bill of sale to Messrs. Solman & Ruford; sgd in text. Dar Oct 10 (197) $950

Ds, 9 Mar 1759. 1 p, 8vo. Promissory note by Robert Porter for £106.12.6 payable to Thomas Hancock; sgd as witness. Illus in cat. sup May 9 (373) $1,850

— 1 July 1775. 1 p, folio. Commission for Reuben Dickinson as Captain. Illus in cat. R June 13 (156) $4,500

— 17 July 1775. 1 p, 4to. Appointment of Donald Campbell as Deputy Quartermaster General. Illus in cat. sup May 9 (375) $5,250

— 10 Dec 1776. 1 p, 4to. Military appointment. Framed. P Dec 12 (108) $3,000

— 10 Sept 1779. 2 pp, 4to. Report & resolution of the Massachusetts House of Representatives regarding an application by the Falmouth selectmen for a reduction of their taxes. Sgd 3 times; also sgd by Samuel Adams & John Avery. Illus in cat. Spiro collection. CNY May 14 (77) $8,000

— 1 July 1781. 1 p, folio. As Governor of Massachusetts, appointment of Caleb Swan as captain in the militia. Dar Oct 10 (198) $3,250

— 1 July 1781. 1 p, folio. Appointment for A. Cushman as Lieutenant of Militia. Def. sup Oct 15 (1203) $1,575

— 14 Aug 1783. 1 p, 4to. Certification that Nathan Cushing is judge of the Massachusetts Maritime Court. With related document attached. Illus in cat. sup Oct 15 (1206) $4,000

— 11 May 1784. 1 p, folio. Commission for Fredrick Breed as Captain of militia. R June 13 (157) $4,200

— 11 Sept 1784. 1 p, folio. Appointment of Joseph Greenleaf as Justice of the Peace. R Nov 9 (114) $3,800

— 14 Apr 1785. 2 pp, folio. Power of attorney

to William Tudor in a case involving a mortgage on a piece of land. CNY June 9 (238) $2,500

— 25 June 1789. 1 p, folio. As Governor of Massachusetts, registration for the brigantine Success. Framed. P June 16 (222) $6,000

— 1 July 1789. 1 p, folio. Appointment of Chambers Russell as justice of the peace. P Dec 12 (109) $2,750

— 29 Nov 1790. 2 pp, folio. Sale of land in Braintree to John Sprange. Also sgd by Dorothy Hancock. Silked. Illus in cat. sup May 9 (377) $2,600

— 18 Feb 1791. 1 p, folio. Appointment of Samuel Barrett & Edward Gray as Justices of the Peace. CNY June 9 (239) $2,100

— 19 Oct 1792. 1 p, folio. Appointment of Benjamin Wares as Lieutenant of Militia. Imperf. sup Oct 15 (1207) $2,900

— 13 May 1793. 1 p, 4to. Summons addressed to Joseph B. Varnum to attend a session of the General Court. Illus in cat. sup May 9 (376) $1,850

Autograph endorsement, sgd, [n.d.]. 31mm by 88mm. Note of approval, cut from unidentified document. Framed with engrved port. P June 16 (223) $1,200

Cut signature, 3 June 1783. Size not stated. Fragment of a document, countersgd by John Avery. Illus in cat. R Mar 7 (189) $2,500

— Anr, 14 May 1784. 1 p, 8vo. Countersgd by John Avery. R June 13 (158) $1,900

— Anr, 15 June 1784. 7.5 by 3.25 inches. Countersgd by John Avery. R Nov 9 (115) $1,500

— Anr, [n.d.]. Size not stated. Mtd with engraved port. sup Oct 15 (1208) $1,000

Hancock, John, 1737-93 —& Hancock, Ebenezer

Autograph Ms, penmanship exercises, comprising 8 pp in John Hancock's & 24 pp in Ebenezer Hancock's hand, [1753-58]. 36 pp, 4to, in def blue stiff paper covers. Sgd & dated at bottom of each page. CNY Dec 5 (59) $18,000

Hancock, Winfield Scott, 1824-86

ALs, 24 Aug 1880. 1 p, 8vo. To Col. H. B. Carrington. Thanking for a book. wa Oct 19 (219) $100

Handke, Peter

Typescript, fragment from his story Der Chinese des Schmerzes, 26 Nov 1982. 1 p, folio. With ALs below, 18 Sept 1984; note of transmittal. star Mar 26 (210) DM480

Handy, William Christopher, 1873-1958

Ls, 31 Mar 1955. 3 pp, 4to. To Mrs. Cravens. Form letter (2 pp), & thanking for an invitation. Dar Apr 9 (217) $170

Autograph quotation, 2 bars of music, St. Louis Blues, sgd; 1 Aug [19]41. 6 by 3.25 inches (hexagon). Framed with a photograph. Dar Dec 26 (204) $425

— Anr, 2 bars of music, St. Louis Blues, sgd; 1 Aug 1941. Matted, 6 by 3.25 inches. Framed. Dar Aug 6 (116) $600

Hardee, William Joseph, 1815-73 —& Wharton, John Austin, 1829?-65

[An exchange of A Ls s, 21 Dec 1862, 3 pp, 4to, on a single lettersheet, battlefield letters regarding troop movements near Murfreesboro, sold at CNY on 5 Dec 1991, lot 60, for $2,600.]

Hardenberg, Karl August, Fuerst von, 1750-1822

ALs, 19 Aug 1795. 1 p, 4to. Recipient unnamed. Requesting that he purchase Buffon's own copy of his Histoire naturelle for him. star Mar 27 (1434) DM280

— 4 Sept 1818. 1 p, 4to. To an unnamed count. Informing him about his travel plans. star Mar 27 (1435) DM220

Harding, Warren G., 1865-1923

ALs, 22 Apr [1917?]. 3 pp, 8vo. To [James E. Phillips]. Appealing for help in silencing Carrie Phillips's pro-German statements. Sang & Spiro collections. CNY May 14 (81) $7,000

Ls s (2), 28 Mar 1921 & 9 Apr 1923. 2 pp, 4to. To Millard Hunt. Acknowledging a rent check, & reporting about his wife's health. sg Sept 12 (102) $800

Ls, 14 May 1903. 1 p, 4to. To J. E. Messenger. Responding to an invitation. Dar June 11 (213) $300

— 19 Oct 1918. 1 p, 4to. To George W. Upton. Insisting that the war must "end with Germany so reduced in power that she cannot again make warfare in two or three generations". Illus in cat. sup May 9 (237) $3,800

— 22 Mar 1921. 1 p, 8vo. To O. S. Rapp. Referring to the economic situation & hoping for "railway restoration". Dar Oct 10 (199) $500

— 15 Dec 1921. 1 p, 4to. To Millard Hunt. Regarding Hunt's occupancy of Harding's house in Marion. sg Sept 12 (103) $375

— 19 Aug 1922. 1 p, 4to. To his wife's grandson George DeWolfe. Expressing sympathy with his misfortunes. Illus in cat. sup May 9 (238) $1,050

— 14 Sept 1922. 1 p, 4to. To Rachel Harding Russell. Regarding his wife's illness. sup

May 9 (239) $900

Ds, 28 Sept 1896. 1 p, 8vo. Proof of publication of a legal notice (attached) in The Marion Star; sgd twice. Matted with philatelic envelope. Dar June 11 (212) $130

Check, sgd, 12 June 1908. On The Marion Star newspaper account, payable to the NY Sun. Dar Apr 9 (218) $225

— Anr, sgd, 11 May 1921. Payable to Cooper's Art Shop. Uncancelled. Illus in cat. sup Oct 15 (1773) $850

Photograph, sgd, [n.d.]. 9 by 12 inches. Framed. Dar June 11 (211) $325

Photograph, sgd & inscr, [n.d.]. 11.25 by 16.25 inches. Inscr to George H. Carter on mat. With related material. k Sept 29 (188) $500

— Anr, [n.d.]. Size not stated. Inscr to Admiral H. Rodman. By Harris & Ewing. sup Oct 15 (1612) $650

Ptd photograph, 27 Sept 1920. 6 by 9 inches. Sgd. sup Oct 15 (1613) $160

Hardy, Oliver, 1892-1957. See: Laurel, Stan & Hardy

Hardy, Thomas, 1840-1928

ALs, 13 Oct 1877. 1 p, 8vo. To the Ed of Harper's Magazine. Sending the 1st part of a story for publication. Inlaid. wd June 12 (314) $300

— 24 Oct 1900. 1 p, 8vo. To [Frederick Whelen?]. Regretting he will not be in London for some performances. pn June 11 (80) £190 [Wilson]

— 28 Aug 1908. 1 p, 12mo. To Mr. Jacks. Agreeing to meet him. Dar Oct 10 (201) $325

Ls, 20 Aug 1925. 1 p, 8vo. To Mr. Lucas. Agreeing to meet Reginald Roe. Dar Oct 10 (200) $200

Hardy, Sir Thomas Masterman, 1769-1839

ADs, 20 Oct 1805. 1 p, 8vo, torn from larger sheet. Bequest to Capt. Sutton in case of his death at the Battle of Trafalgar. pn June 11 (51) £1,200 [Wilson]

Haring, Keith

Photograph, sgd, [n.d.]. Postcard. Dar June 11 (214) $200

Signature, [6 May 1988]. On 1st Day Cover. Including small sketch. wa Oct 19 (18) $250

Harlow, Jean, 1911-37

ANs, [n.d.]. 1 p, 4to. To Blanche. Stating that she has a script with her. With a photograph. sup Oct 15 (1307) $550

Harraden, Beatrice, 1864-1936

Autograph Ms, novel, The Scholar's Daughter, [n.d.]. 180 pp, 4to, in orig cloth gilt. Inscr to A. P. Watt, 28 Jan 1913. L Nov14 (358) £450

Harris, Bucky

Group photograph, sgd, 30 Aug 1952. 8 by 10 inches. With Connie Mack. Illus in cat. sup July 10 (981) $75

Harrison, Anna Symmes, 1775-1864

ALs, 4 Nov 1846. 2 pp, size not stated. To her nephew Cleves. Informing him about the death of his aunt Mrs. Short. Illus in cat. sup May 9 (317) $1,050

— 12 June 1849. 2 pp, 4to. To Mrs. Reeve. Reporting about the death of 2 grandchildren. Dar June 11 (215) $600

Franking signature, [12 June 1849]. On autograph address leaf to Mrs. Thebe R. Reeve. Dar June 11 (216) $550

Harrison, Benjamin, 1833-1901

ALs, 12 Sept 1879. 1 p, 8vo. To Gen. Gilmore. Concerning the expense accounts of the members of the Mississippi River Commission. Illus in cat. R Mar 7 (122) $600

— 30 Sept 1892. 1 p, 8vo. To John Sherman. Responding to a recommendation for an appointment. Illus in cat. sup May 9 (221) $5,000

— 25 Oct 1899. 1 p, 8vo. To his sister Bettie H. Eaton. Sending a check & reporting about a visit to London. Matted with ptd port. Dar June 11 (218) $200

Ls, 17 Dec 1883. 1 p, 8vo. To R. S. Taylor. Suggesting he come to Indianapolis to see him. Illus in cat. sup Oct 15 (1571) $280

— 30 Nov 1891. 1 p, 12mo. To Gen. Henry B. Carrington. Thanking for a book. Matted with engraved port. Dar June 11 (217) $180

— 24 Oct 1895. 1 p, 8vo. To Funk & Wagnalls. About some books sent to him. R Nov 9 (11) $250

— 11 Feb 1897. 1 p, 8vo. To C. B. Ryan. Confirming that he had a comfortable trip. sup Oct 15 (1574) $260

— 5 Mar 1898. 1 p, 4to. To F. S. Bright. Responding to a request for patronage. sg Feb 27 (85) $175

Ds, 4 Apr 1889. 1 p, folio. Appointment of William A. Mercer as 1st Lieutenant of Infantry. Dar Aug 6 (165) $140

— 4 June 1889. 1 p, 9 by 3 inches. Appointment for J. E. Fitch "to receive subscriptions for the relief of the Johnstown sufferers." Illus in cat. sup Oct 15 (1572) $1,400

— 23 Jan 1890. 1 p, folio. Appointment of F. W. James as postmaster. sup Oct 15 (1573) $480

— 23 May 1890. 1 p, folio. Appointment of H. P. Rucker as commissioner for the Columbian Exposition. Countersgd by Sec of State Blaine. R Nov 9 (12) $380

— 22 Oct 1890. 1 p, 4to. Order to affix the US Seal to letters to the King of Siam. sg Sept 12 (104) $550

— 12 Jan 1891. 1 p, folio. Military commission. R Nov 9 (10) $480

— 7 Jan 1892. 1 p, size not stated. Appointment of Everett E. Benjamin as 1st Lieutenant of Infantry. sg Sept 12 (105) $400

— 8 Mar 1892. 1 p, folio. Appointment of a postmaster at East Greenwich, Rhode Island. sg Sept 12 (106) $275

Check, sgd, 1 May 1873. Payable to P. G. C. Hunt. O May 26 (89) $160

— Anr, sgd, 17 Feb 1900. Payable to Reed & Robinson. Cancellation affecting signature. Dar Apr 9 (220) $325

Photograph, sgd & inscr, [n.d.]. 4.9 by 6.9 inches (image). Sgd on mat. Illus in cat. sup May 9 (222) $900

Harrison, William Henry, 1773-1841

ALs, 29 Mar 1826. 1 p, 4to. To P. Hagner. Requesting papers from the Treasury Department for a Congressional inquiry. CNY Dec 5 (61) $400

— 13 Jan 1837. 1 p, 4to. To the Phrena Kosmian Society of the Pennsylvania College. Thanking for his election as honorary member. Spiro collection. CNY May 14 (82) $2,400

ADs, 11 Aug 1795. 1 p, 8vo. Receipt for beef. Illus in cat. sup Oct 15 (1509) $1,350

Ds, 17 Feb 1795. 1 p, 6 by 2.12 inches. Order addressed to the quartermaster to issue rations of whiskey at Greenville. Framed with engraved port. Dar Feb 13 (196) $850

— 1 Aug 1795. 1 p, 12mo. Order to issue rations to 2 men returned from captivity. Framed with engraved port. Dar June 11 (219) $1,000

— 17 Oct 1813. 2 pp, folio. Pay order in favor of Capt. John A. Rodgers; at foot of Rodgers' statement of transportation costs. Illus in cat. sup Oct 15 (1510) $1,250

Autograph check, sgd, 24 Mar [n.y.]. Drawn on the Bank of the US, Washington. Illus in cat. sup Oct 15 (1762) $2,100

See also: Austin, Moses & Others

Hart, Julius, 1859-1930

ALs, [n.d.]. 2 pp, 8vo. Recipient unnamed. Sending a poem (present; 21 lines, sgd.). star Mar 26 (212) DM240

Hart, Marvin, 1876-1931

Ds, 4 Oct 1909. 1 p, 8vo. Permission to Frank G. Fullgraff to use his photograph for publication. Illus in cat. Dar Feb 13 (111) $3,000

Hart, William Surrey, 1862?-1946

ALs, 29 May 1934. 2 pp, 4to. To Scoop. Stating he "cant see [his] way to oblige..." sup Oct 15 (1311) $210

Harte, Bret, 1836-1902

ALs, 10 Dec [n.y.]. 1 p, 8vo. To "Friend Avery". Inquiring about an English inventor. sg Sept 12 (108) $110

Hartmann, Eduard von, 1842-1906

A Ls s (2), 24 Nov 1887 & 15 Sept 1889. 5 pp, 8vo. Recipient unnamed. About a review of a book & the return of some journals. star Mar 26 (661) DM220

Hasidism

[A group of 59 leaves in various hands, [n.d.], in modern bds, requests from Hasidim for the intercession of Rabbi Isaac of Bojan in spiritual affairs, sold at sg on 19 Dec 1991, lot 57, for $175.]

Hassell, Ulrich von, 1881-1944

ALs, 7 Jan 1929. 3 pp, 4to. To Mrs. Wallroth. Expressing condolences on the death of her husband. star Mar 27 (1752) DM550

Hastings, Warren, 1732-1818

— Trial.- Letter, 1 Oct 1795, 1 p, 48 by 24 inches, sgd by 178 officers of the Bengal Army. To Hastings. Congratulating him on his acquittal. S July 21 (212) £900 [Green]

Hauch, Johannes Carsten, 1790-1872

Ms, Robert Fulton. A Historical Novel, trans by Paul C. Sinding; [ptd 1868]. 2 parts in 1 vol, in def later 3-quarter calf. With extensive Ms corrections. wd June 12 (315) $100

Hauer, Josef Matthias, 1883-1959

Autograph music, Zwoelftonspiel, [n.d.]. 2 pp, size not stated. 10 bars, scored for 2 pianos. Sgd on tp. Illus in cat. star Mar 27 (1026) DM1,300

Hauptmann, Gerhart, 1862-1946

Collection of 2 Ls s & 5 cards, sgd (3 autograph), 12 Jan 1930 to 23 Nov 1938. 7 pp, 4to & 8vo. To Oswald von Hoyningen-Huene & his wife. Hoping to find a house in Grunewald, & commenting on the "new powers". With related material. star Mar 26 (219) DM1,550

Ls, 17 Mar 1890. 1 p, 4to. To Gottfried Doehler. Criticizing his poems. star Mar 26 (215) DM520

— 29 Nov 1893. 2 pp, 8vo. To an unnamed

lady. Declining to lecture in Vienna. star Mar 26 (216) DM600

Photograph, sgd, June 1930. 207mm by 154mm (image). By Geiringer & Horovitz. star Mar 26 (220) DM520

Hausmann, Manfred, 1898-1986

Typescript, fragment of his story Der Huettenfuchs, 23 Apr 1978. 4 pp, folio. Including autograph corrections; sgd. With ALs, note of transmittal. star Mar 26 (221) DM330

Hawn, Goldie

Ds, 19 June 1979. 1 p, 4to. Contract for the title role in Private Benjamin. Dar Apr 9 (221) $250

Hawthorne, Nathaniel, 1804-64

ALs, 5 Jan 1859. 4 pp, 8vo. To Franklin Pierce. Sending family news from Europe & discussing American politics. CNY June 9 (82) $8,000

Ds, 23 Oct 1846. 1 p, 8vo. As port collector, certification of payment of duties. Also sgd by 2 others. sg Feb 27 (86) $225

— 1846. 1 p, 8vo. As surveyor for the port of Salem, certification of an invoice. sg Sept 12 (109) $500

— 22 Oct 1856. 1 p, 4to. As Consul at Liverpool, attestation of a bill of lading (on verso). sg Sept 12 (110) $600

— 18 Nov 1861. 1 p, 3 by 7.5 inches. Endorsement on verso of check by Ticknor & Fields, payable to Hawthorne. sg Sept 12 (111) $325

Hay, John Milton, 1838-1905

ALs, 20 July 1862. 7 pp, 8vo. To Miss Jay. About the progress of the war & Lincoln's policy on abolition. Sang & Spiro collections. CNY May 14 (109) $22,000

— 5 Aug 1862. 1 p, 8vo. To Mrs. Ames. Humorous letter, sending a photograph (not included). R June 13 (131) $350

Hayakawa, Sessue, 1889-1973

Ds, 16 May 1949. 1 p, 8 by 3.5 inches. Certificate of Alien Claiming Residence in the United States. Dar Apr 9 (223) $130

Haydn, Franz Joseph, 1732-1809

Autograph music, sketches for the Andante of his unfinished string quartet, Op. 103; [c.1802]. 2 pp, 8vo. Inscr by Aloys Fuchs. Illus in cat. Searles-Rowland collection. C June 24 (1) £18,000 [Reicher-Wertitsch]

ALs, 3 Feb 1784. 1 p, 4to. To the pbr Artaria. Promising to send the rest of his songs [XI Lieder fuer das Clavier] soon. Illus in cat. S May 29 (556) £9,000 [L'Autographe]

— 19 Dec 1794. 1 p, 4to. To Giovanni Battista Viotti. Asking him to procure a ticket to hear the singer Brigida Banti. In Italian. Illus in cat. S May 29 (554) £11,000 [Wertitsch]

— 11 May 1800. 1 p, 4to. To [J. J. Hummel?]. Acknowledging receipt of payment for the score of The Creation & reporting on progress on the score of The Seasons. Framed with a port. Illus in cat. P June 17 (34) $18,000

Ds, 6 Dec 1801. 1 p, 8vo. Declaration that Breitkopf & Haertel hold the German copyright for his oratorio The Seasons. star Mar 27 (1027) DM17,000

Haydon, Benjamin Robert, 1786-1846

ALs, 27 Apr 1831. 1 p, 4to. To S. J. Dyer. Regretting he cannot travel to Plymouth for the election. Ingilby collection. pn Nov 14 (77) £65 [Autograph House]

Hayes, Helen

Ds, 24 Oct 1949. 2 pp, 4to. Contract with The Theatre Guild Radio Division; carbon copy. Dar Feb 13 (197) $100

Hayes, Rutherford B., 1822-93

ALs, 24 July 1869. 1 p, 8vo. To A. J. Goodman. As Governor of Ohio, informing him that he is unable to secure the papers of Arthur St. Clair for Ohio. wa Oct 19 (297) $350

— 23 Oct 1873. 1 p, 8vo. To "Uncle Scott". Commenting on party politics. R Nov 9 (13) $650

— 12 Mar 1880. 1 p, 8vo. To Andrew Dickson White. Letter of introduction for the Dymond family. Framed with a photograph. P June 16 (225) $500

— 12 Dec 1883. 1 p, 12mo. To James F. Rodgers. Complying with a request [for his autograph]. Matted with engraved port. Dar June 11 (220) $110

— 7 June 1885. 1 p, 4to. To Frank Seaman. About the date of a forthcoming military reunion. Illus in cat. R Mar 7 (124) $450

— 8 June 1889. 1 p, 8vo. To Henry Phillips. Confirming that he took the oath of office in the White House on 3 Mar 1877. Dar Dec 26 (205) $4,250

— [n.d.]. 1 p, 8vo. To Mr. Bell. Introducing Major Butterworth & requesting him to "do something for Capt. Higdon". Illus in cat. sup May 9 (215) $1,150

ANs, 12 Feb 1880. On White House card. To Judge Porter. Introducing Gen. Leske. rs Oct 17 (8) $300

Ds, 1870. Size not stated. As Governor of Ohio, appointment of John Sprague as Justice of the Peace. k Sept 29 (190) $160

— 10 Nov 1877. 1 p, 4to. Order to affix the US Seal to a pardon warrant. Dar Oct 10 (202) $250

— 15 Nov 1877. 1 p, 4to. Order to affix the US Seal to a pardon warrant. Dar Aug 6 (167)

$400

— 14 Aug 1878. 1 p, 4to. Order to affix the US Seal to a pardon warrant. Dar June 11 (221) $475

— 21 June 1880. 1 p, folio. Appointment of George S. Haskell as commissioner for the centennial of the peace treaty of 1783. Dar Oct 10 (203) $400

Check, accomplished & sgd, 13 Apr 1866. Drawn on his account at the House of Representatives; payable to himself. Illus in cat. Dar Apr 9 (222) $900

Signature, [n.d.]. 16mo. Including subscription. Matted with engraved port. Dar Feb 13 (198) $150

— Anr, [n.d.]. Card, size not stated. Framed. wa Oct 19 (298) $90

Hazart, Cornelius, 1617-90

Ms, Breve compendium historiae ecclesiasticae. [Germany, c.1695]. 430 pp, 8vo, in contemp calf. Covering countries with Jesuit missions, & including Itinerarium of Kilian Stumpf on flyleaves, 24 Mar 1691. S Nov 21 (357) £1,500 [Maggs]

Hearn, Lafcadio, 1850-1904

ALs, [c.1891]. 5 pp, 8vo. To his sister Elizabeth. Speaking of his life in Japan. Sgd LH. sg Nov 7 (88) $7,000

Heath, William, 1737-1814

ALs, 7 Feb 1777. 2 pp, 4to. To Major Gen. Wooster. Giving instructions for troop movements the next day. Illus in cat. R Mar 7 (192) $1,000

Ds, 6 Oct 1807. Size not stated. Legal estate document. Framed with engraved port. R June 13 (159) $110

Hebbel, Friedrich, 1813-63

ALs, 2 Mar 1862. 1 p, 4to. To [Julius Pabst?]. Insisting that he return the Ms of his Nibelungen. star Mar 26 (222b) DM1,300

Hebel, Johann Peter, 1760-1826

ALs, 1 Dec 1809. 3 pp, 4to. To the pbr Engelmann. Declining to edit a journal for the less educated classes. star Mar 26 (223) DM10,000

Hebrew Manuscripts

Ms, Isaiah. [Germany, early 14th cent]. Parts of 4 leaves, vellum, up to 255mm by 225mm. In a large Hebrew script with nikud. Def. S Dec 17 (46) £850 [Maggs]

— Ms, Megillah Esther. [Italy, c.1800]. 3 vellum membranes joined, 25cm by 206.5cm. In brown ink in square Sephardic script. With ornamental borders throughout in colors & 11 floral bars separating columns. HH Nov 5 (802) DM3,800

— Ms, Megillah Esther. [20th cent]. Scroll of 3 vellum skins, 295mm wide. In Ashkenazi square script. With elaborate scroll-work throughout. sg Dec 19 (177) $500

— Ms, Megillah Esther. [Western Europe, 18th cent]. 4 membranes of vellum stitched together, 185cm by 20cm. In sq Sephardic script & blessings in Rabbinic hand. With engraved illusts framing text & pilasters between columns with trompe l'oeil floral bas-reliefs, bases with landscape scenes. sg June 25 (247) $13,000

— Ms, Megillah-Psalms 114, 137 (twice), 1, 23, 17 & 48 [in that order]. [Northern Italy or Austria?, 1804]. Scroll, vellum, 405mm by 900mm. In 2 sizes of unvocalised square Hebrew script with Sephardic & Ashkenazic features. Illuminated; with 10 historiated columns. Illus in cat. C June 24 (68) £6,000 [Smith]

— Ms, micrographic circular Book of Esther conceived as an amulet. [East European?, late 19th cent]. 1 leaf, 310mm by 205mm. Including Hebrew aphorisms & port of Esther & Ahasverosh. sg June 25 (251) $375

— Ms, Minchath Todah Ulemizkereth Ahavah, songs for Hanukkah. [Hungary, c.1850]. 1 p, 264mm by 390mm. Presented to Judah Aszod by Meir Eisenstadter. sg Dec 19 (170) $550

— Ms, prayer for the benefit of Joseph Stalin. [Russia, 1950]. 345mm by 550mm. Including newspaper port at center. sg Dec 19 (215) $225

— Ms, Sepher Hazkaroth Neshamoth. [Schtamppen?, 19th cent]. 29 pp, 170mm by 250mm, in worn contemp gilt-stamped sheep. In Ashkenazi square & cursive scripts in more than one hand. Memorializing the dead of the community; last entry dated 1883. sg Dec 19 (169) $500

— Ms, Sepher Seder Haselichoth, according to the rite of Castile. [Turkey?, 1788]. 65 pp & blanks, 125mm by 180mm. Extra contemp calf gilt bdg. In Turkish square Hebrew script. With 2 ornamental borders. sg Dec 19 (165) $1,600

— Ms, Shir She'omrim Betephilath Arvith Veshacharith. [Padua, 1797]. 4 pp, 165mm by 225mm. Poem celebrating delivery of the Padua Community from a fire. sg Dec 19 (119) $110

Document, Ketubah, marriage contract. [Tunis, 1890]. 1 p, 270mm by 395mm. In Sephardic Hebrew script. Illuminated. Framed. sg Dec 19 (142) $650

— Almosnino, Moses ben Baruch. - Ms, Bet Elohim & Sha'ar Ha'Shamayim, a cosmography & geography of the world, including detailed account of the discovery of America. [Salonika, Greece, 1551]. 162 leaves (6 missing) & 7 flyleaves, 268mm by 187mm. Repaired (contemp?) Greek blindstamped goatskin over pastebds. In an elegant near-eastern Spanish rabbinic cursive script by the scribe Chaim Luzio for Peretz ben Yehuda Mintz Ashkenazi. With c.144 astronomical & mathematical diagrams, 8 in colors. Illus in cat. S Dec 17 (47) £32,000 [Schoenberg]

— BONFILS, IMMANUEL BEN JACOB. - Shesh-Kenafayim. [Italy?, 1509]. 54 pp, vellum, 119mm by 164mm. Modern half calf bdg. In an Italian square & cursive Hebrew script by Joseph ben Isaac Gallico. Including 42 pp of astronomical tables. sg Dec 19 (161) $8,000

— RIETI, MOSES BEN ISAAC DA. - Ms, Mikdash Me'at. [Italy, 16th cent]. 70 pp, 154mm by 208mm. Modern vellum bdg. In Italian square & cursive Hebrew scripts. Incomplete; dampstained. sg Dec 19 (162) $325

— SOFER JUDA BEN SCHEMMEL. - Ms, astrological & cabalistic treatise. [Fulda, Germany, 1626-42]. 88 leaves, 190mm by 155mm. Def contemp lea bdg. Including numerous drawings in pen-&-ink & watercolors. HH Nov 5 (514) DM11,500

Hecht, Ben, 1894-1964 —& MacArthur, Charles, 1895-1956

Ds s (2)15 Jan 1947. 4 pp, 4to. Contract, in English & in French, giving Marcel Duhamel the right to adapt their play The Front Page into French. Dar Aug 6 (168) $250

Ds, 30 Nov 1945. 2 pp, 4to. License to broadcast their play Front Page; sgd by both. Dar June 11 (222) $350

Hedin, Sven, 1865-1952

ALs, 6 Dec 1921. 2 pp, 8vo. To his pbr Perthes. Discussing the publication of a work on Tibet. With photograph, sgd. HH Nov 6 (2047) DM240

— 10 Apr 1932. 1 p, 4to. To Hamilton Holt. About his stay in America before going to China. star Mar 26 (662) DM280

Hegar, Friedrich, 1841-1927

Autograph music, Walpurga, choral music to a text by Carl Spitteler, [n.d.]. 1 p, folio. 13 bars, sgd at head. With covering ALs, 11 July 1911. star Mar 27 (1028) DM260

Hegel, Georg Wilhelm Friedrich, 1770-1831

ALs, 3 Dec 1802. 1 p, 4to. To Ramann. Ordering wine. S May 28 (177) £2,000 [Mandl]

— 6 Dec 1802. 1 p, 4to. To Messrs. Ramann. Ordering wine. C Dec 16 (435) £750 [L'Autographe]

Heidegger, Martin, 1889-1976

ALs, 7 Sept 1965. 1 p, 8vo. To Albert Theile. Thanking for a projected article in the journal Humboldt. HH Nov 6 (2049) DM340

Photograph, sgd & inscr, 25 Sept 1961. 8vo. Inscr on verso with a long autograph sentiment regarding the importance of reading. star Mar 26 (663) DM1,500

Heiller, Anton, 1923-79

Autograph music, sketches for his music for organ, Victimae paschali laudes, sgd & inscr; 19 Jan 1978. 4 pp, 34cm by 27cm. star Mar 27 (1029) DM440

Heine Family

[A group of 13 letters from various members of Heinrich Heine's family, 1835 to 1861, 15 pp, 4to & 8vo, mostly to other family members & mentioning Heinrich, sold at C on 16 Dec 1991, lot 401, for £1,000 to Rosenthal.]

Heine, Heinrich, 1797-1856

[A disbound copy of the 1st Ed of his Ueber die franzoesische Buehne. Vertraute Briefe an August Lewald, [pbd 1838], 8vo, with substantial autograph corrections & additions throughout for a new Ed [pbd 1840], sold at C on 16 Dec 1991, lot 354, for £2,200 to Rosenthal.]

[A group of 7 Mss (6 autograph), drafts of articles for the Augsburger Allgemeine Zeitung, later repbd under the title Lutezia, [c.1852 - 54], 15 pp, 4to, sold at C on 16 Dec 1991, lot 372, for £9,000 to Rosenthal.]

Autograph Ms (2), Les Dieux en Exil, [c.1853], 5 pp, 4to; & Goetter im Exil, [c.1853], 1 p, 4to. Partly with corrections in the hand of Richard Reinhardt. Gottschalk collection. C Dec 16 (369) £4,200 [Rosenthal]

Autograph Ms, 2 poems from the cycle Kitty, [c.1834]. 2 pp, 4to. 8 four-line stanzas. Gottschalk collection. C Dec 16 (346) £7,000 [Rosenthal]

— Autograph Ms, 2 poems from the cycle Kitty, [c.1834]. 2 pp, 4to. 6 four-line stanzas. Gottschalk collection. C Dec 16 (347) £6,000 [Rosenthal]

— Autograph Ms, 3 brief aphorisms, [n.d.]. 1 p, 115mm by 210mm, torn from larger sheet. 8 lines. Gottschalk collection. C Dec 16 (375) £1,100 [Rosenthal]

— Autograph Ms, 4 poems from his Lyrisches Intermezzo (nos 5, 22, 34 & 35), [Jan or Feb 1822]. 2 pp, 4to. Fair copy with a few autograph corrections. star Mar 26 (224) DM32,000

— Autograph Ms, A Prosper Enfantin en Egypte, dedication to his book De l'Allemagne; [1835]. 1 p, 4to. Sgd. Gottschalk collection. C Dec 16 (350)

£3,500 [Rosenthal]
— Autograph Ms, article about the political situation in France, 4 Feb [1840]. 14 pp, 4to. Including ANs to Gustav Kolb. Gottschalk collection. C Dec 16 (355) £7,000 [Rosenthal]
— Autograph Ms, article, Allianz zwischen Russland und Frankreich, [c.1843]. 2 pp, 4to. Including numerous revisions. Gottschalk collection. C Dec 16 (361) £3,000 [Rosenthal]
— Autograph Ms, article discussing his pride at the fame of his poems, [c.1854]. 1 p, 4to. Gottschalk collection. C Dec 16 (371) £1,800 [Rosenthal]
— Autograph Ms, article, Lutezia LIV, 2 Feb 1843. 10 pp, mostly 4to. Incomplete. Including revisions & draft of an insertion. Gottschalk collection. C Dec 16 (360) £4,500 [Rosenthal]
— Autograph Ms, Atta Troll, verses from Caput XIX & Caput XX, [c.1842]. 2 pp, 4to. 55 lines, including revisions. Gottschalk collection. C Dec 16 (358) £7,000 [Rosenthal]
— Autograph Ms, Deutschland ein Wintermaerchen, Caput XXIII, [c.1844]. 1 p, 4to. 6 four-line stanzas. Working draft; differing from ptd version. Gottschalk collection. C Dec 16 (362) £5,000 [Rosenthal]
— Autograph Ms, draft for 3 verses of Caput VI of Atta Troll, [c.1847]. 1 p, folio. 12 lines, including revisions. Framed. C Dec 16 (427) £4,000 [Rosenthal]
— Autograph Ms, draft of 5 quatrains from Deutschland. Ein Wintermaerchen, [1843-44]. 1 p, folio. With revisions; including 2 stanzas not ptd in final text. With authentication on verso. S May 28 (179) £8,000 [Symonds]
— Autograph Ms, Elementargeister, draft of a passage relating to the transmission of Tannhaeuser; [c.1836]. 1 p, 4to. Gottschalk collection. C Dec 16 (352) £1,700 [Rosenthal]
— Autograph Ms, essay about French attitudes to money & religion, [c.1841?]. 4 pp, 4to. Working draft; probably unpbd. Gottschalk collection. C Dec 16 (357) £10,000 [Rosenthal]
— Autograph Ms, notes from Geschichte der Regierung Ferdinands des Ersten, vol 5, by Bucholtz; [c.1834]. 3 pp, 4to. Gottschalk collection. C Dec 16 (348) £2,400 [Rosenthal]
— Autograph Ms, poem, beginning "Sorge nie, dass ich verrathe...", [c.1830]. 1 p, 4to. Draft of 3 quatrains. Illus in cat. Mannheim collection. S Dec 5 (459) £7,500 [Rosenthal]
— Autograph Ms, poem, Citronia, lines 46 - 59; [1854]. 2 pp, folio. 30 lines, including revisions. Unpbd version. Gottschalk collection. C Dec 16 (370) £4,000 [Rosenthal]
— Autograph Ms, poem, Dich fesselt mein Gedankenbaum, [1855]. 2 pp, folio. 60 lines, with numerous revisions. In pencil. Gottschalk collection. C Dec 16 (374) £35,000 [Rosenthal]
— Autograph Ms, poem, Geoffroy Rudel und Melisende von Tripoli, [c.1846]. 4 pp, 4to. 17 four-line stanzas. Signature at end crossed out. Gottschalk collection. C Dec 16 (363) £14,000 [Rosenthal]
— Autograph Ms, poem, Gleich Merlin dem eitlen Weisen, [24 Apr 1833]. 1 p, 4to. 4 four-line stanzas. Including ANs to Ferdinand Hiller at foot. Gottschalk collection. C Dec 16 (345) £8,000 [Rosenthal]
— Autograph Ms, poem, Helena, [c.1846-47]. 1 p, 4to. 10 lines, including revisions. Gottschalk collection. C Dec 16 (367) £15,000 [Rosenthal]
— Autograph Ms, poem, Katharina, [c.1837]. 2 pp, 4to. 5 four-line stanzas. Gottschalk collection. C Dec 16 (353) £6,000 [Rosenthal]
— Autograph Ms, poem, Lobgesaenge auf Koenig Ludwig, no III, [Dec 1843]. 2 pp, 4to. 9 four-line stanzas, including corrections. Gottschalk collection. C Dec 16 (359) £10,000 [Rosenthal]
— Autograph Ms, poem, Neuer Fruehling XXXII, final draft, [1830]. 1 p, folio. 3 four-line stanzas. Including revisions. Gottschalk collection. C Dec 16 (344) £7,000 [Rosenthal]
— Autograph Ms, poem, Ramsgate I, [c.1827]. 2 pp, 4to. 3 four-line stanzas, with an explanation in prose. Gottschalk collection. C Dec 16 (343) £10,000 [Rosenthal]
— Autograph Ms, poem, Sie schifften wohl ueber das salzige Meer, [c.1835]. 13 pp, 4to, on rectos only. 73 four-line stanzas, with revisions. Gottschalk collection. C Dec 16 (351) £20,000 [Rosenthal]
— Autograph Ms, poem, Weltverschlimmerung, [n.d.]. 2 pp, 4to. 5 four-line stanzas, sgd; fair copy. star Mar 26 (226) DM26,000
— Autograph Ms, preface to Uebersetzung eines lapplaendischen Gedichts, [c.1855]. 8 pp, folio. Gottschalk collection. C Dec 16 (373) £8,000 [Rosenthal]
— Autograph Ms, sonnet, Mein Tag war heiter, [1852 or later]. 2 pp, folio. Working Ms. star Mar 26 (225) DM24,000
— Autograph Ms, Zur Geschichte der Religion und Philosophie in Deutschland, drittes Buch; [c.1834]. 14 pp, 4to. Draft of a section about Fichte & his school. Gottschalk collection. C Dec 16 (349) £3,800 [Rosenthal]

Ms, article, Irische Rebellion und Landung der

Franzosen in Irland, [pbd 1841]. 16 pp, 4to. Copy in the hand of Richard Reinhardt for an Ed planned in 1852; incomplete. Including AN by Heine at head. Gottschalk collection. C Dec 16 (356) £300 [Rosenthal]

— Ms, corrections for the 2d Ed of Zur Geschichte der Religion und Philosophie in Deutschland, [c.1852]. 9 pp, 8vo. Inserted in incomplete ptd copy of 1st Ed, with Heine's autograph marks throughout. Gottschalk collection. C Dec 16 (368) £1,700 [Rosenthal]

— Ms, Der Doktor Faust. Ein Tanzpoem, [c.1851]. 74 pp, 4to. In 4 scribal hands, with Heine's autograph corrections throughout. Ptr's copy. Gottschalk collection. C Dec 16 (364) £15,000 [Rosenthal]

— Ms, Goetter im Exil, part of the introduction; [c.1852]. 2 pp, 4to. In the hand of Richard Reinhardt, with autograph revisions by Heine. Gottschalk collection. C Dec 16 (366) £550 [Rosenthal]

— Ms, Nachgelesene Gedichte, [n.d.]. 85 pp, 4to. 29 poems, mostly in the hand of Richard Reinhardt; including 8 autograph corrections by Heine. Gottschalk collection. C Dec 16 (376) £10,000 [Rosenthal]

ALs, [12] Oct 1823. 1 p, 4to. To his sister Charlotte Embden. Family letter. Gottschalk collection. C Dec 16 (378) £3,600 [Rosenthal]

— 30 Mar 1824. 2 pp, 4to. To his sister Charlotte Embden. About his projected journey to Berlin & her pregnancy. Gottschalk collection. C Dec 16 (379) £4,000 [Rosenthal]

— 30 Nov 1824. 1 p, 8vo. To Friedrich Wilhelm Gubitz. Asking him to publish an essay by Dr. Peters. Gottschalk collection. C Dec 16 (377) £2,800 [Rosenthal]

— 12 Nov 1825. 2 pp, 4to. To Christian Sethe. Referring to money borrowed from Sethe & hoping to settle in Hamburg. With related material. star Mar 26 (227) DM24,000

— [1 Jan 1827]. 3 pp, 4to. To Friedrich Merckel. Discussing suggestions for changes in poems, his current work, etc. Gottschalk collection. C Dec 16 (380) £7,000 [Rosenthal]

— 23 Apr 1827. 3 pp, folio. To Friedrich Merckel. About his stay in London. Gottschalk collection. C Dec 16 (381) £7,000 [Rosenthal]

— 15 Dec 1827. 1 p, 4to. To Rudolph Christiani. Reminding him to deliver a promised article. Gottschalk collection. C Dec 16 (382) £1,800 [Rosenthal]

— 1 Mar 1828. 1 p, 4to. To Friedrich Merckel. Discussing his financial arrangements with Cotta & Campe. Gottschalk collection. C Dec 16 (383) £3,800 [Rosenthal]

— 15 July 1833. 2 pp, 4to. To Rudolph Christiani. Congratulating him on his forthcoming marriage to Heine's cousin. Gottschalk collection. C Dec 16 (384) £5,000 [Rosenthal]

— 7 May 1834. 2 pp, 8vo. To Pierre-Martinien Bocage. Regarding the Ms of a tragedy by Kleist. Gottschalk collection. C Dec 16 (385) £3,500 [Rosenthal]

— [15 May 1840]. 1 p, 4to. To Gustav Kolb. Referring to the torture of Jews in Damascus. Gottschalk collection. C Dec 16 (386) £2,800 [Rosenthal]

— [26 Feb 1842]. 1 p, 8vo. To Giacomo Meyerbeer. Asking for tickets for a performance of Les Huguenots. star Mar 26 (228) DM16,000

— 24 May 1842. 4 pp, 4to. To [Giacomo Meyerbeer]. Referring to his efforts to establish a good relationship between Meyerbeer & E[scudier]. C Dec 16 (428) £6,500 [Rosenthal]

— 2 Nov 1842. 2 pp, 4to. To Amalie Beer. Expressing condolences on the death of her son Heinrich. Gottschalk collection. C Dec 16 (387) £3,800 [Rosenthal]

— 21 Feb 1843. 3 pp, 4to. To his mother Betty Heine. Referring to his own & recipient's health problems, & discussing Atta Troll. Gottschalk collection. C Dec 16 (388) £5,000 [Rosenthal]

— [28 Feb 1845]. 1 p, 8vo. To Cyprien Marie Tessie du Motay. Expecting his visit & mentioning George Sand. star Mar 26 (229) DM10,000

— 24 June 1845. 2 pp, 4to. To his mother Betty Heine. Describing the house where he has just moved. Gottschalk collection. C Dec 16 (390) £4,000 [Rosenthal]

— 13 Apr 1847. 1 p, 4to. To Moritz Carriere. Asking him to take some autographs to Varnhagen v. Ense. Gottschalk collection. C Dec 16 (391) £3,000 [Rosenthal]

AL, 8 Apr 1843. 1 p, 4to. To his sister Charlotte Embden. Congratulating her on the marriage of her daughter. Foot of letter cut off. Gottschalk collection. C Dec 16 (389) £1,500 [Rosenthal]

— [12 June 1848]. 2 pp, 4to. To his sister Charlotte Embden. Describing his paralysis. Incomplete at beginning & end. Gottschalk collection. C Dec 16 (392) £6,000 [Rosenthal]

Ls, 6 Sept 1852. 1 p, 4to. To the banker Homberg. Asking for money & inquiring about his railway shares. C Dec 16 (429) £2,000 [Rosenthal]

— 5 Feb 1853. 3 pp, 8vo. To Francois Buloz. Thanking for support in his controversy with the pbr Renduel. star Mar 26 (231a) DM9,000

ANs, 28 Mar 1846. On verso of visiting card. To Franz Dingelstaedt. Introducing Felix Bamberg. star Mar 26 (230) DM2,200

Corrected page proofs, Doktor Faust, ptr's proofs; [1851]. 106 pp, size not stated. Including corrections in several hands. With related material. Gottschalk collection. C Dec 16 (365) £1,900 [Rosenthal]

— CAMPE, JULIUS. - ALs, 15 Dec 1826. 4 pp, 4to. To Heinrich Heine. Discussing the publication of Heine's works. Gottschalk collection. C Dec 16 (393) £1,800 [Rosenthal]

— DINGELSTEDT, FRANZ VON. - Autograph Ms, article Pfizer gegen Heine, [pbd 3 May 1838]. 28 pp, 4to. Defending Heine. Including annotations. Gottschalk collection. C Dec 16 (397) £400 [Rosenthal]

— FURTADO, ELIE. - ALs, 1 Jan 1841. 3 pp, 4to. To his daughter Cecile Heine. Mostly about the reduction of Heinrich Heine's pension paid by his uncle Salomon Heine. star Mar 26 (231b) DM1,300

— GIERE, JULIUS. - Lithographed port of Heine, 478mm by 367mm. Sgd by Heine & inscr to his brother Gustav, 25 Aug 1851. C Dec 16 (431) £17,000 [Rosenthal]

— HOFFMANN & CAMPE. - Ds, 11 May 1854. 1 p, 4to. Contract with Heine for 3 vols of his works. Gottschalk collection. C Dec 16 (403) £2,800 [Rosenthal]

Heine, Mathilde, 1815-83

Ls s (2), 2 Sept 1859 & 16 Feb 1883. 4 pp, 8vo. To the pbr Julius Campe, & to Hoffmann & Campe. Regarding one of her husband's Mss, & the payment of her pension. Gottschalk collection. C Dec 16 (399) £1,400 [Rosenthal]

Ls, 13 May 1856. 4 pp, 4to. To Julius Campe. Expressing thanks that Campe will pay her a regular pension, & discussing the Ed of her husband's posthumous works. C Dec 16 (430) £4,000 [Rosenthal]

Heine, Thomas Theodor, 1867-1948

Collection of 11 A Ls s & ANs, 1922 to 1931. 13 pp, folio, & visiting card. To the Ed of the journal Simplizissimus. Discussing financial matters. With related material. HH Nov 6 (2050) DM1,000

Heinrich, Prince of Prussia, 1726-1802

ALs, 7 Apr 1761. 1 p, folio. To [Padre Martini]. About Johannes Ritschel's training in composition. star Mar 27 (1604a) DM850

— 10 Oct 1789. 3 pp, 4to. Recipient unnamed. Commenting on the Revolution in France. star Mar 27 (1604b) DM1,100

Heinse, Wilhelm, 1746-1803

ALs, [n.d.]. 2 pp, 4to. Recipient unnamed. About his trans of Petronius, & mentioning Wieland & Gleim. star Mar 26 (232) DM3,200

Heiseler, Bernt von, 1907-69

Collection of ALs & Ls, 9 Mar 1936 & 1937. 3 pp, folio. To Bruno Schneider. Thanking for a book mentioning his father, & contents not stated. star Mar 26 (233) DM220

Heisenberg, Werner, 1901-76

Autograph Ms, fragment (pp 7 & 8) from a scientific paper, [2 Oct 1961]. 2 pp, folio. With photograph, sgd, & secretarial letter of transferral. star Mar 26 (664) DM650

Hellman, Lilian, 1905-84. See: Bernstein, Leonard & Hellman

Helmholtz, Hermann von, 1821-94

A Ls s (2), 18 May & 5 Nov 1872. 3 pp, 8vo. Recipient unnamed. About a proposed lecture to be given at Cologne. With a photograph. hen Nov 12 (2533) DM440

— A Ls s (2), 11 & 13 Feb 1876. 5 pp, mostly 8vo. To the pbrs Paetel. Concerning corrections to an essay. Including 2 drawings. star Mar 26 (666) DM900

ALs, 12 Oct 1875. 1 p, 8vo. To an unnamed colleague. Arranging a meeting in Rome the next day. star Mar 26 (665) DM320

Hemingway, Ernest, 1899-1961

[A cyclostyled copy of Peter Viertel's revised temporary script for the film The Sun Also Rises, 25 June 1956, 150 pp, 4to, in red mor bdg, with revisions in Viertel's hand & extensive autograph annotations & comments by Hemingway on c.50 pp, sold at S on 21 July 1992, lot 134, for £9,500 to Plunket.]

Collection of 4 A Ls s & 7 Ls s, 21 Dec 1935 to 5 Feb 1940. 22 pp, 4to. To Abner Green (1 to Paul Harris). About his literary endeavors & recipient's fight for asylum for political refugees. P Dec 12 (47) $22,500

— Collection of 35 A Ls s & Ls s, 20 Feb 1948 to 31 Dec 1958. About 70 pp, mostly 4to. To Peter Viertel (2 to his wife Deborah Kerr). Discussing mutual writing interests, commenting on friends, reporting about his activities, etc. S July 21 (133) £3,000 [Houle]

A Ls s (2), 28 June 1949 & 23 July 1954. 2 pp, 4to. To C. W. Wilcox at Scribner's. Ordering books. CNY June 9 (90) $2,000

ALs, 1 Dec 1929. 1 p, 4to. To Mrs. Wolfenstein. Thanking for a letter of praise. CNY June 9 (89) $1,300

— 24 June 1952. 1 p, 4to. To C. W. Wilcox at Scribner's. Ordering books & referring to his own new book. Illus in cat. CNY June 9

(91) $3,800

— 18 Sept 1955. 2 pp, 8vo. To C. W. [Wilcox]. Ordering books. On verso of calendar leaves. sg Feb 27 (88) $1,600

— 5 Nov 1958. 3 pp, 8vo. To Wendell Palmer. About various book orders. Illus in cat. sg Feb 27 (89) $3,800

Ls, 27 Oct 1955. 1 p, 4to. To C. W. Wilcox at Scribner's. Ordering books. CNY June 9 (92) $1,400

— 15 Jan 1961. 2 pp, 8vo. To Roy P. Gates. Sending his son's address. CNY Dec 5 (247) $900

Autograph sentiment, sgd, 1936. 3 by 1.5 inches (card). Expressing good wishes. Framed with a photograph. Dar Feb 13 (200) $750

Hendrix, James Marshall ("Jimi"), 1942-70

Autograph Ms, diary, with entries for 19 to 23 Mar, 28 & 29 Mar, & 1, 2 & 7 Aug 1968. 5 by 7.5 inches. Including private observations & feelings regarding friends, activities relating to his concert tour, etc. P Dec 17 (477) $4,000

— Autograph Ms, essay, As I looked into my crystal ball; [c.1968]. 6 pp, 4to. On airline letterhead. Illus in cat. P Dec 17 (394) $3,000

— Autograph Ms, essay, New Drylands, [c.1969]. 8 pp, 8vo. In green ball point pen. P Dec 17 (387) $3,000

— Autograph Ms, financial notes regarding his concert tour in America, 1968. 4 pp, size not stated. Illus in cat. P Dec 17 (463) $2,000

— Autograph Ms, list of 26 songs for records, [c.1970]. 3 pp, 8vo. Illus in cat. P Dec 17 (385) $3,250

— Autograph Ms, lyrics for the song Trashman, [1969]. 13 pp, 8vo. On hotel letterhead. P Dec 17 (397) $3,500

— Autograph Ms, lyrics for the song Room Full of Mirrors, [1968]. Framed with a photograph, 28 by 18 inches. With orig note pad including notes & drawings. Illus in cat. P Dec 17 (444) $8,000

— Autograph Ms, lyrics for the song Imagination, [c.1969]. 2 pp, size not stated. On hotel letterhead. P Dec 17 (471) $1,200

— Autograph Ms, movie script treatment, Moondust; [1969-70]. 33 pp, size not stated. With typescript detailing complete film treatment, 30 pp. P Dec 17 (479) $15,000

— Autograph Ms, poetical text, Forget of my Name; [c.1968]. 1 p, size not stated. On hotel letterhead. Illus in cat. P Dec 17 (392) $800

— Autograph Ms, thoughts in prose, beginning "Sticks and stones can't break my soul..."; [c.1969]. 1 leaf, 4to. P Dec 17 (481) $700

ANs, [May 1969]. On fragment of a sheet, framed, 18 by 17 inches. To [Roland Robinson]. Giving his phone no & address. Illus in cat. P Dec 17 (439) $1,000

Ds, Dec 1966. 2 pp, size not stated. Contract with Pall Mall Ltd. regarding rights to the song Stone Free. Illus in cat. P Dec 17 (390) $2,500

— 1968. Receipt, in Swedish. Framed with concert tickets, 16 by 15 inches. Illus in cat P Dec 17 (445) $900

Autograph sentiment, sgd, [c.1967]. Framed with L.P. cover, 28 by 17 inches. Inscr to Jeanette. Also sgd & inscr by others. Illus in cat. P Dec 17 (453) $2,000

Group photograph, [n.d.]. Jimi Hendrix Experience promotional postcard, sgd & inscr to Sue on verso, with his address. Illus in cat. P Dec 17 (459) $1,200

Ptd photograph, sgd & inscr, [1969]. In Woodstock movie program, size not stated. P Dec 17 (447) $600

Signature, [1968]. 13 by 8.5 inches. On xerox copy of a drawing by Hendrix. P Dec 17 (449) $400

— Anr, [1968]. On port drawing in record album, framed, 25 by 13 inches. Also sgd by others. Illus in cat. P Dec 17 (450) $1,800

Henry, Patrick, 1736-99

ALs, 20 Aug 1796. 2 pp, 4to. To his daughter Anne Rouse. Explaining that he disagrees with some members of Congress but has not changed his political principles. Framed. Illus in cat. sup May 9 (379) $3,400

Ls, 20 Oct 1785. 1 p, 8vo. To "Gentlemen". Ptd circular regarding returns of disabled persons receiving pensions. Illus in cat. sup May 9 (378) $2,500

ADs, 23 Mar 1788. 1 p, 4to. Receipt by Richard Allen for 2 guineas from P. Henry. Sgd by Henry in text. sg Sept 12 (113) $425

Ds, 8 Feb 1786. 1 p, folio. Land grant in Montgomery County. Dar Oct 10 (204) $1,000

— 8 Apr 1786. 1 p, folio. Land grant. R Mar 7 (190) $1,200

Cut signature, 19 May 1784. 12mo. Cut from a receipt book. R June 13 (160) $600

Henry VIII, King of England, 1491-1547

Ls, 14 July 1524. 1 p, 4to. To Antonioto Adorno, Duke of Genoa. Thanking for his dealings with Cardinal Wolsey & his secretaries Richard Pace & Bryan Tuke. Illus in cat. pn June 11 (46) £5,000 [Wilson]

Ds, 30 Dec 1546. 1 p, vellum, 270mm by 335mm. Life grant to John Gate of offices & estates in Southwark formerly belonging to the Duke of Suffolk, & elsewhere. With annotations in a later hand on attached vellum leaf. C June 24 (369) £2,900 [Browning]

Henschke, Alfred, 1890-1928. See: Klabund, 1890-1928

Hensel, Fanny, 1805-47

Autograph music, song, Die fruehen Graeber, Op. 9, no 4, to a text by Klopstock, [n.d.]. 2 pp, 4to, on blue paper. Notated in black & gold ink on four systems of 3 staves each. Including headpiece illus in pen & ink wash. Illus in cat. S May 29 (588) £2,300 [Haas]

— Autograph music, song in G minor to Heine's poem Der Sturm, scored for soprano & piano; [n.d.]. 4 pp, 4to. 54 bars, sgd & inscr to Maria Stantzler. Gottschalk collection. C Dec 16 (424) £3,800 [Rosenthal]
See also: Mendelssohn-Bartholdy, Felix

Hensel, Wilhelm, 1794-1861

Autograph Ms, poem, beginning "Muendlich hiess es ja...", [n.d.]. 10 lines, sgd. star Mar 27 (898) DM400

Series of 3 A Ls s, 18 June to 17 July 1838. 3 pp, 8vo. To R. A. & A. Solly. Regarding meetings. star Mar 27 (899) DM400

Henson, Jim, 1936-90

Photograph, sgd, [n.d.]. 8 by 10 inches. With puppets. Dar Apr 9 (225) $275

Signature, on front cover of program for World Science Fiction Convention, 1 to 5 Sept 1983. 4to. wa Oct 19 (196) $80

Henson, Matthew Alexander, 1866-1955

Signature, [1948]. On philatelic envelope honoring Edmund Kennedy. Dar June 11 (107) $650

Henze, Hans Werner

Autograph quotation, 7 eighth notes, sgd, 20 Jan 1984. 1 p, folio. star Mar 27 (1030) DM320

Hepburn, Katharine

Ls, 15 July 1987. 1 p, 8vo. Recipient unnamed. Stating that she does not sign photos. Matted with a photograph. R Mar 7 (169) $160

Ds, 15 May 1934. 2 pp, 4to. Contract with RKO Studios; carbon copy. wa Oct 19 (10) $250

— 16 Dec 1948. 1 p, 4to. Contract for a radio version of the play The Game of Love and Death. Dar June 11 (223) $200

Heraldic Manuscripts

Ms, A Catalogue of the five Conquerors of this Island and theire Armes..., 1606. 13 leaves, vellum, 180mm by 140mm. Late 17th-cent English red mor gilt. With 13 full-page armorials in gold & colors. C June 24 (65) £1,400 [Finch]

— Ms, genealogical scroll of the Vander Gheenste, Mer-Roels & Van Steelandt families, 1551 to 1660. Vellum, 69cm by 80cm; framed. In Dutch. Including 3 large & 88 smaller coats-of-arms. b June 22 (141) £180

— Ms, William Fox, His Ms Book of Coats of Armes, Crests &c. ..., [c.1759-70]. 105 pp, 4to, in contemp vellum. Including c.50 coats-of-arms in pen, ink & watercolor, & 3 pen-&-ink sketches. Ck Sept 6 (73) £130

— BERKELEY FAMILY. - Ms, illuminated pedigree prepared for William Lord Berkeley of Stratton, 1697. Vellum scroll, c.13.5 feet by 32.75 inches. Including more than 200 coats-of-arms. S Dec 12 (266) £700 [Heraldry Today]

— RADETZKY, JOHANN VON. - Ms, Der Herold der Ostsee-Provinzen...[Riga, 1864-65]. 892 pp in 2 vols, 290mm by 210mm. Contemp half lea bdg. Including 292 paintings of coats-of-arms of Baltic nobility; incomplete. HH May 12 (13) DM5,500

— WODEHOUSE OF KIMBERLEY. - Ms, illuminated pedigree of the family of Sir Philip Wodehouse & related families, [17th cent]. Vellum, 10.5 feet by 24 inches. Including emblazoned coats-of-arms. With related material. S Dec 12 (300) £600 [Fiske]
See also: Ernst von Bayern, 1583-1612

Herbert, Victor, 1859-1924

ALs, 17 Apr 1922. 1 p, 4to. To "My dear little Misses". Regretting he will not be able to attend a performance. Dar Feb 13 (201) $120

Ds, 11 July 1908. 1 p, 8vo. Receipt for payment for music at Willow Grove Park. Dar Oct 10 (205) $100

Herder, Johann Gottfried von, 1744-1803

Autograph Ms, poem, Das Alter; [n.d.]. 1 p, 4to. 10 lines. star Mar 26 (234) DM2,400

ALs, [4 Mar 1784]. 1 p, 8vo. To Friedrich Heinrich Jacobi. Expressing condolences on the death of his wife. star Mar 26 (236) DM2,000

— 29 Oct 1796. 1 p, 4to. To Freiherr von Breitenbach. Inquiring about autograph material by Lessing. Illus in cat. S Dec 5 (518) £850 [Rosenthal]

Hermine, Consort of Emperor Wilhelm II of Germany, 1887-1947

Series of 3 Ls s, 1940 to 1944. 5 pp, 4to & 8vo. To Ada Haseloff. Mostly about her husband. star Mar 27 (1319) DM650

Ls, 17 Dec 1933. 1 p, folio. Recipient unnamed. Thanking for congratulations on her birthday. star Mar 27 (1318) DM340

Herschel, Sir John Frederick William, 1792-1871

ALs, 25 June 1841. 3 pp, 4to. To Col. Sabine. Introducing the Spanish astronomer S. Montajo. Including ANs by recipient at foot. bba May 28 (174) £70 [Kunkler]

Herschel, Sir William, 1738-1822

Autograph Ms, "Observations of the 71 of the Connois", account of a cluster of stars observed 1783 to 1807. 1 p, 8vo. Framed with engraved port. Dar Feb 13 (202) $225

Hertz, Heinrich, 1857-94

ALs, 17 July 1892. 1 p, 8vo. Recipient unnamed. Agreeing to a suggestion. star Mar 26 (669) DM1,100

Herwegh, Georg, 1817-75

ALs, 7 Nov [c.1862]. 7 pp, 8vo. To Ernst Dohm. Discussing Swiss politics. star Mar 26 (238) DM2,200

ANs, 31 May 1845. 1 p, 8vo. To Mr. Brockhaus. Ordering books. star Mar 26 (237) DM380

Herz, Henriette, 1764-1847

ALs, Dec [1818]. 2 pp, 8vo. To Nanna Arndt. About her stay in Rome. Sgd H. star Mar 26 (239) DM1,900

Herz, Markus, 1747-1803

ALs, 28 Apr 1797. 1 p, 4to. To [a pbr?]. Concerning his port. star Mar 26 (240) DM570

Herzl, Theodor, 1860-1904

Ls, [5?] May 1887. 1 p, 8vo. To Paul Reichard. Inviting contributions to his journal. star Mar 27 (1437) DM1,900

Hess, Rudolf, 1894-1987

Photograph, sgd, [25 July 1936]. Postcard. With secretarial letter of transmittal. HH May 13 (1963) DM500

Hesse, Hermann, 1877-1962

Autograph Ms, 12 poems, [c.1930s]. 12 bifolia, 225mm by 167mm. With 13 watercolor illusts; dedicated to Bryher. Illus in cat. P June 17 (233) $6,500

— Autograph Ms, story, Der Weltverbesserer, [ptd 1911]. 73 pp, 8vo, on rectos only, in blue half lea bdg. Fair copy of 1st version. star Mar 26 (241) DM26,000

Original drawing, view of the Casa Camuzzi, in watercolor over pencil, 12 Aug 1930. 253mm by 194mm. Sgd. star Mar 26 (247) DM18,000

Autograph transcript, 12 poems, [c.July] 1949. 24 pp, 4to. Including 12 pen-&-ink drawings & watercolored tp; sgd on tp. star Mar 26 (243) DM15,000

— Autograph transcript, poem, Blume, Baum und Vogel, [n.d.]. 1 p, 4to. With watercolored pen-&-ink drawing. star Mar 26 (244) DM2,600

— Autograph transcript, poem, Trost, sgd; [25 July 1943]. 2 pp, 8vo. 4 stanzas. FD Dec 3 (1431) DM520

Typescript, poem, Dienst; [4 Aug 1942]. 2 pp, 8vo. Sgd. With a photograph. HH May 13 (1964) DM260

Typescript carbon copy, poem, Seifenblasen, 14 to 16 Jan 1937. 1 p, 8vo. Including ANs to Dr. Feilke at bottom. star Mar 26 (242) DM220

Collection of ALs, 2 Ls s & autograph postcard, sgd, 15 Feb 1935 to 2 Jan 1944. 6 pp, 8vo, & card. To the bookseller A. Buerdeke. Giving permission to use his name in an advertisement, inquiring about an apprenticeship for his nephew, etc. star Mar 26 (249) DM420

— Collection of ALs, Ls, 5 typescripts, sgd (3 carbon copies), & photograph, sgd, 1935 to 1949. 9 pp, 8vo, & 85mm by 115mm. To Erich Kroker. About his health problems, his admiration for Thomas Mann, etc. Typescripts of poems. HH Nov 6 (2054) DM1,300

— Collection of 3 A Ls s, AL, 8 Ls s, Ls, 10 postcards, sgd (5 autograph), & typescript, sgd, 28 July 1939 to 15 July 1958. 37pp, mostly 8vo. To Kitty de Josselin de Jong. Personal correspondence, & 4 poems with watercolor. With related material. C June 24 (370) £1,800 [Tenschert]

ALs, 21 Apr 1929. 2 pp, 8vo. To Herr Rath. Stating conditions for a lecture at Regensburg. HH Nov 6 (2052) DM450

Collection of Ls & 3 postcards, sgd (1 autograph), [12 Sept 1909 to 11 June 1938]. 4 pp, 8vo. To the booksellers A. Buerdeke. About some publishing matters. star Mar 26 (245) DM320

— Collection of 7 Ls s, & 2 typescripts, sgd, 1943 to 1962. 13 pp, 4to & 8vo. To Erich Kroker. About his work & publications. Typescripts of poems, 1 with watercolor at head. HH Nov 6 (2053) DM1,700

Letter, 15 Nov 1951. 2 pp, 4to. To Thomas Mann. Carbon copy, expressing satisfaction about Mann's comments on the publication of Hesse's letters. Including autograph postscript, sgd, addressed to a lawyer. FD Dec 3 (1432) DM280

Autograph postcard, sgd, [19 Oct 1912]. To Boerries von Muenchhausen. Informing him of the date of a lecture in Weimar. With related material. HN Nov 28 (1719) DM420

— [7 Feb 1950]. 1 p, 8vo. Recipient unnamed. Referring to the death of his sister. HN June 26 (922) DM420

Heuss, Theodor, 1884-1963

Ls, 9 Sept 1949. 1 p, 4to. To a former student. Mentioning his literary & political activities. HN Nov 28 (1723) DM260

— 19 June 1954. 1 p, folio. To Hermann Jung. Declining to write a contribution to a special issue of a journal. star Mar 27 (1440) DM620

Hewitt, John, 1807-78

Autograph Ms, Journal of a Tour thro Belgium, 26 June to 8 July 1839. 28 pp, 4to; interleaved with 50 leaves illus with pen-&-ink sketches, engravings & woodcuts; in contemp half calf album. Account of his travels with J. P. Dyott. C June 24 (371) £1,000 [Royal Armouries]

Heydrich, Reinhard, 1904-42

Ds, 1 Mar 1936. 2 pp, 4to. Personnel record for SS member Julius Plaichinger. Dar Apr 9 (226) $550

Heyne, Christian Gottlob, 1729-1812

A Ls s (2), 6 June 1795 & 24 Aug 1807. 6 pp, 8vo. To Friederike Lohmann. About her problems with booksellers & the situation at Goettingen. star Mar 26 (670) DM750

Heyse, Paul, 1830-1914

Autograph Ms, poem, beginning "Dem Mann, der um des Maerzen Mitte..."; 17 Mar 1890. 1 p, 4to. 32 lines, sgd. HH May 13 (1965) DM420

Higgons, Theophilus, 1578?-1659 —& Others

Ds, 27 Nov 1637. 1 sheet of vellum, size not stated. The Ancient Customs of the Parrish of Huntington als. Hunton in the County of Kente...; deed listing tithes, rights of pensioners, charges for marriages, burying, etc. Also sgd by Christopher Crispe & 12 others. pn Nov 14 (15) £380 [Quaritch]

Hille, Peter, 1854-1904

Autograph Ms, aphorisms, [n.d.]. 3 pp, 4to. Mtd. star Mar 26 (255) DM480

ALs, [June 1898]. 4 pp, 8vo. Recipient unnamed. Asking for his help in obtaining financial aid from the Schiller Foundation. star Mar 26 (256) DM600

Hiller, Johann Adam, 1728-1804

ALs, 30 Aug 1781. 2 pp, 4to. To [Friedrich Koepken]. Planning concerts in Magdeburg. star Mar 27 (1032) DM1,300

Himmler, Heinrich, 1900-45

ANs, 4 Nov 1937. 1 p, 12mo. Recipient unnamed. Asserting that a child is being coached by a private tutor as well as by himself & his wife. Illus in cat. Dar June 11 (225) $425

Ns, [1936]. 1 p, 12mo. Recipient unnamed. Ptd message of thanks for congratulations on his appointment as Chief of the German Police; with autograph subscription. Illus in cat. Dar Apr 9 (227) $950

Ds, 31 Jan 1944. 2 pp, 4to. Investigation concerning the ancestry of Bronislawa Schwertfeger. Also sgd by Wilhelm Stuckart & Ernst Kaltenbrunner. Dar June 11 (224) $750

Photograph, sgd, [3 Apr 1934]. Postcard. With secretarial letter of transmittal. HH May 13 (1966) DM500

Hindemith, Paul, 1895-1963

Autograph Ms, instructions for playing his Martinslied, Op. 45, no 5; [1928/29]. 1 p, 4to (2 parts glued together). Sgd. star Mar 27 (1033) DM520

Hindenburg, Paul von, 1847-1934

Collection of 2 A Ls s & Ls, 4 Nov 1886 to 1919. To his "comrade" Becker & Mrs. Becker (1). Reporting about his activities & common friends, & expressing condolences. star Mar 27 (1442) DM550

ALs, 15 Jan 1873. 4 pp, 8vo. To his sister-in-law Lina. Family letter. Dar Feb 13 (203) $140

— 12 Apr 1915. 1 p, 4to. To [Gen. von Mueller]. Expressing thanks. star Mar 27 (1444) DM420

Series of 7 Ls s, 10 Apr 1926 to 22 Mar 1932. 8 pp, folio. To Richard Leutheusser. Official letters to the Minister-President of Thuringia. With related material. star Mar 27 (1446a) DM1,300

Ds, 1 June 1934. 1 p, folio. Military appointment for Curt Kroecher. Countersgd by von Blomberg. star Mar 27 (1446b) DM320

Hirohito, Emperor of Japan, 1901-89

Ls, 1936. 2 pp, 4to. To the President of Honduras. Announcing the appointment of Yoshiatsu Hori as envoy to Honduras. Countersgd by Foreign Minister Koki Hirota. With trans. Dar Dec 26 (206) $7,000

Hirohito, Emperor of Japan, 1901-89 —& Nagako Kuni, Empress of Hirohito of Japan

[A state port photograph of each, sgd, [c.1926], 11.25 by 8 inches (images), in matching silver frames, sold at wd on 12 June 1992, lot 316, for $8,250.]

Hirsch, Samson Raphael, 1808-88

ALs, 1884. 1 p, 4to. To the Rabbi of Nikolsburg. Enclosing his exegesis to the Book of Psalms. sg Dec 19 (109) $850

His Comets. See: Haley, Bill & His Comets

Hitchcock, Alfred, 1899-1980

Ls, 6 Sept 1979. 1 p, 4to. To Elsie Randolph. About his wife's health, & wondering about the possibility of a knighthood. Dar Aug 6 (17) $350

Autograph endorsement, sgd, 23 Feb 1960. 1 p, 4to. On a letter from Gabor Rona requesting consent to use a photograph; giving permission. Matted with a photograph. Illus in cat. sup Oct 15 (1313) $300

Self-caricature, sgd, [n.d.]. 5.5 by 3 inches (card). Profile. Dar June 11 (226) $550

Hitler, Adolf, 1889-1945

Original drawings, (2), pencil sketch for a theatre at Bayreuth & sketch of floor plan, [26 June 1936]. 1 p, 4to. With note of authenticity, sgd, by Albert Speer, 3 Jan 1979. Illus in cat. Dar Apr 9 (228) $2,250

— Original drawings, (3), pencil sketches of a bell tower & of 2 bridges, [1934]. 2 pp, 12mo (card). Illus in cat. Dar Apr 9 (229) $1,100

Original drawing, watercolor of a mansion in a rural setting, sgd, inscr to Gen. Schleicher on verso & dated 1922. 130mm by 160mm. Framed. HH Nov 6 (2056) DM12,000

Christmas card, sgd, 23 Dec 1930. 80mm by 140mm. Recipients unnamed. b June 22 (110) £300

Photograph, sgd, [1933]. 3.5 by 5.5 inches. With letter of transmittal. Dar Dec 26 (209) $1,300

— Anr, [n.d.]. 4.25 by 5.75 inches. Bust port. b&b Feb 19 (153) $650

— Anr, [n.d.]. 5 by 7 inches. Dar Dec 26 (208) $2,000

— Anr, [n.d.]. Postcard. Sgd in pencil. HH May 13 (1969) DM600

— JUNGE, GERTRAUD. - Ls & typescript, 6 Mar 1980. 22 pp, mostly 4to. To Herr Schneider. Responding to questions about Hitler, Eva Braun, his associates, events in Hitler's bunker, etc. Dar June 11 (196) $600

Hodges, Gil, 1924-72

Signature, [n.d.]. On ptd charcoal bust drawing by Volpe, 8 by 10 inches. Dar Dec 26 (61) $170

Hoelty, Ludwig Christoph Heinrich, 1748-76

Autograph Ms, poem, An einen Canarienvogel, [1772]. 2 pp, 8vo. 7 four-line stanzas. star Mar 26 (273) DM7,000

Hoelz, Max, 1889-1933

ALs, 4 Dec 1927. 6 pp, folio. To Hedwig. From prison, about efforts for a retrial, & insisting that there is no woman in Europe who can understand him. star Mar 27 (1448) DM1,500

Hoffmann, Ernst Theodor Amadeus, 1776-1822

ALs, [1817?]. 1 p, 7cm by 12 cm, cut from larger leaf. To [his pbr G. A. Reimer?]. Fragment, subscription & postscript only, referring to 2 stories & his current work on a fairy tale. star Mar 26 (257) DM1,400

Hoffmann, Friedrich, 1660-1742

Ls, 15 Mar 1694. 4 pp, 4to. To Philipp Mueller. Explaining his basic opinions about medicine, discussing medicinal plants, etc. In Latin. star Mar 26 (671) DM700

Hoffmann, Josef, 1870-1956

Collection of 2 A Ls s & photograph, sgd, 22 Dec 1948 & [n.d.]. 3 pp, 4to, & 8vo. To an unnamed lady. About his situation in Vienna, making plans to travel, etc. star Mar 27 (901) DM420

Hoffmann von Fallersleben, August Heinrich, 1798-1874

Autograph Ms, poem, Trinklied, 9 Mar [n.y.]. 3 pp, 8vo. 3 nine-line stanzas, sgd HvF. star Mar 26 (260) DM1,300

Autograph transcript, 3 poems, An der See, Im Flachland, & Jugend im Alter, 16 July 1871 to 5 Oct 1873. 10 pp, 4to. Inscr to an unnamed friend. star Mar 26 (259) DM1,250

— Autograph transcript, poem, Deutschland, Deutschland ueber alles, 8 May 1843. 1 p, 8vo. 1st stanza, sgd. 1 line differing from orig version. Mtd. star Mar 26 (258) DM8,800

Collection of ALs & autograph Ms, 28 July 1855. 2 pp, 8vo. Recipient unnamed. Sending a poem (included; quatrain, sgd). Mtd. HH May 13 (1970) DM800

ALs, 17 Apr 186[7]. 2 pp, 8vo. To Carl Ruempler. Regarding the publication of his autobiography. star Mar 26 (261) DM500

Hofmannsthal, Hugo von, 1874-1929

Autograph Ms, draft for the libretto of Der Rosenkavalier, Act II, duet Sophie & Octavian, [June 1909]. 1 p, folio. 12 lines each. With autograph Ms by Richard Strauss on verso, draft for Rosenkavalier, Act II, discussion between Ochs, Sophie & Octavian. star Mar 26 (262) DM10,000

— Autograph Ms, poem, beginning "Nicht zu der Sonne fruehen Reise...", [ptd 1911]. 1 p, 4to. 8 lines, sgd H.H. star Mar 26 (263) DM3,000

Collection of ALs & Ls, 23 Sept 1928 & 9 Jan 1929. 2 pp, 4to. Recipient unnamed. About his use of antique sources for his plays. With related material. star Mar 26 (267) DM1,700

A Ls s (2), [13 Apr 1922] & 10 Feb 1924. 6 pp, 4to & 8vo. To Rudolf Kassner. Praising Kassner's new book, & commenting on his contribution to a festschrift. star Mar 26 (264) DM5,500

ALs, 16 Jan 1894. 2 pp, 8vo. To the Ed of the journal Simplizissimus. Offering a contribution. HH Nov 6 (2057) DM400

— 12 Apr [19]18. 1 p, 8vo. Recipient unnamed. Expressing thanks. On hotel letterhead. Mtd with a port. JG Sept 27 (366) DM460

— [1922]. 2 pp, 8vo. To his daughter Christiane. Requesting that she contact Felix Somary, convey a message to Max Pallenberg, etc. On concluding leaf of a letter by his wife. star Mar 26 (266) DM850

— 21 Aug [n.y.]. 1 p, 4to. Recipient unnamed. Sending a letter by Richard Strauss. star Mar 26 (268) DM370

Hofmeister, Friedrich, 1782-1864

Series of 14 A Ls s, 1813 to 1825. 21 pp, 8vo. To his son Adolph Moritz. Regarding family affairs & business matters. With related family papers. HH May 13 (1971) DM2,100

Holden, William, 1918-81

Ds, 20 Jan 1947. 1 p, 4to. Contract with The Theatre Guild Radio Division. Dar Feb 13 (205) $100

Holiday, Billie, 1915-59

Ds, 23 Dec 1953. 3.75 by 6 inches. United States Passport No 15460, sgd Eleanor G. McKay (twice) & Billie Holiday. Illus in cat. P Dec 17 (303) $2,500

— 3 Apr 1954. 1 p, 4to. Authorization to Bill Robinson to deduct monies from her salary at the Oasis Club. Illus in cat. P Dec 17 (302) $400

Holliday, Judy, 1921-65

Ls, 28 Mar 1958. 1 p, 4to. To The Theatre Guild, Bells are Ringing Company. Confirming the extension of a contract. Dar June 11 (229) $120

Ds, 28 Mar 1958. 1 p, 4to. Confirmation of an extension of a contract with The Theatre Guild Radio Division. Dar Feb 13 (206) $250

Hollis, Thomas, 1720-74

A Ls s (2), 5 Nov 1763 & 15 Jan 1765. 2 pp, 4to. To Catharine Macaulay. Thanking for the 1st & the 2d vol of her History of England. With retained draft of a letter from Macaulay to Hollis, 9 Jan 1769, 2 pp. pn June 11 (10) £1,500 [Quaritch]

Holly, Charles Hardin ("Buddy"), 1936-59

Autograph postcard, sgd, [21 Aug 1952]. To his sister. Reporting about his trip to Colorado. Framed with a photograph. Illus in cat. P Dec 17 (524) $1,000

Holmes, Oliver Wendell, 1809-94

ALs, 21 Jan 1856. 2 pp, 8vo. Recipient unnamed. Thanking for a gift. sg Sept 12 (114) $90

— 27 May [n.y.]. 1 p, 12mo. To "little Gertie". Sending his autograph. Dar Feb 13 (207) $100

— 7 Oct [n.y.]. 1 p, 16mo. To [E. P.] Whipple. Thanking for his new vol. sg Sept 12 (118) $55

Autograph quotation, quatrain, beginning "Enough of speech!..."; 25 July 1868. 1 p, 32mo. Sgd. sg Feb 27 (90) $120

— Anr, quatrain, beginning "A few can touch the magic string..."; 17 Apr 1878. 1 p, 32mo. Sgd. Mtd with a photograph. sg Sept 12 (115) $375

Holmes, Oliver Wendell, 1841-1935

ALs, 9 June 1931. 1 p, 8vo. To Francis D. Donoghue. Expressing thanks. Dar Dec 26 (210) $500

Holtei, Karl von, 1798-1880

Autograph Ms, poem, Die Wuensche, [n.d.]. 2 pp, 8vo. 40 lines, sgd. Trimmed. star Mar 26 (269) DM320

ALs, 4 Jan 1872. 4 pp, 8vo. To [Paul Lindau]. Responding to a request for contributions to the journal Die Gegenwart. star Mar 26 (270) DM560

Ls, 28 Jan 1872. 3 pp, 8vo. Recipient unnamed. Ptd letter of thanks, with autograph postscript, sgd, thanking for a port. star Mar 26 (271) DM200

Holz, Arno, 1863-1929

ALs, 7 Oct 1916. 1 p, 4to. To Georg Reicke. Sending a copy of his Phantasus. star Mar 26 (274) DM220

Homer, Winslow, 1836-1910

Signature, [8 Mar 1900]. On envelope addressed in anr hand. Dar Apr 9 (230) $200

Honegger, Arthur, 1892-1955

ALs, [c.1925]. 1 p, 8vo. To Georges Dandelot. About his tour in Belgium & the singer Mme Deboute. HN Nov 28 (1728) DM300

— [c.June 1939]. 1 p, 4to. To the director of the theater at Basel. Listing works that might be suitable for performance. star Mar 27 (1034) DM560

Hoover, Herbert, 1874-1964

ALs, 13 Feb 1949. 1 p, 4to. To Peggy Fabian. Encouraging note to a child. Illus in cat. sup Oct 15 (1623) $1,650

— 7 Jan 1954. 1 p, 8vo. To Wallace B. Amsbary. Sending his autograph. Illus in cat. Dar Aug 6 (171) $2,250

— [n.d.]. 1 p, 8vo. To Munn. Giving instructions about some business matters. Framed with a port. Dar June 11 (230) $650

Series of 4 Ls s, 16 June 1943 to 17 Jan 1947. 4 pp, 4to. To D. M. Reynolds. Discussing politics. sg Sept 12 (119) $425

Ls, 28 Feb 1925. 1 p, 4to. To Gertrude Lane. Concerning plans for a women's series. sup Oct 15 (1619) $200

— 20 Dec 1926. 1 p, 8vo. To John Van Oosten. Thanking for cooperation during the year. Matted with engraved port. Dar June 11 (231) $120

— 12 Aug 1933. 1 p, 8vo. To Margaret Blackman. Thanking for birthday wishes. Matted with ptd port. Dar Aug 6 (172) $100

— 8 Aug 1934. 2 pp, 4to. To George Olmsted. Worrying about the future of the Republican Party & party organization. Illus in cat. sup Oct 15 (1621) $1,000

— 11 Jan 1950. 1 p, 4to. To John Black. Thanking for a communication. Dar Apr 9 (231) $110

— 18 Aug 1955. 1 p, 4to. To Paul Dent. Thanking for a special Ed of a newspaper. wa Oct 19 (299) $60

— 13 Feb 1959. 2 pp, 4to. To Herbert S. Bailey. Angrily commenting on the rejection by Princeton Press of his publication project on relief activities. sup Oct 15 (1624) $500

— [n.d.]. 1 p, size not stated. Recipient unknown. Commenting on the Russian dumping of wheat on the European market. Trimmed at head. Dar Dec 26 (213) $225

Ds, 5 Mar 1932. 1 p, folio. Appointment of Hannibal Hopkins as postmaster. sup Oct 15 (1620) $385

Menu, sgd, American Legion reception, NY, 20 Sept 1937. Size not stated. Also sgd by 15 others. R June 13 (180) $70

Photograph, sgd, [n.d.]. 8 by 10 inches. By Harris & Ewing. sup Oct 15 (1625) $150

Photograph, sgd & inscr, 20 Dec 1925. 8.25 by 11.25 inches. Dar Oct 10 (207) $190

— Anr, [n.d.]. 9.75 by 7.5 inches. Inscr to Howard A. Engel. Dar Apr 9 (232) $110

— Anr, [n.d.]. 9 by 7.5 inches. Inscr to Peter Hoguet. Framed. wd Dec 12 (319) $150

Hoover, J. Edgar, 1895-1972

Ls s (2), 1937 & 1941. 2 pp, 4to. Recipient unnamed. About the fingerprint classification of twins, & thanking for information. Dar June 11 (233) $150

Photograph, sgd & inscr, 10 June 1969. 4to. Framed. wa Oct 19 (129) $80

Hopkins, Stephen, Signer from Rhode Island

Ds, Nov 1755. 1 p, 6.25 by 3 inches. Pay order in favor of Thomas Vernon. sup Oct 15 (1209) $420

— 22 Mar 1765. 1 p, 8vo. Fragment; sgd twice as Governor. Dar Oct 10 (210) $325

Hopkinson, Francis, Signer from New Jersey

ALs, 2 May 1785. 1 p, 4to. To Clement Biddle. Ordering him to deliver the sloop Fair Trader to Thomas Unthauk. Dar June 11 (234) $550

Ds s (2)2 Dec 1778 & 20 Sept 1779. 12mo. Continental sight drafts. R Mar 7 (193) $800

Ds, 12 Mar 1779. Size not stated. Sight draft, countersgd by John Lawrence. With a port. R June 13 (161) $320

— 12 Sept 1780. Size not stated. Sight draft, sgd as Treasurer of Loans. Partly ptd. rf Sept 21 (8) $300

Hopkinson, Joseph, 1770-1842

Ds, 9 May 1802. 2 pp, 4to. Power to examine witnesses in the case of Webster v. Hollins. Also sgd by others. Dar Feb 13 (212) $150

Horae B.M.V.

— [Paris?, c.1290-1300]. Of unstated use. 138 leaves, vellum (c.30 lacking), 135mm by 90mm. 16th-cent Italian calf gilt. In a small gothic hand. With several hundred 1- or 2-line initials & linefillers in red & blue on a gold background. Ownership inscr of Edmund Colborne & Sydney Cockerell. bba June 25 (114) £3,500 [Feldman]

— [Eastern? France, Metz?, late 14th cent]. Single leaf, vellum, 206mm by 166mm. With 16 lines of text, small illuminated initials & large historiated initial extending into 3-quarter ivyleaf bar border. Framed. S Dec 17 (20) £3,000 [Quaritch]

— The Hours of Agnes de Pont-Saint-Maxence. [Normandy, c.1405-10]. 383 leaves (3 blank, 3 lacking), vellum, 212mm by 163mm. Modern dark brown mor over wooden bds. In 2 sizes of a gothic liturgical hand. With illuminated borders throughout in a variety of styles, filled with animals, birds, grotesques, etc., 16 large initials enclosing coats-of-arms, 12 historiated initials, 12 Calendar miniatures, & 31 large miniatures in rectangular compartments above 3 lines of text. Illus in cat. S Dec 17 (77) £75,000 [Moore]

— [Paris?, 1410-20]. Of unidentified use. 225 leaves (8 lacking) & 4 flyleaves, vellum, 156mm by 105mm. Late 16th-cent French calf bdg. In a gothic liturgical hand. With 2- to 4-line initials throughout in pink & blue with white tracery on burnished gold grounds extending into borders with sprays of ivyleaves & bezants, some burnished gold bar borders, & 5 large miniatures within full borders. Worn. S Dec 17 (78) £6,500 [Neumann-Walter]

— [Picardy?, 1st half of 15th cent]. Use of Rome. 81 leaves (1 lacking) & 2 flyleaves, vellum, 112mm by 85mm. Dark red velvet over pastebds with late 14th-cent ivory on upper cover. In a small gothic liturgical hand. With 2-line initials throughout in burnished gold on red & blue cusped grounds, & 12 large illuminated initials with full borders in colors & gold. Some 16th-cent additions. S June 23 (84) £5,000 [Dunn]

— [Franche Comte, c.1440]. Use of Besancon. 153 leaves, vellum, 220mm by 150mm. Late 18th-cent French mottled calf gilt. In black & red ink in a fine textura script. Decorated only in 1 quire with initials & linefillers in colors & burnished gold, including 15 initials with floral ornaments etxtending into margins, & pen-drawn design for a miniature; blank spaces for initials & miniatures in all other quires. C Nov 27 (1) £13,000 [Sawyer]

— [Brittany?, c.1440]. Use of Paris. In Latin, with Calendar in French. 152 leaves, vellum, 196mm by 135mm. Late 15th-cent French blindstamped brown calf over wooden bds. In black ink in a gothic bookhand. With small illuminated initials throughout, 8 large miniatures with full-page borders, & 13 three-quarter borders. C Dec 16 (10) £8,000 [Byrne]

— [Bruges, c.1440]. Use of Rome. 221 leaves, vellum, 86mm by 69mm. 17th-cent gilt-tooled red calf bdg. In a liturgical minuscule bookhand. With bar borders on most pages in burnished gold, 15 fine illuminated initials within 3-quarter baguette borders surrounded by full borders of gold ivy leaves & acanthus inhabited by fabulous beasts, & 15 full-page arched miniatures within similar borders. All borders cropped. C June 24 (60) £15,000 [Mirandola]

— [Bruges, c.1440]. Single leaf, vellum, 192mm by 136mm. In a gothic liturgical hand. With large miniature in an arched compartment above 4-line illuminated initial & within full border of flowers & leaves. Illus in cat. S June 23 (14) £3,500 [Johnson]

— [Utrecht, c.1448]. Use of Utrecht. In Dutch. 229 leaves (3 blank) & flyleaf, vellum, 167mm by 115mm. Contemp panel-stamped bdg of polished calf over bevelled wooden bds. In a small gothic liturgical hand. With c.30 larger initials in highly burnished gold with full-length bar borders, 6 very large initials in leafy designs on highly burnished gold cusped panels, & 6 full-page miniatures within full borders. S Dec 17 (90) £70,000 [Tenschert]

— [France, c.1450]. 143 leaves (some lacking), vellum, 98mm by 76mm, in modern mor gilt by Riviere. In brown ink in a gothic textura. With small initials in gold on colored grounds with white tracery & 3 illuminated initials with marginal extensions forming 3-quarter borders. pn Nov 14 (240) £1,700 [Maggs]

— The Cornwallis Hours. [London?, c.1450]. Use of Rome. 260 leaves (4 blank, c.4 lacking) & 2 flyleaves, vellum, 197mm by 142mm. Modern quarter brown mor bdg. In 2 sizes of an English gothic liturgical hand by more than one scribe. With large illuminated initials throughout with borders of sprays of gold flowers on hairline stems, & large armorial initial & full illuminated bar border. S Dec 17 (66) £11,000 [Fogg]

— [Flanders or Hainault, c.1450]. Use of Tournai. In Latin, with prayers in Flemish. 114 leaves (2 blank), vellum, 121mm by 78mm. 18th-cent calf bdg. In a gothic liturgical hand. With 2-line initials throughout in burnished gold with full-length bar borders, & 9 very large illuminated initials with full borders in a variety of styles. S Dec 17 (86) £2,600 [Tolman]

— [Flanders?, c.1450]. Use of Rome. 42 leaves, vellum, 67mm by 53mm. Old blindstamped calf over wooden bds. In a very small gothic liturgical hand. With 2-line initials in burnished gold on red & blue grounds, & 3 very large initials in leafy designs on burnished gold panels with full borders of colored flowers & acanthus leaves. S Dec 17 (87) £1,500 [Ferrini]

— [Bruges?, c.1450]. Use of Sarum. 104 leaves, vellum, 166mm by 112mm. Late 17th-cent English black mor profusely gilt. In a gothic liturgical hand. With 5 large illuminated initials with full borders, 9 very large historiated initials with half-page borders, & 4 full-page miniatures within burnished gold rectangular compartments & full borders. Miniatures damaged. S Dec 17 (88) £6,200 [Schuster]

— [Eastern Netherlands, Zwolle?, c.1450]. Use of Utrecht. In Dutch. 162 leaves (2 lacking), vellum, 146mm by 102mm. 19th-cent blindstamped mottled sheep bdg. In a small gothic bookhand. With 30 illuminated initials, mostly with full-length bar borders sprouting into leaves in upper & lower margins, & 5 large illuminated initials (1 historiated) with 3-quarter borders of flowers & leaves on hairline stems. S Dec 17 (91) £5,000 [Forum]

— [Southern Netherlands, Bruges?, c.1450]. Use of Rome. 151 leaves (1 lacking), vellum, 92mm by 64mm. Late 19th-cent vellum gilt. In a small gothic liturgical hand. With small initials throughout in burnished gold on blue & pink grounds with white tracery, & 14 large illuminated initials with full illuminated borders. S June 23 (85) £3,400 [Sindelfinger]

— [Italy, 15th cent]. Use of Rome. 140 leaves, vellum, 105mm by 75mm. Old wooden bds with blindstamped lea spine & metal clasps. In 2 sizes of a rounded liturgical hand. With 7 large illuminated initials with leafy borders extending into all 4 margins, 2 large historiated initials (repainted or retouched), & 6 full-page miniatures on leaves originally left blank. Worn. S June 23 (95) £1,000 [Maggs]

— [Brittany?, c.1460]. Use of Rome. In Latin, with Calendar in French. 144 leaves (4 lacking) & 2 flyleaves, vellum, 179mm by 127mm. 17th-cent French mor gilt bdg. In a gothic textura. With 2- & 3-line initials in blue on gold ground with scrolled foliate decoration, outer panel borders of gold ivy leaves & painted flowers throughout, 3 full borders, & 10 large miniatures with full borders. Searles-Rowland collection. C June 24 (52) £11,000 [Simpson]

— [Bruges, c.1460]. Use of Sarum. 128 leaves, vellum, 212mm by 155mm. Extra red-brown mor of c.1890 by Riviere & Son. In a gothic textura. With numerous illuminated initials, 20 large historiated initals in gold & colors, & 20 large miniatures (4 lacking) in the style of William Vrelant above large illuminated initials & within full borders. HH Nov 5 (808) DM90,000

— [Netherlands, c.1460-70]. Use of Utrecht. 131 leaves (6 lacking), vellum, 185mm by 135mm. 18th-cent calf bdg. In a gothic textura. With numerous small initials & linefillers in gold & colors, & 8 large miniatures above large illuminated initials & within full foliate borders, partly incorporating angels & grotesques. HH May 12 (14) DM22,000

— [Paris, c.1460]. Use of Paris. In Latin, with Calendar in French. 283 leaves (1 blank, 1 lacking), vellum, 175mm by 114mm. Mid 18th-cent French olive mor gilt bdg. In 2 sizes of a gothic liturgical hand. With small illuminated initials & 3-quarter illuminated borders throughout, & 17 large miniatures in arched compartments above large initials & within full borders. S Dec 17 (67) £32,000 [Mirandola]

— [Hainault or Brabant, c.1460, & Flanders, c.1500]. Use of Rome. 150 leaves (8 lacking), vellum, 154mm by 110mm. Modern red velvet bdg. In a fine lettre batarde. With 13 three-quarter illuminated borders of flowers & leaves including snails, birds, etc., 25 Ghent/Bruges borders including 24 Calendar roundels, 20 historiated initials with three-quarter borders, & 10 large miniatures with full borders. S Dec 17 (89) £13,000 [Mirandola]

— [Bruges, c.1460]. Use of Sarum. 114 leaves (some lacking), vellum, 222mm by 152mm. Def contemp panel-stamped calf over bevelled wooden bds. In a gothic liturgical hand. With 17 very large illuminated initials with full borders (some borders cut away), 22 large historiated initials with 3-quarter illuminated borders, & 4 half-page miniatures with full borders. 1 miniature cut out; further inserted miniatures removed. S June 23 (88) £11,000 [Newman Walter]

— [1461?]. Use not stated. 198 leaves, vellum, 12mo. Old calf bdg. With illuminated initial, illuminated 3-quarter border, & 3 miniatures. wd June 12 (318) $8,000

— [Troyes, c.1465]. Use of Troyes. In Latin, with Calendar & prayers in French. 103 leaves (7 lacking), vellum, 198mm by 140mm. Contemp French blindstamped calf over wooden bds. In a gothic bookhand. With 2-line initials of burnished gold on colored grounds with sprays of gold ivy-leaves, & 11 large miniatures with full-page foliate borders. C Dec 16 (11) £9,000 [Mirandola]

— [Northern France, Rouen?, c.1465]. 2 leaves only, vellum, 170mm by 113mm. With 2 large miniatures above illuminated initials (1 historiated) & within full borders. S Dec 17 (37) £3,000 [Mirandola]

— [Southern Netherlands, Bruges?, 3d quarter of 15th cent]. Use of Sarum. 139 leaves (some lacking), vellum, 110mm by 73mm. Def late 17th-cent calf gilt. In a small gothic liturgical hand. With small initials throughout in burnished gold on red & blue grounds with white tracery, & 5 large initials (2 cut out) with full illuminated borders. S June 23 (86) £1,700 [Rouse]

— [Poitiers?, c.1470]. Use of Rome. In Latin, with Calendar in French. 117 leaves (incomplete), vellum, 123mm by 89mm. Late 17th-cent black mor gilt. In a skilful lettre batarde. With small illuminated initials throughout, panel borders on every page in designs of blue & gold acanthus leaves & colored flowers & fruit, 24 Calendar miniatures in borders, 25 large miniatures within full borders, & full-page coat-of-arms. S Dec 17 (79) £11,000 [Burden]

— [Rouen, c.1470-90]. Use of Lisieux. In Latin, with Calendar in French. 167 leaves (5 lacking) & flyleaf, vellum, 178mm by 120mm. French calf gilt bdg of c.1600. In several different gothic liturgical hands. With 2- to 4-line initials throughout in blue heightened with white enclosing flowers on panels of burnished gold, panel borders on almost every page in designs of flowers, fruit & leaves, & 8 large miniatures within full borders. S Dec 17 (80) £11,000 [Burden]

— [Netherlands, Delft?, c.1475]. Use of Utrecht. In Dutch. 200 leaves, vellum, 160mm by 115mm. Contemp calf rolled in blind. In a gothic liturgical hand. With 30 large initials in red & blue with marginal penwork decoration, & 6 very large initials with full or 3-quarter borders of penwork ornamented with gold & colored flowers, birds, scrolls, etc. bba June 25 (117) £7,000 [Quaritch]

— [Northern France or Flanders, c.1475]. Use of Tournai. In Latin, with Calendar & prayers in French. 88 leaves (1 lacking), vellum, 185mm by 130mm. Repaired 18th-cent calf gilt. In a regular gothic hand. With 7 large initials in red, blue & gold, & 4 very large miniatures each with 4-line initial including flowers, & borders in outer & lower margins of colored fruit & foliage. bba June 25 (118) £2,000 [Feldman]

— [Haarlem & Zwolle, c.1470-80]. Use of Utrecht. In Dutch. 165 leaves & flyleaf, vellum, 195mm by 143mm. Repaired contemp blindstamped brown calf over wooden bds. In a gothic textura. With 41 three- & four-line initials with outer baguette borders & upper & lower borders of sprays of gold petals, flowers & leaves, 8 larger initials within 3-quarter baguette frames & full borders containing angels, birds & grotesques, & 7 very fine full-page miniatures in arched compartments with full borders; illuminated by the Masters of the Zwolle Bible. Searles-Rowland collection. C June 24 (53) £130,000 [Tenschert]

— [Italy, Naples?, c.1475]. Use of Rome. 194 leaves (4 lacking), vellum, 120mm by 81mm. 19th-cent Spanish vellum gilt. In 2 sizes of a regular rounded gothic hand. With illuminated initials throughout in highly burnished gold on colored panels, 3 large initials on burnished gold panels, & 4 historiated initials. Worn. S Dec 17 (93) £1,700 [Feldman]

— [Le Mans, 2d half of 15th cent]. Use of Le Mans. 166 leaves (7 lacking), 172mm by 116mm. 18th-cent French calf. In a well-formed gothic liturgical hand. With linefillers & 1-line initials throughout in designs of liquid silver and gold on red & blue grounds, & 2- to 4-line colored initials throughout enclosing flowers on panels of gold & silver. Spaces left blank for 6 large miniatures. S June 23 (91) £2,200 [Schuster]

— [Rouen, c.1480]. Use of Rouen. In Latin, with Calendar & prayers in French. 126 leaves, vellum, 165mm by 110mm. 19th-cent brown mor decorated in blind. In a handsome lettre batarde. With panel borders in outer margins throughout of colored & gold fruit, flowers & foliage, many small initials in red, blue & gold, & 14 full-page miniatures with panel borders in outer & lower margins in the style of the Master of the Geneva Latini. bba June 25 (120) £22,000 [Finch]

— [Western France, c.1480]. Use of Lisieux. In Latin, with Calendar in French. 117 leaves, vellum, 177mm by 126mm. Def early 19th-cent French red velvet. In a gothic liturgical hand. With 2-line initials in gothic leafy designs on burnished gold grounds, & 15 large miniatures in arched compartments above 3 or 4 lines of text with large initials & within full borders. S June 23 (90) £9,000

— [East central Italy, 2d half of 15th cent]. Use of Rome. 164 leaves (at least 18 lacking), vellum, 144mm by 99mm. Early red velvet over wooden bds. In a small rounded gothic liturgical hand. With c.180 two-line illuminated initials & 5 very large illuminated initials with partial borders in the style of Cristoforo Cortese. Some later additions including 2 pp of impressions of pilgrim badges. Miniatures removed. S June 23 (96) £2,600 [Feldman]

— [Picardy, Peronne?, c.1483-98]. Use of Rome. In Latin, with Calendar in French. 198 leaves (3 blank), 192mm by 128mm. 19th-cent dark blue velvet bdg. In 2 sizes of a skilful gothic liturgical hand. With small initials throughout in burnished gold on colored grounds, panel borders on every page with a 2-line initial, & 14 large miniatures within elaborate historiated architectural borders. S Dec 17 (83) £26,000 [Quaritch]

— [London?, late 15th cent]. Use of Sarum. 126 leaves & 2 flyleaves, vellum, 189mm by 128mm. Contemp wooden bds covered with later vellum. In 2 sizes of a gothic liturgical hand. With small initials throughout in burnished gold with partial foliate borders, & 12 very large initials with 3-quarter or full borders, some including birds & animals. S June 23 (92) £10,000 [Fogg]

— [Northern France, c.1490]. Single leaf, vellum, 218mm by 144mm. In a slightly sloping gothic textura. With 2 small illuminated initials, 2 bar borders, & 2 miniatures. Illus in cat. HH May 12 (38) DM1,600

— [Amiens, late 15th cent]. Use of Rome. 144 leaves & 6 flyleaves, vellum, 257mm by 173mm. 18th-cent French calf bdg. In a compressed gothic liturgical hand. With 3- & 4-line initials in colors enclosing colored flowers on liquid gold ground, & 52 large miniatures (mostly 12 lines high) with full borders of flowers & acanthus leaves on geometrically divided parti-colored liquid gold & colored grounds. S Dec 17 (84) £18,000 [Mirandola]

— [Lorraine?, late 15th cent]. Use of Rome. In Latin, with Calendar in French. 137 leaves (4 lacking) & flyleaf, vellum, 148mm by 105mm. Worn blind-ruled calf over pastebds of c.1600. In a small current lettre batarde. With small initials throughout in blue & gold, larger initials in colors enclosing colored flowers & on gold grounds, 4 full borders with flowers & fruit on gold grounds, & 8 large or full-page miniatures in a provincial style. Unfinished, with spaces left for 18 further miniatures. S Dec 17 (85) £6,500 [Schwing]

— [Northern Netherlands, Leiden?, c.1490]. Use of Utrecht. In Dutch. 131 leaves, vellum, 181mm by 122mm. Contemp blind-stamped polished calf over wooden bds. In a small gothic bookhand. With 28 illuminated initials with full-length bar borders, 5 very large initials in rich blue scrolling designs on highly burnished gold grounds with 3-quarter borders of acanthus leaves & flowers, & 5 full-page miniatures with full borders with exotic birds, a bearded man, monkeys, angels & insects. S Dec 17 (92) £24,000 [Tenschert]

— [Northern France, Paris?, c.1490]. Use of Rome. 55 leaves only, vellum, 191mm by 123mm. Def contemp English blind-stamped calf over pastebds. In 2 sizes of a neat lettre batarde. With panel borders throughout, 4 small miniatures with 3-quarter illuminated borders, & 12 large miniatures with full borders enclosing smaller miniatures. S June 23 (89) £9,000 [Fogg]

— [Paris or Rouen, c.1495]. Use of Paris. In Latin, with prayers in French. 173 leaves, vellum, 166mm by 115mm. 19th-cent vellum bdg. In black ink in a gothic bookhand. With small initials of burnished gold with penwork decoration, panel borders in each outer margin many with birds, mermaids & grotesques, & 22 large miniatures with full borders. C Dec 16 (12) £15,000 [Mirandola]

— [Flanders or Northern France, c.1500]. Use of Rome. 149 leaves, vellum, 155mm by 115mm. 19th-cent calf bdg. In a gothic liturgical hand. With 13 four-line initials in white on gold, 6 with full-page gold borders decorated with fruit, flowers, birds, & a human figure, & 17th-cent painting pasted in. bba June 25 (119) £2,000 [Feldman]

— [Tours?, c.1500]. In Latin, with Calendar in French. 110 leaves, vellum, 142mm by 95mm. 19th-cent brown mor decorated in blind. In a gothic liturgical hand. With 5 four- or five-line initials in red & blue with tracery in gold. Seriously misbound. bba June 25 (121) £950 [Feldman]

— [Southern France?, c.1500]. 2 leaves only, vellum, 224mm by 148mm. In a gothic textura. With 2-line initials in grisaille on pink ground & semi-architectural half-border on each page depicting scenes of a fabulistic character. C June 24 (73) £1,200 [Manour]

— [Northern France, c.1500]. Use not stated. 115 leaves (4 lacking), vellum, 122mm by 76mm. Late 16th-cent calf bdg a la fanfare. In 2 sizes of a lettre batarde. With numerous initials in red or blue & gold, & 9 large miniatures within full borders in gold & colors depicting the Passion of Christ. HH May 12 (15) DM28,000

— [Abbey of Maria Troon, Flanders, c.1500]. Use of Cambrai. In Latin, with Calendar in Flemish. 112 leaves, vellum, 183mm by 124mm. Modern vellum over pastebds. In a handsome calligraphic lettre batarde. With eleven large illuminated initials in leafy designs with delicate tracery in liquid gold, one including a picture of the Holy Dove, & full border in the Ghent/Bruges style incorporating plants & birds. S Dec 17 (69) £6,000 [Maggs]

— [Netherlands, c.1500-20]. Use of Rome. In Latin, with Calendar, Litany & prayers in Dutch. 196 leaves & 2 flyleaves, vellum, 160mm by 110mm. Contemp calf over wooden bds. In a gothic textura. With 8 five- or six-line initials decorated with extensive penwork flourishes, 8 large foliate initials with full borders of flowers, foliage & insects, & 8 full-page miniatures with full borders by 4 different artists. C June 24 (61) £17,000 [Tenschert]

— [Bruges, c.1510-15]. Use of Rome. 224 leaves & flyleaves, vellum, 142mm by 98mm. 19th-cent olive-brown mor gilt by Thivet. In a flamboyant calligraphic lettre batarde by Johann de Bomalia. With small illuminated initials throughout, 8 large illuminated initials with full borders in Ghent/Bruges designs of naturalistic flowers & leaves or in imitation of carved wooden frames, 24 Calendar miniatures, 2 historiated initials, & 35 small, 1 half-page, & 5 full-page miniatures, all within full borders. Miniatures partly attibutable to the Master of Sir George Talbot. Illus in cat. S June 23 (93) £62,640

Horn, Gustav, Count, 1592-1657

Ds, 19 July 1655. 1 p, folio. Pay order. star Mar 27 (1449) DM400

Hornsby, Rogers, 1896-1963

Photograph, sgd, [n.d.]. 6 by 2.5 inches, cut from larger photograph. Dar Oct 10 (80) $250

Signature, 1958. 16mo (card). Dar Dec 26 (90) $130

Houdini, Harry, 1874-1926

Ls, 28 May 1923. 1 p, 8vo. To Melville E. Stone. Sending a ticket for a banquet (included). Illus in cat. sg Feb 27 (92) $1,400

— 19 Mar 1925. 1 p, 4to. Recipient unnamed. Referring to his campaign against the spiritualists. bba Oct 10 (481) £160 [Daniels]

— 2 June 1925. 1 p, 8vo. To Remigius Weiss. Inquiring about his wife's health. In extra frame with related material. Dar Aug 6 (174) $1,300

Autograph sentiment, expressing good wishes, 8 Apr 1911. 5 by 7 inches (card). Sgd & initialled. Ck Nov 15 (133) £210

Photograph, sgd, [n.d.]. 6 by 7.25 inches. In paper frame. Illus in cat. sup Oct 15 (1317) $650

Ptd photograph, sgd, [n.d.]. 4.5 by 3.5 inches, cut from a program. Dar Feb 13 (213) $225

Housman, Alfred Edward, 1859-1936

ALs, 26 Aug 1922. 1 p, 8vo. To Mrs. Smith. Granting permission to publish a setting of a poem. sg Sept 12 (120) $200

— 23 Dec 1923. 1 p, 4to. To Charles Walston. Thanking for a letter & enclosure. pn Mar 19 (136) £100 [Wilson]

Housman, Laurence, 1865-1959

Collection of 250 A Ls s, 74 Ls s, 102 postcards, sgd (100 autograph), 2 autograph Mss, typescript & 5 telegrams, May 1922 to Nov 1955. 570 pp, various sizes. To the Society of Authors & the League of British Dramatists. Detailing his literary business affairs. With related material. CNY Dec 5 (249) $8,000

Houston, Samuel, 1793-1863

Collection of ALs & transcript, 25 Aug 1842 & 10 Jan 1843. 5 pp, 4to & folio. To Col. Thomas Ward. Predicting peace with Mexico & the Indian tribes. Message to the Texas House of Representatives warning of the consequences of an exposure of the Texas archives to a Mexican attack. CNY June 9 (277) $7,000

Ds, 10 May 1838. 2 pp, folio. Receipt for goods delivered to Col. Bowls. Illus in cat. sup May 9 (380) $3,200

— 25 Feb 1861. 1 p, folio. Land grant to the heirs of Alfred Bynum. Dar Aug 6 (175) $750

Howard, Sidney Coe, 1891-1939

Ds, 8 July 1937. 30 pp, 4to. Contract with The Theatre Guild for a production of his play The Ghost of Yankee Doodle. Dar June 11 (235) $100

Howard, Thomas, 1st Earl of Suffolk, 1561-1626

ADs, 7 Apr 1607. 1 p, 12mo. As Lord Chamberlain, pay order in favor of Mr. Bingley. Dar Oct 10 (212) $110

Howe, Julia Ward, 1819-1910

ALs, 2 July 1903. 1 p, 12mo, on verso of cash receipt form. To Annie J. Perkins. Returning the check. Illus in cat. Dar Aug 6 (176) $130

— 11 May [n.y.]. 1 p, 8vo. To Miss Moulton. Informing her that she has "chosen 'Of old sat Freedom on the heights' by Alfred Tennyson". Dar Apr 9 (233) $110

Howe, Richard Howe, Earl, 1726-99

Autograph Ms, Observations on the Report from the Board of the Artillery officers..., 1790. 2 pp, folio. Discussing the use of powder. Sgd by Howe & 8 others. With engraved port. Ck Apr 3 (87) £140

ALs, 29 Oct 1790. 1 p, 4to. To [the future King William IV]. Transmitting alterations to the signal book. Spiro collection. CNY May 14 (83) $700

Howe, Robert, 1732-86

ALs, 17 Jan 1779. 3 pp, 4to. To Gen. Lincoln. Providing information about troops, & regretting that he has been given a different command. Illus in cat. R Mar 7 (194) $2,500

— 15 Feb 1779. 4 pp, 4to. To Lieut. Col. John F. Grimkie. War letter, reflecting their friendship. Silked. CNY June 9 (240) $3,800

Howe, Sir William, 1729-1814

ALs, 17 May 1772. 2 pp, 4to. To Charles Townshend. Recommending Mr. Parkyns for a military appointment. Spiro collection. CNY May 14 (85) $900

Howells, Herbert, 1892-1983

Autograph music, Magnificat & Nunc Dimittis in B minor, for organ & 4-part chorus; 25 & 26 Dec 1955. 14 pp, folio. Ptr's copy. S May 29 (555) £1,050 [Macnutt]

Howells, William Dean, 1837-1920

A Ls s (2), 6 Sept 1887 & 17 Mar 1888. 4 pp, 8vo & 4to. To Dr. Albert Leffingwell. Regarding his daughter Winifred's stay at recipient's sanatorium. With related material. CNY June 9 (95) $260

Single sheet ptg, Clemency for the Anarchists. A Letter from Mr. W. D. Howells ..., 4 Nov 1887. 193mm by 133mm. Proof copy, with 3 autograph corrections; including ANs to Dr. Albert Leffingwell at head. With related letters by or relating to Howell. Illus in cat. CNY June 9 (94) $3,500

Hudson, Rock, 1925-85

Collection of ALs & photograph, 17 Nov 1945. 4 pp, 8vo & 3.5 by 4 inches. To Mrs. L. Hattley. On his 20th birthday, reporting about activities in the Navy. Photograph inscr on verso. Dar Feb 13 (215) $550

ALs, 23 Oct 1945. 5 pp, 8vo. To Mrs. L. Hattley. Chatting about "weekend liberty" with the Navy in the Philippines. Dar Feb 13 (214) $450

Huerta, Victoriano

Ds, 27 June 1913. 1 p, folio. Appointment of Agustin Figueroa as Lieut. Colonel. sup Oct 15 (1375) $400

Hufeland, Christoph Wilhelm, 1762-1836

ALs, 2 Mar 1816. 1 p, 4to. To Dr. Voigtel. About a recent government appointment in Magdeburg. HN Nov 28 (1729) DM500

Huggins, Miller James, 1879-1929

Signature, endorsement on verso of salary check, sgd by Jacob Ruppert & E. G. Barrow, 1 Sept 1925. 9 by 3.25 inches. Dar Dec 26 (91) $2,250

Hughes, Charles Evans, 1862-1948

Series of 4 Ls s, 14 Sept 1921 to 17 Aug 1922. 8 pp, 4to. To Federico Alfonso Pezet. Regarding matters pertaining to relations with Peru. Dar Aug 6 (177) $250

— Series of 4 Ls s, 1921 to 1923. 4to. To Federico Alfonso Pezet. Concerning various matters pertaining to relations with Peru. With related material. Dar Apr 9 (234) $275

Photograph, sgd, [n.d.]. Framed; overall size 19 by 27 inches. By Harris & Ewing. sup Oct 15 (1320) $525

Hughes, Howard, 1905-76

ANs, [n.d.]. 1 p, 2 by 4 inches (card). Recipient unnamed. Sending a gift on opening night. Illus in cat. sup Oct 15 (1321) $775

Hugo, Jean

Original drawing, Shakespeare's England, to illus Shakespeare's Cotswolds, L, 1964. 27cm by 36cm. In pen-&-ink. Sgd & inscr to Boris [Kochno], Easter 1966. Boris Kochno collection. SM Oct 11 (149) FF4,500

Series of 27 A Ls s, 18 June 1933 to 12 Aug 1983. 33 pp, mostly 8vo. To Boris Kochno. About a variety of personal & professional matters. SM Oct 12 (371) FF10,000

Hugo, Victor, 1802-85

ALs, 30 July 1869. 1 p, 8vo. To R. Roettger. Responding to recipient's work. HH May 13 (1973) DM440

— 19 Sept [n.y.]. 1 p, 4to. To a "vieux compagnon d'exil". Assuring him that he is well. star Mar 26 (277) DM550

— [n.d.]. 1 p, 8vo. Recipient & contents not stated. Framed with a port. Illus in cat. sup Oct 15 (1322) $525

Huizinga, Johan, 1872-1945

A Ls s (2), 13 May & 27 July 1937. 5 pp, 8vo. To Antonio Aita. Expecting a "rapprochement spirituel" between Europe & South America. star Mar 26 (674) DM650

Humboldt, Alexander von, 1769-1859

Series of 4 A Ls S, 11 Apr 1839 to 24 Sept 1854. 4 pp, 8vo. To Adolph Theodor von Kupffer. Regarding several scientific projects, sending a publication, recommending Lieut. Pim, etc. star Mar 26 (677) DM1,250

ALs, 9 Nov 1796. 4 pp, 4to. To [Johann Friedrich Reichardt]. Reporting about his current research projects & sending 2 articles. star Mar 26 (675) DM8,000

— 24 May 1805. 3 pp, 8vo. To Karl Friedrich von Dacheroeden. Promising an article about guano & mentioning Schiller's death. star Mar 26 (676) DM3,800

— 10 Nov 1843. 2 pp, 4to. To Marshal [Soult]. Letter of recommendation for Baron von Willisen. star Mar 26 (679) DM540

— [c.Feb 1849]. 1 p, 8vo. To [Friedrich Adolf Trendelenburg]. Sending letters of recommendation for Jeppe Prehn (not present). star Mar 26 (680) DM360

— 3 Aug 1854. 2 pp, 4to. Recipient unnamed. Letter of recommendation for M. Sudre. Trimmed. star Mar 26 (681) DM420

— [n.d.], "Thursday". 1 p, 8vo. Recipient unnamed. Regretting being unable to advise [Julius] Minding about the staging of his play. star Mar 26 (678) DM320

— [n.d.]. 1 p, 8vo. To [J. C. L. Gerhard]. Hoping to see him on Sunday. With related material. star Mar 26 (683) DM320

ANs, [n.d.]. 1 p, 12mo. Recipient unnamed. Sending copies of 2 letters (included). star Mar 26 (684) DM200

Humboldt, Wilhelm von, 1767-1835

ALs, [c.1798]. 1 p, 8vo. Recipient unnamed. Announcing his visit with his brother Alexander. In French. HN Nov 28 (1730) DM1,000

— 13 June 1800. 1 p, 4to. To the bookseller La Garde. Inquiring about a shipment. star Mar 26 (685) DM500

Ls, 9 Apr 1830. 2 pp, 4to. To Friedrich Schlosser. Sending a lithographic port of his wife. star Mar 26 (686) DM420

Hummel, Johann Nepomuk, 1778-1837. See: Chopin, Frederic

Humperdinck, Engelbert, 1854-1921

Autograph music, song, Weihnachten, to a text by Adelheid Wette, 7 Dec 1898. 3 pp, 35cm by 26cm. Complete composition, scored for voice & piano; sgd at head. Illus in cat. star Mar 27 (1035) DM6,500

Autograph quotation, theme from Act I of his opera Koenigskinder, [1910?]. On verso of an unnamed person's visiting card. Sgd. star Mar 27 (1037) DM500

Hund, Friedrich

Autograph Ms, draft of a lecture about the theory of relativity, 1960. 39 pp, 8vo. star Mar 26 (687) DM480

Hunt, Henry Jackson, 1819-89. See: Bragg, Braxton & Hunt

Hunt, William Holman, 1827-1910

ALs, 9 Aug 1857. 4 pp, 8vo. To Tom [Woolner?]. About Edward Lear & an invitation to see the Tennysons. Ingilby collection. pn Nov 14 (82) £200 [Quaritch]

Hunter, John, 1738-1821

Ds, 22 Dec 1795. 1 p, 4to. Certificate of service for David Collins as Judge-Advocate in New South Wales. In modern quarter mor bdg with engraved portraits of both. Longueville collection. S June 25 (137) £2,200 [Stokes]

— 18 Dec 1799. 2 pp, 410mm by 320mm. Grant of land at Toongabbie in New South Wales to Patrick Brennan; later conveyed to Elizabeth Paisley. Also sgd by others. Longueville collection. S June 25 (145) £2,200 [Simpson]

— 26 Mar 1800. 2 pp, folio. Grant of land at Parramatta, New South Wales, to Elizabeth Dougal; later made over to D'Arcy Wentworth. Illus in cat. Longueville collection. S June 25 (152) £1,600 [Simpson]

Hunter, Robert Mercer Taliaferro, 1809-87

ALs, [c.1860]. 2 pp, 8vo. To J. Clancy Jones. Regarding reform of the currency & the presidential election. wa Oct 19 (220) $160

Huntington, Samuel, Signer from Connecticut

ALs, 16 July 1783. 1 p, folio. To Thomas Shaw. Requesting that Darius Peck be reimbursed for the support of prisoners. CNY June 9 (241) $800

Ls, 5 Aug 1786. 1 p, 8vo. To Gov. John Collins. Retained copy, acknowledging a communication. Dar June 11 (236) $225

Ds, 18 Jan 1773. 2 pp, 4to. Nomination of Tavern Keepers; sgd twice. Also sgd by others. Dar Aug 6 (179) $225

— Mar 1775. 1 p, 4to. Account of money due Huntington from the Colony of Connecticut. With similar accounts on attached sheet. Dar Aug 6 (178) $160

— 26 Jan 1790. 1 p, 4to. Order to "attach the Goods or Estate of David Huntington..." sup Oct 15 (1210) $340

Huston, Walter, 1884-1950

Ds, 13 Sept 1946. 2 pp, 4to. Contract with The Theatre Guild Radio Division; carbon copy. Dar Feb 13 (216) $100

Huxley, Aldous, 1894-1963

Typescript, review of Modern American Poetry, Ed by Louis Untermeyer, [n.d.]. 4 pp, size not stated. With numerous autograph corrections; sgd. Ck Apr 3 (53) £220

Series of 7 A Ls s, 28 Apr 1930 to 10 Sept 1962. 12 pp, various sizes. To Antonio Aita. Concerning PEN meetings, & sending a paper (present, typescript carbon copy). star Mar 26 (278) DM2,200

ALs, 10 Nov [19]24. 4 pp, size not stated. To Henry Major Tomlinson. Recommending some gramophone records. Ck Apr 3 (52) £240

— 22 Aug 1962. 2 pp, 4to. To Mr. Shrady. Returning photographs. Dar Oct 10 (213) $120

Hyrtl, Joseph, 1810-94

ALs, 16 Apr 1847. 4 pp, 8vo. To an unnamed colleague. Discussing an academic appointment. star Mar 26 (688) DM720

I

Ibsen, Henrik, 1828-1906

ALs, 29 Jan 1867. 1 p, 8vo. To Julie von Kjerulff. Thanking for an invitation. star Mar 26 (279) DM880

— 12 June 1883. 4 pp, 8vo. To Georg Brandes. Discussing 3 of his works. Framed with a port. P June 17 (36) $4,750

Iffland, August Wilhelm, 1759-1814

ALs, 25 June 1799. 2 pp, 4to. To the pbr Goeschen. Reporting about his recent travels. HH May 13 (1974) DM400

— 8 June 1804. 1 p, folio. To the Rev. Luedeke. Responding to a request for a contribution to a charity. star Mar 27 (1216) DM420

Ls, 24 Nov 1804. 1 p, 4to. Recipient unnamed. Sending a letter for Herr Weitzmann. star Mar 27 (1217) DM340

India

— FORSTER, THOMAS. - Ms, A Digest of the Different Castes of India, 1841. 48 pp & 83 watercolor over ink or pencil drawings captioned in ink, 8vo, in contemp calf gilt. Including presentation inscr to Francis Crawshay. S Nov 21 (358) £650 [Farel]

— VERNER, LIEUT. GEORGE. - 57 A Ls s, 25 Aug 1834 to 26 Dec 1851. 255 pp, 4to & 8vo. To his father or mother. Mostly reporting from India. bba Jan 30 (289) £190 [Knowles]

— WALTER, EMMA MARY. - Autograph Mss, journal detailing her life in India & Afghanistan as the wife of a colonel of the 3d Bombay Light Cavalry, 11 Oct 1838 to 22 Mar 1850, & commonplace & cookery book. About 530 pp, 4to, in 6 vols. With a typed transcript of the journal. S Dec 12 (306) £1,000 [Bristow]

Indian Manuscripts

Ms, legend of Krishna, from the Bhagavata Purana. [Kashmir, 18th cent]. 138 leaves, 225mm by 135mm. Green cloth bdg of c.1900. In nasta'liq script. With 12 miniatures in gold & colors. Incomplete. HH Nov 5 (879) DM3,200

Ionesco, Eugene —& Others

[An archive of 206 carbons & other copies of letters concerning law suits brought against each other by Ioneso & Leo Kertz regarding the Broadway production of the play Rhinoceros, 1961 to 1963, sold at Dar on 9 Apr 1992, lot 235, for $100.]

Ippolitov-Ivanov, Mikhail, 1859-1935

Photograph, sgd & inscr, 10 May 1907. Cabinet size. Inscr to F. S. Hastings. Illus in cat. sg Feb 27 (93) $1,900

Ireland

— DIGGES, THOMAS. - Ms, journal of his tour of Britain & Irland, 21 July to 23 Oct 1798. 82 pp, 4to, in calf bdg. Including extensive descriptions of Ireland after the recent rebellion. S July 21 (214) £1,300 [Rowan]

Irving, Washington, 1783-1859

ALs, 23 Oct 1829. 1 p, 4to. To his brother. Informing him that he is sending a Cheddar cheese by ship. bba Sept 19 (336) £80 [Sakmyster]

— 6 Apr 1854. 7 pp, 8vo. To Helen [Irving]. Charming family letter. CNY Dec 5 (253) $950

— 7 Dec [n.y.]. 1 p, 8vo. To Mr. Otway. Inviting him to dinner. pn Nov 14 (225) £70

Isabella I, Queen of Spain, 1451-1504

Ls, 2 Sept 1483. 1 p, 8vo. To Sancho de Vergara. Recommending Juan de Luxan. S May 28 (25) £1,200 [Polido]

Ds, 20 Jan 1501. 1 p, folio. Pay order in favor of Diego Martinez. Illus in cat. sg Feb 27 (183) $2,000

See also: Ferdinand V & Isabella I

Isolani, Johann Ludwig, Graf von, 1586-1640

Ls, [Aug 1634]. 1 p, 4to. To officials of Lower Austria. About his taxes for the years 1633 & 1634. star Mar 27 (1450) DM640

Israel Meir ha-Kohen ("Hafez Hayyim"), 1838-1933

ALs, 1888. 1 p, 8vo. To [Elijah Schick?]. About an exchange of publications. Imperf. Illus in cat. sg Dec 19 (56) $1,600

Istrati, Panait, 1884-1935

ALs, 22 Nov 1927. 3 pp, 8vo. To Jourdain. Saying he misses his company. star Mar 26 (280) DM260

Italy

— PAGANICO, TUSCANY. - Ms, statutes of the town of Paganico, in Italian, with a few sections in Latin. [Tuscany, c.1471-83]. 37 leaves (11 lacking), vellum, 285mm by 202mm; stitched. In a well-formed rounded upright humanistic bookhand. Some later additions. S June 23 (71) £4,800 [Freuler]

— PIEDMONT. - Letter, 20 June 1827. 1 p, 4to. Addressed to the Provincial Jewish Administration of Vercelli by the Special Committee for Jewish Affairs in Piedmont, sending instructions regarding the management & audit of accounts at the University. sg Dec 19 (122) $100

— TREVISO. - Ms, rules & statutes of the Confraternity of the Church of Santa Maria de Zero, 25 Mar 1562. 14 leaves, vellum, 268mm by 199mm. Fine gold-tooled contemp Venetian bdg. With illuminated frontis. Some later additions. Searles-Rowland collection. C June 24 (56) £9,000 [Lyon]

— URBINO. - Letter, [c.1814?]. 2 p, folio. Addressed to Girolamo Venezianelli by Tomasso Felici & Girolamo Bigliotti, complaining about encroachments of Jews into Christian areas. With related Ms map, 1 p, folio. sg Dec 19 (120) $500

— VENICE. - Ms, De multiplici Venetor[um] errore, quare a S. Pontifice Paulo V. excommunicantur... [Italy, c.1606]. 29 leaves, 196mm by 132mm; in bds. Commentary on the Pope's interdict; possibly unpbd. HH Nov 5 (827) DM320

Itten, Johannes, 1888-1967

A Ls s (2), 7 Oct & 30 Nov 1938. 2 pp, 4to. To Mrs. Sothmann. About his call to Zurich, & ordering a work by Lavater. HN June 26 (923) DM520

Iturbide, Agustin de, 1783-1824

Ls, 19 Apr 1822. 3 pp, 4to. To Domingo Luaces. Ordering an investigation. Illus in cat. sup Oct 15 (1376) $800

J

Jackson, Andrew, 1767-1845

ALs, 23 June 1828. 1 p, 4to. To Levi Woodbury. Introducing Henry Lee. Dar Oct 10 (214) $4,000

— 15 June 1829. 1 p, 4to. To Daniel Garland. Promising to issue "an order for the delivery of John Dungy". Illus in cat. sup Oct 15 (1502) $2,100

— 30 Apr 1830. 2 pp, folio. To John C. McLemore. Discussing a financial matter & hoping to return to Tennessee in the summer. Illus in cat. sup May 9 (177) $6,200

— 3 Feb 1831. 2 pp, 4to. To Sec of War John H. Eaton. Giving instructions for a treaty with the Menominees. Including postscript, initialled. Illus in cat. sup Oct 15 (1504) $18,500

— 4 Mar 1834. 1 p, 4to. To Moses Dawson. Hinting at the termination of the charter of the Bank of the US. Framed with engraved port. P June 16 (229) $14,000

— 18 Jan 1844. 1 p, size not stated. To William Donelson. Asking for a meeting. Illus in cat. wd Dec 12 (320) $1,600

— 8 July [n.y.]. 1 p, 4to. To Ann Ross. Mentioning Van Buren. Def. R Mar 7 (125) $700

AL, [1831?]. 2 pp, 8vo. To Sec of the Treasury [S. D. Ingram]. Requesting information on the nation's finances for a repoprt to Congress. Spiro collection. CNY May 14 (86) $5,000

Ls, 2 Jan 180[7]. 2 pp, 4to. To Gov. John Sevier. Informing him that the Tennessee militia "can be brought in good order into the field in ten days". CNY Dec 5 (63) $6,000

— 3 June 1829. 2 pp, 4to. Recipient unnamed. Declining the suggestion that Mr. Colden be appointed minister to the Netherlands. P June 16 (228) $2,750

— 25 July 1835. 3 pp, 4to. To 12 members of the Democratic Committee of Pennsylvania. Refusing to be drawn into the governor's race in Pennsylvania. Illus in cat. sup Oct 15 (1505) $2,100

ANs, 25 Apr [1827?]. 1 p, 4to. To Major Graham. Sending papers relating to the "Complaint of James Alleson". CNY Dec 5 (64) $1,100

ADs, 31 Jan 1823. 1 p, 4to. Affidavit regarding the settlement of the estate of Severn Donelson. With related schedule of apportionment of slaves. CNY June 9 (242) $14,000

Ds, 8 Mar 1813. 1 p, folio. Provision return for the Tennesse voluntary cavalry. Illus in cat. sup May 9 (178) $1,100

— 13 May 1814. 1 p, 4to. Pay order in favor of Dr. Roane for visits to a wounded soldier. Including Roane's statement at head. Illus in cat. sup May 9 (179) $1,450

— 7 Mar 1829. 1 p, folio. Appointment of John McLean as Associate Justice of the Supreme Court. Framed. P June 16 (227) $2,250

— 14 Dec 1830. 2 pp, folio. Patent to Archibald Little for an "improvement in the mode of making spoons." Countersgd by Van Buren. Framed with engraved portraits of both. Illus in cat. sup Oct 15 (1503) $2,400

— 8 Feb 1831. 1 p, folio. Land grant in Indiana. R Mar 7 (125A) $650

— 27 July 1831. 1 p, folio. Land grant to John Danielly. Framed. Dar Apr 9 (238) $650

— 3 May 1834. 1 p, folio. Appointment of J. Dunlop, Wm. O'Neale & Th. Carbery as Inspectors of the Penitentiary in the District of Columbia. Imperf. CNY Dec 5 (65) $1,100

— 28 June 1834. 1 p, 4to. Appointment of Eugene Boyle as Midshipman. wa Oct 19 (301) $500

— 1 Nov 1834. 1 p, folio. Endorsement on verso of partly ptd land transfer from the Creek nation in Alabama. Repaired. sg Sept 12 (121) $400

— 2 May 1835. 1 p, folio. Patent issued to Thomas Pierce for an "inclined floated wheel and a horizontal Rotary Water Pitch for propelling the same". Illus in cat. sg Feb 27 (94) $1,900

— 1836. 1 p, folio. Appointment of Albion Parris as Assistant Comptroller. sup Oct 15 (1506) $775

Autograph endorsement, sgd, on ANs by Thomas Hinds, 8 Mar 1815, 1 p, 12mo, ordering the Quartermaster to furnish money to Lieut. Dunbar for transportation; note of approval. Illus in cat. Dar June 11 (237) $550

Check, accomplished & sgd, 7 Apr 1836. Payable to A. J. Donelson. Illus in cat. Dar Apr 9 (237) $1,700

— MAUD, HENRY. - ADs, 11 Sept 1835. 1 p, 12mo. Sight draft addressed to Andrew Jackson. With autograph endorsement, sgd, 14 Sept 1835, by Jackson on verso; recording payment. Dar Apr 9 (236) $750

Jackson, Henry, d.1909

Ls, 3 Sept 1872. 1 p, 4to. To R. Seyboth. Giving instructions regarding "old bulletin boards". Framed. Illus in cat. Armstrong collection. sup Oct 15 (1116) $100

Jackson, Michael

Ds, 21 Jan [19]77. 2 pp, folio. Contract assigning rights to Jackson Opening (part of Musical Score for TV Series Jan 1977) to Peacock Music Publishing Co.; also sgd by his father & 4 brothers. Illus in cat. sup Oct 15 (1325) $440

— 20 June 1978. 2 pp, folio. Contract assigning rights to the song You Push me Away to Peacock Music Publishing Co. Also sgd by his father & 4 brothers. wa Apr 9 (287) $600

— 1 Aug 1978. 2 pp, folio. Contract assigning rights to the song Bless His Soul to Peacock Music Publishing Company. Also sgd by his father & 4 brothers. Illus in cat. R June 13 (208) $700

Photograph, sgd, [n.d.]. 8.5 by 11 inches. Framed. Dar Dec 26 (214) $200

— Anr, [n.d.]. 8 by 10 inches. Dar Apr 9 (240) $200

Jackson, Thomas J. ("Stonewall"), 1824-63

Group photograph, [n.d.]. Oval, 7.75 by 5.25 inches; mtd. Composite photograph with central image of Jackson surrounded by 10 members of his staff. By Vannerson & Jones. R June 13 (278) $1,000

Jacob, Max, 1876-1944

Autograph Ms, short story, Le petit homme des eglises, 21 Jan 1920. 5 pp, folio. Sgd. Boris Kochno collection. SM Oct 12 (372) FF22,000

Jacobi, Johann Georg, 1740-1814

ALs, 23 May 1803. 1 p, 4to. To Friedrich Matthisson. Inquiring about contributions for his almanach Iris. star Mar 26 (690) DM1,100

Jagemann, Christian, 1735-1804

ALs, 20 July 1777. 1 p, 4to. To his pbr. Sending a Ms, & ordering books for the library at Weimar. HH May 13 (1953) DM200

Jahn, Friedrich Ludwig, 1778-1852

ALs, 31 May 1830. 2 pp, 4to. To [Jakob Fries?]. Letter of recommendation for Herr Stockmer. star Mar 27 (1457) DM1,000

Jahnn, Hans Henny, 1894-1959

ALs, [n.d.]. 1 p, 8vo. To Hans Leip. Apologizing for leaving early due to anr commitment. FD Dec 3 (1434) DM320

James, Frank, 1843-1915

ALs, 19 Mar 1884. 2 pp, folio. To his wife & Rob. Family letter from jail. Illus in cat. R Mar 7 (222) $3,800

— 19 Apr 1909. 2 pp, 4to. To "Friend Blackmore". Requesting that he refrain from using his name in advertising shows at local fairs. sup May 9 (448) $1,500

James, Frank, 1843-1915 —& Others

[A photograph containing 3 oval images of Frank & Jesse James, & Cal Carter, [c.1870s], carte size, by Dan Chamberlain, sold at R on 7 Mar 1992, lot 223, for $8,500.]

James, Henry, 1843-1916

ALs, 7 July 1888. 6 pp, 8vo. To R. U. Johnson. About a "disaster in Union Square" & the US Copyright Bill. S July 21 (57) £600 [Hoyle]

— 9 Aug 1888. 1 p, 8vo. Recipient unnamed. Transmitting "a contribution to the portrait of Mr. Gladstone". sg Feb 27 (95) $375

— 9 Jan 1891. 8 pp, 8vo. To R. U. Johnson. Declining to go abroad in the spring & promising to write an article about Paris. S July 21 (62) £600 [Stodolski]

— 4 Apr [1893]. 6 pp, 8vo. Recipient unnamed. Commenting on the hopelessness of his task with respect to Dagnan-Bouveret. S July 21 (59) £550 [Stodolski]

— 5 May 1895. 6 pp, 8vo. To R. U. Johnson. About his inability to write for Century Magazine, & giving news of friends. S July 21 (58) £650 [Humphries]

— 20 June [n.y.]. 2 pp, 8vo. To Mrs. Gurney. Regretting he cannot see her. Ingilby collection. pn Nov 14 (83) £110 [Dupre]

— SARGENT, JOHN SINGER. - A photograph of his port of James, [1913], 330mm by 265mm, framed, sgd by both. CNY June 9 (99) $2,400

James I, King of England, 1566-1625

Document, 17 June 1603. 4 membranes of vellum, c.725mm by 820mm. Grant to Meriell Littleton of the reversal of the attainder of her late husband & the restoration of his estates. Illuminated, with large initial-letter port. C June 24 (65A) £7,500 [Manour]

James II, King of England, 1633-1701

Ls, 27 Jan 1688. 2 pp, folio. To Landgraf Karl von Hessen-Kassel. Requesting the immediate recall of his envoy Jean Blancard. In Latin. star Mar 27 (1427) DM2,200

Ds, 18 Jan 1686/87. 1 p, 4to. Warrant to the Commissioners of the Navy for reducing the crew of a ship. Also sgd by Samuel Pepys. S Dec 12 (251) £750 [Ridge]

— DESPORCELLETS. - Ms, La Renommee qui publie de bonheur de L'Europe sous le memorable Reigne de Jacques Auguste Deuxieme...; [1689?]. 12 leaves, 4to. Orig Parisian gold-tooled red mor with the arms of James II. Including engraved port of James II & mezzotint of his wife Mary of Modena. C June 24 (78) £10,000 [Quaritch]

James, Jesse, 1847-82 —& Others
[A group of 10 letters & documents relating to the capture of the James Gang, 1874 to 1876, sold at sup on 9 May 1992, lot 449, for $6,000.]

Jandl, Ernst
Autograph transcript, poem, der fruehling, 4 Dec 1985. 1 p, folio. Sgd & inscr. star Mar 26 (284) DM550

Janssen, Horst
Collection of ALs & orig drawing, sgd, 7 May 1983 & 1/2 Mar 1985. 2 pp, 8vo & 4to. To Balduin Baas. Referring to a joint project. Drawing of a frog. HN June 26 (924) DM800

Jarvis, Greg, 1944-86
Ls, [n.d.]. 1 p, 4to. To Jamie. Referring to the projected Challenger shuttle flight. Dar Apr 9 (60) $750

Jaspers, Karl, 1883-1969
ALs, 4 Feb [19]65. 1 p, 4to. To Albert Theile. Discussing a contribution to the journal Humboldt. HH Nov 6 (2062) DM200

Jay, John, 1745-1829
ALs, 26 May 1798. 1 p, 4to. To Daniel Hale. Directing him to prepare a pardon warrant. P Dec 12 (111) $1,600
— 3 July 1799. 2 pp, folio. To his son Peter Augustus Jay. Regarding his purchase of wigs & a search for the family of a deceased British sailor. Spiro collection. CNY May 14 (87) $1,400
— 12 Sept 1807. 1 p, 4to. To his daughter Maria Banyer. Family letter. Spiro collection. CNY May 14 (88) $1,300
Ls, 1 Jan 1811. 1 p, 4to. To G. W. Featherstonhaugh. Regarding the estate of Mr. Duane. Illus in cat. sup May 9 (382) $1,250
ADs, 15 Feb 1799. 1 p, 6.5 by 8 inches. As Governor of NY, approval of 2 acts. Illus in cat. sup Oct 15 (1328) $1,650
Ds, [1778-79]. 1 p, folio. Ptd broadside of "Instructions to the Commanders of Private Ships or Vessels of War," dated 3 Apr 1776. Sgd as President of the Congress. R Mar 7 (196) $3,800

Jean Paul. See: Richter, Jean Paul Friedrich

Jeanneret, Charles Edouard, 1887-1965. See: Le Corbusier

Jefferson, Thomas, 1743-1826
ALs, 26 Sept 1785. 1 p, 6.5 by 4 inches. To Mr. Stockdale. In 3d person, promising to send maps of North America. Framed. Illus in cat. sup Oct 15 (1482) $3,600
— 10 Sept 1789. 1 p, 4to. To [Nathaniel] Cutting. Seeking a ship to return home. Illus in cat. Spiro collection. CNY May 14 (89) $32,000
— 28 Apr 1791. 1 p, 4to. To William Smith. Outlining areas of study John W. Eppes wishes to pursue in Philadelphia. P June 16 (179) $15,000
— 18 Feb 1793. 1 p, 4to. To Beverley Randolph. Offering him the appointment to a commission to parley with the Indian tribes at Sandusky. Including franking signature. CNY Dec 5 (66) $37,000
— 23 Oct 1799. 1 p, 4to. To Daniel Call. Regarding legal proceedings against his neighbors for damage to his property. Framed with a port. P Dec 12 (113) $9,000
— 12 July 1801. 3 pp, 4to. To Elias Shipman & others. Explaining his policy on appointments & removals from office. P Dec 12 (114) $40,000
— 9 Nov 1802. 1 p, 8vo. To Daniel Rapin. In 3d person; ordering books. Framed with engraved port. P June 16 (231) $4,250
— 14 Nov 1802. 1 p, 4to. To the Institut National de France. Thanking for his election as associate member. Illus in cat. CNY May 14 (5) $35,000
— 20 Dec 1802. 1 p, 8vo. To Mr. Elliott. In 3d person, thanking for a poem. Illus in cat. sup Oct 15 (1485) $5,000
— 1 Mar 1806. 1 p, 4to. To Samuel Mitchell. Correcting a misunderstanding regarding a case involving Gen. Armstrong. Framed with a port. Illus in cat. P June 16 (232) $16,000
— 16 Nov 1808. 1 p, 4to. To John McAlister. Asking him to furnish a pair of glasses & giving detailed instructions. Illus in cat. P June 16 (233) $27,000
— 29 Nov 1820. 1 p, 12mo. To [Charles] Vest. In 3d person, arranging for his mail to be forwarded to Poplar Forest. Illus in cat. CNY June 9 (243) $5,000
ADs, 30 July 1817. 1 p, 4to. Promissory note for $150 in repayment of money received for the cancelled sale of a negro girl named Sally. bbc Dec 9 (168) $21,000
Ds, 3 Mar 1791. 1 p, folio. As Sec of State, ptd Act establishing the US Mint. Illus in cat. sup Oct 15 (1483) $30,000
— [after 12 Apr 1792]. 1 p, 4to. Ptd Act of Congress "supplementary to the Act for the Establishment and Support of Light-Houses..." Framed. P June 16 (230) $4,750
— 14 Apr 1792. 3 pp, 7 by 11.5 inches. As Sec of State, ptd Act concerning Consuls and Vice Consuls under the convention with France. Illus in cat. sup Oct 15 (1484) $13,500
— 28 Feb 1793. 4 pp, 4to. Ptd "Act making appropriation for the support of the Gov-

ernment", sgd as Sec of State. sg Sept 12 (123) $6,000

— 1 July 1801. 1 p, folio. Military land grant to William Ruggles. Countersgd by Madison. CNY Dec 5 (67) $2,400

— 18 Mar 1803. 1 p, folio. Patent to John Staples for "a power obtained by the rising and falling of the Tide..." Countersgd by Madison. Framed with engraved port. Illus in cat. sup Oct 15 (1486) $6,500

— 21 May 1804. 1 p, folio. Ship's papers in 4 languages for the ship Commerce. Countersgd by Madison. R Nov 9 (16) $5,500

— 1 Jan 1805. 1 p, folio. Land grant to Henry Weaver. Countersgd by Madison. Trimmed. P Dec 12 (116) $2,250

— 9 Aug 1805. 1 p, folio. Mediterranean Pass for the brig Sally Tracy of New York. Countersgd by Madison. rf Sept 21 (9) $6,250

— 15 Aug 1805. 1 p, folio. Land grant in Ohio. Countersgd by Madison. R Mar 7 (126) $4,200

— 14 Sept 1805. 1 p, folio. Customs declaration in 4 languages; countersgd by James Madison. Framed. b&b Feb 19 (159) $4,250

— 8 Dec 1806. 1 p, folio. Ship's papers in 4 languages for the schooner Evander. Countersgd by Madison. Illus in cat. R June 13 (181) $3,200

— 3 Feb 1807. 1 p, folio. Land grant in the Northwest Territory to Nicholas Yeager. Countersgd by Madison. Dar Dec 26 (215) $2,000

— 27 Apr 1807. 1 p, folio. Military land grant to Ebenezer Owen. Countersgd by Madison. Endorsed by Henry Dearborn on verso. Framed. Dar Apr 9 (243) $2,000

— 28 Dec 1807. 1 p, folio. Mediterranean Pass for the schooner Lone. Countersgd by Madison. Imperf. rf Sept 21 (10) $3,250

— 3 Mar 1809. 1 p, folio. Appointment of Leonard Covington as Lieut. Colonel of Light Dragoons. R June 13 (182) $1,900

Autograph endorsement, sgd, on verso of legal document, 20 Dec 1766, 2 pp, 8vo, regarding a suit for damages payable to Richard Harvie by John Eue; stating that nothing is due. Framed with engraved port. Illus in cat. Dar Feb 13 (218) $3,000

Franking signature, [27 Aug 1802]. On autograph address leaf to Gen. Bradley. P Dec 12 (115) $3,500

— Anr, [28 Nov 1818]. On autograph address leaf, 5 by 6.5 inches, addressed to Henry E. Watkins. Def. Illus in cat. Dar Apr 9 (242) $600

Jeffries, James Jackson, 1875-1953

Signature, [n.d.]. 4.75 by 2.5 inches. Dar Feb 13 (110) $250

Jennings, Hugh, 1869-1928

Signature, [n.d.]. 4.5 by 1.25 inches. In pencil. Dar Aug 6 (96) $500

Joachim, Joseph, 1831-1907

ALs, 21 Jan [n.y.]. 2 pp, 8vo. Recipient unnamed. Explaining his use of the metronome. star Mar 27 (1041) DM1,100

Autograph quotation, Allegretto, 2 May 1850. 1 p, 4to. 10 bars in B-flat major, scored for violin & piano. star Mar 27 (1040) DM1,200

Johann Georg II, Kurfuerst von Sachsen, 1613-80

Ms, Acta der Churfuerstl. Jaegerey Auffwartung, Ausritt und Einholung frembder Herrschafften..., [2 Feb 1669]. 156 pp, folio. In several hands. Orders, plans & memoranda regarding festivities on the occasion of the baptism of Prince Johann Georg IV. JG Sept 27 (373) DM1,100

ALs, [n.d.]. 1 p, folio. To Bartolomeo Sorlisi. Wishing him a speedy recovery. star Mar 27 (1693) DM600

Johann Wilhelm, Kurfuerst von der Pfalz, 1658-1716

ALs, 5 Feb 1696. 4 pp, 4to. To an unnamed prince. Negotiating the purchase of a diamond. star Mar 27 (1568) DM1,400

John II, King of Castile, 1405-54

Ds, 12 July 1435. 1 p, 4to. Order addressed to Juan Ruiz de Narvaez to join forces with other troops to conquer Granada. Def. sg Feb 27 (182) $1,300

John Paul I, Pope, 1912-78

Signature, [n.d.]. On ptd religious card, 5 by 7.5 inches. As Cardinal. Illus in cat. Dar Apr 9 (244) $750

John V, King of Portugal, 1689-1750

Ds, 22 Feb 1739. 1 p, folio. Appointment of Cardinal Corsini as envoy to the Holy See. star Mar 27 (1577) DM220

John XXII, Pope, 1245-1334

Document, [1 Nov] 1330. 1 p, vellum, 22.5cm by 36cm. Papal Bull for the convent of Premonstratensian nuns at Reusche [near Olmuetz]. Including seal. star Mar 27 (1541) DM3,600

Johnson, Andrew, 1808-75

[An unused ticket to his impeachment, 1 Apr 1868, 5 by 3 inches, sgd in facsimile by Sergeant at Arms George T. Brown, sold at Dar on 6 Aug 1992, lot 181, for $400.]

ALs, 17 Aug 1849. 1 p, 4to. To Messrs.

Clayton, Johnson & Collamer. Regarding the projected census. CNY June 9 (244) $3,200

— 12 Sept 1850. 3 pp, 4to. To William M. Laury. Discussing recipient's removal from office by the Fillmore administration. Including franking signature. sup May 9 (206) $6,250

Ls, 30 Sept 1864. 2 pp, size not stated. To President Lincoln. Introducing J. J. Sears. Illus in cat. sup May 9 (207) $4,600

— 27 Aug 1866. 1 p, 4to. To Sec of the Navy [Gideon Welles]. Requesting him to appoint John Preston Auger to the Naval Academy. CNY Dec 5 (70) $2,500

— 26 Aug 1867. 2 pp, 4to. To Brevet Major Gen. E. R. S. Canby. Ordering him to relieve Major Gen. Sickles of the command of the 2d Military District. Illus in cat. sup May 9 (208) $4,000

Ds, 1 June 1865. 1 p, folio. Appointment of John Jackson as Capt. of Infantry. Framed. sup Oct 15 (1544) $900

— 15 Nov 1865. 1 p, 4to. Order to affix the US Seal. sup Oct 15 (1545) $725

— 19 Mar 1867. 1 p, folio. Appointment of Benjamin F. Robinson as Assessor of Revenue. Dar June 11 (239) $550

— 26 Feb 1868. 1 p, folio. Letters of credence for Alexis Robert as Consul of the Papal States at New Orleans. Countersgd by Seward. R Nov 9 (17) $600

— 25 July 1868. 1 p, folio. Appointment of Charles P. Wannall as Justice of the Peace. Countersgd by Seward. wd Dec 12 (321) $450

— 1 Aug 1868. 1 p, folio. Exequatur for Enrique Aniz as Consul of Spain at Key West. Dar June 11 (238) $1,300

Franking signature, [c.1857]. On autograph envelope to R. M. Price. Dar June 11 (240) $325

— Anr, [n.d.]. On autograph envelope addressed to G. C. Whiting. Dar Oct 10 (215) $375

Johnson, Byron Bancroft, 1864-1931

Ds, 10 Jan 1922. 3 pp, 4to. Approval of a contract between Robert A. Tecarr & the NY Yankees. Also sgd by Tecarr & Jacob Ruppert. Dar Dec 26 (92) $250

Johnson, Jack, 1878-1946

Ls, 18 Mar 1914. 1 p, 4to. To C. F. Bertelli. Agreeing to write about a forthcoming fight for the NY American. Illus in cat. Dar Feb 13 (114) $2,250

Johnson, John Mordaunt, 1776?-1815

[A collection of papers, c.1791 to 1815, c.70 items in a cloth vol, relating mainly to his missions to Prussia & the Low Countries, sold at S on 12 Dec 1991, lot 262, for £1,000 to Duran.]

Johnson, Lady Bird

Check, sgd, 10 June 1987. Payable to Gerald Earl. wa Oct 19 (303) $70

Johnson, Lyndon B., 1908-73

[A typescript of his oath of office, sgd, 22 Nov 1963, on Air Force One stationery, 8vo, with a group photograph, sgd, of Johnson taking the oath of office, 4to, & copy of authentication, sold at sup on 15 Oct 1991, lot 1709, for $10,250.]

[Two signatures in green ink on a single sheet, 4 by 4 inches, attached to a typed note on White House letterhead, 12mo, sold at Dar on 11 June 1992, lot 244, for $130.]

Original drawing, sketch of what is happening in the Vietnam War, [17 May 1966]. 8vo. With letter of authentication. sup Oct 15 (1715) $300

Typescript (duplicated), message to Congress regarding immigration, 13 Jan 1965. 3 pp, folio. Sgd & inscr at head. Illus in cat. sup May 9 (282) $1,550

ALs, 22 Oct [19]63. 1 p, 12mo (card). To Dorothy Nichols. Sending a birthday present. Sgd Lady Bird and Lyndon Johnson. Illus in cat. sup Oct 15 (1708) $3,500

Series of 20 Ls s, 20 July 1954 to 21 Dec 1972. 20 pp, 4to. To Yolanda Boozer or members of her family. Personal letters to a long-time secretary, about a variety of matters. With related material. sup Oct 15 (1721) $3,200

— Series of 5 Ls s, 1970 to 1972. 5 pp, 8vo. To Adrian A. Spears. Contents not stated. Dar Aug 6 (186) $325

Ls, 31 Jan 1939. 1 p, 4to. To Mrs. Henry Bales. Informing her that he "contacted the Bureau of Fisheries" for her. Dar June 11 (242) $250

— 20 May 1940. 1 p, 4to. To Louise Goodwin. Expressing congratulations on her graduation from high school. Dar Apr 9 (245) $200

— 15 June 1949. 1 p, 4to. To Adrian A. Spears. Declining to "influence state officials regarding legislation". Dar Dec 26 (216) $300

— 18 Oct 1951. 1 p, 4to. To Adrian A. Spears. Forwarding a communication from Claude Wickard [present]. Dar Oct 10 (216) $225

— 18 June 1953. 1 p, 4to. To President Eisenhower. Carbon copy; hoping he can attend the State Fair in Dallas. With engraved philatelic port. Dar Apr 9 (246) $250

— 16 July 1953. 1 p, 4to. To Price [Daniel].

Expressing thanks for attention paid to his mother. sg Feb 27 (96) $130

— 1 Dec 1953.9. 1 p, 4to. To Adrian A. Spears. Advising that Sgt. Adams should apply for transfer to an air field near San Antonio. Dar Dec 26 (217) $300

— 26 Mar 1954. 1 p, 4to. To Adrian A. Spears. Regarding an upcoming election. Dar Dec 26 (218) $160

— 24 July 1956. 1 p, 4to. To Adrian A. Spears. Looking forward to the Democratic National Convention. Dar Feb 13 (219) $150

— 7 Aug 1956. 1 p, 4to. To Adrian A. Spears. Planning a caucus of the Texas delegation at the beginning of the Democratic National Convention. Dar Feb 13 (220) $190

— 5 Nov 1956. 1 p, 4to. To Dorothy Nichols. Informing her of a pay raise. sup Oct 15 (1705) $350

— 22 Jan 1957. 1 p, 4to. To Lawrence C. Laskey. Concerning the celebration of Eddie Cantor's 65th birthday. sg Sept 12 (125) $350

— 6 Apr 1957. 1 p, 4to. To Lloyd Hayes. Concerning "a commemorative stamp for the Texas Longhorn." Dar June 11 (243) $150

— 7 Oct 1959. 1 p, 4to. To William L. Cowan. Insisting that he is not a candidate for executive office. Dar June 11 (245) $300

— 24 May 1960. 1 p, 4to. To Adrian A. Spears. Declining an invitation. Matted with philatelic envelope. Dar June 11 (241) $110

— 30 Oct 1961. 1 p, 4to. To Adrian A. Spears. Expressing confidence that he "will add much distinction to the Federal Bench". Dar Oct 10 (217) $325

— 1 Feb 1964. 1 p, 4to. To Curt Schiffeler. Referring to the John F. Kennedy Center for the Performing Arts. sup Oct 15 (1711) $1,000

— 20 Feb 1964. 1 p, 4to. To Harry N. Burgess. Commending the work of the District of Columbia Manuscript Society. sup Oct 15 (1712) $1,050

— 1 Sept 1965. 1 p, 4to. To Cardinal McIntyre. Responding to a telegram concerning riots in Watts, Los Angeles. With related material. Illus in cat. sup May 9 (285) $2,450

— 25 Aug 1967. 1 p, 4to. To Chris Nichols. Responding to a letter from his secretary's son. Illus in cat. sup Oct 15 (1716) $600

— 1 Dec 1967. 1 p, 8vo. To Adrian A. Spears. Thanking for 2 encouraging letters. Dar Feb 13 (221) $450

— 1 July 1968. 1 p, 8vo. To Adrian A. Spears. Concerning Homer Thornberry's nomination as Supreme Court Justice. Dar Oct 10 (218) $800

— 10 Sept 1968. 1 p, 8vo. To Adrian A. Spears. Thanking for an article about Father Schneider. Dar Aug 6 (182) $550

— 13 Jan 1969. 2 p, 8vo. To Adrian A. Spears. Expressing satisfaction that he has been able "to appoint wise and devoted men like yourself to the bench." Illus in cat. Dar Feb 13 (222) $650

— 16 Jan 1969. 1 p, 4to. To Dorothy Nichols. Expressing thanks, & looking forward to his retirement. Illus in cat. sup Oct 15 (1718) $2,050

— 19 Jan 1969. 1 p, 8vo. To Harold Russell. Thanking for his work during the last 4 years. With a group photograph of both. Dar Aug 6 (185) $700

— 12 Nov 1969. 1 p, 8vo. To Adrian A. Spears. Declining an invitation to address the Rotary Club. With autograph postscript. Dar Oct 10 (219) $475

ANs, [c.1 June 1965]. 1 p, 4to. To Bill & Jack. At foot of a memorandum addressed to him by Richard Goodwin; regarding Robert Lowell's disagreement with the Vietnam policy. Illus in cat. sup May 9 (280) $5,000

Ds, 18 Apr 1964. 1 p, folio. Appointment of Harold Russell as Chairman of the Committee on Employment of the Handicapped. Dar Aug 6 (183) $1,900

Autograph endorsement, sgd, on a memorandum addressed to him by Dick Goodwin, 1 Sept 1964, 2 pp, 4to, suggesting general outlines & specific topics for political speeches; agreeing with suggestions. Illus in cat. sup May 9 (283) $1,250

Group photograph, [1957]. 10.25 by 13.25 inches. With Adrian Spears; sgd by Johnson & inscr to Sally Spears. Dar Dec 26 (219) $350

— Anr, addressing a joint session of Congress, 27 Nov 1963. Size not stated; framed. Sgd & inscr to Dorothy Nichols. Illus in cat. sup Oct 15 (1710) $1,550

— Anr, with Harold Russell & 4 others; [n.d.]. 11.5 by 7.5 inches (image). Inscr in calligraphy to Harold Russell & sgd. Dar Aug 6 (184) $300

— Anr, [n.d.]. 8 by 10 inches. With his cabinet & Vice President Humphrey. Sgd LBJ & inscr to Pierre. sup Oct 15 (1724) $200

Photograph, sgd & inscr, 18 Oct 1964. 8 by 10 inches. Inscr to Abbie Rowe. Dar Dec 26 (220) $450

Ptd photograph, [n.d.]. On folio sheet with reprint the Education Bill & of Johnson's remarks made on the signing of the Bill, 11 Apr 1965. Sgd & inscr to Joseph Clark. Illus in cat. sup Oct 15 (1714) $700

Signature, [n.d.]. On unused presidential bookplate. wa Oct 19 (304) $130

Johnson, Samuel, 1709-84

Autograph Ms, 6-word quotation in Greek & 7-word phrase in English; [n.d.]. 1 p, 4to. With note of authenticity. CNY Dec 5 (266) $850

ALs, 19 Nov 1774. 1 p, 4to. To Dr. Lawrence. Sending the "result of [his] negotiation" & mentioning Lord Sandwich. Illus in cat. sg Nov 7 (110) $6,000

— 25 Feb 1775. 1 p, 4to. To [Lucy Porter]. Describing his journey to North Wales & Anglesey. C Dec 16 (300) £7,000 [Quaritch]

ANs, [1768 or earlier]. 1 p, 16mo. To [Andrew Millar]. In 3d person, requesting a book. With note of authenticity at bottom. CNY Dec 5 (265) $3,600

AN, [May 1765?]. 32mo (card). To [David Garrick]. Inquiring about Shakespeare plays. pn Mar 19 (12) £5,500

See also: Boswell, James

Johnson, Uwe, 1934-84

Ls, 2 July 1968. 1 p, folio. Recipient unnamed. Analyzing the current unrest among the younger generation. star Mar 26 (287) DM550

Johnson, Walter Perry, 1887-1946

Signature, [n.d.]. 16mo (card). Dar Dec 26 (93) $350

— Anr, [n.d.]. 3.75 by 1 inches. Stained. Dar Feb 13 (85) $200

Johnston, Albert Sidney, 1803-62

ALs, 18 Mar 1857. 4 pp, 4to. To Col. S. Cooper. Strongly complaining of problems with the Quartermaster. Spiro collection. CNY May 14 (91) $2,800

Ls, 4 Apr [1862]. 2 pp, 8vo. To [J. C. Breckinridge]. Ordering troop movements prior to the Battle of Shiloh. CNY June 9 (245) $11,000

Jolson, Al, 1886-1950

Photograph, sgd & inscr, [n.d.]. 8 by 10 inches. Framed. sup Oct 15 (1330) $525

Signature, 1928. On program for the opening of the Warner Brothers Theatre in Hollywood. R Mar 7 (171) $60

Jones, Robert T. ("Bobby"), 1902-71

Photograph, sgd, [n.d.]. 8 by 10 inches. On golf course. Dar Feb 13 (189) $1,100

Signature, [n.d.]. 5 by 3 inches (card). Mtd. Illus in cat. Dar Aug 6 (164) $400

Jones, Samuel, 1820-87

ALs, 3 Mar 1870. 4 pp, 4to. To P. G. T. Beauregard. Recalling a meeting with Jefferson Davis regarding troop movements prior to "our signal victory at Manassas". Endorsed & initialled by Beauregard. CNY Dec 5 (71) $900

Jones, Spike

Photograph, sgd, [n.d.]. 8vo. Group photograph with band, with individual port inset at corner. wa Oct 19 (163) $75

Joplin, Janis, 1943-70

Ds, 29 Apr 1969. 1 p, folio. Contract for the Woodstock Music Festival. Framed with a photograph. Illus in cat. P Dec 17 (367) $4,750

Joplin, Scott, 1868-1917

Signature, [n.d.]. 7.25 by 6.25 inches. Dar Dec 26 (222) $2,250

Jordan, Pascual, 1902-80

Autograph Ms, fragment from a scientific paper, 21 Oct 1961. 2 pp, folio. Dealing with "Dirac's second hypothesis". With ANs. star Mar 26 (692) DM220

Joseph I, Emperor, 1678-1711

Ls, 26 Feb 1709. 2 pp, folio. To Archbishop Franz Ludwig of Trier & Elector Palatine Johann Wilhelm. Requesting permission for troops to pass through their territories. star Mar 27 (1650) DM700

Joseph II, Emperor, 1741-90

Ls, 25 Feb 1789. 1 p, 4to. To Count Kollowrat. Sending stipulations for insertion in a contract regarding shipments of mercury. star Mar 27 (1667) DM220

Ds, 4 Aug 1777. 2 pp, folio. Writ of execution in the case of D. H. C. Gischer. HN Nov 28 (1735) DM340

— 1 Sept 1781. 6 pp, folio. Ptd act specifying penal authority of feudal lords; in Czech. Numbered 15; sgd Jozehf. Illus in cat. HN Nov 28 (1736) DM2,300

Josephine, Empress of the French, 1763-1814

Endorsement, sgd, 17 Nov 1810. 1 p, 4to. On a report by Bonpland recommending the purchase of land in the Cote d'Or region; approuving acquisition. Framed. P June 17 (38) $1,900

Josephus, Flavius, 37-100?

Ms, De Bello Judaico, book IV:xi:5 to book V:i:5. [France, late 12th cent]. 2 leaves, vellum, 385mm by 218mm. In a small proto-gothic bookhand. With large & 3 small initials in red. Mtd. S Dec 17 (10) £1,500 [Quaritch]

Jourdan, Jean Baptiste de, 1762-1833

ALs, [23 Apr 1795]. 1 p, folio. To an army board in Paris. Notification that Gen. Tilly has arrived at Bonn. Also sgd by Tilly. star Mar 27 (1369) DM320

— [23 Sept 1795]. 1 p, 4to. To Gen. Kleber. Regarding damages committed in Prussian territory. sg Feb 27 (98) $200

Joyce, James, 1882-1941

ALs, 24 Feb 1933. 2 pp, size not stated. To Hubert Foss. Thanking for copies of the Joyce Book. Ck Apr 3 (16) £1,900

— 14 July 1934. 1 p, 4to. To Mr. MacFinlay. Sending a record & enclosing a typed poem, Molly Bloomagain (present, on conjugate leaf). P Oct 11 (183) $15,000

ANs, 14 Mar 1924. Card, 65mm by 102mm. Recipient unnamed. Sending congratulations on recipient's birthday. sg Dec 12 (184) $750

Photograph, sgd & inscr, 1 Sept 1925. 9 by 6 inches. Inscr to Herbert Gorman. Framed. sg June 11 (185) $6,500

Juarez, Benito, 1806-72

ALs, 13 Aug 1869. 2 pp, 8vo. To Dr. Gasser. Explaining that he cannot intervene in the case of debts incurred by Delfin Sanchez. sg Sept 12 (127) $1,000

Ds, 17 Jan 1856. 1 p, folio. Notification regarding orders "to gather data related to the establishments of public benefits" in Oaxaca. Illus in cat. sup Oct 15 (1378) $625

Photograph, sgd & inscr, [c.1868]. Carte size. Inscr to Kurd von Schloezer. star Mar 27 (1488) DM1,300

Judson, Edward Zane Carroll, 1823-86

Photograph, sgd & inscr, 31 Jan 1878. Cabinet size. By J. A. Benjamin. R Nov 9 (150) $450

Juenger, Ernst

Autograph Ms, Parerga zu 'Zahlen und Goetter"; 27 June 1974. 13 pp, folio. Working Ms, sgd & inscr. star Mar 26 (289) DM3,800

Collection of 6 A Ls s, 4 Ls s, & 5 postcards, sgd (4 autograph), 1 Oct 1936 to 20 June 1943. 23 pp, various sizes. To Ulrike Litzmann. About his works, the war, etc. star Mar 26 (290) DM4,000

Ls, 6 Apr 1948. 1 p, folio. To Bruno Schneider. Interpreting his work Sprache und Koerperbau. With related material. star Mar 26 (292) DM350

Juenger, Friedrich Georg, 1898-1977

Collection of 6 A Ls s & 8 autograph postcards, sgd, 1963 to 1976. 8 pp, 8vo, & cards. Recipient unnamed. About his works. star Mar 26 (294) DM620

Julius, Herzog von Braunschweig-Wolfenbuettel, 1528-89

Ls, [after 1576]. 1 p, folio. To an unnamed prince. Fragment, referring to the university at Helmstedt & difficulties with the city of Braunschweig. HN Nov 28 (1737) DM500

Julius II, Pope, 1443-1513

Document, 25 Apr 1506. 1 p, folio. Papal Bull; contents not stated. R Nov 9 (56) $320

Jung, Carl Gustav, 1875-1961

Ls, 16 June 1938. 3 pp, folio. To Benjamin Mendelsohn. Giving his detailed views on crime & punishment. In French. S Dec 5 (522) £1,500 [Sakmyster]

— 4 June 1955. 1 p, 4to. To Dr. John Gruesen. Responding to recipient's findings on basic patterns of behavior. Framed with a port. P June 17 (39) $2,250

Jung-Stilling, Johann Heinrich, 1740-1817

ALs, 18 Jan 1795. 2 pp, 12mo. To Friedrich Matthisson. About the birth of his son. star Mar 26 (288) DM950

K

Kaestner, Abraham Gotthelf, 1719-1800

AL, [c.1791]. 4 pp, 4to. To Christian Gottlob Heyne. About errors in an Ed of tables pbd by the Rev. Grosse. star Mar 26 (694) DM750

Kaestner, Erich, 1899-1974

A Ls s (2), 24 Jan 1929 & 30 July 1930. 2 pp, 4to & 8vo. To the Ed of the journal Simplizissimus. Regarding contributions. HH Nov 6 (2063) DM400

Kagan, Rachel Cohen

Signature, in English & Hebrew, at bottom of a copy of the Israeli Proclamation of Independence, 14 May 1948. 1 p, 4to. R Mar 7 (172) $650

Kalashnikov, Mikhail Timofeevich

Ls, [n.d.]. 1 p, 8vo. Recipient unnamed. Expressing thanks for hospitality. Dar Apr 9 (289) $100

Kalb, Johann, 1721-80

ALs, 9 July 1780. 2 pp, folio. To Major Gen. Richard Caswell. Informing him that he is unable to join him due to a lack of provisions. CNY June 9 (247) $8,000

Kanoldt, Alexander, 1881-1939

Collection of 3 Ls s & 2 autograph postcards, sgd, 1934 & 1935. 3 pp, 4to, & cards. Recipient unnamed. About the sale of his works. FD Dec 3 (1436) DM200

Kant, Immanuel, 1724-1804

ALs, 27 Jan 1777. 1 p, 4to. To an unnamed bookseller. Reporting about subscriptions for an Ed of Cicero. star Mar 26 (693) DM5,500

Kapodistrias, Ioannis Antonios, Count, 1776-1831

ALs, 28 Jan/9 Feb 1828. 2 pp, 8vo. To his brother Augustin. Reporting about his arrival in Greece. star Mar 27 (1459) DM900

Karl August, Grossherzog von Sachsen-Weimar, 1757-1828

ALs, 28 May 1798. 1 p, 4to. To Ludwig Ernst von Benckendorf. Expressing thanks. star Mar 26 (187) DM600

Karl I Ludwig, Kurfuerst von der Pfalz, 1617-80

ALs, 1/10 Apr 1638. 2 pp, folio. To Henry Rich, Earl of Holland. Referring to the King of England's support of his efforts & recipient's help. HN Nov 28 (1745) DM2,600

— 14 May 1657. 1 p, folio. To Luise von Degenfeld. About his efforts to have their union recognized by the church. Sgd with paraph. Illus in cat. star Mar 27 (1562a) DM1,700

— LUISE VON DEGENFELD, RAUGRAEFIN. - ALs, [1675/76]. 2 pp, 4to. To her son Karl Ludwig. Hoping to see him on his march with the army. star Mar 27 (1563) DM1,150

Karl Theodor, Kurfuerst von Bayern, 1724-99

Ls, 24 Mar 1787. 1 p, 4to. To Marchesa M. Zambeccari Scappi. Expressing satisfaction about her safe return to Italy. HN Nov 28 (1747) DM240

Document, 2 Sept 1790. 10 leaves (1 lacking), 345mm by 265mm. Patent of nobility for Caspar Kandler. With pen-&-ink border at head. HH Nov 5 (845) DM600

Karl Wilhelm Ferdinand, Herzog von Braunschweig-Wolfenbuettel, 1735-1806

Ls, 16 Oct 1804. 2 pp, 4to. To an unnamed court councillor. Agreeing to provide financial support for a teacher at Blankenburg. star Mar 27 (1293) DM320

Karloff, Boris, 1887-1969

Cut signature, [n.d.]. Size not stated. Framed with a photograph, overall size 16 by 26 inches. sup Oct 15 (1332) $220

Signature, [n.d.]. 12mo (card). Matted with related material. Dar Dec 26 (189) $250

— Anr, [n.d.]. 4 by 2.5 inches. In extra frame with a port. Dar Aug 6 (18) $450

Karsch, Anna Luise, 1722-91

Autograph Ms, poem, beginning "Der Erde Gueter sind am sterbebette...", [Nov 1783]. 1 p, 4to. End rhymes inserted in anr hand. star Mar 26 (296) DM1,200

ALs, 14 Apr 1777. 4 pp, 8vo. To Johann Martin Miller. Commenting on his novel Siegwart & reporting about a visit with Daniel Chodowiecki. star Mar 26 (297) DM2,500

Kaunitz-Rietberg, Wenzel Anton, Fuerst von, 1711-94

ALs, 17 June 1757. 1 p, 8vo. To an unnamed lady. Conveying the Emperor's invitation to a meeting at Schoenbrunn. HN Nov 28 (1749) DM380

Kearny, Philip, 1814-62

ALs, 7 May 1851. 2 pp, 4to. To Major Gen. R. Jones. Requesting letters of reference for Col. De Peyster. rf Sept 21 (11) $425

Keaton, Buster, 1896-1966

Photograph, sgd, [n.d.]. 9 by 14 inches. By Melbourne Spurr. Framed. Illus in cat. sup Oct 15 (1333) $210

Signature, [n.d.]. 5 by 2.75 inches. Dar Feb 13 (238) $100

Keaton, Diane

Ds, [n.d.]. 2 pp, 4to. Contract for her role in the film The Godfather, Part II. Dar Apr 9 (251) $225

Keefe, Timothy J., 1857-1933

Cut signature, [n.d.]. Matted with related material, 8 by 10 inches. Dar Dec 26 (94) $500

Keeler, Willie, 1872-1923

Signature, [n.d.]. 4 by 2 inches. Matted with Hall of Fame card. Dar June 11 (86) $225

Keitel, Wilhelm, 1882-1946

Ls, Feb 1944. 1 p, 4to. To Albert Speer. Requesting him to replace the roof of army headquarters with fireproof material. Dar Apr 9 (252) $550

Keller, Gottfried, 1819-90

ALs, 27 Aug 1881. 4 pp, 8vo. To the Ed of the journal Nord und Sued. Offering the poem Der Apotheker von Chamonix for print & referring to Heine's Romanzero. Gottschalk collection. C Dec 16 (405) £2,400 [Rosenthal]

— 25 Nov 1881. 1 p, 8vo. To [Paul Lindau]. About a port & a contribution to the journal Nord und Sued. star Mar 26 (300) DM1,600

Keller, Helen, 1880-1968

Ls, 10 Feb 1928. 1 p, 4to. To Mr. Solday. About the American Foundation for the Blind. sup Oct 15 (1334) $420

— 8 Oct 1942. 1 p, 8vo. To E. Earle Moore. Thanking for financial support. sg Sept 12 (130) $200

Photograph, sgd & inscr, 14 June 1938. 9.5 by 7 inches. Inscr to Perry Finkelstein. Dar Oct 10 (238) $400

Kellermann, Francois Christophe, Duc de Valmy, 1735-1820

Ls, 17 Aug 1807. 1 p, folio. To Gen. Rouget. Regarding the arrest of 4 soldiers at Mainz. star Mar 27 (1370) DM380

— 31 May 1808. 1 p, 4to. To Gen. Leclaire. Conveying an order regarding military banners. star Mar 27 (1371) DM220

Kelly, Grace, 1929-82. See: Grace, 1929-82

Kelly, Walt, 1913-73

Original drawing, charcoal drawing of Pogo, [1950s]. 18 by 22 inches; rolled. Sgd & inscr with thanks. With authentication. Dar June 11 (261) $550

Kemble, Fanny, 1809-93

ALs, [n.d.], "Thursday". 8 pp, 8vo. To Lady Georgiana. Describing her friendships & ambitions. Ingilby collection. pn Nov 14 (84) £55

Kendall, Amos, 1789-1869

Photograph, [n.d.]. 1/6 plate daguerreotype. R Nov 9 (172) $300

Kennedy, Edward M.

Ls, 26 Jan 1979. 1 p, 4to. To Michael Levy. Regarding speculations about the death of his brothers. With related material. Illus in cat. sup Oct 15 (1704) $525

Kennedy, John F., 1917-63

Autograph Ms, brief pen & pencil doodles & notes, referring to Berlin; 1963. 1 p, 12mo, on ptd letterhead. Illus in cat. sup Oct 15 (1697) $1,100

— Autograph Ms, doodles & initials HEW, [Jan 1961]. 1 p, 8.5 by 10 inches. In black ink. Illus in cat. sup Oct 15 (1698) $800

— Autograph Ms, speech about Nato politics, delivered at Holy Cross College, 15 Nov 1955. On verso of his reading copy of a speech given at South Weymouth Naval Air Station, 18 Oct 1955. 6 pp, 4to. Illus in cat. Dar June 11 (26) $11,000

ALs, [25 Oct 1951]. 4 pp, 4to. To Broke Mickey. Thanking for assistance in Karachi & commenting on Americal periodicals pbd in Pakistan. Spiro collection. CNY May 14 (92) $4,800

— [n.d.]. 1 p, 4to. Recipient unnamed. Requesting that Miss Desrosiers be permitted "to use the Kennedy apartment". Illus in cat. Dar Apr 9 (40) $1,600

Ls, 21 Oct 1949. 1 p, 8vo. To M. W. Espy. Responding to a request for his autograph. Dar Dec 26 (23) $950

— 25 Nov 1952. 1 p, 8vo. To Harold [Russell]. Thanking for congratulations on his election to the Senate. Dar Aug 6 (190) $900

— 8 May 1953. 1 p, 4to. To Fred Martin. Requesting mailing lists of nationality groups to send information to Massachusetts. Including autograph postscript. Illus in cat. sup Oct 15 (1683) $800

— 4 June 1953. 1 p, 4to. To an unnamed Senator. Sending statements by Congressman Heselton regarding air mail subsidies. Illus in cat. sup Oct 15 (1684) $700

— 6 Oct 1953. 1 p, 4to. To Walter J. McCann. Responding to recipient's inquiry about a job. Illus in cat. sup Oct 15 (1685) $900

— 4 Nov 1953. 1 p, 4to. To Helen Sullivan. Asking her to help find a job for Walter McCann. Illus in cat. sup Oct 15 (1686) $725

— 23 Mar 1954. 1 p, 4to. To Commander Clem Steffanello. Regarding "special recognition of racial or religious veterans' groups." wa Oct 19 (312) $425

— 12 May 1954. 1 p, 4to. To James Wiseman. Discussing the McCarthy-Army hearings. Illus in cat. sup Oct 15 (1687) $890

— 7 Jan 1955. 1 p, 8vo. To Arthur Z. Silver. Acknowledging a message received in hospital. Dar June 11 (23) $1,300

— 7 Jan 1955. 1 p, 8vo. To Arthur Z. Silver. Thanking for a message received in hospital. Illus in cat. sup Oct 15 (1688) $800

— 3 June 1955. 1 p, 4to. To Joseph Finn. Concerning a promotion for a post office clerk. wa Oct 19 (311) $800

— 2 Dec 1955. 1 p, 4to. To John G. DiCroce. Informing him that he has protested against curtailment of personnel at the Charlestown Navy Yard. Dar June 11 (24) $700

— 24 May 1956. 1 p, 8vo. To Lillian Sargeant Safstrom. Assuring her of his support of rehabilitation programs. Dar June 11 (25) $550

— 26 Feb 1957. 1 p, 4to. To Louise R. Palci. Forwarding a letter of the American Consul in Havana (included) about her husband's immigrant visa. Including autograph postscript, sgd J.K. Dar Apr 9 (39) $1,500

— 26 Feb 1957. 1 p, 4to. To Louise Palci. Forwarding a carbon copy of a letter from the American Embassy in Cuba (included) regarding her husband's visa. Illus in cat. sup Oct 15 (1691) $1,200

— 30 July 1957. 1 p, 4to. To Harold Russell. Regarding Russell's recommendation of Thomas Burke for a position in the Social Security Administration. Dar Aug 6 (191) $475

— 26 Dec 1961. 1 p, 4to. To Nate White. Reflecting on American policy towards the Common Market in Europe. Illus in cat. sup May 9 (276) $7,100

— 14 Aug 1963. 1 p, 8vo. To Kenneth J. Gray. Thanking for condolences on the death of his son. Dar June 11 (27) $2,250

Letter, 29 Apr 1963. 1 p, 4to. To Leon

Keyserling. Typed draft, expressing anger at recipient's vituperative remarks & arranging a meeting with Ted Sorensen. Including autograph addition. Illus in cat. sup Oct 15 (1696) $725

ANs, [n.d.]. 1 p, folio. Recipient unnamed. Memorandum regarding information to be given to Pierre [Salinger] about a telephone call & a cable to Churchill. Sgd J.K. Illus in cat. sup May 9 (274) $6,750

Ns, 5 Sept 1962. 1 p, 4to. To Bill Martin. Memorandum requesting his opinion on an article on Japanese economic growth. sup May 9 (277) $2,475

Ds, 25 Aug 1961. 1 p, folio. Appointment of Frederick Gutheim to the Advisory Board of the National Capital Transportation Agency. Countersgd by Dean Rusk. Framed. wa Dec 19 (253) $1,500

— 3 Apr 1962. 1 p, folio. Appointment of Harold Russell as Vice Chairman of the Committee on Employment of the Handicapped. Dar Aug 6 (192) $3,750

Menu, [n.d.]. From US Senate restaurant, size not stated. Sgd & inscr to Tad. sup Oct 15 (1694) $525

New Year's card, sgd, [late 1963]. 8vo. Also sgd by Jacqueline Kennedy. sup May 9 (278) $2,200

Photograph, sgd, [4 Mar 1963]. Size not stated. Also sgd by Jacqueline Kennedy. With secretarial letter of transmittal. LH Dec 11 (13) $400

— Anr, [n.d.]. 10 by 8 inches. Ck Apr 3 (126) £220

Photograph, sgd & inscr, [c.1962]. 10 by 8 inches. Inscr to Frank Scott. By Bachrach. P Dec 12 (117) $1,500

— Anr, [c.1962]. 9.12 by 7.12 inches. Inscr to Mr. Ball. Framed. P Dec 12 (118) $1,400

Signature, [n.d.]. 3.5 by 2.5 inches. Framed with a photograph. Dar Feb 13 (19) $650

— RUBY, JACK. - ANs, [n.d.]. 1 p, 12mo. To a Deputy Sheriff in the Dallas jail. Insisting that he is "being used as a political scapegoat." Illus in cat. Dar Apr 9 (49) $8,500

— RUBY, JACK. - Check, accomplished & sgd, 17 Dec 1950. For the Silver Spur night club, payable to Jimmy Belken. Dar Dec 26 (33) $650

— RUBY, JACK. - Check, accomplished & sgd, 30 Dec 1960. Payable to the Dallas Times Herald. Dar Dec 26 (34) $600

— RUBY, JACK. - Check, sgd, 11 Nov 1953. Payable to National Screen Service. Dar Feb 13 (20) $500

— RUBY, JACK. - Check, sgd, 25 Feb 1960. Payable to Sigels Liquor. Dar Feb 13 (21) $350

— RUBY, JACK. - Check, accomplished & sgd, 8 Feb 1951. Payable to Pearl Dist. Co. Dar Apr 9 (44) $500

— RUBY, JACK. - Check, sgd, 2 Apr 1960. Payable to Ted Stanford. Also sgd by Joe E. Slatin. Dar Apr 9 (46) $450

— RUBY, JACK. - Check, accomplished & sgd, 10 Apr 1961. Payable to the Dallas Power & Light Co. Dar June 11 (49) $400

— RUBY, JACK. - Check, accomplished & sgd, 10 Apr 1961. Payable to the Dallas Times Herald. Illus in cat. Dar June 11 (50) $275

— RUBY, JACK. - Ds, 15 May 1957. 1 p, 4to. Waver of Notice for a stockholders' meeting for Min-I-Ron Co., Inc. Dar Dec 26 (31) $300

— RUBY, JACK. - Ds, 4 Feb 1952. 3 pp, 4to. Agreement with Hyman Fader to establish a night club. Also sgd by Fader. Dar Dec 26 (32) $750

— RUBY, JACK. - Ds, 24 Aug 1953. 1 p, 9.25 by 4 inches. Promissory note no 89831 payable to the Republic National Bank of Dallas. Dar Apr 9 (45) $375

— RUBY, JACK. - Ds, 18 Mar 1952. 5 pp, 4to. Agreement to act as business manager of Ben Estes Nelson; also sgd by Columbus L. Nelson. Dar Apr 9 (47) $400

— RUBY, JACK. - Signature, [n.d.]. On guest card to Club Latino in Dallas, 16mo. Dar Dec 26 (30) $350

— SHAW, CLAY. - Ls, [30 Jan 1968]. 1 p, 4to. To Tom Dawson. Hoping for a speedy trial "to prove [New Orleans District Attorney Jim Garrison] is mad". Dar Apr 9 (50) $800

— SHAW, ROBERT R., M.D. - ALs, 18 June 1984. 2 pp, 4to. To David. Eyewitness account describing the wounds received by Kennedy & Gov. Connolly. Dar Dec 26 (29) $475

— SMATHERS, GEORGE. - Ls, 28 July 1956. 1 p, size not stated. To J. F. Kennedy. Reporting Johnson's reaction to Kennedy's supportive telegram. With some brief unrelated notes in Kennedy's hand on verso. sup Oct 15 (1690) $700

— YAMASHIRO, CAPT. KATSUMARI. - Autograph Ms, The True Story of Pres. John F. Kennedy's PT109 Collision, [n.d.]. 1 p, 4to. Eyewitness account by the commander of the Japanese destroyer Amagiri; including drawing of a map at bottom. With a photograph of Yamashiro, sgd. Dar Dec 26 (27) $1,000

Kennedy, Robert F., 1925-68

Ls s (2), 17 Mar & 1 Sept 1961. 2 pp, 4to. To Gene Schoor. Thanking for books & promising to contact him next week. Dar Oct 10 (240) $325

Ls, 2 Sept 1965. 1 p, 4to. To Rabbi Jay R. Brickman. Referring to the way his brother John F. Kennedy used to quote a poem by

Robert Frost. Dar Feb 13 (240) $425

Photograph, sgd, [n.d.]. 5 by 7 inches. Dar Dec 26 (238) $300

— Milton Academy. - 2 documents, report cards for Robert F. Kennedy, 23 Sept to 14 Nov 1942 & 15 Nov 1943 to 28 Jan 1944; retained carbon copies. 13 pp in 2 stapled booklets, 12mo. With related material. Dar Oct 10 (241) $375

Kent, Rockwell, 1882-1971

Ls s (2), 8 Dec 1957 & 8 Mar 1960. 3 pp, 4to. To the Ed, Chicago Daily News. About his legal efforts to obtain a passport, & urging Americans to support disarmament. sup Oct 15 (1335) $420

Kenton, Simon, 1755-1836

Ds, 28 Sept 1782. 1 p, 8vo. Bond for /24500 to William Montgomery in a land transaction. Framed. Illus in cat. sup May 9 (365) $1,350

Kentucky

[A photo album kept by the Louisville, Ky., Police Department, c.1860s & 1870s, 120 pp, folio, containing 470 photographs of outlaws & criminals with handwritten descriptions, sold at R on 9 Nov 1991, lot 148, for $9,000.]

Kerensky, Alexander Fyodorovich, 1881-1970

Transcript, excerpt, predicting that the democratic regime will prevail over the Russian dictatorship, 25 Nov 1959. 1 p, 12mo (card). Sgd. Dar Dec 26 (239) $350

Kern, Jerome, 1885-1945

ANs, [n.d.]. 1 p, 12mo. To Rudy. "As promised, here we are." In pencil; framed with a port. Dar Apr 9 (256) $225

Kerner, Justinus, 1786-1862

Collection of 56 A Ls s & 13 Ls s, 27 Sept 1848 to 12 Oct 1860. 163 pp, various sizes. To Gustav v. Pfaff & his wife. About personal matters, family problems, his son Theobald's incarceration, etc. star Mar 26 (301) DM28,000

Kerouac, Jack, 1922-69

Ls, 22 Oct 1948. 1 p, 4to. To Bob Strange of Little, Brown. Offering his novel The Town and the City for print. With related material. CNY June 9 (103) $2,600

Key, Francis Scott, 1779-1843

ALs, 18 Jan 1838. 2 pp, 4to. To Franklin Bache. Inquiring about legal procedures. bbc Dec 9 (169) $400

— 3 Aug 1842. 1 p, 4to. Recipient unnamed. Informing him of his son's intention to start a law practice in Iowa. Illus in cat. R Mar 7 (173) $700

Ds, 2 May 1807. 1 p, folio. Plea in a case regarding payment of a debt; sgd as attorney for plaintiffs. Illus in cat. sup Oct 15 (1336) $1,000

Keyserling, Hermann, Graf von, 1880-1946

Collection of 22 A Ls s, 4 Ls s, & 4 autograph postcards, sgd, 1934 to 1939. About 79 pp, various sizes. To Antonio Aita. Important letters about his philosophy, his work, the political situation, etc. star Mar 26 (696) DM2,400

Khachaturian, Aram, 1903-78

Collection of ALs, photograph, sgd, & signature, 28 Nov 1966 & [n.d.]. 2 pp, folio & 8vo, & size not stated. To Pavel Eckstein. About a recent biography, & commenting on a list of his works. star Mar 27 (995) DM1,200

Khevenhueller, Ludwig Andreas, Graf von, 1683-1744

Ls, [c.Aug 1743]. 2 pp, 8vo. Recipient unnamed. Expecting recipient's visit, & commenting on the state of the war. HN Nov 28 (1752) DM800

Khomeini, Ruhollah, Ayatollah, c.1900-89

Photograph, sgd, [n.d.]. 3.5 by 5 inches. Illus in cat. Dar Feb 13 (241) $675

Khrushchev, Nikita Sergeyevich, 1894-1971

Ls, 11 June 1960. 1 p, folio. To the General Secretary of the Communist Party of Great Britain John Gollan. Sending the text of his discussions with De Gaulle, Macmillan & Eisenhower in Paris. With related Russian pamphlet. S May 28 (213) £500 [Franks]

Kienzl, Wilhelm, 1857-1941

Collection of ALs, autograph postcard, sgd, & signature, 3 Apr 1907, 27 June 1930, & [n.d.]. 2 pp, 8vo, & visiting card. To Leo Slezak & his wife. About a performance of Der Evangelimann, & contents not stated. star Mar 27 (1043) DM220

Kieser, Dietrich Georg, 1779-1862

Ls, 24 Nov 1860. 4 pp, 4to. To Theodor von Heuglin. Asking that he look into recent theories about the descent of man when traveling in Africa. star Mar 26 (697) DM1,100

Killigrew, Sir William, 1606-95

Ds, 3 July 1675. 1 p, 4to. Receipt for quarterly payment of his pension. bba Sept 19 (359) £60 [Sutherland]

Kilmer, Joyce, 1886-1918

ALs, 11 Feb 1910. 1 p, 4to. To Russell. Informing him that she has not received his book of verses. Dar Feb 13 (242) $150

King, Martin Luther, Jr., 1929-68

Ls, 18 Jan 1966. 1 p, 4to. To William A. Bennett. Reflecting on the meaning of the words "dark skinned American". Dar Dec 26 (241) $3,750

King, Philip Gidley, 1758-1808

Ds, 1 Jan 1806. 2 pp, folio. Acknowledging the right of William Pascoe Crook to a plot of land at Parramatta, New South Wales; later made over to Rowland Hassall. Illus in cat. Longueville collection. S June 25 (160) £1,400 [Simpson]

King, Stephen

[An archive of material covering his literary career, early 1971 to May 1978, consisting of 48 letters (mostly Ls s) to William G. Thompson & others at Doubleday & Co., copies of replies, autograph Ms & 7 typescripts, etc., sold at CNY on 9 June 1992, lot 104, for $22,000.]

Kinkel, Gottfried, 1815-82

ALs, 2 June 1852. 1 p, 8vo. To an unnamed lady. Concerning German classes for her son. star Mar 27 (1460) DM520

— 19 Mar 1881. 8 pp, 8vo. To an unnamed lady. Pessimistic reflections on his life and the times. star Mar 27 (1461) DM800

Kino, Eusebio Francisco, 1645-1711

Autograph Ms, report of baptisms in San Ignacio de Caborica & San Joseph de los Hymeres, Nov 1690. 4 pp, 8vo. sup May 9 (140) $950

Kipling, Rudyard, 1865-1936

Typescript, The Muse among the Motors, [1919]. 32 pp, folio. With autograph revisions; also annotated in anr hand. With proofs of the work in the Seven Seas Ed of his works, with autograph corrections; 1919, 40 pp. S July 21 (143) £2,000 [Zimmerman]

Series of 34 A Ls s, 1886 to 1890. 55 pp, mostly 8vo. Green levant gilt by Sangorski & Sutcliffe. To the pbrs Thacker, Spink & Co. Regarding the publication of his 1st books. P Dec 12 (59) $27,000

ALs, 20 Feb 1920. 1 p, 8vo. To the Chairman of the Zeebrugge Memorial Fund. Agreeing to become a Vice Patron. bba June 25 (128) £90 [Silverman]

Ls, 7 Sept 1934. 1 p, 4to. To G. E. Chambers. Replying to an inquiry about the history of Bateman's. bba June 25 (129) £80 [Wilson]

— 8 May 1935. 1 p, 8vo. To William Drew. Expressing thanks. Matted with ptd port. Dar June 11 (262) $225

Corrected galley proof, 5 articles, The War in the Mountains, [1917]. 2 complete sets, 20 pp of long sheets in all. Including autograph corrections & revisions. S July 21 (146) £1,100 [Sawyer]

Corrected proof, 2 sets of proof sheets for the 1st English Ed of The Years Between, both with autograph corrections, 1918, 33 sheets in all. S July 21 (144) £1,300 [Sawyer]

Photograph, sgd, [n.d.]. 8.5 by 11.5 inches. Mtd. wd Dec 12 (322) $600

Signature, [n.d.]. 3.75 by 3 inches. Dar Feb 13 (243) $250

Kirchhoff, Gustav Robert, 1824-87

ALs, 6 June 1882. 2 pp, 8vo. To A. L. Besser. Responding to recipient's lecture "Was ist Empfindung?" hen Nov 12 (2536) DM210

Kisch, Egon Erwin, 1885-1948

ALs, 5 Nov 1910. 1 p, 4to. To Herr Schmidt. Returning an old railway ticket (present). star Mar 26 (304) DM220

— 16 Mar 1930. 2 pp, 4to. Recipient unnamed. Responding to critical remarks about his book Paradies Amerika. star Mar 26 (305) DM340

Kitchener, Horatio Herbert, Earl Kitchener of Khartoum & of Broome, 1850-1916

ALs, 1906. 4 pp, 4to. To Mr. Macartney. Asking him to inquire about Chinese porcelain for his collection. b June 22 (113) £85

Klabund, Pseud. of Alfred Henschke, 1890-1928

ALs, [n.d.]. 1 p, 4to. To an unnamed pbr. Agreeing to contribute to a projected journal. star Mar 26 (305) DM340

Klaproth, Martin Heinrich, 1743-1817

ALs, [10 Jan 1801]. 2 pp, 4to. To Johann Bartholomaeus Trommsdorff. Thanking for a publication & reporting about his recent research. star Mar 26 (698) DM1,600

Klebe, Giselher

Autograph music, sketches for his Quadrofonica & for his 5th Symphony, [n.d.]. 2 pp, folio & 8vo. Both sgd & inscr later. star Mar 27 (1044) DM380

Kleber, Jean Baptiste, 1753-1800

Ds, [13 Oct 1794]. 1 p, folio. List of brigades employed for the attack on Maastricht. star Mar 27 (1372) DM620

Kleist von Nollendorf, Friedrich, Graf, 1762-1823

Ls, 16 July 1807. 2 pp, 4to. To [Gen. Ribbentrop]. Discussing the military & political situation after the battle at Eylau. star Mar 27 (1463) DM650

— 2 May 1815. 1 p, folio. To Major von Boyen. Expressing congratulations on his military promotion. star Mar 27 (1464) DM220

Klem, William J., 1874-1951

ALs, 23 Jan 1948. 1 p, 4to. To Ross Wetzsteon. Stating that John H. Wagner is the baseball player he admires most. Dar Dec 26 (95) $1,300

Klinger, Friedrich Maximilian von, 1752-1831

ANs, [1802]. 1 p, 8vo. To Herr Busse. Inviting him for dinner. star Mar 26 (307) DM550

Klinger, Max, 1857-1920

ALs, 23 Aug 1910. 2 pp, 8vo. To an unnamed lady. Regarding photographs & an exhibition at the Academy. HH May 13 (1980) DM220

Klopstock, Friedrich Gottlieb, 1724-1803

Autograph Ms, fragment of a poem, beginning "Der Andern Heere werden nicht abgedankt..."; [n.d.]. 1 p, 55mm by 155mm. 4 lines. With authentication on verso. HH May 13 (1981) DM280

Knebel, Karl Ludwig von, 1744-1834

ALs, 15 Jan 1829. 2 pp, 4to. To Goeschen. Discussing a new Ed of his poems. HH May 13 (1954) DM340

Knerr, Harold H.

Photograph, sgd & inscr, [1930]. 7.25 by 9.25 inches (image). Inscr to Mr. & Mrs. Frank Seaman. Dar Oct 10 (114) $100

Knox, Henry, 1750-1806

Ls, 26 Aug 1789. 2 pp, folio. To the President & Directors of the Bank of NY. Requesting a loan to negotiate treaties with the Indians. Spiro collection. CNY May 14 (93) $2,400

Koch, Robert, 1843-1910

ALs, 20 May 1884. 2 pp, 8vo. Recipient unnamed. Expressing thanks. star Mar 26 (699) DM1,100

— 14 Nov 1909. 2 pp, 8vo. To Dr. Conradi. About recipient's application for the title of professor. star Mar 26 (701) DM950

Autograph postcard, sgd, 18 Aug 1884. To Lieut. Boehmer. Respoonding to an inquiry about a work on bacteriology. star Mar 26 (700) DM520

Kochno, Boris

[A large and important archive comprising over 70 autograph notebooks, Mss of his libretti, working papers for his books, & a vast collection of letters, c.1918 to 1987, sold at SM on 12 Oct 1991, lot 373, for FF650,000.]

See also: Diaghilev, Sergei Pavlovich & Kochno

Kodaly, Zoltan, 1882-1967

ALs, 17 Feb [1962]. 4 pp, 8vo. To Erno Balogh. About personal & musical matters. sg Sept 12 (133) $350

— 24 Mar 1962. 2 pp, 8vo. To Erno Balogh. About his recent travels, & requesting a book. sg Sept 12 (134) $250

— 26 Aug [1964]. 2 pp, 8vo. To Erno Balogh. About his travel plans, & mentioning Toscanini. sg Sept 12 (135) $175

Koerner, Theodor, 1791-1813

ALs, 26 Sept [1812]. 1 p, 4to. To his family. Announcing the completion of his play Hedwig. Kuenzel collection. star Mar 26 (309) DM320

Kohlrausch, Friedrich Wilhelm Georg, 1840-1910

Ls, 1 July 1897. 1 p, 4to. To Franc von Liechtenstein. Concerning a certificate for a mechanic. star Mar 26 (702) DM200

Kokoschka, Oskar, 1886-1980

ALs, 20 Feb 1914. 2 pp, 8vo. To Kurt Wolff. Promising to send a requested work, & inquiring about exhibits at the Leipzig Book Fair. star Mar 27 (904) DM750

Kolb, Annette, 1875-1967

ALs, 9 May 1954. 4 pp, 8vo. To [Hans Ulbricht?]. Asking for a copy of an essay. star Mar 26 (308) DM210

Kollwitz, Kaethe, 1867-1945

Collection of ALs & Ls, 13 Jan & 13 Oct 1915. 3 pp, 4to. To Georg Reicke. Regarding her projected war memorial, & inquiring about the sale of works by members of the Freie Sezession at Berlin. star Mar 27 (906) DM800

— Collection of ALs & 2 A Ns s, 15 Mar [19]23 to 24 Aug 1926. 1 p, 8vo, & 2 cards. Recipient unnamed. Concerning a fee & a reproduction of an etching. FD Dec 3 (1440) DM350

ALs, 2 Apr 1902. 2 pp, 8vo. To Julius Bab. Commenting on recipient's remarks about crowds of people. star Mar 27 (905) DM1,700

— [n.d.]. 2 pp, 8vo. To Capt. Gutschmidt. Responding to a request for some works for an exhibition. star Mar 27 (907) DM750

Autograph postcard, sgd, [23 June 1919]. To Dora Menzler. Responding to a request for a bookplate. HN Nov 28 (1753) DM480

Kollwitz, Kaethe, 1867-1945

ANs, 15 Dec [1927?]. 1 p, 12mo. To Herr Unger. Responding to a request for her autograph. Mtd with a port. JG Sept 27 (383) DM340

Kopp, Georg von, Cardinal, 1837-1914

ALs, 29 June 1901. 2 pp, 8vo. To [Franz von Reichenau]. About recipient's health. star Mar 27 (1465) DM320

Koran

— [North Africa, 8th/9th cent]. 4 leaves, vellum, 120mm by 190mm. In kufic script. HH Nov 5 (864) DM10,000

— [Arabia?, 9th cent]. Single leaf, vellum, 207mm by 295mm. In kufic script with diacritics in red & green. With sura heading in red within a panel of interlaced knotwork. Illus in cat. S Apr 30 (318) £1,600

— [Arabia, 9th cent]. Single leaf, vellum, 210mm by 294mm. In kufic script with diacritics in red & red roundels or commas between verses. Illus in cat. S Apr 30 (319) £1,000

— [North Africa, 9th cent]. Single leaf, vellum, 189mm by 250mm. In dispersed kufic script with diacritics in red & green, & red roundels or green commas between verses. Frayed. Illus in cat. S Apr 30 (321) £850

— [North Africa, 9th/10th cent]. Single leaf, vellum, 320mm by 394mm. In elongated kufic script with diacritics in red & colored markers between verses. Illus in cat. S Apr 30 (317) £13,000

— [Quairawan, 10th cent]. Single leaf, vellum, 146mm by 208mm. In gold kufic script with diacritics in red, green & blue, & gold florets outlined in blue between verses. Illus in cat. S Apr 30 (323) £6,000

— [Persia, Mashhad?, c.A.H.393/A.D.1002]. Juz XVIII only. 152 leaves, 100mm by 75mm, in contemp patterned brown mor bdg. On brown paper in eastern kufic script. With sura headings in ornamental kufic in gold or white on illuminated panels. With [autograph?] inscr by Abu'l Qasim Mansur, 1002. Illus in cat. S Apr 30 (331) £48,000

— [Andalusia, Valencia?, A.H.556/A.D.1160]. 134 leaves, vellum, 170mm by 160mm. Def brown mor bdg tooled in blind. In maghribi script by Abdullah bin Muhammad bin Ali. With sura headings in ornamental kufic in gold with circular devices infilled with interlocking strapwork in foliate design, & full-page illuminated panel richly decorated with geometric motifs. Illus in cat. S Apr 30 (336) £240,000

— [Ottoman?, 15th cent]. Surat al-Baqara, part 2, verses 142 - 252. 42 leaves, 350mm by 250mm. Contemp brown mor bdg tooled in gold & silver. In muhaqqaq script in gold & blue, with titles written in floriated kufic in white. With gold rosettes between verses & double page of fine illumination in orange, white & gold. Illus in cat. S Apr 30 (343) £35,000

— [Ottoman, 16th cent]. 431 leaves, 81mm by 60mm. 19th-cent red mor bdg. In naskhi script. With gold dots between verses, sura headings in gold, & double page of illumination preceded by an illuminated shamsa. S Apr 30 (341) £800

— [Istanbul?, A.H.1215/A.D.1800-01]. 77 leaves, 158mm by 102mm. European olive mor gilt in Islamic style. In naskhi script by 'Abd al-Qadir al-Shukri. With 5 illuminated panels & 2 headpieces with floral decoration in colors. sg Nov 7 (158) $850

— [Qajar, c.1825]. 353 leaves (2 blank), 67mm by 42mm. Contemp floral lacquer bdg. In naskhi script. With gold discs between verses, sura headings in white thuluth on gold panels, & double page of illumination. S Apr 30 (338) £2,800

— [Qajar, 19th cent]. 270 leaves, 77mm by 45mm. Contemp floral lacquer bdg. In naskhi script. With gold roundels between verses, sura headings in red on illuminated panels, & double page of illumination. S Apr 30 (339) £1,400

— [Ottoman, A.H.1270/A.D.1853]. 309 leaves, 140mm by 94mm. Def contemp red mor gilt. In naskhi script by Hafiz Saleh Rami. With sura headings in white on gold panels & double page of illumination. Imperf. S Apr 30 (329) £200

— [Ottoman, A.H.1270/A.D.1853]. 309 leaves, 182mm by 115mm. Contemp red mor. In naskhi script by al-Rifa'ti. With illuminated markers between verses, sura headings in white on illuminated panels, & 2 double pages of fine illumination. S Apr 30 (333) £1,500

— [Qajar, A.H.1273/A.D.1856]. 379 leaves (6 blank), 283mm by 172mm. Contemp floral lacquer bdg. In naskhi script by Abul-Hasan al-Rezavi for Jami al-Mirza-i Mirza Muhammad Ali. With Persian glosses in shikasteh within illuminated cartouches, illuminated markers between verses, sura headings in gold thuluth within illuminated panels, & 8 pages of illumination. Illus in cat. S Apr 30 (344) £9,000

— [Qajar, A.H.1292/A.D.1875]. 217 leaves, 109mm by 67mm. Contemp floral lacquer bdg. In naskhi script by Ibn Aqa Muhammad for Aqa Haji Mirza Muhammad Mehdi. With illuminated markers between verses, sura headings in gold thuluth on illuminated panels & double page of illumination. S Apr 30 (334) £1,000

Ms, album page with Koranic verses. [Tabriz, c.1539]. 466mm by 296mm. In nasta'liq script on gold-sprinkled paper, with naskhi script in outer border. Attributed to Shah Mahmud Nishapuri. Framed. Illus in cat. S Apr 30 (324) £1,300

— Ms, album page with surat a-Fatiha. [Persia, A.H.1082/A.D.1671]. 230mm by 127mm. In nasta'liq script in gold, interspersed with gold bands decorated with floral motifs, by Hasan Kirmani. Illus in cat. S Apr 30 (325) £1,100

— Ms, Koranic scroll. [Persia, early 19th cent]. 510cm in length, in silver box. In minute ghubari script forming geometric & floral motifs, written diagonally in outer borders. With sura headings in red & illuminated headpiece. Illus in cat. S Apr 30 (327) £2,400

Koreff, Johannes Ferdinand, 1783-1851

ALs, [n.d.]. 2 pp, 4to. To an unnamed lady. Explaining why he did not send some material promised earlier. star Mar 26 (703) DM950

Kosciuszko, Tadeusz, 1746-1817

ALs, 4 Apr 1784. 2 pp, 4to. To Mrs. Lewis Morris. Introducing Mr. Benard. CNY June 9 (248) $3,200

Kossel, Albrecht, 1853-1927

ALs, 8 Apr 1915. 1 p, 4to. To W. Kuemmel. Sending condolences on the death of his wife. star Mar 26 (704) DM560

Kovacs, Ernie, 1919-62

Ls, 13 Apr 1957. 1 p, 8vo. To 20th Century Fox. Ptd letter authorizing MCA Artists to collect his fees. Dar Apr 9 (257) $180

Kraus, Karl, 1874-1936

Autograph Ms, notes comparing incidents in Franz Wittels's novel Ezechiel der Zugereiste with real events, [c.1910]. 6 leaves, 4to. HN Nov 28 (1757) DM560

Collection of 5 A Ls s & autograph postcard, sgd, 8 Sept 1907 to 1908. 6 pp, 4to & 8vo. To Irma Karczewska. Worrying about her illness, giving advice in a financial matter, etc. HN Nov 28 (1754) DM6,400

ALs, [1907]. 1 p, 4to. To Herr von Haselhoff. Comparing Neulengbach & Gmunden as summer resorts. HN Nov 28 (1755) DM950

— 12 Dec 1910. 6 pp, 8vo. To an unnamed judicial official. Sending information concerning his suit against Franz Wittels. HN Nov 28 (1758a) DM4,000

Series of 3 A Ls, [8] to 17 June 1910. 6 pp, 4to. To Franz Wittels & his father-in-law A. Pick. Drafts prepared for his lawyer, trying to prevent the publication of Wittels's roman a clef Ezechiel der Zugereiste. HN Nov 28 (1756) DM2,700

— Series of 3 A Ls, 13/14 Oct to 10 Dec 1910. 14 pp, 4to & folio. To his lawyer. Concerning his controversy with Franz Wittels about the publication of Ezechiel der Zugereiste. HN Nov 28 (1758) DM3,800

Krenek, Ernst, 1900-91

Typescript, essay, Composing as a Calling, [n.d.]. 8 pp, 4to. Sgd at end. star Mar 27 (1045) DM220

Kropotkin, Petr Alekseevich, Prince, 1842-1921

Collection of 9 A Ls s & 3 autograph postcards, sgd, 10 Feb 1898 to 27 Feb 1913. 30 pp, 8vo, & cards, in half lea box. To Herbert Grinling. Mostly about recipient's work as a journalist supporting the Labour Party. With related material. star Mar 27 (1466) DM1,750

Krupp, Alfred, 1812-87

ALs, 21 May 1869. 4 pp, 8vo. To M. Sazile. Concerning an order of carriages. Dar Apr 9 (258) $325

— 9 Jan 1884. 2 pp, 8vo. To Carl Julius Schulz. Sending papers regarding a "canal question". HN June 26 (931) DM320

— [c.1885]. 2 pp, 8vo. To Fritz Schulz. Requesting advice concerning a response to Mrs. Schulz. HN June 26 (933) DM360

Krupp, Friedrich, 1820-1901

Series of 3 Ls s, 12 Dec 1840 to 11 June 1841. 6 pp, 4to. To Christian Friedrich Brendel. Concerning an order of steel. star Mar 26 (705) DM750

Krupp, Friedrich Alfred, 1854-1902

Ls s (2), 26 Mar & 15 Apr 1899. 3 pp, 4to. Recipient unnamed. About corrections to a zoological dictionary. sg Feb 27 (105) $275

Krupskaya, Nadezhda Konstantinovna, 1869-1939

ALs, 14 Sept 1914. 4 pp, 8vo. To Hermann Diamant. Enlisting his help in refuting accusations that her husband is a spy. S Dec 5 (526) £8,000 [Fox Glove]

Krushchev, Nikita Sergeyevich, 1894-1971

Cut signature, 1961. 8 by 5 inches. Cut from a document; including countersignature. Illus in cat. Dar Apr 9 (353) $600

Kubin, Alfred, 1877-1959

Collection of 2 A Ls s, 4 autograph postcards, sgd, & ANs, 7 Apr 1924 to 10 Apr 1933 & [n.d.]. 4 pp, 4to, & cards. To Irene Heberle. About personal matters, Klabund, the political situation, etc. Including pen-&-ink sketch. star Mar 27 (909) DM1,900

— Collection of ALs & autograph postcard, sgd, 8 Oct 1934 & [n.d.]. 2 pp, 8vo, & card. To G. von Wolfenau. Concerning the sale of a work. star Mar 27 (911) DM900

ALs, 2 Oct 1952. 1 p, 8vo. To Hans von Goetz. Responding to the news of Roderich von Ompteda's death. star Mar 27 (912) DM360

Autograph postcards (2), sgd, 25 May 1925 & [29 Mar 192?]. To Wolfgang Goetz. About a health problem & a new publication. star Mar 27 (910) DM320

— Autograph postcards (2), sgd, 26 Feb [19]36 & 10 Apr [19]37. To Hans Leip. Inquiring about a publication, & sending greetings. FD Dec 3 (1443) DM360

Autograph quotation, 6 lines, sgd; 2 July 1939. 1 p, 8vo. Mtd with a port. JG Sept 27 (388) DM280

Kuernberger, Ferdinand, 1821-79

Series of 13 A Ls s, Oct 1864 to Sept 1870. Over 50 pp, 8vo. To Emil Kuh. Literary correspondence, discussing Keller, Hebbel, political events, etc. With related material. star Mar 26 (314) DM2,200

Kurz, Isolde, 1853-1944

A Ls s (2), 30 July 1917 & 16 Oct [1918]. 9 pp, 4to. To [Max Friedlaender]. About a competition for a national hymn & the publication of a song written by her father. star Mar 26 (315) DM250

Kussmaul, Adolf, 1822-1902

Autograph Ms, medical report, 28 July 1882. 2 pp, 4to. Sgd. star Mar 26 (707) DM370

L

La Perouse, Jean Francois Galaup de, 1741-88

Ds, Sept 1779 to Feb 1780. 2 pp, folio. List of armourer's supplies for the frigate Amazone; sgd 6 times. Also sgd by 2 others. Illus in cat. CNY June 9 (249) $1,000

— ENTRECASTEAUX, ANTOINE DE BRUNI D'. - ALs, 10 Mar 1784. 1 p, 4to. To unidentified cousins. Informing them that he is sending a bill of exchange. Longueville collection. S June 25 (57) £180 [McCormick]

La Roche, Sophie von, 1731-1807

ALs, 29 Dec 1786. 1 p, 4to. Recipient unnamed. Worrying about her son's whereabouts. star Mar 26 (318) DM1,200

Labarraque, Antoine Germain, 1777-1850

ALs, 2 Nov 1825. 3 pp, 4to. To L. J. M. Robert. Discussing the ptg of recipient's work & the use of chloride. star Mar 26 (708) DM240

Lachenmann, Helmut

Autograph music, sketches for his String Trio, sgd & inscr; 2 Apr 1966. 2 pp, folio. In pencil. star Mar 27 (1046) DM340

Lachner, Franz, 1803-90

ALs, 24 Feb 1856. 2 pp, 4to. To Heinrich Sczadrovsky. Suggesting some of his compositions for performance at St. Gallen. star Mar 27 (1047) DM340

Lactantius, Lucius Caecilius Firmianus, c.240-c.320

Ms, Divinarum Institutionum Libri VII, with De Dei Liber I & De Opificio Liber I. [Italy, 14th cent]. 202 leaves, vellum, 285mm by 205mm. 19th-cent russia-backed wooden bds. In 2 sizes of a gothic bookhand. With 18 large & c.70 two-line initials. bba June 25 (115) £24,000 [Quaritch]

Laemmle, Carl, 1867-1939

Ls, 20 Feb 1935. 1 p, 4to. To R. R. Brookner. Commenting on recipient's idea for a plot on race relations. Dar Aug 6 (117) $200

Lafayette, Gilbert du Motier, Marquis de, 1757-1834

ALs, 18 July [c.1789]. 1 p, 12mo. To the Duc de Rochefoucauld-Liancourt. Discussing events of the French Revolution. With engraved port. Illus in cat. wd Dec 12 (323) $2,600

— 25 Aug 1816. 1 p, 4to. Recipient unnamed. Sending "communications of Mr. Madison". CNY Dec 5 (72) $1,200

— 15 Sept 1816. 1 p, 4to. To Bushrod Washington. Introducing Col. Bernard & his family. P June 16 (236) $1,100

— 26 Oct 1823. 1 p, 4to. To James Brown. Expressing disgust with European politics & mentioning his land grant in Louisiana. Illus in cat. Spiro collection. CNY May 14 (95) $6,000

— 13 Oct 1825. 2 pp, 4to. To William Tudor. Thanking for "testimonies of kindness and approbation" & recalling his friendship with recipient's father. Dar Oct 10 (244) $1,900

— 18 Oct 1827. 1 p, 4to. To the Rev. John J. Palfrey. Commenting on a newspaper. Illus in cat. sup Oct 15 (1339) $775

— 4 Sept 1829. 2 pp, 4to. To M. Andre Paccard. Regretting that he will not be able to visit Chalons-sur-Saone. Spiro collection. CNY May 14 (96) $1,500

— 19 Feb [n.y.]. 1 p, 4to. To an unnamed lady. On personal matters. sg Feb 27 (107) $450

— 25 Mar [n.y.]. 1 p, 8vo. To an unnamed general. Mentioning Mr. Bowring. sg Feb 27 (108) $425

Ls, 22 Nov 1801. 3 pp, 4to. To James McHenry. About the future of France, his own retirement, & Bushrod Washington's plan to write a history of the American Revolution. Duplicate. Thorek & Spiro collections. CNY May 14 (94) $12,000

— 11 Aug [1830]. 1 p, 8vo. To an unnamed general. Regarding troops. Imperf. With engraved port. R Mar 7 (197) $320

— 21 Aug 1830. 2 pp, 4to. To Gen. Guglielmo Pepe. Explaining that he has had difficulty in reaching him, & referring to a request. Spiro collection. CNY May 14 (97) $650

Franking signature, [n.d.]. On envelope addressed to Gen. Gourgaud. R Mar 7 (198) $300
See also: Adams, John Quincy & Lafayette

Lagerloef, Selma, 1858-1940

Collection of 2 A Ls s & Ns, 20 May 1920, 11 Feb 1921 & [1928?]. 4 pp, 8vo. To Kaethe Heinicke. Thanking for a letter, explaining the function of protagonists in fiction, & acknowledging congratulations on her birthday. HN Nov 28 (1760) DM300

Lahr, Bert, 1895-1967

Photograph, sgd, [Aug 1966]. 8 by 10 inches. Dar Aug 6 (19) $700

Lamarck, Jean Baptiste de, 1744-1829

ADs, 30 Sept 1797. 1 p, 4to. Receipt for 300 livres from his pbr. HH May 13 (1983) DM200

Lamb, Charles, 1775-1834

ALs, [30 June 1821]. 3 pp, 4to. To John Taylor. Referring to C. A. Elton's poem Epistle to Elia. P Dec 12 (181) $3,500

Lameth, Theodore, Comte de, 1756-1854

ALs, 24 Dec 1834. 8 pp, 4to. Recipient unnamed. Discussing military honor & the treatment of officers. star Mar 27 (1373) DM320

Landauer, Gustav, 1870-1919

ALs, 28 Dec 1907. 2 pp, 4to. To Julius Bab. Discusssing the origin of an idiomatic phrase. star Mar 27 (1326) DM540

Landis, Carole

Photograph, sgd & inscr, [n.d.]. 4to. Studio pose; inscr to Herb. wa Oct 19 (11) $95

Landis, Kenesaw Mountain, 1866-1944

Ls, 6 Apr 1922. 1 p, 4to. To Francis T. Hayes. Concerning an invitation to Cleveland. Dar Dec 26 (96) $450

— 21 Sept 1939. 1 p, 4to. To Warren Giles. Regarding press tickets for the World Series. Illus in cat. sup July 10 (999) $650

Lang, Fritz, 1890-1976

Ds, 29 Jan 1975. 1 p, 4to. Annual filing for the Directors Guild of America. Dar Apr 9 (179) $150

Langenbeck, Bernhard von, 1810-87

ALs, 30 Nov 1880. 3 pp, 8vo. To an unnamed lady. About congratulations on his 70th birthday. star Mar 26 (710) DM330

Lanner, Joseph, 1801-43

Ds, 24 May 1842. 1 p, folio. Contract with Tobias Haslinger for his waltz Die Vorstaedtler. Text in Haslinger's hand. star Mar 27 (1048) DM750

Lansing, Robert, 1864-1928

Series of 4 Ls s, 20 Nov 1916 to 11 Oct 1917. 6 pp, size not stated. To an unnamed Peruvian official. Concerning the minting of Peruvian coins in the US. Dar Aug 6 (219) $150

Lapacci, Bartolomeo, 1402-66

Ms, De Divinitate Sanguinis Christi. [Florence, 1462]. 42 leaves, vellum, 197mm by 125mm, in modern vellum. In a small neat humanistic minuscule. With 11 large white-vine initials, large historiated initial showing the author presenting his book to Pope Pius II, & full inhabited border. S June 23 (74) £24,000

Larrey, Dominique Jean, 1766-1842

Ls, 16 Aug 1825. 2 pp, 4to. To Hyppolite Larrey. Urging him to take lessons during the school holidays. star Mar 26 (712) DM310

Las Casas, Bartolome de, 1474-1566. See: Casas, Bartolome de las

Lasalle, Ferdinand, 1825-64

ALs, [16 Mar 1864]. 2 pp, 8vo. To his pbr Schlingmann. Protesting about the ptg of parts of his speech in the wrong order. star Mar 27 (1467) DM800

Lasker-Schueler, Else, 1869-1945

Autograph Ms, poem, Der Tempel, [Feb 1915]. 1 p, 4to. 3 three-line stanzas, sgd. Fair copy. star Mar 26 (319) DM5,500

— Autograph Ms, poem, Ein Lied an Gott, [1933]. 2 pp, 8vo. 7 four-line stanzas, sgd at head & inscr to Otto Falckenberg. star Mar 26 (320) DM3,200

Collection of ALs, 2 autograph postcards, & ANs, 8 Sept 1937 to 22 Jan 1942. 9 pp, 4to & 8vo. To Andreas Meyer. Regarding a position for recipient, her literary circle Kraal, etc. Including self port on ALs. star Mar 26 (322) DM2,500

ALs, 30 Aug 1926. 2 pp, 4to. To Otto Pick. Recommending Paul Leppin & mentioning her play Die Wupper. star Mar 26 (321) DM1,300

Lauder, Sir Harry, 1870-1950

Self-caricature, sgd, [n.d.]. 3.5 by 5.5 inches (card). Framed. Dar Aug 6 (20) $120

Laughton, Charles, 1899-1962

Ds, [c.1946]. 2 pp, 4to. Fragment of contract for the film The Paradine Case. With related telegram. Dar Apr 9 (259) $150

Laurel, Stan, 1890-1965

ALs, 6 Apr 1948. 1 p, 4to. To Miss Mendelsohn. Enclosing a statement sent by mistake. Dar Oct 10 (245) $225

Ls, 2 July 1959. 1 p, 4to. To Jeannie & Jack. Chatting about friends. wa Oct 19 (6) $100

Ns, 22 Apr 1963. 1 p, postcard. To Paul & Bluma. Expressing thanks. Matted with a photograph of Laurel & Hardy. Illus in cat. sup Oct 15 (1340) $125

Laurel, Stan, 1890-1965 —& Hardy, Oliver, 1892-1957

Group photograph, [n.d.]. 10 by 8 inches. Sgd by both & inscr to Bill in Laurel's hand. Imperf. Dar Dec 26 (242) $600

Laurens, Henry, 1724-92

ALs, 30 Oct 1792. 1 p, 4to. To Samuel Johnston. Regarding his accounts. Illus in cat. sup Oct 15 (1343) $2,000

Ds, [1 Nov 1777 - 10 Dec 1778]. 1 p, 4to. As President of the Continental Congress, ptd appointment for an army officer; unaccomplished. Countersgd by Charles Thomson. Spiro collection. CNY May 14 (98) $1,100

Lautensack, Heinrich, 1881-1919

ALs, 30 Dec 1903. 1 p, 4to. To Axel Juncker. Inquiring about the publication of his play Medusa. star Mar 26 (323) DM240

Lavater, Johann Kaspar, 1741-1801

ALs, 8 Nov 1776. 1 p, 8vo. To Johann Martin Miller. Poem, apologizing for not having read his novel Siegwart yet, & mentioning Hoelty's death. star Mar 26 (324) DM2,200

— 23 July 1778. 2 pp, 4to. To Rheinhard. About his visit with an exorcist, his new position, Lessing's new book, etc. star Mar 26 (325) DM1,400

ANs, 4 Dec 1800. 1 p, 80mm by 105mm. To Barbara Hess-Wegmann. Sentiment of encouragement. HH May 13 (1985) DM220

Lawrence, David Herbert, 1885-1930

Collection of ALs & autograph postcard, sgd, 24 May & 23 July 1920. 2 pp, 4to, & card. To Hubert James Foss. Hoping that The Queen will publish his work The Lost Girl, & inquiring about the Ms. Ck Apr 3 (20) £1,100

Cut signature, [n.d.]. 4 by 3 inches. Endorsement on portion of a check. Dar Aug 6 (194) $120

Lawrence, Jeffrey

Signature, [n.d.]. On stationery with logo of International Military Trials, Nurnberg; size not stated. sup Oct 15 (1344) $110

Lawrence, Thomas Edward, 1888-1935

Typescript carbon copy, The Mint, [c.1936]. 260 pp, 4to. Inscr by Doubleday, Doran & Co. S July 21 (151) £500 [Blakeney]

ALs, 20 Jan 1927. 1 p, 8vo. To Mr. Bain. Ordering books. Framed with a port. P June 17 (42) $2,750

— 19 Feb [19]30. 2 pp, size not stated. To H. M. Tomlinson. Discussing recipient's book All Our Yesterdays. Ck Nov 15 (45) £1,500

— 3 May [19]30. 2 pp, size not stated. To H. M. Tomlinson. Discussing his reluctance to write prefaces. Illus in cat. Ck Nov 15 (44) £1,600

— 4 Apr 19[34]. 2 pp, 8vo. To [A. E. Chambers]. Encouraging him to stay at his cottage with a friend. Sgd T.E.S. C Dec 16 (304) £500 [Wilson]

Lawrence, William J.

Photograph, sgd & inscr, 1875. 4.25 by 6.25 inches. Inscr to Thomas W. Custer on verso. Illus in cat. Armstrong collection. sup Oct 15 (1117) $200

Le Corbusier, 1887-1965

[A collection of 63 items including 10 A Ls s & 3 Ls s, [n.d.]., length not stated, documenting the relationship between Le Corbusier & Marguerite Tjader-Harris, sold at CK on 15 Nov 1991, lot 24, for £750.]

Le Fort, Gertrud von, 1876-1971

Autograph Ms, poem, Kleines Lied, [n.d.]. 1 p, 8vo. 4 four-line stanzas, sgd & inscr. star Mar 26 (328) DM480

Leacock, Stephen Butler, 1869-1944

Autograph Ms, "My Particular Aversion", essay on his literary peeves; [n.d.]. 9 pp, 4to, on rectos only. Sgd 3 times. sg Feb 27 (109) $900

League of Nations

Document, 2 Oct 1924, 11 pp, folio, stitched. Ptd Protocole pour le Regelement pacifique des differences internationaux..., in English & French. Sgd by 49 delegates to the convention at Geneva. star Mar 27 (1745) DM2,600

Lear, Edward, 1812-88

A Ls s (2), 9 June 1854 & 4 June 1860. 7 pp, 8vo. To Willie [Beadon]. Describing his travels in Egypt & in Italy to a very young friend. Including 4 pen-&-ink sketches. b June 22 (114) £1,200

Lectionary

Ms, The Lectionary of Philippe de Levis. In Latin. [Mirepoix, Languedoc, c.1511-12]. 74 leaves, vellum, 298mm by 198mm. In a large formal gothic liturgical hand. With 35 large illuminated initials in designs of colored leaves & flowers on highly burnished gold panel grounds, & 2 small & 14 very large miniatures & full-page frontis all within full borders of colored acanthus leaves and flowers on liquid gold or colored grounds. S Dec 17 (71) £48,000 [Mirandola]

Lee, Bruce, 1940-73

Original drawing, fire-breathing dragon, in pencil; [n.d.]. 4.5 by 6 inches, on pale green paper. Sgd Lee Shiu Loong & inscr to Dianne. Dar Dec 26 (246) $600

ALs, [n.d.]. 1 p, 12mo. To Dianne. Aphoristic reflections on knowledge, magnanimity, & energy. In English & Chinese. Dar Dec 26 (245) $500

Photograph, sgd & inscr, [n.d.]. 3.25 by 2.5 inches. Inscr to Diane with orig quatrain. Dar Dec 26 (244) $500

Lee, Charles, 1731-82

AL, [n.d.]. 3 pp, folio. Recipient unnamed. Draft, calling for an immediate redress of grievances & restriction of the power of Congress. Silked. R Mar 7 (195) $2,200

Lee, Edwin G., 1835-70. See: Civil War, American

Lee, Henry, 1691-1747

Document, 22 Feb 1747/48. 2 pp, folio. Invoice of Sundry Goods Loaded on board the Ship Portland ... for the Account ... of the Estate of the late Henry Lee. sup Oct 15 (1345) $250

Lee, Henry ("Light-Horse Harry"), 1756-1818

ALs, 6 Mar 1782. 6 pp, 4to. To Nathanael Greene. Complaining about problems caused by a command consisting of Continentals & militia. CNY Dec 5 (74) $5,500

— 23 Dec 1783. 1 p, 8vo. Recipient unnamed. Regarding a land survey. Illus in cat. sup Oct 15 (1346) $290

ADs, 12 July 1812. 3 pp, 4to. Answer to a complaint filed against him in a case regarding land mortgaged to Bushrod Washington. Dar Aug 6 (195) $850

Ds, 3 Apr 1793. 1 p, folio. Contents not stated. R Mar 7 (200) $320

— 5 June 1802. 2 pp, 8vo. Transaction relating to land near Mobile Bay. Dar Oct 10 (246) $120

Lee, Richard Bland, 1761-1827

Autograph Ms, The Seat of Government, [c.1815]. 5 pp, 4to. Memorial regarding the establishment of the District of Columbia as the seat of government. R Mar 7 (199) $3,500

Lee, Richard Henry, Signer from Virginia

ALs, 30 Mar 1770. 1 p, 4to. To Catharine Macaulay. Expressing admiration for her work. pn June 11 (11) £1,900

Lee, Robert E., 1807-70

ALs, 13 Mar 1855. 3 pp, 8vo. To Capt. G. W. Cullum. About his departure from West Point & his appointment to cavalry duty. Illus in cat. Sang & Spiro collections. CNY May 14 (99) $22,000

— 12 July 1858. 2 pp, 4to. To William A. Winston. Arranging for the hire of slaves from his father-in-law's estate. Illus in cat. CNY June 9 (250) $11,000

— 13 May 1861. 3 pp, 4to. To Col. Philip St. George Cocke. Explaining recent changes in rank & command in the Confederate army. Illus in cat. Spiro collection. CNY May 14 (103) $35,000

— 4 Feb 1865. 1 p, 8vo. To [John C. Breckinridge]. Warning him of the possibility of an attack on Salisbury by W. T. Sherman. P June 16 (238) $18,000

— 28 July 1865. 3 pp, 8vo. To John B. Cocke. Thanking for good care given to his horse, & reporting about various family members. Illus in cat. Spiro collection. CNY May 14 (106) $17,000

Ls, 3 May 1861. 2 pp, 4to. To Col. Philip St. George Cocke. Giving orders for the organization of the Virginia forces. Spiro collection. CNY May 14 (100) $38,000

— 7 May 1861. 1 p, 4to. To Col. Philip St. George Cocke. Regarding the mustering of volunteer companies in Virginia. Spiro collection. CNY May 14 (101) $11,000

— 10 May 1861. 2 pp, 4to. To Col. Philip St. George Cocke. Giving instructions for the training of troops in northern Virginia. Spiro collection. CNY May 14 (102) $16,000

— 5 Sept 1861. 2 pp, 4to. To Col. A. C. Moore. Sending marching orders for his regiment. CNY June 9 (251) $14,000

— 13 July 1863. 1 p, 4to. To Col. [John D.] Imboden. Instructing him to protect the retreating Confederate army crossing the Potomac. Spiro collection. CNY May 14 (104) $38,000

— 13 Apr 1869. Length not stated. To R. G. Johnson. Discussing "the little progress made by [recipient's] brother ... in his studies." wd June 12 (319) $2,000

Ds, 13 Aug 1863. 2 pp, size not stated. General

Orders no 85, proclaiming a day of penance & prayer. Including 3 small autograph corrections. Sang & Spiro collections. CNY May 14 (105) $48,000

— 10 Apr 1865. 3 pp, 8vo. Copy of his General Order No 9. Illus in cat. CNY June 9 (252) $42,000

Cut signature, [late 1860s]. 1.5 by 2.5 inches, oblong. sg Sept 12 (136) $1,300

Signature, [n.d.]. 4.25 by 1.5 inches. With a port. Dar Dec 26 (247) $1,500

— Anr, [n.d.]. 2.1 by 4.4 inches. With a port. sg Feb 27 (110) $1,600

Lefebvre, Francois Joseph, Duc de Danzig, 1755-1820

Ls, [22 Sept 1799]. 1 p, 4to. To Gen. Verrieres. Asking that he keep as many cannoneers as possible in caserns. sg Feb 27 (111) $150

Legal Manuscripts

Ms, manual of miscellaneous legal memoranda. [England, c.1520]. 178 leaves, 177mm by 95mm, in recent pigskin. In English, Latin, & Law French in a small Secretary hand. P June 17 (196) $1,300

Document, statement by Artuicus & Gabriel, son of Wido, of Porcia near Udine in Italy, of properties sequestered from them by Conradus Wedephaf, governor of Pordenone, as evidence for arbitration, 1 Aug 1273. Roll of 3 vellum membranes, 1812mm by 95mm. In a minute notarial hand. S Dec 17 (40) £400 [Johnson]

Lehar, Franz, 1870-1948

Autograph quotation, one bar of music, sgd, [n.d.]. Size not stated. Matted with a photograph. wa Oct 19 (164) $160

Photograph, sgd & inscr, 29 Sept 1910. Postcard. Inscr to Oskar Stohandl. HN Nov 28 (1762) DM250

Signature, [n.d.]. On postcard reproduction of a port painting. Dar Feb 13 (247) $180

Lehmann, Lotte, 1888-1976

Ls s (2), 5 June 1949 & Mar 1951. 2 pp, 4to. To Dr. Ernst Schwarz. About her honorary doctorate & her farewell recital. sg Sept 12 (137) $300
See also: Toscanini, Arturo & Lehmann

Leibniz, Gottfried Wilhelm, 1646-1716

ALs, 5 Jan 1691. 2 pp, 4to. To Herzog Ernst August von Braunschweig-Lueneburg. Informing him about his work on the history of the Guelphs. In French. star Mar 26 (713) DM9,500

Leigh, Vivien, 1913-67

ALs, 28 Dec 1966. 1 p, 4to. To George. Thanking for a Christmas present. Framed with a photograph. sup Oct 15 (1347) $550

Ds, 4 Feb 1966. 1 p, 4to. Contract for "the part of Anna in a play now called 'Ivanov'"; carbon copy. Dar Feb 13 (248) $300

— 4 Feb 1966. 1 p, 4to. Contract for the part of Anna in the play Ivanov. Dar Aug 6 (21) $225

Photograph, sgd, [n.d.]. 8 by 10 inches. As Scarlett O'Hara. Dar Dec 26 (196) $850

Photograph, sgd & inscr, [n.d.]. 5 by 6.75 inches. Inscr to John. Dar Oct 10 (247) $225

Leip, Hans, 1893-1983

Autograph Ms, poem, beginning "Was ist mit meinen Sinnen"; 1917. 1 p, 8vo. 2 eight-line stanzas, sgd. FD Dec 3 (1446) DM280

Lenau, Nikolaus, 1802-50

Autograph Ms, poem, Niagara, [n.d.]. 2 pp, 8vo. 7 four-line stanzas, including corrections. star Mar 26 (329) DM4,500

ALs, 15 Aug 1835. 3 pp, 8vo. To Karl Mayer. Reporting about his work on his Fruehlingsalmanach & on Faust. star Mar 26 (330) DM3,800

— 22 Aug 1839. 3 pp, 8vo. To Sophie Loewenthal. About his relationship with Caroline Unger. star Mar 26 (331) DM3,600

Lenbach, Franz von, 1836-1904

Collection of 7 A Ls s, 4 A Ns, & ADs, 1882 to 1888. 26 pp, mostly 8vo. To Alexander Guenther. About a variety of matters, & receipt for a loan. star Mar 27 (913) DM520

Lenin, Vladimir Ilyich, 1870-1924

ALs, 1 Nov 1911. 3 pp, 8vo. To Anton Nemec. Asking for assistance in organizing a secret party meeting in Prague. In German. With related material. Illus in cat. C June 24 (374) £8,000 [Batchelder]

AL, [c.Aug 1915]. 6 pp, 8vo. Recipient unknown. Draft, discussing preparations for the Zimmerwald conference. S May 28 (210) £9,000 [Sawyer]

Lenne, Peter Joseph, 1789-1866

ALs, 12 July 1829. 1 p, 4to. To [August Wilhelm Francke]. Asking that he procure fresh figs for the King of Prussia. star Mar 26 (714) DM500

Lennon, John, 1940-80

Ls, 1973. 1 p, 4to. To John Gill. Regarding a lawsuit. Framed with related material, overall size 16 by 19.5 inches. Illus in cat. P Dec 17 (311) $1,000

Ds, 6 Dec 1974. 2 pp, 4to. Certificate of change of address of Apple Music, Inc. Illus in cat.

sup Oct 15 (1348) $850

— 1976. NY police fingerprints card. Framed with a caricature, overall size 12 by 15 inches. Illus in cat. P Dec 17 (313) $3,750

Ptd photograph, [n.d.]. 12 by 12 inches (album cover). Sgd & inscr to Pete. Framed. Illus in cat. P Dec 17 (312) $800

Signature, [1970s]. Including caricature. Framed with a poster, overall size 22 by 31 inches. Illus in cat. P Dec 17 (345) $1,000

— Anr, [n.d.]. On ptd lyrics of the song I am the Walrus. Framed with group photograph, overall size 20 by 34 inches. Illus in cat. P Dec 17 (340) $1,200

— SPECTOR, PHIL. - Ls, Mar 1972. 1 p, 4to. To Jay. Photocopy; enclosing a record of the Immigration Department's proceedings against Lennon & Yoko Ono (included). Dar Apr 9 (260) $150

Lennon, John, 1940-80 —& Ono, Yoko

[Their signatures on a Cinema Club program, 1969, including a caricature, framed with a group photograph, overall size 22 by 16 inches, sold at P on 17 Dec 1991, lot 331, for $1,000.]

[Their signatures, framed with a group photograph, overall size 18.5 by 16 inches, sold at P on 17 Dec 1991, lot 314, for $500.]

Lenz, Oskar, 1848-1925

Autograph Ms, article about his travels in Central Africa, 30 Nov 1889. 6 pp, 8vo. Sgd at head. In French. With letter of transferral. star Mar 26 (715) DM500

Leo XIII, Pope, 1810-1903

Document, 10 May 1889. 1 p, folio. Papal Brief granting permission to Julius Campori to read Mass at his own house. Sgd by Cardinal Ledochowski; endorsed in anr hand on verso. star Mar 27 (1550) DM420

Leoncavallo, Ruggiero, 1858-1919

ALs, 24 July 1902. 4 pp, 4to. Recipient unnamed. Inquiring about an old "marche typique et nationale" for his opera Der Roland von Berlin. star Mar 27 (1051) DM600

Autograph postcard, sgd, 17 Dec 1917. To Valentino Soldani. Informing him about his holiday plans & inquiring about recipient's films. Dar Feb 13 (249) $250

Autograph quotation, sgd, "Ridi Pagliaccio" in musical quotation, 15 Oct 1911. On card; size not stated. wd June 12 (320) $125

Leopold, Prince of Bavaria, 1846-1930

ALs, 15 Feb 1916. 2 pp, 8vo. To Archduke Karl. Making plans for recipient's visit on the eastern front. star Mar 27 (1268) DM260

Leopold I, Fuerst von Anhalt-Dessau ("Der alte Dessauer"), 1676-1747

Ds, 8 Dec 1700. 1 p, folio. Exemption from feudal duties granted to Friedrich Koerber. star Mar 27 (1240) DM210

Leopold I, Emperor, 1640-1705

ALs, 2 Sept 1690. 2 pp, folio. To his sister [Eleonora]. Informing her about the campaign against the Turks. star Mar 27 (1648) DM620

Ls, 4 Jan 1670. 2 pp, folio. To Cardinal Sforza Pallavicino. Responding to an offer of services. star Mar 27 (1647) DM400

— 10 Dec 1703. 2 pp, folio. To the mayor & town council of Friedberg in Hesse. Ordering them to redress grievances put forth by the Jewish community. Illus in cat. HN Nov 28 (1766) DM720

— 17 Mar 1701. 1 p, folio. To Wolfgang Dietrich Graf zu Castell. Instructing him to continue a judicial inquiry. HN Nov 28 (1765) DM260

Ds, 8 Feb 1662. 1 p, folio. Ptd order addressed to Wolfgang Georg Graf zu Castell & Heinrich Friedrich Graf von Hohenlohe to attend the Imperial Diet at Regensburg. HN Nov 28 (1764) DM340

— 14 Dec 1694. 2 pp, size not stated. Order that Carl Ignatius Jonnar take the oath of allegiance. HH Nov 6 (2069) DM280

Leopold I, King of the Belgians, 1795-1865

ALs, 15 July 1861. 4 pp, 8vo. To Queen Augusta of Prussia. Referring to a recent attempt on her husband's life. star Mar 27 (1272) DM500

Leopold II, Emperor, 1747-92

ALs, 27 Dec [c.1785]. 1 p, 4to. To [Count Colloredo]. Expressing satisfaction at his son's progress. Illus in cat. star Mar 27 (1668) DM2,200

— [1791]. 2 pp, 4to. To his sister Marie Antoinette. Informing her that he has prevented the Comte d'Artois from acting rashly & wishing he could be of more help in her difficult situation. S May 28 (130) £1,400 [Cox]

Leopold II, King of the Belgians, 1835-1909

Ls, 18 Nov 1876. 1 p, 4to. To the President of Chile. Congratulating him on his election. Dar Apr 9 (261) $170

Leopold, Nathan F., 1904-71

Ls, 14 Mar 1958. 1 p, 4to. To Carl Haverlin. Thanking for his friendship during his years in prison. With carbon copy of reply. Dar Apr 9 (170) $400

Lepsius, Richard, 1810-84

ALs, 21 Oct 1873. 3 pp, 8vo. To [Georg Schweinfurth?]. Sending a map for recipient's travels in Arabia & inquiring about copper deposits on Sinai. star Mar 26 (716) DM320

Lerner, Alan Jay, 1918-86 —& Loewe, Frederick, 1901-88

Ds, 8 Aug 1950. 2 pp, 4to. Permission to broadcast their play Brigadoon. Sgd by both. Dar June 11 (263) $200

Lesseps, Ferdinand de, Viscount, 1805-94

Autograph quotation, "fais ce que dois, advienne que pourra"; 15 Feb 1888. 1 p, 16mo (card). Sgd. star Mar 26 (717) DM210

Photograph, sgd, 1891. Cabinet size. By Nadar. sg Sept 12 (138) $425

Lessing, Gotthold Ephraim, 1729-81

ALs, 5 July 1773. 1 p, folio. To Christoph Heinrich Haeseler. About his inability to repay his debts. star Mar 26 (333) DM11,000

Autograph quotation, excerpt from Shaftesbury, The Moralists, Part I, sgd & dated 1755. 1 p, 8vo. star Mar 26 (332) DM5,000

Levett-Yeats, Sidney Kilner

Autograph Ms, novel, The Honour of Savelli, [pbd 1895]. 137 pp, folio. Limp green mor gilt bdg. Inscr to A. S. Watt, 3 May 1899. Incomplete. L Nov14 (359) £80

Levin, Yizhak Meir

ALs, 1933. 1 p, 4to. To Aharon (Harry) Goodman. Regarding immigration certificates [to Eretz Israel]. sg Dec 19 (153) $140

Lewes, George Henry, 1817-78

ALs, 12 Dec [1877]. 2 pp, 8vo. To [Charles Waldstein]. Defending George Eliot against Swinburne. pn Mar 19 (142) £520 [Quaritch]

Lewis, Sinclair, 1885-1951

ALs, 14 June [1917]. 4 pp, 8vo. To Mrs. Finch. About his life & writings. sg Sept 12 (139) $700

Photograph, sgd & inscr, [n.d.]. 10 by 8 inches. Inscr to W. S. Leeds. LH Dec 11 (14) $100

Leydig, Franz von, 1821-1908

ALs, 17 Nov 1865. 4 pp, 8vo. To an unnamed French pbr. Giving permission for a trans of his Lehrbuch der Histologie. star Mar 26 (718) DM260

Lichtenberg, Georg Christoph, 1742-99

ALs, [c.1780]. 1 p, 4to. To Christiane Dieterich. Thanking for her hospitality. star Mar 26 (336) DM2,200

— 26 July 1792. 1 p, folio. To Christian Gottlob Heyne. Explaining that health & family problems have prevented him from announcing his forthcoming lectures. star Mar 26 (337) DM3,800

Lie, Trygve, 1896-1968

Ls, 31 Dec 1935. 1 p, 4to. Recipient unnamed. Concerning civilian assistance to military staffs. Dar Apr 9 (262) $100

Liebermann, Max, 1847-1935

Collection of 8 A Ls s & 5 autograph postcards, sgd, 1911 to 1926. 13 pp, 8vo, & cards. To Hermann Mueller. Mostly about additions to recipient's art collection. star Mar 27 (919) DM9,000

ALs, 19 July 1894. 3 pp, 8vo. To Paul Hildebrandt. Giving his views about nature & art. HN Nov 28 (1769) DM480

— 12 Mar 1902. 3 pp, 8vo. To Otto Seeck. Commenting on Julius Langbehn's book about Rembrandt. star Mar 27 (915) DM900

— 2 Dec 1908. 2 pp, 8vo. To the publishing house Stella. Discussing obscenity in art. star Mar 27 (918) DM1,300

— 13 Dec 1915. 1 p, 8vo. To Hermann Mueller. Asking him to change the date of his visit. star Mar 27 (920) DM220

Autograph postcard, sgd, 10 May 1918. To the head clerk of the art dealer Arnold. Sending his summer address. Including pen-&-ink sketch. Illus in cat. star Mar 27 (921) DM1,300

Liebig, Justus von, 1803-73

ALs, 1 Nov 1849. 4 pp, 8vo. To Dr. [Eben] Horsford. Discussing scientific matters & recipient's experiments. sg Sept 12 (140) $750

— 18 July 1853. 1 p, 8vo. To Professor Alexander. In 3d person, letter of introduction. With engraved port. Dar Dec 26 (248) $140

— 29 Sept 1864. 3 pp, 8vo. To "cher Luna". About phosphate deposits in Spain. star Mar 26 (719) DM1,100

— 15 June 1869. 3 pp, 8vo. To his wife. Informing her about discussions regarding a medal named after him. star Mar 26 (720) DM800

— [n.d.]. 1 p, 8vo. To Camille Demarcay. Regretting that a letter for recipient's father was not delivered in person. With a lithographic port. star Mar 26 (721) DM850

Liebknecht, Wilhelm, 1826-1900

ALs, 30 Mar 1872. 1 p, 8vo. Recipient unnamed. Setting a date for a visit. star Mar 27 (1468) DM435

— 11 June 1900. 1 p, 8vo. To the pbr of The Independent. Acknowledging a fee. star Mar 27 (1469) DM340

Lifar, Sergei Mihailovich, 1905-86

Collection of c.50 A Ls s & postcards, sgd, 1929 to 1977. 90 pp, various sizes. To Boris Kochno. About the Ballets Russes, Diaghilev's archives, theatrical matters, etc. SM Oct 12 (375) FF13,000

Series of c.40 A Ls s, 1924 to 1928. 100 pp, mostly 4to. To Diaghilev. About his education in Italy & his ballet studies. With related material. Boris Kochno collection. SM Oct 12 (374) FF65,000

Liliencron, Detlev von, 1844-1909

Series of 4 A Ls s, 7 May 1886 to 4 Jan 1909. 9 pp, 8vo. To the Schiller Foundation. Regarding applications for financial aid. star Mar 26 (339) DM1,000

A Ls s (2), 12 & 18 June 1905. 2 pp, 8vo. To Moritz Diesterweg. Concerning contributions for a textbook. star Mar 26 (341) DM500

ALs, 11 July 1892. 3 pp, 8vo. To the presiding officers of a society. Regretting he cannot come to a projected meeting. HH Nov 6 (2070) DM240

Lillie, Gordon William, 1860-1942

ALs, 14 June 1921. 1 p, 4to. To Alexander Hill. Informing him that he cannot "use the lithos of the buffalo". Dar Apr 9 (34) $150

Group photograph, sgd, [n.d.]. 3.5 by 6 inches. With his wife. With anr signature on card. Dar June 11 (15) $200

Lincoln, Abraham, 1809-65

ALs, 27 June 1848. 1 p, 4to. To [David B.?] Campbell. Reporting about his stand on the Mexican War & other congressional matters. P Dec 12 (122) $85,000

— 27 June 1853. 2 pp, 8vo. To Thomas J. Turner. Discussing a legal case. Framed with engraved port. Illus in cat. P June 16 (239) $9,500

— 11 Nov 1853. 1 p, 8vo. To L. M. Hays. Sending a draft for $100 & explaining the delay. Imperf. sg Sept 12 (141) $7,000

— 13 June 1861. 1 p, 8vo. To Simon Cameron. Ordering "that Col. W. H. Emory be allowed to withdraw what purports to be his resignation". Illus in cat. Spiro collection. CNY May 14 (108) $30,000

— 13 June 1861. 1 p, 8vo. To Sec of War Cameron. Instructing him "to accept a fifth Regiment from Michigan". Framed with a port. Illus in cat. P Dec 12 (124) $19,000

— 15 July 1861. 1 p, 8vo. To Montgomery Blair. Requesting a nomination for John Armstrong as postmaster. Illus in cat. sup Oct 15 (1527) $7,750

— 28 Dec 1861. 1 p, 8vo. To Quartermaster Gen. [M. Meigs]. Giving instructions for the removal of Capt. Eddy from service in Springfield. Illus in cat. sup May 9 (195) $20,000

— 9 Aug 1862. 1 p, 8vo. To Sec of the Navy [Gideon Welles]. Correcting an error regarding the appointment of midshipmen. CNY Dec 5 (76) $17,000

— 6 Nov 1862. 1 p, 4to. To Major Gen. [Benjamin F.] Butler. Inquiring about free black labor & the forthcoming elections in Louisiana. Illus in cat. Sang & Spiro collections. CNY May 14 (110) $55,000

— 8 Jan 186[3]. 3 pp, 4to. To Major Gen. [John Alexander] McClernand. Refuting fears that it is his "purpose to enslave, or exterminate, the whites of the South" but insisting he cannot retract the Emancipation Proclamation. CNY Dec 5 (77) $680,000

— 24 Nov 1863. 1 p, 8vo. To Sec of State [Wm. H. Seward]. Informing him that news have been received about a battle at Knoxville. CNY Dec 5 (78) $26,000

— 2 May 1864. 1 p, 8vo. To the California Delegation in Congress. Requesting them to "please take this case off [his] hands". Illus in cat. P June 16 (246) $15,000

Ls, 16 Oct 1862. 2 pp, 4to. To H. M. Rice. Requesting his aid for J. P. Usher's peace mission to the Minnesota Indians. Illus in cat. sup May 9 (196) $34,000

— 19 June 1863. 3 pp, folio. To Messrs. Malhiot, Johnson & Cottman. Responding to an appeal by Louisiana planters for reinstatement of the pre-war state constitution. Illus in cat. Spiro collection. CNY May 14 (112) $40,000

— 1 June 1864. 1 p, 8vo. To Henry Bill. Thanking for a copy of [J. C.] Abbott's History of the Civil War. Illus in cat. Dar Aug 6 (196) $9,000

ANs, 7 Nov 1862. 1 p, 8vo. To Sec of the Navy Gideon Welles. Informing him that Mrs. Lewis is seeking a promotion for her husband. Spiro collection. CNY May 14 (111) $14,000

— 27 July 1863. 1 p, 8vo. Recipient unnamed. Stating that Jackson Grimshaw is requesting a military promotion for his brother. Illus in cat. sup May 9 (197) $9,000

— 10 Mar 1864. 1 p, 3 by 2 inches (card). Recipient unnamed. Ordering that a boy be discharged from military service. Framed with a port. Illus in cat. sup May 9 (199) $4,400

— 30 June 1864. 2 pp, 12mo (card). Recipient unnamed. Giving permission for Annie P. Shepherd to visit prisoners at Point Lookout. Illus in cat. sup May 9 (200) $5,250

— 26 Oct 1864. 1 p, 3.5 by 3.5 inches. Recipient unnamed. Ordering the release of the Indian Big Eagle confined at Davenport. In pencil. Illus in cat. sup May 9 (198) $12,500

— 14 Dec 1864. Size not stated (card). To the Surgeon General. Regarding a discharge. With a photograph. rs Oct 17 (24) $3,500

— 21 Dec 1864. 1 p, 12mo. Recipient unnamed. Order that a man "take the oath of Dec. 8, 1863 & be discharged." Illus in cat. Dar Apr 9 (264) $5,500

— 7 Mar 1865. 1 p, 51mm by 85mm (card). To Gen. [Richard] Delafield. Requesting maps for his son Tad. Illus in cat. CNY June 9 (260) $70,000

Ns, 19 Nov 1860. 1 p, size not stated. To F. W. Bowen. Sending his autograph. Framed with engraved port. P June 16 (240) $3,250

Note, [c.Feb 1865]. 1 p, 12mo. To Senator & Mrs. Foster. Engraved invitation to a dinner on 13 Feb [1865]. Illus in cat. R June 13 (124) $5,500

ADs, 26 Sept 1846. 1 p, 4to. Legal brief in the case of Hawks v. Sands; sgd twice. Framed with a port. Illus in cat. P Dec 12 (121) $5,000

Ds, 19 Mar 1861. 1 p, folio. Appointment of Benjamin F. Trumbull as Receiver at Omaha. CNY Dec 5 (75) $4,800

— 20 Mar 1861. 1 p, folio. Appointment of L. L. Weld as Secretary of the Colorado Territory. Repaired; framed. sg Sept 12 (142) $5,600

— 6 Aug 1861. 1 p, folio. Appointment of Augustus V. Barriger as Commissary of Subsistence of Volunteers. Countersgd by Lorenzo Thomas & Thomas A. Scott. Framed with engraved port. Dar June 11 (265) $6,000

— 7 Aug 1861. 1 p, folio. Appointment of Augustus Morse as Capt. of Volunteers. With portraits of Lincoln & Morse. sup Oct 15 (1529) $5,650

— 27 Aug 1861. 1 p, folio. Appointment of William McLean as Lieutenant of Cavalry. Illus in cat. sup May 9 (201) $5,000

— 26 Nov 1861. 1 p, folio. Appointment for George Heister as Lieutenant in the Marine Corps. Illus in cat. R June 13 (120) $5,500

— 26 Dec 1861. 1 p, folio. Appointment of Richard Brindley as 1st Lieutenant of Infantry. Countersgd by Stanton at a later date. Dar Feb 13 (250) $5,500

— 6 Feb 1862. 1 p, folio. Appointment of John M. Brannon as Brigadier Gen. of Volunteers. Countersgd by E. M. Stanton. CNY June 9 (256) $8,500

— 24 Feb 1862. 1 p, folio. Military commission. sup Oct 15 (1530) $3,700

— Feb 1862. 1 p, folio. Appointment for Ormsby M. Mitchell as Brigadier General. Framed with a photograph. Illus in cat. R June 13 (119) $11,000

— 4 Mar 1862. 1 p, folio. Appointment of Lawrence S. Babbitt as Lieutenant. Illus in cat. sup Oct 15 (1531) $5,500

— 11 Mar 1862. 1 p, folio. Appointment of William M. Smith as Additional Paymaster of Volunteers. CNY June 9 (257) $6,500

— 2 May 1862. 1 p, folio. Appointment of Edward O. C. Ord as Major Gen. of Volunteers. Framed. Illus in cat. sup Oct 15 (1532) $10,000

— 14 June 1862. 1 p, folio. Appointment of Thomas W. Leach as surgeon in the Navy. Countersgd by Gideon Welles. rs Oct 17 (25) $3,600

— 26 July 1862. 1 p, folio. Appointment of Louis H. Pelinze as Major. Framed. Illus in cat. sup Oct 15 (1533) $3,800

— 10 Jan 1863. 1 p, 4to. Order to affix the US Seal to a pardon warrant for Henry Fort. Framed with a port. Illus in cat. R June 13 (121) $6,500

— 21 Feb 1863. 1 p, folio. Appointment of Abner Read as Commander in the Navy. Countersgd by Gideon Welles. Illus in cat. sup May 9 (202) $4,600

— 22 Feb 1863. 1 p, folio. Appointment of David S. Glaringer as Assistant Surgeon of Volunteers. Framed with a port. Illus in cat. sup Oct 15 (1534) $4,000

— 26 Mar 1863. 1 p, folio. Ship's paper in 4 languages for the barque The Roscius. Framed with a port. Illus in cat. P June 16 (242) $13,000

— 4 Apr 1863. 1 p, folio. Appointment of N. C. McLean as Brigadier General of Volunteers. With related material. P June 16 (243) $5,500

— 5 June 1863. 1 p, folio. Appointment of Thomas McGregor as 2d Lieut. of Cavalry. Illus in cat. CNY June 9 (258) $5,500

— 15 July 1863. 1 p, 4to. Order to draft troops in the State of NY. Mtd. P June 16 (245) $13,000

— 21 Jan 1864. 1 p, folio. Appointment for Sebastian S. Marble as Customs Collector. Countersgd by S. P. Chase. O May 26 (117) $3,100

— 23 Feb 1864. 1 p, folio. Appointment of A. C. Tavis as paymaster. Framed. R June 13 (122) $4,000

— 20 Apr 1864. 1 p, folio. Appointment of Frank L. Hays as Additional Paymaster. Countersgd by E. M. Stanton. Illus in cat. sup May 9 (203) $3,700

— 25 Apr 1864. 1 p, folio. Appointment of

Edward Dale as Capt. of Volunteers. Illus in cat. sup Oct 15 (1535) $5,250

— 1 July 1864. 1 p, folio. Appointment of Edward J. Whitney as Surgeon of Volunteers. Countersgd by E. M. Stanton. Dar June 11 (266) $3,750

— 7 July 1864. 1 p, folio. Appointment of E. A. Clark as Surgeon of Volunteers. Countersgd by Stanton. Dar Apr 9 (263) $4,750

— 23 Aug 1864. 2 pp, c.17 by 11 inches. Ordering the sale of lands in the Winnebago Indian Reservation. Folds strengthened. Illus in cat. Sang & Spiro collections. CNY May 14 (115) $60,000

— 28 Feb 1865. 1 p, folio. Appointment of A. M. Hayes as additional paymaster. Framed. sup Oct 15 (1536) $4,000

— 16 Mar 1865. 1 p, oblong folio. Appointment of Watson Stewart as Register of the Land Office at Humboldt, Kansas. Countersgd by J. P. Usher. Spotting & staining, affecting L in Lincoln's name. Framed. wa June 25 (125) $3,400

— 21 Mar 1865. 1 p, folio. Appointment of C. C. Hewitt as Chief Justice of the Supreme Court of the Territory of Washington. Countersgd by Seward. Framed. Illus in cat. b&b Feb 19 (150) $5,000

— [n.d.]. 1 p, folio. Plea in the case of Emmett v. Barrett; sgd Lincoln & Herndon. Endorsed in anr hand at foot. Framed. S July 21 (311A) £2,400 [Stodolski]

Autograph endorsement, sgd, 4 May 1861. 1 p, 83mm by 80mm, cut from larger sheet. Recommending that "the Division named within be admitted into the new corps of volunteers". Framed with etched port. P June 16 (241) $3,000

— Anr, sgd, 13 Sept 1861. 1 p, 103mm by 84mm, cut from larger sheet. Agreeing to a judicial appointment for New Mexico. Illus in cat. CNY June 9 (255) $5,500

— Anr, sgd, 14 Jan 1864. 1 p, size not stated, cut from larger document. Pardoning David B. Fry. Framed with a port. R Nov 9 (96) $6,000

— Anr, sgd, 14 Jan 1865. On verso of a letter from P. Golden to John H. Rice, 2 pp, 8vo, regarding a prisoner of war; ordering that the prisoner take the oath of Dec 8, 1863, & be discharged. Also sgd by Hannibal Hamlin. Framed. CNY June 9 (259) $7,500

Autograph quotation, sgd, excerpt from his annual message promising not "to retract or modify the emancipation proclamation..."; 20 Dec 1863. 1 p, 8vo. Addressed to Henry C. Wright in John Hay's hand. In mor gilt album with Wright's address in Lincoln's hand & further related material. Illus in cat. Sang & Spiro collections. CNY May 14 (113) $420,000

Autograph telegram, 25 May 1862. 1 p, 8vo. To Gen. Rufus Saxton. Inquiring if recipient can assist Gen. Banks after his retreat to Martinsburg. Illus in cat. sup Oct 15 (1528) $32,000

— Anr, sgd, 15 June 1864. 1 p, 4to. To Ulysses S. Grant. Approving of his assault on Petersburg & predicting its success. Illus in cat. Sang & Spiro collections. CNY May 14 (114) $380,000

Cut signature, 16 Apr 1863. 46mm by 102mm. Framed with a port. P June 16 (244) $2,750

— Anr, [1864 or 1865]. 4to. Cut from a document countersgd by William T. Otto. wa Oct 19 (314) $2,600

— Anr, [n.d.]. 44mm by 137mm. Clipped from ptd document; countersgd by Seward. With collector's authentication on verso, 1865. CNY Dec 5 (79) $3,200

— Anr, [n.d.]. Mtd with a port, overall size 8.5 by 11 inches. Dar Feb 13 (251) $750

Franking signature, [14 Jan n.y.]. On autograph envelope addressed to J. M. McLean. Illus in cat. Dar Apr 9 (265) $4,000

Photograph, sgd, [1862]. 101mm by 61mm. By Brady; sgd on verso. CNY Dec 5 (80) $19,000

— Anr, [c.17 Apr 1863]. Carte size. Full length. By Thomas LeMere, Brady Studio. Illus in cat. R June 13 (90) $25,000

— Anr, [1864]. 83mm by 61mm. By Brady. Imperf. Illus in cat. P June 16 (247) $14,000

Photograph, [c.1858]. 1.75 by 1.25 inches, oval. Ambrotype, by O. A. Alexander. On engraved mount. Illus in cat. R June 13 (115) $1,600

— Anr, 24 Feb 1861. Carte size. By Alexander Gardner. R Nov 9 (99) $300

— Anr, 9 Feb 1864. 5.25 by 3.75 inches. Reading to his son; by Anthony Berger. R Nov 9 (100) $650

— Anr, [c.1885]. 8.25 by 6.25 inches. Later ptg of 1860 photo. R Nov 9 (101) $650

— Anr, [n.d.]. 1/16 plate tintype. Semiprofile, with beard. R Nov 9 (98) $1,900

— Anr, [n.d.]. 8 by 6 inches (image). Artist's rendition of Lincoln holding Emancipation Proclamation; by Holyland. In orig frame. R June 13 (127) $200

Signature, [n.d.]. 3 by 1.75 inches. Illus in cat. Dar June 11 (264) $1,900

— ASSASSINATION. - Photograph, 7 July 1865, 6.5 by 9 inches. Hanging of Lincoln conspirators at Fort McNair; by Alexander Gardner. R Nov 9 (102) $3,000

— BILLINGS, GRACE BEDELL. - ALs, 8 May 1918. 4 pp, 8vo. To J. E. Boos. Responding to an inquiry about her correspondence with Lincoln in 1860. Illus in cat. sup Oct 15 (1539) $4,600

— CARROLL, WILLIAM. - 6 Mss, day books kept

at Wolcottville, Connecticut, 30 Apr 1861 to 1878. Legal size. Recording sales to Abraham & Robert Lincoln, Peter Cooper, Benjamin F. Butler, & others. R June 13 (128) $100

— Corbett, Boston. - Signature, [n.d.]. 64mm by 195mm. CNY June 9 (261) $300

— Daggett, Albert J. - ALs, 15 Apr [1865]. 3 pp, folio. To Julie Truman. Extensive & agitated eyewitness account of Lincoln's assassination. CNY Dec 5 (81) $30,000

— Gourlay, Jeannie Struthers. - Autograph Ms, eyewitness account of Lincoln's assassination by an actress at Ford's Theatre, [n.d.]. 1 p, 8vo. Sgd. Dar Feb 13 (253) $2,250

— Smith, Webster. - ALs, 1916. 1 p, 4to. To John Boos. Remembering Lincoln. sup Oct 15 (1540) $100

— Stevens, John. - ALs, 1913. 2 pp, 4to. To John Boos. About his Civil War service & Lincoln's assassination. sup Oct 15 (1542) $240

See also: Lincoln, Mary Todd

Lincoln, Abraham, 1809-65 —& Stanton, Edwin M., 1814-69

[Their signatures, [n.d.], on a sheet of light blue paper, 7 by 9 inches, sold at Dar on 9 Apr 1992, lot 266, for £750.]

Lincoln, Mary Todd, 1818-82

ALs, 13 Mar 1864. 4 pp, 8vo. To Mrs. Alexander. Expressing condolences & mourning the death of her son. With franking signature by Abraham Lincoln. R Nov 9 (97) $38,000

Lincoln, Robert Todd, 1843-1926

Ls, 16 May 1881. 3 pp, 8vo. To Joseph H. Barrett. Concerning "the detail of officers to receive instruction in the Signal Service." Dar Apr 9 (267) $190

— 20 Oct 1916. 1 p, 4to. To The Neale Publishing Company. Explaining why he has not acknowledged receipt of a book yet. Dar June 11 (270) $110

Ds, 13 Feb 1884. 1 p, 4to. Appointment of James Theodore Dean as cadet of the US Military Academy. Dar Aug 6 (197) $180

Lind, Jenny, 1820-87

Series of 3 A Ls s, 1 Nov 1841 to 12 Aug 1848. 7 pp, 8vo. To George Blumm. About an excursion to Versailles, & planning a visit to Paris. star Mar 27 (1052) DM1,000

Lindbergh, Charles A., 1902-74

ALs, [1938]. 2 pp, 8vo. To Annie von Cramer-Klett. Fragment, expressing condolences on the death of her husband. HH May 13 (1990) DM550

Ls, 23 Dec 1937. 1 p, 4to. To Lester D. Gardner. Thanking for arranging a ceremony for the Wright Brothers. CNY Dec 5 (133) $1,400

— 28 May 1956. 1 p, 4to. To Samuel Williamson. Giving permission to use a letter in a book. Dampstained. sg Sept 12 (144) $130

— 19 Mar 1963. 1 p, 4to. To Joe. Declining an invitation to a reunion. Illus in cat. sup Oct 15 (1350) $1,700

AN, [19 May 1927]. 1 p, 8vo. "I am taking off for Paris with a combination of the finest aeronautical equipment in the world." Framed with cut signature. With related material. Dar Apr 9 (70) $6,000

Autograph sentiment, sgd, inscr to Betty Schinger, 30 Oct 1960. On verso of airline postcard. Framed with a photograph. Dar June 11 (271) $750

Photograph, sgd & inscr, 12 June 1927. 7.25 by 9.25 inches. Inscr to Fred Buckholz. Dar Apr 9 (71) $2,250

— Anr, [n.d.]. 9 by 7 inches. Inscr to Mrs. Whiting. Framed. Illus in cat. P June 17 (44) $1,200

Signature, [15 Aug 1927]. On poster welcoming him to Springfield, 8 by 13 inches. Inscr to Ray Bahr in anr hand. Illus in cat. Dar June 11 (273) $1,000

— Anr, Aug 1956. Framed with a photograph, overall size 18.5 by 15 inches. Dar Dec 26 (250) $500

— Lindbergh, Charles A., Sr. - Check, accomplished & sgd, 1 Oct 1919. Payable to his wife. Sgd by Mrs. Lindbergh on verso & endorsed to her son. Also sgd by C. A. Lindbergh, Jr. on verso. Matted with a ptd photograph. Dar June 11 (272) $750

Lindbergh Kidnapping Case

— Curtis, John H. - Ds, 30 Jan 1935. 1 p, 12mo. Pass no 939 admitting 4 people to the trial of Bruno Hauptmann. Dar June 11 (274) $325

Lindpaintner, Peter Joseph von, 1791-1856

ALs, 27 July 1853. 1 p, 4to. Recipient unnamed. Expressing his conviction that the enthusiasm for Wagner's music will pass. star Mar 27 (1053) DM800

Linnaeus, Carolus, 1707-78

ALs, 14 Dec 1759. 1 p, folio. Recipient unnamed. Letter of introduction for Clas Alstroemer. In Latin. S May 28 (131) £1,100 [Solomon]

Lintner, Max

Collection of 3 A Ls s & Ds, 1925. 7 pp, 8vo. To the Ed of the journal Simplizissimus. Information & power of attorney concerning an indictment for publishing an obscene poem. With 5 related opinions by various authors. HH Nov 6 (2071) DM650

Lipton, Sir Thomas Johnstone, 1850-1931
[A photograph of the yacht Shamrock IV, 15 by 12 inches (image), sgd by Lipton & inscr to Melville Stone, 22 Aug 1914, sold at sg on 27 Feb 1992, lot 260, for $450.]

Lister, Joseph Lister, Baron, 1827-1912
ALs, 27 Jan 1897. 1 p, 12mo. To Mr. Hart. Declining an invitation. Illus in cat. Dar Apr 9 (268) $450

Liszt, Franz, 1811-86
Autograph music, 3 Liebestraeume, [late 1840s]. 15 pp, folio. Working Ms, sgd on tp, & including AN to the ptr. S May 29 (569) £28,000 [Haas]

— Autograph music, Angelus! Priere aux Anges gardiens, [1883]. 4 pp, 35cm by 27cm. 34 bars, scored for harp. Initialled & inscr to [Wilhelm] Posse. With a sgd copy of the ptd work. star Mar 27 (1056) DM3,500

— Autograph music, corrections to several compositions for piano, [1847]. 2 pp, 250mm by 325mm. star Mar 27 (1054) DM2,000

— Autograph music, corrections to an unspecified work, fragment; [n.d.]. 1 p, 8vo, cut from larger sheet. 12 bars. star Mar 27 (1057) DM1,100

— Autograph music, fragment of the Cantico del Sol, [n.d.]. 1 p, 4to. Correction sheet; 20 bars, scored for voice, chorus & orchestra. S Dec 6 (116) £500 [Macnutt]

— Autograph music, opening instrumental introduction to the Benedictus of his Hungarian Coronation Mass, [n.d.]. 2 pp, 7.5cm by 15.5cm. Abridgment of orig version; 6 (instead of 36) bars, scored for violin, clarinet & voices. Illus in cat. S Dec 6 (107) £650 [Macnutt]

— Autograph music, Papst Hymnus, from his oratorio Christus, [1863]. 6 pp, folio. Working Ms in full score; sgd on tp. Illus in cat. S May 29 (573) £4,000 [Saunders]

— Autograph music, song, O lieb, o lieb, so lang du lieben kannst, to a text by Freiligrath, [n.d.]. 3 pp, 35cm by 27cm. 43 bars, scored for harp. Sgd & inscr to Wilhelm Posse. Illus in cat. star Mar 27 (1055) DM6,500

— Autograph music, transcription for piano of Berlioz's Danse de Sylphes from La Damnation de Faust, [c.1860]. 3 pp, folio. Working Ms, notated on up to 5 systems per page, 2 staves each. S May 29 (570) £4,200 [Billington]

Series of 4 A Ls s, 28 Apr 1884 to 13 Jan 1886. 7 pp, 8vo. To Wilhelm Posse. Admiring recipient's harp play, planning a concert, etc. star Mar 27 (1059) DM3,800

ALs, 24 Nov [18]39. 4 pp, 8vo. To [Count Festetics?]. Describing his excitement at the propect of visiting Hungary & expressing his feelings of patriotism. S May 29 (560) £1,800 [Macnutt]

— 4 Dec [1840]. 5 pp, 4to. To Count Leo Festetics. Describing his longing for Hungary, mentioning several of his works, his concert tour, etc. S May 29 (562) £2,200 [Macnutt]

— 2 Apr [1842]. 10 pp, size not stated. To Count Leo Festetics. Reminiscing about his visit to Hungary, outlining travel plans, etc. S May 29 (565) £2,200 [Macnutt]

— 25 Mar 1849. 3 pp, 8vo. To the pbr Karl Friedrich Kistner. About a visit by H. W. Ernst, publishing matters, & a projected concert. star Mar 27 (1058) DM1,500

— 9 Nov [18]71. 3 pp, 8vo. To Marie von Schleinitz. Expressing pleasure at her acceptance of a dedication, & mentioning Lohengrin, Bayreuth & his daughter Cosima. S Dec 6 (114) £550 [Diamond]

— 23 Jan [18]76. 3 pp, 8vo. To Eduard Liszt. Referring to his religious feelings & his symphonic poem Hunnenschlacht. S May 29 (574) £600 [Macnutt]

— 21 Nov [18]84. 3 pp, 8vo. To Marie von Saar. Praising von Buelow's concerts with the Meiningen orchestra. S Dec 6 (105) £600 [Haas]

— 17 Nov 1885. 3 pp, 8vo. Recipient unnamed. Regarding a performance of his 12 symphonic poems in Munich & sending a schedule of concerts (included, 1 p in anr hand). Framed with a port. P June 17 (45) $1,700

— 26 May 1886. 4 pp, 8vo. To Lina Schmalhausen. About his failing eyesight, his problems in writing down his music, & plans for a visit. S May 29 (575) £900 [Macnutt]

— [n.d.], "Saturday". 1 p, 8vo. To Cardinal [von Hohenlohe?]. About a meeting the next morning. Illus in cat. sg Feb 27 (112) $800

— [n.d.], "Saturday". 1 p, 8vo. To an unnamed Cardinal. Announcing his visit at the Borghese chapel the next morning. In French. Illus in cat. sup Oct 15 (1354) $800

— [n.d.]. 1 p, 8vo. To Mme de Moukhanoff. Announcing the arrival of Hans von Buelow. S Dec 6 (115) £550 [Maggs]

Ls, 1 Nov 1852. 2 pp, 8vo. To Caroline von Perin. Describing efforts to secure the publication of Alfred Becher's quartets. S Dec 6 (109) £500 [Schneider]

Liturgical Manuscripts

Ms, choirbook. [Spain, 16th cent]. Single leaf, vellum, 848mm by 563mm. With 5 lines each of text & of music on 5-line red staves on verso, & large historiated initial with 3 lines of music & 4 lines of text within elaborate foliate border on recto. pn Nov 14 (242) £1,600 [Schuster]

— Ms, choirbook. [Spain, 16th cent]. Single leaf, vellum, 850mm by 568mm. With 5 lines each of text & of music on 5-line red staves & large historiated initial. pn Nov 14 (247) £950 [Schuster]

— Ms, choirbook. [Spain, 16th cent]. Single leaf, vellum, 860mm by 595mm. With 5 lines each of text & of music on 5-line red staves within elaborate foliate border & very large historiated initial; verso blank. pn Nov 14 (248) £1,800 [Schuster]

— Ms, choirbook. [Spain, 16th cent]. Single leaf, vellum, 860mm by 570mm. With 5 lines each of text & of music on 5-line red staves within elaborate foliate border & large miniature. Corner def. pn Nov 14 (249) £950 [Schuster]

— Ms, Das puch der schopfunge an dem xxii capitel x des helfungs die heilig drivaltig-kaft...Item als dem Gerren sein seittem geoffnet ward.... Nordlingen, 1475. 1st text in the hand of S. Barrnian; 2d text by anr southern German hand. 168 leaves, 4to, in contemp calf over wooden bds tooled inblind. With 1 full page miniature on vellum & with crudely illuminated opening initial. Milne Ms Ck June 12 (140) £1,600

— COLLECTARY. - Ms, Collectary & calendar, in Latin. [Savoy, Aosta, 15th cent]. 89 leaves (1 lacking) & flyleaf, vellum, 263mm by 185. Def contemp blindstamped brown lea over wooden bds. In a rather rounded gothic liturgical hand. With large & small painted initials throughout. Worn. S June 23 (76) £1,200 [Enlumineures]

Livingston, Philip, Signer from New York

Ds, 29 Nov 1760. 1 p, folio. Bill of sale for 2 slave girls; also sgd by 2 others. CNY June 9 (274) $1,300

Livingston, Robert R., 1746-1813

ALs, 20 Jan 1806. 3 pp, 4to. To M. [Decree?]. Congratulating him on Napoleon's recent victories. In French. Spiro collection. CNY May 14 (117) $3,800

Livingston, William, 1723-90

Ls, 22 Sept 1769. 4 pp, folio. To Catharine Macaulay. Praising her work & declaring that America should have its own constitution. pn June 11 (12) £3,800

Ds, 5 June 1781. 7 pp, folio. Act "to preserve the buildings in [New Jersey] belonging to the United States..." R Nov 9 (117) $550

— 26 Dec 1782. 2 pp, folio. Act for payment of itemized expenses. R Nov 9 (118) $400

Livingstone, David, 1813-73

ALs, 21 Jan 1858. 2 pp, 4to. Recipient unnamed. Discussing supplies & medicine for his upcoming expedition. sup May 9 (413) $1,600

— 3 Mar 1858. 4 pp, 8vo. To John Laird. About the projected departure of HMS Pearl. Ingilby collection. pn Nov 14 (87) £440

— 31 May 1859. 4 pp, folio. To his son Robert. Outlining his religious principles, the role of Europeans in Africa, & his hope to abolish slave labor. S July 21 (268) £4,000 [Wilson]

— Nov 1871. 2 pp, folio. To Dr. Edwin Seward. Describing his encounter with Stanley & his plight during the preceding months. With related ALs by H. M. Stanley. C Dec 16 (305) £8,200 [Sawyer]

— [n.d.]. 3 pp, 8vo. To the Duchess of Sutherland. Thanking for permission to visit her. CNY Dec 5 (82) $600

Lloyd George, David, 1863-1945

Ls, 1 Nov 1909. 1 p, 4to. To Lady Grove. Regretting being unable to talk to her about the women's suffrage movement. With autograph postscript, expressing support. star Mar 27 (1470) DM650

Lloyd, John Henry, 1884-1964

Signature, [n.d.]. 3.5 by 2 inches. With Hall of Fame card. Dar June 11 (87) $650

Loerke, Oskar, 1884-1941

ALs, 16 Jan [19]28. 1 p, 8vo. To a literary society. Regretting being unable to travel to Hungary. FD Dec 3 (1448) DM240

Loewe, Carl, 1796-1869

Autograph music, draft of his song O dolce far niente; [n.d.]. 1 p, 4to. Differing from final version. Sgd at head. With letter stating provenance. hen Nov 12 (2491) DM550

Loewe, Frederick, 1901-88. See: Lerner, Alan Jay & Loewe

Log Books

— BARNE, MICHAEL. - Autograph Mss (2), covering his services on HMS Camperdown, Barfleur, Cordelia & Crescent in the Mediterranean, the West Indies & off Newfoundland, Feb 1894 to Feb 1898. About 450 pp, folio, in canvas wraps. S Feb 11 (761) £400 [Toscani]

— "CERES". - Log of the Ceres on a whaling voyage from Wilmington, Delaware, along western Africa, the Cape Verde Islands, & in the Pacific Ocean, 31 July 1841 to 2 Jan 1845. 176 pp, folio, in contemp half sheep & marbled paper bds. In the hand of William

Eakins. CNY Oct 8 (230) $6,500

— FRANCIS, JOHN. - Ms, journal kept on a voyage from New York to the West Indies on the ship Mercury, 1 May to 13 June 1791. 140 pp, 4to. Including Ms map of Eastern seaboard, pencil drawings of the islands, wildlife, etc. R Mar 7 (241) $3,500

— "LA FAYETTE". - Log of the La Fayette on a whaling voyage from New Bedford to the Pacific Ocean, 22 Oct 1840 to 20 May 1843. 120 pp, folio, in contemp half sheep & paper bds. Including numerous small drawings of animals, ships, coastlines, etc. CNY Oct 8 (229) $6,500

— "MIDAS". - Log of the bark Midas of New Bedford on a whaling voyage in the Indian Ocean, off New Zealand & in the Pacific, 22 Mar 1861 to 1 Aug 1864. 103 pp, folio, in worn contemp half black roan & marbled paper bds. In the hand of William F. Keyser. Including 2 related documents. CNY Oct 8 (231) $3,800

— NELSON, CHARLES G. - 2 autograph Mss, logs of HMS Rattler & HMS Vengeance on voyages along the coast of West Africa & in the Mediterranean, July 1850 to Dec 1852. 340 pp in 2 vols, folio. Including 7 orig watercolor drawings. sg Feb 27 (28) $650

— "TALBOT". - Log of HMS Talbot on an expedition along the northern coast of Greenland & Baffin Island, 28 Feb to 25 Oct 1854. 200 pp, folio, in orig bds. b June 22 (134) £170

— "VOLAGE". - Ms, log of HMS Volage in the eastern Mediterranean, kept by John F. Wyer, 1 May 1847 to 15 Dec 1848. Length not stated, folio, in contemp half roan. Including 2 orig drawings of a temporary rudder. With a history of the Wyer family in anr hand at end. L Nov14 (355) £60

See also: Whaling Manuscripts

Lombard, Carole, 1908-42

Photograph, sgd & inscr, [n.d.]. Size not stated. Inscr to Bud Davis. sup Oct 15 (1356) $725

Lombardi, Vincent Thomas, 1913-70

Check, sgd, 19 Sept 1959. As Coach, payable to Bobby Dillon. Dar June 11 (183) $300

Signature, [n.d.]. 5 by 3 inches (card). Dar Feb 13 (176) $170

Signature, [n.d.]. 16mo (card). Dar Dec 26 (184) $224

London, Jack, 1876-1916

Autograph Ms, notes for his novel Adventure, [c.Aug - Oct 1908]. 42 pp, 8vo, removed from a notebook. In pencil. CNY June 9 (112) $11,000

ALs, 5 Feb 1902. 4 pp, 4to. To an Ed of the Magazine Youth's Companion. Defending various aspects of his story To Build a Fire. CNY Dec 5 (275) $5,500

— [n.d.]. 1 p, 4to. Recipient unnamed. Fragment, referring to his new novel. sup Oct 15 (1359) $750

Check, sgd, 5 Dec 1909. 6 by 2.75 inches. Payable to Imperial Cash Store. Dar Oct 10 (249) $325

— Anr, accomplished & sgd, 14 Sept 1912. Drawn on the Merchants National Bank of San Francisco for $5.00 payable to W. H. Smith. Framed. sg Sept 12 (146) $275

Longfellow, Henry Wadsworth, 1807-82

Autograph Ms, poem, beginning "The night shall be filled with music...", [n.d.]. 1 p, 12mo. 4 lines, sgd. Framed. Dar Apr 9 (269) $650

Collection of ALs & Ls, 3 Nov 1858 & [n.d.]. 3 pp, 16mo. To [E. P.] Whipple. Inviting him to dine, & thanking for a review. sg Sept 12 (147) $375

ALs, 23 Nov 1860. 3 pp, 16mo. To the pbr Fields. About proofs & corrections. sg Feb 27 (113) $450

— 1 June 1862. 4 pp, 8vo. To Miss Bernard. Thanking for a copy of her Legendes Canadiennes. pn Nov 14 (226) £240

— 23 May 1863. 3 pp, 8vo. Recipient unnamed. Thanking for a book. Dar Dec 26 (251) $225

— 6 Sept 1873. 3 pp, 8vo. To [Dr. Charles Waldstein]. Suggesting that he translate some stories from Aftermath instead of Hiawatha. pn June 11 (84) £180

— 27 May 1879. 3 pp, 8vo. To the Marquise de Saffray. Acknowledging receipt of her poems. Framed with 2 portraits. sg Sept 12 (148) $350

ANs, 31 Dec 1866. 1 p, 12mo. To [J. T. Fields]. Requesting a copy of his [Tales of a] Wayside Inn. Dar June 11 (275) $500

Longstreet, James, 1821-1904

ALs, 20 Sept [1863]. 2 pp, 12mo. To Gen. Thomas C. Hindman. Battlefield letter, praising the performance of his troops at Chickamauga. CNY Dec 5 (83) $3,800

Ls, 3 July 1855. 1 p, 4to. To Col. H. K. Craig. Transmitting vouchers. Framed with a photograph. Dar June 11 (276) $900

Loos, Anita, 1893-1981

Typescript, Darling-Darling, [n.d.]. 150 pp, 4to. Comedy in 3 acts. sg June 11 (208) $60

— Typescript, Zazu Pitts' Play, [n.d.]. 125 pp, 4to. 1st version of an unpbd play. sg June 11 (210) $70

Loos, Anita, 1893-1981 —& Styne, Jule, 1905-81

Ds, 10 Mar 1952. 33 pp, 4to. Contract with 20th Century Fox for the film Gentlemen Prefer Blondes; carbon copy. Dar Aug 6 (40) $225

Lopez, Aaron, 1731-82

ALs, 17 July 1764. 2 pp, size not stated. To Capt. William Pinninger. Giving instructions for a trading voyage to the coast of Africa & Jamaica. With related material. CNY Dec 5 (84) $950

Lorre, Peter, 1904-64

Photograph, sgd, [c.1950s]. 5 by 7 inches. Dar Aug 6 (22) $225

— Anr, [n.d.]. 8 by 10 inches. Dar Feb 13 (254) $120

Lortzing, Albert, 1801-51

ALs, 22 Dec 1847. 1 p, 4to. To Louis Huth. About a financial mattter. star Mar 27 (1060) DM1,800

— 20 Nov 1850. 1 p, 4to. To Louis Brassin. Informing him that the director of the Friedrich Wilhelmstaedtische Theater is not hiring opera singers. star Mar 27 (1061) DM2,500

Loti, Pierre, Pseud. of Julien Viaud, 1850-1923

ALs, [n.d.]. 2 pp, 8vo (lettercard). Recipient unnamed. Refusing to write a preface for recipient's work. HH May 13 (1992) DM200

Louis Ferdinand, Prince of Prussia, 1772-1806

Ls, 2 Dec 1794. 1 p, 4to. To Dr. Voigtel. Congratulating him on an appointment. star Mar 27 (1610) DM480

Louis, Joe, 1914-81

Photograph, sgd & inscr, [n.d.]. 8 by 10 inches. In boxing pose. Dar Dec 26 (127) $375

Signature, [n.d.]. 3 by 4 inches. Framed with a photograph. Dar June 11 (110) $200

Louis Philippe, King of France, 1773-1850

Ls, 20 Nov 1844. 1 p, 4to. To the Duc Decazes. Requesting him to attend "l'ouverture de la Session des Chambres" on Dec 26. HN Nov 28 (1770) DM260

Louis XIV, King of France, 1638-1715

ALs, 17 May 1678. 3 pp, 8vo. To King Charles II of England. Discussing the repercussions of the war with Holland. Framed with a port. Illus in cat. P June 17 (46) $6,000

Ls, 20 Sept 1713. 1 p, 4to. To Queen Maria Anna of Spain. Informing her of the recall of his envoy Marquis de Bonnac. star Mar 27 (1349) DM2,000

Louis XV, King of France, 1710-74

Letter, 17 May 1728. 2 pp, folio. To Archduchess Marie Elisabeth, Regent of the Netherlands. Assuring her of his friendship. With secretarial signature. HN Nov 28 (1774) DM240

Ds, 19 Feb 1743. 38 pp, 330mm by 21mm; stitched. Marriage contract of Jules Hercules de Rohan & Jeanne de la Tour d'Auvergne. Also sgd by the Queen, the Dauphin & over 50 others. C June 24 (375) £1,000 [Saggiori]

Louis XV, King of France, 1710-74 —& Others

Ds, Jan 1774. 12 pp, folio. Marriage contract of Louis Joseph, Comte d'Ailly, & Anne Bonne Genevieve Antoinette Le Camus. Also sgd by Louis XVI, Marie Antoinette, other members of the Royal family, & numerous court members. Illus in cat. Stefan Zweig collection. star Mar 27 (1353) DM15,000

Louis XVI, King of France, 1754-93

Ds, 23 Feb 1776. 1 p, folio. Commending Nicholas Degaux as valet de chambre to Mme Sophie. rs Oct 17 (87A) $300

— 4 Oct 1789. 1 p, folio. Appointment of Philippe de Marigny to the Ordre Militaire de St. Louis. Framed. rs Oct 17 (89) $175

— 14 Oct 1791. 1 p, folio. Pay order. sg Sept 12 (149) $350

Louis XVIII, King of France, 1755-1824

Ms, instructions to the Comte du Moustier, stating his intentions towards the people of France & his political aims, 20 Mar 1796. 17 pp, folio. In the hand of du Moustier. sg Sept 12 (150) $2,600

Lowell, James Russell, 1819-91

Series of 5 A Ls s, 1882 to 1885 & [n.d.]. 6 pp, various sizes. To Lady Marian [Alford]. Mostly about plans for meeting with recipient. wa Oct 19 (51) $210

ALs, 18 Oct 1881. 4 pp, 8vo. To Lady Marian [Alford]. Giving a light-hearted assessment of Anglo-American relations. wa Oct 19 (52) $210

— 12 Feb 1889. 1 p, 12mo. To James Grant Wilson. Declining an invitation. Framed with related material. Dar Oct 10 (250) $100

Lowell, John, 1743-1802. See: Morris, Robert

Lowry, Malcolm, 1909-57

ALs, May 1931. 1 p, 8vo. To Kenneth Wright. Commenting on an essay. With related material. sup Oct 15 (1361) $180

Ludendorff, Erich, 1865-1937

ALs, 24 Mar 1925. 2 pp, 8vo. To Dr. Hermann. Justifying his political position. star Mar 27 (1473) DM850

— 6 Aug 1934. 1 p, 8vo. Recipient unnamed. Stressing the need for the continuation of his political work. star Mar 27 (1474) DM320

Autograph postcard, sgd, [26 Sept 1914]. To Lieut. Mueller-Kranefeldt. Mentioning the battles at Tannenberg & in Masuria. star Mar 27 (1472) DM500

Ludwig, Carl, 1816-95

ALs, 10 Sept 1885. 3 pp, 8vo. To A. G. Dew-Smith. Inquiring about research projects at Cambridge. star Mar 26 (724) DM300

Ludwig I, King of Bavaria, 1786-1868

ALs, 2 June 1818. 2 pp, 4to. To Fuerst Wrede. Commenting on the new Bavarian constitution. star Mar 27 (1256) DM750

Ls s (2), 14 & 15 Nov 1841. 2 pp, 4to. To Karl von Abel. Giving instructions regarding the period of mourning for his stepmother. star Mar 27 (1258) DM420

Ludwig II, King of Bavaria, 1845-86

ALs, 5 Nov 1869. 7 pp, 8vo. To Friedrich Brandt. Describing their friendship in impassioned terms. Illus in cat. star Mar 27 (1263) DM14,500

Ls, 27 July 1864. 1 p, 4to. To his Ministry of the Interior. Notifying officials of a projected journey. star Mar 27 (1260) DM1,200

— 23 Sept 1865. 1 p, 4to. To his Ministry of the Interior. Giving instructions to respond to rumors about his wish to live in seclusion. star Mar 27 (1261) DM1,700

Ds, 31 July 1869. 1 p, folio. Permission that Julius Friedrich Spitta be declared of legal age. HH Nov 5 (847) DM420

— 21 Mar 1883. 1 p, folio. Summons to a meeting of the diet, addressed to Count Karl zu Castell-Castell. star Mar 27 (1264) DM700

— 14 May 1885. 3 pp, folio. Extension of retirement for Ferdinand von Inama-Sternegg. HH May 13 (1994) DM900

Ludwig III, King of Bavaria, 1845-1921

ALs, 21 Mar 1919. 4 pp, 4to. To his daughter Helmtrud. About life after his abdication & the death of his wife. star Mar 27 (1266) DM2,800

Ds, 26 Nov 1914. 1 p, folio. Administrative appointment for Eduard Faber. star Mar 27 (1265) DM500

Ludwig, Otto, 1813-65

ALs, 27 Mar 1862. 1 p, 8vo. Recipient unnamed. Asking for financial aid from the Schiller Foundation. With related letter of recommendation. star Mar 26 (344) DM680

Luetzow, Adolf, Freiherr von, 1782-1834

Ls, 15 Jan 1815. 1 p, folio. To August Froebel. Ptd circular, sending a medal commemorating the campaign of 1813/14. star Mar 27 (1476) DM470

Luise, Queen of Friedrich Wilhelm III of Prussia, 1776-1810

ALs, [24 Apr 1804]. 2 pp, 8vo. To Countess Voss. Chatting about her activities. Illus in cat. star Mar 27 (1615) DM2,500

Ls, 12 Oct 1804. 1 p, 8vo. To Karl Friedrich Muechler. Expressing thanks. hen Nov 12 (2492) DM380

Lukacs, Georg, 1885-1971

Autograph Ms, notes for the preface of a Spanish Ed of his book Der junge Hegel, [n.d.]. 1 p, 8vo. star Mar 26 (725) DM210

Lully, Jean Baptiste, 1632-87

Ms, opera, Alceste, [late 17th cent]. 148 leaves, folio. Early mottled sheep bdg. In a scribal hand, with interlinear libretto by Philippe Quinault. P June 17 (262) $1,600

Lummer, Otto, 1860-1925

Autograph Ms, opinion on a memorial of Friedrich Archenhold regarding the construction of a lens, [1894]. 3 pp, folio. Sgd. Endorsed in anr hand at foot. star Mar 26 (726) DM370

Lunt, Alfred, 1892-1977 —& Fontanne, Lynn, 1887-1983

Ds, 14 Oct 1949. 2 pp, 4to. Contract with The Theatre Guild Radio Division; carbon copy. Dar Feb 13 (255) $100

Luther, Martin, 1483-1546

Ls, [28 Mar] 1532. 1 p, folio. To Georg Vogler. Letter of recommendation for Bernhard Ziegler. Illus in cat. sup Oct 15 (1362) $27,500

Lutoslawski, Witold

Autograph music, sketches for Les espaces du sommeil, 1975. 2 pp, 175mm by 250mm. Sgd later, 13 July 1984. star Mar 27 (1063) DM850

Lvov, Georgy Yevgenyevich, Prince, 1861-1925 —& Others

Ls, Dec 1920. 3 pp, 4to. To the President of the Belgian Chamber of Deputies. Pleading for assistance to Russian refugees. Also sgd by

N. W. Tchaikovsky, J. Rubinstein, J. Polner & N. Axietieff. In French. Dar Oct 10 (251) $950

Lynch, Thomas, 1727-76 —& Others

Ds, 1 May 1775. 4.75 by 6 inches.£50 note certificate authorized by the Provincial Congress of South Carolina; also sgd by Th. Middleton, B. Huger & M. Brewton. R Nov 9 (119) $3,000

M

McAdam, John Loudon, 1756-1836

ALs, 27 Oct 1826. 3 pp, 4to. To J. Bittan. Ingilby collection. pn Nov 14 (88) £160

MacArthur, Charles, 1895-1956. See: Hecht, Ben & MacArthur

MacArthur, Douglas, 1880-1964

Transcript, excerpt from his address on 2 Sept 1945 after Japan's surrender; [n.d.]. 1 p, 12mo (card). Sgd. Dar Oct 10 (253) $375

Ls, 1 May 1933. 1 p, 4to. To Basil O'Connor. As Acting Sec of War, about reforestation on Long Island. sg Sept 12 (151) $200

— 9 Oct 1945. 1 p, 4to. To John V. Ireland. Circular letter to parents of officers who died in action, expressing condolences. CNY Dec 5 (85) $2,200

Group photograph, sgd, [31 Oct 1944]. 7 by 10.5 inches. With Lieut. Gen. Walter Krueger. With cut signature. Dar Feb 13 (256) $275

Photograph, sgd, [c.1945]. 8 by 10 inches. Bust pose, in uniform. sg Sept 12 (152) $400

— Anr, [n.d.]. 8 by 10 inches. Imperf. R June 13 (210) $160

Macaulay, Catharine, 1731-91

— "SOPHRONIA". - 3 A Ls s, 25 Apr 1769 to 24 Mar [1770]. 6 pp, folio & 4to. To Catharine Macaulay. Referring to patriotic principles & women in New England, & introducing John Adams. With copies of 2 replies by Macaulay (1 autograph). pn June 11 (17) £7,000

See also: Adams, John
See also: Dickinson, John
See also: Hollis, Thomas
See also: Warren, Mercy Otis
See also: Wollstonecraft, Mary

Macaulay, Zachary, 1768-1838

ALs, 24 Sept 1824. 1 p, 4to. To D. Hodgsen. Introducing an American inventor. bba May 28 (178) £90 [Wilson]

McCarthy, Joe

Group photograph, sgd, 8 Sept 1951. 10 by 8 inches. With Ed Barrow. Illus in cat. sup July 10 (979) $75

— Anr, sgd, 22 July 1957. 10 by 8 inches. With Casey Stengel & Sam Crawford. Illus in cat. sup July 10 (980) $75

Photograph, sgd, 8 Sept 1951. 8 by 10 inches. Shouting instructions to his team. Illus in cat. sup July 10 (978) $75

McCartney, Paul

Autograph Ms, lyrics for the song Giddy, [1977]. Framed with a photograph, overall size 24 by 23 inches. Illus in cat. P Dec 17 (332) $3,000

McCaskey, William S.

Ds, 20 Aug 1876. 2 pp, 8 by 9.5 inches. Military discharge for John Weis. Sgd 3 times. Armstrong collection. sup Oct 15 (1119) $200

McClellan, George B., 1826-85

ALs, 21 May 1862. 4 pp, 4to. To Gen. Ambrose Burnside. Expressing pride in his past victories & preparing for battle at Richmond. CNY Dec 5 (86) $5,500

Photograph, sgd, [n.d.]. Carte size. In uniform. By Appleton & Co. Illus in cat. R June 13 (108) $450

Signature, [n.d.]. 4.25 by 2.5 inches (card). Including subscription. Framed. Armstrong collection. sup Oct 15 (1120) $350

McCormick, Cyrus H., 1809-84

Check, sgd, 14 May 1871. Payable to J. I. Adams. Dar Apr 9 (282) $225

MacDonald, James Ramsay, 1866-1937

Collection of 3 Ls s & autograph postcard, sgd, 19 May 1931 to 10 Jan 1934. 5 pp, size not stated. To Sean O'Casey. About a variety of matters. C Dec 16 (306) £200 [Doran]

MacDonald, Jeanette

Ls, 28 Sept 1944. 1 p, 8vo. To Miss Gerberg Legault. Thanking for roses. Framed with a photograph. Illus in cat. sup Oct 15 (1363) $130

MacDonald, Sir John, d.1850

Autograph Ms, Particulars of Genl. Ladrizabel's affair..., 5 Mar 1811. 11 pp, 4to. Report on Spanish conduct at the Battle of Barossa. pn Nov 14 (146) £240 [Maggs]

McDowell, Irvin, 1818-85

Photograph, sgd, [n.d.]. Carte size. In uniform. By Anthony, from a Brady negative. Illus in cat. R June 13 (109) $600

McGinnity, Joe, 1871-1929

Signature, [n.d.]. 4.5 by 1.5 inches. With Hall of Fame card. Dar June 11 (88) $200

McIntosh, Lachlan, 1725-1806

ALs, 15 Nov 1774. 1 p, 8vo. To George Houstoun. Requesting a receipt for 150 acres of land. Illus in cat. sup May 9 (385) $1,200

McKean, Thomas, Signer from Delaware

Ds, 4 Feb 1797. 1 p, folio. Deed for land in Philadelphia sold by Mary Allen to John Olden. Dar June 11 (288) $325

Mackensen, August von, 1849-1945

Ls, 24 June 1915. 1 p, folio. To Gen. von Francois. Sending decorations for his soldiers after the campaign in Galicia. star Mar 27 (1477) DM450

Mackenzie, Sir Morell, 1837-92

ALs, [18 Apr 1888]. 2 pp, 8vo. To Frau von Bunsen. Informing her that "the Emperor is decidedly worse this afternoon." star Mar 27 (1311) DM380

McKinley, William, 1843-1901

[3 police documents relating to the assassination of McKinley, Sept 1901, 3 pp, folio, sold at R on 13 June 1992, lot 183, for $6,000.]

ALs, 21 May 1881. 1 p, 4to. To Allen Carnes. About his publishing business. CNY June 9 (263) $500

ALs, 5 Feb 1882. 4 pp, 4to. To Allen Carnes. Denying that he had promised not to seek re-election. CNY Dec 5 (87) $2,600

— 11 Apr 1882. 4 pp, 4to. To Allen Carnes. Denying a secret deal with anr office-seeker. CNY Dec 5 (88) $1,500

— 25 Feb 1893. 1 p, 4to. To William M. Duncan. Informing him about a personal financial crisis. Spiro collection. CNY May 14 (119) $950

— 29 May 1894. 1 p, 8vo. To Gartrie. Enclosing a warrant. Dar Oct 10 (257) $250

— 24 Apr 1896. 1 p, 4to. To H. H. Kohlsaat. Hoping that "Maj. Handy [will] go to Springfield for the Convention." sg Sept 12 (163) $350

— 10 May 1896. 1 p, 8vo. To Henry L. Stoddard. Arranging a meeting. R Nov 9 (22) $350

Collection of 4 Aug 1900. 1 p, 4to. To Gen. Thomas L. Rosser. Expressing thanks. Illus in cat. sup Oct 15 (1580) $450

Ls, 13 Nov 1894. 1 p, 4to. To J. B. Allen. Notifying him of his appointment to the commission to indicate positions of regiments at the Battle of Antietam. Dar Oct 10 (256) $325

— 11 July 1895. 1 p, 4to. To A. C. Powers. Acknowledging receipt of a communication. Framed with a port. Dar Dec 26 (259) $250

— 7 Nov 1895. 1 p, 4to. To Gov. Levi P. Morton. Letter of recommendation for Robert H. Folger. Framed with ptd photograph. Dar June 11 (291) $150

— 16 June 1896. 1 p, 8vo. To George M. Vickers. Thanking for a copy of a campaign song. Dar Apr 9 (283) $300

— 24 June 1896. 1 p, 8vo. To William C. Lyon. Thanking for a congratulatory telegram. Dar Dec 26 (258) $160

— 24 Sept 1896. 1 p, 4to. To Moses Handy. Commenting on "the work of the American Honest Money League". R Nov 9 (23) $600

— 19 Nov 1896. 1 p, 8vo. To C. B. Watson. Thanking for good wishes. Dar Aug 6 (202) $250

— 9 Nov 1897. 2 pp, folio. To Rafael Iglesias, President of Costa Rica. Informing him of the recall of the US Envoy Baker. Illus in cat. sup Oct 15 (1575) $1,325

ANs, 15 Jan 1889. 1 p, 8vo. To W. B. Thompson. Concerning a railway mail service appointment. Dar Feb 13 (261) $180

Ds, 8 Sept 1893. 1 p, folio. As Governor of Ohio, appointment of William H. Marlatt as Notary Public. Matted with a port. Dar June 11 (289) $130

— 11 June 1898. 1 p, folio. Appointment of William Stackpole as postmaster. sup Oct 15 (1577) $610

— 11 July 1898. 1 p, folio. Appointment of Chambers McKibbin as Brigadier General of Volunteers. Framed. Dar Oct 10 (258) $350

— 18 July 1898. 1 p, folio. Appointment of James T. Dean as Chief Ordnance Officer of Volunteers. Dar Aug 6 (203) $300

Ds, 3 Jan 1899. 2 pp, folio. Pardon warrant for the Indian Bay-bah-Maush. CNY Dec 5 (90) $1,700

— 24 Jan 1899. 1 p, folio. Approval of an act of the Chickasaw Legislature (attached, 3 pp, folio). Illus in cat. sup Oct 15 (1578) $2,400

— 4 Mar 1899. 1 p, folio. Appointment of Stuart Heintzelman as 2d lieutenant of cavalry. sg Sept 12 (164) $350

— 5 Apr 1899. 1 p, folio. Appointment of Frederick Rogers as Rear Admiral. R June 13 (186) $500

— 13 Apr 1899. 1 p, folio. Appointment of James T. Dean as Captain of Infantry. Countersgd by D. Merklejohn. Dar Aug 6 (204) $160

— 17 Aug 1899. 1 p, size not stated. Military commission. Framed. F Mar 26 (808) $110

— 26 Dec 1899. 1 p, folio. Appointment of James T. Dean as Captain of Infantry. Countersgd by Elihu Root. Dar Aug 6 (205) $425

— 26 Dec 1899. 1 p, folio. Appointment of

Charles L. Farnsworth as Capt. of Infantry. sup Oct 15 (1579) $360

— 24 June 1901. 1 p, folio. Appointment of Isaac Martin as 2d Lieut. of Cavalry. Framed with engraved port. Illus in cat. sup Oct 15 (1584) $525

— [n.d.]. 1 p, folio. Military commission; countersgd by Elihu Root. R Nov 9 (24) $380

Autograph telegram, 25 Dec 1900. 1 p, 8vo. To Mr. & Mrs. Williams. Sending Christmas greetings. Illus in cat. sup Oct 15 (1582) $600

Check, accomplished & sgd, 13 Mar 1882. Drawn on his account at the House of Representatives; payable to himself. Dar Apr 9 (284) $600

— Anr, sgd, 1 Feb 1898. Payable to Helen McKinley. Endorsed by recipient on verso. Illus in cat. sup Oct 15 (1770) $750

— Anr, sgd, 8 Oct 1898. Payable to his sister Helen McKinley. Endorsed by recipient on verso. wa Oct 19 (316) $500

Executive Mansion card, sgd, July 1900. With secretarial letter of transferral. bbc Sept 23 (26) $125

— Anr, sgd, [n.d.]. 4.25 by 2.75 inches. Dar Aug 6 (201) $450

Group photograph, [1898]. 9.9 by 13.12 inches. With his cabinet. Illus in cat. sup Oct 15 (1585) $210

Photograph, sgd, [1900]. 4 by 5.5 inches (image). By George Prince. R Nov 9 (21) $480

— Anr, [n.d.]. 5 by 7 inches. Dar June 11 (290) $1,000

Photograph, sgd & inscr, [n.d.]. 4.25 by 6.5 inches. Illus in cat. sup Oct 15 (1586) $460

Signature, [n.d.]. 3.5 by 1 inches. Matted with engraved port. Dar Feb 13 (262) $140

— Anr, [n.d.]. As Governor of Ohio, on Executive Chamber Card. wa Oct 19 (317) $170

McLaglen, Victor, 1886-1959

Photograph, sgd, [n.d.]. 7 by 9.25 inches. Dar Apr 9 (285) $110

MacLeay, Alexander, 1767-1848

Ls, 5 Oct 1829. 1 p, folio. To W. C. Wentworth. Acknowledging receipt of his application for a grant of land at Sydney. Longueville collection. S June 25 (192) £140 [McCormick]

McNair, Ronald E., 1950-86

ANs, [n.d.]. 1 p, 4to. Recipient unnamed. At the bottom of a letter addressed to him, responding to questions on his interest in the space program. Dar Oct 10 (94) $400

Photograph, sgd & inscr, [n.d.]. 8 by 10 inches. Inscr to Peter Rubinstein. Dar Dec 26 (260) $160

McQueen, Steve, 1930-80

Ds, 19 May 1971. 2 pp, 4to. Contract regarding the film Junior Bonner; photocopied typescript. Dar Dec 26 (261) $400

— 31 Jan 1972. 1 p, 4to. Approving the use of a picture. Dar Apr 9 (286) $120

Madison, Dorothy Payne Todd ("Dolley"), 1768-1849

ALs, 10 Feb 1807. 2 pp, 4to. To Dr. Thomas Park. Reporting the arrest of Aaron Burr. Including franking signature by James Madison. Illus in cat. Spiro collection. CNY May 14 (120) $9,000

Autograph quotation, citing Dickens, [19] Apr 1842. 1 p, 8vo. Sgd. With contemp note of authenticity. CNY Dec 5 (91) $1,700

Madison, James, 1751-1836

Collection of ALs & Ls, 26 Sept 1788 & 15 May 1835. 4 pp, 4to. To John Brown. Responding to a request for his views on the form of government for Kentucky & quoting congressional resolutions, & enclosing a letter for Mann Butler regarding discussions in 1788 (text copied on integral leaf). Including franking signature. P June 16 (253) $23,000

ALs, 15 Dec 1814. 1 p, 4to. To Benjamin W. Crowninshield. Offering him the Secretaryship of the Navy. CNY Dec 5 (93) $11,000

— 7 Jan 1830. 1 p, 8vo. To Mr. Featherstonhaugh. About receipient's son's "views towards Westpoint". Illus in cat. sup Oct 15 (1494) $6,750

Ls, 17 June 1801. 1 p, 4to. To David Lenox. Transmitting papers concerning a seaman impressed by the British. Illus in cat. sup May 9 (171) $2,700

— [c.5 Mar 1804]. 1 p, 4to. To Aaron Burr. Responding to Burr's request for the papers of an unidentified voyage. Illus in cat. sup Oct 15 (1491) $3,000

ADs, 9 Feb 1782. 1 p, 8 by 2 inches, cut from larger sheet. Bond "to discharge the above Bond in specie". Sgd by Strother Jones as witness. Illus in cat. Dar Aug 6 (199) $700

Ds, 4 Jan 1810. 1 p, folio. Ship's passport for the brig George Washington. CNY Dec 5 (92) $480

— 8 Nov 1810. 1 p, folio. Ship's papers in 4 languages for the schooner Lydia. R Mar 7 (134) $1,200

— 8 Jan 1811. 1 p, folio. Ship's passport for the Garland of New York. R Mar 7 (133) $950

— 27 Apr 1811. 1 p, folio. Ship's papers in 4 languages for the brig Fox. R June 13 (187) $1,300

— 7 Oct 1811. 1 p, folio. Ship's papers for the schooner Purse of New York. R Nov 9 (18)

$900

— 12 Dec 1811. 1 p, folio. Ship's papers in 4 languages for the schooner Lone. Countersgd by Monroe. rf Sept 21 (15) $1,400

— 4 Jan 1812. 1 p, folio. Ship's papers in 4 languages for the ship Martha of Boston. Countersgd by Monroe. R Nov 9 (20) $1,600

— 23 July 1812. 1 p, size not stated. Military commission. Faded. F Mar 26 (809A) $130

— 4 Nov 1812. 1 p, folio. Appointment of Asa Axtell as 2d Lieutenant of Volunteers. sup Oct 15 (1492) $600

— 20 Nov 1812. 1 p, folio. Naval commission for Barton W. Halsey. Imperf. Framed. wd Dec 12 (324) $350

— 13 Dec 1812. 1 p, folio. Ship's papers in 4 languages for the schooner Sea Nymph. Countersgd by Monroe. R Mar 7 (135) $1,700

— 24 Dec 1814. 1 p, folio. Naval commission for Bernard Henry. Framed. wd Dec 12 (325) $650

— 13 Feb 1817. 1 p, folio. Grant of land at Marietta. sg Sept 12 (153) $400

Document, 4 Mar 1815. 2 pp, 4to. Proclamation declaring a national day of thanksgiving after the war. Official transcript in the hand of James Graham, addressed to the National Intelligencer. CNY June 9 (265) $2,000

Check, accomplished & sgd, 24 Apr 1813. Drawn on the Bank of Columbia. Illus in cat. sup Oct 15 (1756) $925

— Anr, accomplished & sgd, 16 Nov 1814. Payable to bearer. Dar Apr 9 (271) $1,700

Cut signature, [n.d.]. 1 by 5.5 inches. With concluding words from an ALs. Dar Dec 26 (252) $600

— Anr, [n.d.]. 5.5 by 1 inches. With concluding line of ALs. Dar June 11 (277) $350

— Anr, [n.d.]. 5.75 by 2 inches. Mtd. Dar June 11 (278) $450

Franking signature, 6 Aug [n.y.]. On autograph address leaf to Richard Peters, 4to. R Nov 9 (19) $480
See also: Gerry, Elbridge
See also: Madison, Dorothy Payne Todd ("Dolley")

Magritte, Rene, 1898-1967

ALs, 15 Jan 1957. 1 p, 8vo. Recipient unnamed. Informing him "que des travaux pourraient commencer le 18 Mars..." star Mar 27 (922) DM300

Mahler, Gustav, 1860-1911

[His copy of the works of Johann Sebastian Bach, 49 vols, Leipzig 1851-99, with extensive annotations & re-orchestrations in Mahler's hand & including 5 autograph pages on additional leaves, sold at S on 29 May 1992, lot 577, for £24,000 to Kohn.]

Autograph music, sketches for the Rondo Burleske, 3d movement of his 9th Symphony, [c.1909]. 2 pp, folio. 24 bars in full & short score. Illus in cat. S May 29 (578) £8,000 [Billington]

ALs, [c.Apr 1885]. 1 p, 8vo. To Eugen Gruenberg. Inquiring about his chances for a position at Leipzig. star Mar 27 (1064) DM5,500

— [1886]. 2 pp, 8vo. To Eugen Gruenberg. Requesting him to send a book to Frau von Weber. Illus in cat. S Dec 6 (118) £1,000 [Haas]

— [n.d.]. 2 pp, 8vo. Recipient unnamed. Regarding a performance of Figaro at Koblenz. Framed with a port. Illus in cat. P June 17 (48) $3,000

Autograph quotation, 3 bars of the opening of the 3d movement of his 2d Symphony, Jan 1897. 1 p, 8vo. Sgd & inscr to "Winifeld Ker Seymer". Illus in cat. S Dec 6 (119) £3,000 [Kaplan]

Signature, [n.d.]. 16mo. With subscription. Mtd with a port. JG Sept 27 (403) DM530

Mahler-Werfel, Alma, 1879-1964

ALs, 12 Dec 1932. 1 p, 4to. To Lotte Czarniawski. Asking for a phone call, & sending Christmas greetings. HN Nov 28 (1779) DM360

— 14 Mar 1953. 2 pp, 8vo. Recipient unnamed. About her move to NY. star Mar 27 (1065) DM280

Autograph postcard, sgd, [n.d.]. To an unnamed lady. Expressing thanks. HH May 13 (1997) DM460

Mailer, Norman

Ls, 7 Oct [1946]. 1 p, 4to. To Mr. Cameron. Discussing his use of profanity in The Naked and the Dead. With sgd copy of 1st Ed of the book. CNY June 9 (119) $2,600

Mainwaring, Sir Henry, 1587-1653

Ms, The Sea-Man's Dictionary [here: An Abstract, and Exposition of all things pertayning to the Practicque of Navigation], [c.1620-23]. About 320 pp, folio, in contemp London bdg with the arms of Charles I as Prince of Wales. In the hand of Ralph Crane, with dedication to Edward, Baron Zouche, sgd by Mainwaring. S July 21 (271) £12,000 [Quaritch]

Malamud, Bernard, 1914-86

A Ls s (2), 1966 & [n.d.]. 2 pp, 4to & 8vo. To Jay Martin. Thanking for an invitation to stay with him, & discussing a projected lecture. Dar June 11 (279) $170

Malenkov, Georgy Maksimilianovich, 1902-88

Signature, 22 Mar [19]56. 4 by 6 inches. Framed with ptd port. Dar Apr 9 (354) $225

Mallarme, Stephane, 1842-98

ALs, Apr 1894. 2 pp, 12mo (card). To Bouyer. Commenting on recipient's book. star Mar 26 (346) DM700

Manet, Edouard, 1832-83

ALs, [n.d.], "Monday". 2 pp, 0vo. To Masenede. Inviting him for dinner. Illus in cat. Thorek collection. sup Oct 15 (1364) $1,250

Manetti, Lorenzo

Ms, poem, beginning "O Glorioso et triumfante Amore". [Italy, late 15th cent]. 14 leaves, vellum, 198mm by 142mm. Later vellum bdg. 50 three-line stanzas; last 5 pp with later texts. C Dec 16 (13) £900 [Jackson]

Mann, Heinrich, 1871-1950

ALs, 22 Dec 1925. 1 p, 8vo. To Dr. Sinsheimer. Regarding a controversial poem ptd in the journal Simplizissimus. HH Nov 6 (2073) DM220

— 8 May 1929. 1 p, 8vo. To [a literary agent?]. Regarding negotiations for fees. star Mar 26 (348a) DM750

Autograph postcard, sgd, [15 Mar 1930]. To the Deutscher Theaterdienst. Responding to a poll regarding the crisis of the German theater. star Mar 26 (348b) DM750

Mann, Klaus, 1906-49

A Ls s (2), 12 May 1929 & 7 July 1930. 3 pp, 4to & 8vo. To the Ed of the journal Simplizissimus. Concerning contributions. HH Nov 6 (2074) DM700

Mann, Thomas, 1875-1955

Collection of 2 A Ls s & Ls, 14 Nov 1926 to 6 Aug 1927. 3 pp, 4to & 8vo. To Dr. Sinsheimer. About contributions to the journal Simplizissimus & requesting a correction. HH Nov 6 (2075) DM1,100

— Collection of 2 A Ls s & 2 A Ns s, 25 Oct 1938 to 30 July 1946. Length not stated. To Martin Gumpert. About a recent pamphlet, an ear ailment, recipient's health problems, etc. sg Feb 27 (116) $900

— Collection of 2 A Ls s, 4 Ls s, 2 postcards, sgd (1 autograph), & autograph sentiment, sgd, 28 Dec 1945 to 3 July 1955. 10 pp, 8vo & 4to. To Mrs. Sothmann. Commenting on Germany after the war, planning meetings, etc. With related material. HN June 26 (943) DM7,400

Series of 6 A Ls s, 20 Jan to 20 May 1948. 12 pp, 8vo. To S. Singer. Reporting about his work on his novel Der Erwaehlte & requesting recipient's help regarding medieval sources. HH Nov 6 (2080) DM13,000

A Ls s (2), 17 June 1946 & 10 Nov 1947. Length not stated, 8vo. To Martin Gumpert. About health matters & recipient's 50th birthday. sg Feb 27 (117) $800

ALs, 9 Dec 1904. 2 pp, 8vo (lettercard). To Georg Hirschfeld. Regretting he was unable to see him in Berlin. star Mar 26 (349) DM460

— 18 Nov 1910. 3 pp, 8vo. Recipient unnamed. Sending his poem Monolog (included) for publication. star Mar 26 (350) DM2,600

— 7 June 1919. 2 pp, 8vo (lettercard). To [Friedrich von Oppeln-Bronikowski?]. About recipient's books & his efforts to finish a work begun before the war. star Mar 26 (351) DM1,000

— 14 Aug [19]34. 1 p, 4to. To Walter Hofstoetter. Discussing projected lectures. HH Nov 6 (2077) DM1,600

— 15 July [19]35. 1 p, 4to. To Walter Hofstoetter. Discussing lectures & hotel arrangements. HH Nov 6 (2078) DM1,800

— 3 Oct 1936. 2 pp, 4to. To Frida Strindberg. Explaining why he is unable to review her book about her husband. star Mar 26 (356) DM2,600

— 12 May [19]41. 1 p, 8vo. To S. Singer. Thanking for comments on his Lotte in Weimar. HH Nov 6 (2079) DM2,000

— 5 Nov 1952. 1 p, 4to. To William Matheson. Sending a chapter from his Felix Krull for a special Ed. star Mar 26 (358) DM1,300

Series of 8 Ls s, 24 Oct 1935 to 3 July 1954. 14 pp, various sizes. To Antonio Aita. About a PEN meeting, his own & recipient's works, biographies, etc. star Mar 26 (355) DM5,500

Ls s (2), 15 Jan 1928 & 1 Oct 1929. 2 pp, 4to & 8vo. To Ludwig Rath. About an invitation to Regensburg. HH Nov 6 (2076) DM440

Ls, 28 Dec 1929. 2 pp, 4to. To Ogden W. Heath. Responding to recipient's comments on Der Zauberberg. star Mar 26 (353) DM850

— 8 Feb 1953. 1 p, 8vo. To the publishing house Hundt. Giving permission to quote from a letter (copy included). star Mar 26 (359) DM320

Autograph postcard, sgd, 30 Dec 1919. To Karl Ernst. About a meeting. star Mar 26 (352) DM420

— 18 Sept 1927. To the Ed of Die literarische Welt. Explaining why he is unable to write a contribution. Dar Apr 9 (272) $200

— 17 June 1950. To Hans Muehlestein. Thanking for a birthday present. star Mar 26 (357) DM360

Photograph, sgd, [n.d.]. 7.75 by 9.5 inches. sg Sept 12 (154) $130

— MANN, KATIA. - 2 Ls s, 13 & 21 Dec 1929. 4 pp, 4to. To the pbr Storch-Marien. Concerning trans rights for her husband's works. star Mar 26 (360) DM320

Mansfield, Joseph K. F., 1803-62

Photograph, sgd, [n.d.]. Carte size. Sgd recto & verso. Full length, in dress uniform. By Anthony, from a Brady negative. Illus in cat. R June 13 (98) $420

Manson, Charles

Signature, [n.d.]. On official 1980 FBI fingerprint card, 8 by 8 inches. Dar June 11 (280) $375

Mao Tse-tung, 1893-1976

Signature, [1942]. On Chinese currency note. Also sgd by others. Illus in cat. Dar Aug 6 (200) $3,000

Maps & Charts

— DOSSAIGA, JAIME. - Ms, portolan atlas of Europe & the Mediterranean, sgd & dated 1590. 10 leaves (2 blank), pasted together to form 4 double-page maps, 367mm by 238mm, in brown levant mor bdg by Lortic fils. With red & green rhumb-lines, 4 scale bars, several large windroses, coastlines in gold wash, & hundreds of place names in red & brown ink in a slightly sloping italic minuscule. CNY Oct 8 (211) $20,000

— GREAM, THOMAS. - Ms, A survey of a Farm in the Parish of Felpham in the County of Sussex belonging to Sir Richard Hotham, 1791. 19 by 29 inches. In ink & watercolor; including cartouche. b Nov 18 (268) £350

— SOUTHERN IRELAND. - Ms, survey of 2 divided thirds of the Manor of Dunshauglin, with the lands of Lishamstown & Howth Park in the Barony of Ratoath & County of Meath ..., 1823. 1520mm by 1445mm; rolled. In ink & colors. S Feb 11 (664) £280 [Maggs]

— SUFFOLK. - Ms, A survey & description of Chilton in the County of Suffolk, 1597. 2 joined sheets, 850mm by 1235mm. S Feb 11 (632) £460 [Quaritch]

Maranville, Walter James Vincent ("Rabbit"), 1891-1954

Ls, [n.d.]. 1 p, 4to. Recipient unnamed. Form letter, thanking for a message received after an accident. Dar Dec 26 (98) $200

Signature, [n.d.]. 16mo (card). Including subscription. Dar Dec 26 (97) $200

Marciano, Rocky, 1923-69

Photograph, sgd, [n.d.]. 4 by 5 inches. Dar Dec 26 (128) $325

— Anr, [n.d.]. 4 by 5 inches. With punching bag. Dar Dec 26 (129) $275

Marconi, Guglielmo, 1874-1937

ALs, 1 Aug 1913. 2 pp, 8vo. To [Melville E.] Stone. Introducing Basil Foster. Illus in cat. sg Feb 27 (118) $475

Ls, 4 July 1922. 2 pp, 8vo. To Melville E. Stone. Agreeing to lunch at the Plaza Hotel. sg Feb 27 (119) $200

— March 1927. 1 p, 4to. To F. L. Minnigerode. Thanking for an article. sg Feb 27 (120) $375

Margaret, Duchess of Parma, Regent of the Netherlands, 1522-86

Ls, 13 Sept 1583. 1 p, folio. To King Philip II of Spain. Suggesting the appointment of Jerome le Franc as President of the council of the Netherlands. star Mar 27 (1641) DM650

Maria Alexandrovna, Empress of Alexander II of Russia, 1824-80

Collection of 29 A Ls s & A Ls, 1836 to 1849 & [n.d.]. 116 pp, 8vo. To her brother Karl von Hessen-Darmstadt. Reporting about her life at the Russian court. Partly incomplete. star Mar 27 (1688) DM3,200

Maria Carolina, Queen of Naples, 1752-1814

Ls, 24 Sept 1805. 1 p, 4to. To A. J. von Stifft. Thanking for news about her daughter's recovery after giving birth to a son. star Mar 27 (1663) DM200

Maria Theresa, Empress, 1717-80

ALs, [1768]. 1 p, 8vo. To Prince Nikolaus Joseph Esterhazy von Galantha. Asking him to confirm a decision of her council. HN Nov 28 (1782a) DM1,300

Ls, 20 Jan 1742. 1 p, folio. To Count Palffy. Fragment, regarding the recruitment of a new regiment. Countersgd by Count Harrach. star Mar 27 (1657) DM310

— 28 July 1744. 2 pp, folio. To Nikolaus von Esterhazy. Discussing the possibility of an alliance with Saxony, Russia & England. star Mar 27 (1658) DM1,100

ANs, [c.1760]. 1 p, 8vo. Recipient unnamed. Referring to arrangements for the funeral of a general. Sgd M. HN Nov 28 (1781) DM230

Ds, 12 Apr 1766. 21 pp, 4to, in red velvet bdg. Patent of nobility for Johann Nepomuk Franz & Ernst Johann von der Goltz. Including full-page painting of the arms in gold & colors. star Mar 27 (1660) DM1,700

— 10 Apr 1769. 1 p, folio. Judicial appointment for Mathias Neumann. HH Nov 6

(2082) DM650

— 9 Feb 1773. 3 pp, folio. Receipt issued to the province of Moravia for a payment for military purposes. Repaired. star Mar 27 (1661) DM420

Marie de Medicis, Queen of France, 1573-1642

Ls, 13 Jan 1607. 1 p, folio. To M. de Bourgtouronde. Reminding him of orders given previously. Silked. star Mar 27 (1343) DM700

Marie Louise, Empress of the French, 1791-1847

Autograph Ms, diary, 20 Oct 1800 to 24 Jan 1801. 49 pp, 8vo, in marbled bds. Recording daily activities, in French. Including corrections & comments by her governess Mme de Poutet. S Dec 5 (533) £950 [Lanfranchi]

Series of 24 A Ls s, 1 May 1809 to 6 Feb 1817 & [n.d.]. 55 pp, 8vo. To her brother Ferdinand. Family correspondence. star Mar 27 (1506) DM14,000

ALs, 13 Nov 1821. 1 p, 4to. To King Ferdinand of the Two Sicilies. As Duchess of Parma, letter of recommendation for Christoph von Bach. star Mar 27 (1507) DM600

Maris, Roger Eugene, 1934-85

Ls, 14 Jan 1980. 1 p, 4to. To Louie Requena. Ordering photographs of "the Yankee Old Timers game last summer". Dar Oct 10 (81) $350

Cut signature, [n.d.]. Framed with a photograph, overall size 16 by 24 inches. Illus in cat. sup July 10 (991) $300

Photograph, sgd, [n.d.]. 8 by 10 inches. Dar Dec 26 (62) $180

Ptd photograph, sgd, [n.d.]. 3.3 by 5.3 inches (collector's card). Dar Apr 9 (98) $150

Maris, Roger Eugene, 1934-85 —& Others

Photograph, sgd, [c.1961]. 8 by 10 inches. Also sgd by 34 other players of the NY Yankees. Dar Dec 26 (63) $1,000

Markevich, Igor, 1912-83

Series of 3 A Ls s, April & July 1929. 12 pp, 4to. To Diaghilev. Discussing his compositions, Stravinsky's music, etc. With related material. Boris Kochno collection. SM Oct 12 (377) FF5,000

— Series of 13 A Ls s, 1929 to 1948. 24 pp, various sizes. To Massine & Boris Kochno. Discussing professional matters. Boris Kochno collection. SM Oct 12 (376) FF13,000

Marlborough, John Churchill, 1st Duke, 1650-1722

ALs, 3 Apr 1703. 2 pp, 4to. To Landgraf Karl von Hessen-Kassel. Urging him to send Hessian troops for the siege of Bonn. star Mar 27 (1480) DM2,700

Marschner, Heinrich, 1795-1861

ALs, 28 Jan 1836. 1 p, 4to. To Herr Rietz. Responding to a request for the score of his opera Hans Heiling. HH May 13 (2001) DM500

— 7 Aug 1838. 1 p, 4to. To Ludwig Cramolini. About a song. With a photograph. HH May 13 (2002) DM240

— 14 Jan 1841. 1 p, 4to. To Joseph Menter. Planning a concert. star Mar 27 (1067) DM220

Martin, Hugh —& Others

Ds, 11 Mar 1960. 9 pp, 4to. Agreement with MGM regarding a stage adaptation of Meet Me in St. Louis. Carbon copy; also sgd by Ralph Blane & Sally Benson. Dar Apr 9 (274) $120

Martin, Hugh —&
Blane, Ralph

Ds, 11 Oct 1946. 3 pp, 4to. Agreement regarding songs pbd jointly that were actually the individual work of either one. Dar Apr 9 (273) $100

— 1 Apr 1960. 3 pp, 4to. Contract with Leo Feist, Inc., for an adaptation of Meet Me in St. Louis; carbon copy. Dar Oct 10 (254) $110

Martini, Johann Paul Aegidius ("il Tedesco"), 1741-1816

ALs, [17 Apr 1799]. 1 p, 4to. To Gen. Jube. Inquiring about an unspecified request. star Mar 27 (1068) DM260

Martinu, Bohuslav, 1890-1959

Series of 5 A Ls s, Apr to Sept 1935. 5 pp, size not stated. To Boris Kochno. About the ballet The Judgment of Paris. 1 letter unopened. SM Oct 12 (378) FF12,000

Marvin, Lee, 1924-87

Ds s (2)10 Jan 1957. 4 pp, 4to. Contracts with The Theatre Guild. Dar Feb 13 (258) $100

Marx Brothers

[The signatures of Groucho, Chico & Harpo Marx on a card, [n.d.], 5 by 3 inches, matted with a group photograph, sold at Dar on 13 Feb 1992, lot 259, for $550.]

[The signatures of Groucho, Harpo & Chico on a single sheet, c.3 inches square, sold at sup on 15 Oct 1991, lot 1367, for $525.]

Marx, Groucho, 1890-1977

Ls, 1 Feb 1951. 1 p, 4to. To Edwin K. Zittell. Commenting on Tallulah Bankhead. sg Sept 12 (155) $1,100

— 2 Apr 1968. 2 pp, 4to. Recipient unnamed. Making jokes. Dar Apr 9 (275) $450

— 29 July 1968. 2 pp, 4to. Recipient unnamed. Joking about jogging, dental problems of the elderly, etc. Dar Apr 9 (276) $600

— 8 Nov 1968. 2 pp, 4to. Recipient unnamed. Joking about an invitation to NY. Dar Apr 9 (277) $700

— 11 Aug 1970. 1 p, 4to. To F. Randolph Swartz. Declining an invitation to Philadelphia. Dar June 11 (282) $500

Autograph sentiment, inscr, sgd, [n.d.], on a poster publicizing his book The Secret Word is Groucho, 18 by 24 inches. Illus in cat. Dar Apr 9 (278) $250

Marx, Harpo, 1893-1964

Ls, 26 Nov 1943. 1 p, 8vo. To J. Wallace Fassman. Thanking for pictures. Framed with a photograph. Dar Apr 9 (279) $250

Marx, Karl, 1818-83

ALs, 3 Feb 1875. 2 pp, 16mo. To [Just Vernouillet]. Complaining about the slow progress made with the ptg of the French Ed of Das Kapital. Illus in cat. Mannheim collection. S Dec 5 (461) £5,500 [Fritz-Denneville]

— 13 Dec 1879. 1 p, 8vo. To Charles Waldstein. Inviting him to lunch with a guest from Russia. pn Mar 19 (98) £4,000 [Wilson]

— 26 Jan 1880. 1 p, 8vo. To Charles Walstein. Announcing his visit, weather permitting. pn June 11 (39) £1,300 [Wilson]

Marx, Wilhelm, 1863-1946 —& Others

Signature, 19 Feb 1925. 1 p, 4to. Attendance list of a meeting of the Prussian cabinet; also sgd by 8 others. star Mar 27 (1481) DM400

Mary, Queen of Scots, 1542-87

Document, 31 Mar 1558. 1 p, size not stated. Warrant addressed to John Menzie to issue letters patent to Alexander Menzie, Baron of Lynton; issued by the Lords in Council in the Queen's name. pnE May 13 (178) £220

Mary, Queen of George V of England, 1867-1953

ALs, 16 Aug 1919. 2 pp, 8vo. To Cecil H. Smith. Offering a Chinese lacquer table & chair for display in the Victoria & Albert Museum. Dar Dec 26 (255) $110

Masaryk, Thomas Garrigue, 1850-1937

ALs, 13 Oct [1930?]. 2 pp, 8vo. To Professor Hlavac. Responding to an inquiry about his political acitivities & about relations with the National Socialists. star Mar 27 (1482) DM1,000

— 17 Oct 1932. 3 pp, 4to. To Willa Cather. Discussing Cather's book. In English. sg Sept 12 (156) $1,100

Autograph postcard, sgd, 21 Dec [191]3. To Professor Wiener. Discussing the possiblity of an American Ed of his book. sup Oct 15 (1368) $300

Ds, 25 Jan 1934. 1 p, folio. Appointment of Victor Braf to a position in the Ministry of Foreign Affairs. Countersgd by Eduard Benes. Illus in cat. sg Feb 27 (51) $800

Mascagni, Pietro, 1863-1945

Autograph music, song, Tu lo sai, Lilia, to a text by Giovanni Marradi, 14 Aug 1894. 2 pp, 4to. 19 bars, sgd. Including autograph Ms by Marradi at head; text of the song, sgd. Illus in cat. star Mar 27 (1069) DM1,900

ALs, 15 May 1906. 2 pp, 8vo. To Leonino. About a financial matter & the premiere of his Amica at Cologne. With a photograph. HH May 13 (2003) DM280

Autograph quotation, sgd, 3 bars from Cavalleria Rusticana, 8 Nov 1899. 1 p, 16mo. sg Sept 12 (157) $550

— Anr, 4 bars from his Cavalleria rusticana, 20 Apr 1907. 1 p, 8vo (lettercard). Sgd. star Mar 27 (1070) DM1,100

Massachusetts

— CHARLESTOWN. - Document, 1 July 1717. 2 pp, 8vo. List of Innholders & Retailers, as submitted to the Selectment of Charlestown. Framed. wa Oct 19 (235) $200

Massena, Andre, 1758-1817

Ls, [23 Apr 1799]. 1 p, folio. To the Minister of War. Concerning the defense of fortifications on the Rhine. sg Feb 27 (122) $200

— 15 Sept 1809. 2 pp, 4to. To an unnamed general. About several military matters. sg Feb 27 (121) $275

Massenbach, Christian von, 1758-1827

Ms, list of books in his possession, 27 Oct 1820. 3 pp, folio. Sgd. star Mar 27 (1483) DM320

Massenet, Jules, 1842-1912

Autograph music, Chant Provencal, to a text by Michel Carre, 23 July [18]71. 3 pp, folio, cut from larger sheet. Scored for voice & piano, on 8 systems, 3 staves each. Sgd & inscr to Mme Carre. S Dec 6 (127) £500 [Macnutt]

Autograph quotation, sgd, 4 bars from Thais, 10 June 1904. On picture postcard of his manor house. Inscr to Antoinette Legier. sg Sept 12 (160) $350

— Anr, sgd, 2 bars from Herodiade, [n.d.]. 1 p, 16mo. sg Sept 12 (159) $325

Massine, Leonide, 1895-1979

Collection of 3 A Ls s, 6 Ls s & telegram, [c.1932-1948]. 11 pp, various sizes. To Boris Kochno. About various ballets. SM Oct 12 (379) FF6,500

Mata Hari, Pseud. of Geertruida Zelle McLeod, 1876-1917

ALs, 8 Aug 1915. 8 pp, 8vo. To her lawyer Hijmans. About problems with the furnishing of her house at The Hague. On hotel letterhead. Illus in cat. sup Oct 15 (1369) $2,600

Mather, Cotton, 1663-1728

Autograph Ms, The Answer of the Administrator Upon the Estate of Nathan Howell, [n.d.]. 1 p, folio. Response to a court summons; sgd. Spiro collection. CNY May 14 (122) $2,000

ALs, 8 Sept 1722. 1 p, 8vo. To the Rev. Thomas Foxcroft. Discussing epitaphs. Illus in cat. Middendorf collection. sup May 9 (384) $2,400

Mathewson, Christopher, 1880-1925

Check, accomplished & sgd, 20 Apr 1922. Payable to Reynolds & Klug. Illus in cat. Dar Feb 13 (87) $2,250

Mathey, Edward Gustave

Ds, 5 Jan 1878. 2 pp, 8.5 by 7.5 inches. Special Requisition of brooms for the 7th Regiment of Cavalry. Framed. Illus in cat. Armstrong collection. sup Oct 15 (1118) $200

Matisse, Henri, 1869-1954

Collection of 10 A Ls s & 2 Ls s, 1931 to 1944 & [n.d.]. 10 pp, folio. To Boris Kochno & Leonide Massine. About his decors for ballets. Boris Kochno collection. SM Oct 12 (380) FF40,000

Matthias, Emperor, 1557-1619

Ds, 25 Feb 1579. 1 p, folio. As Governor of the Southern Netherlands, bond to Gotthart von Wollmereckhausen for payment for his cavalry unit during the current campaign. star Mar 27 (1646) DM950

Matthisson, Friedrich von, 1761-1831

Autograph Ms, poem, Raphsodie im Herbste, [1773/77]. 4 pp, 4to. 43 lines, with later AN at head; sgd M. star Mar 26 (363) DM420

ALs, 4 Apr 1770. 1 p, 4to. To his mother. Reporting from school. With later AN, sgd M. at bottom. star Mar 26 (364) DM320

Maugham, William Somerset, 1874-1965

Series of 3 Ls s, [n.y.]. 3 pp, 4to & 8vo. To Joseph Shipley. Declining to contribute articles. sg Feb 27 (123) $325

Ls, 25 Nov 1924. 1 p, 4to. To Charlie. Concerning his use of a living person's name in his novel The Painted Veil. CNY June 9 (125) $600

— 1 Dec 1961. 1 p, 8vo. Recipient unnamed. Saying he does not feel like writing any-more. Framed with port drawing, sgd by Maugham. Dar Apr 9 (280) $350

Maupassant, Guy de, 1850-93

ALs, [n.d.]. 1 p, 12mo. To Messrs. Brunel & Rousset. Declining to receive them at his home. Dar Apr 9 (281) $325

— [n.d.]. 1 p, 8vo. Recipient unnamed. Sending a document. star Mar 26 (365) DM380

ANs, [7 Dec 1891]. 2 pp, on visiting card. To J. Koff. Referring him to his pbr Ollendorff. HH Nov 6 (2083) DM200

Maupertuis, Pierre Louis Moreau de, 1698-1759

Collection of 2 A Ls s & 3 A Ls, 9 to 30 Nov 1750. 6 pp, 4to. To Friedrich II of Prussia (3) & Leonhard Euler. Retained drafts, regarding the nomination of Nathanael Grischow to the academy at St. Petersburg. With related material. Illus in cat. star Mar 26 (728) DM4,500

Mauriac, Francois, 1885-1970

Ms, article, "Why Shouldn't the Future Pope be an American?", sgd; [c.1940s]. 9 pp, 4to. In French, with autograph additions & revisions. sg Sept 12 (162) $400

Maximilian, Prince of Baden, 1867-1929

ALs, 5 Feb 1913. 2 pp, 4to. To [August Bassermann]. About a point of etiquette. star Mar 27 (1243) DM330

Maximilian I Joseph, King of Bavaria, 1756-1825

Ls, 12 Apr 1803. 1 p, folio. To Herzog Friedrich zu Sachsen-Hildburghausen. Sending condolences on the death of his son. HN June 26 (956) DM270

Ds, 27 Aug 1823. 4 leaves, 366mm by 290mm. Patent of nobility for Peter Anton Kreusser. With full-page painting of the arms. HH Nov 5 (849) DM1,500

Maximilian II, Emperor, 1527-76

Ls, 4 Jan 1564. 1 p, folio. To the mayor & magistrate of Sprottau in Silesia. Postponing a decision in the case of Georg von Schoenaich's widow. HN June 26 (949) DM260

— 23 Aug 1564. 2 pp, folio. To the mayor & magistrate of Sprottau in Silesia. Ordering them to come to Prague for a hearing in the case of Georg von Schoenaich's widow. HN

June 26 (950) DM280

Maximilian II, King of Bavaria, 1811-64

Ls s (2), [1860] & 19 Feb 1861. 2 pp, 4to. To von Neumayr. Giving instructions to investigate a recent carnival parade at Nuernberg, & discussing a financial matter. star Mar 27 (1259) DM420

Maximilian II Emanuel, Kurfuerst von Bayern, 1662-1726

Ds s (2)11 Nov 1715 & 14 Feb 1721. 2 pp, folio. Financial grants to members of the von Preysing family. star Mar 27 (1251) DM220

Maximilian of Mexico, Emperor, 1832-67

ADs, Aug 1866. 1 p, 8vo. Safe-conduct for Jose M. Iturralde. Illus in cat. sup Oct 15 (1380) $500

Ds, 12 Jan 1866. 1 p, 4to. Order to his Minister of Foreign Affairs to issue blank commissions for a mission to Constantinople. Illus in cat. sup Oct 15 (1381) $625

— 31 May 1866. 1 p, 4to. Appointing a sub-prefect. Illus in cat. sg Feb 27 (124) $2,000

— 31 May 1866. 1 p, 4to. Appointment of Juan Devincentis as sub-prefect. Illus in cat. sup Oct 15 (1382) $525

May, Karl, 1842-1912

ALs, 4 Oct 1906. 3 pp, 8vo. To Ludwig Carriere. About problems with his pbr. Illus in cat. hen Nov 12 (2494) DM3,400

— 10 Aug [190]8. 2 pp, 8vo. To the Ed of the Saechsische Volkszeitung, Rauer. Sending contributions. JG Mar 27 (194) DM1,600

Autograph postcard, sgd, [17 Jan 1907]. To R. Kraemer. Sending greetings. star Mar 26 (368) DM780

ANs, [n.d.]. 1 p, 12mo. Recipient unnamed. Promising to write the following day. Mtd with a port. JG Sept 27 (406) DM900

Mayer, Louis B., 1885-1957 —& Gilbert, John, 1897-1936

Ds, 11 Jan 1933. 2 pp, size not stated. Carbon copy, agreement stating dates for the completion of a projected film. Dar Dec 26 (229) $140

Mayo, Charles Horace, 1865-1939 —& Mayo, William Jones, 1861-1939

[A cut signature of each, framed with reproduced portraits, size not stated, sold at wa on 19 Dec 1991, lot 255, for $170.]

Mayo, William Jones, 1861-1939. See: Mayo, Charles Horace & Mayo

Mazarin, Jules, Cardinal, 1602-61

Ls, 29 June 1656. 1 p, 4to. To representatives of Dijon. Refusing to intercede in their behalf. star Mar 27 (1351) DM470

Mazzini, Giuseppe, 1805-72

ALs, 20 Jan 1842. 1 p, 8vo. To a post office official. Inquiring & complaining about foreign postage. pn Nov 14 (172) £90 [Autograph House]

Mboya, Tom, 1930-69

Transcript, excerpt from his speech at Chicago, 27 Apr 1959. 1 p, 12mo (card). Sgd. Dar Dec 26 (256) $110

Meade, George Gordon, 1815-72

ALs, 2 Nov 1863. 4 pp, 8vo. To Major Gen. Henry W. Halleck. Outlining his strategy against Lee's movements. CNY Dec 5 (94) $3,800

— 29 Apr 1865. 3 pp, 8vo. To an unnamed general. Informing him that he cannot spare his cavalry, & discussing the possibility of an armed black insurrection in Virginia. CNY Dec 5 (95) $1,600

— 27 Apr 1868. 3 pp, 8vo. To Gen. W. B. Franklin. Asking him to raise funds to rebuild a church. sg Feb 27 (125) $325

Meagher, Thomas Francis, 1823-67

Photograph, sgd, [n.d.]. Carte size. In uniform. By Anthony, from a Brady negative. Illus in cat. R June 13 (105) $500

Medical Manuscripts

Ms, Allerley Secreta...; medical recipes. [Germany, c.1700]. 194 leaves & blanks, 205mm by 160mm, in def contemp bds. Including 3 pen-&-ink drawings. HH May 12 (18) DM320

— Ms, anthology of pharmaceutical & medical information. [Germany, c.1500]. 156 leaves, vellum & paper, 190mm by 138mm. Black vellum bdg. In Latin & Low German in several hands. HH May 12 (17) DM14,000

— Ms, Arzneibuch; medical recipes in German with a few items in Latin. [Germany, 2d half of 15th cent]. 305 leaves (1 lacking), 148mm by 100mm. Old limp vellum incorporating a 15th-cent liturgical Ms. In German cursive bookhands by several scribes. S June 23 (67) £4,000 [Enluminneures]

— Ms, Delineations of the Cutaneous Diseases comprised in the Classification of the late Dr. Willan together with a New Series which will comprehend the remainder of the System completed by Dr. Bateman. [N.d.] 186 leaves, 235mm by 190mm, in old half lea. In cursive script in black ink on wove paper. With 80 full-page dermatological watercolors. sg May 14 (39) $1,000

— Ms, journal kept by a rural physician at Springfield [Pennsylvania?], 1845 to 1849. 247 pp, 6 by 15 inches; disbound. Recording services performed, medicines, treatments, etc. sg Sept 12 (165) $500

— Ms, medical recipe book. [England, 1663]. 204 pp, folio, in contemp calf. Comprising c.450 recipes in several hands. bba Jan 30 (291) £460 [Johnson]

— Ms, Moritz Buchners Buch von Artzneien und Allerleay Kunststueckhenn. [Eisleben, Germany, 1559 to 1612]. 292 leaves, folio. 16th-cent limp lea bdg. Medical recipes, in the hands of Moritz Buchner, Sebaldt Buchner, & others. Including penwork decoration. FD Dec 2 (1) DM2,750

— Ms, prescriptions & recipes for infusions, pills, tinctures, etc. [England, c.1750?]. About 150 pp, 8vo; disbound. Including prayers at end. Ownership inscr of J. Bayly. pn June 11 (36) £100

— Alberto, Giuseppe. - Ms, Il Raggio dall'ombra, ovvero cognizioni di vari arcani, specifici e secreti sin ora occultati..., dedicata al Sig. D. Franc. Perez Navarretta; 9 Mar 1700. 434 pp, 8vo, in contemp vellum over pastebds. Compilation of medical knowledge, including contributions by late 17th-cent physicians. C June 24 (82) £1,300 [Mediolanum]

— Clapham, William. - Ms, physician's notebook, 28 Sept 1775 & later. 120 pp & blanks, folio, in orig vellum. Including several hundred medical prescriptions for patients. bba June 25 (140) £240 [Wellcome Institute]

Mehring, Walter, 1896-1981

Series of 3 A Ls s, [n.d.]. 3 pp, 4to & 8vo. To the Ed of the journal Simplizissimus. About a request for contributions. HH May 13 (2006) DM380

Mehul, Etienne Nicolas, 1763-1817

ALs, 20 June 1817. 1 p, 4to. To Mme Kreutzer. About recipient's journey to Bourbonne. HH May 13 (2007) DM220

Meidner, Ludwig, 1884-1966

ALs, 10 Sept [1918]. 1 p, 8vo. To Rose Friedrich. Describing the importance of intensity for his artistic production. star Mar 27 (928) DM360

Meir, Golda, 1898-1978

Transcript, excerpt from an interview with the NY Times, 1973; sgd. 1 p, 12mo. Dar Dec 26 (231) $450

Ls, 17 July 1953. 1 p, 8vo. To Mordecai Namir. Carbon copy to Moshe Sharett, welcoming a decision to join the International Organization of Free Trade Associations. Dar Dec 26 (230) $400

— 12 Sept 1955. 1 p, 8vo. To Beba Eidelson. Carbon copy addressed to Moshe Sharett, stressing the need to further women's rights in Israel. Dar Oct 10 (236) $1,000

— 22 Dec 1969. 1 p, 4to. To Rabbi Isadore Breslau. Announcing the visit of emissaries to explain the problems Israel is facing. wa Mar 5 (289) $400

Melvill, Thomas, 1751-1832

Ds, 17 Aug 1807. 1 p, 8vo. Certificate of Importation of a shipment of wine. Countersgd by Benjamin Lincoln. With related material. wd June 12 (321) $200

Melville, Herman, 1819-91

ALs, 12 June [1854]. 1 p, 8vo. To George P. Putnam. Agreeing to terms for the publication of his novel Israel Potter. CNY Oct 8 (174) $9,500

— 13 Jan 1872. 1 p, 8vo. To Miss Coffin. Regretting that he does not "recall where [he] got the fact alluded to". P Oct 11 (227) $5,500

Cut signature, [n.d.]. 15mm by 70mm. CNY Oct 8 (175) $2,200

Mencken, Henry Louis, 1880-1956

Series of 6 Ls s, 1941 to 1948. 6 pp, 8vo. To Joseph Shipley. Declining requests for literary contributions. sg Feb 27 (126) $300

Ls, 26 June [c.1935]. 1 p, 8vo. To Caroline. Suggesting a date for a meeting. bbc Dec 9 (172) $85

Mendelssohn, Arnold, 1855-1933

ALs, 8 Sept 1918. 1 p, 4to. Recipient unnamed. Discussing a projected concert. Including musical quotation, 9 bars. star Mar 27 (1072) DM480

Mendelssohn, Moses, 1729-86

Autograph Ms, essay, Ueber Wunder u wunderbar, [n.d.]. 2 pp, 8vo. Illus in cat. star Mar 26 (734) DM7,500

ALs, 17 July 1767. 4 pp, 4to. To Herzog Ludwig Eugen von Wuerttemberg. Responding to critical remarks about his work Phaedon. star Mar 26 (735) DM7,000

Mendelssohn-Bartholdy, Fanny, 1805-47. See: Hensel, Fanny

Mendelssohn-Bartholdy, Felix, 1809-47

Autograph Ms, diary kept in Paris, 17 Dec 1831 to 6 Apr 1832. 12 pp, 8vo, & blanks, in embroidered silk covers. Day-by-day account of compositions, correspondence, meetings, expenses, etc. Including a bar of autograph music, & a 3-page musical Ms in his sister Fanny's hand of her Duett fuer Tenor und Sopran in D major. Illus in cat. S May 29 (584) £9,000 [Haas]

Autograph music, song, Wasserfahrt, to a text

by Heinrich Heine; [c.1830]. 2 pp, folio. Notated for 2 voices & piano. Ptr's copy. Illus in cat. HN June 26 (959) DM15,000

Autograph transcript, 3 arias from Bach's St. Matthew Passion, 1841. 9 pp, folio. Arranged for voice & keyboard, with numerous dynamic & phrase markings. Including autograph tp. Illus in cat. Mannheim collection. S Dec 6 (12) £12,500 [Sawyer]

Ms, full score of his oratorio Elijah, [1846]. About 500 pp, 326mm by 246mm, in green half mor. In the hand of Eduard Henschke. With Mendelssohn's autograph annotations in c.200 places & notes in other hands, including the organist at 1st performance. C Dec 16 (335) £98,000 [Quaritch]

ALs, 6 Dec 1823. 4 pp, 8vo. To Herr [Latzel]. About a recent concert in Silesia, the summer in Berlin, a tragical accident, etc. Silked. Illus in cat. star Mar 27 (1073) DM7,500

— 16 Sept 1835. 3 pp, 8vo. To Julius Schubring. Important letter about his situation in Leipzig, his recent compositions, etc. star Mar 27 (1074) DM5,000

— 24 June 1836. 3 pp, 4to. To Dr. Clarus. Praising the choir of the Frankfurt Cecilien-Verein, reporting about a meeting with Rossini, etc. Gottschalk collection. C Dec 16 (409) £3,200 [Rosenthal]

— [c.Oct 1837]. 2 pp, 8vo. To Ulrike von Pogwisch. Thanking for a wedding present. Including postscript in his wife's hand. star Mar 27 (1075) DM5,000

— 26 June 1838. 2 pp, 4to. To Franz von Piatkowski. Discussing 4 symphonic works. Illus in cat. S Dec 6 (128) £2,500 [Schneider]

— 25 Mar 1839. 1 p, 8vo. To the pbr Karl Friedrich Kistner. Requesting him to forward 2 packages. star Mar 27 (1076) DM3,600

— 9 May 1840. 2 pp, 4to. To Raymund Haertel. Concerning the 1st performance & publication of Lobgesang, Op. 52. C Dec 16 (334) £1,600 [Haas]

— 15 May 1843. 1 p, 4to. Recipient unnamed. Letter of recommendation for Alfred Doerffel. star Mar 27 (1077) DM2,300

— 7 Jan 1844. 1 p, 8vo. Recipient unknown (name cut out). Letter of recommendation for a music teacher. In English. cb Feb 12 (159) $550

— 14 June 1844. 1 p, 4to. To Wilhelm Taubert. Sending the remaining parts of his incidental music to Athalie, & giving instructions for the performance. Illus in cat. S Dec 6 (130) £2,200 [Schneider]

— 16 Aug 1845. 1 p, 8vo. To Johanna Jeanrenaud. Expressing condolences on the death of her sister. Postscript to ALs by his wife Cecile (included). star Mar 27 (1078) DM3,500

— 12 Oct 1846. 7 pp, 8vo. To Jenny Lind. Giving his views on the English & British musical life, & offering advice on her projected visit in England. Illus in cat. S May 29 (586) £4,000 [Haas]

Mendez de Carmona, Luiz

Ms, Libro de la destreza berdadera de las armas, 1640. 240 leaves, 4to, in old vellum. sg Mar 26 (202) $1,300

Menotti, Gian Carlo

Photograph, sgd, [n.d.]. 7.5 by 11 inches. Matted. Dar Dec 26 (262) $110

Menuhin, Yehudi —& Others

ALs, Apr 1935. 2 pp, 8vo. To Maitre Ciampi. Reporting from Australia. Also sgd by his sisters Hephzibah & Yaltah. HN Nov 28 (1788) DM260

Menzel, Adolph von, 1815-1905

Autograph sketchbook, 1863. 70 leaves (a few lacking), 8vo. Dark green cloth bdg. Domestic scenes, mostly depicting babies & small children; in pencil. Sgd on verso of front cover. HN Nov 28 (1789) DM46,000

A Ls s (2), 18 Jan & 12 May 1869. 12 pp, 8vo & 12mo. To Heinrich Julius Campe. Thanking for a medallion of Heine, & responding to the offer to make a bust of Heine. Gottschalk collection. C Dec 16 (410) £750 [Rosenthal]

ALs, 25 Mar [18]57. 1 p, 8vo. Recipient unnamed. Sending a ticket for a musical event. Illus in cat. FD June 2 (1274) DM270

— 14 Sept [18]61. 1 p, 8vo. Recipient unnamed. Expressing thanks. FD Dec 3 (1453) DM340

— 5 Jan [1869]. 2 pp, 12mo. To Theodor Spitta. Informing him that his watercolors have been returned from Ghent. HN Nov 28 (1790) DM750

— 22 May [18]69. 3 pp, 8vo. Recipient unnamed. About a meeting the next evening. FD June 2 (1275) DM270

— 27 Dec 1878. 2 pp, 8vo. Recipient unnamed. Giving permission to reprint a biographical notice. star Mar 27 (929) DM580

— 21 Nov [18]93. 2 pp, 8vo. Recipient unnamed. Transmitting a letter by Fontane. FD June 2 (1276) DM270

— 5 Jan 1904. 3 pp, 8vo. To Hugo Martini. Family letter, & sending New Year's wishes. star Mar 27 (930) DM550

Merard de Saint Just, Simon Pierre, 1749-1812

Ms, Voltaire. Ode, & other poems, plays & prose; [after 1783]. 84 leaves & 4 flyleaves, 141mm by 81mm, in orig gold-tooled red mor by Pierre Joseph Bisiaux. In Roman book script in imitation of ptd type by F. F. Fyot, written for the author & sgd by him in several places. C June 24 (66) £8,500 [Halwas]

Mercadante, Saverio, 1795-1870

ALs, 22 Apr 1834. 1 p, 8vo. To Louis Duprez. Praising his singing in I Normanni a Parigi. star Mar 27 (1079) DM500

Meredith, George, 1828-1909

Collection of 4 A Ls s & A Ns s, [1861] to 1895. 12 pp, 8vo. To Bonaparte [Wyse] & his wife. Thanking for a publication, promising to help find a pbr, giving family news, etc. S July 21 (65) £450 [Rota]

Merimee, Prosper, 1803-70

ALs, [n.d.]. 3 pp, 8vo. To an unnamed lady. Complaining about censorship in Spain. star Mar 26 (370) DM300

Meshullam Solomon ha-Kohen, d.1823

ALs, 1806. 1 p, 145mm by 185mm. To Tevele Hirsch. Concerning financial difficulties of a widow. Stained. sg Dec 19 (102) $425

Methfessel, Albert, 1785-1869

ALs, 9 Jan 1850. 4 pp, 8vo. To Karl Krebs. Asking for a contribution to a projected journal. star Mar 27 (1080) DM550

Metternich, Klemens Wenzel Nepomuk Lothar von, 1773-1859

ALs, 24 June 1816. 2 pp, 4to. To an unnamed baron. Informing him that the Emperor is donating the castle of Johannisberg to him. With related material. HN June 26 (960) DM550

— 18 Apr 1820. 7 pp, 8vo. To Aurore. Worrying about his daughter's illness, & discussing events in Vienna & Paris. star Mar 27 (1485) DM620

— 29 May 1825. 2 pp, 4to. To an unnamed general. Declining to speculate about recipient's future. star Mar 27 (1486) DM520

Mexican War

— Palmer, Lieut. John. - Autograph Ms, diary of his experiences in the American army during the war, 10 Oct 1846 to 7 June 1847. 132 pp, 4to, in orig blindstamped mor bdg. Including account of the Battle of Buena Vista. CNY Dec 5 (96) $6,500

Mexico

— Baja California. - ALs by Francisco Maria Piccolo, 12 Sept 1700. 2 pp, 12 by 8.25 inches. To Joseph de Miranda y Villaizan. From the mission at Loreto Concho, sending condolences on the death of his mother. Illus in cat. cb Feb 12 (66) $1,300

— Betanzos, Domingo de. - Ds, 3 July 1527. 2 pp, folio. As Vicar General of Mexico City, sentence in the trial of Francisco de Orduna for blasphemy. Also sgd by others. P Dec 12 (130) $5,500

— Cordoba, Juan Fernandez de. - 5 Ls s, 1703 to 1706. 34 pp, folio. To the Counts of Sessa & of Cabra. Discussing his disagreements with the Duke of Albuquerque over the affairs of New Biscay. Partly with autograph postscripts. S Dec 5 (537) £2,000 [Quaritch]

Meyer, Conrad Ferdinand, 1825-98

ALs, [Jan 1875]. 3 pp, 8vo. To Ernest Naville. Expressing thanks for recipient's pamphlet on church questions in Geneva. star Mar 26 (371) DM1,900

— 31 July 1889. 3 pp, 8vo. To S. Schottlaender. About an album sent to his home in his absence. star Mar 26 (372) DM850

Meyerbeer, Giacomo, 1791-1864

Autograph music, song in F major to Heine's poem Die Rose, die Lilie, die Taube, scored for voice & accompaniment; 8 Mar [18]38. 2 pp, folio, in contemp buckram covers. 47 bars, sgd & inscr to Karl Karkel. Gottschalk collection. C Dec 16 (423) £1,800 [Rosenthal]

— Autograph music, song, La Marguerite du Poete, to a text by Henri Blaze, 29 May 1842. 2 pp, folio. Scored for voice & piano; sgd. Trimmed. Illus in cat. star Mar 27 (1081) DM2,600

ALs, 23 July 1831. 1 p, 8vo. To Heinrich Heine. Informing him that his brother has just brought Heine's new book. With related material. Gottschalk collection. C Dec 16 (411) £480 [Rosenthal]

— 15 Aug [18]42. 1 p, 8vo. To Franz Liszt. Sending a letter (not present) which he must discuss with him. S May 29 (590) £400 [Haas]

— 1 Nov 1853. 2 pp, 4to. To his daughter Caecilie. Sending an article about his mother as benefactor. star Mar 27 (1083) DM1,000

— 12 Mar [n.y.]. 1 p, 8vo. To his brother. Promising to come to Dresden for Henriette Sontag's concert. HN June 26 (961) DM480

— [n.d.]. 2 pp, 8vo. To [Carl Stoer?]. Declining permission to perform some parts of his opera Dinorah in a concert. star Mar 27 (1082) DM750

Autograph sentiment, sgd, [n.d.]. 1 p, 16mo. In Italian, inscr to Maestro Mariani. Dar Apr 9 (288) $200

Meyrink, Gustav, 1868-1932

ALs, 7 Mar 1912. 12 pp, 4to. To an official at the Schiller Foundation. Informing him about his past work & his current financial situation. star Mar 26 (373) DM1,700

Ls s (2), 17 Jan [1929] & 4 Apr 1930. 2 pp, 4to. To the Ed of the journal Simplizissimus. Requesting books & discussing a possible contribution. HH Nov 6 (2084) DM360

Middendorf, Alexander Theodor von, 1815-94

ALs, 21 Jan 1856. 4 pp, 8vo. To Richard von Koenig-Warthausen. Sending a painting of a lark's egg. star Mar 26 (736) DM250

Miegel, Agnes, 1879-1964

Autograph Ms, poem, Trost, 10 Apr 1961. 1 p, folio. 8 lines, sgd. Including ALs at head. star Mar 26 (375) DM650

Mifflin, Thomas, 1744-1800

Ds, 6 Mar 1789. 1 p, folio. Land grant to Patrick McGee. sg Feb 27 (129) $80

— 10 Oct 1796. 1 p, folio. Land grant to Henry Drinker. Dar June 11 (292) $300

Miles, Nelson Appleton, 1839-1925

Signature, [n.d.]. 3 by 1.75 inches (card). Framed. Armstrong collection. sup Oct 15 (1121) $140

Milhaud, Darius, 1892-1974

ALs, [c.1935]. 2 pp, 4to. Recipient unnamed. Refusing to play a Mozart sonata & suggesting a composition by Baptiste Anet. HN Nov 28 (1791) DM220

— 19 Aug [n.y.]. 1 p, 8vo. Recipient unnamed. Stating that he has not composed a trio yet. Dar Feb 13 (264) $150

Military Manuscripts

Ms, account of the application of mathematical & geometrical principles to military architecture on the Vauban model. [France, 2d half of 17th cent]. 2 vols, 150 & 72 leaves, folio & 4to. Contemp calf. In more than one hand. Including c.137 diagrams & fortification plans. S June 25 (196) £600 [Quaritch]

— Ms, Exercitium fuer die Kayl: Konigl: Sammentliche Cavallerie, 1771. Length not stated, 8vo, in orig mottled calf. 58 diagrams of cavalry manoeuvres, mostly in red & black. Including colored arms of Count J. N. Esterhazy. bba Sept 19 (392) £400 [Shapero]

— Ms, Rapid battle formations of a company of soldiers in a line against the enemy. [China, 19th cent]. 26 pp on native paper, size not stated, in yellow brocade silk-covered bds. Including 10 drawings of military formations in ink & colors. S Feb 11 (633) £400 [Sotheran]

— GUNNERY. - Ms, notes on various aspects of gunnery, [c.1780]. 56 pp, folio, in orig vellum. bba May 28 (235) £80 [Ball]

— WEST POINT. - Document, 11 June 1897. 1 p, folio. Diploma for Francis H. Pope, sgd by 11 professors. Matted. Dar June 11 (11) $130

Millay, Edna St. Vincent, 1892-1950

Series of 4 A Ls, 17 Dec 1928 to 8 Oct 1929. 17 pp, various sizes. To George Dillon. Love letters. Illus in cat. P June 17 (276) $10,000

Miller, Glenn, 1904-44

Photograph, sgd, [n.d.]. 8 by 6 inches. With trombone. Illus in cat. R Mar 7 (174) $220

Signature, [n.d.]. 3.5 by 1.3 inches (card). Dar Apr 9 (290) $150

Miller, Guillermo, 1795-1861. See: Miller, William

Miller, Henry, 1891-1980

Autograph Ms, Order and Chaos chez Hans Reichel, [Dec 1937 to Feb 1938]. 81 leaves, 8vo, in paper wraps. Illus with numerous collages, watercolor sketches & text illusts. Sgd by Miller & inscr to Reichel. With a copy of the ptd work & further related material. sg Dec 12 (288) $8,000

Collection of 17 A Ls s, 2 Ls s, 11 autograph postcards, sgd, & typescript, 1952 to 1975. 40 pp, 8vo & 4to. To Lucy Schimek-Reichel (4 postcards to Hans Reichel). About various matters. 2 typescript drafts of a introduction to a Reichel exhibition cat, with autograph revisions. sg Dec 12 (296) $3,800

ALs, [15 Feb 1936]. 4 pp, 8vo. To Belvina Slotinkoff. Responding to her article on social work. CNY June 9 (128) $110

Miller, Marilyn, 1898-1936

Photograph, sgd & inscr, [n.d.]. 8 by 10 inches. Inscr to Quinn Martin. Dar Oct 10 (259) $110

Miller, William, 1795-1861

A Ls s (2), 24 Apr 1820 & 3 May 1822. 3 pp, folio. To Jose Ignacio Zenteno. Sending a report (included) about soldiers present at the capture of Valdiva, & interceding in favor of Manuel de Bera. HN Nov 28 (1792) DM420

Milloecker, Carl, 1842-99

Autograph music, 6 piano works, 1891 to 1895. 19 pp, size not stated. On 16-stave paper, including some alterations. Sgd. S May 29 (591) £1,000 [Wertitsch]

— Autograph music, Irische Volkslieder, a setting of 7 folksongs; [n.d.]. 11 pp, size not stated. S Dec 6 (133) £500 [Wertitsch]

Milne, Alan Alexander, 1882-1956

Autograph Ms, dialogue between 2 comic characters, 1917. 8 pp, 4to, on rectos only. Sgd & inscr to H. J. Wrench. C June 24 (376) £450 [Wilson]

Series of 4 A Ls s, 28 Nov 1928 to 28 Dec 1929. 4 pp, 8vo. To George Sutcliffe. Concerning book bindings. With related material. CNY Dec 5 (280) $2,200

ALs, 12 Aug 1926. 2 pp, 8vo. To Puddock, a young girl. About the advantages of being a bear & the forthcoming publication of Winnie-the-Pooh. pn Nov 14 (227) £1,800 [Sawyer]

— [n.d.]. 1 p, size not stated. To Miss King. Referring to his novel Mr. Pim. k Mar 22 (269) $225

Mineo, Sal, 1939-76

ALs, 5 Mar 1960. 1 p, 4to. To Mr. Quirk. Expressing satisfaction with recipient's story. R Mar 7 (175) $100

Ds, 8 Dec 1964. 12 pp, 4to. Contract for the film Who Killed Teddy Bear? Dar Apr 9 (291) $190

— 8 Dec 1964. 2 pp, size not stated. Contract for the film Who Killed Teddy Bear? Carbon copy; sgd & initialled. Dar Aug 6 (24) $130

Mirabeau, Honore Gabriel Victor Riqueti, Comte de, 1749-91

ALs, 13 Apr 1778. 1 p, 8vo. To his wife. Accusing her of failing to send news of their son. C June 24 (377) £350 [L'Autographe]

Miranda, Carmen, 1913-55

Photograph, sgd & inscr, [n.d.]. 8 by 10 inches. Inscr to Winnie. Imperf. Dar Feb 13 (265) $160

Miro, Joan, 1893-1983

ALs, 11 July 1950. 1 p, 4to. To an unnamed art collector. Discussing the possibility of an exhibition. sg Sept 12 (166) $400

Ls, 6 May 1956. 1 p, 4to. To Jim Tillett. Granting permission to use his works on textiles. Also sgd by others. Framed with a port. sup Oct 15 (1399) $210

Ptd photograph, sgd, [n.d.]. 9.5 by 12.75 inches. Dar June 11 (293) $120

Missal

— [England, c.1035]. Fragment, vellum, 267mm by 90mm. In 2 sizes of a slightly sloping English Caroline minuscule. With 4 large initials in red. Recovered from a bdg. S Dec 17 (4) £3,200 [Quaritch]

— The Calvi Missal. [Milan, c.1440-50]. 235 leaves & flyleaf, vellum, 307mm by 228mm. 18th-cent vellum over pastebds. In 2 sizes of a rounded liturgical hand. With 13 pages of music on a 4-line red stave, 21 large historiated initials in full colors & burnished gold with leafy extensions, full border including coat-of-arms, & very large frontis. 3 pp added later. S Dec 17 (75) £40,000 [Mirandola]

— [Savoy, Aosta, 15th cent]. 181 leaves (c.18 lacking), vellum, 323mm by 224mm. Early calf over pastebds. In several sizes of a gothic liturgical hand, with music throughout on a 4-line red stave. With calligraphic initials & red & blue painted initials throughout. Worn. S June 23 (77) £2,600 [Fogg]

Mitchell, Margaret, 1900-49

Ls, 28 Dec 1937. 1 p, folio. To Mr. Neudecker. Sending a pamphlet about Gone with the Wind (present) & confirming that her characters & locations are ficticious. CNY June 9 (129) $2,200

— 9 Dec 1938. 1 p, 4to. To Dr. Mayos. Informing him that work has started on the film Gone With the Wind. Dar Apr 9 (292) $1,900

— 2 May 1944. 2 pp, 4to. To E. C. Mayos. Commenting on a poem & a medical paper. Dar Dec 26 (197) $1,300

Letter, 23 Feb 1944. 3 pp, 4to. To C. E. Mayos. About her health problems & wondering why people in Sweden should be interested in Gone With the Wind. Sgd M.M. in type. Dar Dec 26 (198) $500

Cut signature, [n.d.]. 4 by 4 inches. With letter of transferral. Dar June 11 (295) $275

Mitchell, William, 1879-1936

ALs, 9 Apr 1925. 6 pp, 4to. To Lester D. Gardner. Stressing the development of air power for national defense. CNY Dec 5 (137) $3,800

Ls s (2), 6 July 1918 & 24 Oct 1924. 2 pp, 4to. To Lester D. Gardner. Referring to American military aircraft, & expressing hopes for a separate air service. CNY May 14 (13) $900

Ls, 7 Feb 1921. 1 p, 4to. To Lester D. Gardner. Predicting airpower's domination of naval fleets. CNY Dec 5 (134) $1,200

— 23 Feb 1921. 1 p, 8vo. To Lester D. Gardner. Referring to "a list of questions prepared by Captain Eddie Rickenbacker".

CNY May 14 (10) $900

— 1 Mar 1921. 1 p, 4to. To Lester D. Gardner. Referring to the publication of some controversial material under his signature. CNY Dec 5 (135) $900

— 26 July 1924. 2 pp, 4to. To Lester D. Gardner. Expressing bitterness at the neglect of military aviation & warning of the threat of Japanese militarism. CNY Dec 5 (136) $6,000

ADs, Oct 1919. 2 pp, 8.5 by 14 inches. Agreement regarding shares in the Army & Navy Air Service Association. sup Oct 15 (1406) $500

Mitscherlich, Alexander, 1908-82

Autograph Ms, fragment from a work on psychopathology & collective behavior, [n.d.]. 4 pp, folio. star Mar 26 (738) DM360

Moebius, Karl August, 1825-1908

Series of 17 A Ls s, 1878 to 1887. 34 pp, mostly 8vo. To Julius Viktor Carus. About various scientific & publishing matters. star Mar 26 (739) DM1,000

Moerike, Eduard, 1804-75

Autograph Ms, poem, beginning "Mit hundert Fenstern steht ein stattlich Haus...", 20 Mar 1855. 1 p, 8vo. 12 lines, sgd. Written for a student at the Katharinenstift at Stuttgart. Inscr in anr hand on verso. star Mar 26 (378) DM6,200

— Autograph Ms, poem, Scherz, Sept 1855. 1 p, 8vo. 2 stanzas, sgd. Including AN at head. In the album of Ida Gugler, containing c.70 entries by friends & teachers at the Katharinenstift at Stuttgart, in cloth bdg. star Mar 26 (379) DM7,500

Moholy-Nagy, Laszlo, 1895-1946

Ls, 22 Sept [19]27. 1 p, 4to. Recipient unnamed. Regarding arrangements for a stay in Braunschweig. FD Dec 3 (1454) DM430

Moleschott, Jacob, 1822-93

ALs, 28 Mar 1859. 1 p, 4to. To the pbr C. W. Leske. Sending a Ms. star Mar 26 (741) DM200

Molnar, Ferenc, 1878-1952

Ds s (2)28 Aug 1950. 9 pp, 4to. Agreement with Paramount Pictures concerning the production of his play The Good Fairy. 2 copies; also sgd by others. Dar Aug 6 (206) $200

Moltke, Helmuth, Graf von, 1800-91

ALs, 21 Apr 1851. 2 pp, 4to. To his brother Ludwig. About family matters, financial affairs, & the humiliation of Prussia [at Olmuetz]. Illus in cat. star Mar 27 (1490) DM1,600

— 26 May 1880. 2 pp, 4to. Recipient unnamed. Letter of introduction for the musician Knudson-Nielsson. hen Nov 12 (2497) DM200

ADs, 20 Dec 1865. 1 p, 8vo. Receipt for charts of fortifications. star Mar 27 (1491) DM240

Mommsen, Theodor, 1817-1903

ALs, 7 Dec 1873. 3 pp, 8vo. Recipient unnamed. Declining to be a candidate for the Reichstag. star Mar 26 (744) DM850

Monck, George, 1st Duke of Albemarle, 1608-70

Series of 38 Ls s, 7 Aug 1656 to 12 Sept 1667. 50 pp, folio. To Sir Thomas Morgan. Mostly regarding military preparations for the Restoration of Charles II. With related material. S July 21 (216) £4,500 [Quaritch]

Ds, 3 Nov 1651. 1 p, 8vo. Safeguard for Sir John Drummond. bba May 28 (207) £240 [Maggs]

Monet, Claude, 1840-1926

ALs, 1 Oct 1888. 3 pp, 8vo. To [Georges] Jeanniot. Seeking assistance in releasing his son from military duty. Imperf. sg Sept 12 (167) $1,700

— 15 Jan 1890. 3 pp, 8vo. To Dr. Bellio. About his improving health, & thanking for a prescription. Illus in cat. sup Oct 15 (1408) $1,625

— 19 Oct 1901. 2 pp, 8vo. Recipient unnamed. Apologizing for his tardy response & commenting on recipient's paintings. Illus in cat. sup Oct 15 (1409) $1,750

Monk, William Henry, 1823-89

Autograph music, working Ms containing over 70 hymns composed or transcribed by Monk, [c.1870-86]. 87 pp, 8vo, in an album. Sgd in several places. Including some examples in other hands. S Dec 6 (135) £450 [Haas]

Monroe, James, 1758-1831

Autograph Ms, remarks on the embargo & the importance of maintaining American rights, if necessary by war; [c.1808?]. 1 p, 8vo. Illus in cat. Dar Aug 6 (207) $4,000

ALs, 29 Mar 1808. 1 p, 8vo. Recipient unnamed. Sending "the treaty, Mr. Madison's letter respecting it, & [his] answer." Spiro collection. CNY May 14 (123) $1,500

— 21 July 1815. 1 p, 4to. To Lieut. John Moore. Letter of recommendation for a discharged soldier. Illus in cat. sup May 9 (172) $1,250

— 19 Apr 1821. 3 pp, 4to. To Thomas Jefferson. About a fund for the University of Virginia, the revolt in Naples, negotiations with France, etc. Docketed in Jefferson's hand. Illus in cat. Spiro collection. CNY

May 14 (124) $16,000
— 2 Nov 1823. 1 p, 4to. To [John McLean?]. Requesting a report about the postal service. Framed with a port. P June 16 (257) $2,000
— 25 Mar 1829. 1 p, 4to. To James. Family news. Illus in cat. sup Oct 15 (1500) $3,050
Ls, 26 May 1800. 1 p, c.5.5 by 5.5 inches. As Governor of Virginia, ptd circular regarding vacancies on county courts. sg Feb 27 (130) $475
— 24 Oct 1814. 1 p, 4to. To C. Irvine. Informing him of a remittance. Illus in cat. sup Oct 15 (1496) $800
ADs, 21 July 1812. 1 p, 6.5 by 2.5 inches. Pay order addressed to Mr. Smith. Illus in cat. Dar Apr 9 (295) $550
— 2 July 1813. 1 p, 5.5 by 3 inches. Fragment of a pay order. Dar Apr 9 (293) $300
Ds, 1 Aug 1801. 1 p, 4to. Appointment of Duncan McLauchlin as Sheriff. sup Oct 15 (1495) $480
— 6 Feb 1812. 1 p, 4to. Certification of a copy. Matted with engraved port. Dar June 11 (296) $475
— [after 26 June 1812]. 3 pp, folio. Ptd Instructions for the Private Armed Vessels of the United States, addressed to Capt. Edward Dearey of the schooner Baltimore. Including Act concerning Letters of Marque, etc. Illus in cat. R June 13 (190) $1,200
— 7 Nov 1812. 1 p, 4to. As Sec of State, ptd "Additional Instruction to the Public and Private Armed Vessels" that British unarmed vessels bound to Sable Island are not to be interrupted. Illus in cat. R Mar 7 (136) $800
— [c.1813]. 1 p, 4to. Ptd instructions for private armed vessels of the U.S.A., issued to Capt. F. Boyle of the brig Chasseur. Framed. sg Sept 12 (168) $900
— 1817. 9 by 13 inches. Land grant. LH Dec 11 (14A) $375
— 14 Feb 1818. 1 p, folio. Land grant to Gideon Aldrick. wa Oct 19 (354) $400
— 28 Feb 1818. 1 p, folio. Patent to John L. Sullivan for a "Steam-Engine boiler". Countersgd by J. Q. Adams. sup Oct 15 (1497) $800
— 14 Mar 1818. 1 p, folio. Land grant to Henry Wilkins & Jacob Miller. Dar Apr 9 (294) $600
— 20 Apr 1818. 1 p, folio. Appointment of Samuel Hodges as Consul. Countersgd by J. Q. Adams. sup Oct 15 (1498) $1,100
— 31 May 1819. 1 p, folio. Military land grant in Missouri Territory. sg Sept 12 (169) $325
— 30 June 1820. 1 p, folio. Land grant to Thomas Gaskins & others. wd June 12 (323) $400
— 29 June 1821. 1 p, folio. Grant of land at Cincinnati. R Nov 9 (25) $320
— 1 Aug 1821. 1 p, folio. Land grant to John French. cb Feb 12 (92) $275
— 14 Sept 1821. 1 p, folio. Ship's passport for the brig William Henry of Boston. Countersgd by J. Q. Adams. R June 13 (188) $1,200
— 14 Nov 1822. 1 p, folio. Land grant. Framed with engraved port. Illus in cat. sup Oct 15 (1499) $700
— 13 Dec 1822. 1 p, folio. Ship's papers for the brig Venus. Countersgd by J. Q. Adams. Trimmed; framed. R Nov 9 (26) $650
— 1 Jan 1824. 1 p, folio. Grant of land in Indiana. sg Sept 12 (170) $400
— 25 June 1824. 1 p, folio. Land grant. R Mar 7 (137) $400
— 5 July 1824. 1 p, folio. Ship's passport for the brig William Thacher of New Bedford. Countersgd by J. Q. Adams. Illus in cat. R June 13 (189) $1,500
— 10 Nov 1824. 1 p, folio. Grant of land in Indiana. Dar June 11 (297) $325
— 3 Mar 1825. 1 p, folio. Patent issued to Thomas Pierce for an improved shovel. Countersgd by J. Q. Adams. Illus in cat. sg Feb 27 (131) $2,000

Monroe, Marilyn, 1926-62
Ls, 31 Jan 1952. 1 p, 4to. To Wald Krasno Productions. Giving permission to use her name for sheet music from the film Clash by Night. Also sgd by others. Framed with a photograph. Illus in cat. sup Oct 15 (1414) $3,600
— 16 May 1952. 1 p, 4to. Recipient unnamed. Regretting that a fan club has come to an end. bbc Sept 23 (27) $900
Ds, 11 May 1950. 1 p, 4to. Addendum to a contract with 20th Century-Fox of 2 May 1950. Illus in cat. sup May 9 (51) $2,800
Autograph sentiment, sgd, [n.d.]. On National Institute of Arts & Letters Ceremonial card. Inscr to Margaret McGuire. Framed with a photograph. P Dec 17 (280) $1,300
Check, sgd, 5 July 1953. Payable to Russ Wynn's Service. Framed with a photograph. wa Oct 19 (12) $2,200
Group photograph, 14 Jan 1954. 7.5 by 10 inches. With Joe DiMaggio on their wedding day; sgd by Monroe. Illus in cat. sup Oct 15 (1412) $5,250
Photograph, sgd, [n.d.]. Postcard. Full length; sgd in red. FD Dec 3 (1455) DM700
Photograph, sgd & inscr, [n.d.]. 8 by 10 inches. Illus in cat. sup Oct 15 (1413) $3,600
— Anr, [n.d.]. 8 by 10 inches. Inscr to Richard C. Illus in cat. sup May 9 (52) $3,800
Signature, [n.d.]. On index card. Framed with a photograph, overall size 16 by 20 inches.

Dar June 11 (298) $950

Montefiore, Sir Moses, 1784-1885

Ls, 1855. 1 p, 8vo. To 3 Rabbis in Israel. Transmitting money on behalf of an American donor. In the hand of his secretary Dr. Lowe. sg June 25 (253) $150

— Loewe, Louis. - 2 Ls s, 1886. 2 pp, 4to. To Chief Rabbis Samuel Salant & Raphael Meir Panzil. Ptd letters sgd over Montefiore's ptd signature, sending money for charitable causes. sg Dec 19 (181) $225

Montgomery, Bernard Law, 1st Viscount Montgomery of Alamein, 1887-1976

Typescript (duplicated), address to the Mothers' Union, London, 15 July 1948. 21 pp, folio. Including brief autograph corrections & AN, initialled, at head. sup Oct 15 (1416) $125

ALs, 14 Dec 1946. 2 pp, 12mo. To Miss Storey. Thanking for sending supplies to soldiers in Palestine. Dar Oct 10 (225) $200

Ls, 5 June 1944. 1 p, 4to. Ptd message distributed to officers prior to D-Day invasion; also sgd in facsimile. Illus in cat. Dar Apr 9 (296) $1,300

— 11 June 1956. 1 p, 4to. Recipient unnamed. Sending his photograph (not included). star Mar 27 (1763) DM210

Montmorency, Anne, Duc de, 1493-1567

Ls, 16 Sept 1550. 1 p, 4to. To the Seneschal of Agenois. Sending 20 archers & instructing him to report to the King about the Queen's & the Dauphin's health. star Mar 27 (1341) DM750

Moon, Keith

Ptd photograph, sgd, [n.d.]. 4to. Framed. wa Oct 19 (147) $140

Moore, Douglas Stuart, 1893-1969

Autograph quotation, Willow Song from The Ballad of Baby Doe, 9 bars; [20 May 1963]. 1 p, 4to. Sgd & inscr to James Van Heusen. Dar Feb 13 (266) $110

Moore, George, 1852-1933

Series of 3 A Ls s, 21 June 1923 & [n.d.]. 5 pp, 4to. To Athene Seyler. About a production of The Coming of Gabrielle. bba May 28 (208) £85 [Evans]

Moore, Thomas, 1779-1852

ALs, 2 Sept 1816. 1 p, 4to. To [James] Power. Promising him 2 melodies. Ingilby collection. pn Nov 14 (90) £110 [Quaritch]

More, Sir Thomas, 1478-1535

Ms, A Treatise to receyve the Blessed Bodye of our Lorde, sacramentally and virtually both...; [2d half of 16th cent]. 13 pp; incomplete. In a vol containing a compilation of several English Catholic devotional works, 65 pp, 4to, in orig bdg of a vellum bifolium from a 13th-cent English choirbook. In a secretarial hand. With Ms copy of an indulgence, 6 Feb 1575, inserted in cover. C June 24 (77) £3,800 [Smith]

Moreau, Jean Victor, 1763-1813

ALs, [n.d.]. 1 p, 8vo. To Gen. Grenier. Announcing his visit to discuss army mouvements in Italy. star Mar 27 (1375) DM220

Moreno, Francisco (Dr. Moorne)

Autograph Ms, Historia de la esgrima en Espana, 1900. 149 leaves, 4to, on rectos only. Unbound. sg Mar 26 (208) $200

Morgan, John Pierpont, 1837-1913

Ls, 21 Apr 1908. 1 p, 8vo. To Mr. Conant. Expressing reluctance "to have any biography published, even after I have passed away". Illus in cat. sup May 9 (417) $1,050

Morgan, Sir Thomas, d.1679?

[An archive of Morgan's papers, including 47 letters & documents sent to him (6 by Charles II), 1655 to 1677, c.50 pp, folio, sold at S on 21 July 1992, lot 215, for £4,200 to National Army Museum.]

Morgenstern, Christian, 1871-1914

ALs, 31 Dec 1906. 2 pp, 8vo. To an unnamed pbr. Concerning several publications. star Mar 26 (377) DM550

Moritz von Sachsen, Graf, 1696-1750

Ls, 17 Nov 1747. 1 p, folio. Recipient unnamed. Sending the copy of a letter concerning the shipment of grains in the Netherlands. star Mar 27 (1354) DM370

Morley, Christopher, 1890-1957

Autograph Ms, story, Human Being, 1931. About 425 pp, 4to, on rectos only. Including a few pages in typescript. With galley proof sheets, a copy of 1st Ed, & further related material. sg June 11 (231) $4,600

Typescript, Rudolph and Amina, or the Black Crook, [n.d.]. 2 versions of 76 pp each, 4to; 1 bound. Including related ALs. sg June 11 (233) $750

ALs, [n.d.]. 1 p, 4to. To Juliet. Sending a cartoon by A. E. Goldsmith (included). sg June 11 (252) $600

Morris, Gouverneur, 1752-1816

Ds, 13 Feb 1776. 1 p, 8vo. Promissory note. Dar Oct 10 (260) $275

Morris, Robert, Signer from Pennsylvania

Transcript, budget for 1783 with letter of transmittal to Congress, & speech before Congress, [Aug 1782]. 4 pp, folio. Copy in the hand of John Lowell. sup May 9 (383) $6,250

ALs, 7 Aug 1793. 2 pp, 4to. To James Constable. Requesting his assistance for J. Bonnett. sup Oct 15 (1212) $520

— 30 Mar 1795. 9 pp, 4to. To Sylvanus Bourne. Outlining his plan to sell, manage & settle frontier lands. CNY June 9 (266) $8,500

— 25 Aug 1796. 1 p, 4to. To James Carey. About his financial problems & a legal certificate. R Nov 9 (120) $400

— 4 Jan 1799. 1 p, 4to. To Garrett Cottninger. Regarding the North American Land Company. sup Oct 15 (1214) $420

Ls, 29 Aug 1760. 1 p, 4to. To William Patterson. Sending the trans of a paper about a financial matter. Illus in cat. sg Feb 27 (132) $450

Series of Ds s, 6 Ds s, May & June 1795. 6 pp, 8vo. Promissory notes to John Nicholson. wd June 12 (324) $850

Ds, 1 July 1793. 1 leaf, size not stated. Land deed. Framed. F Mar 26 (807) $275

— 20 Feb 1795. 1 p, folio. Certificate for 4 shares in the North American Land Company. sup Oct 15 (1213) $440

— 16 Mar 1795. 1 p, folio. Certificate of entitlement to shares in the North American Land Company, issued to Bird, Savage & Bird; sgd as president. Framed with a port. R June 13 (164) $600

— 18 Apr 1795. 1 p, 4to. As President of the North American Land Company, certification that Enoch Edwards owns a share. Framed. Dar June 11 (299) $425

— 18 Apr 1795. 1 p, folio. Certificate of entitlement to shares in the North American Land Company, issued to William Temple Franklin; sgd as president. R June 13 (162) $700

— 18 May 1795. 1 p, folio. Certificate of entitlement to shares in the North American Land Company, issued to John Barber Church; sgd as president. Framed with a port. R June 13 (163) $700

— 10 Nov 1795. 1 p, 8vo. Promissory note to John Nicholson. Endorsed by Nicholson & others on verso. Dar Dec 26 (264) $550

Morris, Robert Hunter, c.1700-64

Ds, 29 Apr 1756. 1 p, folio. Commission of Thomas Ogle as captain of militia. Dar Apr 9 (297) $100

Morris, William, 1834-96

ALs, 25 Nov [1872]. 6 pp, 8vo. To Aglaia Ionides Coronio. Complaining about the behavior of Dante Gabriel Rossetti [who was having an affair with Morris's wife]. Repaired. S July 21 (67) £1,500 [Swales]

Morrison, Jim, 1943-71

Autograph Ms, Keep Opening the Doors, or Los Angeles Notebook No 2, [c.1969]. Over 40 pp, size not stated. Composition notebook including poetry & drawings. Illus in cat. P Dec 17 (419) $23,000

Signature, endorsement on verso of check sgd by R. L. Greene, payable to Morrison, 5 Feb 1968. With ptd photograph. Dar Dec 26 (266) $550

— Anr, 19 Feb 1968. Endorsement on verso of check made out to him. Illus in cat. R Mar 7 (176) $700

— Anr, [c.26 Feb 1968]. On verso of check on the Johnson & Harband Management Account, payable to Morrison. Dar Aug 6 (208) $500

— Anr, endorsement on verso of check sgd by R. L. Greene, payable to Morrison, 24 Apr 1969. With ptd photograph. Dar Dec 26 (265) $550

Morrissey, John, 1831-78

Signature, [n.d.]. 4 by 1 inches. Illus in cat. Dar Feb 13 (105) $700

Morse, Samuel F. B., 1791-1872

ALs, 10 Mar 1843. 1 p, 4to. To Sec of the Treasury John C. Spencer. Informing him of his departure & his intention to collect preliminary information regarding his assignment to construct a telegraph line. Dar Aug 6 (209) $2,750

— 1 May 1843. 1 p, 4to. To Sec of the Treasury John C. Spencer. Giving information about the cost of wire for the telegraph line. Illus in cat. Dar Aug 6 (210) $1,600

— 18 May 1843. 1 p, 4to. To Sec of the Treasury John C. Spencer. Stating costs for his laboratory & office. Dar Aug 6 (211) $1,900

— 13 June 1843. 1 p, 4to. To Sec of the Treasury John C. Spencer. Requesting permission to dispose of cotton not needed for preparing the telegraphic wire. Dar Aug 6 (212) $1,600

— 7 Mar 1844. 1 p, 4to. To Sec of the Treasury John C. Spencer. Transmitting the copy of a letter concerning a lead pipe contract. Dar Aug 6 (213) $1,600

— 18 Mar 1844. 1 p, 4to. To Sec of the Treasury John C. Spencer. Responding to an inquiry about the furnishing of pipes by Messrs. Tatham. Dar Aug 6 (214) $1,900

— 1 June 1844. 1 p, 4to. To Acting Sec of the Treasury McClintock Young. Recommending an increase of salary for his assistant Alfred Vail. Dar Aug 6 (215) $3,000

— 20 July 1853. 1 p, 4to. To Samuel Colgate. Inviting him & his wife. Illus in cat. sup Oct 15 (1417) $800

— 1 Mar 1855. 1 p, 4to. To Kennedy

[Fruloúy?]. Responding to an inquiry about a painting. Illus in cat. sup Oct 15 (1418) $900

— 15 Feb 1867. 2 pp, 8vo. To E. S. Sanford. Sending newspaper clippings about the telegraph (present) & stating terms for a purchase of the telegraph by the US government. CNY Dec 5 (98) $4,500

Photograph, sgd & inscr, 10 Mar 1871. 17.5 by 20.5 inches. Inscr with 1st Morse Code message & explanatory note, sgd. Illus in cat. sup Oct 15 (1419) $8,500

Morton, John, Signer from Pennsylvania

Ds, 1769. 1 p, folio. Indenture, sgd 3 times. R Nov 9 (121) $300

— 3 June 1774. 1 p, folio. Order to the Sheriff of Lancaster County to bring all prisoners before the court. Also sgd by Benjamin Chew. Dar June 11 (300) $750

Morton, Levi Parsons, 1824-1920

ALs, 19 June 1860. 8 pp, 8vo. To Justin Morrill. Explaining the potential negative impact of a proposed tariff bill. wa Oct 19 (245) $75

Mosby, John Singleton, 1833-1916

ALs, 11 Apr 1916. 1 p, 4to. To Philip Strous. Denying he ever heard of the John S. Mosby who wrote a letter (copy present) to recipient in 1858 proposing a sale of slaves. Dar Dec 26 (267) $425

Moscheles, Ignaz, 1794-1870

Autograph music, Heimweh, andantino expressivo; 22 Apr 1850. 1 p, 4to. 32 bars in F major, sgd. star Mar 27 (1084) DM800

Moser, Koloman, 1868-1918

Collection of 2 autograph postcards (1 sgd), [27 Jan 1910? & 16 Dec 1913]. To Ditha Moser. Reporting from journeys. Each with a small sketch. star Mar 27 (931) DM800

Moses, Anna Mary Robertson ("Grandma"), 1860-1961

ALs, 23 Nov [19]44. 1 p, 8vo. To Cole Porter. Sending Thanksgiving turkeys. In pencil. sg Sept 12 (171) $600

ANs, [n.d.]. 1 p, 12mo. Recipient unnamed. Expressing birthday congratulations. On notepaper with reproduction of a painting. Dar June 11 (301) $180

Moszkowski, Moritz, 1854-1925

Autograph quotation, Romance, 4 bars; 7 June 1892. 1 p, 8vo. Sgd. star Mar 27 (1085) DM400

Mott, Sir Neville Francis

Autograph Ms, review of the book Kapitza in Cambridge and Moscow, to be ptd in the journal Nature; [n.d.]. 8 pp, 4to, on verso of photocopies. Sgd at end. star Mar 26 (745) DM460

Mountbatten, Louis, 1st Earl Mountbatten of Burma, 1900-79

Ls s (2), 22 Jan 1959 & [n.d.]. 2 pp, 8vo. To Mr. Bilanikin. Regarding his relations with Lord Beaverbrook. Framed with a port & a related newspaper article. P June 17 (53) $500

Ls, 7 Oct 1941. 1 p, 4to. To Mr. Mannix. Thanking for a gift. Framed with a photograph. sup Oct 15 (1421) $250

Mozart, Wolfgang Amadeus, 1756-91

Autograph Ms, part of the libretto of Die Entfuehrung aus dem Serail, comprising 1st two scenes of Act 1; [c.Aug - Sept 1781]. 2 pp, 4to. Passages changed from the libretto originally offered to him. Illus in cat. Mannheim collection. S Dec 6 (15) £94,000 [Haas]

Autograph music, Church Sonata in C major, K.329/317a, for full orchestra & organ, [1779]. 21 pp, 4to. Full score of the complete work, including some corrections & revisions. Some annotations in anr hand. Illus in cat. S Dec 6 (137) £180,000 [Haas]

— Autograph music, draft of the opening of a slow movement of a piano concerto [in G major, K.453?], [c.Apr 1784]. 1 p, 4to. 10 bars, laid out in full score, but with musical notation entered only for violins & bass. Illus in cat. Mannheim collection. S Dec 6 (14) £13,500 [Haas]

— Autograph music, sketch of the beginning of an incomplete & unpbd fugue & trio, [c. 1766 & c.1772]. 2 pp, 4to. 31 & 12 bars. Inscr by Georg von Nissen. Illus in cat. C June 24 (12) £10,000 [L'Autographe]

ALs, 10 Apr 1789. 2 pp, 8vo. To his wife Constanze. About his activities in Prague, plans for a new opera, etc. Illus in cat. Searles-Rowland collection. C June 24 (2) £55,000 [Haas]

— 30 Sept 1790. 2 pp, 4to. To his wife Constanze. Expressing high hopes for success with his performances in Frankfurt, discussing a financial transaction, & expressing his longing for her. Illus in cat. S Dec 6 (138) £58,000 [Pickering & Chatto]

— [c.21 - 27 Apr 1791]. 1 p, 12.5cm by 21.5cm. To Michael Puchberg. Requesting some instruments for a concert, & explaining why he did not repay a loan. Illus in cat. Mannheim collection. S Dec 6 (13) £25,000 [Gledson]

Signature, 1780. On fragment of a tp of a musical score, 83mm by 118mm. Including 2 notes of authentication at bottom. Framed with a port. Illus in cat. P June 17 (54) $25,000

Mucha, Alphonse, 1860-1939

ALs, [n.d.]. 2 pp, 4to. Recipient unnamed. Promising to send a work the next day. star Mar 27 (932) DM1,100

Muehsam, Erich, 1878-1934

ALs, 5 Oct 1932. 2 pp, 8vo. To Herr Schoenberger. Requesting instructions regarding a contribution to the journal Simplizissimus. HH Nov 6 (2085) DM710

Mueller, Johannes Peter, 1801-58

ALs, 3 Nov 1833. 2 pp, 4to. To an unnamed colleague. Returning a case history & discussing the illness. star Mar 26 (747) DM680

Mueller, Johannes von, 1752-1809

ALs, 16 Sept 1788. 2 pp, 4to. To Georg Forster. Informing him about efforts to finance his move to Mainz. Endorsed by Forster. star Mar 26 (746) DM850

Mueller, Max, 1823-1900

Autograph Ms, fragment of a text dealing with Christian & Buddhist myths, [n.d.]. 2 pp, 4to. Sgd. star Mar 26 (749) DM340

ALs, 5 Nov 1882. 3 pp, 8vo. Recipient unnamed. Thanking for a review of his Second Cambridge Lecture. star Mar 26 (750) DM360

Muellner, Adolf, 1774-1829

ALs, 6 Mar 1827. 2 pp, 4to. To Philippine von Reden. Hoping for Mss from the papers of her father, Baron Knigge. star Mar 26 (380) DM320

Muenter, Gabriele, 1877-1962

Collection of 2 A Ls s & autograph postcard, sgd, 26 Mar to 26 Apr 1958. 4 pp, mostly folio. To Leo Wagner. Regarding preparations for an exhibition. HH May 13 (2012) DM550

Muhammad, Elijah, 1897-1975

Check, sgd, 31 July 1971. Payable to Musical Products. Dar Aug 6 (118) $180

Munch, Edvard, 1863-1944

ALs, [5 Oct 1908]. 1 p, 8vo. To Hermann Struck. Promising to finish an engraving in a few days. star Mar 27 (933) DM1,000

ANs, [n.d.]. 2 pp, 12mo (card). Recipient unnamed. Expressing thanks & hoping they will meet. Dar Apr 9 (298) $450

Murat, Joachim, 1767-1815

Ls, [14 Nov 1804]. 1 p, folio. To the War Department. Describing the duties of a medical officer seeking promotion. sg Feb 27 (133) $200

Murphy, Audie, 1924-71

Ds, 19 Apr 1949. 10 pp, 4to. Film contract; carbon copy. Dar Dec 26 (268) $250

Murray, Sir George, 1772-1846

ALs, 6 Oct 1813. 2 pp, 4to. To Major Gen. Lord Aylmer. Giving instructions concerning troop movements. pn Nov 14 (148) £85 [Quaritch]

Murry, John Middleton, 1889-1957

Collection of 12 A Ls s & A Ns s, & 3 autograph Mss, 1920 to 1925 & [n.d.]. Length not stated. To Henry Major Tomlinson. About a variety of matters, & 3 reviews for The Nation. Ck Apr 3 (56) £550

Muscharello, Pietro Paolo, fl.1478

Ms, Algorismus; treatise on practical arithmetic, in Italian. [Italy, Nola, 1478]. 113 leaves (2 lacking), vellum, 211mm by 154mm. 18th-cent mottled calf bdg. In a small semi-cursive sloping bookhand. With decorated initials throughout, historiated initial & full illuminated border, & 54 colored drawings. Possibly autograph. Illus in cat. S June 23 (73) £42,000 [Lawrence]

Musical Manuscripts

Ms, 240 works for lute. [Bavaria, c.1625 - 1655]. 87 pp, folio (some lacking), in modern limp vellum. In brown ink on up to 12 hand-ruled 6-line tablature staves per page, probably in the hand of Albrecht Werl. Mainly dance movements by French lutenists. Cortot collection. S May 29 (576) £16,000 [Haas]

— Ms, c.60 instrumental pieces & accompaniments to songs for seven-course lute & eleven-course theorbo. [Northern? Italy, c.1600-1620]. Over 170 pp (1 missing), 4to, in contemp vellum bdg. Notated in Italian lute tablature, mostly in a professional hand. Many instructions & explanations added. S Dec 6 (117) £8,000 [Schneider]

— Ms, carol, beginning "...which desolatly, leste here in wylderness alone..." [England, mid-16th cent]. 2 pp, 11cm by 13.5cm, on ptd music paper. Possibly a song for Holy Week. Recovered from a bdg. S Dec 6 (218) £1,100 [Quaritch]

— Ms, collection of music for the mandolin. [Italy, early 18th cent]. 30 pp & blanks, 8vo, in contemp wraps. Notated in tablature on 4 four-line staves per page; including composers' names & titles. S Dec 6 (121) £1,400 [Cox]

— Ms, Musique pour la Guitare a Eugene Robert. [Philadelphia?, 1847]. 36 pp & blanks, folio, in bds. Mostly scored for voice & guitar. O May 26 (2) $110

Mussolini, Benito, 1883-1945

ALs, 10 Feb 1924. 2 pp, 8vo. To Orano. Commenting on the progress of his newspaper. Framed with a port. P June 17 (55) $1,700

Ds, 2 Dec 1928. 1 p, folio. Decree regarding the Italian Scout organization. sg Sept 12 (174) $425

Autograph telegram, sgd, [28 Dec 1941]. 1 p, folio. To Senatore di Crollanza. Expressing condolences. star Mar 27 (1496) DM500

Photograph, sgd, Jan 1927. Postcard. Half length. star Mar 27 (1495) DM600
See also: Vittorio Emanuele III, 1869-1947

Muybridge, Eadweard, 1830-1904

Ls, 11 Nov 1887. 1 p, 4to. To Edward H. Greenleaf. Circular letter, inviting subscriptions for his work on animal locomotion. CNY Dec 5 (99) $750

N

Nabokov, Nicolas, 1903-78

Series of c.30 A Ls s, 1927 to 1929. 70 pp, various sizes. To Boris Kochno. About his ballet Ode & other matters. SM Oct 12 (381) FF9,000

Nabokov, Vladimir, 1899-1977

Collection of 74 A Ls s, 10 Ls s, 6 autograph postcards, sgd, & autograph Ms, sgd, 25 May 1941 to 9 Jan 1971. 118 pp, various sizes. To George Hessen. Letters to a close friend, covering a wide variety of personal & professional matters. P Dec 12 (73) $30,000

Nagako Kuni, Empress of Hirohito of Japan.
See: Hirohito & Nagako Kuni

Nansen, Fridtjof, 1861-1930

ALs, 26 June 1892. 1 p, 8vo. To [C. R.] Markham. Referring to a visit & the building of his ship Fram. bba May 28 (210) £160 [Damms]

Ls, 27 Sept 1927. 1 p, 4to. To an unnamed lady. Agreeing to support her charitable cause. star Mar 26 (751) DM360

Napier, Sir Charles James, 1782-1853

ALs, 18 May 1809. 2 pp, 4to. To Francis Freeling. Complaining about unsolicited mail. Ingilby collection. pn Nov 14 (92) £65 [Browning]

Napier, Sir William, 1785-1860

ALs, 20 Mar 1825. 1 p, 4to. To Andrew Rutherford. Asking for his assistance in securing sources for his History of the Peninsular War. pn Nov 14 (155) £180 [Quaritch]

Napoleon I, 1769-1821

Series of 28 Ls s, 9 Apr to 5 Dec 1809. 34 pp, 4to. To Gen. Clarke. Concerning campaigns in Germany & the Peninsula, events in the Netherlands, etc. C Dec 16 (311) £8,500 [L'Autographe]

Ls, [17 Apr 1799]. 3 pp, folio. To Admiral Ganteaume. Giving orders for Vice-Admiral Perree to sail to Crete or Cyprus. C Dec 16 (310) £700 [L'Autographe]

— [20 Nov 1799]. 1 p, folio. Recipient unnamed. Regarding money for prisons. Illus in cat. sup Oct 15 (1032) $1,150

— [6 Mar 1805]. 1 p, 4to. To Marc Gaudin. Sending letters regarding mismanagement in the administration of forests. star Mar 27 (1498) DM1,050

— 7 Apr 1806. 1 p, 4to. To Eugene de Beauharnais. Giving instructions on a variety of matters. Framed with a port. Illus in cat. P June 17 (58) $3,500

— 17 May 1806. 1 p, 4to. To Eugene de Beauharnais. Approving of his decision to annull some nominations. Framed with a port. P June 17 (59) $1,000

— 16 Nov 1806. 1 p, 4to. To Nicolas Francois Mollien. Ordering him to send 500,000 francs to the King of Naples. star Mar 27 (1500) DM1,700

— 1 Apr 1807. 3 pp, 4to. To Count Molien. Discussing which revenues should be used to pay the army. S Dec 5 (539) £650 [Sakmyster]

— 4 Dec 1807. 1 p, 4to. To Eugene de Beauharnais. Making preparations for the war in Italy. Framed with a port. P June 17 (60) $1,600

— 16 Mar 1811. 1 p, 4to. To the Duc de Feltre. Giving instructions for the fortification of Ragusa. Numbered 3 at head. Illus in cat. sup Oct 15 (1034) $1,700

— 22 Aug 1811. 1 p, 7 by 7 inches. To Eugene Beauharnais. Giving permission to establish 2 camps. Framed with a port. sup Oct 15 (1035) $1,450

— 23 Apr 1813. 1 p, 4to. To Bertrand. Criticizing that his letter from Coburg does not provide news about the enemy. Illus in cat. star Mar 27 (1503) DM1,700

— 14 Sept 1813. 3 pp, 4to. To Gen. de Nansouty. Giving orders for the preparation of the campaign in Germany. star Mar 27 (1504) DM2,300

Ds, [20 Oct 1795]. 2 pp, 4to. Confirmation that Lieut. Chambon remained on duty during the insurrection against the National Convention. Framed with a port. P June 17 (57) $1,700

— [1799]. 12.75 by 9.25 inches. Appointment of Citizen Loiseau as lieutenant. Also sgd by others. rs Oct 17 (88) $750

— 10 Apr 1813. 2 pp, 49cm by 35cm. Licence for an unnamed American ship to unload goods in Bordeaux. S May 28 (186) £650 [Sandstrom]

— [n.d.]. Size & contents not stated. Fragment; countersgd by Maret & Lucien Bonaparte. With engraved port. wd Dec 12 (327) $950

Autograph endorsement, sgd, 24 July 1805. On a letter addressed to his wife Josephine by Marianne de Letto, 1 p, folio, concerning a petition; instructing M. Celli to look into the matter. Framed with a port. Illus in cat. sup Oct 15 (1033) $2,300

— Anr, sgd, 7 Jan 1808, on a report addressed to him by Gen. Glarke, 29 Nov 1807, 2 pp, folio. Agreeing that the 23rd Regiment of Dragoons will not be required to provide soldiers for the Imperial Guard. star Mar 27 (1501) DM650

— Anr, sgd, 10 Aug 1813. About 3 by 3 inches. 11 words on fragment of a report dealing with evaluations of the Duc de Castiglione. Illus in cat. sg Feb 27 (136) $650

— Anr, sgd, on a list submitted by Gen. Drouot proposing decorations & rewards for numerous officers, 27 Mar 1815. 1 p, folio. Ordering payment of higher sums. star Mar 27 (1505) DM2,100

Endorsement, sgd, on a letter addressed to him by M. Bossi, 26 June 1797, 2 pp, folio, requesting permission for troop movements in Italy; forwarding letter to headquarters. sup May 9 (460) $1,500

— Anr, sgd, 6 Mar 1799. In the margin of a letter addressed to him by Dominique Jean Larrey, 1 p, folio, asking assistance for orphans; ordering a report. sg Sept 12 (176) $1,600

— Anr, sgd, on minute submitted to him by Petiet, French Minister at the Cisalpine Republic, [6 July 1800]. 1 p, folio; trimmed. Regarding the Brigade of Engineers. pn Nov 14 (175) £170 [Dupre]

— Anr, sgd, on a letter sgd by the Duc de Feltre, 8 June 1811, 2 pp, folio, requesting removal of 3 regiments; refusing request. rf Sept 21 (16) $800

— Anr, sgd, 5 Apr 1812, on a report regarding the employment of prisoners of war, addressed to him by Gen. Glarke, 1 Apr 1812, 2 pp, folio. Deciding that his earlier orders must be executed. star Mar 27 (1502) DM1,200

— Anr, sgd, 5 Oct 1813. 1 p, size not stated. Note of approval on a letter addressed to him by Gen. Mepierez asking him to authorize a military promotion. Ck Apr 3 (90) £280

— Crown Jewels. - Ms, Inventaire General des Diamans et Roses Pierres Precieuses et Perles... composant le Tresor de la Couronne, sgd by Barthelemi Alphonse Lecoulteux de Canteleu & others, 15 May 1811, with supplements 1812 & 1813. 175 pp, folio, in contemp red mor. C June 24 (378) £7,000 [Paradise]

— Prefecture de Police. - Ms, report on an assassination attempt upon Napoleon, [n.d.]. 8 pp, folio. sup Oct 15 (1036) $400

— Tamanti, F. - Ms, description of events during Napoleon's stay at Potsdam, 24 Oct 1806. 21 pp, 4to, in half lea bdg. star Mar 27 (1499) DM1,200

Napoleon III, 1808-73

Collection of 2 A Ls & 2 photographs, 27 Dec 1838 & 9 Jan 1839. 2 pp, 8vo & 12mo, & photographs. To Lord & Lady Eastnor. Thanking for invitations. star Mar 27 (1518) DM200

AD, 19 May 1859. 1 p, folio. Order for troop mouvements. Endorsed by others. Illus in cat. star Mar 27 (1519) DM600

Napoleonic Wars

Ms, A Journey occasioned by my emigration from Mosco, which was villainously taken ... by Bonaparte..., Oct 1812. 21 leaves, 4to; stitched. In epistolary form; sgd T.C. Imperf. bba Sept 19 (437) £70 [Kunkler]

— Ms, account by a Midshipman on HMS Shannon of his capture by the French in 1803, imprisonment, escape & travels through Germany back to England, [c.1805]. 86 pp, 8vo, in calf. Illus with a water-color & 2 ptd maps tipped in. S July 21 (272) £500 [Browning]

— Burch, John. - Autograph Ms, diary; 20 May 1803 to 22 Dec 1813. 62 leaves, 16mo, in lea bds. Describing his capture at sea & detention in Belgium & Northern France. C Dec 16 (291) £160 [McAlear]

Narbrough, Sir John, 1640-88

Ds, 28 Oct 1686. 1 p, folio. As Commissioner of the Navy, order to supply canvas to Chatham yard. Also sgd by others. Longueville collection. S June 25 (26) £500 [Renard]

Nash, John, 1752-1835

ALs, 28 Dec 1799. 2 pp, 4to. Recipients unnamed. Asking permission to present designs for their new warehouses although the date for presentation has passed. bba May 28 (219) £350 [R.I.B.A.]

Nast, Thomas, 1840-1902

Signature, 31 May 1884. 3 by 1.75 inches (card). Framed with a reproduction of a cartoon. Dar Feb 13 (270) $130

Nathan, Isaac, 1790-1864

ALs, 29 June 1840. 1 p, 4to. Recipient unnamed. Offering him the ptg plates of his Hebrew Melodies. S Dec 6 (145) £1,300 [Haas]

Nathanson, Joseph Saul, 1810-75

ALs, 1864. 1 p, 4to. To Jacob Solomon Halperin. Halakhic matter. sg Dec 19 (184) $550

Natural History

Ms, Abbildungen Naturhistorischer Gegenstaende. [Liegnitz, Germany, 1803-06]. 385 pp, 240mm by 185mm. Contemp half lea bdg. Watercolors of flowers, birds, amimals & plants, with subscriptions in German & Latin; sgd F. S. Illus in cat. HH Nov 5 (513) DM16,000

— Ms, Abbildungen Naturhistorischer Gegenstaende. [Liegnitz, Germany, 1811]. 57 pp, 276mm by 235mm. Contemp half lea bdg. Watercolors of flowers, birds, fish & plants, with subscriptions in German & Latin; sgd F. S. HH May 12 (1) DM3,100

Naval Manuscripts

Ms, protest concerning damage to the schooner Washington during a voyage from Newport to Norfolk, 1827. 16 pp, various sizes. sg June 18 (346) $225

— Ms, Remark Book of HMS Ganymede, HMS Owen Glendower & HMS Naiad commanded by Capt. R. C. Spencer on surveying expeditions in the Mediterranean & in South America, 1818 to 1825. 48 pp, folio, in wraps. bba Sept 19 (438) £170 [Hodgson]

Document, 8 Feb 1850. 7 pp, folio. Court record of Joseph Coe v. John Church, Master of the ship William & Henry, detailing grievances. Sgd by Stephen Cooper, judge in the District of Sonoma, California. sg June 18 (343) $325

— TANNER, CAPT. WILLIAM. - ALs, 19 Mar 1774. 2 pp, folio. To Samuel & William Vernon & Company. Advising of damage to vessel & cargo. sg June 18 (341) $175

Nees von Esenbeck, Christian Gottfried Daniel, 1776-1858

ALs, 11 July 1855. 1 p, 4to. To an unnamed colleague. Regarding a prize awarded to Professor Senft. star Mar 26 (754) DM200

Nehru, Jawaharlal, 1889-1964

Transcript, excerpt from a speech given in the US, Dec 1956. 1 p, 12mo (card). Sgd. Dar Dec 26 (269) $150

Ls, 5 Mar 1929. 1 p, 4to. To Sailendra Nath Ghosh. Informing him that he has discussed his letter (carbon copy included) with other politicians. Dar Feb 13 (271) $100

Nelson, Horatio Nelson, Viscount, 1758-1805

ALs, 12 Mar 1794. 2 pp, 4to. To John Udny. Giving his views as to the best way of defeating the French in Corsica. With related material. Ingilby collection. pn Nov 14 (94) £1,100

— 27 Nov 1795. 6 pp, 4to. To Francis Drake. Justifying his recent conduct to counteract accusations that the Austrian retreat is due to lack of cooperation of the British squadron. S Dec 12 (312) £1,100 [Sakmyster]

— 7 Apr [1798]. 1 p, 4to. To his wife. Expressing his wish for peace & referring to financial matters. Illus in cat. Longueville collection. S June 25 (144) £2,200 [Stokes]

— 27 Mar 1803. 1 p, 8vo. To Mr. Willet. In 3d person, declining an invitation. Framed with a port. P June 17 (62) $1,100

— 27 Sept 1803. 2 pp, 4to. To Sir Richard Strachan. Discussing naval movements, & hoping the French will leave Toulon. Illus in cat. star Mar 27 (1520) DM8,500

— 30 Dec 1804. 1 p, 239mm by 187mm. To the Hon. C. Boyce. Ordering him to join the fleet. P Dec 12 (74) $2,500

— 9 May 1805. 3 pp, 4to. To Sir John Acton. Announcing that he is going to the West Indies. C Dec 16 (314) £1,400 [McAlear]

— 9 Oct 1805. 1 p, 4to. To Admiral Collingwood. Discussing supplies at Gibraltar for the Canopus & other ships. Illus in cat. b Nov 18 (270) £1,600

Ls, 30 June 1804. 2 pp, folio. To Commissioner Otway. Ordering naval stores. Including draft of reply on verso. S July 21 (273) £650 [Maggs]

Ds, 20 May 1803. 1 p, folio. Agreement between Capt. S. Sutton & Capt. T. M. Hardy to share prize money; sgd as witness. Also sgd by others. pn June 11 (52) £1,500

Cut signature, 4 Apr 1805. Size not stated. pn Nov 14 (160) £220

Netherlands

— GHOIAUS, INGERANNUS. - Document, Sept 1265. 1 p, vellum, folio. Deed donating tithes at Roberghes & Surkes to the church at Liskes. Lacking seal. star Mar 27 (1522) DM300

Nettelbeck, Joachim, 1738-1824

Ls, 12 Mar 1810. 1 p, folio. To governmental officials at Kolberg. Concerning a fire inspection. Also sgd by others. star Mar 27 (1521) DM600

New Jersey

— HARDY, JOSIAH. - Ds, 10 Mar 1762. 18 pp, folio. Act "to compleat the New Jersey Regiment to [666] effective Volunteers". R Nov 9 (116) $320

New York

Document, 31 Jan 1848. 15 by 22 inches. Appointment of Joseph Mezzetti as fireman, sgd by the Clerk & Treasurer of the Department. R Mar 7 (272) $50

— LONG ISLAND. - Document, 10 Apr 1753. 1 p, folio. True copy, sgd by Jacob Reeder, of a deed by J. Th. Wandall, conveying land in Queens County to Richard Allsup, 1685. Dar Oct 10 (17) $160

— MAYLE, JACOB. - Document, 19 Aug 1699. 1 p, folio. Deed conveying land on the south side of Wall Street to William Nicoll. With related document on verso, 1721. sup May 9 (424) $2,900

— TAMMANY SOCIETY. - Ms, Tammanial Laws, 24 Aug 1789. 50 pp, size not stated, in worn contemp half sheep. sg Dec 5 (246) $650

Newbolt, Sir Henry John, 1862-1938

Series of 4 A Ls s, 24 Apr 1900 to 2 Sept 1908. 12 pp, 8vo. To Thomas & Lucy Hodgkin. About various matters. bba May 28 (179) £65 [Wise]

Newman, Paul

Ds, 19 Dec 1952. 2 pp, 4to. Contract with The Theatre Guild for the play Picnic. Dar Feb 13 (273) $250

Newton, John, 1725-1807

ALs, 1779. 4 pp, 4to. To John Ryland. Discussing the ptg of Olney Hymns. bba May 28 (180) £240 [Wilson]

Ney, Michel, Prince de la Moskowa, 1769-1815

Ls, [2 Sept 1804.] 1 p, 4to. To Gen. Dutaille. Transmitting letters concerning uniforms. R Nov 9 (59) $170

— 11 Feb 1815. 1 p, 4to. To Minister of War Brune. About troops requesting permanent leave. Docketed by Brune. sg Feb 27 (142) $275

Nicholas I, Emperor of Russia, 1796-1855

Ds, 20 Feb 1830. 1 p, folio. Appointment of Roman Furman as State Councilor. Illus in cat. sg Feb 27 (143) $1,000

— 23 Aug 1832. 4 pp, folio. Appointment of Ludwig Sabin Ignatz Tengoborski as Russian commissoner at Krakau. Countersgd by Nesselrode. star Mar 27 (1684) DM210

— 5 Oct 1840. 2 pp, folio. Order addressed to Prince Golitsyn, awarding a decoration to Privy Councilor Furman. R Nov 9 (60) $380

Nichols, Charles ("Kid"), 1869-1953

ALs, 12 July 1949. 1 p, 4to. To John J. Smith. Thanking for a message. Dar Dec 26 (99) $900

Nicolai, Otto, 1810-49

Autograph music, song, Des Freiwilligen Abschied, to a text by Robert Prutz, [1848]. 4 pp, folio. Scored for 2 voices & piano. Illus in cat. star Mar 27 (1101) DM2,800

Niembsch, Nikolaus, Edler von Strehlenau, 1802-50. See: Lenau, Nikolaus

Nietzsche, Friedrich, 1844-1900

Collection of 22 A Ls s & letter, 16 Nov 1868 to Oct 1887. 62 pp, 8vo. To Gustav Krug. Important letters to a close friend, dealing with his work & activities, his health, compositions, Wagner, etc. With related material. star Mar 26 (755) DM180,000

— FOERSTER-NIETZSCHE, ELISABETH. - Collection of ALs, 20 Ls s, 1 letter & 6 A Ns, 31 May 1926 to 3 June 1935. 48 pp, mostly 8vo. To R. Leutheusser & his wife. About the Nietzsche archives, Hitler, etc. star Mar 26 (756) DM1,500

Nightingale, Florence, 1820-1910

ALs, [29 June 1857]. 4 pp, 8vo. To Augustus Stafford. On the health of the army in the Crimea. Incomplete. pn June 11 (41) £120

— 3 Oct 1860. 7 pp, 8vo. To Mrs. Gaskell. Enlisting her support for soldiers' homes in Gibraltar. Ingilby collection. pn Nov 14 (95) £520

— 19 Apr 1886. 1 p, 8vo. To Lydia Norman. Suggesting that she go directly to Holloway. sup Oct 15 (1451) $700

Nijinska, Bronislava, 1891-1972

A Ls s (2), [1923-1924]. 4 pp, size not stated. To Boris Kochno. Announcing completion of the choreography for ballets by Stravinsky & Poulenc. SM Oct 12 (382) FF6,000

Nijinsky, Vaslav, 1890-1950

Ptd photograph, sgd, July 1913. 8 by 5 inches. In floral ballet costume. Framed. Ck Nov 15 (81) £1,000

See also: Stravinsky, Igor

Nikolai Alexandrovich, Crown Prince of Russia, 1843-65

Series of 8 A Ls s, 6 July 1856 to 12 Sept 1857. 16 pp, 8vo & 4to. To his mother Maria Alexandrovna. Charming family letters. 2 in French. HH May 13 (2016) DM650

Nimitz, Chester W., 1885-1966

Photograph, sgd, [n.d.]. 5 by 7 inches. Full length, in uniform. Dar Oct 10 (264) $225

Nixon, Richard M.

Transcript, copy of his letter of resignation of 9 Aug 1974, addressed to the Secretary of State. 1 p, 8vo, on White House stationery. Sgd. Illus in cat. sup Oct 15 (1728) $4,600

— Transcript, copy of his letter of resignation of 9 Aug 1974, addressed to the Secretary of State. 1 p, 8vo. Sgd. Framed with a port. Illus in cat. sup Oct 15 (1729) $1,250

— Transcript, letter of resignation, 9 Aug 1974; souvenir copy. 1 p, 8vo. Sgd. With related material. Dar Dec 26 (272) $900

Collection of Ls & photograph, sgd & inscr, 6 Sept 1951 & [n.d.]. 1 p, 4to, & postcard. To Nellie Thompson. Concerning "treatment of the mentally ill at Sawtelle." sg Sept 12 (179) $120

Ls, 31 Dec 1958. 1 p, 4to. To Walter Winchell. Commenting on a visit to a dentist. Illus in cat. R Mar 7 (138) $1,200

— 1 June 1963. 1 p, 4to. To Walter Winchell. Correcting an inaccurate statement in a newspaper. R Mar 7 (139) $380

— 23 Aug 1984. 1 p, 4to. To Don Lee. Thanking for a letter & promising to send a book. Dar Apr 9 (300) $150

— 11 Feb 1986. 1 p, 4to. To L. L. King. Thanking for a document sgd by President Wilson. Dar Feb 13 (276) $225

— 3 May 1989. 1 p, 4to. To Harold Russell. Praising his services as chairman of the Committee on Employment of the Handicapped. Dar Aug 6 (217) $300

— 2 Feb 1990. 1 p, 4to. To Gov. Mike Hayden. Paying tribute to Dwight Eisenhower. With a photograph. Illus in cat. sup Oct 15 (1731) $800

Ns, May 1969. 1 p, 12mo (card). To Senator Baker. Dinner invitation (engraved). Illus in cat. Dar Feb 13 (275) $375

Ds, 19 Aug 1960. 12 pp, 10 by 15 inches, in lea bdg. Tribute to Mark A. Trice in ptd booklet The US Senate. Illus in cat. sup Oct 15 (1726) $400

— 18 Sept 1967. 1 p, 4to. Permission to Michigan State University to use his "Checkers Speech" in a textbook. sg Feb 27 (144) $250

Group photograph, sgd, [n.d.]. 10 by 8 inches. With President Eisenhower, Justice William J. Brennan & 2 cabinet members. Also sgd by Brennan. Dar Apr 9 (299) $140

Menu, New England Nixon for Goldwater Dinner, Wentworth-by-the-Sea Restaurant, 1 Oct 1964. Size not stated. Sgd on front cover. sup Oct 15 (1727) $150

Photograph, sgd, [1960s]. 5.5 by 6.5 inches. Dar Aug 6 (216) $120

— Anr, [n.d.]. 7.5 by 8.5 inches. Dar Dec 26 (270) $140

Photograph, sgd & inscr, [c.1965]. 8 by 10 inches. Inscr to Judy Palmer. Dar Dec 26 (271) $150

— Anr, [n.d.]. 8 by 10 inches. Inscr to Leslie K. King. Dar Feb 13 (277) $150

— Anr, [n.d.]. 8 by 10 inches. By John Engstead. Dar June 11 (303) $200

Signature, [c.1952]. On senatorial card. wa Oct 19 (325) $160

— Anr, [20 Jan 1969]. On philatelic envelope. Matted with group photograph. Dar Oct 10 (265) $275

— Anr, [24 July 1969]. On philatelic cover. wa Oct 19 (324) $110

Nixon, Richard M. —& Others

[The signatures of Nixon, 15 Jan 1990, & of Gerald R. Ford, Henry A. Kissinger & John B. Connally, on an invitation to the Inaugural ceremonies on 20 Jan 1969, 8vo, sold at Dar on 26 Dec 1991, lot 273, for $300.]

Nobel, Alfred, 1833-96

ALs, [n.d.], "Monday". 1 p, 8vo. To an unnamed lady. About his bronchitis, & hoping he will be able to attend a performance on Wednesday. star Mar 26 (757) DM1,700

AN, [n.d.]. 1 p, on visiting card. Recipient unnamed. Expressing condolences. star Mar 26 (758) DM380

Nolde, Emil, 1867-1956

A Ls s (2), 8 & 21 Dec 1902. 3 pp, 8vo. To Messrs. Fischer & Franke, Jungbrunnen-Gesellschaft. Regarding his friend Heise's suicide. JG Mar 27 (196) DM1,000

ALs, 17 June 1944. 1 p, 8vo. To Johann Reiher. Complaining about his persecution by the Nazis. star Mar 27 (934) DM1,100

Ls, 12 Sept 1954. 1 p, 4to. To Mrs. Sothmann. Declining a request. HN June 26 (968) DM220

Nono, Luigi, 1924-90

Collection of 5 Ls s, photograph, & signature, 21 Jan 1960 to 1 Jan 1965 & [n.d.]. 8 pp, mostly 4to, & photograph. To Pavel Eckstein. Interesting letters about musical & political contacts, a lecture, etc. In German. star Mar 27 (1103) DM2,200

Norblin, Stefan Juliusz, 1892-1952

Original drawing, a cossack on a spotted horse, to illus Adam Mickiewicz's Pan Tawardowski, 1922. 8.5 by 8.75 inches. In pen-&-ink & watercolor, heightened with varnish. Sgd. Illus in cat. Ck Dec 11 (47) £

Nordau, Max, 1849-1923

ALs, 22 Mar 1882. 4 pp, 8vo. To Sara Hutzler. Assuring her of his love, & regretting that their relationship has come to an end. star Mar 27 (1438) DM470

Norris, Frank, 1870-1902

Autograph Ms, fragment of his novel McTeague: A Story of San Francisco, [ptd 1899]. 1 p, folio. Corresponding to pages 58 - 60 of 1st Ed. CNY Dec 5 (304) $1,000

Nossack, Hans Erich, 1901-77

Autograph Ms, sonnet, Das Stifterpaar, [n.d.]. 1 p, folio. Sgd. star Mar 26 (382) DM400

Nussbaum, Johann Nepomuk von, 1829-90

ALs, 18 Mar 1881. 2 pp, 8vo. Recipient unnamed. About a new dressing for surgical wounds. star Mar 26 (759) DM220

O

Oakley, Annie, 1860-1926

ALs, 26 [Dec 1902]. 1 p, 4to. Recipient unnamed. Thanking for a Christmas present. Illus in cat. sup Oct 15 (1453) $3,600

ANs, 11 Feb 1926. 1 p, 12mo, on verso of Valentine's card. To Mrs. Dunlevy. Thanking for a saber. Illus in cat. sup May 9 (451) $2,300

Photograph, [n.d.]. Cabinet size. By Stacy. R Nov 9 (158) $700

Oberth, Hermann, 1894-1989

Collection of ALs, 44 Ls s & 36 cards, sgd (6 autograph), 1948 to 1989. To Jupp Gerhards. About a variety of private, political & scientific matters. With related material. JG Sept 27 (417) DM8,000

Ls, 9 Feb 1978. 9 pp, folio. Recipient unnamed. About his teaching methods. star Mar 26 (761) DM270

O'Casey, Sean, 1880-1964

Autograph Ms, play, Juno and the Peacock [sic], 1st draft, [1923]. 72 pp, 4to, written in 2 directions in a school exercise book. In ink; some pencil notations & 2 small sketches. Newspaper cutting, 8 May 1923, pasted inside cover. With near-final typescript of the play, [1923], 90 pp, 4to; some autograph revisions. P Oct 11 (244) $36,000

— Autograph Ms, play, The Plough and the Stars, full 1st draft, [1924-25]. In ink & pencil, with numerous alterations, 3 pen-&-ink sketches of the flag, 2 pencil sketches of stage sets, & several doodles. 72 pp, in a 4to school exercise book with autograph Ms of parts of chapters 1-3 of Rose and Crown, being part of vol 2 of his autobiography, & 3 caricatures of G. B. Shaw; 36 pp. P Oct 11 (245) $38,000

Collection of ALs & Ls, 12 Mar & 11 Apr 1955. 3 pp, 8vo. To Patrick Galvin. Informing him that a record was received broken, & acknowledging receipt of replacement. sg Sept 12 (181) $300

— Collection of ALs & photograph, sgd & inscr, 14 May 1961. 1 p, 8vo, & 7.75 by 9.5 inches. Recipient unnamed. Sending his photograph. sg Sept 12 (183) $300

ALs, 1 Feb 1946. 6 pp, size not stated. To Angela Barry. Discussing questions of health, the Irish Labour Party, a new magazine, etc. Ck Nov 15 (12) £150

Ls, 31 May 1956. 1 p, 8vo. To Eve Salisbury. About his illness, & advising her on how to cope with loneliness. sg Sept 12 (182) $175

Occult Manuscripts

Ms, treatise on sympathetic magic & divination. [England, early 18th cent]. 169 pp, 325mm by 195mm. Late 19th-cent mor bdg. In a cursive hand, with numerous diagrams in ink. C June 24 (86) £1,200 [Mediolanum]
See also: Hebrew Manuscripts

Ochs, Peter, 1752-1821

A Ls s (2), 9 Apr 1772 & 6 Feb 1775. 13 pp, 4to. To an unnamed lady. About his youth & prospects. star Mar 27 (1247) DM1,000

ALs, [28 Jan 1798]. 1 p, 4to. To [Jean] Perregaux. Sending news about the revolution at Basel. star Mar 27 (1248) DM1,100

O'Connell, Daniel, 1775-1847

ALs, 24/25 June 1839. 3 pp, 4to. To Fitzpatrick. Denouncing English anti-Catholic bigotry. pn Nov 14 (203) £260

Oehlenschlaeger, Adam, 1779-1850

ALs, 28 Jan 1829. 1 p, 4to. To Edvard Hvidt. Warning him of an epidemic of typhus. star Mar 26 (383) DM400

Oersted, Hans Christian, 1777-1851

Ls, 20 Apr 1847. 1 p, 4to. To Wilhelm von Struve. Thanking for a description of the observatory at Pulkova. star Mar 26 (764) DM320

Offenbach, Jacques, 1819-80

Autograph music, 60 bars "en fa" [for the horn part of the song Liebchen, hat dich Schlaf umfangen; 1848]. 1 p, 4to, cut from larger sheet. With authentication. star Mar 27 (1105) DM650

— Autograph music, Marche villageoise, sketches for 10 voices; [n.d.]. 8 pp, folio. star Mar 27 (1104) DM3,600

ALs, [n.d.]. 1 p, 8vo. To Clemenceau. Arranging for a rehearsal. sg Feb 27 (146) $300

— [n.d.]. 3 pp, 8vo. To Auguste Pittaud-Deforges. Hoping for a performance of his music to recipient's libretto at the Theatre Francais. star Mar 27 (1106) DM950

ADs, 19 Mar 1878. 1 p, 8vo. Receipt to the pbr Meyer for a fee for his Maitre Peronnilla. star Mar 27 (1107) DM550

Officium

Ms, Office of the Dead, with Masses for various liturgical seasons, Psalms, & Litany, in Latin. [Florence, c.1400]. 72 leaves (some later), vellum, 307mm by 210mm. Def 17th-cent blindstamped calf over wooden bds. In a rounded gothic hand, with music on a 4-line red stave. With decorated initials throughout & full-page drawing added later. S Dec 17 (74) £900 [Mazza]

— Ms, offices for advent & Christmas, in Latin. [Southern Netherlands, c. 1400]. 27 leaves only, vellum, 242mm by 175mm. Late 19th-cent lea bdg. In a gothic textura. With many penwork initials in colors (3 large) & 3-quarter border. HH Nov 5 (812) DM4,400

— Ms, Officium B.M.V secundum consuetudinem romane, with Psalms, Litany & Office of the Dead. [Northern Italy, c.1485]. 140 leaves, vellum, 105mm by 80mm. Contemp blindstamped brown lea over wooden bds. In black ink in a gothic rotunda. With hundreds of small penwork initials, 10 illuminated initials (2 historiated), & 6 large miniatures within scrolling borders. HH Nov 5 (814) DM5,200

— Ms, Officium B.M.V, with Office of the Dead, Officium S. Crucis, Officium S. Spiritu, & Psalms. [Northern Italy, c.1485]. 157 leaves, vellum, 88mm by 70mm. Late 16th-cent red-brown mor bdg. In an elegant humanistic rotunda. With 7 small & 5 large illuminated initials (4 historiated) & 5 borders in gold & colors. HH Nov 5 (813) DM4,000

Offredus, Apollinaris, fl.15th cent

Ms, Commentary on the Posterior Analytics of Aristotle, & other texts. [Lombardy, Chiaravalle Abbey?, c.1442]. 96 leaves (10 blank), 405mm by 287mm. Rebacked vellum over pastebds of c.1700. By several scribes in a variety of hands. With large painted initial & large historiated initial with full border. S June 23 (68) £9,000 [Symonds]

Ohm, Georg Simon, 1789-1854

ALs, 27 Feb 1846. 1 p, 4to. To Traugott Leberecht Ertel. Requesting a replacement for a faulty instrument. Illus in cat. star Mar 26 (762) DM2,400

O'Keeffe, Georgia, 1887-1986

ALs, 7 Jan 1960. 4 pp, 4to. To Anita O'Keeffe Young. Describing winter at her place. Dar June 11 (304) $850

Ls, 27 Aug 1971. 2 pp, 4to. To her sister Anita Young. Carbon copy, confirming agreements regarding the disposal of her paintings in her sister's possession. With photocopies of 3 lists stating paintings to be given to museums. Dar Aug 6 (221) $1,600

Oland, Warner, 1879-1938

Photograph, sgd & inscr, [n.d.]. 5 by 9.75 inches. Dar Feb 13 (280) $100

Onassis, Jacqueline Bouvier Kennedy

ALs, [11 Mar 1958]. 3 pp, 6 by 6 inches. To Ada Latham. Thanking for a present for her baby & mentioning Bobby Kennedy. Dar Aug 6 (189) $550

ANs, [c.1962]. 1 p, 8vo (card). Recipient unnamed. Sending a copy of the 1st Ed of the White House guide book. Illus in cat. sup Oct 15 (1701) $580

Christmas card, [15 Dec 1983]. Including facsimile signature. With autograph envelope. wa Oct 19 (307) $110

Group photograph, sgd, [21 Jan 1961]. 10 by 8 inches. Chief Justice Warren swearing in the members of President Kennedy's cabinet. Also sgd by Robert S. McNamara. Dar Apr 9 (255) $200

Photograph, sgd, [n.d.]. 4.75 by 6.75 inches. Dar Feb 13 (239) $150

O'Neill, Eugene, 1888-1953

Series of 3 Ls s, 16 Aug [19]41 to 1 Nov [19]46. 3 pp, 4to. To Joseph Shipley. Declining to contribute to a dictionary, commenting on his plays, etc. sg Feb 27 (147) $1,500

Ls, 21 May 1926. 2 pp, 4to. To Mr. Rumsey. Regarding negotiations to buy a house in Bermuda. CNY June 9 (162) $500

— 5 May 1927. 1 p, 4to. To Ruth Mason. Referring to his play Strange Interlude. Mtd. wd Dec 12 (330) $225

Check, accomplished & sgd, 7 Nov 1921. 7 by 2.75 inches. Dar Oct 10 (268) $500

Photograph, sgd, 1937. 8 by 10 inches. wd Dec 12 (329) $1,000

Onizuka, Ellison, 1946-86

ALs, 12 Dec 1978. 1 p, 8vo. To Ms. Tucker. Responding to questions on his interest in the space program. Dar Oct 10 (35) $350

Signature, [n.d.]. On philatelic cover, [cancelled 29 Dec 1990]. Dar Oct 10 (36) $140

Ono, Yoko. See: Lennon, John & Ono

Opper, Frederick Burr, 1857-1937

Original drawing, cartoon, in ink; sgd & dated 12 Jan 1923. 6.25 by 4 inches. Illus in cat. Dar Feb 13 (281) $110

Orff, Carl, 1895-1982

Autograph music, fragment of his musical drama Antigonae, 2d scene; [c.1949?]. 4 pp, folio. Full score. HH May 13 (2017) DM1,500

— Autograph music, fragment of his musical drama Die Bernauerin; [c.1947?]. 2 pp, folio; paginated 87 & 88. Full score. HH

May 13 (2018) DM1,000

Orlik, Emil, 1870-1932

ALs, [c.1902]. 2 pp, 8vo. To an unnamed Ed. Regretting being unable to accept a commission. star Mar 27 (935) DM480

— 1 Jan 1919. 1 p, 4to. To Frau Mainzer. Confirming payment for a port. HN June 26 (970) DM220

Orwell, George, 1903-50

Series of 25 A Ls s, 14 Sept [1911] to 17 Nov 1912. 58 pp, 8vo. To his mother Ida Blair. Reporting from boarding-school. C Dec 16 (317) £5,500 [Wilson]

Orwell, George, 1903-50 —& Blair, Ida Muriel, 1875-1943

[2 autograph Mss, 1 diary each by Orwell, 12 Sept 1947 to 24 Dec 1948, 59 pp, 4to, & by his mother Ida Blair, 1905, in 8vo Pocket Diary, with related material, sold at C on 16 Dec 1991, lot 318, for £2,500 to University College London.]

Osler, Sir William, 1849-1919

ALs, [n.d.], "Tuesday". 1 p, 12mo. To Mrs. Randall. Hoping that a voyage will "help in the convalescence." wa Oct 19 (137) $500

Ls, 21 Apr 1915. 1 p, 8vo. To [Dr. Henry Hun]. Thanking for the 2d Ed of his book. Dar Apr 9 (306) $750

Cut signature, [n.d.]. Size not stated. Including brief autograph statement. Framed with a port. wa Dec 19 (256) $180

Oswald, Lee Harvey, 1939-63

ALs, [17 Dec 1956]. 1 p, 4to. To his brother Robert. Mentioning a sharpshooting contest at the U.S. Marine camp. Illus in cat. Dar June 11 (28) $8,000

— [6 June 1959]. 1 p, 8vo. To his brother Robert. Looking forward to leaving the Marines. Dar June 11 (30) $5,000

— [11 Dec 1959]. 1 p, 8vo. To his brother Robert. Informing him that he is starting a new life in Russia. Illus in cat. Dar June 11 (34) $14,000

— 20 Dec [1961]. 1 p, 8vo. To his mother. Thanking for books & sending his new address. Illus in cat. Dar June 11 (37) $5,500

— [17 Feb 1962]. 2 pp, 8vo. To his brother Robert. About the birth of his daughter & the release of Francis Gary Powers. Illus in cat. Dar June 11 (39) $6,500

— 17 Nov [1962]. 1 p, 8vo. To his brother Robert. Accepting an invitation for Thanksgiving. Illus in cat. Dar June 11 (42) $5,000

— 15 Mar [1963]. 2 pp, 8vo. To his brother Robert. About recipient's move to Arkansas, his own job situation, etc. Illus in cat. Dar June 11 (45) $5,500

Autograph postcard, sgd, [10 Oct 1962]. To his brother Robert. Sending his new address. Illus in cat. Dar June 11 (41) $6,500

— 10 Jan [1963]. To his brother Robert. Thanking for a Christmas present. Dar June 11 (44) $4,500

Ds, 3 Sept 1959. 1 p, 4to. Orders given to Oswald by the Marines in preparation for his release; sgd in receipt. With related material. Dar June 11 (32) $9,000

Autograph sentiment, sgd, 25 May 1955. In a school autograph book. 4 lines of doggerel verse. sup Oct 15 (1702) $4,200

— Oswald, Marina. - Ls, 28 July 1961. 1 p, 8vo. To Robert & Vada Oswald. Thanking for a present. Text in her husband's hand. Dar June 11 (36) $5,000

Otis, James, 1725-83

ALs, 27 July 1769. 8 pp, 4to. To Catharine Macaulay. Praising her work & commenting on the state of affairs in America. pn June 11 (15) £3,400

ANs, 12 Oct 1764. 1 p, 8vo. To B. & E. Davis. Concerning an account of sales of goods. On verso of a Ls by his father. sup Oct 15 (1454) $200

ADs, 1769. 2 pp, 4to. Order to the sherriff to attach goods. Also sgd by others. Dar Aug 6 (44) $120

Ott, Melvin Thomas, 1909-58

Signature, [n.d.]. 4.25 by 5.12 inches. In green ink. Dar Feb 13 (88) $130

— Anr, [n.d.]. Size not stated. Mtd with a port. sup July 10 (992) $150

Otto II, Herzog von Braunschweig-Lueneburg, 1528-1603

Ls, 5 Jan 1599. 1 p, folio. To the magistrate of Braunschweig. Introducing a messenger. HN Nov 28 (1801a) DM700

Ouimet, Francis Desales, 1893-1967

[A card honoring outstanding golfers, filled out & sgd by Ouimet, [n.d.], 5 by 3 inches, sold at Dar on 13 Feb 1992, lot 190, for $500.]

Our Gang

Typescript, orig MGM script for an episode entitled Gang Insurance (released as Cousin Wilbur), 2 Mar 1939. 36 leaves, 4to, in yellow wraps. Working copy of the character Porky. With photograph, sgd, of Gordon "Porky" Lee, 4to. wa Oct 19 (118) $160

Outcault, Richard Felton, 1863-1928

Original drawing, watercolor of a girl in white dress, sgd & inscr; [n.d.]. Mtd, 6.5 by 6.5 inches. Def. Dar June 11 (305) $190

Oxenstierna, Johan, Count, 1611-57

Ls, 7/17 Oct 1644. 2 pp, folio. To Georg Friedrich Graf zu Castell. Sending copies of papers relating to the peace negotiations in Westfalia. HN Nov 28 (1802) DM880

P

Pacini, Giovanni, 1796-1867

Autograph music, cantata, La felicita di Lario, [c.1816]. 220 pp, folio, in contemp marbled bds. Working Ms of the full score. S Dec 6 (150) £2,800 [Macnutt]

See also: Bellini, Vincenzo

Paderewski, Ignace Jan, 1860-1941

ALs, 23 Feb 1898. 1 p, 8vo. To [Friedrich] Rehberg. Thanking for a "gracieuse demarche". star Mar 27 (1110) DM380

Photograph, sgd & inscr, [n.d.]. Cabinet size. By Elliott & Fry. Dar Oct 10 (270) $375

— Anr, [n.d.]. 10.25 by 7 inches (image). Inscr to Madeline [Mason] on mount. sg Sept 12 (187) $300

Paganini, Nicolo, 1782-1840

Ms, Capricci per Violino, [n.d.]. 7 pp, 4to. 5 pieces; in a scribal hand, with autograph tp. S Dec 6 (155) £750 [Haas]

Ls, 6 Feb 1828. 1 p, 4to. To Gaetano Ciandelli. Regarding recipient's search for a new job. Framed with a port. Illus in cat. P June 17 (63) $2,750

— 5 Apr 1829. 1 p, 4to. To Herr Brueggemann. Regarding arrangements for concerts at Magdeburg. star Mar 27 (1111) DM2,400

Paige, Satchel, 1906-82

Signature, [12 June 1979]. On philatelic envelope. Dar June 11 (89) $110

— Anr, [n.d.]. On Hall of Fame card, 5.5 by 3.5 inches. Dar Apr 9 (107) $160

Paine, Thomas, 1737-1809

ALs, 30 Oct 1777. 1 p, folio. To Timothy Matlack. Providing information on Burgoyne's surrender & conditions at Gen. Greene's headquarters. Framed with a port. P June 16 (259) $26,000

— [28 Dec 1797]. 1 p, 4to. To "Citizen President". Transmitting reports respecting the state of affairs in England. Endorsed by Barras. Including French trans in a scribal hand. Illus in cat. Spiro collection. CNY May 14 (126) $24,000

— 20 Nov 1803. 1 p, 4to. To Anthony Taylor. About the death of Mr. Kirkbridge & riots at Trenton. With engraved port. Illus in cat. sup Oct 15 (1455) $12,000

— 20 June [n.y.]. 2 pp, 4to. To John Hall. Regarding the completion of a painting project. Framed with a port. Illus in cat. P June 16 (260) $9,500

Paisiello, Giovanni, 1740-1816

Ls, 3 Apr 1812. 1 p, folio. To the Minister of the Interior. Informing him that the painter Mattioli has continued work on a painting. star Mar 27 (1113) DM850

Palmerston, Henry John Temple, 3d Viscount, 1784-1865

ALs, 8 Dec 1842. 4 pp, 8vo. To Lord Auckland. Giving his views on the behavior of Lord Ellenborough. pn Nov 14 (166) £60

— 4 May [n.y.]. 2 pp, 8vo. To an unnamed count. Asking him to convey an invitation to Prince Oscar of Sweden. HN Nov 28 (1803) DM420

Papen, Franz von, 1879-1969

Typescript, responding to questions on the Nuremberg War Trials, sgd P; 28 July [1956]. On Ls addressed to him by George Sylvester Viereck, 23 July 1956, 1 p, 4to. R Nov 9 (61) $320

Parker, Ely Samuel, 1828-95

ALs, 27 May 1863. 1 p, 4to. To Lieut. Col. J. R. Smith. About "getting into the Regular Army." sup Oct 15 (1456) $275

Parrish, Maxfield, 1870-1966

ALs, 1 Mar 1904. 1 p, 4to. To R. H. Paget. Sending some writing about himself (not included). Dar Apr 9 (307) $325

Pasternak, Boris, 1890-1960

Typescript carbon copy, Poems from Novels in Prose, comprising 10 of his Zhivago poems, 15 May 1948. 20 pp, 8vo, in limp bds. Inscr to Olga Petrovska on flyleaf. S Dec 5 (554) £1,200 [Mandl]

Collection of 3 A Ls s & photograph, sgd & inscr, 24 Sept to 2 Oct 1959. 7 pp, folio. To Karl Pawek. Responding to a circular letter requesting a definition of man ("What is man?"). In German. star Mar 26 (384) DM6,000

ALs, 5 Sept 1941. 4 pp, 4to. To Boris Livanov. Discussing a forthcoming production of Hamlet, & giving an account of his life & work. Illus in cat. S Dec 5 (547) £5,000 [Fox Glove]

— 23 Apr 1945. 5 pp, folio. To John Gielgud. Draft of a joint letter by Pasternak & Boris Livanov, praising recipient's portrayal of Hamlet. S Dec 5 (548) £1,100 [Mandl]

— 7 Feb 1960. 2 pp, 4to. To Basil Ashmore. Informing him that his new play is at least half a year from completion. sup Oct 15 (1457) $1,200

— 24 Feb 1960. 1 p, folio. To Blanche Wagstaff. Doubting that her poem would be ptd in a Russian trans. CNY June 9 (163) $600

Photograph, sgd & inscr, 11 Apr 1949. Postcard. Inscr with ANs to Evgenia Livanov, on verso. Illus in cat. S Dec 5 (550) £800 [Mandl]

Pasteur, Louis, 1822-95

ALs, 17 Nov 1879. 2 pp, 8vo. Recipient unnamed. Discussing the spreading of anthrax. CNY Dec 5 (101) $2,800

Ls, 24 Dec 1892. 2 pp, 4to. To Friedrich Due. Thanking for the notification that he has been awarded a Swedish decoration. star Mar 26 (765) DM950

Patterson, Robert, 1792-1881

Signature, on ptd Orders No 19, 22 June 1848, bidding farewell to his troops. rf Sept 21 (36) $80

Patton, George S., 1885-1945

ALs, 17 July 1910. 4 pp, 4to. To his father. About family matters & life at the base. Illus in cat. sup Oct 15 (1458) $3,000

— 29 July 1916. 2 pp, 4to. To "Aunt Nonnie". Reporting about his activities with the army in Mexico. sup May 9 (487) $3,200

Ds, [c.3 July 1920]. 1 p, 4to. Promotion of William F. Fiederlien to Corporal in the Tank Corps. Framed with a port. Illus in cat. sup Oct 15 (1459) $2,600

Signature, [31 Mar 1944]. Censorship signature on envelope addressed to Suzanne Miner. With related material. Dar Dec 26 (274) $850

Paul, Bruno, 1874-1968

ALs, 9 Apr 1933. 4 pp, 4to. To the collaborators of the magazine Simplizissimus. Discussing changes after Hitler's seizure of power. HH May 13 (2022) DM1,000

Paul I, Emperor of Russia, 1754-1801

Ls, 30 Jan 1797. 3 pp, folio. To an unnamed German prince. Informing him of the appointment of Count Gustav Stakelberg as envoy to Frankfurt. star Mar 27 (1683) DM360

— 12 Aug 1800. 1 p, 4to. To the Landgrave of Hessen-Darmstadt. Expressing congratulations on the marriage of his daughter. Inlaid. sg Sept 12 (188) $400

Paul II, Pope, 1417-71

Document, 4 [June?] 1465. 1 p, folio. Letter of indulgence for the church of St. Margaretha at Heidenreich. HN June 26 (971) DM560

Paul VI, Pope, 1897-1978

Ds, [n.d.]. 2 pp, folio. As Pope, contents not stated. sup Oct 15 (1467) $360

Pavlov, Ivan Petrovich, 1849-1936

Photograph, sgd & inscr, 1928. 85mm by 58mm (image). Inscr to Ismar Boas on mount. Illus in cat. star Mar 26 (766) DM2,800

Pavlova, Anna, 1882-1931

Photograph, sgd & inscr, 20 May 1919. 278mm by 226mm. Inscr to Vincenzo Bellezza. S Dec 6 (157) £550 [Villa]

Payne, John Howard, 1791-1852

Autograph transcript, song, Home, Home! Sweet Home!, 6 Aug 1850. 1 p, 4to. 2 seven-line stanzas, sgd & inscr to Alice Stetson. Spiro collection. CNY May 14 (127) $11,000

Peabody, George, 1795-1869

Photograph, sgd, [n.d.]. Carte size. By Disderi. R Nov 9 (62) $200

Peary, Robert Edwin, 1856-1920

Photograph, sgd & inscr, 1909. 7 by 9 inches (image). By Benjamin Hampton. sup Oct 15 (1462) $550

Pechstein, Max, 1881-1955

ALs, 19 Mar 1921. 1 p, 4to. To [Wilhelm?] Geyer. Correcting an error in an account. HN Nov 28 (1804) DM320

Autograph postcards (2), sgd, [2 Sept 1919 & n.d.]. To Carl Steinbart. Expecting recipient's visit, & confirming receipt of a shipment. HN June 26 (972) DM230

Autograph postcard, sgd, [29 Apr 1911]. To R. Dietze. Sending regards. Including full-page drawing on verso in india ink & colored crayon. Illus in cat. star Mar 27 (937) DM14,000

Pemberton, Sir Max, 1863-1950

Autograph Ms, Love the Harvester. A Story of the days when George the Third was King; [c.1900]. 132 pp & blanks, 4to, in contemp mor. Early draft, initialled & inscr to T. J. B[arratt]. bba June 25 (143) £60 [Johnson]

Peninsular War

— ANDERSON, CAPT. ALEXANDER. - ALs, 24 Feb 1813. 4 pp, folio. To Sir William Wynn. Describing his life "wandering over the Peninsula" & a visit to King Joseph's villa. pn Nov 14 (136) £65 [Browning]

— DE LANCEY, COL. WILLIAM HOWE. - ALs, 5 Sept 1813. 1 p, 8vo. To Major Gen. Lord Aylmer. Conveying Sir Thomas Graham's orders regarding troop movements. pn Nov 14 (141) £75

— DUCKWORTH, LIEUT. COL. G. H. - ALs, 14 May 1810. 4 pp, 4to. To his father, Admiral

Sir John Duckworth. Giving news of French advances. pn Nov 14 (142) £85 [Browning]

— GORDON, LIEUT. STEPHEN. - ALs, [28 July 1813]. 3 pp, 4to. To J. W. Gordon. Preparing for Wellington's invasion of France. pn Nov 14 (143) £55 [Browning]

— HARE, CAPT. RICHARD G. - ALs, 27 July 1812. 2 pp, 4to. To his parents. Reporting about the battle of Salamanca. pn Nov 14 (144) £80 [Browning]

Penn, Thomas, 1702-75

Series of 51 A Ls s, 14 May 1754 to 8 Mar 1770. Over 100 pp, 4to. To William Smith. Regarding proprietary interests in Pennsylvania, affairs of the College of Philadelphia, etc. Some duplicates. With related material. P June 16 (180) $12,000

Penn, William, 1644-1718

ALs, 5 July 1699. 3 pp, folio. To Joseph Pike. Preparing for his trip to America & hinting at financial problems. Spiro collection. CNY May 14 (129) $7,000

Ds, 23 Mar 1681/82. 1 p, vellum, 577mm by 677mm. Sale of 5,000 acres of land in Pennsylvania to Robert Turner for £100. Also sgd by others. Spiro collection. CNY May 14 (128) $4,000

— 2 Mar 1684. 1 p, folio. Sale of land bordering on the Delaware River to Thomas Hudson. Framed with engraved port. Illus in cat. sup May 9 (393) $2,500

— 15 May 1684. 1 p, folio. Indenture to Richard Wall for land in Philadelphia County. Framed. P June 16 (261) $2,750

Pennock, Herbert J., 1894-1948

Signature, endorsement on verso of salary check, sgd by Jacob Ruppert & E. G. Barrow, 15 Sept 1927. 9 by 3.25 inches. Cancellation affecting signature. Dar Dec 26 (100) $1,000

Pepys, Samuel, 1633-1703

ALs, 3 Dec 1700. 4 pp, folio. To his nephew [John Jackson]. Draft, on personal & commercial matters. Sgd SP. Silked. sg Sept 12 (189) $1,500

— 4 Mar 1700/01. 1 p, folio. To John Jackson. Granting his request to return to Madrid. bba June 25 (131) £1,900 [Maggs]

See also: Charles II, 1630-85
See also: James II, 1633-1701

Perignon, Dominique C., Marquis de, 1754-1818

ALs, [21 Apr 1801]. 1 p, 4to. To Citizen Cotte. Promising to recommend the son of an associate. sg Feb 27 (149) $120

Peron, Juan Domingo, 1895-1974

Ls, 26 Apr 1963. 1 p, 4to. To Hans E. Schiener. Sending his autograph. Dar Apr 9 (308) $120

Peron, Maria Eva Duarte ("Evita"), 1919-52

Ls, 26 Apr 1949. 1 p, 4to. To Otto Ruhle. Thanking for some antibiotics. sg Sept 12 (190) $475

Perry, Matthew Calbraith, 1794-1858

ALs, 9 Jan 1846. 4 pp, folio. To Sec of the Navy George Bancroft. Responding to an inquiry "as to the propriety of an increase of steamers" in the Navy. Illus in cat. sup Oct 15 (1461) $2,000

Ls, 16 Mar 1844. 1 p, 4to. To Lieut. Commander T. T. Craven. Transmitting a copy of charges & sentence in the case of John Stewart (present). sg Sept 12 (191) $650

Ds, [29 Oct 1843]. 2 pp, folio. General Order no 8 regarding supplies for vessels of the African Squadron. sg Feb 27 (150) $375

— 19 Aug 1844. Length not stated. General Order no 17 addressed to commanding officers of vessels attached to the African Squadron, referring to the Texas question. R Nov 9 (63) $1,700

Perry, Oliver H., 1785-1819

Ds, 22 July 1815. 1 p, 8vo. Approval, on receipt for naval pay. sg Sept 12 (192) $500

Perse, St. John, Pseud. of Alexis Saint-Leger Leger, 1887-1975

ALs, 25 Apr 1960. 2 pp, 4to. To his pbr. Announcing 2 Mss. star Mar 26 (433) DM320

Pershing, John J., 1860-1948

Transcript, excerpt from radio address of 4 Aug 1940, [n.d.]. 1 p, 12mo (card). Sgd. Dar Oct 10 (271) $225

Autograph sentiment, 13 Sept 1924. 1 p, 8vo. Testimony to Lieut. Gen. Robert L. Bullard. sup Oct 15 (1463) $250

Persian Manuscripts

Ms, Anthology. [Herat, c.1550-60]. 44 leaves only, 238mm by 160mm. 18th-cent black shagreen bdg. In 2 columns of nasta'liq script by Shah Mahmud Nishapuri. With headings in white within illuminated panels, illuminated headpiece preceded by illuminated shamsa, & 19th-cent ink drawing. S Apr 30 (345) £1,200

— Ms, Schahnama. [Persia, A.H.1121/ A.D.1709]. 276 leaves, 323mm by 205mm. Contemp dark brown lea bdg. In nasta'liq script. With illuminated headpiece & 6 large miniatures in gold & colors. HH Nov 5 (863) DM1,900

— ALLAH-YAR IBN ALLAH-QULI AL-BUKHARI. - Maslak al Muttaquin. [A.H.1232/

A.D.1816]. 243 leaves (25 blank), 254mm by 147mm. Repaired blindstamped half lea bdg. In nasta'liq script by Mitza Sayyid Ahmed Khoquandi. With illuminated headpiece. FD June 1 (24) DM1,010

— AMIR KHUSRAU DIHLAVI. DIVAN. [PERSIA OR TURKEY, C.1500]. 321 LEAVES, 212MM BY 126MM. 19TH-CENT INDIAN BROWN MOR BDG. IN NASTA'LIQ SCRIPT BY MUHAMMAD BIN MUHAMMAD NAFAL. WITH SEAL IMPRESSION OF SULTAN BAYAZID II. S Apr 30 (351) £1,400

— NIVAI. - Divan. [Tabriz, c.1540]. 194 leaves, 267mm by 166mm. 19th-cent brown mor tooled in blind. In nasta'liq script by Halabi al-Qani. With double page of illumination & 6 miniatures. S Apr 30 (350) £1,400

— NIZAMI. - Khamsa. [Shiraz, A.H.928/A.D.1521]. 392 leaves (some lacking), 315mm by 175mm. Repaired black mor bdg. In 4 columns of nast'liq script by Murshid al-Katib known as Attar. With 5 illuminated headpieces & 16 miniatures. S Apr 30 (353) £5,000

— NIZAMI. - Khusrau u Shirin. [Afghanistan or Kashmir?, 18th cent]. 133 leaves, 202mm by 113mm. 19th-cent limp lea bdg. In 2 columns of nasta'liq script, with diagonal glosses in margins. With 3-quarter borders & vignettes throughout, 7 miniatures in gold & colors, & double page of illumination. HH Nov 5 (886) DM4,400

— NIZAMI. - Khusrau va Shirin. [Provincial Persia or India, A.H.985/A.D.1577]. 46 leaves, 280mm by 193mm. Brown mor bdg with gilt lea onlay. In 4 columns of nasta'liq script. With illuminated headpiece & 3 miniatures. S Apr 30 (346) £500

— NIZAMI. - Layla va Majnun, & Haft Paykar. [Isfahan, A.H.1007/A.D.1598]. 85 leaves, 295mm by 199mm. Def red mor bdg. In 4 columns of nast'liq script by Muhammad Jan al-Kermani. With 2 illuminated headpieces & 5 miniatures. S Apr 30 (347) £600

— RUMI. - Mathnavi. [Qajar, A.H.1264/A.D.1847]. 277 leaves, 292mm by 180mm. Black shagreen bdg with lea onlay. In 4 columns of nasta'liq script. With 2 illuminated headpieces. S Apr 30 (357) £400

— SA'DI. - Khusrau va Shirin. [Qajar, 19th cent]. 69 leaves, 286mm by 190mm. Green mor bdg with stamped central medallions. In nasta'liq script. With illuminated headpiece & 11 miniatures. S Apr 30 (358) £300

Perutz, Max Ferdinand

Autograph Ms, article, Rothschild + the MRC, [n.d.]. 6 pp, 4to, on rectos only. star Mar 26 (767) DM420

Pestalozzi, Johann Heinrich, 1746-1827

ALs, 7 Oct 1803. 3 pp, 4to. To Wilhelm von Klewitz. About Joseph Jeziorowski's inspection of his school, & explaining the advantages of his methodological approach. star Mar 26 (769) DM9,000

Peter Friedrich Ludwig, Herzog von Oldenburg, 1755-1829

A Ls s (2), 11 Dec 1785 & 15 Mar 1787. 8 pp, 4to. To Frau von Ompteda. About the death of his wife & taxes for purposes of social security. star Mar 27 (1525) DM360

Peter I, Emperor of Russia, 1672-1725

Ls, 15/26 June 1716. 1 p, folio. To Landgraf Karl von Hessen-Kassel. Acknowledging the mission of recipient's envoy Friedrich von Kettler. Countersgd by Count Golovkin. With German trans. star Mar 27 (1680) DM3,700

Ds, 10 May 1723. 1 p, 8vo. Order to pay Gen. Golitsin's salary. Framed with a port. P June 17 (64) $2,750

Peter II, Emperor of Russia, 1715-1730

Ls, 29 Nov 1728. 2 pp, folio. To Landgraf Karl von Hessen-Kassel. Notifying him of the death of his sister. Countersgd by Count Golovkin. With German trans. star Mar 27 (1681) DM3,600

Petermann, August, 1822-78

ALs, 15 Apr 1867. 2 pp, 8vo. Recipient unnamed. Regarding Karl Mauch's exploration of Central Africa. star Mar 26 (770) DM220

Peters, Carl, 1856-1918

ALs, 23 Nov 1891. 8 pp, 8vo. To an unnamed colonial official. Discussing German politics & military actions in Southeast Africa. star Mar 27 (1558) DM1,100

Petrarca, Francesco, 1304-74

Ms, I Trionfi. [Florence?, early 16th cent]. 42 leaves & 2 flyleaves, vellum, 250mm by 140mm. Late 19th-cent French red mor gilt by Trautz-Bauzonnet. In a very fine slightly sloping italic cursive minuscule. With 6 large illuminated initials with full borders in architectural & classical trompe l'oeil designs. S June 23 (75) £90,000 [Schiller]

Pettenkofer, Max von, 1818-1901

ALs, 21 June 1869. 1 p, 8vo. To the publishing house Vieweg & Son. Expressing interest in a new journal. star Mar 26 (771) DM400

— 9 Nov 1877. 1 p, 8vo. To Herr Duerck. Returning a book. HH May 13 (2023) DM200

Pfeffel, Gottlieb Konrad, 1736-1809

Ls, 1 Feb 1775. 1 p, 4to. Recipient unnamed. Forwarding a package. In the hand of his wife. star Mar 26 (387) DM360

Ds, 8 Oct 1779. 1 p, 4to. Receipt for expenses of his student Karl von Wartensleben. In French. star Mar 26 (388) DM280

Pfitzner, Hans, 1869-1949

Collection of 2 A Ls s, Ls, 2 autograph postcards, sgd, & photograph, 13 July 1913 to [18 Feb 1949]. 6 pp, various sizes. To Wolfgang Geist. Personal news. star Mar 27 (1115) DM750

ALs, 19 Sept 1897. 3 pp, 8vo. To [Emil Steinbach]. About a recent performance of one of his works & a new project. star Mar 27 (1114) DM700

Philadelphia

Ms, property tax record book for Philadelphia & its environs, 1774 & 1775. 236 leaves (4 lacking), folio, in rebacked contemp marbled bds. P June 16 (263) $2,750

Philip, Prince, Duke of Edinburgh. See: Elizabeth II & Philip

Philip II, King of Spain, 1527-98

Ls, 22 Mar 1555. 1 p, folio. To the Duke of Alba. Supporting the claim of Luis de Gayano for an increase in salary. S Dec 5 (557) £700 [Maggs]

— 15 Jan 1580. 1 p, folio. To the Conde del Villar. Announcing his intention to unite the crowns of Spain & Portugal. With retained copy of Villar's reply. S May 28 (58) £2,200 [Sawyer]

— Council of War. - Ms, minute book of the Spanish Council of War, 25 Oct 1560 to Dec 1567. About 340 pp, folio, in vellum wraps. In a variety of scribal hands. S May 28 (65) £4,500 [Maggs]

Philipp Wilhelm, Kurfuerst von der Pfalz, 1615-90

Ls s (2), 27 Dec 1677 & 5 Feb 1678. 2 pp, folio. To Francesco Alberti di Poja, Bishop of Trient. Acknowledging New Year's wishes, & thanking for the bestowal of a prebend on his son. star Mar 27 (1567) DM380

Piccard, Jean Felix, 1884-1963

Signature, [Oct 1934]. On an airmail cover carried by balloon; also sgd by his wife Jeannette. Illus in cat. sg Feb 27 (20) $325

Piccolo, Brian, 1943-70

Signature, [n.d.]. 12mo (ptd collector's card). Dar Dec 26 (185) $600

Piccolomini, Enea Silvio, 1405-64. See: Aeneas Sylvius Piccolomini, 1405-64

Piccolomini, Ottavio, 1599-1656

ALs, 11 May 1647. 2 pp, folio. Recipient unnamed. Requesting repayment of a debt. star Mar 27 (1571) DM1,700

Ls, 18 Nov 1638. 2 pp, folio. To Luther von Boenninghausen. Giving instructions regarding winter quarters & further recruiting for his army. star Mar 27 (1570) DM860

— 14 Dec 1648. 1 p, 4to. Recipients unnamed. Informing them about the occupation of the castles at Wettau & Frain. HN Nov 28 (1806) DM1,300

Pickering, Timothy, 1745-1829

ALs, 17 Jan 1800. 2 pp, 4to. To William Eaton. Giving instructions regarding demands for tribute by the Bey of Tunis. Partly in cipher. Illus in cat. CNY June 9 (267) $1,500

— 19 Mar 1800. 1 p, 4to. To George Latimer. Informing him that the ship Benjamin Franklin will be permitted to leave for France with passengers. Dar June 11 (306) $100

— 17 Dec 1810. 2 pp, 4to. To James McHenry. Expressing his conviction that the United States have no legal title to West Florida, & sending related documents. Including franking signature. Tipped onto autograph transcript by Pickering of a letter addressed to him by G. Duval. Spiro collection. CNY May 14 (130) $3,500

— 28 Feb 1828. 3 pp, folio. To Col. Robert Troup. Thanking for details on the Conway Cabal & commenting on Washington & other statesmen he has known. Spiro collection. CNY May 14 (131) $7,000

Franking signature, [before 9 May 1798]. 1 p, 12 by 15 inches. On verso of ptd broadside of proclamation by President John Adams, establishing a day of fasting & prayer. sup Oct 15 (1480) $480

Pierce, Franklin, 1804-69

ALs, 17 Jan 1834. 4 pp, 4to. To an unnamed cousin. Family letter, & reporting about his schedule in Washington. Including franking signature. sup May 9 (191) $1,550

— 25 Apr 1842. 1 p, folio. Recipient unnamed. Reporting about a trial. Spiro collection. CNY May 14 (133) $500

— 14 Apr 1847. 1 p, 4to. To St. George Bowns. Sending new recruits. Dar June 11 (307) $800

— 12 Apr 1856. 2 pp, 4to. To his brother H. D. Pierce. Urging him not to postpone his visit to Washington. CNY June 9 (268) $2,200

— 18 Sept 1869. 2 pp, 8vo. To Fitz-John Porter. Commenting on recipient's court martial. Illus in cat. sup May 9 (192) $1,900

Ds, 25 Mar 1853. 1 p, folio. Appointment of John L. Smith as Justice of the Peace.

Framed. Dar Oct 10 (273) $350
— 7 Apr 1855. 1 p, 4to. Order to affix the US Seal to a treaty with the Cherokee Indians. Illus in cat. sup Oct 15 (1518) $1,450
— 11 July 1856. 1 p, folio. Commission of Louis H. Pelouze as Lieut. of Artillery. Countersgd by Jefferson Davis. Framed. Illus in cat. sup Oct 15 (1519) $1,100

Franking signature, [16 Jan 1857]. On fragment of an autograph envelope to T. H. Herbert. Dar June 11 (308) $250

Pietsch, Ludwig, 1824-1911

Series of 6 A Ls s, 1868 & 1869. 7 pp, 8vo. To an Ed at the Vossische Zeitung. Concerning contributions. star Mar 27 (938) DM1,300

Pinto, Francisco Antonio, 1785-1858

Collection of ALs & Ls, 16 & 29 May 1823. 5 pp, folio. To Jose Ignacio Zenteno. Concerning troops to serve in Peru. HN Nov 28 (1807) DM640

Piozzi, Hester Lynch Thrale, 1741-1821

Signature, [1778]. 32mo. Including address. Visiting card left with David Garrick. pn Mar 19 (62) £220

Pirogov, Nikolai Ivanovich, 1810-81

ALs, 4 Dec 1865. 10 pp, 8vo. Recipient unnamed. Discussing the importance of Russian & other languages for the reception of scholarship. star Mar 26 (773) DM680

Pissarro, Camille, 1830-1903

ALs, 6 Aug 1894. 3 pp, 8vo. To his wife Julie. Worrying about the health of the family. Illus in cat. sup Oct 15 (1465) $1,750
— 25 May [18]97. 2 pp, 16mo. To Julie. About family matters. With a photograph. sg Sept 12 (193) $600
— 15 July 1897. 2 pp, 8vo. To an unnamed doctor. Saying he wants to bring his son for a consultation. bba Sept 19 (363) £380 [Shapero]

Pitt, William, 1759-1806

ALs, [n.d.], "Wednesday". 2 pp, 4to. Recipient unnamed. Informing him about a threat of revolution. pn Nov 14 (205) £160

Pius II, Pope, 1405-64. See: Aeneas Sylvius Piccolomini, 1405-64

Pius IX, Pope, 1792-1878

ALs, 12 Sept 1827. 2 pp, 4to. To Luigi Filippani. As Archbishop of Spoleto, referring to the archives of a monastery. hen Nov 12 (2500) DM300

Document, 17 Mar 1848. 1 p, folio. Papal Brief addressed to the Archbishop of Torino, granting permission for Octavio Thaon de Revel to have Mass read at his house. star Mar 27 (1549) DM280

Pius VII, Pope, 1742-1823

Ls, 14 Nov 1790. 1 p, 4to. To Alfonso Bonfilioli Malvezzi. Expressing thanks. Dar Feb 13 (269) $170

Endorsement, sgd, 15 Nov 1809. 1 p, folio, on address leaf of a petition addressed to him by the Lomellini Family; granting privileges to the family chapel. star Mar 27 (1547) DM650

Pius X, Pope, 1835-1914

Autograph endorsement, sgd, 21 Feb 1910. 1 p, folio. Decision at foot of a petition by Anna Villar de Blancas for permission to have Mass read at her own house. star Mar 27 (1551) DM1,250

Pius XI, Pope, 1857-1939

ALs, 18 Nov 1915. 2 pp, 8vo. To an unnamed lady. Expressing condolences. star Mar 27 (1552) DM900

Photograph, sgd, 16 Apr 1924. 4 by 5.5 inches. Inscr to J. M. Gershberg in anr hand. Mtd. Dar Apr 9 (309) $300

Photograph, sgd & inscr, [n.d.]. 335mm by 185mm (including mount). Inscr to Alfredo Caprile & the Accion Catolica Argentina, with apostolic benediction. star Mar 27 (1553) DM900

Pius XII, Pope, 1876-1958

Ls, 20 Jan 1939. 1 p, 4to. To Truman Talley. As Cardinal, conveying the Pope's appreciation of a film on the funeral of Cardinal Hayes. Illus in cat. sup Oct 15 (1468) $450

Document, 15 Mar 1958. 1 p, folio. Bull granting income from the parish of San Maurizio in the diocese of Casale to Hugo Garoglio. star Mar 27 (1554) DM450

Planck, Max, 1858-1947

A Ls s (2), 1 July 1914 & 12 July 1919. 3 pp, 4to & 8vo. To [Max Friedlaender]. Discussing music to be played at an academic ceremony, & inquiring about teachers at a conservatory. star Mar 26 (775) DM2,200

ALs, 4 Dec 1886. 4 pp, 8vo. To Max Rubner. About his forthcoming marriage to Marie Merck. With related material. star Mar 26 (774) DM1,700
— 1 Jan 1911. 1 p, 8vo. To F. S. Archenhold. Advising against the ptg of an article by Prof. Rudolph, & declining to give a lecture about the theory of relativity. hen Nov 12 (2546) DM950
— 5 July 1926. 1 p, 4to. To [Conrad Cichorius]. Accepting an invitation. star Mar 26 (776) DM680

Platen, August, Graf von, 1796-1835

Autograph Ms, 3 poems, An einen Ultra, 9 stanzas; Luca Signorelli, 11 stanzas; & Zobir, 17 stanzas; [n.d.]. 4 pp, folio. star Mar 26 (389) DM2,400

ALs, 27 [Aug 1827]. 1 p, 4to. To August Kopisch. Requesting his help in a financial matter & in procuring a book. star Mar 26 (390) DM1,200

— 19 Oct 1828. 2 pp, 4to. To Conrad Schwenck. Wondering if Cotta will publish his Oedipus with the references to Heine. Gottschalk collection. C Dec 16 (412) £1,100 [Rosenthal]

Pleasonton, Alfred, 1824-97

Telegram, 8 June 1863. 1 p, 8vo. To Gen. Alpheus S. Williams. Informing him of an impending cavalry attack. Illus in cat. Armstrong collection. sup Oct 15 (1122) $775

Plekhanov, Georgy Valentinovich, 1856-1918

Collection of ALs & autograph postcard, sgd, 8 June 1910 & 18 June 1916. 4 pp, 8vo, & card. To Alexander Amfiteatrov. Promising to send books. star Mar 27 (1573) DM400

Poe, Edgar Allan, 1809-49

Autograph Ms, poem, Spiritual Song. 4 lines including title. Written on verso of anonymus submission to the Southern Literary Messenger [William Maxwell's Sacred Song, which was ptd in the August, 1836 issue]. Unsgd. Illus in catalogue. Z Oct 26 (206) $12,500

ALs, 6 Nov 1840. 1 p, 8vo. Recipient unnamed. Responding to a request for a transcription of a sonnet (below, To Zante). Sgd EAP. Illus in cat. sup May 9 (59) $36,000

— 9 Aug 1845. 1 p, 4to. To Thomas W. Field. Responding to a request for an interview. Repaired. Illus in cat. sup May 9 (60) $15,000

Cut signature, [n.d.]. 4 by 1 inches. Including subscription. In extra frame with engraved port. Dar Aug 6 (225) $4,750

— Fisher, E. Burke. - ALs, 10 June 1839. 2 pp, 4to. To Poe. Inviting him to contribute to The Pittsburgh Literary Examiner. Docketed & annotated in Poe's hand. Illus in cat. sg Feb 27 (154) $1,000

Polk, James K., 1795-1849

ALs, 11 Jan 1835. 1 p, 4to. Recipient unnamed. Regarding a "note from one of your subscribers in Tennessee". Silked. wa Oct 19 (327) $700

— 18 July 1836. 2 pp, 4to. To John W. Childress. Describing his travel plans. Illus in cat. sup Oct 15 (1511) $3,000

— 24 Apr 1838. 1 p, 8vo. To Sec of the Treasury Levi Woodbury. Supporting the application of R. I Powell for a clerkship. Margin def. Dar Dec 26 (275) $1,000

— 18 July 1844. 2 pp, 4to. To Gov. William C. Bouck. Declining an invitation to visit NY. Framed with a port. Illus in cat. P June 16 (264) $4,500

— 8 Apr 1847. 1 p, 4to. Recipient unnamed. Letter of introduction for Henry M. Field. Silked. Illus in cat. sup May 9 (188) $2,500

— 26 Feb 1849. 2 pp, 4to. To J. L. Hutchinson. Accepting an invitation to stop at Charleston on his way to Nashville. P Dec 12 (133) $3,500

Ds, 17 Feb 1840. 1 p, 4to. As Governor of Tennessee, approval of the erection of 2 toll gates near Franklin. Illus in cat. sup May 9 (189) $1,150

— [c.1849]. 1 p, folio. Ship's papers; unaccomplished. Countersgd by James Buchanan. CNY Dec 5 (102) $1,000

Cut signature, [1845-49]. 2 by 9.75 inches. Cut from a document; countersgd by Sec of State James Buchanan. sg Sept 12 (194) $500

Pomare IV, Queen of Tahiti, 1813-77

Ls, 31 Mar 1843. 1 p, folio. To a British commodore. Requesting the release of Charles Wilson. rf Sept 21 (18) $425

— 12 Feb 1845. 1 p, folio. To Gen. [William] Miller. Welcoming him at Tahiti. With contemp trans. rf Sept 21 (19) $425

Pontano, Giovanni, 1426-1503

Ms, De Principe. [Central Italy, c.1480-90]. 58 leaves & 2 flyleaves, vellum, 180mm by 110mm, in contemp blindstamped dark brown mor over thin wooden bds. In a fine rounded slightly clubbed humanist minuscule by Federico Veterano for Ambrogio Landriano. With illuminated opening page with large initial & 3-quarter border incorporating coat-of-arms. S Dec 17 (60) £7,000 [Giorgio]

Pope, Alexander, 1688-1744

ALs, [1735]. 1 p, 12mo. To Mr. Richardson. Announcing his visit. Dar Oct 10 (274) $1,400

Portal, Antoine de, 1742-1832

Autograph Ms, medical report, [13 Apr 1801]. 4 pp, 4to. Sgd. star Mar 26 (778) DM320

Porter, Cole, 1893-1964

Series of 23 A Ls s, Sept 1925 to Mar 1926. 50 pp, various sizes. To Boris Kochno. Expressing his feelings for Kochno, reporting about his travels, plans, friends, etc. SM Oct 12 (384) FF55,000

Collection of Ls & photograph, sgd, 2 Nov 1962. 1 p, 8vo, & size not stated. To Marshall. Sending his photograph (included). Framed. Illus in cat. wd Dec 12 (332) $775

Document, [n.d.]. 5 pp, folio. Contract for a French production of Anything Goes, sgd for Porter by Guy Bolton. Also sgd by others. wa Oct 19 (150) $55

Signature, [n.d.]. Framed with cover of sheet music for Kiss Me Kate, overall size 12 by 15 inches. Dar Apr 9 (310) $140

Porter, David Dixon, 1813-91

Ls, 18 Sept 1863. 1 p, 4to. To E. C. Williams. Declining a request for leave. Dar June 11 (309) $130

Porter, Fitz-John, 1822-1901

Group photograph, [n.d.]. Size not stated. With A. Lincoln & a group of generals in front of a tent. Sgd by Porter & inscr to Mrs. Eddy on verso. Post-Civil War silverprint from a Gardner negative. Illus in cat. R Mar 7 (217) $500

Photograph, sgd, [n.d.]. Carte size. Outdoors, with flag. Illus in cat. R June 13 (100) $650

Porter, Horace, 1837-1921

Ls, 12 July 1876. 2 pp, 4to. To George M. Pullman. Informing him about negotiations with Mr. Bishop concerning railway routes. Dar Aug 6 (132) $120

— 7 June 1878. 4 pp, 8 by 11 inches. To George M. Pullman. Reporting about the opening of the Metropolitan railway system in NY. Dar Aug 6 (241) $325

Porter, Peter Buell, 1773-1844

ALs, 15 Nov 1824. 1 p, 4to. Recipient unnamed. Reporting about the appointment of Presidential electors in NY. Dar Apr 9 (193) $800

Poulenc, Francis, 1899-1963

Autograph music, song, Nuage, to a text by Lawrence de Beylie, Sept 1956. 3 pp, 348mm by 268mm. Notated on 3 & 4 systems of 3 staves each; sgd 3 times & inscr to Rose [Dercourt-Plaut] twice. Illus in cat. P June 17 (305) $2,500

Collection of 6 A Ls s & AL, 1923 & later. 13 pp, various sizes. To Boris Kochno. About Diaghilev, his ballet Les Biches, etc. SM Oct 12 (387) FF12,000

— Collection of 3 A Ls s & 2 autograph postcards, sgd, Feb & Apr 1947 & [n.d.]. 8 pp, 8vo. To Christian Berard. About Les Mamelles de Tiresias & the Opera Comique. With autograph note of a scenario. Boris Kochno collection. SM Oct 12 (388) FF9,500

ALs, [autumn 1923]. 6 pp, 4to & 16mo. To Boris Kochno. About Stravinsky & the designs for Les Biches. Including list of designs for set & costumes. SM Oct 12 (389) FF9,500

— [c.1923/24]. 2 pp, 4to. To Boris Kochno. Discussing orchestration & choreography for the ballet Les Biches. SM Oct 12 (386) FF6,000

— 1 Jan [1941]. 2 pp, 8vo. To Nora Auric. Explaining how he had become affected by the occupation, & mentioning his incidental music to Anouilh's Leocardia. Sgd Fr. S May 29 (608) £500 [Van Lauwe]

Pound, Ezra, 1885-1972

ALs, [n.d]. 2 pp, 4to. Recipient unnamed. Brief cryptic message. Sgd EP. In pencil; framed. sg Sept 12 (197) $700

Collection of Ls & 4 letters, [1955-1956]. 9 pp, size not stated. To Ronald L. Perry. About a variety of political matters. With related material. S July 21 (166) £500 [Reuter]

Ls, 13 Sept [1935]. 2 pp, 4to. To "Dear Crate". About literary matters & the political ramifications of the assassination of Huey P. Long. Some holograph additions. sg Sept 12 (195) $900

— 14 Sept [1935]. 2 pp, 4to. To [Luther] Whiteman. About literary & political matters. Some holograph additions; sgd EP. sg Sept 12 (196) $900

Signature, [n.d.]. 8 by 4 inches. Dar Apr 9 (311) $110

Powell, Anthony

Collection of ALs, 3 Ls s, & 4 autograph postcards, sgd, 21 Oct 1970 to 12 Nov 1977. 9 pp, various sizes. To Dennis Wheatley & his wife (1). Discussing various vols in his A Dance to the Music of Time, sending condolences, etc. CNY June 9 (165) $380

Powell, Colin L.

Photograph, sgd, [n.d.]. 14 by 11 inches. Speaking before a microphone. Dar Apr 9 (312) $250

Power, Tyrone, 1914-58

Ls, 1 Apr 1944. 2 pp, 8vo. To Maynard. About his plans for movies after the war. Framed with a photograph. wd Dec 12 (333) $350

Pownall, Thomas, 1722-1805

Ds, 4 Feb 1760. 1 p, folio. Appointment of Stephen Miller as Lieut. Colonel. R June 13 (165) $450

Prayer Books

Ms, Bett-buch Worinnen Unterschiedliche schoenne gebetter Zu finden seind. [Upper Austria, 1765]. 119 pp, 158mm by 100mm. Contemp lea gilt. Including numerous small & 2 full-page drawings. HH May 12 (4) DM1,300

— Ms, in Latin & French. [Paris?, c.1700]. 96 leaves, vellum, 110mm by 65mm. Dark red mor gilt by Middleton, 1970. In a calligraphic roman hand, with 2 pp written in gold & 1 p on burnished gold background. With gold borders throughout, many 2-line initials in red, blue & gold, & 7 full-page miniatures. bba June 25 (122) £1,300 [Mazza]

— Ms, Morgen u. Abend Gebetter, bey dem Ambt der Heil: Meess... [Southern Germany or Austria, 1788]. 340 leaves, 161mm by 96mm. Contemp lea gilt. Including numerous small & 4 full-page drawings. HH May 12 (10) DM1,700

— Ms, passion prayerbook, in Dutch & Latin. [Northern Netherlands, Utrecht or Guelders?, late 15th cent]. 51 leaves, vellum, 140mm by 100mm. Contemp blindstamped fold-over bdg of calf lined with vellum. In a small gothic hybrid bookhand. With 32 large initials in a variety of styles, 30 full-page miniatures in gently arched compartments in soft colors & liquid gold, & full-page frontis with the arms of Adolphus, Duke of Guelders & his wife Catherine of Cleves. Illus in cat. S June 23 (82) £48,000 [Tenschert]

— Ms, prayerbook for a Bridgettine nun, in Latin & Middle English. [Syon Abbey, Middlesex, early 16th cent]. 136 leaves, vellum & 13 paper leaves, 154mm by 107mm. Modern quarter mor bdg incorporating sides of a 16th-cent Flemish panel-stamped bdg. In a magnificent calligraphic liturgical hand. With 2-line initials throughout in blue or red. S Dec 17 (64) £8,500 [Quaritch]

— Ms, prayers for use at Mass, in German. [Southern Germany, Regensburg?, early 16th cent]. 8 leaves only, 147mm by 113mm; stitched. In a flamboyant German gothic hybrida. With 5 large illuminated initials & 2 full-page miniatures with architectural borders, 1 based on a composition by Albrecht Altdorfer. S June 23 (87) £800 [Schwing]

— Ms, Prayers, with Psalms, etc, in Latin & German. [Germany, 15th cent] 209 leaves, on vellum, 8vo size, in 16th-cent calf over wooden bds, tooled in blind, with 1 remaining metal clasp. In a gothic script in red & black; with 4 crudely illuminated initials; other initials & capitals in red & blue; musical notation in a few margins. Leighton-Milne Ms Ck June 12 (139) £1,700

Prelog, Vladimir

Autograph Ms, notes taken from works on chemistry, beginning with Das optische Drehungsvermoegen, by H. Landolt; [n.d.]. 5 pp, 4to. Sgd at head. star Mar 26 (779) DM450

Preminger, Otto, 1906-86. See: Spoliansky, Mischa & Preminger

President of the United States

Group photograph, Presidents Reagan, Carter, Ford & Nixon in the White House, Oct 1981. 8 by 10 inches. Sgd by all 4. sg Feb 27 (155) $2,200

Presidents of the United States

[A complete set of Presidential autographs from Washington to Reagan, mostly A Ls s & Ls s, sold at sup on 15 Oct 1991, lot 1471, for $40,000.]

[A collection of 34 A Ls s, A Ds s & Ds s of 33 Presidents from Washington to Eisenhower, including duplicates of Garfield, Cleveland & F. D. Roosevelt & 2 others jointly sgd, framed, sold at CNY on 5 Dec 1991, lot 103, for $28,000.]

[The signatures of Presidents Nixon, Ford, Carter & Bush, [n.d.], on a card with an illus of the White House portico, 6.25 by 3.5, sold at Dar on 13 Feb 1992, lot 285, for $800.]

[A collection of Presidential signatures from Washington to Hoover, each mtd with engraved port, 4to, in red mor bdg, with signatures of Bess & Harry Truman & Ls by Eisenhower, sold at R on 13 June 1992, lot 195, for $14,000.]

[A set of 40 Presidential signatures from Washington to Bush, framed, with porcelain portraits, sold at sup on 9 May 1992, lot 310, for $17,300.]

Group photograph, Presidents Reagan, Carter, Ford & Nixon in the White House, with drink in hand, 8 Oct 1981. 10 by 8 inches. Sgd by all 4. Illus in cat. Dar Feb 13 (283) $2,500

— Anr, Presidents Reagan, Ford, Carter & Nixon in the White House, Oct 1981. 8 by 10 inches. Sgd by all 4. Dar Oct 10 (275) $1,600

— Anr, Presidents Reagan, Ford, Carter & Nixon in the White House, Oct 1981. 8 by 10 inches. Sgd by all 4. Dar Dec 26 (282) $1,400

— Anr, Presidents Reagan, Carter, Ford & Nixon in the White House, with Rosalynn Carter in background, [Oct 1981]. 10 by 8 inches. Sgd by all 4. Illus in cat. Dar Aug 6 (227) $2,500

— Anr, Presidents Reagan, Carter, Ford & Nixon in the White House, with glasses in their hands, [Oct 1981]. 10 by 8 inches. Sgd by all 4. Dar Aug 6 (228) $1,800

— Anr, Presidents Reagan, Carter, Ford & Nixon in the White House, Oct 1981. 8 by 10 inches. Sgd by all 4. sg Sept 12 (198) $1,100

— Anr, Presidents Reagan, Ford, Carter &

Nixon in the White House, Oct 1981. 9 by 13 inches. Sgd by all 4. Illus in cat. sup Oct 15 (1732) $2,400

— Anr, Presidents Reagan, Ford, Carter & Nixon in the White House, Oct 1981. 4to. Sgd by all 4. wa Oct 19 (315) $1,500

— Anr, Presidents Reagan, Nixon, Bush & Ford at the dedication of the Nixon Library, 9.5 by 7.5 inches. Sgd by Nixon, Bush & Ford, with autopen signature of Reagan. Illus in cat. Dar Apr 9 (315) $1,100

Presley, Elvis, 1935-77

Autograph Ms, excerpt from an essay on leadership by Theodore F. MacManus, written down from memory, [Dec 1976]. 1 p, 8vo, on hotel letterhead. With signature on postcard & related material. Dar Oct 10 (290) $1,100

— Autograph Ms, prayer, beginning "Lead me Lord to a higher Place...", [Dec 1976]. 1 p, 8vo, on hotel letterhead. Crumpled. Illus in cat. Dar Aug 6 (236) $3,750

ALs, [1959]. 3 pp, size not stated. To Janet. Personal letter written when stationed in Germany. Illus in cat. P Dec 17 (381A) $2,000

— [24 Jan 1961]. Size not stated. To a British fan. Thanking for a card. Framed with a photograph, overall size 23 by 22 inches. Illus in cat. P Dec 17 (375) $1,500

Ls, 18 Sept 1956. 1 p, 4to. To Special Projects, Inc. Carbon copy, threatening to sue unauthorized users & imitators of his name & style. Also sgd by Tom Parker. Dar Aug 6 (237) $1,100

— 26 Jan 1977. 1 p, 4to. To Lane. Responding to a child's request for advice about finding a job for his mother. Also sgd by Vernon Presley. Dar June 11 (315) $550

Concert program, sgd, 1961. Folies Bergere, Tropicana Hotel, Las Vegas. R Mar 7 (178) $220

— Anr, sgd, [n.d.]. Size not stated. Hank Snow souvenir photo program, also sgd by others. P Dec 17 (376) $500

Menu, [c.1975]. Las Vegas Hilton menu; inscr to Janet. Size not stated. P Dec 17 (374) $500

Photograph, sgd, [n.d.]. Postcard; sgd on verso. Dar June 11 (317) $400

— Anr, [n.d.]. 8 by 10 inches. sup Oct 15 (1778) $525

Photograph, sgd & inscr, [1967]. 3.5 by 5.5 inches. Inscr to Joy. Bearing ptd Season's Greetings. Illus in cat. Dar Aug 6 (238) $350

— Anr, [1973]. Postcard size; sgd on verso. Dar June 11 (316) $475

— Anr, [n.d.]. 8 by 10 inches. P Dec 17 (377) $300

Ptd photograph, sgd, [5 Dec 1975]. On magazine cover announcing his tour. Dar June 11 (318) $550

— Anr, [1975]. 4to. Las Vegas Hilton Tour Photo. Dar Feb 13 (295) $550

— Anr, sgd & inscr, [n.d.]. On front cover of his Souvenir Photo Album, 4to. wa Oct 19 (148) $425

Signature, [3 Dec 1976]. On a magazine advertising his performances at the Las Vegas Hilton, 20 pp, 4to. Dar Feb 13 (294) $350

— Anr, [n.d.]. On postcard of the marquee at the Las Vegas Hilton. Dar Feb 13 (292) $500

— Anr, [n.d.]. 3 by 1.25 inches (card). Mtd with 2 photographs. Dar Aug 6 (239) $425

Prevert, Jacques, 1900-77

Autograph Ms, scenario for the ballet Le Rendez-vous, 2 versions; [c.1945]. 6 pp, folio. Boris Kochno collection. SM Oct 12 (392) FF5,500

Processional

— [Syon Abbey, Middlesex, c.1460-80]. Of Bridgettine use. In Latin, with additions in Middle English. 117 leaves & 6 endleaves, vellum, 192mm by 125mm. Modern half brown mor bdg. In a gothic liturgical hand. With c.50 large calligraphic initials including 20 incorporating grotesque faces, & c.40 large blue initials with penwork in red extending up & down margins. S Dec 17 (63) £8,000 [Quaritch]

Procter, George H.

ALs, 24 Dec 1868. 1 p, 4to. To Francis B. Thurber. Suggesting a meeting to discuss a trip to Europe, etc. On Procter & Gamble letterhead. Dar Aug 6 (240) $1,600

Prokofiev, Sergei Sergeevich, 1891-1953

ALs, 14 May 1929. 1 p, 16mo. To Boris Kochno. About an interview to be given by Diaghilev. SM Oct 12 (391) FF6,500

Series of 4 autograph postcards, sgd, 15 Oct to 9 Nov 1909. To Aleksandr Borisovich Goldenweiser. Thanking for agreeing to play chess with him, & sending moves of a game. Illus in cat. S May 29 (609) £2,000 [Haas]

Photograph, sgd & inscr, 1930. 218mm by 164mm. Inscr to Alexander Smallens with a bar of music. Framed. P June 17 (67) $2,750

Proudhon, Pierre-Joseph, 1809-65

ALs, 1 Feb 1856. 1 p, 8vo. To [Hippolyte Tisserant]. Accepting the offer of a theater ticket. star Mar 27 (1633a) DM450

Prudhomme, Rene Francois Armand, 1839-1907. See: Sully Prudhomme, 1839-1907

Psalms & Psalters

Ms, in German, the Psalter of St. Bonaventura & other prayers. [Germany, late 15th cent]. 174 leaves (2 lacking), 151mm by 106mm. Contemp blindstamped calf over wooden bds with metal clasp & catch. In German cursive bookhands by more than one scribe. With headings & initials throughout in red. S June 23 (79) £1,520 [Fogg]

— Ms, in Latin, Psalter. [France, late 15th cent]. 128 leaves, vellum, 310mm by 200mm. Contemp calf tooled in blind. In a regular gothic liturgical hand, with music in square neums on a 4-line red stave. With very many 1- to 4-line initials in red & blue. bba June 25 (118A) £2,200 [Symonds]

— Ms, in Latin, Psalter. [Eastern Europe, 15th cent]. 83 leaves, vellum, 245mm by 175mm. Late 19th-cent lea bdg. In a gothic textura. With numerous small initials in red & blue & 3 large penwork initials. HH Nov 5 (815) DM4,500

— Ms, in Latin, Psalter. [Germany, Mainz?, 13th cent]. Single Calendar leaf, vellum, 178mm by 131mm. With illuminated initial, 3-quarter border, & miniature. Recovered from a bdg. Illus in cat. HH May 12 (39) DM3,800

— Ms, in Latin, Psalter & Horae B.M.V. [Lower Lorraine, c.1275]. 4 leaves only, vellum, 177mm by 136mm. In 2 sizes of a gothic hand. With 8 historiated initials. S Dec 17 (14) £1,400 [Weaver]

— Ms, in Latin, Psalter, with Canticles & Litany. [Flanders, c.1275]. 182 leaves, vellum, 127mm by 96mm. Worn 16th-cent [German?] blindstamped calf over wooden bds. In a gothic liturgical hand. With 3-line initials throughout, over 100 small historiated initials, & 10 very large historiated initials (1 full-page) with branching borders round 2 or 3 margins. Illus in cat. S Dec 17 (54) £11,000 [Marcus]

— Ms, in Latin, Psalter. [Strasbourg?, c.1225]. Single leaf, vellum, 238mm by 139mm. In 2 sizes of a gothic liturgical hand. With full-page miniature in 2 compartments in full color on burnished gold ground with borders in color & foliate tracery. Illus in cat. S June 23 (9) £68,000 [Quaritch]

— Ms, in Latin, with French verse; Psalter, with short Hours of the Virgin. [South Eastern France, Grenoble?, c.1484]. 218 leaves (7 lacking), vellum, 273mm by 190mm. Repaired contemp blind-tooled panelled calf over wooden bds. In a lettre batarde. With 15 calligraphic initials with grotesques, small initials in gold on red & blue ground, 4 larger initials in red or blue on gold ground, 5 historiated initials, 10 large miniatures with historical borders, later calendar miniatures, & 4 small miniatures possibly added in the 16th cent. Searles-Rowland collection. C June 24 (54) £30,000 [Mirandola]

— Ms, in Slavonic, Psalter. [Serbia or Bulgaria, late 15th cent]. 124 leaves, vellum, 152mm by 108mm. Contemp wooden bds overlaid with later stamped vellum. In a semi-cursive hand. With illuminated headpiece incorporating fantastic beasts, 150 five- or six-line initials, some with fantastic animals, & end-piece. C June 24 (63) £9,500 [Fogg]

Puccini, Giacomo, 1858-1924

Autograph music, Madama Butterfly, act 2, Pinkerton's farewell, 1st version; [c.1902/03]. 4 pp, folio, in modern half black mor. Draft in short score, with interlinear libretto. Illus in cat. P June 17 (307) $13,000

— Autograph music, sketches for Act 2, scene 1 of Madama Butterfly, [c.1902]. 1 p, 34cm by 27cm. Short score, notated on 4 systems, 3 staves each. S May 29 (611) £2,600 [Sawyer]

ALs, 28 Aug 1912. 1 p, 8vo. To "Signor Capitano". Explaining why he cannot stop over in Munich. pn Mar 19 (121) £220 [Macnutt]

— 22 Dec 1913. 1 p, 4to. To Sybil Seligman. Making inquiries about the author of a comedy. Illus in cat. sup Oct 15 (1779) $2,273

Autograph quotation, opening staves of Mi chiamano Mimi, from La Boheme, 1905. 13cm by 21.5cm. Sgd. Illus in cat. S May 29 (617) £800 [Wilson]

Cut signature, [n.d.]. Mtd with ptd photograph, overall size 13 by 7.5 inches. Ck Nov 15 (31) £80

Photograph, sgd, 1920. Postcard. By Glantz. star Mar 27 (1119) DM420

Photograph, sgd & inscr, Jan 1895. 30cm by 18.5cm. Inscr to Elvira Ceresoli. Illus in cat. S Dec 6 (164) £3,000 [Tancil]

— Anr, 18 July 1905. 180mm by 95mm. Inscr to Bruno Cittadini. By Armini. C June 24 (22) £250 [Lavers]

— Anr, 3 Nov 1905. Postcard. Inscr to Nellie Heath. With autograph address on verso. S May 29 (613) £500 [Macnutt]

— Anr, 1909. Postcard. Inscr with 2 musical quotations. Illus in cat. S Dec 6 (163) £1,300 [Burkill]

Pueckler-Muskau, Hermann, Fuerst von, 1785-1871

Autograph Ms, fragment (pp 113 - 116) from his book of travels Aus Mehmed Ali's Reich, [n.d.]. 4 pp, 4to. star Mar 26 (394) DM700

ALs, 3 Jan 1832. 2 pp, 4to. To Herr Lehmann or Consul Gen. Schwarz. Confirming receipt of a shipment of cigars. HH May 13 (2028) DM240

— 10 Mar 1848. 3 pp, 8vo. Recipient unnamed. About political developments in France. star Mar 26 (395) DM500

— 5 Dec 1853. 1 p, 8vo. To an unnamed general. Informing him about his travel plans. HH May 13 (2029) DM360

Pugin, Augustus Charles, 1762-1832

ALs, 2 Aug 1826. 3 pp, 4to. To Rudolph Ackermann. Referring to a dispute between John Nash & Ackermann. bba May 28 (219A) £180 [R.I.B.A.]

Purrmann, Hans, 1880-1966

ALs, 7 Dec 1954. 7 pp, 4to. To Mr. Rosin. About Mr. Vollmoeller's suicide & his own health. HH May 13 (2031) DM1,300

— 26 Dec 1955. 4 pp, 4to. To Mr. Rosin. Discussing George Grosz. HH May 13 (2032) DM1,100

— 4 Apr 1956. 2 pp, 4to. To Mr. Rosin. About their forthcoming meeting in Italy. HH May 13 (2034) DM200

Series of 4 Ls s, 4 Dec 1950 to 13 Jan 1953. 5 pp, 4to. To Mr. Rosin. About his travels & the situation in Germany. HH May 13 (2030) DM1,400

Ls, 28 Mar 1956. 1 p, 4to. To Mr. Rosin. About a recent journey to Germany & a projected meeting in Italy. HH May 13 (2033) DM400

Pyle, Howard, 1853-1911

ALs, 12 June 1903. 2 pp, 8vo. To William Lock. Concerning the medical exam of his nephew. Including orig drawing in margin, sgd & inscr. R Nov 9 (64) $800

Q

Quatrefages de Breau, Jean Louis Armand de, 1810-92

ALs, [n.d.]. 3 pp, 8vo. To an unnamed colleague. Discussing the conservation of some prehistoric finds. star Mar 26 (780) DM210

Quayle, J. Danforth

Photograph, sgd & inscr, [n.d.]. 4to. Inscr to Kathleen John. wa Oct 19 (329) $75

Signature, [n.d.]. On vice presidential card. wa Oct 19 (330) $65

— Anr, [n.d.]. On vice presidential card. wa Oct 19 (331) $65

R

Raabe, Wilhelm, 1831-1910

Collection of ALs & autograph postcard, sgd, 2 Aug 1903 & 14 June 1905. 1 p, 8vo, & card. To Moritz Diesterweg. Giving permission for reprints. star Mar 26 (397) DM520

ANs, 23 Dec 1881. 1 p, 8vo. Recipient unnamed. Sending Christmas greetings. star Mar 26 (396) DM280

Rabener, Gottlieb Wilhelm, 1714-71

Ds, 12 Sept 1767. 1 p, folio. Receipt to Johann Gottlieb Grellmann for a bond for 225 thalers. star Mar 26 (398) DM220

Rabinowitz, Shalom ("Sholem Aleichem"), 1859-1916

Autograph postcard, sgd, 1 Apr 1905. Recipient unnamed. Commenting on a trans. Illus in cat. Dar June 11 (252) $1,100

Rachel Felix, Elisa, 1821-58

ALs, [1838]. 3 pp, 8vo. To an unnamed marquis. Thanking for his port. star Mar 27 (1220) DM1,300

Rachmaninoff, Sergei, 1873-1943

Autograph quotation, 3 bars from his 3d piano concerto, sgd; 5 May 1922. 1 p, 8vo. sup Oct 15 (1781) $2,800

Photograph, sgd, [1904]. 167mm by 105mm. By Brodovsky. Illus in cat. S Dec 6 (168) £1,400 [Tancil]

— Anr, [n.d.]. 222mm by 176mm. P June 17 (68) $800

Rackham, Arthur, 1867-1939

ALs, 10 Mar [19]13. 7 pp, 8vo. To D. G. Doty. Complaining about damage to his drawings. sg Sept 12 (199) $600

Radbourne, Charles, 1854-97

Signature, [n.d.]. Matted with related material, 8 by 10 inches. Dar Dec 26 (101) $750

Radiguet, Raymond, 1903-23

Autograph Ms, poem, beginning "Quand je suis au bord de la mer...", [n.d.]. 1 p, 4to. 3 four-line stanzas. star Mar 26 (399) DM750

Rain-in-the-Face

Photograph, [n.d.]. Cabinet size. Full length; by Barry. Illus in cat. R June 13 (288) $550

Rains, Claude, 1889-1967

Ds, 27 June 1932. 1 p, 4to. Permission by The Theatre Guild for Rains to appear in a play in NY; carbon copy. Dar Feb 13 (297) $100

Rambert, Marie, 1888-1982. See: Stravinsky, Igor

Ramsay, James, 1733-89

A Ls s (2), 3 June 1771 & 7 July 1774. 6 pp, 4to. To Catharine Macaulay. Describing the persecution he is suffering, praising her work & discussing political news. pn June 11 (16) £900 [Quaritch]

Randolph, Peyton, c.1721-75 —& Others

Ds, 1 Apr 1773. 1 p, 3 by 6.5 inches. £12 note, drawn on the Virginia James River Bank; also sgd by John Blair & Robert Carter Nicholas. Illus in cat. R June 13 (166) $1,900

Ranke, Leopold von, 1795-1886

ALs, 24 Apr 1830. 4 pp, 4to. To an unnamed Austrian official. Asking for a letter of introduction. star Mar 26 (781) DM800

Collection of Ls & ANs, 12 Nov 1882 & [n.d.]. 4 pp, 8vo. To Eduard von Tempeltey. Praising his play Cromwell, & contents not stated. star Mar 26 (782) DM220

Rapp, Jean, Comte, 1771-1821

ALs, [11 June 1804]. 1 p, 4to. To the merchant Wolff. Requesting him to settle his accounts at Strasbourg. star Mar 27 (1376) DM620

Rasputin, Grigory Efimovich, 1872?-1916

ALs, [c.1915]. 2 pp, 8vo. To Prince Obolenskii. Complaining that he is not allowed to leave Petrograd. C Dec 16 (320) £3,000 [Batchelder]

Rathbone, Basil, 1892-1967

Photograph, sgd, [n.d.]. 7.25 by 9.5 inches. Dar Feb 13 (299) $300

Rathenau, Walther, 1867-1922

Collection of ALs & autograph Ms, 1 Aug 1915. 4 pp, folio. To [Maximilian Harden]. Sending an imaginary discussion among wartime enemies (included). star Mar 27 (1635) DM1,300

Ls, 24 Jan 1916. 2 pp, 4to. To Eugen Bracht. Requesting his cooperation in a commission for art. Also sgd by 11 other members of the Kulturbund. star Mar 27 (1636) DM1,000

Rauch, Christian Daniel, 1777-1857

ALs, 25 Oct 1836. 3 pp, 4to. To Pierre Jean David d'Angers. Acknowledging receipt of a marble sculpture. star Mar 27 (939) DM1,300

Ravel, Maurice, 1875-1937

ALs, 22 Oct 1925. 2 pp, 8vo. To Jean Aubry. Inquiring about arrangements for concerts in England & Scandinavia. S May 29 (630) £700 [Giesen]

— 18 Apr 1926. 1 p, 8vo. To Louis Fleury. Announcing completion of the 2d song of his Chansons Madecasses. S May 29 (632) £700 [Macnutt]

Ls, 26 Sept 1911. 1 p, 12mo. To the Countess de Chalamers. Sending greetings. Also sgd by others. Illus in cat. Dar Aug 6 (243) $350

— 2 Dec 1924. 1 p, 8vo. To Jean Aubry. Referring to the premiere of his Tzigane. Dar Aug 6 (242) $600

Autograph quotation, 3 bars of music, 3 June [19]14. 1 p, 8vo. Sgd & inscr to Madame de Menuel; in pencil. Sgd in anr hand on verso. Dar Oct 10 (292) $1,300

— Anr, 2 bars from L'Enfant et les Sortileges, sgd; [n.d.]. 171mm by 125mm. Framed with a port. P June 17 (69) $1,800

Signature, 15 Mar [19]29. Framed with a photograph, overall size 10.5 by 16 inches. Dar Apr 9 (319) $300

Ray, James E.

ALs, 8 July 1991. 1 p, 4to. To Ernest E. Quinn. Explaining that the FBI & the NAACP acted "to eliminate the Rev. King." Illus in cat. Dar Apr 9 (171) $650

Raymond, John T., 1836-87. See: Clemens, Samuel Langhorne & Raymond

Reach, Alfred James, 1840-1928

ALs, 20 Mar 1889. 2 pp, 4to. To Harry [Wright]. Referring to baseball schedules, balls, etc. Including postscript. Dar Dec 26 (64) $1,900

Reagan, John Henninger, 1818-1905

ALs, 15 July 1904. 2 pp, 4to. To W. F. McCaleb. Admitting that he willingly joined the secession movement. With a port. Dar June 11 (319) $225

Reagan, Nancy. See: Reagan, Ronald & Reagan

Reagan, Ronald

Original drawing, sketch of a man, sgd; [n.d.]. 1 p, on engraved card. sup Oct 15 (1744) $360

Transcript, quotation ptd in the Los Angeles Herald-Examiner on 2 Dec 1971 concerning self-proclaimed revolutionaries; 1 p, 8vo. Sgd. Framed with a port. Illus in cat. sup Oct 15 (1742) $625

Typescript, tribute to Dwight Eisenhower; [n.d.]. 1 p, 8vo. Sgd. sup Oct 15 (1743) $460

Collection of 5 A Ls s, 2 Ls s & photograph, sgd, 15 Nov 1940 to 12 Dec 1966. 8 pp, 4to, & postcard. To Tressie Masocco. Friendly letters to a fellow classmate at Eureka College. sup Oct 15 (1739) $5,250

ALs, 1 Apr [1962]. 1 p, 4to. To Miss White. Promising to show her play to anr producer. Dar Oct 10 (295) $800

— [7 Nov 1967]. 1 p, 4to. To Luis G. Aguilera. Hoping recipient's nephew will soon be home from Vietnam. Dar June 11 (320) $600

— [c.1972?]. 2 pp, 8vo. To Ray. Returning a script & speculating about his return to the screen. Spiro collection. CNY May 14 (138) $2,000

— 9 Apr [1981]. 1 p, 4to. To Mr. Wild. Offering a date for an appearance in Lubbock. Probably draft. Illus in cat. sup May 9 (301) $6,750

Ls, 6 Nov 1945. 3 pp, 4to. To Walter Winchell. About G. L. K. Smith & "the re-birth of Naziism" in Los Angeles. Illus in cat. sup May 9 (302) $1,100

— 13 Sept 1968. 2 pp, 4to. To Lowell Martin. Explaining employment opportunities in California. wa Oct 19 (333) $280

— 17 June 1971. 1 p, 4to. To Joe E. Brown & his wife. Thanking for a note of support. sup Oct 15 (1741) $190

— 12 Jan 1983. 1 p, 8vo. To Jean & Bill Thompson. Promising to sign some pictures. Dar Oct 10 (294) $450

— 28 Sept 1988. 1 p, 8vo. To Bill Thompson. Referring to a visit of Soviet visitors in Illinois. Dar Dec 26 (286) $325

ANs, [c.Oct 1981]. On mount of a newspaper article; folio. To Jack Drummey. Thanking for a lesson [in drawing caricatures, given in a newspaper article]. Including caricature of Reagan & anr sketch, sgd, by Drummey. sup Oct 15 (1745) $500

— [Dec 1983]. 1 p, 8vo, on ptd Christmas card. To Jean & Bill [Thompson]. Thanking for Christmas gifts. Dar Oct 10 (296) $900

Ds, 10 Aug 1943. 2 pp, 4to. Leave of absence granted to a 1st Lieutenant. Illus in cat. sup Oct 15 (1738) $110

Check, accomplished & sgd, 1 June 1948. Payable to "Cash". Dar Apr 9 (322) $475

— Anr, sgd, 4 Oct 1948. Payable to Murray & Gee Inc. wa Oct 19 (335) $650

Photograph, sgd, [n.d.]. 10 by 8 inches. Ck Apr 3 (128) £70

— Anr, [n.d.]. 11 by 14 inches. Dar Apr 9 (320) $225

Photograph, sgd & inscr, [2 Oct 1941]. Postcard. Inscr, sgd twice & addressed to Harry Heuschkel. Dar Apr 9 (321) $200

— Anr, [1941?]. 9.75 by 7.75 inches. Inscr to Jane. Dar Feb 13 (300) $225

Ptd photograph, [n.d.]. 10 by 13 inches. Magazine ad for the film Desperate Journey; sgd by Reagan, sgd & inscr by Raymond Massey. Dar Dec 26 (287) $250

Signature, [n.d.]. On presidential "post-it note". wa Oct 19 (334) $180

— HINCKLEY, JOHN. - ALs, 22 July 1982. 1 p, 4to. To Ed [Richardson]. Referring to his shooting of President Reagan & his plans to kill Jodie Foster. Dar Oct 10 (206) $1,700

Reagan, Ronald —& Others

Group photograph, [1981]. 9.5 by 8.5 inches. With members of the Supreme Court on the day Sandra O'Connor became a Justice; sgd by all 10 on mat. Dar Oct 10 (334) $2,250

— Anr, [c.1981]. 20 by 16 inches. With members of the Supreme Court; sgd by all 10 on mat. Dar Dec 26 (312) $2,750

Reagan, Ronald. See: Gorbachev, Mikhail Sergeyevich & Reagan

Reagan, Ronald —& Reagan, Nancy

Group photograph, [c.1952]. 10 by 8 inches. Sgd by both. Dar Apr 9 (323) $225

— Anr, [c.1990]. 8 by 10 inches. Sgd by both. Dar Apr 9 (324) $225

Reaumur, Rene Antoine Ferchault de, 1683-1757

ALs, 30 May 1755. 2 pp, 4to. Recipient unnamed. Explaining that he was unable to write due to an inheritance & to health problems. star Mar 26 (783) DM900

Redford, Robert. See: Streisand, Barbra & Redford

Reger, Max, 1873-1916

Collection of 21 A Ls s & 25 autograph postcards, sgd, 30 Jan 1894 to [10 Apr 1912]. 70 pp, 4to & 8vo, & cards. To Waldemar Meyer. About his compositions, reviews of his music, concerts, etc. star Mar 27 (1120) DM18,000

ALs, 1 Apr 1909. 4 pp, 8vo. To Max Brockhaus. About recent concerts & some hostile reviews. star Mar 27 (1122) DM900

Autograph postcard, sgd, [21 Feb 1905]. To Wilhelm von Wymetal. Expressing thanks. star Mar 27 (1121) DM320

— [16 Dec 1910]. To Philipp Wolfrum. Sending congratulations on recipient's birthday. star Mar 27 (1123) DM450

Lithographed port, 6 Jan 1911. 4to. Sgd & inscr to P. Toeche with a musical quotation. Mtd. star Mar 27 (1124) DM1,700

Regnier, Henri Francois Joseph, 1864-1936

Autograph Ms, Litterature, [1901]. 9 pp, 4to, in half cloth bdg. Reviews of 8 works, sgd. Ptr's copy. star Mar 26 (401) DM230

Reibold, Ferdinand von, 1786-1858

Autograph Ms, diary of a journey from Dresden to Constantinople & Malta, 9 Apr to 3 July 1839. 141 leaves, 240mm by 193mm; stitched. HH May 12 (20) DM650

Reichardt, Johann Friedrich, 1752-1814

A Ls s (2), 14 & 27 Apr 1804. 6 pp, 4to & 8vo. To Herr Stelzer & to Mrs. Stelzer. About professional opportunities for Stelzer & a relative. star Mar 27 (1125) DM1,900

Reichenbach, Heinrich Gottlieb Ludwig, 1793-1879

ALs, 5 Mar 1831. 5 pp, 8vo. Recipient unnamed. Responding to a review of his Flora germanica excursiora. HN Nov 28 (1811) DM360

— 1 Nov 1852. 4 pp, 8vo. To an unnamed scientist. Thanking for specimens gathered in Australia. star Mar 26 (784) DM250

Reichstein, Tadeusz

Autograph Ms, scholarly paper, Asplenium nesii Christ..., [n.d.]. 8 pp, folio. With covering ALs, 8 Feb 1982. star Mar 26 (785) DM330

Reinecke, Carl, 1824-1910

Collection of ALs & 4 autograph postcards, sgd, 23 Aug 1891 to 4 Apr 1892. 7 pp, 8vo. To August Marten. Regarding arrangements for a concert in Kiel. HN June 26 (974) DM340

ALs, 19 Mar 1854. 1 p, 4to. To Theodor Kirchner. Recommending a musical academy, & worrying about Schumann's health. star Mar 27 (1126) DM1,000

— 7 July 1900. 4 pp, 8vo. Recipient unnamed. Commenting on the draft of a biographical sketch. star Mar 27 (1127) DM340

Reinhardt, Max, 1873-1943

ALs, [1 Oct 1928]. 1 p, 8vo. To Hans Thimig. Draft, informing him that [Elisabeth] Bergner refuses to have him play the part of Romeo. star Mar 27 (1221) DM850

Remarque, Erich Maria, 1898-1970

ALs, 4 Apr 1968. 1 p, folio. To unnamed friends. About work on his new book. In English. star Mar 26 (404) DM430

Remington, Frederic, 1861-1909

Series of 19 A Ls s, 1902 to 1909. 29 pp, various sizes. To Joel Burdick. About a variety of matters. Including several sketches. P Dec 12 (139) $25,000

ALs, 13 Jan 1890. 1 p, 8vo. To Fred B. Schell. Sending some drawings of the Battle at Wounded Knee for publication. Dar June 11 (324) $500

— [n.d.]. 1 p, 4to. To Mr. Albi. Looking forward to a meeting, & speculating about the use of the bicycle in war. Illus in cat. sup Oct 15 (1783) $1,050

— [n.d.]. 1 p, 4to. Recipient unnamed. Planning a vacation. Including self port on the beach at head. Illus in cat. sup May 9 (61) $2,400

Remy, Claude

Autograph Ms, Traite des Elemens Presente a M. Raoul de Choiseul-Gouffier, 1786. 192 pp, 8vo. Contemp red mor by Derome. With ornamental headpieces. b Nov 18 (271) £110

Renaulme, Matthieu de, fl.1530

Autograph Ms, Anacreontos Lexicon. [Blois, c.1530]. 100 leaves, 8vo, in 19th-cent red mor. In a humanistic greek script. With colored architectural title-border incorporating armorial devices. C June 24 (76) £11,000 [Kraus]

Reno, Marcus A., 1834-89

Ls, 26 Aug 1864. 1 p, 12mo. To George A. Custer. Carbon copy, giving instructions for troop movements. Illus in cat. Armstrong collection. sup Oct 15 (1123) $900

Photograph, sgd & inscr, [n.d.]. Carte size. In Dragoon uniform. Framed. Illus in cat. Armstrong collection. sup Oct 15 (1124) $5,750

Resnik, Judith A., 1949-86

Photograph, sgd, [n.d.]. 8 by 10 inches. With space shuttle model. Dar Oct 10 (237) $150

— Anr, [n.d.]. 8 by 10 inches. Dar Dec 26 (234) $160

Photograph, sgd & inscr, [n.d.]. 8 by 10 inches. Inscr to Brian. Dar Feb 13 (233) $300

Reuter, Fritz, 1810-74

ALs, 25 Mar 1869. 2 pp, 4to. To his pbr in Kopenhagen. About the Danish trans of his work Franzosentid. star Mar 26 (405) DM1,500

Revels, Hiram Rhoades, 1822-1901

Franking signature, [n.d.]. On envelope addressed to George Evans. sup Oct 15 (1026) $275

Reynolds, John Hamilton, 1796-1852

Series of 10 A Ls s, 19 June 1816 to 19 Aug 1821 & [n.d.]. 21 pp, 8vo & 4to. To his publishers Taylor & Hessey. Discussing his own writings & mentioning other authors. CNY Dec 5 (317) $1,400

Rezzori, Gregor von

Autograph Ms, fragment, describing the buying of milk in Hamburg, [n.d.]. 1 p, folio. With ALs, 1986; letter of transferral. star Mar 26 (406) DM240

Rhinfeld, Mathilde de

Autograph Ms, Floriana, or The Method of Constructing Artificial Flowers, [c.1833]. 254 pp, 4to. Contemp calf, rebacked. Including 48 watercolor drawings (28 full-page), 3 pen-&-ink sketches, 2 folding pen-&-wash drawings, & pen-&-ink head & tail pieces to chapters. C Oct 30 (227) £900

[Spelman]

Rice, Sam, 1890-1974. See: Gehringer, Charles & Rice

Richard, 3d Duke of York, 1411-60

Document, 20 Dec 1448. 1 p, vellum, 196mm by 360mm. Grant of the manor of Cressege to Ralph, Lord Cromwell, & others. S June 23 (47) £900 [Quaritch]

Richardson, Samuel, 1689-1761

ALs, Oct 1760. 1 p, 8vo. To [Catherine Lintot]. Affectionate letter to a young business partner; inviting her for a visit. CNY Dec 5 (318) $800

Richelieu, Armand Emmanuel du Plessis, Duc de, 1766-1822

ALs, [n.d.], "Thursday". 1 p, 8vo. Recipient unnamed. Concerning a conference of diplomats. Dar Apr 9 (326) $100

Richelieu, Armand-Jean du Plessis, Cardinal de, 1585-1642

Ds, 1623. 1 p, folio. Bond to Claude de Bouthillier for 36,000 livres. Endorsed by Bouthillier on verso. star Mar 27 (1347) DM2,700

Richter, Hans Werner

Autograph Ms, Nachruf fuer Uwe Johnson, [1984]. 14 pp, folio. Sgd & inscr. star Mar 26 (407) DM450

Richter, Jean Paul Friedrich, 1763-1825

Collection of 12 A Ls s & 2 A Ls, [18 Sept 1808] to 4 May 1825. 15 pp, 8vo, in half vellum bdg. To Johann Chr. Martin Miedel. About recipient's garden, presents, family activities, etc. star Mar 26 (408) DM16,000

ALs, 7 Nov 1817. 3 pp, 8vo. To Sophie Paulus. Sending a copy of his latest work. With related material. star Mar 26 (411) DM2,800

AL, 22 Apr 1814. 4 pp, 4to. To Czar Alexander of Russia. Draft, petitioning for a pension & sending his pamphlet Mars und Phoebus. star Mar 26 (409) DM3,000

Rickenbacker, Edward Vernon, 1890-1973

Signature, 1946. 8vo. On photo after a pencil port by Paul Trehm. wa Oct 19 (68) $100

Rickover, Hyman G., 1900-86

Transcript, excerpt from a 1957 article entitled "Talented Children"; [n.d.]. 1 p, 12mo (card). Sgd. Dar Oct 10 (303) $200

A Ls s (2), 25 Oct & 14 Nov 1966. 2 pp, 4to. To William Ryan. Reporting about tests of 2 ships. sup Oct 15 (1786) $675

Ls, 18 Aug 1969. 1 p, 4to. To Bob Wilson. Reporting on nuclear-powered submarines. sg Feb 27 (160) $1,700

Riemer, Friedrich Wilhelm, 1774-1845

[A visiting card for August von Goethe in Riemer's hand sold at HN on 28 Nov 1991, lot 1708, for DM220.]

Rieti, Vittorio

Collection of c.50 A Ls s & autograph Ms, 1925 to 1947. 90 pp, mostly 4to. To Boris Kochno (1 to Diaghilev). Charting his working relationship with the Ballets Russes. Ms, scenario for the ballet Le Bal. SM Oct 12 (393) FF6,000

Riis, Jacob August, 1849-1914

[An archive containing 29 A Ls s, 3 Ls s, & ANs by Riis, with 19 letters addressed to or concerning him, 1882 to 1914, sold at sg on 12 Sept 1991, lot 202, for $1,100.]

Riley, James Whitcomb, 1849-1916

Autograph Ms, poem, beginning "We say and we say and we say...", [n.d.]. 1 p, 4.5 by 3 inches. 4 lines, sgd. Framed with a photograph. Dar Feb 13 (307) $120

Rilke, Rainer Maria, 1875-1926

Autograph Ms, poem, Die Liebende, [n.d.]. 1 p, 4to. 15 lines. star Mar 26 (412) DM6,500

Autograph transcript, poem, Rodin, 10 Nov 1902. 1 p, 4to. 2d version, written in his elegant calligraphic hand, partly in red ink. Illus in cat. S May 28 (216) £1,100 [Symonds]

Collection of 9 A Ls s & AN, 7 Nov 1907 to 2 May 1924. To Count Alexander Dietrichstein-Mensdorff (4) & Princess Olga Dietrichstein. About a variety of personal & literary matters. C Dec 16 (322) £7,000 [Rosenthal]

Series of 3 A Ls s, 14 Jan 1912 to 26 Apr 1922. 14 pp, 4to. To Hedwig Fischer. Important personal letters about his work, feelings & activities. star Mar 26 (415) DM5,500

— Series of 4 A Ls s, [1916/17] to 23 Jan 1919. 4 pp, 4to. To Kerstin Strindberg. About recipient's engagement & marriage, the situation after the war, etc. star Mar 26 (417) DM4,800

A Ls s (2), 7 Feb 1906 & 17 Dec 1907. 3 pp, 4to & 8vo. To Hugo Salus. Sending his Stunden-Buch, & mentioning the birth of his daughter. star Mar 26 (414) DM2,600

ALs, 10 Dec 1913. 2 pp, 8vo (lettercard). To Lia Rosen. Praising her acting in a recent performance, & sending 3 photographs (included). star Mar 26 (416) DM1,800

Rimsky-Korsakov, Nikolai Andreevich, 1844-1908

ALs, 18 Jan [18]98. 4 pp, 8vo. To Mikhail Delin. Discussing the influence of Wagner on music in Russia & France. Illus in cat. S May 29 (633) £3,000 [Scriptorium]

Autograph sentiment, inscr to Frank Seymour Hastings, 27 May 1907. 1 p, 12mo. Framed with related material. Dar Oct 10 (304) $1,300

Ringelnatz, Joachim, Pseud. of Hans Boetticher, 1883-1934

Autograph Ms, poem, beginning "Wenn man das zierlichste Naeschen...", Mar 1926. 1 p, 12mo. 6 lines, sgd. Mtd with a port. JG Sept 27 (436) DM600

ALs, 17 Oct 1924. 1 p, 8vo. To the Ed of the journal Simplizissimus. Sending a contribution. HH Nov 6 (2093) DM420

— 23 Feb 1928. 2 pp, 8vo. To W. Buller. Agreeing to lecture. HN Nov 28 (1813) DM340

Ptd photograph, sgd, [n.d.]. Postcard. Was mtd. With related material. star Mar 26 (418) DM300

Rinser, Luise

Series of 7 A Ls s, 1946 to 1949. 13 pp, 4to. To W. Dengler. About various publication matters. HN Nov 28 (1814) DM400

Ritchie, Joseph, 1788?-1819

ALs, 28 Aug 1818. 1 p, 4to. To Mr. Wishaw. Recommending a Tripolitan who has given useful information about Africa. Dawson Turner collection. pn Nov 14 Sawyer (132) £80

Rittenhouse, David, 1732-96

Ds, 25 Apr 1786. 1 p, 4to. Pay order in favor of Benjamin Barton. Also sgd by others. R Mar 7 (179) $350

Robbe-Grillet, Alain

A Ls s (2), 15 Jan & 1 Mar 1973. 2 pp, 8vo & 4to. To Putnam's Sons. Giving information about his earliest works. star Mar 26 (419) DM300

Robeson, Paul, 1898-1976

Concert program, sgd, for a concert of the National Symphony Orchestra in Washington, 25 June 1943. 16 pp, 8vo. Dar Feb 13 (308) $170

Robespierre, Maximilien, 1758-94 —& Others

Ds, [29 Dec 1793]. 1 p, folio. Order by the Comite de Salut Public to transfer 4 generals held at Arras to Paris. Also sgd by Carnot, Barere & Collot d'Herbois. Illus in cat. S Dec 5 (560) £2,200 [Fritz-Denneville]

— [n.d.]. 1 p, 8vo. Decree of the Comite de Salut Public that Marie-Louise Rhaimbault should continue to work as midwife. Also sgd by Carnot, Charere & Thierry. bba Jan 30 (279) £540 [Benjamin]

Robinson, Jackie, 1919-72

Photograph, sgd, [23 July 1962]. 8 by 10 inches. Holding Hall of Fame plaque. Illus in cat. sup July 10 (963) $1,200

Ptd photograph, sgd, [1949]. 6.25 by 9 inches. Framed. Dar Oct 10 (82) $170

Signature, [13 Nov 1952]. 5 by 3 inches, on verso of trimmed postcard. Dar Dec 26 (102) $200

— Anr, [n.d]. Size not stated. Framed with related material. Dar Oct 10 (83) $200

Robinson, Michael Massey, 1744-1826

Endorsement, sgd, in the margin of an assignment by Robert Forrester at Sydney to secure debts to Simeon Lord & Thomas Rickerby, 28 Aug 1801. 2 pp, folio. Longueville collection. S June 25 (150) £450 [Quaritch/Hordern]

Robinson, William Heath, 1872-1944

Original drawing, Interesting Sidelights in the Wig Industry, to illus Hutchinson's Magazine, May 1926. 16 by 11.75 inches. In pencil, pen-&-ink, & wash. Sgd. Illus in cat. Ck Dec 11 (109) £

— Original drawing, Mrs. Bloggs at the Football Match, to illus The Bystander Magazine, 10 Nov 1926. 15 by 10.5 inches. In pencil, pen-&-ink, & wash. Sgd. Illus in cat. Ck Dec 11 (108) £

— Original drawing, "The Little Old Cupid", to illus Walter de la Mare's Peacock Pie, 1916. 10.25 by 7.5 inches. In pen & black ink; initialled. Ck Dec 1! (41) £

Rochow, Friedrich Eberhard von, 1734-1805

ALs, 18 Mar 1805. 3 pp, 4to. To Heinrich Gottlieb Zerrenner. Referring to a work by [Jakob] Hoogen. star Mar 26 (786) DM300

Rockefeller, John D., 1839-1937

Ds, 31 Mar 1875. 1 p, folio. Stock Certificate for 100 shares in the Standard Oil Company. Illus in cat. sup May 9 (421) $7,600

Rockwell, Norman, 1894-1978

Ls s (2), 13 Feb 1961 & 8 Oct 1968. 2 pp, 8vo. Recipient unnamed. Stating that he is not doing covers for the Saturday Evening Post any more, & contents not stated. R June 13 (212) $280

Photograph, sgd & inscr, [n.d.]. 10.75 by 14 inches. Inscr to Hedda Hopper. Dar Oct 10 (307) $250

Signature, on cover of The Saturday Evening Post, 23 Apr 1938, illus by Rockwell. Framed, overall size 18.75 by 20.5. Dar Feb 13 (309) $200

— Anr, [8 Feb 1960]. On philatelic cover. Dar Aug 6 (248) $120

— Anr, [26 Oct 1963]. On philatelic cover. Dar Aug 6 (249) $110

— Anr, [13 Oct 1973]. On philatelic cover. Dar Aug 6 (250) $160

— Anr, [16 Nov 1973]. On 1st Day Cover. wa Oct 19 (20) $95

— Anr, [n.d.]. On reproduction from his illus Ed of The Adventures of Huckleberry Finn. wa Oct 19 (21) $140

Rodenberg, Julius, 1831-1914

ALs, 8 Mar 1855. 1 p, 4to. To Josef Dessauer. Praising Dessauer's compositions of his poems. Including poem, 5 stanzas. star Mar 26 (420) DM350

Rodgers, Richard, 1902-79

Ds, 5 Dec 1950. 2 pp, folio & 4to. Agreement with designer Jo Mielziner for the play Anna and the King of Siam. sup Oct 15 (1789) $545

Rodin, Auguste, 1840-1917

ALs, 3 May 1914. 1 p, 8vo. To [Dr. Charles Waldstein]. Thanking for an honorary Cambridge doctorate. pn June 11 (66) £120 [Wilson]

— [n.d.]. 2 pp, 12mo (card). Recipient unnamed. Expressing sympathy. Dar June 11 (325) $225

— [n.d.]. 2 pp, 8vo. Recipient unnamed. About recipient's wish to see his drawings. star Mar 27 (942) DM340

Ls, 9 Oct 1910. 2 pp, 4to. To Alexander Amersdorffer. Inquiring about the date of an exhibition. star Mar 27 (940) DM360

— 11 Oct 1912. 2 pp, 8vo. Recipient unnamed. Declining a suggestion. star Mar 27 (941) DM360

Roebling, Washington Augustus, 1837-1926

Series of 5 A Ls s, 24 Feb to 17 Mar 1913. Length not stated. To his son John. About the strike at his wire plant. 4 initialled. k Mar 22 (403) $500

A Ls s (2), 4 Aug 1908 & 6 Aug [19]16. 2 pp, 4to & 8vo. To his son John. About business matters. Illus in cat. sg Feb 27 (161) $600

ALs, 4 Jan [19]13. 2 pp, 8vo. To his son John. About business matters, & mentioning Brooklyn Bridge. With related material. sg Feb 27 (162) $600

Roehm, Ernst, 1887-1934

Photograph, sgd, [11 June 1934]. Postcard. With secretarial letter of transmittal. HH May 13 (2037) DM950

Roentgen, Wilhelm Conrad, 1845-1923

AN, 7 Jan 1908. 1 p, on ptd visiting card. Recipient unnamed. Sending rent & requesting a receipt. Illus in cat. star Mar 26 (788) DM730

Roethke, Theodore, 1908-63

Autograph Ms, poem, beginning "With all the freshness gone...", [c.1935]. 2 pp, size not stated. Sgd. Ck Nov 15 (13) £100

Rogers, Ginger. See: Astaire, Fred & Rogers

Rohan, Louis Rene Edouard de, Cardinal, 1734-1803

ALs, 18 Mar 1780. 3 pp, 4to. To the Bishop of Aralty. Concerning counterfeit money tendered to Jewish creditors in Alsace. Dar Dec 26 (235) $275

Ls, 18 Mar 1780. 3 pp, 4to. To the Bishop of Arath. Concerning counterfeit money tendered to Jewish creditors in Alsace. sg Sept 12 (128) $325

Roland de la Platiere, Jean Marie, 1734-93

Ls, 6 Sept 1792. 1 p, folio. To the Tresorerie Nationale. Sending pay orders. With engraved port. star Mar 27 (1387) DM320

Rolland, Romain, 1866-1944

ALs, 19 July 1900. 2 pp, 8vo. To the Conservatory at Naples. Requesting information about Mss by Luigi Rossi. HH May 13 (2039) DM240

Rolle, Richard, 1290?-1349

Ms, Commentary on the Psalms. [London?, c.1400-1430]. Fragment of a bifolium, 310mm by 230mm. In a good Anglicana script. With large illuminated initial & extensive illuminated border along upper margin. Recovered from a bdg. S Dec 17 (9) £1,300 [Quaritch]

Rolling Stones, The

[The signatures of all 5 orig members of the band on a single sheet, [c.1964], framed with an early photograph, 10.5 by 14.5 inches, sold at P on 17 Dec 1991, lot 482, for $500.]

[The signatures of all 5 orig members of the band on an album cover, [1967], framed, 35 by 21 inches, sold at P on 17 Dec 1991, lot 494, for $1,200.]

Group photograph, [c.1965]. Framed, 26 by 19 inches. Sgd by all 5 orig members of the band. Framed. Illus in cat. P Dec 17 (489) $800

— Anr, [n.d.]. Postcard. Sgd by all 5 orig members of the band. Framed. Illus in cat. P Dec 17 (487) $600

Romberg, Sigmund, 1887-1951

Photograph, sgd & inscr, 6 Mar [19]36. 7.25 by 9.25 inches. Inscr to Jenny Lind Bothe. With related telegram. Dar Apr 9 (328) $180

Rommel, Erwin, 1891-1944

ALs, 9 Oct 1911. 2 pp, 4to. To [his future wife] Lucia. Making plans for a meeting. Illus in cat. sup Oct 15 (1794) $1,700

— 16 Oct 1911. 3 pp, 4to. To [his future wife]. Reporting from the military academy. Illus in cat. sup Oct 15 (1793) $1,600

— 2 Jan 1912. 4 pp, 8vo. To his [future] wife. Reporting about his Christmas vacation. sup May 9 (489) $1,300

— 10 Apr 1912. 6 pp, 8vo. To [his future wife] Lucia. Love letter. Illus in cat. sup Oct 15 (1796) $2,450

— 13 May 1912. 4 pp, 8vo. To [his future wife]. Love letter. Illus in cat. sup Oct 15 (1797) $2,700

— 10 Sept 1912. 4 pp, 4to. To his [future] wife. Love letter, regretting he did not kiss her in the park. sup May 9 (488) $1,550

— 22 Feb 1913. 8 pp, 8vo. To Lucia [Mollin]. Very personal letter describing his life in the army. Dar Dec 26 (294) $2,500

AL, 11 Oct 1913. 4 pp, 4to. To [his future wife] Lucia. Reporting about an illness, & thanking for a photograph. Incomplete. Illus in cat. sup Oct 15 (1799) $900

Ls, [n.d.]. 1 p, 4to. Recipient unnamed. Ptd circular expressing thanks for congratulations & reporting about his campaign in North Africa. Including typed postscript. star Mar 27 (1764) DM2,800

Ds, 14 Feb 1942. 1 p, 4to. Award of the War Service Cross 2d Class to 6 soldiers. Illus in cat. Dar Aug 6 (251) $2,750

Photograph, sgd, [n.d.]. 3.5 by 5.5 inches. Dar Dec 26 (293) $1,700

— MOLLIN, LUCIA. - Autograph postcard, sgd, [n.d.]. To [her future husband] E. Rommel. Reminding him of an invitation. On verso of port postcard. sup Oct 15 (1800) $430

Romulo, Carlos P., 1899-1985

Ls, 9 Sept 1969. 1 p, 8vo. To Morris Cotkin. Recalling an incident in World War II involving Gen. McArthur. Matted with ptd port of McArthur. Dar June 11 (369) $475

Roosevelt, Eleanor, 1884-1962

Autograph Ms, poem, The History of a blue Sweater, [n.d.]. 1 p, 8vo. 12 lines, sgd. On White House letterhead. Dar Oct 10 (310) $1,000

Collection of 40 A Ls s, 4 Ls s & 3 telegrams, 16 May 1931 to 15 Dec 1934. Mostly 8vo. To George Marvin. Supportive letters to an old friend. sup May 9 (348) $2,100

ALs, 24 Sept [n.y.]. 2 pp, 8vo. To Esther. Thanking for clippings. Sgd E.R. sup Oct 15 (1639) $160

Ls s (2), 19 & 25 July 1949. 2 pp, 8vo. To Mr. Vars. Responding to inquiries about plane travel accidents. Dar Apr 9 (329) $130

Ls, 26 Apr 1945. 1 p, 4to. To [Basil O'Connor]. Discussing plans for a memorial to her husband & enclosing carbon copy of a letter to President Truman (present). sg Sept 12 (205) $550

— 11 July 1947. 1 p, 8vo. To [Basil O'Connor]. Requesting information about some financial contributions. R Nov 9 (27) $280

— 2 July 1948. 1 p, 4to. To Mr. Paley. Soliciting support for the United Jewish Appeal. F Mar 26 (663) $175

Photograph, sgd & inscr, [c.1933-34]. 6 by 8.25 inches. With anr, def. sg Sept 12 (204) $80

— THOMPSON, MALVINA C. - Ls, 12 Apr 1945. 1 p, 8vo. To Stella Hoyt. Informing her that Mrs. Roosevelt is unable to accept an invitation. Dar Feb 13 (311) $150

Roosevelt, Eleanor, 1884-1962 —& Others

Group photograph, [n.d.]. 10 by 8 inches. With Morton Dean Joyce & Thomas Steinway; sgd by all 3. Dar June 11 (326) $110

Roosevelt, Franklin D., 1882-1945

Collection of ALs & autograph endorsement, 19 Nov [n.y.] & 31 Dec 1940. 3 pp, 4to & 8vo. To Mr. Crowley. Sending checks for the Georgia Warm Springs Foundation. Endorsement on verso of check. sg Sept 12 (210) $650

ALs, 1 Jan 1913. 1 p, 4to. To Governor William Sulzer. Recommending John C. Otis as State Health Commissioner. Illus in cat. Dar Apr 9 (331) $2,250

— 30 June 1917. 1 p, 8vo. To Aymar Johnson. Thanking for a log book. Illus in cat. Dar June 11 (328) $900

— 31 July 1926. 1 p, 4to. To Mr. Crowley. Sending a check for the Georgia Warm Springs Corporation. Illus in cat. Dar June 11 (329) $850

— 5 May 1927. 1 p, 4to. To Mr. Crowley. Asking that a check be sent to the Warm Springs Foundation. R Nov 9 (28) $650

— 18 Nov 1927. 1 p, 4to. To Mr. Leanley. Sending checks for deposit to the credit of the Georgia Warm Springs Foundation. Dar Dec 26 (296) $750

— 1 Mar [n.y.]. 1 p, 4to. To [Mr. Savernor?]. Introducing an official of the American Construction Council. Illus in cat. sup Oct 15 (1631) $1,900

— [n.d.]. 1 p, 4to. To Senator Smith. Suggesting that his amemdments [to the Agricultural Adjustment Act] would defeat the bill. Illus in cat. sup May 9 (245) $6,750

Ls, 1 Sept 1915. 1 p, 4to. To Rear Admiral Charles F. Pond. As Acting Sec of the

Navy, informing him that Wm. F. Fullam will replace him. Endorsed by Pond. Dar Dec 26 (298) $225

— 6 Oct 1920. 1 p, 4to. To Victor G. Perrin. Sending his autograph. Dar Apr 9 (338) $350

— 5 Dec 1924. 2 pp, 4to. To John Callahan. Outlining principles of the Democratic Party, differences between Democrats & Republicans, & party strategy. wa Oct 19 (337) $1,300

— 16 Aug 1927. 1 p, 4to. To H. T. Morningstar. Expressing reluctance to run for Governor of NY. Spiro collection. CNY May 14 (140) $1,000

— 8 Oct 1928. 1 p, 8vo. To A. M. Chambers. Thanking for a telegram. Framed with engraved port. wa Oct 19 (336) $240

— 18 Nov 1928. 1 p, 4to. To Basil O'Connor. Regarding a tax application. Including 8-line autograph postscript, sgd F.D.R., about political plans. sg Feb 27 (164) $750

— 30 Jan 1930. 1 p, 4to. To Miss Monahan. About his interest in ship pictures. With related material. sg Sept 12 (208) $325

— 22 Oct 1931. 1 p, 4to. To Charles J. McDermott. About an appointment. With related material. Dar Oct 10 (313) $200

— 16 Feb 1932. 1 p, 4to. To Harold W. Fisher. Referring to a "recent statement by former Governor Smith". Dar Dec 26 (299) $250

— 9 Apr 1932. 1 p, 4to. To Basil O'Connor. Sending a check as "the result of a poker party" to be donated to the [Warm Springs] Foundation. Dar Apr 9 (334) $375

— 9 Apr 1932. 1 p, 4to. To Basil O'Connor. Sending a check as "the result of a poker party". R Nov 9 (33) $280

— 13 Apr 1932. 1 p, 4to. To William H. Fales. Responding to an inquiry (present, carbon copy) about his economic policy. Dar Oct 10 (311) $250

— 21 May 1932. 1 p, 4to. To Glenn B. Ralston. Acknowledging a letter. R Nov 9 (31) $220

— 9 June 1932. 1 p, 4to. To Edward I. Wade. Confirming that he will act promptly "on all evidences of official wrong-doing properly submitted to me." Spiro collection. CNY May 14 (141) $480

— 23 Dec 1932. 1 p, 4to. To Basil O'Connor. Humorously suggesting that a night in a cold storage plant "will restore [recipient] to health." R Nov 9 (30) $1,200

— 22 Mar 1933. 1 p, 8vo. To Mrs. Aymar Johnson. About her husband's sending a child to Georgia for treatment. With related material. Dar June 11 (331) $180

— 26 Mar 1934. 1 p, 8vo. To Alvin V. Baird. Planning a meeting. Dar Oct 10 (314) $350

— 27 June 1934. 1 p, 8vo. To Mr. & Mrs. John B. Allen. Congratulating them on their 60th wedding anniversary. Dar Oct 10 (316) $200

— 29 Dec 1934. 1 p, 8vo. To Dr. L. S. Rowe. Thanking for a trans of an article by Manuel Ugarte. Dar June 11 (332) $250

— 9 Jan 1935. 1 p, 8vo. To Postmaster General [Farley]. Memorandum instructing him to discontinue the issuance of unperforated or ungummed sheets of stamps. Illus in cat. sup May 9 (247) $4,400

— 26 Feb 1936. 1 p, 8vo. To Mrs. Aymar Johnson. About the death of Harry Roosevelt. Dar June 11 (327) $200

— 28 Apr 1936. 1 p, 4to. To Walter Trumbull. Thanking for condolences on the death of Louis Howe. R Nov 9 (32) $300

— 17 Sept 1936. 1 p, 4to. To Eugene Klein. Sending greetings to the annual convention of the American Philatelic Society. Illus in cat. sup May 9 (248) $1,000

— 16 Dec 1936. 1 p, 4to. To Walter P. Chrysler. Thanking for a message. sup Oct 15 (1627) $700

— 1 Apr 1937. 2 pp, size not stated. To Aymar Johnson. Expressing the wish to resign as trustee of the NY Cathedral. Dar Apr 9 (333) $2,000

— 18 June 1937. 1 p, 8vo. To Marshall. Expressing thanks for philatelic covers. Framed with engraved port. Dar Dec 26 (297) $300

— 21 Mar 1938. 1 p, 4to. To Louis N. Robinson. Acknowledging a report on prisons in the District of Columbia. Illus in cat. sup Oct 15 (1628) $1,550

— 15 Sept 1938. 1 p, 8vo. To Aymar Johnson. Saying his son is "progressing well". Dar June 11 (330) $325

— 22 Sept 1939. 1 p, 4to. To William E. Dodd. Thanking for comments on the situation in Europe. pn June 11 (43) £280

— 2 July 1941. 1 p, 4to. To Aymar Johnson. Thanking for his letter, & mentioning problems with the Bermudian Government. Dar Apr 9 (337) $400

— 16 Aug 1941. 1 p, 4to. To Col. W. Don Jones. Responding to an offer to organize disabled veterans for service. Illus in cat. sup May 9 (250) $800

— 13 Mar 1942. 1 p, 4to. To Mrs. Anthony J. Drexel Biddle. Referring to a present & the governorship pf Pennsylvania. Spiro collection. CNY May 14 (143) $400

— 17 Mar 1942. 1 p, 4to. To an unnamed attorney. Approving of a suggestion regarding his mother's estate. R Mar 7 (142) $500

— 28 Dec 1943. 1 p, 4to. To Emil Ludwig. Thanking for comments on his Christmas address. star Mar 27 (1676) DM850

— 10 Mar 1944. 1 p, 4to. To Harry L. Hopkins.

About recipient's recovery from an operation. Spiro collection. CNY May 14 (142) $500

— 15 Mar 1944. 1 p, 4to. To Harry L. Hopkins. Forwarding condolences from Churchill on the death of Hopkins's son. Spiro collection. CNY May 14 (144) $800

— [n.d.]. 1 p, 4to. Recipient unnamed. Expressing thanks. R Mar 7 (143) $180

ANs, [n.d.]. 16mo (card). Recipient unnamed. Sending his autograph. Illus in cat. Dar Apr 9 (335) $1,400

— [n.d.]. 1 p, 12mo. To Mary. Aboard R.M.S. Aquitania, asking her to see him after dinner. Framed with a port. Dar Apr 9 (336) $425

Collection of Ds & autograph Ms, 10 Feb 1923 & [1924]. 9 pp, 4to & 8vo. Last will & testament, & memorandum addressed to John Hackett outlining changes to be made to the will. P June 16 (270) $25,000

Ds, 13 June 1916. 1 p, 4to. Orders to Rear Admiral Charles F. Pond that his divison has been renamed. Dar Apr 9 (332) $275

— 15 Mar 1929. 1 p, 4to. As Governor, veto of a bill "to amend the penal law, in relation to punishment for receiving deposits in insolvent banks." Dar Oct 10 (312) $1,300

— 14 Apr 1930. 1 p, 4to. As Governor of NY, veto of an act regarding an avenue in Ogdensburg. Dar Aug 6 (252) $275

— 7 Dec 1934. 1 p, folio. Appointment of Thomas Rickert as board member of Federal Prison Industries. R June 13 (192) $300

— 25 July 1938. 1 p, folio. Humorous certification that E. G. Esperancilla, U.S.N., has crossed the equator. Illus in cat. sup Oct 15 (1629) $1,000

Autograph endorsement, sgd, 14 Apr 1930. As Governor of NY, on ptd Assembly bill no 2160, 1 p, 5.75 by 10.5 inches; vetoing the bill. Illus in cat. Dar Feb 13 (310) $400

— Anr, sgd, on Ls addressed to him by Sec of Labor Frances Perkins, suggesting that a committee be sent to England to study the handling of industrial differences, 22 Apr 1938. 1 p, 4to; agreeing with suggestion. With related material. Dar Oct 10 (315) $400

— Anr, sgd, [31 Dec 1940]. On verso of check sgd by Basil O'Connor. Dar Dec 26 (301) $450

Check, sgd, 3 Apr 1944. Payable to Merchants' National Bank & Trust Co. Illus in cat. sup Oct 15 (1775) $800

Engraving, [n.d.]. 4to. Sgd. sg Sept 12 (206) $300

Photograph, sgd & inscr, 6 July 1932. 197mm by 145mm. Inscr to M. A. L[e Hand]. P June 16 (279) $4,500

— Anr, [c.1933-34]. 8.25 by 9.75 inches, oblong. Inscr to Harry Braum. sg Sept 12 (209) $350

— Anr, Jan 1935. 252mm by 232mm. Close-up of his hands, inscr to M. A. L[e Hand]. Framed. P June 16 (280) $3,000

— Anr, [8 Jan 1943]. 4to. Inscr to Lynn U. Stambaugh. Framed with forwarding letter. wa Oct 19 (339) $350

— Anr, [n.d.]. 18 by 13 inches. At desk. Inscr to the National Democratic Club of America. b&b Feb 19 (162) $600

— Anr, [n.d.]. 18 by 13 inches. Full face. Inscr to the National Democratic Club of America. b&b Feb 19 (163) $700

— Anr, [n.d.]. 10 by 8 inches. Inscr to Charley Hand. Framed. Dar Dec 26 (300) $350

— Anr, [n.d.]. Framed; overall size 22 by 20 inches. Inscr to C. Simopoulas. sup Oct 15 (1636) $700

Signature, [n.d.]. On card with scene of the White House. Framed with engraved port. sup Oct 15 (1634) $725

Roosevelt, Franklin D., 1882-1945 —& Others

[The signatures of Roosevelt, Vice President Garner & 10 members of his cabinet on a sheet of 100 stamps, 1933, sold at sup on 15 Oct 1991, lot 1633, for $750.]

Roosevelt, Franklin D., 1882-1945 —& Garner, John Nance, 1868-1967

Group photograph, 13 June [19]38. Size not stated. Sgd & inscr to Dr. Calver by both. sup Oct 15 (1635) $500

— Anr, [n.d.]. 14 by 11 inches. Sgd & inscr to Dr. Caloer by both. Dar Dec 26 (302) $950

Roosevelt, Franklin D., 1882-1945. See: Truman, Harry S.

Roosevelt, Sara Delano, 1854-1941

A Ls s (2), 1906 & 1907. Length not stated. To W. J. Fontein. Referring to her son Franklin D. Roosevelt. With a photograph. sg Sept 12 (211) $600

Roosevelt, Theodore, 1858-1919

Autograph Ms, draft of an introduction to a book on R. E. Peary's expedition to the North Pole, 12 Mar 1910. 2 pp, folio. Including revisions; sgd. Illus in cat. Sang & Spiro collections. CNY May 14 (145) $11,000

— Autograph Ms, fragment from his work The Winning of the West; [n.d.]. 1 p, folio. Paginated 98. Illus in cat. sup Oct 15 (1588) $2,000

ALs, 10 Nov 1888. 1 p, 8vo. Recipient unnamed. Granting a request. Illus in cat. R Mar 7 (140) $650

— 30 Sept 1889. 2 pp, 8vo. To Louis Butterfield. About his wish to get a transfer from

Ghent to Nice. Framed with a photograph. Dar Apr 9 (341) $700

— 15 July 1916. 1 p, 12mo. To Mr. Reynolds. Requesting him to send the clippings with his letters in the future. Illus in cat. Dar Feb 13 (314) $650

— 27 Aug 1916. 2 pp, 8vo. To Miss Treadwell. Praising her work during the war & denouncing pacifists. Illus in cat. sup May 9 (225) $3,800

— 7 Mar 1917. 1 p, 8vo. To Mr. Wolcott. Introducing [Rock] Channing & Mr. Dolge. CNY Dec 5 (112) $800

— 7 Mar 1917. 1 p, 8vo. To Mr. Wolcott. Introducing Mr. Channing & Mr. Dolge. Illus in cat. Dar June 11 (333) $800

— [n.d.]. 1 p, 8vo. To Mr. Cortelyou. Hoping he "can do as Mr. Wolf writes". CNY Dec 5 (111) $1,000

Collection of Ls & photograph, 26 Aug 1898 & [n.d.]. 1 p, 4to, & 8 by 10 inches. To J. B. Allee. Thanking for a letter. Dar June 11 (334) $250

Ls, 21 Feb 1895. 1 p, 4to. To the Wallihan family. About photography of wild game. With autograph postscript. sg Sept 12 (212) $1,100

— 14 Mar 1896. 1 p, 4to. Recipient unnamed. Protesting against faked photographs used in a book. R Nov 9 (35) $600

— 16 Mar 1896. 1 p, 8vo. To Leslie Carter. Informing him about articles pbd in various magazines. Dar Feb 13 (312) $300

— 17 June 1901. 1 p, 4to. To Miguel A. Otero. Congratulating him on his appointment as Governor of New Mexico Territory. Dar Aug 6 (254) $500

— 6 July 1901. 1 p, 4to. Recipient unnamed. Referring to problems in procuring saddles & guns. R Nov 9 (34) $600

— 27 Aug 1901. 1 p, size not stated. To Walter Jennings. Concerning arrangements made by Mrs. Roosevelt. wd Dec 12 (335) $425

— 26 Jan 1904. 1 p, 4to. To Robert Worthington. Wishing the citizens of Santa Cruz success with their new library. Illus in cat. sup Oct 15 (1589) $700

— 12 May 1904. 1 p, 4to. To E. E. Garrison. Informing him that he will introduce Mr. Cooke to Mr. Coolidge. Some holograph additions. R Nov 9 (37) $450

— 12 Feb 1906. 1 p, 4to. To Christine Walton Dunlap. Supporting "the movement for the restoration of the McLean farmhouse at Appomattox". Illus in cat. sup May 9 (226) $1,600

— 1 Oct 1907. 1 p, 8vo. To R. S. Taylor. Acknowledging receipt of 2 pamphlets. Dar Feb 13 (313) $550

— 12 Feb 1908. 1 p, 4to. To Charles Waldstein. Thanking for a kind letter. pn Mar 19 (100) £140 [Revter]

— 12 Nov 1908. 1 p, 8vo. To William H. Hunt. Saying he "was pleased that Montana went for Taft." Dar Apr 9 (339) $600

— 25 Dec 1908. 1 p, 4to. To Mrs. John M. Glenn. Inviting her to a conference concerning care for destitute children. wa Oct 19 (341) $650

— 24 May 1912. 1 p, 4to. Recipient unnamed. Congratulating recipient "on being a delegate for the Sixth District". R Nov 9 (36) $280

— 7 Apr 1913. 1 p, 4to. To John Bleicher. About the political campaign of 1912. sg Feb 27 (167) $2,600

— 1 Apr 1915. 1 p, 4to. To Oscar King Davis. Enclosing a letter [of recommendation]. R Mar 7 (141) $320

— 29 Apr 1918. 1 p, 4to. Recipient & contents not stated. F Sept 26 (586) $125

— 27 July 1918. 1 p, 4to. To Rock H. Channing. Regretting being unable to participate in the war, since "the old should not live when the young die". With autograph addition. CNY Dec 5 (113) $6,000

ANs, 27 June 1906. 1 p, 16mo (card). To the War Department. Requesting that Major Flagler be appointed to the Delaware Canal Commission. Illus in cat. sup May 9 (227) $1,300

Ds, 31 Oct 1900. 1 p, 2.4 by 8 inches. As Governor of NY, receipt for some federal aid. sg Feb 27 (166) $250

— 29 Mar 1902. 1 p, folio. Naval commission for Charles W. Littlefield. sup Oct 15 (1590) $355

— 7 Nov 1902. 1 p, folio. Certification of an Act of the Chickasaw Legislature. CNY Dec 5 (110) $950

— 18 Dec 1902. 1 p, folio. Military commission, countersgd by Elihu Root. R Nov 9 (29) $450

— 6 June 1903. 1 p, folio. Appointment of Rand Crandall as surgeon in the Navy. sg Sept 12 (213) $425

— 23 May 1904. 1 p, folio. Appointment of A. V. Vogdes as Brigadier General, retired. Dar June 11 (336) $300

— 20 Dec 1904. 1 p, folio. Appointment of Daniel Pearson as lieut. colonel of cavalry. Countersgd by Wm. H. Taft. Framed. sg Sept 12 (214) $850

— 2 Feb 1906. 1 p, folio. Appointment of William H. Tyrrell as postmaster. Framed with a photograph. sup Oct 15 (1591) $360

— 17 Mar 1906. 1 p, folio. Appointment of George E. Terry as Notary Public. sup Oct 15 (1592) $355

— 2 May 1907. 1 p, folio. Appointment of D. C. Cubbison as Lieut. of Artillery. Countersgd by W. H. Taft. Framed. sup

Oct 15 (1593) $675

— 7 Jan 1908. 1 p, folio. Military commission. Countersgd by W. H. Taft. R Nov 9 (39) $950

Autograph sentiment, 28 Dec 1916. 1 p, 4to. Expressing good wishes; sgd. Illus in cat. sup Oct 15 (1597) $750

— Anr, sgd, [n.d.]. 6.25 by 3.25 inches. Inscr to George K. Cherrie on portion of a page removed from his book Through the Brazilian Wilderness. Dar Apr 9 (342) $200

Check, sgd, 3 Jan 1913. Payable to Von Lengerke & Detmold. Dar Apr 9 (340) $600

Franking signature, [8 Nov 1898]. As Governor of NY. bbc Sept 23 (29) $95

Menu, sgd, for a dinner in his honor given by the Commercial Interests of NY City at the Waldorf Astoria, 10 Mar 1900. 4 pp, 6 by 9 inches. Dar June 11 (335) $275

Photograph, sgd & inscr, 19 Nov 1904. Size not stated; oval. Inscr to Henry W. Taft. Framed. Illus in cat. wd Dec 12 (336) $1,100

— Anr, 18 Sept 1905. 4 by 5.5 inches. By Bell. sup Oct 15 (1595) $860

— Anr, 30 Jan 1909. 7.5 by 9 inches. Inscr to Leo Mielziner. With related material. sg Sept 12 (215) $700

White House card, sgd, 25 May 1908. With centered engraved vignette. R Nov 9 (38) $900

Rose, Billy, 1899-1966

Ds, 6 Feb 1963. 6 pp, 4to. Contract with Theatre Guild Productions Inc. for The Jack Benny Show; carbon copy. Dar Feb 13 (315) $250

Photograph, sgd & inscr, [n.d.] 8 by 10 inches. Inscr to Maurice. Dar Aug 6 (26) $110

Rosecrans, William Starke, 1819-98

Photograph, sgd, [n.d.]. Carte size. In uniform. By Anthony, from a Brady negative. Illus in cat. R June 13 (101) $450

Rosegger, Peter, 1843-1918

Autograph Ms, poem, beginning "Auf alle Wiegen sollt' man's schreiben...", [n.d.]. 1 p, 8vo. Quatrain, sgd. HH Nov 6 (2095) DM360

ALs, 2 Jan 1882. 3 pp, 8vo. To unnamed friends. Thanking for New Year's wishes; in dialect. With 2 photographs. star Mar 26 (422) DM300

Series of 16 autograph postcards, sgd, 8 Aug 1871 to 24 Dec 1886. To Hugo Hirt. About meetings, lectures, family news, etc. HH May 13 (2040) DM800

Autograph postcard, sgd, 15 Jan 1893. Recipient unnamed. Requesting permission to reprint an essay. HH Nov 6 (2096) DM220

Rosenberg, Alfred, 1893-1946

Photograph, sgd, [n.y.]. Postcard. HH May 13 (2041) DM400

Rosenheim, Jakob, 1870-1965

ALs, 1900. 1 p, 4to. To Joseph Hayyim Sonnenfeld. Regarding matters of charitable concern. sg Dec 19 (203) $130

Rosenkranz, Johann Karl Friedrich, 1805-79

ALs, 19 July 1854. 4 pp, 4to. Recipient unnamed. Explaining that logic is fundamental to mathematics. star Mar 26 (790) DM650

Rosser, Thomas Lafayette, 1836-1910

Cut signature, [n.d.]. 4.25 by 1 inches. Framed. Illus in cat. Armstrong collection. sup Oct 15 (1125) $300

Rossetti, Dante Gabriel, 1828-82

Ms, poem, Ave; [c.1869]. 4 pp, folio. 146 lines, representing an intermediate stage between the 1st draft & the ptd version of 1870. Probably in Christina Rossetti's hand. C June 24 (380) £650 [Maggs]

Series of 3 A Ls s, 1862. 3 pp, size not stated. To C. F. Hayward. Concerning a proposed commission for decorating a cabinet. With related ALs by Hayward. Ck Nov 15 (27) £550

ALs, 30 Mar 1865. 4 pp, 8vo. To G. Lucas. Suggesting that Swinburne write an article on [Ford Madox] Brown. Ingilby collection. pn Nov 14 (97) £380 [Quaritch]

— [n.d.], "Monday". 2 pp, 8vo. To Thomas Woolner. Saying he will bring Mr. Marshall to see Woolner's bust of Tennyson. Ingilby collection. pn Nov 14 (96) £460

Rossini, Gioacchino, 1792-1868

ALs, [c.1824]. 3 pp, 8vo. To Carlo Severini. Discussing a program comprising parts of La gazza ladra & Otello. S Dec 6 (177) £1,800 [Franks]

— 3 Feb 1838. 1 p, 8vo. To Andrea Ghedini. Urging him to come to Milan, & giving advice on his passport. S Dec 6 (176) £500 [Tamura Shoten]

— 2 Nov 1841. 2 pp, 4to. To Gaetano Donizetti. Urging him to accept the directorship of the Liceo Musicale in Bologna. S May 29 (640) £3,800 [Franks]

— 12 Feb 1844. 1 p, 4to. To Felice Romani. Reporting the alterations he has made to the Chorus of the Bards from La donna del lago. S May 29 (637) £2,800 [Franks]

— 3 Feb 1846. 1 p, 4to. To Prince Giuseppe Coniatosti. Discussing details of his opera Matilde. Framed with a port. P June 17 (71) $2,500

— 17 Jan 1859. 3 pp, 4to. To Angelo Mignani. Discussing his financial affairs. S Dec 6

(178) £1,000 [Caverzasio]

— 1 Sept 1863. 2 pp, 12mo. To Victor Masse. Letter of recommendation for M. Sauza. Searles-Rowland collection. C June 24 (9) £580 [L'Autographe]

— 1 Aug 1866. 1 p, 4to. To "Conte Giuseppe". Describing his difficult position in Paris during the war against the Austrians. S Dec 6 (173) £1,000 [Tamura Shoten]

— [n.d.]. 1 p, 8vo. To an unnamed general. Reporting that the piano is ready. bba Sept 19 (378) £400 [Sakmyster]

AL, [n.d.]. 2 pp, 4to. To the Fratelli Dacci. Draft, praising their invention to improve a musical instrument. star Mar 27 (1129) DM750

Photograph, sgd & inscr, [1860]. 10cm by 6cm. Inscr to Mme Richards. S May 29 (638) £1,200 [Pulido]

— Anr, 1861. Carte size. Inscr to Aristide Farrenc. Illus in cat. S Dec 6 (179) £1,800 [Burkill]

Roth, Eugen, 1895-1976

Autograph Ms, poem, beginning "Ein Mensch hats nunmehr schwarz auf weiss...", [1965]. 14 lines, sgd. With related material. HH Nov 6 (2097) DM330

Roth, Rudolf von, 1821-95

ALs, 6 Nov 1846. 1 p, 8vo. To Theodor Benfey. Discussing a Vedic Ms. Endorsed by recipient. star Mar 26 (791) DM650

Rousseau, Jean Baptiste, 1671-1741

ALs, 29 June 1720. 3 pp, 4to. To M. de Cronsaz. Reflecting on literature & politics. sg Sept 12 (216) $750

Rousseau, Jean Jacques, 1712-78

ALs, 2 Apr 1765. 1 p, 4to. To Samuel Meuron. Expressing thanks "pour la besogne que vous avez faite". star Mar 26 (424) DM6,000

Rousseau, Theodore, 1812-67

ALs, 22 Mar 1867. 1 p, 8vo. To an unnamed colleague. Inviting him to a dinner with other members of a panel. star Mar 27 (943) DM400

Rowe, John, 1726-76

Autograph Ms, Introduction to the Doctrine of Fluxions, 5 July 1757. 177 pp, 4to, in contemp calf. Ms prepared for the 2d Ed, including copious additions to 1st Ed & c.74 diagrams. Sgd. Ck Apr 3 (24) £320

Rubens, Peter Paul, 1577-1640

ALs, 4 May 162[8]. 2 pp, folio. To Pierre Dupuy. Discussing the wars & dynastic conflicts in Northern Italy. In Italian. Illus in cat. Mannheim collection. S Dec 5 (462) £7,000 [Stad]

Rubinstein, Anton, 1829-94

Autograph music, 6 songs to poems by Heine, Goethe, Tieck, Uhland, etc., Op.31, scored for tenor & bass; [n.d.]. 13 pp, folio. Gottschalk collection. C Dec 16 (425) £1,600 [Rosenthal]

ALs, 1876. 1 p, 8vo. To Mimi Katler. About projected productions of Nero in Hamburg & Berlin. sup Oct 15 (1801) $350

Autograph quotation, sgd, 9 Dec 1842. 1 p, 4to. Musical quotation. HN June 26 (975) DM360

— Anr, seven bars of a song, scored for 2 voices, 23 Nov 1883. 1 p, 8vo. Sgd. star Mar 27 (1130) DM650

Photograph, sgd, [1857?]. 8vo. By Alviach. HN June 26 (975a) DM200

Ruby, Jack, 1911-67. See: Kennedy, John F.

Rudolf II, Emperor, 1552-1612

Ds, 24 Oct 1576. 1 p, 527mm by 679mm. Patent of nobility & grant of arms for Hans, Gregor & Leonhard Hueber. Including painting of the arms in gold & colors. Illus in cat. HH May 12 (62) DM2,600

— 23 Aug 1597. 1 p, folio. Ptd order addressed to Counts Heinrich & Georg zu Castell to attend the Imperial Diet at Regensburg. HN Nov 28 (1817) DM480

Rudolf IV, Duke of Austria, 1339-65

Ds, [25 Nov] 1362. 1 p, vellum, folio. Confirmation of privileges granted to the Carthusian monastery at Seitz by Duke Leopold VI, 1227. star Mar 27 (1527) DM5,500

Rueckert, Friedrich, 1788-1866

Autograph Ms, poem, beginning "Ich bin die Blum' im Garten...", Feb 1857. 5 stanzas (1 incomplete), sgd. star Mar 26 (425) DM950

— Autograph Ms, poem, beginning "Zweihundert Jahr alt war geworden Abraham...", [n.d.]. 1 p, 8vo. 18 lines. star Mar 26 (426) DM700

Series of 11 A Ls s, 6 Feb 1838 to [15 May 1852]. 13 pp, 4to & 8vo. To Ferdinand Scheler. About negotiations with publishers, legal matters, his publications, etc. With related material. star Mar 26 (427) DM4,000

Ruetimeyer, Ludwig, 1825-95

A Ls s (2), 20 Sept 1883 & 12 Aug 1885. 4 pp, 8vo. To Henri & Alphonse Milne-Edwards. Discussing a paleontological question, & expressing condolences. star Mar 26 (792) DM360

Ruge, Arnold, 1803-80

ALs, 18 July 1850. 3 pp, 12mo. To an unnamed lady. Commenting on a work by [Alexander] Herzen. star Mar 27 (1677) DM480

Rundstedt, Gerd von, 1875-1953

Autograph postcards (2), sgd, 22 Apr & 25 July 1942. To his wife Luise. Rewporting from the front. star Mar 27 (1765) DM1,200

Rupprecht, Crown Prince of Bavaria, 1869-1955

ALs, 21 Apr 1930. 2 pp, 4to. To [Hermann] Schmitz. Responding to an inquiry about old paintings in his family's possession. star Mar 27 (1269) DM400

Rush, Benjamin, Signer from Pennsylvania

A Ls s (2), 20 July & 10 Aug 1802. 5 pp, 4to. To William Smith. Returning a letter Smith had written on the death of his wife (included, 22 Oct 1793) & assuming that "a gallery of portraits of sick people" could help in the study of medicine. P June 16 (181) $3,750

Rusk, Thomas Jefferson, 1803-57

ALs, 23 Sept 1843. 3 pp, folio. To Thomas Ward. Discussing local elections & the general temper of the people in Texas. CNY June 9 (280) $2,100

— 13 Feb 1845. 1 p, 4to. To John A. Quitman. About a letter of introduction. R Nov 9 (153) $320

Ruskin, John, 1819-1900

ALs, [1856?]. 1 p, 8vo. Recipient unnamed. Giving instructions on how to pack a picture. pn Nov 14 (215) £80 [Quaritch]

— 4 July 1867. 1 p, 8vo. To Woodward. Sending a mineralogical paper for publication. bba June 25 (133) £75 [Kunkler]

— 10 May 1884. 2 pp, 8vo. To Miss Willett. Thanking for the gift of an opal from her father. bba Sept 19 (367) £75 [Hetherington]

— [n.d.]. 4 pp, size not stated. To Mr. Cuff. Discussing corrections to be made to an engraving. Ck Apr 3 (82) £140

— [n.d.]. 1 p, 8vo. To Mrs. Gaskell. Saying how puzzling he finds some aspects of women's work. Ingilby collection. pn Nov 14 (99) £160 [Quaritch]

Russell, Bertrand, 3d Earl, 1872-1970

Ls s (2), 9 & 16 March 1965. 2 pp, 8vo. To Miss Bedford. Making arrangements for a meeting. bba Sept 19 (368) £60 [Rivlin]

Russell, John Scott, 1808-82

[A group of engineering notebooks, including records of trials on steam carriages & registers relating to the Great Eastern constructed in partnership with I. K. Brunel, 1834 to 1867, c.585 pp in 7 vols, sold at pn on 11 June 1992, lot 61, for £1,800 to Quaritch.]

Ruth, George Herman ("Babe"), 1895-1948

Ls, 12 Apr 1930. 1 p, 8vo. To D. F. Cusick. Informing him that he will write articles for the NY Evening Journal. Illus in cat. Shaw collection. sup July 10 (859) $2,000

— 13 Apr 1934. 1 p, 4to. To J. A. Donan. Expressing appreciation for the work of recipient's advertising agency. Illus in cat. Shaw collection. sup July 10 (858) $3,500

Check, accomplished & sgd, 6 June 1937. 8.5 by 3.25 inches. Also endorsed on verso. Dar Oct 10 (84) $1,000

— Anr, sgd, 5 Jan 1941. Drawn on the Chemical Bank & Trust Co. of NY. wa Oct 19 (82) $1,700

Photograph, sgd, 1932. 3 by 5 inches. Shaw collection. sup July 10 (851) $625

— Anr, [1947]. 5 by 6.5 inches. Inserted in a banquet program. Illus in cat. Shaw collection. sup July 10 (864) $750

Photograph, sgd & inscr, [1920s]. 5 by 6.75 inches. Illus in cat. Shaw collection. sup July 10 (848) $1,350

— Anr, [early 1930s]. 8 by 10 inches. Inscr to Jack Thomas. Illus in cat. Shaw collection. sup July 10 (840) $2,700

— Anr, [early 1930s]. 6 by 10 inches. Inscr to Rosa M. Morison. Framed. Illus in cat. Shaw collection. sup July 10 (852) $950

— Anr, [5 Apr 1947]. 8 by 10 inches. Inscr to Bugs Bear. Including ANs by Christy Walsh on verso. Dar Dec 26 (104) $1,500

— Anr, 25 Dec 1947. 9 by 7 inches. Inscr to Domenico Facci. CNY Dec 5 (115) $2,000

— Anr, [n.d.]. 10.25 by 13.25 inches. Inscr to Harry Brown. Dar Dec 26 (103) $2,250

— Anr, [n.d.]. 8 by 10 inches. Inscr to Gordon Lowenstein. Illus in cat. Shaw collection. sup July 10 (841) $2,100

— Anr, [n.d.]. 8 by 10 inches. Inscr to Jimmy. Illus in cat. Shaw collection. sup July 10 (842) $1,800

— Anr, [n.d.]. 8 by 10 inches. Inscr to Edgar A. Moss. Imperf. Illus in cat. Shaw collection. sup July 10 (847) $650

— Anr, [n.d.]. 8 by 10 inches. Framed. Illus in cat. Shaw collection. sup July 10 (853) $2,000

Ptd photograph, sgd, Aug [1929]. 7.5 by 4.5 inches. Visiting patients injured in Yankee Stadium accident. Dar Dec 26 (105) $850

— Anr, sgd & inscr, [1932]. Size not stated. Illus in cat. Shaw collection. sup July 10 (867) $1,100

— Anr, sgd, [1930s]. 3.5 by 4 inches. Illus in cat. Shaw collection. sup July 10 (845)

$1,100

Signature, [c.31 May 1922]. On verso of check payable to him, sgd by J. Ruppert as president of the NY Yankees, with a fine noted on verso. Illus in cat. Shaw collection. sup July 10 (861) $4,000

— Anr, [1930]. On football program. Also sgd by Frank Frisch. sup July 10 (866) $340

— Anr, 23 May [19]35. 4to. Including note of authentication & ptd photograph pasted on. Sgd by R. Maranville on verso. Illus in cat. Shaw collection. sup July 10 (849) $750

— Anr, 12 Feb 1936. 8vo. On golf score card. Illus in cat. sg Feb 27 (169) $1,100

— Anr, [c.1939]. Card, mtd on 16mo leaf. sg Sept 12 (217) $500

— Anr, [c.1943]. On Press Parade program. F Sept 26 (588) $450

— Anr, [c.11 Mar 1944]. On verso of check payable to him; sgd twice. Illus in cat. Shaw collection. sup July 10 (863) $850

— Anr, [n.d.]. 3.5 by 2 inches (card). In violet ink. Dar Oct 10 (85) $600

— Anr, [n.d.]. On cover of a matchbook, 1.5 by 4 inches. Imperf. Framed with related material. Dar Feb 13 (89) $100

— Anr, [n.d.]. 3.25 by 2 inches. Matted with Hall of Fame card. Illus in cat. Dar June 11 (90) $800

— Anr, [n.d.]. 2 by 1 inches. Dar June 11 (91) $375

— Anr, [n.d.]. 2 by 3.5 inches (card). R Mar 7 (79A) $450

— Anr, [n.d.]. Framed with orig pencil port, overall size 14 by 18 inches. Illus in cat. Shaw collection. sup July 10 (855) $1,000

— Anr, [n.d.]. Size not stated. On typescript of 18-line poem by a fan. Illus in cat. Shaw collection. sup July 10 (860) $700

— Anr, [n.d.]. 3 by 5 inches (card). Illus in cat. Shaw collection. sup July 10 (872) $625

— HERRIN, M. H. - Orig drawing, pencil port of Ruth, 17 Apr 1934. 6.5 by 10 inches. Sgd by both. Framed. Illus in cat. Shaw collection. sup July 10 (854) $1,100

Ruths, Valentin, 1825-1905

Collection of 24 A Ls s & AL, 20 Mar 1847 to 3 Aug 1892. 77 pp, 4to & 8vo. To his brother Eduard. Family correspondence, & about his travels, his paintings, etc. hen Nov 12 (2502) DM3,000

Ryan, John, 1845-1926. See: Custer, George Armstrong

Ryder, Albert Pinkham, 1847-1917

Signature, [1896]. 16mo. On a page from his account book. Dar Apr 9 (345) $100

S

Sacher-Masoch, Leopold von, 1836-95

A Ls s (2), 28 July 1877 & 15 Oct 1893. 8 pp, 8vo. To the Schiller Foundation. Applying for financial aid. With related material. star Mar 26 (432) DM1,100

ALs, 10 Jan 1869. 7 pp, 8vo. To the Ed of the Salon fuer Literatur, Kunst und Gesellschaft. Refuting criticism of his novel Soldaten Christi. star Mar 26 (431) DM530

— 18 Aug 1888. 2 pp, 8vo. Recipient unnamed. About recipient's interest in his Contes Juifs. Dar Apr 9 (346) $400

Sadat, Anwar El, 1918-81

Transcript, excerpt from an interview, referring to the necessity of a permanent settlement in the Middle East; 6 Feb 1977. 1 p, 12mo. Sgd. Dar Dec 26 (303) $375

Sade, Donatien Alphonse Francois, Marquis de, 1740-1814

ALs, 29 Oct 1763. 2 pp, 4to. To Antoine-Raimond de Sartine. Desperately pleading to be released from prison. CNY Dec 5 (321) $3,000

Saint-Saens, Camille, 1835-1921

Collection of 7 A Ls s & AN, 1913 to 1922. 12 pp, 4to & 8vo. To Adolphe Boschot. About a variety of musical matters. S May 29 (641) £450 [Mazzucchetti]

ALs, 28 Jan 1901. 1 p, 8vo. Recipient unnamed. Telling him that he has written to people on his behalf. sg Feb 27 (170) $100

Autograph quotation, 8 bars from his 5th Concerto, 1913. 1 p, 8vo. Sgd. star Mar 27 (1131) DM1,100

Salieri, Antonio, 1750-1825

Autograph music, Agnesina's aria, Son'io semplice fanciulla, for the 1st act of an unidentified opera, [n.d.]. 12 pp, 23cm by 32cm. 243 bars in full score. Illus in cat. star Mar 27 (1132) DM8,500

Salinger, Jerome David

ALs, 22 Jan 1967. 1 p, 8vo. To James Ciletti. Thanking for a letter. Illus in cat. sup Oct 15 (1803) $1,800

Salk, Jonas

Ls, 25 Feb 1963. 1 p, 4to. To Dr. Herman Harvey. Regretting that he cannot participate in a conference. Framed with a photograph. sup Oct 15 (1804) $380

Salomon, Haym, c.1740-85

Ds, 25 Oct 1781. 1 p, folio. Conveyance of property in Philadelphia to Peter Woglom. Also sgd by his wife Rachel. Illus in cat. CNY May 14 (6) $19,000

Salzmann, Christian Gotthilf, 1744-1811

ALs, 6 Feb 1795. 2 pp, 4to. To Archenholz. Suggesting that he publish a review of one of his works in the journal Minerva. star Mar 26 (793) DM330

San Martin, Jose de, 1778-1850

[A letter addressed to him by 11 inhabitants of Valdiva, 9 Dec 1817, 2 leaves, folio, professing their patriotic motives, sold at HN on 28 Nov 1991, lot 1822, for DM200.]

ALs, 27 Aug 1817. 1 p, 4to. To Luis de la Cruz. Asking for the arrest of Exequiel Juelt. HN Nov 28 (1818) DM1,000

— [1824]. 1 p, 4to. To J. B. Robinson. Sending compliments. Dawson Turner collection. pn Nov 14 (133) £320

Ls, 15 Nov 1817. 1 p, 4to. To the Sec of State for the Department of the Interior. Acknowledging receipt of a dispatch. Dar Oct 10 (317) $550

— 29 Jan 1821. 1 p, folio. To Jose Ignacio Zenteno. Referring to the change of name of the frigate Esmeralda. Including autograph endorsement, sgd, by Bernardo O'Higgins. HN Nov 28 (1821) DM400

Ds s (2)11 Feb & 20 Dec 1820. 2 pp, 8vo & 4to. Lists of staff of the Peruvian army. HN Nov 28 (1820) DM340

Sand, George, Pseud. of Amandine, Baronne Dudevant, 1804-76

ALs, [c.1830s]. 1 p, 8vo. To Florestan Bonnaire. Thanking for money & a letter. star Mar 26 (435) DM900

— [23 Nov 1854]. 2 pp, 8vo. To Josef Dessauer. Assuring him of her friendship & referring to Heine. With letter of transferral by Dessauer. Gottschalk collection. C Dec 16 (415) £380 [Rosenthal]

— 6 Oct [1867]. 1 p, size not stated. Recipient unnamed. Explaining that she is unable to intervene in a situation. Ck Apr 3 (25) £200

— 9 Oct [n.y.]. 1 p, 8vo. To Gen. Pepe. Changing the date of an appointment. wd June 12 (332) $225

Sandburg, Carl, 1878-1967

Ls, 8 July 1933. 1 p, 4to. To Miss Bullard. Informing her that Henry Holt & Company own the copyright to his Chicago Poems. Dar Oct 10 (318) $350

Santa Anna, Antonio Lopez de, 1794-1876

Ls, 14 Oct 1847. 1 p, 4to. To his godson. Congratulating him on his engagement to G. Flores. Framed with a port. sup May 9 (146) $800

— 2 Nov 1853. 1 p, 4to. To Percy W. Doyle. About the railroad between Veracruz & Acapulco. sup Oct 15 (1384) $900

Ds, 13 Oct 1853. 2 pp, folio. Proclamation ordering seats to be reserved for for himself, the Governor of the district & others at theaters in Mexico City. Illus in cat. sup May 9 (149) $950

— 3 Jan 1854. 1 p, folio. Patent for a machine for the making of chocolate issued to Manuel Gutierrez de Rozes. Dar Oct 10 (320) $800

— Feb 1854. 2 pp, folio. Contents not stated. R Mar 7 (235) $650

— 8 June 1866. 1 p, folio. Bond no 786/1500 for $500, to be secured by land in Mexico. Framed with a port. Illus in cat. sup Oct 15 (1385) $950

— 28 June 1866. Folio. Mortgage bond dealing with land sales in Vera Cruz, St. Thomas, & New Granada. Framed. R Mar 7 (236) $600

Santayana, George, 1863-1952

ALs, 12 Dec 1950. 1 p, 4to. To Martin Gumpert. About an interview & his autobiography. sg Feb 27 (171) $275

Autograph postcard, sgd, 11 Feb 1932. To Emmanuel Horowitz. Declining to contribute to recipient's "proposed discussion on Liberalism." Imperf. Dar Aug 6 (256) $120

Saphir, Moritz Gottlieb, 1795-1858

A Ls s (2), 13 Nov 1821 & 4 Oct 1824. 4 pp, 4to. To Adolf Baeuerle. About contributions to the Wiener Theaterzeitung. star Mar 26 (436) DM240

Sassoon, Siegfried, 1886-1967

Autograph Ms, poem, A Defence of Idealism; [n.d.]. 1 p, size not stated. 3 stanzas. Ck Apr 3 (62) £350

— Autograph Ms, poem, Concert-interpretation (le Sacre du Printemps); [c.1922]. 1 p, size not stated. 7 stanzas. Illus in cat. Ck Apr 3 (58) £200

— Autograph Ms, poem, On Finding Phoenixes; [c.1921]. 1 p, size not stated. 5 rhyming couplets; initialled. Ck Apr 3 (61) £240

— Autograph Ms, poem, Sheldonian Soliloquy (during Bach's B minor Mass); [c.1922]. 1 p, size not stated. 4 stanzas, sgd Cyprinoid. Illus in cat. Ck Apr 3 (59) £200

— Autograph Ms, poem, Villa d'Este Gardens; [c.1922]. 1 p, size not stated. 4 stanzas, sgd. Illus in cat. Ck Apr 3 (60) £280

— Autograph Ms, Wonted Themes, a group of 14 poems, 1952. Length not stated, in wraps. Initialled. With ALs, 1 Jan [19]53, sending these poems to Henry Major Tomlinson. Ck Apr 3 (67) £3,200

Collection of 7 A Ls s & A Ns s, 1 May [19]28 & [n.d.]. Length not stated. To Henry Major Tomlinson & Hugh Massingham. About a variety of private & literary matters. Ck Apr 3 (64) £700

A Ls s (2), 19 Mar [19]39 & 21 July [19]41. Length not stated. To Henry Major Tomlinson. Discussing the war, his projected book, etc. Ck Apr 3 (65) £280

ALs, 20 Oct [19]47. 2 pp, size not stated. To Henry Major Tomlinson. Expressing frustrations with his critics & international publishing policies. Ck Apr 3 (66) £180

— 4 Mar [19]55. 2 pp, size not stated. To Henry Major Tomlinson. Discussing T. E. Lawrence & Thomas Hardy. Ck Apr 3 (70) £500

— 20 Feb [19]56. 2 pp, size not stated. To Henry Major Tomlinson. About the harsh winter, Thomas Hardy, his own work, etc. Ck Apr 3 (71) £260

— 15 Mar [19]56. 2 pp, size not stated. To Henry Major Tomlinson. Referring to Thomas Hardy & musing about the long winter. Ck Apr 3 (72) £450

— 26 Feb [n.y.]. 1 p, size not stated. Recipient unnamed. Rejecting John Middleton Murry's assertion that Wilfried Owen was the greater war poet. Ck Apr 3 (63) £280

Satie, Erik, 1866-1925

ALs, 24 Apr 1913. 1 p, 12mo. To M. D. Calvocoressi. Thanking for an article. Framed with a port. P June 17 (73) $1,400

Sauguet, Henri

Autograph music, draft of the ballet Le Prince et le mendiant, Mar to May 1965. 38 pp, 20.5cm by 26.5cm. Short score, written on up to 5 systems per page, 2 & 3 staves each. Sgd & inscr to Boris [Kochno]. Boris Kochno collection. SM Oct 12 (395) FF13,500

— Autograph music, sketches for the ballet Paris, 1964. 51 pp, 8vo. Extensive working draft, written on up to 20 staves per page. Sgd on tp. With related ALs to Boris Kochno. Boris Kochno collection. SM Oct 12 (394) FF15,000

Collection of 16 A Ls s & A Ls, 1927 to 1965. 40 pp, various sizes. To Boris Kochno. About several of his ballets. Including 3 autograph musical quotations. SM Oct 12 (396) FF6,000

— Collection of 5 A Ls s & 2 postcards sgd, 1927 to 1934. 15 pp, 4to & 16mo. To Christian Berard. About his ballet La Nuit, the opera La Chartreuse de Parme, & other works. With related material. Boris Kochno collection. SM Oct 12 (397) FF5,000

Savigny, Friedrich Karl von, 1779-1861

ALs, 15 Nov 1832. 1 p, 4to. To E. G. Friedlaender. Responding to an inquiry about J. Brippius. star Mar 26 (794) DM480

Scanzoni von Lichtenfels, Friedrich Wilhelm, 1821-91

ALs, 20 Apr 1859. 2 pp, 8vo. To an unnamed colleague. About a date for a consultation. star Mar 26 (795) DM210

Schadow, Johann Gottfried, 1764-1850

Autograph Ms, minutes of a meeting with Karl Friedrich Schinkel concerning the study of architecture at the Berlin Academy of Arts, 19 Feb 1824. 3 pp, folio. Sgd. Including half-page autograph addition by Schinkel, sgd. Illus in cat. star Mar 27 (944) DM2,000

ALs, 1 Apr 1828. 1 p, 8vo. To an unnamed bookseller. Sending engravings. star Mar 27 (945) DM320

— 9 June 1831. 2 pp, 8vo. To a friend in Denmark. Introducing the painter Wilhelm Krause. hen Nov 12 (2503) DM320

Ls, 22 May 1849. 1 p, 4to. To Francois Auber. Notifying him of his election as member of the Berlin Academy of Arts. star Mar 27 (946) DM250

Schalk, Ray, 1892-1970

ALs, [n.d.]. 1 p, 8vo. To Tom. Replying to his questions about memorable moments in his career. Dar Dec 26 (106) $225

Scharnhorst, Gerhard von, 1755-1813

ALs, 9 Aug 1802. 3 pp, folio. To an unnamed Lieut. General. Sending 2 papers regarding the artillery. Def. star Mar 27 (1706) DM370

— 29 Dec 1805. 2 pp, 4to. To [Ludwig von Ompteda]. Discussing troop movements of the several armies in the Kingdom of Hannover. Illus in cat. star Mar 27 (1707) DM2,600

Scheerbart, Paul, 1863-1915

Autograph Ms, novella, Der Aufgang zur Sonne, 17 June 1900. 62 pp, 4to, on rectos only, in half vellum bdg. Including revisions. Sgd on tp & at end. star Mar 26 (437) DM5,200

Schefer, Leopold, 1784-1862

A Ls s (2), 15 July 1850 & 8 Nov 1856. 2 pp, 8vo. To J. J. Weber. Offering works for print. star Mar 26 (439) DM220

Scheffel, Joseph Victor von, 1826-86

ALs, 2 Mar 1868. 2 pp, 8vo. Recipient unnamed. Thanking for a publication. HN Nov 28 (1824) DM280

— 27 Nov [18]71. 1 p, 8vo. To the bookseller Brissel. Promising to send 50 copies of one of his works. HH May 13 (2044) DM240

Schelling, Friedrich Wilhelm Joseph von, 1775-1854

ALs, 27 Oct 1802. 4 pp, 8vo. To [the winesellers Ramann]. Complaining about a recent shipment. star Mar 26 (796) DM700

Schenkendorf, Max von, 1783-1817

Autograph Ms, poem, beginning "Schoenes Gestern, leeres Heute...", [n.d.]. 1 p, 8vo. 3 four-line stanzas; sgd with paraph. star Mar 26 (441) DM340

Schikaneder, Emanuel, 1751-1812

Ds, 1 Apr 1799. 1 p, 4to. Fragment, contract with Joseph von Seyfried. Also sgd by others. star Mar 27 (1228) DM1,700

Schiller, Friedrich von, 1759-1805

ALs, 20 June 1799. 2 pp, 4to. To Christian Gottfried Koerner. Sending part of his Wallenstein, & discussing recipient's review of a work. Sgd S. star Mar 26 (442) DM22,000

— 2 May 1802. 1 p, 4to. To Siegfried Lebrecht Crusius. Reminding him of a promised advance payment. Mtd. star Mar 26 (443) DM16,500

Schillings, Max von, 1868-1933

ALs, 4 Dec 1921. 2 pp, 4to. To Max Friedlaender. Complaining about his work load & the music scene in Berlin. star Mar 27 (1139) DM260

Schinkel, Karl Friedrich, 1781-1841. See: Schadow, Johann Gottfried

Schlecht, Ignatius Christophorus

Ms, Rechenbuch ... von Vielen Nutzlichen Kauffmans Reglen in allen Handtirungen... [Augsburg, Germany, 1 Apr 1691]. 232 leaves, 210mm by 172mm. Contemp red vellum bdg. Arithmetics, weights & measures, etc. HH Nov 5 (816) DM850

Schlegel, August Wilhelm von, 1767-1845

Autograph Ms, essay, Ueber den Nahmen der Kunst; [n.d.]. 2 pp, 8vo. Illus in cat. HH May 13 (2046) DM600

— Autograph Ms, monologue, Der Narr; [n.d.]. 2 pp, 4to. With instructions for the ptr in margin. Illus in cat. HH May 13 (2045) DM900

— Autograph Ms, poem, Ein Portraet ohne Namen, [n.d.]. 1 p, 8vo. 7 lines. star Mar 26 (444) DM750

ALs, 15 Apr 1824. 2 pp, 4to. To Graves Champney Haughton. About recipient's forthcoming book about "les lois de Manu" & their joint interest in Sanskrit. In French. star Mar 26 (445) DM420

Schlegel, Friedrich von, 1772-1829

ALs, 1 June 1804. 3 pp, 8vo. To Friedrich Wilmans. Promising to finish the new issue of the journal Europa in a few days. star Mar 26 (446) DM1,300

Schleiden, Matthias Jacob, 1804-81

ALs, 1 Jan 1848. 3 pp, 8vo. To Marshall. Asking for recipient's opinion about his recent book. hen Nov 12 (2547) DM300

Schleiermacher, Friedrich, 1768-1834

Series of 6 A Ls s, 12 July 1829 to 2 Jan 1834. 17 pp, 4to & 8vo. To unnamed friends in Biala. Mostly about financial problems of his widowed sister, the care of her children, family news, etc. star Mar 26 (802) DM3,800

ALs, 14 Mar 1826. 1 p, 4to. To his pbr Heinrichshofen. Sending 3 sermons for print. star Mar 26 (801) DM460

Ls, 8 Dec 1815. 1 p, folio. To the Academy at Goettingen. As Secretary of the Berlin Academy, sending a publication. Partly ptd. star Mar 26 (800) DM240

Schliemann, Heinrich, 1822-90

ALs, 13 Aug 1884. 1 p, 8vo. To Dr. Krueger. Declining an invitation to a conference. star Mar 26 (803) DM650

— 13 Aug 1886. 1 p, 8vo. To Herr Merkens. About recipient's collection of Roman glass. star Mar 26 (804) DM1,500

— 22 Feb 1890. 1 p, 8vo. To Eduard Prell-Erckens. In 3d person, responding to an inquiry about the Greek relatives of Mrs. Buresch. In Greek. With related material. star Mar 26 (805) DM600

Autograph sentiment, "Es liegt um uns herum gar mancher Abgrund..."; 6 Aug 1884. 1 p, 4to. Sgd. HN Nov 28 (1827) DM620

Schloezer, August Ludwig von, 1735-1809

ALs, 15 Feb 1781. 2 pp, 4to. To [Dr. Stein]. Thanking for some presents, & requesting material for a publication. star Mar 26 (807) DM1,100

Schlosser, Friedrich Christoph, 1776-1861

Autograph Ms, Neueste Geschichte, fragment of a scholarly work; [n.d.]. 8 pp, 4to. Working Ms. star Mar 26 (806) DM440

Schmidt, Helmut

Autograph Ms, commentary on recent political developments, [c.1990]. 1 p, folio. In pencil. HH Nov 6 (2102) DM300

Schmidt-Rottluff, Karl, 1884-1976

ALs, 22 Feb 1911. 2 pp, 8vo. To an unnamed lady. Thanking for an invitation. HN June 26 (979) DM300

Schneersohn, Joseph Isaac, 1880-1950

Ls, [19 Nov] 1929. 1 p, 8vo. To Isaac. Inviting him to the wedding of his daughter. With related material. sg Dec 19 (210) $2,000

Schneider, Louis, 1805-78

A Ls s (2), 24 Jan & 6 Oct 1845. 8 pp, 8vo. To an unnamed pbr. Discussing a projected work about the history of Prussia & a bilingual Ed of Shakespeare's works. star Mar 26 (447) DM220

Schnitzler, Arthur, 1862-1931

Autograph Ms, poem, Am Fluegel, [c.1930]. 8 four-line stanzas, sgd. star Mar 26 (448) DM2,600

ALs, 5 Dec 1897. 3 pp, 4to. Recipient unnamed. Agreeing to a French trans of his play Freiwild. star Mar 26 (449) DM800

— 24 Feb 1917. 2 pp, 8vo (lettercard). To Lydia Winternitz. Sending condolences on the death of her husband. HN Nov 28 (1829) DM340

Photograph, sgd, 29 Dec 1920. Postcard size. By Franz Loewy. star Mar 26 (451) DM350

Schnyder von Wartensee, Xaver, 1786-1868

ALs, 4 Mar 1855. 1 p, 4to. To Joseph Greith. Thanking for a score & sending anr. star Mar 27 (1140) DM700

Schoenberg, Arnold, 1874-1951

ALs, 15 Oct 1913. 1 p, 8vo. To the Wiener Volksbildungsverein. Responding to their invitation to give an address. S Dec 6 (181) £650 [Villa]

Ls s (2), 21 Dec 1944 & 16 Jan 1945. 2 pp, 4to. To Gottfried Bermann Fischer. About a contribution to the Neue Rundschau in honor of Thomas Mann. star Mar 27 (1141) DM2,000

Ls, 6 Jan 1950. 2 pp, 4to. To Jacques Martet. Expressing pleasure that an amateur musician has managed to acquaint himself with his music, & mentioning the forthcoming recording of Pierrot Lunaire. S May 29 (642) £950 [Macnutt]

ADs, Aug 1941. 2 pp, 4to. American Composers Alliance - ASCAP Survey for his Gurre Lieder. Dar Oct 10 (321) $550

Schoenlein, Johann Lukas, 1793-1864

ALs, 11 Mar 1848. 2 pp, 8vo. To [Salomon Friedrich Stiebel]. Expecting the German Parliament to meet at Frankfurt in a few days. star Mar 26 (808) DM950

Schroeder, Friedrich Ludwig, 1744-1816

ALs, 10 Sept 1814. 1 p, 4to. To Friedrich Heinrich Germar. About the death of Duke Friedrich Christian von Holstein-Sonderburg-Augustenburg. star Mar 27 (1229) DM450

Schubert, Franz, 1797-1828

Autograph music, 3 songs (nos 7, 8, & 9) from Die schoene Muellerin, [c.1824]. 7 pp, 22.5cm by 30cm. Notated on up to 4 systems per page, 3 staves each, with corrections. Including ANs at end. Illus in cat. S May 29 (643) £110,000 [Wertitsch]

— Autograph music, 3 songs, Sehnsucht, Mignon, & Der Zufriedene, with opening bars of a rondo, sgd; 16 to 23 Oct 1815. 6 pp, folio. Notated on 4 systems per page, 3 staves each, with numerous revisions; partly differing from ptd versions. Illus in cat. Mannheim collection. S Dec 6 (18) £40,000 [Wertitsch]

— Autograph music, 4 songs, Blumenlied, Klage, Der Leidende, & Seligkeit, with an [unrecorded] canon in B flat major; Jan & May 1816. 6 pp, folio. Working Ms, notated on up to 4 systems per page, 3 staves each. Some annotations in other hands. Illus in cat. Mannheim collection. S Dec 6 (20) £40,000 [Wertitsch]

— Autograph music, Fantasia in F minor for piano duet, comprising a substantial working draft of the final section; [1828]. 4 pp, folio. Notated on up to 12 systems per page; differing from final version. Illus in cat. Mannheim collection. S Dec 6 (19) £20,000 [Wertitsch]

— Autograph music, Quartet in B flat major (no 8), D.112; 5 to 13 Sept 1814. 36 pp, 4to. Working Ms, notated on 4 four-stave systems per page. Sgd. C June 24 (16) £270,000 [Schneider]

— Autograph music, song, Grenzen der Menschheit, to a text by Goethe, Mar 1821. 5 pp, 24cm by 31.5cm. 159 bars, scored for voice & piano; sgd at head. Illus in cat. star Mar 27 (1143) DM160,000

— Autograph music, songs, An die Musik, Der Juengling und der Tod, & Trost im Liede; Mar 1817. 8 pp, 235mm by 315mm. Including alterations; each sgd. Some annotations in other hands. Illus in cat. S May 29 (644) £50,000 [Haas]

— Autograph music, songs, Von Ida, & Die Erscheinung, to texts by Kosegarten, 7 July 1815. 2 pp, 4to. Scored for voice & accompaniment, with extensive corrections. Sgd twice. Some annotations in other hands. S May 29 (645) £22,000 [Saggiori]

Schubert, Richard von, 1850-1933

Collection of ALs & typescript, sgd, 19 Oct 1914. 32 pp, folio. To Gen. von Hindenburg. Sending a report (included) about the activities of the troops under his command in East Prussia. Including sketch of a map. star Mar 27 (1447) DM440

Schumann, Clara, 1819-96

Collection of 2 A Ls s & AN, 23 Apr 1858, 24 Apr 1873, & [n.d.]. 2 pp, 8vo, & visiting card. Recipient unnamed. Thanking for a shipment, & inquiring about the score of her husband's opera Genoveva. hen Nov 12 (2505) DM550

ALs, 17 Nov 1838. 2 pp, 8vo. To Frau von Nass. Accepting an invitation. star Mar 27 (1144) DM1,300

— 24 Oct 1862. 3 pp, 8vo. To Frau Rieter-Biedermann. About a recent concert, & sending Brahms's address in Vienna. star Mar 27 (1146) DM1,500

AN, 26 Oct 1891. On ptd visiting card. To Herr Ruebner. Sending material for Dagmar Gade. HN Nov 28 (1832) DM220

Autograph quotation, 6 bars in F major, 1 Mar 1850. 1 p, 4to. Sgd. star Mar 27 (1145) DM1,400

— WIECK, MARIE. - Collection of 10 A Ls s & AL, 18 Oct 1893 to 3 Jan 1897 & [n.d.]. 68 pp, 8vo. To Richard Batka. About her sister Clara's relationship with her father, the Wieck family & Robert Schumann, etc. 3 fragments. star Mar 27 (1147b) DM4,200

Schumann, Robert, 1810-56

Autograph Ms, draft for the title of 20 songs from Heine's Buch der Lieder, Op. 29, dedicated to Mendelssohn-Bartholdy; [c.1840]. 1 p, 153mm by 135mm. Unpbd. Gottschalk collection. C Dec 16 (416) £4,200 [Rosenthal]

ALs, 2 Sept 1838. 1 p, 8vo. To Julius Stern. Promising to publish 2 of recipient's songs. Imperf. Illus in cat. hen Nov 12 (2506) DM3,600

— 5 Sept 1839. 3 pp, 4to. To Heinrich Dorn. Explaining his troubles with Friedrich Wieck, acknowledging Clara as the inspiration of his recent work, & complaining about some criticism. Illus in cat. Mannheim collection. S Dec 6 (24) £3,500 [Giesen]

— 10 July 1840. 1 p, 8vo. Recipient unnamed. Assuring him that he would be pleased to receive a song composed by recipient & referring to his own songs to texts by Heine. Gottschalk collection. C Dec 16 (417) £3,500 [Rosenthal]

— 8 Sept 1840. 3 pp, 8vo. To Emilie List. Inviting her to his wedding, sending some songs to be presented to Clara, & mentioning the cycle Myrthen. Illus in cat. S May 29 (649) £4,000 [Tamura]

— 6 Jan 1849. 1 p, 8vo. To Julius Rietz. Discussing problems with a projected performance of his opera Genoveva. star Mar 27 (1148) DM5,000

— 15 Sept 1850. 2 pp, size not stated. To C. F. Peters. Regarding proofs of his opera Genoveva & plans for further performances. S Dec 6 (182) £1,500 [Schneider]

— 16 Jan 1851. 1 p, 8vo. To C. F. Peters. Discussing terms for the publication of 2 overtures. S May 29 (652) £1,300 [Macnutt]

— 28 Jan 1851. 3 pp, 8vo. To C. F. Peters. Discussing arrangements for the publication of the overtures to Genoveva & Die Braut von Messina. S Dec 6 (183) £1,700 [Schneider]

— 20 Apr [18]53. 1 p, 8vo. To Carl Reinecke. Informing him that Liszt may perform Des Saengers Fluch at a later date, & giving news of the music festival at Duesseldorf. Illus in cat. S May 29 (651) £1,600 [Harrison]

Schumpeter, Joseph, 1883-1950

Ls, 3 July 1931. 2 pp, 4to. To an unnamed official in Berlin. Discussing work ethics & the financial situation in historical perspective. star Mar 26 (810) DM1,100

Schurz, Carl, 1829-1906

ALs, 5 Mar [n.y.]. 2 pp, 8vo. Recipient unnamed. Inquiring about a horse. star Mar 27 (1708) DM480

Schuyler, Philip John, 1733-1804

ALs, 7 Aug 1776. 1 p, folio. To Gov. Jonathan Trumbull & Gen. David Waterbury. Requesting money & supplies for the army. sup May 9 (395) $2,000

— 11 Jan 1786. 4 pp, 4to. Recipient unnamed. Giving [Alexander] Hamilton's opinions on recipient's affairs & political questions. R Nov 9 (122) $450

Ls, 27 Oct 1776. 1 p, folio. To Col. Elias Dayton. Informing him of a possible change in his marching orders. Spiro collection. CNY May 14 (146) $1,800

Schwarzenberg, Karl Philipp, Fuerst zu, 1771-1820

Ls, 4 Feb 1814. 2 pp, folio. To Bluecher. Concerning the reorganization of the administration of the occupied French provinces. star Mar 27 (1711) DM480

Schweinfurth, Georg, 1836-1925

ALs, 16 Mar 1900. 4 pp, 8vo. To [Joseph von Knopf]. Reporting from Egypt. star Mar 26 (812) DM360

Schweitzer, Albert, 1875-1965

[A photograph of a port drawing, sgd & inscr, 17 Oct 1962, 20cm by 13.5cm, mtd, sold at star on 26 Mar 1992, lot 813, for DM320.]

Collection of ALs & autograph postcard, sgd, 4 Feb 1933 & 2 Apr 1945. 2 pp, 4to & 8vo. To the Rev. S. A. Alexander. About his hospital. bba May 28 (213) £220 [Sakmyster]

— Collection of 10 A Ls s & 5 A Ns s, 1949 to 1964. 17 pp, mostly 4to. To Anita Daniel. About events at Lambarene, etc. sg Feb 27 (174) $3,000

ALs, [n.d.]. 2 pp, 8vo. Recipient unnamed. Requesting information about the time of Mrs. Lingenfelder's arrival. Dar Apr 9 (347) $160

Autograph sentiment, sgd, 20 Nov 1952. 5 by 3 inches (card). With typed quotation below. Dar June 11 (337) $200

Photograph, sgd & inscr, 15 June [19]51. 6.75 by 7 inches (image). In canoe; inscr in French. sg Feb 27 (172) $250

— Anr, 1954. Postcard. Framed. HH May 13 (2047) DM210

Schweitzer, Albert, 1875-1965 —& Others

Signature, 7 July [19]49. In program for the Goethe Bicentennial Convocation & Music Festival at Aspen, Colorado, 160 pp, 8vo. Inscr by Schweitzer to Dora Pondell. Also sgd by Thornton Wilder, Ortega y Gasset, & others. Dar Oct 10 (322) $180

Schwind, Moritz von, 1804-71

ALs, 26 Apr 1854. 2 pp, 4to. To Freiherr von Arnswald. Planning his arrival at Eisenach. star Mar 27 (951) DM780

Scobee, Dick, 1939-86

Transcript, quoting Virgil Grissom on the hazards of space flight, [n.d.]. 1 p, 8vo. Sgd. Dar Dec 26 (49) $650

ALs, [n.d.]. 1 p, 4to. To Susan. Responding to questions on his interest in the space program. Dar Oct 10 (39) $500

Photograph, sgd, [n.d.]. 10.5 by 8 inches. In front of NASA jet. Dar Apr 9 (62) $250

Photograph, sgd & inscr, [n.d.]. 10.5 by 8 inches. In front of NASA jet. Dar Oct 10 (41) $130

Signature, on philatelic envelope, [24 May 1983]. Dar Apr 9 (61) $100

— Anr, on philatelic cover, [5 June 1983]. Dar Oct 10 (40) $180

Scott, Charles, 1779-1813. See: American Revolution

Scott, Sir Walter, 1771-1832

Series of 3 A Ls s, 29 May & 16 Nov [1822] & [n.d.]. 4 pp, 4to. To Messrs John & Thomas Smith. About the enlargement of Abbotsford House. Including 2 small pencil sketches. C June 24 (381) £650 [Quaritch]

ALs, 24 Oct 1811. 4 pp, 4to. To Matthew Weld. Discussing research for his Ed of Swift's works. CNY Dec 5 (322) $1,300

— 18 June 1814. 2 pp, 4to. To James Ellis. Referring to postal arrangements & sending "some verses on Otterbourne". bba Sept 19 (341) £520 [Jarndyce]

— Aug 1822. 1 p, 4to. To an unnamed lawyer. Thanking for advice. star Mar 26 (456) DM320

— 7 June 1827. 1 p, 4to. To William Scott. Referring to a contested election & his current work. bba Sept 19 (342) £380 [Jarndyce]

— 11 Aug 1827. Length not stated. To Andrew Lang. Requesting game certificates for his son. Framed. pnE May 13 (181) £300

— 17 Apr 1830. 1 p, 4to. To [Harriet?] Hunter. Thanking for a flattering poem. C Dec 16 (324) £260 [Quaritch]

— 22 Jan [n.y.]. 2 pp, 8vo. To Mrs. Hamilton. Sending a copy of The Lay of the Last Minstrel for Miss Carmichael. Ingilby collection. pn Nov 14 (101) £420 [Quaritch]

Scott, Winfield, 1786-1866

ALs, 7 Feb 1819. 4 pp, 4to. To an unnamed officer. Referring to his public quarrel with Andrew Jackson. With contemp newspaper reprinting the correspondence between Jackson & Scott. Spiro collection. CNY May 14 (147) $1,700

Photograph, sgd, [n.d.]. Carte size. In uniform. By Anthony, from a Brady negative. Illus in cat. R June 13 (104) $900

Scriabin, Alexander, 1872-1915

Photograph, sgd & inscr, [1914]. 222mm by 144mm (image). Sgd & inscr to Fedor Borisovich Keil with a musical quotation from his 3d Symphony. Illus in cat. star Mar 27 (1153) DM3,800

Seaman, Elizabeth Cochrane ("Nellie Bly"), 1867-1922

ALs, [n.d.]. 2 pp, 8vo. To the Ed of the Omaha Herald. Sending a copy of her novel. R Mar 7 (162) $400

Searle, Ronald

Original drawing, A Night in a London Coffee House, to illus A. Atkinson's & R. Searle's The Big City, 1958. 9.5 by 6 inches. In pen-&-ink. Sgd. Ck Dec 11 (58) £

Collection of ALs & ANs, [late 1940s]. 2 pp, 8vo. To Irving [Hoffman]. Thanking for clippings, & sending Christmas greetings. Both illus with a sketch. sg Feb 27 (175) $325

Seberg, Jean, 1938-79

Collection of ALs, 3 Ls s, & ANs, 1965. 5 pp, various sizes. To Ruth Hancock. About her life in Paris, film projects, New Years wishes, etc. Dar Dec 26 (304) $325

Seddon, James Alexander, 1815-80

Ls, 26 Aug 1863. 1 p, 4to. To Dr. J. W. King. Notifying him of his appointment as Surgeon in the Confederate Army. Dar June 11 (338) $600

Seeckt, Hans von, 1866-1936

ALs, 19 Oct 1926. 1 p, 4to. To Max Warburg. Thanking for words of praise. star Mar 27 (1720) DM450

Seewald, Richard, 1889-1976

Collection of ALs & 2 autograph postcards, sgd, 1967 to 1970. 3 pp, 8vo. Recipient unnamed. About an order for church windows. HN Nov 28 (1836) DM450

Seidel, Ina, 1885-1974

Autograph Ms, poem, Vorfruehling, [n.d.]. 1 p, 8vo. 8 lines, sgd. With Ls, 1961; letter of transmittal. star Mar 26 (457) DM460

Selznick, David O., 1902-65

Ls, 30 Dec 1957. 1 p, 4to. To Daniel T. O'Shea. Regretting that recipient was unable to attend the premiere of A Farewell to Arms. Dar Oct 10 (323) $140

— 20 Nov 1958. 1 p, 4to. To Daniel T. O'Shea. Requesting legal advice concerning an exchange of letters. Dar Dec 26 (200) $250

— 1 Apr 1959. 1 p, 4to. To Dan & Helen O'Shea. About the death of his mother. Dar Apr 9 (348) $120

— 3 Aug 1959. 1 p, 4to. To Daniel T. O'Shea. Expressing condolences on the death of his father. Dar Feb 13 (319) $200

— 1 Oct 1962. 1 p, 4to. To Arnold Weissberger. Referring to contracts for the film The Shattered Glass. Dar Aug 6 (27) $130

— 11 Feb 1965. 1 p, 4to. To Daniel T. O'Shea. Inquiring about the names of distributors of some films. Dar June 11 (339) $130

Check, sgd, 20 May 1941. Payable to E. J. Mannix. Dar Aug 6 (28) $100

Semper, Gottfried, 1803-79

ALs, [n.d.]. 1 p, 8vo. To Herr Gans. Arranging an appointment. HH May 13 (2048) DM220

Senghor, Leopold Sedar

Collection of Ls & photograph, sgd & inscr, 15 Oct 1969 & [n.d.]. 1 p, 4to, & 8vo. To an unnamed journalist. Thanking for an article about his poems. star Mar 26 (458) DM220

Sennett, Mack, 1880-1960

Ds, 24 Apr 1918. 1 p, folio. Lease assignment by Woodley Theatre Co. to Riviera Theatre Co.; retained carbon copy. sg Sept 12 (219) $300

Serling, Rod, 1924-75

Ds, 28 July 1955. 1 p, 4to. Contract for a television script. Dar June 11 (340) $225

Sermini, Gentile, fl.1425

Ms, untitled novella. [Italy, late 18th cent]. 350 pp, stitched. HH May 12 (27) DM700

Sermons

Ms, Lenten Sermons, in Latin. [Eastern France, 15th cent]. 90 leaves, 281mm by 205mm. Contemp calf over wooden bds, rebacked in vellum. In a gothic bookhand with cursive features. With c.50 painted initials in red. Dampstained. S June 23 (64) £2,000 [Enlumineures]

— Ms, Sermones ad Fratres in Eremo Commorantes, attributed to St. Augustine. [Northern Italy, 2d half of 15th cent]. 100 leaves (2 blank), 215mm by 144mm. Modern bdg incorporating lower cover of contemp blindstamped brown goatskin over wooden board. In a small regular cursive bookhand with gothic features. With 42 decorated initials & 4-line historiated initial. S June 23 (70) £2,000 [Enlumineures]

Seton, Ernest Thompson, 1860-1946

ALs, 12 Oct 1920. 1 p, 4to. To Arthur. About a hand sign to be used by the Woodcraft Indians. sup Oct 15 (1810) $300

Seume, Johann Gottfried, 1763-1810

ALs, [summer 1805]. 1 p, 4to. To Johann Heinrich von Busse. Declining an invitation. star Mar 26 (459) DM2,600

Sevier, John, 1745-1815

ADs, 18 Apr 1778. 1 p, 8vo. As Clerk of the Supreme Court of North Carolina, warrant to arrest James Coleson. Dar Dec 26 (305) $850

Ds, 2 Dec 1783. 1 p, 8vo. Summons. R Nov 9 (123) $600

Seward, William Henry, 1801-72

ALs, 23 May 1841. 1 p, 4to. To Gary V. Sackett. As Governor of NY, regarding accounts. sup Oct 15 (1811) $210

Collection of Ls & Ds, 27 Feb 1869. 2 pp, 4to. To the Governor of Nebraska. Circular letter, sending a certified copy of the Congressional resolution proposing the 15th Amendment (present). Illus in cat. sup Oct 15 (1546) $13,500

Series of 3 Ls s, 8 Dec 1863 to 30 Sept 1865. 7 pp, size not stated. To an official at the Peruvian Embassy. Regarding matters pertaining to relations with Peru. Dar Aug 6 (257) $900

Sexton, Anne, 1928-74

ALs, 19 Mar 1969. 1 p, 12mo (card). To Mr. Seward. Thanking for his interest in her poems. Dar Aug 6 (258) $160

Shackleton, Sir Ernest Henry, 1874-1922

Autograph transcript, Spitsbergen, a poem by an anonymous author; sgd & dated 24 July 1918. 6 by 7.5 inches. 4 lines. Ck Apr 3 (29) £190

Series of 3 A Ls s, 19 Sept to 29 Nov 1914. 3 pp, 8vo & 4to. To Molly Bridgeman & her father (2). Thanking for a present & bidding farewell before leaving on his expedition. pn June 11 (53) £520

ALs, [c.13] Sept 1909. 4 pp, 8vo. To Mr. Gwatkin. Declining an invitation & announcing Scott's new expedition to the South Pole. C Oct 30 (79) £400 [Sotheran]

— [29 Sept] 1911. 2 pp, 8vo. To Charles Waldstein. Asking him to return a paper. pn Mar 19 (109) £75 [Wilson]

Shalom Aleichem, 1859-1916. See: Rabinowitz, Shalom ("Sholem Aleichem")

Shapira, Hayyim Eleazar, 1872-1937

Ls, 1933. 2 pp, 8vo. Recipient unnamed. Appeal for funds for the Munkacs Yeshiva. sg Dec 19 (212) $450

Shapiro, Abraham Duber Cahana

ALs, [28 Mar] 1927. 2 pp, 8vo. To Jacob Bauman. Answering a Talmudic inquiry. sg Dec 19 (214) $250

Sharett, Moshe, 1894-1965

ALs, 22 Dec 1937. 1 p, 8vo. Recipient unnamed. Letter of sympathy. Dar Feb 13 (234) $100

Shaw, George Bernard, 1856-1950

Autograph Ms, responses in a ptd journalist's questionnaire, 13 May 1946. 2 pp, size not stated. Sgd. Illus in cat. Ck Nov 15 (14) £420

— Autograph Ms, The Presentation of Shakespeare in Modern Dress, replies on a typewritten questionnaire; 12 Nov 1940. 32 lines on 2 leaves, 8vo. Sgd. C June 24 (382) £750 [Wilson]

Typescript, menu for a dinner at the Waldorf Hotel London, 17 Nov 1932. 1 p, 4to. Sgd by Shaw in approval. pn June 11 (89) £95 [Wilson]

Collection of 9 A Ls s, cards, sgd, & Ns s, 30 May 1945 to 16 Feb 1949. 15 pp, mostly 8vo & 4to. To R. Palme Dutt. On election policies, socialism, his own political activities, etc. With related material. S July 21 (175) £3,800 [Dupre]

A Ls s (2), 13 Feb 1933 & 3 Dec 1942. 2 pp, size not stated. To Arthur Hanson. Discussing vaccination & the description of Shaw as "freethinker". With related material. b June 22 (133) £650

ALs, 11 Nov 1887. 2 pp, 8vo. To [Edith] Bland. Asking for her opinion about a story "suited for a Xmas annual". star Mar 26 (460) DM1,300

— 3 Jan 1893. 2 pp, size not stated. To Ernest White. On the prospects of a career as a dramatic critic. Ck Apr 3 (30) £800

— 20 June 1902. 2 pp, 4to. To Frederick Whelen. Describing the achievements of the Theatre de l'Oeuvre & praising Maeterlinck. pn June 11 (87) £1,200

— 3 Nov 1906. 2 pp, 8vo. To Francis J. Hart. Giving details of his career as a music critic. pn June 11 (88) £500 [Wilson]

— 10 Dec 1908. 10 pp, 4to. Recipient unnamed. Discussing the proposed statutes for a National Shakespeare Theatre. With anr, letter of transmittal. S July 21 (176) £2,800 [Dupre]

— 26 Oct 1916. 2 pp, 8vo. To Thomas Burke. Insisting that his book is not "fit for general circulation". Dar Dec 26 (306) $1,600

— 13 Mar 1919. 1 p, size not stated. To H. M. Tomlinson. Thanking for praising his book. Ck Nov 15 (19) £180

— 18 June [19]19. 1 p, size not stated. To H. M. Tomlinson. Explaining his "special vindictiveness against S.". Ck Nov 15 (20) £190

— [24 Nov 1921]. 1 p, size not stated. To H. M. Tomlinson. Complaining about the excessive use of quotation marks. Ck Nov 15 (16) £380

— 24 Oct 1932. 1 p, 8vo (card). To Mme Chan Toon. Returning a forgery (included). bba Jan 30 (280) £90 [Ulysses]

— 22 Mar 1944. 1 p, 12mo. To Messrs. J. Thomlinson. Placing an order. Dar Oct 10 (325) $325

— [25 Dec] 1949. 1 p, size not stated. To Mr. MacGeochlin. Discussing happiness. With recipient's reply. Ck Apr 3 (33) £750

Ls, 12 May 1908. 3 pp, 4to. To the Rev. John Oliver. Responding to questions on free love & marriage. Framed with a port. P June 17 (74) $2,750

— 1 Apr 1932. 2 pp, 8vo. To Karl Musek. Sending a copy of a book & inquiring about copyright expirations. sg Sept 12 (221) $550

— 1 Nov 1937. 1 p, 8vo. To David Clarke. Maintaining that there is "a set of class dialects" in English. pn Nov 14 (229) £520 [Dupre]

Autograph postcard, sgd, 1 July 1900. To Frederick Whelen. Apologizing for not attending a theatrical supper the previous night. pn June 11 (85) £280 [Wilson]

— 6 Dec 1900. To Frederick Whelen. Securing a box for Ellen Terry for Captain Brassbound's Conversion. pn June 11 (86) £300 [Wilson]

— 13 Apr 1905. To H. Greenhaugh Smith. Informing him that he gave his Shakespeare lecture without notes. Illus in cat. Dar June

11 (341) $500
— 7 Mar 1929. To Lewis Casson. Commenting on the production of a play. bba June 25 (134) £400 [Dupre]
— 13 Aug 1941. To Joseph Shipley. Declining to write an article on criticism. Illus in cat. sg Feb 27 (177) $475
— 30 Mar 1946. To Arthur Rank, Jr. Agreeing to the deletion of a reference to Jews in a film. sg Sept 12 (220) $950
— 13 Mar 1950. To Kenneth Barnes. Refusing to let one of his plays be cut. bba Jan 30 (281) £70 [Ulysses]
ANs, 28 Jan 1923. 1 p, size not stated. To H. M. Tomlinson. Promising to write a contribution. Ck Nov 15 (18) £170
— 18 May 1927. 1 p, 4to. To F. L. Minnigerode. Giving permission to quote a letter. At bottom of letter addressed to him. With secretarial letter. sg Feb 27 (176) $450
Ds, 28 Feb 1914. 1 p, 8vo. Receipt for a fee for Plays Pleasant & Unpleasant. star Mar 26 (461) DM400
Check, sgd, 15 May 1947. Drawn on the Westminster Bank Ltd. for £20 payable to himself. Also sgd on verso. wa Oct 19 (55) $280
Photograph, sgd, 1930. Postcard. With separate inscr. Ck Nov 15 (15) £420

Shawn, Ted, 1891-1972
ALs, 24 July 1918. 6 pp, 8vo. To Eddie O'Day. About the similarity of army drill to "the system of virile dance I have been an adherent of for some years." wd Dec 12 (337) $50

Shelley, Mary Wollstonecraft, 1797-1851
ALs, 19 July [1828]. 2 pp, 4to. To Isabella [Baxter Booth]. Describing her unhappiness. With related material. Ingilby collection. pn Nov 14 (102) £3,400 [Pickering & Chatto]
Cut signature, [n.d.]. 4.25 by 1.25 inches. Dar Apr 9 (349) $400

Shelley, Percy Bysshe, 1792-1822
ALs, 7 Nov 1812. 3 pp, 8vo. To John Williams. Promising his continued assistance for the building of a model town. Framed with a port. Illus in cat. P June 17 (75) $5,500
Autograph check, sgd, [n.d.]. 70mm by 188mm. Drawn on Messrs. Brookes & Co. for £50 payable to Mr. Cox. CNY Dec 5 (331) $1,600

Sheridan, Philip Henry, 1831-88
Signature, [n.d.]. 3.5 by 2 inches. Framed. Armstrong collection. sup Oct 15 (1130) $260
Telegram, 1875. 1 p, 8vo. To Capt. G. W. Yates. Approving of recipient's arrangements. Armstrong collection. sup Oct 15 (1129) $300
— Sheridan, Michael V. - Ls, 20 June 1888. 1 p, 4to. As aide-de-camp on his brother's staff, transmitting letters of introduction. Framed. Armstrong collection. sup Oct 15 (1128) $170
See also: Grant, Ulysses S. & Sheridan

Sheridan, Richard Brinsley, 1751-1816
Collection of 42 A Ls s & 4 A Ns s, 5 Dec 1777 to 23 Nov 1807 & [n.d.]. 46 pp, various sizes. To Richard Peake. Mostly about financial matters; often desperate pleas for money. With related material. CNY Dec 5 (332) $3,500
ALs, 27 Oct [1802]. 3 pp, 4to. Recipient unnamed. Concerning a comedy submitted to the Drury Lane Theatre by Lumley Skeffington. pn Nov 14 (230) £300 [Sotheran]
— 25 June [1812]. 1 p, 4to. To C. Ward. Urgently requesting a loan. C Dec 16 (325) £180 [Maggs]

Sherman, Roger, Signer from Connecticut
Ds, Oct 1767. 1 p, 4to. Debenture of the Connecticut Assembly; also sgd by 10 others. sup Oct 15 (1215) $420

Sherman, William Tecumseh, 1820-91
ALs, 16 Mar 1863. 3 pp, 4to. To Gen. S. A. Hurlbut. About new orders from Grant for manoeuvres around Vicksburg. Illus in cat. Sang & Spiro collections. CNY May 14 (148) $30,000
— [29 May 1863]. 1 p, 4to. To Admiral David D. Porter. Predicting that "the capture of Vicksburg is a dead sure thing". In pencil. CNY Dec 5 (117) $4,500
— 19 Jan 1864. 4 pp, 4to. To Ulysses S. Grant. Reporting about his own & the Confederate Army's forces & suggesting strategy for the spring campaign. Illus in cat. CNY June 9 (272) $14,000
— 5 Apr 1865. 3 pp, 4to. To Admiral John A. Dahlgren. Reflecting about his campaign in the Carolinas. CNY May 14 (7) $32,000
— 4 Aug 1868. 3 pp, 8vo. To David Dixon Porter. Interceding in favor of a cadet appointed to the Naval Academy. CNY June 9 (273) $850
— 22 Apr 1876. 2 pp, 4to. To J. Pierpont Morgan & al. Declining an invitation. Framed. Armstrong collection. sup Oct 15 (1131) $380
ANs, [c.12 July 1861]. 1 p, 8vo. Recipient unnamed. Forwarding a letter by William Arthur (at head) who is seeking a military appointment. Framed with engraved port. Dar Feb 13 (321) $500
— 27 Nov 1865. 1 p, 4to. To Admiral David D. Porter. Forwarding a a letter by Jervis Wolfery (present, on verso) & discussing 2

appointments. CNY Dec 5 (118) $500

Photograph, sgd & inscr, 6 Nov 1887. Cabinet size. Inscr to J. M. Brown. P June 16 (285) $2,250

Signature, [n.d.]. Framed with ptd visiting card & photograph, overall size 16 by 14 inches. sup Oct 15 (1813) $300

Sherwood, Robert Emmet, 1896-1955

Ds, 1947. 1 p, 4to. Permission to The Theatre Guild to broadcast his play Abe Lincoln in Illinois. Dar June 11 (342) $130

Shields, James, 1806-79

ALs, 3 Mar 1852. 1 p, 4to. To Sec of the Interior A. H. H. Stewart. Requesting that Mrs. Ann Rogers be given part of her husband's salary for the maintenance of her children. With engraved port. Dar June 11 (343) $150

Shostakovich, Dimitri, 1906-75

Series of c.150 A Ls s, Sept 1923 to 1931, & 1957. Over 500 pp, various sizes. To Tanya Glivenko. About his early compositions, his political & artistic beliefs, their relationship, etc. S Dec 6 (184) £65,000 [Hochhauser]

ALs, 26 Mar 1966. 1 p, 4to. To Abram Lobkovsky. Thanking for some medicine. cb Feb 12 (117) $1,200

Autograph postcard, sgd, 26 Sept 1965. To Abram Lobkovsky. Thanking for congratulations on his birthday. cb Feb 12 (119) $550

ANs, 28 Nov 1947. 1 p, 8vo. To the pbrs Muzgiz. Stating that a concert by A. M. Lobkovsky should be pbd. Illus in cat. cb Feb 12 (118) $900

Photograph, sgd, 21 Mar [19]74. Framed, 39.5cm by 30cm. With covering ANs. Illus in cat. S Dec 6 (185) £1,100 [Friedman]

Photograph, sgd & inscr, 1940, 1942, & c.1953. 265mm by 180mm. Inscr to Boris Livanov with 10 musical quotations & sgd at 3 different times. Illus in cat. S Dec 6 (187) £4,000 [Tancil]

Siam

Ms, letterbook kept by George Swinton, containing accounts of Siam & reports on the 1st Burmese War, Sept 1824 to July 1825. 220 pp, folio. Half cloth over marbled bds. In several hands. S June 25 (462) £1,000 [Randall]

Sibelius, Jean, 1865-1957

Autograph music, Impromptu, Op. 5 no 4; [c.1893]. 2 pp, folio. Early working Ms of the complete piece; differing from pbd version. Illus in cat. S Dec 6 (194) £1,800 [Dreesman]

— Autograph music, song, Aus banger Brust, Op. 50 no 4, to a text by Richard Dehmel; [c.1906]. 8 pp, folio. Working Ms scored for voice & piano; sgd. Text written in anr hand. S Dec 6 (192) £3,500 [Haas]

— Autograph music, song, Die stille Stadt, Op. 50 no 5, to a text by Richard Dehmel; [c.1906]. 4 pp, folio. Scored for voice & piano; sgd. Text written in anr hand. S Dec 6 (192) £3,500 [Saunders]

Collection of 20 A Ls s & 19 Ls s, 8 Dec 1905 to 15 Dec 1955. 69 pp, 4to & 8vo. To his pbr Robert Heinrich Lienau. Mostly about the publication of his works. With carbon copies of Lienau's replies. star Mar 27 (1150) DM23,000

ALs, 23 Oct 1905. 1 p, 4to. To Robert Lienau. Agreeing to the publication of a piano arrangement for 4 hands of the 2d movement of his violin concerto. S May 29 (653) £1,200 [Macnutt]

— 10 July 1907. 2 pp, 8vo. To Robert Lienau. Promising to deliver a symphony at the end of the month & discussing financial matters. S May 29 (654) £550 [Harding]

— [1907]. 2 pp, 4to. To Robert Lienau. About the symphonic poem Pohjola's Daughter, conducting commitments, a new cantata, etc. S Dec 6 (191) £750 [Leach]

— 11 Jan 1910. 1p, 4to. To an unnamed conductor. Sending a membership fee. star Mar 27 (1151) DM900

— 25 Nov 1934. 1 p, 4to. To Nils Hopeglund. Declining an invitation. Illus in cat. Dar Apr 9 (350) $550

Ls, 30 Dec 1949. 1 p, 8vo. To Katherine Cornell. Thanking for a birthday gift. Framed with a port. P June 17 (77) $250

Sidney, Algernon, 1622-83

Collection of 6 A Ls s & 4 A Ls, 29 Nov [1677] to 8/18 Apr [1678]. 17 pp, various sizes. To Benjamin Furly. About his reasons for returning to England & other matters. bba May 28 (216) £400 [Johnson]

Siebold, Karl Theodor Ernst von, 1804-85

A Ls s (2), 26 Nov 1877 & 28 May 1881. 5 pp, 4to & 8vo. To Heinrich Abegg. About the reproduction of jellyfish & other scientific matters. star Mar 26 (816) DM530

Siege of Babylon

Ms, A Relation of the Late Siege and taking of the City of Babylon, by the Turk, as it was written from thence by Zarain Aga ... & Englished, by W:J:L; [late 18th cent?]. 48 pp, 12mo, in contemp wraps. bba May 28 (245) £200 [Loman]

Siemens, Werner von, 1816-92

Autograph Ms, scientific paper, Zur Frage der Ursachen der atmosphaerischen Stroemungen; [n.d.]. 4 pp, 4to. Sgd at head. Possibly incomplete. star Mar 26 (817) DM1,100

ALs, 14 Sept 1886. 1 p, 8vo. To Adolf von Eye. Disagreeing with recipient's journal Pionier. star Mar 26 (818) DM640

Sigel, Franz, 1824-1902

ALs, 14 Feb 1877. 3 pp, 8vo. To Edward Lester. Praising recipient's book "as a Centennial gift to the American people". star Mar 27 (1722) DM220

Signac, Paul, 1863-1935

Series of 28 A Ls s, 1918, 1919 & 1927. 60 pp, 8vo. To Louis Gustave Cambier & his wife Juliette. About their own & other people's painting, the war, politics, etc. Including a pencil drawing. S Dec 5 (562) £9,000 [Fox Glove]

Silcher, Friedrich, 1789-1860

ALs, 19 Aug 1836. 2 pp, 4to. To the piano manufacturer [Schiedermayer?]. Ordering a piano for the bookseller Osiander. star Mar 27 (1152) DM750

Silverheels, Jay, 1919-80

Ds, 25 Sept 1957. 1 p, 4to. Contract with Lone Ranger Pictures; carbon copy. Dar Oct 10 (328) $700

Simmel, Georg, 1858-1918

ALs, 5 Dec 1892. 1 p, 8vo. To an unnamed colleague. Promising to send a copy of his new book for review. star Mar 26 (819) DM360

Simmons, Aloysius Harry ("Al"), 1903-56

Photograph, sgd, [21 Jan 1953]. 8 by 10 inches. 2-in-1 photograph, with D. Dean. Illus in cat. sup July 10 (973) $290

Simon, Neil

Ls, 15 Mar 1971. 1 p, 8vo. To Arnold Weissberger. Declining to contribute to the New Dramatists Building Fund. With related material. Dar Aug 6 (259) $150

ANs, [n.d.]. 1 p, 3 by 5 inches (card). Recipient unnamed. Referring to his play Brighton Beach Memoirs. wa Oct 19 (200) $80

Sinatra, Frank

Ls, 19 Feb 1949. Length not stated. To Louis Sobel. Thanking "for that Sunday feature". Dar Apr 9 (351) $250

Ns, 20 Jan 1955. 1 p, 5 by 4 inches. To Martin Lowitz. Thanking for comments. sup Oct 15 (1815) $190

Ds, 8 Oct 1951. 2 pp, 4to. Permission to use a double in the film Ma and Pa Kettle in Paris; carbon copy. Dar Dec 26 (307) $350

Photograph, sgd, [n.d.]. 8 by 10 inches. LH Dec 11 (516) $80

Sinatra, Frank —& Others

[The signatures of Frank Sinatra, Jack Benny, Rochester, Betty Grable, Don Ameche, Deanna Durbin & Van Johnson, Thanksgiving 1944, on a postcard of the Earl Carroll Theatre at Hollywood, sold at Dar on 9 Apr 1992, lot 8, for $160.]

Sinoviev, Alexander

Autograph Ms, fragment from a paper about Soviet literature & his own works, [n.d.]. 3 pp, folio. Sgd later. In German. star Mar 26 (462) DM600

Sippy, Ben

Photograph, [n.d.]. 1/6 plate tintype. R Nov 9 (156) $1,200

Siringo, Charles A., 1855-1928

ALs, 10 Oct 1928. 5 pp, 4to. To William E. Hawks. Discussing his home, his neighborhood, & a publication project. Dar Feb 13 (8) $500

Sisler, George Harold, 1893-1973 —& Others

[The signatures of Sisler, Rogers Hornsby, Bert Haas, Cy Young, Jesse Haines & Jigger Statz on a 12mo sheet, [n.d.], sold at Dar on 13 Feb 1992, lot 49, for $275.]

Sismondi, Jean Charles Leonard Simonde de, 1773-1842

ALs, [Oct 1837]. 3 pp, 8vo. To Fr. Cusani. Welcoming Cesare Cantu's forthcoming Storia universale. star Mar 26 (821) DM320

Sitting Bull, 1834?-90

Signature, [6 Oct 1884]. 52mm by 84mm (card). Including authentication on verso. CNY Dec 5 (5) $2,500

Sitting Bull, 1834?-90 —& Cody, William F. ("Buffalo Bill"), 1846-1917

Group photograph, 1885. 6.75 by 11 inches. Sgd by both. Framed. sup Oct 15 (1141) $23,500

Sitwell, Dame Edith, 1887-1964

Autograph Ms, 3 poems, Romance, Interlude, & Popular Song, [n.d.]. 15 pp, mostly 4to. Each sgd. S July 21 (178) £500 [Blackwells]

ALs, 25 Oct 1923. 2 pp, size not stated. To Miss Rittenhouse. Giving permission to reprint a poem. sg Feb 27 (180) $80

Signature, on detached tp of program for the Society of Twentieth Century Music, 19 May 1952. Size not stated. Framed with a photograph. Ck Apr 3 (129) £50

Sitwell, Sir Osbert, 1892-1969

Autograph Ms, poem, Ultimate Judgement - (For Edith); 21 Aug 1920. 20 lines, sgd. Ck Apr 3 (73) £120

Skoda, Joseph, 1805-81

ALs, 30 July 1879. 2 pp, 8vo. To an unnamed colleague. Thanking for flowers. star Mar 26 (822) DM220

Slavery

AL, 18 Nov 1826. 2 pp, 4to. To Sarah Lucas from her niece in Missouri. Giving family news, & mentioning the price of negroes. sg Sept 12 (225) $225

Document, 16 Jan 1802. 1 p, 8vo. Acknowledging the sale of a slave named Judith in North Carolina. sg Dec 5 (232) $200

— 5 Mar 1808. 1 p, 8vo. Bill of sale for the slave Tom from Joshua Owings to J. Boswell; sgd by Owings. sg Sept 12 (227) $200

— 28 Aug 1809. 1 p, 8vo. Bill of sale for the slave Lucy from James Fishbach to J. Boswell; sgd by Fishbach. sg Sept 12 (226) $200

— 28 Mar 1825. 2 pp, 4to. Acknowledging the sale of 9 slaves in Orange County. sg Dec 5 (233) $150

— 21 Mar 1837. 1 p, folio. Legal charge against Abner Blaisdell for selling liquor to a slave in Lawrence County, Alabama. sg Dec 5 (234) $150

— 16 Sept 1842. 2 pp, folio. Acknowledging the sale of a slave named James in Washington. sg Dec 5 (235) $140

— 5 Dec 1850. 7.5 by 4 inches. Receipt for payment "for a Negro Boy named Henry", sold to P. R. Hoyle. Framed. Dar Feb 13 (101) $300

— 17 Dec 1850. 1 p, 4to. Certification of ownership of 3 slaves, issued at New Orleans. In French. Dar June 11 (105) $160

— 27 Nov 1858. 1 p, folio. Acknowledging the sale of 2 slaves named Mary & Judith in Washington. sg Dec 5 (236) $150

— 6 Jan 1860. 1 p, 8 by 4.25 inches. Receipt, sgd Griffin & Pullum, for payment for 2 slaves sold to John Johnson. Dar Aug 6 (121) $120

See also: Civil War, American
See also: Livingston, Philip

Slavonic Manuscripts. See: Psalms & Psalters

Slevogt, Max, 1868-1932

Collection of 58 A Ls s & 27 autograph postcards, sgd, 29 June 1910 to 4 Nov 1922 & [n.d.]. Length not stated. To Carl Steinbart. About a wide variety of personal & professional matters. Including 6 small drawings. HN June 26 (981) DM32,000

ALs, [1918]. 1 p, 4to. To [Max Friedlaender]. Expressing satisfaction with a publication. Including pen-&-ink sketch. star Mar 27 (953) DM770

Smetana, Bedrich, 1824-84

Photograph, sgd, [c.1880]. Cabinet size. By Mulac. Illus in cat. star Mar 27 (1155) DM4,700

Smith, Abigail Adams, 1765-1813

Series of 3 A Ls s, 3 Jan 1782 to 27 Apr 1783. 10 pp, 4to. To Mr. Thaxter. Chatting about mutual friends, expressing concern about her father's health, regretting her brothers' absence, etc. sup May 9 (313) $300

Smith, Algernon Emory, d.1876

Cut signature, [n.d.]. 3.75 by 2 inches. As Lieut., 7th Regiment of Cavalry. Framed. Armstrong collection. sup Oct 15 (1132) $240

Smith, Isaac, 1752-1831

ALs, 13 Nov 1821. 1 p, 4to. To J. D. Blake. About legal matters, & referring to Mrs. Cook. Longueville collection. S June 25 (77) £700 [Arnold]

Smith, Joseph, 1805-44

Ds, 7 Feb 1837. 7 by 3 inches. Kirkland Safety Society Bank note no 1328 for $5.00, payable to I. Perkins. Also sgd by Sidney Rigdon. Illus in cat. Dar Apr 9 (352) $850

Smith, Samuel F., 1808-95

Autograph transcript, 4 stanzas of America, sgd & dated 1 Oct 1892. 1 p, folio. Dar Dec 26 (11) $1,500

— Autograph transcript, 4 stanzas of America, sgd; 1880. 2 pp, 8vo. With related ALs. Illus in cat. R Mar 7 (181) $600

— Autograph transcript, 4 stanzas of America, sgd, 27 Feb 1888. 2 pp, 8vo. Mtd. Illus in cat. sup May 9 (66) $1,550

ALs, [n.d.]. 2 pp, 8vo. To C. D. Kellogg. Sending some verses (not present). Dar Oct 10 (330) $225

Smith, Sidney, 1877-1935

Original drawing, cartoon, [n.d.]. 2.25 by 3.25 inches (card). Sgd. Illus in cat. Dar Feb 13 (323) $100

Smith, William, 1727-1803

Autograph Ms, 12 workbooks containing copies of poems, transcriptions of letters, the draft of an article, inventories, etc., [1750-1800]. About 300 pp, various sizes, bound together in a half mor vol. P June 16 (182) $8,000

ALs, 4 July 1792. 3 pp, folio. To Col. Benjamin Walker. Regarding trade between the US & Britain. Seal hole. R Nov 9 (124) $150

Smith, William Farrar, 1824-1903

ALs, 1 Nov 1892. 2 pp, 8vo. To Capt. Hunter. Explaining changes in a new Ed of a work on the Civil War. Dar June 11 (131) $150

Smyth, Dame Ethel, 1858-1944

Collection of 36 A Ls s & postcards, sgd, 24 Jan 1933 to 19 Feb 1934. Length not stated. To Alice Jones. Concerning the typing of several of her works. S July 21 (180) £500 [Rota]

Soane, Sir John, 1753-1837

ALs, 5 Apr 1797. 1 p, 4to. To Henry Holland. Refusing to attend a meeting because of the conduct of some club members. bba May 28 (220) £200 [Soane Museum]

— [1811]. 1 p, 4to. To T. Tyrell. Expressing the wish to succeed Robert Mylne as Surveyor of St. Paul's Cathedral. bba May 28 (221) £220 [Soane Museum]

Soemmering, Samuel Thomas von, 1755-1830

ALs, 16 Sept 1814. 1 p, 4to. To Friedrich von Matthisson. About scientific matters. star Mar 26 (823) DM950

ANs, [n.d.]. 1 p, 8vo. Recipient unnamed. Sending a present. star Mar 26 (824) DM240

Sokolow, Nahum, 1859-1936

ALs, [1879]. 1 p, 8vo. To Mr. Margolin. Protesting against "awful copy-editing" of his writings. Dar Feb 13 (235) $350

Solzhenitsyn, Alexander

Transcript, typescript of opening lines of One Day in the Life of Ivan Denisovich, Sept 1980. 1 p, 4to. Sgd & with typed inscr to Earl Porter. Dar Aug 6 (260) $250

Ls, 24 Aug 1983. 1 p, 8vo. Recipient & contents not stated. With a port. Illus in cat. R June 13 (213) $160

Somdelat Phra-Paramendr Maha Mongkut, King of Siam

Letter, 11 June 1863. 7 pp, 8vo. To Sir James Brooke, Rajah of Sarawak. Referring to the good relationship between them & the reception of Malay traders. bba June 25 (135) £2,200 [Kunkler]

Sophie Dorothea, Queen of Friedrich Wilhelm I of Prussia, 1687-1757

Ls, 26 July 1727. 1 p, folio. To Matthias von der Schulenburg. Acknowledging condolences on the death of her father. star Mar 27 (1586) DM750

Sorabji, Kaikhosru, 1892-1988

Collection of 2 A Ls s & 13 Ls s, 13 Jan 1949 to 10 Mar 1956. To Gordon Watson. Mostly about musical matters. C Dec 16 (339) £750 [Haas]

Soubise, Charles de Rohan, Prince de, 1715-87

Ls, 12 Oct 1761. 1 p, 4to. To the Prince de Turenne. Recommending the promotion of 3 officers. HN Nov 28 (1838) DM480

Soult, Nicolas Jean, Duc de Dalmatie, 1769-1851

Ls, 27 Sept 1808. 1 p, 4to. To L. P. E. Bignon. Returning 2 letters. star Mar 27 (1377a) DM220

Sousa, John Philip, 1854-1932

Autograph music, fragmentary opening of a melody march; [n.d.]. 2 pp, folio. Sgd. P June 17 (364) $1,500

— Autograph music, The Thunderer March, sgd J.P.S. & dated 21 Sept 1889. 1 p, folio. Complete working Ms; 90 bars. Framed. Dar Dec 26 (308) $8,000

ALs, 27 Sept 1899. 1 p, 8vo. To Mr. Murney. Inquiring about scores, & hoping he can come to a concert in New Haven. Dar June 11 (345) $250

Group photograph, sgd, [n.d.]. 9.5 by 7.5 inches. With 6 others, sgd by each. Illus in cat. R June 13 (214) $320

Signature, [19]08. On a card. Framed with a photograph, overall size 11 by 7 inches. Dar June 11 (344) $120

Autograph quotation, 4 bars from Stars and Stripes Forever, sgd;. [n.d.]. 1 p, 8vo. Illus in cat. R Mar 7 (182) $550

South Africa

— CRADOCK (CARADOC), SIR JOHN FRANCIS. - 2 Mss, military general orders issued from Cape Colony headquarters by Lieut. Gen. Sir J. Cradock & others, Sept 1811 to Jan 1814, 900 pp in 2 calf vols. S Dec 12 (309) £450 [Sawyer]

— RUSSELL, ANNE EMILY. - Autograph Ms, diary kept in South Africa, 28 Mar 1852 to 11 Mar 1853. 238 pp, 8vo. Sgd on flyleaf. S Feb 11 (786) £240 [Sawyer]

South Carolina

[A group of 5 letters from Charleston, 1767 to 1773, to Newton & Gordon, Madeira, regarding business matters, shipping of wine, etc., sold at R on 13 June 1992, lot 168, for $150.]

Southern, Terry

[The autograph & typed working drafts of his novel The Magic Christian, [pbd 1959], 265 pp (70 autograph), 4to & folio, sold at CNY on 9 June 1992, lot 178, for $6,500.]

Spain

— INQUISITION. - Ms, eyewitness account of an auto-da-fe held in Valladolid, 8 Oct 1559. 16 pp, folio; stitched. Detailed account of proceedings, charges, etc. S Dec 5 (570) £3,000 [Ragone]

— INQUISITION. - Ms, account of an investigation into the murder of the Inquisitor Pedro de Arbues, [after 1485]. 150 pp, folio, in vellum wrap. In 2 neat scribal hands. S May 28 (66) £1,100 [Maggs]

— MORISCOS. - Ms, notarial documents recording the redistribution of land belonging to the moriscos of Ugixar in southern Spain, 1572 to 1575. About 1000 pp, folio, in modern bds. In scribal hands. S May 28 (64) £1,600 [Maggs]

Spalatin, Georg, 1484-1545

ALs, [9 Jan] 1536. 1 p, 4to. To Heinrich von Einsiedel. Sending Melanchthon's sermon on angels in his own German trans. Illus in cat. star Mar 27 (1723) DM4,200

Spalding, Albert Goodwill, 1850-1915

Cut signature, [n.d.]. Matted with Hall of Fame card, overall size 8 by 10 inches. Dar Feb 13 (90) $500

Speaker, Tris E., 1888-1958. See: Cobb, Ty & Speaker

Spiegel zum Desenberg, Ferdinand August, Graf, Erzbischof von Koeln, 1764-1835

ALs, 23 Feb 1831. 3 pp, 4to. Recipient unnamed. Confidential letter discussing theological & historical works & current political affairs. star Mar 27 (1415) DM250

Spielhagen, Friedrich, 1829-1911

ALs, 6 Feb 1888. 4 pp, 8vo. To an unnamed actress. Referring to the premiere of his play Die Philosophin. HN Nov 28 (1839) DM220

Spohr, Louis, 1784-1859

ALs, 20 May 1828. 2 pp, 4to. To A. C. Prell. Offering to arrange a concert for him at Kassel. star Mar 27 (1157) DM580

— 24 Feb 1856. 2 pp, 4to. To Heinrich Sczadronsky. Suggesting that his 3d Symphony might be easier to perform at Sankt Gallen than his 4th Symphony. star Mar 27 (1159) DM1,300

ADs, 17 June 1851. 1 p, 4to. Attestation for his student, the violinist Hueni. star Mar 27 (1158) DM600

Spoliansky, Mischa, 1898-1985 —& Preminger, Otto, 1906-86

Ds, 18 Jan 1957. 1 p, 4to. Contract for music for Saint Joan. Dar Oct 10 (331) $110

Spontini, Gaspare, 1774-1851

ALs, [n.d.]. 1 p, 8vo. To Herr Baader. Suggesting that his opera Agnes be performed on Sunday. In French. FD Dec 3 (1465) DM200

Springer, William McKendree, 1836-1903

Autograph Ms, resolution submitted to the Democratic Caucus, US House of Representatives, "that an enabling act for the Territories of Dakota, Montana, Washington & New Mexico should be passed at this session"; 1888. 1 p, 4to. With authentication on verso. bbc Dec 9 (174) $2,500

Stadion, Johann Kaspar von, 1567-1641

Ls, 4 Mar 1620. 1 p, folio. To Count Karl von Buquoy. Inquiring about Simon Schroetl. Also sgd by Ferdinand II & Gerhard von Questenberg. HN Nov 28 (1841) DM1,000

Stael-Holstein, Anne Louise Germaine, Baronne de, 1766-1817

A Ls (2), 9 & 30 Jan 1812. 8 pp, 8vo. To [Karl Viktor von Bonstetten]. Complaining about her stay at Geneva, & reporting about her activities, books, friends, etc. 1 leaf def. star Mar 26 (468) DM2,200

Stalin, Joseph, 1879-1953

Ds, 7 Sept 1950. 2 p, 12mo. Ptd form from the Council of Ministers, countersgd by A. Gromyko. Framed with a port. Illus in cat. P June 17 (78) $4,750

Cut signature, [n.d.]. 7 by 2.5 inches. Also sgd by Andrei Gromyko. Framed with a photograph. Dar Apr 9 (355) $2,250

Stamitz, Carl, 1745-1801

ALs, 26 May 1786. 7 pp, 4to. To [the Rev. Sievers?]. Reporting vividly about his successful concerts in Berlin. Illus in cat. star Mar 27 (1161) DM19,000

Stanhope, Lady Hester Lucy, 1776-1839

ALs, [n.d.], "Thursday". 3 pp, 8vo. To [Thomas Pitt]. Asking him to dine & mentioning her quarrel with Stratford Canning. Ingilby collection. pn Nov 14 (105) £160 [Browning]

Stanislas II Augustus Poniatowski, King of Poland, 1732-98

Ls s (2), 30 July & 8 Aug 1794. 2 pp, folio. To L. S. I. Tengoborskij. Regarding letters to Mr. Jagnin. star Mar 27 (1576) DM230

Stanley, Sir Henry Morton, 1841-1904

Series of 14 A Ls s, 12 Apr to 5 Nov 1869. 32 pp, 8vo & 4to. To Katie Gough-Roberts & her father Thomas (2). Letters from Spain to his fiancee, & discussing their engagement with her father. With related material. Illus in cat. C June 24 (383) £7,000 [Chalmers]

ALs, 25 Jan 1878. 3 pp, 8vo. To Samuel White Baker. Expressing pride that his "work meets such flattering approbation from practical travellers like yourself". CNY Dec 5 (119) $1,600

— 28 Jan 1878. 4 pp, 8vo. To Agnes Livingstone Bruce. About his trans-African expedition, & referring to her father. C Oct 30 (86) £850 [Sawyer]

— 15 Oct 1890. 4 pp, size not stated. To Messrs. Forrest & Son. Praising the boat their company built for his recent trip to Africa. Illus in cat. sup May 9 (423) $1,250

Stanton, Edwin M., 1814-69

ALs, 26 Sept 1864. 1 p, 4to. To Major Gen. W. T. Sherman. Giving news of a change in the Confederate command & the Mobile campaign. Spiro collection. CNY May 14 (149) $1,600

See also: Lincoln, Abraham & Stanton

Starhemberg, Konrad Balthasar, Graf von, 1612-87

Ls, 1 June 1640. 1 p, folio. To the magistrate of Upper Austria. Inquiring about the accounts of officers quartered in their territory. HN Nov 28 (1843) DM900

Stauffer, Karl, 1857-91

ALs, 10 Oct 1886. 2 pp, 8vo. To [Max Friedlaender]. Hoping to meet Wilhelm Unger. star Mar 27 (954) DM360

Stauffer-Bern, Karl, 1857-91. See: Stauffer, Karl

Steigentesch, August Ernst von, 1774-1826

ALs, 22 July 1815. 2 pp, 4to. To Georg Joachim Goeschen. Expecting an increased importance of the German language for literature & the sciences after the defeat of Napoleon. star Mar 26 (469) DM220

Stein, Charlotte von, 1742-1827

ALs, 21 Feb 1824. 3 pp, 8vo. Recipient unnamed. About her deafness, a recent masquerade, etc. Illus in cat. HH May 13 (1955) DM2,200

— STEIN, LUISE VON. - ALs, [c.Dec 1826]. 4 pp, 4to. To Fritz von Stein. In the name of her grandmother, giving news. Beginning 4 lines in Charlotte vom Stein's hand. star Mar 26 (195) DM2,200

Stein, Gertrude, 1874-1946

ALs, [1907]. 5 pp, 8vo. To Jeane Boiffard. Chatting about recent visitors. In French. P June 17 (366) $800

— [1926]. 2 pp, 16mo (card). To unnamed friends. About a projected meeting. sg Feb 27 (197) $400

— [n.d.]. 2 pp, 8vo. To [her friend's dog] Curly. About her own pets. Illus in cat. sg Feb 27 (196) $400

Autograph postcard, sgd, 28 Jan 1945. To Myron Wood. Explaining her book How to Write. sg Sept 12 (232) $475

Stein, Karl, Freiherr vom und zum, 1757-1831

ALs, 17 Sept 1830. 1 p, 4to. To Mlle. Schroeder. Asking that she bring his account book to Cappenberg. star Mar 27 (1732) DM400

Ls, 15 Dec 1807. 1 p, folio. To von Scharnhorst. Notifying him of a decision concerning the "Warsaw frontier". star Mar 27 (1731) DM380

Steinbeck, John, 1902-68

ALs, [2 Mar 1962]. 1 p, 4to. To [Robert & Cynthia Wallsten]. Complaining about the cold weather in Italy. Dar Apr 9 (357) $1,300

— [26 Apr 1962]. 5 pp, 4to. To Robert & Cynthia Wallsten. Giving advice on Robert Wallsten's problems with Judith Anderson's autobiography. Dar Oct 10 (332) $2,250

Autograph postcard, sgd, 28 Aug 1962. To Mrs. Frank McKowne. Thanking for catalogues. Illus in cat. sg Feb 27 (198) $650

Stengel, Charles Dillon ("Casey"), 1889-1975

Ds, 1930. 1 p, 4to. Contract with the Toledo Baseball Club. Illus in cat. sup July 10 (1003) $800

Group photograph, sgd, 1949. 10 by 8 inches. With Burt Shotton. Illus in cat. sup July 10 (976) $125

Stengel, Charles Dillon ("Casey"), 1889-1975 —& Others

Group photograph, 27 July 1964. 5.5 by 3.5 inches. Talking to Joe McCarthy & Elmer Flick. Sgd by Stengel on recto, by Flick & McCarthy on verso. Dar Dec 26 (108) $130

Stengel, Charles Dillon ("Casey"), 1889-1975 —&
Williams, Theodore Samuel

Group photograph, 1966. 5.5 by 3.5 inches. Sgd by both on recto & on verso. Dar Dec 26 (121) $100

Stephan, Heinrich von, 1831-97

ALs, [n.d.]. 4 pp, 8vo. To an unnamed lady. Informing her that her request has been granted. HH May 13 (2051) DM220

ADs, 21 Mar 1886. 1 p, 8vo. Confirmation of a cadet's visit. hen Nov 12 (2508) DM340

Stephens, Alexander H., 1812-83

Franking signature, [27 Sept n.y.]. On autograph address leaf to John L. Stephens, 6 by 3.25 inches. Dar June 11 (346) $110

Stephenson, George, 1781-1848

Ls, 21 Sept 1844. 1 p, 8vo. Recipient unnamed. About the worries of railway business. pn Mar 19 (114) £300 [Wilson]

Ds, 18 May 1822. 1 p, folio. Patent application for modifications to the steam engine; incorporating ink-&-watercolor drawing of the invention. CNY Dec 5 (120) $4,500

Stephenson, Robert, 1803-59

ALs, [n.d.]. 1 p, 8vo. To Thomas Page. Informing him that he is "not sure about being able to attend the Atheneum on Monday". star Mar 26 (826) DM220

Sternheim, Carl, 1878-1942

ALs, 11 Dec 1938. 2 pp, 4to. To his niece Gretel Fritz. Deploring the general decline of civilization in Europe. star Mar 26 (470) DM350

Stevens, Clement Hoffman, 1821-64

Ds, 19 Jan 1853. 1 p, 7 by 3 inches. $5.00 bill, sgd as Cashier of the South Carolina Planters & Mechanics Bank. Matted. Dar June 11 (132) $400

Stevenson, Robert Louis, 1850-94

ALs, [1884?]. 1 p, 8vo. To Mrs. F. A. Cox. Listing his pbd works. CNY Oct 8 (241) $1,400

— [Oct 1887]. 4 pp, 8vo. To Miss Boodle. Describing atrocious conditions he has to endure [at Saranac Lake]. Ingilby collection. pn Nov 14 (106) £2,200 [Dupre]

Ds, 13 Apr 1887. 1 p, 8vo. Draft on the Wilts & Dorset Banking Co. sg Sept 12 (233) $425

Stewart, James

Ds, 24 Sept 1969. 1 p, 4to. Contract to play "the part of Elwood P. Dowd in the play now called 'Harvey'". Dar Apr 9 (358) $425

Stieglitz, Alfred, 1864-1946

ALs, 9 Feb 1930. 2 pp, folio. To Frank J. Hermann. About the success of his new gallery. On verso of 2 lithographic flyers for exhibitions. Framed. CNY Dec 5 (122) $1,000

Stieglitz, Charlotte, 1806-34

ALs, 15 Jan 1834. 4 pp, 8vo. To Theodor Mundt. Accusing him of abandoning her. Gottschalk collection. C Dec 16 (418) £280 [Rosenthal]

Stieler, Joseph, 1781-1858

ALs, 10 Jan 1829. 2 pp, 4to. To Johann Adam Ackermann. Thanking for a drawing. HH May 13 (2053) DM650

Stifter, Adalbert, 1805-68

Autograph Ms, poem, beginning "Du duerstend Herz! sag an, was soll dein Muehen?", Apr 1833. 2 pp, 8vo. 4 four-line stanzas; possibly unpbd. star Mar 26 (471) DM8,500

Stiles, Ezra, 1727-95

ALs, 15 Apr 1775. 3 pp, folio. To Catharine Macaulay. Discussing the political situation & predicting the future greatness of America. pn June 11 (18) £2,300

Stoker, Bram, 1847-1912

ALs, 2 Sept 1841. 2 pp, 8vo. To F. R. Rogers. Informing him of Sir Henry Irving's travel arrangements. wa Oct 19 (56) $180

Stolberg, Christian, Graf zu, 1748-1821

ALs, 1 Dec 1802. 4 pp, 4to. To an unamed lady. Suggesting that her daughter needs a rest & should not be urged to see her mother at this point. In French. star Mar 26 (473) DM1,900

Stolberg, Friedrich Leopold, Graf zu, 1750-1819

ALs, [Nov 1788]. 3 pp, 4to. To Frau von Ompteda. Informing her of the death of his wife. star Mar 26 (474) DM2,600

— 9 Aug 1806. 4 pp, 4to. Recipients unnamed. Regretting being unable to participate in a project honoring Gellert. star Mar 26 (475) DM3,800

Storm, Theodor, 1817-88

Autograph transcript, poem, Spruch des Alters 2, 31 May 1886. 1 p, 8vo. 6 lines, sgd. star Mar 26 (477) DM3,000

ANs, 21 Dec 1880. 1 p, 125mm by 135mm, cut from larger leaf. Recipient unnamed. Note of transferral. star Mar 26 (476) DM580

AN, [n.d.]. On ptd visiting card. To Emil Palleske. Inviting him for lunch. star Mar 26 (478) DM900

Stowe, Harriet Beecher, 1811-96

Collection of ALs, photograph, sgd, & group photograph, [1851?] & [n.d.]. 1 p, 8vo, & cabinet size. To Dr. Stone. Requesting him not to mention her "Uncle Tom project". Bust port & group photograph with her husband. Spiro collection. CNY May 14 (150) $3,500

ALs, 29 Mar 1852. 2 pp, 4to. To Prince Albert. Presenting a copy of Uncle Tom's Cabin to Prince Albert & Queen Victoria. Repaired; silked. Illus in cat. Spiro collection. CNY May 14 (151) $16,000

— 29 Dec 1855. 3 pp, 4to. To Mrs. S. C. Hall. About the hardships of a black woman singer & the innate musicality of blacks. Spiro collection. CNY May 14 (152) $4,200

— [1856]. 4 pp, 8vo. To [Sampson] Low. Outlining emendations to her novel Dred.

Including ALs by her husband on same sheet. Ingilby collection. pn Nov 14 (107) £750
— 14 Feb [1864]. 1 p, 12mo. To Sarah Green. Requesting her to oversee her move from Andover to Hartford. wa Dec 19 (274) $260

Strachey, Lytton, 1880-1932

ALs, 16 June 1918. 1 p, 4to. To Mr. Bradshaw. Discussing his Eminent Victorians & a putative 2d series of Lives. bba June 25 (136) £140 [Silverman]

Strassmann, Fritz, 1902-80

Autograph Ms, lecture about atomic energy, given at Cologne, 22 Jan 1957. 10 pp, folio. Sgd later, at head. With ALs, 6 Jan 1962. star Mar 26 (827) DM8,000

Strauss, Johann, 1825-99

ALs, [26 Oct 1882]. 4 pp, 12mo. To Adele Strauss. Love letter. star Mar 27 (1163) DM4,300

Autograph quotation, 4 bars from Der Zigeunerbaron, 5 Jan [18]85. 1 p, 85mm by 170mm. Sgd. Illus in cat. S Dec 6 (201) £800 [Macnutt]

Photograph, sgd & inscr, 1867. Carte size. Inscr with a musical quotation. Framed. Illus in cat. P June 17 (79) $2,750
— Anr, 29 Mar 1892. 165mm by 105mm. Sgd & inscr to Emil Diesterweg with a musical quotation. star Mar 27 (1164) DM2,200
— Anr, 14 Oct 1894. 105mm by 65mm. Inscr to Frau Kretschmann. Illus in cat. S Dec 6 (204) £500 [Macnutt]

Strauss, Johann, 1866-1939

Autograph quotation, 2 bars from a waltz, sgd; 4 Dec [19]26. 12mo. Mtd with a port. JG Sept 27 (462) DM350

Strauss, Richard, 1864-1949

Autograph music, draft for the finale of his "Duettconcertino", Op. 147, [c.Oct 1947]. 1 p, 339mm by 269mm. Sgd & inscr to Willi Schuh. Illus in cat. star Mar 27 (1167) DM11,000
— Autograph music, sketches for the 3d act of his opera Die schweigsame Frau, [1933]. 46 pp, 13cm by 17.5cm, in bds. Sgd & inscr to Willi Schuh, 12 June 1936. star Mar 27 (1166) DM46,000
— Autograph music, song, Erschaffen und beleben, to a text by Goethe; [c.Dec 1922]. 2 pp, folio. Incomplete draft, in pencil; sgd. Trimmed. S Dec 6 (208) £1,000 [Biba]

Typescript, essay, Erfahrungen mit klassischen Meisterwerken, [1934]. 14 pp, 4to, in quarter vellum bds. Including extensive autograph revisions & 2 autograph musical quotations. Some additions in anr hand. S May 29 (660) £2,200 [Haas]

ALs, 16 Apr 1902. 1 p, 8vo. To Adolf Goettmann. Recommending [Arnold] Schoenberg. star Mar 27 (1169) DM3,000
— 21 Feb 1908. 2 pp, 8vo. To [Ernst von Schuch?]. Urging him to visit to discuss the first performance of his opera Elektra. star Mar 27 (1170) DM1,600
— 15 Jan 1912. 1 p, 4to. To Arthur Bernstein. Responding to an inquiry about the best interpreters of his compositions. star Mar 27 (1171) DM1,900

Autograph postcard, sgd, 22 Feb [18]97. 1 p, 8vo. To Gustav Mahler. Thanking for the score of his 2d Symphony & commenting on it. Illus in cat. S Dec 6 (206) £900 [Kaplan]
— 12 Nov 1913. To Otto Lohse. Promising to attend a performance of Elektra at Leipzig. R Nov 9 (65) $300

Autograph quotation, 4 bars from his Don Quixote, sgd; [1896/97]. 1 p, 12mo. Framed with a port. P June 17 (80) $1,200

Photograph, sgd, 5 Jan 1926. 233mm by 172mm (image). Sgd on mount. Illus in cat. star Mar 27 (1172) DM1,700

See also: Hofmannsthal, Hugo von

Stravinsky, Igor, 1882-1971

[A group of 12 autograph musical Mss written by British composers to celebrate Stravinsky's 85th birthday, 1967, 20 pp, various sizes, marked for the ptr, sold at S on 29 May 1992, lot 666, for £800 to White.]

Autograph music, fragment of 3 bars, scored for orchestra; [n.d.]. 1 p, 35cm by 11cm, cut from larger sheet. In pencil. SM Oct 12 (406) FF6,500

ALs, 18 Apr 1919. 2 pp, 4to. To Misia Sert. About Diaghilev, Petroushka, his financial situation, etc. Boris Kochno collection. SM Oct 12 (398) FF13,000
— [19 Nov 1921]. 2 pp, 4to. To Vera Sudeikina. Suggesting that living away from her husband is probably not advisable. Boris Kochno collection. SM Oct 12 (403) FF11,000
— [19 Nov 1921]. 3 pp, 4to. To Vera Sudeikina. Responding to her question whether he will love her whatever happens. Boris Kochno collection. SM Oct 12 (404) FF10,000
— [30 Nov 1921]. 3 pp, 8vo. To Vera Sudeikina. Describing his heartache caused by their separation. Boris Kochno collection. SM Oct 12 (400) FF10,000
— [n.d.]. 2 pp, 8vo. To Vera Sudeikina. Comparing the expressive qualities of words & of music. Possibly incomplete. Boris Kochno collection. SM Oct 12 (405) FF8,000

Ls, 10 May 1941. 1 p, 8vo. To Paul Stoes. Discussing a projected concert tour. Framed with a photograph. sup Oct 15

(1820) $340

— 17 July 1964. 1 p, 4to. Letter of introduction for Arnold Weissberger. Dar Dec 26 (310) $250

ANs, 18 June 1958. 1 p, size not stated. To "Sis" & "Bob". Expressing thanks. Including 1 bar of music. Ck Nov 15 (32) £480

Corrected proof, Epitaphium fuer das Grabmal des Prinzen Max Egon zu Fuerstenberg, 1959. 6 pp, folio. Comprising 2 versions of the title, including Stravinsky's own design, & 4 proofs of the music, heavily annotated. S May 29 (665) £2,200 [Fuerstenberg]

Cut signature, 1954. Size not stated. Including subscription. Framed with a photograph. sg Sept 12 (234) $250

Photograph, sgd, [c.1936]. 17cm by 23cm. Illus in cat. S Dec 6 (213) £500 [Kaplan]

Photograph, sgd & inscr, 1940. 7 by 5 inches. Inscr to Boaz Piller. Dar Oct 10 (333) $425

— Anr, 1940. 10 by 8 inches. Inscr to Morris Miller. Illus in cat. sg Feb 27 (201) $750

Signature, [n.d.]. On envelope bearing his port. Dar Apr 9 (359) $200

— RAMBERT, MARIE. - A copy of the 1st Ed of the piano reduction of Le Sacre du Printemps, extensively annotated in Marie Rambert's hand recording Nijinsky's choreography for the ballet, 1913, with Rambert's typed introduction & trans of her annotations, 1967. S Dec 6 (210) £11,000 [Library of Congress]

Stravinsky, Igor, 1882-1971 —& Others

Concert program, Opening Gala Concert of the Seattle World's Fair, 21 Apr 1962. 8 pp, 4to. Sgd & inscr by Stravinsky, Van Cliburn, Milton Katims, & Robert Craft. sup Oct 15 (1821) $455

Streisand, Barbra —&
Redford, Robert

Group photograph, [n.d.]. 10 by 8 inches. Film scene; sgd by both. Dar Dec 26 (311) $160

Strickland, Charlotte, 1759-1833 —&
Strickland, Juliana Sabina, 1765-1849

Ms, Specimens of British Plants, [c.1803]. Length not stated, folio, in contemp blue/green roan. 53 watercolor botanical studies interleaved with descriptive text. C Oct 30 (230) £5,000 [Maggs]

Strickland, Juliana Sabina, 1765-1849. See: Strickland, Charlotte & Strickland

Strindberg, August, 1849-1912

Autograph Ms, play, Kronbruden, [1901]. 95 pp, size not stated; stitched, in calligraphic wrap. Including autograph emendations, a pen-&-ink drawing, autograph musical settings of songs, & instructions to the ptr. S May 28 (217) £30,000 [Swedish Royal Library]

Autograph transcript, excerpts from Honore de Balzac's novel Louis Lambert, [1895?]. 7 pp, 8vo. About Swedenborg. star Mar 26 (480) DM2,600

ALs, 23 May 1895. 3 pp, 8vo. To [Robert Fuchs]. Regarding his separation from his wife (recipient's client). star Mar 26 (481) DM1,500

Strozzi, Pietro, 1510-58 —&
Este, Ippolito d', Cardinal, 1509-72

Ms, copies of their correspondence, 11 Jan 1554 to 28 Apr 1555; [later 16th cent]. 78 leaves, 330mm by 228mm, in modern vellum. Comprising 68 letters by Strozzi & 34 by Cardinal d'Este, including details relating to the War of Siena. sg Nov 7 (238) $425

Struensee, Johann Friedrich, Graf von, 1737-72

Ls, 6 Oct 1771. 1 p, 4to. To the Count of Holstein. Ordering him to officiate as judge. star Mar 27 (1734) DM640

Stuart, James Ewell Brown, 1833-64

Photograph, [n.d.]. Oval, 6.25 by 5.25 inches; mtd. Seated, in uniform. Illus in cat. R June 13 (277) $1,700

Studebaker, Clement, 1831-1901

ALs, 25 Nov 1868. 1 p, 4to. To C. F. Hatch. Negotiating the shipment of sleighs to Chicago. Dar Aug 6 (263) $1,400

Sturgis, Samuel Davis, 1822-89

Signature, [n.d.]. 3 by 1.5 inches (card). Framed. Armstrong collection. sup Oct 15 (1133) $100

Styne, Jule, 1905-81. See: Loos, Anita & Styne

Sullivan, Sir Arthur, 1842-1900

Autograph music, anthem, Hearken unto Me, My People, sgd; Dec 1876. 16 pp, 4to, in modern half green calf. Marked by the ptr. P June 17 (379) $5,500

Sullivan, John, 1740-95

ADs, 28 Oct 1778. 1 p, 4to. To Benjamin Steel. Pay order in favor of Aaron Lopez for articles supplied to the army. Spiro collection. CNY May 14 (153) $500

Sullivan, John Lawrence, 1858-1918

Signature, [n.d.]. 5 by 3 inches (card). Including subscription. Illus in cat. Dar Feb 13 (106) $550

Sully Prudhomme, Pseud. of Rene Francois Armand Prudhomme, 1839-1907

ALs, 30 Dec 1881. 3 pp, 12mo. Recipient unnamed. Mentioning Abraham Dreyfus. Dar Apr 9 (317) $150

Sulzer, Johann Georg, 1720-79

ALs, [n.d.]. 1 p, 4to. Recipient unnamed. About an order for some scholarly works. star Mar 26 (829) DM650

Sunday, William Ashley ("Billy"), 1862?-1935

Ls, 5 Dec 1911. 1 p, 8vo. To James E. Sullivan. Concerning a book about baseball by A. G. Spalding. Trimmed. Dar Dec 26 (65) $600

Supervielle, Jules, 1884-1960

Series of 7 A Ls s, 23 Oct 1933 to 12 Feb 1945. 13 pp, 4to & 8vo. To Antonio Aita. About his works, current projects, etc. star Mar 26 (482) DM320

Sutermeister, Heinrich

Collection of 2 Ls s, photograph, & cut signature, 16 May 1964 & 16 Mar 1967. 4 pp, various sizes, & photograph. To Pavel Eckstein. About his recent projects & the premiere of his Madame Bovary. star Mar 27 (1177) DM480

Sutter, John A., 1803-80

Photograph, sgd, 1867. 3 by 4.5 inches. Sgd on verso. By Ulke. sup Oct 15 (1056) $400

Suttner, Bertha von, 1843-1914

Collection of 8 A Ls s & 9 autograph postcards, sgd, 15 Oct 1891 to 27 Jan 1900. 11 pp, mostly 8vo, & cards. To Moritz Adler. About contributions to her journal, her own & recipient's works, etc. star Mar 26 (483) DM1,300

Swanson, Gloria, 1899-1983

Ls, 5 July 1949. 1 p, 8vo. To Leslie. Referring to the film Sunset Boulevard. Framed with 2 photographs. Illus in cat. wd Dec 12 (339) $300

Swift Bear

Photograph, [n.d.]. 5.4 by 3.75 inches (image). By Gardiner. Illus in cat. R June 13 (287) $300

Swift, Jonathan, 1667-1745

ALs, 17 Dec 1734. 2 pp, 8vo. Recipient unnamed. Declining an invitation. Def. sup Oct 15 (1823) $1,500

Swinburne, Algernon Charles, 1837-1909. See: Calligraphy

Switzerland

— Cantons of Uri, Schwyz, Unterwalden, Lucerne, & Zug. - Letter, [26 July 1563]. 1 p, folio. To the Duke of Sessa. Letter of recommendation for their envoy Walter Roll. S Dec 5 (572) £3,000 [Fox Glove]

Sylva, Carmen, Pseud. of Elisabeth, Queen of Carol I of Romania, 1843-1916

Ls, 20 Mar 1902. 3 pp, 4to. To Georgina Max Mueller. About her artwork & other activities. Dar Aug 6 (151) $110

Symons, Arthur, 1865-1945

Typescript, The Tragedians, [1890s?]. 73 pp, folio, in contemp wraps. Some Ms corrections. bba Sept 19 (369) £300 [Y. & S. Company]

Collection of ALs, Ls, & 2 autograph Mss, sgd, 9 June 1892 to 4 Aug 1927. 5 pp, 4to & 8vo. To Yvette Gilbert. Regarding a piece he has written about her, & proposing to trans her book. Poems, Faint Love, & Yvette: her wonder. CNY Dec 5 (340) $650

Szold, Henrietta, 1860-1945

Ls, 18 Nov 1932. 1 p, 8vo. To Mrs. M. Skivin. Requesting information about a boy caught by the Jerusalem police. Illus in cat. Dar Feb 13 (236) $190

— 11 Nov 1936. 1 p, 4to. To David Umansky. Welcoming him to a committee. Dar June 11 (259) $140

T

Taft, William Howard, 1857-1930

Autograph Ms, testimony to Major Archibald W. Butt, sgd; 19 Apr 1912. With a photograph, sgd, & further material relating to Butt in a disbound lea vol. sup Oct 15 (1603) $800

Typescript, extract from Four Aspects of Civic Duty; [n.d.]. 1 p, 4to. Sgd. Framed with a port. Illus in cat. sup Oct 15 (1600) $1,300

ALs, 26 Sept 1920. 1 p, 4to. Recipient unnamed. Declining an invitation to speak at Williamsport. R Mar 7 (147) $250

— 20 Jan 1921. 1 p, 8vo. Recipient unnamed. Declining a request. Illus in cat. R Mar 7 (146) $220

— 26 May 1923. 1 p, 8vo. To D. Pierson Ricks. Stating that he prefers "the Bench to Executive office". Dar Feb 13 (329) $1,000

— 18 Dec 1925. 1 p, 8vo. To Mr. Wolf. Referring to a handkerchief he forgot to return. R Mar 7 (145) $250

— 4 Apr 1929. 1 p, 8vo. To Mrs. Ernest Ibsen. Concerning her husband's port of Taft. With related material. sup Oct 15 (1605) $850

Series of 3 Ls s, 2 Jan 1914 to 21 June 1916. 3 pp, 4to. To John Wesley Hill. About luncheon dates, & expressing thanks. R June 13 (193) $2,200

Ls, 8 Feb 1905. 2 pp, 4to. To John Dalzell. Urging his support for a bill. R Nov 9 (40) $900

— 1 May 1905. 1 p, 8vo. To J. Warren Keefer.

Concerning an appointment in the Secretary of War's office. Dar Aug 6 (264) $150
— 10 July 1906. 1 p, 8vo. To J. Kemp Bartlett. Sending a memorandum concerning recipient's company. Including brief autograph addition. Dar Aug 6 (265) $200
— 30 Apr 1907. 1 p, 8vo. To Wesley Hook. Responding to an inquiry about opportunities for the practice of law in the Philippines. Including autograph postscript, sgd WHT. Dar Feb 13 (326) $425
— 4 Mar 1908. 1 p, 8vo. To M. D. Fritz. Thanking for clippings. Including autograph postscript. Dar Apr 9 (360) $160
— 28 Nov 1908. 1 p, 8vo. To A. B. Hagner. Thanking for congratulations on his election. wa Oct 19 (344) $130
— 8 Mar 1909. 1 p, 4to. To F. A. Pezet. Expressing the wish to see him in Washington. Dar Apr 9 (361) $450
— 11 May 1910. 1 p, 8vo. To Frank P. MacLennan. Hoping he will come to a garden party. Dar Oct 10 (336) $160
— 4 June 1912. 2 pp, 4to. To C. S. Woodruff. Angrily denying that he ever "had any conference with Judge Archibald" concerning violations of the Anti-Trust Act. R Nov 9 (42) $850
— 8 Aug 1912. 1 p, 4to. To Marcus P. Knowlton. Thanking for some information. Dar Apr 9 (362) $275
— 2 Dec 1915. 1 p, 8vo. To W. M. Van Der Weyde. Declining an invitation. Dar Oct 10 (337) $150
— 15 July 1921. 1 p, 4to. To J. Strouse. Thanking for congratulations. sup Oct 15 (1604) $160
— 12 Mar 1925. 1 p, 4to. To James Beck. Informing him about Supreme Court schedules. R Mar 7 (148) $450
— 26 Oct 1926. 1 p, 4to. To Mr. De Forest. Denying that Cecile de Wenthworth ever painted his port. R Nov 9 (41) $250
— [n.d.]. 1 p, 8vo. To J. B. Henderson. Responding to criticism of a statement concerning President McKinley & the Philippines. Dar June 11 (349) $400

Ds, 8 Apr 1909. 1 p, folio. Appointment of Clyde S. McDowell as Lieutenant. Dar Feb 13 (327) $225
— 1 July 1909. 1 p, folio. Appointment of H. H. Malvin as 2d Lieut. of Artillery. sup Oct 15 (1601) $500
— 20 Oct 1910. 1 p, folio. Appointment of James T. Dean as Major of Infantry. Dar Aug 6 (266) $250
— 7 Nov 1910. 3 pp, folio. Lease for Peabody Cottage. Illus in cat. sup Oct 15 (1599) $700
— 19 Dec 1910. 1 p, folio. Appointment of James T. Dean as Major of Infantry. Including vignettes. Dar Aug 6 (267) $300
— 6 Mar 1911. 1 p, folio. Naval commission for John Bailey. sg Sept 12 (235) $275

Autograph sentiment, sgd, 22 Apr 1922. 4.5 by 3 inches. Matted with photograph of port painting. Dar Apr 9 (364) $150

Check, sgd, 19 Nov 1917. Payable to Katherine S. Witz. wa Oct 19 (345) $400
— Anr, accomplished & sgd, 20 Dec 1920. Payable to Martha Bowers Taft. Dar Apr 9 (363) $500

Engraving, sgd & inscr, [n.d.]. 10.75 by 13.5 (image). Framed. Dar Oct 10 (335) $350

Photograph, sgd & inscr, 1 Mar 1912. 8 by 12 inches. Inscr to William T. Tilden. sup July 8 (68) $600
— Anr, 2 Dec 1915. 7.25 by 10.75. Inscr to Harry O. Knerr. Dar Oct 10 (338) $180
— Anr, 30 Apr 1921. 7.5 by 9 inches. Inscr to Charles S. Lecky. Dar Aug 6 (268) $375
— Anr, [n.d.]. 5.5 by 7.2 inches. Inscr to Mrs. John Addison Porter, on mat. Dar Feb 13 (330) $200

Signature, 19 Jan 1913. Size not stated. Including subscription. Framed. wa Oct 19 (346) $100

Tagore, Rabindranath, 1861-1941

Photograph, sgd, 30 Mar 1922. 3.75 by 5.5 inches. Framed. Dar Feb 13 (331) $225

Talleyrand-Perigord, Charles Maurice de, 1754-1838

ALs, 6 July 1833. 2 pp, 8vo. To Miss Fox. Arranging to visit her. With ANs by recipient on verso. pn Nov 14 (176) £80

Ls, [15 Dec 1800]. 1 p, folio. To a Swedish commissioner. Asking him to renew some passports. star Mar 27 (1736) DM240

Ds, [8 July 1798]. 2 pp, folio. Appointment for Citoyen Chepy as Consul. sup Oct 15 (1824) $160
— [22 Aug 1799]. 1 p, 4to. Certification of a baptismal record (present). star Mar 27 (1735) DM320

Talma, Francois Joseph, 1763-1826

ALs, 9 May 1817. 2 pp, 4to. To M. Champion. Informing him that he is unable to accept an engagement in Brussels. star Mar 27 (1232) DM280

Tandy, Jessica —& Cronyn, Hume

Ds, 4 Feb 1948. 2 pp, 4to. Contract with The Theatre Guild Radio Division; carbon copy. Dar Feb 13 (332) $100

Taney, Roger B., 1777-1864

Ds, 11 Oct 1818. 1 p, 4to. Deposition in the case of Joseph Smith v. Barton Philpott. Dar Oct 10 (339) $180

Photograph, sgd, [n.d.]. Carte size. Full length, with hat & cane. By Benidann Bros. Ltd. Illus in cat. R June 13 (96) $950

Tarkington, Booth, 1869-1946

Series of 3 A Ls s, Aug & Sept 1923. 10 pp, 8vo. To Martha Bryan Allen. Discussing her roles in various plays. With related material. wd June 12 (335) $400

Tasso, Torquato, 1544-95

ALs, 3 Jan 1588. 3 pp, folio; stitched. To Prince Ranuccio of Parma. Elaborate plea for patronage. Illus in cat. Phillips Ms 8086 & Mannheim collection. S Dec 5 (463) £4,000 [Roma]

Taylor, Elizabeth

Photograph, sgd & inscr, [17 Mar 1981]. 8 by 10 inches. Inscr to Dana. Dar Dec 26 (313) $250

Taylor, Tom, 1817-80

ALs, 9 May [n.y.]. 3 pp, 8vo. To Mrs. Holland. Suggesting she contact the pbr Lacey about plays for performance. sup Oct 15 (1541) $150

Taylor, Zachary, 1784-1850

ALs, 7 Jan 1826. 1 p, 4to. To Col. R. Jones. Transmitting his monthly return of enlistments, etc. Illus in cat. wd June 12 (336) $800

Ds, 29 June 1833. 1 p, 8vo. Receipt for goods received at Fort Crawford. Framed with engraved port. sup Oct 15 (1514) $700

Franking signature, [10 Sept n.y.]. On def cover. rf Sept 21 (31) $675

— Anr, [n.d.]. On fragment of envelope, 2.75 by 0.5 inches. Dar Dec 26 (314) $475

Tchaikovsky, Peter Ilyich, 1840-93

[An autograph musical quotation, 3 bars from The Queen of Spades, [n.d.], mtd with a photograph, sgd, overall size 180mm by 255mm, sold at S on 29 May 1992, lot 670, for £5,200 to Mandl.]

ALs, 22 July 1892. 4 pp, 8vo. To Katerina Ivanovna Laroche. Reporting about his travels with his nephew & about his current work. S May 29 (667) £3,800 [Haas]

— 1 Aug [1893]. 8 pp, 8vo. To Katerina Ivanovna Laroche. Describing his Pathetique Symphony as his masterpiece, & urgently requesting a loan. S May 29 (671) £5,000 [Scriptorium]

— [n.d.]. 2 pp, 8vo. To Eduard Frantsevich. Letter of introduction for O. B. Baits. In Russian. P Dec 12 (90) $2,750

Photograph, sgd & inscr, 1891. 160mm by 105mm. Inscr to Alexander Gordon with a musical quotation. Illus in cat. S Dec 6 (217) £4,000 [Tancil]

Tchelitchev, Pavel, 1898-1957

Series of 37 A Ls s, 1923 to 1953 & [n.d.]. 76 pp, 4to. To Boris Kochno (1 to Massine). About his designs for the ballet Ode & his later exhibitions. SM Oct 12 (408) FF7,000

Teilhard de Chardin, Pierre, 1881-1955

Ls, 11 Dec 1947. 2 pp, 4to. Recipient unnamed. Expressing his conviction "que nous allons inevitablement a une unification de la Terre..." star Mar 26 (831) DM1,700

Telemann, Georg Philipp, 1681-1767

ALs, 11 Oct 1755. 2 pp, 4to. To Elias Kaspar Reichard. Expressing condolences on the death of his wife, & inquiring about a passion play. Illus in cat. star Mar 27 (1178) DM27,000

Temple, Shirley

[2 signatures, [1940s], on cover & 1st page of the sheet music of Animal Crackers In My Soup, 9 by 12 inches, sold at Dar on 11 June 1992, lot 350, for $400.]

Ds, 12 Mar 1938. 1 p, 12mo. Subscription to the Motion Picture Relief Fund of America. Dar Apr 9 (366) $300

Photograph, sgd, [1943]. 7 by 9 inches. Mtd. Dar Dec 26 (315) $170

Tennant, Stephen

Collection of 24 A Ls s & cards, sgd, 1940 to 1952. 40 pp, 4to & 8vo. To Boris Kochno. Discussing his life, friends, travels, etc. Including some pen-&-ink & watercolor illusts. SM Oct 12 (409) FF12,500

Tenniel, Sir John, 1820-1914

[20 color-ptd wood engravings, proofs for the 1st Ed of The Nursery Alice, L, 1889, with Tenniel's autograph corrections & annotations, bound in a copy of the 1st Ed of the book in blue mor gilt by Riviere & Son, sold at P on 12 Dec 1991, lot 172, for $40,000.]

Tennyson, Alfred, Lord, 1809-92

ALs, 16 Apr [1847]. 4 pp, 8vo. To [Drummond] Rawnsley. Acknowledging the importance of old friends. With related material. Ingilby collection. pn Nov 14 (108) £360 [Wilson]

— [c.1852]. 1 p, 8vo. To Sir Alexander & Lady Duff-Gordon. Inviting them to a christening. bba Sept 19 (344) £180 [Jarndyce]

— [1867]. 1 p, 8vo. To [Robinson Ellis]. Thanking for his Ed of Catullus. pn Mar 19 (143) £110 [Wilson]

— 1 Nov 1869. 2 pp, 8vo. To Philpott. About

the death of John Coningham. pn Nov 14 (232) £360 [Quaritch]

Photograph, [n.d.]. 9.5 by 7.5 inches. By Julia Margaret Cameron. Faded. Ck Nov 15 (22) £150

Terry, Ellen, 1847-1928

— LUCAS, E. V. - Autograph Mss (2), A Memory of Ellen Terry, & about Terry's country home; [c.1929]. 42 pp, 4to. With extensive revisions. Both sgd. sg Sept 12 (237) $950

Texas

— MUSQUIZ, RAMON. - Ds, 28 Nov 1831. 2 pp, 4to. Order addressed to the Alcalde of Goliad, regarding theft of horses by the Comanche Indians. R Mar 7 (237) $60

— REILY, JAMES. - ALs, 29 Apr 1842. 4 pp, 4to. To Col. Thomas Ward. Weighing the possibility of a full-scale war with Mexico. CNY June 9 (278) $3,200

— REILY, JAMES. - ALs, 31 Dec 1843. 1 p, 4to. To Col. Thomas Ward. Expressing doubts that Texas will be annexed to the United States. CNY June 9 (279) $2,800

Textile Designs

— REICHENHEIM, J. - Ms, Cours de theorie. [France?, 1857-58]. 2 vols, contemp half mor. Describing types of weaving machinery & techniques, & including fabric samples, design samples, & illusts of equipment. S Nov 21 (102) £1,400 [Quaritch]

Thackeray, William Makepeace, 1811-63

Autograph Ms, fragment of Vanity Fair, [c.Feb 1848]. 1 p, 8vo, in red mor gilt. With orig drawing for the plate showing J. Sedley escaping from Brussels, 8vo. P Dec 12 (193) $4,000

A Ls s (2), 18 May 1852 & [n.d.]. 2 pp, 8vo. Recipient unnamed. About lectures to be given at Manchester. 1 in 3d person. sg Sept 12 (238) $350

ALs, 1 Apr [n.y.]. 1 p, 8vo. To an unnamed relative. Declining a dinner invitation. Dar Dec 26 (316) $180

Thalberg, Irving G., 1899-1936

Check, sgd, 8 Dec 1923. Drawn on the account of the Louis B. Mayer Studios; payable to John M. Stahl. Endorsed by Stahl. Dar Aug 6 (31) $150

Thatcher, Margaret

Typescript, comments expressing admiration for President Reagan, Mar 1990. 1 p, 4to. 1 autograph line; sgd. Dar Oct 10 (341) $700

Theological Manuscripts

Ms, fragment of a text of exegesis of Scriptural history, [France, late 9th cent]. Fragment of a bifolium, vellum, 240mm by 152mm, in fitted mor case. Part of 19 lines in a very fine small Carolingian minuscule. Recovered from a bdg. S Dec 17 (2) £1,400 [Quaritch]

— Ms, Tractatus de Christo, seu de Deo Incarnato, 1758. 105 leaves, 8vo, in orig bds. bba Sept 19 (397) £50 [Quaritch]

— Ms, unidentified theological tract, [c.1300]. Bifolium, vellum, 330mm by 215mm. Final part of the tract, explicit & part of the index. Recovered from a 16th-cent bdg. HH May 12 (39a) DM3,800

— SHIMEALL, REV. R. C. - Ms, The Book of the Revelation St. John the Divine Made Plain.... [NY, 1873]. Over 600 pp, 405mm by 265mm, in def half sheep bdg. Profusely illus with related engravings excised from other works & with visionary pen-&-ink drawings. sg Nov 7 (9) $325

Thiers, Louis Adolphe, 1797-1877

Series of 3 A Ls s, 11 Aug 1871 to 27 May 1873. 9 pp, 8vo. To the Comte de Harcourt. Touching diplomatic relations with the Holy See, Great Britain & Russia. star Mar 27 (1399) DM310

Thiess, Frank, 1890-1977

Collection of ALs, 2 Ls s & autograph postcard, sgd, 12 Apr 1947 to 28 Mar 1950. 8 pp, 8vo & 4to. To Wilhelm Buller. About lectures, his work, etc. Postcard on verso of photograph, sgd. HN Nov 28 (1845) DM200

Thoma, Hans, 1839-1924

Collection of 2 A Ls s & AN, 30 Oct & 12 Nov 1899 & [n.d.]. 4 pp, mostly 8vo. To the pbr Diesterweg. Concerning publications. star Mar 27 (955) DM240

A Ls s (2), 10 & [27] May 1917. 3 pp, 4to & 8vo. To Max Friedlaender. Concerning a call for a German hymn. star Mar 27 (957) DM280

ALs, 22 Jan 1907. 2 pp, 8vo. To an unnamed art collector. About the sale of 2 pictures. star Mar 27 (956) DM250

— 8 June 1922. 1 p, 8vo. To Max Liebermann. Giving permission to exhibit one of his pictures at The Hague. star Mar 27 (958) DM240

Thoma, Ludwig, 1867-1921

ALs, 23 July 1914. 1 p, 4to. To his pbr. Regarding the publication of a new column. HH May 13 (2056) DM340

— 15 Mar 1918. 2 pp, 4to. To an unnamed Ed. Sending his poem Marinefest for print (included, 18 lines). star Mar 26 (486) DM650

Thomas Aquinas, Saint, 1225?-74

Ms, Le Livre de l'Information des Roys et Princes, opening of Book IV. [Bruges, c.1480]. Single leaf, vellum, 388mm by 278mm. In a lettre batarde. With very large miniature above large illuminated initial & within full border of acanthus leaves & flowers. Illus in cat. S Dec 17 (30) £6,000 [Simmen]

Thomas, Dylan, 1914-53

Series of 12 A Ls s, [c.1929-1932]. 36 pp, 4to. To Percy Eynon Smart. Important letters to a friend about his literary projects, a school magazine, his work as a reporter, etc. S July 21 (182) £9,500 [Quaritch]

ALs, [n.d.], "Monday". 2 pp, 12mo. To his wife Caitlin. Love letter, & informing her about a BBC program. CNY June 9 (187) $2,000

Signature, [n.d.]. 2.25 by 1 inches. Illus in cat. Dar Apr 9 (367) $250

Thomas, Lorenzo, 1804-75

Ds, 21 May 1848. 1 p, 4to. Order no 101 regarding troop movements to accompany US Commissioners A. H. Sevier & N. Clifford. Dar Apr 9 (368) $225

Thomson, Charles, 1729-1824

Ds, 5 Oct 1780. 2 pp, folio. As Secretary of the Continental Congress, resolution agreeing with the declaration of the Empress of Russia regarding rights of neutral vessels. CNY June 9 (283) $3,200

Thomson, Richard, 1794-1865

Autograph Ms, "Geoffrey Barbican", Chronicles of London Bridge, 1824. 387 leaves & blanks, 4to, in orig half mor. Including 10 ink & wash drawings, 7 proof engravings, & further related material. bba June 25 (144A) £700 [Johnson]

Thomson, Virgil, 1896-1989

Typescript, essay, Mozart, One Musician's Best Friend, sgd; [early 1940s]. 11 pp, 4to. Account of the effects of the war on cultural circles in Paris. P June 17 (388) $200

Autograph quotation, 8 bars from The Mother of Us All, [n.d.]. 1 p, 8 by 5 inches. Sgd & inscr to Martin Riskin. Dar Feb 13 (333) $300

Thoreau, Henry David, 1817-62

ALs, 30 June 1858. 4 pp, 8vo. To Daniel Ricketson. Regarding a trip to the White Mountains, the nature of his friendships, & his "preaching ... in the Walden strain". With related material. Illus in cat. CNY June 9 (188) $9,000

— [n.d.]. 1 p, 8 by 2.5 inches. Recipient unnamed. Fragment, stating that he is at present living in Mrs. Emerson's house. sup May 9 (68) $2,000

Thorpe, James Francis, 1888-1953

Signature, [14 Nov 1951]. 5 by 2.5 inches, on verso of trimmed postcard. Dar Dec 26 (186) $400

Thorpe, Rose Hartwick, 1850-1939

Autograph transcript, poem, Curfew Must Not Ring Tonight, sgd; Oct 1930. 6 pp, 8vo. sup Oct 15 (1827) $150

Three Stooges

Group photograph, [n.d.]. 3 by 5 inches. Sgd by all 3 & inscr to Eugene on verso. Dar Aug 6 (32) $130

Photograph, sgd, [1959]. 8 by 10 inches. Motion picture still, sgd by all 3. Dar Oct 10 (211) $275

Tieck, Ludwig, 1773-1853

Autograph Ms, poem, Einsamkeit, [c.1800]. 2 pp, folio. 9 eight-line stanzas. star Mar 26 (487) DM3,200

Tilden, William Tatem ("Big Bill"), 1893-1953

Autograph Ms, The Heart of a Champion, [n.d.]. 35 pp, size not stated. In pencil. Revised last chapter of his autobiography. With a copy of the book. sup July 8 (59) $440

Autograph Ms, article, Tournament Manager of Movieland, [n.d.]. 9 pp, size not stated. Sgd at head in 3d person. Regarding a tournament at Charlie Chaplin's home. sup July 8 (83) $380

— Autograph Ms, Pancho Gonzales - Tennis Bonanza, [1948]. 7 pp, 4to. Sgd at head. With typed transcript & related letter. sup July 8 (73) $1,000

Typescript, short story, Advantage Receiver, [early 1930s]. 54 pp, size not stated. Sgd at head. Unpbd. sup July 8 (80) $900

— Typescript, short story, Freeze Out, [n.d.]. 49 pp, size not stated. Sgd at head. sup July 8 (82) $725

Series of 50 A Ls s, 1949. Length not stated. To Art Anderson & his mother Marrion. Written from Saugus Correctional Farm. sup July 8 (75) $1,300

ALs, [n.d.], "Sunday". Length not stated. To Katharine Hepburn. Concerning tennis lessons. sup July 8 (63) $300

Ds, 2 Mar 1915. Length not stated. Last will & testament; sgd on each page. sup July 8 (61) $525

Autograph sentiment, sgd, 1943. On front of 16 pp tennis program. Inscr to Art. Illus in cat. sup July 8 (65) $425

Group photograph, 1927. 8 by 12 inches. With Francis T. Hunter; sgd by both & inscr by

Tilden. Illus in cat. sup July 8 (67) $675

Photograph, sgd & inscr, 1931. 8 by 10 inches. Inscr to "Auntie". Illus in cat. sup July 8 (71) $480

— Anr, [n.d.]. 8 by 10 inches. Inscr to Art. Illus in cat. sup July 8 (70) $400

Tilghman, William Matthew, 1854-1924

Ds, 11 Feb 1897. 2 pp, 4to. Summons. Also sgd by others. sup Oct 15 (1828) $1,450

— 11 Feb 1897. 2 pp, 8vo. Summons. Also sgd by others. Illus in cat. sup May 9 (453) $1,100

Tilly, Johann Tserclaes, Graf von, 1559-1632

Ls, 22 Sept 1631. 1 p, folio. To the magistrate of an unnamed town. Sending Lorenz Muench von Stainach with a request. star Mar 27 (1739) DM1,700

Tinker, Joseph Bert, 1880-1948

ALs, 29 Oct 1945. 1 p, 8vo. To Mr. Smith. Sending his autograph & suggesting that he write to other players. Dar Dec 26 (109) $1,500

Signature, [n.d.]. 3 by 5 inches (card). Illus in cat. Shaw collection. sup July 10 (878) $400

Titanic Disaster

[The signatures of 6 survivors of the disaster on a postcard of R.M.S. Titanic, 5.5 by 3.5 inches, sold at Dar on 26 Dec 1991, lot 317, for $160.]

— SHUTES, ELIZABETH W. - Autograph postcard, sgd, 16 Apr [1912]. To Mrs. Irving G. Mills. Aboard the ship Carpathia, reporting about the sinking of the Titanic. With related material. Illus in cat. Ck Nov 15 (54) £800

— W. J. R. - Autograph postcard, sgd, 11 Apr 1912. To James Day. Sending greetings; posted at Queenstown. On colored card depicting the ship. S July 21 (278) £500 [Wilson]

Tolkien, John Ronald Reuel, 1892-1973

Collection of 3 A Ls s, Ls & AN, 1955 to 1959. 10 pp, various sizes. To Patricia. Sending news. sup May 9 (69) $2,400

Corrected page proofs, The Lord of the Rings, 3 vols, 1953 to 1955. 8vo. With numerous corrections by the ptr, & many queries marked & answered in Tolkien's hand. Complete; with some related material. S July 21 (183) £11,000 [Joseph]

Tolstoy, Leo, 1828-1910

ALs, [n.d.]. 1 p, 4to. Recipient unnamed. Suggesting that some farmers have been sentenced unfairly & should see a lawyer. star Mar 26 (488) DM1,400

Ls, 10/23 July 1901. 5 pp, 4to. To Prince Mirza Reza Khan Arfa. Outlining his philosophy of life. In French. Framed with a port. Illus in cat. P June 17 (83) $12,000

Photograph, sgd, 18 Apr 1907. 5 by 3 inches. Framed. P June 17 (84) $1,200

Tompkins, Daniel D., 1774-1825

Ls, 11 Nov 1812. 1 p, 4to. Recipients unnamed. Response to a war address. Dar Apr 9 (369) $200

Tomson Family

[A group of 28 documents & letters pertaining to the Tomson family of Halifax, Massachusetts, 1700 - 1850, including documents sgd by John Hancock, Samuel Adams & John C. Calhoun, sold at sg on 12 Sept 1991, lot 100, for $6,500.]

Torrington, Sir Alfred —& Briton, George Andrew

Ms, Remarks on the History of England, address'd to the rising Generation of the British Youth..., 1780. 180 pp, 4to. Contemp calf. bba Jan 30 (295) £200 [Johnson]

Torstenson, Lennart, Count, 1603-51

Ds, 25 Nov 1642. 1 p, folio. Safeguard for Simon Schmidt's house at Halle. star Mar 27 (1742) DM800

Toscanini, Arturo, 1867-1957

Autograph quotation, 3 bars of music, sgd, 27 Nov 1933. 57mm by 98mm. Framed with a port. P June 17 (85) $400

Autograph sentiment, referring to music that appeals to "small-minded and vulgar people"; [n.d.]. 1 p, 8vo. Sgd. In Italian. Framed with a port. sg Feb 27 (207) $600

Photograph, sgd, 29 Oct 1933. Postcard. HN Nov 28 (1847) DM280

Photograph, sgd & inscr, [n.d.]. 6 by 8 inches. Inscr to Morris Stouzek. Dar Apr 9 (370) $475

Toscanini, Arturo, 1867-1957 —& Lehmann, Lotte, 1888-1976

Group photograph, [n.d.]. 8 by 10 inches. Seated, in formal attire. Sgd by both. Illus in cat. sup Oct 15 (1829) $900

Tracy, Spencer, 1900-67

Photograph, sgd, [n.d.]. 5 by 7 inches. Dar Apr 9 (371) $350

Travel

Ms, journal of a tour through Belgium, Germany, Austria & Italy, 5 July to 20 Dec 1844. 221 pp, 8vo, in panelled calf. bba Jan 30 (297) £150 [Bristow]

— PARKINSON, JOHN. - Autograph Ms, journal of his tour of Norway, Sweden, Finland & Russia, 24 Aug 1792 to 15 Mar 1793. About 500 pp, size not stated, in 2 vols of 19th-cent half red calf & marbled bds. S

Dec 12 (304) £800 [Quaritch]

— READE, H. F. - Ms, Journal of a Tour from Brighton to Ilfracombe, 1834. 66 pp, 4to, in orig wraps. Illus with 16 sketches in watercolor, pastel, or pen-&-ink. bba May 28 (243) £300 [Howes]

Traynor, Pie, 1899-1972

Signature, [n.d.]. On postcard picturing Hall of Fame plaque. Dar Feb 13 (91) $130

Treitschke, Heinrich von, 1834-96

ALs, 28 Mar 1873. 3 pp, 8vo. To Heinrich Ulmann. Disapproving of Schlosser's moralizing tendencies & Ranke's purported objectivity in historical scholarship. star Mar 26 (838) DM550

— 3 Jan 1875. 2 pp, 8vo. To [A. Gaedeke]. Expressing reservations about Gregorivius's new book. star Mar 26 (839) DM260

Treves, Sir Frederick, 1853-1923

ALs, 2 Jan 1915. 2 pp, size not stated. To Lord Sudeley. About his son's death in the war. Dar Feb 13 (263) $160

Trollope, Anthony, 1815-82

ALs, [n.d.]. 1 p, 8vo. To [George] Smith. Inquiring about the whereabouts of an Ed. Ingilby collection. pn Nov 14 (110) £600 [Sawyer]

Trommsdorff, Johann Bartholomaeus, 1770-1837

Autograph Ms, alphabetical list of autographs prepared for a collector, [16 Mar 1808]. 2 pp, 4to. star Mar 26 (841) DM280

Trotsky, Leon (Lev Davydovich Bronstein), 1879-1940

ALs, [Jan 1918]. 1 p, 4to. To Lenin. Suggesting that negotiations for peace at Brest-Litovsk be broken off for tactical reasons. sup May 9 (483) $27,000

Ls, 22 Nov 1933. 1 p, 8vo. To [Harold J.] Laski. Discussing 2 publication projects. star Mar 27 (1743) DM1,600

Truman, Bess Wallace

ALs, [n.d.]. 3 pp, 8vo. To Hildegarde. About family photographs. wd Dec 12 (341) $150

ALs, [3 Aug 1950]. 1 p, 8vo. To Charles Tucker. Informing him that her husband believes "the Ambassador would do everything in his power to get Bob out along with himself". Dar June 11 (351) $120

Truman, Harry S., 1884-1972

Typescript, statement on the 10th anniversary of the Philippine Commonwealth, 15 Nov 1945. 1 p, 4to. Sgd. Illus in cat. sup Oct 15 (1641) $1,100

ALs, 17 July 1946. 1 p, 8vo. To Edward D. McKim. Responding to comments about the OPA. sg Feb 27 (218) $425

— 25 Jan 1955. 1 p, 4to. To Dean Acheson. Inviting him to discuss his forthcoming memoirs. With related material. Illus in cat. sup Oct 15 (1648) $2,000

— 30 Nov 1956. 2 pp, 4to. To Dean Acheson. Discussing the situation in the Near East & in Hungary. Framed. P June 16 (292) $9,000

— 1 June 1957. 4 pp, 4to. To Dean Acheson. Insisting that Dean & Alice Acheson attend the opening of his Presidential Library, & chatting about his activities. Illus in cat. sup May 9 (254) $5,000

— 24 Jan 1959. 1 p, 4to. To Edward D. McKim. Regarding a forthcoming Battery reunion. sg Sept 12 (256) $1,600

— 19 Mar 1961. 2 pp, 8vo. To Edward D. McKim. About health & the family. sg Sept 12 (257) $1,800

Collection of 3 Ls s & letter, 1940 to 1944. 4 pp, 4to. To Edward D. McKim. On a variety of matters. Including 2 autograph postscripts. sg Feb 27 (213) $900

— Collection of Ls & photograph, sgd & inscr, 17 Nov & 22 Dec 1966. 1 p, 4to & 8 by 10 inches. To Robert A. Browne. Thanking for a Christmas message. sup Oct 15 (1659) $305

Series of 3 Ls s, 15 Mar 1946 to 7 Feb 1947. 3 pp, 8vo. To Edward D. McKim. About Presidential appointments. sg Sept 12 (249) $800

— Series of 3 Ls s, 10 to 29 Mar 1947. 3 pp, 4to. To Edward D. McKim. About a judicial appointment. sg Sept 12 (251) $750

— Series of 10 Ls s, 1947 to 1966. 10 pp, 4to. To Edward D. McKim. Expressing thanks. 1 initialled. sg Sept 12 (259) $1,100

— Series of 3 Ls s, 10 Feb to 13 May 1949. 3 pp, 8vo. To Edward D. McKim. About various personal & political matters. sg Feb 27 (222) $800

— Series of 4 Ls s, 7 to 30 Apr 1948. Length not stated. To Edward D. McKim. About various political matters. sg Sept 12 (252) $800

— Series of 3 Ls s, 12 to 23 July 1949. 3 pp, 4to. To Edward D. McKim. Acknowledging communications. sg Sept 12 (253) $550

— Series of 3 Ls s, 16 Mar 1950 to 6 Mar 1952. 3 pp, 4to. To Edward D. McKim. About McKim's becoming a Director of the Panama Railroad. sg Sept 12 (250) $600

— Series of 5 Ls s, May 1951 to 1967. 5 pp, 8vo. To Edward D. McKim. Acknowledging birthday wishes. sg Sept 12 (260) $1,100

— Series of 6 Ls s, 1953 & 1954. 6 pp, 8vo. To Edward D. McKim. About appointments, photographs, etc. sg Feb 27 (224) $650

— Series of 6 Ls s, 1955 & 1956. 6 pp, 8vo. To Edward D. McKim. About personal matters. sg Feb 27 (225) $650
— Series of 6 Ls s, 1957 to 1971. 6 pp, 8vo. To Edward D. McKim. Acknowledging Christmas greetings. sg Sept 12 (261) $650
— Series of 4 Ls s, 1965 to 1969. 4 pp, 4to. To Edward D. McKim. Commenting on friends' and relatives' ailments. sg Feb 27 (229) $600

Ls s (2), 11 Dec 1944 & 11 Jan 1945. 2 pp, 4to. To Edward D. McKim. Sending personal news. sg Feb 27 (215) $400
— Ls s (2), 3 Feb & 8 Mar 1945. 2 pp, 8vo. To Edward D. McKim. Acknowledging receipt of cartoons, & enclosing a letter. sg Sept 12 (247) $275
— Ls s (2), 18 Sept & 20 Nov 1945. 2 pp, 8vo. To Edward D. McKim. About personal matters & politics in Nebraska. sg Feb 27 (216) $475
— Ls s (2), 23 Mar & 29 June 1946. 2 pp, 8vo. To Edward D. McKim. About personal matters & political gossip. sg Feb 27 (217) $550
— Ls s (2), 30 Apr & 16 June 1947. 2 pp, 8vo. To Edward D. McKim. Sending personal & political news. sg Feb 27 (219) $700
— Ls s (2), 7 July & 10 Dec 1948. 2 pp, 8vo. To Edward D. McKim. About a mutual friend & health matters. sg Feb 27 (221) $300
— Ls s (2), 11 & 18 Dec 1953. 2 pp, 8vo. To Edward D. McKim. Concerning letters of introduction. sg Sept 12 (255) $350

Ls, 3 Feb 1933. 1 p, 4to. To Glen B. Woods. Hoping to "get something done in your case." wa Oct 19 (347) $130
— 13 Feb 1935. 2 pp, 4to. To Edward D. McKim. About a meeting with Franklin D. Roosevelt, the Appropriations Committee, & personal matters. With autograph postscript. sg Sept 12 (242) $2,200
— 27 Sept 1940. 1 p, 4to. To Edward D. McKim. As Senator, reporting on the start of his reelection campaign. sg Feb 27 (210) $475
— 22 Nov 1941. 1 p, 4to. To Edward D. McKim. Expressing condolences, & giving his views about John L. Lewis. sg Sept 12 (243) $1,400
— 16 Dec 1941. 1 p, 4to. To Edward D. McKim. Commenting on Pearl Harbor & security on the West Coast. sg Feb 27 (211) $1,000
— 5 Feb 1942. 1 p, 4to. To Edward D. McKim. Giving advice on how to help the war effort. Illus in cat. sg Feb 27 (212) $900
— 21 Feb 1942. 2 pp, 4to. To Edward D. McKim. Explaining his New Deal philosophy. With autograph postscript. sg Sept 12 (244) $1,900
— 21 Sept 1942. 1 p, 4to. To Donald C. Cubbison. Thanking for a recent discussion about the artillery. Dar Oct 10 (346) $325
— 13 Mar 1944. 1 p, 4to. To James A. Wade. Thanking for a resolution from the American Legion Post at Ironton & promising support. Dar Aug 6 (273) $250
— 22 May 1944. 1 p, 4to. To Edward D. McKim. About his mother's accident & saying he is not a candidate for the Vice Presidency. With autograph postscript. sg Sept 12 (245) $3,000
— 21 Dec 1944. 1 p, 4to. To Edward D. McKim. Sending news about Joe Fraser. sg Feb 27 (214) $425
— 10 Feb 1945. 1 p, 4to. To the President of a fraternity at George Washington University. Regretting he will be in Missouri on the date suggested. Dar Oct 10 (347) $300
— 25 May 1945. 1p, 4to. To Janie Chiles. Thanking for a copy of the annual of his old high school. Spiro collection. CNY May 14 (154) $600
— 20 Sept 1945. 1 p, 6.5 by 6.5 inches. To Brigadier Gen. Frank T. Hines. Accepting his resignation as Reemployment Administrator because of his appointment as Ambassador. Framed with a photograph. Dar Apr 9 (373) $275
— 23 Sept 1946. 1 p, 8vo. To Edward D. McKim. Stating he has "the Commerce thing well out of the way". With autograph postscript. sg Sept 12 (248) $425
— 20 Mar 1948. 1 p, 4to. To Dave Morgan. Thanking for a letter. Including autograph postscript saying that he is "a mile deep in decisions". Illus in cat. sup May 9 (257) $1,200
— 24 June 1948. 1 p, 8vo. To Edward D. McKim. Commenting on several pending matters. sg Feb 27 (220) $425
— 12 May 1949. 1 p, 8vo. To Albert West. Thanking for a hand-tooled vol of Mozart's Sonatas. Dar Dec 26 (318) $275
— 18 May 1949. 1 p, 4to. To Elmer F. Strain. Returning a letter from the Grand Master of a Masonic Lodge in Mexico. sup May 9 (256) $1,350
— 12 July 1949. 1 p, 4to. To Edward D. McKim. Expressing pleasure that McKim's son-in-law "got the job", & promising to receive Gov. Val Peterson. Dar June 11 (353) $400
— 14 July 1949. 1 p, 8vo. To Edward D. McKim. Thanking for a note concerning Leo Coleman. Dar Apr 9 (375) $325
— 10 July 1950. 1 p, 8vo. To Harold Russell. Thanking for a telegram conveying the thoughts of the Veterans of World War II on the Korean question. Dar Aug 6 (271) $500

— 16 Apr 1951. 1 p, 8vo. To Nathan Straus. Justifying his dismissal of Gen. MacArthur. Framed with a photograph. P June 16 (291) $3,250

— 27 Nov 1951. 1 p, 8vo. To Edward D. McKim. Commenting on Churchill. Illus in cat. sg Feb 27 (223) $650

— 8 Apr 1952. 1 p, 8vo. To Fred Bowman. Thanking for a baseball glove & ball. Dar Apr 9 (372) $325

— 12 Sept 1952. 1 p, 4to. To Edward D. McKim. Regretting he will not be able to make a trip to Panama. sg Sept 12 (254) $750

— 10 Nov 1952. 1 p, 4to. To Donald O'Toole. Insisting that the Democratic Party "is not dead by any means." Illus in cat. sup Oct 15 (1644) $1,250

— 16 Jan 1953. 1 p, 4to. To Lynn U. Stambaugh. Thanking for his valuable services. Framed. wa Oct 19 (348) $170

— 19 Jan 1953. 1 p, 4to. To Phil Regan. Thanking for a telegram. Illus in cat. sup Oct 15 (1645) $850

— 7 Feb 1953. 1 p, 4to. To Dean Acheson. Thanking for a luncheon. sup Oct 15 (1646) $300

— 24 Apr 1953. 1 p, 4to. To Dean Acheson. Commenting on the new administration. Dar Oct 10 (343) $1,800

— 9 Apr 1954. 1 p, 4to. To Dean Acheson. Thanking for a memorandum on atomic arrangements with England. Including autograph postscript. Illus in cat. sup Oct 15 (1647) $1,050

— 7 June 1954. 1 p, 4to. To Joe Gleason. Thanking for a record. With related Ls by his daughter Margaret, 1984. Dar Feb 13 (336) $110

— 5 Dec 1955. Size not stated. To George Killion. Expressing appreciation for his reception in San Francisco. R June 13 (194) $180

— 30 Nov 1956. 1 p, 4to. To Dean Acheson. Expressing apprehension "about the foreign situation" & Eisenhower's re-election. Illus in cat. sup Oct 15 (1651) $960

— 16 Jan 1958. 1 p, 4to. To Mary & Eddie McKim. Thanking for Christmas greetings. With long autograph postscript. Dar June 11 (355) $300

— 27 Jan 1958. 1 p, 4to. To Edward D. McKim. Explaining why he could not call him during a meeting with Paul-Henri Spaak. sg Feb 27 (226) $325

— 6 May 1958. 1 p, 4to. To John A. Blomgren. Reflecting about his Presidency. Illus in cat. sup Oct 15 (1653) $1,550

— 11 June 1959. 1 p, 4to. To Edward D. McKim. Talking about medical problems. sg Feb 27 (227) $325

— 31 Aug 1960. 1 p, 4to. To James F. Yoham. Thanking for "automatic bookmarks". Dar Oct 10 (348) $110

— 9 Aug 1961. 1 p, 4to. To Earl Shackelford. Informing him about a meeting with the American Legion in Wichita. Including autograph postscript. R Mar 7 (150) $200

— 3 Oct 1961. 1 p, 4to. To M. A. Mott. Responding to an inquiry about the dates of his Presidential term. Illus in cat. sup Oct 15 (1657) $575

— 15 June 1962. 1 p, 4to. To Edward D. McKim. Thanking for a note. With autograph postscript. sg Sept 12 (258) $275

— 15 Oct 1963. 1 p, 4to. To Edward D. McKim. Giving his views on aging. Illus in cat. sg Feb 27 (228) $550

— 30 Aug 1967. 1 p, 4to. To Harold Russell. Expressing concern for the handicapped. Dar Aug 6 (272) $250

— 6 Jan 1969. 1 p, 4to. To John W. McCormack. Thanking for Christmas greetings & congratulating on his reelection as Speaker. Dar Feb 13 (335) $170

— 22 Jan 1969. 1 p, 4to. To Bill & Mrs. Simmons. Returning Christmas wishes. Framed with a photograph. Dar Dec 26 (319) $110

ANs, [19 Feb 1942]. 1 p, 4to, removed from a book. Stating that [Zachary] Chandler was Chairman of the Committee on the Conduct of the War during the Civil War. Also inscr by Wallace M. White. Illus in cat. Dar Apr 9 (376) $500

— 6 Dec 1963. 1 p, 12mo. To Grace Shackelford. Wishing her a speedy recovery. Illus in cat. R Mar 7 (149) $750

Ns, 11 Sept 1947. 1 p, 4to. To division officers of the US Navy. Aboard USS Mississippi, approving "of the conduct of the officers and men ... during the recent visit to Rio de Janeiro". With 12 related photographs. R Mar 7 (151) $350

— [1968]. Size not stated (card). Recipient unnamed. Ptd card thanking for congratulations on his birthday. wa Oct 19 (349) $90

Autograph sentiment, sgd, [n.d.]. Inscr to Capt. J. H. Kesers on a photograph of USS Williamsburg. Framed; overall size 27 by 20 inches. sup Oct 15 (1662) $180

Autograph telegram, sgd, 21 July 1944. 8vo. To Franklin D. Roosevelt. Saying he is "happy to be [his] running mate." Sgd again & inscr to Ed McKim. Mtd below ptd telegram from Roosevelt to Truman, 21 July 1944, congratulating on his nomination; sgd by Truman & inscr to McKim. sg Sept 12 (246) $14,000

Group photograph, sgd & inscr, [n.d.]. 9.5 by 8 inches. With Ed McKim & 2 others.

Framed. Dar June 11 (352) $350

Photograph, sgd, [n.d.]. 8 by 10 inches. By Harris & Ewing. R Mar 7 (152) $320

— Anr, [n.d.]. 19 by 15 inches (image). Mtd. sg Feb 27 (209) $150

Photograph, sgd & inscr, showing Truman holding 3 Nov 1948 issue of Chicago Daily Tribune with headline "Dewey Defeats Truman". 15 by 18 inches. Inscr "Too bad!" LH Dec 11 (19) $1,400

— Anr, showing Truman holding 3 Nov 1948 issue of Chicago Daily Tribune with headline "Dewey Defeats Truman". 14 by 12.5 inches. Inscr to Courteney Barber, 12 Aug [19]56. LH Dec 11 (21) $1,700

— Anr, [n.d.]. 14 by 11 inches. Inscr to A. F. Ruppenthal. Dar Oct 10 (349) $350

— Anr, [n.d.]. 6.5. by 9 inches. Inscr to E. D. McKim. Framed. Dar June 11 (354) $300

— Anr, [n.d.]. Framed; overall size 11 by 14 inches. Inscr to Al Cohn. sup Oct 15 (1663) $400

Signature, 18 Sept 1943. On Senate Chamber admission card. Dar Oct 10 (345) $140

— Anr, [20 Jan 1949]. On philatelic cover. Illus in cat. Dar Aug 6 (270) $250

Truman, Harry S., 1884-1972 —& Others

Group photograph, [c.1930]. 8 by 10 inches. With John Snyder & Harry Vaughan, in uniforms. Sgd by all 3. sg Sept 12 (241) $300

Trumbull, John, 1756-1843

ALs, 15 Jan 1807. 1 p, folio. To John Ormrod. Requesting him to collect subscriptions for engravings of Revolutionary battle scenes. bbc Dec 9 (175) $850

Trumbull, Jonathan, 1710-85

ADs, 24 Nov 1767. 1 p, folio. Deed conveying 88 acres in Connecticut. sg Feb 27 (232) $200

Trumbull, Jonathan, 1740-1809

ALs, 1 Nov 1782. 1 p, folio. To Col. Richard Varick. Conveying Washington's request to authenticate a copy. R Nov 9 (125) $400

— 30 Sept 1797. 2 pp, 8vo. To Andrew Kingsbury. Discussing payment of a debt owed the State of Connecticut by Mr. Tisdale. Dar Aug 6 (275) $150

— 26 Mar 1804. 1 p, 4to. To Andrew Kingsbury. Requesting him to make arrangements for preachers on Election Day. Dar Aug 6 (276) $110

Truth, Sojourner, 1797?-1883

Photograph, [c.1864]. Carte size. Seated beside a table. bbc Dec 9 (18) $490

Tucholsky, Kurt, 1890-1935

Ls, 12 Oct 1926. 1 p, 4to. To the Ed of the journal Simplizissimus. Responding to a request for contributions. HH Nov 6 (2106) DM1,000

Turgenev, Ivan, 1818-83

ALs, 21 Mar 1874. 3 pp, 8vo. Recipient unnamed. Praising a trans & suggesting that recipient translate his latest novella into German. In German. star Mar 26 (490) DM2,200

— 4 May 1875. 2 pp, 8vo. To [Jules Claretie]. Regretting that he was not informed about his visit earlier. star Mar 26 (491) DM550

Turkish Manuscripts

Ms, Berat of Sultan Selim III, confirming Shaykh Isma'il in his posts. [Constantinople, A.H.1209/A.D.1795]. 93cm by 49cm. In diwani script, with illuminated tughra within an arch decorated with a flame motif. Framed. Illus in cat. S Apr 30 (315) £4,000

— Ms, Firman of Sultan Selim III, addressed to the deputy cadi of Tokat. [Constantinople, A.H.1215/A.D.1801]. 88cm by 51cm. In diwani script, with tughra in gold within a gold arched motiv culminating in a burst of trophies. Framed. Illus in cat. S Apr 30 (313) £1,300

— Ms, Firman of Sultan Selim III, addressed to the deputy cadi of Selanik. [Constantinople, A.H.1209/A.D.1795]. 76cm by 51cm. In diwani script, with tughra in gold within a gold arch decorated with a flame motif. Framed. Illus in cat. S Apr 30 (314) £800

— NIZAMI. - Layla va Majnun. [Azerbaijan, c.1900]. 92 leaves, 193mm by 115mm, in def lea. In nasta'liq script in black with Persian headings in red. With 45 large miniatures in a naive late Qajar style. sg Nov 7 (148) $350

Turner, Dawson, 1775-1858

Ms, anthology, Miscellanea curiosa, being a collection of Original unpublished Manuscripts in Verse & Prose; [c.1800-1833]. About 235 pp, folio, in half roan marbled bds. Containing c. 35 texts on various subjects. S July 21 (326) £1,000 [Browning]

Turner, Lana

Ds, 24 Apr 1950. 2 pp, 4to. Permission to Universal Pictures to use her name in the lyrics of a song. Dar Dec 26 (321) $110

Twain, Mark, 1835-1910. See: Clemens, Samuel Langhorne & Raymond

Tyler, John, 1790-1862

ALs, 8 May 1842. 3 pp, 4to. To his wife. Chatting about social life in Washington, politics, family matters, etc. Illus in cat. sup May 9 (186) $7,500

— 20 July 1854. 2 pp, size not stated. To Capt. J. Lester. Mentioning the acquisition of Texas & California. Including franking signature on integral leaf. rf Sept 21 (23) $2,100

— 8 Mar 1859. 3 pp, 4to. To his son Robert. Discussing current political problems & predicting the failure of the Democrats. CNY Dec 5 (125) $8,000

— 27 Aug 1860. 3 pp, 4to. To his son Robert. Discussing Lincoln's chances for election. CNY Dec 5 (126) $19,000

Ls, 26 Apr 1841. 2 pp, 4to. Recipient unnamed. Giving information regarding the defense of Alexander McLeod. Countersgd by Sec of State Webster. With related material. Illus in cat. sup May 9 (185) $9,000

— 30 Mar 1843. 2 pp, folio. To King Ferdinand II. Sending condolences on the death of his brother. Countersgd by D. Webster. P June 16 (293) $1,800

Cut signature, [n.d.]. 3 by 1 inches. Dar Apr 9 (377) $130

Franking signature, [21 Jan n.y.]. rf Sept 21 (32) $180

— Anr, [6 July n.y.]. rf Sept 21 (34) $180

— Anr, [26 July n.y.]. rf Sept 21 (33) $190

Franking signature, [22 Oct 1856]. On autograph address leaf to Margaret G. Beekman. With concluding 7 lines of ALs on verso. Dar June 11 (356) $250

Tyrwhitt-Wilson, Gerald Hugh, 14th Baron Berners, 1883-1950

Series of 5 A Ls s, 1930 to 1939 & [n.d.]. 14 pp, various sizes. To Boris Kochno. About the ballet Luna Park & other matters. SM Oct 12 (351) FF4,500

U

Udet, Ernst, 1896-1941

Photograph, sgd & inscr, 30 June 1934. Postcard. HH May 13 (2058) DM360

Uhland, Ludwig, 1787-1862

ANs, 31 Dec 1841. 1 p, 8vo. Recipient unnamed. Ordering books. Mtd. star Mar 26 (492) DM240

United States

— ROBBERY BROADSIDE. - Ptd reward broadside, 9 Apr 1838. 11.75 by 7.75 inches. Referring to a robbery at Mount Vernon. With extensive Ms notation at foot decribing suspects. Addressed to the postmaster at Jackson, Ohio, on verso. Illus in cat. R Mar 7 (228) $280

— SENATE. - Broadside, (Bristol 10561); four-article proposal to amend Article II of the Constitution, [1798]. 1 p, folio. Including additional [unrecorded] article added in an unidentified contemp hand. CNY Dec 5 (20) $3,800

— SUPREME COURT. - Group photograph, 1937. 12 by 10.5 inches. Sgd by Chief Justice Charles E. Hughes & 8 Associate Justices. Illus in cat. sup May 9 (428) $3,700

— SUPREME COURT. - Group photograph, [n.d.]. 11 by 10.5 inches. Sgd by Chief Justice Burger & 8 Associate Justices. Illus in cat. sup May 9 (429) $2,000

Urban III, Pope, d.1187

Document, [9 Jan 1186/87]. 1 p, vellum, 4to. Confirmation of grants bestowed on the Abbess & convent of Sancta Maria at Messines by Count Philip of Flanders. Including seal. Illus in cat. star Mar 27 (1540) DM5,800

Urey, Harold Clayton, 1893-1981

Ls, 20 June 1975. 1 p, 4to. To an unnamed lady. Describing his reaction to winning the Nobel Prize. star Mar 26 (842) DM220

V

Valentin, Gabriel Gustav, 1810-83

ALs, 7 Apr 1836. 1 p, 4to. Recipient unnamed. Sending a list of items to be procured. star Mar 26 (843) DM300

Valentino, Rudolph, 1895-1926

ALs, [n.d.]. 1 p, 8vo. To Mr. Romano. Declining an invitation. Framed with a photograph. Illus in cat. sup Oct 15 (1835) $1,850

Ls, 7 Feb 1924. 1 p, 4to. To H. S. Jacobs. Giving instructions in a financial matter. Framed with a photograph. Illus in cat. sup Oct 15 (1836) $800

Valery, Paul, 1871-1945

Autograph postcard, sgd, 8 Apr 1933. To the Ed of the journal Kunst und Kuenstler. Giving permission for the publication of Max Liebermann's trans of his work Triomphe de Manet. HH May 13 (2059) DM240

Van Buren, Martin, 1782-1862

ALs, 8 Feb 1848. 1 p, 4to. To H. D. Gilpin. Expressing condolences. Dar Aug 6 (277) $500

— 18 Dec 1857. 1 p, 8vo. To Mr. Boltwood. Giving information about a former clerk. Illus in cat. R Mar 7 (155) $450

— 25 May [n.y.]. 1 p, 8vo. To Mr. Woods. In 3d person, regarding an invitation. R Mar 7 (154) $250

ADs, 21 Sept 1808. 5 pp, 4to. Plea as attorney for Junis Van Pelt seeking judgment for $200. Dar Aug 6 (278) $300

Ds, 27 Aug 1817. 1 p, 4to. As Attorney General of NY; contents not stated, Sgd twice. R Mar 7 (156) $380

— 24 Jan 1829. 1 p, folio. Appointment of W. P. Buffit as master in chancery. R Nov 9 (43) $180

— 18 June 1839. 1 p, 4to. Order to affix the US Seal to "a letter to the acting President of the Mexican Republic." sup Oct 15 (1508) $525

— 30 Mar 1840. 1 p, folio. Ship's passport for the brig Inga. sg Sept 12 (267) $300

Check, sgd, 22 May 1856. Drawn on The Bank of Kinderhook. Corner def. Dar Apr 9 (378) $900

Cut signature, 29 July 1837. 4to. Lower portion of document, countersgd by John Forsyth & Samuel Swartwout. wa Oct 19 (350) $180

Franking signature, [19 Jan n.y.]. On Department of State envelope. sup Oct 15 (1507) $210

Van Vogt, Alfred Elton

Typescript, story, Slan, [1950-51]. 297 pp, 4to. Ptr's copy of revised version, with numerous autograph emendations. Including autograph inscr, sgd, to Forrest Ackerman. With a copy of the ptd work. P Oct 11 (300) $3,250

Varick, Richard, 1753-1831

ALs, 10 Oct 1777. 11 pp, folio. To Richard Henry Lee, John Adams, & Henry Lawrence. Reporting on the loss of Fort Ticonderoga. Sgd R. V. CNY May 14 (8) $9,500

Varnhagen von Ense, Karl August, 1785-1858

Autograph Ms, fragment from a review of a biography of Frederick the Great, [n.d.]. 1 p, 4to. star Mar 26 (495) DM400

ALs, 16 Aug 1858. 1 p, 8vo. To Gustav Wiemann. Thanking for a biographical sketch of Friedrich Friesen. star Mar 26 (496) DM380

— Assing, Rosa Ludmilla. - 2 A Ls s, 14 Aug 1859 & 12 Mar 1860. 3 pp, 8vo. To Wilhelmine Stintzing. About her Ed of the correspondence of her uncle Varnhagen with Alexander von Humboldt. star Mar 26 (497) DM750

Varnhagen von Ense, Rahel, 1771-1833

ALs, 17 July 1823. 2 pp, 8vo. To Fouque. Informing him that she has forwarded his letter to her husband in Hamburg. star Mar 26 (494) DM2,800

Varnum, Charles Albert

Ds, May 1878. 2 pp, size not stated. Tobacco Return, sgd as 2d Lieutenant, 7th Regiment of Cavalry. Sgd by Samuel D. Sturgis on verso. Framed. Illus in cat. Armstrong collection. sup Oct 15 (1134) $210

Vedder, Elihu, 1836-1923

Photograph, sgd & inscr, [1877]. Cabinet size. By W. Kurtz. wa Oct 19 (23) $95

Veeck, William Louis, 1914-86

ALs, [6 Oct 1965]. 1 p, 12mo (card), To John. Responding to an inquiry about the most exiting moment in his career. Dar Dec 26 (110) $275

Ls, 1 Aug 1978. 1 p, 4to. To Gary Zimet. Informing him that the Chicago White Sox are overstaffed. Dar Dec 26 (111) $150

Venice

Ms, collection of decrees & edicts of the Doge Bertuccius Valerio & later Councils, 1498 to 1656; [18th cent]. 200 leaves, 4to, in contemp red velvet bdg. Mostly in Italian; 7 pp in Latin. Including decorated tp. Ck Mar 6 (249) £450

Verdi, Giuseppe, 1813-1901

Autograph music, "Scena ed Aria Rolando", from La battaglia di Legnano, [c.1848]. 2 pp, folio, in half mor bdg. 8 bars; sketch of full score. Sgd. Illus in cat. C June 24 (50) £7,000 [Franks]

— Autograph music, song, beginning "Sgombra, a gentil, dall' ansia menti i terrestri ardori...", 20 Apr 1858. 1 p, 365mm by 265mm. 22 bars, scored for voice & piano; sgd & inscr to [Melchiorre] Delfico. Illus in cat. star Mar 27 (1180) DM26,000

Series of 4 A Ls s, 28 Feb 1844 to 21 Mar 1847. 4 pp, 8vo. To Giuseppina Appiani. Referring to his operas Ernani, Attila, & Macbeth. C June 24 (25) £3,800 [Franks]

— Series of 13 A Ls s, 5 Mar 1861 to 13 Dec 1862. 24 pp, 8vo. Mostly to Enrico Tamberlik. Relating to the contract, casting, composition & production of La forza del destino in St. Petersburg. Including a copy predominantly in the hand of his wife. C June 24 (36) £18,000 [Franks]

— Series of 3 A Ls s, 27 Apr 1868 to 7 July 1875. 3 pp, 8vo. To Giovanni Maloberti. Instructing him to recruit coachmen, a cook, etc. C June 24 (37) £1,400 [Schneider]

A Ls s (2), 10 Nov 1848. 3 pp, 8vo. To Ferdinand Gravrand & [Leon] Escudier. Regarding the ballet music for the 1st performance of Nabucco in Brussels. C June 24 (32) £2,000 [Franks]

ALs, 20 Mar 1845. 1 p, 8vo. To Francesco Lucca. About the publication of his album of songs Sei Romanze. C June 24 (26) £550 [Haas]

— 1 Aug 1846. 1 p, 8vo. To Francesco Guidi. Politely declining to collaborate with him. C June 24 (28) £550 [L'Autographe]

— 25 Mar 1848. 1 p, 8vo. To Giovanni Ricordi. Worrying about the situation in Milan. C June 24 (30) £950 [Franks]

— 21 May 1848. 1 p, 8vo. To Eroteide Soldati. Expressing pleasure that she is recovered from her illness. C June 24 (31) £550 [Wilson]

— 21 May 1853. 2 pp, 8vo. To Marie Escudier. Insisting that he will not agree to a poor French production of Ernani. C June 24 (34) £900 [Macnutt]

— 10 Sept 1872. 2 pp, 8vo. To Antonio Ghislanzoni. Expressing pleasure at the success of Aida. C June 24 (39) £1,900 [Franks]

— 15 Apr 1874. 1 p, 8vo. To Parmigiani. Insisting that the Requiem should be performed properly. C June 24 (38) £1,200 [Franks]

— 26 May 1875. 2 pp, 8vo. To [Richard Peyton?]. Declining to write a cantata for the Birmingham Festival of 1876. C June 24 (41) £900 [Macnutt]

— 7 Feb 1880. 4 pp, 8vo. To Giulio Ricordi. About the piano reduction of his Ave Maria, expressing his admiration for earlier Italian composers, & regretting the modern craze for Bach's music. C June 24 (42) £3,800 [Franks]

— 20 Aug 1884. 2 pp, 8vo. To Commendatore Beccaro. Thanking for sending a garden chair. C June 24 (43) £450 [Wilson]

— 15 May 1887. 2 pp, 8vo. To Signor Castignani. Giving instructions for interviewing 2 cooks. C June 24 (44) £280 [Wilson]

— 12 Feb 1890. 2 pp, 8vo. To Gen. Corvetto. Interceding for a young officer requesting a transfer to be near his aged mother. C June 24 (45) £280 [L'Autographe]

— 5 Oct 1891. 2 pp, 8vo. To Achille de Lauzieres. Stating that he is writing some notes in Boito's libretto of Falstaff for his own pleasure only. C June 24 (46) £2,400 [Franks]

— 20 Nov 1894. 1 p, 8vo. Recipient unnamed. About Gounod. C June 24 (47) £1,000 [Macnutt]

— 20 Feb 1895. 8vo (card). To Edoardo Mascheroni. Reporting about his wife's illness. C June 24 (48) £360 [Schneider]

— 28 Aug 1897. 1 p, 8vo. To Giuseppe de Amicis. Reporting about his wife's illness. S May 29 (673) £2,600 [Mazzucchetti]

— 5 May 1898. 1 p, 8vo. Recipient & contents not stated. On hotel letterhead. Illus in cat. sup Oct 15 (1839) $1,100

— [n.d.]. 2 pp, 8vo. To Erminia Frezzolini. Requesting an answer concerning a new project. C June 24 (35) £1,400 [Franks]

— [n.d.]. 1 p, 4to. To Antonio Ghislanzoni. Fragment, discussing the libretto for the triumphal scene in Aida. Illus in cat. C June 24 (40) £2,800 [Franks]

AD, [c.1848]. 1 p, 4to. Draft for a contract with the Paris Opera. Illus in cat. C June 24 (33) £2,000 [Franks]

Ds, 14 Aug 1845. 3 pp, 8vo. Contract assigning the British rights to his opera Alzira to Beale & Chappell. Including 16 musical quotations from the opera. Illus in cat. C June 24 (27) £3,600 [Franks]

Autograph quotation, 3 bars from Les Vepres siciliennes, sgd; 23 July 1855. Framed with engraved port, overall size 36cm by 23.5cm. Illus in cat. S Dec 6 (219) £2,000 [Dr. Sam]

— Anr, 2 bars from the Agnus Dei of his Requiem, sgd; 24 May 1875. 1 p, 8vo. Illus in cat. S Dec 6 (222) £2,400 [Dr. Sam]

Veronese, Paolo Caliari, 1528-88

ALs, 8 June 1578. 1 p, folio. To Marcantonio Gandini. Discussing a property which he hopes to buy. Margins trimmed. S May 28 (68) £1,500 [Saggiori]

Veterinary Manuscripts

Ms, Ein bewehrtes Newess Buch von der Ross:Artzeney...; [Germany, early 18th cent]. 184 leaves, 4to. Contemp brown lea over wooden bds. In 2 hands. Including pen-&-ink sketch. JG Sept 27 (424) DM1,100

Viardot, Pauline, 1821-1910

Autograph music, Berceuse, [n.d.]. 3 pp, 4to, in marbled bds. Scored for voice & piano, with interlinear text ascribed to Stephan Bordese. Sgd. P June 17 (398) $1,100

Victoria, Duchess of Kent, 1786-1861

ALs, 21 Nov 1841. 3 pp, 8vo. To the Duchess of Gloucester. About the birth of her 1st grandchild. pn Nov 14 (180) £80

Victoria, Queen of England, 1819-1901

Series of 6 A Ls s, 29 Jan 1864 to 24 Oct 1869. 33 pp, 8vo. To Lord Derby (1 to Lady Derby). Discussing various political matters, inviting him to form a new administration, etc., & letter of condolence. S July 21 (205) £2,200 [Cunningham]

ALs, 29 Oct 1852. 6 pp, 12mo. To the Duchess of Sutherland. Mentioning Uncle Tom's Cabin & the death of Wellington. Spiro collection. CNY May 14 (156) $2,300

— 12 Jan 1855. 1 p, 8vo. To Sir G. Grey. In 3d person, approving of the appointment of Sir Henry Ward as Governor of Ceylon. Framed. Dar June 11 (357) $300

— 4 June 1863. 9 pp, 8vo. Recipient unnamed. Mourning her husband, giving family news, & hoping for a meeting. sup May 9 (484) $3,300

— 3 Apr 1870. 9 pp, 8vo. To Mrs. Grey. Personal letter of condolence. sg Sept 12 (268) $425

— 14 Sept 1872. 3 pp, 8vo. To Lady Shaftesbury. About her god-daughter's marriage to Lord Templemere. Initialled. sup Oct 15 (1842) $170

— 4 Sept 1886. 6 pp, 8vo. To Alexander I of Bulgaria. Worrying about his safety after the recent revolt, & promising support against Russia. Im German. star Mar 27 (1433) DM1,350

Ds, 10 July 1854. 1 p, folio. Appointment of G. A. H. Falconer as Major. sup Oct 15 (1841) $250

— 10 Feb 1897. 1 p, folio. Appointment of Albany St. Leger Fetherstonhaugh as Lieut. in the militia. Matted with a port. sup Oct 15 (1843) $460

— [n.d.]. Size not stated. Conditional pardon granted to Joseph Bevis. Def. pn June 11 (49) £170

Document, 1 Nov 1864. 3 membranes of vellum, c.28 by 38 inches each. Letters Patent appointing John Lord Wodehouse as Lieutenant General of Ireland. Illuminated. With related material. S Dec 12 (259) £600 [Heraldry Today]

— 4 Jan 1872. Folio. Patent to John Low. Including wax seal. bbc Sept 23 (28) $260

Signature, 1897. On composite photo of the Royal Family, made from an engraving. R Mar 7 (183) $280

Viereck, George Sylvester, 1884-1962. See: Papen, Franz von

Villa, Francisco ("Pancho"), 1878-1923

ALs, 14 Jan 1919. 1 p, 4to. To Federico Jacobby. Informing him that the bearer is coming to collect $20,000. Illus in cat. sup Oct 15 (1389) $1,750

— 10 Nov 1919. 1 p, 4to. To the manager of the Alvarado Mining & Milling Co. Reminding him of the payment of protection money. Illus in cat. sup Oct 15 (1390) $2,300

— 4 Mar 1920. 1 p, 4to. To Mr. Miller of the Alvarado Mining & Milling Co. Referring to a circular letter to the managers of mining companies. Illus in cat. sup Oct 15 (1391) $1,550

— 4 Mar 1920. 3 pp, 4to. To the managers of the American Smelting & Refining Co. & others. Requesting a loan & threatening to disrupt business operations. Illus in cat. sup Oct 15 (1393) $5,500

Virchow, Rudolf, 1821-1902

ALs, 29 Dec 1871. 1 p, 8vo. Recipient unnamed. Concerning a meeting. star Mar 26 (844) DM550

— 6 Feb 1873. 1 p, 8vo. To [Georg von Bunsen?]. Thanking for an invitation. Illus in cat. hen Nov 12 (2552) DM380

Vischer, Friedrich Theodor, 1807-87

ALs, 1 Feb 1851. 1 p, 8vo. To Eduard Boas. Responding to an inquiry about the works of Gotthold Staeudlin. star Mar 26 (498) DM350

Vittorio Emanuele III, King of Italy, 1869-1947

Ls, 28 July 1939. 1 p, folio. To Aurelio Mosquera Narvaez. Congratulating him on his election as President of Ecuador. Countersgd by Mussolini. HH May 13 (2060) DM1,000

Ds, 8 Feb 1937. 2 pp, folio. Military retirement order. Countersgd by Mussolini. sg Sept 12 (175) $400

Vivaldi, Antonio, 1678-1741

ALs, 26 Nov 1737. 4 pp, 4to. To Marchese Guido Bentivoglio. About his operas in Ferrara, his relationship with Anna Giro, & the reasons why he no longer celebrates mass. Illus in cat. Mannheim collection. S Dec 6 (25) £54,000 [Riskin]

Vogeler, Heinrich, 1872-1942

ALs, [13 Feb 1924]. 8 pp, 8vo. To Karl & Marie Jaenichen. Important letter analyzing the situation in the Soviet Union. star Mar 27 (959) DM5,500

Autograph sentiment, sgd, political statement referring to Marx & Lenin; [n.d.]. 1 p, 8vo. Mtd with a port. JG Sept 27 (474) DM400

Vogler, Georg Joseph, 1749-1814

ALs, 26 May 1811. 1 p, 4to. Recipient unnamed. Sending one of his works & mentioning Meyerbeer. star Mar 27 (1181) DM1,400

Vogt, Karl, 1817-95

ALs, 28 May 1866. 2 pp, 8vo. Recipient unnamed. Discussing German politics on the eve of war. star Mar 26 (845) DM800

Voltaire, Francois Marie Arouet de, 1694-1778. See: Friedrich II, 1712-86

Voltaire, Francois Marie Arouet de, 1694-1778

Ls, 17 Nov 1738. 3 pp, 4to. To the Rev. Charles Poree. Giving his assessment of Newton & Descartes. CNY Dec 5 (343) $3,500

— 10 Mar 1769. 1 p, 4to. To Joseph Audra. Discussing the judicial persecution of the Sirven family. star Mar 26 (500) DM1,700

— 3 July [1770]. 3 pp, 4to. To his nephew d'Hornoy. Regarding recipient's marriage. Final page autograph; sgd v. star Mar 26 (501) DM2,600

Letter, 2 Apr 1765. 1 p, 4to. To Elie Bertrand. Praising Stanislaus II of Poland. With secretarial signature. pn Nov 14 (177) £300

Autograph endorsement, 2 dockets on ALs addressed to him by Andre Dacier, 25 Sept 1714, 3 pp, 4to, commenting on his drama Oedipe & mentioning Racine. star Mar 26 (499) DM670

Voss, Johann Heinrich, 1751-1826

ALs, 28 Sept 1793. 1 p, 8vo. To Friedrich Matthisson. Sending his new almanach & chatting about his recent activities. star Mar 26 (502) DM3,000

W

Waddell, George Edward ("Rube"), 1876-1914

Signature, [n.d.]. Matted with Hall of Fame card, overall size 8 by 10 inches. Dar Feb 13 (92) $500

Wagner, Cosima, 1837-1930

ALs, 19 Aug 1855. 8 pp, 8vo. To her half-sister Claire. Describing a visit to her father Franz Liszt in Weimar. S May 29 (676) £500 [Giesen]

Wagner, Ernst, 1769-1812

ALs, 5 Apr 1811. 2 pp, 4to. To Christoph Wilhelm Hufeland. Thanking for medical advice & a treatise on magnetism. star Mar 26 (503) DM600

Wagner, John Peter ("Honus"), 1874-1955

Ls, 8 Jan 1929. 1 p, 4to. To W. J. Foley. Regarding a baseball game for the benefit of Lou Criger. Dar Dec 26 (112) $1,000

Check, accomplished & sgd, 26 May 1917. Payable to Al B. Wagner. Cancellation affecting signature. Illus in cat. sup July 10 (937) $675

— Anr, accomplished & sgd, 25 July 1918. Payable to Fred L. Fox. Cancellation affecting signature. Illus in cat. sup July 10 (936) $1,450

Photograph, sgd, [n.d.]. 7 by 9 inches. Illus in cat. sup July 10 (938) $750

Signature, 1948. On verso of postcard. Dar Oct 10 (86) $275

Wagner, Richard, 1813-83

Autograph music, Prelude to Act III of his opera Siegfried, with opening bars of 1st scene, 22 June 1869. 2 pp, folio. In short score; heavily revised. Illus in cat. Mannheim collection. S Dec 6 (26) £18,000 [Sawyer]

— Autograph music, sketches for Siegfrieds Tod, the 1st version of Goetterdaemmerung, 12 Aug [18]50. 2 pp, folio. Over 150 bars in short score, comprising early drafts of the Valkyrie motif, the 1st scene of the Prologue, the Norns' scene, etc. Illus in cat. S May 29 (682) £3,800 [Lussato]

— Autograph music, untitled piano piece in A flat major (WWV 93) presented to his wife with the complete score of Parsifal, 25 Dec 1881. 1 p, 4to. 13 bars. Inscr in his daughter Eva's hand. With related ALs by Eva Chamberlain-Wagner. Illus in cat. S Dec 6 (236) £9,000 [Mayer]

ALs, 19 Dec 1842. 1 p, 4to. To Ferdinand David. Apologizing for the confusion caused by the unnecessary search for a score. Repaired. star Mar 27 (1182) DM2,200

— 6 Feb 1850. 4 pp, 4to. To Franz Liszt. Important letter about his move to Zurich & Paris, his cooperation with Belloni, current projects, etc. Illus in cat. star Mar 27 (1183) DM8,500

— 27 Apr [18]53. 1 p, 8vo. Recipient unnamed. Inquiring about arrangements for the forthcoming Wagner festival in Zurich. S May 29 (683) £1,200 [Zentralbibliothek Zurich.]

— 20 July 1853. 3 pp, 8vo. To Carl Grabowsky. About a recent performance of Lohengrin at Dessau. star Mar 27 (1184) DM3,600

— 8 Nov 1853. 1 p, 8vo. To Theodor Kirchner. Conveying a message from E. Merian-Koechlin. star Mar 27 (1185) DM4,000

— 13 Nov 1853. 1 p, 8vo. Recipient unnamed. Reporting about financial arrangements with the double-bass player Weber. S May 29 (685) £750 [L'Autographe]

— 2 Dec [18]53. 1 p, size not stated. Recipient unnamed. Arranging the program for a concert. S May 29 (684) £1,100 [Mazzucchetti]

— [c.1860]. 1 p, 8vo. Recipient unnamed. Arranging a meeting & hoping he will introduce him to M. Bertin. S Dec 6 (227) £650 [Dr. Sam]

— 16 Oct 1863. 1 p, 8vo. To [Johann Friedrich Kittl]. Forwarding letters & promising to send some scores. star Mar 27 (1186) DM3,200

— 4 Oct 1864. 1 p, 4to. To Ludwig Nohl. Inviting him to a rehearsal of a work composed for the King's birthday. Illus in cat. S Dec 6 (230) £1,100 [Schneider]

— 31 May 1865. 1 p, 4to. To [Ludwig Nohl]. Accepting the dedication of Nohl's Ed of the letters of Beethoven. Illus in cat. S Dec 6 (231) £1,500 [Benjamin]

— 31 May 1868. 1 p, 8vo. To M. von Meysenbug. Inviting her to the premiere of Die Meistersinger von Nuernberg. S Dec 6 (232) £1,300 [Schneider]

— 26 Dec 1871. 2 pp, 8vo. To an unnamed pbr. Refusing to deal with him regarding the publication of his collected writings. S May 29 (697) £800 [Mazzucchetti]

— 29 June 1873. 3 pp, 8vo. Recipient unnamed. Reporting about the building of the festival hall at Bayreuth. star Mar 27 (1188) DM2,800

— 6 Dec 1876. 1 p, 8vo. To Karl Voltz. Requesting him to send money. S Dec 6 (229) £750 [Caverzasio]

Ls, 12 Jan 1875. 3 pp, 4to. To an unnamed conductor. Discussing a performance at the Bayreuth Festival. Repaired. cb Feb 12 (171) $1,100

Ds, 1877. 1 p, 108mm by 272mm. Receipt for royalty payments from Carl Voltz. S May 29 (692) £500 [Haas]

— [4 Dec 1881]. 1 p, 8vo. Receipt for registered mail. star Mar 27 (1189) DM1,200

Autograph quotation, 16 bars from Rienzi's Prayer, 14 Apr 1869. 7cm by 11cm. Sgd. Illus in cat. S May 29 (691) £5,500 [Harding]

— Anr, 4 bars of music from his opera Siegfried, sgd; [n.d.]. 1 p, 8vo. Including lyrics; inscr to Onkel Lueders. Framed with a port. Illus in cat. P June 17 (89) $4,500

Photograph, sgd & inscr, 1882. 19.5 by 27 inches; oval. Illus in cat. sup Oct 15 (1846) $3,100

Wagner, Robert —& Wood, Natalie, 1938-81

Ls, 22 Sept 1959. 2 pp, size not stated. To Walter Winchell. Explaining that they refuse to cooperate with fan magazines because they "insult the intelligence of the personalities they cover" as well as of their readers. Dar Feb 13 (2) $275

Wain, Louis William, 1860-1939

ALs, 15 Dec 1900. 4 pp, 8vo. To Hamon. About the amount of work he has been doing, & incorporating a pen-&-ink sketch of a piratical cat. bba June 25 (137) £100 [Spademan]

Waite, Morrison Remick, 1816-88

ALs, 2 July 1872. 2 pp, 8vo. Recipient unnamed. Declining an invitation to a dinner & ball in Geneva. Dar Aug 6 (281) $170

Waldeyer, Wilhelm, 1836-1921

ALs, 7 May 1866. 2 pp, 8vo. Recipient unnamed. Regarding specimens for a medical collection. star Mar 26 (847) DM480

Walker, Mary Edwards, 1832-1919

ALs, 15 Dec 1879. 1 p, 8vo. Recipient unnamed. Requesting theater seats. R Nov 9 (83) $380

Wallenberg, Raoul, 1912-1947?

Ls, 21 Aug 1943. 1 p, 4to. Recipient unnamed. Regarding the delivery of machinery. Illus in cat. sg Feb 27 (238) $3,800

Wallenstein, Albrecht von, Herzog von Friedland & Mecklenburg, 1583-1634

Ls, 23 Apr 1625. 2 pp, folio. To Vincenz Muschinger. Requesting him to assist Augustin Moranda in an unspecified matter. star Mar 27 (1746) DM2,600

— 4 June 1630. 1 p, folio. To Emperor Ferdinand II. Supporting a request by the mayor of Nuernberg concerning Andreas Harsdoerffer. HN Nov 28 (1852) DM3,400

Waller, Thomas W. ("Fats"), 1904-43

Autograph music, song, Anita; [1939]. 2 pp, 4to. Complete final draft; sgd. Framed. Dar Dec 26 (322) $4,750

Autograph sentiment, [n.d]. 5.25 by 4 inches. Inscr to Frank Sebastian. Dar Oct 10 (95) $300

Photograph, sgd & inscr, [n.d.]. 7.5 by 10 inches. Inscr to Charles Silvia. Framed. Dar Dec 26 (323) $950

Signature, June 1939. On hotel register leaf, 9 by 7 inches. sup Oct 15 (1847) $220

Walpole, Horace, 4th Earl of Orford, 1717-97

ALs, 31 Jan 1778. 3 pp, 4to. To Catharine Macaulay. Commenting on the French Enlightenment & comparing the ideal of a free America to that of Israel. Imperf. pn June 11 (19) £3,600

Walser, Martin

Autograph Ms, draft, reflections on apologies; 18 July 1972. 2 pp, folio. On verso of photocopies. star Mar 26 (504) DM850

— Autograph Ms, essay, Zum Glueck kein Sieg, [June 1991]. 5 pp, 4to. Responding to questions regarding the future capital of Germany. HH Nov 6 (2107) DM420

— Autograph Ms, fragment, Kafka - jetzt; 1 July 1983. 3 pp, 4to, on verso of galleys. Sgd & inscr. star Mar 26 (505) DM500

Walser, Robert, 1878-1956

ALs, 4 Sept 1926. 1 p, 8vo. To the Ed of the journal Simplizissimus. Offering a novella for print & stating his fee. HH Nov 6 (2109) DM3,000

— [n.d.]. 1 p, 8vo. To the Ed of the journal

Simplizissimus. Offering a contribution. HH Nov 6 (2108) DM3,000

Walter, Bruno, 1876-1962

Collection of 8 A Ls s & Ls s, 1912 to 1936. 16 pp, various sizes. To Nathalie Bauer-Lechner & Mary Komorn-Rebhahn. Mostly about Bauer-Lechner's book of reminiscences of Gustav Mahler. S May 29 (698) £550 [Haas]

Ls, 15 Apr 1936. 1 p, 4to. To Rosa Mayreder. Inviting her to a rehearsal of the opera Der Corregidor. star Mar 27 (1192) DM280

Walton, George, Signer from Georgia

Ds, 8 Oct 1802. 1 p, 6 by 7 inches. Witness' invoice for time & travel to attend a court case. Also sgd by others. sup Oct 15 (1216) $625

Walton, Sir William, 1902-83

Series of 3 A Ls s, Nov 1949 & 5 Feb 1950. 4 pp, size not stated. To Boris Kochno. About the Ballet Devoir de Vacances, & the newly composed Galop Final. With related material. SM Oct 12 (411) FF8,500

Waner, Paul Glee, 1903-65

Autograph sentiment, sgd, inscr to "The Rileys", [n.d.]. On Hall of Fame card, 5.5 by 3.5 inches. Dar Apr 9 (109) $110

War of 1812

— Hamilton, Paul. - ALs, 18 June 1812. 1 p, size not stated. To Commodore John Rodgers. Informing him of the declaration of war & giving instructions for the vessels under his command. rf Sept 21 (24) $14,500

— Marshall, Capt. John. - ALs, 10 Apr 1813. 10 pp, 4to. To William Phillips. Giving an account of the capture of HMS Java by the USS Constitution. With ptd minutes of related Admiralty Court-martial. Spiro collection. CNY May 14 (48) $10,500

Ward, Artemas, 1727-1800

ALs, 6 Feb 1792. 2 pp, 4to. To his daughter Maria. Complaining that Philadelphia "is unhealthy, the people immoral and disagreeable..." CNY June 9 (284) $900

Warhol, Andy, d.1987

Photograph, sgd, [n.d.]. 8 by 10 inches. Dar Apr 9 (379) $200

Signature, [n.d.]. On art postcard with his self port. Dar Aug 6 (282) $200

— Anr, [n.d.]. On art postcard. Dar Aug 6 (283) $140
See also: Capote, Truman & Warhol

Warren, Earl, 1891-1974

Transcript, quotation from Supreme Court decision in Brown v. Board of Education, 17 May 1954. 1 p, 12mo (card). Sgd. Dar Dec 26 (123) $600

Warren, Mercy Otis, 1728-1814

Series of 4 A Ls s, 29 Dec 1774 to 20 Sept 1789. 15 pp, folio & 4to. To Catharine Macaulay. Discussing the state of the American colonies, the war, the signing of the American Constitution, & the struggles of the young republic. With retained copies of 2 letters from Macaulay to Warren, 1790 & 1791. pn June 11 (20) £5,500

Warren, Robert Penn

Ls, 8 Oct 1962. 1 p, 4to. To Mr. Wilder. Responding to a note on school prayer & William Faulkner. wa Mar 5 (271) $85

Washington, Booker T., 1856-1915

Ls, 12 June 1909. 1 p, 4to. To Rev. H. N. Vaz. Regarding recipient's son's illness. sup Oct 15 (1849) $140

Washington, Bushrod, 1762-1829

ALs, 17 June 1800. 1 p, 4to. To Mr. Lewis. Regarding his uncle's estate. sup Oct 15 (1478) $950

Washington, District of Columbia

Ms, plat book displaying the extensive real estate holdings of Thomas Law in Washington, 1801. About 40 leaves, folio, stitched. Annotated with owner's names of lots, & interleaved with smaller sheets providing details of purchases, leases, etc. Incomplete. wa Nov 21 (144) $4,000

— Blodget, Samuel. - Ds, 25 Feb 1792. 1 p, folio. Sale of a lot of land in the Jamaica district of Washington to John Dewhurst. Illus in cat. sup May 9 (387) $1,900

Washington, George, 1732-99

[An autograph address leaf, [28 Mar 1766], 1 p, 4to, addressed to Robert Cary & Co., with related material, sold at sg on 12 Sept 1991, lot 269, for $500.]

Autograph Ms, fragment from the 1st draft of his 1st Inaugural Address, [c.April 1789]. 2 pp, 4to; numbered 57 & 58. Referring to the nation's commerce, internal improvements, & new immigrants. Illus in cat. Spiro collection. CNY May 14 (158) $75,000

ALs, 21 Jan 1776. 2 pp, 4to. To Jonathan Trumbull. Discussing plans to provide for the soldiers involved in the Canadian campaign. Illus in cat. R Mar 7 (159) $22,000

— July 1776. 1 p, folio. To [Benjamin Franklin]. Informing him that his letter [regarding peace initiatives of the Howe Brothers] has been sent to Lord Howe, & promising to support an inventor's project. Illus in cat. Spiro collection. CNY May 14 (157) $125,000

— 20 Mar 1779. 4 pp, 4to. To Henry Laurens. Responding to the suggestion to arm slaves. Severely stained. Illus in cat. P Dec 12 (145) $9,000

— 13 June 1779. 1 p, 4to. To Henry Knox. Circular, sending instructions (not included) "in case the enemy march against West Point". Illus in cat. sup Oct 15 (1473) $24,000

— 15 Aug 1786. 1 p, 4to. To David Gordon Stuart. Inviting him to dinner with Gen. Du Plessis. CNY Dec 5 (129) $26,000

— 28 Sept 1788. 2 pp, 4to. To John Polson. Responding to an inquiry about land on the Great Kanawha. P Dec 12 (144) $23,000

— 31 Mar 1796. 2 pp, 4to. To George W. Lafayette. Extending an invitation. Framed. Illus in cat. P Dec 12 (146) $21,000

— 27 June 1796. 1 p, 8vo. To George Lewis. Explaining that he has sent letters to other family members through Lewis. Framed with a port. P June 16 (304) $13,000

— 31 Dec 1798. 3 pp, 4to. To Bushrod Washington. Commenting on the Alien & Sedition Acts. Silked. Illus in cat. Spiro collection. CNY May 14 (159) $70,000

— 14 Feb 1799. 1 p, 4to. To William A. Washington. Requesting the delivery of more corn. P June 16 (305) $18,000

Ls, 19 May 1777. 1 p, folio. Recipient unnamed. Introducing M. Colerus, "who is to fill a Majority in Colo. Hazen's Regiment". Illus in cat. sup May 9 (166) $17,000

— 25 Sept 1778. 2 pp, 4to. To Benjamin Tallmadge. Regarding the shortage of horses. Including franking signature. Illus in cat. P June 16 (300) $16,000

— 9 Sept 1782. 1 p, folio. To Brig. Gen. David Forman. Acknowledging 2 letters & requesting him to watch the movements of the British fleet. Imperf. CNY June 9 (285) $11,000

— 11 Nov 1782. 1 p, folio. To Lieut. Col. Ebenezer Gray. Granting leave for 8 weeks. CNY Dec 5 (127) $9,500

— 16 Dec 1782. 2 pp, folio. To Lieut. Col. [William Stephens]. Considering the strength of fortifications at Dobbs Ferry. CNY Dec 5 (128) $26,000

— 6 Jan 1790. 1 p, folio. To Miss C. Goddard. Explaining his position on appointments. Framed. Illus in cat. P June 16 (302) $14,000

Note, [May 1792]. 1 p, 12mo (card). To Mr. Gilbert. Dinner invitation. Partly engraved; accomplished in Washington's hand. R Nov 9 (128) $3,000

ADs, 23 Mar 1750/51. 1 p, folio. Survey of land in Frederick County for John Grub; including plat drawing. P Dec 12 (142) $17,000

— 2 Apr 1751. 1 p, 4to. Survey of land in Frederick County for Samuel Isaac. With plat drawing on integral leaf. Illus in cat. P Dec 12 (143) $8,000

— 3 Aug 1770. 1 p, folio. Agreement with George Muse regarding Muse's claim for a military land grant. Sgd 5 times (4 times in text). Also sgd by others. Framed with a port. Illus in cat. sup May 9 (164) $22,000

— 15 Nov 1771. 1 p, 12mo. Receipt, sgd by James Cleveland, for £115 from Washington (sgd in text). Dar Dec 26 (324) $5,000

— 12 May 1799. 1 p, 8vo. Receipt to David Stuart for the annuity due from the estate of John Parke Custis. Framed with engraved port. Illus in cat. P June 16 (306) $10,000

AD, 22 Jan 1755. 1 p, folio. Receipt, sgd by Adams Stephen & Thomas Cowper, for payment for tools delivered to Mount Vernon. Sgd by Washington 3 times in text. Illus in cat. sup May 9 (163) $15,000

Ds, 8 June 1783. 1 p, folio. Army discharge for Cornelius Hendrickson. Framed. LH Dec 11 (22) $7,500

— 9 June 1783. 1 p, folio. Discharge certificate for John Thayre. P June 16 (301) $4,000

— 3 Aug 1790. 1 p, folio. Appointment of John Stokes as district court judge for North Carolina. Countersgd by Jefferson. Framed with ports of both. P June 16 (303) $6,500

— 13 June 1794. 1 p, folio. Ship's papers in 3 languages for the ship Mary of Norfolk. Countersgd by Jefferson. Illus in cat. CNY June 9 (286) $15,000

— 11 Apr 1795. 1 p, folio. Appointment of William Simmons as Accountant in the War Department. Countersgd by E. Randolph. Illus in cat. sup Oct 15 (1475) $3,400

— 17 Sept 1796. 1 p, folio. Land grant to James Murray. Countersgd by Pickering. Illus in cat. sg Feb 27 (239) $8,500

— 16 Nov 1796. 1 p, folio. Ship's papers for the Fanny. Framed with engraved port. Illus in cat. sup Oct 15 (1476) $8,800

— [n.d.]. 1 p, folio. Membership certificate for the Society of the Cincinnati; unaccomplished. P Dec 12 (147) $5,550

— [n.d.]. 1 p, folio. Membership certificate in the Society of the Cincinnati for William Stuart. Framed with a port. Imperf. Illus in cat. sup May 9 (165) $8,500

Cut signature, [n.d.]. 31mm by 79mm. Framed with engraved port. P June 16 (307) $3,250

— FORGERY. - Ls, 12 Sept 1796, 2 pp, 4to. To James Wood. Offering him the job as Surveyor General. Probably by Charles

Weisberg, forging Washington's hand. bbc Sept 23 (33) $130

— OTIS, SAMUEL A. - Autograph transcript, report of the Senate committee charged with making arrangements for Washington's taking of the oath of office, sgd & addressed to [Robert R. Livingston], 25 & 27 Apr 1789. 2 pp, folio. P June 16 (308) $8,000

Watson, Sir William, 1858-1935

Collection of 20 A Ls s & Ls, 18 Sept 1914 to 28 Feb 1928. About 65 pp, 4to & 8vo. To J. Cartwright Frith. About recipient's poetry, current publishing, critics, etc. With related material. S July 21 (185) £750 [Rota]

Watt, James, 1736-1819

ALs, 25 Oct [1817]. 1 p, 8vo. To [Samuel] Tertius Galton. Introducing the French scientist Biot. pn Nov 14 (207) £240

Waugh, Evelyn, 1903-66

Typescript (duplicated), The Cynic, a magazine for distribution at Heath Mount School, Ed by Waugh & Derek Hooper; 5 issues, 21 Jan to Sept 1916. 40 pp, 210mm by 165mm, on rectos only; mimeographed. Including orig watercolor drawing, sgd by Waugh. Complete series. Illus in cat. C June 24 (386) £2,200 [Maggs]

— Typescript (duplicated) The Cynic, a magazine for distribution at Heath Mount School, Ed by Waugh & Derek Hooper; vol I no 2, 8 Feb 1916 (3 copies), & vol I no 5, Sept 1916. 32 pp, 210mm by 165mm, on rectos only; mimeographed. Including orig watercolor drawing, sgd by Waugh. C June 24 (387) £950 [Maggs]

Wayne, Anthony, 1745-96

Autograph Ms, 8 memoranda recording proceedings of the Supreme Executive Council of Pennsylvania, 1777 to 1780. About 18 pp, folio & 4to. CNY June 9 (287) $4,200

— Autograph Ms, notes on proceedings of the E[xectutive] C[ommittee], 6 Jan to 9 June 1780; [probably made 1784-85]. 2 pp, 4to. R Nov 9 (126) $150

A Ls s (2), 9 June & 20 Sept 1780. 3 pp, 4to. To his wife Polly. Reporting from camp. With 4 A Ls s by Polly Wayne & ALs by his mother Elizabeth, 1776 to 1779, to Antony Wayne. CNY June 9 (288) $17,000

ALs, 30 Dec 1777. 3 pp, 4to. To Richard Peters. Reporting on the poor state of his troops & requesting a leave of absence. Encapsulated. P June 16 (309) $800

— 18 Dec 1792. 1 p, 4to. To Elliot & Williams. Strongly complaining about lack of provisions for the army. Illus in cat. R Mar 7 (203) $1,900

Ds, [24 Dec 1796?]. 1 p, 4to. Request addressed to the Clothier General for articles of clothing for 3 officers. Framed. P Dec 12 (148) $700

— WILCOCKS, ALEXANDER. - ADs, 18 Oct 1784. 1 p, folio. Confirmation of A. Wayne's title to Waynesborough; also sgd by Wm. Lewis. Endorsed in anr hand; docketed by Wayne on integral leaf. R Nov 9 (127) $800

Wayne, John, 1907-79

Collection of 2 Ls s & telegram, 1 to 9 June 1960. 4 pp, mostly 4to. To Gerald Ashford. Concerning his film The Alamo. Dar Dec 26 (325) $1,100

Ds, 3 Jan 1972. 1 p, 4to. Consent of shareholders to the election to wind up & dissolve John Ford Productions. Also sgd by Ford & B. Benjamin. Illus in cat. sup Oct 15 (1850) $675

Group photograph, [n.d.]. Size not stated. With 2 others at a firing range. Sgd by Ford & inscr to Jim. sup Oct 15 (1851) $250

— Anr, [n.d.]. 4to. With Kirk Douglas; sgd by Wayne. wa Oct 19 (8) $425

Photograph, sgd & inscr, [1970]. 8 by 10 inches. Inscr to Dennis. Dar Apr 9 (380) $425

— Anr, [n.d.]. 8 by 10 inches. Inscr to William. Illus in cat. R June 13 (215) $320

Ptd photograph, 1970. 9.5 by 8.25 inches. Inscr to Albert. Illus in cat. Dar Aug 6 (33) $325

Signature, [n.d.]. On cover of Princess Cruises ticket holder. sup Oct 15 (1852) $210

Weare, W. K., 1823-94?

Autograph Ms, autobiography, poetry, prose & letters, [1880s]. 662 pp, size not stated. R Nov 9 (164) $1,000

Webb, Sidney, 1859-1947

Series of 3 A Ls s, 3 to 15 Dec 1906. 10 pp, 8vo. To Thomas Hodgkin. About a subscription & publication matters. 1 also sgd by Beatrice Webb. bba May 28 (195) £100 [Ball]

Webber, Andrew Lloyd

Photograph, sgd, [n.d.]. 8 by 10 inches. Dar June 11 (361) $200

Weber, Andreas Paul, 1893-1980

Collection of ALs, 2 autograph postcards, sgd, & ANs, 2 Jan [1969] to 1971. 5 pp, 8vo. Recipient unnamed. About his calendar, sending New Year's wishes, etc. JG Mar 27 (203) DM300

Weber, Bernhard Anselm, 1766-1821

Series of 4 A Ls s, 8 Mar 1818 to 20 Aug 1819. 7 pp, 4to & 8vo. To Johann Daniel Sander. About some musical projects, Kotzebue's assassination, etc. star Mar 27 (1193) DM1,300

Weber, Carl Maria von, 1786-1826

Autograph Ms, part of the libretto of Euryanthe, 17 lines; [n.d.]. 120mm by 168mm. Mtd with autograph address leaf to his wife. Searles-Rowland collection. C June 24 (5A) £1,700 [Schneider]

ALs, 24 Sept 1810. 1 p, 4to. To Hans Georg Naegeli. Asking that he return a score. star Mar 27 (1194) DM3,200

— [summer 1816]. 1 p, 8vo, cut from larger sheet. To Caroline Brandt. Expressing disappointment about his failure to secure an appointment in Berlin, & outlining his travel plans. Possibly incomplete. S Dec 6 (240) £1,800 [Haas]

— 22 Oct 1817. 1 p, 4to. To Carl Stuermer. Complaining that he has had no news, & mentioning the repayment of a loan. S Dec 6 (238) £1,000 [Haas]

— 17 Jan 1820. 2 pp, 4to. To Herr [Teichmann]. Commenting on an opera by Konrad Kocher, & looking forward to the premiere of his Freischuetz in Berlin. star Mar 27 (1195) DM4,000

— 25 Mar 1821. 2 pp, 4to. Recipient unnamed. Discussing his opera Der Freischuetz, especially Agathe's Cavatina & the Bridal Chorus. S May 29 (700) £3,200 [Haas]

— 6 Sept 1824. 2 pp, 4to. To [Karl August von Lichtenstein?]. Responding to a request for a new composition. Illus in cat. star Mar 27 (1196) DM5,500

— 24 Feb 1825. 1 p, 4to. To C. Bachmann. Informing him that he has no works available for sale at the moment. S May 29 (699) £1,000 [Haas]

Ls, 22 May 1826. 1 p, 4to. To an unnamed musician. Inviting him to a rehearsal for a projected concert. S Dec 6 (239) £1,700 [Schneider]

Autograph sentiment, "Beharrlichkeit fuehrt zum Ziel!"; sgd & dated 8 June 1821. 1 p, 8vo. S Dec 6 (237) £550 [Giesen]

Weber, Gottfried, 1779-1839

ALs, 1 May 1807. 1 p, 4to. Recipient unnamed. Thanking for his election as honorary member of the Schweizerische Musikgesellschaft. star Mar 27 (1197) DM500

Weber, Max, 1864-1920

ALs, 11 Dec 1906. 4 pp, 8vo. To [Camilla Jellinek?]. Concerning Karl Diehl's cooperation in the journal Archiv fuer Sozialwissenschaft und Sozialpolitik. star Mar 26 (848) DM1,500

Weber, Wilhelm, 1804-91

ALs, 6 July 1838. 1 p, 8vo. To Edward Solly. About a joint scientific project. Illus in cat. star Mar 26 (849) DM750

Webern, Anton von, 1883-1945

Collection of ALs & 2 autograph postcards, sgd, 1921 to 1923. 3 pp, 8vo & 4to. To Karl Rankl. Arranging appointments, mentioning Schoenberg, etc. S May 29 (701) £600 [Van Lauwe]

ALs, 18 Jan 1926. 1 p, 8vo. To Karl Rankl. Giving news of Schoenberg. S Dec 6 (241) £450 [Pickering & Chatto.]

ANs, 16 Aug 1939. 2 pp, 65mm by 105mm, on ptd visiting card. To Leonard Gross. Expressing relief that recipient may be able to help his pupil Filip Gershkovich. S Dec 6 (242) £450 [Haas]

Webster, Daniel, 1782-1852

ALs, 27 Sept [18]50. Length not stated. To Daniel Dickinson. Referring to recipient's leaving the Senate. Framed. b&b Feb 19 (319) $200

— 26 Sept [n.y.]. 1 p, 8vo. To Dr. Hodgkin. Acknowledging a letter of introduction. bba May 28 (196) £75 [Wilson]

Franking signature, [n.d.]. Size not stated. As Senator. sup Oct 15 (1853) $140

Webster, Noah, 1758-1843

Autograph Ms, definitions of blood & words including the term blood for his American Dictionary of the English Language, [n.d.]. 2 pp, 4to (2 smaller sheets pieced together). Illus in cat. P June 16 (310) $4,250

Wedekind, Frank, 1864-1918

ALs, 19 Sept 1895. 3 pp, 8vo. To Otto Eisenschitz. Asking that he submit his play Der Schweigerling to the Raimund-Theater in Vienna. star Mar 26 (507) DM550

— 5 July 1905. 4 pp, 8vo. To an unnamed lady. Suggesting that she come to Munich, & commenting on life in the city. star Mar 26 (508) DM900

Weedon, George, c.1730-c.1793

ALs, 13 Oct 1783. 3 pp, folio. To an unnamed colonel. Inquiring about the fate of a petition for lands "between the little and great Miamis". R Nov 9 (129) $1,500

Weelkes, Thomas, d.1623

Ms, Weelks his ffa la's, [n.d.]. 24 pp, 8vo, in later bds. Contemp copy of the Quintus part from the 24 Balletts and Madrigals for 5 voices of 1598. C June 24 (10) £400 [Macnutt]

Weill, Kurt, 1900-50

Collection of ALs & Ls, 5 Apr & 20 June 1933. 3 pp, 4to. To Boris Kochno. Explaining his aims in The Seven Deadly Sins, & announcing he will start working with Brecht. SM Oct 12 (412) FF15,000

Ls, 10 Dec 1929. 1 p, 4to. To Jolly. Agreeing with recipient's suggestion of a "Dreigro-

schenmusik for 2 Klaviere". star Mar 27 (1198) DM1,300
— 27 May 1949. 2 pp, 4to. To Heinz Jolles. Giving an assessment of his life & achievements in America. Illus in cat. S May 29 (702) £1,400 [Macnutt]

Weinberger, Jaromir, 1896-1967

ALs, 15 Nov 1929. 2 pp, folio. To Nikolai Malko. Hoping that he will direct one of his works in Vienna. star Mar 27 (1199) DM400

Weinheber, Josef, 1892-1945

ALs, 22 Jan 1944. 2 pp, folio. Recipient unnamed. Analyzing the difference between Rilke's & his own works. star Mar 26 (510) DM800

Weir, Thomas Bell, d.1876

Photograph, sgd, [n.d.]. Carte size. Framed. Armstrong collection. sup Oct 15 (1135) $360

Weismann, Julius, 1879-1950

Autograph music, Conzert fuer Klavier u. Orchester. B-Dur. Neue Fassung. Opus 33; [Jan to 15 July 1936]. 150 pp, 4to, in bds. Sgd. HN Nov 28 (1853) DM460

Weiss, George, 1895-1972

Photograph, sgd, [n.d.]. 8 by 10 inches. Dar Dec 26 (113) $250

Weizsaecker, Heinrich, 1862-1945

Series of 5 A Ls s, 1898 to 1902. 13 pp, 8vo. To Otto Harnack. About Goethe & art. star Mar 26 (850) DM340

Welch, Mickey, 1859-1941

Signature, [n.d.]. Matted with Hall of Fame postcard, overall size 8 by 10 inches. Illus in cat. Dar Aug 6 (97) $650

Welles, Gideon, 1802-78

Autograph Ms, 8 lines referring to the reinforcement of Fort Sumter, [c.1861]. 1 p, 4to. sg Feb 27 (39) $400

Welles, Orson, 1915-85

Ls, 2 June 1969. 1 p, 4to. To Donald A. Koos. Saying he does not have a photograph at the moment. sup Oct 15 (1855) $200

Ds s (2)12 June 1969. 4 pp, 4to. Agreement with Manheim Fox Enterprises to use the orig broadcast of The War of the Worlds; 2 identical copies. Dar Aug 6 (42) $550
— Ds s (2)21 June 1980. 12 pp, 4to. Contract for commercials for Paul Masson Wines & related affidavit. Dar Aug 6 (34) $275

Ds, 22 Aug 1978. 2 pp, 4to. Contract for voice recordings for the cartoon Lord of the Rings. Dar Aug 6 (35) $300

Photograph, sgd, [n.d.]. 3 by 5 inches. LH Dec 11 (551) $90

Photograph, sgd & inscr, [n.d.]. 5 by 7 inches. Inscr to Arnold [Weissberger]. Dar Dec 26 (326) $120

Wellington, Arthur Wellesley, 1st Duke, 1769-1852

ALs, 9 June 1804. 4 pp, 4to. To Lieut. Gen. James Stuart. Giving an account of the state of his supplies. pn Nov 14 (162) £160
— 2 Feb 1811. 1 p, 4to. To the Conde de Penne Villeneur. Informing him that the Spanish troops in Spain will be furnished with victuals. pn Nov 14 (151) £85 [Autograph House]
— 28 May 1811. 8 pp, 8vo. Recipient unnamed. Referring to the "notion of the omniscience and occult omnipotence of Bonaparte." With authentication. wd June 12 (337) $750
— 15 Sept 1811. 1 p, 4to. To Admiral George Berkeley. Informing him that he has informed the Prime Minister that "we ought ... to have a larger fleet in the Tagus". pn Nov 14 (152) £160 [Maggs]
— 26 May 1817. 1 p, 8vo. To C. Stewart. Planning to arrive in Paris in a few days. star Mar 27 (1749) DM550
— 14 Nov 1818. 1 p, 8vo. To Gen. von Boyen. Asking for a meeting. star Mar 27 (1750) DM360

Ds, 14 Apr 1814. 1 p, 4to. Safe-conduct issued to Col. St. Simon. pn Nov 14 (153) £130 [Maggs]

**Wells, Henry, 1805-78 —&
Fargo, William George, 1818-81**

Ds, 27 Apr 1854. 1 p, 4to. Stock certificate in the American Express Company, issued to Julius Candee. Illus in cat. Dar Aug 6 (284) $2,000
— 23 Dec 1861. 1 p, folio. Stock certificate in the American Express Company. sup Oct 15 (1857) $1,000
— 28 July 1864. 1 p, folio. Stock certificate in the American Express Company. Repaired. Dar Dec 26 (327) $450

Wells, Herbert George, 1866-1946

Autograph Ms, sgd, statement on race & the progress of civilization; [c.1911]. 1 p, folio. Written for the Modern Historic Records Association. sg Sept 12 (271) $500

Collection of 4 A Ls s & Ls, 1926 to 1928. 10 pp, various sizes. To Col. Minnigerode. On literary matters, publishing arrangements, etc. sg Feb 27 (242) $450

ALs, [25 Apr 1911]. 1 p, 4to. To an unnamed lady. Thanking for praise & recommending other works. sg Sept 12 (270) $300
— [n.d.]. 1 p, 4to. To [Mr. Melville?]. Inquiring about an invitation. star Mar 26 (511) DM220

— [n.d.]. 4 pp, 4to. To the Ed of the magazine Nation. Expressing anger at the response his articles have received. sup Oct 15 (1856) $575

Werdenberg, Johann Baptist von, d.1648

Ls, 10 Jan 1629. 2 pp, folio. To Margrave Friedrich von Savorgnano. Regarding a dispute between Hieronymus Savorgnano & some Jesuits. Also sgd by Emperor Ferdinand II. In Latin. HN Nov 28 (1854) DM1,200

Werfel, Franz, 1890-1945

Autograph Ms, poem, Couplet eines Verdammten, [n.d.]. 2 pp, 4to. 19 lines. star Mar 26 (513) DM500

— Autograph Ms, poem, Der Reim, [n.d.]. 1 p, 4to. 15 lines. star Mar 26 (512) DM850

Ls, 23 Aug 1939. 1 p, 4to. To Georg Moenius. Reporting that he has just finished his new work Der veruntreute Himmel. star Mar 26 (514) DM380

Werner, Anton von, 1843-1915

Autograph Ms, diary kept during his journey from Berlin to Karlsruhe, Oct 1862. 130 pp, 8vo, in half lea bdg. Including 25 drawings. Sgd on front cover. star Mar 27 (961) DM2,800

Wesley, John, 1703-91

ALs, 2 May 1766. 2 pp, 8vo. To "My Dear Sister". Expressing his need for her prayers, especially for his work in Ireland. Illus in cat. bba Sept 19 (346) £1,500 [Mandl]

West Indies

— BARBADOS. - 2 Mss, ledgers recording accounts for the Mangrove Plantation, 1825 to 1841. 330 pp in 2 vols, folio, in worn calf bdg. With related family letters. S Dec 12 (305) £550 [Appelbaum]

West, Mae, 1892-1980

Photograph, sgd & inscr, [n.d.]. 5 by 7 inches. Inscr to Bill Sorrs. Illus in cat. sup Oct 15 (1858) $200

West, Rebecca, 1892-1983

[An archive containing 50 letters, postcards & notes, mostly autograph, to Maboth Moseley & Vera Watson, 1 Oct 1931 to 1982, with related material, relating to family problems & literary matters, sold at CNY on 5 Dec 1991, lot 348, for $3,200.]

Collection of 7 A Ls s & 4 Ls s, 1934 to 1958 & [n.d.]. 18 pp, size not stated. To A. S. Frere & Pat Frere. About a variety of matters. S Feb 11 (390) £200 [Rota]

Westinghouse, George, 1846-1914

Ds, 27 May 1871. 2 pp, folio. Agreement concerning payment for the sale of rights & interest in the partnership G. Westinghouse & Co. from his father to Westinghouse. Sgd by both. Illus in cat. sg Feb 27 (244) $1,000

— WESTINGHOUSE, GEORGE, SR. - Ds, 27 May 1871. 1 p, folio. Bill of sale of rights & interest in the partnership G. Westinghouse & Co. to his son George. sg Feb 27 (243) $700

Wetzel, Friedrich Gottlob, 1779-1819

Autograph Ms, 3 poems, Die Verhuellte, Aus einem Mayentag 1822, & Huldigung; [1821/22]. 2 pp, 4to. Working Ms. star Mar 26 (515) DM6,500

A Ls s (2), 28 Feb & 10 Mar 1806. 4 pp, 4to. To the medical faculty of the university at Erfurt. Applying for the doctorate, outlining his studies & works, etc. star Mar 26 (516) DM4,200

Wezel, Johann Karl, 1747-1819

ALs, 23 Feb 1780. 1 p, 4to. To [Friedrich Nicolai?]. Submitting a "project" & requesting his help. star Mar 26 (517) DM1,300

Whale, James, 1886-1957

Signature, [n.d.]. 3 by 1.5 inches (card). With 2 photographs, 8 by 10 inches. Dar Aug 6 (39) $150

Whaling Manuscripts

Ms, log of the ship Cambria of New Bedford, 2 June 1836 to 1838, on a voyage to the South Atlantic & Indian Ocean; kept by George W. Gray. 170 pp, legal size. R June 13 (307) $7,000

Wharton, John Austin, 1829?-65. See: Hardee, William Joseph & Wharton

Wheat, Zachary Davis, 1886-1972

ANs, [n.d.]. 1 p, 8vo. Recipient unnamed. Responding to an inquiry about the "greatest thrill" in his career. Dar Dec 26 (114) $140

Whistler, James Abbott McNeill, 1834-1903

ALs, [n.d.]. 1 p, size not stated. To Mr. Wallace. Commenting on an article. Framed. Ck Apr 3 (83) £550

Signature, [n.d.]. 8vo. Including butterfly. Ingilby collection. pn Nov 14 (112) £100

White, Edward H., 1930-67

Ls, 24 Aug 1964. 1 p, 4to. Recipient unnamed. Thanking for congratulations on his Gemini assignment. wa Oct 19 (188) $300

Whitman, Walt, 1819-92

Autograph Ms, lecture, Death of Abraham Lincoln, Feb 1879. 17 leaves of various sizes, mtd on 4to sheets. In half mor bdg with related material. P June 16 (316) $30,000

ALs, 1 Oct 1861. 1 p, 8vo. To James Russell Lowell. Offering his poem 1861 for print. Illus in cat. sup Oct 15 (1861) $2,500

— 18 May 1884. 1 p, 8vo. Recipient unnamed. Thanking for a picture of Father Taylor. CNY June 9 (195) $950

— 16 Dec 1884. 1 p, 12mo. Recipient unnamed. Asking him to convey his thanks to the Marquis de Leuville. Framed with a port. P June 16 (315) $1,000

Autograph postcard, sgd, 20 Apr 1883. To Karl Knortz. Thanking for the "German renderings". sg Sept 12 (272) $400

ANs, 16 Apr 1886. 1 p, 12mo. To T. W. Acknowledging receipt of money. Framed with a port. wd Dec 12 (343) $1,200

Photograph, [c.late 1880s]. 230mm by 180mm. Mtd with ptd poem, sgd. CNY June 9 (196) $500

Whittier, John Greenleaf, 1807-92

Autograph transcript, 10-line poem, beginning "O Englishmen! In hope & creed...", 22 May 1861. 1 p, 8vo. Sgd. sg Sept 12 (273) $250

ALs, 13 [Mar] 1837. 2 pp, 4to. To "Friend May". Urging him to attend an anti-slavery meeting. CNY Dec 5 (350) $600

— 26 Dec 1875. 4 pp, 8vo. To Lucy Larcom. Discussing "Songs" they are publishing jointly. sg Sept 12 (274) $400

— 10 Oct 1883. 1 p, 8vo. Recipient unnamed. Agreeing to meet Col. Bow. bba May 28 (197) £60 [Wilson]

— 12 Dec 1884. 3 pp, 8vo. To Lucy Larcom. About his health & travel plans, & enclosing money. sg Sept 12 (275) $325

— [n.d.]. 1 p, 8vo. Recipient unnamed. Expressing thanks. wa Oct 19 (57) $120

Who, The

Concert program, [summer 1968]. 26 pp, 4to. Sgd by John Entwistle, Peter Townshend & Roger Daltrey; inscr to Howard by Keith Moon. wa Oct 19 (149) $250

Whymper, Edward, 1840-1911

ALs, 5 Dec 1888. 3 pp, 8vo. To F. F. Tuckett. Commenting on a pair of barometers. bba May 28 (198) £120 [Mandl]

Widmann, Josef Viktor, 1842-1911

ALs, 8 Oct 1889. 3 pp, 4to. To an unnamed pbr. Offering a vol of stories for print. star Mar 26 (518a) DM360

Widor, Charles-Marie, 1844-1937

ALs, 10 Apr 1887. 3 pp, 8vo. To A. W. Gottschalk. About an article which is shortly to appear. sg Sept 12 (276) $150

Wiechert, Ernst, 1887-1950

Series of 3 A Ls s, 2 Jan to 12 July 1940. 3 pp, 8vo. To [Arnold Petzet?]. Thanking for some catalogues, describing his life in the country, etc. star Mar 26 (518b) DM320

Wieghorst, Olaf, 1899-1988

ALs, 31 May 1969. 1 p, 8vo. To Catherine & Strohm. Sending a drawing "for the celebration". Including pen-&-ink sketch, sgd, of coonskin hatted man's head, at head. Illus in cat. Dar Feb 13 (9) $375

Wiehl, Emil Karl Joseph

[A collection of 32 documents tracing his career in the German artillery, in law & the diplomatic service, 1909 to 1944, sold at b on 22 June 1992, lot 109, for £1,300.]

Wieland, Christoph Martin, 1733-1813

Autograph Ms, bibliographical description of the journal Alruna, [c.1808]. 1 p, 12mo. star Mar 26 (522) DM420

— Autograph Ms, fragment from his Geschichte des Agathon, book 16, chapter 3, [1793/94]. 2 pp, 4to. Working Ms. star Mar 26 (520) DM8,000

— Autograph Ms, title (in Latin) of lectures in theology given by Wilhelm Schmarger at Klosterbergen, & a few notes, 1748. 2 pp, 4to, on detached cover. Sgd. star Mar 26 (519) DM620

ALs, 18 Nov 1780. 4 pp, 8vo. To Johann Christian Schmohl. Refusing to publish his rejoinder to a polemical article ptd in the journal Deutsches Museum. star Mar 26 (521) DM7,500

— 21 Aug 1786. 1 p, 4to. To Herr von Hillern. About financial matters. sg Sept 12 (277) $1,100

— Wieland, Thomas Adam. - 3 A Ls s, 9 Dec 1746 to 11 Apr 1747. 8 pp, 4to & folio. To Abbot Steinmetz at Klosterbergen. About his son Christoph Martin Wieland's admission to the school at Klosterbergen, his previous schooling, etc. star Mar 26 (523) DM1,800

Wigner, Eugene Paul

ALs, 5 Sept 1964. 2 pp, 4to. To an unnamed lady. Responding to a suggestion to collect autobiographies of scientists. star Mar 26 (853) DM380

Wigston, William Bacon, 1782-1872?

Ms, journal of a round trip from Suffolk, through the Cotswolds, Monmouthshire, Oxfordshire & Berkshire, 1833. 55 pp & blanks, 8vo, in orig calf. bba Jan 30 (298) £60 [Bristow]

Wilde, Oscar, 1854-1900

ALs, [c.Aug 1893]. 2 pp, 8vo. Recipient unnamed. Refusing to "allow any extracts from my works to be quoted as examples of Irish humour." CNY Dec 5 (352) $1,400

— [n.d.]. 1 p, 8vo. To Auguste Monod. Explaining that he already has a trans for his book. Framed with a port. P June 17 (90) $1,700

— [n.d.]. 4 pp, 8vo. Recipient unnamed. Commenting on recipient's book & giving his views about art & the aesthetic life. wa Oct 19 (58) $2,300

Signature, [n.d.]. In extra frame with engraved port, overall size 20 by 23 inches. Including subscription. Dar Aug 6 (285) $550

— SHERARD, ROBERT HARBOROUGH. - Ls, 8 May 1935. 7 pp, 8vo. To [Arthur] Symons. Referring to evidence at Wilde's trial regarding his homosexuality. C Dec 16 (330) £1,400 [Maguire]

Wilhelm I, Deutscher Kaiser, 1797-1888

ALs, 7 Apr 1855. 3 pp, 8vo. To an unnamed major. About the death of Nicholas I & the situation in Russia. HN June 26 (987) DM400

— 24 Feb 1859. 2 pp, 4to. Recipient unnamed. Criticizing the marching order of a military unit during a funeral cortege. star Mar 27 (1622) DM220

— 12 Jan 1879. 3 pp, 8vo. Recipient unnamed. Thanking for sympathy and support after a recent attempt on his life. star Mar 27 (1303) DM2,000

— 4 Nov 1879. 4 pp, 8vo. To [Gen. von Werder]. Sending a letter for the Czar concerning the Russian constitution. Including postscript. star Mar 27 (1304) DM900

Ds, 10 Jan 1871. 1 p, folio. Contents not stated. sup Oct 15 (1862) $220

Wilhelm II, Deutscher Kaiser, 1859-1941

Autograph Ms, Greek school trans, 1 Aug 1876. 2 pp, 8vo. Sgd at head. star Mar 27 (1312) DM200

Typescript, "Book - Religion and oral tradition"; [c.1920s]. 10 pp, folio. Reply to an essay by Dr. Kessler submitted for comments; sgd. With postcard port. sg Feb 27 (247) $600

Collection of 5 A Ls s, Ls, ANs & photograph, sgd, 30 July 1926 to 8 Apr 1939. 7 pp, 8vo, & photograph. To Kurt Jagow. Mostly about recipient's books & other publications. With related material. star Mar 27 (1317) DM1,300

ALs, 29 Dec 1896. 3 pp, 8vo. To an unnamed uncle. Concerning a coin commemorating his grandfather's 100th birthday. star Mar 27 (1313) DM650

Ls, 4 Aug 1897. 1 p, 4to. To Emile Quinette de Rochemont. Contents not stated. Dar Oct 10 (352) $170

— 29 Nov 1915. 2 pp, 4to. To [the future Emperor] Karl of Austria. Appointing him to the German navy. star Mar 27 (1316) DM950

A Ns s (2), 4 May [19]20 & 6 July [19]37. 3 pp, 8vo. To an unnamed aunt. About his move to Doorn & a projected sculpture. FD Dec 3 (1472) DM750

Ds, 20 Oct 1906. 1 p, 4to. Contents not stated. Dar June 11 (192) $275

— 18 Jan 1910. 1 p, 4to. Appointment of Otto Steinmeister. Dar Apr 9 (381) $170

Photograph, sgd, 11 Feb [19]39. 295mm by 210mm. FD Dec 3 (1472A) DM280

Wilkes, Charles, 1798-1877

Photograph, sgd, [n.d.]. Carte size. Seated, in civilian dress. By Anthony, from a Brady negative. Illus in cat. R June 13 (99) $550

Wilkinson, Sir Geoffrey

Autograph Ms, scientific paper, Synthesis of Two-Carbon Components by Homogeneous Fischer-Tropsch Type reactions, [n.d.]. 7 pp, 4to. Sgd at head. star Mar 26 (854) DM250

Willdenow, Karl Ludwig, 1765-1812

ALs, 20 Sept 1796. 2 pp, 4to. To an unnamed colleague. About the decription & identification of plants. In Latin; sgd at head. star Mar 26 (855) DM360

William, Comte de Champagne, Cardinal, 1135-1202

Document, 1182. 1 p, vellum, 4to. Confirmation of land grants in Flanders to the church at Messines. Including seal (restored). Illus in cat. star Mar 27 (1340) DM2,400

William IV, King of England, 1765-1837

Ds, 1 Dec 1830. 1 p, folio. Appointment of Alexander Dickson as Colonel in the Army. Countersgd by Lord Melbourne. Dar Apr 9 (382) $110

— 20 Dec 1833. 1 p, folio. Appointment of A. S. Dickson as 2d Lieutenant of Artillery. Dar Aug 6 (286) $120

Williams, Eleazar, c.1789-1858

ALs, 27 Mar 1820. 2 pp, 4to. To Jasper Parish. Discussing the westward removal of the Six Nations. CNY Dec 5 (6) $1,100

Williams, Roger, 1603?-83

ALs, 7 June [16]40. 1 p, folio. To Gov. John Winthrop. Regarding hostages held by the Connecticut Indians. Illus in cat. Sang & Spiro collections. CNY May 14 (160) $26,000

Williams, Theodore Samuel ("Ted") —& DiMaggio, Joseph Paul ("Joe")

Group photograph, [n.d.]. 16 by 20 inches. Sgd by both. sup July 10 (993) $440

— Anr, [n.d.]. 16 by 12 inches. Sgd by both. sup July 10 (994) $275

Williams, Theodore Samuel. See: Stengel, Charles Dillon ("Casey") & Williams

Williams, William, Signer from Connecticut

Ds, May 1766. 10 pp, 4to. Debenture of the Connecticut Assembly. sup Oct 15 (1217) $340

— 8 Apr 1789. 1 p, 8vo. Summons. Dar Dec 26 (328) $120

Wilson, Dooley, 1894-1953

Signature, [n.d.]. On orig sheet music (incomplete) of As Time Goes By, from the film Casablanca. 4 pp, 4to. With a photograph. Dar Feb 13 (131) $400

Wilson, Henry, 1812-75

ALs, 1860. 2 pp, 8vo. Recipient unnamed. Offering to speak in recipient's city. sup Oct 15 (1863) $210

Wilson, James, Signer from Pennsylvania

ALs, 27 May 1798. 2 pp, 4to. To William B. Giles. Regarding a debt & the sale of crops. wd June 12 (338) $200

Wilson, Woodrow, 1856-1924

ALs, 30 May 1903. 1 p, 8vo. To Mr. West. Requesting him to fill out a form. Illus in cat. R Mar 7 (158) $750

— 11 Nov 1903. 1 p, 8vo. Recipient unnamed. Sending his autograph. R Mar 7 (157) $550

Collection of 3 Ls s & 2 letters, 23 Jan to 9 Nov 1912. 5 pp, 4to. To Herman Bernstein. Expressing thanks. Letters with stamped signatures. sg Feb 27 (248) $275

Ls s (2), 4 Aug 1913 & 18 Mar 1915. 2 pp, 4to. To Herman Bernstein. Thanking for a letter, & discussing the reprinting of an essay. sg Feb 27 (251) $450

Ls, 24 Jan 1901. 1 p, 4to. To Charles C. Nott. Thanking for a copy of his paper on The Immutability of the Constitution. Illus in cat. sup Oct 15 (1607) $300

— 28 Mar 1901. 1 p, 4to. To Charles Bell Burke. Responding to the suggested conferring of a degree on Prof. Corson. wa Oct 19 (352) $130

— 30 Aug 1907. 1 p, 8vo. To the Cashier, Princeton Bank. Asking for a loan. Dar Oct 10 (353) $160

— 3 Feb 1911. 1 p, 8vo. To C. F. Robinson. Declining a speaking engagement. Trimmed. Dar Feb 13 (340) $110

— 6 Apr 1911. 1 p, 4to. To William C. Liller. Promising to telegraph his arrival time in Indianapolis. Dar Aug 6 (287) $150

— 7 Nov 1912. 1 p, 4to. To William F. Sheehan. Thanking for congratulations on his election. sg Sept 12 (279) $130

— 3 Jan 1913. 1 p, 4to. To F. R. Pemberton. Acknowledging receipt of his letter (carbon copy included) describing William G. McAdoo's shady financial dealings. Dar Dec 26 (329) $250

— 21 Apr 1914. 1 p, 4to. To the Rev. Remensnyder. Hoping "that we will have no war." sg Sept 12 (280) $650

— 9 June 1914. 1 p, 4to. To Herman Bernstein. Insisting that he did not discriminate against Judaism in recent remarks. sg Feb 27 (249) $425

— 29 June 1914. 2 pp, 4to. To Joseph Johnson. Asking that commercial attaches be assigned to the Department of Commerce, not the State Department. Illus in cat. sup Oct 15 (1609) $1,200

— 7 Oct 1914. 1 p, 4to. To Herman Bernstein. Praising recipient's projected newspaper. sg Feb 27 (250) $425

— 21 Aug 1915. 1 p, 8vo. To Mr. Howard. Insisting that publication of his interview with Mr. Shepherd "would very much embarrass [him] in several ways." Illus in cat. sup May 9 (233) $825

— 20 Sept 1916. 1 p, 4to. To Herman Bernstein. About the Jewish role in America. sg Feb 27 (252) $4,000

— 29 Nov 1923. 1 p, 4to. To Mrs. George W. Nichols. Thanking for biscuits. Dar Aug 6 (290) $300

Ds, 10 July 1894. Size not stated. Certification that John I. McLeish has taken courses in general law. k Sept 29 (447) $100

— 22 Oct 1913. 1 p, folio. Appointment of John P. Jackson as Lieutenant Commander in the Navy. Dar June 11 (362) $650

— 22 Feb 1915. 1 p, folio. Appointment of W. Coffin as consul general. R Nov 9 (44) $400

— 24 Jan 1916. 1 p, folio. Appointment of Willard Williams as postmaster. Dar Apr 9 (384) $140

— 1 July 1916. 1 p, folio. Appointment of E. Hunt as Capt. of Infantry. Framed with a photograph. Illus in cat. sup Oct 15 (1610) $800

— 24 July 1916. 1 p, folio. Appointment of J. T. Dean as Lieut.-Colonel of Infantry. With related document. Dar Aug 6 (288) $425

— 17 Aug 1916. 1 p, folio. Appointment of C. H. Wash as Lieut. of Cavalry. sup Oct 15 (1611) $525

— 18 Sept 1916. 1 p, folio. Appointment of Asa Margrave Lehman as lieutenant in the Medical Reserve Corps. Dar Oct 10 (354) $300

— 16 Feb 1917. 1 p, folio. Appointment of John H. Holmead as Notary Public. Framed. wa Oct 19 (351) $75

— 22 Aug 1917. 1 p, folio. Appointment of J. T. Dean as Brigadier General. Dar Aug 6 (289) $550

Group photograph, [n.d.]. 9.5 by 13.5 inches. With King Vittorio Emmanuele of Italy; sgd by Wilson. Dar Apr 9 (383) $250

Photograph, sgd, 7 Apr 1913. 18 by 11 inches. By Harris & Ewing. Framed. Dar June 11 (363) $425

Signature, [1901]. Size not stated. On ptd schedule of classes at Princeton for H. J. Rendell. Also sgd by 7 other professors. sup Oct 15 (1608) $130

Wilson, Woodrow, 1856-1924 —& Others

Group photograph, [c.1913]. 9.9 by 13 inches (image). With his entire cabinet, seated around a table in the White House; sgd by all 11. Illus in cat. sg Feb 27 (253) $2,400

Windsor, Edward, Duke of, 1894-1972

[A theater program, The Bathroom Door. A Farce in One Act, c.1925, sgd by all members of the cast including Prince Edward, with 3 related photographs, sold at Ck on 15 Nov 1991, lot 82, for £280.]

A Ls s (2), [13] & 27 Oct 1924. Length not stated. To Embree McBride. Discussing a party the night before, & responding to her request for his port. Ck Apr 3 (97) £400

ALs, 29 Apr 1936. 4 pp, 8vo. To Grand Duchess Xenia. About an "Easter Egg from [her] Russian monk friend". Illus in cat. sup Oct 15 (1237) $1,300

Photograph, sgd, 10 June 1911. 10 by 7 inches. In ceremonial dress. Framed. Ck Apr 3 (110) £130

— Anr, [c.1911]. 10 by 7 inches. In ceremonial dress. Illus in cat. Ck Apr 3 (109) £140

— Anr, 1939. 12.5 by 10.5 inches. In Admiral's uniform; by Hugh Cecil. Framed. Ck Nov 15 (83) £380

Windsor, Edward, Duke of, 1894-1972 —& Windsor, Wallis Simpson, Duchess of, 1896-1986

[Their signatures on a card, [n.d.], 12mo, sold at Dar on 26 Dec 1991, lot 176, for $300.]

Group photograph, [1950s]. 5 by 7 inches. On board the S.S. United States. Sgd by both. Ck Apr 3 (111) £450

— Anr, [n.d.]. 8 by 10 inches. In front of a limousine; sgd by both. Illus in cat. R Mar 7 (166) $400

Windsor, Wallis Simpson, Duchess of, 1896-1986

Collection of ALs & photograph, 2 Feb [n.y.]. 2 pp, 8vo, & 6.5 by 8.5 inches. To Rosie [Chisholm]. Sending her photograph & mentioning a projected ball. Dar Apr 9 (188) $200

ALs, 15 Dec 1946. 2 pp, 8vo. To Frances Perkins. Regretting they did not see her the day before. Dar Aug 6 (149) $400

See also: Windsor, Edward & Windsor

Winner, Septimus, 1827-1902

ALs, 22 Dec 1888. 1 p, 8vo. To J. C. Green. Giving information about his song Listen to the Mocking Bird. Dar Oct 10 (355) $250

Winslow, John Ancrum, 1811-73

ALs, 13 Apr 1866. 2 pp, size not stated. To David H. Ingraham. Sending his autograph for a charity & paying tribute to deceased soldiers. Dar Aug 6 (133) $275

Winterhalter, Franz Xaver, 1805-73

ALs, 25 Feb 1862. 3 pp, 8vo. To the art dealer Sachse. Informing him that a painting will be finished soon. star Mar 27 (962) DM240

Wise, Henry Alexander, 1806-76

ALs, 16 July 1862. 1 p, 4to. To an unnamed lady. Contents not stated. Def. wa Oct 19 (223) $60

Ds, 26 June 1859. 1 p, 4to. As Governor of Virginia, appointment of B. J. Bruckinbrough as Justice of the Peace. wa Oct 19 (224) $60

Wittgenstein, Ludwig, 1889-1951

— ANON. - Typescript, notes on Wittgenstein's lectures on the philosophy of psychology at Cambridge, 1946/47. 164 pp, 4to. S Dec 12 (321) £1,500 [Price]

Wittgenstein, Paul, 1887-1961

ALs, [n.d.]. 1 p, 4to. To his brother Ludwig. Regretting that he could not play for him. star Mar 27 (1202) DM520

Wladyslaw IV Vasa, King of Poland, 1595-1648

Ls, 24 Sept 1641. 1 p, folio. To Landgraf Wilhelm VI von Hessen-Kassel. Requesting that he allow a shipment of wine to pass through his territories dutyfree. star Mar 27 (1574) DM480

Woehler, Friedrich, 1800-82

ALs, 30 July 1861. 2 pp, 4to. To Jakob Henle. Concerning a defect in the gas supply system of the Goettingen anatomical museum. star Mar 26 (856) DM1,900

— 14 July 1872. 1 p, 4to. To a library society in Vienna. Regretting he is unable to send books. star Mar 26 (857) DM550

Wolcott, Oliver, Signer from Connecticut

ADs, 19 June 1760. 1 p, 5.75 by 3 inches. Notice that the defendant Fisher has been arrested "for Want of Estate". sup Oct 15 (1219) $350

Ds, 20 Jan 1753. 1 p, 4to. As Lichfield County Sheriff, notice that a writ (on verso) regarding a debt has been executed. sup Oct 15 (1218) $360

— 1781. Size not stated. Pay order for the State of Connecticut, sgd as Auditor. rf Sept 21 (26) $80

Wolf, Hugo, 1860-1903

Autograph music, song, beginning "Das ist ein Brausen und Heulen...", to a text by Heinrich Heine, 31 May 1878. 2 pp, 32cm by 25cm. Scored for voice & piano; sgd at head. Stichvorlage. Illus in cat. star Mar 27 (1203) DM17,000

— Autograph music, song, beginning "Wie glaenzt der helle Mond...", to a text by Gottfried Keller, [n.d.]. 3 pp, 34cm by 26cm. Scored for voice & piano; sgd at head. Stichvorlage. Repaired. Illus in cat. star Mar 27 (1204) DM16,000

— Autograph music, song, Singt mein Schatz wie ein Fink, to a text by Gottfried Keller; [c.1890]. 3 pp, folio. Scored for voice & piano; sgd. Ptr's copy. HN June 26 (995) DM16,000

ALs, [6 July 1894]. 6 pp, 8vo. To Melanie Koechert. Quoting from last year's diary, & reporting about his activities. star Mar 27 (1205) DM2,600

— 18 Aug 1897. 3 pp, 8vo. To [Heinrich Potpeschnigg?]. About a discussion with Mahler regarding his opera Der Corregidor. star Mar 27 (1206) DM3,100

Wolff, Christian von, 1679-1754

ALs, 20 Sept 1736. 2 pp, 4to. To an unnamed bookseller. Concerning rumors about his return to Halle. star Mar 26 (859) DM1,100

Wolfgang, Herzog von Braunschweig-Grubenhagen, 1531-95

Ls, 4 Dec 1574. 2 pp, folio. To the magistrate of an unnamed town. About problems with the purchase of wine for his court. HN Nov 28 (1862) DM320

Wolfgang Wilhelm, Pfalzgraf von Neuburg, 1578-1653

Ls, 10 Nov 1609. 1 p, folio. To Engelbert von Orsbeck & Paul Hahn. Raising taxes at Neuenahr, Sinzig & Remagen. Also sgd by Margrave Ernst zu Brandenburg-Ansbach. star Mar 27 (1565) DM550

— 21 Oct 1628. 1 p, folio. To Johann Adolf von Brembt. Ptd circular, inviting him to the funeral of his wif. star Mar 27 (1566) DM320

Wolfram, Robert Hieron

Autograph Ms, Ferien-Reise ins Meissner Hochland und nach Boehmen, 1 to 14 Aug 1840. 94 leaves, 177mm by 107mm, in contemp bds. Including 5 small pen-&-ink drawings & 2 pen-&-ink maps. HH May 12 (23) DM500

Wollstonecraft, Mary, 1759-97

ALs, [30 Dec 1790]. 1 p, 4to. To Catharine Macaulay. Presenting her with a copy of her Vindication of the Rights of Man. With autograph copy of Macaulay's reply on integral leaf. Imperf. pn June 11 (21) £5,500 [Edwards]

Wood, Grant, 1892-1942

Autograph sentiment, 1937. 8 by 9 inches. Inscr to Mrs. & Mrs. R. D. Smith, on ptd reproduction of a painting. Dar Aug 6 (291) $160

Wood, Natalie, 1938-81. See: Wagner, Robert & Wood

Wood, Thomas John, 1823-1906

Autograph Ms, report about the Battle of Murfreesboro, 11 Jan 1863. 12 pp, 4to. Sgd. sup Oct 15 (1073) $3,600

Wool, John Ellis, 1784-1869

Photograph, sgd, [n.d.]. Carte size. In uniform. By Anthony, from a Brady negative. Illus in cat. R June 13 (106) $350

Woolf, Leonard Sidney, 1880-1969

Ms, A Gentile & the Jews, [n.d.]. 6 pp, size not stated. Review of Hilaire Belloc's The Jews. Ck Apr 3 (77) £240

Woolf, Virginia, 1882-1941

ALs, 12 May 1923. 1 p, 8vo. To Mr. Temple. Thanking for forwarding a jacket. sg Feb 27 (254) $175

Ls, 20 Mar 1929. 2 pp, 4to. To Quentin Bell. Chatty letter, saying she wants to write "an entirely new kind of book". With autograph conclusion. Sgd Virginia. CNY June 9 (205) $1,600

— 3 Dec [1933]. 2 pp, 4to. To Quentin Bell. Chatting about T. S. Eliot & other visitors. CNY June 9 (206) $1,500

— 21 Dec 1933. 2 pp, 4to. To Quentin Bell.

Commenting on the homosexuality of some acquaintances. CNY June 9 (208) $1,500
— 24 Jan [1934]. 2 pp, 4to. To Quentin Bell. Chatting about her activities. P June 17 (413) $1,000
— 5 Dec 1935. 2 pp, 4to. To Antonio Aita. Declining an invitation to a PEN conference in Argentina. star Mar 26 (525) DM1,600
Letter, 13 Dec [1933]. 2 pp, 4to. To Quentin Bell. About Miss Hutchinson's "marriage to the richest Jew in Europe" & various acquaintances. CNY June 9 (207) $700

Woolworth, Frank Winfield, 1852-1919
ALs, 28 Dec 1889. 1 p, 8vo. To John Quevedo. Announcing his own & Mr. Hessel's visit. Illus in cat. Dar June 11 (364) $700

Wordsworth, William, 1770-1850
Series of 4 A Ls s, 8 June [1842], 28 Oct [1844] & [n.d.]. 9 pp, 12mo & 8vo. To Charles Pasley. About a variety of matters. CNY Dec 5 (356) $2,800
ALs, 8 Oct 1836. 1 p, 4to. To Thomas Attwood. Giving permission to set his poems to music. pn June 11 (90) £780 [Browning]
Autograph quotation, sgd, Oct 1834. 16mo. Quoting Akenside on the function of the poet. Ingilby collection. pn Nov 14 (114) £360

World War II
— Atomic Bomb. - Document, 6 Aug 1945. 10 by 8 inches. Ptd certification by Sec of War Stimson that John L. Priest participated in the production of the Atomic Bomb. Sgd by Edward Teller & 6 crew members of atomic bomb flights. Dar June 11 (56) $500
— Fuchida, Capt. Mitsuo. - Autograph postcard, sgd, [14 Dec 1962]. To Mr. & Mrs. Ray Votaw. Sending Christmas greetings. Dar Dec 26 (333) $200
— Germand Air Force. - Document, 5 May 1945. 1 p, 4to. Minute agreeing to terms of unconditional surrender; sgd by Major Gen. Uebe for the German Air Force, Northern Zone. With related documents. pn June 11 (44) £1,100
— Holocaust. - Ms, detailed family, medical & work record kept by an unnamed Jewish doctor at the temporary work-camp of Lundenburg, Czechoslovakia, 1944-45. 144 pp (7 blank), 4to, in half cloth bdg (exercise book). sg Dec 19 (110) $650
— Nagasaki. - Autograph Ms by Fred J. Olivi, co-pilot of the B-29 on 9 Aug 1945, 8 pp, 4to. Diary of the bombing. With authentication in Olivi's hand. Dar June 11 (58) $8,000
— Rosenthal, Joe. - Signature, [11 July 1945]. On philatelic envelope bearing stamps reproducing his Iwo Jima photograph. Dar June 11 (368) $100
— Zakhaym, Tchyil. - Ls, 25 Apr 1947. 1 p, 4to. To Trygve Lie. Requesting that he be allowed to leave the camp in the American zone of Germany to go to Palestine. Partly ptd. Dar Oct 10 (223) $325

Wrangel, Carl Gustav, Graf von Salmis, 1613-76
Ls, 1 Feb 1662. 1 p, folio. To M. de Lubienietz. Promising to give orders for a payment to recipient's wife. With engraved port. star Mar 27 (1753) DM250

Wrede, Karl Philipp, Fuerst, 1767-1838
Collection of ALs & Ls, 18 Mar 1831 & 31 Aug 1836. 5 pp, 4to. To Quartermaster Gen. von Bangold. About an office to be established at Speyer & the importance of railways for defense. star Mar 27 (1754) DM320
ALs, 19 Nov [n.y.]. 1 p, 4to. To an unnamed baron. About an audience with the King of Bavaria. star Mar 27 (1755) DM200

Wright, Frank Lloyd, 1869-1959
Collection of 12 A Ls s, 6 Ls s, postcard, sgd, & 2 telegrams, 1909 to 1954. 51 pp, various sizes. To his daughter Catherine Baxter, her husband & daughter, & to his 1st wife Catherine Tobin Wright. Documenting the difficulty of his relationship with his family. CNY June 9 (209) $10,000
Ls, 22 May 1958. 2 pp, 4to. To Lewis Mumford. Inviting him to Taliesin. Illus in cat. sup Oct 15 (1866) $1,750

Wright, Henry, 1835-95
ADs, 2 Apr 1887. 1 p, 8vo. As manager of the Philadelphia Ball Club, agreement with pitcher Charles J. Ferguson. Dar Oct 10 (87) $8,500

Wright, Orville, 1871-1948
Ls, 8 Jan 1904. 2 pp, 4to. To Carl Dienstbach. Describing their 1st powered flight & including a newspaper clipping (present). Lester D. Gardner collection. CNY Dec 5 (138) $55,000
— 11 Oct 1918. 1 p, 4to. To William H. Kelly. Explaining why "no gain in efficiency is to be secured by using [recipient's] design" for a new propeller. Dar Dec 26 (334) $5,000
— 31 Oct 1921. 2 pp, 4to. To Lester D. Gardner. Discussing the influence of S. P. Langley & O. Lilienthal on their own aerodynamic experiments. CNY Dec 5 (144) $9,500
— 10 Nov 1921. 1 p, 4to. To Lester D. Gardner. Regarding the controversy over Glenn Curtiss & Samuel Langley's flying machine. CNY May 14 (24) $2,000
— 28 Nov 1923. 2 pp, 4to. To Lester D. Gardner. Protesting against the use of an earlier misleading article in a projected

publication. CNY Dec 5 (146) $4,000
— 4 Apr 1935. 1 p, 4to. To Willard Dickerson. Requesting data for a report on an estate. Framed with a photograph. Dar June 11 (370) $1,000
— 2 Dec 1943. 9 pp, 4to. To Lester D. Gardner. Describing his investigations of the Manly-Langley engine & concluding "that the basic design of the motor was [S. M.] Balzer's". Illus in cat. CNY May 14 (27) $8,000
— 11 Dec 1943. 2 pp, 4to. To Lester D. Gardner. Discussing a letter by Carl Dienstbach written in 1903. CNY Dec 5 (147) $4,500

Ds, 1926. 5 by 4 inches. Aviation License issued to Adolph P. Kerr. Illus in cat. sup Oct 15 (1868) $1,250
— [n.d.]. 4 pp, 3 by 4 inches. Aviator's Certificate issued to John Francis Gill. sup Oct 15 (1869) $800

Photograph, sgd & inscr, [c.1920-1930]. 230mm by 167mm (image). Inscr to Roy G. Fitzgerald. CNY Dec 5 (149) $1,000

Signature, [Sept 1946]. On airline booklet, 4 pp, 8vo. Dar Aug 6 (301) $475

Wright, Orville, 1871-1948 —& Others

Group photograph, 1943. 11 by 8 inches. With Igor Sikorsky & Frank Gregory in front of 1st helicopter delivered to the army. Sgd by all 3; inscr to D. Levy by Gregory. Illus in cat. sup Oct 15 (1870) $2,100

Wright, Orville, 1871-1948 —& Wright, Wilbur, 1867-1912

[A photograph of the 1st flight at Kitty Hawk, sgd by Orville Wright, framed with a photograph of Orville & a photograph of Wilbur Wright sgd & inscr by him to William Berri, [n.d.], overall size 17 by 15 inches, sold at Dar on 9 Apr 1992, lot 72, for $5,000.]

Ls, 21 Dec 1904. 2 pp, 4to. To Carl Dienstbach. Reporting about their flight experiments at Huffman Prairie. Sgd Wilbur & Orville Wright, in Orville's hand; initialled O.W. Lester D. Gardner collection. CNY Dec 5 (139) $18,000
— 17 Nov 1905. 1 p, 4to. To Carl Dienstbach. Reporting on their 3d season of test flights. Sgd Wilbur and Orville Wright per O.W., in Orville's hand. Lester D. Gardner collection. CNY Dec 5 (140) $18,000
— 17 Nov 1905. 2 pp, 4to. To Carl Dienstbach. Giving names of independent witnesses to their flights. Sgd for both by O. Wright. CNY May 14 (17) $13,000
— 27 Mar 1907. 1 p, 4to. To Carl Dienstbach. Declining to make an exhibition flight for the Aero Club of America. Sgd Wright Brothers/ O.W., in Orville's hand. Lester D. Gardner collection. CNY Dec 5 (141) $3,800

Letter, 28 Dec 1903. 2 pp, 4to. To Carl Dienstbach. Reporting about their 1st flights. With related material. Illus in cat. CNY May 14 (15) $14,000

Group photograph, 1 May 1909. 3.5 by 5.5 inches. Sgd by both & inscr to Elizabeth in Wilbur's hand. Illus in cat. sup Oct 15 (1867) $8,250
— Wright, Milton. - ALs, 22 Dec 1903. 3 pp, 8vo. To Carl Dienstbach. Giving news about his sons' first flights at Kitty Hawk. CNY May 14 (14) $12,000

Wright, Wilbur, 1867-1912

ALs, 4 Mar 1910. 1 p, 4to. To Hart O. Berg. Referring to Mr. Peartree's departure & new German motors. Including pencilled notes in other hands. CNY May 14 (18) $5,500
— 18 July 1911. 2 pp, 8vo. To Hart O. Berg. About the abrogation of a contract. Illus in cat. CNY May 14 (21) $4,500

Ls, 5 July 1910. 1 p, 4to. To Hart O. Berg. About their patent suit against Glenn Curtiss & Louis Paulhan, new flight records, etc. Lester D. Gardner collection. CNY Dec 5 (142) $8,000
— 16 Nov 1910. 2 pp, 4to. To Hart O. Berg. Giving an account of recent competitions with other airplanes. Illus in cat. CNY May 14 (20) $12,000
— 3 Feb 1912. 1 p, 4to. To Robert J. Collier. Agreeing not to enforce their patents to permit the race for the Gordon Bennett Cup. Lester D. Gardner collection. CNY Dec 5 (143) $4,000

See also: Wright, Orville & Wright

Wundt, Wilhelm, 1832-1920

ALs, 28 Feb 1883. 4 pp, 8vo. To an unnamed colleague. Discussing the "cosmological problem". Ammann collection. star Mar 26 (861) DM420

Wyatt, Sir Thomas, 1503?-42

Ds, 10 Mar 1535. 2 pp, vellum, 8vo. Receipt by Lord Vaux for £280 from Roger Cholmley for the manor of Newyngton Luces; sgd as witness. Also sgd by others. pn Nov 14 (235) £4,800 [Sawyer]

Wyeth, Andrew

Signature, [n.d.]. On verso of art postcard. Illus in cat. Dar Aug 6 (302) $225

Wykeham, William of, 1324-1404

— Atkinson, George. - Ms, A True and Most exact Pedigree descending from the Antient Family of the Strettons to William de Wickham Lord Bishop of Winchester... and from thence to this present yeare 1694.

Scroll, vellum, 17 by 64 inches. Showing descendants of the bishop's sister Agnes. Including illuminated coats-of-arms. L Nov14 (357) £150

Wylie, Philip, 1902-71

Typescript, story, An Emergency Mate, 1952. 20 pp, 4to. Sgd & inscr to Jack Leonard. With related ALs. sg Feb 27 (258) $300

— Typescript, story, Crunch Finds the Body, 1952. 20 pp, 4to. Sgd & inscr to Jack Leonard. sg Feb 27 (259) $300

Wyndham, John, Pseud. of John Wyndham Parkes Lucas Beynon Harris, 1903-69

Collection of 350 A Ls s & Ls s, 3 Sept 1939 to 26 June 1945. Over 1000 pp, various sizes. To his [future] wife Grace. Covering various aspects of the war. Including 21 poems (20 autograph), 2 Christmas cards, & a later letter. S July 21 (186) £3,800 [Rota]

Y

Yawkey, Thomas Austin, 1903-76 —& Griffith, Clark Calvin, 1869-1955

Ds, 8 May 1951. 1 p, 4to. Transfer of the contract of Fermin R. Guerra from the Boston Red Sox to the Washington Senators. Dar Aug 6 (108) $160

Yeats, William Butler, 1865-1939

ALs, 20 June 1935. 1 p, 4to. Recipient unnamed. Thanking for a message. sup Oct 15 (1871) $400

— 26 May [n.y.]. 2 pp, 8vo. To Cynthia Asquith. Responding to her request for a poem for children. S July 21 (189) £380 [Cunningham]

Yevtushenko, Yevgeny Aleksandrovich

Autograph Ms, poem, 4 six-line stanzas; [n.d.]. 1 p, folio. Sgd. star Mar 26 (285) DM700

Yorck von Wartenburg, Ludwig, Graf, 1759-1830

ALs, 11 Dec 1811. 3 pp, folio. To Capt. von Boyen. About some military appointments. star Mar 27 (1757) DM750

Ls, 20 Mar 1812. 3 pp, folio. To the military administration of Eastern Prussia. Sending a survey of horses & servants. star Mar 27 (1758) DM360

York, Alvin Cullum, 1887-1964

Ls, 16 Aug 1929. 1 p, 4to. To James Vance. Inquiring about secondhand books. Matted with a photograph. Dar June 11 (367) $450

Youmans, Vincent, 1898-1946

ALs, 10 June 1944. 1 p, 8vo. To Mr. Manfred. Sending his autograph. Dar Feb 13 (342) $100

Young, Brigham, 1801-77

Ds, 23 May 1846. 1 p, 9.75 by 8 inches. Appointment for Oliver B. Huntington as missionary; addressed to Elder Reuben Hedlock. In the hand of & also sgd by Willard Richards. Illus in cat. cb Feb 12 (91) $2,750

Young, Denton True ("Cy"), 1867-1955

Signature, [1938]. On official Boston National League score card, 12 pp, 6.5 by 10 inches. Dar Aug 6 (98) $160

— Anr, [19]47. 4 by 2.25 inches (card). Dar Apr 9 (110) $160

— Anr, [n.d.]. 16mo (card). Dar Dec 26 (115) $300

Younger, Thomas Coleman, 1844-1916 —& Others

Group photograph, [n.d.]. Carte size. Composite photograph of 6 members of the Younger Gang. Illus in cat. R June 13 (283) $1,300

Z

Zadkine, Ossip, 1890-1967

A Ls s (2), 4 & 17 Dec 1954. 3 pp, 8vo. To Mrs. Sothmann. Declining to participate in exhibitions. HN June 26 (997) DM380

Zangwill, Israel, 1864-1926

Collection of 3 A Ls s & 3 Ls s, 1898 to 1904. 6 pp, various sizes. To Herman Bernstein. Dealing with Jewish literature & recipient's poems. sg Feb 27 (262) $150

Series of 6 A Ls s, 8 Feb 1899 to 29 Aug 1913. 10 pp, various sizes. To Professor Wiener. Mostly about meetings. sup Oct 15 (1872) $320

Zapata, Emiliano, 1879-1919

Ls, 20 July 1916. 1 p, 4to. To Gen. Francisco Mendoza. Ordering that weapons taken from soldiers be returned to their owners. Faded. sup Oct 15 (1392) $450

Zelter, Karl Friedrich, 1758-1832

ALs, 5 June 1803. 1 p, 4to. To [Friedrich Matthisson]. Returning some contributions with Herder's requests for corrections. star Mar 27 (1207) DM3,000

Zhukovskii, Vassilii Andreevich, 1783-1852

Series of 5 A Ls s, 13 June 1842 to 6 Oct 1849. 11 pp, 4to. To Nestor von Schloezer. Requesting his help concerning the shipment of paintings & other objects to the Czarina & her son. star Mar 26 (454) DM1,300

Ziegfeld, Florenz, 1869-1932

Autograph telegram, sgd, [n.d.]. 1 p, 8vo. To Cochran, Cockranus, Piecy. Offering a theater contract. Dar Apr 9 (386) $180

Zieten, Hans Joachim von, 1699-1786

Ls, 10 Aug 1780. 1 p, 4to. To an unnamed chaplain. Congratulating him on the birth of a son. star Mar 27 (1760) DM900

Zille, Heinrich, 1858-1929

Series of 3 A Ls s, 14 Apr 1924, 2 Jan 1925 & [n.d.]. 8 pp, 4to & 8vo. To K. Lemmer. About his health problems, lack of incentive to work, etc. star Mar 27 (964) DM620

A Ls s (2), 3 Oct 1924 & 29 June 1926. 3 pp, folio & 8vo. To the Ed of the journal Simplizissimus. Sending contributions, & discussing the seizure of a drawing. HH Nov 6 (2113) DM850

ALs, 26 Apr [19]17. 1 p, 8vo. To the Ed of the journal Ulk. Informing him that he will not be sending a caricature his week. FD Dec 3 (1473) DM270

Autograph postcard, sgd, 8 Jan 1921. To F. Doerfler. Explaining that he hopes to be able to send the promised engravings next week. star Mar 27 (963) DM270

Zimmermann, Johann Georg, 1728-95

ALs, 18 May 1783. 5 pp, 4to. To [Gottlieb Fritze]. Regarding the position of physician to the Landgrave of Hesse-Kassel. Illus in cat. star Mar 26 (862) DM1,250

Zola, Emile, 1840-1902

ALs, 12 Dec 1865. 1 p, size not stated. Recipient unnamed. Discussing the impossibility of stretching the Librairie Hachette's budget to the sending of books overseas. With engraved port. Ck Apr 3 (37) £240

— 7 Oct [18]92. 1 p, 8vo. To an unnamed pbr. Requesting that a journal be sent to Paris. sg Feb 27 (264) $225

— 18 May 1901. 1 p, 8vo. Recipient unnamed. Promising to send a copy of his work La verite en marche to Dr. Engel. HH May 13 (2066) DM320

— 9 Oct 1901. 2 pp, 8vo. Recipient unnamed. About a delivery of coal. Framed with a photograph. Dar June 11 (260) $600

Zrinyi, Miklos, 1620-64

Ls, 29 Oct 1656. 4 pp, folio. To Emperor Ferdinand III. Defending his conduct of war in Croatia. In Latin. star Mar 27 (1761) DM1,800

Zuckmayer, Carl, 1896-1977

Typescript, poem, Wintervoegel, 19 Jan [19]52. 1 p, 4to. 7 stanzas, sgd & with holograph inscr to Kurt Triemel. HH Nov 6 (2115) DM320

Collection of 2 A Ls s, 9 Ls s, & ANs, 27 July 1934 to 19 Nov 1960. 15 pp, various sizes. To his friend Rudolf Joseph. Personal correspondence, chatting about meetings, his own & recipient's work & projects, etc. star Mar 26 (528) DM1,500

— Collection of 2 A Ls s, AL & Ls, 24 Apr 1960 to 24 Jan 1972. 14 pp, folio & 8vo (partly on verso of picture postcards). To Albrecht Joseph. Chatting about his travels & activities, reminiscing, etc. star Mar 26 (531) DM650

ALs, 8 Apr 1926. 1 p, 4to. To the Ed of the journal Simplizissimus. Offering a poem for print. HH Nov 6 (2114) DM200

— 10 Nov 1955. 6 pp, 8vo. To Hella Jacobowski. Expressing apprehension about political developments & the communist threat. star Mar 26 (530) DM700

Series of 14 Ls s, 1 Oct 1941 to 22 Feb 1951. 25 pp, 4to & 8vo. To Gottfried Bermann Fischer & his wife. Interesting letters about his work in exile, his reception in Germany immediately after the war, etc. star Mar 26 (529) DM3,200

— Series of 4 Ls s, 1956. 7 pp, mostly 8vo. To Hella Jacobowski. About a variety of professional & private matters. HH May 13 (2073) DM260

— Series of 3 Ls s, 1957. 3 pp, 8vo & folio.. To Hella Jacobowski. About a variety of organizational matters. HH May 13 (2074) DM260

Zweig, Arnold, 1887-1968

Series of 3 A Ls s, 28/30 June 1918 to 31 Aug 1947. 12 pp, 4to & 8vo. To Martin & Sophie Moerike. Commenting on the political & intellectual situation in Germany & Europe, Jews & "the Palestinian option", etc. star Mar 26 (532) DM2,600

Zweig, Stefan, 1881-1942

Typescript, poem, Matkowskys Othello, 1909. 2 pp, folio. 11 four-line stanzas, sgd. Some autograph corrections. star Mar 26 (533) DM520

Collection of 14 A Ls s, 28 Ls s, letter, 25 postcards, sgd (24 autograph), & 5 telegrams, 1918 to 1939. 70 pp, mostly 4to, & cards. To Carl Seelig. Interesting letters about his work, literary plans, other authors, the political situation, etc. star Mar 26 (536) DM14,000

— Collection of 58 A Ls s, 38 Ls s & 14 autograph postcards, sgd, 1928 to 1941. 143 pp, 4to & 8vo, & cards. To Heinrich

Eisemann. About his autograph collection, the political situation, the war, his emigration, etc. In German & English. star Mar 26 (537) DM20,000

ALs, 18 Sept 1900. 1 p, 4to. To [R. M. Werner]. Sending information about Hebbel autographs not recorded in recipient's list. star Mar 26 (534) DM540

— [13 Oct 1939]. 1 p, 4to. To Olga Torbe. About his move into his house in Bath. star Mar 26 (541) DM320

Ls s (2), 9 Oct 1936 & 7 June 1937. 3 p, 4to. To Paul Zech. Commenting on Zech's novel. 1 Ls on verso of a letter addressed to him. star Mar 26 (539) DM900

Ls, 5 Dec 1938. 2 pp, 4to. To an unnamed author. Giving his opinion on recipient's Ms about Hitler & Austria. star Mar 26 (540) DM240

Autograph postcard, sgd, [29 Nov 1934]. To Cyril Lakin. Regretting he could not see him in London. star Mar 26 (538) DM210

Autograph quotation, 2 lines from Verwirrung der Gefuehle, [1926?]. 8vo. Mtd with a port. JG Sept 27 (491) DM300

PART II

Books

ATLASES, BOOKS, BROADSIDES, AND MAPS & CHARTS ARE REPORTED IN THIS SECTION

A

Aa, Cornelis van der

— Atlas van de Zeehavens der Bataafsche Republiek.... Amst., [c.1970]. Folio, half cloth; soiled. With engraved title & 31 double-page plates.. Reprint of 1805 Ed. B May 12 (2036) HF500

Aa, Pieter van der, 1659-1733

— Atlas du monde. [Leiden, c.1710]. Folio, contemp calf over bds; worn. With c.141 (of 194) maps only. Lacking titles. cb Oct 10 (112) $3,750

— La Galerie agreable du monde...tome troisieme d'Amerique. Leiden, [1729]. Folio, modern half calf. With double-page engraved map, 19 double-page views, 1 folding view & 24 plates. Some water-staining at upper margins, affecting engraved surface. S June 25 (447) £1,300 [Silva]

Abarbanel, Henry

— English School and Family Reader, for the Use of Israelites.... NY, 1883. 1st Ed. 8vo, cloth. sg June 25 (6) $150

Abbad Lasierra, Inigo

— Historia geografica, civil y politica, de la Isla de S. Juan Bautista de Puerto Rico. Madrid, 1788. 4to, modern sheep gilt. sg Dec 5 (1) $800

Abbadie, Jacques

— Traite de la verite de la religion chretienne.... Rotterdam, 1689. 3d Ed. 2 vols. 12mo, contemp mor. bba Nov 28 (150) £400 [Pickering & Chatto]

Abbe, Dorothy

— The Dwiggins Marionettes, a Complete Experimental Theatre in Miniature. NY, [1970]. Folio, cloth. K July 12 (180) $75

Anr copy. Cloth, in d/j. O Sept 24 (1) $80

Abbey Collection, John R.

— The Italian Manuscripts in the Library of Major J. R. Abbey. L, 1969. 4to, orig cloth, in d/j. sg Oct 31 (186) $60

— Life in England in Aquatint and Lithography. L, 1953. One of 400. 4to, cloth, in d/j. bba Feb 27 (418) £130 [Pagan]

Anr Ed. L, 1972. 4to, orig cloth, in soiled d/j. Reprint of the 1953 Ed. bba Dec 19 (244) £65 [Cline]

Anr copy. Orig cloth in frayed d/j. Reprint of the 1953 Ed. DW Jan 29 (290) £75

— [Sale Catalogue] Catalogue of Valuable Printed Books and Fine Bindings. L, 1965-89. 11 vols. 4to, orig bds or wraps. With price lists. bba May 28 (546) £130 [Dawson]

Parts 1-7. 4to, 2 in wraps; others, bds. O Sept 24 (2) $225

Parts 1-9 only. Orig bds or wraps. With price lists. bba May 28 (547) £120 [Heuer]

— Scenery of Great Britain and Ireland in Aquatint and Lithography. L, 1952. One of 500. 4to, orig cloth in worn d/j. bba Feb 27 (416) £110 [Pagan]

Anr copy. Orig cloth; extremities rubbed. Ck Oct 18 (36) £220

Anr copy. Orig cloth in worn d/j. DW Oct 2 (84) £160

Anr copy. Cloth in frayed d/j. DW Jan 29 (291) £115

Anr Ed. L, 1972. 4to, orig cloth, in d/j. Reprint of 1952 Ed. bba Feb 27 (417) £65 [Whatman]

— Travel in Aquatint and Lithography. L, 1972. 2 vols. 4to, orig cloth, in d/js. Reprint of 1956-57 Ed. bba May 28 (478) £80 [Graves-Johnston]; pnE Dec 4 (223) £190

Abbildung...

— Abbildung und Beschreibung derer saemtlichen Berg-Wercks-Beamten und Bedienten.... Nuremberg, 1721. With 25 plates. Bound with: Abbildung und Beschreibung derer saemtlichen Schmeltz-Huetten.... Nuremberg, 1721. With 25 plates. 4to, old bds. Library stamp on 1st title. S Dec 5 (446) £2,800 [Watson]

Abbondanza, Vincenzo

— Dizionario storico delle vite di tutti i monarchi ottomani.... Rome, 1786. 4to, contemp vellum. With frontis, 2 plates, 2 folding plans & folding map hand-colored in outline. S June 30 (221) £1,300 [Atabey]

Abbot, Abiel, 1770-1828

— Letters Written in the Interior of Cuba.... Bost., 1829. 1st Ed. 8vo, orig half cloth; worn, lacking front free endpaper. sg June 18 (1) $50

Abbott, Berenice

— The World of Atget. NY, [1964]. 1st Ed. 4to, cloth, in d/j. bbc Feb 17 (173) $55

Abbott, Berenice —& McCausland, Elizabeth

— Changing New York. NY, 1939. 4to, orig cloth, in d/j; worn. bbc Feb 17 (163) $250

Anr copy. Cloth, in chipped d/j. sg Oct 8 (1) $350

Abbott, Edwin Abbott

— Flatland. L, 1884. 1st Ed. 8vo, ptd vellum. Browned. sg June 11 (1) $450

Abbott, George

— Views of the Forts of Bhurtpoore & Weire. L, 1827. Folio, contemp half mor gilt; rubbed. With litho title, dedication & 11 plates on india paper mtd. Letterpress plate list tipped onto front free endpaper; some spotting. Ck Nov 29 (1) £380

Abbott, Gorham D.

— Mexico and the United States. NY, 1869. 8vo, orig cloth; worn & spotted. With 2 ports & folding hand-colored map. O Jan 14 (1) $770

Abbott, Henry

— Antiquities of Rome.... L, [early 1820s]. Folio, modern cloth. With 24 plates; this Ed without panoramas. Library stamps on plate versos; some soiling. S Nov 15 (763) £450 [Elliott]

Abbott, Jacob, 1803-79

— Rollo's Travels.... Bost., 1840. 1st Ed. 12mo, orig cloth. Epstein copy. sg Apr 29 (3) $500

A'Beckett, Gilbert Abbott, 1811-56

— The Comic History of England. L, 1846-48. Illus by John Leech. In orig 20/19 parts. 8vo, orig wraps; rebacked, front cover of Part 1 loose. Epstein copy. sg Apr 29 (1) $850

1st Ed in orig 20/19 parts. 8vo, orig pictorial wraps; some spine panels def, some edges chipped. Not collated for ads. sg Mar 5 (1) $275

1st Ed in Book form. L, 1847-48. 2 vols. 8vo, later mor gilt by Riviere, orig cloth covers & spines bound in at end. With 20 hand-colored plates.. Extra-illus with 22 ink & pencil drawings by John Leech mtd to size opposite the relevant plate of illust, 21 of these heightened with watercolor. Gardner-Aykroyd copy. C May 20 (3) £4,800 [Marlborough]

Anr copy. Contemp half mor; spines scuffed; some joints cracked. cb Sept 26 (145) $60

Anr copy. Calf gilt; rubbed. sg Mar 5 (2) $80

Anr Ed. [L]: Punch Office, 1855-53. 2 vols in 1. 8vo, contemp half calf; rubbed, loose. With 20 hand-colored plates. F Sept 26 (261) $50

Anr Ed. L, [c.1880]. 2 vols in 1. 8vo, contemp calf gilt. F Mar 26 (77) $170

Ed on Japanese vellum. L, [1897]. 2 vols. 4to, contemp mor gilt by Cox, his own copy with his library ticket. With 10 hand-colored plates & illusts, all on india paper mtd. Ck Oct 18 (206) £320

— The Comic History of Rome. L, [1852]. 1st Ed in Book form. Illus by John Leech. 8vo, contemp half calf; scuffed & worn. With engraved title & 10 hand-colored plates. cb Sept 26 (144) $60

Abel, Clarke

— Narrative of Journey in the Interior of China. L 1818. 4to, 19th-cent half calf by Leighton, using orig cloth bds. With 4 maps & 19 plates, 8 hand-colored. S May 14 (1281) £750 [Baring]

Abel, Niels Henrik

— Oeuvres. Christiana, 1839. Bound with: Memoire sur un propriete generale d'une classe tres-etendue de fonctions transcendantes. Berlin, 1826. 2 vols in 1. 4to, 19th-cent half mor. Ck Nov 29 (116) £240

Abelin, Johann Philipp, d.c.1634

— Histor. Chronick oder Beschr. der merckwuerdigsten Geschichte, so sich von Anfang der Welt.... Frankfurt, 1743-59. Vol I only. Contemp lea; worn & wormed. With engraved title & 31 plates. HH May 12 (709A) DM2,100

— Historische Chronica, oder Beschreibung der Fuernehmsten. [Frankfurt], 1674. Folio, contemp pigskin over wooden bds with brass catches; lacking clasps, some wear. With folding world map, folding plate & 31 full-page plates. Frontis trimmed & mtd; some soiling & stains; minor tears; opening leaves loose. sg Oct 24 (137) $850

Abercrombie, Lascelles, 1881-1938. See: Gregynog Press

Abert, James W.

— Report and Map of the Examination of New Mexico. [Wash.], 1848. 1st Ed. 8vo, modern cloth. With folding map & 24 plates. Senate Exec. Doc. 23, 30th Congress, 1st Session. cb Feb 12 (1) $225

— Western America in 1846-1847. San Francisco, 1966. Folio, cloth. With 14 color plates & 2 folding maps. NH May 30 (553) $55

Abraham a Sancta Clara, 1644-1709

— Etwas fuer Alle, das ist: Eine kurtze Beschreibung allerley Stands- Amkbts- und gewerbs-Persohnen.... Wuerzburg, 1711. Bound with: Gack, Gack, Gack, Gack, a Ga. Einer wunderseltzamen Hennen in dem Hertzogthumb Bayrn. Munich, 1687 8vo, contemp pigskin over wooden bds; wormed & worn. Some browning; lacking 4 leaves in 1st work. HH May 12 (1094) DM1,600

Abravanel, Judah, d.1535

— Dialogi di amore. Venice: Aldus, 1541. 2d Ed. 8vo, later half calf; rubbed. Some marginal staining. bba Sept 19 (279) £340 [Hesketh & Ward]

Anr Ed. Venice, 1549. 8vo, old vellum. Margins trimmed; front free endpaper excised; marginal scrawls on several leaves. sg Oct 24 (1) $225

Abstract...

— An Abstract of the Evidence...on the Part of the Petitioners for the Abolition of the Slave Trade. L, 1791. 1st Ed. 8vo, orig bds; rebacked in calf, soiled, joints & corners worn. With folding map & folding diagram. Diagram with early repairs to tear in blank corner & 1 tear into image. b June 22 (218) £360

Abul-Farajius, Gregorius. See: Grighor, Abu al-Faraj

Academie des Sciences, Paris

— Memoires de mathematique et de physique.... Paris, 1692-94. 3 vols in 1. 4to, contemp calf; covers detached. Some spotting. Ck Nov 29 (118) £50

Academie Royale des Sciences, Paris

— Divers ouvrages de mathematique et de physique. Paris, 1693. Folio, contemp calf; joints rubbed. Ck Nov 29 (119) £680

Accademia del Cimento. See: Essayes...

Accademia della Crusca

— Vocabolario degli Accademici della Crusca.... Venice, 1741. Folio, contemp vellum. SI June 9 (285) LIt380,000

Account...

— An Account of the Automaton, constructed by Orffyreus, in two Letters, the one from Professor Gravesande to Sir Isaac Newton, the other from Baron Fischer to Dr. Desaguliers. L, 1770. 4to, disbound. Ck Nov 29 (134) £320

— Account of the Terrific and Fatal Riot at the New-York Astor Place Opera House.... NY, 1849. 1st Ed. 8vo, orig wraps worn. O Jan 14 (2) $60

Anr copy. Orig wraps; soiled & wrinkled. wd Dec 12 (352) $50

Accum, Friedrich Christian, 1769-1838

— Culinary Chemistry; Exhibiting the Scientific Principles of Cookery. L: R. Ackermann, 1821. 12mo, modern cloth. With colored frontis & colored engraved title. Library markings. bba Oct 24 (84) £180 [Hughes]

Acerbi, Giuseppe, 1773-1846

— Travels through Sweden, Finland, and Lapland, to the North Cape.... L, 1802. 1st Ed. 2 vols. 4to, contemp calf; spines faded. With folding map & 15 plates. bba Sept 19 (128) £350 [Hannas]

Anr copy. Half lea; covers detached. With map (torn at fold) & 16 plates, 5 hand-colored. Lacking half-titles; stamp on verso of titles. bba June 11 (365) £70 [Lib. Naturalistica Bolognese]

Achdjian, Albert

— A Fundamental Art, the Rug.... Paris, 1949. Ltd Ed. 4to, wraps; spine torn. In French & English. sp Feb 6 (226) $75

Anr copy. Orig wraps; tear to base of spine. In French & English. sp June 18 (274) $60

Achilles Tatius

— The Love of Clitophon and Leucippe. Oxford: Shakespeare Head Press, 1923. One of 498 on Batchelor's Kelmscott handmade paper. Trans by Wm. Burton. 4to, half cloth; unopened. sg Jan 30 (1) $110

Ackerman, Phyllis. See: Pope & Ackerman

Ackermann Publications, Rudolph—London

— Cambridge. 1815. ("A History of the University of Cambridge.") 2 vols. 4to, contemp russia gilt; rebacked. With port & 95 hand-colored plates (including the 16 Founders plates). C May 20 (233) £2,600 [Schuster]

Anr copy. Contemp russia gilt; rubbed, rebacked. P Dec 12 (3) $2,000

Anr copy. Contemp russia gilt with cipher of Sir Henry Charles Englefield; joints broken. Subscriber's copy. S Nov 21 (116) £2,200 [Yamanaka]

— Engravings after the Best Pictures of the Great Masters. [N.d.]. Folio, contemp half mor; broken, rubbed. With 20 plates. Dampstain in margins; drawing loosely inserted. bba Nov 7 (16) £150 [Barker]

— The History of Eton College. 1816. 4to, orig bds; broken; stained. With 10 colored plates. sg Nov 7 (1) $800

— The History of Rugby School. 1816. 4to, orig bds; rubbed. With 5 hand-colored plates. Some spotting. Ck Oct 18 (37) £300

— The History of the Abbey Church of St. Peter's Westminster.... 1812. With: A History of the University of Cambridge. 1815. 1st Ed. 4 vols. 4to, uniformly bound in contemp russia gilt. With all the plates, including the colored ports of the Founders. C May 20 (6) £10,500 [Quaritch]

2d Issue. 2 vols. 4to, 19th-cent half sheep; worn. Scattered foxing to plates. sg Jan 9 (1) $400

Issue not specified. Contemp russia gilt; joints weak. With port, plan & 81 hand-colored plates. Text spotted. Ck July 10 (77) £350

Anr copy. Contemp calf gilt; worn, rebacked retaining orig spine, recornered, 1 new cover. S Nov 15 (904) £160 [Clegg]

— The Microcosm of London. 1808-10. 3 vols. 4to, contemp half mor gilt; joints & corners rubbed. With 104 hand-colored plates. C Oct 30 (123) £2,500 [Marshall]

Anr copy. Mor gilt by Sangorski & Sutcliffe. With 3 wood-engraved title, 3 engraved dedications & 104 hand-colored plates, 4 in Abbey's 1st state. One text leaf torn & repaired. C May 20 (4) £5,200 [Hedge]

Anr copy. Orig bds, unopened; rebacked, bd edges & corners repaired. With 104 hand-colored plates. Some stains. McCarty-Cooper copy. CNY Jan 25 (1) $6,500

Anr copy. Half mor gilt by Riviere. With 104 hand-colored plates. With only 1 of the 13 errata corrected; watermarks are 1806, 1807 & 1808 Some soiling. P Dec 12 (2) $4,000

Anr copy. Contemp calf gilt; rebacked, rubbed. With engraved titles, dedications & 104 hand-colored plates. Some browning; a few plates misbound; lacking half-titles; 1 dedication trimmed. pn Apr 23 (252) £2,600

Anr copy. Contemp russia gilt. S June 25 (272) £4,800 [Tulip]

Anr copy. Contemp mor. With engraved titles, engraved dedications & 104 hand-colored plates. S June 25 (273) £3,000 [Nicholson]

Anr copy. Contemp calf gilt; rebacked with modern calf. With 104 hand-colored plates. Some foxing. wd June 12 (361) $4,000

Tooley's 2d Issue. Contemp russia gilt; joints & corners repaired, spines chipped. With engraved dedications & 104 hand-colored plates. Lacking half-titles; some browning of text; Freemasons Hall plate in Vol II with tear to lower blank margin. C Oct 30 (1) £4,200 [Woods]

— Oxford. 1814. ("A History of the University of Oxford....") 2 vols. 4to, orig bds, unopened; joints weak. With uncolored port & 81 colored plates. With list of plates in 1st state & without the Founders ports. C May 20 (7) £2,400 [Schuster]

Anr copy. Contemp russia gilt by Rowe & Waller. With port, 70 hand-colored aquatints on 64 sheets, 17 hand-colored costume plates & list of subscribers. Without half-titles & Founders plates; list of plates is in 1st state; frontis to Vol I & plate of Corpus Christi College in 1st state, the 8 others mentioned by Tooley in 2d state. S June 25 (271) £2,000 [George]

— Poetical Sketches of Scarborough. 1813. 1st Ed. Illus by Thomas Rowlandson. 8vo, modern mor gilt by Bayntun-Riviere. With 21 colored plates. C May 20 (101) £280 [Spelman]

— The Repository of Arts, Literature, Commerce.... Series 1-3. L, 1809-28. First Series only. Vols I-XII, Parts 1-72 only. 12 vols. 8vo, contemp calf; rebacked. Many plate captions tightly bound in; some imprints or numerals cropped; some staining. McCarty-Cooper copy. CNY Jan 25 (2) $2,000

— View of the Great Falls of Niagara. [1927]. Oblong folio, orig paper-backed wraps; spotted, marginal loss. With litho title & 5 litho plates on chine colle mtd. Marginal loss to last few plates. P June 16 (297) $8,500

— Winchester, Eton and Westminster. 1816. ("The History of the Colleges of Winchester, Eton, and Westminster....") 4to, modern mor gilt. With 44 hand-colored plates. Lacking half-title. sg May 7 (1) $2,200

1st Ed, 1st Issue, 2d state. 4to, mor gilt by Sangorski & Sutcliffe, ptd wraps to orig 12 parts bound in. With 48 hand-colored plates. C May 20 (8) £3,200 [Marlborough]

Early Issue, with Plate 23 in 1st state & Plate 26 in 2d state. Later mor gilt for Sawyer. With 48 colored plates. C Oct 30 (3) £1,600 [Sifton Praed]

Issue not stated. 19th-cent half mor gilt; corners renewed, bd edges worn, upper inner joint cracked. With 48 hand-colored plates. Minor foxing & stains; old library stamp on tp verso. McCarty-Cooper copy. CNY Jan 25 (4) $2,600

Acosta, Jose de, 1539?-1600

— Histoire naturelle et moralle des Indes.... Paris: Marc Orry, 1598. 8vo, old vellum; soiled. Some worming without loss; minor browning. S Feb 26 (714) £480 [Voltaire]

— The Naturall and Morall Historie of the East and West Indies.... L, 1604. 1st Ed in English. Trans by Edward Grimstone. 4to, contemp calf; rebacked, worn, upper cover detached. Marginal foxing; dampstaining to quire Cc. CNY Oct 8 (1) $1,600

Acta...

— Acta Eruditorum. Leipzig, 1682-1731. 62 vols. 4to, half lea. Browned. SI Dec 5 (2) LIt200,000

Acta Sanctorum...

— Acta Sanctorum, quotquot toto orbe coluntur, collegit, digessit.... [Various imprints], 1643-1902. 49 vols. Folio, contemp blind-stamped pigskin, final 2 vols in cloth. Ck Nov 29 (2) £600

Actius, Thomas

— De Ludo Scacchorum in legali methodo tractatus.... Pesaro, 1583. 4to, modern vellum. Burn-hole in title, affecting device. Ck May 8 (15) £450

Acton, Harold

— This Chaos. Paris: Hours Press, [1930]. One of 150. Orig half calf; rubbed & soiled, loose. Inscr, 1944. S Nov 14 (533) £160 [Hassan]

Acuna, Christoval, 1597-1676?

— Voyages and Discoveries in South America. L, 1698. 8vo, contemp calf; covers detached. With 2 folding maps. Some browning. CNY Oct 8 (2) $1,100

Adair, James, 1709?-1783?

— The History of the American Indians.... L, 1775. 1st Ed. 4to, contemp calf; rebacked. With folding map. S Nov 21 (320) £600 [Beeleigh]

Adalbert, Prince of Prussia, 1811-73

— Aus meinem Tagebuch 1842-1843. Berlin, 1847. 4to, orig cloth; worn. Inscr to his cousin Friederike. HH May 12 (612) DM14,000

Adam, Eugen & Franz

— Erinnerungen an die Feldzuege der K. K. Oester. Armee in Italien. Munich, [1851]. Folio, orig cloth. With litho title & 24 plates on india paper. Some spotting or waterstaining. S Nov 21 (178) £1,200 [Christoph]

Adam, Robert, 1728-92

— Ruins of the Palace of the Emperor Diocletian at Spalatro in Dalmatia. L, 1764. Folio, contemp bds; spine repaired. With 61 plates on 54 sheets. Some dust-soiling to edges. C Oct 30 (4) £2,200 [Sotheran]

Anr copy. Contemp calf gilt; worn. With 55 (of 61) plates on 46 (of 54) sheets, several double-page or folding. Plate XXVIII creased; some dust-soiling. S June 25 (89) £1,050 [Toscani]

Adam, Robert Borthwick, 1833-1904

— The R. B. Adam Library relating to Samuel Johnson and his Era. Buffalo, 1929-30. 4 vols. Cloth & half cloth. George Milne copy. CNY Dec 5 (264) $350

Adams, Ansel Easton

— Born Free and Equal. NY, 1944. Wraps; frayed. cb Feb 12 (1) $190

Anr copy. Wraps; worn & soiled. sg Apr 13 (3) $400

— The Four Seasons in Yosemite National Park. [Los Angeles, 1936]. 1st Ed. 4to, wraps. bbc Feb 17 (166) $110; K Sept 29 (1) $60

— Making a Photograph.... L & NY, 1935. Half cloth. cb Jan 16 (1) $65

— My Camera in Yosemite Valley. Yosemite National Park & Bost., 1949. 1st Ed. Folio, spiral bound with pictorial wraps; worn & soiled. bbc Feb 17 (167) $90

— My Camera in the National Parks.... Yosemite National Park & Bost., 1950. 4to, bds, spiral bound; cover dampstained & with soft creases, corners bumped. With 30 photos, inset on gloss paper. Foxing on front free endpaper & tp. sg Apr 13 (4) $175

— Yosemite and the Range of Light. Bost.: New York Graphic Society, 1979. Special Ed, with mtd ptd label sgd by Adams. Intro by Paul Brooks. Oblong 4to, cloth, in d/j. cb Dec 19 (1) $85; wa Sept 26 (643) $90

Anr copy. Cloth; soiled, terminal leaf & rear free endpaper creased. wa Apr 9 (258) $55

Adams, Frederick B., Jr.

— Radical Literature in America. Stamford CT, 1939. One of 650. Worn. O Sept 24 (3) $85; sg May 21 (123) $80

Adams, George, 1720-73

— A Treatise Describing and Explaining the Construction and Use of New Celestial and Terrestrial Globes. L, 1769. 2d Ed. Dedication by Samuel Johnson. 8vo, contemp sheep; rubbed. With 14 plates. Opening leaves wormed in blank lower margins. sg May 14 (258) $300

Adams, Hannah

— An Alphabetical Compendium of the Various Sects.... Bost., 1784. 8vo, contemp sheep. Some foxing. sg Dec 5 (2) $100

Adams, Henry, 1838-1918

— Mont Saint Michel and Chartres. Wash., 1904. 1st Ed. 4to, orig cloth; spine ends and lower joint repaired. Inscr. Epstein copy. sg Apr 29 (5) $2,600

Adams, Herbert Mayow

— Catalogue of Books Printed on the Continent of Europe, 1501-1600, in Cambridge Libraries. Cambr., 1967. 2 vols. 4to, orig cloth, in d/js. Ck Nov 1 (326) £250

Anr copy. Cloth; worn. O Sept 24 (4) $450

Anr copy. Cloth; Vol II rear joint and edges of cover discolored. sg Oct 31 (1) $900

Anr copy. Orig cloth, in d/js. sg Nov 7 (2) $425

Adams, John, Topographer, fl.1680

— Index Villaris. L, 1690. ("Index Villaris or an Exact Register of All the Cities, Market Towns, Parishes....") Folio, contemp calf. With folding map. 1 signature misbound. bba Oct 24 (294) £80 [Elliott]

Adams, Ramon F.

— Burrs Under the Saddle. A Second Look at Books and Histories of the West. Norman: Univ. of Oklahoma Press, [1964]. In d/j. cb Oct 17 (3) $95

— The Rampaging Herd: a Bibliography. Norman, [1959]. 1st Ed. In d/j. cb Oct 17 (4) $90

Anr Ed. Norman, Okla., [1959]. In d/j. O Sept 24 (5) $70

— Six-Guns & Saddle Leather: a Bibliography.... Norman, [1954]. 1st Ed. In d/j. cb Oct 17 (5) $80

Anr Ed. Norman, Okla., [1969]. In d/j. O Sept 24 (6) $50

Adams, Richard, Novelist

— Watership Down. L, 1972. 1st Ed. In d/j with vertical tear. bbc June 29 (354) $410

Review copy with accompanying press release. In d/j. bba Dec 119 (157) £550 [C. Edwards]

Adams, Robert, Sailor

— The Narrative of Robert Adams, a Sailor, who was Wrecked on the Western Coast of Africa. L, 1816. 1st Ed. 4to, recent half mor. Map def and laid down; some repaired tears. cb Oct 10 (1) $50

Anr copy. Modern cloth. Library markings. O Apr 28 (144) $120

Adamson, Michel

— A Voyage to Senegal, the Isle of Goree, and the River Gambia. L, 1759. 8vo, modern half calf. With folding map. pnE Aug 12 (29) £170

Addison, Charles Greenstreet, d.1866

— Damascus and Palmyra. L, 1838. Illus by Wm. Makepeace Thackeray. 2 vols. 8vo, cloth. With 10 hand-colored plates. sg Jan 9 (2) $450

Early Issue with 8 plates omitted from the 2d Issue. Later mor gilt by Riviere; upper covers detached. With hand-colored frontises & 16 plates. Some spotting. With ADs, 22 Dec 1837, tipped onto inserted leaf. Ck Nov 29 (319) £700

Addison, Joseph, 1672-1719

See also: Spectator...

— The Free-Holder. Or Political Essays. L, 1716. 12mo, old calf; worn. O Jan 14 (3) $110

— Works. L, 1721. 4 vols. 4to, calf gilt; rubbed. O Feb 25 (2) $100

Anr copy. Contemp calf. rs Oct 17 (77) $125

Anr copy. Contemp sheep; rebacked, worn. Some foxing & browning. sg Oct 17 (107) $60

Anr Ed. L, 1761. 4 vols. 4to, contemp calf gilt; joints cracked. LH May 17 (632) $150

Anr Ed. NY, 1811. 6 vols. 12mo, contemp calf gilt; joints worn. pn Apr 23 (62) £80 [Pordes]

Ade, George, 1866-1944

— People You Know. NY, 1903. Illus by John T. McCutcheon. Orig cloth; front hinge starting. Inscr by both Ade & McCutcheon, 1941 & 1942. sg Dec 12 (1) $150

— The Strenuous Lad's Library. Phoenix: Bandar Log Press, 1903-4. One of 674 & 374. 3 vols. 16mo, orig wraps; chipped & split. sg Sept 26 (12) $650

Adhemar, Jean

— Toulouse-Lautrec: His Complete Lithographs and Drypoints. NY, [1965]. 4to, cloth, in d/j. sp Sept 22 (346) $60

Adrianus Carthusiensis

— De remediis utriusque fortunae. [Cologne: Ulrich Zel, c.1470]. 4to, later calf. Gothic letter; rubricated. Stains in 1st 3 leaves & in a few margins; last leaf with 12 lines replaced in Ms. 160 leaves. Goff A-54. B Nov 1 (533) HF3,200

Adrichomius, Christianus, 1533-85

— Theatrum terrae sanctae et biblicarum historiarum. Cologne, 1682. Folio, modern calf; rubbed. With engraved title, folding map & 10 double-page or folding maps. Lacking plan of Jerusalem; spotted & stained throughout; general map repaired with 2 tears. S July 1 (823) £420 [Sofer]

Adventures...

See also: Clemens, Samuel Langhorne; White, James

— The Adventures of a Parrot. L: G. Margin, [c.1810]. 8vo, orig wraps. With 16 colored plates. bba July 23 (159) £600

Advice. See: Osborne, Francis

Adye, Sir John Miller

— [Grecian Costumes] L: J. Aresti, [c.1850]. Folio, contemp half mor gilt. With 17 litho costume plates, 12 hand-colored, captioned in ink in lower margin. S July 1 (538) £4,500

Aelian (Aelianus Tacticus)

— The Tactiks of Aelian or Art of Embattailing an Army.... L, 1616. 1st Ed in English. Trans by John Bingham. Folio, contemp calf; rubbed. With engraved title & 50 plates. Some shaving & tears; some staining. S July 1 (1199) £450 [Poole]

Aelian (Aelianus Tacticus) —& Polybius, 205?-125? B.C.

— La milice des grecs et romains. Paris, 1615. Folio, later calf; rubbed. S July 9 (1200) £200 [Poole]

Aelianus, Claudius

— De animalium natura libri XVII. Geneva, 1616. 16mo, contemp calf; head of spine lacking. In Greek & Latin. bba Jan 30 (311) £60 [Bifolco]

— De natura animalium libri XVII. L, 1744. 1 vol in 2. 4to, contemp calf; rubbed, joints split. In Greek & Latin. S July 1 (507) £280 [Thecharaki]

Aemilius, Georgius

— Biblicae historiae...depictae.... Frankfurt: Christian Egenolph, [1539]. Illus by Hans Sebald Beham. 8vo, 19th-cent calf. Tp trimmed & inlaid to size; stamp on next leaf. sg May 7 (23) $2,000

Aeneas Sylvius, Pope Pius II, 1405-64

— De curialium miseria. [Rome: Bartholomaeus Guildenbeck, not after Aug], 1475. 4to, 18th-cent mor; spine laid down. 29 lines; type 1:108R; capitals supplied in yellow, some in faint wash only. Minor foxing. 22 leaves. Goff P-662. Milne copy. CNY Dec 5 (308) $1,800

Aero...

— Aero Digest. NY, 1928-29. Vols 12-15. 4 vols. Library bdgs. Z Nov 23 (274) $55

Vols 16-21. NY, 1930-32. 5 vols. Library bdgs. Z Nov 23 (275) $55

Vols 22-33. NY, 1933-38. 9 vols. Library bdgs. Z Nov 23 (276) $95

Aeschylus, 525-456 B.C.

— Opera. Venice: Aldus, 1518. ("Tragoediae.") 8vo, 19th-cent lea gilt; worn. Greek type; early marginalia throughout in a humanist hand. British Museum cancellation stamp. Heber copy. C June 24 (263) £5,500 [Rosenthal]

Anr Ed. Paris: Henri Estienne, 1557. ("Aeschyli Tragoediae VI....") 4to, contemp mor gilt; rubbed, corners & head & foot of spine slightly damaged. Inner margin of title reinforced. bba Jan 16 (219) £750 [Stamatoyannopoulos]

Anr copy. 18th-cent russia gilt; rebacked retaining orig spine. S July 1 (509) £700 [Thecharaki]

Aesop, c.620-560 B.C.

See also: Gregynog Press; Limited Editions Club

Fables

— 1505. - Vita et fabellae.... Venice: Aldus. Folio, 19th-cent mor gilt by Bedford; extremities rubbed. Upper outer corner of 1st 11 leaves repaired; tp repaired. Crawford-Harris copy. C June 24 (264) £17,000 [Thomas Scheler]

— 1651. - The Fables. L. Trans by John Ogilby. 4to, contemp calf; extremities repaired, later endpapers. With frontis & 80 plates. Margins of F2 & Aa1 torn & repaired; outer margin of 4H3 tattered. C Dec 16 (176) £3,200 [Schiller]

Anr copy. Lev gilt by Lortic; front cover detached. With frontis, port & 79 (of 80) plates numbered 1-81. Lacking plate 69; washed. sg Oct 24 (2) $750

— 1667. - Fabularum Aesopiarum libri

quinque. Amst. 8vo, old sheep gilt; scuffed. Some browning. sg Mar 12 (248) $200

— 1668. - The Fables. L. Bound with: Aesopics, or a Second Collection of Fables. L, 1668. 2 parts in 1 vol. 2d Ed of 1st part; 1st Ed of 2d part. Paraphrased in verse by John Ogilby. Folio, contemp lea; needs rebacking. With port & 148 plates. Opening leaves of 1st work gnawed in upper margin; a few plates torn & repaired on verso; clean tears in 2 plates in 2d work; lacking 1 port. Sold w.a.f. sg Sept 19 (160) $1,800

— 1687. - Fables.... L: H. Hills for Francis Barlow. Folio, later calf gilt; rebacked, spine ends torn. With engraved title, dedication leaf, 31 plates & 110 illusts in text. Illust on 2T2 double-printed; Plate 1, dedication, 2Y2 & last leaf with small tears, mostly repaired; some staining & browning. pn Nov 14 (255) £850 [Poole]

— 1694. - L. Vol I. Folio, contemp calf; rubbed, corners worn, upper joint split. Tp spotted. bba July 23 (4) £75 [Ginnan]

— 1745. - Phaedri fabularum Aesopiarum libri quinque. Leiden: S. Luchtmans. 8vo, contemp vellum gilt, prize bdg, 1759. wa Sept 26 (37) $80

— c.1780. - Select Fables. L. Ed by Robert Dodsley. 12mo, orig Dutch floral bds; joints wearing. bba July 23 (5) £200 [Miles]

— 1818. - The Fables of Aesop and Others. Newcastle Illus by Thomas Bewick. 8vo, contemp bds; rebacked. bba Oct 24 (227) £160 [Ash Rare Bks]

— 1883. - Some of Aesop's Fables with Modern Instances. L. Illus by Randolph Caldecott. 4to, contemp calf gilt, orig covers bound in. Heavily foxed throughout. wd June 12 (375) $150

— 1909. - Fables. L. One of 750. Illus by Edward Detmold. 4to, orig cloth; rubbed. With 25 mtd color plates. DW Mar 4 (345) £290

— 1912. - L. Trans by V. S. Vernon Jones; illus by Arthur Rackham. 4to, orig lea; rubbed. DW May 13 (466) £50

One of 1,450, sgd by the artist. Orig cloth; soiled. With 13 colored plates. Ck Dec 11 (175) £350

— 1912. - L & NY One of 1,450. Illus by Arthur Rackham. Mor gilt by Bayntun-Riviere; soiled, stains on front free endpaper. With 13 color plates Dampstain affecting Rackham's signature. Ck Nov 1 (492) £400

Anr copy. Vellum over bds by Zaehnsdorf. With a pen-and-ink and watercolor drawing, sgd. CNY Dec 5 (315) $800; sg Nov 7 (161) $1,300

Anr copy. Soiled, stains on front free endpaper. sg May 7 (179) $1,200

— [1931]. - Paris: Harrison of Paris One of 50 with orig drawing tipped in at front. Illus by Alexander Calder. 4to, orig bds. bbc Sept 23 (429) $4,750

One of 495 on Auvergne handmade paper. Orig wraps over bds. K Sept 29 (189) $375

One of 595 on Auvergne handmade paper. Orig bds. Manney copy. P Oct 11 (38) $5,000

— 1936. - L. One of 525. Trans by Sir Roger L'Estrange; illus by Stephen Gooden. Vellum gilt; bowed. Ck Dec 11 (156) £400

— 1954. - 12 Fables of Aesop. NY Ltd Ed. Illus by Antonio Frasconi. 4to, half cloth. Sgd by Frasconi, Wescott & Joseph Blumenthal, the ptr. sg Jan 30 (55) $200

— 1968. - Fables. L. One of 250, sgd by the artist. Illus by Elizabeth Frink. Folio, orig mor gilt, unopened. Ls, sgd by Frink, inserted. S Nov 14 (110) £380 [Stone]

— 1973. - The Fables: The First Three Books of Caxton's Aesop. Verona: Officina Bodoni One of 160. 2 vols. Orig half mor. bba June 25 (214) £1,700 [P & P Books]

— 1976. - History and Fables...translated and printed by William Caxton, 1484. L. One of 50. 4to, mor. sg May 21 (241) $350

Aevolus, Caesar

— De causis antipathiae, & sympathiae rerum naturalium. Venice: F. Zilettum, 1580. Bound with: De divinis attributis, quae Sephirot at Hebraeis nuncupata. Venice, 1573. 4to, half vellum. SI June 9 (6) LIt1,400,000

Affiches...

— Les Affiches etrangeres illustrees.... Paris, 1897. 4to, modern mor. Epstein copy. sg Apr 30 (383) $1,500

Affo, Ireneo

— Vita di Luigi Gonzaga.... Parma, 1780. 4to, bds. SI Dec 5 (14) LIt250,000

Africanus. See: Leo, Johannes

Agee, James, 1909-55

— A Death in the Family. NY, [1957]. In d/j. sg Dec 12 (5) $140

— A Way of Seeing. NY, [1965]. Illus by Helen Levitt. In d/j. sg Oct 8 (46) $250

Agocchie, Giovanni dall'

— Dell'arte di scrimia libri tre.... Venice: Giulio Tamborino, 1572. 4to, old vellum. Contemp inked marginal notations throughout. sg Mar 26 (2) $400

Agostini, Giovanni degli

— Notizie istorico-critiche intorno la vita, e le opere degli scrittori Viniziani. Venice, 1752-54. 2 vols. 4to, contemp vellum. SI Dec 5 (15) LIt550,000

Agostini, Leonardo

— Gemmae et sculpturae antiquae. Franeker: Leonardum Strik, 1694. 2 parts in 1 vol. 4to, contemp calf gilt; extremities worn. With 269 plates Some wear along extremities; old stamp on tp. sg Oct 24 (3) $500

— Le gemme antiche figurate di Leonardo Agostini. Rome, 1657-69. 2 parts in 1 vol. 4to, contemp vellum; upper hinge worn, backstrip def. bba Jan 16 (228) £420 [Etching]

Anr copy. 2 vols. 4to, contemp vellum, not uniform. bba Jan 30 (313) £360 [Nibris]

Agricola, Georgius, 1494-1555

— De l'arte de metalli. Basel: Froben & Bischof, 1563. Folio, contemp vellum. Some browning & foxing. SI Dec 5 (17) LIt12,500,000

— De re metallica. Basel: Froben, 1556. 1st Ed. Folio, 19th-cent mor; rubbed. With 273 woodcuts by Hans Deutsc. Stamp on tp verso. S Dec 5 (348) £6,500 [Martayan]

Anr Ed. L, 1912. Trans by Herbert C. & Lou Hoover. Folio, orig half vellum. bba Sept 5 (185) £340 [Hobbes]

Anr copy. Vellum. Tp with stamp on verso. bba June 11 (210) £380 [Henly]

Anr copy. Orig half vellum. Worn; a few leaves clumsily opened. O Aug 25 (2) $375

Anr copy. Orig vellum. Institutional handstamps. wa Sept 26 (498) $350

Agricola, Rudolphus

— De inventione dialectica libri tres.... Paris: Apud Ioannem Lodoicum Tiletanum, 1542. 4to, 17th-cent calf; rebacked, worn. Early leaves heavily annotated. bba Sept 5 (186) £280 [M. Phelps]

Agrippa, Camillo

— Trattato di scientia d'arme. Rome: Antonio Blado, 1553. 4to, later vellum gilt. With port & 56 illusts. sg Mar 26 (3) $4,000

Anr copy. Contemp vellum. Lacking privilege leaf, 1 index leaf & final blank; marginal worming & staining. SI June 9 (8) LIt600,000

Anr Ed. Venice: Antonio Pinargenti, 1568. ("Trattato di scienza d'arme.") 4to, modern mor gilt. sg Mar 26 (4) $2,200

Agrippa, Henricus Cornelius, 1486?-1535

— De incertitudine & vanitate scientiarum declamatio invectiva. [N.p.], 1537. 8vo, later calf; rebacked. sg Mar 12 (196) $425

Aguilar y Santillan, Rafael, 1863-1940

— Bibliografia geologica y minera de la Republica Mexicana. Mexico, 1898. Folio, new cloth. Some corners repaired. sg Oct 31 (4) $250

Aiken, Conrad

— Earth Triumphant. NY, 1914. In d/j. sg Dec 12 (6) $225

Aikin, John, 1747-1822

— England Delineated.... L, 1795. 8vo, calf; worn. pnE Oct 1 (312) £90

Anr Ed. L, 1804. 2 vols in 1. 8vo, half lea. With 2 engraved title & 148 plates. Ink annotations; small tear to corner of 1 page of text. pn Dec 12 (307) £90

Aikin, Lucy, 1781-1864

— Memoirs of the Court of King Charles the First. L, 1833. 2 vols. 8vo, calf gilt; scuffed, joints tender. F Dec 18 (59) $60

Aimoinus, Monachus Floriacensis

— De regum procerumque Francorum origine gestisque clarissimis.... [Paris]: Johannes Parvus & Badius Ascensius, 1514. Folio, half mor; broken. Old ink marginalia; foxed. K Dec 1 (7) $350

Ainsworth, William Francis

— Travels and Researches in Asia Minor, Mesopotamia, Chaldea, and Armenia. L, 1842. 2 vols. 12mo, orig cloth; spine and cover edges faded. sg Jan 9 (3) $175

Ainsworth, William Harrison, 1805-82

— Merry England; or, Nobles and Serfs. L, 1874. 1st Ed. 3 vols. 8vo, orig cloth; spine ends rubbed. O July 14 (3) $60

— Old Saint Paul's. L, 1841. 1st Ed. Illus by John Franklin. 3 vols. 12mo, mor gilt extra. Hoe copy. cb Oct 31 (2) $800

— The Spendthrift. L, 1857. Illus by Hablot K. Browne. 8vo, orig cloth. sg Mar 5 (4) $140

— The Tower of London. L, 1840. 1st Ed in Book form. Illus by George Cruikshank. 8vo, orig cloth; front hinge cracked. With 40 plates. bbc June 29 (372) $80

Anr copy. Calf gilt by Zaehnsdorf; joints worn. With 40 steel etchings & 58 woodcuts. Some browning. Inscr. wa Mar 5 (23) $220

— Windsor Castle. L, 1843. 8vo, half calf. LH May 17 (593) $300

— Works. L, [n.d.]. 16 vols. 8vo, contemp half calf; spines faded & rubbed. bba Oct 10 (276) £90 [Sotheran]

Aircraft...

— Aircraft Year Book.... NY, 1919. For 1919. In d/j. Tp stamped. cb Nov 7 (4) $150

For 1920. Garden City, 1920. In d/j. Tp stamped. cb Nov 7 (5) $140

For 1921. Bost., 1921. In d/j. Tp stamped. cb Nov 7 (6) $90

For 1922. NY, 1922. In d/j. Tp stamped. cb Nov 7 (7) $50

Aiton, William, 1731-93

— Hortus Kewensis. L, 1810-13. 5 vols. 8vo, modern cloth. wa Dec 9 (568) $425

Alabama

— The Constitution of the State of Alabama.... Montgomery, 1861. 8vo, orig wraps. Pages numbered 73-112, but wraps made for this volume. sg Dec 5 (75) $600

Alain-Fournier, Henri, 1886-1914

— Le Grand Meaulnes. Paris, 1913. 12mo, mor gilt by Devauchelle, orig wraps bound in. S May 28 (255) £700 [Holinger]

Alamanni, Luigi, 1495-1556

— La Coltivatione. Paris: Estienne, 1546. 1st Ed. 8vo, 18th-cent mor gilt. With the 2-leaf privilege & 2-leaf dedication to Catherine de Medicis at the end; errata ptd on U2 verso. Short tear in fore-margin of tp repaired. S Dec 5 (34) £850 [Kaiser]

— Gyrone il cortese. Paris, 1548. 1st Ed. 4to, 18th-cent mor gilt; some restoration. Italic type; double-column. C June 24 (89) £1,100 [Wood]

Anr Ed. Venice: Comin da Trino di Monferrato, 1549. ("Girone il cortese.") 4to, 19th-cent half lea. SI Dec 5 (734) LIt200,000

— Opere Toscane. Lyons: S. Gryphius, 1532. 8vo, 18th-cent calf. Some leaves browned. SI Dec 5 (735) LIt600,000

Alarcon, Pedro Antonio de

— Le Tricorne. Paris, [1958]. One of 140 with additional suite of 13 etchings. Illus by Salvador Dali. Folio, loose in wraps as issued; edges worn. With 10 color lithos. sg Sept 26 (79) $3,400

— Le Tricorne. Paris, [1958]. One of 140, with an additional suite of the etchings. Folio, loose as issued. With 10 (of 20) color lithos, each sgd in pencil by Dali. sg Jan 30 (33) $1,300

Albee, Edward

— Who's Afraid of Virginia Woolf? NY, 1962. In d/j. sg June 11 (4) $90

Albers, Josef

— Interaction of Color. New Haven, 1963. 2 vols. 4to, orig cloth-covered box. With 79 folding plates, many with overslips. P June 18 (603) $1,700

Anr copy. Text orig cloth, commentary in orig wraps & boxed with plates, unbound as issued. With 80 double-page plates. sg Sept 6 (1) $1,900

Albert, King of the Belgians

— King Albert's Book. L, 1914. 4to, cloth; soiled. sg Jan 30 (150) $150

Albert Victor, Prince —& George, Prince of Wales

— The Cruise of her Majesty's Ship "Bacchante" 1879-1882. L, 1886. 2 vols. 8vo, cloth; rubbed. kh Nov 11 (475) A$100

Alberti, Giuseppe Antonio

— Istruzioni pratiche per l'ingegnero civile.... Venice, 1761. 2 parts in 1 vol. 8vo, later half vellum. With 37 folding plates. bba Feb 27 (401) £220 [Thorp]

— La Pirotechnia ossia trattato dei fuochi d'artificio. Venice, 1749. 4to, contemp half vellum; worn. With 21 folding plates. Plate 21 repaired; some staining & soiling. S July 1 (1201) £250 [American Mus.]

Anr copy. Contemp vellum. With 20 folding plates. SI June 9 (9) LIt1,300,000

Alberti, Leandro, 1479-1552

— Descrittione di tutta Italia.... Venice: Giovanni Maria Leni, 1577. 2 parts in 1 vol. 4to, contemp vellum. With 20 plates. SI June 9 (9) LIt1,300,000

Alberti, Leon Battista, 1404-72

— L'Architettura. Venice, 1565. 4to, 18th-cent sheep; extremities worn. sg Feb 6 (1) $2,400

— Hecatomphila. Venice: V. Ruffinelli, 1545. Bound with: Deiphira. Venice, 1545. 8vo, modern mor. Outer margin of 1st title restored; some light staining; lacking final blank to 2d work. C Dec 16 (16) £500 [Franks]

— I Dieci Libri di architettura. Rome, 1784. 4to, contemp half sheep; fore-edges damp-damaged. With 35 folding plates. bba Feb 27 (273) £180 [Hetherington]

Anr copy. Contemp vellum; soiled. S June 25 (182) £550 [Gorini]

Anr copy. Half lea; worn. Some foxing & marginal spotting; brown stain on frontis. SI Dec 5 (736) LIt420,000

Alberti, Lodewyk

— De Kaffers aan de Zuidkust van Afrika.... Amst., 1810. 2 vols. 8vo & folio, bds, Atlas in contemp wraps. Text with folding hand-colored map, engraved title & 2 hand-colored plates; Atlas with 4 hand-colored plates. bba Sept 19 (53) £4,200 [Sawyer]

Alberti, Rafael

— El Negro. Bedford NY: Tyler Graphics, 1983. One of 51 on hand-made paper. Illus by Robert Motherwell. Variously sized folding sheets bound into a folding case. With 19 orig lithos. Schlosser copy. P June 17 (628) $9,500

— X Sonetos Romanos. Buenos Aires, [1964]. One of 100. 4to, cloth. sg Sept 26 (5) $110

Albin, Eleazar, fl.1713-59

— Birds. L, 1738-40. ("A Natural History of Birds.") 3 vols. 4to, contemp calf gilt; spines chipped. With 306 hand-colored plates. Some browning. C Oct 30 (252) £4,200 [Schuster]

— Insects. L, 1749. ("A Natural History of English Insects.") 4to, contemp calf gilt; spine chipped. With 100 hand-colored plates. Without Derham's text or index; some browning. C Oct 30 (253) £1,400 [Dunbar]

Anr copy. Contemp calf gilt; spine ends & joints repaired. Bound without Derham's notes & the index at end; some discoloration. S June 25 (1) £1,200 [Junk]

Albinus, Bernard Siegfried, 1697-1770

— Dissertatio de arteriis et venis intestinorum hominis.... Leiden: Theodore Haak, 1736. Bound with: Dissertatio secunda de sede et caussa coloris Aethiopum.... Leiden, 1737 4to, early bds; corners bumped. Each tract with a 3-color mezotint plate sgd by Jan L'Admiral. Schlosser copy. P June 17 (439) $6,500

— Explicatio tabularum anatomicarum Bartholomaei Eustachii.... Leiden, 1761. 1 vol in 2. Folio, early 19th-cent bds; backstrips & corners imperf. With 37 plates, with duplicates in outline. sg Nov 14 (1) $1,100

— Icones ossium foetus humani.... Leiden, 1737. 4to, calf; back & corners renewed. With 16 plates, each with accompanying outline plate. B Nov 1 (380) HF1,100

Albrecht, Kurt

— Nineteenth Century Australian Gold and Silver Smiths. Melbourne, 1969. kh Nov 11 (2) A$80; kh Nov 11 (3) A$120; kh Nov 11 (4) A$100

Albrizzi, Giovanni Battista

— Forestier illuminato intorno le cose piu rare e curiose, antiche, e moderne, della citta di Venezia. Venice, 1765. 8vo, old bds. Piece missing from table at p. 54; some soiling & browning; D3 def. SI Dec 5 (694) LIt450,000

Album...

— L'Album: Aquarelles et Dessins Inedits. Paris: Tallandier, [1902]. 4to, orig cloth with orig covers bound in; hinges starting. sg Apr 2 (227) $700

Albumasar, 805-886

— Flores astrologiae. Augsburg: Erhard Ratdolt, 18 Nov 1488. 4to, modern calf; scratched. Marginal soiling. 20 leaves. Goff A-356. CNY Dec 5 (152) $5,000

Alcarez, Ramon

— The Other Side, or Notes for the History of the War between Mexico and the United States. NY, 1850. 12mo, orig cloth; worn, soiled, spine chipped. With 10 ports & 14 folding maps. Some dampstaining. NH May 30 (353) $120

Alchimia...

— Alchimia, das ist, alle Farben, Wasser, Olea, Salia unnd Alumina. Frrankfurt: heirs of C. Egenolff, 1589. Bound with: Bauhin, J. De plantis absynthii nomen habentibus. Montbeliard, 1593. And: Duno, T. Epistolae medicinales locis multis auctae. Zurich, 1592. And: anr work. 8vo, contemp vellum; stained. S Dec 5 (349) £1700 [Lib. Scheler]

Alciatus, Andreas, 1492-1550

— Duello de lo eccellentissimo e clarissimo. Venice, 1552. 8vo, old vellum. sg Mar 26 (5) $175

— Los Emblemas. Tracudidos en rhimas Espanolas. Lyons: G. Roville, 1549. 8vo, contemp vellum. Lacking B8, Q3 & last leaf. Sold w.a.f. bba Apr 30 (254) £180 [Bernard]

— Emblematum. Lyon, 1566. ("Emblemata....") 8vo, later vellum with yapp edges. With 211 woodcut emblems. Tp & prelims soiled & stained; F1 repaired at lower margin. Ck Oct 31 (82) £350

Anr Ed. Antwerp: Christopher Plantin, 1574. ("Omnia...emblemata.") Bound with: Junius, Hadrianus. Emblemata. Antwerp, 1575. 2 vols in 1. 16mo, contemp vellum. sg Mar 12 (74) $1,300

Anr Ed. Leiden: Plantin, 1581. ("Emblemata.") 8vo, vellum; joints def. Some staining. B Nov 1 (327) HF1,100

Alcide. See: Gamiani...

Alcoholics Anonymous

— The Story of How More Than Eight Thousand Men and Women Recovered from Alcoholism. NY, 1943. 4th Ptg. In d/j. cb Dec 5 (1) $1,000

Alcott, Louisa May, 1832-88

— Little Men. Bost., 1871. 1st American Ed, 1st Issue. 12mo, orig cloth; some rubbing & soiling. Manney copy. P Oct 11 (1) $200

— Little Women. Bost., 1868. With: Little Women...Part Two. Bost., 1869. 1st Eds. 8vo, orig cloth; spine ends & 1 fore-corner repaired. Hinges in Vol I renewed; title re-hinged. Epstein copy. sg Apr 29 (6) $2,400

Aldam, W. H.

— A Quaint Treatise on "Flees...." L, 1876. 4to, orig cloth; worn, upper joint broken. With 2 colored plates & the series of 22 specimen flies on sunken mounts. Some foxing. Marston-Koopman copy. O Oct 29 (1) $1,100; pn Mar 19 (374) £680

Anr copy. Orig cloth; corners chipped, spine ends chipped. Some pencil annotations by a previous owner. S Feb 26 (832) £550 [Montague]

Alden, John. See: Brown Library, John Carter

Alder, Joshua—& Hancock, Albany

— A Monograph of the British Nudibranchiate Mollusca. L: Ray Society, 1845. In orig 8 parts. 4to, orig half cloth; rubbed & partly loose. With 83 plates, most partly colored. Sold w.a.f. bba May 14 (460) £190 [Lib. Naturalistica Bolognese]

Aldington, Richard, 1892-1962

— All Men are Enemies. L, 1933. 1st Ed, one of 110. Orig half cloth. sg Dec 12 (7) $100

— Death of a Hero. L, 1929. Orig cloth, in d/j. sg Dec 12 (8) $70

Aldini, Giovanni

— Essai theorique et experimental sur le galvanisme.... Paris, 1804. 2 vols in 1. 8vo, early 19th-cent half cloth; spine faded. With 10 folding plates. sg Nov 14 (209) $800

Aldrich, Thomas Bailey, 1836-1917

— Friar Jerome's Beautiful Book. [Bost., 1896]. One of 250 L.p. copies on handmade paper. 12mo, vellum. cb Oct 17 (12) $70

Aldrovandi, Ulisse, 1522-1605

— De piscibus libri V et de cestis lib. unis. Bologna, 1613. Folio, modern calf incorporating early calf covers. Upper margin of 1 leaf & outer margin of colophon leaf repaired; some browning or spotting. C Oct 30 (169) £1,200 [Pirages]

— De reliquis animalibus exanguibus libri quatuor.... Bologna: Giovanni Battista Bellagamba, 1606. Folio, old blind-tooled calf; spine chipped, front joint cracked. Upper outer corner excised from title. sg Nov 7 (3) $3,400

— Monstrorum historia.... Bologna, 1642. Folio, contemp vellum; spine worn. Lacking 1 prelim leaf; tp torn at outer margin with some loss to border; D1-2 stained at lower margin; E2 torn & repaired; index leaves soiled. Ck Nov 29 (13) £700

Anr copy. Some browning & waterstaining. SI June 9 (10) LIt750,000

Aleman, Mateo, 1547?-1610?

— The Rogue: or the Life of Guzman de Alfarache. L, 1656. 4th Ed. 2 parts in 1 vol. Folio, contemp calf; rebacked, extremities rubbed. Tp repaired; browned throughout. Milne copy. Ck June 12 (3) £80

Alembert, Jean le Rond d', 1717?-83
See also: Diderot & Alembert

— Opuscules mathematiques.... Paris, 1761-80. 8 vols. 4to, orig half calf; spines worn at head. With 30 folding plates & half-titles to Vols IV-VIII. Tp to Vol I soiled at upper margin; some browning & spotting. Ck Nov 29 (173) £1,200

— Reflexions sur la cause generale des vents. Paris, 1747. 2 parts in 1 vol. 4to, contemp calf gilt. With 2 folding plates. Tp browned at margins; section torn from lower margin of b1. Ck Nov 29 (170) £240

Alencar, Jose Martiniano, 1829-77

— Iracema, the Honey-Lips, a Legend.... L, 1866. Bound with: Pereira da Silva, J. M. Manuel de Moraes.... L, 1886. First work trans by Isabel Burton; 2d work trans by both Burtons. 8vo, orig wraps. S June 25 (408) £350 [Quaritch]

Alexander, J. J. G.

— A Survey of Manuscripts Illuminated in the British Isles. L, 1975-82. Vols I-IV (of 6). Folio, cloth, in d/js. sg Oct 31 (187) $500

Alexander, Sir James Edward, 1803-85

— Narrative of a Voyage of Observation among the Colonies of Western Africa. L, 1837. 1st Ed. 2 vols. 8vo, recent mor gilt. Library markings. DW Jan 29 (1) £54

— Salmon-Fishing in Canada, by a Resident.

L, 1860. Ed by Alexander. 8vo, orig cloth; worn. Koopman copy. O Oct 29 (2) $90

— Transatlantic Sketches, comprising Visits to the most interesting Scenes in North and South America.... L, 1833. 1st Ed. 2 vols. 8vo, half mor; rubbed. With map & 10 plates. bba Mar 26 (320) £110 [Eccles]

Alexander, L.

— Alexander's Hebrew Ritual, and Doctrinal Explanation.... L, 1819. 8vo, calf; rubbed. sg June 25 (149) $225

Alexander, Samuel, Publisher

— Photographic Scenery of South Africa. [L, 1880]. 4to, orig mor gilt; rubbed. With tinted litho title & 98 photographs mtd on 49 sheets. Ck May 15 (65) £190

Alexander, William, 1767-1816

— Austrians. L, 1813. ("Picturesque Representations of the Dress and Manners of the Austrians.") 4to, contemp half mor; head of spine torn, hinges def. With 50 hand-colored plates. Plate 1 detached & frayed at margins; minor spotting to 2 plates. b June 22 (146) £200

— Chinese. L, 1814. ("Picturesque Representations of the Dress and Manners of the Chinese.") 4to, contemp mor gilt, orig backstrip retained. With 50 hand-colored plates. sg May 7 (3) $850

Anr Ed. L, 1814 [plates watermarked 1829]. 4to, modern lev. With pictorial title & 49 hand-colored plates. Pearl Buck's copy. bbc Dec 9 (318) $975

— Russians. L, [c.1823]. ("Picturesque Representations of the Dress and Manners of the Russians....") 8vo, contemp mor gilt; rubbed. With 64 hand-colored plates. Some browning. SI June 9 (15) LIt1,000,000

— Turks. L, 1814. ("Picturesque Representations of the Dress and Manners of the Turks.") 4to, contemp mor gilt; rubbed. With 60 hand-colored plates, some finished with gum-arabic. some creases & thumbmarks. S June 30 (125) £600 [Gonul]

Alexandre, Arsene

— L'Art decoratif de Leon Bakst. Paris, 1913. Folio, orig half vellum gilt; spine tape-repaired. With port & 73 (of 77) plates, 46 in color. sg Oct 17 (7) $350

— Jean-Francois Raffaelli, peintre, graveur.... Paris, 1909. 4to, contemp half mor; spine ends chipped, loose. sg Feb 6 (236) $200

Alexandre, Arsene —& Others

— The Modern Poster. NY: 1895. One of 1,000. 8vo, cloth. Lacking the Bradley poster. sg Apr 2 (228) $110

Alfieri, Francesco Fernando

— La Scherma.... Padua, 1640. 2 parts in 1 vol. Oblong 4to, later half calf. With engraved title, port & 35 plates. sg Mar 26 (6) $2,000

Alfonso X, King of Castile & Leon

— Lapidario.... Madrid, 1881. 4to, modern half calf; new endpapers. With 264 color plates. bba June 25 (1A) £130 [Polites]

Alfonso XI, King of Castile & Leon

— Chronica del muy esclarecido Principe.... Valladolid: Medina del Campo, 1551. Folio, mor gilt by Chambolle-Duru. Double column, gothic letter. C May 28 (250) £4,500

Alford, Lady Marianne Margaret

— Needlework as Art. L, 1886. 8vo, orig half vellum; soiled. bba Oct 24 (104) £50 [Besley]

Anr copy. Cloth; soiled. DW Oct 9 (799) £65

Anr copy. Orig cloth. L Feb 27 (92) £70

Alger, Horatio, 1832-99

— Ragged Dick; or, Street Life in New York with the Boot-Blacks. Bost.: Loring, [1868]. 1st Ed, 1st Issue. 8vo, orig cloth; some rubbing & wear, small segments along upper & lower inner hinges lost from insect damage. Some soiling & staining. Manney copy. P Oct 11 (2) $5,500

— Timothy Crump's Ward. Bost., 1866. Ptd wraps; worn. NH May 30 (252) $3,100

Alibert, Jean Louis, 1766?-1837

— Description des maladies de la peau.... Paris, 1833. ("Clinique de l'Hopital Saint-Louis....") Folio, modern calf preserving orig bds. With hand-colored frontis & 63 hand-colored plates. Some foxing. sg May 14 (2) $1,100

Alison, Sir Archibald, 1792-1867

— History of Europe from the Commencement of the French Revolution in 1789 to the Restoration of the Bourbons.... Edin. & L, 1847-48. 20 vols; without Atlas. 8vo, half mor. W Mar 6 (15) £220

Anr Ed. Edin. & L, 1849-50. 14 vols. 8vo, contemp calf gilt; rubbed & soiled. bba Jan 30 (206) £260 [Corbett]

Anr copy. Contemp calf gilt; rubbed. bba Feb 27 (133) £220 [Harrington]

Anr copy. Contemp calf; rubbed. bba July 9 (196) £70 [Axe]

Anr copy. Half mor; extremities rubbed.

sg Oct 17 (108) $80

Anr copy. Atlas only. Contemp sheep; worn. With frontis & 108 maps, most with hand-coloring. sg Feb 13 (127) $175

Alken, Henry, 1784-1851

— A Collection of Sporting and Humourous Designs.... L: Thomas M'Lean, 1824. 2 vols. Folio, 19th-cent mor gilt, bound for Henry Arthur Johnstone, with his shield. With 3 hand-colored titles & 208 plates only, 4 folding, 2 loosely inserted. Cut round (with occasional loss of imprint) & mtd or inalid; interleaved throughout. Sold w.a.f. C May 20 (9) £11,000 [Marshall]

— Driving Discoveries. L, 1817. Oblong 4to, later mor gilt by Riviere. With 7 hand-colored plates. C May 20 (10) £850 [Marlborough]

— Hunting, or Six Hour's Sport.... L, 1823. Folio, modern mor gilt by Bayntun. With 6 hand-colored plates. Small hole in Plate I. C May 20 (11) £1,800 [Marlborough]

— The National Sports of Great Britain. L, 1823. Folio, contemp mor gilt; joints split, upper cover detached. With hand-colored aquatint title & 50 hand-colored plates. Frontis detached; some soiling. C May 20 (140) £4,500 [Shapero]

Anr Ed. L, 1903. Folio, orig half cloth; worn. With 50 colored plates. Ck Sept 6 (1A) £550

Anr copy. Orig cloth; rubbed & soiled, joints split, shelf mark on spine. With additional colored title & 50 colored plates. Stamp on verso of additional title; contents leaf soiled. pn Mar 19 (355) £850 [Map House]

— Sporting Notions. L, [1832]. Oblong folio, orig half mor; broken. With 36 uncolored plates. Some soiling & marginal tears; lacking text. DW May 13 (106) £280

— Sporting Sketches. L, [1817-19]. 6 parts. Oblong folio, contemp bds. With title & 48 plates. bba Dec 19 (59) £1,300 [Etching]

— Symptoms of Being Amused. L, 1822. Vol I (all pbd). Oblong folio, later half mor. With 41 hand-colored plates & hand-colored litho title. C Oct 30 (6) £280 [Traylen]

Anr copy. Contemp half mor gilt; worn. With 41 hand-colored plates. L Feb 27 (176) £500

Alken, Samuel

— Sixteen Views of the Lakes in Cumberland and Westmorland. L, [n.d. - plates watermarked 1794]. 4to, modern half calf, orig wraps preserved. bba Feb 27 (335) £650 [E. Robinson]

All...

— All the Year Round. L, 1859-1868. 20 vols in 10. Conducted by Charles Dickens. 8vo, later half calf; rubbed. bba Feb 27 (124) £240 [Grant & Shaw]

New Series, Vols II-XXIII, Nos 27-573. L, 1869-79. 8vo, bound by vol in half calf; worn & scuffed. bbc Dec 9 (452) $200

Allan, John Harrison

— A Pictorial Tour in the Mediterranean. L, 1843. Folio, orig cloth; def. With litho title & 40 tinted lithos. Most plates becoming detached; several plates showing waterstains or spotting in margins. S Nov 15 (1169) £450 [Kutluoglu]

Anr copy. Orig cloth; worn. With pictorial title & 40 plates. Some staining in lower margins; some spotting. S May 14 (1189) £300 [Bailey]

Allason, Thomas, 1790-1852

— Picturesque Views of the Antiquities of Pola, in Istria. L, 1819. 1st Ed. Folio, contemp half lea; spine broken, worn. With frontis & 9 plates. Some foxing. SI June 9 (20) LIt1,100,000

Allemagne, Henry Rene d'

— Les Accessoires du costume et du mobilier depuis le treizieme jusqu'au milieu du dixneuvieme siecle. Paris, 1928. 3 vols. Folio, orig half cloth; tear along 1 joint. Eva Le Gallienne's copy. sg Feb 6 (4) $550

— Les Anciens Maitres serruriers et leurs meilleurs travaux. Paris, 1943. One of 600. 2 vols. Folio, text in orig wraps, plates loose as issued in bd folder. With 168 plates. S July 1 (1234) £180 [Angelini]

— Les Cartes a jouer du XIVe au XXe siecle. Paris, 1906. 2 vols. 4to, rebound in cloth. sg Oct 31 (6) $1,000

Anr copy. Later cloth, orig wraps bound in. sg Nov 7 (5) $1,200

— Histoire du luminaire depuis l'epoque romaine.... Paris, 1891. One of 1,000. 4to, half mor gilt, orig wraps bound in; covers stained. With 80 color plates. sg Feb 6 (3) $600

— Musee le Secq des Tournelles a Rouen. Ferronerie Ancienne. Paris, 1924. 2 vols. 4to, orig half cloth; worn & dampstained. With 206 plates. cb Sept 5 (57) $55

Allen...

— The Allen Press Bibliography. [Greenbrae, 1981]. One of 450. Folio, half cloth. cb Nov 21 (5) $130

— The Allen Press Bibliography. A Facsimile with Original Leaves and Additions to Date.... San Francisco: Book Club of California, 1985. One of 750. Folio, cloth. bbc Apr 27 (87) $100

— The Allen Press Bibliography. San Francisco: Book Club of CA, 1985. One of 750. Folio, half cloth. cb Jan 16 (4) $100

— The Allen Press Bibliography: A Facsimile with Original Leaves and Additions to Date.... San Francisco: Book Club of California, 1985. One of 750. pba July 23 (3) $110

Allen, A. J.

— Ten Years in Oregon. Ithaca, NY, 1848. 1st Ed, 2d Issue. 8vo, contemp sheep gilt; stained, spine chipped, rear joint split. Some dampstaining. wa Mar 5 (391) $100

Issue with the Fremont extracts. Cloth. Some foxing. sg June 18 (443) $90

Allen, Albert H. See: McMurtrie & Allen

Allen, Charles Dexter, 1865-1926

— American Book-Plates. A Guide to their Study.... L, 1894. Ltd Ed. 8vo, orig vellum wraps. With 41 plates. cb Oct 17 (16) $70

Anr copy. Cloth. O Sept 24 (7) $170

Allen, Jay. See: Quintanilla, Luis

Allen, John, 1660?-1741

— Synopsis Medicinae, or a Summary View of the Whole Practice of Physick.... L, 1761. 4th Ed. 2 vols. 8vo, contemp calf; rubbed. bba Sept 5 (260) £55 [Maggs]

Allen, John Fisk

— Victoria regia; or the Great Water Lily of America. Bost., 1854. Folio, orig wraps; spine reinforced & torn, a little loose. With 6 color plates. Schlosser copy. P June 18 (505) $16,000

Allen, Lewis M.

— Printing with the Handpress. Kentfield: Allen Press, 1969. One of 140. pba July 23 (2) $1,100

Allen, Thomas, 1803-33

— Lancashire Illustrated. L, 1832. 4to, half mor; worn, covers loose. bba Feb 13 (28) £130 [B. Bailey]

— The Picturesque Beauties of Great Britain: Kent. L: George Virtue, [c.1830]. 4to, orig mor; spine worn. With frontis, folding map & 126 views on 63 plates. DW Mar 4 (80) £190

Anr Ed. L: George Virtue, [c.1832?]. 4to, contemp half calf; worn, backstrip lacking, upper cover detached. With engraved title, frontis, folding map & 126 views on 63 plates. bba Sept 19 (258) £130 [E. Hill]

Allen, Thomas, 1813-82

— The Commerce and Navigation of the Valley of the Mississippi. St. Louis, [1847]. 8vo, modern half cloth folder, orig wraps bound in. sg June 18 (3) $375

Allen, William, 1793-1864

— Picturesque Views on the River Niger.... L, 1840. Oblong folio, orig wraps. With 22 plates on 10 sheets, including folding panorama. pnE May 13 (188) £350

Alley, Ronald

— Francis Bacon. L, [1964]. Intro by John Rothenstein. 4to, later half mor gilt. With 27 mtd colored plates. DW Mar 11 (460) £640

Allgaier, Johann, 1763-1823

— Neue theoretisch-praktische Anweisung zum Schachspiel. Vienna, 1795-96. 2 vols. Vol I in contemp calf, Vol II in half cloth. With 5 plates, 1 hand-colored. Some browning. Ck May 8 (82) £200

Allibone, Samuel Austin, 1816-89

— A Critical Dictionary.... Phila., 1874-91. 3 vols, without Supplement. Half mor gilt; supplement loose. bbc Sept 23 (66) $65

Anr Ed. Phila., 1882-91. 5 vols, including 2-vol Supplement. 4to, bdg not given. cb Oct 17 (19) $160

Anr Ed. Phila., 1891-92. 5 vols, including 2-vol Supplement. 4to, half mor by Bradstreet; rubbed. K Dec 1 (8) £160

Anr Ed. Phila., 1908. 5 vols, including 2 Supplements. Half calf. cb Feb 27 (1) $140

Allingham, Helen. See: Huish, Marcus Bourne

Allingham, William, 1824-89

— In Fairyland.... L, 1870 [1869]. 1st Ed. Illus by Richard Doyle. 4to, orig cloth; prelims loose. With 16 colored plates. Some spotting. bba July 23 (48A) £520 [Ginnan]

Anr copy. Orig cloth; extremities rubbed. Ck July 10 (235) £260

Anr copy. Orig bds; spine detached, corners bumped. Ck July 10 (236) £160

Anr copy. Orig cloth; extremities worn. Soiled & frayed. DW Nov 6 (540) £310

Anr Ed. L, 1870. Folio, orig cloth; worn. With frontis & 15 plates. Margins soiled. DW Dec 11 (415) £180

Anr copy. Orig cloth; worn, backstrip def. Some soiling & marking. DW Dec 11 (416) £160

2d Ed. L, 1875. Folio, orig cloth. With 16 colored plates. Some leaves frayed. S Apr 28 (29) £150 [Besley Bks]

Alliot, Hector

— Bibliography of Arizona. Los Angeles, 1914. One of 500. Bdg worn. sg Oct 31 (7) $200

Allison, Charles Elmer

— The History of Yonkers.... NY, [1896]. 4to, orig lea; rebacked, rubbed. Met Apr 28 (453) $70

Allison, Thomas

— An Account of a Voyage from Archangel in Russia.... L, 1699. 8vo, contemp calf; rebacked. With 2 charts. Rust-holes in margins; small hole in inner margin of 1 plate. S Nov 21 (370) £4,500 [Walcot]

Allom, Thomas, 1804-72
See also: Rose, Thomas

— Constantinople ancienne et moderne.... Paris & L, [c.1850]. 3 vols in 1. 4to, contemp half calf; def. With engraved title, 2 maps & 95 plates & views. S June 30 (85) £600 [Consolidated Real]

— Views in the Tyrol. L, [1836]. 4to, contemp half calf gilt; worn. With folding map & 45 plates. lower margin spotted & dampstained; lacking frontis. DW Mar 4 (1) £80

Almanacs
See also: Miniature Books

— Almanach royal. Paris, 1764. 8vo, contemp mor gilt with large central ciphers ADM. P Dec 12 (156) $3,750

— The Book-Lover's Almanac. NY: Duprat, 1893-97. Ltd Ed. 5 vols. cb Oct 17 (110) $190

— Hand-Book Almanac for the Pacific States. San Francisco, 1863. 12mo, cloth. cb Sept 12 (104) $110

— Nautical Almanac and Astronomical Ephemeris. L, 1769-99. Compiled by Nevil Maskelyne. 23 vols in 21. 8vo, contemp calf; some worn and disbound; some def. Sold w.a.f. bba Jan 30 (411) £70 [M. Clarke]

Alpheraky, Sergius

— The Geese of Europe and Asia. L, 1905. 4to, orig cloth; rubbed. With colored litho frontis & 24 plates. C May 20 (141) £400 [Mitchell]

Anr copy. Orig cloth; badly dampstained. Scattered spotting. DW Dec 11 (134) £190; DW Apr 8 (145) £300

Alphonsus de Spina

— Fortalitium fidei. Nuremberg: Anton Koberger, 10 Oct 1485. 4to, new half calf over wooden bds. 159 (of 160) leaves; lacking initial blank. Goff A-541. B Nov 1 (534) HF3,200

Alpinus, Prosperus, 1553-1617

— De medicina Aegyptiorum. Venice, 1591. 4to, later half vellum. Tp soiled; some spotting. Ck Oct 18 (1) £220

Anr Ed. Paris, 1645. 2 parts in 1 vol. 4to, contemp vellum. Marginal staining & browning. SI Dec 5 (26) LIt600,000

— De praesagienda vita, et morte aegrotantium libri septem.... Bassano: Remondini, 1774. 4to, contemp vellum. Some foxing. SI Dec 5 (28) LIt320,000

Alter, J. Cecil

— James Bridger. Salt Lake City, [1925]. Ltd Ed, sgd. cb Feb 12 (2) $140

Al'tman, Natan

— Lenin. Petersburg, 1921. 4to, orig wraps; recased, spine ends restored. With cover design & 9 plates. sg Nov 7 (182) $150

Alunno, Francesco, d.1556

— Della fabrica del mondo.... Venice: Porta, 1584. 2 parts in 1 vol. Folio, contemp vellum. Marginal spotting. SI June 9 (25) LIt480,000

— Le Ricchezze della lingua volgara.... Venice: Sons of Aldus Manutius, 1551. 2d Ed. 4to, 16th-cent vellum. Short tear in F2. S Dec 5 (35) £1,100 [Quaritch]

Alvares, Francisco, c.1465-1541

— Historiale Description de l'Ethiopie. Antwerp: Plantin, 1558. 8vo, 18th-cent mor gilt. Gennadius-Clements copy. S Nov 21 (347) £2,800 [Maggs]

Alvord, Clarence W., 1868-1928

— The Mississippi Valley in British Politics. Cleveland, 1917. 2 vols. K Sept 29 (6) $170

Alvord, Thomas G. See: Derrydale Press

Amadis de Gaul

— Le Premiere Livre de Amadis de Gaule.... Paris, 1546-54. Books 1-3 & 6-11 (of 12), in 4 vols. Folio, 16th-cent vellum gilt; 2 spines def. Lacking I3-4 in Book 8; some dampstaining at the beginning of Book 6. S Dec 5 (36) £1,800 [Quaritch]

Amadon, Dean. See: Brown & Amadon

Amateur Flagellant, Pseud.

— A Series of Remarkable Instances of Whipping inflicted on Both Sexes.... L: Pvtly ptd, 1885. 8vo, orig cloth; lacking backstrip. sg Mar 5 (109) $150

Amati, Carlo

— Regole del chiar-oscuro in architettura. Milan, 1802. Folio, contemp half lea. With engraved title & 13 plates. Some foxing & marginal spotting. SI Dec 5 (29) LIt500,000

Amazing Stories
— Amazing Stories. NY, Apr 1926. Vol I, No 1. Ed by Hugo Gernsback. 4to, pictorial wraps; edges chipped. sg June 11 (6) $200

Ambert, Joachim, 1804-90
— Esquisses historiques des...l'armee francaise. Saumur, 1835. 2 vols. Folio, plate vol in contemp mor with gilt initial H on upper cover, text vol in contemp wraps with orig upper wrap bound as title. With hand-colored litho & 13 (of 16) plates. Some text leaves with clean tears. C Oct 30 (7) £700 [Toscani]

Ambrose, Poet
— L'estoire de la Guerre Sainte histoire en vers de la troisieme croisade.... Paris, 1897. 4to, later cloth. S June 30 (5) £650 [Bank of Cyprus]

Ambrosius, Saint, 340?-397
— De officiis. Milan: Christophorus Valdarfer, 7 Jan 1474. 4to, 16th-cent bds. Roman type; 28 lines. Some annotations; Ms note dated 23 Apr 1565; marginal spotting at end. 128 leaves. Goff A-560.. SI June 9 (27) LIt5,000,000

Amedeo, Luigi, of Savoy. See: Luigi Amedeo of Savoy

Amelung, Peter
— Der Fruedruck im deutschen Suedwesten, 1473-1500. Stuttgart, [1979]. 4to, wraps. sg Oct 31 (144) $80

American...
— American Architecture of the Twentieth Century, NY, [1927]. Ed by Oliver Reagan. Vols I-II, Parts 1-6, in 5. Loose in orig bd folders. With 120 plates. Minor edge wear to plates, some staining. bbc Apr 27 (481) $110
— American Artist and Their Works: A Series of Etchinge, Photo-Etchings.... Bost., [1889]. 2 vols 8vo, orig half mor; worn, joints cracking. cb Nov 21 (6) $130
— American Book Prices Current. NY, 1959-79. Vols 65-85. 21 vols. Ck Nov 29 (49) £50

Indexes for 1965-87. NY, 1966-88. 8 vols. NH Aug 23 (350) $675

Vols 72-84. NY, 1969-75. Worn, shaken. O Sept 24 (13) $175

11 vols for 1969-71, 1974-76, and 1978-82. NY, 1972-82. sg Oct 31 (9) $600

Index vol for 1965-70. NY, 1974. 2 vols. Worn, shaken; Vol II loose in bdg. O Sept 24 (11) $80; sg Oct 31 (11) $110

Vols 80-86. NY, 1974-80. cb Feb 27 (3) $275

Index, 1970-75. NY, 1976. 2 vols. Worn, inner joints broken. O Sept 24 (12) $130

Anr copy. Vol I loose in bdg. sg Oct 31 (13) $200

Vols 83-96, with Indexes for 1970-87. NY, 1976-90. Together, 21 vols. Cover of Vol 96 damaged. bba Apr 30 (368) £750

Vols 82 & 84-91. Together, 9 vols. NY, 1977-86. O Apr 28 (145) $250

Index for 1975-79. NY, 1980. 2 vols sg Oct 31 (14) $250; sg Oct 31 (15) $175

Index for 1979-83. NY, 1984. 2 vols. sg Oct 13 (16) $375

Vols 92-94. NY, 1986-88. O Aug 25 (5) $200

Index for 1983-87. NY, 1988. 2 vols. sg Oct 31 (17) $375
— The American Mercury: A Monthly Review. NY, 1924-30. Vols I-XIX. Ed by H. L. Mencken. Bound in 19 vols. 8vo, half cloth, orig wraps bound in; bdgs worn. O Aug 25 (9) $100
— The American Remembrancer; or an Impartial Collection of Essays, Resolves, Speeches, &c. relative...to the Treaty with Great Britain. Phila., 1795-96. Ed by Mathew Carey. Nos 1-12 (complete) in 3 vols. 8vo, contemp calf; rubbed & dried. Library markings. O Apr 28 (157) $120
— The American Review: A Whig Journal. NY, 1845. Vol I, Nos 1-6. 6 issues. 8vo, bound together in modern half mor gilt. Contains the first appearance of Poe's The Raven. sg Mar 5 (267) $850
— The American Wanderer through Various Parts of Europe.... L, 1783. 1st Ed. 8vo, modern half calf. Foxed & browned; dampstain to fore-edge affecting text. wa Sept 26 (540) $70

American Aeroplane Supply House
— Bleriot Type Monoplanes. Hampstead NY, 1912. 8vo, wraps. cb Nov 7 (63) $225

American, An. See: Robinson, Alfred

American Farmer. See: Forsyth, William

American Philosophical Society
— Transactions of the American Philosophical Society.... Phila, 1789-1804. Vols I-VI. 4to, orig bds; spines chipped, some staining & foxing. Some internal foxing. P June 16 (152) $10,000

American Type Founders Company
— Specimen Book and Catalogue, 1923. NY: Pvtly ptd, 1910. One of 100. cb Oct 17 (882) $55

Ames, Joseph, 1689-1759
— Typographical Antiquities. L, 1749. 1st Ed. 4to, contemp calf; rebacked. With 8 plates. cb Jan 16 (8) $275

Ames, Joseph, 1689-1759 —& Herbert, William, 1718-95

— Typographical Antiquities. L, 1785-90. 3 vols. 4to, modern half cloth. Vol III lacking last leaves of index; last 3 leaves of Vol I reinforced at outer edge. bba Dec 19 (246) £95 [Rix]

Amherst, J. H.

— The Burmese War; a Grand Naval and Military Melo-Drama, in Three Acts. L, [n.d.]. Illus by Robert Cruikshank. 8vo, half calf; edges worn. With hand-colored frontis. Cohn copy. sg Oct 17 (192) $200

Amici, Domenico

— Raccolta delle principali vedute di Roma. Rome, 1834-37. Oblong folio, contemp half lea. With engraved title & 39 plates. SI June 9 (28) LIt1,100,000

— Raccolta di trenta vedute degli obelischi, scelte fontane.... Rome, 1839. Bound with: Raccolta delle vedute dei contorni di Roma. Rome, 1847. Oblong folio, contemp half mor. With engraved title & 71 plates in 1st work & engraved title & 12 plates in 2d work. Ck Nov 29 (289) £550

Amico, Bernardino

— Trattato delle piante & immagini de sacri edifizi di Terra Santa. Florence: Pietro Cecconcelli, 1620. Plates engraved by Jacques Callot. 4to, contemp mor gilt with gilt arms of Peiresc; slightly waterstained. With engraved title & 34 double-page plates showing 46 plans & views. Lower margins stained & affected by damp throughout; 2 plates with minor tears at lower fold. C Dec 19 (18) £5,000 [Panini]

Anr copy. Wraps; torn. With 33 double-page plates only. Sold w.a.f. SI June 9 (29) LIt380,000

Ammirato, Scipione, 1531-1601

— Istorie Fiorentine. Florence, 1647-41. 2 vols in 3. Folio, 19th-cent vellum. Some browning. SI June 9 (30) LIt1,700,000

Amos, William

— Minutes of Agriculture and Planting.... Bost., 1810. 4to, half mor. With 9 plates & 3 leaves with 10 mtd specimens of grass types. bba Apr 9 (194) £400 [Hollander]

Amphiareo, Vespasiano

— Opera di frate Vespiasiano Amphiareo da Ferrara...nella quale si insegna a scrivere varie sorti di lettere.... Venice, 1559. Oblong 4to, modern mor. Hole affecting a few letters in 1 text leaf; some staining; F3 torn & restored & lower half in facsimile; marginal tear in last leaf. C June 24 (222) £1,900 [Franks]

Anr Ed. Venice: Marco Bindoni, 1596. Oblong 4to, contemp wraps. C June 24 (223) £800 [Franks]

Amuchastegui, Axel

— Some Birds and Mammals of South America. L, 1966. One of 50 with an orig drawing. Text by Carlos Selva Andrade. Folio, orig vellum gilt by Zaehnsdorf. W Mar 6 (93) £570

Amundsen, Roald, 1872-1928

— The South Pole: an Account of the Norwegian Antarctic Expedition in the "Fram." L, 1912. 2 vols. Orig cloth. DW Nov 6 (3) £350

Anr copy. Cloth; worn & shaken. O Aug 25 (11) $160

Anr copy. Orig cloth. sg Jan 9 (5) $650

— Sydpoten den Norske Sydpolsfaerd Med Fram. Kristiania, 1912. 2 vols. Half mor gilt; rubbed. Some underscoring in Vol I. DW Nov 6 (5) £50

— "The North West Passage": Record of a Voyage of Exploration on the Ship "Gjoa...." NY, 1908. 2 vols. Orig cloth; rubbed & soiled. DW Nov 6 (4) £120

Anr copy. Orig cloth; corners worn. DW Jan 29 (4) £165

Amundsen, Roald, 1872-1928 —& Ellsworth, Lincoln

— First Crossing of the Polar Sea. NY, 1927. In d/j. Sgd & dated by Amundsen just before he disappeared. cb Nov 7 (1) $250

Amyntor. See: Belknap, Jeremy

Anabaptisticum...

— Anabaptisticum et Enthusiasticum Pantheon.... [Coethen, 1705?]. 15 parts in 1 vol. Folio, contemp vellum. With 31 ports; 17 plates. sg May 7 (4) $2,400

Anacreon, 572?-488? B.C.

See also: Nonesuch Press

— Recueil de compositions dessinees par Girodet, et Gravees par M. Chatillon.... Paris, 1825. Folio, contemp half mor; worn at extremities. With 52 plates. Ck Dec 11 (194) £110

— 1791. - Odaria.... Parma: Bodoni Press. 8vo, contemp calf gilt. SI June 9 (29) LIt380,000

— 1800. - Odes. L. Trans by Thomas Moore. 4to, later half mor; stained. With 29 plates. cb Sept 26 (160) $120

Anania, Giovanni Lorenzo d'

— L'Universale Fabrica del mondo, overo cosmografia. Venice: Andrea Muschio, 1596. 4to, contemp vellum; upper joint split. With 4 folding maps. Tp & dedications dampstained; marginal worming. Ck Oct 18 (40) £400

Anburey, Thomas

— Travels through the Interior Parts of America. L, 1789. 1st Ed. 2 vols. 8vo, half calf; rubbed. With folding map (hand-colored in outline) & 6 plates. Some plates split. O Jan 14 (7) $325

Anr Ed. L, 1791. 2 vols. 8vo, contemp half calf; rubbed, broken. With folding map & 6 plates. Some foxing. O Aug 25 (12) $160

Ancient. See: Lockhart, John Gibson

Andersen, Hans Christian, 1805-75

See also: Limited Editions Club

— Danish Fairy Legends and Tales. L, 1846. 8vo, half mor; rubbed. Bound without half-title. DW May 13 (247) £75

— Eventyr, fortalte for Born. Copenhagen: Bianco & Schneider for C. A. Reitzel, 1837 [ptd 1835-37]. 3 parts in 1 vol. 8vo, contemp bds; rubbed. Manney copy. P Oct 11 (3) $8,500

— Eventyr og Historier. Copenhagen: Reitzel, 1862-63. 1st Collected Ed. Vol I only, bound from parts. Contemp half lea, orig upper wraps for Parts 1 & 3 bound in. Without prelims. Inscr to Paul Bloch on 2 of the wraps. C Dec 16 (20) £2,000 [Schiller]

— Fairy Tales. L, [1924]. Illus by Kay Nielsen. 4to, orig cloth; rear bd stained; minor stain to corner of front bd. pnL Nov 20 (198) £65

Anr copy. Orig cloth. Inscr. wa Dec 9 (439) $325

One of 500. Vellum gilt, orig cloth wrap; frayed. With 12 mtd colored plates. b Mar 11 (120) £850

Anr copy. Vellum. b June 22 (61) £800

Anr copy. Orig cloth, in d/j. bba Apr 9 (290) £150 [Fox]

Anr copy. Orig cloth; spine stained. With 12 plates. Ck July 10 (82) £220

Anr copy. Mor gilt; upper joint cracked. With 12 mtd colored plates. P Oct 11 (242) $1,700

Anr copy. Orig cloth; upper joint split, spine chipped. With 12 colored plates. S Nov 14 (124) £300 [Droller]

Anr Ed. L, [1932]. Illus by Arthur Rackham. 4to, cloth, in d/j; upper cover torn. bba Jan 16 (378) £160 [Sotheran]; bba Apr 9 (325) £320 [W. White]

Anr copy. Half lea. br May 29 (184) $175

One of 525. Orig vellum gilt. With 12 colored plates. S Nov 14 (128) £500 [Richardson]

Anr Ed. NY, 1932. Illus by Kay Nielsen. In d/j. sg Jan 30 (137) $225

Anr Ed. Phila., [1932]. Illus by Arthur Rackham. 4to, orig cloth, in d/j. S Apr 28 (44) £220 [Marks]

Anr Ed. L, 1935. ("Fairy Tales and Legends.") Illus by Rex Whistler. In frayed & def d/j. bba July 23 (309) £55 [Sotheran]

One of 150. b Nov 18 (117) £190; bba Mar 26 (202) £200 [Thorp]; wa Sept 26 (676) $140

— Het leelijke jonge eendje. Amst., 1893. Proof copy. Illus by Theo van Hoytema. Folio, orig half cloth; worn, upper joint split, backstrip def. With tp & 31 plates with accompanying text, each mtd on large sheets of paper, colored by hand. Edges of some sheets torn or stained. S Nov 14 (140) £150 [Schiller]

— Stories. L, 1911. ("Stories from Hans Andersen.") Illus by Edmund Dulac. 4to, orig cloth; rubbed. bba Jan 16 (374) £65 [Harrington]

One of 750. Orig vellum gilt. With 28 colored plates. sg Sept 26 (96) $700

Anr copy. Mor gilt by Bayntun. sg Nov 7 (72) $950

Anr copy. Orig vellum gilt. sg Jan 30 (41) $1,800

— Stories for the Household. L: Routledge, 1866. Trans by H W. Dulcken; illus by the Dalziel Brothers after A. W. Bayes. 8vo, later calf. Extremities rubbed. cb Sept 26 (5) $190

— Wonderful Stories for Children. L: Chapman & Hall, 1846. Trans by Mary Howitt. 16mo, orig cloth; extremities rubbed & the color there retouched, lower free endpaper restored at tail-edge. With 4 hand-finished color plates. Manney copy. P Oct 11 (4) $2,250

Anderson, Adam, 1692?-1765

— An Historical and Chronological Deduction of the Origin of Commerce.... L, 1764. 2 vols. 4to, contemp calf; worn. With 3 folding maps. Marginal worming; some dampstaining to fore-margins of Vol I. DW Nov 6 (285) £100

Anr Ed. L, 1801. 4 vols. 4to, later cloth. With 2 folding maps. Library markings. bba June 11 (79) £150 [Quaritch]

Anderson, George William

See also: Cook, Capt. James

— A New, Authentic, and Complete Collection of Voyages Round the World. L: Alex. Hogg, [1784-86]. 2d Ed. Folio, contemp calf; def. With port & 146 maps & plates only. Part of general map lacking; tears with loss; soiling; 4NI & final list lacking. Sold w.a.f. pnL Nov 20 (118) £350 [Bailey]

Anderson, James

— The New Practical Gardener. L: William Mackenzie, [1872-74]. 8vo, contemp half calf; worn, upper cover detached, backstrip loose. With 25 color plates. bba June 11 (251) £110 [Mason]

Anderson, James, 1662-1728

— Selectus diplomatum et numismatum Scotiae thesaurus. Edin., 1739. Folio, modern half calf. With frontis, extra title & 179 plates, 12 folding. bba Nov 28 (271) £170 [Bernard]

Anderson, James, 1680?-1739

— Constitutions of the Antient Fraternity of Free and Accepted Masons. L, 1784. 4to, contemp mor gilt; rubbed. bba May 28 (49) £400 [Bunout]

Anderson, James, 1739-1808

— An Account of the Present State of the Hebrides and the Western Coasts of Scotland. Dublin, 1786. 8vo, contemp calf; rubbed, joints broken. With folding map. Library markings. O Jan 14 (8) $50

— The New Practical Gardener and Modern Horticulturist. L, [c.1875]. 4to, contemp half mor; worn, lacking upper cover. With 22 plates only. Some plates loose. bba Jan 16 (342) £95 [Mason]

Anderson, Joseph, 1832-1916 —& Drummond, James, 1816-77

— Ancient Scottish Weapons. L, 1881. One of 500. 4to, orig half mor; rubbed. pnE Aug 12 (107) £190

Anderson, Sherwood, 1876-1941

— Dark Laughter. NY, 1925. One of 350. Half vellum. sg Dec 12 (9) $50

— Home Town. NY, [1940]. 4to, cloth, in d/j. Some soiling. F June 25 (488) $75

— Tar: a Midwest Childhood. NY, 1926. 1st Ed. Half vellum, in d/j. sg Dec 12 (10) $70

— Windy McPherson's Son. NY, 1916. 1st Ed. sg Dec 12 (11) $200

— Winesburg, Ohio. NY, 1919. 1st Ed, 1st Issue. Front hinge cracked. sg Dec 12 (12) $80

1st Ptg. In ptd white d/j; top edge stained yellow. Doheny-Manney copy. P Oct 11 (5) $5,500

Andersson, Charles John, 1827-67

— Lake Ngami, or Explorations and Discoveries.... NY, 1857. 1st American Ed. 8vo, orig cloth; rubbed. sg May 21 (1) $70

— The Okavango River: A Narrative of Travel.... NY, 1861. 8vo, modern half calf gilt. With extra title with port & 16 plates. DW Apr 8 (2) £100

Andrae, Walter

— Coloured Ceramics from Ashur. L, 1925. Folio, orig cloth; rubbed. DW Oct 9 (804) £145

Andreini, J. M.

— J. Winfred Spenceley: His Etchings and Engravings in the Form of Book Plates. NY: Torch Press, 1910. One of 1,000. cb Oct 17 (27) $55

Andreossi, Antoine Francois, 1761-1828

— Constantinople et le Bosphore de Thrace. Paris, 1828. Atlas only. Folio, orig wraps; frayed, backstrip def. With 10 double-page plates & maps. S June 30 (87) £700 [Consolidated Real]

Andrews, Henry C., fl.1799-1828

— The Botanist's Repository, for New, and Rare Plants. L, 1797-[1813?]. Vols I-VII only. Contemp calf gilt; extremities rubbed. With engraved titles & 491 hand-colored plates only. Some plates just shaved. Sold w.a.f. C Oct 30 (254) £3,500 [Cherrington]

Anr copy. Vols I-VI only. Contemp calf; worn & rubbed. With 6 engraved titles & 432 hand-colored plates, some ptd in green. Plate 157 detached. Sold w.a.f. C May 20 (143) £3,800 [Schuster]

Anr copy. Vols I-VI (of 10) bound in 3 vols. Contemp mor gilt with initials SG; rubbed. With 6 engraved titles & 432 hand-colored plates. Some ink stains; library stamps; 3 plates cropped & 1 or 2 shaved; 2 plates with small paper adhesions; 1 or 2 plates with small ink stains. pn Mar 19 (252) £3,000 [Bailey]

— Coloured Engravings of Heaths. L, [1794]-1802-9. Vols I-II only. Contemp mor gilt; extremities scuffed. With 144 hand-colored plates. C Oct 30 (255) £1,300 [Jeffrey Sharpe]

Anr Ed. L, [1794]-1802-9-[30]. 4 vols. Folio, modern half mor; stamps on edges, shelf marks on spines. Some soiling, browning & foxing. pn Mar 19 (253) £3,400 [Junk]

— The Heathery, or a Monograph of the Genus Erica. L, 1804-6. Vols I-III (of 6). 8vo, contemp half calf; extremities rubbed. With hand-colored title to Vol I and 149 (of 150) plates. Occasional spotting. Ck July 10 (377) £200

Andrews, James

— Flora's Gems or the Treasures of the Parterre. L, [1830]. Folio, orig cloth; lacking spine. With hand-colored additional title & 9 plates (of 12). Some spotting; 3 plates cut down & loosely inserted. Ck May 15 (3) £400

Andrews, William Loring, 1837-1920

— Among My Books. 1894. One of 2 copies ptd on vellum. 8vo, lev gilt extra by Club Bindery with mosaic pattern of mor inlays. CNY Dec 5 (373) $16,000

— An Essay on the Portraiture of the American Revolutionary War. NY, 1896. One of 185. 8vo, cloth; spine soiled. K Sept 29 (25) $95

— The Iconography of the Battery and Castle Garden. NY, 1901. One of 135. cb Oct 17 (30) $110

— New Amsterdam, New Orange, New York. NY, 1897. One of 170. 4to, contemp mor extra; spine rubbed & patched. Ck Nov 29 (25) £50

— Paul Revere and his Engravings. NY, 1901. One of 135. 8vo, lev gilt extra by Marius-Michel. CNY Dec 5 (411) $1,400

— A Prospect of the Colledges in Cambridge in New England. NY, 1897. One of 115. 8vo, cloth; spines frayed & split. wa Sept 26 (381) $55

Andriveau-Goujon, J.

— Atlas de Geographie ancien et moderne.... Paris: J. Andriveau-Goujon, [c.1855]. Folio, half mor; spine & edges worn. With 30 double-page maps, hand-colored in outline. cb Jan 30 (144) $550

Anduaga y Garimberti, Joseph de

— Arte de escribir por reglas y sin muestras.... Madrid, 1781. 4to, contemp vellum. With 53 plates. bba May 28 (287) £180 [Poel]

Anesaki, Masaharu

— Buddhist Art in its Relation to Buddhist Ideals.... Bost. & NY, 1915. 1st Ed. 4to, half cloth; corners bumped, worn. With 47 plates. sg Apr 2 (204) $100

Angas, George French, 1822-86

— South Australia Illustrated. L, 1846. 1st Ed. Folio, later 19th-cent half lea; worn, joints cracked. With additional colored litho title, litho dedication, ptd title, list of subscribers & 59 hand-finished colored plates. sg May 7 (5) $9,500

Anr Ed. Sydney, 1967. Ltd Ed. Folio, orig half mor. Facsimile of the 1847 Ed. kh Nov 11 (411) A$440

Angelita, Giovanni Francesco

— I Pomo d'oro.... Ricanati: Antonio Braida, 1607. 4to, 17th-cent mor gilt, with arms of Cardinal Alderano. Some browning & staining. C Dec 16 (21) £1,600 [Mediolanum]

Angelo, Domenico, 1717?-1802

— L'Ecole des Armes, avec l'explication generale.... L, [1763]. Oblong folio, contemp calf; split. With 44 plates. pnE Oct 1 (325) £700

Anr copy. 18th-cent half sheep; needs rebdg. With 47 plates, 2 hand-colored. sg Mar 26 (8) $4,400

— The School of Fencing.... L, 1787. Oblong 8vo, later half calf; rubbed. With 47 (on 44) plates. Some plates trimmed to platemark; some foxing & soiling. pn July 16 (1) £380

Anr copy. Later calf. With 44 (of 47) plates. Upper fore-edge corners excised on 2 leaves, not affecting pagination or text. sg Mar 26 (9) $250

Anr copy. Old sheep; needs rebdg. With 47 (on 44) plates. 2 plates excised & trimmed. sg Mar 26 (10) $500

Angelo, Henry

— Angelo's Pic Nic; or, Table Talk. L, 1834. Illus by George Cruikshank. 8vo, later half mor gilt. sg Mar 26 (11) $120

Anr Ed. L, 1905. One of 50 L.p. copies. 4to, half mor; needs rebdg. With 24 plates. sg Mar 26 (12) $110

One of 500. sg Mar 26 (13) $110; sg Mar 26 (14) $90

Angelo, Henry Charles William, 1760-1839?

— Instructions for the Sword Exercise.... L, 1835. 8vo, 19th-cent cloth. With frontis & 9 plates. sg Mar 26 (15) $175

— Reminiscences. L, 1828-30. 2 vols. 8vo, half sheep. Dedication & preface leaves loose in Vol I. sg Mar 26 (16) $90

Anr Ed. L, 1904. 2 vols. 4to, orig cloth; Vol I bdg spotted. wd June 12 (362) $75

One of 1,000. Cloth. sg Mar 26 (17) $90

Anr Ed. Phila., 1904. 2 vols. 4to, orig cloth. With 68 plates. sg Mar 26 (19) $375

— A Treatise of the Utility and Advantages of Fencing. L, 1817. Oblong folio, contemp sheep; spine def, front cover loose. With 53 plates. sg Mar 26 (20) $1,700

Angelo, Valenti

— A Battle in Washington Square. NY: Golden Cross Press, 1942. One of 200. cb Jan 16 (9) $90

— Valenti Angelo: Author, Illustrator, Printer. San Francisco: Book Club of Calif., 1976. One of 400. Folio, half cloth. pba July 23 (6) $250

Angelus de Clavasio, 1411-95?

— Summa angelica de casibus conscientiae. Venice: Georgius Arrivabenus, 4 June 1492. 4to, half lea. 516 (of 540) leaves; lacking 8 prelims, 265-68 & 12 unnumbered leaves at end. Goff A-723. SI June 9 (36) LIt550,000

Anghiera, Pietro Martire d'. See: Martyr, Peter

Angler, An. See: Davy, Sir Humphry

Anglers' Club of New York

— The Best of the Anglers' Club Bulletin 1920-1972. NY, 1972. One of 1,000. O Mar 31 (9) $110

Angus, William, 1752-1821

— The Seats of the Nobility and Gentry.... L, 1787. Vol I only. Oblong 4to, contemp cloth; soiled & worn. With engraved title & 48 plates. Dampstained throughout. DW Nov 20 (1) £150

Anr copy. Oblong 4to, contemp mor gilt; worn. With title & 63 plates. Spotted, some corners dampstained. DW Mar 4 (56) £240

Anr Ed. L, 1787 [but reissue of 1815]. Oblong 4to, later half lea. With engraved title & 63 plates. Library stamps. Extra-illus with orig watercolor by Humphry Repton of Sundridge Park in Kent. C Oct 30 (72) £1,700 [Woodruff]

Anker, Jean Thore Hojer Jensen

— Bird Books and Bird Art. Copenhagen, 1990. One of 300. 4to, cloth. Reprint of 1938 Ed. sg May 21 (128) $150

Annabel, Russell

See also: Derrydale Press

— Hunting and Fishing in Alaska. NY, 1948. 4to, cloth; spine faded. sg Jan 9 (209) $140; sg May 21 (2) $80

Annan, Thomas

— The Old Closes and Streets of Glasgow. Glasgow, 1900. One of 50. Folio, orig cloth. With 49 (of 50) plates. pnE Mar 11 (120) £210

Anne, Saint

[-] Hec est quedam rara et ideo cara legenda de sanctam Anna.... Strassburg: Kysteler, 1501. 4to, contemp vellum over wooden bds. With colored woodcut title & 3 other colored woodcuts. FD Dec 2 (24) DM4,550

Annesley, George, Viscount Valentia & Earl of Mountmorris

— Voyages and Travels to India, Ceylon.... L, 1809. 3 vols. 4to, contemp calf gilt; rubbed & faded. With 9 folding maps & 60 plates. 1 plate torn. bba Sept 19 (79) £520 [Dawson]

Anr copy. Contemp calf gilt; rubbed & worn. With 3 engraved vignettes & 69 plates, incluyding folding maps. Spotted; many plates in Vol II faintly stained pink. DW Mar 4 (47) £600

2d Ed. L, 1811. Atlas vol only. 4to, contemp half calf; rubbed, upper joint worn & front of spine def. With 72 maps, plates & plans. pn Nov 14 (410) £240

Annesley, James

— Memoirs of an Unfortunate Young Nobleman, Return'd from a Thirteen Years Slavery in America where he had been sent by the Wicked Contrivances of his Cruel Uncle. L, 1743. 2 vols. 12mo, calf; worn, front cover detached. NH May 30 (44) $100

Anonymous. See: Cook, Capt. James

Ansaldis, Ansaldo de

— Decisiones sacrae rotae romanae. Rome: Camera Apostolica, 1711. Folio, contemp mor gilt with arms of Pope Clement XI. Dedication copy. S Dec 5 (255) £1,600 [Breslauer]

Ansidei, Giuseppe

— Trattato cavalleresco contra l'abuso del mantenimento delle private inimicitie. Perugia, 1691. 8vo, old vellum. sg Mar 26 (21) $175

Anson, George, 1697-1762

— A Voyage Round the World.... L, 1748. 1st Ed. 4to, contemp calf gilt; rebacked, corners repaired. With 42 folding maps, charts & plates. Foxed & soiled. bba Apr 9 (145) £440 [Erlini]

Anr copy. 18th-cent calf gilt; rebacked, corners repaired but renewal lea dry & brittle, later endpapers. With 42 maps & plates. Each of the 2 large folding maps with a single tear, 1 repaired. CNY Oct 8 (5) $1,300

Anr copy. Later bds; crudely rebacked. With 42 folding maps, charts & plates. DW Nov 6 (7) £390

Anr copy. Calf gilt; rebacked. With folding frontis map & 42 plates. pnE Oct 2 (490) £650

Anr copy. Contemp calf gilt; rubbed, rebacked & recornered. With 42 folding maps, charts & plates. S June 25 (35) £450 [Renard]

Anr copy. Later half calf; rejointed & worn. Some plates creased & soiled; a few with crudely repaired folds & small areas of backing. wa Apr 9 (108) $850

3d Ed. 4to, modern half calf. With 2 (of 3) folding charts. cb Jan 30 (5) $140

Anr Ed. Edin., 1776. 2 vols in 1. 4to, old

bds with modern calf back; worn. With folding map. O Dec 17 (11) $60
15th Ed. L, 1776. 4to, contemp calf; rubbed, covers detached. With 40 (of 43) folding plates. Some plates stained, some pp loose. Sold w.a.f. bba Feb 27 (2) £260 [B. Bailey]

Ansted, David T.
— The Ionian Islands in the Year 1863. L, 1863. 8vo, contemp half mor; rubbed, rebacked retaining orig spine. With tinted frontis & 4 maps. S June 30 (224) £300 [Consolidated Real]

Answer. See: Company of Royal Adventurers

Anthony, Gordon
— Ballet: Camera Studies.... L, 1937. 4to, orig cloth; stained at bottom edge. With frontis & 95 mtd illusts. K July 12 (46) $100
— Russian Ballet: Camera Studies. L, 1939. 4to, orig cloth; worn & soiled. O Mar 31 (10) $50

Antichristus...
— Antichristus; sive, Prognostica finis mundi. Basel: Petrus Perna, [1570?]. 4to, vellum; spine head chipped. sg Mar 12 (197) $225

Antique...
— Antique Gems from Greek & Latin. Phila.: George Barrie & Son, [1902]. One of 1,000 on japan vellum. 13 vols. 8vo, lev extra. Library stamps. CNY Dec 5 (359) $1,600

Antiquities...
— Antiquities of the Russian Empire. L, 1855 & Moscow, 1849-53. ("Drevnosti Rossiiskago Gosydarstva.") 6 vols in 7 parts, folio & 6 text vols bound in 1, 4to, half syn. sg Nov 7 (198) $5,000

Antolini, Giovanni Antonio
— Opera d'Architettura ossia Progetto sul Foro che doveva eseguirsi in Milano. Milan: Fratelli Bettalli, [early 1800s]. Folio, contemp bds; joints & spine ends worn. With 16 double-page plates & 8 double-page plans. sg Feb 6 (5) $7,500

Antonini, Carlo
— Manuale de vari ornamenti tratti dalle fabbriche e trammenti antichi. Rome, 1781-90. 2 vols in 1. Folio, contemp half vellum; soiled. With frontis & 100 plates. Some discoloration. S May 14 (1075) £370 [Rose]
— Manuale di vari ornamenti componenti la serie de' vasi antichi. Rome, 1821. 3 vols. Folio, contemp vellum gilt. With titles with engraved vignettes, 3 engraved tail-pieces, 3 section titles & 193 plates. Section title & Plate 3 to Vol III bound in at end of Vol I. Rootes copy. C June 24 (211) £1,150 [Ursus]

Antoninus Florentinus, Saint, 1389-1459
— Chronicon. Nuremberg: Anton Koberger, 31 July 1484. ("Summarium primi voluminis partis hystorialis.") 3 vols. Folio, contemp blind-stamped pigskin over wooden bds with vellum title labels on upper covers of each vols, brass clasp plates, bound by the Benedictines of Nuremberg (Kyriss shop 20); formerly chained & restored. 68 lines & headline; double column; types 8:83G (text), 9:165G (titling). Elaborately rubricated, the major initials of each vol incorporating grotesque figures & accompanied by fine penwork borders, including the arms of St. Giles of Nuremberg. Scattered waterstaining. 772 leaves. Goff A-778. Schoyen copy. P Dec 12 (1) $9,000
— Confessionale. Florence: Laurentius de Morgianis et Johannes Petri pour Piero Pacini, 22 Feb 1496. 4to, 19th-cent half calf. 36 lines; roman letter. 114 leaves. Goff A-836. S Dec 5 (2) £2,000 [Schafer]
— Summa moralis. Nuremberg: Anton Koberger, 1478-79. 4 vols. Folio, contemp sheepskin over wooden bds, blind-stamped including gilt letter-stamping at top of each cover, a Nuremberg bdg (Kyriss shop 113); wormed, scraped & rubbed. 59 lines & headline; double column; types 3:110G (text) & 4:160G (titling). Elaborately rubricated & with illuminated initials Some worming in each vol. 254 leaves, 322 leaves, 464 leaves & 338 leaves. Goff A-871. Schoyen copy. P Dec 12 (2) $25,000
— Summa theologica. Strassburg: Johann (Reinhard) Grueninger, 24 Apr-4 Sept 1496. Parts 1 & 2 only (of 4) & index. Folio, contemp German pigskin over wooden bds; stains on front cover, front joint cracked; lacking catches & clasps. 67 lines plus headlines; gothic letter in 2 columns; initials & initial strokes supplied in red & blue; major capitals with penwork decoration. Minor marginal worming at beginning & end; Part 1 has tp trimmed close & mtd on front free endpaper & clean tear in n2. 485 (of 486) leaves; lacking last blank of Part 2. Goff A-878. sg Oct 24 (5) $1,100

Anville, Jean Baptiste Bourguignon d', 1697-1782
— A Complete Body of Ancient Geography. L, 1795. Folio, contemp half calf; def. With 13 maps, colored in outline. First 3 maps with trimmed margins occasionally causing some loss to plates. pn June 11 (297) £150
— L'Empire turc. Paris, 1772. 12mo, contemp calf gilt. S July 1 (589) £300 [Atabey]

Apel, Johann August

— Der Freischuetz. Travestie.... L, 1824. Illus by George Cruikshank. 8vo, mor gilt; worn. With 12 hand-colored plates. sg Oct 17 (154) $300

Aperture

— Aperture. Rochester, 1970-85. Nos 3-80. 34 Issues; lacking Vol 19, Nos 2-3 & No 80 (numbering changed during this period). Wraps; rubbed. bbc Feb 17 (170) $160

Apianus, Petrus, 1495-1552

— Astronomicum Caesareum. Leipzig, 1969. One of 750. 2 vols. with commentary. Folio & 8vo, orig pigskin & half cloth. Facsimile of 1540 Ed. sg Nov 7 (8) $550

— Cosmographicus liber. Antwerp: A. Berckman, 1540. ("Cosmographia....") Bound with nearly identical Ed. Antwerp: G. Bontius, 1550. 4to, old vellum from a 16th-cent Ms. With woodcut on title, 51 other woodcuts (6 with volvelles) & some smaller woodcuts. B Nov 1 (483) HF6,500

Anr copy. Vellum. With 4 (of 5) volvelles. sg May 7 (7) $2,200

— Libro dela cosmographia.... Antwerp: Gregorius Bontius, 1548. 4to, contemp vellum; rebacked, wormed. Lacking world map, E2, G1, G4 & H3; 4 later volvelles present but 1 detached; worming affecting endpapers, tp & last leaf; some foxing. Sold w.a.f. pn Dec 12 (1) £90

Apicius Coelius, fl.14-37 A.D.

— De re coquinaria libri decem. Lyons: S. Gryphius, 1541. ("De re culinaria libri decem....") 8vo, 18th-cent calf. Some browning. SI June 9 (44) LIt1,000,000

Apollinaire, Guillaume, 1880-1918

— Alcools. Paris, 1913. 1st Ed. Half mor, orig wraps bound in. With frontis by Picasso. sg June 11 (7) $1,000

Anr copy. With frontis by Pablo Picasso. Orig wraps. Epstein copy. sg Apr 29 (9) $3,400

— Calligrammes. Paris, 1918. 8vo, orig wraps. Epstein copy. sg Apr 29 (10) $1,300

— L'Enchanteur pourrissant. Paris, [1909]. One of 75. Illus by Andre Derain. 4to, mor in style of illusts by Creuzevault, orig wraps bound in. S May 28 (224) £16,000 [Rosenthal]

Apollo...

— Apollo. A Journal of the Arts. Nendeln, 1976. Vols 1-20 in 15 vols. 4to, orig cloth. Reprint Ed. bba Mar 26 (107) £140 [Ashmolean Library]

Apollodorus Atheniensis

— Bibliotheces, sive de deorum origine.... Rome, 1555. 1st Ed. 8vo, 18th-cent vellum. Some browning. SI Dec 5 (743) LIt320,000

Apollon...

— Apollon. St Petersburg, 1909-17. Ed By S. Makovsky. 82 issues in 68 (complete set), bound in 22 vols. 4to, various cloths, most of orig wraps bound in. S Dec 5 (319) £800 [Lewinson]

Apollonius Pergaeus, fl.225 B.C.

— Conicorum.... Bologna: Alexander Benacius, 1566. Ed by Federicus Commandinus. 2 parts in 1 vol. Folio, contemp calf; upper cover detached & secured with adhesive tape. Tp & 3 prelims detached; tp repaired & the following 3 leaves with repaired tears. Ck Nov 29 (136) £850

Apollonius Rhodius, 240-186 B.C.

— Argonautica. Florence: [Laurentius (Francesci) de Alopa, Venetus], 1496. 1st Ed. 4to, mor gilt. 172 leaves. Goff A-924. Fitzwilliam copy. C Nov 27 (5) £14,000 [Quaritch]

1st Aldine Ed. Venice: Aldus, Apr 1521. 8vo, mor gilt by Gruel. Marginal tears mended. C June 24 (258) £1,400 [Mediolanum]

Anr copy. Contemp calf; rebacked, clasps def. Some dust-soiling; wormhole in margins at beginning; contemp annotations. S June 30 (510) £1,250 [St. Andrews]

Apostol

— Apostol. Lvov: Ivan Federov, 1573. Folio, old blind-stamped calf over wooden bds; rebacked with cloth. 25 lines; cyrillic letter; full-page woodcut of St. Luke on f.2v. Many tears & repairs; stained; last 7 leaves def; some loss in other leaves. Sold w.a.f. 13 (of 15) unnumbered leaves; 259 numbered leaves; 3 leaves of Epilogue. S Dec 5 (39) £5,500 [Franklin]

Apotheose...

— L'Apotheose du beau-sexe. Londres: chez Van Der Hoek, 1712. 8vo, old half sheep; frontis & title loose. sg Oct 24 (6) $80

Appalachia

— Appalachia. The Journal of the Appalachian Mountain Club. Bost., 1879-1929. Vols 1-17. 17 vols. Orig cloth. Tears to folding map in Vol I. NH Oct 6 (210) $1,350

Apperley, Charles J., 1777?-1843

— The Chace, the Turf, and the Road. L, 1837. 8vo, modern half mor gilt by Morrell, orig cloth covers and spine bound in. With frontis & 13 hand-colored plates. sg Jan 9 (210) $225

— The Life of a Sportsman; by Nimrod. L, 1842. 1st Ed. 8vo, contemp mor; joints rubbed. With hand-colored engraved title, frontis & 34 hand-colored plates. 3 plates trimmed to images and laid down; others with imprints shaved or cropped. cb Dec 5 (4) $200

1st Issue. Orig cloth. With hand-colored title & 35 plates, 4 mtd. C May 20 (14) £3,100 [Steedman]

Anr copy. Mor gilt by Riviere; upper joint cracking. With hand-colored title & 35 plates. Dampstained; lacking ad leaves at end; some imprints cropped. pn Apr 23 (216) £400

Anr copy. Orig cloth; joints worn. With hand-colored engraved title & 36 hand-colored plates. S Nov 15 (730) £950

2d Issue. Modern mor gilt, orig cloth upper cover & spine bound in. With hand-colored additional title & 35 plates. With 2 plates shaved with slight loss to imprint. C May 20 (15) £900 [Marlborough]

Anr Ed. L, 1914. Calf gilt by Riviere with sporting tools as cornerpieces. sg Oct 17 (109) $425

Anr copy. Mor gilt by Riviere with multi-colored lea inlays depicting the hunt; joints partly worn, front cover soiled & with some stains & scrapes. With 36 hand-finished color plates. wa Mar 5 (21) $120

Anr copy. Contemp half mor gilt; some wear & soiling, front hinge cracking. wa Mar 5 (79) $220

— Memoirs of the Life of the Late John Mytton, Esq. L, 1851. 3d Ed. Illus by Henry Alken. 8vo, modern mor gilt by Zaehnsdorf, orig cloth bound in at back. With engraved title & 18 hand-colored plates. C Oct 30 (171) £700 [Grahame]

Anr Ed. L, 1877. ("The Life of John Mytton.") 8vo, contemp half mor. With engraved title & 18 colored plates. bba Jan 30 (381) £110 [Wm. Dawson]

— Sporting; Embellished by Large Engravings and Vignettes Illustrative of Field Sports.... L, 1838. 4to, orig cloth; upper hinge weak. With engraved title & 22 plates. Some foxing. bba July 23 (326) £150 [York Gallery]

Appian of Alexandria

— Delle Guerre civile et esterne de Romani. Venice: Aldus, 1551. 3 parts in 2 vols. 8vo, later sheep; spine wormed, tear to head of 1 spine. Some stains & soiling; tp of 1st part backed; old marginalia. wa Dec 9 (456) $120

— Des Guerres des Romains.... Lyons: Antoine Constantin, 20 Oct 1544. Folio, 16th-cent calf gilt; worn. Some worming in tp touching border. S Dec 5 (40) £450 [Poile]

— Historia Romana. Venice: Bernhard Maler, Erhard Ratdolt & Petrus Loeslein, 1477. Vol I. Folio, 18th-cent mor gilt; rebacked with orig spine. Type 1:109R, 32 lines. Some worming at beginning & end. 132 leaves. Goff A-928. C June 24 (91) £2,600 [Wood]

Anr copy. 2 vols in 1. Folio, vellum. 32 lines; roman letter.. 205 (of 344) leaves; lacking a1 blank & m1-o10 in the first part & 1-110 in the 2d part. Goff A-928. SI June 9 (45) LIt1,000,000

— The History.... L, 1679. Trans by John Davies. Folio, calf; rebacked. W July 8 (81) £110

— Romanarum historiarum Celtica. Paris: Charles Estienne, 1551. ("Romaikon Keltike.") Folio, 19th-cent half lea. SI June 9 (48) LIt600,000

Appier, Jean, called Hanzelet

— La Pyrotechnie.... Pont a Mousson, 1630. 4to, 19th-cent half mor. Lacking Y2-3; 2K4 def; tp def, repaired & mtd on stub. S July 1 (1205) £190 [American Mus.]

Anr copy. Contemp vellum; soiled, inner hinge broken. Some browning & staining; a few marginal wormholes. S July 1 (1373) £500 [American Mus.]

Appleton & Co., Daniel

— Appleton's Cyclopaedia of American Biography. NY, 1887-89. Ed by J. G. Wilson & John Fiske. 6 vols. 4to, cloth. Some dampstaining. sg June 18 (587) $175

Anr Ed. NY, 1888-89. 6 vols plus 1900 Supplement. 4to, orig half calf; worn. bbc June 29 (70) $290

— Appleton's General Guide to the United States and Canada. NY, 1882. 8vo, orig sheep; scuffed. With 2 maps loose in rear pocket. cb Nov 14 (4) $70

— Appleton's Journal of Literature, Science, and Art. NY, 1869-73. Vols 1-10, Nos 1-249. 10 vols. 4to, half mor; rubbed, extremities worn, joints starting in 3 vols. sg Feb 13 (145) $550

Apponyi, A.

— Hungarica, Ungarn Betreffende im Auslande Gedruckte Buecher.... Munich, 1903-27. 4 vols in 3. 4to, contemp half mor. Ck Nov 1 (337) £160

Anr copy. 4 vols. Newly bound in cloth, orig front wraps bound in. sg Oct 31 (21) $275

Apuleius, Lucius

See also: Limited Editions Club

— De l'Asino d'Oro. Venice: Francesco de Leno, [1565]. 8vo, contemp vellum. Some dampstaining at margin. Ck Nov 29 (40) £650

— The Golden Ass. Paris: Pvtly ptd, 1904. One of 750. Illus by Martin von Maele. Half mor. O July 14 (14) $80

Aquinas, Thomas, Saint. See: Thomas Aquinas

Arabian Nights

— 1839-41. - The Thousand and One Nights L. Edward William Lane's trans. 3 vols. 8vo, half calf gilt. L Nov 14 (419) £65

— 1883. - L. 3 vols. 8vo, mor. sg Mar 5 (5) $175

— 1885-88. - The Book of the Thousand Nights and a Night, with Supplemental Nights. Benares: Kamashastra Society Sir Richard F. Burton's trans. 16 vols. 8vo, mor gilt extra with lion of Persia on cover of each vol; spines discolored or stained. With colored frontises on satin. Facsimile of copy made for the Prince of Wales. cb Dec 5 (5) $2,000

Anr copy. Orig cloth; spines & joints worn. S June 25 (407) £800 [Maggs]

— 1894-[97]. - L. 12 vols. 8vo, orig cloth; spines bumped. pn July 16 (70) £170

— 1899-1904. - Le Livre des mille nuits et une nuit. Paris One of 25 on japon. J. C. Mardrus's trans. 16 vols. 8vo, half mor gilt, orig wraps bound in. S May 28 (401) £600 [Shapero]

— [1908]. - Contes des mille et une nuits. Paris Illus by Edmund Dulac. 4to, mor gilt by Ourvand. With 50 mtd color plates. bbc Sept 23 (44) $650

Anr copy. Contemp half mor gilt by Durvand; rubbed & corners bumped, orig wraps preserved. With 50 mtd colored illusts. DW May 13 (430) £75

Anr copy. Orig wraps; spine ends worn. sg Jan 30 (42) $275

— [n.d.]. - The Book of the Thousand Nights and a Night, with Supplemental Nights. L: Burton Club One of 1,000. Sir Richard F. Burton's trans. 17 vols. 8vo, orig cloth; worn & soiled. cb Oct 17 (9) $110

Anr copy. Orig cloth; spines rubbed & faded. cb Dec 19 (3) $140

Anr copy. Cloth; rubbed. O May 26 (3) $140

— The Adventure of Hunch-Back, and the Stories connected with it.... L, 1814. Illus by Wm. Daniell after Robt. Smirke. Folio, old bds; worn, rebacked. With 17 mtd india-proof plates. sg Oct 17 (110) $90

— Aladdin; or the Wonderful Lamp. L, [c.1815]. 8vo, contemp wraps; loose. With folding hand-colored frontis (cropped). bba July 23 (6) £75 [Miles]

— Princess Badoura. Retold by Laurence Housman. [L, 1913]. Illus by Edmund Dulac. DW Apr 8 (494) £55

Anr copy. 4to, orig cloth; rear cover & spine stained. With 10 tipped-in color plates. wa Mar 5 (571) $210

One of 750, sgd by artist. Orig cloth. With 10 tipped-in colored plates. pn July 16 (75) £210

— La Princesse Badourah. Paris, 1914. One of 500, sgd by Dulac. Illus by Edmund Dulac. 4to, contemp half mor gilt by Durvand; rubbed & corners bumped. With 10 colored plates. DW May 13 (429) £50

— Sinbad the Sailor. L, [1911]. Illus by Edmund Dulac. 4to, orig cloth. With 23 colored plates. F Sept 26 (76) $180

Anr copy. Orig cloth; worn. pn July 16 (74) £160 [Sotheran]

Anr copy. Orig cloth; tear to bottom edge of front bd. pnL Nov 20 (197) £90

Anr copy. Orig cloth; extremities worn. sg Sept 26 (98) $150

Anr copy. Half cloth; edges browned; front hinge cracked. sg Jan 30 (49) $130

Anr Ed. L, [1914]. 4to, orig cloth; extremities rubbed. cb Jan 19 (46) $190

Anr copy. Cloth; worn & shaken. O Mar 31 (166) $130

Aracandam, Pseud.

— De veritatibus & praedictionibus astrologiae.... Paris: Denis Janot, 1542. 8vo, contemp calf; rebacked. Some stains & soiling; outer margin of title next 2 leaves & last leaf torn & restored with loss. sg Mar 12 (198) $350

Aragon, Louis

See also: Peret & Aragon

— Le Paysan de Paris. Paris, 1926. Orig wraps, unopened. Inscr to Boris Kochno, 1945. SM Oct 12 (416) FF1,600

— Shakespeare. NY: Abrams, [1965]. Illus by Picasso. Folio, orig cloth, in worn d/j. With 13 plates. bbc Dec 9 (283) $100

Arber, Agnes

— Herbals. Their Origin and Evolution. Cambr., 1912. Cloth; spine ends chipped, worn. bbc June 29 (83) $50

Arber, Edward, 1836-1912

— The First Three English Books on America.... Birm., 1885. 4to, cloth; worn. K Sept 29 (29) $65

Arbogast, Louis Francoise Antoine

— Du calcul des derivations. Strassburg, 1800. 4to, contemp calf; upper cover detached. Ownership inscr erased from tp. Ck Nov 29 (117) £260

Arbuthnot, John, 1667-1735

— Law is a Bottomless Pit.... L, 1712. 8vo, contemp calf gilt; upper cover stained, extremities worn. Milne copy. Ck June 12 (4) £75

Archaeological...

— The Archaeological Journal. L, 1846-99. Vols 1-56 and Index for Vols 1-25. Together, 57 vols. 8vo, all but 4 in orig cloth. bba Jan 30 (74) £190 [Quaritch]

Archdall, Mervyn, 1723-91

— Monasticon Hibernicum; or, an History of the Abbies, Priories and other Religious Houses in Ireland. L, 1786. 4to, orig bds; rubbed, rebacked. With folding map & 18 plates. S July 1 (1406) £150 [Gamble]

Archenholtz, Johann Wilhelm von, 1743-1812

— Memoires concernant Christine, Reine de Suede.... Amst., 1751-60. 4 vols. 4to, 18th-cent sheep gilt; worn. With folding map, hand-colored in outline in Vol III. sg Oct 24 (66) $110

Archer, Sir Geoffrey Francis —& Godman, Eva M.

— The Birds of British Somaliland and the Gulf of Aden.... L, 1937-61. 4 vols. 4to, orig cloth, 2 vols in d/js. Stamp on front pastedown of Vol I. pn Mar 19 (203) £220 [Greyfriars]

Anr copy. Orig cloth. With 2 ports, 34 colored plates & 4 folding maps (1 strengthened at hinge). pn May 14 (161) £300

Anr Ed. L, 1961. Vols 3 & 4 only (of 4). 4to, cloth. With 2 folding maps & 12 color plates. sg May 14 (187) $120

Archer, Thomas

— Pictures and Royal Portraits Illustrative of English and Scottish History. L, 1878. 2 vols. 4to, contemp half calf; scuffed. sg Oct 17 (111) $70

Archer, William George

— Indian Miniatures. L, 1960. Folio, orig cloth, in d/j. sg Apr 2 (144) $50

Archer, William Henry, b.1825

— The Statistical Register of Victoria.... Melbourne, 1854. 8vo, early calf. kh Nov 11 (412) A$140

Archimbaud, Theodore

— Les Soliloques de pecheur penitent avec Jesus souffrant. Lyons: Jacquenod pere & Rusand, 1766. 12mo, contemp red mor gilt with arms of Marie Leczinska [Olivier 2507, fer 3]. Stamp of an unidentified religious house on titles. S May 28 (100) £500 [Shapero]

Archimedes, 287?-212 B.C.

— Opera. Basel: J. Hervagius, 1544. 2 (of 4) parts only. Folio, modern mor. Some leaves damaged with loss. Sold w.a.f. Ck June 18 (1) £280

Archives...

— Archives de l'Orient Latin. Paris, 1884. Vol II only. Orig ptd wraps. S June 30 (8) £600 [Bank of Cyprus]

Arctic...

— Arctic Bibliography. Wash. & Montreal, 1953-59. Vols I-III bba July 9 (1) £60 [Grigor-Taylor]

Anr Ed. Wash. & Montreal, 1953-57. Vols I-VII O Dec 17 (12) $375

Arcussia, Charles d', 1545-1617

— La Fauconnerie.... Paris: Jean Houze, 1605. 8vo, contemp vellum; rubbed & stained. With 7 full-page illusts in text. Some staining & soiling; portions torn from tp & A3 just affecting text; repaired; lacking a4 blank. S Feb 26 (898) £1,400 [Kyd]

Anr Ed. Rouen, 1643-44. 2 parts in 1 vol. 4to, contemp vellum. With 11 full-page illusts of hawks & 1 double-page plates of hawking equipment only (of 5). 2T1 to 3Y4 dampstained at outer margin; some spotting & soiling. Jeanson 1278. Ck Sept 6 (2) £280

Arents Collection, George, Jr.

— Tobacco: Its History Illustrated in the...Library. NY, 1937-52. By Jerome E. Brooks. One of 300. 4to, cloth. With Supplementary Catalogue, Parts I-VII, compiled by Sarah A. Dickson & Parts VIII-X compiled by Perry H. O'Neil. 4to, orig cloth. O Sept 24 (16) $2,100

Aretaeus

— Medici insignis ac vetustissimi libri septem.... Venice: Junta, 1552. 4to, contemp vellum. Some headlines inked out & oxidized. sg May 14 (6) $1,800

Aretino, Pietro, 1492-1556

— Abbattimento Poetico del divino Aretino.... [Milan: F. M. Calvo], 1539. 4to, late 19th-cent half calf. C Dec 16 (22) £2,800 [Quaritch]

— Lettere scritte al signor Pietro Aretino.... Venice: Francesco Marcolini, 1551. 2 vols in 1. 8vo, 19th-cent vellum gilt. Lower margin of 1st title repaired. S Dec 5 (41) £950 [Burgess Browning]

— Les Ragionamenti ou dialogues. Paris, 1882. One of 100. 6 vols. 8vo, half mor gilt by Lanscelin. With plates in 2 states. S Feb 11 (540) £240 [American Book Store]

— The Ragionamenti or Dialogues. Paris, 1889-90. 6 vols in 2. 4to, half mor; worn. K July 12 (50) $80

— Il sesto delle scritte lettere volume. Venice: Gabriel Giolito, 1557. 8vo, modern mor gilt. Annotations in an 18th-cent hand. C Dec 16 (23) £4,800 [Jackson]

Arfe de Villafane, Juan

— Varia commensuracion para la escultura, y arquitectura.... Madrid, 1773. Folio, contemp vellum; crinkled. Dampstained throughout; O3 & Y6 torn. Ck Nov 29 (138) £190

Argens, Jean Baptiste de Boyer, Marquis d'

— The Jewish Spy: Being a Philosophical, Historical and Critical Correspondence.... L, 1766. 5 vols. 12mo, lea. br May 29 (53) $110

Argensola, Bartolome Leonardo y, 1562-1631

— Conquista de las Islas Malucas. [Madrid: Alonso Martin, 1609]. 4to, contemp vellum. Engraved title shaved along fore-margin & cropped at foot affecting imprint; A4-5 transposed; some thumb-marks. S Nov 21 (355) £2,000 [Beeleigh]

Argenville, Antoine Joseph Dezallier d'. See: Dezallier d'Argenville, Antoine Joseph

Arias Montanus, Benedictus, 1527-98

— Naturae historia.... Antwerp: Plantin, 1601. 4to, contemp vellum; stained, upper cover repaired. Browned. A few ink marginalia. bba Sept 5 (1A) £240 [Poole]

Arif Pacha, Mushir

— Les Anciens Costumes de l'Empire Ottoman. Paris, [1863]. Vol I (all pbd). Folio, later half mor gilt; worn. With litho port & 16 color lithos. Litho title waterstained; interleaves torn & repaired, some spotting. S July 1 (539) £6,800 [Kutluoglu]

Aringhus, Paulus

— Roma subterranea novissima. Paris, 1659. 2 vols in 1. Folio, contemp calf. SI June 9 (60) LIt420,000

Anr copy. Contemp calf; worn. SI June 9 (61) LIt1,200,000

Ariosto, Ludovico, 1474-1533

— Il Negromante, comedia. Venice, 1535. 8vo, mor gilt by Hardy-Mennil. C Dec 16 (24) £1,000 [Ghezzi]; C June 24 (92) £500 [Panini]

— Opere. Venice, 1730. 2 vols in 1. Folio, contemp vellum. Lacking 4 plates. SI June 9 (67) LIt420,000

— Orlando furioso. Venice: Domenego Zio, Apr 1539. 4to, old vellum with initials IL stamped on both covers. Upper margin of 1st 2 leaves repaired with slight loss on 2d leaf; early note of purchase at head of title. S Dec 5 (43) £1,500 [Mediolanum]

Anr Ed. Venice: Giolito, 1542. 2 parts in 1 vol. 4to, 16th-cent mor gilt; rubbed, 1 corner cracked, later 18th-cent spine lettered & tooled, laid down & repaired in the early 19th cent. Heber-Beckford copy. C Dec 16 (25) £3,800 [Mediolanum]

Anr Ed. Venice: V. Valgrisi, 1558. 4to, 18th-cent calf gilt; extremities rubbed, front joint cracking at head. With 46 full-page woodcuts. Tp shaved at fore-edge & foot; lower fore-edge corner of Y7 repaired at an early date; minor repairs; some soiling. P Dec 12 (4) $800

Anr Ed. Venice: Vincenzo Valgrisi, 1562. 4to, 18th-cent half vellum; free endpapers wormed. Some fingersoiling; minor repairs. Ck Oct 31 (16) £420

Anr Ed. Venice: Valgrisi, 1568. 2 parts in 1 vol. 4to, contemp calf gilt; rebacked. With 51 full-page woodcuts. Final part of stanza 5 of Canto X in a contemp italic hand on front endpaper. S May 13 (800) £330 [P & P]

Anr copy. 18th-cent vellum. Some marginal repairs; some browning. SI June 9 (64) LIt550,000

Anr Ed. Venice: V. Valgrisi, 1572. 4to, 17th-cent calf; rebacked, worn. Some browning. SI June 9 (65) LIt1,100,000

Anr Ed. Venice, 1580. 4to, early vellum; soiled. Some dampstaining at top; some running heads shaved; institutional handstamp on front blank. wa Sept 26 (493) $290

Anr copy. Later vellum gilt. Marginal dampstain to 1st 10 leaves. wa Mar 5 (472) $550

Anr Ed. Venice: Francesco de Franceschi Senese, 1584. Bound with: Alberto Lavezuola. Osservationi...sopra il Furioso.

Venice, 1584 4to, later calf; broken, worn. bba Feb 27 (241) £260 [Tosi]

Anr copy. 3 parts in 1 vol. 4to, 18th-cent mor gilt. With 3 engraved titles & 51 plates Lacking final blank; some soiling; last 4 leaves with wormholes affecting a few letters. C Dec 16 (98) £1,800 [Ghezzi]

Anr Ed. Venice, 1603. 4to, contemp vellum. Some soiling & browning. SI June 9 (66) LIt650,000

Anr Ed. Birm.: Baskerville, 1773. 4 vols. 4to, contemp calf; rebcked in mor, extremities rubbed. With port & 46 plates. Some spotting & browning to text. Ck Oct 31 (26) £450

Anr copy. Contemp calf gilt; rebacked & recornered, edges rubbed. pn Apr 23 (64) £550

Anr copy. Contemp mor gilt. Some spotting. S July 21 (21) £1,100 [Maggs]

Anr Ed. L, 1783. 5 vols. 8vo, contemp calf; hinges cracking. wd June 12 (363) $300

Anr Ed. L, 1823-31. 8 vols. 8vo, 19th-cent calf; rubbed & soiled. sg Mar 5 (6) $200

Aristides, Aelius

— Logoi. Orationes. Florence: P. Giunta, 1517. Folio, contemp vellum; soiled. A few leaves with stains toward inner margin; tp soiled. C Dec 16 (26) £2,000 [Quaritch]

Aristophanes, 448?-380? B.C.
See also: Limited Editions Club

— Comoediae undecim. Leiden: Raphelengius, 1600. 16mo, contemp mor gilt with arms of Jacques-Auguste de Thou & his 1st wife. S May 28 (69) £700 [Shapero]

— Komodiai ennea. Comoedia novem. Venice: Aldus, 15 July 1498. Folio, 19th-cent half sheep; rubbed. 42 lines & head-line; Greek letter; woodcut floral & interlaced headlines & initials. 347 (of 348) leaves. Lacking final blank. Goff A-958. C Nov 27 (6) £12,000 [Hart]

Anr Ed. Florence: Filippo Giunta, 1515. 8vo, modern mor gilt. Partly misbound; tp margin restored; lacking 1 blank; some worming in text towards the end; annotations. S May 13 (738) £600 [Theocharaki]

— Lysistrata. L, 1896. One of 100. Illus by Aubrey Beardsley. 4to, bds; worn, spine def. bba Dec 19 (61) £1,700 [Frew MacKenzie]

Anr Ed. L: Fanfrolico Press, 1926. One of 725. Trans by Jack Lindsay; illus by Norman Lindsay. 4to, half mor; worn. sg Sept 26 (109) $130

Aristotle, 384-322 B.C.

— Ethica. Paris: Henri Estienne, 5 Feb 1514. ("Decem libri ethicorum seu moralium....") 8vo, contemp mor gilt; damaged. Some headlines shaved; annotations & underlining. S Dec 5 (44) £950 [Schafer]

— Ethicorum ad Nichomachum. Venice: Aldus, 1536. ("Eustratii et aliorum... commentaria in libros decem Aristotelis de moribus ad Nicomachum....") Folio, 19th-cent mor gilt. Repair to inner margin of title. Syston Park copy. S July 1 (511) £1,600 [Thecharaki]

— Ethicorum ad Nichomachum.... Frankfurt: heirs of Andreas Wechel, 1591. ("Ethicorum, sive de moribus, ad Nichomachum libri decem.") 8vo, old half lea. Woodcut device on tp partly hand-colored. Some underscoring & marginalia. sg Oct 24 (8) $150

— Opera. Venice: Aldus, 1495-98. 1st Ed in Greek. 5 vols. Folio, 18th-cent calf gilt; worn, joints split. 30 lines & head-line; Greek letter; woodcut initials & headpieces. Has the cancel-strip in Part 3 kk10v emending last line & catchword & the uncancelled blank that is conjugate with the inserted leaf sgd PP. Small hole in penultimate leaf of Part 3, affecting 1 letter; some dampstaining towards end of Parts 2 & 5. 1,852 leaves. Goff A-959. C Nov 27 (7) £80,000 [Mediolanum]

Anr Ed. Frankfurt: Heirs of Andreas Wechel, 1585. 4to, contemp vellum. Library stamp on tp; browned. bba June 11 (4) £190 [Poole]

Anr Ed. Paris, 1629. 2 vols. Folio, contemp vellum. Some dampstaining. bba Oct 10 (499) £220 [Stamatoyannopoulos]

— Positiones circa libros physicorumque et de anima Aristotelis. [Cologne: Heinrich Quentell, 16 May 1494. Folio, modern half vellum. Gothic type. Marginal repairs on 2 leaves. First 29 (of 47) leaves only. Goff P-946. sg Oct 24 (10) $950

— Problemata. Frankfurt: heirs of Andreas Wechel, 1585. 4to, contemp glind-tooled pigskin over wooden bds with panel stamps showing arms of Holy Roman Empire on front cover & Friedrich III, Elector Palatine, on rear cover; lacking clasps & catches. Some browning throughout. sg Oct 24 (9) $750

— Rettorica, et Poetica. Florence: L. Torrentino, 1549. 4to, old calf gilt; worn. K Sept 29 (33) $225

Arkham House

— [Complete run of the publications of Arkham House]. Sauk City, 1939-82. 172 titles in 173 vols. In d/js. Manney set. P Oct 11 (6) $15,000

Arland, Marcel

— Antares. Paris, 1944. One of 300. Illus by Marie Laurencin. 4to, unsewn in orig wraps. CGen Nov 18 (302) SF3,000

Arlington, Lewis Charles

— The Chinese Drama from the Earliest Times Until Today. Shanghai, 1930. One of 750. 4to, half cloth. With frontis & 115 colored plates. sg Oct 17 (1) $200

Armes...

— Armes et armures du Moyen Age et de la Renaissance. Paris, 1864. Folio, half mor; worn. With litho title & 54 tinted plates. sg Feb 6 (7) $250

Armitage, Merle

— The Lithographs of Richard Day. NY, 1932. One of 500. Folio, orig bds; worn & soiled, lacking backstrip. wa Sept 26 (580) $65

Armory Show

— Catalogue of International Exhibition of Modern Art...at the Armory of the Sixty-ninth Infantry, Lexington Avenue, Twenty-fifth and Twenty-sixth Streets, New York. NY, 1913. Orig wraps; scuffed. sg Sept 6 (8) $1,900

Arms, Dorothy Noyes

— Churches of France. NY, 1929. 4to, cloth, in d/j. wd Dec 12 (350) $225

Armstrong, Edmund Archibald

— Axel Herman Haig and his Work. L, 1905. 4to, later cloth. Library markings. F Dec 18 (298) $70

Armstrong, Elizabeth

— Robert Estienne: Royal Printer. Cambr., 1954. 4to, cloth; worn. O Sept 24 (17) $60

Armstrong, John, 1709-79

— The Art of Preserving Health: a Poem. L, 1744. 4to, disbound. bba Jan 16 (114) £55 [Murray Hill]

Armstrong, Mostyn John

— An Actual Survey of the Great Post-Roads between London and Edinburgh. L, 1776. 8vo, disbound. With engraved title, general map frontis & 44 maps, some colored in outline. Soiled. Library markings. DW Mar 4 (57) £95

Armstrong, Nevill Alexander Drummond

— After Big Game in the Upper Yukon. L, [1937]. Koopman copy. O Oct 29 (10) $100

Armstrong, Robert Bruce

— Musical Instruments. Part 1: The Irish and the Highland Harps. Part 2: English and Irish Instruments. Edin., 1904-8. One of 180. 2 vols. 4to, orig cloth gilt; edges rubbed. Some soiling. Inscr. pn Oct 24 (310) £280

Armstrong, Sir Walter, 1850-1918

— Gainsborough and his Place in English Art. L, 1898. 4to, lev gilt by Zaehnsdorf, dated 1898; rubbed. sg Feb 6 (93) $425

Arndt, Johann, 1555-1621

See also: Franklin Printing, Benjamin

— Postilla; oder Ausslegung und Erklaerung der Evangelien. Luneburg: Johann Stern, 1712. Folio, contemp sheep; worn, joints cracked. Browned. sg Oct 24 (13) $110

Arnold, Matthew, 1822-88

— New Poems. L, 1867. 1st Ed. 8vo, orig cloth. Inscr. Epstein copy. sg Apr 29 (11) $850

— Works. L, 1883-89. 11 vols. 12mo, early half calf. bbc Dec 9 (201) $400

Arnoux, Alexandre

— La Legende du Roi Arthur. Paris, [1920]. One of 1,500. Illus by Arthur Rackham. 4to, half mor gilt; extremities worn. sg Jan 10 (138) $350

Arnoux, Charles Albert d'

— Les Communeux 1871. Paris & L, [1871]. 4to, orig cloth; rebacked. With 40 hand-colored plates. SI Dec 5 (75) LIt250,000

Aronson, Boris

— Sovremyennaya Evreiskaya Grafika. Berlin, 1924. Out-of-series copy. Folio, orig wraps. sg Dec 19 (131) $750

Arp, Jean (or Hans), 1887-1966

— I, rue Gabrielle; douze eaux-fortes originales. Paris, 1958. One of 60. Preface by Michel Seuphor. Oblong 4to, loose in orig wraps as issued. sg Jan 26 (9) $1,600

— Le Siege de l'air. Paris, 1946. One of 1,000. 4to, orig wraps. With cover design & 8 full-page illusts by Arp & Sophie Tauber-Arp. CGen Nov 18 (305) SF320

— Le Volier dans la foret. [Paris:] Louis Broder, [1957]. One of 130. 4to, orig wraps. sg Nov 7 (10) $1,800

Arrianus, Flavius
— Arriani & Hannonis Periplus [& other works]. Basel: Froben & Episcopius, 1533. 4to, contemp blind-stamped pigskin over wooden bds, with 2 clasps & catches. Upper margins at beginning & end dampstained. S Dec 5 (49) £700 [Maggs]

Arrighi, Ludovico degli, called Vicentino. See: Vicentio, Ludovico degli Arrighi

Arrowsmith, Aaron
— Orbis Terrarum. A Comparative Atlas of Ancient and Modern Geography.... L, 1828. Folio, modern half mor. With engraved title & 53 colored maps. pn Apr 23 (289) £90

Arrowsmith, Aaron, the Younger
— An Atlas of Modern Geography.... L, 1830. 8vo, early half lea; worn, front bd detached. With 30 maps, hand-colored in outline. wa Apr 9 (164) $220

Arrowsmith, H. W. & A.
— The House Decorator and Painter's Guide.... L, 1840. 4to, contemp half calf; rebacked. With 61 plates, including 26 hand-colored. Lacking ad leaf. pn Sept 12 (60) £500 [Traylen]

Art...
See also: Great...
— Art and Song. L, 1867. Ed by Robert Bell. 4to, contemp calf; rubbed & soiled. With 30 plates. cb Jan 9 (11) $55
— Art decoratif et industriel de l'URSS. Moscow, 1925. 4to, bdg not described but cover design by A. Rodchenko. S Apr 28 (1) £400 [Gilbert]
— The Art Journal. NY, 1875-80. New Series, Vols 1-6. 6 vols. 4to, orig half lea; rubbed. O July 14 (18) $400
— Art Work of Seattle & Alaska. Racine: W. D. Harney, 1970. 4to, orig calf; rebacked. With 80 leaves having 1 or a pair of gravure reproductions. Some smudging. bbc Feb 17 (172) $400

Artaud de Montor, Alexis Francois
— The Lives and Times of the Popes. NY: The Catholic Publication Society of America, 1910-[11]. Lateran Ed, one of 1,000, this copy specially made for Cardinal George W. Mundelein & with his 18-line Ms endorsement of the work on a vellum leaf. 15 vols plus 2 boxes of 20 Papal Bulls. Folio, mor extra by Riviere, with upper cover having oval medallion of St. Michael (by Alberto Sangorski) overcoming Satan & lower cover a smaller medallion of Our Lady of the Heavens, each upper cover set with 4 garnets & 4 chalcedonies, each upper doublure set with an oval port miniature of a Pope. Extra-illus with 307 letters & documents by Popes, kings & other historical figures & with other related material. CNY Dec 5 (389) $90,000

Arte. See: Anduaga y Garimberti, Joseph de

Artemidorus
— De somniorum interpretatione libri quinque. Venice, 1518. 8vo, mor gilt by Cape. Washed. C June 24 (259) £3,000 [Jackson]

Articulen...
— Articulen van Vrede ende Verbondt [Treaty of Breda]. The Hague, 1667. 1st Ed. 4to, bds. B Nov 1 (276) HF300

Artis, Edmund Tyrell, 1789-1847
— Antediluvian Phytology, Illustrated.... L, 1838. 4to, modern half calf. With 24 plates. bba Sept 5 (2) £85 [S.Baldwin]

Artistes...
— Les Artistes du livre. Paris: Henry Babou, 1928-33. Ltd Ed. 24 vols (complete set). 4to, orig wraps. Sold w.a.f. S July 1 (1181) £380 [Maggs]

Artistic...
— Artistic Houses; being a Series of Interior Views.... NY, 1883-84. One of 500. 2 vols in 4. Folio, half mor; rubbed. Some vols with marginal dampstaining. O Feb 25 (14) $2,100

Artsibushev, Y.
— Tipy voennoplennykh 1915 g. [Moscow, n.d.]. Folio, loose in orig paper folder; worn, partly separated at folds. With 8 litho plates. sg Nov 7 (183) $800

Arundell, Francis Vyvyan Jago, 1780-1846
— A Visit to the Seven Churches of Asia.... L: J. Rodwell, 1828. 8vo, contemp calf; rebacked. With 13 folding plates & folding map. S June 30 (229) £150

Arundo. See: Beever, John

Arvieux, Laurent d'
— Memoires...contenant ses voyages a Constantinople.... Paris, 1735. 6 vols. 12mo, contemp calf. W. H. Lewis's copy. S June 30 (227) £600 [Ther]

Asbjornsen, Peter Christen, 1812-85 —& Moe, Jorgen I, 1813-82
— East of the Sun and West of the Moon. L, [1914]. One of 500. Illus by Kay Nielsen. 4to, orig cloth; soiled. With 24 colored plates. cb Jan 16 (111) $130
Anr copy. With 25 colored plates. sg Jan 30 (110) $250
Anr Ed. NY: Doran, [1927?]. Orig cloth, in torn d/j. With colored frontis & 24 tipped-in colored plates. pn Dec 12 (202) £80

Ascham, Roger, 1515-68

— The Scholemaster.... L: John Daye, 1570. 1st Ed. 4to, 19th-cent calf gilt; rebacked. Title & colophon leaves laid down on heavy paper with loss to 3 letters of colophon; rust-hole to E4; repaired tear to H2, affecting 6 lines of text. George Milne copy. CNY Dec 5 (156) $1,500

Anr copy. Contemp calf gilt; rebacked preserving much of old spine. Some spotting. STC 832. S July 21 (1) £6,000

— Toxophilus. L: A Jeffes, 1589. 4to, mor. Portion of 1 leaf torn & restored with a few letters in Ms. sg May 7 (9) $2,400

Asder, H. See: Sinclair de Rochemont, H. A.

Ash, Edward Cecil

— Dogs: their History and Development. Bost., [1927]. 2 vols. 4to, cloth; tear to head of spine of Vol I. b June 22 (343) £120

Anr Ed. L, 1927. 2 vols. 4to, cloth; covers dampstained. sg Jan 9 (247) $130

Ashbee, Charles Robert

— The Masque of the Edwards of England. L & NY, 1902. One of 300. Illus by Edith Harwood. Oblong folio, orig bds; soiled. bba July 9 (258) £80 [Wand]

Ashbee, Henry Spencer, 1834-1900

— Bibliography of Prohibited Books. NY, 1962. 3 vols. cb Dec 19 (4) $50; cb Feb 27 (7) $75

Ashendene Press—London

— A Descriptive Bibliography of the Books... 1935. One of 390. bba July 9 (242) £700 [Collinge & Clark]; Ck July 10 (181) £550

— Cervantes Saavedra, Miguel de. - Don Quixote. 1927-28. One of 225. 2 vols. bba July 9 (329) £750 [Marks]; HH May 12 (2139) DM1,600; pnE Mar 11 (185) £360

— Longus. - Les Amours pastorales de Daphnis et Chloe. 1933. One of 290. pnE Oct 2 (433) £400

— More, Sir Thomas. - Utopia. 1906. ("A Fruteful and Pleasaunt Worke....") One of 100. DW Apr 8 (475) £210

— Thucydides. - The History of the Peloponnesian War. 1930. One of 260. cb Oct 31 (11) $1,600

Ashley, Clifford Warren

— Whaleships of New Bedford. Bost. & NY, 1929. One of 1,000. 4to, cloth. With 60 plates. sg May 21 (4) $175

Anr copy. Cloth, in torn d/j. wa Mar 5 (426) $110

Ashley, William H. See: Morgan, Dale Lowell

Ashley-Cooper, John

— A Line on Salmon. L: Witherby, [1983]. One of 35. Half calf. Koopman copy. O Oct 29 (11) $600

— A Salmon Fisher's Odyssey. L: Witherby, [1982]. One of 20. 4to, half mor. Koopman copy. O Oct 29 (12) $1,000

Ashmole, Elias, 1617-92

— The Institution, Laws & Ceremonies of the Most Noble Order of the Garter. L, 1672. 1st Ed. Folio, contemp calf; worn, covers detached. With port & 28 plates, including 12 double-page or folding & 5 double-sided. bba Oct 24 (50) £200 [Land]

Anr copy. Contemp calf with Signet arms; modern spine. With port & 31 plates. Tp repaired & rehinged. W July 8 (43) £170

— Memoirs of the Life of that Learned Antiquary.... L, 1717. 12mo, 19th-cent sheep gilt; extremities rubbed. Browned; outer corners of half-title restored. sg Mar 12 (199) $550

Ashton, John

— The Legendary History of the Cross. NY, 1887. 8vo, orig pictorial vellum, with metal catches & clasps. With 64 woodcuts from a 1483 Dutch book. sg Oct 31 (160) $60

— Social Life in the Reign of Queen Anne. L, 1882. One of 100. 4to, lea. br May 29 (156) $120

Asiatic Society of Bengal

— Asiatic Researches; or, Transactions of the Society.... L, 1799-1808. Vols I-V only. Contemp half russia; extremities rubbed, most joints weak. Some browning. C May 20 (234) £100 [Scott]

Asiatick...

— Asiatick Researches, or Transactions of the Society.... L, 1799-1801. Vols I-VI. Contemp calf gilt; rubbed & soiled. Some dampstaining & soiling. Ck Sept 6 (96) £150

Asimov, Isaac

— Earth is Room Enough. Garden City, 1957. In d/j. cb Sept 19 (4) $100

— The End of Eternity. Garden City, 1955. In d/j with edge wear. sg June 11 (8) $140

— Foundation. NY: Gnome Press, 1951. In 1st d/j with 3 titles on rear panel. cb Sept 19 (4) $100

— Foundation and Empire. NY: Gnome Press, [1952]. 1st Ed. 1st state bdg & 1st d/j with wear at ends of spine panel & corners. sg June 11 (9) $200

— I, Robot. NY: Gnome Press, 1950. In chipped d/j. sg June 11 (10) $400

— Lucky Starr and the Oceans of Venus. Garden City, 1954. In d/j. pba July 9 (8) $225

— Pebble in the Sky. Garden City, 1950. In chipped d/j. sg June 11 (10) $400

— The Stars, Like Dust. Garden City, 1951. In d/j with minor wear to spine panel. sg June 11 (12) $150

Aspin, Jehoshaphat

— The Naval and Military Exploits.... L, 1820. 1st Ed. 12mo, 19th-cent half mor; rubbed. With 34 plates. Soiled & stained. bba Dec 19 (62) £400 [Cave]

Anr copy. Contemp calf gilt by Atkinson. With hand-colored frontis & 35 circular plates (has the 2 additional plates of Pampelona & Vittoria). C May 20 (16) £550 [Old Hall]

Aspley, John

— Speculum nauticum. L, 1638. 4to, calf by Riviere; joints rubbed. Inner margins of last 3 leaves renewed; I4 lacking. STC 861.6. DuPont copy. CNY Oct 8 (6) $10,000

Assaraco, Andrea

— Historiae novae ac veteres. Milan: Gottardo da Ponte, 24 Dec 1516. Folio, vellum. Woodcut shaved; lacking initial blank; tp repaired; hole in text of final leaf; annotations. S Dec 5 (47) £2,000 [Mediolanum]

Assiette...

— L'Assiette au beurre. Paris, 1901-12. Nos 1-594. Folio, half calf or wraps. HH May 12 (2140) DM12,000

Astle, Thomas, 1735-1803

— The Origin and Progress of Writing. L, 1784. 1st Ed. 4to, modern half mor. With 31 plates on 28 leaves. bba Jan 30 (60) £140 [Bernard]

2d Ed. L, 1803. 4to, needs rebdg. With port & 32 plates. Some foxing. sg May 21 (267) $150

Astley, Philip

— Astley's System of Equestrian Education. L, [1801]. 3rd Ed. 8vo, contemp half calf; rebacked. With port & 9 plates. Some dampstaining. S Nov 14 (262) £500 [Tibbals]

Astley, Thomas

— A New General Collection of Voyages and Travels.... L: Thomas Astley, 1745-47. 4 vols. 4to, modern half calf. W July 8 (97) £420

Atanagi, Dionigi

— Delle lettere facete, et piacevoli di diversi huomini.... Venice, 1582-75. 2 vols in 1. 8vo, contemp vellum. Some gatherings browned. bba Feb 27 (240) £85 [Poel]

Atget, Eugene

— Atget: Photographe de Paris. Paris, 1930. 4to, cloth. With 96 plates. sg Oct 8 (3) $600

— A Vision of Paris. NY, 1963. Text by Marcel Proust. 4to, cloth. sg Apr 13 (6) $110

Anr copy. Orig cloth; rubbed. wa Apr 9 (257) $110

Athenaeus

— Deipnosophistarum. Venice: Aldus, Aug 1514. 1st Ed in Greek. Folio, 18th-cent blind-stamped vellum; Lacking B8 blank; inner margin of tp strengthened; some dampstain; Ms marginalia. Gaisford copy. C June 24 (266) £8,000 [Segal]

Anr Ed. Lyons: Sebastianus Bartolomaeus Honoratus, 1556. 8vo, 17th-cent calf; front cover loose. Some dampstaining at end; some underscoring & marginalia. sg Mar 12 (4) $250

Athenian...

— The Athenian Gazette: or Casuistical Mercury. L, 1691-97. Vols 1-20 (lacking parts of Vols 9-11).. Folio, modern cloth. Frontis damaged; browned & with old repairs. Milne copy. Ck June 12 (56) £300

— Athenian Letters or the Epistolary Correspondent of an Agent to the King of Persia.... L, 1741-43. 4 vols. 8vo, orig bds; needs rebacking. With folding map & 14 plates. Map foxed. sg Mar 5 (9) $60

Atherton, Gertrude

— The Splendid Idle Forties.... Kentfield: Allen Press, 1960. One of 150. Folio, cloth. cb Oct 31 (3) $300; cb Jan 16 (5) $130

Atherton, John

— The Fly and the Fish. NY, 1951. One of 222. Koopman copy. O Oct 29 (13) $400

Atkinson, A.

— A Set of Four. Poet, Miser, Virtuoso, Hypochondriac. L, 1824. Folio, orig wraps; rebacked, bottom of rear cover torn. sg May 7 (10) $1,100

Atkinson, G. M. W.

— Sketches in Norway Taken During a Yachting Cruise in...1852. [Cork, 1853]. Oblong folio, contemp mor gilt; corners rubbed, spine def. With map & 21 plates. Minor soiling, mainly in margins. C Oct 30 (5) £550 [Hannas]

Atkinson, Geoffroy

— La Litterature geographique francaise de la renaissance. Paris, 1927. One of 550. 4to, orig wraps. K July 12 (444) $80

Atkinson, George Francklin

— The Campaign in India. L, 1859. Folio, disbound. With litho title & 25 plates on 21 sheets. Tears to titles of 2 plates. W Mar 6 (17) £200

— "Curry & Rice" on Forty Plates.... L, [1859]. 4to, loose in orig cloth; rubbed. DW Nov 6 (9) £110

Anr copy. Later half mor. kh Nov 11 (30) A$200

2d Ed. L, [1860]. 4to, orig cloth; rubbed. With litho title & 39 plates. Some waterstaining to upper margins. bba May 28 (353) £60 [Bailey]

Atkinson, James, 1780-1852

— Sketches in Afghaunistan. L, 1842. Folio, contemp half mor; rubbed & soiled. Lacking port; tp torn & frayed; 1 plate with marginal tear. Ck Dec 11 (195) £280

Anr copy. Bds. With pictorial title & 23 (of 25) tinted plates. Some spotting & marginal dampstains; some marginal tears; 1 tear tape-repaired. DW Mar 4 (2) £300

Atkinson, John Augustus, 1775-1831

— Characteristic Groups, Scenery, and Costumes of Great Britain. L, 1808. Folio, unsewn as issued in orig wraps. With 16 hand-colored plates. C May 20 (235) £1,200 [Marlborough]

— A Picturesque Representation of the Naval, Military and Miscellaneous Costumes of Great Britain. L, 1807. 1st Issue, with title falsely promising one hundred plates and ptd Vol I. Vol I (all pbd). Folio modern mor gilt by Zaehnsdorf. With 33 hand-colored plates. Repair to lower blank margin of Sand Boy; hole in Rigged Lighter. C May 20 (17) £2,000 [Marlborough]

Atkinson, Thomas Witlam, 1799-1861

— Oriental and Western Siberia. L, 1858. 8vo, recent cloth. With folding map. Library markings. DW Apr 8 (5) £55

Atkinson, William

— Views of Picturesque Cottages with Plans. L, 1805. Folio, orig wraps; soiled & worn. With engraved title & 19 plates, 12 hand-colored. DW Oct 9 (808) £360

Atkyns, Sir Robert, 1647-1711

— The Ancient and Present State of Glocestershire. L, 1768. 2d Ed. Folio, contemp calf gilt; rubbed, head of spine worn. With double-page maps, 8 plates of arms & 64 folding views. bba June 25 (244) £2,000 [Heald]

Anr copy. Contemp calf; rubbed, front cover detached. With 73 plates. Marginal dampstaining, occasionally extending into image. F Mar 26 (764) $4,700

Atlante...

— Atlante dell' America contenente le migliori carte geografiche, e topografiche delle principali citta.... Livorno, 1777. Folio, contemp half sheep; rubbed, corners abraded, loss to lea on lower cover near joint. With 43 maps, plans & views Repair to fore-edge of Plate 13; soiling to Plate 26. CNY Oct 8 (7) $1,600

Atlas

— Arbuckles' Illustrated Atlas of the Fifty Principal Nations of the World. NY, [1889]. Oblong 4to, pictorial wraps; upper cover detached. With 48 chromolitho maps. S May 14 (1165) £450 [Quaritch]

— Asher & Adams' New Commercial, Statistical and Topographical Atlas.... NY, [1872]. Folio, orig cloth; worn & broken. Some staining & chipping. Sold w.a.f. O Dec 17 (13) $260

— Asher and Adams' New Statistical and Topographical Atlas of the United States. NY, [1872]. Folio, orig half lea; worn & soiled, hinges split. With 28 double-page hand-colored maps. Some spotting. wa Nov 21 (17) $250

— Atlas moderne ou collection de cartes sur toutes les parties du globe terrestre. Paris: Lattre & J. T. Herissant, [1762-83]. Part 1 only. disbound. With engraved title & 35 double-page maps & 1 double-page plate, the maps in contemp outline color. S Feb 26 (700) £1,400 [Vilsuet]

— Atlas of Frederick County, Maryland.... Phila., 1873. Folio, half sheep; spine tape-repaired. With 30 hand-colored maps, some double-page. bbc Dec 9 (8) $270

— Atlas to Accompany the Official Records of the Union and Confederate Armies. Wash., 1891-95. 2 vols. Folio, half mor; worn. With 175 maps. Library markings. sg June 18 (173) $325

— Atlas usuel de geographie moderne. Paris: E. Andriveau-Goujon, [c.1865]. Folio, orig half mor. With 31 (of 32) double-page hand-colored maps. Tp creased; some maps splitting at central crease. cb Oct 10 (114) $550

— Colton's Atlas of the World. NY, 1855-56. 2 vols. Folio, half mor; worn, Vol I needs rebdg. Vol I lacking Georgia. sg Sept 19 (31) $1,600

Anr Ed. NY, 1856-57. 2 vols. Folio, contemp half calf; needs rebackingn. Most maps hand-colored. Some foxing & staining, mainly to margins.. sg Sept 19 (32) $1,200

Anr Ed. NY, 1856. 2 vols. Folio, half mor; def. Some marginal chips & tears. Sold w.a.f. sg Feb 13 (115) $1,300

Anr copy. Half mor; worn. Tp trimmed &

rehinged. sg Feb 13 (116) $1,100

Anr Ed. NY, 1857. 2 vols. Folio, modern lea. With 2 litho frontises, 101 mostly hand-colored maps & 2 plates. Some browning & repaired tears to margins. S May 14 (1169) £900 [Map House]

— Colton's General Atlas.... NY, 1857. Folio, orig half mor gilt; worn. With frontis & 96 colored maps. Some spotting & discoloration; frontis torn & foxed. S June 25 (304) £1,200 [Nicholson]

Anr copy. Disbound. With 170 colored maps & plans on 100 sheets. Margins browned, with occasional damping that affects images at rear. wa Nov 21 (18) $1,200

Anr Ed. NY, 1864. Folio, orig half mor gilt; joints weak. With engraved title & 110 (of 113) mapsheets, most hand-colored. Short tear in additional title. S July 9 (1413) £800 [Nicholson]

— Family Cabinet Atlas.... Phila.: Carey & Lea, 1832. 12mo, cloth; rebacked & loose. With 52 maps, most hand-colored. sg Feb 13 (122) $650

— Il Gazzettiere Americano contenente un distinto regguaglio di tutte le parti del Nuovo Mondo.... Livorno, 1763. 3 vols. 4to, 19th-cent half calf. With 21 maps & 57 plates. HH May 12 (617) DM5,200

— Gray's Atlas of the United States. Phila., 1875. Folio, half mor; worn. With 70 colored maps & plans. Some maps loose; marginal browning. S June 25 (428) £450 [Map]

— Johnson's New Illustrated Family Atlas. NY, 1862. Folio, orig half mor; worn, joints tender. With 62 hand-colored maps. wa Mar 5 (438) $750

Anr copy. Orig cloth; broken, worn. Stain to margin of pp. 1-20, not affecting images; also stain to margin of text at end. Z Nov 23 (211) $400

Anr Ed. NY, 1864. Folio, disbound. With 63 hand-colored maps. NY state map torn; prelims & last leaves frayed; vignette title def; some dampstaining. wa Nov 21 (19) $650

Anr Ed. NY, 1865. Folio, orig half lea; worn & broken. Some foxing & soiling; 4 maps splitting at center crease; long tear in 1 map. wa Mar 5 (439) $550

Anr Ed. NY, 1866. Folio, bdg not described. Map of NY State damaged, as is 2-page plate of world flags; marginal dampstaining. NH May 30 (32) $600

Anr Ed. NY, 1869. Folio, orig half mor; worn. With 59 hand-colored maps. Double-page map of Ontario detached & with margins chipped; marginal browning. wa Nov 21 (20) $550

— Mitchell's New Universal Atlas. Phila., 1862. ("Mitchell's New General Atlas.") Folio, disbound. Some spots & smudges. wa Mar 5 (440) $850

Anr Ed. Phila., 1863. Folio, orig half mor; worn. With 49 hand-colored maps & town plans. bbc June 29 (26) $475

Anr Ed. Phila., 1864. Folio, orig half sheep; lacking backstrip, worn. With 50 hand-colored maps. Boston street map with corner crease into image. bbc June 29 (24) $450

Anr Ed. Phila., 1873. Folio, orig half lea; worn. With 61 hand-colored maps. bbc Dec 9 (10) $425

Anr Ed. Phila., 1878. Folio, orig half mor gilt; corners & edges worn. With 69 hand-colored maps. bbc June 29 (25) $400

— The Modern County Atlas of England & Wales. L: Johnston, 1889. 4to, modern half mor gilt. With 57 color maps. sg Feb 13 (121) $275

— The National Atlas; Containing Elaborate Topographical Maps of the United States and the Dominion of Canada.... Phila., 1875. Folio, half sheep; extremities worn. Inked owner's stamps on several prelims. sg Sept 19 (87) $850

— Neues Kriegs-Theater oder Sammlung der Merkwuerdigsten Begebenheiten des gegenwaertigen Krieges in Teutschland. Leipzig, 1757-[62]. 18th-cent half vellum; soiled. With engraved title & 80 town & battle-plans, several hand-colored. With 2 Ms plans inserted. Tp stamped. S Nov 21 (155) £1,050 [Haas]

— The Royal Illustrated Atlas of Modern Geography. L & Edin.: Fullarton, [1864]. Folio, contemp half lea. With 76 colored maps numbered as 74, 44 of them double-page. Some soiling. pn Apr 23 (305) £600

Anr copy. 26 (of 27) parts. Folio, orig wraps; worn. With 68 hand-colored maps. Some tears; most maps stained. Sold w.a.f. S Nov 15 (1049) £620 [Seibu]

— West Point Atlas of American Wars, 1689-1953. NY, [1959]. Ed by Vincent J. Esposito. 2 vols. Folio, orig cloth; minor defs. wa Feb 20 (27) $50

Attendolo, Dario

— Il Duello. Venice, 1562. 8vo, 18th-cent sheep. sg Mar 26 (25) $250

Anr Ed. Venice, 1564. 8vo, old vellum. sg Mar 26 (26) $110

Atwood, George, 1746-1807

— A Treatise on the Rectilinear Motion and Rotation of Bodies.... Cambr., 1784. 8vo, 19th-cent half mor. With 8 folding plates. A few annotations. bba Sept 5 (188) £340 [Dawson]

Aubery, Antoine

— Memoires pour l'histoire du Cardinal Duc de Richelieu. 2 vols. Folio, orig calf; rebacked in cloth with portion of 1 backstrip laid down. Some browning; stain at bottom right corner of Vol II. bbc Dec 9 (294) $70

Aublet, Jean B. C. Fusee

— Histoire des plantes de la Guiane francoise.... L, 1775. 4 vols. 4to, modern half mor. With frontis & 350 (of 392) plates. Massachusetts Horticultural Society copy. sg Sept 19 (162) $1,400

Anr copy. Modern half mor. Massachusetts Horticultural Society copy, presented to it by Turell Tufts, Sept 1839. sg Feb 13 (158) $2,000

Aubrey, John, 1626-97

— Wiltshire. The Topographical Collection of John Aubrey.... Devizes, 1862. Continued by John Edward Jackson. 4to, orig cloth; rubbed, spine worn. DW Apr 8 (120) £68

Auden, Wystan Hugh, 1907-73

See also: Moore & Auden

— Another Time: Poems. NY, 1940. 1st Ed. Sgd. sg June 11 (14) $80

— The Double Man. NY, [1941]. 1st Ed. In d/j. Sgd. cb Dec 12 (3) $55

— For the Time Being. NY, [1944]. In soiled d/j. Sgd on tp. cb Dec 12 (4) $55

— The Orators, an English Study. L, 1932. 1st Ed. Sgd. Epstein copy. sg Apr 29 (12) $225

— Poems. L, 1930. 1st Trade Ed. 4to, orig wraps; chipped. With ALs to Frederic Prokosch inserted. pn June 11 (184) £180

Anr copy. Orig wraps; rear joint torn. Epstein copy. sg Apr 29 (13) $475

Auden, Wystan Hugh, 1907-73 —& Isherwood, Christopher

— The Ascent of F6. L, 1936. Inscr by Isherwood, Sept 1936. S Nov 14 (536) £280 [Quaritch]

Audiguier, Vital D'

— A Tragi-Comicall History of our Times.... L, 1635. Folio, contemp sheep; rebacked, worn. Small portion of center of title cut away & repaired; A2 also cut; waterstained. bba Nov 28 (225) £75 [Rix]

— Le vray et ancien usage des duels. Paris, 1617. 8vo, later half cloth. sg Mar 26 (27) $275

Audot, Louis Eustache

— L'Arte di fare i fuochi d'artifizio.... Milan: Fratelli Sonzogno, 1823. 12mo, orig wraps. With 10 plates. Some foxing. sg Nov 14 (280) $200

Audsley, George Ashdown, 1838-1925

— The Art of Organ-Building. NY & L, 1905. 2 vols. 4to, orig cloth; rubbed. pn Oct 24 (311) £140 [Archive]

Audubon, John James, 1785-1851

— The Birds of America. L, 1827-38. 4 vols. Elephant folio, contemp half russia gilt; rebacked & corners renewed with gilt-tooled calf in replication of the orig & with the orig stitching preserved, by Aquarius of London. With 435 hand-colored plates bound by families. Fries's 1st variant of Prothonotary Warbler, Bonaparte's Flycatcher, Wild Turkey, Brown Lark, White-throated Sparrow, Selby's Flycatcher & Brown Titlark, Wild Turkey (Plate VI) & Purple Grackle; 2d variant of Yellow-billed Cuckoo Plates 426 & 531 have vertical hard creases, minor repair & are on new guards; 10 other plates with minor soft creases; occasional foxing, offsetting or show-through affecting 40 plates; Plate 121 with small inkstain; Plate 44 with 3-inch repaired tear to blank margin; other minor nicks to edges repaired; Plate 1 on an old guard; small ink library stamp on each tp & on verso of Plate 17. Sold with: The Ornithological Biography, 1831-39, 5 vols, with unrecorded copy of the Prospectus for The Birds of America bound in; Synopsis of the Birds of North America, 1839. University of Edinburgh (original subscriber) set. CNY Apr 24 (2) $3,700,000

1st 8vo Ed. NY, 1840-44. Vol V only. Half lea; worn & broken. With 69 colored plates only. Some plates torn with loss; some text leaves def. Sold w.a.f. O Dec 17 (14) $400

Anr Ed. NY & Phila., 1840-44. 7 vols. Contemp half mor gilt; some scuffing. With 500 hand-colored plates. DuPont copy. CNY Oct 8 (8) $22,000

Anr copy. Contemp mor gilt; spines worn & faded; hinges & extremities rubbed. 1 plate misbound; 1 cropped. CNY Dec 5 (284) $20,000

Anr copy. Half mor; worn, both covers of Vol I and upper cover of Vol V detached. CNY Dec 5 (285) $12,000

Anr copy. Contemp mor gilt; inner hinges renewed. Vols 3-7 without subscribers' lists; 4-inch tear to text pp.435-36 in Vol VI; numerals of Plates 442 & 465, caption of Plate 141 & image of Plate cropped; Plate 496 bound in upside down; lacking half-titles; minor foxing & browning. CNY Apr 24 (3) $22,000

Anr copy. Orig 100 parts. Orig wraps; most parts rebacked, some spines chipped, Parts 43-56 reassembled into parts from a trimmed & bound copy that preserved the wraps. Some foxing. Manney copy. P Oct 11 (7) $27,000

Anr copy. 7 vols. Contemp half lea; worn, joints rubbed. Text foxed; some offsetting onto plates in first few vols. sg Nov 7 (12) $16,000

Anr Ed. NY, 1856-57. 7 vols. 8vo, orig mor; joints & corners worn or restored. With 500 hand-colored plates. Dampstaining; some soiling. P June 16 (190) $9,500

Anr Ed. NY, [1856-60]. Vol II only. Orig mor; extremities worn. With 70 hand-finished color plates. Some foxing. sg Sept 19 (163) $1,300

2d Folio Ed. NY, 1860. Atlas vol only. Old half mor gilt; spine & corners restored, some scraping to covers, repairs to end-papers & flyleaves. With litho title & 150 chromolitho plates on 105 sheets (all pbd), some finished by hand. Tp, 1st 3 plates & final plate with inner margins & most outer margins renewed; a few plates with tear to edge of image & vertical crease; Plates 19 & 257 with tear just entering image; most other plates with minor marginal repair & occasional short marginal tears. CNY Apr 24 (4) $70,000

Anr Ed. NY, 1861. 7 vols. 8vo, orig lea; extremities rubbed. With 500 hand-colored plates. Opening text leaves & plates in Vol 7 dampwrinkled; corner of 1 plate browned. sg May 7 (11) $13,000

Anr Ed. NY, [1870-71]. 8 vols. 8vo, contemp half mor; rubbed, library book-plates on front pastedowns. With 500 colored plates. Some soiling. P June 16 (191) $17,000

Anr Ed. NY, 1937. Text by Wm. Vogt. Folio, orig cloth. With port & 500 colored plates. K Sept 29 (48) $50

Anr copy. Half cloth. NH Aug 23 (65) $80

Anr Ed. NY & Amst., 1971-72. One of 250. Folio, orig half calf. With 435 color plates. C Oct 30 (276) £8,000 [Kenyon]

Anr copy. Loose in 2 wooden crates. With 430 (of 435) colored lithos plus duplicates of 5 plates. S June 25 (2) £4,800 [Clark]

— The Birds of America: A Selection of Plates... L: Ariel Press, 1972-73. One of 1,000. 2 vols. Folio, cloth; soiled. bba Sept 5 (131) £600 [Ginnan]

Anr copy. Orig half cloth. C Oct 30 (172) £550 [Schuster]; DW Dec 11 (173) £260

— The Original Water-Colour Paintings by John James Audubon for the Birds of America. NY & L, 1966. 2 vols. 4to, cloth. bba Sept 5 (132) £50 [Ginnan]; bba June 11 (232) £50 [Sotheran]; bbc Dec 9 (358) $140; cb Dec 19 (5) $60; cb Feb 27 (9) $50; DW Jan 29 (112) £52; K Mar 22 (25) $75; L Feb 27 (77) £80; LH Dec 11 (60) $70; O Jan 14 (11) $50; sg Sept 6 (14) $50; sg Nov 14 (159) $130; sg Feb 6 (9) $60

— Ornithological Biography.... Edin., 1831-39. 5 vols. 8vo, modern cloth. Lacking half-titles. S Feb 26 (899) £420 [St. Annes Books]

Audubon, John James, 1785-1851 —& Bachman, John, 1790-1874

— The Viviparous Quadrupeds of North America. NY, 1845-48. 1st Ed. 3 plate vols only. Folio, contemp half russia; very worn, covers detached. With 100 (of 150) colored plates. Title of Vol III damp-stained. CNY Dec 5 (286) $22,000

Anr copy. Orig mor gilt; Vol III rebacked with orig spine laid down. With 150 hand-colored plates. Repair to 6-inch tear in Plate 59 & to 1-inch tear in Plates 87 & 98; vertical creases to tp of Vol III & contents leaves of Vols I & II; all prelim text leaves marginally foxed. Redwood Library and Athenaeum copy. CNY Apr 24 (5) $100,000

Anr Ed. NY, 1849-51-54. ("The Quadrupeds of North America.") Orig 31 parts. 8vo, orig wraps; front wrap of Part 1 with small stain, some other parts stained or soiled, rear wrap of Part 14 detached, rear wrap of Part 31 with lower corner restored. With 155 hand-finished color plates. Half-titles for Vols I & III; indexes in Parts 10, 20 & 31. Manney copy. P Oct 11 (8) $7,500

Anr copy. 3 vols. 8vo, half mor; rubbed. With 155 hand-colored plates. Some soiling; marginal dampstaining in Vol I. P June 16 (192) $3,250

Anr copy. Half mor, ptd wraps for the orig 31 parts bound in rear, rubbed, covers detached from Vols I & III, library book-plates on front pastedowns. Vol II lacking half-title; some staining & foxing; Plate 35 severely stained. P June 16 (193) $2,750

1st 8vo Ed. NY, 1849-54. 3 vols. Contemp half mor; rubbed, front inner hinges of Vols I & III broken. With 155 hand-colored plates. Lacking half-titles; library stamps on titles & 1 or 2 text pages in each vol; regulations & borrowers' slip pasted down on lower endpapers; tiny tears to inner margin of Plate 19; some foxing to titles & last pages. Redwood Library and Atheneum copy. CNY Apr 24 (6) $6,500

Anr copy. Contemp half mor; extremities rubbed. Manney copy. P Oct 11 (9) $6,000

Anr copy. Orig lea; rubbed. sg May 7 (12) $6,000

Anr copy. Mor gilt; rubbed. wd Dec 12 (353) $5,200

Anr Ed. NY, 1852-54-54. 3 vols. 8vo, contemp half mor; front cover of Vol II detached, spines repaired or def. With 155 colored plates. Some foxing. P Dec 12 (6) $4,000

Anr Ed. L, 1854-54-[n.d.]. 3 vols. 8vo, orig mor; rubbed, joints & corners restored. With 155 hand-colored plates. Some dampstaining & soiling. P June 16 (194) $2,500

Anr copy. Contemp mor gilt; 1 joint split. Occasional spotting. S July 25 (3) £2,800 [Mackin]

Audubon, John Woodhouse, 1819-62

— The Drawings of John Woodhouse Audubon Illustrating his Adventures Through Mexico.... San Francisco: Book Club of California, 1957. One of 400. b&b Feb 19 (199) $125

Audubon, Maria R.

— Audubon and his Journals. NY, 1897. 2 vols. 8vo, cloth; hinges starting. Library markings. sg June 18 (6) $50

Augustine, Saint, 354-430
See also: Limited Editions Club

— Certaine Select Prayers gathered out of S. Augustines Meditations. L: John Day, 1575. 2 parts in 1 vol. 8vo, 18th-cent mor gilt with name A. Bunbury in gilt letters on upper cover. Black letter. Tp laid down; gathering A soiled; A4 repaired at outer margin; some soiling. STC 924. Ck Oct 31 (21) £300

— Confessions. L, 1900. One of 30 ptd on vellum. Vellum, loose in sheets & untrimmed; worn. O Dec 17 (15) $160

— De civitate Dei. Venice: Gabriele di Pietro, 1475. Folio, later calf with brass catches; lacking clasps. Rubricated, with initials at beginning of each book in blue and red. Some dampstains. 295 (of 296) leaves; lacking 1 blank. Goff A-1236.. sg May 7 (13) $4,800

Anr Ed. Basel: Michael Wenssler, 25 Mar 1479. Folio, contemp blind-stamped over wooden bds with brass clasps & edging strips; once chained, spine worn, some scratching. 56 lines of text, 73 lines of commentary; double-column; type 1B:121G (text), 2:92G (commentary), quire 10 & 1st 3 leaves of quire 11 ptd with Richel type 3:120G. rubricated. Quire 28 bound before 27; stains on 1st page; worming at from & back. 248 leaves; lacking initial blank. Goff A1241. Schoyen copy. P Dec 12 (3) $11,000

Anr Ed. Basel: Johann Amerbach, 13 Feb Bound with: Augustine. De trinitate. [Basel]: Johann Amerback, 1489. 1489. Folio, later bds. 54 lines & headlines; gothic letter; double column; large woodcut. Some wormholes; dampstaining in some lower margins. 268 leaves, Goff A-1243; 86 leaves, Goff A-1343. S May 28 (14) £1,700 [Zioni]

Anr Ed. Venice: Bonetus Locatellus for Octavianus Scotus, 18 Feb 1489. Folio, contemp Italian blind-tooled goatskin over wooden bds; spine ends & corners repaired, some worming & other defs clasps & catches removed. 51 lines of text & 65 lines of commentary; types 4:92G (text), 1:74G (commentary), 2:130G (titles & headlines); double column. Some worming at beginning & end; some staining; inner margin of tp strengthened. 264 leaves. Goff A-1245. C Nov 27 (8) £2,800 [Mediolanum]

Anr copy. Old half sheep gilt; occasional browning or staining. 2 holes in title repaired; lacking K8. 256 (of 264) leaves. Goff A-1245. sg Mar 12 (114) $1,200

— De la cita di Dio. [Venice: Antonio di Bartolommeo (Miscomini), c.1476-78]. Folio, 19th-cent russia gilt; rebacked, joints cracked. Marginal dampstaining with some spotting from fungus. 322 (of 324) leaves; lacking blanks. Goff A-1248. George Milne copy. CNY Dec 5 (157) $1,700

— Epistolae. Basel: Johann Amerbach, 1493. Folio, 18th-cent half sheep. 52 lines & headline; double column for the index; types 14:285G (title), 8:115R (headlines), 17:87R (text), 19:62G (marginalia), 28:120G (index headlines). Minor worming at beginning & end. 328 leaves. Goff A-1268. C Nov 27 (9) £2,000 [O'Keefe]

— Of the Citie of God.... L, 1610. Folio, contemp calf gilt; rebacked. STC 916. W July 8 (16) £310

2d Ed in English. L, 1620. Folio, contemp calf; rebacked, broken. STC 917. LH Dec 11 (61) $250

— Opera. Antwerp: Plantin, 1576-77. 10 vols in 5. Folio, 18th-cent half calf; very worn. Some browning & soiling; a few headlines cropped in Vol VII; some annotations. S Feb 25 (471) £300 [Maggs]

— Sermones ad heremitas. [Strassburg: George Husner, c.1493-94]. 8vo, 19th-cent half mor; extremities rubbed, 8 leaves with headlines shaved; Q3 with 2 small holes. 108 leaves. Goff A-1318. George Milne copy. CNY Dec 5 (158) $850

Augustus II, Duke of Brunswick-Lueneburg.
See: Selenus, Gustavus

Auldjo, John, d.1857

— Journal of a Visit to Constantinople.... L, 1835. Illus by George Cruikshank. 8vo, contemp half mor gilt; rubbed. With 7 plates. Inscr. bba Sept 19 (114) £80 [Morrell]

Anr copy. 19th-cent half calf. S June 30 (231) £300 [Consolidated Real]

— Sketches of Vesuvius.... L, 1833. 8vo, contemp half lea. SI June 9 (87) LIt850,000

Aulnoy, Marie Catherine LaMothe, Comtesse d', 1650?-1705

— Les Contes des Fees. Trevoux, 1698. Pirated Ed. 2 vols. 12mo, 18th-cent calf; Vol II lacking spine, Vol I lacking spine ends. Library stamp on titles; browned & dampstained throughout; lower edge of Vol II wormed throughout. S Dec 5 (222) £900 [Schiller]

Anr Ed. Paris, 1725. 2 vols in 1. 12mo, later calf. Some browning. bba July 23 (164) £400 [Bodleian Library]

Anr Ed. Paris, 1810. 5 vols. 12mo, contemp calf gilt; worn, some backstrips loose or lacking. With 28 plates. 1 waterstained. bba Oct 10 (8) £80 [Ginnan]

Auriferae...

— Auriferae artis, quam chemiam vocant, antiquissimi authores, sive turba philosophorum.... Basel: Petrus Perna, 1572. Vol I (of 2) only. 8vo, blindstamped pigskin. Lacking the frontis. SI June 9 (89) LIt750,000

Aurora...

— Aurora Australis. East Antarctica, [pbd at the Winter Quarters of the British Antarctic Expedition], 1908. Ed by Sir Ernest H. Shackleton; illus by George Marston. 4to, orig half calf; joints restored. Inscr by the ptr. Manney copy. P Oct 11 (274) $24,000

Ausbund...

— Ausbund, das ist, eitliche schoene Christliche Lieder.... Germantown: Sauer, 1751. Bound with: Fuenff Schoene Geistliche Leider. Germantown, 1752. 8vo, contemp calf; rebacked. Library Company of Philadelphia duplicate. sg Dec 5 (223) $500

Austen, Jane, 1775-1817

— Emma. L, 1816. 1st Ed. 3 vols. 8vo, later half calf. Lacking 2 half-titles; partially misbound; 1 leaf repaired. bba June 25 (196) £2,000 [Finch]

Anr copy. Orig bds; rebacked, orig spines laid down, short crack along top of spine in Vol I. Manney copy. P Oct 11 (11) $9,500

Anr copy. 19th-cent half calf; worn, rebacked preserving old spines. Lacking half-titles; E1 in Vol I repaired; some staining & spotting. S Dec 12 (26) £800 [Harries]

— Mansfield Park. L, 1814. 1st Ed. 3 vols. 12mo, contemp half calf. Vol II, pp. 95-98 & Vol III, pp. 227-30 supplied in early Ms. Sold w.a.f. b Mar 11 (95) £360

Anr copy. Contemp calf; rebacked. Half-titles in Vols II & III only; ad leaf in Vol III; lacking final blank in Vol II; some spotting, staining, tears & repairs, occasionally just affecting text. S Dec 12 (23) £700 [Harries]

— Northanger Abbey and Persuasion. L, 1818. 1st Ed. 4 vols. 12mo, orig bds; rebacked with portions of orig spines laid down, endpapers affected in rebdg. Minor pencil markings. Kern-Manney copy. P Oct 11 (12) $10,000

Anr copy. 19th-cent half calf. Half-title in Vol I only; ad leaf in Vol I; Vol IV lacking final blanks; some spotting. S Dec 12 (25) £700 [Harries]

— Pride and Prejudice. L, 1813. 1st Ed. 3 vols. 12mo, 19th-cent half calf; worn, rebacked preserving old spines & recornered. With half-titles. Some spotting & soiling. S Dec 12 (22) £5,500 [Rocklin]

3d Ed. L, 1817. 2 vols in 1. 12mo, variant brown pbr's-remainder cloth; rebacked, orig spine laid down. Some dampstaining. pn Sept 12 (240) £380 [Jarndyce]

— Sense and Sensibility. L, 1811. 1st Ed. 3 vols. 12mo, orig bds; rebacked, portions of orig spine laid down, restored, spines stained, bookplates removed from endpapers. Some browning; marginal pencil lines; some marginal tears. With half-titles, that in Vol II watermarked 1808. Newton-Manney copy. P Oct 11 (10) $21,000

Anr copy. Contemp half calf; worn, rebacked preserving old spines gilt. With half-titles. Some spotting. S Dec 12 (21) £6,200 [Harcourt-Williams]

2d Ed. L, 1813. 3 vols. 12mo, contemp calf gilt; rebacked, orig spines laid down, chipped. With the half-titles. pn Sept 12 (242) £1,300 [Jarndyce]

Anr copy. 19th-cent half calf. Lacking half-titles & final blanks. S Dec 12 (24) £750 [Emmerson]

Anr Ed. L: H. G. Clarke, 1844. 2 vols. 8vo, orig mor gilt, with front wraps bound in; 1 corner worn. pn Sept 12 (243) £140 [Louise Ross]

— Three Evening Prayers. San Francisco: Colt Press, [1940]. One of 300. cb Jan 16 (12) $85

— Works. L, 1833. 5 vols. 8vo, 1st issue bdgs of plum-colored linen bds; rubbed, spine of

Northanger Abbey soiled & slightly torn. Lacking 2 ad leaves but with additional 12-page pbr's cat at end of Persuasion. pn Sept 12 (232) £440 [Jarndyce]

Anr Ed. L, 1892. 10 vols. Half mor. pnE Oct 2 (373) £320

Anr Ed. NY: Atheneum Society, [1892]. 6 vols. 8vo, cloth; worn. O Aug 25 (16) $70

Anr Ed. L, 1898. ("Novels.") Ed by R. B. Johnson; illus by C. E. & H. M. Brock. 10 vols. 8vo, half mor. Some soiling & browning. P June 17 (327) $800

Anr Ed. NY,1906. One of 1,250. 12 vols. Orig cloth; extremities frayed. F Dec 18 (55) $60

Chawton Ed. ("Novels and Letters.") 12 vols. 8vo, cloth. br May 29 (54) $125

Winchester Ed. Edin., 1911-12. 12 vols. Half mor gilt. Fragment of an ALs bound into Vol I. P June 17 (103) $2,250

Anr Ed. Oxford, 1923. One of 1,000 L.p. copies. Ed by R. W. Chapman. 5 vols. contemp half mor gilt by Birdsall. DW Oct 2 (429) £360

Austin, A. B.

— An Angler's Anthology. L, 1930. One of 100, sgd by author & artist. Illus by Norman Wilkinson. 4to, half mor by Bayntun-Riviere. Koopman copy. O Oct 29 (14) $120

Austin, Mary Hunter, 1868-1934

— The Land of Little Rain. Bost. & NY, 1903. 4to, cloth. sg June 18 (37) $130

Anr Ed. Bost., 1950. Illus by Ansel Adams. 4to, cloth, in frayed d/j. bbc Feb 17 (165) $160

— Taos Pueblo. Bost., 1977. One of 950. Illus by Ansel Adams. With 12 plates. sg Apr 13 (5) $800

Austin, Sarah

— The Story without an End. L, 1868. Illus by Eleanor Vere Boyle. 8vo, orig cloth. With tinted litho frontis & 15 chromolithos. Minor marginal spotting. b Nov 18 (47) £60

Australia

— A Concise History of the English Colony in New South Wales.... L, [1804]. 8vo, modern half calf. Tp laid down & with upper outer corner cut away; repair in fore-margin of dedication leaf. C June 25 (155) £2,600 [Arnold]

— Historical Records of New South Wales. Sydney, 1892-1901. 7 vols in 8 without the 4to vol of chart facsimiles. 8vo, cloth, in d/js. kh Nov 11 (592) A$160

— Report from the Select Committee on the state of Gaols.... L, 12 July 1819. Folio, contemp half calf. With folding litho chart & 4 folding litho plates. C June 25 (179) £650 [Quaritch/Hordern]

— The Resources of Australia, and the Prospects and Capabilities of the New Settlements.... L, 1841. 8vo, orig wraps; worn. cb Jan 30 (6) $325

— New South Wales Agricultural Society. - Prospectus, List of Subscribers, and Rules and Regulations. Sydney: Robert Howe, 1822. 12mo, modern half mor. C June 25 (186) £500 [Carlisle]

Austria

— Katalog der datierten Handschriften in Oesterreich. Vienna, 1969-88. Vols I-VIII in 16. 4to, cloth, in d/js. sg Oct 31 (229) $800

Avedon, Richard

— Observations. NY, [1959]. Text by Truman Capote. Folio, bds; spine spotted. bbc Feb 17 (174) $110

Anr copy. Bds; rubbed. sg Oct 8 (5) $375

Anr copy. Some staining. sg Apr 13 (7) $175

Anr copy. Bds; box worn. sg June 11 (57) $130

Aventinus, Joannes, 1477-1534

— Annalium Boiorum libri septem. Ingolstadt: A. & S. Weissenhorn, 1554. Folio, 18th-cent half calf. Small portion of woodcut surface on t4r rubbed with loss; a few stains at beginning & end. S Dec 5 (206) £500 [Reiss & Auvermann]

Avicenna, 980-1037

— Liber canonis. Venice: Junta, 1562. ("Liber canonis de medicinis cordialibus, cantica....") Folio, 18th-cent vellum. Repaired wormhole in 1st title; index to 3d book of 1st part misbound at end. C June 24 (290) £1,700 [Hakimzadeh]

— Libri canonis. Venice: Luc'Antonio Giunta, [1527]. Folio, modern half lev gilt. sg Nov 14 (3A) $2,200

Avila y Zuniga, Luis de, c.1500-64

— Comentario de la guerra de Alemana.... Antwerp: Juan Steelsia [ptd by Jean Grapheus?], 1550. 116 pp, 8vo, mor. With 4 woodcut maps & plates, 2 folding, 1 double-page. Some stains; a few marginal wormholes. B May 12 (11) HF1,100

Aviler, Augustin Charles d', 1653-1700

— Cours d'architecture.... Paris, 1691-93. Mixed Ed. 2 vols in 1. 4to, mor gilt by Bauzonnet; soiled. With 2 engraved titles & 117 plates. Lacking text. Sold w.a.f. Yemeniz copy. S Feb 11 (290) £320 [Klein]

Avirett, James B. —& Others

— Memoirs of General Turner Ashby and his Compeers. Balt., 1867. 12mo, cloth; worn. NH May 30 (154) $280

Avison, Charles, 1710?-70

— An Essay on Musical Expression. L, 1752. 8vo, contemp sheep; worn, joints cracked. Tp browned. pn Oct 24 (313) £130 [Johnson]

Axe, John Wortley

— The Horse: Its Treatment in Health and Disease. L, 1908. 3 vols. 4to, orig cloth. kh Nov 11 (318) A$240

Ayer Collection, Edward Everett

— A Bibliographical Check List of North and Middle American Indian Linguistics in the Ayer Collection. Chicago, 1941. 2 vols. 4to, cloth. bbc Apr 27 (92) $55

— Narratives of Captivity among the Indians of North America. Chicago, [1912]-28. 2 vols (including Supplement One). Wraps. cb Oct 17 (47) $80

Ayers, Paul. See: Baur Collection

Ayme, Marcel

— Gustalin. Paris, 1937. One of 45 on velin pur fil Lafuma Navarre. 12mo, mor by Devauchelle, orig wraps bound in. S May 28 (264) £550 [Saxhof]

— Le Vaurien. Paris, 1931. One of 9 hors commerce on papier verge Lafuma-Navarre. 4to, mor by Devauchelle, orig wraps bound in. S May 28 (262) £500 [Saxhof]

Ayres, Atlee Bernard

— Mexican Architecture. NY, 1926. Folio, cloth, in d/j. LH Dec 11 (149) $70

Ayres, Philip, 1638-1712

— The Voyages and Adventures of Capt. Barth. Sharp...in the South Sea. L, 1684. 8vo, contemp calf; spine repaired with ends renewed, 3 corners recapped. Marginal worming in tp & next few leaves; a few upper margins cut close. CNY Oct 8 (201) $1,700

Anr copy. Contemp calf; rebacked, corners worn, inner hinges strengthened with white linen tape, 1 rear flyleaf def. CNY Oct 8 (202) $950

Ayres, W. P. See: Gardeners'...

Ayrton, William

— The Adventures of a Salmon in the River Dee. L: Whittaker & Co., [1853]. 12mo, contemp half mor; rubbed. bba Nov 28 (8) £90 [Hereward Books]

Ayton, Richard, 1786-1823. See: Daniell & Ayton

Aytoun, William Edmondstoune

— Lays of the Scottish Cavaliers.... Edin. & L, 1863. 4to, orig mor gilt. cb Sept 26 (10) $70

B

B., L. J. D. See: Du Blar, L. J.

B., R. See: Burton, Robert

Babbage, Charles, 1792-1871

— The Ninth Bridgewater Treatise. A Fragment. L, 1838. 2d Ed. 8vo, contemp half mor; front joint cracked, rubbed. Library stamp on title. bba July 9 (55) £75 [Bickersteth]

— Passages from the Life of a Philosopher. L, 1864. 1st Ed. 8vo, recent half mor. With frontis. Title ink-marked; some spotting & soiling. DW Nov 6 (186) £105

— Reflections on the Decline of Science in England. L, 1830. 1st Ed. 8vo, contemp half sheep gilt; worn, backstrip detached. sg Nov 14 (210) $350

— Thoughts on the Principles of Taxation.... L, 1848. 8vo, wraps. Inscr to Henry Goulburn. sg Nov 14 (211) $850

Babcock, Harold L.

— The Turtles of New England. Bost., 1919. 4to, loose in wraps; worn. With 16 plates. O Jan 14 (12) $90

Babcock, Havilah

— Tales of Quails 'n Such. NY, [1951]. One of 299. Illus by William Schaldach. Inscr. cb Jan 30 (7) $90

Babcock, Philip H. See: Derrydale Press

Babington, John

— Pyrotechnia or, a Discourse of Artificiall Fire-Works. L 1635. Folio, contemp calf; rebacked, endpapers renewed. A few leaves torn; Qq3.4 folded backwards. Lacking the 2 folding plates. sg Nov 14 (281) $600

Babington, William, 1757-1833

— A New System of Mineralogy.... L, 1799. 4to, modern cloth. Lacking half-title or initial blank; library markings. sg Nov 14 (212) $400

Babson Collection, Grace K.

— A Descriptive Catalogue of the...Collection of the Works of Sir Isaac Newton. NY, 1950-66. One of 750 and of 450. 2 vols, including Macomber's Supplement O Sept 24 (26) $250

Bachman, John, 1790-1874. See: Audubon & Bachman

Back, Sir George, 1796-1878

— Narrative of the Arctic Land Expedition.... L, 1836. 8vo, contemp half calf; rubbed & frayed. With folding map & 16 plates.. DW Nov 6 (10) £140

Anr Ed. L, 1837. 8vo, orig bds; worn, some dampstains. With folding map; plate count not given. Some dampstains, soiling & foxing. O May 26 (4) $130

2d Ed. Phila., 1837. 8vo, orig half cloth; rubbed, hinges split. With folding map. NH Oct 6 (14) $50

— Narrative of an Expedition in H.M.S. Terror. L, 1838. 1st Ed. 8vo, modern calf, orig cloth bound in. With folding map & 12 plates. Some plate captions trimmed. W July 8 (237) £200

Backer, Augustin de & Alois de

— Bibliotheque de la Compagnie de Jesus.... Louvain, 1960. 12 vols. 4to, orig cloth. Reprint of 1890 Ed. Ck Nov 1 (343) £800

Bacon Collection, Edward R.

— Getz, John. - Catalogue of Chinese Art Objects. 4to, half mor; broken. sg Feb 6 (10) $225

Bacon, Sir Francis, 1561-1626

See also: Eragny Press

— The Charge of Sir Francis Bacon Knight, His Maiesties Attourney Generall, touching Duells.... L, 1614. 1st Ed. 4to, mor gilt by Riviere. Washed; margins trimmed. sg May 7 (14) $1,000

— The Essayes or Counsels, Civill and Morall. L, 1625. 1st Ed, 1st Issue. 4to, calf gilt by Francis Bedford. Washed; lacking initial blank. Gibson 13; STC 1147. sg Nov 7 (13) $2,200

2d Issue. Modern mor gilt by Riviere. Tp repaired with rule borders supplied in facsimile; A3 with similar repair to lower margin; V1 with small rusthole. STC 1148. C Dec 16 (178) £450 [Paradise]

Anr Ed. L, 1639. 4to, modern mor gilt by Bernard Middleton. Some headlines shaved; lacking initial & final blanks; worming towards end. STC 1151. bba June 25 (175) £140 [Thomas Plume's Library]

Anr copy. Old calf; repaired, lower cover detached. Some old dampstaining; repairs to blank margins of tp & 1st few leaves; lacking initial blank. STC 1151. C Dec 16 (179) £140 [Rix]

Anr copy. Modern half calf. Lacking A1; S2 with ragged tear & a large section in facsimile. STC 1157. Milne copy. Ck June 12 (8) £120

Anr Ed. L: James Knapton, 1691. 8vo, modern calf with fragments of old calf covers & spine laid on. cb Oct 25 (3) $75

— The Historie of the Raigne of King Henry the Seventh. L, 1622. 1st Ed. Folio, contemp calf gilt; small split to upper section of lower joint. Gibson 116a; STC 1159. C Dec 16 (180) £320 [Finch]

Anr copy. Old calf rebacked with modern calf; worn with patches & slits. Gibson 116a; STC 1159. cb Oct 25 (4) $650

Anr copy. Old calf; adhesive stains on spine & covers, which are detached. Lacking frontis. Gibson 116a; STC 1159. K July 12 (44) $130

Anr copy. Later half calf. Tp rebacked; port mtd. rs Oct 17 (85) $750

Anr copy. Contemp calf; rebacked. Some underscoring; opening leaves partly dampstained. Gibson 116a; STC 1159. sg Oct 24 (14) $400

Anr copy. Lea; broken. Gibson 116a; STC 1159. sp June 18 (289) $160

— Resuscitatio.... L, 1657. 1st Ed. 4to, library cloth; soiled. Library stamps. bba Oct 24 (46) £95 [R. Clark]

2d Ed. L, 1661. Folio, contemp calf; upper cover detached. Some stains & soiling. O Aug 25 (19) $160

— Sylva Sylvarum. L, 1626. 1st Ed, 1st Issue. 2 parts in 1 vol. Folio, contemp calf gilt with initials H.G.; spine rubbed & repaired at ends. Old marginal dampstaining.. Gibson 170 but variant collation. STC 1168. C Dec 16 (181) £1,900 [Quaritch]

Anr Ed. L, 1639. Folio, lea. sp Apr 16 (331) $300

9th Ed. L, 1670. Folio, old calf; rebacked, rubbed. Lacking engraved title; some stains & soiling. Sold w.a.f. O Aug 25 (20) $100

— The Twoo Bookes of Francis Bacon. Of the Proficience and Advancement of Learning.... L, 1605. 1st Ed. 4to, modern mor gilt by Riviere; upper joint split. Tp soiled; final blank lacking; no errata leaves; some repairs at ends. STC 1164. C Dec 16 (182) £700 [Rix]

2d Ed. L, 1629. 4to, modern calf. Tp damaged & strengthened on verso; some leaves supplied from anr copy; M3-2M3 wormed at outer edge. STC 1165. Milne copy. Ck June 12 (7) £120

3d Ed. Oxford, 1633. 4to, old sheep rebacked with modern calf; worn. cb Oct 25 (5) $140

Anr Ed. L, 1674. ("Of the Advancement and Proficience of Learning....") Folio, 18th-cent calf; upper joints cracked, spine torn at head. Rust-hole in 2F1-2. Milne copy. Ck June 12 (9) £140

Anr copy. Lea; worn & broken. Browned.

wa Mar 5 (476) $110

— Works. L, 1753. 3 vols. Folio, contemp calf; rubbed, rebacked preserving orig spines, joints split. Some browning & spotting. pn June 11 (140) £190 [Shapero]

Anr Ed. L, 1765. Ed by Thomas Birch. 5 vols. 4to, contemp calf gilt; rubbed, spines chipped. Titles browned. L Nov 14 (365) £180

Anr copy. Contemp calf. LH Dec 11 (62) $170

Bacon, Sir Francis, 1561-1626 —& Godwin, Bishop Francis, 1562-1633

— The History of the Reigns of Henry the Seventh, Henry the Eighth, Edward the Sixth and Queen Mary. L, 1676. 2 parts in 1 vol. Folio, contemp calf; upper joint cracked, rubbed. Some browning & spotting. pn Mar 19 (172) £110 [Clarke]

Badcock, John. See: Hinds, John

Badeslade, Thomas —& Toms, William Henry

— Chorographia Britanniae, or a Set of Maps of all the Counties in England and Wales.... L, 1742. 8vo, contemp calf; upper cover detached, extremities rubbed. With engraved title, dedication leaf, 7 tables & 46 double-page maps. 2 maps spotted. Ck July 10 (339) £420

Badger, Mrs. C. M.

— Wild Flowers. NY, 1859. 4to, orig mor; upper joint cracking, extremities worn. With 22 colored plates. pn Apr 23 (222) £550

Anr copy. Orig mor gilt; extremities rubbed, front hinge cracked. Plate count not given. Some foxing & browning. sg Sept 19 (164) $950

Badius, Jodocus

— Navis Stultifera. Paris, 26 Sept 1505. 4to, 18th-cent vellum. Holes to 4 leaves; 1 leaf torn; some worming or soiling; early marginalia. C June 24 (291) £2,200 [Wood]

Badminton...

— Badminton Magazine of Sports and Pastimes. L, 1895-1900. Vols 1-11. 8vo, half mor. S Feb 26 (837) £300 [Najera]

Vols 1-30. L, 1895-1919. 4to, contemp half calf. Ck Dec 11 (123) £280

Baedeker, Karl, Publishers

— Russia, with Teheran, Port Arthur, and Peking.... L, 1914. With 40 maps & 78 plans, some folding. General map of Russia detached & torn. DW Oct 2 (9) £320

Baer, Elizabeth

See also: Fowler & Baer

— Seventeenth Century Maryland: a Bibliography. Balt., 1949. One of 300. 4to, cloth; worn. O Sept 24 (27) $140

Baer, Karl Ernst von, 1792-1876

— [Drawings to the Investigation of the Caspian Sea Fisheries.] St. Petersburg, 1861. 4to, half calf. With 86 double-page & folding plates, ptd in color. Prelims foxed. wd June 12 (365) $1,500

Baglione, Giovanni

— Le Vite de' pittori, scultori.... Naples, 1733. 4to, modern half vellum. Title cropped at foot; a few leaves browned. bba Sept 19 (308) £180 [Bifolco]

Bagrow, Leo

— History of Cartography. L, 1964. Revised by R. A. Skelton. 4to, cloth; worn. O Sept 24 (28) $90; O Sept 24 (28) $90

Anr copy. Cloth, in d/j. sg Oct 31 (68) $100

Anr copy. Cloth, in torn d/j. wa Mar 5 (455) $65

Baif, Lazare de, d.1547

— Annotationes in legem II de captivis, et postliminio reversis. Basel: Froben & Episcopius, 1537. 4to, contemp vellum; soiled. Tp waterstained & restored at lower margin; some browning. Ck Nov 29 (46) £180

— De re navali libellus.... Paris: F. Estienne, 1537. 8vo, new bds. B Nov 1 (547) HF1,400

Anr copy. Modern half mor. bba Sept 19 (278) £220 [Pickering & Chatto]

Baigell, Matthew

— Thomas Hart Benton. NY, [1973?]. In d/j. sg Sept 6 (23) $225

Baigent, William

— A Book on Hackles for Fly Dressing. [Newcastle upon Tyne, c.1941]. 2 vols, including box of specimens. 4to, lea. With 10 cards of mtd specimens. Koopman copy. O Oct 29 (15) $950

Bailey, Liberty Hyde, 1858-1954

— Cyclopedia of American Horticulture. NY, 1900-2. 4 vols. 8vo, cloth; worn & shaken. O Mar 31 (13) $60

Anr Ed. NY, 1907. 4 vols. 8vo, orig cloth; soiled, spine ends frayed, some corners worn. wa Dec 9 (513) $110

— The Standard Cyclopedia of Horticulture. NY, 1925. 3 vols. 4to, cloth; worn. With 24 color & 96 uncolored plates. wa Dec 9 (563) $85

Anr Ed. NY, 1933. 3 vols. cb Jan 16 (13) $50

Bailey, Nathan, d.1742

— An Universal Etymological English Dictionary. L, 1773. 23rd Ed. 8vo, contemp sheep; rebacked, joints & spine ends worn, endpapers renewed. sg Oct 24 (15) $175

Bailey, Rosalie F.

— Pre-Revolutionary Dutch Houses and Families in Northern New Jersey and Southern New York. NY, 1936. One of 334. 4to, cloth. Library stamp inked-out. cb Feb 12 (8) $50

Baillie, Matthew, 1761-1823

— The Morbid Anatomy of Some of the Most Important Parts of the Human Body. Albany, 1795. 1st American Ed. 8vo, contemp calf; worn, 1 pair of leaves partly detached. Browned. bbc Sept 23 (265) $140

Baillie Scott, M. H.

— Houses and Gardens. L, 1906. 4to, cloth. sg Sept 6 (15) $225

Baillie-Grohman, William Adolph

— Sport in Art. L, [1913]. 1st Ed. 4to, orig cloth; bumped. sp June 18 (163) $65

Bailliere, F. F.

— Bailliere's Victorian Gazetteer and Road Guide.... Melbourne, 1865. 8vo, bdg not described but worn & with backstrip split. Folding map with tear. kh Nov 11 (695) A$140

Baily's Magazine...

— Baily's Magazine of Sports and Pastimes. L, 1860-88. Vols 1-48, but lacking Vol 5. 8vo, orig cloth; spines rubbed, covers dampstained; Vol 29 misnumbered 24. W Mar 6 (96) £160

Bainbridge, George Cole

— The Fly Fisher's Guide.... Liverpool, 1816. 1st Ed. 8vo, mor; rebacked, rubbed. With 8 hand-colored plates. Koopman copy. O Oct 29 (17) $325

Bainbridge, Henry Charles

— Peter Carl Faberge.... L, 1949. One of 1,000. 4to, orig cloth, in d/j. Some soiling. F Mar 26 (317) $140

Baines, Thomas, 1806-81

— Yorkshire, Past and Present.... L, [1871-77]. 2 vols in 4. 4to, orig cloth; tear in spine of Division 2. With folding map & 27 plates. Some spotting. pnL Nov 20 (91) £80

Baines, Thomas, 1822-75

— Explorations in South-West Africa. L, 1864. 8vo, orig cloth. With colored frontis, 3 folding map & 8 wood-engraved plates. Some tears at folds. pn Apr 23 (234) £290 [Baring]

Baird, Joseph Armstrong. See: Grabhorn Printing

Baird, Spencer Fullerton, 1823-87 —& Others

— A History of North American Birds. Bost., 1875. 3 vols. 4to, orig cloth. HH May 12 (482) DM1,200

— The Water Birds of North America. Bost., 1884. 2 vols. 4to, orig cloth. HH May 12 (483) DM1,800

Baker...

— The Baker Street Journal. NY, 1946-47. Vols I-II. 8 parts. Orig wraps; edge wear. bbc Sept 23 (398) $60

Baker, Charles Henry Collins. See: Derrydale Press

Baker, Charlotte Alice

— True Stories of New England Captives.... Cambr., 1897. 1st Ed. 8vo, orig cloth. Tp coming loose. NH Oct 6 (163) $50

Baker, Edward Charles Stuart

— The Indian Ducks and their Allies. L, 1908. 8vo, half mor. With litho title & 30 colored plates. S Feb 26 (901) £280 [Montevecchi]

Baker, Ezekiel

— Remarks on Rifle Guns.... L, 1804. ("Twenty-Six Years Practics and Observations with Rifle Guns.") 2d Ed. 8vo, later cloth. With 6 hand-colored plates & 2 uncolored charts. S Feb 26 (838) £260 [Montague]

Baker, George Percival

[-] A Memorial. NY, 1939. L.p. copy sgd by the contributors. sg Oct 17 (6) $175

Baker, Oliver

— Black Jacks and Leather Bottells. Stratford, [1921]. Ltd Ed, sgd. 4to, cloth; rubbed. DW Oct 2 (430) £70; sp June 18 (311) $80

Baker, Sir Richard, 1568-1645

— A Chronicle of the Kings of England.... L, 1643. 1st Ed. Folio, old calf; rebacked, recently oiled, front joint cracked, bottom of backstrip partly detached. With engraved title & port. sg Oct 24 (16) $350

Ed not specified. Folio, later half lea; worn, stained. A few leaves loose. Sold w.a.f. O Dec 17 (18) $100

Anr Ed. L, 1665. Folio, contemp mor gilt with arms of Edward Hyde, Earl of Clarendon added before Dec 1667, from Samuel Mearne's workshop. C Dec 16 (183) £4,800 [Quaritch]

Baker, Sir Samuel White, 1821-93
— Cyprus as I Saw It in 1879. L, 1879. 8vo, orig cloth. With frontis & half-title (both reattached). S June 30 (234) £300 [Caramondanis]
— Eight Years' Wanderings in Ceylon. L, 1855. 1st Ed. 8vo, later half calf; rubbed, upper joint split. With 6 colored plates. Ck May 15 (71) £140
— Ismailia. NY, 1875. 8vo, cloth; extremities worn. NH May 30 (544) $60
— The Nile Tributaries of Abyssinia. L, 1867. 1st Ed. 8vo, orig cloth; rebacked, orig spine preserved. With port, 2 maps & 23 plates. bba Jan 16 (286) £110 [Scott]

Baker, Thomas, 1625?-90
— The Geometrical Key.... L, 1684. 4to, contemp vellum; soiled. With 10 folding plates. One leaf with small hole. Ck Nov 29 (139) £260

Baker, Thomas, 1656-1740
— Reflections upon Learning. L, 1700. 2d Ed. 8vo, lea. Text dampstained. sp Apr 16 (330) $70

Baker, Warren. See: John & Baker

Baker, William S., 1824-97
— The Engraved Portraits of Washington. Phila., 1880. 4to, orig cloth. F Mar 26 (392) $100
One of 500. Cloth. Extra-illus with 19 ports of Washington. sg June 18 (540) $250
— Medallic Portraits of Washington.... Phila., 1885. 1st Ed. 4to, later cloth. Library markings. F Dec 18 (293) $80

Bakst, Leon, 1866?-1924
See also: Levinson, Andre
— The Inedited Works. NY: Brentano's, 1927. One of 600. Oblong folio, half cloth; worn. Library markings. Sold w.a.f. sg Mar 5 (206) $325

Balbus, Joannes
— Catholicon. Mainz: [Johann Gutenberg], 1460. Single leaf. Folio. Laid into a copy of Stilwell's Gutenberg and the Catholicon of 1460. P June 17 (105) $2,000

Baldi, Bernardino, 1553-1617
— Heronis Ctesibii Belopoeeca, hoc est Telifactiva.... Augsburg: D. Frank, 1616. 4to, modern half calf. S July 9 (1208) £320 [Poole]

Baldini, Baccio, 1436?-1487?
— Vita di Cosimo Medici. Florence: Bartolomeo Sermatelli, 1578. Folio, 19th-cent vellum. Some foxing. SI Dec 5 (749) LIt400,000

Baldinucci, Filippo, 1624-96
— Opere. Milan, 1808-12. 11 vols. 8vo, contemp vellum; soiled. S Feb 11 (6) £340 [Mannocci]
— Vocabolario Toscano dell'arte del disegno.... Florence: Santi Franchi, 1681. 4to, old half vellum; rubbed & soiled. Some browning. S Feb 11 (7) £260 [Sagelli]
— Vocabulario Toscana dell'arte del disegno. Florence, 1681. 4to, contemp bds; worn. Old marginal annotations; some browning. SI Dec 5 (55) LIt500,000

Baldo, Camillo
— Delle Mentite. Venice: Bartolomeo Fontana, [1633]. Bound with: Delle considerationi & dubitationi sopra la materia delle mentite. Venice, 1634. 4to, old vellum. sg Mar 26 (30) $225

Baldwin, James
— Giovanni's Room. NY, 1956. In torn d/j. wa Sept 26 (123) $90
— If Beale Street Could Talk. NY, 1974. Ltd Ed, sgd. wa Dec 9 (169) $130

Baldwin, Joseph G.
— The Flush Times of Alabama and Mississippi. NY, 1853. 8vo, cloth. sg June 18 (7) $80

Baldwin, Thomas, of Chester
— Airopaidia. Chester, 1786. 1st Ed. 8vo, orig bds; rebacked. With 3 plates, 2 hand-colored. Marginal holes; some spotting. L.p. copy. pn May 14 (72) £600 [Joseph]

Baldwin, Thomas, b.1750?
— Narrative of the Massacre, by the Savages, of the Wife and Children of Thomas Baldwin.... NY, 1835. 1st Ed. 8vo, modern cloth. Some browning & foxing; hole to tp; some tape repairs. wa Dec 9 (275) $190

Bale, John, 1495-1563
— Illustrium maioris Britanniae scriptorum.... Gippeswici [Ipswich]: Joannes Overton [but Wesel?: Dietrich van den Straten?], August 1548. 1st Ed, Issue not given. 4to, contemp half pigskin over wooden bds; recased. Title mtd; wormed throughout with some text loss in first half of vol. sg Oct 31 (22) $850

Balfour, J. O.
— A Sketch of New South Wales. L, 1845. 8vo, cloth. kh Nov 11 (426) A$120

Ball, Charles
See also: Stafford & Ball
— The History of the Indian Mutiny. L, [c.1875-1900]. 2 vols. 4to, mor gilt; extremities rubbed. Sold w.a.f. sg Jan 9 (123) $130

Ball, Katherine M.

— Decorative Motifs of Oriental Art. L & NY, 1927. 4to, cloth. Inscr. b&b Feb 19 (272) $125

Anr copy. Cloth; top of spine worn. Bottom of rear leaves damp-wrinkled. K Sept 29 (51) $65

Ballantyne, James

— Homes and Homesteads in the Land of Plenty.... Melbourne, 1871. 8vo, orig cloth. kh Nov 11 (427) A$100

Ballard, George, 1706-55

— Memoirs of Several Ladies of Great Britain.... L, 1775. 8vo, contemp calf; worn. bba Aug 13 (123) £55 [Crawford]

Ballou, John

— The Lady of the West, or, the Gold Seekers. Cincinnati, 1855. 12mo, cloth. Foxed. sg June 18 (39) $70

Baltazarini. See: Beaujoyeulx, Baltasar de

Baltimore Museum of Art

— 2000 Years of Calligraphy. Balt., 1965. 4to, half cloth. sg Oct 31 (189) $150

Balzac, Honore de, 1799-1850

See also: Limited Editions Club

— Les Contes drolatiques. Paris, 1861. One of 25 on chine. Illus by Gustave Dore. 12mo, 19th-cent mor gilt. With port, woodcut frontis & 425 illusts in the text. With ALs of Barbey d'Aurevilly to Dutacq, complaining of the poor quality of Dore's illusts. S May 28 (266) £3,400 [Beres]

— The Hidden Treasures.... Kentfield: Allen Press, 1953. One of 160. Illus by Malette Dean. Bds. b&b Feb 19 (303) $300

— Oeuvres. Paris, 1869-76. 20 vols. 8vo, mor gilt. DW Nov 6 (430) £155

Vols 1-39 (of 40). Paris, 1912-38. Half mor gilt by Canape. B Nov 1 (1129) HF1,000

— Petites Miseres de la vie conjugale. Paris: Chlendowski, [1845]. 1st Ed. Illus by Bertall. 8vo, 19th-cent half lea; joints rubbed. sg Oct 17 (113) $150

— Works. Phila., [1895-1900]. Definitive Ed, One of 1,000. 53 vols. 8vo, mor gilt by Bayntun. F Sept 26 (241) $1,150

Bancroft, Edward

— An Essay on the Natural History of Guiana.... L, 1769. 1st Ed. 8vo, contemp half calf; joints weak. Ms index at end. bba June 25 (250) £200 [Waggett]

Bancroft, George, 1800-91

— History of the United States.... Bost., 1885. 6 vols. 8vo, calf gilt; minor wear. wa Mar 5 (3) $260

— Memorial Address on the Life and Character of Abraham Lincoln.... San Francisco: Book Club of California, 1929. One of 325. cb Jan 16 (14) $60

Bancroft, Hubert Howe, 1832-1918

— The Book of the Fair. Chicago & San Francisco, 1893. Columbian Ed. 10 parts. Folio, wraps. cb Feb 12 (151) $275

— History of California. San Francisco, 1884-90. Vols I-VI (of 7). Orig calf; spines stained. cb Sept 12 (11) $160

— Popular Tribunals. San Francisco, 1887. 1st Ed. 2 vols. 8vo, orig cloth. cb Sept 12 (15) $100

— Works. San Francisco, [1882]. Vols I-IV: The Native Races. Half calf; 1 spine dampstained. cb Sept 12 (16) $95

Anr Ed. San Francisco, 1883-90. 39 vols. 8vo, sheep, 2 vols in half calf; worn. sg June 18 (8) $950

Bancroft, Laura. See: Baum, L. Frank

Bandar Log Press

— All About the Bandar Log Press. Phoenix, 28 Oct 1903. Out-of-series copy. Illus by Frank Holme. sg Sept 26 (13) $225

Bandello, Matteo, 1480?-1562

— La Prima [-quarta] parte de la novelle. L [Italy ptd], 1740. 4 vols in 3. 4to, modern half mor. Lacking frontises. bba Sept 19 (310) £50 [Barker]

Anr copy. 4 vols. 4to, contemp calf. SI June (93) LIt400,000

Bandini, Angelo Maria, 1726-1803

— Vita e lettere di Amerigo Vespucci. Florence, 1745. 1st Ed. 4to, contemp calf; rebacked. With frontis & folding table. SI June 9 (94) LIt450,000

Bandini, Ralph. See: Derrydale Press

Bangs, John Kendrick, 1862-1922

— Portals West: A Folio of Late Nineteenth Century Architecture in California. San Francisco: California Historical Society, [1960]. Folio, cloth, in d/j. cb Sept 12 (17) $95

Bankes, Henry

— Lithography; or, the Art of Taking Impressions from Drawings and Writing Made on Stone.... L, 1816. 8vo, modern bds with vellum spine. With 4 litho plates. Some spotting. Schlosser copy. P June 17 (508) $800

Bankes, Thomas —& Others

— A New Royal Authentic and Complete System of Universal Geography. L, [c.1790]. 2 vols in 1. Folio, contemp calf; broken & def. With frontis, 87 plates & 20 maps only. Frontis torn & soiled; a few plates repaired; folding maps creased &

torn; some staining throughout. Sold w.a.f. S July 1 (1459) £450 [Bailey]

Banks, Sir Joseph, 1743-1820

— The Endeavour Journal of Joseph Banks 1768-1771. Sydney, 1962. Ed by J. C. Beaglehole. 2 vols. 8vo, cloth, in d/j. kh Nov 11 (428) A$160

— The Journal of Joseph Banks in the Endeavour.... Guildford, 1980. One of 500. Commentary by A. M. Lysaght. 2 vols. Orig half calf. Facsimile of orig Ms. S June 25 (86) £130 [Kahn]

Banks Library, Sir Joseph

— DRYANDER, JOHN. - Catalogus bibliothecae historico-naturalis Josephi Banks. L, 1798-96-99. One of 250. Vols I-IV (of 5). 8vo, contemp half calf gilt. S June 25 (71) £900 [Maggs]

Banks, Sir Joseph, 1743-1820 —& Solander, Dr. Daniel

— Illustrations of the Botany of Captain Cook's Voyage round the World...in 1768-71. L, [1900]-1905. 3 vols. Folio, loose in orig half cloth. With 2 folding maps & 320 plates. S June 25 (84) £5,800 [Graham]

Bannerman, David Armitage

— Birds of the Atlantic Islands. L, 1963-68. 4 vols. Orig cloth, in d/js. pn May 14 (163) £300

Anr copy. Orig cloth. sg May 14 (190) $450

Bannerman, David Armitage —& Bannerman, Winifred Mary

— Birds of Cyprus. L, 1958. Orig cloth in frayed d/j. DW Nov 6 (150) £85

Bannerman, David Armitage —& Lodge, George E.

— The Birds of the British Isles. Edin. & L, 1953-63. 12 vols. Orig cloth. With 390 color plates. B May 12 (1950) HF1,000

Anr copy. With 387 colored plates. Ck July 10 (378) £125

Anr copy. Orig cloth, in d/js. James Robertson-Justice's copy, with his comments. pn May 14 (164) £260 [Grahame]

Anr copy. Vols I-III & XII (of 12). Together, 4 vols. sg Nov 14 (161) $90

Anr copy. 12 vols. Orig cloth, in d/js. With 1 uncolored & 386 colored plates. W July 8 (349) £180

Bannerman, Helen

— Sambo and the Twins... NY, 1936. 1st Ed. 16mo, orig cloth, in d/j. F Sept 26 (390) $90

— The Story of Little Black Sambo. L, 1899. 1st Ed. 16mo, orig cloth. Epstein copy. sg Apr 29 (14) $7,000

Bannerman, Winifred Mary. See: Bannerman & Bannerman

Bar Hebraeus. See: Grighor, Abu al-Faraj

Bara, Jerome de

— Le Blason des armoiries.... Paris, 1628. Folio, modern calf. Title soiled. bba Apr 9 (212) £100 [Elliott]

Barbaro, Daniello, 1513-70

— La Pratica della perspettiva. Venice, 1569 [colophon dated 1568]. Folio, 19th-cent vellum. With woodcut title-border, 17 pictorial woodcuts & numerous woodcut diagrams. C Nov 27 (29) £4,000 [Maggs]

Barbault, Jean, 1705?-66

— Denkmaeler des Alten Roms. Augsburg, 1782. Folio, contemp half calf; rubbed. With 104 plates on 60 leaves. S Nov 21 (64) £600 [Barker]

— Vues des plus beaux Restes des Antiquites Romaines.... Rome, 1770. 4 parts in 1 vol. Folio, early 19th-cent half sheep; backstrip def. With 99 plates on 61 leaves. Dampstaining in lower margin throughout, entering image on some leaves. sg Feb 6 (11) $1,100

Barbe-Marbois, Francois, Marquis de, 1745-1837

— The History of Louisiana. Phila., 1830. 8vo, contemp half sheep; rubbed. Browned throughout. sg Dec 5 (146) $250

Barber, John Thomas

— A Tour throughout South Wales.... L, 1803. 1st Ed. 8vo, contemp half calf; worn. With folding map. DW Oct 2 (87) £60

Barber, John Warner, 1798-1885

— History and Antiquities of New Haven.... New Haven, 1831. 1st Ed. 12mo, cloth; worn & shaken. Foxed & stained. O Apr 28 (148) $50

Anr copy. Orig cloth; worn. With frontis map, plan & 6 plates, all colored. Some foxing. O July 14 (22) $110

Barber, Thomas

— Picturesque Illustrations of the Isle of Wight. L, [1834]. 8vo, orig cloth; worn, inner joints tape-repaired. With engraved title, folding map & 40 views. O Jan 14 (13) $70

Barbey d'Aurevilly, Jules, 1808-89

— Un Pretre marie. Paris, 1865. 2 vols. 12mo, mor gilt by Carayon, orig wraps bound in. ALs bound in. S May 28 (269) £2,000 [Beres]

Barbie du Bocage, Jean Denis. See: Barthelemy, Jean Jacques

Barbier, Antoine Alexandre

— Dictionnaire des ouvrages anonymes. Paris, 1822-27. 2d Ed. 4 vols. 8vo, contemp half mor. Ck Nov 1 (344) £150

Anr Ed. Paris, 1872-89. 4 vols. 8vo, half lea; rubbed, spines worn. O Sept 24 (29) $150

Barbier, Georges

— Falbalas et Fanfreluches: Almanach des modes presentes, passees et futures, 1922 [-26]. Paris, [1921-25]. 5 vols. Pictorial wraps. Each vol with 12 plates & cover design by Barbier, colored through stencils. Z Oct 26 (8) $3,700

— La Guirlande des Mois. Paris, 1917-18. Vols I & II only. 16mo, orig bds; joints of Vol II split. Ck July 10 (156) £140

Barbiere, Joe

— Scraps from the Prison Table. Doylestown, 1868. 8vo, orig cloth; worn & repaired. Some foxing & dampstaining. wa Dec 19 (388) $200

Barbusse, Henri, 1873-1935

— Le Feu. Paris, 1916. One of 33 on japon. 8vo, mor extra by Madeleine Noulhac, orig wraps bound in. With ALs inserted. S May 28 (272) £650 [Lardancheet]

Barbut, Jacques

— Les Genres des insectes de Linne. L, 1781. 4to, contemp calf; rubbed, joints weak. With hand-colored title & 21 (of 22) plates only, 19 hand-colored, 2 folding & uncolored. Tp & a few other leaves spotted. Sold w.a.f. C Oct 30 (235) £200 [Elvidge]

Barcia Carballido y Zuninga, Andrew Gonzalez de. See: Gonzales de Barcia, Andres

Barclay, James

— A Complete and Universal Dictionary of the English Language. Bungay, 1813. ("The Bungay Edition of Barclay's Dictionary.") 4to, disbound. With engraved title & frontis (def), 20 hand-colored maps & 14 plates. Sold w.a.f. L Nov 14 (137) £90

Anr Ed. L, [1848?]. 4to, modern half calf. With engraved title, frontis, 50 county maps & town plans & 11 plates. Some spotting. bba May 14 (259) £600 [Burden]

Anr copy. Contemp calf gilt; worn, joints cracked. With engraved title & 84 plates & maps, some hand-colored in outline. Some plates spotted; some map margins shaved; lacking part of appendix. pn May 14 (194) £650 [Ventnor]

Anr copy. 19th-cent calf; joints weak. With engraved title & frontis, 50 engraved maps, plans & plates & 10 ports. Some shaving. S Feb 26 (701) £650 [Burden]

Barclay, John, 1582-1621

— Argenis. L, 1625. Trans by Kingsmill Long. Folio, contemp calf; rubbed & worn, rebacked. Library markings. bba Oct 24 (44) £70 [Rix]

Anr Ed. L: Felix Kyngston for Richard Meighen & Henry Seile, 1629. 4to, old calf gilt; recently oiled, rebacked, endpapers renewed. sg Oct 24 (17) $200

— Argenis: or, the Loves of Poliarchus and Argenis. L, 1636. Trans by Kingsmill Long. 4to, modern calf; new endpapers. Some browning. STC 1395. bba June 11 (68) £110 [Aspin]

Barclay, Patrick

— The Universal Traveller, or a Complete Account.... L, 1735. Folio, orig calf; broken. Some foxing; front & rear blanks wrinkled. bbc June 29 (103) $350

Barclay, Robert, 1648-90

See also: Franklin Printing, Benjamin

— An Apology for the True Christian Divinity.... Birm.: Baskerville, 1765. 8th Ed. 4to, contemp calf; rubbed. bba Jan 16 (124) £90 [Whetman]

Anr copy. Lea; rebacked. NH Aug 23 (346) $115

Bard, Samuel

— A Compendium of the Theory and Practice of Midwifery.... NY, 1808. 1st Ed, 2d Issue. 8vo, contemp vellum. sg Nov 14 (4) $600

Bardi, Luigi

— Galerie du Palais Pitti. Florence, 1842-45. 4 vols. Half mor. Some foxing & dampstaining. Met Apr 27 (3) $975

— L'Imperiale e reale galleria Pitti.... Florence, 1837-42. 4 vols. Folio, contemp half lea gilt; worn & broken. With 498 (of 500) plates. HH May 12 (895) DM2,400

Bardswell, Monica. See: Tristram & Bardswell

Barduzzi, Bernardino

— A Letter in Praise of Verona (1489). Verona: Officina Bodoni, 1974. One of 150. Half vellum. bba July 9 (364) £140 [Marks]

Barham, Richard Harris, 1788-1845

— The Ingoldsby Legends. L: Bentley, [1870]. 8vo, mor extra by Kelliegram with varicolored pictorial mor inlays, orig front cover & spine bound in at end. O May 26 (5) $700

Anr Ed. L, 1898. Illus by Arthur Rackham. Orig cloth. With 12 color plates. F Sept 26 (277) $130

Anr copy. Bdg not described but rubbed. K Dec 1 (376) $150

Anr copy. Orig cloth; worn. Tp foxed. K Mar 22 (376) $95; sp June 18 (149) $100

Anr Ed. L & NY, 1907. 4to, cloth. With 24 colored plates. bba Jan 16 (380) £110 [Hughes-Games]

Anr copy. Cloth; faded. bba Apr 9 (277) £50 [Blumenkron & Ramirez]

Anr copy. Orig cloth; rubbed, worn. K Sept 29 (366) $85

Anr copy. Cloth; worn, spotted. O Jan 14 (158) $100; sg Jan 30 (139) $150

One of 560, sgd by Rackham. Orig vellum gilt. With 24 tipped-in colored plates & 12 tinted plates. b Nov 18 (99) £280

Anr copy. Mor gilt by Sangorski & Sutcliffe. sg Nov 7 (162) $900

Anr Ed. L, 1919. 4to, orig cloth; rubbed. With 24 colored plates. bba Oct 10 (150) £50 [Ginnan]

Anr Ed. L, 1920. 4to, cloth, in worn d/js. kh Nov 11 (36) A$140

Anr Ed. L, 1929. 4to, orig cloth. DW Oct 2 (386) £60; DW Mar 4 (376) £90

Baring, Daniel Eberhard

— Clavis diplomatica tradens specimina veterum scripturarum.... Hanover, 1737. 1st Ed. 4to, contemp half calf. With 33 plates. SI Dec 5 (57) LIt380,000

Baring-Gould, Sabine

— The Life of Napoleon Bonaparte. L, 1897. 4to, mor extra by Morrell, each cover inset with 2 rectangular color port miniatures on ivory of Napoleon. sg Nov 7 (15) $4,000

Barker, Benjamin —&
Fielding, Theodore Henry, 1781-1851

— The Fine Arts. Forty-Eight Aquatint Colored Engravings...Views in and Near Bath. Bath, 1824. Oblong 4to, modern mor gilt. With 48 hand-colored plates, mtd on orig brown paper & framed wwith an ink rule. small tears in mounts, some repaired. C May 20 (18) £1,100 [Denniston]

Barker, Lucy D. Sale

— Kate Greenaway's Birthday Book for Children. L, [1880]. 1st Ed. 16mo, orig cloth, in d/j lacking large fragment. With 12 color plates.. cb Sept 5 (41) $110

Barker, Matthew Henry, 1790-1846

— Greenwich Hospital. L, 1826. Illus by George Cruikshank. 4to, 19th-cent calf gilt; joints split, rubbed. With 12 hand-colored plates. Marginal dampstaining, not affecting text or plates. S Feb 25 (442) £340 [Marlborough]

Barker, Thomas, 1769-1847

— Forty Lithographic Impressions.... Bath, 1813. 1st Ed, one of 200. Folio, 19th-cent bds with recent sheep spine. With 40 lithos, 30 on tinted paper, with sepia wash & white highlights added by hand. Schlosser copy. P June 18 (510) $2,250

Anr copy. Orig bds; spine renewed. With 40 lithos, 21 on tinted maper, mtd. P June 18 (511) $600

Barlaeus, Caspar, 1584-1648

— Medicea hospes, sive descriptio publicae gratulationis.... Amst., 1638. Folio, later mor gilt; rubbed. With port & 16 folding plates. Title repaired. bba Oct 24 (278) £440 [Erlini]

Anr copy. Contemp calf, armorial bdg; rebacked. With port & 16 double-page plates, 1 folding. One plate trimmed & mtd. W July 8 (95) £440

Barlow, Edward, b.1642

— Meteorological Essays concerning the Origin of Springs.... L, 1715. 8vo, disbound; some leaves loose at beginning & end. With 12 folding & double-page maps & plans. Some browning; a few small holes affecting text; 1 plate torn & def at fore-margin; anr plate shaved at fore-margin. S Nov 14 (499) £150 [Mason]

Barlow, Francis

— Livre de plusieurs animaux.... Paris: De Poilly, [c.1675]. Oblong 4to, 19th-cent vellum. With engraved title & 11 plates. Tp stained at lower margin; some spotting. Sold w.a.f. Ck Oct 18 (3) £650

— Severall Wayes of Hunting, Hawking and Fishing.... L, [c.1740]. Illus by Wenceslas Hollar. 4to, modern half calf. With 12 plates. bba June 25 (215) £750 [Sabin]

Barlow, Jane, 1860-1917

— The End of Elfintown. L, 1894. Illus by Laurence Housman. 8vo, orig cloth; corners rubbed. DW Apr 8 (522) £90

Barlow, Percival

— The General History of Europe and Entertaining Traveller. L, [c.1790]. Folio, contemp calf; worn, rebacked. With frontis, 50 (of 51) plates & 18 (of 19) folding maps. Some browning & soiling; a few tears; tp & frontis cut down & mtd. Sold w.a.f. S May 14 (1190) £440 [Bailey]

Barlow, William, d.1625

— The Navigators Supply.... L: G. Bishop, R. Newbery & R. Barker, 1597. 4to, disbound. With engraved title & 7 folding plates. Tp cut close at top & with marginal tears; a few headlines cut into. STC 1445. DuPont copy. CNY Oct 8 (10) $8,500

Barman, Christian

— The Bridge.... L & NY, 1926. One of 125. Illus by Frank Brangwyn. 4to, orig half cloth. pnE Oct 2 (537) £60

Barnard, George, 1807-90

— Switzerland. Scenes and Incidents of Travel in the Bernese Oberland. L, 1843. Folio, contemp half mor; worn & loose. With litho title & 27 lithos on 25 plates. bba Nov 7 (241) £1,000 [Hildebrandt]

Barneby, William Henry

— Life and Labour in the Far, Far West. L, 1884. 8vo, cloth. With folding map in rear pocket. sg June 18 (9) $70

Barnes, Joseph K.

— The Medical and Surgical History of the War of the Rebellion. Wash., 1870-88. Vols I-II only. 4to, orig cloth; spine ends worn, joints frayed or torn. Some foxing to text only. bbc Feb 17 (93) $175

Vol I, Part 2 & Vol II, Part l (of 6 vols) only. Wash., 1870-79. 4to, orig cloth; shaken & discolored. Marginal dampstaining throughout; inked-over stamps on tp. sg May 14 (8) $200

Barnes, Joshua, 1654-1712

— The History of that most Victorious Monarch Edward IIId. Cambr., 1688. Folio, contemp calf; rebacked. With port-frontis & 2 other ports. W July 8 (44) £125

Barnett, Percy Neville

— Armorial Book-Plates. Sydney: Pvtly ptd, 1932. One of 120. 4to, cloth; tape marks to rear endpapers. kh Nov 11 (37) A$100

Barozzi, Giacomo, called Vignola, 1507-73

— Le Due Regole della prospettiva practica.... Rome: Zanetti, 1583. 1st Ed. Folio, modern vellum. With architectural title & 29 illusts (1 or 2 just shaved). A few marginalia & annotations in a contemp hand. S Nov 21 (65) £2,500 [Panini]

Anr copy. Half vellum gilt. Some worming. SI June 10 (1064) LIt850,000

Anr Ed. Rome, 1611. Folio, 19th-cent half lea; worn. Lacking last leaf; some repairs. SI Dec 5 (709) LIt400,000

Anr copy. 18th-cent half calf; worn. SI June 10 (1065) LIt900,000

— Regola delli cinque ordini d'architettura. Amst.: Willem Janssz, 1619. Folio, contemp vellum. Engraved throughout. Lacking port; ink stain in upper inner margins at beginning; some tears. Sold w.a.f. bba June 25 (216) £320 [MacDowell]

Anr Ed. Rome, [c.1620]. Folio, vellum; worn. Engraved throughout. K July 12 (29) $250; S Dec 5 (223) £600 [Maggs]

Barratt, Francis

— The Magus.... L, 1801. 4to, contemp half lea; worn. With port & 22 plates, 5 hand-colored. bba Jan 16 (154) £50 [Bunout]

Anr copy. Recent antique calf. With port & 23 plates, 5 hand-colored. DW Mar 4 (186) £300

Barratt, Thomas James

— The Annals of Hampstead. L, 1912. One of 550. 3 vols. 4to, orig cloth; edges rubbed. pn Nov 14 (399) £160 [Marlborough]

Barraud, Charles Decimus —& Travers, William T. L., 1819-1903

— New Zealand Graphic and Descriptive. L, 1877. Folio, modern half calf preserving orig bds. With colored title, map, 6 plain & 24 color plates. S June 25 (486) £700 [Zhang]

Anr copy. Some fraying; a few plates becoming loose. S June 25 (487) £550 [Zhang]

Barre, Louis, 1799-1857

— Herculaneum et Pompei. Paris, 1840-39-40. 7 vols, lacking the suppressed Musee secret. 8vo, half mor. Minor foxing. sg Sept 6 (143) $275

Anr Ed. Paris, 1875-77. 8 vols, including the suppressed Musee secret. 8vo, bds; worn. Some foxing. sg Sept 6 (143) $275

Barrett, Charles Golding

— The Lepidoptera of the British Islands. L, 1892-1907. 11 vols plus index. 8vo, orig cloth, index in orig wraps; joints rubbed or torn. With 504 hand-colored plates. Marginal annotations in ink & pencil. S Feb 26 (902) £720 [Johnson]

Barrett, Ellen C.

— Baja California: A Bibliography.... Los Angeles, 1957-67. One of 550. 2 vols. cb Oct 17 (55) $50; sg Oct 31 (23) $150

Barrett, Joseph Hartwell

— Life of Abraham Lincoln.... Indianapolis: Asher, 1865. 8vo, orig half calf. bbc June 29 (193) $50

Barrie, Sir James Matthew, 1860-1937

— The Admirable Crichton. L, [1914]. Illus by Hugh Thomson. 4to, cloth. kh Nov 11 (40) A$60

Anr copy. Vellum. With 20 mtd color plates. sg Jan 30 (175) $300

One of 500. Orig vellum gilt. With 20 mtd color plates. L Nov 14 (85) £80

— The Little White Bird. L: Hodder & Stoughton, 1902. 1st Ed. cb Sept 5 (7) $50

— Peter and Wendy. NY, [1911]. 1st American Ed. In d/j. Epstein copy. sg Apr 29 (17) $1,800

— Peter Pan in Kensington Gardens. L, 1906. One of 500. 4to, mor gilt by Bayntun. sg Nov 7 (163) $850

Anr copy. Illus by Arthur Rackham. Orig cloth; head of spine worn. With 50 colored plates. Frontis detached. b Nov 18 (94) £120

Anr copy. Orig cloth; rubbed, backstrip frayed. bba Apr 9 (278) £140 [Ginnan]; DW Apr 8 (543) £210

One of 500, sgd by Rackham. Orig vellum gilt. With 50 colored plates. b Nov 18 (93) £900

One of 500. Orig vellum gilt. With 50 mtd color plates. Manney copy. P Oct 11 (259) $3,000

— Peter Pan [in Dutch]. Amst., 1907. One of 320. Illus by Arthur Rackham. 4to, mor gilt; needs rebdg. sg Sept 26 (261) $400

— Peter Pan in Kensington Gardens. L, 1907. Illus by Arthur Rackham. 4to, orig cloth; hinges weak. bba Jan 16 (381) £180 [Ginnan]

Anr Ed. L, [1912]. 4to, orig vellum gilt. With 50 colored mtd plates. sg Jan 30 (140) $175

— Quality Street. [L, 1913]. Illus by Hugh Thomson. 4to, orig cloth, in d/j. With 22 colored plates. bba Apr 9 (347) £70 [Ulysses]

Anr copy. Cloth; worn. O Jan 14 (14) $60

One of 1,000. Cloth. Some foxing. kh Nov 11 (41) A$50

— Works. NY, 1929-31. One of 1,030. 14 vols. Half cloth, unopened. O Aug 25 (24) $120

Barriere, Dominique, d.1678

— Villa Aldobrandina Tusculana.... Rome, 1647. Folio, contemp calf; spine worn & patched, corners recapped, joints & lea of covers cracking. With engraved title & 17 plates only. Lacking Plates 15 & 16; vertical crease to Plate 8; tp & 1st dedication leaf marginally discolored. McCarty-Cooper copy. CNY Jan 25 (5) $1,300

Barrington, Daines, 1727-1800

— Miscellanies. L, 1781. 1st Ed. 4to, later half calf; rubbed. With 2 folding maps, 2 plates & 5 tables. Marginal tears; some foxing. pn Oct 24 (316) £460 [Macnutt]

— The Possibility of Approaching the North Pole Asserted. L, 1818. 8vo, modern half calf. With folding map. W July 8 (238) £125

Barrington, George, 1755-c.1840

— The Life, Amours, and Wonderful Adventures of that most Notorious Pickpocket, George Barrington. L: W. Mason, [1790]. 8vo, disbound. Some spotting. C June 25 (117) £200 [Joachim]

— The Memoirs of George Barrington.... L, [c.1790]. 8vo, modern half mor. S June 25 (118) £180 [Joachim]

— A Voyage to Botany Bay. L, 1969. Facsimile Ed. Old calf; broken & def. Some soiling; marginal defs; library markings. kh Nov 11 (431) A$300

Barrois, Jean

— Bibliotheque Prototypographique; ou, Librairies des Fils du Roi Jean.... Paris, 1830. One of 200. 4to, modern wraps. Some foxing. sg Oct 31 (190) $120

Barrow, Albert Stewart

— More Shires and Provinces. L, 1928. Illus by Lionel Edwards. 4to, cloth; spine rubbed, corners bumped. wd Dec 12 (356) $150

— Shires and Provinces. L, 1926. With 16 mtd plates. DW Dec 11 (141) £200

Barrow, Isaac, 1630-77. See: Euclid

Barrow, John, fl.1735

— A New Universal Dictionary of Arts and Sciences.... L, 1751. Folio, contemp calf; worn, joints loose. With frontis (loose) & 61 plates. pn Nov 14 (390) £80

Barrow, Sir John, 1764-1848

— An Account of Travels into the Interior of Southern Africa. L, 1806. ("Travels into the Interior of Southern Africa.") 2d Ed. 2 vols. 4to, contemp calf; spine def, worn. With 8 colored plates & 8 (of 10) folding maps. Lacking half-titles; dampstaining & soiling throughout. pn Dec 12 (347) £70

— A Chronological History of Voyages into the Arctic Regions. L, 1818. 1st Ed. 8vo, modern half calf. With folding map. W July 8 (239) £165

— The Eventful History of the Mutiny and Piratical Seizure of H.M.S. Bounty. L, 1831. 1st Ed, 2d Issue. 8vo, old calf gilt; relined, rubbed, hinges tender. With frontis & 5 plates. Thumbed; some stains. Manney copy. P Oct 11 (13) $400

— Travels in China. L, 1806. 2d Ed. 4to, modern half calf. With 8 plates, 5 of them hand-colored. Imprint cropped from frontis. C Oct 30 (8) £280 [Roscigno]

— A Voyage to Cochinchina.... L, 1806. 4to, old bds; disbound, spine missing. With 19 (of 21) plates & maps. Lacking 2 plates. Some soiling and staining. Sold w.a.f. O Mar 31 (14) $120

Anr copy. Contemp calf; rebacked. With

19 hand-colored plates & 2 double-page maps. S Nov 15 (1136) £380 [Beeleigh Abbey]

Barrows, John A. See: Waterman & Barrows

Barrucand, Victor

— Le Chariot de terre cuite. Paris, [1920]. One of 910. Illus by Leon Carre. 4to, mor gilt extra, orig wraps bound in; spine scuffed. cb Oct 25 (6) $275

Barth, Heinrich, 1821-65

— Reisen und Entdeckungen in Nord- und Central- Afrika. Gotha, 1859-60. Abridged Ed. 2 vols. 8vo, early half-cloth; worn. Some foxing; minor marginal damping at rear; stamp & owner's signature on each title. wa Apr 9 (104) $140

Barth, Johann August

— Pacis annis MCCCCXIV et MDCCCXV foederatis armis restitutae monumentum. Vratislav, 1816. Folio, orig ptd wraps; spine torn. Schlosser copy. P June 17 (513) $1,300

— Pacis annis MCCCCXIV et MDCCXV foederatis armis restitutae monumentum.... Vratislaviae, [c.1818]. Ed by Barth. Folio, orig bds; rubbed, rebacked. With 64 leaves with color litho borders & vignettes in as many as 5 colors. Some foxing. Schlosser copy. P June 18 (514) $4,250

Barth, John

— Giles Goat-Boy. Garden City, 1966. One of 250. sg Dec 12 (14) $250; sg June 11 (15) $120

Barthelemy, Jean Jacques, 1716-95

— Maps, Plans, Views and Coins, Illustrative of the Travels of Anacharsis.... Dublin, 1795. 8vo, sheep. With 31 double-page maps & plans. sg Feb 13 (110) $110

Anr Ed. L, 1825. Atlas vol only. 4to, modern cloth. With port & 38 plates, some hand-colored in outline. pn Apr 23 (290) £75 [Bailey]

— Travels of Anacharsis the Younger in Greece.... L, 1791. Atlas vol only. 4to, contemp russia; lacking backstrip. With 31 double-page maps & plates, 11 of them hand-colored in outline. One plate foxed. pn Dec 12 (392) £80 [Bailey]

Anr Ed. L, 1806. 7 vols; lacking Atlas. 8vo, contemp half calf; rubbed. bba July 9 (132) £85 [Hay Cinema]

— Voyage du jeune Anacharsis en Grece. Paris: Didot jeune, [1799]. 8 vols. 8vo & 4to, contemp calf; joints cracked. With port & 40 maps & views. Milne copy. Ck June 12 (12) £150

Barthelme, Donald

— Come Back, Dr. Caligari. Bost., [1964]. In d/j. pba July 9 (13) $75

Bartholdy, Jakob Ludwig Salomon, 1779-1825

— Voyage en Grece. Paris: Dentu, 1807. 8vo, contemp calf. With folding map, 10 hand-colored costume plates & 7 other plates. Some dampstaining towards end of Vol I. S June 30 (235) £550 [Consolidated Real]

Anr copy. 19th-cent half calf with Signet arms. S July 1 (544) £400 [Chelsea]

Bartholinus, Thomas, 1616-80

— Orationes varii argumenti. Copenhagen, 1668. 8vo, contemp vellum. sg Nov 14 (5) $275

Bartholomaeus degli Albizzi de Rinonichi

— Opus auree & inexplicabilis bonitatis & continentie. Milan: Zanotus Castilioneus, 18 Aug 1513. 2d Ed. Bound with: Clichtove, Josse. Elucidatorium ecclesiasticum, ad officium ecclesiae.... Paris: H. Estienne, 1516. Folio, contemp mor over wooden bds; rubbed, bottom of backstrip off, lacking catches & clasps. Prelims marginally wormed & dampstained; lacking final blank. sg Oct 24 (18) $650

Bartlett, Edward

— A Monograph of the Weaver-Birds.... [Maidstone, 1888-89]. Parts 1-5 (all pbd) in 1 vol. 4to, recent half mor gilt. With 31 plates, 12 hand-colored. Title & 1st leaf cut away; some corners chewed or nicked. DW Oct 2 (129) £150

Bartlett, Edward Everett

— The Typographic Treasures in Europe. NY & L, 1925. One of 585. Folio, orig half cloth; spine soiled. pba July 23 (216) $65

Bartlett, Henrietta Collins —& Pollard, Alfred William

— A Census of Shakespeare's Plays in Quarto...(1594-1709). New Haven, 1916. 4to, half cloth. K Sept 29 (394) $50

Anr Ed. New Haven, 1939. 4to, cloth. cb Sept 17 (59) $50

Bartlett, John, 1820-1905

— A Collection of Familiar Quotations. Cambr., 1855. 1st Ed. 12mo, orig cloth; ends rubbed, front hinge cracked. ALs laid in. sg May 21 (133) $300

Bartlett, John Russell, 1805-86

— Personal Narrative of Explorations and Incidents in Texas.... NY, 1854. 1st Ed. 2 vols. 8vo, orig cloth; extremities worn. With folding map & 16 plates. cb Feb 12 (3) $600; sg Dec 5 (5) $325

Bartlett, William Henry, 1809-54. See: Beattie, William

Bartlett, William Henry, 1809-54
See also: Finden, William
— The History of the United States of North America. NY, [1856]. In Book form. 3 vols. 8vo, mor gilt. With 86 (of 88) plates, 3 engraved titles & hand-colored folding map. K Sept 29 (54) $300
— The Nile Boat.... NY, 1851. 8vo, orig cloth; extremities worn. Lacking frontis & final plate. cb Oct 10 (7) $90
— Pictures from Sicily. L, 1862. 8vo, cloth. bba Sept 19 (132) £110 [Pordes]
— Walks about the City and Environs of Jerusalem. L, [c.1845]. 2d Ed. 4to, orig cloth; front cover detached, some fraying & chipping, lacking front free endpaper. With engraved title, frontis, 2 folding maps & 25 plates. bbc Dec 9 (321) $85

Bartoli, Cosimo, c.1503-72
— Del Modo di misurare, le distantie.... Venice, 1564. ("Del modo di misurare le distantie, le superficie, i corpi, le piante....") 1st Ed. 4to, later half calf. Tp shaved at foot; some staining at end; stamp of Stonyhurst College on tp. S May 28 (1) £800 [Zioni]
Anr Ed. Venice, 1589. 4to, contemp vellum. Ms sidenotes; some staining. pn Nov 14 (259) £380 [Robertshaw]

Bartoli, Daniello, 1608-85
— Del ghiaccio e della coagulatione. Rome, 1681. 4to, contemp vellum. Marginal spotting; some browning. SI Dec 5 (59) LIt750,000

Bartoli, Pietro Santi & Francesco
— Le pitture antiche delle grotte di Roma. Rome, 1706. Folio, contemp calf; joints splitting. With 75 engraved plates. bba Dec 19 (64) £320 [Etching]

Bartoli, Pietro Santi, c.1635-1700
— Admiranda Romanarum antiquitatum ac veteris sculpturae vestigia. Rome, 1693. Oblong folio, half calf; badly worn, front cover nearly detached. With 84 plates, including title & dedication. Tp browned & rebacked with sheet containing ink notations; marginal dampstaining & soiling. sg Sept 6 (19) $275
— Le Antiche Lucerne sepolcrali figurate. Rome, 1691. Folio, contemp calf gilt. With 3 engraved titles & 116 plates. Lacking tp. b June 22 (149) £230
Anr copy. Contemp vellum; hinges cracking. With 117 plates. bba Apr 30 (330) £260 [Thorp]
— Gli antichi sepolcri, ovvero mausolei Romani.... Rome, 1697. Folio, modern cloth. Dampstained throughout. sg Feb 13 (146) $275
Anr Ed. Rome, 1727. Folio, half calf; worn. With 113 plates. sg Sept 6 (17) $275
— Columna Antoniniana. Rome, [1672]. Oblong folio, modern half lea. With engraved title & 76 plates. Sold w.a.f. SI Dec 5 (607) LIt150,000
— Columna cochlis M. Aurelio Antonino Augusto dicata.... Rome, 1704. Folio, old mor; front cover detached. With 77 plates. Some foxing & staining. wd Dec 12 (357) $200
— Museum Odescalchum, sive Thesaurus antiquarum gemmarum. Rome, 1751-52. 2 vols in 1. Folio, contemp vellum; worn. With 104 plates. sg Nov 7 (16) $350
— Picturae Antiquissimi Virgiliani Codicis Bibliothecae Vaticanae. Rome: Monaldini, 1782. 4to, contemp half vellum; spine worn. With engraved title, port & 124 plates. Without text; Plate XXXV soiled; some spotting. Ck Nov 29 (291) £300

Bartolozzi, Francesco —& Others
— Italian School of Design. L, 1835. 2 vols. Folio, half mor; rubbed. With 152 plates. bba Feb 13 (178) £2,800 [Vitale]
Anr copy. Contemp half mor; worn, detached. With 151 plates. Some dampstaining; Vol I tp frayed & with date added in pen. Sold w.a.f. S May 14 (919) £550 [Shapero]

Barton, Rose
— Familiar London. L, 1904. One of 300. 4to, orig cloth; upper cover stained, corners scuffed. With colored frontis & 60 plates. Ck Dec 11 (143) £180

Bartram, William, 1739-1823
— Reizen door Noord-en Zuid-Carolina.... Haarlem, 1794-97. 3 vols in 1. 8vo, modern half mor. With folding map. Lacking the 3 plates; library stamp on 1st text leaf. sg Dec 5 (7) $350

Bartsch, J. Adam von, 1757-1821
— Le Peintre graveur. Wuerzburg, 1920. 21 vols in 13. 8vo, contemp half mor; some spines repaired, some def. pn Dec 12 (119) £80 [Bifolco]

Basan, Pierre Francois, 1723-97
— Receuil d'estampes gravees d'apres les tableaux du Cabinet de Monseigneur le Duc de Choiseul. Paris, 1771. 4to, contemp calf. With engraved title & 123 plates only. SI June 9 (104) LIt2,100,000
— [Sale Catalogue] Catalogue raisonne differens objets de curiosites dans les sciences et arts qui composoient le cabinet de feu M. Mariette. Paris, 1776. 8vo, contemp calf gilt with Stirling arms on

upper cover; joints split, worn. With Ms prices & buyers' names in a contemp hand. S Feb 11 (8) £400 [Apoloni]

Basile, Giovanni Battista, c.1575-1632

— Stories from the Pentamerone. L, 1911. Illus by Warwick Goble. 4to, cloth. With 32 colored plates. cb Jan 16 (56) $110

One of 150. Orig vellum gilt, in rubbed d/j. With 32 colored plates. P Oct 11 (150) $700

Baskin, Leonard

— Ars Anatomica: A Medical Fantasia. NY, [1972]. Folio, loose as issued in portfolio. With 13 plates. sg Sept 26 (15) $150

— Demons, Imps & Fiends. Northampton: Gehenna Press, 1976. One of 450. 4to, bds. cb Feb 12 (9) $140; sg Sept 26 (16) $60

— Drawings for the Iliad. NY, 1962. One of 60 with an extra suite of 6 etchings on japan nacre, but this copy lacking the drawing. Folio, loose as issued. sg Sept 26 (19) $800

— Figures of Dead Men. Amherst MA, 1968. One of 200, sgd. Preface by Archibald MacLeish. Laid in is an orig sgd woodcut by Baskin. sg Sept 26 (17) $175

Basnage, Jacques, 1653-1725

— 't Groot waerelds tafereel en met vaersen verrykt d. A. Alewyn. Amst., 1721. Illus by Romeyn de Hooghe. Folio, modern calf. With 2 double-page maps. Tp torn. sg Oct 24 (19) $300

Bassereau, Leon

— Traite des affections de la peau symptomatiques de la syphilis. Paris, 1852. 8vo, contemp half sheep; scuffed. Some browning. sg Nov 14 (6) $200

Bastelaer, Rene van

— Les Estampes de Peter Bruegel l'ancien. Brussels, 1908. 4to, modern half calf, orig upper wrap bound in. Some leaves frayed. bba Jan 30 (347) £85 [Bifolco]

Bateman, James, 1811-97

— A Monograph of Odontoglossum. L, [1864]-74. Folio, orig cloth; rubbed & soiled, small tears to upper cover. With 30 hand-colored plates. pn Mar 19 (256) £3,200 [Shapero]

— The Orchidaceae of Mexico and Guatemala. L, [1837]-43. One of 125. Folio, contemp half mor gilt; rubbed, spine ends chipped. With 40 hand-colored lithos & 1 uncolored plan. Lacking orig litho title, supplied in facsimile (a title-leaf or wrap from anr copy); lacking Addenda et Corrigenda & Directions to the Binder slips; dedication leaf backed & with old marginal repairs; marginal repairs to subscribers list; prelims creased; Plate 40 with gutter renewed & traces of old tape at inner margin; some foxing. CNY June 9 (139) $44,000

— A Second Century of Orchidaceous Plants. L, 1867. 4to, orig cloth; extremities worn, inner joints cracked. With 100 uncolored plates, numbered 101 to 200. Some text leaves spotted. CNY Jan 25 (84) $2,200

Anr copy. Orig cloth; extremities rubbed, loose. With 100 uncolored plates. Some foxing to text. CNY June 9J (141) $2,300

Bateman, Thomas, 1778-1821

— Delineations of Cutaneous Diseases.... L, 1817. 1st Ed. 4to, contemp calf; backstrip chipped, rubbed. With 76 color plates. Some browning. bba May 14 (447) £300 [Phillips]

Bates, George Washington

— Sandwich Island Notes. By a Haole. NY, 1854. 12mo, orig cloth; spine ends chipped. cb Jan 30 (10) $110; sg Dec 5 (117) $100

Bates, Henry Walter, 1825-92

— The Naturalist on the River Amazon. L, 1863. 1st Ed. 2 vols. 8vo, orig cloth; spotted. kh Nov 11 (321) A$50

Bates, Joseph D.

— Atlantic Salmon Flies and Fishing. Harrisburg: Stackpole, [1970]. One of 600. Half cloth. Koopman copy. O Oct 29 (23) $300

— Streamer Fly Tying and Fishing. Harrisburg, [1966]. Ltd Ed. Half cloth. Koopman copy. O Oct 29 (24) $225

— Streamers and Bucktails. NY, 1979. One of 36. Lea gilt. Koopman copy. O Oct 29 (25) $700

Bates, William, d.1884

— George Cruikshank.... L & Birm., 1879. 2d Ed. 4to, orig half cloth; rebacked, rubbed. With 17 plates, all but 2 on india paper. bba Aug 13 (322) £60 [Sabin]

Bateson, William, 1861-1926

— Materials for the Study of Variation. L, 1894. 1st Ed. 8vo, orig cloth; rubbed & soiled. DW Nov 6 (323) £105

— Mendel's Principles of Heredity. Cambr., 1913. 8vo, cloth; rubbed & faded. bba Sept 5 (189) £100 [Ramer]

Batsch, August Johann Georg Karl, 1761-1802

— Elenchus fungorum. Halle, 1783-89. 3 vols. 4to, orig bds; rubbed & soiled. With 42 hand-colored plates. Some browning of text. Ck Oct 31 (95) £1,700

Battershall, Fletcher
— Bookbinding for Bibliophiles: Being Notes on Some Technical Features.... Greenwich CT, 1905. One of 350. cb Oct 17 (61) $130

Battey, Thomas C.
— The Life and Adventures of a Quaker among the Indians. Bost. & NY, 1875. 1st Ed. 8vo, cloth. sg June 18 (10) $80

Batti, Cristoforo
— Miracula quae mense Decembri in Pannonia visa sunt.... Rome, 1524. 4to, modern bds. S July 1 (546) £680 [Reiss & Auvermann]

Battingius, Rodolphus
— Nova quaedam & compendiosa usus astrolabii methodus. Paris: Jacques du Pays, 1557. 1st Ed. 8vo, later vellum. Some staining; a3 torn & repaired; Q2 with small burnholes affecting text. bba June 11 (213) £550 [Rogers & Turner]

Batty, Elizabeth Frances
— Italian Scenery. L, 1820. 4to, contemp mor gilt. With engraved title & 60 plates. HH May 12 (719) DM1,400

Anr copy. Contemp half mor; rubbed. Some foxing. W July 6 (195) £420

Batty, Robert, d.1848
— French Scenery. L, 1822. 4to, disbound. With engraved title & 64 plates. Some spotting. pn Dec 12 (348) £140
— German Scenery.... L, 1823. Folio, contemp half mor gilt; rubbed. With frontis & 60 plates. Some discoloration throughout. S July 1 (1441) £750

Anr copy. Half lea gilt; rubbed. With 600 plates. Library markings. sp Apr 16 (255) $475
— Hanoverian and Saxon Scenery. L, 1829. Folio, orig cloth. With engraved title, dedication & 61 plates. 1 plate & 2 text leaves loose. L Feb 27 (160) £1,150
— Scenery of the Rhine, Belgium and Holland. L, 1826. 4to, contemp calf; worn. With engraved title & 61 plates. S May 14 (1191) £450 [Garwood & Voigt]

Baud-Bovy, Daniel —& Boissonas, Fred
— En Grece par monts et par vaux. Geneva, 1910. Folio, orig wraps. With 40 plates & map. S July 1 (547) £670 [Chelsea]

Baudelaire, Charles, 1821-67
— Les Fleurs du mal. Paris, 1910. One of 80 on japon imperial. 4to, mor gilt by Pagnant. wa Mar 5 (10) $375

Anr Ed. Stockholm, [1946]. Illus by Hallman. Folio, half mor gilt, orig wraps bound in. sg Sept 26 (20) $120
— Oeuvres posthumes et correspondances inedites.... Paris, 1887. 8vo, half mor, orig wraps bound in. Epstein copy. sg Apr 29 (19) $800
— Le Voyage. Paris, 1922. One of 16 with sketch used in preparation of an illust, plates in 3 states, an additional suite of plates in color & a color suite of woodblock designs. 4to, loose as issued, lacking bdg. Marginal dampstaining to some plates. Sold w.a.f. sg Jan 30 (6) $150

Baudement, Emile
— Les Races bovines au concours universel agricole de Paris en 1856.... Paris, 1861. 2 vols. Oblong folio, contemp half mor. With 5 colored maps & 87 plates. bba June 25 (217) £600 [Thorp]

Bauderies...
— Bauderies Parisiennes. Les Rassemblements: Physiologies de la Rue. Paris, 1896. One of 220. 4to, half mor, orig wraps bound in. With 30 full-page illusts. Kochno copy. SM Oct 12 (413) FF13,000

Baudier, Michel, 1589?-1645
— Histoire generalle du serrail.... Paris, 1631. 2 parts in 1 vol. 4to, contemp vellum with initials HL beneath coronet on covers; hole in spine repaired. With engraved title & full-page illust of a giraffe. S June 30 (237) £420 [Maggs]

Bauer, Ferdinand. See: Stearn, William T.

Bauer, Franz Andreas, 1758-1840
— Illustrations of Orchidaceous Plants.... L, 1830-38. Folio, 19th-cent mor gilt; extremities worn. With 15 plain & 20 hand-colored plates. A few plates foxed. Derby —de Belder—McCarty-Cooper copy. CNY Jan 25 (85) $3,800

Bauer, Frederick. See: Bollinger & Bauer

Bauhinus, Caspar, 1560-1624
— Pinax theatri botanici. Basel, 1671. Bound with: Prodromos Theatri Botanici. 4to, later mor gilt; rubbed. Some worming with loss. Sold w.a.f. bba Sept 5 (5) £190 [Bifolco]

Baum, L. Frank, 1856-1919
— Aunt Jane's Nieces on Vacation. By Edith Van Dyne. Chicago: Reilly & Britton, [1912]. 1st Ed, 1st State with ad on verso of half-title listing 7 titles. In d/j. cb Dec 12 (8) $300
— By the Candelabra's Glare. Chicago, 1898. One of 99. 8vo, cloth; soiled. Preliminary gatherings detached. Inscr. cb Sept 19 (6) $6,500
— Dorothy and the Wizard in Oz. Chicago, [1908]. 1st Ed, 1st Issue. bbc Apr 27 (266)

$220

Anr copy. Orig cloth, 2ndary bdg; hinges cracked, front free endpaper loose. Dampstaining & chipping. F June 25 (184) $85; K Mar 22 (303) $200

2d Issue. K Mar 22 (304) $95

— The Emerald City of Oz. Chicago, [1910]. 1st Ed, 1st State. K Mar 22 (305) $250

Anr copy. In d/j. sg May 7 (20) $7,500
2d State. sg Oct 17 (328) $150

— Father Goose: His Book. Chicago: Hill, [1899]. 1st Ptg. 4to, bds; soiled & worn. Inscr by W. W. Denslow, the artist. Epstein copy. sg Apr 29 (20) $2,800

8th Ptg. Chicago: Donohue, [c.1913]. 4to, orig bds; soiled & stained, hinges cracked, lacking front free endpaper. bbc Dec 9 (100) $50

— The Gingerbread Man. Chicago, [1917]. Bds. NH May 30 (311) $55

— John Dough and the Cherub. Chicago, [1906]. 1st Ed. sg Oct 17 (329) $80
2d State. Orig cloth; front hinge cracked, lower hinge split, some wear. With the detachable contest blank. bbc Apr 27 (267) $120

— The Life and Adventures of Santa Claus. Indianapolis, [1902]. 1st Ed. Orig cloth; spine ends and fore-corners worn. Fore-edge ink-stained. Inscr. Epstein copy. sg Apr 29 (21) $5,000
1st State. Corners of bdg rubbed, hinges cracked. bbc Dec 9 (106) $80

Anr copy. Bdg with spine ends frayed, hinges cracked. bbc Dec 9 (107) $80

— The Lost Princess of Oz. Chicago, [1917]. 1st Ed, 1st State. In edgeworn d/j with several short tears. With 12 color plates. wa Apr 9 (215) $900

— The Magic of Oz. Chicago, [1919]. 1st Ed. In chipped d/j. rs Oct 17 (15A) $75

— The Marvelous Land of Oz. Chicago, 1904. 1st Ed, 1st State. Orig cloth. With 16 colored plates. Inscr, presumably to Mary "L" (for Louise) Brewster, Baum's sister. sg May 7 (18) $15,000

— The Master Key. Indianapolis, [1901]. 1st Ed. sg Oct 17 (330) $90

— Mother Goose in Prose. Chicago: Way & Williams, [1897]. 1st Ed, 1st Issue. 4to, orig cloth; spine darkened. Epstein copy. sg Apr 29 (22) $3,000
1st State. Cloth; foot of spine worn; some soiling; front hinge starting. Inscr to his mother. With illust from Three Wise Men of Gotham, sgd by Maxfield Parrish, laid in. sg May 7 (16) $58,000

— Ozma of Oz. Chicago, [1907, but later]. Popular Ed. In chipped d/j. pba July 9 (14) $60
1st Ed, 1st State. Chicago, [1907]. Orig cloth. Inscr to Katharine Elizabeth Hubbard. sg May 7 (19) $17,000

— The Patchwork Girl of Oz. Chicago, [1913]. 1st Ed, 1st State. Rubbed & soiled. cb Sept 19 (7) $65

Anr copy. Rubbed, hinges starting. sg Oct 17 (333) $120
2d State. Orig cloth; rubbed. K Mar 22 (310) $130

— Policeman Bluejay. Chicago, [1907]. 1st Ed. Half cloth; rubbed, corners worn through, shaken. With 8 inserted color plates. bbc June 29 (357) $180

— Queen Zixi of Ix. NY, 1905. 1st Ed, 1st State. Cloth; front free endpaper gone, traces of removed pocket. Ink number on tp. K Mar 22 (311) $85

— Rinkitink in Oz. Chicago, [1916]. 1st Ed, 1st State. K Mar 22 (312) $200

Anr copy. Extremities worn, hinges cracked. sg Oct 17 (334) $200

— The Road to Oz. Chicago, [1909]. 1st Ed, 1st State. K Mar 22 (313) $225

— The Scarecrow of Oz. Chicago, [1915]. 1st Ed, 1st State. sg Oct 17 (335) $375

— Sky Island. Chicago, [1912]. 1st Ed. Cloth; soiled, frayed, front joint opening. K Mar 22 (314) $150

— The Songs of Father Goose. Chicago, 1900. 1st Ed. 4to, half cloth; soiled, corners bumped. K Sept 29 (55) $140

Anr copy. Cloth; rubbed, corners bumped. K Mar 22 (315) $150

— Tik-Tok of Oz. Chicago, [1914]. 1st Ed, 1st State. sg Oct 17 (336) $250

— The Tin Woodman of Oz. Chicago, [1918]. 1st Ed, 1st State. K Mar 22 (316) $200

— The Woggle-Bug Book. Chicago, 1905. 1st Ed, 2d Issue. 4to, half cloth with yellow background on front cover & yellow lettering on rear cover; vertical crease in front cover, small chip from outer edge of rear cover. sg Mar 5 (50) $500

— The Wonderful Wizard of Oz. Chicago & NY, 1900. 1st Ed. 8vo, orig cloth. With rubber-stamped copyright notice on title verso and first state plates. Inscr to Elizabeth Hubbard. sg May 7 (17) $36,000

Later state. Pictorial cloth; extremities rubbed. sg Oct 17 (337) $1,700
1st State. Orig cloth, 1st bdg; spine end frayed, some rubbing. Manney copy. P Oct 11 (14) $25,000

Anr copy. Cloth in 1/3 of orig d/j. Epstein copy. sg Apr 29 (23) $19,000
Blanck's State Z. Cloth; soiled. Epstein copy. sg Apr 29 (24) $1,600

3d Ed, 2d State. Chicago: M. A. Donohue, [c.1915]. ("The New Wizard of Oz.") Orig cloth; some wear. bbc Apr 27 (268) $60

Anr Ed. West Hatfield MA: Pennyroyal Press, 1985. One of a few copies with a pencil drawing by Moser, sgd. Folio, bds. With 63 wood-engraved illusts. sg Jan 10 (126) $1,200

Baur Collection—Geneva

— Chinese Ceramics. Geneva, 1968-77. Compiled by John G. Ayers. Vols I-III. Orig cloth, in d/js. sg Apr 2 (43) $1,500

— Japanese Ceramics. Geneva, [1982]. Ltd Ed. Compiled by Paul Ayers. 4to, cloth, in d/j. cb Nov 21 (17) $150

Baurenfeind, Michael

— Vollkommene Wieder-Herstellung der... Schreib-Kunst. [Nuremberg, 1716]. 1st Ed. Oblong folio, contemp half pigskin; new endpapers. With engraved title, folding table & 59 plates. S May 28 (153) £500 [Uceta]

— Der zierlichen Schreib-Kunst vollkommener Wiederherstellung anderer Theil. Nuremberg: Lorenz Bieling, 1736. Oblong folio, half cloth. With engraved title & 66 plates. Tp shaved at head. S May 28 (154) £500 [Uceta]

Bavaria

— Reformacion in der baeyrischen Landrecht. Munich: J. Schobser, 1518. Folio, later bds. Woodcut shaved at fore-edge; dampstaining in margins. S May 13 (739) £450 [Schwing]

Baxter, Andrew, 1686?-1750

— Matho: or, the Cosmotheroria Puerilis.... L, 1745. 2d Ed. 2 vols. 8vo, contemp calf; worn. Lacking a prelim leaf. ESTC t100525. bba July 23 (167) £65 [Laywood]

Baxter, James Phinney, the Elder, 1831-1921

— A Memoir of Jacques Cartier, Sieur de Limoilou.... NY, 1906. One of 335. Library markings. bbc Sept 23 (216) $50

Baxter, William, 1787-1871

— British Phaenogamous Botany.... Oxford, 1834-43. Vols I-V (of 6). 8vo, contemp half mor; worn, some covers detached. Library markings. bba Oct 10 (195) £80 [Barker]

Anr copy. 6 vols. 8vo, contemp half calf. With 509 hand-colored plates. Margin of Plate 331 repaired with tape. L Nov 14 (209) £550

Anr copy. Contemp half calf; worn, spines def, stamps on upper covers & edges, shelf labels on spines. Some spotting; Plate 280 shaved; stamps on tp verso, 1st & final leaf of text & versos of 10 plates. pn Mar 19 (258) £360 [Titles]

Bayard, Hippolyte

— Bayard. Paris, 1943. One of 150 on papier verge. 4to, cloth. Lacking the suite of 2 photographs. sg Oct 8 (6) $300

Bayardi, Ottavio Antonio

— The Antiquities of Herculaneum. L, 1773. Vol I in 2 parts (all pbd). 4to, contemp calf; joints split. With engraved title & 48 (of 50) plates. Some fold tears. Sold w.a.f. bba May 28 (44) £260 [Elliott]

Anr copy. 4to, contemp calf; worn, rebacked with orig spine laid down. With map & 50 plates. Some foxing, heavy on Plate XXI. sg Sept 6 (141) $225

Anr copy. Half russia gilt, c.1800; worn, covers detached. sg Feb 6 (128) $500

Bayf, Lazare de. See: Baif, Lazare de

Bayle, Pierre, 1647-1706

— Dictionaire historique et critique. Rotterdam, 1720. 3d Ed. 4 vols. Folio, contemp calf; rubbed. bba Jan 16 (237) £160 [Thoemmes]

Anr Ed. Amst., 1734. 5 vols. Folio, contemp calf; worn, joints split, upper cover of 2 vols detached. bba Jan 16 (104) £120 [J. Bailey]

— The Dictionary. L, 1734-38. 5 vols. Folio, contemp calf; rebacked, extremities worn, hinges reinforced with cloth tape. sg Oct 24 (20) $250

Anr copy. Contemp calf; worn & soiled. W Mar 6 (37) £160

Bayley, John Whitcomb, d.1869

— History and Antiquities of the Tower of London. L, 1821-25. 1st Ed. 2 vols. Folio, contemp half mor; joints & extremities rubbed. With port & 28 plates. Library markings; some foxing. F Dec 18 (463) $70

Bayly, Thomas, d. 1657?

— Herba Parietis: or, the Wall-flower.... L, 1650. Folio, contemp calf; def. bba Jan 30 (134) £180 [R. Clark]

Bazin, Gilles Augustin, d.1754

— Histoire naturelle des Abeilles. Paris, 1744. 2 vols. 8vo, contemp calf. With 15 folding plates (Plates 9-11 supplied in duplicate). Ms notes in margins; names erased from titles, leaving smallholes. pn Dec 12 (90) £70

— The Natural History of Bees.... L, 1744. 8vo, contemp calf; rubbed, rebacked. With 12 folding plates. 1st leaves marginally stained. bba Sept 5 (6) £85 [Elliott]

Be Merry...

— Be Merry and Wise; or the Cream of the Jests and the Marrow of Maxims....By Tommy Trapwit, Esq. L: Carnan & Newbery, 1770. 32mo in 8s, early Dutch floral bds. Roscoe-Schiller-Manney copy. P Oct 11 (1237) $5,500

Beach, William Nicholas. See: Derrydale Press

Beadle, John Hanson

— The Undeveloped West; or, Five Years in the Territories.... Phila.: National Publishing Co, [1873]. 8vo, cloth. sg June 18 (12) $90

— Western Wilds, and the Men Who Redeem Them. San Francisco, 1878. 8vo, orig half mor; extremities rubbed. cb Feb 12 (4) $50

Beale, Joseph Henry

— A Bibliography of Early English Law Books. Cambr. MA, 1926-43. 2 vols, including Supplement sg Oct 31 (25) $200

Beale, Thomas

— The Natural History of the Sperm Whale.... L, 1839. 2d Ed. 8vo, cloth. sg June 18 (560) $500

Beall, Karen F.

— Cries and Itinerant Trades. Hamburg, [1975]. One of 750. Folio, cloth. K Dec 1 (36) $325

Beamish, North Ludlow, 1797-1872

— The Discovery of America by the Northmen. L, 1841. 8vo, cloth, unopened. sg June 18 (15) $110

Beard, Mark

— Manhattan Third Year Reader. NY, 1984. One of 35. Folio, mor extra with mor onlays, collage elements & crushed & rusted tin can, by Gerard Charriere. Schlosser copy. P June 17 (607) $5,000

Beardsley, Aubrey, 1872-98

— The Early Work. L, 1899. With: The Later Work. L, 1901. 2d ptg. Together, 2 vols. 4to, orig cloth; worn. First signature in 1st work detached, 2d work inscr by John Lane. wd Dec 12 (358) $250

— An Issue of Five Drawings Illustrative of Juvenal and Lucian. L, 1906. Out-of-series copy. Folio, loose as issued in orig wraps; torn & faded. With 5 plates. S Nov 14 (93) £260 [Riex]

— The Later Work. L, 1930. 4to, orig cloth, in d/j. bba Apr 9 (292) £110 [Ulysses]

— Morte Darthur Portfolio. L, 1927. One of 300. 4to, orig lea-backed vellum. O May 26 (7) $190

Anr copy. Orig calf-backed vellum; spine rubbed & chipped. S Nov 14 (95) £200 [Riex]

— A Portfolio of Aubrey Beardsley's Drawings Illustrating "Salome" by Oscar Wilde. [L: John Lane, 1920]. Folio, loose in portfolio; soiled. With 16 plates & cul de lampe. bba Apr 9 (272) £85 [Frew Mackenzie]

— Six Drawings Illustrating Theophile Gautier's Romance, Mademoiselle de Maupin. L, 1898. One of 50. Folio, loose as issued in portfolio. Tp browned & frayed. bba July 9 (243) £290 [Marks]

Anr copy. Loosely inserted is an additional copy of the tp & contents page. Prelims & margins of 1 plate spotted. S Nov 14 (91) £340 [Riex]

— The Story of Venus and Tannhaeuser. L, 1907. One of 50 on Japan vellum. 4to, orig vellum gilt; browned & stained. S Nov 14 (94) £240 [Riex]

— The Uncollected Work. L, 1925. Intro by C. Lewis Hind. 4to, orig cloth, in d/j. bba Apr 9 (292) £110 [Ulysses]

Anr copy. Later half mor; worn. O Aug 25 (26) $100

Anr copy. Cloth, in def d/j. Frontis detached. sg Sept 6 (20) $50

Anr copy. Cloth; minor blistering & soiling. sg Feb 6 (12) $120

Beaton, Cecil

— The Book of Beauty. L, 1930. 4to, orig cloth; soiled & marked. DW Oct 9 (550) £135

Anr copy. Bds; some edge wear. Inscr to William Odom. sg Oct 8 (7) $275

— Cecil Beaton's New York. Phila., [1938]. In repaired d/j. sg Apr 13 (8) $90

Beattie, James, 1735-1803

— Poems on Several Occasions. Edin., 1776. 8vo, contemp calf gilt; rubbed & scuffed. A3 with tear to lower edge; some fingersoiling. Inscr with a poem to Susan Logan Park. Adam-Fleming-Manney copy. P Oct 11 (32) $6,000

Beattie, William, 1793-1875

— The Danube. L, [c.1840]. Illus by William H. Bartlett. 4to, contemp calf; extremities worn. With frontis, engraved title, 2 maps & 80 views. Prelims waterstained; margins browned. DW Nov 20 (3) £210

Anr copy. Bound with: Pardoe, Julia. The Beauties of the Bosphorus. L, [c.1845]. contemp half mor gilt; rubbed & soiled, upper hinge split. With 2 engraved titles, 2 ports & 168 maps & plates. Some spotting; 2d engraved title loose & frayed. pn May 14 (210) £500 [Dupont]

Anr Ed. L, [1844]. Illus by W. H. Bartlett. 4to, contemp half lea; worn. With port, pictorial title, 2 maps & 80 plates. Some foxing & soiling. bba Apr 30 (25) £210 [Gorwood & Voigt]

Anr copy. Modern cloth. With port, pictorial title, 1 map & 80 plates. Lacking 1 plate. FD Dec 2 (294) DM1,000

Anr copy. 19th-cent half calf; worn. With port, pictorial title, 2 maps & 80 plates. S Nov 15 (1090) £280 [Orssich]

— Scotland Illustrated.... L, 1838. 2 vols. 4to, orig wraps; a few covers detached. With 2 engraved titles, folding map & 118 plates. Foxed. bba Sept 19 (234) £120 [Martinez]

Anr copy. Vol II (of 2) only. 4to, orig half mor gilt; worn. With engraved title & 77 plates. Some spotting throughout. DW Nov 6 (113) £50

Anr copy. 2 vols. 4to, contemp half calf; worn. With 2 engraved titles, folding map & 118 plates; some spotting. DW Jan 29 (66) £130

Anr copy. Vol II only. Mor. pnE Oct 2 (486) £60

Anr copy. 2 vols. 4to, 19th-cent mor gilt. With 2 engraved titles, folding map & 121 plates. pnE May 13 (48) £210

Anr copy. Contemp mor gilt; needs rebdg. sg Feb 13 (149) $325

Anr copy. Contemp half calf; rubbed. With engraved titles, 133 plates & folding map. W Mar 6 (18) £105

Anr Ed. L, 1842. 2 vols. 4to, contemp mor gilt. With engraved titles, folding map & 118 plates. b Nov 18 (334) £180

— Switzerland Illustrated.... L, 1836. Illus by W. H. Bartlett. 2 vols. 4to, contemp mor gilt by G. Winstanley of Manchester; extremities worn. With folding map, 2 engraved titles & 106 plates. Ck May 15 (72) £400

Anr copy. Contemp calf gilt; rubbed, extremities worn. DW Oct 2 (11) £330

Anr copy. Contemp half mor; rubbed. DW Jan 29 (13) £260

Anr copy. Half mor; rebacked, orig spines retained. With engraved titles, folding map & 106 plates. K Sept 29 (56) $475

Anr copy. Half mor; 1 joint cracked, spines detaching, rubbed. Some foxing. K Sept 29 (57) $425

Anr copy. Contemp half mor by David Condie. With folding map, 2 engraved titles & 106 plates.. pn Nov 14 (412) £360

Anr copy. Contemp half calf; corners rubbed. With engraved titles, folding map & 106 plates.. pn May 14 (211) £320 [Bailey]

Anr copy. Contemp lea gilt; worn, spine of Vol I torn & lacking section. With 2 engraved titles, map & 79 plates only. Some browning & marginal dampstaining. pn May 14 (212) £110 [Bailey]

Anr copy. 2 vols in 1. 4to, contemp half mor; worn. With folding map, 2 engraved titles & 106 plates. Some spotting or browning. S Feb 26 (715) £380 [Poole]

Anr copy. 2 vols. 4to, contemp half mor; rubbed. S Feb 26 (716) £380 [Poole]

Anr copy. 2 vols in 1. 4to, disbound. S May 14 (1193) £300 [Papakonstantinou]

Anr copy. 2 vols. 4to, contemp mor gilt. S May 14 (1194) £320 [Bailey]

Anr copy. Lea; rubbed. Library markings. sp Apr 16 (256) $210

Anr Ed. L, 1838. 2 vols. 4to, contemp mor gilt; spine worn. With engraved titles, folding map & 106 plates. DW Nov 9 (17) £320

Beatty Library, Sir A. Chester

— [Sale Catalogue] Catalogue of the Renowned Collection of Western Manuscripts.... L, 1932-33. 2 vols. 4to, orig wraps. bba May 28 (549) £50 [Symonds]

Beauchamp, J. de, Pseud. of Jules le Petit —& Rouveyre, Edouard

— Guide du Libraire-Antiquaire et du Bibliophile. Paris, 1882-86. 16 parts. 8vo, loose as issued in wraps. With 60 plates. sg Oct 31 (26) $70

Beauclerk Library, Topham

— [Sale Catalogue] Bibliotheca Beauclerkiana. A Catalogue of the Large and Valuable Library.... L, 1781. 2 parts in 1 vol. 8vo, later half calf. bba June 25 (9) £180 [Spelman]

Beaufort, Emily Anne, Viscountess Strangford

— Egyptian Sepulchres and Syrian Shrines. L, 1861. 2 vols. 8vo, orig cloth; rubbed, spines faded. With 6 color plates & folding map in pocket at end of Vol I, hand-colored in outline. bba Feb 27 (5) £120 [Dawson]

Beaufort, Francis, 1774-1857

— Karamania, or a Brief Description of the South Coast of Asia-Minor. L: R. Hunter, 1817. 8vo, contemp half calf. With folding map & 6 plates & plans. Some spotting & browning. S June 30 (238) £480 [Maggs]

Beaufort, Henry Somerset, Duke of —& Watson, A. E. T.

— The Badminton Library of Sports and Pastimes. L, 1885-96. Vol I is 2d Ed. 29 vols. 8vo, orig cloth. L Nov 14 (366) £980

Anr Ed. L, 1889-1902. 28 vols. 4to, orig cloth; worn & soiled. Library markings. F Dec 18 (596) $625

Beaujour, Louis Felix, baron de, 1763-1836
— Tableau du commerce de la Grece. Paris; Renouard, 1800. 8vo, contemp half mor. S June 30 (239) £550 [Atabey]

Beaujoyeulx, Baltasar de, d.1587
— Balet comique de la Royne.... Paris, 1582. Illus by Jacques Patin. 4to, 17th-cent vellum. With 27 illusts, 6 folding. Some plates shaved; some wormholes; minor spotting. C Nov 27 (30) £26,000 [Librairie Thomas-Scheler]

Beaulieu, Luke de
— The Holy Inquisition, wherein is represented.... L: Joanna brome, 1681. 8vo, contemp calf; covers detached, endpapers renewed. Some browning & dampstaining. sg Oct 24 (21) $300

Beaumarchais, Pierre Auguste Caron de, 1732-99
— Le Barbier de Seville. Paris, 1963. One of 270. Illus by Andre Derain. Folio, unsewn in orig wraps. With 2 plain & 54 colored illusts. SM Oct 11 (420) FF1,800

Beaumont, Cyril William
— The History of Harlequin. L, 1926. One of 325. 4to, orig half vellum; minor tear to lower corner of upper cover. Inscr. pn Dec 12 (22) £140

Beaumont, Cyril William —& Sitwell, Sacheverell
— The Romantic Ballet.... L, 1938. 4to, orig cloth, in d/j. bba Apr 9 (293) £150 [Ulysses]

Anr copy. Orig silver cloth; corners bumped. With 81 tipped-in plates, some colored. pn Oct 24 (319) £95

Beaumont de Perefixe, Hardouin de, 1605-70
— Histoire de Roy Henry le Grand.... Paris, 1662. 4to, early calf; joints worn & cracked. Tp soiled. wa Dec 9 (486) $50

Beaumont, Edouard de
— L'Epee et les femmes. Paris, 1881. One of 500. 4to, half mor. sg Mar 26 (33) $150

Beaumont, Francis, 1584-1616 —& Fletcher, John, 1579-1625
— Works. L, 1647. ("Comedies and Tragedies.") 1st Collected Ed, 2d state of port. Modern half calf incorporating old bds with vellum corners; rubbed. Tp damaged & repaired; tp & frontis laid down; some text leaves remargined, with small loss to pp. 9-10 of the Tragedy of Valentinian. W July 8 (18) $125

Anr Ed. L, 1679. ("Fifty Comedies and Tragedies.") Folio, contemp calf; joints split, spine def. Lacking M3-P3; hinges broken. bba Jan 16 (76) £75 [Gammon]

Anr copy. 19th-cent bds using contemp bds. Lacking port. LH Dec 11 (63) $200

Anr Ed. Edin., 1812. 14 vols. 8vo, contemp mor gilt; rubbed. S July 1 (968) £200 [Holleyman/Treacher]

Anr Ed. L, 1843-46. 11 vols. 8vo, calf; rubbed. O Feb 25 (18) $300

Anr copy. Mor by Zaehnsdorf; rubbed. O Aug 25 (27) $700

Beaumont, William, 1785-1853
— Experiments and Observations on the Gastric Juice.... Plattsburgh, 1833. 1st Ed. 8vo, contemp bds; rebacked retaining most of orig backstrip. Title repaired; some stains. With ANs from Harvey Cushing, 10 June 1899, pasted in. O Nov 26 (17) $2,400

Anr copy. Orig half cloth; worn, covers detached. Some foxing & soiling. O Aug 25 (28) $800

2d Ed. Burlington VT, 1847. ("The Physiology of Digestion....") 8vo, orig cloth; worn. Some foxing. O Aug 25 (29) $200

Beaunier, Stanislas
— Traite-Pratique sur l'Education des Abeilles. Vendome, 1806. 8vo, contemp half calf; rubbed. With 4 plates. Some browning. Inscr. pn Dec 12 (92) £90

Beauvallet, Pierre Nicolas
— Fragmens d'ornemens dans le style antique.... Paris, 1820. 24 cahiers in 2 vols. Folio, 19th-cent half mor gilt. With 144 plates. Lower corners of last few plates in Vol I damaged without loss of surface. S Nov 21 (66) £500 [Shapero]

Beauveau, Henri de
— Relation iournaliere du voyage du Levant. Nancy, 1619. 6 parts in 1 vol. 4to, old calf; worn & broken. Some fraying & soiling; a few minor tears. O July 14 (24) $1,500

Becattelli, Lorenzo
— I riti nuziali degli antichi Romani.... Bologna, 1762. Folio, bds. Some foxing. SI Dec 5 (314) LIt450,000

Becher, Henry C. R.
— A Trip to Mexico.... Toronto, 1880. 8vo, cloth; rubbed. With 13 mtd albumen prints. bba Jan 16 (407) £90 [Graves-Johnston]

Becker, Felix. See: Thieme & Becker

Becker, Robert H. See: Grabhorn Printing

Becket, Thomas a, Saint. See: Thomas a Becket

Beckett, Samuel

— En attendant Godot. Paris, 1952. One of 35 on velin superieur. Orig ptd wraps, unopened. Inscr to William Targ. CNY June 9 (9) $17,000

— Ill Seen, Ill Said. Northridge CA, 1982. One of 299. sg June 11 (17) $150

Anr Ed. Northridge: Lord John Press, 1982. Half mor. pba July 9 (17) $95

— The North. L: Enitharmon Press, 1972. One of 137, sgd by Beckett. Illus by Avigdor Arikha. Folio, unbound as issued in orig cloth portfolio. With 3 sgd etchings. DW Mar 11 (468) £340

Beckford, Peter, 1740-1811

— Thoughts on Hunting. L, 1796. ("Thoughts upon Hare and Fox Hunting.") 2 vols. 8vo, contemp calf; rubbed. With 20 plates. Foxed. pnE Oct 1 (284) £130

Anr Ed. L, 1847. 8vo, orig cloth; lower joint cracked. bbc Apr 27 (502) $65

Beckford, William Thomas, 1760-1844

See also: Nonesuch Press

— Recollections of an Excursion to the Monasteries of Alcobaca and Batalha. Phila., 1835. 1st American Ed. 8vo, old half calf. wd Dec 12 (360) $200

— Vathek. L, 1786. ("An Arabian Tale.") 1st Ed. 8vo, 19th-cent calf; joints rubbed. Lacking a prelim leaf; tp restored at upper margin; a2 & a3 exchanged; B6 spotted & with corner restored. Ck Oct 31 (27) £120

Beckford Library, William Thomas

— [Sale Catalogue] The Valuable Library of Books in Fonthill Abbey. L, 1823. 8vo, contemp half mor; rubbed. Priced in ink. bba May 28 (564) £180 [Dawson]

Beckovsky, Frantisek Jan

— Poselkyne starych prjbehuw Czeskych.... Prague, 1700. Folio, contemp blind-stamped pigskin over wooden bds; partly loose. Soiling & dampstaining to margins; hole in K1 with loss; clean tear in R2 repaired; lower half of last index leaf torn out. sg Oct 24 (22) $250

Becmanus, Christianus

— De originibus Latinae linguae.... Wittenberg: Paulus Helwichius, 1613. 8vo, contemp vellum. Some foxing. sg Oct 24 (23) $225

Becon, Thomas, 1512-67

— The Sicke Mans Salve wherin the faythfull Christians may learn both how to behave them selves.... L: John Daye, 1579. 8vo, contemp blind-tooled calf over wooden bds with Crucifixion panel stamp on front cover; lacking clasps, front cover chipped & detached. Black letter. Tp soiled & chipped; next leaf torn in outer margin with loss of text; B1.8 suppied in Ms. STC 1762.3. sg Oct 24 (24) $250

Bede, The Venerable, 673-735

— The History of the Church of Englande. Antwerp: Laet, 1565. 1st Ed in English. Trans by Thomas Stapleton. 4to, inserted in earlier bdg of calf over wooden bds with large heraldic panel in 4 compartments with Tudor emblems, metal clasps; rebacked, lacking head of spine, joints split. Lacking 6 prelims; 3 17th-cent Ms leaves inside lower cover; tp torn at corners with loss of text. STC 1778. S Feb 25 (476) £280 [Rix]

Anr copy. Old vellum. Tp soiled & stained. sg Mar 12 (10) $3,600

Bede, Cuthbert. See: Bradley, Edward

Bedford, George

— Art Sales: A History of Sales of Pictures.... L, 1888. 2 vols. 4to, orig cloth; rubbed & soiled. S Feb 11 (177) £260 [Zwemmer]

Beebe, Charles William, 1877-1962

— A Monograph of the Pheasants. L, 1918-22. One of 600. 4 vols. Folio, orig cloth; scuffed. With 90 color plates, 87 photogravures & 20 distribution maps. C Oct 30 (277) £2,200 [Greyfriars]; CNY Dec 5 (287) $1,700

Anr copy. Mor gilt; rubbed. With 90 color plates, 88 photogravures & 20 distribution maps. Some soiling. P June 17 (109) $3,250

— Pheasants, their Lives and Homes. NY, 1931. 2 vols. In chipped d/js. K Sept 29 (58) $55

Beebe, Lucius Morris, 1902-66

— The Central Pacific & The Southern Pacific Railroads. Berkeley, 1963. In d/j. cb Feb 13 (27) $50

— Mansions on Rails: The Folklore of the Private Railway Car. Berkeley, Calif., 1959. Ltd Ed. 4to, orig bdg. cb Feb 13 (32) $75

Beebe, Lucius Morris, 1902-66 —& Clegg, Charles M.

— The Age of Steam. NY, 1957. One of 400. cb Feb 13 (23) $80

— Cable Car Carnival. Oakland, 1951. 1st Ed. Sgd by both authors. cb Feb 13 (25) $50

Beebe, Lucius Morris, 1902-66 —& Clegg, Charles M.

— Narrow Gauge in the Rockies. Berkeley, 1958. In d/j. cb Feb 13 (34) $50

One of 850. cb Feb 13 (35) $170

— Virginia & Truckee: A Story of Virginia City and Comstock Times. Oakland, 1949. One of 950. In d/j. cb Feb 13 (39) $75

Beechey, Frederick William, 1796-1856
See also: Grabhorn Printing

— Narrative of a Voyage to the Pacific and Beering's Strait.... L, 1831. 1st Ed. 2 vols. 4to, modern calf. With 3 maps & 23 plates. Some discoloration. S Nov 15 (1320) £280 [Longenbough]

Anr copy. 2 vols in 1. 4to, modern calf gilt. With 23 plates & 3 folding charts. Repairs to 2 leaves of intro. W July 8 (240) £540

New Ed. 2 vols. 8to, modern half mor. Prelims bound out of order in Vol I; small repair to fore-edge of 1 title & to several maps. kh Nov 11 (322) A$350

Anr copy. 2 vols. 8vo, contemp calf; rebacked retaining part of orig spines. With 25 maps & plates. Folding maps repaired on verso. sg June 18 (16) $550

1st American Ed. Phila., 1832. 8vo, half cloth. Library stamp on tp & front flyleaf. sg Dec 5 (8) $175

Beechey, Frederick William, 1796-1856 & Henry William

— Proceedings of the Expedition to Explore the Northern Coast of Africa. L, 1828. 1st Ed. 4to, half cloth. With folding map, 8 plans & 13 plates. bba Apr 30 (43) £140 [Folios Ltd]

Anr copy. Old bds. Library markings. DW Oct 2 (12) £55

Beedham, Ralph

— Wood Engraving. Ditchling: St. Dominic's Press, 1920. 1st Ed. Intro by Eric Gill; illus by Eric Gill & Desmond Chute. Orig half cloth. DW Apr 8 (462) £55

Beerbohm, Sir Max, 1872-1956

— Caricatures of Twenty-Five Gentlemen. L, 1896. 8vo, orig cloth; upper bd soiled. With 25 plates. pn Sept 12 (127) £120 [Traylen]

— Fifty Caricatures. L, 1913. 4to, orig cloth. sg Dec 12 (17) $140

— The Happy Hypocrite. L & NY, 1897. 1st Ed. 16mo, half mor, orig wraps preserved. Some dampstaining. ANs to Desmond MacCarthy inserted. S July 1 (970) £200 [Brown]

Anr Ed. L, [1915]. Illus by George Sheringham. 4to, orig bds; rubbed. bba Mar 26 (194) £60 [Dawson]

Anr copy. Orig cloth; rubbed. kh Nov 11 (43) A$80

Anr copy. Orig cloth, in d/j. sg Dec 12 (19) $200

Anr Ed. NY, 1931. With ALs to John Mason Brown laid in. Met Apr 28 (560) $140

— More. L & NY, 1899. 1st Ed. 12mo, cloth. cb Sept 19 (10) $75

— Observations. L, 1925. 1st Ed. 4to, orig cloth; soiled. With colored frontis & 51 plates. sg Sept 26 (24) $70

— The Poet's Corner. L, 1904. 1st Ed. Folio, orig bds; slight tears to edges & foot of spine. With 20 colored plates. pn Sept 12 (130) £140

— Rossetti and his Circle. L, 1922. Orig cloth; extremities worn. F June 25 (268) $70; sg Dec 12 (20) $110

— Seven Men. L, 1919. Inscr to ABW, 1919. Met Apr 28 (562) $200

Anr copy. Calf gilt; rubbed. ALs to Desmond MacCarthy inserted. S July 1 (969) £340 [Chelsea]

— A Survey. L, 1921. 1st Ed, one of 250. 4to, cloth. pnE Mar 11 (124) £75

One of 275. Orig cloth. With colored frontis & 51 plates. pn Sept 12 (126) £65 [Traylen]

Anr Ed. NY, 1921. Cloth; worn, spine ends torn. Met Apr 28 (561) $70

— Things New and Old. L, 1923. 1st Ed, One of 380. 4to, orig cloth; worn & soiled. With extra sgd color plate inserted into rear cover pocket. O May 26 (8) $150

— Works. L, 1896. 1st Ed. 4to, orig cloth. cb Sept 19 (11) $110

— Zuleika Dobson. L, 1911. sg Dec 12 (21) $110

1st Ed, Issue not stated. bba Apr 30 (188) £75 [Elvidge]

Beeson, John

— A Plea for the Indians. NY, 1858. 3d Ed. 8vo, ptd wraps; worn & soiled. Some margins dampstained. NH May 30 (292) $100

Beethoven, Ludwig van, 1770-1827

— [Symphony No 9], Opus 125. Mainz & Paris: A. Schott, [1826]. 1st Ed of full score, 1st Issue, with subscribers' list. Folio, 19th-cent mor gilt; extremities rubbed. Without the list of subscribers & with the addition of metronome markings. Plate No 2322. Litho tp, music engraved throughout. P Dec 12 (8) $2,000

Beeton, Isabella Mary

— The Book of Household Management. L, 1861. 1st Ed. 22 (of 24) orig parts; lacking Parts 1 & 15. 8vo, orig wraps. Lacking additional title & frontis. S May 14 (970) £320 [Petta]

Anr copy. 2 vols in 1. 8vo, contemp half calf; rubbed, rebacked. With colored frontis, additional title & 12 plates. Some dampstaining; frontis & some leaves with fore-margin shaved; small hole in 3Q1 & tears in last leaf with slight loss. S May 14 (1007) £400 [Petta]

Anr Ed. L, [c.1869]. 8vo, orig half calf; hinges cracked, some wear. Vertical crease to 1 plate. bbc Apr 27 (215) $85

Beets, Johannes, d.1476

— Expositio decem decalogi praeceptorum. Louvain: Aegidius van der Heerstraten, 19 Apr 1486. Folio, 19th-cent calf; formerly chained with rustmarks of hasps at foot of old endleaf at front & at top of G7. 50 lines; double column; type 1:75G; partially rubricated. Commendatory words about Heerstrated in colophon censored; repaired tear on a2 & repaired holes on 67. 296 (of 298) leaves; lacking first & final blanks. Goff B-296. Schoyen copy. P Dec 12 (4) $7,000

Beever, John

— Practical Fly Fishing.... By Arundo. L, 1849. 16mo, contemp half lea; worn. Koopman copy. O Oct 29 (26) $475

Begin, Menachem

— The Revolt: Story of the Irgun. NY, [1951]. Inscr. sg June 25 (25) $225

Beham, Hans Sebald, 1500-50

— Biblia Veteris Testamenti Historie... Biblische Historien, Kuenstlich Fuergemalet. Frankfurt: C. Egenolph, [1557]. 16mo, early 19th-century bds; worn. With 171 half-page woodcuts. Tp & next few leaves severely wormed with varying loss. Some woodcuts crudely tinted. Blank margins of some leaves cropped. Sold w.a.f. sg Mar 12 (11) $375

Beissel, Johann Conrad

— Deliciae Ephratenses, Pars I.... Ephrata, 1773. Bound with: Urstandliche. Ephrata, 1745. 8vo, contemp sheep. 2d work lacking title & preface. sg Dec 5 (9) $400

Beit-Arie, Malachi —& Sirat, Colette

— Manuscrits medievaux en caracters hebraiques.... Jerusalem, 1972-79. Vols I-II in 5. 4to & folio, orig bdgs. sg Oct 31 (191) $90

Bekker, Balthazar, 1634-98

— De Betoverde Wereld, zijnde een grondig onderzoek van 't gemeen gevoelen aangaande de Geeste.... Amst., 1691-93. 4 parts in 1 vol. 4to, calf; worn, front joint splitting. Some waterstaining at beginning. B May 12 (1037) HF500

— Le monde enchante.... Amst., 1694. 3 (of 4) vols. 12mo, contemp calf. Some browning. SI June 9 (109) LIt260,000

Bel Geddes, Norman

— A Project for theatrical Presentation of the Divine Comedy of Dante Alighieri. NY: Theatre Arts, 1924. Sgd. Met Apr 27 (641) $170

Belcher, Sir Edward, 1799-1877

— The Last of the Arctic Voyages. L, 1855. 2 vols. 8vo, orig cloth. Lacking 1 folding map. DW Jan 29 (143) £195

Anr copy. Contemp half calf. With 36 plates (12 colored) & 4 maps (2 folding). W July 8 (241) £720

— Narrative of the Voyage of H.M.S. Samarang.... L, 1848. 1st Ed. 2 vols. 8vo, cloth, unopened; worn & shaken. With 3 folding maps inside front cover pocket. O Feb 25 (19) $650

Belidor, Bernard Forest de, 1693?-1761

— Architecture hydraulique.... Paris, 1737-53. 4 vols. 4to, 3 vols in contemp calf, 1 in contemp vellum. With 2 frontises & 219 folding plates. Some browning & spotting. SI Dec 5 (66) LIt2,600,000

— La Science des ingenieurs.... Paris, 1729. 4to, contemp calf; extremities rubbed, lower cover with small piece of lea torn away. Ck Oct 18 (148) £220

Anr copy. Contemp calf; worn, upper joint cracked. DW Oct 9 (814) £110

Belknap, Jeremy, 1744-98

— The Foresters, an American Tale.... Bost., 1796. 8vo, calf; rebacked, extremities worn, endpapers replaced. Some foxing & dampstaining. NH Oct 6 (101) $75

— The History of New Hampshire.... Phila & Bost, 1784-92. 3 vols. Cloth. With folding map. Lacking blanks; trimmed; tp repaired in vols I & III; map repaired. NH May 30 (387) $350

Bell, Benjamin, 1749-1806

— A Treatise on the Theory and Management of Ulcers.... Edin., 1784. 8vo, contemp calf; rebacked, new endpapers. pba Aug 20 (13) $80

Bell, Sir Charles, 1774-1842

— A Series of Engravings, Explaining the Course of the Nerves.... Phila., 1818. 1st American Ed. 4to, contemp bds; rebacked in cloth, spine imperf. With 9 plates. Some foxing. sg May 14 (10) $400

Bell, Charles Dent

— The Four Seasons at the Lakes. L: Marcus Ward, [c.1865]. Chromolithographed throughout from illuminated designs by Blanche de Montmorency Conyers Morrell. Folio, orig cloth; rubbed. cb Sept 26 (14) $110

Bell, Clive, 1881-1964 —& Others

— Euphrosyne, a Collection of Verse. Cambr., 1905. Orig cloth-backed wraps; worn. With ALs of Duncan Grant to Lady Aberconway, 12-19 July 1962, presenting the book & with the authors' names by the poems in Lady Aberconway's hand. S July 21 (107) £950 [Edwards]

Bell, Ellis. See: Bronte, Emily

Bell, James

— A New and Comprehensive Gazetteer of England and Wales. Glasgow, 1837. 3 vols. 8vo, contemp calf gilt; rubbed. With 44 maps. bba Jan 30 (107) £260 [Burden]

Bell, James Stanislaus

— Journal of a Residence in Circassia.... L, 1840. 2 vols. 8vo, contemp half mor gilt; corners worn. With folding map & 12 plates, 3 colored. DW Dec 11 (7) £155

Bell, John, 1691-1780

— Travels from St. Petersburg in Russia to Diverse Parts of Asia. Glasgow: Foulis, 1763. 1st Ed. 2 vols. 4to, contemp calf gilt; rubbed, spines broken. Some Ms annotations; map with platemark partly cropped; library markings. S Nov 15 (1283) £160 [Waggett]

Bell, John, 1745-1831

See also: British Poets

— Bell's British Theatre. L, 1792-97. 33 vols; lacking Vol 34. Contemp half mor; some corners bumped, some joints starting, rear cover of Vol I detached. wa Sept 26 (34) $250

— Bell's New Pantheon; or, Historical Dictionary. L, 1790. 2 vols. 4to, contemp calf gilt. bba Jan 30 (61) £160 [Thorp]

Bell, John, 1763-1820

— Discourses on the Nature and Cure of Wounds. Edin., 1795. 3 parts in 1 vol. 8vo, contemp half calf; rubbed & soiled, upper joints split. With 2 plates. Some spotting & staining. S Feb 25 (581) £260 [Phillips]

Bell, Malcolm

— Edward Burne-Jones, a Record and Review. L, 1892. One of 390. Folio, orig cloth; rubbed. DW Mar 11 (7790) £60

Bell, William Abraham

— New Tracks in North America. L, 1869. 1st Ed. 2 vols. 8vo, cloth, unopened; spines blistered. Some foxing. sg June 18 (17) $225

Bellamy, Daniel

— Ethic Amusements. L, 1768. 1st Ed. 2 parts in 1 vol. 4to, later half calf gilt; worn, covers almost detached. bba Oct 10 (15) £340 [Miles]

Bellamy, Edward, 1850-98

See also: Limited Editions Club

— Equality. NY, 1897. 8vo, orig cloth, in d/j. Theodore Roosevelt's copy. CNY June 9 (11) $800

— Looking Backward.... Bost., 1888. 1st Ed, 1st Issue. 12mo, orig cloth. With ALs laid in. Epstein copy. sg Apr 29 (29) $450

1st State. Cloth; spine frayed & chipped at top. Library markings. bbc Sept 23 (375) $65

Anr copy. Orig cloth; rubbed. Smith-Jefferson-Manney copy. P Oct 11 (16) $550

Bellantius, Lucius

— Defensio Astrologiae contra Ioannem Picum Mirandulam. Venice: Bernardinum venetum de Vitalibus, 1502. Folio, contemp vellum; crinkled, spine worn. Tp & address to the reader cut down & mtd; some browning; soiled at lower margins. Ck Nov 29 (141) £750

Bellarmino, Roberto Francesco Romolo, Cardinal, 1542-1621

— De scriptoribus Ecclesiasticis. Rome, 1613. 2 parts in 1 vol. 4to, contemp vellum; foot of spine chipped. Blank lower margin of title restored; some dampstaining. sg Oct 31 (27) $225

— De translatione imperii Romani.... Cologne: Joannes Gymnicus, 1599. 2 parts in 1 vol. 8vo, contemp blind-tooled pigskin over wooden bds, armorial bdg. sg Mar 12 (12) $225

— Institutiones Linguae Hebraicae. Rome: Zanetti, 1580. 8vo, contemp vellum; worn. Stamps. SI Dec 5 (68) LIt220,000

Bellasis, George Hutchins

— Views of St. Helena. L, 1815. Oblong folio, orig ptd upper wrap with title within Etruscan border, laid down & soiled, lower wrap renewed. With 6 colored plates. Minor dust-soiling in outer margins. C May 20 (19) £600 [Arader]

Anr copy. Orig half lea wraps; backstrip def. S Nov 15 (1263) £400 [Druett]

Bellicard, Jerome Charles, 1726-86. See: Cochin & Bellicard

Bellin, Jacques Nicolas, 1703-72

— Description geographique des Isles Antilles possidees par les Anglois. Paris, 1758. 4to, contemp mor gilt, with Turgot arms. With engraved title & 13 maps. Some spotting or dampstaining. S June 25 (444) £2,000 [Baskes]

Bellini, Lorenzo, 1643-1704

— Discorsi di anatomia.... Florence, 1741. 3 parts in 2 vols. 8vo, contemp vellum; 1 cover damaged at edge. S May 13 (876) £440 [Rieux]

Bellini, Vincenzo, 1708-83

— De monetis Italiae medii aevi. Ferrara, 1755-79. 4 vols. 4to, contemp vellum. SI Dec 5 (755) LIt1,100,000

Bellmer, Hans, 1902-75 —& Eluard, Paul, 1895-1952

— Les Jeux de la Poupee. Paris, 1949. One of 119. 4to, wraps; repaired. With 15 hand-colored silver prints & 1 hand-colored silver print mtd on front cover & the identical image mtd on tp. sg Oct 8 (71) $20,000

Belloc, Hilaire, 1870-1953

— The Highway and its Vehicles. L, 1926. One of 1,250 numbered copies. 4to cloth. bba Jan 16 (184) £70 [Hay Cinema]

Anr copy. Cloth over bevelled bds. kh Nov 11 (44) A$130

— Verses and Sonnets. L, 1896. 1st Ed. 8vo, orig cloth. bba Apr 30 (189) £150 [C. Johnson]

Bellori, Giovanni Pietro, 1636?-1700

— Veterum illustrium philosopharum, poetarum, rhetorum.... Rome, 1685. Folio, contemp calf gilt. With 3 engraved titles, frontis & 92 plates. b June 22 (150) £160

Bellow, Saul

— Dangling Man. NY, 1944. 1st Ed. Orig cloth, in d/j with fraying at top. CNY June 9 (12) $320

Anr copy. Orig cloth, in d/j. Inscr. sg Dec 12 (22) $600

Anr copy. Orig cloth, in d/j. Inscr. Epstein copy. sg Apr 29 (30) $1,000

— Nobel Lecture. NY: Targ, [1979]. One of 350. pba July 9 (18) $55; wa Dec 9 (170) $65

Bellows, George Wesley

— His Lithographs. NY, 1927. 1st Ed. 4to, cloth. Plate count not given. sg Apr 2 (20) $60

Anr copy. With 195 plates. sp June 18 (164) $90

Revised Ed. NY, 1928. 4to, cloth. sg Sept 6 (21) $80

— The Paintings. NY, 1929. Folio, half cloth, in d/j. With color frontis & 143 plates. sg Apr2 (21) $175

Anr copy. Bds. Some wrinkling. sp June 18 (166) $110

Bell's. See: British Poets

Belot, Jean

— Oeuvres.... Lyons: Claude de la Riviere, 1649. 8vo, contemp sheep; spine ends chipped, joints cracked. Some browning & dampstaining; folding woodcut of hand partly separated along center fold. sg Mar 12 (200) $140

Anr Ed. Rouen: Pierre Amiot, 1688. 8vo, 19th-cent half sheep; front cover detached. Margins trimmed; tear in H1 repaired. sg Mar 12 (201) $110

Belzoni, Giovanni Battista, 1778-1823

— Narrative of the Operations and Recent Discoveries...Egypt and Nubia. L, 1820. 2 vols, including Atlas vol. 4to & folio, contemp half mor & modern half calf. Text vol with frontis port & plate of inscrs; Atlas with 44 plates on 34 sheets, all but 4 hand-colored. Tp supplied by front wrap of a french trans; frontis & tp of text vol foxed; Atlas with wrap & list of plates restored at edges. With a copy of the 1821 2d Ed of the text vol, which has the Appendix. Manney copy. P Oct 11 (17) $3,500

2d Ed. L, 1821-22. 2 vols in 1. Folio, later half mor; rubbed. With 40 hand-colored plates. Ck May 15 (75) £4,500

Beman, David

— The Mysteries of the Trade.... Bost., 1825. 8vo, contemp calf; rubbed. O Jan 14 (16) $190

Bembo, Pietro, 1470-1547

See also: Borgia & Bembo

— Gli Asolani. Venice: Aldus, 1505. Issue without dedication to Lucrezia Borgia. 8vo, mor extra with arms of the Duke of Sutherland, by Thouvenin. Italic letter; guide letters in capital spaces. First 2 & last 3 leaves with marginal tears repaired; tp & last 2 leaves soiled; upper cover of m4&5 torn away. Sutherland copy. C Dec 16 (101) £3,200 [Ghezzi]

Anr Ed. Venice: Sabbio, 1530. 4to, modern mor. bba Sept 19 (276) £240 [Maggs]

— Epistolarum Leonis decimi.... Venice: G. Padoano & V. de Rofinellis, [1535]. Folio, later vellum. Possibly lacking a 2d section. Foxed throughout & with ink underscoring. Sold w.a.f. cb Dec 5 (11) $55

— Opere. Venice, 1729. 4 vols in 2. Folio, 19th-cent half lea. SI June 9 (115) LIt650,000

— Prose.... Venice: G. Tacuino, 1525. 1st Ed. Folio, contemp vellum. S Dec 5 (52) £1,800 [Jackson]

Bemelmans, Ludwig

— Hotel Splendide. NY, 1941. One of 350. Bound in "the draperies of a famous New York hotel". sg Dec 12 (23) $200

— Now I Lay Me Down to Sleep. NY, 1945. One of 400. sg Dec 12 (24) $100

Bemmel, Abraham van

— Beschryving der Stad Amersfoort. Utrecht, 1760. 2 vols. 8vo, half calf; defs, 1 bdg stained. With 9 folding plates. Some waterstaining. B Nov 1 (298) HF1,000

Bendire, Charles Emil, 1836-97

— Life Histories of North American Birds. Wash., 1892-95. 2 vols. 4to, half lea; worn, hinges weak. With 19 color plates. K Sept 29 (81) $100

Anr copy. Cloth; Vol I needs re-sewing. sp Apr 16 (294) $150

Benesch, Otto

— The Drawings of Rembrandt. L, 1954-57. 6 vols. 4to, orig cloth, in d/js. sg Feb 11 (9) £320 [Cantini]

Anr Ed. L, 1973. 6 vols. 4to, orig cloth. S May 13 (518) £180 [Sims, Reed]

Benet, Stephen Vincent, 1898-1943

— Johnny Pye and the Fool-Killer. Weston VT, [1938]. One of 750. Illus by Charles Child. K Sept 29 (59) $50

Benezit, Emmanuel, 1854-1920

— Dictionnaire critique.... Paris, 1911-19. 3 vols. Contemp half calf. Browned. F June 25 (303) $150

Anr Ed. Paris, 1924. 3 vols. 4to, orig bdg; worn. SI June 9 (118) LIt800,000

Anr Ed. Paris, 1948-55. 8 vols. sg Sept 6 (22) $250

Anr Ed. Paris, [1954]-59. 8 vols. Some covers detached. DW Oct 9 (815) £60; DW Nov 6 (499) £105; S Feb 11 (293) £150 [Ippocrate]; SI Dec 5 (756) LIt500,000

Anr Ed. Paris, 1959-62. 8 vols. Orig cloth; rubbed. bba June 11 (300) £110 [Camal]; pn Dec 12 (120) £160

Anr copy. Orig cloth; some wear with tears, several hinges cracked. sg Apr 2 (22) $200

Anr Ed. Paris, 1960. 8 vols. Orig cloth; spine torn. Library markings. pn July 16 (95) £170

Anr Ed. Paris, 1966. 8 vols. bba Jan 16 (257) £180 [Frew Mackenzie]; bbc Apr 27 (432) $220; Ck July 10 (87) £260; DW Mar 11 (791) £110; S Feb 11 (292) £160 [Ippocrate]

Anr Ed. Paris, 1976. 10 vols. Ck Feb 14 (103) £300; sp June 18 (315) $325

Bennet, Henry Grey, 1777-1836

— Letter to Viscount Sidmouth, Secretary of State...on the Transportation Laws, the State of the Hulks, and of the Colonies in New South Wales. L, 1819. 8vo, modern half calf. With folding table. Lacking half-title; somewhat browned throughout. S June 25 (177) £800 [Quaritch/Hordern]

Bennett, Arnold, 1867-1931

See also: Limited Editions Club

— The Old Wives' Tale.... L, 1908. 1st Ed. Orig cloth. sg Dec 12 (25) $150

Manuscript Facsimile Ed. L, 1927. One of 500, sgd. 2 vols. 4to, orig half vellum. Ck July 10 (164) £55; K July 12 (48) $100

— Venus Rising from the Sea. L, 1931. One of 350. Illus by E. McKnight Kauffer. 4to, orig cloth. bba May 14 (335) £140 [Hannan]

Bennett, Frederick Debell

— Narrative of a Whaling Voyage Round the Globe. L, 1840. 2 vols. 8vo, orig cloth. sg Jan 9 (30) $1,300

Bennett, George, 1804-93

— Gatherings of a Naturalist in Australasia.... L, 1860. 8vo, modern syn. Tape repairs to tp. kh Nov 11 (436) A$120

— Wanderings in New South Wales.... L, 1834. 2 vols. 8vo, contemp half calf. With frontises & errata slip. S June 25 (124) £650 [Barbernin]

Bennett, John C.

— The History of the Saints: or an Expose of Joe Smith and Mormonism. Bost., 1842. 1st Ed. 12mo, orig cloth, rebacked. cb Oct 25 (99) $225

Bennett, John Whitchurch

— A Selection of the Most Remarkable and Interesting Fishes found on the Coasts of Ceylon.... L, 1828-30. 4to, contemp half mor; extremities rubbed. With 30 hand-colored plates, heightened with gum arabic. Ck May 15 (7) £2,600

Benois, Alexandre

— Azbuka v kartinakh. [St. Petersburg, 1904 but probably a 1930s reissue]. folio, half cloth; endpapers browned. With cover designs & 35 full-page illusts in color, including title. sg Nov 7 (186) $2,600

Benoist, Philippe & Felix

— Rome dans sa grandeur. Paris, 1870. 3 vols. Folio, orig mor gilt (has arms of Pope Pius IX); some outer corners bumped. With colored map & 99 plates. Some spotting. C Oct 30 (9) £1,800 [Bifolco]

Benoist, Rene. See: Michel & Benoist

Benoit, Pierre, 1886-1962

— Ne changer. Ales, 1955. One of 99. 87mm by 87mm, unsewn in orig wraps. SM Oct 12 (421) FF2,000

Benson, Arthur Christopher, 1862-1925

— The Book of the Queen's Dolls' House. [The Book of the Queen's Dolls' House Library]. L, 1924. One of 1,500. 2 vols. 4to, half cloth; chipped. DW Mar 11 (712) £70

Anr copy. Bds, in d/js. Some foxing. wd Dec 12 (361) $225

Bentham, James, 1707-76

— The History and Antiquities of the Conventual and Cathedral Church of Ely. Cambr., 1771. 4to, contemp calf; rubbed, rebacked. With 48 plates on 46 sheets. bba Sept 19 (172) £95 [Traylen]

Bentivoglio, Guido, Cardinal, 1579-1644

— The History of the Wars of Flanders.... L, 1678. Folio, modern cloth. Some browning, stains & foxing; map with old reverse paper repairs; tp laid down. bbc Dec 9 (313) $120

Benton, Joseph Augustine, 1818-92

— The California Pilgrim.... Sacramento, 1853. 1st Ed. 8vo, orig cloth. Sgd. sg June 18 (42) $100

Benton, Thomas Hart, 1782-1858

— Fath, Creekmore. - The Lithographs of Thomas Hart Benton Austin: U of Texas Press, 1969. Orig bdg; soiled. ALs of Rita P. Benton affixed to front free endpaper. cb Feb 27 (13) $50

Beowulf

— Beowulf. NY, 1932. One of 950. Illus by Rockwell Kent; trans by W. E. Leonard. Folio, cloth. With 8 lithos. sg Sept 226 (144) $140

Anr copy. Cloth, in def d/j. sg Jan 30 (92) $225

Berain, Jean

— Ornemens du peinture et de sculpture.... [Paris, c.1710]. Folio, 19th-cent half mor; worn. With engraved title & 29 plates. Some dust-soiling. S Nov 21 (67) £700 [Price]

Beraudiere, Marc de la

— Le Combat de seul a seul en camp clos. Paris, 1608. 4to, old vellum. sg Mar 26 (35) $275

Berenger, Charles Random de. See: Random de Berenger, Charles

Berenger, Richard, d.1782

— The History and Art of Horsemanship. L, 1771. 4to, contemp calf. With 2 frontises & 15 plates. Some worming in Vol II, affecting frontis but not affecting text. S May 14 (1014) £340 [Grigoropoules]

Berenson, Bernard, 1865-1959

— The Drawings of the Florentine Painters. Chicago, 1938. 3 vols. 4to, orig cloth, 2 vols in d/js. bba Feb 13 (250) £200 [Halwas]

Anr copy. 3 vols. Folio, cloth, in worn d/j. sg Feb 6 (13) $325

— I Disegni dei pittori fiorentini. Milan, 1961. 3 vols. 4to, contemp half mor. Ck Feb 14 (69) £650

— Italian Pictures of the Renaissance. L, 1957-68. 5 (of 7) vols: Venetian & Central & North Italian schools. Orig cloth, in d/js. Ck Feb 14 (68) £600

Anr copy. 7 vols. 4to, S Feb 11 (13) £1,300 [Messaggeria]

— Italian Pictures of the Renaissance....Venetian School. NY, [1957]. 2 vols. 4to, orig cloth, in d/js. DW Oct 9 (816) £150

— Italian Pictures of the Renaissance....Florentine School. L, [1963]. 2 vols. 4to, orig cloth, in d/js. cb Dec 19 (10) $275

— Italian Pictures of the Renaissance. L, 1968. 7 vols. SI Dec 5 (70A) LIt4,000,000

Berenson Collection, Bernard

— Russoil, Franco. - The Berenson Collection. Milan, [1964]. Preface by Nicky Mariano. Folio, cloth, in d/j. sg Feb 6 (14) $225

Beresford, James, 1764-1810

— The Miseries of Human Life. L, 1806. 8vo, modern half mor. With title & 49 plates. Soiled & spotted. bba Oct 10 (191) £650 [Mandl]

Berettini, Pietro. See: Berrettini, Pietro

Berganus, Georgius Jodocus

— Benacus. Verona: A. Putelleto, 1546. 1st Ed. 4to, 19th-cent half vellum. Some browning. SI June 9 (125) LIt950,000

Berger, Christoph Heinrich von

— Commentatio de personis, vulgo larvis seu mascheris. Frankfurt & Leipzig: G. M. Knock, [1723]. 4to, contemps bds; dampstained. With 84 plates. sg Nov 7 (19) $200

Berger, Klaus

— Odilon Redon, Fantasy and Colour. L, 1964. 4to, cloth, in d/j. bba May 14 (546) £70 [Zwemmer]

Bergk, Johann Adam

— Ansichten von der Tuerkei. Leipzig, 1812. Oblong folio, half calf. With 20 plates. S June 30 (10) £1,500 [Atabey]

Bergman, Ray

— Trout. Phila., 1938. One of 149. Lea gilt; worn, cover detached. Koopman copy. O Oct 29 (28) $475

— With Fly, Plug, and Bait. NY, 1947. One of 249. Contemp calf; rebacked. Koopman copy. O Oct 29 (29) $325

Bergstrom, I.

— Dutch Still-Life Painting in the Seventeenth Century. L, 1956. pn May 14 (128) £55

Berington, Joseph, 1746-1827

— The History of the Lives of Abeillard and Heloisa. Birm., 1788. 2d Ed. 4to, contemp calf; rebacked, bumped, front hinge cracked. pba Aug 20 (15) $60

Berkeley, George, 1685-1753

— Alciphron: or, the Minute Philosopher. L, 1732. 2 vols. 8vo, contemp calf; rubbed, joints split. Some browning. S May 13 (594) £240 [Hannas]

1st Ed. 2 vols. 8vo, contemp calf; worn, covers of Vol I detached. O Mar 31 (17) $90

Berlese, Laurent, 1784-1863

— Iconographie du genre Camellia. Paris: Cousin, [1839]-41-43. Orig 150 parts in 96. Folio, orig ptd wraps. With 300 hand-finished colored plates. C Oct 30 (174) £20,000 [Vieux Livres d'Europe]

Berliner, Rudolf. See: Halm & Berliner

Berling, Karl

— Festive Publication to Commemorate the 200th Jubilee of the Oldest European China Factory: Meissen. [Dresden], 1910. Folio, cloth; hinges cracked. sg Apr 2 (44) $275

Anr copy. Cloth; worn. sp June 18 (316) $160

Berlinghieri, Francesco

— Geographia. [Florence: Nicolaus Laurentii Alemanus, before Sept 1482]. Issue with title ptd in red & with the register & colophon. Folio, mor gilt by Trautz-Bauzonnet; rubbed. 51 lines & headline; double column; types 4A:115RA; 4B:115RB 6:111RA. With 31 maps on 30 mapsheets. Washed; world map cropped; maps 9, 10, 11 & 31 possibly supplied; Italy with severe repaired tears & portions in facsimile;l repairs to maps 4, 14, 19, 24 & 31 with affected portions supplied in facsimile. 126 leaves (plus 2 extra inserted leaves). Goff B-342. DuPont copy. CNY Oct 8 (12) $42,000

Anr Ed. Amst., 1966. Folio, cloth, in d/j. Facsimile of the 1482 Ed. sg Oct 31 (69) $110

Bernanos, Georges. See: Limited Editions Club

Bernard, Saint (Bernardus Claravallensis), 1091-1153

— Floretus. [Cologne: Heinrich Quentell, not after 1491]. 4to, 19th-cent calf; rubbed, head of spine chipped. 45 lines of commentary & headline; types 3:180 (title, headlines), 7:80 (text); 6:63 (commentary). Some worming with minor text loss; corner of tp torn; 1st few leaves discolored; some foxing; marginal dampstaining. 56 leaves. Goff B-392. Milne copy. CNY Dec 5 (163) $1,000

— Modus bene vivendi. Venice: Bernardinus Benalius, 30 May 1494. 8vo, 16th-cent calf; rebacked. 27 lines, double column, gothic letter. Some browning. 106 leaves. Goff B-414. SI June 9 (127) LIt2,500,000

— Opuscula. Venice: Simon Bevilaqua, 17 Oct 1495. 8vo, modern vellum. 40 lines; double column; roman & gothic letter. First leaf reconstructed & def; marginal repairs; browning & dampstaining. 346 leaves. Goff B-365. SI June 9 (128) LIt750,000

Bernard, Claude, 1813-78

— De la physiologie generale. Paris, 1872. 1st Ed. 8vo, half mor gilt. Some foxing at beginning & end. sg May 14 (13) $130

— Lecons de physiologie operatoire. Paris, 1879. 1st Ed. 8vo, contemp half sheep; front cover detached. Some foxing. sg May 14 (15) $225

— Lecons sur les proprietes physiologiques et les alterations pathologiques des liquides de l'organisme. Paris, 1859. 2 vols. 8vo, half mor, orig wraps bound in. Some foxing. sg May 14 (12) $275

— La Science experimentale. Paris, 1878. 1st Ed. 12mo, modern half lea. Some foxing. sg May 14 (14) $200

Bernard, Pierre Joseph

— Oeuvres. Paris: Didot, 1797. One of 150. Illus by Pierre Paul Prud'hon. 4to, modern mor by Riviere. With 4 plates. sg Nov 7 (20) $850

Bernard, Pons Joseph, 1748-1816

— Nouveaux Principes d'hydraulique appliques a tous les objets d'utilite.... Paris, 1787. 4to, contemp sheep gilt. With 3 folding plates. Library stamp on tp. sg Nov 14 (214) $225

Bernard, Tristan, 1866-1947

— Amants et voleurs. Paris, 1927. One of 350. Illus by Dignimont. 4to, orig wraps. With 16 plates in 2 states, plain & hand-colored by pochoir. wa Sept 26 (593) $110

Bernardini, Pietro. See: Pietro da Lucca

Bernardus Carthusiensis

— Dialogus Virginis Mariae misericordiam elucidans. Leipzig: Melchior Lotter, 1497. 4to, old bds. Gothic type. Browned; dampstained at beginning & end; contemp underscoring throughout; last leaf mtd. 56 leaves. Goff B-361. sg Oct 24 (25) $900

Bernatz, Johann Martin
See also: Schubert & Bernatz

— Scenes in Ethiopia. L, 1852. 2 vols in 1. Oblong folio, orig half mor. With 2 litho titles & 47 color-tinted or tinted views. Some foxing. S Nov 21 (348) £1,800 [Maggs]

Berners, Dame Juliana, b.1388?

— Book of St. Albans. L: for Humfrey Lownes, 1595. ("The Gentlemans Academie. Or, the Book of S. Albans....") 4to, 19th-cent mor gilt. Lacking the medial & final blank leaves L4 & 2D4; some foxing; marginal wormhole in A1-2 filled; top margin of D3 repaired without loss. Britwell-Schwerdt copy. P Dec 12 (149) $6,000

Anr Ed. L, 1810 [1811]. ("The Book Containing the Treatises of Hawking, Hunting....") One of 150. 4to, contemp mor gilt by Charles Clarke. pn Mar 19 (367) £360

— A Treatyse of Fysshynge wyth an Angle.... L, 1883. ("An Older Form of the Treatyse of Fysshynge wyth an Angle.") One of 200. 4to, orig bds; rubbed, spine worn. bba Nov 28 (11) £110 [Hereward Bks]

Anr Ed. NY: Gillis Press, 1903. One of 106. Vellum. O Jan 14 (17) $160

Berni, Francesco, 1497-1536

— Orlando innamorato.... Venice, 1545. 2d Ed. 4to, contemp vellum. Some dampstaining in margins at end. SI Dec 5 (72) LIt450,000

Bernier, Francois, 1620-88

— Voyages de Francois Bernier contenant le description des etats du Grand Mogol, de l'Hindoustan.... Amst., 1699. 2 vols. 12mo, contemp calf; joint split, head of 1 spine worn. With frontises, 3 maps & 8 plates. Some lower margins stained. b June 22 (152) £240

Bernoulli, Daniel, 1700-82

— Hydrodynamica, sive de viribus et motibus fluidorum commentarii. Strassburg, 1738. 1st Ed. 4to, early 19th-cent bds. With engraved title & 12 folding plates. Plates spotted; 2A3-4 dampstained. Ck Nov 29 (142) £1,200

Bernoulli, Jean, 1667-1748
See also: Leibnitz & Bernoulli

— Opera. Geneva, 1742. 4 vols. Contemp calf. Without stamps but with accession numbers. Ck Nov 29 (144) £1,600

Beron, Eugene

— La Troisieme Invasion. Paris, 1876. One of 50 on hollande. 2 vols. Folio, mor by Marius Michel; rubbed & soiled. P June 17 (116) $200

Berosus

— Reliquiorum consimilis argumenti autorum.... Lyons: Joannes Temporalis, 1554. Vol I (of 2). 16mo, contemp vellum; front hinge split. Dampstaining in lower margins throughout. sg Mar 12 (14) $300

Berquin, Arnaud, 1749?-91

— The Children's Friend. L, 1793. 6 vols. 12mo, contemp calf; rubbed. bba Oct 10 (19) £60 [James]

Berr de Turique, Marcelle

— Raoul Dufy. Paris, 1930. 4to, orig wraps; backstrip def. With etched frontis & unspecified number of plates, some in color. sg Apr 2 (106) $225

Berrettini, Pietro, 1596-1669

— Tabulae anatomicae.... Rome, 1741. Folio, contemp calf gilt; worn. With 27 plates. Some dampstaining & browning; last plate with margin reinforced. SI Dec 5 (759) LIt4,000,000

Berriman, Algernon E.

— Aviation. L, [1913]. Marginal notations & underlining. cb Nov 7 (22) $70

Berry, Wendell

— November Twenty Six Nineteen Hundred Sixty Three. NY, [1964]. Ltd Ed. Illus by Ben Shahn. sg Jan 30 (162) $700; wa Sept 26 (662) $60

Berry, William, 1774-1851

— The History of the Island of Guernsey. L, 1815. 4to, contemp half calf. With folding map & 29 plates. Some waterstaining to upper margins. S Feb 26 (820) £200 [Shapero]

Bertall. See: Arnoux, Charles Albert d'

Bertaud, Jean

— Encomium trium Marium cum earundem cultus defensione adversus Lutheranos. Paris: Josse Bade & Galliot du Pre, 1529. 1st Ed, 1st Issue. 4to, early 19th-cent blind-stamped calf; joints worn. With 4 woodcuts in Part 1, 16 full-page woodcuts in Part 2, & 7 other woodcuts in Part 3. Lacking 2 unsgd leaves of verse between Parts I & III. S Dec 5 (54) £5,000 [Libsalvador]

Bertelli, Pietro

— Aggiunta al Theatro delle citta d'Italia. Padua, 1629. Oblong 4to, disbound. With 60 (of 67) plates. Several plate versos repaired, affecting some text. Sold w.a.f. sg Sept 19 (7) $3,400

— Theatro delle citta d'Italia.... Padua, 1629. 2 parts in 1 vol. Oblong 4to, contemp calf; worn & chipped. With engraved title & 75 maps & plates only. Edges of additional title frayed; lower margin of tp closely cropped, affecting text. P June 17 (119) $8,000

Bertini, A.

— Costumi di Roma e dei contorni. Rome, 1846. 8vo, orig bds; joints scuffed. With hand-colored engraved title & 29 plates. Ck Dec 11 (218) £260

Bertram, Bonaventura Cornelius, d.1594

— De republica Ebraeorum.... Leiden, 1651. 12mo, later vellum. Some spotting & browning; tp detached; bottom margin of 1st leaf of preface clipped. wa Dec 9 (490) $75

Bertram, Charles

— Isn't It Wonderful? A History of Magic and Mystery. L, 1896. 8vo, cloth; worn. Inscr. sg Oct 17 (10) $100

Bertran, Marcos Jesus

— El Gran Teatro del Liceo de Barcelona.... Barcelona, 1931. One of 850. Folio, orig half vellum; soiled & shelfworn. wa Dec 9 (508) $160

Bertrand, Alfred

— Au Pays des Ba-Rotsi Haut-Zambeze.... Paris, 1898. 4to, orig cloth. bba Sept 19 (54) £65 [Maggs]

Bertrandi, Giovanni Ambrogio Maria

— Traite des operations de chirurgie.... Paris, 1769. 8vo, contemp sheep gilt. With 4 folding plates. Marginal foxing throughout. sg Nov 14 (9) $175

Bertuch, Friedrich Johann Justin, 1747-1822

— Bilderbuch fuer Kinder. Weimar, 1798-1830. 12 vols. 4to, contemp half calf. With 1181 (of 1186) colored plates. HH May 12 (1746) DM15,000

Anr Ed. Weimar, 1810. Vols 1-3 & 5-7 (of 12). 4to, 19th-cent half mor; needs rebdg. Minor foxing. sg Feb 13 (150) $3,400

— Naturgeschichtliche Belustigungen oder Abbildungen naturgeschichtlicher Gegenstaende aus Bertuchs Bilderbuche fuer Kinder. Weimar, [c.1811[. 6 (of 7) parts in 1 vol. Contemp half mor, orig front wrap bound in. With 35 (of 42) hand-colored plates. Some leaves torn with loss; tears to several plates. cb Feb 27 (14) $130

Berwick, Jacobo Maria del Pilar, Duque de

— Mapas Espanoles de America, Siglos XV-XVII. Madrid, 1951. One of 312. Folio, unbound as issued in half cloth portfolio. With 78 maps, numbered 1-79. sg Oct 31 (70) $1,400

Besnier, Ernest —& Others

— Le Musee de l'Hopital Saint-Louis. Iconographie des maladies cutanees.... Paris, [c.1890]. Folio, contemp half mor gilt. With 50 chromolitho plates. sg Nov 14 (10) $250

Besoldus, Christophorus, 1577-1638

— Historia Constantinopolitana.... Strassburg, 1634. 12mo, contemp vellum. With engraved title. Repair at C3 touching text; minor flaws. S Nov 21 (237) £500 [Maggs]

Bessarion, Joannes, Cardinal, d.1472

— Lettere & orazioni...scritte a principi d'Italia intorno al collegarsi.... Florence: Filippo Giunta, 1594. Bound with: Ammirato, Scipione. Orazione.... Florence, 1594. 4to, old vellum; worn. Some leaves dampstained. S July 1 (550) £600 [Consolidated Real]

Besson, Jacques

— Teatro de los Instrumentos y Figuras matematicas y mechanicas.... Lyon: Horatio Cardon, 1602. Folio, modern vellum. Minor tears; browned. C May 28 (251) £1,600

Anr copy. With 60 plates. Browned. SI Dec 5 (80) LIt4,000,000

— Theatrum instrumentorum et machinarum.... Lyons: Barth. Vincentium, 1582. Folio, 19th-cent calf gilt; rebacked, corners worn. Ink stamp on tp & dedication. pn Mar 19 (187) £900 [Bifolco]

Best, Thomas

— A Concise Treatise on the Art of Angling.... L, 1787. 1st Ed. 12mo, early 19th-cent bds; worn. Koopman copy. O Oct 29 (30) $450

2d Ed. L: C. Stalker, [1789?]. 12mo, early 19th-cent bds; worn. Koopman copy. O Oct 29 (31) $160

Bestelmeier, Georg Hieronimus

— Systematisches Verzeichnis eines magazins von verschniedenen Kunst- und anderen nuezlichen Sachen.... Nuremberg, 1803. Parts 1-7 in 1 vol. Oblong 4to, contemp bds; rubbed. With 70 plates. Some short tears; some staining. S Dec 5 (258) £2,600 [Quaritch]

Bester, Alfred

— The Demolished Man. Chicago: Shasta, [1953]. 1st Ed, one of 200. In chipped d/j. sg June 11 (19) $350

Besterman, Theodore

— A World Bibliography of Bibliographies. Geneva, [1955-56]. 3d Ed. 4 vols. Bdg worn. O Dec 17 (20) $70

4th Ed. Lausanne, [1966]. 4 vols. O Sept 24 (30) $275

Anr Ed. L, 1980. 5 vols. 4to, cloth. sg Oct 31 (28) $350

Bestiary

— A Medieval Bestiary. Bost.: Godine, 1971. One of 100. Illus by Gillian Tyler. 4to, half mor. sg Sept 26 (228) $90

Bethel, Slingsby, 1617-97

— The Interest of Princes and States. L, 1680. 1st Ed. 8vo, modern half calf. Lacking A1; tp torn with loss to lower margin; some browning. bba May 14 (63) £190 [Clark]

Beveren, Jacques Joseph van —& Dupressoir, Charles

— Costume du moyen age.... Brussels, 1847. 2 vols in 1. 8vo, early half mor; worn & scuffed. With 145 plates with contemp hand-coloring. Institutional stamp at top edge of text. bbc June 29 (266) $160

Beveridge, Albert J., 1862-1927

— Abraham Lincoln. Bost., 1928. One of 1,000. With leaf of orig Ms tipped-in. O Aug 25 (30) $150

Beveridge, Erskine, 1851-1920

— Coll and Tiree: their Prehistoric Forts.... Edin., 1903. Ltd Ed. 4to, orig half mor; rubbed. bba Sept 19 (172) £80 [V. Fleming]

Beverley, Robert, c.1673-c.1722

— The History of Virginia. L, 1705. ("The History and Present State of Virginia.") 4 parts in 1 vol. 8vo, contemp calf. With armorial frontis, folding table & 14 plates. Frontis partly detached; some browning. Ck Oct 31 (7) £320

Bewick, Thomas, 1753-1828

[-] Bewick Gleanings.... Newcastle, 1886. 2 parts in 1 vol. 4to, orig mor; rubbed. bba Feb 27 (338) £160 [Dawson]; bba Feb 27 (339) £100 [Books & Prints]

— Figures of British Land Birds.... Newcastle, 1800. Vol I (all pbd). 8vo, orig bds. bba (336) £240 [Feb 27] [Sanderson]

— A General History of Quadrupeds. Newcastle, 1790. 8vo, pigskin gilt. Piece torn from blank margin of A8; some dampstaining affecting last 2 gatherings. pn June 11 (228) £220 [Russell]

Anr copy. Calf gilt by Riviere. Washed. sg May 7 (25) $300

2d Ed. Newcastle, 1791. 8vo, later mor gilt; rubbed. bba Jan 30 (87) £220 [Way]

Anr copy. Contemp half calf; rubbed, upper joint crcked. DW Apr 8 (148) £75

3d Ed. Newcastle, 1792. 8vo, later 19th-cent half calf gilt. Tp spotted. sg May 14 (193) $200

4th Ed. Newcastle, 1800. 8vo, mor gilt by J. Clarke. bba Sept 5 (8) £280 [Ventnor Bks]

Anr copy. Later calf. Ck May 15 (8) £110

8th Ed. Newcastle, 1824. 8vo, orig lea; rebacked. NH Oct 6 (34) $75

— A History of British Birds. Newcastle, 1797-1804. 1st Ed. 2 vols, each vol with 2d Ed of Supplement bound at end later mor gilt. bba Jan 30 (88) £360 [Jacob]

1st Ed. 2 vols. 8vo, contemp mor gilt by Bedford. Vignette on p. 285 inked over by hand. Watercolor drawing inserted as a frontis, apparently by Thomas Bewick. S July 22 (400) £800 [Steadman]

Anr copy. 3 vols, including Supplement. 8vo, later 19th-cent calf gilt & contemp bds; joints weak. Vol II prelims dampstained. sg May 7 (26) $700

1st Ed, variants A & B, respectively. 2 vols. 8vo, mor gilt. Minor defs. pn June 11 (229) £220 [Russell]

Anr Ed. Newcastle, 1804-5. 2 vols. 8vo, half lev gilt by Fazakerly; edge-wear, rubbed. bbc Sept 23 (245) $300

Anr Ed. Newcastle, 1804. 2 vols. 8vo, calf gilt; 1 joint broken. O Jan 14 (20) $170

Anr Ed. Newcastle, 1821. 2 vols. 8vo, half lea; rubbed, 1 cover detached. Some foxing; tp of Vol II dust-soiled. K Sept 29 (61) $110

Anr copy. Orig cloth; worn. Some leaves soiled or spotted. Sold w.a.f. Inscr to Mr. Bustin. S Feb 26 (903) £150 [Tattesfield]

Anr Ed. Newcastle, 1826. 2 vols. 8vo, contemp half calf; front cover of Vol II nearly detached. Some foxing at beginning & end. wa Mar 5 (631) $110

— A Memoir of Thomas Bewick. Newcastle & L, 1862. 8vo, orig cloth; spine faded. cb Jan 9 (13) $100

— Select Fables. Newcastle, 1820. 7th Ed. 4to, half calf; stained. bba Feb 27 (337) £110 [Sotheran]

— The Watercolors and Drawings of.... Cambr. MA: MIT Press, [1981]. 2 vols. Oblong 8vo, orig cloth. sg Sept 6 (24) $70

— Works. Newcastle, 1885-87. Memorial Ed, One of 750. 5 vols. 8vo, contemp half mor; rubbed. Some marginal stains. bba May 14 (464) £120 [Books & Prints]

Beyer, August

— Memoriae historico-criticae librorum variorum, accedunt Evangeli Cosmopolitani.... Dresden, 1734. 8vo, modern half vellum. Some browning at end. Ck May 8 (19) £150

Beyer, Edward

— Album of Virginia. [Richmond: Beyer], 1858. Oblong folio, orig half mor gilt; extremities rubbed. With litho title & 40 sheets of plates. Some dampstaining at upper fore-edge corner; foxed; a few plates with marginal tears; tear to final plate closed on verso with transparent tape. P June 16 (195) $7,500

Beyle, Marie Henri ("Stendhal"), 1783-1842

— Le Rouge et le noir.... Paris, 1831. 1st Ed. 2 vols. 8vo, later half calf. Margins in Vol II restored. S May 28 (446) £8,000 [Holinger]

Bezold, Gustav F. T. von. See: Dehio & Bezold

Bianchini, Giuseppe Maria

— Dei Gran Duchi di Toscana della Real Casa de' Medici.... Venice, 1741. Folio, contemp calf; rubbed, upper cover detached, spine def. With frontis & 10 ports. bba Sept 19 (311) £380 [Kunkler]

Anr copy. Contemp half vellum. SI Dec 5 (762) LIt1,800,000

Bianco, Margery Williams, 1881-1944

— Poor Cecco. L, 1925. Illus by Arthur Rackham. 4to, orig cloth; soiled. With 7 colored plates. bba Jan 16 (382) £80 [Harrington]

Bibelot...

— The Bibelot: A Reprint of Poetry and Prose for Book-Lovers. Portland ME, 1895-1915. Ed by Thomas B. Mosher. 21 vols, including Index, 1925. 16mo, half mor gilt. rs Oct 17 (3) $275

Bible in Arabic

— 1671. - Biblia Sacra Arabica.... Rome: Sacra Congregatio de Propaganda Fide. 3 vols. Folio, early 19th-cent half lea; spine ends & corners damaged, Vol II front cover loose. Vol I lacking tp. D & M 1652. sg Oct 24 (26) $600

— [Gospels]. Rome: Typographia Medicea, 1590 [colophon dated 1591]. Folio, 17th-cent vellum; stained, spine worn & restored, covers warped. Some spotting & staining; without title & prelims as issued. C June 24 (94) £650 [Wood]

Bible in Arabic & Latin

— 1774. - [Four Gospels]. Florence Folio, half vellum. Some stains in margins; some browning. S June 30 (309) £420 [Rota]

Bible in Basque

— Evangeloia San Lucasen Guissan. El evangelio segun S. Lucas.... Madrid, 1838. 8vo, contemp calf; rubbed. D & M 1946. S Feb 11 (718) £380 [Orssich]

Bible in Bohemian

— 1488, Aug. - Prague: Johann Kamp. Folio, calf; scuffed, upper hinge split. Some leaves misbound; many leaves damaged & repaired, a few with loss; some leaves supplied in Ms; marginal annotations in at least 5 hands. Sold w.a.f. 578 (of 610) leaves. Goff B-620. C Nov 27 (31) £12,000 [Rosenthal]

Bible in Cherokee

— 1860. - [New Testament]. NY 12mo, cloth; worn. With contemp broadside key to Cherokee alphabet inserted. O Nov 26 (19) $350

Bible in Chinese

— 1823. - New Testament. Malacca: Anglo-Chinese Press. Paris 1-16; lacking Part 17, Daniel to Malachi. 8vo, sewn into ptd wraps. Xylographic printing throughout on 1 side of folded sheets. S July 1 (1516) £1,100 [Quaritch]

Bible in Choctaw

— 1848. - [New Testament] NY 12mo, contemp calf. Margins dampstained. Inscr by translator. O Nov 26 (20) $275

Bible in Cree

— 1861-62. - L. 2 vols in 1. 8vo, contemp sheep; extremities worn. D & M 3130. sg Dec 5 (13) $110

Bible in Dutch

— 1657-46. - Antwerp: Pieter J. Paets. 2 parts in 1 vol. Folio, blind-stamped calf over wooden bds; worn, spine def. Black letter; double-column; over 1,000 woodcuts by Christoffel van Sichen. Tear along inner margin of 1st page of Genesis; small tear in leaf Ss1 of NT. D & M 3314. K July 12 (279) $1,200

— 1660. - [States General Version]. Amst. Folio, contemp lea over wooden bds with brass cornerpieces and clasps; spine ends chipped, joints cracked. sg Mar 12 (15) $550

— 1710. - Dordrecht Folio, old blind-stamped calf, with brass fittings; rebacked at an early date, spine damaged. Black letter. Browned; clean tears in maps; penultimate leaf of Apocrypha def. Sold w.a.f. sg Oct 24 (28) $400

— 1721. - Amst. Folio, 18th-cent lea over wooden bds with brass fittings; lacking clasps, joints cracked, foot of spine chipped. sg Oct 24 (29) $800

— 1729. - Dordrecht Folio, contemp calf over wooden bds, with brass fittings. With engraved title, 6 double-page maps, & 51 plates. Some marginal dampstaining of text leaves; minor marginal tears in 4 maps; lacking front free endpaper. sg Oct 24 (30) $700

— 1729. - Biblia, dat is, de gantsche heylige Schrift.... Dordrecht: Pieter & Jacob Keur. Folio, contemp calf over wooden bds. Marginal dampstaining; minor marginal tears in 4 maps, lacking front free endpaper. sg Oct 24 (30) $700

— 1736. - De Kleine Print-Bybel. Amst. 8vo, contemp calf; upper cover almost detached. With frontis & 150 plates, each with small illusts replacing words of text. Some stains. bba Oct 10 (21) £360 [Quaritch]

— 1748. - [States General version]. Gorinchem: N. Goetzee. 3 parts in 1 vol. Folio, contemp calf; worn. With 9 double-page maps & 127 plates. Sold w.a.f. b June 22 (69) £350

— Taferelen der voornaamste geschiedenissen van het Oude en Nieuwe Testament. Amst., 1728. Vols I-II. Contemp calf gilt; rubbed. With engraved titles & 142 plates. Some browning. Ck Sept 6 (82) £400

Bible in English

— 1535, 4 Oct. - [Miles Coverdale's version]. Cologne: Eucharius Cervicornus & Johannes Soter. 1st Ed of 1st complete Bible in English. Folio, 19th-cent mor gilt. Gothic letter; with 158 woodcut illusts. Lacking 7 text leaves (4 supplied in facsimile) & 2 blanks; without the 2-page woodcut map of Palestine; shaved, affecting headlines & sidenotes; several leaves supplied; some tears & stains, affecting text. Doheny-Manney copy. P Oct 11 (18) $50,000

— 1539. - L: John Bydell for Thomas barthelet. Folio, old lea; worn & rebacked, lacking clasps. Black letter Titles & 17 other leaves at beginning & end lacking but supplied in facsimile; B3-4 remargined with loss; M2 repaired with loss; NT lacking 31 leaves; repaired, with stains & worming; some marginalia cropped. Sold w.a.f. Herbert 45; STC 2067. S July 21 (294) £4,200 [Thomas]

— 1540, Apr. - [Great Bible] L: Edward Whytchurche. 2d Ed of this version. Folio, old calf; worn & rebacked. Black letter. Lacking tp & following 3 leaves; marginal tears; final leaf frayed; some staining. Herbert 53; STC 2070. S July 21 (296) £3,400 [Smith]

— 1541, May. - 5th Ed of this version. L: Edward Whitchurch. Folio, modern mor. Black letter; 62 lines; double column. General title & final leaf in facsimile; some other leaves with restoration, occasionally affecting text; a few leaves with tears & wormholes; upper margin trimmed occasionally affecting headline & pagination; 4th title torn with loss at foot & mtd. Herbert 61; STC 2074. C June 24 (95) £5,000 [Smith]

— 1549. - L: T. Raynalde & W. Hyll. Folio, mor gilt by Bedford; soiled. General title & last 3 leaves in facsimile; some leaves remargined with occasional headline partly supplied in Ms; some worming. Herbert 75; STC 2078. C June 24 (96) £4,000 [Smith]

— 1551. - The Byble, that is to say, al the holy Scripture.... L: John Day. 4to, old calf; def. Black letter; double column Lacking tp & all efore last 6 leaves of the table; also lacking 3D1, blank V4 & all after 4R5; most leaves before Genesis frayed & torn with loss; 1st leaf of Genesis with very slight loss; substantial portion of f1 torn away;l 4H1 & 4R5 torn with loss; other defs. Herbert 93. S July 21 (295) £2,400 [Thomas]

— 1557. - The Newe Testament [Version ascribed to Wm. Whittingham]. Geneva:

Conrad Badius. 8vo, calf; rubbed. Lacking all before c1, y1, Y8, Bb1, Cc7, Dd3 & 6, Ee3 & all after Kk7; H1 loose; some worming, occasionally touching text; some staining; some scribblings in the text. Herbert 106; STC 2871. S July 21 (304) £3,400 [Smith]

— 1560. - [Geneva version] Geneva: Rouland Hall. 1st Ed of this version. 4to, 19th-cent calf; rebacked. With 5 folding woodcut maps & plans (2 imperf). Some cropping, affecting headlines; lacking 3 (of 4) prelims, final leaf & 89 leaves of the Apocrypha. STC 2093; Herbert 107. S Nov 15 (771) £1,200 [Truppa]

— 1562. - The Bible in Englishe.... L: Richard Harrison. 2 parts in 1 vol. Folio, mor gilt by Pratt. Black letter; double column. Lacking final leaf; outer margin of 1st 2 & last 3 gatherings strengthened; outer margins trimmed affecting sidenotes; some other small tears, mostly marginal; some leaves stained or soiled. Herbert 117. Chadwyck-Healey copy. C June 24 (97) £3,000 [Smith]

— 1566. - [Great Bible]. Rouen: R. Carmarden. Folio, contemp calf; rubbed, rebacked. Lacking 1st 3 and last leaf (supplied in photocopy); 6 leaves with margins restored; some staining. Sold w.a.f. bba Oct 24 (41) £2,200 [Aspin]

Anr copy. 19th-cent calf gilt; rubbed, upper joint cracked. Black letter; double column. Tp restored with some portions in facsimile; NT title with tear repaired; final table leaf in facsimile; some soiling & repaired tears; marginal dampstains. Herbert 119; STC 2098. C June 24 (98) £2,600 [Smith]

— [1568]. - [Bishops' Bible] L: R. Jugge. 1st Ed of this version. Folio, old calf with metal clasps. With 2 ports & map. Soiled; some leaves torn; imperf at beginning & end. STC 2099; Herbert 125. S Feb 25 (478) £3,400 [Aspin]

Anr copy. Old calf; wormed & worn. Black letter. Lacking engraved title (supplied in facsimile); woodcut title to NT torn & repaired affecting image; lacking some leves; tears & repairs, occasionally affecting text; some staining & worming with loss. Herbert 125; STC 2099. S July 21 (297) £3,500 [Smith]

— 1582. - [1st Ed of the Douai New Testament] Rheims: John Fogny. 4to, contemp calf; spine split, joints cracked. Lacking front free endpaper; some pp repaired; margin wormed. Sold w.a.f. STC 2883; Herbert 177. bba Mar 26 (125) £460 [M. Thomas]

Anr copy. Old calf; rubbed, rebacked & recornered. Tp border torn with loss & affecting text on verso & remargined; first few corners with lower outer corners torn away just affecting marginalia of 1 leaf; Pp1 repaired affecting text; last leaf torn & repaired; some staining. STC 2883; Herbert 177. S July 21 (305) £650 [Cresswell]

— 1583. - [Geneva version] L: Christopher Barker. Folio, old calf with brass corner & centerpieces on covers; worn, surface def; crudely rebacked. First 6 pp loose, creased & frayed with some loss; next 2 gatherings loose; last few pp creased. Sold w.a.f. bba Feb 27 (316) £850 [Lachman]

Anr copy. 18th-cent calf gilt with brass cornerpieces; rebacked with mor. Black letter; double column. Lacking initial blank; some soiling; minor marginal tears, most repaired. Herbert 178; STC 2136. C June 24 (99) £2,800 [Smith]

— 1589. - [New Testament] L: Deputies of Christopher Barker. Folio, early calf gilt; rubbed & repaired. Tp may be from anr copy; Sig. 3S4 & 5 torn with loss; 4L5 torn; 4K3 & 4 misbound. Sold w.a.f. Herbert 202. bba Aug 13 (84) £260 [Ohlausen]

— 1599. - [Geneva version] L: Deputies of C. Barker. 4to, contemp calf; worn. bba Feb 27 (317) £60 [D. Smith]

Anr copy. Modern half pigskin. Has Book of Common Prayer (lacking A1) & Metrical Psalms, both undated. Lacking last leaf of OT; general title def at lower inner corner, as is leaf to the Christian Readerk; some shaving or soiling; old scribbles. Sold w.a.f. Herbert 247. L Nov 14 (257) £160

Anr copy. 17th-cent mor; needs rebdg; fore-edges gnawed. Lacking 1st & 4th prelims. sg Mar 12 (17) $250

— 1601. - The Text of the New Testament of Jesus Christ Translated...by the Papists of the Traiterous Seminarie at Rhemes.... L: Robert Barker. Folio, late 18th-century sheep gilt; worn, covers detached. Herbert 265. sg Mar 12 (18) $250

— 1603. - [Geneva version] L: Robert Barker. 2 vols in 1. 4to, later calf; worn, covers detached. 1st few leaves frayed & repaired with some loss; some staining & soiling. Sold w.a.f. Herbert 274. bba Jan 16 (199) £80 [Hilton]

Anr copy. 4to, contemp calf; short tear to head of spine. Leaf listing books in the Bible def; corner torn off Fff4; Bound in Book of Common Prayer & Metrical Psalms both incomplete. Sold w.a.f. Herbert 274. L Nov 14 (372) £170

— 1606. - L: R. Barker. Bound with: Two Right Profitable and Fruitfull Concordances, 1605, and The Whole Booke of Psalmes, 1606. 4to, later sheep; worn, joints cracked. Lacking initial leaf. sg Mar 12 (19) $475

— 1607. - L: R. Barker. 4to, early 19th-cent russia gilt; front cover detached. Title cropped; scattered marginal repairs. Herbert 289. sg Mar 12 (20) $475

— 1611. - [Authorized Version] L: Robert Barker With "he" reading in Ruth III, 15. Folio, 17th-cent calf with metal fittings; rebacked, orig spine laid down, 2 cornerpieces missing, endpapers renewed. Tp inserted from anr copy, soiled, repaired & remargined; repair to next 7 leaves, mostly marginal; some soiling; map cut close, soiled & strengthened at inner margin; last leaf remargined & soiled; c.18 headlines shaved; marginal repairs towards end. STC 2216; Herbert 309. Newton-Doheny-Manney copy. P Oct 11 (19) $55,000

Anr copy. 17th-cent calf; backed with reversed calf, lacking clasps, worn. Black letter. Woodcut border to general title torn with loss; some stains & creases; small hole at A4 of NT, affecting text. Herbert 309; STC 2216. S July 21 (298) £17,500 [Finch]

— 1612. - L: Robert Barker. 2 parts in 1 vol. 4to, contemp calf; rebacked, fore-edges restored. Title trimmed. Herbert 312. DW Oct 2 (258) £120

— 1613. - L: Robert Barker. 2 parts in 1 vol. 4to, 18th-cent calf gilt; rebacked with orig spine laid down, rubbed. Black letter; double column; variant leaf of A4 bound in. Lower margin of B2 torn away just affecting text; small rusthole in FF6 touching a few letters; tear in FFF3 & UUU3 torn & repaired; upper margin of 2d title repaired; final leaf with small rustholes & tears repaired. Herbert 322; STC 2226. Chadwyck-Healey copy. C June 24 (102) £2,800 [Smith]

— 1613-11. - L: Robert Barker With "she" reading in Ruth III, 15. Folio, contemp calf; upper joint worn. Corner of map torn away with loss; OT tp backed; 3 leaves supplied from other copies or Eds. Herbert 319. b June 22 (71) £4,200

Anr copy. 19th-cent calf; rubbed, spine partly detached. Black lettter; double column Lacking 1st title (supplied in facsimile); inner margin of 1st 5 leaves restored; A1-2 torn & repaired; other minor tears, mostly repaired. Herbert 319; STC 2224. Chadwyck-Healey copy. C June 24 (101) £4,200 [Smith]

— 1616. - L: Robert Barker. Bound with: John Speed. The Genealogies recorded in the Sacred Scriptures. [n.p., n.d.] And: John Downame. A Concordance or Table to the Bible. L, 1639. Folio, cloth; worn, lacking backstrip. Lacking Apocrypha, corner torn from title; A4 def. STC 2244. bba Nov 28 (221) £130 [Aspin]

— 1617. - L: R. Barker. Folio, mor gilt by Bedford. Black letter; double-column. Lower margin of A2 restored; folding map trimmed; 1 leaf with rust-hole affecting 3 letters; minor marginal tears repaired. Herbert 353; STC 2245. C June 24 (103) £6,500 [Smith]

— 1630. - L. Bound with: contemp Eds of The Book of Common Prayer & Psalms, both incomplete. 4to, old sheep; worn, needs rebacking. Sold w.a.f. sg Oct 24 (32) $200

— 1630. - L: Robert Barker & John Bill. Bound with contemp editions of The Booke of Common Prayer & The Whole Booke of Psalms, incomplete at beginning & end, respectively. 4to, old sheep; worn, needs rebacking. Black letter. Margins trimmed, affecting some sidenotes; corners gnawed with occasional loss. Sold w.a.f. Herbert 430. sg Oct 24 (32) $200

— 1637. - Cambr. 4to, calf. Included Book of Common Prayer with tp & A2 def. Sold w.a.f. L Nov 14 (375) £200

Anr copy. Later bds; rebacked. pnE Dec 4 (12) £80

Anr copy. 3 parts in 1 vol. 4to, old lea; lacking catches & clasps, front free endpaper adhered to pastedown. Lacking NT tp & rear free endpaper. Herbert 513. sg Oct 24 (33) $250

— 1637. - Cambr.: Thomas Buck & Roger Daniel. Bound with: The Whole Book of Psalmes. Cambr., 1637. 3 parts in 1 vol. 4to, old lea; lacking catches & clasps, front free endpaper adhered to pastedown. Lacking NT title. Herbert 513. sg Oct 24 (32) $200

— 1640-39. - [Authorized version] L: R. Barker & the Assignes of John Bill. Folio, mor gilt by Bedford. Black letter; double column. First title remargined; some waterstaining; upper margin of last leaf repaired; marginal tears, mostly repaired. Herbert 543; STC 2339. C June 24 (104) £2,800 [Smith]

— 1648. - Cambr. 18mo, contemp tortoiseshell bdg with 4 gold hinges & gold clasp; spine repaired by lower hinge; lacking an inset shaped head of a king on upper cover. Herbert 612. C June 24 (109) £400 [Papper]

— 1660-59. - Cambr. 3 vols in 1. Folio, contemp calf; rubbed. Last few pp wormed in margin. Herbert 668. bba Apr 9 (73) £350 [Krown & Spellman]

Anr copy. 3 parts in 1 vol. Folio, contemp blind-stamped reversed calf; lower joint split, lower cover scuffed. Lacking map of Jerusalem; some worming to outer margins; minor marginal tears; some soiling. Herbert 668. Ck Sept 6 (74) £70

Anr copy. 2 vols. Folio, 19th-cent mor gilt; worn, Vol II loose in bdg & with spine split at joint. With engraved title, dedication & 113 double-page folding plates. Tears to 2 plates, anr plate def; some marginal fraying at folds; lacking title to 2d vol after Job. Sold w.a.f. Herbert 668. L Nov 14 (376) £950

Anr copy. 2 vols in 1. Folio, mor gilt with Royal Arms; rubbed, worn & split. Some repairs & tears; lacking tp to Vol II; front titles torn & loose. Herbert 668. pnE May 13 (205) £330

Anr copy. 2 vols. Folio, mor gilt; edges rubbed. Small hole to engraved title & Eden plate. Herbert 668. S July 1 (738) £700 [Tooley Adams]

— 1676. - L: Bill & Barker. 16mo, contemp mor gilt in "manner reminiscent of the Queen's Binders"; rubbed. Soiled & stained; a few leaves repaired or strengthened. Sold as a bdg. With Book of Common Prayer bound in. O Nov 26 (86) $500

— 1717-16. - ["Vinegar" Bible]. Oxford: John Baskett. 2 vols. Folio, 18th-cent mor gilt, armorial bdg; rubbed, some coloring added. Herbert 942. P June 17 (123) $3,250

Anr copy. 2 vols in 1. Folio, contemp mor gilt. Some leaves torn & repaired; last leaf def & repaired; additional title torn at inner margin. Herbert 942. S July 1 (939) £450 [Humber]

— 1723. - Oxford: John Baskett. 2 vols in 1. 4to, contemp English mor gilt; rebacked & repaired, orig spine laid down but head & foot torn. With engraved title 5 (of 6) folding maps & 127 plates. Flyleaves at front with copious fmaily notes; some fold tears. Sold w.a.f. pn Dec 12 (4) £85

— 1763. - Cambr.: Baskerville With list of subscribers in 3d State. Folio, contemp mor gilt; minor worming in upper cover, extremities worn. pn Sept 12 (17) £340 [Maggs]

— 1769-71. - Birm.: Baskerville. Folio, bds; rebcked in mor. With 10 plates.. LH May 17 (590) $100

— 1791. - Worcester, Mass.: Isaiah Thomas. 2 vols in 1. Folio, orig calf; rebacked in calf. First frontis worn & chipped; without Concordance. Herbert 1356. bbc June 29 (260) $210

— 1794. - A New Hieroglyphical Bible, for...Children.... Bost.: W. Norman. 1st American Ed. 8vo, orig bds; rubbed, spine lacking, tear to lower endpaper. bba July 23 (78) £90 [Stone]

— 1800. - L: Thomas Macklin. 6 vols. Folio, contemp mor gilt; rubbed. bba Jan 16 (200) £1,200 [Thorp]

Anr copy. 6 vols in 7. Folio, contemp calf gilt; rubbed, some hinges broken. bba Jan 30 (168) £480 [Bifolco]

— 1808. - Phila.: Jane Aitken. 4 vols. 8vo, orig bds, unopened; spines def. Some dampstains. D & M 1006. sg Dec 5 (11) $2,000

— 1867. - The Holy Scriptures. Plano 12mo, orig mor gilt; extremities rubbed. Some text underlinings by previous owner. sg June 18 (388) $650

— 1936. - [King James Version] NY 5 vols. sg Sept 26 (179) $50

— 1949. - Cleveland One of 975. Designed by Bruce Rogers. Folio, cloth. sg Nov 7 (22) $600

— The Apocalypse. San Francisco: Arion Press, 1982. One of 150. Illus by Jime Dine. Orig half pigskin. Schlosser copy. P June 17 (604) $3,000

— The Book of Esther. NY: Golden Cross Press, 1935. One of 135. Designed & illuminated by Angelo Valenti. Pigskin. pba July 23 (15) $200

— The Book of Tobit and the History of Susanna. L, 1929. One of 875. 4to, bds. With 4 colored plates by W. Russell Flint. sg Sept 26 (111) $60

— Ecclesiastes.... L, 1849. ("The Words of the Preacher.") Illus by Owen Jones. 4to, orig decorated wooden bds; rebacked, rubbed. With ornamental title & 33 pp of illuminated text by Jones, ptd in colors & gold. pn Dec 12 (63) £120

Anr Ed. NY: Spiral Press, 1965. One of 285. Illus by Ben Shahn. Folio, half vellum. sg Sept 26 (278) $175

Anr Ed. L: Trianon Press, 1967. ("Ecclesiastes, or, the Preacher.") One of 26 on arches grand velin with 2 orig lithos, an extra suite of plates & a series of progressive states of 1 plate. Mor gilt by Engel, Malakoff. P June 17 (360) $1,500

Anr Ed. Paris: Trianon Press, 1967. One of 200. 4to, orig mor. S Nov 14 (139) £290 [Stone]

— The First Tome or Volume of the Paraphrase of Erasmus upon the Newe Testamente. L: E. Whitchurche, 31 Jan 1548. 2 parts in 1 vol. Folio, 19th-cent calf; rubbed, rebacked. First Tome with some dampstaining, some headlines cropped, P3 & a2-4 def & lacking tp & final blank; Second Tome with some dampstaining & worming, part of St. John misbound, tp torn & repaired & mtd. Sold w.a.f. S Feb 25 (477) £1,500 [Lachman]

— Genesis. L: Riccardi Press, 1914. One of 500. Illus by F. Cayley Robinson. Half cloth. With 10 colored plates. O Jan 14 (162) $80

— The Gospels. Wash., 1930-34. One of 475. 4 vols. sg Sept 26 (27) $50

— A Harmonie upon the Three Evangelists, Matthew, Mark and Luke.... L, 1611. 2d Ed. 2 parts in 1 vol. 4to, orig calf; worn, front hinge starting, back cover detached. Lacking 1st 4 leaves, including tp. NH May 30 (454) $90

— The Parables from the Gospel. L: Vale Press, 1903. One of 310. Illus by Charles Ricketts. Orig vellum; soiled. bba July 9 (320) £280 [Collinge & Clark]

— The Sermon on the Mount. L, [1861]. Illus by W. & G. Audsley & Charles Rolt. 4to, half mor with ptd silk bds & endleaves; rubbed. With chromolitho frontis mtd on chromo-border & 26 leaves of chromolitho illusts. Schlosser copy. P June 18 (507) $600

Anr copy. Orig cloth; worn & soiled, hinges cracked. wa Sept 26 (565) $150

— The Song of Songs which is Solomon's. L, 1886. ("The Song of Songs.") One of 250. Illus by Bida. 4to, orig half mor; worn, joints cracked. cb Sept 26 (20) $110

Anr Ed. L: Circle Press, 1968. ("The Song of Solomon.") One of 15 artist's proofs. Illus by Ronald King. Folio, loose as issued in cloth. sg Sept 26 (28) $250

— The Story of the Exodus. Paris: Leon Amiel, 1966. One of 285. Illus by Marc Chagall. Folio, orig wraps. CNY May 11 (351) $1,500

Bible in French

See also: Francoise

— Le Cantique des cantiques. Paris, 1886. One of 10 on china with an additional impression of the frontis etching on velin. Illus by Alexandre Bida. Folio, mor extra with onlays in an Art Nouveau design by Marius Michel, from his early period. CNY Dec 5 (413) $26,000

Bible in German

— 1562. - Biblia; das ist, die gantze heilige Schrifft. Wittenberg: Hans Lufft. Folio, contemp bilnd-tooled pigskin over wooden bds; front cover detached with 1st several leaves adhered, lacking 6 brass cornerpieces & clasps. Marginal soiling; 1st 10 leaves remargined & repaired with loss; some other tears repaired; lacking general title, which has been replaced with facsimile from anr Ed; also lacking last prelim leaf & final blank. sg Oct 24 (34) $1,700

— 1630. - Sacra Biblia, das ist, die gantze H. Schrifft Alten und Newen Testament.... Cologne: Johann Creps. Folio, old tooled bdg with brass mts & clasps. D & M 4217 note. rs Oct 17 (99A) $700

— 1662. - Nuremberg Folio, contemp pigskin over wooden bds with metal fittings. With port of Luthor & 12 ports of dukes of Saxony, engraved table & armorial plate, 4 double-page maps & 2 plans & 14 full-page illusts. Some browning & spotting; some worming. B Nov 1 (505) HF1,500

— 1668. - Frankfurt: T. Falkeysen. 4 parts in 1 vol. Folio, contemp blind-panelled pigskin over oak bds with remnants of brass clasps; soiled & worn. With engraved architectural title, engraved double-page plan of Jerusalem & 3 double-page maps. 3 plates detached. Sold w.a.f. b June 22 (70) £220

— 1720. - Nuremberg Folio, contemp calf gilt over wooden bds with metal fittings. With engraved title, 12 ports, 6 double-page maps & plans, 29 plates & 1 double-page plate. Some foxing & spotting; 1 map with tear repaired. S May 28 (99) £4,8800 [Symonds]

— 1729. - Tuebingen Folio, lea. Heavily annotated. b&b Feb 19 (100) $175

— 1730. - Tuebingen: Cotta. 2 vols in 3. Folio, blindstamped lea over contemp wooden bds. Some spotting & staining. FD Dec 2 (46) DM1,300

— 1733. - Nuremberg Folio, contemp pigskin over wooden bds with brass fittings; Lacking 3 bosses & clasps, lea torn off rear cover, front hinge cracked. Small hole through last several leaves; last leaf loose. sg Oct 24 (35) $200

— 1775. - Das Neue Testament. Germantown: Christoph Sauer. 12mo, contemp calf. Minor dampstaining & browning. Evans 13837. sg Dec 5 (225) $275

— 1776. - ["Gun-Wad" Bible] Germantown, Pa.: Christoph Saur. 4to, contemp sheep; extremities rubbed, rear cover loose, lacking 2 hinges & both clasps. Tp loose & with tear into text; library markings. sg June 18 (486) $300

— Jesus Syrach, Spiegel der Hausszucht genandt.... Nuremberg: Dietrich Gerlach, 1571. Folio, contemp blind-tooled pigskin over wooden bds, with brass fittings; lacking 1 clasp, contemp notes on end-papers. sg Oct 24 (37) $550

Bible in Gothic & Anglo-Saxon

— [Gospels]. Dordrecht: Junianis, 1665. 2 parts in 1 vol. 4to, calf; rebacked. Some waterstaining. D & M 1604. B May 12 (1029) HF3,500

Bible in Greek

— 1545. - Basel: Hervagius. 2 parts in 1 vol. Folio, mor gilt by Bedford. A few leaves towards end with small tear repaired in outer margin. DM 4614. C June 24 (105) £600 [Waxman]

— 1550. - [Gospels] Venice: Andrea Spinelli. Folio, 16th-cent vellum; spine def. With 4 full-page woodcuts of the Evangelists. Lacking final blank; some fraying at end. S Dec 5 (60) £4,000 [Jackson]

— 1587. - Rome: Francisco Zanetti. Folio, 17th-cent mor gilt; joints split, lower headband torn. D & M 4647. Howe copy. C June 24 (268) £1,400 [Quaritch]

— 1624. - Kaine diatheke [New Testament]. Leiden: Elzevir. 12mo, late 18th-cent mor gilt; front cover starting. Tp browned. D & M 4669. sg Oct 24 (38) $120

— 1632. - [New Testament] Cambr.: Thomas & John Buck. 8vo, 18th-cent sheep; worn, needs rebacking. D & M 4678. sg Oct 24 (39) $175

— 1638. - [Geneva] 4to, contemp vellum; upper joint cracked. D & M 4958. S July 1 (514) £650 [Chelsea]

— 1653. - [Old Testament] L: Roger Daniel. 8vo, contemp calf. Some browning. SI Dec 5 (81) LIt240,000

— 1800. - Kaine diatheke [New Testament]. Wigorniae [Worcester], Mass.: Isaiah Thomas, Jr.. 12mo, lea; scuffed. D & M 4775. sp Nov 24 (99) $90

— The Four Gospels in the Original Greek. Oxford: Clarendon Press, 1932. 4to, orig half cloth. bba June 25 (7) £130 [Lehrer]

— [Gospels] Venice, 1847. 8vo, contemp silver bdg with 5 applied niello plaquettes. Sold as a bdg. S July 1 (523) £650 [D. Smith]

— Josua-Rolle. Graz: Akademische druck- und Verlagsanstalt, 1983. One of 700. Roll, 300mm by 10,040mm, laced to wooden rollers at either end in cloth display case with accompanying vol of explanatory text by otto Mazal. Facsimile of Codex Vaticanus palatinus graecus 431. sg Nov 7 (23) $1,400

Bible in Hawaiian

— 1860. - Ke Kauoha Hou. NY 12mo, mor; front cover loose. Judd 378. sg June 18 (283) $100

Bible in Hebrew

— 1543-46. - Paris: Estienne. Bound in 6 vols. 16mo, French red mor gilt fanfare bdg of c.1575; spines restored, several joints cracked. Catholic Univ. of America copy. St. 115. C June 24 (106) £21,000 [Litup]

— 1566. - Antwerp: Plantin. 2 vols. 8vo, later half mor; joints & extremities rubbed. With 63 plates. F Sept 26 (476) $160

— 1573-74. - Antwerp: Plantin. 8vo, old mor; worn. Some browning & soiling; a few leaves loose. St. 227, col. 39. S Feb 25 (480) £280 [Landau]

— 1587. - Hamburg: Johann Saxo. Folio, modern mor. Lacking 5 prelim leaves; repaired at beginning & end with some loss; wormed; portion of 3I1 torn away with loss. S July 1 (1057) £500 [Granader]

— 1700-5. - Amst.: David Nunes Torres & Immanuel Athias. 2 vols. 12mo, contemp calf extra; spine cracked, front cover loose. Browned. D & M 5140. sg Dec 19 (30) $375

— 1720. - Halle Ed by Johann Heinrich Michaelis. 2 vols. 8vo, old bds; broken, spine gone. Some foxing. D & M 5144. O May 26 (14) $250

Bible in Hebrew & Greek

— 1584. - Antwerp: Plantin. 3 parts in one vol. Folio, contemp Antwerp calf gilt with F. M. monogram; rebacked, extremities rubbed, later endpapers. OT with hebrew & roman type; NT with greek & roman type. D & M 5106 & 4645. C June 24 (267) £600 [Speeckaert]

Bible in Italian

— 1937. - La Bibbia di Borso d'Este. Milan One of 500. Ed by Giovanni Treccani & Adolfo Venturi. 2 vols. Folio, orig calf with metal fittings; rubbed. SI Dec 5 (82) LIt700,000

— 1961. - La Bibblia di Borso d'Este. Bergamo: Banco Popolare. 2 vols. Folio, mor gilt extra with metal plaque of Este arms on front cover. With reproductions of the orig Ms leaves. sg Nov 7 (24) $600

Bible in Latin

— c.1459-60. - Biblia Latina. Bamberg: Ptr of the 36-line Bible (Albrecht Pfister). Folio, mor gilt by Charles Hering. 36 lines; gothic textura quadrata type 1. Rubricated by 2 hands. 480 (of 884) leaves; lacking quires 28-45 (now part of John Rylands Library set), quires 46-67 (lost) & folios 89/5-6 (blanks cancelled by a binder). GKW 4202. Liverpool copy. C Nov 27 (50) £1,000,000 [Kraus]

— [c.1473]. - Strassburg: R-Press type 1. Folio, contemp blind-stamped calf over wooden bds, with 2 brass fore-edge clasps & remains of lea index tabs; rebacked in the 18th cent. 56 lines, type 1:103R, double column. Some minor staining. 425 (of 426) leaves; lacking initial blank. Goff B-534. Doheny-Schoyen copy. P Dec 12 (6) $29,000

— 1478, 14 Apr. - Nuremberg: Anton

Koberger. Folio, contemp blind-stamped pigskin over wooden bds, with 2 fore-edge brass clasps, brass bosses, a large drawing of a rosette on each edge, remains of tawed lea index tabs, an Amorbach bdg, using the name stamp of the monastery; upper hinge split but firm. 51 lines & headline; double column; types 3:110G (text) & 4:160G (headline, incipits of chapters); rubricated. First leaf loose; green stains on the outside of sheet 7/2.9. 468 leaves. Goff B-557. Doheny-Schoyen copy. P Dec 12 (7) $16,000

— 1479. - Venice: Nicolaus Jenson. Folio, modern mor gilt. 51 lines & headline; double column; types 8:93G (text), 7:150G (headlines & book incipits); & 9:50G (guide letters); rubricated; illuminated with a miniature of the creation of Eve on a5r; book initials on gilt grounds in magenta, green & blue with border extensions including gold dotting; initial for Jerome's first prologue historiated with port, & for the 4 Gospels with the Evangelist symbols. First 8 leaves on guards; restorations & repaired tears at lower margins of ff. 1-3; clean tear repaired on I10; repaired tear on E7 affecting a few letters; minor wormholes; waterstaining to inner & lower margins of some quires. 451 (of 452) leaves; lackling initial blank. Goff B-563. General Theological Seminary—Schoyen copy. P Dec 12 (8) $11,000

Anr copy. 19th-cent mor gilt in cathedral style; rubbed. 51 lines, double column, gothic letter. Repairs & soiling; some staining. 451 (of 452) leaves; lacking 1st blank. Goff B-563. SI June 9 (138) LIt5,000,000

— not after 1480. - Strassburg: Adolf Rusch for Anton Koberger. Vol III (of 4). Folio, contemp blindstamped pigskin over wooden bds, with brass fore-edge clasps, an Eichstaett bdg (Kyriss shop 175). 73 lines & headline; double column; types 2:106G (text, commentary incipits), 3:92G (commentary), 1:180G (headlines, text incipits), 4:68G (interlinear commentary. Some staining. 340 leaves. Part of Goff B-607. Schoyen copy. P Dec 12 (11) $3,500

— 1482, 31 Dec. - Nuremberg: Anton Koberger. Folio, 15th-cent blindstamped pigskin over wooden bds; lacking 1 clasp. 53 lines & headline; double column; gothic letter; rubricated. First leaf remargined; other marginal repairs; some leaves with damage to edge of text; 1 leaf with repaired tear. 460 (of 462) leaves; lacking fol. VII & initial blank. Goff B-575. S Dec 5 (8) £1,600 [Aspin]

— 1486. - [Basel: Johann Amerbach]. Folio, 18th-cent sheep; abraded. 48 lines & headlines; double column; types 3B:92G (text), 10:82G (Interpretationes), & 1:185G (headlines & book incipits); rubricated. Worming at ends, rather heavy in final quire; stain in upper corner of 1st dozen leaves; stain in outer margin of the Interpretations; 7 leaves in the Apocalypse & Index of Lessons with loss from outer margin, affecting a number of ptd marginalia. 536 (of 538) leaves; lacking initial & final blanks. Goff B-581. Schoyen copy. P Dec 12 (10) $2,250

— 1487, 3 Dec. - Nuremberg: Anton Koberger. Parts I & II (of 4) in 2 vols. Folio, later pigskin over bds with central panel port of Martin Luther on upper cover & port of Philip Melanchthon on lower cover; worn. Library markings. Some staining & worming; corrosion in gutter of first leaf in Part II with slight loss. 467 (of 468) leaves, lacking 1st blank in Part I. Goff B-614. O Nov 26 (23) $2,800

— 1489, 8 Aug. - Venice: [Bonetus Locatellus for] Octavianus Scotus. 4 vols. Folio, 17th-cent vellum. 74 lines & headline; double column; types 4:92G (text), 1:74G (commentary), 2:130G (headlines), some Roman capitals in commentary; 3 woodcut historiated initials; 47 woodcuts; rubricated, colored & illuminated; Creation cut & 2 historiated initials hand-colored; frontis page of each vol illuminated with floral border in colors & gilt, incorporating at foot of each a Sibyl port. Extensive wormhole in 1st leaves of Vol I, touching a portion of the border & with considerable textual loss; single wormholes at front & back of Vol II & front of Vol III; stain in upper corner of 1st leaves of Vol IV, affecting border; some browning & staining. 1,106 (of 1,107) leaves; lacking initial blank in Vol I. Goff B-616. Schoyen copy. P Dec 12 (12) $12,000

— 1491, 27 June. - Basel: Johann Froben. 8vo, 19th-cent mor over wooden bds with metal clasp & catch. Double column; 56 lines & headline; gothic letter; initials supplied in red & blue. First few leaves stained in foremargin; some other small stains; small wormhole in final leaf repaired with minimal loss. 495 (of 496) leaves; lacking 2 blanks. Goff B-592. S May 28 (16) £3,000 [Franklin]

— 1493. - Nuremberg: Anton Koberger. Part IV (of 4). Folio, contemp calf over wooden bds; worn. 71 lines & headline; double column; gothic letter; initials & paragraph-marks supplied in red. Some worming & staining; first & last few leaves frayed; 1 leaf torn. 350 (of 352) leaves; lacking a4 & final blank. Goff B-618. S May 13 (742) £380 [Aspin]

— 1497, 6 Sept. - Biblia com postillis Nicolai de Lyra.... Nuremberg: Anton Koberger. 4 vols. Folio, contemp Nuremberg bdg of blind-stamped calf over wooden bds; worn & torn, lacking clasps & catches. 58 lines & headline; double-column; gothic letter; initials supplied in red & blue. Portions of margins of Ac5 & Bg8 of Vol I torn away with small loss in 1 case; tear in Dv8 of Vol II; small stain on ii7r of Vol IV, obscuring some text; some worming at beginning & end of each vol; some browning & staining; early Ms annotations in margins. 1,432 leaves. Goff B-619. S Dec 5 (10) £2,500

— 1498, 8 May. - Venice: Simon Bevilaqua. 4to, old vellum; soiled & repaired. 51 lines & headline; double column; types 4,10:130G, 19:107R, 21:85G, 20:63G; woodcut floral black on white & historiated initials; with 72 woodcut illusts, including 1 half-page & 1 full-page. B1 torn in half but repaired with upper outer corner of half-page woodcut supplied in Ms facsimile; bb5 holed at inner margin; v2 & X8 with small hole affecting 1 or 2 characters. 528 leaves. Goff B-603. C Dec 16 (102) £1,700 [Bifolco]

— 1522. - Lyons: Jacob Sacon for A. Koberger. Folio, 18th-cent bds; worn. Wormed throughout; some staining & soiling. Sold w.a.f. O Nov 26 (21) $550

Anr copy. Some worming & staining. Lacking 2 leaves. Sold w.a.f. O Jan 14 (19) $160

— 1526. - Lyons: Jacobum Mareschal als Roland. 8vo, vellum; rebacked, hinges & joints split. Lacking pp 241-48 & 250-53. Waterstained & browned throughout. Sold w.a.f. bba Oct 24 (3) £240 [Royston]

— 1565. - Antwerp: C. Plantin. 8vo, later calf; upper joint cracked, spine ends chipped, metal clasps. Earlier leaves with Ms annotations in margins. S July 1 (1059) £150 [Bentley]

— 1573. - Paris: Nicolaus Brusle for Sebastian Nivellius. Folio, later half calf. A few pp def. Darlow & Moule 6158. bba Feb 27 (321) £120 [Bifolco]

— 1578. - Venice 4to, 19th-cent cloth; spine faded. Remains of woodcut title relaid. Spotted & soiled. DW Nov 6 (433) £60

— 1593. - Testamenti Veteris Biblia Sacra, sive, Libri Canonici.... L. Folio, 18th-cent mor gilt; rubbed. Lacking final blanks to Parts 1 & 6; some soiling or dampstaining; a few rust-holes & tears; some contemp marginalia. STC 2061.5; D & M 6185. C Dec 16 (103) £380 [Sokol]

— 1608. - Venice: E. Deuchinum & J. B. Pulciani. 4to, old half calf; worn. Tp repaired on verso along lower edge; minor stains & soiling. O July 14 (27) $120

— 1629. - Biblia Sacra. Antwerp 16mo, old sheep; worn, rear joint cracked. sg Mar 12 (25) $50

— 1645. - Antwerp: Plantin. 8vo, calf over bds with metal fittings & remnants of clasps; worn. First few leaves with some stains & soiling. O May 26 (13) $250

— 1748. - Venice 2 vols. Folio, old vellum. With frontis in Vol I. sg Oct 24 (40) $110

— 1961. - Paterson & NY: Pageant Books One of 1,000. 2 vols. Folio, orig mor; Vol I spine scraped. Facsimile of the Gutenberg Bible of c.1450-55. sg Oct 31 (146) $800

— The Lorsch Gospels. NY, [1967]. Ltd. Folio, half vellum. sg Oct 31 (232) $150

One of 1,000. Half vellum. sg May 21 (275) $110

Out-of-series copy. Half vellum. K Dec 1 (282) $160

Bible in Latin & English

— 1538. - Newe Testament both Latine and Englyshe.... Southwarke: James Nicolson. 2d 4to Ed of Coverdale's Diglot New Testament, 2d Issue. 4to, 19th-cent mor gilt; extremities rubbed. Roman type & black letter. Lacking tp, following 5 & last 2 leaves (supplied in facsimile); some leaves remargined; Aa1 & some other leaves torn & repaired; occasional stains. STC 2816.7; Herbert 38. S July 21 (303) £1,500 [Smith]

Bible in Malayan

— 1677. - Jang ampat Evangelia.... Oxford: H. Hall. 4to, contemp sheep; worn, needs rebacking. Lacking tp & dedication. D & M 6492. sg Mar 12 (23) $60

Bible in Old Church Slavonic

— 1581. - Biblia sirech' knigy vetxavo i novago saveta, po jazyku slovensku. Ostog: Ivan Theodorov Issue with colophon dated 12 Aug 1581. Folio, 19th-cent half sheep; extremities rubbed. Some marginal soiling & stains; repaired wormholes with small loss; tp in facsimile; prelims frayed & inlaid to size with occasional minor loss; c.12 leaves supplied in Ms; 2d leaf in 2d part supplied from shorter copy; lacking some leaves. D & M 8370. sg Oct 24 (41) $12,000

Bible in Slavonic

— 1692. - Psaltyr i Novyi zavet. Kiev: Monastery of the Caves. 4to, contemp calf with gilt Crucifixion plaque on both cover & cornerpieces depicting the evangelists on front cover. Some soiling & repairs, causing slight text loss on 2 leaves. sg Nov 7 (188) $2,800

Bible in Spanish

— 1569, Sept. - [Basel: S. Apairius for Thomas Guarinus]. 1st Ed of complete Bible in Spanish. 3 parts in 1 vol. 4to, old calf with initials TH stamped in gilt on both covers; rebacked, new endpapers. Stain on tp; minor worming. D & M 8472. S May 28 (35) £1,200 [Polido]

— 1602. - Amst.: Lorenco Jacobi. 3 parts in 1 vol. Folio, later calf. Without the leaf of address sometimes inserted after title; some browning & spotting throughout; dampstaining at beginning & end. S May 28 (74) £700 [Montero]

Bible in Syriac

— 1555. - [New Testament] Vienna: Michael Cymbermannus 1st Issue, with 1st 4 lines of Syriac title ptd in red with vowel points in black. 4to, old calf; worn, bumped. D & M 8947. S Nov 21 (290) £3,400 [Quaritch]

— 1664-67. - Hamburg 3 parts in 1 vol. 8vo, contemp vellum; soiled. In Peshitta letters. D & M 8966(d). bba Jan 16 (204) £90 [Loman]

Bible in Welsh

— 1588. - Y Beibl Cyssegr-lan. L: deputies of Christopher Barker. Folio, old calf; worn, rebacked, recornered & repaired. Lacking general title & 5 following leaves, A1-2, G6, 3Y1-4C6, 4E3-4F2 & all after 4Z1, all supplied in facsimile; tears & repairs; stained. Sold w.a.f. S July 21 (299) £900 [Smith]

Bible, Polyglot

— 1599. - Biblia Sacra, Ebraice, Chaldaice, Graece, Latine, Germanice, Italice.... Nuremberg Folio, contemp vellum; front joint restored. D & M 1427. sg May 7 (27) $1,200

Bibliander, Theodorus

— De fatis monarchiae Romanae somnium vaticinium Esdrae prophetae. Basel, [1553]. Bound with: Ad illustrissimos Germaniae principes.... Basel, 1553. 4to, contemp blind-tooled sheep over pastebd; spine & corners worn. Traces of mold at end of 2d work. sg Oct 24 (42) $700

Bibliographica...

— Bibliographica: Papers on Books, their History and Art. L, 1895-97. 12 parts in 3 vols. 8vo, contemp half mor, orig wraps bound in. cb Oct 17 (78) $350

Anr copy. 12 parts. 8vo, orig wraps; Part 1 split at spine & rear wrap detached. cb Jan 16 (16) $325

Facsimile reprint of 1895-97 Ed. Westport, [1970]. 12 parts in 3 vols. cb Feb 27 (15) $90

Bibliographical Society of the University of Virginia

— Studies in Bibliography. Charlottesville, 1948-75. Vols 1-28. Vols I-III, wraps; others, cloth or bds. O Sept 24 (237) $170

Vols 1-44, but with 16 of first 19 vols reissues. Charlottesville, 1948-76. bba Apr 30 (373) £80 [Makrocki]

Bibliophile...

— Le Bibliophile francais. Gazette illustree des amateurs de livres. Paris, 1868. Vols I-II. 2 vols. 8vo, contemp half mor. Some foxing. SI Dec 5 (84) LIt360,000

Biblioteca Casanatense, Rome

— Catalogo dei Manoscritti della Biblioteca Casanatense. Rome, 1949-58. 5 vols in 1. 4to, new cloth, orig front wraps bound in. sg Oct 31 (249) $250

Bibliotheque Nationale

— Les Plus Belles Reliures.... Paris, 1929. One of 20 on japon imperiale. Folio, mor gilt by Halpin-Weitz, orig wraps preserved. With 42 plates. CNY Dec 5 (400) $1,600

Bickel, Karl A.

— The Mangrove Coast.... NY, [1942]. Illus by Walker Evans. Cloth, in d/j. With 32 plates. sp Feb 6 (352) $110

Bickham, George, the Elder, d.1769

— The Musical Entertainer. L: Charles Corbett, [c.1739]. 2 vols in 1. Folio, later half calf. With engraved title & table of songs in each vol, plus 200 plates of music. First engraved title laid down; first table of contents with small repair to lower corner; some soiling. W July 8 (3) £960

Bidpay

— La moral filosophia del Doni.... Venice: Francesco Marcolini, 1552. 2 parts in 1 vol. 4to, contemp vellum. With 38 woodcuts. Small wormhole in last few leaves. S Dec 5 (62) £2,800 [Quaritch]

Biel, Gabriel, 1425?-95

— Sacri canonis misse Expositio.... Tuebingen: [Johann Otmar for Friedrich Meynberger, 29 Nov] 1499. Folio, contemp pigskin over wooden bds with remains of clasps. 53 lines & headline, double column, types 12:75G (text), 10:76G (headings), 7:170G (titling); 1 woodcut. Early annotations; waterstain on final leaf. 334 leaves. Goff B-660. Schoyen copy. P Dec 12 (14) $5,500

Bierbaum, Otto Julius

— Das schoene Maedchen von Pao. Munich, 1910. One of 600. Illus by Franz von Bayros. Folio, orig mor. With 7 lithos. HH May 12 (2147) DM1,000

Bierce, Ambrose, 1842?-1914
See also: Limited Editions Club

— Battle Sketches. Oxford: Shakespeare Head Press, 1930. One of 350. Illus by Thomas Derrick. 4to, orig vellum. Some spotting. bba July 9 (250) £55 [Deighton Bell]

— Black Beetles in Amber. San Francisco, 1892. 1st Ed. 8vo, orig cloth; spine darkened, soiled. cb Dec 8 (9) $100

— Cobwebs from an Empty Skull. L & NY, 1874. 12mo, cloth; spine split from joint; some discoloration. cb Dec 12 (10) $50

— The Cynic's Word Book. NY, 1906. 1st Ed, 1st Issue, without frontis. cb Dec 12 (11) $90

— The Dance of Death. By William Herman. San Francisco: Henry Keller, 1877. 2d Ed. Cloth; worn, corners bumped. cb Dec 12 (12) $110

— The Fiend's Delight. L: John Camden Hotten, [1873]. 8vo, orig cloth; hinges cracked. Epstein copy. sg Apr 29 (31) $550

— A Horseman in the Sky.... San Francisco: John Henry Nash, 1920. One of 400. Half cloth. cb Jan 16 (17) $110

— The Letters.... San Francisco: Book Club of California, 1922. One of 415. Half cloth. cb Jan 16 (18) $110

— The Shadow on the Dial.... San Francisco, 1909. Endpapers discolored. cb Sept 19 (12) $80; cb Dec 12 (17) $70

— A Son of the Gods.... San Francisco: Paul Elder, [1907]. One of 1,000. Half vellum, in d/j. cb Dec 12 (18) $55

Bierce, Ambrose, 1842?-1914 —& Danziger, G. A.

— The Monk and the Hangman's Daughter. Chicago: F. J. Schulte, 1892. 8vo, cloth; discolored. cb Dec 12 (15) $225

Bigelow, Horatio. See: Derrydale Press

Bigelow, Jacob, 1787-1879

— American Medical Botany.... Bost., 1817-18-20. 3 vols. 8vo, disbound. With 60 hand-colored plates. Occasional worming. cb Feb 12 (13) $1,800

Bigges, Walter. See: Drake, Sir Francis

Bigmore, Edward Clements —& Wyman, Charles William Henry

— A Bibliography of Printing. NY, 1945. 3 vols in 2. Worn. Facsimile of the 1880-86 Ed. O Sept 24 (33) $70; O Dec 17 (22) $60; wa Mar 5 (132) $65

Bilder...

— Bilder zum Anschauungs-Unterricht fuer die Jugend. Esslingen, 1873. 2 vols in 1. 4to, disbound. With 30 color plates. Met Apr 28 (567) $80

Bildermann....

— Der Bildermann. Berlin: Paul Cassirer, 1916. Nos 1-18. 4to, contemp half vellum; worn. With 8 single-leaf songsheets & 10 supplementary leaves. S Feb 11 (249) £1,700 [Ursus]

Billings, John D.

— Hardtack and Coffee, or the Unwritten Story of Army Life. Bost., 1887. 8vo, cloth; shaken. K Mar 22 (76) $60

Billings, Robert William, 1813-74

— The Baronial and Ecclesiastical Antiquities of Scotland. Edin. & L, [1848-52]. 4 vols. 4to, contemp half calf; worn. With 240 plates. Titles stamped. DW Apr 8 (83) £85

Anr copy. Orig bds; rebacked. pnE May 13 (58) £180

Anr copy. Calf. With 240 plates. pnE Aug 12 (50) £130

Bilson, Thomas

— The Perpetual Government of Christes Church. L: Deputies of Christopher Barker, 1593. 1st Ed. 4to, later calf; rubbed, rebacked. Stained; corner torn from 2 leaves. bba Dec 19 (339) £80 [Hilton]

Anr copy. Calf. Margins trimmed, affecting some sidenotes; some marginal dampstaining; tp soiled, with blank upper margin restored. STC 3065. sg Oct 24 (43) $275

Bing, Samuel, 1838-1905

— Le Japon artistique. Paris, [1888]. 36 parts. Folio, orig half cloth; joints strengthened. bba Mar 26 (87) £160 [Wood]

Bingham, Hiram, 1789-1869

— A Residence of Twenty-One Years in the Sandwich Islands.... Hartford & NY, 1847. 1st Ed. 8vo, modern cloth; spine repaired. With folding map & 6 plates. sp Feb 6 (419) $90

2d Ed. Hartford & NY, 1848. 8vo, orig cloth. sg June 18 (273) $80

Bingley, William, 1774-1823

— A Tour Round North Wales.... L, 1800. 1st Ed. 2 vols. 8vo, 19th-cent cloth; faded. bba Sept 5 (9) £55 [Hay Cinema]

Binns, W. Moore

— The First Century of English Porcelain. L, 1906. One of 100. 4to, orig cloth; worn. Library markings. sg Feb 6 (15) $150

Binyon, Laurence, 1869-1943
See also: Eumorfopoulos Collection, George

— The Art of Botticelli. L, 1913. One of 275. Folio, mor gilt. With sgd frontis by Muirhead Bone & 23 colored plates. Sgd. sp Nov 24 (251) $400

— The Drawings and Engravings of William Blake. L, 1922. Folio, half vellum; rubbed & soiled. bba Dec 19 (29) £60 [Kurita]

— The Engraved Designs of William Blake. L & NY, 1926. 4to, half cloth; extremities worn. sg Feb 6 (27) $80

Anr copy. Orig half cloth; spine soiled. Some foxing. wa Dec 9 (494) $60

— The Wonder Night. NY: Rudge, 1927. One of 27. Illus by Barnett Freedman. Orig wraps. Ariel Poem No. 3. sg June 11 (20) $60

Binyon, Laurence, 1869-1943 —& Sexton, J. J. O'Brien

— Japanese Colour Prints. L, 1923. 4to, cloth, in d/j. With 16 colored plates. kh Nov 11 (47) A$220

Biographia...

— Biographia Britannica: or, the Lives of the most Eminent Persons.... L, 1747-66. 6 vols. Folio, contemp calf; rubbed, joints broken. O July 14 (30) $300

Biographie...

— Biographie universelle, ancienne et moderne. Paris, 1811-28. Vols 1-52. Ed by J. F. Michaud. 8vo, contemp calf gilt. Ck July 10 (192) £380

Biologia...

— Biologia Centrali-Americana: Contributions to the Knowledge of the Fauna and Flora of Mexico and Central America. L, 1879-1901. Pisces. 4to, modern half mor. With 26 plates. bba Sept 5 (100) £770 [R. & G. Way]

Bion, Nicolas, 1652?-1733

— The Construction and Principal Uses of Mathematical Instruments. L, 1723. 1st Ed in English. Trans by Edmund Stone. Folio, contemp sheep; rubbed, joints cracked. With 25 (of 26) folding plates. Some browning. sg May 14 (265) $600

— Traite de la construction et des principaux usages des instrumens de mathematique. Paris, 1752. 4th Ed. 4to, contemp calf. With frontis, port & 37 folding plates. 1 plate torn. bba Sept 5 (190) £320 [Rogers Turner]

Birago, Francesco

— Cavalleresche decisioni. Milan, 1637. 8vo, old vellum. sg Mar 26 (41) $275

Birch, A. G.

— The Moon Terror and Other Stories.... Indianapolis: Popular Fiction Co., [1927]. In chipped d/j. sg June 11 (21) $110

Birch, Thomas, 1705-66

— The Heads of Illustrious Persons of Great Britain.... L, 1743-51. 1st Ed. 2 vols. Contemp mor & half mor; worn. DW Oct 2 (261) £250

Anr Ed. L, 1747-52. 2 vols in 1. Folio, early 19th-cent mor gilt; extremities rubbed, spine discolored. Ck July 10 (186) £550

Birch, William, 1755-1834

— The Country Seats of the United States.... Springfield PA, 1808 [1809]. Oblong 4to, half sheep; worn. With 20 hand-colored views. Some foxing & staining; marginal tears in 2 leaves. P June 16 (196) $18,000

— Delices de la Grande Bretagne. L, 1791. Oblong 4to, contemp mor gilt. With 36 plates. W July 8 (200) £360

Birkbeck, Morris, 1764-1825

— Notes on a Journey in America. L: James Ridgway, 1818. Bound with: Letters from Illinois. L, 1818. 2 vols in 1. 8vo, old bds; rebacked in mor. cb Oct 10 (8) $65

Anr copy. 8vo, modern half mor. With folding map with outlines hand-colored & with 4 pages of ads not mentioned in Howes. wd June 12 (368) $150

Birken, Sigmund von

— Der Donau-Strand. Nuremberg, 1674. 12mo, modern half vellum. With 26 plates. sg Jan 9 (33) $325

Birrell, Augustine, 1850-1933

— Frederick Locker-Lampson; a Character Sketch.... NY, 1920. wa Mar 5 (127) $50

Bischoff, James, 1776-1845

— Sketch of the History of Van Diemen's Land. L, 1832. 8vo, contemp half calf. With engraved frontis & view of Emu Bay (both foxed) & folding map hand-colored in outline. S June 25 (126) £550 [Koch]

Bischoff, Jan de. See: Episcopius, Johannes

Bishop Collection, Cortlandt Field

— [Sale Catalogue] Library: Parts 1-4. NY, 1938-39. 4 parts in 2 vols. 4to, cloth. Priced in margins. O Sept 24 (34) $50

Bishop, George, d.1668

— New-England Judged...Sufferings of the People call'd Quakers in New-England. L, 1702-3. 2 parts in 1 vol. 8vo, lea; bdg tape-repaired. sp Nov 24 (104) $175

Bishop, Richard Evett

— Bishop's Birds. Phila., 1936. One of 1,050. 4to, cloth; worn. With 73 plates. F Sept 26 (325) $150

— Bishop's Wildfowl. St. Paul, 1948. 4to, lea. bbc Apr 27 (506) $65; K Dec 1 (44) $90

Bisschop, Jan de. See: Episcopius, Johannes

Bisset, James

— Bisset's Magnificent Guide, or Grand Copperplate Directory, for the Town of Birmingham. Birm., 1808. 8vo, orig bds; joints & hinges cracked, some wear at extremities. With 51 plates. sg Mar 5 (17) $750

Bitting, Katherine Golden

— Gastronomic Bibliography. San Francisco, 1939. Spine faded. sg Oct 31 (29) $225

Anr Ed. San Francisco, 1981. Reprint of 1939 Ed. bbc Apr 27 (217) $75

Anr copy. In d/j. Reprint of 1939 Ed. O Dec 17 (23) $50

Bivero, Pedro de

— Sacrum oratorium piarum imaginum immaculatae Mariea et animae creatae.... Antwerp: Plantin, 1634. 4to, contemp lea gilt. With engraved title & 58 plates. HH May 12 (879) DM2,200

Bizarri, Pietro

— Cyprium Bellum.... [Basel: S. Henricpetri, 1573]. Bound with: Pannonicum bellum, sub Maximiliano II. Basel, [1573] And: Geuffroy, Antoine. Aulae Turcicae.... Basel, [1573. 8v, contemp vellum. S Nov 21 (241) £3,000 [Christodolou]

Bizot, Pierre, 1630-96

— Histoire metallique de la Republique de Hollande. Paris, 1687. Folio, contemp calf; spine worn. DW Dec 11 (260) £55

Anr Ed. Amst., 1688. 8vo, vellum. pnE Oct 2 (588) £85

Anr Ed. Paris, 1788. Folio, contemp calf; rubbed. F Mar 26 (771) $120

Blaauw, Frans Ernst

— A Monograph of the Cranes. Leiden & L, 1897. One of 170. Folio, orig cloth; rubbed. With 22 colored plates. C May 20 (145) £3,200 [Marshall]

Anr copy. Orig cloth; extremities and hinges rubbed. CNY Dec 5 (288) $4,200; S Nov 21 (1) £3,500 [Forum Antiq.]

Black, Adam & Charles

— General Atlas of the World. Edin. & L, 1844. Folio, contemp half mor. With 61 colored maps. DW Nov 6 (20) £150

Blacker, J. F. See: Gorer & Blacker

Blacker, William

— Art of Angling, and Complete System of Fly-Making. L, Mar 1842. 1st Ed. 16mo, orig lea; rubbed. With engraved title & 2 plates. Sgd. Koopman copy. O Oct 29 (37) $1,600

Anr Ed. L, 1855. ("Art of Fly Making....") 12mo, contemp half calf gilt; rubbed. With engraved title & 20 plates of flies, all but 3 hand-colored. Koopman copy. O Oct 29 (34) $950

Anr copy. Orig cloth; worn, spine frayed. With engraved title & 20 uncolored plates of flies. Koopman copy. O Oct 29 (35) $400

Anr copy. Lea; rubbed. With engraved title & 16 plates of flies, all but 3 hand-colored. Koopman copy. O Oct 29 (36) $500

Blackmore, John

— Views on the Newcastle and Carlisle Railway. Newcastle, 1837 [engraved title dated 1836]. 4to, orig cloth; ends of spine restored. With engraved title & 23 plates. DW Apr 8 (84) £270

Blackmore, Richard Doddridge, 1825-1900

— Lorna Doone. L, 1869. 1st Ed. 3 vols. 8vo, orig cloth; spines & corners worn. Epstein copy. sg Apr 29 (34) $1,800

Blackstone, Sir William, 1723-80

— Commentaries on the Laws of England. Oxford, 1765-69. 1st Ed. 4 vols. 4to, 19th-cent russia; rebacked, rubbed, some chipping. Underlining in red on pp. 40-43 in Vol I; some pencil & ink markings, generally marginal; lacking final blank in Vol I; some staining & browning. P Dec 12 (14) $7,000

Anr copy. Early 19th-cent calf; spines rebacked. Vol III marginaly dampstained in front. Epstein copy. sg Apr 29 (35) $8,500

Mixed Ed. 4 vols. 4to, contemp calf; joints cracked, scuffed. LH Dec 11 (68) $1,300

Vols I & II, 2d Ed; Vols III & IV, 1st Ed. Oxford, 1766-67-68-69. 4 vols. 4to, contemp calf; rubbed, joints broken. Marginal worming in Vol II. O Nov 26 (24) $1,200

4th Ed. Oxford, 1770. 4 vols. 4to, early calf; joints repaired, worn. Dampstain through lower portion of all vols. bbc June 29 (278) $330

Anr copy. Contemp calf; spines worn, backstrips loose, joints cracked or split. Dampstained in lower portion of letterpress, more so in Vols I & IV. wa Mar 5 (527) $325

7th Ed. Oxford, 1775. 4 vols. 8vo, contemp calf; rubbed, joints splitting. bba Jan 16 (3) £80 [J. Rees]

Blackwall, John, 1790-1881

— A History of the Spiders of Great Britain and Ireland. L, 1861. Bound in 2 vols. Folio, modern half mor. With 29 hand-colored plates. pn July 16 (141) £100 [Proctor]

Blackwell, Elizabeth, c.1700-58

— A Curious Herbal. L, 1739. Vol I (of 2) only. Folio, old calf; worn, broken. With 198 plates. Lacking many plates & some portions of text. Some plates sliced into 3 horizontal portions. O Jan 14 (22) $1,850

Blackwell, Henry

— The English Fencing-Master.... L, 1702. 8vo, modern half calf. Tp soiled; hole in each of 2 final leaves, causing loss of 3 words of text; lacking leaf B3. sg Mar 26 (44) $375

Blackwood, Algernon

— Day and Night Stories. L, [1917]. In d/j. sg June 11 (22) $600

— Tales of the Uncanny and Supernatural. L, [1949]. In d/j with edge wear. Sgd. sg June 11 (24) $80

Blackwood, Lady Alicia

— Scutari, the Bosphorus and the Crimea. Ventnor, Isle of Wight, 1857. 2 vols. Folio, orig wraps; Vol II lacking lower cover. With 2 pictorial litho titles & 19 litho plates. A few plates frayed. bba Oct 24 (306) £440 [Demetzy]

Anr copy. With 2 tinted litho titles & 19 tinted plates. Some margins scuffed. S July 1 (551) £400 [Gonul]

Blades, William, 1824-90

— The Biography and Typography of William Caxton, England's First Printer. L & Strassburg, 1877. 1st Ed. 8vo, orig cloth; spine chipped. cb Jan 16 (21) $110

— A Catalogue of Books Printed by...William Caxton. L, 1865. 4to, contemp calf relievo bdg, the upper cover with a panel of brown calf molded & pressed to a design of a woodsman carrying firewood. CNY Dec 5 (423) $850

— The Life and Typography of William Caxton. L, 1861-63. 2 vols. 4to, later cloth. Some spotting. sg May 21 (243) $175

Blaes, Gerhard. See: Blasius, Gerardus

Blaeu, Willem, 1571-1638

— Institution astronomique de l'usage des globes et sphere celestes et terrestres. Amst., 1642. 4to, contemp vellum. Dampstaining in upper margins. sg May 14 (266) $650

— The Light of Navigation.... Amst., 1612. 3 parts in 1 vol. 4to, old half sheep; worn. With 2 working volvelles & 41 double-page charts. Clean tear in 1st D3; 2d volvelle loose; charts trimmed near or to platemarks; some dampstaining in upper margin; lacking general title & engraving of hydrography lesson. STC 3110. sg Sept 19 (11) $12,000

Blaeu, Willem, 1571-1638 & Jan, 1596-1673

— Atlas major, sive cosmographia Blaviana. Amst., 1662. 1st Ed. 11 vols. Folio, orig vellum gilt; spines soiled, a few hinges weak. With 7 engraved frontises only & 592 maps & plates (of 597), colored throughout in a contemp hand, the frontises fully colored & some heightened with gold. Lacking 4 leaves of Blaeu to the reader; some maps from anr copy; some maps discolored or waterstained; marginal repairs; a few light creases. Mailhos copy. S June 25 (292) £75,000 [Frick]

Anr copy. Orig vellum gilt; worn & rubbed, vol VI spine torn. With 9 (of 11) engraved titles & 597 plates, colored throughout by a contemp hand, including fully colored frontises & sub-title (heightened with gold). Library stamps on titles, frontises, some text leaves & each mapsheet, mostly just touching image; some browning & minor flaws; some marginal tears. Royal Scottish Geographical Society copy. S June 25 (293) £60,000 [Arader]

— Kaert-boeck van alderhande generale en particuliere Landt ende Zee-kaerten en Kusten van de geheele Werelt. Amst., [c.1665-72]. Bound with: Loon, Jan van. Klaer Lichtende Noort-ster ofte Zee Atlas. Folio, orig vellum gilt; worn, joints splitting, upper cover abraded, warped, endpapers renewed. Part 1 has world map, 4 continents, a 2d map of Europe, 37 maps of Germany & the low Countries, 19 maps of European countries, 4 maps of Middle-Eastern & Asian regions, 1 maps of Straits of Magellan & 1 of the Florida coast & the Caribbean & Central America. Part 2 has 37 navigational charts. Lacking final map; on guards throughout; lower margin of the van Loon text leaves extended; 12 maps with tears, repairs or adhesive damage incurring some loss; marginal tears or fold breaks; some maps creased & with edges frayed & chipped; some foxing & staining.

CNY Dec 5 (165) $24,000

— Novum ac magnum theatrum urbium Belgicae.... Amst.: J. Blaeu, [1649]. 2 vols. Folio, contemp vellum gilt; corners rubbed. With 2 hand-colored engraved titles with arms heightened in gilt & 226 plates, colored throughout in a contemp hand. Some worming affecting outer margins of a few early leaves & final quires of Vol I, not affecting text or plates; some browning to margins. C Oct 30 (143) £40,000 [Sourget]

— Novum Italiae Theatrum sive accurata descriptio urbium.... The Hague, 1724. 4 vols. Folio, later half russia; extremities rubbed, joints weak, upper cover of Vol IV detached. With 285 maps & plates. Some worming to 4 plates in Vol I, 2 with image area affected; tear to the folding view of Genoa in Vol I; some plates creased; some browning or spotting. Koeman I, Bl 103-6. C Oct 30 (144) £28,000 [Giunta]

— Novum Theatrum Pedemontii et Sabaudiae.... The Hague, 1726. In 4 vols. Folio, later half russia; extremities rubbed, joints weak. With 141 plates & maps & 4 engraved titles. Some marginal tears; small hole in margin of Plate 64 in Vol II, part 2; some spotting or browning. C Oct 30 (145) £14,000 [Toscani]

— Novus Atlas.... Amst., 1642. Vol III only [Italy]. Folio, contemp vellum. With 48 maps. Soiled. Many maps repaired. Sold w.a.f. German text. cb Jan 30 (145) $850

Anr Ed. Amst., 1655. Vol VI only [China]. Folio, orig vellum gilt; soiled. With engraved title & 17 double-page maps, colored throughout in a contemp hand. Some browning. German text. Koeman I, Bl 55. S June 25 (458) £2,600 [Arader]

— Theatrum orbis terrarum. Amst., 1647-56. ("Novus Atlas. Das ist, Weltbeschreibung.") Vol I only. 18th-cent blind-stamped calf; rubbed. With ptd title on overslip within allegorical border colored in a contemp hand & heightened with gold & with 82 (of 103) maps, colored in a contemp hand. Cologne damaged near centerfold; some shaving near upper neatlines; a few splits repaired without loss; stamp of Kunstgewerbemuseum Strassburg on tp verso. S June 25 (291) £3,800 [DeJonge]

Vol VI only [China]. Amst., 1655. Folio, orig vellum gilt; lower corners of both covers abraded. With engraved title heightened with gold and 17 double-page maps hand-colored in outline. 1 map with vertical crease causing printing def; minor creasing to a few other maps. CNY Dec 5 (164) $7,500

— Toonneel des Aerdriicx, ofte Nieuwe Atlas. Amst., 1649-50-54. ("Sevende Stuck der Aedrycks Beschryving....") Vol III only. Folio, contemp vellum. With 65 maps, hand-colored in outline. Title slip lacking. sg Feb 13 (110A) $14,000

Blagden, Charles Otto. See: Skeat & Blagden

Blagdon, Francis William, 1778-1819
See also: Orme, Edward

— A Brief History of Ancient and Modern India. L, 1805. Folio, orig bds. With uncolored engraved general title, engraved title to 24 views, hand-colored plate of the Native Judges port of Tippoo Sultan & 64 hand-colored plates. Some soiling to outer blank margins; 1 plate with vertical crease. C May 20 (20) £6,500 [Marlborough]

Blainville, —— de

— Travels through Holland, Germany, Switzerland.... L, 1767. 3 vols. 4to, half calf; rebacked, orig backstrips retained. Lacking maps. bba Apr 30 (28) £50 [Tosi]

Blainville, H. M. D. de

— Manuel de malacologie et conchyologie. Paris & Strasbourg, 1825-27. Plate vol only. Orig bds; worn. With 86 plates. Some soiling & foxing. O Aug 25 (52) $90

Blair, David

— The History of Australasia.... Glasgow, 1879. 4to, orig mor gilt. kh Nov 11 (439) A$140

Blair, Eric Arthur. See: Orwell, George

Blair, Hugh, 1718-1800

— Lectures on Rhetoric and Belles Lettres. L, 1783. 1st Ed. 2 vols. 4to, modern half calf; new endpapers. Some foxing. bba July 9 (121) £60 [Hay Cinema]

Blair, John, d.1782

— The Chronology and History of the World. L, 1768. Folio, contemp calf; covers detached, rubbed. bba Mar 26 (230) £220 [B.Bailey]

Anr copy. Half calf; def, upper cover detached. Some browning; most maps loose. Sold w.a.f. S Feb 26 (703) £280 [Burden]

Blair, Robert, 1699-1746

— The Grave.... L, 1808. 4to, modern cloth. With frontis, pictorial title & 12 plates. Prospectus for Blake's Chaucer's Pilgrims bound in at end. P June 18 (442) $700

Anr Ed. L, 1813. 4to, bds; bumped. With engraved title & 11 plates after William Blake & port after T. Phillips, all engraved by Schiavonetti. Met Apr 28 (392) $350

Blake, William, 1757-1827
See also: Nonesuch Press

— All Religions are One. L: Trianon Press, 1970. One of 36 for the Trustees of the Blake Trust & the pbrs. 4to, orig mor. With 10 facsimile plates plus a set of proofs showing the progressive stages. S Nov 14 (103) £140 [Clark]

One of 600. Orig half mor. bba Dec 19 (20) £80 [Poetry Bookshop]

Anr copy. Half mor; spine faded. sg Sept 26 (32) $90

— America: a Prophecy. L: Trianon Press, 1963. One of 526. Folio, orig half mor. sg Sept 26 (33) $425

— Bible. L: Trianon Press, 1957. ("Illustrations to the Bible.") One of 506. Folio, half mor. With 9 colored plates. sg Sept 26 (51) $700

Anr copy. Orig half mor. sg Sept 26 (51) $700

Anr copy. Half mor; rubbed. sg Feb 6 (25) $350

— The Book of Ahania. Paris: Trianon Press, 1973. One of 32 for the Trustees of the Blake Trust & the pbrs. 4to, mor gilt. S Nov 14 (102) £140 [Clark]

One of 750. Half mor. sg Sept 26 (35) $150

— The Book of Los. L, 1976. One of 480. 4to, orig half mor gilt. bba Dec 19 (23) £95 [Poetry Bookshop]

Anr copy. Half mor. sg Sept 26 (36) $140

— The Book of Thel. Paris: Trianon Press, 1965. One of 20. 4to, orig mor gilt. With added proofs, guide-sheet & stencil. Facsimile of Keynes and Wolf's Copy O. S Nov 14 (100) £140 [Clark]

One of 380. Half mor gilt. Facsimile of Keynes and Wolf's Copy O. bba Dec 19 (18) £160 [Bookworks]

Anr copy. Half mor. Facsimile of Keynes and Wolf's Copy O. sg Sept 26 (37) $225

— The Book of Urizen. L: Trianon Press, 1958. One of 480. 4to, orig half mor. With 27 colored plates. sg Sept 26 (38) $300

— The Complete Portraiture.... L: Trianon Press, 1977. One of 500. 4to, half mor. sg Sept 26 (58) $175

— Dante. L, 1922. ("Illustrations to the Divine Comedy of Dante.") One of 250. Folio, loose in orig portfolio. With 103 plates. sg Feb 6 (18) $400

Anr Ed. NY, 1968. One of 1,000. Folio, half mor. sg Sept 26 (34) $450

Anr Ed. L: Trianon Press, 1978. ("Illustrations of Dante.") One of 376. Oblong folio, half mor. With 12 plates. bba Dec 19 (25) £220 [Kurita]

— Designs for Gray's Poems. L, 1922. One of 650. Folio, orig cloth; worn & shaken. sg Feb 6 (19) $60

Anr Ed. Clairvaux: Trianon Press, 1972. ("Water-Colour Designs for the Poems of Thomas Gray.") One of 100 for Paul Mellon. Ed by Geoffrey Keynes. Half mor gilt. Schlosser copy. P June 18 (635) $800

— Europe, a Prophecy. L, 1969. One of 480. Folio, half mor. With 18 colored plates. sg Sept 26 (39) $140

— The Gates of Paradise. L, 1968. One of 650. 3 vols. bba Dec 19 (19) £110 [L. Kerr]

Anr copy. With uncolored illusts. sg Sept 26 (40) $350; sg Feb 6 (26) $150

— Jerusalem. [L, 1877]. One of 100. 4to, calf gilt; front cover partly detached. With 100 plates. sg Oct 8 (17) $175

Anr Ed. L: Trianon Press, [1951]. One of 516. Folio, cloth; extremities worn. sg Sept 26 (42) $850

Anr Ed. L: Trianon Press, 1974. One of 32 for the Trustees of the Blake Trust & the pbrs. sg Sept 26 (43) $850

One of 516. Half mor. O Dec 17 (224) $160

— Job. L, 1906. ("Illustrations of the Book of Job.") 4to, orig cloth. With facsimile title & 21 plates. bba Dec 19 (28) £50 [Kurita]

Anr Ed. NY: Pierpont Morgan Library, 1935. 6 parts. Folio, half cloth. sg Sept 26 (41) $600; sg Feb 6 (23) $800

— The Marriage of Heaven and Hell. [L: Trianon Press, 1960]. One of 526. Folio, half mor. With 27 colored plates. Facsimile of the Rosenwald Ms.. sg Sept 26 (44) $325

— Milton, a Poem. Paris: Trianon Press, 1967. One of 380. 4to, half mor gilt. sg Sept 26 (45) $225

— Poems.... L & NY, 1893. Ed by W. B. Yeats. 8vo, orig cloth; spine rubbed & faded. bba Dec 19 (11) £60 [Books & Prints]

Anr copy. Orig cloth; spine ends torn. Paper-clip stains on frontis, tp verso & 1st contents leaf. K Dec 1 (47) $80

— Poetical Sketches. L, 1927. 4to, half cloth; rubbed & faded. bba Dec 19 (31) £85 [Kiefer]

— The Song of Los. Paris: Trianon Press, 1975. One of 400. 4to, half mor. bba Dec 19 (22) £140 [Bookworks]; sg Sept 26 (46) $130

Anr copy. Orig half mor; spine nicked. wa Sept 26 (48) $160

— Songs of Innocence. L: Trianon Press, 1954. One of 1,600. Orig half cloth. With 31 colored plates. Facsimile of the Rosenwald copy of the 1789 Ed. bba Dec

19 (16) £80 [Kurita]

Anr copy. Orig mor; 1 signature loose. Facsimile of the Rosenwald copy of the 1789 Ed. sg Sept 26 (47) $100

— Songs of Innocence and Experience. [L: Trianon Press, 1955]. One of 526. Mor; spine darkened. sg Sept 26 (48) $475

Anr copy. Orig mor. sg Feb 6 (24) $375

— There is no Natural Religion. L: Trianon Press, 1971. One of 616. 2 vols. 4to & 8vo, half mor. bba Dec 19 (21) £100 [Poetry Bookshop]; sg Sept 26 (49) $120

— Vala, or the Four Zoas. Oxford: Clarendon Press, 1963. Ed by G. E. Bentley. Folio, orig cloth; soiled & frayed. DW Dec 11 (344) £100

— Visions of the Daughters of Albion. [L: Trianon Press, 1959]. One of 446. Folio, half mor. With 11 hand-colored plates. sg Sept 26 (50) $300; sg Sept 26 (50) $300

— Works. L, 1893. One of 500. Ed by Ellis & Yeats. 3 vols. 8vo, orig cloth; rubbed. Library markings. bba Dec 19 (10) £300 [Fellner Antiquariat]

— Young's Night Thoughts. Cambr. MA & L, 1927. ("Illustrations to Young's Night Thoughts.") One of 500. Folio, loose as issued in cloth folder. With 5 colored & 25 plain plates. sg Feb 6 (20) $175

Blake, William, 1757-1827 —& Gray, Thomas, 1716-71

— Poems by Mr. Gray. L: Trianon Press, 1972. One of 518. 3 vols sg Sept 26 (52) $1,100

Blake, William O.

— The History of Slavery and the Slave Trade.... Columbus OH, 1858. 8vo, orig mor; scuffed. F Mar 26 (125) $80

Anr Ed. Columbus, Ohio, 1858. 8vo, modern cloth. sg June 18 (506) $60

Blakeway, John Brickdale, 1765-1826. See: Owen & Blakeway

Blakey, Dorothy

— The Minerva Press 1790-1820. L, 1939. 4to, orig half cloth. bba May 28 (484) £65 [Dawson]

Blakey, J. W.

— The Northern Angler: A Weekly Newspaper devoted to All-Round Angling [later The Angler...]. Scarborough, 1892-94. Vols 1-4. 4to, orig cloth. With 11 colored plates. S Feb 11 (835) £380 [Montague]

Blakston, W. A. —& Others

— The Illustrated Book of Canaries and Cage-Birds.... L, [1877-80]. 4to, orig cloth; worn. With 56 colored plates. Some text leaves foxed. K July 12 (95) $250

Anr copy. Half calf. Some repairs. pnE Mar 11 (247) £140

Anr copy. Contemp half lea gilt; spine ends & front joint worn; front hinge cracked. With frontis & 55 color plates. sg Nov 14 (163) $225

Blanchet, Paul

— Notices sur quelques tissus antiques.... Paris, 1897. Folio, loose as issued in half cloth folder. With 37 heliogravure plates. Some foxing. sg Feb 6 (278) $130

Blanck, Jacob Nathaniel

— Bibliography of American Literature. New Haven, 1955-83. Vols I-VII. Cloth. sg May 21 (137) $400

Vols I-IV. cb Sept 19 (14) $225

Vols I-VII. NH Aug 23 (353) $425

— Peter Parley to Penrod.... NY, 1938. One of 500. Inscr. O Dec 17 (25) $110

Anr Ed. NY, 1956. Bdg worn. sg Oct 31 (30) $80

4th ptg. Waltham, 1974. K Sept 29 (86) $85

Bland, Humphrey, 1686?-1763

— A Treatise of Military Discipline.... L, 1762. 8vo, old calf; upper cover detached, worn. With 7 folding plates. Browned. Shippen copy, with Ms notation about James Buchanan in the War of 1812. bbc Sept 23 (225) $200

Bland, Jane Cooper

— Currier & Ives: A Manual for Collectors. Garden City, [1931]. 4to, cloth; worn. O Mar 31 (18) $80

Anr copy. Cloth; spine stained. sg Sept 6 (79) $50

Blaquiere, Edward

— The Greek Revolution. L, 1824. 8vo, modern half mor. With frontis, hand-colored in outline. S June 30 (236) £380 [Atabey]

Blasius, Gerardus, 1626?-92?

— Anatome animalium. Amst., 1681. 1st Ed. 4to, contemp calf; upper cover detached, head of spine torn. With frontis & 65 plates. Minor worming to blank margin of a few leaves; marginal tear in M3. b June 22 (154) £580

Blaue. See: Kandinsky & Marc

Blckmantle, Bernard. See: Westmacott, Charles Molloy

Bledsoe, Anthony J.
— Indian Wars of the Northwest.... San Francisco, 1885. 1st Ed. 8vo, cloth; rubbed. cb Sept 12 (21) $110
Anr copy. Cloth; worn. With the errata slip. sg June 18 (44) $90

Blegny, Etienne de
— Les Elemens, ou premieres instructions de la jeunesse. Paris, 1751. 8vo, contemp calf gilt; joints split, rubbed. bba Oct 10 (24) £3380 [Miles]

Bleiler, Everett F.
— The Checklist of Fantastic Literature. Chicago, 1948. In d/j. Sgd. cb Oct 17 (95) $75

Blengini, Cesare Alberto
— Trattato teorico-pratico di spada e sciabola. Bologna, 1864. 8vo, modern bds. sg Mar 26 (45) $225

Bles, Joseph
— Rare English Glasses of the XVII & XVIII Centuries. L, 1925. 4to, orig cloth, in worn d/j. kh Nov 11 (48) A$340

Blew, William C. A.
— Brighton and its Coaches. L, 1894 [1893]. 1st Ed. 8vo, orig cloth. pnE Dec 4 (197) £140
Anr copy. Half mor. With 20 hand-colored plates. pnE Mar 11 (34) $100

Blewitt, Mary
— Surveys of the Seven Seas.... L, 1957. Folio, cloth. With 67 illusts on 61 leaves, some in color. sg Oct 31 (71) $50

Bligh, William, 1754-1817
See also: Golden Cockerel Press
[-] An Account of the Mutinous Seizure of the Bounty.... L: for Robert Turner, Mar 1791. 8vo, modern calf. Lacking a half-title or initial blank; lower inner corner of 3d leaf torn away & repaired with loss of a few letters; 2 short tears in margin of final leaf repaired. C June 25 (66) £4,400 [Tulip]
— A Narrative of the Mutiny on Board his Majesty's Ship Bounty.... L, 1790. 1st Ed. 4to, orig bds; rebacked, worn & stained. With folding plan & 3 charts, 2 folding. Some creasing. DuPont copy. CNY Oct 8 (13) $3,600
Anr copy. Contemp half calf. S June 25 (63) £6,500 [Quaritch/Hordern]
— A Voyage to the South Sea.... Dublin, 1792. 1st Irish Ed. 4to, contemp sheep; needs rebdg. With port, folding plate & 6 folding maps. Foxed & browned throughout. sg Jan 9 (34) $375
Anr Ed. L, 1792. 4to, modern mor. Tp repaired. kh Nov 11 (440) A$3,500
1st Ed. 4to, contemp bds; rebacked but upper cover detached, corners worn. With port, folding plate & 6 folding maps. Upper margins stained at end, affecting largest chart. DuPont copy. CNY Oct 8 (14) $3,400
Anr copy. Modern half calf. S Feb 26 (719) £2,000 [Toscani]
Anr copy. Contemp calf; joints repaired. Joints repaired. S June 25 (64) £3,200 [Tulip]
Anr copy. Contemp calf; worn. With port, plate & 6 folding map. Dampstains. S June 25 (127) £1,100 [Barberini]

Blind. See: Pinchard

Blish, James Benjamin
— Earthman, Come Home. NY: Putnam, [1955]. In d/j; Ink mark at bottom of endpapers. pba July 9 (23) $60
— The Seedling Stars. Reading, 1957. In d/j. sg June 11 (25) $60

Bliss, Douglas Percy
— A History of Wood-Engraving. L, 1928. Cloth, in def d/j. kh Nov 11 (49) A$50

Bloch, Jean-Richard
— Dix filles dans un pre. Paris, 1926. One of 995. Illus by Marie Laurencin. Orig wraps. With 4 plates. HH May 12 (2384) DM1,600

Bloch, Robert
— The Opener of the Way. Sauk City: Arkham House, 1945. 1st Ed, Ltd Ed. Inscr. bbc Dec 9 (553) $200; sp Nov 24 (320) $60
Anr copy. In pictorial d/j, which is browned along spine & rear. wa Sept 26 (294) $110
— Psycho. NY, 1959. In chipped d/j. sp Apr 16 (361) $65

Blome, Richard, d.1705
— Britannia: or a Geographical Description.... L, 1673. 1st Ed. Folio, contemp calf; joints weak. With 47 (of 50) maps, full-page plan of London & 12 leaves containing 24 plates showing 812 coats of arms, the last torn & repaired. Map of the smaller islands cropped at fore-margins; erasure at foot of title; some dust-soiling. S June 25 (264) £2,500 [Wells]
— A Description of the Island of Jamaica.... L, 1672. 8vo, contemp calf; worn, front outer joint broken. With 3 folding maps. Jamaica backed with linen & 3 margins cut to border; Carolina with tear in blank area repaired. DuPont copy. CNY Oct 8 (15) $5,500
— A Geographical Description of the Four Parts of the World.... L, 1670. Folio,

contemp calf; worn, spine def. With 25 mostly double-page or folding maps. Lacking engraved dedication to the Travel supplement; some maps torn & repaired affecting image; rust-marks & thumbing to text. S Nov 21 (209) £2,000 [Faupel]

— The Present State of His Majesties Isles and Territories in America.... L, 1687. 8vo, early calf; spine worn, outer joints cracked. With frontis, plate & 7 folding maps. New York bound upside down; Jamaica with small stains & a tear in blank area repaired. CNY Oct 8 (16) $2,400

Blondel, Francois, 1618-86

— Cours d'architecture enseigne dans l'Academie Royale d'Architecture. Paris, 1675-83. 5 parts in 2 vols. Folio, contemp calf; rubbed. C June 24 (112) £1,000 [Dreesman]

Blondel, Jacques Francois, 1705-74

— Cours d'architecture. Paris, 1675-83. 5 parts in 2 vols. Folio, modern half calf. With 2 frontises & 81 plates. Some waterstaining; minor repairs without loss. S May 14 (1076) £900 [Bifolco]

Anr Ed. Paris, 1771-77. Vols I-IV only, with plate vols I-IV in 2. Together, 6 vols. 8vo, contemp sheep gilt; spine ends chipped. Sold w.a.f. sg Feb 6 (33) $550

— De la distribution des maisons de plaisance et de la decoration des edifices en general. Paris, 1737-38. 1st Ed. 2 vols. 4to, modern half calf; joints & extremities rubbed. With frontis (2d Issue) & 155 plates. Vol I half-title lacking; Vol II half-title & leaf with errata for both vols misbound in index; several plates with stains. McCarty-Cooper copy. CNY Jan 25 (6) $2,000

Anr copy. Contemp calf gilt, armorial bdg. With frontis & 155 plates. Short tears occasionally affecting image, 1 repaired; blank corner of Y1 torn away. pn June 11 (141) £900 [Marlborough]

Blondus, Flavius, 1388-1463

— Historium ab inclinatione Romanorum imperii decades. Venice: Octavianus Scotus, 16 July 1483. Folio, 19th-cent half vellum; almost entirely disbound. Occasional worming with minor text loss; lower gutter of last 30 leaves badly dampstained & wormed. 372 leaves. Goff B-698. George Milne copy. CNY Dec 5 (168) $850

Anr copy. 19th-cent half vellum. 42 lines, roman letter. Wormed; old marginal annotations; some browning. 371 (of 372) leaves; lacking initial blank. Goff B-698. SI June 9 (144) LIt2,600,000

Bloomfield, Robert, 1766-1823

— The Farmer's Boy: a Rural Poem. L, 1800. Bound with: Rural Tales, Ballads, and Songs. L, 1802. 1st Eds. 4to, calf gilt. With Autograph Ms, poem, Address to the British Channel, incorporated in an ALs, 2 Nov 1806. S Nov 14 (511) £150 [Maggs]

Blossfeldt, Karl

— Urformen der Kunst. Berlin, [c.1929]. 4to, cloth; worn. With 120 photogravures. O Mar 31 (19) $70

Blouet, Guillaume Abel

— Expedition scientifique de Moree. Paris, 1831-38. 3 vols. Folio, contemp half mor gilt. With engraved titles & 262 plates, 5 hand-colored. Some discoloration to text. S July 1 (552) £7,200 [Consolidated Real]

Anr copy. 3 vols in 4. Folio, contemp calf gilt; worn. With 3 engraved titles & 262 plates, 6 double-page or folding of which 5 are hand-colored. Some discoloration; hole in Plate 19 of Vol I without loss. S July 1 (553) £6,500 [Chelsea]

Blount, Sir Thomas Pope, 1649-97

— A Natural History.... L, 1693. 1st Ed. 8vo, contemp calf. b June 22 (155) £380

Bluemel, Johann Daniel

— Gruendliche Anweisung zur Lust-Feuerwerkerey. Strassburg, 1771. 4to, bds; worn. With 10 folding plates. Some browning & staining. S July 1 (1211) £280 [American Mus.]

Blum, Andre

— The Origins of Printing and Engraving. NY, 1940. In d/j. cb Oct 17 (97) $50

Blume, Karl Ludwig, 1796-1862

— Collection des orchidees les plus remarquables de l'Archipel Indien et du Japon. Amst., 1858-[59]. Vol I (all pbd). Folio, library cloth. With litho title & 70 plates, 56 hand-colored. A few soiled. bba Feb 27 (407) £1,800 [Greyfriars]

Blunden, Edmund Charles

— Masks of Time. A New Collection.... L: Beaumont Press, 1925. One of 310. bba July 9 (249) £60 [Deighton Bell]; O Dec 17 (27) $70

— To Themis: Poems on Famous Trials. L: Beaumont Press, 1931. One of 80. O Dec 17 (28) $70

Blundeville, Thomas, fl.1561

— His Exercises.... L: John Windet, 1594. 1st Ed. 6 parts in 1 vol. 4to, 19th-cent vellum. Mostly black letter. Woodcut on U1r without volvelle but intact; Sexagenarie table dampstained & with folds reinforced & lower edge cropped; tear to inner edge of folding diagram of the Mariners Card;

some inkstains in quire C partially obscuring some letters. Sold w.a.f. STC 3146. CNY Oct 8 (17) $3,200

Blunt, Lady Anne, 1837-1917. See: Gregynog Press

Blunt, Wilfrid Jasper Walter

— The Art of Botanical Illustration. L, 1950. In d/j. bbc Apr 27 (105) $80

Anr copy. Pigskin gilt. pn June 11 (162) £120

— Tulips and Tulipomania. L: Basilisk Press, 1977. One of 500. Illus by Rory McEwen. 4to, orig half lea. With 16 mtd colored plates & 8 large colored plates. bba Sept 5 (11) £260 [Atkins]

Blunt, Wilfrid Jasper Walter —& Jones, Paul

— Flora superba. L, 1971. One of 405. Illus by Paul Jones. Folio, half vellum by Zaehnsdorf. With 16 color plates. bba Feb 13 (365) £140 [Rose]

Anr copy. Orig half vellum by Zaehnsdorf. With 16 colored plates. Ck Sept 6 (28) £140

Blunt, Wilfrid Scawen, 1840-1922. See: Gregynog Press; Kelmscott Press

Boaden, James, 1762-1839

— An Inquiry into the Authenticity of Various Pictures and Prints. L, 1824. 4to, lev gilt extra by Riviere & Son; upper cover set with 5 oval port miniatures of Shakespeare. With 5 plates. CNY Dec 5 (425) $3,800

— Memoirs of the Life of John Philip Kemble. L, 1825. 1st Ed. 2 vols. 8vo, half mor gilt; rubbed. O Feb 25 (25) $100

Anr copy. Calf; worn. sg Oct 17 (14) $50

Boate, Gerard

— A Natural History of Ireland.... Dublin, 1725-26. 4to, old calf; scuffed & soiled. With 11 plates, 7 folding. wd June 12 (370) $275

Boazio, Baptista. See: Drake, Sir Francis

Boccaccio, Giovanni, 1313-73

See also: Limited Editions Club

— Amorous Fiammetta. L: Mandrake Press, 1929. One of 550. Folio, vellum gilt. O Jan 14 (24) $90

— De claris mulieribus. Bern: Matthias Apiarius, 1539. Folio, later vellum. Marginal tears repaired. C June 24 (293) £650 [Pizey]

Anr copy. Later bds. Some browning. S May 28 (37) £1,500 [Bossi]

— Genealogie deorum gentilium. Venice: Manfredus de Bonellis, de Monteferrato, 25 Mar 1497. Folio, later vellum. 63 lines & headline; types 6:142G (title), 6:18R (text) & 81R. Small slit in lower blank margin of q1; some browning or dampstaining; light worming to most leaves. 162 leaves. Goff B-754. C Dec 16 (105) £1,700 [Bifolco]

Decameron in English

— 1620. - The Decameron.... L.2d Ed in English of Vol I, 1st Ed in English of Vol II. 2 vols. Folio, 19th-cent calf; rebacked. Tp of 1st part shorter at fore-edge; lacking initial blank; some tears repaired; small holes in text, affecting a few letters. P June 17 (134) $2,250

— 1928. - Phila. One of 1,500. Trans by John Payne. 2 vols. 4to, mor gilt. K Sept 29 (68) $375

— 1934-35. - The Decameron. Oxford: Shakespeare Head Press One of 325. 2 vols. 4to, half mor. S Nov 14 (76) £160

— 1949. - Garden City One of 1,500. Illus by Rockwell Kent. 2 vols. 4to, cloth. With 32 colored plates. cb Dec 19 (83) $140

Decameron in Italian

— 1557. - Venice 4to, modern vellum. SI June 9 (146) LIt600,000

— 1573-74. - Florence: Giunti. 4to, 19th-cent vellum. Some browning; frontis repaired. SI June 9 (147) LIt450,000

— 1729. - Venice 4to, orig calf; worn. Library markings. Reprint of Florence, 1527, Ed. F June 25 (670) $170

— 1729. - Venice: Pasinello. 4to, contemp vellum; worn. SI June 9 (149) LIt800,000

— 1757. - L [but Paris] 5 vols. 8vo, contemp mor gilt; Vol IV not uniform. With 5 engraved titles, 1 port & 110 plates. C Dec 16 (106) £900 [Kaiser]

Anr copy. 19th-cent mor gilt by Berthand; joints & extremities scuffed, front cover of Vol I detached. F June 25 (607) $1,100

Anr copy. 18th-cent calf gilt; lower cover of Vol IV repaired. With 5 engraved titles, 1 port & 110 plates. Small hole in lower margin of 1st plate in Vol III. S May 28 (102) £800 [Gregorio]

Anr copy. Contemp calf gilt. With 5 frontises, port & 110 plates. Marginal repair to 1 leaf; tear in margin of E3. SI Dec 5 (86) LIt2,100,000

Boccalini, Trajano, 1556-1613

— I Ragguagli di Parnasso, or Advertisements.... L, 1656. 1st Ed in English. Folio, old calf; rubbed. Browned & stained. Lacking the port. O Apr 28 (150) $60

Boccioni, Umberto, 1882-1916

— Pittura scultura futuriste. Milan, 1914. Orig wraps; chipped. SI Dec 5 (88) LIt750,000

Bock, Carl A.

— The Head-Hunters of Borneo. L, 1882. 2d Ed. 8vo, contemp half calf; extremities rubbed. With folding map & 30 colored plates. Tp spotted. Ck May 15 (76) £400

Bock, Elfried, 1875-1933

— Die deutschen Meister. Berlin, 1921. 2 vols. 4to, orig cloth. S Feb 11 (18) £400 [Creed]

— Die Zeichnungen in der Universitaets-bibliothek Erlangen. Frankfurt, 1929. 2 vols. 4to, orig half vellum; rubbed & soiled. S Feb 11 (20) £440 [Creed]

Bock, Elfried, 1875-1933 —& Rosenberg, J.

— Die niederlandischen Meister. Frankfurt, 1931. 2 vols. Folio, orig cloth; spine & edges soiled. S Feb 11 (20) £480 [Bennett]

Bock, Hieronymus, 1489?-1554

— De stirpium. Strassburg: Vendelinus Rihelius, 1552. 4to, 19th-cent mor; rubbed & discolored. Tp with tear repaired in lower margin & library stamp; S5-6 torn; some staining. S Nov 21 (2) £1,500 [Bifolco]

— Kraeuterbuch. Strassburg, 1551. Folio, orig pigskin over wooden bds stamped with scenes from the Life of Christ; rubbed. With c.450 hand-colored woodblock illusts. Sold w.a.f. K Mar 22 (181) $2,300

Bode, Wilhelm von, 1845-1929

— Italian Bronze Statuettes of the Renaissance. L & Berlin, 1907-12. 3 vols. Folio, cloth. O Dec 17 (29) $80

Bodenehr, Gabriel, 1664-1758

— Force d'Europe.... Augsburg, [c.1720-26]. Oblong folio, 18th-cent half vellum over patterned paper bds; soiled. With engraved title, index & 200 plans. Lacking the supplements; foremargins of a few plates scuffed; stamp on tp. S Nov 21 (153) £3,000

Bodfrey, John

— A Treatise upon the Useful Science of Defence.... L, 1747. 4to, contemp half calf. sg Mar 26 (131) $175

Bodin, Jean, 1530-96

— Daemonomania, oder ausfuehrliche Erzehlung des wuetenden teuffels.... Hamburg, 1698. 3 parts in 1 vol. 8vo, contemp blind-stamped pigskin with initials ASAC & date 1711. P June 16 (198) $1,000

— De la demonomanie des sorciers. Antwerp: chez Arnould Coninx, 1593. 8vo, contemp calf gilt, armorial bdg; spine rubbed. Ck Oct 31 (40) £400

— Demonomania de gli stregoni. Venice: Aldus, 1592. 4to, contemp vellum. Some browning. SI June 9 (155) LIt1,400,000

Bodoni, Giovanni Battista, 1740-1813

— Le Piu insigni pitture Parmensi.... Parma: Bodoni, 1809 [1816]. 4to Ed. Contemp half lea; worn. SI June 9 (158) LIt1,300,000

Boeckler, Georg Andreas

— Architectura civilis nova & antiqua.... Frankfurt: Johann Georg Spoerlin, [1663]. Folio, vellum bdg from an antiphoner leaf; soiled. With 40 plates. Small stamp on title; some worming at inner margin without loss. S Nov 21 (69) £600 [Barker]

Boehme, Jacob, 1575-1624

— Works. L, 1764-81. 4 vols. 4to, recent mor. With port & 25 plates (1 in facsimile). Lacking subtitle to a plate in Vol I, errata-leaf & 2 leaves in Vol IV; several plates & 1 text leaf misbound; pencil notes. B Nov 1 (669) HF13,500

Boehn, Max von, 1850-1921

See also: Fischel & Boehn

— Dolls and Puppets. L, [1932]. In def d/j. With 30 colored plates. kh Nov 11 (50) A$100

Boelker, Homer H.

— Portfolio of Hopi Kachinas. Hollywood, [1969]. One of 1,000. 4to, cloth plus 16 loose plates in wraps. cb Nov 14 (14) $140

Boerhaave, Hermann, 1668-1738

— Methodi studii medici.... Amst., 1751. 2 vols. 4to, contemp calf; rebacked, rubbed. bba Sept 5 (265) £190 [Bickersteth]

Boethius, Anicius Manlius Torquatus Severinus, 480?-524?

— De consolatione philosophie. [Westminster:] William Caxton, [c.1478]. 1st Ed in English. Trans by Geoffrey Chaucer. Folio, 19th-cent mor gilt by Bedford. 29 lines; types 2:135B (text) & 3:135G (Latin incipits & epitaph on Chaucer); rubricated. Lower corner of 1st 2 leaves restored; repairs to inner margin of several leaves, not touching text. 94 leaves. Goff B-813. Hamilton-Thomas-Stetson copy. P Dec 12 (159) $130,000

Anr Ed. Strassburg: Pruess, 1491. 4to, later calf. Black letter. Early marginal annotations; some lower corners damaged; some stains. 190 leaves. Goff B-792. B Nov 1 (623) HF5,000

Anr Ed. Florence, 1521. 8vo, contemp vellum; worn. Browned; old annotations; old stamp. SI Dec 5 (92) LIt320,000

— Della consolatione de la filosofia. Florence:

Lorenzo Torrentino, 1551. Trans by Cosimo Bartoli. 8vo, contemp vellum. SI Dec 5 (764) LIt650,000

Anr copy. Some staining. SI Dec 5 (765) LIt650,000

— Opera. Basel: Henricus Petrus, 1546. Folio, 19th-cent half calf. Some dampstaining & marginal worming; final leaves singed at outer margin. Ck Oct 31 (41) £550

Boffito, Giuseppe

— Biblioteca Aeronautica Italiana Illustrata.... Florence, 1929-37. 2 vols, including Supplement. 4to, new cloth. sg Oct 31 (32) $850

— Scrittori Barnabitici, o della Congregazione dei Chierici Regolari di San Paolo.... Florence, 1933-37. One of 240. 4 vols. 4to, orig bds; Vol I rear hinge cracked. sg Oct 31 (33) $1,000

Bogeng, Gustave Adolf Erich

— Geschichte der Buchdruckerkunst: der Fruehdruck. Hellerau bei Dresden, [1930]. Folio, orig half mor; rubbed. First 2 leaves in Vol II repaired. bba May 28 (604) £220 [Dawson]

— Die Grossen Bibliophilen. Leipzig, 1922. 3 vols. 4to, cloth; worn & shaken. sg Oct 31 (34) $200

Boggs, Mae Helene Bacon

— My Playhouse was a Concord Coach.... Oakland, Calif., [1942]. 4to, cloth. Inscr. K July 12 (60) $140

Bohatta, Hanns

— Bibliographie des livres d'heures horae B.M.V., officia...des XV. und XVI. Jahrhunderts. Vienna, 1924. Cloth, orig wraps bound in. sg Oct 31 (35) $400

— Liturgische Bibliographie des XV. Jahrhunderts.... Vienna, 1911. One of 300. 4to, old half calf, orig front wrap bound in; lacking backstrip. Inscr. bbc Sept 23 (104) $90

Bohny, Nicholas

— The New Picture Book.... Edin., 1873. 6th Ed. Oblong folio, orig cloth & pictorial bds; rebacked, rubbed. With 36 litho pages each with hand-colored illusts. Some repaired, occasionally affecting plate. bba Oct 10 (25) £240 [Stevenson]

Boiardo, Matteo Maria, 1434-94

— Orlando Innamorato...Orlando Furioso... with an Essay on the Romantic Narrative Poetry of the Italians.... L: Wm. Pickering, 1830-34. 9 vols. contemp half mor. SI Dec 5 (766) LIt350,000

— Sonnetti e canzone. Venice: Manfredus de Bonellis for Giovanni Battista Sessa, 26 June 1501. 8vo, late 19th-cent mor gilt. Lower margin of H1 restored. C Dec 16 (27) £4,700 [Jackson]

Boillot, Joseph

— Modelles, artifices de feu, et divers instrumens de guerre.... Chaumont, 1598. 1st Ed. 4to, old vellum. Some dampstaining in margins towards end. S July 1 (1212) £600 [Maggs]

Boissard, Jean Jacques, 1528-1602

— Emblematum Liber. Metz: Faber, 1588. 4to, half calf. B Nov 1 (329) HF5,000

— Leben und Contrafeiten der Tuerckischen und Persischen Sultanen.... Frankfurt: Dietrich de Bry, 1596. 4to, contemp vellum stamped ASA 1596 on upper cover. With port, engraved arms on dedication & 47 ports. S July 1 (555) £4,200 [Quaritch]

Boissiere, Claude de

— Nobilissimus et antiquissimus ludus Pythagoraeus.... Paris: G. Cavellat, 1556. 8vo, later 18th-cent half calf; upper cover detached. Lower margins wormed; outer margins shaved, affecting text of diagrams; dampstains in lower part of page. Ck May 8 (21) £320

Boissonas, Fred. See: Baud-Bovy & Boissonas

Boitard, Pierre, 1787-1859

— Traite de la composition et de l'ornement des jardins.... Paris, 1825. 3d Ed. Oblong 4to, recent half mor. With 97 plates, 1 hand-colored. McCarty-Cooper copy. CNY Jan 25 (7) $700

Bolingbroke, Henry St. John, Viscount, 1678-1751

— Works. L, 1754. 5 vols. 4to, contemp calf; rebacked. A few leaves spotted. bba Oct 24 (69) £150 [Land]

Anr copy. Modern half lea; worn. O Aug 25 (36) $225

Bollinger, Edward T. —& Bauer, Frederick

— The Moffat Road. Denver, 1962. In d/j. Sgd by both. cb Feb 13 (43) $65

Bolton, Arthur T.

— The Architecture of Robert and James Adam. L, 1922. 2 vols. Folio, orig cloth; rubbed. DW Mar 11 (793) £220

Anr copy. Orig cloth; spine ends ragged, tear on front joint of 1 vol; initial gathering of Vol II loose. Eva Le Gallienne's copy. sg Feb 6 (34) $250

Bolton, Edmund, 1545?-1633?

— The Elements of Armouries. L: George Eld, 1610. 4to, contemp vellum; worn. Woodcut illus on p 198 lacking orig moveable overslips. Last few leaves brittle & marginally torn. bba Oct 24 (171) £340 [Land]

Bolton, Ethel S. —& Coe, Eva J.

— American Samplers. [Bost.], 1921. K July 12 (16) $120

Anr copy. With 127 plates, some in color. sg Apr 2 (3) $100

Bolton, Herbert Eugene

[-] New Spain and the Anglo-American West. Historical Contributions Presented to.... Los Angeles, [1932]. 1st Ed, one of 500. 2 vols. sg June 18 (19) $175

Bolton, James, d.1799

— Geschichte der merckwuerdigsten Pilze. Berlin, 1795-1820. 1st Ed in German. 4 vols in 2. 8vo, orig bds; spines rubbed. With 2 hand-colored engraved titles & 138 (of 182) plates only. Sold w.a.f. Ck Oct 31 (97) £500

— A History of Fungusses, Growing about Halifax. Halifax & Huddersfield, 1788-91. 4 vols in 2, including Supplement. 4to, later cloth; joints weak. With engraved title & 182 plates. Stamps on versos of titles & plates; some browning. pn Nov 14 (424) £420

Bolton, Theodore

— American Book Illustrators. NY, 1938. One of 1,000. sg May 21 (139) $60

Bolus, Harry, 1835-1911

— Icones orchidearum Austro-Africanarum extratropicarum. L, 1896-1913. 3 vols in 4. 8vo, orig cloth; extremities worn, inner joints of Vol III cracked. With port & 300 plates, some colored. Port in Vol II with upper blank margin dampstained; very faint dampstaining at top towards end of Vol III. CNY Jan 25 (86) $850

Bombelli, Rafael

— L'Algebra opera. Bologna: Giovanni, Rossi, 1579. 8vo, 18th-cent half calf; spine worn at extremities. Tp & following leaf waterstained. Ck Nov 29 (147) £900

Bonacini, Claudio

— Bibliografia delle arti scrittorie et della calligrafia. Florence, 1953. Orig wraps. sg Oct 31 (194) $130

Bonafous, Louis Abel de. See: Fontenai, Abbe de

Bonanni, Filippo, 1638-1725

— Gabinetto Armonico, pieno d'Istromenti sonori indicati, e spiegati. Rome: Giorgio Placho, 1722. 2d Issue, with text to the appendix. 4to, contemp calf. With frontis & 151 plates, plus additional frontis bound in. C June 24 (114) £2,200 [Kraus]

— Numismata summorum pontificum templi Vaticani fabricam indicantia.... Rome, 1696. Folio, contemp lea. With engraved title & 90 plates. Some worming. HH May 12 (730) DM1,800

Anr copy. Contemp half lea; worn. With 88 (of 91) plates, most folding. Some browning. S May 14 (1077) £360 [Bifolco]

Anr Ed. Rome, 1715. Folio, contemp calf; joints & spine ends worn, 2 small strips torn from lower cover. With double-page plate of medals & 91 plans & views. Tp & 1 leaf creased; waterstain in blank foremargin of tp & a few leaves at the front. b June 22 (156) £520

Bonannius, Philippus. See: Bonnani, Filippo

Bonaparte, Charles Lucien, 1803-57
See also: Wilson & Bonaparte

— American Ornithology. Phila., 1825-33. 1st Ed. 3 (of 4) vols. Lacking Vol IV. Folio, half mor; disbound. With 21 hand-colored plates. Some leaves browned. CNY Dec 5 (299) $400

Anr copy. 4 vols. Folio, contemp half lea gilt; spine ends rubbed. With 27 hand-colored plates. Text foxed. sg May 7 (32) $2,200

— Iconographia della fauna italica. Rome, 1832-41. 3 vols in orig 30 parts. Folio, unbound in orig ptd wraps; some spines worn. With 181 hand-colored plates, including a duplicate in Part 25 Single wormhole through Part 1. S June 25 (4) £5,500 [Lib. Bolognese]

Bonaventura, Saint, 1221-74

— Dieta salutis. Venice: Arrivabene, 1518. 8vo, later calf. Some stains; stamp of the National Library, Lisbon, on tp. S Nov 14 (451) £200 [Franks]

Anr copy. Vellum. SI June 9 (168) LIt420,000

— Opuscula. Strassburg: [Printer of the 1483 Jordanus de Quedlinburg (Georg Husner)], 1495. 2 vols. Folio, 19th-cent half pigskin. Vol I lacking final blank; Vol II marginally wormed; some passages scored; lacking 1st 8 leaves. 381 (of 382) & 362 (of 370) leaves. Goff B-928. sg Mar 12 (115) $800

— Quaestiones super IV libros sententiarum Petri Lombardi cum textu. Nuremberg: Anton Koberger, 1500. Part 2 (of 4) only. Contemp calf over wooden bds; worn, restored, def catches & clasps. 192 leaves.

Goff P-488. sg Oct 24 (47) $1,100

Bond, Frederick Bligh —& Camm, Bede

— Roodscreens and Roodlofts. L, 1909. 2 vols. 4to, orig cloth; faded & rubbed. With 132 plates. Some foxing. sg Feb 6 (35) $80; sg Apr 2 (25) $100

Bond, George

— A Brief Account of the Colony of Port Jackson in New South Wales.... L, 1806. 4th Ed. 8vo, modern half calf. Title repaired with slight loss of text. S June 25 (164) £1,700 [Maggs]

Bond, Henry

— The Longitude Found.... L, 1676. 1st Ed. 4to, contemp calf; rebacked, corners renewed, sides worn. With 8 plates, including the extra plate of the inclinatory needle & with the extra leaf "This treatise...hath been examined..." Without the inclinatory needle plate. CNY Oct 8 (18) $950

Bond, John Walpole

— A History of Sussex Birds. See: Walpole-Bond, John

Bone, Muirhead

— Glasgow. Fifty Drawings.... Glasgow, 1911. One of 200. Folio, orig cloth. With 50 plates. pnE Mar 11 (121) £70

Anr copy. Cloth. pnE Mar 11 (260) £85

Bone, Muirhead & Gertrude

— Old Spain. L, 1936. One of 265. 2 vols & 1 (of 2) portfolios with 2 drypoints. Folio, pigskin. bba Mar 26 (177) £460 [Orssich]

Bonfils, Winifred Black

— The Life and Personality of Phoebe Apperson Hearst. San Francisco: John Henry Nash, 1928. One of 1,000. Vellum. sg Sept 26 (241) $60

Boni, Mauro

— Lettere sui primi libri a stampa di alcune citta' e terre dell' Italia superiore. Venice, 1794. 4to, old wraps; spine worn. bba May 28 (485) £110 [Maggs]

Bonifaccio, Giovanni

— Istoria di Trivigi. Venice, 1744. Folio, contemp vellum. SI Dec 5 (99) LIt1,200,000

Anr copy. 19th-cent half vellum. SI Dec 5 (769) LIt900,000

Boniface VIII, Pope, 1235?-1303

— Liber sextus decretalium. Mainz: Peter Schoeffer, 5 Apr 1473. Folio, contemp Viennese blind-stamp calf with pierced brass clasp plates; bosses removed, spine ends repaired, lower cover with some scratches & vertical crack in lea. 66 lines; double-column; types 5:118G (text) & 6:92G (commentary); rubricated; 1st initial illuminated. 161 (of 162) leaves; lacking final leaf with colophon, which is supplied in vellum facsimile. Goff B-981. Schoyen copy. P Dec 12 (15) $32,500

Bonnani, Filippo, 1638-1725

— Museum Kircherianum sive Musaeum a P. Athanasio Kirchero in Collegio Romano Societatis Jesu iam pridem incoeptum. Rome: Georgii Plachi, 1709. Folio, contemp vellum; spine worn. With 172 plates, 2 folding. Lacking port. C June 24 (113) £1,800 [Huber]

Bonnard, Camille

— Costumes des XIIIe, XIVe, et XVe Siecles.... Paris, 1845. ("Costumes historiques des XIIIe, XIVe et XVe siecles.") 2 vols. 4to, later cloth. With 200 hand-colored plates. Some dampstaining, affecting plates. bbc Apr 27 (188) $110

— Costumes historiques des XIIe, XIIIe, XIVe, et XVe siecles. Paris, 1860-61. Vols I & III only. Contemp half mor; worn, Vol I covers detached. sg Feb 13 (170) $275

Anr copy. 3 vols. 4to, contemp mor gilt; worn. Library markings. sg Feb 13 (171) $300

Bonnard, Pierre, 1867-1947

— Correspondances. Paris, 1944. 1st Ed, One of 1,025. CGen Nov 18 (309) SF200

Anr copy. Orig wraps. pn May 14 (104) £50; sg Sept 6 (30) $300

Bonnat, Leon

— Les Dessins de la Collection Leon Bonnat. Paris, 1925-26. 3 vols. Folio, loose as issued in half cloth; rubbed. With 180 plates. S Feb 11 (21) £150 [Creed]

Bonne, Rigobert, 1727-94

— Atlas moderne ou collection de cartes sur toutes les parties du globe terrestre. Paris: Chez Lattre...et Delalain, [1771]. Folio, contemp calf; rubbed. With engraved title & 73 double-page maps & 1 double-page diagram. S Nov 21 (137) £1,500 [Map House]

Bonnefoy, Yves

See also: Chagall, Marc

— Pierre Ecrite. Paris: Maeght, 1958. Out-of-series copy with an extra suite of plates & a proof. Illus by Raoul Ubac. Folio, unsewn in orig wraps. With 10 colored lithos. Frontis sgd by Ubac. CGen Nov 18 (310) SF6,500

Bonner, James

— A New Plan for Speedily Increasing the Number of Bee-Hives in Scotland.... Edin., 1795. 8vo, contemp bds; worn, upper cover detached. Some browning. pn Dec 12 (95) £120

Anr copy. Calf. pnE Oct 1 (278) £160

Anr copy. Cloth. pnE Mar 11 (23) $80

Bonner, T. D.

— The Life and Adventures of James P. Beckwourth, Mountaineer.... NY, 1856. 1st Ed. 12mo, orig cloth; some wear to ends, cloth damaged on lower rear bd. Some foxing; mold soiling at end. wa Mar 5 (395) $85

Bonnet, Charles, 1720-93

— Oeuvres d'histoire naturelle et de philosophie. Neuchatel, 1779-83. 8 vols. 4to, contemp calf; rubbed, spines chipped. Titles stamped. O Apr 28 (103) $600

— Recherches sur l'usage des feuilles dans les plantes. Goettingen & Leiden, 1754. 1st Ed. 4to, contemp calf with modern calf back; rubbed. With 31 folding plates. Lacking engraved title. O Jan 1 4 (26) $140

Bonnycastle, John, 1750?-1821

— An Introduction to Astronomy.... L, 1787. 2d Ed. 8vo, contemp calf. With 20 plates. 1 plate soiled & creased. bba Sept 5 (192) £150 [Bowers]

Bonnycastle, Sir Richard Henry, 1791-1847

— Spanish America.... L, 1818. 1st Ed. 2 vols. 8vo, contemp calf; spines dry & worn, joints cracked, 1 bd nearly detached, anr rejointed. With 2 fold-out maps & 1 fold-out plate. Some dampstain to lower gutter of Vol I, especially at beginning. wa Dec 9 (339) $130

Bontius, Jacobus

— De medicina Indorum libri IV. Leiden: F. Hackius, 1642. 12mo, modern calf; marked. Some worming, occasionally affecting text; repaired; some dampstaining. S Nov 15 (693) £150 [Erlini]

Bonvalot, Gabriel

— Across Thibet.... L, 1891. 2 vols. 8vo, orig cloth. sg Jan 9 (37) $150

— Through the Heart of Asia. L, 1889. 2 vols. 8vo, orig cloth. sg Jan 9 (38) $250

Bonwick, James, 1817-1906

— Daily Life and Origins of the Tasmanians.... L, 1870. 8vo, orig cloth. Foxed. kh Nov 11 (444) A$500

— Port Phillip Settlement. L, 1883. 8vo, orig cloth. With map & 36 plates. Lacking copy of old newspaper at p. 475. bba June 25 (245) £70 [Dawes]

Boodt, Anselmus Boetius de, 1550?-1634

— Gemmarum et lapidum historia. Leiden, 1647. In 1 vol. 8vo, orig vellum. pnE Dec 4 (26) £380

Book, Booke, or Boke

— Book Auction Records. Folkestone, 1976-87. Vols 72-84. 4to, orig cloth; worn. O Apr 28 (151) $120

Vols 86-87. Folkestone, 1989-90. 4to, orig cloth. DW Mar 4 (275) £85

— A Book of Sweethearts: Pictures by Famous American Artists. Indianapolis, [1908]. 4to, half cloth. With 12 colored plates. sp Apr 16 (161) $85

— The Book of the Homeless. NY, 1916. 1st American Ed, One of 50 on French handmade paper. Ed by Edith Wharton. 4to, half cloth. Lacks portfolio. sg Dec 12 (409) $225

— The Book of Trades, or Library of the Useful Arts. L, 1805-6. Mixed Ed. 3 vols. 12mo, orig cloth; Vol I marked. With 67 plates. bba Oct 10 (27) £340 [Rainford]

Book of Common Prayer

See also: Franklin & Dashwood

— 1549, 7 Mar. - [The Book of Common Prayer] L: Edward Whitchurche. 1st Ed, 1st Issue. Folio, early 18th-cent calf; rebacked preserving old spines. Black letter. Lacking 4 leaves & final blank; tear to margin of K3; rusthole in 2F5; 3 headlines shaved; wormed at margins affecting sidenotes; some stains. STC 16267. S July 21 (302) £1,300 [Rix]

— 1637-36. - Edin.: R. Young. 2 parts in 1 vol. Folio, contemp calf; marginal soiling & dampstaining. Stain and minor repair on M2; free endpapers torn & restored. STC 16607. sg Mar 12 (32) $650

— 1665. - Cambr.: J. Field. 2 parts in 1 vol. 12mo, contemp mor gilt; rubbed. In Greek. bba May 28 (18) £95 [Aspin]

— 1717. - L: John Sturt. 8vo, old mor gilt; rebacked, orig spine used. bba Apr 9 (81) £280 [R. Clark]

Anr copy. Contemp mor gilt; joints rubbed. Engraved throughout & ruled in red; volvelle on page v but no pointers. S May 14 (936) £320 [Cox]

— 1760. - Cambr.: Baskerville. 1st 8vo Ed. Contemp mor gilt; joints & extremities rubbed. F Mar 26 (697) $500

— 1761. - Cambr.: Baskerville. 8vo, contemp mor gilt; corners rubbed, head of spine damaged. bba Jan 16 (206) £220 [Bickersteth]

— 1844. - L: William Pickering. Folio, unbound. Foxed & browned at edges. bbc Apr 27 (186) $325

— 1845. - L. Designed by Owen Jones. 8vo,

orig mor gilt. cb Sept 26 (129) $150

— 1892. - NY 16mo, mor extra jewelled bdg by Sangorski & Sutcliffe. CNY June 9 (174) $4,600

— 1903. - Campden: Essex House Press One of 400. Folio, half mor gilt over oak bds, with metal clasps. sg Sept 26 (62) $1,200

— 1930. - Bost.: Merrymount Press One of 500. Folio, orig pigskin. sg Sept 26 (232) $350

Bookman's...

— Bookman's Price Index. Detroit, [1964-81]. Vols I-XV & XVII-XXII. Together, 21 vols. Cloth. sg Oct 31 (45) $550

Boole, George, 1815-64

— An Investigation of the Laws of Thought.... Cambr. & L, 1854. 8vo, orig cloth; rebacked. With the 2 errata leaves. With related material. DW Nov 6 (287) £3,900

Boone and Crockett Club. See: North American...

Boosey, Thomas

— Piscatorial Reminiscences and Gleanings, by an Old Angler and Bibliopolist. L, 1835. 2 parts in 1 vol. 8vo, cloth; worn. Koopman copy. O Oct 29 (39) $100

Booth, Edward Thomas

— Rough Notes on the Birds.... L, 1881-87. 3 vols. Folio, modern half mor gilt. With 2 hand-colored maps & 114 hand-colored plates. b June 22 (345) £2,800

Anr copy. Moder half mor. With 2 maps & 114 hand-colored plates. A few plates loose. bba Sept 5 (133) £3,200 [Swinley]

Anr copy. Contemp half mor gilt. With 114 hand-colored plates & 2 hand-colored maps. C Oct 30 (173) £3,600 [Radel]

Anr copy. Half calf. With 2 maps & 114 hand-colored plates. C May 20 (145A) £3,000 [Kelly]

Booth, Edwin Carton

— Australia. L, [1873-76?]. 2 vols. 4to, contemp half lea; rubbed. With 108 plates & 8 colored maps. Some dampstaining, mostly marginal. S May 14 (1314) £540 [Lochtenberg]

Booth, John

— The Battle of Waterloo. L, 1817. 10th Ed. 2 vols. 4to, contemp calf gilt; rebacked. With port, e6 folding plans & maps, colored folding panorama & 34 plates. Some folds torn, many repaired; 1 plate lacking section at edge. pn Nov 14 (372) £85

Booth, Stephen

— The Book Called Holinshed's Chronicles.... San Francisco: Book Club of California, 1968. Ltd Ed. 4to, half cloth. With orig leaf from the 1587 Ed. b&b Feb 19 (283) $90

Borchgrevink, Carsten Egeberg, 1864-1934

— First on the Antarctic Continent. L, 1901. 1st Ed. Orig cloth; loose. With port & 3 colored folding maps. Some tears. Library markings. bba Sept 19 (40) £150 [Maggs]

Anr copy. Frontis & port detached. cb Jan 30 (13) $425

Bordona, Jesus Dominguez. See: Dominguez Bordona, Jesus

Bordone, Benedetto

— Libro de Benedetto Bordone nel qual si ragiona de tutte l'isole del mondo. Venice: Nicolo de Aristotile, detto Zopppino, June 1534. ("Isolario....") Folio, contemp vellum; soiled. With 7 double-page maps & a double-page plan. Minor spotting to margins. C Dec 16 (28) £4,500 [Panini]

Borelli, Giovanni Alfonso, 1608-79

— De motu animalium. Rome, 1680-81. 1st Ed. 2 vols. 4to, contemp calf; worn. With 18 plates. Edges trimmed & creased; some staining to inner margins at beginning of Vol I; tp to Vol I soiled. S Dec 5 (358) £2,500 [Casey]

Anr Ed. The Hague, 1743. 2 parts in 1 vol. 4to, contemp half lea; worn. With engraved title & 19 plates. Some browning. SI Dec 5 (101) LIt1,400,000

Borges, Jorge Luis

See also: Limited Editions Club

— Ficciones. [N.p., 1984]. Illus by Sol Lewitt. Calf by Lewitt. Sgd by Lewitt. sg Sept 26 (164) $350

Borghi, Camillo Ranier

— L'Oplomachia pisana, ovvero la battaglia del Ponte di Pisa. Lucca, 1713. 4to, contemp vellum. Some leaves browned. SI Dec 5 (102) LIt1,200,000

Borghini, Vincenzo Maria

— Discorsi.... Florence: Giunta, 1584-85. 2 vols. 4to, contemp vellum. Lacking 1 blank; some browning. SI Dec 5 (771) LIt1,600,000

Borgia, Girolamo

— Ad carolum Caesarem Opt. Max. Monarchia. [Rome, 1525]. 4to, later bds; spine chipped. Some soiling & foxing. O May 26 (17) $700

Borgia, Lucrezia —& Bembo, Pietro, 1470-1547

— Messer Pietro Mio. Letters between Lucrezia Borgia & Pietro Bembo. Marlborough: Libanus Press, 1985. One of 135. Mor extra by Denise Lubett. CNY June 9 (114) $1,000

Borlase, William, 1695-1772

— The Natural History of Cornwall. Oxford, 1758. 1st Ed. Folio, contemp calf; rebacked, orig spine preserved. With folding map & 28 plates. Map torn at fold. bba Jan 30 (12) £380 [Shapero]

Anr copy. Contemp calf; worn, spine def. With folding map & 28 plates, but map is substitution by Morden for the missing map by Jackson issued with the book. wa Sept 26 (465) $210

Anr copy. Contemp calf; rebacked, worn & chipped. With folding map & 28 plates. Some browning. wd June 12 (371) $550

— Observations of the Antiquities Historical and Monumental, of the County of Cornwall. Oxford, 1754. 1st Ed. Folio, contemp calf; spine worn, joints broken, bds loosely secured by cords. With 24 full-page plates & map of Cornwall. wa Sept 26 (464) $210

— Observations on the Ancient and Present State of the Islands of Scilly.... Oxford, 1756. 4to, modern half calf. With 4 folding plates. bba Jan 30 (11) £190 [J. Smith]

Anr copy. Calf gilt; spine & corners chipped. With 5 plates, 3 folding. L Nov 14 (95) £180

— Observations of the Antiquities Historical and Monumental, of the County of Cornwall. L, 1769. ("Antiquities Historical and Monumental of the County of Cornwall.") 2d Ed. Folio, contemp calf; corners repaired. With 2 maps (1 folding) & 25 plates. bba Jan 30 (13) £340 [Thorp]

Anr copy. Later half sheep. With 2 maps & 25 plates. bba Jan 30 (367) £170 [Collinge]

Born, Ignaz von, 1742-91

— Travels through the Bannat of Temeswar, Transylvania, and Hungary.... L, 1777. 1st Ed in English. 8vo, contemp calf; rubbed. bba Sept 19 (133) £320 [Morrell]

Borneman, Henry Stauffer

— Pennsylvania German Illuminated Manuscripts: a Classification.... Norristown, 1937. Folio, orig cloth; scratched & marked. K Dec 1 (348) $180

Anr copy. Cloth; worn. NH May 30 (409) $150; sg Oct 31 (195) $200

Borroni, Fabia

— Bibliographia dell'archeologia classice dell'arte italiana. Florence, 1954-67. One of 666. 2 vols in 12. New cloth, orig wraps bound in. O Sept 24 (38) $400

Borrow, George Henry, 1803-81

— Lavengro. L, 1851. 1st Ed. 3 vols. 8vo, orig cloth; scuffed. Some foxing. O July 14 (32) $80

Anr copy. Orig cloth; worn. O July 14 (32) $80

Borthwick, John Douglas

— Three Years in California. Edin. & L, 1857. 8vo, cloth; spine repaired without loss. sg June 18 (45) $300

Bory de Saint Vincent, Jean Baptiste G. M., 1778?-1846 —& Schneider, Antoine

— Histoire et description des iles Ionniennes. Paris, 1823. Atlas vol only. Folio, contemp half vellum. With 16 litho plates & maps & 2 plates showing coins. S June 30 (244) £450 [Frew Mackenzie]

Bory de Saint-Vincent, Jean Baptiste G. M., 1778?-1846

— Expedition scientifique de Moree. Paris & Strasbourg, 1835. Atlas vol only. Folio, modern cloth; soiled. With port & 141 plates & maps only, 65 of them hand-colored. Some spotting. S July 1 (556) £3,800 [Constantelopoulos]

Bosa, Eugene

— Soggetti pittoreschi e costumi di Venezia. Venice, [1835?]. Folio, contemp bds. With 23 (of 24) plates. Marginal spotting. SI Dec 5 (104) LIt800,000

Boscar, Professor. See: Ceillier, Remi

Boschini, Marco, 1613-78

— L'Arcipelago. Con tute le Isole, Scogli secche, e Bassi fondi.... Venice: Francesco Nicolini, 1658. 4to, bds. With arms, folding general map of the Archipelago (damaged with loss at fold), folding maps of Crete & Negroponte & 47 plates. Corner of Tinos plate torn away; small hole in map of Cerigo; lacking half-title. S Nov 21 (236) £1,600 [Maggs]

— Le Minere della pittura.... Venice, 1664. 12mo, contemp vellum; soiled, lacking free endpapers. With frontis & 6 plates. Some dampstaining. S Feb 11 (23) £320 [Zioni]

Boscovich, Ruggiero Giuseppe, 1711-87

— Theoria philosophiae naturalis.... Venice, 1763. 4to, contemp vellum bds; rubbed. With 4 folding plates. Library stamps. bba Nov 28 (146) £400 [Quaritch]

Bosio, Giacomo

— Histoire des chevaliers de l'ordre de S. Jean de Hierusalem.... Lyon: G. Rouille, 1612. Folio, contemp vellum. Portion torn from head of engraved title & conjugate leaf with some loss of surface & letters. S June 30 (11) £950 [Severis]

Anr Ed. Paris: J. d'Allin, 1643. 4 parts in 1 vol. Folio, contemp calf; repaired. With 3 engraved title & 4 maps. Worming to 1st engraved title & some margins; 1 map with splits; some margins shaved. S June 30 (12) £2,700 [Christodoulou]

— Historia della Sacra Religione et Illustrissima Militia di S. Giovanni Gierosolomitano. Rome, 1676 [but Venice & Naples, 1695-84]. 3 vols. Folio, contemp calf. With engraved titles (2 shaved at foot) & double-page view. Some leaves discolored. S June 30 (13) £1,100 [Ganado]

Bosman, Willem

— A New and Accurate Description of the Coast of Guinea.... L, 1705. 8vo, contemp calf; rebacked, rubbed. With folding map & 7 plates. Map repaired at margin, affecting corner of engraved framed. b June 22 (229) £300

Anr copy. Modern cloth. Some dampstaining & browning; H1 repaired at outer margin; 1 plate torn at outer margin, affecting image. Ck May 15 (77) £140

Bosse, Abraham

— La Pratique du trait a preuves de Mr. Desargues...pour la coupe des pierres en l'architecture. Paris, 1643. 1st Ed. Vol I (all pbd). 8vo, 18th-cent calf; worn. SI June 9 (172) LIt750,000

Bossert, Helmuth Theodor

— An Encyclopaedia of Colour Decoration.... L, 1928. 4to, cloth, in d/j. Some foxing. kh Nov 11 (57) A$180

Bosset, C. P. de

— Parga, and the Islands.... L, 1821. 8vo, contemp half calf; rubbed. With 2 maps, 1 folding, both browned. S June 30 (245) £400 [Spink]

Bossi, Luigi

— Vita di Cristoforo Colombo.... Milan, 1818. 1st Ed. 8vo, orig half calf; worn & faded, worm holes in spine. With 6 plates. Some foxing. wa Dec 9 (283) $60

Bossoli, Carlo, 1815-84

— The War in Italy. L, 1859-60. 4to, sewn; disbound. With tinted litho title & 39 plates & 2 maps. Some spotting. Ck May 15 (78) £550

Bossuet, Francois

— De Natura aquatilium carmen. Lyon: Matthiam Bonhome, 1558. 2 vols in 1. 4to, contemp calf; rebacked & recornered. Some soiling, browning & staiing; final leaf torn with some loss. Ck Oct 31 (42) £600

Bost, Pierre

— Electricite. Paris, 1931. One of 500. Illus by Man Ray. 4to, loose as issued. CGen Nov 18 (311) SF10,500

Boston Museum of Fine Arts

— American Church Silver of the Seventeenth and Eighteenth Centuries.... Bost., 1911. 8vo, half cloth. sp Feb 6 (231) $60

Boswell, Henry

— Historical Descriptions.... L: A. Hogg, [c.1790]. Folio, contemp calf; worn. With 224 plates & maps. Library stamps on plate versos, some with show-through. S Nov 15 (776) £700 [Brigantian]

Anr copy. Bound in 2 vols. Folio, W July 8 (201) £680

Boswell, James, 1740-95

— An Account of Corsica. Glasgow, 1768. 1st Ed. 8vo, contemp calf; rebacked, corners rubbed, upper cover detached & repaired at inner hinges. With cancelled E2 & Z3 as usual; E2 with Istria divided. Milne copy. Ck June 12 (17) £200

Anr copy. Contemp vellum. Lacking final blank. sg Nov 7 (97) $475

2d Ed. L, 1768. 8vo, library half mor. bba Jan 16 (129) £150

Anr copy. Contemp calf gilt; old calf, rebacked with modern calf. With folding map. cb Oct 25 (7) $140

Anr copy. Contemp calf; joints cracked. Last 2 leaves browned at margins. Milne copy. Ck June 12 (18) £90

— Dr. Johnson's Table-Talk. L, 1798. 8vo, modern half calf. sg Mar 12 (141) $200

— The Journal of a Tour to the Hebrides.... L, 1785. 1st Ed. 8vo, contemp sheep; covers detached. sg Nov 7 (98) $650

2d Ed. 8vo, modern calf. sg Mar 12 (138) $275

— The Life of Samuel Johnson. L, 1791 1st Ed, with the "give" reading on p. 135 of Vol I. 2 vols. 4to, contemp calf. Bound in are the Principal Corrections and Additions...1793, & the folding map from the Tour of the Hebrides. K July 12 (69) $2,900

1st Ed. L, 1791. Issue not given. 2 vols. 4to, contemp half russia; covers detached. Lacking port; some spotting. Milne copy. Ck June 12 (20) £300

With the "give" reading on p. 135 of Vol I. Modern calf. CNY Dec 5 (169) $1,900

Anr copy. Contemp half mor gilt; rubbed, bd edges worn. With port, 2 facsimiles & 7 cancels. Stub of 2d plate affixed to leaf 4F with some discoloration; pencil lines in margins; small hole in T1 of Vol II affecting a word in each page; inked word on Z3r. Manney copy. P Oct 11 (20) $13,000

With the "gve" reading. Modern calf gilt by Birdsall. With port & 2 plates. Vol II lacking front blank. C Dec 16 (185) £1,500 [Paradise]

Anr copy. Contemp half sheep; spines rubbed, joints starting. sg Nov 7 (99) $2,6000

Anr copy. Contemp calf gilt; endpapers renewed. sg Mar 12 (140) $1,600

Anr copy. 19th-cent calf gilt; rear cover and last few pp of Vol I detached. A few marginal repairs and pencil scrawls in some margins of Vol II. Epstein copy. sg Apr 29 (36) $3,000

2d Ed. L, 1793. 3 vols. 8vo, contemp calf; worn, Vols I & III covers detached. bba Jan 30 (166) £650 [Harrington]

Anr copy. Contemp calf; rebacked, orig spines preserved. With port & folding facsimile at end of Vol III. bba Apr 9 (9) £320 [Gammon]

Anr copy. Contemp calf; rubbed, rebacked. With port & 2 folding plates. S Nov 14 (512) £250 [Beeleigh Abbey]

Anr Ed. Bost., 1807. 3 vols. 8vo, calf; worn. Margins of Vol I tp badly frayed; frontis hinged; some foxing. NH Aug 23 (113) $75

Anr copy. Orig bds, Vol III in variant marbled bds; some chipping & tearing of spines. Some browning & soiling; marginal tears. P Dec 12 (160) $1,900

Anr Ed. L, 1822. 4 vols. 8vo, half mor gilt. Extra-illus with c.200 ports & views. sg May 7 (34) $400

Anr Ed. L, 1831. 5 vols. 8vo, orig bds; spine ends worn. sg Mar 5 (22) $200

Anr copy. Modern half calf gilt. Extra-illus with c.150 ports. sg Mar 5 (23) $550

Anr Ed. L, 1835. 10 vols. 8vo, later mor gilt by Bayntun; scuffed. F Mar 26 (82) $275

Anr copy. Mor gilt. NH May 30 (79) $340

Reynolds Ed. L, 1885. One of 500. 5 vols. 8vo, mor gilt by Root. Extra-illus with c.150 ports. O May 26 (18) $950

Anr Ed. Oxford, 1887. Ed by George Birkbeck Hill. 6 vols. 8vo, mor gilt by Morell; spine rubbed & chipped. Extra-illus with c.290 etched & engraved plates. CNY Dec 5 (388) $1,100

Anr copy. Half mor gilt. pnE Aug 12 (278) £160

Temple Bar Ed. NY, 1922. Ed by Clement Shorter. 10 vols. 8vo, pigskin gilt extra; some spines discolored or stained. cb Dec 5 (13) $375

Anr copy. Contemp half mor by Sangorski & Sutcliffe. Ck July 10 (191) £420

Anr copy. Bds, in chipped d/js (2 lacking). Frank Frisch's copy. K July 12 (70) $160

— Private Papers from Malahide Castle in the Collection of Ralph Heyward Isham. L, 1928-37. Ed by Geoffrey Scott. Vols 7-9 only. 4to, cloth. sg Oct 31 (49) $150

Botanic...

— The Botanic Garden.... L, 1825-[51]. Ed by Benjamin Maund. Vols I-XIII (complete set), plus The Fruitist, The Floral Register & the Auctarium. 8vo, contemp mor gilt. With engraved titles & 312 hand-colored plates in the Botanic Garden Fruitist with 72 hand-colored illusts. C Oct 30 (210) £4,000 [Marshall]

Anr copy. Vols I-III. Contemp half lea; worn, 1 spine def, anr repaired with tape. Vol II lacking ptd title; engraved title loose; some spotting. pn Apr 23 (229) £600 [Russell]

Vol XII only. Contemp half calf; rubbed. With engraved title & 47 hand-colored plates. Ck May 15 (37) £350

Vols I-IX. 9 vols. modern cloth. With 216 hand-colored plates. Sold w.a.f. S Nov 21 (34) £1,600 [Kiefer]

Vols I-V. 5 vols plus The Auctarium. Half mor gilt; rubbed. With 120 hand-colored plates. Sold w.a.f. S Nov 21 (32) £1,300 [Burden]

Vols I-XII (of 13) in 11. 11 vols. Contemp half mor gilt; final vol not uniform & with upper cover detached. With 290 hand-colored plates. Plate 39 soiled; Plate 101 stained. Sold w.a.f. L.p. copies excapt for Vols XI & XII. S Nov 21 (33) £3,200 [Burden]

Botanical. See: Loddiges, Conrad & Sons

Botanist...

— The Botanist: Containing Accurately Coloured Figures of Tender and Hardy Ornamental Plants. L, [1837-42]. Ed by Benjamin Maund & J. S. Henslow. 5 vols. 4to, contemp half mor. With 3 engraved titles & 250 hand-colored plates. Ck Oct 6 (33) £1,800

Botero, Giovanni, 1540-1617

— Aggiunta alla quarta parte dell'Indie.... Venice: Alessandro Vecchi, 1622. 4to, vellum bds. S July 1 (826) £700 [Martayan Lan]

— Allgemeine historische Weltbeschreibung. Munich: Nicolaus Heinrich, 1611. Folio, contemp blind-stamped pigskin over wooden bds painted sepia, brass clasps & catches. With 5 folding maps.. Tp stamped; L1 & tp damaged & repaired touching letters; some discoloration to text. S Nov 21 (210) £2,300 [Maggs]

Botkin, Mikhail Petrovich, 1839-1914

— Sobranie M. P. Botkina. St. Petersburg, 1911. 4to, contemp half lea; rear joint cracked, spine ends & corners chipped. With 103 plates, some colored. sg Apr 2 (26) $375

Bottomley, William Lawrence

— Great Georgian Houses of America. NY, 1933-37. 2 vols. sp Feb 6 (163) $210

Bottu de Limas, J.

— Six Mois en Orient. Lyons, 1861. 8vo, contemp half mor. With engraved double-page plan & 18 plates, 1 folding. S June 30 (93) £400 [Kanaan]

Bouche, Henri. See: Dollfus & Bouche

Boucher, Francois

— Les Enseignes de Paris. Paris: Le Goupy, [1924-25]. One of 100. Illus by Jean-Jules Dufour. 2 vols in 1. 4to, contemp half lea; spine ends chipped, rear joint cracked. With 10 sgd etchings. sg Feb 6 (74) $150

Boudinot, Elias, 1740-1821

— Journal, or Historical Recollections of American Events.... Phila., 1894. Out-of-series copy. 4to, mor gilt by Oldach. Extra-illus with ports, views & ALs from Boudinot to his brother, 1 Apr 1782. K Dec 1 (53) $1,500

Boue, Ami

— La Turquie d'Europe. Paris, 1840. 8vo, contemp calf gilt by J. Clark, with Fitzwilliam crest on covers; 1 cover detached. With folding map. Lacking half-title in Vol I. S June 30 (246) £1,300 [Atabey]

Boufflers, Stanislas Jean de

— Aline, Reine de Golconde. Paris: Societe des Amis des Livres, 1887. One of 115. 8vo, bdg not described. br May 29 (16) $525

Bougainville, Louis Antoine de, 1729-1811

— Voyage autour du monde.... Paris, 1771. 1st Ed. 4to, contemp calf gilt; joints cracked, spine repaired. With 20 folding maps & 3 plates. S June 25 (47) £900 [Quaritch/ Hordern]

— A Voyage Round the World.... L, 1772. 4to, contemp half calf; rebacked & corners restored. With 5 folding maps & 1 folding plate. Marginal tear to tp;l 2 other 1-inch marginal tears; short tears to 3 inner margins of 3 maps; tp soiled. CNY Oct 8 (19) $1,500

Anr copy. 19th-cent calf; upper cover detached, lower joint cracked, top compartment of spine torn away. Small stains to 2d map; 3 maps with 1-inch tears at inner margins; 1 stain partly obscuring a letter; world map foxed. CNY Oct 8 (20) $850

Anr copy. Early calf; minor defs, rebacked. Maps torn & repaired. kh Nov 11 (446) A$1,500

Anr copy. Contemp calf; rebacked, orig spine preserved, lower cover detached. With 5 folding maps. Lacking plate of the canoes; dampstaining to lower margins of 1st few leaves; some spotting. pn June 11 (284) £280

Anr copy. Calf; rebacked. With 6 folding maps & 1 folding plate. S Nov 21 (375) £700 [Clark]

Anr copy. Contemp calf; joints restored. With 6 folding maps & plates. S June 25 (48) £950 [Arnold]

Bougard, R.

— The Little Sea Torch. L, 1801. Folio, contemp half calf; rubbed, spine ends torn with loss. With 20 hand-colored plates & 24 hand-colored charts on 12 sheets. Ck May 15 (79) £1,100

Bouillon, Pierre, 1776-1831

— Musee des antiques. Paris, [1811-27]. Vols I-II only. Contemp half mor gilt; some wear. With 181 plates. Some dampstaining. S Feb 11 (295) £500 [Shapero]

Boulger, Demetrius Charles

— History of China. L, 1881-84. 3 vols. 8vo, orig cloth; head of spine chipped. With frontis & folding map. sg May 21 (8) $150

Boulton, William B.

— The Amusements of Old London. L, 1901. 2 vols. 4to, orig cloth. With 12 hand-colored plates. K Dec 1 (17) $90

Bourgoing, Jean Francois de, 1748-1811
— Travels in Spain.... L, 1789. 3 vols. 8vo, modern half calf; worn. With 12 plates, maps & plans. O Jan 14 (27) $300

Bourke, John Gregory, 1843-96
— The Snake-Dance of the Moquis of Arizona. NY, 1884. 8vo, orig cloth. With 33 plates & diagrams. Underscored in red. DW Nov 20 (4) £105

Bourke-White, Margaret
— "Dear Fatherland Rest Quietly" A Report on the Collapse of Hitler's "Thousand Years." NY, 1946. 4to, cloth; spine ends bumped. sg Apr 13 (12) $150
— Photographs of U.S.S.R. Albany: Argus Press, [1934]. One of 1,000. Folio, cloth-backed bd portfolio; dampstaining on covers. With 24 photogravures. Intro curling at fold with small tear; creases & curling on 3 mats. sg Apr 13 (13) $2,600
— Portrait of Myself. NY, 1963. Inscr to Sid Kramer. wa Dec 9 (264) $65

Bourke-White, Margaret —& Caldwell, Erskine
— Say, Is This the U.S.A. NY, [1941]. 1st Ed. Folio, orig bds, in d/j. Some spotting & soiling. F June 25 (490) $70

Anr copy. Cloth; spine ends worn. Some soiling. sg Oct 8 (9) $150
— You Have Seen Their Faces. NY, [1937]. 4to, orig cloth, in d/j. Some soiling. F June 25 (489) $90

Bourne, George
— Picture of Slavery in the United States of America. Middletown, Conn., 1834. 1st Ed. 12mo, orig cloth; spine ends chipped. Some foxing & browning. bbc Feb 17 (122) $50

Bourne, John C.
— The History and Description of the Great Western Railway.... L, 1846. Folio, contemp half mor; rubbed. With litho title, dedication leaf & 47 plates on 33 sheets & 2 maps, 1 colored in outline. Title to A2 dampstained at lower margin. Ck Sept 6 (104) £3,200

Anr copy. With litho title & 47 plates on 33 sheets & 2 maps, 1 hand-colored. A1-U2 holed affecting text; some dampstaining to plate margins; 1 plate frayed. Ck Oct 18 (45) £1,300

Bourne, John C. —& Britton, John, 1771-1857
— Drawings of the London and Birmingham Railway. L, 1839. Folio, orig half mor; spotted. With litho title, 2 maps on 1 sheet & 34 plates on 29 sheets. Ck Oct 18 (43) £1,300

Anr copy. Parts III & IV only. Folio, orig half cloth; worn. With litho title & 14 plates on 12 sheets. Tp with small section at bottom excised; some fraying; text browned. Ck Oct 18 (44) £200

Bourne, William, d.1583
— A Booke Called the Treasure for Traveilers.... L: Thomas Woodcocke, 1578. 1st Ed. 4to, old sheep; upper cover detached. Small hole to tp & dedication leaf with loss to 1 letter of dedication; sidenotes & errata leaf cropped. CNY June 9 (134) $5,500

Bourrienne, Louis Antoine Fauvelet de. See: Fauvelet de Bourrienne, Louis Antoine

Boutet de Monvel, Maurice
— Jeanne d'Arc. Paris, [1896]. Oblong 4to, orig cloth; spine worn. sg Jan 30 (12) $100

Boutet, Henri
— Pointes seches. Paris, 1898. One of 50 on Japan imperial with orig drypoint, sgd, & with additional suite of the plates on China. 4to, contemp half mor by Meunier. Ck Dec 11 (134) £260

Bovis, Marcel —& Saint-Julien, Francois
— Nus d'autrefois.... Paris, 1953. 4to, wraps; spine end torn. sg Apr 13 (15) $50

Bowdich, Thomas Edward, 1791-1824
— Mission from Cape Coast Castle to Ashantee.... L, 1819. 4to, contemp half calf gilt; rubbed. With 2 maps & 12 plates, 7 hand-colored. Repair to 1 plate. bba June 25 (21) £380 [Lawson]

Bowditch, Nathaniel, 1773-1838
— The New American Practical Navigator. Newburyport MA: Edmund M. Blunt, 1802. 8vo, contemp calf; spine perished, upper cover detached. With folding map & 7 plates. Some staining; H3 torn; hole in ad leaf; browned. CNY Oct 8 (22) $2,200

Anr copy. Contemp sheep; joints broken & repaired, portion of backstrip & corners renewed. Fore-edge of frontis renewed; 2 small tears into plate; Dd1 with lower edge ragged & signature mark def; browned; some dampstaining. CNY Oct 8 (23) $2,600

Anr Ed. Newburyport, 1807. 8vo, contemp sheep; first gathering loose. With folding map & 11 plates. Short tear to map fold; some foxing. sg June 18 (22) $350

Bowen, Emanuel, d.1767
See also: Owen & Bowen
— A Complete System of Geography. L, 1744. 2 vols. Folio, orig bds; worn & split. With 45 maps only, some loose & torn. Sold

w.a.f. pnE May 13 (100) £620

Anr copy. Vol I (of 2). Folio, calf; worn. With 27 mostly folding maps, hand-colored in outline, & 2 plates. Tp laid down. S June 25 (300) £900 [Storey]

Bowen, Emanuel, d.1767 —& Bowen, Thomas

— Atlas Anglicanus, or a Complete Sett of Maps of the Counties of South Britain. L, 1777. Folio, orig calf; worn & def, broken. With 45 hand-colored maps. Lacking engraved title; some leaves loose; some browning & spotting. S May 14 (1133) £1,100 [Tooley Adams]

Bowen, Frank Charles

— The Golden Age of Sail: Indiamen, Packets and Clipper Ships. L, 1925. One of 1,500. 4to, cloth. sg Jan 9 (39) $150

— The Sea, its History and Romance. NY, 1927. 4 vols. 4to, cloth; worn. O July 14 (35) $50

Bowen, Thomas. See: Bowen & Bowen

Bowerbank, James Scott

— A Monograph of the British Spongiadae. L: Ray Society, 1864-82. 4 vols. 8vo, cloth; worn. Library markings. O Apr 28 (69) $60

Bowes, James Lord, 1834-99

— Japanese Pottery. Liverpool, 1890. 4to, orig cloth; rubbed, rear joint starting. cb Nov 21 (50) $90

Bowler, George

— Chapel and Church Architecture.... Bost., 1856. Folio, half lea; edges worn. With 47 lithos, 32 in color. sg Sept 6 (6) $750

Bowles, Samuel, 1797-1851

— Across the Continent: A Summer's Journey to the Rocky Mountains.... Springfield MA, 1865. 8vo, orig cloth; extremities worn. cb Feb 12 (6) $80

— Across the Continent. Springfield, Mass., 1866. 12mo, bdg not stated. O Feb 25 (28) $80

Bowlker, Charles, d.1779

— The Art of Angling.... Birm.: M. Swinney, 1783. 3d Ed. 12mo, half calf; rubbed. Thomas Best's copy. Koopman copy. O Oct 29 (40) $475

Bownas, Samuel, 1676-1753 —& Richardson, John, 1667-1753

— The Journals of the Lives and Travels of.... Phila., 1759. 2 parts in 1 vol. 8vo, contemp sheep; worn. sg June 18 (23) $175

Bowring, Sir John, 1792-1872

— The Kingdom and People of Siam. L, 1857. 2 vols. 8vo, bds; crudely rebacked. Sold w.a.f. O Apr 28 (155) $70

Bowyer, Robert, 1758-1834

— The Campaign of Waterloo. L, 1816. Folio, contemp half mor gilt; upper cover detached. With map, hand-colored plate of the Battle of Waterloo, single-page plate & 4 half-page plates. DW May 13 (6) £130

Anr copy. Old half mor; rebacked. With 2 plates of ports & 6 (on 4) hand-colored views. Small marginal repair. L Nov 14 (49) £180

— An Illustrated Record of Important Events in the Annals of Europe.... L, 1816. Folio, orig cloth; worn. With 6 hand-colored plates. Torn along folds. bba Oct 24 (232) £260 [Erlini]

— An Impartial Historical Narrative.... L, 1823. Folio, contemmp half mor gilt; spine worn. With 7 plates only, 3 hand-colored. DW Oct 2 (90) £95

— The Triumphs of Europe.... L, 1814. Bound with: Bowyer. An Illustrated Record of Important Events in the Annals of Europe. L, 1815. And: Bowyer. The Campaign of Waterloo. L, 1816. Folio, modern half mor gilt by Bayntun-Riviere. With engraved map & 2 plates & 19 hand-colored aquatint plates. Short marginal tears at the fold of 2 plates; sold w.a.f. C May 20 (21) £1,100 [Litup]

Boyd, James, 1888-1944

— Drums. NY, 1925. One of 525. With ALs, 13 Jan 1926. sg Dec 12 (27) $60

Anr Ed. NY, [1928]. 4to, orig cloth, in d/j. K Mar 22 (460) $150

One of 500. Orig cloth. bbc Apr 27 (423) $460

Anr copy. Orig cloth, in worn & chipped d/j. NH Aug 23 (455) $70

Boydell, John & Josiah

— Graphic Illustrations of the Dramatic Works of Shakespeare. L, [plates dated 1798-1802]. Folio, contemp mor gilt; rubbed, spine worn at head. With engraved title, frontis, port (mtd) & 98 plates, 10 cut down & remtd. pn July 16 (126) £150

Anr copy. Contemp mor gilt; worn. With engraved title & 100 plates. Small tear in lower outer corner of 1st few leaves. S Feb 25 (446) £750 [Golden Legend]

Anr Ed. NY, 1852. ("Illustrations of the Dramatic Works of Shakespeare....") 2 vols. Folio, disbound. With 100 plates. Some foxing & staining. Sold w.a.f. O Nov 26 (27) $2,200

Anr copy. Half sheep; extremities worn.

With 2 engraved title vignettes & 98 plates. sg Feb 13 (167) $2,000

Anr copy. Folio, half sheep; worn. Some dampstaining, occasionally affecting extremities of images. sg Apr 2 (166) $1,200

Anr copy. Contemp half sheep; worn. With 2 title vignettes & 98 plates. Some plates foxed; prelims creased. sg May 7 (36) $2,200

— An History of the River Thames. L, 1794-96. 2 vols. Folio, 19th-cent half mor; corners scuffed. With folding map bound as 2 separate sheets & 65 plates. Lacking general titles & dedication to George III;; spotting affecting frontis, 2 plates & a few text leaves. C Oct 30 (124) £3,000 [Joseph]

Anr copy. Half mor gilt by Bayntun. With frontis, map on 2 folding sheets (1 in each vol) & 76 hand-colored plates, including 3 double-page. Lacking general titles & dedication to George III; some spotting to text. C May 20 (23) £2,800 [Simon Finch]

Anr copy. Contemp mor gilt; Vol I lower cover stained. With frontis, folding map & 76 hand-colored plates & with the dedication to George III. Vol I with light marginal waterstain touching 1 or 2 plates. S June 25 (275) £3,400 [Marlborough]

Boyer, Jean Baptiste de, Marquis d'Argens.
See: Argens, Jean Baptiste de Boyer

Boyle, Kay

— Short Stories. Paris: Black Sun Press, 1929. One of 150. Wraps. Epstein copy. sg Apr 29 (37) $450

Boyle, Robert, 1627-91

— Hydrostatical Paradoxes Made Out by New Experiments. Oxford, 1666. 1st Ed. 8vo, contemp calf; needs rebacking. With 3 folding plates. sg May 14 (267) $800

— Medicinal Experiments.... L, 1703. "4th Ed". 3 parts in 1 vol. 12mo, contemp calf; broken, lacking front free endpaper. Some words of text inked out. sg May 14 (21) $200

— New Experiments Physico-Mechanicall, Touching the Spring of the Air and its Effects.... Oxford, 1662. 2d Ed. 3 parts in 1 vol. 4to, sheep; worn. Folding plate detached & laid in. P June 17 (137) $1,900

Boyle, Roger, 1st Earl of Orrery, 1621-79

— A Treatise of the Art of War.... L, 1677. 1st Ed. Folio, later half calf; rubbed, joints split. With frontis & 6 plates. Lacking final blank; outer corner of P1 torn away; some staining & fraying at margins of last few leaves. S July 1 (1217) £260 [Dennistoun]

Boym, Michael

— Flora Sinensis, Fructus Floresque Humillime Porrigens.... Vienna, 1656. Folio, contemp vellum; restored. With 23 plates in contemp hand-coloring. Lower part of fore-margins repaired throughout without loss. C May 20 (147) £29,000 [Israel]

Boynton, Edward C., 1824-93

— History of West Point.... NY, 1871. 8vo, cloth. Orange Judd's copy. O Aug 25 (38) $60

Boys, Thomas Shotter, 1803-74

— Original Views of London as It Is. L, 1842. Folio, orig half mor gilt; rubbed. With 26 tinted lithos, hand-colored. Schlosser copy. P June 18 (520) $9,000

— Original Views of London.... L, 1954-55. 2 vols. Folio, orig half mor; rubbed. Facsimile of the 1842 Ed. pn July 16 (184) £60

— Picturesque Architecture in Paris, Ghent, Antwerp, Rouen. L, 1839. Folio, contemp mor with silk onlay; hinges cracked. With 26 tinted & chromolitho plates, including title. Interleaved; tp loose; fore-edge lightly soiled. Schlosser copy. P June 18 (519) $4,250

Anr copy. Half mor gilt, with orig gilt blocked upper cover; rubbed. Lacking 3 leaves of plates & Descriptive Notice; 3 plates frayed & soiled at edges; Plate 13 stained, cut down & mtd; some dampstaining to lower margins. pn Sept 12 (255) £600 [Sotheran]

Brackenridge, Henry M., 1786-1871

— Voyage to South America.... Balt., 1819. 1st Ed. 2 vols. 8vo, contemp sheep; needs rebdg. sg Dec 5 (16) $60

Bradbury, Frederick

— History of Old Sheffield Plate. L, 1912. 4to, cloth. sg Apr 2 (27) $130

Bradbury, Ray

See also: Limited Editions Club

— Dandelion Wine. Garden City, 1957. In d/j. cb Dec 12 (187) $110

— Dark Carnival. Sauk City, 1947. Cover with stains, in d/j. sp Sept 22 (125) $325

One of 300. sg Apr 29 (38) $600

Anr copy. In d/j. sp Sept 22 (125) $325

— Fahrenheit 451. NY: Ballantine Books, [1953]. One of 200 bound in Johns-Manville Quinterra asbestos. P Oct 11 (22) $1,900

— Genie Trouble. Los Angeles, 1940. Orig wraps. In: The Damned Thing. pba July 9 (27) $100

— The Illustrated Man. NY, 1951. In frayed d/j. bba Aug 13 (240) £55 [Pearson]

— The Martian Chronicles. Garden City, 1950. 1st Ed. In green bdg, in d/j with edge wear. sg June 11 (29) $450

Anr copy. In d/j. wa Sept 26 (299) $350

— The October Country. NY: Ballantine Books, [1955]. 1st Ed. In d/j with small chips. wa Mar 5 (150) $160

Bradford, John, 1749-1830. See: Grabhorn Printing

Bradford, Sarah H.

— Scenes in the Life of Harriet Tubman. Auburn, 1869. 12mo, orig cloth; stain to upper cover. bbc Dec 9 (419) $300

Bradford, Thomas Gamaliel, 1802-87

— A Comprehensive Atlas.... Bost.: American Stationers Co., [1835]. 4to, old bds with modern mor back; worn. O Nov 26 (28) $600

Bradford, Thomas Lindsley, 1847-1918

— The Bibliographer's Manual of American History.... Phila., 1907-10. 5 vols. 4to, bdg not described. Wilberforce Eames's set. K Sept 29 (91) $60

Bradford, William, Artist

— The Arctic Regions Illustrated with Photographs.... L, 1873. Folio, orig mor gilt by Leighton; rebacked. With 141 albumen prints. Some discoloration. Manney copy. P Oct 11 (23) $12,000

Bradford, William, 1755-95

— An Enquiry how far the Punishment of Death is Necessary in Pennsylvania. Phila., 1793. 8vo, 19th-cent mor; extremities worn. Staining throughout in lower margin. sg June 18 (24) $225

Bradford, William, c.1779-1857

— Sketches of the Country, Character, and Costume in Portugal and Spain.... L, 1809-10. 2 parts in 1 vol. 4to, modern half mor. With 53 hand-colored plates. Lacking frontis found in some copies. S Nov 21 (161) £800 [Marlborough]

Anr Ed. L, 1812. 4to, contemp half calf by Lancashire of Huddersfield. With 53 handcolored plates. Lacking frontis. S June 25 (166) £650 [San Lorenzo]

Anr Ed. L [plates watermarked 1823-24]. Folio, contemp mor gilt; rebacked. With 55 hand-colored plates. sg May 7 (38) $1,500

Bradley, Edward, 1827-89

— Photographic Pleasures, Popularly Portrayed with Pen & Pencil. L, 1855. 1st Ed. 8vo, orig cloth; worn, spine ends frayed, shaken. With pictorial title & 24 plates. Old tape repair at tp gutter; some foxing & browning. bbc Feb 17 (182) $310

Bradley, Katherine Harris, d.1914 —& Cooper, Edith Emma

— Fair Rosamund. L: Vale Press, 1897. One of 210. 8vo, orig bds. bba July 9 (306) £180 [Bookworks]

— The Race of Leaves. L, 1901. One of 280. Orig bds. bba July 9 (315) £120 [Bookworks]

Bradley, Martha

— The British Housewife: or, the Cook, Housekeeper's and Gardiner's Companion. L, 1755. 2 vols. 8vo, modern half mor by Sangorski & Sutcliffe. With frontis & 7 plates. S May 14 (973) £520 [Cooks]

Bradley, Omar N.

— A Soldier's Story. NY, [1951]. In later d/j. wa Oct 19 (238) $65

One of 750. wa Dec 9 (257) $140

Bradley, Richard. See: Furber & Bradley

Bradley, Richard, d.1732

— New Improvements of Planting and Gardening. L, 1731. 3 parts in 1 vol. 8vo, contemp sheep; worn. With 13 (of 14) plates. A few plates frayed with loss. sg Nov 14 (165) $175

Bradley, Will H.

— Bradley: His Book. Springfield Mass., 1896-97. Vol I only. 4to, half mor, orig wraps bound in. K Sept 29 (92) $140

Anr copy. Vol I, Nos 1 & 4 and Vol II, Nos 1-4, orig wraps bound together in def bds. sg Oct 17 (119) $350

— Peter Poodle, Toy Maker to the King. NY, 1906. Orig pictorial bds; worn & scuffed, shaken, lacking front free endpaper & front blanks. bbc Dec 9 (443) $70

— A Record and Review of Some Printing and Drawing.... Cambr. MA, [1898]. 8vo, orig wraps; frayed & soiled. Z Oct 26 (29) $625

Braght, Tieleman Jans van

— Der blutige Schau-Platz.... Ephrata, 1748-49. 1st Ed. 2 vols in 1. Folio, old stamped sheep; rubbed. Lacking frontis; ink damage from calligraphic fraktur bookplate; some foxing; marginal waterstains. K Sept 29 (251) $800

— Het bloedigh Tooneel; of, Martelaars Spiegel der Doops-Gesinde of Weereloose Christenen.... Amst.: J. vander Deyster, 1685. Illus by Jan Luyken. Foli, contemp blind-stamped vellum. Black letter. sg Oct 24 (50) $550

Braine, Sheila E.

— Pleasant Surprises: A Novel Picture Book with Verses. L: Ernest Nister, [c.1885]. Folio, chromolitho bds. With 6 revolving chromolitho plates. Tp detached but present. cb Sept 26 (26) $600

Braive, Michel

— The Photograph: A Social History. NY, [1966]. 4to, cloth, in torn & chipped d/j. sg Apr 13 (16) $90

Bramah, Ernest

— Kai Lung's Golden Hours. L, 1924. One of 250. In d/j, unopened copy. cb Dec 12 (26) $100

Braman, D. E. E.

— Braman's Information about Texas. Phila., 1858. 2d Ed. 12mo, orig cloth; worn. Foxed. NH May 30 (508) $210

Bramston, James, 1694-1744

— The Man of Taste.... L, 1733. 1st Ed. Folio, calf by Riviere; rear cover detached, spine worn. K July 12 (71) $65

Brandt, Bill

— Perspective of Nudes. NY, 1961. 4to, bds. sp Feb 6 (353) $145

Brandt, Geeraert, 1626-85

— Het leven en bedryf van Michiel de Ruiter. Amst., 1701. Folio, later blind-stamped vellum; upper joint split. Piece torn from 2B3 & a corner repair to 5Y4, both without loss. Ck May 15 (81) £160

— Historie der vermaerde zee- en koop-stadt Enkhuisen. Enkhuisen: E. van den Hoof, 1666. 4to, vellum with gilt arms of Enkhuizen on sides; spine def. With engraved title, 5 ports & folding plate. Lacking plan; some waterstains. B May 12 (1534) HF800

Brangwyn, Frank, 1867-1956

— Bookplates. L, 1920. Foreword by Eden Phillpotts. 4to, orig cloth. pba Aug 20 (31) $55

Anr copy. Orig cloth; worn. sg May 21 (144) $130

— Catalogue of the Etched Work.... L: The Fine Art Society, 1912. 4to, orig cloth. cb Oct 17 (124) $170

Brannon, George

— Vectis Scenery.... Wooton-Common, Isle of Wight, 1849. 4to, contemp half mor; rubbed, spine worn. With engraved title, frontis, map & 30 plates. 2 additional plates from a later Ed loosely inserted. DW Apr 8 (85) £145

Brantome, Pierre de Bourdeille, Sieur de, 1535?-1614

— Oeuvres. The Hague, 1740. 15 vols. 12mo, mor gilt by Thouvenin. With 14 frontises & 1 port. S May 28 (279) £1,400 [Lardanchet]

Braque, Georges, 1882-1963

— Braque lithographe. Monte Carlo, 1963. Text by Francis Ponge; notices & catalogue by Fernand Mourlot. Folio, orig wraps. bba Oct 24 (352) £160 [Sims Reed]

Anr copy. Lacking tp & 2 lithos. sg Feb 6 (40) $175; sg Apr 2 (29) $275

[-] Hommage a Georges Braque. Paris, 1964. One of 350. Folio, loose as issued in orig wraps; soiled with short tear. Derriere Le Miroir, Nos 144-46. sg Apr 2 (31) $250

— The Intimate Sketchbooks. NY, 1955. Folio, orig bds. Verve Nos 31/32. bba May 14 (346) £160 [Roe & Moore]

Anr copy. Orig bds, in torn d/j. Verve Nos 31/32. sg Sept 6 (36) $500

Anr copy. Orig bds, in d/j. Verve Nos 31/32. sg Apr 2 (30) $275

Anr copy. Orig bds; lacking lower inch of spine, backstrip loose. Verve Nos 31/32. wa Apr 9 (189) $260

Brasher, Rex, 1869-1960

— Birds and Trees of North America. Kent CT, 1929-32. 12 vols. Oblong folio, half calf gilt; worn, rubbed & scuffed; a few spines nearly detached. With 867 hand-colored plates. cb Feb 12 (15) $4,500

Anr copy. Half sheep; rubbed. With 865 (of 867) hand-colored plates. sg Nov 7 (28) $4,800

Anr Ed. NY, 1961-62. 4 vols. Oblong folio, half lea. With 875 colored plates. NH Aug 23 (66) $175

Anr copy. Orig cloth. wa Dec 9 (524) $200

Brassai, Pseud. of Gyula Halsz

— Histoire de Marie. Paris, 1949. One of 136 with sgd etching. Orig wraps, unopened. Inscr to Boris Kochno. SM Oct 12 (424) FF3,000

Brassington, William Salt

— A History of the Art of Bookbinding. L, 1894. 8vo, orig cloth. bba May 28 (488) £140 [Ventnor]

Brauer, Heinrich —& Wittkower, Rudolf

— Die Zeichnungen...Bernini. Berlin, 1931. 2 vols. Folio, orig cloth. S Feb 11 (24) £420 [Ars Libri]

Braun, Georg —& Hogenberg, Franz

— Civitates orbis terrarum. Plochingen, 1965-70. ("Beschreibung und Contrafactur der vornembster Staet der Welt.") Facsimile Ed. 6 vols. Folio, syn gilt. German text ptd in Gothic letter on verso of 360 double-page colored plans & views. Facsimile of the 1st German Ed of 1574. C Oct 30 (147) £1,300 [Litup]

Anr Ed. Plochingen, 1965. 6 vols. Folio, orig lea. German text ptd in Gothic letter on verso of 360 double-page colored plans & views. Facsimile of the 1st German Ed of 1574. HH May 12 (694) DM1,400

Anr Ed. NY, 1966. 6 parts in 3 vols. Folio, cloth, in d/js. With 369 plates, including 6 colored duplicate plates. sg May 7 (39) $450; wa Apr 9 (174) $260

— Theatre des cites du monde. Cologne, 1579. 4 parts in 2 vols. Folio, contemp mor gilt; joints & corners rubbed. With engraved titles & 236 plates colored by a contemp hand. Small section at centerfold of the map of Conil rubbed; occasional discoloration. C Oct 30 (146) £68,000 [Litup]

Braunschweig, Hieronymous. See: Brunschwig, Hieronymus

Bray, Anna Eliza Stothard, 1790-1883

— Life of T. Stothard. L, 1851. 4to, contemp mor gilt. cb Sept 26 (194) $70

Bray, William. See: Manning & Bray

Braybourne, Wyndham W. Knatchbull-Hugessen, Baron —& Chubb, Charles

— The Birds of South America. L, [1912]-17. Atlas vol only. 4to, contemp half mor, 5 orig wraps bound in; joints cracked, corners rubbed. With 38 hand-colored plates. Plate 20 with minor indentations; 2 plates ink-marked by ptr. pn May 14 (167) £180

Braybrooke, Richard Griffin, Baron. See: Griffin, Richard

Brayley, Edward Wedlake, 1773-1854

See also: Britton & Brayley; Nash & Brayley

— Ancient Castles of England and Wales. L, 1825. 2 vols. 4to, contemp calf; edges rubbed. With frontises, engraved titles, 92 plates, & 13 plans. Some spotting. pn Dec 12 (304) £180

— London and Middlesex. L, 1810-16. 4 vols in 5. 8vo, contemp half calf; worn, some covers detached. With 147 (of 148) plates. Spotted & soiled. DW Jan 29 (69) £125

Brea, Manuel Antonio de

— Principios universales y reglas generales de la verdadera destreza del Espadin.... Madrid, 1805. 1st Ed. 8vo, 19th-cent sheep. With 18 plates. sg Mar 26 (50) $275

Breasted, James Henry, 1865-1935

— The Edwin Smith Surgical Papyrus.... Chicago, 1930. 2 vols. 4to, cloth. sg May 14 (22) $350

Brebeuf, Jean de, 1593-1649. See: Golden Cockerel Press

Bredero, Gerbrand Adriaensz, 1585-1618

— Boertigh, amoreus, en aendachtigh groot liedt-boeck. Amst., 1622. 3 parts in 1 vol. Oblong 8vo, later vellum. With engraved title, port, 3 full-page engravings & 17 half-page engravings. Tear in 1 leaf repaired. B Nov 1 (318) HF3,800

— Wercken. Amst., 1638. 14 parts in 1 vol. 4to, vellum. B Nov 1 (313) HF1,000

Bree, Charles Robert, 1811-86

— A History of the Birds of Europe.... L, 1859-63. 4 vols. 8vo, contemp half mor; rubbed. With 238 colored plates. bba Sept 5 (134) £480 [St. Ann's Books]

Anr copy. Orig cloth; spine ends chipped. Great Grey Shrike with clean tear into image; plates distributed 59, 60, 60, 59 in this set. C Oct 30 (175) £200 [Bifolco]; C Oct 30 (241) £300 [Radclyffe]

Anr copy. Contemp calf gilt. Ck May 15 (10) £500

2d Ed. L, 1875-76. 5 vols. 8vo, later cloth. With 1 plain & 252 hand-colored plates. Library markings. bba Sept 5 (135) £190 [W. Fleming]

Anr copy. Orig cloth; spine of Vol V worn, others rebacked. Library stamps on plate versos; some ink marks in Vol I. S Nov 15 (778) £280 [Elliott]

Brees, Samuel Charles

— Pictorial Illustrations of New Zealand. L, 1849. 4to, contemp half mor; rubbed. With engraved title & 20 (of 21) plates. 1 plate cropped and mtd. Sold w.a.f. bba Apr 30 (57) £220 [Grosvenor Prints]

Breeskin, Adelyn D.

— The Graphic Work of Mary Cassatt. A Catalogue Raisonne. NY, 1948. One of 550. 4to, recent half lea. Tear repaired on pp. 26/27. wa June 25 (447) $750

— Mary Cassatt.... Wash., 1970. 4to, cloth, in torn d/j. bba Feb 13 (68) £850 [Zwemmer]

Anr copy. Cloth, in d/j. F Sept 26 (122) $1,100

Brehm, Alfred Edmund, 1829-84

— Cassell's Book of Birds.... L, [1869-73]. 4 vols in 2. 4to, contemp half mor; recased, rubbed. DW Apr 8 (166) £100

Bremer Press—Toelz, Munich, etc.

— EMERSON, RALPH WALDO. - Nature. [Munich: Bremer Press, 1929]. One of 250. Half vellum. sg Jan 30 (13) $90

— FIELD, W. B. OSGOOD. - John Leech on my Shelves. 1930. One of 155. bba May 28

(248) £320 [Dawson]

— VESALIUS, ANDREAS. - Icones anatomicae. 1934. One of 615. sg May 14 (172) $4,000

Brenchley, Julius L., 1816-73. See: Remy & Brenchley

Brennan, Christopher John

— The Burden of Tyre. Sydney, 1953. One of 300. Cloth, in d/j. kh Nov 11 (447) A$60

Brentius, Andreas

— Caesaris oratio Vesontione habita. [Rome: Stephen Plannck, c.1481-84]. 4to, modern half vellum. Gothic type. 8 leaves. Goff B-1110. sg Mar 12 (116) $750

Brentz, Johann, 1499-1570

— Esaias propheta, commentariis explicatus. Frankfurt: Petrus Brubachius, 1550. Folio, contemp blind-tooled pigskin over wooden bds. Some foxing & contemp marginalia. sg Mar 12 (33) $400

— Evangelion quod inscribitur, secundum Joannem.... Frankfurt: Petrus Brubachius, 1551. Folio, contemp blind-tooled pigskin over wooden bds; lacking clasps & catches. Early marginalia; dampstaining in corner of opening leaves. sg Mar 12 (34) $225

Breslauer, Bernard. See: Grolier Club

Bretez, Louis

— Plan de Paris. Paris, 1739. Folio, 19th-cent half mor. With general plan & 20 double page or folding plans. With the index sheet. S June 25 (215) £2,200 [Tulip]

Breton, Andre, 1896-1966

— L'Air de l'Eau. Paris, 1934. Special copy for Christian Zervos, ptd on a buff hand-made linen-textured paper. Illus by Alberto Giacometti. Folio, orig ptd wraps. With 4 orig engravings. P June 17 (216) $6,000

— Nadja. Paris, 1928. One of 100 on 4to format on papier verge Lafuma-Navarre. Orig wraps. Epstein copy. sg Apr 29 (39) $3,600

— Le Surrealisme et la peinture. Paris: NRF, 1928. Ltd Ed. 4to, orig cloth; rubbed. pn Sept 12 (74) £150 [Armero]

— Young Cherry Trees Secured against Hares. NY: View Editions, 1946. One of 1,000, but with the 2 orig drawings by Arshile Gorky. In d/j. sg Apr 2 (79) $250

Breton, Andre, 1896-1966 —& Duchamp, Marcel

— Exposition Internationale du Surrealisme... Le Surrealisme en 1947. [Paris, 1947]. 4to, orig wraps. sg Apr 2 (84) $175

Breton, Andre, 1896-1966 —& Peret, Benjamin

— Almanach surrealiste du demi-siecle. Paris, 1950. One of 65. Illus by Max Ernst. 8vo, orig wraps; chipped. Copy lacking 1 color litho. sg Apr 2 (77) $550

Breton de la Martiniere, Jean Baptiste Joseph

— China: Its Costume, Arts, Manufactures.... L, 1812-13. 2d Ed of Vol II, 5th Ed of other vols. 4 vols in 2. 12mo, contemp mor gilt; Vol I lacking piece at top of spine. With 80 hand-colored plates. Some browning. b June 22 (157) £380

Anr Ed. L, 1824. 4 vols in 2. 12mo, contemp mor gilt; not quite uniform. Some soiling. bba June 25 (252) £200 [Hildebrandt]

Breton, Ernest Franeois Pierre Hippolyte

— Athenes decrite et dessinee. Paris, 1862. 8vo, contemp half mor; dampstain on upper cover. With tinted frontis & 8 plates, 7 tinted. S July 1 (559) £300 [Chelsea]; S July 1 (560) £350 [Consolidated Real]

Breton, Nicholas, 1545?-1626?. See: Golden Cockerel Press

Brett, William Henry, 1818-86

— The Indian Tribes of Guiana. L, 1868. 8vo, orig cloth. With folding map, 10 uncolored & 8 color plates. sg May 21 (12) $80

Breuil, Henri —& Burkitt, Miles Crawford

— Rock Paintings of Southern Andalusia. Oxford, 1929. 4to, orig cloth. bba Dec 19 (411) £65 [Hay Cinema]

Breval, John Durant, 1680?-1738

— Remarks on Several Parts of Europe.... L, 1726. 2 vols. Folio, contemp calf; re-backed; upper joints of Vol II tape-repaiared. With folding map & 42 plates. cb Jan30 (14) $325

Breviary...

— The Breviary Treasures. Bost.: Pvtly ptd, 1903-5. Olympic Ed, one of 12 on royal japanese vellum paper. Ed by Nathan H. Dole. 10 vols. 4to, mor extra by the Adams Bindery. With orig watercolor frontises & watercolor head- & tail-pieces by A. C. Learned. Boyle copy. P June 17 (329) $3,500

Brewer, James Norris, fl.1799-1829

— A Descriptive and Historical Account of Various Palaces.... L, 1821. 4to, contemp russia gilt; covers detached, spine def. With 25 plates. sg Apr 2 (33) $150

Brewer, Luther

— My Leigh Hunt Library...the First Editions. Cedar Rapids, Iowa, 1932. One of 125. cb Oct 17 (125) $140

Brewington, Marion Vernon & Dorothy

— Kendall Whaling Museum Prints. Sharon MA, 1969. 4to, cloth; worn. O Sept 24 (39) $50

Brewster, John

— The Parochial History and Antiquities of Stockton upon Tees. Stockton, 1796. 4to, contemp half mor; rubbed. With port & 8 plates, 1 folding. bba Sept 19 (174) £150 [Traylen]

Breydenbach, Bernard von

— Peregrinationes in terram sanctam. [Speier]: Peter Drach, 29 July 1490. ("Peregrinatio in terram sanctam.") 2d Ed in Latin. Folio, contemp blind-tooled goatskin but a remboitage; worn & rebacked, clasps lacking. Types 10:146G (headings) & 13:80G (text). Some damage & restoration the folding views, 2 with loss; some worming at beginning & in 1 section of Palestine view; large folding view of Venice made up from several copies. Sold w.a.f. 120 leaves, including the 18 additional leaves needed to extend the folding views. Goff B-1190. C Dec 16 (110) £14,000 [Salamon]

Briano, Giorgio

— La Siria e l'Asia Minore illustrate. Turin, 1841. 8vo, contemp half mor, orig ptd wraps bound in. With engraved title, map & 120 plates. Some foxing. bba July 23 (344) £260 [Nolan]

Brice, Germain, 1652-1727

— Description de la ville de Paris. Paris, 1752. 4 vols. 12mo, contemp calf gilt. sg May 7 (40) $300

Bridgens, Richard

— Furniture with Candelabra and Interior Decoration. L: Pickering, 1838. Folio, contemp half mor; rubbed. With 60 hand-colored plates, including title & 1 double-page with 2 numerals. b Nov 18 (242) £750

Anr copy. Modern mor over old bds; new endpapers. With 59 hand-colored plates, including title. Last 10 plates cockled from damp; final 2 plates with some with some running of color. McCarty-Cooper copy. CNY Jan 25 (8) $1,000

— Sketches Illustrative of the Manners and Costumes of Italy, Switzerland and France. L, 1821. 4to, half lea. With engraved title & 49 plates, all hand-colored. Some browning. SI June 9 (181) LIt1,700,000

Bridges, Robert, 1844-1930

See also: Gregynog Press

— The Tapestry. L, 1925. One of 150. bba July 9 (251) £90 [Cox]

Brieger, Lothar

— E. M. Lilien: eine kuenstlerische Entwickelung um die Jahrundertwende. Berlin & Vienna, 1922. 4to, half calf; minor damage. sg June 25 (138) $400

Briggs, Henry, 1561-1630

— Trigonometria Britannica.... Gouda, 1633. Folio, contemp half calf; worn. Half-title spotted; some browning. Ck Nov 29 (154) £500

Briggs, Richard

— The English Art of Cookery. L, 1791. 2d Ed. 12mo, contemp calf; rebacked. With 12 plates. S May 14 (971) £360 [Lerner]

Brigham, Clarence Saunders

— History and Bibliography of American Newspapers, 1690-1820. Worcester MA, 1947. 2 vols. 4to, cloth. sg Oct 31 (51) $120

— Paul Revere's Engravings. Worcester, Mass., 1954. 1st Ed. 4to, cloth, in d/j. With 77 plates. O Sept 24 (40) $60

Anr copy. Orig cloth, in d/j. sp June 18 (319) $80

Brigham, William Tufts

— The Volcanoes of Kilauea and Mauna Lao.... Honolulu, 1909. 4to, cloth. Library markings. Inscr by "the Author". sg June 18 (274) $140

Bright, Richard, 1789-1858

— Clinical Memoirs on Abdominal Tumours and Intumescence. L, 1860. 1st Ed in Book form. 8vo, orig cloth; spine ends worn, front joint partly cracked. Inked-over stamp on tp. sg May 14 (24) $110

Brillat-Savarin, Jean Anthelme, 1755-1826

See also: Limited Editions Club

— Gastronomy as a Fine Art..... L, 1877. 8vo, orig cloth; rubbed. bbc Apr 27 (219) $300

Brinckle, Gertrude. See: Morse & Brinckle

Brindejont-Offenbach, Jacques

— Les Divertissements d'Eros. Paris, 1927. One of 235. Illus by Tsuguharu Foujita. 4to, unsewn in orig wraps. With 9 colored plates. CGen Nov 18 (312) SF900

Brindesi, Jean

— Elbicei atika; musee des anciens costumes Turcs de Constantinople. Paris [1855]. Folio, orig cloth; worn, spine def. With 22 colored plates. Some spotting to plates. S July 1 (562) £1,400 [Heriri]

Anr copy. Orig mor-backed cloth; edges

worn. With chromolitho title & 22 plates ptd within gold-ptd borders. Tp & Plate 21 spotted; waterstain near upper blank margin of last few plates. S Nov 21 (59) £2,200 [Beeleigh Abbey]

Brinkley, Frank, 1841-1912

— Japan. Described and Illustrated by the Japanese. Bost. [1897-98]. Edition de Grand Luxe, One of 50. 10 vols. Folio, silk-covered bds. wd June 12 (373) $800

1st Ed in Book form, One of 750. 10 vols. Folio, cloth; worn. Library markings. Some larger plates removed. Sold w.a.f. O Mar 31 (24) $170

Edition De Luxe. 10 vols. Folio, orig crepe paper over bds; worn. With 10 orig color woodblock prints, 10 chromolithographs from photographs in paper mats, 60 large hand-colored photographs & 197 smaller hand-colored photographs. Vol V with some photos wrinkled & bubbled. cb Feb 12 (16) $1,400

Yedo Ed, One of 1,000. 10 vols. Folio, cloth. sg Jan 9 (100) $600

— Oriental Series: Japan and China. Bost. & Tokyo, 1901-2. Library Ed, One of 1,000. 15 vols. Lev gilt extra with lea onlays. CNY Dec 5 (368) $7,500

Anr Ed. L, 1903-4. one of 500. 12 vols. Orig cloth. W July 8 (168) £170

Brinton, Christian

— Polo, Six Impression of a Chukker. NY: Rudge, [n.d.]. Illus by C. Moorepark. 4to, unbound as issued in orig cloth. Ck Nov 29 (250) £800

Brion de la Tour, Louis

— Atlas general.... Paris, 1782. 4to, contemp half calf; rubbed. With double-page engraved title & 58 double-page or folding mapsheets, hand-colored. A few maps cut close; some soiling. S Nov 21 (140) £1,300 [Map House]

Briquet, Charles Moise, 1839-1918

— Les filigranes.... Amst., 1968. Facsimile of 1907 Ed. 4 vols. 4to, cloth. DW Dec 11 (346) £250

Anr Ed. NY, 1985. 4to, cloth. sg Oct 31 (50) $225

Brisbin, Gen. James S., 1837-92

— The Beef Bonanza; or, How to Get Rich on the Plains. Phila., 1881. 8vo, orig cloth; water-stained. sp Nov 24 (14) $50

Briscoe, John

— A Discourse on the late funds of the Million-Act, Lottery-Act and Bank of England.... L, 1696. 3d Ed. 8vo, contemp calf; joints weakened, backstrip repaired. With 1 folding table. bba May 14 (69) £360 [Edwards]

Briseux, Charles Etienne

— Architecture moderne or l'art de bien batir. Paris, 1728. 1st Ed. 5 parts in 2 vols. 4to, contemp calf gilt; rubbed. With frontis, double-page additional title & 150 plates on 113 sheets. Plate 131 cut into; some browning. S June 25 (187) £550 [Gorini]

— L'Art de batir des maisons de campagne. Paris, 1743. 2 vols. 4to, contemp calf; rebacked. With frontis & 260 plates. Some worming in blank lower margin of 1st 12 pp of Vol II & affecting margins of plates 138 & 139. CNY Jan 25 (9) $1,000

Britannia...

— Britannia Delineata: comprising Views of...Kent. L, 1822. Folio, half calf; rebacked. With litho title & 25 plates, the coloring possibly later. Prelims with foxing; edges browned; small marginal dampstain at end. Schlosser copy. P June 18 (553) $2,700

British...

— British Apollo, or Curious Amusements for the Ingenious.... L, 1708-10. Vols I-II in 1 vol. Folio, contemp calf; rebacked, corners repaired. Ck June 12 (22) £120

— The British Essayists. L, 1817. 45 vols. 12mo, contemp half calf; some backstrips lacking or def; some covers detached. bba Oct 10 (342) £100 [Landry]

Anr Ed. L, 1823. Ed by Alexander Chambers. 38 vols. 12mo, half mor gilt; some wear to tips & joints. wa Dec 9 (6) $500

— British Hunts and Huntsmen.... L, 1908-11. 4 vols. Folio, contemp half mor; edges rubbed. Stained; 1 plate creased; foxed. pnL Nov 20 (169) £130

— The British Plutarch; or, Biographical Entertainer. L, 1762. 12 vols. 12mo, contemp calf; rebacked retaining orig backstrips, covers detached or starting, corners restored. With engraved titles & 63 plates. sg Oct 24 (51) $175

— British Sports and Sportsmen. L: Sports and Sportsmen Ltd., [1908-33?]. One of 1,000. 1914 vol only. Orig mor gilt. LH Dec 11 (257) $90

British and Foreign Bible Society

— Specimens of some of the Languages and Dialects, in which the Distribution, Printing, or Translation of the Scriptures...has been promoted by the...Society. L, 1852. 4to, orig cloth; spine lacking. Some annotations. S Feb 11 (721) £380 [Questor]

— Specimens of Some of the Languages and Dialects.... L, 1852. 4to, orig cloth; worn, backstrip partly detached. Lacking specimens of Basque, Latin, Tschuwaschian, Khasse & Amharic.. sg May 21 (146) $300

British Library. See: British Museum

British Museum —London

Catalogues

— Ivory Carvings of the Christian Era.... 1909. Compiled by O. M. Dalton. 4to, orig cloth, rubbed. With 125 plates. bba June 25 (39) £70 [Howes]

— The Book of the Dead. 1890. Ed by E. A. Wallis Budge. Folio, orig half mor; rebacked, orig spine preserved. With 37 colored double-page plates. DW Nov 6 (21) £115

— List of Catalogues of English Book Sales 1676-1900 Now in the British Museum. L, 1915. 8vo, cloth; worn. O Sept 24 (43) $130; sg May 21 (148) $250

— WARNER, SIR GEORGE FREDERIC. - Queen Mary's Psalter. 1912. 4to, half mor; scuffed. sg Oct 31 (264) $225

Catalogues

— Books, Manuscripts, Maps and Drawings...(Natural History). [NY: Martino, 1991]. 8 vols, including the 3-vol Supplement, in 4. 4to, orig cloth; worn. O May 26 (20) $120

— Books Printed in the XVth Century.... 1963-[62]. 11 vols. Folio, orig bds. Ck Nov 1 (364) £800

Anr copy. Vols I—IX and 2 vols of facsimiles bound in 12. Folio, half cloth. O Sept 24 (42) $1,150

Anr Ed. 1963-85. Vols 1-10 & 12 in 13 vols. Folio, half cloth and cloth. sg Oct 31 (148) $1,300

— British and American Book Plates.... 1903-4. Compiled by E. R. J. Gambier Howe. 3 vols. 8vo, orig cloth; worn. O Sept 24 (41) $60; O May 26 (19) $400

— Collection of Birds' Eggs.... 1901-12. Compiled by E. W. Oates & S. G. Reid, with Vol V compiled by W. R. Ogilvie-Grant. 5 vols. With 79 plates. sg Nov 14 (166) $600

— The Collection of English Pottery.... 1903. Compiled by Robert Lockhart Hobson. 4to, orig cloth. With 42 plates, some in color. sg Sept 6 (147) $200

— Dated and Datable Manuscripts c.700-1600.... 1979. Compiled by Andrew G. Watson. 2 vols. 4to, cloth, in d/js. sg Oct 31 (265) $200

— A Description of the Collection of Ancient Marbles.... 1812-61. 11 vols. 4to, contemp half lea; worn, Vol III in modern cloth, 2 spines def, shelf marks on spines, library labels on some pastedowns. With 375 (of 377) plates, 1 hand-colored. Some spotting & browning; a few plates shaved; Plate 3 in Vol VIII repaired; stamps on versos of titles & versos of many plates. pn Mar 19 (146A) £220 [Tilleke]

— Drawings by Dutch and Flemish Artists.... 1915-32. Compiled by Arthur M. Hind & A. E. Popham. 5 vols. 8vo, orig cloth. S Feb 11 (26) £400 [Sims Reed]

— Early Italian Engravings.... 1910-9. Compiled by Arthur M. Hind. 2 vols. Some annotations in pencil. S Feb 11 (27) £200 [Sims Reed]

— Engraved British Portraits.... 1908-25. Compiled by Freeman O'Donoghue & Henry M. Hake. 6 vols, including Supplements & Indexes. Orig cloth; covers of Vol II stained. Library markings. bba May 14 (575) £170 [Grosvenor Prints]

— General Catalogue of Printed Books. NY: Readex, 1956-75. 10 Supplments. 4to, orig cloth. bba Feb 27 (423) £260 [Quaritch]

Anr Ed. NY: Readex, 1967. 37 vols, including Supplements. 4to, orig cloth. bba Apr 30 (375) £480 [Thorp]

Anr copy. 37 vols, including 10 supplements to 1975. 4to, bba May 28 (536) £800 [Zaal]

Anr Ed. NY: Readex, 1967-80. 37 vols, including 4 Supplements in 10 vols. 4to, orig cloth. Ck July 10 (182) £420

Anr copy. 37 vols, including Supplements. DW May 13 (354) £500

Anr Ed. NY: Readex, 1967. 27 vols and Supplements 1-3 in 8 vols. Together, 35 vols. 4to, orig cloth. With accompanying magnifying glass. O Nov 26 (30) $550

Anr copy. 27 vols plus Supplements 1-3, in 8 vols. Together, 35 vols. 4to, O May 26 (21) $675

Anr Ed. NY: Readex, 1967-80. 32 vols, including 5-vol Supplement. 4to, orig cloth. sg Oct 31 (59) $900

Anr Ed. NY: Readex, 1967. Vols 2 & 3 (of 27) only. 4to, orig cloth; spines faded and spotted. sg Oct 31 (60) $400

Anr copy. 27 vols. 4to, wa June 25 (30) $240

— Italian Drawings.... 1950. Compiled by A. W. Popham & P. Pouncey. 2 vols. In d/js. S Feb 11 (28) £300 [Faldella]

— Ivory Carvings of the Christian Era.... 1909. Compiled by O. M. Dalton. 4to, orig cloth. Library stamp on front ocver. bba Mar 26 (36) £100 [Zwemmer]

— List of Catalogues of English Book Sales, 1676-1900. L, 1915. sg May 21 (148) $250

— Liturgies. 1899. 3 parts in 1 vol. Folio, contemp half lea gilt; worn. Library markings. sg Oct 31 (54) $50

— The Manuscripts in the Cottonian Library.... 1802. Compiled by Joseph Planta. Folio, contemp half russia; worn, covers detached. Sig. 7Q repeated; some foxing &

browning. bba May 28 (588) £75 [Bennett & Kerr]

— Printed Maps, Charts and Plans. 1967. 15 vols plus 2 issues of corrections & additions. Folio, cloth. DW Jan 29 (301) £350

Anr copy. 15 vols. Folio, DW Jan 29 (302) £210

— Short-Title Catalogue of Books Printed in France.... 1924. Cloth; spine ends nicked, front hinge cracked. sg Oct 31 (55) $100

— Short-Title Catalogue of Books Printed in Italy and of Italian Books printed in Other Countries from 1465 to 1600. 1958. O Sept 24 (46) $110

Anr copy. Spine faded, joints partly torn. sg Oct 31 (56) $80; sg May 21 (149) $70

— Short-title Catalogue of Books Printed in the German-Speaking Countries..... 1958. sg May 21 (150) $90

Anr Ed. 1962. O Sept 24 (45) $90; sg Oct 31 (57) $100

— Short-Title Catalogue of Books Printed in the Netherlands.... 1965. sg May 21 (151) $60

— Short-Title Catalogues of Spanish, Spanish-American, and Portuguese Books.... 1966. In d/j. sg Oct 31 (58) $80

— Short-Title Catalogue of Books Printed in France.... 1966. sg May 21 (152) $130

— Short-Title Catalogues of Spanish, Spanish-American, and Portuguese Books.... [1966]. sg May 21 (153) $110

— A Short-Title Catalogue of French Books 1601-1700.... 1969-73. 7 fascicles. 4to, ptd wraps; worn. O Sept 24 (47) $80

British Poets

— The Poets of Great Britain.... L & Edin., 1776-84. 112 vols. 12mo, contemp calf. LH Dec 11 (64) $600

Anr copy. 109 vols. 12mo, calf. W July 8 (19) £1,100

Britton, John, 1771-1857

See also: Bourne & Britton

— The Architectural Antiquities of Great Britain.... L, 1807-26. 5 vols. 4to, contemp mor gilt, cathedral bdg; endpapers rehinged, some wear to spine & corners. With 7 etched title & 353 plates, 4 double-page. Lacking 1 folding plate; adhesive stain to 1 leaf affecting a few letters; occasional minor marginal dampstaining. McCarty-Cooper copy. CNY Jan 25 (10) $900

Anr Ed. L, 1835. 5 vols. 4to, contemp half mor gilt; rebacked, orig spines preserved. With extra titles & 354 plates. bba Jan 30 (384) £100 [Jeffery]

Anr copy. Half mor; rubbed. Some dampstains throughout. O Feb 25 (31) $200

— The Beauties of Wiltshire.... L, 1801-25. 3 vols. 8vo, contemp half mor. Extra-illus with engraved & litho plates. DW Apr 8 (126) £260

— The Fine Arts of the English School.... L: Chiswick Press, 1812. 1st Ed. Folio, contemp half mor; rubbed. L.p. copy. DW Oct 9 (823) £60

— Picturesque Antiquities of the English Cities. L, 1830. One of 12 L.p. copies. 4to, contemp half mor; rubbed. With 60 plates. Ck Dec 11 (206) £450

— The Pleasures of Human Life. L, 1807. Illus by Thomas Rowlandson. 8vo, half calf; worn & marked. With engraved title & 6 hand-colored plates. Title browned; some spotting. bba Oct 10 (163) £50 [Coupe]

— The Union of Architecture, Sculpture, and Painting.... L,l 1827. 4to, contemp half calf. With color frontis & 22 uncolored plates. sg Sept 6 (40) $375

Britton, John, 1771-1857 —& Brayley, Edward Wedlake, 1773-1854

— The Beauties of England and Wales.... L, 1801-18. 18 vols in 26; with Brewer's Introduction. 8vo, contemp half lea; rubbed. With engraved titles in all vols except Brewer & with c.695 plates & 2 folding maps. Some stains or spotting. S Nov 15 (892) £750 [Sotheran]

Anr copy. In 18 vols; without Brewer's Introduction. 8vo, contemp half calf; worn, joints cracked or starting, Vol IV back cover torn, 5 covers detached. Some dampstaining. Extra-illus with c.800 plates. wa Apr 9 (278) $600

— Devonshire and Cornwall Illustrated. L, [1829]-32. 2 vols in 1. 4to, contemp half calf; worn, crudely rebacked. With engraved titles, 2 maps & 138 views on 69 plates. bba Sept 19 (176) £140 [Russell]

Anr copy. Contemp half mor gilt; worn. DW Jan 29 (71) £260

Anr Ed. L, 1832-37. 2 vols in 1. 4to, contemp calf gilt; rubbed. With engraved titles, 2 maps & 136 views on 68 plates. Lacking general title. C Oct 30 (13) £200 [Cherrington]

Britton, John, 1771-1857 —& Robson, George Fennell

— Picturesque Views of the English Cities. L, 1828. 4to, contemp mor gilt; stained & rubbed, joints split. With engraved title & 31 plates. Marginal foxing. pn June 11 (274) £400 [Map House]

Broadley, Alexander Meyrick

— Napoleon in Caricature 1795-1821. L, 1911. Ltd Ed. 2 vols. Folio, incompletely bound. sg Jan 9 (139) $475

Broadsides

— Grand Celebration! Of the Abolition of the Slave Trade. General Order. To da Culur Peeple Ob Ebery Occupation...[Racist satire]. [Bost., 1817]. Folio, laid onto cardbd. Some stains & fraying. O Mar 31 (5) $2,800

— The Representatives of the United States of America, in Congress Assembled [call to arms to defend Philadelphia against the British]. [Phila.: John Dunlap, 1776]. Folio. 2 small holes. CNY June 9 (215) $6,000

— To the Inhabitants of Pennsylvania [announcing a public meeting to oppose the landing at Philadelphia of a shipment of East India Company tea]. [Phila., 1773]. 100mm by 204mm. Browned. CNY June 9 (212) $2,200

— American Revolution. - Bucks County, December 14, 1776. The Progress of the British and Hessian Troops through New Jersey, has been attended with such scenes of Desolation and Outrage.... [Phila., 1776]. 4to. Some patches at folds. CNY June 9 (217) $4,200

— American Revolution. - By His Excellency Sir William Howe...a free and general Pardon to all such Officers and private Men, as shall voluntarily come and surrender themselves.... [Phila: James Humphreys, Jr., 1777]. Folio. CNY June 9 (220) $4,000

— American Revolution. - Epitaph. Indignant Reader, Whoever thou art, more especially an American....[George III, Mock epitaph]. Phila, 1782. 408mm by 315mm, backed with linen. Some staining & abrasion at folds. CNY May 14 (2) $4,500

— American Revolution. - The following Remonstrance, was this Day presented to the President and Council...Israel Pemberton, John Hunt, and Samuel Pleasants... [about the arrest and detention of several suspected Tories]. Phila: Robert Bell, [1777]. Folio. A few tears at left edge affecting a few letters. CNY June 9 (221) $3,000

— American Revolution. - Mason's Lodge, September 9th, 1977, 10 o'clock P.M. [appeal from 22 residents of Philadelphia imprisoned on political grounds in the Free-Mason's Lodge]. [Phila.: Robert Bell, 1777]. Folio. Ptd on both sides CNY June 9 (222) $3,200

— American Revolution. - Pennsylvania War-Office, April 13th, 1777. This board think it their duty to publish a letter received from Mr. Henry Fisher [notice of the presence of British warships in Delaware Bay]. Phila.: John Dunlap, [1777]. Folio. Small dampstain at extreme right edge. CNY June 9 (218) $3,500

— American Revolution. - Philadelphia. June 10, 1777. [Call to a public meeting with reference to defensive measures against Gen. Howe's army]. Phila.: Styner & Cist, [1777]. 210mm by 157mm. Fold tears. CNY June 9 (219) $4,500

— American Revolution. - Philadelphia, February 6, 1779 [George III's address to Parliament on French intervention in America]. Phila.: Hall & Sellers, [1779]. 4to. CNY June 9 (223) $3,200

— American Revolution. - To the Commissioners Appointed by the East-India Company, for the Sale of Tea, in America. [Phila., 1773]. Folio. Lght stains at right-hand margin. CNY June 9 (213) $3,200

— American Revolution. - The Twelve United Colonies, by Their Delegates in Congress, To the Inhabitants of Great Britain...[An appeal for reconciliation]. NY: John Holt, [1775]. Ptd on recto & verso. 409mm by 254mm. Framed. Silked with central fold separation mended; some spotting. P June 16 (294) $2,500

— Boker, George Henry. - The Second Louisiana. [N.p.], 27 May 1863. 8.5 by 5.5 inches. Rhyming promotion of the bravery of the black regiment during 1 battle in the Civil War. cb Nov 21 (72) $325

— Corfu. - Declaration de monsieur general commissaire du roi [concerning military provisions & the treasury]. Corfu, 10 June 1814. Folio size. S July 1 (577) £450 [Spink]

— Corfu. - Nel nobile teatro di San Giacomo in Corfu per le due prossime stagioni di Autunno 1827 e Carnevale 1828. Corfu, 1827. 427mm by 312mm, framed. S July 1 (579) £320 [Spink]

— Corfu. - Noi James Campbell maggior generale, regio commissionario civile [concerning shipping between Malta & the Ionian Islands]. Dalla publica Stamperia delle Isole Ionie liberate, 19 May 1815. Folio size. Traces of wax. S July 1 (578) £800 [Spink]

— Goddard, William. - No. I. Philadelphia, June 10th, 1773. To My Fellow Citizens. Friends of Liberty [protesting the erection of "shambles or stalls" in the streets of Philadelphia]. [Phila., 1773]. Folio size. Small holes at fold intersections. CNY June 9 (211) $2,400

— Lincoln Assassination. - $30,000 Reward. Description of John Wilkes Booth! Wash., 16 Apr 1865. 254mm by 201mm. Creased & with several fold separations not affecting text. P Dec 12 (127) $16,000

— PUTNAM, ISRAEL. - Head-Quarters, Philadelphia, December 13th, 1776 [trying to counter rumors that the Continentals would burn & destroy Philadelphia]. [Phila.: John Dunlap, 1776]. 177mm by 207mm. CNY June 9 (216) $2,400

Brocardus

— Le Premier (second) volume de la mer des histoires. Paris: Arnoul L'Angelier for Oudin Petit, [1555]. Bound with: LeGendre, Jean. tiers livre de la fleur et mer des hystoires. Paris, 20 Dec 1550. Folio, 16th-cent vellum; spine def. First work with 2 double-page woodcut map. Lacking 2 leaves in 1st work; 2d work with upper margins dampstained affecting text in last few leaves. S Nov 21 (211) £4,000 [Burden]

Brock, Michael John. See: Lardner & Brock

Brockedon, William, 1787-1854

— Illustrations of the Passes of the Alps.... L, 1828-29. 2 vols. 4to, contemp half mor; worn. With 99 plates & maps. DW Nov 6 (22) £320

Anr copy. Contemp half mor; rubbed. L.p. copy with India proof plates. O Nov 26 (31) $1,400

Broderies...

— Broderies chinoises. Paris: Henri Ernst, [19--?]. Folio, loose in half cloth portfolio. With 36 hand-colored plates on 32 leaves. kh Nov 11 (92) A$100

Anr copy. Library markings on text & a few mounts. sg Apr 2 (111) $100

Brodhead, L. W.

— The Delaware Water Gap. Phila., 1870. 8vo, cloth; worn & shaken. Inscr. Koopman copy. O Oct 29 (45) $180

Brome, Alexander, 1620-66

— Songs and Other Poems. L, 1664. 2d Ed. 8vo, contemp calf; lower cover peeling. Lacking A-a8. Sold w.a.f. bba Oc 24 (49) £60 [R. Clark]

Bromley, George W. —& Walter, S.

— Atlas of the City of New York.... Phila., 1908. Folio, bdg not described. With 50 color plates. NH May 30 (31) $350

Bronsted, Peter Oluf

— The Bronzes of Siris. L, 1836. Folio, calf gilt; broken. With frontis & tailpiece vignettes & 6 plates. Some spotting to plates. sg Sept 6 (132) $70

Bronte, Charlotte, 1816-55

— Jane Eyre. L, 1847. 1st Ed. 3 vols. 8vo, orig cloth; rubbed, spines & inner hinges restored. Some spotting & soiling. P Oct 11 (24) $13,000

Anr copy. Calf gilt by Riviere. Lacking ads in Vol I. sg Apr 29 (40) $6,000

4th Ed. L, 1850. 8vo, late 19th-cent half mor gilt. Lacking ads. Inscr by Charlotte Bronte's father to her grandfather, 20 Jan 1853. P Dec 12 (161) $6,000

— The Professor. L, 1857. 1st Ed, Issue not given. 2 vols. 8vo, loose in orig cloth; soiled & worn. DW Dec 11 (262) £145

Remainder Issue. 2 vols in 1. 8vo, orig cloth; rebacked, orig backstrip retained; corners worn. sg Oct 17 (121) $150

— Shirley. L, 1849. 1st Ed. 3 vols. 8vo, orig cloth; spine ends worn, new rear endpaper in Vol II. Jones-Newton-Doheny-Manney copy. P Oct 11 (25) $3,250

Anr copy. Later half mor by Root, orig cloth bound in; Vol I spine partly split. Some foxing. wa Mar 5 (13) $425

— Villette. L, 1853. 1st Ed. 3 vols. 8vo, orig cloth; extremities rubbed. Chip in fore-edge of Vol I tp. Doheny-Manney copy. P Oct 11 (26) $3,500

Bronte, Charlotte, Emily & Anne

— Poems by Currer, Ellis and Acton Bell. L, 1846. 1st Ed, 2d Issue. 8vo, orig cloth; torn along inner hinges. Without the catalogue of books at end. Manney copy. P Oct 11 (28) $1,200

— Works. L, 1893. 12 vols. 8vo, half calf. pnE Oct 2 (373) £240

Anr Ed. Edin., 1905. 12 vols. Orig cloth; worn, hinges repaired. F Dec 18 (619) $110

Thornton Ed. 12 vols. 8vo, cloth. pnE Mar 11 (203) £120

Anr copy. Orig cloth; Vol II of Agnes Grey partly dampstained. wa Mar 5 (151) $95

Anr Ed. L, 1905. Illus by Edmund Dulac. 10 vols. 8vo, cloth. Sold w.a.f. O Jan 14 (30) $70

Thornton Ed. Edin., 1924. Ed by Temple Scott. 12 vols. Orig cloth; rubbed. DW May 13 (423) £100; sg Mar 5 (24) $250

Bronte, Emily, 1818-48

— Wuthering Heights. NY, 1848. 8vo, later half mor; repaired, upper joint wearing, rubbed. Some spotting & soiling. Hover-Manney copy. P Oct 11 (27) $900

Anr Ed. NY, 1931. One of 450, sgd by the artist. Illus by Clare Leighton. 4to, cloth. DW Apr 8 (533) £90

Brontius, Nicolaus

— Libellus compendiariam tum virtutis. Antwerp: Symon Cocus, 1541. 1st Ed. 8vo, calf gilt; rebacked. With large woodcut on title, large coat-of-arms on last page & 7 emblems (some repeated) for the 12 arts. Lower corner of tp repaired; small wormhole in blank corner. B May 12 (6) HF5,500

Brook, Richard

— The Cyclopaedia of Botany.... L, [c.1865?]. 2 vols in 1. 8vo, contemp half mor; lacking backstrip, front cover detached. With hand-colored title, frontis & 99 hand-colored plates. bba Aug 13 (356) £80 [Lloyd's of Kew]

Brooke, Sir Arthur de Capell

— Travels through Sweden, Norway and Finmark, to the North Cape. L, 1823. 1st Ed. 4to, orig cloth; rubbed; shaken, front hinge cracked. Waterstained; lacking a prelim leaf. bba May 14 (288) £70 [Eng]

— A Winter in Lapland and Sweden.... L, 1827. 4to, orig bds; upper cover detached. With 24 tinted lithos on india paper mtd. Lacking maps. Inscr. C Oct 30 (11) £500 [Hannas]

Brooke, E. Adveno

— The Gardens of England. Rome, 1821. Folio, contemp half mor. With chromolitho title & frontis & 24 chromolitho plates, several finished by hand. Lacking dedication; 4 plates shaved affecting imprints; 3 plates trimmed & mtd on paper; title & plates backed on linen. C June 24 (213) £4,800 [Marlborough]

Brooke, Henry, 1703?-83. See: Moore & Brooke

Brooke, Jocelyn

— The Wild Orchids of Britain. L, 1950. One of 1,140. Folio, orig cloth. With 40 colored plates. bba Sept 5 (15) £55 [Henly]

Brooke, Ralph, 1553-1625

— A Catalogue and Succession of the Kings, Princes...of England.... L, 1662. Folio, modern calf. W July 8 (82) £120

Brooke, Rupert, 1887-1915

— 1914 and Other Poems. L, 1915. 1st Ed. 4to, orig cloth, in d/j. Epstein copy. sg Apr 29 (41) $800

— Lithuania. Chicago, 1915. Wraps. sg Dec 12 (28) $200

— Poems. L, 1911. 1st Ed, One of 500. sg Dec 12 (30) $225

Brookes, Richard

— The Art of Angling, Rock and Sea-Fishing. L, 1740. 1st Ed. 12mo, later calf; rubbed. bba Nov 28 (15) £260 [Ash Rare Bks]

Anr copy. Old calf; rebacked, rubbed. Koopman copy. O Oct 29 (46) $300

Anr Ed. L, 1766. 12mo, contemp calf; rubbed, rebacked. 1 gathering loose; soiled & browned. bba Nov 28 (16) £65 [Hereward Bks]

Brooks, Hugh Cecil

— Compendiosa bibliographia di edizioni Bodoniane. Florence, 1927. One of 700 on carta a mano vergata. 4to, half cloth. Ck Dec 12 (277) £220

Brookshaw, George

— Groups of Flowers [Groups of Fruit...Six Birds...]. L, 1819. 2d Ed. 3 works in 1 vol. Folio, cloth; rebacked. With 18 plates in 2 states, 1 hand-colored. Most plates with imprints cropped; text foxed; some soiling or discoloration. S June 25 (5) £1,600 [Lack]

— A New Treatise on Flower Painting.... L, 1816. 1st Ed. 5 parts. 4to, orig wraps; 1 split at fold. With 12 plates, each in 3 states. P June 18 (445) $700

— Pomona Britannica.... L, 1817. 2 vols in 1. 4to, contemp half mor by Harding; extremities rubbed, upper joint of Vol II holed. With 60 plates ptd in color & finished by hand. Some spotting. C Oct 30 (176) £4,800 [Galleria Etching]

Anr copy. 2 vols. 4to, contemp mor gilt; extremities scuffed. Some soiling & smudging to plates. C Oct 30 (256) £3,800 [Shapero]

Brosses, Charles de, 1709-77

— A Collection of Voyages to the Southern Hemisphere. L, 1788. Trans by John Callander. 8vo, contemp sheep; rebacked. Some discoloration. S June 25 (128) £500 [Renard]

— Histoire des navigations aux terres Australes. Paris, 1756. 2 vols. 4to, contemp calf; rebacked. With 7 folding maps. 1 leaf in Vol II torn with minimal loss. S June 25 (39) £1,300 [Arnold]

Brouckner, Isaac

— Nouvel Atlas de Marine.... Berlin, 1749. Folio, unbound & uncut. With double-page engraved World chart serving as sheet index & 12 double-page engraved charts, all hand-colored in outline. Waterstaining along top of 9 map sheets, 2 also soiled. S Nov 21 (141) £2,200

Brough, Robert Barnabas, 1828-60

— The Life of Sir John Falstaff. L, 1858. Illus by George Cruikshank. 8vo, later calf gilt by Zaehnsdorf. With 20 plates. Richard Ellis's copy, with related material. F June 25 (164) $140

— Shadow and Substance. L, 1860. Illus by Charles Bennett. 8vo, mor gilt by Riviere, orig cloth bound in at rear; some wear. wa Sept 26 (4) $375

Broughton, Alice

— Photographing the Famous. NY, 1928. Ltd Ed. 4to, half cloth; rubbed. Inscr. O July 14 (34) $150

Broughton, William Robert, 1762-1821

— A Voyage of Discovery to the North Pacific Ocean. L, 1804. 1st Ed. 4to, 19th-cent mor gilt; rebacked. With 9 plates & maps. First folding map & 2 folding plates linen-backed to reinforce fold tears; 3d folding map with insufficient fold repairs; 1st leaves washed, thin & with marginal repairs. CNY Oct 8 (25) $3,000

Brown, Sir Arthur Whitten

— Flying the Atlantic in Sixteen Hours. NY, [1920]. In worn d/j. cb Nov 7 (23) $75

Brown, Bob

— Readies for Bob Brown's Machine. Cagnes sur Mer: Roving Eye Press, 1931. Later half cloth, orig front wrap bound in; corners bumped. cb Dec 12 (27) $110

— Words. Paris; Hours Press, 1931. Out-of-series copy. Some browning. sg Dec 12 (35) $120

Brown, Charles Brockden

— Works. Bost., 1827. 7 vols in 6. 12mo, orig half cloth; rubbed & soiled. Manney set. P Oct 11 (29) $700

Brown, Eleanor & Bob

— Culinary Americana. NY, [1961]. bbc Apr 27 (220) $130

Anr copy. In d/j. O Dec 17 (34) $85

Brown, Frederic

— What Mad Universe. NY, 1949. In d/j with edge wear. sg June 11 (31) $110

Brown, Fredric

— The Bloody Moonlight. NY, 1949. In d/j. cb Sept 19 (17) $50

Brown, Glenn

— History of the United States Capitol. Wash., 1900-2. 2 vols. Folio, orig cloth; worn. O May 26 (22) $150

Anr copy. Cloth; extremities worn, hinges weak. sg June 18 (27) $90

Brown Library, John Carter

— Bibliotheca Americana. Providence, 1961-31. Vols I-III (of 7). 8vo, cloth; worn. Vols I & II, reprint of the orig; Vol III, orig Ed. O Sept 24 (32) $100

Anr Ed. NY, 1975-63 & Providence, 1973. Bound in 6 vols. Orig cloth. Ck Nov 1 (331) £320

— European Americana: A Chronological Guide.... NY, 1980. Ed by John Alden & Dennis C. Landis. 2 vols. 4to, cloth. sg Oct 31 (5) $225

Brown, John Ednie

— The Forest Flora of South Australia. L, 1882-[90]. Folio, contemp half calf; worn. With title with colored vignette & 45 color plates. S June 25 (83) £800 [Renard]

Brown, John Henry, 1810-1905. See: Grabhorn Printing

Brown, John J.

— The American Angler's Guide.... NY, 1857. 8vo, cloth; worn. Koopman copy. O Oct 29 (47) $75

Brown, Keith Macarthur

— Medical Practice in Old Parramatta. Sydney, 1937. kh Nov 11 (450) A$60

Brown, Leslie —&
Amadon, Dean

— Eagles, Hawks and Falcons of the World. [NY, 1968]. 2 vols. 4to, orig cloth. DW Nov 6 (153) £85; wa Apr 9 (110) $150

Brown, Louise Norton

— Block Printing & Book Illustration in Japan. L & NY, 1924. Folio, orig half cloth; worn, hinges cracked. Library markings. sg Feb 6 (42) $175

Brown, Paul. See: Derrydale Press

Brown, Peter, fl.1776

— New Illustrations of Zoology. L, 1776. 4to, modern half mor. With 50 hand-colored plates. FD Dec 2 (255) DM2,900

Anr copy. Contemp mor gilt; rubbed, upper cover rehinged with tape. S Nov 21 (3) £1,100 [Shapero]

Brown, Richard

— The Rudiments of Drawing Cabinet and Upholstery Furniture.... L, 1822. 4to, orig half cloth; rubbed, lacking spine. With 32 plates, some with hand-coloring. Sold w.a.f. S Feb 11 (299) £600 [Sims Reed]

Brown, Robert, 1773-1858

— The Miscellaneous Botanical Works of.... L, 1866-68. 3 vols, including Atlas. 8vo & folio, orig cloth & half cloth; worn. Library markings. bba Feb 13 (366) £50 [Maggs]

Brown, Capt. Thomas

— The Book of Butterflies, Sphinxes and Moths. L, 1832-34. 3 vols. 8vo, contemp half mor. With 144 hand-colored plates (1 detached). b Mar 11 (217) £115

Anr copy. Vols I-II only (of 3). Orig cloth; recased with orig backstrips laid down, new endpapers. With engraved titles & 96 hand-colored plates. Engraved titles foxed; 2 plates misbound. bbc Apr 27 (509) $220

— Illustrations of the Land and Fresh Water Conchology of Great Britain and Ireland. L & Edin., 1845. 4to, orig cloth. With 27 hand-colored plates Library markings. bba Sept 5 (17) £80 [Lib. Naturalistica Bolognese]

Anr copy. Contemp calf gilt; rubbed, backstrip def. bba Oct 10 (199) £110 [Mason]

Anr copy. Orig cloth; lacking section of spine, hinges splitting. bba May 14 (465) £80 [Henly]

— Illustrations of the Fossil Conchology of Great Britain and Ireland. L, 1849. 4to, early half lea; worn, backstrips def. With 118 plates, 15 hand-colored. Plate 69 reinserted & frayed; some marginal staining. kh Nov 11 (332) A$240

Browne, Alexander

— Ars Pictoria, or an Academy Treating of Drawing, Painting.... L, 1669. 1st Ed. 2 parts in 1 vol. Folio, calf. With frontis & 30 plates. Tp soiled; Plate 22 soiled & with repairs. P June 18 (446) $600

Browne, Daniel Jay, b.1804

— The Sylva Americana.... Bost., 1832. 8vo, orig cloth with modern cloth back. O Jan 14 (31) $70

Browne, Edward, 1644-1708

— An Account of Several Travels through a Great Part of Germany. L, 1677. 1st Ed. 4to, later calf. With 6 plates, some double-page. bba Jan 30 (140) £170 [Rogers Turner]

— A Brief Account of some Travels in Divers Parts of Europe. L, 1687. 2d Ed. Folio, contemp calf; rebacked, worn. With 16 plates, some folding. Some tears to folds, 1 repaired, anr with significant loss. S June 30 (247) £250 [Longworth]

Browne, Hablot K., 1815-82

— A Run with the Stag-Hounds. By Phiz. L, [c.1864]. Oblong folio, orig pictorial bds; worn. With 12 tinted lithos, a few with added hand-coloring. Some plates spotted or becoming detached. S July 9 (912) £320

Browne, Irving, 1835-99

— Ballads of a Book-Worm. East Aurora: Roycrofters, 1899. One of 850. 8vo, bds. cb Oct 17 (131) $65

— Iconoclasm and Whitewash. NY, 1886. 4to, later half mor gilt; scuffed. With sgd albumen print frontis. Extra-illus with c.50 19th-cent plates & with ALs. sg Mar 5 (25) $225

Browne, John, 1642-1700

— Verteutschte neue Beschreibung derer in dem menschlichen Coerper befindlichen Musculen.... Berlin, 1704. Folio, modern half vellum. With engraved title & 45 plates. Some browning. S Feb 25 (582) £420 [American Book Store]

Browne, John Ross, 1817-75

— Adventures in the Apache Country.... NY, 1869 [1868]. 1st Ed. Contemp half mor; extremities scuffed. cb Feb 12 (8) $180

Anr Ed. NY, 1869. 12mo, cloth. sg June 18 (28) $175

— Crusoe's Island.... NY, 1864. 1st Ed. 12mo, cloth. sg June 18 (29) $100

Browne, Richard, fl.1674-94

— Medicina musica; or, a Mechanical Essay on the Effects of Singing.... L, 1729. 8vo, contemp calf; rebacked, upper joint spit, upper cover split. Some browning. Owner's inscr saying book was gift of the author. pn Oct 24 (329) £320

Browne, Sir Thomas, 1605-82

— Pseudodoxia Epidemica.... L, 1646. 1st Ed. Folio, modern calf. Hole repaired on p. 185, affecting text on both sides. W July 8 (22) £165

2d Ed. L, 1650. Folio, later calf gilt; rebacked & corners repaired. Tp cut down & mtd. bba June 25 (178) £130 [Thorp]

6th Ed. L, 1672. 4to, contemp calf. Contemp Ms annotations on endpapers concerning Brown & Sir Kenelm Digby. L Nov 14 (381) £150

— Religio Medici..... Strassburg, 1665. 8vo, modern half calf. bba Jan 16 (68) £60 [Thorp]

Anr Ed. L: Vale Press, 1902. One of 300. Folio, half mor gilt. sg Jan 30 (181) $130

— Works. L, 1686. Folio, later calf gilt; rebacked, corners repaired. Tp to 1st work cut down & mtd. bba June 25 (178) £130 [Thorp]

Anr Ed. L, 1836-35. 4 vols. 4to, calf by Tout; rubbed. O Feb 25 (33) $160

Browne, W. H.

— The Art of Pyrotechny. L: The Bazaar Office, [c.1873]. 8vo, orig cloth. sg Nov 14 (282) $200

Anr Ed. L: The Bazaar Office, [1885]. 8vo, orig cloth; worn. sg Nov 14 (283) $60

Anr Ed. L: L. Upcott Gill, [1888]. 8vo, orig wraps; spine reinforced. sg Nov 14 (285) $80

Browne, William George

— Travels in Africa, Egypt and Syria.... L, 1799. 1st Ed. 4to, recent half mor. With 2 folding maps (few tears & repairs), frontis view (edge tears) & engraved sketch plan. Tear in gutter of tp; some ink numerals to reverse of frontis & 1st leaf of preface. wa Apr 9 (152) $425

Browne, William Henry James

— Ten Coloured Views Taken During the Arctic Expedition of Captain Sir James C. Ross. L, 1850. Folio, orig cloth; soiled, modern spine. With 10 lithos on 7 plates. First plate on cloth guard. W July 8 (242) £700

Brownell, Charles De Wolf

— The Indian Races of North and South America. Cincinnati & Hartford, 1853. 1st Ed. 8vo, half lea. sg Dec 5 (31) $175

Browning, Elizabeth Barrett, 1806-61

See also: Limited Editions Club

— Poems Before Congress. L, 1860. 1st Ed. 8vo, orig cloth. bba June 25 (204) £65 [Dailey]

— The Seraphim and Other Poems. L, 1838. 1st Ed. 12mo, orig cloth. rs Oct 17 (58B) $275

— Sonnets from the Portuguese. NY, 1901. Saint Dunstan Ed, out-of-series copy. 6 vols. Mor extra, with inlays, by Trautz-Bauzonnet. Ptd on vellum & lavishly illuminated throughout. P June 17 (124) $2,500

Anr Ed. San Francisco, 1927. 2 vols, including facsimile. Folio & 8vo, half vellum bds. bba July 9 (252) £65 [Cox]

Browning, Robert, 1812-89

— The Pied Piper of Hamelin. L, [c.1903]. Illus by Kate Greenaway. 4to, orig half cloth; chipped. kh Nov 11 (110) A$60

Anr Ed. L, [1934]. Illus by Arthur Rackham. Orig wraps, in d/j. Lacking 3 plates. sg Sept 26 (262) $175

One of 410. Vellum; covers and endpapers buckled. sg Jan 30 (141) $600

1st American Ed. Phila., [1934]. In d/j. K Mar 22 (377) $70

— The Ring and the Book. L, 1868-69. 1st Ed. 4 vols. 8vo, half calf. LH Dec 11 (75) $80

— Works. L, 1888-94. ("The Poetical Works.") One of 250 L.p. copies. 17 vols. 8vo, half mor gilt; extremities scuffed, rubbed. F Mar 26 (81) $200

Centenary Ed. L, 1912. one of 526. 10 vols. With 10 ports. pn July 16 (28) £110 [Thorpe]

Bruant, Aristide

— L'Argot au XXe Siecle. Paris, 1901. One of 25 on japon. Half mor, orig wraps bound in. With ALs inserted. Kochno copy. SM Oct 12 (428) FF2,400

— Dans la Rue. Paris, 1889-92. Vols I-II. Half mor, orig wraps bound in. SM Oct 12 (426) FF3,000

— Le Mirliton. Paris, 1885-1906. Vols 1-22, No 22. 194 issues bound in 4 vols. 4to & folio, wraps. S May 28 (237) £750 [Benjamins]

Bruccoli, Matthew J.

— F. Scott Fitzgerald. A Descriptive Bibliography. Pittsburgh, 1972-80. 2 vols, including Supplement. O Sept 24 (48) $70

— First Printings of American Authors. Detroit: Gale, [1977-79]. 4 vols. 4to, cloth. cb Nov 21 (51) $130

Bruce, Sir James, 1730-94

— Travels to Discover the Source of the Nile. L, 1790. 5 vols. 4to, contemp half calf; worn. With 2 (of 3) folding maps & 58 plates. 1 map torn. Sold w.a.f. DW Jan 29 (18) £100

3d Ed. Edin., 1813. Atlas vol only. 4to, contemp half mor; rubbed. With 79 plates & 3 folding maps. Some tears & repairs to maps. bba Sept 19 (56) £200 [L. Young]

Bruce, Peter Henry, 1692-1757

— Memoirs.... L, 1782. 4to, half calf using old bds; worn. S June 30 (248) £150 [Anderson]

Bruff, Joseph Goldsborough

— Gold Rush. NY, 1944. 4to, orig half cloth. sg June 18 (47) $150

Bruin, Cornelis de. See: Le Brun, Cornelius

Brulart de Genlis, Stephanie Felicite, 1746-1830. See: Genlis, Stephanie Felicite de

Brune, Johannes de, 1589-1658

— Emblemata of Zinne-werck; voorghestelt in Beelden.... Amst.: Hans vander Hellen, 1624. With 51 emblems. Lower outer corner of Tt2 repaired; a few inner margins at the end wormed. S May 13 (743) £160 [Cigognini]

— Emblemata of Zinne-werck. Amst., 1661. 3d Ed. 4to, vellum; worn, spine torn. Some foxing & soiling. O May 26 (23) $750

Brunel, Isambard Kingdom
— The Thames Tunnel. L, 1833. 4to, contemp mor gilt. Inscr. S July 9 (1402) £380 [Sotheran]

Brunet, Jacques Charles, 1780-1867
— Dictionnaire de geographie ancienne et moderne.... Paris, 1870. 8vo, half lea; worn, covers detached. Library markings. O Sept 24 (49) $70
— Manuel du libraire et de l'amateur de livres. Paris, 1820. 3d Ed. 4 vols. 8vo, contemp calf; worn. Browned. SI Dec 5 (114) LIt250,000
Anr copy. 4 vols plus 3-vol Supplement. 8vo, contemp half vellum. SI June 9 (186) LIt600,000
Anr Ed. Brussels, 1839. 5 vols. Modern cloth. bba June 25 (146) £100 [Old Times]
Anr Ed. Paris, 1842-44. 5 vols in 10. 8vo, contemp half mor. bba Jan 30 (328) £140 [Bifolco]
Anr copy. 5 vols. 8vo, modern bds. bba Apr 30 (374) £160 [Grigoropoulos]
Anr Ed. Paris, 1860-65. 6 vols plus 1880 Supplement in 2 vols. 8vo, contemp half mor; some joints worn. Ck Nov 1 (368) £360
Anr Ed. Paris, 1860-80. 8 vols, including 2 Supplements. 8vo, cloth. O Sept 24 (50) $350
Anr Ed. Paris, 1860-65. 6 vols plus 1880 Supplement in 1 vol. 8vo, contemp half mor gilt; spine ends rubbed. sg Oct 31 (62) $700
Anr Ed. Berlin, 1922. 9 vols, including supplement. 8vo, contemp half mor; worn. SI Dec 5 (776) LIt1,100,000
Anr copy. 8 vols, including Supplement. 8vo, orig cloth, in d/js. SI June 9 (187) LIt550,000
Anr Ed. Copenhagen, 1966-68. 9 vols. Reprint of the Paris 1860-80 Ed. bba Dec 19 (260) £280 [Burden]

Brunfels, Otto, 1488?-1534
— Onomastikon medicinae. Strassburg: Joannes Schott, 1534. Folio, old vellum bds; worn. Some dampstaining in outer margins. S Dec 5 (360) £1,300 [Martayan Lan]

Bruni, Leonardo Aretinus, 1369-1444
— De bello Italico adversus Gothos.... Venice: Nicolaus Jenson, 1471. 4to, mor gilt by Katharine Adams. Wormed at beginning & end, touching letters. 64 leaves. Goff B-1235. Schoyen copy. P Dec 12 (16) $19,000
— Historia fiorentina. Florence: Bartolommeo di Libri, 5 June 1492. ("Le Historie Eiorentine.") Folio, later sheep gilt; scuffed. Type 2:qq4R2; capital spaces with guide letters. Some old dampstaining or spotting at beginning & end; table of contents bound at beginning. 222 leaves. Goff B-1248. C Dec 16 (97) £1,100 [Bifolco]
— Libro della Guerra de Ghotti. Florence: Giunta, 1526. 8vo, modern vellum. Lacking last leaf; some browning & marginal annotations. SI Dec 5 (115) LIt110,000

Bruno, Guido
— Adventures in American Bookshops, Antique Stores and Auction Rooms. Detroit, 1922. In d/j. cb Oct 17 (133) $50

Bruns, Henry P.
— Angling Books of the Americas. Atlanta, 1975. 4to, cloth; worn. O Feb 25 (34) $100

Brunschwig, Hieronymus, c.1450-c.1512
— The Noble Experyence of the Vertuous Handy Warke of Surgeri.... [Southwark: Peter Treveris, 26 Mar 1525]. 4to, sewn. Black letter; 42 woodcut illusts only. Lacking C2 & T2-6; B2 supplied from a taller copy; various small tears to first & last few years. C Dec 16 (32) £850 [Sokol]

Brunus Aretinus, Leonardus. See: Bruni, Leonardo Aretinus

Brussel, Isidore Rosenbaum
— A Bibliography of James Branch Cabell. Phila., 1932. One of 100. Half cloth. cb Oct 17 (134) $55

Bruyn, Abraham de
— Omnium Poene Gentium Imagines.... Cologne: I. Rutus, 1577. Folio, contemp vellum. With engraved title & 50 double-page plates depicting 206 figures. Some browning & staining. S July 1 (563) £7,500 [Kutluoglu]

Bruyn, Cornelius le
— A Voyage to the Levant.... See: Le Brun, Cornelius

Bry, Johann Theodor de, 1561-1623, & Johann Israel de
— [Little Voyages]. Frankfurt, 1598-1613. Parts 1-3 only, in 1 vol. Contemp vellum; soiled, spine def. Part 1 with folding map & 10 (of 14) plates in the text; Part 2 with 2 large folding maps, prot & 34 (of 38) plates in text; Part 3 with 2 folding maps (of 4) & 57 (of 58) plates & maps in text. Sold w.a.f. S July 9 (1460) £1,200 [Antiques Orient]
German Ed. ("Zehender theil der Orientalischen Indien begreiffende...ein Duscurs an ihr Kon. Maj. in Spanien wegen des funfften Theils der Welt Terra Australis

Incognita gennant von einem Capitein Petro Ferdinandes de Quir.") Part 10 only. Folio, Modern bds. S June 25 (9) £1,300 [Maggs]

Bry, Theodor de & Johann Theodor de

— [Great Voyages] Collectiones peregrinationum in Indiam Orientalem et Indiam Occidentalem. Frankfurt & Oppenheim, 1590-1625. Latin Ed. Parts 1-12 only bound in 2 vols. With: [Little Voyages] Parts 1-10 only in 2 vols. Frankfurt & Oppenheim, 1598-1619. 1st Ed. Together, 4 vols plus separate pigskin-backed folder containing the Appendix Regni Congo, 1625, & Indiae Orientalis pars undecima, 1619. Folio, contemp blind-stamped pigskin over wooden bds with central panel of the Virgin & Child with elaborate blind-stamped floral borders. Barbet set. C Oct 30 (15) £130,000 [Sourget]

Anr Ed. Frankfurt & Oppenheim, 1590-1625 [1620-25]. Parts 4-6 only. Mor; worn & broken. K Sept 29 (99) $4,600

Bry, Theodore de, Johann Theodor de & Johann Israel de

— [The duPont set of Great Voyages, 14 parts in 4 vols, & of the Small Voyages, 13 parts in 3 vols, bound by Sangorski & Sutcliffe] CNY Oct 8 (26) $14,000

Bryan, Michael, 1757-1821

— Brian's Dictionary of Painters and Engravers. Port Washington NY: Kennikat Press, 1964. One of 400. 5 vols. DW Nov 6 (505) £60

— Dictionary of Painters and Engravers. L, 1889. Bound in 8 vols. 8vo, half mor gilt by Tout. Extra-illus with c.700 plates & 1 Dutch 17th-cent drawing. S Feb 11 (300) £1,100 [Bauer]

Anr Ed. L, 1903-5. 5 vols. 4to, orig cloth; worn & soiled. F Dec 18 (305) $120

Anr copy. Later cloth; worn. Library markings. F June 25 (353) $50

Bryant and May Museum

— The Bryant and May Museum of Fire-Making Appliances. Catalogue of the Exhibits. L, 1926-28. 2 vols, including Supplement Half cloth & wraps. sg Nov 14 (286) $200

Bryant, Edwin, 1805-69

— What I Saw in California.... NY & Phila., 1848. 1st Ed. 8vo, orig cloth. Library markings. sg June 18 (48) $110

2d Ed. NY, 1849. 8vo, orig cloth; spine chipped, front hinge cracked. cb Sept 12 (31) $90

Bryant, Jacob, 1715-1804

— A New System; or, an Analysis of Ancient Mythology. L, 1775-76. Vols I & II, 2d Ed; Vol III, 1st Ed. 3 vols. 4to, contemp calf; joints cracked, rubbed. bba Dec 19 (1) £220 [Bookworks]

Bryant, William Cullen, 1794-1878

See also: Picturesque...

— Poems. Cambr. MA, 1821. 1st Ed. 12mo, contemp mor; rubbed, joints worn. O Nov 26 (33) $375

One of 750. Orig bds; rebacked. Epstein copy. sg Apr 29 (44) $1,000

Bryant, William Cullen, 1794-1878 —& Gay, Sydney H., 1814-88

— A Popular History of the United States. NY, 1876-81. 4 vols. 8vo, half mor; rubbed. O Feb 25 (35) $100

Bryden, Henry Anderson

— Gun and Camera in Southern Africa. L, 1893. 8vo, contemp half mor; spine rubbed, scuffed. Library markings. F Dec 18 (413) $60

Brydone, Patrick, 1743-1818

— A Tour through Sicily and Malta. L, 1775. 2 vols. 8vo, contemp calf gilt; rebacked. With folding map. DW Mar 4 (8) £115

Bryson, Charles Lee. See: Gilbert & Bryson

Buchan, John, 1875-1940

— Scholar Gipsies. L & NY, 1896. 1st Ed. Illus by D. Y. Cameron. 8vo, orig half cloth. With ALs in pencil, 21 Oct 1925, to W.N. Roughead. bba Apr 30 (158) £180 [FouFou]

Anr copy. Orig half cloth; spine split, rubbed, rear endpaper torn. With etched title & 6 plates. bba July 23 (430) £100 [Bickersteth]

— Sir Quixote of the Moors. L, 1895. 1st Ed. 8vo, orig cloth. bba Apr 30 (157) £100 [Bannatyne]

Buchan, William, 1729-1805

— Domestic Medicine.... Phila.: Folwell for J. & J. Crukshank, 1797. 8vo, contemp sheep; worn. Lacking free endpapers. sg Nov 14 (16) $80

Buchanan, Francis Hamilton, 1762-1829

— A Journey from Madras through the Countries of Mysore, Canara, and Malabar. L, 1807. 1st Ed. 3 vols. 4to, contemp calf; worn, recased. With frontis, folding colored map, 5 folding tables & 38 plates (1 colored). pn Nov 14 (415) £190

Buchanan, George, 1506-82

— De Maria Scotorum Regina.... L: John Day, 1571. 12mo, 19th-cent mor gilt. bba Jan 30 (127) £160 [Rix]

— Histoire de Marie Royne d'Escosse.... Edin., 1572. 8vo, 19th-cent mor gilt by Bedford; joints splitting. Repair to rusthole in margin of D4; lower outer corner of Y2 repaired. STC 3979. C June 24 (295) £200 [Shapero]

Buchanan, John Lanne

— Travels in the Western Hebrides.... L, 1793. 8vo, contemp calf gilt; joints cracked, rubbed. bba Apr 9 (152) £160 [Fort]

Anr copy. Contemp calf; upper joint cracked. kh Nov 11 (334) A$160

Bucher, Francois

— The Pamplona Bibles: a Facsimile compiled from Two Picture Bibles with Martyrologies Commissioned by King Sancho el Fuerte of Navarra. New Haven & L, 1970. 2 vols. 4to, cloth. sg Oct 31 (196) $150

Buchinskaja, Nadezhda Aleksandrovna. See: Teffi, N. A.

Buchon, J. A. C.

— Recherches historiques sur la principaute franease de Moree.... Paris, 1845-43. 2 vols in 4. 8vo, orig wraps, unopened; 1 def. Some loss to blank margins of half-title & title of last part. S June 30 (14) £220 [Apostalkis]

Buc'hoz, Pierre Joseph, 1731-1807

— Premiere [Seconde] Centurie enluminees et non enluminees representant au naturel... les Animaux les Vegetaux et les Mineraux pour servir d'intelligence a l'Histoire Generale des Trois Regnes de la Nature. Paris, 1778-81. 2 vols. Folio, modern half mor. With 200 plates in uncolored & hand-colored states. Tp creased & repaired; Vol II tp creased & strengthened. L.p. copy. wd June 12 (374) $9,750

Buck, Pearl, 1892-1973

— East Wind; West Wind. NY, 1930. In d/j. Inscr. sg Dec 12 (36) $550

— The Good Earth. NY, [1931]. 1st Ed, 1st Issue. In d/j. Inscr to Mrs. H. Kanti. Epstein copy. sg Apr 29 (45) $1,900

Buck, Walter J. See: Chapman & Buck

Buckell, George Teasdale Teasdale. See: Teasdale-Buckell, George Teasdale

Buckingham, Nash

See also: Derrydale Press

— Game Bag. Tales of Shooting and Fishing. NY, [1945]. One of 1,250. Orig cloth. F Mar 26 (63) $70

Buckland, William, 1784-1856

— Reliquiae diluvianae. L, 1823. 1st Ed. 4to, orig bds; rubbed & worn. With 27 plates & maps, 1 folding, 3 hand-colored. Title cut at head. bba Feb 13 (367) £80 [Ballantyne & Date]

2d Ed. L, 1824. 4to, contemp half calf; rubbed. With 27 maps & plates. bba Nov 28 (102) £140 [Collicott]

Buckland Wright, John

— Fourteen Wood-Engravings to Illustrate "Le Sphinx." Antwerp, 1960. One of 250. 4to, orig folder. With text & with A. A. M. Stols' book on Wright, for which this set was ptd. Lacking 4 (of 9) illusts in the Stols book. S Apr 28 (23) £520

Buckler, John Chessell, 1793-1894

— Sixty Views of Endowed Grammar Schools. L, 1827. 4to, contemp half mor; lacking spine, both covers detached. With 60 plates. bba Dec 19 (67) £150 [Croft]

Buckley, Arabella B.

— Life and her Children.... Bost., 1884. Folio, half sheep. Text in relief lettering to be read by touch. bbc Sept 23 (198) $325

Buckley, Wilfred, 1878-1933

— Notes on Frans Greenwood and the Glasses that he Engraved.... L, 1930. One of 250. 4to, orig half cloth; corners rubbed. bba July 23 (443) £100 [Hetherington]

Buckton, George Bowdler

— Monograph of the British Cicadae or Tettigidae. L, 1890-91. 2 vols. 8vo, half calf; worn, spines singed. O Apr 28 (70) $140

Budge, Sir Ernest Alfred Wallis, 1857-1934

— From Fetish to God in Ancient Egypt. L, 1934. 1st Ed. Corners bumped. DW Dec 11 (14) £135

— The Life of Takla Haymanot L, 1906. One of 250. Trans & Ed by Budge. One vol in 2. Folio, orig cloth. With 165 colored plates. bba June 25 (24) £140 [Cumming]

Buel, Clarence Clough. See: Johnson & Buel

Buenting, Heinrich, 1545-1606

— Itinerarium Sacrae Scripturae, Das ist, Ein Reisebuch.... Magdeburg: Kirchner, 1594. 5 parts in 1 vol. Folio, contemp blind-stamped pigskin over wooden bds; lacking 1 metal mount. With 4 double-page woodcut maps & 1 full-page woodcut map only. Lacking tp & some text; some browning & staining. Sold w.a.f. S July 1 (739) £600 [Martayan Lan]

Anr Ed. Magdeburg, 1595. Folio, contemp vellum; rubbed & worn, lower joint split. With 10 double-page woodcut maps &

views & 2 full-page maps. Tp restored in 2 places; a few maps with short tears at fold; browned throughout; some worming. S June 25 (290) £3,200 [Franks]

Buffet, Bernard

— Lithographies, 1952-1966. Paris, 1967. Text by Fernand Mourlot. 4to, orig wraps; minor edge-wear. bbc Apr 27 (431) $400

— Lithographs, 1952-1966. NY, [1968]. Text by Fernand Mourlot. 4to, orig wraps, in d/j. With 11 plates. cb Sept 19 (13) $750

Anr copy. Orig wraps. sg Sept 6 (41) $450

— Venise. Paris, 1986. One of 150. Folio, in frames. Lacking text but accompanied by a small bound vol which reproduces the entire portfolio. CNY May 12 (342) $2,800

Buffon, Georges Louis Marie Leclerc, Comte de, 1707-88

— Histoire naturelle des oiseaux. Paris, 1770-86. 10 vols. Folio, contemp calf gilt; joints split. With 973 (of 1008) hand-colored plates; lacking the 35 plates of insects. Small tear to lower margin of Vol V tp; Plate 227 in Vol VII with numeral smudged. L.p. copy. C May 20 (148) £34,000 [Marshall]

— Histoire naturelle generale et particuliere. Paris, 1785-91. 54 vols. 8vo, contemp calf. Ck May 15 (14) £1,200

— Natural History.... L, 1791. 9 vols. 8vo, contemp calf gilt; spine ends soiled & rubbed. Ck May 15 (13) £350

Anr Ed. L, 1797-1808. 16 vols. 8vo, contemp half calf; rubbed & worn. With 145 plates, mostly hand-colored. DW Apr 8 (154) £200

Anr Ed. L, 1797. 10 vols. 8vo, contemp half sheep; joints cracked, rubbed. With port & 135 (of 145) plates. Some damp-staining & soiling. pn July 16 (142) £55

Anr Ed. L, 1808. 6 vols. 8vo, later half mor; rubbed. Foxed & stained. O Nov 26 (34) $325

— Oeuvres. Paris, [1853-57]. 12 vols. 4to, contemp half lea gilt; spine ends chipped. Some foxing to text. sg Sept 19 (167) $600

Anr copy. Contemp half cloth. With 160 hand-colored plates. sg Nov 14 (167) $1,700

Buffum, Edward Gould

— Six Months in the Gold Mines.... Phila., 1850. 12mo, orig cloth; spine ends frayed. sg June 18 (31) $250

Buhler, Kathryn C.

— American Silver, 1655-1825, in the Museum of Fine Arts, Boston. NY, 1972. 2 vols. Orig wraps. sp Feb 6 (240) $80

Anr copy. Half cloth. sp Apr 16 (125) $60

Buhler, Kathryn C. —& Hood, Graham

— American Silver in the Yale University Art Gallery. New Haven, 1970. 2 vols. 4to, cloth. K July 12 (17) $160

Bukowski, Charles

— Crucifix in a Deathhand. NY, [1965]. In d/j, orig ptd band torn & laid in. Sgd. bbc Apr 27 (273) $95

Bulfinch, Thomas

See also: Limited Editions Club

— The Age of Chivalry. Bost., 1859. 12mo, orig cloth; extremities worn. NH Oct 6 (59) $125

— The Age of Fable, or Studies of Gods and Heroes. Bost., 1855. 1st Ed, 1st Issue, with names of both ptr & stereotyper on copyright page. Orig cloth; rubbed & frayed. Manney copy. P Oct 11 (30) $700; sg Oct 17 (124) $375

Bulkeley, John —& Cummins, John

— A Voyage to the South Seas.... L, 1743. Issue with authors' names on tp. 8vo, contemp calf gilt; rebacked, corners worn. Some browning. CNY Oct 8J (27) $950

Anr copy. Contemp calf gilt; rebacked & recornered. S June 25 (36) £500 [Kahn]

Bull, Henrik Johan

— The Cruise of the "Antarctic" to the South Polar Regions.... L & NY, 1896. 8vo, contemp half mor; scuffed. Library markings. F Dec 18 (451) $130

Bull, Henry Graves. See: Hogg & Bull

Bullen, Frank Thomas, 1857-1915

— The Cruise of the "Cachalot". L, 1898. 1st Ed. 8vo, cloth. With an ALs. 19 Dec 1905. cb Oct 10 (10) $160

Anr copy. Orig cloth; rubbed. K July 12 (79) $180

Anr copy. Cloth. sg Jan 9 (43) $60

Buller, Sir Walter Lawry, 1838-1906

— A History of the Birds of New Zealand. L, [1872]-73. 1st Ed. 4to, contemp calf gilt; rebacked. With litho frontis & 35 hand-colored lithos. Some spotting. S June 25 (84) £1,300 [Mackin]

2d Ed. L, [1887]-1888. 2 vols plus 1905-6 Supplement in 2 vols. 4to, contemp half mor gilt by Henderson & Bisset; joints rubbed. With 2 plain & 48 colored plates plus port & 12 hand-colored lithos in the Supplement. C May 20 (149) £2,100 [Baring]

Anr copy. 2 vols. 4to, contemp half mor gilt, orig wraps bound in. With 2 plain & 48 colored plates. Some spotting at beginning & end not affecting plates. S June 25 (8) £1,000 [Shapero]

Anr copy. Orig half mor gilt; worn, corners bumped & frayed. Some spotting. wa Dec 9 (472) $1,400

Bulliet, Clarence Joseph

— Venus Castina: Famous Female Impersonators Celestial and Human. NY, 1928. One of 960. Illus by Alexander King. 4to, mor; rubbed. O May 26 (24) $550

Bullokar, John

— An English Expositor.... L, 1695. 12mo, old lea; rebacked, joints worn. Margins trimmed close; some soiling & minor stains; tp loose; tear in lower margin of a few leaves at end; lacking final leaf. sg Oct 24 (52) $600

Bullot, Maximilien, d.1748. See: Helyot & Bullot

Bulychev, Ivan Dem'ianovich

— Voyage dans la Siberie Orientale...Premier Partie. Voyage au Kamchatka. [St. Petersburg, 1855]. Folio, contemp calf gilt; extremities rubbed. With tinted litho title & 63 plates only, some colored; engraved map of the Russian Empire bound in. Spotted; 1 plate detached with minor marginal tears. C May 20 (320) £2,200 [Arader]

Bunbury, Henry W., 1750-1811

— An Academy for Grown Horsemen. L, 1787. 1st Ed. Folio, orig bds; joints split, soiled. With 12 hand-colored plates. Lacking B1. Ck July 10 (197) £95

Anr Ed. L, 1809. Illus by Thomas Rowlandson. 8vo, modern mor gilt by Riviere; rubbed. With 29 hand-colored plates. Lightly soiled. bba Sept 5 (175) £200 [Worthing]

Anr Ed. L, 1812. With 12 plates. Bound with: Bunbury. Annals of Horsemanship. L, 1812. With 17 plates. 4to, later mor gilt. With 17 hand-colored plates. Ck Dec 11 (112) £420

— Annals of Horsemanship. L, 1812. Illus by Thomas Rowlandson. 2 parts in 1 vol. 8vo, contemp half lea; rubbed, upper joint split. With hand-colored frontis (cropped, affecting image) & 16 hand-colored plates. Stain to 1 plate; 1 text leaf with short marginal tear. pn Mar 19 (368) £150

— Twenty-Two Plates Illustrative of Various Interesting Scenes in the Plays of Shakspeare. L, [c.1792-95]. Folio, contemp half mor; worn. Some spotting & waterstaining. Sold w.a.f. S May 14 (920) £240 [Shapero]

Bunce, Daniel

— Australasiatic Reminiscences of Twenty-Three Years' Wanderings in Tasmania.... Melbourne, 1857. 8vo, recased in orig bds with newer lea backstrip; some external silverfish damage. kh Nov 11 (453) A$100

Anr copy. Orig bds; worn. S June 25 (238) £160 [Quaritch/Hordern]

Bunch, Mother, Pseud.

— Mother Bunch's Fairy Tales.... L: Dean & Munday, [c.1820]. ("Mother Bunch's Entertaining Fairy Tales....") 8vo, orig wraps; worn. Hand-colored frontis frayed; some soiling. bba July 23 (267) £110 [Quaritch]

Bunyan, John, 1628-88

See also: Cresset Press; Limited Editions Club; Nonesuch Press

— The Pilgrim's Progress. L, 1830. Intro by Robert Southey; illus by John Martin. 8vo, mor by Root; worn. With 2 plates. Extra-illus with c.300 plates. O May 26 (25) $650

Anr Ed. Honolulu, 1842. ("Ka hele malihini ana mai keia ao aku a hiki i kela ao.....") 12mo, orig sheep; front cover loose. Lower margin browned throughout, with some chipping & other defs. sg June 18 (280) $325

Anr Ed. L, 1881. 12mo, lea inlaid with wood from oak tree of Elstow church. sp Nov 24 (253) $60

Buomattei, Benedetto

— Descrizione delle Fesste Fatte in Firenze per la Canonizzazione di Sto. Andrea Corsini. Florence: Aznobi Pignoni, 1632. 4to, contemp vellum; recased. With engraved title & 19 illusts by Stefano della Bella. Washed. Ck Oct 31 (46) £1,200

Buonarroti, Filippo

— Osservazioni istoriche sopra alcuni medaglioni antichi all'altezza serenissima di Cosimo III.... Rome, 1698. Folio, contemp vellum; soiled. With engraved title, 30 numismatic plates, 1 port & 2 double-page or folding plates. Some discoloration. S July 9 (1446) £300 [Maggs]

Buovo d'Ancona

— Libro chiamato Buovo de Ancona. Venice: Francesco Venetiano, 1557. 8vo, late 19th-cent mor; joints rubbed. Some staining. C Dec 16 (33A) £1,900 [Bredford]

Burbank, Luther, 1849-1926

— Luther Burbank: His Methods and Discoveries and their Practical Application. NY: Luther Burbank Press, 1914-15. 12 vols. Lea; bumped. Ltd Ed, sgd. Met Apr 28 (478) $160

Burchell, William John, 1782-1863

— The South African Drawings of William J. Burchell. Johannesburg, 1938. One of 300. Folio, orig half mor by Chivers. bba Feb 13 (353) £200 [Sotheran]

Burchett, Josiah, 1666-1746

— A Complete History of the Most Remarkable Transactions at Sea. L, 1720. 1st Ed. Folio, contemp calf; worn. With frontis, port & 9 folding or double-page maps by Herman Moll. Ck July 10 (198) £280

Anr copy. Contemp calf; rebacked & restored, new endpapers. CNY Oct 8 (30) $1,200

Burckhardt, John Lewis, 1784-1817

— Travels in Arabia. L, 1829. 4to, contemp russia gilt; rebacked in matching calf. With folding map & 4 plates. Some discoloration. S July 1 (829) £1,300 [Folios]

— Travels in Syria and the Holy Land. L, 1822. 4to, contemp half mor; rubbed. With port & 6 maps, 2 folding. A few early leaves browned; lacking half-title. S July 1 (828) £750 [Sotheran]

Burford, Robert, 1791-1861

— Description of a View of the Town of Sydney, New South Wales.... L, 1829. 8vo, wraps. Lacking ads. S June 25 (193) £300 [Marlborough]

— Description of a View of Hobart Town, Van Diemen's Land.... L, 1831. 8vo, bds. S June 25 (194) £280 [Quaritch/Hordern]

Burgess, Anthony

— A Clockwork Orange. L: Heinemann, [1962]. In chipped d/j. wa Dec 9 (172) $220

Anr copy. In d/j with several adhesive stains & slight paper lift on reverse. wa Mar 5 (152) $260

— Coaching Days of England. L, 1966. Oblong folio, orig cloth, in d/j. L Nov 14 (183) £50

Anr copy. Cloth, in d/j. sp June 18 (251) $60

Burgess, Henry W.

— Eidodendron. Views of the General Character & Appearance of Trees.... L, 1827. Folio, contemp half mor gilt; rubbed. With 2 litho titles, port & 54 mtd plates. Some spotting, mainly in margins. C Oct 30 (261) £350 [Riepera]

Burgoyne, Sir John, 1722-92

— A State of the Expedition from Canada.... L, 1780. 1st Ed. 4to, half calf. With folding map & 5 folding plans with outline color. S Nov 21 (321) £700 [Arader]

2d Ed. 4to, contemp calf; upper hinge worn. With 6 maps & plans (partly hand-colored), 2 with engraved overlays, & with folding table. One plate with short split in blank fold. b June 22 (158) £700

Anr copy. Contemp calf gilt; joints split, spine chipped. With 6 maps & plans, hand-colored in outline, 2 with overslips. Small tears at folds. C May 20 (239) £450 [Maggs]

Burgundia, Antonius A.

— Mundi Lapis Lydius.... Antwerp, 1639. 4to, contemp vellum with unidentified arms. With 50 emblematic text engravings. Lacking tp; some soiling. Sold w.a.f. sg Oct 24 (54) $200

Burke, Edgar

— American Dry Flies and How to Tie Them. NY, 1931. One of 500. Koopman copy. O Oct 29 (71) $275

Burke, Edmund, 1729-97

— An Impartial History of the War in America, between Great Britain and her Colonies. L, 1780. 1st Ed. 8vo, contemp calf; rebacked. With folding map & 13 ports. Some soiling. P June 16 (200) $1,600

— A Philosophical Enquiry in to the Origin of our Ideas of the Sublime and Beautiful. L, 1759. 8vo, contemp sheep; spine darkened, joints weak. sg Mar 12 (35) $90

Anr Ed. L, 1767. 8vo, calf; rubbed. bba Mar 25 (227) £85 [Kerpel]

— Reflections on the Revolution in France. L, 1790. Bound with: Burke. A Letter from Mr. Burke...in answer to Some Objections to His Book on French Affairs. L, 1791. 2d Ed. 8vo, contemp calf; joints worn. 1st Ed. Epstein copy. sg Apr 29 (50) $800

7th Ed. Bound with: Burke. Letter to a Member of the National Assembly; In Answer to Some Objections to his Book on French Affairs. L, 1791. 8vo, contemp calf; rubbed. O Dec 17 (37) $100

— Speech of Edmund Burke, Esq. on American Taxation, April 19, 1774. L, 1775. Bound with: Speech...for Conciliation with the Colonies. L, 1775. 2d Ed. And: Tucker, Josiah. A Letter to Edmund Burke... .Glocester, 1775 2d Ed. And: Burke. Speech...on Directions for Changing the Nabob of Arcot's Private Debts.... L, 1785 8vo, old calf; spine split. Contents list in hand of Charles James Fox on free front endpaper. wd Dec 12 (367) $700

1st Ed. 8vo, modern calf. Epstein copy. sg Apr 29 (49) $1,200

2d Ed. 8vo, modern wraps. sg Dec 5 (34) $175

— Works. L, 1899. 12 vols. 8vo, orig cloth; joints of 3 vols frayed, some hinges weakened. With 1 frontis. bba May 14 (171) £70 [Lawbook Exchange]

Burke, Russell. See: Gerdts & Burke

Burkitt, Miles Crawford. See: Breuil & Burkitt

Burlington, Charles —& Others
— The Modern Universal British Traveller. L, 1779. Folio, contemp calf; rebacked, worn. With frontis, 2 folding maps & 105 plates. Prelims, index maps, 2 plates & some text leaves repaired & backed with loss. S May 14 (1139) £360 [Brigantian]

Burlington Fine Arts Club—London

Catalogues of Exhibitions
— Collection of Italian Sculpture. 1912. Folio, orig cloth; front joint cracked. Marginal stains to a few leaves. bba May 14 (606) £50 [Pearl]

Burmannus, Johannes, 1706-79
— Rariorum Africanorum plantarum.... Amst., 1738-39. 10 parts in 1 vol. 4to, modern half lea. With 100 plates. bba Sept 5 (18) £750 [Shapero]

Burn, Richard, 1709-85. See: Macquarie's copy, Lachlan

Burnet, Gilbert, 1643-1715
— History of his Own Time. L, 1724-34. 1st Ed. 2 vols. Folio, contemp calf; broken, worn. LH Dec 11 (77) $80
Anr Ed. Oxford, 1823. 6 vols. 8vo, late 19th-cent half mor gilt; scuffed, 1 rear cover partly mottled. With 2 ports. Some foxing & pencilling to text. wa Mar 5 (30) $55
— The Memoires of the Lives and Actions of James and William, Dukes of Hamilton and Castleherald.... L, 1677. Folio, later calf; worn, covers loose. bba Jan 16 (75) £55 [Land]
Anr copy. Modern half calf. Frontis cut round & mtd & from anr work. W July 8 (46) £60

Burnet, John
— A Practical Treatise on Painting. L, 1850. ("A Treatise on Painting.") 4 parts in 1 vol. 4to, modern half mor; worn. O Jan 14 (33) $120
Anr copy. Half mor; rubbed. O Feb 25 (36) $80

Burnet, Thomas, 1635?-1715
— De statu mortuorum et resurgentium liber. L, 1723. 4to, contemp calf gilt; rebacked, edges rubbed. pn Mar 19 (173) £260 [Marlborough]
— The Theory of the Earth. The Two First Books. L, 1697. 3d Ed. 3 parts in 1. Folio, contemp calf, rebacked. Old marginalia in pencil. DW Mar 4 (194) £190

Burnett, Frances Hodgson, 1849-1924
— Little Lord Fauntleroy. L, 1886. 1st English Ed. 4to, orig cloth; back cover soiled, inner joints opening. K Mar 22 (49) $70
1st Ed. NY, 1886. 1st Issue. 4to, orig cloth; rubbed. P Oct 11 (31) $2,250

Burnett, M. A.
— Plantae Utiliores; or, Illustrations of Useful Plants Employed in the Arts and Medicine. L, [1839]-42-47-50. Vol I only. orig cloth. With 60 hand-colored plate. pnE Oct 2 (429) £250

Burnett, Peter Hardeman, 1807-95
— Recollections and Opinions of an Old Pioneer. NY, 1880. 1st Ed. 12mo, cloth. sg June 18 (49) $110

Burnett, William. See: Dugdale & Burnett

Burnett, William Riley
— The Asphalt Jungle. NY, 1949. In d/j with edge wear. sg June 11 (33) $70

Burney, Charles, 1726-1814
— An Account of Musical Performances in Westminster-Abbey.... L, 1785. 1st Ed. 4to, contemp half calf; rubbed, rebacked, old spine preserved. With engraved frontis & 7 plates.. Some plates stained; tp soiled. pn Oct 24 (269) £170 [Biblio]
Anr copy. Contemp calf; rebacked. pn Oct 24 (334) £120 [Archive]
— A General History of Music. L, 1776-89. 4 vols. 4to, 19th-cent russia gilt; joints split, worn. With 4 frontises & 9 plates, mtd on new guards. Some foxing. pn Oct 24 (335) £550
Anr copy. Early 19th-cent half calf; rebacked, orig backstrips retained. With 12 plates. sg Nov 7 (100) $800
2d Ed. L, 1789. 4 vols. 4to, later half mor gilt; rubbed. bba Mar 26 (286) £260 [Tosi]

Burney, Frances, 1752-1840
— Camilla: Or a Picture of Youth. L, 1796. 1st Ed. 5 vols. 12mo, contemp calf; rebacked. bba July 9j (127) £110 [Harlow]
Anr copy. Contemp calf; rubbed, spines chipped, joints worn. O Mar 31 (26) $60
— Diary and Letters. L, 1854. 7 vols. 8vo, half lea. br May 29 (137) $260
— Fanny Burney and her Friends. L: Seeley, [c.1890]. One of 150. 1 vol extended to 2. 8vo, mor gilt by Snford. Extra-illus with 245 plates. O May 26 (26) $900
— Memoirs of Doctor Burney, Arranged from his own Manuscripts.... L, 1832. 3 vols. 8vo, contemp sheep gilt with Signet Library arms; rebacked. Lacking half-titles. sg Mar 5 (27) $110
— The Wanderer; or, Female Difficulties. L, 1814. 1st Ed. 5 vols. 12mo, orig bds. rs Oct

17 (83A) $150

Burney, James, 1750-1821

— A Chronological History of the Discoveries in the South Sea.... L, 1803-17. Parts 1 & 2 (of 5) in 1 vol. Later half lea; old backstrip preserved. With 5 maps in Vol I, 10 maps in Vol II & 3 additional maps. K Sept 29 (304) $700

Anr copy. 5 vols. 4to, early 19th-cent calf gilt; rebacked, old spines retained; a few stains. With 28 maps & charts & 13 plates. B1 of Vol I repaired in upper margin. S June 25 (73) £5,000 [Quaritch/Hordern]

Burns, Jabez

— Satirical and Panegyrical Instructions to Mr. William Hogarth...by A. Marvell, Jun. L, 1740. Bound with: Smith, John. A Poetical Description of Mr. Hogarth's Election Prints.... And: Christie, Sharp & Harper, auctioneers. A Catalogue of the Most Complete Collection of Hogarth's Works ever offered to the public, the property of a gentleman [Samuel Ireland]. L, 1797. And: Young, John. A Descriptive Catalogue of the Works of Hogarth Placed in the Gallery of the British Institution for Exhibition. L, 1814 4to, later vellum; spotted & soiled. With port by Samuel Ireland, after Hogarth, bound in at front. Some staining to lower margin; some spotting. Milne copy. Ck June 12 (87) £1,700

Burns, John, 1774-1850

— Obstetrical Works.... NY, 1809. 8vo, old calf; worn. Some staining. bbc Sept 23 (267) $75

Burns, Robert, 1759-96

See also: Fore-Edge Paintings

— The Cotter's Saturday Night. L, [1908]. bba Apr 9 (279) £55 [Richardson]

— Poems, Chiefly in the Scottish Dialect. Kilmarnock, 1786. 1st Ed. 8vo, calf gilt; rebacked. Lacking tp, prelims & pp. 175 onwards, which have been replaced by pages from a facsimile Ed. pnE May 13 (211) £120

2d (1st Edin.) Ed. Edin, 1787. 8vo, mor gilt by Bayntun. pnE Oct 1 (201) £310

Anr copy. Later mor gilt. Foxed. pnE May 13 (27) £330

3d (1st London) Ed. L, 1787. 8vo, mor gilt by Bayntun. pnE Oct 1 (211) £160

— Works. L, 1834. 8 vols. 8vo, half mor; rubbed. O Feb 25 (38) $110

Anr copy. Half lea; scuffed. sp Feb 6 (508) $95

Anr Ed. Edin., 1877-79. 6 vols. 8vo, mor gilt extra by Harcourt Bindery. CNY Dec 5 (369) $1,400

Burnside, Wesley

— Maynard Dixon, Artist of the West. Provo: Brigham Young U Press, [1974]. In d/j. cb Feb 12 (18) $75

Burr, Aaron, 1756-1836 —& Hamilton, Alexander, 1757-1805

[-] Particulars of the late Duel, Fought at Hoboken, July 11.... NY, 1804. 8vo, later half sheep; spine torn. Some browning; old stain at center of leaves; library markings. bbc Sept 23 (297) $150

Burr, Frederic Martin

— Life and Works of Alexander Anderson, the First American Wood Engraver. NY, 1893. One of 725, sgd by Burr. 4to, half mor. Upper fore-edge corner excised on tp. sg Dec 5 (35) $110

Burrard, Sir Gerald

— The Modern Shotgun. L & NY, 1931-32. 3 vols. O Mar 31 (27) $60

Burritt, Elijah H., 1794-1838

— Atlas, Designed to Illustrate the Geography of the Heavens. Hartford, 1833. 2d Ed. Folio, ptd wraps; rubbed & soiled. With 7 hand-colored plates Some foxing. NH May 30 (69) $250

New Ed. Folio, ptd wrap; worn & soiled. With 8 hand-colored plates. Some foxing; ink stain in top margin. NH May 30 (70) $225

Anr Ed. NY, 1835. Folio, orig wraps; worn, soiled & frayed, front cover def. With 9 maps & charts. Plate I with 6-inch tear; other plates with some surface rubbing. wa Mar 5 (433) $150

Burrough, Edward

— A Declaration of the Sad and Great Persecution and Martyrdom of the People of God, called Quakers.... L: for Robert Wilson, [1660]. 4to, modern calf. sg June 18 (33) $550

Burroughs, Edgar Rice, 1875-1950

— Back to the Stone Age. Tarzana CA, [1937]. 1st Ed. In repaired d/j. sg June 11 (34) $275

— The Beasts of Tarzan. Chicago, 1916. Orig cloth; spine ends rubbed. pba July 9 (35) $110

— Carson of Venus. Tarzana, [1939]. In d/j. bbc Dec 9 (557) $180; sg June 11 (35) $325

— The Chessmen of Mars. Chicago, 1922. Illus by J. Allen St. John. In d/j with surface scrubbed on spine panel, paper-lined on verso reinforcing chips & splits. sg June 11 (36) $1,100

— The Deputy Sheriff of Comanche County. Tarzana, [1940]. In d/j. bbc Dec 9 (558) $240

Anr copy. In chipped d/j. wa Mar 5 (156) $210

— The Efficiency Expert. NY, 1921. In: the 4 issues pbd in Oct 1921 of Argosy All-Story Weekly. cb Sept 19 (19) $60

— Escape on Venus. Tarzana, [1946]. In edge-worn d/j. bbc Dec 9 (559) $70

— Jungle Tales of Tarzan. Chicago, 1919. Illus by J. Allen St. John. Inscr. sg June 11 (37) $400

— Land of Terror. Tarzana, 1944. In d/j. bbc Dec 9 (564) $230

— Llana of Gathol. Tarzana, [1948]. In d/j. bbc Dec 9 (565) $70

— The Oakdale Affair - The Rider. Tarzana, [1937]. In d/j with minor wear at ends of spine panel. sg June 11 (39) $425

— Pirates of Venus. Tarzana, [1934]. In d/j with head of spine panel reinforced on verso. sg June 11 (40) $225

— A Princess of Mars. Chicago, 1917. Cloth; marked, spine cloth rippled. K July 12 (83) $180

Advance review copy. Orig wraps; upper wrap supplied. Manney copy. P Oct 11 (35) $3,500

— Swords of Mars. Tarzana: Burroughs, [1936]. In worn d/j with tape along top & bottom edges. bbc Dec 9 (566) $75

— Synthetic Men of Mars. Tarzana, Calif., [1940]. 1st Ed. In d/j. bbc Dec 9 (567) $275; sg June 11 (41) $350

— Tarzan and the Jewels of Opar. Chicago, 1918. Orig cloth; warped, front endpaper pasted down. With 8 plates. K Mar 22 (52) $60

— Tarzan and the Golden Lion. Chicago, 1923. Orig cloth; soiled, front joint starting, inked rhyme & signature on front pastedown. Some foxing. K July 12 (84) $60

Anr copy. In chipped d/j. Epstein copy. sg Apr 29 (53) $1,800; sp Apr 16 (363) $250

— Tarzan and the Lost Empire. NY: Metropolitan, [1929]. 1st Ed. In repaired & lined d/j. Some foxing. sg June 11 (45) $375

— Tarzan and the Lion Men. Tarzana, [1934]. 1st Ed. In d/j with edge wear. sg June 11 (44) $425

— Tarzan and the Leopard Men. Tarzana, Calif., [1935]. 1st Ed. Illus by J. Allen St. John. In d/j. sg June 11 (43) $600

— Tarzan and the Forbidden City. Tarzana: Burroughs, [1938]. In d/j with wear to spine ends. sg June 11 (42) $400

— Tarzan and the Foreign Legion. Tarzana, [1947]. In d/j with tear. bbc Dec 9 (568) $60

Anr copy. In repaired d/j. pba July 9 (38) $50

— Tarzan and the Castaways. NY: Canaveral Press, 1965. In d/j. cb Sept 19 (22) $65

— Tarzan, Lord of the Jungle. Chicago: A. C. McClurg, 1928. In d/j. Epstein copy. sg Apr 29 (54) $1,900

— Tarzan of the Apes. NY, 1912. 1st Ed. Orig wraps; some restoration. In: The All-Story. Vol 24, No 2. Manney copy. P Oct 11 (33) $10,000

Anr Ed. Chicago, 1914. Orig cloth; recased, new endpapers. sg June 11 (47) $325

1st Ptg. Orig cloth; repaired & recased. sg June 11 (46) $900

1st Ed in Book form, 2d Issue. Orig cloth; spine ends frayed. Manney copy. P Oct 11 (34) $1,200

Anr Ed. NY: A. L. Burt, 1914 [but 1915]. Cloth, in d/j. cb Dec 12 (192) $225

Anr Ed. NY, [n.d.]. Cloth. Inscr, 1928. sg June 11 (48) $250

— Tarzan the Invincible. L, [1935]. In d/j. pba July 9 (40) $275

— Tarzan the Magnificent. Tarzana, [1936]. In d/j. sg June 11 (49) $400

— Tarzan the Untamed. Chicago, 1920. In chipped d/j. Inscr. Epstein copy. sg Apr 29 (52) $1,600

— Tarzan Triumphant. Tarzana, [1932]. In chipped d/j. Inscr. sg June 11 (50) $550

— Tarzan's Quest. Tarzana, [1936]. In chipped d/j. sg June 11 (51) $550

— Thuvia, Maid of Mars. Chicago, 1920. Orig cloth; spine frayed, rubbed. With 10 plates. Some smudges & spots. bbc Sept 23 (380) $60

Anr copy. Orig cloth, in frayed & chipped d/j. O May 26 (27) $800

— The Warlord of Mars. Chicago, 1919. 1st Ed, 1st Issue. Cloth. pba July 9 (42) $80

Burroughs, John, 1837-1921

— Works. Bost., 1904-22. Autograph Ed, One of 750. 23 vols. Half mor gilt. sg Mar 5 (28) $900

Burroughs, Stephen

— Memoirs.... Hanover NH, 1798. 1st Ed. 8vo, disbound. Lacking half-title & blanks; browned; library markings. bbc Sept 23 (298) $300

Burroughs, William S.

— The Naked Lunch. Paris, [1959]. 1st Ed. Wraps. bba Jan 16 (185) £55 [Virgo]

Burton, John, 1710-71

— Monasticon Eboracense: and the Ecclesiastical History of Yorkshire. York, 1758. Folio, contemp calf; rebacked. With 3 folding plans (1 repaired). pnL Nov 20 (86) £55 [Miles]

Burton, Sir Richard Francis, 1821-90

— Abeokuta and the Camaroons Mountains. L, 1863. 1st Ed. 2 vols. 8vo, orig cloth. With mtd frontis to Vol I & 4 plates. Lacking map. bba Jan 16 (288) £65 [Travel Bookshop]

Anr copy. With port, 4 plates & folding map. S June 25 (382) £2,600 [Baring]

— The Book of the Sword. L, 1884. 8vo, orig cloth; rubbed & soiled. bba Jan 16 (272) £190 [Mayou]

Anr copy. Orig cloth; soiled. Contents leaf carelessly opened causing tear to upper margin. S June 25 (406) £400 [Skiathos]; S July 1 (1221) £170 [Nat. Army Mus.]

Anr copy. Orig cloth; worn, stained. sg Mar 26 (54) $650

— The City of the Saints, and Across the Rocky Mountains to California. L, 1861. 1st Ed. 8vo, orig cloth; lower inner hinge broken. Last few leaves & endpapers stained. S June 25 (380) £1,100 [Asprey]

2d Ed. L, 1862. 8vo, half lea gilt. b&b Feb 19 (1) $125

— Explorations of the Highlands of the Brazil. L, 1869. 1st Ed. 2 vols. 8vo, cloth & contemp calf; covers detached. With engraved titles, frontises & folding map. bba Mar 26 (324) £140 [Harrington]

Anr copy. Later half mor; rubbed. Some spotting & staining. DW Mar 4 (9) £100

Anr copy. Half calf; rubbed; spine of Vol II water-damaged & wormed. With frontises & 2 folding maps. O Feb 25 (39) $550

Anr copy. Orig cloth. Lacking folding map. S Nov 15 (1237) £200 [Maggs]; S June 25 (388) £900 [Quaritch]

— Falconry in the Valley of the Indus. L, 1852. 1st Ed. 12mo, orig cloth; spine ends worn. S June 25 (375) £1,000 [Quaritch]

— First Footsteps in East Africa. L, 1856. 8vo, orig cloth; stitching weak, rubbed. With 2 maps & 4 colored plates Lacking the 4th Appendix as usual. S Feb 26 (723) £540 [Shapero]

— A Glance at the "Passion-Play." L, 1881. 8vo, orig cloth. With Burton's ptd card pasted to front free endpaper. S June 25 (403) £700 [Quaritch]

— The Gold-Mines of Midian.... L, 1878. 8vo, orig cloth; worn & soiled. Folding map just shaved. S june 25 (398) £750 [Folios]

— The Guide-Book. A Pictorial Pilgrimage to Mecca and Medina. L, 1865. 8vo, orig wraps. S June 25 (371) £15,000 [Sotheran]

— The Kasidah.... L, 1880. 1st Ed. 4to, orig wraps; dust-soiled. S June 25 (401) £1,000 [Quaritch]

— The Lake Regions of Central Africa. L, 1860. 1st Ed. 2 vols. 8vo, orig cloth; spines worn. With 12 color plates. Spotting. DW Apr 8 (16) £420

Anr copy. With 12 tinted plates & folding map. S June 25 (379) £2,600 [Baring]

— The Land of Midian Revisited. L, 1879. 1st Ed. 2 vols. 8vo, orig cloth; soiled. With 16 plates (6 colored) & folding map. S June 25 (399) £950 [Skiathos]

— The Lands of Cazembe, Lacerda's Journey to Cazembe in 1798. L, 1873. 1st Ed. 8vo, orig cloth. With folding map. bba May 28 (25) £110 [Spademan]

— Letters from the Battlefields of Paraguay. L, 1870. 1st Ed. 8vo, orig cloth; some wear & soiling. With engraved title, frontis & folding map. S June 25 (390) £600 [Quaritch]

— A Mission to Gelele, King of Dahome. L, 1864. 1st Ed. 2 vols. 8vo, orig cloth; spines worn at head. Pbr's presentation copy, as from Burton. S June 25 (384) £1,150 [Baring]

— A New System of Sword Exercise for Infantry. L, 1876. 8vo, orig cloth; lower cover stained. S June 25 (394) £2,500 [Quaritch]

— The Nile Basin. L, 1864. 1st Ed. 8vo, orig cloth; spine ends worn. With 3 maps. Martin copy. S June 25 (386) £1,000 [Quaritch]

— Personal Narrative of a Pilgrimage to El-Medinah and Meccah. L, 1893. Memorial Ed. 2 vols. 8vo, orig cloth; spine ends chipped, corners worn. cb Oct 10 (11) $120

Anr copy. Orig cloth; worn, Vol II stained on lower edges of covers. With 5 color plates & 8 lithos. wa Mar 5 (554) $95

— Scinde; or, the Unhappy Valley. L, 1851. 2d Ed. 2 vols. 8vo, orig cloth; bookplates removed from pastedowns. S June 25 (373) £3,200 [Baring]

— The Sentiment of the Sword. L, 1911. 8vo, orig bds; worn & soiled. S June 25 (414) £600 [Sotheran]

— Sind Revisited. L, 1877. 2 vols. 8vo, orig cloth; worn & soiled. Half-title in Vol I only. S June 25 (397) £800 [Hosains]

— Sindh, and the Races that Inhabit the Valley of the Indus. L, 1851. 8vo, orig cloth. With large folding map on blue paper. S June 25 (374) £3,200 [Skainthos]

— Terminal Essay to The Thousand and One

Nights. L: Pvtly ptd, 1901. One of 50 duplicated typescripts. 4to, calf gilt by Zaehnsdorf. S June 25 (413) £700 [Quaritch]

— Two Trips to Gorilla Land. L, 1876. 2 vols. 8vo, orig cloth; spine ends worn. Some spotting at beginning & end. S June 25 (395) £1,900 [Baring]

— Ultima-Thule, or a Summer in Iceland. L, 1875. 1st Ed. 2 vols. 8vo, orig cloth; worn. bba Apr 30 (26) £130 [R. Clark]

— Vikram and the Vampire. L, 1870. 1st Ed, 2d Issue. 8vo, orig cloth by Edmonds & Remnants; upper joint split. L Feb 27 (202) £70

Anr copy. Mor gilt; worn. O May 26 (28) $250

Anr copy. Orig cloth; spine ends worn. With 16 plates. S June 25 (389) £300 [Quaritch]

— Wanderings in West Africa.... L, 1863. 2 vols. 8vo, orig cloth. With folding map in Vol I & frontis in Vol II. S June 25 (383) £750 [Quaritch]

— Zanzibar: City, Island and Coast. L, 1872. 1st Ed. 2 vols. 8vo, orig cloth; extremities worn, inner hinges weak. With 2 frontises, 9 plates, 4 plans & folding map. S June 25 (392) £3,000 [Remington]

Burton, Sir Richard Francis, 1821-90 —& Cameron, Verney Lovett, 1844-94

— To the Gold Coast for Gold. L, 1883. 1st Ed. 2 vols. 8vo, orig cloth; soiled. With 2 folding maps & 1 colored plate. S June 25 (405) £1,200 [Quaritch]

Burton, Sir Richard Francis, 1821-90 —& Drake, Charles F. T.

— Unexplored Syria. L, 1872. 2 vols. 8vo, orig cloth. With 2 frontises & 25 plates (11 folding) & folding map. S June 25 (391) £1,300 [Quaritch]

3d Issue. Orig cloth; rubbed, Vol I with corners repaired. With 2 frontises, 25 plates & folding map. S July 1 (740) £550 [Kangan]

Burton, Robert, 1577-1640

See also: Nonesuch Press

— The Anatomy of Melancholy. Oxford, 1621. 1st Ed. 4to, contemp vellum; worn & soiled, modern reinforcement of inner hinges with partial loss of early 19th-cent presentation inscr. With the errata leaf 3D4; repairs to lower extremities of tp & 1st few leaves; last few leaves dampstained; minor worming in last half. Manney copy. P Oct 11 (36) $20,000

2d Ed. Oxford, 1624. Folio, contemp calf; rebacked & recornered. Leaf d2 with burn-hole. bba Nov 28 (223) £320 [Poole]

Anr copy. Contemp calf; spine repaired, joints split. STC 4160. C Dec 16 (187) £1,100 [Coulson]

8th Ed. L, 1676. Folio, contemp calf; rebacked & recornered. Some worming; rusthole in Ee3 with slight loss. bba June 25 (179) £180 [Thorp]

Burton, Robert, 1632?-1725?

— The English Hero; or, Sir Francis Drake Reviv'd. By R. B. L, 1687. 1st Ed. 12mo, contemp calf; upper cover gouged. Corner of F10 torn with loss to catchword; small perforation fo I9 affecting woodcut & 2 letters; some catchwords shaved. CNY Oct 8 (99) $1,900

Burton, William, 1575-1645

— The Description of Leicester Shire.... Lynn, 1777. 2d Ed. Folio, calf gilt; joints cracked. With 2 frontises & folding map. DW Dec 11 (90) £90

Burton, William, 1609-57

— A Commentary on Antoninus his Itinerary.... L, 1658. Folio, contemp calf; rebacked. With port & double-page map. W July 8 (47) £150

Burton, William, b.1863

— A General History of Porcelain. L, 1921. 2 vols. F Mar 26 (238) $70

Anr copy. In d/js. kh Nov 11 (62) A$90

Anr copy. With 80 uncolored & 32 colored plates. sg Sept 6 (42) $50

— A History and Description of English Earthenware and Stoneware. L, 1904. One of 1,450. kh Nov 11 (63) A$50

— Josiah Wedgwood and his Pottery. L, 1922. One of 1,500. With 72 plain & 32 colored plates. sp Feb 6 (241) $65

Burton Library, William Evans

— [Sale catalogue] Bibliotheca Dramatica. Catalogue of the Theatrical and Miscellaneous Library of.... [NY, 1860]. Compiled by Joseph Sabin. 4to, bdg not given. cb Oct 17 (144) $275

Burton's...

— Burton's Gentleman's Magazine. Phila., 1840. Vol V, Jan-June. 8vo, modern half mor gilt. Contains 1st ptgs of Poe's The Journal of Julius Rodman & of his Some Account of Stonehenge. sg Mar 5 (269) $275

Bury, Mrs. Edward

— A Selection of Hexandrian Plants.... L, 1831-34. Folio, contemp half calf; rubbed & soiled. With engraved title & 51 hand-finished colored aquatint plates. Plate 1 with foxmarks; Plate 51 spotted at lower edge; Plate 19 with ptd caption on a pasted overslip; library stamps, not affecting plates. pn Mar 19 (262) £28,000 [Arader]

Bury, Priscilla Susan. See: Bury, Mrs. Edward

Bury, Richard de, 1287-1345
See also: Grolier Club

— The Philobiblon. L, 1888. One of 50 L.p. copies. Ed & trans by Ernest C. Thomas. 8vo, half mor gilt. Inscr by Ralph Thomas & sgd by the ptr, Charles Whittingham. sg May 21 (156) $400

Bury, Thomas Talbot, 1811-77

— Coloured Views of the Liverpool and Manchester Railway. L, 1831. 4to, contemp russia; rebacked. With 13 hand-colored plates & 2 the double-page hand-colored folding plates A Train of the First and Second Class with the Mail etc. and A Train of Waggons with Goods, etc (both of these with small split at fold). C Oct 30 (14) £2,600 [Arader]

Anr copy. Orig wraps. With 7 hand-colored plates (as the work originally appeared), 5 in 1st State. S June 25 (277) £900 [Arader]

Bussing, Caspare

— Einleitung zu der Herolds-Kunst.... Hamburg, 1694. 3 parts in 1 vol. Oblong 8vo, old calf; rubbed, 1 cover cracked. Foxed & browned. O Nov 26 (35) $250

Busti, Bernardinus de

— Mariale. Nuremberg: Anton Koberger, 15 Apr 1503. Folio, contemp vellum. Gothic letter. Marginal annotations; browned throughout. SI Dec 5 (119) LIt200,000

Butcher, Edmund —& Haesler, H.

— Sidmouth Scenery, or Views of the Principal Cottages and Residences of the Nobility and Gentry.... Sidmouth, [1816-17]. 8vo, contemp calf gilt; corners rubbed, joints weak. Some leaves marginally frayed & reinserted. Sir Joseph Scott's subscriber's copy. C May 20 (26) £600 [Old Hall]

Buten, Harry M.

— Wedgwood ABC, but Not Middle E. Merion PA: Buten Museum of Wedgwood, 1964. Ltd Ed. 4to, syn with Wedgwood medallion mtd on front cover. Inscr to Byron & Elaine Bone. sg Sept 6 (294) $130

Anr copy. Syn with Wedgwood medallion mtd on front cover. Inscr to Anne Reese Wedgwood. sg Feb 6 (304) $110

Buteo, Joannes, c.1485-c.1560

— Opera geometrica. Lyons: T. Bertellus, 1554. 4to, modern bds. Some sidenotes shaved; lower forecorners stained. S May 28 (2) £700 [Hellwig]

Butler, Arthur Gardiner, 1844-1925

— Birds of Great Britain and Ireland. Order Passeres. L, [1904-8]. 2 vols. 4to, cloth; spines frayed. With 115 colored plates. DW Dec 11 (138) £150

— Birds of Great Britain and Ireland. L, [1907-8]. 2 vols. 4to, orig cloth; rubbed. With 107 colored plates of birds & 8 colored plates of eggs. Library markings. bba Oct 10 (202) £160 [Marco]

Anr copy. Contemp half russia gilt; lower joint of Vol II split, spines chipped. L Nov 14 (212) £180

— Foreign Finches in Captivity. L, 1894-[96]. 1st Ed. 4to, orig cloth. With 60 hand-colored plates. S Nov 21 (5) £1,000 [Cherrington]

2d Ed. L, 1899. 4to, half mor. With 60 color plates. b June 22 (348) £150

Anr copy. Orig half lea; rubbed. With 60 colored plates. pn Dec 12 (274) £110

Butler, Arthur Gardiner, 1844-1925 —& Others

— British Birds, their Nests and Eggs. L, [1896-99]. 6 vols. 4to, orig cloth. b Nov 18 (362) £50

Butler, Arthur Stanley George

— The Architecture of Sir Edward Lutyens. L, 1950. With: Hussey, Christopher E. C. The Life of Sir Edward Lutyens. L, 1950. Together, 4 vols. Folio & 4to, orig cloth, in chipped d/js. sg Feb 6 (170) $800

Anr Ed. Woodbridge, 1984. 3 vols. Folio, cloth, in d/j. wd Dec 12 (369) $250

Butler, Benjamin Clapp

— Lake George and Lake Champlain, from their First Discovery.... Albany, 1868. 12mo, orig cloth. With 4 folding maps. NH Aug 23 (1) $90

Butler, Charles, d.1647

— The Feminin Monarchi, or the Histori of Bees. L, 1623. 2d Ed. 4to, contemp vellum. Some staining; last few leaves frayed, affecting a few letters. STC 4193. pn Dec 12 (97) £440

Butler, Ellis Parker, 1869-1937

— Pigs Is Pigs. Garden City, 1913. Inscr & with a small pig sketch. Epstein copy. sg Apr 29 (55) $700

Butler, Henry

— South African Sketches. L, 1841. Folio, orig cloth. With litho title & 15 litho plates, each with 2 vignettes, 1 hand-colored & the other in outline, except Plate 11 which has 2 colored vignettes. C Oct 30 (177) £350 [Grahame]

Butler, John, 2d Marquis of Ormonde, 1808-54

— An Autumn in Sicily.... Dublin, 1850. 8vo, orig cloth; extremities worn. With folding map & 16 plates. DW Oct 2 (19) £75

Butler, Joseph, 1692-1752

— The Analogy of Religion, Natural and Revealed.... L, 1736. 4to, contemp calf gilt; rubbed. Marginal worming. bba July 9 (100) £95 [Wilbraham]

Butler, Lewis

— The Annals of the King's Royal Rifle Corps. L, 1913-32. 6 vols, including Appendix. Bdg of Appendix perished with some leaves loose. bba Oct 24 (185) £150 [Austen]

Butler, Samuel, 1612-80

— Hudibras. L, 1663-78. 1st Ed, 2d Issue of Part 3, 1st Issue of Parts 1-2. 3 parts in 1 vol. 8vo, 19th-cent half mor gilt. Inscr by Charles II to Walter Charleton. Ck Nov 29 (63) £420

Anr Ed. L, 1710. Illus by Wm. Hogarth. 3 parts in 1 vol. 12mo, contemp calf; spine worn & dry. wa Dec 9 (483) $75

Anr Ed. L, 1822. Illus by J. Clark. 2 vols. 8vo, contemp half lea; rubbed. With 12 hand-colored plates. O Jan 14 (35) $80

Anr copy. Mor gilt; worn at edges. rs Oct 17 (48A) $125

Butler, Samuel, 1835-1902

See also: Gregynog Press; Limited Editions Club

— Erewhon. L, 1872. 1st Ed. 8vo, orig cloth; rubbed. Some leaves carelessly opened causing marginal defs. bba May 14 (164) £75 [Korn]

Anr copy. Orig cloth; soiled, spine darkened & with ends worn, joints partly split, hinges cracked, front free endpaper partly split at gutter. wa Mar 5 (157) $160

— The Way of All Flesh. L, 1903. 1st Ed. sg Dec 12 (38) $60

Butlin, Martin

— The Paintings and Drawings of William Blake. New Haven: Yale Univ., 1981. 2 vols. 4to, orig cloth, in d/js. DW Mar 11 (798) £75

**Butlin, Martin —&
Joll, Evelyn**

— The Paintings of J. M. W. Turner. New Haven: Yale Univ., 1977. 2 vols. 4to, orig cloth. bba Jan 16 (260) £90 [Hetherington]

Butterfield, Consul Willshire, 1824-99

— History of Brule's Discoveries and Explorations.... Cleveland, 1898. 8vo, cloth. With frontis & 6 plates. bbc Sept 23 (299) $75

**Butterworth, Edwin —&
Tait, Arthur Fitzwilliam**

— Views on the Manchester and Leeds Railway. L, 1845. Folio, orig cloth; rubbed. With litho title & 19 plates. Some spotting. Ck Oct 18 (47) £850

Butterworth, William

— Three Years Adventures of a Minor, in England, Africa, the West Indies.... Leeds, 1831. 12mo, modern half calf. sg June 18 (34) $300

Buxtorf, Joannes, 1564-1629

— Lexicon Hebraicum et Chaldaicum. Basel, 1621. 3d Ed. 8vo, contemp vellum; worn, backstrip & front endpaper gone. Old ink annotations on tp; some wear to tp & front matter with loss of text. F June 25 (589) $100

Byblis

— Byblis. Miroir des arts du livre et de l'estampe. Paris, 1921-31. Nos 1-40, One of 100. 4to, unsewn as issued in orig wraps. Sold w.a.f. S July 1 (1182) £550

Byerley, Frederick John

— Narrative of the Overland Expedition...from Rockhampton to Cape York.... Brisbane, 1867. 8vo, orig cloth; worn & discolored. With folding map. Some spotting. S June 25 (256) £3,200 [Quaritch/Hordern]

**Byington, Lewis Francis —&
Lewis, Oscar**

— The History of San Francisco. Chicago & San Francisco, 1931. 3 vols. Inscr by Lewis. cb Nov 14 (19) $110

**Byne, Arthur —&
Stapley, Mildred**

— Decorated Wooden Ceilings in Spain. NY, [1920]. Folio, unbound. With 56 plates. Tp soiled & with small hole. sg Apr 2 (36) $100

Bynner, Witter. See: Knish & Morgan

Byrd, Richard Evelyn, 1888-1957

— Alone. NY, 1938. One of 1,000. Illus by Richard E. Harrison. In torn d/j. Inscr. sg Jan 9 (13) $50

— Discovery: the Story of the Second Byrd Antarctic Expedition. NY, 1935. 1st Ed, Dedication copy, numbered 1 & lettered Edsel Ford. With related material, including flag & photographs. Manney copy. P Oct 11 (37) $1,800

Out-of-series copy. DW Jan 29 (19) £100

— Little America: Aerial Exploration in the Antarctic.... NY, 1930. In d/j. Inscr to Harold Jensen. cb Nov 7 (24) $75

Anr copy. Inscr. wa Oct 19 (115) $80

First Issue. With Ls from pbr attesting to

Issue. cb Nov 7 (25) $80

One of 1,000. sg May 21 (13) $90

— Skyward. NY, 1928. One of 500. 4to, half cloth. With a piece of the Josephine Ford. cb Nov 7 (26) $325

Byrne, Muriel Saint Clare. See: Sayers & Byrne

Byrnes, Thomas

— Professional Criminals of America. NY, [1886]. 1st Ed. 8vo, orig clothh; edges worn, loose, bookplate at front pastedown. bbc Feb 17 (187) $285

Anr copy. Half mor; rebacked with portion of orig spine retained, 1st gathering loose. sg Dec 5 (83) $175

Byrom, John, 1692-1763

— The Universal English Short-Hand. Manchester, 1767. 1st Ed. 8vo, contemp calf; rebacked. With 13 plates. bba Jan 16 (127) £75 [Rainford]

Byron, George Gordon Noel, Lord, 1788-1824

[-] Bibliographical Catalogue of First Editions, Proof Copies and Manuscripts of Books by Lord Byron Exhibited by The First Edition Club January 1925. L, 1925. Ltd Ed. 4to, orig cloth. bba May 28 (503) £50 [Ogino]

— Childe Harold's Pilgrimage. L, 1812-16-18. 1st Ed. Cantos I-IV. Contemp mor gilt; joints & extremities rubbed. F Sept 26 (108) $210

Anr Ed. Paris, 1931. One of 35. 4to, half mor. bbc Sept 23 (430) $55

— Don Juan. L, 1819-23. 1st Eds. In 6 vols. 4to (Cantos I-II) & 8vo, mor gilt. Lacking some ads, 1 half-title & 1 blank. Lady Byron ALs inlaid in Part 1. P June 17 (144) $1,800

— English Bards and Scotch Reviewers. L, [1809]. 2d Ed. 12mo, early calf; worn & scuffed. Some browning. bbc Apr 27 (274) $80

— Hebrew Melodies. L, 1815. 1st Ed, 1st Issue. 8vo, orig wraps; spine chipped. Epstein copy. sg Apr 29 (57) $1,100

— Hours of Idleness. Newark, 1807. 1st Ed. 8vo, mor gilt by Riviere; rebacked, new endpapers, inner hinges strengthened; some rubbing & soiling. P June 17 (143) $900

Anr copy. Mor gilt by Riviere; rebacked, new endpapers, inner hinges strengthened. P June 17 (143) $900

Anr copy. Orig bds. rs Oct 17 (78) $400

— Manfred, a Dramatic Poem. L, 1817. 1st Ed, 2d Issue. 8vo, contemp German bds. Lacking the ads. sg Oct 17 (125) $200

— Mazeppa. L, 1819. 1st Ed, 2d Issue. 8vo, orig wraps. Epstein copy. sg Apr 29 (58) $275

— Oeuvres. Paris, 1822-25. 8 vols. 8vo, contemp calf extra by Charles Blaise. CNY Dec 5 (365) $400

— The Prisoner of Chillon.... L, 1816. 1st Ed, 1st Issue. 8vo, orig wraps. Epstein copy. sg Apr 29 (59) $200

— Sardanapalus, a Tragedy. The Two Foscari, a Tragedy. Cain, a Mystery. L, 1821. 1st Ed. 8vo, orig bds; inner hinges reinforced. LH May 17 (592) $100

— The Siege of Corinth.... L, 1816. 1st Ed. 8vo, half mor; rubbed. K July 12 (87) $80

— Works. Paris, 1825. 7 vols. 8vo, modern half mor gilt; extremities worn. sg Mar 5 (30) $175

Anr Ed. L, 1832-33. 17 vols. 12mo, later half calf; spine darkened; 1 spine head nicked. cb Dec 5 (20) $550

Anr copy. 17 vols. 8vo, contemp half mor; joints & extremities rubbed. F Mar 26 (159) $90

Anr copy. 17 vols. 12mo, half mor. Met Apr 28 (511) $130

Anr copy. Orig cloth; rubbed. With engraved titles & frontises. Some spotting. pn Apr 23 (131) £50

Anr copy. Later calf gilt. pnE Oct 2 (371) £320

Anr copy. Orig cloth; worn & soiled, spine ends chipped, 3 covers detached. Foxed. wa Dec 9 (174) $80

Anr Ed. L, 1833. 17 vols. 8vo, contemp mor gilt; soiled. S Nov 14 (543) £220 [Joseph]

Anr Ed. L, 1855-56. 6 vols. 8vo, calf gilt. pnE Aug 12 (284) £200

Anr Ed. Bost.: F. A. Niccolls, 1900. One of 750 for America. 16 vols. Half mor gilt; spines faded; 9 with heads chipped. cb Dec 5 (21) $425; sg Mar 5 (31) $850

Byron, John, 1723-86

— The Narrative of the Honourable John Byron.... L, 1768. 1st Ed. 8vo, modern half mor; rubbed. Title spotted. DW Jan 29 (20) £1100

Anr copy. Contemp calf. S June 25 (38) £650 [Quaritch/Hordern]

Anr Ed. L, 1785. 8vo, later half calf gilt; rubbed. Fore-margins wormed. DW Apr 8 (19) £115

[-] A Voyage Round the World, in His Majesty's Ship The Dolphin. L, 1767. 8vo, contemp calf gilt; worn, rebacked & recornered. With 3 plates. S June 25 (44) £350 [Renard]

C

C., T. See: Carwell, Thomas

C., V. See: Skues, G. E. M.

Cabala...

— Cabala, sive Scrinia sacra, Mysteries of State and Government.... L, 1691. 3d Ed. 2 parts in 1 vol. Folio, 18th-cent mor gilt. pn Apr 23 (114) £220

Anr copy. Contemp calf; rubbed. W July 8 (73) £90

Cabell, James Branch, 1879-1958

— From Hidden Way. NY, 1916. 1st Ed, One of 610. Orig cloth, 1st bdg. Inscr to Vincent Starrett. bbc Apr 27 (275) $80

— Jurgen: a Comedy of Justice. NY, 1919. 1st Ed, 1st State. Orig cloth, in d/j. Inscr. Epstein copy. sg Apr 29 (60) $475

— Works. NY, 1927-30. Storisende Ed, one of 1,590. O Aug 25 (44) $170

Cabell forgery, James Branch

— Poor Jack; a Play in One Act. Richmond: Pvtly ptd, 1906. Wraps. sg Dec 12 (40) $200

Cabeus, Nicolaus

— Philosophia magnetica.... Ferrara: Francesco Succhi, 1629. 1st Ed. Folio, contemp calf, prize copy; worn. Engraved title shaved at outer edge; without Cologne tp; repairs to D4-5 affecting text; a few leaves creased at outer edges towards end. S Dec 5 (361) £1,300 [Jackson]

Cabinet...

— The Cabinet of Genius. L, 1787. 2 vols. 4to, mor gilt by Root; rubbed. O May 26 (29) $550

Anr copy. Contemp calf. With engraved titles, 82 (of 84) ports & 10 plates. Soiled & dampstained; a few leaves loose or cropped. pn Dec 12 (35) £360

Cabinet-Maker's...

— The Cabinet-Maker's Guide; or, Rules and Instructions in the Art of Varnishing, Dying.... Concord, 1827. 12mo, orig bds; worn. Some marginal chipping; some foxing. sg Apr 2 (37) $375

Cable, George Washington, 1844-1925

— Old Creole Days. NY, 1879. 1st Ed. 12mo, orig cloth. sg Oct 17 (126) $120

Caesar, Caius Julius, 100-44 B.C.

See also: Limited Editions Club

The Commentaries

— 1499, 13 Apr. - Commentarii. Venice: Philippus Pincius for Benedictus Fontana. Folio, modern vellum. 45 lines & headline; type 16:108R; a2 with 7-line woodcut white on black initial. Some old dampstaining; with contemp Ms gloss with notes in same hand on recto & verso of tp. 134 leaves. Goff C-25. C Dec 16 (111) £550 [Bifolco]

— 1517, 30 Nov. - Commentaria. Venice: Bernardino de Vitali. Folio, contemp Northeast Italian bdg of mor over pastebds with knotwork border tooled in blind & small gilt fleurons at inner corners & in center & title lettered in gilt at head of upper cover; small tear at head & foot of spine. S Dec 5 (74) £6,000 [Jackson]

— 1655. - L. 3 parts in 1 vol. Folio, contemp calf; rebacked. With engraved title, port & 14 plates. Some leaves lacking from 3d part; 2 leaves holed. Sold w.a.f. bba Oct 10 (296) £55 [Gammon]

Anr copy. Contemp calf; cover panels detached. With port & 13 plates. Some edge tears, minor stains & foxing. bbc Dec 9 (297) $150; LH Dec 11 (78) $130

— 1661. - Opera. Amst.: Elzevir. 8vo, contemp vellum. With 3 folding maps. sg Mar 12 (39) $175

— 1677-76. - L. Trans by Clement Edmonds. Folio, contemp calf; extremities worn. With frontis & 14 plates. cb Oct 25 (11) $400

Anr copy. Contemp calf; rebacked. cb Dec 5 (22) $225

— 1712. - L: Tonson. 2 vols. Folio, contemp mor gilt. With 87 plates & maps. Tears entering image on engraved title; port of Marlborough & a few other plates; last 10 double-page plates pasted together to create a single long frieze. Schlosser copy. P June 18 (447) $2,750

— 1753. - L. Folio, contemp sheep gilt; worn, joints cracked. With 86 plates, maps & plans. Some plates toned or spotted; 2 plates with fold breaks & frayed; piece torn out of upper margin of tp touching top line of text. sg Oct 24 (57) $800

Cafky, Morris

— Colorado Midland. Denver: Rocky Mountain Railroad Club, 1965. In d/j. Sgd & with related material. cb Feb 13 (52) $140

— Rails Around Gold Hill. Denver: Rocky Mountain Railroad Club, 1955. In d/j. Sgd. cb Feb 13 (53) $120

— Steam Tramways of Denver. Denver: Rocky Mountain Railroad Club, 1950. cb Feb 13 (54) $60

Cahiers...

— Cahiers d'Art. Paris, 1948. Vol 23: Picasso au Musee d'Antibes. 4to, orig wraps; worn & chipped. Inscr to Maria Martins. F June 25 (311) $800

Cahill, Holger

— Max Weber. NY: Downtown Gallery, 1930. One of 250, sgd by Weber. Cloth; rubbed. With orig sgd litho as frontis. bbc Dec 9 (290) $250

Cahoon, Herbert. See: Slocum & Cahoon

Caillet, Albert Louis

— Manuel bibliographique des sciences psychiques ou occultes. Paris, 1912 [1913]. 3 vols. Cloth; worn. O Sept 24 (51) $275

Caimo, Pompeo

— Parallelo Politico delle Republiche Antiche.... Parua: Pietro Paolo Tozzi, 1627. 4to, old vellum. Some foxing; outer margin of tp cropped. sg Oct 24 (58) $300

Cain, James M.

— Mildred Pierce. NY, 1941. 1st Ed. 8vo, cloth, in chipped d/j. Sgd by Orson Welles. pba Aug 20 (42) $250

— The Postman Always Rings Twice. NY, 1934. In d/j. Epstein copy. sg Apr 29 (61) $500

— Serenade. NY, 1937. In chipped d/j. Inscr. sg Dec 12 (41) $375

Anr copy. In tape-repaired d/j. sg June 11 (54) $50

Cain, Julien

[-] Humanisme actif. Melanges d'art et de litterature offerts a Julien Cain. Paris, 1968. 2 vols. 4to, orig wraps. With a litho by Chagall, an etching by Dunoyer de Segonzac & 112 other illusts. K Dec 1 (246) $325

Cala, Marcello

— Istituzioni di pirotecnia. Naples, 1819. 2 parts in 1 vol. 4to, contemp half mor. With 2 engraved titles & 24 plates & 1 folding table. Some browning. S July 9 (1223) £480 [American Museum]

Calandri, Filippo

— Aritmetica. Florence: Lorenzo Morgiani & Johannes Petri, 1 Jan 1492. 8vo, modern vellum. 28 lines; type 3:81G; single & double column; with 58 woodcuts, including 3 full-page. Minor marginal repairs at beginning & end, affecting a few signatures. 104 leaves. Goff C-34. C Nov 27 (32) £10,000 [Halwas]

Calarone, Costantino

— Scienza prattica necessaria all'huomo.... Rome, 1714. 8vo, later vellum. sg Mar 26 (59) $425

Caldecott, Randolph, 1846-86

— The Complete Collection of Pictures and Songs. L, 1887. One of 800. Folio, half cloth. pnE Oct 1 (266) £100

Anr copy. Cloth; rubbed & soiled. sg Jan 30 (17) $225

— Picture Books. L, [c.1878-84]. 16 vols bound in 2. 4to, contemp half calf, orig wraps bound in; rubbed. bba Apr 9 (253) £120 [Ginnan]

Anr copy. 16 vols. 4to, cloth, orig wraps for each part bound in. Epstein copy. sg Apr 29 (62) $1,100

— The Queen of Hearts. L: Routledge, [1881]. 4to, orig wraps; chipped & soiled. sg Jan 30 (18) $70

Calder, Alexander, 1898-1976

— Gouaches et Totems. Paris: Galerie Maeght, 1966. One of 150 on velin de Rives. Folio, loose as issued in wraps. Derriere le Miroir, No 156. Sgd by Calder. sg Sept 26 (67) $650

— Stabiles. Paris: Galerie Maeght, 1963. Folio, loose as issued. Derriere le Miroir, No 141. Sgd by Calder. sg Sept 26 (66) $600

One of 150. Loose as issued in orig wraps. Derriere le Miroir, No 141. sg Sept 6 (46) $850

Anr copy. Loose as issued in wraps. With 8 color lithos, including wrap. Derriere le Miroir, No 141. sg Apr 2 (38) $500

— Three Young Rats. NY, 1944. one of 700. 4to, half cloth, unopened, in d/j. sg Sept 26 (65) $200

Anr copy. Half cloth, in d/j. sg Jan 30 (19) $375

Calderini, Emma

— Il Costume popolare in Italia. Milan: Sperling & Kupfer, [1934]. Folio, cloth; shaken, joints partly frayed. With 200 plain & 14 color plates. Library markings but plates unmarked. sg Apr 2 (71) $175

Caldesi & Montecchi, Photographers

— Photographs of the Gems of the Art Treasures Exhibition. Manchester, 1857. L: Colnaghi & Agnew, 1858. 2 (of 5) vols in 1. Folio, mor gilt dated 1870. With litho dedication & 99 (of 100) mtd albumen photographs of paintings by contemp English artists. Lacking tp, plate list & Plate 98. sg Feb 6 (48) $275

Caldwell, Erskine. See: Bourke-White & Caldwell

Calendario...

— Calendario manual y guia universal de forasteros en Venezuela. Caracas: Matthew Gallagher & James Lamb, [1810]. 8vo in 4s, oversewed & unbound, as issued. Lacking pp. 57-64; indistinct watermark in quires C, E, F & G; headlines cropped; first lines of text imperf on pp 3-6, 43-48 & 51-54; 1st & last leaves frayed & soiled without loss. P Dec 12 (97) $12,000

Calepinus, Ambrosius, 1435-1511

— Dictionarium.... Lyons, 1667. 2 vols. Folio, contemp mor gilt with unidentified crowned monogram on covers; some wear. sg Oct 24 (59) $1,100

— Dictionarium copiosissimum. Strassburg: M. Schurer, Dec 1516. Bound with: Dictionarium decem linguarum. Lyons, 1585. And: Il Dittionario dalla lingua latina.... Venice, 1552. Folio, 16th-cent pigskin. Some worming; upper margin of tp cut away. S Dec 5 (76) £1,500 [Quaritch]

— Dictionarium undecim linguarum. Basel: Henricpetri, 1590. 2 vols in 1. Folio, contemp blind-stamped pigskin over wooden bds; worn & soiled, lacking clasps insect-damage to lower bd. Tp lacking inch strip from lower edge. wa June 25 (148) $200

California

— Message from the President...on the Subject of California and New Mexico. Wash., 1850. 8vo, cloth. With 5 (of 7) maps. House Exec. Doc. No. 17. sp Feb 6 (51) $130

— Proceedings of a Public Meeting of the Democratic Members of the Legislature of California, Opposed to the Election of a United States Senator.... San Francisco, 1854. 8vo, modern half mor. cb Nov 14 (25) $50

— Gold Rush. - A List of Persons from Nantucket Now in California, or on Their Way Thither.... Nantucket: Jethro Brock, 1 Jan 1850. 24mo, orig wraps; restitched. sg June 18 (96) $900

California Historical Society

— Quarterly of the California Historical Society. San Francisco, 1922-75. Vol I, No 1 to Vol LIV, No 4. Orig wraps. cb Nov 14 (23) $2,250

Callahan, Harry

— Color, 1941-1980. Providence: Matrix, [1980]. 4to, orig cloth. bbc Feb 17 (188) $70

Callander, John

— Terra Australis Cognita, or Voyages to the Terra Australis, or Southern Hemisphere. Edin., 1766-68. 3 vols. 8vo, contemp calf. With 3 folding maps. S June 25 (43) £9,600 [Quaritch/Hordern]

Calliat, Victor

— Encyclopedie d'architecture. Paris, 1851-62. 12 vols. 4to, contemp half mor. Some dampstaining. S July 9 (1224) £380 [Arnold]

Callimachus

— Hymni, epigrammata, et fragmenta.... Amst.: Christopher Pantin, 1584. 2 parts in 1 vol. 16mo, contemmp calf; rubbed, lower cover def. bba June 11 (7) £130 [Kent]

Calmet, Augustin, 1672-1757

— Dictionnaire historique, critique, chronologique, geographique et litteral de la Bible. Paris, 1722-28. 4 vols. Folio, modern half mor. With frontis & 208 plates & maps. bba Apr 30 (273) £170 [Crossley]

Caloprese, Gregorio

— Lettura sopra la concione di Marfisa a Carlo Magno. Naples, 1691. Part 1 (all pbd). 4to, contemp mor gilt with arms of Clement XI; rubbed. SI June 9 (201) LIt850,000

Calvert, Frederick, Artist

— The Isle of Wight Illustrated. L, 1846. 4to, orig cloth gilt; rebacked preserving orig backstrip. With hand-colored map, frontis & 20 hand-colored plates; Plate 4 is titled Ryde plate I. C May 20 (27) £450 [Traylen]

Calvert, Samuel

— A Memoir of Edward Calvert. L, 1893. One of 350. 4to, orig cloth. With 35 plates on 31 leaves. bba Feb 27 (442) £2,600 [Sims Reed]

Calvete de Estrella, Juan Christobal

— El Felicissimo Viaie d'el...Principe Don Phelippe.... Antwerp: Martin Nucio, 1552. 1st Ed, with title having woodcut of imperial coat of arms. Folio, contemp calf. Some worming; a few stains. B Nov 1 (305) HF4,400

Calvin, John, 1509-64

— A Harmonie upon the Three Evangelists.... L, 1611. 8vo, orig calf; worn, front hinge starting, back cover detached. Lacking 4 leaves, including tp; some foxing. STC 2963. NH May 30 (454) $90

— Institutio christianae religionis. Geneva: Franciscus Perrinus, 6 June 1568. Folio, later half calf; rubbed. Title stained & torn in inner margin. bba Feb 27 (238) £90 [Hartley]

— The Institution of Christian Religion.... L: R. Wolfe & R. Harison, 1561. 1st Ed in English. Trans by Thomas Norton. Folio, contemp calf; backstrip torn. Inner margin wormed. bba Nov 28 (175) £180 [Axe]

Anr copy. Contemp calf; front bd detached. STC 4415. LH Dec 11 (79) $400

Anr Ed. L: Henrie Middleton, for William Norton, 1582. 4to, old sheep. Dampstained at beginning & end. Tp soiled & frayed. sg Mar 12 (40) $375

Cambray, —— de, Chevalier

— Maniere de fortifier de Mr. de Vauban. Amst., 1689. 8vo, contemp calf. With frontis & 30 folding diagrams. Minor worming to Part 2. b June 22 (223) £320

Cambridge...

— Cambridge Bibliography of English Literature. Cambr., 1940-57. 5 vols, including Index & Supplement. pn Sept 12 (27) £70 [Pordes]

Anr copy. Vol I rear cover frayed; Vol II hinge cracked. sg Oct 31 (65) $70

Anr Ed. NY, 1941. Ed by F. W. Bateson. 4 vols. sg May 21 (157) $50

Anr Ed. Cambr., 1966. 5 vols, including Supplement. bbc Sept 23 (77) $130

Anr Ed. Cambr., 1969-77. Ed by F. W. Bateson. 5 vols, including Index and Supplement. In d/js. cb Nov 21 (54) $190

Ed by George Watson. Cambr., 1974-77. ("The New Cambridge Bibliography of English Literature.") 5 vols. In d/js. bba Dec 19 (293) £220 [Ogino]; O Sept 24 (182) $250

— The Cambridge History of English Literature. Cambr., 1907-16. Ed by A. W. Ward & A. R. Waller. 14 vols. b Nov 18 (285) £60

— The Cambridge Medieval History. NY, 1911-36. Ed by J. B. Bury & others. 8 vols. Orig cloth; shaken. Library markings. F Dec 18 (385) $275

— Cambridge Modern History. Cambr., 1934. 13 vols. O May 26 (31) $110

Cambridge, Richard Owen, 1717-1802

— The Scribleriad. L, 1751. 1st Ed. 6 parts in 1 vol. 4to, contemp half calf; upper cover detached. With 7 plates. Some leaves frayed; B2 torn in margin. L.p. copy. pn May 14 (30) £55

Camden, William, 1551-1623

— Annals. L, 1625-29. ("Annales. The True and Royall History of the Famous Empresse Elisabeth [i.e., Parts 1-3] * Tomus Alter & Idem; or, the History of...that Famous Princesse, Elizabeth [i.e., Part 4].") Parts 1-3 only. Contemp calf; rubbed, joints splitting. With engraved frontis port & title. Lacking prelim leaf; C2 & B4 torn with loss; other tears; some cropping. Sold w.a.f. STC 4497. bba July 9 (82) £75 [Gammon]

Anr copy. ("Annales. The True and Royall History of the Famous Empresse Elisabeth [i.e., Parts 1-3] × Tomus Alter & Idem; or, the History of...that Famous Princesse, Elizabeth [i.e., Part 4].") Contemp half calf; worn. Soiled. STC 4497. DW Mar 4 (195) £85

— Britannia: or a Chorographical Description.... L, 1610. ("Britain....") 1st Ed in English. Trans by Philemon Holland. 2 parts in 1 vol. Folio, modern half calf. With extra title & c.12 orig maps. Most maps supplied in crude photocopy. Sold w.a.f. STC 4509. bba Jan 30 (109) £300 [Kentish]

Anr copy. Later half mor. With engraved title (laid down) & 13 double-page maps. Some worn. Some text leaves def. Sold w.a.f. STC 4509. bba Apr 30 (4) £200 [Crossley]

Anr copy. Contemp calf; worn, upper joint weak. With engraved title (torn, laid down & repaired), 57 double-page maps & 8 plates showing coins, frontis & 1st map partly colored. Some spotting & marginal discoloration throughout; a few pages torn; 5 maps torn at fold; Cornwall cut close at side margins; Gloucester badly torn & browned. STC 4509. S June 25 (263) £3,500 [Wayman]

1st Ed of Gibson's trans. L, 1695. ("Britannia....") Folio, later calf. With port (torn at inner margin) & 51 maps & 9 plates of coins. Devonshire def at 2 corners, torn & mtd; 2 maps repaired; Roman Britain stained. L Feb 27 (132) £1,080

Anr copy. Contemp calf; worn, upper cover detached. With port, 50 double-page & folding map & 9 plates of coins. Some dampstain to port & prelims; a few maps wormed; Hertfordshire & Scotland with shaved margins; some tears. pn May 14 (242) £1,600

Anr copy. Modern mor. With port, 9 full-page plates of coins & 50 double-page maps. Some staining. pnE Oct 2 (532) £1,600

Anr copy. Contemp calf; rebacked. With port, 8 full-page plates of coins & 50 double-page maps. Kent & Hertfordshire shaved. S June 25 (265) £1,600 [Higgins]

Anr copy. Contemp calf; rebacked, spine def. With port (repaired), 50 double-page or folding maps & 9 plates of coins. Some maps with short splits at fold; Kent & Hampshire torn at fold; Norfolk & Cambridge with worming affecting engraved surface at lower fold. S July 1 (1396) £1,500 [Burden]

Anr copy. Old calf; soiled & worn. Extensive marginal repairs; some maps with holes, both extant & repaired; some maps with leading edges shaved; in a dishevelled condition. W July 8 (205) £270

2d Ed of Gibson's trans. L, 1722. 2 vols. Folio, contemp calf; spines & joints worn. With frontis, 51 maps & 10 plates. Waterstain in some margins T1 in Vol I repaired. b Mar 11 (194) £1,500

Anr copy. Later half calf. With port, frontis to Vol I & 51 double-page maps. DW Dec 11 (91) £1,500

Anr copy. Contemp calf; worn. With frontis, 51 maps & 10 plates. Some browning. S Nov 15 (955) £1,800 [Tooley Adams]

Anr copy. Contemp calf; worn, rebacked & repaired. With port, 51 double-page or folding maps & 10 plates. Tear to 1 text leaf. S Feb 26 (704) £1,750 [Barron]

Anr Ed. L, 1753. 2 vols. Folio, contemp calf; worn. With port, 51 double-page or folding maps & 10 plates. Spotted & browned. DW Mar 4 (63) £1,450

Anr copy. With port, 51 double-page or folding maps & 10 plates of coins. Hertfordshire cut close; Norfolk cut close and holed near fold. S June 25 (267) £1,500 [Burden]

2d Ed of Gough's trans. L, 1806. 4 vols. Folio, contemp russia; joints worn, some covers detached. bba Jan 30 (349) £850 [Bernard]

Anr copy. Contemp calf; rebacked & recornered, rubbed. With port, 57 maps & 104 plates. Library markings, with ink stamps on plate & map versos, with some show-through; some foxing. Sold w.a.f. bba May 14 (260) £420 [J. & D. Clarke]

Anr copy. Vols I-II (of 4). Half mor; worn, Vol II becoming disbound. With 77 plates. wa Mar 5 (446) $450

— Britannia, sive florentissimorum regnorum Angliae.... L, 1607. Folio, bound for John Evelyn in mid-17th-cent calf gilt with Evelyn's monogram in gilt repeated 6 times. With engraved title, 57 maps & 8 plates of coins. Cornwall & Sussex shaved at fore-margins; Q3 side-margin def; some browning. STC 4508. S June 25 (269) £5,500 [Quaritch]

Anr Ed. Amst.: Blaeu, 1639. 12mo, contemp vellum; worn. With 19 miniature double-page maps, 1 with colored border. Tear at fold of 1 map; side edges cropped of map of islands; some browning at edges & folds. S Nov 15 (954) £300 [Tooley Adams]

— The Historie of the Most renowned and Victorious Princesse Elizabeth.... L, 1675. ("The History of the Life and Reign of the...Princess Elizabeth....") Folio, contemp calf; rebacked. With port. W July 8 (48) £100

3d Ed. Folio, modern half mor. bba Oct 10 (300) £90 [Shapero]

Camera Work

— 1903. - NY No 4. cb Oct 25 (25) $250

— 1904. - NY 5 & 6. Cloth. sg Oct 8 (13) $550

— 1905. - NY No 10. sg Oct 8 (14) $425

No 12. Orig wraps; spine lacking. sg Apr 13 (19) $1,000

— 1906. - NY No 14. Lacking 1 plate. cb Oct 25 (26) $800; sg Oct 8 (15) $2,200

No 15. cb Oct 25 (17) $300; sg Apr 13 (20) $600

No 16. Lacking 1 halftone. cb Oct 25 (19) $150

— 1907. - NY No 17. cb Oct 25 (18) $200; sg Oct 8 (16) $250

— 1909. - NY No 25. Copy lacking Brigman's The Source. sg Apr 13 (21) $950

No 26. cb Oct 25 (20) $350

Anr copy. Disbound, soiled. sg Oct 8 (17) $650

No 28. cb Oct 25 (22) $500

— 1910. - NY No 31. sg Apr 13 (22) $325

No 32. sg Apr 13 (23) $425

— 1913. - NY No 42/43. cb Oct 25 (16) $700

Special No for 1913. cb Oct 25 (13) $150

— 1914. - NY No 44. sg Oct 8 (19) $900

Anr copy. Lacking 1 plate. Inscr by Abraham Walkowitz. sg Apr 13 (25) $275

No 45. cb Oct 25 (24) $200; sg Apr 13 (26) $550

No 46. Bdg worn & chipped. Title detached but present. cb Oct 25 (14) $190

— 1916. - NY No 48. cb Oct 25 (15) $3,750; sg Oct 8 (20) $6,000

— 1917. - NY No 49/50. sg Oct 8 (21) $10,000

Cameron, Verney Lovett, 1844-94. See: Burton & Cameron

Camm, Bede. See: Bond & Camm

Camocio, Giovanni Francesco

— Isole famose porti fortezze e terre maritime.... Venice: Libreria del segno di S. Marco, [c.1572]. Oblong folio, modern half mor. With 60 plates & maps. Lacking tp & without the regional maps except for Zenoi's map of Europe & the Mediterranean; some surface dirt; a few maps cut close. S Nov 21 (231) £4,200 [Foros]

Camoens, Luis de, 1524?-80

— The Lusiad, or, Portugal's Historicall Poem.... L, 1880-84. ("The Lusiad.") 1st Ed, 1st Issue of Sir Richard F. Burton's trans. 6 vols. 8vo, orig cloth; worn & soiled. Inscr. S June 25 (400) £800 [Mandl]

Camp, Charles L.

— James Clyman: American Frontiersman. San Francisco, 1928. 1st Ed. sg June 18 (163) $175

Camp, Walter

— American Football. NY, 1891. 8vo, orig cloth; spine & rear cover partly discolored, hinges cracked. sg May 21 (15) $120

Campanella, Tommaso, 1568-1639

— De sensu rerum et magia, libri quatuor.... Frankfurt, 1620. 1st Ed. 4to, modern half vellum. Laminated where tattered at margins & with library stamp on tp verso; some browning. Ck Oct 31 (50) £1,000

— Prodromus philisophiae instaurandae.... Frankfurt, 1617. Bound with: De sensu rerum et magia.... Frankfurt, 1620. And: Apologia pro Galileo. Frankfurt, 1622. 4to, modern vellum. Ck Oct 31 (49) £2,800

Campbell, Albert H. —& Others

— Report upon the Pacific Wagon Roads.... [Wash.], 1859. Senate Issue. 8vo, modern half mor. With 6 folding maps. Some maps torn. cb Feb 12 (10) $200

Anr copy. Disbound. Tear in blank margin of 2 maps; 2 others with linen backing. K July 12 (92) $225

Campbell, Alexander, 1764-1824

— A Journey from Edinburgh through Parts of North Britain. L, 1802. 1st Ed. 2 vols. 4to, orig bds; spines worn, Vol I def. With 44 hand-colored lithos. bba Sept 19 (237) £140 [Vine]

Anr copy. 2 vols in 1. 4to, half calf. L Nov 14 (98) £120

Anr Ed. L, 1811. 2 vols. 4to, contemp calf gilt; spines worn. With 42 hand-colored lithos. Some spotting. DW Jan 29 (71) £90

— The Sequel to Bulkeley and Cummins's Voyage to the South-Seas.... L, 1747. 8vo, bds; rebacked. C June 25 (37) £2,500 [Quaritch/Hordern]

Campbell, Archibald, 1726-80

— Lexiphanes, a Dialogue.... L, 1767. 1st Ed. 8vo, 19th-cent half sheep; rubbed. A few leaves missing blank corner. sg Mar 12 (144) $175

Campbell, Archibald, 1764-1824

— A Voyage Round the World.... Edin., 1816. 1st Ed. 8vo, contemp calf; rubbed. With folding chart. Some browning. Inscr to Count P. Rivedin by the Editor, James Smith. S Feb 26 (724) £500 [Baring]

Campbell, Colin, d.1720 —& Others

— Vitruvius Britannicus. L, [1715]-17-31-67-71. Vols I-III only. contemp calf. With 2 engraved titles, 1 dedication & 231 plates. Library stamp on each plate; marginal tear to 1 folding plate. Nottingham Reference Library copy. C Oct 30 (16) £2,200 [Rojas]

Anr copy. 5 vols. Folio, 19th-cent half mor; edges rubbed. With 5 engraved titles, 4 engraved dedications & 390 plates, 101 of them double-page or folding. Tp, dedication & 1st leaf of introduction of Vol I trimmed & mtd. C June 24 (214) £4,500 [Shapero]

Anr copy. Vols I-III only. Folio, contemp calf; not quite uniform. With engraved titles in Vols I-II, engraved dedication & 231 plates & with 11 additional plates from other works & 4 Ms plans & elevations in ink & washes inserted at the end of Vol III. A few plates torn at fold; some soiling. S June 25 (91) £6,500 [Pagan]

Anr Ed. L, 1717. Vols I-II. Folio, contemp calf; worn, rebacked & repaired. With 2 engraved titles, 1 dedication & 158 plates. Library stamps on plates. Sold w.a.f. S Nov 15 (780) £1,200 [Mason]

Campbell, John, 1708-75

— Lives of the Admirals, and other eminent British Seamen. L, 1761. 3d Ed. 4 vols. 8vo, contemp calf gilt; rubbed. O Jan 14 (36) $150

— A Political Survey of Britain. L, 1774. 1st Ed. 2 vols, without Index. 4to, contemp calf; corners bumped, hinges weak. bba Jan 16 (135) £50 [Wilbraham]

Anr copy. 2 vols. 4to, later half calf. cb Feb 12 (21) $300

2d Ed. Dublin, 1775. 4 vols. 8vo, contemp calf; rubbed. O Jan 14 (37) $110

Campbell, John, 1766-1840

— Travels in South Africa [2d Journey].... L, 1822. 2 vols. 8vo, old half calf. With 12 hand-colored plates & 1 hand-colored folding map. Vol II lacking half-title; map torn. L Nov 14 (139) £160

Campbell, John, Baron Campbell, 1779-1861

— The Lives of the Lord Chancellors and Keepers of the Great Seal of England.... L, 1846-69. Vols I-VII. Later half calf; rubbed. CG Oct 7 (474) £60

Anr Ed. Phila., 1848. 7 vols. 8vo, half mor. cb Jan 16 (29) $225

Campbell, John W., 1910-71

— Islands of Space. Reading: Fantasy Press, 1956. One of 50. In d/j with minor stains to rear panel. wa Mar 5 (160) $300

— Who Goes There? Seven Tales of Science Fiction. Chicago: Shasta, 1948. In rubbed d/j. sg June 11 (55) $225

Campbell, Joseph, Critic

— The Mythic Image. Princeton, [1974]. One of 200. bbc Dec 9 (296) $230

Campbell, Roy, 1901-57

— Poems. Paris: Hours Press, 1930. One of 200, sgd. Folio, orig half lea. sg Dec 12 (43) $150

Campbell, William J.

— A Collection of Franklin Imprints in the Museum of the Curtis Publishing Company. Phila., 1918. One of 475. 4to, later cloth. bbc Apr 27 (128) $55

Anr copy. Cloth; shaken. sg Oct 31 (66) $70

Camphuysen, Dirk

— Stichtelycke Rymen om te lesen ofte singhen. Amst.: I. Colom, 1647. Oblong 8vo, calf gilt. With folding port & 61 emblematic illusts. B Nov 1 (319) HF1,600

Camus, Albert

— La Chute. Paris, 1956. One of 35 on hollande Van Gelder. Mor, orig wraps bound in. S May 28 (283) £4,000 [Beres]

— L'Etranger. Paris: Gallimard, 1942. Mor, orig wraps bound in, by Alix. Review copy. S May 28 (280) £1,000 [Sims Reed]

— L'Exil et le Royaume. Paris, 1957. One of 45 on hollande Van Gelder. Mor gilt, orig wraps bound in, by A. & R. Maylander. S May 28 (284) £800 [Holinger]

— Oeuvres. Paris, [1962]. 6 vols. 4to, wraps. DW Mar 11 (479) £260

— La Peste. [Paris]: Gallimard, [1947]. One of 30 on velin de Hollande. Mor by Maylander, orig wraps bound in. S May 28 (281) £4,200 [Lardanchet]

1st Ed. Orig wraps. Epstein copy. sg Apr 29 (64) $1,400

Canadian...

— The Canadian Handbook and Tourist's Guide. Montreal, 1867. 4to, orig cloth; worn. With 6 albumin prints by W. Notman. Frontis & last plate loose. sg Oct 8 (52) $110

Canal, Antonio. See: Canaletto

Canaletto, 1697-1768

— Urbis Venetiarum prospectus celebriores. Venice: Giovanni Battista Pasquali, 1742. 3 parts in 1 vol. Oblong folio, contemp half calf over marbled bds; worn. With double port & 38 plates. Stamp on tp; a few short tears without loss; some thumb-marks. S Nov 21 (163) £8,500 [Bifolco]

Candolle, Augustin Pyramus de, 1778-1841

— Organographie vegetale, ou description raisonee des organes des plantes. Paris, 1827. 2 vols. 8vo, contemp half sheep gilt. With 60 plates. Title & a few plates browned. sg Nov 14 (168) $150

— Plantarum succulentarum historia, ou Histoire naturelle des plantes.... Paris, [1799-1805]. 2 vols. Folio, old bds with orig ptd wraps pasted on covers, completely uncut; rebacked & recornered with mor. With 144 hand-finished color plates. Tear to 1 plate repaired. Bound without titles, prelims & indexes but with 2 orig ptd wraps bound in as titles. Sold w.a.f. L.p. copy. C May 20 (150) £8,000 [Gallup]

Canfield, Chauncey L.

— The Diary of a Forty-Niner. San Francisco, 1906. 1st Ed. Half cloth. cb Feb 12 (11) $130

Canina, Luigi, 1795-1856

— Particolare genere di architettura domestica. Rome, 1852. Folio, modern bds. With 40 plates. Some dampspotting. SI Dec 5 (133) LIt300,000

Canny, James R. See: Heartman & Canny

Canova, Antonio, 1757-1822

— Works. L, 1824. 2 vols. 4to, half mor; rubbed. With port & 100 plates. Some foxing. K July 12 (96) $65

Anr Ed. Bost., 1876. 2 vols. 4to, half mor; hinge cracked & endpaper torn in vol II. With frontises & 162 plates. sg Apr 2 (40) $225

Cantemir, Demetrius, 1673-1723

— Geschichte des osmanischen Reichs nach seinem Anwachse und Abnehmen. Hamburg, 1745. 4to, contemp vellum. With 22 ports & folding plan. S June 30 (110) £600 [Reiss & Auvermann]

— The History of the Growth and Decay of the Othman Empire.... L, 1734-35. 2 parts in 1 vol. Folio, modern half mor. With port, folding plan & 22 plates. Soiled at beginning & end; port repaired; plan torn with loss. S June 30 (253) £280 [Ozbek]

Cantone, Oberto

— L'Uso prattico dell' aritmetica.... Naples: Tarquinio Longho, 1599. 1st Ed. 4to, modern vellum bds. Prelims wormed; some browning & staining. S May 28 (3) £750 [Lib.Casella]

Cantu, Federico

— Obra realizada de 1922 a 1948. Mexico, 1948. Wraps. With an inscr engraving. sg Feb 6 (49) $110

Capella, Galeazzo Flavio, 1487-1537

— De rebus nuper in Italia gestis libri octo. Antwerp: Martinus Caesar [de Keyser], 1533. 8vo, calf gilt. B May 12 (18) HF1,000

Capgrave, John

— The Book of the Illustrious Henries. L, 1858. 8vo, mor gilt by Oldach. Extra-illus with ports & views. K Dec 1 (219) $250

Capitan, Louis, 1854-1929

— La Caverne de Font-de-Caume aux Eyzies (Dordogne). Monaco, 1910. Folio, half cloth; soiled & shaken. sg Apr 2 (42) $225

Capitula...

— Capitula dominorum helvetiorum xii cantonum contra impios et blasphemos lutheranos. [N.p., n.d.]. 4 leaves. 4to, modern wraps. Erasure on title causing holes; marginal repairs. S Dec 5 (170) £850 [Schumann]

Capobianco, Alessandro

— Corona e palma militare di artiglieria. Venice: Francesco Bariletti, 1618. Folio, old lea-backed limp bds. Some worming at beginning & end. S July 9 (1225) £300

Capodivaca, Paolo

— Massime et avvertimenti da praticarsi nella scherma. Padua, 1704. 4to, later wraps. Some dampstaining. sg Mar 26 (62) $100

Capote, Truman

See also: Avedon, Richard

— Breakfast at Tiffany's. NY, [1958]. 1st Ed. In d/j sg Dec 12 (44) $130

— The Grass Harp. NY, [1951]. In d/j. sg Dec 12 (45) $80

— Other Voices, Other Rooms. NY, [1948]. 1st Ed. In d/j. Sgd on front free endpaper. bbc Apr 27 (276) $180

Anr copy. In torn d/j. Met Apr 28 (581) $60

Anr copy. In d/j. sg Dec 12 (46) $130

Anr copy. In d/j with edge-tears. sg June 11 (58) $175

Captain...

— The Captain: a Magazine for Boys & "Old Boys." L, 1899-1907. Vols XIII-XXIII. 4to, orig cloth; spines dulled. bba Feb 27 (177) £100 [Willilams]

Caracciolus, Robertus, 1425-95

— Sermones de laudibus sanctorum. Naples: Mathias Moravus et socii, 31 Jan 1489. 4to, contemp vellum; worn, 2 holes in upper cover. 50 lines; double column; gothic letter. Early Ms annotations in margins. 224 leaves. Goff C-143. S Dec 5 (11) £3,000 [Quaritch]

— Sermones quadrigesimales de poentenia. [Venice: Bartholomaeus Cremonensis, 1472]. Folio & 4to, later vellum. Stain in lower margin of last 20 leaves; 1 margin frayed. 340 (of 344) leaves; lacking initial & final blanks & tables. Goff C-169. bba Aug 13 (53) £750 [Bernard]

Anr copy. Modern calf; rubbed. 33 lines; roman letters; capital letters in red & blue. Some spotting & dampstaining; worming towards end; 3 additional Ms leaves in a modern hand at beginning. 336 (of 344) leaves; lacking initial & final blanks & 4 other leaves. Goff C-169. S Feb 25 (489) £650 [Anastassakis]

Anr Ed. [Venice]: Vindelinus de Spira, 20 July 1472. Part 1 (of 2). 4to, 15th-cent half vellum. Marginal spotting & foxing. 290 leaves. Goff C-165. SI June 9 (209) LIt13,000,000

Caradoc of Llancarfan, Saint

— The Historie of Cambria, now called Wales. L, 1774. ("The History of Wales...") 8vo, contemp russia gilt; joints cracking. bba Nov 28 (289) £50 [Bennett & Kerr]

Carcano, Francesco, called Sforzino. See: Giorgi, Federigo

Carcano, Michael de

— Sermonarium de peccatis.... Basel: Michael Wenssler, 29 May 1479. Folio, contemp Austrian pink deerskin with brass fittings, from the cloister bindery of the Benedictines of Lambach. 60 lines; double column; types 1B:121G (headings, colophon) & 2:92G (text; rubricated; 1st major initial in blue with red Maiblumen penwork, the 2d in red with green Maiblumen penwork & a partial violet ground. Single wormhole in text of 1st quire; several wormholes in last few quires; some marginal tears; a few waterstains. 272 (of 274) leaves; leaves 102 & 111 supplied in contemp Ms. Goff C-195. Schoyen copy. P Dec 12 (17) $12,000

Carcciolo, Antonio

— Opere. Milan: Gottardo da Ponte for Joannes Jacobus da Legnano & brothers, 23 Sept-20 Nov 1518. 8vo, 19th-cent vellum. Ee1 supplied in facsimle; upper margins cropped with a few short tears affecting text; small repairs at head of text in Parts 1 & 2. S Dec 5 (78) £1,500 [Jackson]

Carco, Francis, Pseud., 1886-1958

— Ces Messieurs-Dames.... Paris, 1926. One of 25 for friends of the author, with illusts in colored & uncolored state. Illus by H. Dignimont. 4to, orig wraps. Inscr to Henri Barthelemy, with 4 drawings by Dignimont & with a large gouache illust inscr by Dignimont to Boris Kochno. SM Oct 12 (436) FF7,000

— Jesus la Caille. Paris, 1914. One of 20 on hollande. Mor extra by P. L. Martin, orig wraps bound in. Inscr to Pierre MacOrlan & with ALs laid in. S May 28 (285) £1,700 [Saxhof]

Anr Ed. Paris, [1929]. One of 833. Illus by Andre Dignimont. 4to, orig wraps, unopened. Inscr to Boris Kochno, with full-page watercolor drawing inscr in 1947. SM Oct 11 (438) FF7,000

— Vertes. NY, [1946]. One of 1,200. 4to, pictorial wraps. sg Sept 6 (280) $200

Cardanus, Hieronymus, 1501-76

— Artis magnae, sive de regulis algebraicis. Nuremberg: Johannes Petreis, 1545. Foli, 18th-cent bds. Tp soiled, with repairs at margins; D4 repaired at lower margin; final leaves dampstained & wormed at inner margins; lacking final leaf. Ck Nov 29 (157) £3,000

— De rerum varietate libri XVII. Basel: Sebastianus Henricpetrus, 1581. 8vo, contemp blind-stamped calf; spine ends repaired. Sold w.a.f. Ck June 18 (9) £350

— De subtilitate libri XXI. Lyon: Philibert Rolletium, 1554. 8vo, modern vellum preserving an early vellum bdg. Some dampstaining & repairs. Sold w.a.f. Ck June 18 (8) £500

Anr Ed. Lyons: G. Roville, 1559. 8vo, old vellum; rear joint cracked. Inscr on tp & some text passages inked out; marginal dampstaining. Sold w.a.f. sg May 14 (268) $550

Anr Ed. Basel: Sebastianum Henricpetri, [c.1582]. Folio, contemp vellum. Marginal repairs to p1-A1; other marginal defs. SI June 9 (210) LIt400,000

— In Cl. Ptolemaei Pelusiensis iiii de astrorum judiciis...commentaria. Basel: Heinrich Petri, 1554. 8vo, contemp blind-stamped sheep, dated 1557; rubbed & soiled, joints split. P June 17 (145) $3,500

Care, Henry

— English Liberties, or the Free-born Subject's Inheritance.... Bost., 1721. 1st American Ed. 12mo, contemp sheep; rubbed, spine ends chipped. Some browning; 1 leaf loose; some corners rubbed. P June 16 (2) $1,800

Carew, Richard, 1555-1620

— The Survey of Cornwall. L, 1602. 1st Ed. 4to, modern calf gilt. Lacking 1 prelim leaf; Z1 torn; small burn-hole causing slight loss. bba Jan 30 (14) £120 [Rix]

Anr Ed. L, 1723. 4to, modern calf. bba Jan 30 (15) £130 [Shapero]

Carey, David, 1782-1824

— Life in Paris. L, 1822. 1st Ed in Book form. Illus by George Cruikshank. 8vo, later mor gilt by J. Larkins; upper joint with small split. With engraved title & 20 hand-colored plates. Without the to the binder leaf; some plate titles shaved. C Oct 30 (17) £280 [Roseigno]

1st Issue. Later mor gilt by Riviere, upper wraps to orig parts bound in. With 21 hand-colored plates. Without the leaf of directions to the binder. L.p. copy. C May 20 (28) £580 [Marlborough]

Anr copy. Half calf; worn & stained. With 20 (of 21) colored plates. pnE Oct 1 (328) £50

Carey, Henry, d.1743. See: Golden Cockerel Press

Carey, Henry Charles, 1793-1879 —& Lea, Isaac

— Atlas.... Phila., 1822. Folio, contemp half calf; worn, broken. With 46 hand-colored double-page maps, all linen-backed on guards, view & hand-colored table. Some discoloration. Below date on tp is the addition of the London: John Miller imprint. C May 20 (241) £1,600 [Arader]

— A Complete Historical, Chronological, and Geographical American Atlas.... L, 1823. Folio, later half mor gilt. With 18 hand-colored folding maps & plates. Small tear to 1 map. sg Dec 5 (44) $700

Carey, Mathew, 1760-1839

— Carey's General Atlas. Phila., 1811. Folio, later cloth; worn. Lacking some maps; some creasing & foxing. NH Aug 23 (27) $1,500

Caricature

— La Caricature. Paris, 1830-32. 78 Nos in 3 vols. Folio, contemp half mor gilt, orig wraps bound in. With 160 lithos, 50 of them hand-colored. Plate 19 & letterpress text for No 35 lacking; some browning &

staining. Schlosser copy. P June 17 (521) $4,750

Carion, Johannes, 1499-1537

— Chronicon Carionis expositum et auctum multis et veteribus et recentioribus historiis.... Lyons: Petrus Santandreanus, 1576. 8vo, contemp blind-tooled pigskin over wooden bds with panel stamps dated 1565. sg Oct 24 (61) $400

Carleton, James Henry. See: Caxton Club

Carlyle, Thomas, 1795-1881

— The French Revolution. L, 1837. 1st Ed. 3 vols. 8vo, contemp mor gilt extra; extremities rubbed. cb Oct 25 (28) $250

— History of Friedrich II of Prussia.... L, 1858-65. 1st Ed. 6 vols. 8vo, contemp mor gilt by Horser and Storey; spines rubbed. DW Nov 6 (440) £100

— The Life of John Sterling. L, 1851. 1st Ed. 8vo, cloth; worn, inner joint broken. O July 14 (47) $90

— Sartor Resartus. L, 1834. 1st Ed in Book form. 8vo, contemp half calf; worn, spine chipped. Tp & final leaves spotted; lacking ad leaf at end; ads on verso P2 pasted over. Inscr to Benjamin Nelson. C June 24 (117) £450 [Spademan]

Carman, Bliss, 1861-1929

— A Seamark: A Threnody for Robert Louis Stevenson. Bost., 1895. 12mo, ptd wraps; chipped. Some foxing. sg Dec 12 (47) $120

Carmena y Millan, Luis

— Catalogo de la Biblioteca Taurina. Madrid, 1903. One of 50. Newly bound in cloth. sg Oct 31 (63) $425

Carne, John, 1789-1844

— Letters from the East. L, 1826. 8vo, contemp half calf; rubbed. With frontis. S June 30 (15) £280 [Severis]

Anr copy. 2 vols. 8vo, 19th-cent half sheep; rubbed. S June 30 (254) £220 [Popular Bank]

— Syria, the Holy Land, Asia Minor. L, [1836-38]. 3 vols in 2. 4to, half mor gilt; rubbed. With 3 engraved titles, 2 maps & 117 plates. bba June 11 (353) £220 [Hutchins]

Anr copy. Contemp mor; worn. With engraved titles, 2 maps & 117 plates. DW Oct 2 (20) £110

Anr copy. 3 vols in 1. 4to, contemp half calf; spine worn. DW Oct 2 (21) £140

Anr copy. Contemp half mor gilt; rubbed. DW Nov 6 (26) £220

Anr copy. 3 vols. 4to, half lea. LH Dec 11 (80) $275

Anr copy. 3 vols in 1. 4to, contemp calf; rebacked. With port, 3 engraved titles, 3 maps & 117 plates. Some spotting. pn May 14 (213) £220 [Ozbek]

Anr Ed. L, [1842]. Illus by W. H. Bartlett. 3 vols. 4to, contemp half mor; soiled, spines rubbed. With engraved titles, 117 plates & 2 maps. Library stamps on versos. S Nov 15 (781) £200

Anr copy. 3 vols in 2. 4to, cloth; worn. With 3 engraved titles, 2 maps & 117 plates. Some spotting & soiling. S Nov 15 (1172) £220 [Dimakarkos]

Carnegie, Dale

— Lincoln the Unknown. NY, 1932. Mor extra with port miniature of Lincoln by Anker Kjerulff after J. Pound mtd in front doublure; minor wear at foot of spine. Inscr by Carnege & with clipped Lincoln signature affixed to front flyleaf. P June 16 (249) $800

Carnegie, David Wynford

— Spinifex and Sand...Pioneering and Exploration in Western Australia. L, 1898. 8vo, orig cloth. S June 25 (273) £2,200 [Quaritch/Hordern]

Caro, Annibale, 1507-66

— Commento di Ser Agresto da Ficarvolo sopra la prima ficata del padre Siceo. [Rome: A. Blado?], 1539. 4to, 19th-cent mor gilt; joints wormed. S Dec 5 (77) £1,000 [Jackson]

Carpenter, George N.

— History of the Eighth Regiment Vermont Volunteers. Bost., 1886. 8vo, orig cloth; worn & shaken. NH May 30 (157) $95

Carpenter, Percy

— Hog Hunting in Lower Bengal. L, 1861. Folio, orig half mor gilt. With litho title with hand-colored vignette & 8 hand-colored lithos mtd on card. Some spotting, chiefly affecting mounts & text leaves. S June 25 (105) £2,000 [Quaritch]

Carpenter, Thomas

— The American Senator. Phila., 1796-97. 3 vols. 8vo, contemp sheep; worn & loose. Owner's name excised from upper margin of titles. sg Dec 5 (45) $110

Carpenter, William

— The Angler's Assistant. L, 1852. 2d Ed. 12mo, cloth; worn. Koopman copy. O Oct 29 (48) $140

Carpue, Joseph Constantine, 1764-1846

— An Account of Two Successful Operations for Restoring a Lost Nose.... L, 1816. 1st Ed. 4to, orig bds; spine def, covers detached. With 5 plates, 4 of them partly colored. Some spotting & discoloration. S

Dec 5 (364) £7,800 [Phelps]

Carr, Alice

— North Italian Folk Sketches... L, 1878. One of 400 with hand-colored illusts. Illus by Randolph Caldecott. 8vo, orig half cloth; rubbed & soiled. bba Oct 10 (34) £80 [Ball]

Carr, Mrs Comyns. See: Carr, Alice

Carr, Sir John, 1772-1832

— Caledonian Sketches, or a Tour through Scotland.... L, 1809. 1st Ed. 4to, modern half calf. With folding frontis & 11 plates. Frontis repaired. pnE Dec 4 (155) £70

— A Northern Summer or Travels Round the Baltic.... L, 1805. 4to, contemp calf gilt. With 11 sepia tinted plates, 1 folding. bba June 25 (27) £220 [Howes]

Anr copy. Old half calf; rubbed, rebacked. With 11 hand-colored plates. Folding plate torn at fold; repaired; 2 prelim leaves from anr copy. S Nov 15 (1105) £350 [Porter]

— The Stranger in Ireland. L, 1806. 1st Ed. 4to, later half calf; front bd detached, rear joint starting. With uncolored map & 16 hand-colored plates, 5 folding. Margins foxed. wa Sept 26 (569) $450

— A Tour through Holland, along the Right and Left Banks of the Rhine, to the South of Germany.... L, 1807. 1st Ed. 4to, contemp half calf gilt; rubbed, hinges tender. With map & 20 tinted plates. Bound without index. DW Mar 4 (10) £210

Carranza, Domingo Gonzalez

— A Geographical Description of the Coasts, Harbours and Sea Ports of the Spanish West Indies. L, 1740. 8vo, modern calf. With engraved folding map & 4 folding plans. CNY Oct 8 (33) $2,400

Carre de Montgeron, Louis Basile

— La Verite des miracles operes a l'intercession de M. de Paris et autres appellans. Paris, 1737-41. 2 vols. 4to, contemp calf. Some browning. SI Dec 5 (140) LIt480,000

Carrera, Pietro

— Il Gioco de gli scacchi.... Militello, 1617. 4to, contemp calf gilt. Some dampstaining of prelims. Ck May 8 (23) £1,700

Carroll, Lewis. See: Dodgson, Charles Lutwidge

Carroll, W.

— The Angler's Vade Mecum.... Edin., 1818. 1st Ed. 8vo, modern half lea. With 12 hand-colored plates. Koopman copy. O Oct 29 (49) $300

Carson, James, 1772-1843

— An Inquiry into the Causes of the Motion of the Blood.... Liverpool, 1815. 1st Ed. 8vo, disbound. bba Apr 30 (300) £190 [N. Phillips]

Carson, Rachel. See: Limited Editions Club

Cartari, Vincenzo

— Les Images des dieux.... Lyons: Guichard Juleron for B. Honorat, 1581. 4to, modern cloth. Browned & stained. bba Nov 28 (178) £70 [Wilbraham]

— Imagines deorum.... Lyon: apud Estienne Michel, 1581. 4to, later calf; rubbed. Minor wound to 1 leaf. F Mar 26 (701) $210

— Le Imagini de i Dei degli antichi.... Lyons, 1624. 4to, 17th-cent calf; front joint restored. sg Mar 12 (203) $550

Anr Ed. Venice: Evangelista Deuchino, 1625. 4to, old calf; worn. Italic letter. With 87 large engraved illusts in text. Some dampstaining; tp & following leaf torn & repaired. S Feb 11 (38) £180 [Erlini]

Anr Ed. Venice, 1647. ("Imagini delli Dei de gl'antichi....") 4to, 19th-cent half lea. Some browning. SI Dec 5 (141) LIt560,000

Anr copy. Contemp vellum; rubbed. With 2 folding plates. Marginal repairs. SI June 9 (210) LIt400,000

Carte...

— La Carte Surrealiste. [Paris, 1937]. Nos 1-21 (complete set). Ptd on pale green card sg Apr 2 (78) $750

Carter, Charles

— The Compleat City and Country Cook.... L, 1732. 1st Ed. 8vo, contemp calf; new endpapers. With 49 plates. Some dampstaining in margins. S May 14 (975) £480 [Rainsford]

Carter, George, 1737-94

— A Narrative of the Loss of the Grosvenor East Indiaman.... L, 1791. 8vo, orig bds; rebacked, sides stained, portion of front free endpaper lacking. With folding frontis & 3 plates (2 foxed). CNY Oct 8 (34) $300

Carter, Harry. See: Morison & Carter

Carter, John, 1748-1817

— The Ancient Architecture of England. L, 1806-7. 2 parts in 1 vol. Folio, early 19th-cent half lea; rubbed. With frontis, titles & 106 plates. S May 14 (1140) £50 [Marlborough]

Carter, John Waynflete, 1905-75

— Binding Variants in English Publishing, 1820-1900. L & NY, 1932. 1st Ed. Bds. sg May 21 (158) $80

One of 500. Orig half vellum. bbc Apr 27 (111) $110

Carter, John Waynflete, 1905-75 —& Muir, Percy H.

— Printing and the Mind of Man. NY, 1967. 4to, In d/j. cb Oct 17 (151) $95

Anr copy. Mor gilt by Bernard Kiernan. L Nov 14 (12) £80

Anr copy. In d/j. O Dec 17 (148) $95

Anr copy. 4to, sg Oct 31 (67) $175

Anr copy. Cloth, in smudged d/j. Pencillings in margins. wa Apr 9 (12) $70

1st American Ed. 4to, orig cloth, in d/j. sg May 21 (159) $50

2d Ed. Munich, 1983. Folio, orig cloth, in d/j. bba Apr 9 (3) £55 [Adrian]

Anr copy. 4to, O Aug 25 (146) $95; sg May 21 (160) $100

Carter, John Waynflete, 1905-75 —& Pollard, Graham

— An Enquiry into the Nature of Certain Nineteenth Century Pamphlets. L & NY, 1934. In d/j. F Dec 18 (185) $80; sg May 21 (161) $120

Carteret, Leopold

— Le tresor du bibliophile.... Paris, 1924-28. 4 vols. Cloth, orig front wrap to Vol I bound in. Ck Nov 1 (371) £140

Anr Ed. Paris, 1946-48. ("Le Tresor du bibliophile: livres illustres modernes, 1875 a 1945.") 5 vols. 4to, half mor, orig wraps bound in. S May 13 (555) £220 [Vecchi Libri]

Anr copy. Ptd wraps; spine ends worn. sg May 21 (162) $250

One of 150. Half mor, orig wraps bound in. S July 1 (1184) £200

Cartier-Bresson, Henri

— The Decisive Moment. NY, [1952]. Folio, bds, in d/j. With separate pamphlet of captions laid in. cb Dec 5 (24) $190

Anr copy. Pamphlet of captions not mentioned. CGen Nov 17 (320) SF1,000

Anr copy. Bds. With separate pamphlet of captions laid in. sg Oct 8 (23) $550

Anr copy. Bds; front hinge torn. Inscr to Manuel Manrique. sg Oct 8 (24) $450

Anr copy. Bds, in d/j. With separate pamphlet of captions. sg Apr 13 (29) $400

Anr copy. Orig bds; lower front tip worn, lower inch of spine split. Pamphlet of captions bound in. wa Mar 5 (612) $200

— The Europeans. NY, [1955]. Folio, bds; spine ends chipped, with short cracks. With separate pamphlet of captions in English laid in. bbc Feb 17 (189) $155

Anr copy. Bds; head of spine pulling away. F Mar 26 (688) $120; sg Oct 8 (25) $375

Anr copy. Bds; joints inexpertly repaired, rubbed. sg Oct 8 (26) $300

Anr copy. With separate pamphlet of captions in English laid in. sg Apr 13 (30) $400

Anr copy. Bds. Epstein copy. sg Apr 29 (70) $400

— Les Europeens. Paris: Verve, [1955]. Folio, bds with design by Miro. CNY June 9 (319) SF1,900

Cartwright, George, 1739-1819

— A Journal of Transactions and Events during a Residence of Nearly Sixteen Years on the Coast of Labrador. Newark, 1792. 3 vols. 4to, contemp half sheep; worn. With port & 3 folding charts. One map repaired on verso; scattered foxing to maps & text. sg Jan 9 (47) $850

Caruso, Enrico, 1873-1921

— Caricatures. NY, 1914. Folio, orig bdg. b&b Feb 19 (308) $100

Carvalho, Solomon N.

— Incidents of Travel and Adventure in the Far West with Col. Fremont's Last Expedition.... NY: Derby & Jackson, 1857. 2d Ed. 8vo, orig cloth; worn. Some foxing. NH Oct 6 (372) $130

Carwell, Thomas

— The New Atlas or, Travels and Voyages in Europe, Asia, Africa, and America.... L, 1698. 1st Ed. 8vo, contemp calf; front outer joint cracked, worn. CNY Oct 8 (35) $3,800

Cary, Elisabeth Luther, 1867-1936

— The Art of William Blake.... NY, 1907. 1st Ed. 4to, half cloth; rubbed. bba Dec 19 (35) £50 [Kurita]

Cary, John, c.1754-1835

— New and Correct English Atlas. L, 1787. 4to, modern half calf. With 2 engraved titles & 45 maps. Some spotting. bba June 11 (375) £420 [Baskes]

Anr copy. Contemp half calf; worn. With 47 maps, hand-colored in outline. Marginal dampstaining & soiling; some corners creased. DW May 13 (72) £600

Anr copy. Contemp calf; upper cover detached, worn. With engraved title & dedication & 47 maps hand-colored in outline. First map, tp & dedication offset. S Nov 15 (958) £550 [Brigantian]

Anr copy. Contemp half calf gilt; worn.

With engraved title, engraved dedication & 46 maps hand-colored in outline. Some spotting at text margins. Subscriber's copy. S June 25 (95) £500 [Nicholson]

Anr Ed. L, 1793. 4to, contemp half calf; rubbed, rebacked. With engraved title & 47 maps, hand-colored in outline. pn Apr 23 (292) £550 [Kidd]

Anr copy. Cloth. pnE Mar 11 (41) £540

Anr copy. Contemp half calf; worn. With engraved title & 46 maps, hand-colored in outline. S July 1 (1397) £420 [Nicholson]

Anr Ed. L, 1809. Folio, cloth; soiled & worn. With engraved title & 47 maps, hand-colored in outline. some browning. L Feb 27 (133) £340

Anr Ed. L, 1818. 4to, modern half calf. With engraved title & 47 maps, hand-colored in outline. Tear to index leaf; p. 5-6 torn at inner margin with small loss. pn Nov 14 (433) £520 [Marsden]

— New Map of England and Wales.... L, 1794. 4to, contemp russia; covers detached, spine def. With engraved title & dedication, hand-colored general map & map in 77 sections numbered to 81. Some staining. pn Apr 23 (294) £150 [Franks]

Anr copy. Half lea; worn, upper cover detached. pn June 11 (299) £160

Anr copy. Contemp bds; worn, covers detached. S Nov 15 (957) £150 [Nichols]

Anr copy. Contemp calf; worn, covers detached. S Feb 26 (705) £160 [Ross]

— Survey of the High Roads from London. L, 1790. 4to, contemp calf; rebacked preserving orig spine, corners repaired. With engraved title, hand-colored general plan, general map & 80 strip maps on 40 sheets, all hand-colored. Some spotting. S Nov 15 (956) £330 [Baskes]

— Traveller's Companion, or a Delineation of the Turnpike Roads of England and Wales.... L, 1814. 8vo, contemp calf; covers detached. bba Mar 26 (326) £110 [B. Bailey]

Casa, Giovanni della, 1503-56

— Il Galathea. Milan, 1559. ("Trattato... cognominato Galatheo.") 2 parts in 1 vol. 8vo, 19th-cent vellum. C Dec 16 (35) £1,400 [Quaritch]

Casanova de Seingalt, Giacomo Girolamo
See also: Limited Editions Club

— Histoire de ma fuite des prisons de la republique de Venise. Leipzig, 1788. 8vo, contemp half calf gilt; scuffed. C Dec 16 (36) £3,200 [Mediolanum]

— Memoirs. [N.p.]: Aventuros, 1925. One of 1,000. Trans by Machen; illus by Rockwell Kent. 12 vols. 4to, cloth; worn. O July 14 (48) $70

Casas, Bartolome de las, 1474-1566

— An Account of the First Voyages and Discoveries made by the Spaniards in America. L, 1699. 8vo, contemp calf; upper cover detached & scraped, lower cover gouged. With 2 double-page plates. Conjugate leaves A1.4 & quire S supplied; foxed. CNY Oct 8 (36) $1,200

— The Spanish Colonie, or Briefe Chronicle... L: William Brome, 1583. 4to, recent mor. Black letter & roman types. Last 2 leaves lacking & supplied in photo-facsimile; headlines cropped. STC 4739. P June 16 (203) $2,500

Casati, Gaetano, 1838-1902

— Ten Years in Equatoria. L, 1891. 2 vols. 8vo, orig cloth; edges rubbed. pn Mar 19 (388) £85 [Sawyer]

Cash, John. See: Pool & Cash

Casler, Walter. See: Taber & Casler

Casper, Johann Ludwig, 1796-1864

— A Handbook of the Practice of Forensic Medicine. L, 1861-65. 4 vols. 8vo, orig cloth; spine ends worn, some joints frayed. sg Nov 14 (18) $140

Cassas, Louis Francois

— Voyage pittoresque de la Syrie.... Paris, 1799-1800. 3 vols in 2. Folio, later half calf, with Signet arms; rubbed. With 180 plates before letters. Lacking text. S July 1 (745) £3,400 [Maggs]

Cassavetes, John

— Minnie & Moskowitz. Los Angeles, 1973. One of 50. sg Oct 17 (15) $100

Cassell's...

— Cassell's Picturesque Australasia.... L, 1887. Ed by Edward Ellis Morris. 4 vols. 8vo, orig cloth; hinges strengthened or repaired. kh Nov 11 (586) A$200

Anr Ed. L, etc., 1887. 4 vols in 2. 4to, contemp half calf gilt; rubbed. With 40 colored maps & 40 wood-engravings. DW May 13 (2) £105

— Cassell's Popular Natural History. L, [1863-67]. 4 vols. 8vo, contemp half calf gilt; spines rubbed. DW Oct 2 (132) £60

Cassin, John, 1813-69

— Illustrations of the Birds of California.... Phila., [1853]-56. 1st Ed. 8vo, modern half mor gilt. With 50 hand-colored plates. Staining & paper discoloration mostly affecting text. S Nov 21 (4) £850 [Maggs]

Cassini, Jacques, 1677-1756

— Tables astronomiques du soleil, de la lune.... Paris, 1740. 2 parts in 1 vol. 4to, contemp sheep; rubbed & wormed. With 5 folding plates. Lacking errata leaf. bba Nov 28 (147) £180 [Tolomei]

Anr copy. 18th-cent mor gilt, armorial bdg; corners rubbed. Horblit copy. S July 1 (1105) £800 [Quaritch]

Castellan, Antoine Laurent, 1772-1838

— Lettres sur la Grece, l'Hellespont et Constantinople. Paris, 1811. 2 vols in 1. 8vo, contemp calf. With 2 folding maps & 20 plates. S June 30 (255) £250 [Consolidated Real]

— Moeurs, usages, costumes des Othomans. Paris, 1812. 6 vols. 18mo, later half mor gilt, sections of orig wraps mtd at the beginning of Vol I. With 73 hand-colored plates. C Oct 30 (18) £750 [Roscigno]

Anr copy. Vols I-V (of 6). Contemp mor gilt. With 45 hand-colored plates. Half-titles stamped. S June 30 (111) £360 [Spink]

Castelli, Pietro, d. c.1657

— Hyaena Odorifera. Messina: G. F. Bianco, 1638. 8vo, 18th-cent calf. With engraved title, port & 8 engraved illusts of Hyenas. C Dec 16 (37) £750 [Mediolanum]

Anr copy. 18th-cent calf gilt. With engraved title, port & 8 engraved illusts. Lacking 4 prelim leaves. C June 24 (119) £260 [Wood]

Castelnau, Michel de, 1526?-92

— Les Memoires.... Brussels, 1731. 3 vols. Folio, contemp calf gilt. Waterstaining & browning. SI June 9 (221) LIt220,000

Castiglione, Baldassare, 1478-1529

Il Cortegiano

— 1528, Apr. - Il Libro del cortegiano. Venice: Aldus. 1st Ed. Folio, contemp calf; repaired, worn, upper joint split. Marginal wormholes in 2d half; some spotting. C Nov 27 (10) £7,000 [Mediolanum]

Anr copy. Contemp mor; rubbed, head of spine restored. Margins stained & affected by damp; outer margin of later leaves wormed. C Dec 16 (38) £7,000 [Jackson]

— 1538. - Venice: Giovanni Paduano for Federico Torresano d'Asola. 8vo, 16th-cent calf over bds with Tudor rose & royal crown surmount; worn, pastedowns lifted, free endpapers lost. Hopetoun-Amherst of Hackney copy. P June 17 (125) $1,000

— 1539. - Venice: Alvise de Tortis. 8vo, 19th-cent half calf; worn, front hinges cracking. Some dampstaining to tp & prelims. cb Dec 5 (75) $225

— 1727. - Il Cortegiano; or The Courtier.... L. 4to, half lea; worn & broken. Pencil marginalia at beginning of book. wa Mar 5 (499) $140

Castiglioni, Arturo, 1874-1953

— A History of Medicine. NY, 1947. 2d Ed. Cloth. sg May 14 (30) $100

Castillo, Antonio del

— El devoto peregrino, viage de Tierra Santa. Madrid, 1756. 8vo, contemp vellum. With engraved title & 4 folding plates. Jerusalem def & laid down; 1 text engraving defaced; E torn with loss of text; M3 with small hole affecting text; some repairs. S July 1 (746) £200 [Menican]

Castle, Egerton, 1858-1920

— L'Escrime et les escrimeurs, depuis le moyen age jusqu'au XVIIIe siecle. Paris, 1888. 8vo, cloth; stain on rear cover. sg Mar 26 (63) $175

Anr copy. Cloth; front cover dampstained. sg Mar 26 (64) $130

Anr copy. Cloth; extremities rubbed, hinges weak. sg Mar 26 (65) $300

Castlereagh, Frederick William Robert Stewart, Viscount. See: Stewart, Frederick William Robert

Castlman, Riva

— Technics and Creativity. II. Gemini Gel. NY: Museum of Modern Art, [1971]. Illus by Jasper Johns. 4to, wraps, in orig syn case. Target 1970 mtd inside front half of case & sgd by Johns. sg Apr 2 (152) $200

Castro, Casimiro

— Album of the Mexican Railway. Mexico, 1877. Oblong folio, orig cloth; minor rubbing to extremities. With colored frontis, double-page map & 24 colored plates. Plates I-V spotted in margins. In English, Spanish & French. S Nov 21 (331) £2,400 [Cristobal]

Castro, Joseph de

— Directorio para informaciones de los pretendientes de el Santo Habito de N. Seraphico P. S. Francisco. Mexico, 1737. 8vo, old vellum. Lacking port. sg June 18 (367) $325

Caswall, Edward

— Sketches of Young Ladies, by "Quiz." L, 1837. 1st Ed. 16mo, mor gilt; corners worn. sg May 7 (72) $450

Catalogo...

— Catalogo dei manoscritti in scrittura latina datati o databili per indicaszione di anno, di luogo, o di copista. Turin, 1971-82. Vols I-II in 4. 4to & folio, orig bdgs. sg Oct 31 (197) $500

Catalogue. See: Burns, John

Cataneo, Pietro

— I Quattro Primi Libri di architettura. Venice: Aldus, 1554. 1st Ed. Folio, contemp vellum. Some waterstaining at top. SI Dec 5 (143) LIt6,200,000

Catelan, Laurens

— Ein schoener newer historischer Discurs, von der Natur, Tugenden, Eigenschafften und Gebrauch dess Einhorns.... Frankfurt, 1625. 8vo, wraps. B Nov 1 (690) HF1,200

Catesby, Mark, 1679?-1749

— The Natural History of Carolina, Florida, and the Bahama Islands.... L, 1754. 2d Ed. 2 vols. Folio, contemp calf gilt; upper cover of Vol I detached & spine broken. With 220 hand-colored plates & hand-colored map in Vol II. Occasional marginal soiling. CNY Dec 5 (289) $60,000

Anr copy. Contemp russia gilt; spine & upper hinges cracked spine ends & corners chipped. With 220 hand-colored plates & folding hand-colored map. Plate 53 in Vol II creased; minor soiling, mostly marginal. Lonsdale-Clay-Roman Catholic Diocese of Lexington copy. CNY Apr 24 (1) $70,000

Cather, Willa, 1873-1947

— April Twilights. Bost., 1903. 1st Ed. Orig bds; rubbed, dampstains to front endpapers. P Dec 12 (19) $1,000

Anr copy. Orig bds; spine ends chipped. Some leaves roughly opened. sg June 11 (59) $1,100

Anr Ed. NY, 1923. One of 450, sgd. wa Dec 9 (177) $130

— Death Comes for the Archbishop. NY, 1927. 1st Ed. sg Dec 12 (50) $140

One of 175, sgd, on rag paper. Epstein copy. sg Apr 29 (71) $1,200

— A Lost Lady. NY, 1923. 1st Ed, One of 200 L. p. copies. Joints broken. O Apr 28 (158) $75

— Lucy Gayheart. NY, 1935. 1st Ed, one of 749, sgd. Orig cloth; endpapers browned. sg June 11 (60) $130

— My Antonia. Bost., 1918. 1st Ed, 1st Issue. sg Dec 12 (51) $250

— My Mortal Enemy. NY, 1926. One of 220 on Japanese vellum, sgd. Half cloth; backstrip browned. sg June 11 (61) $200

— Sapphira and the Slave Girl. NY, 1940. One of 520. In d/j with small portion lacking from spine panel. sg June 11 (62) $130

1st Ed. In d/j. bbc Dec 9 (447) $220; sg Dec 12 (52) $325

— The Song of the Lark. Bost., 1915. 1st Ed, 1st Issue. sg Dec 12 (53) $150

Catherine of Siena, Saint, d.c.307

— D. Catharinae senesis virginis vita ac miracula selectoiora formis aeneis expressa. [N.p., c.1650]. 4to, 18th-cent calf; rebacked. With engraved title & 33 plates. S Dec 5 (227) £550 [Franks]

Catlin, George, 1796-1872

— Letters and Notes on the Manners, Customs, and Condition of the North American Indians. L, 1841. 2d Ed. 2 vols. 8vo, cloth; rebacked with orig spines retained. Some crude hand-coloring. sg Dec 5 (46) $225

5th Ed. 2 vols. 8vo, contemp half mor. This set has Plates 113/114 (but lacking Plates 1/2). cb Nov 14 (27) $325

1st American Ed. NY, 1841. 2 vols. 8vo, half calf; worn. With 3 maps, frontis & 308 plates on 176 leaves & with portion only of the errata slip. One plate bound in upside down. K July 12 (98) $450

Anr copy. Orig cloth. This set has Plates 113/114. With errata slip tipped in. Epstein copy. sg Apr 29 (72) $1,500

Anr Ed. L, 1842. 2 vols. 8vo, orig cloth; rebacked with portions of spines preserved. With frontis, 3 maps & 306 plates on 175 leaves. Lacking the leaf with plates 123 & 124; 1 plate with small tear. K July 12 (99) $225

7th Ed. L, 1848. ("Illustrations of the Manners, Customs, and Condition of the North American Indians....") 2 vols. 8vo, calf; extremities worn. sg Dec 5 (47) $200

Anr Ed. L, 1851. 2 vols. 8vo, orig cloth; tear across backstrip on Vol I, hinges cracked. With contemp Ms list of plates inserted at rear of each vol. Vol II dampstained. bbc Dec 9 (364) $170

Anr Ed. Phila., 1857. 2 vols. 8vo, orig cloth; spines tape-repaired. Considerable foxing & dampstaining; a few loose pp. sp Nov 24 (16) $275

Anr Ed. L, 1876. ("Illustrations of the Manners, Customs, and Condition of the North American Indians.") 2 vols. 8vo, orig cloth; extremities worn, rebacked. Some plates & text leaves loose. Sold w.a.f. sg June 18 (168) $130

— Notes of Eight Years' Travels and Residence in Europe.... L, 1848. 2 vols. 8vo, 19th-cent half mor gilt; extremities rubbed. With 24 plates. Unaccomplished presentation copy, inscr & sgd. Manney copy. P Oct 11 (39) $900

Catlow, Agnes, 1807?-89 and Maria E.

— Sketching Rambles; or Nature in the Alps.... L, [1861]. 8vo, orig cloth. With 19 tinted litho plates. bba Sept 19 (134) £190 [Sotheran]

Cato, Marcus Porcius, 234-149 B.C.

— Cato's Moral Distichs. San Francisco: Book Club of California, 1939. One of 250. Facsimile of the Benjamin Franklin Ed of 1735, with an orig leaf from a Franklin-ptd work tipped in. Doheny copy. cb Jan 16 (52) $120

— Moralissimus Cato cum elegantissimo commento. Basel: Johann Amerbach, 14 June 1486. 4to, 17th-cent vellum with initials of Placidius Hieber & date 1659 stamped on upper cover; recased, with new endleaves. Lineation variable; types 5:106G (headings, text), 3:92G (commentary), 19:62G (interlinear text); woodcut Maiblumen initial; rubricated. Minor stains. 48 leaves. Goff C-297. Schoyen copy. P Dec 12 (18) $5,500

Cato, Varro, Columella & Palladius

— Scriptores rei rusticae. Bologna: Benedicti Hectoris, 1504. ("Opera agricolationum.") Folio, 18th-cent vellum. SI Dec 5 (616) LIt900,000

Anr Ed. Venice: Aldus & Andreas [d'Asola], May 1514. ("Libri de re rustica.") 4to, contemp vellum. bba Sept 5 (19) £700 [Soave]

Anr copy. 19th-cent mor gilt; worn. Tp soiled; tears repaired. wa Sept 26 (474) $400

Cattani da Diacetto, Francesco de

— Panegirico. Rome: Ludovico Vicentino, 1526. 4to, modern half vellum. Some spotting. C Dec 16 (39) £1,600 [Halwas]

Catullus, Caius Valerius, 84?-54 B.C.

— The Carmina. L, 1894. One of 18 on japan vellum with proofs of frontis in 2 states before letters. 8vo, orig half vellum; rubbed & soiled. S June 25 (411) £300 [Maggs]

— Complete Poetry. L: Fanfrolico Press, [1929]. Ltd Ed. Trans by Jack Lindsay; illus by Lionel Ellis. 8vo, orig mor; spine darkened. With 30 illus. sg Sept 26 (110) $120

Ltd Ed. L: The Fanfrolico Press, 1929. Orig mor; spine faded. bba Dec 19 (130) £65 [Hay Cinema]

Catullus, Tibullus & Propertius

— Opera. Parma: Andreas Portilia, 12 May 1479. Folio, modern vellum. 36 lines; type 110R. First leaf soiled & with small section of lower blank margin torn away. 196 (of 208) leaves; lacking 1st blank & leaves after x7. Goff V-161. C Dec 16 (171) £3,500 [Quaritch]

Anr Ed. Cambr.: Tonson, 1702. 4to, contemp calf; joints cracking. bba Apr 9 (13) £140 [C.L. Edwards]

Cauchy, Augustin Louis, Baron, 1789-1857

— Exercises d'analyse et de physique mathematique. Paris, 1840-47. 4 vols. 4to, contemp half mor; extremities rubbed. Some spotting. Ck Nov 29 (161) £220

Caulfield, James, 1754-1826

— Memoirs of the Celebrated Persons composing the Kit-Kat Club. L, 1821. Folio, contemp mor gilt; edges & joints scuffed. With 47 (of 48) plates; lacking Plate 46. cb Dec 5 (25) $425

Caumont de la Force, Charlotte Rose de

— Histoire de Marguerite de Valois. Paris: Didot l'aine, 1783. 6 vols. 12mo, 18th-cent mor gilt. S Feb 11 (546) £550 [Shapero]

Caussin, Nicolas, 1583-1651

— De symbolica Aegyptiorum sapientia.... Cologne: Joannes Kinchius, 1654. 8vo, contemp vellum. sg Mar 12 (204) $200

Cavalca, Domenico, d.1342

— Frutti della lingua. Florence, [Bartolommeo di Libri, c.1494]. 4to, 19th-cent half mor. 33 lines; roman letter. A few stains in margin. 142 leaves. Goff C-332. S Dec 5 (12) £2,000 [Mediolanum]

Cavalcanti, Bartolomeo

— La Retorica. Venice: Gabriel Giolito de' Ferrari, 1560. Folio, disbound. Some dampstaining, mainly at end. sg Oct 24 (62) $500

Cavalieri, Bonaventura, 1598-1647

— Exercitationes geometricae sex. Bologna, 1647. 4to, 19th-cent half mor. Some browning. Ck Nov 29 (163) £650

— Geometria indivisibilibus continuorum nova quadam ratione promota. Bologna, 1653. 4to, contemp calf gilt. Tp stamped; A4 of 3d part restored at upper margin. Ck Nov 29 (162) £1,600

— Trattato della ruota planetaria perpetua...di Silvio Filomantio. Bologna, 1646. 4to, contemp vellum; soiled & wormed. With engraved folding plate mtd at p.14 & with folding table at end. Some worming. Sold w.a.f. Ck June 18 (12) £240

Cavallo, Tiberius, 1749-1809

— The History and Practice of Aerostation. L, 1785. Bound with: Walker, Thomas. A Treatise upon the Art of Flying.... Hull, 1810. 8vo, contemp bds; upper cover detached, spine worn. With 2 folding plates in 1st work, 1 repaired & the other with marginal tear. pn May 14 (76) £620

Cavazzoni Zanotti, Giovanni Pietro
— Le Pitture di Pellegrino Tibaldi ed di Niccolo Abbati esistenti nell'Instituto di Bologna. Venice, 1756. Folio, contemp half calf; hinges cracked. With engraved title, frontis, 2 ports & 41 plates. Spotted. DW Oct 9 (828) £520

Cave, Francis Oswin —& Macdonald, James David
— Birds of the Sudan. Edin. & L, 1955. Cloth, in d/j. bba Feb 13 (354) £90 [St. Ann's Books]

Cave, Roderick
— The Private Press. L, [1971]. In def d/j. wa Mar 5 (133) $50

Cave, William, 1637-1713
— Apostolici. L, 1677. ("Antiquitates Apostolicae, or the History of the Lives, Acts and Martyrdoms of the Holy Apostles....") 3d Ed. Vol I only. 4to, contemp mor gilt; extremities worn. With engraved titles & 23 ports. DW Jan 29 (219) £54

Cavendish, William, Duke of Newcastle. See: Newcastle, William Cavendish

Caxton Club—Chicago
— CARLETON, JAMES HENRY. - The Prairie Logbooks. Dragoon Campaigns.... 1943. One of 350. sg May 21 (166) $70
— CHARLEVOIX, PIERRE FRANCOIS XAVIER DE. - Journal of a Voyage to North America. 1923. One of 200. sg May 21 (168) $130
— DAVENPORT, CYRIL. - Roger Payne: English Bookbinder of the Eighteenth Century. 1929. 1st Ed, One of 250. sg May 21 (173) $300
— DAVENPORT, CYRIL. - Samuel Mearne, Binder to King Charles II. 1906. One of 252. sg May 21 (172) $225
— DAVENPORT, CYRIL. - Thomas Berthelet, Royal Printer and Bookbinder to Henry VIII. 1901. One of 252. sg May 21 (171) $170
— DEARBORN, HENRY. - Revolutionary War Journals, 1775-83. 1939. One of 350. sg May 21 (174) $70
— DERBY, GEORGE H. - Phoenixiana. 1897. One of 165. 2 vols. sg May 21 (175) $60
— DUFF, EDWARD GORDON. - William Caxton. 1905. One of 252. Folio, half cloth. LH May 17 (649) $50; sg May 7 (100) $350; sg May 21 (176) $175
— ESTIENNE, HENRI. - The Frankfort Book Fair. 1911. One of 303. Ed by James Westfall Thompson. sg May 21 (178) $200
— JOUTEL, HENRI. - Journal of La Salle's Last Voyage. 1896. One of 203. sg May 21 (180) $375
— LA SALLE, NICOLAS DE. - Relation of the Discovery of the Mississippi River. 1898. One of 269. sg May 21 (182) $130
— LA SALLE, RENE ROBERT CAVELIER. - Relation of the Discoveries and Voyages.... One of 227. sg May 21 (183) $140
— LAUFER, BERTHOLD. - Paper and Printing in Ancient China. 1931. One of 250. sg May 21 (184) $70
— MANSFIELD, HOWARD. - A Descriptive Catalogue of the Etchings and Dry-Points of James Abbott McNeill Whistler. 1909. One of 300. In repaired d/j. One leaf roughly opened. bbc Dec 9 (292) $275
Anr copy. Some foxing. O May 26 (32) $110
— OWENS, HARRY J. - Doctor Faust. 1953. One of 350. sg May 21 (191) $150
— POLLARD, ALFRED WILLIAM. - An Essay on Colophons. 1905. One of 252. sg May 21 (193) $200
— STEELE, JOHN. - Across the Plains in 1850. 1930. One of 350. sg May 21 (198) $80; sg June 18 (516) $70
— TONTI, HENRI DE. - Relation of Henri de Tonty concerning the Explorations of La Salle.... 1898. One of 197. sg May 21 (199) $175
— UZANNE, OCTAVE. - The French Bookbinders of the Eighteenth Century. 1904. One of 252. sg May 21 (200) $225
— WAKEFIELD, JOHN ALLEN. - History of the Black Hawk War. 1908. One of 203. sg May 21 (201) $120
— WILKINS, ERNEST HATCH. - The Trees of the Genealogia Deorum of Boccaccio. 1923. One of 160. sg May 21 (202) $150
— ZWEIG, STEFAN. - The Old-Book Peddler and Other Tales for Bibliophiles. 1937. One of 200. sg May 21 (203) $130

Caxton, William, 1422?-91
— The Dictes and Sayings of the Philosophers: A Facsimile.... Detroit: Cranbrook Press, 1901. One of 244, unopened. Folio, bdg not stated. cb Oct 17 (242) $110
— [Group of 4 discontinuous leaves from the Caxton Ed of Voragine's Golden Legend, including 2 with woodcuts] Westminster, 1483. Folio. Goff J-148. sg Nov 7 (39) $1,900
— The Life of St. George.... L: De la More Press, [not before 1919]. One of 21 ptd on vellum. Contemp half mor; rubbed. wa Sept 26 (105) $120

Cayet, Pierre Victor Palma, 1525-1610
— Chronologie septenaire de l'histoire de la paix entre les Roys de France et d'Espagne. Paris, 1611. 4to, 18th-cent bds; spine rubbed. With engraved title. Some headlines shaved; minor browning. Phillipps copy. S Feb 26 (725) £150 [Maggs]

Caylus, Anne Claude Philippe, Comte de, 1692-1765
— Recueil d'antiquites egyptiennes, etrusques, grecques.... Paris, 1752-67. Vols VI-VII only. Contemp calf; spine worn. With frontis & 230 plates. sg Sept 6 (49) $200

Cazabon, M. H.
— Views of Trinidad. Paris: Lemercier, [1851]. Oblong folio, half mor; scuffed. With 18 plates. 1 torn & scuffed, 6 waterstained. bba Mar 26 (327) £4,400 [Hanton]

Cazotte, Jacques. See: Laboureur & Cazotte

Cecil, Robert A. T. G., 3d Marquess of Salisbury, 1830-1903
[-] Calendar of the Manuscripts of...the Marquess of Salisbury, preserved at Hatfield House, Hertfordshire. L, 1930-72. Vols 15-22. 8vo, Vols 1-3, orig half cloth; others, orig cloth. DW Mar 4 (355) £55

Cecil, William, Baron Burghley, 1520-98
— The Copy of a Letter Sent Out of England.... L: R. Field, 1588. ("Certaine Advertisements Out of Ireland....") Part 2 (of 2) only. 4to, wraps. W July 8 (102) £420

Cecina Rica y Fergel, Pablo
— Armas contra la espada y broquel. Madrid 1819. 8vo, contemp sheep. sg Mar 26 (68) $130

Ceillier, Remi
— Manuel pratique d'illusionisme et de prestidigitation. Paris, 1935-36. 2 vols. sg Oct 17 (16) $110

Celarie, Henriette
— Behind Morocco Walls. Ny, 1931. Illus by Boris Artzbasheff. 4to, cloth. sg Jan 9 (49) $100

Celestina...
— [Celestina] The Spanish Bawd, Represented in Celestina.... L, 1631. Trans by James Mabbe. Folio, old calf; rebacked. Tp damaged & repaired with loss of part of text & with ink stains. W July 8 (26) £70

Celine, Louis Ferdinand
— Mort a credit. Paris, [1936]. Uncensored copy. With a copy of the 2d Issue & Boris Kochno's holograph list of pages from which text has been omitted. SM Oct 11 (461) FF4,200

One of 25 on japon. Mor by Paul Bonet, 1968, with an abstract design of colored onlays, orig wraps bound in. With related material bound in. S May 28 (292) £8,000 [Beres]

— Voyage au bout de la nuit. Paris, 1932. 1st Ed, 1st Issue. Half mor, orig wraps bound in. Inscr to Francis Carco. Epstein copy. sg Apr 29 (73) $4,000

One of 100. Half mor by Semet & Plumelle, orig wraps bound in. SM Oct 11 (460) FF23,000

Cellarius, Christoph, 1638-1707
— Notitia orbis antiqui sive Geographia Plenior.... L, 1703-6. 2 vols. 4to, contemp vellum. With engraved title, port, plate & 20 maps. DW Apr 8 (394) £310

Cellini, Benvenuto, 1500-71
See also: Limited Editions Club
— The Autobiography.... Garden City, 1946. One of 1,000. Illus by Salvador Dali. sg Sept 26 (81) $200
— The Life of Benvenuto Cellini.... L: Vale Press, 1900. One of 300. Trans by J. A. Symonds. 2 vols. Folio, half cloth; worn, spines frayed. O Jan 14 (39) $50
— Vita.... Cologne: P. Martello [Naples, 1728]. 1st Ed. 4to, contemp English russia gilt; rubbed. bba Feb 27 (266) £400 [Grant & Shaw]

Anr copy. Contemp vellum. Some browning; margins dampstained; F3 holed with loss. Ck Oct 31 (53) £280

Anr copy. Some staining; small tear at inner margin of tp. P Oct 11 (40) $3,250

Anr copy. Contemp calf. Some foxing. SI Dec 5 (800) LIt650,000

Celtic...
— Celtic Ornaments from the Book of Kells. Dublin & L, 1895 [1892-95]. 9 parts in 3 vols. 4to, orig cloth. With 50 plates. bba Aug 13 (2) £300 [Cathach]

Cendrars, Blaise, 1887-1961
— Dix-neuf poemes elastiques. Paris, 1919. Out-of-series copy on hollande with 2 ports by Modigliani. Mor extra by Mercher, orig wraps bound in. S May 28 (288) £1,600 [Pettini]
— J'ai Tue. Paris, [1918]. One of 353. Illus by Fernand Leger. 4to, mor-backed perspex by Mercher with painted design in the style of Leger; spine def. Inscr. S May 28 (287) £2,600 [Beres]
— Moravagine. Paris, 1926. One of 30 on japon. Mor-backed perspex by Mercher, orig wraps bound in. S May 28 (289) £800 [Sims Reed]
— Profond aujourd'hui. Paris, 1917. One of 50 on japon with a suite of the illusts in bistre. Illus by A. Zarraga. Oblong 4to, mor gilt by Canape, orig wraps bound in. S May 28 (286) £1,400 [Beres]

Cennini, Cennino
— A Treatise on Painting.... L, 1844. 8vo, orig cloth by Remnant & Edmonds. DW Oct 9 (829) £100

Ceremonial

— Caeremoniale Episcoporum Clementis VIII. Primum nunc denuo Innocentii Papae X. Rome: Typis Rev. Camerae Apostolicae, 1651. 4to, contemp mor gilt with arms of a Cardinal & initials AR. Doheny copy. Ck Oct 31 (258) £480

Ceremonials

— 1582. - Sacrarum caeremoniarum, sive rituum ecclesiasticorum S. Rom. ecclesiae.... Venice: Giuntas. 4to, half vellum. Marginal repairs & browning. SI June 10 (898) LIt450,000

Cereta, Laura

— Epistolae iam primum e Ms in lucem.... Padua: Sebastian Sardi, 1640. 8vo, old sheep; spine head chipped. sg Mar 12 (45) $500

Cerri, Giuseppe

— Bastone. Milan, 1854. ("Trattato teorico-pratico della scherma de bastone.") Oblong 8vo, half calf. Owner's stamp on tp. sg Mar 26 (69) $275

— Sciabola. Milan, 1861. ("Trattato teorico-pratico della scherma per sciabola.") Oblong 8vo, half cloth, orig front wrap bound in. With port & 28 plates. Inked stamp of Cerri on tp. sg Mar 26 (70) $275

Certain or Certaine...

— Certaine Sermons or Homilies. Oxford, 1683. Folio, later half lea. STC 13659, 13675. O Mar 31 (35) $60

Cerutus, Benedictus

— Musaeum Franc. Calceolari Jun. veronensis a B. Ceruto medico incaeptum.... Verona, 1622. Folio, 17th-cent calf; joints cracked. With engraved title, folding plate & 8 full-page illusts. Evelyn copy. sg Nov 7 (40) $3,400

Cervantes, Enrique A.

— Hierros de Oaxaca. Oaxaca, 1932. 4to, loose as issued in embroidered cloth folder. sg Feb 6 (138) $225

Cervantes Saavedra, Miguel de, 1547-1616

See also: Ashendene Press; Limited Editions Club; Nonesuch Press

Don Quixote in Spanish

— 1780. - El Ingenioso Hidalgo Don Quixote de la Mancha. Madrid: Joaquin Ibarra. 4 vols. 4to, contemp calf gilt. With 4 frontises, port, double-page map & 31 plates. Small hole in s3 of Vol IV. S May 28 (104) £2,000 [Uceta]

English Versions

— 1675. - L. Folio, modern cloth. Kk2 & 3 misbound; some tears & repairs with slight loss of text. bba Nov 28 (244) £55 [Aspin]

— 1742. - L. Trans by Charles Jarvis. 2 vols. 4to, contemp calf; rubbed, soiled & worn. With port & 68 plates. W July 8 (307) £230

— 1801. - The Life and Exploits of.... L. 4 vols. 8vo, half calf by Brentano's. K Sept 29 (116) $190

— 1818. - L. Trans by Mary Smirke; illus by Robert Smirke. 4 vols. 8vo, later half mor; worn & rubbed. Some dampstaining in Vols III & IV. cb Oct 31 (22) $550

— 1820. - L: Hurst, Robinson. 4 vols. 8vo, early mor gilt; scuffed. With engraved titles & 19 plates, all with contemp hand-coloring Foxed. bbc Apr 27 (55) $120

— 1879-84. - Edin. Illus by Ad. Lalauze. 4 vols. 8vo, half calf. pnE Oct 1 (201) £95

One of 50 L.p. copies. Cloth; worn, joints & hinges cracked. With plates in 2 states. Sold w.a.f. sg Mar 5 (36) $200

— 1885. - L. 4 vols. 8vo, half mor gilt by Henry Young & Sons. bba Oct 10 (371) £170 [Baring]

George Cruikshank Ed, one of 50 with an extra suite of plates on japon. 4 vols. 8vo, orig half calf; spine rubbed. Richard Ellis's copy, with related material. F June 25 (165) $90

— 1900. - Don Quixote of the Mancha, retold by Judge Parry. L. Illus by Walter Crane. 8vo, orig cloth; worn. With colored frontis, pictorial title & 10 plates. cb Sept 26 (42) $90

— 1906-7. - NY One of 840. 4 vols extended to 8. 4to, mor gilt; joints cracking, rubbed. Extra-illus with plates & with 8 orig sgd watercolors by Robert Smirke used for the 1817 Ed. Joyce copy. P June 17 (147) $3,500

— 1906-7. - The History of the Valorous and Witty Knight-Errant Don Quixote.... NY One of 140 with an extra suite of the plates before letters. 5 vols. 4to, orig half vellum gilt; marked. wa Sept 26 (558) $450

— 1910. - The History of the Ingenious Gentleman Don Quixote.... Edin.: John Grant. 4 vols. 8vo, contemp half mor gilt with chivalric device. wa Mar 5 (19) $280

— 1922. - The History of Don Quixote de la Mancha. Illus by Jean de Bosschere. 4to, half mor by Frost. O Jan 14 (41) $70

French Versions

— Pages choisies de Don Quichotte de La Manche. Paris, 1957. One of 25 on arches with 2 extra suites of plates. Illus by Salvador Dali. Folio, orig wraps in folder & slipcase. P June 17 (171) $3,750

— Les Principales Avantures de l'admirable Don Quichotte. The Hague, 1746. 4to, contemp calf gilt; rebacked & cornered, old spine laid down. With 31 plates in 1st state. C June 24 (300) £480 [Montero]

Anr copy. 18th-cent calf gilt. Some text leaves browned. S Dec 5 (256) £1,500 [Knill]

— 1776. - Les Principales aventures de l'admirable Don Quichotte. Liege 4to, contemp calf gilt; rubbed. With 31 plates. ba Oct 10 (511) £160 [Maggs]

Cescinsky, Herbert

— English Furniture of the Eighteenth Century. L, [1909-11 & n.d.]. 3 vols. 4to, contemp half mor. Titles spotted. bba May 14 (586) £130 [Deighton Bell]

Anr copy. Orig half mor gilt; spines rubbed & faded. DW Apr 8 (329) £115

Anr copy. Half mor. pnE Oct 2 (483) £140

Anr copy. Orig half mor; rubbed. pnE Aug 12 (160) £130

Anr copy. Contemp half calf; dry & worn, 1 joint split. wa Mar 5 (585) $95

— The Gentle Art of Faking Furniture. L, 1931. 4to, cloth, in d/j. pnE Oct 1 (267) £85

Cescinsky, Herbert —& Gribble, Ernest

— Early English Furniture and Woodwork. L, 1922. 2 vols. Folio, contemp half mor; rubbed. DW Mar 11 (716) £80

Anr copy. Orig cloth. LH Dec 11 (81) $160

Anr copy. Orig cloth; rubbed. W Mar 6 (3) £85

Anr copy. Orig cloth; spines rubbed. wa Mar 5 (583) $140

Cescinsky, Herbert —& Webster, Malcolm R.

— English Domestic Clocks. L, [c.1915]. 4to, contemp half mor; rubbed. DW Mar 11 (715) £70

Chabans, Louis de

— Advis et moyens pour empescher les desordre des duels. Paris, 1615. 8vo, old vellum. sg Mar 26 (71) $110

Chabert, Joseph Bernard, Marquis de

— Sur l'usage des horloges marines, relatiement a la navigation.... Paris, 1785. 4to, contemp calf gilt, with arms of the Comte d'Estaing as Admiral; spine head chipped. Offprint from the Memoires of the Academie Royale des Sciences for 1783. CNY Oct 8 (37) $4,800

Chaffers, William, 1811-92

— Hall-Marks on Gold and Silver Plate. L, 1905. 9th Ed. 8vo, half mor gilt. sg Apr 2 (48) $50

— Marks and Monograms on European and Oriental Pottery and Porcelain. L, 1886. 8vo, half mor by the Rose Bindery; rubbed. O Feb 25 (48) $90

Anr copy. Cloth; hinges cracked. sg Sept 6 (50) $120

Chagall, Marc

See also: Bible in English; Meyer, Franz

— The Biblical Message. NY, [1973]. 4to, orig cloth, in d/j. bba May 14 (321) £110 [Ginnan]

Anr copy. Cloth, in d/j. bbc Apr 27 (34) $100

Anr copy. Cloth, in repaired d/j. A few leaves at center loose. bbc Apr 27 (435) $80

— Chagall. Paris, 1962. Text by Yves Bonnefoy. Folio, unsewn in orig wraps. Derriere le Miroir, No 132. Met Apr 28 (15) $250

Anr Ed. Paris, 1969. One of 150 on velin de Rives. Text by Claude Esteban. Folio, unsewn as issued in orig wraps. Sgd by Chagall on rear cover. Derriere le Miroir, No 182. sg Apr 2 (54) $500

— Chagall. Dessins et lavis. Paris: Galerie Maeght, 1964. Folio, loose as issued. With 3 orig lithos, including cover. Derriere le Miroir, No 147. Met Apr 28 (16) $225

— Chagall; Gouaches, 1957-1968. NY, 1968. 4to, wraps. sp Sept 22 (339) $80

— Chagall lithographe. Monte Carlo: Andre Sauret, 1960-63-69-74. Text by Fernand Mourlot. Vols I-IV. 4to, orig cloth, in d/js. bba Mar 26 (4) £1,700 [Sims Reed]

— Drawings for the Bible. NY, 1960. Folio, bds, in d/j. With 24 color lithos. Verve No 37/38. P Dec 12 (20) $3,250

Anr copy. Bds, in def d/j. Verve No 37/38. sg Sept 6 (61) $3,000

Anr copy. Bds; edges worn, ink writing on front free endpaper. With 24 color lithos & 96 uncolored plates. Verve No 37/38. sg Apr 2 (50) $3,200

— Glasmalerein fuer Jerusalem. Monte Carlo, 1962. Folio, cloth. HH May 12 (2168) DM1,600

— Hommage a Marc Chagall. [Paris, 1969]. Folio, cloth, in d/j. Sgd on tp. sg Sept 6 (62) $175

Anr copy. With 1 orig litho. sg Feb 6 (55) $250

Anr copy. Cloth, in torn d/j. sg Apr 2 (61) $80

— Illustrations for the Bible. NY, 1956. Folio, orig bds. Verve No 33/34. b Nov 18 (245) £2,800; S May 28 (222) £2,800 [Panini]

— The Jerusalem Windows. NY, 1962. Text by Jean Leymarie. Folio, orig cloth, in chipped d/j. bbc Apr 27 (437) $800

Anr copy. Orig cloth; soiled. CG Oct 7 (456) £300

Anr copy. Cloth, in d/j. sg Nov 7 (41) $1,100

Anr copy. Cloth, in d/j. Claudio Arrau's copy. sg Jan 30 (21) $700

Anr copy. Owner's inscr on front endpaper. Sold w.a.f. sg May 7 (57) $800

Anr copy. 4to, orig cloth, in torn & repaired d/j. wa Sept 26 (559) $1,000

— The Lithographs of Chagall. Monte Carlo & NY or Bost., 1960-84. 5 vols. 4to, orig cloth, in d/js. CNY May 11 (370) $3,200

Vol II only. Met Apr 28 (63) $900

Anr copy. Orig cloth; upper cover stained. Loosely inserted is a litho, sgd by Chagall in pencil. S Nov 14 (8) £600 [Primrose Hill]

Vol IV only. 4to, orig cloth, in d/j. bba Oct 24 (355) £140 [Hildebrandt]; wa Sept 26 (560) $300

Vols I-III. 3 vols. 4to, orig cloth, in d/js; some rubbing. P Dec 12 (21) $4,250

Vol III only. Text by Fernand Mourlot. Orig cloth, in d/j. bbc Sept 23 (144) $300; sg Sept 26 (72) $325

— Ma Vie. Paris, [1931]. One of 1,683. Orig wraps; spine browned. sg Apr 2 (53) $80

— Vitraux pour Jerusalem. Monte Carlo, 1962. 4to, orig cloth, in d/j. P June 17 (150) $900

Anr copy. Cloth, in d/j. sg Feb 6 (51) $850

Anr copy. Orig wraps. wd Dec 12 (373) $2,400

Chalcondylas, Laonicus
See also: Gregoras & Chalcondylas

— L'Histoire de la decadence de l'Empire Grec.... Paris, 1650. 6 parts in 2 vols. Folio, modern calf. With 2 engraved titles, 24 ports & 78 plates. Constantinople torn & repaired with loss; some index leaves damaged & repaired with loss; Vol II plate at D3 torn away; some leaves repaired in margins. Sold w.a.f. S June 30 (114) £2,200 [Consolidated Real]

Chalkley, Thomas, 1675-1741. See: Franklin Printing, Benjamin

Challenger Expediton

— Report on the Scientific Results of H.M.S. Challenger during the Years 1873-76.... L, 1880-95. Ed by C. Wyville Thomson & John Murray. 40 vols only; lacking Zoology vols 8, 13, 15, 16, 17, 22, 23, 26, 27 & 28. orig cloth; some vols loose in bdgs, worn. Library markings. Sold w.a.f. sg May 14 (198) $3,600

Chalmers, Alexander, 1759-1834. See: British...

Chalmers, Patrick Reginald

— Birds Ashore and A-Foreshore. L, [1935]. One of 150. Illus by Winifred Austen. 4to, orig half mor; rubbed. With 16 colored plates. bba Jan 30 (418) £50 [Freddie]

— Gun-Dogs. L, 1931. One of 125. 4to, orig cloth, in torn d/j; rubbed & soiled. pnE May 13 (24) £55

Chamberlain, Henry

— A New and Compleat History and Survey of London.... L, [1769]. Folio, contemp calf; repaired. bba Apr 9 (154) £380 [Land]

Anr copy. Modern half calf. With frontis, 66 plates & 2 folding maps. Frontis, tp & dedication leaf def & laid down; a few plates shaved; some leaves loose; some soiling & browning; marginal worming. pn June 11 (275) £110

Chamberlain, Julian Ingersoll. See: Higginson & Chamberlain

Chamberlaine, John, 1745-1812. See: Holbein, Hans

Chamberlin, Clarence D.

— Record Flights. Phila., [1928]. One of 500. Unopened. Sgd on front free endpaper. cb Nov 7 (29) $160

Chamberlin, Harry D. See: Derrydale Press

Chambers, Ephraim, d.1740

— Cyclopaedia: or, an Universal Dictionary of Arts and Sciences. L, 1738. 2d Ed. 2 vols. Folio, contemp calf; worn. With double-page engraved title & 19 plates. Some spotting. Milne copy. Ck June 12 (31) £220

Anr Ed. L, 1778-86. 5 vols. Folio, contemp calf; spines torn. With 133 (of 135) plates. Tears to folds of 2 plates; bottom margins of 2 other plates torn. Ck Dec 11 (208) £140

Anr Ed. L, 1786. 5 vols. Folio, contemp calf. DW Mar 4 (197) £230

Anr copy. Vol V only. Disbound. F Sept 26 (719) $110

Chambers, Robert, 1802-71

— Vestiges of the Natural History of Creation. L, 1844. 2d Ed. 8vo, orig cloth; worn, spine ends frayed, repaired tears at heads of joints. Inscr to Lady Lovelace from Worowzow Grieg & from her to him in return. bbc Sept 23 (251) $250

Chambers, Robert William, 1865-1933

— The Maker of Moons. NY, 1896. Orig bds. Inscr to Mrs. Henry M. Tod. Manney copy. P Oct 11 (41) $300

Chambers, Sir William, 1726-96

— Designs of Chinese Buildings, Furniture.... L, 1757. Folio, contemp calf gilt; rehinged, spine & corners restored, a few gouges & wormed spot to covers. With 21 plates. Minor worming to fore-margins; Plate 5 with 11-inch repaired tear; 2-inch marginal tear to fol. E; last plate foxed. McCarty-Cooper copy. CNY Jan 25 (12) $2,800

— A Dissertation on Oriental Gardening. L, 1772. 1st Ed. 4to, contemp calf; rebacked. bba Feb 27 (88) £400 [Thorp]

— Plans, Elevations, Sections and Perspective Views of the Gardens and Buildings at Kew.... L, 1763. 1st Ed. Folio, disbound. With 43 plates. Lacking tp; text frayed & soiled; staining throughout. S Feb 11 (301) £400 [Shapero]

— A Treatise on Civil Architecture. L, 1768. 2d Ed. Folio, orig half calf; worn. With 50 plates. S June 25 (90) £700 [Camden]

Chameleon...

— The Chameleon: a Bazaar of Dangerous and Smiling Chances. L: Gay & Bird, [1894]. Vol I, No 1 (all pbd). 4to, mor by Riviere, orig wraps preserved; lacking backstrip. Endpapers stained. CNY Dec 5 (351) $950

Chamisso, Adelbert von, 1781-1838

See also: Grabhorn Printing

— Werke. Leipzig, 1836-39. 6 vols. 12mo, contemp bds; worn. With 2 maps, 2 ports, 4 plates & folding table. HH May 12 (1180) DM1,600

Chamouin, J. B. M.

— Collection de vues de Paris prises au daguerreotype. Paris, [c.1850]. Oblong folio, contemp cloth; worn, spine chipped. With engraved title & 25 plates. Some foxing & soiling. O May 26 (33) $180

Champion, Pierre

— Le Roman de Tristan et d'Iseult. Paris, 1928. One of 95. Illus by J. G. Daragnes. Folio, mor extra by Marius Michel, orig wraps bound in. S May 28 (290) £3,800 [Quaritch]

Champlain, Samuel de, 1567-1635

— Les Voyages de la Nouvelle France Occidentale.... Paris, 1632. 2d Issue. 4to, 17th-cent calf with arms of Claude du Sauzay (Olivier 2383); scraped. With large folding map. Foxing & browning; dampstains to upper margins of most leaves, extending into text of c.30 leaves; stains of G4-H3 of Part 1 blotting out up to 7 letters; marginal repairss, in 1 case affecting text with 9 letters in facsimile; minor worming; folding map with repaired tear. DuPont copy. CNY Oct 8 (39) $48,000

— Les Voyages du Sieur de Champlain... Paris, 1613. 1st Ed. 2 parts in 1 vol. 4to, contemp vellum. With folding map of Nouvelle France, 7 smaller folding maps & 3 folding plates. Repaired tear to large folding map; 4-inch repair to N3, touching letters; 2E2 & 2F4 each with tiny burn-hole, affecting letters; some creasing; last 3 leaves frayed & dampstained at top. DuPont copy. CNY Oct 8 (38) $90,000

Champlain Society—Toronto

— Publications. Toronto, 1907-86. Vols I-LV and Works of Samuel de Champlain in 7 vols. Together, 62 vols. O Jan 14 (45) $4,600

Champollion-Figeac, Jacques Joseph, 1778-1867

— Monographie du Palais de Fontainebleau. Paris, 1863-85. Illus by Rudolph Pfnor. 3 vols. Folio, bdg not described. With 230 plates, some in color. NH May 30 (22) $775

Chandler, Raymond, 1888-1959

— The Big Sleep. NY, 1939. Orig cloth, in d/j. Epstein copy. sg Apr 29 (75) $3,000

Anr copy. In d/j with minor nicks. sg June 11 (63) $6,500

Advance copy. Orig wraps; spine def at bottom. bbc Apr 27 (277) $2,500

— Farewell, My Lovely. NY, 1940. In tired d/j. NH Oct 6 (96) $525

Anr copy. In d/j. Epstein copy. sg Apr 29 (76) $1,500

Anr copy. In chipped & soiled d/j. wa June 25 (47) $280

— Killer in the Rain. Bost., 1964. In d/j. cb Dec 12 (30) $180

1st American Ed. In d/j. cb Sept 19 (23) $160; cb Dec 12 (30) $180

— The Long Good-Bye. L, [1953]. In soiled d/j. cb Sept 19 (24) $150

Anr copy. In d/j. Epstein copy. sg Apr 29 (77) $325

— Playback. L, [1958]. 1st Ptg in 1st State bdg. In worn d/j. wa Sept 26 (134) $75

— Raymond Chandler Speaking. L, 1962. 1st Ed, Uncorrected proof. Wraps; soiled. cb Sept 19 (25) $100

— The Simple Art of Murder. Bost.: Houghton Mifflin, 1950. In d/j. cb Sept 19 (26) $180

Chandler, Richard, 1738-1810

— Marmora Oxoniensia. Oxford, 1763. 3 parts in 1 vol. Folio, early 19th-cent mor gilt with Oxford arms, presentation copy to Charles Abbot, 1st Baron Colchester. With engraved title & 76 plates. With inscr to Baron Colchester from the University. sg Feb 6 (58) $750

— Travels in Asia Minor.... Oxford, 1775. 1st Ed. 4to, contemp calf; upper joint weak. With folding map. S June 30 (113) £550 [Consolidated Real]

2d Ed. L, 1776. 4to, contemp calf; upper cover detached. With folding map. Tp holed with small loss. S July 1 (570) £380 [Chelsea]

— Travels in Asia Minor and Greece. Oxford, 1825. 2 vols. 8vo, contemp mor gilt, with Grenville arms. With 6 folding maps. S June 30 (256) £650 [Dallegio]

— Travels in Greece. Oxford, 1776. 4to, contemp half calf; scuffed. With 7 maps. Fold tear to 1 map. Ck Oct 18 (49) £480

Anr copy. Contemp half calf; rubbed. Ck Dec 11 (209) £180

Anr copy. Contemp calf; upper cover detached. With 7 maps & plans. S July 1 (571) £600 [Chelsea]

Channing, William Ellery, 1780-1842

— Slavery. Bost.: James Munroe, 1835. 12mo, orig cloth. Some foxing, small piece torn away from edge of front pastedown. Horace Mann's copy, sgd twice. bbc Dec 9 (366) $160

Chaplin, Charles

— My Trip Abroad. NY: Harper, [1922]. Bds; front cover stained. sg Oct 17 (17) $100

Chapman, Abel, 1851-1929 —& Buck, Walter J.

— Wild Spain (Espana Agreste): Records of Sport with Rifle.... L, 1893. Half mor gilt. sg Jan 9 (219) $140

Chapman, Frederik Henrik af

— Traite de la construction des vaisseaux. Paris, 1781. 4to, calf. With 20 plates, 19 folding. B Nov 1 (554) HF1,100

Chapman, George, 1559?-1634. See: Marlowe & Chapman

Chapman, Henry, Numismatist. See: Jenks Collection, John Story

Chapman, James

— Travels in the Interior of South Africa. L, 1868. 2 vols. 8vo, orig cloth. Library markings. sg Jan 9 (219) $140

Chapman, Robert William

— Cancels. L, 1930. One of 500. K Sept 29 (117) $75

Chappell, Edward, 1792-1861

— Voyage of His Majesty's Ship Rosamond to Newfoundland and the Southern Coast of Labrador. L, 1818. 1st Ed. 8vo, calf; front cover loose. sg Jan 9 (50) $225

Chappell, George S.

— A Basket of Poses. NY, 1924. Illus by Hogarth Jr [Rockwell Kent]. 4to, half cloth. Inscr. sg Sept 26 (145) $60

Chappell, William

— Old English Popular Music. L, 1893. One of 100. 2 vols. 8vo, orig half vellum; soiled. pn Oct 24 (342) £60

Chappon, Lajos

— Theoretisch-pratische Anleitung zur Fecht-Kunst. Budapest, 1839. Oblong 4to, contemp half cloth; hinges reinforced, orig wraps bound in. With 80 plates. sg Mar 26 (74) $375

Chapuis, Alfred —& Jaquet, Eugene

— Histoire et technique de la montre suisse. Basel & Olten, 1945. 4to, orig cloth. LH May 17 (674) $70

Chapuy, Nicolas Marie Joseph, 1790-1858. See: Moret & Chapuy

Char, Rene

— Dent prompte. Paris & NY, 1969. One of 240. Illus by Max Ernst. 4to, unsewn in orig wraps. SM Oct 11 (434) FF8,000

— L'Inclemence lointaine. Paris, 1961. One of 130. Illus by de Vieira da Silva. Folio, loose as issued in orig folder. CGen Nov 18 (323) SF7,500

— Le Soleil des eaux, spectacle pour une toile des pecheurs. Paris, 1949. One of 200, sgd by author & artist. Illus by Georges Braque. 4to, unsewn, in orig wraps. With 4 plates, including colored title. CGen Nov 18 (325) SF15,000

Chardin, Sir John, 1643-1713

— Journal du voyage du Chevalier Chardin en Perse et aux Indes Orientales. Amst., 1735. ("Voyages en Perse et autres lieux de l'Orient.") 4 vols. 4to, 18th-cent russia; rubbed, rebacked, hinges reinforced with tape. Plate count not given. Spotted & soiled. S Feb 26 (728) £500 [Voltaire]

— The Travels.... L, 1686. Vol I (all pbd). Folio, contemp calf; rebcked with old spine laid down. Some browning; some plates torn at folds; old repairs. Ck Oct 31 (54) £380

Anr copy. Contepm calf; rebacked & repaired, rubbed. With engraved title, folding map & 15 (of 17) plates. A few plates torn & repaired; tear in 4M. S June 30 (258) £260 [Nicholas]

— Voyages du Chevalier Chardin, en Perse, et autres lieux de l'Orient. Paris, 1811. Atlas vol only. Folio, contemp half calf. With port & 64 plates, including map. Ck Dec 11 (247) £600

Chardon, Francis A.

— Journal at Fort Clark, 1834-1839. Pierre, 1932. NH May 30 (232) $70

Charlemagne. See: Tower, Charlemagne

Charles'...

— Charles' Wain: A Miscellany of Short Stories. L, [1933]. One of 95, sgd by all 18 contributors. O Dec 17 (39) $120

Charles de Valois, Duc d'Orleans

— Poemes. Paris, 1950. One of 1,230. Illus by Matisse. Folio, orig wraps. Inscr by Matisse. S May 28 (229) £1,400 [Gal. Arenthon]

Charles I, King of England

— Eikon Basilike. The Pourtraicture of His Sacred Majestie.... L, 1649. 8vo, contemp calf; joints cracked. With folding frontis trimmed; later ink inscr on front free endpaper. bba May 14 (60) £55 [Taylor]

— The Kings Maiesties Declaration to His subjects, Concerning Lawfull Sports to be Used. L, 1633. 4to, modern cloth. cb Sept 5 (18) $180

— Koenigs Caroli letze Reden.... [N.p.], 1649. Bound with: Koeniglich Gebett. So Carolus Koenig von Gros-Britannien in seiner Gefangnuss gethan.... Frankfurt: Philipps Fievet, 1649. 2 works in 1 vol. 4to, modern wraps. A2-3 in 1st work loose & tp with small repair. S Dec 12 (246) £600 [Quaritch]

— A Large Declaration Concerning the Late Tumults in Scotland. L, 1639. Folio, contemp calf; upper joint worn. DW Jan 29 (220) £150

Anr copy. Calf; rebacked. Tp & frontis repaired. pnE May 13 (29) £85

— Works. L, 1662. ("Basilika. The Workes of....") 2 vols. Folio, contemp calf; worn, rebacked with royal arms. With engraved title, 2 frontises & 3 double-page plates. W July 8 (23) £170

Charles II, King of England

[-] Relation en forme de journal, du voyage et sejour que...Charles II...a fait en Hollande.... The Hague, 1660. Bound with: Kevchenius, Robert. Anglia Triumphans.... Hagenau: Adrian Vlacq, 1660. Folio, contemp vellum. Some stains & repairs. S May 28 (75) £700 [Gatino]

Charlet, Nicolas Toussaint

— Costumes militaires francais. [Paris: Delpech, 1817-18]. Folio, loose as issued. With 28 hand-colored lithos. Some foxing & soiling. Schlosser copy. P June 17 (522) $2,750

Charlevoix, Pierre Francois Xavier de, 1682-1761

See also: Caxton Club

— Journal of a Voyage to North-America. L, 1761. 1st Ed in English. 2 vols. 8vo, contemp calf; spines rubbed or worn. With folding map. b June 22 (160) £280

Anr copy. Contemp calf; some wear to some extremities. CNY Oct 8 (41) $950

Charlot, Jean

— Picture Book. NY: John Becker, 1933. One of 500. Inscriptions by Paul Claudel. 4to, wraps, in d/j. With 32 plates. sg Feb 6 (59) $700

Charnock, John, 1756-1807

— An History of Marine Architecture. L, 1800-2. 1st Ed. 3 vols. 4to, modern half mor gilt. With engraved title & 99 plates. Some imprints & captions cropped. S July 1 (1226) £1,550 [San Lorenzo]

Charnois, Jean Charles Le Vacher de

— Recherches sur les costumes et sur les theatres de toutes les nations.... Paris, 1790. 2 vols in 1. 4to, recent half mor. With frontis & 54 plates, 47 in color aquatint ptd from 4 plates each, with added watercolor wash. Tp & frontis soiled. Schlosser copy. P June 18 (475) $2,750

Charpentier, Toussaint de, 1779-1847

— Libellulinae Europaeae. Leipzig: Leopold Voss, 1842. 4to, contemp half calf. With 2 uncolored & 46 hand-colored plates. Browned. C Oct 30 (178) £600 [Grahame]

— Orthoptera descripta et depicta. Leipzig, 1841-45. 4to, contemp half calf. With 60 hand-colored plates. C Oct 30 (179) £600 [Junk]

Chartier, Alain

— Delectable Demaundes, and Pleasaunt Questions.... L, 1596. 4to, modern calf. Tp browned & frail; repaired at margins & with library stamp on verso; a2 repaired at outer margin; dampstains; verso of final leaf soiled. STC 5060. Ck Oct 31 (55) £600

— Les Oeuvres. Paris, 1617. 4to, contemp calf; rebacked preserving old spine. Worming to upper margins from tp to 2F1; some browning at end. Ck Oct 31 (56) £90

Chase, Owen. See: Golden Cockerel Press

Chassepol, Francois de

— Histoire des grands vizirs Mahomet Coprogli Pacha et Ahcmet Coprogli Pacha. Paris: Estienne Michallet, 1676. 12mo, contemp calf; rubbed. With engraved title & folding plan. Corner of plan def; some spotting. S June 30 (259) £350 [Kutluoglu]

Chateaubriand, Francois Rene de, 1768-1848

— Genie du christianisme ou Beautes de la religion chretienne. Paris, [1802]. 5 vols. 8vo, contemp half calf; rubbed. bba Apr 9 (232) £100 [Abdullah]

— Itineraire de Paris a Jerusalem et de Jerusalem a Paris. Paris, 1812. 2d Ed. 2 vols. 8vo, contemp calf; becoming disbound. With folding map. A few leaves in Vol I dampstained. S June 30 (261) £150 [Lemos]

Anr copy. 3 vols. 8vo, later half lea; joints cracked & tape-reinforced. sg Jan 9 (51) $90

Chateauneuf, Francois de

— Dialogue sur la musique des anciens. Paris, 1725. 12mo, contemp calf; rubbed, upper cover detached. With 7 plates. Some browning. pn Oct 24 (270) £95 [Robertshaw]

Chatelain, Henri Abraham

— Atlas historique ou nouvelle introduction a l'histoire.... Paris, 1705-8. Vols I & II, Parts 1 and 2. Together, 3 vols. Folio, orig half calf; scuffed & rubbed. With 103 double-page plates. cb Jan 30 (146) $2,000

Anr Ed. Amst., 1708-19. Vol IV (of 7). Folio, contemp sheep gilt. With engraved title & 34 maps. Sold w.a.f. sg Feb 13 (114) $600

Mixed Ed. 7 vols in 3. Folio, contemp calf gilt; rubbed. With 280 maps & plates. Worming in Vol III affecting plates & 1 or 2 maps with small loss; stamps on titles. S Nov 21 (133) £6,800 [Burden]

3d Ed of Vol I, 2d Ed of Vols II-III, 1st Ed of Vols IV-VII. Amst., 1718-21. 7 vols. Folio, contemp calf gilt; worn, some covers stained. With engraved title to 5 vols & 280 plates & maps. Minor worming in Vol I without loss; a few splits without loss; some discoloration to text. With Vols I-IV dated 1718. S June 18 (297) £8,500 [Map House]

Chatelain, Jean

— Le Message Biblique. Paris: Fernard Mourlot, 1972. Illus by Marc Chagall. Folio, cloth. sg Apr 2 (58) $110

Chater Collection, Sir Catchick P.

— The Chater Collection. Pictures Relating to China, Hongkong, Macao.... L, 1924. One of 750. Ed by James Orange. 4to, orig cloth. pnE Mar 11 (108) £330; S Feb 11 (349) £350 [Cumming]

Chatterton, Edward Keble, 1878-1944

— Ship-Models. NY, [c.1945]. Reprint of the 1923 Ed. bbc Sept 23 (218) $70

Chatto, William Andrew, 1799-1864

See also: Jackson & Chatto

— The Angler's Souvenir. L, 1835. 8vo, half lea; rubbed. Koopman copy. O Oct 29 (51) $160

— Facts and Speculation on the Origin and History of Playing Cards. L, 1848. 1st Ed. 8vo, orig cloth; dampstained, spine ends worn, hinges cracked. sg Oct 17 (131) $175

Chaucer, Geoffrey, 1340?-1400

See also: Golden Cockerel Press; Kelmscott Press; Limited Editions Club

— Canterbury Tales. NY, 1930. Illus by Rockwell Kent. 2 vols. Folio, orig cloth. sg Sept 26 (147) $100

One of 924. Orig cloth. sg Sept 26 (146) $275

— The Prologue from the Canterbury Tales. Surrey: Circle Press, [1978]. One of 250. Illus by Ronald King. Folio, orig cloth. wa Sept 26 (60) $120

— Works. L: Jhon Kyngston for Jhon Wight, 1561. 5th Ed, 2d Issue. Folio, old calf; rebacked, orig backstrip retained; clasps restored. Black letter. Washed; title rehinged; scattered marginal repairs. STC 5076. sg Nov 7 (43) $4,000

Anr Ed. L: Adam Islip, 1598. Folio, old calf; joints repaired but split. Black letter. Lacking 1st & last blanks; repair to lower margin of 1st leaf of dedication; some worming with occasional loss; tears to b6 & C3-5. STC 5078. C Dec 16 (189) £1,100 [Maggs]

Anr Ed. L, 1721. Folio, contemp calf; rebacked. With 2 ports. Some soiling, affecting tp. Ck Nov 29 (67) £260

Anr copy. Contemp calf; rebacked retaining orig backstrip. sg Oct 24 (63) $475

Anr Ed. Cleveland: World Publishing Co., [1958]. Folio, orig cloth, in d/j. Facsimile of the Kelmscott Chaucer. LH Dec 11 (82) $80

Anr Ed. L: Basilisk Press, 1975. One of 515. 2 vols. Folio, orig cloth. Facsimile reprint of Kelmscott Chaucer, with companion vol by Duncan Robinson. L Nov 14 (270) £320

Chauchard, Jean Baptiste Hippolyte

— A General Map of the Empire of Germany.... L, 1800. Folio, contemp half calf; scuffed. With index map & map on 25 sheets. Ck May 15 (84) £140

Anr copy. Contemp half calf; worn. DW Oct 2 (22) £135

Anr copy. Half calf; worn. Minor spotting & soiling. DW May 13 (13) £120

Chaumeton, Francois Pierre, 1775-1819

— Flore medicale. Paris, 1828-32. Illus by Lambert, chiefly after Turpin. 6 (of 8) vols. 8vo, contemp bds; rebacked in cloth, inner hinges strengthened. With 349 hand-colored plates. Ck Nov 29 (68) £1,100

Cheeseman, Thomas Frederick, 1846-1923 —& Hemsley, W. B.

— Illustrations of the New Zealand Flora. Wellington, 1914. 2 vols. 4to, orig cloth; rubbed. bba Nov 28 (104) £110 [Lloyds of Kew]

Cheever, Henry Theodore, 1814-97

— The Island World of the Pacific. NY, 1851. 8vo, orig cloth; worn, front joint splitting. cb Jn 30 (16) $90

— Life in the Sandwich Islands. NY, 1851. 1st Ed. 12mo, orig cloth. With 7 plates. cb Jan 30 (15) $150

Cheever, John

— The Way Some People Live. NY, [1943]. 1st Ed. In d/j. CNY Dec 5 (180) $420

Chemnitz, Martin

— Examinis concilii Tridentini.... Frankfurt, 1606. 8vo, contemp vellum; front cover damaged along fore-edge. Some browning & contemp underscoring. sg Oct 24 (64) $200

Chenier, Andre Marie de, 1762-94

— Les Bucoliques. Paris, 1905. One of 12 with silver plaque by Denys Peuch on bdg. Illus by Henri Fantin-Latour. 4to, mor gilt extra by Meunier, 1907. With 12 lithos, each in 3 states. CNY Dec 5 (419) $6,000

Chenu, Jean Charles, 1808-79

— Encyclopedie d'histoire naturelle.... Paris, 1873-77. 18 (of 22) vols only. Contemp half sheep; 1 front hinge def. Some foxing. sg Sept 19 (169) $750

— Lecons elementaires d'histoire naturelle.... Paris, 1847. 4to, contemp calf; rubbed, spine repaired at head. bba May 14 (467) £80 [Lib. Naturalistica Bolognese]

Cherry-Garrard, Apsley

— The Worst Journey in the World. L, 1922. 2 vols. Orig half cloth; soiled. DW Apr 8 (21) £360

1st Ed. L, 1922-23. Later Issue. 3 vols, including Supplement. Modern calf. W July 8 (243) £360

2d Ed. L, 1929. 2 vols. Orig cloth; spine worn. DW Nov 6 (27) £85

Cherubin d'Orleans, Pere

— La Dioptrique oculaire.... Paris, 1671. Folio, contemp calf; rebacked. With 60 plates. SI June 9 (233) LIt6,000,000

Cheselden, William, 1688-1752

— The Anatomy of the Human Body. L, 1750. 7th Ed. 8vo, contemp calf; lower joint split. With engraved title, frontis & 40 plates. b June 22 (74) £120

— Osteographia, or the Anatomy of the Bones. L, 1733. 1st Ed. Folio, modern half lea. With 56 plates & port. K Sept 29 (256) $75

— A Treatise on the High Operation for the Stone. L, 1723. 8vo, contemp calf; rebacked. With 17 plates. S Feb 25 (583) £500 [Wein]

Chesnutt, Charles Waddell, 1858-1932

— The Conjure Woman. NY, 1899. 1st Ed. 8vo, orig cloth. NH May 30 (91) $165

Chesterfield, Philip Dormer Stanhope, 4th Earl of, 1694-1773

— Letters written by the Late Right Honourable Philip Dormer Stanhope, Earl of Chesterfield, to his Son.... L, 1774. 1st Ed. 2 vols. 4to, modern calf. Epstein copy. sg Apr 29 (79) $600

5th Ed. 2 vols. 8vo, calf; rebacked, contemp spines & covers laid down. F Mar 26 (17) $110

Chesterton, George Laval

— Peace, War and Adventure: An Autobiographical Memoir. L, 1853. 2 vols in 2. 12mo, later calf; joints & edges worn. wa Mar 5 (419) $190

Chesterton, Gilbert Keith, 1874-1936

— Gloria in Profundis. NY: Rudge, 1927. 1st American Ed, One of 27. Wraps. sg Dec 12 (55) $140

— Magic: A Fantastic Comedy. L, [n.d.]. One of 150. Bds. sg Dec 12 (56) $140

Chetham, James, 1640-92

— The Angler's Vade Mecum.... L, 1681. 1st Ed. 8vo, later half mor. Final leaf remtd & repaired, with loss; 1 or 2 other leaves repaired; other minor stains & soiling. Koopman copy. O Oct 29 (52) $700

2d Ed. L, 1689. 12mo, calf. With 2 plates. pnE Aug 12 (39) £210

3d Ed. L, 1700. 8vo, newer calf; rubbed, rear cover detached. Dean Sage-Koopman copy. O Oct 29 (53) $550

Chevalier, Guillaume de

— Le decez ou fin du monde.... Paris: Robert le Fizelier, 1584. 4to, mor gilt. Final leaf with repaired hole at lower margin. Ck Oct 31 (58) £450

Chevalier, Ulysse, 1841-1923
— Repertoire des sources historiques du moyen age. Bio-bibliographie. Paris, 1877-86. 4to, contemp half lea. Tp & next leaf loose. sg Oct 31 (84) $80

Chevallier, Guillaume Sulpice. See: Gavarni

Cheyneius, Jacobus
— De priore astronomiae parte, seu de sphaera.... Douai, 1575. 3 parts in 2 vols. New half vellum. B Nov 1 (484) HF1,100

Chicago
— CHICAGO TRIBUNE TOWER. - The International Competition for a New Administration Building for the Chicago Tribune.... Chicago, [1923]. Folio, cloth, in d/j. With 282 plates. sg Sept 6 (70) $1,200

Chicago, Burlington & Quincy Railroad
— Dedication of the New Burlington Terminal, Cheyenne U.S.A. May 17, 1929. Chicago, 1929. cb Feb 13 (63) $55

Chicago Tribune Tower. See: Chicago

Children's...
— The Children's Tableaux, a Novel Colour Book. L: Ernest Nister & NY: E. P. Dutton, [1895]. 4to, orig half cloth; worn. With 5 double-page colored plates, lifting to form 3-dimensional views. All plates damaged. W Mar 6 (123) £60

Chinese Woodblock Books
— Ta ts'ang ching. [N.p., c.1200]. Sung Ed. With: Ta ts'ang ching. [China, c.1300]. 2 vols. Narrow folio, in folding silk chemise with bone clasps. First work with 71 block-ptd pages; 2d work with 34 block-ptd pages Some worming. cb Feb 12 (128) $3,000

Chippendale, Thomas, 1718?-79
— The Gentleman and Cabinet-Maker's Director. L, 1754. 1st Ed. Folio, old calf gilt; rebacked with old backstrip laid down, corners restored. With 161 plates. Some staining. McCarty-Cooper copy. CNY Jan 25 (13) $2,000

Anr copy. Later half calf. Lacking half-title, tp, preface & subscribers list; some staining. Sold w.a.f. pnE Oct 2 (526) £480

Anr copy. Modern calf. Title silked & possibly supplied from anr copy; Plate 28 edge shaved; corner of plate 71 torn & repaired. sg Nov 7 (44) $5,000

Anr copy. Contemp sheep; joints cracked. Plate 34 torn in blank lower margin & repaired. sg May 7 (59) $4,200

2d Ed. L, 1755. Folio, modern half calf. With engraved dedication & 161 plates. Outer margins of tp & first 5 leaves restored, with loss to dedication leaf; other repairs; Plates CXXXIX-XLXIX stained at upper outer corners. Sold w.a.f. C May 20 (242) £1,600 [Rex Art Galleries]

Anr copy. Orig calf; worn. With engraved dedication & 161 plates, including plate 25 bis. Small wormholes at extreme lower edge. S Feb 11 (302) £2,200 [Ursus]

Anr Ed. L, 1910. Folio, orig half cloth; worn. SI June 9 (244) LIt200,000

Anr Ed. NY, 1938. Folio, cloth. Facsimile of the 1762 Ed. sp June 18 (327) $55

Chiquet, J.
— Le Nouveau et curieux Atlas geographique et historique.... Paris, [c.1720]. Oblong 4to, old bds; worn & soiled. With engraved title, 3 astronomical diagrams & 24 maps, most hand-colored in outline. Tp worn & soiled & pasted on verso of 1st diagram; marginal browning & staining throughout. S May 14 (1168) £620 [Shapero]

Chisholm, C. R.
— Chisholm's All Round Route and Panoramic Guide of the St. Lawrence.... Montreal, 1875. Orig cloth; spine rubbed. With 4 folding maps & 1 folding plate. bba Sept 19 (21) £85 [Scott]

Chittenden, Hiram Martin, 1859-1917
— History of Early Steamboat Navigation on the Missouri River.... NY, 1903. One of 950. 2 vols. With 16 plates. cb Nov 14 (29) $225

Chodzko, Leonard
— La Pologne, scenes historiques, monumens.... Paris, [c.1835]. 3 vols. 4to, half mor with Mr de Nantois lettered in gilt on upper covers; rubbed. With engraved titles & 116 plates & maps & 8 pp of engraved music. Some spotting. S Feb 26 (729) £290 [Shapero]

Choiseul-Gouffier, Marie Gabriel F. A., Comte de, 1752-1817
— Voyage pittoresque de la Grece. Paris, 1782-1822. 2 vols in 5, comprising Vol I & Vol II in 4 livraisons as issued. Folio, orig bds, uncut; rubbed, some backstrips def. With 3 half-titles & engraved title, port, 7 double-page of folding maps & 283 plates & maps on 168 sheets. Small hole in 1 plate without loss; some spotting & discoloration; a few leaves in Vol II, part 2 wormed at inner margin. S July 1 (573) £3,500 [Keskiner]

2d Issue of Vol I. 3 parts in 2 vols. Folio, contemp half mor; worn, Vol I loose in bdg, front cover of Vol II, Part 1 detached. With 3 engraved titles, port, 2 double-page maps & 285 plates on 168 leaves, some double-page, including 8 bis & the double-page view 76 bis. Some foxing & spotting.

P June 17 (156) $5,500

Choulant, Ludwig, Johann, 1791-1861

— History and Bibliography of Anatomic Illustration.... NY, [1962]. O Sept 24 (54) $120

Anr copy. In d/j. sg Oct 31 (87) $90

Christie, Agatha

— The Hound of Death and Other Stories. L: Odhams Press, [1933]. In chipped d/j. cb Sept 19 (30) $160

— The Murder of Roger Ackroyd. L, 1926. S May 13 (646) £240 [Grigor]

Anr copy. Epstein copy. sg Apr 29 (82) $350

— The Mysterious Affair at Styles. L, 1921. 1st English Ed. Bdg worn. 1 outer margin holed. Epstein copy. sg Apr 29 (83) $1,100

— Passenger to Frankfort. L, [1970]. In d/j. Staining to lower edges & bottom of tp. Inscr. cb Sept 19 (31) $250

— Towards Zero. L, [1944]. In soiled & rubbed d/j, with edge tears. cb Sept 19 (35) $110

Christie, James, 1773-1831

— An Inquiry into the Ancient Greek Game.... L, 1801. 4to, contemp half cloth; rebacked in sheep, extremities rubbed. With 5 plates & 3 aquatints. With 2 plates wormed at lower margins; British Museum duplicate. Ck May 8 (96) £280

Chronicles

— Coronica llamada Las dos Conquistas del Reyno de Napoles. Zaragoza: Miguel Capila, 1559. Folio, old vellum; soiled. Border of port with tear; repair at upper inner margin of tp; N8 torn without loss; last leaf of index holed touching letters; some browning or waterstaining. S May 13 (760) £2,800 [Delstereis]

— Cronica breve de i fatti illustri de' Re di Francia. Venice: Bernardo Giunta, 1590. 4to, contemp vellum gilt with Il. Sig. Nicolo on upper cover & Perotti on lower cover; worn. With 62 plates. Washed; some staining. bba May 28 (436) £340 [P & P Books]

— Die Cronica van der hilliger Stat van Coellen. [Cologne]: Johann Koelhoff the Younger, 23 Aug 1499. Folio, later calf; rubbed. 50 lines & headline; gothic letter. Portions of text supplied in Ms facsimile on 4 leaves; repairs & tears occasionally affecting text (supplied in Ms facsimile); some soiling & staining. 362 (of 368) leaves; lacking first A1, A6, nn2 & nn4 (all but nn2 supplied in facsimile). Goff C-476. S Dec 5 (12) £2,000 [Mediolanum]

Chronicon. See: Fleetwood, William

Chrusanthos, Notaras, Patriarch of Jerusalem

— [Historia et descriptio terrae sanctae, in Greek] Paris, 1716. Folio, modern half calf. With port, map (repaired) & 3 plates. Dampstaining, causing softening & fraying. S July 1 (575) £2,200 [Franks]

Chubb, Charles. See: Braybourne & Chubb

Chubb, Thomas

— The Printed Maps in the Atlases of Great Britain and Ireland. L, 1927. 4to, orig cloth; worn. bbc Sept 23 (86) $90

Chukhovskij, Kornej

— Telefon...3-'e izdanie. [Leningrad: Raduga, [1930s]. 4to, orig wraps. sg Nov 7 (194) $250

Church, Benjamin, 1639-1718

— The History of the Great Indian War of 1675 and 1676. Dayton, NY, 1859. 8vo, cloth. With 12 plates, 6 hand-colored. sp Apr 16 (9) $65

Church Library, Elihu Dwight

— A Catalogue of Books Relating to the Discovery and Early History of North and South America.... NY, 1951. Compiled by George Watson Cole. 5 vols. 4to, cloth. DW Dec 11 (349) £160

Church, Jerry

— Journal of Travels, Adventures, and Remarks. Harrisburg, 1845. 8vo, contemp mor; worn, rebacked. Dampstaining throughout; some leaves stained; lacking ad leaf. sg Dec 5 (50) $1,000

Church, John

— A Cabinet of Quadrupeds. L, [1794]-1805. 2 vols. Folio, contemp mor gilt; rubbed & soiled. With 2 engraved titles & 84 plates, 3 plates from anr work tipped in Some library stamps; some foxing. pn Mar 19 (264) £360 [Shapero]

Church of Scotland. See: Franklin Printing, Benjamin

Church, Willis Humphry. See: Hoak & Church

Churchill, Awnsham & John

— A Collection of Voyages and Travels. L, 1732. 6 vols. Folio, contemp calf; worn. With ports, engraved titles & 159 plates. First few leaves in Vol II torn & repaired. S Feb 26 (730) £1,850 [Voltaire]

Anr Ed. L, 1744-46. 6 vols. Folio, contemp sheep; rejointed, some joints cracked. With 230 plates Some corners dampstained; Vol IV wormed. sg Nov 7 (45) $2,600

Churchill, Charles, 1731-64
— The Rosciad and The Apology. L, 1891. One of 400. 4to, half mor gilt. Extra-illus with c.40 plates. sg Mar 5 (62) $250

Churchill, G.C. See: Gilbert & Churchill

Churchill, James Morss. See: Stephenson & Churchill

Churchill, Sir Winston L. S., 1874-1965
See also: Grabhorn Printing
— Arms and the Covenant. L, 1938. 1st Ed. cb Dec 5 (29) $110
Anr copy. Inscr to Sumner Welles & with related material. CNY June 9 (16) $67,500
Anr copy. In repaired d/j. Inscr to Kathleen Hill. S July 21 (226) £1,300 [Spencer]
— The Collected Works. L, 1973-76. 35 vols, including proof copy of Vol I. With: The Collected Essays. L, 1976. 4 vols. Together, 39 vols. Orig vellum gilt. Some staining. bba July 9 (157) £1,300 [Taylor-Smith]
— The Dawn of Liberation. L, etc., 1945. 1st Ed. Lea with initials K.H. on spine; upper cover stained. Inscr to Kathleen Hill, 1946. S July 21 (232) £1,000 [Wilson]
— The End of the Beginning. L, 1943. Lea with spine lettered in gilt with initials K. H.. Inscr to Mrs Kathleen Hill, 1943. S July 21 (230) £900 [Wilson]
— Great Contemporaries. L, 1937. 1st Ed. Orig cloth, in d/j. cb Dec 5 (30) $350
— A History of the English-Speaking Peoples. L, 1956-58. 1st Ed. 4 vols. In d/js. bba Dec 19 (171) £80 [Tholstrup]
Anr copy. Half mor gilt. DW Oct 2 (434) £75
Anr copy. In d/js. Inscr. S July 21 (235) £1,350 [Wilson]
— Into Battle. L, 1941. Lea with initials K.H.. Inscr to Kathleen Hill, 1942. S July 21 (227) £950 [Finch]
— London to Ladysmith via Pretoria. L, 1900. 1st Ed. 8vo, orig cloth; light soiling & wear. Inscr. cb Dec 5 (32) $700
Anr copy. Orig cloth; rubbed, soiled & stained; joints worn. cb Dec 5 (33) $85
Anr copy. Orig cloth; rubbed. A few leaves roughly opened; tear in 1 map. wa June 25 (48) $210
— Lord Randolph Churchill. L, 1906. 1st Ed. 2 vols. bba Apr 9 (125) £65 [W. White]
Anr copy. Inscr. cb Dec 5 (34) $150
Anr copy. In d/j with short tears. Inscr to Kathleen Hill, 1952. S July 21 (234) £890 [Pinch]
2d Ed. L, 1907. Crudely rehinged. Sgd, 24 July 1924. DW Nov 6 (210) £360
— Marlborough, his Life and Times. L, 1933-38. 1st Ed. 4 vols. Orig cloth; rubbed & faded. DW Dec 11 (467) £105
Anr copy. Orig cloth, 2 vols in d/js. Inscr to Kathleen Hill, 27 July 1946. S July 21 (223) £1,400 [Spencer]
Mixed Ed. 4 vols. Inscr to Gerald Cole-Deacon. S July 21 (239) £850 [Finch]
— My African Journey. L, 1908. 1st Ed. b June 22 (53) £160
Anr copy. Orig pictorial cloth with Churchill standing over a dead rhinoceros. cb Dec 5 (36) $500
Anr copy. Half mor gilt. Some foxing. pn Dec 12 (351) £130
— My Early Life. A Roving Commission. L, 1930. 1st Ed. Mor gilt by Sangorski & Sutcliffe. Inscr Kathleen Hill. S July 21 (221) £800 [Spencer]
2d Issue. In tape-repaired d/j. cb Dec 5 (37) $450
— Onwards to Victory. L, 1944. Lea with spine lettered in gilt with initials K. H.. Inscr to Mrs Kathleen Hill, 1944. S July 21 (231) £1,000 [Wilson]
— Painting as a Pastime. L, 1949. 3d Impression. Inscr to Eunice Simeon & with related material. S July 21 (241) £500 [Wilson]
1st American Ed. NY, [1950]. In d/j. cb Dec 5 (38) $50
— The River War. L, 1899. 1st Ed. 2 vols. 8vo, orig cloth; rubbed & stained. cb Dec 5 (39) $1,600
2d Impression. Orig cloth. b June 22 (54) £350
— Savrola. NY, 1900. 1st Ed. 8vo, orig cloth. cb Dec 5 (40) $600
— The Second World War. Bost., 1948-53. 1st American Ed. Vols I-V (of 6). In d/js, that of Vol IV def. bbc Dec 9 (298) U85
Anr copy. 6 vols. br May 29 (91) $775
Anr copy. In d/j with a few tears. Inscr in 1st 2 vols to Kathleen Hill, 1945, 1954. S July 21 (233) £1,600 [Wilson]
Anr copy. In torn d/j. Inscr to Anne Triggs. S July 21 (240) £1,200 [Wilson]
1st English Ed. L, 1948-54. 6 vols. In chipped d/js. bbc June 29 (264) $80
Anr copy. In d/js. cb Dec 5 (41) $130
Vol I, 3d Ed; Vol II, 2d Ed; Vols III-VI, 1st Eds. L, 1950-54. 6 vols. Ck July 10 (210) £150
— Secret Session Speeches. L, 1946. 1st Ed. Lea with initials K. H.. Inscr to Kathleen Hill, 1948. S July 21 (225) £900 [Wilson]
— Step by Step. L, 1939. 1st Ed. cb Dec 5 (42) $160
— The Story of the Malakand Field Force. L, 1898. 1st Ed. 8vo, orig cloth; worn. This

copy has neither errata slip nor 32-page catalogue. cb Dec 5 (43) $2,250

Anr copy. Orig cloth; upper cover stained. Some spotting. S July 21 (237) £1,200 [Spencer]

— Thoughts and Adventures. L, 1932. 1st Ed. In d/j with tear. Inscr to Kathleen Hill, 1945. S July 21 (222) £1,000 [Weber]

— The Unrelenting Struggle. L, 1942. Mor with spine lettered in gilt with initials K. H.. Inscr to Mrs Kathleen Hill, 1942. S July 21 (229) £900 [Wilson]

— The War Speeches.... L, 1941-46. 1st Eds. 7 vols. Orig cloth in soiled & frayed d/j. DW Oct 2 (435) £60

— The World Crisis. L, 1942. Mor gilt by Sangorski & Sutcliffe. Inscr to Kathleen Hill, Christmas 1942. S July 21 (228) £700 [History Merchant]

Churton, Edward, 1800-74. See: Richardson & Churton

Ciampini, Giovanni Giustino

— Vetera monumenta.... Rome, 1747. 3 vols. Folio, contemp calf; joints weak. With port & 165 full-page or folding plates. Library stamps on titles. S June 25 (188) £900 [Shapero]

Cibber, Theophilus, 1703-58

— An Epistle from Mr. Theophilus Cibber, to David Garrick.... L, 1755. 8vo, cloth. sg Mar 5 (210) $350

Ciceri, Eugene

— Souvenirs des Pyrenees. L, [c.1871]. 2 parts in 1 vol. Oblong folio, orig cloth; def. With 60 plates, only, 18 folding or double-page. Some spotting; 1 folding panorama torn at folds. pn Nov 14 (416) £320

Cicero, Marcus Tullius, 106-43 B.C.

— Cato major. Leipzig: Johannes Steinmann, [1584]. Bound with: Fabricius, Georgius. Epitomes prosodiae et elegantiarum poeticarum liber.... Leipzig, 1579. 8vo, contemp blind-stamped pigskin over wooden bds, dated 1596. Browned throughout; dampstained at beginning & end; blank corner of 1st title repaired. sg Oct 24 (68) $500

Anr Ed. L, 1778. 8vo, modern calf; soiled. O Dec 17 (42) $130

— De natura deorum.... Florence: Filippo Giunta, Oct 1516. 8vo, 18th-cent mor gilt; joints & spine ends worn. sg Mar 12 (47) $300

— De officiis. [Mainz]: Johann Fust & Peter Schoeffer, 1465. 1st Ed. Folio, 18th-cent mor gilt. 28 lines; type 511G (headings, colophon), 3:91G. 88 leaves. Goff C-575. Engel-Dresden Koenigliche Bibliothek-Vickery copy. P Dec 12 (163) $110,000

Anr Ed. Venice: Bonetus Locatellus for Octavianus Scotus, 27 May 1494. 3 parts in 1 vol. Folio, contemp vellum, with vellum endleaves from an antiphonary; worn & rubbed, holes punched in lower cover. 63 lines of commentary & headline; types 6:105R, 5:80R, 105Gk & 80 Gk. Short tear to 1 leaf just entering text; a few worm tracks to gutters, 1 grazing a few letters on O74, anr touching text on q7 with loss to 8 letters on verso; corner of k3 repaired touching sidenotes on verso; small inkstain to k1r partially obscuring a few words. 158 leaves. Goff C-609. Milne copy. CNY Dec 5 (181) £1,000

— De Oratore. Venice: Thomas de Blavis de Alexandria, 1488. Folio, 18th-cent calf gilt; extremities worn. 53 lines; type 5:84R & 8:104R; illuminated initial C at beginning of text in gold with green, blue & red scroll & floral decoration; other initials & some capitals in red & blue. A few leaves with minor stains; small wormholes mainly in 1st & last leaves; a few minor marginal tears. 210 (of 212) leaves; lacking g4-5. Goff C-663. C Dec 16 (113) £1,000 [Bossi]

— De philosophia. Venice: Aldus, 1523. 2 vols. 8vo, later calf; rebacked. Repairs to 2d tp; lacking 3 blanks at end. rs Oct 17 (39) $400

Anr Ed. Lyons: Jean Frellon, 1562. 2 vols in 1. 16mo, 18th-cent sheep gilt; front joint starting. Ptr's device on Vol I title hand-colored. sg Mar 12 (49) $110

— The Familiar Epistles.... L, [1620]. Trans by J. Webbe. 12mo, contemp calf; rubbed, rebacked, bound tight. Some dampstaining; short tear in K4. STC 5305. S Nov 14 (457) £170 [Lawson]

— In Omnes de arte rhetorica. Venice: Aldus, 1551-[46]. Folio, modern bds. Marginal repairs. SI Dec 5 (159) LIt280,000

— Opera. Leiden: Elzevir, 1642. 10 vols. 12mo, 18th-cent mor gilt. Ink stains on tp of Vol VIII. S May 28 (76) £800 [Shapero]

Anr Ed. Paris, 1740-42. 9 vols. 4to, contemp calf gilt; worn. bba Aug 13 (65) £200 [Bkyrne]

Anr Ed. Paris, 1768. 14 vols. 12mo, contemp mor gilt; a few corners rubbed. S Feb 25 (547) £400 [Delbridge]

— Orationes. Venice: Adam de Ambergau, 1472. Folio, contemp Bavarian blind-tooled lea over wooden bds, with remains of 2 brass fore-edge clasps, Kyriss shop 154; endpapers renewed. 37 lines; type 2:116R; rubricated; occasional early marginalia. Some spotting & staining; slight worming in first several quires, touching a few letters; 1 marginal tear. 296 (of 298) leaves; lacking initial & final blanks. Goff C-543. Schoyen copy. P Dec 12 (19)

$18,000

Anr Ed. Venice: Aldus, 1554. ("Orationum.") 3 vols. 8vo, early calf; head and foot of spine chipped. cb Dec 5 (48) $60

Anr copy. Old vellum; crinkled. A2 torn with loss & repaired; tp with erased ownership inscr. Ck Nov 29 (6) £95

— Orationes Philippicae. Venice: Joannes Tacuinus de Tridino, 22 Mar 1494. Folio, later calf. 60 lines of commentary surrounding text & headline; types 3:108R (text), 1:80R (commentary), 80Gk (commentary). Some worming. 78 leaves. Goff C-557. C Dec 16 (114) £950 [Sokol]

— Rhetorica ad C. Herennium. Venice: Aldus, 1514. ("Rhetoricerum ad C. Herrenium [& other works].") 4to, 17th-cent mor gilt; worn. Lacking final leaf; tp soiled & torn at inner margin; some staining & marginal soiling throughout; H5 restored. Ck Nov 29 (4) £150

Cicognara, Leopoldo, 1767-1834

— Catalogo ragionato dei libri d'arte e d'antichita. Pisa, 1979. 2 vols in 1. 8vo, cloth. Reprint of 1821 Ed. sg Oct 31 (88) $80

— Storia della scultura dal suo risorgimento in Italia. Prato, 1823-24. 2d Ed. 7 vols. 8vo, contemp half lea; rebacked. SI June 9 (257) LIt1,400,000

Cilham, William

— Manual of Instruction for the Volunteers and Militia of the Confederate States. Richmond, 1861. 12mo, cloth; rebacked with orig spine retained. Browned. sg Dec 5 (77) $275

Cinderella...

— Cinderella, or the Little Glass Slipper. L, 1814. Sq 16mo, wraps; worn, tape-repaired. With hand-colored heads on almost all figures. cb Jan 9 (44) $70

Cioni, Alfredo

— Bibliografia delle Sacre Rappresentazioni. Florence, 1961. One of 666. Wraps. sg Oct 31 (89) $50

Cioranescu, Alexandre

— Bibliographie de la litterature francaise.... Paris, 1965-66. 3 vols. 4to, cloth; worn. O Sept 24 (55) $180

— Bibliographie de la Litterature Francaise du Siezieme Siecle. Geneva, 1975. Syn. sg Oct 31 (90) $80

Cipriani, Giovanni Battista, 1727-85

— Monumenti di fabbriche antiche estratti dai disegni dei piu celebri autori. Rome, 1796-1803-[7]. 3 vols. 4to, contemp bds; worn. With 3 engraved titles & 267 (of 268) plates. Text engraved. Some spotting throughout. S May 14 (1079) £360 [Nicolas]

Ciranna, Alfonso

— Giorgio de Chirico, Catalogo delle opere grafiche 1921-1969. Rome, 1969. One of 1,500. Folio, orig cloth. SI Dec 5 (161) LIt750,000

Circinianus, Nicolaus

— Ecclesiae anglicanae trophaea. Rome: Bartolommeo Grassi, 1584. 4to, later vellum. Lower margins cropped with some loss to captions; lacking 2d part. sg Oct 24 (70) $225

Cirni, Anton Francesco

— Comentarii...ne quali si descrive la guerra ultima di Francia...e l'historia dell' assedio di Malta. Rome: Giulio Accolto, 1567. 4to, contemp vellum; worn. With folding woodcut map. Repair to foot of N4 with text in facsimile. S July 1 (646) £1,800 [Ganado]

Clairaut, Alexis Claude, 1713-65

— Elemens de geometrie. Paris, 1753. 8vo, contemp calf; corners & spine ends worn. With 14 folding plates; scattered spotting. DW Jan 29 (222) £80

Anr Ed. Paris, 1765. 8vo, contemp calf. With 14 plates. cb Oct 25 (30) $70

Clamorgan, Jean de

— La Chasse du loup.... Lyon: Gabriel Cartier, 1597. 8vo, 19th-cent half vellum. B May 12 (1741) HF1,600

Clancy, Tom

— The Hunt for Red October. Anapolis: Naval Institute Press, [1984]. In chipped d/j. cb Dec 12 (31) $350

Anr Ed. Annapolis: Naval Institute Press, [1984]. Orig cloth, in d/j; bds bowed. Sgd. wa Mar 5 (163) $500

— The Sum of All Fears. NY, [1991]. One of 600. pba July 9 (52) $75

— The Hunt for Red October. Annapolis: Naval Institute Press, [1984]. In d/j. Inscr. bbc June 29 (367) $650

Clappe, Louise A.K.S., 1819-1906. See: Grabhorn Printing

Clappe, Louise Amelia Knapp Smith, 1819-1906

— The Shirley Letters from California Mines.... San Francisco, 1922. One of 450. Half cloth. Frontis loose. sg June 18 (51) $110

Clapperton, Capt Hugh. See: Denham & Clapperton

Clare, John, 1793-1864

— The Village Minstrel and Other Poems. L, 1821. 2 vols. 12mo, 19th-cent mor gilt; spines soiled & rubbed. S Apr 28 (597) £450 [Joliffe]

Clarendon, Edward Hyde, 1st Earl of, 1609-74

— A Brief View and Survey of the Dangerous and Pernicious Errors...in...Leviathan. Oxford, 1676. 1st Ed. 4to, 20th-cent half calf; rubbed. Frontis inkstained; tp soiled & dampstained at inner margin. Ck Oct 18 (120) £160

— The History of the Rebellion and Civil Wars in England.... Oxford, 1702-4. 1st Ed. 3 vols. Folio, contemp calf; rubbed. bba Nov 28 (233) £150 [Gammon]

Claret de Flerieu, Charles Pierre, comte, 1738-1810. See: Fleurieu, Charles Pierre Claret de

Claretie, Jules

— Le Pietons de Paris. Paris: Le Livre contemporain, 1911. One of 100, with an extra suite of plates, vignettes & decorative initials bound in. 4to, mor gilt by Rene Kieffer, 1917. Bound in are 8 orig watercolor drawings by Luigi Loir, all sgd. Front wrap sgd by Claretie. Manney copy. P Oct 11 (42) $2,250

Clark, Arthur Henry

— A Bibliography of the Publications of the Rowfant Club. Cleveland, 1925. One of 140. cb Oct 17 (164) $140

Clark, Edwin

— The Britannia and Conway Tubular Bridges. L, 1850. Atlas vol only. Loose in orig half calf. With 46 plates. Some dampstains. pnE Mar 11 (132) £240

Clark, J. H.—&
Dubourg, M.

— An Historical Memento Representing the Different Scenes of Public Rejoicing...Peace of 1814. L, 1814. 4to, modern cloth. 1 leaf torn & creased at outer margin; some soiling. Ck Sept 6 (138) £180

Clark, J. O. M. See: Noel & Clark

Clark, John Heaviside, 1770-1863

— Field Sports of the Native Inhabitants of New South Wales. L, 1813. 4to, contemp half mor. S June 25 (172) £2,000 [McCormack]

— A Practical Illustration of Gilpin's Day.... L, 1811. Folio, old bds with section of orig wraps mtd on upper cover. With 30 hand-colored plates. C May 20 (31) £1,100 [Spelman]

Clark, Sir Kenneth MacKenzie

— A Catalogue of the Drawings of Leonardo da Vinci...at Windsor Castle. Cambr., 1935. 2 vols. 4to, cloth. O July 14 (54) $50

Clark, Robert S.—&
Sowerby, Arthur de C.

— Through Shen-Kan: The Account of the Clark Expedition in North China, 1908-9. L, 1912. 4to, cloth. sg Jan 9 (53) $325

Clark, Roland. See: Derrydale Press

Clark, Sterling B. F., 1825-52

— How Many Miles from St. Jo? San Francisco, 1929. Half cloth. sg June 18 (52) $60

Clark, Thomas Dionysius

— Travels in the Old South. A Bibliography. Norman, [1956-59]. 3 vols. In d/js. cb Oct 17 (165) $170; K Sept 29 (126) $180; O Sept 24 (57) $170

Anr copy. In d/js. sg Oct 31 (91) $275

Anr Ed. Norman, 1969. 3 vols. cb Oct 17 (166) $160

Clark, Walter van Tilburg

— Ten Women in Gale's House and Shorter Poems. Bost.: Christopher Publishing House, [1932]. In chipped & stained d/j. With ALs & ACs. cb Dec 12 (34) $100

Clark, William, 1770-1838

See also: Lewis & Clark; Limited Editions Club

— The Field Notes of Captain William Clark, 1803-1805. New Haven, 1964. Folio, cloth, in d/j. Z Nov 23 (58) $55

Clark, William P., 1845?-84

— Indian Sign Language, with Brief Explanatory Notes of the Gestures.... Phila., 1885. 1st Ed. 8vo, orig cloth; worn, spine faded. With folding map.. Map reinserted with tape. cb Nov 14 (31) $60

Clarke, Adam, 1760?-1832

— A Bibliographical Dictionary. L, 1802-6. 1st Ed. 8 vols, including Supplement, in 4. 12mo, contemp calf gilt; rubbed. Marginal worming at start of Vol IV. bba Jan 30 (2) £170 [Vine]

Anr copy. 8 vols, including Supplement. 12mo, contemp vellum; spine of Vol VIII chipped. bba May 28 (504) £260 [Dawson]

Clarke, Arthur C.

— Against the Fall of Night. NY: Gnome Press, [1953]. sp Apr 16 (372) $50

Anr Ed. NY: Harcourt Brace, [1956]. ("The City and the Stars.") In d/j with edge tear. wa Mar 5 (164) $85

Clarke, Brian. See: Goddard & Clarke

Clarke, Edward Daniel, 1769-1822

— Travels in Various Countries of Europe, Asia and Africa. L, 1810-23. 1st Ed. 6 vols. 4to, contemp half russia gilt; rubbed. With 187 plans, maps & plates, 1 hand-colored. S Nov 15 (1138) £620 [Finch]

Anr Ed. L, 1816-18. 8 vols. 8vo, contemp half calf; worn, some covers detached. With port, 17 maps & 3 plates. Some flyleaves detached or lacking. cb Oct 10 (15) $350

Clarke, Hermann Frederick

— John Coney, Silversmith, 1655-1722. Bost., 1932. One of 365. sp June 18 (328) $150

Clarke, James Stainier, 1765?-1834. See: Fore-Edge Paintings

Clarke, James Stanier, 1765?-1834 —& McArthur, John, 1755-1840

— The Life of Admiral Lord Nelson. L, 1809. 2 vols. 4to, mor gilt cathedral bdg by George Mullen of Dublin, with his ticket. With 12 plates & 5 plans. Some foxing. CNY Oct 8 (42) $3,200

Anr copy. Contemp mor gilt; corners bumped. DW Dec 11 (264) £240

Anr copy. Contemp mor gilt; rebacked preserving spines, worn. With frontis & 16 plates & plans. One folding plate frayed at edges; some spotting & soiling. pn Apr 23 (18) £200 [Storey]

Anr copy. Calf; split. pnE Oct 1 (336) £140

Clarke, R. M.

— The Angler's Desideratum, containing the Best and Fullest Directions.... Edin., 1839. 1st Ed, 2d Issue. 16mo, half calf; rubbed. Koopman copy. O Oct 29 (54) $275

Clarke, Samuel, 1599-1683

— A General Martyrologie, containing a Collection of all the Greatest Persecutions.... L: A.M. for Thomas Underhill & John Rothwell, 1651. Folio, crude half cloth. Minor marginal worming not affecting text; small hole in T4; lacking 2C4. sg Oct 24 (71) $275

Clarke, Samuel A.

— Pioneer Days of Oregon History. Cleveland [Portland]: A. H. Clark, 1905. 1st Ed. 2 vols. Cloth. sg June 18 (444) $90

Clarke, William, Editor of The Monthly Magazine

— Three Courses and a Desert. L, 1830. Illus by George Cruikshank. 8vo, modern half mor gilt; extremities rubbed. With 5 plates. Sgd George Cruikshank and Eugene Field by Eugene Field II. sg Oct 17 (224) $130

Clarke, William, 1640?-84

— The Natural History of Nitre: or, a Philosophical Discourse.... L, 1670. 1st Ed. 8vo, contemp sheep; worn, covers detached. Some browning & soiling. S July 1 (1227) £300 [Knohl]

Clarke, William, fl.1819

— Repertorium Bibliographicum: or, Some Account of the Most Celebrated British Libraries. L, 1819. 2 vols in 1. 8vo, bdg not given. cb Oct 17 (168) $170

Clarkson, Paul S.

— A Bibliography of William Sydney Porter. Caldwell, Idaho, 1938. One of 600. In d/j. cb Oct 17 (169) $120

Clarkson, Thomas, 1760-1846

— A Portraiture of Quakerism as Taken from a View of the Moral Education.... L, 1806. 1st Ed. 3 vols. 8vo, orig bds. sg Mar 5 (63) $150

Anr copy. Contemp sheep. sg June 18 (468) $60

Claude Lorrain (Claude Gelee), 1600-82

— The Beauties of Claude Lorraine. L, 1825. Folio, contemp half lea; worn. With engraved title, port & 24 plates. C Oct 30 (98) £450 [Cormier]

— Liber Veritatis, or a Collection of Prints.... L, 1777-1819. Vols I-II. Contemp mor gilt by H. Walther; spine rubbed. With port & 200 plates. Some browning. C Oct 30 (99) £4,200 [Garisenda]

Anr copy. Contemp half russia gilt; covers detached. 2 plates creased; 1 repaired. DW Mar 11 (800) £3,300

Anr copy. Vols I-II only. Contemp calf gilt; spines rubbed. Minor discoloration, chiefly in margins. S Nov 21 (73) £4,000 [Burgess Browning]

Anr copy. 3 vols. Folio, early 19th-cent calf gilt with Signet arms; rebacked preserving orig spine. With 3 ports & 300 plates. Two plates inverted; some spotting. S Feb 11 (43) £4,600 [Gilgermann]

Anr copy. 19th-cent calf gilt; rubbed, upper cover of Vol III detached. With 2 (of 3) ports & 300 plates. Some spotting, mostly in margins. S June 25 (171) £4,500 [Bifolco]

Anr Ed. L, [c.1840]. 3 vols. Folio, 19th-cent half mor by J. Wright; rubbed. With 3 frontises & 300 plates. Some spotting. S May 14 (921) £2,800 [Maggs]

Claudianus, Claudius

— De raptu Proserpinae. [Venice: Albertinus Rubeus, c.1510]. Folio, early vellum. Some soiling & spotting; 3 leaves browned. C Dec 16 (115) £400 [Paradise]

Clavigero, Francesco Saverio, 1731-87

— Historia antigua de Mexico y de su conquista. L, 1826. 2 vols. 8vo, half calf; spine ends chipped, corners worn & bumped. With 2 folding maps & 19 (of 20) plates. Lacking large piece of 1 map; 1 plate missing upper right portion. Sold w.a.f. wa Apr 9 (86) $65

— The History of Mexico. Collected from Spanish and Mexican Historians.... L, 1787. 1st Ed in English. 2 vols. 4to, modern half calf gilt. With 2 folding maps & 25 plates. Some browning & spotting. FD Dec 2 (447) DM1,100

Anr copy. Modern calf. Penciled marginalia. sg June 18 (176) $1,000

Clavius, Christophus, 1537-1612

— Geometria Practica. Rome: Zannetti, 1604. 4to, contemp vellum; rebacked. Small hole in title; some browning. Inscr. Ck Nov 29 (164) £500

— In sphaeram Joannis de Sacro Bosco commentarius. Rome: Domenico Basa, 1585. 4to, later calf; rubbed. Title & last leaf stained. bba Feb 27 (392) £300 [Bifolco]

Clay, Enid. See: Golden Cockerel Press

Clayden, P. W.

— Rogers and his Contemporaries. [L, 1889]. 4 vols. 8vo, mor gilt; hinges cracked. Lacking titles. Extra-illus with 287 mtd photographs. sg Oct 17 (357) $550

Cleaver, Arthur H. See: Hatton & Cleaver

Clegg, Charles. See: Beebe & Clegg

Clegg, Charles M. See: Beebe & Clegg

Cleland, Thomas Maitland

[-] The Decorative Work of T. M. Cleland. A Record and Review. NY, 1929. One of 55. 4to, half vellum. With a sgd color print by Cleland bound in. With 1 ALs & 2 Ls s & 10 plates of ads by Cleland laid in. sg Sept 26 (75) $400

Clemenceau, Georges

— Au pied de Sinai. Paris, 1898. One of 355 on velin d'Arches. Illus by Toulouse Lautrec. 4to, orig wraps; loose, backstrip cracked. Prelim & final leaves browned; a few leaves spotted. S May 28 (236) £1,600 [Sims Reed]

Clemens, Samuel Langhorne, 1835-1910

See also: Limited Editions Club

— The £1,000,000 Bank-Note and Other Stories. NY, 1893. 1st Ed. 8vo, cloth. cb Dec 12 (144) $90; K Mar 22 (87) $75

— 1601, or, a Fireside Conversation. San Francisco: Windsor Press, 1929. One of 40. Half mor. b&b Feb 19 (304) $125

— The American Claimant. NY, 1892. 1st Ed. 8vo, orig cloth; spine worn. K Sept 29 (128) $55

— Les Aventures de Tom Sawyer. Paris: Bibliotheque Nouvelle de la Jeunesse/ A. Hennuyer, [n.d.]. 4to, orig cloth; hinges tender. 1 margin holed. Epstein copy. sg Apr 29 (465) $1,600

— The Celebrated Jumping Frog of Calaveras County.... NY, 1867. 1st Ed, 1st Ptg. 12mo, orig terra cotta cloth, the frog in lower left corner; rebacked. Inscr, May 9, 1867. CNY Dec 5 (182) $8,500

Anr copy. Orig green cloth, with frog in lower left corner; slight fraying at heel of spine. Arthur Swann-Jules Merron copy. CNY June 9 (17) $8,000

Anr copy. Orig plum cloth, with frog in center; minor restoration at extremities. Manney copy. P Oct 11 (43) $12,000

Anr copy. Orig cloth, frog in lower left corner; extremities worn; rebacked, most of orig spine retained. Title soiled; front free endpaper & ad leaf torn. sg Oct 17 (388) $1,3000

Anr copy. Orig brown cloth, with frog in center with head pointed up; spine ends worn, hinges cracked. Epstein copy. sg Apr 30 (466) $7,000

2d State. Orig green cloth, with frog in lower left corner; small piece of cloth torn from lower front corner. cb Feb 12 (134) $2,000

Anr Ed. NY, 1869. 12mo, cloth; worn. Lacking front free endpaper. Sgd as S. L. Clemens (Mark Twain)), Bret Harte, and Eugene Field by Eugene Field II. sg Oct 17 (245) $375

— Christian Science. NY, 1907. 1st Ed. Orig cloth; some stains. Inscr to Dr. Robert Halsey. CNY June 9 (30) $2,400

— Concerning Cats. Two Tales by Mark Twain. San Francisco: Grabhorn Press for the Book Club of California, 1959. One of 450. 4to, half cloth, in d/j. cb Oct 31 (60) $120; cb Feb 27 (98) $90

— A Connecticut Yankee in King Arthur's Court. NY, 1889. 1st Ed. 8vo, orig cloth; endpapers cracked at inner hinges. Inscr to George L. Bell, 1889. Merron copy. CNY June 9 (26) $7,000

Anr copy. Orig half mor; joints & extremities rubbed, endpapers loose. F June 25 (225) $110

Anr copy. Modern half mor gilt, orig covers bound in. Sgd as S. L. Clemens (Mark Twain) and Eugene Field by Eugene Field II. sg Oct 17 (246) $450

2d Issue. Orig cloth; soiled & rubbed. wa Mar 5 (252) $100

Salesman's Dummy. Cloth. Merron copy. CNY June 9 (25) $2,200

Anr Ed. NY, 1890. 8vo, orig cloth; very worn, inner hinges broken. With extensive sgd pencilled annotations by Dan Beard regarding his illusts. CNY June 9 (33) $3,000

— A Dog's Tale. NY & L, 1904. With 4 plates. cb Dec 12 (133) $50

— A Double Barrelled Detective Story. NY & L, 1902. 1st Ed. Illus by Lucius Hitchcock. Spine faded. cb Dec 12 (134) $; sp Nov 24 (288) $90

— English as She Is Taught.... Bost., [1900]. 1st American Ed, 2d State of p.16, line 5. Wraps. cb Dec 12 (135) $50

Anr copy. Cloth. cb Feb 12 (136) $55

— Following the Equator. Hartford, 1897. 1st Ed. 8vo, orig cloth; rubbed, hinges cracked. bbc Apr 27 (282) $90

Anr copy. Cloth. Salesman's dummy with title, 1 frontis, and a sampling of pages & plates. cb Dec 12 (138) $600

Anr copy. Cloth; front hinge repaired. cb Jan 30 (125) $100

One of 250. Orig cloth; hinges cracked. Epstein copy. sg Apr 30 (467) $3,200

Only known copy in orig 2 vols. 2 vols. 8vo, orig cloth. Consists of sheets of the trade Ed bound up in 2 vols with identical inserted titles, with the frontis & other illusts in the text; Vol I contains text through end of Chapter XXXVIII. Merron copy. CNY June 9 (29) $8,000

Anr Ed. L, 1897. ("More Tramps Abroad.") 8vo, cloth. K Mar 22 (90) $75

— Huckleberry Finn. L, 1884. 1st Ed. 8vo, orig cloth; front cover discolored. cb Feb 12 (131) $600

Anr copy. Orig cloth; front inner hinge torn. Manney copy. P Oct 11 (49) $2,250

Anr copy. Orig cloth; spine chipped. S May 13 (598) £160 [Pearson]

1st American Ed. NY, 1885. 8vo, orig cloth; worn, soiled. Inscr by Twain as Huckleberry Finn. O Nov 26 (183) $150

1st Issue. Orig cloth; corners bumped. K Sept 29 (129) $1,500

Anr copy. Orig cloth; worn. rs Oct 17 (62) $450

Anr copy. ("The Adventures of Huckleberry Finn.") Orig cloth; spine ends chipped, extremities worn, rear hinge cracked. Some foxing & soiling. sg Mar 5 (308) $140

Anr copy. Orig cloth; spine ends frayed, extremities worn. sg Mar 5 (309) $325

Anr copy. Orig cloth; spine ends & bd tips worn, a few marks to covers. With the receipt stamp of The Merchants general agent, W. Gus Chittenden, dated Feb 23, 1885, on front free endpaper. wa Sept 26 (257) $2,300

Early Issue. Orig pictorial green cloth; front cover a little bowed. Merron copy. CNY June 9J (23) $8,000

Anr copy. Orig blue pictorial cloth. Merron copy. CNY June 9 (24) $8,500

Anr copy. Orig cloth; bottom edge of bdg lightly worn, corners bumped. K July 12 (134) $1,100

Anr copy. Orig sheep; rebacked with orig spine preserved, corners restored, inner hinges reinforced. Inscr as a Christmas present to his wife, 1884. Manney copy. P Oct 11 (51) $90,000

Anr copy. Orig cloth; hinges tender. Epstein copy. sg Apr 30 (462) $2,800

Anr copy. Orig cloth; soiled, hinges cracked, ink marks on fore-edge. wa Sept 26 (256) $220

Issue not indicated. Orig cloth; rubbed. S July 1 (1027) £120 [Bentley]

Late Issue. Orig cloth; spine ends chipped, corners showing. pba Aug 20 (218) $150

Mixed Issue. Orig cloth; rubbed, spine ends frayed. K July 12 (135) $250

Anr copy. Orig cloth; worn & soiled. NH Aug 23 (413) $725

Anr copy. Orig cloth; front free endpaper clipped out, extremities rubbed. Sgd, 1886. Manney copy. P Oct 11 (50) $8,000

Anr Ed. West Hatfield MA: Pennyroyal Press, 1985. One of 350 with an extra suite of plates in separate portfolio. Illus by Barry Moser. Folio, orig mor gilt. O Nov 26 (184) $650; sg Jan 30 (127) $1,400

— The Innocents Abroad. Hartford, 1884. 8vo, modern half mor gilt. Sgd as S. L. Clemens (Mark Twain) and Eugene Field by Eugene Field II. sg Oct 17 (248) $350

— Is Shakespeare Dead? NY & L, 1909. 1st Ed, Issue not stated. Cloth, in d/j, unopened. cb Dec 12 (139) $120

— Life on the Mississippi. Bost., 1883. 1st American Ed. 8vo, orig cloth; spine frayed, 1 signature sprung. F Dec 18 (109) $140

1st State. Orig sheep; extremities rubbed. Manney copy. P Oct 11 (48) $2,750

1st State. Orig cloth; lower extremities lightly rubbed. Manney copy. P Oct 11 (47) $2,750

Anr copy. Orig cloth. With "The Suppressed Chapter" laid in. Epstein copy. sg Apr 30 (469) $850

1st Ed. L, 1883. 1st Issue. 8vo, orig cloth; spine faded. bba Feb 27 (150) £190 [Huntley]

Anr copy. Orig cloth. Manney copy. P Oct 11 (46) $1,600; sg Oct 17 (389) $300; sg Oct 17 (390) $425

Anr copy. Orig cloth; front hinge cracked. sg Mar 5 (313) $200

Anr copy. Orig cloth; spine ends chipped, worn, hinges tender. Signature on tp; some stains. wa Sept 26 (258) $120

Salesman's Dummy. Orig cloth. Merron copy. CNY June 9 (22) $2,800

— The Man that Corrupted Hadleyburg.... NY & L, 1900. 1st Ed, 1st state. bbc June 29 (370) $175

— Mark Twain's Autobiography. NY, 1924. 1st Ed. 2 vols. In d/js. sg Oct 17 (391) $80

Anr copy. Orig cloth. sg Mar 5 (314) $110

— Mark Twain's (Burlesque) Autobiography and First Romance. NY, [1871]. 1st Ed, 1st State. 12mo, orig cloth. cb Feb 12 (137) $150

— Mark Twain's Sketches, New and Old. Hartford & Chicago, 1875. 1st Ed, 2d State. 8vo, orig cloth; worn & shaken. O Dec 17 (181) $60

— Mark Twain's Speeches. NY & L, 1910. 1st Ed. Cloth, in d/j. cb Dec 12 (142) $75

— Merry Tales. NY, 1892. 1st Ed. 12mo, cloth; spine rubbed. cb Dec 12 (143) $60

— The Prince and the Pauper. Bost., 1882. 1st American Ed. 8vo, orig cloth; corners rubbed; hinges strengthened. cb Feb 12 (138) $325

Anr copy. Cloth; worn. O May 26 (191) $300

Anr copy. Orig cloth, 1st bdg; spine ends worn. pba Aug 20 (220) $200

Anr copy. Orig cloth; worn, shaken. rs Oct 17 (63) $225

— Pudd'nhead Wilson's Calendar for 1894. Dawson's Landing MO [but NY: The Century Co, 1893]. BAL form C. 76mm by 62mm, orig ptd wraps, wire-stitched as issued. Merron copy. CNY June 9 (27) $2,000

— Pudd'nhead Wilson. Hartford, 1894. 1st American Ed in Book form. 8vo, cloth. cb Dec 12 (145) $110

Anr copy. Orig cloth. cb Dec 12 (150) $375; K Sept 29 (127) $160

Anr copy. Orig cloth; worn & soiled; rear cover stained. O Dec 17 (182) $70; rs Oct 17 (61) $150

Anr copy. Orig cloth; faded. sp Nov 24 (291) $130

— Punch, Brothers, Punch! and other Sketches. NY, [1878]. 1st Ed in Book form, 1st Issue. 16mo, cloth. sg Oct 17 (392) $275

Anr copy. Wraps; corners chipped. Epstein copy. sg Apr 30 (4770) $350

— The Quaker City Holy Land Excursion.... NY: M. Harzof, 1927. One of 200. Wraps. cb Dec 12 (146) $225

— Roughing It. Hartford, 1877. Eighty-Fifth Thousand. 8vo, orig cloth; rubbed. Some foxing. bbc Apr 27 (283) $50

Anr Ed. Kentfield CA, 1953. One of 200. Wood veneer over bds backed with a red paper spine. cb Oct 31 (8) $140

— The Stolen White Elephant, etc. Bost., 1882. 1st American Ed. 16mo, orig cloth; spine ends worn, 1 signature starting. Inscr to his nephew, Will M. Clemens. Merron copy. CNY June 9 (21) $4,000

Anr copy. Orig cloth; rubbed. Leaf 2.1 with short tear at lower margin. Inscr to U. S. Grant, Jr. Manney copy. P Oct 11 (45) $6,500

— Tom Sawyer. Hartford, 1876. 1st American Ed, 1st Ptg. 8vo, orig cloth with gilt edges (748 so bound); minor rubbing, endpapers cracked at inner hinge. Merron copy. CNY June 9 (18) $9,000

Anr copy. Orig half mor gilt (200 so bound); minor rubbing at extremities, small stain at front upper joint. Merron copy. CNY June 9 (19) $11,000

Anr copy. Orig mor gilt; spine & corners repaired, inner hinges reinforced, spine & corners with minor repair, inner hinges reinforced, contemp newpaper clippings mtd on front flyleaves. Manney copy. P Oct 11 (44) $13,000

Anr copy. Orig cloth; hinges cracked. Epstein copy. sg Apr 30 (463) $8,500

2d Ptg. Orig cloth; front hinge splitting, spine frayed, bottom corner of front free endpaper torn off. Some smudges & edge tears. bbc Apr 27 (284) $300

— Tom Sawyer Abroad.... NY, 1894. 1st Ed. 8vo, orig cloth. cb Feb 12 (139) $500

— Tom Sawyer Abroad, Tom Sawyer Detective.... NY, 1896. 8vo, orig cloth; soiled. With frontis & 45 plates, 1 plate in the text Tp soiled & wrinkled. F Sept 26 (517) $90

— A Tramp Abroad. Hartford & L, 1880. 1st Ed. 8vo, orig cloth; worn. cb Dec 12 (151) $140

Anr copy. Orig cloth; faded, spine ends frayed. cb Feb 12 (141) $150

Anr copy. Orig cloth; rubbed & worn, inner hinges starting. Stain on blank side of port. K July 12 (133) $55

Anr copy. Orig cloth; spine ends chipped. NH Oct 6 (81) $55

Anr copy. Later calf; chipped. rs Oct 17 (60) $375

Anr copy. Modern mor gilt, orig cloth covers bound in. Sgd as S. L. Clemens

(Mark Twain)and Eugene Field by Eugene Field II. sg Oct 17 (249) $550

Anr copy. Orig cloth. Epstein copy. sg Apr 30 (471) $1,500

— Works. NY, [1907]. Author's National Ed. 25 vols. b&b Feb 19 (131) $125

Definitive Ed, one of—1,024. NY, 1922-25. 37 vols. Orig half cloth; spines soiled, scuffed. A few leaves badly opened. wa Mar 5 (253) $1,000

Stormfield Ed. NY, [1929]. 37 vols. Half mor gilt; upper joint of Vol 37 cracked, head of spine on Vol 36 chipped. P June 17 (331) $4,250

Clemens's copy, Samuel Langhorne

— Giles, Herbert A. - Great Religions of the World. NY, 1901. Sgd, 15 Sept 1901 & with c.69 words of annotation in his hand in pencil on 18 pages. CNY Dec 5 (183) $3,000

— Kingsley, Charles. - The Heroes or Greek Fairy Tales for My Children. Chicago: Donohue, Henneberry, [1900?]. 12mo, orig cloth. Tp detached; leaves browned. Annotated by Clemens. Doheny copy. P June 17 (160) $2,500

— Lecky, William Edward Hartpole. - History of European Morals from Augustus to Charlemagne. NY, 1874. 2 vols. 8vo, orig cloth; worn, shaken. Sgd in each vol & with c.78 annotations totalling c.929 words in pencil & inks on 68 pages. CNY Dec 5 (184) $11,000

— Trevelyan, Sir George Otto. - The Life and Letters of Lord Macaulay. NY, 1876. 1 vol (of 2). 8vo, orig cloth; portions of spine lacking, front cover with 1st 80 pages detached. With some 67 annotations in pencil totalling c.304 words on 44 pages. CNY Dec 5 (186) $3,500

Clemens, Samuel Langhorne, 1835-1910 —& Harte, Bret, 1836-1902

— Sketches of the Sixties.... San Francisco, 1926. 1st Ed, One of 2,000. Half cloth, in tattered d/j. cb Oct 31 (42) $160

Anr copy. Half cloth, in chipped d/j. cb Dec 12 (148) $80

Clemens, Samuel Langhorne, 1835-1910 —& Warner, Charles Dudley, 1829-1900

— The Gilded Age. Hartford, 1874. 8vo, orig cloth; rubbed, front free endpaper lacking. bbc Apr 27 (280) $60

Anr copy. Half mor; rubbed. O Mar 31 (183) $85

Anr Ed. Hartford, 1884. 8vo, modern half mor gilt. Sgd as S. L. Clemens (Mark Twain) and Eugene Field by Eugene Field II. sg Oct 17 (247) $350

Clement, of Alexandria

— Opera. Florence: Laurentius Torrentinus, 1550. 1st Ed. Folio, 16th-cent pigskin over pastebds.. Tp browned; wormholes in final leaf. S Dec 5 (84) £1,500 [Jackson]

Clement, Hal, Pseud.

— Mission of Gravity. Garden City, 1954. In d/j with spine & corners worn. sg June 11 (64) $200

Clement-Janin, Noel

— Essai sur la bibliophilie contemporaine de 1900 a 1928. Paris, [1931-32]. One of 500. 2 vols. Folio, half mor, orig wraps bound in. This copy reserved for the pbr in his own hand & sgd by him. S July 1 (1185) £250

Clerk, John, 1728-1812

— An Essay on Naval Tactics. L, 1790-97. 1st Ed. 2 vols. 4to, orig bds; Vol I backstrip cracked. sg May 7 (61) $450

2d Ed. Edin., 1804. 4to, contemp calf; upper joints split. With 52 folding plates. Some spotting. bba Oct 24 (188) £150 [Lewcock]

Clouet Jean Baptiste Louis

— Geographie moderne.... Paris, 1787. Folio, half calf; worn, front cover detached, spine def. cb Oct 10 (117) $450

Clouzot, Henri

— Le Style moderne dans la decoration interieure. Paris, [c.1925]. Folio, loose in half cloth portfolio as issued. With 36 plates. sg Apr 2 (145) $200

Clouzot, Henri —& Follot, Charles

— Histoire du papier peint en France. Paris, 1935. 4to, orig wraps; spine ends chipped with some tears. sg Sept 6 (288) $300

Clowes, Sir William Laird, 1856-1905

— The Royal Navy. L, 1897-1903. 7 vols. 4to, orig cloth; Vol III hinge worn, covers stained. b June 22 (237) £350

Club. See: Puckle, James

Cluverius, Philippus, 1580-1622

— Introductionis in universam geographiam.... Amst.: Elzevir, 1661. 12mo, contemp calf. With engraved title, folding chart & 38 double-page maps. cb Dec 5 (50) $750

Anr Ed. Wolffenbuettel, 1694. ("Introductio in omnem geographiam.") 4to, contemp vellum bds; stained. With engraved title, 3 plates, 43 folding maps & 2 folding tables. Some Ms sidenotes & underlinings; browned. pn Nov 14 (434) £420

Anr Ed. Amst.: Johannes Wolters, 1697. 4to, contemp vellum; soiled. With engraved title & 43 double-page or folding maps & 3 engraved diagrams. Blindstamp on title; some soiling; 1 map torn without loss. pn Mar 19 (415) £1,400

— Italia antiqua. Leiden: Elzevir, 1624. 1st Ed. In 2 vols. Folio, contemp vellum bds; spines worn. With 15 double-page maps. DW May 13 (264) £470

Coates, Charles, 1746?-1813

— The History and Antiquities of Reading. L, 1802-[10]. 2 parts in 1 vol. 4to, contemp calf. With folding plan & 7 plates, including 1 folding. Lower margins of 2 plates trimmed. Inscr. bba Sept 19 (181) £240 [Princeton Rare Books]

Cobbett, William, 1763-1835
See also: Forsyth, William

— The American Gardener. L, 1821. 12mo, orig bds; spine lacking. Some spotting. bba June 11 (83) £50 [Henly]

Anr copy. Modern half cloth. Some browning & foxing. sg June 18 (178) $70

— Cobbett's Tour in Scotland; and in the Four Northern Counties of England.... L, 1833. 12mo, orig half cloth. bba June 11 (94) £90 [Quaritch]

— The English Gardener.... L, 1829. 8vo, contemp half calf; spine lacking, upper cover detached. Tp & front free endpaper waterstained. bba June 11 (90) £75 [Sotheran]

2d Ed. L, 1833. 8vo, orig half cloth; rubbed. Inscr by the author's son. bba June 11 (95) £130 [Fetzer]

— Rural Rides in the Counties of Surrey, Kent, Sussex.... L, 1930. One of 1,000. Illus by John Nash. 3 vols. Orig half cloth. pnE Oct 1 (314) £60; pnE Mar 11 (39) $95

— A Treatise on Cobbett's Corn, Containing Instructions for Propagating and Cultivating the Plant.... L, 1828. 1st Ed. 12mo, contemp calf. bba June 11 (89) £110 [Fellner]

— The Woodlands. L, 1825 [but 1828]. 1st Ed. 8vo, contemp half calf; worn, covers detached. bba June 11 (88) £70 [Sotheran]

— A Year's Residence in the United States of America.... L, 1822. 8vo, contemp calf; rubbed. Last leaf cropped affecting text; folding map repaired. bba June 11 (86) £50 [Sotheran]

Cobden-Sanderson, Thomas James, 1840-1922

— Ecce Mundus. Industrial Ideals and the Book Beautiful. Hammersmith, 1902. Orig half vellum. cb Oct 17 (175) $75

— The Journals.... NY, 1926. One of 1,000. 2 vols. cb Oct 17 (176) $150

Coburn, Alvin Langdon

— London. L & NY, 1909. Folio, bds; lea spine flaked & very worn. With 20 mtd plates. sg Apr 13 (32) $3,600

— Men of Mark. L, 1913. 4to, cloth; spine soiled. With 33 tipped-in photogravures. cb Feb 12 (25) $900

Cochin, Charles Nicolas, 1699-1773. See: Gravelot & Cochin

Cochin, Charles Nicolas, 1715-90 —& Bellicard, Jerome Charles, 1726-86

— Observations sur les antiquities d'Herculanum. Paris, 1755. 2d Ed. 12mo, contemp sheep gilt; spine ends chipped. With 40 on 33 plates. sg Oct 24 (72) $150

Anr copy. Contemp sheep; extremities rubbed, joints cracked. Some foxing, generally not affecting plates. sg Feb 6 (60) $150

Cochrane, George

— Wanderings in Greece. L, 1837. 2 vols. 8vo, orig cloth; joints torn. With 3 litho folding maps & plans & 6 litho plates. S June 30 (263) £550 [Chelsea]

Cochrane, John Dundas

— Narrative of a Pedestrian Journey through Russia and Siberian Tartary. L, 1825. 3d Ed. 2 vols. 8vo, recent cloth. With 2 folding maps. DW Apr 8 (22) £50

Cockburn, Sir George, 1772-1853

— A Voyage to Cadiz and Gibraltar. L, 1815. 1st Ed. 2 vols. 8vo, recent calf gilt. With 2 engraved titles, 3 folding maps. 3 emgraved plates & 23 plain plates. Title & folding map of Sicily in Vol II relaid. DW Mar 4 (12) £190

Cockburn, James Pattison, 1779?-1847. See: Donaldson & Cockburn

Cockburn, John, 1652-1729

— The History and Examination of Duels. L, 1720. 1st Ed. 8vo, later 18th-cent calf gilt. sg Mar 26 (81) $350

— The History of Duels. Edin.: Pvtly ptd, 1888. One of 275. 2 vols in 1. 8vo, cloth. sg Mar 26 (82) $80

Cocker, Edward, 1631-75

— Magnum in parvo, or the Pens Perfection. L, [1675]. Oblong 4to, mor by Bumpus. With engraved title & 25 plates. Pages 3-8 only of ptd text at end; browned; a few leaves with marginal repairs, just touching illust on tp. C Dec 16 (247) £550 [Franks]

Cockerell, Sir Sydney C.

— Old Testament Miniatures: a Medieval Picture Book.... NY, [1969]. Folio, cloth. K Dec 1 (249) $100

Anr copy. Cloth, in d/j. sg Oct 31 (198) $50; sg Dec 19 (35) $120; sg Feb 6 (61) $50

Cocles, Bartholomaeus

— La Physionomie naturelle, et la chiromancie. Rouen, 1698. 12mo, contemp calf; spine ends chipped, corners worn. sg Mar 12 (206) $325

Cocteau, Jean, 1889-1963

— Dessins. Paris, 1923. One of 400. 4to, contemp mor gilt, orig wraps bound in. DW Oct 9 (561) £640

Anr Ed. Paris, 1924. 4to, vellum gilt. CGen Nov 18 (341) SF1,500

— Essai de critique indirecte, le mystere laic.... Paris, 1932. One of 300. 4to, orig wraps, unopened. Inscr to Boris Kochno. SM Oct 11 (448) FF5,800

— Le Grand Ecart. Paris, 1923. Half mor by Gras, orig wraps bound in. Inscr to Henri Massis, May 1923 & with later ALs. S May 28 (296) £650 [Lardanchet]

— Leone. Paris, 1945. One of 40 hors commerce. 4to, orig bds. Inscr to Boris Kochno, 1962. SM Oct 12 (452) FF13,000

— Le Livre blanc. Paris, 1928. Out-of-series copy. 4to, orig wraps, unopened. With 2 photographs of Cocteau. Kochno copy. SM Oct 12 (444) FF17,000

— Maison de Sante. Paris: Briant-Robert, 1926. One of 100 on japon imperial. Bds; spines worn. With 31 plates. With orig drawing on verso of half-title, inscr to the Marquise de Polignac. CGen Nov 18 (340) SF60,000

— Les Monstres sacres. Paris, 1940. One of 20 hors commerce. Orig wraps, unopened. Inscr to Christian Berard. Kochno copy. SM Oct 12 (451) FF4,200

— Le Mystere de Jean L'Oiseleur. Paris: Edouard Champion, 1925. One of 142. 4to, loose as issued. CGen Nov 18 (337) SF8,000

— Mythologie. Paris, 1934. One of 130, with 10 plates numbered & sgd by artist. Illus by Giorgio di Chirico. 4to, orig half cloth folder. CGen Nov 18 (343) SF20,000

— Oedipe-Roi, Romeo et Juliette.... Paris, 1928. Orig wraps, unopened. Inscr to Boris Kochno. SM Oct 12 (445) FF2,500

— Orphee. L, 1933. One of 100. Trans by Carl Wildman; illus by Picasso. Orig cloth; marked. S Nov 14 (9) £420 [Leutsch-Dorner]

— Poesie 1916-1923. Paris, [1925]. Mor by Devauchelle with design featuring 2 multicolored faces, orig wraps bound in. Inscr with an ink drawing of a head on half-title. S May 28 (297) £900 [Beres]

— Poesies 1917-1920. Paris, 1920. One of 1,032. Mor extra by Devauchelle, orig wraps bound in. With ALs, 18 Sept 1919 & with later inscr with an ink drawing of a face on a prelim leaf. S May 28 (294) £500 [Saxhof]

— Reines de la France. Paris, 1949. Copy XIV, ptd for Boris Kochno. Illus by Christian Berard. 4to, unbound in orig wraps. With series of 51 proofs, including 17 duplicates, 17 of the sheets initialled by the artist, some hand-colored. SM Oct 11 (519) FF10,000

— Renaud et Armide. Paris, 1945. One of 5 hors commerce on Madagascar. Illus by Christian Berard. 4to, orig wraps, unopened. Inscr to Boris Kochno & with related material. SM Oct 11 (520) FF15,000

— Le Sang d'un Poete. Paris, 1948. One of 20 on velin d'Arches hors commerce. Illus by Sacha Masour. 4to, mor by Micheline de Bellefroid, orig wraps bound in. With 50 photographic illusts. With related material bound in, including 27 photographs by Sacha Masour, all of them prints from which illusts were reproduced. S May 28 (298) £1,200 [Filipacchi]

Codex

— Codex Barberini. Balt., 1940. ("The Badianus Manuscript: an Aztec Herbal of 1552.") Trans by Emily W. Emmart. 4to, orig cloth. Library markings. sg May 14 (35) $120

— Codex Durmachensis. Lausanne & Freiburg, 1960. ("Evangeliorum quattuor Codex Durmachensis.") One of 650. 2 vols. Folio, orig mor. CG Oct 7 (532) £700

Anr copy. Orig pigskin. S July 1 (1167) £550

Anr copy. Lea. sg Nov 7 (25) $225

— Codex Lindisfarnensis. Evangeliorum quattuor. Oltun & Lausanne, 1956-60. One of 680. 2 vols. Folio, orig half vellum. pn May 14 (48) £480 [Forster]; S July 1 (1168) £900

Codice...

— Codice diplomatico del sacro militare ordine Gerosolimitano oggi di Malta. Lucca, 1733-37. 2 vols. Folio, vellum. With 3 folding maps, folding table & 13 plates. S June 30 (67) £2,600 [Bank of Cyprus]

Codrington, Kenneth de Burgh

— L'Inde ancien des origins a l'epoque gupta.... Paris, [1928]. Folio, orig cloth; shelf number on spine. With 76 plates. Library markings. K July 12 (286) $75

Cody, William F., 1846-97
See also: Inman & Cody

— The Life of Hon. William F. Cody. Known as Buffalo Bill.... Hartford: Frank E. Bliss, [1879]. 8vo, orig cloth; joints & extremities restored, gilding retouched. Doheny-Manney copy. P Oct 11 (54) $3,250

Coe, Eva J. See: Bolton & Coe

Coghlan, Margaret

— Memoirs.... Dublin, 1794. 1st Ed. 2 vols. 12mo, contemp calf; rubbed. O Mar 31 (36) $110

Cohn, Albert Mayer

— A Bibliographical Catalogue of the Printed Works Illustrated by George Cruikshank. L, 1914. Bdg extremities rubbed. sg Oct 31 (92) $150; sg Nov 7 (46) $175

Cohn, David L.

— New Orleans and its Living Past. Bost., 1941. One of 1,000. Illus by Clarence John Laughlin. 4to, cloth. sg Apr 13 (59) $325

Coignet, Matthieu

— Politique Discourses upon Trueth and Lying. L: Ralfe Newberie, 1586. 4to, modern calf. Tp cropped at head & repaired at inner margin; a few other headlines cropped; small hole in contents leaf affecting text; foot of O1 burned just affecting signature; lacking last 3 leaves. STC 5486. S Feb 11 (495) £260 [Clarke]

Coit, Daniel Wadsworth, 1787-1876. See: Grabhorn Printing

Coke, Sir Edward, 1552-1634

— The First Part of the Institutes of the Lawes of England.... L, 1639. 4th Ed. Folio, contemp calf; worn. Some dampstaining; tear in 2D3. STC 15787. S July 1 (1078) £180 [Feinberg]

— The Second Part of the Institutes.... L, 1662. Folio, contemp sheep; worn, needs re-backing. sg Mar 12 (52) $475

Coke, Henry John

— A Ride over the Rocky Mountains to Oregon and California.... L, 1852. 1st Ed. 8vo, modern half mor. Some foxing. sg June 18 (179) $225

Colahan, Colin

— Max Meldrum; his Art and Views. Melbourne, [n.d.]. Wraps. kh Nov 11 (69) A$220

Colange, Leo de

— Voyages and Travels or Scenes in Many Lands. Bost.: Walker, [1887]. 4 vols. 4to, orig bdg; corners bumped. sp June 18 (253) $65

Colardeau, Charles Pierre

— Le Temple de Gnide. Paris, [1773?]. 8vo, contemp sheep gilt. Some plates browned. sg Mar 12 (53) $90

Colbatch, Sir John, d.1729

— Novum Lumen Chirurgicum: or, a New Light of Chirurgery. L, 1695. 8vo, Modern half calf. Lacking a1. bba Sept 5 (269) £300 [Keys]

Colden, Cadwallader, 1688-1776

— The History of the Five Indian Nations of Canada.... L, 1747. 2 parts in 1 vol. 8vo, contemp calf; upper cover detached. With folding map. S Nov 15 (1222) £350 [Ruddell]

2d English Ed. L, 1750. 8vo, contemp calf; joints weak. With folding map. S Nov 15 (1221) £200 [Beeleigh Abbey]

Colden, Cadwallader David, 1769-1834

— Memoir, Prepared at the Request of a Committee...Celebration of the Completion of the New York Canals. NY, 1825. 4to, mor gilt by Wilson & Nichols tooled with arms of City of New York in both center panels; rubbed, joints worn, covers bowed. First few leaaves dampstained & with marginal corrosion. Sold w.a.f. Richard Riker's copy, inscr to his daughter, 1839. With ALs from Riker to Charles Rhind, 1826, inserted. O Nov 26 (40) $850

Coldewey, Jan. See: Keulemans & Coldewey

Cole, G. —&
Roper, J.

— The British Atlas. L, 1810. Folio, contemp half mor; worn. With 58 maps, colored in outline & 21 city plans. DW Apr 8 (91) £860

Anr copy. Syn. Some browning & soiling. pn Apr 23 (296) £750

Anr copy. 19th-cent half calf; worn, covers detached. With 58 hand-colored maps & 21 town plans. Occasional spotting. S July 1 (1399) £900 [Nicholson]

Cole, George Watson. See: Church Library, Elihu Dwight

Cole, Timothy, 1852-1931

— Old Dutch and Flemish Masters. NY, 1895. One of 65. Folio, bds; worn. NH Aug 23 (22) $100

Colebrook, Robert H.

— Twelve Views of Places in the Kingdom of Mysore.... L, 1793. Oblong folio, half calf; def. With 12 plates. Title & text leaves to 1st 4 plates punctured within neatlines. S May 14 (1285) £760 [R. S. Books]

2d Ed. L, 1805. Folio, contemp half calf; rebacked preserving orig backstrip. With 12 hand-colored plates. C Oct 30 (19) £1,200 [Shapero]

Coleridge, Henry Nelson, 1798-1843

— Six Months in the West Indies. L, 1826. 2d Ed. 8vo, contemp calf gilt. With map. Ck May 15 (85) £120

Coleridge, Samuel Taylor

— Works. L, 1835-73. 23 vols. 8vo, later mor gilt by Zaehnsdorf; extremities rubbed. One of the 2 litho frontises detached. Ck Nov 29 (70) £550

Coleridge, Samuel Taylor, 1772-1834

See also: Wordsworth & Coleridge

— Christabel; Kubla Khan, a Vision; the Pains of Sleep. L, 1816. 1st Ed. 8vo, mor gilt; spine darkened. CNY Dec 5 (204) $1,000

Anr copy. Recased in wraps. Marginal repair. Epstein copy. sg Apr 29 (85) $1,200

— The Literary Remains. L: Pickering, 1836-38. 1st Ed. 4 vols. 8vo, half lea. Met Apr 28 (874D) $80

— Poetical Works. L, 1840. 3 vols. 8vo, contemp mor gilt. S Apr 28 (599) £200 [Papper]

— The Rime of the Ancient Mariner. L, 1876. Illus by Gustave Dore. Folio, orig cloth; spine crudely tape-repaired. With frontis & 38 plates. cb Sept 26 (76) $95

Anr Ed. L, 1903. One of 150. Orig vellum; soiled & with a few brown stains at lower corner. Ptd on vellum. wa Sept 26 (67) $160

Anr Ed. L, [1910]. Illus by Willy Pogany. 4to, orig mor gilt. With 20 colored plates. bba Apr 9 (320) £190 [M. Edwards]; K July 12 (415) $65

Anr Ed. Bristol: Douglas Cleverdon, 1929. One of 400. Illus by David Jones. 4to, half cloth; rubbed. DW Mar 11 (515) £520

Anr Ed. L, 1945. One of 700. Illus by Duncan Grant. Bound in ostrich hide. With 5 colored plates. cb Oct 31 (84) $100

— Works. L, 1847-53. 22 vols. 8vo, contemp calf; rebacked, some corners repaired. pn Apr 23 (77) £500 [Holleyman & Treacher]

— Zapolya: a Christmas Tale. L, 1817. 1st Ed. 8vo, contemp cloth. Lacking half-title; tp soiled. Milne copy. Ck June 12 (36) £80

Colette, Sidonie Gabrielle, 1873-1954

— Bella-Vista. Paris, 1937. Orig wraps. Inscr to Christian Berard. Kochno copy. SM Oct 12 (457) FF3,000

— Cheri. With: La Fin de Cheri. Paris, 1920-26. 2 vols. 12mo, mor gilt by L. Leveque, orig wraps bound in. Both inscr to Rachide. Bound at end of 2d work is fair copy of 50 Ms pages which were omitted from the first 1,000 ptd. S May 28 (302) £1,200 [Lib. Panini]

— La Treille muscate. Paris, 1932. One of 20 with a suite of the 36 illusts & a further 11 etchings, all on japon. Mor extra by P. L. Martin, 1963. Inscr by Segonzac. S May 28 (233) £16,000 [Lardanchet]

Coley, Henry, 1633-95?

— Clavis Astrologiae Elimata: or, a Key to the Whole Art of Astrology.... L, 1676. 2d Ed. 3 parts in 1 vol. 8vo, old half sheep; rubbed. End matter of Part 3 incomplete; old annotations; tp cut down with minor loss of text. F Sept 26 (613) $60

Collado, Luigi

— Pratica Manuale di arteglieria. Venice: Pietro Dusinelli, 1586. Folio, later vellum. With 2 folding woodcut plates & 35 woodcuts in text. Some spotting. S July 1 (1229) £450 [American Mus.]

Anr Ed. Milan: Filippo Ghisolfi, 1641. Folio, 19th-cent half calf. With 26 folding woodcut plates. S July 1 (1228) £300 [Toscani]

Collaert, Adriaen, d.1618

— Florilegium.... [Antwerp, c.1650]. Folio, disbound. With 23 (of 25) plates, including title & frontis. Lacking plates 7 & 14. S June 25 (10) £950 [Franks]

Collection....

— Collection de peintre antiques qui ornoient les palais...des Empereurs Tite, Trajan.... Rome, 1781. Folio, old wraps; rebacked, worn. With 33 hand-colored plates. bba Apr 9 (262) £380 [Erlini]

— Collection de Costumes Suisses. [Lucerne, c.1830]. 8vo, early cloth; spine worn & def. With 30 hand-colored plates. bbc Dec 9 (83) $2,100

— A Collection of Pretty Poems for the Amusement of Children Three Foot High. By Tommy Tagg, Esq. L: Newbery, 1756. 12mo, calf. With 62 woodcuts. Tears on A2 damaging a letter, on B1 costing 3 words, on F4 touching a letter, & on I6 damaging the page numbers; some soiling & early ink marks on a few cuts. Schiller-Manney copy. P Oct 11 (1236) $5,500

— A Collection of the Dresses of Different Nations, Ancient and Modern.... L, 1757-72. Vols I-II (of 4). Calf; lacking backboard of Vol I and front cover of Vol II; others detached. With 240 uncolored plates. 1 plate torn, a few pp loose. bba Mar 26 (169) £350 [Finney]

Anr copy. Early 19th-cent half mor; worn, bds detached & crudely mended with tape. With 234 plates only, all hand-colored. Marginal crimp to a few plates; a few repaired marginal tears to text; library markings not affecting text or plates. wa Sept 26 (574) $1,100

— A Collection of Old Ballads. L, [n.d.]. Facsimile reprint. 3 vols. 8vo, contemp half calf. bba Apr 9 (53) £120 [Abdullah]

Collier, Jeremy, 1650-1726

— Essays upon Several Moral Subjects. L, [c.1700]. 8vo, contemp calf. sg Mar 26 (83) $100

— A Short View of the Immorality and Profaneness of the English Stage. L, 1699. 8vo, later cloth. Preface misbound; tp mtd on a stub. K July 12 (176) $80

Collier, John
See also: Nonesuch Press

— No Traveller Returns. L, 1931. One of 210. 8vo, orig velveteen gilt. Presentation copy, sgd. bba Apr 30 (163) £110 [Axe]

Collier, John, 1708-86

— Human Passions Delineated, by Timothy Bobbin, Esq. L, 1810. ("The Passions Humourously Delineated by Timothy Bobbin....") 4to, contemp half calf; rubbed. With extra title, port & 25 plates. Corner of 1 plate torn & repaired. bba Oct 10 (166) £200 [Hildebrandt]

Collier, John Payne, 1789-1883
See also: Limited Editions Club

— Farther Particulars regarding Shakespeare and his works. L, 1839. One of 50. 8vo, orig half lea; spine ends chipped. Inscr to the Rev. Joseph Hunter, to whom the work was addressed. sg Mar 5 (211) $475

— Punch and Judy. L, 1828. Illus by George Cruikshank. 8vo, mor gilt by Riviere; edges worn, front hinge cracked. With 24 plates in 2 states, 1 state hand-colored. sg Oct 17 (157) $650

2d Ed. 8vo, mor by Morrell; rubbed. With 24 hand-colored plates. Some staining & foxing. O Feb 25 (159) $325

Colling, James Kellaway

— Details of Gothic Architecture. L, [1856]. 2 vols. 4to, half mor; worn. Library markings. sg Apr 2 (5) $175

— Suggestions in Design. Being a Comprehensive Series.... L, [1880-81]. 4to, orig cloth; hinge cracked. With frontis & 100 plates. cb Sept 26 (149) $250

Collins, ——

— The Chapter of Kings.... L, 1818. 16mo, orig half lea; worn. Engraved throughout, with pictorial title & 37 hand-colored illusts. bba July 23 (30) £140 [Sotheran]

Collins, Arthur, 1690?-1760

— The Peerage of England. L, 1756. 8 (of 9) vols. 4to, lea. sp Apr 16 (262) $90

Anr Ed. L, 1812. 9 vols. 8vo, lea; some covers detached; spines chipped. sp Feb 6 (145) $200

Collins, David, 1756-1810

— An Account of the English Colony in New South Wales. L, 1798-1802. 1st Ed. Vol I only in 2 vols. Contemp half calf; worn, repaired. With 2 maps & 18 plates. Small burnhole in L11 touching text. Gov. Philip Gidley King's copy, sgd, interleaved & annotated; extra-illus with 2 folding maps (both torn) & 17 extra plates. S June 25 (110) £12,500 [Maggs]

Anr copy. 2 vols in 1. 4to, contemp calf gilt; rebacked. With 24 plates & maps. S June 25 (129) £900 [Arnold]

2d Ed. L, 1804. 4to, contemp calf; rebacked. With port, 2 maps, plan & 22 plates, 3 hand-colored. Lacking ad leaf; several uncolored plates reversed at rebacking, obscuring imprints. S Nov 21 (376) £500 [Shapero]

Collins, Capt. Greenville

— Great Britain's Coasting Pilot. L, 1693. 1st Ed. Parts 1 & 2 in 1 vol. Folio, contemp calf; rubbed, upper cover scored, joints weak. With frontises & 48 charts. Some worming; small hole in margin of b1. Ck Dec 11 (210) £2,600

Anr Ed. L, 1792. Folio, modern calf. With 48 charts, 45 of them double-page. Some spotting & staining. C May 20 (243) £2,400 [Burgess]

Collins, Samuel, 1619-70

— The Present State of Russia. L, 1671. 8vo, contemp calf; rubbed. With port & 6 plates. Rust-hole in E8, affecting text; some browning; a few holes & tears. S Nov 15 (1111) £400 [Kunkler]

Collins, Wilkie, 1824-89

See also: Dickens & Collins

— The Moonstone. L, 1868. 1st Ed. 3 vols. 8vo, orig cloth; color retouched, upper cover of Vol I buckling with some abrading & repair in lower portion. Minor defs; a few gatherings in Vol II slightly sprung. Slater-Manney copy. P Oct 11 (56) $11,000

Anr copy. Early 20th-cent half calf by Birdsall; rubbed, joints split, covers loose. Some spotting & staining; lacking some ads. S May 13 (601) £650 [Johnson]

— No Name. L, 1862. 1st Ed. 3 vols. 8vo, orig cloth; soiled, extremities rubbed. bba July 23 (412) £700 [Valentine]

— The Queen of Hearts. L, 1859. 1st Ed. 3 vols. 8vo, orig cloth; rubbed. Epstein copy. sg Apr 29 (86) $9.500

— Rambles Beyond Railways. L, 1851. 1st Ed. 8vo, contemp cloth; rebacked, rubbed, new endpapers. With 12 color plates. Head of tp cropped. bba July 23 (410) £75 [Jarndyce]

— The Woman in White. NY, 1860. 3 vols. 8vo, orig cloth; extremities worn. bba July 23 (411) £320 [Spademan]

Anr copy. Orig cloth; spine ends & edges worn. bbc Apr 27 (287) $340

Anr copy. Orig cloth; minor rubbing. Manney copy. P Oct 11 (55) $5,000

Anr copy. Orig cloth; worn, hinges tender. Text spotted. sg Oct 17 (133) $450

Collis, J.

— The Builders' Portfolio of Street Architecture.... L, 1837. Folio, cloth. With litho title & 30 plates. Some stains & foxing. O Dec 17 (45) $160

Collodi, Carlo, Pseud., 1826-90

— Le Aventure di Pinocchio. Florence, 1883. 1st Ed. 8vo, orig cloth; recased with endpapers renewed, joints repaired, rubbed. Some browning & soiling; p. 65 repaired across page with slight misalignment; marginal tears & repaired; illust on p. 101 partially inked in. Manney copy. P Oct 11 (57) $13,000

— The Story of a Puppet, or the Adventures of Pinocchio. L, 1892. 8vo, orig cloth; spine soiled. bba July 23 (251) £650 [Valentine]

Anr copy. Orig cloth. Marginal tear in P1 affecting 1 letter; some browning at back. Manney copy. P Oct 11 (58) $3,250

Colloquium...

— Colloquium zu Altenburgk, in Meissen, vom Artikel der Rechtfertigung vor Gott. Jena, 1569. Folio, contemp blind-tooled pigskin over wooden bds. Some browning. sg Oct 24 (73) $650

Colman, Benjamin

— It is a fearfyl thing to fall into the hands of the Living God. A Sermon Preached to some miserable Pirates July 15, 1726. Bost., 1726. 12mo, half mor gilt by Bennett. Marginal repairs; browned; fore-margins of B2 & B3 frayed with loss; top margins of F1 & F2 renewed, affecting 3 headlines & 1 pagination; lacking half-title. DuPont copy. CNY Oct 8 (203) $350

Cologne

— Christlicher und Catholische Gegenberichtung eyns Erwirdigen Dhomcapittels zu Coellen. Cologne: Jaspar von Gennep, 1544. Foli, blind-tooled calf over pastebds. Wormhole in inner margin of 1st few leaves. S Dec 5 (87) £650 [Schwing]

Colonna, Francesco, d.1527

— Hypnerotomachia Poliphili. Venice: Aldus, Dec 1499. Folio, 18th-cent calf; joints & 2 corners restored; head of spine chipped; corners rubbed. Title and a few other leaves supplied; gutters of c.15 leaves renewed; some leaves with repaired tears. 234 leaves. CNY Dec 5 (211) $38,000

Anr Ed. Venice: Aldus Manutius, Dec 1499. Folio, 18th-cent mor gilt; hinges rubbed. Worming at beginning & end. 234 leaves. Goff C-767. bba June 25 (162) £52,000 [Beres]

Anr Ed. [L: Eugrammia Press, 1963]. One of 315. Folio, mor gilt. Facsimile of the 1499 Ed. sg Oct 31 (149) $275

Colophon...

— The Colophon: A Book Collector's Quarterly. NY, 1930-50. Set comprising: First Series, 20 parts * New Series, 12 parts * New Graphic Series, 4 parts * The New Colophon, Vols I & II in 8 parts & Vol III, and Index, 1930-35, in 2 vols. Together, 47 vols. Ck Oct 10 (183) £250

Anr copy. Complete set: First Series, 20 parts* New Series, 12 parts* New Graphic Series, 4 parts* The New Colophon, Vols I & II in 8 parts & Vol III* Index, 1930-35* Annual of Bookmaking, 1938. Together, 47 vols. 4to & 8vo, bds & cloth. sg Nov 7 (47) $850

Anr copy. Set composed of: First Series, 20 parts* New Series, 12 parts* New Graphic Series, 4 parts* The New Colophon, Vols I & II in 8 parts. Together, 45 vols. 4to & 8vo, bds & cloth. Lacking only Index & Annual of Bookmaking. SP Sept 22 (469) $425

Colophons...
— Colophons de manuscrits occidentaux des origines au XVIe Siecle. Fribourg, 1965-82. 6 vols. 8vo, cloth, orig wraps bound in. sg Oct 31 (200) $600

Colt, Miriam Davis
— Went to Kansas: A Thrilling Account.... Watertown NY, 1862. 12mo, orig cloth; worn & soiled, rebacked preserving orig spine. wa Apr 9 (77) $170

Colton, George Woolworth. See: Atlas

Colton, Walter, 1797-1851
— Deck and Port. NY, 1850. 1st Ed, Mixture of 1st & 2d Issues. 12mo, cloth. With frontis & 4 colored plates. cb Sept 12 (39) $110

Columna, Franciscus. See: Colonna, Francesco

Columna, Guido de
— Historia Troiana. Medina: Francisco del Canto for Benito Boyer, 1587. ("Cronica Troyana.") Bound with: Resende, Garcia. Chronica dos Valerosos e Insignes Feitos del rey Dom Joao II. Lisbon: Antonio Alvarez, 1622. Folio, 17th-cent sheep; rubbed, portion of front pastedown torn away, front free endpaper loose. Lower margin of tp of 2d work restored; lacking L4.8. sg Nov 7 (48) $1,400
— Ein huebsche histori von der kunngelichenn stat Troy.... Strassburg: Johann Knoblauch, 1510. Folio, modern bds. Lacking at least 10 leaves; repaired tear in N2; some browning. Sold w.a.f. S May 13 (755) £460 [Dijksman]

Combattimento...
— Combattimento, e balletto a cavallo rappresentato di notte in Fiorenza a'serenissimi Arciduchi & Archiduchessa d'Austria. Florence: Stamperia di S.A.S. alla Condotta, 1652. 8vo, recent half mor. C Dec 16 (40) £1,700 [Jackson]

Combe, George, 1788-1858
— Notes on the United States of North America, during a Phrenological Visit.... Phila., 1841. 1st American Ed. 2 vols. 8vo, orig cloth; rubbed. bba Sept 19 (22) £55 [Hay Cinema]

Combe, William, 1741-1823
— The Dance of Life. L: R. Ackermann, 1817. Illus by Thomas Rowlandson. 8vo, contemp calf; rubbed, rebacked. With frontis, additional title & 24 hand-colored plates. Lacking ptd title. bba Jan 30 (388) £70 [Hildebrandt]

Anr copy. Contemp half calf; rubbed. With 26 hand-colored plates, some with imprints shaved. S May 14 (939) £170 [Forsyth]

— English Dance of Death * Dance of Life. L, 1815-17. 3 vols. 8vo, cloth, remainder bdgs from c.1840. Death with hand-colored frontis, additional title & 72 plates; Life with hand-colored frontis, additional title & 24 plates. C May 20 (34) £1,800 [Bibermuehle]
— The English Dance of Death. L, 1815-16. 1st Ed in Book form. Illus by Thomas Rowlandson. 2 vols. 8vo, contemp calf gilt; rebacked preserving orig spine, hinges reinforced with tape. With 74 hand-colored plates, including title to Vol I. Some plates cropped; 2 leaves & 1 plate repaired; plate opposite p.199 smaller & from anr copy. S may 14 (938) £400 [Saville]

Anr copy. Later calf; extremities worn. With 74 hand-colored plates. Some foxing. sg Mar 5 (64) $600

— A History of Madeira. L: Ackermann, 1821. 4to, orig orange cloth, remainder bdg. With hand-colored title vignette & 27 plates. C May 20 (37) £850 [Old Hall]
— Journal of Sentimental Travels in the Southern Provinces of France. L: Ackermann, 1821. Illus by T. Rowlandson. 8vo, orig bds. With 18 colored plates. C May 20 (36) £600 [Quaritch]

Anr copy. Orig cloth, remainder bdg of c.1840. Occasional spotting. C May 20 (38) £380 [Old Hall]

— The Tour[s] of Doctor Syntax in Search of [1] the Picturesque; [2] Consolation; [3] a Wife. L: Ackermann, [1812]-20-[21]. 1st Ed of Vols II & III; 7th Ed of Vol I. Illus by Thomas Rowlandson. 3 vols. 8vo, contemp half mor. With 2 engraved titles & 78 hand-colored plates. Ck July 10 (213) £220

1st Ed of Vols I & III; 2d Ed of Vol II. 3 vols. 8vo, modern mor gilt; covers loose. sg Oct 17 (135) $650

1st Eds. 3 vols. 8vo, later calf gilt by Riviere. 1st Tour with text & plate numbered 4 in 1st states; 2d Tour has Skimmington Riders plate in 2d state. Lower margin of hand-colored aquatint title shaved; Plate 12 in 1st Tour with minor surface damage. C Oct 30 (117) £650 [Toscani]

3d Eds. L: Ackermann, [1813]-20-[21]. 3 vols. 8vo, mor gilt. rs Oct 17 (45) $600

9th Ed of 1st Tour; 3d Ed of 2d Tour; 1st Ed of 3d Tour. L, 1819-20-21. 3 vols. 8vo, half lea; hinges cracked. LH May17 (584) $225

Anr copy. Calf gilt by Root. O May 26 (37) $425

3d Ed. L, [c.1820]. 3 vols. 8vo, mor gilt by Root. wd Dec 12 (376) $500

Miniature Ed. L: Ackermann, 1823. Illus

by Thomas Rowlandson. 3 vols. 12mo, contemp cloth; soiled. With 80 color plates. bba Aug 13 (320) £100 [Kiefer]

Anr copy. Orig bds; most covers loose. sg Mar 5 (65) $225

Anr copy. Mor gilt by Root, each front cover with small gilt equestrian vignette of Dr. Syntax; joints rubbed. With 2 engraved titles & 78 hand-colored plates. Lacking Vol II engraved title & ads; directions to binder in Vol I only. wa Mar 5 (60) $500

4th Ed. L, 1828. 3 vols. 8vo, orig cloth; spine ends worn. With 2 engraved titles & 78 hand-colored plates. bba July 23 (330) £120 [Ginnan]

"9th" Ed. L, 1855. 3 vols. 8vo, orig cloth; worn. With 2 engraved titles & 74 (of 78) hand-colored plates. A few leaves loose. Sold w.a.f. bba Apr 30 (346) £110 [Gyldenlak]

Anr copy. Half calf; worn & rubbed, joints cracked. With 2 engraved titles & 78 hand-colored plates. cb Sept 5 (20) $200

Anr copy. Old half calf; worn & broken. K Sept 29 (135) $300

Anr Ed. L, [c.1885]. 8vo, cloth; heavily worn. Sold w.a.f. sg Oct 17 (360) $225

1st Tour

— 1819. - L: Ackermann. 8th Ed. Illus by Thomas Rowlandson. 8vo, 19th-cent sheep gilt; worn. Sgd as Eugene Field & Frederic Remington by Eugene Field II. sg Oct 17 (223) $250

2d Tour

— 1820. - L: Ackermann. In the 8 orig parts. 8vo, orig wraps; stained & frayed, those of Part 8 detached. With 24 hand-colored plates. C Dec 16 (248) £140 [Spademan]

Syntax Imitations, not by Combe

— Doctor Syntax in Paris. L, 1820. 1st Ed. 8vo, later mor gilt by Riviere. sg Oct 17 (136) $350

— The Grand Master or Adventures of Qui Hi in Hindostan. L, 1816. Illus by Thomas Rowlandson. 8vo, mor gilt by Wallis; rejointed but new joints chipped. With 28 hand-colored plates, including title. Repaired tear to 1 plate just affecting corner of image. wa Sept 26 (660) $260

— The Life of Napoleon. L, 1815. 1st Ed. Illus by George Cruikshank. 8vo, modern mor gilt by Morrell. With 30 colored plates. Some repairs & browning. C May 20 (33) £320 [Page]

Anr copy. Contemp half calf gilt; rebacked. Fore-margins repaired. DW Apr 8 (228) £155

Anr copy. Mor gilt with arms of the Duke of Newcastle; rubbed. Some soiling & foxing. O May 26 (38) $350

Anr copy. Half mor; browned & worn, hinges cracked, front cover nearly detached. Some soiling & foxing of plates. sg Oct 17 (158) $325

— The Tour of Doctor Syntax through London. L, 1820. 8vo, calf gilt. With engraved hand-colored title & 19 colored plates. LH May 17 (585) $475

Anr copy. Contemp calf; rubbed. O Jan 14 (185) $275

Anr copy. Mor gilt; extremities worn. Some foxing. sg Mar 5 (66) $200

Anr copy. Early half calf; soiled & worn, front inner hinge cracked. wa Sept 26 (661) $180

Combefis, Francois, 1605-79

— Bibliotheca Patrum Concionatoria.... Venice, 1749. 7 vols. Folio, contemp vellum. bba Jan 16 (243) £120 [Incisioni]

Combrune, Michael

— An Essay on Brewing. L, 1758. 8vo, disbound. Minor soiling. pn May 14 (32) £95

Comestor, Petrus. See: Petrus Comestor

Comiers, Claude

— La Nature et presage des cometes. Lyons: Charles Mathevet, 1665. 8vo, old vellum. Foxed; marginal stains; half-title loose. sg Mar 12 (207) $500

Comines, Philippe de, Seigneur d'Argenton

— The Historie.... L: for J. Norton, 1596. 1st Ed in English. Folio, later half lea; rubbed. Browned & soiled. Closely trimmed throughout, with some headlines and page numbers shaved. Sold w.a.f. O Mar 31 (39) $300

Anr Ed. L, 1614. Folio, contemp calf gilt; rebacked, recornered. Lacking final leaf; some worming. bba Oct 10 (291) £80 [Trotman]

Anr copy. Contemp calf; rebacked. Some stains. STC 5604. S June 30 (19) £280 [Bank of Cyprus]

Comites, Natalis

— Mythologiae sive explicationes fabularum.... Padua: P. P. Tozzius, 1615-16. 4to, contemp vellum; spine worn. Ck Oct 18 (142) £260

Commelin, Isaac, 1598-1676

— Begin ende Voortgang vande Vereenigde Neederlantsche Geoctroyeerde oost-Indische Compagnie. [Amst.], 1646. 11 parts in 1 vol (of 2). Oblong 8vo, contemp calf. With engraved title & 160 maps, plans & plates, 3 folding. B Nov 1 (573) HF6,500

Commentarii...

— Commentarii Academiae Scientiarum Imperialis Petropolitanae. St. Petersburg, 1728-32. Vols I-VII. 4to, contemp half calf; extremities rubbed. With 173 plates. Ck Nov 29 (132) £500

Commission Royale de Pomologie

— Annales de pomologie Belge et etrangere.... Brussels, 1853-60. Vols II, V, VII & VIII. 4to, contemp half mor; rubbed & worn. With 188 hand-colored plates. Sold w.a.f. C Oct 30 (169A) £6,400 [Shapero]

Commodianus

— Octavius et Caecilli Cypriani De Vanitate Idolorum.... See: Minucius Felix, Marcus

Communications...

— Communications to the Boards of Agriculture; on Subjects Relative to the Husbandry, and Internal Improvement of the Country. L, 1796-1811. 7 vols. 4to, calf & half calf; worn, some joints broken. Title of Vol I def, with loss. Sold w.a.f. O Jan 14 (48) $110

Company of Royal Adventurers

— Answer of the Company of Royal Adventurers of England Trading into Africa. L, 1667. 4to, later half lea. Some cropping, affecting text & numerals. K Dec 2 (146) $250

Compton, Thomas

— The Northern Cambrian Mountains, or a Tour through North Wales. L, 1817. Orig 10 parts in 1 vol. Oblong folio, mor gilt by Zaehnsdorf. With 30 hand-colored plates. Text leaves & tissue-guards browned. P Dec 12 (164) $800

2d Ed. L, 1820. Oblong folio, contemp half calf; rebacked preserving orig backstrip. With 40 hand-colored plates, including 1 litho. Inscr. C May 20 (40) £1,300 [Maggs]

Compton-Burnett, Ivy

— Brothers and Sisters. L, 1929. In d/j. sg Dec 12 (57) $225

— Dolores. Edin. & L, 1911. 1st Ed. bba Feb 277 (180) £80 [C. Robinson]

Anr copy. Orig cloth; extremities rubbed, pencil notes inside back cover. bba July 9 (210) £130 [Scott]

Comstock, John Lee, 1789-1858

— The Illustrated Botany.... NY, 1847. Vol I (all pbd). 8vo, contemp lea gilt. With 48 (of 50) hand-colored plates. Some foxing; lacking pp.19-30. sg Feb 13 (159) $250

Comte, Auguste, 1798-1857

— Cours de philosophie positive. Paris, 1864. 6 vols. 8vo, contemp half calf; rubbed. bba Feb 27 (285) £120 [Camden Books]

Concordantiae...

— Concordantiae maiores sacrae Bibliae. Basel: Froben & Episcopius, Mar 1531. Folio, old blind-tooled vellum over wooden bds with brass fittings; joints cracked. Stains on tp & last page. sg Oct 24 (74) $425

Concordia

— Christliche, widerholete, einmuetige Bekenntnues nachbenanter Churfuersten, Fuersten und Stende augspurgischer Confession.... Dresden: Matthes Stoeckel & Gimel Bergen, 1580. Folio, 19th-cent sheep; scuffed. Browned; some dampstaining; tp mtd. sg Oct 24 (75) $375

Anr copy. Bound with August I. Ordnung, wie es in seiner...Landen, bey den Kirchen.... Leipzig, 1580. contemp blind-tooled pigskin over wooden bds; worn, front joint cracked, lacking clasps. 2d work with lower portion torn off last leaf of preface. sg Oct 24 (76) $500

Conder, Claude Reignier —& Kitchener, Horatio Herbert, Earl Kitchener of Khartoum & of Broome

— [Map of Western Palestine in 26 sheets from Surveys conducted for the Committee of the Palestine Exploration Fund...during the years 1872-1877] L: Ordnance Survey, 1880. Folio, orig half mor. Tp & some sheet margins dust-soiled. S Nov 21 (287) £500 [Ferber]

Conder, Josiah, b.1852

— The Flowers of Japan and the Art of Floral Arrangement. Tokyo, 1891. Folio, orig wraps; worn & soiled. O Mar 31 (41) $325

Condillac, Etienne Bonnot de, 1715-80

— Essai sur l'origine des connaissances humaines. Amst.: Pierre Mortier, 1746. 8vo, Contemp calf. S Nov 14 (429) £550 [Drury]

— Traite des sensations. L, 1754. 2 vols. 4to, contemp calf gilt. S May 13 (827) £450 [Shapero]

Confederate States of America

— Register of the Commissioned and Warrant Officers of the Navy of the Confederate States.... [Richmond, 1863]. 8vo, wraps. sg Dec 5 (81) $375

Confucius

See also: Limited Editions Club

— Confucius sinarum philosophus, sive scientia sinensis latine exposita.... Paris: Daniel Horthemels, 1687. Folio, contemp red mor with arms of Louis XIV (Olivier

2494[10]); rubbed. Britwell Court copy. C Dec 16 (117) £4,200 [Bjorck & Borjesson]

Congreve, William, 1670-1729
See also: Nonesuch Press
— Works. Birm.: Baskerville, 1761. 3 vols. 8vo, calf by J. Larkins; rubbed, joints worn. O Feb 25 (53) $130

Congreve, William, 1772-1828
— A Treatise on the General Principles...of the Congreve Rocket System.... L, 1827. 4to, modern cloth; soiled. With 12 folding plates. Stained; Sion College stamp on tp verso. S July 1 (1230) £300 [Weiner]

Conjurers'...
— Conjurers' Monthly Magazine. NY, 1906-8. Ed by Harry Houdini. Vols I & II. 8vo, cloth, orig wraps bound in; Lacking upper cover of Vol I, No 12. S Nov 14 (275) £100 [Hackhofer]

Conlin, Albert Joseph
— Der Christliche Welt-Weise beweinent die Thorheit der neu-entdeckten Narren-Welt.... Augsburg, 1710. 4to, contemp vellum; worn. With frontis & 20 plates. HH May 12 (1185) DM700

Connelley, William Elsey, 1855-1930
See also: Root & Connelley
— Doniphan's Expedition and the Conquest of New Mexico and California. Topeka, 1907. 1st Ed. 8vo, cloth; extremities rubbed. Some soiling. Inscr. sg June 18 (188) $80

Connelly, Marc
— The Green Pastures. NY, 1930. One of 550, sgd. 4to, orig bds. sg Jan 30 (22) $70

Connett, Eugene V. See: Derrydale Press

Connick, Charles Jay
— Adventures in Light and Color. NY, [1937]. 4to, orig cloth. sg Apr 2 (270) $130

Connoisseur...
— Connoisseur: An Illustrated Magazine for Collectors. L, 1901-18. Vols 1-52. Cloth. bba Feb 27 (454) £120 [Lobo]

Vols 1-25. L, 1901-09. 4to, contemp mor gilt; last 3 vols, mor. bba Jan 16 (273) £170 [Harrington]

Vols 1-34. L, 1901-12. 4to, orig cloth; rubbed. pn Sept 12 (79) £65 [Gull]

Vols 1-44. L, 1901-13. 4to, contemp mor gilt; corners rubbed. bba Apr 30 (431) £450 [Grigoropoulos]

Connolly, Cyril V.
— Enemies of Promise. L, 1938. Orig cloth; spine frayed. DW Apr 8 (489) £50
— The Rock Pool. Paris: Obelisk Press, 1936. 1st Ed. Orig ptd wraps. bba Aug 13 (244) £220 [Burgess Browning]

Conolly, Arthur, 1807-42?
— Journey to the North of India.... L, 1834. 1st Ed. 2 vols. 8vo, orig cloth; rubbed. Folding map torn & repaired; frontis & flyleaves of Vol II detached. cb Ooct 10 (17) $225

Conrad, Joseph, 1857-1924
See also: Limited Editions Club
— Almayer's Folly. L, 1895. 1st Ed. 8vo, orig cloth; edge wear. sg June 11 (65) $425

1st American Ed. NY, 1895. 8vo, half mor gilt; front endpaper cracked at inner hinge. Ink drawing by Conrad tipped in before title. CNY Oct 8 (43) $1,500

Anr copy. Orig cloth; sides marked. CNY June 9 (48) $800

— The Arrow of Gold. Garden City, 1919. 1st Ed in Book form. Orig cloth; soiled. b Nov 18 (289) £65; sg Dec 12 (58) $70

1st English Ed. L, [1919]. Orig cloth; lower fore-corners jammed. Inscr to Harriet Capes, 1919. CNY Oct 8 (63) $1,200

— Chance. L, [1913]. 1st Ed in Book form, 1st Issue. Orig cloth; sides soiled, light staining on free endpapers. Inch tear in half-title. CNY June 9 (50) $950

Anr Ed. L, 1914. 2d Issue. Orig cloth; extremities rubbed. Sgd on half-title. CNY Oct 8 (58) $450

2d Issue, this copy with a spurious 1913 tp tipped in. Sgd. sg June 11 (67) $120

— Conrad's Manifesto: Preface to a Career. Phila., 1966. One of 1,100 on Fabriano paper. DW May 13 (425) £50
— Geography and Some Explorers. L: Pvtly ptd, 1924. One of 30. Orig wraps. CNY Oct 8 (68) $1,000
— Last Essays. Toronto & L, 1926. In d/j. cb Dec 12 (36) $65
— Laughing Anne. L, 1923. One of 200. bba July 9 (253) £220 [Collinge & Clark]

Anr copy. Vellum; covers buckled. sg June 11 (69) $225

— Lord Jim. NY, 1900. 1st American Ed. Inscr to Mr & Mrs J. Spiridion, Nov 1900. CNY Oct 8 (48) $2,200
— The Mirror of the Sea. L, 1906. 1st Ed. Orig cloth; endpapers cracking at inner hinges. Inscr to Harriet Capes, Oct 1906. CNY Oct 8 (52) $1,400; sg Dec 12 (61) $175
— The Nigger of the "Narcissus." NY, 1897. ("The Children of the Sea.") 1st Pbd Ed. 8vo, orig cloth; inner hinge cracked. Ls tipped in, 26 Jan 1922. CNY Oct 8 (45) $650

Anr copy. Cloth; rubbed. sg Dec 12 (59) $275

1st English Ed. L, 1898. 8vo, contemp half mor. Ck July 10 (214) £100

Anr copy. Orig cloth; extremities rubbed, endpaper cracked at front inner hinge. ALs tipped in. CNY Oct 8 (46) $1,300

Anr copy. Cloth. sg Dec 12 (62) $200

Anr Ed. [Hyth: Pvtly ptd for the Author by J. Lovick, 1902]. One of 100. Wire stitched. Inscr, also sgd on final page, 18 Mar 1919. C June 24 (121) £1,900 [Zia]

Anr copy. Wire stitched; lacking staple but inner margins stained by it. sg June 11 (70) $2,200

— Nostromo: A Tale of the Seabord. L: Dent, [1918]. Presentation bdg of mor gilt by Sangorski & Sutcliffe. Inscr to Edmund Gosse, June 1918. CNY Oct 8 (62) $1,500

Anr Ed. L, 1919. Inscr (sgd with initials). bba Oct 10 (391) £190 [Fior]

— Notes on Life and Letters. L, 1921. 1st Ed, 1st Pvd Issue, 2d state of contents page. Orig cloth; hinges tender. Inscr to Mr & Mrs G. F. W. Hope, 1921. CNY Oct 8 (65) $1,100

— Notes on my Books. L, 1921. One of 250. Orig bds; soiled, spine ends chipped. K July 12 (145) $80

Anr copy. Half vellum; hinges tender. sg June 11 (71) $130

— Oeuvres. Paris, 1918-34. Various limitations, all but 2 are L.p. copies on verge Lafuma-Navarre. 18 works in 20 vols. 4to & 12mo, all but 1 uniformly bound in half mor, orig wraps bound in, Typhoon bound in mor, orig wraps bound in. Sold w.a.f. S May 28 (305) £1,300 [Beres]

— One Day More. L: Beaumont Press, 1919. 1st Pbd Ed, one of—250. bba July 9 (247) £60 [Deighton Bell]

Anr Ed. Garden City, 1920. One of 377, sgd. Bds; soiled, spine ends rubbed. wa Sept 26 (135) $150

— An Outcast of the Islands. NY, 1896. 1st American Ed. Inscr, 10 Mar 1896. CNY Oct 8 (44) $1,300

Anr copy. 8vo, cloth; front cover spotted. sg June 11 (73) $60

— The Point of Honor. NY, 1908. 1st Ed. sg June 11 (74) $130

— The Rescue.... L & Toronto, 1920. 1st English Ed. In d/j. cb Dec 12 (37) $130

Anr copy. Orig cloth; inner hinges strengthened. Inscr to Sir Sidney & Lady Colvin, 1920. CNY Oct 8 (64) $1,100

Anr copy. Orig cloth; needs rebdg. Inscr to Miss Allen. sg June 11 (75) $250

Anr copy. In d/j with edge wear. sg June 11 (76) $70

— The Rover. Garden City, 1923. Out-of-series copy. Bds, in d/j. Presentation copy, sgd & with ANs to Mr. and Mrs. Arthur Curtiss James, 10 May 1923, bound in. Epstein copy. sg Apr 29 (88) $750

Anr Ed. L, [1923]. sg June 11 (77) $60

1st English Ed. In d/j. cb Dec 12 (38) $90

Anr copy. Inscr to Fountaine & Nellie Hope, 1923. CNY Oct 8 (66) $1,400

— The Secret Agent. L, 1907. 1st Ed. Orig cloth. Inscr to Mr & Mrs Hope, Sept 1907. DuPont copy. CNY Oct 8 (53) $7,000

Anr copy. Orig cloth. Epstein copy. sg Apr 29 (89) $950

— The Secret Agent: A Drama in Three Acts. L, 1923. One of 1,000. 4to, half vellum; rubbed. K July 12 (147) $130

— A Set of Six. L, 1908. 1st Ed. Inscr to Mr & Mrs Hope, 1908. CNY Oct 8 (54) $1,400

— The Shadow Line. L, [1917]. Orig cloth; inner hinges cracked. Inscr to Mr & Mrs G. F. W. Hope, 1917. CNY Oct 8 (61) $1,200

Anr Ed. L, [1920]. In worn & chipped d/j. Inscr & initialled by Conrad to Hugh Walpole. Epstein copy. sg Apr 29 (91) $750

— Some Reminiscences. L, 1912. 1st Ed. Orig cloth. Inscr to Sidney Colvin. CNY Oct 8 (56) $1,200

— Tales of Unrest. L, 1898. 1st Ed. Orig cloth; rubbed & soiled, endpaper cracked at front inner hinge. ALs, 1919, tipped in. CNY Oct 8 (47) $1,200

Anr copy. Cloth; front joint cracked. sg Dec 12 (64) $175

— The "Torrens." A Personal Tribute. L: Pvtly ptd, Oct 1923. One of 20. 4to, orig wraps. DuPont copy. CNY Oct 8 (67) $1,000

[-] Twenty Letters to Joseph Conrad. L, 1926. One of 220. 12 separately bound pamphlets. 8vo, wraps, in half cloth folder as issued. sg Dec 12 (67) $175

Anr copy. 4to, orig folder. sg June 11 (79) $200

— 'Twixt Land and Sea. L, 1912. 1st Ed. Orig cloth, 2d issue bdg. Inscr to John Quinn, 1912. CNY Oct 8 (57) $1,600

Anr copy. Orig cloth, 1st bdg. sg June 11 (80) $750

1st Issue, with Freya of the Secret Isles on front cover. Orig cloth; rear cover marked. Marginal foxing. Hugh Walpole's copy, dated Oct 1912. CNY June 9 (49) $1,600

— Typhoon. NY, 1902. ALs tipped in. CNY Oct 8 (50) $850

— Typhoon and Other Stories. L, 1903. 1st English Ed in Book form. sg Dec 12 (65) $120

— Under Western Eyes. L, 1911. 1st Ed. Orig cloth. Inscr to Sidney Colvin, 1911. DuPont copy. CNY Oct 8 (55) $4,200

— Victory. L, [1915]. Orig cloth; soiled. Inscr to Sir Sidney & Lady Colvin, 1915. CNY Oct 8 (60) $1,800

Anr copy. In orig pictorial d/j (frayed). Sutton-Manney copy. P Oct 11 (59) $1,800

— Within the Tides. L, 1915. 1st Ed. Orig cloth; rear inner hinge cracked. Inscr to Harriet M. Capes. CNY Oct 8 (59) $850

— Works. Garden City, 1920-28. Standard Ed, one of 735. 19 (of 24) vols. wa Mar 5 (167) $210

Anr Ed. L, 1921-27. One of 780. 20 vols. Half mor gilt; rubbed. Some browning & soiling. P June 17 (332) $3,000

Memorial Ed. Garden City, 1925-26. One of 400. 23 vols. 8vo, half mor gilt; dampstained & scuffed. Some internal dampstaining. Cut signature mtd to blank in Vol I. F Mar 26 (83) $400

Medallion Ed. L, 1925. 20 vols. In frayed d/js. DW Oct 2 (439) £210

— Youth. Edin. & L, 1902. 1st Ed. Orig cloth. Inscr to Miss H. Capes, 20 Nov 1902. DuPont copy. CNY Oct 8 (51) $5,500

Anr copy. Orig cloth. Epstein copy. sg Apr 29 (91) $750; sg June 11 (81) $350

Anr Ed. Kentfield CA, [1959]. One of 140. Bds. K Sept 29 (4) $160

Conrad, Joseph, 1857-1924 —& Ford, Ford Madox, 1873-1939

— The Inheritors. An Extravagant Story. NY, 1901. 1st Ed, 2d Issue, with the dedication in corrected state. Orig cloth; endpapers cracked at inner hinges. CNY Oct 8 (49) $600

— Romance. L, 1903. 1st Ed. Orig cloth; minor wear. sg June 11 (83) $50

Conradus de Alemania. See: Contraus de Halberstadt

Consett, Matthew

— A Tour through Sweden, Swedish-Lapland.... L, 1789. Issue with 7 engravings & 1 woodcut. 4to, contemp calf; worn. bba Sept 19 (135) £150 [Scott]

Anr copy. Orig bds; worn. bba Oct 24 (307) £260 [Shapero]

Considerations...

— Considerations Touching Trade, with the Advance of the Kings Revenue, and Present Reparation of His Majesty. L, 1641 [but 1642]. 4to, disbound, resewn. sg Mar 12 (55) $225

Constable, John, 1776-1837

— English Landscape Scenery. L, 1855. Folio, disbound. With 40 plates.. Ck July 10 (89) £350

Constable, William George

— Canaletto. Oxford, 1962. 2 vols. Orig cloth, in d/js. S Feb 11 (46) £150 [Bocca]

Constantine, Mildred

— Tina Modotti: A Fragile Life. NY & L, 1975. 4to, cloth, in torn d/j. sg Apr 13 (67) $150

Constitution of the United States of America

— The Constitution of the United States of America.... Phila.: John Fenno, 1791. 12mo, contemp sheep. F Mar 26 (496) $130

— The New Plan for a Federal Government Proposed by the Convention. Phila., 1787. 8vo, contemp sheep; lacking rear bd, worn & soiled. Contents with stains & foxing but the issue for Sept 1787 complete, though folding plates have tears & creases. In: Columbian Magazine for Sept 1787, contained in a vol containing 16 issues from Sept 1786-Dec 1787. wa Sept 26 (400) $1,100

Anr copy. Contemp sheep bds; rebacked in cloth. Some foxing. In: Columbian Magazine for Sept 1787, which is here bound with 15 other issues. wa Mar 5 (334) $1,900

Constitutions...

— The Constitutions of the Several Independent States of America.... Phila., 1781. One of 200. 12mo, contemp sheep; rubbed, free endpaper rubbed. Dampstaining to bottom fore-edge corners; ink mark on imprint date; cut down. F June 25 (673) $1,300

— Constitutions des treize Etats-Unis de l'Amerique. Phila. & Paris, 1783. One of 50 bound in calf & lettered. 8vo, orig calf; extremities rubbed. Tp soiled; first & last few leaves spotted. P June 16 (144) $2,500

Contact...

— Contact Collection of Contemporary Writers. [Paris: Contact Publishing Co., 1925]. One of 300. Ed by Robert McAlmon. Orig wraps, in d/j with tear to spine. bba Aug 13 (317) £180 [Blackwell]

Anr copy. Orig wraps, unopened, spine ends frayed, 2-inch tear in rear outer joint. CNY June 9 (88) $500

Contatore, Dominico Antonio

— De historia terracinensi libri cinque. Rome, 1706. 4to, contemp red mor gilt with arms of Pope Clement XI. Library stamp of the Albani library on tp. S May 28 (106) £1,250 [Tolomei]

Contes...

— Contes du temps jadis. Paris, 1912. Illus by U. Brunelleschi. 4to, orig wraps; spine darkened. With 20 colored plates. sg Jan 30 (14) $130

Conti, Natale

— Delle historie de' suoi tempi. Venice: Damian Zenaro, 1589. 2 vols. 4to, 18th-cent vellum. S Nov 21 (239) £2,200 [Bank of Cyprus]

Continental...

— The Continental Tourist: Belgium and Nassau. L: Black & Armstrong, [1883-84]. 8vo, orig cloth; spine darkened & rubbed. With 62 plates & 2 folding maps. Prelims spotted. DW Dec 11 (17) £150

Anr copy. Orig cloth; torn at head of spine with some loss. With 62 plates. Lacking maps.. DW Dec 11 (18) £120

Anr copy. Orig cloth; soiled. Lacking maps & front endpaper; frontis & title detached. DW Dec 11 (19) £125

Contraus de Halberstadt

— Concordantie maiores biblie tam dictionum declinabilium.... Basel: J. Froben, 1496. 2 parts in 1 vol. Folio, contemp calf; rebacked, remnants of clasps. Some soiling, staining & fraying; some leaves with tears; last leaf trimmed & strengthened on verso; paper flaws in tp repaired, affecting a few letters on verso. 463 leaves. Goff C-853. O May 26 (41) $1,600

Conway, Sir William Martin, 1856-1937

— The Alps. L, 1904. One of 300. Illus by A. D. McCormick. 4to, orig cloth; spine darkened. With 70 colored plates. DW Apr 8 (397) £200

— Climbing and Exploration in the Karakoram Himalayas. L, 1894. 8vo, cloth; rubbed. With folding map. DW Jan 29 (23) £135

Anr copy. Cloth; hinges starting. sg Jan 9 (284) $325

One of 150, sgd. 2 vols. 8vo, contemp cloth. With many illusts in 2 states, 1 on India proof paper. Without the 3 maps issued as a supplement. cb Jan 30 (33) $800

— The First Crossing of Spitsbergen.... L, 1897. 4to, contemp half mor; joints & extremities rubbed. Library markings. F Dec 18 (445) $90

Cook, Cyril

— The Life and Work of Robert Hancock. L, 1948. sp Feb 6 (221) $70

Cook, Henry

— Recollections of a Tour in the Ionian Islands, Greece and Constantinople. L, 1853. Folio, orig half mor gilt; def, text & plates detached. With litho dedication & 21 (of 30) tinted litho plates. Some fraying, affecting some plate titles; a few tears with loss. S July 1 (574) £6,200 [Conslidated Real]

Cook, Capt. James, 1728-79

See also: Limited Editions Club; Stokes's copy, John Lort

[-] Captain Cook's Florilegium.... L: Lion & Unicorn Press, 1973. One of 100 on handmade paper. 4to, bound by Zaehnsdorf in goatskin & silk. With 30 plates. S June 25 (85) £4,200 [Graham]

First Voyage

— ANONYMOUS. - A Journal of a Voyage Round the World, in his Majesty's Ship Endeavour.... L, 1771. 1st Ed, 1st Issue, with the dedication leaf. 4to, contemp calf gilt; rebacked, corners repaired. Some spotting. Attributed to James Matra or Magra. DuPont copy. CNY Oct 8 (70) $17,500

— HAWKESWORTH, JOHN. - An Account of the Voyages.... L, 1773. 1st Ed. 3 vols. 4to, library cloth. With 52 plates & maps. A few plates torn. Library markings. bba Feb 27 (7) £420 [Lewis]

Anr copy. Half mor gilt. Some foxing & soiling. kh Nov 11 (464) A$2,000

2d Ed. 3 vols. 4to, contemp mor; spines soiled. With 52 plates & maps. Old repair along fore-margins of plate at pp. 322-23. S June 25 (113) £3,200 [Quaritch]

Ed not indicated. 3 vols. 4to, contemp calf; scuffed. With 51 (of 52) plates & maps. Ck Oct 18 (62) £1,000

Anr Ed. NY, 1774. ("A New Voyage round the World....") 2 vols. 8vo, contemp sheep; abraded. With folding map & 2 folding plates. Browned; 2 leaves with small tears; lower corner & catchword of R4 lost; Vol II with small tear to T2. DuPont copy. CNY Oct 8 (71) $5,500

— PARKINSON, SYDNEY. - A Journal of a Voyage to the South Seas.... L, 1773. 1st Ed. 4to, contemp calf; rebacked with old spine laid down, upper joint split, corners repaired. With port & 27 plates. L.p. copy. DuPont copy. CNY Oct 8 (73) $4,200

L.p. Issue. 19th-cent half calf. With port & 26 plates and with extra prelim half-sheet. Lacking final blank. S June 25 (49) £4,500 [Heuer]

Second Voyage

— A Second Voyage Round the World.... L, 1776. 4to, modern half calf. Some spotting at end; stamp of Admiralty Office Library, London. DuPont copy. CNY Oct 8 (75) $5,000

— A Voyage towards the South Pole and Round the World. L, 1777. 1st Ed. 2 vols. 4to, contemp half calf; worn. With engraved port frontis to Vol I & folding table to Vol II. Frontis dampstained. DW Dec 11 (21) £180

Anr copy. Half mor gilt. kh Nov 11 (465) A$1,400

Anr copy. Modern half calf. With port & 63 plates & charts. Some browning; ink library stamps; 3B1 in Vol II with small tear, affecting text; a few plates & maps shaved affecting imprint; Vol I lacking final blank. pn Apr 23 (236) £1,050 [Baring]

Anr copy. Contemp calf gilt; worn, Vol II upper cover detached. With port & 63 maps & plates. Port cut within plate-mark along upper margin; some dust-soiling. S Nov 21 (372) £1,600 [Remington]

2nd Ed. 2 vols. 4to, contemp calf; re-backed. With port & 63 maps & plates & folding table. A few imprints soiled; small repair to 1 plate; repaired tear to margin of O4 in Vol I; other short tears in 2R2 & 2Y2. S Nov 21 (373) £1,500 [Mandl]

4th Ed. L, 1784. 2 vols. 4to, contemp mor; spines soiled. With port & 63 charts & plates. A few imprints shaved. S June 25 (114) £3,000 [Remington]

Third Voyage

— A Voyage to the Pacific Ocean. L, 1784. 4 vols including Atlas. 4to & folio, contemp calf gilt; worn. With 4 plates & folding map. pnE Dec 4 (159) £230

Anr copy. 3 vols (lacking Atlas). 4to, contemp calf gilt; joints cracked. With 24 charts. Some dust-soiling. S Nov 21 (377) £1,000 [Remington]

1st Ed. 3 vols; lacking Atlas vol. 4to, contemp calf; rubbed & scratched. With 24 charts & plates. bba Sept 19 (6) £1,200 [Sotheran]

2d Ed. L, 1784-85. 4 vols. Folio, contemp mor, Atlas in 19th-cent half calf with upper cover detached. With 82 plates & maps only. S June 25 (115) £3,000 [Remington]

3 text vols only. L, 1784. Folio, modern cloth. With 23 (of 24) maps, charts & views. 1 leaf torn & repaired. cb Oct 10 (18) $1,700

3 vols. Folio, contemp calf; worn, spine repaired. With 24 maps & charts, including 13 folding. Some foxing & staining. DW Dec 11 (20) £260

4 vols. Folio, contemp calf. With 49 plates & 2 folding charts. Small hole in 2d title. cb Jan 30 (34) $450

Abridged Ed. 4 vols. Contemp calf; some covers detached, worn. Hole in 1 leaf & corner of anr torn in anr. K Sept 29 (306) $400

Anr Ed. L, 1785. Atlas only. Half calf. kh Nov 11 (466) A$3,400

Anr copy. Half mor. This copy with Death of Cook plate. kh Nov 11 (467) A$4,000

Anr copy. Old bds; worn. With 60 plates & 1 map only. Versos repaired; map with surface repaired; lacking General Chart. kh Nov 11 (468) A$1,300

2d Ed. 3 vols; lacking Atlas vol. 4to, 19th-cent russia gilt; rebacked, corners repaired, rubbed. With 24 charts & plates; Occasional spotting. bba Sept 19 (5) £300 [Traylen]

Anr copy. 3 vols. 4to, contemp calf; rubbed, joints worn. Lacking Atlas vol. O Nov 26 (45) $700

Anr copy. Atlas vol only. With 2 folding charts & 61 (of 62) plates. Lacking Death of Cook plate; larger chart shaved at head & torn at lower folds; smaller chart torn & repaired at folds with surface wear; 3 plates cut down & mtd, 1 with margin trimmed; some staining & tears. pn Nov 14 (435) £1,300 [Hinchliffe]

2d Ed of Vols I & III, 1st Ed of Vol II. L, 1785-84-85. 3 vols. 4to, contemp calf; rebacked, worn, some covers detached. With 20 maps, 6 folding panoramas & 58 (of 61) plates. A1 repaired in Vol II; A1 torn in Vol III. Sold w.a.f. bba Sept 19 (4) £1,100 [Mandl]

Anr Ed. Perth, 1785-87. 4 vols. 12mo, contemp calf; worn. sg Jan 9 (57) $550

— LEDYARD, JOHN. - A Journal of Captain Cook's Last Voyage.... Hartford: Nathaniel Patten, 1783. 1st Ed. 8vo, contemp calf; rubbed. Lacking map; browned & dampstained throughout; prelims torn with loss. Ck Oct 18 (51) £1,700

— RICKMAN, JOHN. - Journal of Captain Cook's Last Voyage.... L, 1781. 1st Ed. 8vo, modern half calf. With folding map & 5 plates. Map torn & repaired. S June 25 (52) £1,500 [Quaritch/Hordern]

Third Voyage in French

— Cartes et figures du troisieme voyage.... Paris, 1785. 4to, contemp bds; worn. with 86 (of 88) plates & maps. Some foxing & soiling. Sold w.a.f. O Nov 26 (44) $1,000

— Troixieme Voyage de Cook ou voyage a l'Ocean Pacifique.... Paris, 1785. Atlas vol only. 4to, contemp bds; def. With 87 maps & plates. Lacking all text except title & privilege leaf. sg Jan 9 (55) $900

Three Voyages

— [Set of Hawkesworth, South Pole & Pacific Ocean]. L, 1773-77-84. 1st Eds. 10 vols, including Webber's Views. 4to & folio, text vols in calf gilt (rebacked), the Atlases in matching half mor. DuPont set. CNY Oct 8 (76) $28,000

Anr copy. 8 vols (lacking Atlas to 3d Voyage). 4to & folio, early 19th-cent russia, blind-tooled with cathedral-style decoration enclosing the arms of the 6th Earl of Harborough; joints rubbed. 1st Voyage lacking 1 plate; 2d Voyage with small repaired tears; 2 plates shaved. Sold w.a.f. kC Oct 30 (100) £4,800 [Remington]

Anr copy. 9 vols. 4to & folio, text vols in contemp calf gilt, Atlas bound to style; some vols rebacked, others with minor restoration. Some fold separations & repairs. Manney set. P Oct 11 (60) $30,000

1st Voyage, 1st Ed, early issue; 2d Voyage, 1st Ed; 3d Voyage, 3d Ed. L, 1773-77-85. 10 vols. 4to & folio, 4to vols in 19th-cent russia gilt, Atlas in matching half-russia. Atlas to 3d Voyage extra-illus with 25 additional plates including the death of Cook plate & a full set of 16 hand-colored plates from the Boydell Ed of Webber's Views in the South Seas. C Oct 30 (20) £14,000 [Shapero]

2d Ed of 1st & 3d voyages, 1st Ed of 2d voyage. 10 vols, including a composite Atlas vol to the first 2 voyages. 4to & folio, modern half mor. Some maps & plates repaired; a few frayed. bba June 11 (341A) £4,800 [Freddie]

2d Ed of 3d Voyage, 1st Ed of others. L, 1773-77-84. 9 vols, including Kippis but lacking Atlas to 3d Voyage. 4to, half mor; worn, most front covers detached. Some foxing. P June 17 (163) $4,000

4th Ed of 2d Voyage, 2d Ed of 3d Voyage, 1st Eds of 1st Voyage & of Kippis's biography. L, 1773-77-84-88. 10 vols, including Kippis's Life. 4to & folio, contemp calf, Atlas in half-sheep; some bdgs dampstained. Some foxing; tear in crease of 2d map in Vol I of 1st Voyage. sg Nov 7 (49) $10,000

2d Ed of 1st Voyage; 1st Ed of 2d & 3d Voyage. L, 1777-77-84. 9 vols. 4to & folio, uniform 19th-cent mor gilt. A few minor tears & repairs. S June 25 (50) £23,000 [Quaritch/Hordern]

— The Three Voyages.... L, 1821. 7 vols. 8vo, modern half calf. With folding map, 2 folding tables & 25 plates. A few leaves worn; map & 1 folding plate backed. cb Oct 10 (29) $600

— ANDERSON, GEORGE WILLIAM. - A Collection of Voyages round the World.... L, 1790. 8 vols. 8vo, modern half calf. With 131 plates, some folding, and 24 folding charts. Contents soiled. Several charts torn & repaired; chart of Magellan's strait lacking portion. cb Feb 12 (26) $850

Anr copy. 6 vols. 8vo, contemp calf; worn, bds of Vol IV detached. With 129 plates & 29 folding maps. Frontis of Vol II lacking; Vol VI lacks directions to the binder. Ck Oct 18 (53) £280

Cook, Moses

— The Manner of Raising, Ordering, and Improving Forest and Fruit-Trees.... L, 1679. 4to, modern half calf. With 4 plates. C Oct 30 (263) £200 [Arader]

Cooke, Capt. Edward

— A Voyage to the South Sea, and Round the World.... L, 1712. 1st Ed. 8vo, contemp calf; rebacked. With 4 maps & plans & 16 plates. Stamp on tp, 1 plate & 4 other pages. CNY Oct 8 (77) $850

2d Ed of Vol I, 1st Ed of Vol II. 2 vols. 8vo, contemp calf; rebacked with orig spines laid down, corners worn. With 6 maps, 1 with stain & margin cut close with los of some latitude degree numerals. CNY Oct 8 (78) $1,200

Cooke, Edward William, 1811-80

— Landscapes, British and Foreign.... L, 1874. Oblong folio, orig cloth; spine ends & corners scuffed. With 30 plates on india paper mtd. C Oct 30 (21) £200 [Abbott & Holder]

Cooke, George Alexander

— Modern and Authentic System of Universal Geography...forming a Complete Collection of Voyages and Travels. L, 1817-22. 2 vols. 4to, contemp calf gilt; scuffed, upper joint of Vol I split. Ck May 15 (87) £170

Cooke, John Esten, 1830-86

— A Life of Gen. Robert E. Lee. NY, 1871. 8vo, bdg not described; chipped. With frontis, 23 plates & folding map. Inscr, Mar 1871. K Sept 29 (229) $150

Cooke, Philip St. George, 1809-95

— The Conquest of New Mexico and California. NY, 1878. One of 600. cb Nov 14 (35) $50

Cooke, William Bernard, 1788-1855

— A New Picture of the Isle of Wight. L, 1808. 8vo, contemp russia gilt; spine rubbed. With frontis, hand-colored folding map & 35 plates. Some browning & marginal spotting. pn May 14 (195) £120 [Ventnor]

Coolbright, Ina, 1842-1928

— California. San Francisco: Book Club of California, 1918. One of 500. Half cloth. cb Jan 16 (36) $80

Coolidge, Calvin, 1872-1933

— Autobiography. NY, 1929. 1st Ed, one of 1,000 L.p. copies. Half cloth; front joint & lower hinges wormed. sg Sept 12 (55) $70

Coomaraswamy, Ananda Kentish

— Catalogue of Indian Collections in the Museum of Fine Arts, Boston. Bost., 1923. Parts 1 & 2 only in 1 vol. Folio, half cloth. O Mar 31 (43) $50

Cooper, Sir Astley Paston, 1768-1841

— A Treatise on Dislocations and on Fractures.... L, 1823. 2d Ed. 4to, half calf; corners worn. With 30 plates. S Feb 25 (585) £360 [Voltaire]

Cooper, Edith Emma. See: Bradley & Cooper

Cooper, Edward Joshua, 1798-1863

— Views in Egypt and Nubia. L: John Murray, [1824-27]. 4to, contemphalf calf gilt; worn. With 43 plates & folding litho map at rear. Without tp; some spotting. DW May 13 (17) £200

Cooper, James Fenimore, 1789-1851
See also: Limited Editions Club

— The Deerslayer. Phila., 1841. 1st Ed. 2 vols. 12mo, orig cloth; spines & extremities worn. Manney copy. P Oct 11 (63) $1,500

Anr copy. Orig cloth; worn, lightly stained. Epstein copy. sg Apr 29 (92) $850

— The Last of the Mohicans. Phila., 1826. 2 vols. 12mo, orig bds; spines renewed. Large tear on text leaf in Vol II repaired with tape. Manney copy. P Oct 11 (61) $9,000

Anr copy. Contemp calf; rebacked, orig spines laid down. Epstein copy. sg Apr 29 (93) $2,000

— The Pathfinder.... Phila., 1840. 1st American Ed. 2 vols. 12mo, orig bds, in d/j; corners worn, hinges tender. "An excellent copy". Epstein copy. sg Apr 29 (95) $2,600

1st State. Orig cloth; Vol I spine chipped. Manney copy. P Oct 11 (62) $1,700

— The Prairie. L, 1827. 1st Ed. 3 vols. 12mo, contemp half calf; rubbed. O Jan 14 (50) $110

— Works. NY, 1856. 20 vols. Orig half mor. cb Oct 31 (25) $450

Mohican Ed. NY: Appleton, [n.d.]. one of 250. 32 vols. 8vo, half mor; scuffed. Marginal dampstaining at rear of 1 vol. wa Sept 26 (5) $700

Cooper, John Butler

— The History of Malvern from its First Settlement.... Melbourne, 1935. Bds; some adhesion. kh Nov 11 (272) A$160; kh Nov 11 (272) A$160

Cooper, Thomas, 1517-94

— Thesaurus Linguae Romanae et Britannicae. L, 1584. 2 parts in 1 vol. Folio, 19th-cent calf; upper cover & spine detached. Tp laid down & remargined; repair to tail edge of 7D6 & 7M5 extended; lacking 7M6; some spotting. STC 5689. Milne copy. Ck June 12 (41) £50

Coornhert, Dirck Volckertszoon, 1522-90

— Recht ghebruyck ende misbruyck, vantijdlicke Have. Amst., 1610. 4to, bds. With port & 25 emblems. Soiled throughout. B Nov 1 (330) HF1,200

Coppard, Alfred Edgar, 1878-1957
See also: Golden Cockerel Press

— Yokohama Garland, and other Poems. Phila., 1926. One of 500. Illus by Wharton Esherick. 4to, half cloth. F Dec 18 (40) $80

Copway, George, 1818-63

— The Traditional History and Characteristic Sketches of the Ojibway Nation. L, 1850. 1st Ed. 12mo, wraps; chipped. sg June 18 (172) $70

Corancez, Louis Alexandre Olivier de, 1770-1832

— Itineraire d'une partie peu connue de l'Asie Mineure. Paris, 1816. 8vo, contemp calf gilt; rubbed. With folding map. Some browning. S June 30 (264) £380 [Maggs]

Corbesier, Antoine J.

— Principles of Squad Instruction for the Broadsword. Phila., 1869. 12mo, orig cloth; front hinge starting, lacking rear free endpaper. sg Mar 26 (85) $100

Corbett, Col. Edward

— An Old Coachman's Chatter. With some Practical Remarks on Driving.... L, 1890. Illus by John Sturgess. 8vo, orig cloth; rubbed. bba Feb 27 (369) £100 [Collezionista]

Corbin, Bernard —& Kerka, William

— Steam Locomotives of the Burlington Route. Red Oak IA, 1960. In d/j. cb Feb 13 (77) $70

Cordelois

— Lecons d'armes. Paris, 1862. 8vo, half mor; extremities worn. Sgd. sg Mar 26 (86) $350

Cordier, Henri

— Bibliotheca Sinica: Dictionnaire bibliographique des ouvrages relatifs a l'Empire Chinois. Paris, 1904-24. 2d Ed. 5 vols, including Supplement/Index. Half cloth; worn. sg Oct 31 (94) $800

Cordiner, Charles, 1746?-94

— Antiquities and Scenery of the North of Scotland in a Series of Letters to Thomas Pennant. L, 1780. 4to, contemp calf; rubbed. With title & 20 plates. L.p. copy. bba Sept 19 (238) £140 [Dawson]

Corfu

— Relacam diaria do sitio de Corfu com a descripcam desta importante Praca.... Lisbon, 1716. 4to, half calf. S July 1 (580) £600 [Spink]

Corio, Bernardino, 1459-1519?

— Historia di Milano.... Venice, 1554. ("L'Historia de Milano....") 4to, 17th-cent mor gilt. SI June 9 (277) LIt1,500,000

Anr Ed. Padua, 1646. 2 parts in 1 vol. 4to, contemp bds. Some marginal spotting toward end. SI Dec 5 (171) LIt1,000,000

Cornazzano, Antonio, 1429-84

— De re militari. Venice, 1536. 8vo, 18th-cent calf; spines worn. DW Nov 6 (442) £65

Corneille, Pierre, 1606-84

— Le Theatre. [Geneva], 1764. 12 vols. Contemp calf gilt; some wear. With frontis & 34 plates. B May 12 (661) HF800

Anr Ed. Geneva [Berlin], 1774. Ed by Voltaire. 8 vols. 4to, 18th-cent calf; spine of Vol I chipped. With 35 plates. Some foxing. S Feb 25 (548) £600 [American Book Store]

Cornelius Scribonius, Grapheus. See: Grapheus, Cornille

Cornwall, Barry

— Charles Lamb: a Memoir. L, 1866. 4to, mor extra by Bayntun Riviere with inset miniature of Lamb on upper cover. Extra-illus with hand-colored port & 21 plates, 4 hand-colored. Ck Dec 11 (118) £650

Anr copy. Mor gilt by Bayntun, upper cover inlaid with miniature port of Lamb; rubbed. S Feb 25 (409) £320 [Shapero]

Cornwallis, Charles, 1st Marquis, 1738-1805

— Answer to That Part of the Narrative of Lieutenant-General Sir Henry Clinton.... L, 1783. 1st Ed. 8vo, contemp calf gilt; upper joint cracked. Hole in the margin of E3 & K4; 4 leaves with trimmed margins. pn Mar 19 (389) £120

Coronado, Francisco Vasquez de, 1510-54. See: Grabhorn Printing

Coronelli, Vincenzo Maria, 1650-1718

— Corso geografico universale. Venice, 1692. Folio, contemp sheep gilt; worn. With frontis & 97 (of 118) maps only plus 3 extra maps. Sold w.a.f. CNY June 9 (135) $15,000

— Description geographique et historique de la Moree.... Paris: Nicolas Langlois, 1687. Folio, contemp calf; worn. With 48 (of 50) plates. Some tears, 1 with loss; lacking large folding map. Presentation copy. S July 1 (584) £2,800 [Apostolakis]

Anr copy. Modern calf. With folding map & 50 plates. Repairs at fore-margins; some leaves at end recornered; library stamp of the Marquis de Preaulx. S July 1 (585) £1,900 [Chelsea]

— Epitome cosmografica.... Coloniia [Venice]: Andrea Poletti, 1693. 4to, contemp vellum. With 22 (of 37) double-page plates. SI June 9 (278) LIt1,100,000

— An Historical and Geographical Account of the Morea.... L, 1687. 12mo, contemp calf; worn. With 42 folding plates. Minor tears; plate opposite p.117 torn with loss, that opposite p 221 torn. S June 30 (267) £1,250 [Consolidated Real]

— Libro Dei Globi. Amst.: Theatrum Orbis Terrarum, 1969. Folio, cloth, in d/j. Facsimile of Venice 1701 Ed. sg Oct 31 (72) $110

Anr copy. Cloth, in d/j. Facsimile of the 1701 Venice Ed. sg Feb 13 (117) $250

— Ordinum equistrium, ac militarium brevis narratio.... Venice, 1715. Folio, later half mor; old dark stain along spine & joints, worn. With 141 plates, 12 pages of crests & 67 ports Dampstained; 1 plate repaired. bbc Sept 23 (226) $110

Corpus...

— Corpus francicae historiae veteris et sincerae. Hanau: heirs of Joannes Aubrius, 1613. Folio, contemp blind-tooled pigskin with brass catches & clasps. Some browning, with early owner's partial table of contents added in ink on tp. sg Oct 24 (78) $275

Corrozet, Gilles, 1510-68

— Les Antiquitez croniques et singularitez de Paris.... Paris: Nicolas Bonfons for Galiot Corrozet, 1586-88. 2 vols in 1. 8vo, 19th-cent calf gilt; joints rubbed. DW Nov 6 (443) £110

Cortes, Balbino

— El Palo e el sable. Madrid, 1851. Bound with: Merelo y Casademunt, Jaime. Manual de esgrima. Madrid, 1878. Oblong 8vo, half calf. sg Mar 26 (87) $200

Cortes, Hernando, 1485-1547

— The Despatches of.... NY & L, 1843. 8vo, later half mor. cb Oct 10 (27) $60

Cortesao, Armando. See: Zuzarte Cortesao, Armando

Cortissoz, Royal

— The Architecture of John Russell Pope. NY, [1925-30]. 3 vols. Orig half mor; stained. Some gnawing. NH May 30 (15) $350

Cory, Charles B., 1857-1921

— The Birds of Haiti and San Domingo. Bost., 1885. One of 300. 4to, contemp cloth. With map & 22 colored plates. C May 20 (164) £300 [Shapero]

— The Birds of the Bahama Islands. Bost., 1890. 4to, orig cloth. With 8 hand-colored plates (colored in 1964). Frontis loose. sg May 14 (201) $250

Cosmo III, Grand Duke of Tuscany

— Travels of Cosmo the Third through England.... L, 1821. 4to, contemp half calf; rubbed, joints splitting, spine detached. With port & 39 plates. bba Jan 30 (391) £340 [Bifolco]

Cossley-Batt, Jill

— The Last of the California Rangers. NY, 1928. sg June 18 (56) $130

Costa, Enrico

— Album di costumi sardi. Sassari: Giuseppe Dessi, 1898-[1901]. Folio, 19th-cent cloth; worn. With 10 color plates. SI Dec 5 (173) LIt2,000,000

Costalius, Petrus. See: Coustau, Pierre

Costello, Augustus E.

— Our Firemen: A History of the New York Fire Departments.... NY, 1887. Folio, bdg not described but rubbed & shaken. Met Apr 28 (481) $110

Anr copy. Cloth; worn, foot of spine reinforced with cloth tape, hinges weak. sg Dec 5 (188) $120

Costume...

— The Costume of the Russian Empire. L, 1803. Folio, contemp mor; rubbed, extremities worn. With 73 hand-colored plates, including title. Title soiled. DW Oct 2 (81) £280

Anr Ed. L, 1804. Folio, contemp mor gilt; rebcked preserving orig spine. With 73 hand-colored plates, including title. CG Oct 7 (538) £425

Anr copy. Syn. With 73 hand-colored plates. sg Nov 7 (195) $350

Anr Ed. L, 1811. Folio, contemp mor gilt; covers stained. With engraved title & 72 handcolored plates. S Feb 26 (731) £420 [American]

— The Costume of Yorkshire. L, 1814 [plates watermarked 1811-13]. 4to, contemp half mor; soiled & scuffed. With frontis & 40 colored plates With set of duplicate plates. 1 small tear repaired, anr with margin tear repaired; 1 plate with paint splashes at edge. pnL Nov 20 (101) £1,800

Anr Ed. Leeds, 1885. One of 100 with proofs on japan paper. 4to, orig half vellum gilt; rubbed & soiled, upper hinge cracked. With chromolitho frontis & 40 plates (2 rubbed). S Nov 15 (921) £190

One of 600. Orig half mor; rubbed. With frontis & 40 colored plates. pnL Nov 20 (88) £260 [Dawson]

Anr copy. Half mor; worn. Some spotting to titles & text only. S May 14 (1159) £150 [Eliot]

Costumes...

— Costumes Europeens du XVIIe au XIXe siecle tires des documents les plus authentiques.... Paris: Librairie Centraled'Art et d'Architecture, [c.1910]. Folio, loose as issued with text in portfolio; worn. With 60 hand-colored plates. Plate 7 with marginal tape repair, touching image. cb Dec 5 (52) $450

Costumi. See: Bertini, A.

Cotarelo y Mori, Emilio, 1857-1936

— Diccionario biografico y bibliografico de caligrafos espanoles. Madrid, 1914-16. 2 vols. 4to, cloth, orig wraps bound in. O Sept 24 (60) $275

Coterie....

— Coterie. L, 1919-21. Nos 1-6/7 (all pbd) in 6 vols. Unopened. bba Apr 9 (126) £140 [Robinson]

Cotman, John Sell, 1782-1842

— Architectural Antiquities of Normandy. L, 1822. 2 vols. Folio, orig cloth; rubbed. With 96 plates. bba Jan 30 (392) £280 [Thorp]

Anr copy. 2 vols in 1. Folio, contemp half mor; rubbed, upper joints cracked. With 100 plates. Ck July 10 (90) £120

Anr copy. 2 vols. Folio, half mor. With 50 plates. Some foxing & dampstaining. Met Apr 28 (10) $300

Anr copy. 2 vols in 1. Folio, contemp half mor gilt. With 100 plates. S Nov 15 (1093) £420 [Sims]

— Specimens of Architectural Remains in Various Counties of England.... L, 1838. 5 series in 2 vols. Folio, 19th-cent half mor gilt; rubbed. With etched additional titles & 278 plates. Minor foxing. S Nov 21 (72) £550 [Sims Reed]

Cotterell, Howard Herschel
— Old Pewter, its Makers and Marks.... NY, 1929. 4to, cloth; worn. With 6 folding plates. O May 26 (42) $50

Cotton, Charles, 1630-87
See also: Limited Editions Club; Walton & Cotton
— Burlesque upon Burlesque: or, the Scoffer Scoft. L, 1675. 8vo, modern half calf. bba Jan 16 (72) £220 [Thomas Plume's Library]

Cotton, Henry, 1789-1879
— Editions of the Bible and Parts Thereof in English.... Oxford, 1852. 2d Ed. cb Oct 17 (185) $60

Cotton, John, 1584-1652
— The Way of Life.... L, 1641. 4to, contemp calf; rubbed, crudely repaired. Dampstained & soiled. F Mar 26 (191) $100

Cotton, Sir Robert Bruce, 1571-1631
— A Short View of the Long Life and Raigne of Henry the Third. [L], 1627. 4to, old calf; rebacked. STC 5864. W July 8 (52) £95

Cotugno, Domenico, 1736-1822
— De sedibus variolarum syntagma. Vienna, 1771. 8vo, bds. SI Dec 5 (174) LIt1,100,000

Couch, Jonathan, 1789-1870
— A History of the Fishes of the British Islands. L, 1862-65. 4 vols. 8vo, contemp half mor; spine worn. With 201 hand-colored plates only. Some foxing; marginal dampstaining; some annotations. pn Dec 12 (276) £90 [Elliott]

Anr copy. Half mor gilt. With 252 hand-colored plates. Some foxing. pnE Aug 12 (30) £250

Anr copy. Contemp half mor. With 252 colored plates. Some spotting. S May 14 (1021) £380 [Seragnoli]

Anr copy. Contemp half lea gilt; extremities rubbed. With 248 colored plates. sg May 7 (62) $2,000

Anr Ed. L, 1867. 4 vols. 8vo, contemp half mor; spines rubbed. With 252 colored plates. DW Oct 2 (133) £320

Anr Ed. L, 1868-69. 4 vols. 8vo, half mor gilt. bba Jan 30 (89) £480 [Corbett]

Anr copy. Orig cloth; spines worn. DW Nov 6 (156) £320

Anr Ed. L, 1877-78. 4 vols. 8vo, cloth. Vol IV lacking title. Library markings. Sold w.a.f. bba Sept 5 (22) £180 [Bifolco]

Anr copy. Orig cloth; hinges reinforced, spine worn at head & foot. With 252 hand-colored plates. bba May 14 (470) £320 [K. Books]

Anr copy. Orig cloth; soiled & rubbed, rebacked. Library stamps on plate versos. S Nov 15 (784) £280 [Barker]

Coudray, Jean Baptist du. See: Le Perche

Coues, Elliott, 1842-99
— Forty Years a Fur Trader on the Upper Missouri...Charles Larpenteur, 1833-1872. NY, 1898. One of 950. 2 vols. cb Feb 12 (14) $325

Courboin, Francois, 1865-1926 —& Roux, Marcel
— La Gravure francaise: essai de bibliographie. Paris, 1927-28. One of 525. 3 vols in 2. 4to, recent cloth. sg Sept 6 (77) $250

Court de Gebelin, Antoine, 1725-84
— Histoire naturelle de la parole. Paris, 1776. Bound with: Comte d'Albon. Eloge de Court de de Gebelin. Amst., 1785. 8vo, contemp calf gilt. With frontis, folding table & folding plate ptd in colors. sg Mar 12 (208) $850

Court, Pieter de la
— Sinryke Fabulen, verklaart en toegepast tot alderley Zeedelessen. Amst.: H. Sweerts, 1685. 4to, vellum. With frontis & 100 emblematic engravings. B May 12 (863) HF1,500

Courtship...
— The Courtship and Marriage of Jerry and Kitty. L: J. Harris, 1814. 16mo, contemp wraps. With engraved title & 15 hand-colored illusts. Tp & 1 other leaf backed. bba July 23 (36) £300 [Sotheran]

Coustau, Pierre
— Pegma. Lyons: Matthiam Bonhomme, 1555. 8vo, calf gilt by Francis Bedford. sg May 7 (63) $3,400

Couts, Joseph
— A Practical Guide for the Tailor's Cutting-Room.... Glasgow, [1848]. 4to, contemp half sheep; spine scuffed. With 4 plain & 13 hand-colored fashion plates & 18 diagrammatic plates. Plates & diagrams foxed & dampstained. sg Feb 6 (64) $500

Covarrubias, Miguel
— The Eagle, the Jaguar, and the Serpent.... NY, 1954. 4to, cloth, in frayed d/j. With 68 plates. wa Sept 26 (575) $65
— Negro Drawings. NY, 1927. In def d/j. With frontis & 56 plates. sg Sept 6 (78) $325

Anr copy. 4to, cloth, in chipped d/j. With color frontis & 56 uncolored plates. sg Feb 6 (65) $400

Covel, John, 1638-1722

— Some Account of the present Greek Church... Cambr.: for Cornelius Crownfield, 1722. Folio, contemp calf; rubbed, repaired. With 4 plates & 1 engraved plan in text. S June 30 (268) £150 [Consolidated Real]

Coventry, Francis

— The History of Pompey the Little.... L, 1751. 1st Ed. 12mo, contemp calf; joints weak. Some spotting. bba July 9 (105) £50 [Wilbraham]

Coveny, Christopher

— Twenty Scenes from the Works of Charles Dickens. Sydney, 1883. 4to, orig half calf; rubbed. With added title & 21 plates. bba Oct 10 (167) £100 [Thorp]

Cowan, Robert Ernest & Robert G.

— A Bibliography of the History of California, 1510-1930. San Francisco, 1933. cb Oct 17 (189) $75

1st Ed. 3 vols. 4to, orig bdg. b&b Feb 19 (309) $225

Anr copy. Half cloth. cb Feb 12 (15) $170

2d Ed. 3 vols. 4to, half cloth; Vol I spine holed. sg Oct 31 (95) $275

Anr Ed. Columbus, 1952. cb Oct 17 (188) $90

Anr copy. 4to, cloth; worn. O Sept 24 (61) $110

Coward, Noel

— Present Indicative. Garden City, 1937. 1st Ed, one of 301 L.p. copies. sg Dec 12 (69) $200

— Pretty Polly and Other Stories. NY, 1965. In d/j. Sgd. sg Dec 12 (70) $150

Anr copy. In soiled d/j. Sgd. wa Dec 19 (179) $85

— The Rat Trap. L, 1924. In d/j. Laid in is typescript carbon copy of Coward's intro to Three Plays. sg Dec 12 (71) $225

Cowley, Abraham, 1618-67

— The Third Part of the Works. Being his Six Books of Plants. L, 1708. 8vo, half lea. Bronson Alcott's copy. O Aug 25 (3) $300

— Works. L, 1668. 8vo, early 18th-cent mor gilt; joints weak. Port shaved at fore-edge, torn & repaired; ownership stamp partially removed from title; e1 & e2 shorter. pn Nov 14 (261) £320 [Quaritch]

Anr Ed. L, 1700. Folio, old calf; worn, rebacked. K July 12 (148) $90

Cowley, John. See: Dodsley & Cowley

Cowley, John Lodge

— An Appendix to the Elements of Euclid. L: T. Cadell, [1765?]. 2d Ed. 4to, contemp half calf; joints cracked, corners rubbed. With 42 engraved cut-out plates mtd on guards; interleaved. Schlosser copy. P June 17 (451) $2,750

Cowper, William, 1731-1800

— Poems. L, 1808. 2 vols. 8vo, recent half mor gilt. DW Mar 4 (202) £50

Anr Ed. L, 1811. 2 vols. 8vo, contemp mor gilt; joints weak. With 7 plates. Some spotting. bba July 9 (136) £220 [Kunkler]

Anr Ed. L, 1820. 2 vols. 8vo, orig mor gilt, with fore-edge paintings; Vol II rebacked. LH May 17 (601) $700

Anr Ed. L, 1864. 8vo, contemp calf gilt. cb Nov 21 (75) $50

— Works. L, 1835-37. 15 vols. 8vo, contemp calf gilt. bba Feb 27 (118) £260 [Aspin]

Cowper, William, 1731-1800 —& Newton, John, 1725-1807

— Olney Hymns. L, 1779. 12mo, contemp sheep; worn. ESTC t018634. bba June 25 (190) £110 [Land]

Cox, David, 1783-1859

— A Treatise on Landscape Painting.... L, 1813-14. Issue not indicated. 12 parts in 1 vol. Oblong folio, contemp half calf; rebacked. With 16 hand-colored views & 49 views on 40 sheets. DW Mar 11 (805) £460

— The Young Artist's Companion.... L, 1825. Oblong 4to, contemp half mor; front inner hinge split; extremities rubbed. With hand-colored frontis, 52 plain & 12 colored plates. With autograph 9-page Ms dictated by the author and specially produced to accompany and illustrate the text. Ck July 10 (91) £800

Cox, E. H. M. See: Gosse Library, Sir Edmund W.

Cox, Edward Godfrey

— A Reference Guide to the Literature of Travel. NY, 1969. Vols I-III. 4to, cloth. cb Nov 21 (76) $160

Cox, Marian Roalfe

— Cinderella: Three Hundred and Forty-five Variants.... L, 1893. Vol 31 of the Publications of the Folk-lore Society. cb Oct 17 (193) $50

Cox, Ross, 1793-1853

— Adventures on the Columbia River.... L, 1831. 2 vols. 8vo, half calf. sg June 18 (190) $450

Coxe, William, 1747-1828

— Account of the Russian Discoveries Between Asia and America. L, 1780. 2d Ed. 4to, calf; worn, joints broken; spine dried & corroded. With plate & 4 folding maps. O Nov 26 (48) $475

3d Ed. L, 1787. 8vo, contemp calf gilt; rebacked, orig spine preserved. With 5 maps & plates. A few short tears. S June 25 (54) £400 [Quaritch/Hordern]

— Memoirs of Horatio Lord Walpole. L, 1802. 4to, old calf; rebacked with orig spine retained. With frontis & 20 other ports. Inscr to the 3d Viscount Hampden. K July 12 (149) $110

Coykendall, Frederick

— Arthur Rackham: A List of Books Illustrated by him. NY, 1922. One of 175. Orig bds; spotted. Martin Birnbaum's annotated copy. wd Dec 12 (377) $225

Coyne, Joseph Stirling, 1803-68. See: Willis & Coyne

Coyner, David H.

— The Lost Trappers: A Collection of Interesting Scenes and Events in the Rocky Mountains. Cincinnati, 1847. 1st Ed. 12mo, orig cloth; rebacked, corners worn down, soiled. Foxed; old dampstain at top & margins of last 50 pages. bbc Apr 27 (579) $110

Cozio, Carlo, Conte

— Il Giuoco degli scacchi, o sia nuova idea d'attacchi.... Turin, 1766. 2 vols. 8vo, early 19th-cent mor gilt; rubbed. Ink spots on tp to Vol I. Ck May 8 (99) £800

Cozzens, Samuel Woodworth

— The Marvellous Country. Bost., 1873. 1st Ed. 8vo, orig cloth. sp Sept 22 (24) $75

Crabb, George, 1778-1851

— Universal Technological Dictionary.... L, 1823. 2 vols. 4to, later half cloth. With 60 plates plus 1 duplicate. Foxed. bba May 14 (434) £70 [Ventnor]

Crabbe, George, 1754-1832

— The Library. A Poem. L, 1781. 4to, modern cloth; new endpapers. Lacking half-title. bba July 9 (120) £130 [Hannas]

Craddock, Harry

— The Savoy Cocktail Book. NY, 1930. Half cloth. O Jan 14 (52) $80

Anr copy. Half cloth; spine ends frayed. sg Sept 6 (10) $130

Craig, Clifford

— The Engravers of Van Diemen's Land. [Hobart], 1961. kh Nov 11 (72) A$200

Craig, Clifford —& Others

— Early Colonial Furniture in New South Wales and Van Diemen's Land. Melbourne, 1972. 4to, cloth, in d/j. kh Nov 11 (73) A$120

Craig, Edith N. See: Robertson & Craig

Craig, Edward Gordon, 1872-1966

— Books and Theatres. L & Toronto, 1925. Orig half cloth. With ANs laid in. Met Apr 28 (605) $70

— Ellen Terry and her Secret Life. L, [1931]. One of 256. Orig bds; spine worn, hinges cracked. sg Oct 17 (22) $70

— Fourteen Notes. Seattle, 1931. One of 350. 4to, half cloth; worn, hinges starting. Library markings. sg Oct 17 (20) $100

— Henry Irving. Ellen Terry. A Book of Portraits. Chicago, 1899. Orig bds; worn & soiled, spine perished. Marginal tears. pba Aug 20 (52) $140

Anr copy. Orig bds; rebacked & rubbed. With 19 mtd plates. sg Mar 5 (214) $130

— Paris Diary, 1932-1933. North Hills: Bird & Bull Press, 1982. One of 350. Orig half mor. bbc Apr 27 (99) $110; K July 12 (58) $60; pba July 23 (29) $110

— A Production, being Thirty-two Collotype Plates of Designs...for The Pretenders of Henrik Ibsen. L, 1930. One of 650. Folio, orig half vellum; spine rubbed at head. With 32 plates, 12 colored. pn May 14 (109) £110

— Scene. L, 1923. 4to, orig bds. Met Apr 28 (607) $130

— Woodcuts and Some Words. L, 1924. 4to, cloth. pba Aug 20 (51) $70

Craig, Maurice James

— Irish Book Bindings, 1600-1800. L, 1954. Folio, orig cloth, in d/j. With colored frontis & 58 plates. bba July 23 (445) £100 [Whetman]

Craig, Robert H.

— Rules and Regulations for the Sword Exercise of the Cavalry.... Balt., 1812. 8vo, contemp calf. With 26 plates; some def. Some browning & foxing. sg Mar 26 (89) $175

Craik, Dinah Maria Mulock, 1826-87

— The Adventures of a Brownie.... NY, 1872. 8vo, orig cloth; spine & corners worn. Epstein copy. sg Apr 29 (97) $250

— John Halifax, Gentleman. L, 1856. 1st Ed. 3 vols. 8vo, orig cloth; worn. O May 26 (134) $250

Cram and Ferguson

— The Work of Cram and Ferguson Architects. NY, 1929. Intro by Charles D. Maginnis. Folio, cloth; spine ends worn. sg Apr 2 (11) $225

Cramer, Johann Andreas, 1710-77

— Elements of the Art of Assaying Metals.... L, 1741. 8vo, contemp calf; rubbed. With 6 folding plates. Browned. bba Sept 5 (196) £140 [Nibris Books]

Cramer, Patrick

— The Illustrated Books of Joan Miro. Geneva, 1989. 4to, cloth, in d/j. Inscr by Cramer. sg Apr 2 (183) $250

Cranach Press—Weimar

— SHAKESPEARE, WILLIAM. - Hamlet. 1930. One of 300. bba July 9 (254) £1,500 [Watson]; CNY Dec 5 (214) $1,800

— VERGILIUS MARO, PUBLIUS. - Eclogae & Georgica. 1926. Ed in Latin & German, One of 36 with an extra suite plates in sanguine, 1 sgd by Maillol. Illus by Aristide Maillol. 4to, mor gilt by O. Dorfner. Schlosser copy. P June 18 (434) $9,000

— VERGILIUS MARO, PUBLIUS. - The Eclogues. 1927. One of 25 hors commerce. Illus by Aristide Maillol; trans by J. H. Mason. Unopened copy. S Dec 5 (311) £1,000 [Pirages]

One of 33 on Imperial japon. S Dec 12 (182) £2,000 [Rassam]

Anr copy. Mor gilt by Sangorski & Sutcliffe, orig upper wrap bound in. S July 22 (395) £1,200 [Maggs]

Cranbrook Press—Michigan

— The Dictes and Sayings of the Philosophers. 1901. One of 244. cb Oct 17 (242) $110

Cranch, Christopher Pearse, 1813-92

— The Last of the Huggermuggers.... Bost., 1856. 8vo, cloth. pba Aug 20 (53) $60

Anr copy. Cloth. With holograph poem, sgd, laid in. Epstein copy. sg Apr 29 (98) $200

Crane, Hart, 1899-1932

— The Bridge. Paris, 1930. One of 200. 4to, orig wraps. With 3 photographic plates by Walker Evans. Epstein copy. sg Apr 29 (99) $2,400

— White Buildings. NY: Boni & Liveright, 1926. 1st Ed, 2d Issue. pba Aug 20 (55) $65

Anr copy. In d/j. sp Nov 24 (239) $600

Crane, Stephen, 1871-1900

See also: Grabhorn Printing

— George's Mother. NY, 1896. 1st Ed. 12mo, cloth; endpapers browned. sg Mar 5 (69) $120

— Legends. Ysleta TX: Edwin B. Hill, 1942. One of 45. Pictorial wraps. sg Dec 12 (72) $90

— The Little Regiment and Other Episodes of the American Civil War. NY, 1896. 1st Ed, 1st Ptg. 8vo, orig cloth. sg Mar 5 (70) $70

Anr copy. Orig cloth, in d/j. Epstein copy. sg Apr 29 (100) $1,200

2d Ptg. Orig cloth, in d/j with minor tears at edge. Manney copy. P Oct 11 (65) $600

— Maggie, a Girl of the Streets. [NY, 1893]. 1st Ed. 8vo, orig wraps; soiled, extremities restored. Manney copy. P Oct 11 (64) $7,000

1st Pbd Ed. NY, 1896. 12mo, orig cloth; spine darkened & frayed. K Mar 22 (106) $100

— The Monster & Other Stories. NY, 1899. 1st Ed. 8vo, orig cloth. sg Mar 5 (72) $175

— The Red Badge of Courage. NY, 1895. 1st Ed, 1st Issue. 8vo, orig cloth; torn along front joint. Epstein copy. sg Apr 29 (101) $1,400

2d Issue. Cloth; soiled & spotted. sg Oct 17 (138) $450

— The Third Violet. NY, 1897. 1st Ed. 12mo, orig cloth, in d/j; spine ends chipped. Manney copy. P Oct 11 (66) $1,200

Anr copy. Cloth; spine ends worn. Possibly washed. sg Mar 5 (74) $80

— War is Kind. NY, 1899. 1st Ed. 8vo, orig bds; worn, clipping removed from endpaper. K July 12 (151) $400

Anr copy. Orig bds; front outer joint splitting. Epstein copy. sg Apr 29 (102) $225

Anr copy. Orig bds; spine ends & forecorners worn. sg June 11 (88) $325

— Wounds in the Rain.... L, 1900. 1st Ed. 8vo, cloth; some wear at extremities, front hinge starting. sg Mar 5 (75) $90

Crane, Walter, 1845-1915

See also: Greenaway & Crane

— The Absurd A.B.C. L: Routledge, [c.1873]. 4to, wraps. sg Jan 30 (23) $250

— Columbia's Courtship: A Picture History of the United States in Twelve Emblematic Designs in Color with Accompanying Verses. Bost.: L. Prang, [1893]. Folio, cloth; worn & rubbed, endpapers soiled. With 12 chromolitho plates. Corner crease to 1 plate. cb Sept 26 (38) $200

— The First of May, a Fairy Masque. L, 1881. One of 200. Oblong folio, cloth; rebacked. With 56 proof plates on india paper Marginal dampstaining throughout. sg Oct 17 (140) $150

One of 300. Mor gilt. With 56 proof plates on india paper. S Apr 28 (26) £190 [James]

— Flora's Feast, a Masque of Flowers. L, 1889. 4to, orig half cloth. b Nov 18 (55) £60

Anr Ed. L, 1895. 4to, orig half cloth. With 40 colored illusts. cb Sept 26 (40) $75

— Flowers from Shakespeare's Garden. L, 1906. Orig half cloth, in chipped d/j. bba Dec 19 (103) £130 [Ginnan]

— India Impressions. L, [1907]. Pictorial cloth. Inscr. sg Jan 30 (24) $275

— Of the Decorative Illustration of Books Old and New. L, 1896. Bdg not given. cb Oct 17 (196) $85

One of 130. 8vo, contemp mor gilt. bbc Apr 27 (114) $200

— Panpipes: A Book of Old Songs. L, 1883. Half cloth; corners worn. sg Jan 30 (27) $150

— Red Riding Hood's Picture Book. L, [1898]. sg Jan 30 (28) $130

— Triplets. L, 1899. One of 750. Oblong 4to, half vellum. pnE Dec 4 (259) £90

Anr copy. 4to, orig half vellum; soiled. sg Oct 17 (141) $90

[-] The Work of Walter Crane: With Notes by the Artist. L, 1898. 4to, half cloth, orig wrap bound in. In: The Easter Art Annual for 1898 (an Extra Number of The Art Journal). sg Jan 30 (29) $110

Crane, William H.

— Rocky Mountain Views on the Rio Grande.... Denver, 1913. cb Feb 13 (80) $120

Crantz, David, 1723-77

— The History of Greenland. L, 1767. 1st Ed in English. 2 vols. 8vo, old calf; rebacked, worn. With 2 folding maps & 7 plates. Browned & spotted. O Aug 25 (49) $350

Anr Ed. L, 1820. 2 vols. 8vo, contemp half mor; rubbed. With 2 maps & 7 plates. bba June 25 (258) £140 [Lewis]

Crashaw, Richard, 1613?-49

— Steps to the Temple.... L, 1648. 2d Ed. 12mo, contemp calf; detached covers secured with adhesive tape. Later leaves waterstained; b3 & C8 torn at outer margins. Ck Nov 29 (73) £100

Crastonus, Johannes

— Dictionarium graecum cum interpretatione latinum. Venice: Aldus, Dec 1497. ("Lexicon Graeco-Latinum.") Folio, russia over pastebd by Charles Hering; rebacked & rubbed. 42 lines; greek & roman letter. Some worming at beginning & end; lower blank margin of t7 renewed. 243 (of 244) leaves; lacking final blank. Goff C-960. C Nov 27 (11) £4,200 [Mediolanum]

Anr copy. 19th-cent calf; rubbed. 42 lines; 2 columns, index in 3 columns; greek & roman letter; capital spaces with guide letters. Tear in upper margin of quires k-B, touching text on 4 leaves. 244 leaves. Goff C-960. C Dec 16 (41) £5,000 [Fletcher]

Crato von Krafftheim, Johannes

— Consiliorum et epistolarium medicinalium.... Hanover 1609-19 & Frankfurt, 1620. 7 vols in 4. 8vo, old vellum. Some browning; titles of vols VI & VII repaired. Ck Oct 18 (9) £200

Craven, Lady Elizabeth, 1750-1828

— A Journey through the Crimea to Constantinople. L, 1789. 4to, half calf. With folding map & 6 plates. Tear to map. pn Sept 12 (328) £110

Anr copy. Modern half calf. With folding map (2 short tears at fold) & 6 plates, 1 folding. S July 1 (586) £550 [Hunersdorff]

Anr copy. Contemp calf; rebacked, edges worn. With folding map & 6 plates. Repair to map. S July 1 (587) £550 [Consolidated Real]

Anr copy. Orig bds; worn, later spine. S July 1 (588) £280 [Kutluoglu]

Craven, Tunis Augustus Macdonough

— A Naval Campaign in the Californias...Journal of.... San Francisco: Book Club of California, 1973. One of 400. cb Sept 12 (43) $70

Crawford, James Ludovic Lindsay, Earl of

— Bibliotheca Lindesiana. A Catalogue of the Printed Books. Aberdeen, 1910. One of 200. 4 vols. Folio, orig cloth. bba Jan 30 (326) £160 [Kent]

Crawfurd, George

— The Peerage of Scotland. Edin., 1716. Folio, modern half calf. With 10 plates Title torn & repaired. O Mar 31 (45) $100

Crawhall, Joseph, b.1821

— Chap-book Chaplets. L, 1883. 4to, orig bds; joints split, worn. bba Oct 10 (46) £60 [Biltcliffe]

Anr copy. Orig bds; rubbed, joints split. Illusts hand-colored. bba May 28 (275) £60 [Cox]

— Chorographia, or a Survey of Newcastle upon Tyne: 1649. Newcastle, 1884. 4to, orig bds; rebacked, rubbed. bba May 28 (373) £50 [Sanderson]

— The Compleatest Angling Booke that Ever was Writ. Newcastle, 1881. One of 100. 4to, contemp half mor. bba Nov 28 (22) £280 [Baylis]

Anr copy. Calf gilt by Reid; inner hinges

strengthened. Inscr & with ALs inserted. pn Mar 19 (377) £600
— Izaak Walton: his Wallet Booke. L: Leadenhall Press, 1885. 8vo, orig bds, unopened. S Feb 26 (848) £180 [Montague]
— A Jubilee Thought. Newcastle, 1887. 4to, orig wraps; chipped & spotted. bba May 28 (87) £50 [Cox]
— Olde Ffrends Wyth Newe Faces. L, 1883. 4to, orig bds; rebacked & recornered, old spine preserved. Ck July 10 (219) £100

Crayon, Geoffrey. See: Irving, Washington

Crealock, Henry Hope
— Deer-Stalking in the Highlands of Scotland. L, 1892. One of 250. Folio, orig cloth; spine ends worn. L Nov 14 (391) £440
Anr copy. With 40 plates. A few leaves with waterstaining. S Feb 26 (906) £650 [McEwan Gall.]

Creasy, Sir Edward Shepherd, 1812-78. See: Limited Editions Club

Crebillon, Claude Prosper Jolyot de, 1707-77
— La Nuit et le moment. Paris, 1946. One of 15 for the artist with 2 extra suites. Illus by Louis Icart. 4to, loose as issued. CGen Nov 18 (346) SF3,300
— Oeuvres. L, [Paris], 1777. 14 vols. 12mo, 19th-cent calf. Ck July 10 (220) £280

Creeley, Robert
— Poems, 1950-1965. L, [1966]. One of 100 on handmade paper, sgd. Half vellum; front cover repaired. sg June 11 (89) $90

Crescentiis, Petrus de, 1230?-1310?
— Commodorum ruralium. Florence: Cosimo Giunti, 1605. ("Trattato dell' agricoltura....") 4to, 18th-cent vellum; soiled. Some browning & foxing. SI Dec 5 (181) LIt650,000
— De agricultura, omnibusque plantarum, & animalium generibus, libri XII. Basel: H. Petrus, Aug 1538. 4to, contemp blind-stamped pigskin; worn. Some dampstaining. SI Dec 5 (180) LIt550,000

Cresset Press—London
— The Apocrypha. 1929. One of 450. b Mar 11 (123) £70; LH May 17 (643) $160; wa Sept 26 (62) $170
— Bunyan, John. - The Pilgrim's Progress. 1928. One of 195. 2 vols. bba May 28 (251) £200 [Cox]; pnE Mar 11 (186) £90
— Gogol, Nicolai Vasil'evich. - The Diary of a Madman. 1929. One of 30 with an extra suite of engravings. Orig half mor; joints split, rubbed. bba May 28 (252) £130 [Kam]
One of 250. b&b Feb 19 (99) $50
— Johnson, Alfred Forbes. - Decorative Initial Letters. 1931. One of 500. bba May 28 (529) £50 [Maggs]; DW Apr 8 (353) £60
— Lawrence, D. H. - Birds, Beasts, and Flowers. 1930. One of 500. pnE Mar 11 (236) £75; sg Jan 30 (30) $175
— Milton, John. - Paradise Lost; Paradise Regained. 1931. One of 195. S Apr 28 (32) £220 [Dimakarakos]
— Ovid (Publius Ovidius Naso). - The Heroycall Epistles. 1928. One of 375. bba July 9 (295) £90 [Bookworks]
— Painter, William. - The Palace of Pleasure. 1929. One of 500. 4 vols. pnE Mar 11 (253) £95
— Spenser, Edmund. - The Shepheards Calendar. 1930. One of 350. sg Sept 26 (77) $90
— Swift, Jonathan. - Gulliver's Travels. 1930. One of 195. Illus by Rex Whistler. 2 vols. With 12 hand-colored plates & 5 maps. CNY Dec 5 (215) $2,500

Cresswell, Beatrix Feodore
— The Royal Progress of King Pepito. L: S.P.C.K., [1889]. 1st Ed. Illus by Kate Greenaway. 8vo, orig bds; nick to upper bd edge, spine chipped at foot. Inscr & with orig pencil sketch, sgd with initials, tipped in. wa Mar 5 (597) $1,300

Creswell, Keppel A. —& Others
— The Mosques of Egypt. Giza, 1949. 2 vols. Folio, orig lea. With colored titles & frontises, plates (count not given but several colored), 2 folding maps & Index in pocket at end of Vol I. S Nov 15 (1194) £300 [Folios]

Crevecoeur, Michel Guillaume St. Jean de, 1735-1813
— Letters from an American Farmer.... L, 1782. 8vo, contemp bds; broken, spine gone. With 2 folding maps. Minor foxing & soiling. O May 26 (43) $2,000
— Voyage dans la Haute Pensylvanie et dans L'Etat de New York.... Paris, 1801. 3 vols. 8vo, half calf gilt. pnE Dec 4 (80) £110

Crevel, Rene
— Feuilles eparses. Paris, 1965. One of 150, sgd by 11 artists. Illus by Bellmer, Ernst, Giacometti, Arp, Miro & others. 4to, unsewn as issued in orig wraps. With 14 plates. CGen Nov 18 (347) SF9,000

Crevier, Jean Baptiste Louis
— Histoire des Empereurs Romains. Paris, 1750-56. 6 vols. 4to, contemp calf; worn. SI June 9 (284) LIt380,000

Cries...

— The Cries of London as They are Daily Exhibited.... L: F. Newbery, 1775. 32mo, early Dutch floral bds; spine worn, endleaves renewed. Some staining. Manney copy. P Oct 11 (238) $5,500

— The Cries of London as They are Daily Practiced.... L: J. Harris, [1815]. 16mo, half vellum. Some staining & spotting. bba July 23 (184) £130 [Excell]

Cripps-Day, Francis Henry

— A Record of Armour Sales, 1881-1924. L, 1925. Folio, orig cloth. Some pencil annotations. bba May 14 (608) £60 [Goddard]

Anr copy. Cloth; worn. O May 26 (44) $80

Anr copy. Orig cloth; soiled. pn Dec 12 (137) £50 [Elliott]

Crisp, Sir Frank, 1843-1919

— Mediaeval Gardens. L, 1924. One of 1,000. 2 vols. 4to, orig cloth. rs Oct 17 (54) $225

Croall, Alexander. See: Johnstone & Croall

Crocker, Henry Radcliffe

— Atlas of the Diseases of the Skin. Edin. & L, 1896. 1st Ed. Folio, loose as issued in paper folders in 2 cloth portfolios; worn & split. With 96 plates in 16 paper folders, each with text. wa Sept 26 (511) $200

Croft, P. J.

— Autograph Poetry in the English Language. L, 1973. One of 1,500. 2 vols. Folio, orig half cloth, in d/js. DW Jan 29 (307) £55

Anr copy. Cloth, in d/js. sg Oct 31 (97) $80

Crofts, Master. See: Drake, Sir Francis

Crofts, Freeman Wills

— Inspector French and the Cheyne Mystery. L, [1970]. Lea gilt. Inscr. cb Sept 19 (41) $150

Croker, John Wilson

— The Croker Papers. L, 1885. 2d Ed. 3 vols. 8vo, contemp half mor. bba Feb 27 (154) £50 [The Bookroom]

Croll, Robert Henderson

— Tom Roberts, Father of Australian Landscape Painting. Melbourne, 1935. 4to, cloth. kh Nov 11 (75) A$650

Crombie, Benjamin William

— Modern Athenians. A Series of Original Portraits. L, 1882. 4to, contemp half mor; rubbed. With litho frontis & 48 hand-colored double-page plates. bba June 25 (37) £85 [Cox]

Anr copy. Orig half mor; rubbed. With frontis & 48 double-page plates; 1 stained. bba Aug 13 (321) £95 [Finney]

Anr copy. Half mor. pnE May 13 (94) £110

Crome. See: Morin, Lazare

Cromer, Martin

— De origine et rebus gestis Polonorum libri XXX.... Basel: Joannes Oporinus, Sept 1558. Folio, later half calf. Lacking last blank. bba Nov 28 (179) £300 [Robertshaw]

Crosby, Sylvester Sage, d.1914

— The Early Coins of America.... Bost., 1875. 4to, half mor. With 12 plates. Inked stamp on tp. sg Dec 5 (193) $400

Cross, John Walter, 1840-1924

— George Eliot's Life as Related in her Letters and Journals. L, 1885. 3 vols. 8vo, contemp calf gilt; rubbed. bba July 23 (459) £50 [Books & Prints]

Cross, Joseph, Printer

— Journals of Several Expeditions made in Western Australia.... L, 1833. 1st Ed. 12mo, orig cloth. With folding map. S June 25 (218) £4,400 [Baring]

Crossen, Forest

— The Switzerland Trail of America. Boulder: Pruett Press, 1962. In d/j. Sgd. cb Feb 13 (82) $70

Crouch, Nathaniel, 1632?-1725?. See: Burton, Robert

Crowley, Aleister

— 777 Revised. L: Nepture Press, 1955. One of 1,100. Orig half vellum. bba Aug 13 (265) £70 [Houle]

— Carmen Seculare. [N.p.], 1901. 1st Ed. Orig wraps; frayed. bba Aug 13 (248) £170 [Blakeney]

— The City of God, a Rhapsody. L, 1943. One of 200. Orig wraps. bba Aug 13 (263) £160 [Houle]

— Household Gods, a Comedy. Pallanza, 1912. bba Aug 13 (256) £180 [Blackwell]

— Jephthah and other Mysteries.... L, 1899. 8vo, orig half cloth; broken. bba Aug 13 (247) £50 [Bokladan]; DW Apr 8 (490) £50

— Little Essays towards Truth. L, 1938. bba Aug 13 (259) £60 [Houle]

— Magick in Theory and Practice. L: Pvtly ptd, 1929. 1st Ed. 4to, orig cloth, in d/j. bba Oct 10 (492) £120 [Andersson]

— Olla: An Anthology of Sixty Years of Song. L, [1947]. One of 500. Orig cloth, in d/j. bba Aug 13 (264) £100 [Shah]

— Oracles.... Inverness, 106. Orig wraps; chipped. Ad leaf repaired. bba Aug 13 (251) £70 [Blakeney]

— Orpheus. Inverness, 1905. One of a few sets on India paper & bound as 2 vols in 1. Orig bds, unopened. bba Aug 13 (252)

£260 [Blakeney]

— The Rites of Eleusis. Chiswick Press, [1910]. Loose in orig wraps; chipped & repaired. bba Aug 13 (255) £190 [Blakeney]

— Rosa Coeli, a Poem. Chiswick Press, 1907. One of 10 on chine. 4to, orig wraps. bba Aug 13 (253) £340 [Blakeney]

— The Scientific Solution of the Problem of Government. L, [1937]. Orig wraps; soiled. bba Aug 13 (258) £95 [Houle]

— Seven Lithographs by Clot from the Watercolours of Auguste Rodin with a Chaplet of Verse. L, 1907. 1st Ed, One of 500. 4to, orig cloth; soiled. bba Aug 13 (254) £200 [Houle]

— The Soul of Osiris: A History. L, 1901. 1st Ed. Orig half cloth. bba Aug 13 (249) £90 [Hart]

— The Spirit of Solitude: An Autohagiography.... L: Mandrake Press, 1929. 1st Ed. 2 vols. 4to, orig cloth; soiled. bba Aug 13 (257) £340 [Bokladan]

— Temperance, a Tract for the Times. L, 1939. Out-of-series copy. Orig wraps. bba Aug 13 (260) £55 [Houle]

Crowne, William

— A True Relation of all the Remarkable Places and Passages Observed in the Travels of...Thomas Lord Howard.... L, 1637. 1st Ed. 4to, later calf bds with modern spine. Lacking final blank; port cut round & mtd. STC 6097. W July 8 (96) £135

Crowninshield, Francis Boardman

— The Log of Cleopatra's Barge II, 1928-1942. Bost., 1948. 4to, half mor. K July 12 (537) $60

Crowther, Samuel. See: Ford & Crowther

Cruikshank, George, 1792-1878

See also: Dolly...; Stock...

— Cruikshank's Water Colours. L, 1903. One of 300 L.p. copies, sgd by pbr. Intro by Joseph Grego. 4to, lev extra by Morrell, with inlaid borders & with scenes from Oliver Twist on both covers.. With 67 colored plates. CNY Dec 5 (420) $5,000

— England's Prime Minister Murdered.... L, [c.1812]. 12mo, orig wraps. With hand-colored frontis by Cruikshank. Title is same as Cohn 637, but pagination & frontis differ in this copy. sg Mar 5 (78) $275

— History of the Late War; including Sketches of Buonaparte, Nelson, and Wellington. L, 1832. Illus by George Cruikshank. 12mo, calf gilt. With 2 full-page woodcuts. Salomons copy. sg Oct 17 (167) $150

— The Humourist: a Collection of Entertaining Tales.... L, 1822-19-19-20. Re-issue of Vol I; Vols II-IV 1st Ed. 4 vols. 8vo, mor gilt by Riviere, orig upper wraps bound in. With hand-colored titles & 36 plates. Locker-Lampson—Bruton copy. C May 20 (42) £1,150 [Marlborough]

Anr copy. 4 vols in 2. 8vo, calf gilt by Sangorski & Sutcliffe. With 4 engraved titles with hand-colored vignettes & 36 hand-colored plates. Some browning & foxing; frontis in Vol I torn without loss; lacking plate list. pn Sept 12 (258) £120

Anr Ed. L, 1892. One of 70 with a duplicate set of the plates in hand-colored state. 4 vols. 4to, orig cloth. bba Apr 9 (258) £220 [Ulysses]

— Illustrations of Time. L, 1827. Oblong folio, orig wraps; chipped. Some foxing. rs Oct 17 (47A) $125

— Metropolitan Grievances; or, a Serio-Comic Glance and Minor Mischiefs in London...By One who Thinks for Himself. L, 1812. 12mo, calf, orig wraps bound in. With hand-colored folding frontis. Salomons copy. sg Oct 17 (146) $550

— Omnibus. L, 1842. 1st Ed in Book form. 8vo, later calf gilt. bba June 25 (220) £70 [Thorp]

Anr copy. Orig cloth; worn. With port & 21 plates. sg Oct 17 (147) $130

— Phrenological Illustrations. L, 1826. 1st Ed, 1st Issue. Oblong folio, cloth folder, orig rear wrap preserved. With 6 plates on india paper. Title soiled. sg Oct 17 (148) $250

Anr Ed. L, 1873. Oblong folio, mor gilt. Inscr & with pen-and-ink sketch, sgd. sg Nov 7 (50) $650

— The Pigeons—Dedicated to all the Flats.... L, 1817. 6th Ed. 12mo, orig cloth; worn, hinges tender. With 6 hand-colored plates. sg Oct 17 (176) $300

— Points of Humour. L, 1823-24. 2 parts in 1 vol. 8vo, mor by Tout. Plates hand-colored. Bound at end is Westmacott's Points of Misery, L, 1823. O May 26 (45) $550

Anr copy. Mor with onlaid figures after Cruikshank designs. With 20 plates. sg Oct 17 (149) $450

— A Pop-Gun Fired Off by George Cruikshank in Defence of the British Volunteers of 1803.... L, 1860. 8vo, calf, orig wraps bound in. Presentation copy, inscr. With Ms leaf containing Cruikshanks' notes for the work and 3 watercolor studies for the title design. sg Oct 17 (150) $850

— The Road to the Derby. L: Raphael Tuck & Sons, [1882]. 6 punch-out chromolitho panels, each c.88mm by 312mm, hinged onto cardbd sheets With Ns describing this as 1 of 2 proof copies given to John van Oost by Raphael Tuck. sg Oct 17 (151) $1,500

— Scraps and Sketches. L, 1828. Bound with:

Illustrations of Time. L, 1827. And: Phrenological Illustrations. L, 1826. Oblong folio, half mor. Oblong folio, 19th-cent half sheep; def. Some foxing. sg Feb 13 (185) $150

— A Slice of Bread and Butter. L, [1857]. 1st Ed. 8vo, half calf. With 3 woodcuts. Salomons copy. sg Oct 17 (179) $150

— Sunday in London.... L, 1833. 8vo, half calf; spine stained. cb Sept 26 (51) $50

— Table-Book. L, 1845. Ed by G. A. a Beckett. 8vo, orig cloth; edges worn, hinges cracked. With 12 plates. Some foxing. sg Oct 17 (152) $100

— The Wonderful Life and Adventures of Three-Fingered Jack, the Terror of Jamaica! L 1829. Allman's Ed. Bound with: Burdett, William. A New and Tenth Edition of the Life and Exploits of that Daring Robber, Three-finger'd Jack.... L, [n.d.] 12mo, calf gilt. 1st work with hand-colored folding frontis by Cruikshank; 2d work with frontis not by Cruikshank. sg Oct 17 (182) $275

Cruikshank, Isaac Robert & George

— The Cruikshankian Momus. L, 1892. One of 520. 4to, orig cloth; soiled. With 52 hand-colored plates. bba May 14 (354) £150 [Thorp]

Cruise, Richard Alexander

— Journal of a Ten Months' Residence in New Zealand. L, 1823. 1st Ed. 8vo, later half mor gilt. With hand-colored frontis. DW Apr 8 (23) £185

Crull, Jodocus, d.1713?

— The Antiquities of St. Peters, or the Abbey Church of Westminster.... L, 1713. 2 parts in 1 vol, including Supplement. 8vo contemp calf; rebacked. With folding frontis & 24 plates. bba Apr 9 (2) £130 [Land]

Crump, Spencer

— Redwoods, Iron Horses and the Pacific.... Los Angeles: Trans-Anglo Books, 1963. One of 400. In d/j. cb Feb 13 (87) $75

— Ride the Big Red Cars.... Los Angeles: Crest Publications, 1962. In d/j. cb Feb 13 (88) $55

Cruttwell, Clement

— A Gazetteer of France, containing Every City.... L, 1793. 3 vols in 1. 12mo, contemp sheep. With folding map, partly hand-colored in outline & with short tear. sg Oct 24 (79) $150

Cruveilhier, Jean

— Anatomia patologica del corpo umano. Florence, 1838-43. 4 vols of text & Atlas. 8vo & folio, text in half vellum, Atlas in later half vellum. With 232 litho plates, many colored. Tear in Plate 111; Plate 42 stained; some plates stained in inner margins; a few plates ink-stained in extreme outer margins. S May 13 (879) £2,300 [Riex]

— Anatomie pathologique du corps humain.... Paris, 1829. Vol I (of 2). only. Livraisons 1-12 (of 20) only. Folio, contemp cloth; worn. With 72 plates. Lacking titles. Spotting & dampstaining. DW Nov 6 (338) £150

Cruz, Martin de la. See: Codex

Cuala Press—Churchtown & Dublin

— FENOLLOSA, ERNEST F. - Certain Noble Plays of Japan.... 1916. One of 350. sg June 11 (90) $325

— YEATS, WILLIAM BUTLER. - Discoveries. 1907. One of 200. DW May 13 (496) £80

— YEATS, WILLIAM BUTLER. - A Packet for Ezra Pound. 1929. One of 425. Bookplate roughly removed from pastedown. wa Dec 9 (236) $70

— YEATS, WILLIAM BUTLER. - Stories of Michael Robartes and his Friends. 1931. One of 450. wa Dec 9 (237) $55

Cucala y Bruno, Jose

— Tratado de esgrima. Madrid, 1854. 8vo, calf. With 24 plates. Inscr. sg Mar 26 (91) $225

Anr copy. Orig wraps. sg Mar 26 (92) $110

Cudworth, Ralph, 1617-88

— The True Intellectual System of the Universe. L, 1743. 2d Ed. 2 vols. 4to, contemp sheep; worn. With folding frontis in Vol I. sg Oct 24 (80) $70

Cuitt, George, 1779-1854

— Wanderings and Pencillings amongst Ruins of the Olden Time. L, 1848. Folio, contemp half mor; rubbed, joints cracked. With 73 plates. Ck May 15 (92) £190

Cullen, Countee, 1903-46

— The Ballad of the Brown Girl. NY, 1927. 8vo, half cloth. bbc Apr 27 (290) $200

— Color. NY, 1925. Half cloth; edges worn. sg Dec 12 (73) $110

Culpeper, Nicholas, 1616-54

— The English Physician Enlarged.... L, 1790. ("Culpeper's English Physician and Complete Herbal.") 4to, old lea; worn, spine def. With 40 plates. Ink numerals at bottom of tp & verso of frontis; whiteout marks at foot of some text leaves; 1 plate tipped-in with tape; other minor defs. K July 12 (256) $450

Anr Ed. L, [1798?]. 2 vols in 1. 4to, contemp calf; rubbed. With 2 frontises, 12 tinted anatomical plates & 29 plates of plants. Tp dampstained. Ck Oct 18 (10) £120

Anr Ed. L, 1824. ("Culpeper's Complete Herbal....") 4to, contemp calf; def. With port & 40 colored plates. Some browning; lacking prelims. Sold w.a.f. pn Sept 12 (290) £85

— Pharmacopoeia Londinensis: or the London Dispensatory.... L, 1659. 8vo, 19th-cent calf; rubbed & worn. Torn & repaired. DW Mar 4 (203) £100

Culver, Henry Brundage

— The Book of Old Ships. NY, 1924. One of 750. 4to, orig bds; worn & stained. With engraved extra frontis, sgd. O Jan 14 (57) $60

— Contemporary Scale Models of Vessels of the Seventeenth Century. NY, [1926]. One of 1,000. Folio, half vellum; worn, spine frayed. O Apr 28 (163) $60

— Forty Famous Ships: their Beginnings, their Life Histories.... Garden City, NY, 1936. One of 501, sgd. Illus by Gordon Grant. 4to, cloth. O July 14 (59) $50

Cuming, Edward William Diron. See: Gilbey & Cuming

Cummings, Edward Estlin, 1894-1962

— 50 Poems. NY, [1940]. In d/j. Inscr to William Chapman Goodson. sg June 11 (92) $300

— Christmas Tree. NY: Pvtly ptd, 1928. Ltd Ed. Orig half cloth, unopened. Inscr to Montgomery Evans. pn Dec 12 (210) £110

— Complete Poems. Bristol, [1968]. One of 150. 2 vols. sg Dec 12 (74) $300

— The Enormous Room. NY, [1922]. 1st Ed, p 219 censored. sp Sept 22 (118) $90

Anr copy. Clipped signature mtd to tp. wa Sept 26 (142) $120

P 219 uncensored. Orig cloth, unopened, in def d/j. Sgd on front free endpaper. CNY June 9 (56) $350; sg Dec 12 (76) $50

Anr copy. Orig cloth, in d/j. Sgd. Epstein copy. sg Apr 29 (104) $650

Anr copy. In def d/j. sg June 11 (91) $110

— Him. NY, 1927. 1st Ed, one of 160. Bds. sg Dec 12 (77) $200

— Is 5. NY, 1926. 1st Ed. Half cloth. sg Dec 12 (78) $50

One of 77, sgd. sg June 11 (93) $375

— No Thanks. [NY, 1935]. Inscr. sg June 11 (94) $175

— Poems: 1923-1954 NY, 1954. Mor gilt. sg Dec 12 (80) $225

— Tulips and Chimneys. NY, 1923. 1st Ed. Half cloth. sg Dec 12 (81) $110

— W. NY, 1931. ("Viva: Seventy New Poems.") 1st Ed. In d/j. sg Dec 12 (82) $175

Cummins, John. See: Bulkeley & Cummins

Cunard, Nancy

— Negro. L, 1934. 1st Ed. Ed by Cunard. With contribs by Beckett, Langston Hughes, Pound, W. C. Williams & Dreiser. 4to, orig cloth; some wear, affected by damp. S Dec 12 (51) £700 [Horne]

— Poems (Two) 1925 L, 1930. One of 150. Sgd. cb Dec 12 (40) $50

Cundall, Herbert Minton, 1848-1940

— Birket Foster. L, 1906. One of 500. bba Dec 19 (104) £80 [Thorp]

Anr Ed. L, 1910. 4to, orig cloth; lower cover rubbed & stained. With frontis & 73 colored plates. pn May 14 (134) £90 [Proctor]

Cunningham, Eugene

— Triggernometry: a Gallery of Gunfighters. NY, 1934. 8vo, cloth; rubbed. cb Nov 14 (37) $65

Cunningham, Peter, 1816-69

— The Story of Nell Gwyn. L, 1862. 8vo, mor gilt by Kaufmann; upper joint starting on Vol I. Extra-illus with c.100 plates. O May 26 (46) $325

Cunningham, Peter Miller, 1789-1864

— Two Years in New South Wales.... L, 1828. 3d Ed. 2 vols. 8vo, orig cloth; worn, lacking backstrips, covers detached. Last leaves detached. bba Apr 30 (61) £80 [C. Smith]

Cunnington, Cecil Willett

— English Women's Clothing in the Nineteenth Century. L, 1937. 1st Ed. Folio, cloth. Sgd. pn Sept 12 (80) £55 [J. C. Books]

Cunynghame, Sir Arthur Augustus Thurlow, 1812-84

— An Aide-de-Camp's Recollections of Service in China.... L, 1844. 2 vols. 8vo, orig cloth. bba June 25 (254) £300 [Heywood Hill]

Cupid's...

— Cupid's Vagaries, or the Lover's Panorama for St. Valentine's Day. L, [1822]. Illus by George & Robert Cruikshank. 12mo, orig wraps. With 12 hand-colored illusts. Salomons copy. sg Oct 17 (187) $450

Cureus, Joachim
See also: Aimoinus, Monachus Floriacensis
— Schlesische und der weitberuembten stadt Bresslaw General Chronica. Wittenberg, 1587. Folio, contemp blind-tooled pigskin over wooden bds dated 1595; lacking clasps & catches. Browned. sg Oct 24 (81) $750

Curie, Marie, 1867-1934
— Traite de radioactivite. Paris, 1910 [i.e., 1911]. 1st Ed, Later Issue. 2 vols. Orig wraps; worn. With 8 plates. sg Nov 14 (221) $800

Curione, Carlo Lodovico
— Lanatomia delle Cancellaresche corsive.... Rome, 1588. Oblong 4to, modern vellum. 48 engraved leaves. Title & plates numbered 32-39 supplied from a smaller copy; some soiling; 7th line of title excised & replaced by blank slip. C June 24 (230) £300 [Gherucci]

Curle, Richard H. P.
— Collecting American First Editions. Indianapolis, [1930]. Ltd Ed. With 50 plates. cb Feb 27 (21) $50; K Sept 29 (145) $55

Curley, Lucy Matilda
— The Hills and Plains of Palestine. L, 1860. 4to, orig cloth; new endpapers. With tinted litho frontis & additional title & 28 tinted litho plates. Some browning. S July 1 (749) £340 [Maggs]

Curling, Bill. See: Graham & Curling

Curr, Edward Micklethwaite
— Recollections of Squatting in Victoria.... Melbourne & L, 1883. 8vo, orig cloth; spine rubbed. With folding map (torn at fold). bba June 25 (247) £70 [Dawes]

Currier, Ernest M., 1867-1936
— Marks of Early American Silversmiths.... Portland: Southworth-Anthoensen Press, 1938. One of 750. 4to, cloth; worn. sp June 18 (334) $120

Curschmann, H.
— Klinische Abbildungen. Berlin, 1894. 4to, half lea; spine def, corners bumped. With 57 heliogravure plates. Some foxing to text. sg Apr 13 (66) $550

Curtis, Edward S., 1868-1952
— In the Land of the Head-Hunters. Yonkers, 1915. Half cloth; worn, hinges cracked. bbc Feb 17 (195) $160
— Indian Days of the Long Ago. Yonkers NY, 1914. Photos by Curtis; drawings by F. N. Wilson. bbc Feb 17 (196) $65
— The North American Indian. Cambr., Mass., 1907-30. Mixed set, with most photogravures in the rarest state, ptd on Japanese tissue. Ed by F. W. Hodge; foreword by Theodore Roosevelt. 40 vols. 4to & folio, Text, orig half mor gilt; portfolios, library cloth. With 1,505 photogravures (34 hand-colored), 4 maps & 2 diagrams in text vols. 723 photogravures in sepia; 9 plates issued out of sequence. Perforated library stamps on titles & ink stamps on following leaves and versos of large plates. CNY Dec 5 (216) $180,000

Curtis, John, 1791-1862
— British Entomology. L, 1824-39 [1823-40]. 16 vols. 8vo, contemp half mor; rubbed. With 700 hand-colored plates. Text spotted. Library markings. bba Sept 5 (23) £1,500 [Rainer]

Anr copy. Bound in 16 vols. 8vo, half mor gilt. With 770 hand-colored plates. pnE Mar 11 (22) $2,100

Anr copy. 16 vols. 8vo, orig bds; spines missing or def. Minor staining; plates in Vol I are reissues. S June 25 (11) £1,400 [Elvidge]
— Farm Insects: Being the Natural History.... L, 1860. 8vo, orig cloth. With 16 hand-colored plates. Library markings. bba Sept 5 (24) £50 [Ginnan]

Curtis, Natalie
— The Indians' Book. An Offering by the American Indians of Indian Lore, Musical and Narrative. NY & L, 1907. 4to, orig cloth; rubbed. K Mar 22 (195) $90

Curtis, William, 1746-99
— The Botanical Magazine; or Flower Garden Displayed. L, 1787-1926. Vols 1-152, lacking Vol 147. Bound in 152 vols plus 2 index vols. Vols 1-100 in contemp half calf, the remainder in library cloth; various defs. With c.9,050 hand-colored plates. Some plates cropped affecting imprints & image in a few cases; library stamps, not affecting plates. Sold w.a.f. pn Mar 19 (269) £20,000 [Schuster]

Vols 1-300. L, 1787-1809. Bound in 15 vols. Contemp half mor gilt; extremities worn. With 1,238 plates, all but 2 hand-colored. sg May 7 (66) $16,000

Vols 1-6. L, 1787-93. Bound in 3 vols. Contemp calf; worn. With 216 hand-colored plates. Some soiling & spotting. Ck Sept 6 (11) £1,600

Vols 1-26. L, 1792-1807. Bound in 13 vols. 8vo, contemp mor gilt; upper cover of final vol scuffed. With 1,061 plates, 1,059 of them hand-colored. C Oct 30 (257) £5,000 [Mason]

Vol 7. L, 1794. 8vo, orig bds; spine worn. With 36 hand-colored plates. bba Nov 7 (100) £320 [Princeton Rare Books]

Vols 18-20 in 1 vol. L, 1803-4. 8vo, contemp calf; worn. With 172 hand-colored plates. Tp & Plate 645 soiled; hand-coloring to Plate 666 smudged. Ck May 15 (19) £1,100

Vols 26 & 27. L, 1807-8. Contemp sheep gilt; worn. sg Feb 13 (160) $1,500

Vols 28-29. L, 1807-9. 2 vols in 1. Contemp sheep gilt. sg Feb 13 (161) $1,300

Vols 30-31. L, 1809. Bound in 1 vol. Contemp sheep gilt; worn. sg Feb 13 (162) $1,600

Vol 45. L, 1818. 8vo, contemp half calf; broken. With 81 hand-colored plates. pn May 14 (169) £360

— Flora Londinensis. L, 1817-28. 5 vols. Folio, contemp mor gilt; worn. With 647 hand-colored plates. Some spotting, mainly confined to text. S June 25 (13) £5,800 [Junk]

— Lectures on Botany. L, 1805. 3 vols in 2. 8vo, contemp calf gilt; rebacked. With port & 119 hand-colored plates. Some spotting & discoloration. S June 25 (12) £600 [Titles]

— Practical Observations on the British Grasses.... L, 1812. 5th Ed. 8vo, modern half calf. With folding colored frontis & 7 colored plates. bba Jan 16 (346) £80 [Ginnan]

Curtis, Winifred. See: Stones & Curtis

Curtiss, Glenn Hammond —& Post, Augustus

— The Curtiss Aviation Book. NY, [1912]. Orig cloth. Inscr. cb Nov 7 (30) $450; cb Nov 7 (31) $80

Curtius (Quintus Curtius Rufus)

— Historia Alexandri magni Regis Macedonum.... Delft & Leiden, 1724. ("De rebus gestis Alexandri magni.") 4to, early vellum; soiled. With frontis, folding map & 14 plates. wa Apr 9 (107) $180

Curwen Press—London

— A Specimen Book of Pattern Papers.... L, 1928. Ed by Paul Nash. Orig cloth; rubbed. With 31 specimens Library markings. bba Oct 24 (219) £400 [Collinge & Clark]

Curzon, George Nathaniel

— Persia and the Persian Question. L, 1892. 2 vols. 8vo, cloth; several hinges starting. sg Jan 9 (61) $300

Cusack, Capt. George

[-] The Grand Pyrate: Or, the Life and Death of Capt. George Cusack the great Sea-Robber. L, 1676. 2 parts in 1 vol. 4to, half lea; spine ends worn. Dampstained; some cropping at bottom. DuPont copy. CNY Oct 8 (204) $1,300

Cushing, Harvey, 1869-1939

— Meningiomas: their Classification, Regional Behaviour.... Springfield IL, 1938. Library markings. sg May 14 (36) $300

Cuspinianus, Joannes

— De Caesaribus atq[ue] imperatoribus Romanis. [Strassburg: C. Mylius], 1540. Folio, contemp blind-stamped pigskin; rebacked, clasps lacking. Tp wormed at outer margin affecting inscr; wormhole at upper margin of prelims; verso of X3 soiled; ink stain on 2H4; final leaf restored at corner. Ck Oct 31 (72) £800

Cussans, John Edwin, 1837-89

— History of Hertfordshire. L, 1870-81. 3 vols. Folio, contemp half mor gilt; rubbed. With map & 22 plates. bba Oct 24 (295) £260 [C. Smith]

Anr copy. Contemp half lea; some bds detached, lacking spine, Vol I rebacked. With 3 frontises, 1 double-page map, 1 estate plan, 19 plates (17 tinted) & some spotting. pn Apr 23 (258) £95 [Spake]

One of 75 L.p. copies. Contemp half mor; hinges repaired. With 21 plates. bba June 25 (38) £240 [Culley]

Custer, Elizabeth Bacon, d.1933

— Tenting on the Plains, or General Custer in Kansas and Texas. NY, 1889. 8vo, orig cloth. cb Nov 14 (39) $70

Custos, Raphael

— Emblemata amoris. Augsburg: Lucas Schultes, 1622-31. 2 parts in 1 vol. 4to, contemp vellum. With 2 engraved titles & 73 engraved emblems. Some staining & a few short tears. S Dec 5 (229) £750 [Forum]

Cutler, Nathaniel —& Halley, Edmund

— Atlas Maritimus & Commercialis: or, a General View of the World. L, 1728. 2 vols. Folio, contemp calf; worn, joints split on text vol; Atlas with upper cover detached. With 54 engraved sheets froming 50 double-page & folding charts & 5 diagrams tipped-in to text. Some tears at folds & margins; dampstaining; some shaving & pencil marginalia. pn June 11 (301) £3,200 [Franks]

Cyllenius, Domenicus

— De vertere & recentiore scientia militari.... Venice: Francesco Portonari, 1559. Folio, later bds. Tp browned; some dampstaining throughout. S May 13 (762) £300 [Casa d'Arte]

Cynwal, William. See: Golden Cockerel Press

Cyprian, Saint

— Opera. Venice: Vindelinus de Spira, 1471. Folio, 19th-cent sheep; joints repaired. 37-38 lines; types 1:110R (text) & 110Gk (chapter numbers in Book 2 of Ad Quirinum. First leaf with marginal def & anr small def affecting a single letter; minor staining. 182 (of 184) leaves; 2 final blanks. Goff C-1011. C Nov 27 (12) £3,000 [Mediolanum]

Cyrano de Bergerac, Savinien, 1619-55

— The Comical History of the States and Empires of the Worlds of the Moon and Sun. L 1687. 1st Ed in English. Trans by A. Lovell. 2 parts in 1 vol. 8vo, modern calf gilt by Bayntun. Some dampstaining; short tears without loss. Manney copy. P Oct 11 (69) $3,000

— Histoire comique...contenant les Estats & Empires de la Lune. Lyons: Pierre Compagnon & Robert Taillandier, 1672. 12mo, contemp sheep; worn, spine ends chipped. Tp & next leaf browned & brittle; some foxing. sg Oct 24 (83) $850

Cyril of Alexandria, Saint

— In Evangelium Ioannis. Paris: V. Hopyl, 1508. Bound with: Praeclarum opus thesaurus. Paris: W.Hopyl, 1514 [1513]. And: Eximii commentarii in Leviticum. Paris: W. Hopyl, 20 May 1514. Folio, 16th-cent blind-stamped pigskin over wooden bds; lacking 2 clasps, some rubbing & worming to bdg. Duplicate stamp of the Royal Library at Munich. S Dec 5 (95) £800 [Salvador]

Czwiklitzer, Christophe

— Picasso's Posters. NY, 1970-71. 4to, orig cloth, in d/j. DW Mar 11 (485) £95

Anr Ed. NY, 1970. Folio, cloth; corners worn, rear hinge cracked. sg Feb 6 (226) $200

Anr Ed. NY, [1971]. In d/j. cb Nov 21 (187) $75

D

D., ——

— Le Grand Livre de la nature, ou l'apocalypse philosophique et hermetique. Midi, [1790?]. 8vo, modern sheep. sg Mar 12 (211) $175

D., C. See: Deval, Charles

D., H. See: Doolittle, Hilda

Dacier, Emile —& Others

— Jean de Jullienne et les graveurs de Watteau au XVIIIe siecle. Paris, 1929-21-22. 4 vols, including portfolio of plates. Folio, orig wraps. Some pencil & ink annotations. bba Feb 13 (255) £150 [Sims Reed]

Anr copy. 4 vols in 2. Folio, half mor; joints split, spines chipped. S Feb 11 (51) £200 [Lanfranchi]

Dagley, Richard, d.1841

— Gems, Selected from the Antique. L, 1804. One of 25. 4to, contemp mor gilt. With 20 plates. bba Oct 10 (168) £200 [Demtzy]

Daglish, Eric Fitch

— Birds of the British Isles. L, 1948. Ltd Ed. Orig cloth. DW Apr 8 (402) £55

Dahl, Roald

— The Gremlins.... L: Collins, [1944]. Illus by Walt Disney Studios. 4to, orig half cloth; corners bumped. DW Dec 11 (411) £160

Dahlberg, Erik Johnsson, Count, 1625-1703

— Suecia antiqua et hodierna. [Stockholm, 1693-1713, but later]. 3 vols in 1. Oblong folio, 19th-cent half mor; rebacked in calf. With 350 plates & maps. Some outer margins soiled; several lower corners rodent-damaged. Additional folding plate bound in at end. Sold w.a.f. C Dec 16 (42) £2,200 [Kafka]

Anr Ed. [Paris or Stockholm, 1667-1716]. 3 vols in 2. Oblong folio, 18th-cent half calf; worn. With 354 (of 359) plates plus additional plate of the Swedish Church in London dated 1728 inserted at end. Tp in facsimile. S June 25 (318) £2,700 [Toscani]

Anr Ed. [Stockholm, 1693-1713]. 3 vols in 1. Oblong folio, contemp calf gilt, reportedly by Kristoff Schneidler of Stockholm; minor rubbing at corners, joints & spine extremities. With 353 plates & ports & maps cut round & mtd as issued plus extra plate of the Swedish Church in London. Some browning; tear to blank lower margin of Plate 146 in Part 1; smudge to Plate 10 in Part 2. McCarty-Cooper copy. CNY Jan 25 (15) $6,500

Daily...

— The Daily Citizen. Vicksburg, 4 July 1863. 442mm by 265mm, ptd on floral wallpaper. Trimmed close at top, shaving 1 letter of masthead & bit of border rule; some marginal tears; some browning & soiling. P June 16 (206) $3,500

Dainelli, Giotto

— Buddhists and Glaciers of Western Tibet. L, 1933. sg Jan 9 (285) $110

Dakota Territory

— The Resources of Dakota—1887. Sioux Falls, 1887. 8vo, cloth; front hinge starting. sg Dec 5 (86) $150

Dalby, Isaac. See: Mudge & Dalby

Dale, Anthony, 1638-1708

— Dissertationes de origine ac progressu idololatriae et superstitionum.... Amst., 1696. 4to, contemp vellum; rear joint gnawed. sg Mar 12 (209) $300

Dalence, Joachim, d.1707

— Trattato curioso di matematica.... Venice: Giovanni Battista Recurti, 1753. 4to, contemp bds. O Dec 17 (47) $190

Dali, Salvador

— Les Metamorphoses erotiques. L, 1969. One of 300. 4to, loose in orig cloth folder as issued. S July 1 (1172) £190 [MacDonald]

One of 1,200. Loose in orig silk covered bds. DW Mar 11 (486) £55

— Le Mythe tragique de l'Angelus de Millet. [Paris], 1963. 4to, cloth in form of notebook secured by integral belt & buckle; rubbed. wa Sept 26 (578) $75

— La Quete du Graal. Paris, 1975. One of 25 on velin d'Arches with 2 extra suites of plates. Folio, loose as issued. CGen Nov 18 (350) SF20,000

Dalla Bona, Giovanni

— Dell' use e dell' abuso del caffe.... Livorno, 1762. 4to, contemp wraps; rubbed. bba Nov 28 (106) £90 [Il Collezionista]

Dallaway, James, 1763-1834

— Constantinople. L, 1797. 4to, half calf; repaired, rebacked, orig backstrip preserved. With engraved title, map & 9 plates. Library markings. bba Sept 19 (115A) £160 [Scott]

Anr copy. Later half calf; covers rubbed. With engraved title & 10 plates. Ck Oct 18 (57) £320

Anr copy. Contemp russia gilt. S June 30 (272) £600 [Dallegio]

Anr copy. Contemp calf; worn & broken. With engraved title, map & 9 plates. S July 1 (590) £280 [Consolidated Real]

— Inquiries into the Origin and Progress of the Science of Heraldry in England. Gloucester, 1793. 2 parts in 1 vol. 4to, contemp calf gilt; corners, rubbed, rebacked, hinges reinforced. With frontis & 26 plates, 8 colored by hand. S July 1 (1233) £160 [C. Smith]

Anr copy. Old calf; rebacked, worn. With 26 plates, 8 in color. wa June 25 (490) $210

Dalrymple, Alexander, 1737-1808

— A Collection of Voyages Chiefly in the Southern Atlantick Ocean. L, 1775. 4to, modern half calf, orig bds retained. With 3 plates. 2 leaves spotted. S June 25 (46) £4,200 [Quaritch/Hordern]

— An Historical Collection of the Several Voyages and Discoveries in the South Pacific Ocean. L, 1770-71. 2 vols in 1. 4to, modern half calf; Vol II shorter. With 5 folding maps & 12 plates. Some browning; 4th folding map in Vol I with 2 small tears. Cuvier-duPont copy. CNY Oct 8 (81) $4,500

Anr copy. 18th-cent calf gilt; rebacked. With 4 folding maps & 12 plates. Lacking 1 (of 2) half-titles. S June 25 (45) £3,200 [Quaritch/Hordern]

— A Plan for Extending the Commerce of this Kingdom and of the East India Company. L, 1769. 8vo, modern mor gilt. With folding map. C June 25 (40) £3,200 [Randall]

Dalrymple Library, Alexander

— [Sale Catalogue] A Catalogue Part II of the Library...sold by Auction by Messrs. King & Lochee...Covent-Garden, on Monday, Nov. 6, 1809.... L: J. Barker, [1809]. 8vo, modern calf. Tp soiled; a few leaves torn in margins. C June 25 (74) £380 [Quaritch/Hordern]

Dalton, James, Novelist

— The Gentleman in Black. L, 1831. Illus by George Cruikshank. 12mo, later calf gilt, orig cloth covers & spine bound in. bba Apr 9 (257) £60 [Dawson]

Anr copy. Later calf gilt by Zaehnsdorf. F Sept 26 (102) $90

Dalton, Richard, 1715?-91

— Antiquities and Views in Greece and Egypt.... L, 1751-52. 2d Ed. Folio, contemp half russia gilt; upper cover detached. With 43 plates. George Milne copy. CNY Dec 5 (217) $1,000

Dalton, William Hugh

— The New and Complete English Traveller. L, [1794]. Folio, disbound. With frontis, 46 views & 16 maps. Some leaves & plates with worm-tracing; some spotting & browning. Sold w.a.f. DW Apr 8 (93) £400

Dalvimart, Octavien. See: Alexander, William

Daly, James. See: Gray, Frank S.

Daly, T. A. See: Morley & Daly

Dalziel, George & Edward

— The Brothers Dalziel, a Record of Fifty Years Work...1840-1890. L, 1901. cb Sept 26 (69) $100

— The Brothers Dalziel, a Record of Fifty Years' Work. 1840-1890. L, 1901. 1st Ed. 4to, modern mor; upper hinges splitting. bba May 28 (276) £70 [Pickering & Chatto]

Anr copy. Orig cloth; rubbed. cb Sept 26 (69) $100

Dame...

— Dame Wiggins of Lee and her Seven Wonderful Cats.... L: Dean & Munday, 1823. 4to, orig ptd wraps; detached, worn & stained. With frontis & 16 plates, all colored. Some discoloration. bba July 23 (291) £300 [Ribose]

Anr Ed. Orpington: George Allen, 1885. Ed by John Ruskin. 8vo, orig cloth. bba July 23 (232) £70 [Kinokuniya]

Damhouderius, Jodocus, 1507-81

— Praxis rerum criminalium. Antwerp: Joannes Bellerus, 1562. 4to, contemp blind-tooled pigskin over pastebd, stamped 1565 on front cover. Tear in 1 leaf. sg May 7 (67) $1,400

Damiano da Odemira

— Libro da imparare giochare a scachi. [Rome, c.1525]. 8vo, 19th-cent lea gilt; spine worn. 28 lines; roman type. Ck May 8 (25) £4,600

Anr Ed. [Rome, c.1528]. 8vo, contemp vellum. Short tear in tp affecting cut; tears in last 2 leaves affecting text. Ck May 8 (27) £1,500

Anr Ed. [Rome, c.1530]. 8vo, contemp vellum. Tp cropped & with holes; Blass library-stamp offset onto title & text; last leaf soiled. Ck May 8 (26) £1,600

Dampier, William, 1652-1715

— A Collection of Voyages. L, 1729. 4 vols. 8vo, contemp calf; outer joint cracked, some wear. With 63 plates & maps. Marginal chip in 1 plate; fore-margin of 1 map cropped. DuPont copy. CNY Oct 8 (82) $4,000

Anr copy. With 62 (of 63) maps & plates. S June 25 (33) £2,500 [Stokes]

— A New Voyage Round the World. L, 1697. 2d Ed. 8vo, 18th-cent calf; worn. With 5 maps, 4 foldin. Some dampstaining; frontis map stained & frayed along outer margin. DW May 13 (19) £160

Dana, James Dwight, 1813-95

— Corals and Coral Islands. NY, 1872. 8vo, contemp calf; minor wear. kh Nov 11 (476) A$180

Anr copy. Cloth; worn. With 2 folding maps. O Jan 14 (58) $110

Dana, Richard Henry, Jr., 1815-82

See also: Grabhorn Printing; Limited Editions Club

— The Seaman's Friend: Containing a Treatise on Practical Seamanship. Bost., [1841]. 8vo, orig sheep. sg May 7 (68) $1,100

— Two Years Before the Mast. NY, 1840. 1st Ed, 1st Issue. 12mo, orig cloth, BAL's bdg A but this copy in brown cloth; front free endpaper lacking. Some foxing. McCutcheon-duPont copy. CNY Oct 8 (83) $1,900

Anr copy. Orig cloth; some soiling, spine restored, with orig spine laid down. Some rubbing. Manney copy. P Oct 11 (70) $5,500

Anr copy. Orig cloth; some fraying or surface tears on spine & corners. P June 17 (172) $900

Anr copy. Orig cloth; rebacked. Soiled & rubbed. Epstein copy. sg Apr 29 (105) $2,600

Anr copy. Orig cloth, BAL bdg B, State 1. Some foxing. sg June 18 (57) $550

Anr Ed. L, 1841. 8vo, orig cloth; spine def. Browned. bbc Sept 23 (309) $160

Anr Ed. Chicago, 1930. One of 1,000. Cloth. sg Jan 30 (34) $80

Anr copy. Illus by Edward A. Wilson. Cloth; worn. K Sept 29 (147) $60

Dance. See: Douce, Francis

Dance, George, 1741-1825

— A Collection of Portraits Sketched from the Life...in Imitation of the Original Drawings by William Daniell. L, 1809 [1808]-14. 2 vols. Folio, contemp half calf; spines worn, covers of Vol I detached, joints of Vol II split. With 72 plates. Lacking tp in Vol I. S Feb 11 (304) £320 [Edmonds]

Daneau, Lambert

— Geographiae poeticae, id est, universae terrae descriptionis.... Geneva: Jacob Stoer, 1580. 1st Ed, 2d Issue. 8vo, contemp vellum. Some dampstaining in corners. sg Mar 12 (59) $200

Danet, Guillaume

— L'Art des armes. Paris, 1746-47. 2 vols in 1. 8vo, contemp sheep. With frontis & 43 folding plates. sg Mar 26 (93) $700

Anr Ed. Paris, 1766-67. 2 parts in 1 vol. 8vo, contemp sheep gilt. With port & 33 (of

43) plates. Lacking 10 plates. sg Mar 26 (94) $90

Anr Ed. Paris, 1788. 2 parts. 8vo, ucontemp sheep. With frontis & 43 folding plates. sg Mar 26 (95) $200

Danfrie, Philippe

— Declaration de l'usage du graphometre.... Paris, 1597. 1st Ed, 2d Issue. 8vo, vellum; worn. Some staining; marginal worming. S May 28 (4) £2,000 [Pickering]

Daniel, Gabriel, 1649-1728

— Histoire de la milice francoise. Paris, 1721. 2 vols. 4to, contemp calf; worn. With frontises & 68 plates. Some blank corners cut away. S July 1 (1235) £250 [Booth]

Anr copy. Contemp sheep; spines derf. sg Jan 9 (128) $200

— Voiage du monde de Descartes. Paris, 1691. 12mo, contemp vellum. Title soiled & frayed. DW Jan 29 (225) £80

Anr copy. Contemp vellum; soiled. DW Mar 4 (204) £50

— A Voyage to the World of Cartesius. L, 1692. 1st Ed in English. 8vo, modern half mor. Tears repaired in upper corners of E3, H2-3, T5 & U1, affecting some page numerals; lower corner of tp & 1st few pages chipped & soiled; tear in text of G6 not affecting legibility. Manney copy. P Oct 11 (71) $250

Daniel Library, George

— [Sale Catalogue] Catalogue of the most valuable, interesting and highly important Library.... L, 1864. 8vo, contemp calf. Priced in Ms throughout. cb Oct 17 (215) $150

Anr copy. Half calf; worn. O Dec 17 (48) $770

Daniel Press—Oxford

— Memorials of C. H. O. Daniel with a Bibliography of the Press.... 1921. One of 500. 4to, half cloth, unopened. cb Oct 17 (563) $95

Anr copy. Orig half cloth; rubbed. DW May 13 (358) £50

Daniel, Samuel, 1562-1619

— The Collection of the Historie of England. L, [1618]. Folio, old calf; rebacked. kh Nov 11 (340) A$100

— The Collection of the History of England. L, 1634. With the 1636 continuation bound in Folio, contemp mor gilt with crest of Charles II as Prince of Wales; spine & corners repaired, later free endpapers. C Dec 16 (188) £4,800 [Quaritch]

Daniel, William Barker, 1753?-1833

— Rural Sports. L, 1801-2. 2 vols plus 1813 Supplement. 4to, contemp calf; Vol I joint cracked, Vol II rebacked preserving orig spine. With engraved titles, frontis & 67 plates & tables. Some spotting. S Feb 26 (847) £320 [Hughes]

Anr Ed. L, 1812. 4 vols including 1813 Supplement. 4to, calf gilt. With 73 (of 75) plates. bba Jan 30 (427) £180 [Kafka]

Anr copy. 3 vols. 4to, contemp calf. Lacking title & 3 plates for Vol I. DW Oct 2 (135) £100

Anr copy. 4 vols including 1813 Supplement. 4to, half mor. LH Dec 11 (90) $190

Anr copy. 3 vols plus 1913 Supplement. 4to, contemp calf gilt. pnE Oct 1 (283) £220

Daniell, Samuel, 1755-1811

— Sketches Representing the Native Tribes.... L, 1820. Oblong 4to, contemp half mor; rubbed. With 48 plates. bba Sept 19 (57) £600 [Sharp]

Daniell, Thomas, 1749-1840 & William, 1769-1837

— A Picturesque Voyage to India.... L, 1810. Oblong folio, recent half mor. With 50 colored plates. C Oct 30 (23) £2,200 [R. S. Books]

Anr copy. With 50 hand-colored plates on thick paper, mtd on guards. C May 20 (248) £33,200 [Strover]

Anr copy. Later half calf gilt; rubbed. With 50 hand-colored plates on thick paper. DW Mar 4 (15) £1,600

Anr copy. 19th-cent half pigskin; rubbed & faded. With 48 (of 50) hand-colored plates; lacking 3 & 49. Lacking tp & introduction; some soiling. S Nov 15 (1286) £900 [Shapero]

Daniell, William, 1769-1837

— Interesting Selections from Animated Nature. L, [1809-11]. Vol I only. Cloth; rubbed. b Nov 18 (363) £200

Anr copy. Contemp russia bilt; rebacked, old spine preserved. With 50 plates. pn Mar 19 (390) £160

— Select Views of Windsor Castle and Adjacent Scenery. L, [mounts watermarked 1831-35]. Oblong folio, unbound as issued in contemp half mor portfolio. With 12 hand-colored plates, each cut to edge of image & mtd on card within a single-line ruled ink border. Without the dedication/title leaf; 7 of the plates have small engraved title labels mtd on verso, 4 are titled in pencil on the mounts, 1 is untitled. C May 20 (44) £5,500 [Heywood Hill]

— A Voyage Round the North and North-

West Coast of Scotland.... L: W. Lewis, [c.1820]. Folio, orig wraps; upper cover torn. With etched & aquatint title & 26 plates. Some spotting & marginal soiling. Ck Oct 18 (58) £150

Daniell, William, 1769-1837 —& Ayton, Richard, 1786-1823

— A Voyage Round Great Britain.... L, 1814-25. Vol I only. Contemp half russia gilt; worn. With 26 hand-colored plates. Dedication leaf loose & frayed. Sold w.a.f. bba May 14 (356) £950 [Kinnaird]

Anr copy. 8 vols. 4to, half mor gilt by Sawyer. With aquatint dedication & 308 hand-colored plates ptd on card & mtd on guards. Without index map & the uncolored Kemaes Head plate. C May 20J (45) £19,000 [Litup]

Anr copy. 8 vols in 4. 4to, contemp mor gilt; rebacked. With engraved dedication leaf, folding map & plate of Kemaes-Head on Vol I, & 308 hand-colored plates. Clean tear at 1 fold of the map; some foxing. Morgan-Schlosser copy. P June 18 (453) $18,000

Vol VII here is dated 1826. L, 1814-26. 8 vols in 4. 4to, half mor gilt by Lauriat; rubbed, spine ends repaired. With 308 hand-colored plates. Without the map & the uncolored Kemaes Head plate. C Oct 30 (24) £8,500 [Marshall]

Danielson, Richard Ely. See: Derrydale Press

Dante Alighieri, 1265-1321

See also: Limited Editions Club; Nonesuch Press

— Opere. Venice, 1757. Vol II (of 3) only. 4to, contemp vellum. Some leaves inkstained. bba Apr 9 (23) £140 [Abdullah]

Anr Ed. Florence, 1830. 6 vols. 8vo, bds; spines soiled or frayed. Some spotting. pn Sept 12 (192) £60 [American Bookstore]

Anr copy. Contemp half vellum. SI Dec 5 (820) LIt550,000

— La Vita nuova. New Rochelle: G. D. Sproule, 1902. Saint Dunstan Ed, Out-of-series copy of vellum, illuminated throughout in gold and colors. 2 vols. 4to, mor extra by Trautz-Bauzonnet. CNY Dec 5 (445) $2,600

Divina Commedia in Italian

— 1491, 18 Nov. - Venice: Petrus de PLasiis Cremonensis called Veronensis. Folio, 19th-cent vellum. 45 lines of text, 61 lines of commentary; types 6:109R (text) & 7:80R (commentary); 100 woodcut illusts. Leaf g8 torn & inserted from anr copy; damage to cut on a6r; also to b4 affecting text; small tear in g7; some worming & staining. 323 (of 324) leaves; last leaf in facsimile. Goff D-33. C Dec 16 (43) £2,200 [Mazza]

— 1502. - Le Terze Rime. Venice: Aldus Issue with inverted V in colophon. 8vo, 19th-cent calf. Italic letter. Some waterstaining. C Dec 16 (119) £2,500 [Soave]

— 1507. - Dante Aligheri Fiorentino historiado.... Venice: Bartholomeo de Zanni da Portese. Folio, 19th-cent vellum painted with port of Dante on front cover. With full-page woodcut port. Marginal dampstaining throughout. sg Oct 24 (84) $2,400

— 1515. - Venice: Aldus. 8vo, vellum bds; upper joints split, loose. Italic letter. Some staining; some leaves cropped, affecting headlines; some leaves at end repaired in inner margins; lacing a1, a7 (supplied in facsimile) & H7 & 8. Sold w.a.f. pn July 16 (11) £320

— 1564. - Venice: Marchio Sessa & fratelli Ed by Francesco Sansovino. Folio, modern pigskin. 3 leaves holed in upper margins. SI June 9 (291) LIt3,000,000

— 1578. - Venice: G. Marchio Sessa. Folio, old bds; worn, backstrip missing. Title marked and witht small holes & repaired tears; last leaf marked. bba Jan 30 (307) £400 [Bifolco]

Anr copy. 18th-cent mor gilt with arms of Jacques-Claude Claret de la Tourrette; spine worn at head. Some browning; 1st 8 leaves with marginal dampstain at foot. C Dec 16 (118) £2,200 [Ghezzi]

Anr copy. Modern vellum; upper joint split. Some soiling & browning; marginal annotations. Milne copy. Ck June 12 (45) £400

— 1596. - Dante con l'espositioni di Christoforo Landino et d'Alessandro Vellutello. Venice: G. B. Sessa. Folio, old vellum; spine repaired, front joint cracking. First few leaves mtd on stubs; old repairs, especially to tp; last numeral of date supplied from colophon; tear in leaf CC2; some browning. K Mar 22 (111) $425

— 1815-17. - Rome: De Romanis. 4 vols. 12mo, contemp half lea. SI Dec 5 (186) LIt320,000

— 1902. - La Divina Commedia. Florence 3 vols. Folio, modern half lea, orig wraps bound in. SI Dec 5 (188) LIt300,000

Divina Commedia in Italian & German

— 1921. - Vienna, etc. One of 1,100. Illus by F. von Bayros. 3 vols. 4to, half vellum gilt. With 60 mtd color plates heightened with gilt. Sgd by illustrator in Vol I. HH May 12 (2148) DM550

English Versions

— [c.1860]. - L. Trans by Henry Francis Cary; illus by Gustave Dore. 4to, contem half mor; rubbed. bba Apr 9 (301) £110 [Percy]

— 1866. - L. Trans by Henry Francis Cary; illus by Gustave Dore. 4to, contemp half mor; rubbed. bba Apr 9 (302) £110 [Percy]

Anr copy. Mor gilt. Met Apr 28 (394) $350

— 1867. - Bost. Trans by Henry Wadsworth Longfellow. 3 vols. 8vo, contemp half mor; worn. cb Oct 25 (34) $60

— 1867. - L. Trans by Henry Wadsworth Longfellow. 3 vols. 8vo, half calf gilt; extremities scuffed. sg Mar 5 (81) $120

— 1929. - San Francisco: John Henry Nash One of 250 on handmade paper. 4 vols, including The Florence of Dante, in 2. Folio, later half mor. cb Oct 31 (277) $475

— 1949. - The Comedy of Dante Alighieri, the Florentine. Harmondsworth: Penguin Books Trans by Dorothy L. Sayers. Wraps, in d/j. Inscr. cb Sept 19 (188) $130

— 1955. - NY One of 300. Trans by Charles Eliot Norton. Folio, mor gilt. O Nov 26 (153) $85; pba July 23 (191) $350; sg Sept 26 (82) $175

— 1969. - NY Trans by Thomas G. Bergin; illus by Leonard Baskin. 3 vols. Folio, half cloth. sg Sept 26 (18) $50

Dapper, Olfert, d.1690

— Asia.... Amst., 1680. Folio, contemp calf gilt; worn. With engraved title & 11 (of 15) double-page maps & plates. Some stains & tears, affecting text. Sold w.a.f. S July 1 (831) £500 [Rieden]

Anr Ed. Nuremberg, 1681. 2 parts in 1 vol. folio, contemp calf; worn, crudely repaired. With engraved title, 11 double-page or folding maps, 20 double-page or folding plates & 8 full-page plates. Jerusalem slightly torn; some spotting. S July 1 (748) £1,050 [Baum]

— Description de l'Afrique. Amst., 1686. 1st Ed in French. Folio, contemp calf; crudely rebacked. With extra title, 11 double-page maps (1 folding) & 32 double-page plates. Some soiling. DW Nov 6 (32) £420

— Description exacte des isles de l'archipel.... Amst., 1703. Folio, calf. With engraved title, 7 folding maps, 11 folding plates & 16 single plates. S Nov 21 (246) £2,400 [Athanassiou]

Anr copy. Modern half calf; rubbed. With engraved title, 17 (of 18) folding maps & plates & 16 full-page plates. Some leaves towards end dampstained at foot. S July 1 (595) £2,600 [Consolidated Real]

Anr Ed. The Hague, 1730. Folio, contemp calf gilt; upper joint split. With 29 maps & plates. Extra-illus with 5 additional plates. bba Sept 19 (136) £2,200

— Naukeurige beschrijvinge der Afrikaensche gewesten van Egypten.... Amst., 1676. Folio, later half vellum; slight defs. With engraved title, 46 maps & 56 engravings. With 3 extra maps by J. B. Nolin, colored in outline. Title of Part 3 misbound; small tear in 1 map repaired; some foxing. B May 12 (1289) HF4,500

— Naukeurige Beschryving van Morea.... Amst., 1688. Folio, contemp calf. With 20 maps, views & plates. CNY Dec 5 (218) $700

— Naukeurige beschryving der Eilanden, in de Archipel der Middelantische Zee.... Amst., 1688. Folio, contemp calf; spine ends chipped, rear joint cracked. With engraved title & 15 (of 17) plates & maps. Some soiling & stains; some tears. Sold w.a.f. sg May 21 (21) $800

Daran, Jacques

— Observations chirurgicales sur les maladies de l'urethre.... Paris, 1748. Illus by Jacques Gautier d'Argoty. 12mo, contemp mor gilt with the arms of the Dauphin; rubbed, hinges weak. With 1 folding plate ptd in colors. Schlosser copy. P June 18 (454) $700

Darbee, Harry

— Catskill Flytier. My Life, Times and Technique. Phila., [1977]. One of 125. 4to, cowhide. With a salmon fly, "Little Inky Boy," tipped to limitation leaf. Koopman copy. sg Oct 29 (58) $500

Darby, Charles

— Bacchanalia: or a Description of a Drunken Club. L, 1680. 1st Ed. Folio, modern half mor. Some soiling. bba July 9 (90) £160 [Hannas]

Dares Phrygius. See: Dictys Cretensis & Dares Phrygius

Daressy, Henri

— Archives des maitres d'armes. Paris, 1888. One of 620. 8vo, later half cloth, orig wraps bound in. Sgd by Gabriel Letainturier. sg Mar 26 (96) $120

Darlow, Thomas Herbert —& Moule, Horace Frederick

— Historical Catalogue of the Printed Editions of the Holy Scripture.... NY, 1963. 4 vols. 4to, orig cloth; worn. Facsimile reprint of the 1903 Ed. O Sept 24 (64) $550

Darmstaedter, Ludwig

— Handbuch zur Geschichte der Naturwissenschaften und der technik. [N.p.], 1960. 4to, cloth. Reprint of 1908 Ed. O Sept 24 (65) $140

Darrah, Henry Zouch

— Sport in the Highlands of Kashmir. L, 1898. 8vo, orig cloth. Lacking map in rear pocket. sg Jan 9 (224) $325

Anr copy. With 2 maps & 52 photographic illusts. sg May 21 (22) $300

Darrell, Paul. See: Hardy & Darrell

Darrow, Clarence, 1857-1938

— The Story of My Life. NY & L, 1932. Ltd Ed. Orig cloth; rubbed. Presentation copy, inscr, to Capt. & Mrs. Frderick J. Horne. Epstein copy. sg Apr 29 (106) $2,200

Darton, F. J. Harvey. See: Sawyer & Darton

Darwin, Charles, 1809-82

See also: Limited Editions Club

— The Descent of Man and Selection in Relation to Sex. L, 1871. 1st Ed, 1st Issue. 2 vols. 8vo, contemp calf gilt; rebacked. bba Feb 13 (393) £160 [Scott]

Anr copy. Orig cloth; upper hinge in Vol I broken. T5-T8 carelessly opened; small hole in title to Vol II not affecting text; some spotting. S May 14 (1026) £200 [Goldman]

Anr copy. Orig cloth; spine ends rubbed; Vol II front hinge cracked. sg Nov 14 (27) $600

— The Expression of the Emotions in Man and Animals. L, 1872. 1st Ed. 8vo, orig cloth; rubbed. bba Feb 13 (394) £90 [Mollon]

Anr copy. Orig cloth; rubbed, spine ends frayed. DW Apr 8 (157) £100

— Geological Observations on South America. L, 1846. 8vo, orig cloth; rebacked, most of orig spine laid down, corners bumped. Folding map with tear repaired; some discoloration. Sabine-Quayle copy. P June 17 (173) $2,250

— Insectivorous Plants. L, 1875. 1st Ed. 8vo, orig cloth; rubbed. bba Feb 13 (395) £150 [Sanderson]

— Journal of Researches into the Geology and Natural History of the Various Countries.... L, 1840. 1st Ed, 3d Issue. 8vo, orig cloth; upper joint frayed; spine worn. Bound without maps. DW Dec 11 (24) £140

— The Life and Letters of C. Darwin. L, 1887. 3 vols. 8vo, orig cloth; rubbed. bba Dec 19 (372) £55 [L. Kerr]

— On the Origin of Species.... L, 1859. 1st Ed. 8vo, orig cloth, Freeman's A bdg; spine ends & corners frayed, hinges rubbed, loose, lacking front free endpaper. Publisher's catalogue in Freeman's state 3 Half-title torn at gutter; tp creased; some fraying. CNY June 9 (136) $8,500

3d Issue, with ads dated June 1859. Orig green cloth, Freeman variant b; spine ends with some wear. Occasional stains. S Dec 5 (372) £4,000 [Phillips]

Issue not stated. Orig cloth. Half title repaired along inner margin. Epstein copy. sg Apr 29 (107) $16,000

Anr Ed. L, 1860. 8vo, orig cloth; rebacked, orig spine preserved. bba Feb 13 (391) £130 [Scott]

5th Thousand. 8vo, orig cloth. b Nov 18 (277) £140

Anr Ed. NY, 1860. 8vo, orig cloth; upper joint cracked. Some spotting. S July 1 (915) £200 [Kohler]

Anr copy. Orig cloth; lacking rear free endpaper. sp June 18 (234) $250

— The Variation of Animals and Plants under Domestication.... L, 1868. 1st Ed, 1st Issue. 2 vols. 8vo, orig cloth. Bookplate & stamp of the English Rooms, Funchal. S Feb 26 (910) £150 [American Book Store]

Anr copy. 19th-cent half calf gilt; rubbed. Lacking the inserted ads in Vol I. S Feb 26 (911) £190 [Thorp]

2d Issue. Contemp half calf; rubbed. bba Feb 13 (392) £130 [Ginnan]

— The Zoology of the Voyage of H.M.S. Beagle. Wellington, [1980]. 3 vols. 4to, contemp half mor. Facsimile of 1840-43 Ed. bba June 11 (236) £160

Darwin's copy, Charles

— WORDSWORTH, WILLIAM. - Poetical Works. L, 1840. 6 vols. 8vo, contemp half calf by Hawes; extremities rubbed. Annotated & sgd in each vol by Darwin. C June 24 (123) £1,600 [Franklin]

Darwin, Charles, 1809-82 —& Others

— Narrative of the Surveying Voyages of his Majesty's Ships Adventure and Beagle.... L, 1839. 1st Ed. 4 vols. 8vo, recent half mor. With 47 plates, & 9 maps & charts, including 8 folding charts loose in pockets. Plates waterstained; library stamp of the Inner Temple on titles & some text leaves; stamp on title versos. C May 20 (250) £2,000 [Mitchell]

1st Issue of Vol III. Half mor; spines chipped, extremities rubbed. With 47 plates & 9 folding maps, 8 loose in pockets. Short tear to inner edge of South America in Vol I; tp of Vol II foxed; some spotting & foxing. DuPont copy. CNY Oct 8 (84) $4,800

Anr copy. Orig cloth, Freeman variant b; spines worn, some joints repaired. Marginal stains; some foxing. S Dec 5 (373) £2,500 [Schumann]

2d Issue of Vol III. 19th-cent calf gilt by C. Lewis with arms of Earl of Acheson. With 56 plates & maps. Some discoloration to text. S June 25 (130) £3,900 [Quaritch]

Darwin, Erasmus, 1731-1802

— The Botanic Garden. L, 1791. 1st Ed of Part 1; 2d Ed of Part 2. 2 vols in 1. 4to, modern half mor. With frontises & 18 plates. A few leaves & 1 plate repaired. bba Dec 19 (2) £140 [Bickersteth]

1st Ed of Part 1; 3d Ed of Part 2. 2 vols. 4to, contemp half russia gilt; joints cracked. With 21 plates. sg Nov 14 (172) $450

Anr Ed. NY, 1798. 8vo, contemp sheep gilt; head of spine chipped. sg Nov 14 (273) $60

— A Plan for the Conduct of Female Education in Boarding Schools. Derby, 1797. 8vo, contemp half calf; rubbed, soiled. Ck Oct 18 (144) £580

— The Poetical Works. 1806. 3 vols. 8vo, orig bds; spine worn. DW Oct 2 (272) £95

— The Temple of Nature or the Origin of Socity.... Balt.: John W. Butler, 1804. 8vo, calf; joints starting, worn. With frontis & 3 plates. Browned; 1 plate detached, anr lacking lower corner. wa Mar 5 (505) $80

— Zoonomia; or, the Laws of Organic Life. L, 1794-96. 1st Ed. 2 vols. 4to, contemp calf; rebacked, rubbed. With 6 hand-colored & 4 plain plates. bba Sept 5 (31) £260 [Bickersteth]

Dasent, George Webbe, 1817-96

— The Vikings of the Baltic. L, 1875. 1st Ed. 3 vols. 8vo, orig cloth. O July 14 (60) $80

Dashwood, Sir Francis, Lord le Despencer. See: Franklin & Dashwood

Dauberville, Jean & Henry

— Bonnard.... Paris, 1966-74. One of 1,000. 4 vols. 4to, bdg not described. CGen Nov 18 (353) SF5,800

— Bonnard...Catalogue raisonne de l'oeuvre peint. Paris, 1965-74. 4 vols. In d/js. S Dec 5 (301) £3,200 [Pillar]

Anr copy. Vol I only. In d/j. S Dec 5 (302) £1,000 [Holstein]

Anr copy. 4 vols. In d/js. S July 1 (1143) £3,200 [Seibel]

Daudet, Alphonse, 1840-97

— Avantures prodigieuses de Tartarin de Tarascon. Paris, 1872. 1st Ed. 12mo, mor extra by Huser, orig wraps bound in. S May 28 (308) £2,800 [Beres]

— Contes du lundi. Paris, [1873]. 12mo, orig ptd wraps. S May 28 (309) £800 [Holinger]

— Le Petit chose. Paris, 1868. 1st Ed. 12mo, mor by Charles Septier, orig wraps bound ing wraps bound in. S May 28 (307) £50 [Beres]

— Sapho, Moeurs Parisiennes. Paris, 1884. 12mo, half mor, orig wraps bound in. Epstein copy. sg Apr 29 (108) $150

D'Audiguier, Vital. See: Audiguier, Vital D'

Daulby, Daniel

— A Descriptive Catalogue of the Works of Rembrandt.... Liverpool, 1796. One of 50. 8vo, contemp calf; worn, rebacked. DW Mar 11 (807) £180

Daulier Deslandes, Andre

— Les Beautez de la Perse. Paris, 1673. 4to, contemp calf. With engraved title (shaved at foot), folding map & 7 plates. One plate shaved at foot. Lascarides copy. S July 1 (834) £350 [Maggs]

Daulte, Francois

— Alfred Sisley. Catalogue raisonee de l'oeuvre peint. Lausanne, 1959. One of 1,200. 4to, orig cloth, in torn d/j. S July 1 (1144) £980

Daumier, Honore, 1808-79

— Married Life: Twenty-Four Lithographs. NY, [1944]. 4to, bdg not stated. With 24 plates. Met Apr 28 (128) $80

Davenant, Charles, 1656-1714

— The Political and Commercial Works.... L, 1771. 5 vols. 8vo, modern cloth. Library markings. S Nov 14 (403) £450 [Quaritch]

Davenant, Sir William, 1606-68

— Gondibert. L: for John Holden, 1651. 4to, later calf; rubbed. Cropped; some pencil markings. Wing D326. bba July 9 (85) £60 [Poetry Bookshop]

Davenport, Cyril

See also: Caxton Club

— English Embroidered Bookbindings. L, 1899. 4to, orig cloth. cb Oct 17 (219) $180

Anr copy. Orig cloth; worn, spine scuffed. O Sept 24 (66) $65

— English Heraldic Book-Stamps. L, 1909. 4to, orig cloth; flecked. kh Nov 11 (76) A$120

Davenport, Guy

— The Bowmen of Shu. NY: Grenfell Press, [1983]. One of 115. 4to, half mor. With 12 illusts. sg Sept 26 (128) $90

David, Francois Anne

— Antiquites d'Herculanum.... Paris, 1780. Vols I-X (of 12) only. 4to, contemp calf; Vol IV not uniform. Sold w.a.f. bba Oct 10 (169) £550 [Burden]

Anr copy. Vols I-VIII (of 12) only. Calf; some covers detached, 1 lacking. With engraved titles & 636 plates. Some foxing. sg Sept 6 (82) $425

Davidson, Allan A.

— Journal of Explorations in Central Australia by the Central Australian Exploration Syndicate.... Adelaide, 1905. Folio, modern cloth, orig ptd upper wrap bound in. With 2 folding colored maps. C June 25 (276) £450 [Renard]

Davidson, Jo

— Between Sittings: an Informal Autobiography. NY, 1951. One of 74. Cloth. bbc Apr 27 (446) $100

Davies Arthur Bowen, 1862-1928. See: Price, Frederic Newlin

Davies, G. Christopher, 1849-1922

— Norfolk Broads and Rivers. [N.p., early 1890s]. Oblong folio, contemp half mor gilt. With 48 photogravures by Anna after Davies. Some spotting with traces of mildew. sg May 21 (23) $325

Davies, Hugh William

— Catalogue of Early French Books in the Library of C. Fairfax Murray. L, 1961. 2 vols. 4to, orig cloth, in d/js. bbc Dec 9 (182) $85

— Devices of the Early Printers, 1457-1569. L, 1935. 1st Ed. cb Oct 17 (221) $80

Davies, Thomas, 1712-85

— Memoirs of the Life of David Garrick Esq. L, 1780. 1st Ed. 2 vols. 8vo, half mor; corners rubbed. bba Apr 30 (94) £130 [Land]

Anr copy. Contemp calf. sg Mar 5 (218) $225

Davies, Valentine

— Miracle on 34th Street. NY, [1947]. In d/j. Sgd by Davies, Edmund Gwenn & George Seaton. sg Oct 17 (26) $250

Davies, William Henry, 1871-1940
See also: Gregynog Press

— True Travellers. L, 1923. One of 100. Illus by William Nicholson. 4to, orig half cloth; soiled & worn. DW Apr 8 (491) £65

Davila, Enrico Caterino, 1576-1631

— The Historie of the Civill Warres of France.... L, 1647. 1st Ed in English. Folio, contemp calf; worn. LH Dec 11 (91) $90

Anr copy. Contemp sheep; worn, loose. License leaf torn & repaired on recto. sg Oct 24 (85) $175

Anr copy. Lea gilt; rebacked. Privilege leaf backed at corners with repaired tear; corner of final leaf also backed. wa Feb 20 (180) $130

Davillier, Jean Charles, Baron, 1823-83

— Recherches sur l'orfevrerie en Espagne.... Paris, 1879. One of 500. 8vo, half mor; bumped. b Mar 11 (45) £60

Davis, Charles Henry, 1807-77

— Narrative of the North Polar Expedition. Wash., 1876. 4to, cloth; joints & edges rubbed, ends worn, front hinge cracked. With 2 steel ports, 6 maps & 38 wood-engravings, most full-page. Library markings removed. wa Sept 26 (526) $80

Anr copy. Cloth; spine ends chipped & frayed, corners bumped. With 34 plates & 6 maps. wa Mar 5 (542) $70

1st Ed. 4to, orig cloth; spine ends frayed. bbc Dec 9 (323) $110

Davis, Edmund Walstein

— Salmon-Fishing on the Grand Cascapedia. [NY], 1904. One of 100. 8vo, mor gilt by W. Roach. Koopman copy. O Oct 29 (59) $800

Davis, Jefferson, 1808-89

— The Rise and Fall of the Confederate Government. NY, 1881. 1st Ed. 2 vols. 8vo, lea; some covers detached. sp Nov 24 (112) $110

Anr copy. Cloth. Foxed. sp Apr 16 (82) $170

Davis, John, 1774-1854

— Travels of Four Years and a Half in the United States of America.... Bost.: The Bibliophile Society, 1910. ("Travels in the United States of America....") One of 487. Ed by J. V. Cheney. 2 vols. 8vo, orig half vellum; soiled. wa Mar 5 (413) $80

Davis, Col. John, of the Second Royal Surrey Militia

— The History of the Second, Queen's Royal Regiment. L, 1887-1961. 10 vols, including Atlas. 8vo, orig cloth; worn. DW Apr 8 (24) £75

Davis, John King

— With the "Aurora" in the Antarctic, 1911-1914. L, [1919]. 4to, cloth; rubbed & soiled. With folding map at rear. DW Nov 6 (35) £120

Davis, Matthew Livingston, 1773-1850

— Memoirs of Aaron Burr. NY, 1836. 2 vols. 8vo, orig cloth; soiled & frayed. ALs of Burr, sgd with initials, 1795, to his daughter, tipped in. wd Dec 12 (368) $375

Davis, William Morris, c.1815-90

— Nimrod of the Sea, or the American Whaleman. L, 1874. 8vo, spine worn, front hinge cracked with half-title & frontis starting. bbc June 29 (112) $50

Anr copy. Cloth. cb Jan 30 (38) $95

Davis, William Watts Hart, 1820-1910

— El Gringo, or New Mexico and her People. NY, 1857. 1st Ed. 12mo, orig cloth; rubbed. Marginal pencil markings & notes. bbc Apr 27 (580) $85

Davis, Winfield J. See: Illustrated...

Davy, Henry

— A Series of Etchings Illustrative of the Architectural Antiquities of Suffolk. L, 1827. Folio, contemp half calf; rubbed. With 71 plates, including the cancelled plate of Orford Castle. Sold w.a.f. L.p. copy. Extra-illus with plates, drawings, offprints & other material. pn Apr 23 (259) £180

Davy, Sir Humphry, 1778-1829

— Salmonia: or, Days of Fly Fishing. L, 1828. 1st Ed. 8vo, half calf; rubbed. O Oct 29 (60) $175

2d Ed. L, 1829. 8vo, orig cloth; rubbed. bba Jan 16 (360) £90 [Ginnan]

1st American Ed. Phila., 1832. 12mo, old calf; rubbed. O Oct 29 (61) $60

Dawe, George, 1781-1829

— The Life of George Morland. L, 1807. 8vo, contemp calf; smoke damage, joints cracked. Some browning & foxing. bbc Apr 27 (471) $55

Anr Ed. L, 1904. Ltd Ed. Folio, orig cloth. With 52 plates. Foxed. K July 12 (352) $150

Dawson, Charles

— Pioneer Tales of the Oregon Trail. Topeka, 1912. Cloth; scuffed, bookseller's description mtd to front free endpaper. sg June 18 (194) $300

Dawson, Charles C.

— A B C's of Great Negroes. Chicago, 1933. 4to, orig wraps. Inscr, 1956. bbc Apr 27 (430) $600

Dawson, George, 1813-83

— Angling Talks: Being the Winter Talks on Summer Pastimes. NY, 1883. 12mo, cloth; worn. Koopman copy. O Oct 29 (62) $140

— Pleasures of Angling with Rod and Reel for Trout and Salmon. NY, 1876. 1st Ed. 8vo, cloth; worn. Koopman copy. O Oct 29 (63) $250

Dawson, Warren Royal. See: Smith & Dawson

Dawson, William Leon

— The Birds of California. San Diego, 1923. One of 350. 4 vols. 4to, orig cloth; worn & shaken. O Apr 28 (25) $200

Anr copy. Later cloth. With 110 color plates after paintings & 149 (of 150) plates from photographs. Library markings, but plates unmarked. Sold w.a.f. sg May 14 (204) $1,300

One of 1,000. Orig cloth; rubbed. wa Apr 9 (111) $210

Day, Charles Russell, 1860-1900

— The Music and Musical Instruments of Southern India. L, 1891. One of 700. 4to, orig vellum gilt; soiled. pn Oct 24 (347) £120

Day, Francis, 1829-89

— British and Irish Salmonidae. L & Edin., 1887. One of 25 for private circulation. 8vo, contemp calf gilt. With 12 plates, including 9 chromolithos. bba May 14 (471) £190 [Thorp]

— Fishes of Great Britain and Ireland. L, 1880-84. 2 vols. 8vo, orig cloth; rubbed & soiled, inner hinges broken. With 179 plates. DW Oct 2 (136) £90

Day, Martin

— Doomes-Day: or, a Treatise of the Resurrection of the Body. L: Nathanael Butter, 1636. 3 parts in 1 vol. 4to, calf. Lacking A2; p.279 supplied in facsimile. STC 6427. cb Feb 12 (30) $225

Day, Richard, 1552-1607?

— A Booke of Christian Prayers.... L: John Daye, 1581. 4to, contemp calf gilt with royal badge of crowned Tudor rose with sprays of rose leaves; rebacked & cornered. Some leaves creased; a few leaves with repaired tears; some soiling. STC 6431. Violet Trefusis's copy. C Dec 16 (250) £1,300 [Pirages]

Anr Ed. L, 1590. Bound with: The Whole Booke of Psalmes collected into English Meetre... L: John Windet for the Assignes of Richard Daye, 1602. 4to, 17th-cent calf gilt; rebacked, worn. Tp of 1st work soiled & frayed & with margins def; some fraying; 2d work lacking Ff4 & Ff2-3 with large portion torn away with loss. STC 6431 & 2506.5. S Nov 14 (460) £340 [Clark]

Day, Thomas, 1748-89

— The History of Sandford and Merton. L, 1783-89. 1st Ed. 3 vols. 8vo, contemp calf. With 2 frontises. Vol II lacking an ad leaf. bba July 23 (185) £520 [Hannasa]

Days...

— Days of the Dandies. L: Grolier Society, [after 1900]. Ed des Amateurs, One of 100. 15 vols. 8vo, mor gilt; some spines chipped. Some plates in 2 states. P June 17 (333) $2,750

Dayton Wright Airplane Company
— An Achievement. Dayton, [c.1917]. Pictorial wraps. cb Nov 7 (35) $85

De Belder Library, Robert
— [Sale Catalogue] A Magnificent Collection of Botanical Books.... L: Sotheby's, 1987. 4to, cloth. wa Sept 26 (458) $80

De Brahm, William Gerard, 1717-99
— The Atlantic Pilot. L, 1772. 8vo, orig wraps; rebacked. Some fraying & browning; several fold breaks to the charts & table, affecting border of 1st chart; 4-inch repaired tear to 2d chart; 3d chart cleanly torn from mount; table marginally dampstained. DuPont copy. CNY Oct 8 (85) $8,000

De Camp, L. Sprague
— The Wheels of If. Chicago, 1948. In d/j. sg June 11 (97) $80

De Camp, L. Sprague —& Pratt, Fletcher
— The Castle of Iron. NY: Gnome Press, [1950]. In d/j. sp Nov 24 (347) $70
— Land of Unreason. NY, [1942]. In d/j. Inscr by both. sg June 11 (271) $150
— Walls of Serpents. NY: Avalon Books, [1960]. Label sgd by de Camp affixed to front free endpaper. pba July 9 (65) $60

De Carava, Roy —& Hughes, Langston
— The Sweet Flypaper of Life. NY, [1955]. Wraps; rubbed. sg Oct 8 (31) $110

1st German Ed. Brandt, [1956]. ("Harlem Story.") Pictorial bds. sg Apr 13 (35) $150

De Gouy, Louis Pullig. See: Derrydale Press

De Guignes, Joseph. See: Guignes, Joseph de

De Guillebon, Regine de Plinval. See: Plinval de Guillebon, Regine de

De Jonghe, Adriaan. See: Junius, Hadrianus

De la Mare, Albina. See: Garzelli & De la Mare

De la Mare, Walter, 1873-1956
— Desert Islands and Robinson Crusoe. L, 1930. wa Sept 26 (147) $80

One of 650. K July 12 (158) $75; LH May 17 (644) $80
— Memoirs of a Midget. L, [1921]. 1st Ed. Orig cloth, in d/j. Inscr. Epstein copy. sg Apr 29 (109) $200
— Peacock Pie. L, 1913. 1st Ed. Inscr with holograph poem. sg Dec 12 (84) $130

Anr Ed. L, [1924]. One of 250. Illus by Claud Lovat Fraser. Half cloth. sg Dec 12 (85) $225
— The Riddle and Other Stories. L, 1923. Out-of-series copy. Inscr to J. St. L. Strachey, May 1923. sg Dec 12 (86) $300
— Songs of Childhood. L, 1902. 1st Ed. Orig half vellum. Ck July 10 (320) £50

Anr copy. Orig half vellum; some soil. Inscr with a holograph poem to J. N. Hart & with ALs. Epstein copy. sg Apr 29 (110) $700

De Long, George Washington
— The Voyage of the Jeannette. Bost., 1883. 2 vols. 8vo, orig cloth. cb Oct 10 (34) $275

1st English Ed. L, 1883. 2 vols. 8vo, orig cloth; rubbed & soiled. DW Nov 6 (36) £135

De Marinis, Tammaro
— Il Castello di Monselice, raccolta degli antichi libri venetiani figurati. Verona, 1941. One of 310. 4to, orig half vellum. bba Mar 26 (184) £1,100 [Quaritch]; bba July 9 (362) £1,200 [Franks]
— Catalogue d'un collection anciens livres a figures italiens. Milan: Ulrich Hoepli, [1925]. One of 440. Folio, wraps; soiled. sg Oct 31 (267) $300
— La Legatura artistica in Italia nel secoli XV e XVI. Florence, 1960. One of 300. 3 vols. Folio, orig half mor. Ck Nov 1 (450) £1,500

Anr copy. Orig half lea. SI June 9 (306) LIt3,600,000

De Moivre, Abraham, 1667-1754
— The Doctrine of Chances. L, 1718. 1st Ed. 4to, contemp calf gilt. Lower margins wormed throughout. L Nov 14 (392) £420

De Quille, Dan. See: Wright, William

De Quincey, Thomas, 1785-1859
See also: Limited Editions Club
— Confessions of an English Opium-Eater. L, 1822. 1st Ed. 12mo, orig bds; joints rubbed. P Oct 11 (74) $4,500

Anr copy. Later calf gilt. Sgd Mark Twain and James Whitcomb Riley by Eugene Field II. sg Oct 17 (225) $425

Anr copy. Contemp half calf. With half title. Lacking ads. Epstein copy. sg Apr 29 (111) $600

2d Ed. L, 1823. 12mo, contemp half calf gilt; spine chipped. wa Feb 20 (57) $50
— Works. Edin., 1878. 16 vols. 8vo, half mor. pn Sept 12 (193) £210 [Traylen]

De Ricci, Seymour
— Catalogue raisonne des premieres impressions de Mayance, 1445-1467. Mainz, 1911. New cloth; shaken. Upper margins at end stained. sg Oct 31 (150) $60
— A Census of Caxtons. Oxford, 1909. 4to, cloth, orig wraps bound in. sg May 21 (245) $130

De Ricci, Seymour —& Wilson, W. J.

— Census of Medieval and Renaissance Manuscripts in the United States and Canada. NY, 1935-40-62. 3 vols, including Index and Supplement. 4to, cloth; Vol I backstrip blistered; hinges cracked. sg Oct 31 (203) $650

De Roos, Frederick Fitzgerald, 1804-61

— Personal Narrative of Travels in the United States and Canada.... L, 1827. 1st Ed. 8vo, contemp half calf; rubbed. With folding frontis & 13 plates. bba Sept 19 (23) £150 [Felcone]

Anr copy. Contemp half calf; rubbed, some staining & soiling. With folding frontis & 12 plates. 1 plate loose. O Jan 14 (59) $180

De Rossi, Giovanni Gherardo. See: Rossi, Giovanni Gherardo de

De Smet, Pierre Jean, 1804-73

— Oregon Missions and Travels over the Rocky Mountains.... NY, 1847. 1st Ed. 12mo, cloth. Some leaves wormed; foxed. Sold w.a.f. sg June 18 (196) $200

De Soto, Hernando. See: Grabhorn Printing

De Tavera, T. H. Pardo

— Biblioteca Filipina. Wash., 1903. Unopened. cb Oct 17 (227) $65

De Tolnay, Charles

— Michelangelo. Princeton, 1943-60. 5 vols. 4to, orig cloth, 4 vols in d/js. S Feb 11 (53) £220 [Mayer]

De Vinne, Theodore Low, 1828-1914

— The Invention of Printing: a Collection of Facts and Opinions. NY, 1876. 8vo, cloth. cb Oct 17 (229) $50

De Wald, Ernest T.

— The Illustrations in the Manuscripts of the Septuagint. Princeton, 1941. Vol III: Psalms and Odes. Parts 1-2: Vaticanus Graecus 1927. 2 vols. Folio, cloth, in d/js. sg Oct 31 (205) $275

De Wint, Peter, 1784-1849. See: Light & De Wint

De Wit, Frederick

— Atlas. [Amst.?, 1680]. Folio, contemp vellum. With 49 (of 51) double-page maps, hand-colored in outline. Extensive Ms Lation annotations in margin & on surface of about a third of the maps; some fold breaks. sg Feb 13 (119) $9,000

Anr Ed. Amst.: F. de Wit, [c.1705]. Folio, contemp blind-stamped vellum with large central ornament enclosing an armillary sphere, yapp edges. With engraved title & 152 maps & charts, on guards throughout, all colored by a contemp hand. Tp holed & repaired & with margins frayed; a few maps creased, others with clean tears to folds, most neatly repaired. C Oct 30 (168) £24,000 [Marshall]

— Atlas maior. Amst.: Covens & Mortier, [c.1725]. Folio, modern calf; rubbed. With engraved title (hand-colored & heightened with gold) & 79 (of 80) double-page maps, hand-colored in a contemp hand. With Ms index. Some fold breaks; some waterstains. S Nov 21 (138) £9,000 [Potter]

Dean Collection, Bashford

— The Bashford Dean Collection of Arms and Armor, in the Metropolitan Museum of Art. Portland ME, 1933. One of 250. 4to, half cloth. sg Apr 2 (14) $90

— Catalogue of European Daggers. NY, 1929. One of 900. 2 vols. 4to, cloth. sg Mar 26 (97) $150

Anr copy. Later cloth. Plate count not given. sg Apr 2 (16) $130

Anr copy. Cloth. wd Dec 12 (379) $75

— Catalogue of European Court Swords and Hunting Swords.... NY, 1929. One of 900. 2 vols. 4to, later cloth. Plate count not given. sg Apr 2 (15) $100

Dearborn, Henry. See: Caxton Club

Dearden, Robert R., Jr. See: Grabhorn Printing

Deasy, Henry Hugh Peter

— In Tibet and Chinese Turkestan. NY, 1901. Frontis loose. sg Jan 9 (63) $175

Debret, Jean Baptiste

— Voyage pittoresque et historique au Bresil.... Paris, 1834-35-39. 3 vols. Folio, orig half mor gilt; worn. With half-title in Vol III only, port & 140 hand-colored plates, 3 maps & plans & litho facsimile letter. Some discoloration; a few plates with short margins. With livraison wrap containing 14 duplicate plates, 14 mtd working drawings & lithographer's tracings, 8 mtd sketches & drawings & 11 small leaves with pencil or watercolor or ink sketches & trials. S June 25 (450) £24,000 [Silva]

Decastro, Jacob, b.1758

— The Memoirs. L, 1824. 1st Ed. 12mo, 19th-cent cloth. With port & 2 folding facsimiles. Port discolored; some contemp annotations. S Nov 14 (282) £1,400 [Tibbals]

Decker, Malcolm. See: Decker, Peter

Decker, Paul, the Elder

— Fuerstlicher Baumeister, oder Architectua civilis.... Augsburg, 1711-16. 3 vols in 1. Oblong folio, 18th-cent bds; worn. With frontis & 130 plates. Some fraying & creasing; occasional stains; small stamp on tp. S Nov 21 (74) £3,600 [Lyon]

— Fuerstlicher Baumeister oder Architectura civilis. Augsburg, 1711-16. 3 parts in 1 vol. Oblong folio, 18th-cent bds; worn. With frontis & 130 plates. Some plates frayed at fore-margins or heavily creased at folds with occasional loss of engraved surface; occasional stains; stamp on tp. S June 25 (172) £1,800 [Shapero]

Decker, Peter

See also: Soliday Library, George W.

— Descriptive Checklist.... NY, 1940-45. 4 parts in 1 vol. cb Feb 12 (16) $225

— A Descriptive Check List...of Western Americana.... NY, 1960. 4to, cloth; worn. O Sept 24 (67) $80

Declaration of Independence

See also: Pennsylvania Gazette; Pennsylvania Magazine...; Remembrancer...

— Im Congress, den 4ten July, 1776. Eine Erklaerung durch die Repraesentanten der Vereinigten Staaten von America.... Phila.: Gedruckt bey Steiner und Cist, 6-8 July 1776. 410mm by 334mm. Double column; fraktur types; on paper with 16 horizontal chainlines watermarked V. With 3 small holes costing a total of c.7 words; a few other tiny holes costing a total of c.7 words; a few other tiny holes not affecting text; browned; some stains. P June 16 (208) $300,000

— In Congress. July 4, 1776. A Declaration.... [NY: Samuel Loudon, 10-20 July 1776]. 365mm by 245mm. Mtd on bd. Double column. Browned; hole costing portion of 1 letter of line 44 in 1st column. P June 16 (209) $80,000

Anr Ed. Charles-Town: Peter Timothy, [after 2 Aug 1776]. 425mm by 303mm. Slightly creased at center when ptd, affecting 1st 8 words of line 35; some creasing; short closed tear at upper left not affecting text; light staining at edges; mtd on bd. P Dec 12 (101) $270,000

Anr Ed. [Phila.: Benjamin Owen Tyler, 1818]. Single sheet, 29.5 by 23 inches. LH May 17 (726) $2,400

Defoe, Daniel, 1659?-1731

See also: Johnson, Capt. Charles; Limited Editions Club

— A Journal of the Plague Year.... L, 1754. ("The History of the Great Plague in London, in the Year 1665....") 8vo, contemp calf; rebacked. Some dampstaining throughout, with occasional traces of mold. sg Oct 24 (86) $150

— Jure Divino: a Satyr. L, 1706. 1st Ed. Folio, half calf. bba Apr 9 (78) £85 [R. Clark]

— Memoirs of a Cavalier. L: A. Bell, J. Osborn, W. Taylor & T. Warner, [1720]. 1st Ed. 8vo, contemp calf gilt; rubbed, joints repaired. bba Nov 28 (261) £100 [Ash Rare Books]

— Moll Flanders. L, MDDCXXI [sic, for 1722]. ("The Fortunes and Misfortunes of the Famous Moll Flanders.") 1st Ed. 8vo, contemp calf; rebacked. Litchfield-Manney copy. P Oct 11 (73) $11,000

— Robinson Crusoe. L, 1719-20. ("The Life and Strange Surprizing Adventures of Robinson Crusoe....* The Farther Adventures....* Serious Reflections....") 1st Ed. 3 vols. 8vo, calf; rebacked, rubbed. Newton-Hersholt-Manney copy. P Oct 11 (72) $22,000

Anr copy. Contemp calf; not uniform, 2 vols rebacked, 1 repaired. Vol I with 1st state of tp, 3d state of preface & 2d state of text; Vol II the 1st issue, 1st variant. Some spotting & staining. S July 21 (22) £7,000 [Joseph]

Anr copy. Old calf; front bd detached, rear joint cracked. wa Dec 9 (477) $120

Anr Ed. Dublin, 1789. ("The Life and Surprising Adventures of Robinson Crusoe.") 12mo, contemp calf. LH Dec 11 (92) $200

Anr Ed. L: John Stockdale, 1790. ("The Life and Strange Surprising Adventures of Robinson Crusoe.") 2 vols. 8vo, old calf gilt by Tout; broken, spine ends worn. K July 12 (159) $100

Anr copy. Contemp calf; rubbed. pnE Oct 1 (225) £70

Anr Ed. L, 1804. Illus by Medland after Stothard. Parts 1 & 2 only in 2 vols. 8vo, contemp mor gilt with fore-edge paintings. LH May 17 (605) $650

Anr Ed. L, 1831. ("The Life and Surprising Adventures of Robinson Crusoe.") Parts 1 & 2 in 2 vols. 8vo, orig calf; modern half mor gilt. Sgd A. Lincoln by Eugene Field II. With note "authenticating" them by Lincoln's coachman. sg Oct 17 (226) $375

Anr Ed. NY, 1884. One of 100. Illus by George Cruikshank. 4to, cloth; spine worn, head torn, hinges cracked. sg Oct 17 (160) $60

Anr Ed. L: Basilisk Press, 1979. One of 515. Illus by Edward Gordon Craig. 4to, orig half mor gilt. With 2 plates & an orig etching by Craig. sg Sept 26 (83) $400

— A Tour thro' London about the Year 1725....

L, 1929. One of 350. Folio, orig cloth; some wear. K Sept 29 (149) $75

— A True Collection of the Writings of the Author of the True Born Englishman. L, 1703. 1st Authorized Ed. 8vo, contemp calf; rebacked, rubbed. bba Jan 16 (86) £80 [Bickersteth]

1st Authorized Ed of Vol I; 3d Ed of Vol II. L, 1703-[13]. 2 vols. 8vo, contemp calf gilt & contemp calf, uniformly rebacked. bba Jan 16 (87) £120 [R. Clark]

— Works. Oxford [ptd] & L, 1840-41. ("The Novels and Miscellaneous Works.") 20 vols. 8vo, contemp half calf gilt. With port. Some browning. pn Apr 23 (78) £420

Anr Ed. NY: Jenson Society, 1907. Out-of-series copy. 16 vols. 8vo, pigskin gilt; some scuffing. wa Mar 5 (25) $200

Anr Ed. Oxford: Shakespeare Head Press, 1927-28. ("Novels and Selected Writings.") One of 750. 14 vols. Orig cloth. wa Mar 5 (136) $190

DeFontaine, Felix G.

— Marginalia, or Gleanings from an Army Note-Book by "Personne." Columbia, 1864. 8vo, wraps. sg Dec 5 (76) $130

Degas, Edgar

— Catalogue des tableaux, pastels et dessins par Edgar Degas a Galerie Georges Petit. Paris, 1918-19. 4 vols in 2. 4to, later cloth, orig wraps bound in at end. S Feb 11 (254) £550 [Doll]

— Monotypes. Paris, [1948]. One of 1,000. Text by Denis Rouart. Folio, ptd wraps. sg Feb 6 (67) $100

Degering, Hermann

— Die Schrift.... L, [Berlin ptd], 1929. 4to, cloth; foot of spine chipped. With 240 plates. sg Oct 31 (201) $90

Dehio, Georg Gottfried —& Bezold, Gustav F. T. von

— Die Kirchliche baukunst des Abendlandes: Historisch und Systematisch Dargestellt. Stuttgart, 1887-1901. 2 text vols & 8 portfolios with 603 plates numbered 1-600. 8vo & folio, text in half calf. B May 12 (297) HF650

Deidier,——, Abbe, 1696-1740

— Manuel de l'artificier. Neuchatel, 1755. 12mo, contemp calf; rubbed, worming in lower cover. With 11 plates & 5 folding ptd tables. S July 1 (1299) £380 [American Mus.]

Dejean. See: Hornot, Antoine

DeKay, James E., 1792-1851

— Zoology of New-York. Part III- Reptiles and Amphibia. Albany, 1842. 2 vols. 4to, cloth; spine chipped. With 79 plates. sp Feb 6 (375) $50

— Zoology of New-York. Parts V (Mollusca) & VI (Crustacea). Albany, 1843-44. 4to, cloth; covers dampstained. With 53 hand-colored plates. Several plates dampstained & def. sg Sept 19 (172) $400

— Zoology of New-York. Part II—Birds. Albany, 1844. 4to, contemp half sheep; def. With 141 color plates. Some foxing to plates. sg Sept 19 (180) $550

Dekker, Eduard Douwes, the Elder. See: Multatuli

Delacour, Jean Theodore

— The Waterfowl of the World. L, 1954-64. 4 vols. 4to, Orig cloth, in d/js. bba July 9 (255) £130 [Cumming]

Anr copy. Orig cloth, in torn d/js. With 66 color plates & 108 maps. pn Sept 12 (293) £120 [Head]

Delacour, Jean Theodore —& Jaboille, Pierre

— Les Oiseaux de l'Indochine francaise. Paris, 1931. 4 vols. Half cloth. With 67 plates, all but 2 colored. S Nov 15 (734) £320 [Greyfriars]

Delafield, Richard, 1798-1873

— Report on the Art of War in Europe.... Wash.: George W. Bowman, 1860. 4to, cloth. Many folding maps & plates torn. 36th Congress, 1st Session, Sen Exec Doc 59. sp Nov 24 (113) $110

Anr copy. Cloth; rebacked. Foxed throughout; some tears; 1 map detached. 36th Congress, 1st Session, Sen Exec Doc 59. wa Feb 20 (30) $80

Delano, Alonzo, 1806-74

— Life on the Plains and among the Diggings. Auburn, 1854. 12mo, cloth. With 4 plates. sg June 18 (60) $140

Delany, Mary Granville

— The Autobiography and Correspondence of.... L, 1861-62. 1st & 2d Series. 6 vols. 8vo, half mor gilt by Henderson & Bisset. Light pencilling in Vol I. wa Apr 9 (33) $65

Delaunay, Henri

— Les Evangiles des dimanches et fetes de l'annee. Paris: L. Curmer, 1864. 2 vols, including Appendix. 4to, contemp mor with brass monogram on front cover. With hundreds of full-page & text illuminations, borders, initials, etc., in gold & colors. 2d vol has over 70 mtd photos of etchings by the Wierix brothers. sg May 7 (28) $1,200

Delisle, Guillaume, 1675-1726

— Atlante novissimo che contiene tutte le parti del mondo. Venice, 1740-50. 2 vols in 1. Folio, contemp half vellum; extremities worn, edges frayed. With 2 engraved titles & 78 mapsheets, all on guards, the world map colored in outline & 3 other maps with traces of outline coloring. Marginal repair to 1st engraved title (becoming detached); ownerschip markings excised from both letterpress titles, just cropping vignette of Vol I tp; 21 maps in Vol I & most maps in Vol II with short fold breaks or tears, incurring minor loss to c.13 maps; Map 16 in Vol I split along fold & repaired; 5-inch tear to Map 17 in Vol II; Map 12 in Vol II with neatly repaired 4-inch tear; Map 23 in Vol II cropped with loss to longitude scale; 10 other map borders shaved; small stain to Map 43; occasional faint marginal dampstaining. CNY June 9 (137) $4,000

Delisle, Leopold

— Le Cabinet des manuscrits de la Bibliotheque Imperiale. NY, 1973. 4 vols. 4to, cloth. sg Oct 31 (202) $110

Delius, Christoph Traugott

— Anleitung zu der Bergbaukunst. Vienna, 1773. 4to, contemp half calf; worn, upper cover detached. With 24 folding plates. Library stamps on plate versos & on titles; some browning & soiling. S May 13 (884) £240 [Hasbach]

Delkeskamp, Friedrich Wilhelm

— Vues du Rhin. Frankfurt: Friedrich Wilmans, [c.1840]. 8vo, orig mor gilt; rubbed. With 35 hand-colored plates, seeral heightened with gum-arabic. A few margins discolored. S June 25 (323) £700 [Lorenzo]

Della Bella, Stefanino

— A Collection of Etchings. L, 1818. Ed by Thomas Dodd. Folio, contemp mor gilt; rubbed, spine worn at head & foot. With frontis & 179 etchings on 96 plates. S Feb 11 (305) £1,900 [L'Arte Antica]

Delord, Taxile, 1815-77

— Un Autre monde. Paris, 1844. Illus by J. J. Grandville. 4to, modern half mor. With frontis & 36 hand-colored plates. Some browning & foxing. SI Dec 5 (284) LIt95,000

— Les Fleures animees. Paris, 1847. Illus by J. J. Grandville. 2 vols in 1. 8vo, contemp mor gilt; extremities worn. With 2 engraved titles & 41 hand-colored and 2 plain plates. DW Jan 29 (226) £155

Anr copy. 2 vols. 8vo, orig half mor gilt; worn. With 54 plates including 2 titles, all but 2 hand-colored. Library stamp to verso of titles. DW May 13 (272) £300

Anr copy. Contemp half mor; rubbed. With hand-colored title, 2 uncolored & 40 hand-colored plates. S July 1 (1121) £200

Anr Ed. Brussels, 1852. 2 vols. 8vo, orig cloth; extremities rubbed. With hand-colored engraved titles & 52 plates. Ck Dec 11 (157) £400

Delteil, Joseph

— Allo! Paris! Paris: Editions des Quatre Chemins, [1926]. One of 300. Illus by Robert Delaunay. 4to, orig wraps; minimal wear. P June 17 (178) $2,500

Delteil, Loys, 1869-1927

— Manuel de l'amateur d'estampes des XIXe et XXe siecles. Paris, [1925-26]. 4 vols, including plate vols. Recent cloth, orig wraps bound in. sg Sept 6 (87) $550

— Le Peintre-graveur illustre. Paris, 1908. Vol III: Ingres & Delacroix. 4to, contemp half mor; rubbed, orig wraps bound in. bba Feb 13 (255) £150 [Sims Reed]

Demachy, R. —&
Puyo, C.

— Les Procedes d'Art en Photographie. Paris, 1906. 4to, bdg not described but chipped. With 41 plates. some foxing & mildew. sg Oct 8 (32) $750

Demidoff, Anatole de, 1813-70

— Travels in Southern Russia and the Crimea. L, 1853. 1st Ed. 2 vols. 8vo, orig cloth; Vol I spine def. sg Jan 9 (64) $200

Demortain, G.

— Les Plans, profils, et elevations, des ville et chateau de Versailles.... Paris, [1716]. Folio, calf gilt. With 56 plates. Ms alterations in ink & pencil to the numbering of the plates. W July 8 (5) $1,300

Demosthenes, 385?-322 B.C.

— Opera. Venice: Aldus, 1554. ("Orationes.") 3 vols. 8vo, later half calf; rubbed, some covers detached. Titles detached; Vol II lacking final blank; some headlines shaved; some waterstaining. bba Aug 13 (55) £350 [K. Books]

— Orationes duae & sexaginta.... Venice: Aldus, Nov 1504. Folio, 18th-cent vellum. Marginal worming at beginning & end. C June 24 (269) £5,500 [Pregliasco]

— The Orations. L: W. Johnson, 1770. 4to, contemp russia gilt; joints cracked, surface imperfection on front cover. sg Oct 24 (88) $140

— Orationum. Basel: Joannes Hervagius, [1547]. Parts 1-2 (of 3) in 1 vol. 8vo, old vellum. First title dusty. sg Oct 24 (87) $175

Demotte, G. J.

— La Tapisserie gothique. Paris, 1924. Folio, half pigskin; needs rebdg. With 100 mtd colored plates. Sold w.a.f. sg Feb 6 (68) $90

Anr copy. Unbound as issued in cloth portfolio. sg Apr 2 (100) $600

Dempster, Thomas, 1579?-1625

— De Etruria regalia libri VII. Florence, 1723-24. 2 vols. Folio, contemp calf. With 2 ports, folding map, 83 plates & an additional 7 plates reproducing Mss. bba Jan 16 (238) £650 [Erlini]

Denham, Maj. Dixon —& Clapperton, Capt. Hugh

— Journal of a Second Expedition into the Interior of Africa.... L, 1829. 1st Ed. 4to, orig bds; rebcked. With port & folding map. bba June 25 (240) £200 [Bonham]

Anr copy. Orig bds; spine worn. DW Oct 2 (24) £220

— Narrative of Travels and Discoveries in Northern and Central Africa. L, 1828. 3d Ed. 2 vols. 8vo, half calf; extremities faded. Tear to 1 map. sg Jan 9 (65) $250

Denham, Sir John, 1615-69

— Poems and Translations, with Sophy. L, 1668. 1st Ed. 8vo, contemp mor gilt; rebacked retaining orig backstrip. Margins trimmed affecting some headlines & touching text on B3; paper fault in 2E5 causing loss; some stains & soiling; N7 bound after A4. sg Oct 24 (89) $120

Denis, Georges

— Isadora Duncan. Paris, [1928]. One of 475. Illus by Jose Clara. 4to, loose as issued in half cloth. With 72 plates. Eva Le Gallienne's copy. sg Mar 5 (223) $500

Denis, Michel

— Wiens Buchdruckergeschicht bis M. D. L. X. Vienna, 1782. 4to, contemp sheep; worn. Some foxing & browning; large portion of 4C3 cut out with loss. bba May 28 (609) £55 [Mytze]

Dennis, Jack H.

— Western Trout Fly Tying Manual. Jackson Hole: Snake River Books, [1974]. One of 150. 4to, half syn. Koopman copy. O Oct 29 (65) $120

Denon, Dominique Vivant, Baron, 1747-1825

— Travels in Upper and Lower Egypt. L, 1803. 3 vols. 8vo, contemp half mor; rebacked. With 61 maps & plates, many folding. DW Mar 4 (16) £175

— Voyage dans la basse et la haute Egypte.... L, [1807]. 3 vols. 4to & folio, contemp half cloth; scuffed & soiled. With 109 plates. Library stamp on versos of each plate; margins of Vol II frontis & half-title repaired; some foxing; dampstains to a few plates. Sold w.a.f. pnL Nov 20 (124) £210 [Kinnaird]

Denslow, William Wallace

— Pictures from the Wonderful Wizard of Oz. Chicago: George W. Ogilvie, [c.1903]. Text by Thomas Russell. Orig cloth-backed pictorial wraps; child's scrawl on verso of front wrap. sg Oct 17 (338) $130

Dent, John

[-] [Sale Catalogue] Catalogue of the Splendid, Curious, and Extensive Library.... L, 1827. 2 vols in 1. 8vo, modern bds. Priced throughout in ink. bba May 28 (553) £140 [Dawson]

Anr copy. Old half vellum; worn, top half of spine missing. Priced in ink. Part 2 misbound before Part 1. Dawson Turner's copy. W Mar 6 (4) £95

Denton, Sherman Foote

— As Nature Shows Them. Moths and Butterflies of the United States East of the Rocky Mountains. Bost., 1898-1900. One of 500. 2 vols. 8vo, half mor gilt; joints rubbed, hinge broken. With 56 nature-ptd plates, with hand-colored engraving by the author. Schlosser copy. P June 17 (487) $1,000

Anr Ed. Bost., [1900]. 2 vols. 4to, contemp mor gilt. With 56 color transfer plates, mtd. Ck Nov 29 (19) £400

Denver & Rio Grande Railroad

— The Opinions of the Judge and the Colonel as to the Vast Resources of Colorado.... Denver: Passenger Department of the Denver & Rio Grande R. R., 1895. cb Feb 13 (92) $85

— Slopes of the Sangre de Cristo. Denver: Carson-Harper Co., 1896. cb Feb 13 (281) $110

Depero, Fortunato

— Depero Futurista. Milan, 1927. One of 1,000. 4to, bds with leaves held by large aluminum bolts. CGen Nov 18 (354) SF10,000

Depping, George Bernhard. See: Rechberg & Depping

Derby, George H. See: Caxton Club

Derleth, August William

— In re: Sherlock Holmes, the Adventures of Solar Pons. Sauk City, 1945. In d/j. cb Sept 19 (43) $55

— Not Long for this World. Sauk City, 1948. In d/j. F Dec 19 (159) $80

— Someone in the Dark. [Sauk City], 1941. Inscr & with Ls to Harold Dahl, 13 Oct

1941. pba July 9 (72) $425
— Something Near. Sauk City: Arkham House, 1945. In d/j. cb Sept 19 (44) $70
— Still Is the Summer Night. NY, 1937. In d/j. Inscr to Else Reisenberg. sg June 11 (99) $90

Dernieres. See: Matisse, Henri

Derrydale Press—New York
— A Decade of American Sporting Books & Prints by the Derrydale Press 1927-1937. 1937. One of 950. K July 12 (162) $80
— Some Early American Hunters. 1928. One of 375. F Sept 26 (447) $50
— ALVORD, THOMAS G. - Paul Bunyan, and Resinous Rhymes of the North Woods. 1934. One of 332. wa Sept 26 (63) $85
— ANNABEL, RUSSELL. - Tales of a Big Game Guide. 1938. One of 950. Koopman copy. O Oct 29 (66) $240
— BABCOCK, PHILIP H. - Falling Leaves: Tales from a Gun Room. [1937]. Out-of-series review copy. Koopman copy. O Oct 29 (67) $70
— BAKER, CHARLES HENRY COLLINS. - The Gentleman's Companion. 1939. One of 1,250. 2 vols. sg Jan 9 (225) $120
— BANDINI, RALPH. - Veiled Horizons... [1939]. One of 950. Koopman copy. O Oct 29 (68) $120
— BEACH, WILLIAM NICHOLAS. - In the Shadow of Mount McKinley. 1931. One of 750. sg Jan 9 (226) $350
— BIGELOW, HORATIO. - Gunnerman. [1939]. One of 950. Inscr. wa Apr 9 (116) $70
— BROWN, PAUL. - Aintree: Grand Nationals —Past and Present. 1930. One of 850. sg Jan 9 (228) $110
— BUCKINGHAM, NASH. - Blood Lines... [1938]. One of 1,250. Koopman copy. O Oct 29 (69) $100

Anr copy. Inscr. wa Mar 5 (506) $85
— BUCKINGHAM, NASH. - De Shootinest Gent'man and Other Tales. [1934]. One of 950. bbc Apr 27 (511) $95
— BUCKINGHAM, NASH. - Mark Right! [1936]. One of 1,250. F Mar 26 (54) $90

Anr copy. Koopman copy. O Oct 29 (70) $140; wa Mar 5 (507) $100
— BUCKINGHAM, NASH. - Ole Miss'. 1937. One of 1,250. wa Mar 5 (508) $130
— CHAMBERLIN, HARRY D. - Training Hunters, Jumpers, and Hacks. 1937. One of 1,250. wa Mar 5 (509) $50
— CLARK, ROLAND. - Etchings. 1938. One of 800. wa Dec 9 (507) $375
— CLARK, ROLAND. - Gunner's Dawn. 1937. One of 900. Koopman copy. O Oct 29 (72) $425; O Oct 29 (73) $300

Anr copy. With orig sgd etching in uncolored state. wa Mar 5 (510) $260
— CONNETT, EUGENE V. - Fishing a Trout Stream. [1934]. One of 950. Koopman copy. O Oct 29 (74) $100
— CONNETT, EUGENE V. - Random Casts. 1939. One of 1,075. Koopman copy. O Oct 29 (75) $150
— CONNETT, EUGENE V. - Upland Game Bird Shooting in America. 1930. O Apr 28 (165) $275

One of 850. sg May 21 (26) $200
— DANIELSON, RICHARD ELY. - Martha Doyle and other Sporting Memories. [1938]. One of 1,250. Koopman copy. O Oct 29 (76) $70
— DE GOUY, LOUIS PULLIG. - The Derrydale Cook Book of Fish and Game. 1937. One of 1,250. 2 vols. Koopman copy. O Oct 29 (77) $165
— FOOTE, JOHN TAINTOR. - Jing. [1936]. One of 950. wa Apr 9 (117) $75
— GAMBRILL, RICHARD V. N. & MACKENZIE, JAMES C. - Sporting Stables and Kennels. 1935. One of 950. F Mar 26 (49) $100
— GRAND, GORDON. - The Silver Horn and Other Sporting Tales of John Weatherford. 1932. One of 950. Joints rubbed. sg Jan 9 (232) $50
— GRAY, PRENTISS N. - Records of North American Big Game. 1932. One of 500. Koopman copy. O Oct 29 (81) $950
— HAIG-BROWN, RODERICK L. - The Western Angler.... 1939. One of 950. 2 vols. Koopman copy. O Oct 29 (82) $750
— HARKNESS, WILLIAM HALE. - Temples and Topees. 1936. One of 200. sg Sept 26 (88) $50
— HAWKER, PETER. - Colonel Hawker's Shooting Diaries. [1931]. In d/j. Koopman copy. O Oct 29 (83) $110
— HERBERT, HENRY WILLIAM. - My Shooting Box. 1941. One of 250. bbc Dec 9 (324) $70; wa Apr 9 (118) $65
— HOOD, THOMAS. - The Epping Hunt. 1930. One of 490. O July 14 (63) $50
— HUNT, LYNN BOGUE. - An Artist's Game Bag. 1936. De Luxe Ed, One of 1,250. sg Jan 9 (235) $175
— KIRMSE, MARGUERITE. - Dogs. 1930. One of 750. L Nov 14 (192) £220
— LANIER, HENRY W. - A.B. Frost: the American Sportsman's Artist. [1933]. One of 950. O Jan 14 (62) $110; sg Jan 9 (238) $150; wd Dec 12 (381) $100
— LEE, AMY FREEMAN. - Hobby Horses. 1940. One of 200. Marginal tape stains. Inscr but recipient's name crossed out & inscr affected by damp. pba July 23 (58) $70
— LITTAUER, VLADIMIR S. - Be a Better Horseman: an Illustrated Guide to the Enjoyment of Modern Riding. 1941. One of 1,500. sg Jan 9 (239) $50
— LITTAUER, VLADIMIR S. - Jumping the Horse. 1931. One of 950. F Mar 26 (52) $50

— Lytle, Horace. - Point! A Book about Bird Dogs. [1941]. One of 950. wa Apr 9 (119) $55
— Manchester, Herbert. - Four Centuries of Sport in America, 1490-1890. 1931. One of 850. K Sept 29 (151) $110; O Sept 24 (157) $60
— Montgomery, Rutherford G. - High Country. 1938. One of 950. sg May 21 (27) $90
— O'Connor, Jack. - Game in the Desert. [1939]. One of 950. bbc Apr 27 (513) $240

Anr copy. Koopman copy. O Oct 29 (85) $425; O Oct 29 (86) $300
— Palmedo, Roland. - Skiing: The International Sport. 1937. One of 60. wd Dec 12 (382) $700

One of 950. Koopman copy. O Oct 29 (87) $250
— Phair, Charles. - Atlantic Salmon Fishing. 1937. One of 950. Koopman copy. O Oct 29 (88) $550; O Jan 14 (63) $225
— Pickering, Harold G. - Merry Xmas. Mr. Williams. 20 Pine St. N.Y. 1940. One of 267. Inscr. pba July 23 (59) $180
— Santini, Piero. - Riding Reflections. 1932. One of 850. sg May 21 (28) $70
— Sheldon, Harold P. - Tranquillity. 1936. One of 950. sg May 21 (29) $80
— Sheldon, Harold P. - Tranquillity Revisited. 1940. One of 485. sg May 21 (30) $150
— Smith, Edmund Ware. - The One-Eyed Poacher of Privilege. [1941]. One of 750. Koopman copy. O Oct 29 (89) $155
— Smith, Harry Worcester. - Life and Sport in Aiken.... 1935. One of 950. bbc Apr 27 (514) $60
— Spiller, Burton L. - Firelight. [1937]. One of 950. wa Mar 5 (513) $110
— Stone, Herbert L. & Loomis, Alfred F. - Millions for Defense. [1934]. One of 950. sg Jan 9 (242) $130
— Streett, William B. - Gentlemen Up. 1930. One of 75 L.p. copies. Inscr. sg Jan 9 (243) $850
— Sturgis, William B. - New Lines for Flyfishers. 1936. One of 950. Koopman copy. O Oct 29 (91) $90
— Walden, Howard T. - Big Stony. 1940. One of 550. O Oct 29 (92) $150
— Watson, Frederick. - Hunting Pie. 1931. One of 750. Covers soiled, front hinge shaken. sg Jan 9 (245) $50
— White, Frederick. - The Spicklefisherman and Others. 1928. One of 740. K July 12 (161) $60
— Williams, Ben Ames. - The Happy End. [1939]. One of 1,250 & with a specially prepared half-title for the Clove Valley Rod and Gun Club. Koopman copy. O Oct 29 (93) $160

One of 1,250. Koopman copy. O Oct 29 (94) $85

One of 1,250, but this 1 of a lesser number for the Clove Valley Rod and Gun Club. wa Sept 26 (65) $150

Des Barres, Joseph F. Wallet, 1722-1824

— A Statement Submitted by Lieutenant Colonel Desbarres.... [N.p., 1796]. Folio, contemp calf; rebcked, some wear. With extensive holograph annotations, forming a gloss for over 150 of the numbered paragraphs; a further 77 entries in red ink giving names of various military & other gentlemen; c.48 textual corrections. DuPont copy. CNY Oct 8 (88) $13,000

Des Murs, Marc Athanase Parfait Oeillet, 1804-78?

— Iconographie ornithologique. Nouveau recueil general de planches peintes d'oiseaux.... Paris, [1845]-49. 4to, contemp half mor gilt; rubbed. With 72 hand-colored plates. bba Nov 28 (107) £2,200 [Shapero]; C Oct 30 (182) £3,800 [Marshall]

Desaguliers, John Theophilus, 1683-1744

— A Course of Experimental Philosophy. L, 1763. 2 vols. 4to, contemp calf; rubbed. Ck Dec 11 (213) £280

Desarnod, A. See: Sayger & Desarnod

Desaulses de Freycinet, Louis Claude. See: Freycinet, Louis Claude Desaulses de

Desault, Pierre Joseph, 1744-95

— The Surgical Works, or Statement of the Doctrine and Practice. Phila., 1814. 2 vols. 8vo, contemp calf; head of Vol II chipped. With 12 plates. sg May 14 (40) $375
— A Treatise on Fractures, Luxations, and other Affections of the Bones. Phila., 1811. 8vo, contemp calf; rubbed. With 3 plates. Foxed. K July 12 (337) $70

Desbarres, Joseph Frederick Wallet, 1722-1824. See: Des Barres, Joseph F. Wallet

Descamps-Scrive, Rene

— [Sale Catalogue] Bibliotheque.... Paris, 1925. 3 vols. 4to, half calf, orig wraps bound in. A few prices marked in ink in Vol I. S Feb 11 (308) £180 [Klein]

Descartes, Rene, 1596-1650

— De homine. Amst., 1677. ("Tractatus de homine, et de formatione de foetus.") 4to, contemp calf; rebacked, old spine preserved. bba Sept 5 (271) £400 [Poole]
— Opera philosophica. Amst., 1672. 5th Ed. 3 parts in 1 vol. 4to, contemp calf; worn. Library markings. bba Sept 5 (201) £80 [Greenwood]

Anr copy. Contemp calf; extremities repaired. Some dampstaining; 1 leaf with rusthole; some soiling & staining. Ck Oct 18 (118) £120

— Les Principes de la philosophie.... Paris: Pierre Des Hayes for Henry le Gras, 1647. 4to, contemp calf gilt; rebacked, old spine laid down. With engraved folding title & 25 folding plates, including duplicates of plates 15-20. Sig. Aaa wrongly set & therefore misbound. C June 24 (302) £600 [Shapero]

— Principia philosophiae. L, 1664. 3 parts in 1 vol. 8vo, contemp calf; rebacked, rubbed. bba Sept 5 (200) £240 [Poole]

Desclozeaux, Adrien

— Gabrielle d'Estrees. L: Arthur L. Humphreys, 1907. 18mo, lev extra with royal cypher of Henry of Navarre & monogram of Gabrielle d'Estrees enclosed in laurel wreath on front cover, miniature port on ivory of Gabrielle d'Estrees in doublure, by Sangorski & Sutcliffe. P June 17 (126) $1,400

Descourtilz, Jean Theodore

— Ornithologie Bresilienne, ou histoire des oiseaux du Bresil.... Rio de Janeiro [L ptd]: Thomas Reeves, [1852-56]. Folio, half mor gilt, orig ptd upper wraps bound in. With 44 chromolitho plates finished in colors by hand. Some plates foxed. P Dec 12 (27) $16,000

— Pageantry of Tropical Birds. L, 1960. 2 vols. Folio, cloth, in d/j with lamination bubbled. With 60 full-page plates. wa Dec 9 (466) $60

Descourtilz, M. E.

— Flore (pittoresque et) medicale des antilles, ou traite des plantes usuelles des colonies francaises.... Paris, 1821-29. Plate vol only. contemp calf; rubbed. With 232 hand-colored plates only (of 600). Ck Nov 29 (75) £1,300

Descriptio...

— Descriptio Alcahirae urbis quae Mizir, et Mazar dicitur. Venice: Mathio Pagan, 1549. 8vo, old wraps. Fore-edge shaved. S Nov 21 (291) £500 [Burgess Browning]

Description...

— Description de l'Egypte, ou Recueil des observations et des recherches...pendant l'expedition de l'armee francaise. Paris, 112-17. 3 (of 12) vols. Folio, cloth; def. With c.165 plates. Some foxing. Sold w.a.f. sg Feb 13 (173) $175

— Description des festes donnees par la ville de Paris, a l'occasion du mariage de Madame Louise-Elisabeth de France, et Dom Philippe, Infant...d'Espagne. Paris, 1740. Folio, contemp red mor gilt armorial bdg. With engraved title & 13 plates, 8 double page. Some discoloration. S June 25 (216) £900 [Tulip]

— Description de l'Egypte ou recueil des observations et des recherches...pendant l'expedition de l'armee francaise. Paris, 1809-22. 3 (of 12) vols. Folio, cloth; def. Some foxing. sg Feb 13 (187) $3,400

— Description exacte de tout ce qui s'est passe dans les guerres.... Amst., 1668. 4to, old bds; rebacked in calf. Ck Oct 31 (9) £200

Anr copy. Later half vellum. With engraved title vignette & 9 other illusts, 8 of naval encounters. Some browning & dampstaining; C3 holed with small loss. Ck Nov 29 (18) £300

Descrizione...

— Descrizione delle feste celebrate in Parma l'anno MDCCLXIX per...nozze di...Don Ferdinando colla Reale Arciduchessa Maria Amalia. Parma, [1769]. Folio, contemp calf; rebacked. With frontis & 32 (of 36) plates. SI June 10 (756) LIt1,600,000

Deseine, Francois Jacques, d.1715

— Beschryving van oud en nieuw Rome. Amst., 1704. Folio, calf; minor defs. With 3 engraved titles, 8 double-page or folding maps & plans & 94 plates. B May 12 (1358) HF2,400

Desfontaines, Pierre Francois Guyot

— Relation de l'expedition de Moka.... Chaubert, 1739. 8vo, 19th-cent calf gilt. With folding map. S June 30 (127) £1,200 [Atabey]

Desgodetz, Antoine, 1653-1728

— Les Edifices antiques de Rome. Paris, 1695. 2d Issue. Folio, contemp mor gilt; worn. With engraved title & 137 plates. Some staining. Jeudwine—McCarty Cooper copy. CNY Jan 25 (16) $2,000

Anr Ed. Paris, 1779. Folio, 19th-cent half lea; spine def at head. With engraved title & 136 (of 137) plates, some folding. Some spotting. HH May 12 (813) DM2,100

Deshairs, Leon

— L'Art Decoratif Francais. Paris: Albert Levy, [c.1925]. Folio, half cloth; worn, becoming disbound. sg Apr 2 (17) $275

— Exposition des arts decoratifes: interieurs en couleurs. Paris, [1925]. 4to, loose as issued in half cloth portfolio; worn. With 50 color plates. sg Sept 6 (158) $425

Desmarets de Saint Sorlin, Jean, 1595-1676

— Ariana. L: John Dawson for Thomas Walkeley, 1641. Folio, contemp sheep; rebacked, worn. With extra title. Title & 1 other leaf repaired; dampstained. bba Nov 28 (227) £60 [Rix]

— Clovis, ou la France chrestienne. Paris, 1657. 1st Ed. 4to, contemp calf; worn. bba Feb 27 (251) £180 [Thorp]

Desmurs, Marc Athanase Parfait Oeillet. See: Des Murs, Marc Athanase Parfait Oeillet

Desnos, Robert

— Contree. Paris: Godet, 1944. One of 200. Illus by Pablo Picasso. Mor gilt, orig covers bound in. With 4 etchings ptd different colors. CGen Nov 18 (355) SF7,000

Desor, Edouard

— Excursions et sejour de M. Agassiz sur la Mer de Glace du Lauteraar et du Finsteraar.... [Geneva, 1841]. 8vo, contemp bds. Operning leaves foxed. Inscr. Offprint from the Bibliotheque Universelle de Geneva, Mar/Apr 1841. sg Nov 14 (174) $300

Destrez, Jean

— La Pecia dans les manuscrits universitaires du XIIIe et du XIVe Siecle. Paris, 1935. Folio, wraps. sg Oct 31 (204) $250

Deutsche Akademie der Wissenschaften

— Miscellanea Berolinensia. Berlin: Johann Christoph Papenius, 1710. Vol I. 4to, contemp vellum. With 30 folding plates only. Dampstaining in upper margin throughout; text browned; lacking front free endpaper & frontis. sg Nov 14 (223) $350

Deval, Charles

— Deux annees a Constantinople et en Moree.... L & Paris, 1828. 8vo, contemp half mor. With 14 (of 16) hand-colored plates, some heightened with gold. Some waterstaining. S Nov 21 (251) £500 [Kutluoglu]

Deventer, Hendrik van, 1651-1724

— Manuale Operatien I. Deel zijnde een nieuw ligt voor Vroed-Meesters en Vroed-Vrouwen. The Hague, 1701. Bound with: Nader vertoog van de sware baringen. Delft, 1719. Chapter 49 only (pp. 351-442). 4to, contemp vellum. With frontis & 35 plates in 1st work & port in 2d work. Ck Sept 6 (66) £300

— Operationes chirurgicae novum lumen exhibentes obstetricantibus.... Leiden, 1701. 1st Ed in Latin. 4to, early 19th-cent German bds. With engraved title & 35 plates. Some foxing. sg Nov 14 (29) $2,200

Devol, George H.

— Forty Years a Gambler on the Mississippi. NY, 1892. 2d Ed. 8vo, cloth; rubbed & faded; hinge cracked. cb Sept 12 (49) $160

Dewar, George Albemarle Bertie

— The Book of the Dry Fly. L, 1897. 1st Ed. 8vo, cloth; worn. With 2 plain & 3 color plates. Koopman copy. O Oct 29 (95) $100

Dewees, W. B.

— Letters from an early Settler of Texas.... Louisville, 1852. 12mo, modern mor. Some foxing. NH May 30 (515) $325

Dewees, William Potts

— A Treatise on the Physical and Medical Treatment of Children. Phila., 1836. 8vo, bdg not described. K Dec 1 (288) $90

Dewey, Melvil

— A Classification and Subject Index for Cataloguing and Arranging the Books and Pamphlets of a Library. Amherst, 1876. 8vo, later cloth. Perforated stamp on tp. sg May 7 (70) $250

Dexter, Elisha

— Narrative of the Loss of the Whaling Brig William and Joseph, of Martha's Vineyard.... Bost., 1848. 2d Ed. 12mo, orig wraps; small stains on covers. sg June 18 (561) $900

Dezallier d'Argenville, Antoine Joseph, 1680-1765

— L'Histoire naturelle eclaircie dans deux de ses parties principales. La Lithologie et la conchyliologie. Paris, 1757. 4to, contemp calf gilt; worn. With 41 plates. FD Dec 2 (258) DM650

— La Theorie, et la pratique du jardinage. The Hague, 1739. 4to, contemp calf. With 42 double-page or folding plates. Sold w.a.f. S Feb 26 (912) £320 [American]

Dial...

— The Dial. L, 1889-97. Ed by C. S. Ricketts & C. H. Shannon. Nos. 1-5 (all pbd). 4to, orig wraps, No 1 in contemp cloth with orig wraps bound in. S July 22 (389) £600 [Perrin]

Dialogue. See: Morin, Lazare

Diaz del Castillo, Bernal, c.1492-1581?. See: Limited Editions Club

Dibble, Sheldon, 1809-45

— History of the Sandwich Islands. Lahainaluna, 1843. 8vo, contemp half calf; rebacked, chipped. With folding map. Lacking the 3 plates; tear in folding map repaired; some foxing. S May 14 (1315) £550 [Blackburn]

Dibdin, Thomas Frognall, 1776-1847

— Aedes Althorpianae.... L, 1822. Vol I only. Half mor. sg Mar 5 (84) $60

— The Bibliographical Decameron. L, 1817. 3 vols. 4to, calf by Tout; rubbed. O Feb 25 (63) $325

Anr copy. 3 vols. 8vo, contemp russia gilt; rebacked. Some plates foxed. sg Oct 17 (193) $450

One of 50 L.p. copies. 3 vols. 4to, contemp calf gilt; rebcked, joints weak, lower cover of Vol I detached. Ck Nov 1 (377) £300

— A Bibliographical, Antiquarian, and Picturesque Tour in France and Germany. L, 1821. 1st Ed. 3 vols. 4to, calf by Tout; rubbed; Vol III water-damaged. Vol III internally stained. Sold w.a.f. O Feb 25 (61) $425

Anr copy. Mor gilt with gilt badge of the Carlton Club; rebacked. Extra-illus with ports & plates. S July 1 (1186) £260 [Bickersteth]

2d Ed. L, 1829. 3 vols. 8vo, bdg not given. cb Oct 17 (235) $110

Anr copy. Bdg not stated. cb Oct 17 (235) $110

— A Bibliographical, Antiquarian and Picturesque Tour in the Northern Counties of England and in Scotland. L, 1838. 1st Ed. 2 vols. 8vo, bds; worn. O Feb 25 (63) $325

Anr copy. Half mor. pnE Oct 2 (430) £190

— The Bibliomania.... L, 1809. 1st Ed. 8vo, contemp russia gilt; broken. Some foxing. sg May 21 (207) $175

2d Ed. L, 1811. 8vo, mor by Hathaway; rubbed. Dampstained. O Feb 25 (64) $450

Anr copy. Contemp half russia gilt; extremities worn. Inscr. sg Oct 17 (194) $850

Anr Ed. L, 1842. 2 vols in 1. 8vo, contemp calf gilt; rebacked with orig spine laid down. DW Apr 8 (232) £50

Anr Ed. L, 1876. 8vo, bdg not described. cb Oct 17 (236) $65

Anr Ed. Bost., 1903. 4 vols. 4to, mor gilt. cb Oct 17 (237) $450

One of 483. Orig bds. sg Mar 5 (85) $200

— An Introduction to the Knowledge of Rare and Valuable Editions of the Greek and Latin Classics. L, 1827. 4th Ed. 2 vols. 8vo, bdg not given. cb Oct 17 (238) $150

Anr copy. Half lea; worn. Library markings. O Sept 24 (68) $180

— The Library Companion. L, 1824. 1st Ed. 2 vols. 8vo, half mor; worn. K Dec 1 (141) $160

2d Ed. L, 1825. 2 vols. 8vo, bdg not stated. cb Oct 17 (240) $60

— Reminiscences of a Literary Life. L, 1836. 1st Ed. 2 vols. 8vo, bdg not stated. cb Oct 17 (241) $140

Anr copy. Later cloth. K Dec 1 (140) $75

Dibdin, Thomas John, 1771-1841

— The Reminiscences. L, 1827. 1st Ed. 2 vols. 8vo, later half mor; extremities rubbed. Extra-illus with "a profusion" of plates. sg Oct 17 (27) $425

Dichter, Harry —& Shapiro, Elliott

— Early American Sheet Music, its Lure and its Lore. NY, 1941. 4to, orig cloth, in chipped d/j. F Mar 26 (460) $55

Dick, Harris Saint John

— Flies and Fly Fishing for White and Brown Trout.... L, 1873. 8vo, cloth; worn. Koopman copy. O Oct 29 (96) $100

Dick, Philip K.

— The Man in the High Castle. NY: Putnam, [1962]. 1st Ed, with code D36 at base of p 239. wa Mar 5 (169) $260

— Time Out of Joint. Phila., [1959]. In d/j with spine ends worn. sg June 11 (100) $175

— UBIK. Garden City, 1969. In d/j. wa Mar 5 (170) $200

Dick, Stewart

— The Cottage Homes of England. L, 1909. One of 500. Illus by Helen Allingham. 4to, orig cloth; 1 corner bumped. Marginal browning. bba May 14 (316) £90 [Vandeleur]

Anr copy. Orig cloth; rubbed & soiled. DW Mar 4 (99) £210

Dickenmann, R.

— Souvenir du Lac de Lucerne. Zuerich, [c.1830s]. Oblong 8vo, orig cloth. With 14 hand-colored plates heightened with gum-arabic. S Nov 21 (199) £900 [Mandl]

Dickens, Charles, 1812-70

[An assembled set of 1st Eds in Book form of the Works, L, 1836-84, in 29 vols] wd Dec 12 (384) $6,000
See also: All...; Caswall, Edward; Grabhorn Printing; Kyd; Limited Editions Club; Nonesuch Press

— American Notes for General Circulation. L, 1842. 1st Ed, 1st Issue. 2 vols. 8vo, orig cloth; spines sunned; upper cover of Vol I wrinkled. DW Dec 11 (271) £210

Anr copy. Orig cloth; recased with new endpapers. O July 14 (64) $250

Anr copy. Orig cloth. Headline of contents page (A5r) incorrectly spaced as CONTENTS T OVOLUME I & leaf slit for cancellation. Manney copy. P Oct 11 (87) $2,500

Anr copy. Mor gilt; corners worn. sg May 7 (78) $475

1st American Ed. NY, 1842. 2 vols. 8vo, orig wraps; spine chipped. sg Oct 17 (195) $425

Anr Ed. NY, Nov 1842. 2d Version. 4to, old half calf; worn. Some foxing. In: The New World, Extra Series, Vol II, Nos 8-9. bbc Apr 27 (292) $110

— Barnaby Rudge. L, 1841. 1st Ed in Book form. 8vo, orig cloth; rubbed. Without preface leaf. Manney copy. P Oct 11 (86) $1,000

Anr copy. Later half mor. Soiled. sg Oct 17 (196) $120

— The Battle of Life. L, 1846. 1st Ed, 2d Issue. 8vo, orig cloth; corners worn. Manney copy. P Oct 11 (92) $700

— Bleak House. L, 1852-53. 1st Ed in orig 20/19 parts. 8vo, wraps; last part rebacked. cb Nov 7 (60) $850

Anr copy. Orig wraps; several spines faded. Ck July 10 (228) £300

Anr copy. Orig wraps; some spines repaired. CNY Dec 5 (223) $750

Anr copy. Bound in 2 vols. 8vo, later half mor, orig wraps bound in. With frontis, additonal title & 38 plates. Part 1 lacking W. Mott & Norton's Camomile Pills ads; Part 2 lacking Ford's Eureka Shirts slip; Part 11 lacking New Sporting Newspaper slip & Handley Cross slip; Part 13 lacking Grace Aguilar's Works slip; Part 14 lacking New Geographical & Educational Works ad; Part 16 lacking Grace Aguilar's Works slip; Part 18 lacking Treasure of the Desert slip & W. Mott ad; Part 19/20 lacking p13-20 of Bleak House Advertiser, p3-14 of Ransome's Patent Stone Filters, Samuel Warren slip, W. Mott ads & The Newcomes slip; Household Words slip lacking from 8 parts & Crochet Cotton slip lacking from 6 parts. S May 13 (609) £220 [Thorp]

Anr copy. 8vo, orig wraps; some spines chipped. Epstein copy. sg Apr 29 (117) $1,000

1st Ed in Book form. L, 1853. 8vo, contemp half mor; rubbed. bba Jan 30 (201) £60 [Pordes]

Anr copy. Contemp half lea; rebacked, orig spine preserved. bba Apr 9 (31) £60 [Pordes]

Anr copy. Half calf gilt. O Mar 31 (52) $170

Anr copy. Orig cloth; rubbed, short tear at head of rear joint. Ewing-Manney copy. P Oct 11 (97) $1,400

Anr copy. Disbound. With additional title, frontis & 38 plates. Lacking half-title; spotted. Inscr to John Tenniel, 3 Oct 1853. S July 21 (49) £7,200 [Lindseth]

Anr copy. Mor gilt; some edges worn. sg May 7 (182) $275

— A Child's History of England. L, 1852-54. 1st Ed. 3 vols in 1. 16mo, early half calf. Lacking the frontis. kh Nov 11 (257) A$50

— The Chimes. L, 1845. 1st Ed. 8vo, calf gilt; joints rubbed. With 13 plates. cb Sept 5 (26) $55

1st Issue. Orig cloth; inner hinges splitting. Pforzheimer-Manney copy. P Oct 11 (90) $800

Anr copy. Mor gilt. With 13 plates. sg May 7 (779) $250

2d Issue. Orig cloth; front hinge split. With 13 plates. Dampstain at bottom corner of extra title. bbc Apr 27 (293) $60

Anr copy. Orig cloth; spine ends bumped. sg Nov 7 (56) $175

— [Christmas Books]. L, 1843-48. 1st Eds, A Christmas Carol, 2d Ed, 1st state; The Chimes, 1st Issue; The Battle of Life, 4th Issue.. 5 vols. 12mo, mor gilt. Lacking ads; washed. P Dec 12 (28) $1,200

— A Christmas Carol. L, 1843. 1st Ed, 1st Issue. 8vo, orig cloth; stained. With 4 hand-colored plates. CNY Dec 5 (222) $4,500

Anr copy. Pictorial inlaid mor gilt, orig cloth covers preserved. CNY Dec 5 (361) $2,000

Anr copy. Orig cloth; upper joint split, stain on upper cover. Pforzheimer-Manney copy. P Oct 11 (88) $7,500

Issue not given. Orig cloth; spine broken & def. Some foxing. rs Oct 17 (16) $650

Anr Ed. L, 1915. One of 525. Illus by Arthur Rackham. 4to, mor gilt by Bayntun with design after Rackham; spotted. sg Sept 26 (264) $400

Anr copy. Orig vellum gilt. sg Nov 7 (165) $1,100

Anr Ed. Phila.: Lippincott, [1915]. 4to, orig cloth; water damage on front pastedown. kh Nov 11 (79A) A$140

Anr Ed. Chicago: Monastery Hill Press, [1940]. Mor gilt, the front cover inset with a Dickensian character in vari-colored mor. sg Mar 5 (86) $200

— The Cricket on the Hearth. L, 1846 [1845]. 1st Ed. 8vo, cloth. bba Apr 9 (28) £80 [Hart]

Anr copy. Orig cloth; rubbed, stain to front free endpaper. Pforzheimer-Manney copy. P Oct 11 (91) $700

1st American Ed. NY, 1846. 8vo, orig wraps; spine chipped, front cover stained. Several leaves dampstained. sg Oct 17

(198) $70

— David Copperfield. L, 1849-50. 1st Ed in orig 20/19 parts. 8vo, orig wraps; No 2 lacking rear wrap; No 3 torn horizontally; No 16 lacking front wrap & with portion of last page missing; No 19 lacking front wrap. LH Dec 11 (98) $1,200

Anr copy. Orig wraps; most parts with spines restored, many with marginal chipping or repair, last part with small portions of front wrap supplied. Some plates spotted, browned or stained; lacking 2 slips in Part 13, the single slip in Part 14 & the Household Words slip in Part 16. Manney copy. P Oct 11 (95) $3,750

Anr copy. Orig wraps; some backstrips chipped, minor soiling. sg Mar 5 (87) $4,200

Anr copy. Orig wraps; some covers soiled; several with spines repaired. Epstein copy. sg Apr 29 (116) $3,000

1st Ed in Book form. L, 1850. 8vo, later half mor gilt; rubbed. bba Apr 9 (30) £65 [Ash]

Anr copy. Lev gilt Cosway-style bdg; upper cover set with oval port miniature of Dickens as a young man. With 40 plates. CNY Dec 5 (362) $1,600

Anr copy. Orig cloth; inner hinges split. Frontis & vignette title stained from inserted clipping; U2 with short tear at fore-edge; bound later, as copy includes notes for Bleak House & Hard Times. Manney copy. P Oct 11 (96) $1,100

Anr copy. Mor gilt by Bayntun with inset port of young Dickens on front cover. sg Nov 7 (59) $2,400

Anr copy. Cloth. With 39 plates. Foxed. sp Apr 16 (378) $80

— Dombey and Son. L, 1846-48. 1st Ed in orig 20/19 parts. 8vo, orig wraps; some spines chipped or cracked, several covers starting. A few plates browned. sg Nov 7 (58) $650

Anr copy. Orig wraps; many wraps soiled. sg May 7 (80) $800

1st Ed in Book form. L, 1848. 8vo, modern half lea; front joint splitting. cb Jan 16 (39) $90

Anr copy. Later half calf. Foxed. sg Oct 17 (199) $70

— Great Expectations. L, 1861. 1st Ed. 3 vols. 8vo, mor gilt. sg May 7 (83) $5,000

1st Ed in Book form. 3 vols. 8vo, orig cloth; some wear, some waterstain to Vol II bdg. Some dampstaining. O Mar 31 (54) $8,500

Anr copy. Orig cloth; inner hinges, joints & extremities restored. Doheny-Manney copy. P Oct 11 (101) $29,000

Anr copy. Calf gilt by Riviere, orig cloth bound in. Titles spotted. S Nov 14 (553) £4,000 [Johnson]

— The Great International Walking-Match of February 29, 1868. [Bost., Mar 1868]. Single sheet, 530mm by 583mm. Framed. Sgd by Dickens & the other participants. CNY June 9 (57) $13,000

— Hard Times. L, 1854. 1st Ed in Book form. 8vo, orig cloth; backstrip frayed, small tears. bba June 25 (41) £50 [Dewar]

Anr copy. Orig cloth, Carter's A bdg; extremities rubbed, small stain on front cover. Manney copy. P Oct 11 (98) $1,000

Anr copy. Orig cloth; recased, spine ends reinforced. sg Nov 7 (61) $275

— The Haunted Man and the Ghost's Bargain. L, 1848. 1st Ed. 12mo, orig cloth. bba Feb 27 (122) £60 [Dawson]

Anr copy. Later half mor; rubbed. cb Sept 5 (27) $85

Anr copy. Mor gilt by the Club Bindery for James W. Ellsworth, orig cloth bound in. Inscr to Anna Maria Hall, 14 Dec 1848. Manney copy. P Oct 11 (94) $9,000

Anr copy. Mor gilt; 2 forecorners bumped. sg May 7 (81) $250

— Hunted Down: A Story. L: Hotten, [1870]. 8vo, half mor. bba Feb 27 (123) £90 [Thorp]

— The Lamplighter. L, 1879. One of 250. 8vo, mor gilt; some corners worn. sg May 7 (86) $300

— Little Dorrit. L, 1855-57. 1st Ed in orig 20/19 parts, 1st Issue. 8vo, orig wraps; front wrap detached from Nos 19 & 20; some chipping. LH Dec 11 (95) $600

Anr copy. Orig wraps; spines restored; Part 1 with portion at fore-edge of front wrap supplied in ink facsimile, several rear wraps from other parts, though only 1 of these from anr set. Lacking The Eclectic Review in Part 2, The London Stereoscope in Part 6 & the 2 front slips in Part 13. Pforzheimer-Manney copy. P Oct 11 (99) $400

Anr copy. Contemp half mor, some orig wraps bound in at end. Lacking all ads. S May 13 (605) £140 [Thorp]

Anr copy. Orig wraps; some spine ends restored. Plates foxed; those in Part 13 dampstained. sg Nov 7 (62) $750

Issue not indicated. Orig wraps. With extra Part 2 & some plates. b&b Feb 19 (312) $650

1st Ed in Book form. L, 1857. 8vo, contemp calf gilt; rebacked, orig spine preserved. bba Apr 9 (32) £75 [Tholstrup]

Anr copy. Contemp half mor; rubbed.

Some spotting. bba May 14 (145) £55 [Culley]

Anr copy. Calf gilt; rubbed. O Mar 31 (56) $170

— Martin Chuzzlewit. L, 1843-44. 1st Ed in orig 20/19 parts, 1st Issue. 8vo, mor gilt by Zaehnsdorf, wraps & ads bound in at end. Part 1 lacking lower wrap & slips for Bentley's Hand-books & Wyld's Globes; Part 2 lacking Thomas Boys prospectus; Part 7 lacking Neatly bound in cloth slip; Parts 9-11 lacking E. Moses booklets; Part 15 with Chuzzlewit Advertiser cropped along fore-edge with loss; Part 16 lacking pp. 3-14 of Chuzzlewit Advertiser & E. Moses booklet. S May 13 (618) £380 [Aspin]

1st Ed in Book form. L, 1844. 8vo, orig cloth; extremities rubbed, inner hinges restored. Manney copy. P Oct 11 (89) $2,750

1st Issue. Contemp calf; spine detached, joints weak. bba Nov 28 (356) £50 [Ogino]

1st American Ed. Phila., 1844. 8vo, bdg not described but repaired. sp June 18 (416) $110

— Master Humphrey's Clock. L, 1840-41. 1st Ed, 1st Issue, in 88 weekly parts. 8vo, orig wraps; covers of Part 1 detached. Epstein copy. sg Apr 29 (115) $1,200

1st Ed in Book form. 3 vols. 8vo, contemp half calf; worn. b Mar 11 (100) £80

Anr copy. Orig cloth; rubbed. bba Feb 27 (121) £55 [Hilton]

Anr copy. 3 vols in 2. 8vo, contemp half calf; rubbed. Lacking title to Vol III. Sold w.a.f. bba Apr 9 (25) £50 [Abdullah]

Anr copy. 3 vols. 8vo, orig cloth; rebacked with orig spines laid down. Some spotting. bba July 9 (153) £55 [Kay Books]

Anr copy. 3 vols in 1. 8vo, calf; rubbed. O Mar 31 (57) $120

Anr copy. 3 vols. 8vo, orig cloth gilt; joint of Vol II split at foot & repaired. Marginal soiling. Manney copy. P Oct 11 (84) $800

Anr copy. Mor gilt; edges worn. sg May 7 (77) $475

[-] Memoirs of Joseph Grimaldi. L, 1838. 1st Ed, 1st Issue. Ed by Dickens; illus by George Cruikshank. 2 vols. 8vo, calf by Morrell, orig cloth retained at rear of each. With port & 12 plates. DW Mar 4 (205) £145

Anr copy. Calf gilt; rubbed, joints repaired. O May 26 (50) $300

Anr copy. Orig cloth, Carter's A bdg; rubbed. Minor foxing. Manney copy. P Oct 11 (82) $1,500

— The Mystery of Edwin Drood. L, 1870. 1st Ed in Book form. 8vo, mor gilt by Cedric Chivers; upper cover with medallion of arms of city of Rochester. Extra-illus with 15 pencil and watercolor drawings of Rochester scenes, Dickens's bookplate, & related material. CNY Dec 5 (385) $800

Anr copy. Later calf; spine rubbed. sg Mar 5 (89) $130

Anr copy. Cloth. With port & 12 plates. sp Sept 22 (104) $80

6 orig parts. 8vo, orig wraps; Parts I and VI slightly torn. With port, engraved title (in part 6) & 12 plates. Sold w.a.f. Ck July 10 (229) £160

Anr copy. Orig wraps; Nos 1 & 2 rebacked. LH Dec 11 (99) $550

Anr copy. Orig wraps; chipped with some loss. Part 2 lacking Gaimes...Cork Hats; Part 4 with uncalled for 8-page Chapman & Hall catalogue; Part 5 with Our Farm of Four Acres slip. S May 13 (617) £240 [Pearson]

6 orig parts bound together. 8vo, mor gilt by Riviere. sg Oct 17 (204) $225

6 orig parts. 8vo, orig wraps; spine ends chipped; some edges worn. With port, engraved title (in part 6) & 12 plates. sg Nov 7 (65) $300

Anr copy. Orig wraps; some spine ends chipped; front wrap torn. Epstein copy. sg Apr 290 (118) $600

— Nicholas Nickleby. L, 1838-39. 1st Ed, in orig 20/19 parts. 8vo, orig wraps; spines worn, some chipping. Plates stained in Nos 4, 6, 10 & 11. LH Dec 11 (97) $800

1st Ed in Book form. L, 1839. 1st Issue. 8vo, modern half calf; new endpapers. Lacking half-title. bba June 11 (111) £60 [Sanerson]

Anr copy. Contemp half calf; worn, joints broken. Foxed. O Aug 25 (56) $90

Anr copy. Mor gilt; corners worn. sg May 7 (75) $350

Anr copy. Half lea. Foxed. sp Apr 16 (379) $75

Anr copy. Early half calf; worn, joints splitting at ends, 1 gathering sprung. Some plates browned; 1 plate with small brown stain. wa Sept 26 (148) $60

Issue not given. Orig cloth. sg Oct 17 (202) $950

Later Issue. Orig cloth; joints & corners rubbed. Some foxing; marginal chip from 1 plate. Manney copy. P Oct 11 (83) $9,500

— The Old Curiosity Shop. L, 1841. 8vo, orig cloth; rubbed. Lower margins of leaves 2b-2K with small gouge. Manney copy. P Oct 11 (85) $1,000

— Oliver Twist. L, 1838. 1st Ed in Book form, 1st Issue. Illus by George Cruikshank. 3 vols. 12mo, contemp half mor; rubbed.

Lacking ad leaf. bba Feb 27 (119) £320 [Ash Rare Books]

Anr copy. Orig cloth; most inner hinges split, no pbr's imprint on spines. Minor foxing; lacking plate list. Manney copy. P Oct 11 (81) $3,750

Anr copy. Mor gilt. sg May 7 (73) $1,800

2d Ed in Book form. L, 1839. 3 vols. 12mo, orig cloth; worn & shaken. With inserted clippings. K Dec 1 (144) $90

Anr copy. Contemp half calf gilt; rubbed. L Nov 14 (277) £100

— Our Mutual Friend. L, 1864-65. 1st Ed, in orig 20/19 parts. 2 vols. 8vo, orig wraps; marginally worn & chipped. cb Feb 12 (32) $425

Anr copy. Orig wraps; front wrap to Part 1 detached & chipped, bottom edge of front wrap for Part 2 chipped, 11 parts with early signature neatly scratched out. Lacking 4 ads & with 1 ad not called for by Hatton & Cleaver. K Mar 22 (116) $425

Anr copy. Orig wraps; some chipping to wraps. LH Dec 11 (96) $700

Anr copy. Orig wraps; most parts rebacked. sg Nov 7 (64) $650

1st Ed in Book form. L, 1865. 2 vols. 8vo, orig cloth. bba Apr 9 (33) £80 [Grujicic]

Anr copy. 2 vols in 1. 8vo, mor gilt by Bayntun-Riviere with central port of Dickens on front cover. sg Oct 17 (206) $300

Anr copy. 2 vols. 8vo, contemp half calf; some leaves sprung, rear inside hinge of Vol I broken. With 20 full-page plates. wa Dec 9 (180) $110

[-] The Pic Nic Papers. L, 1841. 1st Ed. Ed by Dickens. 3 vols. 8vo, calf by Tout; rubbed. O Mar 31 (59) $250

Anr copy. Orig cloth; recased with new endpapers, hinges of Vol III cracked. wd June 12 (378) $350

— [Pickwick Papers]. L, 1836-37. 1st Ed, in orig 20/19 parts. 8vo, wraps; spines worn and repaired, some staining. With 43 plates (mixed states). CNY Dec 5 (220) $1,000

Anr copy. Orig wraps (most 1st issue); soiled, most spines frayed or restored, marginal fraying & repair, rear wrap of Part 2 is supplied by an orig from Part 1, front wrap of Part 3 evidently a contemp reprint wrap with part number altered by hand, Parts 4 & 5 wraps are contemp reprints. With additional title & frontis by Phiz, 41 plates by Seymour, Buss & Phiz. Plates & text leaves with minor marginal repairs or closed tears. Pforzheimer-Manney copy. P Oct 11 (78) $6,500

Anr copy. Wraps; some covers soiled. sg Nov 7 (54) $3,400

1st Ed in Book form. L, 1837. 8vo, calf; rubbed. O Mar 31 (60) $170

1st English Ed in Book form, 2-vol Issue. Contemp half mor; rubbed. With additional title & frontis & 41 plates. Extra-illus with duplicate, variant state plates of the vignette title, frontis & 7 other Phiz plates,the 2 Phiz etchings for the cancelled Buss plates & 27 plates from Thomas Onwhyn's Illustrations to the Pickwick Club. Crawford-Manney copy. P Oct 11 (79) $2,750

Early Issue. 8vo, half calf; rubbed. With 43 plates, including the 2 suppressed plates by Buss. Some foxing & soiling; minor edge tears. O July 14 (66) $130

Anr copy. Later half mor. Plates in mixed states; upper wrap from Part 15 bound in. Extra-illus with 24 Illustrations to the Pickwick Papers by F. W. Pailthrope and Sam Weller's Illustrations to the Pickwick Club. S May 13 (610) £180 [Culley]

Issue not given. Half mor gilt. sg Oct 17 (207) $275

Later Issue. Orig cloth; lower joints splitting. With 43 plates. Some browning to plates. Manney copy. P Oct 11 (80) $4,000

Bound from the orig parts. 8vo, later mor; rubbed. With 7 plates by Seymour, 2 by Buss & 34 by Browne in mixed states. Lacking all ads. Extra-illus with 40 plates by Alfred Crowquill & 20 plates by W. Heath. S May 13 (607) £220 [Thorp]

Bound from the orig parts in 2 vols, First Issue text with plates in 1st and 2d states and some examples of later issue plates. 8vo, mor gilt by Stikeman (lacking orig wraps). With engraved title & 42 plates. Sold w.a.f. CNY Dec 5 (221) $600

Anr Ed. L, 1910. Illus by Cecil Aldin. 2 vols. Folio, orig cloth. With 24 colored plates. bba Oct 10 (143) £50 [Lobo]; DW Dec 11 (396) £90

Anr copy. Half cloth. kh Nov 11 (80) A$180

Anr Ed. L, 1930. Illus by C. E. Brock. Lev gilt extra with lea inlays illustrating a plate in the book. CNY Dec 5 (426) $1,300

— Pictures from Italy. L, 1846. 1st Ed. 8vo, orig cloth; spine rubbed. bba Apr 9 (26) £95 [Harlow]; sg Nov 7 (57) $225

— Sketches by "Boz." L, 1836. First Series only. 2 vols. 12mo, orig cloth; outer joints split. Epstein copy. sg Apr 29 (112) $3,200

1st Ed in Book form of First Series; 1st Ed of 2d Series. L, 1836-37. 2 vols. 12mo, orig cloth; corners bumped. Ewing-Manney copy. P Oct 11 (75) $11,000

1st Ed in Book form of 1st Series; 1st Ed of 2d Series. 3 vols. 12mo, orig cloth. With 10 plates, including frontis & extra title. Jerome Kern copy. sg Nov 7 (53) $3,600

2d Ed in Book form of First Series; 1st Ed of 2d Series. 3 vols. 12mo, 19th-cent calf gilt, armorial bdg; rubbed. With 3 frontises, pictorial title & 22 plates in 2 states, 1 hand-colored. Lacking ad leaves at end; some spotting. pn Sept 12 (195) £300 [Dyce]

Anr Ed. L, 1837. 2d Series only. 12mo, cloth; rebacked. Sgd George Cruikshank and Eugene Field by Eugene Field II. sg Oct 17 (227) $300

— Sketches by "Boz." Second Series. L, 1837-39. 1st Ed, 2d Issue. 8vo, orig cloth; spine repaired. Manney copy. P Oct 11 (76) $2,250

— Sketches by "Boz." L, 1839. 8vo, half lea; rubbed. sp Nov 24 (200) $60

— Speeches: Literary and Social. L, [1870]. 8vo, mor gilt; 1 corner bumped. sg May 7 (85) $300

— Sunday under Three Heads. L, 1836. 1st Ed. 8vo, orig wraps; rebacked, repair. P Oct 11 (76) $2,250

Anr copy. Orig wraps; rebacked. Upper fore-edge corners stained. P Oct 11 (77) $1,900

Anr copy. Orig wraps; torn with some loss, spine cracked & shaken. Some spotting. S May 13 (619) £380 [Alatrist]

— Sunday under Three Heads. By Timothy Sparks. L, 1836. 1st Ed. 8vo, half mor, orig front wrap bound in. Inscr to Thomas Mitton. Epstein copy. sg Apr 29 (113) $7,000

— A Tale of Two Cities. L, 1859. 1st Ed in Book form, 1st Issue. 8vo, orig cloth; inner hinges cracking. Dickens-Perkins-Ewing-Manney copy. P Oct 11 (100) $14,000

Anr copy. Orig cloth; worn, rear joint torn; rear cover stained. sg Nov 7 (63) $1,300

1st American Ed in Book form. Phila.: T. B. Peterson, [1859]. 8vo, orig cloth; frayed. bbc Dec 9 (456) $175

— Works. L, 1861-[c.1885]. Illustrated Library Ed. 27 (of 30) vols. 8vo, later half mor. cb Dec 5 (55) $325

Anr copy. 30 vols plus Forster's Life & the Letters. 8vo, half mor gilt by Zaehnsdorf. pn Sept 12 (197) £2,200 [Dyce]

Anr Ed. NY, 1864-67. 48 vols. 8vo, half mor; some wear. bbc Dec 9 (208) $700

Anr Ed. L, 1874-76. 30 vols. 8vo, later half mor by Bayntun Riviere. Ck Dec 11 (122) £1,100

Anr copy. Contemp half calf gilt; rubbed. S Nov 14 (518) £300 [Cox]

Anr copy. Half mor gilt by Morrell. sg Mar 5 (90) $1,700

Anr copy. 32 vols. 8vo, half mor gilt by Blackwell-Bennett; some scuffing to joints, some soiling. wa Mar 5 (26) $500

Anr Ed. L, 1881-82. 30 vols. Orig cloth; soiled. bba Oct 10 (351) £120 [Ferret Fantasy]

Ed de Luxe. 30 vols. 4to, half mor gilt; rubbed. Envelope sgd & addressed by Dickens tipped in. P June 17a (335) $2,750

Illustrated Library Ed. L, 1889-90. 32 vols. 8vo, orig cloth; rubbed. DW Oct 2 (442) £260

Anr Ed. L, 1890-95. 20 vols, including Dickens Dictionary and Life. 8vo, contemp half mor; some joints rubbed. bba Oct 24 (128) £420 [Spademan]

Gadshill Ed. L, 1897-1903. American Issue. 34 vols only. Half mor gilt by Zaehnsdorf. NH May 30 (80) $1,200

Anr Ed. L, 1900. One of 25. 32 vols. 8vo, mor gilt; 1 spine dry; 1 bdg cracked along gutter with a few leaves loose & some leaves restitched. With plates & some orig water-color drawings of characters. P June 17 (334) $3,750

Extra Illustrated Ed of the Chapman & Hall Large Paper Dickens. L: Caxton Society, [n.d.]. One of 15, the Star copy. 60 vols. 8vo, mor extra; 4 leaves in Vol 34 bound upside down. With engravings on india paper mtd, from the orig blocks, numerous ink drawings from the novels by Kyd & H. C. Green. CNY Dec 5 (380) $42,000

Dickens, Charles, 1812-70 —& Collins, Wilkie, 1824-89

— The Wreck of the Golden Mary.... Kentfield, Calif.: Allen Press, 1956. One of 200. cb Oct 21 (4) $140

Dickeson, Montroville Wilson

— American Numismatic Manual.... Phila., 1860. 4to, orig cloth; detached with frontis, backstrip lacking. With port, frontis & 21 colored plates. bbc Apr 27 (581) $70

Anr copy. Cloth; def. With 21 tinted lithos. sg June 18 (441) $110

Dickinson, Emily, 1830-86

— Letters of.... Bost., 1894. Ed by Mabel Loomis Todd. 2 vols. 16mo, orig cloth; worn. pba July 9 (73) $110

— Poems by Emily Dickinson...Second Series. L, 1891. 1st English Ed. 8vo, orig cloth; soiled; joints separating. sg Oct 17 (209) $175

— Poems by Emily Dickinson Edited by Mabel Loomis Todd. Third Series. Bost., 1896. 8vo, mor. sg Oct 17 (210) $150

Dickson, Martin Bernard. See: Firdausi

Dickson, R. W.

— A Complete Dictionary of Practical Gardening. L, 1807. 2 vols. 4to, contemp calf; rebacked. With 13 uncolored & 61 hand-colored plates. Text spotted; some staining to plates. C May 20 (167) £1,500 [Ramsay]

Anr copy. Modern half calf. With 46 hand-colored plates only. Lacking tp of Vol II. Sold w.a.f. W July 8 (360) £600

Anr Ed. L, 1812. ("The New Botanic Garden.") Illus by Sydenham Edwards. 2 vols. 4to, contemp mor gilt; some scuffing. With 61 hand-colored plates. Tear to blank margin of final leaf of text. C Oct 30 (189) £2,200 [Junk]

— Practical Agriculture; or, a Complete System of Modern Husbandry. L, 1805. 2 vols. 4to, contemp calf gilt; joints broken, 1 cover detached. With folding plan & 86 plates. Some spotting & dampstaining. S Nov 15 (735) £150 [Freeman]

Dickson, Robert, 1828-93

— Introduction of the Art of Printing into Scotland. Aberdeen: Edmond & Spark, 1885. One of 50 L.p. copies. 8vo, pictorial cloth; rubbed. bba May 28 (609) £50 [Forster]

Dickson, Robert, 1828-93 —& Edmond, John Philip, 1850-1906

— Annals of Scottish Printing. L, 1890. 1st Ed, one of 500. 4to, orig cloth; worn. F Mar 26 (367) $100

Dictionary...

— Dictionary of American Biography. NY, 1928-73. 23 vols, 3 Supplements. 4to, orig cloth. Library markings. bba May 28 (146) £220 [Quaritch]

Anr Ed. NY, 1928-44. 22 vols, including Index & Supplement I. 4to, bdg not described but rebacked. Sold w.a.f. K Mar 22 (118) $375

Anr copy. Cloth. O Sept 24 (69) $650

Anr Ed. NY, 1928-58. 23 vols, including Index & Supplements I & II. 4to, orig cloth. Library markings. wa Mar 5 (93) $500

— The Dictionary of National Biography. L, 1885-1904. 63 vols plus 3-vol Supplement, Index and Epitome, & Errata, & 3-vol Second Supplement. Together 72 vols. 8vo, orig cloth; some spines torn. F Dec 18 (381) $80

Anr Ed. L, [1950]. 22 vols, including Supplement. wa June 25 (23) $325

Anr Ed. L, 1967-68-70. 23 vols, including Supplement and 1931-40 Supplement All but last vol in d/js. bba Apr 9 (122) £720 [Abdullah]

Anr copy. 21 vols, lacking Supplement In d/js. Ck Nov 1 (379) £380

Compact Ed. L, 1975. 28 vols in 2. 4to, orig cloth. bba May 14 (175) £250 [Books & Prints]

Anr copy. Cloth. First few leaves in each vol creased. bba May 14 (176) £220 [Barkhorn]

Anr copy. Cloth, boxed with magnifying glass. DW Jan 29 (310) £310; DW Mar 4 (284) £360; DW Apr 8 (336) £280; DW Apr 8 (403) £210; L Nov 14 (19) £250

Anr copy. Cloth, lacking slipcase & glass. pn Apr 23 (21) £250

Anr copy. Cloth, boxed with magnifying glass. A few leaves creased. sg Oct 31 (100) $500

— Dictionary of Scientific Biography. NY, [1970-72]. Vols I-VI (of 16). 4to, cloth, in d/js. DW Dec 11 (362) £70

Dictionnaire...

— Dictionnaire de l'Academie Francaise. Lyon, 1776. 2 vols. 4to, contemp sheep; worn. sg Mar 5 (92) $100

— Dictionnaire des sciences naturelles. Paris & Strassburg, 1816-30. Plates for 2d Part, Botanique only. 4to, later cloth. With 8 ports & 94 plates, all but 3 hand-colored. Library markings. DW Jan 29 (135) £300

Dictys Cretensis —& Dares Phrygius

— Historia Troiana. Venice: Christophorus de Pensis, de Mandello, 1 Feb to 20 Mar 1499. ("De Historia belli Troiani et Dares Phrygius de eadem....") 4to, 18th-cent half vellum. 61 lines & headline; type 7:109R. Some soiling & dampstaining. 74 leaves. Goff D-187. C Dec 16 (120) £550 [Schilt]

Diderot, Denis, 1713-84

— Essais sur la peinture. Paris, 1796. 8vo, contemp calf gilt; head of spine chipped, joints weak. Prelims foxed. sg Apr 2 (103) $425

— Jacques le fataliste et son maitre. Paris, [1797]. 2 vols in 1. 8vo, modern half mor. Lacking final blank in Vol I. bba Oct 10 (456) £220 [Maggs]

— Oeuvres philosophiques. Amst., 1772. 5 vols. 8vo, contemp calf gilt; extremities rubbed. C June 24 (303) £700 [Quaritch]

Diderot, Denis, 1713-84 —& Alembert, Jean le Rond d', 1717?-83

— Diderot Encyclopedia: The Complete Illustrations, 1762-1777. NY: Harry Abrams, [1978]. 5 vols. 12mo, half syn. With 3,115 plates. Library markings. sg Feb 6 (69) $200

— Encyclopedie.... Livorno, 1770-75. 17 vols only. Folio, half vellum. HH May 12 (846) DM1,700

— Recueil de Planches. Paris, 1762-77. Bound in 12 vols, including Supplement. Folio, contemp half lea. With 3,099 (of 3,129) plates. HH May 12 (847) DM2,000

Anr Ed. Lausanne, 1966. 12 vols in 6. Folio, sheep gilt. Facsimile of the 1764-66 Ed. sg Nov 7 (66) $550

Didymus

— Interpretatio in Odysseam. Venice: Aldus, June 1528. 8vo, contemp lea. SI June 9 (313) LIt1,700,000

Diedo, Giacomo

— Storia della repubblica de Venezia. Venice, 1751. 4 vols. 4to, contemp vellum bds; soiled, minor repairs. Some dampstaining. S June 30 (25) £700 [Bank of Cyprus]

Anr copy. Contemp half vellum. SI June 9 (314) LIt500,000

Diehl, Edith

— Bookbinding: its Background and Technique. L & NY, 1946. 2 vols. cb Oct 17 (243) $80; cb Nov 21 (81) $65

Anr copy. Worn. O Sept 24 (70) $70; pba July 23 (60) $60

Diemerbroeck, Isbrandus de, 1609-74

— The Anatomy of Human Bodies.... L, 1689. Folio, later calf; worn, hinges cracked. With port & 15 (of 16) plates. Plate 4 def; lacking 2 leaves. Sold w.a.f. bba Oct 10 (229) £120 [Rix]

Diesel, Matthias

— Erlustierende Augenweide in Vorstellung herrlicher Garten und Lustgebauede. Augsburg: Jeremias Wolff [c.1720-30]. Part 1 only. Contemp sheep; rubbed. With engraved title & 50 plates. Thumb-marks; tp stamped. S Nov 21 (76) £1,800 [Dal Mondo]

Diesel, Rudolf, 1857-1913

— Die Entstehung des Dieselmotors. Berlin, 1913. 8vo, orig cloth; edge wear. bbc Sept 23 (254) $55

— Theory and Construction of a Rational Heat Motor. L & NY, 1894. 8vo, cloth; repaired. With 3 folding plates. K July 12 (171) $190

Dietrich, Nathanael Friedrich David

— Flora universalis. Jena, 1831-[56]. Division II, Part 4 & Division III, Part 1 in 2 vols. Contemp half calf; worn & wormed, 2 covers detached. With c.860 hand-colored plates. Sold w.a.f. C May 20 (170) £3,000 [Schuster]

Anr Ed. Jena: August Schmid, 1838-52. Division I, Parts 1-2 in 2 vols. Folio, contemp half calf; spines wormed, worn. With c.860 hand-colored plates. Sold w.a.f. C May 20 (168) £3,000 [Burgess]

Dietrich, Veit

— Summaria ueber die gantze Bibel. Nuremberg: Johann vom Berg & Ulrich Neuber, 1548. Folio, contemp blind-tooled pigskin over wooden bds. Some foxing & marginal stains. sg Oct 24 (92) $475

Dietterlin, Wendel, 1550-99

— Architectura und Ausstheilung der V Seuln. Das Erst Buch. Nuremberg, 1598-99. Folio, recent calf by Middleton. With etched title & 185 plates, including 4 duplicates. Lacking 4 part tiles; some browning. bba June 25 (221) £1,500 [Shapero]

Digby, Sir Kenelm, 1603-65

— The Closet of the Eminently Learned Sir Kenelme Digbie Kt. Opened.... L, 1671. 2d Ed. 8vo, later half calf; rubbed, some wear to head of spine. Port & tp laid dow, with slight loss along inner edge of port; some spotting & dampstaining; a few page numerals cropped; wormhole in upper margin affecting some words. Joseph Crawhall's copy with his signature & a presentation inscr to Charles Keene. S Nov 15 (695) £400 [Shapero]

Anr copy. Contemp calf; rebacked & repaired. L5 supplied in facsimile; verso of A2 with running title cropped. S May 14 (978) £400 [Lerner]

— Two Treatises in the One of Which the Nature of Bodies, in the Other the Nature of Mans Soule is Looked into. L, 1665. 4to, contemp calf; rebacked, front free endpaper renewed. Lacking port. sg May 14 (42) $225

— Two Treatises. In the one of which, the Nature of Bodies.... L, 1669. ("Of Bodies, and of Mans Soul....") 4to, contemp calf; rubbed. Lacking port. bba Jan 16 (70) £170 [Gammon]

Digges, Leonard, d.1571?

— An Arithmeticall Militare Treatise, named Stratioticos.... L, 1579. 1st Ed. 4to, 19th-cent calf; worn. Some headlines & sidenotes shaved or cropped; portion cut from inner margin of title, with loss to coat-of-arms. STC 6848. S July 1 (1238) £850 [Knohl]

Dill & Collins Co.

— Some Examples of the Work of American Designers. Phila. & NY, [1918]. 4to, pictorial bds; worn & soiled, spine chipped. With specimens of 30 varieties of paper produced by Dill & Collins. NH Aug 23 (329) $65

Dillin, John G. W.

— The Kentucky Rifle. Wash., 1924. 4to, cloth; spine worn, inner hinges tender. Foxed. K Sept 29 (153) $55

Dimand, Maurice S.

— The Ballard Collection of Oriental Rugs in the City Art Museum of St. Louis. St. Louis, 1935. sp June 18 (275) $325

Dimsdale, Thomas, d.1866

— The Vigilantes of Montana.... Helena MT, [1915]. ("The Vigilantes of Montana, or Popular Justice in the Rocky Mountains.") 3d Ed. 12mo, orig cloth. Spine head torn. cb Sept 12 (50) $65

Dinesen, Isak

— Out of Africa. NY: Random House, [1938]. In chipped d/j. F Dec 18 (251) $70

Anr copy. In d/j with edge wear. sg June 11 (101) $140

Dinet, Etienne, 1861-1929 —& Suliman Ben Ibrahaim Baemer

— La Vie de Mohammed, Prophete d'Allah. Paris, 1918. One of 925. 4to, contemp half mor; rubbed, backstrip def. Some foxing. Ptd in colors & gold. F June 25 (715) $110

Dio Cassius, b.1557

— Neruae & Traiani, atque Adriani Caesarum vitae. Venice: Aldus, Aug 1519. 8vo, early 19th-cent half sheep. Tp rehinged. sg Mar 12 (72) $175

Diodorus Siculus

— Bibliothecae.... Venice: Joannes Tacuinus, de Tridino, 20 Sept 1496. ("Bibliothecae historicae libri VI.") Trans by Poggio Bracciolini. Folio, later bds; extremities rubbed. Small tears in outer margin of title; a2 with old repair; inner lower margin of leaves a3-4 strengthened; some soiling & dampstaining. 78 leaves. Goff D-213. C Dec 16 (121) £450 [Bifolco]

Anr Ed. Basel: J. Operinus, 1539. ("Historiarum libri aliquot....") Bound with: Pollux, Julius. Onomasticon. Basel: Balthasar Lasius & Thomas Platter, 1536. 4to, contemp pigskin over wooden bds with brass fittings. Old stamps on titles. sg Oct 24 (94) $700

Anr Ed. Lyon: S. Gryphius, 1552. ("Bibliothecae Historicae Libri XVII.") 16mo, contemp calf gilt; spine worn. DW Dec 11 (275) £65

Anr Ed. Amst.: H. Wetsten, 1746. ("Bibliothecae historicae.") 2 vols. Folio, vellum gilt with arms of Utrecht. B May 12 (1651) HF700

— The History.... L, 1653. Folio, needs rebdg. Stamp on leaf after title. sg Oct 24 (95) $150

Diogenes Laertius

— Vitae et sententiae philosophorum. Venice: Nicolaus Jenson, 14 Aug 1475. ("Vitae et sententiae eorum qui in philosophia probati fuerunt.") Folio 18th-cent sheep; spine chipped at foot. 34 lines; types 1:115(111)R, 115GK; Ms initials in red & blue. repairs to 1st 10 & last 13 leaves with a few characters in Ms facsimile; wormhole through outer blank margin of final 40 leaves & repaired in all but last leaf. 186 (of 187) leaves; lacking last blank. Goff D-220. C Dec 16 (122) £2,000 [Tenschert]

Anr Ed. Brescia: Jacobus Britannicus, 23 Nov 1485. Folio, later vellum. 40 lines & headline; roman letter. Some worming at beginning; early Ms annotations, some initialled MAV with penwork scrolls. 124 leaves. Goff D-221. S May 28 (20) £1,300 [Zioni]

Diomedes

— Ars grammatica. Venice: Theodorus de Ragazonibus de Asula, 12 June 1495. ("De arte grammatica....") Folio, 18th-cent half calf; corners rubbed. Some worming. 84 lines. Goff D-238. From the Monastery of San Faustino in Brescia. Sussex copy. S May 28 (22) £650 [Zioni]

Dionis, Pierre, d.1718

— Cours d'operations de chirurgie, demontrees au jardin royal. Paris, 1714. 2d Ed. 8vo, contemp calf. With folding frontis & 10 plates. b Nov 18 (278) £90

Dionysius Areopagiticus

— Opera. Strasbourg, 1502. 2 parts in 1 vol. Folio, half vellum. Some foxing. SI June 9 (316) LIt1,200,000

Dionysius Halicarnassus

— Antiquitates romanae. Treviso: Bernardinus Celerius, [24 or 25 Feb] 1480. Folio, modern vellum. Type 1:13R, 37 lines.. 299 (of 300) leaves; lacking initial blank. Goff D250. SI June 9 (317) LIt4,000,000

Anr Ed. Paris: R. Stephanus, 1546-47. ("Antiquitatum Romanarum lib. X.") 2 parts in 1 vol. Folio, 16th-cent calf gilt; upper cover detached. Chatsworth copy. S July 1 (526) £2,600 [Jackson]

Diophantus Alexandrinus

— Arithmeticorum libri sex. Paris: Hieronymus Drouart, 1621. Folio, 19th-cent half calf; upper joint cracked. Tp wormed at outer margin; some browning; appendix leaves wormed with some loss. Ck Nov 29 (175) £900

Dioscorides, Pedacius

— De materia medica. Frankfurt: C. Egenolph, [1549]. ("De medicinali materia libri sex.") Folio, contemp calf; worn, spine backed with paper. Lacking 4 leaves of prelims; some dampstaining. S Nov 21 (8) £1,200 [Burgess Browning]

Diringer, David

— The Hand-Produced Book. NY, [1953]. In d/j. cb Oct 17 (245) $50

— The Illuminated Book: its History & Production. L, 1967. In d/j. O Sept 24 (71) $75; sg Oct 31 (206) $110

Disher, Maurice Wilson

— Clowns & Pantomimes. L, 1925. 4to, half mor. Some browning. bba June 11 (151) £120 [Ulysses]

Disher, Wilson. See: Disher, Maurice Wilson

Disney Studios, Walt

— The Adventures of Mickey Mouse. L, 1931. Orig bds. sp Feb 6 (344) $225

Anr Ed. Phila.: David McKay, [1931]. Orig bds; spine ends worn. K Mar 22 (120) $550

Anr copy. Orig wraps; scraped. K Mar 22 (121) $225

Anr copy. Orig cloth. Epstein copy. sg Apr 29 (119) $2,000

— The Pop-up Minnie Mouse. NY, [1933]. Orig bds. K Mar 22 (126) $250

— Walt Disney's Snow White and the Seven Dwarfs. NY, 1937. Orig half cloth; worn & shaken. Sgd on tp by Walt Disney. bbc Sept 23 (394) $425

Disraeli, Benjamin, 1st Earl of Beaconsfield, 1804-81

— Endymion. L, 1880. 1st Ed. 3 vols. 8vo, orig cloth; rubbed. O July 14 (70) $80

— Works. L, 1926-27. ("Novels and Tales.") Bradenham Ed. 12 vols. pn Apr 23 (130) £110

Disraeli, Isaac, 1766-1848

— Curiosities of Literature. Bost., 1858. 8vo, half mor gilt; rubbed. O Jan 14 (65) $90

Distinta...

— Distinta Relazione di un caso assai funesto avvento in Costantinopoli e sentenze terribile pronunziata dal primo visire.... Venice, 1768. 4to, bds; spine worn. S July 1 (600) £350 [Consolidated Real]

District of Columbia

— Acts Concerning the Territory of Columbia and the City of Washington. [Phila: Francis Childs & John Swaine, 1791]. 8vo, sewn. Some browning. bbc Dec 9 (432) $600

Dixon, Charles, 1858-1926

— The Game Birds and Wild Fowl of the British Islands. Sheffield, 1900. 2d Ed. 4to, orig cloth; extremities rubbed, soiled. With 41 chromolitho plates. Tp spotted. Ck May 15 (21) £160

Anr copy. Orig half vellum; spine worn. With 41 mtd color plates. pnL Nov 20 (180) £200 [Manger]

Anr copy. Orig cloth. With 41 colored plates. S Feb 26 (914) £190 [Agazzi]

Dixon, Capt. George, 1755?-1800

— A Voyage Round the World.... L, 1789. 1st Ed. 4to, contemp mor; spine soiled. With half-title, large folding map & 21 maps & plates, 4 folding; natural history subjects hand-colored. Soiling on verso of folding chart. S June 25 (118) £3,200 [Quaritch]

Large & thick paper Issue. Half mor gilt by Bayntun; joints cracked. With 5 folding maps & 17 plates, 3 folding, 7 colored by hand. Repaired tear to Aa2; 2d & 4th folding maps torn & repaired; margins cut down by binder. CNY Oct 8 (89) $2,400

2d Ed. 4to, half calf. With folding chart, engraved leaf of music & 20 plates & maps. Tear to folding chart at fold; 1 map with tear repaired; some foxing to plates. S Nov 15 (1224) £400 [Ruddell]

Anr copy. Contemp calf; rebacked. With half-title, large folding map (short tear at fold) & 20 maps & plates & engraved leaf of music. Some foxing to plates; wormholes affecting extremities of upper margins at end. S Nov 21 (323) £550 [Ruddell]

Anr copy. Half calf. With folding chart (with tear at fold), engraved leaf of music & 20 plates & maps. Tear in 1 plate repaired; some foxing. S Feb 26 (733) £420 [Swigert]

Dixon, Joseph Kossuth

— The Vanishing Race.... Garden City, 1913. 1st Ed. Illus by R. Wanamaker. 4to, orig cloth. With 80 sepia plates. Inscr. F Sept 26 (337) $160

Dixon, Maynard

— Images of the Native American. San Francisco: California Academy of Sciences, [1981]. cb Feb 12 (18) $75

Dlandol, —

— Le Contre'Espion; ou, les clefs de toutes les correspondances secrettes. Paris, 1794. 8vo, contemp wraps; backstrip chipped. sg Oct 24 (97) $200

Dobai, Johannes

— Die Kunstliteratur des Klassizismus und der Romantik in England. Bern, [1974-84]. 4 vols. In d/js. O Sept 24 (72) $70

Dobie, James Frank, 1888-1964

— The Ben Lilly Legend. Bost., 1950. Presentation Issue. In d/j. cb Sept 12 (55) $140

— Coyote Wisdom. Austin, 1938. Sgd. cb Sept 12 (53) $50

— Legends of Texas. Austin, 1924. Texas Folk-Lore Society Publication 3. Inscr to Helen Evans, 1932. sg Dec 5 (90) $175

— Mustangs and Cow Horses. Austin: Texas Folk-lore Society, 1940. In d/j. cb Nov 14 (44) $80

Dobneck, Johann

— Vita Theoderici regis quondam ostrogothorum.... Ingolstadt: A. Weissenhorn, 1544. Bound with: Felicius, C. De coniuratione L.Catilinae. Leipzig, 1535. And: Libri duo. Leipzig, 1535. And: Antiqua et insignis epistola Nicolai Pape I.... Leipzig, 1536. And: Dobneck. Ad Paulum III congratulatio super eius electione. Leipzig, 1535. 4to, 16th-cent blind-tooled calf. S Dec 5 (96) £3,000 [Halwas]

Dobson, Austin, 1840-1921

— William Hogarth. L, 1902. Copy without the duplicate plate vol. 4to, cloth; hinges cracked. sg Feb 6 (134) $60

Dobuzhinskij, Mstislav

— Veselaja azbuka. Leningrad, 1925. Orig wraps. sg Nov 7 (197) $550

Dodd, James Solas

— The Ancient and Modern History of Gibraltar.... L, 1781. 8vo, contemp sheep; spine rubbed, front joint cracked. sg May 21 (31A) $110

Dodd, William, 1729-77

— A Commentary on the Old and New Testament. L, 1770. 3 vols. Folio, modern half syn. bba Jan 30 (53) £50 [Jeffery]

Doddridge, Sir John, 1555-1628

— The Lawes Resolutions of Womens Rights.... L, 1632. 4to, contemp calf gilt. Black letter. STC 7437. sg Nov 7 (67) $1,500

Dodge, Mary Mapes, 1831-1905

— Hans Brinker; or, The Silver Skates. NY, 1866. 1st Ed, State not given. 12mo, orig cloth; recased with orig backstrip laid down, some soiling, a few gatherings sprung. wa Sept 26 (562) $50

Anr Ed. Phila., [1925]. 8vo, mor gilt by Asprey. sg Oct 17 (211) $90

Dodgson, Campbell

— A Catalogue of Etchings & Engravings by Robert Austin. L, 1930. Ltd Ed. 4to, cloth; worn. O July 14 (72) $50

— Contemporary English Woodcuts. L, 1922. One of 550. Folio, half cloth, in soiled d/j; free front endpaper showing silverfish damage. kh Nov 11 (82) A$100

— The Etchings of James McNeill Whistler. L, 1922. Folio, half vellum bds; endpapers browned. bbc Dec 9 (291) $130

— Old French Colour-Prints. L, 1924. One of 1,250. 4to, half vellum; spine stained. sp June 18 (172) $95

— Woodcuts of the XV Century in the Department of Prints and Drawings British Museum. L, 1934-35. 2 vols. Folio, orig cloth. DW Oct 9 (850) £175

Dodgson, Charles Lutwidge, 1832-98

See also: Limited Editions Club

— Alice's Adventures in Wonderland. L, 1866 [1865]. 2d (1st Pbd) Ed. 8vo, recent mor gilt, orig cloth covers bound in. DW Apr 8 (234) £1,450

Anr copy. Mor gilt by Riviere, orig bdg preserved & bound at end. Inscr to Una Taylor. Kern copy. P Dec 12 (169) $13,000

Anr Ed. L, 1866. ("Alice's Adventures Under Ground.") 8vo, orig cloth. cb Sept 19 (28) $1,300

1st American Ed, comprising the sheets of the 1st (suppressed) English Ed with a cancel title. NY: D. Appleton & Co., 1866. 8vo, orig cloth; rubbed. Molstad-Manney copy. P Oct 11 (106) $17,000

Anr copy. Mor gilt. With ALs to Thomas Kish. P June 17 (183) $4,000

Anr copy. Orig cloth; covers marked, upper joint split. S Nov 14 (151) £2,600 [Kendall]

Anr copy. Orig cloth; 1-inch tear along rear joint; front hinge cracked. Epstein copy. sg Apr 29 (65) $7,000

Anr Ed. Bost., 1869. 8vo, orig cloth; spine ends & corners worn. bbc Dec 9 (459) $375

21st Thousand. L, 1870. 8vo, orig cloth; back cover bumped, soiled & rubbed. bba July 23 (46) £50 [Hollander]

Anr Ed. L, 1872. Illus by Sir John Tenniel. 8vo, orig cloth; joints split, soiled. Inscr to Percy Fitzgerald. Ck Dec 11 (146) £1,100

75th thousand. L, 1885. 8vo, orig vellum gilt; soiled. Prelims & final leaves spotted. Inscr to Emmie Wyper. S Apr 28 (63) £2,500 [Dr. J-Stern]

Anr Ed. L, 1886. ("Alice's Adventures Under Ground.") 8vo, orig cloth; spine worn. bba May 14 (163) £75 [Harlow]

Anr copy. Contemp mor gilt; upper joint

cracked. Inscr, "almost certainly" to Alice's mother, Mrs. Henry George (Lorina) Liddell. CNY Dec 5 (225) $22,000

Anr copy. Orig cloth, with black glazed endpapers. Inscr to Marie Louise Butterfield. P Dec 12 (171) $2,750

Anr Ed. L, 1890. ("The Nursery Alice.") 4to, orig half cloth; worn & soiled. Some spotting. S Nov 14 (156) £150 [M. James]

Anr copy. Orig half cloth; edges worn. Inscr. Epstein copy. sg Apr 29 (68) $3,200

Anr Ed. L, [1907]. One of 1,130. Illus by Arthur Rackham. 4to, orig cloth; some browning of endpapers. With 13 colored plates. Manney copy. P Oct 11 (260) $1,300

Anr copy. Orig cloth; browned & soiled. Prelims browned. S Nov 14 (132) £320 [Joseph]

Anr copy. Cloth. With autograph proem by Austin Dobson used in the vol. sg Nov 7 (164) $3,200

Anr Ed. L, 1927. Illus by Alice B. Woodward. 8vo, contemp mor gilt. Some dampstaining & warping. F Mar 26 (78) $170

Anr Ed. NY, 1969. Illus by Salvador Dali. Folio, loose as issued in cloth folder. With 13 colored plates. bbc Sept 23 (395) $1,200

Anr copy. Loose as issued in cloth folder. With 12 colored plates. Sgd in pencil. cb Feb 12 (29) $1,200

Anr copy. With 13 colored plates. sg Nov 7 (34) $1,100

Anr copy. Loose as issued in cloth folder. Sgd in pencil. Epstein copy. sg Apr 29 (66) $1,200

Anr Ed. NY, [n.d.]. Illus by Arthur Rackham. cb Jan 16 (130) $50

— La Chasse au Snark. Chapelle-Reanville: Hours Press, 1929. One of 360. Trans by Louis Aragon. 4to, orig wraps. cb Dec 5 (66) $160

— Curiosa mathematica: Part I, A New Theory of Parallels. L, 1888. 12mo, orig cloth; front joint cracked. sg Mar 5 (33) $500

— Feeding the Mind. L, 1907. 8vo, bds; soiled. K July 12 (174) $50

— The Game of Logic. L, 1886. 8vo, orig cloth. With the card board & 2 counters. cb Sept 5 (29) $2,250

— The Hunting of the Snark. L, 1876. 1st Ed. 12mo, orig cloth; rebacked preserving orig spine, rubbed. Lacking half-title; tp foxed. bba July 23 (450) £50 [Ginnan]

Anr copy. Orig cloth; upper joint split, some fraying & chipping, hinges cracked. bbc Dec 9 (461) $80

Anr copy. Orig cloth, in orig ptd d/j. Manney copy. P Oct 11 (108) $4,750

Anr copy. Orig cloth. With Easter Greeting tipped on blank recto of frontis. Inscr to Nina Harper, 29 Mar 1876. P Oct 11 (109) $3,250

Anr copy. Orig cloth, in stained & torn d/j. S Nov 14 (153) £1,200 [Ash]

One of 100 in red & gold deluxe bdg. Orig cloth; front hinge cracked. Inscr. Epstein copy. sg Apr 29 (67) $2,600

— The Hunting of the Snark: Die Jagd nach dem Schnark. Stuttgart, 1968. One of 130, sgd by the artist. Illus by Max Ernst. 4to, loose as issued in cloth folder. With 19 plates. sg Nov 7 (37) $2,600

— Phantasmagoria, and Other Poems. L, 1869. 1st Ed, 2d Issue. 8vo, orig cloth; rubbed. bbc Apr 27 (295) $160

— Sylvie and Bruno. With: Sylvie and Bruno Concluded. L, 1889-93. 1st Eds. Illus by Harry Furniss. 2 vols. 8vo, orig cloth. bba July 23 (451) £120 [Ginnan]

Anr copy. Orig cloth. Both inscr to May Wilcox. P Dec 12 (173) $1,700

Anr copy. Mor gilt extra by Bayntun, orig cloth covers bound in. sg Nov 7 (36) $350

Anr copy. Orig cloth, Vol II in d/j. Epstein copy. sg Apr 29 (69) $225

— Symbolic Logic. Part I: Elementary [all pbd]. L, 1897. 4th Ed. 12mo, orig cloth; worn & soiled, spine chipped at head, endpapers browned. Inscr to the Clarendon Press Institute & with inscr booklabel as Dodgson. S Apr 28 (61) £1,400 [Dr. J-Stern]

— Through the Looking Glass. L, 1872 [1871]. 1st Ed, 1st Issue. 8vo, orig cloth; rebacked preserving orig spine, rubbed & stained. A few leaves soiled. bba July 23 (449) £170 [Demetzy]

1st Issue, with "wade" on p. 21. Orig cloth; worn, spine ends restored. Some smudging & foxing; ink squiggle on ad leaf at rear. bbc Apr 27 (298) $500

Anr copy. Orig cloth; endpapers split along the hinges, lower hinge tender. Inscr to Mrs Edgcombe, Christmas 1871. Manney copy. P Oct 11 (107) $10,000

Anr copy. Mor gilt by Riviere, orig cloth bound in. Inscr to Una M. Taylor. Kern copy. P Dec 12 (170) $5,500

1st American Ed. Bost. & NY, 1872. 12mo, later mor gilt; backstrip def. DW Jan 29 (412) £110

1st Ed. L, 1872. 1st Issue, with "wade" on p. 21. 8vo, later calf gilt by Zaehnsdorf. Ck Dec 11 (114) £600

Anr copy. Orig cloth; rubbed, extremities worn. DW Dec 11 (414) £200

2d Issue. Mor gilt with vignettes depicting the Red & White Queens, by Sangorski & Sutcliffe. Some soiling. pn Apr 23 (168) £160 [Harrington]

Issue not given. Mor gilt by Zaehnsdorf, orig cloth bound in at end; joints worn. pn June 11 (180) £200 [Book Room]

1st American Ed. NY, 1872. 8vo, orig cloth; rubbed & shaken. NH Oct 6 (66) $115

Anr Ed. NY, 1902. Illus by Peter Newell. In def d/j. With 40 plates. sg Oct 17 (129) $60

Anr Ed. West Hatfield MA: Pennyroyal Press, 1982. One of 350. Illus by Barry Moser. Folio, orig half mor. With an extra suite of the engravings, each sgd. sg Nov 7 (35) $1,300

One of 350, with an additional suite of the wood engravings. Half mor. sg Nov 7 (38) $700

Dodoens, Rembert, 1518-85

— Cosmographica in astronomiam et geographiam isagoge. Antwerp, 1548. 8vo, new bds. Waterstains; a little short; some annotations on verso of last leaf; lacking volvelle on D1 recto & D8 verso. B Nov 1 (485) HF1,300

— Histoire des plantes. Antwerp, 1557. Folio, calf; rebacked. B Nov 1 (466) HF8,000

— A Niewe Herball. L [Antwerp ptd], 1578. ("A Niewe Herball, or Historie of Plantes.") Folio, bds detached. Lacking tp. STC 6984. LH Dec 11 (101) $500

Anr Ed. L: Ninian Newton, 1586. ("A New Herball, or Historie of Plants....") 8vo, old sheep; new spine. Mostly black letter. Some loss to running heads toward rear; some dampstain, principally to margins; repairs to margins of tp & other leaves, obscuring some text of index. STC 6985. wa Sept 26 (470) $400

— Purgantium aliarumque eo facientium.... Antwerp: Plantin, 1574. Bound with: Florum, et coronariarum odoratarumque nunnullarum herbarum historia. Antwerp, 1569. 8vo, vellum. B Nov 1 (468) HF2,800

Anr copy. 2 parts in 1 vol. 8vo, Stain in lower margin. B Nov 1 (469) HF1,000

Dodsley, Robert, The Oeconomy of Human Life.

— The Oeconomy of Human Life. See: Oeconomy...

Dodsley, Robert, 1703-64 —& Cowley, John

— The Geography of England.... L, 1744. 8vo, contemp calf; joints split, worn. With 56 maps. Some dampstaining. S Nov 15 (910) £850 [Basket]

Dodsworth, Roger, 1585-1654. See: Dugdale & Dodsworth

Dodsworth, William

— An Historical Account of the Episcopal See.... Salisbury, 1814. 4to, orig bds; rebacked, old spine preserved. With engraved title & 19 plates. bba Sept 19 (184) £130 [Traylen]

Anr copy. Later half mor; rubbed. With 20 plates. Some spotting. bba Sept 19 (185) £60 [Traylen]

Dodwell, Edward, 1767-1832

— A Classical and Topographical Tour through Greece.... L, 1819. 2 vols. 4to, contemp calf; worn. With folding map & 66 plates, including 2 colored by hand. Some stains. S nov 15 (1092) £800 [Theocharaki]

Anr copy. 19th-cent calf; stained & rubbed, rebacked, 1 cover detached. With 1 folding map & 66 plates. S June 30 (280) £650 [Consolidated Real]

— Views in Greece, from Drawings by.... L, 1821. 5 orig parts. Folio, unsewn in orig card folder with lea spine. With 30 hand-colored plate each mtd on card with ptd slip on verso giving plate information. Lacking preface & text to Plate 5; foremargins of a few text leaves soiled; card mount of Plate 6 spotted; ptd slip on verso of Plate 10 corrected in Ms. C Oct 30 (126) £7,000 [Athanassiou]

Anr copy. Folio, later half mor gilt. With 30 hand-colored plates, each mtd on card. Some spotting. C May 20 (251) £5,500 [Joseph]

Doe, Janet

— A Bibliography of the Works of Ambroise Pare. Chicago, 1937. Folio, cloth; rubbed. bba Dec 19 (267) £50 [Weiner]

Doegen, Mathias

— L'architecture militaire moderne, ou fortification.... Amst.: Elzevir, 1648. 2 parts in 1 vol. Folio, old vellum bds. With engraved title & 70 double-page plates. Blank corner torn from F2; stain in 3G1 with loss of text. S July 9 (1240) £400 [Dennistoun]

Doesticks, Q. K. Philander. See: Thomson, Mortimer

Dog of Knowledge...

— The Dog of Knowledge, or Memoirs of Bob, the Spotted Terrier L: J. Harris, 1801. 12mo, contemp cloth. With hand-colored frontis. sg Mar 5 (45) $200

Doheny Collection, Estelle

— Catalogue of Books and Manuscripts.... Los Angeles: Ward Ritchie Press, 1940-46-55. One of 100, this copy 1 of 3 bound in mor. 3 vols. P Oct 11 (110) $1,200

— [Sale Catalogue] The Estelle Doheny Collection.... NY: Christie's, 1987-89. 7 vols, including Index. Folio, orig cloth. Price lists (1 in photocopy) loosely inserted. bba Jan 16 (253) £160 [Kent]

Anr copy. Parts 1-2 only. bbc Sept 23 (69) $90

Anr copy. Parts 1-6; without Index vol. Folio, orig cloth. Price lists loosely inserted in 5 vols. sg May 21 (209) $140

Anr copy. 7 vols. Folio, SI Dec 5 (223) LIt250,000; wa Mar 5 (101) $200

Dolby, Edwin Thomas

— Dolby's Sketches in the Baltic 1854. L, 1854. Folio, orig half lea; rubbed. With litho title & 17 plates, some colored. Ck Dec 11 (215) £450

Dolce, Lodovico, 1508-68

— Dialogo della pittura.... Florence, 1735. 8vo, contemp bds; worn. Some foxing. SI Dec 5 (214) LIt150,000

— Dialogo nel quale si ragiona del modo.... Venice: G. & M. Sessa, 1562. 8vo, contemp vellum; sides crinkled & soiled, hole in spine & upper cover. Title affected by damp. Ck Oct 31 (75) £480

Anr Ed. Venice: Sessa, 1562. 8vo, contemp vellum. With 23 full- or half-page woodcuts. Some stains; repair in blank margin of K4. sg Oct 24 (99) $850

Anr Ed. Venice: G. Sessa, 1586. 8vo, modern bds. Lower margin of tp cut away & repaired; short tear at head of C6 repaired; some stains. S May 28 (42) £650 [Lib. Casella]

— Didone, tragedia. Venice: Aldus, 1547. 8vo, 19th-cent mor. S Nov 14 (462) £600 [P & P Books]

— Epistole de G. Plinio, di M. Franc. Petrarca...et d'altri Eccellentiss. Huomini. Venice: G. Giolito, 1548. Trans by Dolce. 8vo, 19th-cent half lea. Some dampstaining. SI Dec 5 (211) LIt150,000

— L'Ulisse.... Venice: Gabriel Giolito de'Ferrari, 1573. 4to, old vellum; turn-ins sprung. Some stains. sg Nov 7 (68) $500

Dollfus, Charles —& Bouche, Henri

— Histoire de l'aeronautique. Paris, 1942. Folio, half cloth. bbc Dec 9 (338) $80

Dolly...

— Dolly and the Rat, or the Brisket Family. L, 1823. 1st Ed. Illus by George Cruikshank. 8vo, mor gilt. With hand-colored frontis. Salomons copy. sg Oct 17 (161) $350

Domenech, Emmanuel, 1825-86

— Seven Years' Residence in the Great Deserts of North America. L, 1860. 2 vols. 8vo, contemp calf; scuffed. With folding map & 58 plates. Folding map tape-repaired. cb Nov 14 (46) $225

Anr copy. Calf gilt. pnE May 13 (20) £220

Domesday-Book...

— Domesday Book, seu Liber censualis.... L, 1783-1816. 4 vols. Folio, contemp half calf; rubbed, 3 covers loose. bba Jan 30 (59) £600 [Quaritch]

Dominguez Bordona, Jesus

— Die spanische Buchmalerei.... Leipzig, 1930. 2 vols. 4to, orig cloth. sg Oct 31 (207) $250

Dominguin, Luis Miguel

— Toros y Toreros. NY, 1961. Illus by Picasso. Folio, orig cloth; some wear. sg Sept 6 (220) $300

Dominici, Bernardo de

— Vite de' pittori, scultori ed architetti napoletani. Naples, 1752-53. 3 vols in 2. 4to, contemp vellum; rubbed. bba Feb 13 (161) £340 [Erlini]

Donaldson, Alfred Lee, 1866-1923

— A History of the Adirondacks. NY, 1921. 1st Ed. 2 vols. O Jan 14 (66) $70

Donaldson, Thomas C., 1843-98

— The George Catlin Indian Gallery in the U. S. National Museum. Wash., 1886. 8vo, cloth; worn & shaken. Folding map torn in gutter. O Jan 14 (67) $70

Anr copy. Bound with: Report of the United States National Museum...1885. sg June 18 (169) $140

Donaldson, Thomas Leverton, 1795-1885

— A Collection of the Most Approved Examples of Doorways from Ancient Buildings in Greece and Italy. L, 1833. 4to, half calf; worn & rubbed. With 25 plates. ALs to Richard Westmacott inserted. K July 12 (27) $140

Donaldson, Thomas Leverton, 1795-1885 —& Cockburn, James Pattison, 1779?-1847

— Pompeii, Illustrated with Picturesque Views. L, 1827. 1st Ed. 2 vols in 1. Folio, 19th-cent half mor; worn, upper cover detached. With 80 plates & plans, 5 hand-colored, most ptd on india paper. Library stamps on plate versos. S Nov 15 (786) £550 [Shapero]

Donatus, Aelius

— Erotemata grammatices rudibus.... Rome: M. Silber, 1516. Cantalicio, Giovanni Battista. Summa perutilis in regulas distinctas totius artis grammatices.... Rome: S. Guilereti, 6 Oct 1517. 4to, old vellum; spine def. S Dec 5 (98) £4,200 [Jackson]

Doni, Antonio Francesco, 1513?-74

— La Zucca del Doni en Spanol. Venice, 1551. 8vo, old vellum, in later mor d/j. With 18 woodcut illusts. Tp cropped at upper margin affecting border; some spotting of margins. Ck Nov 29 (79) £750

Donne, John, 1573-1631

— Biathanatos. A Declaration of that Paradoxe.... L: John Dawson, [c.1647]. 1st Ed. 4to, later calf gilt. Lacking 1st blank; some lower margins wormed. bba Jan 16 (61) £1,000 [Kunkler]

— Devotions upon Emergent Occasions.... L, 1624. 1st Ed. 12mo, orig vellum. Lacking C2; S1 & S4 with torn margins; lower marginal extremities towards end are stained red. Sold w.a.f. STC 7033. L Nov 14 (281) £260

— LXXX Sermons. L, 1640. 1st Ed. Folio, contemp calf; rebacked & repaired, rubbed. Lacking initial & final blanks, later endpapers; engraved title remargined. S Nov 14 (463) £400 [Knohl]

— Poems, by J. D..... L, 1633. 1st Ed. 4to, modern calf. Washed; A4 holed affecting 3 letters of text; short tear on V1. James Russell Lowell-Epstein copy. sg Apr 29 (120) $4,800

3d Ed. L, 1639. 8vo, 19th-cent calf gilt by Pratt. Port repaired; O4 & O5 shorter; small hole in Dd1. STC 7047. L Nov 14 (282) £550

Anr copy. Modern calf gilt. Frontis torn at blank margin & bound tightly; X2-3 torn with loss to page numerals; Dd2 with lower margin torn away with loss of catchword. STC 7047. S Dec 12 (3) £700 [Dawson]

Donneau de Vize, Jean

— Relation veritable da siege de Vienne. Lyon: Thomas Amaulry, 1684. 8vo, contemp vellum; soiled. With port & folding engraved plan. Some browning. S July 1 (602) £380 [Kutluoglu]

Donnet, Fernand

— Coup d'Oeil sur l'Histoire Financiere d'Anvers au Cours des Siecles. [Brussels, 1927]. Folio, half mor; rebacked. Ptd for J. P. Morgan. sg May 7 (88) $200

Donovan, Edward, 1768-1837

— An Epitome of the Natural History of the Insects of China. L, 1798. 4to, modern half mor gilt with spine lettered Pattern Plates. With 48 (of 50) hand-colored plates. Some staining & soiling; several plates trimmed to plate-mark at outer edge; marginal repairs. S June 25 (15) £1,600 [Lack]

— An Epitome of the Natural History of the Insects of India.... L, 1800-[4]. 4to, modern half calf. With 58 hand-colored plates. With the errata slip. Some discoloration. S June 25 (16) £2,700 [Dillon]

— Fishes. L, 1802-[8]. ("The Natural History of British Fishes.") 5 vols in 3. 8vo, later half lea; shelf marks on spine, rubbed. With titles to Vols I & II only & 120 hand-colored plates. Some dampstaining. pn Mar 19 (273) £1,400 [Burden]

— The Natural History of British Birds. L, 1794-1819. 10 vols in 5. 8vo, contemp mor gilt. With 244 hand-colored plates. C Oct 30 (242) £3,800 [Cockell]

— The Naturalist's Repository, or Monthly Miscellany of Exotic Natural History.... L, [c.1835]. ("The Naturalist's Repository of Exotic Natural History.") 2 vols. 8vo, contemp cloth; worn. With 72 hand-colored plates. Reissue of Vols I-II. F June 25 (603) $750

Doolittle, Hilda, 1886-1961

— Kora and Ka. Dijon: Pvtly ptd, 1934. 1st Ed, one of 100. Wraps, unopened. sg Dec 12 (87) $200

Doppelmayr, Johann Gabriel

— Globus Coelestis in tabulas planas redacti.... Nuremberg, 1730. Folio, half cloth. With 6 double-page maps with hand-colored borders. With 3 similar double-page celestial maps laid in, partly colored. K Sept 29 (115) $1,300

— Historische Nachricht von den Nuernbergischen Mathematicis und Kuenstlern.... Nuremberg, 1730. Folio, contemp bds. With 15 plates including map. HH May 12 (580) DM1,200

Doran, John, 1807-78

— Annals of the English Stage.... L, 1888. One of 300 L.p. copies. 3 vols. 8vo, orig cloth; soiled. pn Sept 12 (32) £60 [Rix]

— Table Traits with Something on Them. L, 1854. 1st Ed. 8vo, orig cloth; spine ends chipped. bbc Apr 27 (225) $65

Dorat, Claude Joseph, 1734-80

— Les Baisers. Rouen, 1880. One of 50 on papier de chine with illusts in 3 states. 8vo, contemp lev gilt by Pagnant. sg Mar 5 (93) $200

Dore, Gustave, 1833-83 —&
Jerrold, William Blanchard, 1826-84

— London. L, 1872. Folio, contemp half mor; corners bumped. With 180 wood-engravings, including 54 full-page plates. Some foxing. Schlosser copy. P June 18 (421) $1,600

Doring, Ernest

— How Many Strads? Our Heritage from the Master. Chicago, 1945. One of 1,400. Orig syn gilt. Inscr to Hill & Sons. pn Oct 24 (260) £2,000

Dornbusch, C. E.

— Regimental Publications & Personal Narratives of the Civil War. NY, 1961-62. 7 vols, including Index. Wraps. sg Dec 5 (55) $250

Dorra, Henri —&
Rewald, John

— Seurat...L'Oeuvre Peint, Biographie et Catalogue Critique. Paris, 1959. 4to, orig cloth. DW Mar 11 (490) £65

Dorset, Catherine Ann, 1750?-1817?

— The Peacock "at Home." L, [c.1820]. 8vo, orig wraps; soiled, backstrip frayed. With 4 hand-colored plates. bba July 23 (48) £80 [Demetzy]

Dortu, M. G.

— Toulouse-Lautrec et son oeuvre. NY, 1971. One of 1,450. 6 vols. 4to, orig cloth. DW Mar 11 (491) £400

Anr copy. Orig cloth, in d/js. sg Sept 6 (278) $800

Anr copy. Orig cloth. sg Feb 6 (285) $1,100

Anr copy. Cloth. sg Apr 2 (277) $900

Dos Passos, John

— 1919. NY, [1932]. In d/j. cb Dec 12 (43) $170

— The 42nd Parallel. NY, 1930. In torn & chipped d/j. cb Dec 12 (42) $170

— Most Likely to Succeed. NY, [1965]. One of 1,000. In d/j. sg Dec 12 (89) $150

— One Man's Initiation - 1917. L, [1920]. One of 1,250. In d/j. Epstein copy. sg Apr 29 (121) $225

— Orient Express. NY, 1927. Half cloth; in chipped d/j, tape-repaired at spine ends. Inscr. sg Dec 12 (90) $200

— U.S.A. Bost., 1946. One of 365, sgd by author & artist. Illus by Reginald Marsh. 3 vols. Cloth. sg Sept 26 (224) $200

Anr copy. Cloth. Sgd by author & artist. Epstein copy. sg Apr 29 (122) $450

Dosio, Giovanni Antonio, 1553-1609?

— Urbis Romae aedificiorum illustrium.... [Florence] 1569. Oblong 4to, 16th-cent vellum. With engraved title & 49 plates. Thumb-marks at lower forecorners. S Nov 21 (77) £1,700 [Marlborough]

Dossie, Robert, d.1777

— The Elaboratory Laid Open.... L, 1758. 8vo, old calf; joints worn. Tp soiled. DW May 13 (273) £100

Dostoevsky, Fyodor, 1821-81

See also: Limited Editions Club

— Brat'ya Karamazovy. St. Petersburg, 1881. 2 vols. 8vo, contemp half mor gilt; Vol II rebacked & with upper free endpaper lost. Lacking final blank in Vol I; some stains; Vol I p. 77 stained in outer margin; pencil scribbles in Vol II, pages 311 & 315. P Dec 12 (30) $2,000

Anr copy. Contemp half lea; Vol I rebacked, orig spine laid down; rear cover of Vol II nearly detached. Epstein copy. sg Apr 29 (124) $12,000

Douat, Dominique

— Methode pour faire une infinite des desseins differens avec des carreaux mi-partis de deux couleurs. Paris, 1722. 4to, contemp calf. With 28 plates. bba Feb 27 (328) £480 [Robertshaw]

Douce, Francis

— The Dance of Death.... L, 1833. 8vo, mor gilt by Bayntun with pictorial mor inlay. Extra-illus with plates & an orig watercolor by P. Mayr. O May 26 (52) $1,200

— Illustrations of Shakspeare and of Ancient Manners.... L, 1807. 2 vols. 8vo, contemp calf; rebacked, extremities rubbed. Ck Oct 18 (214) £140

Dougall, John

— The Cabinet of the Arts. L: R. Ackermann, [1821]. 2 vols in 1. 4to, cloth. With 132 plates. Dampstain to 1st 2 plates & traces of it to several others. P June 18 (533) $400

Doughty, Charles Montagu, 1843-1926

— Travels in Arabia Deserta. Cambr., 1888. 1st Ed. 2 vols. 8vo, orig cloth. bba Jan 16 (310) £600 [Folios]

Anr copy. With small hole at fold of colored map in pocket at end of Vol I. L Feb 27 (161) £850

Anr Ed. NY & L, 1923. Intro by T. E. Lawrence. 2 vols. cb Oct 10 (36) $50

Doughty, Dorothy

— The American Birds of Dorothy Doughty. Worcester MA, [1962]. One of 1,500. Folio, lea gilt. With 70 mtd color plates. sg Feb 6 (229) $200

Douglas, Lord Alfred, 1870-1945

— Poems. Paris, 1896. 1st Ed. 18mo, contemp cloth; soiled. In English & French. Siegfried Sassoon's copy. S July 1 (981) £350 [Stevens]

Douglas, George Mellis

— Lands Forlorn. NY & L, 1914. sg Jan 9 (67) $200

Douglas, John, Bishop of Salisbury

— A Letter Addressed to Two Great Men.... L: A. Millar, 1760. 8vo, wraps, sewn as issued; later thread, some chipping & browning. wa Mar 5 (336) $130

Douglas, Norman, 1868-1952

— The Angel of Manfredonia. San Francisco, 1929. One of 225. Half cloth. bba Apr 30 (241) £85 [Casella]

— Capri, Materials for a Description of the Island. Florence, 1930. 1st Ed, one of 103. 4to, orig cloth; soiled. bba Apr 30 (242) £280 [Casella]

One of 525. Half cloth; faded. bba Apr 30 (243) £260 [Casella]

— D. H. Lawrence and Maurice Magnus, a Plea for Better Manners. [Florence: Pvtly ptd], 1924. Orig wraps. Pink ad slip mtd to half-title. With ALs to unnamed recipient. sg Dec 12 (92) $60

— Experiments. [Florence]: Pvtly ptd, 1925. One of 300. 4to, orig bds. bba Apr 30 (231) £120 [Deighton Bell]

— Fabio Giordano's Relation of Capri. Naples, 1906. One of 250. Contemp half vellum, orig upper wrap bound in. Presentation copy, sgd. bba Apr 30 (215) £130 [Casella]

— In the Beginning. [Florence], 1927. 1st Ed, one of 700. Bds. sg June 11 (102) $100

— London Street Games. L, [1916]. 1st Ed, One of 500. Inscr. bba Apr 30 (222) £180 [Blackwell]

— Looking Back.... L, 1933. 1st Ed, One of 535. Orig half cloth. bba Apr 30 (248) £50 [Goddard]

— Nerinda. Florence: G. Orioli, 1929. 1st Ed, One of 475, sgd. bba Apr 30 (237) £100 [Casella]

— On the Herpetology of the Grand Duchy of Baden. L, 1894. 8vo, orig wraps. bba Apr 30 (209) £300 [Blackwell]

— One Day. Chapelle-Reanville: The Hours Press, 1929. 1st Ed, One of 300 on Verge. Orig bds. bba Apr 30 (238) £120 [Deighton Bell]

— Paneros. L, 1930. 1st Ed, One of 250. Inscr. bba Apr 30 (244) £160 [Blackwell]

— Report on the Pumice Stone Industry of the Lipari Islands. L, 1895. 8vo, later half mor. bba Apr 30 (210) £320 [Casella]

2d Ed. L, 1928. 8vo, sewn. Presentation copy, sgd. bba Apr 30 (211) £320 [Casella]

— Some Limericks. [Florence]: Pvtly ptd, 1928. ("Some Limericks Collected for the Use of Students....") One of 110. bba Apr 30 (236) £160 [Blackwell]; sg Dec 12 (93) $375

— South Wind. L, [1922]. One of 150 L.p. copies, sgd. Orig cloth, in worn d/j. bba Apr 30 (224) £170 [Blackwell]

4th American Ed. Chicago, 1929. Illus by John Austen. 2 vols. In d/js. bba Apr 30 (225) £85 [Virgo]

Anr copy. Contemp half mor by Whitman Bennett; scuffed at edges & corners. bbc Apr 27 (62) $60

— Summer Islands. NY, 1931. 1st American Ed, one of 550. 4to, cloth. bba Apr 30 (246) £90 [Casella]; bba Apr 30 (247) £100 [Casella]

Anr Ed. L: Corvinus Press, 1942. one of 30 on handmade paper. 4to, orig half cloth. bba Apr 30 (245) £280 [Casella]

— Three Monographs. L, 1906. One of 250. Orig wraps. bba Apr 30 (217) £120 [Casella]

— Together. L, 1923. 1st Ed, One of 275 L.p. copies, sgd. In torn d/j. bba Apr 30 (229) £110 [Virgo]

— Unprofessional Tales by Normyx. L, 1901. One of 750. bba Apr 30 (214) £75 [Rassam]

Douglas, Richard John Hardy

— The Works of George Cruikshank. L, 1903. One of 1,000. 4to, half lea; bumped. Met Apr 28 (33) $80

Douglas, William

— Mercurius Nov-Anglicanus: or, An Almanac. By William Nadir. Bost., 1743. 12mo, later calf. Inner margins of a few leaves repaired; tp soiled. sg Dec 5 (3) $150

Douglass, Frederick, 1817?-95

— My Bondage and My Freedom. NY & Auburn, 1855. 1st Ed. 8vo, orig cloth; soiled. With frontis & 2 plates. lower corners dampstained; foxed. wa Apr 9 (62) $150

— Narrative of the Life of.... Bost., 1845. 1st Ed. 12mo, cloth; bound upside down, covers torn. cb Nov 21 (31) $130

Dover, Thomas

— The Ancient Physician's Legacy to his Country.... L, 1733. 4th Ed. 8vo, contemp calf; rebacked. Some browning. sg May 14 (44) $130

Doves Press—London

— The English Bible. 1903-5. One of 500. 5 vols. sg Nov 7 (21) $3,200

— In Principio. 1911. One of 200. Orig mor by Doves Bindery. sg May 7 (96) $400

— Pervigilium Veneris. 1910. One of 150. bba July 9 (257) £130 [Collinge & Clark]

— EMERSON, RALPH WALDO. - Essays. 1906. One of 25 on vellum. Orig vellum. sg May 7 (91) $2,800

— GOETHE, JOHANN WOLFGANG VON. - Auserlesene Lieder, Gedichte und Balladen.... 1916. One of 10 on vellum. Orig vellum. sg May 7 (98) $3,200

One of 175. B Nov 1 (1141) HF1,200

— GOETHE, JOHANN WOLFGANG VON. - Faust. 1906-10. One of 300 & 250. Vol I only. bba July 9 (256) £180 [Cox]

Anr copy. 2 vols. CNY Dec 5 (236) $800

Vol I, 1 of 25 on vellum; Vol II, one of 275. Mor by Kieffer with cover panels formed by 24 wooden discs affixed with metal bosses. sg May 7 (93) $4,000

— GOETHE, JOHANN WOLFGANG VON. - Iphigenie auf Tauris ein Schauspiel.... 1912. One of 12 on vellum with gold initials. Mor gilt by the Doves Bindery, 1912. The von Hirsch copy. sg May 12 (97) $3,600

— GOETHE, JOHANN WOLFGANG VON. - Torquato Tasso ein Schauspiel.... 1913. One of 200. Orig mor sgd 19 C-S 19. HH May 12 (2214) DM2,200

— MILTON, JOHN. - Areopagitica. 1907. One of 25 on vellum. sg May 7 (94) $2,800

— MILTON, JOHN. - Paradise Lost. 1902. One of 25 on vellum. Orig vellum. sg May 7 (90) $3,800

— MILTON, JOHN. - Paradise Regain'd. 1905. b&b Feb 19 (311) $500

— RUSKIN, JOHN. - Unto this Last. 1907. One of 300. cb Sept 5 (30) $325

— SHAKESPEARE, WILLIAM. - Hamlet. 1909. One of 250. Inscr by T. J. Cobden-Sanderson to Eric Gill. cb Sept 5 (31) $1,100

— TACITUS, PUBLIUS CORNELIUS. - De vita et moribus Julii Agricolae liber. 1900. Ck Nov 29 (80) £50

One of 225. sg May 7 (89) $325

— WINSHIP, GEORGE PARKER. - William Caxton. 1909. One of 300. Inscr. O Jan 14 (68) $80

Dow, George Francis, 1868-1936

— Slave Ships and Slaving. Salem MA: Marine Research Society, 1927. sp Apr 16 (118) $130

— Whale Ships and Whaling. Salem, 1925. Marginal dampstaining to last several signatures. bbc June 29 (116) $55; sg Dec 5 (91) $100

Downey, W. & D.

— The Cabinet Portrait Gallery. L, 1890-94. 1st-5th Series. 5 vols. 4to, cloth; spine ends bumped. With 72 Woodburytypes. Foxed throughout but plates unaffected. sg Apr 13 (36) $350

Downie, William

— Hunting for Gold: Reminiscences.... San Francisco, 1893. 8vo, half mor; extremities worn. sg June 18 (61) $175

Doyle, Sir Arthur Conan, 1859-1930

— The Adventures of Sherlock Holmes. L, 1892. 1st Ed in Book form. 8vo, orig cloth; soiled, hinges weak. W July 8 (309) £180

Anr copy. With: The Memoirs of Sherlock Holmes. L, 1894. Illus by Sidney Paget. 2 vols. 8vo, orig half cloth; rubbed; hinges starting in both vols. Epstein copy. sg Apr 29 (125) $2,800

1st Ed in Book form. 8vo, orig cloth, in ptd d/j; spine bumped. Manney copy. P Oct 11 (115) $49,000

1st American Ed. NY, [1892]. 8vo, pictorial cloth; some browning to covers. sg Mar 5 (95) $175

Anr Ed. L, 1893. Illus by Sidney Paget. 8vo, cloth; rubbed. kh Nov 11 (343) A$50

— The Case-Book of Sherlock Holmes. L, [1927]. 1st Ed. Front panel & flap of orig d/j tipped in. Epstein copy. sg Apr 29 (126) $300

— Danger! And Other Stories. L, 1918. 1st Ed, Colonial Issue. In chipped d/j. Manney copy. P Oct 11 (121) $500

— A Duet, with an Occasional Chorus. L, 1903. Calf gilt. With Eugene Field II forgeries of the signatures of the author & of C.M. Russell. sg Oct 17 (228) $225

— The Firm of Girdlestone, a Romance of the Unromantic. L, 1890. 1st Ed. 8vo, cloth; hinges cracked. cb Sept 19 (45) $190

— The History of Spiritualism. L, 1926. 2 vols. bba Jan 30 (248) £85 [Kitazawa]

Anr copy. In d/js. Some spotting. ANs to Mrs. Carmichael loosely inserted. S Nov 14 (627) £360 [Whiteson]

— The Hound of the Baskervilles. L, 1902. 1st Ed. Orig cloth. cb Sept 19 (46) $850; Ck July 10 (234) £130

Anr copy. Bdg rubbed & soiled. DW Jan 29 (413) £170

Anr copy. Orig cloth; small inkstains on spine & upper cover. Inscr. Manney copy. P Oct 11 (117) $17,000

Anr copy. Orig cloth; upper hinge cracked, endpapers & half-title spotted. S Nov 14 (625) £350 [Beeleigh Abbey]; S Apr 28 (648)

£550 [Orskey]

Anr copy. Epstein copy. sg Apr 29 (127) $1,600

Anr copy. Orig cloth. With frontis & 15 plates. W July 8 (310) £200

1st Issue. Orig cloth; soiled, spine & edges worn. pn June 11 (187) £110

1st American Ed. NY, 1902. 2d State. Orig cloth; warped, some wear. F June 25 (223) $60

— The Land of Mist. L, [1926]. 1st Ed. Inscr to Mrs Langworth. b Nov 18 (293) £140

— The Lost World. L, [1912]. 1st Ed. Orig cloth; rubbed. Inscr to his wife, Jean, 16 Oct 1912 & With AC, inscr, laid in. P Oct 11 (119) $4,500

— The Maracot Deep and Other Stories. L, 1929. Inscr to W. B. Maxwell. Epstein copy. sg Apr 29 (128) $1,000

— The Memoirs of Sherlock Holmes. L, 1894 [1893]. 1st Ed. Illus by Sidney Paget. 12mo, orig cloth. cb Sept 19 (47) $700

Anr copy. 8vo, orig cloth; upper endpaper splitting along hinge. Manney copy. P Oct 11 (116) $2,000

Anr copy. 12mo, orig cloth; spine rubbed & soiled. S May 13 (650) £340 [Frew Mackenzie]

1st American Ed. NY, 1894. 1st Issue. 12mo, orig cloth. Epstein copy. sg Apr 29 (129) $700

— Micah Clarke his Statement. L, 1889. 1st Ed. 8vo, calf gilt; joints rubbed. Sgd A. Conan Doyle and C.M. Russell by Eugene Field II. sg Oct 17 (229) $225

— The Mystery of Cloomber. L, 1889. 8vo, orig wraps; rebacked with much of orig spine preserved & laid down. Manney copy. P Oct 11 (113) $1,200

— The Return of Sherlock Holmes. L, 1905. 1st Ed. Orig cloth; partly resewn, extremities rubbed. Manney copy. P Oct 11 (118) $1,500

Anr copy. Orig cloth; rubbed. Epstein copy. sg Apr 29 (130) $1,900

— Round the Red Lamp. L, 1894. 1st Ed. 8vo, orig cloth. sp Nov 24 (277) $55

— The Sign of Four. L, 1890. 1st Separate Ed in Book form. 8vo, orig cloth. Manney copy. P Oct 11 (114) $2,500

— A Study in Scarlet. L, [1887]. 8vo, orig wraps; restored, with part of upper wrap, most of spine, & all of lower wrap supplied in facsimile. From: Beeton's Christmas Annual, 28th Season. Manney copy. P Oct 11 (112) $21,000

Ward, Lock's Colonial Ed. 8vo, orig cloth; bubbled. Ink port of Holmes by George Hutchinson, sgd, pasted in opposite contents leaf. S May 13 (649) £400 [Rosenbaum]

— The Valley of Fear. NY: George H. Doran, [1914]. pba July 9 (79) $80

1st Ed in Book form. L, 1915. Orig cloth. Inscr, 16 June 1915. P Oct 11 (120) $15,000

— The Wanderings of a Spiritualist. NY: Doran, [1921]. Inscr to Harry Houdini & inscr by Houdini about the circumstances of the book's presentation. P Dec 12 (31) $5,500

— Works. L, 1903. Author's Ed, One of 1,000, sgd. 12 vols. Some fore-edges spotted. P June 17 (337) $1,600; pnE May 13 (127) £720

Anr copy. 11 vols. S Feb 25 (398) £380 [Montague]

Doyle, James W. E., 1822-92

— A Chronicle of England.... L, 1864. 1st Ed. 4to, later mor gilt. bba July 9 (165) £320 [de Beaumont]

Anr copy. Orig cloth; worn & rubbed. cb Sept 26 (83) $60

Anr copy. Cloth; joints cracking. With 80 color plates. K Sept 29 (154) $80

Anr copy. Lev gilt by Bayntun with lea onlays of a knight in armor. sg May 7 (99) $2,000

— The Official Baronage of England. L, 1886. 3 vols. 4to, half mor; rubbed & worn. DW Apr 8 (236) £70

Doyley, Edward

— A Narrative of the Great Success God hath been pleased to give His Highness Forces in Jamaica.... L: Henry Hills & John Field, 1658. 4to, calf gilt; head of spine worn. DuPont copy. CNY Oct 8 (91) $950

D'Oyly, Sir Charles, 1781-1845

See also: Smith & D'Oyly

— Behar Amateur Lithographic Scrapbook. Patna: Behar Lithographic Press, [1828]. Oblong folio, orig wraps; worn, torn & dampstained. With 42 plates. cb Sept 26 (152) $475

— Tom Raw, the Griffin.... L: Ackermann, 1828. 8vo, later mor gilt by Riviere. With 25 hand-colored plates. C May 20 (46) £380 [Strover]

Drake, Charles F. T. See: Burton & Drake

Drake, Daniel, 1785-1852

— A Systematic Treatise, Historical, Etiological, and Practical, on the Principal Diseases of the Interior Valley of North America. Cincinnati, 1850-54. 1st Ed. Vol I (of 2). 8vo, rebound in syn, orig lea spine labels preserved. With 19 plates. Plates browned, text foxed. sg Nov 14 (30) $200

Drake, Edward Cavendish

— A New Universal Collection of Authentic and Entertaining Voyages and Travels. L, 1768. Folio, contemp calf; joints cracked, worn. With 54 plates & 8 maps. DW Dec 11 (27) £310

Drake, Francis, 1696-1771

— Eboracum: or the History and Antiquities of the City of York. L, 1736. 2 vols. Folio, contemp calf; rebacked & recornered, new endpapers. With 60 maps & plates. Margin tear to 1 plate. 7 related invoices & bdg directions bound in contemp calf. pnL Nov 20 (43) £160 [Almar]

Drake, Sir Francis, c.1545-95

— Sir Francis Drake Revived.... L, 1653 [1652]. Bound with: Clarke, Samuel. The Life and Death of...Drake. L, 1671. 4to, 18th-cent calf gilt; spine head chipped, joints & extremities rubbed. Frontises with margins restored; lower corner of E1 in Part 1 torn; some shaving; lacking 2 blanks; rust-hole to G4 of Part 1 affecting 2 letters; repaired hole to D1 affecting 1 letter; tp of 2d work with marginal repair & frayed fore-edge; marginal hole to L2. CNY Oct 8 (96) $2,200

Anr copy. Mor gilt janseniste by the French Binders. Frontis washed; repair to K1 of Part 1 affecting 10 letters; title-border & headline of B1v shaved; minor worming through gutter of a few quires; marginal repairs & wormholes. CNY Oct 8 (97) $2,400

— Le Voyage de l'Illustre Seigneur et Chevalier Francois Drach.... Paris: Jean Gesselin, 1627. 8vo, mor gilt by R. Petit. With the folding map showing the route of Drake's circumnavigation of the globe, on thin paper. DuPont copy. CNY Oct 8 (94) $65,000

— The Voyages and Travels of that Renowned Captain.... L, 1683. 4to, disbound. Mostly black letter. Hole in quire C with partial loss to 15 letters this quire in smaller typeface than the 1st 2 quires & on different paper, thus from anr Ed or issue. DuPont copy. CNY Oct 8 (98) $1,300

— The World Encompassed by Sir F. Drake.... L, 1635. 2d Ed. 4to, half mor. Frontis lacking & supplied in facsimile; lacking final blank; some dampstaining; map with small stains, affecting 11 letters of the engraved text & engraver's signature; 3 headlines shaved. STC 7162. CNY Oct 8 (95) $2,000

— Bigges, Walter & Crofts. - Expeditio Francisci Draki Equitis Angli in Indias occidentales. Leiden: Fr. Raphelengius, 1588. 4to, 19th-cent mor gilt; rubbed. Bound with blanks; variant with type ornament vignette on tp. Lacking the 4 accompanying folding maps (stubs remaining) & the final blank; washed; upper margins restored. DuPont copy. CNY Oct 8 (92) $8,000

— Boazio, Baptista. - [5 hand-colored maps or view-plans made to illustrate Bigges & Croftes at the end of the 1580s, each c.422mm by 557mm, from the duPont collection]. CNY Oct 8 (93) $210,000

Drake, Francis Samuel, 1828-85

— The Indian Tribes of the United States.... Phila., 1884. 2 vols. 4to, orig half mor. With 100 plates. cb Feb 12 (20) $250

Drake, Leah Bodine

— A Horn Book for Witches. Sauk City: Arkham House, 1950. One of 553. In d/j. Inscr. Epstein copy. sg Apr 29 (131) $1,100

Drake, Samuel Gardner, 1798-1875

— Indian Biography.... Bost., 1833. ("The Book of the Indians of North America.") 5 parts in 1 vol. 8vo, contemp calf; worn, upper joint becoming tender. Sokme foxing; old dampstain across half of frontis, tp & 1st 2 signatures. bbc Sept 23 (311) $55

Drayton, Michael, 1563-1631

— Poems. L, 1630. 8vo, later mor. Lacking final blank; a few headlines shaved; H1 repaired with a few letters supplied in ink; small repair to G8 affecting 2 letters; marginal repair to A4 & hole in O8; some foxing & soiling. STC 7224. pn Dec 12 (6) £150 [Clark]

— Poly-Olbion. L, 1622. ("A Chorographicall Description....") 1st Ed, Mixed Issue. Bound with: The Second Part. L, 1622. Folio, later calf gilt. With engraved title, port of Prince Henry & 30 double-page maps. The 18 maps in Part 1 shorter & with new guards; maps in Part 2 restored at margins with occasional loss, especially to Norfolk & Northumberland; washed; tp restored. Sold w.a.f. STC 7227-9. pn Mar 19 (175) £1,500 [Burden]

Dreams...

— Dreams and Derisions. NY, 1927. One of 200. 4to, half mor. cb Dec 5 (71) $190

Dreier, Katherine S.

— Shawn the Dancer. NY, 1933. 4to, In d/j. cb Jan 16 (37) $75

Dreiser, Theodore, 1871-1945

See also: Limited Editions Club

— An American Tragedy. NY, 1925. 1st Ed, 1st Issue. 2 vols. Cloth; hinges cracked & tender. Inscr, 1925. wa Sept 26 (149) $55

One of 795. In d/js. Epstein copy. sg Apr 29 (132) $650

— Dawn. NY, [1931]. 1st Ed, One of 275, sgd. O Mar 31 (62) $90

— Epitaph: a Poem. NY, [1929]. One of 800, sgd. O Aug 25 (57) $60

— A Gallery of Women. NY, 1929. 1st Ed, One of 560, sgd. 2 vols. Cloth. cb Dec 12 (46) $120

Anr copy. Orig half vellum; spine scuffed, cover bumped. F Sept 26 (331) $60

Anr copy. Orig half vellum; spines soiled. pn Dec 12 (190) £50 [Bookroom]

1st Trade Ed. 2 vols. In chipped d/js. sp June 18 (420) $50

— Sister Carrie. NY, 1900. 1st Ed. 8vo, orig cloth; edges rubbed. Epstein copy. sg Apr 29 (133) $3,200

Dresser, Christopher

— Studies in Design. L, [1874-76]. Folio, later cloth. With 60 plates. Some chipping. F Dec 18 (690) $625

Anr copy. Contemp cloth, orig wrap bound in at end; lacking section of spine, shelf mark on spine. With litho title & 60 litho plates. Some soiling. pn Mar 19 (166) £650 [Pagan]

Anr copy. Orig cloth; rubbed & soiled. With 54 (of 60) plates. Lacking all before p.3. Sold w.a.f. S May 14 (922) £220 [Pagan]

Dresser, Henry Eeles, 1838-1915

— Eggs of the Birds of Europe. L, [1905]-10. 2 vols. 4to, contemp half mor, orig wraps bound in. C Oct 30 (185) £600 [Grahame]

Anr copy. Contemp half mor. With 106 colored plates. Repaginated & bound under the author's supervision, with the orig 13 wraps to Parts 1-24 bound in at the end of Vol II. S May 14 (1027) £200 [Cumming]

Anr copy. Modern half mor. With 106 colored plates. A few plates soiled. S May 14 (1028) £250 [Seragnoli]

— A History of the Birds of Europe. L, 1871-96. 9 vols, including Supplement. 4to, contemp half mor; rebacked, old spines preserved. With 721 (of 722) plates. bba Sept 5 (136) £3,800 [Shapero]

Anr copy. 8 vols. 4to, With engraved titles & 633 lithos, most colored by hand. Without the supplement. C Oct 30 (184) £4,000 [Greyfriars]

Anr copy. 9 vols, including Supplement. 4to, contemp half mor, orig wraps bound in. With 721 hand-colored plates & 2 plain plates. C Oct 30 (278) £7,600 [Radclyffe]

Anr copy. 20th-cent half mor gilt. Occasional foxing or spotting to plates. CNY Dec 5 (290) $13,000

Anr copy. 8 vols, without Supplement. 4to, half mor gilt. With engraved title, 631 hand-colored plates & 2 uncolored plates. S June 25 (17) £5,400 [American]

— A Monograph of the Coraciidae, or Family of the Rollers. Farnborough, 1893. 4to, modern half lev; front inner hinge cracked. With 27 hand-colored plates. C Oct 30 (279) £3,000 [Grahame]

— A Monograph of the Meropidae or Family of the Bee-Eaters. L, 1884-86. 5 parts in 1 vol. 4to, contemp half mor gilt. With 34 colored plates. Some leaves with minor soil or spotting. C Oct 30 (280) £4,800 [Grahame]

Anr copy. 4to, contemp half mor. With 34 hand-colored plates. C May 20 (172) £4,800 [Grahame]

Dreux du Radier, Jean Francois

— L'Europe Illustre, contenant l'histoire abregee des souverains.... Paris, 1777. 6 vols. 8vo, early 19th-cent calf gilt. C June 24 (304) £350 [Ursus]

Drinkwater, John, 1762-1844

— A History of the Late Siege of Gibraltar. L, 1785. 1st Ed. 4to, contemp calf gilt; joints cracked. With folding map & 9 folding plates & charts. DW Dec 11 (28) £160

Anr copy. Contemp calf; broken, spine ends chipped. With 4 folding maps & 6 folding plates. Some maps torn, 1 with several crude paper repairs on verso; marginal notes. pba Aug 20 (67) $190

Anr copy. Contemp half sheep; front cover loose. With folding map & 9 folding plates & charts. sg Jan 9 (130) $90

2d Ed. L, 1786. 4to, contemp calf; rebacked, orig spine preserved. DW Apr 8 (25) £170

Anr copy. Modern half calf incorporating old bds. Some foxing & soiling. O Aug 25 (58) $225

Anr Ed. L, 1790. 4to, contemp calf; joints weak, rubbed. With 9 (of 10) folding maps & plates. Some spotting; 2 plates with marginal tears. bba July 9 (124) £95 [Kay Books]

Anr copy. Half calf gilt; hinges cracked. With folding map & 9 folding plates. DW Nov 6 (38) £170

Drummond, Alexander, d.1769

— Travels through Different Cities of Germany, Italy, Greece.... L, 1754. 1st Ed. Folio, contemp calf gilt; rubbed. With frontis & 34 plates & maps. Some tears at folds without apparent loss; frontis dust-soiled. S Nov 21 (248) £1,000 [Shapero]

Anr copy. Modern calf. Some repairs to text & plates; some spotting & soiling. S June 30 (282) £650 [Severis]

Drummond de Melfort, Guy, Comte de
— Traite de cavalerie, propre a conduire l'homme de guerre.... Paris, 1776. 2 vols. Folio, contemp calf gilt; worn. With frontis & 1 single & 9 double-page plates in text vol; with 32 double-page or folding plates bound as 36 & 9 full-page plates. Some creases, tears & repairs. S June 25 (88) £1,900 [Marshall]

Drummond, James, 1816-77
See also: Anderson & Drummond
— Old Edinburgh. Edin. & L, 1879. One of 500. Folio, half mor. pnE May 13 (119) £130

Drummond, William Henry, 1845-79
— The Large Game and Natural History of South and South-East Africa. Edin., 1875. 8vo, orig cloth. With colored frontis & 12 color plates. bba Feb 13 (356) £150 [Baring]

Drury, Dru, 1725-1803
— Illustrations of Natural History. L, 1770-82. 3 vols. 4to, contemp half russia; Vol I rebacked with orig spine laid down. With 150 hand-colored plates & 1 uncolored schematic plate. Ownership blindstamps removed from titles. C Oct 30 (186) £2,400 [Junk]

Anr copy. Part 1 only. 19th-cent calf; rubbed, joints broken. With 50 hand-colored plates & 1 uncolored plate. S Nov 15 (737) £650 [Mason]

Anr Ed. L, 1837. ("Illustrations of Exotic Entomology.") 3 vols. 4to, contemp half lea; edges rubbed. With 1 uncolored & 152 plates, including 1 additional plate. pn Mar 19 (278) £1,200 [Shapero]

Dryander, John. See: Banks Library, Sir Joseph

Dryden, John, 1631-1700
See also: Fore-Edge Paintings; Golden Cockerel Press; Nonesuch Press
— Absalom and Achitophel. L, 1681. 1st Ed, 1st Issue of Part 1; 2d Issue of Part 2. Parts 1 & 2 in 1 vol. Folio, modern calf gilt by Riviere. Lacking initial blank in 1st part; tp to 2d part with crease & some soil. C Dec 16 (191) £250 [Pirages]
— Alexander's Feast. L: Essex House Press, 1904. One of 140 on vellum. Orig vellum; bowed, endpapers soiled. Margin of opening text leaf soiled. wa Sept 26 (68) $210
— The Hind and the Panther. L, 1687. 1st Ed. 4to, modern half calf gilt. sg May 7 (175) $275
— Marriage a-la-Mode, a Comedy. L, 1673. 1st Ed. 4to, modern mor extra. cb Oct 25 (36) $180
— Works. L, 1760. ("Miscellaneous Works.") 4 vols. 8vo, contemp calf gilt; hinges rubbed. DW Jan 29 (228) £220

Anr Ed. L, 1821. Ed by Sir Walter Scott. 18 vols. 8vo, contemp half mor over bds. With port. bba July 9 (198) £320 [Jarndyce]

Anr copy. Contemp half calf; rubbed. Marginal dampstaining. pn apr 23 (79) £100

Anr copy. 19th-cent mor gilt; rubbed. Some spotting & browning. S July 1 (978) £380 [Jarndyce]

Du
— Du. Zurich: Verlag Conzett & Huber, [1959]. August Sander issue. 4to, pictorial wraps; soiled. With 48 plates. sg Apr 13 (37) $150

Du Bartas, Guillaume de Saluste, 1544-90
— His Devine Weekes and Workes. L, 1621. ("His Divine Weekes and Workes") Folio, contemp calf; rebacked. STC 21653. W July 8 (37) £145

Du Bellay, Guillaume
— Instructions sur le faict de la guerre. Paris: Michel de Vascosan, 1549. 8vo, bound in Paris in 1556 for Fuerst Peter Ernst von Mansfeld in calf over pastebds gilt with areas painted black, green, red & silver & with arms, motto & name Mansfelt on both covers. Inscr cut out of the center of tp & with a short tear in the text; a few margins wormed. S Dec 9 (172) £280,000 [Maggs]

Du Bellay, Joachim, 1522?-60
— Les Oeuvres francoises.... Rouen, 1597. 12mo, contemp calf gilt, armorial bdg. Ck Oct 31 (79) £750

Du Blar, L. J.
— Coup-d'oeil sur la lithographie...par L. J. D. B..... Brussels, 1818. 8vo, contemp sheep gilt; inner hinges broken. With 4 additional pages about lithography written by Du Blar bound in. Schlosser copy. P June 17 (534) $3,500

Du Bois, Henri Pene
— Four Private Libraries of New York. NY, 1892. Ltd Ed. First Series. 8vo, cloth. cb Oct 17 (257) $130

Du Bois, John Van Deusen. See: Grabhorn Printing

Du Bosc, Jacques, d.1660
— The Excellent Woman Described by her True Characters.... L: Joseph Watts, 1692. 8vo, contemp calf gilt; extremities rubbed, front joint cracked. Some stains & browning. sg Oct 24 (101) $650

Du Chaillu, Paul Belloni, 1831-1903

— Explorations and Adventures in Equatorial Africa. L, 1861. 1st Ed. 8vo, orig cloth; soiled. With folding frontis & folding map. bba Sept 19 (59) £130 [Crabtree]

Anr copy. Modern half calf. With 22 plates & 1 folding map. Some spotting. pn Mar 19 (393) £85

— A Journey to Ashango-Land. L, 1867. 8vo, half lea gilt. b&b Feb 19 (26) $70

Du Fouilloux, Jacques, 1521?-80

— La Caccia. Milan, 1615. 8vo, contemp vellum; soiled. Some staining; tp washed. S May 28 (77) £850 [Lib. Casella]

— La Venerie. Angers: C. Lebosse, 1844. 8vo, contemp half lea gilt; head of spine chipped. sg Oct 17 (212) $60

Du Fresnoy, Charles Alphonse, 1611-65

— De Arte Graphica. The Art of Painting. L, 1716. ("The Art of Painting.") 2d Ed of Dryden's trans. 8vo, contemp calf; rubbed, joints cracked. F Sept 26 (422) $50

Du Halde, Jean Baptiste, 1674-1743

— The General History of China.... L, 1736. 4 vols. 8vo, modern calf; worn. Library stamps on titles. O May 26 (54) $750

Du Roure,

— Analectabiblion, ou Extraits Critiques de Divers Livres Rares.... Paris, 1836-37. One of 90. 2 vols. 8vo, contemp half calf; rebacked. bba Oct 10 (524) £80 [Vine]

Du Vignau, —, Sieur des Joannots

— L'Etat present de la puissance ottomane.... Paris, 1687. 8vo, contemp calf; rubbed, upper joint weak. S Nov 21 (250) £700 [Kutluoglu]

Dube, Jean-Paul

— Let's Save our Salmon. Ottawa: Dube, [1972]. One of 850. Lea. Inscr. Koopman copy. O Oct 29 (99) $80; O Oct 29 (100) $70

Dubin, Arthur D.

— Some Classic Trains. Milwaukee, 1964. In d/j. cb Feb 13 (104) $65

Dubois, Georges

— Essai sur le traite d'escrime de Saint-Didier publie en 1573. Paris, 1918. One of 60. Wraps. Inscr. sg Mar 26 (105) $200

Dubois, Urbain

— Artistic Cookery. L 1870. 4to, orig cloth; broken & loose. With 80 plates, some spotted. bba Oct 24 (86) £360 [J. Clarke]

Anr copy. Orig cloth; bubbled. With frontis, port & 68 plates. S May 14 (980) £800 [Lerner]

Dubourg, M. See: Clark & Dubourg

Dubourg, Matthew

— Views of the Remains of Ancient Buildings in Rome and its Vicinity. L, 1820. Folio, unbound. With 26 hand-colored plates. Some text margins frayed; tp mtd on gray paper. S May 14 (1197) £650 [Bifolco]

Anr copy. Orig half lea gilt. S June 25 (98) £1,100 [Toscani]

Anr Ed. L, 1844. Folio, contemp half mor. With 16 (of 26) hand-colored plates. Some plates loose. NH May 30 (9) $350

Anr copy. Orig cloth; worn, spine def. With 26 hand-colored plates. Marginal stain to frontis & tp; some imprints cropped or shaved; date erased from tp. pn Mar 19 (391) £950

Dubravius, Janus, Bishop of Olmutz

— Historia regni Boiemiae.... Prossnitz: Joannes Gunther, 1552. Folio, old lea; rubbed, 2 prelims rehinged. Marginal dampstaining; lacking tp & 4th prelim leaf; small piece excised from 2d prelim leaf. sg Oct 24 (102) $200

Dubuffet, Jean

— Catalogue des travaux de Jean Dubuffet. Paris, [1966-9]. Fascicules 1-37. 4to, pictorial wraps; spine ends worn. sg Sept 6 (97) $1,300

— Elements, Moments. [N.p.], 1959. One of 20. Folio, loose as issued. CGen Nov 18 (361) SF7,500

— Le Preneur d'empreintes. [N.p.], 1958. One of 22. Folio, loose as issued. CGen Nov 18 (360) SF7,500

— Tables Rases. [N.p.], 1962. One of 24. Folio, loose as issued. CGen Nov 18 (362) SF7,500

Ducarel, Andrew Coltee, 1713-85

— Anglo-Norman Antiquities Considered in a Tour through Part of Normandy. L, 1767. Folio, contemp mor gilt. With 20 plates. Lacking port. Extra-illus with 25 plates & 3 orig drawing. Author's copy. C Oct 30 (101) £1,100 [Marlborough]

Anr copy. Lea. sg Oct 24 (103) $250

Ducchi, Gregorio

— Il Giuoco de gli scacchi ridotto in poema eroico.... Vicenza, 1607. 4to, later cloth. Ck May 8 (30) £220

— La Scaccheide. Vicenza: Perin & Giorgio Greco, 1586. 4to, 18th-cent half vellum; rubbed, spine wormed. Some leaves torn & repaired; minor worming with loss. Ck May 8 (29) £280

Duchamp, Marcel
See also: Breton & Duchamp

— Not Seen and/or Less Seen of/by Marcel Duchamp/ Prose Selavy 1904-64. Mary Sisler Collection. NY, 1965. 4to, pictorial wraps. sg Apr 2 (82) $120

One of 100. Pictorial wraps. sg Apr 2 (81) $700

— Notes and Projects for the Large Glass. L, 1969. Folio, orig cloth; rubbed & soiled. DW Mar 11 (492) £50

Duchesne, Andre, 1584-1640

— Historiae Normannorum scriptores. Paris, 1619. Folio, contemp calf; worn. Some browning. SI Dec 5 (838) LIt400,000

Duchesne, Jean, 1779-1855

— Museum of Painting and Sculpture.... L, 1828. 17 vols. 16mo, contemp half calf; spines worn, 2 vols rebacked. DW Mar 4 (313) £65

Duchow, John Charles

— The Duchow Journal: a Voyage from Boston to California, 1852. [Kentfield, Calif.]: Allen Press, 1959. One of 200. Folio, half cloth. b&b Feb 19 (299) $60

Dudevant, Maurice. See: Sand, Maurice

Dudley, Robert. See: Russell & Dudley

Duer, William Alexander, 1780-1858

— A Reply to Mr. Colden's Vindication of the Steam-Boat Monopoly. Albany, 1819. 1st Ed. 8vo, modern bds; def. sg June 18 (167) $80

Duerer, Albrecht, 1471-1528
See also: Grolier Club; Senefelder, Alois

— Albert Durers Designs of the Prayer Book. L: Ackermann, 1 Sept 1817. Folio, orig bds. With frontis, litho title & 44 plates. P June 17 (537) $700

— De Symmetria partium in rectis formis humanorum corporum.... Nuremberg, 1532. Folio, 19th-cent mor. Lacking final blank; small stain on tp. S May 28 (5) £5,200 [Phelps]

Anr Ed. [Nuremberg: in aedib. viduae Durerianae, 1532]. Folio, 19th-cent vellum with yapp edges. Tp remargined; some marginal closed tears; some foxing; lacking last blank. Schlosser copy. P June 18 (424) $4,250

— Hierinn sind begriffen vier Bucher von menschlicher Proportion. Nuremberg: Hieronymus Formschnyder, Oct 1528. Folio, 18th-cent half lea gilt; worn & wormed. FD Dec 2 (13) DM2,800

Duff, Edward Gordon, 1863-1924
See also: Caxton Club

— Early Printed Books. L, 1893. One of 150. cb Oct 17 (258) $55

Dufy, Raoul, 1877-1953

— Croquis de Modes. Paris, Feb 1920. Loose as issued in wraps. With 8 color plates. Supplement to the Gazette du Bon Ton. sg Feb 13 (173) $175

Dugdale, Thomas —& Burnett, William

— England and Wales Delineated. L, [1845?]. 8 (of 11) vols. Orig cloth. Sold w.a.f. bba May 28 (370) £160 [Angle Books]

Anr copy. ("Curiosities of Great Britain.") 8 (of 11) vols. 8vo, With 58 double-page maps, hand-colored in outline & 183 plates. 1 map cropped with pin holes in margin; some browning & dampstains to margins. pnL Nov 20 (120) £250 [Kinnard]

Dugdale, Sir William, 1605-86

— The Antient Usage in Bearing of Such Ensigns of Honour as are Commonly Call'd Arms. Oxford, 1682. 8vo, old calf; rubbed, joints broken. O Dec 17 (50) $90

— The History of Imbanking and Drayning of Divers Fenns and Marshes.... L, 1662. 1st Ed. Folio, contemp calf; rubbed, upper joint cracked. With 11 double-page or folding maps. bba Sept 19 (186) £800 [Elton Engineering Books]

— The History of St. Paul's Cathedral.... L, 1658. 1st Ed. Folio, contemp calf; front joint cracked. With port & 12 plates. Corner of a few text leaves dampstained. sg Nov 7 (71) $950

— Origines juridicales, or Historical Memorials of the English Laws. L, 1671. 2d Ed. Folio, modern bds; lacking spine. bba Jan 16 (8) £160 [J. Rees]

— A Short View of the late Troubles in England. Oxford, 1681. Folio, contemp calf; hinges weak. LH Dec 11 (103) $100

Dugdale, Sir William, 1605-86 —& Dodsworth, Roger, 1585-1654

— Monasticon Anglicanum. L, 1655-73. 3 vols. Folio, contemp calf; rubbed, joints split. With engraved title & 107 (of 111) plates. Some browning. Sold w.a.f. pn July 16 (12) £220 [Thorpe]

Anr Ed. L, 1718. ("Monasticon Anglicanum, or the History of the Ancient Abbeys....") 3 parts in 1 vol. Folio, contemp calf; rebacked in mor, scuffed, rubbed. With frontis & 103 plates. Some waterstaining. bba Aug 13 (99) £90 [Gleeson]

Anr copy. Contemp calf; rebacked. With frontis & 102 plates. Some browning. pnL Nov 20 (98) £190 [Riley]

Dugmore, Arthur Radclyffe, 1870-1955
— Camera Adventures in the African Wilds.... L, 1910. 1st Ed. 4to, cloth; inner joints weak. K Sept 29 (156) $60
— The Romance of the Newfoundland Caribou.... Phila. & L, 1913. 4to, cloth. cb Jan 30 (42) $95; sg Jan 9 (69) $120

Duhamel du Monceau, Henri Louis, 1700-81?
— De l'exploitation des bois, ou moyens de tirer un parti avantageux.... Paris, 1764. 2 parts in 1 vol. 4to, contemp calf gilt, armorial bdg; joints split. With 36 folding plates. wa Sept 26 (467) $300
— A Practical Treatise of Husbandry. L, 1759. 4to, calf; rebacked. pnE Dec 4 (165) £110

Duhamel, Georges, 1884-1966
— Maurice de Vlaminck. Paris, 1927. One of 875. 4to, lea. With 28 plates, including 4 etchings. Met Apr 28 (35) $190

Duke, Thomas S.
— Celebrated Criminal Cases of America. San Francisco, 1910. Orig cloth; water damage to spine, front hinge cracked through. Mold to inner margins at hinges; some leaves detached. pba Aug 20 (68) $55

Dulac, Edmund, 1882-1953
— Fairy Book: Fairy Tales of the Allied Nations. L, [1916]. One of 350. 4to, orig cloth in def d/j; spine ends frayed. sg Sept 26 (92) $200
— Lyrics, Pathetic and Humorous, from A-Z. L, [1906]. 4to, orig half cloth; broken. kh Nov 11 (84) A$340

Anr Ed. L & NY, 1908. 4to, half cloth; rubbed. sg Sept 26 (95) $400

Anr copy. Loose as issued in folding case. A few plates loose or detached. sg Jan 30 (40) $225
— Picture Book for the French Red Cross. L, [1915]. 4to, orig cloth, in d/j. With port & 19 colored plates. sg Sept 26 (93) $275; sg Jan 30 (39) $90

Dullaert, Johannes, 1470-1530. See: Johannes de Janduno

Dumas, Alexandre, 1802-70, pere
— Celebrated Crimes. Phila., [1895]. 8 vols. 8vo, half lea. sp June 18 (468) $160
— The Corsican Brothers. NY, [c.1850]. 8vo, half cloth. Heavily annotated & interleaved prompt copy used by J. B. Roberts for a mid-19th-cent production at Memphis TN. sg Oct 17 (84) $325
— The Count of Monte-Cristo. L, 1846. 2 vols. 8vo, orig cloth; extremities rubbed. With 3 small inkstains. Manney copy. P Oct 11 (125) $4,750
— The Three Musketeers. L, 1894. One of 775. Illus by Maurice Leloir. 2 vols. 4to, half mor gilt; some nicks or scuffs. wa Mar 5 (28) $200
— Les Trois Mousquetaires. Paris, 1894. Illus by Maurice Leloir. 2 vols. Folio, half mor by Vauthman. O Aug 25 (59) $80
— Works. NY: Sproul, 1903. ("The Romances of Alexandre Dumas.") Louvre Ed, one of 1,000. 32 vols. Half lea; some rubbing. O May 26 (55) $300

Ed de Medicis. Bost: Dana Estes & Co, [n.d.]. 47 vols. Half mor; rubbed. Library stamp on Chapter 1 in 1st vol; some browning. P June 17 (338) $1,300

Dumas, Alexandre, 1824-95, fils
See also: Limited Editions Club
— Rapport sur les prix de vertu. Paris: Firmin-Didot, 1877. Unique copy. 18 vellum leaves, 4to, orig vellum; soiled. Some browning to front blank. wa Sept 26 (106) $350
— Theatre complet.... Paris 1874-98. 25 vols. 12mo, contemp half mor gilt; spine worn. sg Mar 5 (95A) $275

Dumolinet, Claude, 1620-87
— Historia summorum pontificum a Martino V. ad Innocentium XI. Paris, 1679. 1st Ed. Folio, contemp calf; hinges cracked. DW Mar 4 (207) £100

Dumont d'Urville, Jules Sebastien Cesar, 1790-1842
— Voyage au pole Sude et dans L'Oceanie.... Paris, 1846. 2 vols (Atlas pittoresque) only in 1. Folio, contemp half mor; scuffed, inner hinges split. With 2 tinted litho titles, 198 plates & 9 double-page maps. Some mounts browned; 4 plates detached; 8 plates with marginal tears. C Oct 30 (27) £5,500 [Hinchcliffe]

Dumont, Jean, Baron de Carlscroon
— Batailles gagnees par le Prince Eugene de Savoye. The Hague, 1720. Folio, contemp calf gilt. With port, 10 double-page plates & 4 double-page maps. Ck May 15 (94) £1,700
— A New Voyage to the Levant. L, 1702. 3d Ed in English. 8vo, 19th-cent half mor; worn. With frontis & 8 folding plates. Lacking A1; tp soiled. S June 30 (284) £90 [Consolidated Real]
— Nouveau voyage du Levant. The Hague: Etienne Foulque, 1694. 8vo, contemp calf; worn. With 8 folding plates. S July 1 (836) £1,100

Dunbar, Paul Laurence, 1872-1906
— Poems of Cabin and Field. NY, 1913. Orig bdg; rubbed. Met Apr 28 (405) $50

Duncan, Archibald

— The Mariner's Chronicle; or, authentic and complete History of Popular Shipwrecks. L, 1805-12 & [n.d.]. 6 vols. 8vo, contemp half mor; rubbed. With 50 plates. Hole in p.253 of Vol II; p.127 in Vol V cropped; tear in p.85 of Vol VI. S May 14 (1066) £360 [Remington]

Duncan, Isadora, 1878-1927

— The Art of the Dance. NY, 1928. 4to, half cloth; covers marked, rubbed. K Sept 29 (157) $75

Anr copy. Half cloth. John Mason Brown's copy, with his sgd attestation that Duncan sgd & corrected this copy & with pencil corrections, sgd ID in ink. Met Apr 28 (621) $1,400

Anr copy. Half cloth; worn. O Dec 17 (51) $100; O Apr 28 (167) $70

Anr copy. Half cloth. With ALs to Eva Le Gallienne. sg Mar 5 (221) $650

Duncumb, John

— Collections towards the History and Antiquities of the County of Hereford. Hereford, 1804-12. 1st Ed. 2 vols. 4to, contemp half mor. Some foxing; annotated in a contemp hand. bba June 25 (46) £190 [Howes]

Dunkle, John

— Prison Life During the Rebellion.... Singer's Glen VA, 1869. 1st Ed. 8vo, orig wraps; worn at edges. bbc Feb 17 (52) $110

Dunlap, William, 1766-1839

— A History of the American Theatre. NY, 1832. 1 vol extended to 3. 8vo, mor gilt; extremities rubbed, hinges cracked. Assembled from at least 3 copies & misbound. Extra-illus with ports, playbills & A Ls s. sg Dec 5 (93) $500

— History of the Rise and Progress of the Arts of Design in the United States. NY, 1834. 1st Ed. 2 vols. 8vo, later half mor; joints & extremities rubbed. Some foxing; library markings. F Dec 18 (323) $90

Anr Ed. Bost., 1918. 3 vols. F Dec 18 (322) $60

— The Life of George Fred. Cooke. L, 1815. 2d Ed. 2 vols. 8vo, modern half mor. Library stamps. sg Oct 17 (29) $110

Duns Scotus, Johannes, 1265?-1308?

— Quaestiones in Aristotelis Metaphysicam. Venice: J. Hamman for A. Torresanus, 20 Aug 1499. Folio, old vellum; spine imperfect. Marginal dampstains throughout; blank portion of title excised. 233 (of 234) leaves; lacking a2. Goff D-373. sg Mar 12 (117) $600

Dunsany, Edward Plunkett, 18th Baron
See also: Golden Cockerel Press

— The Gods of Pegana. L, 1911. One of 500. Illus by S. H. Sime. 4to, orig half cloth. sg June 11 (105) $70

— Time and the Gods. L, 1922. One of 250. Illus by S. H. Sime. 4to, orig half vellum. With 10 plates. K July 12 (179) $250

Dunscomb, Guy L. See: Stindt & Dunscomb

Dunthorne, Gordon

— Flower and Fruit Prints of the 18th and Early 19th Centuries. L, 1938. Anr Issue. 4to, orig cloth; backstrip torn. bba Aug 13 (361) £100 [Lloyd's of Kew]

Anr Ed. Wash., 1938. 4to, orig cloth. Met Apr 28 (622) $190; sg May 21 (211) $400

Dupaty de Clam, ——

— La Science et l'art de l'equitation. Paris, 1776. 4to, contemp sheep gilt; worn. With 9 plates. Some foxing & dampstaining. sg May 21 (33) $300

Dupin, Jacques

— Fits and Starts. Selected Poems. Salisbury: Compton Press, 1973. One of 100 with sgd color litho by Calder. Trans by Paul Auster; illus by Alexander Calder. 4to, cloth. sg Sept 26 (68) $1,400

— Miro: Life and Work. NY, 1962. In d/j. Met Apr 27 (36) $140

Duplessis, Georges V. A. Gratet, 1834-99
See also: Schongauer, Martin

— Costumes historiques des XVIe, XVIIe et XVIIIe siecles.... Paris, 1867. 2 vols. 4to, half cloth; rubbed. With 150 colored plates. Some spotting. pn Sept 12 (263) £220 [Talanti]

Duppa, Richard

— The Life and Literary Works of Michel Angelo Buonarroti. L, 1806. One of 50 L.p. copies. Folio, half calf; rebacked, rubbed. Some repairs to folding plate. O Dec 17 (52) $190

Dupre, Louis

— Voyage a Athenes et a Constantinople. Paris, 1825. Folio, modern half mor. With 40 colored plates, partly hand-colored double-page facsimile of a Turkish passport & 12 uncolored litho illusts in the text. Half-title & 4 plates with marginal tears repaired; a few plates with dicoloration; 4 plates cut round & inlaid to size. C Oct 30 (29) £28,000 [Basket]

Dupressoir, Charles. See: Beveren & Dupressoir

Durand-Ruel Galeries

— Recueil d'estampes gravees a l'eau-forte. L, 1873. 4to, contemp half mor; rubbed. With 300 plates. sg Feb 6 (76) $350

Duranti, Guillelmus, 1237?-96

— Rationale divinorum officiorum. [Mainz]: Johannes Fust & Peter Schoeffer, 6 Oct 1459. Single leaf ptd on vellum. Formerly used as a pastedown; 1 small hole in text. Goff D-403. S Dec 5 (15) £850 [Maggs]

Duranty, Louis Emile Edmond, 1838-80

— Theatre des marionnettes du jardin des Tuileries. Paris, 1863. 4to, half mor; worn. Several text leaves repaired. sg Oct 17 (70) $300

Durazzo, Ippolito

— Elogj storici di Cristoforo Colombo e di Andrea D'Oria. Parma: Stamperia Reale, 1781. 4to, later half mor; worn, new endpapers. Some worming & soiling. bba June 25 (35) £80 [Bernard]

Anr copy. Contemp bds; rebacked. Library stamp on tp. Ck Oct 31 (10) £380

Durelli, Gaetano & Francesco

— La Certosa di Pavia. Milan, 1823-53. Folio, half calf. With 70 plates. Some spotting. S May 13 (803) £300 [Casa d'Arte]

Duret, Theodore, 1838-1927

— Histoire d'Edouard Manet et de son oeuvre. Paris, 1906. One of 600. Contemp half mor. ALs of Manet & ALs of Monet, both to Duret, tipped in on front free endpapers. Ck Oct 18 (288) £1,700

— Histoire des peintres impressionistes. Paris, 1906. 4to, cloth. With 26 plates, some in color. S Feb 11 (275) £1,550 [Sims Reed]

— Die Impressionisten. Berlin, 1914. 4to, orig half vellum; soiled. S Feb 11 (255) £520 [Klein]

— Manet and the French Impressionists. L & Phila., 1910. With 4 etchings by Manet, Morisot & Renoir (2).. pn Sept 12 (84) £320 [Sims & Reed]

— Renoir. Paris, 1924. 1st Ed, Out-of-series copy. 4to, half mor, orig wraps bound in. S Feb 11 (287) £240 [Gilgemann]

D'Urfey, Thomas, 1653-1723

— The Songs to the New Play of Don Quixote. L: J. Heptinstall for Samuel Briscoe, 1694. Part I (of 3) only. Folio, modern half calf. Lacking A2 & M2; lower margin of E2 shaved with slight loss; some browning. C Dec 16 (194) £250 [Pickering & Chatto]

Durfort, Claire de

— Ourika. Austin: W. Thomas Taylor, 1977. One of 500. Half mor. wa Dec 9 (188) $75

Durling, Richard J.

— A Catalogue of Sixteenth Century Printed Books in the National Library of Medicine. Bethesda, 1967. 4to, orig cloth. cb Oct 17 (261) $70

Durnford, Edward

— A Soldier's Life and Work in South Africa.... L, 1882. 8vo, orig cloth; worn & dampstained. With frontis & folding map. O Feb 25 (66) $140

Durno, J.

— A Description of a New-Invented Stove-Grate.... L, 1753. 8vo, modern wraps. Tp & final page soiled. P June 16 (56) $800

Durrell, Lawrence

— The Alexandria Quartet. L, 1962. 1st Collected Ed, one of 500. Orig cloth; soiled. S Nov 14 (628) £250 [Words]

— Panic Spring by Charles Norden. L, 1937. In soiled d/j. S Feb 25 (396) £250 [Sawyer]

— The Red Limbo Lingo: A Poetry Notebook. L, 1971. bba Apr 29 (128) £65 [Ulysses]

Durrie, Daniel Steele, 1819-92

— A History of Madison.... Madison WI, 1874. 8vo, modern half lea; worn. With 19 mtd albumen prints. Soiled & stained. O Mar 31 (64) $200

Dusseldorf...

— The Dusseldorf Artist's Album. Dusseldorf: Arnz, 1854. Ed & trans by Mary Howitt. 2 vols. 4to, orig lea; rubbed, joints weakening. With 27 plates including extra title. K July 12 (263) $75

Duthuit, Georges

See also: Reverdy & Duthuit

— La Sculpture copte. Paris, 1931. Folio, wraps. sg Apr 2 (68) $150

Duval, Elizabeth W.

— T. E. Lawrence. A Bibliography. NY, 1938. One of 500. wa Apr 9 (45) $140

Duveen, Denis Ian

— Bibliotheca alchemica et chemica: an Annotated Catalogue of Printed Books. L, 1949. One of 200. 4to, orig cloth; worn. O Sept 24 (74) $325

Duvilliers, Francois

— Les Parcs et jardins. Paris, 1871-78. 2 parts in 2 vols. Folio, orig half cloth; minor rubbing & discoloration, front inner hinges cracked, Vol II shaken. With port & 80 hand-colored plans. Some foxing at ends. McCarty-Cooper copy. CNY Jan 25 (17) $5,000

Duyckinck, Evert Augustus, 1816-78

— History of the World.... NY, [1871]. 4 vols. 4to, orig half mor; scuffed. cb Feb 27 (23) $50

— National Portrait Gallery of Eminent Americans. NY, [1864-67]. 2 vols. 4to, half mor; 1 cover loose, others worn. sg Dec 5 (94) $130

Anr copy. Orig half mor; worn. With 151 plates. Some foxing. wa Sept 26 (588) $80

Anr copy. Mor gilt; worn, spines cracked, joints scuffed. With 119 plates. wa Feb 20 (125) $85

— Portrait Gallery of Eminent Men and Women of Europe and America. NY, [c.1873]. 2 vols. 4to, orig mor; scuffed. With 119 plates. F June 25 (722) $65

Dwiggins, William Addison. See: Limited Editions Club

Dwight, Timothy, 1752-1817

— Travels in New-England and New-York. L, 1823. 4 vols. 8vo, 19th-cent half calf; spines def. With port & 3 folding maps. sg June 18 (204) $80

Dyer, Frederick Henry

— A Compendium of the War of the Rebellion.... NY: Thomas Yoseloff, [1959]. 3 vols. 4to, cloth. bbc Feb 17 (55) $100

Dyer, Thomas H., 1804-88

— Pompeii Photographed. L, 1867. 4to, orig cloth; spine partly detached. With 18 mtd photos. Ck May 15 (95) £110

Anr copy. Orig cloth; hinges cracked, frontis partly detached. Some staining at end; half-title soiled. wa Mar 5 (613) $80

Dykes, E. Katherine. See: Dykes & Dykes

Dykes, Jeff

— Billy the Kid: The Bibliography of a Legend. Albuquerque, 1952. cb Oct 17 (267) $70

Anr copy. Wraps. sg Oct 31 (101) $110

— Fifty Great Western Illustrators: A Bibliographic Checklist. Flagstaff, [1975]. One of 200. 4to, cloth. sp Apr 16 (501) $60

Dykes, William Rickatson —& Dykes, E. Katherine

— Notes on Tulip Species. L, 1930. Folio, cloth, in worn d/j. With 54 colored plates. sg May 14 (210) $200

Anr copy. Orig cloth, in worn d/j with tape repairs on verso; edges rubbed & bumped. wa Dec 9 (654) $280

E

Eadmer, Monk of Canterbury, d.1124?

— Historiae novorum sive sui saeculi libri VI.... L, 1623. Folio, later calf; rebacked & corners repaiared. D1 and K4 with burnholes; E4 holed, all with slight loss. bba Nov 28 (222) £75 [Land]

Eardley-Wilmont, John Eardley. See: Wilmont, Sir John Eardley Eardley

Earhart, Amelia M., 1898-1937

— 20 Hrs. 40 Min.: Our Flight in the Friendship. NY & L, 1928. 1st Ed. In d/j. cb Nov 7 (38) $65

One of 150, sgd. Unopened. cb Nov 7 (37) $1,200

Earle Collection, Cyril

— The Earle Collection of Early Staffordshire Pottery. L, [1915]. One of 250. Folio, orig cloth; rubbed & marked. DW Oct 9 (855) £120

Anr copy. Cloth. Library markings. sg Sept 6 (51) $300

Early, Jubal Anderson, 1816-94

— A Memoir of the last Year of the War for Independence, in the Confederate States.... Toronto, 1866. 1st Ed. 8vo, modern cloth, orig paper wraps bound in. wa Dec 9 (367) $150

East India Company

— A True Relation of the Unjust, Cruell, and Barbarous Proceedings against the English at Amboyna.... L: H. Lownes for Nathaniel Newberry, 1624. 4to, modern half calf. Tp holed; A-A2 frayed; some discoloration. STC 7451. S May 14 (1283) £600 [Randall]

Eastern...

— Eastern Love [Oriental Tales]. L, 1927-30. One of 1,000. Trans by E. Powys Mathers; illus by Hester Sainsbury. 12 vols. Half lea gilt; spines soiled. K Sept 29 (253) $70

Anr copy. Half cloth. pnE Mar 11 (72) £55

Eastman, Mary Henderson, b.1818

— American Aboriginal Portfolio. Phila., [1853]. 4to, orig cloth; lower cover with discoloration, spine ends & corners worn. With engraved title & 26 plates. bbc Sept 23 (312) $475

Anr copy. Disbound; stained & soiled. With 26 plates. Sold w.a.f. O Feb 25 (68) $400

Anr copy. Orig cloth gilt; worn. With engraved title & 26 plates. Foxing throughout to text & plates. sg Dec 5 (95) $375

— Dahcotah; or, Life and Legends of the Sioux around Fort Snelling. NY, 1849.

12mo, orig cloth; front cover spotted, discoloration to lower left corner of lower cover, spine ends & corners worn with some chipping. Foxed. bbc Sept 23 (313) $160

— The Iris: an Illuminated Souvenir for MDCCCLII. Phila., 1852. 8vo, mor gilt; scuffed. Lacking presentation plate & frontis. cb Sept 26 (103) $770

Eaton, Amos, 1776-1842

— An Index to the Geology of the Northern States.... Leicester MA, 1818. 1st Ed. 8vo, contemp wraps. With folding plate. Some dampstaining. sg June 18 (206) $60

Eaton, Elon Howard

— Birds of New York. Albany, 1910-14. 1st Ed. 2 vols. 4to, cloth; bumped. Met Apr 28 (459) $80

Anr copy. Orig cloth. With 106 colored plates. NH Oct 6 (43) $80

Anr copy. Cloth. NH Aug 23 (68) $55

Anr copy. Cloth; worn. O Mar 31 (66) $50

Anr copy. Cloth; shaken. With 106 colored plates. sg Nov 14 (176) $225; sg May 14 (211) $225

Eaton, John Matthews

— A Treatise on the Art of Breeding and Managing ...Pigeons. L, 1858. 8vo, later cloth. With hand-colored frontis & 16 plates. K Mar 22 (345) $180

Anr copy. Later bdg. With hand-colored frontis & 16 plates only. K July 12 (506) $190

Eaton, Seymour

— More About Teddy B. and Teddy G. Phila., 1907. Illus by R. K. Culver. 4to, half cloth; bumped. sp Sept 22 (259) $120

— The Roosevelt Bears. Their Travels and Adventures. Phila., 1906. Illus by V. Floyd Campbell. 4to, bds; bumped. sp Sept 22 (260) $95

Eber, Paul, 1511-69

— Calendarium historicum.... Wittenberg: Georg Rhau, 1564. 8vo, contemp blind-tooled pigskin over wooden bds, with 1 catch. Tp soiled; wormed at end. sg Oct 24 (105) $650

Eberlein, Harold Donaldson. See: Richardson & Eberlein

Ebers, Georg —&
Guthe, Hermann

— Palaestina in Bild und Wort. Stuttgart & Leipzig, 1883-84. 2 vols. Folio, orig cloth. With 2 engraved titles, 2 frontises & 35 plates. bba Oct 24 (321) £170 [Khatib]

Anr copy. With frontises & 2 double-page maps. S July 1 (750) £200 [Ferber]

Eberstadt, Charles

— Lincoln's Emancipation Proclamation. [NY, 1950]. One of 200. 4to, bds. cb Sept 5 (131) $225

Eberstadt, Edward

— The Annotated Eberstadt Catalogues of Americana. NY, 1965. One of 750. 4 vols, including Index. cb Feb 27 (24) $325

Anr copy. Nos 103-138 (1935-1956). 4 vols. O Sept 24 (77) $200

Eccleston, Robert

— The Mariposa Indian War, 1850-1851.... Salt Lake City, 1957. One of 500. K Sept 29 (159) $50

Eckel, John C.

— The First Editions of the Writings of Charles Dickens. L, 1913. One of 250. 4to, orig half vellum. S May 13 (557) £120 [Crizen]

Anr copy. Orig half vellum, in chipped d/j. sg Oct 31 (102) $130; sg May 21 (212) $140

One of 750. Cloth, in d/j. cb Oct 17 (269) $150

Anr copy. Cloth. sg Oct 31 (103) $140

Anr Ed. NY & L, 1932. One of 250. Orig half mor gilt; extremities worn. DW Jan 29 (312) £160

Anr copy. Cloth, in d/j; worn. O Sept 24 (78) $160

One of 750. Orig mor, in d/j. bba Apr 9 (4) £150 [Tholstrup]

Anr copy. In d/j. cb Oct 17 (270) $250; sg Oct 31 (104) $150

— Prime Pickwicks in Parts.... NY & L, 1928. One of 400. Foreword by A. Edward Newton. sg Oct 31 (105) $100

Eckert, Allan W.

— The Owls of North America (North of Mexico). Garden City, 1974. One of 250. Illus by Karl Karalus. 4to, orig lea. bbc Sept 23 (247) $90

Eckert, H. A. —&
Monten, D.

— Das Deutsche Bundesheer. [Munich & Wurzburg, 1838-43]. 3 vols. Folio, Vol I in contemp mor gilt, Vols II & III in similar contemp calf gilt; rubbed. With 2 litho dedication leaves, 16 hand-colored plates of insignia Schemas & 401 hand-colored lithos of uniforms (the plates comprising 376 of the 385 German uniforms listed by Colas & 25 additional plates). Most plates with margins cut away & mtd; lacking tp & contents leaf; tp & most plates in Vol I stamped with initials P.P.V. surmounted by the Emperor's crown; a few plates soiled; 1 plate damaged in corners. Sold w.a.f. C May 20 (252) £5,800 [Schuster]

Eddison, E. R.

— The Worm Ouroboros. L: Jonathan Cape, [1922]. 1st Ed. In repaired d/j. sg June 11 (106) $200

Eddy, Mary Baker Glover, 1821-1910

— Science and Health. Bost., 1875. 1st Ed. 12mo, orig purple cloth; extremities worn. Library markings. sg Mar 5 (98) $425

Anr copy. Orig green cloth; spine ends repaired. Epstein copy. sg Apr 29 (135) $1,600

Subscription Ed. Bost, [1941]. one of 1,026. 4to, orig mor. sg Sept 26 (105) $850

Ede, Harold Stanley

— A Life of Gaudier-Brzeska. L, 1930. One of 350. Folio, cloth. Eva Le Gallienne's copy. sg Feb 6 (78) $90

Eden, Frederic Morton, 1766-1809

— The State of the Poor. L, 1797. 1st Ed. 3 vols. 4to, contemp calf gilt; rubbed. Lacking half-titles; some spotting; margins annotated. S July 21 (313) £7,000 [Quaritch]

Edgar, Matilda

— Ten Years of Upper Canada in Peace and War...the Ridout Letters. Toronto, 1890. 8vo, orig cloth. cb Jan 30 (45) $50

Edgerton, Harold E. —& Killian, James R.

— Flash! Seeing the Unseen by Ultra High-Speed Photography. Bost., [1939]. 4to, cloth. Frontis detached. bbc Feb 17 (203) $70

Anr copy. Cloth, in d/j. sg Oct 8 (34) $140

Edgeworth, Maria, 1767-1849

— Castle Rackrent, an Hibernian Tale. L, 1801. 3d Ed. 8vo, contemp calf gilt. bba July 23 (399) £80 [Jarndyce]

— The Parent's Assistant, or Stories for Children. L, 1820. 6 vols. 12mo, contemp half mor; lacking lower endpaper to Vol VI. Some spotting. bba July 23 (52) pS120 [Kitazawa]

— Patronage. L, 1814. 1st Ed. 4 vols. 12mo, contemp half calf; rubbed, joints worn. O May 26 (56) $70

Edinburgh...

— The Edinburgh Journal of Natural History, and of the Physical Sciences. Edin., [1835-40]. Ed by Wm. Macgillivray. 6 parts only. Folio, contemp half mor; rubbed. With 129 hand-colored plates. One plate partly detached. b Nov 18 (365) £150

Edmond, John Philip, 1850-1906. See: Dickson & Edmond

Edmondes, Sir Clement, 1564?-1622

— Observations upon the Five First Bookes of Caesars Commentaries. L, 1609 [engraved title dated 1604]. Issue without the 2 dedicatory leaves. Folio, contemp calf; rebacked. Tp stamped. STC 7491. W July 8 (104) £55

Edmonds, Harfield H. —& Lee, Norman N.

— Brook and River Trouting. Bradford: Pvtly ptd, [1916]. One of 1,000. Koopman copy. O Oct 29 (102) $85

Edmondson, John Ludlam. See: Sugden & Edmondson

Edmondson, Joseph, d.1786

— A Complete Body of Heraldry. L, 1780. 1st Ed. 2 vols. Folio, later half mor; worn. With port & 24 plates. DW Oct 2 (273) £55

Anr copy. Contemp calf; rubbed, joints split. S May 14 (948) £300 [Elliott]

Anr copy. Contemp calf; rebacked, worn, loose. S July 1 (1244) £180 [Milkain]

Edmunds, William H.

— Pointers and Clues to the Subjects of Chinese and Japanese Art. L, [1934-38]. One of 1,000. Prelims foxed. sg Feb 6 (79) $120

Out-of-series copy. In torn d/j. sg Apr 2 (205) $90

Education...

— The Education of a French Model...Alice Prin. NY, 1950. Trans by Samuel Putnam; intro by Ernest Hemingway. 4to, cloth, in d/j. cb Oct 25 (50) $80

Edward, P. I. See: Whitehead & Edward

Edward VI, King of England. See: Clement

Edward VIII, King of England. See: Windsor, Edward

Edwards, Bryan, 1743-1800

— An Historical Survey of the French Colony in the Island of St. Domingo. L, 1797. 1st Ed. 4to, recent cloth. Tp chipped; some foxing; map browned & foxed. bbc Dec 9 (326) $130

— The History, Civil and Commercial, of the British Colonies in the West Indies. L, 1793. 2 vols. 4to, disbound. With 2 frontises & 3 folding maps (some tears) & other maps & plates. Some foxing & soiling. Sold w.a.f. O Aug 25 (61) $250

2d of Vol III, 1st Ed of Vols I-II. L, 1793-1801. 3 vols. 8vo, modern calf. With 22 maps & plates. Several maps with tears at gutters. sg June 18 (207) $750

Anr Ed. L, 1801. 3 vols. 8vo, contemp calf; rubbed, joints of Vol I broken & crudely repaired, spine torn at edges. With port, 10 folding plates & 11 folding maps. pn Apr 23 (237) £400 [Storey]

Edwards, Edward, 1812-86

— Memoirs of Libraries: including a Handbook of Library Economy. L, 1859. 2 vols. 8vo, contemp half lea; Vol I backstrip partly detached. Library markings. sg May 21 (213) $80

Edwards, Edwin

— Old Inns. L, 1873-81. Ltd Ed. 3 vols in 2. Folio, contemp vellum gilt, 2 orig front wraps bound in; 1 wrap cut down & mtd, Vol II rebacked, soiled & rubbed. With 2 additional titles, dedication & 132 sheets of plates. pn Apr 23 (260) £400 [Hay]

Edwards, Elza Ivan

— Desert Voices: A Descriptive Bibliography. Los Angeles: Westernlore Press, 1958. One of 500. In d/j. cb Oct 17 (274) $95

Edwards, Ernest, Photographer

— Portraits of Men of Eminence.... L, 1863-64. Vols I-II. 8vo, mor gilt. With 48 photographs. K Dec 1 (366) $550

Edwards, Frank S.

— A Campaign in New Mexico with Colonel Doniphan. Phila., 1847. 1st Ed. 12mo, orig half cloth. With folding map. cb Sept 12 (58) $450

Edwards, George, 1694-1773

— Gleanings of Natural History. L, 1758-64. 1st Ed. Vols II & III only. Calf gilt. With 102 hand-colored plates. Sold w.a.f. C Oct 30 (188) £2,400 [Marshall]

— A Natural History of Uncommon Birds. L, 1743-76. ("A Natural History of Birds * Gleanings of Natural History.") 7 vols. 4to, contemp mor gilt. With uncolored plate of a Samoed & 362 hand-colored plates. Lacking frontis & port; subscribers lists in vols IV, VI & VII. C Oct 30 (264) £20,000 [David Ker]

Anr copy. With colored frontis & 362 hand-colored plates; port of a Samoyed (repeated) in Vol II; port of Edwards in Vol V. Text in English & French throughout. Lacking list of subscribers in Vols I & II; Vol I lacking last leaf, A Catalogue of the Birds Names..... S Nov 21 (9) £13,500 [Travers]

Anr copy. Modern mor gilt or contemp mor gilt. Repairs to Plates 223, 232, 242 & 246; Plate 229 with lower margin renewed; stamp of Glasgow Philosophical Society on a few titles & prelims; seems to be English text only. S Nov 21 (10) £8,500 [Germundson]

Anr Ed. L, [c.1752]-47-64. 7 vols in 4. 4to, contemp calf gilt; some joints split, spine & corners worn. With port & 362 hand-colored plates; port of a Samoyed in Vol II. Lacking frontis; tp to Vol III stained. Text in English & French throughout. S June 25 (18) £7,500 [Koromvokis]

Edwards, James

— A Companion from London to Brighthelmston in Sussex. L, 1801. 4to, 19th-cent half lea. With 6 plates & 13 maps, 10 double-page. Additional map bound in; dampstaining & foxing affecting some maps & plates; 1 plate laid down. pn May 14 (197) £260 [Burden]

Edwards, Jonathan, 1703-58

— A Careful and Strict Enquiry into the Modern Prevailing Notions of that Freedom of Will.... Bost.: S. Kneeland, 1754. 1st Ed. 8vo, contemp sheep; joints & spine ends rubbed. Marginal dampstaining at beginning. sg June 18 (208) $700

— Some Thoughts concerning the Present Revival of Religion in New-England. Lexington, 1803. 8vo, contemp sheep; rebacked with tape. Library markings. sg June 18 (209) $250

Edwards, Lionel

— My Hunting Sketch Book. L, 1928. One of 250. 2 vols. 4to, orig cloth. pnL Nov 20 (159) £150 [Nelson]

— A Sportsman's Bag. L, [1926]. One of 650. Folio, orig cloth, in d/j. With 18 mtd color plates. L Nov 14 (184) £370

Edwards, Lionel —& Wallace, Harold Frank

— Hunting & Stalking the Deer.... L, 1927. 4to, orig cloth. With 8 color plates. b Mar 11 (224) £110

Anr copy. Orig cloth; rubbed. Inscr by Sir Herbert Maxwell to his son. pn Mar 19 (369) £120 [Dawson]

Edwards, Philip Leget, 1812-69

— California in 1837. Sacramento, 1890. 1st Ed. 12mo, orig wraps; front wrap loose but intact. sg June 18 (63) $110

Edwards, Ralph. See: Macquoid & Edwards

Edwards, Sydenham Teak, 1769?-1819

— The Botanical Register. L, 1815-47. Vols 1-16. Contemp mor gilt; rubbed. With 3 uncolored & 1,392 hand-colored plates. Lacking plates 481, 818, 1081 & 1389. Sold w.a.f. S Nov 21 (11) £4,200 [Faupel]

Vols 1-7. L, 1815-21. Contemp half mor gilt. With 633 hand-colored plates, some folding. DW Mar 4 (106) £3,000

— Cynographia Britannica, Consisting of Coloured Engravings of...Dogs.... L, 1800. 4to, contemp calf; rubbed, new endpapers.

With 8 (of 12) hand-colored plates & with orig composite watercolor of 4 dogs inserted as frontis. Text of mastiff ends abruptly; plates not of uniform size; some spotting & staining. pn May 14 (170) £900

Edwards, William Frederic

— De l'influence des agens physiques sur la vie. Paris, 1824. 8vo, contemp half sheep gilt. Old stamp on tp. sg Nov 14 (32) $650

Edwords, Clarence E.

— Bohemian San Francisco.... San Francisco, 1914. cb Dec 19 (51) $75

Efros, Abram

— Kamerny Teatr. Moscow, 1934. 4to, orig cloth. DW Mar 11 (493) £200

Egan, Pierce, 1772-1849

— Boxiana; or Sketches of Antient & Modern Pugilism. L, 1818-29. Vols I-IV (of 5) only. 8vo, half mor gilt. sg Jan 9 (250) $275

— Finish to the Adventures of Tom, Jerry and Logic.... L, [1871]. Illus by Robert Cruikshank. 8vo, 20th-cent mor extra. With 36 hand-colored plates. cb Dec 5 (56) $130

Anr copy. Modern lea. With 36 plates. Frontis & tp mtd on stubs. K July 12 (184) $160

Anr Ed. L, 1889. 1st Issue. 8vo, modern mor gilt by Zaehnsdorf, orig wraps bound in; lacking upper wrap to Part 1. With hand-colored frontis & 35 plates. C May 20 (50) £580 [Drizen]

— Life in London. L, 1823. 8vo, orig bds; worn, upper cover detached. With 36 colored plates. Half-title torn. With ANs from George Cruikshank, 5 July 1868. O Nov 26 (56) $375

— The Life of an Actor. L, 1892. 8vo, half lea; rear hinge & front joint starting. sp Apr 16 (473) $125

Egan Imitations not by Egan

— Real Life in London. L, 1821-22 [but 1826?]. 1st Ed. 16 vols in 15. 8vo, contemp calf or half calf; some vols def. bba Jan 30 (394) £450 [Going]

Anr Ed. L, 1821-22. 2 vols. 8vo, later half mor gilt. With 29 (of 30) hand-colored plates. 1 badly pen-marked; all somewhat browned. DW Apr 8 (95) £135

Anr copy. Lea; rubbed, spines worn, 3 covers detached. With 32 hand-colored plates. K Mar 22 (130) $200

Anr copy. Cloth; worn & shaken. O Feb 25 (69) $120

— Real Life in Ireland. L, 1821. 1st Ed. 8vo, modern mor gilt by Riviere. With colored frontis & 17 (of 18) hand-colored plates. Offsetting from several plates. Sold w.a.f. sg Oct 17 (215) $225

Egan, William M.

— Pioneering the West, 1846-1878: Major Howard Egan's Diary.... Richmond UT: Howard R. Egan estate, 1917. Modern cloth. cb Nov 14 (52) $50

Ege, Otto F.

— Original Leaves from Famous Bibles, Nine Centuries 1121-1935 A.D. Cleveland, Ohio, [c.1950]. Compiled by Ege. Folio, loose in cloth box. With Preface leaf, 4 Ms & 56 ptd mtd leaves, each with descriptive caption.. With vellum leaf from a 13th-cent English Psalter with illuminated initial Q. Ck Nov 29 (81) £1,300

One of 50. Loose in cloth box. With 40 ptd & Ms leaves, each hinged to overmat. sg Nov 7 (78) $2,600

Egerton, Francis, Earl of Ellesmere, 1800-57

— Views in Palestine and Lebanon. [L, c.1845]. Oblong folio, contemp half mor; rebacked preserving orig spine. With 13 hand-colored plates, 7 before letters. Lacking tp & letterpress; some foxing. Holland House copy. S July 1 (752) £1,500 [Folios]

Egger, Hermann. See: Huelsen & Egger

Eginhartus

— Vita et gesta Karoli Magni. Cologne: I. Soter, 1521. 4to, contemp vellum with later paper jacket. C June 24 (306) £650 [Rosenthal]

Eglauer, Anton

— Die Missionsgeschichte spaeterer Zeiten. Augsburg: Nicolaus Doll, 1794-95. 3 vols. 12mo, contemp half sheep gilt. sg May 21 (35) $250

Ehninger, John W.

— Illustrations of Longfellow's Courtship of Miles Standish. NY, 1859. Oblong 4to, orig mor gilt. With 8 mtd albumen prints by Brady. Some foxing. O Aug 25 (39) $90

Ehrenburg, Ilya, 1891-1967

— Shest' poviestei olegkikh kontsakh. Moscow & Berlin, 1922. Illus by El Lissitzky. Half cloth; worn. With 6 illusts. sg Jan 30 (98) $1,400

Eiffel, Gustave, 1832-1923

— Nouvelles Recherches sur la resistance de l'air et l'aviation.... Paris, 1914. 2 vols. 4to, cloth; backstrips torn. bba Jan 30 (410) £200 [Greenwood]

Eight...

— Eight Harvard Poets. NY, 1917. 1st Ed. Inscr by John Dos Passos to Henry Tatnoll; also sgd by E. E. Cummings in 1939. Epstein copy. sg Apr 29 (123) $750

Einstein, Albert, 1879-1955

— Out of My Later Years. NY, [1950]. In chipped d/j. With cut signature dated 1952 mtd on tp. sg Nov 14 (233) $275

— Relativity.... L: Methuen, [1920]. Cloth; spine faded. sg Nov 14 (229) $200

Anr Ed. NY, 1920. sg Nov 14 (230) $120

— Zur einheitlichen Feldtheorie. Berlin, 1929. 4to, wraps. sg Nov 14 (232) $60

Einstein, Alfred, 1880-1952

— The Italian Madrigal. Princeton, 1949. 1st Ed. 3 vols. With 12 plates. LH May 17 (677) $140; pn Oct 24 (352) £110 [Cox]

Eisen, Gustav, 1847-1940

— The Great Chalice of Antioch.... NY, 1923. 2 vols. Folio, half mor. b June 22 (33) £90

Eisen, Gustav, 1847-1940 —& Kouchakji, Fahim

— Glass: its Origin, History.... NY, 1927. One of 525. 2 vols. 4to, orig half cloth; 1 joint broken. pn Sept 12 (85) £120

Anr copy. With 188 photographic plates. sg Feb 26 (80) $400

Anr copy. Orig half cloth; smudged. wa Dec 9 (427) $150

Eisenhower, Dwight David, 1890-1969

— Crusade in Europe. Garden City, 1948. One of 1,426. bbc Dec 9 (375) $600

Anr copy. Epstein copy. sg Apr 29 (136) $1,000

— Mandate for Change, 1953-56. NY, 1963. One of 1,434. br May 29 (82) $325

Anr copy. Inscr to C. D. Jackson. br May 29 (83A) $450

Eisler, Max

— Gustav Klimt. Eine Nachlese. Vienna, 1931. One of 200. Folio, loose as issued. With 15 plain & 30 color plates. Color plates 9 & 28 with margins trimmed to image & pasted down on bd; Plate 9 chipped at corner; some foxing. sg Sept 6 (170) $900

Eitner, Robert

— Bibliographie der Musik-Sammelwerke des XVI und XVII Jahrhunderts. Berlin, 1877. 8vo, contemp half lea; extremities worn, backstrip partly detached; marginalia. Yale Music Library release stamp; some marginalia. sg Oct 31 (107) $120

— Biographisch-bibliographisches Quellen Lexikon der Musiker und Musik-gelehrten.... Leipzig, 1900-4. 10 vols plus the 3-vol Supplement, 1912-16, by Springer et al. Together, 13 vols. Yale Music Library release stamp. sg Oct 31 (108) $225

Elements...

— Elements of Natural History: Being an Introduction to the Systema Naturae of Linnaeus. L, 1801-2. 2 vols. 8vo, orig bds; worn. With 12 folding plates. Some foxing & soiling. O Jan 14 (71) $50

Elgood, George S.

— Italian Gardens. L, 1907. Folio, orig cloth; sides discolored. L Nov 14 (396) £65

Elias, Julius

— Max Liebermann zu Hause. Berlin, 1918. Ltd Ed. Folio, orig half calf. With 2 orig sgd etchings by Liebermann. cb Sept 5 (59) $750

Eliot, George, 1819-80

— Adam Bede. Edin. & L, 1859. 1st Ed. 3 vols. 8vo, orig cloth; soiled, corners bumped. Ck July 10 (241A) £420

Anr copy. Orig cloth; rubbed. Lacking 16-page publisher's catalogue. Ewing-Manney copy. P Oct 11 (129) $3,750

Anr copy. Orig cloth; rubbed, color re-freshed. Ewing-Manney copy. P June 17 (191) $1,500

— Daniel Deronda. Edin. & L, 1876. 1st Ed in Book form, 1st Issue. 4 vols. 8vo, contemp half calf; spines very worn, extremities rubbed. Ck July 10 (241G) £60

2d Issue of Vols II & IV. Orig cloth; rubbed. Unopened copy. Manney copy. P Oct 11 (135) $7,500

— Felix Holt the Radical. Edin. & L, 1866. 1st Ed. 3 vols. 8vo, orig cloth; soiled. Some spotting. Ck July 10 (241E) £120

Anr copy. Orig cloth, Carter's B bdg. Manney copy. P Oct 11 (133) $1,300

— Middlemarch. Edin. & L, 1871. 1st Ed in Book form. 4 vols. 8vo, contemp half mor; extremities rubbed, corners bumped. Ck July 10 (241F) £190

Anr copy. Orig cloth; some inner hinges repaired, color renewed at extremities. Borowitz-Manney copy. P Oct 11 (134) $5,500

Anr copy. Mor gilt by Bedford; some joints splitting. S Nov 14 (558) £450 [Frew MacKenzie]

— The Mill on the Floss. Edin. & L, 1860. 1st Ed. 3 vols. 8vo, orig cloth; rubbed, 2 spines wrinkled. bba July 23 (416) £170 [Scott]

Anr copy. Orig cloth; soiled, corners bumped. Ck July 10 (241B) £260

Anr copy. Orig cloth, Carter's B bdg; inner hinges & spines repaired. ALs, sgd "MELewes" laid in. Manney copy. P Oct

11 (130) $2,500

1st American Ed. NY, 1860. 8vo, orig cloth. NH Oct 6 (108) $105

— Romola. L, 1863. 2 vols in 1. 8vo, orig cloth; soiled, extremities rubbed. Ck July 10 (241D) £380

1st Ed in Book form. 3 vols. 8vo, orig cloth; inner hinges repaired, some color renewed on extremities. Manney copy. P Oct 11 (132) $1,500

Anr Ed. Leipzig: Tauchnitz, 1863. 2 vols. 12mo, orig vellum gilt. LH Dec 11 (107) $60

— Scenes of Clerical Life. Edin., 1858. 1st Ed. 2 vols. 8vo, modern half mor gilt by Bayntun. bba July 23 (454) £480 [Jarndyce]

Anr copy. Orig cloth; front hinge of Vol I split. Ck July 10 (241) £1,300

Anr copy. Orig cloth; some color renewed on extremities. Manney copy. P Oct 11 (128) $14,000

— Silas Marner. Edin. & L, 1861. 1st Ed. 8vo, orig cloth. bba June 25 (205) £1,000 [Jarndyce]

Anr copy. Orig cloth; worn & rubbed. cb Dec 19 (52) $65

Anr copy. Orig cloth; soiled, corners bumped. Ck July 10 (241C) £500

Anr copy. Orig cloth, Carter's B bdg; extremities rubbed. Half-title torn at inner margin. Manney copy. P Oct 11 (131) $2,750

— Works. Bost., 1887. 12 vols. 8vo, half calf by MacDonald. Plates in 2 states. wa Mar 5 (29) $425

Illustrated Cabinet Ed. NY, [c.1900]. 24 vols. 8vo, half calf. sg Mar 5 (100) $450

Anr Ed. Bost., 1908. 10 vols. 8vo, half calf. LH May 17 (626) $325

L.p. Ed, one of 750. 25 vols. 8vo, half mor gilt; dampstained. sg Oct 17 (217) $700

Eliot, Thomas Stearns, 1888-1965

— Animula. [L, 1929]. 1st Ed, one of 400 L.p. copies. Illusts by Gertrude Hermes. Orig bds; soiled. sg Dec 12 (96) $250

— Ash Wednesday. L & NY, 1930. One of 600. In worn d/j. S Nov 14 (629) £350 [Shepherd]

Anr copy. Epstein copy. sg Apr 29 (138) $650

— Ezra Pound: His Metric and his Poetry. NY, 1917 [pbd Jan 1918]. 1st Ed. Orig bds. K July 12 (186) $180

— Four Quartets. NY: Harcourt Brace, [1943]. 1st Ed, 1st ptg, with the words "first American edition" on verso of tp. In d/j. Epstein copy. sg Apr 29 (140) $1,200

Anr Ed. L, [1960]. One of 290, sgd. Folio, orig parchment-backed bds. S July 21 (110) £650 [Barnitt]

— Journey of the Magi. NY: Rudge, 1927. 1st American Ed, One of 27. Orig wraps. sg Dec 12 (97) $900

— Murder in the Cathedral. Canterbury, 1935. 1st Acting Ed, one of 750. Orig wraps; soiled, torn at backstrip. S May 13 (652) £450 [Jolliffe]

— Old Possum's Book of Practical Cats. L, 1939. 1st Ed. In d/j; stained. bba Oct 10 (436) £85 [Ball]

— Poems. L: Hogarth Press, 1919. 1st Ed, 1st State, with "capitaux" on p. 13. Orig wraps; "A fine copy". Epstein copy. sg Apr 29 (141) $5,400

— Poems 1909-1925. L, 1925. In d/j. sg Dec 12 (99) $175

— Prufrock and Other Observations. L: The Egoist, 1917. 1st Ed, one of 500. Very skillfully reset into the orig wraps. Epstein copy. sg Apr 29 (142) $6,000

— The Sacred Wood. L, [1920]. 1st Ed. sg Dec 12 (100) $50

— Selected Essays, 1917-1932. L, 1932. One of 115. Orig vellum; backstrip faded. Epstein copy. sg Apr 29 (143) $1,600

— A Song for Simeon. L, [1928]. 1st Ed, 2d Issue. One of 500 L.p. copies. Orig bds; browned at edges. sg June 11 (109) $200

— Triumphal March. [L, 1931]. 1st Ed, one of 300. Orig bds. DW Oct 2 (340) £75

— The Waste Land. L, 1922. Wraps. In: The Criterion, Oct 1922, Vol I, No 1. sg June 11 (110) $425

1st Ed in Book form, 1st Issue. NY, 1922. one of 1,000. In d/j. Epstein copy. sg Apr 29 (144) $3,000
2d State. In d/j with small chips. pba July 9 (82) $2,500
Later State. sg Dec 12 (1001) $650

Elizabeth, Princess, Daughter of George III

— A Series of Etchings, Representing the Power and Progress of Genius. L, 1806. Folio, later half mor. With dedication (sgd) & 25 plates. Foxed. pn Apr 23 (200) £130 [Finney]

Elkus, Richard J. See: Grabhorn Printing

Elliot, Daniel Giraud, 1835-1915

— Bucerotidae. L, 1877-82. ("A Monograph of the Bucerotidae, or Family of the Hornbills.") Folio, modern half mor by Sangorski & Sutcliffe, orig wraps bound in. With 3 uncolored plates, each in duplicate, & with 57 lithos in uncolored & colored states, the latter being pattern plates before letters; also 6 additional proof plates on india paper. Pattern plates soiled or stained; a few leaves of text in facsimile. Unique copy with orig pattern plates. S Nov 21 (13) £3,000 [Aristophanous]

— Felidae. [L], 1878-83. ("A Monograph of the Felidae or Family of the Cats.") 1st Ed. Folio, mor gilt by Zaehnsdorf; extremities rubbed. With 43 hand-colored plates. Some foxing & dust-soiling. P June 17 (192) $35,000

— The New and Heretofore Unfigured Species of the Birds of North America. NY, [1866]-69. 2 vols. Folio, contemp half mor gilt. With 72 hand-colored plates plus additional plate of Parus Occidentalis bound at beginning of Vol I. Plate of Baird's Cormorant torn across center & repaired. C Oct 30 (190) £4,000 [Shapero]

Anr copy. Contemp half lea gilt; extremities worn, Vol II rear cover detached. With 72 hand-colored plates. sg Feb 13 (152) $8,500

— Paradiseidae. [L], 1873. ("A Monograph of the Paradiseidae, or Birds of Paradise.") Folio, later half mor gilt; extremities rubbed. With 1 plain & 36 hand colored plates, mtd on guards throughout. Repaired tears to blank lower margins of 2 prelim leaves. C May 20 (174) £11,500

Anr copy. Contemp mor gilt by S. Hogg, with monogram AEK in center of each cover. With 1 plain & 36 hand colored plates. S June 25 (64) £10,000 [Wheldon]

— Phasianidae. NY, [1870]-72. ("A Monograph of the Phasianidae, or Family of the Pheasants.") 2 vols in 1. Folio, contemp mor gilt by S. Hogg with large monogram AEK in center of each cover. With 79 hand-colored plates & 2 uncolored plates. Plate of feathers in Vol I folded at foot & with short tear. S June 25 (53) £44,000 [Wheldon]

— Pittidae. L, [1861]-63. ("A Monograph of the Pittidae, or Family of Ant Thrushes.") 1st Ed. 5 (of 6) parts; lacking Part 6 orig half mor; covers detached; lacking lower cover of Part 1 and upper cover of Part 3. With 23 (of 31) hand-colored plates. CNY Dec 5 (292) $2,000

— Tetraoninae. NY, [1864]-65. ("A Monograph of the Tetraoninae, or Family of Grouse.") 5 parts in 4. Folio, orig half mor; broken. With 27 hand-colored plates and 2 plates of eggs. CNY Dec 5 (293) $5,500

Elliot, John, 1791-1868

— An Account of the Nature and Medicinal Virtues of the Principal Mineral Waters of Great Britain and Ireland.... L, 1781. 8vo, contemp calf; rebacked. Spotted. DW Nov 6 (345) £90

Elliot, Capt. Robert

— Views in the East Comprising India, Canton, and the Shores of the Red Sea. L, 1833. 2 vols in 1. Folio, contemp mor gilt by S. Wright. Some spotting. Ck May 15 (97) £900

Anr copy. 19th-cent calf gilt; front cover loose. sg Jan 9 (71) $2500

Elliott, Charles Boileau

— Travels in the Three Great Empires of Austria, Russia, and Turkey. L, 1838. 2 vols. 8vo, contemp calf gilt. With frontises & 2 maps. S June 30 (286) £600 [Maggs]

Elliott, Mary Belson

— Rural Employments, or a Peep into Village Concerns. L: Wm. Darton, 1820. 12mo, contemp half calf; worn. With frontis & 17 plates. Plates cropped; 1 leaf with marginal tear; some leaves loose. bbc Apr 27 (337) $200

Ellis, Edward Sylvester, 1840-1916

— Seth Jones; or the Captives of the Frontier. NY: Irwin P. Beadle, [1860]. 12mo, orig ptd wraps; spine chipped. Some foxing. Epstein copy. sg Apr 29 (146) $600

Ellis, Frederick Startridge

— The History of Reynard the Fox. L, 1897. Illus by Walter Crane. 8vo, cloth; soiled. Inscr to John Lane, 2 Jan 1901. sp June 18 (145) $60

Ellis, Havelock, 1859-1939. See: Grabhorn Printing

Ellis, Henry, 1721-1806

— Voyage de la Baye de Hudson. Paris, 1749. 12mo, contemp sheep; worn. With folding map & 10 folding plates. sg June 18 (210) $250

— A Voyage to Hudson's Bay.... L, 1748. 1st Ed. 8vo, contemp calf; rebacked. With folding map & 9 plates. tear in map repaired. S Nov 15 (1225) £300 [Walcot]

Anr copy. With folding map & 9 plates, 5 folding. Split in 1 plate repaired. S Feb 26 (735) £450 [Baring]

Anr copy. Tp & folding map washed. S May 14 (1251) £360 [Beeleigh Abbey]

Anr copy. Some discoloration. S May 14 (1309) £320 [Walcot]

Anr copy. Contemp half calf; front hinges cracked, worn, some leaves starting. Foxed throughout. wd June 12 (379) $400

Anr copy. Modern calf gilt. With folding map & 9 plates. wd June 12 (380) $800

Ellis, Sir Henry, 1777-1869

— Original Letters Illustrative of English History. L, 1825-46. 2d Ed of 1st Series, 1st Eds of 2d & 3d Series. 1st-3d Series. 11 vols. 8vo, mor gilt by Winstanley. sg Mar 5 (102) $350

Ellis, John, Cartographer

— English Atlas, or a Complete Choreography of England and Wales. L, 1766. Oblong 4to, contemp calf; rubbed. With 54 maps on 27 leaves.folding Some repairs & browning; 1st 2 maps def. pn Apr 23 (298) £550

Ellis, John, 1710-76

— An Essay towards a Natural History of the Corallines.... L, 1755. 4to, contemp calf; rebacked, old spine preserved. With frontis & 38 plates, 4 folding. 1 or 2 plates waterstained in outer margin. bba Sept 5 (38) £250 [Hay Cinema]

— An Historical Account of Coffee. L, 1774. 4to, later half vellum. With 2 copies of the folding plate, 1 hand-colored. bba Sept 5 (37) £1,700 [Kunkler]

— The Natural History of Many Curious and Uncommon Zoophytes.... L, 1786. 4to, contemp half calf; rubbed, head of spine repaired. With 63 plates. Browned; some spotting & cropping. bba May 14 (473) £100 [Elliott]

Ellis, William, 1794-1872

— A Journal of a Tour Around Hawaii.... Bost., 1825. 12mo, orig half cloth; needs rebdg. With folding map & 5 plates. Some foxing & browning. sg Dec 5 (118) uS110

— Narrative of a Tour through Hawaii. L, 1826. 1st Ed. 8vo, later half calf; modern cloth. With folding map & 7 plates. cb Jan 30 (46) $170

Anr copy. Early calf; rebacked. Some scorch marks; occasional discoloration. kh Nov 11 (478) A$100

Anr copy. Modern half mor gilt. With folding map & 7 plates. sg June 18 (276) $550

— Polynesian Researches.... NY, 1833. 4 vols. 12mo, orig cloth. Library markings. sg June 18 (211) $90

Ellison, Fred E.

— Etchings of Bath. Bristol, 1888. Ltd Ed. Folio, orig cloth; worn. With 24 plates. DW Nov 6 (117) £55

Ellison, Harlan

— Dangerous Visions. Garden City, 1967. In chipped d/j. pba July 9 (83) $150

— Shatterday. Bost., 1980. In d/j. Sgd. cb Sept 19 (50) $50

Ellison, Ralph

— Invisible Man. NY, [1952]. In repaired d/j. sg June 11 (107) $275

Ellms, Charles

— The Pirates Own Book, or Authentic Narratives of...Sea Robbers. Portland ME, 1856. 12mo, cloth. sp Feb 6 (403) $70

Ellsworth, Lincoln. See: Amundsen & Ellsworth

Elman, Robert

— The Great American Shooting Prints. NY, 1972. One of 450. Oblong folio, half lea; worn. With 72 colored plates. Koopman copy. O Oct 29 (103) $140

Elmes, James, 1782-1862. See: Shepherd & Elmes

Elrington, J. F.

— Practical Hints on Pyrotechny.... Dublin, 1850. 12mo, orig cloth. With 6 lithos. sg Nov 14 (287) $140

Elton, Charles I. & Mary A.

— The Great Book-Collectors. L, 1893. One of 150. 8vo, bdg not stated. cb Oct 17 (280) $55

Eluard, Paul, 1895-1952
See also: Bellmer & Eluard

— Capitale de la Douleur. Paris, 1926. One of 109 on papier verge Lafuma-Navarre. 4to, mor extra by H. Duhayon, orig wraps bound in. Inserted is autograph draft of a poem of 3 stanzas by Eluard. S May 28 (314) £800 [Beres]

— Le Dur Desir de Durer. Paris, 1946. One of 25, sgd by author & artist. Illus by Marc Chagall. Folio, unsewn in orig wraps. With colored frontis & 25 illusts. With orig sgd ink drawing laid in; Chagall's signature on limitation page embellished with a small ink drawing of a woman's head & a cow's head. P June 17 (148) $3,500

One of 330. Mor gilt by Bayntun Riviere. With colored frontis & 25 illusts. S Dec 5 (304) £450 [Panini]

— Poesie et verite 1942. Paris, 1947. One of 184. Illus by Oscar Dominguez. 4to, Loose as issued. CGen Nov 18 (371) SF3,000

— Voir. Geneva & Paris, 1948. Folio, wraps. sg Feb 6 (82) $110

— Les Yeux fertiles. Paris, 1936. One of 200 hors commerce. Illus by Pablo Picasso. Inscr by Eluard. CGen Nov 18 (370) SF3,400

Elwes, Henry John, 1846-1922

— A Monograph of the Genus Lilium. L, [1877]-80. With: Grove, Arthur & Cotton, A. D. A Supplement to Elwes' Monograph of the Genus Lilium. L, 1933-40. 2 vols. Folio, contemp half mor gilt & half mor. Monograph with 48 hand-colored lithos, map & photographic plate (detached & spotted); Supplement with 30 hand-colored lithos. S Nov 21 (16) £6,500

Anr copy. Without supplements. Folio, later half mor gilt; soiled. With map, photographic plate, map & 48 hand-colored lithos. S June 25 (19) £5,500 [Ogasawava]

Elwes, Henry John, 1846-1922 —& Henry, Augustine

— The Trees of Great Britain and Ireland. Edin., 1906-13. 8 vols, including index. 4to, half mor gilt by Sotheran, ptd wraps to the parts bound at end of index vol. C Oct 30 (265) £600 [Hayley]

Emblemata...

— Emblemata Selectiora. Amst.: Franciscus van der Plaats, 1704. 4to, 19th-cent half mor gilt; extremities rubbed. With 38 plates. Plate 28 trimmed & mtd; minor marginal repairs on a few text leaves. sg Mar 12 (75) $475

Embury, Emma C.

— American Wild Flowers in Their Native Haunts. NY, 1845. 4to, orig mor gilt; spine lacking. With 20 colored plates. F Sept 26 (172) $140

Emerson, Ralph Waldo, 1803-82

See also: Bremer Press; Doves Press; Limited Editions Club

— An Address Delivered before the Senior Class in Divinity College, Cambridge. Bost., 1838. 8vo, orig wraps; hole in rear wrap. sg Mar 5 (103) $225

— Essays [First Series]. Bost., 1841. 1st Ed. 8vo, orig cloth; spine ends worn. Epstein copy. sg Apr 29 (147) $750

— Poems. Bost., 1847. 1st American Ed. 12mo, Modern cloth; worn. O Aug 25 (63) $100

— [Seven Essays] L, 1908. 8vo, mor gilt by Zaehnsdorf, orig upper wrap preserved. CNY Dec 5 (450) $750

— Society and Solitude: Twelve Chapters. Bost., 1870. 1st Ed, 1st Issue. 12mo, orig cloth; spine chipped. Inscr to Charles W. Dabney, 4 Mar 1870. P June 17 (193) $1,800

— Works. L, 1882-93. Riverside Ed, One of 25; Vol 12 is 1 of 250. 12 vols. 8vo, calf extra by Zaehnsdorf; extremities rubbed. sg Mar 5 (105) $1,200

Emerson, William, b.1873 —& Gromort, Georges

— Old Bridges of France: A Series of Historical Examples.... NY, 1925. One of 1,000. 4to, bdg not described. Some waterstaining to bdg & front matter. sp June 18 (206) $65

Emmons, Ebenezer, 1799-1863

— Agriculture of New-York. Albany, 1851. Vol III (of 5) only, in 2 vols. 4to, orig cloth; worn. With engraved titles & 100 hand-colored plates. Many plates stained. S May 14 (1029) £520 [Elliott]

Emmons, Samuel Franklin

— Map of Alaska showing Known Gold-Bearing Rocks. Wash., 1898. 8vo, modern cloth. With large folding map. Library markings. sg June 18 (375) $250

Emory, William Hemsley

— Notes of a Military Reconnoissance, from Fort Leavenworth...to San Diego.... Wash., 1848. House Issue. 8vo, cloth. With folding map in front pocket. Library markings. 30th Congress, 1st Session, H of R Exec. Doc 41. sg June 18 (212) $375

Senate Issue. Orig cloth; worn. With 40 plates, 3 full-page maps & large folded map in rear pocket. Some foxing; large map with fold breaks; a few plates detached. 30th Congress, 1st Session, Sen. Exec. Doc. 7. bbc Sept 23 (315) $225

Anr copy. With 40 plates & 3 battle-plans. Lacking large folding map from rear pocket. cb Nov 14 (55) $110

Anr copy. Orig cloth; rebacked. Lacking the first map. 30th Congress, 1st Session, Sen. Exec. Doc. 7. cb Feb 12 (11) $200

Anr copy. Lacking the 2 folding maps. cb Feb 12 (21) $350

Anr copy. Later calf; extremities worn. 30th Congress, 1st Session, Sen. Exec. Doc. 7. sg June 18 (213) $150

— Report on the United States and Mexican Boundary Survey.... Wash., 1857-59. House Issue. 3 vols. Modern half lea. cb Feb 12 (23) $2,000

Anr copy. 2 vols in 1. Some plates loose. sp Sept 22 (25) $130

Encyclopaedia...

— Encyclopaedia of Sport. L, 1897-98. Bound in 2 vols. Half mor gilt by Bumpus, 2 orig wraps bound in. b June 22 (374) £100

Anr copy. 4 vols. 8vo, contemp half mor, orig upper covers bound in. Ck Sept 6 (18) £90

— Encyclopaedia Judaica. Das Judentum in Geschichte und Gegenwart. Berlin, [1928-34]. Vols I-X (all pbd). 4to, orig half lea;

def. HH May 12 (934) DM1,100

Encyclopaedia Britannica

— Encyclopaedia Britannica. Edin., 1771. 1st Ed. 3 vols. 4to, contemp lea. With 160 plates & 3 chemical tables. Lacking the grammatical table. sg May 7 (101) $11,000

3d Ed. Dublin, 1790. 18 vols. 4to, contemp calf; worn, covers detached. Many defects, including loss of leaves at front & rear of some vols. Sold w.a.f. DW Jan 29 (229) £105

Anr Ed. Edin., 1797-1803. 18 vols of text & 2 vols of plates. 4to, contemp calf; rubbed. With port & 542 plates; lacking plates 25, 58, 59, 418 & 503 but with 5 additional plates. S July 1 (941) £750 [Lerner]

4th Ed. L, 1815. 20 vols. 4to, contemp half calf; worn, some spines or covers detached. Some foxing. Sold w.a.f. O Aug 25 (64) $200

9th Ed. L, 1875-1903. 35 vols. 4to, orig half mor; rubbed, some covers detached. b Nov 18 (208) £100

Anr copy. Orig half mor; 1 cover detached, rubbed. b Nov 18 (209) £110

Anr Ed. L, 1910-22. 29 vols. Folio, orig lea; worn, some hinges cracked. sg May 21 (214) $60

11th Ed. L, 1910-11. 29 vols, including Index. Cloth. br May 29 (77) $175

Anr copy. Orig half mor gilt. DW Mar 4 (287) £105

Anr Ed. NY, 1910-22. 29 vols plus 4 supplements, in 16 vols. Orig half mor; rubbed, some spines worn with loss. bba May 14 (177) £110 [Corbett]

Anr copy. 29 vols. Orig mor. cb Sept 5 (33) $140

Anr copy. Lea gilt. sg Oct 31 (109) $400

13th Ed. NY, 1910-29. 29 vols plus 3 Supplements. Orig mor, Supplements in dif bdg; some spine ends frayed. wa Mar 5 (104) $300

Anr Ed. Chicago, 1974. 30 vols. 4to, orig syn. W July 8 (6) £120

Encyclopedia...

— Encyclopedia of World Art. NY, 1959-68. 15 vols. 4to, orig cloth. LH May 17 (673) $275

Anr copy. Orig cloth; soiled & marked, ends rubbed. wa Apr 9 (269) $375

Enders, John Ostrom

— Random Notes on Hunting. Hartford: Pvtly ptd, 1955. One of 300. Inscr. Koopman copy. O Oct 29 (104) $50

Endters, Johann A. See: Ernesti, Johann Heinrich Gottfried

Enemy...

— The Enemy: A Review of Art and Literature. L, 1927-29. Ed by Wyndham Lewis. Nos 1-3 (all pbd). Orig wraps; soiled. DW Apr 8 (534) £65

Enfield, William, 1741-97

— Institutes of Natural Philosophy.... L, 1785. 4to, contemp half calf; rubbed, rebacked. With 11 folding plates. bba Sept 5 (204) £110 [P & P Books]

2d Ed. L, 1799. 4to, contemp calf; rubbed, rebacked. With 11 folding plates. bba Nov 28 (156) £75 [Howard]

Engel, Samuel, 1702-84

— Essai sur cette question: Quand et comment l'Amerique a-t-elle ete peuple d'hommes et d'animaux? Amst., 1767. 5 vols in 4. 4to, contemp mor gilt. Ck Oct 31 (11) £350

Engelbach, Lewis

— Naples and the Campagna Felice. L: Ackermann, 1815. 8vo, later half mor gilt. With hand-colored additional title, 15 plates, 2 hand-colored maps & additional mtd port of the author. C May 20 (51) £480 [Spelman]

Engelhardt, Zephyrin, 1851-1934

— The Franciscans in California. Harbor Springs MI, 1897. 8vo, modern half mor. sg June 18 (64) $70

Engelmann, Godefroy

— Manuel du dessinateur lithographe. Paris, 1822. 8vo, wraps. With litho half-title & title & 13 litho plates. Some spotting. Schlosser copy. P June 17 (540) $1,600

— Recueil d'essais lithographiques dans les differents genres de dessin.... Paris: chez l'auteur, [1816]. Bound after: Institut Royal de France: Academie des Beaux-Arts. Rapport sur la lithographie et particulierement sur un recueil de dessins lithographies, par M. Engelmann. Paris, 1816. 4to, early wraps. With 10 litho plates. Schlosser copy. P June 17 (539) $1,400

Engelmann, Gustav. See: Sazerac & Engelmann

Engels, Friedrich

— Der Ursprung der Familie, des Privateigenthums und des Staats.. Zurich: Hottingen, 1884. 8vo, orig cloth. Margins of 1st gathering strengthened. Sheets of the 1st Ed bound with other works as Vol XI of the Internationale Bibliothek. C June 24 (127) £800 [Shapero]

England

— A Complete Collection of State Trials, and Proceedings for High Treason. L, 1719. 4 vols in 5. Folio, library cloth. Library stamps. bba Feb 27 (42) £130 [Lawbook Exchange]

— A List of all the Officers of the Army and Royal Marines. L, [1801-02]. 2 vols. Folio, contemp mor gilt; Vol I dampstained & with def stitching. L.p. copy on thick paper. S June 25 (151) £220 [McCormick]

— Rules and Regulations for the Sword Exercise of the Cavalry. L, 1796. 8vo, contemp bds; needs rebdg. With 29 plates. sg Mar 26 (279) $140

Laws & Statutes

— An Act for Granting certain Duties in the British Colonies and Plantations in America.... L, 1764. Folio, disbound. 4 George III, cap. 15. sg Dec 5 (21) $200

— An Act for the Abolishing the Kingly Office in England, Ireland, and the Dominions.... L: for Edward Husband, 19 Mar 1648/49. Single sheet, folio, framed. Wing E-1086. Ck Oct 18 (137) £300

Anr copy. In cloth folder; rebacked. Wing E-1086. S July 1 (1096) £220 [Quaritch]

— An Act for the Preservation of...Pine-Trees growing in Her Majesties Colonies of New Hampshire, the Massachusetts-Bay...for the Masting Her Majesties Navy. L, 1711. Folio, disbound. 9 Anne, cap. 22. sg Dec 5 (18) $450

— [George III] An Act for Granting and Applying certain Stamp Duties...in America.... [Bost: R. & S. Draper & Green & Russel, 1765]. 11 leaves. Folio, disbound. Some fraying; final leaf with marginal tear touching 1 letter. Manney copy. P Oct 11 (1287) $4,750

— The Statutes Made and Established from the Time of Kyng Henry the Thirde, unto...Henry VIII.... [L: T. Berthelet, 1543]. Vol I (of 2) only. Folio, contemp calf; rebacked, rubbed. Lacking colophon leaf; library markings. bba Feb 27 (37) £580 [Sokol]

Parliament

— An Ordinance by the Lords and Commons for the Preservation and Keeping Together for Publique Use, such Books, Evidences, Records and Writings Sequestred.... L, 1643. 4to, modern half mor. bba June 25 (83) £300 [Johnson]

— Speeches and Passages of this Great and Happy Parliament. L: W. Cooke, 1641. 4to, lea; rebacked, extremities worn. Tp soiled & frayed; minor damage to several leaves. NH Aug 23 (168) $120

— George III. - His Majesty's most gracious Speech...Thursday October 31, 1776 [news of the war in America, commenting on the audacity of the Declaration of Independence]. Phila.,[1776]. Single sheet, 8vo. CNY June 9 (214) $1,300

Proclamations

— [George III] Declaring the Cessation of Arms...agreed upon between His Majesty, the...King of Spain, the States General of the United Provinces, and the United States of America.... L: Eyre & Strahan, 1783. 483mm by 337mm, framed. A few holes where formerly folded, costing 1 letter & touching a few others; some repairs & stains. P June 16 (217) $15,500

Englefield, Sir Henry Charles, 1752-1822

— A Description of the Principal Picturesque Beauties...of the Isle of Wight. L, 1816. 1st Ed. 4to, contemp half mor; worn. With 74 plates (9 folding, 1 hand-colored) & 3 folding maps (1 hand-colored). W July 8 (211) £450

— Ancient Vases from the Collection.... L, 1848. Illus by Henry Moses. 4to, orig cloth; edges worn. With engraved title, port & 51 plates. sg Feb 6 (83) $475

— Ancient Vases from the Collection.... L, 1848. Illus by Henry Moses. 4to, orig cloth; spine ends worn, hinges tended. With frontis & 51 plates. sg Sept 6 (100) $225

Anr copy. Some foxing. sg Apr 2 (112) $400

— Vases from the Collection.... L, 1819. By Henry Moses. 4to, old bds; broken, lacking spine. With 39 plates. O Mar 31 (67) $310

English...

— English Cyclopaedia: a New Dictionary of Universal Knowledge. L, [n.d.]. Ed by Charles Knight. 2 vols. 4to, half lea. sp Apr 16 (301) $95

— The English Dialect Dictionary. L, 1898-1905. Ed by J. Wright. 6 vols, including Supplement. 4to, library cloth. bba Nov 28 (390) £120 [Bernard]

Anr copy. Contemp half mor; worn, some covers almost detached. Lacking half-title; library markings. bba June 11 (67) £100 [C. Smith]

— The English Pilot. L, 1689. ("The English Pilot. The Fourth Book, Describing the West-India Navigation, from Hudsons-Bay to the River Amazones....") Folio, modern calf by Sangorski & Sutcliffe. With 15 charts. Lacking A1 blank & at least 7 charts; long tear to a fold of the large folding chart. DuPont copy. CNY Oct 8

(101) $36,000

English, Harriet

— Conversations and Amusing Tales. L, 1799. 4to, contemp half calf; joints split. With frontis, 12 plates & 2 engraved leaves of music. Lacking half-title; some soiling. ESTC t034058. bba July 23 (192) £150 [James]

English Poets

— The Works of the English Poets. L, 1790. Prefaces by Samuel Johnson. 74 (of 75) vols (lacking Vol VI). 8vo, 18th-cent mor gilt; spines rubbed. DW Mar 4 (223) £270

Anr Ed. L, 1810. 21 vols. 8vo, 19th-cent sheep gilt; extremities rubbed. sg Mar 5 (145) $475

Enlart, Camille, 1862-1927

— L'Art gothique et la renaissance en Chypre. Paris, 1899. 8vo, orig ptd wraps; spines weak. Inscr to the Count de Barthelemy. S June 30 (27) £1,300 [Bank of Cyprus]

Enschede, Charles, 1855-1919

— Typefoundries in the Netherlands.... Haarlem, 1978. Folio, orig half pigskin. pba July 23 (66) $250

Ensko, Stephen G. C.

— American Silversmiths and Their Marks. NY: Pvtly ptd, 1927-48. 3 vols. Half cloth. Library markings. sp Feb 6 (251) $200

Entick, John, 1703?-73

— The General History of the Late War.... L, 1763-64. 5 vols. 8vo, contemp calf; rubbed. With 8 folding maps & 41 ports. Some foxing. O May 26 (58) $550

Ephemera. See: Fitzgibbon, Edward

Epictetus.

— Manuall. L, 1616. 2 parts in 1 vol. 12mo, contemp vellum; rehinged & soiled. Lacking final blank; some marginalia; tp & some other leaves frayed; H12 holed without loss. STC 10426. P June 17 (386) $800

— Morals. L, 1694. ("Epictetus his Morals, with Simplicius his Comment.") 8vo, contemp calf. Rebacked. Library copy. bba Feb 27 (51) £50 [W. Poole]

Epicurus, 342?-270 B.C. See: Limited Editions Club

Epiphanius, Saint, 315?-403

— Contra octoginta haereses. Basel, 1544. Bound with: Contra octoginata haereses, trans. by J. Cornarius. Basel, 1578. Folio, later calf. bba Jan 16 (217) £480 [Nicolas]

Episcopius, Johannes, 1646-86

— Paradigmata Graphices Variorum Artificum. Amst.: Nicolas Visscher, [n.d.]. 2 parts in 1 vol. Folio, contemp mor gilt with red wash & gilt floral endpapers. Engraved throughout, with title, fly-title & 157 plates. C Dec 16 (104) £2,500 [Halwas]

— Signorum veterum icones. [N.p., c.1670]. With 100 plates. Bound with: Episcopius. Paradigmata graphices variorum artificum.... The Hague, 1671. With 57 plates. Folio, later half calf bba Mar 26 (165) £800 [Mason]

Epistolae...

— Epistolae claro virorum selectae.... Venice: Aldus, 1556. 8vo, 17th-cent mor gilt; spine rubbed, piece of adhesive tape on lower cover. Ck Nov 29 (7) £110

— Epistolae diversorum philosophorum, oratorum, rhetorum. Venice: Aldus, [29] Mar & [not before 17 Apr] 1499. Part 2 only. 4to, vellum. Marginal soiling. 180 leaves only. SI June 9 (340) LIt600,000

Epistolai. See: Epistolae...

Epithalamia...

— Epithalamia exoticis linguis reddita. Parma: Bodoni, 1775. Folio, late 18th-cent calf; sides repaired. With 139 engraved headpieces, culs-de-lampe & initials & 26 specimen verses ptd in exotic types. Some browning. S Dec 5 (254) £5,000 [Controlfida]

Epopeia

— Epopeia. Literaturnyi ezhemesiachnik pod redaktsiei Andreia B'lago. Moscow, Apr 1922. 8vo, prd wraps designed by El Lissitzky; front cover & 1st signature nearly detached. Foxed; some chipping. sg Sept 6 (178) $250

Epstein, Jacob, 1880-1959

— Seventy-Five Drawings. L, 1929. One of 220. Oblong 4to, orig vellum; rubbed. DW Oct 9 (567) £190

Anr copy. Orig vellum; front hinge starting. pba July 23 (67) $130

Equinox

— The Equinox. The Official Review of the A. A. L, [1910-15]. Vol I, Nos 4-9. Ed by Aleister Crowley. 6 vols. 4to, half cloth; worn. sg Oct 17 (25) $275

Eragny Press—London

— BACON, SIR FRANCIS. - Of Gardens: an Essay. 1902. One of 226. sg Jan 30 (51) $250

— JONSON, BEN. - Songs by Ben Jonson. 1906. One of 175. S Nov 14 (59) £200 [Moulenacker]

— RONSARD, PIERRE DE. - Choix de Sonnets de

Pierre de Ronsard. 1902. One of 226. Orig bds; rubbed. bbc June 29 (382) $140

— VILLON, FRANCOIS. - Autres Poesies. 1901. One of 222. O Dec 17 (57) $160

— VILLON, FRANCOIS. - Les Ballades. 1900. One of 222. O Dec 17 (58) $100

Erasmus, Desiderius, 1466?-1536

— Adagia. Basel: Episcopus, 1574. ("Adagiorum chiliades quatuor.....") Folio, contemp blind-stamped calf over wooden bds; lacking 1 clasp. Title lettered in ink across fore-edge. S Dec 5 (102) £450 [Schwing]

— Antibarbarorum...liber unus. Basel: Johannes Froben, May 1520. 4to, 19th-cent calf; worn. Roman type; woodcut title border by Hans Holbein. Stain to title; some marginal dampstaining; early marginalia in 2 hands. Milne copy. CNY Dec 5 (229) $1,500

— Apophthegmatum opus. Lyons: Sebastian Gryphius, 1534. 8vo, contemp blind-tooled pigskin over wooden bds; lacking clasps. Marginal stains. sg Oct 24 (108) $600

— De duplici copia verborum. Lyons: Seb. Gryphium, 1550. 8vo, bdg not described but def. F Mar 26 (702) $150

— Le Mariage Chretien. Paris: Francois Barbuty, 1715. 12mo, contemp mor gilt; spine head chipped. sg Oct 24 (109) $250

— The Praise of Folie.... L, 1709. ("Moriae Encomium: or, a Panegyrick upon Folly.") 8vo, old calf; rubbed & soiled. O Dec 17 (59) $90

Anr Ed. L: Essex House Press, 1901. Out-of-series copy. Folio, vellum bds. sp Sept 22 (146) $50

— Precatio dominica in septem portiones distributa. [Basel: Johann Froben, 1523?]. 8vo, modern cloth. S July 9 (1067) £400

Ercilla y Zuniga, Alonso de

— Araucana. Madrid, 1632. 8vo, contemp vellum; discolored. Natural flaw in a few pp. bba Feb 27 (250) £300 [Montero]

Ercker, Lazarus, d.1593

— Aula subterranea domini dominantium subdita subditorum.... Frankfurt, 1703. Folio, old bds; spine def. Browned throughout; engraved title shaved. S May 13 (885) £420 [Phelps]

Ericson, A. W.

— Redwood and Lumbering in California Forests. San Francisco, 1884. 4to, orig cloth. With 24 photographs. pba July 23 (230) $50

Erinnerung...

— Erinnerung der verschulten plagen, des Teutschlands, sampt ainer getrewen ermanung zu Christenlicher bekerung, unnd sculdiger hilff, wider des Tuercken.... [Augsburg: Philipp Ulhart, 1529]. 4to, loose in recent bds. Black letter. Outer edges soiled. S July 1 (604) £620 [Reiss & Auvermann]

Ernesti, Johann Heinrich Gottfried, 1664-1723

— Die Woleingerichtete Buchdruckerey.... Nuremberg, 1721. 1st Ed. Oblong 4to, contemp calf; rebacked. With frontis & 13 ports. HH May 12 (1069) DM2,500

Anr copy. Contemp calf; rebacked & worn, corners bumped. Some leaves at beginning & end restored in inner margin; some soiling. P Dec 12 (37) $1,200

Ernst, Henri

— Tapisseries et etoffes coptes. Paris, [c.1925]. Folio, unbound as issued in half cloth. With 48 mtd plates, most colored. Some browning to text & mounts. wa Sept 26 (667) $150

Ernst, Max

— Histoire Naturelle. [N.p.]: Niggli, [1972]. One of 200. Intro by Hans Arp. Folio, loose as issued in cloth folding case. With 34 plates. sg Apr 2 (85) $110

— Le Musee de l'homme. [Paris, 1965]. One of 99 with both etchings. 4to, wraps. sg Jan 30 (52) $950

— ZU: At Eye Level, Poems and Comments.... Beverly Hills: Copley Galleries, 1949. One of 22 with etching, on wove paper. Orig bds. With ptr's proofs of 2 of the typographical illusts, laid down on bd. CNY May 12 (377) $38,000

Eros

— Eros. NY, 1962. Ed by Ralph Ginzburg. Vol I, Nos 1-4 (all pbd). Bds. K Sept 29 (163) $55

Anr copy. Bds; soiled & worn. sp Apr 16 (204) $75

Erpenius, Thomas, 1584-1624

— Grammatica Arabica. Amst.: J. Janson, 1636. 3 parts in 1 vol. 4to, contemp calf; rebacked. Early annotations obscuring or affecting text; some waterstaining. b June 22 (76) £65

Erskine, John Elphinstone, 1806-87

— Journal of a Cruise...The Western Pacific. L, 1853. 8vo, modern half mor. Map repaired at folds. kh Nov 11 (479) A$100

Anr copy. Orig cloth. With tinted frontis, map & 7 plates, some colored. pnE Aug 12 (44) £180

Eschenbach, Andreas Christian

— Epigenes de poesi Orphica.... Nuremberg, 1702. 4to, old half vellum. Prelim leaf loose. sg Oct 24 (110) $200

Escholier, Raymond

— Delacroix.... Paris, 1926-29. One of 200. 3 vols. 4to, orig wraps. sg Apr 2 (99) $110

Esmerian Library, Raphael

— [Sale Catalogue] Bibliotheque Raphael Esmerian. Paris, 1972-74. 5 vols in 6. 4to, cloth. sg Oct 31 (38) $700; sg May 21 (215) $325

Espouy, Hector d'

— Monuments antiques.... Paris: Ch. Massin, [1910-12]. 3 vols plus supplement. 4to, half mor. S Nov 15 (880) £220 [Krupp]

Esquemeling, Alexandre Olivier. See: Exquemelin, Alexandre Olivier

Essay. See: Bancroft, Edward

Essayes...

— Essayes of Natural Experiments made in the Academie del Cimento. L, 1684. 1st Ed in English. Trans by Richard Waller. 4to, contemp sheep; worn, covers detached. With frontis & 19 plates. S Feb 25 (579) £550 [P & P]

Essling, Victor Massena, Prince d', 1836-1910

— Les Livres a figures venitiens de la fin du XVe siecle.... Torino, 1967. 3 parts in 6 vols. 4to, orig half lea. SI Dec 5 (222) LIt1,300,000

Estaban, Claude

— Comme un sol plus obscur. Paris, 1979. One of 15 hors commerce. Illus by Raoul Ubac. Folio, loose as issued. CGen Nov 18 (374) SF6,000

Estaugh, John. See: Franklin Printing, Benjamin

Esteban, Claude. See: Chagall, Marc

Estienne, Charles, 1504-64

— Praedium Rusticum. Paris, 1554. 8vo, later calf; rubbed. bba Sept 5 (40) £280 [Poole]

Estienne, Charles, 1504-64 —& Liebault, Jean, d.1596

— L'Agriculture et maison rustique.... Rouen, 1668. Bound with: Clamorgan, Jean de. La Chasse du Loup.... Lyon, 1668 4to, modern mor; rubbed. Waterstained at inner margin. bba Sept 5 (41) £130 [Hughes]

Estienne, Henri, 1528?-98

See also: Caxton Club

— Dictionarium medicum, vel, expositiones vocum medicinalium.... [Geneva]: H. Estienne, 1564. 8vo, vellum. B Nov 1 (385) HF1,300

— L'Introduction au traite de la conformite des merveilles anciennes avec les modernes. [Geneva], 1566. 3d Issue. 8vo, 18th-cent calf. S May 13 (763) £300 [Hantzis]

Estienne, Robert, 1503-59

— Dictionaire francoislatin, autrement dict les mots francois.... Paris: Robert Estienne, 27 July 1549. Folio, 16th-cent calf; joints split. Some margins wormed. S Dec 5 (105) £1,400 [Quaritch]

— Hebraea, Chaldaea, Graeca, et Latina nomina virorum, mulierum.... Antwerp: C. Plantin, 1560. 12mo, 19th-cent sheep; extremities rubbed. Lower corners dampstained. sg Dec 19 (74) $400

Etchison, Dennis. See: Lord John Press

Etherton, Percy Thomas

— Across the Roof of the World. L, 1911. 8vo, cloth. sg Jan 9 (74) $300

Anr copy. Library markings. sg Jan 9 (254) $300

Ettmueller, Michael

— Opera Medica Theoretico-Practica. Frankfurt: Officina Zunneriana, 1708. 2 vols in 3. Folio, contemp vellum; 1 rear cover gnawed. Some browning. sg Nov 14 (33) $200

Euclid

Elementa

— 1574. - Rome: Vincentius Accoltus. 2 vols. 8vo, contemp vellum. Dampstaining, severe in Vol I. Ck Nov 29 (178) £260

— 1575. - Urbino: Domenico Frisolino. Folio, contemp vellum. Marginal repairs; some foxing. SI Dec 5 (227) LIt650,000

— [1594]. - Rome: Typographia Medicea. 4to, later 18th-cent half vellum over bds. Tp in Arabic only. Library stamp & accession number on privilege page only; some browning & dampstaining. Ck Nov 29 (179) £3,400

— 1678. - Euclidis elementorum libri XV.... L. Ed by Isaac Barrow. 2 parts in 1 vol. 8vo, lea; broken. Annotated. b&b Feb 19 (112) $90

— 1686. - L: for Christopher Hussey & E.P.. 12mo, contemp calf; covers detached. With 14 folding plates. sg May 14 (277) $250

— 1847. - L. 4to, later 19th-cent half mor; joints & corners rubbed. Corner of opening leaves dampstained. sg May 7 (102) $1,600

— 1847. - The First Six Books of Euclid in which Coloured Diagrams and Symbols are used.... L. 4to, contemp half sheep. Tp & half-title soiled; tear in upper margin repaired; pp. 1-48 with a waterstain, not affecting text; some foxing. Schlosser copy. P June 17 (419) $3,000

Euler, Leonhard, 1707-83

— Letters to a German Princess.... L, 1795. 2 vols. 8vo, contemp calf; joints cracked, corners bumped. With 20 plates. Ck Nov 29 (182) £130

— Methodus inveniendi lineas curvas maximi minimive proprietate gaudentes.... Lausanne & Geneva, 1744. 1st Ed. 4to, contemp half calf; spine cracked at head. With 5 folding plates. Some staining to upper margins; tp soiled. C June 24 (128) £800 [Palinurus]

— Tentamen novae theoriae musicae.... St. Petersburg, 1739. 1st Ed. 4to, modern half mor. With engraved title, engraved table, 2 folding ptd tables & 3 folding plates. Titles repaired; library stamp. S May 13 (725) £240 [Tosi]

— Theoria motus lunae. St. Petersburg & Berlin [ptd], 1753. 4to, 19th-cent half calf. With folding plate. Tp browned & waterstained at outer margin; plate waterstained at upper margin & spotted; some browning of text. Ck Nov 29 (180) £1,000

— The True Principles of Gunnery Investigated and Explained.... L, 1777. 4to, modern half calf gilt. With folding table & 5 folding plates. S July 1 (219) £2220 [Nat. Army Mus]

Eumorfopoulos Collection, George

— BINYON, LAURENCE. - Catalogue of the Chinese Frescoes.... L, 1927-28. Each one of 585. 2 vols. Folio, half cloth; edges worn. sg Apr 2 (206) $400

Euripides

See also: Gregynog Press

— Opera. Venice: Aldus, Feb 1503. ("Tragoediae septendecim.") 2 vols in 1. 8vo, early 19th-cent mor; rubbed. Lacking 1 blank & 1 signature in Vol II; signature Xi Xi to TT of Vol II misbound in Vol I. bba Jan 16 (214A) £1,700 [Stamatoyannopoulos]

Anr Ed. Basel, 1551. ("Tragoediae octodecim.") 8vo, contemp vellum; loose. Tp soiled. sg Mar 12 (86) $70

— The Tragedies.... L, 1781-83. Trans by Robert Potter. 2 vols. 4to, contemp sheep; worn, joints cracked. With frontis in Vol II. Marginal worming in Vol I. sg Oct 24 (112) $150

Eusebius Pamphili, 260?-340?

— De evangelica praeparatione. Paris: Antoine Augereau & Simon de Colines, 1534. 4to, contemp blind-tooled calf; rebacked. Early marginalia; marginal stains. sg Mar 12 (87) $750

— Historia ecclesiastica. Strasbourg: [Georg Husner], 14 Mar 1500. ("Ecclesiastica historia divi Eusebii et ecclesiastica historia gentis Anglorum venerabilis Bedae.") Folio, 19th-cent calf; worn, rebacked. 50 lines & headline; double column; types 5:156G (titles, headlines) & 6:80G (text). Tp mtd & with a few holes & tears; several stains at beginning & end. 160 leaves. Goff E-129. S Nov 27 (13) £900 [Pickering & Chatto]

Anr Ed. Paris: R. Stephanus, 1544. ("Ecclesiasticae historiae.") Folio, contemp vellum. C June 24 (271) £950 [Franklin]

Eustachius, Bartolomaeus, 1524?-74

See also: Albinus, Bernard Siegfried

— Tabulae anatomicae. Venice, 1769. Folio, modern half vellum. With engraved title, port & 21 plates. Some spotting. SI Dec 5 (847) LIt800,000

Eustathius, Archbishop of Thessalonica

— Commentarii in Homeri Iliadem et Odysseam [in Greek]. Rome: Antonio Blado, 1542-50. 4 vols, including index. Folio, russia; rebacked. A number of leaves in Vol III repaired with small loss; tp to Vol III repaired; some staining & foxing; 1 leaf torn in margin. Adams E1107. S Dec 5 (108) £2,000 [Theocharaki]

Eustratius, Archbishop of Nicaea

— Commentaris in secundum librum Posteriorum Resolutiuorum Aristotelis. Venice, 1542. Folio, modern bds; rubbed. Adams E1107. DW Dec 11 (279) £130

Euw, Anton von —& Plotzek, Joachim M.

— Die Handschriften der Sammlung Ludwig. Cologne, 1979. 4 vols. Folio, cloth, in d/js. sg Oct 31 (211) $400

Evans, Charles Seddon

— Cinderella. Phila. & L, 1919. Illus by Arthur Rackham. 4to, orig half cloth. bba Jan 16 (383) £60 [Sotheran]

Anr copy. Orig half cloth; soiled. With tipped-in color frontis. bba May 14 (341) £60 [Glynn]

Anr copy. Orig half cloth, in def d/j. K Mar 22 (379) $65

One of 525. Half cloth; corners bumped, spots on front cover. K Mar 22 (378) $200

— The Sleeping Beauty. L, [1920]. Illus by Arthur Rackham. 4to, half cloth. bba Jan 16 (384) £60 [Sotheran]

One of 625. Bds; spotted & bumped. Soiled. Met Apr 28 (417) $300

Anr copy. Orig half vellum gilt; soiled, worn at corners. S Nov 14 (126) £760

1st American Ed. Phila., [1920]. 4to, half cloth, in chipped d/j. K Mar 22 (380) $110

Evans, David. See: Harrison & Evans

Evans, Frederick W.

— Tests of Divine Inspiration.... New Lebanon PA, 1853. 1st Ed. 12mo, wraps. Z Oct 26 (244) $70

Evans, George William

— A Geographical, Historical and Topographical Description of Van Diemen's Land.... L, 1824. ("History and Description of the Present State of Van Diemen's Land....") 2d Ed. 8vo, contemp calf gilt; joints split. S June 25 (189) £400 [Baring]

— Voyage a la terre de Van Diemen.... Paris, 1823. 8vo, uncut in wraps as issued. With folding plate & folding map, colored in outline. kh Nov 11 (484) A$600

Evans, Lewis, 1700?-56. See: Franklin Printing, Benjamin

Evans, Lady Maria Millington

— Lustre Pottery. NY, [1920]. 4to, cloth; worn. Prelims browned. sg Sept 6 (107) $90

Evans, Oliver, 1755-1819

— The Young Mill-Wright's and Miller's Guide. Phila., 1834. 8vo, contemp sheep; worn. With 28 plates. bbc June 29 (136) $65

Evans, Walker

— American Photographs. NY, [1938]. Text by Lincoln Kirstein. 4to, cloth, in d/j. Met Apr 28 (90) $50

— Many are Called. NY, 1966. 1st Ed. In d/j. sg Apr 13 (39) $300

— Message from the Interior. NY, [1966]. Folio, cloth. With 12 photos. sg Apr 13 (40) $425

Evelyn, John, 1620-1706

— Kalendarium Hortense: or, the Gardners Almanac. L, 1699. 9th Ed. 8vo, calf; rubbed. K Mar 22 (141) $200

— Memoirs.... L, 1819. 2d Ed. 2 vols. 4to, contemp calf. LH Dec 11 (109) $140

Anr copy. Mor gilt. sg Mar 5 (108) $150

— Navigation and Commerce, their Origin and Progress. L, 1674. 1st Ed. 8vo, contemp sheep; spine & corners worn. Some worming to lower inner margins. CNY Oct 8 (102) $1,300

— A Philosophical Discourse of Earth. L, 1676. 1st Ed. 8vo, contemp sheep; rebacked, rubbed. Lacking final blank; some ink annotations. bba Sept 5 (42) £400 [Kinokuniya]

— Sculptura.... L, 1662. ("Sculptura: or the History and Art of Chalcography and Engraving in Copper....") 1st Ed. 8vo, contemp calf gilt; rebacked. With frontis, engraving on p. 121 & folding mezzotint by Prince Rupert of the Rhine. Some spotting & browning. Schlosser copy. P June 18 (456) $3,250

— Sylva.... L, 1664. 1st Ed. 3 parts in 1 vol. Folio, 19th-cent sheep; front joint starting. Washed. sg May 7 (103) $800

3d Ed. L, 1679. Folio, contemp calf; rebacked, rubbed. Some rehinging at beginning & end. bba June 11 (237) £100 [Lloyd's of Kew]

4th Ed. L, 1706. Folio, later sheep gilt; rebacked, corners repaired. bba Jan 30 (90) £120 [Hughes]

5th Ed. L, 1729. Folio, calf; rebacked. pnE May 13 (93) £240

Anr Ed. York, 1776. 4to, contemp calf; upper cover detached, lower joint split. bba Sept 5 (44) £170 [Freddie]

Anr copy. Contemp calf; rebacked, rubbed. Some foxing & soiling. bba Nov 28 (110) £190 [Lloyd's of Kew]

Anr copy. Contemp sheep gilt; rubbed. bba Jan 303 (419) £240 [Ceri]

Anr copy. Modern half mor gilt. With 40 plates. Lacking port. pn June 11 (230) £110 [Russell]

Anr Ed. York, 1786. 2 vols. 4to, contemp calf. H3 of Vol I torn & repaired. bba Mar 26 (229) £140 [Williams]

Everard, Anne

— Flowers from Nature. L, 1835. Folio, orig cloth; spine chipped. With hand-colored frontis & 12 plates. C Oct 30 (191) £300 [Gerits]

Everard, Harry Stirling Crawfurd

— A History of the Royal & Ancient Golf Club St. Andrews from 1754-1900. Edin., 1907. 4to, orig cloth. Ns of the Club Secretary, Henry Gullen, 1919, tipped in. b Mar 11 (225) £350

Everard, Major Hugh Edmund Elsden

— History of Thos. Farrington's Regiment, the 29th (Worcestershire) Foot. L, 1891. 2 vols. 4to, orig cloth; rubbed. bba Oct 24 (190) £75 [A. Thompson]

Everard, John

— Some Gospel Treasures, or the Holiest of all Unvailing.... Germantown: Christopher Sower, 1757. 2 vols in 1. 8vo, contemp calf; extremities worn. sg Dec 5 (227) $200

Everest, Sir George

— An Account of the Measurement of Two Sections of the Meridional Arc of India. L, 1847. 2 vols. Folio, orig cloth. With frontis & 2 diagrammatic plates in Vol I & 29 plates, double-page map & 2 folding plans in Vol II. Marginal tear in pp. 413-14. Inscr to the Royal Society of Edinburgh. Manney copy. P Oct 11 (1138) $4,250

Everett, Edward. See: Lincoln, Abraham

Everett, Horace, 1780-1851

— Regulating the Indian Department: Report. [Wash.], 1834. 8vo, later half mor; worn, rear bd detached. With folding map hand-colored in outline. Library markings. 23rd Congress, 1st Session, H of R Report 474. wa Apr 9 (72) $160

Everitt, Graham

— English Caricaturists and Graphic Humourists of the Nineteenth Century. L, 1886. 4to, orig cloth; front hinge cracked. Library markings. sg Sept 6 (108) $70

Everson, William

— A Privacy of Speech. Berkeley: Equinox Press, 1949. One of 100. Half vellum. cb Feb 12 (36) $800

Evrardus de Valle Scholarum, d.c.1272

— Sermones de Sanctis. Heidelberg: [Eponymous press but perhaps Heinrich Knoblochtzer], 21 Jan 1485. Folio, bound at the Benedictine Abbey of St. Peter at Salzburg in contemp blind-tooled lea over wooden bds, with vellum liners & sewing guards cut from an Austrian romanesque liturgical Ms. 44-46 lines & headline; types 1:180G & 2:90G (text); double column; rubricated in red & green by a contemp hand. Minor worming at end. 286 leaves Goff H-513. C Nov 27 (34) £9,000 [Nakles]

Evreinov, Nikolae Nicolaevich

— Tamara Platonovna Karsavina. [St. Petersburg, 1914]. One of 200. 4to, orig cloth-backed pictorial wraps. SM Oct 11 (534) FF8,500

Ewald, Mrs. ——

— Jerusalem and the Holy Land. L, 1854. Oblong folio, orig cloth; worn. With 12 tinted or color plates. Some spotting. S July 1 (839) £500 [Sofer]

Ewald, Alexander Charles

— The Life and Times of Prince Charles Stuart. L, 1875. 2 vols. 8vo, mor extra by Bayntun-Riviere, the upper covers set with oval port miniatures of Prince Charles Stuart & Flora Macdonald. Extra-illus with 38 ports & views, some colored. P Dec 12 (11) $1,000

Ewald, Ernest

— Decorations Polychromes. Paris, [n.d.]. 2 vols. Folio, cloth; worn. Some marginal soiling; a few plates detached with margins worn; marginal dampstaining in Vol II. sg Apr 2 (114) $350

Ewbank, J. —&
Lizars, William Home, 1788-1859

— Picturesque Views of Edinburgh. Edin., [1825]. 4to, contemp half mor over bds; worn. With engraved title & 51 plates. Foxed; gutter split. bba July 23 (360) £100 [Grant & Shaw]

Ewbank, Thomas, 1792-1870

— Life in Brazil.... NY, 1856. 8vo, orig cloth; front hinge weak. Top corner of 1st 25 leaves dampstained. sg Dec 5 (97) $110

Anr copy. Cloth. sg June 18 (214) $90

Examiner...

— The Examiner. Or, Remarks upon Papers and Occurrences. L, 1710-12. Vol I, Nos 1-52 & Vol II, Nos 1-39 only, bound in 1 vol. Folio, modern cloth. Some annotations in a late 18th-cent hand; some drophead titles cropped or shaved. Milne set. Ck June 12 (57) £550

Excellency...

— The Excellency of the Pen and Pencil.... L: Dorman Newman, 1688. 8vo, early calf; rubbed, spine split. With frontis & 2 plates, 1 folding, anr misbound. Tp shaved at fore-edge. Schlosser copy. P June 18 (457) $2,500

Experienced Artist. See: Whole...

Exquemelin, Alexandre Olivier, 1645?-1707

— Bucaniers of America.... L, 1684-85. 1st Ed in English of Parts 1-3, 1st Ed of Part 4. Vol I (Parts 1-3). 4to, contemp sheep; extremities rubbed, joints split, spine chipped at head & foot. With 4 ports & 4 plates & 1 folding map. Some worming or old dampstaining to margins. Portland copy. C June 24 (311) £450 [Waxman]

Anr copy. 2 vols in 1. 4to, mor gilt by Riviere; joints cracked. With 8 ports & plates (2 double-page), 1 doublepage map & 1 text engraving in Vol I (Parts 1-3) & 1 folding chart & 15 maps & charts in Vol II. CNY Oct 8 (103) $2,600

Anr copy. 2 vols. 4to, mor gilt by Riviere; upper cover detached. With 4 ports, 3 double-page or folding maps, 13 maps & charts, & 4 plates, 2 double-page. Repair to 3F2 efacing c.11 words; repair to 3K1 affecting a few letters; 2 charts shaved; washed. CNY Oct 8 (104) $1,600

Anr copy. 4 parts in 1 vol. 4to, 18th-cent calf; upper cover detached. With 4 ports, 3 folding maps & 4 plates.. Inscr in verse by John Masefield. S June 25 (451) £900 [Remington]

Abridged Ed. L, 1684. ("The History of the Bucaniers....") 12mo, contemp calf; rubbed, lea of spine cracking, endpapers becoming detached. jWith port & 1 folding plate. Some soiling; a few corners creased; tear to C4 not affecting text. CNY Oct 8 (105) $2,800

Anr copy. Mor gilt by R. Bedford; extremities rubbed. With port & 1 folding plate. Repaired 1-inch tear to tp; smaller tear to A2; rust hole to G12 affecting 2 letters; frontis & folding plate on new guards. CNY May 14 (58) $1,000

Exsteens, Maurice

— L'Oeuvre grave et lithographie de Felicien Rops. Paris, 1928. One of 500. 4 vols plus portfolio of plates. Folio, orig wraps, spine ends torn, a few signatures loose. sg Sept 6 (250) $750

Eyre, Edward John, 1815-1901

— Journals of the Expeditions of Discovery into Central Australia.... L, 1845. 2 vols. 8vo, orig cloth; spines worn. With 22 plates & 2 folding maps (1 with fold repair) in pocket in Vol I. R. J. Maria copy. C June 25 (227) £3,200 [Maggs]

Anr copy. Orig cloth; 1 vol rebacked, retaining orig backstrip. Some plates foxed; lacking the 2 folding maps. kh Nov 11 (487) A$1,200

Eyton, Robert William, 1815-81

— Antiquities of Shropshire. L, 1854-60. Ltd Ed. 12 vols. 8vo, contemp half vellum; soiled. DW Dec 11 (101) £540

Eyton, Thomas Campbell, 1809-80

— A History of the Rarer British Birds.... L, 1836. 2 parts in 1 vol. 8vo, contemp cloth; rebacked preserving orig backstrip. With both versions of pp 25/26. C Oct 30 (243) £150 [Cockell]

F

F., W. See: Fleetwood, William

Faber du Faur, Kurt von

— German Baroque Literature: a Catalogue of the Collection in the Yale University Library. New Haven, 1958. 4to, cloth; worn. O Sept 24 (83) $130

Faber, John, 1660?-1721. See: Kneller & Faber

Fabre, Francois, 1766-1837

— Nemesis medical illustree. Paris, 1840. Illus by Daumier. 2 vols in 1. 8vo, half mor, orig wraps bound in, uncut. With 30 wood-engraved vignettes in text. Schlosser copy. P June 17 (529) $2,000

Fabre, Jean Henri, 1823-1915

— Fabre's Book of Insects. L, [1921]. Illus by E. J. Detmold. 4to, orig cloth; worn, front hinge cracked. sg Sept 26 (108) $70

— Souvenirs entomologiques. Paris, 1924. 11 vols. 8vo, half calf; spines rubbed. S Nov 15 (740) £50 [Dunbar]

Fabre, Jean Raymond Auguste

— Histoire du siege de Missolonghi. Paris, 1827. 8vo, contemp half calf; rubbed. S June 30 (289) £280 [Finnopoulos]

Fabricius von Helden, Wilhelm, 1560-1634

— Wund-artzney. Hanau, 1652. Folio, contemp vellum; stained. Some browning; lacking final blank. S Dec 5 (379) £1,700 [Preidel]

Fabris, Salvator

— Scienza e pratica d'arme. Leipzig, 1677. 4to, contemp sheep; worn. sg Mar 26 (110) $1,200

Anr Ed. Leipzig: E. Hynitzsch, 1677. Folio, wraps. With 2 ports. S Dec 5 (263) £700 [Mediolanum]

Fabrizzi, Girolamo, 1537-1619

— Wund-Artznei. Nuremberg, 1672. 2 vols in 1. 4to, contemp vellum bds. With engraved title, port & 9 folding or double-page plates. Some shaving. S Dec 5 (380) £950 [Preidel]

Fabyan, Robert, d.1513

— The Chronicle.... L: John Kynston, 1559. 2 parts in 1 vol. Folio, later calf gilt, armorial bdg; rebacked. W July 8 (54) £700

Faden, William

— Atlas minimus universalis. L, 1798. Oblong 8vo, contemp mor; rebacked. Engraved throughout. With 55 maps, hand-colored in outline. Ck July 10 (340) £600

Faernius, Gabriel, d.1561

— Centum Fabulae ex antiquis auctoribus delectae. Antwerp: Plantin, June 1567. 16mo, calf; def. Upper margin short. B May 12 (30) HF1,200

Fahey, Herbert. See: Grabhorn Printing

Fairbairn, James

— Crests of the Families of Great Britain and Ireland. Edin., 1892. ("Fairbairn's Book of Crests of the Families of Great Britain and Ireland.") 2 vols. 4to, cloth. kh Nov 11 (347) A$220

Anr Ed. L, 1905. 2 vols. 4to, orig cloth;

head of spine of Vol I gone. Library markings. F Dec 18 (335) $50

Anr copy. Orig cloth; shaken. sp June 18 (255) $125

Fairy...

— A Fairy Garland. L, [1928]. One of 1,000. Illus by Edmund Dulac. 4to, orig half vellum. With 12 color plates. sg Jan 30 (43) $400

Anr Ed. NY, [1928]. 4to, orig half vellum. With 12 color plates. sg Sept 26 (94) $250

Faithorne, William, 1616-91

— The Art of Graveing, and Etching.... L, 1662. 8vo, calf; rebacked, edges worn. With engraved title & 10 plates. Some spotting. P June 18 (458) $2,000

Falconer, Richard

— The Voyages, Dangerous Adventures and Imminent Escapes.... L, 1720. 1st Ed. 3 parts in 1 vol. 8vo, contemp calf gilt; rubbed. With frontis. Tear in 1 leaf repaired, affecting text. S Feb 26 (736) £280 [Grants & Shaw]

Falconer, William, 1732-69

— The Shipwreck, a Poem. L, 1804. 8vo, mor by Riviere. Some foxing & soiling. O May 26 (60) $180

Anr Ed. L, 1808. 4to, loose in contemp calf; crudely rebacked. With engraved dedication, folding map & 18 plates. Lacking text. Sold w.a.f. DW Jan 29 (230) £65

3d Ed. L, 1811. 4to, contemp calf by Edwards of Halifax with Greek key pattern borders. With 3 plates. With a fore-edge painting of a large country house. Ck July 10 (247) £260

— A Universal Dictionary of the Marine. L, 1789. 4to, contemp calf; worn. With 12 folding plates. S July 1 (1247) £200 [Middleton]

Falda, Giovanni Battista

See also: Rossi & Falda

— Le Fontane di Roma, nelle piazze e luoghi publici della citta. Rome: Giovanni Giacomo di Rossi, [1691]. 4 parts in 1 vol. Oblong 4to, contemp half vellum; scuffed. With 4 titles, 4 dedications & 99 plates. Small tear to 1 folding plate; 4 others shaved with loss. Engraved throughout. C Oct 30 (102) £4,000 [Baskett]

Anr copy. Contemp mor gilt; rubbed. With 4 engraved titles, 4 dedications & 73 plates. S June 25 (198) £7,000 [Ursus]

Anr copy. 18th-cent half vellum. Some dampstaining & browning. SI Dec 5 (230) LIt3,600,000

— Li Giardini di Roma.... Rome: G. G. Rossi, [c.1683?]. Oblong folio, 18th-cent half calf over paper bds; rubbed. With engraved title, engraved dedication & 19 plates & plans. Library stamp on dedication; some spotting. S June 25 (194) £2,800 [Shapero]

Faletus, Hieronymus

— De bello Sicambrico libri IIII. Venice: Aldus, 1557. 4to, old vellum; soiled, recased. Tp with tape mark at upper margin; tp & prelims soiled. Ck Nov 29 (8) £220

Falke, Otto von, 1862-1942

— Decorative Silks. L, 1936. 3d Ed. Folio, cloth; extremities worn, lacking front free endpapers. sg Sept 6 (109) $140

Falkner, Frank

— The Wood Family of Burslem.... L, 1912. One of 450. 4to, orig cloth. DW Mar 11 (751) £90

Famous...

— The Famous Tommy Thumb's Little Story-Book.... L, [1760?]. 16mo, orig wraps; spines torn. Manney copy. P Oct 11 (67) $7,500

Fanning, Edmund, 1769-1841

— Voyages & Discoveries in the South Seas. Salem MA; Marine Research Society, 1924. With 32 plates. sg Jan 9 (76) $50

Fantin-Latour, Henri, 1836-1904

[-] Catalogue de l'oeuvre complete, 1849-1904. Amst. & NY, 1969. Reprint of the Paris, 1911, Ed. wa Apr 9 (229) $140

Faraday, Michael, 1791-1867

— Experimental Researches in Electricity. L, 1839-55. 3 vols. later calf gilt by Sayer & Wilson; spines rubbed & faded. DW Nov 6 (348) £100

— Experimental Researches in Chemistry and Physics. L, 1859. 1st Ed. 8vo, orig cloth; rubbed. With 3 plates. DW Nov 6 (347) £150

Farington, Joseph, 1747-1821

— Views of the Lakes. L, 1789. Oblong folio, contemp half mor; rubbed & worn. With 20 plates, including 8 relaid. DW Jan 29 (74) £270

Farmer, Fannie Merritt, 1857-1915

— The Boston Cooking-School Cook Book. Bost., 1896. 1st Ed. 8vo, cloth; worn & shaken; inner joints broken. Some staining. O Nov 26 (57) $180

Farmer, John Stephen —& Henley, William Ernest, 1849-1903

— Slang and its Analogues. L, 1890-1904. Out-of-series copy. 7 vols. 4to, half mor gilt. S July 1 (1188) £220 [Holleyman/

Treacher]

Farmer, Philip Jose

— The Green Odyssey. NY: Ballantine, [1957]. In d/j. Epstein copy. sg Apr 29 (148) $850

Farnham, Thomas Jefferson, 1804-48

— Travels in the Great Western Prairies.... Ploughkeepsie [sic], 1843. 8vo, modern half calf gilt. sg June 18 (215) $175

Farquhar, Francis Peloubet

— The Books of the Colorado River & the Grand Canyon.... Los Angeles, 1953. cb Oct 17 (293) $70

— The Grizzly Bear Hunter of California: A Bibliographic Essay. San Francisco, 1948. One of 200. Wraps. cb Sept 12 (60) $65

— History of the Sierra Nevada. Berkeley, 1965. In d/j. Inscr to Warren Howell. cb Sept 12 (61) $100

— Yosemite, the Big Trees, and the High Sierra: a Selective Bibliography. Berkeley, 1948. 1st Ed. Cloth, in d/j. cb Oct 17 (294) $150

Farquhar, George, 1678-1707

— Sir Harry Wildair. L: for James Knapton, 1701. 4to, disbound. Tp & prelims creased; final leaf soiled on verso. Milne copy. Ck June 12 (59) £140

Farquharson, Martha. See: Finley, Martha

Farrar, Timothy

— Report of the Case of the Trustees of Dartmouth College against William H. Woodward. Portsmouth, N.H., [1819]. 8vo, contemp sheep; rubbed. Foxed. O Mar 31 (69) $140

Farrell, Henry

— What Ever Happened to Baby Jane? NY, [1960]. In d/j. Sgd by Bette Davis, Victor Buono & others. sg Oct 17 (30) $200

Farren, Robert

— The Granta and the Cam from Byron's Pool to Ely. Cambr., 1880. 1st Ed. Folio, orig cloth; soiled & worn. With 36 plates. DW Nov 6 (118) £125

Farrington, S. Kip, Jr.

— Atlantic Game Fishing. NY, 1937. Cloth; worn. Intro by Hemingway. sg May 21 (37) $225

Fath, Creekmore. See: Benton, Thomas Hart

Faujas de Saint-Fond, Barthelemi, 1741-1819

— Description des experiences de la machine aerostatique de M. de Montgolfier.... Paris, 1783-84. 1st Ed. 2 vols. 8vo, contemp half calf; vols misnumbered on spines. With 14 plates & folding table. bba Sept 5 (207) £1,200 [Mandl]

Anr copy. Bound with: Premier Suite de la Description..... With 14 plates but lacking leaf T5. And: Bourgeois, David. Recherches sur l'Art de Voler.... 8vo, contemp calf; rubbed. bba June 25 (168) £500 [Pegliasco]

Anr copy. Vol I only. 8vo, modern half calf. With 9 plates & 1 folding table. Tear in T1 without loss; some browning & staining at beginning. S July 1 (1248) £400

Faulkner, William, 1897-1962

See also: Limited Editions Club

— Absalom, Absalom! NY, 1936. In rubbed d/j. bbc Sept 23 (399) $300

Anr copy. In d/j. Library stamped. sg Dec 12 (102) $120

Anr copy. Orig bds. Epstein copy. sg Apr 29 (149) $1,800

2d ptg. In repaired d/j. Sgd twice. wa Sept 26 (155) $1,100

— An Address delivered...at the Seventeenth Annual Meeting of Delta Council, May 15, 1952. Cleveland MS, 1952. Orig wraps; staples rusted. wa Sept 26 (156) $650

— As I Lay Dying. NY, [1930]. 1st Ed. Orig cloth, in def d/j. wd Dec 12 (386) $425

1st State. Orig cloth, in d/j. sg Dec 12 (103) $275

— Decline to Accept the End of Man. Rochester: Press of the Good Mountain, 1950. One of 100. 4to, orig bdg. Met Apr 27 (633) $190

— Doctor Martino and other Stories. NY, 1934. 1st Trade Ed. In rubbed d/j. bbc Sept 23 (401) $225

One of—360. Orig cloth; worn. wa Sept 26 (157) $350

— A Fable. NY, [1954]. In d/j. cb Dec 12 (54) $600

1st Ed, one of 1,000. Sgd. cb Dec 12 (53) $450; sg Sept 12 (77) $400; sg Dec 12 (104) $400

— Father Abraham. NY: Red Ozier Press, 1983. Half cloth by Twelfth Night Bindery. cb Dec 12 (55) $70

— Go Down, Moses. NY, [1942]. 1st Ed. In chipped d/j. bbc Sept 23 (402) $150

— A Green Bough. NY, 1933. One of 360. bbc Sept 23 (403) $450; cb Feb 12 (37) $475

One of 360, sgd. CNY Dec 5 (231) $650

— The Hamlet. NY, 1940. One of 250, sgd. Half cloth; worn. bbc Dec 9 (464) $875

One of 250. CNY Dec 5 (233) $1,700

— Idyll in the Desert. NY, 1931. 1st Ed, one of 400. bbc Sept 23 (405) $350

One of 400, sgd. Bds. CNY Dec 5 (230) $450

One of 400. Unopened copy. CNY June 9 (64) $700

— Intruder in the Dust. NY, [1948]. 1st Ed.

In d/j with vertical fold at spine. bbc Sept 23 (406) $55

Anr copy. Orig cloth, in d/j. bbc Dec 9 (465) $85; bbc Apr 27 (302) $90

— Knight's Gambit. NY, [1949]. 1st Ed. Cloth, in def d/j. bbc Apr 27 (303) $60

— Light in August. [NY, 1932]. 1st Ed. Cloth; spine ends chipped. pba July 9 (86) $120

1st Issue. In d/j. sg Dec 12 (105) $750; wd Dec 12 (388) $425

Issue not stated. In chipped d/j. bbc Sept 23 (407) $55

— The Marble Faun. Bost.: The Four Seas Company, [1924]. 1st Ed. Orig bds, in d/j lined with Japanese tissue; spine ends of bdg restored. Inscr to Hilda Lester & sgd on tp, 30 Dec 1924. Manney copy. P Oct 11 (139) $10,000

— Mosquitoes. NY, 1927. 1st Ed. sg Dec 12 (107) $80

1st Issue. In d/j. CNY June 9 (63) $1,100; sg Dec 12 (106) $1,400

— Pylon. NY, 1935. In d/j with vertical crease along spine. bbc Sept 23 (409) $130

— The Reivers. NY, [1962]. 1st Ed, one of 500, sgd. bbc Sept 23 (410) $350; sg Dec 12 (108) $400

— Requiem for a Nun. NY, 1951. One of 750, sgd. bbc Dec 9 (466) $350

1st Trade Ed. In d/j. cb Sept 19 (52) $50

— Salmagundi; and a Poem ["Ultimately"] by Ernest M. Hemingway. Milwaukee, 1932. 1st Ed, one of 525. Bds; with bottom edge trimmed. O May 26 (61) $225

Anr copy. Orig wraps; sppine soiled & rubbed. wa Mar 5 (178) $290
2d State of bdg. Orig wraps. CNY June 9J (65) $300

— Sanctuary. NY, [1931]. 1st Ed. In repaired d/j. wd Dec 12 (387) $425

1st Ptg. Orig bds, in d/j. Epstein copy. sg Apr 29 (152) $850

Anr Ed. Paris, 1932. Wraps; worn & with gouge in center of front cover. wd Dec 12 (364) $100

— Soldiers' Pay. NY, 1926. 1st Ed. sg Dec 12 (109) $100

— The Sound and the Fury. NY, [1929]. 1st Ed. Orig half cloth; hinges cracked. cb Sept 19 (54) $160

Anr copy. Orig half cloth, in d/j. Epstein copy. sg Apr 29 (153) $2,200

Anr copy. Orig half cloth. sp Sept 22 (120) $120

— These 13. NY, [1931]. One of 299. sg Sept 12 (76) $500

— This Earth: a Poem. NY, 1932. Wraps, unopened. sg Dec 12 (110) $110

Anr copy. Illus by Albert Heckman. Wraps; broken, chipped. bbc Sept 23 (412) $65

— The Unvanquished. One of 250, sgd. bbc Dec 9 (467) $1,000

Anr Ed. NY, [1938]. CNY Dec 5 (232) $1,000

— The Wild Palms. NY, [1939]. one of 250. In d/j with edge wear & small tears. bbc Sept 23 (413) $150

One of 250, sgd. bbc Dec 9 (468) $800

Fausto da Longiano

— Duello...regolato a le leggi de l'honore. Venice, 1552. 8vo, 19th-cent half calf. Some dampstaining. sg Mar 26 (111) $110

Fauvelet de Bourrienne, Louis Antoine, 1769-1834

— Memoirs of Napoleon Bonaparte. L, 1885. 3 vols. 12mo, half mor gilt. wa Mar 5 (63) $220

Favre, N. de, Abbe

— Les Quatres Heures de la toilette des dames.... Paris, 1779. 8vo, half mor; rubbed. O Dec 17 (61) $110

Favyn, Andre, b.c.1560

— The Theater of Honour and Knight-hood. L, 1623. 2 vols in 1. Folio, contemp calf; rebacked in lea, upper joints weak. Some browning. STC 10717. Ck Nov 29 (91) £450

Anr copy. Contemp calf; rebacked, worn. S June 30 (28) £750 [Knohl]

Fay, Bernard. See: Grolier Club

Fazellus, Thomas, 1498-1570

— De rebus Siculis decades duae. Palermo: apud Joannem Matthaeum Maidam & Franciscum Carraram, 1558. 1st Ed. Folio, bound c.1595 for Jacques-Auguste de Thou in red mor gilt with his arms & those of his first wife blocked in the center. C Nov 27 (14) £3,500 [Panini]

Fearnside, William Gray. See: Tombleson & Fearnside

Fearon, Henry Bradshaw

— Sketches of America. A Narrative of a Journey.... L, 1818. 1st Ed. 8vo, modern half mor. cb Oct 10 (44) $60

Feather, John

— English Book Prospectuses: An Illustrated History. Newton PA: Bird & Bull Press, 1984. One of 325. Half mor. With 24 folding facsimiles loose in paper folder as issued. NH Aug 23 (51) $155

Anr copy. With 14 folding facsimiles loose in paper folder as issued. O Sept 24 (84) $110

Anr copy. Half mor by Gray Parrot. pba July 23 (30) $75

Featherstonhaugh, George W., 1780-1866

— Excursion through the Slave States.... NY, 1844. 1st American Ed. Orig wraps Spine def. sg June 18 (216) $80

Febres, Andres, 1734-90

— Arte de la lengua general del reyno de Chile.... Lima, 1765. 1st Ed. 8vo, contemp vellum. S Feb 26 (737) £300 [Maggs]

Federalist...

— The Federalist: A Collection of Essays Written in Favour of the New Constitution [by Hamilton, Madison & Jay]. NY, 1788. 1st Ed. 2 vols. 12mo, mor gilt by Alfred Matthews; upper covers detaching, lower joints & extremities worn. Vol II lacking a1 blank. Sonneborn copy. CNY May 14 (60) $13,000

Anr copy. Contemp calf; rebacked, fore-corners renewed. Inner margin repaired on G6 & tear repaired on L3 in Vol I. Epstein copy. sg Apr 29 (203) $19,000

Feldmann, Josef

— Leitfaden zum Unterrichte im Stock-, Rapier-, Saebel- und Bayonnett-Fechten. Vienna, 1886. 4to, mor gilt. sg Mar 26 (113) $200

Felibien, Andre, 1619-95

— Des principes de l'architecture, de la sculpture.... Paris, 1690. 2d Ed. 4to, contemp calf gilt; foot chipped. With 65 plates. bba Sept 19 (305) £420 [Kunkler]

3d Ed. Paris, 1697. 4to, contemp vellum; loose in bdg. With 65 plates. sg Feb 6 (87) $400

— Description de la Grotte de Versailles. Paris, 1679. Folio, contemp calf gilt with royal arms; 1 corner damaged. With 20 numbered plates & 28 un-numbered plates (35 full-page, 13 double-page). Occasional discoloration. Sold w.a.f. S June 25 (202) £2,200 [Maggs]

— Description Sommaire du Chasteau de Versailles. Paris: Guillaume Desprez, 1674. 12mo, 19th-cent half vellum. With etched plan. sg Oct 24 (115) $140

Feliciano, Felice

— Alphabetum Romanum. Verona: Officina Bodoni, [1960]. One of 400. cb Oct 17 (297) $4775

Anr copy. Orig half mor. sg May 7 (104) $750

Fellowes, William Dorset

— A Visit to the Monastery of La Trappe. L, 1818. 1st Ed. 8vo, contemp half calf. With 3 plain & 12 hand-colored plates. DW Nov 6 (42) £60

3d Ed. L, 1820. 8vo, contemp mor gilt. With 3 uncolored & 12 colored plates. Tp spotted. Ck Dec 11 (219) £130

4th Ed. L, 1823. 8vo, contemp mor gilt; joints rubbed, later endpapers. With 2 uncolored & 13 hand-colored plates. L.p. copy. C May 20 (52) £180 [Thornhill]

Anr copy. Contemp mor. With 2 plain & 13 colored plates. L.p. copy. Ck July 10 (257) £160

Anr copy. Orig cloth; spine faded. DW Oct 2 (27) £50

Anr copy. Orig cloth; extremities worn. With 13 plates. DW May 13 (22) £55

Fellows, Sir Charles, 1799-1860

— An Account of Discoveries in Lycia. L, 1841. Later cloth. With 37 plates & 2 hand-colored maps. S June 30 (133) £700 [Kalafat]

— A Journal Written During an Excursion in Asia Minor. L, 1839. 4to, orig cloth; some wear. With frontis, double-page map & 20 plates. Some spotting. Bibliotheca Lindesiana copy. S June 30 (132) £700 [Kalafat]

— Lycia, Caria, Lydia. L, 1847. Illus by George Scharf. Folio, unbound. With 7 tinted litho plates. Some margins bumped or soiled. S Nov 21 (253) £1,100 [Talbot]

Fenelon, Francois de Salignac de la Mothe, 1651-1715

— Les Avantures de Telemaque. Amst. & Rotterdam, 1734. Folio, 18th-cent mor gilt. With port, double-page map & 24 plates. S Dec 5 (261) £2,500 [Livres d'Europe]

Fenice, Giovanni Antonio

— Dictionnaire francois & italien. Morges & Paris, 1585. 8vo, old vellum. Dampstaining through 1st half; some marginalia; tp repaired. sg Mar 12 (65) $225

Fenollosa, Ernest F., 1853-1908

See also: Cuala Press

— Epochs of Chinese & Japanese Art. NY, [1913]. 2 vols. 4to, half cloth, in d/js. Eva Le Gallienne's copy. sg Feb 6 (88) $120

Fenton, James

— A History of Tasmania. Hobart, 1884. 8vo, orig cloth; head of spine repaired. With folding map & 5 ports, all but 1 chromolithos. bba June 11 (342) £100 [Deighton Bell]

Ferber, Edna, 1887-1968

— Cimarron. Garden City, 1930. Advance proofs. Orig wraps. Sgd. sg Dec 12 (113) $120

Ferchl, Franz Maria

— Uebersicht der einzig bestehenden, vollstaendigen Incunabeln-Sammlung der Lithographie und der uebrigen Senefelder-Erfindungen.... Munich, 1856. 8vo, orig wraps. With 3 lithos, 2 folding. Schlosser copy. P June 17 (541) $1,600

Ferentilli, Agostino

— Discorso Universale.... Venice: Gabriel Giolito de'Ferrari, 1570. 4to, 19th-cent calf gilt; front joint cracked, head of spine chipped. sg Nov 7 (79) $400

Ferguson, Adam, 1723-1816

— An Essay on the History of Civil Society. Edin., 1767. 1st Ed. 4to, contemp calf; worn, spine wormed. DW Dec 11 (282) £700

— The History of the Progress and Termination of the Roman Republic. L, 1783. 3 vols. 4to, contemp calf. bba Aug 13 (126) £160 [Byrne]

— Principles of Moral and Political Science. Edin., 1792. 2 vols. 4to, contemp calf; worn & split. Library markings. pnE Aug 12 (237) £900

Ferguson, James, 1710-76

— The Art of Drawing in Perspective Made Easy. L, 1775. 1st Ed. 8vo, contemp calf; worn. With 9 folding plates. sg Sept 6 (110) $150

— Lectures on Select Subjects in Mechanics.... L, 1760. 8vo, contemp calf gilt. With 23 folding plates. b June 22 (168) £110

Anr copy. Contemp sheep; rubbed. With 36 folding plates. Some plates creased or frayed. bba Sept 5 (208) £65 [Raiklen]

Ferguson, John, 1837-1916

— Bibliographical Notes on Histories of Inventions and Books of Secrets. L, 1959. One of 350. DW Dec 11 (359) £80; O Sept 24 (85) $160

— Bibliotheca Chemica: a Catalogue of...the Collection of the late James Young. Glasgow, 1906. 2 vols. 4to, orig cloth. B May 12 (102) HF640

Anr Ed. L, 1954. ("Bibliotheca Chemica. A Bibliography of Books on Alchemy Chemistry and Pharmaceutics.") 2 vols. Reprint of the Glasgow 1906 Ed. bba Dec 19 (268) £100 [Montero]; bba June 25 (149) £100 [Kiefer]; O Sept 24 (86) $140; sg Nov 14 (238) $110

Ferguson, John Alexander, 1881-1969

— A Bibliography of Australia.... Sydney & L, 1951-75. Mixed Ed. 7 vols. 6 vols in d/js. kh Nov 11 (492) A$225

Anr Ed. Canberra, 1975-77. One of 500. 7 vols. In frayed d/js. DW Dec 11 (360) £300

Anr Ed. Canberra, 1977-86. Facsimile Ed. 7 vols. bba Apr 30 (377) £320 [Montero]

Fergusson, James, 1808-86

— Illustrations of the Rock Cut Temples of India. L, 1845. Atlas only. Folio, contemp half calf; rubbed. With litho title & 18 plates. Foxed & waterstained. bba Sept 19 (86) £200 [Mansoor]

Anr copy. Orig half mor; worn. Some foxing; library stamp on tp. P June 17 (205) $800

— One Hundred Stereoscopic Illustrations of Architecture and Natural History in Western India. L, 1864. 8vo, cloth; worn & loss. With 100 mtd stereoscope photographs. O Feb 25 (79) $350

— Picturesque Illustrations of Ancient Architecture in Hindostan. L, 1848. 4 orig parts. Folio, orig wraps. With engraved title, hand-colored map & 23 tinted plates, some with added hand-coloring. Dust-soiled. S May 14 (1288) £1,000 [R. S. Books]

Fergusson, W. N.

— Adventure, Sport and Travel on the Tibetan Steppes. NY, 1911. 4to, cloth. sg Jan 9 (77) $140

Fermat, Pierre de, 1601-65

— Oeuvres. Paris, 1891-1922. 4 vols, including Supplement. 4to, later cloth. DW Nov 6 (349) £220

Fernandez de Navarrete, Martin

— Coleccion de los viages y descubrimientos, que hicieron por mar los Espanoles desde fines del sigo XV.... Madrid, 1825-37. 5 vols, but Vols IV & V are photocopies. Cloth. Sold w.a.f. K Dec 1 (222) $110

Fernandez de Queiros, Pedro

— Account of a Memorial Presented to his Majesty.... Sydney: T. Richards, 1874. 4to, contemp half mor. Facsimile of 1610 text. C June 25 (14) £380 [Maggs]

— Copie de la Requeste presentee au Roy d'Espagne par le capitaine Pierre Ferdinand de Quir. Paris, 1617. 8vo, mor gilt by Lortic. DuPont copy. CNY Oct 8 (106) $23,000

— Historia del descubrimiento de las regiones australes. Madrid, 1876-82. 3 vols in 2. 8vo, bdg not stated. With 5 folding maps. 2 vols spotted. S June 25 (15) £800 [Quaritch/Hordern]

— Senor. El Capitan Pedro Fernandez de Quiros. Cincuenta meses ha que estoy en esta Corte suplicando a V.M. se sirua mandar.... [Madrid, 1611]. 4 leaves. Folio, unbound. Upper portion of final blank browned; horizontal crease across all 4 leaves. C June 25 (5) £55,000 [Quaritch/Hordern]

— Terra Australis Incognita, or a New Southerne Discoverie.... L: for John Hodgetts, 1617. Issue without "translated by W. B." on tp. 4to, mor by Huser. A few marginal repairs. S June 25 (11) £22,000 [Quaritch Hordern]

Anr Ed. L: for William Bray, [1723]. 4to, modern wraps. Reprint of 1617 Ed. S June 25 (13) £2,200 [Quaritch/Hordern]

Fernandez Ferreira, Diego

— Arte de caca da altaneria. Lisbon, 1616. 4to, vellum. Upper margin of frontis shaved; small stain affecting tp; margin of final leaf restored. C Dec 16 (44) £5,000 [Hodgson]

Fernel, Jean, 1497-1558

— Universa medicina.... Leyden, 1645-44. 5 pts in 2 vols. 8vo, later calf gilt; rubbed. bba Sept 5 (2776) £100 [Quaritch]

Anr Ed. Utrecht, 1656. 4to, contemp sheep gilt; joints cracked. Marginal dampstaining & foxing. sg Nov 14 (34) $175

Fernow, Berthold, 1837-1908

— The Records of New Amsterdam from 1653 to 1674. NY, 1897. 7 vols. 8vo, orig cloth; worn. NH Oct 6 (83) $80

Fernyhough, Thomas

— Military Memoirs of Four Brothers.... L, 1829. 8vo, later half calf gilt. With 8 plates. pn Dec 12 (353) £190

Fernyhough, William Henry

— A Series of Twelve Profile Portraits of Aborigines of New South Wales.... Sydney: J. G. Austin, 1836. 4to, orig wraps; spine torn & frayed & with 2 tears into upper cover. With 13 plates. pn Dec 12 (354) £4,100 [Baring]

Ferrara. See: Italy

Ferrari, Giovanni Battista, 1584-1655

— De florum cultura. Rome, 1633. 1st Ed. 4to, contemp vellum. With engraved title & 45 plates. Waterstained at end. SI Dec 5 (857) LIt2,400,000

— Flora, overo cultura di fiori. Rome, 1638. 1st Ed in Italian. 4to, contemp vellum. SI June 9 (362) LIt3,100,000

— Flora seu de florum cultura. Amst., 1646. 4to, 18th-cent calf; some wear at joints. With port & 45 plates. Minor foxing. O May 26 (62) $1,200

— Hesperides, sive de malorum aureorum cultura et usu.... Rome, 1646. 1st Ed. Folio, contemp vellum; worn. With engraved title & 101 plates on 100 sheets. Lacking engraved title & colophon; some spotting & staining; text browned. Sold w.a.f. C June 24 (130) £3,200 [Shapero]

Anr copy. Later vellum. With engraved title & 94 plates. Marginal repairs; some browning. SI Dec 5 (858) LIt5,500,000

Ferrariis, Theophilus de

— Propositiones ex omnibus Aristotelis libris excerptae. Venice: Joannes & Gregorius de Gregoriis, de Forlivio, 3 Aug 1493. 1st Ed. 4to, modern half lea. Dampstaining & marginal repairs at ends; some traces of mold; scattered marginalia; minor worming at beginning. 342 (of 344) leaves; lacking tp & final blank. Goff F-117. sg Oct 24 (116) $900

Ferrario, Giulio

— Le Costume anciene et moderne.... Milan, 1815. Asie, Vol 1 only. Folio, modern cloth. With 2 maps & 87 hand-colored plates. Library markings; lacking world map. sg Feb 13 (174) $325

Ferreira, Christovao. See: Jesuit Relations

Ferrell, Mallory Hope

— A Description of Locomotives Manufactures by the Grant Locomotive Works of Paterson, N.J. Boulder: Pruett Publishing Co., 1971. One of 1,500. Facsimile of 1871 Ed. cb Feb 13 (123) $50

— Silver San Juan. Boulder: Pruett Publishing Co., 1931. One of 750. In d/j. cb Feb 13 (126) $85

Ferrer de Valdecebro, Andres, 1620-80

— Govierno general, moral y politici. Madrid: Juan de Zuniga for Francisco Medel del Castillo, [c.1728?]. 4to, contemp vellum; spine damaged, partly loose in bdg; lacking S1 with woodcut of wild boar. sg Mar 12 (76) $275

Ferrerio, Pietro

— Palazzi di Roma.... [Rome, 1655]. 2 parts in 1 vol. Folio, later calf; worn. With engraved titles & 103 plates. Plates unnumbered. Lacking plates 44 in Part 1 & 27 in Part 2; small adhesive stain to Plate 3 in Part 1; marginal worming. McCarty-Cooper copy. CNY Jan 25 (19) $2,200

Anr Ed. Rome: Giovanni Giacomo de Rossi, [c.1690]. Bound with: Disegno d'una delle facciate de real palazzo che si fa nella citta di Napoli. Rome., c.1680. And: Falda, Giovanni battista. Li Giardini di Roma... Rome, c.1683. And: Passarini, Filippo. Nuove inventioni d'ornamenti d'architettura e d'intagli diversi utili ad argentieri intagliatori ricamatori et altri professori delle buone arti. Rome, 1698. Bound with: Opere per argentieri et altri. Rome, 1632. Oblong folio, contemp calf; corners, head & foot of spine worn, split to foot of joints. With engraved titles & 101 (of 103) plates. Library stamp in blank corner of 1st title. b June 22 (169) £2,900

Ferrero di Lavriano, Francesco Mario

— Augustae regiaeque sabaudae domus arbor gentilitia. Turin: G. B. Zappata, 1702. Folio, 18th-cent calf gilt; rebacked. With frontis & 34 ports. Small hole in 1 plate. S May 13 (834) £420 [Shapero]

Ferriar, John, 1764-1815. See: Fore-Edge Paintings

Ferrier, J. P.

— Caravan Journeys and Wanderings in Persia, Afghanistan, Turkistan, and Beloochistan. L, 1856. 8vo, orig cloth; rubbed. With port, 2 plates & folding engraved maps. S Nov 15 (1288) £300 [Baring]

Ferrier, Susan Edmonstone, 1782-1854

— Destiny; or, the Chief's Daughter. Edin., 1831. 1st Ed. 3 vols. 12mo, calf by Riviere; rubbed. Some foxing. O Aug 25 (69) $170

— The Inheritance. Edin. & L, 1824. 1st Ed. 3 vols. 8vo, calf by Riviere; rubbed. Some foxing. O Aug 25 (70) $170

Ferrieres Sauveboeuf, Louis Francois, Comte de

— Memoires historiques, politiques, et geographiques des voyages...faits en Turquie, en Perse et en Arabie.... Paris, 1790. 2 vols. 8vo, contemp half calf. Some spotting or browning. S June 30 (293) £650 [Dallegio]

Fessenden, Thomas Green, 1771-1837

— The Register of Arts, or a Compendious View.... Phila., 1808. orig calf Upper joint repaired, spine gouged, worn. Browned; some foxing; tp stamped. bbc Dec 9 (342) $170

Feyerabend, Sigmund

— Reysbuch des heyligen Lands.... Frankfurt, 1584. Folio, contemp blind-stamped pigskin; wormed, soiled. Some worming, touching letters; stamp on tp. S Nov 21 (299) £1,050 [Reiss & Auvermann]

Ffoulke Collection, Charles M.

— The Ffoulke Collection of Tapestries. NY, 1913. One of 250. Folio, lea; rebacked, corners torn, doublures loose. wa Apr 9 (275) $70

Ffoulkes, Charles John, 1868-1947

— Inventory and Survey of the Armouries of the Tower of London. L, 1916. 2 vols. 4to, orig cloth; soiled. S July 1 (1249) £180 [Trentman]

Fialetti, Odoardo

— De gli habiti delle religioni. Venice, 1626. 4to, contemp vellum; soiled, Ms title on spine. Engraved throughout. C Dec 16 (45) £480 [Panini]

Fiaschi, Cesare

— Trattato dell'imgrigliare, atteggiare e ferrare cavalli. Venice: Vicenzo Somascho, 1614. 2 parts in 1 vol. 4to, contemp vellum. Some staining. S Nov 21 (17) £600 [Schuster]

Ficino, Marsilio, d1433-99

— De triplici vita.... Florence: Antonio di Bartolommeo Miscomini, 3 Dec 1489. Folio, old half vellum. Scattered dampstaining; some margins wormed; 2 leaves rehinged. Lacking first 2 leaves and last 5 leaves. 83 (of 90) leaves. Goff F-158. sg Nov 14 (35) $550

Ficke, Arthur Davison. See: Knish & Morgan

Ficoroni, Francesco de', 1664-1747

— Dissertatio de larvis scenicis, et figuris comicis antiquorum Romanorum.... Rome, 1754. 2d Ed. 4to, contemp half lea; worn. With 85 plates. SI June 9 (368) LIt450,000

Fiddes, Richard, 1671-1725

— The Life of Cardinal Wolsey. L, 1724. 1st Ed. Folio, modern half lea. cb Feb 12 (39) $190

Fidell, Thomas

— A Perfect Guide for a Studious Young Lawyer. L, 1654. 4to, disbound. sg Mar 12 (88) $300

Field...

— The Field of Mars.... L, 1781. 2 vols. 4to, contemp calf; hinges & joints split; Vol II covers detached. bba Oct 24 (78) £120 [Erlini]

Field, Barron, 1786-1846

— Geographical Memoirs on New South Wales.... L, 1825. 8vo, contemp half calf. With 3 plates & 4 folding maps. S June 25 (213) £800 [Bonham]

Field, Eugene, 1850-95

— Field Flowers. Chicago, [1896]. 4to, cloth. With Eugene Field II forgery of a Frederic Remington signature & sketch. sg Oct 17 (230) $225

— My Book. To William C. Buskett.... [St. Louis: Pvtly ptd for William K. Bixby, 1905]. 1st Ed, Ltd Ed. 4to, half vellum; extremities rubbed. Sgd as Frederic Remington by Eugene Field II & with a

pen-and-ink sketch of a bucking bronco. sg Oct 17 (231) $175
— Poems of Childhood. NY, 1904. Illus by Maxfield Parrish. In chipped d/j with tape repairs on verso. With frontis & 8 colored plates. K Mar 22 (325) $130
— With Trumpet and Drum. NY, 1892. Out-of-series copy. 8vo, half vellum. Inscr as Eugene Field to his wife Julia by Eugene Field II.. sg Oct 17 (231) $175
— Works. NY, 1914. 12 vols. 8vo, mor gilt; extremities scuffed. sg Oct 17 (221) $550

Field, Michael. See: Bradley & Cooper

Field, Stephen Johnson, 1816-99
— Personal Reminiscences of Early Days in California.... [Wash.: Privately ptd, c.1893]. 8vo, cloth. Inscr. sg June 18 (67) $200

Field, Thomas W., 1820-81
— An Essay towards an Indian Bibliography.... NY, 1873. 1st Ed. 8vo, later cloth; worn, front hinge split. Some pencil notations; corner of 1 leaf lacking. bbc Sept 23 (93) $190

Field, W. B. Osgood. See: Bremer Press

Fielding, Henry, 1707-54
See also: Limited Editions Club
— Amelia. L, 1752 [1751]. 1st Ed. 4 vols. 12mo, modern calf. bba Nov 28 (276) £280 [Scott]

Anr copy. Modern half calf. bba Jan 16 (109) £100 [Books & Prints]

Anr copy. Old calf; worn, spines dried. Title in Vol I trimmed & restored in upper margin. Sold w.a.f. O Dec 17 (62) $110
— An Enquiry into the Causes of the Late Increase of Robbers.... L, 1751. 2d Ed. 8vo, disbound. Small tear to 2 upper margins; 1 lower margin soiled. Milne copy. Ck June 12 (64) £320

Anr copy. Tp dusty. sg Mar 12 (90) $175
— The History of the Adventures of Joseph Andrews.... L, 1742. 1st Ed. 2 vols. 12mo, contemp calf. Some browning & soiling. Milne copy. Ck June 12 (62) £400
— The History of Tom Jones.... L, 1749. 1st Ed. 6 vols. 12mo, old calf; worn. Some soiling & staining. Sold w.a.f. O Dec 17 (63) $160

Anr copy. Contemp calf gilt; crack in spine of Vols III & VI, some upper joints cracked. With the usual cancels except that N8 in Vol V is uncancelled. Hole in margin of B10; lacking final blank in Vols III & V; marginal tear in D10 of Vol V affecting a letter; some browning & soiling. Kauffman-Manney copy. P Oct 11 (140) $8,500

Anr copy. Contemp calf; joints cracked, some worming in lower portion of the bdg of Vol I. Lacking final blanks in Vols I & V; tears into text on D10 of Vol I & D3 of Vol II; marginal tears; some spotting & soiling. P Dec 12 (174) $4,750

Anr copy. Contemp calf; worn. S May 13 (621) £380 [Hall]

2d Issue. Calf gilt; spines worn. With the appropriate cancels. P June 17 (206) $600

Mixed Issue. Contemp calf; worn. With the appropriate cancels. M2 torn; some staining & soiling. Sold w.a.f. bba Nov 28 (275) £380 [Scott]

Anr Ed. New-Brentford: P. Norbury for G. Thompson, [c.1800]. ("The Remarkable History of Tom Jones.") 32mo, orig Dutch floral wraps. S Apr 28 (65) £280 [Quaritch]
— The Journal of a Voyage to Lisbon. L, 1755. 1st Pbd Ed. 12mo, contemp sheep; rebacked, rubbed. bba Jan 16 (110) £650 [Murray Hill]

Anr copy. Orig wraps; backstrip def. bba Jan 16 (111) £120 [Thorp]

Anr copy. Lev gilt by Riviere; joints rubbed. bba Jan 19 (112) £130 [Thorp]

2d Ptd Ed (1st Pbd Ed). 12mo, modern half calf. Dampstained. cb Oct 10 (45) $150
— The Life of Mr. Jonathan Wild the Great. L, 1754. 1st Separate Ed. 12mo, modern calf. S Feb 25 (402) £300 [Axe]
— The Miser. A Comedy. L, 1733. 1st Ed. 8vo, 19th-cent calf gilt; joints rubbed. cb Oct 25 (39) $225
— The Mock Doctor; or, The Dumb Lady Cur'd. L, 1771. 8vo, contemp half sheep; spine worn, front cover loose. Interleaved, with Ms stage directions & supplementary dialogue in the hand of William Warren, with his signatures & Warren & Wood Prompt Book written on tp. sg Oct 17 (32) $1,100
— Pasquin: A Dramatick Satire of the Times. L, 1736. 1st Ed. 8vo, later mor gilt by Root. Lacking final leaf. Ck Oct 31 (93) £190

Anr copy. Half mor; edges rubbed. K July 12 (213) $150

Anr copy. Later calf; rubbed. O Dec 17 (64) $140
— A Proposal for Making an Effectual Provision for the Poor.... L, 1753. 8vo, sewn. With folding plate. Tp & verso of final leaf browned. Milne copy. Ck June 12 (67) £600
— Select Works. Ediin, 1807. 5 vols. 8vo, calf by Bayntun. Extra-illus with plates. O May 26 (64) $500
— Tom Thumb. L, 1730. 8vo, 19th-cent calf gilt. Some foxing. cb Oct 25 (40) $350
— Works. L, 1766. 3d Ed. 12 vols. 12mo, orig calf; rubbed. Foxed. b&b Feb 19 (119)

$250

Anr Ed. L, 1771. 8 vols. 8vo, contemp calf; some joints split, rubbed. bba Jan 30 (55) £95 [Harrington]

Anr Ed. L, 1783. 12 vols. 12mo, early half calf; worn. wa Mar 5 (35) $350

Anr Ed. L, 1784. 10 vols. 8vo, contemp mor. Ck July 10 (260) £280

Anr copy. 19th-cent calf gilt. S July 1 (1032) £380 [Toscani]

Anr Ed. L, 1893. One of 250. Ed by George Saintsbury. 12 vols. 8vo, orig cloth; rubbed. bba May 14 (168) £85 [Books & Prints]

Anr Ed. L, 1898-99. One of 750. 12 vols. 8vo, cloth; worn. LH May 17 (627) $50

Ed de Bibliophile. NY, [1902-3]. one of 20 on Japon (this the Samuel Johnson copy). 16 vols. 8vo, mor extra with water lily and dragonfly onlays. With frontises in 3 states: on japan vellum, color-ptd or hand-colored & sgd in pencil by the colorist, or mtd on china paper. Plates in 2 states: on japan vellum & color-ptd. CNY June 9 (68) $2,300

Fielding, Mantle

See also: Morgan & Fielding

— Gilbert Stuart's Portraits of George Washington. Phila., 1923. One of 350. Cloth, in soiled d/j. F Mar 26 (394) $60

Fielding, Theodore Henry, 1781-1851

See also: Barker & Fielding

— British Castles. L, 1825. Oblong 4to, later half mor. With 25 hand-colored plates, mtd on guards. Lacking half-title; tp laid down; some browning. C May 20 (56) £180 [Thornhill]

— Cumberland, Westmoreland and Lancashire Illustrated. L, 1822. Folio, modern half mor gilt. With 44 colored plates. Repairs to small tears in blank margins of some plates. L.p. copy. C May 20 (55) £900 [Spelman]

— Painting in Oil and Water Colours. L, 1839. 4to, contemp cloth; rubbed & soiled. With 4 hand-colored & 6 plain plates. DW Mar 11 (811) £55

— Picturesque Description of the River Wye. L, 1841. Folio, orig cloth. With 12 hand-colored plates. C May 20 (57) £900 [Bradley]

Fielding, Theodore Henry, 1781-1851 —& Walton, J.

— A Picturesque Tour of the English Lakes. L: Ackermann, 1821. 4to, modern half mor gilt by Bayntun. With hand-colored title vignette & 48 hand-colored plates. Some spotting. L.p. copy. C May 20 (54) £1,800 [Joseph]

Anr copy. Modern half mor. CNY Dec 5 (236) $950

Anr copy. Contemp half mor; stained & rubbed. pn Sept 12 (313) £900

Anr copy. Half mor gilt. A few stains in text. S Nov 21 (117) £750 [Fraser]

Anr copy. Contemp half mor; edges worn, front hinge cracked. sg Nov 7 (80) $1,200

Fielding-Hall, H.

— Margaret's Book. L, [1913]. Illus by Charles Robinson. 8vo, cloth. With 12 color plates. sp Nov 24 (223) $65

Figatelli, Giuseppe Maria

— Retta linea gnomonica. Forli: G. Cimatti, 1667. 1st Ed. 4to, 18th-cent bds; rebacked. With 4 folding plates. Marginal waterspotting. SI Dec 5 (242) LIt900,000

Figdor Collection, Albert

— [Sale catalogue] Die Sammlung Dr. Albert Figdor. Berlin, 1930. 5 vols. Folio, orig wraps; spines worn & soiled. S Feb 11 (62) £50 [Campion]

Figgis, Darrell, 1882-1925

— The Paintings of William Blake. L, 1925. One of 1,150. 4to, half cloth; rubbed. bba Dec 18 (37) £110 [Kurita]

Anr copy. Half cloth, in d/j. sg Feb 6 (31) $120

Filhol, Antoine Michel

— Galerie du Musee Napoleon.... Paris, 1804-15. Vols I-IV (of 10). 8vo, contemp calf; rubbed. Some soiling. O Aug 25 (72) $150

Anr copy. 10 vols. 8vo, 19th-cent half sheep gilt; brittle, rubbed; Vol 3 joint starting. sg Nov 7 (81) $600

Filippi, Filippo de, 1869-1938

— The Ascent of Mount St. Elias, Alaska, by H.R.H. Prince Luigi Amadeo de Savoia.... L, 1900. 8vo, orig cloth; extremities frayed, warped; some soiling. Library markings. F Feb 18 (420) $140

— Karakoram and Western Himalaya. L, 1912. Without Atlas vol. 4to, cloth; spine torn, hinges cracked. Library markings. sg May 21 (38) $110

— Ruwenzori: an Account of the Expedition of Prince Luigi Amedeo of Savoy.... L, 1908. Orig cloth. With 5 folding maps. Scattered spotting. DW Nov 6 (43) £270

Anr Ed. NY, 1908. Recent half mor gilt. DW Oct 2 (29) £90

Anr copy. Front hinge starting. sg Jan 9 (62) $300

Filomantio, Silvio. See: Cavalieri, Bonaventura

Filson, John, 1747?-88

— Histoire de Kentucke, Nouvelle Colonie. Paris: Buisson 1785. 8vo, bdg not described but spine lacking. Met Apr 27 (634) $650

Finaughty, William

— The Recollections of William Finaughty, Elephant Hunter, 1864-1875. Phila., [1916]. One of 250. 8vo, orig cloth; soiled. sg Jan 9 (256) $750

Fincham, Henry Walter

— Artists and Engravers of British and American Book Plates. L, 1897. One of 1,050. 4to, half cloth. cb Oct 17 (300) $100

Finden, William, 1787-1852 & Edward Francis, 1791-1857

— Findens' Tableaux of National Character.... L, 1843. 2 vols. Folio, orig cloth; worn & soiled. b Nov 18 (336) £180

— Illustrations to the Life and Works of Lord Byron. L, 1833-34. 3 vols. 4to, contemp mor gilt. With 3 engraved titles & 123 plates. HH May 12 (1825) DM750

Anr copy. Contemp calf gilt; 1 cover detached. With engraved titles & 123 plates. Some foxing. pn Dec 12 (44) £190 [Mackenzie]

Anr copy. Contemp half lea gilt; soiled. With 3 engraved title & 153 (of 157) plates & ports. pn Apr 23 (238) £320

Anr copy. Contemp half mor; upper hinge in Vol I cracked. With frontis, 3 engraved titles & 123 plates & ports. S May 14 (923) £260 [MacKenzie]

— Views of Ports and Harbours, Watering Places, Fishing Villages...on the English Coast. L, 1838. 4to, contemp half mor; rubbed. With engraved title & 49 plates. Some foxing. bba May 28 (372) £150 [Harlow]

Anr Ed. L, 1842. ("The Ports, Harbours, Watering Places and Coast Scenery of Great Britain.") Illus by W. H. Bartlett. 2 vols. 4to, contemp half mor; rubbed, corners worn. Lacking 1 plate. S Nov 15 (914) £440 [Map House]

Anr copy. Contemp calf; rubbed. With engraved titles, port & 123 plates. S May 14 (1143) £400 [Walford]

Anr Ed. L, 1844. 2 vols. 4to, orig cloth; edges rubbed, joints torn. With engraved titles & 122 plates. pn Mar 19 (392) £360 [Burden]

Anr Ed. L, [1874]. 2 vols. 4to, orig cloth; rubbed. With 2 frontises, 2 engraved titles & 142 plates; some waterstaining & foxing. bba Sept 19 (191) £300 [Russell]

Anr copy. 2 vols in 6 parts. Folio, cloth; rubbed. With 2 frontises, 2 engraved titles & 143 plates. bba Sept 19 (191) £300 [Russell]

Anr copy. Vol I (of 2) only. 4to, orig cloth; rubbed. With title & 61 plates. bba Dec 19 (74) £180 [Thorp]

Anr Ed. L, [n.d.]. 2 vols. 4to, orig cloth; hinges weak. Library markings, including ink stamps on titles & verso of some plates. bba May 14 (267) £320 [Nolan]

Finden, William, 1787-1852 & Edward Francis, 1791-1857 —& Horne, Thomas Hartwell, 1780-1862

— Landscape Illustrations of the Bible.... L, 1836. 2 vols. 4to, half mor gilt; scuffed & rubbed. With 96 plates. cb Sept 26 (87) $275

Findlater, Charles 1754-1838

— General View of the Agriculture of the County of Peebles. Edin., 1802. 8vo, orig bds. With frontis map. pnE Oct 1 (305) £120

Fine Print

— Fine Print: The Review for the Arts of the Book. San Francisco, 1979-90. Vol V, No 1-Vol XVI, No 2. 46 issues. 4to, wraps; some wear. O Sept 24 (87) $130

Finlayson, Duncan. See: Grabhorn Printing

Finley, Anthony

— A New General Atlas. Phila., 1824. Bound with: Finley. Atla Classsica. Phila., 1818. Folio, half calf; spine & rear bd lacking. Lacking 1 hand-colored plate in 2d work. wa Mar 5 (441) $2,100

Finley, Martha, 1828-1909

— Elsie Dinsmore. NY, 1867. 1st Ed. 12mo, orig cloth. Parsons-Epstein copy. sg Apr 29 (155) $6,500

Finn, Edmund

— Chronicles of Early Melbourne. Melbourne, 1888. Centennial Ed. 2 vols. 4to, orig mor gilt. kh Nov 11 (280) A$450

Anr copy. Vol I in orig bdg, 2d vol in later rebdg. Margins of 2d tp stained. kh Nov 11 (281) A$250

Finney, Charles Grandison, b.1905

— The Circus of Dr. Lao. NY, 1935. Illus by Boris Artzybasheff. In chipped d/j, with tear at top right of front panel. bbc Sept 23 (415) $80

Anr copy. In d/j. sg Dec 12 (114) $80

Finsch, Otto, 1839-1917

— Die Papageien.... Leiden, 1867-68. 2 vols in 3. 8vo, contemp calf-backed bds, 1 vol in contemp cloth. With folding map & 6 lithos. pn May 14 (173) £240

Fioravanti, Leonardo

— Corona oder Kron der Artzney. Frankfurt: N. Hoffmann, 1604. 8vo, contemp vellum; worn & soiled. Some browning; repair to f.4. S May 13 (889) £200 [Phelps]

Firbank, Ronald, 1886-1926

— The Flower Beneath the Foot. L, 1923. 1st Ed. sg Dec 12 (115) $50

Firdausi

— Shahnama. Cambr. MA, 1981. ("The Houghton Shahnameh.") One of 750. Ed by Martin Bernard Dickson & Stuart Cary Welch. 2 vols. Folio, cloth. bba Mar 26 (180) £460 [J. Randall]

Fireworks...

— Fireworks and How to Make Them. L, 1871. 12mo, orig bds; spine ends chipped, joints & corners worn. sg Nov 14 (288) $100

Firmicus Maternus, Julius

— De nativitatibus. Venice: Aldus, June 1499. ("Astronomicorum libri octo.") Folio, 18th-cent calf; small wormholes in spine, hinges split. 38 lines & headline; 40 lines of Greek surrounding text. 376 leaves. Goff F-191. C Nov 27 (36) £9,000 [Mediolanum]

Anr copy. 18th-cent mor gilt. 38 lines & headline, 40 lines of Greek surrounding text; types 2:114R, 115R, 7:114Gk. N1-T8 & tp all trimmed to edge of text & mtd to size. 374 (of 376) leaves; lacking 2 blanks. Goff F-191. Wodhull-Cromer copy. C Dec 16 (123) £6,500 [Tenschert]

Firmin-Didot, Ambroise, 1790-1876

— Les Graveurs de portraits en France. L, 1875-77. One of 750. 2 vols. 8vo, orig wraps, unopened; soiled. F Mar 26 (424) $60

— Notes d'un voyage fait dans le Levant. Paris, [1826]. 8vo, modern half mor gilt. S June 30 (279) £900 [Dallegio]

Anr copy. Orig wraps, unopened. S July 1 (597) £1,800 [Chelsea]

Fischel, Oscar —&
Boehn, Max von, 1850-1921

— Modes and Manners of the Nineteenth Century. L, 1927. 4 vols. lea; worn. br May 29 (64) $125

Fischer, Joseph —&
Von Wieser, F. R.

— Die aelteste Karte mit dem Namen Amerika aus dem Jahre 1507. Innsbruck, 1903. Folio, contemp half sheep; worn, needs rebacking. With 27 double-page facsimile plates. sg May 21 (218) $350

Fischer von Erlach, Johann Emmanuel

— Anfang einiger vorstellungen der vornehmsten Gebaude.... Vienna, [1719]. Oblong folio, contemp calf. With engraved title, privilege leaf & 29 plates. Lacking Plate 2. S June 25 (200) £2,400 [Pagan]

Fish, Daniel

— Lincoln Bibliography. Rock Island, Ill., 1926. ("A Reprint of the Books and Pamphlets Relating to Abraham Lincoln....") One of 102. Orig half mor. bbc June 29 (205) $75

Fisher, Albert Kenrick, 1856-1948

— The Hawks and Owls of the United States.... Wash., 1893. 8vo, orig cloth. With 26 color plates (1 detached). b June 22 (354) £90

Fisher, Alexander

— A Journal of a Voyage of Discovery to the Arctic Regions, in His Majesty's Ships Hecla and Griper.... L, 1821. 3d Ed. 8vo, contemp half calf; rubbed. With 2 maps. W July 8 (246) £140

Fisher, Frederick George

— A Catalogue of the Various Articles contained in Clara Fisher's Shaksperean Cabinet. L, 1830. 8vo, orig wraps; chipped. Inscr. sg Oct 17 (33) $325

Fisher, Harrison

— The American Girl. NY, 1909. Folio, half cloth; worn. With 12 plates plus port. kh Nov 11 (94) A$240

— The Harrison Fisher Book. NY, 1907. 4to, orig cloth; a few small stains or spots to rear bd. with 21 color ports. wa Sept 26 (589) $110

Fisher, J. B.

— Poetical Rhapsodies. L, 1818. Illus by George Cruikshank. 8vo, mor gilt. Frontis inserted. sg Oct 17 (162) $140

Fisher, James. See: Philip & Fisher

Fisher, John, Saint & Cardinal, 1459-1535

— De causa matrimonii serenissimi regis angliae liber. Alcala de Henares: Miguel de Eguia, Aug 1530. 4to, modern vellum bds. Short tear in E7 repaired; sme underlining in text & a few early Ms annotations in margins. S Dec 5 (115) £1,400 [Quaritch]

Fisher, P. See: Chatto, William Andrew

Fisher, Thomas, 1781-1836

— Monumental Remains and Antiquities in the County of Bedford. Hoxton, 1828. One of 50. Folio, half mor; dampstained, corners rubbed. Lithographed throughout, with hand-colored title & 36 hand-colored plates. Schlosser copy. P June 17 (542)

$1,500

Fiske, John, 1842-1901

— Works. [Cambr., Mass., 1902]. Ltd Ed. 24 vols. 8vo, half mor gilt; rubbed. O Feb 25 (80) $325

Fiske, Willard, 1831-1904

— The Book of the First American Chess Congress. NY, 1859. 12mo, orig cloth; spine worn at head. With colored frontis. Ck May 8 (171) £220

— Chess in Iceland and in Icelandic Literature. Florence, 1905. sg Oct 17 (251) $50

Fitzclarence, George Augustus, Earl of Munster

— Journal of a Route Across India.... L, 1819. 4to, 19th-cent half calf by Leighton using orig cloth bds. With 2 maps, 6 engraved plates & 11 aquatint plates, 9 hand-colored. Lacking half-title & final blank. S May 14 (1289) £260 [Baring]

FitzGerald, Edward Arthur

— Climbs in the New Zealand Alps. L, 1895. 2d Ed. 8vo, cloth; marked & stained. Folding map mtd on linen in pocket at end. Map taped at folds on verso. kh Nov 11 (496) A$120

Anr Ed. L, 1896. One of 60, sgd. 8vo, modern mor with orig lea spine. Folding map mtd on linen in pocket at end. sg Jan 9 (286) $400

Fitzgerald, F. Scott, 1896-1940

— All the Sad Young Men. NY, 1926. 1st Ed. In d/j. K July 12 (219) $1,300

Anr copy. In frayed & soiled orig cloth, in tape-repaired d/j; stamp on free endpaper. Some browning & staining; half title creased. P June 17 (207) $1,600

Anr copy. In d/j. Epstein copy. sg Apr 29 (156) $1,400

— The Beautiful and Damned. NY, 1922. 1st Ed. sg June 11 (115) $60

1st Ptg. In d/j with a few tears at upper edge. CNY June 9 (69) $3,200

Anr copy. Orig cloth; worn. F June 25 (20) $60

Anr copy. In restored d/j; Orig white lettering with black outlines on front cover filled in with black ink. Manney copy. P Oct 11 (142) $2,750

Anr copy. Cloth; discoloration to title on front cover. pba July 9 (93) $50

Anr copy. In d/j. Epstein copy. sg Apr 29 (157) $3,400; sp June 18 (424) $50; wa Dec 9J (186) $70

[-] A Book of Princeton Verse II. Princeton & L, [1919]. 1st Ed. cb Sept 19 (60) $50

— Flappers and Philosophers. NY, 1920. 1st Ed. bbc Dec 9 (470) $80

— The Great Gatsby. NY, 1925. 1st Ed, 1st Ptg. Orig cloth, in restored d/j; rear endpapers browned. Manney copy. P Oct 11 (143) $13,000

Anr copy. Orig cloth. sg Dec 12 (116) $425

Anr copy. Orig cloth; front hinge cracked. Epstein copy. sg Apr 29 (158) $700

Anr copy. Orig cloth; minor wear. sg June 11 (116) $425

Anr copy. Orig cloth; soiled & rubbed. wa Dec 9 (187) $240

Anr copy. Orig cloth; spine worn. wa Mar 5 (179) $200

[-] Nassau Herald: Class of Nineteen Hundred and Seventeen: Princeton University. Princeton, 1917. Vol I. Cloth; rubbed. With short biographical sketch & photograph of Fitzgerald in 1917. cb Sept 19 (61) $50

— Tales of the Jazz Age. NY, 1922. 1st Ed. Orig cloth; spotted, front hinge cracked. bbc Sept 23 (416) $55; cb Sept 19 (58) $80

Anr copy. Minor paint spots on upper cover. O Jan 14 (75) $60

Anr copy. In d/j. sg Apr 29 (159) $2,200

1st Ptg. K Dec 1 (226) $60; pba July 9 (94) $110

— Taps at Reveille. NY, 1935. 1st Ed, 1st State. In d/j. CNY Dec 5 (237) $750

Anr copy. In d/j. Epstein copy. sg Apr 29 (160) $1,200

Anr copy. In chipped d/j. sg June 11 (117) $550

— Tender is the Night. NY, 1934. 4 vols. 4to, pictorial wraps. In: Scribner's Magazine, Jan-Apr 1934. sg Dec 12 (119) $425

1st Ed. In d/j. Epstein copy. sg Apr 29 (161) $2,400

— This Side of Paradise. NY. 1920. 1st Ed, 1st Ptg. In d/j, restored & lined with Japanese tissue. Manney copy. P Oct 11 (141) $4,250

3d Ptg, one of 500 with "Author's Apology" leaf, sgd, tipped in. Epstein copy. sg Apr 29 (162) $1,600

1st Ptg. Orig cloth; front cover soiled. K July 12 (220) $250

Ptg not stated. Orig cloth, in def d/j. Inscr to Florence Griffiths. S July 21 (112) £2,100 [Joseph]

— The Vegetable. NY, 1923. 1st Ed. cb Sept 19 (59) $60

Anr copy. In chipped & tape-repaired d/j. Some browning & soiling. With related material, including an ALs. P June 17 (208) $2,250

Anr copy. Sgd by Orson Welles. pba Aug 20 (78) $150

Anr copy. Ad page chipped. sp Feb 6 (461) $65

Fitzgerald, Percy Hetherington, 1834-1925
— The History of Pickwick. L, 1891. 1 vol extended to 2. 8vo, half mor; rebacked. Extra-illus with a Dickens letter, plates, illusts & drawing. P June 17 (182) $1,300

Fitzgerald, Robert
— Salt-Water Sweetned.... L: W. Cademan, 1683. 4to, recent mor. bbc Dec 9 (343) $900

Fitzgerald, Robert D., 1830?-92
— Australian Orchids. [East Melbourne]: Lansdowne Eds, 1977. Facsimile Ed, One of 350. 2 vols. Folio, orig half calf gilt. wa Dec 9 (629) $280

Fitzgerald, "Scottie"
— The Romantic Egoists. NY, [1974]. Ltd Ed, sgd. Folio, half cloth. bbc Apr 27 (304) $50

Fitzgerald, Zelda
— Save Me the Waltz. NY, 1932. 1st Ed. Orig cloth, in d/j; spine faded. CNY Dec 5 (238) $900

Fitzgibbon, Edward, 1803-57
— The Book of the Salmon. By Ephemera. L, 1850. 16mo, orig cloth. With 1 plain & 8 hand-colored plates. Minor dampstain on tp & frontis. pn Mar 19 (378) £190
— A Handbook of Angling: Teaching Fly-Fishing.... By Ephemera. L, 1847. 8vo, cloth; worn, spine ends chipped. Koopman copy. O Oct 29 (115) $90

Flanagan, Hallie
— Shifting Scenes of the Modern European Theatre. NY, 1928. ANs tipped in. Met Apr 27 (636) $50

Flaubert, Gustave, 1821-80
See also: Golden Cockerel Press
— Bouvard et Pecuchet. Paris, 1881. 1st Ed, one of 55 on Hollande. 12mo, half mor, orig wraps bound in. Epstein copy. sg Apr 29 (163) $700
— L'Education sentimentale. Paris, 1870. 1st Ed, One of 25 on Hollande. 2 vols. 8vo, mor extra by Noulhac. S May 28 (318) £10,000 [Sims Reed]
— Madame Bovary. Paris: aux bureaux de la Revue de Paris, [1856-57]. 1st Ed. 8vo, 19th-cent mor gilt. Extracted from the Revue de Paris, Vols 39-40 & bound with half-title & title for Vol 39. Manney copy. P Oct 11 (144) $2,500

1st Ed in Book form. Paris, 1857. 2 vols. 12mo, orig wraps. S May 28 (316) £2,600 [Beres]
— Trois contes.... Paris, 1877. 1st Ed, one of 100 on hollande. 12mo, mor extra by Charles Meunier, 1899, orig wraps bound in. S May 28 (317) £2,400 [Lardanchet]
— Works. NY, [1904]. Saint-Beuve Ed, one of 100. 10 vols. NH May 30 (81) $210

Flaxman, John, 1755-1826
— Compositions from the Works Days and Theogony of Hesiod. L, 1817. Illus by William Blake. Oblong folio, orig bds; rebacked, rubbed. With engraved title & 36 plates. bba Dec 19 (4) £360 [Bookworks]
— Compositions from the Tragedies of Aeschylus. L, [c.1831]. Oblong folio, half lea; worn. With 36 outline-engraved plates, including title. Some marginal browning & foxing. sg Sept 6 (112) $60

Flechier, Valentin Esprit
— Oraisons funebres. Paris: Renouard, 1802. Only copy ptd on vellum. 2 vols. 12mo, mor extra by Bozerian. Renouard's copy. C June 24 (131) £1,000 [Shapero]

Fleetwood, William, Bishop, 1656-1725
— Chronicon Preciosum: or, an Account of English Money.... L, 1707. 8vo, contemp calf; rebacked, worn, upper cover detached. Library markings. bba Oct 24 (60) £95 [Rainford]

Fleming, Sir Alexander, 1881-1955
— Penicillin: its Practical Application. L, 1946. 1st Ed. cb Nov 21 (87) $120

Fleming, George
— Travels on Horseback in Mantchu Tartary. L, 1863. 8vo, half lea; rubbed, spine gouged. O Feb 25 (81) $375

Fleming, Ian
See also: Plomer, William
— Casino Royale. L, 1953. 1st Ed. In d/j. bba Apr 9 (130) £800 [Frew MacKenzie]; DW Apr 8 (499) £50

Anr copy. In d/j. Inscr to Ian Munro. Manney copy. P Oct 11 (145) $14,000
— The Diamond Smugglers. L, [1957]. 1st Ed. In d/j. cb Sept 19 (64) $90

Anr copy. Inscr to Sir Percy Sillitoe. S Dec 12 (57) £750 [Pickard]
— Diamonds Are Forever. L, 1956. In d/j. cb Sept 19 (63) $325; pn June 11 (188) £190 [McKenzie]
— Dr. No. L, [1958]. 1st Ed, Advance proof. Wraps; soiled. cb Sept 19 (65) $425
— Live and Let Die. L, 1954. 1st Ed. In d/j with tear. pn June 11 (191) £420 [McKenzie]

Anr Ed. NY, 1955. sp Apr 16 (383) $85
— Moonraker. L, [1955]. 1st Ed. Bds, in rubbed & torn d/j. pn June 11 (192) £300 [McKenzie]
— On Her Majesty's Secret Service. L, 1963. In d/j; bdg cocked. wa Mar 5 (182) $65
— You Only Live Twice. [L, 1964]. Advance proof. Wraps; soiled. cb Sept 19 (66) $275

Flers, Robert de, 1872-1927

— Ilsee, Princesse de Tripoli. Paris, 1897. One of 252. Illus by Alphonse Mucha. 4to, half mor gilt, orig wraps bound in; marbled paper almost detached from lower bd. With 129 color illusts, 4 full-page. Dampstained at end; spotted & slightly stained at beginning. S Feb 11 (285) £650 [Marlborough]

Fletcher, George U.

— The Well of the Unicorn. NY, [1948]. In d/j. sg June 11 (119) $70

Fletcher, John, 1579-1625. See: Beaumont & Fletcher

Fletcher, John, 1579-1625 —& Shakespeare, William, 1564-1616

— The Two Noble Kinsmen. L, 1634. 1st Ed. 4to, mor gilt by Bedford. B2 shaved, costing most of signature but preserving catchwords; B3 repaired in lower margins partly obscuring catchword. Roxburghe-Manney copy. P Oct 11 (281) $7,500

Fletcher, John William, 1729-85

— American Patriotism Farther Confronted with Reason, Scripture, and the Constitution.... Shrewsbury, 1776. 1st Ed. 12mo, old half lea; rubbed. Fly-title cut down; lower blank margin of tp cut away; some soiling & fraying. K July 12 (222) $95

Fletcher, Phineas, 1582-1650

— The Purple Island, or the Isle of Man.... Cambr., 1633. 1st Ed. 4to, 19th-cent calf gilt; rebacked. STC 11082. W July 8 (28) £220

Fletcher, Samuel

— Emblematical Devices with Appropriate Mottos. L, 1810. 8vo, later half calf. With frontis, engraved title & 64 plates. cb Sept 26 (88) $150

Fletcher, William Younger, 1830-1913

— Foreign Bookbindings in the British Museum. L, 1896. One of 500. Folio, orig cloth; worn, head of spine bumped. O Sept 24 (88) $90

Fleurieu, Charles Pierre Claret de, Comte, 1738-1810

— Decouvertes des Francois...dans le Sud-Est de la Nouvelle Guinee. Paris, 1790. 4to, contemp calf gilt with arms of Louis XVI. With 12 folding plates & maps. S June 25 (41) £2,200 [Quaritch/Hordern]

— Discoveries of the French in 1768 and 1769, to the South-East of New Guinea.... L, 1791. 4to, orig bds; joints split & portions of spine missing. S June 25 (42) £1,200 [Quaritch/Hordern]

— Voyage autour du monde, pendant...1790-92.... Paris, 1798-1800 [Ans VI-VIII]. 4 vols, including Atlas. 8vo & 4to, contemp half calf; spine ends repaired. With folding tables in text & 1 plate & 15 folding maps in atlas. Library stamps on titles; Vols II & III lacking blanks before title. C Oct 30 (32) £1,000 [Gerits]

Fleuron...

— The Fleuron: A Journal of Typography. L & Cambr., 1923-30. Ed by Oliver Simon & Stanley Morison. Nos 3-7 only. orig cloth. L Nov 14 (38) £70

Anr copy. Nos 1-7 (all pbd). 4to, orig cloth or half-cloth. S Nov 14 (62) £320 [Forster]; wd June 12 (383) $700

Anr Ed. L & Cambr., 1924-26. Nos 3-5. 4to, Nos 3-4 in d/j. cb Oct 17 (308) $150

Flick, Arthur B.

— Art Flick's New Streamside Guide to Naturals and Their Imitations. NY, [1969]. One of 250. Koopman copy & inscr to him. O Oct 29 (116) $150

Flinders, Matthew

— A Voyage to Terra Australis.... L, 1814. 1st Ed. 2 vols plus Atlas vol. 4to & folio, modern half mor gilt. With 9 plates in text vol & 16 charts and 12 plates in Atlas vol. A few leaves in both vols spotted. S June 25 (199) £8,000 [Quaritch/Hordern]

Flora...

— Flora and Sylva: A Monthly Review. L, 1903-5. 3 vols (all pbd). Orig cloth; hinges rubbed. DW Oct 2 (140) £130

Floral...

— The Floral Magazine: Comprising Figures and Descriptions of Popular Garden Flowers. L, 1861-71. Ed by Thomas Moore. 10 vols. 8vo, half mor; rubbed. With 544 hand-colored plates. Stamps on plates. bba Aug 13 (360) £3,500 [Neale]

Anr copy. Vols I-III only. Half mor gilt; not uniform, spines rubbed, 1 split at foot. With 192 hand-colored plates. Title of Vol III torn & repaired; some oxidation to plates. C Oct 30 (216) £1,500 [Dinan & Chighine]

Flore...

— La Flore industrielle. Fleurs de fantaisie. Paris, 1888. Folio, loose in orig portfolio. With 20 colored plates. Sopme marginal soiling & tears. Sold w.a.f. Ck July 10 (120) £240

Florence

— Le dieci mascherate delle bufole mandate in Firenze.... Florence: Giunta, 1566. 8vo, 19th-cent mor gilt. S Dec 5 (116) £750 [Goldschmidt]

Flores, Juan de

— Comptes amoureux, touchant la punition que faict Venus.... Lyons, [n.d.]. Bound with: Martial d'Auvergne. Droictz nouveaux publiez par messieurs les Senateurs du temple de Cupido.... [N.p., 1542] 2 works in 1 vol. 8vo, contemp vellum; loose. S Dec 5 (112) £4,500 [Halwas]

Floriani, Pietro Peolo

— Alla Maestra Caesarea di Feerdinando II.... Venice: Francesco Baba, 1654. ("Difesa et offesa delle piazze....") Folio, orig bds; soiled. With engraved title, port & 51 plates & folding plate. S June 25 (192) £600 [Gorini]

Anr copy. Modern half pigskin. With engraved title, port, 43 plates & 1 folding plan only. Engraved title wormed & with paper cut-out arms affixed with seal to verso. S July 1 (1250) £180 [Toscani]

Florilegium. See: Greek Anthology

Florio, John, 1553?-1625

— Florio his First Fruites.... L: Thos. Dawson for Thos. Woodcocke, 1578. With: Florio. Florios Second Frutes. L: Thos. Woodcocke, 1591. 2 parts in 1 vol. 4to, 17th-cent calf gilt; repaired. Small hole to 1st title, 2d shaved at head, 3d cut close at foot; lacking final blank; some tears, spotting & staining; 2 small holes below the colophon to the 1st work. STC 11096, 11097. S July 21 (4) £3,000 [Knohl]

— Queen Anna's New World of Words.... L, 1611. Folio, contemp calf; rebacked, worn. STC 11099. S July 1 (1068) £350 [Thomson]

Anr copy. Contemp vellum. With port inserted after prelims. Lacking final blank; about half of prelim blank torn away; Qqq1 remargined; minor spots or stains. STC 11099. S July 21 (5) £1,000 [Knohl]

— Vocabulario Italiano & Inglese. A Dictionary.... L, 1659. 1st Ed. 2 parts in 1 vol. Folio, 18th-cent mor gilt; rebacked preserving old spine, rubbed. S July 1 (1251) £220 [American Mus.]

Florist...

— Florist and Pomologist... L, 1862-64. Vols 1-3. Ed by Robert Hogg & Thomas Moore. Half calf. b Nov 18 (366) £600

Florist's...

— The Florist's Journal. L, 1840-42. 3 vols. 8vo, various half calf. With 36 hand-colored plates. Ck May 15 (1) £300

Anr Ed. L, 1840-51. 12 vols. 8vo, contemp half calf; spines faded. With 146 (of 147) plates. Some spotting or adhesion damage. DW Oct 2 (141) £420

Anr Ed. L, 1840. Vols I. 8vo, bdg not described but waterstained. With 10 hand-colored plates. kh Nov 11 (96) A$90

Florus, Publius Annaeus

— Florus, Cl. Salmasius addidit. Leiden: Elzevir, 1638. 1st 1638 Elzevir Ed, with the siren headpiece. 12mo, later mor gilt; worn, hinges cracked. Some browning. bbc Sept 23 (210) $50

Flower-Garden. See: Furber & Bradley

Fly-Fishing...

— Fly-Fishing in Salt and Fresh Water. L: Van Voorst, 1851. 8vo, orig cloth. With 1 plain & 5 hand-colored plates. L Feb 27 (187) £180

Anr copy. worn. O Oct 29 (122) $375

Foa, Edouard

— After Big Game in Central Africa. L, 1899. 8vo, orig cloth. bba Jan 16 (361) £80 [Gramm]

Fogg, William Perry

— "Round the World." Cleveland, 1872. 8vo, half mor; scarred. With port & 10 other albumen prints. Port inscr. sg Apr 13 (99) $425

Foglietta, Uberto

— Historiae genuensium libri xii. Genoa: G. Bartolo, 1585. 4to, mor gilt by Niccolo Franzese c.155, with arms of Cozza in center with name Clemens Cozza lettered above & below arms. Sold w.a.f. S Dec 5 (113) £3,200 [Mediolanum]

Foley, Edwin

— The Book of Decorative Furniture. L, 1910-11. 2 vols. 4to, cloth. sg Apr 2 (117) $50

Anr copy. Orig cloth; some fraying. With 100 tipped-on color plates. wa Mar 5 (587) $85

Folkard, Henry Coleman

— The Wild-Fowler; a Treatise on Ancient and Modern Wild-Fowling.... L, 1864. 2d Ed. 8vo, contemp half calf gilt; rubbed. L Nov 14 (400) £85

Folkes, Martin, 1690-1754

— A Table of English Silver Coins from the Norman Conquest to the Present Time.... L, 1763. ("Tables of English Silver and Gold Coins....") 4to, 19th-cent half calf; rubbed, inner hinges repaired with tape. With 67 plates. W Mar 6 (22) £120

Follot, Charles. See: Clouzot & Follot

Folter, Roland. See: Grolier Club

Foltz, F.
— Halenza's Rheinisches Album. Mainz, [c.1860]. Oblong 4to, orig cloth. With 22 plates. Minor spotting. bba May 14 (291) £160 [Davies]

Fonderie G. Peignot & Fils
— Specimen. Paris, 18896. 8vo, orig cloth. Foxed. cb Sept 5 (110) $150

Fonderie Gustave Mayeur
— Caracteres d'Imprimerie Gustave Mayeur. Paris, 1883. Folio, orig cloth; rebacked. Some dampstaining. cb Sept 5 (111) $325

Fonderie Van Loey-Nouri
— Fonderie Typographique. Maison Van Loey-Nourie. Brussels, [c.1905]. 8vo, orig cloth; worn, front hinge cracked. cb Sept 5 (112) $110
— Gravures et Fonderies Typographiques. Brussels, [c.1897]. Folio, orig cloth. cb Sept 5 (113) $225

Fondin, Jean. See: Remise & Fondin

Fontaine, Nicolas, Sieur de Royaumont
— L'Histoire du Vieux et du Nouveau Testament. Paris, 1752. 2 parts in 1 vol. 8vo, early 19th-cent half mor gilt; corners worn. Some soiling & stains. sg Oct 24 (119) $140
— The History of the Old and New Testament. L, 1690-88. Vol I (of 2) only. Folio, contemp calf; worn. With 154 plates & 2 maps. Some text leaves & plates torn or def. bba Jan 16 (211) £120 [Ceri]

Anr Ed. L, 1705. Trans by Robert Blome. Folio, contemp calf; rubbed, roughly rebacked. bba Feb 27 (323) £220 [D. Smith]

Anr copy. Contemp mor gilt; worn. Some browning & foxing; minor repairs. SI June 10 (890) LIt800,000

4th Ed. L, 1711. 4to, contemp calf; rubbed. With folding maps & 234 plates. Frontis frayed. DW May 13 (276) £60

Fontaine, Pierre Francois Leonard, 1762-1853. See: Percier & Fontaine

Fontana, Giacomo
— Les Eglises de Rome les plus illustres et venerees. Turin, [1887]. 6 vols in 3. Folio, half mor. With engraved title & 302 plates; 3 pictorial livraison titles bound in. Vol VI, Plate XXX soiled & repaired at margins. S June 25 (193) £500 [Shapero]

Fontanier, Victor, 1796-1857
— Voyages en Orient. Paris, 1829. 8vo, contemp half calf gilt. With folding map & 8 plates & plans. Short tear in map; some spotting. S June 30 (134) £190 [Kutluoglu]

Anr copy. 2 vols. 8vo, contemp bds; rubbed. With folding map & 8 plans plates. Stamps removed from titles; some staining. S June 30 (294) £200 [O'Neill]

Fontanus, Jacobus
— De bello Rhodio libri tres. Hagenau: Johann Secer, Aug 1527. 4to, contemp calf; lower cover wormed. Margins dampstained; wormholes in margins of the final leaf. S Dec 5 (117) £1,200 [Halwas]

Fontenai, Abbe de
— Galerie du Palais Royal. Paris, 1786-1808. Illus by J. Couche. 3 vols. Folio, contemp half calf gilt; worn & scuffed, spine ends frayed. With 129 plates. bbc Sept 23 (148) $450

Anr copy. Modern half calf. Sold w.a.f. S Feb 11 (68) £1,000 [Doll]

Fontenelle, Bernard le Bovier de, 1657-1757. See: Nonesuch Press

Foord, Jeanie
— Decorative Flower Studies. NY, 1901. Folio, orig cloth; rubbed. With 37 (of 40) plates. Sold w.a.f. DW Apr 8 (340) £100

Foot, Mirjam M.
— The Henry Davis Gift; a Collection of Bookbindings. L, 1982-83. One of 250 & 750. 2 vols. 4to, orig cloth. O Sept 24 (89) $150; pba July 23 (41) $225

Foote, John Taintor. See: Derrydale Press

Forabosco
— La Gigantea insieme con la Nanea. Florence: Alessandro Ceccherelli, 1566. 4to, late 19th-cent half lea. Lower corners stained. C Dec 16 (46) £5,200 [Quaritch]

Forbes, Edward, 1815-54 —&
Hanley, Sylvanus, 1819-99
— A History of British Mollusca. L, 1853. 4 vols. 8vo, orig cloth. With 203 plates, all but 2 hand-colored. 2 plates repaired at outer margins. bba Feb 13 (374) £540 [Finbar MacDonnell]

Forbes, Edwin, 1839-95
— Life Studies of the Great Army. NY, [1876]. Folio, in orig portfolio; broken & worn. With 40 plates. Marginal waterstains; 2 plates chipped. K Dec 1 (122) $475

Forbes, Henry O.
— A Naturalist's Wanderings in the Eastern Archipelago. L, 1885. 8vo, orig cloth; worn & stained; upper cover gouged. O Feb 25 (83) $180

Forbes, James, 1749-1819
— Oriental Memoirs. L, 1813. 1st Ed. 4 vols. 4to, contemp half calf; worn, joints split, pieces missing from spine. With port & 92 plates, 26 of them hand-colored, a few heightened with varnish. Some staining; a few leaves creased. pn June 11 (246)

£1,200

Anr copy. Bds; worn & soiled. Some foxing; 1 plate loose; marginal tear. wa Dec 9 (450) $2,500

Forbes, James David, 1809-68

— Norway and its Glaciers.... Edin., 1853. 8vo, orig cloth; worn & shaken. O Feb 25 (84) $80

Anr copy. With 2 colored maps, 10 colored lithos & 1 uncolored plates. One gathering loose. S Nov 15 (1095) £220 [Bookroom]

Forbin, Louis, Comte de, 1777-1841

— Voyage dans le Levant en 1817 et 1818. Paris, 1819. 2 vols, including Atlas. 8vo & folio, half calf & later half mor; not uniform. With folding plan & 80 plates. Lacking tp to Atlas; 9 plates holed & repaired affecting image. S June 30 (136) £4,000 [Consolidated Real]

Force, Peter, 1790-1868

— American Archives. Fourth and Fifth Series. Wash., 1837-53. 5 (of 9) vols. 4th Series, Vols 1,3 & 4; 5th Series, Vols 2 & 3. Folio, contemp bds; water-damaged. sp Nov 24 (25) $85

Ford, Ford Madox, 1873-1939

See also: Conrad & Ford

— The Good Soldier. NY, 1905. 1st American Ed. sg Dec 12 (121) $325

Ford, Henry, 1863-1947 —& Crowther, Samuel

— Edison As I Know Him. NY, 1930. In chipped d/j. cb Nov 7 (122) $50

Ford Motor Company

— Lift Up Your Eyes. Dearborn MI, [1929]. Folio, half cloth. With related Ls by F. L. Black about the Ford Tri-Motor. cb Nov 7 (41) $120

Ford, Paul Leicester, 1865-1902

— The New England Primer: a History of its Origin and Development. NY, 1897. One of 425. 4to, bdg not stated. cb Oct 17 (313) $75

Ford, Thomas, 1800-50

— A History of Illinois, from the Commencement.... Chicago, 1854. 8vo, orig cloth; spine ends frayed. Title soiled. cb Sept 12 (64) $60

Ford, Worthington Chauncey, 1858-1941

— George Washington. NY & Paris, 1900. One of 1,250. 2 vols. 4to, mor gilt. b&b Feb 19 (15) $175

Forde, William

— A Sermon Preached at Constantinople.... L: Edward Griffin for Francis Constable, 1616. 4to, modern half mor. Lacking M2; cropped at head with some loss to line border & headlines. STC 11176. S June 30 (292) £850 [Ther]

Fore-Edge Paintings

See also: Milton, John; Vaniere, Jacques

— Biblia Sacra vulgatae editionis. Antwerp, 1603. Folio, 18th-cent mor gilt, with exposed fore-edge painting, Evil Tidings: Job, Ch. 1, sgd by John T. Beer; spine worn, corners bumped. Epstein copy. sg Apr 29 (164) $4,200

— The Book of Common Prayer. L, 1787. 8vo, mor gilt with painting of a Hartfordshire scene. LH May 17 (620) $500

— Elegant Extracts from the Most Eminent Prose Writers. L, 1810. With: Elegant Epistles. L, 1810. Bound in 12 matching mor gilt bdgs each with a fore-edge view of an English scene. LH May 17 (606) $3,000

— The Greek Tragic Theatre.... L, 1809. Vols I-IV (of 5). 8vo, contemp mor gilt, each vol with a painting of a view in London. S Feb 11 (455) £1,000 [Graton & Graton]

— The Tatler. L, 1797. 4 vols. 8vo, contemp mor gilt with paintings of London scenes. CNY Dec 5 (398) $2,600

— BURNS, ROBERT. - Poetical Works. NY: American News, [c.1875]. Orig cloth with painting of the market at Surrey. cb Feb 27 (28) $110

— CLARKE, JAMES STAINIER & MCARTHUR, JOHN. - The Life of Admiral Lord Nelson.... L, 1809. 2 vols. 4to, mor gilt by Bayntun with paintings of Trafalgar & Portsmouth. CNY Oct 8 (107) $2,300

— DRYDEN, JOHN. - Poetical Works. NY: Thomas Y. Crowell, [c.1875]. Orig cloth with painting of a ship at port. cb Feb 27 (27) $110

— FERRIAR, JOHN. - Illustrations of Sterne. L, 1798. 8vo, contemp mor gilt with painting of Dawson Street; joints & extremities rubbed. CNY Dec 5 (392) $550

— HAWKESWORTH, JOHN. - The Adventurer. L, 1805-7. 4 vols. 12mo, contemp mor gilt with paintings of Old Hungerford Market, Tebard Inn, Sadlers Wells & London Bridge. CNY Dec 5 (393) $1,100

— LUCAS, EDWARD VERRALL. - Highways and Byways in Sussex. L, 1921. Mor gilt with painting of Cowdray ruins, Midhurst, by C. B. Currie. CNY Dec 5 (391) $3,000

— MILTON, JOHN. - Paradise Lost. With: Paradise Regained. L, 1795-96. 2 vols. 8vo, contemp mor gilt, prize bdg of Trinity College, Dublin, with paintings of Milton's cottage & of his birthplace, St. Giles

Cripplegate. CNY Dec 5 (394) $700

— Moore, Thomas. - Lalla Rookh.... L, 1817. 8vo, contemp mor gilt with double painting of an angling & a coaching scene. CNY Dec 5 (395) $350

— Petrarca, Francesco. - Le Rime. Florence, 1821. 2 vols. 8vo, contemp vellum, each cover with painted panel of views, fore-edge paintings of Verona & Rome. CNY Dec 5 (396) $650

— Pollok, Robert. - The Course of Time. Edin., 1832. 12mo, 19th-cent mor with painting of a castle. sg Mar 5 (112) $225

— Rogers, Samuel. - Poems. L, 1854. 8vo, contemp mor gilt with painting of Westminster Abbey; scuffed. cb Oct 25 (42) $550

— Scott, Sir Walter. - Marmion; a Tale of Flodden Field. Edin., 1808. 8vo, contemp mor gilt, with painting of Norham Castle. CNY Dec 5 (397) $400

— Shakespeare, William. - The Plays. L: Cassell, [c.1885]. 3 vols. Orig mor gilt with paintings from Richard II, Lear & Rosalind. cb Dec 5 (58) $700

— Somervile, William. - The Chase, a Poem. L, 1796. 4to, contemp mor gilt with painting of a fox-hunting scene. L.p. copy. C May 20 (175) £360 [Traylen]

— Swinburne, Algernon Charles. - Essays and Studies. L, 1876. 8 vols. Mor gilt with double-views of Florence & Naples. LH May 17 (610) $600

— Thomas a Kempis. - The Christian's Pattern: or, a Treatise of the Imitation of Jesus Christ. L, 1733. 8vo, 19th-cent mor gilt with painting of Gloucester with sailing ships in the foreground; lower cover scuffed. S July 9 (945) £380

— Trimmer, Mary. - Trimmer's Natural History. L, 1830. 2 vols in 1. 12mo, mor gilt with painting of a whaling scene. cb Feb 12 (41) $850

— Wordsworth, William. - Poetical Works. Edin: Gall & Inglis, [c.1880]. Orig cloth with painting of an American privateer sailing ship. cb Feb 27 (29) $110

— Worlidge, Thomas. - A Specimen of a Select Collection of Drawings, from the Curious Antique Gems.... L, 1766. 3 vols. 4to, contemp mor gilt, each vol with a double painting, of which the first is in 2 scenes, all of the scenes being English, except for 1 of Florence. CNY Dec 5 (399) $6,500

Foreest, Pieter van, 1522-97

— Observationum et curationum medicinalium.... Leiden: Plantin, 1596. 8vo, contemp vellum. Some browning. SI Dec 5 (249) LIt200,000

Foreign...

— Foreign Field Sports: Fisheries, Sporting Anecdotes.... L, 1814-13. 1st Ed. 4to, 19th-cent half mor; rubbed. With 110 hand-colored plates. Plate 89 short at lower margin; text to Plate 50 torn & crudely repaired; some spotting. S Nov 21 (213) £950 [Schuster]

2d Ed. L, 1819. 4to, contemp mor gilt. With 110 hand-colored plates. Some discoloration in text & on some plate versos; lacking half-title. S Nov 21 (378) £1,150 [Schuster]

Anr Ed. L, [some plates watermarked 1823]. 4to, contemp mor gilt; rubbed. With 110 hand-colored plates. Some soiling; frontis & tp on new guards. pn Apr 23 (218) £950 [Bifolio]

Anr Ed. L: W. Gilling, [plates dated 1823]. 4to, later half lea; piece torn from head of spine, upper joint torn. With 110 hand-colored plates. Library stamps, not affecting text; some soiling. pn Mar 19 (356) £1,200

Anr Ed. L: Edward Orme [c.1825]. Folio, mor gilt. With 110 hand-colored plates. L.p. copy. C May 20 (58) £4,200 [Maggs]

Fore's...

— Fore's Sporting Notes and Sketches: A Quarterly Magazine. L, 1885-1907. 24 vols. Half mor; A few covers detached. cb Jan 30 (50) $375

Foresi, Bastiano

— Libro chiamato ambizione. [Florence: Antonio di Bartolommeo Miscomini, c.1485]. 4to, 19th-cent mor gilt. 86 (of 90) leaves; lacking a1-4. Goff F-243. SI June 9 (386) LIt800,000

Fores's...

— Fores's Sporting Notes & Sketches L, 1884-1912. Vols 1-29 (complete set). 8vo, cloth; worn. O Dec 17 (68) $325

Forester, Cecil Scott

— Captain Horatio Hornblower. Bost., 1939. 3 vols. Half mor; rubbed, spine head of Vol II chipped. cb Sept 19 (68) $70

Forester, Johann Georg Adam. See: Forster, Georg

Forester, Thomas

— Norway in 1848 and 1849. L, 1850. 8vo, half mor gilt. Some foxing. sg Jan 9 (79) $130

— Rambles in the Islands of Corsica and Sardinia. L, 1858. 8vo, half mor. DW Apr 8 (30) £78

Forman, Harry Buxton, 1842-1917

— The Books of William Morris. Chicago, 1897. 8vo, bdg not stated. cb Oct 17 (317) $100

Forrest, Charles Ramus

— A Picturesque Tour along the Rivers Ganges and Jumna. L, 1824. 4to, mor gilt by Zaehnsdorf. With folding map & 24 plates, all hand-colored. L.p. copy with orig watercolor drawing by Forest of the Palace of delhi, sgd with initials, pasted to front free endpaper. C May 20 (59) £3,800 [Fida Ali]

Anr copy. Contemp cloth. C May 20 (60) £1,900 [Shapero]

Anr copy. Half mor by Sangorski & Sutcliffe. Some spotting & smudging. wa Dec 9 (451) $2,300

Forrest, John, 1847-1918

— Explorations in Australia. L, 1875. 8vo, old half mor; rubbed. Library markings; maps & plates laid down on linen; soiling & discoloration; bound without final book ads. kh Nov 11 (500) A$300

Anr copy. Orig cloth. With 2 ports, 6 plates & 4 folding maps. S June 25 (262) £1,300 [Brooke-Hitching]

Forshaw, Joseph Michael

— Parrots of the World. Melbourne, 1973. Folio, orig cloth, in d/j. S Feb 26 (915) £150 [Shapero]

Forster, Edward Morgan, 1879-1970

— Alexandria: A History and a Guide. Alexandria, 1922. 1st Ed. With 3 maps, 1 colored & in pocket at end. DW Apr 8 (501) £70

— Anonymity, an Enquiry. L: Hogarth Press, 1925. Inscr to D. H. Lawrence. P June 17 (209) $700

— The Longest Journey. L, 1907. Some spotting. Siegfried Sassoon's copy. S Feb 25 (403) £60 [Sotheran]

Anr copy. Front hinge cracked. sg Dec 12 (122) $275

— A Passage to India. L, 1924. One of 200 L.p. copies, sgd. Half cloth, unopened; spine ends bumped. Epstein copy. sg Apr 29 (165) $1,900

1st Ed. In torn d/j. F Dec 18 (92) $120

One of 200 L.p. copies. Orig half cloth. Ck Dec 11 (155) £280

Anr copy. Orig half cloth; covers browned, endpapers foxed. wd Dec 12 (389) $650

Forster, Georg, 1754-94

— A Voyage Round the World.... L, 1777. 2 vols. 4to, 19th-cent calf; joints cracked, spine rubbed. Some staining to titles & early leaves of both vols. Ck May 15 (102) £1,300

Anr copy. Modern half syn. Marginal repairs to folding chart & some text leaves; tp of Vol II def & laid down; some foxing & dampstaining, mainly to Vol II. pn June 11 (285) £300

Anr copy. Contemp calf; rebacked. With folding chart & errata leaf (with short tear repaired). S Nov 21 (374) £900 [Bifolco]

Anr copy. Modern half mor gilt by Sangorski & Sutcliffe. With large folding chart (short tear repaired). S June 25 (492) £1,00 [Afsentus]

Forster, George, d.1792

— A Journey from Bengal to England. Calcutta 1790 & L, 1798. 2 vols. 4to, contemp half calf; worn, upper covers detached. DW Dec 11 (31) £145

Forster, Johann Reinhold, 1729-98

— History of the Voyages and Discoveries made in the North. L, 1786. 4to, contemp half calf; spine & joints rubbed. With 3 folding maps. Small tear to b4; 3-inch marginal tear to 3P2; 1st & 3d folding maps lightly creased & foxed & with small tears at inner margin. CNY Oct 8 (108) $1,400

— Indische Zoologie, oder systematische Beschreibungen seltner und undbekannter Thiere aus Indien. Halle: Johann Jacob Gebauer, 1795. Folio, contemp bds; rubbed. With 15 hand-colored plates, 1 folding (repaired at outer edge). Text browned; 2 stamps on tp. S June 25 (20) £1,700 [Marshall]

Forster, John, 1812-76

— The Life of Charles Dickens. L, 1872-74. 3 vols. 8vo, contemp half calf. bba June 11 (119) £95 [Aspin]

Anr copy. Mor gilt by Riviere; each upper cover with recessed panel containing painted badges of English cities. Extra-illus with c.500 ports & plates & 58 autographs by Dickens, Forster & their contemporaries. CNY Dec 5 (386) $5,000

Forsyth, Frederick

— The Day of the Jackal. [L, 1971]. In d/j. Inscr. sg Dec 12 (123) $200

Forsyth, Robert, 1766-1846

— The Beauties of Scotland. Edin., 1805-8. 5 vols. 8vo, contemp calf; rubbed. bba Sept 19 (239) £100 [Martinez]

Forsyth, William, 1737-1804

— An Epitome of Mr. Forsyth's Treatise on the Culture and Management of Fruit Trees. Paris, 1803. 8vo, contemp sheep; shabby. With 15 plates. Tp torn along gutter; contents partly dampstained. wa Dec 9 (492) $60

— A Treatise on the Culture and Management of Fruit-Trees. L, 1803. 3d Ed. 4to, contemp sheep; some wear, joints starting, front free endpaper detached. With 13 folding plates. Some foxing & browning. wa Mar 5 (352) $80

Fort, Paul, 1872-1960

— Le Livre des ballades. Paris: H. Piazza, [1921]. One of 1,300. Illus by Arthur Rackham. 4to, half mor; worn, front cover loose. Sold w.a.f. sg Jan 30 (143) $175

Fortescue, Sir John William, 1858-1933

— A History of the British Army. L, 1910-35. 13 vols in 14, plus 6 map vols. Together, 20 vols. Library markings. bbc Sept 23 (227) $330

Anr Ed. L, 1935-30. 13 vols plus 6 map vols. Together, 19 vols. In d/js. pnE Oct 1 (319) £600

Fortescue, Sir John William, 1859-1933. See: Gregynog Press

Fortitudo...

— Fortitudo leonina in utraque fortuna Maximiliani Emmanuelis...Comitis Palatini Rheni...et electoris. Munich, 1715. 2 parts in 1 vol. Folio, 18th-cent calf; spine head damaged. With frontis, 16 plates (1 double-page) & 64 engraved emblems. S Dec 5 (265) £1,000 [Halwas]

Fortsas...

— The Fortsas Catalogue. North Hills: Bird & Bull Press, 1970. One of 225. 4to, half cloth. bbc Apr 27 (100) $110; F Dec 18 (191) $80

Fortune, Robert, 1813-80

— A Journey to the Tea Countries of China.... L, 1852. 8vo, orig cloth. With additional title, map & 3 plates. bba June 25 (255) £240 [Heywood Hill]

— A Residence among the Chinese. L, 1857. 8vo, orig cloth. bba June 25 (256) £240 [Cumming]

Forty-Four...

— Forty-Four Turkish Fairy Tales. NY: Thomas Y. Crowell, [n.d.]. Illus by Willy Pogany. Orig cloth; rubbed. With 16 mtd color plates. Manney copy. P Oct 11 (255) $400

Fosbroke, Thomas Dudley, 1770-1842

— Encyclopaedia of Antiquities; and Elements of Archaeology, Classical and Mediaeval. L, 1825. 1st Ed. 2 vols. 4to, contemep calf gilt; extremities rubbed, Vol I rear joint cracked. Some plates foxed. sg Oct 17 (254) $100

Foskett, Daphne

— A Dictionary of British Miniature Painters. L, 1972. 2 vols. 4to, cloth, in d/js. DW Mar 11 (812) £85

Fossati, Gaspard, 1809-83

— Aya Sophia, Constantinople, as Recently Restored.... L, [1852]. Folio, orig half mor gilt; def. With litho title & 25 tinted plates. Plates & text loose & some edges frayed. S July 1 (607) £3,800 [Consolidated Real]

Fossati, Giorgio

— Raccolta di varie favole. Venice, 1744. 6 vols in 3. Folio, contemp vellum gilt, Vol I in half vellum. With 213 plates ptd in colors. Lacking plates 3, 32 & 17; hole in Plate 5 repaired with some loss; Plate 19 scratched; Plate 20 with overpainting. Schlosser copy. P June 18 (459) $1,300

Fossett, Frank

— Colorado: its Gold and Silver Mines, Farms, and Stock Ranges.... NY, 1879. 12mo, orig cloth. With 5 maps & 50 plates. sg Dec 5 (98) $50

Foster, Joshua James, 1847-1923

— Concerning the True Portraiture of Mary, Queen of Scots. L, 1904. Folio, half mor gilt; worn & soiled. wa Feb 20 (221) $55

One of 45. Lea with Stuart arms. With 57 plates. K Dec 1 (228) $120

— Miniature Painters British and Foreign. L & NY, 1903. One of 175 de luxe copies. 2 vols. 4to, orig vellum bds; worn & warped. F Mar 26 (413) $100

— The Stuarts. L, 1902. One of 175. 2 vols. Folio, orig cloth. K Dec 1 (229) $80

Foster, William Harnden

— New England Grouse Shooting. NY, 1942. 4to, cloth; worn. O Mar 31 (77) $50

Fothergill, John, 1712-80

— The Fothergill Omnibus. L, 1931. One of 250. Mor gilt. Sgd by Fothergill & all 17 contributors. pba July 9 (100) $100

— Some Anecdotes of the Late Peter Collinson. L, 1775. Folio, half calf over contemp bds; rubbed. P June 16 (127) $500

Foucquet, Jehan, 1415?-80?

— Oeuvres. Paris: L. Curmer, 1866-67. 2 vols. 4to, mor gilt. Ck July 10 (264) £240

Anr copy. Mor; rubbed. O Mar 31 (78) $700

Fougasses, Thomas de

— The General Historie of the Magnificent State of Venice.... L, 1612. 2 vols. Folio, 17th-cent calf; rebacked. A few rust-holes touching letters; minor worming from upper fore-corner of 5C6 onwards. STC 11207. S Nov 21 (300) £3,800 [Bank of Cyprus]

Anr copy. Contemp calf; repaired. With woodcut view of Venice on title & 90 woodcut ports. Title slightly creased & dust-soiled. STC 11207. S June 30 (29) £3,400 [Kutluoglu]

Fouilloux, Jacques du. See: Du Fouilloux, Jacques

Fouquier, Marcel

— De l'art des jardins. Paris, 1911. Presentation copy. 4to, contemp half mor by Ourvand, orig wraps bound in. wa Sept 26 (469) $200

Fourquevaux, Raimond de. See: Du Bellay, Guillaume

Fowler, Christopher

— Daemonium Meridianum. Satan at Noon.... L, 1655. 4to, later bds; worn. O Dec 17 (70) $160

Fowler, Jacob, 1765-1850

— The Journal of Jacob Fowler. Narrating an Adventure from Arkansas through the Indian Territory.... NY, 1898. One of 950. 8vo, cloth. bbc Sept 23 (306) $80

Fowler, John

— Journal of a Tour in the State of New York. L, 1831. 12mo, cloth. sg June 18 (433) $50

Fowler, Lawrence Hall —& Baer, Elizabeth

— The Fowler Architectural Collection of the Johns Hopkins University: Catalogue. Balt., 1961. 4to, orig cloth; worn. sg Oct 31 (111) $275

Fowles, John

— The Collector. Bost., [1963]. 1st American Ed, Advance copy. Orig wraps; cocked, spine soiled, scratch to front cover. wa Mar 5 (183) $100

Anr Ed. L, [1963]. Bds in d/j. bba Dec 19 (180) £160 [Great NW Bookstore]

Anr copy. Orig cloth, in d/j. Epstein copy. sg Apr 29 (166) $550

Advance copy. Orig wraps. cb Feb 12 (45) $150

Advance proof copy. Orig wraps, in d/j. P Oct 11 (146) $1,600

— The Magus. L: Jonathan Cape, [1966]. 1st English Ed, Advance proof. Wraps. cb Sept 19 (70) $225

Fowles, Joseph

— Sydney in 1848.... Sydney: D. Wall, [1848]. 4to, modern cloth. Lacking half-title; photostat typescript index added. kh Nov 11 (498) A$100

Fox, Charles James, 1749-1806

— A History of the Early Part of the Reign of James the Second. L, 1808. 4to, lea. With port-frontis. K July 12 (225) $65

Fox, George Henry

— Photographic Illustrations of Skin Diseases. NY, 1887. 4to, orig half mor; hinges reinforced. With 48 plates by Edward Bierstadt, colored by Dr. Joseph Gaertner. bbc Feb 17 (208) $170

— Photographic Atlas of the Diseases of the Skin. Phila., [1905]. 4to, cloth; worn. With 96 color plates. bbc Feb 17 (207) $80

Fox, John William, 1863-1919

— The Little Shepherd of Kingdom Come. NY, 1931. One of 500. Illus by N. C. Wyeth. Half vellum. sg Jan 30 (190) $600

Foxe, Luke, 1586-1635

— North-west Fox, or, Fox from the North-West Passage. L, 1635. 4to, mor gilt by Bedford; joints rubbed. With woodcut frontis, folding circumpolar map & full-page woodcut map; cancel leaf u2.3 inserted between V2 & V3 but paginated 172, 170, 171 & with errata on u3v. Folding map with clean tear at mount & fold at mount reinforced; T4 & Kk2 repaired, affecting last letter of each catchword; other marginal repairs; washed. STC 11221. DuPont copy. CNY Oct 8 (109) $22,000

Foxon, D. F.

— English Verse 1701-1750. Cambr., 1975. 2 vols. 4to, cloth, in d/js. bba June 25 (151) £85 [Forster]

Fracker, George

— A Voyage to South America, with an Account of a Shipwreck in the River la Plata.... Bost, 1826. 12mo, modern bds. Tp repaired; library markings. sg June 18 (221) $175

Fradin, Gabriel

— Le Duel. [N.p.], 1886. 8vo, half mor, orig front wrap bound in. Lithographed throughout. sg Mar 26 (169) $150

Fragmenta...

— Fragmenta poetarum veterum latinorum quorum opera.... Geneva: Henricus Stephanus, 1564. 8vo, contemp vellum. Tear in blank corner of tp. sg Oct 24 (120) $375

Francais...

— Les Francais peints par eux-memes. Paris, 1840-42. 9 vols. 8vo, contemp half mor; 3 backstrips detached; others rubbed & chipped with loss. bba Apr 30 (290) £300 [Maggs]

France, Anatole, 1844-1924

— Clio. Paris, 1900. One of 150. Illus by Alphonse Mucha. 8vo, half lea. K Sept 29 (278) $250

Anr copy. Half mor; worn. Extra title & front endpapers loose. sg Sept 26 (240) $90

Anr copy. Half mor, orig wraps bound in; worn. sg Jan 30 (107) $150

— Les Contes de Jacques Tournebroche. Paris, [1909]. Half mor. cb Jan 16 (51) $70

— Les Dieux ont soif. Paris, 1912. 1st Ed, One of 100 on japon. 4to, mor gilt, orig wraps bound in. S May 28 (322) £1,300 [Holinger]

— The Life of Joan of Arc. L, 1909. One of 500. 2 vols. Half lev gilt; spot on front cover of 1st vol. cb Oct 31 (57) $325

— Le Lys Rouge. Paris, 1894. 1st Ed, one of 30 on japon imperial. 12mo, mor gilt, orig wraps bound in. S May 28 (320) £800 [Beres]

— Mystere du sang. Paris, 1942. Unique copy with 5 orig gouaches by Exter. 4to, loose as issued. CGen Nov 18 (375) SF2,500

— Le Petit Pierre. Paris, 1923. One of 400. Illus by Pierre Brissaud. 4to, mor extra by Pierre Legrain. CGen Nov 18 (381) SF1,800

— Works. NY, 1924. Autograph Ed, one of 1,075. 30 vols. Half cloth; spines faded. cb Dec 19 (60) $250

Anr copy. Half cloth, in d/js; minor defs. wa Apr 9 (42) $200

Anr Ed. Paris, [1924]. 30 vols. Half calf; spines faded. cb Dec 19 (61) $100

Franceschi, Domenico de

— Solyman the Magnificent going to Mosque.... Edin: Pvtly ptd, 1877. One of 100. Folio, orig half mor. With ports on recto & verso of tp, 9 double-page plates & 1 page of woodcut. S June 30 (296) £200 [Quaritch]

Francesco III, Duke of Modena

— Della storia e della ragione d'ogni poesia. Bologna, 1739-52. 5 vols in 7. 4to, 19th-cent half vellum. Some worming. SI Dec 5 (987) LIt300,000

Franchere, Gabriel, 1786-1863

— Narrative of a Voyage to the Northwest Coast of America.... NY, 1854. 1st American Ed. 8vo, orig cloth. With 3 plates. cb Feb 12 (25) $375

Anr copy. Cloth. Some foxing. sg June 18 (322) $130

Franchetti, Gaetano

— Storia e descrizione del Duomo di Milano. Milan, 1821. 4to, contemp half lea; worn. ALs inserted. SI Dec 5 (251) LIt850,000

Francia, Francois L. T.

— Progressive Lessons Tending to Elucidate the Character of Trees.... L, 1835. 4to, half russia; worn. With hand-colored table, 1 plain & 12 hand-colored plates. bba Feb 27 (3347) £200 [Spelman]

Francis, Austin M.

— Catskill Rivers. Birthplace of American Fly Fishing. NY: Beaverskill Press, 1983. One of 300. 4to, lea. Koopman copy. O Oct 29 (131) $225

Francis, Dick

— The Sport of Queens. L, 1957. bba Dec 19 (182) £65 [Wilfred]

Francis, Francis

— A Book on Angling: a Complete Treatise.... L, 1867. 1st Ed. 8vo, contemp calf; rubbed, head of spine chipped. With 15 plates, including 5 hand-colored. Koopman copy. O Oct 29 (132) $325

Francis, Grant R.

— Old English Drinking Glasses. L, 1926. 4to, orig cloth; spine faded. bba Oct 24 (395) £100 [Demetzy]

Anr copy. Orig cloth; some wear. Former owner's address label affixed to tp. O May 26 (69) $190

Francis, H. R.

— The Fly-Fisher and his Library. L, 1856. 8vo, half mor; rubbed. Koopman copy. O Oct 29 (133) $375

Francis, J. G.

— A Book of Cheerful Cats and Other Animated Animals. NY, 1892. Orig pictorial bds in chipped d/j. Epstein copy. sg Apr 29 (168) $425

Francis of Assisi, Saint, 1182-1226. See: Limited Editions Club

Franciscus de Retza. See: Retza, Franciscus de

Franck, Sebastian, 1499-1543?

— Die Guldin Arch darein der kehrn und die besten hawptspruech der heyligen Schrifft.... Augsburg: Heinrich Steiner, 1538. Folio, contemp blind-tooled pigskin over wooden bds; lacking catches & clasps.

Tp creased & loose; small wormhole through last several leaves. sg Oct 24 (121) $800

Franco, Giacomo

— Raccolta di Essemplari di piu famosi Scrittori. [Venice, c.1594]. Oblong 4to, contemp vellum. With 42 plates plus additional plate inserted at end Plate numbered 15 with repaired tear; some ink or waterstain. Nicolo Manassi's copy. C June 24 (234) £2,800 [Franks]

Francoise

— La Plus Vieille Histoire du monde, mise en images par Francoise. Paris: Les Jardin des Modes, [c.1930]. Oblong 4to, ptd on linen with outer pages forming cover; minor soiling on covers. sg Mar 5 (42) $325

Frank, Robert

— Les Americains. Paris, 1958. Texts by Alain Bosquet. Pictorial bds with Saul Steinberg illust; hinges starting. sg Apr 13 (44) $1,800

Frankau, Julia, 1864-1916

— The Story of Emma, Lady Hamilton. L, 1911. One of 250. 2 vols. Folio, orig vellum. Ck July 10 (265) £260

Frankland, Charles Colville

— Travels To and From Constantinople. L, 1830. 2d Ed. 2 vols. 8vo, 19th-cent half mor; rubbed. With 2 hand-colored frontises, 14 aquatint & 11 wood-engraed plates & 4 maps & plans. Lacking half-titles. S June 30 (135) £800 [Consolidated Real]

Franklin, Benjamin, 1706-90

See also: Limited Editions Club

— Briefe von der Elektricitat. Leipzig: for Gottfied Keisewetter, 1758. 8vo, contemp half vellum; soiled & rubbed. Marginal loss to 2d leaf not affecting text. P June 16 (45) $1,000

— Cool Thoughts on the Present Situation of our Public Affairs. Phila.: W. Dunlap, 1764. 8vo, calf. Lacking half-title & terminal blank; tp & several other leaves extended; marginal repairs. S June 16 (90) $1,500

— Enskildta Lefverne. Stockholm, 1792. 8vo, contemp bds; worn. Lower fore-edge cut from final text leaf, with loss. sg Dec 5 (98A) $300

— The Examination of Doctor Benjamin Franklin...relating to the Repeal of the Stamp-Act. [Phila.: Hall & Sellers, 1766]. 1st Ed. 8vo, disbound. Repaired tear on initial leaf; some browning. sg Dec 5 (98B) $3,000

— Experiments and Observations on Electricity. L, 1751-53. 1st Ed. Part 1 only. Calf. Lacking terminal leaf of ads. P June 16 (43) $6,500

4th Ed. L, 1769. 4to, contemp calf gilt; rebacked with orig spine preserved. With 7 plates. P June 16 (46) $3,000

— Memoires de la vie privee.... Paris, 1791. 1st Ed. 2 parts in 1 vol. 8vo, early 19th-cent bds. sg Dec 5 (98C) $450

Anr copy. Contemp bds; corners chipped. Epstein copy. sg Apr 29 (169) $1,900

Anr copy. Old bds. wd Dec 12 (390) $1,000

— Narrative of the Late Massacres in Lancaster County.... [Phila.: Franklin & Hall], 1764. 8vo, half mor. Foxed. Library Company of Philadelphia duplicate. P June 16 (92) $3,000

— Opere politiche. Padua, 1783. 8vo, contemp half calf. P June 16 (140) $200

Anr copy. Contemp paper covers; spine & corners worn, becoming loose with 1st gathering sprung. Minor stains & annotations. wa Dec 9 (289) $180

— Philosophical and Miscellaneous Papers.... L, 1787. 8vo, contemp calf; rubbed. With 4 folding plates. Some foxing. P June 16 (157) $1,800

— A Pocket Almanack for the Year 1765. Phila.: Franklin & Hall, [1764]. 24mo, orig wraps; rubbed, 1 corner restored. A10,11 with hole costing 3 characters; small inkstain at lower fore-edge corner of first few leaves. P June 16 (94) $2,250

— Political, Miscellaneous, and Philosophical Pieces.... L, 1779. 8vo, contemp calf; extremities rubbed, joints repaired. With port & 3 plates. L.p. copy. P June 16 (139) $1,500

Anr copy. Half calf. sg Dec 5 (99) $600

Anr copy. Old calf; worn, hinges weak. Some foxing. wd Dec 12 (391) $800

Anr copy. Old half calf; front cover detached. Foxed throughout. L.p. copy. wd June 12 (384) $500

— Poor Richard Phila.: B. Franklin, [1736]. ("Poor Richard, 1737. An almanack for the Year of Christ 1737....") 8vo, sewn as issued. Marginal tears not affecting text; final leaf detached. P June 16 (8) $12,000

Anr Ed. Phila.: Franklin and Hall, [1752]. ("Poor Richard Improved, being an Almanack...for 1753.") 8vo, sewn as issued. Some marginal tears & fraying; F1.2 with long tear into text closed with transparent tape costing several words on F1. P June 16 (51) $5,500

Anr Ed. Phila.: Franklin and Hall, [1753]. ("Poor Richard Improved, being an Almanack...for 1754.") 12mo, disbound, restitched. Browned; some staining; some marginal tears into text. P June 16 (57)

$5,000

Anr Ed. Phila.: Franklin and Hall, [1757]. ("Poor Richard Improved, being an Almanack...for 1758.") 12mo, newly restitched. Bottom quarter of final leaf supplied; some corners lost; a few closed tears & marginal repairs; some staining. P June 16 (174) $5,000

Anr Ed. Paris, 1795. ("The Way to Wealth, or Poor Richard Improved.") 12mo, contemp half calf; front joint cracked. Frontis foxed. P June 16 (135) $800

— Proposals Relating to the Education of Youth in Pensilvania. Phila., 1749. 8vo, calf. Some browning & dampstaining; tp & D3 with early marginal repairs. P June 16 (38) $2,500

— La Science du Bonhomme Richard.... Phila. & Paris, 1777. 12mo, orig wraps; spine frayed. P June 16 (127) $500

— La scuola della economia e della morale. Pavia, 1825. 12mo, wraps. sg Dec 5 (98D) $120

[-] The Universal Asylum, and Columbia Magazine. Phila., Apr 1790. 8vo, modern cloth. Contains contemp account of Franklin's final illness & funeral.. P June 16 (159) $400

— The Way to Wealth.... [L: J. Johnson, 1779 or 1780]. Single sheet, 387mm by 199mm, framed. P June 16 (133) $1,500

— Works. Phila., 1808-18. ("Memoirs of the Life and Writings....") 6 vols. 8vo, contemp sheep; rubbed. With engraved title, 2 facsimiles & 12 plates & maps. Some browning & foxing. P June 16 (165) $500

Anr Ed. Bost., 1840. 10 vols. 8vo, cloth; some stains & wear, some hinges cracked. With 23 plates. wa Mar 5 (347) $65

Franklin Printing, Benjamin

— The American Magazine and Historical Chronicle for February, 1744. Bost., 1744. 8vo, side-stitched in wraps; chipped with loss & 2-inch tear into woodcut. P June 16 (20) $800

— The Charter, Laws and Catalogue of Books, of the Library Company of Philadelphia. Phila., 1764 [1765]. 8vo, 19th-cent half mor; rubbed, head of spine chipped. Some browning; some headlines shaved. P June 16 (109) $1,800

Anr copy. 19th-cent half lea; extremities worn. Endpapers dampstained. sg May 7 (140) $1,700

— The Charters of the Province of Pensilvania and City of Philadelphia.... Phila.: B. Franklin, 1742 [but 1743]. 3 parts in 1 vol. Folio, contemp half sheep over bds; worn, foot of spine chipped. Some corrections & marginalia; some browning & staining. P June 16 (17) $1,500

— A Confession of Faith, Put forth by the Elders and Brethren of Many Congregations of Christians.... Phila., 1743. 6th Ed. 8vo, contemp calf; front cover worn. Some dampstaining & soiling. P June 16 (18) $2,750

— Contributor Certificate. [Phila.: Franklin & Hall, c.1758]. ("This is to certify, that....") 140mm by 214mm, on vellum. P June 16 (64) $7,500

— Minutes of Conferences, held at Easton, in October, 1758. Phila.: Franklin & Hall, 1758. Folio, resewn. Marginal restoration costing c.10 words; H1 with small portion torn from top costing c.8 words; a few marginal tears; some staining. P June 16 (72) $4,000

— Penn against Ld. Baltimore in Chancery. Copy of Minutes on Hearing. [Phila., 1750]. 8vo, orig wraps. Chew copy. P June 16 (40) $12,000

— Penn against Ld. Baltimore in Chancery. [Phila.: Franklin & Hall for Thomas & Richard Penn, 1750]. 8vo, orig wraps. Chew copy. P June 16 (40) $2,000

— The Pennsylvania General Assembly Laws to Session of January 7, 1750-51. Phila., 1751. Folio, sewn as issued. Browned, a few small marginal chips & tears. P June 16 (49) $800

— A Treaty Held at the Town of Lancaster...with the Indians of the Six Nations, In June, 1744. Phila., 1744. Folio, sewn. Some soiling & browning. P June 16 (25) $7,500

— Votes and Proceedings of the House of Representatives of the Province of Pennsylvania. Phila.: Franklin & Hall, 1752-43-54 & Phila.: Henry Miller, 1774-75-76. Vols I-VI. Folio, Vols I-V in orig sheep; Vol VI in half calf. Sold as a periodical w.a.f. Each vol sgd on tp by John Penn (1729-95). Fleming set. P June 16 (54) $5,000

Anr Ed. Phila.: Franklin & Hall, 1752-43-54 & Phila.: Henry Miller, 1774. Vols I-IV. Folio, various contemp calf; 3 vols rebacked & restored. University of Pennsylvania duplicate. P June 16 (55) $1,500

— ARNDT, JOHANN. - Des Hocherleuchteten Theologi.... Phila. Franklin & Boehm, 1751. 8vo, sheep with remnants of clasps; worn & repaired. With 62 (of 64) plates. Tp frayed at inner margin & with closed tear into text; browned. P June 16 (42) $1,600

— BARCLAY, ROBERT. - The Anarchy of the Ranters, and other Libertines.... Phila., 1757. 8vo, orig sheep; rubbed, spine worn & splitting. K Mar 22 (152) $300

— CHALKLEY, THOMAS. - A Collection of the Works.... Phila., 1749. 1st Ed. 2 parts in 1 vol. 8vo, orig sheep; worn & rubbed. Lacking initial blank; piece missing from p.

319-20, affecting text; anr leaf torn. K Dec 1 (230) $400

Anr copy. 8vo, contemp sheep; worn, spine head chipped, shaken. Browned & soiled. Manney copy. P Oct 11 (147) $1,100

— CHURCH OF SCOTLAND. - The Confession of Faith, the Larger and Shorter Catechisms.... Phila.: B. Franklin, 1745. 8vo, mor gilt by Bedford; extremities rubbed. Several leaves with corners restored or other minor marginal restoration. P June 16 (28) $1,600

— CHURCH OF SCOTLAND. - A Solemn Acknowledgment of Publick Sins.... Phila.: B. Franklin, 1745. 8vo, modern cloth. Browned; headlines of final 2 leaves shaved. P June 16 (29) $200

— ESTAUGH, JOHN. - A Call to the Unfaithful Professors of Truth. Phila.: B. Franklin, 1744. 8vo, contemp wraps; foxed, chipped. Fore-edge of tp chipped not affecting text. P June 16 (21) $1,000

— EVANS, LEWIS. - Geographical, Historical, Political, Philosophical and Mechanical Essays. Phila., 1755. 2d Ed, variant tp with addition of Dodsley to imprint. 4to, half calf, orig wraps bound in. Quire A from 1st Ed. Facsimile of the general Map bound in. P June 16 (66) $1,000

— JERMAN, JOHN. - The American Almanack for the Year of Christian Account 1731. Phila.: Franklin & Meredith, [1730]. 8vo, calf. Tp silked with loss of a few letters; marginal restoration to other leaves, occasionally affecting text. P June 16 (6) $5,000

— JOHNSON, SAMUEL. - Elementa Philosophica, containing chiefly Noetica...and Ethica. Phila.: B. Franklin & D. Hall, 1752. 2 parts in 1 vol. 8vo, orig sheep; worn. Dampstained; browned. P June 16 (52) $1,300

— LAW, WILLIAM. - An Extract from a Treatise by William Law, M.A. called, The Spirit of Prayer.... Phila., 1760. 8vo, later calf. wd June 12 (385) $400

— LETCHWORTH, THOMAS. - A Morning and Evening's Meditation.... Phila.: Franklin & Hall, 1766. Bound with: William Penn, Fruits of a Father's Love. L, 1760. And: John Rutty. Liberty of the Spirit. Phila. ,1759. 8vo, contemp sheep; worn, most of spine lost. E2 ptd with the short title of the poem on 3 lines between rows of typographic ornaments. P June 16 (121) $1,500

— MORGAN, ABEL. - Anti-Paedo-Rantism Defended.... Phila.: Franklin & Hall, 1750. 8vo, orig sheep. sg Dec 5 (100) $475

— PENNSYLVANIA HOSPITAL. - Contributor Certificate. [Phila.: Franklin & Hall, c.1754]. ("This is to certify, that....") 148mm by 192mm, on vellum. Some staining; 2 short tears into text at top. P June 16 (63) $2,500

— RINGOLD, T. - Remarks upon a Message, send by the Upper to the Lower House of Assembly of Maryland, 1762. Phila., 1764. 8vo, modern half mor. P June 16 (95) $2,500

— RUTTY, JOHN. - The Liberty of the Spirit and of the Flesh...in an Address to...the People called Quakers.... Phila., 1759. 8vo, orig wraps; worn. Some browning. P June 16 (77) $600

— SHORT, THOMAS. - Medicina Britannica. Phila.: Franklin & Hall, 1751. 8vo, contemp sheep; loose. sg Dec 5 (101) $1,000

— STEVENSON, JOHN. - A Rare Soul-Strengthning and Comforting Cordial.... Phila.: B. Franklin, 1744. 1st American Ed. 12mo, mor. Tp & final leaf extended. Only known copy. P June 16 (26) $8,500

— WHITEFIELD, GEORGE. - A Continuation of the Reverend Mr. Whitefield's Journal...Vol II. Phila.: Franklin, 1740. 12mo, contemp sheep; rubbed, restored & rebacked preserving most of orig spine. Top fore-edge corners of A3,4 lost costing a few characters; E9,10 & a few other leaves with short marginal tears into text; tp with marginal chipping & small filled hole; some stains & browning. P June 16 (14) $900

— WOOLMAN, JOHN. - Considerations on Keeping Negroes...Part Second. Phila.: Franklin & Hall, 1762. 8vo, mor gilt by Morley. Some soiling & foxing. P June 16 (86) $4,000

— ZINZENDORFF, NIKOLAUS LUDWIG. - Etliche zu dieser Zeit nicht unnutze Fragen ueber einige Schrift-Stellen.... Phila.: B. Franklin, [1742]. 8vo, 19th-cent calf; extremities worn. P June 16 (15) $700

— ZINZENDORFF, NIKOLAUS LUDWIG. - The Remarks which the Author of the Compendious Extract.... Phila.: B. Franklin, 1742. 8vo, disbound, inlaid to larger sheets & bound in mor album with 4 19th-cent ports of Franklin; front cover detached, rubbed, repaired. P June 16 (16) $700

Franklin, Benjamin, 1706-90 —& Dashwood, Sir Francis, Lord le Despencer

— Abridgement of the Book of Common Prayer.... L, 1773. 8vo, contemp mor gilt; extremities rubbed with loss to head of spine, rear joint cracked, front joint restored. P June 16 (124) $8,000

Franklin, Benjamin, 1706-90 —& Jackson, Richard

— The Interest of Great Britain Considered. Phila, 1760. 8vo, modern half mor. Some browning & staining; reinforced at inner folds. P June 16 (79) $1,500

Franklin, Sir John, 1786-1847

— Narrative of a Journey to the Shores of the Polar Sea.... L, 1823. 1st Ed. 4to, old calf; rebacked, worn & chipped. With 4 maps & 30 plates, some in color. Some foxing. wd June 12 (386) $375

Anr Ed. L, 1829. ("Journey to the Shores of the Polar Sea...with a Brief Account of the Second Journey....") 4 vols. 12mo, contemp calf. W July 8 (248) £160

— Narrative of a Second Expedition to the Shores of the Polar Sea.... L, 1828. 1st Ed. 4to, 19th-cent half mor; rubbed. With frontis, 6 folding maps & 30 plates, 1 map hand-colored in outline. Some foxing throughout; frontis heavily foxed. S May 14 (1310) £320 [Hasbach]

Frankum, Richard

— The Bee and the Wasp. L, 1861. 1st Ed. Illus by George Cruikshank. 12mo, calf gilt; joints worn. With 4 proof plates with full margins. sg Oct 17 (144) $400

Franzini, Federico

— Roma antica e moderna. Rome, 1678. 8vo, orig bds; rebacked. bba Sept 19 (317) £190 [Goldschmidt]

Frary, Ihna Thayer

— Thomas Jefferson, Architect and Builder. Richmond, 1931. Cloth; spine bumped & faded. With 96 plates. sp Feb 6 (168) $50

Fraser, Claud Lovat, 1890-1921

— Sixty-Three Unpublished Designs. L, [1924]. One of 500. 16mo, bds; spine rubbed. Z Oct 26 (139) $50

Fraser, James Baillie, 1783-1856

— Journal of a Tour through Part of the Snowy Range of the Himala Mountains.... L, 1820. 1st Ed. 4to, contemp half calf; worn. Final 2 leaves damaged & repaired with some loss. Frontis browned & spotted; latter half of vol progressively dampstained. DW Nov 6 (75) £300

— Narrative of a Journey into Khorasan.... L, 1825. 1st Ed. 4to, modern half calf. bba Sept 19 (117) £380 [Sotheran]

— Views in the Himala Mountains. L, 1820. Folio, disbound. With sepia aquatint title & 17 hand-colored plates (of 20). Waterstain affecting image on some plates. S Nov 21 (359) £3,200 [Sims, Reed]

Frate, Settimo del

— Istruzione pel maneggio e scherma della sciabola. Milan, 1869. 8vo, half cloth. With 20 litho plates. sg Mar 26 (118) $175

Frazer, Mrs.

— The Practice of Cookery, Pastry.... Edin., 1810. 6th Ed. 8vo, orig bds; worn. pnE Dec 4 (57) £55

Frazer, Sir James George, 1854-1941

— Folk-Lore in the Old Testament. L, 1918. 3 vols. 8vo, orig cloth; faded & rubbed. DW Dec 11 (471) £52

— The Golden Bough. L, 1890. 1st Ed. 2 vols. 8vo, orig cloth; corners bumped. Epstein copy. sg Apr 29 (170) $425

Anr Ed. NY, 1935. 12 vols. Orig cloth; worn. wa Apr 9 (125) $190

Anr Ed. L, 1966. 13 vols. In d/js. B May 12 (975) HF800

Freart, Roland, Sieur de Chambray

— A Parallel of the Antient Architecture with the Modern.... L, 1680. ("The Whole Body of Antient and Modern Architecture....") 1st Ed in English, 2d Issue. Trans by John Evelyn. Folio, contemp calf; rebacked, edges renewed, new endpapers. With engraved title & 50 plates. Some dampstaining & worming, catching some plates. CNY Jan 25 (20) $200

Frederick Henry, Prince of Orange

— Memoires.... Amst., 1733. 4to, modern half mor gilt. With engraved title & port. Dampstained throughout. sg Oct 24 (122) $90

Frederick II, Emperor

— The Art of Falconry.... Stanford CA, 1961. 4to, orig cloth, in d/j. With 188 plates. bba Oct 24 (274) £50 [Baring]

— Reliqua librorum Friderici II, Imperatoris, De arte venandi cum avibus. Augsburg: H. Schultes, 1596. 8vo, 18th-cent calf; rebacked preserving orig spine. Some soiling. C Dec 16 (124) £1,300 [Kaiser]

Freeman, Douglas Southall, 1886-1953

— George Washington: a Biography. NY, 1948-54. 6 vols. sp June 18 (22) $95

1st Ed. NY, 1948-57. Vols I-V (of 7). F Dec 18 (52) $50

— Lee's Lieutenants; a Study in Command. NY, 1942-44. 3 vols. Inscr to Col. Percy Howes, Jr. Z Apr 18 (40) $110

— R. E. Lee; a Biography. NY, 1934-35. 4 vols. bbc Feb 17 (61) $210; wa Sept 26 (396) $55

Anr copy. Some foxing. Sgd in Vol I. wa Sept 26 (397) $130

Anr copy. Inscr to Col. Percy Howes, Jr. Z Apr 18 (39) $120

Freeman, John
— Lights and Shadows of Melbourne Life. L, 1888. 8vo, bds; upper bd creased. Signs of use. kh Nov 11 (499) A$140

Freeman, Richard Austin, 1862-1943
— John Thorndyke's Cases. L, 1909. cb Sept 19 (71) $1,000
— The Singing Bone. L, [c.1912]. Inscr to Freeman's agent and with small ink self-caricature. cb Sept 19 (72) $1,000

Freeman, Strickland
— Observations on the Mechanism of the Horse's Foot.... L, 1796. 4to, contemp mor gilt. With 16 hand-colored plates, each with uncolored duplicate in outline. Some outline duplicates foxed. sg Nov 7 (82) $800

Fremantle, Sir Arthur J. L., 1835-1901
— Three Months in the Southern States. Mobile, 1864. 8vo, disbound. sg June 18 (187) $400

Fremont, John Charles, 1813-90
— Geographical Memoir upon Upper California.... Wash., 1849. 8vo, modern cloth. Folding map chipped. 30th Congress, 2d Session, H of R Miscellaneous Doc. 5. sg June 18 (69) $200
— Report of the Exploring Expedition to the Rocky Mountains.... Wash., 1845. 1st Ed, House Issue. 8vo, unbound & unopened gatherings, stab sewn, as issued; folding map at rear pulled loose from sewing cord. wa Dec 9 (293) $475

Anr copy. Modern cloth. With folding map present but not bound in & with 22 plates & 4 other maps (1 detached). Some foxing & fold splits. wa Mar 5 (349) $250

Senate Issue. Later half mor; spine & corners scuffed. With large map in end-paper pocket. cb Sept 12 (66) $550

Anr copy. Later half sheep. With 5 maps and large folding map at rear. cb Feb 12 (27) $550

Anr copy. Orig sheep. cb Feb 12 (28) $325

Anr copy. Orig cloth; worn. Some foxing & soiling. O Nov 26 (70) $550

Anr copy. Orig cloth. Epstein copy. sg Apr 29 (171) $1,100

Anr copy. Cloth; needs rebdg. With 5 maps (including large folding map inserted at rear) & 22 plates. Library markings. sg June 18 (226) $275

Frenaud, Andre
— Le Chemin des devins.... Paris, 1966. Hors commerce copy on Arches. Illus by Eduardo Chillida. 4to, loose as issued. CGen Nov 18 (384) SF7,000
— Le Tombeau de mon pere. [N.p.], 1961. One of 59. Illus by Maurice Esteve. 4to, relief box bdg with geometric design. CGen Nov 18 (383) SF8,500

French, Charles
— A Handbook of the Destructive Insects of Victoria.... Melbourne, 1891-1911. 5 vols. 8vo, orig cloth. One plate damaged by adhesion. kh Nov 11 (502) A$50

French, Edwin Davis
[-] Edwin Davis French: A Memorial.... NY, 1908. One of 50 on japan vellum. cb Oct 17 (276) $180

French, John, 1616?-57
— The Art of Distillation.... L, 1667. 4th Ed. 2 parts in 1 vol. 4to, calf; rebacked & repaired. Some foxing & staining; some margins short. B Nov 1 (636) HF1,300

French, Paul. See: Asimov, Isaac

Freneau, Philip, 1752-1832
— Poems Written between the Years 1768 & 1794. Monmouth, N.J., 1795. 8vo, later half mor; front cover loose. With extraneous port plate bound in. sg Dec 5 (102) $60

Freshfield, Douglas W., 1845-1934
— The Exploration of the Caucasus. L, 1902. 2 vols. sg Jan 9 (80) $250
— Round Kangchenjunga. L, 1903. sg Jan 9 (287) $500
— Travels in the Central Caucasus and Bashan. L, 1869. 8vo, orig cloth; rubbed. With colored frontis & 3 folding maps. DW Oct 2 (33) £135

Freud, Sigmund, 1856-1939
— Die Frage der Laienanalyse: Unterredungen mit einem Unparteiischen. Vienna, 1926. Orig cloth; soiled. Met Apr 28 (326) $70
— Three Contributions to the Sexual Theory. NY, 1910. Orig wraps; loose & crudely secured with cloth tape, some def. sg Nov 14 (37) $375
— Vorlesungen zur Einfuehrung in die Psychoanalyse. Leipzig & Vienna, 1916-17. 1st Ed. Orig wraps; spine taped, chipped. Met Apr 28 (325) $275
— Der Witz und seine Beziehung zum Unbewussten. Leipzig & Vienna, 1905. 1st Ed. 8vo, half cloth. pn Dec 12 (47) £270
— Works. L, [1953-74]. 24 vols. With 20 vols in d/js. bbc Apr 27 (522) $325

Frey, Carroll
— A Bibliography of the Writings of H. L. Mencken. Phila., 1924. One of 85 L.p. copies. Sgd. cb Oct 17 (331) $75

Frey, Johann Michael. See: Gignoux & Frey

Freycinet, Louis Claude Desaulses de, 1779-1842

— Voyage autour du monde...sur les corvettes de S. M. L'Uranie et La Physicienne.... Paris, 1824-[26]. Atlas historique; Histoire naturelle: Zoologie planches; Histoire naturelle: Botanique planches. 3 vols. Folio, 19th-cent mor gilt; worn. Zoologie with engraved title & 96 plates, including 77 ptd in colors & finished by hand; Atlas historique with engraved title & 112 plates, including 41 ptd in colors & finished by hand & 13 maps & charts; Botanique with engraved title & 120 plates. Some spotting. S Nov 21 (379) £4,200 [Quaritch]

— Voyage de decouvertes aux Terres Australes.... Paris, 1811. Part 2 of Atlas vol only. Folio, orig bds. With 2 folding maps & 12 single maps. S June 25 (203) £4,600 [McCormick]

Frezier, Amedee Francois, 1682-1773

— Relation du voyage de la Mer du Sud.... Amst., 1717. 2 vols. 12mo, contemp calf; worn. With 2 frontises & 37 maps & plates. Some browning. S May 14 (1254) £300 [Voltaire]

— La Theorie et la pratique de la coupe des pierres et des bois.... Strassburg, 1738. 2 vols. 4to, contemp half calf; joints cracked, rubbed. With frontis & 69 plates. Some dampstaining. S July 9 (1374) £300 [American Museum]

— A Voyage to the South-Sea.... L, 1717. 2 vols. 12mo, contemp calf; rebacked. With 37 plates & maps. S May 14 (1255) £550 [Dawson]

Frias, Simon de

— Tratado elemental de la destreza del sable. Mexico, 1809. 8vo, 19th-cent calf. With 13 plates. sg Mar 26 (119) $275

Frick, Christoph —& Schewitzer, Christoph

— A Relation of Two Several Voyages Made into the East-Indies. L, 1700. 1st Ed in English. 8vo, modern calf. Tp upper rule-border & some headlines shaved. S Nov 15 (1289) £260 [Beeleigh Abbey]

Friedel, Adam de

— The Greeks, Twenty-Four Portraits of the Principal Leaders and Personages...Greek Revolution.... L, 1827. Folio, bdg not described. With 25 hand-colored plates (with an additional plate, Bobolina) on india paper, 14 mtd. Minor foxing & staining. S July 1 (606) £3,500 [Kedros]

Friedlaender, Johnny

— Oeuvre 1961-1965. NY & Stuttgart: Touchstone, [1967]. Folio, orig cloth. With 14 tipped-in color plates. With orig litho, sgd in pencil, laid in. bbc Dec 9 (272) $55

Friedlaender, Max J., 1852-1934

— Die altniederlandische Malerei. Berlin & Leiden, 1924-37. 13 (of 14) vols; lacking Vol 13. 4to, orig half cloth; rubbed, some corners knocked. bba Feb 13 (203) £220 [Holstein]

Anr copy. 14 vols. 4to, orig half cloth, Vol 14 in half mor. S Feb 11 (73) £400 [Lucas]

— Handzeichnungen deutscher Meister in der herzogl. Anhaltschen Behoerden-Bibliotheck zu Dessau. Stuttgart, 1914. Folio, text booklets & unbound plates loose in cloth case as issued. With 79 mtd reproductions. sg Feb 6 (91) $110

Friedlander, Max J.

— Early Netherlandish Painting. Leiden, 1967-76. Vols I-IV in 16. 4to, orig cloth, in d/j. Ck Feb 14 (46) $2,400

Fries, Waldemar H.

— The Double Elephant Folio: The Story of Audubon's Birds. Chicago, 1973. 4to, half syn. O Apr 28 (32) $120

Frink, Elisabeth

— Etchings Illustrating Chaucer's Canterbury Tales. L, 1972. One of 300. Loose as issued in cloth portfolio. With 19 plates. S Nov 14 (111) £200 [Stone]

Frink, Margaret A.

— Journal of the Adventures of a Party of California Gold-Seekers.... [Oakland, 1897]. 12mo, orig cloth. sg June 18 (70) $1,100

Frisius, Joannes

— Dictionarium latinogermanicum. Zurich: Christopher Froschauer, Mar 1541. Folio, 16th-cent calf; spine damaged, ink-stain on lower cover. S Dec 5 (120) £1,100 [Quaritch]

Frith, Francis

— Lower Egypt, Thebes, and the Pyramids. L, [c.1862]. Folio, orig half mor gilt. With 37 mtd photos. S Feb 26 (739) £500 [Sotheran]

— Sinai and Palestine. L: William Mackenzie, [1862 or later]. Folio, orig half lea. With litho title & 37 mtd plates. Some spotting. S Feb 11 (7400) £240 [Hildebrandt]

— Upper Egypt and Ethiopia. L, [c.1862]. Folio, contemp mor gilt; covers detached, spine def. With 37 actual mtd photos. Marginal spotting. pn Sept 12 (331) £400 [Hildebrandt]

Froes, Luis. See: Jesuit Relations

Frohawk, Frederick William

— Natural History of British Butterflies. L, [1914]. 2 vols. Folio, orig cloth, in chipped d/j. Some soiling. F Mar 26 (450) $175

Frois, Luigi. See: Jesuits

Froissart, Jean, 1333?-1400?

— Chronicles. L, 1844. 4 vols. 8vo, contemp mor gilt; rubbed. O May 26 (70) $600

Anr Ed. Stratford: Shakespeare Head Press, 1927-28. ("Froissarts Cronycles....") One of 350. 8 vols. 4to, orig bds. Some soiling. S July 1 (1190) £180 [Cox]

Fronsperger, Leinhard

— Kriegsbuch. Frankfurt, 1578-73. 3 parts in 1 vol. Folio, 18th-cent pigskin; rebacked retaining orig spine. With 23 folding or double-page plates & 3 double-page woodcuts. Some staining & repairs. S July 9 (1253) £950 [Bracklein]

— Kriegs Ordnund und Regiment. Frankfurt, 1564. Bound with: Von Geschuetz und Fewerwerck. Folio, later vellum bds. Some dampstaining; a few small holes in tp of 1st work; some upper margins wormed. S May 13 (766) £500 [Hasbach]

Frontinus, Sextus Julius

— De aquaeductibus urbis Romae commentarius.... Padua, 1722. 4to, contemp vellum; spine darkened, front hinge cracked. With 15 plates.. sg Nov 14 (240) $450

Frost, Arthur Burdett, 1851-1928

— A Book of Drawings. NY, [1904]. Intro by Joel Chandler Harris; verse by Wallace Irwin. Folio, pictorial half cloth. With 40 plates. K Mar 22 (154) $225

Anr copy. Half cloth; edges chipped. With 39 plates. K Mar 22 (155) $110

Frost, Donald McKay

— Notes on General Ashley, the Overland Trail, and South Pass. Worcester MA, 1945. One of 50 L.p. copies. 4to, half cloth. sg June 18 (227) $150

Frost, John, 1800-59

— History of the State of California.... Auburn, 1850. 1st Ed. 8vo, orig lea; worn, spine partially def. Foxed. sg Dec 5 (103) $60

Frost, Robert, 1874-1963

See also: Limited Editions Club

— A Boy's Will. L: David Nutt, 1913. 1st Ed. Orig cloth, A. Epstein copy. sg Apr 29 (172) $3,600

1st American Ed. NY, 1915. 2d Ptg. NH Oct 6 (132) $100

— Collected Poems. NY, 1930. 1st Ed, one of 1,000. In d/j. Sgd. sg Dec 12 (124) $375

— Collected Poems, 1939. NY, [1939]. Sgd. wa Oct 19 (50) $210

— Come In and Other Poems. NY, 1945. 5th ptg. In chipped & worn d/j. Inscr. NH Aug 23 (191) $175

— From Snow to Snow. NY, [1916]. Ptd wraps. Sgd on half-title. sg Dec 12 (125) $300

— A Further Range. NY, [1936]. One of 803, sgd. sg June 11 (121) $250

— In the Clearing. NY, [1962]. One of 1,500, sgd. sg June 11 (122) $175

— A Masque of Reason. NY, [1945]. 1st Ed. Cloth, in d/j. Inscr to Eleanor Turnbull. sg June 11 (123) $350

One of 800. Half cloth. Met Apr 28 (639) $60

— Mountain Interval. NY, [1916]. 1st Ed, 1st Issue. sg Dec 12 (126) $200; sg June 11 (124) $90

— New Hampshire. NY, 1923. 1st Trade Ed. Half cloth. Inscr. sg Dec 12 (127) $325

— North of Boston. NY, 1914. 1st Ed, 1st Issue. Bdg variant A. Epstein copy. sg Apr 29 (174) $1,900

Issue not given. Half cloth; worn. Inscr. O Dec 17 (71) $180

— A Way Out. NY, 1929. 1st Ed, One of 485, sgd. Half cloth, unopened. Sgd. O Dec 17 (72) $155

Anr copy. Orig half cloth. sg Dec 12 (128) $275

— West-Running Brook. NY, [1928]. Illus by J. J. Lankes. Half cloth; corners worn. Sgd. sg June 11 (126) $200

Anr copy. Contemp half mor gilt by Brentanos. wa Mar 5 (41) $80

One of 1,000 L.p. copies, sgd by author & artist. sg June 11 (125) $275

— A Witness Tree. NY, 1942. One of 735. Half cloth. Inscr with a holograph poem, sgd. sg Dec 12 (129) $800

Froude, James Anthony

— History of England. L, 1858-70. ("History of England from the Fall of Wolsey to the Death of Elizabeth.") 2d Ed. 12 vols. 8vo, contemp calf gilt; rubbed. Sgd envelope tipped in. pn Sept 12 (36) £140 [Freeman]

Anr Ed. L, 1872. 12 vols. 8vo, contemp calf gilt; some vols rubbed. bba Oct 10 (369) £140 [Koziell]

Fryer, John, 1752-1817. See: Golden Cockerel Press

Fuchs, Eduard

— Geschichte der Erotischen Kunst. Munich, [1922-24]. 3 vols. 4to, cloth; worn, hinges cracked. sg Sept 6 (106) $300

— Illustrierte Sittengeschichte. Munich, [1909-12]. Vols I-III, without the Supplements. 4to, cloth. sg Mar 5 (80) $140

Anr copy. Vols I-III, each with Supplement (Ergaenzungsband). Together, 6 vols. 4to, orig cloth; needs rebdg. Browned & repaired. Sold w.a.f. wa Feb 20 (171) $80

— Die Juden in der Karikatur. Munich, [1921]. 4to, orig cloth; soiled, worn, broken. With 32 plates, 12 colored. wa Sept 26 (621) $70

Fuchs, Leonhard, 1501-66

— Compendiaria ac succincta admodum in Medendi... Hagenau: Johann Setzer, 1531. Bound with: Berengario da Carpi, Giacomo. Isagogae Breves et Exactissimae in Anatomiam Humani Corporis. Strassburg: Heinrich Seybold, 1530. And: Schiller, Joachim. De Peste Brittannica Commentariolus vere Aureus. Basel: Heinrich Petri, 1531. And: Galla, Giorgio. De Urinae significatione....Strassburg: Heinrich Seybold, [1528?]. 4 works in 1 vol. 8vo, contemp vellum, wallet-style bdg. C June 24 (132) £7,500 [Quaritch]

— De historia stirpium. Basel: Isingrin, 1542. 1st Ed. Folio, 18th-cent half vellum; worn, spine def. With port of Fuchs, ports of Fuellmaurer & A. Meyer at end & 509 full-page woodcuts, 2 smaller botanical woodcuts & 1 woodcut diagram. Some early marginalia & captioning; a few margins dampstained or cut close; tp soiled; prelims thumbed & 1 blank corner restored without loss; 4 pp stained; leaf Q6 torn & artlessly repaired with part of woodcut restored in pencil facsimile; some worming toward end; 19th-cent English Ms blurb on leaf tipped in before tp. British Museum duplicate; U of Wisconsin at Madison copy. P June 17 (214) $17,000

Anr Ed. Paris, 1546. 16mo, contemp blind-stamped pigskin over wooden bds, upper cover with border of the Virtues & central panel dated 1546; soiled & rubbed. pn June 11 (147) £1,400 [Phelps]

— Neu Kreuterbuch. Basel, 1543. Folio, contemp pigskin with brass cornerpieces, catches & clasps. "Possibly" hand-colored for the pbr. Upper margins dampstained; prelims & final leaves soiled; tp frayed & loose with corner off. sg May 7 (107) $16,000

Fuld, James J.

— A Pictorial Bibliography of the First Editions of Stephen C. Foster. Phila., 1957. Folio, orig cloth. F Mar 26 (459) $60

Fuller, John Frederic Charles

— The Star in the West...Aleister Crowley. L, 1907. bba Aug 13 (269) £60 [Houle]

One of 100. bba Aug 13 (268) £330 [Houle]

Fuller, Ronald. See: Whistler & Fuller

Fuller, Thomas, 1608-61

— Abel redevivus: or the Dead yet Speaking. L, 1651. 1st Ed. 4to, contemp sheep; rebacked. sg Mar 12 (94) $200

— The Church-History of Britain. L, 1655. 1st Ed. Folio, contemp calf; spine damaged. With 5 plates. sg Oct 24 (125) $275

Anr copy. Needs rebdg. Tp soiled; initial on 3F1v excised && restored in Ms; 3b1 torn & repaired. Sold w.a.f. sg Mar 12 (95) $80

— The Historie of the Holy Warre. Cambr., 1647. 3d Ed. Bound with: Fuller. The Holy State. Cambr., 1652. 3d Ed. And: Fuller. The Profane State. L, 1652. 4to, contemp calf; rebacked, rubbed hinges cracked. bba Dec 19 (346) £160 [Thomas Plume's Library]

— The History of the Worthies of England. L, 1662. Folio, modern half lea. Some browning. pn Apr 23 (116) £80 [Clark]

— A Pisgah-Sight of Palestine. L, 1650. 1st Ed. Folio, contemp calf; worn, rebacked with new endpapers. With 18 (of 21) double-page maps & plans & 5 (of 7) double-page plates. Lacking large folding map; several maps repaired. Sold w.a.f. S Feb 26 (741) £380 [Berger]

Anr copy. 19th-cent calf by Pickering; repaired. With armorial plate, engraved title, map bound in 2 sheets, 20 double-page regional maps & 7 double-page plates. Engraved title repaired along inner margin; map cut close & restored affecting surface; some underlinings in red ink; a few small rust-holes. S July 1 (840) £800 [Sofer]

Anr Ed. L, 1662. Folio, modern half mor. Lacking 6 maps; lower left corner of tp & 1 plate torn & repaired with loss; some fore-edges gouged; some plates worn, soiled or torn; lacking Ccc2 & 3. Sold w.a.f. sg June 25 (80) $450

Fulton, John Farquhar

— A Bibliography of the Honourable Robert Boyle. L, 1961. 4to, orig cloth; worn. O Sept 24 (92) $110

Fulton, Robert, of Brockley

— The Illustrated Book of Pigeons. L, etc., [c.1886]. 4to, contemp cloth; extremities worn. With 50 chromolithographed plates, 3 bound out of sequence. Foxed; some margins taped; 1 plate traced in charcoal on verso. bba July 23 (316) £130 [Books & Prints]

Anr copy. Half mor; rubbed. With 50 color plates. Owner stamps on back of each plate. K Mar 22 (347) $300

Anr copy. Orig bdg; inner hinges opening. One plate rehinged with tape; some foxing. K July 12 (407) $180

Fulton, Robert, 1765-1815

— De la machine infernale maritime.... Paris, 1812. 8vo, modern wraps. With 4 folding plates. Marginal dampstaining throughout; tp foxed; old institutional stamp. sg Nov 14 (241) $300

— Torpedo War, and Submarine Explosions. NY, 1810. Oblong 4to, orig wraps; spine chipped & repaired. With 5 plates. Inscr to Gaspard Monge & with autograph draft of a letter from Monge to President Madison & Congress about Fulton's torpedoes. DuPont copy. CNY Oct 8 (110) $15,000

Fulton, Robert Lardin

— Epic of the Overland. Los Angeles, 1954. One of 275. In d/j. cb Feb 13 (135) $55

Fulvio, Andrea

— Antiquitates urbis. [Rome: Marcellus Silber, 1527]. Folio, contemp calf over pastebds with title lettered in gilt on upper cover; worn & wormed. Some worming in 1st & last few leaves. S Dec 5 (122) £1,400 [Goldschmidt]

Fumagalli, Giuseppe

— Lexicon typographicum italiae. Dictionnaire geographique d'Italie. Florence, 1905. 4to, later cloth. O Sept 24 (93) $130

Funck, M—, b.1870

— Le Livre Belge a gravures. Paris & Brussels, 1925. Half mor, orig wraps bound in. bba June 25 (151) £85 [Forster]

Funnell, William

— A Voyage Round the World.... L, 1707. 8vo, contemp calf; rebacked. With 15 maps & plates. S June 25 (28) £750 [Quaritch/Hordern]

Fur Trader. See: Grabhorn Printing

Furber, Robert —&
Bradley, Richard

— The Flower-Garden Display'd. L, 1732. 4to, calf; rebacked. With engraved title & 12 plates, all hand-colored. C May 20 (174A) £1,800 [Heywood Hill]

Furnival, William James

— Leadless Decorative Tiles, Faience, and Mosaic.... Stone, Staffordshire, 1904. Bdg rubbed & soiled. DW Oct 9 (864) £80

Furst, Herbert Ernest Augustus

— The Modern Woodcut. L, 1924. 1st Ed. 4to, orig cloth. K Sept 29 (174) $70

Anr copy. Orig cloth with small burn mark, in worn d/j. kh Nov 11 (100) A$160

Furtenbach, Joseph, 1591-1667

— Architectura martialis.... Ulm, 1630. 3 parts in 1 vol. Folio, old vellum; head of spine missing, foot torn, fragments of newspaper adhering to sides. With double-page frontis & 11 plates & plans. Some worming with loss; some spotting & staining; library stamps on tp. S July 1 (1256) £350 [Bracklein]

— Buechsenmeisterey-Schul, darinnen die newangehende Buechsenmeister und Feurwercker.... Augsburg, 1643. Folio, contemp vellum; worn. With folding engraved title & 44 double-page plates. Lacking the port; some staining; 1 plate cropped. S July 1 (1257) £400 [American Mus.]

Futrelle, Jacques, 1875-1912

— The Thinking Machine. NY, 1907. Orig bdg; cocked, blind stamp on front free endpaper. K July 12 (236) $200; sg June 11 (127) $200

G

Gabory, Georges

— La Cassette de lomb. Paris, 1920. One of 125 on Arches. Illus by Andre Derain. Wraps. CGen Nov 18 (387) SF800

Gabriel, Albert

— Monuments turcs d'Anatolie. Paris, 1931-34. 2 vols. Folio, orig half cloth. With 135 plates. DW Oct 9 (866) £460

Anr copy. With 136 plates. S July 1 (608) £650 [Kutluoglu]

Gaddis, William

— The Recognitions. NY, [1955]. In soiled d/j. F Dec 18 (228) $110

Advance proof copy. Orig wraps. Inscr to Annetta. Manney copy. P Oct 11 (148) $500

Gaffarel, Jacques, 1601-81

— Curiositez inouyes, sur la sculpture talismanique des Persans. [France], 1631. 8vo, 17th-cent calf gilt. sg Mar 12 (215) $750

— Unheard-of Curiosities: concerning the Talismanical Sculpture of the Persians.... L, 1650. 8vo, contemp sheep; rebacked, worn. Lacking folding plate and 1 prelim leaf. Some leaves frayed & stained. Sold w.a.f. bba Sept 5 (210) £55 [Rogers Turner]

Gage, John

— The History and Antiquities of Hengrave in Suffolk. L, 1822. 4to, half vellum. With 30 plates. bba Feb 27 (29) £100 [Land]

Gage, Thomas, d.1656

— The English-American his Travail, by Sea and Land.... L, 1648. 1st Ed. Folio, contemp sheep; spine ends chipped, corners worn, lower cover scuffed & wormed. Small tear to G2. CNY Oct 8 (111) $2,200

Gagnon, Phileas

— Essai de bibliographie canadienne.... Quebec, 1895. 8vo, new cloth. sg Oct 31 (112) $90

Anr Ed. Quebec, 1895 & Montreal, 1913. 2 vols. 8vo, cloth; worn. O Sept 24 (94) $60

Gaguin, Robert, 1433?-1501

— De origine & gestis Francorum...compendium. Paris: Thielman Kerver, for Durand Gerlier & Jean Petit, 13 Jan 1500. ("Compendium de origine et gestis Francorum.") Folio, 17th-cent calf; worn. Types 10:92R (text), 15:79R (index, marginalia), 17:180G (headings, at recto), 45 lines. Some marginal dampstains. 179 (of 180) leaves; lacking F5. Goff G-15. C Nov 27 (15) £600 [Sawyer]

Gaiani, Giovanni Battista

— Discorso del Tornear a Piedi. Genoa: Giuseppe Pavoni, 1619. 4to, modern half vellum. C Dec 16 (47) £200 [Jackson]

Gailhabaud, Jules, 1810-88

— L'Architecture du Vme au XVIIme Siecle.... Paris, 1869-72. 4 vols. Folio, orig half sheep; most backstrips lacking, some covers detached. Vol I with dampstain at top lef corner throughout; some foxing. Sold w.a.f. bbc Apr 27 (454) $550

Gaimard, Paul, 1790-1858

— Voyage en Islande et au Groenland. Paris: A. Bertrand, 1838-[42]. 6 vols: Atlas historique in 2 vols; Histoire du voyage, Vol I only; Physique; & histoire de l'Islande in 2 vols. Folio & 8vo, Atlas vols in contemp half mor gilt, text vols in half calf (def). Stamps of Royal Geographical Society in text vols; sold with a copy of Xavier Marmier's Lettres sur l'Islande, 1837. S June 25 (476) £2,400 [Gustaussan]

Gainsborough, Thomas

— Studies of Figures, Selected from the Sketch Books.... L, 1825. 4to, contemp calf gilt; rubbed. With cover litho, tp with mtd litho port & 24 lithos. Some foxing. Inscr by Richard Lane to William Sharpe. Schlosser copy. P June 17 (544) $300

Gajdar, Arkady

— Skazka o voennoj tajne o mal'chishe-kibal'chishe i ego tverdom slove. Moscow, 1933. Folio, orig bds. sg Nov 7 (200) $550

Galbally, Ann

— Arthur Streeton. Melbourne, 1969. One of 250. 4to, orig bdg, in d/j. kh Nov 11 (226) A$90

Gale, Thomas, 1635?-1702

— Opuscula Mythologica physica et ethica. Amst., 1688. 8vo, calf. B Nov 1 (254) HF375

Galenus, Claudius

— De constitutione artis medicae.... Lione: Rouville, 1552. 16mo, contemp vellum. Some browning. SI June 9 (394) LIt250,000

— Delli mezzi, che si possono tenere per conservarci la sanita. Venice: M. Tramezzino, 1549. 8vo, calf; head of spine chipped. bba Feb 27 (400) £220 [Marlborough]

— Des Tumeurs oultre le coustumier de nature. Lyon: Estienne Dolet, 1542. 8vo, mor by Cortio; rubbed. O May 26 (71) $900

— Opera. Venice: V. Valgrisi, 1562-63. 10 vols in 4. Folio, modern calf. Some dampstaining in blank outer corners, with occasional paper corrosion. sg May 14 (56) $1,600

— Opera omnia. Basel: Froben & Episcopius, 1542. 10 vols bound in 4, including Index. Folio, contemp blind-stamped pigskin over wooden bds. Some discoloration; last leaf in final vol torn in upper margin & partly adhering to pastedown. S Dec 5 (385) £2,300 [Rizzo]

Galerie...

— Galerie Dramatique. Costumes des Theatres de Paris. Paris, [1844-60]. Vols 1-5. 5 vols. 8vo, contemp half lea. With litho titles & 478 litho plates. Some discoloration; 1 plate cut down & mtd. Kochno copy. SM Oct 12 (536) FF50,000

Galilei, Galileo, 1564-1642

— Dialogo di Galileo Galilei Linceo matematico...sopra i due massimi sistemi del mondo Tolemaico e Copernico. Florence, 1632. 1st Ed. 4to, later vellum bds. Some browning. S Dec 5 (386) £6,500 [Scheler]

— Discorsi e dimostrazioni matematiche.... Leiden: Elzevir, 1638. 1st Ed. 4to, vellum gilt; rubbed & wormed, hinges starting. Early Italian marginalia. Manney copy. P Oct 11 (149) $25,000

— Opere. Bologna, 1656-55. 2 vols. 4to, old calf; rebacked. With frontis, port & 1 folding plate. Frontis with outer margin shaved with loss; tear in G6 in the 2d work in Vol II. Bunbury copy. C June 24 (213) £2,000 [Pregliasco]

Gallaccini, Teofilo

— Trattato...sopra gli errori degli architetti. Venice, 1767. Bound with: Visentini, Antonio. Osservazioni...che servono di continuazione al trattato di...Gallaccini. Venice, 1771. Folio, half vellum; rubbed & marked. bba Sept 19 (318) £600 [Bifolco]

Gallatin, Albert, 1761-1849

— Letter from the Secretary of the Treasury...Relating to the Redemption...of the Whole of the Public Debt of the United States. Wash., 1806. 8vo, disbound. sg June 18 (217) $250

Gallatin, Albert Eugene, 1881-1952

— Art and the Great War. NY, 1919. Illus by Childe Hassam. Folio, half cloth. With 100 plates. sg Apr 2 (122) $50

Gallaudet, Thomas Hopkins, 1787-1851

— Hoike Akua: he Palapala ia e hoike ana ma na mea i hanaia aia no he Akua. Lahainaluna, 1842. 12mo, half cloth. sg June 18 (278) $425

Gallonio, Antonio, d.1605

— De SS. Martyrum Cruciatibus.... Paris, 1660. 4to, 18th-cent calf; worn. SI Dec 5 (257) LIt900,000

Gallotti, Jean

— Moorish Houses and Gardens of Morocco. NY, [1926?]. 2 vols. 4to, half cloth; spines darkened. With 136 plates. sg Sept 6 (117) $250

Gallucci, Giovanni Paolo, 1538-1621?

— De fabrica et usu hemisphaerii Uranici. Venice, 1598. 4to, old bds; spine worn. With folding woodcut plate. Lacking folding diagram & volvelles, the latter supplied in facsimile; b4 & d4 holed with loss; d4 repaired at outer margin. Ck Nov 29 (186) £380

Galsworthy, John, 1867-1933

— The Forsyte Saga. L, 1922. 1st Ed, one of 275. Calf. cb Sept 19 (74) $120

— From the Four Winds. 1897. 1st Ed. 12mo, orig cloth. Epstein copy. sg Apr 29 (175) $400

— Jocelyn. L, 1898. 1st Ed, One of 750. 8vo, orig cloth; endpapers cracked. sg Dec 12 (131) $200

— A Man of Devon. L, 1901. 1st Ed. 12mo, orig cloth; scuffed. sg Dec 12 (132) $225

— A Modern Comedy. L, 1929. Compact Ed, one of 500. 6 vols. Orig half mor gilt, in cloth d/js. wa Mar 5 (44) $160

— Works. NY, 1922-36. Manaton Ed, One of 750. 25 vols. 8vo, orig bds; worn torn. F Mar 26 (162) $90

Galton, Sir Francis, 1822-1911

— Finger Prints. L, 1892. 1st Ed. 8vo, orig cloth. With 15 plates, 1 double-page & colored. sg May 14 (59) $375

Galvao, Antonio, d.1557

— The Discoveries of the World.... L, 1601. 4to, 19th-cent mor gilt; extremities rubbed. Mostly black letter. Text browned; lacking final blank. STC 11543. DuPont copy. CNY Oct 8 (112) $21,000

Gamaches, Etienne Simon de

— Astronomie physique ou principes generaux de la nature, appliques au mecanisme astronomique.... Paris, 1740. 4to, contemp calf; worn, spine ends chipped, joints starting. With 22 folding plates. Title holed. bba Sept 5 (211) £160 [Greenwood]

Gamba da Bassano, Bartolommeo, 1776-1841

— Serie des Testi di Lingua e di altere Opera importanti nella Italiana Letteratura scritte dal secolo XIV al XIX. Venice, 1839. 4th Ed. 8vo, half lea; worn. O Sept 24 (95) $50

Gambado, Geoffrey. See: Bunbury, Henry W.

Gambogi, Michele

— Trattato sulla scherma. Milan, 1837. Oblong 4to, 19th-cent half sheep. With port & 38 plates. Minor dampstaining in lower margin throughout. sg Mar 26 (120) $375

Gambrill, Richard V. N. See: Derrydale Press

Gameren, Hannardus

— Veritable recit des choses passees es Pays Bas.... Luxembourg: Martin Marchant, 1577. 4to, contemp vellum. S Dec 5 (124) £2,400 [Kraus]

Gamiani...

— Gamiani, ou deux nuits d'exces. Par Alcide.... Paris, 1926. One of 100. 12mo, mor gilt. With 12 color lithos. HH May 12 (1073) DM2,600

Gamucci, Bernardo, 1522-92

— Le Antichita della citta di Roma. Venice, 1569. 8vo, 18th-cent calf. SI June 9 (398) LIt550,000

Gandee, B. F.

— The Artist, or Young Ladies' Instructor in Ornamental Painting.... L, 1835. 8vo, orig cloth; rubbed. With frontis & 17 plates. bba Feb 27 (348) £80 [Thorp]

Gandhi, Mohandas K., 1869-1948

[-] Gahdhiji; His Life and Work. [Bombay, 1944]. One of 250. 4to, burlap; front hinge cracked, shaken. Inscr to Eleanor Roosevelt by Jawaharlal Nehru. Epstein copy. sg Apr 29 (176) $3,600

Gandy, John Peter. See: Gell & Gandy

Gandy, Joseph

— The Rural Architect. L, 1806. 4to, contemp half russia; worn, joints cracked. With 42 plates. Foxed throughout. sg Feb 6 (95) $275

Gans, Richard

— Muestrario de la Fundicion Tipografica Galvanoplastia y Estereotipia de Richard Gans. Madrid, [c.1880]. Folio orig cloth; rebacked, with orig spine laid down. Some leaves remargined. cb Sept 5 (114) $190

Ganzo, Robert

— Orenoque. Paris, 1942. One of 84. Illus by Jean Fautrier. Folio, loose as issued. CGen Nov 18 (388) SF32,000

Garcia Conde, Pedro

— Verdadera Albeyteria. Barcelona: Joseph Giralt, 1734. Folio, contemp vellum; hole in spine. Some stains & browning. CNY Dec 5 (294) $550

Garcia Franco, Salvador

— Catalogo critico de astrolabios existentes en Espana. Madrid, 1945. 8vo, calf. O Aug 25 (82) $180

Garcia Icazbalceta, Joaquin, 1825-94

— Bibliografia Mexicana del Siglo XVI.... Mexico, 1954. 4to, half sheep; head of spine stainedd. sg Oct 31 (114) $200

Garden...

— The Garden; an Illustrated Weekly Journal.... L, 1872-84. Vols 1-26. 4to, orig cloth. pnE Dec 4 (21) £1,600

Gardeners'...

— The Gardeners' Magazine of Botany. L, 1850-51. Ed by Thomas Moore & W. P. Ayres. 3 vols. 4to, contemp half mor; minor stains to foot of upper covers. With tinted title, 11 plain & 100 hand-colored plates. b June 22 (368) £650

Anr copy. Vol I only. 4to, contemp half mor; rubbed, head of spine torn. With tinted litho title & 32 hand-colored plates. pn Sept 12 (294) £220

Anr copy. Vol III only. Later cloth. With 48 plates, 38 hand-colroed. Some soiling; 1 plate with corner creased. pn Dec 12 (279) £300

Gardens...

— The Gardens and Menagerie of the Zoological Society Delineated. Chiswick, 1830-31. 2 vols. 8vo, modern half cloth. Titles foxed. bba July 23 (461) £190 [Quaritch]

— Gardens Old and New: The Country House & its Garden Environment. L: Country Life Library, [1920]. 3d Ed. 3 vols. Folio, orig cloth. sg Feb 6 (96) $225

Gardilanne, Gratiane de —& Moffatt, Elizabeth Whitney

— Les Costumes regionaux de la France.... NY, 1929. One of 500. 4 vols. Folio, text booklets & plates in 4 cloth folding cases as issued. With 200 colored plates. Library markings, but plates unmarked. sg Feb 6 (97) $750

Gardiner, Allen Francis, 1794-1851

— Narrative of a Journey to the Zoolu Country in South Africa.... L, 1836. 8vo, recent half calf. With 2 folding maps & 26 plates, 2 hand-colored. Scattered spotting. DW Mar 4 (22) £140

— A Visit to the Indians on the Frontiers of Chili. L, 1841. 12mo, cloth; rebacked. sg June 18 (228) $375

Gardiner, J. Stanley

— The Fauna and Geography of the Maldive and Laccadive Archipelagoes. Cambr., 1903-6. 2 vols. 4to, orig cloth. Library markings. O Apr 28 (116) $100

Gardiner, John, Physician

— An Inquiry into the Nature...of Gout. Edin., 1792. 8vo, contemp half calf; spine ends repaired. Gov. Philip Gidley King's copy, inscr by him at head of title. C June 25 (111) £450 [McCormick]

Gardner, John, 1933-82

— Grendel. NY, 1971. Illus by Emil Antonucci. In d/j. Bookplate sgd by Gardner affixed to front flyleaf. pba July 9 (104) $60

— The Resurrection. NY, [1966]. In soiled d/j. Stain to 2 text pages. wa Dec 19 (189) $180

Gardner, Thomas, 1690?-1769

— A Pocket Guide to the English Traveller. L, 1719. 4to, contemp sheep; rebacked. With 100 double-page strip road maps. Some lower margins shaved with loss; lacking engraved title to 2d part. C Oct 30 (151) £720 [Cherrington]

1st Ed. 2 vols in 1. 4to, bds; worn. With 100 double-page maps. Some staining at end. B May 12 (1351) HF2,400

Gardnor, John

— Views Taken On and Near the River Rhine.... L, 1788. 1st Ed. Folio, contemp calf; worn, upper cover detached. With engraved title & 32 plates. Plates spotted. C May 20 (254) £3,000 [Sims Reed]

Anr Ed. L, 1791. 4to, contemp calf gilt. With engraved title & 32 colored plates. C May 20 (63) £550 [Maggs]

Anr copy. 19th-cent half calf. With engraved title & 32 uncolored plates. Some plates shaved, affecting imprint; some spotting. S May 14 (1198) £400 [Eliott]

Garibay y Zamalloa, Esteban de, 1525-99

— Los XL Libros del compendio historial de las chronicas...de los Reynos de Espana. Antwerp: Plantin, 1571. 1st Ed. 2 (of 4) vols. Calf; rubbed. Some waterstaining & worming; 2d title repaired; library stamps. Sgd; also inscr by Robert Southey. bba June 25 (54) £200 [Polites]

Garland, Hamlin, 1860-1940

— The Book of the American Indian. NY, 1923. Illus by Frederic Remington. 4to, half cloth, in d/j. sg Jan 30 (159) $200

Anr copy. Half cloth; extremities rubbed. sg June 18 (229) $90

— Prairie Songs. L, 1905. Inscr to Major J. B. Pond. sg Dec 12 (135) $110

Garner, Thomas, d.1906 —& Stratton, Arthur

— The Domestic Architecture of England during the Tudor Period. L, 1911. 2 vols. Folio, modern half mor. With 131 plates. S Nov 15 (894) £150 [Minaded]

Anr Ed. Bost., 1923. 4to, half cloth. sg Feb 6 (71) $130

Garnet, J. Ros

— Wildflowers of Southeastern Australia. Melbourne, 1974. Out-of-series copy. Illus by Betty Conabere. 2 vols. Folio, cloth. kh Nov 11 (506) A$120

Garnett, Richard, 1835-1906 —& Gosse, Sir Edmund W., 1849-1928

— English Literature: an Illustrated Record.... NY, 1905. 4 vols. cb Oct 17 (339) $65

Garnett, Thomas, 1766-1802

— Observations on a Tour through the Highlands and Part of the Western Isles of Scotland. L, 1800. 1st Ed. 2 vols. 4to, calf; rebacked. With folding map & 52 plates. pnE May 13 (47) £160

2d Ed. L, 1811. 2 vols. 4to, contemp calf gilt; rubbed, joints cracked. With 2 maps & 52 plates. bba Mar 26 (328) £120 [McCormick]

Garnier, Edouard

— The Soft Porcelain of Sevres. L, 1892. Folio, contemp mor; rubbed. With 50 chromolitho plates. Some soiling; library markings. F June 25 (748) $1,900

Garran, Andrew

— Picturesque Atlas of Australasia. Sydney, 1886. 2 vols. Folio, orig half lea; 1 cover damaged along outer edge. kh Nov 11 (507) A$225

Anr copy. Bound in 3 vols. Folio, bdg not described but repaired. Sold w.a.f. kh Nov 11 (508) A$250

Garrard, George, 1760-1826

— A Description of the Different Varieties of Oxen, Common in the British Isles. L, 1800-15. Oblong folio, half lea; worn. With 52 colored plates. Some soiling. S June 25 (86) £3,000 [Temperly]

Garrard, Lewis Hector, 1829-87. See: Grabhorn Printing

Garrick, David, 1717-79

— The Country Girl, a Comedy. L, 1766. 8vo, modern half calf. sg Mar 5 (231) $225

— The Private Correspondence of.... L, 1831-32. 2 vols. 4to, contemp half lea; 1 cover detached. With port. L Feb 27 (211) £90

Anr Ed. L, 1831. 2 vols. 4to, contemp half lea gilt; covers detached. sg Oct 17 (36) $90

Garrick Library, David

— [Sale Catalogue] A Catalogue of the Library, Splendid Books of Prints, Poetical and Historical Tracts.... [L: Saunders, 1823]. 1st Ed, 2d Issue. 8vo, contemp half lea. bba May 28 (55) £280 [Dawson]

Anr copy. Disbound. bba May 28 (556) £200 [Maggs]

Garrison, E. B.

— Studies in the History of Medieval Italian Painting. Florence, 1953-62. Vols I-IV. 4to, cloth. sg Oct 31 (217) $1,400

Garrucci, Raffaele

— Storia della arte Cristiana nei primi otto secoli della chiesa. Prato, 1872-81. 6 vols. Folio, contemp half vellum; soiled. With 500 plates. Ck Nov 29 (94) £220

Garston, Edgar

— Greece Revisited, and Sketches in Lower Egypt in 1840.... L, 1842. 2 vols. 8vo, contemp calf gilt; rubbed. With 3 lithos, 2 stained. Lacking half-title in Vol II. S June 30 (299) £350 [Consolidated Real]

Anr copy. Contemp calf with Signet arms; joints weak. With 3 plates. S July 1 (611) £380 [Atabey]

Garzelli, Annarosa —& De la Mare, Albina

— Miniature Florentina del Rinascimento, 1440, 1525. Florence, 1985. 2 vols. Folio, wraps. sg Oct 31 (218) $175

Gaskell, Elizabeth Cleghorn, 1810-65

— Cranford. L, 1853. 1st Ed. 12mo, orig cloth; front joint torn, hinges cracked. sg Oct 17 (256) $50

Gass, Patrick, 1771-1870

— A Journal of the Voyages and Travels.... Pittsburgh, 1807. 1st Ed. 12mo, half mor by Riviere; rubbed. Soiled & browned. P June 16 (216) $1,200

Gassendi, Pierre, 1592-1655

— Institutio astronomica juxta hypotheses tam veterum.... L, 1653. 3 parts in 1 vol. 8vo, 19th-cent half calf; rubbed. bba Sept 5 (212) £480 [Quaritch]

Gasser, Achilles Pirminius, 1505-77

— Historiarum et chronicorum mundi epitomes libellus. Venice: Melchior Sessa, 1533. 8vo, contemp Ms vellum; worn. 4 leaves torn & restored. sg Mar 12 (97) $225

Gastineau, Henry, 1791-1876

— Wales Illustrated.... L, 1830. 2 parts in 1 vol. 4to, modern cloth. With engraved title & 62 plates. Some foxing. bba Dec 19 (76) £55 [Thorp]

Anr copy. Later half mor gilt; worn. With engraved title & 96 views on 48 sheets. Scattered spotting. DW Nov 20 (34) £75

Anr copy. Orig half mor; worn. With engraved title & 88 views on 44 leaves.. DW Nov 20 (35) £60

Anr copy. Rebacked. With engraved title & 176 views on 88 sheets. Minor spotting. DW Nov 20 (36) £120

Anr copy. Contemp half mor gilt; rubbed. With engraved title & 224 views on 112 sheets.. DW Nov 20 (37) £190

Gates, Eleanor

— Good-Night (Buenas Noches). NY, 1907. Illus by Arthur Rackham. Orig cloth. With 5 color plates. bba July 23 (283) £85 [Spalding]

Gatteri, Giuseppe

— La Stori Veneta. Venice, 1864. 2 vols in 1. Oblong folio, contemp half mor. With frontis & 150 plates. Frontis torn at inner margin; Plate 150 creased. S Nov 21 (254) £2,200 [Christodolou]

— La Storia veneta. Venice, 1862. 2 vols. Oblong folio, orig half mor gilt; spines rubbed, lower cover of Vol II detached. With frontis & 150 plates. S June 30 (31) £1,000 [Severis]

Gatty, Harold. See: Post & Gatty

Gaubil, Antoine

— Le Chou-king, un des livres sacres des chinois. Paris, 1770. 4to, contemp calf gilt; spine chipped at foot. Library stamp on half-title pasted over. S Feb 11 (551) £200 [Thorp]

Gaudier-Brzeska, Henri, 1891-1915

— Henri Gaudier-Brzeska 1891-1915. L: Ovid Press, [1919]. One of 250. Folio, unbound as issued in orig portfolio. With 20 facsimile drawings on 19 plates. S July 21 (115) £500 [Eccles]

Gauguin, Paul, 1848-1903

See also: Grabhorn Printing

— Noa Noa. [Munich, 1926]. One of 320. 4to, orig raffia, in def d/j. Facsimile of the Ms. wa June 25 (482) $425

Anr Ed. Paris, [1926]. One of 100. Folio, burlap. cb Feb 12 (47) $400

Anr Ed. [Stockholm, 1947]. 4to, bds, in frayed. O Aug 25 (83) $110

Anr Ed. [Paris, 1954]. One of 100. Orig straw cloth, in pictorial d/j. S Feb 11 (278) £600 [Ursus]

Gaunt, William

— The Etchings of Frank Brangwyn. A Catalogue Raisonne. L, 1926. 4to, half vellum, in d/j. kh Nov 11 (102) A$140

Anr copy. Half vellum; spine torn at head. sg Feb 6 (39) $130

Anr copy. Orig half vellum; worn & soiled, small tear at head of spine. Some margins soiled. wa Apr 9 (202) $150

Gauricus, Lucas, 1476-1558

— Tractatus astrologicus in quo agitur de praeteritis multorum hominum accidentibus.... Venice: Curtius Troianus Navo, 1552. 4to, contemp calf gilt; spine ends chipped. sg Mar 12 (216) $1,500

Gauss, Karl Friedrich, 1777-1855

— Disquisitiones arithmeticae. Leipzig, 1801. 8vo, orig bds; rubbed, joint cracked, spine ends damaged. Some foxing; library stamps on flyleaf & tp. bba June 25 (171) £3,200 [Quaritch]

Gautier d'Agoty, Jacques, 1717-85

— Exposition anatomique des organes des sens.... Paris: Demonville, 1775. Folio, later bds; sheep spine abraded. With 8 color mezzotints. Tp soiled; some waterstains; K2 with tear into text, repaired. Schlosser copy. P June 17 (463) $20,000

Gautier, Theophile, 1811-72
See also: Golden Cockerel Press

— La Comedie de la mort. Paris, 1838. 1st Ed. 8vo, mor gilt by Mercier, orig wraps bound in. S May 28 (325) £800 [Clapp]

— Emaux et camees. Paris, 1852. 1st Ed. 18mo, lea gilt. S May 28 (326) £1,900 [Sims Reed]

Gavarni

— Le Diable a Paris: Paris et les Parisiens. Paris, 1845-46. 2 vols. 8vo, later half mor gilt. bbc Apr 27 (67) $150

Anr copy. Lea. br May 29 (43) $150

— Gavarni in London, Sketches of Life and Character. L, 1849. Ed by Albert Smith. 8vo, contemp cloth; bumped. With 24 plates. bba July 23 (333) £70 [Cline]

Anr copy. Orig cloth; rubbed. With extra title & 23 plates.. cb Jan 9 (95) $140

— Oeuvres choisies. Paris, 1846. 6 parts. 4to, orig bds; rubbed. wa Sept 26 (556) $55

Gavin, Charles Murray

— Royal Yachts. L, 1932. One of 1,000. 4to, orig cloth; dampstained. L Feb 27 (212) £60

Gay, Jean

— Bibliographie Anecdotique du Jeu des Echecs. Paris, 1864. One of 260. 12mo, modern half cloth preserving contemp bds, which have been laminated. Inscr. Ck May 8 (102) £240

Gay, John, 1685-1732

— The Beggar's Opera. Paris, 1937. One of 1,500. Illus by Mariette Lydis. With 15 plates. sg Sept 26 (174) $110

— Fables. L, 1737-38. Mixed Ed. 2 vols. 4to, early calf gilt; worn. bbc Sept 23 (48) $120

Anr Ed. Newcastle, 1779. 8vo, contemp sheep; worn, lower cover detached. S Apr 28 (16) £380 [Steedman]

Anr Ed. L, 1793. 2 vols. 8vo, contep calf gilt; broken & worn. Lacking 2 plates; some foxing. bbc Sept 23 (419) $170

Anr copy. Contemp calf. cb Jan 9 (96) $85; rs Oct 17 (49) $375

Anr Ed. L: Stockdale, 1793. 2 vols. 8vo, contemp mor gilt with crest of Thomas Hutton. Engraved titles shaved with slight loss. C Dec 16 (196) £420 [Woods]

— Polly: an Opera.... L, 1729. 4to, modern half calf; edges rubbed. Some soiling & foxing. pn Oct 24 (359) £180

Gay, Sydney H., 1814-88. See: Bryant & Gay

Gaya, Louis de

— Traite des armes, des machines de guerre, des feux d'artifice. Paris, 1678. 1st Ed. 12mo, contemp sheep. sg Mar 26 (121) $325

Gaza, Theodorus

— Grammatica introductionis, libri quatuor.... Venice: Aldus, 25 Dec 1495. Bound with other tracts & accompanied by the 1495 Aldus Theocritus & Hesiod. Together, 2 vols. Folio, 18th-cent calf gilt with fore-edge painting of the Sebright arms; damage to headcap of Vol I. Gaza 31 lines; types 1:146G (text), 5:110R (title, colophon); 6:83R (Aldus lectori). Theocritus 30 lines; types 1:146Gk (text), 2:11R (title) & 6:38R (dedication, colophon). Gasa in the state with initial & headpiece on h4v of leafwork rather than strapwork design. Theocritus in corrected state, with sheets E1-2 & quire F reset. Bound in are 18 Ms leaves in contemp or near-contemp hand of additional texts of Theocritus. Many of the initials & headpieces in both vols hatched with brown ink. Gaza partly misbound. Gaza is 198 leaves; Goff G-110. Theocritus is 140 leaves; Goff T-144. P Dec 12 (175) $26,000

Gazette...

— Gazette du Bon Ton. Art, modes & frivolites. Paris, 1914. Vol II, No 7. 8vo, wraps. With 13 colored plates. sg Sept 19 (175) $300

Vol V, No 4. Paris 1922. Ptd paper folder. Z Oct 26 (86) $200

Vol V, No 1. Ptd paper folder; soiled. Z Oct 26 (83) $325

Vol V, No 2. Ptd paper folder. Z Oct 26 (84) $225

Vol V, No 3. Ptd paper folder. Z Oct 26 (85) $225

Vol V, No 5. Ptd paper folder. Z Oct 26 (87) $200

Vol V, No 6. Ptd paper folder. Z Oct 26 (88) $225

Vol V, No 7. Ptd paper folder. Z Oct 26 (89) $225

Vol V, No 8. Ptd paper folder. Z Oct 26 (90) $190

Vol V, No 9. Ptd paper folder. Z Oct 26 (91) $170

Vol V, No 10. Ptd paper folder. Z Oct 26 (92) $150

Gedde, John

— The English Apiary: or, the Compleat Bee-Master. L, 1721-22. 2 parts in 1 vol. 12mo, contemp sheep; rebacked & recased. Lacking both blanks. bba Sept 5 (48) £280 [Lilburn]

Gee, Ernest R.

— The Sportsman's Library: a Descriptive List.... NY, 1940. One of 600. K July 12 (238) $70

— The Sportsman's Library: Being a Descriptive List.... NY, 1940. One of 600. Cloth; soiled. wa Mar 6 (139) $70

Geffroy, Gustave, 1855-1926

— Auguste Brouet: Catalogue de son oeuvre grave. Paris, 1923. One of 100 on on Arches, with orig etching in 2 states, both sgd. 2 vols. 4to, loose as issued in orig wraps. S July 1 (1191) £180 [Sims Reed]

Geiger, Benno

— Alessandro Magnasco. Bergamo, 1949. Ltd Ed. Folio, orig bdg. SI Dec 5 (263A) LIt280,000

One of 1,500. Half lea; spine edges worn. sg Apr 2 (170) $500

Geiler von Kaisersberg, Johann, 1445-1510

— Das irrig Schaf. Strassburg: Mathias Schuerer, [c.1510]. 7 parts in 1 vol. 4to, 16th-cent calf over wooden bds; rebcked, 1 clasp & catch. Some staining; d1 misbound before c6; lacking 2 blanks; hole in B3 with loss of a few letters; some staining; small wormholes in margins at beginning & end repaired. S May 28 (46) £6,800 [Schiller]

— Navicula penitentie. Augsburg: Johann Otmar for G. Diemar, 1511. Folio, contemp blind-stamped pigskin-backed bds. Some worming, mainly in margins; some staining. S Dec 5 (123) £550 [Schwing]

Geisberg, Max

— The German Single-Leaf Woodcut: 1500-1550. NY: Hacker, 1974. 4 vols. Folio, cloth. sg Feb 6 (100) $175

Geisel, Theodore Seuss. See: Seuss, Dr.

Geldner, Ferdinand

— Bucheinbaende aus elf Jahrhunderten. Munich, 1958. Folio, orig half cloth. With 100 plates. bba June 25 (12) £60 [Kaiser]

Gelis-Didot, Pierre —& Laffillee, H.

— La Peinture decorative en France du XVIe au XVIIIe Siecle. Paris: Charles Schmid, [1896]. Folio, bdg not described but def. With 60 chromolitho plates. F Sept 26 (667) $75

Gell, Sir William, 1777-1836

See also: Nibby & Gell

— The Geography and Antiquities of Ithaca. L, 1807. 4to, contemp calf; rebacked. With 2 maps & 13 plates. Some spotting. S July 1 (610) £700 [Chelsea]

— Narrative of a Journey in the Morea. L, 1823. 8vo, contemp half mor; rubbed. With 9 plates. Lacking directions to binder. S June 30 (300) £550 [London Lib.]

— Pompeiana: the Topography, Edifices and Ornaments of Pompeii. L, 1832. 2 vols. 8vo, modern cloth. bba Jan 30 (112) £65 [Tosi]

Anr copy. Half mor; rubbed. bba Feb 27 (23) £140 [Holland]

Anr copy. Contemp half mor; worn & soiled. Plates are all proof impressions on india paper. L.p. copy. W July 8 (214) £70

Anr Ed. L, 1837. 2 vols. 4to, contemp half mor gilt; rubbed & scuffed. With 88 plates. DW Nov 5 (46) £75

— The Topography of Troy and its Vicinity. L, 1804. 1st Ed. Folio, contemp half mor; extremities rubbed, upper cover scuffed. With hand-colored etched title vignette & 26 plates, 7 hand-colored. H2-I2 spotted at upper margin. Extra-illus with 2 double-page plates. Ck May 15 (105) £1,500

Gell, Sir William, 1777-1836 —& Gandy, John Peter

— Pompeiana. L, 1817-19. 1st Ed. 8vo, contemp mor. With 81 plates & maps, 1 in color, 1 ptd in gold. K July 12 (417) $200

Gellert, Hugo. See: Marx, Karl

Gelli, Jacopo

See also: Levi & Gelli

— Bibliografia generale della scherma. Florence, 1890. One of 600. 4to, half mor; spine ends worn. sg Mar 26 (122) $450

— Nuovo codice cavalleresco. Florence, 1888. Parte prima [all issued]. 8vo, later half cloth. Final gathering loose. sg Mar 26 (123) $100

Gellius, Aulus

— Noctes Atticae. Venice: Christophorus de Quaietis & Martinus de Lazaronibus, 17 July 1493. Folio, later vellum; soiled. 43 lines & headline; types 1:111R & 111Gk. Some worming to blank margins of 31-u3; some holes neatly repaired. 126 (of 128) leaves; lacking front & final blanks. Goff G-124. C Dec 16 (125) £850 [Maggs]

Anr Ed. Basel: Cratander, Sept 1519. ("Noctium Atticarum libri xx.") Bound with: Quintilianus, M. F. Oratoriarum institutionum lib. xii.... Cologne: Cervicornus & Fuchs, Mar 1521. And: Macrobius, A.T. In somnium Scipionis libri duo.... Cologne: E. Cervicornus, Aug 1521. Folio, blind-stamped calf over wooden bds, with pastedowns from legal Ms on vellum; foot of spine def. S Dec 5 (125) £1,400 [King]

Anr Ed. Cologne: Ioannem Gymnicum, 1537. 8vo, contemp blindstamped vellum with central blindstamped ports of the Dukes of Saxony; some wear, lacking clasps. Italic letter. Ms notes on tp; some browning. pn Nov 14 (272) £160

Geminus, Thomas

— Compendiosa totius anatomie delineatio. L, 1545. Trans by Nicolas Udall. Folio, 18th-cent calf; rubbed, corners worn. With engraved title & 40 plates, 1 folding. All plates mtd on extending guards; most trimmed within plate-line; tp cropped & laid down; Adam & Eve plate soiled & def with some loss at outer edge; tear in Plate 39; some dampstaining. STC 11714. S Dec 5 (387) £6,000 [Joffe]

Genauer, Emily

— Chagall at the "Met." NY, [1971]. Folio, cloth, in d/j. sg Sept 6 (68) $50; sg Feb 6 (57) $110

General...

— The General Stud Book. L, 1858-1969. 1st few vols later Eds. Vols 1-39 in 43. 2 vols in orig wraps; others, calf or half calf; rubbed. bba Sept 5 (176) £400 [R. & G. Way]

Genest, John, 1764-1839

— Some Account of the English Stage.... Bath, 1832. 1st Ed. 10 vols. 8vo, half lea; rubbed, some bds detached. Met Apr 28 (818) $160

Genet, Jean

— Le Condamne a Mort. Fresnes, 1942. Unsewn in orig wraps. Inscr to Boris Kochno. SM Oct 12 (468) FF13,000

— Journal du voleur. Paris, [1949]. One of 410. Folio, unsewn in orig wraps, unopened. SM Oct 12 (475) FF2,500

— Miracle de la Rose. Lyon: Barbezat, [1946]. One of 475. 4to, orig bds. Inscr to Boris Kochno. SM Oct 11 (472) FF3,500

— Notre Dame des fleurs. Monte Carlo, [1944]. One of 350. 4to, half mor by Semet & Plumelle, orig wraps bound in. Inscr to Boris Kochno, twice. SM Oct 12 (469) FF15,000

One of 350, this copy ptd for Jean Decarnin. Orig wraps; loose & stained. SM Oct 12 (470) FF1,800

— Pompes Funebres. Bikini: Aux Depens de quelques amateurs, 1947. One of 470. Orig wraps. Inscr to Boris Kochno. SM Oct 11 (473) FF4,000

— Querelle de Brest. [Milan, 1947]. 1st Ed, one of 525. Illus by Jean Cocteau. Inscr to Boris Kochno. SM Oct 11 (474) FF22,000

— Vingt Lithographies pou un livre que j'ai lu. Paris, 1945. One of 115. Illus by Roland Caillaux. Foli, unsewn in orig wraps. Lacking 1 illust. Loosely inserted are 3 pencil drawings by Caillaux. Kochno copy. SM Oct 12 (471) FF9,000

Genevoix, Maurice

— Images pour un jardin sans murs. Paris, [n.d.]. One of 144. Illus by Maurice de Vlaminck. Folio, loose as issued in ptd wraps. With 9 color lithos. sg Jan 10 (182) $250

Genlis, Stephanie Felicite de, 1746-1830

— Arabesques mythologiques ou les attributs de toutes les divinites de la fable. Paris, 1810-11. 2 vols. 12mo, later half calf. With 78 plates. Some margins trimmed; Avis au Relieur leaf lacking. pn Dec 12 (129) £180 [Vine]

Genthe, Arnold

— The Book of the Dance. NY, 1916. 1st Ed. 4to, cloth; edges worn. Some foxing. bbc Feb 17 (210) $140

— Impressions of Old New Orleans. NY, [1926]. 1st Ed, one of 200. 4to, half cloth; extremities worn. With 102 plates. Inscr to Thomas J. Watson. sg Apr 13 (47) $225

— Isadora Duncan. NY, 1929. 4to, cloth; several hinges cracked. Pages loose. cb Jan 16 (54) $110; Met Apr 28 (643) $70

Anr copy. Cloth. Eva Le Gallienne's copy. sg Mar 5 (222) $325

— Pictures of Old Chinatown. NY, 1913. ("Old Chinatown.") Text by Will Irwin. cb Sept 13 (71) $100

Gentleman...

— The Gentleman Angler: Containing Short, Plain and Easy Instructions.... L, 1726. 1st Ed. 12mo, later half calf; rubbed. Library markings on title. Koopman copy. O Oct 29 (136) $600

Anr copy. 19th-cent calf. Some margins cropped; some browning. S Feb 26 (853) £320 [Montague]

Gentleman of Elvas. See: Relation...

Gentleman of the Province, A. See: Peters, Samuel A.

Gentleman's...

— The Gentleman's Magazine, or Trader's Monthly Intelligencer [continued as the Historical Chronicle, etc.]. L, 1731-1849. 183 vols only, lacking Vols 19-21. 8vo, 19th-cent half vellum; rubbed & soiled, some spines worn. Sold w.a.f. bba Aug 13 (144) £4,000 [Matthew]

Gentry, Thomas George, 1843-1905

— Nests and Eggs of Birds of the United States. Phila., 1882. 4to, orig mor; extremities rubbed. With port, chromolitho title & 54 chromolitho plates. Some foxing. F Sept 26 (611) $180

Anr copy. Later 3-ring binder; worn, soiled.

A few leaves torn. O Apr 28 (33) $350

Geoffnete Fecht-Boden...

— Der Geoffnete Fecht-Boden auf welchen durch kurtz gefast Regeln.... Hamburg, 1715. 12mo, modern bds. With 10 plates. Sold w.a.f. sg Mar 26 (125) $140

Geographical...

— A Geographical Present: being Description of the Principal Countries of the World. L, 1817. 12mo, contemp half mor; worn. With 60 hand-colored plates. sg July 23 (303) £240 [Bickersteth]

3d Ed. L, 1820. 12mo, contemp half mor. With hand-colored frontis & 59 plates. bba July 23 (143) £180 [Sotheran]

George, Prince of Wales. See: Albert Victor & George

George, Sir Ernest

— Etchings on the Loire, and in the South of France. L, 1875. Folio, cloth; worn. bba Jan 30 (356) £100 [Going]

George III, King of England. See: England

George, Waldemar

— Boris Aronson et l'art du theatre. Paris, 1928. One of 315. 4to, orig wraps. Inscr to John Mason Brown. Met Apr 28 (859) $775

Georgi, Johann Gottlieb, 1738-1802

— Description de toutes les nations de l'empire de Russie.... St. Petersberg, 1776-77. Vols I-III (of 4) bound in 2. Contemp half lea. With 75 plates. Lacking plate lists for Vols I & II; tp to text Vol II stained; plate vol title laid down on verso of Vol III plate list. Sold w.a.f. C Oct 30 (34) £320 [Shapero]

Georgian...

— The Georgian Society: Records of Eighteenth-Century Domestic Architecture and Decoration in Dublin. Dublin, 1909-13. 5 vols. 4to, cloth; soiled & stained. Sold w.a.f. K Sept 29 (210) $110

Georgijevic, Bartholomej

— Opera nova che comprende quattro libretti. Rome: Antonio Barre, 1555. 8vo, later vellum. sg May 7 (108) $1,100

Georgirenes, Joseph, Archbishop of Samos

— A Description of the Present State of Samos.... L, 1678. 12mo, modern calf gilt by Birdsall. Tp repaired at fore-edge; small repair in final leaf; soiled. S June 30 (302) £900 [Chelsea]

Gerard, Jean Ignace Isidore

— Les Metamorphoses du jour. See: Grandville

Gerard, John, 1545-1612

— The Herball.... L, 1597. Folio, old calf; rebacked, corners repaired. With engraved title & port. Colophon leaf laid down; lacking final blank; engraved title soiled, marginal tears repaired & ptd date ringed with indelible ink. STC 11750. C Oct 30 (193) £850 [Bifolco]

Anr copy. 19th-cent calf gilt; worn. Lacking blanks at front & rear; remains of upper part of engraved title; index leaves frayed with loss; marginal repairs. Sold w.a.f. DW May 13 (113) £460

Anr copy. Modern pigskin by Margaret Simeon; upper cover with blindstamped garden design. Lacking tp (supplied in Ms) & c.32 leaves; several others torn & repaired, a few def at beginning & end; some Ms annotations. Sold w.a.f. pn July 16 (148) £320 [Finney]

Anr copy. 18th-cent calf. With engraved title, port & illusts in text, the port & illusts hand-colored. Minor dampstaining; tp, 2d A1 & last leaf def, duct down & mtd; large hole in 3A4 & corner torn from 5C4, with loss of text. STC 11750. S May 14 (1032) £1,900 [Marshall]

Anr copy. Modern half calf preserving an earlier blind-tooled spine. Tp soiled & worn; some loss at edges (supplied); margins mostly restored; occasional stains to text. STC 11750. wa Sept 26 (471) $1,600

2d Ed. L, 1633. Folio, contemp half vellum; worn,spine ends repaired. Tp & some leaves lacking. Sold w.a.f. b June 22 (357) £420

Anr copy. 18th-cent mor gilt; spine scuffed. Engraved title cut down & mtd; lacking 1st & last blanks; dedication cut down & mtd & 4 following leaves with upper margins strengthened; 3 leaves from smaller copies. STC 11751. C Oct 30 (236) £1,200 [Claridge]

Anr copy. Contemp bds; worn. Engraved title mended & soiled. STC 11751. LH Dec 11 (118) $1,200

Anr copy. Contemp calf; rubbed & split. Some repairs to margins & final 2 leaves; engraved title repaired & rebacked. pnE Dec 4 (200) £600

Anr copy. Contemp calf; worn & broken. Engraved title cut round & mtd; some browning & staining; last 3 leaves remargined; tear repaired in D4; other minor marginal tears; lacking 1st & last blanks. STC 11751. S May 14 (1031) £550 [Clark]

Anr copy. Modern half calf. Engraved title def; lacking 3 text leaves & 2 blanks; a number of leaves torn & def, affecting text; some stains & soiling. Sold w.a.f. STC 11751. S May 14 (1033) £450 [Bifolco]

Anr copy. Modern calf; worn. Engraved title soiled; lacking M3 & 7B5 & 1st & last blanks; a few leaves with tears; some staining. STC 11751. S July 1 (916) £400 [Toscani]

3d Ed. L, 1636. Folio, later mor; broken, cover detached. Lacking 1st & last blank & 1st 2 leaves. O Nov 26 (72) $1,100

Anr copy. 18th-cent half calf; rubbed. Lacking engraved title & 1st & last blanks; some dampstaining; a few small holes in text. STC 11752. S Feb 26 (916) £500 [Erlini]

Anr Ed. L, 1927. One of 150. 4to, orig vellum; warped. bba Sept 5 (49) £75 [Atkins]

Gerasch, Franz

— Das Oesterreichische Heer von Ferdinand II.... Vienna, [c.1854]. 4to, loose as issued in portfolio. With 152 (of 153) hand-colored plates. HH May 12 (978) DM2,200

Gerbier, Sir Balthazar, 1592?-1667

— A Brief Discourse concerning the Three Chief Principles of Magnificent Building. L, 1662. 8vo, modern half calf. bba Feb 27 (49) £600 [Knohl]

Gerdts, William H. —&
Burke, Russell

— American Still-Life Painting. NY, [1971]. sp Apr 16 (141) $175

Gerhard, Johann, 1582-1637

— Meditationes sacrae. [N.p.]: Roger Daniel, 1655. 24mo, old sheep; front cover detached. A9 torn with loss. sg Oct 24 (129) $225

Gerli, Agostino

— Opuscoli. Parma: Bodoni, 1785. 5 parts in 1 vol. Folio, orig bds. With 15 plates. SI June 9 (408) LIt2,800,000

Germain, Pierre

— Elements d'orfeverie. Paris, 1748. 4to, calf gilt. With 100 plates, 3 remargined. bba Feb 27 (331) £1,300 [Etching]

Germany

— Bambergische peinliche halszgerichts Ordnung. Bamberg: Johann Wagner, 1580. Folio, old vellum; worn. Ck Nov 29 (47) £1,400

Gerning, Johann Isaac von, 1767-1837

— A Picturesque Tour along the Rhine.... L, 1820. 4to, contemp half mor gilt by D. Condie. With 24 hand-colored plates & colored folding map. Orig tissue guards browned, but plates clean. L.p copy. C May 20 (62) £2,300 [Joseph]

Gernsback, Hugo, 1884-1967

— Ralph 124C41+: A Romance of the Year 2660. Bost., 1925. Orig blue cloth; rubbed. Contents leaf with corner chipped, not affecting text. F June 25 (538) $130

Anr copy. Orig cloth, in d/j. Epstein copy. sg Apr 29 (377) $2,000

Gernsheim, Helmut & Alison

— The History of Photography from the Camera Obscura.... NY, 1969. In d/j. sg Apr 13 (48) $175

Gerritszoon, Hessel

— The Arctic North-East and West Passage. Amst., 1878. 4to, orig bds; worn. S June 25 (80) £120 [Renard]

Gersaint, Edme Francois, d.1750

— Catalogue raisonne considerable de diverses curiosites en tous genres.... Paris, 1744. 12mo, calf; rubbed. bba Mar 26 (60) £140 [Quaritch]

Gershwin, George, 1898-1937
See also: Heyward & Gershwin

— George Gershwin's Song-Book. NY, 1932. 1st Ed, One of 300. Illus by Alajalov. 4to, orig mor gilt; joints worn. Epstein copy. sg Apr 29 (1797) $5,200

— Rhapsody in Blue. NY: Harms, [1927]. Folio, orig wraps. Piano solo score. Inscr to John Galsworthy. Epstein copy. sg Apr 29 (178) $17,000

Gerson, Johannes, 1362-1428?

— Opera. Cologne: Johann Koelhoff the Elder, 1484. Vol IV only. Contemp calf over wooden bds; def. First 2 leaves repaired with loss; some dampstaining at beginning; 303 leaves only, lacking r8, G9-10, K9-10 & all after Q8. Sold w.a.f. S May 13 (768) £260 [Rix]

Anr Ed. Strassburg: Johann Knoblauch, 1514. 5 parts in 4 vols. Folio, 16th-cent blind-stamped pigskin over wooden bds, clasps & catches; rubbed. Short tear in Uu3 of Part 3; some worming at beginning & end of each vol; tp of Part 4 detached; some early Ms annotations in margin of Part 2. S Dec 5 (128) £1,500 [Maggs]

— Super Cantica Canticorum. Nuremberg: Johann Sensenschmidt, 1470. Bound with: Gerson. De Parvulis ad Christum trahendis. Nuremberg: Johann Sensenschmidt, c.1470. And: Gerson. De Arte audiendi Confessiones; De Remediis contra recidivum peccandi. [Nuremberg: Johann Sensenschmidt, c.1470]. 3 works in 1 vol. Folio, early 19th-cent mor gilt. Some marginalia. 40 leaves; Goff G-272. 10 leaves; Goff G-274. 6 leaves. Goff G-191. C June 24 (133) £15,500 [Quaritch]

Gerstaecker, Friedrich, 1816-72
See also: Grabhorn Printing
— Gerstaecker's Travels: Rio De Janeiro... California and the Gold Regions. L, 1854. 1st Ed in English. 12mo, cloth; spine torn at head. sg June 18 (71) $140

Gerstinger, Hans
— Die Wiener Genesis: Farbenlichtdruck-faksimile der Griechischen Bilderbibel aus dem 6. Jahrhundert, Cod. Vindob. Theol. Graec. 31. Vienna: Austrian National Library, [1931]. 2 vols. Folio, half vellum; facsimile vol loose in bdg. With 26 plates plus colored facsimile on 48 pp. sg May 21 (269) $375

Gesamtkatalog...
— Gesamtkatalog der Wiegendrucke. Leipzig, 1925-40. Vols I-IX in 12 vols & Vol I Supplement. Together, 13 vols. 4to. Vol IX, wraps; others, cloth. sg Oct 31 (151) $1,100

Gesner, Conrad, 1516-65
— Bibliotheca Universalis, sive catalogus omnium scriptorum locupletissimus.... Zurich: Christoph Froschauer, 1545. Folio, 16th-cent blind-stamped pigskin over wooden bds. Tear in lower margin of oo2 repaired; some staining, mainly in margins. S Dec 5 (127) £7,000 [Scheler]
— Gesnerus redivivus auctus & emendatus. Oder: Allgemeines Thier-Buch. Frankfurt, 1669-70; Part 6 is Heildeberg, 1613. 6 parts in 1 vol. Folio, old paper-covered vellum bds; worn. Lacking T2-3; some browning; a few leaves shaved, affecting illust. Sold w.a.f. S Nov 21 (18) £1,250 [Bifolco]
— Historiae animalium lib. IV qui est de piscium.... Zurich, 1558. Folio, 18th-cent vellum. SI June 9 (409) LIt3,000,000
— Historiae animalium. Frankfurt, 1617. ("Historiae animalium liber III.") Folio, half vellum with wooden bds. HH May 12 (491) DM2,100

Anr Ed. Zurich: C. Froschouer, 1551-58 & Frankfurt: H. Laurentz, 1621. Books I-IV only in 3 vols. Old blindstamped vellum; soiled, spine ends chipped. Ink library stamps on titles & margins of c.20 text leaves; Book I title creased; Book II title laid down & with small section supplied in Ms facsimile; final leaf of Book III laid down; lacking blanks from Books II & III; old dampstaining. C Oct 30 (194) £3,500 [Pampaloni]
— Vogelbuch: Thierbuch: Fischbuch. Zurich: C. Froschauer, 1557-63-75. Folio, 18th-cent bds; spine worn at head. Colored by a contemp hand. 1st work lacks all before f.25; also ff. 68, 76, 178, 192, 220, 224, 263; 2d work lacks ff. 40, 74, 95, 98, 125, 126; 3d work lacks ff. 30, 97, 98 & 199-202. Many leaves torn & def, sometimes affecting text; dampstained. Sold w.a.f. S Nov 21 (19) £2,900 [Mandl]

Gesta...
— Gesta Romanorum. Nuremberg: Anton Koberger, 8 Sept 1494. ("Gesta romanorum cum applicationibus moralisatis ac misticis....") 4to, contemp blind-stamped half pigskin over wooden bds, unpressed copy. 45 lines, double-column; types 14:130G, 15:91G & 21:74G; rubricated through i2r. 119 (of 120) leaves; lacking final blank. Goff G-294. C Nov 27 (16) £1,900 [Quaritch]

Anr Ed. Paris: Philippe Pigouchet for Jean Petit, 1503. Bound with: Brulefer, Stephanus. Opuscula. Paris, 24 Apr 1500. Goff B-1222. 8vo, contemp blindstamped calf over wooden bds with metal fittings & vellum Ms endpapers; 5 cornerpieces lacking, rebacked. C Nov 27 (38) £1,500 [Quaritch]

Anr Ed. L: Johannes Marion for Constantin Fradin, 11 Jan 1518. 8vo, 19th-cent mor. C Dec 16 (48) £400 [Pickering & Chatto]

Gestes...
— Les Gestes de Chiprois, recueil de chroniques franeaises.... Geneva, 1887. One of 50 L.p. copies, this copy for the Comte Riant. 8vo, orig wraps. S June 30 (35) £550 [Sophoclides]

Getty, Alice
— The Gods of Northern Buddhism. Oxford, 1928. 4to, orig cloth. sg Feb 6 (103) $150

Getz, John. See: Bacon Collection, Edward R.

Ghibbesius, Jacobus Albanus
— Carminum.... Rome: Fabio de Falco, 1668. 8vo, contemp vellum. With engraved title & port. sg Oct 24 (130) $175

Ghirardacci, Cherubino
— Della Historia di Bologna. Bologna, 1596-1657. 2 vols. Folio, 19th-cent half vellum. Some old marginal annotations. SI Dec 5 (876) LIt1,400,000

Giacometti, Francesco
— Nouveau Jeu d'Echecs, ou le jeu de la guerre.... Genova, 1801. 8vo, contemp calf; rubbed, covers discolored. Blank section torn from F1. Ck May 8 (103) £100

Giafferri, Paul Louis de
— L'Histoire du costume feminin.... Paris, [1922-23]. Orig 10 parts. Folio, in cloth portfolio. With 100 pochoir plates. sg Sept 6 (123) $300

Anr copy. Orig pictorial wraps; spines def on 4 parts with covers detached. With 120 colored plates. Some chipping to a few plates. sg Apr 2 (73) $600

Giannotti, Donato, 1492-1573?

— Respublica Venetum. Der grossen Commun, der Statt Venedig.... Neuburg: Hans Kilian, 1557. Folio, modern bds. sg May 7 (109) $1,100

Gianutio, Orazio

— Libro nel quale si tratta della maniera di giuocara scacchi. Turin: Antonio de Bianchi, 1597. Later half calf; rubbed. Some dampstaining throughout; 1st 2 & last leaves repaired in margins; some browning. pn Nov 14 (264) £1,200

Gibb, Elias John Wilkinson, 1857-1901

— Ottoman Poems Translated into English Verse in the Original Forms. L, 1882. One of 345. Mor; stained. cb Feb 27 (32) $55

Gibb, William

— The Royal House of Stuart. L, 1890. Folio, orig half mor; some wear. W July 8 (215) £60

Gibbings, Robert

See also: Golden Cockerel Press

— Fourteen Wood Engravings from Drawings.... L: Golden Cockerel Press, [1933?]. Folio, orig wraps. wa Dec 11 (125) £100

— The Wood Engravings.... L, 1959. 4to, cloth. O Mar 31 (82) $100

Gibbon, Edward, 1737-94

— An Essay on the Study of Literature.... L, 1764. 1st Ed in English. 8vo, contemp calf gilt; rubbed. DW May 13 (280) £740

— The History of the Decline and Fall of the Roman Empire. L, 1776-88. 1st Ed. 6 vols. 4to, contemp calf gilt; rebacked. With port & 2 (of 3) folding maps. A few leaves browned. CNY Dec 5 (241) $4,200

Anr copy. Early 19th-cent russia gilt; spine ends chipped; some joints cracked or starting. With port & 3 folding maps. Port dampstained in corner. sg Nov 7 (101) $4,000

1st State of Vol I. Early 19th-cent russia; rebacked. With port & 3 folding maps. Lacking half-titles. Epstein copy. sg Apr 29 (181) $4,800

2d of Vol I, 1st Ed of Vols II-VI. 6 vols. 4to, early calf; 1 bd detached. With port & 2 folding maps. Repair & foxing to 1 map; some browning or foxing. wa Mar 5 (522) $1,300

3d Ed of Vol I, 1st Ed of Vols II-VI. L, 1777-88. 6 vols. 4to, calf gilt; rebacked. With port & 3 folding maps. Some foxing. wa Dec 9 (488) $850

Vols II and IV-VI, 1st Ed; Vol I, 3d Ed; Vol III, 2d Ed. 6 vols. 8vo, contemp calf gilt; upper joint of Vol I split; foot of spine of Vol VI scuffed. Ck July 10 (270) £750

Anr Ed. L, 1791. Vols I-VI (of 12) only. 8vo, contemp calf; rear cover of Vol I rehinged. 1 folding map repaired. cb Dec 19 (64) $140

Anr Ed. L, 1802. 12 vols. 8vo, contemp calf; rubbed, spine of Vol IX lacking small section. With frontis & 2 folding maps. Some spotting. pn Sept 12 (37) £90 [Freeman]

Anr Ed. L, 1838-39. Bound in 8 vols. 8vo, calf. LH Dec 11 (119) $475

Anr Ed. Bost., 1854-55. 4 vols. 8vo, later half mor by Riviere. Marginal spotting. bbc Dec 9 (214) $290

Anr Ed. L, 1854-55. 8 vols. 8vo, later half calf by Henry Young & Sons. bba Oct 10 (360) £350 [Cumming]

Anr Ed. L, 1887. 8 vols. 8vo, half mor. pnE Aug 12 (286) £350

— Miscellaneous Works. L, 1796-1815. 1st Ed. 3 vols. 4to, contemp calf; rubbed, head of 2 spines worn. With frontis, port & folding table. S Nov 14 (562) £170 [Laywood]

Anr copy. Vols I-II (of 3) only. Contemp calf gilt; covers detached. sg Mar 12 (98) $175

Gibbon, Lardner. See: Herndon & Gibbon

Gibbs, James, 1682-1754

— A Book of Architecture. L, 1728. 1st Ed. Folio, 18th-cent calf; rebacked with old backstrip laid down, corners restored. With 150 plates. Tp dampstained at fore-edge; other dampstains to corners at ends; plates 1 & 19 hsaved; Plate 40 with tear at platemark; plates 35 & 120 with small stains; plate 149 with small abrasions; plate 150 creased. McCarty-Cooper copy. CNY Jan 25 (23) $3,000

Anr copy. Later half calf; worn. pnE Aug 12 (96) £950

Anr copy. Contemp calf; worn. Plate 150 soiled; some soiling. S June 25 (92) £1,700 [Ham]

2d Ed. L, 1739. Folio, later half mor; rubbed & worn. With 143 (of 150) plates. Some plates torn or soiled. pnE Dec 4 (212) £240

— Rules for Drawing.... L, 1753. Folio, contemp bds; worn. LH Dec 11 (120) $110

Gibson, Charles Dana, 1867-1944
— The Education of Mr. Pipp. NY, 1899. 1st Ed. Oblong folio, cloth. Last plate of Vol I creased. sp June 18 (136) $90
— The Gibson Book: a Collection of the Published Works. NY, 1907. 2 vols. Oblong folio, cloth. Last plate of Vol I creased. sp June 18 (137) $80
— London, as seen by Gibson. NY, 1897. 1st Ed. Oblong folio, half cloth. sp June 18 (135) $150
— Sketches and Cartoons. NY, 1898. 1st Ed, One of 250. Oblong folio, half cloth. sp June 18 (130) $230
— Sketches in Egypt. L & NY, 1899. 8vo, orig cloth; spine rubbed, shaken. pba Aug 20 (89) $50

Gibson, Reginald Walter
— Francis Bacon: a Bibliography.... Oxford, 1950-59. 2 vols, including Supplement. 4to, half cloth; worn. O Sept 24 (98) $100

Gibson, Thomas, Physician
— The Anatomy of Human Bodies.... L, 1703. 6th Ed. 8vo, contemp calf. With 20 plates. sg May 14 (61) $275

Gid, Denise
— Catalogue des reliures francaises estampees a froid...de la Bibliotheque Mazarine. Paris, 1984. 2 vols. 4to, wraps. sg Oct 31 (40) $80

Giddings, Joshua Reed, 1795-1864
— The Exiles of Florida: or, the Crimes Committed by Our Government against the Maroons who Fled from South Carolina. Columbus, 1858. 1st Ed. 8vo, orig cloth; spine ends frayed. bbc Sept 23 (317) $75

Gide, Andre, 1869-1951
— Corydon. Bruges, 1920. One of 21 on chandelle. Pigskin by E. & A. Maylander, orig wraps bound in. S May 28 (334) £800 [Poole]
— Les Faux-monnayeurs. Paris: Mercure de France, 1896. One of 15 on hollande. Mor extra by Alix. Inscr to Marguerite Moreno. S May 28 (361) £6,500 [Lib. Valette]

Anr Ed. Paris, 1925. One of 112 on papier verge Lafuma-Navarre, this copy ptd for M. Leboeuf. 4to, mor gilt by Tchekeroul, orig wraps bound in. S May 28 (336) £1,700 [Beres]

— L'Immoraliste. Paris, 1902. 1st Ed. 16mo, half mor, orig wraps bound in. Tear on page 31 crossing 8 lines of text. Inscr. Epstein copy. sg Apr 29 (183) $1,000
— Isabelle. Paris, 1911. 1st Ed, one of 500 on verge d'Arches; this copy 1 of c.10 with colophon dated 29 Mai 1911. 16mo, calf extra by P. L. Martin, orig wraps bound in. Inscr to Gerard d'Houville & Mme Henri de Regnier. S May 28 (332) £4,500 [Holinger]
— Montaigne: an Essay in Two Parts. L & NY, 1929. One of 800. In split & browned d/j. wa Sept 26 (163) $50
— Philoctete. Paris, 1899. One of 300. 8vo, half lea; rubbed. Inscr to Edmund Gosse. O May 26 (72) $400
— Le Voyage d'Urien. Paris, 1893. 1st Ed, one of 300. Illus by Maurice Denis. 4to, half mor gilt by G. Huser, orig wraps preserved. With 30 litho vignettes. Inscr. Schlosser copy. P June 18 (531) $6,500

Anr copy. Mor extra by Canape & Corriez, orig wraps bound in. With 30 plates. Inscr to Paul Adam. With 3 A Ls s, 1 sgd by the author, 1 sgd by the artist & 1 sgd by Adam. S May 28 (329) £4,600 [Rota]

Gieronimo, Rocco
— Vaghe et varie inventioni di caratteri di lettere cancellaresche.... [Pavia or Turin], 1602. Oblong 4to, recent vellum using an early Hebrew Ms leaf. With 53 plates. Outer margin of 1st 4 leaves restored; minor staining. C June 24 (235) £700 [Franks]

Giffard, Edward, 1812-67
— A Short Visit to the Ionian Islands.... L, 1837. 8vo, modern half calf. With frontis, map & 5 plates. Some stains to corners. S June 30 (305) £420 [Spink]

Gift...
— Gift of Flowers. NY, [c.1860]. 8vo, in black lacquer bds, the front cover with hand-painted landscape scene & mother-of-pearl onlays; rebacked in mor. sg Oct 17 (258) $200

Gignoux, Anton Christoph —& Frey, Johann Michael
— Hundert Ansichten und Gegenden an der Donau. [Vienna, c.1782]. 4to, contemp calf; rubbed. With engraved title & 100 plates. Stamps on tp; some discoloration; several plates misbound. S Nov 21 (175) £1,100 [Kiefer]

Gilbert, Charles Sandoe
— An Historical Survey of the County of Cornwall.... Plymouth Dock, 1817-20. 2 vols. 4to, contemp calf; rebacked, orig spines preserved. With 49 plates. bba Jan 30 (18) £360 [Ventnor]

Anr copy. 3 vols in 2. 4to, contemp calf; not uniform. Vol I lacking title; some spotting. Sold w.a.f. DW Jan 29 (76) £100

Gilbert, Frank T.
— History of San Joaquin County, California.... Oakland, 1879. 1st Ed. 4to, orig half mor; worn. With 171 plates & maps. Some plates chipped or torn. cb Nov 14 (189) $425

Gilbert, Josiah —& Churchill, G.C.
— The Dolomite Mountains. L, 1864. 8vo, half calf. With 2 folding maps & 6 colored plates. pn Sept 12 (332) £190 [Grigor-Taylor]

Gilbert, Paul —& Bryson, Charles Lee
— Chicago and its Makers. Chicago, 1929. Cloth; spine rubbed & soiled. wa Mar 5 (322) $100
Out-of-series copy. 4to, lea. LH May 17 (715) $180

Gilbert, Thomas
— Journal of a Voyage to New South Wales. See: White, John

Gilbert, William, 1540-1603
— De Magnete. L: Peter Short, 1600. 1st Ed. Folio, contemp calf; rebacked, rubbed. Corners of pp 209-11 touched by damp; rusthole on R5 just affecting 2 letters of text; a few spots or stains; a few ink smudges. Presentation copy with Ms annotations. pn Mar 19 (189) £20,000 [Martyan Lan]
— Tractatus sive physiologia nova de magnete.... Stettin: Goetzianis, 1628. 4to, contemp half lea. With engraved title & 12 plates. FD Dec 2 (146) DM1,000

Gilbert, Sir William Schwenck, 1836-1911
— Iolanthe. L, 1910. Illus by W. Russell Flint.. 4to, orig cloth. pn Oct 24 (363) £48 [Emery]

Gilbert, Sir William Schwenck, 1863-1911. See: Limited Editions Club

Gilbey, Sir Walter, 1831-1914
— Animal Painters of England.... L, 1900-11. 3 vols. 4to, orig cloth. sg Jan 9 (261) $275

Gilbey, Sir Walter, 1831-1914 —& Cuming, Edward William Diron
— George Morland: his Life and Works. L, 1907. One of 250. 4to, orig cloth. L Nov 14 (25) £100

Gilchrist, Alexander, 1828-61
— Life of William Blake. L, 1863. 2 vols. 8vo, orig cloth; spines rubbed; Vol I broken. bba Dec 19 (38) £100 [Kurita]
Anr copy. Orig cloth; spine faded, corners rubbed. DW Oct 9 (869) £80
Anr Ed. L, 1880. 2 vols. 8vo, orig cloth; slightly stained. S July 1 (985) £190 [Stevens]

Gilchrist, James P.
— A Brief Display of the Origin and History of Ordeals.... L, 1821. 8vo, contemp mor extra. Inscr to the Garrison Library at Gibraltar. sg Mar 26 (128) $375

Gildas, 516?-70?
— Opus Novum Gildae Britannus Monachus...de calamitate excidio.... [L], 1525. 1st Ed. 8vo, 18th-cent calf gilt. Some marginal notes close shaved. STC 11892. C June 24 (315) £350 [Edwards]

Gildon, Charles
— The Post-Boy Robb'd of His Mail.... L, 1706. 2d Ed. 2 vols in 1. 8vo, calf; rebacked. W July 8 (29) £50

Giles, Ernest, 1847-97
— Australia Twice Traversed.... L, 1889. 2 vols. 8vo, cloth; rubbed. With port, frontis, 6 folding maps & 44 plates. Library markings. bba June 11 (343) £340 [Burgess Browning]
Anr copy. Orig cloth; rubbed & soiled. Owner's stamps to prelims; several tears along map folds; corner of 1 text leaf lost; lacking list of plates in Vol II. kh Nov 11 (510) A$400
Anr copy. Contemp half calf. With port, 20 plates & 6 colored folding maps. S June 25 (133) £1,500 [Quaritch]
Anr copy. Orig cloth. With port, frontis, 6 folding maps & 20 plates. S June 25 (265) £3,800 [Arnold]
— Geographic Travels in Central Australia.... Melbourne, 1875. 8vo, orig cloth. With folding map. Some spotting. Inscr by the editor, Ferdinand von Mueller. S June 25 (260) £1,100 [Maggs]

Giles, Herbert A. See: Clemens's copy, Samuel Langhorne

Giles, Phyllis M. See: Wormald & Giles

Gill, Emlyn Metcalf
— Practical Dry-Fly Fishing. NY, 1912. O Oct 29 (137) $80

Gill, Eric, 1882-1940
— Engravings.... L, 1934. 4to, orig cloth, in d/j, unopened. Ck July 10 (170) £550
Anr copy. Orig cloth, in d/j. S Apr 28 (34) £450 [Elliott]
Anr Ed. Wellingborough: Christopher Skelton, 1983. Folio, orig half cloth. bba May 28 (513) £80 [Wand]
— Engravings, a Selection.... Fanfare Press for Douglas Cleverdon, 1929. One of 420. 4to, orig cloth; rubbed, light stain on front cover. sg Feb 6 (104) $500

— An Essay on Typography. [L, 1931]. 1st Ed, One of 500. bba July 9 (265) £160 [Donnithorne]

— First Nudes. L, 1954. Ltd Ed, sgd by Sir John Rothenstein & Gordian Gill. Intro by Rothenstein. Inscr. Ck July 10 (172) £220

— Quia amore langueo. L, 1937. One of 20 ptd on vellum in 2 colors. Ed by H. S. Bennett. 4to, orig vellum. Some spotting. wa Sept 26 (103) $180

Gill, Samuel Thomas, d.1890

— The Australian Sketch-Book. Melbourne, 1974. One of 1,000. Oblong folio, cloth. kh Nov 11 (511) A$100

Gillen, Francis J. See: Spencer & Gillen

Gilles, John

— The History of Ancient Greece.... L, 1786. 2 vols. 4to, lea. br May 29 (168) $195

Gillet-Laumont, Francois

— Note sur les impressions lythographiques. Paris, 1809. Single sheet. 4to, bds. Offprint from the Bulletin de la Societe d'Encouragement, inscr. Schlosser copy. P June 17 (545) $300

Gillett, Charles Ripley. See: Union Theological Seminary

Gillingham, Robert Cameron

— The Rancho San Pedro. Los Angeles, 1961. In d/j. cb Sept 12 (74) $75

Gilliss, James Melville, 1811-65

— The U. S. Naval Astronomical Expedition to the Southern Hemisphere. Wash., 1855-56. Vols I-III (of 4). Recent cloth. With 9 maps, folding panoramic view & 42 (of 43) plates. Some foxing. bbc Apr 27 (526) $150

Anr copy. Vols I-II (of 4) only. 4to, half calf; worn, stained. Lacking 1 plate. Sold w.a.f. O Jan 14 (81) $165

Anr copy. Vols I & II (of 4) only. 4to, half calf; worn. Lacking "some " color plates. Sold w.a.f. O Mar 31 (83) $140

Anr copy. Contemp half calf; worn. Some dampstaining. House Issue. sg Dec 5 (105) $130

Anr copy. Vols I (of 4) only. 4to, lea; front cover detached. With 2 folding mpas & folding panorama. sp Nov 24 (147) $140

Gilliss, Walter. See: Grolier Club

Gillray, James, 1757-1815

— Works. L: Bohn, [c.1849]. Folio, contemp half mor gilt. With port & 588 plates on 153 leaves. pn Nov 14 (394) £800

Anr copy. Contemp half mor; worn & loose. With port & 582 plates on 292 pages. sg Sept 6 (124) $700

Anr Ed. L, [1873]. 4to, loose in orig cloth. DW Mar 4 (289) £60

Anr copy. Contemp half mor; rebacked preserving section of orig spine. With port & 81 plates, 1 double-page. ALs from the publishers tipped-in. pn Dec 12 (86) £80

Gilly, William Stephen, 1789-1855

— Narrative of an Excursion to the Mountains of Piedmond. L, 1824. 4to, contemp half calf; rebacked, rubbed. bba June 25 (57) £260 [Bifolco]

Gilmor, Harry

— Four Years in the Saddle. NY, 1866. 12mo, orig cloth. NH Oct 6 (74) $80

Gilpin, Laura

— The Rio Grande.... NY, 1949. 4to, orig cloth, in chipped d/j with tears. bbc Feb 17 (212) $65

Gilpin, William, 1724-1804

— Observations on the River Wye, and Several Parts of South Wales. L, 1782. 1st Ed. 8vo, contemp calf gilt; rubbed. With 15 plates. pn Apr 23 (262) £65 [Clark]

— Observations Relative Chiefly to Picturesque Beauty...Mountains and Lakes of Cumberland and Westmorland. L, 1788. 2d Ed. 2 vols. 8vo, contemp calf; rebacked & repaired. With 28 (of 30) plates. pnL Nov 20 (103) £48 [Niles]

— Observations relative chiefly to Picturesque Beauty Made in 1776...the Highlands of Scotland. L, 1789. 1st Ed. 8vo, contemp calf; spine faded & rubbed. Some offsetting to text. DW Apr 8 (96) £55

— Observations on the River Wye, and Several Parts of South Wales.... L, 1792. 3d Ed. 8vo, calf. pnE May 13 (56) £70

— Remarks on Forest Scenery.... Edin., 1834. 2 vols. 8vo, contemp half mor. bba June 11 (190) £55 [Archdale]

Gilpin, William, 1822-94

— The Central Gold Region. Phila., 1860. 1st Ed. 8vo, cloth; extremities rubbed, front joint starting. With 6 folding maps, mostly hand-colored. sg June 18 (230) $275

Ginsberg, Allen

— Howl for Carl Solomon. San Francisco: City Lights Pocket Bookshop, [1956]. ("Howl and Other Poems.") 1st Ptd Ed. Orig wraps; label dampstained. Inscr to dedicatee Lucien Carr; also inscr by William Burroughs & sgd by Carl Solomon. CNY June 9 (75) $2,800

Giorgi, Federigo

— Libro del modo di conoscere i buoni falconi, astori, e sparavieri.... Brescia, 1607. Bound with: Carcano, Francesco. Dell'Arte del strucciero con il modo di conoscere e medicare falconi.... Brescia, 1607. Last leaf torn. 12mo, contemp vellum; lacking ties; soiled. At front is contemp watercolor of a nobleman & his wife hawking, with their arms in watercolor on facing page; also crude pencil drawings of hawking on other blank leaves. C Oct 30 (195) £700 [Junk]

Giorgi, Felice

— Descrizione istorica del teatro di Tor di Nona. Rome: Stampe del Cannetti, 1795. 4to, contemp mor gilt with arms of Cardinal Carlo Crivelli; head of spine wormed. S May 28 (120) £850 [Marlborough]

Giovanni Giuseppe di Santa Teresa

— Istoria delle guerre del Regno del Brasile. Rome, 1700. 2 parts in 1 vol. Folio, modern vellum gilt. With engraved title, port & 23 folding maps, plans & views. Without the port of Jorge IV in Part 2. S June 25 (454) £3,200 [Hodson]

Gipps, George

— Copy of a Despatch from Sir G. Gipps [giving the results of Strzelecki's geological exploration]. L, 1841. Folio, unbound. With 6 maps (5 folding), all partly hand-colored. Foremargin of non-folding plate restored affecting neatline. R. J. Maria copy. C June 25 (230) £1,900 [McCormick]

Giraldi Cinthio, Giovanni Battista, 1504-73

— Hecatommithi, overo cento novelle. Venice, 1608. 2 parts in 1 vol. 4to, 18th-cent calf. SI Dec 5 (884) LIt400,000

Giraldus Cambrensis, 1146?-1220?

— The Itinerary of Archbishop Baldwin through Wales.... L, 1806. 2 vols extended to 5. 4to, later half mor. With 52 plates, 3 plans & 5 hand-colored maps. Extra-illus with 360 plates & maps. C Oct 30 (35) £2,000 [National Library of Wales]

Girard, Gabriel, 1677-1748

— The Difference between Words Esteemed Synonymous. L, 1766. 2 vols. 8vo, contemp calf; joints cracked, rubbed. bba Aug 13 (115) £140 [Jarndyce]

Girard, Pierre Jacques Francois

— Traite des armes.... Paris, 1737. 2d Ed. Oblong 4to, contemp sheep; rebacked. With port, engraved title & 116 plates. Some soiling. sg Mar 26 (129) $3,200

Anr Ed. The Hague, 1740. Oblong 4to, 18th-cent half calf. With frontis & 116 plates. Frontis with some soil. sg Mar 26 (130) $3,200

Giraudoux, Jean, 1882-1944

— Amphitryon 38. Paris, 1929. 1st Ed. Mor extra by Paul Bonet, 1951. Interleaved with page proofs containing the author's holograph revisions. S May 28 (344) £4,200 [Rosenthal]

One of 68 on velin d'Arches. Mor extra by Maylander, orig wraps bound in. Inscr to Mme Meyer. S May 28 (346) £550 [Beres]

— Juliette au pays des hommes. Paris, 1924. One of 15 on chine. Mor extra by Semet & Plumelle, orig wraps bound in. S May 28 (342) £800 [Beres]

— Sodome et Gomorrhe. Paris: Grasset, [n.d.]. Illus by Christian Berard. 4to, orig wraps, unopened. With 6 watercolor & gouache illusts, 2 full-page, the remainder double-page. SM Oct 11 (521) FF20,000

Girtin, James

— Seventy-five Portraits of Celebrated Painters. L, 1817. 8vo, 19th-cent half mor. With frontis & 74 plates. Tp & list of plates laid down. pn Sept 12 (87) £90

Girtin, Thomas, 1775-1802

— A Selection of Twenty of the Most Picturesque Views in Paris and its Environs. L, 1803. Folio, half mor; dampstained. With engraved title & 20 plates. Tp with plate stress, repaired; Plate 19 with marginal tear; some foxing throughout; lacking dedication leaf. Schlosser copy. P June 18 (465) $900

Giry, Francois

— Les vies des saints. Paris, 1703. 4 parts in 2 vols. Folio, contemp mor gilt; scraped. S July 9 (1120) £300 [Booth]

Gissing, George, 1857-1903

— Born in Exile. L, 1892. 3 vols. 8vo, orig cloth; extremities rubbed, backstrip of Vol III frayed. bba May 28 (94) £90 [Hilton]

— The Private Papers of Henry Ryecroft. L, 1903. 1st Ed. 8vo, orig cloth. ALs loosely inserted. pn Sept 12 (209) £130 [Silverman]

Giustiniani, Agostino, 1470-1536

— Castigatissimi annali...della eccelsa & illustrissima Republi. di Genoa. Genoa: Antonio Bellono, 1537. 1st Ed. Folio, old vellum. Some browning; early marginalia; some light dampstaining at beginning & end. sg Oct 24 (131) $500

Anr copy. 19th-cent half lea. Some browning. SI Dec 5 (886) LIt300,000

Giustiniani, Hieronimo

— La Description et histoire de l'isle de Scios, ou Chios. Paris, 1506 [but 1606?]. 4to, contemp vellum. Waterstains. S July 1 (612) £6,200 [Franks]

Giustiniani, Vincenzo, d.1637

— Galleria Giustiniani. Rome, [1631]. 2 vols. Folio, 18th-cent calf; worn, spines def. With 317 (of 322) plates. Vol I tp foxed. S Feb 11 (83) £1,800 [Shapero]

Giustiniano, Pompeo

— Della guerre di Fiandra, libri VI. Antwerp, 1609. 4to, vellum. With 29 maps & plans. B Nov 1 (288) HF3,800

Gjerstad, Einar —& Others

— The Swedish Cyprus Expedition. Finds and Results of the Excavations in Cyprus 1927-1931. Stockholm & Lund, 1934-72. 9 vols of text & 3 portfolios of plates. 4to, orig cloth. With 993 plates, 88 maps & plans & 3 folding tables. S Nov 21 (255) £1,200 [Graves-Johnston]

Gladwin, Francis

— The Persian Moonshee. L, 1801. 3 parts in 1 vol. 4to, contemp bds; rebacked, rubbed. In Persian & English. bba Jan 16 (312) £150 [Poole]

Anr copy. Contemp bds; rebacked & rubbed. With 32 plates & ad leaf. Some foxing. bba May 14 (109) £50 [Valentine]

Glaeser, Ludwig. See: Museum of Modern Art

Glaisher, James —& Others

— Travels in the Air. L, 1871. 8vo, orig cloth; extremities worn. DW Oct 2 (35) £70

Glanvill, Joseph, 1636-80

— Essays on Several Important Subjects in Philosophy and Religion. L, 1676. 1st Ed. 4to, contemp calf; rubbed. Hole in H2 affecting text; some spotting & staining. S July 1 (1071) £190 [Lawson]

— Saducismus triumphatus: or Full and Plain Evidence Concerning Witches and Apparitions. L, 1682-81. 8vo, contemp calf; rebacked, rubbed. Some browning & soiling; some headlines shaved; hole in 3E2, affecting text. S July 1 (1070) £220 [Steinbeck]

— Scepsis scientifica. L, 1665. 4to, contemp calf gilt; rubbed. Lacking 1 blank; a2 torn, affecting text. bba Jan 16 (69) £100 [R. Clark]

Anr copy. Contemp calf; rebacked, worn. Some browning; dampstaining in Part 2. S July 1 (1069) £320 [Lawson]

Glasenapp, C. F.

— Life of Richard Wagner. L, 1900-8. 6 vols. pn Oct 24 (469) £50

Glasgow, Ellen, 1874-1945

— Barren Ground. Garden City, 1925. 1st Ed. Cloth; soiled, in d/j separated into 4 pieces. Inscr to Hunter Stagg. wa Sept 26 (167) $60

— The Battle-Ground. NY, 1902. Cloth; soiled & rubbed. Inscr to Hunter Stagg. wa Sept 26 (168) $65

— Works. NY, 1938. Ltd Ed, sgd. Half vellum. K Sept 29 (183) $100

Glasse, Hannah, fl.1747

— The Art of Cookery, Made Plain and Easy.... L, 1758. 8vo, contemp calf gilt; extremities worn. 1st few leaves waterstained. DW Mar 4 (215) £95

Anr Ed. L, 1803. 8vo, recent cloth. Some foxing; tp repaired. bbc Apr 27 (232) $210

— The Compleat Confectioner. L, [c.1760]. 8vo, orig bds; worn & stained; lacking backstrip, covers detached. bba Oct 10 (320) £160 [Demetzy]

Anr Ed. L, 1800. 8vo, orig bds; worn, upper cover detached. Slightly wormed. bba Oct 24 (83) £300 [Stork]

Glauber, Johann Rudolf, 1604-62

— Works. L, 1689. 3 parts in 1 vol. Folio, contemp calf; worn, rebacked. With 4 woodcut plates & 8 engraved plates. Plates sgd by a previous owner; some holes, affecting text; dampstaining at lower edge; lacking frontis. pn June 11 (148) £300 [Phelps]

Gleason's...

— Gleason's Pictorial Drawing Room Companion. Bost., 1851-54. Vol I only. Orig cloth. NH May 30 (608) $170

Gleizes, Albert, 1881-1953 —& Metzinger, Jean, 1883-1956

— Cubism. L, 1913. In chipped d/j; owner's stamps on front endpapers. sg Sept 6 (126) $350

Glissenti, Fabio

— Discorsi morali.... Venice: Bartolomeo Alberti, 1600. 5 parts in 1 vol. 4to, modern vellum. Marginal dampstaining at beginning & end; minor worming in gutters; line of text on L5 scored & oxidized. sg Oct 24 (132) $375

Glover, Dorothy —& Greene, Graham

— Victorian Detective Fiction. L, 1966. One of 500, sgd by John Carter, Glover & Greene. In torn d/j. L Feb 27 (103) £180

Anr copy. In d/j. sg May 21 (220) $250

Glover, Robert, 1544-88

— Nobilitas politica vel civilis.... L, 1608. 1st Ed. Folio, contemp calf; worn & rebacked. With frontis (trimmed & laid down) & 8 plates. Errata leaf trimmed & laid down & marginal note pasted into margin of p. 139; text tired with wormhole in margin & some repairs. W July 8 (64) £100

Gmelin, Frederico, 1745-1821

— Dissertazioni di Tivoli e di Albano. Rome, 1816. Oblong folio, contemp half mor; corners worn. With 12 plates. Kissner —McCarty-Cooper copy. CNY Jan 25 (24) $750

Gobet, Nicolas. See: Pichon & Gobet

Gobier, Charles

— Istoria dell'editto dell'imperatore della Cina.... Turin: Giovanni Battista Zappata, 1699. 8vo, contemp vellum. S July 9 (1509) £300 [Ad Orientem]

Gobius, Johannes

— Scala coeli. Luebeck: Lucas Brandis, 1476. Folio, 18th-cent half calf, the lower bd of blindstamped pigskin over wooden bds; worn. 31 lines & headline; initials & rubrics in red Some soiling; a few leaves with marginal tears. 242 leaves. Goff G-310. C Dec 16 (49) £7,500 [Tenschert]

Gobler, Justin, c.1496-1567

— Chronica der Kriegshaendel...Maximiliani des Namens der Erst. Frankfurt: heirs of Christian Egenolph, 1566. Bound with: Reissner, Adam. Historia Herrn Georgen und Herrn Casparn von Frundesberg. Frankfurt: Georg Raben & the heirs of W. Han, 1572. Folio, contemp blindstamped pigskin over wooden bds, upper cover with blocked panel with arms of Hanns Harrer Cammermeister, the lower cover with those of his wife Barbra Harrerin. Gothic type. C June 24 (317) £800 [Kraus]

Godby, James

— Italian Scenery. L, 1806. 4to, contemp half lea. With 32 colored plates. Some marginal staining & browning. SI June 9 (428) LIt1,600,000

**Goddard, John —&
Clarke, Brian**

— The Trout and the Fly; a New Approach. L, [1980]. One of 25. 4to, mor gilt. With 7 hand-tied flies by Stewart Canham in an oval sunken mount. Koopman copy. O Oct 29 (139) $1,100

Goddard, Robert H., 1882-1945

— Liquid-Propellant Rocket Development. Wash., 1936. 8vo, orig wraps, unopened. Smithsonian Miscellaneous Collections, Vol 95, No 3.. sg May 14 (281) $800

— A Method of Reaching Extreme Altitudes. Wash., 1919. 8vo, orig wraps. sg May 14 (280) $1,800

Godelmann, Johann Georg

— Tractatus de magis, veneficis et lamiis. Frankfurt: N. Bassaeus, 1591. 4to, modern half calf. Lacking final blank to Part 1; some leaves at beginning with waterstains. C Dec 16 (50) £800 [Cooper]

Godey's...

— Godey's Lady's Book. Phila., 1840-41. 2 vols. 8vo, half mor; 1 cover & backstrip loose. With 22 hand-colored plates. wa Feb 20 (126) $110

Godfrey, Masters John

— Monograph & Iconograph of Native British Orchidaceae. Cambr., 1933. 4to, orig cloth; rubbed, corners bumped. bba Sept 5 (50) £320 [Junk Antiquariat]

Godman, Eva M. See: Archer & Godman

Godman, Frederick Du Cane, 1834-1919

— A Monograph of the Petrels.... L, 1907-10. 1st Ed, one of 225. 5 parts in 2 vols. 4to, contemp half mor, orig wraps to the parts bound in. With 106 hand-colored plates. C May 20 (176) £1,900 [Travers]

Godman, John Davidson, 1794-1830

— American Natural History. Phila., 1826-28. Part I: Mastology [all pbd]. 3 vols. 4to, contemp calf; rubbed, joints worn. Foxed. O Jan 14 (82) $80

Godwin, Bishop Francis, 1562-1633
See also: Bacon & Godwin

— Annales of England. L, 1630. Folio, contemp calf. With 2 ports Some damp-staining in upper outer corners throughout. STC 11947. sg Oct 24 (133) $200

Godwin, William, 1756-1836

— An Enquiry Concerning Political Justice. L, 1793. 1st Ed. 2 vols. 4to, recent calf. bbc Apr 27 (528) $3,000

2d Ed. L, 1796. 2 vols. 8vo, calf; worn, hinges broken, front cover of Vol I detached, head of spine of Vol I chipped. NH Oct 6 (311) $300

— Essay on Sepulchres: or, a Proposal for Erecting Some Memorial.... L, 1809. 8vo, orig bds; spine torn. Michael Sadleir's copy. S May 14 (944) £220 [Marlborough]

— Fleetwood or the New Man of Feeling. Alexandria, 1805. 2 vols. 8vo, later half mor. sg June 18 (231) $70

— History of the Commonwealth of England. L, 1824-28. 4 vols. 8vo, contemp calf gilt; rubbed. bba Nov 28 (340) £75 [Drury]

— Life of Geoffrey Chaucer. L, 1803. 1st Ed. 2 vols. 4to, contemp half calf; rubbed. With 3 ports. Some foxing. bba June 11 (80) £320 [Land]

— Lives of the Necromancers. NY, 1835. 1st American Ed. 8vo, later half sheep; rubbed. Lacking half-title & orig blanks; some foxing & browning. bbc Sept 23 (215) $65

Goedaert, Joannes, 1620-68

— De insectis in methodum redactus.... L, 1685. Ed by M. Lister. 8vo, contemp vellum. With 21 folding plates. W July 8 (354) £190

Goemaere, Alfred

— Escrime-Vagabondages a travers les Auteurs.... Antwerp, 1905. Wraps. sg Mar 26 (132) $130

Goerling, Adolf, 1821-77 —& Others

— Art Treasures of Germany. Bost.: Samuel Walker, [c.1870]. 2 parts in 1 vol. 4to, contemp half mor; crudely rebacked, worn. Sold w.a.f. bba Jan 30 (337) £75 [Mason]

Anr copy. Contemp mor gilt by Van Antwerp; scuffed. bbc Dec 9 (202) $190

Goes, Damiano de, 1501-73

— De bello cambaico ultimo commentarii tres.... Louvain, 1549. 1st Ed. 4to, recent bds. B May 12 (68) HF5,000

— Fides, religio, Moresque Aethiopum sub Imperio Pretiosi Ioannis.... Louvain, 1540. 4to, later half lea. Title lined. B May 12 (67B) HF6,000

Goethe, Johann Wolfgang von, 1749-1832
See also: Doves Press

— Faust. Paris, 1828. Illus by Eugene Delacroix. Folio, early half mor. With frontis & 17 plates, some on tinted paper. Schlosser copy. P June 18 (530) $9,500

Anr Ed. L, 1908. One of 250. Illus by Willy Pogany. 4to, mor gilt with interlacing strapwork design with with large central panel of Faust and Margaret in summerhouse in mor onlays. With 31 mtd colored plates. sg Nov 7 (155) $2,000

Anr Ed. NY: Dingwall-Rock, [1925]. One of 1,000. Trans by John Anster; illus by Harry Clarke. 4to, orig half vellum; soiled, rear bd dampstained. With 22 plates. wa Apr 9 (218) $120

— Faust. Eine Tragoedie. Leipzig: Insel-Verlag, 1912. One of 515. b&b Feb 19 (140) $275

— Faust und Urfaust. Darmstadt, 1922-24. 3 vols. 4to, orig vellum. HH May 12 (2229) DM1,000

— Goethes Italienische Reise. Leipzig, 1925. Folio, lea gilt; extremities rubbed; hinges starting. sg Jan 30 (57) $425

— Hermann und Dorothea. Berlin: Friedrich Vieweg the Elder, 1798. 8vo, orig bds; worn. Marginal foxing. SI Dec 5 (276) LIt280,000

— Reineke Fuchs. Munich, 1846. 4to, contemp mor; worn. DW Oct 2 (276) £60

Anr copy. Orig calf gilt; worn, spine chipped. With frontis, pictorial tp & 34 plates. Some leaves affected by damp; some tears. S Nov 14 (23) £180 [Seidman]

— Reynard the Fox. L, 1855. Trans by Thomas J. Arnold; illus by Joseph Wolf. 8vo, orig half lea; rubbed & chipped. With engraved title & 12 plates. NH Aug 23 (177) $50

— Die Wahlverwandtschaften. Tubingen, 1809. 2 vols. 8vo, contemp calf; worn & wormed. Some spotting. HH May 12 (1270) DM1,900

— Werke. Stuttgart & Tuebingen: Cotta, 1815-19. 20 vols. 8vo, orig half calf. B May 12 (664) HF950

Anr Ed. Stuttgart & Tubingen, 1840. 40 vols. 8vo, contemp half mor; scuffed. Ck Oct 31 (112) £180

Anr Ed. Stuttgart: Cotta, [1902-12]. 40 vols, without Index. Half mor; some bdgs with stain at lower corners. bbc Sept 23 (49) $500

— West-oestlicher Divan. Stuttgart, 1819. 1st Ed. 8vo, contemp bdg; rubbed. Some spotting. HH May 12 (1273) DM2,200

— Zur Farbenlehre. Tubingen, 1810. 1st Ed. 3 vols, including Atlas vol. 8vo & 4to, contemp bds & wraps. With 17 plates, 12 colored. L.p.copy. HH May 12 (1280) DM12,000

Goetz von Berlichingen

— Das Leben des Goetz von Berlichingen, von ihm selbst erzaehlt. Berlin, 1920. One of 50 with full-page illusts sgd by the artist. Illus by Lovis Corinth. Folio, contemp vellum; soiled & bowed. With 16 full-page lithos. S Feb 11 (251) £1,200 [Gal Bauer]

Goff, Frederick R.

— Incunabula in American Libraries: A Third Census. NY, 1964. bbc Apr 27 (131) $55

Anr Ed. NY: Kraus, 1973. 2 vols, including 1972 supplement. Facsimile reprint from Goff's copy with his annotations. sg Oct 31 (152) $225

Gogol, Nicolai Vasil'evich, 1809-52
See also: Cresset Press
— The Over-Coat. Verona: Officina Bodoni, 1975. One of 160. Illus by Pietro Annigoni. 4to, orig half vellum. With 6 plates. sg Jan 30 (115) $500

Gold Rush. See: California

Golden Cockerel Press—Waltham Saint Lawrence, Berkshire
— Ecclesiastes, or the Preacher. 1934. One of 247. S Nov 14 (41) £200 [Furber]
— Homeric Hymn to Aphrodite. 1948. One of 650. S Nov 14 (42) £180 [Barnitt]
— Mabinogion. 1948. One of 75 specially bound. Trans by Gwyn Jones & Thomas Jones. bba Dec 19 (139) £450 [Ginnan]
— Roses of Sharon... 1937. One of 125. Ed by O.E. Oesterley. O Dec 17 (78) $90
— Sir Gawain and the Green Knight. 1952. One of 360. Trans by Gwyn Jones. bbc Apr 27 (308) $100
— The Song of Songs... 1936. One of 140. DW Dec 11 (427) £125
One of 64 with 6 extra plates specially bound. S Nov 14 (49) £360 [Marlborough]
— BLIGH, WILLIAM. - Voyage in the Resource. 1937. One of 350. b&b Feb 19 (242) $200
— BLIGH, WILLIAM & FRYER, JOHN. - The Voyage of the Bounty's Launch. 1934. One of 300. S Apr 28 (33) £405 [Aust. Nat. Gall.]
— BREBEUF, JEAN DE. - The Travels & Sufferings...Among the Hurons of Canada. 1938. One of 300. Ck Nov 29 (95) £50; sg Sept 26 (121) $275
— BRETON, NICHOLAS. - The Twelve Moneths. 1927. One of 500. sp Apr 16 (439) $170
— CAREY, HENRY. - Songs & Poems. 1924. One of 350. K July 12 (244) $130
— CHASE, OWEN & OTHERS. - Narratives of the Wreck of the Whale-Ship Essex. 1935. One of 275. S Nov 14 (39) £220 [White]
— CHAUCER, GEOFFREY. - The Canterbury Tales. 1929-31. One of 485. 4 vols. sg Sept 26 (122) $2,800
— CHAUCER, GEOFFREY. - Troilus and Criseyde. 1927. One of 219. P June 18 (427) $3,500
— CLAY, ENID. - The Constant Mistress. 1934. One of 300. b&b Feb 19 (103) $150
— CLAY, ENID. - Sonnets and Verses. 1925. One of 450. DW Apr 8 (412) £170
— COPPARD, ALFRED EDGAR. - Adam and Eve and Pinch Me. 1921. One of 550. Inscr. sg Dec 12 (68) $175
— CYNWAL, WILLIAM. - In Defence of Women. [1960]. One of 100 specially bound. sg Jan 30 (58) $90
— DRYDEN, JOHN. - Songs and Poems. 1957. One of 500. DW Apr 8 (417) £70
— DUNSANY, EDWARD PLUNKETT. - Lord Adrian. 1933. One of 325. sg Sept 26 (123) $150
— FLAUBERT, GUSTAVE. - Salambo. 1931. One of 500. b&b Feb 19 (241) $80
— GAUTIER, THEOPHILE. - Mademoiselle de Maupin. 1938. One of 450. bba Dec 19 (136) £90 [Setra]; DW Apr 8 (415) £90; W July 8 (314) £85
One of 50 specially bound with 4 additional plates. With proofs of 5 of the engravings annotated by the artist & others, proofs of the 1st signature & of the title lettering, paper samples & 3 typed letters. S Dec 12 (172) £500 [Collinge & Clark]
— GIBBINGS, ROBERT. - The Seventh Man, a True Cannibal Tale of the South Seas. 1930. One of 500. sg Sept 26 (124) $100
— KEATS, JOHN. - Endymion. 1947. One of 400. B May 12 (220) HF850; DW Apr 8 (418) £120
One of 500. Ck July 10 (314) £240
— KEATS, JOHN. - Lamia, Isabella, the Eve of Saint Agnes and Other Poems. 1928. One of 485. S Nov 14 (565) £170 [Cox]
— LAWRENCE, T. E. - Crusader Castles. 1936. One of 35 unnumbered copies. 2 vols. S July 21 (153) £500 [Rota]
One of 1,000. cb Oct 25 (771) $375
Anr copy. Lacking folding map. Ck Oct 18 (241) £130; Ck July 10 (326) £450; pnE Mar 11 (238) £160
Out-of-series copy. S July 1 (770) £600 [Chelsea]
— LAWRENCE, T. E. - Men in Print. 1940. One of 500. DW Dec 11 (433) £190
— LAWRENCE, T. E. - Secret Despatches from Arabia. 1939. One of 1,000. F Dec 18 (47) $260; sg May 7 (136) $1,500
— LONGUS. - Daphnis and Chloe. 1923. One of 450. b&b Feb 19 (105) $80
— LUCIAN OF SAMOSATA. - The True Historie.... 1927. One of 275. pnE Oct 2 (434) £240
— MATHERS, E. POWYS. - Love Night. 1936. One of 125. DW Apr 8 (416) £110
One of 85 with 6 extra plates. bba Dec 19 (138) £480 [Heuer]
— MATHERS, E. POWYS. - Procreant Hymn. 1926. One of 175. sg Nov 7 (84) $600
— MILLER, PATRICK. - Women in Detail. 1947. One of 100 specially bound. With an extra suite of 8 plates in rear pocket. DW Apr 8 (414) £75
One of 430. Inscr to W. Russell Flint by Christopher Sandford. Z Oct 26 (97) $50
— POWYS, LLEWELYN. - The Book of Days. 1937. One of 300. cb Feb 12 (49) $110
— RUTTER, OWEN. - The First Fleet. 1937. One of 370. kh Nov 11 (634) A$300
— SHAKESPEARE, WILLIAM. - The Poems & Sonnets. 1960. One of 100. sg Jan 30 (59) $150
— SHELLEY, PERCY BYSSHE. - Zastrozzi. 1955.

One of 60 specially bound, with an extra set of the illusts. sg Jan 30 (60) $350
— STERNE, LAURENCE. - A Sentimental Journey. 1928. One of 500. pnE Oct 1 (261) £75
— SWINBURNE, ALGERNON CHARLES. - Hymn to Proserpine. 1944. sg Jan 30 (61) $150
One of 350. DW Dec 11 (429) £55
— TOUSSAINT, FRANZ. - The Garden of Caresses. [1934]. One of an unspecified number specially bound in vellum gilt & with the extra sgd engravings. pba July 23 (80) $900
— WALPOLE, HUGH. - The Apple Trees. 1932. One of 500. O Aug 25 (92) $80
— WELLS, H. G. - The Country of the Blind. 1939. One of 30 specially bound. Orig vellum over bds by Sangorski & Sutcliffe. Inscr. Epstein copy. sg Apr 30 (488) $1,400
— WHITFIELD, CHRISTOPHER. - Lady from Yesterday. 1939. One of 50. b&b Feb 19 (104) $70

Golden Fleece
— Fundacion, ordenanzas, y constituciones del insigne Orden del Toyson de Oro.... Madrin 1726. 4to, contemp mor gilt, with arms of the Order. Lacking Sig. S, supplied in contemp Ms facsimile. Ck Nov 29 (48) £380
— Ordine del Cavalieri del Tosone.... Venice, 1558. 4to, 19th-cent mor gilt; inner hinges strengthened. Ck Nov 29 (10) £500
— Les Ordonnances de l'Ordre de la Thoyson d'Or. [Antwerp: Balthasar Moretus, 1626?]. 4to, old vellum gilt covered with old velvet; edges worn. S Dec 5 (230) £1,800 [Maggs]

Golding, William
— Lord of the Flies. L, 1954. 1st Ed. In repaired d/j. S Dec 12 (58) £600 [Steedman]
Anr copy. In soiled d/j with short tears. S July 21 (116) £700 [Burgess]

Goldschmid, Edgar
— Entwicklung und Bibliographie der pathologisch-anatomischen Abbildung. Leipzig, 1925. 4to, cloth; worn, rear joint cracked. With 44 plates, 28 in color. sg May 14 (63) $250

Goldschmidt, Ernst Philip
— Gothic & Renaissance Bookbindings.... L, 1928. 2 vols. 4to, orig cloth. Ck Dec 11 (273) £220
Anr copy. Orig cloth; worn. O May 26 (73) $275
2d Ed. Nieuwkoop & Amst., 1967. one of 600. 2 vols. 4to, orig cloth. pn Apr 23 (146) £95
— The Printed Book of the Renaissance. Amst., 1966. 2d Ed. In d/j. cb Jan 16 (57) $90

Goldschmidt, Lucien. See: Grolier Club

Goldsmid, Edmund Marsden
— A Bibliographical Sketch of The Aldine Press at Venice. Edin., 1887. 3 parts in 1 vol. 8vo, new cloth. sg Oct 31 (115) $120
— A Complete Catalogue of all the Publications of the Elzevir Presses. Edin., 1885-88. One of 350. 3 vols in 1. 8vo, orig cloth; rubbed & soiled. Ink annotations. bba May 28 (515) £70 [Dawson]

Goldsmid, Sir Frederic John, 1818-1908
— Eastern Persia: an Account of...the Persian Boundary Commission. L, 1876. 2 vols. 8vo, cloth; worn, 1 vol stained. O Feb 25 (67) $425

Goldsmith, Alfred F. See: Wells & Goldsmith

Goldsmith, Rev J.. See: Phillips, Sir Richard

Goldsmith, Oliver, 1728-74
— The Citizen of the World; Or Letters from a Chinese Phiosopher.... L, 1819. 2 vols. 12mo, 19th-cent sheep; def. Sgd as Abraham Lincoln, Andrew Lang, and Eugene Field by Eugene Field II. sg Oct 17 (233) $200
— The Deserted Village. L, 1842. Illus by The Etching Club. 8vo, orig mor gilt; rebacked, orig spine strip laid on, front joint just splitting again. With 40 mtd plates. Some foxing. cb Sept 26 (95) $140
Anr Ed. San Francisco, 1926. One of 200. 2 vols, including facsimile. Folio & 4to, half vellum bds. b&b Feb 19 (278) $80
— An Enquiry into the Present State of Polite Learning in Europe. L, 1759. 1st Ed. 8vo, contemp sheep; loose. sg Mar 5 (107) $225
— The Good Natur'd Man. L, 1768. 1st Ed, 1st Issue with the 1-page Epilogue. 8vo, modern calf gilt by Riviere; margins trimmed. sg Mar 12 (145) $275
2d Issue with the 2-page Epilogue. Modern cloth. Some stains & foxing; corners off B1; lacking half-title. sg Mar 5 (116) $90
— The Grecian History, from the Earliest State to the Death of Alexander the Great. L, 1774. 1st Ed. 2 vols. 8vo, contemp calf. cb Oct 25 (45) $200
— An History of England, in a Series of Letters.... L, 1764. 2 vols. 12mo, contemp calf; joints cracked, rubbed. With 2 additional ad leaves at end of Vol I. ESTC t146101. bba July 23 (222) £100 [Excell]

— An History of the Earth and Animated Nature. L: Fullerton, 1851. 2 vols. 4to, contemp half mor gilt; worn. With 2 titles, frontis to Vol I & 69 hand-colored plates. DW Apr 8 (161) £80

Anr Ed. L, 1852-53. 2 vols. 8vo, contemp mor gilt; edges scuffed. With port, 2 engraved titles with hand-colored vignettes & 71 (of 72) hand-colored plates. bbc Apr 27 (529) $130

Anr Ed. L: Fullarton, [c.1856]. 2 vols. 4to, contemp half calf gilt; rubbed. With port & 74 hand-colored plates, including titles. DW Nov 6 (161) £70

Anr Ed. L, 1856 [1857]. 2 vols. 8vo, contemp calf gilt; rubbed & marked. bba Oct 100 (204) £120 [Ginnan]

Anr Ed. L, 1857. 2 vols. 8vo, contemp half sheep; extremities worn. With 36 hand-colored plates & with an unspecified number of uncolored plates. sg Sept 19 (185) $130

— History of the Earth and Animated Nature.... L, 1870. 2 vols. 8vo, orig cloth; scuffed. L Nov 14 (216) £70

— The Poetical Works. L, 1820. 4to, orig bds; worn. With engraved dedication & 6 hand-colored plates. bbc Sept 23 (424) $65

— She Stoops to Conquer. L, 1773. 1st Ed, state not mentioned. 8vo, half mor by Sangorski & Sutcliffe. sg Nov 7 (85) $1,000

— The Vicar of Wakefield. Salisbury, 1766. 1st Ed. 2 vols. 12mo, contemp calf; rebacked, portions of orig spines laid down, rubbed. Short tears in inner margins of Vol I. Manney copy. P Oct 11 (151) $2,500

Anr Ed. L: Ackermann, 1817. Illus by Thomas Rowlandson. 8vo, modern mor gilt; upper joint weak, stain on lower cover. pn Apr 23 (201) £150 [Scott]

Anr Ed. L, 1823. 8vo, orig cloth, remainder bdg of c.1840. With 24 colored plates. C May 20 (65) £450 [Maggs]

Anr Ed. L, 1914. One of 500 L.p. copies. Illus by Edmund J. Sullivan. Folio, bdg not described but marked. kh Nov 11 (105) A$50

Anr Ed. L, 1929. Illus by Arthur Rackham. 4to, cloth. bba Jan 16 (385) £65 [Goddard]

Anr copy. Cloth, in d/j. bba Apr 9 (329) £160 [Ulysses]

Anr copy. 8vo, mor with frontis repeated on upper cover. DW Apr 8 (547) £115

Anr copy. 4to, cloth, in worn d/j. K Mar 22 (382) $85

Anr copy. Mor gilt with varicolored mor onlay depicting the frontis illust. sg Jan 30 (145) $375

One of 575. Orig vellum gilt. b Nov 18 (97) £200; sg Nov 7 (167) $550; sg Jan 30 (144) $650

1st American Ed. Phila., [1929]. 4to, cloth, in d/j. K Mar 22 (381) $90

— Works. L, 1854. 4 vols. 4to, later half mor gilt by Riviere. bbc Dec 9 (215) $230

Anr Ed. Bost.: Jefferson Press, [c.1900]. 12 vols. 8vo, half mor gilt; rubbed. O Aug 25 (93) $170

— Works. NY, 1908. Turk's Head Ed, one of 100. 10 vols. Mor gilt. CNY Dec 5 (401) $2,000

Goldsmith, Oliver, 1728-74 —& Parnell, Thomas, 1679-1718

— Poems. L, 1795. Illus by T. & J. Bewick. 4to, half russia; rubbed. bba Feb 27 (341) £150 [Thorp]

Anr copy. Contemp bds. With 5 wood-engraved plates. Foxed; Ms notes in pencil on pastedown. L.p. copy. Schlosser copy. P June 18 (428) $800

Anr Ed. L, 1804. Illus by Thomas & John Bewick. 8vo, later half calf. bba July 23 (400) £50 [Scott]

Goldston, Will

— Great Magicians' Tricks. L, [1931]. Ltd Ed. 4to, orig cloth. Sgd. bba Oct 10 (477) £200 [Carrandi]

Anr copy. Orig cloth; worn, shaken, rear hinge starting. Sgd. sg Oct 17 (39) $300

— More Exclusive Magical Secrets. L, [1920?]. Ltd Ed. 4to, orig cloth. bba Oct 10 (476) £60 [Carrandi]

Goll, Ivan

— Four Poems of the Occult. Kentfield: Allen Press, 1962. One of 130. Folio, 5 folded fascicles, each with wraps. cb Oct 31 (5) $2,000

Goll, Ivan & Claire

— Love Poems. NY: Hemispheres, [1947]. One of 640. Illus by Marc Chagall. Orig wraps. Inscr by the Golls. sg Feb 6 (56) $90

Goloubew, Victor

— Les Dessins de Jacopo Bellini au Louvre et au British Museum. Brussels, 1912-8. 2 vols. Folio, orig half vellum; worn. Inscr. S Feb 11 (85) £260 [Maggs]

Golovnin, Vasilii Mikhailovich

— Zapiski. St. Petersburg: Naval Press, 1816. 3 vols in 2. 4to, contemp calf & contemp half calf. With 2 folding maps, 1 torn. Some leaves spotted; 1 leaf in Vol III torn without loss. C May 20 (321) £2,200 [Quaritch]

Goltzius, Hubert, 1526-83

— Icones imperatorum romanorum, ex priscis numismatibus.... Antwerp, 1645. Folio, contemp sheep gilt. With engraved title & 144 chiaroscuro woodcuts in brown & black. Schlosser copy. P June 18 (430) $3,750

Anr copy. 18th-cent vellum; damaged & stained, hinges cracked & repaired. With 160 plates, many hand-colored. Tp soiled; marginal notes in a contemp hand; heavy offsetting throughout. wd June 12 (387) $500

— Lebendige Bilder gar nach aller keysern.... Antwerp: Gilles Coppens, 1557. Folio, early 19th-cent bds. With tp & 133 plates ptd in chiaroscuro, each from an etched plate & 2 color woodblocks. Foxed throughout. Schlosser copy. P June 17 (429) $4,500

— Sicilia et magna Graecia.... Bruges, Apr 1576. 2 vols in 1. Folio, contemp vellum. With engraved title & 2 full-page ports (1 shaved at fore-margin), 2 full-page maps & 37 plates of numismatics. Lower portion of last leaf torn away & repaired with loss; rust-hole in P4; upper margins dampstained. S Dec 5 (129) £1,050 [Spink]

Gomez Pereya, Juan

— Antoniana Margarita. Opus nempe Physicis.... Medina del Campo, 1572. Folio, modern calf. Ck Oct 31 (113) £480

Goncharova, Natal'ya

— Vojna. Moscow, 1914. Folio, unbound as issued in orig folder. With 14 lithos. sg Nov 7 (201) $3,000

Goncourt, Edmond de, 1822-96 & Jules de, 1830-70

— Journal...Memoires de la vie litteraire. Paris, 1887-96. 1st Ed, one of 50 on hollande. 9 vols. 12mo, half cloth, orig wraps bound in. Inscr to Claude Roger-Marx and with a page of holograph Ms. Epstein copy. sg Apr 29 (185) $4,400

Gonzales de Barcia, Andres

— Ensayo cronologica, para la historia general de la Florida.... Madrid, 1723. 1st Ed. Folio, contemp vellum; soiled. Folding ptd table torn without loss; some stain towards ends; minor worming near inner margin. S Nov 15 (1220) £360 [Ginsberg]

Gonzalez de Mendoza, Juan

— Dell' historia della China. Venice, 1590. 8vo, modern vellum. Marginal repairs. SI Dec 5 (277) LIt180,000

Good, Edward

— The Book of Affinity. L, 1933. One of 525. Illus by Jacob Epstein. 4to, cloth. sg Dec 19 (72) $130

Good, John Mason, 1764-1827 —& Others

— Pantologia. A New Cyclopaedia. L, 1813. 12 vols. 8vo, contemp half calf; def. With c.347 plates, including 164 hand-colored. Some plates loose; some browning. Sold w.a.f. pn Sept 12 (268) £320 [Fleming]

Goodale, George Lincoln, 1839-1923 —& Sprague, Isaac

— Wild Flowers of America. Bost., 1894. 4to, contemp cloth; worn. With 51 chromolithos. 2 plates def. sg Feb 13 (163) $250

Goodhue, Bertram Grosvenor

— A Book of Architectural and Decorative Drawings. NY, 1924. 2d Ptg. Folio, half cloth; worn. sg Feb 6 (107) $140

Goodrich, Samuel Griswold, 1793-1860

— The Tales of Peter Parley about America. Bost., 1827. 16mo, orig half sheep; worn, covers detached. With 32 plates. Endpapers detached and with childish scrawl in ink; scattered dampstaining. Epstein copy. sg Apr 29 (186) $12,000

Goodspeed, Charles Eliot

— Angling in America: its Early History and Literature. Bost., 1939. 1st Ed, one of 795. Koopman copy. O Oct 29 (140) $225; O Feb 25 (88) $130

— Yankee Bookseller: Reminiscences. Bost., 1937. One of 310. In d/j. cb Oct 17 (348) $55

Goodspeed's Book Shop—Boston

— The Month at Goodspeed's. Bost., 1929-69. Vols I-XL and Index for Vols I-XXX. 12mo, half cloth. O Sept 24 (171) $375

Goodwin, Francis, 1784-1835

— Domestic Architecture, Being a Series of Designs.... L, 1843. 2d Ed. 2 vols. 4to, half mor; rubbed. Dampstained throughout. Sold w.a.f. Supplement, Cottage Architecture, bound in. O Feb 25 (89) $400

— Rural Architecture. L, 1835. 2d Ed. 4 vols in 2, including Supplements. 4to, orig cloth; repaired, rebacked. With 99 plates & plans. bba Dec 19 (77) £360 [Heywood Hill]

Goodwin, Joseph

— A New System of Shoeing Horses. L, 1820. 1st Ed. 8vo, contemp mor gilt; rubbed, shelf number at head of spine. With 10 plates. DW May 13 (114) £115

Goodwin, Philip Lippincott —& Milliken, Henry Oothovt

— French Provincial Arhcitecture. NY, 1924. Folio, orig half cloth; worn, old stain at top corner of covers & across top edge of text leaves. Some foxing. bbc Dec 9 (273) $90

Gookin, Frederick William

— Japanese Colour-Prints and their Designers. NY, 1913. Ltd Ed. 4to, orig half cloth; some wear. bbc Dec 9 (274) $110

Gool, Johan van, d. 1763

— De nieuwe Schouburg der Nederlantsche Kunstschilders, en Schilderessen. The Hague, 1750-51. 2 vols. 8vo, calf; hinges weak. With engraved title, port, folding plate & 51 other ports on 21 plates, all hand-colored. B Nov 1 (353) HF1,000

Anr copy. Contemp vellum bds; soiled. With engraved title, port & 21 plates of ports plus an unlisted folding plate opposite p. 518 in Vol II. Some browning. S Feb 11 (88) £320 [Brown]

Goos, Pieter

— De Zee-Atlas, ofte Water-weereld. Amst., 1673. Folio, contemp blind-stamped vellum; shelf number on spine, inner hinges cracked. With 40 double-page or folding charts colored in a contemp hand, on thick paper. Some discoloration; text leaf foxed; lacking dedication leaf & Plate 34. DuPont copy. CNY Oct 8 (114) $29,000

— The Lighting Colomne or Sea-Mirror.... Amst., 1662. 2 parts in 1 vol. Sold with: The Lighting Colom of the Midland-Sea. Amst., 1669. Together, 3 parts in 2 vols. Folio, modern calf by Sangorski & Sutcliffe. With 59 double-page charts in 1st work & 24 double-page charts & 1 full-page chart in 2d work. First work with tp frayed; repaired tear to lower margin of C1 in Part 1, affecting catchword & last 3 lines of verso; some cropping & worming with minor loss; corner of Chart 10 chipped with loss to chart number; corner of Chart 50 repaired. Some foxing & browning to 2d work; tp repaired; hole to 1 leaf of Chart 1; borders of 7 charts shaved with minor loss; tear to last leaf with loss to woodcuts & text; mostly marginal dampstainig; ink-stamps on tp & last page of 2d work. DuPont copy. CNY Oct 8 (113) $24,000

Gordon, Alexander, 1692?-1754?

— Itinerarium Septentrionale, or a Journey thro'...Scotland.... L, 1726. Folio, calf; rebacked. With folding map & 66 plates. pnE Mar 11 (257) £140

Gordon, Capt. Anthony

— A Treatise on the Science of Defence for Sword, Bayonet, and Pike. L, 1805. 4to, orig bds. With 19 plates. Inscr to Frederic Pollock & with holograph notes by Gordon. sg Mar 26 (133) $2,600

Gordon, Patrick, fl.1700

— Geography Anatomized: or, the Geographical Grammar. L, 1744. 8vo, contemp calf; hinges cracked. With 17 folding maps. Spotted & browned. DW Mar 4 (23) £120

Gordon, Sir Robert, 1580-1656

— Genealogical History of the Earldom of Sutherland. Edin., 1813. Folio, contemp half calf; worn & split. pnE May 13 (201) £60

Gordon, Theodore, 1854-1915

— The Complete Fly Fisherman: The Notes and Letters.... NY, 1970. One of 50. 4to, lea; worn. Koopman copy. O Oct 29 (142) $850

[-] The Gordon Garland: A Round of Devotions by his Followers. NY, 1965. One of 1,500. Ed by Arnold Gingrich. 8vo, half lea. Koopman copy. O Oct 29 (141) $130

Gordon, Thomas, 1788-1841

— History of the Greek Revolution. Edin., 1844. 2 vols. 8vo, contemp calf gilt. With 1 plate & 10 maps & plans. Lacking half-titles; 1 plate torn. S June 30 (308) £380 [Valentine]

Gorer, Edgar —& Blacker, J. F.

— Chinese Porcelains and Hard Stones. L, 1911. One of 1,000. 2 vols. 4to, orig cloth. b&b Feb 19 (265) $800

Anr copy. Orig cloth; rubbed & soiled. pn May 14 (137) £140; sg May 7 (110) $800; wd Dec 12 (398) $300

Gorham, George Cornelius, 1787-1857

— The History and Antiquities of Eynesbury and St. Neot's.... L, 1820-24. 1st Ed. 2 vols, including Supplement. 8vo, orig bds; rubbed, rebacked. bba Sept 19 (195) £55 [Robertshaw]

Gori, Antonio Francisco, 1691-1757

— Museum etruscum exhibens insignia veterum etruscorum monumenta.... Florence, 1737-43. 3 vols. Folio, contemp vellum. With port & 300 on 100 plates. SI Dec 5 (887) LIt3,000,000

Goris, Gerard

— Les Delices de la campagne a l'entour de la ville de Leide. Leiden, 1712. 12mo, contemp calf. With engraved title & 12 plates. B May 12 (1549) HF550

Gorringe, Henry H., 1841-85

— Egyptian Obelisks. NY, [1882]. 4to, orig cloth; worn & spotted; inner joints broken; some dampstains. With 51 plates. Sold w.a.f. O Feb 25 (90) $130

Anr copy. Half lea; worn, front cover detached. Library markings. sg Nov 14 (244) $140

Gosse, Sir Edmund W., 1849-1928
See also: Garnett & Gosse

— British Portrait Painters and Engravers of the Eighteenth Century.... L, 1906. Folio, wraps; upper wrap spotted. kh Nov 11 (106) A$60

One of 100. Mor extra by Philippe, orig wraps preserved. CNY Dec 5 (422) $300

Gosse Library, Sir Edmund W.

— The Library of Edmund Gosse. L, 1924. Compiled by E. H. M. Cox. In d/j. cb Oct 17 (192) $50

Gosse, Philip Henry, 1810-88

— A History of the British Sea-Anemones and Corals.... L, 1860. 8vo, later cloth. With 1 plain & 11 colored plates. Library markings. bba Sept 5 (52) £60 [Ginnan]

— Letters from Alabama, chiefly Relating to Natural History. L, 1859. 8vo, cloth. bba Nov 28 (114) £70 [Socolof]

Gosselin, Louis Leon Theodore. See: Lenotre, G.

Gothein, Marie Luise

— A History of Garden Art. L & Toronto, 1928. 2 vols. 4to, cloth. bba Mar 26 (115) £140 [Sotheran]; bba Mar 26 (115) £140 [Sotheran]

Gottlieb, Gerald

— Early Children's Books and their Illustration. NY & Bost., [1975]. 4to, cloth, in d/j. sg Oct 31 (116) $90; sg May 21 (223) $70

Goudy, Frederic William, 1865-1947

— Elements of Lettering. NY: Mitchell Kennerley, 1926. Folio, cloth, unopened. cb Oct 17 (350) $75

— Typologia: Studies in Type Design & Type Making. Berkeley, 1940. One of 300. In d/j. cb Oct 177 (351) $50

Gouffe, Jules, b.1807

— The Royal Cookery Book. L, 1883. 8vo, orig cloth; recased with orig spine laid down, later endpapers. With 16 colored plates. Some foxing & staining. bbc Apr 27 (233) $110

Gould, John, 1804-81

[A nearly complete set of subscriber's copies of Gould's folio works, 14 works in 53 vols, lacking only the 2 cancelled parts of Birds of Australia, the 2d Ed of Ramphastidae, & Pittidae, sold at CNY on 24 April 1992, for –800,000. This was the University of Edinburgh set.] .

— The Birds of Europe. L, [1832]-37. 5 vols. Folio, mor gilt by Riviere; some covers discolored, joints rubbed. With 448 hand-colored plates. Longleat House copy. S June 25 (26) £40,000 [Quaritch]

— The Birds of Great Britain. L, [1862]-73. 5 vols. Folio, contemp half mor gilt; rubbed & scuffed. With 365 hand-colored plates. C Oct 30 (199) £36,000 [Vieux Livres d'Europe]

Anr copy. Mor gilt by de Coverly. With 367 hand-colored plates. About 12 plates spotted. C May 20 (179) £34,000 [Shapero]

Anr copy. Vol III only. Contemp half mor gilt; extremities rubbed. With 76 hand-colored plates. Some spotting to text & plate margins. Ck Sept 6 (19) £8,500

Anr copy. Vol I only. With 37 hand-colored plates. Ck Oct 18 (13) £6,000

Anr copy. Vol II only. Folio, contemp mor gilt. With 78 hand-colored plates. Ck July 10 (383) £8,500

Anr copy. 5 vols. Folio, contemp mor gilt; rebacked, rubbed. With 367 hand-colored plates, many heightened with gum-arabic. Some soiling; corner of 1 plate in Vol II with crease. pn Nov 14 (426) £34,000

Anr copy. With 367 hand-colored plates. Plate of Greenfinch in Vol III slightly discolored. S Nov 21 (42) £44,000 [Sourget]

Anr copy. Mor gilt by Zaehnsdorf, 1910; rubbed. S Nov 21 (43) £38,000 [Quaritch]

Anr copy. Contemp half mor gilt; marked. S June 25 (36) £32,000 [Sims Reed]

Anr copy. Contemp half mor gilt; rubbed. Some spotting to text & tables. S June 25 (37) £30,000 [Marshall]

— A Century of Birds from the Himalaya Mountains. L, [1831]-32. 1st Issue, with backgrounds uncolored. Folio, mor gilt by Riviere. With 80 hand-colored plates. C Oct 30 (196) £8,000 [Grahame]

Anr copy. Modern half mor by Bayntun-Riviere. Some browning to plates; 8 plates spotted; tp mtd on linen; repaired tear to margin of contents leaf. C Oct 30 (258) £4,200 [Mosca]

2d Issue. Half pigskin gilt; worn, spine almomst detached. With 80 hand-colored plates. Marginal foxing to 10 plates; vertical repair to 1 text leaf. CNY Dec 5 (295)

$8,500

— Humming-Birds. L, [1849]-61. ("A Monograph of the Trochilidae or Family of Humming-Birds.") 5 vols plus 1887 Supplement. Folio, contemp mor gilt. With 418 hand-colored plates, many highlighted with gold overpainted with transparent oil colors & varnish. C Oct 30 (198) £66,000 [Marshall]

Anr copy. 5 vols. Folio, contemp mor gilt; rubbed. With 360 hand-colored plates, many highlighted with gold overpainted with transparent oil colors & varnish. Some spotting or soiling. C May 20 (177) £45,000 [Arader]

Anr copy. Part 5 only. Orig half cloth; rubbed, upper section with pasted overlabel advertising the complete work with the supplement. With 15 hand-colored plates, some heightened with transparent oil colors & varnish. Sold w.a.f. C May 20 (178) £2,600 [Marshall]

— Icones Avium, or Figures and Descriptions of New and Interesting Species of Birds.... L, 1837-38. 2 vols. Folio, orig half cloth; stamp on upper covers. With 18 hand-finished colored plates. Soiled & discolored. S June 25 (23) £4,000 [Marshall]

— Partridges. L, [1844]-50. ("A Monograph of the Odontophorinae, or Partridges of America.") Folio, half mor by Gauche. With 32 hand-colored plates. Mtd on guards throughout; tp spotted. Jeanson copy. S June 25 (21) £4,500 [Arader]

Anr copy. Mor gilt by Clyde; rebacked preserving orig spine. Tear to inner margin of Large-tailed Partridge. S June 25 (22) £4,000 [Shapero]

— Toucans. L, [1833]-34-35. ("A Monograph of the Ramphastidae, or Family of Toucans.") Folio, 19th-cent half mor gilt; rubbed & marked. With 1 plain & 33 colored plates. Imprint of 1st plate cropped. S Nov 21 (53) £14,000 [Sourget]

2d Ed. L, 1854. One of 250. Folio, 19th-cent mor gilt. With 1 plain plate and 51 hand-colored plates. S Nov 21 (54) £16,000 [Klein]

— Trogons. L, [1858]-75. ("A Monograph of the Trogonidae, or Family of Trogons.") 2d Ed. Folio, contemp mor gilt; joints rubbed. With 47 hand-colored plates. Inscr to his daughter, 1869. C May 20 (180) £16,000 [Mitchell]

Goupil-Fesquet, Frederic Auguste Antoine

— Voyage d'Horace Vernet en Orient. Paris: Challamel, [1843]. 8vo, contemp half mor; rubbed. With 16 hand-colored plates. Text discolored. S June 30 (138) £420 [Kutluoglu]

Gourmont, Remy de, 1858-1915

— Le Songe d'une femme. Paris, 1925. One of 27 with an additional suite of proofs of the illusts. Illus by J. E. Laboureur. 8vo, mor extra, orig wraps bound in. sg May 7 (111) $3,200

Goury, Jules. See: Jones & Goury

Gower, John, 1325?-1408

— De confessione amantis. L: T. Berthelette, 1532. 2d Ed. Folio, contemp blind-stamped calf over wooden bds; rebacked, spine repaired, clasps lacking. Dampstained; 1st 3 & last 2 leaves with margins repaired; light worming to F3 with occasional loss of characters. STC 12143. C Dec 16 (199) £2,500 [Maggs]

Goya y Lucientes, Francisco, 1746-1828

— Los Caprichos. Munich, 1922. One of 500. 8vo, orig wraps. With 83 plates. Spotted throughout. pn Apr 23 (147) d£55 [Finbar]

— Los Desastros de la guerra. Madrid, 1863. 4to, contemp cloth; rebacked in mor. With litho title & 80 plates before corrections made to captions. Tp soiled; a few plates transposed. Schlosser copy. P June 18 (546) $36,000

Gozzi, Carlo, Conte, 1722-1806

— Turandot. Princessin von China. Tuebingen, 1802. Trans by Friedrich von Schiller. 8vo, contemp half calf; worn & scuffed, spine ends chipped. Some foxing & staining. bbc Apr 27 (401) $70

Gozzini, Vincenzo

— Monumenti sepolcrali della Toscana. Florence, 1819. Folio, contemp half calf; worn. With 47 plates; lacking Plate 43. Some waterstaining & foxing. SI Dec 5 (283) LIt250,000

Graaf, Abraham de

— De Starre-Kunst. Amst., 1659. 2 parts in 1 vol. 4to, calf; small defs. With 8 plates. B Nov 1 (486) HF1,000

Grabhorn, Edwin. See: Grabhorn Printing

Grabhorn, Edwin & Marjorie. See: Grabhorn Printing

Grabhorn, Jane. See: Grabhorn Printing

Grabhorn Printing—San Francisco, etc.

— A California Gold Rush Miscellany... 1934. One of 550. b&b Feb 19 (182) $100; K Sept 29 (106) $50

— Festivals in San Francisco... 1939. One of 1,000. wa Mar 5 (107) $95

— Joan the Maid of Orleans... 1938. One of 525. wa Dec 9 (27) $55

— A Leaf from the King James Bible. With "The Noblest Monument of English Prose"

by J.L. Lowes & "The Printing of the King James Bible" by L.I. Newman. 1937. One of 300. b&b Feb 19 (210) $200
— A Leaf from the 1611 King James Bible. With "The Noblest Monument of English Prose" by J. L. Lowes & "The Printing of the King James Bible" by L. I. Newman. 1937. One of 300. Book Club of California No 51. cb Oct 31 (48) $350
— An Original Issue of "The Spectator," together with the Story of the Famous English Periodical.... 1939. One of 455. 4to, half cloth. With orig leaf from The Spectator tipped in. cb Jan 16 (61) $200
— An Original Leaf...Barclay's English Translation...Brant's Ship of Fools... 1938. One of 260. b&b Feb 19 (197) $100
— An Original Leaf from the Polycronicon printed by William Caxton... 1938. One of 297. b&b Feb 19 (185) $375; cb Dec 5 (26) $275
— Reglamento para el gobierno de la Provincia de Californias...[Regulations for Governing the Province of the Californias...]. 1929. One of 300. 2 vols. cb Feb 12 (9) $170
— The Spectator: An Original Issue of...with the story of the famous English periodical...by Eric Partridge. 1939. One of 455. b&b Feb 19 (220) $60
— BAIRD, JOSEPH ARMSTRONG. - California's Pictorial Letter Sheets 1849-1869. 1967. One of 475. sg June 18 (38) $150
— BECKER, ROBERT H. - Designs on the Land, Disenos of California Ranchos and Their Makers. 1969. One of 500. b&b Feb 19 (246) $175; cb Nov 14 (10) $225; pba July 23 (88) $160
— BECKER, ROBERT H. - Disenos of California Ranchos... 1964. One of 400. b&b Feb 19 (297) $225; cb Sept 12 (18) $475
— BEECHEY, FREDERICK WILLIAM. - An Account of a Visit to California... 1941. One of 350. b&b Feb 19 (196) $80
— BRADFORD, JOHN. - Historical Notes on Kentucky. 1932. One of 500. cb Jan 16 (27) $60
— BROWN, JOHN HENRY. - Reminiscences and Incidents of Early Days of San Francisco. 1933. One of 500. cb Feb 12 (7) $90
— CHAMISSO, ADELBERT VON. - A Sojourn at San Francisco Bay 1816... 1936. One of 250. b&b Feb 19 (208) $100; cb Feb 12 (12) $225
— CHURCHILL, SIR WINSTON L. S. - Addresses Delivered in the Year 1940 to the People of Great Britain... 1940. One of 250. b&b Feb 19 (211) $150
— CHURCHILL, SIR WINSTON L. S. - Broadcast Addresses to the People of Great Britain.... 1941. One of 250. b&b Feb 19 (212) $150; K Dec 1 (67) $150
— CLAPPE, LOUISE A.K.S. - California in 1851 [in 1852] The Letters of Dame Shirley. 1933. One of 500. 2 vols. cb Sept 12 (37) $130
— CLAPPE, LOUISE AMELIA KNAPP SMITH. - California in 1851 [1852]. The Letters of Dame Shirley. 1933. One of 500. 2 vols. cb Nov 14 (30) $110; sg June 18 (233) $70
— COIT, DANIEL WADSWORTH. - An Artist in El Dorado... 1937. One of 325. b&b Feb 19 (218) $50; cb Feb 12 (13) $110
— CORONADO, FRANCISCO VASQUEZ DE. - The Journey of... 1933. One of 550. b&b Feb 19 (180) $80; sg June 18 (234) $100
— CRANE, STEPHEN. - The Red Badge of Courage. 1931. One of 980. b&b Feb 19 (198) $50; sg Jan 30 (64) $50
— DANA, RICHARD HENRY, JR. - Two Years Before the Mast. NY: Random House, 1936. One of 1,000. In d/j. cb Sept 5 (24) $160; sg June 18 (235) $80
— DE SOTO, HERNANDO. - The Discovery of Florida. 1946. One of 280. b&b Feb 19 (193) $100; cb Oct 10 (35) $190
— DEARDEN, ROBERT R. & WATSON, DOUGLAS S. - An Original Leaf from the Bible of the Revolution and an Essay Concerning It. 1930. One of 515. pba July 23 (84) $225
— DICKENS, CHARLES. - A Christmas Carol. 1950. One of 250. b&b Feb 19 (214) $90
— DU BOIS, JOHN VAN DEUSEN. - Campaigns in the West... 1949. One of 300. cb Nov 14 (49) $200
— ELKUS, RICHARD J. - Alamos: A Philosophy in Living. 1965. One of 487. b&b Feb 19 (247) $90
— ELLIS, HAVELOCK. - Marriage Today and Tomorrow. 1929. One of 500. pba July 23 (85) $55
— FAHEY, HERBERT. - Early Printing in California... 1956. One of 400. pba July 23 (68) $180
— FINLAYSON, DUNCAN. - Traits of American Indian Life & Character, by a Fur Trader. 1933. One of 500. cb Feb 12 (24) $100; sg June 18 (251) $90
— GARRARD, LEWIS HECTOR. - Wah-to-Yah & the Taos Trail. 1936. One of 550. cb Sept 12 (70) $110
— GAUGUIN, PAUL. - Letters to Ambroise Vollard & Andrew Fontainas. 1943. sg Feb 6 (99) $120
— GERSTAECKER, FRIEDRICH. - Scenes of Life in California. 1942. One of 500. sg June 18 (238) $90
— GRABHORN, EDWIN. - Figure Prints of Old Japan... 1959. One of 400. cb Oct 31 (30) $425
— GRABHORN, EDWIN. - Landscape Prints of Old Japan. 1960. One of 450. bbc Apr 27 (464) $235; cb Oct 31 (31) $425
— GRABHORN, EDWIN & MARJORIE. - Ukiyo-e, "The Floating World." 1962. One of 400.

b&b Feb 19 (213) $250
— GRABHORN, JANE. - The Compleat Jane Grabhorn... 1968. One of 400. cb Oct 17 (352) $85
— GRABHORN, JANE. - One Hundred & Sixty Cat Proverbs.... 1969. One of 300. cb Jan 16 (58) $85
— GRABHORN, ROBERT. - Nineteenth Century Type Displayed in 18 Fonts.... 1959. One of 300. cb Nov 21 (99) $120
— GRABHORN, ROBERT. - Short Account of the Life and Work of Wynkyn de Worde with a Leaf from the Golden Legend... 1949. One of 375. b&b Feb 19 (217) $175
— HARLOW, NEAL. - The Maps of San Francisco Bay from the Discovery...to the American Occupation. 1950. One of 375. wa June 25 (240) $325
— HARTE, BRET. - The Luck of Roaring Camp. 1948. One of 300. cb Jan 16 (75) $90; sg Jan 30 (66) $100
— HARTE, BRET. - Mliss.... 1948. One of 300. b&b Feb 19 (215) $80; cb Oct 31 (41) $95
— HARTE, BRET. - San Francisco in 1866. San Francisco: Book Club of California, 1951. One of 400. sg June 18 (239) $70
— HAWTHORNE, NATHANIEL. - The Golden Touch. 1927. One of 240. wa Mar 5 (108) $65
— HELLER, ELINOR R. & MAGEE, DAVID. - Bibliography of the Grabhorn Press, 1915-1940. 1940. One of 210. cb Oct 31 (32) $750
— HOLMES BOOK CO. - A Descriptive & Priced Catalogue of Books...on California and the Far West.... 1948. One of 500. Folio, half cloth. sg June 18 (237) $90
— JEFFERS, ROBINSON. - Hungerfield. 1952. One of 32. cb Dec 12 (84) $425
— JEFFERS, ROBINSON. - Solstice and Other Poems. NY: Random House, 1935. One of 320. Sgd. sg Dec 12 (180) $200; wa Mar 5 (210) $90
— KABOTIE, FRED. - Designs from the Ancient Mimbrenos... 1949. One of 250. Half cloth. sg Dec 5 (108) $200
— KAISER, HENRY J. - Twenty-Six Addresses Delivered during the War Years. 1945. One of 30. cb Oct 31 (47) $275
— KANE, THOMAS L. - The Private Papers and Diary of.... 1937. One of 500. cb Sept 12 (98) $60
— KITAGAWA, UTAMARO. - Twelve Woodblock Prints of Kitagawa Utamaro Illustrating the Process of Silk Culture. 1965. One of 450. Intro by Jack Hillier. bbc Apr 27 (466) $100
— LANG, A. - Book Ballades for Roxburghers. [1928]. One of 50. cb Nov 21 (100) $180
— LEIGHLY, JOHN. - California as an Island... 1972. One of 450. b&b Feb 19 (298) $600
— LEWIS, OSCAR. - California in 1846... 1934. One of 550. b&b Feb 19 (181) $60
— LITTLEJOHN, DAVID. - Dr. Johnson and Noah Webster. 1971. One of 500. sg May 21 (262) $200
— MAGEE, DAVID. - The Hundredth Book: a Bibliography of the Publications of the Book Club of California... 1958. One of 400. b&b Feb 19 (205) $175; sg May 21 (264) $60; sg June 18 (240) $90
— MAGEE, DOROTHY & DAVID. - Bibliography of the Grabhorn Press, 1940-56. 1957. One of 225. cb Oct 33 $800
— MANDEVILLE, SIR JOHN. - The Voiage and Travaile. NY: Random House, 1928.. One of 150. Joints rubbed. cb Feb 12 (50) $1,200
— MERCER, ASA SHINN. - The Banditti of the Plains... 1935. One of 1,000. cb Nov 14 (121) $70
— MEYERS, WILLIAM H. - Journal of a Cruise to California and the Sandwich Islands... 1955. One of 400. b&b Feb 19 (200) $125; b&b Feb 19 (201) $100
— MEYERS, WILLIAM H. - Naval Sketches of the War in California. NY, 1939. One of 1,000. Bds; spine scuffed. O Mar 31 (85) $50

Anr copy. Half pigskin. sg Sept 26 (126) $130; sg June 18 (241) $80

Anr copy. Copy with stained & deteriorating bdg. sg June 18 (242) $50
— MEYERS, WILLIAM H. - Sketches of California and Hawaii... 1970. One of 450. Blindstamp on foreleaf. b&b Feb 19 (202) $100; cb Sept 12 (116) $50; pba July 23 (89) $80; sg June 18 (243) $80
— MILLER, HENRY. - 13 California Towns from the Original Drawings. 1947. One of 300. b&b Feb 19 (187) $100; cb Feb 12 (58) $70
— M'ILVAINE, WILLIAM, JR. - Sketches of Scenery and Notes of Personal Adventure in California & Mexico. 1951. One of 400. b&b Feb 19 (186) $60; NH May 30 (136) $75
— OLDFIELD, OTIS. - Aboard the Three Masted Schooner Louise.... 1969. One of 400. O Jan 14 (85) $70
— PARSONS, GEORGE F. - The Life and Adventures of James W. Marshall. 1935. cb Sept 12 (136) $60; cb Nov 14 (157) $50
— PATTISON, MARK. - The Estiennes: A Biographical Essay... 1949. One of 390. b&b Feb 19 (216) $80
— PHILLIPS, CATHERINE COFFIN. - Coulterville Chronicle.... 1942. One of 500. sg June 18 (244) $70
— POE, EDGAR ALLAN. - The Journal of Julius Rodman. 1947. One of 500. cb Oct 31 (52) $95
— ROBERTSON, JOHN WOOSTER. - Bibliography of the Writings of Edgar A. Poe. 1934. One of 350. 2 vols. cb Oct 17 (800) $160
— ROBERTSON, JOHN WOOSTER. - Commentary on the Bibliography of Edgar A. Poe. 1934.

One of 350. cb Jan 16 (121) $350
— ROBERTSON, JOHN WOOSTER. - Francis Drake and Other Early Explorers Along the Pacific Coast. 1927. One of 1,000. cb Oct 10 (91) $150; sg June 18 (245) $100
— ROWLANDSON, THOMAS. - The Beauties of Boswell. 1942. One of 250. b&b Feb 19 (294) $125; cb Sept 5 (93) $80
— SAROYAN, WILLIAM. - Hilltop Russians in San Francisco. 1941. One of 500. In d/j. cb Nov 21 (203) $50

Anr copy. In soiled d/j. F June 25 (425) $70; sg June 18 (246) $90
— SAWYER, EUGENE T. - The Life and Career of Tiburcio Vasquez... 1944. One of 500. sg June 18 (247) $60
— SCAMMON, L. N. - Spanish Missions, California: A Portfolio of Etchings.... 1926. One of 90. 10 orig etchings tipped into individual paper folders, loose as issued, in cloth portfolio. cb Feb 12 (76) $325
— SHAKESPEARE, WILLIAM. - Anthony and Cleopatra. 1960. One of 185. sg Jan 30 (70) $200
— SHAKESPEARE, WILLIAM. - [Henry IV]. The First Part of Henry the Fourth. 1961. One of 180. b&b Feb 19 (190) $125; sg Jan 30 (67) $175
— SHAKESPEARE, WILLIAM. - Julius Caesar. 1954. One of 180. sg Jan 30 (71) $200
— SHAKESPEARE, WILLIAM. - King Lear. [1959]. One of 180. b&b Feb 19 (192) $125
— SHAKESPEARE, WILLIAM. - Macbeth. 1952. One of 180. sg Jan 30 (72) $225
— SHAKESPEARE, WILLIAM. - A Midsommer Nights Dreame. 1955. One of 180. sg Jan 30 (68) $150
— SHAKESPEARE, WILLIAM. - Othello. 1956. One of 185. b&b Feb 19 (209) $125; sg Jan 30 (73) $100
— SHAKESPEARE, WILLIAM. - Richard the Third. 1953. One of 185. sg Jan 30 (74) $200
— SHAKESPEARE, WILLIAM. - The Taming of the Shrew. 1967. One of 375. sg Jan 30 (78) $150
— SHAKESPEARE, WILLIAM. - The Tempest. 1951. One of 160. sg Jan 30 (69) $200
— SHORT, FRANK HAMILTON. - Selected Papers... 1923. One of 250. Front cover ink-spotted. cb Jan 16 (62) $50
— STEVENSON, ROBERT LOUIS. - Silverado Journal. 1954. One of 400. b&b Feb 19 (188) $90
— STODDARD, CHARLES WARREN. - Diary of a Visit to Molokai.... 1933. One of 250. cb Jan 16 (144) $50
— STRATTON, ROYAL B. - Life Among the Indians. 1935. One of 550. cb Feb 12 (82) $170; sg June 18 (248) $60
— SUTTER, JOHN A. - New Helvetia Diary... 1939. One of 950. sg June 18 (249) $80; sg June 18 (250) $50
— TRIPP, C.E. - Ace High the 'Frisco Detective. 1948. One of 500. b&b Feb 19 (195) $50
— UTAMARO, KITAGAWA. - Twelve Wood-Block Prints... 1965. One of 450. b&b Feb 19 (203) $150; cb Oct 31 (62) $200; sp June 18 (181) $150
— VESPUCCI, AMERIGO. - Letter...describing his Four Voyages to the New World... 1926. One of 250. Pages waved. b&b Feb 19 (194) $225
— WAGNER, HENRY RAUP. - The Plains and the Rockies, a Bibliography of Original Narratives of Travel and Adventures. 1937. One of 600. cb Oct 17 (958) $85
— WASHINGTON, GEORGE. - Washington's Farewell Address. 1922. One of 50. Pencil markings on label & part of front cover; sunned & dampstained. cb Jan 16 (63) $70

One of 125. sg Dec 5 (265) $60
— WATSON, DOUGLAS S. - Neighbors of Yesterday. 1934. One of 100. cb Oct 31 (34) $60
— WHEAT, CARL I. - Books of the California Gold Rush.... 1949. One of 500. K Sept 29 (185) $120; sg June 18 (146) $300
— WHEAT, CARL I. - Mapping the Transmississippi West. 1957-63. One of 1,000. Vol I only. b&b Feb 19 (291) $375

Anr copy. 5 vols in 6. O Sept 24 (263) $2,100; sg May 7 (210) $1,600

Anr Ed. 1963. Vol 5/1 (of 6) only. sg Oct 31 (80) $175

Anr Ed. 1967. Vol V only in 2 parts cb Sept 12 (188) $750
— WHEAT, CARL I. - The Maps of the California Gold Region. 1942. One of 300. sg June 18 (253) $1,300
— WHEAT, CARL I. - The Pioneer Press of California. 1948. One of 450. cb Oct 17 (982) $150; cb Nov 14 (235) $190; sg June 18 (254) $90
— WHITMAN, WALT. - Leaves of Grass. NY, 1930. One of 400. Half mor. Inscr by the artist, Valenti Angelo. cb Feb 12 (148) $1,500; P June 18 (431) $900

Anr copy. With 2 trial pp laid in, each inscr by Valenti Angelo. Epstein copy. sr Apr 30 (499) $1,600
— WIERZBICKI, FELIX PAUL. - California as it is... 1933. One of 500. cb Nov 14 (237) $70
— WILTSEE, ERNEST A. - Gold Rush Steamers of the Pacific. 1938. One of 500. sg June 18 (255) $200
— WINDSOR, EDWARD. - Farewell Speech of King Edward the Eighth. 1938. One of 200. b&b Feb 19 (206) $80

Anr copy. Half pigskin. sg Jan 30 (65) $70
— ZEITLIN, JAKE. - For Whispers and Chants. 1927. One of 450. cb Jan 16 (180) $120

Grabhorn, Robert. See: Grabhorn Printing

Grace, William Gilbert, 1848-1915
— Cricket. Bristol & L, 1891. One of 662. 4to, orig half lea; worn, upper cover dampstained. pn July 16 (176) £220 [McKenzie]

Graesse, Johann Georg Theodor, 1814-85
— Tresor de livres rares et precieux.... Berlin, 1922. 7 vols in 4. 4to, later cloth. Ck Nov 1 (406) £420

Anr Ed. Milan, 1950. 8 vols, including Supplement. 4to, orig cloth. O Sept 24 (101) $475; SI Dec 5 (888) LIt850,000

Graevius, Johann Georg, 1632-1703
— Thesaurus antiquitatum romanarum. Utrecht & Leiden, 1694. Vol I only (of 12). Contemp calf; loose. With 2 folding maps & 1 folding numismatic plate. sg Feb 13 (123) $80

Grafton, Richard, d.c.1572
— A Chronicle at Large and Meere History of the Affayres of Englande.... L: Denham for R. Tottle & H. Toye, 1569. 2d Ed. 2 vols in 1. Folio, old calf; rebacked. Marginal repairs. STC 12147. W July 8 (55) £760

Graham, Clive —&
Curling, Bill
— The Grand National. L, 1973. One of 105. 4to, mor extra. W Mar 6 (104) £70

Graham, John Andrew, 1764-1841
— A Descriptive Sketch of the Present State of Vermont.... L, 1797. 1st Ed. 8vo, orig bds. Errata slip pasted to rear endpaper; some spotting. bba May 28 (344) £110 [Robertshaw]

Graham, Maria
— Journal of a Residence in Chile.... L, 1824. 4to, calf. With 14 plates. Contents browned at edges. DW Apr 8 (33) £280

Anr copy. Modern cloth. Front flyleaf def; marginal tears & chips to frontis; inked library stamps. sg Dec 5 (109) $120

Graham, Tom. See: Lewis, Sinclair

Grahame, Kenneth, 1859-1932
— The Golden Age. L & NY, 1900 [1899]. Illus by Maxfield Parrish. 8vo, orig cloth; rubbed & worn; shaken. sg Sept 26 (249) $150; sp Feb 6 (338) $65; sp Feb 6 (339) $75

Anr Ed. L & NY, 1904. 8vo, orig cloth. sp Feb 6 (340) $65

— The Wind in the Willows. L, 1908. 1st Ed. bba Apr 30 (140) £450 [Heuer]

Anr copy. Orig cloth; joints rubbed, bumped, endpapers browned. P June 17 (219) $1,500

Anr copy. Orig cloth; spine chipped & frayed. Inscr to his sister Helen, Oct 1908. S Nov 14 (161) £4,200 [Sawyer]

Anr copy. Orig cloth; rubbed, recased with repairs to spine, new endpapers. Prelims spotted. S Nov 14 (162) £300 [Sotheran]; S Apr 28 (66) £1,100 [Murphy]

Anr copy. Orig half cloth, unopened, in d/j. sg Apr 29 (189) $5,600

Anr Ed. L, 1931. Out-of-series copy, sgd by author & artist. Illus by E. H. Shepard. Orig half cloth; rubbed & soiled. DW Oct 2 (355) £600

Anr Ed. L, 1951. One of 500. Illus by Arthur Rackham. 4to, orig calf; dampstained. With 12 colored plates. S Nov 14 (129) £420 [Richardson]

Anr copy. Mor gilt by Zaehnsdorf with Rackham design on front cover. sg Nov 7 (168) $1,100

Grahame-White, Claude
— The Story of the Aeroplane. Bost., [1911]. cb Nov 7 (45) $55

Graham's...
— Graham's Lady's and Gentleman's Magazine. Phila., 1841. Vol XVII, bound with Graham's Vol XXIX. 8vo, contemp cloth gilt. Contains such Poe stories as Murders in the Rue Morgue. Manney copy. P Oct 11 (253) $2,500

Vol XVIII, No 1 - Vol XIX, No VI. Together, 2 vols (containing 12 issues) in 1. 8vo, half mor. Contains such Poe stories as Murders in the Rue Morgue, A Descent into the Maelstrom, etc.. sg Oct 17 (352) $450

— Graham's Magazine of Literature & Art Phila., 1842. ("Graham's American Monthly Magazine.") Vols XX-XXI. 8vo, orig half calf; worn, broken. Some foxing & browning. bbc June 29 (427) $65

Gram, Hans. See: Slange & Gram

Grancsay, Stephen V. See: Bashford Collection, Dean

Grand. See: D.,

Grand, Gordon. See: Derrydale Press

Grand-Carteret, John, 1850-1927
— Les Almanachs francais: bibliographie, iconographie des almanachs.... Paris, 1896. One of 1,200. 1 vol in 2. 4to, new cloth, orig wraps bound in. sg Oct 31 (117) $300

— L'Histoire, la vie, les moeurs, et la curiosite par l'image, le pamphlet, et le documents. Paris, 1927-29. 5 vols. Folio, orig half lea; rubbed, spines worn. K July 12 (23) $120

Grandville, 1803-47

— Cent Proverbs. Paris, [1887]. 8vo, contemp half lea. SI June 9 (436) LIt380,000

— Les Fleurs animees. Paris, 1867. 2 vols. 8vo, contemp half mor. With 50 hand-colored plates & 2 uncolored plate. Upper margins through much of Vol I stained. S Apr 28 (7) £250 [Tsuboi]

Anr copy. 2 vols in 1. 8vo, contemp half mor; rubbed & chipped. With hand-colored title, 2 uncolored & 40 hand-colored plates. S July 1 (1121) £200

— The Flowers Personified, being a Translation of Les Fleurs Animees. NY, 1847-49. 2 vols. 4to, half lea; rubbed, joints weak. With 2 uncolored & 52 hand-colored plates. Some staining. K Dec 1 (240) $550

— Les Metamorphoses du jour. Paris, 1869. 8vo, contemp lea. SI June 9 (437) LIt1,000,000

Grant, Asahel, 1807-44

— The Nestorians; or, The Lost Tribes. L, 1841. 12mo, contemp half calf. With folding map. S June 30 (310) £180 [Maggs]

Anr Ed. NY, 1841. 12mo, orig cloth; spine lacking. With folding map. Tear at inner margin affecting map; some waterstaining to upper margins. bba May 28 (345) £90 [Folios]

Grant, George Monro, 1835-1902

— Picturesque Canada. A Pictorial Delineation of the Beauties.... Toronto & L, [1882-85]. 6 vols. Folio, cloth; rubbed & marked. bba Sept 19 (24) £50 [Butcher]

Anr copy. 2 vols. Folio, half mor gilt; rubbed. O Jan 14 (150) $135

Grant, James, 1771-1833

— The Narrative of a Voyage of Discovery Performed in his Majesty's Vessel the Lady Nelson.... L, 1803. 1st Ed. 4to, contemp half russia gilt; upper joint cracked. With folding frontis plan, 1 folding map with outline color, 1 hand-colored plate & 5 other plates. Frontis with small tear repaired with tape; other plates browned. CNY Oct 8 (115) $5,500

Anr copy. Contemp wraps; broken. Offsetting from frontis onto title. sg May 7 (112) $3,000

Grant, James, 1822-87

— The Tartans of the Clans of Scotland. Edin., 1886. Folio, later cloth. Library markings. sg Apr 2 (126) $90

Grant, Jedediah

— Three Letters to the New York Herald. [NY, 1852]. 8vo, later half cloth; library markings on spine, endpapers loose or lacking. sg Dec 5 (157) $375

Grant, Maurice Harold

— A Chronological History of the Old English Landscape Painters. Leigh-on-Sea, 1971-74. 8 vols. DW Oct 9 (874) £230

— The Makers of Black Basaltes. Edin. & L, 1910. 4to, cloth; upper cover creased. bba Apr 30 (435) £80 [Oatley]

Anr copy. Cloth; worn, with a few tears & with hinges cracked. Some soiling to prelims. sg Sept 6 (130) $250

Grant, Ulysses S., 1822-85

— Personal Memoirs. NY, 1885-86. 2 vols. 8vo, half mor; worn & scuffed. bbc Feb 17 (69) $60

Anr copy. Lea; scuffed, joints starting. sp Apr 16 (87) $55

Anr copy. Cloth; scuffed & stained with paint. sp June 18 (90) $60

Grant, William —& Murison, David D.

— The Scottish National Dictionary. Edin., [n.d.]-1976. One of 1,000. 10 vols. 4to, half calf. pnE May 13 (103) £120

Granville, Augustus Bozzi, 1783-1872

— St. Petersburgh. A Journal of Travels.... L, 1828. 1st Ed. 2 vols. 8vo, contemp calf; rubbed, rebacked. With 13 hand-colored plates & 24 uncolored plates. Some spots & stains; folding plate torn at folds & repaired; Vol I lacking half-title. S Nov 15 (1118) £350 [Harley Mason]

Grapheus, Cornille

— Spectaculorum in susceptione Philippi Hisp. prin. divi Caroli V. Caes. f. an. MCXLIX Antuerpiae aeditorum, mirificus apparatus. [Antwerp: Gillis van Diest for Pieter Coecke van Aelst, 1550]. Illus by Pieter Coecke. Folio, modern vellum. Lacking final blank. Lower margin of title restored. bba Apr 30 (255) £1,800 [Mandl]

Grass, Gunter

See also: Limited Editions Club

— Drawings and Words 1954-1977. L, 1983. One of 250. In d/j. sg Jan 30 (79) $130

— Inmarypraise. [Munich, 1973]. One of 280. Illus & with an orig etching by Grass. bbc Dec 9 (474) $80

Grasset de Saint-Sauveur, Jacques

— L'Antique Rome ou description historique et pittoresque.... Paris, 1796. 4to, calf; joints & edges worn, front joint partly cracked. With 50 plates. Some foxing to text; lower corner margin dampstained at rear; lacking rear free endpaper. wa Sept 26 (573) $80

Grasset, Eugene

— Plants and their Application to Ornament. L: Chapman & Hall, [1896-97]. Folio, loose as issued in cloth portfolio; spine stained. With 72 colored plates. b June 22 (361) £950

Anr copy. Unbound as issued in orig cloth portfolio. With 67 (of 72) plates pochoir-colored. Tp tattered; Plate 32 soiled; other soiling. Ck Dec 12 (279) £700

Grassineau, James, d.1769

— Musical Dictionary. L, 1740. 1st Ed. 8vo, contemp calf gilt. With 4 plates. Tear in 1 plate. L Nov 14 (407) £75

Gratianus, the Canonist, d.c.1150

— Decretum. Mainz: Peter Schoeffer, 13 Aug 1472. Folio, late 17th-cent sheep. 79 lines; double column; types 5:118G (text), 6:92G (commentary); with 38 miniatures & 39 initials in gilt & colors & 39 pages with borderpieces. Miniature excised from f.162 with loss also of the backing text; c.16 portions of borderwork excised & patched, in a few cases touching letters; a few miniatures rubbed. Ptd on vellum. 411 (of 413) leaves; lacking 48/1.8,the latter of which is blank. Goff G-362. Schoyen copy. P Dec 12 (22) $220,000

Anr Ed. Strassburg: Johann Grueninger, 4 Sept 1489. Folio, 16th-cent German pigskin over wooden bds with 2 brass fore-edge clasps, with binding date 1562; bosses removed. 88 lines; double column; types 11:91G (text), 12:71G (commentary), 1:180G (headline) & 4:52C (reference letters). Stains on first & last leaves & occasionally elsewhere. Ptd on vellum. 254 leaves. Goff G-380. Fuerstenberg-Schoyen copy. P Dec 12 (23) $31,000

Anr Ed. Venice: Baptista de Tortis, 30 Mar 1496. Folio, contemp goatskin over wooden bds, an Augsburg bdg (Kyriss shop 86). 82 lines of gloss surrounding text & headline, double column; types 12:95G (text), 10:82G (commentary), 14:185G (title-page, headlines); rubricated & illuminated with port of Gregory IX in space provided on a2r in colors on a gilt ground. 338 leaves. Goff G-388. Schoyen copy. P Dec 12 (24) $7,000

Gratzl, Emil

— Islamische Buchenbaende des 14. bis 19. Jahrhunderts. Leipzig, 1924. 4to, cloth; shelf-worn. O Sept 24 (103) $180

Graux, Lucien

— L'Agneau du Moghreb. Paris, 1942. One of 125. Illus by F. L. Schmied. 4to, orig wraps; worn. S Nov 14 (32) £300 [Ryken-Skull]

Gravelot, Hubert Francois Bourguignon, 1699-1773 —&
Cochin, Charles Nicolas, 1699-1773

— Iconologie par figures ou traite complet des allegories.... Paris, [1791]. 4 vols. 8vo, contemp calf gilt; 2 spines chipped at foot. With 4 engraved titles, 2 ports & 202 plates. Some margins browned or spotted. S Dec 5 (269) £900 [Kraus]

Graves, Algernon

— The Royal Academy of Arts: A Complete Dictionary of Contributors.... L, 1970. 4 vols. In d/js. sg Apr 2 (127) $120

Graves, John

— The History of Cleveland in the North Riding of the County of York. Carlisle, 1808. 4to, later half vellum; fore-edges worn. With engraved title, folding map, hand-colored in outline, & 9 plates. Some foxing & wear to fore-edges. pnL Nov 20 (61) £85 [Tuston]

Graves, Richard, 1715-1804

— The Spiritual Quixote. L, 1821. 8vo, contemp mor gilt. With port & 2 folding maps. Title spotted. Ck July 10 (271) £650

Graves, Robert

— Country Sentiment. L, 1920. 1st Ed. Orig bds, in worn & repaired d/j. K July 12 (246) $100

— Love Respelt Again. NY, [1969]. One of 1,000, sgd. Cloth, in d/j. sg June 11 (131) $70

— Over the Brazier. L, 1916. 1st Ed, 1st Issue. Orig wraps; worn. Sgd. Epstein copy. sg Apr 29 (190) $1,100

— Poems, 1914-1927. L, 1927. 1st Ed, One of 115. Half vellum. sg Dec 12 (138) $300

— The Shout. L, [1929]. One of 530, sgd. 4to, orig bds, in d/j. sg June 11 (132) $120

— Ten Poems More. Paris: Hours Press, 1930. 1st Ed, one of 200. Half lea; spine faded, ends chipped. cb Dec 12 (63) $130

Gray, Frank S.

— For Love and Bears. Chicago, 1886. 8vo, modern cloth. With mtd albumen photograph. sg June 18 (193) $250

Gray, George John

— A Bibliography of the Works of Sir Isaac Newton. Cambr., 1907. 2d Ed. Half cloth. O Dec 17 (86) $60

Gray, George Robert, 1808-72

— The Genera of Birds.... L, [1837]-44-49. 3 vols. Folio, modern half mor. With 185 hand-colored plates & 150 uncolored plates of detail. Some plates with captions trimmed. C Oct 30J (281) £4,000 [Wheldon & Wesley]

Gray, Henry, 1825-61

— Anatomy, Descriptive and Surgical. Phila., 1859. 8vo, orig sheep; joints & extremities rubbed. sg May 14 (66) $850

Gray, John, F.R.S.

— A Treatise of Gunnery. L, 1731. 8vo, contemp calf; rubbed, joints split. S July 9 (1267) £250 [National Army Museum]

Gray, Prentiss N. See: Derrydale Press

Gray, Thomas, 1716-71

See also: Blake & Gray; Vertue, George

— An Elegy Wrote in a Country Church Yard. San Francisco: John Henry Nash, 1925. ("An Elegy Written in a Country Churchyard.") One of 300. 2 vols. Folio & 4to, half vellum. cb Oct 31 (35) $110

Anr Ed. L: Raven Press, 1938. ("Elegy Written in a Country Churchyard.") Illus by Agnes Miller Parker. K July 12 (192) $110

One of 1,500. sg Jan 30 (230) $140

— An Ode on a Distant Prospect of Eton College. L, 1747. Folio, unbound, unstitched & untrimmed, as issued. Loveday-Robinson copy. P Dec 12 (176) $65,000

— Ode on the Pleasure Arising from Vicissitude. San Francisco, 1933. One of 200. 2 vols. 4to, orig half vellum. bba July 9 (266) £75 [Kunkler]; cb Oct 31 (36) $150

— Works. York, 1778. ("Poems.") 4 vols. 8vo, early calf; recased, worn, old edge stains at endpapers. bbc Dec 9 (216) $75

Graziani, Antonio Maria, 1537-1611

— Histoire de la guerre de Chypre. Lyon: Thomas Amaulry, 1686. 2 vols. 8vo, contemp calf; spines chipped. S June 30 (139) £700 [Sophoclides]

Grazzini, Antonio Francesco, 1503-85

See also: Lasca

— La Prima e la Seconda Cena: novelle.... L, 1756. 8vo, lea. br May 29 (38) $175

— The Story of Doctor Manente.... Florence: Orioli, [1929]. 1st Ed, one of 1,000. Trans by D. H. Lawrence. Orig bds, in d/j with Dottor misprint. pba July 9 (172) $50

Great...

— The Great Chronicle of London. L, 1938. One of 50. Ed by A. H. Thomas & I. D. Thornley. Orig mor gilt with gilt arms of the Corporation of the City of London. With dedication leaf to Viscount Wakefield of Hythe. S Feb 25 (459) £220 [Thorp]

— Great Exhibition, 1851. L, 1851-[52]. ("Official Descriptive and Illustrated Catalogue.") 4 vols. 4to, orig cloth; extremities worn. DW Mar 11 (817) £100

Anr copy. ("The Art Journal Illustrated Catalogue: The Industry of All Nations.") 4to, half lea; some wear. sg Sept 6 (131) $175

— Great Georgian Houses of America. NY, 1933-37. 2 vols. Folio, cloth. Vol II inscr by Stark Young. Met Apr 28 (647) $120

— The Great Operas.... Phila., 1899. New England Ed. 10 vols. Folio, each vol a differently colored mor gilt with center ornaments bearing Verdi's monogram & with upper doublures with gilt monograms LBJ & RJ. Most plates in 2 states. CNY June 9 (77) $4,500

Greatrex, Charles Butler

— Dame Perkins and her Grey Mare.... L, 1866. 1st Ed. 4to, cloth; extremities rubbed. With colored frontis & 7 colored plates. cb Jan 9 (103) $60

Greblinger, Georg

— Wahre Abbildungen der tuerckischen Kayser und persischen Fuersten.... Frankfurt: Johann Ammon, 1648. Illus by J. J. Boissard. 4to, 19th-cent mor gilt by Pratt. With 47 plates. sg Oct 24 (46) $1,000

Greco, Gioachino

— Le Jeu des eschets. Paris, 1669. 12mo, contemp calf; extremities worn. Ck May 8 (34) £350

Anr Ed. Paris, 1689. 12mo, contemp calf; extremities worn. Ck May 8 (35) £180

Anr Ed. Paris, 1713. 12mo, 19th-cent calf; rebacked with old spine preserved. Some browning. Ck May 8 (36) £130

Anr Ed. Paris, 1714. 8vo, contemp half calf; joints cracked. William Lewis's copy. Ck May 8 (37) £180

— The Royall Game of Chesse-Play. L, 1656. 8vo, later calf; rebacked with old spine laid down, extremities rubbed. Title border cropped at lower margin. Ck May 8 (33) £950

Greek Anthology

— Anthologia epigrammatura graecorum libri VII.... Florence: Francisci de Alopa Venetus, 11 Aug 1494. 4to, mor gilt with the arms of John, 3d Duke of Roxburghe. 28 lines; types 5:11Gk (text) Z& 5:116R (dedication). Some dampstaining in a few margins. 280 leaves. Goff A-765. Roxburghe copy. C Nov 27 (4) £19,000 [Turner]

Anr Ed. Venice: Aldus, Nov 1503. ("Florilegium diversorum epigrammatum in septem libros.") 8vo, mor gilt. Greek type. Margins stained. C June 24 (260) £2,500 [Pregliasco]

Greeks...

— The Greeks: A Poem. L, 1817. 17th Ed. Illus by George Cruikshank. 12mo, calf gilt; joints worn. With 6 hand-colored plates. sg Oct 17 (163) $325

Greeley, Horace, 1811-72

— The American Conflict. Hartford, 1865-66. 2 vols. 8vo, orig mor gilt; extremities worn. sg Dec 5 (57) $90

Greely, Adolphus Washington, 1844-1935

— Three Years of Arctic Service. An Account of the Lady Franklin Bay Expedition.... NY, 1886. 1st Ed. 2 vols. 8vo, recent half calf gilt. DW Nov 6 (48) £75

Anr copy. Pictorial cloth; worn. Inscr to Ambrose Swasey & with pencilled note from Swasey telling how he met Greely. O May 26 (74) $170

Anr copy. Pictorial cloth; stained. sg Oct 17 (14) $110

Anr copy. Contemp mor bds; modern spines. W July 8 (250) £100

Green, Anna Katharine

— The Leavenworth Case. NY, 1878. 1st Ed. 8vo, orig cloth; rubbed. "Ellery Queen"-Epstein copy. sg Apr 29 (192) $2,800

Green, Calvin —&
Wells, Seth Y.

— A Summary View of the Millenial Church.... Albany, 1823. 12mo, contemp half calf; rubbed. Some dampstaining. O Jan 14 (179) $80

Green, F. H.

— Old English Clocks: being a Collector's Observations.... Ditchling: St. Dominic's Press, 1931. One of 300. 4to, half cloth, in d/j. cb Dec 5 (61) $250

Green, J. F.

— Ocean Birds. L, 1887. Folio, cloth. With 6 colored plates. DW Oct 2 (142) £50

Green, John Richard, 1837-83

— A Short History of the English People. L, 1892-94. 4 vols. 8vo, contemp half mor gilt. bba Oct 10 (378) £130 [Lobo]

Green, Mowbray A.

— The Eighteenth Century Architecture of Bath. Bath, 1904. One of 500. 4to, orig cloth; rubbed. bba Sept 19 (198) £120 [Camden Books]

Green, William, 1761-1823

— The Tourist's New Guide Containing a Description of...Cumberland, Westmoreland, and Lancashire. Kendal, 1819. 2 vols. 8vo, old half calf; spine on Vol I becoming detached. With folding map & 60 plates. wd Dec 12 (399) $200

Greenaway, Kate, 1846-1901

— Almanack for 1884. L: Routledge, [1883]. 24mo, syn. K Mar 22 (161) $140

— Almanack for 1887. L: Routledge, [1886]. 24mo, syn. K Mar 22 (162) $95

Anr copy. 32mo, orig half cloth; soiled. NH Aug 23 (234) $60

Anr copy. 24mo, orig bds, in orig ptd envelope; minor soiling. Inscr to Mrs Locker Lampson. wa Mar 5 (594) $850

— Almanack for 1894. L: Routledge, [1893]. 32mo, orig syn. K Mar 22 (163) $110

— Almanack for 1895. L, [1894]. 24mo, orig cloth. NH Aug 23 (235) $175

— Almanacks for 1883-1897. L: Routledge, [1882-96]. 13 vols issued to 1895 plus the Almanack & Diary for 1897. 12mo & 24mo, various bdgs. wa Mar 5 (595) $2,400

— [Almanacs for 1883-1895]. L, 1882-94. 16 vols, including variant bdgs. 12mo & 24mo, orig bdgs. With 3 vols inscr to Miss Vyvyan. Herschel Jones copies. P June 17 (223) $3,250

— A Apple Pie. L: Routledge, [1886]. Oblong 4to, orig half cloth; bumped. b Nov 18 (64) £50; bba Oct 10 (67) £90 [Ginnan]

— A Day in a Child's Life. L: Routledge, [1881]. 1st Ed. 4to, orig half cloth; rubbed & soiled. Some foxing. bba July 23 (224) £55 [Ginnan]

— Kate Greenaway's Album. L: Routledge, [1888? Unpbd]. One of 8 (all ptd). 16mo, orig color-ptd wraps; spine chipped & strengthened, extremities rubbed. Gribbel-Manney copy. P Oct 11 (154) $7,500

— Kate Greenaway Pictures from Originals Presented...to John Ruskin.... L, 1921. 4to, half cloth in worn d/j. kh Nov 11 (108) A$280

Anr copy. Cloth, in chipped d/j. sg Oct 17 (261) $100

Anr copy. Cloth, in torn d/j. sg Oct 17 (262) $150

Anr copy. Cloth. sg Jan 30 (80) $300

— Language of Flowers. L: Routledge, [1884]. 1st Ed. 12mo, orig half cloth; rubbed. bba Dec 19 (80) £70 [Ginnan]; bba July 23 (68) £50 [Sotheran]

Anr copy. Bds. cb Sept 5 (43) $65

Anr copy. Syn; worn & soiled. sg Oct 17 (259) $250

1st Issue. Bds; rubbed. cb Sept 5 (42) $110

6th Issue. Orig half cloth. pnE Oct 2 (436) £50

— Marigold Garden. L, [1885]. 1st Ed. 4to, orig half cloth; rubbed. bba Feb 27 (366) £85 [Ginnan]; pnE Oct 2 (388) £75

Anr copy. Pictorial bds; corners worn,

hinges tender. sg Oct 17 (260) $90

— Mother Goose, or the Old Nursery Rhymes. L: Routledge, [1881]. 1st Ed, 2d Issue. 8vo, orig cloth; soiled. bba July 23 (69) £130 [Subun-So]

Anr copy. Orig cloth, in d/j; soiled. cb Sept 5 (44) $120

— Under the Window. L: Routledge, [1878]. 1st Ed, 1st Issue. 4to, half cloth. bba Dec 19 (78) £130 [Ginnan]

Issue not stated. Half cloth. bba Dec 19 (79) £75 [Ginnan]

Anr copy. Half cloth; extemities rubbed. cb Sept 26 (96) $50

1st American Ed. NY: Routledge, [1880?]. 4to, orig half cloth; worn. K Mar 22 (164) $100; NH Oct 6 (144) $135

Greenaway, Kate, 1846-1901 —& Crane, Walter, 1845-1915

— The Quiver of Love; a Collection of Valentines.... L, 1876. 4to, orig cloth; worn. With chromolitho title & 4 mtd color plates only. bba July 23 (233) £60 [Ginnan]

Greene, Graham

See also: Glover & Greene

— Babbling April. Oxford, 1925. Orig ptd bds, in soiled d/j. Vivienne Greene's copy. S Dec 12 (63) £1,200 [Hawthorn Books]

— The Bear Fell Free. L, 1935. One of 285. Orig cloth, in d/j with small holes along foldline. S Nov 14 (638) £550 [Kassam]

Anr copy. Orig cloth. sg Dec 12 (139) $700

— Brighton Rock. L, 1938. 1st English Ed. In chipped d/j. W Mar 6 (55) £3,400

— A Burnt-Out Case. L, 1961. 1st English Ed. In d/j. Inscr to his wife & with Ls to her about criticisms she made of the book. S Dec 12 (81) £550 [Gekoski]

— Carving a Statue. L, 1964. In d/j. Inscr to his wife. S Dec 12 (84) £400 [Gekoski]

— The Complaisant Lover. L, 1959. 1st Ed. In spotted d/j. Inscr to his wife. S Dec 12 (79) £500 [Pieraccini]

— Doctor Fischer of Geneva.... L, 1980. 1st Ed. In d/j. Greene's own copy, with holograph corrections. S Dec 12 (92) £900 [Rocklin]

— The End of the Affair. L, [1951]. In soiled d/j. Inscr to his wife. S Dec 12 (72) £2,600 [Rocklin]

— The Heart of the Matter. L, [1948]. In def d/j. Vivien Greene's copy. S Dec 12 (71) £500 [Englehardt]

— How Father Quixote Became a Monsignor. Los Angeles, 1980. Ltd Ed. 4to, cloth. wa Dec 9 (190) $80

— In Search of a Character.... L, 1961. In soiled d/j. Inscr to his wife. S Dec 12 (82) £400 [Gekoski]

Anr Ed. NY, [1961]. One of 600. Half cloth. pba July 9 (112) $70

— The Lawless Roads. L, 1939. 1st Ed. In frayed d/j. Inscr to his wife. S Dec 12 (68) £1,900 [Maggs]

1st American Ed. NY, 1939. ("Another Mexico.") In d/j. pba July 9 (110) $300

— Loser Takes All. L, 1955. 1st Ed. In soiled d/j. Inscr to his wife. S Dec 12 (73) £1,000 [Pieraccini]

— The Lost Childhood and other Essays. L, 1951. Cloth, in d/j. Inscr to his wife. Below inscr is photograph of Greene as a boy, with caption in Vivien Greene's hand repeating the information in Greene's mother's hand on verso of photograph. S Dec 12 (75) £1,050 [Hitchcock]

— The Man Within. L, 1929. 1st Ed. In d/j. CNY June 9 (78) $550

Anr copy. In d/j. Manney copy. P Oct 11 (155) $2,750

Anr copy. In 2 d/js, 1 soiled. pn June 11 (194) £1,100

Anr copy. In stained & soiled d/j. Inscr to his wife. S Dec 12 (64) £12,000 [Maggs]

Anr copy. In chipped d/j. W Mar 6 (52) £740

1st American Ed. NY, 1929. In d/j. Inscr to his wife as Mrs. Pooze. S Dec 12 (65) £1,200 [Gekoski]

— May We Borrow Your Husband? L, 1967. One of 500. Half cloth. Inscr to his wife on a letterhead loosely inserted. S Dec 12 (85) £500 [Gekoski]; wa Sept 26 (173) $130

— The Name of Action. L, 1930. 1st Ed. Some spotting. pn Sept 12 (152) £90 [Virgo Books]

Anr copy. In soiled & torn d/j. Inscr to his wife. S Dec 12 (67) £10,500 [Maggs]

Anr copy. In chipped d/j. W Mar 6 (53) £960

— Nineteen Stories. L, 1947. In spotted d/j with a few small tears. Inscr to his wife & with his holograph corrections & her note. S Dec 12 (70) £1,000 [Gekoski]

— Our Man in Havana. L, 1958. In soiled d/j. Inscr to his wife. S Dec 12 (78) £1,150 [Blackwell]

— The Potting Shed. NY, 1957. 1st Ed. In d/j. Inscr to his wife. S Dec 12 (76) £1,000 [Englehardt]

1st English Ed. L, 1958. In frayed d/j. Inscr to his wife & with several deletions in his hand & a note by her. S Dec 12 (77) £500 [Gekoski]

— The Power and the Glory. L, 1940. 1st Ed. In d/j. Epstein copy. sg Apr 29 (198) $1,500

Anr copy. In chipped d/j. W Mar 6 (56) £1,000

Anr Ed. NY: Viking, [1940]. ("The Labyrinthine Ways.") In d/j. Dedication copy, inscr to his wife. S Dec 12 (69) £4,500 [Quaritch]

— The Quiet American. L, [1955]. Orig cloth, in d/j. Inscr to his wife. S Dec 12 (74) £1,400 [Gekoski]

— The Return of A. J. Raffles. L, 1975. One of 250. Bds, in d/j. Inscr to his wife. S Dec 12 (86) £700 [Gekoski]

— A Sense of Reality. L, 1963. 1st Ed. In d/j. Inscr to his wife. S Dec 12 (83) £400 [Gekoski]

— Stamboul Train. L, 1932. 1st Ed. bba Jan 16 (191) £50 [Crabtree]

— Travels with My Aunt. L, 1969. 1st Ed. In torn d/j. Inscr to Ernest Stoffberg, 1973. Ck Oct 18 (245) £200

— A Visit to Morin. L, [1959]. 1st Ed in English, one of 250. In stained & soiled d/j. Inscr to John Lehmann, Christmas 1960. S Nov 14 (569) £420 [Hosking]

Anr copy. In scuffed d/j. Inscr to his wife. S Dec 12 (80) £500 [Gekoski]

— Ways of Escape. Toronto: Lester & Orpen Dennys, [1980]. One of 150. S Feb 11 (404) £200 [Sanderson]

Greene's copy, Graham

— Waugh, Evelyn. - Put Out More Flags. L, 1942. In torn & repaired d/j. Sgd by Greene on front free endpaper. S Dec 12 (100) £850 [Blackwell]

Greene, William Thomas

— Parrots in Captivity. L, 1884-87. Vols I-III. Cloth. With 81 hand-finished color plates. Lacking the 9 supplementary plates. bba Sept 5 (141) £1,300 [Shapero]

Anr copy. Later cloth. Lacking the 9 supplementary plates. Library markings. bba Sept 5 (142) £850 [Rostron]

Anr copy. Vol I only. Later cloth; rubbed. With 27 hand-finished color plates. DW Oct 2 (143) £520

Anr copy. Vol III (of 3) only. 8vo, orig cloth; spines worn. With 27 colored plates. DW Nov 6 (164) £400

Anr copy. Vols I-III. Orig cloth; worn, hinges broken, library labels inside front covers. With 81 hand-finished color plates. Library markings; accession numbers on versos of titles. pn Mar 19 (220) £1,300 [L'Aquaforte]

Greenewalt, Crawford H.

— Hummingbirds. Garden City, [1960]. One of 500. 4to, cloth. With 70 mtd color photos. cb Dec 119 (70) $80

Anr copy. Cloth, in worn & repaired d/j. With 69 mtd colored plates. NH Aug 23 (69) $105

Anr copy. Cloth, in torn d/j. O Dec 17 (87) $70

Anr copy. Cloth; worn. With 68 mtd color photos. O Dec 17 (88) $50

Anr copy. Cloth; soiled. With 69 mtd colored plates. sg Nov 14 (180) $110

Anr copy. Cloth, in d/j. sg May 14 (217) $500

Greenfield, John

— A Compleat Treatise of the Stone and Gravel.... L, 1710. 8vo, contemp calf; spine def, covers detached. With 23 plates, 3 folding. S Feb 25 (591) £260 [Philips]

Greenhow, Robert T., 1800-54

— Memoir, Historical and Political, on the Northwest Coast of North America.... L, 1844. ("The History of Oregon and California....") 1st English Ed. 8vo, half calf; front hinge cracked. With folding map mtd on linen. With errata slip. sg June 18 (261) $225

Anr copy. Half calf; def. With folding map, torn along folds. Library stamp on tp. sg June 18 (262) $70

Greenwood, Charles & John

— Atlas of the Counties of England. L, 1834. Folio, maps segmented & mtd on cloth & contained in 4 contemp calf boxes; worn. With hand-colored engraved title & 46 hand-colored double-page maps. C Oct 30 (152) £900 [Traylen]

Greenwood, James, d.1737

— The London Vocabulary, English and Latin.... L, 1791. 20th Ed. 12mo, contemp cloth; rubbed & worn. Some foxing; small dampstain at inner corner. wa Apr 9 (216) $75

Greenwood, James, 1832-1929

— The Hatchet Throwers. L, 1866. 1st Ed. Illus by Ernest Griset. 4to, cloth; hinge broken. With 36 hand-colored illusts (some half-page). With orig pencil drawing by Griset taped to front endpapers. rs Oct 17 (36A) $425

— The Purgatory of Peter the Cruel. L & NY, 1868. 1st Ed. Illus by Ernest Griset. 4to, later calf; joints split, worn. With 36 hand-colored plates. bba Apr 30 (350) £80 [Thorp]

Greenwood, Robert

— California Imprints, 1833-1862. Los Gatos, 1961. One of 750. In d/j. pba July 23 (206) $90

Greg, Robert Hyde, 1795-1875

— Remarks on the Site of Troy.... Manchester, 1823. 4to, contemp calf. With folding map. Inscr to his son Arthur. Sold with the autograph Ms for the work. S July 1 (616) £1,900 [Atabey]

Greg, Sir Walter Wilson, 1875-1959

— A Bibliography of the English Printed Drama to the Restoration. L, 1939-59. 4 vols. 4to, orig half cloth; 1st 2 vols browned. bba Dec 19 (271) £110 [Hay Cinema]

Anr copy. Orig half cloth; rubbed. bbc Sept 23 (95) $90

Anr copy. Orig half cloth; worn. O Sept 24 (104) $100

Gregg, Josiah, 1806-50?

— Commerce of the Prairies, or the Journal of.... NY, 1844. 1st Ed, Mixed Issue. 2 vols. 12mo, orig cloth; worn. With 2 maps & 6 plates. Minor dampstaining. sg Dec 5 (110) $275

Grego, Joseph, 1843-1908

— Cruikshank's Water Colours. L, 1903. One of 300. 4to, orig cloth. DW Dec 11 (343) £100

Gregoras, Nicephoros, 1295-1359 —& Chalcondylas, Laonicus

— Romanae, hoc est byzantinae historiae libri xi.... Basel: Johannes Oporinus, 1562. 2 parts in 1 vol. Folio, contemp pigskin over pastebd; front hinge cracked, front free endpaper def. Some dampstaining on opening leaves, with resulting paper cracks causing slight loss. sg Oct 24 (138) $200

Gregory, Augustus Charles & Francis Thomas

— Journals of Australian Explorations. Brisbane, 1884. 8vo, orig cloth. S June 25 (247) £950 [Arnold]

Gregory IX, Pope, 1147?-1241

— Decretales. Mainz: Peter Schoeffer, 23 Nov 1473. Folio, contemp calf over wooden bds, bound by the Carthusians of Nuremberg (Kyriss shop 23).; rebacked, clasps missing, some scoring of lea. Types 5:118G (decretals, colophon, commendatory verse), 6:92G (gloss), 2 columns with commentary surround, 81 lines of commentary; rubricated. Although on paper, this exceptionally tall copy corresponds in its particulars to the BL and Morgan vellum copies. 305 leaves. Goff G-447. Doheny-Schoyen copy. P Dec 12 (25) $19,000

Anr Ed. Nuremberg: Anton Koberger, 10 Mar 1493. Folio, contemp calf over wooden bds; a vellum leaf pasted inside lower cover with recipes for the colic & the stone & documents relating to the parish church of Hanwell & to the monastery of St. Mary at Wroxton, dated between 1491 & 1528. Foremargins of 1st 11 & last 12 leaves extended; tear in L1-M3 with loss of text in each leaf (supplied in Ms); some stains. 384 (of 386) leaves; lacking a1 & BB8. Goff G-470. S May 28 (24) £1,750 [Burns]

Gregory, John Walter, 1864-1932

— The Great Rift Valley. L, 1896. 1st Ed. 8vo, orig cloth. sg Jan 9 (82) $300

Gregory XIII, Pope, 1502-85

[-] Tomar grigoreann yawitenakan. Rome: Domenico Basa, 1584. 4to, old vellum. In Armenian. With arms of Gregory XIII on title; half-page woodcut of the Last Supper on last leaf recto. Some foxing. sg May 7 (113) $4,600

Gregynog Press—Newtown, Wales

— [Ecclesiastes] Llyfr y Pregeth-wr. 1927. One of 25 specially bound. S July 22 (338) £600 [Sunderland]

One of 223. pnE Oct 2 (450) £130

— The Lamentations of Jeremiah. 1933. One of 15 specially bound. S July 22 (359) £1,300 [Marks]

One of 250. Ck Sept 6 (116) £200

Anr copy. Orig mor. Ck July 10 (322) £380; pnE Oct 2 (464) £400; S July 22 (360) £800 [Sunderland]

— Psalmau Dafydd.... 1929. One of 25 specially bound. S July 21 (343) £620 [Breen]

— The Revelation of St. John the Divine. 1932. One of 250. b Nov 18 (12) £480

Anr copy. Orig calf. pn Nov 14 (335) £800; S July 22 (354) £580 [Marriott]; S July 22 (355) £500 [Uechti]

— Abercrombie, Lascelles. - Lyrics and Unfinished Poems. 1940. One of 20 specially bound. S July 22 (375) £600 [Grossland]

One of 175. pn Nov 14 (328) £140 [Quaritch]; pnE Oct 2 (471) £100

— Aesop. - Fables. 1931. One of 25 specially bound. S July 21 (348) £2,000 [Rosner]

One of 250. pnE Oct 2 (457) £720; S July 22 (350) £750 [Lindseth]; S July 22 (351) £650 [Bankes Chandor]

Out-of-series copy. With inscr by Thomas Jones stating that the colophon in this copy is in orig state. S July 22 (349) £950 [Quaritch]

— Blunt, Lady Anne & Blunt, Wilfrid Scawen. - The Celebrated Romance of the Stealing of the Mare. 1930. One of 25 specially bound. S July 21 (344) £650 [Barnitt]

One of 275. b Mar 11 (143) £180

Anr copy. Inscr to Jelly D'Aranyi by Gwendoline P. Davies & Margaret S.

Davies, founders of the Press. Ck Dec 11 (128) £320; Ck July 10 (188) £220

— BRIDGES, ROBERT. - Eros and Psyche. 1935. One of 15 specially bound. S July 22 (364) £750 [Marks]

One of 300. pnE Oct 2 (468) £240

Anr copy. With Ls on Gregynog letterhead to Graily Hewitt. sg Jan 30 (82) $750

— BUTLER, SAMUEL. - Erewhon. 1932. One of 25 specially bound. S July 22 (353) £950 [Barnitt]

One of 300. bba Apr 30 (351) £60 [McMinn]

— DAVIES, WILLIAM HENRY. - Selected Poems. 1928. One of 310. b Nov 18 (15) £55

— EURIPIDES. - The Eight Plays. 1931. One of 500. 2 vols Ck July 10 (245) £160; DW Dec 11 (475) £95

Anr copy. 2 vols. pnE Oct 2 (456) £110

— FORTESCUE, SIR JOHN WILLIAM. - The Story of a Red-Deer. 1935. One of 15 specially bound. S July 22 (366) £500 [Kay]

One of 250. pn Nov 14 (330) £50

— GREVILLE, FULKE. - Caelica. 1936. One of 15 specially bound. S July 22 (367) £700 [Barnitt]

— GRUFFYDD, W. J. - Caniadau. 1932. One of 25 specially bound. S July 22 (352) £650 [Barrie Marks]

— HABERLY, LOYD. - Anne Boleyn and Other Poems. 1934. One of 300. pnE Oct 2 (466) £60

— HARTZENBUSCH, JUAN EUGENIO. - The Lovers of Teruel. 1938. One of 20 specially bound. S July 22 (370) £800 [Rasan]

— HERBERT OF CHERBURY, EDWARD. - Autobiography. 1928. One of 300. DW Apr 8 (424) £150; pnE Oct 2 (453) £75; sg Sept 26 (127) $80

— JOINVILLE, JEAN. - The History of Saint Louis. 1937. One of 15 specially bound. S July 22 (368) £2,600 [Maggs]

One of 200. S July 22 (369) £650 [Lehrer]

— JONES, THOMAS GWYNN. - Elphin Lloyd Jones. 1929. cb Oct 17 (482) $60

— LAMB, CHARLES. - Elia and the Last Essays of Elia. 1929-30. One of 25 specially bound. 2 vols. pnE Oct 2 (454) £380; S July 21 (345) £650 [Barnitt]

One of 285. pn Nov 14 (332) £100

— MADARIAGA, SALVADOR DE. - Don Quixote, an Introductory Essay in Psychology. 1934. One of 15 specially bound. S July 22 (361) £500 [Barnitt]

— MILTON, JOHN. - Comus.... 1931. One of 25 specially bound. Orig lev by Blair Hughes-Stanton. Ck July 10 (367) £400; S July 21 (347) £850 [Grossland]

Anr Ed. 1934. One of 250. b Nov 18 (17) £180

— MILTON, JOHN. - Four Poems. 1933. One of 250. Orig calf tooled in blind on upper cover. Library stamp on tp verso. Ck Oct 18 (246) £95; pn Nov 14 (333) £200; pnE Oct 2 (462) £160

— PEACOCK, THOMAS LOVE. - The Misfortunes of Elphin. 1928. One of 25 specially bound. S July 21 (341) £650 [Barnitt]

— SAMPSON, JOHN. - XXI Welsh Gypsy Folk-Tales. 1933. One of 15 specially bound. S July 22 (357) £800 [Marks]

One of 250. b Mar 11 (145) £100; pnE Oct 2 (463) £250

— SHAW, GEORGE BERNARD. - Shaw Gives Himself Away. 1939. One of 25 specially bound. S July 22 (371) £800 [Marks]

— THOMAS, EDWARD. - Selected Poems. 1927. One of 25 specially bound. S July 22 (337) £480 [Grossland]

One of 275. bba June 25 (61) £90 [Cox]

— VANSITTART, ROBERT. - The Singing Caravan. 1932. One of 250. bba June 25 (62) £60 [Cox]; DW May 13 (442) £65; O Jan 14 (86) $60

— VAUGHAN, HENRY. - Poems. 1924. One of 500. b Nov 18 (22) £110

— VEGA CARPIO, LOPE FELIX DE. - The Star of Seville. 1935. One of 175. pnE Oct 2 (467) £130

— WYNNE, ELLIS. - Gweledigaethau y Bardd Cwsc. 1940. One of 20 specially bound. S July 22 (373) £700 [Sunderland]

One of 175. pnE Oct 2 (470) £110

— XENOPHON. - Cyropaedia. 1936. One of 15 specially bound. S July 22 (365) £1,700 [Maggs]

Greig, John. See: Storer & Greig

Grelot, Guillaume Joseph

— Relation nouvelle d'un voyage de Constantinople. Paris, 1680. 4to, contemp calf; rubbed, spine worn. With 13 plates, 7 plans, 10 folding or double-page. Some tears. S June 30 (312) £600 [Keskiner]

1st Ed. 4to, contemp calf; worn. With 13 plates & plans (3 detached, short slit to 1 fold). b June 22 (171) £500

Anr copy. Contemp calf gilt; worn. With panorama & 4 (of 12) plates. Panorama creased & torn. Spotted & soiled throughout. DW Oct 2 (36) £55

Anr copy. Contemp calf. With 13 mostly folding plates & 4 engraved illusts. A few tears & wax stains. S June 30 (141) £2,400 [Consolidated Real]

Greville, Charles C. F., 1794-1865

— Greville Memoirs. L, 1874-87. Ed by Henry Reeve. 8 vols. 8vo, half mor gilt by Hatchards; joints scuffed. wa Dec 9 (7) $200

Greville, Fulke, Baron Brooke, 1554-1628. See: Gregynog Press

Greville, Robert Kaye, 1794-1866

— Scottish Cryptogamic Flora. Edin. [1822]-23-28. 6 vols. 8vo, contemp half mor; rubbed. With 360 hand-colored plates. 1 plate torn. Library markings. bba Sept 5 (54) £420 [Elliott]

Grew, Nehemiah, 1641-1712

— The Anatomy of Vegetables Begun. L, 1672. 1st Ed. 8vo, contemp calf; rubbed, joints split. With 3 folding plates. Some spotting. S May 14 (1034) £350 [Porter]

— The Comparative Anatomy of Trunks.... L, 1675. 1st Ed. 8vo, contemp calf; upper joint cracked, spine ends def. With 19 plates, all but 1 folding. 8 leaves misbound. C Oct 30 (266) £700 [Heuer]

Grey, Sir George, 1812-98

— Journals of Two Expeditions of Discovery in North-West and Western Australia.... L, 1841. 2 vols. 8vo, contemp calf gilt; rebacked, rubbed. With 22 plates, 6 hand-colored & with 2 folding maps in pocket at end of Vol II. Marginalia in pencil; lacking ad leaves. bba June 11 (344) £500 [Woodstock]

Grey, William. See: White, William F.

Grey, Zane, 1875-1939

— The Last of the Plainsmen. NY, 1908. Cloth; worn, a few plates loose. Inscr by the book's subject, C. J. Jones, & by Grey. sg June 11 (133) $350

— The Maverick Queen. NY: Harper, [1950]. In d/j. K Mar 22 (167) $60

— Raiders of Spanish Peaks. NY: Grosset & Dunlap, [n.d.]. In d/j. Sgd on front endpaper. wa Dec 9 (191) $80

— Tales of Fishing Virgin Seas. NY & L, 1925. 4to, cloth. sg May 21 (41) $175

— Tales of Fresh-Water Fishing. NY & L, 1928. 4to, cloth, in d/j. sp Feb 6 (388) $240

— Tales of Swordfish and Tuna. NY, 1927. 1st Ed. 4to, cloth; hinges splitting. cb Dec 12 (64) $80; Met Apr 28 (399) $70

— Tales of Tahitian Waters. NY, 1931. In chipped d/j. cb Dec 12 (65) $350

Anr copy. African goatskin with lea onlay design of tropical fish among exotic ocean plants. sg May 7 (114) $1,500

— Tales of the Angler's Eldorado, New Zealand. NY & L, 1926. 4to, cloth. cb Sept 19 (76) $180

Gribble, Ernest. See: Cescinsky & Gribble

Griffin, John, 1769-1834

— Memoirs of Captain James Wilson. Bost., 1822. 1st American Ed. 12mo, contemp sheep. With frontis. Pages dampstained. cb Jan 30 (136) $90

Griffin, Richard, Baron Braybrooke

— The History of Audley End.... L, 1836. Folio, contemp calf gilt, armorial bdg; upper joint weak. With engraved title & 18 plates. b Mar 11 (192) £60

Griffith, Charles

— The Present State and Prospects of the Port Phillip District of New South Wales. Dublin, 1845. 8vo, contemp half calf. With frontis. S June 25 (135) £300 [Quaritch]

Griffiths, Arthur George Frederick, 1838-1908

— Memorials of Millbank, and Chapters on Prison History. L, 1875. 2 vols. 8vo, orig cloth; hinges weak. bba Apr 30 (9) £110 [Bickersteth]

Grighor, Abu al-Faraj

— Historia compendiosa dynastiorum.... Oxford, 1663. 3 parts in 1 vol. 4to, early vellum, armorial bdg. Small holes & 20th-cent writing on tp; small piece missing from terminal blank. wa Mar 5 (467) $170

Grijalva, Juan de

— The Discovery of New Spain in 1518.... Berkeley: Cortes Society, 1942. One of 200. Ed by Henry Raup Wagner. sg Dec 5 (261) $110

Grile, Dod. See: Bierce, Ambrose

Grillandus, Paulus

— Tractatus de hereticis et sortilegiis omnifariam coitu eorumque penis. Lyons: Jacobus Giunta, 1547. 8vo, old limp vellum; loose. Some browning; blank lower margin excised from title; old institutional stamp on tp verso. sg Mar 12 (217) $750

Grilli, Elise

— The Art of the Japanese Screen. NY, [1970]. In torn & chipped d/j. sg Feb 6 (111) $150

Grillparzer, Franz, 1791-1872

— Der arme Spielmann. Vienna, 1915. One of 50. 4to, orig mor gilt. HH May 12 (2556) DM3,200

Grimble, Augustus

— The Deer Forests of Scotland. L, 1896. Ltd Ed. Illus by Archibald Thorburn. 4to, half cloth. With 8 plates. b Mar 11 (227) £65

— Deer-Stalking and the Deer Forests of Scotland. L, 1888. 2d Ed, One of 250. 4to, orig bds; worn & stained. L Nov 14 (186) £90

Anr Ed. L, 1901. 4to, half vellum gilt; soiled. bba Nov 28 (89) £90 [Hereward Bks]

— The Salmon Rivers of Scotland. L, 1899-1900. Ltd Ed. 4 vols. 4to, orig bds; worn. S Nov 15 (738) £200 [Graham]

— The Salmon Rivers of Ireland. L, 1903. One of 250. 2 vols. 4to, orig half vellum; spotted. L Nov 14 (188) £160

— Shooting and Salmon Fishing.... L, 1902. 4to, orig bds; stained. Some spotting, mainly to text; 1 plate with stained margin. L Nov 14 (187) £90

Grimm Brothers

See also: Limited Editions Club

— Fairy Tales. L, 1900. Illus by Arthur Rackham. Later half mor. bba Apr 9 (280) £240 [Sotheran]

Anr Ed. L, 1909. 4to, orig cloth. bba Jan 16 (386) £220 [Frew MacKenzie]

Anr copy. Orig cloth; soiled & worn, lower third of spine missing. With 40 tipped-in color plates. W July 8 (317) £85

Deluxe Ed, One of 750. 4to, orig vellum gilt; spine head nicked. With 40 tipped-in colored plates. b Nov 18 (98) £890

Anr Ed. NY, 1909. 4to, mor gilt by Zaehnsdorf. Sgd & dated by Rackham, 23 Nov 1909. P Oct 11 (261) $1,800

— German Popular Stories. L, 1834. Illus by George Cruikshank. 2 vols. 8vo, contemp calf; rubbed & dampstained. Foxed; 1st 4 pages of Vol II dampstained. W July 8 (318) £60

— Hansel and Gretel and Other Tales. L, 1920. Illus by Arthur Rackham. 4to, orig cloth, in d/j. With 20 colored plates. bba Apr 9 (331) £220 [W. White]

Anr Ed. Garden City, 1923. 4to, orig cloth; spine faded. cb Dec 5 (90) $350

— Hansel and Gretel. L, [1925]. One of 600. Illus by Kay Nielsen. Orig cloth; rubbed. Some spotting. Manney copy. P Oct 11 (243) $2,750

Anr Ed. NY, [1925]. Orig cloth; spine & edges of covers soiled. S July 22 (426) £800 [Joseph]

Anr copy. Half cloth. sg Sept 25 (244) $1,200

— Household Stories. L, 1882. Trans by Lucy Crane; illus by Walter Crane. 8vo, orig cloth; rubbed. bba July 23 (234) £65 [Stevenson]

— Little Brother and Little Sister. L, [1917]. Illus by Arthur Rackham. 4to, orig cloth. bba Jan 16 (387) £170 [Gleeson]

Anr copy. Orig cloth, in d/j. bba Apr 9 (330) £420 [W. White]

Anr Ed. NY: Dodd, Mead,. [n.d.]. 4to, orig cloth; worn. Frontis creased. cb Sept 5 (88) $75

— Snowdrop and other Tales. L, 1920. Illus by Arthur Rackham. Orig cloth, in tape-repaired d/j. With 20 colored plates. bba Apr 9 (332) £280 [Fox]

Grimm, Herman Friedrich, 1828-1901

— Life of Michael Angelo. Bost., 1890. 2 vols in 4. 8vo, half mor gilt. Extra-illus with c.167 plates. sg Mar 5 (189) $475

Grimwade, Arthur Girling

— London Goldsmiths, 1697-1837.... L, 1976. In d/j. sg Apr 2 (131) $60

Grindlay, Robert Melville

— Scenery, Costumes and Architecture, Chiefly on the Western Side of India. L, 1826-30. 2 vols. 4to, 19th-cent calf gilt. With engraved title with hand-colored vignette & 36 hand-colored plates. Lacking litho title to Vol II & both contents leaves; 1 plate laid down. C Oct 30 (37) £3,000 [Hollin]

Anr Ed. L, 1830. Folio, contemp mor gilt; joints & extremities worn. With engraved title with hand-colored vignette & 36 hand-colored plates. bba Sept 19 (87) £1,500 [Russell]

Anr copy. Recent half mor gilt. C May 20 (67) £2,700 [Joseph]

Anr copy. Contemp half calf gilt; worn, backstrip def. Inner margin of frontis strengthened; some text leaves repaired; tp grubby with old library stamp; some soiling to outer plate margins. L Nov 14 (143) £2,000

Grinnell, George Bird, 1849-1938

See also: Roosevelt & Grinnell

— American Big Game in its Haunts. NY, 1904. Ed by Grinnell. Bdg worn & shaken. Koopman copy. O Oct 29 (146) $160

— The Cheyenne Indians: Their History and Ways of Life. New Haven, 1923. 2 vols. Cloth. sg Dec 5 (112) $140

Anr copy. Cloth; rubbed, marked & soiled, ring stain to 1 rear bd. Crease & fraying to margin of 1 leaf. wa Dec 9 (310) $120

— The Indians of Today. Chicago & NY, 1900. Folio, orig cloth; rubbed, hinges cracked. Some old stain along bottom margin; tear to 1 plate. bbc Feb 17 (259) $360

Grinnell, Joseph, 1877-1939 —& Storer, Tracy

— Animal Life in the Yosemite. Berkeley, 1924. Cloth; shaken, institutional bookplate & card pocket. With 60 plates, 12 of them in color. sg May 14 (218) $150

Griset, Ernest
— Griset's Grotesques, or Jokes Drawn on Wood.... L, 1867. 4to, orig cloth; rubbed. bba May 14 (361) £50 [Ginnan]

Grisetti, Pietro. See: Scorza & Grisetti

Grishanin, V. C. See: Zbinevich & Grishanin

Grisier, Augustin
— Les armes et le duel. Paris, 1847. 8vo, mor gilt with Imperial Russian arms. sg Mar 26 (135) $375

Grisone, Federico
— Ordini di cavalcare, et modi di conoscere le nature de' cavalli.... Pesaro: Bartolomeo Cesano, 1557. 4to, old vellum; spine def at head & foot. With 50 full-page woodcuts. Small wormhole in inner margin of first few leaves; some dampstains. S May 28 (47) £900 [Horsemans]

Griswold, Frank Gray, 1854-1937
— Sport on Land and Water. [N.p.]: Plimpton Press, 1913-19. 4 vols. Lea; rubbed. Inscr. cb Oct 25 (47) $100

Groce, George C. See: New York...

Groenveldt, Joannes. See: Greenfield, John

Grohmann, Johann Gottfried
— Ideenmagazin fuer Liebhaber von Gaerten.... Leipzig, 1796-1806. Parts 1-48 bound in 9 vols & the continuation, Neue grosses Ideen-Magazine, Parts 1-12 (or 49-60) in 12 orig parts. 4to, half vellum or ptd wraps. Sold w.a.f. S Nov 21 (80) £2,300 [Shapero]

Grohmann, Will
— Kandinsky. Paris, 1931. One of 8 on japon imperial with orig drawing & sgd engraving. Orig wraps. P June 17 (245) $26,000
— Paul Klee. NY: Abrams, [n.d.]. 4to, cloth, in chipped d/j. sg Feb 6 (149) $110

Grolier Club—New York
— Catalogue of an Exhibition of Illuminated and Painted Manuscripts... 1892. One of 350. O May 26 (77) $80
— Catalogue of...English Writers from Langland to Wither*...Wither to Prior. 1963. 4 vols. O Dec 17 (90) $80
— A Description of the Early Printed Books owned by the Grolier Club... 1895. One of 400. cb Oct 17 (373) $55
— Facsimile of the Laws and Acts of the General Assembly...of New-York... 1894. One of 312. Ed by Robert Ludlow Fowler. sg Dec 5 (175) $130
— Gazette Francoise: A Facsimile Reprint of a Newspaper Printed at Newport on the Printing Press of the French Fleet... 1926. One of 300. O July 14 (89) $60
— One Hundred Books Famous in English Literature. Intro by George E. Woodberry Kent, H.W.-Bibliographical Notes on One Hundred Books... 1902-3. Each, One of 305. 2 vols. sg May 21 (225) $175
— One Hundred Books Famous in English Literature. 1902. One of 305. Intro by George E. Woodberry. bbc Sept 23 (97) $130
— One Hundred Influential American Books Printed Before 1900. 1947. One of 600. sg May 21 (227) $150
— Breslauer, Bernard & Folter, Roland. - Bibliography: its History and Development. 1984. One of 600. O Mar 31 (88) $60; O Apr 28 (170) $120; O July 14 (86) $50; sg May 21 (145) $140
— Bury, Richard de. - Philobiblon. 1889. One of 297. cb Oct 17 (362) $110
— Duerer, Albrecht. - Of the Just Shaping of Letters. 1917. One of 215. Bdg rubbed. cb Oct 31 (28) $225
— Fay, Bernard. - Notes on the American Press at the End of the Eighteenth Century... 1927. One of 325. O July 14 (88) $120
— Gilliss, Walter. - Recollections of the Gilliss Press and its Work during 50 years, 1869-1919. 1926. One of 300. Unopened copy. O May 26 (78) $60
— Goldschmidt, Lucien & Naef, Weston. - The Truthful Lens: a Survey of the Photographically Illustrated Book, 1844-1914. 1980. One of 1,000. O Dec 17 (91) $225
— Haebler, Konrad. - The Study of Incunabula... 1933. One of 350. cb Jan 16 (67) $160; O Dec 17 (92) $170
— Hart, Charles Henry. - Catalogue of the Engraved Portraits of George Washington. 1904. One of 425. 4to, half vellum bds, in worn & dampstained d/j. F Mar 26 (393) $130; K Sept 29 (434) $130
— Henderson, Robert W. - Early American Sport: a Chronological Check-list... 1937. One of 400. sg Jan 9 (263) $70
— Hoe, Robert. - A Lecture on Bookbinding as a Fine Art... 1886. One of 200. O May 26 (79) $170
— Horblit, Harrison D. - One Hundred Books Famous in Science. 1964. One of 1,000. bbc Sept 23 (96) $260; Ck Dec 12 (274) £320; O Sept 24 (107) $325; sg May 21 (237) $325

Anr copy. Inscr to William & Marianne Salloch. Ck Nov 1 (424) £280

— Kennedy, Edward Guthrie. - The Etched Work of Whistler. 1910. One of 402. Text vol & 3 portfolios. Half cloth; minor wear. O Sept 24 (108) $750
— Keynes, Sir Geoffrey. - A Bibliography of William Blake. 1921. One of 250. O May 26 (80) $375
— Keynes, Sir Geoffrey & Wolf, Edwin. -

William Blake's Illuminated Books. A Census. 1953. One of 400. O Sept 24 (109) $80

— KOEHLER, SYLVESTER ROSA. - A Chronological Catalogue of the Engravings, Dry-Points and Etchings of Albert Duerer. 1897. One of 400. O May 26 (81) $80

— LIVINGSTON, LUTHER SAMUEL. - Franklin and his Press at Passy. 1914. One of 300. sp Feb 6 (535) $80

— MORISON, STANLEY. - Fra Luca de Pacioli of Borgo S. Sepolcro. 1933. One of 390. O May 26 (82) $600; P June 18 (618) $800

— PICHON, JEROME. - The Life of Charles Henry Count Hoym. 1899. One of 303. O Aug 25 (95) $50; sg Oct 31 (120) $90

— RUZICKA, RUDOLPH. - New York. 1915. One of 250. wa Dec 9 (449) $550

— TORY, GEOFROY. - Champ Fleury. 1927. One of 390. Copy used to execute the Kraus reprint, with limitation & colophon pages marked to delete. K Sept 29 (415) $200; wd June 12 (390) $500

— WARREN, ARTHUR. - The Charles Whittinghams Printers. 1896. One of 385. Upper cover insect-damaged. O Feb 25 (92) $110

— WROTH, LAWRENCE C. - The Colonial Printer. 1931. One of 300. Bdg worn. O Dec 17 (94) $70

Grolier de Serviere, Nicolas, 1479-1565

— Recueil d'ouvrages curieux de mathematique et de mecanique.... Lyons, 1719. 1st Ed. 4to, contemp calf; spine repaired with adhesive tape. With 85 plates. Ck Nov 29 (189) £1,050

Gromort, Georges. See: Emerson & Gromort

Gronow, Rees Howell, 1794-1865

— Reminiscences: Being Anecdotes of the Camp, the Court, and the Clubs. L, 1889. ("The Reminiscences and Recollections: Anecdotes of Camp, Court, Clubs....") One of 870 with plates in 2 states. 2 vols. 8vo, contemp half mor; tips bumped & worn. wa Sept 26 (3) $325

Grooms, Red. See: Gross & Grooms

Groot, Constantin de

— Voor-Bereidselen tot de Bybelsche Wysheid.... Amst., 1690. 2 vols. Folio, contemp vellum; rubbed. With 47 plates. Some plates torn, some browned. Sold w.a.f. bba Apr 9 (21) £240 [Abdullah]

Groote...

— Het Groote Tafereel der Dwaasheid, vertoonende de Opkomst.... [Amst.], 1720. Folio, contemp calf gilt; some wear. With 75 plates only. Some surface dirt. Sold w.a.f. S Nov 21 (326) £1,400 [Twaalfhoven]

Gropius, Walter

— Bauhausbauten Dessau. Munich, 1930. 4to, orig bdg. DW Oct 9 (576) £170

Grose, Francis, 1731?-91

— The Antiquarian Repertory: A Miscellaneous Assemblage of Topography.... L, 1780-84. ("The Antiquarian Repertory: A Miscellany intended to Preserve and Illustrate Several Valuable Remains of Old Times.") 2d Ed of Vol I, 1st Ed of other vols. 4 vols. 4to, contemp calf gilt; spines worn, 1 torn, joints split. wa Mar 5 (559) $240

— The Antiquities of England and Wales. L, 1773-87. Vols I-III (of 4). Folio, later half calf. bba Jan 30 (113) £130 [Thorp]

Anr copy. 6 vols in 4, including Supplement. With: The Antiquities of Scotland. L, 1789-91 2 vols.. And: The Antiquities of Ireland. L, 1791-95 2 vols. Together, 8 vols. 4to, contemp mor gilt. C Oct 30 (38) £1,600 [Brooke-Hitching]

Anr copy. Vols I-IV. Folio, contemp half calf; worn. DW Nov 6 (120) £180

Anr copy. 4 vols. Without 2-vol Supplement. Folio, contemp calf. DW May 13 (82) £360

Anr copy. 6 vols, including Supplement in 2 vols. 4to, 19th-cent half calf. With 6 engraved titles, 5 (of 5) engraved frontises & 54 (of 55) hand-colored maps & 62 full-page plates. Several tears repaired; some soiling or spotting. S May 14 (1147) £420 [Burden]

Anr copy. 6 vols, including 2-vol Supplement. Folio, later half mor; joints cracked. With folding map (hand-colored in outline), 58 half-page maps in Vol VI (hand-colored in outline) & 63 full-page plates & plans. S July 1 (1268) £500 [Lerner]

Anr Ed. L, [1783]-97. 8 vols. 8vo, contemp calf; several vols broken. With 30 maps. Incomplete & lacking the Welsh section. Sold w.a.f. DW Dec 11 (188) £185

Anr Ed. L, 1785. 7 vols. 4to, contemp calf gilt; worn, some covers detached. With 7 engraved titles & 467 plates. DW Dec 11 (107) £210

— The Antiquities of Scotland. L, 1789-91. 1st Ed. 2 vols. Folio, calf gilt. pnE Dec 4 (185) £100

Anr copy. Contemp calf; rebacked. pnE May 13 (46) £150

— The Antiquities of England and Wales. L, [1790?]. 8 vols, including Supplement. 4to, later half mor; scuffed. With 8 titles, 94 maps (3 folding), & 595 plates. DW Apr 8 (98) £440

— The Antiquities of Ireland. L, 1791-95. Vol

I only. Old half calf; broken, lacking backstrip. Browned, foxed & dampstained. bbc Sept 23 (182) $60

Anr copy. 2 vols. 4to, contemp bds. Some foxing. CG Oct 7 (529) £220

Anr copy. Old mor; rubbed. With engraved titles & 262 plates. DW Apr 8 (97) £270

Anr copy. Contemp half calf; covers detached. With 2 titles, 24 plans & 236 plates. Scattered spotting. DW Apr 8 (99) £100

Anr copy. Contemp calf gilt; hinges cracked, upper cover of Vol I detached. With engraved titles & 264 plates & plans. Lower margins of both titles cut away. DW Apr 8 (425) £130

— The Antiquities of Scotland. L, 1797. 2 vols. 4to, later half mor; rubbed. bba Sept 19 (240) £120 [Martinez]

Anr copy. Later calf. pnE Dec 4 (187) £60

Anr copy. Half calf. pnE May 13 (226) £150

— Military Antiquities Respecting a History of the English Army. L, 1786-88. 2 vols. 4to, contemp calf; 1 vol rebacked. Title & frontis of Vol I dampstained. sg Jan 9 (131) $400

— A Provincial Glossary, with a Collection of Local Proverbs, and Popular Superstitions. L, 1811. 4to, bds; spine worn. bba Aug 13 (147) £55 [Korn]

Grose, John Henry

— A Voyage to the East Indies.... L, 1766. 2d Ed. 2 vols. 8vo, contemp half momr; rubbed & worn. With 6 folding plates. Some browning & worming. DW Oct 2 (37) £105

Grose-Smith, Henley —&
Kirby, William Forsell

— Rhopalocera Exotica, Being Illustrations of...Butterflies. L, 1887-92. 3 vols. 4to, half mor gilt; upper hinge broken. With 180 hand-colored plates. Stamps on endpapers, verso of titles, first & final leaf of text. pn Mar 19 (285) £2,300 [Wheldon & Wesley]

Gross, Chaim

— Fantasy Drawings. NY, [1956]. 4to, cloth, in d/j with chunk missing from top of front panel. Inscr to John Baur. bbc Apr 27 (456) $70

Gross, Mimi —&
Grooms, Red

— A Book of Drawings.... Florence, 1961. One of 700. With drawing entitled Moses with His Hand Up, in ink, 1962, at page opposing title. bbc Apr 27 (457) $175

Grossmith, George & Weedon

— The Diary of a Nobody. Bristol, [1892]. 1st Ed. 8vo, cloth; rubbed. Lacking ad. bba July 9 (179) £130 [Sotheran]

Anr copy. Orig cloth; hinges splitting. bba July 23 (427) £65 [Valentine]

Grosz, Georg, 1893-1959

— 30 Drawings & Watercolours. NY, 1944. Folio, spiral-bound wraps. Inscr. sg Feb 6 (116) $350

Anr copy. Spiral-bound bds. Inscr. sg Apr 2 (135) $275

— 30 Drawings and Watercolours. NY, 1948. 4to, spiral-bound bds. Some browning. sg Sept 6 (134) $250

— Abrechnung Folgt! Berlin: Malik-Verlag, [1923]. Orig wraps; faded. bba Apr 30 (295) £100 [Axe]

— Ade, Witboi. Berlin, [1955]. 4to, cloth, in d/j. Inscr, Dec 1955, & with pencil sketch on facing page. sg Feb 6 (118) $300

— Drawings, with an Introduction by the Artist. NY, 1944. Folio, cloth, in d/j. With 52 plates. sg Apr 2 (133) $110

— Ecce Homo. Berlin, [1923]. 1st Ed, Ausgabe C. Folio, orig bdg. With 84 plain & 16 colored plates. Inscr, 22 Mar 1939. sg Feb 6 (112) $1,800

Anr copy. Wraps. vg May 30 (653) DM8,500

— Die Gezeichneten: 60 Blaetter aus 15 Jahren. Berlin, 1930. 1.-8. Tausend. 4to, orig wraps; worn. sg Feb 6 (113) $400

— Interregnum. NY: Black Sun Press, 1936. Out-of-series copy, sgd on tp. Folio, half mor. Additionally inscr "No 1 of a limited edition of twenty copies George Grosz March 1945". sg Feb 6 (115) $650

Out-of-series copy, unsgd. Loose in half-cloth folding case with text booklet hinged inside front cover, as issued. Lacking plate list. sg Feb 6 (114) $2,600

— A Little Yes and a Big No. NY, 1946. In chipped d/j. sg Sept 6 (133) $70

Anr copy. In d/j with clean tear in spine panel. Inscr, Christmas 1946. sg Feb 6 (117) $150

Anr copy. In d/j with minor wear. sg Apr 2 (134) $70

Grote, George, 1794-1871

— A History of Greece. L, 1862. 8 vols. 8vo, contemp calf gilt, prize bdg of Trinity College Dublin. bba Aug 13 (188) £220 [Shapero]

Anr Ed. L, 1872. 10 vols. 8vo, contemp half calf gilt; some scuffing, 1 spine head worn. wa Mar 5 (4) $130

Anr Ed. L, 1888. 10 vols. 8vo, half calf. cb Jan 16 (65) $475

Grote-Hasenbalg, Werner

— Masterpieces of Oriental Rugs. NY, [1921]. With 2 portfolios containing 120 colored plates. sp June 18 (276) $200

Grotius, Hugo, 1583-1645

— Syntagma arateorum: opus poeticae et astronomiae. Leiden, 1600. 6 parts in 1 vol. 4to, 17th-cent calf; rebacked, rubbed. With 2 plates, 1 folding. bba Sept 5 (216) £720 [J. Franks]

Grove, Sir George, 1820-1900

— Dictionary of Music and Musicians. L, 1879-90. 4 vols, including Index. 8vo, half mor. pn Sept 12 (39) £50 [Fabians]

Anr Ed. NY, 1904-10. 5 vols. Bdg worn & shaken. O Feb 25 (93) $90

Anr Ed. L, 1927. 5 vols. Contemp half mor. pn Oct 24 (55) [Archive]

Anr Ed. L, 1954. 10 vols, including Supplement. In d/js. Library markings. bba Oct 24 (161) £120 [Erlini]

Anr copy. 9 vols. sg Mar 5 (232) $60

Anr copy. 9 vols plus 1961 Supplement. Orig cloth, with d/js that have been overglazed & stuck to the covers. Library markings. W Mar 6 (119) £110

Anr Ed. NY, 1960-61. 10 vols, including Supplement. cloth, in worn d/js. K Dec 1 (304) $190

Gruffydd, W. J. See: Gregynog Press

Gruner, Ludwig, 1801-82

— Specimens of Ornamental Art. L, 1850. Plate vol only. Folio, contemp half mor; worn, spine def, covers detached. With 80 plates. bba Oct 24 (243) £600 [MacDonald]

Gryphius, Otho

— Virgilii centones continentes vitam salvatoris nostri. Ratisbon: A. Burgero, 1593. 4to, 19th-cent calf gilt; joints rubbed. Tp mtd. sg Mar 12 (103) $425

Gsell-Fels, Theodor, 1818-98

— Switzerland: its Scenery and People. L, 1881. 4to, orig cloth; rubbed, spine torn, shaken. bba June 11 (366) £120 [Garwood & Voigt]

Gualterotti, Rafaello, 1543-1638

— Feste nelle nozze del serenissimo Don Francesco Medici Gran Duca di Toscana.... Florence, 1579. 4to, 18th-cent bds. With 16 folding plates & duplicates of 2 plates inserted from anr copy. 1 leaf bound in backwards. George Milne copy. CNY Dec 5 (244) $4,000

Guarini, Camillo Guarino

— Architettura civile...opera postuma. Turin, 1737. Contemp vellum; worn & soiled, endpapers renewed. With port & 79 plates. Some discoloration & soiling. C Oct 30 (39) £2,200 [Fletcher]

Anr copy. Foliio, contemp calf; rubbed. With port & 77 (of 79) plates. Port with margin partly torn away at lower fore-corner, restored with minimal loss; some discoloration. S June 25 (203) £1,500 [Gorini]

Guarinus Veronensis

— Regulae grammatices. [Parma: Angelo Ugoleto, c.1492]. 4to, modern vellum. 27 lines; roman letter. Some staining; early Ms annotations with alterations to the Italian translations. S May 28 (21) £3,000 [Lib. Panini]

Guazzo, Marco

— Historie di tutte le cose degne di memoria quai del anno MDXXIII sino a' questo presente anno sono occorse nella Italia.... Venice, 1540. 4to, modern half lea; spine scuffed. Bottom edge of prelims shaved; lacking last leaf; lower outer corners dampstained. sg Mar 12 (104) $425

Gudlaugsson, Sturla J.

— Geraert Ter Borch. The Hague, 1959-60. 2 vols. 4to, orig cloth, in d/js. S Feb 11 (92) £200 [Phillips]

Guenee, Antoine, 1717-1808

— Letters of Certain Jews to Monsieur Voltaire. Cincinnati, 1845. 8vo, contemp sheep; crudely taped, shaken. Some foxing. sg Dec 19 (15) $175

Guer, Jean Antoine, 1713-64

— Moeurs et usages des Turcs.... Paris, 1747. 2d Ed. 2 vols. 4to, contemp calf; worn. With 28 plates & 2 frontises. Vol I with worming at foremargin of a few leaves; Vol II with 1 plate torn & repaired; 1 plate just shaved along upper neatline. S June 30 (143) £800 [Menicon]

Guericke, Otto von, 1602-86

— Experimenta nova (ut vocantur) Magdeburgica de vacuo spatio. Amst., 1672. 1st Ed. Folio, contemp calf. SI Dec 5 (288) LIt5,500,000

Guerin, Maurice de, 1810-39

— The Centaur. The Bacchante. L: Vale Press, 1899. One of 150. 8vo, orig cloth; soiled. bba July 9 (308) £140 [Blackwell]

Guerra, Francisco

— American Medical Bibliography. NY, 1962. bbc Dec 9 (184) $55; sg Nov 14 (42) $70

— Iconografia Medica Mexicana. Mexico, 1955. One of 550. 4to, loose as issued in wraps. cb Nov 21 (103) $50

Guerre...

— Guerre horrende de Italia. Tutte le guerre & fatti darme seguiti nella Italia comenzando dalla venuta di re Carlo.... Venice: Gulielmo da Fontaneto, 1535. 4to, early 19th-cent russia gilt; joints split at head & foot. Portion of text of penultimate leaf cut away; short tear in title & H8 repaired; some worming at end; some browning. S Dec 5 (149) £900 [Franks]

Guggenheim, Harry Frank

— The Seven Skies. NY & L, 1930. One of 100. In d/j. cb Nov 7 (46) $50

Guglielmini, Domenico, 1655-1710

— Della natura de' fiumi. Bologna, 1697. 4to, contemp vellum. With frontis & 15 folding plates. SI June 9 (445) LIt1,900,000

Guicciardini, Francesco

— La Historia de Italia. Florence, 1561. Folio, 18th-cent vellum. Marginal worming & dampstaining. SI June 9 (446) LIt320,000

Anr Ed. Florence: Torrentino, 1561. Folio, contemp vellum; edges frayed. Some stainig. S Dec 5 (133) £2,600 [Rota]

Anr Ed. Venice: Giolito, 1564. Folio, contemp vellum. Some browning. SI June 9 (447) LIt500,000

Anr Ed. Venice: Gabriel Giolito, 1567. 2 parts in 1 vol. 4to, late 18th-cent calf. Some leaves discolored or stained. S May 13 (806) £260 [Patrino]

Anr Ed. Venice: Giolito, 1567. 4to, contemp vellum. SI June 9 (448) LIt650,000

Anr Ed. Venice, 1738-[40]. ("Della historia d'Italia, libri XX.") 2 vols. Folio, contemp calf; spines cracked on hinges. L.p. copy. DW Apr 8 (243) £125

Anr Ed. Venice, 1738-39. 2 vols. Folio, contemp vellum; soiled. Some browning & marginal dampstains to Vol I. L.p. copy. DW May 13 (284) £270

— The Historie of Giucciardin, Containing the Warres of Italie.... L: Richard Field, 1599. Folio, contemp vellum; soiled. DW Dec 11 (289) £150

Anr copy. Contemp calf; old reback. STC 12459. W July 8 (89) £65

Anr Ed. L, 1618. Folio, later calf; rebacked. bba Oct 10 (293) £120 [Thomas Plume's Library]

Guicciardini, Ludovico, 1521-89

— Belgicae, sive Inferioris Germaniae descriptio. Amst., 1652. 2 parts (of 3) in 1 vol. Vellum; front joint splitting, soiled. With engraved title, frontis, folding map & 20 (of 21) double-page town plans. B May 12 (1494) HF550

— Descrittione...di tutti i Paesi Bassi.... Antwerp, 1588. Folio, contemp calf; worn, stitching broken. With port, 12 double-page maps, 47 double-page town plans & views, 11 full-page plates & 4 other double-page plates, all colored by a contemp hand. Lacking final blank; small hole in 1 map; small tears to the margins of 2 plans & 1 map; minor worming to blank lower margin of K4-P6. C Oct 30 (153) £6,000 [de Jong]

Anr copy. Contemp vellum; soiled. With half-title with engraved allegorical figure (misbound), ptd title with engraved arms on verso, port & 77 (of 78) maps & plates plus 10 unnumbered plates bound in at relevant chapters. Lacking Plate 50; some plates misbound; some waterstaining. S Nov 21 (177) £1,600 [Walmacq]

Guidott, Thomas

— De thermis Britannicis tractatus. L, 1691. 4to, contemp mor gilt, with Strangways crest on spine. Tear to 1 leaf; some foxing. bba June 11 (221) £480 [Maggs]

Guigard, Joannis, 1825-92

— Nouvel Armorial du bibliophile. Paris, 1890. 2 vols. 8vo, contemp half mor; Vol II worn. Ck Nov 1 (410) £140

Guignes, Joseph de

— Voyages a Peking, Manille et l'Ile de France.... Paris, 1808. Atlas only. Folio, 19th-cent half cloth; worn, upper cover loose. With 92 plates on 60 leaves & 6 maps. Some browning. G. E. Morrison's copy. S Nov 15 (1290) £300 [Shapero]

Guignes, Louis de, 1759-1845

— Dictionnaire chinois, francais et latin. Paris, 1813. Folio, contemp half calf; worn. Some soiling; tp & half-title torn & repaired; Ms annotations. S Nov 15 (795) £500 [Brockhaus]

Guillaume, Paul —& Munro, Thomas

— Primitive Negro Sculpture. NY, 1926. 1st Ed. 8vo, half cloth. cb Jan 16 (66) $95

Anr copy. Orig half cloth, in def d/j. sg Sept 6 (135) $50

Guillaumet, Gustave

— Tableaux algeriens. Paris, 1888. 4to, half mor; extremities rubbed. sg Jan 9 (83) $110

Guillebon, Regine de Plinval de. See: Plinval de Guillebon, Regine de

Guillemard, Francis Henry Hill

— The Cruise of the Marchesa to Kamschatka and New Guinea. L, 1886. 1st Ed. 2 vols. 8vo, orig cloth. DW Oct 2 (39) £115

Anr copy. Bdg not described but scuffed. kh Nov 11 (518) A$440

Anr copy. Half calf. pnE Dec 4 (244) £100

Guillet de Saint-George, George

— Les Arts de l'homme d'epee, ou le dictionnaire du gentilhomme. The Hague, 1686. 5th Ed. 12mo, contemp vellum. With frontis & 3 folding plates. Inked library stamp on tp verso. sg Mar 26 (138) $90

— The Gentleman's Dictionary. L, 1705. 8vo, contemp calf; worn. With 3 folding plates. 1 plate soiled & frayed. DW Mar 4 (216) £70

Guillevic, Eugene

— Harpe. Paris: Galanis, 1980. One of 15 hors commerce, with 2 suites. Illus by Jean Bazaine. 4to, loose as issued. CGen Nov 18 (391) SF3,000

Guillim, John, 1565-1621

— A Display of Heraldrie. L, 1679. "5th Ed". Folio, old half calf gilt; broken. Rr3 apparently from a later Ed; 2 plates cut round & mtd. Sold w.a.f. L Feb 27 (171) £150

6th Ed. L, 1724. Folio, modern calf gilt. Portion of title excised & restored with loss; old stamps, not affecting plates. sg Oct 24 (141) $110

Guinot, Eugene, 1812-61

— A Summer at Baden-Baden. L, [c.1870]. 8vo, cloth; rubbed. DW Nov 6 (49) £180

Guischardt, Charles, 1724-75

— Memoires militaires sur les Grecs et les Romains. The Hague, 1758. 2 vols in 1. 4to, contemp calf gilt; rubbed, upper joint split. Some leaves waterstained in upper margin. bba Oct 24 (193) £170 [Graves Johnston]

Guizot, Francois Pierre Guillaume

— A Popular History of France. Bost., [1880?]. 6 vols. 8vo, half calf; rubbed. O May 26 (83) $60

Gumuchian & Cie., Kirkor

— Catalogue de reliures du XVe au XIXe siecle.... Paris, [1930]. 4to, contemp half mor, orig wraps bound in; rubbed. bba May 28 (490) £100 [Maggs]

One of 1,000. Cloth, in chipped d/j. pba July 23 (45) $190

— Les Livres de l'enfance du XVe au XIXe siecle. Paris, [1930]. One of 900. 2 vols. 4to, orig wraps. bba July 23 (236) £130 [Demetzy]

Anr copy. Orig wraps; broken. sg Oct 17 (267) $90

Anr Ed. L, 1979. One of 600. 2 vols. 4to, orig cloth, in d/js. O Sept 24 (110) $60; sg Oct 31 (122) $90

Anr Ed. L, 1985. One of 900. 2 vols. 4to, bds, in d/js. Reprint of 1930 Ed. bbc Apr 27 (150) $60

Gunn, Hugh. See: Ross & Gunn

Gunn, John, fl. 1790

— An Historical Enquiry Respecting the Performance of the Harp in the Highlands of Scotland. Edin., 1807. 4to, contemp bds; rebacked. With 3 plates. Edges of leaves touched by damp; 1st leaf of text annotated; small stamp on tp. pn Oct 24 (372) £260

Gunn, Thom

— The Missed Beat. Sidcot: Gruffyground Press, 1976. One of 170. Ptd wraps; upper corner creased. wa Mar 5 (189) $55

Gunnlaugr, called Ormstunga

— Sagan af Gunnlaugi Ormstungu ok Skalld-Rafni; sive, Gunnlaugi Vermilinguis & Rafnis Poetae Vita. Copenhagen, 1775. 1st Ed. 4to, contemp calf; backstrip chipped, rubbed. With frontis & 1 plate. bba May 14 (11) £140 [Hannas]

Gunsaulus, Helen Cowen

— The Clarence Buckingham Collection of Japanese Prints. Harunobu, Koryusai, Shigemasa.... Chicago, [1965]. One of 1,000. Folio, orig cloth. wa Sept 26 (619) $120

Gunter, Edmund, 1581-1626

— The Description and Use of the Sector.... L, 1636. 2d Ed. 4to, contemp calf; spine cracking, joints rubbed. Lacking 1 woodcut plate; dampstin to tp & fiirst few leaves. STC 12523. CNY Oct 8 (116) £1,100

— Works. L, 1673. 5th Ed. 4to, contemp calf; upper cover detached. With engraved title & 2 folding plates. Illust on p.64 lacking volvelle; some browning of margins. Ck Nov 29 (190) £280

Anr copy. Contemp calf; rubbed, joints splitting. With engraved title, folding plate

& small plate at p. 74; volvelle on I4 verso. Dampstained in lower corner at beginning; small hole in Bbb. S May 13 (887) £360 [Lewcock]

Gunther, Robert William Theodore

— The Astrolabes of the World.... Oxford, 1932. 2 vols. 4to, orig cloth. Ck June 18 (20) £420

— Early Science in Oxford. Oxford, 1923-45. 14 vols. 8vo, Vol I, rebound; others, orig cloth. Library markings. sg Nov 14 (245) $500

Guntherus

— Ligurini de gestis imp. caesaris.... [Augsburg]: Erhardum Oeglin, Apr 1507. 1st Issue, without Duerer woodcut on L6 recto. Folio, later half calf. Contemp ink annotations to first leaves; some worming to margins of last leaves. 83 (of 84) leaves; lacking final blank. Ck Oct 31 (115) £750

2d Issue. Later calf; rebacked, old spine laid down. With full-page woodcut illust by Albrecht Duerer. Tp torn at upper margin with loss of 3 characters (supplied in Ms); 2d leaf also restored at upper margin; wormhole in 2 final leaves affecting text. 83 (of 84) leaves; lacking final blank. Heber copy. Ck Oct 31 (116) £1,800

Guptill, Arthur Leighton

— Norman Rockwell, Illustrator. NY, 1946. Folio, cloth, in def d/j. Inscr to Caroline Haywood. F Sept 26 (133) $100

Gutenberg Jahrbuch

— Gutenberg Jahrbuch. [Mainz, 1926-51]. 40 vols. 4to, various bdgs. Ck Nov 1 (411) £200

— Register...1926-1960. Mainz, 1962. Compiled by Siegfried Joost. 4to, cloth. sg Oct 31 (152A) $110

Guthe, Hermann. See: Ebers & Guthe

Guthrie, Alfred Bertram

— The Big Sky. NY: William Sloan, [1947]. One of 500. In d/j with nicks at edges & with additional ptd d/j for limited issue. bbc Sept 23 (427) $75

Guthrie, William, 1708-70

— A New Geographical, Historical, and Commercial Grammar.... L, 1788. 11th Ed. 8vo, later cloth. With 20 folding maps. Some foxing. wa Nov 21 (24) $220

Guttmann, Oscar, 1855-1910

— The Manufacture of Explosives. L, 1895. 2 vols. 8vo, orig cloth. sg Nov 14 (289) $110

Guyon, Claude Marie

— A New History of the East-Indies.... L, 1757. 1st Ed in English. 2 vols. 8vo, contemp calf gilt; spine rubbed. With 2 folding maps. Sold w.a.f. b June 22 (161) £140

Guys, Pierre Augustin, 1721-99

— Voyage litteraire de la Grece.... Paris, 1776. 2 vols. 8vo, contemp calf gilt; spines worn. With 7 plates. S July 1 (619) £350 [Consolidated Real]

Guzman, Jose Maria

— Breve Noticia que da al Supremo Gobierno del Actual Estado del Territorio de la Alta California.... Mexico, 1833. 8vo, orig wraps; back wrap stained. F Sept 26 (339) $425

Anr copy. Wraps. With folding chart. sg June 18 (78) $650

Anr copy. Orig wraps; chipped, dampstain along top edge of front cover. wa Apr 9 (58) $500

Gwynn, John

— Liber Ardmachanus. The Book of Armagh. Dublin, 1913. One of 400. 4to, orig suede, unopened. CG Oct 7 (534) £280

Anr copy. Orig suede. Inscr to Arthur A. Luce. S July 1 (1166) £280

H

H., E. See: Hickeringill, Edmund

H., H. See: Jackson, Helen Hunt

H., N.

— The Ladies Dictionary; being a General Entertainment for the Fair Sex. L: John Dunton, 1694. 8vo, contemp calf; worn, needs rebacking. Marginal soiling. sg Oct 24 (143) $700

Haberly, Loyd

See also: Gregynog Press

— Mediaeval English Pavingtiles. Oxford: Shakespeare Head Press, 1937. One of 425. 4to, half mor gilt. DW Oct 2 (396) $120

Habington, William, 1605-54

— The Historie of Edward the Fourth, King of England. L, 1640. 1st Ed. Folio, calf. Minor worming in lower outer corner throughout; some browning; tear in I4. STC 12586. sg Oct 24 (144) $150

Hacke, William

— A Collection of Original Voyages. L, 1699. 1st Ed. 3 parts in 1 vol. 8vo, contemp calf; rebacked, front cover detached, spine & corners worn. With 6 maps & plans. CNY Oct 8 (117) $2,000

Anr copy. Half mor gilt by C. Walters. Some browning. CNY Oct 8 (118) $800

Anr copy. Contemp calf; rebacked. With 6 maps & plates. A few leaves dampstained at head. S June 25 (27) £900 [Quaritch/Hordern]

Hackett, John

— A History of the Orthodox Church of Cyprus.... L, 1901. S June 30 (36) £180 [Zeno]

Hacklaender, Friedrich Wilhelm. See: Adam, Eugen & Franz

Haddon, Alfred Cort —& Hornell, James

— Canoes of Oceana. Honolulu, 1936-38. 3 vols, orig wraps. sg Jan 9 (84) $225

Hadeln, Detlev von

— The Drawings of G. B. Tiepolo. Paris, 1928. 2 vols. 4to, cloth, in d/js. sg Feb 6 (280) $200

— Venezianische Zeichnungen des Quattrocento. Berlin, 1925-[26]. Folio, orig cloth; rubbed, 1 cover stained. bba Feb 13 (187) £120 [Halwas]

Haden, Sir Francis Seymour, 1818-1910
See also: Salaman, Malcolm Charles

— About Etching. L, 1879. 2 parts. 4to, half mor; rubbed. With frontis & 15 plates. O Sept 24 (111) $90

Haebler, Konrad
See also: Grolier Club

— Bibliografia Iberica del siglo XV. Leipzig & The Hague, 1903-17. 2 vols. 8vo, later cloth & orig wraps. bba Feb 27 (428) £320 [Montero]

Anr copy. Contemp half lea; Vol I spine faded & rubbed. sg Oct 31 (152) $650

Haedus, Petrus

— De Miseria Humana.... Venice: Academia Veneziana, 1558. 4to, 19th-cent mor gilt by L. C.. Ck Nov 29 (11) £350

Haesler, H. See: Butcher & Haesler

Haestens, Henrik van

— De bloedige ende strenge Belegeringhe der Stadt Oostende in Vlaenderen.... Leiden, 1613. 4to, vellum; def. With 14 double-page plates & coats-of-arms. Lacking port. B May 12 (1313) HF1,800

Hafen, Leroy R.

— The Mountain Men and the Fur Trade of the Far West. Glendale, 1966-72. Vols III-IX (of 10). cb Nov 14 (77) $275

Haggard, Sir Henry Rider, 1856-1925

— Allan Quartermain.... NY, 1887. 8vo, orig ptd wraps; rear cover becoming detached. P Oct 11 (157) $450

— Cetywayo and his White Neighbours. L, 1882. 1st Ed. 8vo, orig cloth; rubbed. Some spotting. bba July 9 (38) £260 [Jarndyce]

— Heart of the World. NY, 1908. 8vo, mor gilt extra, orig cloth covers bound in; front cover loose. Sgd as O. Henry by Eugene Field II.. sg Oct 17 (239) $90

— King Solomon's Mines L, 1885. 2d Issue. 8vo, calf gilt by Bayntun. With colored folding frontis (small tear & repair). pn Dec 12 (240) £80

— The Mahatma and the Hare. L, 1911. Illus by William H. Horton. In d/j. Manney copy. P Oct 11 (158) $450

— The People of the Mist. L, 1894. 8vo, orig cloth. With AMs for the dedication laid in, sgd. Epstein copy. sg Apr 29 (200) $1,200

— She: a History of Adventure. L, 1887. 1st Ed. 8vo, orig cloth; joint starting at head of spine. With 2 color lithos. Hogan-Manney copy. P Oct 11 (156) $1,000

1st Issue, with Godness me on p 269, line 38. Orig cloth; spine ends worn. With 2 color lithos. Inscr to George Saintsbury. Epstein copy. sg Apr 29 (201) $3,600

Haghe, Louis, 1806-85

— Sketches in Belgium and Germany. Third Series. L, 1850. Folio, orig half lea; worn, loose. Inscr to William Simpson by Elizabeth Day. K Dec 1 (241) $190

Hahn, Carl Wilhelm, d.1835 —& Koch, C. L.

— Die Arachniden. Nuremberg, 1831-48. 16 vols in 8. 8vo, bds; worn. With 563 hand-colored plates. Some plates trimmed; library stamps removed from titles; tp to Vol 13 with lower portion cut away. S May 14 (1035) £1,400 [Antik. Junk]

Haig, Douglas Haig, 1st Earl

— Sir Douglas Haig's Despatches.... L, 1920. Ed by J. H. Boraston. 2 vols, orig cloth. With 10 folding maps. cb Jan 30 (53) $100

Haig-Brown, Roderick L.
See also: Derrydale Press

— Return to the River; a Story of the Chinook Run. NY, 1941. One of 520. Illus by Charles DeFeo. Half mor. Koopman copy. O Oct 29 (150) $300

— The Salmon. Ottowa, 1974. Includes text vol & 4 folders, loose as issued, of plates. Koopman copy. O Oct 29 (151) $575

Haile, Martin

— James Francis Edward the Old Chevalier. L, 1907. Cosway bdg in mor gilt by Bayntun Riviere, with miniature hand-painted port of Clementina Walkinshaw inlaid on front cover. Extra-illus with 12 plates. Ck Dec 11 (119) £320

Hain, Ludwig, 1781-1836

— Repertorium bibliographicum in quo libri omnes ab arte typographica inventa usque ad annum MD. Stuttgart, Tuebingen & Paris, 1826-38. 2 vols in 4 plus Copinger's 1926 Supplement & Burger's 1902 Index in 2 vols. Together, 6 vols. 8vo, half vellum. sg Oct 31 (154) $300

Anr Ed. Berlin, 1925. 5 vols in 4, including 1926 Supplement by W. A. Copinger. 8vo, orig half vellum. bba June 25 (13) £140 [Tosi]

Anr Ed. Milan, [1948]. 4 vols plus Copinger & Burger in 3 vols. Together, 7 vols. Library markings. bba Dec 19 (274) £190 [Forster]

Anr copy. 2 vols in 4. 8vo, half mor. Reprint of 1826-38 Ed. bba Feb 27 (429) £130 [Montero]

Anr copy. 4 vols plus Copinger & Burger in 3 vols. Together, 7 vols. Ck Nov 1 (412) £250; O Sept 24 (112) $350

Anr copy. 4 vols, plus Supplement, 1950, in 3 vols. SI Dec 5 (294) LIt750,000

Hajek z Libocan, Vaclav

— Kronyka Czeska. Prague, 1541. 4to, 19th-cent half sheep; worn, front hinge cracked. Tp mtd; some prelims creased or rehinged; lacking leaves 269-72. sg Oct 24 (147) $550

Hake, Henry M. See: British Museum

Hakewill, James, 1778-1843

— The History of Windsor and its Neighbourhood. L, 1813. 4to, contemp calf; rebacked. With frontis & 20 plans & plates. Some browning. L Feb 27 (137) £80

— A Picturesque Tour of Italy.... L, 1820. Folio, contemp mor gilt; rubbed. With engraved title & 63 plates. Some browning. SI June 9 (450) LIt1,000,000

Anr copy. Contemp mor. With 63 plates.. SI June 9 (451) LIt1,100,000

Anr copy. Modern lea. Foxed. SI June 9 (452) LIt780,000

— A Picturesque Tour of the Island of Jamaica. L, 1825. Folio, mor gilt by Zaehnsdorf. With 21 colored plates. C May 20 (69) £5,800 [Arader]

Hakluyt, Richard, 1552?-1616

— The Principall Navigations.... L: G. Bishop & R. Newberie, 1589. 1st Ed. Folio, mor gilt by Pratt; joints rubbed. With the folding map & the 6-leaf Drake insert. Tp with gutter restored & 2 marginal repairs; small tears at gutter of 2d leaf; some holes & repaired tears, affecting a few letters; worm-track to gutter from R2 through Bb5, touching several letters; 3M4-8 remargined on 3 sides; last 5 leaves remargined; antepenultimate leaf with repairs with loss to text, the affected areas supplied in ink facsimile; lacking final blank; world map linen-backed & with repaired tear; washed. STC 12625. DuPont copy. CNY Oct 8 (119) $21,000

Anr copy. Late 19th-cent mor by Pratt. Black letter. With folding map laid on linen; with the Bowes leaves present in both 1st & 2d issues; with the 6 leaves describing Drake's circumnavigation (these & the 2d issue Bowes leaves from a shorter copy margined to size). Lacking final blank. STC 12625. S Nov 21 (216) £14,000 [Clark]

2d Ed. L, 1598-99-1600. Vols I-II (of 3) in 1 vol. 18th-cent calf; spine torn. Black letter. Facsimile tp to Vol I; that to Vol II repaired at margin; marginal repairs throughout; minor worming through upper & lower margins affecting headlines & some text towards the end. STC 12626. pn Nov 14 (274) £100

1st Issue. 3 vols in 2. Folio, mor gilt by Riviere; joints cracking, rubbed. In Vol I, marginal repair to A5, touching text, large repair to fore-margin of Ee1 costing most of a sidenote & 2 letters of text, smaller repairs to Ee2-5 affecting 3 letters of sidenote; some other repairs & cropping;l some worming at end of Vol II, affecting text; washed; titles soiled; some finger-soiling & discoloration; marginal dampstaining; Lenox Library duplicate stamps on versos of titles. STC 12626. DuPont copy. CNY Oct 8 (120) $7,000

Anr Ed. L, 1599-1600. 2d Issue of Vol I. 3 vols in 2. Folio, 19th-cent mor gilt by Kalthoeber; extremities rubbed, small gouge to upper cover of Vol I, scrape to upper cover of Vol II. With cancel tp dated 1599 but with the account of Drake's voyage to Cadiz on pp. 607-19 of Vol I. Lower corners of 1st 2 leaves & margin of tp of Vol I repaired; small holek to 1 leaf affecting 1 letter & border rule; 3 leaves in Vol III stained, affecting 2 or 3 letters; 4 leaves with rust-holes affecting letters; washed; some foxing at ends of vols. STC 12626a. DuPont copy. CNY Oct 8 (121) $8,500

Anr copy. 18th-cent calf; spine ends repaired, worn, stained, joints cracked. With Church's 3d issue of the voyage to Cadiz on pp. 607-19 of Vol I Hole to Ii6 in Vol I with partial loss to 9 words; lower corner of X3 in Vol II torn affecting catchword; headline rule of Ppp2 shaved; Vol III with margins of several leaves cut away; some cropping, affecting rules or headlines; some dampstaining & browning; marginal tears. STC 12626a. DuPont copy. CNY Oct 8 (122) $6,000

Anr Ed. Glasgow, 1903-5. 12 vols. Orig cloth; spines dulled. bba Dec 19 (392) £160 [Shapero]

Anr copy. Orig cloth; spine splitting. cb Oct 10 (48) $225

Hale, Edward Everett, 1822-1909

— Kanzas and Nebraska.... Bost., 1854. 1st Ed. 12mo, cloth. With folding map, which is wrinkled & chipped. Some foxing. sg June 18 (265) $90

— The Man Without a Country. [Bost., 1863]. 8vo, wraps. In: The Atlantic Monthly. Bost., 1863 (December), pp 665-79. With 2 A Ls s laid in. bbc Apr 27 (314) $130

Hale, John Henry

— How to Tie Salmon Flies. L, 1892. 8vo, cloth; some wear. Koopman copy. O Oct 29 (153) $325

Hale, Sir Matthew, 1609-76

— The Primitive Origination of Mankind. L, 1677. 1st Ed. 4to, calf; portion missing from back flyleaf, spine loose. b&b Feb 19 (108) $80

Anr copy. Contemp calf; worn. First leaves dampstained & chipped. cb Sept 5 (46) $110

Hales, Stephen, 1677-1761

— Philosophical Experiments. Containing Useful and Necessary Instructions.... L, 1739. Bound with: Armstrong, John. The Art of Preserving Health. L, 1745. 8vo, contemp half calf; rejointed, spine chipped. sg May 14 (283) $300

— Statical Essays: containing Vegetable Staticks. L, 1769. 4th Ed of Vol I; 3d Ed of Vol II. 8vo, contemp calf; front covers loose. With 19 plates in Vol I. sg May 14 (69) $650

Halevy, Ludovic, 1834-1908

— La Famille Cardinal. Paris, 1938. One of 325 on velin de Rives. Illus by Edgar Degas. 4to, mor gilt extra by Gruel. sg May 7 (69) $5,000

Haley, C. S. See: Price & Haley

Halford, Frederic M., 1844-1914

— Dry Fly Entomology: a Brief Description.... L, 1897. 2 vols. 4to, contemp half lea gilt. L Nov 14 (410) £160

Anr copy. Orig half lea; rubbed, spine worn. With 10 hand-colored plates of flies. Koopman copy. O Oct 29 (154) $150

One of 100. Mor. With 18 plain & 28 hand-colored plates & with 99 (of 100) artificial flies in 12 sunken mounts. Koopman copy. O Oct 29 (155) $1,700

Anr copy. Orig mor gilt; spines def, covers detached. With 18 plain & 28 hand-colored plates & with 100 flies in 12 sunken mounts. Stamps on titles. pn Mar 19 (357) £1,000

— Dry-Fly Fishing in Theory and Practice. L, 1889. 4to, orig cloth; worn. With 25 plates. Koopman copy. O Oct 29 (157) $150

One of 100. Orig cloth; rubbed & soiled. DW Apr 8 (163) £130

— The Dry-Fly Man's Handbook. L, 1913. Koopman copy. O Oct 29 (158) $140

— Floating Flies and How to Dress Them. L, 1886. 8vo, cloth; worn. With 9 hand-colored plates. Koopman copy. O Oct 29 (159) $300

— Modern Development of the Dry Fly. NY: Dutton, [1910]. 8vo, orig cloth; rebacked. bba Nov 28 (36) £110 [Cope]

Anr copy. Orig cloth; worn. Koopman copy. O Oct 29 (160) $140

Halfpenny, William

— The Art of Sound Building. L, 1725. 2d Ed. Folio, contemp sheep; worn, worn, joints cracked. With engraved allegorical plate & 25 architectural plates Tp soiled. sg Apr 2 (136) $600

— A New and Compleat System of Architecture Delineated.... L: for John Brindley, 1749. Oblong 4to, contemp half calf; rebacked, fragments of orig spine laid down, corners restored. With 47 plates, 2 folding. Some foxing. McCarty-Cooper copy. CNY Jan 25 (25) $1,300

Halfpenny, William & John

— Gothic Architecture. L, 1752. ("Rural Architecture in the Gothick Taste.") Bound with: Barton, Cutts. Modern Characters for Pictures...L, 1778. And: Strange, Robert. A Descriptive Catalogue of a Collection of Pictures....L, 1769. 8vo, contemp half calf; rebacked in the 19th cent. 2d & 3d works each lacking a prelim leaf. CNY Jan 25 (26) $1,000

Halkett, Samuel, 1814-71 —& Laing, John, 1809-80

— Dictionary of Anonymous and Pseudonymous English Literature. Edin., 1926-[56]. 8 vols, including Supplement O Nov 26 (78) $300

Anr Ed. L, 1926-62. 7 vols only. 4to, orig cloth. Ck Nov 1 (413) £250

Anr copy. 9 vols, including Index, Supplements & Addenda. 4to, orig cloth; rubbed, 2 vols in frayed d/js. Library markings. DW Jan 29 (318) £420

Anr copy. 9 vols. L Nov 14 (45) £440

Anr copy. Vols 1-7. 4to, cloth, in d/js. sg May 21 (229) $375

Anr Ed. Edin., 19226-34. Vols I-VII. O Sept 24 (113) $400

Hall, B. Fairfax. See: Le Bas Collection, Edward

Hall, Basil

— The Great Polyglot Bibles: Including a Leaf from the Complutensian of Acala, 1514-17. San Francisco: Book Club of Calif., 1966. One of 400. Folio, unbound. cb Oct 31 (6) $275

Hall, Basil, 1788-1844

— Account of a Voyage of Discovery to the West Coast of Corea.... L, 1818. 4to, contemp half calf; spine rubbed, joints split. With 1 plain & 8 hand-colored aquatint plates, 5 maps & 1 uncolored engraving. C Oct 30 (104) £400 [Arader]

Anr copy. Contemp calf; upper joint split. With 5 maps & 10 plates, 8 hand-colored. Some browning. Ck Sept 6 (118) £420

Anr copy. 19th-cent half mor. With 9 aquatint plates (all but 1 hand-colored), 1 engraved plate & 5 maps, 3 folding. Ck May 15 (109) £600

— Extracts from a Journal.... Edin., 1824. ("Extracts from a Journal, Written on the Coasts of Chili, Peru, and Mexico.") 3d Ed. 2 vols. 8vo, old bds; rebacked, worn. O May 26 (84) $100

— Forty Etchings from Sketches Made with the Camera Lucida, in North America. Edin., 1829. 4to, orig bds; covers detached. With 40 plates on 20 sheets & hand-colored folding map. DW May 13 (32) £160

Hall, Carroll Douglas

— Heraldry of New Helvetia.... San Francisco, 1945. One of 250. Half calf, in chipped d/j. sg June 18 (266) $90

Hall, Charles Bryan

— Military Records of General Officers of the Confederate States of America. NY, 1898. Folio, half mor gilt. With 108 plates & frontis. K Sept 29 (137) $2,700

Hall, Charles Francis, 1821-71

— Narrative of the Second Arctic Expedition.... Wash., 1879. 4to, orig cloth. W July 8 (264) £210

Anr copy. Orig cloth; ends frayed, corners bumped, shaken, hinge broken. Color folding map mtd on linen in rear pocket. wa Mar 5 (543) $90

Hall, Edward, d.1547

— The Union of the Two Noble and Illustre Families of Lancastre & Yorke. L: Grafton, [1548]. Folio, old calf; rebacked. Tp cut down & mtd; marginal repairs at beginning & end. STC 12722. W July 8 (58) £680

Hall, Frances & Almira

— Narrative of the Capture and Providential Escape.... [N.p.], 1834. 12mo, unbound. Lacking frontis. sg June 18 (267) $50

Hall, James, 1793-1868. See: McKenney & Hall

Hall, James Norman, 1887-1951. See: Nordhoff & Hall

Hall, Joseph, 1574-1656

— Samson: Selections from a Contemplation on an Historical Passage in the Old Testament. Lexington KY: Victor Hammer, 1972. Foli, Half mor. cb Jan 16 (72) $60

Hall, Lillian Arvilla

— Catalogue of Dramatic Portraits in the...Harvard College Library. Cambr. MA, 1930-34. 4 vols. O Sept 24 (114) $60

Hall, Norman S.

— The Balloon Buster: Frank Luke of Arizona. Garden City, 1928. In repaired d/j. cb Nov 7 (48) $50

Hall, Peter, 1803-49

— Picturesque Memorials of Salisbury.... Salisbury, 1834. 4to, contemp half mor; joints worn. With frontis & 28 plates on india paper, mtd. 1 or 2 plates scorched. bba Oct 24 (296) £65 [C. Smith]

Anr copy. Later cloth. bba Jan 30 (368) £80 [Dawson]

Hall, Samuel Carter, 1800-89

— The Book of Gems, the Poets and Artists of Great Britain. L, 1836-38. 3 vols. 8vo, contemp mor extra. cb Sept 26 (99) $90

Hall, Samuel Carter & Anna Maria

— Ireland, its Scenery, Character.... L, 1841-43. 3 vols. 8vo, Vols I & II, contemp calf gilt; Vol III, contemp mor gilt; Vol III rubbed. With 65 plates & 17 maps. Vol II lacking title & 1st 2 leaves of Index. Sold w.a.f. DW Nov 6 (123) £65

Anr copy. Contemp half mor; edges worn. With 3 frontises, 19 maps & 46 (of 50) plates. pn July 16 (198) £110 [Map House]

Anr copy. Mor gilt. 1 plate loose. sg Jan 9 (86) $150

Hall, Sidney

— A New General Atlas.... L, [1857]. Folio, calf; broken & def. With 53 hand-colored maps. S July 9 (1416) £350 [Nicholson]

Hall, Trevor H.

— A Bibliography of Books on Conjuring in English from 1580 to 1850. Minneapolis, 1957. One of 500. O Dec 17 (95) $70; sg Oct 31 (123) $150

Hall, William Henry

— The New Royal Encyclopaedia. L, [1788?]. 3 vols. Folio, later cloth. Lacking text. A few plates stained. Sold w.a.f. bba Feb 27 (162) £220 [B. Bailey]

Haller, Albrecht von, 1708-77

— Disputationes ad morborum historiam et curiationem facientes. Lausanne, 1757-60. 7 vols. 4to, contemp half calf gilt; corners worn, Vol VI spine chipped at head. With 34 plates. sg May 14 (70) $450

Anr copy. Vols I-VI. Contemp vellum. Some browning & foxing; some repairs. Sold w.a.f. SI Dec 5 (295) LIt200,000

— Elementa physiologiae corporis humani. Lausanne & Leiden, 1757-78. 8 vols. 4to, contemp half sheep; spine ends chipped. sg May 14 (71) $600

— First Lines of Physiology. Troy, 1803. 8vo, contemp sheep; extremities rubbed, end-papers def. sg May 14 (72) $120

Halley, Edmund. See: Cutler & Halley

Hallock, Charles, 1834-1917

— An Angler's Reminiscences. A Record of Sport.... Cincinnati, 1913. Koopman copy. O Oct 29 (161) $85

— The Salmon Fisher. NY, 1890. 16mo, cloth; worn. Koopman copy. O Oct 29 (163) $120

Halm, Philipp Maria —& Berliner, Rudolf

— Das Hallesche Heiltum. Berlin, 1931. 4to, orig cloth. Met Apr 28 (174) $80

Halpin, Warren T.

— Hoofbeats: Drawings and Comments. Phila., 1938. 4to, orig cloth. F June 25 (166) $50

Halsey, Rosalie V.

— Forgotten Books of the American Nursery. Boston, 1911. One of 700. Half cloth. cb Oct 17 (390) $85

Hamconius, Martinus, c.1550-1620

— Frisiae seu de viris rebusque Frisiae illustribus. Franeker, 1620. 4to, vellum. With armorial plate, port of the author, 53 ports of Frisian rulers & 3 woodcuts of coats-of-arms. B May 12 (1626) HF680

Hambourg, Maria Morris. See: Szarkowski & Hambourg

Hamburg...

— Hamburg und seine Umgebungen in 19th Jahrhundert. Hamburg, 1844. Bdg not described. Foxed. Met Apr 27 (321A) $925

Hamerton, Philip Gilbert, 1834-94

— Etching and Etchers. L, 1876. 8vo, orig cloth; rubbed, edges worn. With 12 plates. Some spotting. pn May 14 (140) £50 [Thorp]

3d Ed. L, 1880. 4to, orig half lea; rubbed. pn July 16 (106) £250 [Thorpe]

Anr copy. Half mor; worn. sg Sept 6 (136) $325

— Landscape. L, 1885. One of 525. Folio, half sheep; needs rebacking. sg Feb 6 (121) $90

Hamilton, Alexander, 1712-56

— Hamilton's Itinerarium.... St. Louis, 1907. One of 487. Ed by Albert B. Hart. 4to, half lea; extremities rubbed. Inscr by the pbr. NH Oct 6 (84) $65

Hamilton, Alexander, 1739-1802

— The Family Female Physician.... Worcester, Mass.: Isaiah Thomas, 1793. 8vo, orig sheep; scuffed. F Mar 26 (700) $260

— Outlines of the Theory and Practice of Midwifery. L, 1791. 8vo, contemp calf. bba Sept 5 (280) £85 [Quaritch]

— A Treatise of Midwifery. L, 1781. 8vo, orig bds; rubbed. bba Sept 5 (276) £100 [Quaritch]

Hamilton, Alexander, 1755-1804

— Report of the Secretary of the Treasury...relative to a Provision for the Support of the Public Credit of the United States. NY: Childs & Swaine, 1790. Folio, formerly sewn but thread lost. Some dampstaining & marginal fraying. P Dec 12 (106) $8,000

Hamilton, Alexander, 1757-1805. See: Burr & Hamilton

Hamilton, Anthony, 1646?-1720

— Memoires du Comte de Grammont.... L, [1793]. 4to, 19th-cent mor gilt. With 78 ports. Lonsdale copy. pn Apr 23 (83) £80

— Memoirs of Count Grammont. L, [1794]. 2 vols. 4to, mor gilt by Bayntun; with port miniature of Nell Gwyn and of Charles II on upper covers. CNY Dec 5 (384) $3,800

Anr Ed. L, 1811. 2 vols. 4to, early mor gilt; rebacked. With frontis & 63 mtd ports, india proof prints. Diagonal crease across bottom right of Vol II tp & prelims; some foxing to text. bbc Dec 9 (218) $200

Hamilton, Charles

— American Autographs. Norman, [1983]. 2 vols. 4to. wa Mar 5 (293) $180

Anr Ed. Norman, Okla., [1983]. 2 vols. 4to. Half syn. sg Oct 31 (124) $130

Hamilton, Gavin, 1730-97

— Schola italica picturae.... Rome, 1773 [but 1870 or later]. Folio, modern cloth. With engraved title & 35 plates. Stamp of the Regia Calcografia di Roma on tp & several leaves. sg Sept 19 (208) $375

Hamilton, George, Surgeon

— A Voyage Round the World in his Majesty's Frigate Pandora.... Berwick, 1793. 8vo, contemp half calf; extremities rubbed. DuPont copy. CNY Oct 8 (124) $5,000

Anr copy. Modern calf. Tp stained. CNY Oct 8 (125) $2,600

Anr copy. Modern half mor gilt. S June 25 (67) £4,800 [Quaritch/Hordern]

Anr copy. Contemp half sheep; worn. With frontis. Library mark on front pastedown; frontis & tp soiled. S June 25 (494) £2,400 [Quaritch]

Hamilton, Mary

— The Surprising Adventures of a Female Husband! L, [1813]. Illus by George Cruikshank. 12mo, mor by Riviere. With folding frontis. Salomons copy. sg Oct 17 (165) $1,300

Hamilton, Patrick

— The Resources of Arizona. Prescott, 1881. 8vo, wraps; loose and chipped. sg Dec 5 (4) $110

Hamilton, Sinclair

— Early American Book Illustrators and Wood Engravers.... Princeton, 1958-68. Without Supplement. 4to, cloth. bbc Apr 27 (133) $100

— Early American Book Illustrators and Wood Engravers, 1670-1870.... Princeton, 1958-68. Without Supplement. 4to, cloth. sg Feb 6 (123) $60; sp Sept 22 (458) $140

Hamilton, Sir William, 1730-1803

— Campi Phlegraei. Naples, 1776-79. 2 vols in 1; without Supplement. Folio, contemp half sheep; rubbed & worn. With double-page map & 59 hand-colored plates, all hand-colored. Hamilton shown wearing a red coat. Some spots & stains. Sold w.a.f. C May 20 (256) £11,000 [Bifolco]

Anr copy. 3 vols in 1 including Supplement. Folio, contemp bds; spine lacking, worn. With etched & mezzotint title & 60 plates. Half-title in Vol I only; accession number in margin of p.43. Ck Nov 29 (294) £950

Anr copy. 2 vols & Supplement. Folio, half vellum, Supplement in half sheep; some wear & repairs. With double-page map & 59 hand-colored plates, all hand-colored. Some foxing. McCarty-Cooper copy. CNY Jan 25 (28) $40,000

— Collection of Engravings from Ancient Vases.... Naples, 1791-95. 4 vols. Folio, half calf; edges worn. With 2 engraved titles in English & in French in the first 3 vols, pictorial engraved dedication in Vol I & 249 plates only. Some plates browned; some foxing. sg Sept 6 (137) $2,000

Anr copy. Vols I-II (of 4). Folio, modern half calf & contemp calf. With engraved title & 122 plates. Some browning. SI June 9 (453) LIt1,800,000

— Observations on Mount Vesuvius...and Other Volcanos. L, 1773. 2d Ed. 8vo, modern calf gilt. With 5 plates & 1 folding map. Map & 1 leaf of text torn. bba Sept 5 (217) £220 [Worthing]

Anr copy. Contemp calf; rebacked. SI June 9 (454) LIt1,000,000

Hamilton Collection, Sir William

— Outlines from the Figures and Commpositions upon the Greek, Roman and Etruscan Vases. L, 1814. 8vo, contemp mor gilt; rubbed. With 62 plates. S Feb 11 (315) £240 [Shapero]

— HANCARVILLE, PIERRE FRANCOIS HUGUES D'. - Antiquites etrusques, grecques et romaines.... Paris, 1787. 5 vols. Folio, contemp calf gilt; extremities worn. 16 plates in Vol 3 wormed in blank corner. sg Nov 7 (87) $900

Anr copy. Contemp wraps; worn, spines chipped & cracked, Vol II with spotting in outer margin of titles & dampstaining in blank corner of plates. With 361 plates, about half hand-colored. Vol II with spotting in outer margin of titles & light dampstaining in blank corner of plates. sg Feb 6 (124) $1,500

— HANCARVILLE, PIERRE FRANCOIS HUGUES D'. - Collection of Etruscan, Greek and

Roman Antiquities. Naples, 1766-67. 4 vols. Folio, 2 vols in contemp calf & 2 vols in sheep gilt; some wear. With 2 hand-colored engraved titles in each vol, 5 engraved dedication leaves & 433 (of 436 or 437) plates, 181 hand-colored. One of the double-page colored plates loosely inserted in Vol II & possibly from anr copy; 1 leaf with tear repaired just touching a footnote; foremargin of Plate 25 cut short; large tear to margin of Plate 101; top margin of Plate 106 stained yellow; last plate of Vol II creased; other minor defs. McCarty-Cooper copy. CNY Jan 25 (27) $40,000

Hamilton, William T., b.1822

— My Sixty Years on the Plains.... NY, 1905. Illus by Charles Russell. With port & 6 plates. cb Nov 14 (78) $120

Anr copy. Cloth with port label mtd to front cover. sg June 18 (268) $140

Hamma, Friedolin

— Meisterwerke Italienischer Geigenbaukinst. Stuttgert, [1930]. 4to, orig half vellum; soiled, endpapers discolored. wd Dec 12 (401) $375

Hammar, August. See: Schulz & Hammar

Hammer, Victor

— Concern for the Art of Civilized Man. Lexington KY: Stamperia del Santuccio, 1963. One of 109. Bds. cb Jan 16 (70) $90

— A Theory of Architecture. NY, [1952]. Review copy. cb Jan 16 (69) $60

Hammer-Purgstall, Joseph von, 1774-1856

— Geschichte des Osmanischen Reiches. Pest, 1834-35. 4 vols. 8vo, cloth; worn. With 8 folding maps. S June 30 (319) £250 [Consolidated Real]

Hammett, Dashiell, 1894-1961

— The Dain Curse. NY, 1929. Cloth, with fragment of d/j. bbc Apr 27 (316) $230

— The Glass Key. L, 1931. 1st Ed. Orig cloth with fragment of d/j. bbc Apr 27 (317) $185

1st American Ed. NY, 1931. Orig cloth, in d/j with wear at extremities. Inscr to Katheryn Lyon, 28 Apr 1935. P June 17 (225) $5,000

— The Maltese Falcon. NY, 1930. In rubbed, torn & chipped d/j. bbc Apr 27 (318) $1,850

Anr copy. Orig cloth, in d/j with tears at foot of spine. P Oct 11 (159) $27,000

Anr copy. Orig cloth. sg June 11 (134) $300

— Red Harvest. NY, 1929. sg June 11 (135) $250

— The Thin Man. NY, 1934. 1st Ed, Later state. In d/j, with reviews on front flap. Epstein copy. sg Apr 29 (204) $950

Hammond, Capt. Harold

— Pinkey Perkins, Just a Boy. NY, 1905. In d/j. Epstein copy. sg Apr 29 (205) $425

Hammond, John Martin

— Colonial Mansions of Maryland and Delaware. Phila. & L, 1914. Orig cloth. With 65 plates. wa Mar 5 (373) $85

Hamon, P. G.

— Spinal Deformities Cured and Prevented.... L, 1832. 8vo, 19th-cent calf gilt, orig front wrap bound in. With 8 hand-colored plates. sg Mar 26 (141) $225

Hampton, J. Fitzgerald

— Modern Angling Bibliography. L, 1947. In d/j. Koopman copy. O Oct 29 (164) $70

Hampton, Taylor

— The Nickel Plate Road. Cleveland, 1947. In d/j. cb Feb 13 (163) $55

Hamy, E. T. J. See: Quatrefages de Breau & Hamy

Hanbury, William, 1725-78

— A Complete Body of Planting and Gardening. L, 1770-71. 2 vols. Folio, contemp calf. With 2 frontises & 20 plates. C Oct 30 (267) £1,300 [Hayley]

Hancarville, Pierre Francois Hugues d'

See also: Hamilton Collection, Sir William

— Monumens de la vie privee des douze Cesars.... Caprees [Nancy: Leclerc], 1780. 2d Issue. 4to, contemp calf gilt; some wear. With engraved title & 50 plates. SI Dec 5 (845) LIt1,900,000

Hancke, Erich

— Max Liebermann: sein Leben und seine Werke. Berlin, 1923. 4to, half vellum. sg Dec 19 (156) $100; wd Dec 12 (402) $50

Hancock, Albany. See: Alder & Hancock

Handbook...

— Handbook on Rigid Airship No. 1. L: Admiralty, Nov 1913. Parts I & II & Appendix in 1 vol. Cloth; marked & rubbed. bba Jan 30 (410) £220 [Elton]

Hanfstaengl, Francois

— Die Vorzueglichsten Gemaelde des Koeniglichen Galerie in Dresden. Dresden, 1842. 3 vols. Folio, 19th-cent half mor; upper covers of Vols II & III detached. With 3 litho titles, 3 frontis ports, allegorial plate & 200 litho plates on india paper, several tinted. Spotting affecting several margins. S June 25 (99) £400 [Toscani]

Hanley, Sylvanus, 1819-99. See: Forbes & Hanley

Hanna, Phil Townsend

— Libros Californianos, or Five Feet of California Books. Los Angeles, 1958. One of 1,000, sgd. cb Oct 17 (394) $55

Hannaford, Samuel

— Sea and River-Side Rambles in Victoria. Geelong, 1860. 8vo, upper wrap laid down & lower wrap replaced in stiffened card to match. Some staining. kh Nov 11 (282) A$80

Hanneman, Audre

— Ernest Hemingway: a Comprehensive Bibliography. Princeton, 1969-75. 2 vols, including Supplement. In d/js. O Dec 17 (96) $70; sg Oct 31 (125) $100

Hansard, George Agar

— The Book of Archery, being the Complete History.... L, 1841. 8vo, half calf; rubbed. Some foxing. O May 26 (87) $85

— Trout and Salmon Fishing in Wales. L, 1834. 8vo, cloth; worn. Koopman copy. O Oct 29 (165) $80

Hansard, Thomas Curson, 1776-1833

— Typographia: an Historical Sketch of the Origin and Progress of the Art of Printing. L, 1825. 1st Ed. 8vo calf. L Nov 14 (27) £130

Hanson, Laurence William

— Contemporary Printed Sources for British and Irish Economic History, 1701-50. Cambr., 1963. In d/j. sg Oct 31 (126) $175

Hanway, Jonas, 1712-86

— An Historical Account of the British Trade over the Caspian Sea.... L, 1753. Vols I-II (of 4). 4to, contemp calf gilt; minor surface worming on lower cover of Vol I. With frontises, 14 plates & 8 folding maps. Vol II lacking 3A4. b June 22 (172) £90

Hanzelet. See: Appier, Jean

Haole, A. See: Bates, George Washington

Haraszthy, Agostin, 1812-69

— Grape Culture, Wines, and Wine-Making. NY, 1862. 8vo, orig cloth; worn & soiled. sg Mar 5 (333) $800

Harcourt, John

— Original Jests. L, 1827. 1st Ed, with lettering on frontis. Illus by George Cruikshank. 12mo, orig wraps bound in. sg Oct 17 (166) $60

Hardie, James, 1758-1826

— The American Remembrancer, and Universal Tablet of Memory. Phila., 1795. 1st Ed. 12mo, contemp sheep; lacking front free endpaper. sg June 18 (269) $120

Hardie, Martin

— The Etched Work of W. Lee-Hankey.... L, [1921]. One of 240. 4to, cloth; soiled. kh Nov 11 (112) A$70

— Water-Colour Painting in Britain. L, 1966-68. 3 vols. 4to, orig cloth. DW Oct 9 (878) £100

Anr copy. Orig cloth, 2 vols in frayed d/js. DW Mar 11 (819) £90

Anr Ed. L, 1975-79. 3 vols. 4to, orig cloth, in frayed d/js. DW May 13 (367) £65

Hardin, John Wesley

— The Life of.... Seguin TX, 1896. 1st Issue, with port mislabeled. 8vo, orig wraps. sg Dec 5 (113) $175

Harding, Edward West

— The Flyfisher & the Trout's Point of View. Phila., 1931. 4to, cloth, in frayed d/j. Koopman copy. O Oct 29 (166) $90

Harding, James Duffield, 1798-1863

— The Park and the Forest. L, 1841. 1st Ed. Folio orig half lea gilt by Leighton; rubbed, lower spine torn, corners bumped. With litho title & 25 plates. Interleaved; some foxing, mostly to mounts. Schlosser copy. P June 18 (549) $1,000

— Portfolio. L, [1837]. Folio, disbound. With hand-colored litho title & 23 plates. Some spotting & discoloration to margins. Ck Sept 6 (120) £90

— A Series of Subjects from the Works of the late R. P. Bonington.... L, [1829-30]. Proof copy. 4 parts. Folio, orig wraps; soiled, tears along fold. With 22 lithos, 18 on india paper mtd. Schlosser copy. P June 17 (547) $1,750

— Seventy-Five Views of Italy and France.... L, 1834. Folio, contemp half mor. With 75 plates on india paper mtd. Some spotting. Ck May 15 (110) £450

Harding, John

— The Chronicle of John Hardyng from the First begynnyng...A Continuacion of the Chronicle of England. L: R. Grafton, 1543. 2d Ed. 2 parts in 1 vol. 8vo & 4to, contemp blind-stamped calf over wooden bds; worn, rebacked, lacking clasps, upper cover detached. Black letter. First part lacking 1st 8 leaves & n3-4; 2d part lacking 2P1, 2P6-8, 2S1-6 & last 2 leaves, all but 2P6-8 of 2d part supplied in type facsimile; some browning & soiling; a few headlines cropped. Sold w.a.f. STC 12767. S Nov 14 (468) £280 [Rix]

Hardinge, Charles Stewart, 1822-94

— Recollections of India. L, 1847. Folio, contemp half mor. With 26 hand-colored plates, heightened with varnish. Plates cut round & mtd on card without signatures. C May 20 (257) £5,000 [Fida Ali]

Anr copy. Contemp half mor gilt; rebacked preserving orig backstrip. With 26 plates. Lacking title to Part 2. C May 20 (258) £1,600 [Frida Ali]

Hardwicke, Elizabeth Yorke, Countess of

— The Court of Oberon.... L, 1823. 4to, contemp half lea; worn, broken. With engraved title & 24 plates. Some foxing. bba July 23 (181) £90 [Ginnan]

Hardy, Campbell

— Forest Life in Acadie: Sport and Natural History in the Lower Provinces of the Canadian Dominion. NY, 1869. 8vo, cloth; worn & shaken. Frontis taped. O Jan 14 (88) $70

— Sporting Adventures in the New World. L, 1855. 1st Ed. 2 vols. 8vo, orig cloth. bba June 25 (260) £80 [Thorp]

Anr copy. Orig cloth; worn. Library markings. Koopman copy. O Oct 29 (167) $375

Hardy, Charles

— A Register of Ships, employed in the Service of the Honorable The United East India Company.... L, 1811. 8vo, contemp half calf gilt. sg May 21 (44) $350

Hardy, Grahame —& Darrell, Paul

— American Locomotives, 1871-1881. Oakland, 1950. One of 1,000. cb Feb 13 (165) $100

Hardy, Joseph

— A Picturesque and Descriptive Tour in the Mountains of the High Pyrenees. L, 1825. 8vo, contemp half mor gilt by Simier. With map & 24 mtd hand-colored plates. C May 20 (68) £450 [Montero]

Anr copy. Orig cloth; small split to upper joint. With 24 colored plates, mtd as issued. C May 20 (70) £620 [Quaritch]

Hardy, Robert William Hale, d.1871

— Travels in the Interior of Mexico. L, 1829. 8vo, later half calf; rubbed, spine repaired. Folding map torn. cb Nov 14 (81) $140

Hardy, Thomas, 1840-1928

See also: Limited Editions Club

— The Dynasts: a Drama of the Napoleonic War. L, 1927. One of 525. 3 vols. 4to, orig half vellum. cb Sept 19 (82) $275

— A Group of Noble Dames. [L, 1891]. 1st Ed. 3 vols. 8vo, 1st bdg, orig cloth. Inscr to the Earl of Lytton. CNY Dec 5 (245) $2,400

— Life's Little Ironies. L, 1894. 1st Ed. 8vo, contemp half mor. bba Dec 19 (374) £80 [Davis]

— Old Mrs. Chundle. NY, 1929. One of 742. Z Oct 26 (104) $65

— The Return of the Native. L, 1878. 1st Ed in Book form. 3 vols. 8vo, orig cloth in recent half calf box; rubbed, extremities worn. DW Apr 8 (249) £1,300

Anr copy. Orig cloth; some hinges cracked. Lightly foxed. Epstein copy. sg Apr 29 (206) $2,600

— Tess of the D'Urbervilles.... [L, 1891]. 1st Ed in Book form, 1st Issue. 3 vols. 8vo, orig cloth; inner hinges repaired. Newton-Manney copy. P Oct 11 (161) $2,500; S July 21 (131) £2,000 [Chappel Hill]

Anr copy. Orig cloth; edges rubbed, spines cocked. Epstein copy. sg Apr 29 (208) $2,400

Anr Ed. L, 1892. 2d Issue. 3 vols. 8vo, later half mor by Root & Son. DW Apr 8 (250) £500

Anr Ed. L, 1926. One of 325. Illus by Vivien Gribble. 4to, orig half vellum; corners rubbed. bba Oct 10 (393) £260 [Boz]

Anr copy. Half vellum, in d/j. Epstein copy. sg Apr 29 (209) $800

Anr copy. Bds, in d/j. wd June 12 (392) $375

— Two on a Tower.... NY, 1882. 1st American Ed. 8vo, orig cloth; rubbed. DW Apr 8 (252) £65

— The Well-Beloved. L, 1897. 1st Ed. 8vo, orig cloth; top of spine damaged. Lafcadio Hearn's copy, sgd on tp. K July 12 (251) $70

— Winter Words in Various Moods and Metres. L, 1928. In d/j. cb Dec 12 (67) $55

— Works. NY: Harper, [1895]. Anniversary Ed. 21 vols. 8vo, half mor; some covers soiled. With ALs bound into Vol I. CNY Dec 5 (403) $2,000

Wessex Ed. L, 1912-31. 21 vols. Half mor gilt; rubbed. P June 17 (340) $2,000

— Yuletide in a Younger World. NY: W. E. Rudge, 1927. 1st American Ed, one of 27. Orig wraps. sg Dec 12 (142) $150

Hardy, William John, 1857-1919

— The Handwriting of the Kings and Queens of England. L, 1893. 8vo, cloth. cb Oct 17 (396) $70

Harkness, William Hale. See: Derrydale Press

Harlan, Robert D.

— Bibliography of the Grabhorn Press.... San Francisco: John Howell, 1977. One of 225. Folio, half mor. sg May 21 (230) $300

Harleian Library

— Catalogus Bibliothecae Harleianae. L, 1743-45. Parts 1 & 2 only. sewn. Tp to Part 1 & verso of final leaf of Vol II browned. Milne copy. Ck June 12 (83) £260

Anr copy. 5 vols. 8vo contemp half sheep; joints of 2 vols cracked. George Milne copy. CNY Dec 5 (263) $2,000

Harlow, Neal. See: Grabhorn Printing

Harlow, Vincent Todd

— Raleigh's Last Voyage. L: Argonaut Press, 1932. One of 775. 4to, orig half vellum. sg Dec 5 (114) $70

Harper's...

— Harper's New York and Erie Rail-Road Guide Book. NY, 1855-56. 8th Ed. 12mo, pictorial wraps; spine reinforced. sg June 18 (470) $100

— Harper's Weekly: A Journal of Civilization. NY, 1857. Vol I. Cloth; spine lacking. Z Nov 23 (305) $200

Vol II. NY, 1858. Half lea; worn & chipped. Z Nov 23 (304) $275

Vols V-IX. NY, 1861-65. Modern cloth. Marginal repairs. sg Dec 5 (59) $2,400

Vols V-VIII. NY, 1861-64. 4 vols. Folio, bdgs not described but worn, loose, 1 cover lacking. Some leaves torn; others with eroded margins, occasionally affecting text. Sold w.a.f. K July 12 (249) $1,700

Vols VI. NY, 1862. Cloth; disbound. With 14 Winslow Homer illusts. Minor creasing and staining. Sold w.a.f. O Mar 31 (91) $325

Vol VII. NY, 1863. Folio, disbound. With 8 plates by Winslow Homer. Marginal stains. Sold w.a.f. O Mar 31 (92) $325

Anr copy. Cloth; soiled & worn. Dark stains to final 70 pp; a few leaves stuck together; 1 leaf tattered. Z Nov 23 (303) $225

Vol VIII. NY, 1864. Folio, disbound. With 5 plates by Winslow Homer. Sold w.a.f. O Mar 31 (93) $400

Anr copy. Later bds; worn. Lacking pp 695-96, 347-52 & 769-84. Sold w.a.f. O Aug 25 (97) $225

Vol X. NY, 1866. Half lea; worn, front hinge broken. Some foxing; tear in outer margin of early leaves of Vol VII. NH May 30 (422) $170

Anr copy. Folio, half lea; worn & shaken. Sold w.a.f. O Aug 25 (98) $225

Vol XI. NY, 1867. Folio, old half lea; worn. Some stains & soiling. Sold w.a.f. O Aug 25 (99) $250

Vol XII. NY, 1868. Bound in 2 vols. Cloth. Z Nov 23 (306) $255

Vol XVI. NY, 1872. Folio, half lea; worn. Z Nov 23 (302) $260

Vol XX, Nos 992-1044. NY, 1876. Later cloth. Tp repaired with tape; some leaves with short tears. bbc Dec 9 (377) $275

Vol XXIII, Nos 1149-1200. NY, 1879. Early half mor; stained & frayed, upper joint splitting. Some leaves with short tears. bbc Dec 9 (378) $325

Vol XXVII, Nos 1364-1410. NY, 1883. Contemp half sheep; spine strip partially lacking. Title page rubberstamped. cb Dec 19 (75) $225

Harriman...

— Harriman Alaska Expedition. NY, 1901. Vols I & II (of 14). 4to, cloth. O May 26 (87) $85

Harriot, Thomas, 1560-1621

— Artis analyticae praxis.... L, 1631. Folio, contemp calf; spine rubbed. Some Ms calculations in a 17th-cent hand in text margins & on blank leaves; 2I2 with clean tear near lower margin; 2U2 cropped at lower margin with loss of catch numbers. STC 12784. Ck Nov 29 (191) £2,200

Harris, James, Pirate —& Others

[-] The Lives, Apprehensions, Arraignments, and Executions, of the 19 late Pyrates. L: for John Busby the elder, [1609]. 4to, 19th-cent half lea; top of spine chipped. Tp & last page soiled; hole in B1 partly injuring a few letters; piece torn from upper margin of G4. STC 12805. DuPont copy. CNY Oct 8 (205) $3,200

Harris, Joel Chandler, 1848-1908

— Daddy Jake the Runaway.... NY, [1889]. 1st Ed. Illus by E.W. Kemble. 4to, orig bds, in d/j. Epstein copy. sg Apr 29 (210) $1,200

1st English Ed. L, 1890. 4to, orig cloth; rubbed. K Mar 22 (176) $190

— The Tar-Baby and Other Rhymes.... NY, 1904. 1st Ed. bbc June 29 (395) $60

Anr copy. In d/j. Epstein copy. sg Apr 29 (211) $1,600; sp June 18 (429) $100

— Uncle Remus: his Songs and his Sayings. NY, 1881. 1st Ed. 8vo, lea gilt. Met Apr 28 (429) $270

1st Issue. Orig cloth; rubbed. Tear in blank margin of leaf 3-10. Manney copy. P Oct 11 (163) $2,000; P Oct 11 (164) $2,250; sg Oct 17 (270) $800

Anr copy. Cloth; front hinge tightened. Epstein copy. sg Apr 29 (212) $2,000

Anr Ed. NY, 1895. One of 250 L.p. copies, sgd. Illus by A.B. Frost. 8vo vellum; tp & frontis loose. Library markings. sg Mar 5 (46) $500

Harris, John, 1667?-1719

— The History of Kent. L, 1719. 1st Ed. Vol I (all pbd). Folio disbound. With port, 30 (of 42) double-page plates. Lacking map; port with marginal tears & creasing; some fraying; a few leaves of text lacking. Sold w.a.f. pn Dec 12 (309) £520 [Dinan & Chighine]

— Lexicon Technicum: or an Universal English Dictionary.... L, 1704-10. 1st Ed. 2 vols. Folio, contemp calf; rebacked & rubbed. bba Sept 5 (218) £1,800 [Kinokuniya]

Anr copy. Modern half calf. bba Jan 30 (93) £150 [Rogers Turner]

Anr copy. Modern calf. With 15 plates including port, 8 folding. Some foxing. Schlosser copy. P June 18 (466) $3,500

— Navigantium atque Itinerantium Bibliotheca; or, a Compleat Collection of Voyages and Travels.... L, 1705. 1st Ed. 2 vols. Folio, modern half syn. bba Jan 30 (114) £540 [Page]

Anr copy. 19th-cent half mor; worn, joints cracked. With 9 double-page maps, 3 plates of ports & 20 plates. Some browning; lacking 6H2 in Vol II. Sold w.a.f. CNY Oct 8 (126) $1,200

2d Ed. L, 1744-48. 2 vols. Folio, contemp calf; upper cover of Vol I detached. With 22 maps (15 folding), port & 37 (of 38) plates. Some folding maps torn; 2 signatures misbound. Sold w.a.f. bba Oct 24 (323) £1,300 [Faupel]

Anr copy. Contemp calf; rebacked. With 61 plates & maps. Some discoloration. S June 25 (34) £3,200 [Quaritch/Hordern]

Anr copy. Contemp calf gilt; rebacked. A few maps shaved; some spotting. Bibliotheca Lindesiana copy. S July 1 (1270) £1,800 [Remington]

Harris, Moses, 1731?-85?

— The Aurelian. A Natural History of English Insects.... L, 1766 [but 1839]. Folio, contemp half mor gilt; rubbed & soiled. With hand-colored frontis & key plate & 44 hand-colored plates, some watermarked "Whatman 1837". Possibly a proof copy; final index leaf watermarked Royal 1797. C Oct 30 (200) £2,600 [Colefax & Fowler]

Anr Ed. L, 1840. 4to, contemp half mor; rubbed, spine ends torn. With engraved title, frontis key plate & 44 hand-colored plates. Stamp on tp. pn Mar 19 (287) £2,600 [Shapero]

— An Exposition of English Insects. L, 1782. 4to, contemp mor gilt; rubbed & wormed. With engraved title, hand-colored frontis, key plate & 50 hand-colored plates. FD Dec 2 (262) DM3,000

Anr copy. Early 19th-cent half calf; worn. With engraved title & 51 hand-colored plates. Lacking frontis & plate of anatomical diagrams. S Nov 15 (741) £200 [Cherrington]

2d Ed. 4to, modern half calf. With engraved title, colored frontis & 50 hand-colored plates & plate of anatomical diagrams. U1 & X2 torn. S July 1 (918) £300 [Dunbar]

Harris, Stanley

— The Coaching Age. L, 1885. 8vo later half calf by Bayntun; rubbed & soiled. With 16 litho plates. cb Sept 26 (102) $110

Harris, Thomas Mealey

— Assassination of Lincoln. A History of the Great Conspiracy.... Bost., [1892]. 8vo, orig cloth; rubbed. bbc June 29 (208) $55

Harris, Walter, 1647-1732

— Pharmacologia Anti-Empirica. L: Richard Chiswell, 1683. 8vo, cloth. Lacking initial leaf; corners of a few leaves repaired. Gilbert Redgrave's copy. sg Nov 14 (44) $325

Harris, Walter, 1686-1761

— The History and Antiquities of the City of Dublin.... L, 1766. 8vo, modern calf. With folding plate & folded ptd table. CG Oct 7 (501) £120

Harris, William Charles, 1830-1905

— The Fishes of North and Middle America.... Wash., 1896-1900. 4 vols. 8vo, cloth; worn; Vol I tape-repaired. Library markings. O Apr 28 (121) $100

Harris, Sir William Cornwallis, 1807-48

— The Highlands of Aethiopia. L, 1844. 1st Ed. 3 vols. 8vo, rebound in cloth. With folding map & 3 frontises. DW Mar 4 (26) £190

— Portraits of the Game and Wild Animals of Southern Africa. L, 1840. Folio, contemp half mor gilt. With 30 colored plates. Final 2 text leaves with holes repaired, 1 with loss of text. C Oct 30 (201) £5,500 [Marshall]

Anr copy. Contemp half mor; bdg detached & rubbed. With litho title with hand-colored vignette & 30 hand-colored plates. Foxing & soiling affecting text & several plates; marginal tears or repairs to 7 plates & some leaves of text; additional title extensively repaired along inner margin; Plate 9 mtd on guards; stamps on verso of tp & at foot of last page of text. pn Mar 19 (288) £3,000 [Shapero]

— The Wild Sports of Southern Africa. L, 1841. 3d Ed. 8vo, orig cloth; rubbed. With litho title & 25 hand-colored plates. bba Sept 19 (60) £420 [Sawyer]

Anr Ed. L, 1844. 8vo, orig cloth. With 26 colored plates & folding map. Inscr. pnE Dec 4 (70) £520

Harrison, David

— The Melancholy Narrative of the Distressful Voyage and Miraculous Deliverance of.... L, 1766. 8vo, modern half mor. DuPont copy. CNY Oct 8 (127) $1,200

Harrison, J. C. —&
Evans, David

— The Birds of Prey of the British Islands. L, 1980. One of 275. Folio, orig half mor. With 20 colored plates. pn May 14 (171) £160

Harrison, Jane Ellen —&
MacColl, Donald Sutherland

— Greek Vase Paintings. L, 1894. Folio, later cloth. With color frontis & 43 plates. Library markings; 1 text leaf torn. sg Apr 2 (130) $200

Anr copy. Orig cloth; worn & soiled, endpapers soiled. With 44 plates. Some dampstaining. wa Sept 26 (601) $55

Harrison, Jim

— Selected and New Poems 1961-1981. [NY, 1982]. One of 250. pba July 9 (123) $75

Harrison, John

— Posters & Publicity. L, 1927. Orig wraps; spine chipped, front cover splitting along joint. 1927 Annual of Commercial Art. sg Apr 2 (232) $130

Harrison, Joseph

— The Floricultural Cabinet, and Florist's Magazine. L, 1833. Half calf; corners bumped. With 26 hand-colored plates. Lacking title. cb Jan 9 (113) $170

Anr Ed. L, 1833-47. 15 vols. 8vo, contemp half calf; worn. With 167 hand-colored plates. Ck July 10 (385) £380

Anr Ed. L, 1833-59. Vols I-IV only. Contemp half calf. Sold w.a.f. sg Sept 19 (189) $500

Harrison, Sarah

— The Housekeeper's Pocket Book and Compleat Family Cook. L, 1777. 9th Ed. 8vo, contemp calf; rebacked. S May 14 (986) £320 [Petta]

Harrison, Walter

— A New and Universal History, Description and Survey...of London and Westminster.... L: J. Cooke, [n.d.]. Folio, contemp half calf; rebacked, upper hinge cracked. With engraved frontis, 5 plans & 122 plates on 96 leaves. Frontis, tp & 2 other leaves torn, most repaired; 1 lef def. pn Sept 12 (314) £240

Anr copy. Contemp half lea; def. With frontis & 100 plates & maps. Lacking last leaf of index; a few final leaves def; browned. pn July 16 (189) £100 [Map House]

Harrsen, Meta P.

— Nekcsei-Lipocz Bible: a Fourteenth Century Manuscript from Hungary in the Library of Congress.... Wash., 1949. Ltd Ed. Folio half mor; scuffed. sg May 21 (271) $110

Harsdoerffer, Georg Philipp, 1607-58

— Vollstaendiges und von neuem vermehrtes Trincir-Buch. Nuremberg: Christoph gerhard for Paulus Fuersten, [1665]. 5 parts in 1 vol. Oblong 4to, contemp vellum. With engraved title to Part 2, engraved dedication plate & 58 full-page plates. Lacking frontis to Part 4 & 2 folding plates; repairs to D3-4, Part 1; upper fore-corners ink-stained at end; some browning. S Dec 5 (368) £2,100 [Kraus]

Hart, Charles Henry. See: Grolier Club

Hart, James David

— My First Publication: Eleven California Authors Describe their Earliest Appearances in Print. San Francisco: Book Club of Calif., 1961. One of 475. cb Oct 31 (38) $90

Hart, Lockyer Willis

— Character & Costumes of Affghanistan. L, 1843. Folio, orig half mor; backstrip worn, endpapers replaced. With litho title, map & 26 tinted litho plates. bba Nov 7 (180) £800 [Morrell]

— Character and Costumes of Affghanistan. L, 1843. Folio, orig half mor; backstrip worn, endpapers replaced. With litho title, map & 26 tinted lithos. bba Nov 7 (180) £800 [Morrell]

Harte, Bret, 1836-1902

See also: Clemens & Harte; Grabhorn Printing

— The Heathen Chinee. Chicago, 1870. 1st Ed, 1st Issue. 9 litho cards. Lacking envelope. Some foxing. sg June 11 (136) $200

— The Lost Galleon and Other Tales. San Francisco, 1867. 1st Ed. 12mo, contemp mor; joints rubbed. First and last few pp dampstained. cb Feb 12 (53) $125

— The Luck of Roaring Camp.... Bost., 1870. 1st Ed, 1st Issue. 12mo, orig cloth; spine ends chipped, causing some fraying. bbc Dec 9 (477) $225

Anr copy. Orig cloth; rubbed. cb Sept 19 (84) $250

Anr copy. Orig cloth; spine ends chipped. Marginal dampstaining to fore-edge corners. wa Mar 5 (190) $170

— A Millionaire of Rough-and-Ready. Kentfield CA, 1955. One of 220. Bds. cb Jan 16 (6) $250

— Outcroppings: being Selections of California Verse. San Francisco, 1866. Ed by Harte. Square 8vo, orig cloth. cb Nov 14 (83) $50

— The Queen of the Pirate Isle. Bost. & NY, 1887 [1886]. Illus by Kate Greenaway. 8vo, orig cloth, A bdg. K Mar 22 (165) $85

Anr copy. Orig cloth; marks on back cover. K Mar 22 (166) $120

— Works. Bost. & NY, [1896]-1914. Autograph Ed, One of 350. 21 vols. 8vo, half mor gilt; rubbed. P June 17 (341) $1,600

Anr copy. 14 (of 20) vols. Half mor gilt; some hinges cracked. Many illusts sgd in pencil by the artists. sg Oct 17 (271) $425

Standard Library Ed. 20 vols. 8vo, contemp half mor; spine ends chipped. wa Sept 26 (16) $300

Hartmann, Daniel

— Burgerliche Wohnungs Baw-Kunst. Basel, 1688. Bound with: Wilhelm, Johann. Architectura Civilis. Nuremberg, [later 17th cent]. Folio, contemp vellum; front hinge cracked. First work with engraved title & 18 plates; 2d work with 74 plates on 71 leaves. Some soiling or foxing; tear in Plate 9 of 1st work. sg Sept 6 (139) $2,000

Hartmann, Robert

— Reise des Freiherrn Adalbert von Barnim durch Nord-Ost-Afrika.... Berlin, 1863. 2 vols. 4to & oblong folio, orig cloth. Text vol with port, 3 folding maps & 4 plates; Atlas with colored litho title & 24 tinted or color-ptd plates. S Nov 21 (350) £1,200 [Maggs]

Hartzenbusch, Juan Eugenio, 1806-80. See: Gregynog Press

Harvard University

— The Houghton Library, 1942-1967. Cambr. MA, 1967. Folio, cloth. O Sept 24 (125) $70

Harvey, William, 1578-1657

— Exercitationes de generatione animalium. Amst.: Elzevir, 1651. 2d Ed. 4to, old vellum with yapp edges, painted red & with spine lettered in ink; free endpapers lost, some paint rubbed away. With engraved title. P June 17 (228) $1,500

Anr copy. Contemp sheep; joints cracked. sg Nov 14 (45) $2,000

— Works.... L, 1847. 8vo, orig cloth. Bodleian Library release stamp. sg May 14 (76) $275

Harvey, William Henry, 1811-66

— Phycologia Australica; or, a History of Australian Seaweeds. L, 1858-63. 5 vols in 4. 8vo, half russia. With 300 colored plates. Titles mutilated by removal of inscription, affecting the word Australia in each case; tp to Vol V lacking. S June 25 (27) £800 [Wheldon]

— Phycologia Britannica: or, a History of British Sea-Weeds. L, 1871. 4 vols. 8vo, orig cloth; rubbed & faded. With 360 plates. bba Sept 5 (56) £220 [Maggs]

Hasan ibn Yazid, Abu Zaid, al Sirafi

— Anciennes relations des Indes et de la Chine, par deux voyageurs mahometans.... Paris, 1718. 8vo, new mor gilt. Some browning & worming. DW Oct 2 (73) £65

Haseler, H.

— Scenery on the Southern Coast of Devonshire. L, 1819. Oblong 4to, contemp half calf. With 30 hand-colored plates (Plate 23 with artist's name erased as in Abbey's copy). C May 20 (71) £1,000 [Harley-Mason]

Haskell, Daniel Carl

See also: Stokes & Haskell

— The United States Exploring Expedition, 1838-42, and its Publications. NY, 1942. sg Oct 31 (127) $80

Haskell, Grace C. See: Latimore & Haskell

Haskell, William B.

— Two Years in the Klondike and Alaskan Gold-Fields.... Hartford, 1898. 8vo, cloth; front hinge cracked. sg June 18 (376) $50

Haskins, Charles Waldo, 1852-1908

— The Argonauts of California, being the Reminiscences of Scenes and Incidents that Occurred in California in Early Mining Days. NY, 1890. 1st Ed. 8vo, orig cloth; soiled & worn, hinge cracked. cb Sept 12 (78) $130

Haslem, John

— The Old Derby China Factory. L, 1876. 4to, later cloth. With frontis & 10 plates. Library markings. F Dec 18 (271) $90

Hassall, William Owen

— The Holkham Bible Picture Book. L, 1954. Folio, orig half mor. sg Oct 31 (220) $250

Hassell, John

— Aqua Pictura Illustrated by a Series of Original Specimens.... L, [plates dated 1812-18]. Oblong folio, contemp mor gilt; joints & corners worn. With 19 plates, each in 4 states, each with leaf of text describing the artist's technique with color samples. Tp & last 2 plates with crease; minor staining & spotting to some margins. C May 20 (72) £1,400 [Maggs]

Anr Ed. L, [plates dated 1818]. Oblong folio, contemp mor gilt; rebacked, orig spine retained, corners bumped. With 19 plates, each in 4 states. Prelims with vertical folds; some soiling; occasional foxing. Schlosser copy. P June 18 (467) $800

— Beauties of Antiquity; or, Remnants of Feudal Splendor.... L, 1807 [engraved titles dated 1810]. 2 parts in 1 vol. 8vo, calf gilt; rubbed. With 2 engraved titles & 52 plates. DW Dec 11 (111) £65

— Excursions of Pleasure and Sports on the Thames. L, 1823. 12mo, later mor by Riviere. With hand-colored frontis & 23 plates. Some spotting. C Oct 30 (40) £380 [Maggs]

— Picturesque Rides and Walks, with Excursions by Water, Thirty Miles Round the British Metropolis. L, 1817-18. 2 vols. 8vo, contemp calf gilt; soiled & rubbed. With 2 hand-colored frontises & 118 plates. Some spotting. C Oct 30 (41) £800 [Marlborough]

Anr copy. Later calf gilt. With 120 hand-colored plates. C Oct 30 (128) £650 [Wingham]

Anr copy. Contemp calf gilt. Lacking half-title to Vol I; blindstamp to titles & on 3 final leaves. L.p. copy. C May 20 (73) £700 [Marlborough]

— Tour of the Grand Junction. L, 1819. 8vo, orig bds; rebacked. With hand-colored frontis & 23 hand-colored plates. L.p. copy. C May 20 (260) £300 [Marlborough]

Hasselquist, Frederik, 1722-52

— Iter Palaestinum, eller Resa til Heliga Landet.... Stockholm, 1757. Ed by Linnaeus. 8vo, old half vellum over bds; soiled. Some browning throughout. S Nov 21 (293) £500 [Lepanto]

— Voyages and Travels in the Levant.... L, 1766. 8vo, modern cloth. With folding map. Some early leaves with worming to margins. S July 1 (757) £250 [Menicon]

Anr copy. Contemp calf; rebacked with modern cloth. Some browning. S July 1 (758) £200 [Menicon]

Hasted, Edward, 1732-1812

— The History and Topographical Survey of the County of Kent. L, 1886. Ed by H. M. Drake. Part 1 (all pbd). Folio, orig cloth. 11 plate torn across. Scattered spotting. DW Mar 4 (75) £65

Haswell, Charles H.

— Reminiscences of an Octogenarian of the City of New York. NY, 1897. 1 vol extended to 2. 8vo, half mor; rubbed & soiled. Extra-illus with c.160 plates. sg Dec 5 (181) $350

Hatch, Benton L.

— A Check List of the Publications of Thomas Bird Mosher 1891-1923. Northampton MA: Gehenna Press, 1966. One of 500. 4to, orig half cloth. sg Oct 31 (128) $140

Hatton, Thomas —& Cleaver, Arthur H.

— A Bibliography of the Periodical Works of Charles Dickens. L, 1933. 1st Ed, one of 250 L.p. copies, sgd by both authors. b Nov 18 (300) £190

Hatzveld, Adolf von

— Sommer. Dusseldorf, 1920. One of 60 with 4 lithos on japon pelure. Illus by Marie Laurencin. Folio, loose as issued. CGen Nov 18 (407) SF,6000

Haudicquer de Blancourt, Francois

— The Art of Glass.... L, 1699. 8vo, modern calf. With 9 plates. bba Jan 16 (85) £650 [Chaucer Head]

Hauke, Cesar M. de

— Seurat et son oeuvre. Paris, 1961. One of 1,050. 2 vols. 4to, orig cloth. S July 1 (1150) £1,800 [Schmidt]

Hauy, Rene Just, 1743-1822

— Essai d'une theorie sur la structure des crystaux.... Paris, 1784. 8vo, contemp wraps. With 8 folding plates. sg Nov 14 (246) $3,000

Havard, Henry, 1838-1921

— Dictionnaire de l'ameublement et de la decoration.... Paris: Maison Quantin, [1887-90]. 4 vols. 4to contemp cloth; front inner hinge of Vols I-III split. May lack a plate from Vol IV; some spotting & browning. Ck Oct 18 (283) £100

Anr copy. Contemp mor gilt; lacking spines, edges worn. With 256 plates, 61 in color. Some spotting. wa Mar 5 (569) $75

Havell, William

— A Series of Picturesque Views of the Thames. L, 1818. 2d Ed. Oblong folio, contemp half mor; rebacked preserving orig backstrip. With aquatint title & 12 colored plates, each within buff wash-borders & laid on card. C May 20 (75) £11,000 [Marlborough]

Havens, Munson Aldrich

— Horace Walpole and the Strawberry Hill Press. Canton, Pa., 1901. One of 300. Half cloth, unopened; some wear. O July 14 (91) $70

Haverkamp-Begemann, Egbert —& Others

— Drawings from the Clark Art Institute. New Haven, 1964. 2 vols. 4to, orig half cloth. sg Apr 2 (137) $140

Hawaii

— Ka Mooolelo no ka Ekalesia. NY, 1863. 12mo, cloth. sg June 18 (281) $200

— Ka Palapala Hemolele a iehova Ko Kakou Akua.... Oahu, 1838. 8vo, calf; front cover detached. Some foxing & dampstaining. cb Feb 12 (54) $400

— Ka Wehewehehala. Honolulu, 1847. 12mo, half cloth. sg June 18 (282) $200

— Na Haiao i Kakauia e na Misionari ma Hawaii nei. Honolulu, 1841. 12mo, old wraps. sg June 18 (284) $150

Hawker, Peter, 1786-1853

See also: Derrydale Press

— Instructions to Young Sportsmen.... L, 1824. 3d Ed. 8vo, half mor gilt. rs Oct 17 (53A) $75

Hawkes, John

— Fiasco Hall. Cambr. MA,: Pvtly Ptd, 1943. 1st Ed. Orig wraps. CNY Dec 5 (246) $600

Hawkesworth, John, 1715?-73. See: Cook, Capt. James; Fore-Edge Paintings

Hawkins, Sir Anthony Hope, 1863-1933

— The Dolly Dialogues. L, 1894. Illus by Arthur Rackham. 8vo, orig cloth. bba Apr 9 (281) £55 [Richardson]

Hawkins, Sir John, 1719-89

— The Life of Samuel Johnson. L, 1787. 1st Ed. 8vo 19th-cent half lea; hinges reinforced. Tp & final text leaf trimmed & inlaid to size. Extra-illus with 16 plates. sg Mar 5 (119) $110

2d Ed. 8vo, modern calf. 3 index leaves torn & repaired with loss. sg Mar 12 (147) $110

Hawkins, Laetitia Matilda

— Memories, Anecdotes, Facts, and Opinions. L, 1824. 2 vols. 12mo, contemp calf with Signet Library arms; rebacked. sg Nov 7 (102) $300

Hawkins, Richard

— A Discourse of the Nationall Excellencies of England. L, 1658. 8vo, old calf; spine varnished, front joint cracked. sg Oct 24 (145) $300

Hawkins, Sir Richard, 1562?-1622

— The Observations of Sir Richard Hawkins Knight, in his Voyage into the South Sea. L, 1622. 1st Ed. Folio, 18th-cent calf gilt; spine chipped, lower joint cracked. Marginal dampstains; ink writing on tp cropped by binder; ink stain on final blank. STC 12962. CNY Oct 8 (128) $8,500

Anr copy. Calf gilt by Eedy; covers detached, worn. Some soiling & dampstaining. STC 12962. CNY Oct 8 (129) $6,500

Hawks, Francis Lister, 1798-1866

— Narrative of the Expedition of an American Squadron to the China Seas and Japan. Wash., 1856. 3 vols. 4to orig cloth; head of spine torn; spine faded. sg Jan 9 (87) $200

Hawley Collection, Royal de Forest

— The Hawley Collection of Violins. Chicago, 1904. Ltd Ed. 4to, orig half cloth. With port & 36 plates, 23 colored & mtd. pn Oct 24 (228) £380

Anr copy. Orig half cloth; front hinge splitting. pn Oct 24 (379) £280

Hawthorne, Julian

— Nathaniel Hawthorne and his Wife, a Biography. Cambr. MA, 1884. One of 350 L.p. copies. lev gilt extra. 2 vols in 4. 8vo, Extra-illus with 350 ports, views, etc., & 25 A Ls s, including several of Hawthorne interest. CNY June 9 (83) $2,800

Hawthorne, Nathaniel, 1804-64

See also: Grabhorn Printing; Limited Editions Club

— The House of the Seven Gables. Bost., 1851. 1st Ed. 8vo, cloth; spine ends worn. sg Mar 5 (121) $225

— The Marble Faun. Leipzig: Tauchnitz, 1860. ("Transformation; or, the Romance of Monte Beni.") 2 vols in 1. 12mo, 19th-cent vellum, in cloth wrap. Extra-illus with ports & prints mtd on blank inserted leaves. bbc Feb 17 (224) $90

— The Scarlet Letter. NY, 1850. 8vo, orig cloth; covers dampstained, recased. Inscr to David Roberts of Salem. Webster-Manney copy. P Oct 11 (168) $21,000

Anr copy. Orig cloth; spine ends frayed. Epstein copy. sg Apr 29 (215) $2,800

Anr Ed. L, 1920. Illus by Hugh Thomson. bba Apr 9 (349) £80 [Ulysses]

— Tanglewood Tales.... Bost., 1853. 1st American Ed, 1st Issue. 12mo, cloth. sg Oct 17 (273) $275

Anr copy. Orig cloth; spine ends worn, rubbed. Epstein copysr. sg Apr 29 (216) $1,000

Anr Ed. L, [1918]. One of 500. Illus by Edmund Dulac. 4to, orig half vellum; endpapers creased. With 14 colored plates.

P Oct 11 (124) $1,400

— Twice-Told Tales. Bost., 1837. 1st Ed. 12mo, orig cloth. Some foxing. Manney copy. P Oct 11 (167) $2,250

Anr copy. Orig cloth; rubbed, spine ends worn. Foxed. Epstein copy. sg Apr 29 (217) $3,200

— A Wonder-Book for Girls and Boys. Bost., 1852. 1st Ed, 1st Issue. 8vo, orig cloth; worn. Epstein copy. sg Apr 29 (218) $1,200

Anr Ed. NY, 1910. Illus by Maxfield Parrish. 4to, orig cloth; rubbed, hinges cracked. bbc Sept 23 (465) $100

Anr copy. Cloth; rubbed. With 10 colored plates. K Mar 22 (327) $120; sg Oct 17 (347) $175

Anr copy. With 10 colored plates. sg Jan 30 (119) $150

Anr Ed. L, 1922. Illus by Arthur Rackham. Cloth; spine faded. bba Jan 16 (388) £130 [Ulysses]

Anr copy. In d/j, which is lacking top inch of spine. K Mar 22 (383) $150

One of 600. Orig cloth; extremities rubbed. DW Dec 11 (451) £155; sg Jan 30 (146) $800

Anr copy. Orig cloth; bowed, smudged. With 16 tipped-on color plates, 8 inserted color plates & 20 uncolored illusts. wa Apr 9 (268) $550

— Works. Bost., 1909. 13 vols. 8vo, half calf. bbc Dec 9 (220) $325

Hay, John Milton, 1838-1905. See: Nicolay & Hay

Hay, Robert, 1799-1863

— Illustrations of Cairo. L, 1840. Folio, loose in orig half mor gilt; def. With litho title & dedication & 30 views on 29 plates. Lacking tp & text; 3 plates with marginal tears, 1 with tape repair; some marginal soiling. pn July 16 (199) £800

Anr copy. Modern cloth; soiled. With litho title, dedication & 30 views on 29 plates. Soiled & browned in margins; a few short tears to text leaves repaired. S Nov 21 (294) £1,000 [Wolf]

Hayden, Arthur

— Spode and his Successors. L, 1925. In def d/j. kh Nov 11 (115) A$140

Hayden, Ferdinand V., 1829-87

— Geological and Geographical Atlas of Colorado. NY, 1877. Folio, orig half sheep; worn & broken. With 20 maps & views in color. Last map with 10-inch tear; some soiling & staining. Sold w.a.f. wa Mar 5 (435) $250

Hayes, William, fl.1794

— A Natural History of British Birds. L, [1771]-75. Folio, contemp half lea; rubbed, outer edge of bds worn. With 35 plates only. Tp torn; outer margin affected by damp & worn; some soiling. Ck Dec 11 (224) £950

Hayley, William, 1745-1820

See also: Hopkinson's copy, Francis

— The Life of George Romney. Chichester, 1809. 4to, contemp calf gilt. With frontis & 11 plates. bba Dec 19 (6) £320 [Thorp]

Haynes, F. Jay

— Yellowstone National Park: Photo-gravures from Nature. [Chicago, 1891]. Oblong folio cloth; spine ends repaired, corners bumped, hinges renewed. With 25 photogravures. Lacking tp. sg Apr 13 (49) $175

Haynes, James

— Travels in Several Parts of Turkey.... L, 1774. 8vo, modern half mor. Some browning. S July 1 (759) £300 [Hunersdorff]

Hayter, John, 1756-1818

— A Report upon the Herculaneum Manuscripts. L, 1811. 4to, contemp bds, orig upper wrap bound in; rebacked with old spine laid down. With 1 plain & 5 hand-colored plates. Some spotting & browning. Ck Oct 18 (63) £220

Hayward, John, 1905-65

— English Poetry: an Illustrated Catalogue of First and Early Editions. L, 1950. One of 550. 4to, cloth. sg May 21 (232) $60

Hayward, Sir John, 1564?-1627

— The First Part of the Life and Raigne of King Henrie the IIII. L: J. Wolfe, 1599. 4to, 19th-cent half calf. STC 12997a. W July 8 (59) £80

Hazanas y la Rua, Joaquin

— La Imprenta en Sevilla.... Seville, 1945-49. 2 vols in 1. 8vo, new cloth. sg Oct 31 (130) $275

Hazart, Cornelius

— Kerckelycke historie van de gheheele wereldt.... Antwerp, 1682-68-69-71. 4 vols. Folio, vellum; some defs. With 4 engraved titles & 116 (of 121) plates. Marginal worming; corner of 1 plate torn off. B May 12 (1035) HF650

Hazlitt, William, 1778-1830

— Political Essays, with Sketches of Public Characters. L, 1819. 1st Ed. 8vo, contemp calf; rubbed. Marginal staining at start & finish. bba Nov 28 (329) £130 [H. D. Lyon]

— A View of the English Stage. L, 1818. 1st

Ed. 8vo, modern half lea. Extra-illus with c.60 contemp engravings. sg Oct 17 (44) $275

Hazlitt, William Carew, 1834-1913

— Hand-Book to the Popular, Poetical and Dramatic Literature of Great Britain. NY, 1961. 8 vols. Facsimile re-issue of 1867-93 Ed. O Sept 24 (116) $50

— Old Cookery Books and Ancient Cuisine. L, 1902. Unopened. cb Oct 17 (410) $50

Head, Richard, 1637?-86?

— Proteus Redivivus: or the Art of Wheedling, or Insinuation. L, 1679. 2d Ed. 8vo, modern mor gilt by Lewis & Harris. Tp washed & strengthened at verso & possibly from anr copy; tears & repairs into text on A2; repairs with small loss to C8 & I8; margins of R1 & R5 repaired. Sold w.a.f. pn May 14 (2) £240

Headrick, James

— View of the Mineralogy, Agriculture, Manufactures and Fisheries of the Island of Arran. Edin., 1807. 8vo, later calf. pnE May 13 (6) £80

Heal, Sir Ambrose

— The English Writing-Masters and their Copy-Books. Cambr., 1931. Ltd Ed. Folio, half mor gilt; spine faded & rubbed. sg Oct 31 (221) $250

— London Tradesmen's Cards of the XVIII Century. L, 1925. 4to, half cloth, in d/j. pnE Oct 1 (268) £130

Anr copy. Half cloth; shaken. sp June 18 (350) $75

Healey, Robert C.

— A Catholic Book Chronicle: The Story of P. J. Kenedy & Sons, 1826-1951. NY, 1951. cb Oct 17 (413) $55

Heaney, Seamus. See: Limited Editions Club

Hearn, Lafcadio, 1850-1904

— Exotics and Retrospectives. Bost., 1898. In d/j. sg June 11 (137) $375

— Glimpses of Unfamiliar Japan. Bost., 1894. 1st Ed. 2 vols. 8vo, orig cloth; rubbed. DW Dec 11 (38) £60

Anr copy. Cloth; worn, hinges cracked. sp Feb 6 (429) $55

— Interpretations of Literature. NY, 1915. 2 vols. Half mor. b&b Feb 19 (69) $175

— Japanese Fairy Tales. Tokyo, [1905]. 5 vols. Wraps; stabbed & sewn. Ptd in color by hand from Japanese wood blocks. Epstein copy. sg Apr 29 (219) $1,300

— Kokoro. Hints and Echoes of Japanese Inner Life. Bost.: Houghton Mifflin, [1896]. 8vo, orig cloth; spine stained. sg June 11 (138) $110

— Kotto. NY & L, 1902. 1st Ed, 1st Issue. In chipped d/j. sg June 11 (139) $500

— The Romance of the Milky Way.... Bost. & NY, 1905. 1st Ed. Roughly opened. sg June 11 (140) $120

— Some Chinese Ghosts. Bost., 1887. 1st Ed. 12mo, orig cloth; soiled. Tp & some prelims splitting along inner margin. sg June 11 (141) $150

— Two Years in the French West Indies. NY, 1890. 1st Ed. 12mo, orig cloth; soiled. sg Dec 12 (143) $225

— Youma: the Story of a West-Indian Slave. NY, 1890. 1st Ed. 12mo, orig cloth. bbc Sept 23 (431) $90

Hearne, Thomas, 1744-1817

— Antiquities of Great-Britain, Illustrated in Views of Monasteries, Castles, and Churches. L, 1778-86. Orig parts I, III-IV, VII-XIII only. Orig wraps; some frayed. With 40 plates. Sold w.a.f. S Feb 26 (744) £200 [Brigantian]

Anr Ed. L, 1786-1807. Vol I only. disbound. With 2 frontises, 45 (of 50) plates & 2 additional plates. Plates rearranged by county; 3 plates remtd. bba May 28 (374) £190 [Clarke]

Anr copy. 2 vols in 1. Oblong 4to, conotemp sheep; hinges reinforced. With extra title & 79 (of 83) plates. Vol II lacking title & prelims. sg Jan 9 (88) $275

Anr Ed. L, 1807. 2 vols. Oblong 4to, contemp mor gilt; rubbed. With engraved title & 83 plates. Vol I, Plate 24 as frontis; plates 39/40 & 49/50 transposed; some spotting. S Nov 21 (118) £750 [Kennedy]

Anr Ed. L, 1876-1807. Vol I only. Contemp calf gilt with views on sides & fore-edge. With 50 numbered plates, frontis & view of Stonehenge. LH May 17 (603) $1,000

Heartman, Charles F.

— The New England Primer Issued Prior to 1830. [NY], 1922. One of 265. 4to, half cloth; worn. O Sept 24 (117) $70

— New England Primer Issued Prior to 1830: a Bibliographical Checklist. [NY], 1922. Out-of-series copy. 4to, half cloth; rubbed. Inscr & with Ns to Wilberforce Eames. K Sept 29 (192) $85

Heartman, Charles F. —& Canny, James R.

— A Bibliography of First Printings of the Writings of Edgar Allan Poe. Hattiesburg MS, 1943. cb Oct 17 (415) $85

Heath, Charles, 1785-1848
See also: Pugin & Heath

— Beauties of the Opera and Ballet. L: David Bogue, [1845]. 8vo, orig mor gilt; joints rubbed. With 10 ports. Some staining. S Nov 14 (229) £180 [Quadrille]

Heath, Laban. See: Heath's...

Heath, William, 1795-1840

— Fashion and Folly. L, [c.1822]. 4to, half mor, orig wraps bound in; worn & nearly disbound. With 23 hand-colored plates. K July 12 (252) $250

Heath's...

— Heath's Gallery of British Engravings. L, 1838. Vols 1-4. 8vo, contemp half lea; covers detached or starting. With engraved titles & 215 plates. sg Feb 6 (125) $475

— Heath's Infallible Counterfeit Detector at Sight. Bost., 1864. 8vo, cloth. sg Mar 5 (68) $140

12th thousand. Cloth. With 10 plates, 2 folding. K Mar 22 (105) $95

Heaton, John Aldam, 1830-97

— Furniture and Decoration in England during the Eighteenth Century. L, 1889. 2 vols in 4. Folio, orig cloth. b Mar 11 (51) £50

Heawood, Edward

— The Position on the Sheet of Early Watermarks.... Hilversum, 1950. 4to, orig cloth; spine ends worn. Ck Nov 1 (415) £110

— Watermarks mainly of the 17th and 18th Centuries. Hilversum, [1957]. Folio, cloth. sg Oct 31 (132) $425

Hebel, Johann Peter

— Francisca and Other Stories. Lexington KY: Anvil Press, 1957. One of 175. In d/j. cb Jan 16 (73) $55

Heber, Reginald, 1783-1826

— Narrative of a Journey through the Upper Provinces of India. L, 1828. 3d Ed. 3 vols. 4to, 19th-cent mor. With 27 plates. Ck May 15 (111) £160

Heberden, William, 1710-1801

— Commentaries on the History and Cure of Diseases. L, 1803. 2d Ed. 8vo, contemp sheep; rebacked, orig spine label preserved. sg Nov 14 (46) $400

Hebert, Alexandre

— La Technique des Rayons X. Paris, 1897. 8vo, orig cloth; joints rubbed. With 10 plates. sg Nov 14 (47) $300

Hebrew Books

— Haggadah. Sulzbach: Aaron ben Uri Lipmann, 1711. One of 6 recorded copies ptd on vellum. Folio, contemp lea gilt; bdg rubbed. Yaari 72. C June 24 (139) £17,000 [Walden]

Anr Ed. Metz, 1767. 4to, vellum. Lacking map; some foxing. Yaari 162. sg June 25 (87) $500

Anr Ed. Amst., 1781. 4to, half calf; rubbed. Yaari 199. sg June 25 (88) $1,800

Anr copy. Calf gilt. Lacking map. Yaari 199. sg June 25 (89) $500

Anr Ed. Prague, 1784. 4to, modern cloth. Institutional stamps on opening & closing leaves. Yaari 210. sg Dec 19 (87) $800

Anr Ed. Offenbach: Tsvi Hirsch Segal Spitz, [1795?]. 8vo, contemp half lea; worn & scuffed. Stain on tp. sg Dec 19 (88) $175

Anr Ed. Basel, 1816. 4to, bds; worn, front cover nearly detached. Some foxing & browning. Yaari 399. sg June 25 (95) $175

Anr Ed. Vilna & Grodno, 1836. 4to, modern cloth; stained. Some leaves strengthened. Yaari 545. sg Dec 19 (89) $110

Anr Ed. Livorno, 1847. 8vo, modern cloth. Lacking final leaf; stained. sg Dec 19 (90) $225

Anr Ed. NY: Henry Frank, 1853. 12mo, contemp half cloth. Foxed & stained. Yaari 722. sg Dec 19 (91) $275

Anr Ed. Trieste, 1864. 4to, bds; covers nearly detached. Some foxing. sg June 25 (98) $700

Anr Ed. Livorno, 1867. 4to, modern half cloth. Yaari 958. sg Dec 19 (92) $550

Anr Ed. Poona, 1874. 8vo, later half cloth; rehinged. Some repairs. In Hebrew & Marathi. Yaari 1077. sg Dec 19 (93) $2,000

Anr Ed. L: Beaconsfield Press, [1939]. One of 125, ptd on vellum. Illuminated by Arthur Szyk; ed by Cecil Roth. 4to, orig mor gilt extra by Sangorski & Sutcliffe. Inscr by Szyk. Epstein copy. sg Apr 29 (199) $5,800

Anr Ed. Tel Aviv, 1946. Folio, pictorial bds. With 12 plates. sg Dec 19 (96) $250

Anr Ed. Bost., 1965. Trans by Cecil Roth; illus by Ben Shahn. cb Jan 16 (138) $50

Anr Ed. L: Trianon Press, [1966]. One of 292, sgd by artist. Illus by Ben Shahn. Folio, loose as issued in wraps. Epstein copy. sg Apr 30 (414) $1,200

One of 18 hors commerce in auvergne, with 2 extra suites of color plates, a suite of uncolored plates on arches grand verge, a series of progressive states of 1 plate, 3 orig guide-sheets & stencils, 2 proof states of the litho frontis & 2 specimen pages. Unsewn in orig wraps, in vellum gilt box. P June 17 (359) $1,800

— Kol Meihechal. Jerusalem, 1888. Single sheet, c.245mm by 900mm. Left edge frayed. sg Dec 19 (128) $300

— Machzor mikkol hash-Shanah. Sabbioneta, 1556 & Cremona, 1560. 4to, old lea; gutter split. Heavily stained in plates; many paper repairs; some marginal note; censored; lacking 4 leaves. St. 2452. sg Dec 19 (188) $1,500

— Seder Chamicha Ta-Aniot. Amst.: Schlomo Jacob Judah Leon Timplo, 1726. 8vo, later half lea; worn. sg Dec 19 (190) $150

— Siddur Safa Berura. Roedelheim: Wolf Heidenheim, 1829. Bound with: Psalms & Techinoth for women. 8vo, contemp lea with silver fittings. sg Dec 19 (193) $400

— Sidur Mi'bracha Minhag Italiani. Ferrara, 1693. 12mo, modern cloth. Some foxing; first 2 leaves wormed. sg June 25 (83) $600

— Tephiloth kol Hashanah.... Buenos Aires, [c.1920]. 8vo, cloth. sg Dec 19 (17) $300

— Abravanel, Isak. - Pirush al Nevi'im Rishonim. Hamburg: Thomas Rose, 1687. Folio, later calf; spine worn, corners bumped. Lower outer corner of opening title replaced in Ms; ff.1-2 supplied from anr copy; outer edges dampstained. Cowley 255. sg Dec 19 (2) $100

— Almosnino, Moshe. - Tephilah Le'Moshe. Salonica: Joseph Yavetz, 1563. 4to, later half cloth. Lower outer corners of final 4 leaves repaired; last leaf, final blank & rear endpapers bearing stamp struck out in pen; some dampstaining; censors' signatures but uncensored. sg Dec 19 (4) $650

— Bialik, Chaim Nachman. - Ketina Kol-Bo. Berlin, 1923. 4to, pictorial wraps; spine taped. sg June 25 (48) $350

— Eybeschuetz, Jonathan ben Nathan. - Sepher Ahavath Yohathan. Hamburg, 1765-66. 4to, later half lea. Foxed; institutional stamps. Cowley 324. sg Dec 19 (76) $175

— Gedalia ibn Yahia. - Shalshelet Ha'Kabbalah. Amst., 1697. 8vo, bds. First 5 leaves repaired, not affecting text. sg June 25 (120) $60

— Immanuel ben Solomon. - Sefer Ha-Mahbarot. Brescia: Gershom ben Moses Soncino, 30 Oct 1491. 4to, bds with sheep spine & tips. Waterstained; upper margin shaved on 1st text leaf, affecting several letters. 159 (of 160) leaves; lacking initial blank. Goff Heb-43. P Dec 12 (56) $35,000

— Isaac ben Moses Aramah. - Akedat Yizhak. Venice: Juan di Gara, 1573. Folio, modern cloth. Opening leaf laid down with some loss along inner margin; 2d leaf remargined along outer edge; dampstained; marginalia. St. 5312.7. sg Dec 19 (16) $400

— Jehudah Loeb ben Joseph Rofe. - Kol Yehuda. Prague, 1641. Folio, modern lea. Tp repaired; some browning. sg June 25 (157) $200

— Joseph ben Gorion. - Sepher Yosiphon. Calcutta, 1841. 4to, later half lea. Tp mtd with loss; following 12 leaves with taped repairs not affecting text. sg Dec 19 (113) $175

— Karo, Joseph. - Shulchan Aruch. Amst.: Immanuel ben Joseph Athias, 1697-98. 4 vols. 4to, 3 vols in contemp sheep & 1 in calf. Some leaves loose; some staining; 2 errata leaves lacking. sg Dec 19 (141) $300

— Kipniss, Levin. - Aleph-Bet. Berlin: Hasefer Verlag, 1923. Illus by Ze'ev Raban. Pictorial bds; bumped, shaken, opening free endpaper removed. With 2 pages soiled. sg Dec 19 (198) $225

— Reuven ben Hoeschke. - Yalkut Reuveni. Prague, 1660. 4to, contemp calf; warped & damaged, portions absent. Some browning & staining. sg June 25 (131) $350

— Richietti, Joseph Shalit ben Eliezer. - Igereth Mesapereth Yechasuta Detzadikei De'ara Deyisrael. Mantua, 1676. 4to, modern bds. Outer margin shaved, affecting letters. sg Dec 19 (149) $400

— Shlomo Luria, Maharshal. - Ateret Shlomo. Basel: Conrad Waldkirch, 1598-99. Bound with: Loanz, Elijah. Rinath Dodim. Basel, 1600. 4to, later calf; backstrip scuffed. Opening title worn; stained. sg Dec 19 (159) $700

— Simon Darshan of Frankfurt. - Yalkut Shimoni. Salonica, 1521-26. 2 parts in 2 vols. Folio, modern calf. sg Dec 19 (222) $6,200

— Yakov Emden. - Mitpachat Sefarim. Altona, 1768. 4to, modern bds; stained. sg Dec 19 (69) $1,400

— Zahalon, Yakov. - Otzar Ha'chaim. Venice, 1683. 1st Ed. Folio, modern cloth. Opening 2 leaves torn with loss; some stains. St. 5633.1. sg Dec 19 (173) $1,000

Heddon, Jack

— Scotcher Notes. Bibliographical, Biographical and Historical Notes to George Scotcher's Fly Fisher's Legacy.... L, 1975. One of 150, sgd by Heddon & John Simpson, the artist. Half mor. With 6 hand-colored plates & a hand-tied artifical black gnat by Jack Heddon countersunk as frontis. Koopman copy. O Oct 29 (271) $275

Hedgeland, J. P.

— A Description, Accompanied by Sixteen Coloured Plates, of the Splendid Decorations...Church of St. Neot.... L, 1830. 4to, contemp half calf; rubbed. bba Jan 30 (21) £140 [Brewer]

Hedin, Sven, 1865-1952

— Central Asia and Tibet. L, 1903. 2 vols. 8vo, cloth. LH Dec 11 (124) $130

Anr copy. Orig cloth. sg Jan 9 (89) $225

— Trans-Himalaya: Discoveries and Adventures in Tibet. L, 1909-13. Vols I-II. O Apr 28 (171) $60

Anr copy. 3 vols. Orig cloth; dampstained. W July 8 (222) £160

Vols I & II, reprints; Vol III, 1st Ed. L, 1910-13. 3 vols. bba Mar 26 (329) £120 [Alpha Books]

Hedin, Sven, 1865-1952 —& Others

— History of the Expedition in Asia 1927-1935. Stockholm, 1943-45. Ed by Folke Bergman; trans by Donald Burton. 4 vols. 4to, orig ptd wraps, unopened. Half-title to Vol II inscr in pencil Donald Burton from F.B.. C May 20 (261) £500 [Loose Page]

Hedlund, Monica

— Katalog der datierten Handschriften in lateinischer Schrift vor 1600 in Schweden. Stockholm, 1977-80. Vols I-II in 4. 4to, wraps. sg Oct 31 (222) $200

Hedrick, Ulysses Prentice

— The Cherries of New York. Albany, 1915. Orig cloth; soiled & rubbed. With 56 color plates. wa Dec 9 (548) $75

— The Plums of New York. Albany, 1911. 4to, cloth; stained, bumped. Met Apr 28 (465) $50

Heeres, J. E., 1858-1932

— The Part Borne by the Dutch in the Discovery of Australia.... L, 1899. 4to, later cloth. kh Nov 11 (709) A$200

Hefner-Alteneck, Jakob Heinrich von, 1811-1908

— Deutsche Goldschmiede-Werke des sechzehnten Jahrhunderts. Frankfurt, 1890. Folio, disbound. Plate margins stamped. sp June 18 (351) $175

Hegemann, Werner, 1881-1936 —& Peets, Elbert

— The American Vitruvius: an Architect's Handbook of Civic Art. NY, 1922. Folio, cloth. With 1,203 illusts. K Sept 29 (20) $110

Heiden, Jan van der, the Elder & the Younger

— Beschryving der Nieuwlijks uitgevonden en geoctrojeerde Slang-Brand-Spuiten.... Amst., 1690. Folio, disbound. With 17 plates only. Frayed & frail; text def & imperf. Sold w.a.f. S Feb 26 (745) £160 [Shapero]

Heilner, Van Campen

— Our American Game Birds. Garden City, 1941. Folio, orig cloth; worn. O Aug 25 (101) $50

Heine, Heinrich, 1797-1856

— Ausgewaehlte Lieder. L: Essex House Press, 1903. One of 100. Illus by Reginald Savage. Mor gilt by Rene Kieffer. HH May 12 (2234) DM5,500

— Reisebilder. Hamburg: Hoffmann & Campe, 1826-30. 3 vols. 8vo, contemp half calf; rubbed. With holograph dedications, 2 in verse, to Friedrich Merckel in 3 vols. Gottschalk copy. C Dec 16 (342) £25,000 [Rosenthal]

— Tragoedien, nebst einem lyrischen Intermezzo. Berlin: F. Duemmler, 1823. 8vo, later 19th-cent half mor. Tp & 2 other leaves rehinged. ALs to Rahel Varnhagen tipped in. Gottschalk copy. C Dec 16 (341) £8,500 [Rosenthal]

Heinichen, Johann David

— Der General-Bass in der Composition.... Dresden, 1728. 4to, contemp vellum; hinges cracked, endpapers soiled. With 3 plates. Tp soiled. sg Mar 5 (234) $425

Heink, Johann Anton

— Praktische Bemerkungen ueber die kleine Jagd. Dresden, 1827. 4to, late 19th-cent cloth. With 1 uncolored & 26 hand-colored lithos. Some upper & lower margins shaved, occasionally affecting ptd border & caption. S Feb 26 (863) £900 [Shapero]

Heinlein, Robert A.

— Assignment in Eternity. Reading: Fantasy Press, [1953]. In d/j. Label sgd by Heinlein mtd to front free endpaper. pba July 9 (124) $150; sp Nov 24 (371) $85

One of 500. In d/j with wear at ends of spine panel. Sgd. sg June 11 (143) $375

Anr copy. Orig cloth, Currey's A bdg, in d/j with 1 closed tear. wa Mar 5 (195) $400

— Beyond This Horizon. Reading: Fantasy Press, 1948. In d/j. bbc Dec 9 (576) $200

One of 500. In repaired & soiled d/j. Sgd on bookplate tipped to front free endpaper. pba July 9 (125) $85

Anr copy. In chipped & rubbed d/j with tear along rear flap fold. Sgd on bookplate tipped to front free endpaper. sg June 11 (144) $375

Anr copy. In d/j. Inscr to C. S. Kuhn. wa Mar 5 (196) $425

— The Door into Summer. Garden City, 1957. In d/j. sg June 11 (145) $400

Anr copy. Bdg water-damaged. sp Nov 24 (372) $125

— Farmer in the Sky. NY, 1950. In d/j. sp Feb 6 (466) $130

— Glory Road. NY: Putnam, [1963]. In d/j with edge wear. sg June 11 (146) $250

— The Green Hills of Earth. Chicago: Shasta, [1951]. In d/j with edge wear. sg June 11 (147) $120

— The Man Who Sold the Moon. Chicago: Shasta, [1950]. In chipped d/j. sg June 11 (148) $110

One of 250. In d/j. wa Mar 5 (194) $400

— The Menace from Earth. Hicksville: Gnome, [1959]. In d/j. sg June 11 (149) $90

— The Moon is a Harsh Mistress. NY: Putnam, [1966]. In abraded d/j. Inscr. P Oct 11 (170) $2,250

— Orphans of the Sky. NY: Putnam, [1964]. In d/j. sg June 11 (150) $80

— Revolt in 2100. Chicago: Shasta, [1953]. In d/j. Sgd on tipped-in page. sg June 11 (151) $325

One of 200 pre-publications, sgd. In d/j. wa Mar 5 (192) $550

— Rocket Ship Galileo. NY: Scribner's, [1947]. Orig cloth, in frayed d/j. Inscr. P Oct 11 (169) $1,000

Anr copy. In d/j with small chip & tears & some later coloring. wa Sept 26 (330) $290

— Sixth Column. NY: Gnome, [1949]. In d/j. bbc Dec 9 (577) $190; wa Mar 5 (193) $300

Anr Ed. NY: Gnome Press, [1949]. In d/j with edge wear. sg June 11 (152) $200

— Space Cadet. NY, 1948. In d/j with edge tears. Sgd & dated. sg June 11 (153) $600

— Stranger in a Strange Land. NY: Putnam, [1961]. In d/j. K July 12 (253) $700

Anr copy. In d/j. Epstein cpy. sg Apr 29 (220) $950

— Time for the Stars. NY: Scribner's, [1956]. 1st Ed, with code A-8.56(v) on copyright page. In d/j. sg June 11 (154) $140

— The Unpleasant Profession of Jonathan Hoag. Hicksville: Gnome Press, [1959]. In d/j with chip to spine. sg June 11 (155) $100

— Waldo and Magic, Inc. Garden City, 1950. In d/j. sg June 11 (156) $150

Heins, Henry Hardy

— A Golden Anniversary Bibliography of Edgar Rice Burroughs. West Kingston RI: Grant, 1964. In d/j. F Dec 18 (121) $210

Heldenbuch

— Heldenbuch. [Strassburg: Johann Pruess, c.1480]. Folio, contemp blind-tooled lea over wooden bds with orig brass catches; clasps gone, front cover detached, foot of spine def. 38 lines; double column; type 1:100G. With 163 woodcuts repeated to 230 impressions, including 3 full-page frontises; rubricated in red & blue by a contemp hand. Minor marginal worming at beginning; some dampstaining. 284 leaves. HC 8419. C Nov 27 (49) £320,000 [Rare Books Ltd.]

Helding, Michael, Bishop of Merseburg

— Catechismus Catholicus.... Cologne: heirs of Johannes Quentel & Gerwinus Calenius, 1562. Folio, contemp blind-tooled pigskin over wooden bds, with brass catches & clasps; backstrip cracked. Stamp & ownership inscr of the Carthusians at Buxheim. sg Oct 24 (149) $375

Heller, Elinor R. See: Grabhorn Printing

Heller, Joseph

— Catch-22. NY, 1961. In chipped & soiled d/j. pba July 9 (129) $160

Anr copy. In d/j. Inscr. sg Dec 12 (145) $325

Advance copy. Orig wraps; soiled. CNY June 9 (84) $350

Hellinga, Wytze & Lotte

— An Original Leaf from the Ovid Moralise Bruges 1484. Amst., 1963. One of 40. Folio, in folding blue case with incunable leaf. Ck Oct 31 (202) £400

Hellinga, Wytze Gerbens

— Kopij en Druk in de Nederlanden. Amst., 1962. Folio, orig cloth. bba June 25 (14) £50 [Maggs]

Hellwig, Christoph von

— Nosce te ipsum, vel anatomicum vivum, oder kurtz gefastes...anatomisches Werck. Frankfurt & Leipzig, [1720]. Folio, contemp half vellum; def. With 4 plates, each with numerous overlays. Some browning of text. S Dec 5 (393) £1,000 [Pirages]

Helman, Isidore Stanislas Henri

— Abrege historique des principaux traits de la vie de Confucius. Paris, [1788]. 4to, contemp half mor. With engraved title & 24 plates. Some marginal staining. Ck Oct 31 (119) £170

Helmont, Jan Baptista, 1577-1644

— Ortus medicinae.... Amst.: Elzevir, 1648. 2 parts in 1 vol. 4to, contemp vellum, armorial bdg; dampstained. sg Nov 14 (48) $2,400

Helper, Hinton Rowan, 1829-1909

— The Land of Gold: Reality Versus Fiction. Balt., 1855. 1st Ed. 8vo, orig cloth; worn. Minor marginal stains. O Aug 25 (102) $80

Anr copy. Cloth. sg June 18 (81) $90

Helps, Sir Arthur, 1813-75

— The Spanish Conquest in America and its Relation to the History of Slavery and the Government of Colonies. L, 1855-61. 1st Ed. 4 vols. 8vo, half mor. NH Oct 6 (36) $150

Helvicus, Nicolaus

— Theatrum historiae universalis Catholico-Protestantium. Frankfurt, 1644. 3 parts in 1 vol. Folio, contemp vellum. With engraved title, 39 double-page plates & maps & 102 ports in the text. Some leaves loose; lower blank margin holed in places with loss; tp stamped. Sold w.a.f. S Nov 21 (179) £900 [Haas]

Helyot, Hippolyte

— Geschichte aller geistlichen und weltlichen Kloster-und Ritterorden.... Leipzig, 1753-56. 8 vols. 4to, bds; rubbed. With 810 plates. S Dec 5 (270) £550 [Reiss & Auvermann]

Helyot, Pierre, 1660-1716

— Ausfuhrliche Geschichte aller geistlichen und weltlichen Kloster.... Leipzig, 1753-56. 4to, old wraps; worn, spines perishing. With 807 plates. Some browning & foxing; some leaves loose in Vol IV. wd June 12 (394) $650

Helyot, Pierre, 1660-1716 —& Bullot, Maximilien, d.1748

— Histoire des ordres monastiques, religieux et militaires. Paris, 1714-19. 1st Ed. 8 vols. 4to, contemp calf; rubbed, some joints cracked. bba Dec 19 (82) £260 [Greenwood]

Hemingway, Ernest, 1899-1961

See also: Limited Editions Club; North & Kroch

— Across the River and into the Trees. L, 1950. 1st Ed. In d/j. Sgd by Orson Welles. pba Aug 20 (108) $110

— Death in the Afternoon. NY, 1932. 1st Ed. In worn & chipped d/j. K July 12 (254) $200

— A Farewell to Arms. NY, 1929. 6 issues. 4to, orig pictorial wraps; worn. In: Scribner's Magazine, May-Oct 1929 [Vol LXXXV, Nos 5-6 & Vol LXXXVI, Nos 1-4]. sg Dec 12 (150) $300

1st Ed, 1st Issue, without the legal disclaimer. In 1st d/j, with some chipping. bbc Dec 9 (479) $475

Anr copy. Orig cloth; portion of d/j tipped to front pastedown, covers spotted. Sgd. bbc Apr 27 (322) $1,600

Anr copy. Orig cloth; small portion of rear free endpaper lacking, part of d/j tipped to front pastedown. Sgd. bbc Apr 27 (323) $1,000; NH May 30 (268) $120

Anr copy. Inscr to Ludwig Lewisohn. Manney copy. P Oct 11 (172) $11,500

Anr copy. Inscr. Epstein copy. sg Apr 29 (222) $8,000

Anr copy. Repair to p. 65. sp June 18 (430) $70

Anr copy. In def d/j. wa Mar 5 (197) $130

Anr copy. In d/j with small paper lift to inside front flap. wa Mar 5 (198) $400

One of 510 L.p. copies, sgd. Orig half vellum. P Dec 12 (46) $3,750

Anr copy. Half vellum. Epstein copy. sg Apr 29 (223) $4,000

— The Fifth Column and the First Forty-Nine Stories. NY, 1938. 1st Ed. Orig cloth, in chipped d/j. bbc Dec 9 (480) $550

Anr copy. In frayed d/j. CNY June 9 (86) $650

Anr copy. Orig cloth, in d/j. 1-inch tear at head of spine panel. Epstein copy. sg Apr 29 (224) $300

— For Whom the Bell Tolls. NY, 1940. 1st Ed. Orig cloth. Sgd. cb Dec 12 (70) $350

Anr copy. Orig cloth, in frayed d/j; spine ends and corners worn. Inscr. Epstein copy. sg Apr 29 (225) $4,000

Anr copy. In d/j with edge tears. sg June 11 (160) $225

Anr copy. In d/j. sp Apr 16 (389) $70

Anr copy. Orig cloth, in 1st d/j, which is chipped. wa Sept 26 (188) $120

Anr copy. Orig cloth, in 1st d/j, which is smudged & edge-worn & repaired. With pencilled writing. wa Sept 26 (189) $65

— Green Hills of Africa. NY, 1935. 7 issues. 4to, orig ptd wraps; worn. In: Scribner's Magazine, May-Nov 1935 [Vol XCVII, Nos 5-6 & Vol XCVIII, Nos 1-5]. sg Dec 12 (151) $325

1st Ed. In creased d/j. cb Sept 19 (88) $400

Anr copy. In chipped d/j. cb Dec 12 (71) $350

— In Our Time. Paris: Three Mountains Press, 1924. 1st Ed, one of 170. Orig bds; spine repaired, minor wear to extremities. Inscr to Alma Lloyd. Manney copy. P Oct 11 (171) $22,000

Anr copy. Orig bds; bowed, spine ends worn. Epstein copy. sg Apr 29 (228) $9,500

1st American Ed. NY, 1925. Orig cloth; spine ends def. K Mar 22 (179) $1,300

1st English Ed. L, [1926]. bbc Dec 9 (481) $175

[-] Kiki's Memoirs. Paris: Black Manikin Press, 1930. 1st Ed, Ltd Ed. Trans by Samuel Putnam; intro by Hemingway. Orig wraps. sg Dec 12 (152) $140

— The Old Man and the Sea. L, [1952]. 1st English Ed. In d/j. K Mar 22 (180) $50

Anr Ed. NY, 1952. 1st Ed in Book form Inscr to Wendell Palmer. sg June 11 (161) $3,400

1st Ed in Book form. In d/j. cb Sept 19 (90) $160; cb Dec 12 (72) $110

Anr copy. Orig cloth, in ptd d/j (possibly supplied). With ALs, 12 Apr 1953. P June 17 (231) $3,000

Anr copy. Orig cloth, in chipped d/j. pba July 9 (132) $120

Anr copy. In d/j. sg June 11 (162) $275; sp Feb 6 (468) $100

Anr copy. Bdg soiled, in d/j. sp Apr 16 (390) $85

Anr copy. In 1st d/j. sp June 18 (433) $70

Advance proofs. Unbound as issued. sg Dec 12 (146) $350

— The Spanish Earth. Cleveland, 1938. 1st Ed, 1st Issue, with endpapers illustrating the F.A.I. banner. One of 1,000. Orig cloth. Epstein copy. sg Apr 29 (229) $1,200

— The Spanish War. L, 1938. Ptd wraps. In: Fact, July 1938. sg Dec 12 (147) $90

— The Sun Also Rises. NY, 1926. 1st Ed, 1st Issue. In d/j. Epstein copy. sg Apr 29 (230) $16,000

— Three Stories & Ten Poems [Paris: Contact Publishing Co., 1923]. 1st Ed, one of 300. Orig wraps. P Dec 12 (45) $13,000

Anr copy. Orig wraps; spine ends chipped. P June 17 (230) $10,000

Anr copy. Orig wraps. Epstein copy. sg Apr 29 (231) $8,000

— To Have and Have Not. NY, 1937. 1st Ed. In chipped & scratched d/j. Vertical crease to right side of 1st 2 leaves following disclaimer notice. bbc Dec 9 (483) $160

Anr copy. In worn d/j. bbc Dec 9 (484) $130

Anr copy. In frayed d/j. CNY June 12 (85) $240

Anr copy. In d/j. Inscr. Epstein copy. sg Apr 29 (227) $4,200

— Winner Take Nothing. NY, 1933. 1st Ed. Sgd by Orson Welles. pba Aug 20 (109) $130

Anr copy. Orig cloth, in d/j. sg Dec 12 (148) $225

Anr copy. In d/j with edge wear. sg June 11 (163) $250; sp Feb 6 (469) $50

Hemon, Louis, 1880-1913

— Maria Chapdelaine.... Paris & Montreal, 1916. Illus by Suzor-Cote. 8vo, mor extra by Canape, orig wraps bound in. S May 28 (356) £450 [Beres]

Hemsley, W. B. See: Cheeseman & Hemsley

Henault, Charles Jean Francois, 1685-1770

— Cornelie.... Strawberry Hill, 1768. One of 200. 8vo, mor gilt; rubbed. O Jan 14 (178) $150

Henderson, Alexander, of Melbourne

— Henderson's Australian Families, a Genealogical and Biographical Record. Vol I [all pbd]. Melbourne, 1941. One of 100, sgd. 4to, orig cloth; some wear. kh Nov 11 (520) A$850

Henderson, George —& Hume, Allan Octavian

— Lahore to Yarkand. L, 1873. 8vo, orig cloth; spine frayed at head. With folding map hand-colored in outline, 3 geological plates (2 hand-colored), 26 Heliotype view on 16 sheets, 32 hand-colored bird plates & 6 hand-colored botanical plates. b June 22 (362) £550

Anr copy. Recent half calf gilt. With 4 maps & geological profiles, 16 heliotype plates, 32 hand-colored ornithological plates & 6 hand-colored botanical plates. DW Nov 6 (53) £620

Anr copy. Orig cloth. sg Jan 9 (90) $650

Henderson, Harold Gould —& Ledoux, Louis Vernon

— The Surviving Works of Sharaku. NY, 1939. 4to, cloth. sg Feb 6 (126) $175

Henderson, Robert W.
See also: Grolier Club

— Early American Sport: a Check-List of Books Published in America prior to 1860. NY, 1953. 2d Ed. sg Mar 26 (142) $200

Hendley, Thomas Holbein, 1847-1917

— Indian Jewellery. L, 1909. Folio, half mor. With 167 plates, some in color. sg Apr 2 (138) $650

Henkel, Arthur —& Schoene, Albrecht

— Emblemata: Handbuch der Sinnbildkunst des XVI und XVII Jahrhunderts. Stuttgart, [1967]. Folio, orig half lea. SI Dec 5 (298) LIt400,000

Henkel, Paul

— Der Christliche Catechismus. New Market VA, 1816. 12mo, half cloth. sg June 18 (289) $140

Henley, William Ernest, 1849-1903. See: Farmer & Henley; Stevenson & Henley

Hennepin, Louis, 1640-1705?

— A New Discovery of a Vast Country in America.... L, 1698. 1st Ed in English, Issue with imprint ending "Tonson," with tp of Vol II supplied from the "Bon" issue. 8vo, contemp calf; rebacked, lea cracking, rubbed. With frontis 6 plates & 2 folding maps. Plates with repaired tears & reinforced folds; repaired tear to 1st map; 2d map with fold break affecting caption, supplied in ink facsimile except for 1 letter;l hole to I1 of Part 2 with loss to 7 letters; stain to upper margin of pp. 14-19, partially obscuring pagination of pp. 15-16; some foxing & browning. CNY Oct 8 (130) $2,600

— Nouveau voyage d'un pais plus grand que l'Europe.... Utrecht, 1698. 12mo, contemp calf gilt; split at head of lower joint, 1 corner worn. With folding map & 4 folding plates. Head of tp discolored. b June 22 (175) £1,600

— Nouvelle Decouverte d'un tres grand pays situe dans l'Amerique.... Utrecht, 1697. 8vo, contemp calf; spine nicked, 2 corners rubbed. With engraved title, 2 folding maps, folding view & folding plate. b June 22 (174) £2,000

Henrey, Blanche

— British Botanical and Horticultural Literature before 1800.... L, 1975. 3 vols. 4to, orig cloth. bba May 28 (520) £90 [Laywood]; bba June 25 (152) £100 [Grant]; DW Dec 11 (365) £200

Anr copy. Some stamps in text. pn June 11 (249) £100

Anr copy. Cloth. sg May 21 (234) $200

Anr copy. Orig cloth. SI June 9 (460) LIt200,000; wa Dec 9 (652) $240

Henricus Ariminensis

— De quattuor virtutibus. Strassburg: [Printer of Ariminensis type I, c.1473-74]. Folio, contemp blind-stamped deerskin over wooden bds; formerly chained with marks of hasp at top of lower cover. 34 lines; type 1:120G. 148 leaves. Goff H-19. Schoyen copy. P Dec 12 (26) $16,000

Henry, Alexander, 1739-1824

— Travels and Adventures in Canada and the Indian Territories.... NY, 1809. 8vo, contemp sheep; front joint repaired. Soiled & stained. cb Nov 14 (87) $1,000

Henry, Alexander, d.1814 —& Thompson, David, 1770-1857

— New Light on the Early History of the Greater Northwest.... NY, 1897. Ltd Ed. 3 vols. 8vo, orig cloth. cb Sept 12 (42) $160

Henry, Augustine. See: Elwes & Henry

Henry, David, 1710-92

— An Historical Account of all the Voyages Round the World, Performed by English Navigators.... L, 1774-73. 4 vols. 8vo, modern half calf. With 5 folding maps & 44 plates, 3 with later hand-coloring. Minor tears at folds; some browning. pn Dec 12 (357) £180

Henry, George Morrison Reid

— Coloured Plates of the Birds of Ceylon. L, 1927-35. Parts 1-4 in 1 vol. 4to, cloth. With 64 colored plates. S Feb 26 (921) £180 [Schober]

Anr copy. Parts 1-4. 4to, orig wraps; spine of Part 1 repaired. S Feb 26 (922) £180 [Shapero]

Henry VIII, King of England

— Assertio septem sacramentorum adversus Martin Lutherum.... L: Pynson, 1521. 1st Ed. 4to, 18th-cent russia gilt; rebacked, old spine laid down. Tp torn & repaired with final word supplied in Ms; some other repairs; stained. STC 13078. C June 24 (319) £850 [Rix]

Anr Ed. Rome: Stephani Guillireti, Dec 1521. Bound with: Literarum quibus... Henricus Octavus...respondit ad quandam epistolam Martini Lutheri. Rome: F. Minitium Calvum, 1527. 4to, later mor gilt. B1 & B2 supplied from a smaller copy. bba June 25 (163) £550 [Braunschweig]

— A Necessary Doctrine and Erudition for any Christen Man.... L, 1543. 8vo, 18th-cent mor gilt; upper joint & head & foot of spine repaired but rubbed. Tp repaired in margins with small section of the woodcut border supplied in Ms facsimile; repairs to the 3 preface leaves; repair to V4 with the headlines supplied in Ms facsimile. STC 5168.7. C Dec 16 (201) £450 [Sokel]

Henslow, John Stevens, 1796-1861

— Le Bouquet des souvenirs. L, 1840. 8vo, contemp half mor gilt; stained. With 25 hand-colored plates. Inner margin of frontis cropped. pn Sept 12 (295) £120

Henty, George Alfred, 1832-1902

— The Queen's Cup. L, 1897. 3 vols. 8vo, half lea; upper cover of Vol I loose, trimmed, spine ends chipped. S Apr 28 (69) £250 [Chulos]

Hepplewhite, Alice

— The Cabinet-Maker and Upholsterer's Guide.... L, 1789. 2d Ed. Folio, contemp calf; rebacked. With 127 plates on 126 sheets. Double-page plate with small tears repaired. C Oct 30 (43) £3,200 [Marlborough]

Anr Ed. L, 1897. Folio, orig cloth. Plates 1 & 2 loose. L Nov 14 (32) £90

Heralds'...

— Heralds' Commemorative Exhibition 1484-1934. L, 1936. One of 300. 4to, mor gilt. With 55 plates, some colored. Library markings. sg Oct 31 (133) $50

Heraud y Clavijo de Soria, Antonio

— Manuel de esgrima. Paris, 1864. 12mo, calf. sg Mar 26 (144) $90

Herbal

— Tractus de virtutibus herbarum. [Venice: Simon Bevilaqua, 14 Dec 1499]. 4to, early wooden bds; lea spine replaced, stitching of final quire def. 28-37 lines; types 22, 24:120G (title), 23:112– (ill. text), 18:83R (unill. text); 150 half-page woodcut illusts. Wormed at beginning & end affecting text & cuts. 172 leaves. Goff H-69. C June 24 (141) £7,500 [Mediolanum]

Herbelot, Barthelemy d', 1625-95

— Bibliotheque orientale, ou dictionnaire universel. Paris, 1697. Folio, contemp calf; joints rubbed. Some spotting. S July 1 (835) £350 [Quaritch]

Anr Ed. Paris, 1781-83. 6 vols. 8vo, contemp mor gilt. Some spotting or dustsoiling. C Oct 30 (107) £1,300

Herbert, Frank

— Dune. Phila.: Chilton, [1965]. In d/j. Epstein copy. sg Apr 29 (236) $1,400

Anr copy. In slightly rubbed d/j. wa Sept 26 (332) $650

Herbert, Henry Howard Molyneux, Earl of Carnarvon

— Recollections of the Druses of the Lebanon. L, 1860. 8vo, later calf; rubbed. S July 1 (761) £450 [Kanaan]

Herbert, Henry William, 1807-58
See also: Derrydale Press

— Frank Forester's Horse and Horsemanship of the United States.... NY, 1857. 2 vols. 4to, half mor. sg Jan 9 (264) $225

Anr copy. Orig cloth; shabby. With 11 (of 16) plates. Browned & with dampstained edges. Sold w.a.f. wa Dec 9 (426) $80

Herbert of Cherbury, Edward, Lord, 1583-1648. See: Gregynog Press

Herbert, William, 1718-95. See: Ames & Herbert

Herbert, William, 1778-1847

— Amaryllidaceae. L, 1837. 4to, contemp half mor. With 6 plain & 42 hand-colored plates. With errata leaf. S June 25 (28) £500 [Wheldon]

Herberts, Kurt

— Oriental Lacquer: Art and Technique. NY [1963]. 4to, cloth. With 324 mtd plates. sg Feb 6 (127) $200

Herdman, William Gawin, 1805-82

— Pictorial Relics of Ancient Liverpool. L, 1843. 4to, mor gilt; worn. With litho title & 48 plates. Litho title stained at outer margin. S May 14 (1149) £120 [Cherrington]

Heredia, Jose Maria de, 1842-1905

— Les Trophees. Paris, 1893. One of 25 on Whatman. 8vo, mor extra by Marius Michel, orig wraps bound in. Inscr to James Carleton Young & with ALs to Paul Verlaine inserted & with related material. S May 28 (358) £2,000 [Bonna]

Heresbach, Conrad, 1496-1576

— The Whole Art and Trade of Husbandry.... L, 1614. 4to, later calf gilt; head of upper joint torn, rubbed. Some worming in lower outer margins, touching border on tp; some browning. STC 13201. pn May 14 (34) £320

Hergsell, Gustav

— Talhoffers Fechtbuch aus dem Jahre 1467. Prague, 1887. 4to, half mor. With 268 plates. sg Mar 26 (145) $600

Heriot, George, 1766-1844

— Travels through the Canadas. L, 1807. 4to, orig bds; spine restored preserving orig label. With hand-colored folding map & 27 plates. S June 25 (434) £1,200 [Kahn]

Herman, William. See: Bierce, Ambrose

Hermant, Abel, 1862-1950

— Phili, ou par dela le bien et le mal. Paris, 1921. One of 275. Illus by Brunelleschi. Half mor, orig wraps bound in; spine rubbed. With 12 hand-colored plates. Prelim & final leaves reinserted on stubs. S Nov 14 (4) £240 [Leutsch-Dorner]

Hermes Trismegistus

— Le Pimandre.... Bourdeaux: Simon Millanges, 1579. Folio, contemp lea; spine rubbed, extremities chipped, upper joint split. Some browning; small tears to margins of 1st few leaves. C June 24 (320) £1,700 [Thomas Scheler]

Hermit. See: Longueville, Peter

Herndon, William Henry, 1818-91 —& Weik, Jesse W.

— Herndon's Lincoln; the True Story of a Great Life. Chicago, [1889]. 1st Ed. 3 vols. 12mo, half mor; worn. cb Sept 5 (60) $225

Herndon, William Lewis, 1813-57 —& Gibbon, Lardner

— Exploration of the Valley of the Amazon. Wash., 1854. Vol I only. Modern cloth. With 15 (of 16) plates. 33d Congress, 1st Session, House Exec. Doc. 53. sg Jan 9 (91) $50

Hero of Alexandria

— Gli artifitiosi et curiosi moti spiritali.... Bologna, 1647. 4to, later half vellum; rubbed. bba Sept 5 (220) £260 [P & P Books]

Anr copy. Recased in 17th-cent Roman bdg by the Andreoli brothers for Queen Christina of Sweden. Some staining. S May 28 (84) £1,200 [Zioni]

Herodian

— Der Fuertrefflich Griechisch Geschichtschreiber Herodianus. Augsburg: Heynrich Steyner, 1531. Folio, bound later in antiphonal vellum leaf; stitching weak. Some browning; holes in 2 final leaves. Ck Oct 31 (122) £550

— Historiae de imperio post Marcum. Florence: Giunta, 1517. ("Historiae libri VIII....") 8vo, old calf; worn & broken. Title soiled. O Dec 17 (101) $150

Anr Ed. [Geneva]: Estienne, 1581. ("Historiarum libri VIII...") 4to, vellum. Waterstained to upper margin. bba May 28 (433) £180 [Poole]

Herodotus

See also: Limited Editions Club; Nonesuch Press

— Historiarum libri x. Venice: Johannes & Gregorius de Gregoriis, Mar 1494. ("Historiae Halicarnasei libri novem....") Folio, old vellum sheet form a medieval Italian Ms used as bdg. 45 lines & headline; type 26:110R. Marginal staining. 142 leaves. Goff H-90. C Nov 27 (39) £5,800 [Panini]

— Historiarum libri IX. Venice: Aldus, 1502. ("Libri novem.") Folio, 18th-cent mor gilt; worn. Some staining; 1 leaf with small def; early Ms marginalia faded. C June 24 (273) £3,800 [Mediolanum]

Anr Ed. [Geneva]: H. Estienne, 1566. ("Historiae.") Bound after: Historia, sive historiarum libri IX. Geneva, 1570. Folio, later calf gilt with arms of Cardinal Mazarin; joints split, upper joint & cover repaired. Mazarin College-Thorold copy. C June 24 (274) £750 [Hakimzadeh]

Anr Ed. Frankfurt: A. Wecheli, 1584. 8vo, later calf; rebacked. bba June 11 (16) £85 [Kent]

Anr Ed. Geneva: Paul Estienne, 1618. Folio, contemp vellum. Tp stamped. sg Mar 12 (106) $275

— History. L, 1880. 4 vols. 4to, calf gilt, armorial bdg. bba July 9 (26) £160 [D & D Galleries]

Heroldt, Johannes

— Heydenweldt und irer Gotter anfangcklicher ursprung. [Basel: Henricus Petrus, 1554]. Folio, old bds; lacking spine. Lacking some leaves; tp soiled & creased; final leaves affected by damp & torn with loss at inner margin; some worming of inner margins. Sold w.a.f. Ck Nov 29 (99) £260

Heron-Allen, Edward

— De fidiculis bibliographia: being, an Attempt towards a Bibliography of the Violin.... L, 1890-94. 6 parts bound in 11, including the supplements. 8vo, half lea. pn Oct 24 (229) £160

Anr copy. 2 vols. 4to, orig bds; worn. pn Oct 24 (384) £300

One of 60. Orig bds; spine torn. Inscr to Arthur F. Hill. pn Oct 24 (230) £420 [Macnutt]

Herrera, Antonio de, 1559-1625

— The General History of the Vast Continent and Islands of America. L, 1725-26. 1st Ed in English. 6 vols. 8vo, later half calf; worn. With 2 folding maps, 2 ports & 12 plates only. Sold w.a.f. O May 26 (91) $425

— Historia general de los hechos de los castellanos en las islas y tierra firme del mar oceano.... Madrid, 1726. Parts 4-7 (of 8) in 2 vols. Folio, contemp vellum; def. Sectional title to quarta decada def; that to sexta decada lacking; some leaves def. Sold w.a.f. sg June 18 (291) $225

— Historia general de las Indias occidentales. Antwerp, 1728. 4 vols. Folio, 18th-cent mor gilt. With 5 engraved titles, 53 ports & plates & 3 folding maps mtd on linen. Engraved title to Vol I torn & mtd, those to Vols III & IV trimmed affecting imprint; 2 ports torn & repaired; 1 map cropped at foot with loss. C Oct 30 (108) £1,700 [Braeken]

Herring, Philip

— Paper & Paper Making, Ancient and Modern. L, 1856. 8vo, later cloth. Portion cut out of 1 specimen. bba May 28 (596) £180 [Maggs]

Hersey, John. See: Limited Editions Club

Hershberger, H. R.

— The Horseman; a Work on Horsemanship.... NY, 1844. 1st Ed. 12mo, orig cloth; joints splitting, spine foot frayed. With 30 plates. Some foxing. sg Mar 26 (146) $100

Hertz, Heinrich Rudolph, 1857-94

— Untersuchungen ueber die Ausbreitung der elektrischen Kraft. Leipzig, 1892. 1st Ed. 8vo, orig cloth. Inscr. sg Nov 14 (248) $4,200

Hervas y Panduro, Lorenzo, 1735-1809

— Catalogo de las lenguas de las naciones conocidas.... Madrid, 1800-5. 6 vols in 3. 4to, 19th-cent calf gilt by Clarke & Bedford; worn. S Feb 25 (553) £500 [Quaritch]

Hervey, Charles

— The Theatres of Paris. Paris, 1846. 8vo, later half mor gilt; extremities worn. sg Mar 5 (235) $150

Hervey, Frederic

— The Naval History of Great Britain.... L, 1779. 1st Ed. 5 vols. 8vo, later half calf. With 4 frontises, 44 plates & 9 folding maps. Some tears at folds; some browning. pn Dec 12 (55) £95

Hervey, Thomas Kibble, 1799-1859

— The Book of Christmas. L, 1837. Illus by Robert Seymour. 8vo, later calf. cb Sept 26 (189) $95

Hervieu, Louise

— L'Ame du Cirque. Paris, 1924. One of 403. Folio, unsewn in orig wraps. With 14 plates. S Nov 14 (292) £120 [Garnier]

Herzfeld, Ernst

— Materiaux pour un corpus inscriptionum Arabicarum, deuxieme partie: Syrie du Nord.... Cairo, 1956-54. 3 parts in 2 vols. 4to, modern half mor. Partly misbound. S Feb 11 (354) £320 [Loman]

Herzl, Theodor

— Der Judenstaat. Leipzig & Vienna, 1896. 1st Ed. 8vo, later wraps. Rubbed & soiled. bba Apr 9 (237) £80 [Farfouille]

Anr copy. Rebound in mor. Epstein copy. sg Apr 29 (237) $2,600

Heschusius, Tilemannus

— Zehen Predigten von der Rechtfertigung des Suenders fuer Gott. Laugingen: Emanuel Saltzer, 1568. 4to, early vellum; hinges cracked. sg Oct 24 (153) $750

Hesiod

— Opera. [Leiden]: Plantin, 1603. 2 parts in 1 vol. 4to, contemp vellum; soiled & worn, bowed. Stains on pp. 145-200; penned note along top edge of full-page woodcut. wa Apr 9 (120) $120

Hess, Hans

— Lyonel Feininger. NY, [1961]. Folio, orig cloth, in d/j. DW Mar 11 (507) £185

Hess, Pavel von

— The Album of Greek Heroism, or the Deliverance of Greece. Braila: Pericles Pestemalgiogla, [plates dated 1890]. Folio, orig cloth; worn & def. With frontis with port ptd in colors & silver (torn with significant loss) & 40 tinted lithos. Blank foremargins of last plates def. Sold w.a.f. S July 1 (621A) £1,200 [Sossidis]

Hess, Thomas B.

— Willem De Kooning: Drawings. Lausanne, [1972]. One of 100. Andy Warhol's copy. sg May 7 (48) $1,000

Hetherington, Arthur Londsdale

— The Early Ceramic Wares of China. L, 1922. 4to, orig cloth. Lower corners of several plates damaged by silverfish. kh Nov 11 (117) A$140

Heude, William

— Voyage de la cote de Malabar a Constantinople. Paris, 1820. 8vo, modern half calf. With folding map & 6 hand-colored plates. Small repairs to map. S Nov 15 (1174) £500 [O'Neil]

Heussen, Hugo F. van, 1654-1719 —& Rijn, H. van

— Oudheden en gestichten van Zeeland. Leiden, 1722. 2 vols in 1. 8vo, calf gilt. With folding map & 17 folding plans & plates. B Nov 1 (312) HF650

Heussler, Sebastian

— Kuenstliches Abprobirtes und Nuetzliches Fecht-Buch.... Nuremberg, 1665. Bound with: New Kuenstlich Fechtbuch....Nuremberg, 1630. 8vo, old vellum. Hole in 1 plate. sg Mar 26 (147) $2,600

Hewes, Robert

— Rules and Regulations for the Sword Exercise of the Cavalry. Bost., [1802]. 8vo, contemp sheep; spine ends worn. With 28 plates. Some foxing. sg Mar 26 (148) $175

Hewitson, William Chapman, 1806-78

— British Oology. Newcastle, [1831-38]. 2 vols. 8vo, contemp mor gilt; spine rubbed. With 155 hand-colored plates. DW Oct 2 (146) £110

Hewitt, Edward R.

— Secrets of the Salmon. NY, 1922. 1st Ed, one of 780 L.p. copies. 8vo, mor by Aquarius. Koopman copy. O Oct 29 (171) $250

Hewitt, Graily

— The Pen and Type Design. L, 1928. One of 250. Folio, bdg not stated. cb Oct 17 (419) $150

Anr copy. Orig mor gilt; extremities worn. DW Apr 8 (431) £65

Hewlett, Maurice, 1861-1923

— Quattrocentisteria: How Sandro Botticelli Saw Simonetta in the Spring. NY: Golden Cross Press, 1937. One of 175. Illus by Valenti Angelo. pba July 23 (12) $75

Hexham, Henry, 1585?-1650?

— A Copious English and Netherdutch Dictionary. Rotterdam, 1675-72. 4to, contemp vellum; soiled. bba June 25 (64) £65 [Kunkler]

Heydt, Johann

— Allerneuester Geographisch- und Topographischer Schau-Platz von Africa und Ost-Indien. Willhermsdorff & Nuremberg, 1744. Oblong folio, half cloth; broken. With engraved title & 83 plates only. Lacking 4 leaves; some others loose. HH May 12 (717) DM1,400

Heyl, Edgar

— A Contribution to Conjuring Bibliography.... Balt., 1963. One of 300. 4to, new cloth. sg Oct 31 (134) $200

Heylyn, Peter, 1600-62

— Cosmographie. L, 1666. 3d Ed. Folio, contemp calf; spine ends restored, endpapers renewed. With engraved title & 4 double-page maps. sg May 21 (46) $350

Anr Ed. L: Anne Seile, 1669. 4 parts in 1 vol. Folio, old calf; worn & shaken; spine crudely rebacked. With extra title & 3 (of 4) folding maps. Some tears & fraying. Sold w.a.f. O Mar 31 (97) $140

Heym, G.

— Umbra vitae. Munich, 1924. One of 510. Illus by E. L. Kirchner. Orig cloth. Some spotting. B May 12 (207) HF8,000

Heyward, Du Bose, 1885-1940 —& Gershwin, George, 1898-1937

— Porgy and Bess. NY, 1935. One of 250. 4to, orig wraps backed in black cloth; spine ends frayed. Pencil notes on a few leaves. bbc Sept 23 (422) $90

Anr copy. Orig lea; 3 tiny wormholes in joints. Sgd by George & Ira Gershwin. Epstein copy. sg Apr 29 (180) $6,500

Heywood, Thomas, 1574?-1641

— Troia Britanica: or, Great Britaines Troy. L, 1609. 1st Ed. Folio, contemp vellum; upper joints repaired; soiled & worn. Lacking most of last leaf; stained. bba Nov 28 (220) £95 [Rix]

Hiatt, Charles

— Picture Posters: a Short History. L, 1895. 8vo, cloth. sg apr 2 (233) $100

Hibberd, Shirley, 1825-90

— Familiar Garden Flowers. L: Cassell, [1879-87]. 5 vols. 8vo, half mor gilt; rubbed. DW Apr 8 (436) £125

Hibbert Library, George

— [Sale Catalogue] Catalogue of the Library of.... L, 1829. 8vo, contemp half calf; rebacked, rubbed. Priced throughout. bba Jan 30 (3) £110 [Maggs]

Hickeringill, Edmund, 1631-1708

— Jamaica Viewed. L: for Iohn Williams, 1661. 1st Ed but Variant of Wing H-1816 without "By J. R." given as ptr in imprint. 8vo, contemp sheep; worn, front cover nearly detached. With the folding map (repaired, upper border mostly trimmed). Small tear at gutter on tp; small burn hole in A4 touching a few letters; minor soiling. DuPont copy. CNY Oct 8J (131) $5,800

Hicks, Wilson

— Words and Pictures. NY, [1952]. In d/j. sg Apr 13 (50) $50

Hieronymus, 340?-420

— Buch der Altvater. Augsburg: Anton Sorg, 25 Sept 1482. Folio, 18th-cent calf; rubbed. 35 lines; gothic letter; woodcuts & large initials all hand-colored. Some tears; hole in 1 leaf; anr leaf remargined; fore-margin of final leaf renewed. 382 (of 392) leaves. Goff H-217. S Dec 5 (17) £5,000 [Thoemmes]

— Epistolae. [Strassburg: Johann Mentelin, 25 Sept not after 1469]. Folio, contemp deerskin over wooden bds with brass bosses, 2 fore-edge clasps, trace of chaining staple, 2 (of 4) iron peg-stands preserved, mtd on bottom edge of covers. Bound by the Dominicans of Vienna, with their tooled device; wormed & cracked with early repairs. 50 lines; type 2:111G; double column. 1st leaf strengthened on outer margin; slight staining. 224 leaves. Goff H-162. Doheny-Schoyen copy. P Dec 12 (27) $25,000

— Omnium operum.... Basel: Froben, 1516. 9 vols in 5. Folio, 16th-cent blind-stamped pigskin over wooden bds. Some worming at ends with loss; some staining & browning; annotations. S Dec 5 (138) £2,400 [Salvador]

— Opera. Basel: Froben, 1537-38. 10 vols in 5, including Index. Folio, 16th-cent blind-stamped pigskin over wooden bds; 1 spine damaged at head. Dampstaining at beginning of Vols IV & VIII; worming at end of the Index vol. S Dec 5 (139) £700 [Stanley]

— Le Vite de Sancti Padri.... Vicenza: Hermannus Liechtenstein, 1479. Folio, old vellum. 151 (of 166) leaves. Goff H-228. sg Mar 12 (118) $450

Hietman, Francis B.

— Historical Register and Dictionary of the United States Army. Wash., 1903. 2 vols. 8vo, cloth; extremities worn. sg Dec 5 (151) $120

Higden, Ranulph, c.1299-c.1363

— Polycronicon. Southwark: Peter Treveris, 1527. 3d Ed. Folio, 17th-cent calf gilt with royal arms; laid down, rebacked, joints cracked, rubbed. Black letter; double-column; full-page woodcut on verso of z6. With word "pope" censored throughout; tp in Ms facsimile; some marginal worming; browned & stained. STC 13440. P June 17 (234) $3,000

Higgins, Bryan

— Experiments and Observations Made with the View of Improving the Art of Composing and Applying Calcareous Cements.... L, 1780. 8vo, modern half calf. bba Sept 5 (221) £240 [Kent]

Higginson, Alexander Henry

— British and American Sporting Authors.... Berryville, Va., 1949. 4to, cloth. wa Sept 26 (114) $85; wa Mar 5 (138) $70

Higginson, Alexander Henry —& Chamberlain, Julian Ingersoll

— Hunting in the United States and Canada.... Garden City, 1928. 1st Ed, one of 450. Cloth; spine faded. sg Jan 9 (266) $90

High. See: Perceval le Gallois

Hildeburn, Charles R., 1855-1901

— A Century of Printing: the Issues of the Press in Pennsylvania, 1685-1784. Phila., 1885. Ltd Ed. 2 vols. 4to, cloth; worn. O Sept 24 (118) $100

Hildreth, James

— Dragoon Campaigns to the Rocky Mountains. NY, 1836. 1st Ed. 8vo, orig mor; rubbed. Stained. Inscr twice. O Nov 26 (81) $550

Hill, Arthur George, 1857-1923

— The Organ-Cases and Organs of the Middle Ages and Renaissance. Series I & II. L, 1883-89. 1st Ed. Vol I only. Modern cloth. sg Mar 5 (236) $300

Hill, David Octavius

— Sketches of Scenery in Perthshire. Perth: T. Hill, [c.1821]. Oblong folio, contemp half mor; rebacked, soiled. With 30 chalk lithos, 15 each on brown & white paper. Some foxing; Bridge of Earn plate lacking date called for in Abbey; 1 plate captioned in Pencil. Schlosser copy. P June 18 (550) $1,800

Hill, Fidelia S. T.

— Poems and Recollections of the Past. Sydney, 1840. 8vo, contemp mor gilt. C June 24 (143) £600 [Arnold]

Hill, George Birkbeck

— Footsteps of Dr. Johnson, Scotland.... L, 1890. One of 160. 4to, orig wraps. pnE Oct 1 (240) £55

Hill, Sir George Francis

— Catalogue of the Greek Coins of Cyprus. L, 1904. With map & 26 plates. S June 30 (39) £380

— A Corpus of Italian Medals of the Renaissance before Cellini. L, 1930. 2 vols. Folio, orig cloth; soiled. Author's annotated copy. S Feb 11 (104) £650 [Spink]

Anr copy. With 201 plates. SI Dec 5 (899) LIt1,000,000

Hill, Sir John, 1716?-75

— The British Herbal. L, 1756. Folio, 20th-cent half mor; joints & corners rubbed. With frontis & 75 plates. Library stamps removed, leaving marks on on plate edges. S Nov 15 (800) £550 [Erlini]

— The Construction of Timber, from its Early Growth.... L, 1770. 8vo, contemp calf; rebacked preserving orig backstrip. With 44 plain & 2 hand-colored plates. C Oct 30 (268) £1,000 [Heuer]

— Eden, or a Compleat Body of Gardening.... L, 1757. Folio, mor. With frontis & 60 plates. Some browning & staining; some plates with margins trimmed; Plate 4 repaired. pn June 11 (231) £1,700

Anr copy. Contemp russia gilt; joints split, worn. S June 25 (30) £2,200 [Beaux Arts]

— The Family Herbal. Bungay, 1812. 8vo, old bds; rebacked. With 54 hand-colored plates. DW Nov 6 (166) £60

Anr copy. Calf; joints split. pnE May 13 (21) £75

Hill, Jonathan A.

— The Hill Collection of Pacific Voyages. San Diego, 1974-83. Ed by De Braganza & Oakes; annotated by Hill. Vol I (of 3) only. sg Oct 31 (135) $225

Hill, Joseph J.

— The History of Warner's Ranch.... Los Angeles, 1927. One of 300. Half cloth. cb Feb 12 (31) $110

Anr copy. Half cloth. Cowan-Graff copy. sg June 18 (82) $100

Hill, Lewis Webb. See: Phillips & Hill

Hill, William Henry, Violin Maker —& Others

— Antonio Stradivari, his Life and Work, 1644-1737. L, 1902. 1st Ed. 4to, contemp cloth. With 21 colored plates & 9 uncolored plates of facsimile letters. pn Oct 24 (386) £460 [Macnutt]

— The Violin-Makers of the Guarneri Family.... L, 1931. 4to, orig half vellum; spine soiled. With 53 plates, 17 colored, 3 maps, 2 folding & 4 plates of facsimile labels. Tp & a few leaves soiled. pn Oct 24 (233) £400

Anr copy. With 53 plates, 17 colored, 3 plans & 4 leaves of facsimile labels. pn Oct 24 (234) £380

Anr copy. Orig half vellum; soiled. With 53 plates & 3 plans & 4 plates of facsimiles of labels. pn Oct 24 (385) £320

Japanese Ed. L, 1988. pn Oct 24 (226) £45

Hillary, Edmund

— High Adventure. L, [1955]. In d/j. Sgd. sg Jan 9 (288) $140

Hiller, Lejaren Arthur

— Sutures in Ancient Surgery. [N.p.]: Davis & Geck, 1928. 4to, portfolio; horizontal tear on spine, worn. With 51 plates. sg Apr 13 (52) $275

Hillerman, Tony

— The Great Taos Bank Robbery.... Albuquerque: U of New Mexico Press, [1973]. In 1st-issue d/j. pba July 9 (136) $225

Hills, Margaret Thorndike

— The English Bible in America. NY, 1961. O Sept 24 (1119) $60

Hilton, Harold H. —& Smith, Garden G.

— The Royal and Ancient Game of Golf. L, 1912. One of 900. Orig mor gilt; rubbed. S Feb 26 (923) £580 [McEwan]

Hilton, James

— Goodbye Mr. Chips. L, 1934. In chipped d/j. bbc Apr 27 (325) $220

Hind, Arthur Mayger

See also: British Museum

— The Etchings of D. Y. Cameron. L, 1924. One of 200. Half lea; rubbed. O Aug 25 (104) $110

— An Introduction to a History of Woodcut.... Bost., 1935. 2 vols. 4to, orig cloth. Ink accession number of title versos. bba May 14 (576) £70 [Deighton Bell]; Ck Nov 1 (420) £130

Anr copy. Cloth; worn, spines faded. O Sept 24 (120) $90

Anr copy. Cloth; spines faded. sg Oct 31 (136) $120

Anr copy. Cloth, in d/js. sg Feb 6 (129) $225

— Rembrandt's Etchings; an Essay and a Catalogue. L, 1923. ("A Catalogue of Rembrandt's Etchings.") 2d Ed. 2 vols. Orig cloth, in fragmentary d/js. kh Nov 11 (122) A$100

— Wenceslaus Hollar and his Views of London.... L, 1922. 4to, orig cloth, in d/j. bba Oct 10 (551) £50 [Marsden]

Hind, Henry Youle, 1823-1908

— Narrative of the Canadian Red River Exploring Expedition.... L, 1860. 2 vols. 8vo, contemp calf gilt; rubbed. With 8 maps & 20 plates. bba Sept 19 (26) £340 [Hay Cinema]

Anr copy. Orig blind-stamped cloth, unopened. With 8 colored maps & plans & 20 chromoxylograph plates with tinted borders (borders a little discolored). Printed list pasted at front of Vol I. C Oct 30 (42) £400 [Toscani]

Hindley, Charles, d.1893

— The History of the Catnach Press. L, 1887. 8vo, orig cloth. cb Oct 17 (423) $50

Hinds, John

— The Groom's Oracle. L, 1829. 8vo, orig half cloth. With colored folding frontis by Alken. bba Sept 5 (177) £120 [Worthing]

Hingston, James

— Guide for Excursionists from Melbourne. Melbourne, 1868. 8vo, orig cloth. kh Nov 11 (311) A$600

Hinton, John Howard, 1791-1873

— The History and Topography of the United States.... Bost., 1834. 2 vols. 4to, orig wraps. sp Nov 24 (30) $110

Anr Ed. Bost., 1846. 2 vols. 4to, early sheep gilt; scuffed. With 42 plates. Some foxing & marginal dampspots. wa Apr 9 (69) $160

Anr Ed. L: J. & F. Tallis, [c.1850]. Vol II (of 2) only. 4to, contemp calf gilt; worn. With frontis & 45 plates. DW Dec 11 (41) £75

Anr copy. ("History of the United States of America.") 2 vols in 6. 4to, loose in orig cloth. DW Jan 29 (31) £230

Hipkins, Alfred James, 1826-1903

— Musical Instruments. Edin., 1888. One of 1,040. Folio, later cloth. With 50 chromolitho plates. Library markings but plates unmarked. sg Mar 5 (237) $475

Anr Ed. L, 1921. 4to, orig cloth; spines soiled. With 48 colored plates. pn Oct 24 (388) £60

Hipkiss, Edwin James

— Eighteenth-Century American Arts: the M. and M. Karolik Collection. Bost., 1941. 4to, cloth; rear cover dampstained. sp Sept 22 (300) $250

Hippocrates, 460?-377?B.C.

— Aphorismi. Cambr.: Thomas Buck & Roger Daniel, 1633. 2 parts in 1 vol. 8vo, later sheep; rubbed. STC 13518. bba Sept 5 (281) £130 [N. Phillips]

Anr Ed. Nuremberg, 1641. 8vo, contemp vellum. Some browning; additional title stained. sg May 14 (80) $200

— Opera. Basel: Andreas Cratander, Aug 1526. Folio, modern vellum. Marginal foxing & dampstaining throughout; lower outer corner of c.50 leaves restored. Sold w.a.f. sg Nov 14 (49) $350

Anr Ed. Venice, 1588. Folio, 18th-cent vellum. Old marginal annotations. SI Dec 5 (302) LIt600,000

Hiroshige Ichiryusai, 1797-1858

[-] Catalogue of the Memorial Exhibition of Hiroshige's Works on the 60th Anniversary of his Death. Tokyo, 1918. One of 275. 4to, ptd wraps. Some foxing. sg Apr 2 (203) $200

Hirschfeld, Christian Cayus Lorenz

— Theorie de l'art des jardins. Leipzig, 1779-89. 5 vols in 3. 4to, contemp sheep; rubbed & rebacked. With 7 plates, 1 folding & 229 engraved illusts, 29 full-page. Some spotting & staining. C June 24 (215) £800 [Camden Books]

Anr copy. Contemp half calf; worn. With 7 plates. Some browning or discoloration. S Nov 21 (81) £1,500

Anr copy. Contemp half calf; rubbed. With 11 half-titles, engraved vignettes on titles & 7 plates (1 folding). Tp stamped; some browning. S Nov 21 (82) £1,700 [Reiss & Auvermann]

Hirschfeld, Magnus, 1868-1935

— Sittengeschichte des Weltkriegs. Leipzig & Vienna: Sexualwissenschaft, [1930]. 2 vols. Rubbed. DW Jan 29 (376) £80

Historia...

— Historia von denen Wider Taeuffern. [Coethen, 1705]. 15 parts in 1 vol. Folio, contemp vellum gilt; soiled. With 31 ports. Foremargin of E3 in 1st part neatly repaired; some worming to lower blank margins; some old dampstaining. C Dec 16 (19) £3,600 [Tenschert]

Historiae...

— Historiae Anglicanae Scriptores X.... L, 1652. 1st Ed. Folio, contemp calf; joints weak. John Evelyn's copy. S June 30 (20) £1,000 [Bank of Cyprus]

Historie...

— De Historie der Vromer Martelaren.... Delft: Bruyn Harmanssz. Schinckel, 1593. 4to, contemp blind-tooled calf over wooden bds with brass fittings; lacking catches & clasps. K3.6 & K4.5 transposed. sg Oct 24 (155) $900

History...

See also: Long, Edward

— The History and Adventures of Little Henry. L, 1811. 8th Ed according to front cover; 5th Ed according to tp. 16mo, orig wraps; fore-edge frayed. With 7 figures & movable head. bba July 23 (79) £220 [Blackett]

— The History of Joseph and his Brethren. L, [n.d.]. 4to, contemp half mor gilt; worn and soiled. With 25 illusts by A. Warren after Owen Jones & Henry Warren. Some plates detached. cb Sept 26 (131) $120

— The History of Little Goody Two-Shoes.... L, 1796. 32mo, 19th-cent mor gilt. Corner of 1 leaf repaired. S Nov 14 (171) £340 [Janies]

— The History of New Holland.... L, 1787. 1st Ed. 8vo, corners rubbed, lower joint cracked, joints repaired. S June 25 (94) £1,900 [Quaritch/Hordern]

Anr copy. Contemp calf; rebacked & recornered, orig spine preserved. S June 25 (95) £800 [Quaritch/Hordern]

— The History of Prince Lee Boo, a Native of the Pelew Islands.... L: William Darton, 1823. Oblong 12mo, wraps; def, backstrip renewed. Illusts hand-colored. sg Oct 17 (285) $120

— History of the Connecticut Valley in Massachusetts.... Phila., 1879. 2 vols. Folio, half lea; rubbed & shaken. O Mar 31 (98) $100

Anr copy. Half lea; rubbed, spine tips chipped. O July 14 (96) $80

Hitchcock, Charles H. See: New Hampshire

Hitchcock, Edward, 1793-1864

— Final Report on the Geology of Massachusetts. Amherst & Northampton, 1841. 2 vols. 4to, cloth; worn. O Mar 31 (99) $130

Hitler, Adolf, 1889-1945

— Bilder aus dem Leben des Fuehrers. Hamburg, 1936. 4to, orig half cloth, in d/j. Inscr by Hitler's official photographer. cb Oct 25 (50) $350

— Mein Kampf. Munich, 1925-27. 1st Ed. 2 vols. Orig vellum over bds; soiled. Gothic types. P Oct 11 (173) $10,000

Hittell, John Shertzer, 1825-1901

— The Resources of California. San Francisco, 1863. 1st Ed. 12mo, cloth; spine ends frayed, front cover loose. Library markings. sg June 18 (83) $60

Hittell, Theodore Henry, 1830-1917

— The Adventures of James Capen Adams. Boston, 1860. 12mo, modern cloth. cb Sept 12 (83) $90

— History of California. San Francisco, 1898. 4 vols. 8vo, orig calf; spines rubbed. cb Sept 12 (82) $225

Hoak, Edward Warren —& Church, Willis Humphry

— Masterpieces of Architecture in the United States. NY, 1930. Folio, cloth. Library stamps but plates unmarked. sg Feb 6 (130) $375

Hoare, Sir Richard Colt, 1758-1838

— The Ancient History of South Wiltshire [North Wiltshire]. L, 1812-19. 2 vols. Folio, contemp russia gilt by Bedford; worn, upper cover loose. With 2 ports, 3 engraved titles & 127 plates, 8 double-page. Library stamps; some superficial soiling. pn Apr 23 (264) £220

— A Tour through the Island of Elba. L, 1814. 4to, orig bds. With 7 (of 8) plates. Lacking map. Edward Hoare's copy. S July 1 (1450) £220 [Chelsea]

Anr copy. Contemp bds; spine lacking. With a map. SI Dec 5 (810) LIt1,000,000

Hoare, Sir Richard Colt, 1758-1838 —& Others

— The History of Modern Wiltshire. L, 1822-43. Orig bds; rebacked. Outer margin of title strengthened. bba Oct 24 (297) £65 [Torrance]

Anr Ed. L, 1822-35. 6 (of 11) vols. Folio, orig bds; repaired & restored; soiled & worn. DW Jan 29 (82) £220

Anr Ed. L, 1822-43. 6 vols. Folio, contemp cloth; worn. With 120 plates & 10 maps. Margins dampstained. DW Apr 8 (129) £260

Hobbes, Thomas, 1588-1679

— Behemoth; or an Epitome of the Civil Wars of England.... L, 1682. ("History of the Causes of the Civil-Wars of England.") 8vo, contemp sheep; rebacked, worn; joints cracked. sg Mar 12 (107) $250

[-] Considerations upon the Reputation, Loyalty, Manners, & Religion, of Thomas Hobbes...Written by himself. L, 1680. 2d Ed. 8vo, modern half calf. Title stained; some worming. bba Mar 26 (224) £420 [Malcolm]

— Elementa philosophica de cive. Amst.: Elzevir, 1647. 3d version of Elzevir Ed. 12mo, disbound. Marginal dampstaining throughout. sg Oct 24 (156) $150

Anr Ed. Amst.: Elzevir, 1669. Bound with: L. van Velthuysen. - Epistolica Dissertatio de Principiis Justi.... Amst., 1651. And: R. Blackburne. - Thomae Hobbes Angli Malmeburiensis Philosophi Vita. [L], 1681. 12mo, contemp vellum; soiled. DW Nov 6 (295) £170

— Hobbes's Tripos, in Three Discourses.... L, 1684. 3d Ed. 8vo, modern half calf. Some staining. Ck Oct 31 (132) £100

— Leviathan. L, 1651. 1st Ed, 1st Issue, with "head" ornament on t.p. Folio, modern half calf. Some soiling & browning. Ck Oct 18 (119) £3,000

Anr copy. Bdg not described. In poor condition. LH Dec 11 (127) $400

Anr copy. Half lea; worn, front cover detached. With engraved title & folding table. Dampstain in top margin of early leaves. NH Aug 23 (158) $1,600

Anr copy. Mor gilt by Riviere; minor repair to spine. With engraved title. Folding table bound after F3. P June 17 (235) $3,500

Anr copy. Disbound. Some staining. sp June 18 (292) $1,600

Anr Ed. L: Andrew Crooke, 1651. 1st Issue, with head ornament on title. Folio, contemp calf; spine repaired but joints split. Tear from upper margin into text of Gg2. C Dec 16 (202) £2,500 [Quaritch]

1st Issue, with "head" ornament on t.p. 4to, contemp calf; rubbed, joints split, spine ends worn, inner hinge broken. Small inkstain on C4v. pn Nov 14 (277) £3,400

— Tracts.... L, 1682. 8vo, contemp calf; rubbed, rebcked. Some dampstaining. Sir William Molesworth's copy. S July 1 (1074) £340 [Quaritch]

Anr copy. Contemp half sheep; spine worn. sg Mar 12 (109) $100

Hobhouse, John Cam, 1st Baron Broughton

— A Journey through Albania.... L, 1813. 1st Ed. 4to, contemp half russia; bds & joints rubbed. With 2 folding maps, engraved frontis & 5 plates & 17 hand-colored etched & aquatint plates. Tear in 4L2; 1st map torn & spotted; some plates bound upside down. S June 30 (318) £1,700 [Consolidated Real]

Anr copy. 19th-cent half calf; rubbed, rebacked preserving spine. With frontis, 2 folding maps, 1 plan, 17 hand-colored plates, 2 facsimiles of letters & 2 plates of music. Some soiling; 1 double-page view shaved at left margin. S July 1 (622) £1,300 [Kutluoglu]

2d Ed. 4to, contemp half mor gilt. With frontis, 2 folding maps & 22 plates (some colored) & 5 other plates. 4D4 in Vol II holed with loss of page numerals; some browning. Egremont copy. S June 30 (145) £3,200 [Consolidated Real]

Anr copy. Later bds. With frontis, 2 folding maps, 1 plan, 17 hand-colored plates, 7 costume plates heightened with gold, 10 topographical views (7 double-page), 2 plates of facsimiles & 1 double-page of music. Some browning; 1 costume plate shaved with loss of imprint. S July 1 (623) £1,500 [Gonul]

Hobson, Geoffrey D.

— Thirty Bindings. L, 1926. One of 600. 4to, orig cloth. With 30 plates. bba May 28 (491) £115 [Cox]

Hobson, Robert Lockhart
See also: British Museum

— Chinese Art. L, 1927. 4to, orig cloth, in def d/j. Some foxing. kh Nov 11 (124) A$50

— Chinese Porcelain & Wedgwood Pottery. L, 1928. One of 350. 4to, cloth, in d/j. Record of the Collections in the Lady Lever Art Gallery, Vol II. F Mar 26 (266) $70

— The Wares of the Ming Dynasty. L, 1923. 4to, cloth, in worn d/j. kh Nov 11 (125) A$180

Anr copy. Cloth; hinges starting. sp June 18 (355) $65

Hobson, Robert Lockhart —& Hetherington, Arthur Lonsdale

— The Art of the Chinese Potter. L, 1923. One of 1,500. 4to, orig half vellum; some wear & soiling. F Mar 26 (344) $80; wd Dec 12 (404) $100

Hobson, Robert Lockhart —& Morse, Edward S., 1838-1925

— Chinese, Corean and Japanese Potteries.... NY, 1914. One of 1,500. 4to, orig bds; soiled & warped. F Mar 26 (243) $100

Anr copy. Half cloth; edges & corners worn. Stamp of A. W. Bahr. sg Feb 6 (131) $120

Anr copy. With 27 plates, 2 colored. sg Apr 2 (139) $60

Hochstetter, Ferdinand Christian von, 1829-84

— New Zealand. Stuttgart, 1867. 4to, orig cloth; rubbed. Marginal waterstaining; foxed. bba June 11 (347) £150 [Hay Cinema]

Hockney, David
See also: Spender & Hockney

— Martha's Vineyard and Other Places. NY, [1985]. 2 vols, including text booklet. 4to, half lea. sg Jan 30 (84) $90

— Paper Pools. L, 1980. One of 1,000. 4to, orig cloth. With orig litho in folder. bba Jan 30 (376) £900 [Marks]

Anr copy. Orig cloth. Inscr to Leonard Schlosser. P June 18 (620) $2,000

Hodge, Frederick Webb, 1864-1956

— Handbook of American Indians North of Mexico. Wash., 1907-10. 2 vols. Orig cloth; rubbed & worn. Endpapers rubberstamped. Bureau of American Ethnology Bulletin 30. cb Nov 14 (90) $120

Anr Ed. Wash., 1912. 2 vols. Cloth; worn, shelfmarks. Library markings. Bureau of American Ethnology Bulletin 30. NH Oct 6 (169) $75

2d Ed. 2 vols. K July 12 (259) $100

Hodges, Sir Benjamin. See: Impartial...

Hodges, William, 1744-97

— Travels in India.... L, 1793. 1st Ed. 4to, contemp calf gilt; worn. With 14 plates & 1 folding map. Some spotting. DW Dec 11 (42) £155

Hodgkin, John Eliot

— Rariora. L, [1900]-2. 3 vols. 4to, cloth. kh Nov 11 (126) A$280

Hodgson, A. W.

— Old English China. L, 1913. Folio, cloth, in d/j with some wear. Some foxing. kh Nov 11 (127) A$70

Hodgson, Christopher Pemberton

— Reminiscences of Australia with Hints.... L, 1846. 8vo, orig cloth; joints worn. With folding map. S June 25 (235) £180 [Quaritch/Hordern]

Hodgson, John Edmund

— The History of Aeronautics in Great Britain. L, 1924. One of 1,000. 4to, cloth, in torn d/j. bba Nov 28 (159) £180 [Browning]

Anr copy. Cloth. pn May 14 (85) £220

Hodson, James S.

— An Historical and Practical Guide to Art Illustration. L, 1884. 8vo, orig cloth; loose. With 24 specimens of ptg processes. Plate facing p. 204 bound upside down; some foxing. Schlosser copy. P June 17 (551) $2,500

Hoe, Robert, 1839-1909. See: Grolier Club

Hoe Library, Robert

— One Hundred and Seventy-Six Historic and Artistic Book-Bindings.... NY, 1895. One of 200 on Japan vellum. 2 vols. Folio, mor extra by the Club Bindery; joints cracked. Inscr to his daughter Ruth, 1901. CNY Dec 5 (374) $1,500; CNY Dec 5 (375) $1,800

Anr copy. Half mor gilt by James MacDonald & Co; corners bumped, joints & extremities worn. CNY Dec 5 (405) $1,200

— [Sale Catalogue] Catalogue of the Library.... NY, 1911-12. 8 parts in 4 vols. Cloth, orig wraps bound in. NH May 30 (97) $160

Hoefer, J. C. F.

— Nouvelle Biographie generale depuis les temps les plus recules jusqu'a nos jours. Paris, 1857-66. 46 vols in 23. 8vo, half mor; rubbed. Library markings. Sold w.a.f. O Sept 24 (188) $300

Hoelderlin, Friedrich, 1770-1848

— Gedichte. Stuttgart, 1826. 8vo, modern mor gilt. C Dec 16 (50A) £4,000 [Schumann]

Hoet, Gerard

— Catalogus of naamlyst van Schilderyen met derzelver prysenin. The Hague, 1752-70. 1st Ed. 3 vols. 8vo, calf & half calf; worn. Tear in tp of Vol III. S Feb 11 (107) £220 [Bernet]

Hoffer, Adriaan

— Nederduytsche Poemata. Amst., 1635. 4to, contemp blind-stamped vellum; turn-ins sprung. With engraved title & 21 emblematic illusts. Marginal repairs on last few leaves. sg Oct 24 (157) $1,300

Hoffmann, Ernst Theodor Wilhelm, 1776-1822

See also: Limited Editions Club

— Nachstuecke.... Berlin, 1817. 2 vols. 8vo, contemp half calf gilt. Some browning. HH May 12 (1357) DM2,000

— Prinzessin Brambilla. Breslau, 1821. 8vo, modern bds with parts of orig wraps laid down. With 8 plates by Jacques Callot. Later leaves dampstained at lower outer corners. Ck Oct 31 (133) £650

— Die Serapions-Brueder. Gesammelte Erzaehlungen und Maehrchen. Berlin, 1819-21. 4 vols. 8vo, contemp half calf gilt; rubbed. Some browning. HH May 12 (1360) DM2,000

Hoffmann, Heinrich, 1809-94

— King Nutcracker or the Dream of Poor Reinhold. Leipsig: Friedrich Volckmar, [c.1848]. 4to, orig bds; joints cracked, lacking lower half of backstrip. S Apr 28 (71) £400 [Jones]

Hoffmann, Louis. See: Lewis, Angelo John

Hoffmann, Tassilo

— Jacob Abraham und Abraham Abrahmson 55 Jahre Berliner medaillenkunst. Frankfurt, 1927. One of 350. 4to, later cloth. Some foxing. sg Dec 19 (172) $200

Hofland, Thomas C., 1770-1843

— The British Angler's Manual. L, 1839. 1st Ed. 8vo, modern half mor by Atkinson; worn. Koopman copy. O Oct 29 (172) $130

— The British Angler's Manual.... L, 1848. Ed by E. Jesse. 8vo, lea, orig wraps bound in; joints worn. sp Apr 16 (315) $120

Hofmannsthal, Hugo von, 1874-1929

— Der Kaiser und die Hexe. Berlin, 1900. One of 200. 4to, orig vellum gilt. HH May 12 (2313) DM9,000

Hofstede de Groot, Cornelis, 1863-1930

— Beschreibendes und kritisches Verzeichnis der Werke der...hollandischen Maler. Esslingen, 1907-28. 10 vols. Ck Feb 14 (44) £900

Hogarth, William, 1697-1764

— Works. L, 1801. ("Hogarth Restored.") Folio, contemp half mor; worn. Sold w.a.f. Ck July 10 (97) £1,100

Anr Ed. L, 1806. Folio, contemp half lea; broken. With 96 (on 82) plates only. Some tears & fraying; some plates loose; 1 plate with cropped margins; some foxing. pn May 14 (155) £460 [Bifolco]

Anr copy. Contemp half mor; rubbed. With 111 plates on 95 sheets. Dampstained at beginning, affecting c.20 plates. S May 14 (925) £920 [Bifolco]

Anr Ed. L, 1821. Ed by T. H. Horne. 2 vols. 4to, contemp mor gilt; spine ends worn. With 159 proof plates. Some spotting. L.p. copy. b Nov 18 (253A) £75

Anr Ed. L, 1822. Ed by John Nichols. Folio, half mor; rubbed & bumped. With port & 115 plates. Minor marginal spotting.

b Mar 11 (53) £800

Anr copy. Contemp mor gilt; joints & edges rubbed. With engraved plates on 119 leaves; 2 suppressed plates bound at end. Tp with vertical crease & laid down on linen. C Dec 16 (255) £900 [Bifolco]

Anr copy. Contemp half mor; worn. With port & 115 plates plus 2 suppressed plates in pocket at end. S May 15 (926) £950 [Walford]

Anr copy. Contemp sheep; worn. sg Feb 13 (190A) $1,400

Anr Ed. L, [c.1828]. Folio, contemp half mor; worn & broken. With 153 plates on 116 sheets; Before and After plates loosely inserted. Tp torn across; 1st few leaves & frontis port def; library markings. bba Nov 7 (36) £650 [Talanti]

Anr Ed. L: Baldwin, Cradock & Joy, [c.1830]. Folio, contemp half mor; front cover detached. 1st few pp rumpled. cb Feb 12 (158) $1,050

Anr Ed. L, 1833. 2 vols in 1. 4to, orig half mor; rubbed. Lacking 2 plates & 1 port added. K Mar 22 (183) $55

Anr Ed. L: Baldwin & Cradock, [1835-37]. Folio, orig half mor; worn. With 105 (of 116) plates. Some deep tears, occasionally affecting engraving; dampstaining to upper margin throughout. Sold w.a.f. Ck Sept 6 (124) £650

Anr copy. Orig half mor; extremities rubbed. With port, 115 plates & 2 suppressed plates in pocket at rear. Ck Dec 11 (226) £1,100

Anr copy. Disbound. With port & 115 plates. Prelims, frontis & 2 suppressed plates damaged. sg Sept 6 (148) $1,300

Anr Ed. L, [c.1850]. Ed by Trusler & E. F. Roberts. 2 vols in 1. Folio, orig half mor; rubbed, joints cracked. F Sept 26 (18) $90

Anr Ed. L, [c.1880]. Intro by James Hannay. 4to, cloth; extremities worn, front joint starting. sg Feb 6 (133) $100

Anr copy. 6 vols. 4to, orig cloth; soiled & smudged, ends worn & chipped, corners bumped. With frontis & 149 plates. wa Sept 26 (603) $80

Anr copy. 4to, half mor gilt; scuffed, library number on spine. Some foxing. wa Mar 5 (601) $55

Anr Ed. Phila., 1900. One of 1,000. 10 vols. 4to, cloth. sp Apr 16 (149) $55

Hogenberg, Franz. See: Braun & Hogenberg

Hogg, Edward

— Visit to Alexandria, Damascus, and Jerusalem.... L, 1835. 2 vols. 8vo, contemp half cloth; chipped. With hand-colored frontises. S July 1 (763) £280 [Maggs]

Hogg, James, 1770-1835

— The Jacobite Relics of Scotland.... Edin., 1819-21. 2 vols. 8vo, contemp calf gilt. bba Feb 27 (108) £130 [Ash Rare Books]

— Poetical Works. Edin., 1822. 4 vols. 12mo, contemp calf gilt; rubbed. bba Feb 27 (109) £130 [Aspin]

Hogg, Robert, 1818-97 —& Bull, Henry Graves

— The Herefordshire Pomona. Hereford, 1876-85. 2 vols. 4to, orig cloth; extremities rubbed, corners bumped. With 77 colored plates & 4 plain plates. Marginal browning. C Oct 30 (259) £2,800 [Burden]

Anr copy. Mor gilt. Some spotting, affecting text & plates. S Nov 21 (25) £2,400 [Wheldon & Wesley]

Hogg, Robert, 1818-97 —& Johnson, George William

— The Wild Flowers of Great Britain. L, 1863-68. Vols I-IV (of 11). Orig cloth; spine worn. DW Oct 2 (147) $115

Hohlwein, Ludwig

— Ludwig Hohlwein. Berlin, 1926. Ed by H. K. Frenzel. 4to, cloth; 2 tears along joints, spine darkened. sg Sept 6 (236) $300

Anr copy. Cloth; some wear at extremities. sg Feb 6 (135) $275

Anr copy. Cloth; spine darkened. sg Apr 2 (234) $375

Anr copy. Orig cloth; spine soiled. Minor marginal dampstaining at front. wa Dec 9 (428) $290

Holbach, Paul Henri Thiry, Baron d', 1723-89

— Systeme de la nature.... L [Amst.], 1770. 1st Issue, with comma after Londres on tp. 2 vols. 8vo, contemp calf gilt. Half-title in Vol I only; lacking the 2 errata leaves at end of Vol II. S Nov 14 (425) £950 [Soave]

Holbein, Hans, 1497-1543

— The Dance of Death. L, 1803. 4to, lea; worn, spine def. With engraved prelims & 46 plates. Some foxing. O Aug 25 (51) $85

Anr Ed. L, 1811. 8vo, half calf; needs rebdg. sg Mar 5 (130) $225

— Facsimiles of Original Drawings in the Collection of his Majesty, for the Portraits of Illustrious Persons of the Court of Henry VIII. L, 1884. Folio, half mor gilt. pnE Mar 11 (118) £210

— Historiarum veteris testamenti icones.... Paris: Pierre Regnault, 1544. 4to, contemp calf gilt; spine damaged at head & foot. With 105 metal cuts. Some staining. S Dec 5 (141) £4,500 [Quaritch]

— Icones historiarum Veteris Testamenti. Lyons: Jean Frellon, 1547. French verses by Gilles Corrozet; illus by Holbein. 4to, later vellum. With 94 woodcuts & 4 medallion woodcuts of Evangelists by anr hand. Inner margins stabbed. bba Jan 16 (218) £3,218 [Hartley]

Anr copy. Late 19th-cent mor by A. Chatelain. Lower corner of tp repaired; some soiling of prelims; quires K-N with dampstain in lower margin. Blum copy. P Dec 12 (48) $5,000

— Icones Veteris Testamenti: Illustrations of the Old Testament.... L, 1830. 8vo, 19th-cent mor gilt. sg Nov 7 (91) $3,200

— Imitations of Original Drawings for the Portraits...of the Court of Henry VIII. L, 1792-[1800]. 2 vols. Folio, contemp half mor. With 82 ports, most on india paper mtd, some in proof state before captions. b Nov 18 (254) £2,000

Anr copy. Near-contemp mor gilt with crests of William Beckford. With 84 plates ptd in colors on 83 leaves, 24 of them in 2 states Imprint of 1 plate shaved; 9 plates spotted. Extra-illus with 1 plate on india paper mtd. William Beckford's annotated copy. C May 20 (263) £6,500 [Quaritch]

Anr copy. Mor gilt by J. Wright; rebacked, old spines laid down. With 84 ports on 83 leaves, on white & pink paper, ptd in colors, 83 of the plates with additional uncolored states & a further 8 untitled plates each in 2 uncolored states. Together, 183 plates. 74 plates, the majority uncolored states, trimmed to plate mark & mtd. Derby copy. C June 24 (216) £7,000 [Sims Reed]

Anr copy. 2 vols in 1. Folio, contemp mor gilt; gouged. With 84 color plates; ports on pink or white paper, several mtd with borders in sepia wash. Some foxing; final leaf with marginal tear; creased. P June 18 (469) £15,000

Anr copy. Bound in 1 vol. Folio, 19th-cent half mor gilt. With 92 plates, including the continuation of 8 plates. sg May 9 (117) $7,500

Anr Ed. L, 1812. ("Portraits of Illustrious Personages of the Court of Henry VIII.") 4to, contemp mor gilt; worn. With 1 plain & 83 colored plates. Some dampstaining to upper margins; some spotting. Ck Nov 29 (101) £630

Anr Ed. L, 1828. 4to, contemp half mor; extremities rubbed. With 81 hand-colored plates ptd on pink or white paper. 6 plates dampstained at lower margin. Ck Dec 12 (283) £500

Anr copy. Modern syn. With ports of Holbein & his wife & 82 other plates. sg Sept 6 (151) $700

Anr Ed. L, 1884. ("Facsimiles of Original Drawings....") Folio, half mor gilt; worn, upper hinge cracked with backstrip pulling away, prelims nearly detached. sg Sept 6 (150) $175

Anr copy. Half mor; needs rebdg. About a third of the plates lacking the accompanying text leaves; minor marginal dampstaining & soiling. sg Feb 13 (191) $700

Holbrook, John Edwards, 1794-1871

— North American Herpetology, or a Description of the Reptiles Inhabiting the United States. Phila., 1836-42. Vol I only. Old half mor. With 23 color plates. Some foxing throughout; Ms note in margins of p. 9. wd Dec 12 (405) $325

Holden, George H., 1848-1914

— Canaries and Cage-Birds. NY & Bost., [1883]. 4to, cloth; rubbed. Wit 8 color plates. Occasional spotting. bba Sept 5 (144) £55 [Henly]

Holder, William, 1616-98

— A Treatise of the Natural Grounds and Principles of Harmony. L, 1694. 1st Ed. 8vo, contemp calf; rubbed. With 2 plates, 1 folding. pn Oct 24 (392) £260 [Robertshaw]

Hole, Richard, 1746-1803

— Remarks on the Arabian Nights' Entertainments.... L, 1797. 8vo, contemp half sheep; spine worn. sg Mar 12 (109) $100

Holinshed, Raphael, d.1580?

— The Firste [-Laste] Volume of the Chronicles.... L: John Hunne & Lucas Harrison, 1577. 1st Ed, STC 13568.5. 4 parts in 2 vols. Folio, mor gilt by Riviere. Black letter; double column. A few sidenotes cropped; some worming affecting 1st c.30 leaves; minor soiling & staining. pn Nov 14 (278) £900

Anr Ed. L: John Hunne, [1577]. STC 13568b. 2 vols. Folio, 17th-cent calf, rebacked. A few leaves and folding plan of Edinburgh "probably" supplied from anr copy. Marginal dampstaining. CNY Dec 5 (248) $7,500

2d Ed. L, 1587. ("The First and Second [Third] Volumes of Chronicles.") 4 parts in 1 vol. Folio, later calf; worn, upper cover detached. Some leaves lacking in 1st part & woodcut title laid down & repaired; some other repairs. Sold w.a.f. bba Aug 13 (83) £190 [Gammon]

Anr copy. 3 vols in 2, with a duplicate set of pp. 1419-1574 bound as Vol IV. Folio, 18th-cent calf; upper cover of Vol I detached, scuffed. Sold w.a.f. STC 13569.

Milne copy. Ck June 12 (89) £700

Holkot, Robert

— Super sapientiam Salomonis. Reutlingen: Johann Otmar, 1489. Bound with: Nicolaus de Lyra. Repertorium in postillam super bibliam. Memmingen: Albrecht Kunne, 1492. Folio, later half vellum. 1st work is 50 lines & headline, gothic letter & has a few small wormholes at the beginning; 2d work is 47 lines; gothic letters & with large portins of text in final 7 leaves torn away with paper repairs to the last 2 only. 289 (of 290) leaves; Goff H-292. 122 (of 124) leaves, lacking r1 & final blank; Goff N-148. S Dec 5 (18) £800 [Maggs]

Hollaender, Eugen

— Die Karikatur und Satire in der Medizin. Stuttgart, 1921. Folio, bdg not described. With 11 plates. Met Apr 28 (196) $160

— Wunder, Wundergeburt und Wundergestalt in Einblattdrucken des fuenfzehnten bis achtzehnten Jahrhunderts. Stuttgart, 1921. Folio, cloth. Met Apr 28 (197) $50

Holland, Henry, 1583-1650?

— Herologia Anglica hoc est clarissimorum aliquot Anglorum vivae effigies. Arnheim [L?], 1620. Folio, contemp calf; spine & corners repaired, joints weak. With engraved title, 4 plates & 63 ports, 1 half-page. Tp & a few other leaves with repaired tears; lacking final leaf; 5-6 supplied from a smaller copy. STC 13582. C Dec 16 (203) £100 [Rix]

Holland, Sir Henry, 1788-1873

— Travels in the Ionian Isles.... L, 1815. 4to, contemp calf gilt; joints weak. With map & 12 plates. S June 30 (147) £460 [Maggs]

Anr copy. Modern cloth. Tp soiled; map with imprint shaved. Royal Institution copy. S July 1 (624) £450 [Chelsea]

Anr copy. Contemp half russia gilt; repaired. Tp soiled; map detached. S July 1 (625) £450 [Consolidated Real]

2d Ed. L, 1819. 2 vols. 8vo, contemp half calf. With folding map & 12 plates. Map repaired. cb Oct 10 (51) $160

Anr copy. Half calf. Some imprints cropped or lacking. S June 30 (320) £220 [Consolidated Real]

Holland, John

— The Ruine of the Bank of England.... [N.p.], 1725. 4to, disbound. Margins trimmed, touching a few headlines. sg Mar 12 (110) $250

Hollanders...

— De Hollanders in Iowa. Arnhem, 1858. 12mo, orig bds; chipped, rubbed. bbc Dec 9 (383) $275

Hollar, Wenceslaus, 1607-77

— Muscarum scarabeorum vermiumque variae figura et formae.... Antwerp, 1646. Oblong 8vo, sewn as issued. With engraved title & 11 plates. Some soiling & spotting. Ck May 15 (29) £350

Hollenback, Frank R.

— The Argentine Central. Denver, 1959. One of 300. In d/j. cb Feb 13 (175) $55

— The Laramie Plains Line. Denver, 1960. One of 300. cb Feb 13 (176) $55

Hollis, Thomas, 1720-74

— Memoirs of T. H. L, 1780. 1st Ed. 2 vols. 4to, modern half cloth. With 35 plates. Some browning & foxing. pn Apr 23 (31) £70 [Clark]

Holman, James, 1786-1857

— Travels through Russia, Siberia, Poland, Austria...while Suffering from Total Blindness. L, 1834. 2 vols. 8vo, contemp half calf; rubbed. With frontises & 8 plates. bba July 9 (39) £50 [Deighton Bell]

— A Voyage Round the World. L, 1834-35. 1st Ed. 4 vols. 8vo, orig cloth; rubbed, Vol II rebacked, orig spine preserved. With port & 22 plates & maps. bba Sept 19 (9) £300 [Maggs]

Holman, John Paulison

— Sheep and Bear Trails; a Hunter's Wanderings in Alaska and British Columbia. NY, 1933. 8vo, cloth; worn. Koopman copy. O Oct 29 (174) $110

Anr copy. Cloth. Inscr. sg Jan 9 (267) $550

Holme, Charles, 1848-1923
See also: Modern...

— Art in Photography. L: The Studio, 1905. 4to, remains of orig wraps. Some creases & foxing. Sold w.a.f. bbc Feb 17 (171) $65

— The Art of the Book. L: The Studio, 1914. 4to, orig bds; corners bumped, spine worn. F Mar 26 (370) $70

— English Water-Colour. L: The Studio, 1902. 4to, orig cloth; some wear. SI Dec 5 (304) LIt400,000

— Modern Pen Drawings: European and American. L, 1901. One of 300. Folio, orig cloth; soiled. sg Sept 6 (152) $50

Holmes Book Co. See: Grabhorn Printing

Holmes, John Clellon

— Go. NY, 1952. In d/j with small chips; crayon mark on endpaper. wa Mar 5 (201) $190

Holmes, Oliver Wendell, 1809-94

— Boylston Prize Dissertations for the Years 1836 to 1837. Bost., 1838. 8vo, orig cloth; rebacked retaining orig backstrip, corners worn. Foxed; institutional stamp on tp. sg May 14 (81) $130

— Currents and Counter-Currents in Medical Science.... Bost., 1860. 12mo, orig wraps; chipped & loose. In: Medical Communications of the Mass. Medical Society, Vol 9, No 6. sg Nov 14 (52) $100

Anr Ed. Bost., 1861. 1st Issue. 12mo, orig cloth, 1st bdg; spine ends chipped. sg May 14 (82) $100

— Memorial Bunker Hill. Bost., [1875]. 8vo, orig wraps; lower wrap foxed. Cut signature laid in. bbc Apr 27 (326) $75

— Poems. L, 1846. 16mo, orig cloth. Inscr & with ALs tipped in. rs Oct 17 (17) $150

— Works. Cambr., Mass., 1891-92. One of 275 L.p. copies. 16 vols. 8vo, lev gilt extra; spines faded. cb Dec 5 (64) $900

Standard Library Ed. Bost. & NY, [1892-96]. 15 vols. 8vo, half mor; worn & soiled, spine ends chipped. wa Sept 26 (19) $250

Holmes, Sir Richard Rivington

— Queen Victoria. L & Paris, 1897. One of 350. 4to, orig wraps; rubbed, spine faded. bba Jan 30 (80) £60 [Sanderson]

Holmes, Thomas James

— Cotton Mather. A Bibliography.... Cambr., Mass., 1940. One of 500. 3 vols. 4to, half mor; worn. O Sept 24 (121) $150

— Increase Mather: his Works. Being a Short-Title Catalogue.... Cleveland, 1930. One of 250. 8vo, half mor, in d/j. O Jan 14 (91) $140

Holt, Arden

— Fancy Dresses Described; or, What to Wear at Fancy Balls. L, [1887]. 8vo, orig cloth. sp Feb 6 (361) $55

Holwell, John, 1649-86?

— Catastrophe Mundi, or Europes Many Mutations until the Year 1701.... L, 1682. 4to, early 19th-cent russia; covers detached. Margins trimmed close, causing text loss on some leaves. sg Oct 24 (158) $500

Homann, Johann Baptist, 1663-1724

— Grosse Atlas uber die gantze Welt. Nuremberg: Johann Ernst Adelbulner, 1725. Folio, contemp calf; rebacked, rubbed. With hand-colored frontis, port & 199 maps, plans & views colored in a contemp hand, all double-page. With Ms index. Small tears to folds of 6 maps; outer margin of plan of Naples soiled; inner margin of tp strengthened; outer margin of port shaved. C Oct 30 (154) £15,000 [Gebt Haas]

— Staedt-Atlas, oder: Schauplatz beruehmter Staedte, Vestungen, Prospeckte, Gegenden, Gruendrisse, Belagerungen.... Nuremberg, 1762. Folio, contemp calf; rubbed, spine & corners repaired. With engraved title & 95 double-page mapsheets colored in a contemp hand. Minor discoloration; a few tears repaired without loss of surface. S June 25 (298) £31,000 [Hassold]

Home, Henry, Lord Kames, 1696-1782

— The Gentleman Farmer.... Edin., 1776. 1st Ed. 8vo, contemp calf; upper cover detached, spine cracked. bba Apr 30 (316) £120 [Subunso]

Home, Robert, 1750?-1836?

— Select Views in Mysore.... L, 1794. 1st Ed. 4to, modern half cloth. Lacking maps & plans. b Nov 18 (338) £130

Homer

See also: Limited Editions Club; Nonesuch Press

Iliad & Odyssey in Greek

— 1535. - Ilias kai Odysseia meta tes exegesios. Basel: Joannes Hervagius. Folio, contemp blind-tooled pigskin over pastebd; warped, front joint starting. Dampstained throughout, with traces of mold at beginning; library markings & pocket. sg Oct 24 (160) $375

Iliad & Odyssey in English

— [c.1612-14]. - L: Nathaniel Butter Trans by George Chapman. 2 vols. Folio, calf gilt; rubbed. Iliad with engraved title remargined & with minor repairs & with small hole to first few leaves affecting border & lacking the 2 further leaves of verse to Sir Edward Philips & Viscounts Cranbourne & Rochester at end. Odyssey with slight cropping at inner margin; engraved title repaired with loss & remargined as are following few leaves. S Dec 12 (2) £2,500 [Frew Mackenzie]

— 1763. - L. Trans by Alexander Pope. 7 vols. 12mo, contemp calf; rebacked in modern calf. One map torn with no loss. bba Aug 13 (114) £140 [Houle]

— 1805. - L. Illus by John Flaxman. 2 vols in 1. Oblong folio, half mor gilt. DW Nov 6 (508) £80

— 1905. - The Iliad. Bost. & NY One of 600 L.p. copies. Trans by William Cullen Bryant; illus by Flaxman. 8 vols. 4to, orig cloth; soiled & rubbed. wa Mar 5 (575) $75

Iliad in English

— 1660. - His Iliads Translated, Adorn'd with Sculpture.... L.1st Ed of Ogilby's Iliad. Trans by John Ogilby. Folio, half calf; worn & broken. Lacking ports & tp; some plates with tears & repairs; some dampstaining. Sold w.a.f. pn Nov 14 (279) £110

— 1715-20. - The Iliad. L. Trans by Alexander Pope. 6 vols. Folio, contemp calf; covers detached, rubbed. NH May 30 (243) $290

One of 1,000. Contemp calf gilt; spines chipped at head & foot. Greece map browned; Troy misbound at start of text in Vol II; some browning. C Dec 16 (227) £750 [Maggs]

Iliad in Greek

— 1517. - Homeri interpres pervetustus (seu scholia graeca in Iliadem, in integrum restituta....) Rome: Angeli Collotii. Folio, 18th-cent mor gilt; head of both covers rubbed, upper joint partly split. Stain in upper margin of 1st few leaves; some other margins spotted. Crofts-Wodhull-Gennadius copy. S Dec 5 (142) £3,500 [Kraus]

— 1554. - Ilias. Paris: A. Turnebus. 8vo, old calf; restored & rebacked. DW Jan 29 (239) £100

— 1953. - Ilias Ambrosiana: Cod. F.205 P. Inf., Bibliothecae Ambrosianae Mediolanensis. Berne & Oltun One of 800. Ed by Aristide Calderini. Folio, vellum gilt. With 58 mtd colored plates, with English & Italian captions; 57 pp of Latin text. sg May 21 (273) $275

Odyssey in English

— 1929. - Cambr., Mass. One of 550 L.p. copies. Illus by N. C. Wyeth. 4to, half lea, unopened. With an extra suite of plates, loose as issued. bbc June 29 (449) $900

Anr copy. Half lea. sg Jan 30 (189) $1,100

— 1932. - L. One of 530. Trans by T. E. Lawrence. 4to, contemp mor. Ck July 10 (300) £550

Anr copy. Mor gilt. P Dec 12 (64) $2,250

Anr copy. Orig mor; worn. S July 1 (516) £800 [Chelsea]

Anr copy. Lea; several joints tape-reinforced. sg Jan 30 (85) $1,500

Anr copy. Orig mor; spine scuffed. Sgd by author & inscr by Bruce Rogers and Wilfred Merton. Epstein copy. sg Apr 30 (300) $6,500

Odyssey in German

— 1963. - Fuenf Gesaenge der Odyssee. Hamburg One of 300. Trans by J. H. Voss; illus by G. Marks. Loose in orig wraps. With 60 woodcuts. B May 12 (192) HF600

Odyssey in Italian

— 1582. - L'Odissea. Florence 8vo, vellum. Wormed at beginning & end. S May 13 (806) £260 [Patrino]

Works in English

— [1616]. - The Whole Works of Homer.... L: Nathaniell Butter Trans by George Chapman. 2 parts in 1 vol. Folio, contemp calf gilt with arms of James I; spine repaired, some cracking to lozenge on upper cover. With engraved title & the unsigned leaf of dedicatory sonnets. Final blank lacking; some old dampstaining. STC 13624. C Dec 16 (204) £2,500 [Finch]

Works in Greek

— 1524. - Venice: Aldus. 2 vols. 8vo, Vol II in 19th-cent mor gilt with Aldine device gilt, Vol I in later copy of this bdg. Partly misbound; some browning. S July 1 (517) £700 [Shapero]

— 1756-58. - Glasgow: Foulis. 4 vols in 2. Folio, modern calf. Some leaves foxed; lacking blanks & half-titles & the general title. sg Oct 24 (161) $500

Honan, Michael Burke

— The Andalusian Annual for MDCCCXXXVII. L, 1836. 4to, orig cloth. With 12 hand-colored plates, each heightened with gum-arabic. Occasional discoloration to text. S Nov 21 (60) £800 [Girou]

Hondius, Henrik, the Younger

— Onderwijsinge in de Perspectie conste. The Hague, 1623. Folio, old bds; worn. With engraved title & 35 plates. Parallel French & German texts inserted & possibly from a later Ed; some staining & creasing; lacking figure 41. S June 25 (205) £400 [Ungers]

Hondius, Jodocus, 1563-1611. See: Mercator & Hondius

Hone, William, 1780-1842

— Ancient Mysteries Described, Especially the English Miracle Plays. L, 1823. 8vo, half lea. sp Apr 16 (324) $90

Honey, William Bowyer

— European Ceramic Art. L, 1949-52. 2 vols. 4to, orig cloth; soiled. sg Sept 6 (53) $175

Anr Ed. L, 1949. 4to, cloth. sp Sept 22 (298) $70

Honeyman Collection, Robert

— [Sale catalogue] The Honeyman Collection of Scientific Books and Manuscripts. L, 1978-81. 7 vols. 4to, wraps. Price lists loosely inserted. bba July 9 (11) £50 [Laywood]

Anr copy. Wraps; faded. Includes prices. cb Nov 21 (110) $140

Anr copy. Estimates list loosely inserted in each vol. DW Jan 290 (322) £70

Anr copy. Wraps; worn. Price lists laid in. O Sept 24 (123) $180

Anr copy. Wraps; opening leaves of Vol III loose. Price and estimate lists laid in. sg Oct 31 (138) $90

Anr copy. Price lists laid in all but last part. sg Nov 14 (250) $350

Anr copy. Price lists taped in. sg May 21 (236) $110

Anr Ed. L, 1978-79. 7 vols. 4to, orig bds. SI June 9 (473) LIt320,000

Honorius III, Pope

[-] Gremoire du pape Honorius.... Rome, 1670 [but France, 17th-cent]. 12mo, old sheep gilt; rubbed. With engraved title & 13 plates. Thumbed; 1 plate & pages 67-70 stained. P June 17 (236) $800

Honzo-Zufu

— Kinjunbu. Japan, 1921. 6 vols. 4to, orig wraps. Ck Oct 31 (98) £500

Hood, Graham. See: Buhler & Hood

Hood, Thomas. See: Derrydale Press

Hood, Thomas, 1799-1845

— The Epping Hunt. L, 1829. 1st Ed. 12mo, orig wraps; spotted, lacking backstrip, front cover detached. With 6 india-proof plates by George Cruikshank. sg Oct 17 (168) $150

— Fairy Realm. L, 1865. Illus by Gustave Dore. 4to, cloth; spine worn. cb Sept 26 (78) $60

— The Headlong Career and Woful Ending of Precocious Piggy. L, 1864. 8vo, orig half cloth. Some soiling. bba July 23 (86) £70 [Sotheran]

— Works. L, 1869-73. 10 vols. 8vo, contemp half calf gilt; ends occasionally scuffed or worn. wa Mar 5 (44) $160

Hood, Thomas, 1835-74

— Poems. L, 1872. Illus by Birket Foster. 4to, cloth; worn & rubbed. 1 text leaf torn. cb Jan 9 (94) $110

Hoogewerff, Godefridus Joannes

— De Noord-Nederlandsche Schilderkunst. The Hague, 1936-47. 5 vols. S Feb 11 (110) £220 [Ars Libri]

Hooke, Robert, 1635-1702

— Micrographia, or Some Physiological Descriptions of Minute Bodies Made by Magnifying Glasses. L, 1667. 1st Ed, 2d Issue. Folio, later calf gilt; upper cover detached, worn. With 38 plates, 15 folding. A few plates torn. bba Sept 5 (222) £3,800 [Phelps]

Hooker, Sir Joseph Dalton, 1817-1911

— A Century of Indian Orchids. Calcutta, 1895. Folio, loose in half mor portfolio,; covers abraded. With 101 partly colored lithos. Plates dampstained & spotted. In: Annals of the Royal Botanic Garden, Calcutta, Vol V. McCarty-Cooper copy. CNY Jan 25 (89) $550

Anr copy. Cloth; rubbed. With port & 101 plates. Minor dampstaining. CNY June 9 (143) $350

— The Flora of British India. L, 1875-97. 7 vols. 8vo, orig cloth. wa Dec 9 (543) $55

— The Rhododendrons of Sikkim-Himalaya. L, 1849-[51]. 3 parts in 1 vol. Folio, modern half mor gilt. With 30 hand-colored plates. Part titles, dedication & list of subscribers absent. S Nov 21 (24) £5,500 [Quaritch]

2d Ed of Part 1, 1st Ed of Parts 2 & 3. 3 parts in 1 vol. Folio, contemp mor gilt. With 30 hand-colored plates. C Oct 30 (237) £3,200 [Junk]

Anr copy. 19th-cent cloth; stained, recased, new endpapers. Some spotting. S June 25 (33) £6,500 [Drake]

Hooker, Richard, 1554?-1600

— Works. L, 1662. 1st Ed. Folio, 19th-cent calf; rubbed. With engraved title & frontis; both repaired. bba Oct 10 (299) £90 [Thoemmes]

Anr copy. Contemp calf; hinges broken, rubbed. Lacking dedication leaf. bba Oct 24 (48) £60 [Gammon]

Hooker, Sir William Jackson, 1785-1865

— A Century of Ferns. L, 1854. 8vo, contemp calf; rebacked & corners repaired, rubbed. With 98 hand-colored lithos (2 double-page). bba May 14 (479) £110 [Freddie]

— Journal of a Tour in Iceland.... Yarmouth, 1811. 8vo, contemp half calf; covers detached. With colored frontis & 3 plates (2 folding). Geyser plate, tp & 1 leaf spotted in margins. Inscr "from Dawson Turner". b June 22 (176) £320

Anr copy. Contemp half calf; worn. With hand-colored frontis, folding plan & 2 plates (1 folding). Internal soiling. Folding plan & plate detached. cb Jan 30 (65) $600

Anr copy. Contemp calf; spine & corners worn. With hand-colored frontis & 3 plates. S Nov 15 (1097) £190 [Baring]

2d Ed. L, 1813. 2 vols. 8vo, modern half calf. sg Jan 9 (93) $175

Hooper, William, M. D.

— Rational Recreations. L, 1783-82. 4 vols. 8vo, contemp calf gilt; joints rubbed. With 65 folding plates. S July 1 (1108) £220 [Bickersteth]

4th Ed of Vol I, 2d Ed of the rest. L, 1794-82. 4 vols. 8vo, needs rebdg, Vol I taller; broken. With 65 folding plates. Sold w.a.f. sg May 14 (284) $475

Hooper, William Hulme, 1827-54

— Ten Months among the Tents of the Tuski.... L, 1853. 8vo, orig cloth; rebacked. Several leaves loose. sg Jan 9 (94) $325

Hooton, Charles, 1813?-57

— Colin Clink. L, 1841. Illus by George Cruikshank & John Leech. 3 vols. 12mo, later half calf. bba Apr 30 (118) £110 [Deighton Bell]

Hoover, Herbert Clark, 1874-1964

— The Challenge to Liberty. NY & L, 1934. 1st Ed. Inscr. O July 14 (100) $120

— On Growing Up; Letters to American Boys and Girls. NY, 1962. In d/j. Inscr. K Sept 29 (202) $50

— A Remedy for Disappearing Game Fishes. NY, 1930. One of 990. Half cloth. Koopman copy. O Oct 29 (175) $130; sp Apr 16 (479) $60

Hope, Anthony. See: Hawkins, Sir Anthony Hope

Hope, Thomas, 1770?-1831

— An Historical Essay on Architecture. L, 1840. 3d Ed. 2 vols. 8vo, contemp calf; rubbed. With 97 plates. bba Mar 26 (44) £75 [Sotheran]

— Household Furniture and Interior Decoration. L, 1807. Folio, orig bds; rubbed. With 60 plates. Some foxing. McCarty-Cooper copy. CNY Jan 25 (30) $1,900

Anr copy. Half calf; worn, lacking backstrip, covers detached. With engraved title & 60 plates. Some foxing & edge-darkening. sg Sept 6 (157) $600

Anr copy. Some foxing. sg Sept 6 (157) $600

Hope, Sir William

— A Vindication of the True Art of Self-Defence.... Edin., 1724. 8vo, 18th-cent sheep; front cover & free endpaper loose. sg Mar 26 (150) $275

Hopkins, Albert Allis

— Magic. L, 1897. 8vo, contemp half mor; extremities bumped. Library markings. F Dec 18 (568) $130

Hopkins, Charles, 1664?-1700?

— Pyrrhus King of Epirus. L, 1695. 1st Ed. 4to, modern half calf; new endpapers. bba July 9 (93) £70 [Thorp]

Hopkins, Gerard Manley, 1844-89

— Poems. L, 1918. 1st Ed. Ed by Robert Bridges. Orig half cloth. Epstein copy. sg Apr 29 (238) $1,800

Hopkinson's copy, Francis

— Hayley, William. - Plays of Three Acts. Written for a Private Theatre. L, 1784. 1st Ed. 4to contemp calf; worn, covers detached along with final signature, lacking front endpaper. Sgd by Hopkinson on tp. pba Aug 20 (114) $160

Hopps, Walter —& Others

— Marcel Duchamp: ready-Mades, etc. (1913-1964). Milan: Galeria Schwarz, 1964. One of 100, with sgd proof by Duchamp. Folio, mor. sg Apr 2 (83) $3,800

Horace, 65-8 B.C.

— Odes. Paris, 1939-[42]. One of 50 with 2 extra sets of woodcuts. Illus by Aristide Maillol. 2 vols. Loose as issued in orig wraps. CNY Dec 5 (277) $1,600

— Opera. Venice: Raynaldus de Novimagio, 6 Sept 1483. Folio, contemp blind-stamped calf over oak bds; clasps removed, front joint broken, spine-ends repaired, corners worn. 56 lines of commentary; types 4:105R (text) & 5:83R (commentary). Upper blank corners of 1st 7 leaves renewed; some dampstaining. 163 (of 164) leaves. Goff H-449. C June 24 (323) £1,600 [Wood]

Anr Ed. Venice: Bernardinus Stagninus de Tridino, 1486. Folio, vellum. 56 lines; roman letter. Some spotting & soiling. 174 (of 178) leaves; lacking e2, o1, s8 & t8. Goff H-450. SI June 9 (474) LIt550,000

Anr Ed. Amst., 1713. 4to, vellum gilt with arms of Dordrecht; rubbed, soiled. B May 12 (1654) HF500

Anr Ed. L, 1733-37. Pine's 1st Issue, with "post est" reading on p 108. 2 vols in 1. 8vo, modern mor gilt by Bayntun. Some soiling. Ck No 29 (102) £480

Anr copy. 2 vols. 8vo, contemp mor gilt. P June 18 (489) $1,000

Pine's 2d Issue, with "potest" on p 108. 2 vols in 1. 8vo, contemp calf. bba Jan 16 (103) £350 [Thorp]

Anr copy. 2 vols. 8vo, mor gilt; spines broken, 1 cover detached. F June 25 (608) $175

Anr Ed. L: Pine, 1733-37. Pine's 2d Issue with "postest" reading on p. 108. 2 vols. contemp calf; worn, joints weak; front cover of Vol II detached. cb Feb 12 (60)

$375

Anr Ed. Birm.: Baskerville, 1770. 4to, contemp mor gilt; worn & stained. With frontis & 4 plates. Some foxing & soiling. pn Apr 23 (66) £85

Anr copy. Contemp calf; worn. SI Dec 5 (900) LIt450,000

Anr Ed. Parma, 1793. 8vo, contemp calf; repaired. SI June 9 (447) LIt1,200,000

— Poemata. Venice: Ph. Pincio, 16 May 1509. 8vo, vellum; rebacked. Some dampstaining; short tear in text of x5. S July 1 (1075) £380 [Gatteno]

Horae B. M. V.

— 1499, 20 Mar. - Use of Rome. Lyons: Boninus de Boninis. 8vo, early 19th-cent mor with silver catches & clasps; joints rubbed. Gothic type; ptd on vellum; small initials, penwork decoration, paragraph strokes & line fillers supplied in gold & colors; hand-colored throughout. 80 (of 176) leaves. Goff O-48. sg Mar 12 (119) $3,200

— c.1500. - Paris: Simon Vostre for Philippe Pigouchet. 8vo, modern vellum; rubbed & soiled. Batarde type; ptd on vellum; Ms initials in gold on orange ground throughout. Sold w.a.f. sg Mar 12 (111) $1,200

— [c.1500; Calendar 1500-20]. - Use of Rome. Paris: Guillaume Anabat, for Gilles & Germaine Hardouin. 8vo, 18th-cent calf gilt. With 15 large metalcuts; every page within historiated border (some shaved); initials supplied in gilt on red or blue panels. M2-3 soiled. Ptd on vellum. Bohatta 712; Lacombe 90. S Dec 5 (66) £2,200 [Pirages]

— [c.1515]. - Use of Sarum. Paris: at the expense of Simon Vostre. 8vo, 16th-cent blind-stamped pigskin, upper cover with allegorical panel of Justice on upper cover, Chastity on lower cover, both panels sgd S. R.. Tp rubbed; many leaves close-shaved or shaved with loss to the borders; some soiling. STC 15913. C June 24 (322) £2,200 [Quaritch]

— [c.1520]. - Second Use of Rome. Paris: Gilles Hardouyn. 8vo, old mor. With 21 large & 12 smaller illusts. Ptd on vellum. rs Oct 17 (84) $3,000

— [c.1526; Calendar 1526-41]. - Use of Rome. Paris: Germain Hardouyn. 8vo, old sheep gilt; rubbed, a few corners restored. With initials in gold & colors, each page within a gold frame. 3 full-page & 14 half-page miniatures & 19 painted vignettes. A3r stamped; lacking A2. sg May 7 (118) $7,500

— [c.1537; Calendar 1537-50]. - Paris: G. Hardouyn. 16mo, 17th-cent calf; spine restored at head, covers scratched. 27 lines; gothic letter; 13 metal cut illusts, all colored with liquid gold borders; initials illuminated in gold, red & blue. Tp rubbed; some soiling to fore-margins. Ptd on vellum. C June 24 (146) £1,800 [Hindman]

— 1841 [but 1861]. - Le Livre d'heures de la Reine Anne de Bretagne. Paris: Curmer One of 850. 2 vols. 4to, mor by Riviere; rubbed, upper joints cracking. With 79 full-page chromolitho plates & pages & 314 chromolitho borders. At least 2 plates used for doublures; browned. P June 25 (526) $500

Horam, the Son of Asmar

— The Tales of the Genii. L, 1805. 2 vols. 8vo, calf backed in mor; rubbed. O May 26 (184) $80

Horan, James D.

— The Life and Art of Charles Schreyvogel. NY, [1969]. Folio, orig bdg; shaken. sp June 18 (183) $80

— The McKenney-Hall Portrait Gallery of American Indians. NY, [1972]. One of 249. Half mor. bbc Sept 23 (320) $60

Horblit, Harrison D. See: Grolier Club

Horblit Library, Harrison D.

— [Sale Catalogue] The Celebrated Library.... L, 1974. Parts 1 & 2 (all issued). 2 vols. 4to, cloth. Price lists laid in. cb Nov 21 (111) $55; O Sept 24 (124) $60

Horgan, Paul

— The Return of the Weed. NY, 1936. One of 350. Illus by Peter Hurd. 4to, cloth. bbc Dec 9 (488) $210

Horn, Madeline Darrough

— Farm on the Hill. NY, 1936. In chipped d/j. With 8 color plates. sg Jan 10 (188) $150

Hornaday, William Temple, 1854-1937

— The National Collection of Heads and Horns. NY, 1907-8. 2 vols. 4to, cloth, orig wraps bound in. Library markings. sg Jan 9 (268) $425

Hornby, Lady Emily Bithynia

— Constantinople during the Crimean War. L, 1863. 8vo, orig cloth; soiled, worn. With 5 color plates. S Nov 15 (1175) £260 [Kutluoglu]

Horne, Herbert Percy

— The Binding of Books. L, 1894. One of 150. cb Oct 17 (433) $100

Horne, Thomas Hartwell, 1780-1862

See also: Finden & Horne

— An Introduction to the Study of Bibliography. L, 1814. 2 vols. 8vo, contemp half cloth; rubbed, 1 cover detached. Some foxing. K Dec 1 (245) $120

— The Lakes of Lancashire, Westmorland, and Cumberland. L, 1816. Illus by Joseph Farington. Folio, orig cloth; rebacked, modern endpapers. With double-page hand-colored map & 43 plates. Some spotting. C Oct 30 (30) £320 [Marsden]

Hornell, James. See: Haddon & Hornell

Horneman, Frederich Konrad, 1772-1800

— The Journal of F. Horneman's Travels from Cairo to Mourzouk.... L, 1802. 4to, modern half calf gilt. With 2 folding maps. S July 1 (1497) £180 [Maggs]

Horner, William Edmonds, 1793-1853. See: Smith & Horner

Hornor, William MacPherson, Jr.

— Blue Book. Philadelphia Furniture. William Penn to George Washington. Phila., 1935. One of 400. 4to, cloth; hinges cracked. sg Sept 6 (116) $70

Hornot, Antoine

— Anecdotes americaines ou histoire abregee.... Paris, 1776. 8vo, old calf; rubbed, bottom inch of spine worn, corners bumped. K July 12 (261) $110

Horozco y Covarruvias, Juan de

— Emblemas morales. Madrid: Sanchez, 1610. 8vo, modern vellum. Lacking 4 plates; some repairs. SI Dec 5 (175) LIt380,000

Horsbrugh, Boyd Robert

— The Game-Birds and Water-Fowl of South Africa. L, 1912. Illus by C. G. Davies. 4to, contemp half mor; spine rubbed & faded. With 67 colored plates. S July 1 (919) £400 [Grahame]

Horsfield, Thomas, 1773-1859

— Zoological Researches in Java, and the Neighbouring Islands. L, 1824. 1st Ed. 8 parts in 1 vol. 4to, contemp half mor. With 72 plates, 64 hand-colored. Some text leaves & tp verso stamped. C Oct 30 (203) £1,000 [Wheldon & Wesley]

Horsfield, Thomas Walker, d.1837

— The History, Antiquities, and Topography of the County of Sussex. Lewes, 1835. 2 vols. 4to, disbound. Some stains & foxing; first few leaves of Vol I loose. bba June 11 (290) £130 [MacDonnell]

Horst, Horst P.

— Horst. Photographs of a Decade. NY, [1944]. Ed by George Davis. 4to, cloth; spine soiled. Inscr. sg Apr 13 (53) $200

Horticultural Society of London

— Journal. L, 1846-55. Vols 1-9. 8vo, contemp half mor. With 8 colored & 3 uncolored plates. bba July 9 (64) £140 [Maggs]

— Transactions. L, 1815-30. 2d Ed of Vol I. 7 vols. 4to, half mor gilt; rubbed. With engraved titles (browned) & 133 plates, 69 partly ptd in color & hand-finished. Stains to 3 uncolored plates. L Nov 14 (413) £2,300

First Series I-VII; Second Series I-II. L, 1829-42. 9 vols. 4to, contemp calf; rebacked. Some spotting, mainly affecting engraved titles & a few text leaves; some plates shaved. Sold w.a.f. C May 20 (182A) £2,200

Hortus...

— Hortus Sanitatis. Paris: pour Anthoine Verard, [c.1500]. ("Ortus Sanitatis translate de latin en francois.") 2 vols. Folio, recent vellum. 50 lines; double column; batarde type; with 4 full-page woodcuts & 450 woodcut illusts in the text. Both vols stained & affected by damp & mildwew, causing paper decay & small holes with loss on c.25 leaves; repairs to 1st 3 text leaves in Vol I; 23 leaves with small wormholes at inner margin; 6 leaves in Vol II with tears repaired; 5 leaves inkstained; 7 index leaves decayed at inner margin & repaired. 444 (of 446) leaves; lacking 2 blanks. Goff H-490. C Nov 27 (40) £8,000 [Sawyer]

Horwood, Richard

— Plan of the Cities of London and Westminster.... L, [1792-99]. Folio, contemp half mor; rebacked & recornered, rubbed. Hand-colored map on 32 numbered sheets, joined in 4's to form 8 large folding sheets. Lacking index & list of subscribers; margins soiled with occasional small tears. C Oct 30 (129) £950 [Woodruff]

Anr copy. Later half cloth. On 32 mapsheets. Lacking list of subscribers. C Oct 30 (130) £900 [Marlborough]

Anr Ed. L, 1799. Folio, modern half calf. With 32 mapsheets joined & bound as 8 strips of 4 sheets, fully hand-colored. A1 detached without loss; other sheets frayed at outer margins or cut close; occasional discoloration. Pasted onto front pastedown is a letterpress Reference to each page; reduced single-sheet facsimile of Ogilby's plan of 1676 bound in. S Nov 21 (113) £700 [Schuster]

Hoste, Paul, 1652-1700

— L'Arte des armees navales.... Lyons, 1697. 1st Ed. 2 parts in 1 vol. Folio, contemp calf; rebacked, corners bumped, covers scraped, joints & extremities rubbed. With 145 plates. Repaired marginal tear to tp; some dampstaining & discoloration; last folding plate creased. CNY Oct 8 (133) $2,200

Anr copy. Contemp calf; worn. With 145 plates, 11 folding. Some waterstaining, mainly to margins. S June 25 (167) £1,800 [Stampe]

Houbigant, A. G.

— Moeurs et Costumes des Russes. Paris, 1817. Folio, contemp half calf; joints becoming weak. With 50 hand-colored plates. Some plates handstamped with initials A.G.H. in lower corners; small hole in blank margin of Plate 8; without ad leaf of half-title. S Nov 21 (61) £1,800 [Beeleigh]

Houdart de la Motte, Antoine, 1672-1731

— Fables nouvelles. Paris, 1719. 4to, contemp calf gilt; worn. SI June 9 (505) LIt600,000

Houdini, Harry, 1874-1926

— Magical Rope Ties and Escapes. L: Will Goldston, [c.1920]. 8vo, pictorial bds. sg Oct 17 (48) $130

— A Magician among the Spirits. NY, 1924. 1st Ed. Spine head chipped. cb Jan 16 (79) $160

— The Unmasking of Robert-Houdin. NY, 1908. Inscr to H. Hanson, 1915 & with Ds of Houdini giving Hanson power of attorney in South Africa. S Nov 14 (325) £1,600 [Carrandi]; sg Octt 17 (50) $110

Houghton, William, 1829?-97

— British Fresh-Water Fishes. L, [1879]. 2 vols in 1. Folio, contemp half lea; rubbed, head of spine torn away. With 41 colored plates. Library stamp on tp verso. b June 22 (363) £550

Anr copy. 2 vols. Folio, contemp half mor gilt. Frontis & title spotted. C May 20 (183) £500 [Bifolco]

Anr copy. 2 vols in 1. Folio, contemp half russia; worn. Ck Dec 11 (227) £650

Anr copy. 2 vols. Folio, contemp mor; hinges cracked. With 35 (of 41) color plates. DW Oct 2 (149) £320

Anr copy. Old half mor; rubbed, hole in cloth on front cover, stained. With 41 colored plates. Ink scribbling on lower corner of front blank. K Sept 29 (204) $650

Anr copy. Contemp cloth; Vol I rubbed. Marginal soiling. pn Dec 12 (282) £520 [Bailey]

Anr copy. Orig cloth; rubbed & soiled. Library stamps on half-titles & prelims; marginal soiling. pn Mar 19 (294) £520 [Bifolco]

Anr copy. Contemp half russia; spine worn. Small tear to margin of 1 plate; library stamp on tp & occasionally in text. pnL Nov 20 (163) £420 [Bailey]

Anr copy. Orig cloth; rubbed & soiled. Slight staining to lower edge of text, just affecting most plates; occasional foxing. S May 14 (1040) £480 [Bifolco]

Hourtiq, Louis

— Delacroix, l'oeuvre du maitre. Paris, 1930. 4to, orig cloth. Inscr by Marie-Laure de Noailles to Christian berard & with an ink & wash drawing by Jean Cocteau. Kochno copy. SM Oct 12 (441) FF22,000

House, Homer Doliver, 1878-1949

— Wild Flowers of New York. Albany, 1918. 2 vols. 4to, cloth; some wear. O Mar 31 (101) $50

Anr Ed. Albany, 1923. 2 vols. 4to, cloth. With 264 colored plates. Library markings. sg Nov 14 (181) $60

2d Ptg. Orig cloth. With 264 colored plates. NH Oct 6 (215) $60

Housman, Alfred Edward, 1859-1936

— Last Poems. L, 1922. 1st Ed. In d/j. sg Dec 12 (158) $120

— More Poems. L, 1936. 1st Ed, one of 379. Orig half mor. sg Dec 12 (159) $110

— A Shropshire Lad. L, 1896. 1st Ed, one of 500. 8vo, orig bds, Carter & Sparrow A label; spine soiled. Endpapers spotted & with newspaper clippings pasted in. C June 24 (147) £600 [Dawson]

— A Shropshire Lad, and Last Poems. L: The Alcuin Press, 1929. One of 325. 2 vols sg Dec 12 (160) $110

Housman, Clemence Annie

— The Were-Wolf.... L, 1896. Illus by Laurence Housman. 8vo, orig cloth; head of spine chipped. With frontis & 5 plates. With ALs, 14 Jan 1903, pasted in. sg Oct 17 (276) $60

Housman, Laurence, 1865-1959
See also: Arabian Nights

— Stories from the Arabian Nights. L, [1907]. Illus by Edmund Dulac. 4to, cloth; spine worn. sg Sept 26 (100) $140

One of 350. Orig vellum. With 50 mtd color plates. sg Sept 26 (99) $800

Anr copy. Orig vellum; front joint cracked. sg Jan 30 (44) $375

Houzeau, Jean Charles —& Lancaster, Albert

— Bibliographie generale de l'astronomie. L, 1964. 2 vols in 3. 4to, cloth; worn. O Sept 24 (126) $170

Hovell, William H. —& Hume, Hamilton, 1797-1873

— Journey of Discovery to Port Phillip.... L, 1837. 2d Ed. Ed by William Bland. 8vo, modern calf. With folding map, backed on cloth. R. J. Maria copy. C June 25 (214) £7,500 [Quaritch/Hordern]

How, George E. P. & Jane P.

— English and Scottish Silver Spoons. L, 1952-57. One of 50. 3 vols. Folio, mor gilt by Sangorski & Sutcliffe. pn May 14 (142) £550

One of 550. Cloth, in soiled d/js. S May 13 (530) £280 [Forsyth]

Howard, David Sanctuary

— Chinese Armorial Porcelain. L, 1974. 4to, cloth, in d/j. With colored frontis & 24 colored plates. W July 8 (148) £310

Howard, Henry

— England's Newest Way in all sorts of Cookery, Pastry, and All Pickles that are fit to be Used. L: Chr. Coningsby, 1708. 8vo, modern calf. With 7 plates. Browned; some edge repairs at beginning. S May 14 (987) £750 [Quaritch]

Howard, Henry Charles, 18th Earl of Suffolk. See: Suffolk, Henry Charles Howard

Howard, Henry Eliot

— The British Warblers. L, 1907-14. Parts 1-9. 4to, orig half cloth; rubbed. With 63 plain & 35 colored plates. Ck Sept 6 (23) £140

Anr copy. 10 orig parts, including supplement. 8vo, Ck Sept 6 (24) £190

Anr copy. 2 vols. 4to, contemp half mor by Bumpus. With 12 maps, 51 uncolored & 25 colored plates. Some spotting. S May 14 (1041) £200 [Seragnoli]

Howard, John, 1726?-90

— The State of the Prisons in England and Wales.... Warrington, 1780. 2d Ed. 8vo, calf; front cover detached. With 11 plates, all but 1 folding. bba Mar 26 (228) £110 [Land]

Howard, John Eliot, 1807-83

— The Quinology of the East Indian Plantations. L, 1869-76. 3 parts in 1 vol. Folio, orig cloth; rebacked preserving orig spine, endpapers renewed, corners rubbed. With 3 hand-colored plates, 2 photographic plates, 2 plain & 10 hand-colored lithos. C Oct 30 (204) £550 [Arader]

Howard, Leland Ossian —& Others

— The Mosquitoes of North and Central America and the West Indies. Wash., 1912-17. 4 vols. 4to, cloth. Inscr by 3 authors. K Sept 29 (277) $100

Howard, Oliver O.

— Nez Perce Joseph. Bost., 1881. 8vo, cloth. sg Dec 5 (121) $225

Howard, Robert E.

— Conan the Barbarian. NY: Gnome Press, [1954]. In d/j. sg June 11 (165) $175

— Conan the Conqueror: The Hyborean Age. NY: Gnome Press, [1950]. In d/j. wa Sept 26 (333) $80

— The Dark Man and Others. Sauk City: Arkham House, 1963. In d/j. F Dec 18 (153) $50; sp Nov 24 (394) $85

— King Conan: The Hyborean Age. NY: Gnome Press, [1953]. In d/j. sp Nov 24 (185) $70

— Skull-Face and Others. Sauk City, 1946. 1st Ed. In d/j. Epstein copy. sg Apr 29 (241) $500; sp Nov 24 (392) $250

Howard, W. See: Lowe & Howard

Howard-Bury, Charles Kenneth

— Mount Everest. The Reconnaissance, 1921. L, 1922. Folio, cloth. sg Jan 9 (290) $150

Howe, E. R. J. Gambier. See: British Museum

Howe, James Virgil

— The Modern Gunsmith.... NY, 1945. 2 vols. 4to, cloth. Supplement bound at rear at Vol 2. sp Apr 16 (316) $55

Howell, James, c.1594-1666

— Dendrologia, Dodona's Grove, or the Vocall Forrest. L, 1640. Folio, 19th-cent sheep; needs rebacking. Minor spotting on tp & frontis; border of 2 plates shaved. STC 13872. sg Oct 24 (163) $150

— Epistolae Ho-Elianae. Familiar Letters.... L, 1645. 4to, modern calf gilt. bba Dec 19 (345) £80 [Coupe]

— Lexicon Tetraglotton, an English-French-Italian-Spanish Dictionary. L: J. G. for Samuel Thomson, 1660. 3 parts in 1 vol. Folio, contemp calf; rubbed, spine ends worn. K1 with small burn-hole; c3 with small hole affecting text; some foxing & browning. Wing H-3088. bba June 11 (52) £240 [Clark]

— Londinopolis; an Historicall Discourse.... L, 1657. Folio, contemp calf; rebacked. W July 8 (61) $200

— Lustra Lucovici, or the Life of the Late...King of France, Lewis the XIII. L, 1646. 1st Ed. Folio, calf. W July 8 (90) £60

Howells, William Dean, 1837-1920

— Clemency for the Anarchists. A Letter from Mr. W. D. Howells. To the Editor of the [New York] Tribune.... Dansville NY, Dec 1887. Single sheet, 193mm by 133mm. Corrected proof copy, inscr to Dr. Albert Leffingwell. Sold with related autograph material having to do with his support for clemency for the anarchists. CNY June 9 (94) $3,500

Howe-Nurse, Wilfrid

— Berkshire Vale. Oxford, 1927. One of 250. Folio, orig cloth in torn d/j. Ck July 10 (302) £75

Howes, Wright

— U.S.-iana (1650-1950); a Selective Bibliography.... NY, 1962. Cloth; worn, inner hinge cracked. Library markings. NH Aug 23 (365) $65

Anr copy. Cloth; worn. O sept 24 (127) $80

Anr copy. Colton Storm's copy. sg May 21 (238) $90

Anr copy. Owner's handstamp on front pastedown. wa Sept 26 (430) $55

— U.S.-iana (1700-1950); a Descriptive Check-list.... NY, 1954. 1st Ed. sp Nov 24 (261) $65

Howitt, Samuel, 1765?-1822

See also: Williamson & Howitt

— British Preserve. L, 1824. 4to, modern half calf. With engraved title & 36 plates. bba Nov 28 (122) £170 [A. Cumming]

— A New Work of Animals. L, 1811. Ed with 100 plates. 4to, later half mor gilt. Lacking preface. Ck Dec 11 (228) £260

Anr copy. Contemp mor gilt. Plates hand-colored & interleaved with smaller text. Frontis creased & repaired; 3 plates repaired & laid down; stamps on front pastedown, tp verso & 1st page of text. pn Mar 19 (295) £600 [Shapero]

Howitt, William, 1792-1879

— The Student-Life of Germany. L, 1841. 8vo, calf gilt by Bickers; rubbed. With 7 plates. pn Dec 12 (359) £70 [Bailey]

Howitt, William & Mary

— Ruined Abbeys and Castles of Great Britain. L, 1862-64. Series I only. 2 vols. 4to, orig cloth. kh Nov 11 (347) A$220

Howlett, Bartholomew

— A Selection of Views in the County of Lincoln.... L, 1805. Folio, orig wraps. With engraved title, hand-colored map & 44 views only plus 2 other loose plates from anr work. Sold w.a.f. L Feb 27 (138) £90

Hoyem, Andrew

— Shaped Poetry. San Francisco: Arion Press, 1981. One of 300. Folio, loose as issued in wrap. With 30 prints. Lacking plexiglass display frame. sg Sept 26 (8) $110

Hoym Library, Carl Georg Heinrich von, Count

— [Sale Catalogue] Catalogus librorum bibliothecae.... Paris, 1738. Compiled by Gabriel Martin. 8vo, half mor. Library stamp on tp. Priced in Ms. bba May 28 (557) £65 [Maggs]

Hrabanus Magnentius, 784-856

— Commentaria in Hieremiam Prophetam. Basel: Henricus Petrus, [1534]. Bound with: Roll of Hampole, Richard. In Psalterium Davidicum. Cologne, 1536. Folio, contemp blind-stamped pigskin dated 1562 & sgd CKW. Ck Oct 31 (190) £500

Hsiang Yuan-pien

— Noted Porcelains of Successive Dynasties. Peking, 1931. Folio, orig silk wraps gilt. b&b Feb 19 (273) $175

Hubback, Theodore R.

— To Far Western Alaska for Big Game. L, 1929. Cloth; stain on rear cover. sg May 21 (47) $140

Hubbard, Elbert, 1856-1915

— A Message to Garcia.... East Aurora, 1901. One of 450. 8vo, loose in portfolio, as issued. With 11 pages of Ms notes. sg Jan 30 (86) $375

— Works. East Aurora, N.Y., [c.1908-15]. One of 1,000. Vols I-VI only. Half mor. rs Oct 17 (69) $200

Hubbard, Gurdon Saltonstall

— Incidents and Events in the Life of.... [Chicago], 1888. 1st Ed. Ed by Henry E. Hamilton. 8vo, cloth. sg June 18 (295) $110

Hubbard, L. Ron

— Death's Deputy. Los Angeles: Fantasy Publishing, 1948. Orig cloth, Currey's A bdg, in soiled d/j. wa (203) $120 [Mar 5]

— Dianetics: The Modern Science of Mental Health. NY: Hermitage House, [1950]. In def d/j. bbc Apr 27 (534) $90

Anr copy. In d/j. sg June 11 (166) $250; sp Nov 24 (310) $100

— Final Blackout. Providence: Hadley Publishing, [1948]. In d/j. Sgd. bbc Dec 9 (579) $140

Anr copy. In edge-worn d/j. Sgd. sg June 11 (167) $140

Anr copy. In d/j. wa Sept 26 (334) $140

— The Kingslayer. Los Angeles: Fantasy Publishing, 1949. In d/j with soiled rear panel. sg June 11 (168) $130

Variant issue with Currey's priority A white wove endpapers & ptd on his priority B wove text paper. In d/j. wa Mar 5 (205) $110

— Slaves of Sleep. Chicago: Shasta, 1948. In edge-worn d/j. sg June 11 (169) $150

Anr copy. In d/j. wa Sept 26 (335) $120

— Two Novels.... NY: Gnome Press, [1951]. In soiled d/j with damp-spotting along spine panel that slightly affects covers. Owner's stamp to tp & front free endpaper. wa Mar 5 (206) $90

Hubbard, William, 1621?-1704

— The Present State of New-England, Being a Narrative of the Troubles with the Indians.... L, 1677. 4to, contemp sheep; rebacked, rubbed. Map repaired. Streeter copy. O Nov 26 (88) $22,000

Hubrecht, Alphonse

— Grandeur et suprematie de Peking. Peking, 1928. One of 1,000. 4to, calf; worn. b&b Feb 19 (269) $125

Hudson, Derek

— Arthur Rackham: his Life and Work. L, 1960. 4to, orig bdg, in repaired d/j. K Mar 22 (375) $85

Anr Ed. NY, [1960]. 4to, cloth, in d/j; worn. sg Oct 31 (139) $50

Hudson, William Henry, 1841-1922

See also: Limited Editions Club; Sclater & Hudson

— The Birds of La Plata. L, 1920. 2 vols. 4to, orig cloth. With 22 colored plates. sg May 14 (221) $110

Anr copy. Orig cloth, in chipped & def d/j. Note in ink on 1st page of intro in Vol I. wa Feb 20 (157) $120

Anr copy. Orig cloth, in d/js. wa Mar 5 (490) $65

Huelsen, Christian —& Egger, Hermann

— Die Roemischen Skizzenbuecher von Marten van Heemskerck im Koeniglichen Kupferstichkabinett zu Berlin. Berlin, 1913-16. One of 200. 2 vols text in orig bds, plates loose as issued, both in orig portfolios; 1 cover almost detached. S Feb 11 (114) £360 [Bernett]

Hughes, Griffith

— The Natural History of Barbados. L, 1750. Folio, contemp calf; joints cracked. With folding map & 28 engraved hand-colored plates. LH Dec 11 (131) $1,300

Hughes, John T., 1817-62

— Doniphan's Expedition, Containing an Account of the Conquest of New Mexico. Cincinnati: U.P. James, [1847]. 8vo, modern half calf, orig wraps bound in. sg June 18 (296) $275

Anr Ed. Cincinnati, [c.1851]. 12mo, ptd wrap; both covers partially detached. Some foxing. NH May 30 (386) $100

Hughes, Langston. See: De Carava & Hughes

Hughes, Richard

See also: Limited Editions Club

— A High Wind in Jamaica. L, 1929. In d/j. P Oct 11 (175) $125

Anr copy. Half cloth. sg Dec 12 (162) $60

— The Spider's Palace and Other Stories. L, 1931. One of 110. Half cloth. sg Dec 12 (163) $50

Hughes, Rupert

— The Lakerim Athletic Club. NY, 1898. 1st Ed. 8vo, orig cloth. With frontis & 23 plates. Epstein copy. sg Apr 29 (242) $250

Hughes, Sukey

— Washi; the World of Japanese Paper. Tokyo, [1978]. One of 1,000. 4to, half cloth. bbc Dec 9 (185) $275; cb Feb 27 (61) $250; sg Oct 31 (140) $300

Hughes, Ted

— Crow, from the Life and Songs of the Crow. L, 1973. One of 400. Illus by Leonard Baskin. Folio, orig half cloth. bba Sept 19 (199) £75 [Great NW Bkstore]

— Earth-Moon. L: Rainbow Press, 1976. One of 226. 4to, orig calf. sg June 11 (170) $70

— The Hawk in the Rain. L, [1957]. In d/j. DW Oct 2 (359) £100

Hughes, Thomas Smart, 1786-1847

— Travels in Sicily, Greece and Albania. L, 1820. 2 vols. 4to, contemp calf gilt; joints split, heads of spine chipped. S June 30 (321) £700 [Chelsea]

Hugnet, Georges

— Au depens des mots. Paris, 1941. One of 20. Illus by Valentine Hugo. 16mo, loose as issued. CGen Nov 18 (392) SF1,600

— La Chevre-feuille. Paris, 1943. One of 534. Illus by Picasso. 4to, wraps. With 6 plates. CGen Nov 18 (396) SF800

Anr copy. Wraps. Inscr by Hugnet. sg Jan 30 (128) $250

— Marcel Duchamp. Paris, 1941. One of 20 on verge havane. Unbound as issued. With tipped-in moustache & beard for Mona Lisa. CGen Nov 18 (395) SF7,000

— Non Vouloir. Paris, [1940]. One of 20 on verge antique. Illus by Joan Miro. Unbound as issued. CGen Nov 18 (393) SF3,100

— Onan. Paris, 1934. One of 50. Illus by Salvador Dali. 4to, orig wraps. With watercolor frontis, sgd. CGen Nov 18 (397) SF12,000

— Pablo Picasso. Paris, 1941. One of 20. Illus by Picasso. 16mo, loose as issued. CGen Nov 18 (394) SF13,000

Hugo, Hermannus, 1588-1629

— De prima scribendi origine et universa rei literariae antiquitate. Antwerp, 1617. 1st Ed. 8vo, contemp calf. sg Oct 31 (223) $750

— Pia Desideria: or, Divine Addresses. L, 1686. 8vo, contemp calf; worn, upper cover detached. With engraved title & 46 plates. Some foxing. bba Aug 13 (91) £65 [Wilbraham]

— The Siege of Breda. L, 1627. Folio, contemp vellum; worn. With engraved title & 15 plans. Some surface abrasion affecting images & imprint; G2 & 3 misbound; 1 blank corner torn away. S July 1 (1277) £200 [Knohl]

Hugo, Jean

— Voyage a Moscou et Leningrad. Paris, 1923. Orig cloth. With 19 colored illusts in panoramic form. Inscr to Boris Kochno with illust. SM Oct 12 (479) FF11,000

Hugo, Thomas, 1820-76

— The Bewick Collector: a Descriptive Catalogue.... L, 1866-68. 2 vols, including Supplement. 8vo, bdg not stated. cb Oct 17 (437) $200

Anr Ed. NY, [1970]. 2 vols, including Supplement. 8vo, cloth. sg Oct 31 (141) $50

Hugo, Victor, 1802-85

— L'Homme qui rit. Paris, 1869. 1st Ed. 4 vols. 8vo, half lea. Epstein copy. sg Apr 29 (243) $500

— Les Miserables. Paris, 1862. 1st Ed. 10 vols. 8vo, contemp half mor. Epstein copy. sg Apr 29 (244) $2,200

— Notre Dame; A Tale of the Ancien Regime. L, 1833. 3 vols. 8vo, contemp half calf gilt; rubbed. Manney copy. P Oct 11 (176) $3,000

— Quatre-vingt-treize. Paris, 1874. 1st Ed, one of 50 on hollande. 3 vols. 8vo, half mor. Epstein copy. sg Apr 29 (245) $200

— Works. Bost: Estes & Lauriat, [c.1892]. 30 vols. 8vo, half mor. cb Oct 31 (45) $190

Huish, Marcus Bourne

— British Water-Colour Art. L, 1904. One of 500. 4to, orig cloth; rubbed, front hinge cracking. Prelims foxed. bba May 14 (332) £90 [Thorp]

Anr copy. Orig cloth; spine faded. sg Apr 2 (141) $70

— Happy England, as Painted by Helen Allingham. L, 1903. One of 750 sgd by the artist. Illus by Helen Allingham. 4to, orig cloth; shaken. bba Oct 10 (140) £60 [Harlow]

Anr copy. Half mor. bba Oct 10 (141) £80 [A. Wilson]

Anr copy. Later half vellum. DW Apr 8 (79) £140

Anr copy. Contemp mor gilt; rubbed. DW Apr 8 (80) £140

Anr copy. Orig cloth; spine darkened. DW Apr 8 (385) £320

Anr Ed. L, 1909. 4to, orig cloth; spine faded, lower cover stained. bba Oct 24 (220) £65 [The Bookroom]

Hullmandel, C. See: Pinelli & Hullmandel

Hullmandel, Charles

— The Art of Drawing on Stone. L, [1824]. 1st Ed. 4to, orig bds; rebacked, stained, scored. With litho title & 19 plates. Some spotting; Plate IX with waterstain into image. P June 18 (555) $3,000

Humber, William, 1821-81

— A Practical Treatise on Cast and Wrought Iron Bridges.... L, 1857. Folio, contemp half mor. With 58 plates, including 35 double-page. Some waterstaining & spotting. S May 14 (1080) £160 [Elton]

Humboldt, Alexander von, 1769-1859

— Kosmos. Entwurf einer physischen Weltbeschreibung. Stuttgart & Tuebingen, 1845-58. Vols I-IV (of 5). 8vo, orig bds backed in mor; tips worn. wa Mar 5 (45) $150

— Researches concerning the Institutions & Monuments of the Ancient Inhabitants of America.... L, 1814. 2 vols in 1. 8vo, contemp sheep; rebacked. sg June 18 (297) $325

Hume, Allan Octavian. See: Henderson & Hume

Hume, David, 1711-76

— An Enquiry Concerning the Principles of Morals. L, 1751. 12mo, contemp calf; joints split, worn. L3 uncancelled; errata corrected in an early hand; some browning; small piece cut from blank corner of L6; stain on L7 affecting 2 letters. pn June 11 (152) £600

Anr copy. Contemp calf; rebacked preserving orig spine. S July 21 (314) £850 [Finch]

— The History of England. L, 1806. 5 vols. Folio, contemp half mor gilt; rebacked preserving orig spines. Library markings;

some foxing. bba May 14 (115) £75 [Wilkinson]

Anr copy. 10 vols. Folio, contemp half calf; rubbed, broken. Some foxing. F Mar 26 (767) $80

Anr Ed. Edin., 1810. 13 vols. 8vo, contemp calf; rubbed. bba Feb 27 (102) £120 [Classic Bindings]

Anr Ed. L, 1822. 13 vols, including Smollett's continuation. 8vo, 19th-cent mor gilt; extremities rubbed. sg Mar 5 (132) $700

— Philosophical Essays Concerning Human Understanding.... L, 1750. 2d Ed. 12mo, contemp calf gilt; corners rubbed, head of spine worn. b June 22 (177) £420

— Political Discourses. Edin., 1752. 8vo, contemp calf; rubbed. b June 22 (79) £1,200

Hume, Hamilton, 1797-1873. See: Hovell & Hume

Humelbergius Secundus, Dick, Pseud.

— Apician Morsels; or Tales of the Table, Kitchen and Larder.... NY, 1829. 12mo, bdg not stated. cb Oct 17 (848) $225

Humourist. See: Cruikshank, George

Humphrey, Mabel & Maud

— Children of the Revolution. NY: Stokes, [1900]. 4to, pictorial bds; top third of spine chewed & in need of repair. bbc June 29 (409) $200

Humphrey, Maud

— Maud Humphrey's Book of Fairy Tales. NY: Stokes, 1892. 4to, orig pictorial bds; edges worn, front hinge separating. F Sept 26 (67) $375

Humphreys, Arthur Lee

— Old Decorative Maps and Charts. L & NY, 1926. One of 1,500. 4to, orig cloth. With 79 plates. sg Feb 13 (125) $110

Humphreys, David, 1752-1818

— An Essay on the Life of....Major-General Israel Putnam. Hartford: Hudson & Goodwin, 1788. 1st Ed. 12mo, calf; rubbed. NH May 30 (465) $170

Humphreys, Henry Noel

— The Genera and Species of British Butterflies. L, [1859]. 8vo, orig cloth; worn & rubbed; contents detached. With 33 colored plates, including title. cb Sept 26 (114) $1190

— The Genera of British Moths. L, [1860]. 2 vols. 8vo, orig cloth; spine lacking. With hand-colored additional title & 42 plates. Some spotting. Ck May 15 (31) £360

Anr copy. Orig cloth; worn. With 62 colored plates. 2d title loosely inserted. pn Apr 23 (226) £140

— Illuminated Illustrations of Froissart.... L, 1844-45. 2 vols in 1. 4to, contemp half mor; extremities rubbed. Ck July 10 (183A) £180

Anr copy. 2 vols. 4to, later half mor gilt; worn. With 74 hand-colored lithos, including additional titles. Some foxing. sg Mar 5 (133) $225

— The Miracles of Our Lord. L, 1848. 8vo, orig lea; covers detached. Sold w.a.f. sg Oct 17 (134) $50

— The Origin and Progress of the Art of Writing. L, 1853. 4to, orig papier mache; rebacked with later mor. Soiled & foxed. cb Sept 26 (115) $250

Anr copy. Papier-mache. With 31 plates. Several leaves loose. sg May 7 (119) $300

— Parables of Our Lord. L, 1847. 8vo, orig half calf. b Mar 11 (109) £120

Humphreys, Henry Noel —& Westwood, John Obadiah, 1805-93

— British Butterflies and their Transformations. L, 1841. 4to, contemp calf gilt; spine wormed & torn at head. With hand-colored litho title & 42 plates. Ck May 15 (30) £380

Anr copy. Orig cloth; spine lacking, soiled. Ck May 15 (31) £360

Anr copy. Contemp half mor gilt. DW Mar 4 (112) £460

Anr Ed. L, 1848. 4to, half mor gilt. With hand-colored litho title & 42 plates. S Nov 15 (743) £550 [Graham]

Anr Ed. L, 1849. 4to, orig half mor gilt; scuffed. With chromolitho title & 39 plates. Sold w.a.f. Ck Dec 12 (284) £550

Anr copy. Contemp half calf; rubbed. With hand-colored title & 42 hand-colored plates. Some spotting. pn Dec 12 (283) £400

— British Moths and their Transformations. L, 1843-45. 2 vols. 4to, contemp mor gilt; extremities rubbed. With 124 hand-colored plates. Harrison copy. Ck Nov 29 (103) £280

Anr copy. Contemp half mor gilt; extremities worn. DW Mar 4 (111) £370

Anr Ed. L, 1849. Vol I only. Contemp half calf; rubbed. With 56 hand-colored plates. Some spotting. pn Dec 12 (284) £160

Anr Ed. L, 1857-58. 2 vols. 4to, half mor. With 124 colored plates. S Nov 15 (744) £400 [Thorp]

Humphries, Sydney

— Oriental Carpets.... L, 1910. Folio, orig cloth; rubbed. O May 26 (94) $80

Anr copy. Orig cloth; front hinge starting. sp Feb 6 (219) $150

Hundt, Magnus

— Compendium totius logices.... Rome: Melchoir Lotter, 1511. Bound with: Bede, the Venerable. Authoritates Aristotelis et aliorum philosohorum.... Leipzig, 1510. And: Hispanus, Petrus. Textus septem tractatuum. Leipzig: Melchior Lotter, 1509. 4to, contemp blind-stamped half pigskin over wooden bds; stained. Ck Oct 31 (20) £1,000

Hunt, Aurora

— The Army of the Pacific. Glendale, 1951. cb Sept 12 (87) $110

Hunt, Henry

— Investigation at Ilchester Gaol.... L, 1821. 8vo, calf gilt; minor wear, hinges tender, fore-edges wormed. With hand-colored frontis port by George Cruikshank & 5 hand-colored ports probably by Robert Cruikshank. Salomons copy. sg Oct 17 (169) $200

Hunt, John, Engraver

— British Ornithology. Norwich, 1815-22. 3 vols. 8vo, recent half calf by Bernard Middleton. With 3 engraved titles, 4 anatomical plates & 180 hand-colored plates. Titles & a few plates shaved; lacking 8 uncolored plates. C May 20 (184) £1,900 [Marshall]

Hunt, Leigh, 1784-1859

— A Jar of Honey from Mount Hybla. L, 1848. 8vo, calf, orig covers used as pastedowns; some rubbing. O May 26 (95) $70

— Lord Byron and Some of his Contemporaries. L, 1828. 2d Ed. 2 vols. 8vo, later half mor. cb Feb 12 (62) $225

Anr copy. Cloth. Stained & foxed. LH May 17 (588) $100

— Stories from the Italian Poets.... L, 1846. 1st Ed. 2 vols. 12mo, later calf by Arthur S. Colley; scrape at top of front cover of Vol II. bbc Dec 9 (225) $70

Anr copy. Cloth. br May 29 (57) $50

— The Town; its Memorable Characters and Events. L, 1848. 1st Ed. 2 vols. 12mo, lea. br May 29 (56) $350

Hunt, Lynn Bogue. See: Derrydale Press

Hunt, P. F.

See also: Walford & Hunt

— Orchidaceae. L, 1973. One of 600. Illus by Mary A. Grierson. 4to, vellum gilt. wa Dec 9 (541) $300

Anr copy. Vellum. With 40 color plates. wa Dec 9 (630) $325

Hunt, R. C.

— Salmon in Low Water. NY: Anglers' Club, 1950. One of 500. With 2 hand-colored plates of flies. Koopman copy. O Oct 29 (180) $325

Hunt Collection, Rachel McMasters Miller

— Catalogue of Botanical Books.... NY: Maurizio Martino, [1991]. Reprint, One of 400. 2 vols. bbc Apr 27 (109) $110

Hunt, William Shapter

— Brown's Sporting Tour in India. L, 1865. 4to, orig cloth. With hand-colored frontis & 41 plates. bba Nov 28 (91) £420 [Hooper]

Hunt, William Southworth

— Frank Forester: a Tragedy in Exile. Newark, 1933. One of 200. Koopman copy. O Oct 29 (181) $160

Hunter...

— The Hunter and Angler. NY, 1882. 12mo, pictorial wraps; chipped. sg Jan 9 (269) $140

Hunter, Dard

— Chinese Ceremonial Paper.... Chillicothe, Ohio, 1937. One of 125. Folio, half mor gilt. b&b Feb 19 (529) $5,000

— My Life with Paper. NY, 1958. In d/j. cb Oct 17 (441) $55

— Papermaking by Hand in India. NY, 1939. One of 375. 4to, orig half calf; spine rubbed & chipped at ends. Inscr. S Dec 12 (174) £900 [Forster]

Anr copy. Half cloth. wd June 12 (395) $1,050

— Papermaking by Hand in America. Chillicothe, Ohio, 1950. One of 210. Folio, half cloth. b&b Feb 19 (256) $5,000

— Paper-Making in the Classroom. Peoria: Manual Arts Press, [1931]. NH Aug 23 (309) $190; Z Oct 26 (111) $120

— Papermaking in Southern Siam. [Chillicothe], 1936. One of 115. Folio, bds. b&b Feb 19 (257) $4,000

— Papermaking in Indo-China. Chillicothe, Ohio, 1947. One of 182. 4to, orig half mor. b&b Feb 19 (261) $1,000

Anr Ed. Chillicothe OH, 1947. 4to, orig half mor; joints & corners rubbed. With 16 plates & 2 mtd paper specimens. Ls inserted. S Dec 12 (175) £850

— A Papermaking Pilgrimage to Japan, Korea

& China. NY, 1936. One of 370, sgd by Hunter & Elmer Adler. 4to, lev. With 50 paper specimens. b&b Feb 19 (258) $1,500

Anr copy. Orig half mor. Inscr & with related material. S Dec 12 (173) £900 [Forster]

Anr copy. Half mor; head of spine worn. sg Nov 7 (93) $1,300

— Papermaking through Eighteen Centuries. NY, 1930. Orig cloth, in d/j. cb Oct 17 (442) $130

Anr copy. Orig cloth, in frayed d/j. O Sept 24 (128) $110

Anr copy. Orig cloth, in d/j. sg Oct 31 (142) $60

Anr copy. Orig cloth; rubbed. Folding frontis creased. wa Mar 5 (129) $120

Anr Ed. NY, 1947. sg Oct 31 (143) $120

— Papermaking: the History and Technique of an Ancient Craft. NY, 1943. 1st Ed. In chipped d/j. K July 12 (265) $55

2d Ed. NY, 1947. cb Oct 17 (443) $65

Hunter, Fenley

— Frances Lake, Yukon. Dawson 1887. Hunter 1923. Flushing, 1924. One of 50. 8vo, orig half mor. Inscr. cb Oct 10 (53) $225

Hunter, George Leland

— Decorative Textiles: Coverings for Furniture, Walls and Floors.... Phila., L & Grand Rapids, 1918. 1st Ed. 4to, cloth; worn. With 27 color plates. sg Sept 6 (275) $200

Hunter, John, 1728-93

— The Natural History of the Human Teeth. Phila., 1839. ("Treatise on the Natural History and Diseases of the Human Teeth.") 8vo, contemp sheep; backstrip chewed & def, worn. With 9 plates. Some foxing. bbc Dec 9 (340) $110

— Works. L, 1835-37. 5 vols, including plate vol. 8vo & 4to, contemp cloth; 1 bdg loose, anr with head of spine torn. With engraved port & 61 plates, several folding. Some edges dampstained; some spotting. pn Nov 14 (360) £600

Anr copy. 4 vols; lacking the Atlas. 8v, contemp sheep; needs rebacking. Some foxing. sg May 14 (86) $400

Hunter, Capt. John, 1738-1821

— An Historical Journal of the Transactions at Port Jackson and Norfolk Island.... L, 1793. 4to, old calf; rebacked, covers detached. With 10 plates & 5 maps. Imprint cropped from title; port & title browned; plan of Norfolk Island cropped at fore-edge; tears to each of the folding maps. CNY Oct 8 (13) $1,800

Anr copy. Early 19th-cent calf; rebacked. With engraved title, port & 15 plates, including 4 folding maps. Tear in lower margin of port repaired. S Nov 21 (381) £1,200 [Sotheran]

— Resa til Nya sodra Wallis.... Stockholm: J. Pfeiffer, 197. 8vo, contemp half calf; spine chipped at head. C June 25 (128) £150 [Turner]

Hunter, Norman, Writer

— The Incredible Adventures of Professor Branestawm. L, 1933. 1st Ed. Illus by Wm. Heath Robinson. Orig cloth. bba Dec 19 (112) £80 [Thorp]

Hunter, W. Patison

— Narrative of the late Expedition to Syria. L, 1842. 2 vols. 8vo, orig cloth; library labels pasted on upper covers & spines. With frontises, map, plan & 5 plates. S July 1 (762) £420 [Kanaan]

Hunter, William, 1718-83

— Anatomia uteri humani gravidi.... Birm: Baskerville, 1774. 1st Ed. Folio, modern half sheep; joints rubbed. With 34 plates. Plate 19 with old repaired tear; Plate 18 shaved at outer margin with loss & repaired. C June 24 (148) £3,000 [Joffe]

Anr copy. Contemp French half sheep gilt; extremities worn. Lacking title & text. Sold w.a.f. sg Nov 14 (56) $2,600

Hunter, William Stanley

— Hunter's Ottawa Scenery, in the Vicinity of Ottawa City, Canada. Ottawa, 1855. 4to, orig cloth; upper inner joint broken. With litho title, frontis, folding map & 13 plates. L Nov 14 (146) £750

Hurlbutt, Frank

— Bow Porcelain. L, 1926. F Mar 26 (256) $70

Anr copy. With 56 uncolored & 8 color plates. Library markings & card pocket. sg Sept 6 (153) $60

Hurston, Zora N.

— Their Eyes Were Watching God. Phila., [1937]. In d/j. wa Mar 5 (208) $1,000

Hurter, Johann Christoph

— Geographica provinciarum Sveviae descriptio. Augsburg: Hans Georg Bodenehr, [c.1685?]. Oblong 4to, contemp half calf. With engraved title, index map & 28 maps hand-colored within regional boundaries. S Nov 21 (152) £1,400 [Hassold]

Husain ibn 'Ali, called Al-Tughrai

— Lamiato'l Ajam, Carmen Tograi.... Oxford, 1661. 8vo, old bds; spine head chipped. sg Oct 24 (164) $350

Hussey, Cyrus M. See: Lay & Hussey

Huston, Harvey

— '93/'41: Thunder Lake Narrow Gauge. Winnetka IL: Pvtly ptd, 1961. In d/j. Sgd. cb Feb 13 (187) $65

Husung, Max Joseph

— Bucheinbande aus der Preussischen Staatsbibliothek zu Berlin. Leipzig, 1925. Folio, orig half cloth; rubbed & soiled. With 74 plain & 26 colored plates. bba May 28 (493) £360 [Maggs]

Hutchins, Henry C.

— Robinson Crusoe and its Printing. NY, 1925. One of 350. 4to, cloth; spine ends chipped. sg May 21 (239) $60

Hutchins, John, 1698-1773

— The History and Antiquities of the County of Dorset. L, 1774. 1st Ed. 2 vols. Folio, modern half syn. bba Jan 30 (115) £390 [Shapero]

Anr copy. Contemp calf; 1 cover detached. With folding map & 58 plates. bba June 25 (261) £250 [Smith]

3d Ed. L, 1861-70. 4 vols. Folio, contemp mor gilt; rubbed. With titles & 117 (of c.127) maps & plates. Some foxing. Sold w.a.f. bba Sept 19 (202) £440 [Russell]

Anr copy. Contemp half calf gilt; rubbed, inner hinge of Vol I weak. With 126 (of 133) plates & maps. Some shaving; titles soiled. pn Mar 19 (396) £550 [Proctor]

Hutchinson, Benjamin

— Biographica Medica; or, Historical and Critical Memoirs.... L, 1799. 2 vols. 8vo, modern half mor. 1 leaf repaired. DW Nov 6 (366) £155

Hutchinson, Francis, 1660-1739

— An Historical Essay Concerning Witchcraft. L, 1720. 2d Ed. 8vo, half mor gilt; worn. Some spotting. wa Mar 5 (555) $300

Hutchinson, Horace

— British Golf Links. L, 1897. One of 250. Title cut down at lower margin. pn June 11 (221) £330

— The Golfing Pilgrim on Many Links. NY, 1898. 8vo, orig cloth; spine marked. Inscr to J. A. Harvie-Brown by J. M. W. Cook, with ALs of Cook loosely inserted. S Feb 26 (864) £150 [Sotheran]

Hutchinson, Thomas, 1711-80

— The Case of the Provinces of Massachusetts-Bay and New-York, respecting the boundary Line between the Two Provinces. Bost., 1764. Folio, in cloth slipcase. P June 16 (226) $2,000

Hutchinson, William, 1732-1814

— The History and Antiquities of the County Palatine of Durham. Newcastle & Carlisle, 1785-94. 3 vols. 4to, contemp calf; rubbed, joints split. With watercolor drawing of Raby Castle pasted onto verso of Vol I title. bba Sept 19 (203) £200 [Princeton Rare Bks]

— History of the County of Cumberland. Carlisle, 1794. 2 vols. 4to, modern half calf. With 6 folding maps & 42 plates. 1 map repaired. pnE Dec 4 (154) £95

Huth, Hans

— Abraham und David Roentgen und Ihre Neuwieder Moebelwerkstatt. Berlin, 1928. 4to, cloth. Met Apr 28 (199) $50

Hutten, Ulrich von, 1488-1523

— Epigrammata. Mainz: J. Schoeffer, 1519. 4to, contemp calf; worn. Tp wormed at inner margin & soiled at outer margin. Ck Oct 31 (122) £550

— Outis: Nemo. Leipzig: in officina Schumanniana, [1518]. 4to, modern calf. Some early Ms annotations & underlinings in text in red ink. S May 28 (48) £850 [Symonds]

Huttich, Johann, 1480?-1544

— Die new Welt, der Landschaften unnd Insulen.... Strassburg, 1534. Folio, contemp blind-tooled pigskin over wooden bds with brass catches; lacking clasps. Prelims & last leaf remargined; wormhole through c.30 leaves towards end causing occasional minor text loss. sg May 7 (120) $3,800

Hutton, Alfred

— Cold Steel. L, 1889. 8vo, cloth; hinges cracked. sg Mar 26 (151) $100

Anr copy. Half mor gilt, orig cloth bound in. sg Mar 26 (152) $110

— Fixed Bayonets. L, 1890. 8vo, half mor gilt, orig cloth bound in. sg Mar 26 (153) $350

— Old Sword-Play: the Systems of Fence in Vogue during the XVIth, XVIIth, and XVIIIth Centuries. L & NY, 1892. One of 300. 4to, orig cloth; spine ends frayed, front joint starting, loose at beginning. With 57 plates. sg Mar 26 (154) $275

Out-of-series copy. Orig cloth. With 57 plates. sg Mar 26 (157) $130

— The Sword and the Centuries. L, 1901. sg Mar 26 (156) $150

— The Swordsman.... L, 1891. 8vo, orig cloth. sg Mar 26 (158) $120

Anr copy. Cloth. sg Mar 26 (159) $50

Hutton, Edward
— The Pageant of Venice. L & NY, 1922 [1921]. Illus by Frank Brangwyn. Folio, cloth; corners bumped. sg Sept 26 (63) $80

Hutton, Sir Richard, 1561?-1639
— The Reports of...in Points of Law... L, 1656. Folio, cloth. Tp stained & chipped; some foxing. cb Jan 16 (80) $130

Huxley, Aldous, 1894-1963
See also: Limited Editions Club
— Apennine. Gaylordsville: Slide Mountain Press, 1930. 1st Ed, One of 91. Orig half cloth. Sgd. cb Dec 12 (74) $160
— Arabia Infelix, and Other Poems. NY & L, 1929. 1st Ed, One of 692. cb Dec 12 (75) $85; sg Dec 12 (165) $175; sg June 11 (171) $140
— Brave New World. L, 1932. 1st Ed. In d/j with tape repairs. bbc Dec 9 (489) $275
Anr copy. Orig cloth; soiled. S Nov 14 (643) £340 [Sotheran]
Anr copy. In d/j. sg Dec 12 (166) $600
One of 324 L.p copies. Epstein copy. sg Apr 29 (246) $1,200
— Brief Candles. NY, 1930. one of 842, sgd. Corners bumped. cb Dec 12 (77) $85
— The Burning Wheel. Oxford, 1916. 1st Ed. Wraps. Epstein copy. sg Apr 29 (247) $325
— Eyeless in Gaza. L, 1936. 1st Ed. In d/j. sg June 11 (173) $100
One of 200. Half cloth. Prelims foxed. sg June 11 (172) $250
— Holy Face and Other Essays. L: The Fleuron, 1929. One of 300. 4to, orig cloth. cb Dec 12 (80) $90
— Jonah. Oxford: Holywell Press, 1917. 1st Ed, One of 50. Orig wraps. S July 21 (135) £1,000 [Blackwell]
— Leda. L, 1920. 1st Ed, One of 160. Orig half cloth. sg Dec 12 (167) $250
— Music at Night and Other Essays. NY: Fountain Press, 1931. 1st Ed, one of 842. DW May 13 (447) £50
— Point Counter Point. L, 1928. 1st Ed. Orig cloth; spine ends frayed, rubbed. D. H. Lawrence's presentation copy to Mabel Harrison, inscr by Huxley. b June 22 (59) £650
One of 256. sg June 11 (174) $200
— Texts and Pretexts. L, 1932. 1st Ed, One of 214. Unopened. cb Oct 17 (449) $90

Huxley, Thomas Henry, 1825-95
— Evidence as to Man's Place in Nature. L, 1863. 1st Ed. 8vo, orig cloth; head of spine torn. bba Feb 13 (403) £170 [Ginnan]
— On our Knowledge of the Causes of the Phenomena of Organic Nature. L, 1862. 8vo, orig cloth; stained. bba Sept 5 (60A) £120 [Korn]

Huygens, Christian, 1629-95
— Horologium oscillatorium sive de motu pendulorum Paris, 1673. 1st Ed. Folio, contemp sheep; worn. Blank outer margins wormed; badly dampstained towards end. sg Nov 14 (253) $2,600

Huysmans, Joris Karl, 1848-1907
— La-bas. Paris, 1891. 1st Ed. 8vo, orig wraps. Epstein copy. sg Apr 29 (248) $375
— A rebours. Paris, 1884. 1st Ed. 12mo, half mor, orig wraps bound in. Epstein cpy. sg Apr 29 (249) $950

Hyde, Thomas, 1636-1703
— Historia religionis veterum Persarum, eorumque magorum.... Oxford, 1700. 4to, contemp calf. With 18 plates. bba Jan 16 (316) £420 [Land]
— Historia religionis veterum Persarum.... Oxford, 1760. ("Veterum Persarum et Parthorum et Medorum religionis historia.") 2d Ed. 4to, contemp calf gilt; joints cracked, rubbed. With 20 plates & folding table. Leaf b4 with tear. bba May 14 (88) £180 [Poole]
— Mandragorias seu Historia Shahiludii. Oxford, 1694. 2 parts in 1 vol. 8vo, contemp calf; rubbed, upper joints cracked. With 3 folding plates. Tp torn at outer margin with loss; some browning. Ck May 8 (43) £600

Hyginus, Caius Julius
— Poeticon astronomicon. Venice: Erhard Ratdolt, 14 Oct 1482. 4to, recent vellum. Types 3:91G (text), 7:92G (headings, a2 recto) Some worming, touching letters. 58 leaves. Goff H-560. P Dec 12 (49) $13,000
Anr Ed. Venice: Thomas de Blavis, 1488. 4to, 18th-cent sheep; wormed, extremities rubbed, spine repaired. 34 lines; types 7:84R (text), 6:70G & 7:61G (lettering on diagram on a1v). Some worming & dampstaining. 56 leaves. Goff H-562. C Dec 16 (128) £1,700 [Bifolco]

I

Iamblichus
— De mysteriis Aegyptiorum Chaldaeorum, Assyriorum.... Venice: Aldus, 1497. 1st Ed. Folio, contemp wooden bds with modern lea spine; clasps removed, new endpapers. Tears in d2 & &1 affecting a few letters; minor stains; minor worming. 186 leaves. Goff J-216. C Nov 27 (17) £8,000 [Turner]
Anr Ed. Venice: Aldus, 1516. Folio, 19th-cent mor gilt; repaired. Marginal annotations; corner of frontis repaired. SI June 9 (486) LIt2,800,000

Anr Ed. Oxford, 1678. Folio, later calf gilt; rubbed, joint cracked. bba Sept 19 (3033) £260 [Poole]

Ibsen, Henrik, 1828-1906

— Hedda Gabler. Copenhagen, 1890. 8vo, orig ptd wraps; soiled & frayed. Pencilled marginalia on 14 pages. Manney copy. P Oct 11 (177) $900

— Peer Gynt. L, 1936. Illus by Arthur Rackham. 4to, orig cloth, in d/j. With 12 colored plates. bba Jan 16 (389) £170 [Ulysses]

One of 460. Vellum gilt. With 12 mtd color plates. sg Nov 7 (169) $1,000

— Peer Gynt: a Dramatic Poem. Phila, [1936]. Illus by Arthur Rackham. DW Dec 11 (451) £70

— Works. NY, 1917. 13 vols. 8vo, half mor gilt. sg Mar 5 (134) $475

Icazbalceta, Joaquin Garcia. See: Garcia Icazbalceta, Joaquin

Icones. See: Zorn, Johannes

Igor Svyatoslavich, Prince

— Slovo o polky Igoreve. Moscow, 1934. Illus by Ivan Golikov. Folio, orig cloth. sg Nov 7 (203) $225

Anr copy. Orig cloth, in d/j. With 10 color plates. wa Apr 9 (273) $180

Illinois

— State Register. Springfield, June-Sept 1847. Vol 1, Nos 1-36 plus Supplement. 37 issues. Folio, bound together in cloth. Lacking 1st leaf of No 2. sg Dec 5 (122) $475

Illustrated...

— An Illustrated History of Sacramento County, California. Chicago, 1890. 8vo, mor gilt extra; scuffed, spine faded. cb Sept 12 (47) $120

— Illustrated London News. L, 1842-45. Vols 2-5. Folio, contemp half calf or cloth. bba Apr 30 (354) £350 [Cline]

Anr Ed. L, 1878. July-Dec issues bound in 1 vol. Folio, contemp half calf; rubbed & stained. S June 30 (21) £950 [Caramondanis]

Illustration...

— L'Illustration horticole. Ghent, 1654-86. Ed by Charles Lemaire. Vols 1-33 (Series I-IV). 8vo, various lea bdgs; several spines worn. With 1,233 color plates, some finished by hand. Ck Sept 6 (26) £4,500

Image...

— L'Image: Revue litteraire et artistique. Paris, 1896-97. Nos 1-12 (all pbd). 4to, orig wraps; many covers detached. DW Mar 11 (511) £90

Imago...

— Imago Mundi: A Review of Early Cartography. Berlin & Amst., 1986-89. Vols 38-41. 4to, orig cloth. wa Nov 21 (92) $75

Impartial...

— An Impartial History of Michael Servetus, Burnt Alive at Geneva for Heresie. L, 1724. 8vo, contemp calf; spine ends restored, joints weak. sg May 14 (152) $325

— An Impartial History of the War in America.... L, 1780. 8vo, sheep; rebacked. With folding map & 13 ports. sg June 18 (32) $1,100

Imprensa Nacional

— Provas da Fundicao de Typos da Imprensa nacional. l, 1888. Folio, orig cloth. cb Sept 5 (115) $190

Improvement...

— The Improvement of Human Reason, Exhibited in the Life of Hai Ebn Yokdhan. L, 1708. Tran by Simon Ockley. 8vo, calf; joints cracked, corners repaired. With frontis & 5 plates. Some staining. B May 12 (1975) HF600

Anr Ed. L, 1711. Trans by Simon Ockley. 8vo, later half calf; worn, upper cover detached. bba Jan 30 (152) £140 [Folios Ltd]

Inchofer, Melchior

— Tractatus syllepticus.... Rome: Ludovicus Grignanus, 1633. 4to, contemp vellum; backstrip damaged, hinges wormed. Browning & stains at end; Vatican Library duplicate stamps. sg Nov 14 (254) $2,600

Incunabula...

— Incunabula in Dutch Libraries. A Census. Nieuwkoop, 1983. 2 vols. sg Oct 31 (156) $110

Indagine, Joannes ab

— La Chiromance et phisionomie.... Paris: Pierre Bienfait, 1662. 12mo, old calf gilt; spine ends chipped, front joint cracked. sg Mar 12 (219) $275

— Introductiones apotelesmaticae.... Frankfurt: David Zephel, [1550?]. 8vo, old calf gilt; joints partly restored. Some stains & soiling; lacking S1.8 (supplied in Ms). sg Mar 12 (218) $500

Index...

— Index librorum prohibitorum.... Rome, 1758. 8vo, contemp sheep gilt; spine rubbed & chipped. Some dampstaining in gutters. sg May 21 (252) $250

Indulgence

— Licence by W. Warham, Archbishop of Canterbury, and E. Vaughan, Bishop of St. David's, as papal commissaries, to Duke Mychaell of Paleolog and his proctors to collect money within the province of Canterbury for ransoming captives of the Turks; with indulgences for benefactors, in English. [L: Richard Pynson, c.1512]. Broadside fragment, c.75mm by 135mm. Fragment, 18 partial lines, black letter. Most of text missing, torn & stained. Removed from the pastedown of the bdg on a copy of Pynson's 1499 Ed of Abridgements of English Statutes. STC 14077c.117B. C June 24 (150) £420 [Quaritch]

Industry. See: Great...

Ingelow, Jean, 1820-97

— Poems. L, 1867. 4to, orig cloth elaborately blocked in gold & black with quadrilobe white paper onlay mtd in sunken center panel on covers (see McLean, plate 108). cb Jan 9 (174) $50

Ingen-Housz, Jan, 1730-99

— Experiments upon Vegetables. L, 1779. 8vo, contemp calf. Lacking half-title; some dampstains. pnL Nov 20 (161) £460 [McDowell]

Inghirami, Francesco

— Monumenti etruschi o di Etrosco nome disegnati.... Fiesole, 1821-26. 6 vols bound in 9, including Index. 4to, new half calf gilt. With 466 plates, some tinted, some fully colored, and a few with lacquered color. Occasional plates bound out of sequence. CNY Dec 5 (252) $1,500

— Pitture di vasi etruschi. Florence: Antonio Tozzetti, 1852. 4 vols. 4to, contemp half vellum. With port, hand-colored additional title & 400 plates, 13 ptd in colors. Some spotting; 2 plates detached & tattered in margins. Ck Nov 29 (295) £800

Inglis, Henry David, 1795-1835

— Rambles in the Footsteps of Don Quixote. L, 1837. 1st Ed. Illus by George Cruikshank. 12mo, mor. sg Oct 17 (170) $175

Ingoldsby, Thomas. See: Barham, Richard Harris

Ingram, James, 1774-1850

— Memorials of Oxford. Oxford, 1837. 3 vols. 4to, contemp mor gilt. With map & 100 plates. bba Jan 30 (116) £420 [Wm. Dawson]

Anr copy. Orig cloth; spine ends worn. With 99 plates & folding map. Some spotting. DW May 13 (88) £300

Anr copy. Mor; 1 cover detached, rubbed, spines worn. With 101 plates, including titles. K Mar 22 (196) $450

Inman, Henry, 1837-99

— The Old Santa Fe Trail: The Story of a Great Highway. NY, 1897. Illus by Frederic Remington. 8vo, orig cloth; spine faded. cb Feb 12 (33) $85

— Stories of the Old Santa Fe Trail. Kansas City, 1881. 1st Ed. 12mo, orig cloth; worn. NH May 30 (570) $95

Inman, Henry, 1837-99 —& Cody, William F., 1846-97

— The Great Salt Lake Trail. NY, 1898. 1st Ed. 8vo, orig cloth, Howes' 2d bdg; shaken, front hinge cracked. bbc Dec 9 (382) $100

Anr copy. Orig cloth; hinge cracking. cb Feb 12 (32) $80

Innocent IV, Pope

— Apparatus super quinque libros Decretalium. Venice: Johannes Hebort for Johannes de Colonia & Nicolaus Jenson et socii, 15 June 1481. Folio, contemp wooden bds, spine covered with white goatskin. 66 lines; double column; types 3:93G (text), 4:93G (minor headings) & 5:150G (major headings). 262 leaves. Goff I-9G. Schoyen copy. P Dec 12 (28) $6,000

Instructive. See: Yonge, Charlotte Mary

Interesting...

— Interesting Narrative of the Loss of...the Porpoise and Cato of London.... L, [1808]. 8vo modern wraps. Lower margin of folding frontis cropped; title browned. S June 25 (198) £380 [Renard]

International...

— The International Journal of Psycho-Analysis. L, 1920-39. Vols 1-20. Directed by Sigmund Freud; Ed by Ernest Jones. 20 vols. 4to, orig cloth. bbc Apr 27 (519) $340

International Shooting & Field Sports Exhibition

— Die erste internationale Jagd-Austellung, Wien, 1910. Vienna: Wilhelm Frick, 1912. 4to, orig cloth. HH May 12 (926) DM750

Ionesco, Eugene. See: Limited Editions Club

Irby, Leonard Howard Lloyd

— The Ornithology of the Straits of Gibraltar. L, 1895. 4to, orig cloth; rebacked & recornered. With 2 folding maps & 8 plates. Library markings. bba Oct 10 (206) £210 [Johnson]

Anr copy. Orig cloth; rubbed. With 8 plates & 2 folding maps. Title supplied in facsimile. DW Nov 6 (168) £180

Iredale, Tom

— Birds of New Guinea. Melbourne, 1956. 2 vols. Orig half lea, in d/js. pn May 14 (174) £80 [Way]

— Birds of Paradise and Bower Birds. Melbourne, 1950. 4to, orig half mor, in d/js. With 33 color plates. pn May 14 (175) £70 [Way]

Ireland, Samuel, d.1800

— An Authentic Account of the Shaksperian Manuscripts, &c. L, 1796. 1st Ed. 8vo half mor; upper cover detached, spine worn. b June 22 (81) £80

— Picturesque Views on the River Medway. L, 1793. 4to, contemp mor gilt. With engraved title, folding map, and 28 plates. Scattered spotting. DW Nov 20 (14) £100

— Picturesque Views on the River Thames. L, 1792. 2 vols. 4to half mor; worn, 1 cover detached. With 2 hand-colored titles, 2 maps & 52 plates. Library markings, with some blindstamps extending into plate images. Sold w.a.f. K July 12 (288) $200

Anr Ed. L, 1801-2. 2 vols. 8vo, contemp calf gilt; worn & rebacked. With aquatint titles, 2 maps & 54 plates. DW Mar 4 (77) £220

— Picturesque Views on the Upper, or Warwickshire Avon. L, 1795. 1st Ed. 8vo, contemp vellum gilt in the style of Edwards of Halifax. With frontis, map, 2 ports & 29 sepia aquatint plates. L.p. copy. C May 20 (265) £1,100 [Browning]

Anr copy. Half mor. With frontis, map, 2 ports & 29 hand-colored plates. pnE Dec 4 (152) £130

Ireland, William Henry

— An Authentic Account of the Shakspearian Manuscripts. L, 1796. 8vo, unbound. sg Mar 5 (136) $130

— The Confessions.... L, 1805. 1st Ed. 12mo, contemp half calf; joints repaired. Some spotting. bba Apr 30 (101) £80 [Land]

— The Life of Napoleon Bonaparte. L, 1828. 2d Issue. 4 vols. 8vo, later mor gilt by Riviere. With 4 engraved titles, 2 folding aquatint plates (24 hand-colored) & 1 folding tinted engraved plate. Some plates worn at folds but neatly mtd; most plates lacking the imprint, a few close-shaved at upper margin. C Oct 30 (44) £650 [Taro-Zagnoli]

Irish...

— The Irish Sword. The Journal of the Military History Society of Ireland. Dublin, 1949-70. Vols I-IX. Orig wraps; rubbed & soiled. No 24 supplied in photocopy. DD Mar 4 (79) £280

Irmischer, Johann Conrad

— Handschriften-Katalog der koeniglichen Universitaets-Bibliothek zu Erlangen. Frankfurt, 1852. 8vo, cloth, orig wraps bound in, unopened; some dampwrinkling. sg Oct 31 (226) $90

Irvine, Leigh Hadley

— History of Humboldt County, California.... Los Angeles, 1915. Orig half mor. cb Sept 12 (92) $110

Irving, Washington, 1783-1859

— Astoria, or Anecdotes of an Enterprise beyond the Rocky Mountains. Phila., 1836. 1st Ed, 1st State. 2 vols. 8vo, cloth. sg June 18 (301) $275

Anr copy. Some foxing. sg June 18 (302) $225

Mixed State. Orig cloth; later half mor. Lacking map. cb Nov 14 (95) $60

— Bracebridge Hall: or, the Humourists, by Geoffrey Crayon. NY, 1896. 2 vols. 8vo, cloth; soiled. K Mar 22 (384) $50; sp Apr 16 (180) $55

— A History of New York.... NY, 1900. Illus by Maxfield Parrish. Folio, orig cloth; rubbed, chipped. K Sept 29 (326) $120

Anr copy. Half cloth. sg Jan 30 (120) $375

— A History of the Life and Voyages of Christopher Columbus. L, 1849. ("The Life and Voyages of Christopher Columbus.") 3 vols. 4to, orig cloth; spines faded. bba Apr 9 (41) £55 [Abdullah]

— The Legend of Sleepy Hollow. L, [1928]. Illus by Arthur Rackham. 4to, cloth, in d/j. bba Jan 16 (391) £140 [Sotheran]; bba Apr 9 (334) £120 [Dawson]

One of 375. Vellum. cb Dec 5 (116) $850

Anr copy. Orig vellum bds. CNY June 9 (167) $900

Anr copy. Vellum. sg Jan 30 (147) $700

Anr Ed. Phila., [1928]. One of 125. 4to, orig vellum. With 8 colored plates. K Mar 22 (385) $450

— Life of George Washington. NY, 1855-59. 1st Ed. 5 vols. 8vo, cloth. sp Feb 6 (37) $75

Anr copy. Orig cloth; covers frayed at head & rubbed. wd Dec 12 (409) $100

— Rip Van Winkle. L, 1905. One of 250. Illus by Arthur Rackham. 4to, orig cloth. With 51 tipped-in colored plates. Marginal spotting. b Nov 18 (100) £120; pnE May 13 (218) £120

Anr Ed. L & NY, 1905. 4to, orig cloth. With 51 colored plates. sg Jan 30 (148) $425

Anr Ed. Paris, 1906. 4to, pictorial vellum; covers bowed, front hinge cracked. sg Jan 10 (149) $325

Anr copy. Half vellum; covers bowed, front

hinge cracked. In French. sg Jan 30 (149) $325

Anr Ed. L, 1907. Illus by Arthur Rackham. 4to, orig cloth. With 50 colored plates. bba Jan 16 (390) £100 [B. Bailey]

Anr Ed. L, 1924. 4to, cloth, in d/j. bba Apr 9 (333) £140 [Boris Books]

— The Rocky Mountains.... Phila., 1837. 1st American Ed. 2 vols. 12mo, orig cloth; rubbed, spine ends frayed. With 2 folding maps (a few short tears). Library markings. bbc Sept 23 (325) $100

— The Sketch Book of Geoffrey Crayon. NY, 1895. Westminster Ed, One of 175. Illus by Arthur Rackham. 2 vols. 4to, calf. O Jan 14 (94) $180

Van Tassel Ed. Illus in part by Arthur Rackham. 2 vols. 8vo, cloth; front inner hinge of Vol II separating. K Sept 29 (206) $65

— Tales of a Traveller. NY, [1895]. Buckthorne Ed. 2 vols. 12mo, cloth. With 25 plates. K Mar 22 (386) $65

— A Tour on the Prairies. L, 1835. 1st Ed. 8vo, contemp calf; rubbed. O Jan 14 (95) $50

2d state. Cloth with 2d state of paper spine label. sg June 18 (304) $140

— Works. NY & L, 1901. Joseph Jefferson Ed, one of 250. 40 vols. Mor extra by Stikeman. CNY Dec 5 (406) $3,800

Anr copy. Mor gilt. With ALs to Col. Thomas Aspinwall. CNY June 9 (97) $2,000

Pocantico Ed. NY: Putnam's, [c.18950. One of 1,000. 40 vols. 8vo, half mor; rubbed. cb Oct 31 (46) $500

Irwin, Will. See: Genthe, Arnold

Isaacs, Nathaniel, b.1808

— Travels and Adventures in Eastern Africa.... L, 1836. 2 vols. 8vo, contemp calf; scuffed, hinges cracked. With folding chart & 4 plates. Foxed. sg May 21 (51) $800

Isherwood, Christopher

See also: Auden & Isherwood

— The Berlin Stories. NY: New Directions, [1945]. In chipped d/j. Sgd. sg Dec 12 (168) $110

— Goodbye to Berlin. L, 1939. 1st Ed. In d/j. sg Dec 12 (169) $1,200

— Lions and Shadows. An Education in the Twenties. L: Hogarth Press, 1938. 1st bdg. K Mar 22 (199) $180

— Prater Violet. NY, [1945]. In d/j. sg Dec 12 (170) $80

— Sally Bowles. L: Hogarth Press, 1937. sg Dec 12 (171) $70

Isocrates, 436-338 B.C.

— Oratio de laudibus Helenae. [Venice: Christophorus de Pensis, c.1498-1500]. Folio, modern half vellum. Some dampstaining & marginalia. 142 (of 144) leaves; lacking a3-4 of table. Goff I-212. sg Oct 24 (166) $700

Italy

— Indice generale degli incunaboli delle biblioteche d'Italia. Rome, 1943-81. 6 vols. 4to, later cloth. sg Oct 31 (157) $1,100

— FERRARA. - Statuta urbis Ferrariae nuper reformata. Ferrara: Franciscus Rubeus de Valentia, 1567. Bound with: Gozadini, Lodovico. Praeclara, ac perutili repetito super...omnes populi.... Bologna: Bonardi, 1561. Folio, 18th-cent bds; worn. SI Dec 5 (238) £700,000

— VENICE. - Forastiere Illuminato intorno le cose piu, e curiose, antiche, e moderne della citta di Venezia. Venice, 1740. 8vo, later half calf; rebacked. b Nov 18 (333) £300

Itinerario...

— Itinerario interno e delle isole della citta di Venezia. Venice: Antonelli, 1832. 8vo, contemp bds; broken. With engraved title & 32 plates. Some foxing. SI June 10 (1053) LIt400,000

Ivchenko, Valerian

— Anna Pavlova. Paris, 1922. One of 325. Trans by W. Petroff. 4to, wraps. sg Oct 17 (80) $550

Anr copy. Half mor gilt. sg Mar 5 (248) $550

Ives, Joseph C.

— Report upon the Colorado River.... Wash., 1861. Issue not stated. 4to, rebound, with orig front & rear cover cloth laid on. With 35 plates & maps. Folding maps detached. cb Feb 12 (34) $400

Senate Issue. Orig cloth; worn & shaken. With 36 plates & maps, 8 in color. Lacking 2 geological maps on Part 2. K July 12 (290) $200

Anr copy. Orig cloth; joints split, spine torn. With 4 folding maps (2 torn) & 34 plates, 8 in color. A few plates & text leaves with small stain in 1 corner at beginning of vol. L Nov 14 (148) £150

J

Jaboille, Pierre. See: Delacour & Jaboille

Jack, Alexander

— Six Views of Kot Kangra.... L, 1847. Folio, orig bds; soiled & worn. With tinted litho title & 6 hand-colored plates. Some plates spotted. S May 14 (1291) £1,400 [Lewcock]

Jack the Ripper

[-] The Times. L, 2 July-31 Dec 1888. 157 issues. Folio, bound in 2 quarter-year vols. Disbound. Covering the full period of the Jack the Ripper murders. Manney set. P Oct 11 (1178) $3,750

Jackman, William James —& Russell, Thomas Herbert

— Flying Machines: Construction and Operation. Chicago, 1910. Cloth; worn, hinges repaired with tape. One leaf misptd with partial tear. bbc Sept 23 (242) $50

Jackson, Sir Charles James

— English Goldsmiths and their Marks. L, 1921. 4to, orig cloth; rubbed. O July 14 (104) $60

Anr Ed. NY, 1964. 4to, orig cloth. LH May 17 (667) $60

— An Illustrated History of English Plate. L, 1911. 2 vols. 4to, half mor. pnE May 13 (118) £60

Jackson, Charles Thomas, 1805-80

— Final Report on the Geology and Mineralogy of...New Hampshire. Concord, 1844. 4to, orig half lea. With folding map, 2 colored folding charts & 7 plates. NH Aug 23 (301) $475

Jackson, Clarence S.

— Picture Maker of the Old West: William H. Jackson. NY, 1947. 1st Ed. 4to, cloth. K Sept 29 (355) $55

Jackson, Donald

— Johann Amerbach. Iowa City, 1956. 2 vols. 4to & folio, ptd wraps. With a leaf from Nicolaus Panormitanus de Tudeschis, Lectura super V libris Decretalium, ptd by Amerbach in 1487-88 (Goff P-51). sg Sept 26 (6) $175

Anr copy. Ptd wraps. With a leaf from: Panormitanus. Lectura super V libris Decretalium. 1487-88. Goff P-51. sg Oct 31 (145) $50

Jackson, Emily Nevill

— Ancestors in Silhouette Cut by August Edouart. L & NY, 1921. 1st Ed. 4to, cloth. Foxed; lacking at least 1 plate; split at p. 42. sp June 18 (184) $70

— A History of Hand-Made Lace.... L & NY, 1900. 8vo, mor gilt; rebacked. With 12 specimens of lace mtd on 6 thick cards. sg Sept 6 (162) $550

— The History of Silhouettes. L, 1911. 4to, cloth; spotted. Some browning. kh Nov 11 (143) A$90

Jackson, Sir Frederick John, 1860-1929

— The Birds of the Kenya Colony and the Uganda Protectorate. L, 1938. 3 vols. 4to, orig cloth. Pencil annotations by previous owner. S Feb 11 (924) £320 [Shapero]

— Notes on the Game Birds of Kenya and Uganda. L, 1926. 1st Ed. sg May 14 (223) $110

Jackson, Helen Hunt, 1830-85

— Ah-Wah-Ne Days.... San Francisco, 1971. One of 450. cb Feb 12 (35) $90

Jackson, Holbrook, 1874-1948

— The Anatomy of Bibliomania. L, 1930-31. One of 1,000. In d/js. cb Oct 17 (458) $120

Anr Ed. NY, 1931. cb Oct 17 (459) $50

Jackson, James Grey

— An Account of the Empire of Marocco. L, 1809. 4to, contemp calf; worn, front cover loose. With 2 maps & 11 plates. Frontis map torn at gutter. sg Jan 9 (99) $90

3d Ed. L, 1814. 4to, contemp calf; joints broken & crudely repaired. With port, 2 maps & 12 plates, 3 hand-colored. Some spotting. pn Apr 23 (241) £180 [Grosvenor]

Jackson, John

— The Practical Fly-Fisher; More Particularly for Grayling or Umber. L, 1854. 8vo, half mor; rubbed, inner joint tape-repaired. With 10 hand-colored plates. O Oct 29 (183) $300

Anr copy. Orig cloth; spine ends rubbed. pn Mar 19 (381) £320 [Sotheran]

Jackson, John, Engraver —& Chatto, William Andrew, 1799-1864

— A Treatise on Wood Engraving. L, 1839. 8vo, contemp half mor; extremities rubbed. bba June 25 (69) £55 [Perrucci]; W July 8 (123) £65

Jackson, John Baptist

— An Essay on the Invention of Engraving and Printing in Chiaro Oscuro.... L, 1754. 4to, modern half mor. With 8 woodcut plates, 4 ptd in chiaroscuro tones, 4 in bright oil colors using 6 blocks each. Closed tear on 1 plate; margin repaired on anr. Schlosser copy. P June 18 (433) $7,500

— Titiani Vecelli, Pauli Caliarii, Jacobi Robusti, et Jacobi de Ponte Opera. Venice, 1745. Folio, early pastepaper bds. With 24 plates. Laid in are single-block impressions of 3 of the blocks. Schlosser copy. P June 18 (432) $14,000

Jackson, Richard. See: Franklin & Jackson

Jackson, Robert, 1750-1827

— A Treatise on the Fevers of Jamaica. Phila., 1795. 12mo, calf. NH May 30 (350) $160

Jackson, Shirley

— The Haunting of Hill House. NY, 1959. In d/j. cb Dec 12 (81) $100

— Raising Demons. NY, 1956. In d/j rubbed at spine ends. cb Dec 12 (82) $50

Jackson, William Alexander

— An Annotated List of the Publications of...the Reverend Thomas Frognall Dibdin. Cambr. MA, 1965. One of 500. Folio, orig cloth. bbc Apr 27 (117) $60

Jacob, Giles, 1686-1744

— The Compleat Sportsman. L, 1718. 12mo, contemp calf; upper bd wormed, spine rubbed. Small tear in margin of F3. S Feb 11 (866) £180 [Way]

— A New Law-Dictionary.... L, 1744. Folio, contemp calf; hinges weak. bba Jan 16 (13) £130 [Bernard]

Jacob, Louis, de Saint Charles

— Traicte des plus belles bibliotheques publiques et particulieres. Paris, 1644. 2d Ed. 2 parts in 1 vol. 8vo, contemp vellum; wormed at beginning & end. sg Oct 31 (170) $60

Jacobson, Oscar Brousse

— Kiowa Indian Art: Watercolor Paintings in Color by the Indians of Oklahoma. Nice: C. Szwedzicki, [1929]. One of 750. Folio, loose in orig board folder. With 30 colored plates. Minor wear at a few plate edges. sg June 18 (299) $550

Jacobus de Gruitroede

— Lavacrum conscientiae. [Augsburg: Johann Froschauer, not after 1498]. 4to, early 19th-cent cloth; spine faded. Wormed throughout; some browning & dampstaining; lst few leaves wormed. 88 (of 100) leaves. sg Mar 12 (123) $275

Jacobus Palmerius. See: Le Paulmier de Grentemesnil, Jacques

Jacobus Philippus de Bergamo

— Novissime hystoriarum omnium repercussiones.... Venice: Albertino de Lissona, 1503. Folio, 17th-cent vellum. Tp holed with loss; final leaves wormed affecting text; lacking final blank. Ck Nov 29 (292) £2,300

Jacolliot, Louis

— Occult Science in India and among the Ancients.... NY, [1884]. 8vo, orig cloth; spine ends chipped. Marginal dampstaining. sg Oct 17 (60) $130

Jacquemart, Albert, 1808-75 —& Le Blant, Edmond, 1813-97

— Histoire artistique, industrielle et commerciale de la porcelaine. Paris, 1862. 4to, half lea gilt. With 28 plates. SI June 9 (484) LIt1,000,000

Anr copy. Contemp half mor by Gaillard. W July 8 (184) £240

Jacquin, Joseph Franz von, 1766-1839

— Beytraege zur Geschichte der Voegel. Vienna, 1784. 4to, 19th-cent half calf; rebacked & recornered. With 19 hand-colored plates. C May 20 (186) £1,800 [Shapero]

Jacquin, Nicolaus Joseph von, 1727-1817

— Collectanea ad botanicam, chemiam et historiam.... Vienna, 1786-96. Vols I-II (of 5) in 1 vol. 4to, contemp bds. With 40 plates, 35 colored. Lacking text. FD Dec 2 (194) DM1,600

Jager, Otto. See: Wright & Jager

Jaggard, William

— Shakespeare Bibliography. Stratford, 1911. One of 500. 4to, cloth. cb Oct 17 (467) $55

Jahrbuch...

— Jahrbuch der Auktionspreise fuer Buecher und Autographen. Hamburg, 1950-88. Vols 1-39 & indexes for 1950-79. 43 vols. Ck Nov 1 (433) £1,300

Jalovec, Karel

— Italian Violin-Makers. L, 1964. 4to, cloth; hinges cracked. bbc June 29 (292) $55

Jameray Duval, Valentin

— Numismata cimelii Caesarei Regii Austriaci Vindobonensis. Vienna, 1755. 2 vols in 1. Folio, contemp vellum. With frontis & 137 plates. S Dec 5 (283) £1,400 [Spinks]

James, George Wharton, 1858-1923

— In and Around the Grand Canyon. Bost., 1900. 1st Ed, One of 500. 8vo, orig cloth; rubbed, hinges cracked. bbc Sept 23 (327) $55

One of 500, sgd. Half mor; rubbed. O July 14 (105) $70

James, Henry, 1843-1916

— The Ambassadors. NY & L, 1903. 1st Pbd Ed. Orig bds, in d/j. cb Sept 19 (93) $350; P Oct 11 (180) $5,000; sg Dec 12 (172) $225

— The Awkward Age. L: Heinemann, 1899. 8vo, cloth. cb Sept 19 (94) $85; sp Sept 22 (105) $65

1st American Ed. NY, 1899. 8vo, cloth. Title nearly detached. sg Oct 17 (280) $50

— The Beast in the Jungle. Kentfield: Allen Press, 1963. One of 130. Illus by Blair Hughes-Stanton. b&b Feb 19 (296) $175

— Confidence. Bost., 1880. 1st American Ed. 8vo, cloth; ends frayed. cb Sept 19 (95) $50

— In the Cage. L, 1898. 8vo, orig cloth. cb Sept 19 (97) $70

— Notes on Novelists with Some Other Notes. L, 1914. 1st Ed. In soiled d/j. Inscr to Edmund Gosse. sg Nov 7 (95) $4,000

— A Passionate Pilgrim, and other Tales.... Bost., 1875. 1st Ed. 8vo, orig cloth; spine ends worn. P Oct 11 (179) $1,000

Anr copy. Orig cloth. Epstein copy. sg Apr 29 (252) $1,700

— The Portrait of a Lady. L, 1881. 1st Ed. 3 vols. 8vo, orig cloth; rubbed & stained, inner hinge of Vol I split, upper cover of Vol II with small portion chipped from 1 corner. S July 1 (992) £850 [Jarndyce]

One of 750. Orig cloth; edges & joints worn. Epstein copy. sg Apr 29 (253) $2,200

— The Sacred Fount. NY, 1901. 1st Ed, 1st Ptg. Cloth; soiled. cb Sept 19 (99) $65

— Washington Square.... NY, 1881. 1st Ed, one of 500. 2 vols. 8vo, orig cloth; joints rubbed. cb Sept 19 (1101) $85

— What Maisie Knew. Chicago: Herbert S. Stone, 1897. 1st Ed. 8vo, orig cloth. bbc Apr 27 (334) $85

— Works. NY, 1907-17. ("The Novels and Tales.") New York Ed. 26 vols. Orig half cloth; worn, spines discolored. Lacking ALs called for with Vol I. CNY Dec 5 (407) $3,800

Anr copy. Half mor; rubbed & chipped. P June 17 (342) $3,000

Anr copy. Some vols unopened. sg Nov 7 (94) $3,600

Anr copy. 25 (of 26) vols; lacking Vol XII. Orig cloth; splits at ends. wa Dec 9 (197) $1,100

One of 156 on handmade Ruisdael paper. 26 vols. Half cloth over Italian-paper-covered bds. P Dec 12 (50) $3,250

James, Sir Henry, 1803-77

— Facsimiles of National Manuscripts of Scotland. Edin., 1867-70. 2 vols. Folio, orig cloth; rebacked. K Sept 29 (49) $100

James I, King of England

— Daemonologie, in Forme of a Dialogue. L, 1603. 4to, disbound, broken. Library stamps. Sold w.a.f. STC 14365. bba Feb 27 (45) £160 [Walker]

— A Publication of His Majesties Edict, and Severe Censure against Private Combats and Combatants. L: Robert Barker, 1613. 4to, later half sheep; needs rebdg. Lacking A1. sg Mar 26 (161) $110

— Works. L, 1616-[20]. 1st Ed. Folio, contemp sheep; rebacked, worn. Lacking engraved title & port. Wormed with some loss of text. Sold w.a.f. bba Oct 10 (292) £55 [Gammon]

James I, King of Scotland

— Poetical Remains. L: Vale Press, 1903. ("The Kingis Quair....") One of 260. bba July 9 (318) £65 [Selwyn]

James, John T., 1786-1828

— Journal of a Tour in Germany, Sweden, Russia.... L, 1816. 1st Ed. 4to, modern half calf. With 18 uncolored plates. Some browning. S Nov 15 (1120) £180 [Wagrett]

James, Philip

— Children's Books of Yesterday. L: The Studio, 1933. 4to, cloth. cb Jan 16 (83) $50

James, Robert, 1705-76

— A Medicinal Dictionary. L, 1743-45. 1st Ed. 3 vols. Folio, contemp calf; rebacked & worn. With 63 plates. Title of Vol 2 with clean tear; 1 plate detached & with ragged margins. George Milne copy. CNY Dec 5 (256) $1,600

Anr copy. Vol I only. Folio, cloth; worn. Library markings. Ls from Sir William Osler tipped in. sg Nov 14 (60) $225

— A Treatise on Canine Madness. L, 1760. 8vo, contemp calf; head of spine repaired. ESTC t0571631. bba July 23 (313) £460 [Johnson]

James, Thomas, 1593?-1635?

— The Strange and Dangerous Voyage of Captaine Thomas James.... L, 1633. 4to, 19th-cent calf with arms blind-stamped on sides; krubbed & with a couple of gouges. With folding map. First & last few leaves washed but still discolored; 2 repaired tears to inner edge of folding map; lacking 1st blank; paper damage to D2 from sticky substance, with partial loss to 10 letters, including 2 on facing page; headline of R3r shaved. STC 14444. DuPont copy. CNY Oct 8 (135) $15,000

Anr copy. 19th-cent russia; upper joint broken, extremities rubbed. Some foxing & soiling; repaired tear to folding map; last 2 or 3 leaves foxed & waterstained; lacking 2 blanks; variant with S4v sgd X.Z. STC 14444. DuPont copy. CNY Oct 8 (136) $14,000

Anr copy. 19th-cent calf gilt. Half-title, tp, frontis & last 6 leaves in facsimile. Together with an engraved copy of the frontis dated 1821. Miller-Christy copy, with ALs about his editing the work for the Hakluyt Society Ed. STC 14444. W July 8 (251) £150

James, Gen. Thomas, 1782-1847

— Three Years among the Indians and Mexicans. St. Louis, 1916. One of 365. Marginal notations in ink on 1 page. NH May 30 (234) $100; NH Aug 23 (439) $130; sg June 18 (307) $120

James, Thomas Horton

— Six Months in South Australia. L, 1838. 8vo, orig cloth. With folding map & plan. S June 25 (221) £180 [Quaritch/Hordern]

James, William, d.1827

— The Naval History of Great Britain. L, 1837. 6 vols. 8vo, contemp half calf; 1 spine worn at ends. b Nov 18J (302) £140

Anr Ed. L, 1847. 6 vols. 8vo, various bdgs. Z Apr 18 (271) $50

Jameson, R. C.

— New Zealand, South Australia, and New South Wales. L, 1842. 1st Ed. 8vo, bdg not described but rebacked. One folding map with frayed blank margin & amateur repair of a tear, the other with tear. kh Nov 11 (525) A$70

Jameson, Robert, 1774-1854

— Mineralogy of the Scottish Isles. Edin., 1800. 2 vols in 1. 4to, contemp half calf; worn, covers detached. With 13 maps & plates. Some foxing & waterstaining. bba Oct 24 (283) £190 [Knowles]

Jamieson, Alexander

— A Celestial Atlas, comprising a Systematic Display of the Heavens.... L, 1822. Oblong 4to, contemp half mor; loose. With engraved title & 30 maps. sg Feb 13 (126) $450

Jammes, Andre

— La Reforme de la Typographie Royale sous Louis XIV: Le Grandjean. Paris, 1961. One of 100. Folio, loose as issued with text booklet in half vellum folding case. With 110 engravings on 35 leaves. sg Oct 31 (171) $700

Jamot, Paul, 1863-1939

— Dunoyer de Segonzac. Paris, 1929. 4to, later cloth, orig front wrap bound in. wa Apr 9 (226) $95

Jane's...

— All the World's Fighting Ships. NY, 1899. Oblong 4to, cloth; rubbed & soiled. DW Mar 4 (361) £210

— Jane's All the World's Aircraft. L, 1941. Orig cloth, in soiled & chipped d/j; dampstain to top & lower edges of bdg. wa Sept 26 (516) $60

Janse, Antonius Johannes Theodorus

— The Moths of South Africa. Durban, 1932-60. 6 vols in 18. 8vo, Vols I-III, cloth; others, wraps. O Apr 28 (83) $50

Janson, Charles William

— The Stranger in America: containing Observations Made During a Long Residence.... L, 1807. 4to, half mor; rubbed, new endpapers. With frontis & 9 (of 10) plates. Frontis repaired with some loss to surface; foxed. bba July 9 (40) £85 [Kay Books]

Anr copy. Contemp calf; rebacked preserving spine. With extra engraved title, map & 9 plates. Lacking ad leaves; 2F-2F2 duplicated & misbound; some discoloration or dust-soiling; tp creased. S May 14 (1257) £500 [Waggett]

Anr copy. Modern calf. Inked library stamps on tp, plate versos & elsewhere. Lacking ads. sg Dec 5 (125) $225

Janssonius, Joannes

— Atlantis majoris quinta pars.... Amst.: Jansson, 1657. Folio, contemp vellum gilt with title in ink at head in upper panel; minor soiling. With 32 double-page charts, including anemographic plate, hand-colored in outline in a contemp hand, the title fully colored & heightened with gold. Tp repaired. S Nov 21 (128) £9,000 [Tooley Adams]

Jaquet, Eugene. See: Chapuis & Jaquet

Jardine, Sir William, 1800-74

— The Natural History of Humming Birds. Edin., 1833-34. 2 vols. 8vo, contemp half mor. With ports, hand-colored titles & 64 hand-colored plates. 2 signatures detached; ports & titles browned. b Mar 11 (228) £140

Anr Ed. Edin., 1840. 2 vols. 8vo, orig cloth; rubbed. With 2 ports, 2 extra engraved titles & 64 hand-colored plates. bba Jan 30 (421) £220 [Ginnan]

Anr copy. Contemp mor gilt. With ports of Linnaeus & Pennant on india paper, hand-colored engraved titles & 64 hand-colored plates heightened with varnish. Some spotting, mainly affecting engraved titles & ports. C May 20 (187) £1,300 [Marshall]

— The Naturalist's Library. Edin, 1833-43. 40 vols. 8vo, contemp half mor; rubbed. With 1,355 plates, most hand-colored. Some plates cropped, a few loose, 3 torn; lacking some text leaves. Sold w.a.f. bba Aug 13 (364) £1,400 [Bailey]

Anr copy. Modern pigskin. With port & engraved title in each vol & 1,276 plates, including 1 duplicate, most plates partly hand-colored. Some repairs & shaving. pn

June 11 (232) £1,400 [Kafka]

Anr copy. Vols I-XIV: Ornithology. Imitation snakeskin; extremities rubbed. Witht 452 hand-colored plates. Some plates and text leaves loose. sg Nov 14 (183) $2,400

Anr Ed. Edin., 1843. 40 vols. 8vo, contemp half calf; rubbed, upper joint of vol II cracked, scuffed, some spines chipped. With ports & engraved titles (some hand-colored) & 1,217 plates only (most hand-colored). Some browning & soiling; some plate numbers trimmed; some marginal tears. P June 17 (242) $2,500

Anr copy. Orig cloth; many bdgs def. With engraved ports & titles & 1,275 plates, most partly hand-colored. A few plates shaved; some spotting. Sold w.a.f. pn Nov 14 (427) £1,500

Anr copy. Orig cloth; some spine ends chipped. sg Nov 7 (96) $2,600

Vols XXIV-XXVII [British Birds]. 8vo, orig cloth. bba Oct 24 (265) £95 [Finney]

Vol XXV, an earlier Ed. Edin., 1854-52. 40 vols. 8vo, contemp half mor gilt; rubbed, 1 spine def, 1 or 2 broken. Some plates & text spotted. bba Sept 5 (61) £2,000 [Ginnan]

Jarry, Alfred, 1873-1907

— Ubu roi. Paris: Teriade, 1966. One of 180. Illus by Miro. Unsewn as issued in orig wraps. With 13 double-page chromolithos. S Dec 5 (314) £5,000 [Tannenbaum]; S May 28 (228) £6,500 [Panini]

Jars, Gabriel, 1732-69

— Voyages metallurgiques, ou recherches et observations sur les mines & forges de fer.... Lyon & Paris, 1774. Vol I (of 3) only. 4to, contemp half calf. With 10 folding plates. bba Feb 23 (343) £60 [Hemming]

Jarves, James Jackson, 1818-88

— History of the Hawaiian or Sandwich Islands. Honolulu, 1847. ("History of the Hawaiian Islands....") 3d Ed. 8vo, contemp half sheep; spine rubbed. cb Oct 10 (56) $375

Jarvis, Edward —& Others

— Report on Insanity and Idiocy in Massachusetts.... Bost., 1855. 8vo, orig cloth; spine ends chipped, worn. Handstamp at front free endpaper. Inscr by Jarvis to Thomas S. Kirkbride. bbc Dec 9 (347) $275

Jauna, Dominique

— Histoire generale des roiaumes de chipre de Jerusalem, d'Armenie, et d'Egypte, comprenant les Croisades.... Leiden, 1785. 1st Ed, 2d Issue. 2 vols. 4to, contemp mor gilt. C Oct 30 (108A) £5,500 [Atabey]

Jay's copy, John

— Acts Passed at a Congress of the United States of America.... NY: Francis Childs & John Swaine, [1789]. Folio, contemp NY bdg of calf over pastebds with gilt Greek key roll borders & mor label in center of upper cover gilt lettered Chief Justice of the United States, bound by Thomas Allen. Inscr by Jay at top of tp: "9 Decr. 1789 - Presented by the President of the United States to John Jay" Doheny-Manney copy. P Oct 11 (181) $210,000

Jayne, Caroline Furness

— String Figures: a Study of Cat's Cradle in Many Lands. NY, 1906. Library markings. F Dec 18 (398) $90

Jeake, Samuel, 1623-90

— Logisticelogia, or Arithmetick Surveighed and Reviewed.... L, 1696. Folio, contemp calf; upper cover detached. Tear to table; hole in 3R1. Ck Nov 29 (194) £850

Jeancon, John A. See: Oesterricher, Johann Heinrich

Jeffers, Robinson, 1887-1962

See also: Grabhorn Printing

— Be Angry at the Sun. NY: Random House, [1941]. One of 100. Unopened. CNY Dec 5 (258) $400

Anr copy. Sgd. Epstein copy. sg Apr 29 (254) $600

— Californians. NY, 1916. 1st Ed. In d/j. Some foxing. sg June 11 (175) $100

Advance copy. Orig cloth. Epstein copy. sg Apr 29 (255) $950

Anr copy. Perforated stamp on tp. sg June 11 (177) $130

— Cawdor, and Other Poems. NY, 1928. One of 375. Sgd. sg Dec 12 (175) $175

— Dear Judas. NY, 1929. One of 375. Bds, in d/j. sg Dec 12 (176) $250

— Descent to the Dead. NY, [1931]. One of 500. Bds. sg Dec 12 (177) $225

— The Double Axe, & Other Poems. NY: Random House, [1948]. In d/j. Inscr. Epstein copy. sg Apr 29 (256) $550

— Flagons and Apples. Los Angeles, 1912. 1st Ed, one of 500. CNY Dec 5 (257) $600

Anr copy. Epstein copy. sg Apr 29 (257) $700

— Give Your Heart to the Hawks.... NY, 1933. 1st Ed, One of 200. Half calf. cb Dec 12 (83) $130; sg Sept 12 (122) $225; sg Dec 12 (178) $225

— Poems. San Francisco, 1928. One of 310. Frontis by Ansel Adams. Sgd by Jeffers and Adams. sg Dec 12 (179) $600

— Such Counsels You Gave to Me.... NY, [1937]. One of 300. Half lea; spine rubbed. K Sept 29 (213) $100

Anr copy. Half mor. Sgd. sg Dec 12 (181) $140

— Tamar, and Other Poems. NY, [1924]. 1st Ed, One of 500. Epstein copy. sg Apr 29 (258) $550

— Tragedy has Obligations. [Santa Cruz CA: Lime Kiln Press, 1973. One of 200. Folio, orig half mor. bbc Apr 27 (349) $140

— The Women at Point Sur. NY, [1927]. One of 265. bbc Sept 23 (436) $125

Anr copy. Bdg unopened. Epstein copy. sg Apr 29 (259) $275

Jefferson, Thomas, 1743-1826

See also: Limited Editions Club

— A Manual of Parliamentary Practice. Wash., 1812. 2d Ed. 12mo, contemp sheep; front cover loose. sg Dec 5 (126) $200

— Memoirs, Correspondence, and Miscellanies.... Bost., 1830. 2d Ed. 4 vols. 8vo, half calf; extremities worn. Hamilton Fish's copy. sg June 18 (309) $175

— Message of the President...Relative to Fortifications Erected at the Several Ports and Harbours of the United States.... Wash., 1806. 8vo, disbound. sg June 18 (298) $225

— Notes on the State of Virginia. L, 1787. 8vo, later half mor; rubbed. With folding map hand-colored in outline & folding table. O Nov 26 (93) $4,100

Anr Ed. NY, 1801. 8vo, contemp sheep; front cover loose, worn. Lacking the port. sg Dec 5 (127) $80

Anr Ed. Phila., 1801. 8vo, lea; covers detached. Library markings. sp Apr 16 (22) $80

— The Papers.... Princeton, 1950-71. Ed by J.P. Boyd. Vols 1-18 plus 2 Index vols. cb Sept 5 (51) $110

Vols 1-15. Princeton, 1950-58. bbc June 29 (318) $300

— The Secretary of State, to whom was referred by the House of Representatives the Letter of John H. Mitchell.... [NY: Francis Childs & John Swaine, 1790]. Single sheet, 340mm by 213mm, disbound with old stab holes in margin. Some marginal staining. P June 16 (234) $12,000

— A Summary View of the Rights of British America. Phila.: John Dunlap, 1774. 2d Ed. 8vo, disbound. Some foxing. P Dec 12 (112) $27,500

— Works. NY, 1892-99. One of 750. 10 vols. 8vo, cloth. sg Dec 5 (128) $300

— Writings.... NY, 1853-54. 9 vols. 8vo, orig cloth; spine ends chipped. Foxed. K Sept 29 (214) $70

Jefferson Library, Thomas

— Catalogue of the Library of.... Wash., 1952-59. 5 vols. 4to, cloth; worn. O Sept 24 (228) $250

Anr copy. Compiled by E. Millicent Sowerby. Orig cloth; worn & soiled. Inscr by Sowerby. wa Dec 9 (28) $280

Jefferys, Thomas, d.1771

See also: Kitchin & Jefferys

— The County of York Survey'd. L, 1771-72. Folio, contep half calf; worn. With 20 folding maps, hand-colored in outline. pnL Nov 20 (41) £470 [Manger]

— A Description of the Spanish Islands and Settlements on the Coast of the West Indies. L, 1762. 4to, half calf gilt by Morrell. With 32 folding maps & plans, 2 colored. Browned; 3 tears to 2 folding maps. CNY Oct 8 (137) $2,600

Anr copy. Bound with: The Present State of the West-Indies. L, 1778. contemp calf; rebacked. With 32 folding maps & plans in 1st work & frontis map in 2d work. sg June 18 (310) $1,800

— A Description of the Maritime Parts of France.... L, 1774. 2 vols. Oblong 4to, contemp half lea; rubbed. With 87 maps, charts & plans, 1 folding. Tp creased; some spotting. pn June 1 (302) £1,000

— The West-India Atlas.... L, 1775. Folio, modern half mor. With engraved title & 39 maps. Chart A shaved at foot with loss of neatline. S June 25 (445) £5,800 [Baskes]

Jeffries, David

— A Treatise on Diamonds and Pearls. L, 1751. 2d Ed. 8vo, modern cloth. With 30 plates. Tear to 1 plate. F Mar 26 (314B) $230

Jeffries, John, M.D.

— A Narrative of the Two Aerial Voyages of Doctor Jeffries with Mons. Blanchard... from London into Kent...from England into France. L, 1786. 4to, orig wraps. With port & plate. bbc Dec 9 (335) $2,500

Jekyll, Gertrude, 1843-1932

— Garden Ornament. L, 1918. 1st Ed. Folio, orig cloth; rubbed. bba Aug 13 (365) £120 [Barry]

Anr copy. Library stamps. pn Mar 19 (352) £75 [Sotheran]

— Some English Gardens. L, 1904. Folio, cloth; extremities rubbed, hinges cracked. With 50 color plates. sg Feb 6 (143) $70

Jekyll, Gertrude, 1843-1932 —& Weaver, Sir Lawrence

— Gardens for Small Country Houses. L, 1920. 4to, cloth; some wear. bbc June 29 (126) $55

Jellicoe, Geoffrey Alan. See: Shepherd & Jellicoe

Jenkins, Charles Francis, 1867-1934

— Animated Pictures: an Exposition of the Historical Development of Chronophotography.... Wash., 1898. 1st Ed. 8vo, cloth; joints & edges worn. bbc Feb 17 (241) $240

Jenkins, Sir George Henry

— Victoria, a Short History and Description of the Parliament House, Melbourne. Melbourne, 1886. 4to, early calf; rubbed, some defs. Inscr. kh Nov 11 (527) A$160

Jenkins, James. See: Naval...

Jenkins, William Fitzgerald, 1896-1975. See: Leinster, Murray

Jenks, James

— The Complete Cook: teaching the Art of Cookery in all its Branches. L, 1768. 12mo, contemp calf; spine ends chipped. Some leaves with slight waterstaining in lower margin. S May 14 (989) £450 [Segal]

Jenks Collection, John Story

— Chapman, Henry. - [Sale Catalogue] Catalogue...Collection of Coins. Phila: Davis & Harvey, 1921. Orig cloth; soiled, hinge cracked at rear. With 42 photographic plates; price list bound in. cb Feb 27 (75) $90

Jennewein, J. Leonard

— Black Hills Booktrails. Mitchell SD, 1962. Sgd. cb Oct 17 (469) $110

Jennings, John

— Theatrical and Circus Life. St. Louis, 1882. 8vo, pictorial cloth; extremities worn, 1st signature loose. sg Oct 17 (63) $175

Jennings, Otto Emery

— Wild Flowers of Western Pennsylvania.... Pittsburgh, 1953. 2 vols. Folio, cloth, in d/js. sg Nov 14 (184) $200

Jennings, Samuel

— Orchids: and How to Grow Them in India.... L, 1875. 4to, contemp half calf; worn, split. With 48 hand-colored plates. pnE May 13 (221) £750

Jerdon, Thomas C., 1811-72

— The Birds of India. Calcutta, 1862-[64]. 2 parts in 3 vols. 8vo, later half mor. bba Oct 24 (266) £65 [Lewcock]

Jerman, John. See: Franklin Printing, Benjamin

Jerrold, Douglas, 1803-57

— Mrs. Caudle's Curtain Lectures. L, 1866. Illus by Charles Keene. 4to, orig cloth; rubbed. cb Sept 26 (125) $55

Jerrold, William Blanchard, 1826-84

See also: Dore & Jerrold

— The Life of George Cruikshank in Two Epochs. L, 1882. 1st Ed. 2 vols. 8vo, mor by Morrell; rubbed. Extra-illus with c.90 plates. O Sept 24 (132) $300

Anr copy. Mor gilt by Riviere. Extra-illus with 130 plates, many with coloring added by Jerrold. S Nov 14 (109) £240 [Ash Rare Books]

— London, a Pilgrimage. L, 1872. Illus by Gustave Dore. Folio, cloth; worn. cb Sept 26 (74) $275

Anr copy. Half lea; rubbed. O Mar 31 (61) $160

Jervis, Christopher. See: Freeman, Richard Austin

Jervis, Henry Jervis White, 1825-81

— History of the Island of Corfu.... Colburn, 1852. 8vo, orig cloth; lacking upper free endleaf. With frontis, 2 wood-engraved plates & 1 plan & folding table. Dampstained in lower margin. S June 30 (324) £380 [Spink]

Jesty, Simon

— River Niger, a Novel.... L, 1935. 1st Ed, One of 25. Ck July 10 (307) £180

Jesuit Relations

— Ferreira, Christovao. - Narratio persecutionis adversus christianos excitatae in variis Japoniae regis.... Antwerp: Johannes Meurs, 1635. 8vo, contemp vellum; soiled. Browned; some rust-marks. S June 25 (468) £1,500 [Barberini]

— Froes, Luis. - Lettera annua del Giappone dell'anno M.D.XCVI. Padua: Francesco Bolzetta, 1599. 8vo, contemp vellum. S June 25 (467) £6,500 [Barberini]

Jesuits

— Defences des Jesuites. Contre les requeste & plaidoyez n'agueres imprimez a l'encontre d'eux. Lyons: Guichard Jullieron, 1594. 8vo, disbound. Wormhole in 1st 5 leaves. S Dec 5 (150) £450 [Trinity College]

— Edifying and Curious Letters of some Missioners, of the Society of Jesus, from Foreign Missions. L, 1707. 8vo, contemp sheep; rubbed. Lacking 1st & last leaf & free endpapers. bba June 25 (259) £130 [Rotagan]

— Lettere annue del Giappone dell' anno 1622.... Rome, 1627. 8vo, disbound. Wormholes affecting margins of 1st few leaves. S Nov 21 (360) £2,000 [Maggs]

Jewish...

— Jewish Encyclopedia.... NY, 1925. 12 vols. 4to, cloth. Library markings. bba May 28 (151) £120 [Farfouille]

Jewish Museum, London

— Catalogue of the Jewish Museum London. Hertford, 1974. Ed by R. D. Barnett. Folio, cloth, in d/j. sg Dec 19 (132) $650

Jewitt, Llewellynn, 1816-86

— The Ceramic Art of Great Britain. L, 1878. 2 vols. 8vo, cloth; worn, hinges cracked. Some foxing. sg Sept 6 (165) $60

Jherome of Bruynwyke. See: Brunschwig, Hieronymus

Joannes Isaacus, Hollandus

— Opera mineralia, sive de lapide philosophico.... Middelburg: R. Schilders, 1600. 8vo, later vellum; bdg loose. With 2 small library stamps on verso of tp; some stains. B Nov 1 (640) HF1,600

Jockey Club

— The Jockey Club; or a Sketch of the Manners of the Age. L, 1792. 2 parts in 1 vol. 8vo, later half mor. DW Dec 11 (316) £72

Johandeau, Marcel

— Carnets de Don Juan. Paris, 1947. One of 500 on velin de Condat. 4to, orig wraps. Inscr to Boris Kochno. SM Oct 12 (485) FF1,300

Johannes Chrysostomus, Saint, 345?-407

— In partem multo meliorem Davidici psalterii homiliae. Paris: Sebastian Nivellius, 1550. 8vo, contemp vellum. Some foxing; wormed in blank lower inner corners. sg Oct 24 (168) $200

Johannes de Janduno

— Questiones super duos Libros peri Hermenias Aristotelis. Salamance, 1517. Folio, modern vellum; warped. Gothic type; woodcut title vignette & full-page woodcut on tp verso. Annotated throughout with contemp Ms notes; some stains. Ck Oct 31 (19) £1,500

Johannes de Verdena

— Sermones dominicales cum expositionibus evangeliorum. Strassburg: Johann Grueninger, 1500. Vol 2 (of 2) only. 4to, old half sheep; joints cracked. Some early underscoring & marginalia; lower margins dampstained. Goff J-469. sg Mar 12 (120) $800

John, Augustus, 1878-1961

— Fifty-Two Drawings. L, 1957. Folio, orig half vellum by Zaehnsdorf. bba Feb 27 (385) £240 [Mandl]

John Bull...

— John Bull and Bonaparte: or, Interesting and Important Dialogues.... L, 1803. Illus by Isaac Cruikshank. 8vo, mor, orig wraps bound in. With folding hand-colored frontis. Salomons copy. sg Oct 17 (190) $350

John Taylor & Co.

— Tables showing the Value of Silver and Gold, per Ounce Troy, at Different Degrees of Fineness. San Francisco, [1880s]. 4to, cloth; back cover stained. sg June 18 (134) $200

John, Wilhelm, 1877-1939

— Erzherzog Karl der Feldherr und Seine Armee. Vienna, 1913. 4to, orig cloth. sp Apr 16 (90) $275

John, William David

— Nantgarw Porcelain. Newport, 1948. 4to, mor gilt; rubbed. b June 22 (40) £90

Anr copy. Mor gilt; rubbed, corners scuffed. With 185 illusts, including 42 color plates. DW Mar 11 (760) £110

— Swansea Porcelain. Newport, 1958. 4to. DW Apr 8 (352) £50

John, William David —& Baker, Warren

— Old English Lustre Pottery. Newport, 1951. Folio, orig cloth. F Mar 26 (262) $130

Anr copy. Orig cloth; soiled. sg Sept 6 (54) $175

Anr copy. Orig cloth gilt. Plate count not given. sg Apr 2 (46) $140

Johnson, Alfred Edwin

— The Russian Ballet. Bost. & NY, 1913. 4to, orig cloth. pn Oct 24 (401) £38

Johnson, Alfred Forbes

See also: Cresset Press

— Selected Essays on Books and Printing. Amst., 1970. Ed by Percy H. Muir. In d/j. O Sept 24 (133) $60

Johnson, Alvin Jewett, 1827-84

— Johnson's New Illustrated Family Atlas of the World. NY, 1864. Folio, orig half sheep; worn. With engraved title & 61 hand-colored maps. Corner lacking from 1 chart. bbc Apr 27 (8) $470

Anr Ed. NY, 1879. Folio, half mor; worn & broken. With 52 hand-colored maps. Old dampstain across top edge into plates. bbc June 29 (23) $325

Johnson, C. Pierpoint, d.1893 —& Sowerby, John E., 1825-70

— British Wild Flowers.... L, [1858]-60. 8vo, mor gilt by Leighton. With hand-colored frontis, 2 plain & 80 hand-colored plates. C May 20 (188) £320 [Grahame]

Anr Ed. L, 1894. 8vo, orig cloth; rubbed. With 90 hand-colored & 2 plain plates. Front free endpaper def. bba Sept 5 (63) £120 [W. Fleming]

Anr Ed. L, 1902. 8vo, cloth. With 100 hand-colored plates. sg Sept 19 (215) $90

Johnson, Capt. Charles, Pseud.

— A General History of the Pirates. L, 1925. 2 vols. 4to, orig cloth, in worn d/j. Some foxing. kh Nov 11 (357) A$120

Johnson, Eldridge Reeves

— Tarpomania—The Madness of Fishing. Phila.: Pvtly ptd, 1910. 8vo, mor gilt with silver-painted lea onlay of tarpon on front cover; some scuffing. F Mar 26 (156) $425

Johnson, Frank M.

— Forest, Lake and River: the Fishes of New-England and Eastern Canada. Bost., 1902. One of 350. 2 vols. 4to, orig lea with catches & clasps; metal snaps missing. Owner's correspondence tipped in Vol I. sg May 21 (56) $550

Johnson, George William. See: Hogg & Johnson

Johnson, Jack

— Jack Johnson - in the Ring - and Out. Chicago, 1927. Inscr to Damon Runyon. bbc Apr 27 (538) $475

Johnson, James, 1750?-1811

— The Scots Musical Museum. Edin, [1787-88]. Vols I-II only. Later lea; rubbed. Some foxing. O July 12 (106) $140

Anr Ed. Edin.: James Johnson, [1803 or after]. 6 vols in 2. 8vo, half calf. Engraved throughout. pnE May 13 (224) £60

Johnson, James Rawlins

— A Treatise on the Medicinal Leech. L, 1816. 8vo, newer bds. Library markings. O Apr 28 (84) $110

Johnson, John, 1777-1848

— Typographia, or the Printers' Instructor. L, 1824. 2 vols. 12mo, later half calf. bba Dec 19 (330) £70 [Forster]

Anr copy. Bdg not stated. cb Oct 17 (4773) $160

Anr copy. Orig cloth; worn. DW Mar 4 (300) £50

Johnson, Kenneth M.

— The Sting of the Wasp: Political & Satirical Cartoons.... San Francisco: Book Club of California, 1967. One of 450. Folio, cloth; With 20 colored plates. cb Oct 31 (65) $80

Johnson, Merle

— American First Editions: Bibliographic Check Lists.... NY, 1929. One of 50 L.p. copies, sgd. Mor. sp Apr 16 (504) $130

— A Bibliography of the Work of Mark Twain. NY, 1910. 1st Ed, one of 500. 4to, cloth; spine rubbed. K Sept 29 (131) $90

— High Spots of American Literature. NY, 1929. One of 50. Lev gilt. sg May 21 (256) $60

Johnson, Richard, 1573-1659?

— The Famous History of the Seven Champions of Christendome.... L, 1687. 2 parts in 1 vol. 4to, contemp calf gilt; worn, joints split, upper cover detached. Cut close, affecting some running heads; some worming with loss; some spotting & staining; scribbling at end. Front endpaper with writing that states the book was bought at the sale of Samuel Johnson's books in Feb 1785. S July 21 (27) £1,700 [Stockholm]

Johnson, Robert Underwood, 1853-1937 —& Buel, Clarence Clough

— Battles and Leaders of the Civil War. NY, [1887-89]. 4 vols. 4to, later cloth. bbc Feb 17 (77) $125

Johnson, Samuel, 1696-1772. See: Franklin Printing, Benjamin

Johnson, Samuel, 1709-84

See also: Piozzi, Hester Lynch Thrale

— A Diary of a Journey into North Wales. L, 1816. 8vo, 19th-cent half calf. With 2 facsimile plates of Johnson's handwriting, spotted. Milne copy. Ck June 12 (117) £100

Anr copy. Modern lea. sg Nov 7 (113) $250

— A Dictionary of the English Language. L, 1755. 1st Ed. 2 vols. Folio, contemp calf; scuffed, rebacked. Some soiling & spotting. Ck Oct 18 (155) £4,000

Anr copy. Early 19th-cent russia; rebacked; 3 leaves torn & repaired. George Milne copy. CNY Dec 5 (262) $4,000

Anr copy. Contemp calf; joints cracked, some surface worming. Sheet 19D1 in 2d setting; Sheet 24O1 in 1st setting. Lower margins of some gatherings in Vol I stained; some Ms marginalia in Vol II; gathering 26Y browned; short marginal tears. P Dec 12 (177) $7,000

Anr copy. Tp & prelims to Vol I badly stained; 4 pages def. pnE Mar 11 (113)

£360

Anr copy. Contemp sheep; rebacked, worn, covers detached or starting. Some spotting or dampstaining in corners; some repairs. sg Oct 24 (169) $3,800

Anr copy. Contemp sheep; worn, covers detached or starting. Prelims loose; institutional stamp on titles. sg Nov 7 (107) $5,000

2d Ed. 2 vols. Folio, contemp calf; worn, 1 cover detached. Some spotting. S July 21 (24) £2,600 [Maggs]

Anr copy. Contemp calf; rubbed, joints split. Leaf 17A-17Z misbound after 18D2; 1 leaf torn without loss; some spotting. S July 21 (25) £600 [Grant & Shaw]

Anr copy. Contemp sheep; worn, spines rebacked. A few minor marginal repairs in Vol II. Epstein copy. sg Apr 29 (260) $8,000

Anr Ed. L, 1756. 2 vols. Folio, later half mor; upper joint of Vol I split, extremities rubbed. Lacking Sig. 5R; tp to Vol II laid down. Milne copy. Ck June 12 (101) £350

3d Abridged (8vo) Ed. L, 1766. 2 vols. 8vo, contemp sheep; rubbed, joints starting. sg Mar 12 (66) $175

Anr Ed. Dublin, 1768. 8vo, modern half calf. Some foxing. cb Oct 25 (59) $250

4th Ed. L, 1773. 2 vols. Folio, modern half calf. sg Nov 7 (108) $2,400

Anr Ed. L, 1785. 2 vols. 4to, later half calf gilt. Lacking frontis. DW May 13 (287) £125

Anr copy. Modern half calf gilt. sg May 7 (126) $800

Harrison's Ed. L, 1786. Folio, old half calf; worn, backstrips def, 1 spine split. Port & title dampstained. bba May 14 (97) £70 [Hannar]

Anr copy. Contemp vellum; soiled. With port & 2 folding plates. Tp & port wormed at outer margin; some spotting & browning. Milne copy. Ck June 12 (103) £420

Anr copy. Contemp calf gilt; Covers detached. Titles stamped. sg Mar 12 (67) $450

Anr Ed. L, 1818. 4 vols. 8vo, contemp half calf; rebacked. bba Oct 10 (343) £190 [B. Turner]

Anr copy. 4 vols. 4to, contemp calf gilt; rebacked, orig spines preserved. A few leaves in Vol III repaired. bba Apr 9 (43) £220 [Howell Williams]

Anr Ed. Phila.: Moses Thomas, 1818. 4 vols. 8vo, contemp half calf; rebacked, worn. Port spotted; newspaper cutting bound in. pn Sept 12 (44) £110 [Traylen]

Anr Ed. L, 1819. ("Johnson's Dictionary of the English Language in Miniature.") 12mo, contemp sheep; rebacked. sg Mar 5 (140) $250

Anr Ed. L, 1827. 3 vols. 4to, contemp calf gilt; worn. With port. bba July 9 (150) £90 [Fleisher]

[-] A General Index to the First Twenty Volumes of the Gentleman's Magazine. L, 1753. 8vo, contemp calf; joints rubbed. Provides a list of Johnson's own contributions. Milne copy. Ck June 12 (100) £2,200

— The Idler. Dublin: Peter Wilson, 1762. 12mo, modern bds. sg Mar 12 (149) $350

— Irene. L, 1749. 1st Ed. 8vo, modern half mor. sg Nov 7 (106) $550

[-] Johnsoniana: or Supplement to Boswell.... L, 1836. 1st Ed. 8vo, mor; extremities rubbed. sg Mar 5 (146) $90

— A Journey to the Western Islands of Scotland. L, 1775. 1st Ed, 1st Issue, with the 12-line errata. 8vo, contemp calf; rebacked. Title to E5 with wormholes at outer margin. Milne copy. Ck June 12 (108) £150

Anr copy. Contemp calf; rebacked, endpapers renewed. sg May 21 (57) $200

2d Issue, with the 6-line errata at end. Contemp calf; joints cracked. Verso of final leaf soiled at upper margin. Milne copy. Ck June 12 (109) £160

2d Ed. 8vo, contemp calf. pnE Oct 1 (310) £120

Anr copy. Contemp calf; rebacked. sg May 7 (125) $400

— The Lives of the Most Eminent English Poets. Dublin, 1779-81. ("Prefaces, Biographical and Critical, to the Works of the English Poets.") 3 vols. 8vo, contemp calf; front cover of Vols I & III detached. sg Mar 12 (150) $225

1st Separate (Pirated) Ed. ("The Lifes of the English Poets.") 3 vols. 8vo, contemp calf. sg May 7 (127) $900

1st Separate London Ed. L, 1781. 4 vols. 8vo, contemp calf; rebacked, rubbed. Some foxing. bba June 11 (76) £85 [Clark]

Anr copy. Contemp calf, rebacked with modern calf. cb Oct 25 (60) $350

Anr copy. Orig bds; rebacked. sg Mar 12 (151) $175

Anr Ed. L, 1793. 4 vols. 8vo, contemp calf. With port. W July 8 (322) £75

— London: a Poem. L, 1738. 2d Ed. Folio, half mor by Sangorki & Sutcliffe. George Milne copy. CNY Dec 5 (259) $2,400

— Miscellaneous and Fugitive Pieces. L: for T. Davies, [1773]. 8vo, contemp calf; spines rubbed. Ck June 12 (107) £150

— The Plan of a Dictionary of the English

Language.... L, 1747. 1st Ed, 2d Issue, without Chesterfield's name on A1 recto. 4to, modern bds; covers detached. George Milne copy. CNY Dec 5 (260) $3,500

Anr copy. Modern half cloth. sg Nov 7 (104) $3,200

— The Poetical Works. L, 1785. 1st Collected Ed. 8vo, contemp half calf; rubbed. bba Nov 28 (299) £80 [Jacob]

Anr copy. Contemp calf; rebacked. sg Mar 12 (152) $300

— Political Tracts. L, 1776. 1st Collected Ed. 8vo, contemp calf; rebacked, covers detached. P2 torn at lower margin. Milne copy. Ck June 12 (111) £280

Anr Ed. Dublin, 1777. 8vo, contemp sheep; rebacked. sg Nov 7 (111) $250

— Prayers and Meditations. L, 1785. Bound with: Enfield, W. Prayers for the Use of Families. Warrington, 1785. 8vo, calf; rebacked. pnE Dec 4 (31) £90

1st Ed. 8vo, contemp calf; spine head worn. cb Oct 25 (62) $120

Anr copy. Contemp calf; rebacked, new endleaves, corners bumped. L Feb 27 (215) £160

Anr copy. Contemp calf; spine rubbed, crack along top portion of upper joint, joints rubbed. Ms marginalia; some spotting & soiling. P Dec 12 (178) $400

Anr copy. Orig bds; front joint restored. sg Mar 12 (153) $550

— The Rambler. L, 1751. 2 vols. Folio, 18th-cent half calf with spine monogram MB; covers detached, lacking upper cover of Vol I. Vol I tp soiled; lacking tp in Vol II. British Museum duplicate. Milne copy. Ck June 12 (98) £300

— Rasselas. L, 1759. ("The Prince of Abissinia.") 1st Ed. 2 vols. 8vo, contemp half calf; spines repaired. C Dec 12 (206) £1,000 [Maggs]

Anr copy. Contemp calf; rebacked, orig spines laid down. Some dampstaining; tp of Vol I with tear to upper margin. C Dec 16 (256) £450 [Pickering & Chatto]

Anr copy. 19th-cent calf gilt; upper cover of Vol I detached. A2 of Vol I holed with loss of page numeral on verso. Ck June 12 (104) £150

Anr copy. Lev gilt by Birdsall. Lacking final blank. sg Nov 7 (109) $1,500

2d Ed. 2 vols. 8vo, contemp calf; upper cover of Vol I detached. Milne copy. Ck June 12 (105) £65

— Samuel Johnson's Prologue Spoken at the Opening of the Theatre in Drury-Lane in 1747 with Garrick's Epilogue. A Facsimile... NY, 1902. One of 90 on Van Gelder. Preface by Austin Dobson; Ed by A. S. W. Rosenbach. 4to, bds. sg Mar 5 (144) $200

— A Sermon written by the late...for the Funeral of his Wife.... L, 1788. 8vo, disbound. Ck June 12 (116) £320

— A Sermon Written by the late Samuel Johnson, LL.D. for the Funeral of his Wife. L, 1788. 1st Ed. 8vo, disbound. Milne copy. Ck June 12 (116) £320

— Thoughts on the late Transactions Respecting Falkland's Islands. L, 1771. 1st Ed, Revised Issue with cancelled K2. 8vo, disbound. Lacking half-title & tp; B1 & L2 detached. Milne copy. Ck June 12 (106) £100

— The Vanity of Human Wishes. L, 1749. 1st Ed. 4to, calf gilt by Pratt; joints & extremities rubbed. Tp soiled. Bute copy. C June 24 (324) £1,500 [Phillips]

Anr copy. Mor by Riviere. Extreme gutters of title & last leaf repaired. George Milne copy. CNY Dec 5 (261) $4,800

Anr copy. Modern lea. Margins trimmed; title and last leaf repaired; Page 3 stained. sg Nov 7 (105) $2,600

— Works. L, 1796. 12 vols. 8vo, contemp mor gilt; rubbed. S July 1 (993) £320 [Sossidis]

Anr Ed. Edin., 1806. 15 vols. 12mo, calf gilt; spines scuffed. cb Jan 16 (84) $190

Anr Ed. L, 1806. 12 vols. 8vo, calf gilt; Vol I joints repaired. cb Oct 25 (65) $150

Anr Ed. Oxford, 1825. One of 75 L.p. copies. 11 vols, including 2 vols of Parliamentary Debates. Contemp mor gilt. Some spotting at beginning & end of each vol. S July 21 (26) £800 [Franklin]

— The Works of the English Poets. L, 1790. 8vo, contemp calf gilt; worn, some spines rubbed. sg Mar 12 (155) $1,500

Johnson, Theodore T., b.1818

— Sights in the Gold Region.... NY, 1849. 1st Ed. 12mo, modern cloth. cb Sept 12 (97) $110

Anr copy. Orig cloth; spine faded. cb Feb 12 (36) $225; sg June 18 (85) $250

Johnson, Sir William

— The Papers of Sir William Johnson. Albany, 1921-65. 14 vols. Library markings. K Dec 1 (255) $600

Johnston, Alexander Keith, 1804-71

— The National Atlas of Historical, Commercial, and Political Geography. Edin, 1851. Folio, bdg not described but worn. With engraved title & 41 double-page colored maps. sp June 18 (259) $950

— The Royal Atlas of Modern Geography.... Edin. & L, 1861. Folio, 19th-cent half mor; worn. With 48 colored maps. S July 1 (1418) £150 [Nicholson]

Anr Ed. L, 1868. Folio, half mor; rubbed

& broken. With 48 colored maps. Some blank margins with small stain; 1 map stained. b Mar 11 (11) £80

Johnston, Lt.-Col. George

[-] Proceedings of a General Court-Martial for the Trial of Lt.-Col. G. Johnston.... L, 1811. 8vo, contemp calf; spine repaired at head. Lacking errata leaf. C June 25 (167) £1,800 [Quaritch/Hordern]

Johnston, Sir Harry Hamilton, 1858-1927

— Liberia. L, 1906. 2 vols. bba Feb 13 (358) £90 [Sotheran]

Johnston, Joseph E., 1807-91

— Narrative of Military Operations...War between the States. NY, 1874. 1st Ed. 8vo, orig sheep; joints cracked, loose. bbc Feb 17 (78) $75

Johnston, Robert, A.M.

— Travels through Part of the Russian Empire.... L, 1815. 1st Ed. 4to, modern half calf. With 2 maps, 1 plain & 20 colored plates. Some browning & soiling; tp torn & repaired; some captions shaved. S Nov 15 (1119) £180 [Wagrett]

Anr copy. Half mor; worn. First few leaves loose; some spotting & discoloration throughout. S Feb 26 (752) £160 [Porter]

Johnston, Robert, 1567?-1639

— Historia rerum Britannicarum. Amst., 1655. Folio, contemp calf; rubbed. bba Nov 28 (230) £250 [Land]

Johnston, Samuel Burr

— Letters Written during a Residence of Three Years in Chili.... Erie, [Pa.], 1816. 8vo, orig bds; rebacked, most of orig spine preserved. bba Sept 19 (27) £900 [Felcone]

Johnston, William G., b.1828

— Experiences of a Forty-Niner. Pittsburgh, 1892. 8vo, cloth. With folding blue-print map issued after publication & 13 plates. sg June 18 (86) $400

Johnstone, Charles, 1719?-1800

— Chrysal; or the Adventures of a Guinea. L, 1822. 2d Ed. 3 vols. 8vo, lea. b&b Feb 19 (67) $125

Johnstone, William Grosart —& Croall, Alexander

— The Nature-Printed British Sea-Weeds. L, 1859-60. 4 vols. 4to, half calf; rubbed. Library markings. O Apr 28 (120) $225

Joinville, Jean, Sieur de, 1224?-1317

See also: Gregynog Press

— Histoire de Saint Louis.... Paris, 1761. Folio, half calf; worn. S June 30 (43) £650

Joll, Evelyn. See: Butlin & Joll

Joly, Henri L.

— Legend in Japanese Art. L, 1908. 4to, orig cloth; rubbed & soiled. DW Mar 11 (827) £95

Jombert, Charles Antoine, 1712-84

— Repertoire des artistes, ou receuil de compositions d'Architecture.... Paris, 1765. Vol I only. Folio, contemp calf; worn. With engraved title & 250 illusts on 218 plates, of which 8 are double-page. S Feb 11 (314) £700 [Shapero]

Jomini, Antoine Henri, Baron de

— Tableau analytique des principales combinaisons de la guerre.... Paris, 1830. 8vo, calf gilt. sg Jan 9 (134) $110

Jonas, F. M.

— Netsuke. L, 1928. Sheep. sg Sept 6 (203) $150

Jones & Co.

— Views of the Seats, Mansions, Castles.... L, 1829. 2 vols. 4to, contemp half mor gilt; worn; Vol I spine torn. With 204 plates on 102 leaves. Some spotting. DW Nov 20 (15) £240

Anr copy. Vol II only. Contemp half calf; worn, spine lacking sections. With engraved title & 152 plates on 76 leaves.. pn Sept 12 (316) £190

Anr copy. Vols I & II only. Contemp half lea; worn. With 212 views on 106 leaves only. Some foxing & dampstaining. pn Dec 12 (312) £160 [Bifolco]

Anr Ed. L, [plates dated to 1831]. 2 vols. 4to, half calf; worn, broken. With engraved title & 240 views on 120 leaves, on india paper mtd. b June 22 (250) £80

Anr Ed. L, [n.d.]. 4to, contemp half calf; crudely rebacked. With 120 views on 60 sheets only. Sold w.a.f. bba Apr 30 (12) £130 [Erlini]

Jones Library, Herschel V.

— Adventures in Americana, 1492-1897.... NY, 1964. 3 vols. 4to, orig cloth. bba May 28 (509) £50 [Dawson]

Anr copy. 3 vols, including checklist. 4to, bba July 9 (15) £60 [Zaal]

Jones, Inigo, 1573-1652

— The Designs of Inigo Jones consisting of Plans and Elevations for...Buildings. L, 1727. 1st Ed. 2 vols in 1. Folio, contemp half calf; worn & rubbed. With frontis & 136 plates on 96 leaves. C Oct 30 (47) £2,400 [Pearl]

Anr copy. 2 vols. Folio, contemp calf; spine & corners renewed. With 136 plates on 97 leaves including 24 double-page plates. Lacking frontis; wormhole through gutter of 1st few leaves affecting caption of 1 plate; some creasing or damage at folds; other minor defs. CNY Jan 25 (31) $2,600

Anr copy. 2 vols in 1. Folio, calf; worn & split. With 107 plates. Minor tears or defs. pnE Aug 12 (97) £1,300

— The Most Notable Antiquity of Great Britain, Vulgarly Called Stone-Heng.... L, 1655. Folio, contemp calf; soiled & worn. With 4 large folding views slightly damaged; 1 leaf of introductory memoir torn, with resultant loss of 2 or 3 lines of text on both pp. 5 & 6. W July 8 (299) £120

2d Ed. L, 1725. 3 parts in 1 vol. Folio, contemp calf; rebacked, upper cover detached. With 14 plates, 8 double-page on guards or folding. Browning to frontis port & plates in Part 2; plates at p. 40 cropped with partial loss of scale; 3 plates shaved at tail edge. Milne copy. Ck June 12 (121) £320

Jones, Inigo, 1573-1652 —& Kent, William

— Some Designs of Mr. Inigo Jones and Mr. Wm. Kent.... L, 1744. Folio, 18th-cent calf; rebacked & restored. With engraved title, 2 engraved leaves of text & 53 plates. Some staining. McCarty-Cooper copy. CNY Jan 25 (32) $1,800

Jones, James

— From Here to Eternity. NY, 1951. 1st Ed. In d/j. cb Dec 12 (87) $50

Anr copy. In chipped d/j. F Dec 18 (234) $50

Anr copy. Sgd. sp Apr 16 (393) $70

Jones, John Paul, 1747-92

— Life and Correspondence of.... NY, 1830. 1st Ed. 8vo, orig half cloth; broken. Some foxing, old library bookplate at front pastedown. bbc June 29 (127) $100

Jones, Leslie Webber —& Morey, Charles Rufus

— The Miniatures of the Manuscripts of Terence prior to the Thirteenth Century. Princeton, 1930-31. 2 vols. Folio, cloth. sg Sept 6 (154) $300

Jones, Owen, 1809-74

— Examples of Chinese Ornament...in the South Kensington Museum. L, 1867. Folio, half mor gilt. Fore-edge of Plate 40 cropped; dampstaining to upper corners; marginal foxing. CNY Jan 25 (34) $950

Anr copy. Orig cloth; spotted. Lacking Plate 5. kh Nov 11 (144) A$1,300

— The Grammar of Ornament. L, 1856. Folio, contemp half mor gilt; upper cover stained, rubbed. With 100 colored plates. Some lower margins waterstained. bba June 25 (224) £1,000 [Ginnan]

Anr copy. Modern half mor. With colored additional title & 100 mostly colored plates. Tp torn & repaired; some preface leaves torn; 1 leaf repaired. Ck Dec 12 (285) £950

Anr copy. Late 19th-cent mor extra; scuffed, some corners restored. With chromolitho title & 100 chromolitho plates. Fore-edges of Plates 84 & 86 cropped with loss to plate numeral of Plate 86; 5-inch marginal repaired tear to F1 of Chapter VIII; other short marginal tears or repairs to text leaves; corners of Plates 94-100 bent. McCarty-Cooper copy. CNY Jan 25 (33) $3,000

Anr copy. Half lea. With 111 plates. Stamps on plate versos; marginal tear to 1 plate. pnL Nov 20 (184) £100 [Waxman]

Anr copy. Modern half mor preserving part of orig cloth design on upper cover. With colored additional title & 100 mostly colored plates. S Nov 15 (896) £1,300 [Sotheran]

Anr copy. Orig half mor; rebacked preserving spine. Library stamps on tp, plate versos & some text leaves; additional title strengthened along fore-edge. S Nov 21 (83) £1,100 [Price]

Anr Ed. L, [1865]. Folio, modern half calf. With litho title & 111 plate, hinged throughout. Stamp on tp. b June 22 (41) £80

Anr copy. Orig cloth; spine lacking. With litho title & 111 plate. Several plates dampstained at lower outer margin; section of outer margin of F1 excised. Sold w.a.f. Ck Dec 12 (286) £90

Anr copy. Orig cloth; worn. With chromolitho additional title & 112 plates. pn June 11 (167) £60

Anr copy. Orig cloth; loose. With litho title & 111 plates. pnE Aug 12 (123) £240

Anr Ed. L, 1868. Folio, orig cloth; rubbed. With illuminated title & 112 plates. DW Oct 9 (899) £180

Anr copy. Cloth. LH May 17 (593) $300

Anr copy. Later cloth. Library markings. sg Apr 2 (153) $275

— One Thousand and One Initial Letters. L, 1864. Folio, orig cloth. With engraved title & 27 plates in colors & gold. Occasional spotting. Ck July 10 (310) £280

Jones, Owen, 1809-74 —& Goury, Jules

— Plans, Elevations, Sections, and Details of the Alhambra.... L, 1842-45. 2 vols. Folio, half mor; worn, joints broken. With colored additional titles & 102 plates, many on india paper. Lacking un-numbered tailpiece in Vol II; Vol I additional title mtd; some staining to plate numbers; some surface dirt. S June 25 (175) £1,500 [Lester]

Jones, P. B.

— Photographs of the Eclipse of the Sun, August 7, 1869. Davenport, 1869. Orig half lea. Illus with orig albumen prints. NH Oct 6 (306) $1,600

Jones, Paul. See: Blunt & Jones

Jones, Capt. Robert

— Artificial Fireworks Improved to the Modern Practice. L, 1776. 2d Ed. 8vo, contemp calf. Lacking 4 plates. sg Nov 14 (290) $375

Anr copy. Contemp sheep; worn, rebacked, front cover detached. With 11 (of 12) folding plates. Marginal dampstaining throughout, with traces of mold at end. sg May 14 (285) $250

— A Treatise on Artificial Fireworks. L, 1765. 8vo, contemp mor gilt. With 5 folding plates. S July 9 (1278) £460 [Johnson]

Anr Ed. Chelmsford, 1801. ("Artificial Fireworks.") 8vo, modern half calf. With 20 plates on 10 leaves. Tear with loss to 1 leaf. S July 9 (1279) £220 [American Museum]

Jones, Stephen, 1763-1827. See: Oracles...

Jones, Thomas Gwynn. See: Gregynog Press

Jones, Virgil Carrington

— The Civil War at Sea. NY, [1960-62]. 3 vols. In d/js. sg Dec 5 (61) $200

Jones, Sir William, 1746-94

— Works. L, 1807. 13 vols. 8vo, contemp calf; rubbed. O Feb 25 (115) $300

Jonghe, Adriaan de. See: Junius, Hadrianus

Jonson, Ben, 1573?-1637

See also: Eragny Press

— Volpone: or the Fox. NY, 1898. Out of series copy on japan with an additional set of full-page plates. Illus by Aubrey Beardsley. 4to, orig vellum. Ck July 10 (311) £420

— Works. L, 1616-40. 1st Ed. 3 vols in 2. Folio, 18th-cent calf gilt; spine heads chipped, extremities rubbed. Engraved title in Vol I shaved at outer margin & with repaired tear at inner margin; lacking initial blank; some worming; general title to Vol II with section of lower blank margin excised & small hole at inner blank margin; some repaired tears. STC 14751 & 14754. C June 24 (325) £2,200 [Franklin]

Anr copy. Vol I only. Later calf; rebacked, joints laid down. Tp laid down; 1 prelim leaf lacking; some worming, spotting & soiling; old repairs to tail edge of a few leaves; 4Q4 laid down. STC 14751. Ck June 12 (122) £320

Anr Ed. L, 1640-[41]. Vol I only. later half calf; covers detached. Engraved title damaged; some soiling & browning. STC 14753. Milne copy. Ck June 12 (123) £75

Anr Ed. L, 1640. 2 vols. Contemp calf; Vol I worn. Port def at foot; tp & 1st few leaves frayed at lower margin & wormed. Sold w.a.f. STC 14753. pn Nov 14 (282) £130

Anr Ed. L, 1640-[41]. Vol I only. Folio, modern calf; joints split. 3C6-3E6 mtd on stubs; stained at inner margins; small hole in p. 123 affecting a few letters of text; a few leaves stained; some short tears to margins. STC 14753. S May 13 (774) £140 [Cumming]

Anr Ed. L, 1692. Folio, contemp calf; rebacked, hinges weak, worn. LH Dec 11 (137) $120

Anr Ed. L, 1716. 6 vols. 8vo, lea; spine repaired. sp Apr 16 (335) $90

Anr Ed. L, 1756. 7 vols. 8vo, half calf by Cross; rubbed. O May 26 (100) $550

Anr Ed. L, 1816. 9 vols. 8vo, contemp half sheep; rubbed. bba July 9 (201) £85 [Cox]

Anr copy. Contemp mor; rubbed, joints worn. Some foxing. O Aug 25 (112) $275

Jonston, John, 1603-75

— Historiae naturalis de quadrupetibus. Amst., 1657. Bound with: Historiae Naturalis de Abivus. Amst., 1657 Parts 1-4 (of 6). Folio, contemp calf; worn, upper cover detached. With title & 79 plates in first work; 62 (of 62) plates in second work. 4 plates with marginal tears; a few text leaves torn. Sold w.a.f. bba Sept 5 (65) £420 [Finney]

Anr copy. 6 parts in 2 vols. Folio, contemp mor gilt; worn,. With 4 engraved titles & 250 plates. Some browning; occasional marginal staining; tear in Plate 17 of Part 3; marginal tears & repairs. S June 25 (32) £3,000 [Marshall]

— Theatrum universale omnium animalium quadrupedum. Heilbronn, 1650-1757. 6 parts in 4 vols. Folio, 18th-cent calf gilt. With 4 engraved titles & 249 plates. FD Dec 2 (263) DM7,500

Jordanus de Quedlinburg

— Sermones Dan de sanctis. [Strassburg: Heinrich Knoblochtzer, not after 1481]. Folio, contemp blind-stamped calf over oak bds with remains of 2 brass clasps; damaged, rebacked, lower bd split. 57 lines, double-column; type 2:102G; woodcut Maiblumen initials; rubricated in red. 246

(of 248) leaves; lacking blanks 1 & 188. Goff J-478. P June 17 (244) $6,000

Jorgensen, Poul

— Salmon Flies; Their Character, Style, and Dressing. Harrisburg: Stackpole Books, [1978]. One of 250. 4to, lea. With a salmon fly mtd to limitation page. Koopman copy. O Oct 29 (184) $250

Jortin, John, 1698-1770

— The Life of Erasmus. L, 1758-60. 1st Ed. 2 vols. 4to, contemp half calf; rubbed, joints split. With port & 6 plates. bba Jan 16 (14) £130 [Jarndyce]

Joseph, Adrian M.

— Chinese and Annamese Ceramics Found in the Philippines and Indonesia. L, 1973. One of 1,020. 4to, cloth. With 125 color plates. cb Nov 21 (119) $160

Joseph, Jacques

— Nasenplastik und sonstige Gesichsplastik.... Leipzig, 1931. 4to, orig half lea. FD Dec 2 (240) DM1,400

Joseph, Michael

— A Book of Cats. NY, 1930. One of 500. Illus by Foujita. 4to, orig cloth. sg Jan 30 (54) $3,400

Josephus, Flavius, 37-100?

— De antiquitate Judaica.... Verona: Petrus Mauser, 25 Dec 1480. ("De bello Judaico.") Folio, calf. 211 (of 214) leaves. Goff J-484. sg Mar 12 (120A) $1,800

— Opera. Basel: Froben & Episcopius, 1544. Folio, contemp blind-tooled pigskin over oak bds; rubbed, foot of spine repaired, 1 clasp def. Greek type. Marginal wormhole at beginning & end; some staining. Harewood copy. C June 24 (276) £5,200 [Quaritch]

— Los Siete Libros...los quales contienen las Guerras de los Judios.... Antwerp: Martin Nucio, 1557. 8vo, 17th-cent sheep; spine brittle & worn. Some soiling. sg Mar 12 (161) $300

— Los veynte Libros de las Antiguedades Iudaycas. Antwerp: Martin Nucio, 1554. Folio, later vellum backed witih pigskin. Several leaves wormed in blank lower margin. sg Mar 12 (160) $850

— Works. L, 1609. Folio, old vellum. rs Oct 17 (84A) $150

Anr Ed. L, 1737. Folio, contemp calf; rubbed, rebacked. With 2 folding maps; half-title in Vol II. ESTC t112661. bba Aug 13 (103) £120 [Jacobus]

Anr copy. Old lea; spine worn, covers detached. With folding map & folding chart (3-inch tear in blank portion) & with anr copy of the folding map laid in. L.p. copy. K Mar 22 (205) $225

Josselyn, John

— An Account of Two Voyages to New-England.... L, 1674. 1st Ed. 8vo, contemp sheep; spine wormed with loss to lea at head & tail. DuPont copy. CNY Oct 8 (139) $3,800

Jouffroy, Alain

— Le Septieme Chant. Paris, [1974]. One of 100. Illus by Andre Masson. 4to, loose as issued. With 4 engravings & with an extra suite of the engravings, sgd. sg Jan 300 (101) $500

Jourdain, Margaret —& Lenygon, Francis

— English Decoration and Furniture of... 1500-1650. L, 1924. Folio, orig cloth. K July 12 (190) $75

Jourdan Collection, Carl

— [Sale Catalogue] Porzellan—Kunstgewerbe des XVI bis XVIII Jahrhunderts. Berlin, 1910. 4to, orig wraps; minor wear with a few chips. sg Sept 6 (13) $90

Journal...

— Journal des dames et des modes. Paris, 1829. Vol 23, Nos 1-36. 8vo, half sheep. With 48 hand-colored plates. sg Sept 19 (176) $250

— Journal fuer Ornithologie. Kassel, 1853-1914. Vols 1-62 & 1 Index vol. Various bdgs; 1 vol lacking upper cover & first few leaves. Library markings, including stamp on plates. Sold w.a.f. bba Aug 13 (366) £1,100 [Kiefer]

— Journal of Glass Studies. Corning: Corning Museum of Glass, 1959-81. Vols 1-23 & index for Vols 1-15. Orig wraps; some chipped. S July 1 (1142) £480

— The Journal of Indian Art. L, 1884-1916. Vols I-XVII in 16. Folio, all but 2 in orig cloth; rubbed & soiled. S Nov 15 (1197) £3,000 [R. S. Books]

— Journal of Natural Philosophy, Chemistry, and the Arts. L, 1798-1801. Vols I-IV (of 5). 4to, 19th-cent half vellum; soiled & rubbed. Library stamps on versos; Vols II-IV with half-titles. S Nov 15 (822) £180 [Nielsen]

Journal fuer Fabrik...

— Journal fuer Fabrik, Manufaktur, Handlung und Mode. Leipzig, 1796. 11 issues (lacking Sept). 8vo, ptd wraps; worn. O May 26 (101) $1,300

— Journal fuer Fabrik, Manufaktur und Handlung. Leipzig, 1797-1804. Vols 1-23 & 26-27. Orig bds. With 122 uncolored plates & 4 paper samples Sold w.a.f. S Dec 5 (336) £5,500 [Bucher Kabinett]

Journal-Manuel....
— Journal-Manuel de peintures appliquees a la decoration des monuments, appartements, magasins.... Paris, Mar 1850-Dec 1867. 7 vols. Folio, orig half mor; spines stained & scratched, hinges weak. A few repaired tears in text vols; foxing. McCarty-Cooper copy. CNY Jan 25 (35) $4,000

Joutel, Henri, 1640?-1735
See also: Caxton Club
— A Journal of the Last Voyage perform'd by Monsr. de la Sale, to the Gulph of Mexico.... L, 1714. 1st Ed in English. 8vo, contemp calf; rebacked. Map supplied in facsimile. cb Feb 12 (37) $550

Jovellanos, Gaspar Melchor de
— Informe de la sociedad de esta corte al real y supremo consejo de Castilla.... Madrid: Sancha, 1795. 4to, contemp calf; sides scraped, joints weak. S May 13 (840) £400 [Xilas]

Jovius, Paulus, 1483-1552
— De vita Leonis Decimi Pont. Max. Libri Quatuor. Florence: Laurentii Torrentini, 1549. Folio, 19th-cent half lea. Some browning. SI June 9 (421) LIt500,000
— Le Iscrittioni poste sotto le vere imagini de gli huomini famosi.... Florence: Torrentini, 1552. 4to, later half calf; backstrip def. Lacking last blank. bba Feb 27 (232) £120 [Bifolco]
— Turcicarum rerum commentarius. Antwerp: Johann Steelsius, 1538. 8vo, modern half mor by Sangorski & Sutcliffe. S June 30 (306) £320 [Atabey]

Joyant, Maurice
— Henri de Toulouse-Lautrec. Paris, 1927. Vol II only: Dessins, Estampes, Affiches. 4to, contemp half mor, orig wraps bound in. pn July 16 (111) £300

Joyce, James, 1882-1941
See also: Limited Editions Club
— Anna Livia Plurabelle. NY, 1928. One of 800. S July 21 (136) £900 [Cathach Books]
— Chamber Music. L, 1907. 1st Ed, 1st bdg variant. one of 509. Dannay-Manney copy. P Oct 11 (182) $4,250

Anr Ed. Bost., [1918]. sg Dec 12 (186) $200
— Collected Poems. NY: The Black Sun Press, 1936. 1st Ed, one of 750. sg Dec 12 (187) $375

Anr copy. Orig cloth. Epstein copy. sg Apr 30 (272) $500

Anr copy. Orig bds; edges soiled & rubbed. wa Mar 5 (212) $240
— Dubliners. L, [1914]. 1st Ed. In d/j. Epstein copy. sg Apr 30 (262) $16,000
— Exiles. NY, 1918. 1st American Ed. Flyleaves foxed. B May 12 (219) HF600
— Finnegans Wake. L, 1939. 1st Ed. Rear hinge cracked. cb Sept 19 (105) $550

1st Ed. K Mar 22 (206) $60

Anr copy. In chipped d/j. pn Dec 12 (213) £180 [Mackenzie]

Anr copy. In d/j. sg Dec 12 (188) $250

Anr copy. In d/j. Epstein copy. sg Apr 30 (265) $1,000

One of 425. Orig cloth; small dampstain on rear cover. With Corrections booklet laid in. CNY June 9 (101) $1,500

Anr copy. Backstrip faded. Title creased. Epstein copy. sg Apr 30 (264) $4,800

1st American Ed. NY, 1939. sp June 18 (435) $90
— Haveth Childers Everywhere. Paris, 1930. 1st Ed, one of 100 on japan. Folio, wraps. Epstein copy. sg Apr 30 (266) $3,200

One of 500. Orig wraps. sg June 11 (179) $425; wa Sept 26 (192) $375

[-] The Joyce Book. L: The Sylvan Press, [1933]. 1st Ed, one of 450. 4to, orig cloth; edges & corners worn. b June 22 (60) £190
— The Mime of Mick, Nick and the Maggies. The Hague: Servire Press, 1934. 1st Ed, one of 1,000. Orig wraps. bba Apr 30 (197) £160 [Edrich]; sg Dec 12 (189) $375

Anr copy. Orig wraps. Epstein copy. sg Apr 30 (267) $475

[-] Our Exagmination round his Factification for Incamination of Work in Progress. Paris, 1929. 1st Ed. Modern half mor, orig wraps bound in. Browned; last leaf of text soiled. bba Aug 13 (239) £130 [Catnach]

Anr copy. Wraps; corner chipped, dampstained. sg Dec 12 (197) $120

One of 96 on verge d'Arches. Orig wraps, unopened. Inscr by Sylvia Beach. Epstein copy. sg Apr 30 (268) $4,000
— Pomes Penyeach. Paris: Shakespeare & Co., 1927. 1st Ed. Orig bds; edges chipped, shaken. bbc Dec 9 (492) $60

Anr copy. Orig bds; spine worn. sg Dec 12 (190) $200

Anr copy. Orig bds; spine worn & chipped, shaken. With errata leaf. sg June 11 (180) $110
— A Portrait of the Artist as a Young Man. NY, 1916. 1st Ed. sg Dec 12 (191) $400

Anr copy. Epstein copy. sg Apr 30 (269) $1,000

Anr copy. Cloth; hinges reinforced. Library markings on pastedowns. sg June 11 (181) $275

Anr copy. Cloth; rubbed, hinges weak. Library stamp. wd Dec 12 (411) $350

1st English Ed. L, [1917]. American sheets. Orig cloth; joint torn. sg Dec 12

(192) $325

[-] A Protest. Paris, 2 Feb 1927. Single sheet, 8vo size Petition protesting the unauthorized American publication in Two Worlds Monthly by Sam Roth, with ptd signatures of eminent literary figures who support the protest. sg Dec 12 (198) $900

— Tales Told of Shem and Shaun. Paris: Black Sun Press, 1929. 1st Ed, One of 500. Orig bds. Ck July 10 (312) £220

Anr copy. Orig wraps. sg Dec 12 (193) $850

Anr copy. Orig wraps. Epstein copy. sg Apr 30 (270) $650

Anr copy. Orig wraps; splitting along front joint, stain at foot of spine. sg June 11 (182) $350

— Two Essays: A Forgotten Aspect...and "The Day of the Rabblement...." Dublin, [1901]. 1st Ed. Loose in orig wraps; some wear. S July 21 (137) £1,500 [Cathach Books]

— Ulysse. Paris, 1929. 1st Ed in French, one of 25 on hollande van Gelder. 4to, half mor by L. Leveque, orig wraps bound in. Simonson copy. S May 28 (363) £1,400 [Beres]

— Ulysses. Paris, 1922. 1st Ed, one of 750 on handmade paper. 4to, half deerskin by Hatcherds. C Dec 16 (257) £1,000 [Frohlich]

Anr copy. Orig wraps; rebacked to match, tear at bottom of front cover repaired on verso. Inscr to Lewis Galantiere, 11 Feb 1922 & with Galantiere's notes. CNY June 9 (100) $18,000

Anr copy. Orig wraps; spine ends torn with some loss; a few small stains. pn Dec 12 (214) £2,400

Anr copy. Cloth, orig wraps bound in; worn. Lacking prelim blanks; 1 final blank only. S July 21 (140) £2,200 [Cathach Books]

Anr copy. Orig wraps; one repaired tear on backstrip. Epstein copy. sg Apr 30 (271) $18,000

2d Ptg (1st English Ed). Paris: Pbd for the Egoist Press, L, by John Rodker, 1922. 4to, cloth, orig upper wrap bound in. Lacking blanks & errata leaves; some browning at margins. S Feb 25 (407) £150 [Interagent]

Anr copy. Orig wraps; worn, joints & spine ends rubbed. S July 21 (138) £500 [Cathach Books]

Anr copy. Orig wraps; rebacked, orig spine preserved. sg Dec 12 (195) $450

Anr copy. Orig wraps; split along joints, chipped, worn. sg June 11 (183) $600

Anr copy. Orig wraps; soiled & stained, frayed & chipped, spine tape-repaired, contents broken at p. 350. Browned; lacking errata slip. wa Sept 26 (193) $230

Anr copy. Half calf gilt, orig wraps bound in; extremities rubbed, head of spine chipped. Marginal dampstain at beginning & end. wa Mar 5 (214) $300

4th Ptg. Paris, 1924. 4to, orig wraps; worn, laid down & bound in. Inscr to Alys Eyre Macmillan, 5 Apr 1927. S July 21 (139) £1,500 [Cathach Books]

Anr copy. Sheep; soiled & worn. sg Dec 12 (196) $110

Anr Ed. NY: Two Worlds Publishing, 1926-27. In 9 parts. Orig wraps. In: Two Worlds Monthly, Vol I, Nos 1-9. cb Dec 12 (88) $200

Anr copy. Parts 1-11. 8vo, orig wraps; worn & chipped. In: Two Worlds Monthly, Vol I, No 1 through Vol III, No 3. F June 25 (744) $110

9th Ptg. Paris, 1927. 4to, cloth; upper cover loose. bba Oct 10 (444) £60 [Christian]

Anr copy. Half mor gilt, orig wraps bound in; worn. sg June 11 (184) $50

10th Ptg. Paris, 1928. 4to, orig wraps; soiled, spine lacking 2 fragments. wa Mar 5 (213) $95

1st Ptg in England. L, 1936. one of 900. Orig cloth. bba July 9 (272) £190 [Sotheran]

Anr copy. Orig cloth; rubbed. S Nov 14 (646) £210

Joyce, Jeremiah, 1763-1816

— Scientific Dialogues, Intended for the Instruction and Entertainment of Young People. L, 1815. 7 vols. 12mo, contemp calf; joints cracked, worn. With 24 plates. Corner torn from 1 leaf; some foxing. bba July 23 (245) £80 [Hashimoto]

Jubinal, Achille, 1810-75

— La Armeria Real.... Paris, [c.1840]. 2 vols in 1. Folio, contemp half mor. With titles within hand-colored litho borders & 81 hand-colored plates. Some spotting to text at end. S July 9 (1281) £1,000 [Dennistoun]

Judson, Ann Hamilton

— An Account of the American Baptist Mission to the Burman Empire. L, 1823. 8vo, orig bds; rebacked preserving orig spine-label. Some foxing & soiling. O May 26 (102) $130

Juifs...

— Les Juifs. Temoignages de Notre Temps No 2. Paris, Sept 1933. Designed by Alexander Liberman. Folio, loose in pictorial wraps; worn. sg Oct 8 (75) $250

Jukes, Joseph Beete, 1811-69

— Narrative of the Surveying Voyage of H. M. S. Fly.... L, 1847. 1st Ed. 2 vols. 8vo, contemp mor. With 2 folding maps & 19 plates. S June 25 (142) £1,300 [Quaritch]

Anr copy. 1st Issue bdg of blue cloth; spines faded. S June 25 (210) £4,200 [Quaritch/Hordern]

— A Sketch of the Physical Structure of Australia.... L, 1850. Orig cloth. Phillipps copy. S June 25 (243) £900 [Quaritch/Hordern]

Julianus, Emperor, 331-63

— Opera. Paris: D. Duval, 1583. 1st Collected Ed. 4 parts in 1 vol. 8vo, calf; rebacked. bba May 28 (433) £180 [Poole]

Junius, Pseud.

— Letters of Junius. L, 1796. 2 vols. 8vo, contemp calf gilt. pnE Mar 11 (135) £110

Junius, Franciscus, 1589-1677

— De pictura veterum.... Amst.: Blaeu, 1637. 4to, contemp vellum gilt; minor defs. Some stains; 2 quires misbound. B May 12 (263) HF700

— Etymologicum Anglicanum. Oxford, 1743. Folio, later half calf over bds. With port. bba June 11 (53) £260 [Robertshaw]

Junius, Hadrianus, 1511-75

— Emblemata.... Antwerp: Plantin, 1565. 8vo, recent vellum. With 58 woodcut emblems. B Nov 1 (334) HF3,400

Anr copy. Bdg not stated. bba Sept 19 (283) £280 [Hesketh & Ward]

Anr copy. 19th-cent mor; spine rubbed. With 58 woodcut emblems. Ck Oct 31 (86) £500

Jurine, Louis

— Memoire sur l'angine de poitrine. Paris, 1815. 8vo, contemp half sheep; Foxed at ends. sg Nov 14 (62) $250

Just. See: Kipling, Rudyard

Justin Martyr, Saint

— Opera. Cologne, 1686. Folio, contemp vellum. Title stamped. sg Mar 12 (162) $110

Justinianus I, Emperor, 483-565

— Infortiatum. Nuremberg: Anton Koberger, 1503. Folio, contemp blind-tooled pigskin over wooden bds. Wormed at beginning & end; lacking tp & last leaf. sg Oct 24 (173) $375

— Instituten warhaffte Dolmetschung. Augsburg: A. Weyssenhorn, 1536. Bound with: Instituta Einleytung. Frankfurt: C. Egenolff, 1536. And: Noariatbuch. Frankfurt: C. Egenolff, 1535. And: Die Lehenrechtvergeutscht. Worms, 1536. 8vo, contemp vellum; spine damaged. S Dec 5 (156) £7,000 [Franks]

Justinus, Marcus Junianus

— Epitome in Trogi Pompeii historias. [Venice: Joannes Rubeus Vercellensis & Albertinus Vercellensis, after 1489-90]. Folio modern bds; front joint cracked. sg Mar 12 (121) $750

Anr Ed. Leiden: Elzevir, 1640. ("Justini historiarum ex Trogo Pompeio libri XLIV....") 12mo, early 19th-cent mor gilt by Simier. sg Oct 24 (174) $250

— Nelle Historie de Trogo Pompeio, novamente in lingua toscana tradotto. Venice: Nicolo Zopino & Vincentio Compagno, 1524. 8vo, contemp calf; worn. bba Feb 27 (222) £250 [Marlborough]

Juvenal des Ursins, Jean

— Histoire de Charles VI, Roy de France.... Paris, 1653. Folio, contemp calf; rebacked retaining most of orig backstrip. Some foxing. sg Oct 24 (176) $250

Juvenalis, Decimus Junius, 60-140 A.D. —& Persius Flaccus, Aulus, 34-62 A.D.

— Satirae. Utrecht: Rudolphus a Zyll, 1685. 4to, contemp vellum. With engraved title. sg Oct 24 (175) $120

— Satires. Oxford, 1673. Trans by Barten Holyday. Folio, contemp calf; worn, rebacked, orig spine preserved. With 4 plates. Hinges crudely repaired. bba Oct 24 (51) £60 [Rix]

Anr copy. Old calf; joints weak, covers detaching. K Sept 29 (217) $110

— Satyrae. Venice: Baptista de Tortis, 1482 & Venice: Reynaldus de Novimagio, 1482. Folio, later Italian carta rustica. Some dampstaining at beginning & end; Ms annotations in margins of 1st work (some shaved). 77 (of 78) leaves, lacking final blank, & 22 leaves. Goff J-646 & P-345. S May 28 (26) £600 [Zioni]

Anr Ed. Venice: Johannes Tacuinus de Tridino, 24 July 1498. Folio, 18th-cent vellum. Types 3:108R, 1:82R & 82GK. Repair to lower blank margins of prelims; some dampstaining at beginning. 318 leaves. Goff J-666. C Nov 27 (19) £1,300 [Bifolco]

Anr Ed. Venice: Aldus, Aug 1501. 8vo, modern calf. Tp holed with loss of 2 characters & repaired with missing characters supplied in Ms; Harvard College stamps & release stamps. Ck Oct 31 (2) £380

K

Kabotie, Fred. See: Grabhorn Printing

Kaempfer, Engelbert

— The History of Japan. L, 1727-28. 2 vols. Folio, contemp calf; rebacked. With engraved title & 45 plates & maps. A few plates shaved. S June 25 (466) £400 [Barberini]

Anr Ed. L, 1727-28 [but Kyoto: Bunji Yoshida, 1929]. 2 vols. Folio, orig half cloth; def & nearly disbound. Titles & some other prelims detached. wa Dec 9 (494) $210

Kafka, Franz, 1883-1924
See also: Limited Editions Club

— Amerika. Norfolk CT, [1940]. Trans by Edwin Muir. In d/j. K Mar 22 (211) $65

— In der Strafkolonie. Leipzig, 1919. 1st Ed. Orig half calf. HH May 12 (23434) DM2,200

— The Metamorphosis. L: Parton Press, 1937. 1st Ed in English. Orig cloth, in d/j. Manney copy. P Oct 11 (1184) $4,250

— Die Verwandlung. Leipzig: Kurt Wolff, [1915]. Orig wraps; edge wear. Epstein copy. sg Apr 29 (273) $5,000

Kahnweiler, Daniel Henry

— Les Sculptures de Picasso. Paris, 1948 [1949]. 4to, half cloth. LH May 17 (675) $110

Kaiser, Henry J. See: Grabhorn Printing

Kaler, James Otis

— Toby Tyler or Ten Weeks with a Circus. NY, 1881. 1st Ed. 12mo, orig cloth; soiled & rubbed, shaken. With 1 leaf & 1 plate tape-repaired; some fraying. K July 12 (301) $60

Anr copy. Pictorial cloth; edges worn, hinges tender. sg Oct 17 (287) $60

Kandinsky, Wassily, 1866-1944
See also: Grohmann, Will

— Kandinsky: Bauhaus de Dessau 1927-1933. Paris: Maeght, [1965]. One of 150. Folio, loose in wraps as issued. Derriere le Mirior. sg Apr 2 (156) $500

— On the Spiritual in Art. NY, 1946. sg Apr 2 (155) $200

— Punkt und Linie zu Flaeche. Munich, 1926. 4to, orig wraps. With 26 plates, 1 colored. Bauhausbuecher No 9. DW Oct 9 (582) £135; DW Oct 9 (583) £125

Kandinsky, Wassily, 1866-1944 —& Marc, Franz, 1880-1916

— Der Blaue Reiter. Munich, 1914. 4to, half mor; soiled. With 4 colored plates. S Nov 14 (20) £260 [Mytze]

Kane, Elisha Kent, 1820-57

— Arctic Explorations. NY, 1854. ("The U. S. Grinnell Expedition in Search of Sir John Franklin....") 8vo, half lea. sp Apr 16 (481) $60

Anr Ed. Phila., 1856. 2 vols. 8vo, orig cloth; worn & chipped. With port, 3 maps & 12 plates. Inscr. F Dec 18 (626) $130

Anr copy. Orig cloth; extremities rubbed. With 16 plates, 2 ports & 3 maps. Inscr to Washington Irving. Manney copy. P Oct 11 (194) $1,000; sp Apr 16 (272) $60

Kane, Paul, 1810-71

— Wanderings of an Artist among the Indians of North America. L, 1859. 8vo, orig cloth. With folding map, port & 7 plates. cb Feb 12 (38) $850

Kane, Thomas L. See: Grabhorn Printing

Kanneman, Johannes

— Passio Jesu Christi.... [Nuremberg: Peter Wagner, not after 15 June] 1491. 3d Ed. 4to, early 19th-cent half calf; worn, head of spine chipped. 1st lines of c.13 pp shaved or cropped with loss of an entire line of 1 leaf. 88 leaves. Goff K-8. George Milne copy. CNY Dec 5 (267) $500

Kant, Immanuel, 1724-1804

— Anthropologie in pragmatischer Hinsicht. Koenigsberg, 1798. 1st Ed. 8vo, contemp half calf gilt. HH may 12 (1405) DM1,200

Anr copy. Contemp half sheep; spine brittle & rubbed. sg Mar 12 (165) $350

— Critick of Pure Reason.... L: Pickering, 1838. 8vo, contemp calf; rebacked. DW Nov 6 (299) £65

— Critik der practischen Vernunft. Riga, 1788. 8vo, contemp half calf. HH May 12 (1407) DM1,300

— Critik der reinen Vernunft. Riga, 1781. 1st Ed. 8vo, contemp half calf. HH May 12 (1409) DM8,000

2d Ed. Riga, 1787. 8vo, contemp half calf; rubbed, joints cracked. S Nov 14 (428) £350 [Thoemmes]

3d Ed. Frankfurt, 1791. 8vo, contemp half sheep; worn. sg Oct 24 (179) $250

— Critik der Urtheilskraft. Berlin & Libau, 1790. 1st Ed. 8vo, contemp bds; worn, backstrip chipped. Lacking final blank & rear free endpaper. sg Oct 24 (178) $1,000

— Logik. Konigsberg, 1800. 8vo, contemp half sheep; spine def. sg Oct 24 (180) $175

— Prolegomena zu einer jeden kuenftigen

Metaphysik die als Wissenschaft wird auftreten koennen. Riga, 1783. 8vo, contemp half sheep; extremities worn, lacking backstrip. Tp foxed & soiled. sg Oct 24 (177) $300

Kantz, Caspar

— Die historia des leydens unsers herrn Jesu Christi. Nuremberg: Valentin Geissler, 1555. 8vo, contemp blind-stamped calf; upper cover rubbed, lacking 2 clasps. S May 28 (50) £700 [P & P Books]

Kappel, August Wilhelm —& Kirby, W. Egmont

— British and European Butterflies and Moths. L, [1896]. 8vo, mor gilt. With 30 colored plates. pn June 11 (233) £150 [Phelps]

Anr copy. Pictorial cloth. sg Sept 19 (195) $50

Karaka, Dosabhai Franji

— History of the Parsis.... L, 1884. 2 vols. 8vo, half calf; rubbed. O Feb 242 (116) $275

Karl, Johann Friedrich

— Vue et prospect des differentes parties du parc pres du Chateau de Freundenhaim.... Passau, [c.1770]. Oblong 4to, half calf. With 26 plates. HH May 12 (555) DM1,500

Karolik Collection, M. & M.

— American Paintings 1815 to 1865. Bost., 1949 [but 1951]. 4to, cloth; worn. O Jan 14 (97) $225

Karpel, Bernard

— Arts in America: A Bibliography. Wash., [1979]. 4 vols. Folio, cloth; worn. O Sept 24 (134) $70; O Aug 25 (113) $80

Karpinski, Louis Charles

— Bibliography of Mathematical Works printed in America through 1850. Ann Arbor, 1940. 4to, cloth, in torn d/j. wa Apr 9 (28) $140

Kauffer, E. McKnight

— The Art of the Poster. L, 1924. 4to, orig half cloth. Prelims browned. sg Apr 2 (236) $275

Kavraiskii, Fedor Fedorovich

— Lososevyia Kavkaza. Die Lachse des Kaukasus. Tiflis: Chancery Press, 1896. 8vo, orig cloth. With 10 plates, 9 of them colored. C May 20 (189) £260 [Schober]

Kay, John, 1742-1826

— A Series of Original Portraits and Caricature Etchings. Edin., 1837-38. 2 vols. 4to, half calf. With 230 plates. b&b Feb 19 (45) $90

Anr Ed. Edin., 1842. Vols I & II (of 4). 4to, half mor; rubbed & worn. cb Sept 26 (135) $75

Anr Ed. Edin., 1877. 2 vols. 4to, contemp half mor. With frontis & 360 plates. L.p. copy. Ck May 15 (115) £190

Anr copy. Half mor. With 361 plates, all hand-colored. pnE Dec 4 (68) £280

Kaye, Sir John William, 1814-76

— History of the War in Afghanistan. L, 1851. 1st Ed. 2 vols. 8vo, contemp calf; browned & chipped at edges, rebacked. DW Oct 2 (43) £110

Keate, George, 1729-97

— An Account of the Pelew Islands. Dublin, 1788. 8vo, contemp calf; rebacked. With port, folding map & 15 plates. bba Jan 30 (358) £90 [Zaal]

2d Ed. L, 1788. 8vo, contemp calf; rubbed, covers detached. With port, folding map & 15 plates. Some soiling. S Nov 15 (1325) £150 [Hayes]

Anr Ed. Dublin, 1790. 8vo, contemp calf; rebacked, old spine laid down. With port, folding map & 15 plates, 1 folding. Folding map reinforced on verso; folding plate repaired at outer margin; plates browned. Ck May 15 (116) £180

Anr Ed. L, 1793. 8vo, rebound. With 16 plates & folding chart. Library markings. K Sept 29 (317) $90

Keating Collection, George T.

— A Conrad Memorial Library.... Garden City, 1929. One of 501. 4to, cloth, unopened. cb Oct 17 (489) $110

Keats, John, 1795-1821

See also: Golden Cockerel Press

— The Collected Sonnets. Maastricht: Halcyon Press, 1930. One of 376. Illus by John Buckland Wright. Cloth. With an additional suite of the illusts on japon, each sgd & mtd. S Apr 28 (21) £520 [Aust. Nat. Gall.]

— Endymion. L, 1818. 1st Ed. 8vo, 19th-cent mor gilt by Zaehnsdorf, 1895; head of spine chipped, extremities rubbed. With 5-line errata & the 1-line erratum. Tp soiled. C Dec 16 (209) £1,500 [Finch]

Anr copy. Lev gilt. Lacking half-title; some browning. P Dec 12 (58B) $4,000

Anr copy. Mor by Riviere; joints rubbed, cracked along upper joint. With 1-line erratum leaf & 5-line errata slip (inlaid). P June 17 (246) $1,800

Anr copy. Orig bds; spine separating along upper joint; some rubbing. With 1-line erratum leaf & 5-line errata slip. Half-title in facsimile. P June 17 (247) $1,700

— The Eve of St. Agnes. L: Essex House Press, 1900. One of 125 ptd on vellum. Orig vellum. sg Sept 26 (107) $600

— The Keats Letters...in the Hampstead Public Library. L, 1914. One of 320. Ed by G. C. Williamson. Folio, orig half vellum bds; rubbed & soiled. bba July 23 (437) £80 [Books & Prints]

— Lamia, Isabella, The Eve of St. Agnes, and Other Poems. L, 1820. 1st Ed. 12mo, later mor gilt; rubbed, spine ends worn. bba June 25 (197) £1,800 [Kitzzawa]

Anr copy. Contemp calf gilt; spine soiled & rubbed. C Dec 16 (210) £2,500 [Maggs]

Anr copy. Lev gilt by Zaehnsdorf. P Dec 12 (58C) $4,000

— Life, Letters, and Literary Remains. L, 1848. Ed by Richard Moncton Milnes. 2 vols. 8vo, orig cloth. bba June 25 (198) £220 [Dailey]

Anr copy. Orig cloth; Vol II spine def. NH Aug 23 (236) $50

— Poems. L, 1817. 1st Ed. 16mo, mor gilt; 1st quire a little loose. P Dec 12 (58A) $9,000

— The Poetical Works. L, 1866. 8vo, Mor gilt by Keeliegram. O May 26 (104) $300

— Poetical Works. NY, 1938-39. One of 1,050. Intro by John Masefield. 8 vols. cb Dec 5 (69) $150

Keene, J. Harrington

— Fly-Fishing and Fly-making for Trout.... NY, 1887. 8vo, cloth; worn. With 2 pages of mtd fly-tying materials. O Oct 29 (186) $275

Anr Ed. NY, 1891. 8vo, cloth. cb Jan 30 $90

Keese, John

— Floral Keepsake for 1850. NY, 1850. 4to, cloth; worn. Witth 30 colored plates. O Apr 28 (175) $190

Kehimkar, Haeem Samuel

— The History of the Bene Israel of India. Tel Aviv, 1937. Pictorial bds. sg June 25 (121) $225

Keill, John

— An Examination of Dr. Burnet's Theory of the Earth. L, 1734. 8vo, contemp sheep; worn, joints starting. With 13 folding plates. sg May 14 (286) $275

— An Introduction to the True Astronomy. L, 1730. 2d Ed. 8vo, contemp half calf; detached. With 27 folding plates. cb Sept 5 (52) $75

Keith, E. C.

— Gun for Company. L, 1937. One of 175. Illus by J. C. Harrison. 4to, orig cloth. L Nov 14 (416) £140

Keith, Sir William

— The History of the British Plantations in America. L, 1738. Part I (all pbd). 4to, contemp calf gilt; rebacked, corners restored. With 2 folding maps. First map with small fold tear; text spotted. Signet-duPont copy. CNY Oct 8 (140) $1,700

Anr copy. Calf gilt by Riviere; upper cover detached. Washed; 1st folding map torn & restored; 2d map def at corner. CNY Oct 8 (141) $1,400

Keller, Ferdinand

— The Lake Dwellings of Switzerland.... L, 1878. 2d Ed. 2 vols. 8vo, orig cloth; worn, Vol II shaken, with some plates loose. With 206 plates. O May 26 (105) $100

Keller, Helen

— Midstream. My Later Life. Garden City, 1929. 2d Ed. Inscr. K Mar 22 (214) $70

Anr copy. Sgd in braille & in pencil. K Mar 22 (215) $100

Kelley, J. D. Jerrold, 1847-1922. See: Wagner & Kelley

Kellner, Heinrich

— Chronica. Das ist: Warhaffte eigentliche und kuertze Beschreibung.... Frankfurt: Paul Reffeler for Sigmunt Feyerabend, 1574. Bound with: Feyerabend, Sigmund. Respublica. Das ist: Warhaffte eigentlicheund kuertze Beschreibung, der herrlichen und weitberuempten Statt Venedig. Frankfurt, 1574. Folio, contemp vellum; soiled, spine broken. Hole affecting letters on tp near fore-margin of 1st work; waterstains to 2d work. S Nov 21 (180) £1,600 [Reiss & Auvermann]

Kelly, Arthur

— The Rosebud, and Other Tales. L, 1909. Illus by Walter Crane. 4to, orig cloth. With 20 colored plates. cb Jan 9 (53) $70

Kelly, Charles

— Old Greenwood: the Story of Caleb Greenwood.... Salt Lake City: Pvtly ptd, 1936. One of 350. Cloth, in d/j. cb Nov 14 (98) $110

Anr copy. Cloth, in tattered d/j. NH May 30 (572) $115

— Salt Desert Trails.... Salt Lake City, 1930. Syn. NH Aug 23 (282) $80

Kelly, Christopher

— A New and Complete System of Universal Geography. L, 1814-17. 2 vols. 4to, contemp calf; worn. With engraved titles, frontises & 82 maps & plates, 4 hand-colored in outline. Some spotting & browning. Ck Oct 18 (68) £230

Anr Ed. L, 1833. 2 vols. 4to, orig cloth. With 32 maps & 50 plates. L Nov 14 (151) £160

Kelly, Robert Talbot, 1861-1934

— Egypt: Painted and Described by.... L, 1902. 1st Ed, one of 500. 4to, orig cloth. DW Dec 11 (9) £230

Kelly, William

— A Stroll through the Diggings of California. L, 1852. One of 750. 8vo, half cloth. Bookcase Library, Vol IV. cb Nov 14 (99) $85

Kelman, John

— The Holy Land. L, 1902. Illus by John Fulleylove. 4to, orig cloth; spine darkened. DW Dec 11 (10) £110

Kelmscott Press—London

— Psalmi Penitentiales. 1894. One of 300. Ck July 10 (243) £180

— Syr Perecyvelle of Gales. 1895. One of 350. wa Mar 5 (112) $325

— Blunt, Wilfrid Scawen. - The Love-Lyrics and Songs of Proteus.... 1892. One of 300. Bdg soiled. cb Dec 5 (70) $350; S Nov 14 (66) £360 [Barnitt]

— Chaucer, Geoffrey. - Works. 1896. One of 425. Back bd badly worn. CNY Dec 5 (2770) $20,000; HH May 12 (2355) DM28,000

Anr copy. Epstein copy. sg Apr 29 (78) $32,000

Trial 1st text page (b1 recto).. bba May 28 (256) £350 [Quaritch]

— Mackail, John William. - Biblia Innocentium: Being the Story of God's Chosen People.... 1892. One of 200. Ck July 10 (334) £190

— Meinhold, William. - Sidonia the Sorceress. 1893. One of 300. Rebound in half mor. O May 26 (106) $325

— Morris, William. - Child Christopher and Goldilind the Fair. 1895. One of 600. 2 vols. O May 26 (107) $250

— Morris, William. - A Dream of John Ball and a King's Lesson 1892. One of 11 on vellum. Mor extra by Riviere. Benz copy. CNY Dec 5 (428) $7,500

— Morris, William. - Gothic Architecture.... 1893. One of 1,500. bba Oct 24 (211) £90 [Elstree Books]; bba July 9 (350) £630 [Marks]

Anr copy. With inscr to Edward Burne-Jones in a hand that may or not be that of Morris. K Jul 12 (302) $350

— Morris, William. - News from Nowhere: or, an Epoch of Rest.... 1893. One of 300. John Lehmann's copy. S Nov 14 (577) £350 [Brown]

— Morris, William. - Poems by the Way. 1891. One of 100 L.p. copies. William Morris's copy; later library markings. sg Mar 5 (196) $175

— Morris, William. - The Water of the Wondrous Isles. 1897. One of 250. sg Sept 26 (137) $500

— Morris, William. - The Well at the World's End. 1896. One of 350. bba Apr 30 (355) £550 [Subunso]

— Rossetti, Dante Gabriel. - Sonnets and Lyrical Poems. 1894. One of 310. Vellum. CNY Dec 5 (268) $650

— Shakespeare, William. - The Poems of William Shakespeare. 1893. One of 500. S Nov 14 (65) £400 [Seibu]; sg Sept 26 (138) $500

— Shelley, Percy Bysshe. - The Poetical Works. [1894]-95. One of 250. 3 vols. CNY Dec 5 (269) $1,000

— Swinburne, Algernon Charles. - Atalanta in Calydon. 1894. One of 250. Inscr by William Morris to Sydney Cockerell. Also inscr by Swinburne. With Morris's orig design for title, 12 orig drawings for initials, his 9-line holograph draft for the colophon & his handwritten list of people to receive complimentary copies. Epstein copy. sg Apr 30 (447) $14,000

Kelson, George M.

— The Salmon Fly. L, 1895. 4to, orig cloth; spine & small section of upper cover faded. With 8 chromolithos. S Nov 15 (745) £260 [Thorp]

Anr copy. Orig cloth; upper joint cracked. Some dampstains. S July 1 (922) £150 [Sotheran]

Keltie, Sir John Scott, 1840-1927

— A History of the Scottish Highlands, Clans and Regiments. Edin. & L, 1875. 2 vols. 8vo, modern half calf. pnE May 13 (45) £75

Kemble, John Philip, 1757-1823

[-] An Authentic Narrative of Mr. Kemble's Retirement from the Stage. L, 1817. 4to, 19th-cent half calf; worn, frontis & tp loose. sg Mar 5 (240) $50

— Remarks on the Character of Richard the Third. L, [1801]. 2d Ed. 8vo, self-wraps. Tp & last page soiled. sg Oct 17 (64) $150

Kendall, George Wilkins, 1809-67

— Narrative of the Texan Santa Fe Expedition.... NY, 1844. 1st Ed. 2 vols. 12mo, orig cloth. With folding map & 5 plates. Map repaired. Presentation copy, inscr. cb Nov 14 (100) $750

Anr copy. Contemp half calf. O Nov 26 (95) $475

Anr copy. Orig cloth. Some foxing; tear to map. sg June 18 (312) $350

Anr copy. Map with 90mm tear; some foxing. sg June 18 (313) $250

Anr Ed. L, 1845. 2 vols. 12mo, orig cloth; rubbed. Folding map slightly torn. bba Apr 30 (50) £60 [Zaal]

Anr copy. Orig cloth; spines faded. cb Feb 12 (39) $325

7th Ed. NY, 1856. 2 vols. 12mo, cloth. With folding map & 5 plates. Some foxing. sg Dec 5 (131) $425

— The War Between the United States and Mexico Illustrated. NY, 1851. Folio, wraps, in modern half mor portfolio with portion of orig cloth front cover laid on. With 12 hand-colored plates & map. cb Feb 12 (40) $6,500

— The War between the United States and Mexico.... NY, 1851. Illus by Carl Nebel. Folio, orig half mor; worn, covers detached. With engraved map & 12 hand-colored plates. Plates 2 & 12 discolored; some text leaves including tp with long tears into text mended with tape. P June 16 (236) $1,700

Kendall, Henry Clarence, 1841-82

— Leaves from Australian Forests. Melbourne, 1869. 1st Ed. 8vo, orig cloth. Postal seal laid to verso of half-title. kh Nov 11 (531) A$90

Kenderdine, Thaddeus S.

— A California Tramp and Later Footprints.... Newtown, Pa., 1888. 1st Ed. 8vo, cloth. sg June 18 (87) $50

Kendrick, Albert Frank —& Tattersall, Creassey Edward Cecil

— Hand-Woven Carpets, Oriental & European. L, 1922. 2 vols. 4to, orig cloth. kh Nov 11 (145) A$375

Anr copy. Orig cloth; soiled & worn. W Mar 6 (6) £140

Kendrick, Tertius T. C.

— The Ionian Islands. L, 1822. 8vo, contemp half calf; rubbed, spine head chipped, upper joint split. Folding frontis spotted. S June 30 (327) £380 [Spink]

Kenly, John R., 1822-91

— Memoirs of a Maryland Volunteer: War with Mexico.... Phila., 1873. 1st Ed. 8vo, bdg not described but spine stained. K Sept 29 (261) $55

Kennedy, Sir Alexander Blackie William

— Petra. L, 1925. Orig half cloth; rubbed & soiled. With frontis, 4 maps (1 on 2 sheets in rear pocket), 3 full-page plates & 211 figures on 72 plates. Library stamp on free endpaper & tp verso. wa Apr 9 (109) $120

Kennedy, Archibald

— The Importance of Gaining and Preserving the Friendship of the Indians to the British Interest, Considered.... NY: James Parker, 1751. 8vo, modern mor gilt by Elizabeth Greenhill. Lacking A1; outer corner of A4 torn away without loss. P June 16 (48) $12,000

Kennedy, Edmund B.

— Supplements to the New South Wales Government Gazette...Monday, January 24, 1848, No 9. Sydney: W. W. Davies, 1848. Folio, disbound. Detailing on pp.95-102 the particulars of the expedition undertaken to ascertain the course of the river Victoria [Barcoo]. R. J. Maria copy. C June 25 (241) £450 [Baring]

Kennedy, Edward Guthrie, 1849-1932. See: Grolier Club

Kennedy, John Fitzgerald, 1917-63

— The Strategy of Peace. NY, [1960]. Pictorial wraps. With Cs laid in. pba Aug 20 (126) $550

Kennedy, Joseph P.

— I'm for Roosevelt. NY, 1936. In d/j. Inscr to Missy Le Hand. Also sgd by Franklin D. Roosevelt. P June 16 (274) $4,000

Kenney Library, C. E.

— [Sale Catalogue] Catalogue of Valuable Printed Books. L, 1965-68. 8 (of 10) parts in 2 vols. Price lists laid in. O Sept 24 (135) $160

Kent, Rockwell

— A Birthday Book. [NY], 1931. One of 1,850. Soiled. cb Nov 21 (121) $50; sg Sept 26 (139) $70; sg Jan 30 (88) $150

— The Bookplates & Marks of Rockwell Kent. NY, 1929. One of 1,250. Cloth, in d/j. cb Oct 17 (493) $130; sg Sept 26 (140) $150

Anr copy. Cloth, unopened, in d/j. sg Jan 30 (89) $175

Anr copy. Cloth, in d/j. sg May 21 (258) $150

Anr copy. Orig cloth, in def d/j. wa Apr 9 (238) $75

— Greenland Journal. NY, [1962]. One of

1,000. With a suite of 6 lithos, 1 sgd. bbc Dec 9 (500) $230; sg Sept 26 (141) $150

— N by E. NY, 1930. One of 900. 4to, cloth. sg Sept 26 (143) $70

Anr copy. Orig cloth. Inscr. wa Sept 26 (623) $95

— Rockwellkentiana. NY, 1933. 4to, cloth. sg Jan 30 (90) $50

— This Is my Own. NY, [1940]. 1st Ed. cb Dec 19 (82) $65

— Voyaging Southward from the Strait of Magellan. NY, 1924. 1st Ed. 4to, orig cloth, in def d/j; lower edge of front cover soiled. Tiny hole in gutter. wa Sept 26 (624) $100

One of 110 with an extra sgd woodcut. Bds. Inscr. sg Jan 30 (91) $475

Kent, William. See: Jones & Kent

Kent, William Saville, d.1908

— The Great Barrier Reef of Australia.... L, [1893]. 4to, orig cloth; worn & shaken. Library stamp on tp. K Sept 29 (221) $150

Anr copy. Later calf gilt; marked. Some soiling & remargining. kh Nov 11 (636) A$100

Keppel, George Thomas, Earl of Albemarle, 1799-1891

— Narrative of a Journey across the Balcan. L, 1831. 2 vols. 8vo, half mor; rubbed, new endpapers. With hand-colored frontis & 3 maps. S June 30 (326) £150 [Longworth]

— Personal Narrative of a Journey from India to England. L, 1827. 1st Ed. 4to, orig bds; rebacked using orig backstrip. With folding map & 3 colored plates. bba June 25 (71) £600 [Folios]

Keppel, Sir Henry, 1809-1904

— The Expedition to Borneo of H.M.S. Dido. L, 1846. 2d Ed. 2 vols. 8vo, orig cloth; rebacked, orig spine preserved. With 7 folding maps & charts. cb Oct 10 (60) $180

Anr Ed. L, 1847. 2 vols. 8vo, orig cloth. W July 8 (224) £200

— A Visit to the Indian Archipelago.... L, 1853. 2 vols. 8vo, orig cloth; worn, spines damaged. With 8 litho plates. Lacking folding map. DW Oct 2 (44) £80

Ker, Henry

— Travels Through the Western Interior of the United States.... Elizabethtown NJ, 1816. 8vo, old calf; rebacked. Soem foxing; old markings. bbc June 29 (319) $300

Kercheval, Samuel, 1786-1845?

— A History of the Valley of Virginia. Woodstock VA, 1850. 2d Ed. 8vo, orig calf; worn, upper cover detached. Some foxing. bbc Apr 27 (617) $55

Kerguelen-Tremarec, Yves Joseph de, 1734?-97

— Relation d'un voyage dans la mer du nord.... Paris, 1771. 1st Ed. 4to, orig wraps; spine rubbed. With 18 plates & maps. Some early leaves wormed along inner margin. S Feb 26 (824) £550 [Hannas]

Anr copy. Contemp calf; rubbed, rebacked. With 18 maps & plates. Lacking privilege leaf & directions to binder; rust hole in O3. S Feb 26 (825) £400 [Hannas]

Kerka, William. See: Corbin & Kerka

Kerner, Johann Simon

— Giftige und essbare Schwaemme.... Stuttgart, 1786. 4to, 19th-cent half sheep; spine worn. With 16 plates with later hand-coloring. Text leaves foxed. sg Nov 14 (186) $350

Kerouac, Jack

— Big Sur NY, [1962]. Half cloth, in d/j. cb Dec 12 (89) $65

— The Dharma Bums. NY, 1958. In d/j. sp Nov 24 (281) $60

— Lonesome Traveler. NY, [1960]. Illus by Larry Rivers. Half cloth, in d/j. cb Dec 12 (90) $55

Anr copy. Half cloth, in d/j. Inscr by Rivers. sg Dec 12 (200) $225

— On the Road. NY, 1957. 1st Ed. In d/j. sg Dec 12 (201) $80

1st English Ed. L, 1958. In soiled d/j. DW Oct 2 (362) £80

— The Town and the City. NY, [1950]. 1st Ed. In d/j with short tear. sg June 11 (186) $325

Advance copy. Wraps. sg Dec 12 (202) $300

— Visions of Cody. [NY, 1960]. One of 750. Half cloth. sg Dec 12 (199) $475

Kerr, John, 1852-1920

— The History of Curling. Edin., 1890. 8vo, half mor; rebacked. pnE Mar 11 (33) $100; pnE Mar 11 (69) £55

Kerridge, Philip Markham

— An Address on Angling Literature. Fullerton, [1970]. Ltd Ed. Half lea with trout fly in sunken mount on upper cover. Koopman copy. O Oct 29 (187) $200

Kesey, Ken

— One Flew Over the Cuckoo's Nest. NY, [1962]. In d/j. Epstein copy. sg Apr 30 (275) $500

Kestnerbuch...

— Das Kestnerbuch. Hannover, 1919. Ltd Ed. Ed by Paul Erich Kueppers. 4to, bdg not described. With 12 illusts. Met Apr 28 (126) $825

Keulemans, Tony —& Coldewey, Jan

— Feathers to Brush. Deventer: Pvtly ptd, [1982]. One of 500. Folio, half lea. O Apr 28 (34) $120

Keulen, Joannes van

— De nieuwe groote lichtende Zee-Fakkel.... Amst.: Gerard Hulst van Keulen, 1788-84-[n.d.]. 3 (of 5) vols. Folio, old vellum; worn. With 152 charts. Lacking some text leaves & some charts. Sold w.a.f. cb Oct 10 (120) $3,750

Key, Francis Scott, 1779-1843

— The Star-Spangled Banner. Phila.: Winkle & Wiley, 1814. ("Defence of Fort M'Henry.") Folio, disbound. Lacking terminal leaf & 1 plate, not affecting the Anthem. In: The Analectic Magazine, Vol IV, No 23 (Nov 1814). wa Mar 5 (404) $80

Keyes, Angela M.

— The Five Senses. NY, 1911. Illus by Jessie Willcox Smith. With Christmas card, inscr & sgd by Smith mtd to front pastedown. F Sept 26 (63) $275; F Sept 26 (78) $90

Keynes, Sir Geoffrey

See also: Grolier Club; Nonesuch Press

— A Bibliography of the Writings of Dr. William Harvey. Cambr., 1953. 4to, cloth; worn. O Sept 24 (136) $90

— Blake Studies. L & NY, 1949. Modern half mor. bba Dec 19 (41) £70 [Kurita]

— Siegfried Sassoon: A Bibliography. L, 1962. bba Dec 19 (284) £70 [Dawson]

— A Study of the Illuminated Books of William Blake. L, 1964. One of 525, sgd. 4to, orig half mor. sg Sept 26 (53) $120

— William Blake's Laocoon. L: Trianon Press, 1976. One of 380. 4to, half mor. sg Sept 26 (54) $110

Keynes, John Maynard, 1883-1946

— The General Theory of Employment, Interest and Money. L, 1936. bba Jan 16 (47) £75 [Sotheran]

Anr copy. In d/j. bba Aug 13 (275) £180 [Pickering & Chatto]; DW May 13 (450) £70

Anr copy. Epstein copy. sg Apr 30 (276) $1,000

— Indian Currency and Finance. L, 1913. 1st Ed. 8vo, orig cloth; extremities rubbed. Some pencil underscoring. DW Nov 6 (302) £440

A Treatise on Money. L, 1930. 1st Ed. 2 vols. bba Jan 16 (46) £100 [Sotheran]

Keys, John

— The Antient Bee-Master's Farewell. L, 1796. 8vo, contemp half calf; rubbed. With 2 plates. pn Dec 12 (104) £170

Anr copy. Contemp calf; rubbed, joints splits. Lacking half-title; first few leaves waterstained; some browning. pn Dec 12 (105) £120

— The Practical Bee-Master.... L, 1780. 8vo, later half calf; worn. Tp & ad leaf at end cropped, affecting text. pn Dec 12 (106) £180

Keysler, Johann Georg, 1693-1743

— Travels through Germany, Bohemia, Hungary.... L, 1757. 4 vols. 4to, contemp calf; hinges cracked, worn. LH Dec 11 (139) $150

Khlebnikov, Velemir —& Kruchenykh, A. —& Guro, E.

— Troe. St, Petersburg, [1913]. 4to, orig wraps; soiled, loose. sg Nov 7 (207) $1,300

Kibre, Pearl. See: Thorndike & Kibre

Kidder, Daniel Parish, 1815-91

— Brazil and the Brazilians.... Phila. & NY, 1857. 8vo, orig cloth; rebacked with orig spine retained. With 2 colored & 16 uncolored plates & 2 maps, 1 folding. K July 12 (74) $90

Anr copy. Later half mor; rubbed. Dampstained. O Feb 25 (118) $120

Kidder, Jonathan Edward

— Japanese Temples: Sculpture, Paintings, Gardens, and Architecture. Tokyo, [1964]. 4to, cloth. sp June 18 (260) $55

Anr copy. Orig cloth. wa Dec 9 (566) $70

Kiki...

— Kiki, Souvenirs. Paris: Broca, 1929. Out-of-series copy. O Dec 17 (110) $130

Kiki's Memoirs

— Kiki's Memoirs. See: Hemingway, Ernest

Kikkwa...

— Kikkwa Meeiji-Sen. Tokyo, 1891. Vol I. 4to, orig silk damask bds. With 25 woodblock plates ptd in color, sheets joined & folding into bdg. C May 20 (185) £300 [Hollander]

Kikuchi Sadao

— A Treasury of Japanese Wood Block Prints.... NY: Crown, [1969]. In d/j. bbc Apr 27 (463) $120

Kilburne, Richard, 1605-78

— A Topographie or Survey of the County of Kent. L, 1659. 1st Ed. 4to, calf gilt by Hayday & Mansell. With port. Oo4 torn without loss; marginal worming at end; dampstaining to upper margins of 1st few leaves. pn May 14 (37) £300

Killian, James R. See: Edgerton & Killian

Kilmer, Joyce, 1886-1918

— Summer of Love. NY, 1911. 1st Issue. Some margins chipped. Inscr. sg June 11 (187) $150

— Trees and Other Poems. NY, 1914. Orig bds, in d/j; soiled. 1 page repaired. cb Oct 25 (66) $110; sg Dec 12 (205) $130

Anr copy. Orig bds, in d/j. Epstein copy. sg Apr 30 (277) $650

Anr copy. Orig bds. Inscr. sg June 11 (188) $250

Kilner, Dorothy, d.1836

— The Holiday Present, Containing Anecdotes of Mr. and Mrs. Jennet.... L: John Marshall, [c.1788]. 3d Ed. 12mo, orig bds. ESTC n008413. bba July 23 (90) £340 [Johnson]

Kimball, Charles P.

— The San Francisco City Directory...1850. San Francisco, [1870]. 16mo, cloth. Reprint of 1850 Ed. sg June 18 (88) $100

Kimberley, W. B.

— Bendigo and Vicinity: A Comprehensive History.... Melbourne, 1895. 4to, bdg not described, upper hinge taped. kh Nov 11 (284) A$200

Kindig, R. H.

— My Best Railroad Photographs. L, 1948. cb Feb 13 (195) $170

Kindig, R. H. —& Others

— Pictorial Supplement to Denver South Park & Pacific. Denver: Rocky Mountain Railroad Club, 1959. In d/j. Sgd. cb Feb 13 (196) $225

King, Charles, fl.1721

— The British Merchant. L, 1721. 3 vols. 8vo, contemp calf gilt; Vol I spine worn at head. Lord Lymington's subscriber's copy. b June 22 (179) £2,300

King, Charles William, 1818-88

— Handbook of Engraved Gems. L, 1885. 2d Ed. 8vo, half mor gilt. K Sept 29 (179) $110

— The Natural History, Ancient and Modern, of Precious Stones and Gems. L, 1865. 8vo, new cloth. With 6 plates. Plates dampstained. sg Nov 14 (255) $175

King, Clarence, 1842-1901

— Mountaineering in the Sierra Nevada. Bost., 1872. 8vo, cloth; worn. Number inked on tp. NH May 30 (131) $125

— United States Geological Exploration of the Fortieth Parallel. Wash., 1877. Vol II only. 4to, orig half mor. Front flyleaf & frontis detached. cb Sept 12 (102) $275

Anr copy. Frontis & flyleaf detached. cb Feb 12 (41) $200

King, Daniel, d.1664

— The Vale-Royall of England. Or, the County Palatine of Chester. L, 1656. Folio, contemp calf; rubbed, joints split, spine worn at head. With engraved title, 2 double-page maps & 17 plates & 4 engraved illusts, 1 full-page. Some marginal worming, browning & spotting; tp strengthened at inner margin. pn Apr 23 (119) £300 [Scott]

King, Edward, 1735?-1807

— Munimenta Antiqua; or, Observations on Ancient Castles.... L, 1799-1805. 4 vols. Folio, contemp calf; rebacked, old spines preserved. With 4 frontises & 164 plates & plans. bba Sept 19 (205) £600 [Blake]

King, Edward D.

— The Southern States of North America. L, 1875. 4 parts. 8vo, orig cloth. With double-page colored map & 4 frontises. Part 2 with lower marginal stain. L Nov 14 (152) £60

King, George, Sir —& Pantling, Robert

— The Orchids of the Sikkim-Himalaya. Calcutta, 1898. 4 vols. 4to, half mor gilt by Period Binders. With 453 plates, some partially colored. Some foxing & a few stains. Vol VIII of the Annals of the Royal Botanic Garden Calcutta. McCarty-Cooper copy. CNY Jan 25 (90) $7,000

Anr copy. Half mor; worn, casing of Vol III detached, inner hinges of Vol IV splitting. Plate 118 misbound; foxing; minor marginal dampstains. Vol VIII of the Annals of the Royal Botanic Garden Calcutta. CNY June 9 (146) $3,200

King, James, 1750-84. See: Cook, Capt. James

King, Martin Luther, Jr.

— Where Do We Go from Here? NY, [1967]. 1st Ed. Half cloth, in d/j. Inscr to Mrs. W. H. Scheide. K Dec 1 (257) $700

King, Stephen

See also: Underwood & Miller

— Carrie. Garden City, 1974. Sgd. cb Sept 19 (107) $450

Anr copy. In d/j. Inscr. sg June 11 (189) $650

Anr copy. In d/j; tape mark on rear cover. wa Sept 26 (340) $400

— Christine. NY: Viking, [1983]. In d/j; ink stain at bottom of front endpapers. Inscr. K Mar 22 (218) $70

— Cujo. NY: Viking, [1981]. In d/j. Inscr. K Mar 22 (219) $70

— Danse Macabre. NY: Everest House,

[1981]. In chipped d/j. Label sgd by King affixed to front free endpaper. pba July 9 (155) $50

One of 250. cb Feb 12 (67) $300

— The Dark Tower: The Gunslinger. West Kingston RI: Grant, [1982]. One of 500. In d/j. K Mar 22 (220) $180

— Dolan's Cadillac. Northridge CA: Lord John Press, 1989. One of 250. Half lea. pba July 9 (158) $150

One of 1,000. cb Sept 19 (109) $130; cb Dec 12 (226) $130

— Firestarter. NY: Viking, [1980]. 1st Trade Ed. In d/j. Sgd. cb Sept 19 (110) $250

— The Plant.... Bangor: Philtrum Press, 1982. Out-of-series copy. Wraps. cb Feb 12 (70) $800

— Salem's Lot. Garden City, 1975. In 2d Issue d/j with misprint "Father Cody" and price clipped off, worn & chipped. Label sgd by King affixed to front free endpaper. pba July 9 (162) $300

— The Shining. Garden City, 1977. In d/j. F Dec 18 (194) $140

Anr copy. In d/j. Label sgd by King affixed to front free endpaper. pba July 9 (163) $75; wa Sept 26 (341) $110

Anr copy. In worn d/j. wa Feb 20 (86) $90

— The Stand. Garden City, 1978. In d/j. F Sept 26 (340) $70

Anr copy. In d/j with chip out of back. Label sgd by King affixed to front free endpaper. pba July 9 (164) $90

Anr copy. In d/j. wa Mar 5 (215) $140

Anr Ed. NY, [1990]. One of 1,250. Lea. sg June 11 (190) $450

King, Stephen —& Straub, Peter

— The Talisman. West Kingston: Donald M. Grant, 1984. One of 1,200. 2 vols. cb Sept 19 (112) $140

King, Thomas Butler, 1804-64

— Report of Hon. T. Butler King on California. Wash., 1850. 8vo, modern cloth, front wrap bound in. sg June 18 (89) $110

King, Thomas H.

— The Study-Book of Mediaeval Architecture and Art: Working Drawings.... Edin., 1893. 4 vols. Folio, half lea; needs recased. sp June 18 (211) $95

King, William, 1650-1729

— The State of the Protestants in Ireland.... L, 1691. 1st Ed. 4to, contemp calf; rubbed, upper joint weak. Wormed in lower margin just touching text. pn May 14 (38) £65

King, William, 1663-1712

— Miscellanies in Prose and Verse. L, [1709]. 8vo, contemp calf; upper hinge worn. Fine paper copy. bba Jan 16 (96) £60 [Books & Prints]

King, William Augustus Henry

— Chelsea Porcelain. L, 1922. One of 75. 4to, cloth, in d/j. kh Nov 11 (146) A$100

King, William Ross

— The Sportsman and Naturalist in Canada. L, 1866. 8vo, half mor, orig cloth bound in. With 6 color plates & errata slip. K July 12 (484) $190

Kingdomes...

— The Kingdomes Case; or, The Question Resolved.... L: John Wright, 1643. 4to, 19th-cent half lea; spine worn. sg Oct 24 (181) $100

Kinglake, Alexander William, 1809-91

— Eothen, or Traces of Travel brought Home from the East. L, 1844. 1st Ed. 8vo, half lea; front cover detached. With hand-colored frontis. Title spotted. sg Oct 17 (289) $50

Anr Ed. L, 1913. One of 100. Illus by Frank Brangwyn. 4to, orig half vellum; spine soiled, edges rubbed. pn May 14 (105) £50 [Elliott]

— The Invasion of the Crimea. Edin., 1888-89. 9 vols. 8vo, cloth. sp Apr 16 (92) $65

Kingsley, Charles, 1819-75

See also: Clemens's copy, Samuel Langhorne

— The Water-Babies. L & Cambr., 1863. 1st Ed, 2d Issue. 8vo, half mor gilt by Bayntun-Riviere; soiled & frayed. Last leaf with repair to 1 corner. pn Dec 12 (243) £130 [Sotheran]

Anr Ed. L, 1869. 8vo, contemp half mor. Extra-illus with 8 mtd ink drawings in a circular format by Harold H. Everett. cb Sept 26 (137) $225

Anr Ed. L, 1885. 8vo, mor with onlays by Bayntun, orig cloth bound in. CNY Dec 5 (409) $1,000

— Westward Ho! Cambr., 1855. 1st Ed. 3 vols. 8vo, orig cloth; extremities rubbed, inner hinges split. Manney copy. P Oct 11 (195) $1,600

Anr copy. Orig cloth; rubbed, inner hinges split. Ewing-Manney copy. P Oct 11 (196) $175

— Works. L, 1901-3. One of 525 L.p. sets. 19 vols. 8vo, calf gilt by Zaehnsdorf. sg Mar 5 (148) $1,100

Kingston, William Henry Giles, 1814-80

— Lusitanian Sketches.... L, 1845. 2 vols. 12mo, contemp cloth; soiled & worn. wa Mar 5 (545) $60

Kinloch, Alexander Angus Airlie

— Large Game Shooting in Thibet.... Calcutta & L, 1885. 4to, orig cloth; spine loose & chipped. Sold w.a.f. sg Jan 9 (278) $175

Kinnamos, Joannis, b.1143

— Imperatorii grammatici historiarum libri sex. Paris: Sebastien Cramoisy for Imprimerie royale, 1670. Folio, contemp calf with gilt arms of Compaignon de Marcheville of Beauce; worn & repaired. Blackmer copy. S July 1 (520) £550 [Dimarkarakos]

Kinnell, Galway

— Fergus Falling. Newark VT: Janus Press, 1979. One of 120. bbc June 29 (403) $80

Kinney, Troy

— The Etchings. Garden City, 1929. One of 900, sgd. Folio, half cloth. O Sept 24 (139) $90

Kinsey, William Morgan

— Portugal Illustrated. L, 1828. 8vo, modern calf. With double-page frontis, additional title, double-page map, 16 plates, 9 hand-colored costume plates. A few leaves browned. pn Nov 14 (418) £240

Anr copy. Contemp calf. With folding map, folding frontis on mtd India paper, 15 mtd plates & 9 hand-colored costume plates. wa Dec 9 (452) $290

Kinzie, Juliette A.

— Wau-Bun, the "Early Days" of the North-West.... NY, 1856. 1st Ed. 8vo, orig cloth; worn, ends of spine frayed. With 6 plates. O Dec 17 (111) $70

Anr copy. Orig cloth; spine ends frayed. Some soiling. sg June 18 (315) $110

2d Ed. NY, 1857. 8vo, cloth; rebacked. Some browning & dampstaining. sg June 18 (316) $60

Kip, Joannes

— Britannia Illustrata, or Views of Several of the Queens Palaces.... L, 1709. Folio, contemp calf gilt; def. With engraved title & 75 (of 80) plates. Imprint & date on engraved title blanked off; some plates loose; some dust-soiling; Plate 80 creased & holed near lower plate-mark. Sold w.a.f. S June 25 (173) £3,500 [Nicholson]

Anr copy. Contemp bds; worn. With engraved title, index & 107 views, 2 cut short at lower edge. S June 25 (276) £1,500 [Marlborough]

Kipling, Rudyard, 1865-1936

— 40 nord—50 vest. [Moscow, early 1930s]. Trans by S. Marshak; illus by D. Shterenberg. 4to, orig wraps; rebacked. sg Nov 7 (208) $175

— The Absent-Minded Beggar. [L, 1899]. Single sheet, 11 by 8 inches, folded to form 6 pages Ptd on silk for Lily Langtry. sg Dec 12 (207) $140

— An Almanac of Twelve Sports.... L, 1898. Illus by William Nicholson. 4to, orig half cloth; extremities worn. sg Oct 17 (324) $225

Anr Ed. NY, 1898. 4to, pictorial bds; spine def, other extremities worn. Owner's stamps. Sold w.a.f. sg Sept 19 (204) $200

Anr copy. Orig half cloth; worn, spine partly split. With 12 plates. wa Mar 5 (608) $190

— "Captains Courageous." L, 1897. 1st English Pbd Ed. 8vo, mor gilt by Bayntun, orig cloth covers and spine bound in. sg Oct 17 (290) $250

Anr copy. Cloth. Epstein copy. sg Apr 30 (279) $700

— Collected Verse.... NY, 1910. One of 125. Illus by W. Heath Robinson. 8vo, half vellum. With 17 mtd color plates. sg Dec 12 (208) $950

Anr Ed. L, 1912. Blue mor with inlaid tan mor & snakeskin by Paul C. Delrue, 1963. DW Mar 4 (191) £350

Anr copy. Orig vellum. ALs laid in. pnE Oct 2 (481) £140

— Departmental Ditties and Other Verses. Lahore, 1886. 1st Ed. 8vo, contemp half mor gilt by Zaehnsdorf, orig wraps bound in; lacking the red tape. Certain Maxims of Hafiz leaf shaved at outer margin with loss of a few characters. C Dec 16 (211) £380 [Finch]

Anr copy. Orig wraps; spotted; lacking the red tape. Epstein copy. With An Exhibition of the Works of Rudyard Kipling. Grolier Club, 1929. sg Apr 30 (280) $1,000

2d Ed. Calcutta, 1886. 8vo, orig bds; chipped, lacking backstrip. bba Jan 30 (215) £55 [Ivens]

— The Five Nations. L, 1903. 1st Ed, one of 200. Cloth; worn, front hinge & joint splitting. sg Oct 17 (291) $175

— A Fleet in Being. L & NY, 1898. 1st Ed in Book form. 8vo, orig cloth; spotted. sg Oct 172 (292) $60

Anr copy. Orig wraps. wa Dec 9 (201) $110

— The Fringes of the Fleet. NY, 1915. American Copyright Issue. Complete set of 6 pamphlets. sg Mar 5 (152) $200

— The Jungle Book. With: The Second Jungle Book. L, 1894-95. 2 vols. 8vo, orig cloth;

extremities rubbed. CNY June 9 (105) $900; S Apr 28 (70) £240 [Bickersteth]

Anr copy. Orig cloth; hinges tender. Epstein copy. sg Apr 30 (281) $800

— The Just So Song Book. NY, 1903. Music by Edward German. 4to, orig cloth. Epstein copy. sg Apr 30 (282) $175

— Just So Stories.... L, 1902. 1st Ed. cb Sept 19 (118) $160; Ck July 10 (316) £75

Anr copy. Epstein copy. sg Apr 30 (283) $650

— Kim. L, 1901. 1st English Ed. sg Mar 5 (154) $175

1st English pbd Ed. In d/j. Epstein copy. sg Apr 30 (284) $1,200

1st Ed. NY, 1901. 1st Issue. cb Dec 12 (91) $110

Anr copy. In d/j. Eckel-Parsons copy. P Dec 12 (60) $3,000

— Letters of Marque. Allahabad, 1891. One of 1,000. 8vo, orig cloth; front hinge starting. Epstein copy. sg Apr 30 (285) $600

— Mandalay. San Francisco, [1899]. 8vo, bds; front cover loose. Eugene Field II forgery of the author's & Frederic Remington's signatures, the latter with a drawing. sg Oct 17 (235) $130

— Plain Tales from the Hills. Calcutta & L, 1888. 1st Ed. 8vo, clotht; shaken. Sgd as Rudyard Kipling & Eugene Field by Eugene Field II. sg Oct 17 (236) $140

Anr copy. Cloth; worn. sg Oct 17 (295) $110

Anr copy. Orig cloth; rear hinge cracked. sg Dec 12 (209) $110

— Poems, 1886-1929 L, 1929. One of 525. 3 vols. 4to, orig mor, in worn d/js. F Mar 26 (9) $575

Anr copy. Orig mor, in d/j. sg Nov 7 (123) $900

Anr copy. Orig mor; spine ends worn. sg June 11 (191) $800

One of 525, sgd. Mor. wd June 12 (397) $700

— Puck of Pook's Hill. NY, 1906. Illus by Arthur Rackham. Orig cloth; extremities rubbed; hinge cracking. With 4 colored plates. cb Feb 27 (84) $50

— Rudyard Kipling's Verse. Garden City, 11919. 1st American Ed, One of 250. Orig vellum gilt; front hinge cracked. sg Dec 12 (210) $100

— The Seven Seas. L, 1896. One of 150. 8vo, orig cloth; spine faded. sg Oct 17 (296) $100

Anr copy. Orig cloth; front joint with small tear. sg Mar 5 (155) $60

— Soldiers Three. Allahabad, 1888. 1st Ed. 8vo, wraps; rebacked. Front flyleaf detached. sg Oct 17 (297) $140

Anr copy. Orig wraps; soiled & creased, some chipping, 2 corners supplied, some reinforcement to front inner hinge. wa Dec 9 (201) $110

— Some Notes on a Bill. Little Rock: The Incunabula Bookshop, 1920. 1st American Ed, one of—100. Orig wraps. sg Mar 5 (156) $175

— A Song of the English. L, [1909]. One of 500. Illus by W. Heath Robinson. 4to, orig cloth. DW Oct 2 (388) £60

— Songs of the Sea. L, 1927. One of 500. Illus by Donald Maxwell. 4to, orig half vellum in def d/j. pn July 16 (79) £150

Anr copy. Orig half vellum. sg Dec 12 (211) $250

— Stalky & Co. L, 1899. 1st Ed. 8vo, later calf gilt. sg Mar 5 (157) $50

— Tales of "The Trade." NY, 1916. American Copyright Issue. Complete set of 3 pamphlets. Orig wraps. sg Mar 5 (158) $110

— A Tour of Inspection. NY: Pvtly ptd, 1928. One of 93. Bds, unopened. sg Mar 5 (159) $150

— Under the Deodars. Allahabad & L, [1890]. 1st English Ed. 8vo, wraps; spine def. Front cover and 1st signature detached; tear in inner margin of title. sg Oct 17 (298) $150

— White Horses. L: Ptd for Private Circulation, 1897. 8vo, orig wraps. T. J. Wise piracy. S July 1 (1054) £280 [Tsuboi]

— With the Night Mail: A Story of 2000 A.D. NY, 1909. 1st American Ed. sg Mar 5 (160) $60

— Works. L, 1913-20. Bombay Ed, One of 1,050; Vols 27-31 are 1 of 500. Vols 1-25 only. Orig half cloth. b Nov 18 (304) £250

Anr copy. 31 vols. Lea. br May 29 (25) $1,500

Anr copy. Orig half cloth, some vols in d/js. DW Apr 8 (529) £240

Anr copy. 25 vols only. Half mor gilt; rubbed & scuffed. P June 17 (343) $1,500

Anr copy. 31 vols. Orig half cloth. pnE Dec 4 (144) £460

Sussex Ed. L, 1937-39. one of 525. 35 vols. Orig mor by James Burn. Sgd in Vol I. S July 21 (147) £4,800 [Blackwell]

Kipping, Heinrich

— Antiquitatum Romanarum. Leiden, 1713. 8vo, contemp bds; worn & shaken. O Mar 31 (106) $70

Kippis, Andrew, 1725-95

— The Life of Captain James Cook. Dublin, 1788. 4to, early calf; rebacked, hinges taped. Some foxing & discoloration; some repairs. kh Nov 11 (535) A$180

Kirby, W. Egmont. See: Kappel & Kirby

Kirby, William, 1759-1850

— Monographia apum Angliae. Ipswich, 1802. 2 vols. 8vo, early 19th-cent half cloth; spines faded. With 18 plates. sg Nov 14 (187) $110

Kirby, William F., 1844-1912

— European Butterflies and Moths. L, 1882. 4to, orig cloth; worn. With 1 plain & 61 hand-colored plates. A few leaves loose. bba Sept 5 (70) £220 [C. Mason]

Anr copy. Contemp half mor; spine rubbed. Some soiling. bba Nov 28 (124) £180 [Pordes]

Anr copy. Orig cloth; rubbed, spine detached. S Nov 15 (746) £200 [Thorp]

Anr copy. Contemp half mor; rubbed. Some leaves & plates loose. S Feb 26 (926) £320 [Dornier]

Anr Ed. L, 1898. 4to, later cloth. With 1 plain & 61 hand-colored plates. Library markings. bba Sept 5 (71) £200 [Finney]

Anr Ed. L, 1903. ("The Butterflies and Moths of Europe.") 4to, orig cloth; hinges rubbed. With 54 plates. DW Nov 6 (173) £60

— Natural History of the Animal Kingdom, for the Use of Young People. L, 1903. 4to, later half mor gilt; rubbed. With 90 double-page plates. Some tape repairs. Sold w.a.f. DW Nov 6 (172) £50

Kirby, William Forsell. See: Grose-Smith & Kirby

Kircher, Athanasius, 1601-80

— Arca Noe. Amst., 1675. Folio, mor gilt; rubbed. With engraved title, port, large folding plan of the Ark, 15 plates (1 half-page, 4 single, 10 double-page) & 3 maps (1 single, 2 folding). Browned; folding plan laid down on linen; some leaves torn & mended without loss. P June 17 (248) $2,250

— Ars magna sciendi, in XII libros digesta. Amst., 1669. 2 vols in 1. Folio, contemp vellum; spine def. Some worming & browning. SI June 9 (493) LIt1,650,000

— China monumentis.... Amst., 1667. 1st Ed. Folio, half cloth; broken. SI June 9 (494) LIt1,400,000

— D'onder-aardse wereld. Amst., 1682. 2 vols in 1. Folio, recent vellum. With engraved title, armorial dedication, 14 double-page or folding maps & plates & 8 full-page engravings. Some wormholes & stains. B Nov 1 (665) HF2,300

— Latium, id est nova et parallela Latii.... Amst., 1671. 1st Ed. Folio, old half sheep gilt; joints cracked, spine worn. With engraved title & 26 plates. sg Nov 7 (124) $900

— Magnes, sive de arte magnetica.... Rome, 1641. 1st Ed. 4to, contemp calf gilt; joints cracked, spine worn at ends, lower headband lost, blank leaf laid down over upper pastedown. With engraved title & 33 plates. Some browning; 1 leaf smudged. P Dec 12 (60A) $3,500

3d Ed. Rome, 1654. Folio, contemp bds; spine def. About half the leaves spotted or browned; wormed in margins. S Feb 25 (596) £900 [Erlini]

— Mundus subterraneus.... Amst., 1678. 3d Ed. 2 vols in 1. Folio, contemp blind-stamped calf; head of spine worn, upper cover detached. With engraved titles, port, 17 plates (7 double-page) & 9 maps (6 double-page). Small tear in 3 blank tail-margins at front of Vol II. b June 22 (180) £2,900

Anr copy. Contemp calf; worn. With additional titles, 14 double-page or folding maps & plates, 6 full page; 4 folding or double-page ptd tables. Tp & prelims with small wormhole at lower edge; last 80 pp of Vol II with small wormhole at center; some browning & spotting; small hole in p.145; p. 451 torn at corner; world map with repaired tear & small hole; small hole in South America. S Feb 26 (754) £1,900 [Bolognese]

— Oedipus Aegyptiacus. Rome, 1652-54. 1st Ed. 4 vols. Folio, 18th-cent vellum with yapp edges; stained. With port, 14 plates & 2 maps, all folding. Some spotting; several plates with repaired tears at folds. C June 24 (155) £4,000 [Martayan Lan]

— Polygraphia nova et universalis. Rome, 1663. Folio, contemp vellum. With folding plate & 2 folding tables. Inscr to Count von Auersperg, 2 Mar 1664. S Dec 5 (231) £4,000 [Mandel]

— Prodromus Coptus sive Aegyptiacus. Rome, 1636. 1st Ed, Variant issue with woodcut device on tp. 4to, 19th-cent calf; spine worn. Some leaves browned or spotted; Cc3 cut short at foot; marginal repairs. S Feb 25 (503) £600 [Zioni]

— Scrutinium physico-medicum contagiosae luis.... Leipzig, 1671. 4to, modern half sheep; upper joint cracking. Library markings. bba Sept 5 (284) £140 [Poole]

Kirchweger, Anton Joseph
— Miscroscopium Basilii Valentini sive commentariolum et cribrellum.... Berlin, 1790. 8vo, later cloth. B Nov 1 (643) HF675

Kirkbride, John
— The Northern Angler. Carlisle, 1837. 1st Ed. 8vo, orig cloth; rubbed & faded. bba Nov 28 (42) £110 [Hereward Bks]

Kirkby, John, 1716-74?
— The Capacity and Extent of the Human Understanding.... L, 1745. 12mo, calf gilt; front cover detached. NH Aug 23 (160) $140

Kirkland, Thomas, 1722-98
— A Commentary on Apoplectic and Paralytic Affections. L, 1792. 8vo, contemp calf; rubbed, rebacked. Some spotting. Sgd by Thomas Kirkland Glazebrook on tp. pn Nov 14 (364) £340
— An Inquiry into the Present State of Medical Surgery. L, 1783-86. 2 vols. 8vo, contemp calf & later calf; joints cracked. Inscr to his son. pn Nov 14 (363) £380

Kirmse, Marguerite. See: Derrydale Press

Kitagawa, Utamaro, 1753?-1806. See: Grabhorn Printing

Kitchener, Horatio Herbert, Earl Kitchener of Khartoum & of Broome. See: Conder & Kitchener

Kitchin, Thomas, d.1784
— Geographia Scotiae: being New...Maps of...Scotland.... L, 1751. 8vo, contemp half calf; spine lacking. With 33 double-page maps mtd on guards. No 28 torn at upper margins. Milne copy. Ck June 12 (125) £700

Kitchin, Thomas, d.1784 —& Others
— General Atlas. L: Robert Sayer, [maps dated 1775-90]. Folio, bdg not described but broken. With 23 maps on 35 double-page & folding mapsheets, hand-colored in outline. Some margins torn & frayed, causing plate loss; a few with small tape repairs. pn Mar 19 (416) £1,300 [Schuster]

Anr Ed. L: Laurie & Whittle, 1795. Folio, contemp half calf; worn. With 25 maps on 37 double-page or folding mapsheets, hand-colored in outline. Some margins frayed; a few creases; some dustsoiling. S June 25 (96) £2,200 [Al-Thani]

Anr copy. Some margins affected by damp, occasionally touching surface; slight worming towards end with slight loss of engraved surface. S June 25 (302) £1,400 [Baskes]

— A New Universal Atlas.... L, 198. Folio, contemp calf; worn, spine & corners repaired, upper hinge def, lower hinge repaired. With 55 maps on 70 double-page or folding mapsheets, hand-colored in outline. minor tears & fraying. S June 25 (303) £3,000 [Map House]

Kitchin, Thomas, d.1784 —& Jefferys, Thomas, d.1771
— Small English Atlas. L, 1751. 8vo, contemp calf; rebacked, joints cracked. With double-page engraved title & 50 maps hand-colored in outline. Some dampstains; Staffordshire torn along fold. Milne copy. Ck June 12 (124) £900

Kittenberger, Kalman
— Big Game Hunting and Collecting in East Africa. L, 1929. O Mar 31 (107) $110

Kitton, Frederick George, 1856-1904
— Dickens and his Illustrators. NY: Abner Schram, 1972. 4to, cloth. Reprint of L, 1899 Ed. bbc Apr 27 (119) $50
— John Leech, Artist and Humourist.... L, 1883. 8vo but each leaf inlaid to 4to, half mor gilt. Mor gilt by Bayntun. Extra-illus with c.75 mtd plates from various early eds of vols with Leech illusts. sg Jan 9 (279) $375

Klauber, Laurence Monroe
— Rattlesnakes: Their Habits, Life Histories, and Influence on Mankind. Berkeley, 1956. 2 vols. 4to, cloth. Sgd. sg May 14 (224) $150

Klebs, Arnold Carl
— Incunabula scientifica et medica. Bruges, 1937. Cloth, orig front wrap bound in. sg Oct 31 (158) $60

Klein, William
— New York. Geneva, 1956. 4to, cloth. With Klein's bookmark tourist pamphlet laid in. sg Apr 13 (57) $425

Kleist, Heinrich von, 1777-1811
— Amphitryon. Dresden, [1807]. 8vo, 19th-cent half cloth. S Dec 5 (294) £3,000 [Schumann]
— Das Kaetchen von heilbronn. Berlin, 1810. 8vo, 19th-cent bds; rubbed. Some staining. S Dec 5 (292) £1,700 [Schumann]
— Der zerbrochne Krug, ein Lustspiel. Berlin, 1811. 8vo, wraps, unopened; covers detached. Foxed. S Dec 5 (293) £800 [Schafer]

Kley, Heinrich, 1863-1945
— Skizzenbuch [Skizzenbuch II]. Munich, [1909-10]. 2 vols. 4to, bdg not described. Z Oct 26 (124) $225

Klimt, Gustav, 1862-1918

— Twenty-Five Drawings.... Vienna, 1964. Ed by Alice Strobl. Folio, loose as issued in cloth slipcase. With 25 mtd plates. sg Feb 6 (150) $300

Klinckowstrom, Alex L.

— Bref om de Forenta Staterna Forfattade under en Resa till Amerika.... Stockholm, 1824. 3 vols in 2. 8vo & folio, contemp half calf, orig ptd wraps bound in atlas; extremities rubbed, joints on text vol cracked at head & tender. Each text vol with engraved title; Atlas with 17 plates & maps. Some plates with short marginal tears or repairs. P Dec 12 (119) $5,500

Kluge, Kurt —& Lehmann-Hartleben, Karl

— Die antiken Grossbronzen. Berlin & Leipzig, 1927. 3 vols. 4to, orig cloth. With 34 plates. pn Sept 12 (99) £110

Kneeland, Samuel

— The Wonders of the Yosemite Valley.... Bost., 1871. ("The Wonders of Yosemite Valley and California.") 1st Ed. Illus by John Soule. 8vo, orig cloth. With 10 albumen prints (3 detached). b&b Feb 19 (98) $375

Anr copy. Half lea; extremities worn. NH Aug 23 (116) $325

Kneller, Sir Godfrey, 1646-1723 —& Faber, John, 1660?-1721

— The Kit-Cat Club. L, 1735. Folio, 19th-cent mor gilt; lea surface damaged. With dedication & 47 ports, all cut round outside plate mark & mtd on paper. Currer-Sheepshanks copy. C June 24 (327) £1,800 [Franklin]

Knight, Charles. See: English...

Knight, Charles, 1791-1873

— London. L, 1841-44. Ed by Knight. 6 vols in 3. 8vo, contemp half calf; rubbed. bba Jan 16 (335) £55 [Cline]

— Old England: A Pictorial Museum of Regal, Ecclesiastical, Baronial, Municipal, and Popular Antiquities. L, 1845-[46]. 2 vols. Folio, orig cloth; worn & darkened. cb Jan 9 (129) $150

Anr copy. 2 vols in 1. Folio, calf; scuffed. With 24 color plates. Some foxing. F June 25 (730) $150

— Passages of a Working Life during Half a Century. L, 1864. 3 vols. 8vo, orig cloth; worn. Library markings. O July 12 (109) $80

Knight, Eric

— Lassie Come-Home. L, [1941]. 1st English Ed. In chipped d/j. Epstein copy. sg Apr 29 (289) $550

Knight, Frederick

— Knight's Heraldic Illustrations, Designed for the Use of Heraldic Painters and Engravers. L, [1843]. 4to, old half lea; worn. With engraved title & 19 plates. kh Nov 11 (111) A$90

Knight, Henry Gally

— The Ecclesiastical Architecture of Italy. L: Henry Bohn, 1842-44. 2 vols. Folio, contemp half mor gilt; rubbed, Vol I spine def. Some waterstaining & spotting. bba Apr 30 (335) £1,600 [Toscani]

Anr Ed. L: H. Bohn, 1843. 2 vols. Folio, orig half mor gilt; rubbed. With chromolitho titles & 81 plates, including 74 tinted lithos & 3 chromolithos. Some faint discoloration but no foxing. S Nov 21 (84) £2,200

Anr copy. Orig half mor; rubbed. With 2 chromolitho titles & 80 litho plates. Some spotting. S Feb 26 (755) £2,100 [Perini]

Knight, John —& Slover, John

— Indian Atrocities: Narratives of the Perils and Sufferings of Dr. Knight and John Slover, among the Indians.... Cincinnati, 1867. 12mo, orig wraps; lower wrap & spine chipped. bbc Sept 23 (331) $65

Knight, Richard Payne, 1750-1824

— An Analytical Inquiry into the Principles of Taste. L, 1805. 2d Ed. 8vo, orig bds; backstrip worn. bba Apr 30 (86) £140 [Jarndyce]

— A Discourse on the Worship of Priapus.... L, 1865. 4to, disbound. With 40 extra plates. sg Apr 13 (38) $225

Knight, Sarah Kemble

— The Journal of Madam Knight. Bost., 1920. One of 525. cb Oct 17 (506) $50

Knish, Anne —& Morgan, Emanuel

— Spectra; a Book of Poetic Experiments. NY, 1916. With William Jay Smith's The Spectra Hoax. sg Dec 12 (39) $120

Knolles, Richard, 1550?-1610

— The Generall Historie of the Turkes. L, 1687. ("The Turkish History....") Vol I (of 3). Folio, modern half mor. Frontis & half-title with "unsightly" tape repairs. sg Oct 17 (299) $80

Knoop, Johann Hermann

— Beschrijving en afbeeldingen van de beste Soorten van Appelen en Peeren [van Vruchtboomen en Vruchten; van Plantagie-gewassen]. Amst. & Dordrecht, 1790. 3 works in 1 vol. Folio, contemp half calf; joints & corners rubbed. With 39 hand-colored folding plates. C Oct 30 (206) £900 [Mason]

— Pomologia. Fructologia. Dendrologia. Leeuwarden, [1758-63]. Folio, contemp half calf; rubbed, spine torn. With 39 hand-colored plates. C Oct 30 (282) £1,000 [Watson]

Knopwood, Robert

— The Diary...1803-1838.... Hobart, 1977. Ed by Mary Nicholls. In plasticized d/j. kh Nov 11 (537) A$90

Knorr, Georg Wolfgang, 1705-61

— Verlustiging der Oogen en van den Geest....Hoorens en Schulpen. Amst., 1770-75. 6 vols in 2. 4to, contemp calf gilt; rubbed. With 190 hand-colored plates. C Oct 30 (284) £3,800 [Junk]

Knorr, Georg Wolfgang, 1705-61 —& Walch, Johann Ernst Immanuel

— De natuurlyke historie der Versteeningen.... Amst.: Jan Christiaan Sepp, 1773. 3 vols in 4. Folio, contemp calf gilt; rubbed. With port & 245 plates ptd in colors or colored by hand. C Oct 30 (283) £5,200 [Junk]

Knotts, Benjamin

— Pennsylvania German Designs.... NY: Metropolitan Museum of Art, [1943]. Folio, loose in bd folder. With 20 color plates, each stamped on blank verso. O May 26 (143) $100

Knowles, James Sheridan, 1784-1862

— The Wife: or, Women as They are. L, 1835. Illus by George Cruikshank. 8vo, mor gilt, orig covers & backstrip bound in. With 4 plates. sg Oct 17 (172) $250

Knox, Dudley Wright

— Naval Sketches of the War in California. NY, 1939. One of 1,000. Illus by William H. Meyers. Folio, half pigskin. With 28 colored plates. Inscr to Marguerite A. Le Hand. P June 16 (275) $1,900

Knox, Hugh, d.1790

— The Moral and Religious Miscellany or Sixty-One Aphoretical Essays. NY, 1775. 1st Ed. 8vo, calf; worn. Some worming in margin of 15 leaves near the front. NH May 30 (459) $60

Knox, Kathleen

— Fairy Gifts. L, 1875. Illus by Kate Greenaway. 8vo, orig blue cloth; worn & rubbed, rebacked with orig spine strip laid on, new endpapers. cb Sept 26 (997) $100

Knox, Robert

— Man: His Structure and Physiology. L, 1858. 2d Ed. 8vo, orig cloth. With 6 colored plates, including 5 plates with a total of 10 moveable flaps. Flap on Plate 1 mended. Schlosser copy. P June 17 (471) $1,500

Koch, C. L. See: Hahn & Koch

Koch, Kenneth

— When the Sun Tries To Go On. Los Angeles: Black Sparrow Press, 1969. One of 200. Illus by Larry Rivers. sg June 11 (192) $375

Koch, Rudolf —& Kredel, Fritz

— Das Blumenbuch. [Darmstadt]: Rosel Kuechler, 1923-30. One of 20 of special Ed ptd from orig blocks by Kuechler & sgd by Kuechler, Koch & Kredel. 12 parts. 4to, loose in 12 folders & 2 decorated, vellum-covered boxes. With 248 (of 250) hand-colored woodcuts, each mtd. P June 17 (249) $5,000

Kock, Charles Paul de, 1794-1850

— Adhemar. Bost.: Frederick J. Quinby, [1904]. One of 250. Half mor gilt; lower corner bumped. pba July 23 (122) $85

— Chermai. Bost.: Frederick J. Quinby, [1904]. One of 250. Vol I only. Half mor gilt. pba July 23 (123) $50

— The Child of my Wife. Bost.: Frederick J. Quinby, [1903]. One of 10 on vellum. 2 vols. 8vo, mor extra with onlays by the Harcourt Bindery. Illus with orig drawings, watercolors or sgd etchings by W. J. Sinnott, Charles H. White, Albert de Ford Pitney & Louis Meynelle & with hand-illuminated initials & borders. Vols I & II of the Bibliomaniac Ed of the Works. O May 26 (109) $1,400

— Madame Pantalon. Bost.: Frederick J. Quinby, [1904]. One of 100. Vol I only. Half mor gilt. pba July 23 (125) $50

— Scenes of Parisian Life Bost.: Frederick J. Quinby, [1904]. One of 250. Half mor gilt; 1 corner showing. pba July 23 (124) $50

Koehl, Herman —& Others

— The Three Musketeers of the Air. NY, 1928. One of 260, sgd. Unopened. cb Nov 7 (52) $250

Koehler, Johann David, 1684-1785

— Descriptio orbis antiqui in XLIV tabulis exhibita. Nuremberg: C. Weigel, [c.1720]. Folio, old calf; worn. With 37 (of 44) hand-colored maps. Lacking tp & contents; some marginal browning. S May 14 (1171) £330 [Saville]

Koehler, Sylvester Rosa. See: Grolier Club

Koehler, Sylvester Rosa —& Others

— American Etchings: a Collection.... Bost., 1886. Ltd Ed. 4to, syn. NH Aug 23 (182) $325

Koeler, David

— Descriptio orbis antiqui. Nuremberg: C. Weigel, [c.1720]. Oblong 4to, old half calf; rubbed. With 44 double-page mapsheets, hand-colored. Library stamp on tp verso. S Nov 15 (1050) £500 [Dal Mondo]

Koeman, Cornelis

— Atlantes Neerlandici: Bibliography of Terrestrial, Maritime and Celestial Atlases and Pilot Books.... Amst., 1967-71. Vols I-III bound in 5 vols. Folio, half cloth. Lacking prelims of Vol II & 1st 2 prelims of Vol III. Proof copy, mainly ptd on 1 side only. B May 12 (92) HF525

Anr copy. 5 vols. Folio, orig cloth; soiled. bba Dec 19 (320) £300 [Potter]; pn Apr 23 (148) £320

Anr copy. 5 vols plus Supplement, 1985. Folio, SI Dec 5 (323) LIt850,000

Kogevinas, Lycidas

— Le Mont Athos. Paris, [1922]. One of 25. 4to, ptd portfolio. With 12 sepia plates accompanied by 12 impressions in blue, each numbered & sgd. S July 1 (630) £1,400

Kok, Jacobus, d.1788

— Vaderlandsch woordenboek. Amst., 1785-99. Vols 1-34 (of 35) & without the supplements. Half calf. With frontis, 4 colored folding maps & 132 ports & plates. B Nov 1 (289) HF425

Kolben, Peter

— Description du Cap de Bonne-Esperance.... Amst., 1741. 3 vols. 12mo, contemp calf. sg Jan 9 (101A) $250

— The Present State of the Cape of Good Hope.... L, 1731. 1st Ed. Vol I only. 8vo, contemp calf; upper joint split. With frontis & 17 plates. Lacking ad leaf at front. b June 22 (181) £400

Kolczycki, Franciszek

— Curiosa relatione del viaggio.... Vienna, 1683. 4to, half cloth. Lacking blanks. S June 30 (329) £600 [Hunersdorf]

Kondakov, Nikodim Pavlovich

— Istoriya i Pamyatniki Vozantinskoi Emali. St. Petersburg, 1892. One of 200. 4to, orig half mor, in d/j. sg Nov 7 (209) $1,400

Koning, Jacobus

— Algemeene ophelderende Verklaring van het oud Letterschrift, in Steenplattendruk. Leiden, 1818. 8vo, orig wraps, uncut, with album of 18 lithos. Schlosser copy. P June 17 (560) $300

Konody, Paul George

— The Art of Walter Crane. L, 1902. 4to, modern cloth. Lacking portion of endpaper. sg Oct 17 (143) $200

Anr copy. Cloth. sg Jan 30 (25) $300

One of 100. Bdg soiled. bba Jan 30 (342) £200 [Kitazawa]

Koops, Matthias

— Historical Account of the Substances which have been used to Describe Events.... L, 1800. 1st Ed. 8vo, orig bds; rubbed. Ptd on straw paper. Ck July 10 (174) £650

2d Ed. L, 1801. 8vo, contemp half calf; rebacked. bba Dec 19 (285) £600 [Thorp]

Anr copy. Modern half calf. Some soiling; ink library stamp & note on title; appendix browned. pn Apr 23 (34) £70

Koran

— The Koran. Zurich: Christoph Froschauer, 1550. ("Machumetis Saracenorum Principis, eiusque successorum vitae, doctrina, ac ipse Alcoran....") Folio, 18th-cent mor gilt. C Nov 27 (24) £3,000 [Quaritch]

Anr Ed. L, 1649. ("The Alcoran of Mahomet.") 4to, contemp vellum; warped, edges worn, 1 endpaper torn. Some browning. bbc Dec 9 (306) $55

— Der Koran. Lemgo: Johann Heinrich Meyer, 1746. 4to, contemp calf gilt. With folding plate folding map & 3 folding genealogical tables. Some browning; corner of front blank excised. sg Oct 24 (182) $375

Kotschy, T. See: Unger & Kotschy

Kotzebue, Otto von, 1787-1846

— A Voyage of Discovery into the South Sea and Beering's Straits. L, 1821. 3 vols. in 1 vol. 8vo, contemp half calf. With 7 charts & 9 plates, 8 of which are colored aquatints. Lacking half-titles & plate list; some spotting & discoloration. C May 20 (267) £950 [Shapero]

Kouchakji, Fahim. See: Eisen & Kouchakji

Krafft, Johann Carl, 1764-1833

— Recueil d'architecture civile.... Paris, 1812. Plates only. Folio, contemp bds. With engraved title & 120 plates. Lacking text. Sold w.a.f. bba Apr 30 (336) £120 [Camden]

Kramer, Sidney

— A History of Stone & Kimball and Herbert S. Stone & Co.... Chicago, [1940]. One of 1,000. In d/j; unopened. Sgd. cb Oct 17 (512) $85

Kramm, Christiaan

— De levens en werken der Hollandsche en Vlaamsche kunstschilders, beeldhouwers.... Amst., 1856-64. 6 parts plus Supplement in 3 vols. 4to, modern cloth. S Feb 11 (118) £170 [Brown]

Krantz, Albert, 1448-1517

— Rerum Germanicarum historici clarissimi.... Frankfurt: heirs of Andreas Wechel, 1590. Bound with: Wandalia. De Wandalorum vera origine.... Frankfurt, 1580. Folio, contemp blind-tooled pigskin over pastebd with panel stamps sgd HH 1560. sg Oct 24 (183) $425

Krascheninnikoff, Stephan Petrovich

— Opisanie zemli Kamchatki. St. Petersburg: Academy of Sciences, 1755. 2 vols. 4to, contemp calf. With 25 plates & maps, 19 of the folding. Some leaves dampstained, mostly in upper margin; final leaf of Vol Ii laid down on endpaper; library stamps. C May 20 (324) £3,800 [Remington]

Kratville, William W. —&
Ranks, Harold E.

— Motive Power of the Union Pacific. Omaha: Barnart Press, 1958. In d/j. cb Feb 13 (202) $160

Kraus, Hans P.

— The Cradle of Printing.... NY, 1954. One of 600. Inscr to James Ford Bell. cb Oct 17 (513) $55

[-] Homage to a Bookman; Essays...for Hans P. Kraus on his 60th Birthday. Berlin, [1967]. 4to, pictorial silk. sg May 21 (260) $80

Krauss, Johann Ulrich

— Historischer Bilder Bibel. Augsburg, 1700. 5 parts in 1 vol. Folio, 19th-cent mor gilt; worn. With 5 engraved titles, 5 frontises & 134 (of 136) plates. HH May 12 (867b) DM1,000

Kredel, Fritz. See: Koch & Kredel

Kress...

— Kress Library of Business and Economics: Catalogue.... Bost., 1957-67 & Fairfield, 1977. 4 vols. 4to, orig cloth. Ck Dec 12 (275) £320

Anr copy. 3 vols. 4to, cloth. O Sept 24 (141) $585

Kretschmer, Albert

See also: Rohrbach & Kretschmer

— Deutsche Volkstrachten. Leipzig, [c.1848]. 8vo, contemp half calf; covers detached, spine def. With 50 hand-colored plates. Tp cropped & laid down; some marginal soiling. S July 1 (932) £480 [Shapero]

Kreutzberger, Hans

— Warhafftige und eygentliche Contrafactur und Formen der Zeumung und Gebiss zu allerley Maengeln unnd Undterichtung der Pferdt.... Augsburg, 1562. Folio, contemp sheep over paper bds, tooled in blind, with central stamp in gilt of a galloping horse; rubbed & worn. With 412 woodcut illusts. Tear at fold of 2 leaves; small tear & cropping at f.200; minor burnhole in q3. Bound in at end are 52 leaves in Ms, headed Von erkantnus guter pfert. C June 24 (157) £7,500 [Kraus]

Kriegel, Georg Christoph

— Erb-Huldigung welche der allerdurchleuchtigst-grossmachtigsten Frauen Mariae Theresiae.... Vienna, [c.1740]. Folio, contemp calf gilt; 2 wormholes. With frontis & 11 plates, including 6 double-page & 1 of 2 sheets folding. Some worming. HH May 12 (753) DM5,400

Kristeller, Paul, 1863-1931

— Iter Italicum: A Finding List of Uncatalogued or Incompletely Catalogued Humanistic Manuscripts.... L, 1963-90. Vols I-V plus Vol III inde. sg Oct 31 (230) $200

Kroch, Carl. See: North & Kroch

Krombholz, Julius Vinzenz

— Naturgetreue Abbildungen und Beschreibungen der Schwaemme.... Prague, 1831-[47]. 10 parts in 2 vol, plus Atlas vol. Folio & oblong folio, contemp half calf; rubbed. With 62 hand-colored plates. Some spotting & soiling. Ck Oct 31 (99) £1,100

Kromer, Martin. See: Cromer, Martin

Kronenberg, M. E. See: Nijhoff & Kronenberg

Kruchenykh, A. See: Khlebnikov & Kruchenykh

Krusinski, Judas Thaddeus

— The History of the Revolution of Persia.... L, 1728. 2 vols. 8vo, contemp calf. Short tear to folding map. b June 22 (182) £480

Kuemmel, Otto

— Chinesische Kunst. Berlin, 1930. Out-of-series copy. Folio, cloth. With 150 plates. Library markings but plates unmarked. sg Feb 6 (152) $130

Kuesel, Melchior

— Icones Biblicae Veteris et Novi Testamenti. Augsburg, 1679. 5 parts in 1 vol. 4to, 18th-cent half calf. With 2 engraved titles, 5 engraved subtitles & 243 plates. Tear in Plate 33 in Part 3 repaired; other short tears; some soiling. S Dec 5 (226) £750 [Pirages]

Kume Yasuo

— Fine Handmade Papers of Japan. Tokyo, 1980. One of 200. 3 vols. Orig wraps. bba May 28 (597) £340 [Forster]

Anr copy. Orig wraps, unopened. pn June 11 (168) £300

Anr copy. Orig wraps. sg Nov 7 (127) $700

— Tesuki Washi Shuho. Tokyo: yushodo, 19779. 4 vols. 4to, patterned wraps. With 207 paper specimens. sg Nov 7 (126) $425

Kunz, George Frederick, 1856-1932

— The Book of the Pearl.... L & NY, 1908. 1st English Ed. 4to, modern half lea. Foldouts at pp. 333 & 398 detached at crease but present; plates stamped. sp June 18 (355) $50

1st Ed. NY, 1908. 4to, orig cloth; soiled. Inscr to Henry Ford, 1915. F Mar 26 (314C) $326

— Gems and Precious Stones of North America.... NY, 1890. 4to, orig cloth; soiled. F Mar 26 (313) $50

— Ivory and the Elephant in Art, in Archaeology, and in Science. Garden City, 1916. 4to, cloth; worn & shaken. Some soiling. Inscr. O May 26 (111) $400

— The Magic of Jewels and Charms. Phila. & L, 1915. 1st Ed. F Mar 26 (312) $70

— Rings for the Finger.... Phila. & L, 1917. Eva Le Gallienne's copy. sg Feb 6 (153) $100

Anr copy. Inscr. wa Dec 9 (436) $60

Kunze, Horst

— Geschichte der Buchillustration in Deutschland: Das 15. Jahrhundert. [Leipzig, 1975]. 2 vols. Folio, cloth, in d/js; text vol with front hinge cracked. sg Oct 31 (159) $90

Kuroda, Nagamichi

— Birds of the Island of Java. Tokyo, 1933-36. 2 vols. Folio, orig half cloth. With 34 colored plates & 2 maps. C May 20 (190) £1,200 [Chateau]

Kurth, Willi

— The Complete Woodcuts of Albrecht Duerer. L, 1927. One of 500. Intro by Campbell Dodgson. Folio, cloth; worn, front hinge cracked. sg Feb 6 (73) $250

Kurz, Rudolph Friederich

— The Journal of.... Wash., 1937. 1st Ed. Orig wraps; front cover barely hanging on. NH Oct 6 (134) $65

Anr copy. Wraps. sg June 18 (316) $60

Kyd, Pseud.

— The Characters of Charles Dickens. Paris & NY, [1889]. 4to, contemp half mor gilt; rubbed. With uncolored litho title & illust on verso of final leaf & 24 chromolithos. L Nov 14 (51) £70

L

La Barre de Beaumarchais, Antoine
See also: Picart, Bernard

— Le Temple des muses. Amst., 1742. Folio, 18th-cent mor gilt. With engraved title, engraved coat-of-arms & 60 plates. Some foxing to fore-margins. S Dec 5 (277) £1,000 [Chaponniere]

La Boessiere, T. de

— Traite de l'art des armes. Paris, 1818. 2 vols. 8vo, text vol in half mor; plate vol in contemp half calf. With 20 folding plates & with text vol containing full complement of the plates in facsimile. sg Mar 26 (46) $250

La Branche, George M. L.

— The Salmon and the Dry Fly. Bost., 1924. One of 775. Half calf by Sangorskii & Sutcliffe. Koopman copy. O Oct 29 (196) $160

La Chapelle, George de

— Recueil de divers portraits des principales dames de la Porte du Grand Turc. Paris: le Blond, [c.1658]. Folio, modern half mor. With engraved title & 12 plates. Engraved title cropped at foot & backed; all plates backed & 1 torn in margin & repaired. S June 30 (330) £1,300 [Kutluoglu]

La Chausse, Michel Ange de

— Le Grand Cabinet romain.... Amst., 1706. Folio, contemp calf; repaired. With engraved title & 43 plates. Some browning. S May 14 (1078) £220 [Milkain]

La Combe de Vrigny, — de
— Travels through Denmark and some Parts of Germany. L, 1707. 8vo, half lea; worn, several leaves detached. Cropped, with some loss of running heads; last few lines of caption on map lost. Z Apr 18 (53) $65

La Court, Pieter de. See: Court, Pieter de la

La Crequiniere, — de
— The Agreement of the Customs of the East-Indians.... L, 1705. 8vo, contemp calf; small strip torn from upper cover, short split at head of joint. With 6 plates. A few letters affected on F4 & 5 due to paper adhesion. b June 22 (165) £210

La Feuille, Daniel de
— Devises et emblemes anciennes & modernes.... Amst., 1691. 4to, later mor. With engraved title & 50 plates. Some soiling; a few leaves trimmed just affecting text; ad misptd on N1 verso. pn Sept 12 (8) £220
— Le theatre du monde ou les nouveaux travaux de Mars et de Neptune. Amst., 1703-[4]. 4 parts in 1 vol. 4to, contemp calf; spine ends wormed, sides worn. With 24 double-page or folding maps & town plans. A4 flawed at lower fore-margin without loss of text; E3 shaved at fore-margin touching letters. S May 14 (1073) £500 [Hermans]

La Folie, Louis Guillaume de
— Le Philosophe sans pretention, ou l'Homme rare. Paris, 1775. 8vo, contemp calf gilt. Library stamp on tp & p. 59. C June 24 (159) £400 [Parikian]

La Fontaine, Jean de, 1621-95
— 1678-94. - Fables choisies, mises en vers. Paris 5 vols in 3 plus the 1671 Fables nouvelles. 12mo, contemp calf gilt; not entirely uniform. Manney set. P Oct 11 (1197) $13,000
— 1685. - Contes et nouvelles en vers. Amst 3d Issue. 2 vols in 1. 12mo, modern calf. With frontis & 58 half-page plates. S July 1 (1082) £300 [Caribersa]
— 1688-87. - Fables choisies mises en vers. Antwerp 4 parts in 1 vol. 8vo, contemp calf. Epstein copy. sg Apr 30 (290) $900
— 1755-59. - Paris 4 vols. Folio, contemp calf gilt; corners scuffed, spines restored. Le Singe et le Leopard in 1st state without lettering on the banner. C Dec 16 (132) £2,700 [Bifolco]

Anr copy. Contemp mor gilt; some spine ends chipped, rubbed, some worming. With 275 plates, Le Singe et le Leopard in 1st state. Slade copy. C June 24 (160) £7,000 [Shapero]

Anr copy. 19th-cent calf gilt; joints weak. With frontis, port & 275 plates; Le Singe et le Leopard with legend in the banner. Loose with some discoloration & deterioration of margins through damp. pn Nov 14 (395) £2,000

Anr copy. 18th-cent mor gilt. With frontis & 275 plates, with Le singe et le leopard in its unlettered state. Short tear in lower margin of 1 plate. S May 28 (124) £6,000 [Shapero]

Anr copy. 18th-cent calf gilt. With 275 plates, with Le singe et le leopard in its unlettered state. Short tear in lower margin of plate opposite p. 180 in Vol IV. S May 28 (368) £2,800 [Shapero]
— 1764. - Contes et nouvelles en vers. Amst. 2 vols. 8vo, 18th-cent half calf over bds. With port & 80 plates before letters. S Nov 14 (433) £300 [Chribersa]

Anr copy. 19th-cent mor gilt; rubbed. With 80 plates. Lacking port; some spotting. S May 13 (843) £200 [Shapero]
— 1765-75. - Fables choisies mises en vers. Paris Vols I-II only. Contemp half calf; spine heads worn. Engraved throughout, with 2 titles, frontis & 86 plates. b June 22 (83) £90

Anr copy. 6 vols. 8vo, contemp calf gilt; worming to liners in Vol VI. With frontis, 6 engraved titles & 245 plates. Engraved throughout. C Dec 16 (133) £1,600 [Lyon]
— 1782. - Fables. Paris: Didot l'aine. 2 vols. 18mo, contemp calf, with gilt arms of Emperor Paul I of Russia as Grand Duke. C Dec 16 (135) £300 [Paradise]
— 1786. - Fables choisies, mises en vers. Leiden 6 vols in 3. contemp calf gilt; rebacked, spines worn, joints split. With engraved frontis & 275 plates. Some browning. pn Apr 23 (209) £190 [Shapero]
— An III [1795]. - Contes et nouvelles en vers. Paris 2 vols. 4to, 19th-cent sheep. sg Mar 5 (166) $110
— 1811. - Fables. Paris: A. Renouard. 12mo, contemp calf gilt; Vol II joints cracked. With 266 engraved vignettes in text. The only book ptd in relief using engraved stone blocks. Schlosser copy. P June 17 (473) $600
— 1838. - Paris Illus by J. J. Grandville. 2 vols. 8vo, half lea; spines cracked, rubbed. Some foxing. Met Apr 28 (96A) $100

Anr copy. Contemp lea gilt; rubbed. Some browning. SI June 9 (500) LIt450,000
— 1841. - Bost. 2 vols in 1. 8vo, orig cloth; shelf-number on spine. Some foxing. O Aug 25 (117) $90
— 1867. - Paris Illus by Gustave Dore. 2 vols. Folio, cloth; worn. O Mar 31 (108) $140
— 1868. - Paris: Hachette. Folio, orig half mor gilt. Manney copy. P Oct 11 (111) $900

— 1884. - Tales and Novels in Verse. Paris One of 100. Illus by Eisen. 2 vols. 8vo, half mor by Root. O May 26 (112) $140

— Les Amours de Psyche et de Cupidon. Paris, 1791. 4to, 19th-cent half mor. With 4 colored plates. SI June 9 (502) LIt2,000,000

Anr Ed. Paris: Didot, 1797. 4to, contemp half mor; rubbed. With 5 plates. Some foxing; ee2 with marginal defect. L.p. copy. bba May 28 (467) £320 [Archdale]

— Psyche. Paris, 1880. Unique copy ptd on vellum with an extra suite before letters on papier de chine. 16mo, mor extra by Chambolle-Duru; hinges cracked. CNY Dec 5 (370) $1,200

La Gueriniere, Francois Robichon de

— Ecole de cavalerie.... Paris, 1733. Folio, contemp calf; rubbed, spine blackened & worn, front free endpaper torn with loss. With engraved title & 24 plates & plans. A few plates shaved at head; wormhole affecting outer margin of later leaves. C June 24 (162) £800 [Bifolco]

Anr Ed. Paris, 1754. Folio, contemp calf; spine heads chipped. With frontis & 33 plates. S July 1 (1377) £300 [Booth]

La Harpe, Jean Francois de

— Abrege de l'histoire generale des voyages. Paris, 1780-1825. 45 vols including Atlas & Continuation. 8vo & 4to, contemp calf; not quite uniform. Atlas with 74 (of 75) maps. C May 20 (269) £1,600

Anr Ed. Paris, 1780-1801. 33 vols, including Atlas. 8vo & 4to, contemp calf; worn. Some browning. SI June 9 (504) LIt3,800,000

La Lande, Joseph Jerome le Francais de

— Bibliographie astronomique.... Paris, 1803 [An XI]. 4to, later 19th-cent half mor; worn. Some outer margins waterstained. Ck Nov 29 (203) £160

La Loubere, Simon de

— A New Historical Relation of the Kingdom of Siam.... L: F. L., 1693. 2 vols in 1. Folio, contemp calf; head of spine worn, short split at foot of upper joint. With 11 plates & maps. b June 22 (184) £1,600

La Marche, Olivier de, 1426?-1502

— El Cavallero determinado.... Antwerp: Juan Steelsio, 1553. 4to, 16th-cent calf with small crowned head with initials RA stamped in center of both covers. With 20 full-page woodcuts. S Dec 5 (158) £3,200 [Halwas]

Anr Ed. Antwerp: Plantin, 1591. 8vo, vellum gilt; stained. With 20 plates. Some stains. B May 12 (44) HF3,200

La Motte, Antoine Houdard de la. See: Houdart de la Motte, Antoine

La Motte, Guillaume Mauquet de

— A General Treatise of Midwifry. L, 1746. 1st Ed in English. 8vo, modern half calf gilt. Some browning. S Feb 25 (597) £250 [Dawson]

La Motte-Fouque, Friedrich H. C. de, 1777-1843

— Undine. L, 1909. Illus by Arthur Rackham. 4to, orig cloth. bba Oct 10 (153) £55 [Sotheran]; bba Jan 16 (393) £120 [Ulysses]

Anr copy. Orig cloth; spine rubbed, small tear at top of spine. With 15 color plates. K Mar 22 (388) $80

Anr copy. Orig cloth; endpapers foxed. With 15 tipped-on color plates; 1 detached. wa Dec 9 (447) $100

One of 1,000. Vellum. sg Sept 26 (266) $325

Anr copy. Mor gilt by Bayntun. sg Nov 7 (170) $500

Out-of-series copy. Orig vellum gilt; soiled. pn June 11 (183) £280 [Sotheran]

Anr Ed. L, 1919. 4to, orig cloth, in d/j. bba Apr 9 (336) £180 [Ulysses]

La Mottraye, Aubrey de

— Travels through Europe, Asia and into Part of Africa. L, 1723-32. 3 vols. Folio, contemp calf gilt; rebacked. With 79 plates, maps & plans. Some browning; a few tears; last 2 leaves in Vol III repaired at inner margin. S June 30 (331) £1,200 [Consolidated Real]

Anr copy. Contemp lea. Some fraying & browning. SI June 9 (506) LIt380,000

La Noue, Francois de, 1531-91

— Discours politiques et militaires. Basel, 1587. 4to, contemp vellum. Some dampstain in lower margins. S May 13 (776) £320 [Rouiller]

— The Politicke and Militarie Discourses. L: T. Orwin, 1587. 4to, 19th-cent calf; rubbed. Mostly black letter. Tp soiled & backed; some dampstaining; quire Ff wormed in upper inner margins; lacking final blank. STC 15215. S July 1 (1284) £250 [Knohl]

La Noue, Pierre de

— La Cavalerie francoise et italienne.... Lyons, 1620 [engraved title dated 1621. Folio, contemp vellum; rubbed & stained. bba Sept 5 (178) £700 [Shapero]

La Perouse, Jean Francois Galaup de, 1741-88

— A Voyage Round the World in the Years 1785.... L, 1798. ("The Voyage of M. de la Perouse round the World....") Atlas vol only. Folio, orig bds, uncut. With engraved title & 69 plates & maps. Some creasing; library labels on pastedown. S Feb 26 (707) £600 [Faupel]

Anr Ed. L, 1799. 3 vols including Atlas. 4to & folio, contemp calf & modern half calf; joints of text vols split at head and foot. S June 25 (56) £1,100 [Quaritch/ Hordern]

La Primaudaye, Pierre de

— L'Academie Francoise, de l'homme et de son institution.... Paris, 1602. 8vo, contemp vellum. Small stain through prelims. sg Mar 12 (171) $300

La Quintinye, Jean de

— The Compleat Gard'ner. L, 1693. Trans by John Evelyn. Folio, contemp calf gilt; spine repaired at head & foot. With port & 11 plates. Port, title & dedication with small repaired wormhole in lower blank margin; repaired tear to folding plate. C Oct 30 (238) £500 [Watson]

— Instruction pour les jardins fruitiers et potagers.... Paris, 1697. 2 vols. 4to, contemp calf, armorial bdg; spines worn, joints chipped. With port & 13 plates, 2 folding. wa Sept 26 (473) $290

La Rochefoucauld Liancourt, Francois Alexandre Frederic, 1747-1827

— Voyage dans les Etats-Unis d'Amerique.... Paris, [c.1799]. 8 vols. 4to, half calf; worn. With folding map in Vol I. LH Dec 11 (141) $100

Anr Ed. Paris, 1799. 8 vols. 4to, old calf; worn, corroded & powdered. O Apr 28 (177) $140

La Roque, Gilles Andre de

— Traite de l'Origine des Noms et des Surnoms. Paris: Etienne Michallet, 1681. 12mo, contemp sheep gilt; spine ends & corners worn, front joint cracked. sg Oct 24 (185) $350

La Roque, Jean de

— Voyage de l'Arabie Heureuse.... Amst., 1716. 12mo, 18th-cent sheep; brittle & worn. With frontis, folding map & 3 folding plates. Marginal dampstaining at end. sg Nov 7 (128) $500

La Salle, Nicolas de. See: Caxton Club

La Salle, Rene Robert Cavelier, Sieur de. See: Caxton Club

La Vardin, Jacques de

— Histoire de Georges Castriot surnomme Scanderbeg, roy d'Albanie. La Rochelle: Hierosme Hauultin, 1593. 8vo, contemp vellum; soiled. Minor waterstains. S June 30 (153) £280 [O'Neill]

La Varenne, Francois Pierre

— Le Cuisinier francois.... Rouen, 1700. 12mo, contemp vellum; soiled. Ck Oct 18 (182) £420

Laar, G. van

— Magazijn van Tuin-Sieraaden. Amst., [1814]. 4to, modern half calf. With 190 plates. CNY Dec 5 (341) $2,800

Labacco, Antonio

— Libro...appartenente a l'architettura.... Rome, [1557]. Folio, 19th-cent half mor; worn. With engraved title & 26 plates, 4 double-page or folding, numbered to 36. S Nov 21 (85) £900 [Bifolco]

Labarte, Jules

— Histoire des arts industriels.... Paris, 1864. One of-100 L.p. copies. 6 vols. 4to, contemp mor; extremities rubbed, some soiling. Ck Nov 29 (110) £500

2d Ed. Paris, 1872-75. 3 vols. 4to, contemp half mor; rubbed. With 79 (of 80) plates, mostly in color. S July 1 (1285) £130 [Hetherington]

Labaume, Eugene, 1783-1849

— Relation circonstanciee de la Campagne de Russie en 1812.... Paris, 1815. 8vo, modern half mor gilt. sg Jan 9 (135) $110

Labillardiere, Jacques Julien Houton de, 1755-1834

— Voyage in Search of La Perouse. L, 1800. 2 vols. 8vo, later half calf; joints split. With folding map & 45 plates. Some spotting. S June 25 (58) £750 [Quaritch/Hordern]

Laborde, Alexandre L. J., Comte de, 1774-1842

— Voyage pittoresque et historique de l'Espagne. Paris: Didot, 1806-20. Atlas vol only. 19th-cent half calf; worn, upper cover detached. With engraved title & 159 plates & plans, all torn horizontally in the centre & repaired; some dampstaining. Sold w.a.f. S Feb 26 (758) £550 [Elliott]

Laborde, Jean Benjamin de

— Choix de Chansons, mises en musique. Paris, 1773. 1st Ed. 4 parts in 2 vols. 8vo, contemp calf with gilt arms of Sir John Smith. Engraved throughout. C Dec 16 (129) £1,600 [Franklin]

— Essai sur la musique ancienne et moderne. Paris, 1780. 4 vols. 4to, contemp calf; rebacked, worn. pn Oct 24 (406) £220

Laborde, Leon de, 1807-69

— Journey through Arabia Petraea to Mount Sinai.... L, 1838. 2d Ed. 8vo, orig cloth. sg Jan 9 (102) $175

Laboureur, Jean Emile —& Cazotte, Jacques

— The Devil in Love.... L, 1925. One of 365. 8vo, half cloth. With frontis & 5 plates. sg Sept 26 (71) $130

Lacepede, Bernard de la Ville sur Illon, Comte de, 1756-1825

— Histoire naturelle de Lacepede. Paris, 1847. 2 vols. 8vo, half lea; worn. Foxed & soiled. O Apr 28 (122) $475

Lachevre, Frederic

— Bibliographie des recueils collectifs de poesies.... Paris, 1922. One of 352. 4to, cloth, orig wraps bound in. sg Oct 31 (174) $110

Lacinius, Janus

— Pretiosa Margarita, novella de thesauro.... Venice: Aldus, 1546. 1st Ed. 8vo, later calf. Lacking F44 & G44; some leaves misbound. Sold w.a.f. Ck Oct 31 (5) £400

Lackington, James, 1746-1815

— The Confessions of J. Lackington, Late Bookseller.... L, [1791]. cb Oct 17 (517) $85

— Memoirs of the First Forty-Five Years of the Life of.... L, [1791]. 1st Ed. 8vo, bdg not stated. cb Oct 17 (518) $85

Laclos, Pierre A. F. Choderlos de, 1741-1803

— Les Liaisons dangereuses. L, 1796 [but Paris, 1812]. Counterfeit Ed. 2 vols. 8vo, contemp calf. With 2 engraved frontises & 13 plates. Lacking final blank in Vol II. C Dec 16 (131) £300 [Paradise]

— Les Liaisons dangeureuses. Paris, 1934. One of 650. Illus by George Barbier. 2 vols. 4to, half mor, orig wraps bound in. With 22 illusts, all but 2 full-page. S Dec 5 (300) £800 [Panini]

Lacombe, Paul, 1834-1919

— Livres d'heures imprimes au XVe et au XVIe siecle. Paris, 1907. 8vo, cloth, orig wraps bound in. sg Oct 31 (175) $80

Lacroix de Vimeux, Rene, Comte de Rochambeau. See: Rochambeau, Rene Lacrois de Vimeux

Lacroix, Paul, 1806-84

— Le Moyen Age et la Renaissance. Paris, 1848-51. 5 vols. 4to, contemp half mor; 1 vol not uniform. cb Jan 9 (132) $275

Anr copy. With chromolitho additional title & 253 colored or partly colored plates, many heightened with gold or silver. S July 1 (1287) £300 [San Lorenzo]

Lactantius, Lucius Coelius Firmianus

— Opera. Venice: Andreas de Paltasichis and Boninus de Boninis, 12 Mar 1478 [i.e. 1479]. Folio, 19th-cent vellum. Type 2:112R; 112b Greek, 38 lines. Spaces for initial capitals, a few supplied in ink. Large repairs to first 2 leaves with considerable loss to text, supplied in ink facsimile; 3d leaf repaired with loss to a few letters. 212 (of 214) leaves; lacking blanks. Goff L-8. George Milne copy. CNY Dec 5 (272) $650

Anr Ed. Venice: Theodorus de Ragazonibus, 21 Apr 1490. Folio, later 19th-cent half sheep; spine ends chipped. Lacking table of contents. sg Mar 12 (122) $275

Anr Ed. Venice: Simon Bevilaqua, 4 Apr 1497. Folio, later bds. 45 lines & headline; roman letter. Hole in text of l5; wormholes in some margins; lower outer corners of last few leaves dampstained with some fraying & tearing. 139 (of 140) leaves; lacking initial blank. Goff L-13. S Dec 5 (21) £1,000 [Maggs]

Anr Ed. Venice: Aldus, 1535. 8vo, contep vellum; loose. Hole in 2d leaf with loss; some dampstainig & marginal worming; upper outer corners frayed at end with some text loss on last leaf. sg Mar 12 (166) $325

Lacy, Thomas Hiales

— Male Costumes, Historical, National & Dramatic. L, 1868. 4to, contemp half mor; rubbed & marked. With title & 200 hand-colored plates. bba Oct 10 (179) £360 [E. Nolan]

Ladd, William

— A Letter to Aaron Burr...by Philanthropos. NY, 1810. 8vo, modern wraps. sg Mar 26 (52) $100

L'Admiral, Jacob, 1694-1770

— Naauwkeurige waarneemingen, van veele gestaltverwisselende gekorvene Diertjes.... Amst., 1774. ("Naauwkeurige waarneemingen omtrent de veranderingen van veele insekten of gekorvene diertjes.") Folio, contemp half calf; some wear. With title with hand-colored engraved vignette & 33 hand-colored plates. First 6 leaves with tear in upper margin; a few leaves with soil. C Oct 30 (286) £1,400 [Watson]

Laennec, Rene Theophile Hyacinthe, 1781-1826

— De l'auscultation mediate.... Paris, 1819. 1st Ed. 2 vols. 8vo, contemp half sheep gilt; spines faded. With 4 folding plates. sg Nov 14 (65) $1,600

Laet, Johannes de, 1593-1649

— Nieuwe Wereldt, ofte Beschrijvinghe van West-Indien.... Leiden: Elzevir, 1630. ("Beschrijvinghe van West-Indien.") 2d Ed. Folio, 18th-cent bds; worn, spine missing. With engraved title & 14 double-page maps; 1st 6 maps hand-colored. O Nov 26 (101) $3,100

— Persia, seu Regni Persici Status, variaque itinera in atque per Persiam. Leiden: Elzevir, 1633. 1st Ed. 16mo, contemp vellum with yapp edges. With engraved title & 8 plates. wa Sept 26 (522) $160

Laffan, William MacKay, 1848-1909

— Engravings on Wood.... NY, 1887. Folio, orig cloth; worn & soiled. With 25 plates. F Mar 26 (756) $135

Laffillee, H. See: Gelis-Didot & Laffillee

Lafitau, Joseph Francois, 1670-1740

— Histoire des decouvertes et conquestes des Portugais dans le nouveau monde. Paris, 1733. 1st Ed. 2 vols. 4to, contemp calf. With frontis, folding map & 13 plates. bba Apr 9 (149) £560 [Dawson]

— Moeurs des sauvages ameriquains comparees aux moeurs des premiers temps. Paris, 1724. 1st Ed. 2 vols. 4to, contemp vellum; stained. With frontis, 41 plates & map. Some browning; occasional old repairs to inner margins. Ck Nov 29 (22) £500

Anr copy. Contemp calf. With map & 42 plates. SI Dec 5 (905) LIt1,700,000

LaFrentz, Ferdinand W.

— Cowboy Stuff: Poems. NY, 1927. Out-of-series copy. Illus by Henry Ziegler. 4to, bdg not described. NH May 30 (202) $200

Lahontan, Louis Armand, Baron de, 1666-1715

— New Voyages to North America. L, 1703. 2 vols. 8vo, contemp calf with initials RS branded into each of 4 sides; front outer joint of Vol II cracked. With 4 maps & 20 plates. Final blank wanting in Vol II. CNY Oct 8 (144) $2,500

Anr Ed. Chicago, 1905. One of 75. 2 vols. 8vo, bds. sg Jan 9 (103) $225

— Nouveaux voyages de Mr. le Baron de Lahontan dans l'Amerique septentrionale.... The Hague, 1703. 2 vols. 12mo, contemp calf; extremities rubbed. Writing on tp inked out; 1 plate holed at lower margin; some browning. Ck Oct 31 (13) £480

Laing, John, 1809-80. See: Halkett & Laing

Lairesse, Gerard de, 1641-1711

— The Art of Painting.... L, 1778. 4to, 19th-cent half calf gilt. With frontis & 69 plates (numbered 1-71). sg Sept 6 (173) $325

Laking, Sir Guy Francis

— Sevres Porcelain of Buckingham Palace and Windsor Castle. L, 1907. 4to, orig half mor; spine def, needs rebacking, covers nearly detached. With 63 color plates. sg Sept 6 (228) $250

Lal, Mohan

— The Life of the Amir Dost Mohammed Khan of Kabul. L, 1846. 2 vols. 8vo, 19th-cent calf gilt; joints rubbed. With 19 mtd india-proof ports. sg May 21 (61) $300

LaLoubere, Simon de. See: La Loubere, Simon de

Lamartine de Prat, Marie Louis Alphonse de, 1790-1869

— Souvenirs, impressions, pensees et paysages.... Paris, 1835. 1st Ed. 4 vols. 8vo, contemp half mor gilt; rubbed; head & foot of spines worn. With frontises & 2 folding litho maps. DW Dec 11 (48) £60

Lamb, Charles, 1775-1834

See also: Gregynog Press

— The Adventures of Ulysses. L, 1808. 1st Ed. 12mo, orig bds. With engraved title & frontis. Leaves of gathering I rehinged. Epstein copy. sg Apar 30 (291) $800

— John Woodvil. L, 1802. 8vo, mor gilt by Bedford. Inscr (partially erased) on a leaf from anr copy bound in before tp. C June 24 (163) £380 [Hannas]

— Letters and Writings. L, 1876. Ed by Percy Fitzgerald. 6 vols. 8vo, calf by Kaufmann; rubbed; 1 cover detached. O Feb 25 (120) $110

— A Masque of Days.... L, 1901. Illus by Walter Crane. 4to, orig half cloth, in d/j. sg Jan 30 (26) $120

Anr copy. Half cloth; spine discolored. Library markings. sg Mar 5 (44) $50

— Works. L, 1899-1900. One of 675. Ed by Alfred Ainger. 12 vols. 8vo, cloth. pnE Oct 1 (217) £50

Anr Ed. L, 1903. One of 200 L.p. copies. Ed by William Macdonald. 12 vols. Orig half vellum. O Dec 17 (115) $50

Lamb, Charles & Mary

— Mrs. Leicester's School.... L, 1809. 2d Ed. 12mo, later calf; rubbed. Lacking some ads; some spotting. bba July 23 (95) £120 [Stevenson]

— Tales from Shakespeare. L, 1807. 1st Ed, 1st Issue. 2 vols. 8vo, contemp calf gilt; joints rubbed, upper joint of Vol I repaired, spines scuffed. With 20 plates, including frontises.. C Dec 16 (213) £1,400 [Franklin]

Anr copy. Modern calf. Epstein copy. sg Apr 30 (292) $2,600

2d Ed. L, 1810. 2 vols. 12mo, contemp half sheep; rubbed. With 2 frontises & 18 plates. pn Dec 12 (244) £170

Anr Ed. L, 1909. Illus by Arthur Rackham. 4to, orig cloth. With 12 colored plates. F Sept 26 (80) $80

One of 750. Orig cloth. b Nov 18 (101) £600

Anr copy. Orig cloth; soiled. With 13 color plates. Ck July 10 (321) £280

Anr copy. Orig cloth. With the additional color plate. sg Nov 7 (171) $900

Anr copy. Orig cloth; soiled. sg Jan 30 (151) $700

Lamb, Dana S.

— Bright Salmon and Brown Trout. Barre, [1964]. One of 350. Half mor. O Oct 29 (189) $250

— Green Highlanders and Pink Ladies. Barre, 1971. One of 1,500. Koopman copy. O Oct 29 (190) $120

— Not Far from the River. Barre, 1967. One of 1,500. Koopman copy. O Oct 29 (191) $80

— On Trout Streams and Salmon Rivers. Barre, 1963. Orig cloth; edges soiled. wa Mar 5 (518) $220

One of 1,500. Koopman copy. O Oct 29 (192) $475

— Some Silent Places Still. Barre, 1969. One of 1,500. Koopman copy. O Oct 29 (193) $90

— Where the Pools are Bright and Deep. NY: Winchester, [1973]. One of 250. Half syn. Koopman copy. O Oct 29 (194) $150

— Wood-Smoke and Watercress. Barre, 1965. One of 200. Half calf; worn. O Oct 29 (195) $250

Lamb, Martha J.

— History of the City of New York.... NY, 1921. 3 vols. Lea; rubbed & bumped. Met Apr 28 (471) $60

Lamb, Patrick

— Royal Cookery.... L, 1726. ("Royal Cookery: or, the Compleat Court-Cook.") 3d Ed. 8vo, modern half calf. With 39 (of 40) plates, some folding. Some waterstaining; 1 plate def. S May 14 (990) £240 [Petta]

Lambard, William, 1536-1601

— A Perambulation of Kent.... L, 1596. 2d Ed. 4to, 19th-cent mor. Black letter; tp within typographic border; full-page woodcut map of England & Walers. Folding woodcut map of the beacons in facsimile; small wormhole at inner margin of a few leaves; tp soiled & neatly repaired at edges. STC 15176. S May 14 (1150) £250 [Janbrugh]

Lambert, Charles J.

— The Voyage of the "Wanderer": from the Journals and Letters.... L, 1883. 8vo, modern cloth. With colored folding map. L Nov 14 (153) £70

Lambert, John

— Travels through Lower Canada and the United States of North America in the Years 1806, 1807, and 1808.... L, 1813. 2d Ed. 2 vols. 8vo, contemp half calf; rubbed. With folding map, colored plan & 16 plates, 6 colored. bba Oct 10 (241) £300 [Demetzy]

Anr copy. Early calf; spines worn, Vol II partly split along center. Some foxing; tear in frontis map with tape repair & resulting stain. wa Apr 9 (82) $350

Lambertini, Vittorio

— Trattato di scherma...di spada e sciabola. Bologna, 1870. 8vo, cloth; rebacked with paper. With frontis & 29 folding plates. sg Mar 26 (164) $300

Lambourne, Alfred

— Scenic Utah: Pen and Pencil. NY, 1891. Folio, half cloth; needs rebdg. sg June 18 (320) $60

Lambrazini, Gregorio

— New and Curious School of Theatrical Dancing. L, 1928. One of 300. Inscr by Serge Diaghilev to Georges Balanchine. Kochno copy. SM Oct 12 (530) FF5,000

Lami, Eugene. See: Vernet & Lami

Lami, Giovanni, 1697-1770

— Lezioni di antichita Toscane.... Florence, 1766. 1st Ed. 2 vols. 4to, half vellum. L.p. copy. SI Dec 5 (906) LIt1,100,000

Lamotte, Bernard

— Proust Portfolio: The France of Marcel Proust. NY, 1949. One of 100. Folio, loose as issued in cloth case. With 25 etchings. sg Sept 26 (154) $425

Lamson, J.

— Round Cape Horn.... Bangor, 1878. 1st Ed. 12mo, half cloth; rear cover with defs at edges. sg June 18 (91) $90

Lamy, Bernard, 1640-1715

— Apparatus Biblicus: or, an Introduction to the Holy Scriptures.... L, 1723. 4to, 18th-cent sheep. With 19 plates & 4 maps & plans. sg Mar 12 (168) $275

Lancaster, Albert. See: Houzeau & Lancaster

Lancaster, James

— De Eerste Scheeps-Togt Gedaan na Oost-Indien. Leiden: Pieter van der Aa, [1706]. Folio, modern bds. With folding map. sg Jan 9 (104) $200

Lancelott, F.

— Australia as it is. L, 1852. 2 vols. 8vo, orig cloth; minor wear. kh Nov 11 (705) A$440

Lancisius, Giovanni Maria

— Dissertatio de nativis, deque adventitiis Romani coeli qualitatibus.... Rome, 1711. 4to, contemp vellum. Some foxing. S Nov 14 (503) £480 [Phelps]

— Opera varia in unum congesta. Venice, 1739. 2 vols in 1. Folio, contemp vellum. With 2 folding maps & 10 plates. Corner dampstained throughout. cb Feb 12 (72) $375

Anr copy. Lacking 1 plate. SI Dec 5 (329) LIt550,000

Lancour, A. Harold

— American Art Auction Catalogues, 1785-1942: a Union List. NY, 1944. Wraps. O Sept 24 (142) $275

Landacre, Paul

— California Hills and Other Wood Engravings.... Los Angeles, 1931. One of 500. Orig bds. b&b Feb 19 (292) $650

Lande Collection, Lawrence M.

— The Lawrence Lande Collection of Canadiana in the Redpath Library of McGill University. Montreal, 1965-71. One of 950. Half pigskin. O Sept 24 (143) $150; wd June 12 (398) $125

Lander, Richard, 1804-34

— Records of Captain Clapperton's Last Expedition to Africa. L, 1830. 1st Ed. 2 vols. 8vo, cloth. pnE Oct 1 (315) £110

Landi, Giuseppe Antonio

— Racolta di alcune Facciate di Palazzi e Cortili de piu riguardevoli di Bologna. Bologna: Lelio dalla Volpe, [c.1750]. Folio, contemp bds; rebacked in calf. With double-page engraved title & 29 double-page plates showing 30 numbered subjects & a folding plate at end (torn without loss). S June 25 (176) £1,800 [Pregliasco]

Landis, Dennis C. See: Brown Library, John Carter

Landon, Perceval

— Lhasa. L, 1905. 2 vols. DW Dec 11 (49) £105

Landor, A. Henry Savage

— China and the Allies. L, 1901. 2 vols. Orig cloth; 1 spine repaired. DW May 13 (37) £105

— In the Forbidden Land: An Account of a Journey into Tibet.... NY, 1899. 2 vols. 8vo, cloth. With 8 color plates. O Apr 28 (178) $120

Anr copy. Cloth; soiled & rubbed, splits at spine ends, shaken. With folding map, frontis, 8 chromolithos & other plates. wa Apr 9 (154) $50

Landor, Edward Wilson

— The Bushman: or, Life in a New Country. L, 1847. 8vo, orig cloth; worn & frayed, stain at upper corners of covers, front hinge split, 1 signature sprung. With frontis & 3 plates. Some foxing. bbc Sept 23 (184) $65

Landor, Walter Savage, 1775-1864
See also: Limited Editions Club

— Gebir, Count Julian, and Other Poems. L, 1831. 8vo, cloth; rubbed & marked. bba Nov 28 (347) £50 [Ogino]

Landscape. See: Sands & Kenny

Landseer, Thomas, 1795-1880

— Monkey-ana. L, 1827. 6 parts in 1 vol. 4to, orig cloth; worn & stained. With title & 24 plates. bba Oct 24 (246) £220 [Walford]

Anr Ed. L, 1857. ("Monkey-ana, or Men in Miniature.") Folio, half calf; worn, joints starting. With 24 mtd india-proof plates. Dampstained, not affecting plates. sg Sept 19 (196) $400

Landwehr, John

— Romeyne de Hooghe.... Leiden, 1973. One of 1,000. Oblong folio, cloth. sg Oct 31 (176) $60

Lane, William Coolidge

— A Catalogue of the Washington Collection in the Boston Athenaeum. Bost., 1897. Ltd Ed. 8vo, orig cloth; worn, inner joints open. K Sept 29 (435) $50

Lanery d'Arc, Pierre

— Le Livre d'Or de Jeanne d'Arc.... Paris, 1894. One of 330. 8vo, cloth; worn. O Sept 24 (63) $100

Lang, A. See: Grabhorn Printing

Lang, Andrew, 1844-1912

— Ballads of Books. NY, 1887. One of 100. Ed by Brander Matthews. cb Oct 17 (584) $170

Lang, John Dunmore

— An Historical and Statistical Account of New South Wales. L, & Edin., 1837. 2d Ed. 2 vols. 8vo, early half calf; worn. kh Nov 11 (537A) A$140

— Queensland, Australia: a Highly Eligible Field for Emigration.... L, 1864. 8vo, bdg not described but upper hinge loose. With 2 folding maps. Leaf removed before half-title; 1 folding map loosely inserted. kh Nov 11 (538) A$160

Lang, R. Hamilton

— Cyprus. L, 1878. 8vo, orig cloth. With 4 colored maps (1 folding) & 1 plate. S June 30 (45) £320 [Caramondanis]

Langbaine, Gerard, 1656-92

— An Account of the English Dramatick Poets. Oxford, 1691. 1st Ed. 8vo, old calf; worn. O Feb 25 (123) $160

Langdon, John Emerson

— Canadian Silversmiths, 1700-1900. Toronto, 1966. One of 1,000. In d/j. bba Aug 13 (39) £55 [Hetherington]

Lange, Karl Nikolaus

— Historia lapidum figuratorum Helvetiae.... Venice: J. Tomasini, 1708. Bound with: Appendix, 1735. And: Tractatus de origine lapidum figuratorum. Lucerne, 1709. Methodus nova & facilis testacea marina. Lucerne, 1722. 4to, contemp calf; rubbed. S Dec 5 (403) £1,700 [Schumann]

Lange, Ludwig

— Koeln. Cologne, [c.1870]. 8vo, orig bds. With 22 plates. Some spotting. b June 22 (251) £160

Langeren, Jacob van

— A Direction for the English Traviller. L: T. Jenner, [1643]. 8vo, contemp calf; worn & stained. With 28 maps only. Lacking Bedfordshire, Buckinghamshire, Kent, Northumberland, Norfolk, Somerset, Sussex, Worcestershire, Wiltshire & the 4 folding maps; lacking tp & prelim text; some browning; some maps loose. S Nov 15 (964) £420 [Jackson]

Langland, William, 1332?-1400?

— The Vision of Pierce Plowman. L, 1550. 2d Ed. 4to, early 19th-cent calf gilt by Hering, 1819 (his bill tipped in at the front). Black letter. Tp with repair to upper outer corner & at inner margin with parts of 1st line of the title supplied in Ms facsimile; anr leaf similarly repaired. STC 19907. C Dec 16 (214) £1,200 [Grant & Shaw]

4th Ed. L: O. Rogers, 21 Feb 1561. 4to, modern calf. Lacking the Crede; washed; faint Ms marginalia; some soiling. STC 19908. P June 17 (250) $2,250

Langle, H. F. M.

— Traite d'Harmonie et de Modulation. Paris, 1793. Folio, contemp vellum gilt, with presentation label on upper cover. Ck Oct 31 (144) £750

Langles, Louis Mathieu

— Relation de Dourry Efendy.... Paris, 1810. 8vo, contemp half calf. S June 30 (332) £1,200 [Atabey]

Langley, Batty, 1696-1751

— The City and Country Builder's and Workman's Treasury of Designs. L, 1750. 4to, contemp calf. With 200 plates. Repaired wormtrack in fore-margin of 1st few quires; anr wormtrack affecting lower blank margins of plates 123 to 200, neatly patched. McCarty-Cooper copy. CNY Jan 25 (39) $300

Anr Ed. L, 1756. 4to, modern half mor gilt. With 200 plates. Tp rehinged; lacking at least 2 prelim leaves; library markings. sg Sept 6 (174) $650

— New Principles of Gardening. L, 1728. 1st Ed. 4to, contemp sheep; rebacked preserving orig spine, corners repaired. With 28 folding plates. Prelims, last gathering of plates & some fore-edges foxed; several plates shaved to platemark with loss of numerals or engravers' names. McCarty-Cooper copy. CNY Jan 25 (37) $1,700

Anr copy. Contemp calf; front hinge cracked, 1 endleaf detached. Small ink stain to upper edges of 1st 20 leaves; several plates shaved to platemark with loss of numerals or engravers' names; some plates with repaired tears & other defs. CNY Jan 25 (38) $850

— Pomona: or the Fruit-Garden Illustrated.... L, 1729. Folio, contemp calf; rebacked. With 79 (on 68) uncolored plates. Foremargins of 12 plates shaved; 1 plate with small marginal tear. C Oct 30 (207) £1,400 [Spelman]

Anr copy. Contemp calf; worn, rebacked, new endpapers. Tp & 1st few leaves dampstained; Plates 5 & 56 shaved, affecting platemark; stamps on verso of tp, upper margin of 1st leaf of text & verso of final plate. pn Mar 19 (300) £1,400 [Toscani]

Langley, Batty & Thomas

— Ancient Architecture Restored, and Improved.... [L, 1742]. 4to, contemp calf; rebacked with fragments of orig spine laid down, corners restored. With engraved title & 64 plates. Marginal tear to title; Plates 57-62 & A-B washed & resized. McCarty-Cooper copy. CNY Jan 25 (40) $450

— The Builder's Jewel, or the Youth's Instructor and Workman's Remembrancer.... L,

1757. 16mo, contemp calf; rebacked, loose in bdg. With frontis & 99 plates. Margins trimmed close. sg Feb 6 (157) $300

— Gothic Architecture. L, 1747. 4to, contemp blind-tooled calf; rebacked, 3 corners repaired, covers scratched & chipped. With engraved title & 64 plates. Minor dampstaining to gutters of a few plates; marginal worming; tp edges frayed & browned. McCarty-Cooper copy. CNY Jan 25 (41) $500

Langley, Samuel Pierpont, 1834-1906

— Langley Memoir on Mechanical Flight. Wash., 1911. Cloth; soiled, tape repairs at hinges & gutter of tp. bbc Sept 23 (243) $110

Anr copy. 2 parts in 1 vol. Orig cloth; spine rubbed. With 101 plates numbered as 104. pn May 14 (89) £110 [Nelson]

Langlois, Victor, 1863-1929

— Voyage dans la Cilicie. L, 1861. 8vo, contemp half mor gilt; worn. With port on india paper & 28 plates & folding litho map. Some browning. S June 30 (154) £550 [Maggs]

Langton, Robert, 1825-1900

— The Childhood and Youth of Charles Dickens. L, 1891. One of 300. 4to, cloth; worn, spine ends frayed. bbc Dec 9 (453) $80

Languet, Thomas

— Cooper's Chronicle...unto the Death of Queene Marie. L, 1560. 4to, 18th-cent sheep; broken, worn. Black letter. Tp loose, with gutter frayed; dampstaining in lower margins at end. STC 15218. sg Mar 12 (170) $500

Lanier, Henry W.

See also: Derrydale Press

— Greenwich Village, Today & Yesterday. NY, [1949]. 1st Ed. Illus by Berenice Abbott. In d/j with minor wear & foxing. bbc Feb 17 (164) $110

Anr copy. In d/j. sg Oct 8 (2) $175

Anr copy. In chipped d/j. With postcard, sgd with initials by Abbott, laid in. sg Apr 13 (1) $200

Lantier, Etienne Francois de

— Voyages d'Antenor en Grece et en Asie.... Paris: Belin, 1798. 3 vols. 8vo, calf gilt; extremities worn. With 5 plates. Some foxing. wa Mar 5 (553) $70

Lapie, Pierre & Alexandre Emile

— Atlas universel de geographie ancienne et moderne.... Paris, 1829-[33]. Folio, half sheep; rubbed & worn; front hinge cracked. With 35 colored double-page maps. 2 maps splitting at central crease. cb Jan 30 (148) $550

Laplace, Pierre Simon de, Marquis, 1749-1827

— Mecanique celeste. Bost., 1829-39. Trans by Nathaniel Bowditch.. 4 vols. 4to, contemp half calf; worn. Tp torn at outer margins & soiled. Ck Nov 29 (204) £550

— Theorie analytique des probabilities. Paris, 1820. 3d Ed. 4to, contemp sheep gilt with arms of Balliol College, Oxford; spine rubbed. Some foxing. sg May 14 (288) $2,400

— Traite mecanique celeste. Paris, [1798-99]-1805. Vols I-IV (of 5). 4to, orig wraps; worn. With Supplements to Vol III-IV. bba Apr 9 (187) £220 [Laywood]

Larbaud, Valery, 1881-1957

— 200 Chambres, 200 Salles de Bains. The Hague: Jean Gondrexon, 1927. One of 20 on hollande antique for Dorbon-Aine, this with an extra suite of the engravings on japon. Illus by J. E. Laboureur. Mor extra by Huser, orig wraps bound in. S May 28 (370) £1,100 [Sims Reed]

— Beaute, mon beau souci. Paris, 1920. One of 412. Illus by J. E. Labourer. Mor extra by Semet & Plumelle, orig wraps bound in. Inscr to Adrienne Monnier. S May 28 (369) £2,800 [Rassam]

Lardner, William Branson —& Brock, Michael John

— History of Placer and Nevada Counties California, with Biographical Sketches.... Los Angeles, 1924. Half mor. cb Sept 12 (106) $80

Lark...

— The Lark. San Francisco, 1896-97. 2 vols. 8vo, orig cloth. Vol I inscr; Vol II with ANs from Burgess tipped in. cb Sept 19 (120) $250

Anr copy. Title & added prelims of Vol I chipped and becoming detached; title tape-repaired. cb Feb 12 (43) $100

Larpenteur, Charles

See also: Coues, Elliott

— Forty Years a Fur Trader on the Upper Missouri. NY, 1898. 1st Ed, one of 950. Ed by Elliott Coues. 2 vols. 8vo, orig cloth; extremities worn. NH Aug 23 (442) $170

Out-of-series copy. Orig cloth. sg June 18 (321) $200

Larson, James

— Sergeant Larson 4th Cav. San Antonio, 1935. One of 300. NH May 30 (168) $250

Lartigue, J. H.

— Boyhood Photos of J. H. Lartigue: The Family Album of a Gilded Age. [Lausanne]: Ami Guichard, [1966]. Oblong 4to, orig cloth; minor stains. sg Oct 8 (45) $500

Anr copy. Cloth; head of spine bumped. sp Feb 6 (355) $175

Las Casas, Bartolome de las. See: Casas, Bartolome de las

Las Cases, Emmanuel, Marquis de

— Memorial de Sainte Helene: Journal of the Private Life and Conversations of the Emperor Napoleon at Saint Helena. L, 1823. 8 parts in 4 vols. 8vo, lev gilt with upper cover of each vol set with an oval port miniature. Extra-illus with c.150 ports, plates & maps. CNY Dec 5 (383) $4,800

Anr copy. 4 vols. 8vo, half sheep. Margins of Vol II wormed. sg Jan 9 (140) $60

Lasca, Academico Fiorentino

— Tutti i Trionfi, carri mascheaate o canti carnascialeschi andati per Firenze. Florence, 1559. 8vo, contemp half calf. SI Dec 5 (861) LIt850,000

Lassaigne, Jacques

— The Ceiling of the Paris Opera. NY, [1966]. Illus by Marc Chagall. 4to, cloth, in d/j with stain at base of spine. bbc Apr 27 (438) $200

Anr copy. Cloth, in d/j with edge wear & chipping. bbc Apr 27 (439) $160

Anr copy. Cloth, in d/j. sg Apr 2 (49) $225

— Chagall. [Paris]: Maeght, [1957]. 4to, wraps, in d/j. Met Apr 28 (53) $1,300

— Marc Chagall, Drawings and Water Colors for the Ballet. NY, [1969]. Folio, orig cloth, in d/j. bbc Sept 23 (143) $240

Lassels, Richard, 1603?-68

— The Voyage of Italy.... Paris & L, 1670. 2 parts in 1 vol. 12mo, later vellum. With frontis (browned in margin). C Oct 30 (109) £400 [Grabin]

Anr copy. Contemp calf gilt. sg May 7 (135) $700

Lasteyrie, Charles Philibert de

— Lettres autographes et inedites de Henry IV.... Paris, [1815-16]. Folio, contemp sheep-backed bds. Lithographed throughout; with tp, port, dedication & 10 plates. Some foxing. From the library of Louis-Philippe. Schlosser copy. P June 17 (562) $700

Lastri, Marco, b.1731

— L'Etruria pittrice.... Florence, 1791-95. 2 vols. Folio, contemp bds; worn. With frontis, engraved titles & 121 plates. SI Dec 5 (907) LIt4,200,000

Latham, Charles

— The Gardens of Italy. L, 1905. Descriptions by Evelyn March Phillipps. 2 vols. Folio, orig cloth; worn, top of back cover of Vol I soiled. K Sept 29 (176) $100

Latham, John, 1740-1837

— A General Synopsis of Birds. L, 1781-85. Deluxe Issue with plates ptd in reverse & colored by Sarah Stone. 3 vols in 6. 4to, contemp mor gilt by Walther, with badge of the house of Commons Library gilt; 1 spine damaged at head & cover loose. With 106 hand-colored plates & 6 titles. S Nov 21 (27) £3,000 [Marshall]

Lathy, Thomas Pike

— The Angler; A Poem in Ten Cantos.... L, 1820. 8vo, contemp mor gilt by Thomas Gosden, with a fore-edge painting of an angler. pn Mar 19 (379) £280

Latimore, Sarah B. —& Haskell, Grace C.

— Arthur Rackham: a Bibliography. Los Angeles, 1936. One of 550. Bds. cb Feb 27 (85) $120; sg Jan 30 (157) $200

Latour, Arsene Lacarriere

— Historical Memoir of the War in West Florida.... Phila., 1816. Text vol only; lacking Atlas. 8vo, old half calf; worn. Piece torn from top edge of tp. bbc Sept 23 (332) $140

Latrobe, John H. B.

— Picture of Baltimore. Balt.: F. Lucas, [1832]. 1st Ed. 18mo, orig mor; rebacked. With engraved title, folding map & 41 plates. Some foxing. bbc June 29 (487) $170

Laucevicius, E.

— Popierius Lietuvoje XV-XVIIIa. Vilna, 1967. 2 vols. Folio, cloth, in d/j. O Sept 24 (144) $100

Anr copy. Cloth, in d/js with pieces lacking from spine ends. pba July 23 (163) $100

Lauder, William, d.1771

— An Essay on Milton's Use and Imitation of the Moderns in his Paradise Lost. L, 1750. 1st Issue. 8vo, modern half calf. sg Mar 12 (156) $500

Laufer, Berthold, 1874-1934
See also: Caxton Club

— Jade: A Study in Chinese Archaeology and Religion. South Pasadena, 1946. sg Feb 6 (141) $80

Laughlin, Clarence John

— Ghosts along the Mississippi. NY, 1948. Folio, cloth. LH Dec 11 (142) $250

Laurencin, Marie, 1885-1956

— Le Carnet des Nuits. Brussels, 1942. One of 25 on velin blanc. Orig wraps, in d/j. Inscr. Kochno copy. SM Oct 12 (490) FF3,500

— Petit Bestiaire: Poemes Inedits. Paris, [1926]. One of 100 on verge d'arches. With 2 orig lithos. Inscr to Valentine Jean Hugo. P Dec 12 (62) $1,300

Laurent de l'Ardeche, Paul Mathieu. See: Laurent, Paul Mathieu

Laurent, Paul Mathieu

— Histoire de l'Empereur Napoleon. Paris, 1840. Illus by Horace Vernet. 8vo, orig cloth; extremities worn. With 25 hand-colored plates. F Mar 26 (465) $75

Lauretta...

— Lauretta, the Little Savoyard. L, 1815. 8vo, orig wraps. With complete set of 7 colored figures & the accompanying colored head. 1 detail detached. Salomons copy. sg Oct 17 (286) $750

Lauri, Jacobus

— Antiquae urbis splendor.... Rome, 1612-[14]. Oblong 4to, disbound. With engraved title & 97 plates only. Tp & dedication trimmed & mtd; marginal dampstains; some lower margins renewed; 1 plate with tear repaired. sg Apr 2 (163) $425

Anr copy. Half calf; worn. With port & 167 plates. Some marginal spotting & browning; 1st 2 leaves worn & backed. SI Dec 5 (355) LIt4,000,000

Laurie, Robert —& Whittle, James

— New Traveller's Companion. L, 1813. 7th Ed. Folio, contemp mor; worn. With folding general map of England and Wales & 25 double-page county maps. DW Dec 11 (113) £130

Lauro, Giacomo. See: Lauri, Jacobus

Lavacrum. See: Jacobus de Gruitroede

Lavalee, Joseph, 1717-1816

— Voyage pittoresque et historique de l'Istrie et de la Dalmatie. Paris: Pierre Didot l'Aine, [1802]. Folio, orig half mor; worn. With engraved title, frontis, double-page map & 66 plates. Plate 7 torn & repaired without loss. S July 1 (572) £500 [Consolidated Real]

Lavater, Johann Caspar, 1741-1801

— Essays on Physiognomy. L, 1810. 3 vols in 5. 4to, contemp bds; rebacked, rubbed. Internal dampstaining & soiling. F Mar 26 (772) $150

Anr copy. Contemp calf; worn. Browned. HH May 12 (1851) DM1,300

— Physiognomische Fragmente zur Befoerderung der Menschenkenntnis und Menschenliebe. Leipzig, 1775. Vols II-IV (of 4). 4to, contemp calf; worn. With titles & 273 plates. Some scribbles & stains. bba Oct 10 (180) £300 [Finney]

Laver, James, b.1899

— A History of British and American Etching. L, 1929. 4to, orig cloth; lower corners bumped. With 84 plates. pba Aug 20 (133) $70

Lavoisier, Antoine Laurent, 1743-94

— Traite elementaire de chimie. Paris, 1793. 3d Ed. 2 vols. 8vo, half sheep gilt; fore-edges dampstained throughout & reinforced. With 2 folding tables & 13 folding plates. sg May 14 (290) $350

Law, John, 1796-1873

— Address delivered before the Vincennes Historical and Antiquarian Society.... Louisville, 1839. 8vo, orig wraps; worn & chipped. With folding map. Fold splits to map; stamps to cover & tp verso. Z Nov 23 (201) $50

Law, William, 1681-1751. See: Franklin Printing, Benjamin

Law, William, 1686-1761

— A Serious Call to a Devout and Holy Life. L, 1729. 8vo, modern half calf. B6 torn & repaired. bba Nov 28 (264) £240 [Gammon]

Anr copy. Contemp calf; rubbed, joints split, later endpapers. Some browning & soiling. S Apr 28 (624) £180 [Edwards]; S May 13 (623) £180 [Scot]

Lawrence, D. H., 1885-1930
See also: Cresset Press; Grazzini, Antonio Francesco

— Amores: Poems. L, [1916]. 1st Ed, 1st Issue. Orig cloth; marked. Louie Burrows' copy, annotated in pencil by her. S Nov 14 (652) £200 [Forster]

— Apocalypse. Florence, 1931. 1st Ed, one of

750. bba May 14 (222) £50 [Deighton Bell]

— The Collected Poems. L, 1928. 1st Ed, one of 100, sgd. 2 vols. Orig half vellum, in d/js. Epstein copy. sg Apr 30 (296) $1,600

— David: A Play. L, [1926]. 1st Ed, one of 500. In d/j. sg Dec 12 (213) $60

— The Escaped Cock. Paris: Black Sun Press, 1929. 1st Ed, one of 450. Wraps. sg Dec 12 (214) $475

— Glad Ghosts. L, 1926. 1st Ed, One of 500. Orig wraps; tape stains on wrapper flaps. sg Dec 12 (215) $350

— Lady Chatterley's Lover. Florence, 1928. 1st Ed, one of 1,000. Orig bds; backstrip repaired. bba May 14 (220) £800 [Sotheran]

Anr copy. Orig bds; head and foot of spine damaged with loss. Ck July 10 (323) £450

Anr copy. 4to, orig bds, unopened; wear at heel of spine. CNY June 9 (107) $2,200

Anr copy. Orig bds, in remains of d/j. DW May 13 (452) £55

Anr copy. Bds. Inscr to Frank Curtin. Manney copy. P Oct 11 (198) $7,000

Anr copy. Orig bds; spine ends chipped. pn June 11 (200) £600 [McKenzie]

Anr copy. Half mor; marked. S Dec 12 (113) £950 [Finch]

Anr copy. Orig bds. Epstein copy. sg Apr 30 (297) $3,000; SI Dec 5 (908) LIt1,100,000

— Love Poems and Others. L, 1913. 1st Ed. Roberts A3. sg Dec 12 (216) $200

— New Poems. L, 1918. One of 500. Wraps; spine chipped. sg Dec 12 (217) $150

— The Paintings.... L: Mandrake Press, [1929]. 1st Ed, One of 510. Folio, orig half mor; rubbed. pn May 14 (125) £170

— Pansies. L, 1929. 1st Ed, one of 250. In chipped d/j. sg Dec 12 (218) $400

Anr copy. Orig bds. Epstein copy. sg Apr 30 (298) $475

Definitive Ed, One of 50. Orig vellum (possibly a trial bdg?); discolored. Sylvia Townsend Warner's copy. S Nov 14 (654) £150 [Rota]

One of 500. Ptd wraps. sg Dec 12 (219) $375

— The Prussian Officer and Other Stories. L, 1914. 1st Ed, 1st Issue. Orig cloth. sg Dec 12 (220) $200

— Psychoanalysis and the Unconscious. NY, 1921. Bds, in worn & repaired d/j. NH Oct 6 (193) $140

— Reflections on the Death of a Porcupine. Phila., 1925. 1st Ed, one of 475. F Dec 18 (38) $60

— Sea and Sardinia. NY, 1921. 1st Ed. Half cloth, in chipped d/j. sg Dec 12 (221) $60

— Sons and Lovers. L, 1913. 1st Ed, with cancel title. sg Dec 12 (222) $375

— Sun. Paris: Black Sun Press, 1928. One of 150. Orig wraps. sg Dec 12 (223) $1,200

— Touch and Go. L, 1920. 1st Ed. Wraps. sg Dec 12 (224) $70

— The Virgin and the Gipsy. Florence, 1930. One of 810. DW Apr 8 (532) £70; sg June 11 (193) $90

— The White Peacock. L, 1911. 1st English Ed. Orig cloth; hinges broken. Some staining. S July 21 (150) £700 [Yoshida] 1st State. Orig cloth; joints repaired. bba Mar 26 (272) £60 [Eccles]

Lawrence, John, 1753-1839

— British Field Sports. L, 1818. 8vo, orig cloth. With 32 plates only. Some foxing. bbc Apr 27 (542) $70

Lawrence, T. E., 1888-1935

See also: Golden Cockerel Press

— The Diary of T. E. Lawrence 1911. [L: Corvinus Press, 1937]. 1st Ed, one of 203. 4to, orig half mor. S July 21 (155) £1,300 [Baring]

— An Essay on Flecker. [L]: Corvinus Press, 1937. One of 30 unpublished copies. Folio, orig cloth. S July 21 (156) £2,400 [Enders]

— Revolt in the Desert. L, 1927. 1st Ed, One of 315. Half mor. sg Dec 12 (227) $550

— Seven Pillars of Wisdom. L, 1926. 1st Ed, one of 170 complete copies, so inscr. 4to, mor gilt by Bumpus. Lacking plates "A Prophet's Tomb" & "A Garden". Manney copy. P Oct 11 (199) $38,000

Anr copy. Mor gilt; hinges starting. S July 21 (158) £15,500 [Baring]

1st Trade Ed. L, 1935. cb Jan 30 (75) $90

One of 750. Orig half pigskin. DW Mar 4 (30) £340

Anr copy. Orig half pigskin; lower corner of covers dampstained. With 50 plates, including 3 facsimiles not found in unltd issue & 4 colored plates which are uncolored in unltd issue. S Nov 14 (655) £250 [Sotheran]

— To His Biographer Robert Graves. With: To his Biographer Liddell Hart. L, 1938. One of 1,000, sgd by Graves & Hart. 2 vols. In d/js. cb Oct 25 (74) $300

Anr copy. In d/js which are partly browned, as is spine. wa Sept 26 (198) $230

Lawson, John Parker, d.1852

— Scotland Delineated in a Series of Views.... L, 1854 [engraved title dated 1847]. Folio, contemp calf; rubbed, worn at edges. With tinted litho title & 71 plates. Lacking engraved title. bba Apr 30 (13) £85 [Grant & Shaw]

Lawson, William, fl.1618

— A New Orchard and Garden.... L: George Sawbridge, 1676. 6th Ed. 4to, disbound. Browned & stained. DW Nov 6 (462) £80

Anr Ed. Phila., 1858. 2 parts in 1 vol. 4to, orig cloth; edge wear. bbc Dec 9 (346) $90

Lay, William —& Hussey, Cyrus M.

— A Narrative of the Mutiny on Board the Ship Globe.... New London, 1828. 1st Ed. 8vo, calf gilt by Blackwell; extremities rubbbed. Marginal dampstaining. Tipped in at rear is Ms transcript with notes by William Folger of poem The Young Mutineer by Henry Glover. CNY Oct 8 (145) $1,000

Layard, Sir Austen Henry, 1817-94

— Discoveries in the Ruins of Nineveh and Babylon. L, 1853. 1st Ed. 2 vols. 8vo, orig cloth; rubbed. bba Apr 9 (66) £80 [Ulysses]

Anr copy. 8vo, contemp calf gilt; joints cracked, spine worn. DW May 13 (38) £80

Anr copy. 2 vols. 8vo, orig cloth; rubbed. With folding litho frontis, 10 plates, 2 folding maps & 3 folding plans. Frontis & tp stained & foxed; 1 plate loose. Manney copy. P Oct 11 (200) $300

— The Monuments of Nineveh. L, 1849. Folio, contemp half lea gilt; extremities worn; joints cracked. sg May 7 (138) $500

— Nineveh and its Remains. L, 1849. 2 vols. 8vo, orig cloth. Some foxing & browning. wa Dec 9 (458) $80

Layard, George Somes, 1857-1925

See also: Spielmann & Layard

— Suppressed Plates, Wood Engravings.... L, 1907. cb Oct 17 (528) $55

Le Bas Collection, Edward

— Paintings and Drawings by Harold Gilman and Charles Ginner in the Collection.... L: Pvtly ptd, 1965. One of 105. Text by B. Fairfax Hall. 4to & folio, text in half calf, plates loose in half mor box. bba Feb 13 (46) £90 [Bookworks]

Le Bas, Philippe

— Suede et Norwege. Paris, 1841. 8vo, half mor gilt. Text and plates foxed. sg Jan 9 (108) $50

Le Blant, Edmond, 1813-97. See: Jacquemart & Le Blant

Le Blon, Jacobus Christoph

— L'Art d'imprimer les tableaux. Paris, 1756. 8vo, contemp calf; rebacked. With 3 folding plates with added hand-coloring. First plate torn away at outermost fold with loss of a portion of the palette. P June 18 (474) $1,700

Le Boe, Sylvius Franciscus de, 1614-72

— Opera medica.... Amst.: Elzevir, 1680. 4to, contemp calf; worn. Some browning; stamps. SI Dec 5 (202) LIt250,000

Le Brun, Charles

— A Series of Lithographic Drawings Illustrative of the Relation between the Human Physiognomy and that of the Brute Creation. L, 1827. Folio, contemp half cloth; broken, spine lacking. With port & 37 plates. Some tears & soiling; port & some plates loose. pn May 14 (157) £200 [Shapero]

Le Brun, Cornelius

— Reizen over Moskovie, door Persie en Indie. Amst., 1711. Folio, contemp calf; rubbed. With frontis, port & 117 (of 121) plates. Some creases & discoloration. S June 25 (461) £1,000 [Orient]

— Reizen van C. de Bruyn door de vermaardste deelen van Klein Asia.... Delft, 1698. Folio, contemp calf gilt; worn, joint broken. With frontis, port & 102 plates depicting 210 images. Some soiling & stains; some plates wrinkled at folds. O May 26 (113) $1,500

— Reizen...door de vermaardste Deelen van Klein Asia.... Delft, 1698. 1st Ed. Folio, contemp half calf gilt; worn. With engraved title & 99 plates. Some plates damaged; lacking port & folding map; some plates just cropped at fore-margins; a few creases; some discoloration. S June 30 (94) £900 [Finopoulos]

— Voyage au Levant. Delft, 1700. Folio, contemp calf; upper joint repaired,. With engraved titles, port & 96 plates. Lacking general map; Plate 98 torn with small loss; a few plates creased; some browning. S Nov 21 (298) £1,350 [Hadyipanay]

— A Voyage to the Levant.... L, 1702. Folio, half calf; worn. With engraved title, port, 97 plates & folding general map. Repairs at 3K to end affecting letters & plates between pp. 219-221 & before p. 231, with some loss & restoration; some browning. S Nov 21 (247) £2,000 [Severis]

— Voyages de Corneille Le Brun par la Moscovie, en Perse, et aux Indes orientales. Amst., 1718. 2 vols. Folio, modern mor gilt. With frontis, 3 folding maps & c.100 plates. Lacking half-title to Vol II, port & at least 14 plates; 1 gathering misbound; some small tears. Sold w.a.f. bba Jan 16 (319) £600 [Shapero]

Anr copy. Contemp calf; rebacked preserving orig spines, inner hinges cracked. With frontis, port, 3 double-page maps & 114 plates. Lacking half-title & final blank in Vol II; some leaves soiled or spotted. C Oct 30 (97) £1,400 [Antiques of the Orient]

Anr copy. 18th-cent calf; rebacked. A few plates shaved with minor loss. S June 25 (331) £1,400 [Lindh]

Le Carre, John, Pseud.

— The Spy Who Came In From the Cold. L, 1963. In chipped d/j. With American pbr's overslip on tp. sg June 11 (194) $175

Le Clerc, Daniel, 1652-1728 —& Manget, Jean Jacques, 1652-1742

— Bibliotheca anatomica.... Geneva, 1699. 2 vols. Folio, contemp calf; rubbed, re-backed. With 123 plates. Lacking half-titles; 1 title cropped at foot; some plates cropped; dampstained. S Feb 25 (598) £700 [Voltaire]

Anr copy. Old half vellum; spine ends chipped. With 121 plates. With 2 plates loose. sg Nov 14 (68) $1,000

Le Clerc, Sebastien, 1637-1714

— Pratique de la geometrie, sur le papier et sur le terrain. Paris: T. Jolly, 1669. 1st Ed. 12mo, contemp vellum; rubbed. 1 plate repaired; 1 holed. bba Apr 30 (307) £150 [Wilbraham]

Le Comte, Louis Daniel, 1655-1728

— Memoirs and Observations Topographical made in a late Journey through the Empire of China. L, 1697. 1st Ed in English. 8vo, contemp calf; spine chipped. With port & 3 plates. b June 22 (185) £480

Le Comte, Pierre

— Afbeeldingen van Schepen en Vaartuigen in Verschillende Bewegingen. Amst., 1831. 2 parts in 2 vols. Oblong folio, loose in orig wraps; those of Atlas frayed & spine broken. With 50 plates. Sgd. B May 12 (2039) HF3,800

Le Coq, Albert von, 1860-1930

— Chotscho. Berlin, 1913. Folio, loose in half vellum portfolio. With 75 plates, many in color. Some margins chipped. sg Apr 2 (164) $3,200

Le Corbusier, 1887-1965

— Oeuvre complete. Zurich, 1973-77. 8 vols. In d/js. sg Apr 2 (165) $450

Le Coz, Albert von, 1860-1930

— Die Buddhistische Spaetantike in Mittelasien. Berlin, 1922-24. Parts 3, 5 & 6 only. Half lea; needs rebacking. sg Feb 6 (160) $700

Le Fanu, Joseph Sheridan, 1814-73

— The Fortunes of Colonel Torlogh O'Brien. Dublin, 1847. 1st Ed in Book form. Illus by H. K. Browne. 8vo, orig cloth; top of spine chipped. sp Apr 16 (403) $65

— Ghost Stories and Tales of Mystery. Dublin, 1851. 1st Ed. Illus by H. K. Browne. 8vo, orig cloth, Carter's A bdg; rubbed, some tears along lower inner hinge. With frontis & 3 plates. Slater-Manney copy. P Oct 11 (204) $5,500

Le Gallienne, Richard, 1866-1947

— An Old Country House. NY & L, 1902. Illus by Elizabeth Shippen Green. 4to, half lea gilt; bumped. With tipped-in photo inscr on mount & with 2 A Ls s. Met Apr 28 (55) $150

— The Romance of Perfume. NY & Paris, 1928. Illus by Georges Barbier. 4to, bds. F Sept 26 (83) $110

Anr copy. Bds; soiled. Met Apr 28 (56) $100

Le Gendre, —, Architect

— Description de la Place de Louis XV que l'on construit a Reims.... Paris, 1765. Folio, contemp mor gilt with arms of the City of Rheims; stain along foot. With 8 plates by Moitte after Cochin, 6 double-page. S June 25 (174) £2,200 [Shapero]

Le Grand, Antoine, d.1699

— An Entire Body of Philosophy.... L, 1694. Folio, contemp calf; worn, covers detached. With 99 plates. Lacking at least 2 opening leaves. bba July 23 (336) £80 [Bailey]

Le Hay, ——

— Recueil de cent estampes representant differentes nations du Levant. Paris, 1714. Bound with: Explication de cent estampes...de ceremonies turques. Paris, 1715. Folio, contemp calf gilt; rubbed. With engraved title, plate of music & 102 plates. Some browning; Dervishes plates creased. S June 30 (155) £5,000 [Quaritch]

— Der wahrest und neuesten Abbildung des Tuerckischen Hofes. Nuremberg: C. Weigel, 1721. 4to, contemp calf. With 52 plates, a folding plate of music & 3 further folding plates. Library stamp on tp. S Nov 21 (259) £1,000

Le Keux, John

— Memorials of Cambridge. L, 1845. 2 vols. 8vo, orig cloth; all leaves detached. With folding map & 69 plates. Sold w.a.f. bba Jan 16 (329) £240 [Hark]

Le Long, Isaac, 1683-1744

— Historische Beschryvinge van der Reformatie der Stadt Amsterdam. Amst., 1729. Folio, vellum; front joint damaged. With folding plan, large folding view of the Botermarkt 51 engravings on 28 plate. Some staining. B Nov 1 (300) HF550

Le Maingre de Boucicaut, Jean

— Histoire de Mre. J. de Boucicaut.... Paris, 1620. 4to, calf. S June 30 (47) £2,200 [Atabey]

Le Maire de Belges, Jean, 1473-1513

— Les Illustrations de Gaule et singularitez de Troye.... Lyons: Jean de Tournes, [8 Oct] 1549. Folio, 19th-cent half calf. Later leaves dampstained at upper margins. Ck Oct 31 (147) £170

Le Muet, Pierre, 1591-1669

— Maniere de bastir pour touttes sortes de personne. Paris, 1681. ("Maniere de bien bastir pour toutes sortes de personnes.") 2d Ed. 2 vols in 1. Folio, contemp calf; headcaps & corners worn away, joints & extremities rubbed. With 2 engraved titles, Part 1 with 38 leaves engraved, Part 2 with 31 plates. McCarty-Cooper copy. CNY Jan 25 (42) $600

Le Nestour, Patrik

— The Mystery of Things: Evocations of the Japanese Supernatural. NY & Tokyo, [1972]. One of 183 on handmade paper. Illus by Akeji Sumiyoshi. Folio, half mor. With 17 mtd plates. sg Feb 6 (275) $225

Le Page du Pratz, Antoine Simon

— The History of Louisiana.... L, 1763. 2 vols. 12mo, contemp calf. With 2 folding maps. S Nov 21 (322) £600 [Maggs]

Anr copy. Contemp sheep; several covers loose. Lacking 1 map, the other def. sg June 18 (325) $100

Le Paulmier de Grentemesnil, Jacques

— De Vino et pomaceo libri duo. Paris: Guillaume Auvray, 1588. Bound with: Piemontese, Alessio. De Secretis...editio quarta. Basel: L. Kuenig, 1603 8vo, contemp vellum with yapp edges. C June 24 (185) £800 [Shapero]

Le Peletier de Saint-Fargeau, Amede Louis Michel

— Histoire naturelle des insectes. Hymenopteres. Paris, 1836-46. 4 vols plus Atlas. 8vo, text in contemp half lea, Atlas in contemp cloth. With 48 plates, most hand-colored. About half the plates dampstained. sg Nov 14 (188) $300

Le Pelletier, Jean

— L'Alkaest ou le dissolvant universel de Van-Helmont. Rouen, 1704. 12mo, contemp calf; worn. Some dampstaining & browning. SI June 9 (532) LIt550,000

Le Perche

— L'Exercise des armes ou le maniment du fleuret. Paris, [1676]. Oblong 4to, modern mor gilt. With engraved title & text & 35 plates. sg Mar 26 (88) $1,900

Anr Ed. Paris: V. de F. Chereau, [n.d.]. Oblong 4to, mor gilt by Maillard. With engraved title & 35 plates plus 5 additional fencing plates bound in at end. C Dec 16 (52) £800 [Forum]

Le Petit, Jean Francois

— La Grande Chronique ancienne et moderne.... Dordrecht, 1601. Illus by Christoffel van Sichem. 2 vols. Folio, 18th-cent mor gilt with Hutton crest; rubbed, spine ends of Vol worn. Some leaves browned; some leaves dampstained; minor tears. C Dec 16 (136) £650 [Forum]

Le Prince de Beaumont, Jeanne Marie, 1711-80

— Magasin des enfans, ou dialogues.... Brussels, 1789. 4 vols in 2. 12mo, contemp half calf; new endpapers. bba July 23 (99) £50 [Ginnan]

Le Rouge, Georges Louis

— Description de Chambord dont le modele en carton...a ete presente au Roy.... Paris: Jombert, [1750]. Folio, old bds; worn. With 13 plates. Marginal worming. bba Apr 9 (246) £300 [Galaister]

Le Roux, Hughes, 1860-1925

— Les Jeux du cirque et la vie foraine. Paris, [1889]. 1st Ed. Illus by Jules Garnier. 4to, orig cloth. SI June 9 (533) LIt550,000

One of 50. Orig cloth; soiled & worn. S Nov 14 (297) £200 [Tibbals]

Le Roy, Francois

— Le Livre de la femme forte et vertueuse.... Paris: for Jean Petit, [c.1515]. 8vo, mor gilt by Lortic, with arms of Charles-Louis de Bourbon, Duke of Parma, Count of Villafranca. Washed & pressed. C June 24 (167) £3,000 [Kraus]

Le Roy, Henri

— Fundamenta Physices. Amst.: Elzevir, 1646. 4to, 18th-cent half calf. Some Ms corrections; small rust hole in B4, affecting 2 letters. Schuckburgh-Evelyn copy. b June 22 (206) £400

Le Roy, Jacques, 1633-1719

— Castella & Praetoria Nobilium Brabantiae.... Leiden, 1699. Bound with: L'Erection de toutes les terres, seigneuries & familles titrees du Brabant. Leiden, 1699. 2 works in 1 vol. Folio, orig calf; restored, new endpapers. B Nov 1 (303) HF7,000

Le Roy, Julien David

— Les Ruines des plus beaux monumens de la Grece. Paris, 1758. 2 parts in 1 vol. Folio, contemp mor gilt. With 60 plates & maps. Tp spotted. C June 24 (213) £4,800 [Marlborough]

Le Sage, Alain Rene, 1668-1747

— The Adventures of Gil Blas of Santillane. L, 1819. Trans by Tobias Smollett. 3 vols. 8vo, half calf gilt; rubbed. Some soiling. O Jan 14 (102) $80

Anr copy. Lea; new spines. sp Feb 6 (482) $50

Anr Ed. L, 1836. 2 vols. 8vo, later calf gilt; worn. bbc Sept 23 (51) $95

— Histoire de Gil Blas de Santillane. Paris: Didot le jeune, [1795]. 4 vols. 8vo, modern half calf. bba Nov 28 (201) £85 [Archdale]

Le Vacher de Charnois, Jean Charles

— Recherches sur les costumes et sur les theatres de tout les nations.... Paris, 1790. Illus by Philippe Chery. 2 vols in 1. 4to, modern half mor by Gustav Hedberg. With colored frontis & 54 plates, 43 ptd in colors, some with added hand-coloring. S June 25 (159) £900 [Shapero]

Lea, Isaac. See: Carey & Lea

Lea, Matthew Carey

— A Manual of Photography Intended as a Text Book.... Phila., 1871. 2d Ed. 8vo, orig cloth; spine ends frayed, hinges cracked. bbc Feb 17 (228) $60

Anr copy. Cloth; spine ends frayed, front joint worn, corners bumped. K Sept 29 (356) $50

Lea, Tom

— The King Ranch. Bost., [1957]. 2 vols. cb Nov 14 (106) $75; wa Mar 5 (368) $55

1st ptg. cb Feb 12 (45) $85

Anr Ed. Kingsville TX, 1957. Ltd Ed. 2 vols. Cloth facsimile of King Ranch saddle blankets. cb Feb 12 (44) $550

— A Picture Gallery: Paintings and Drawings by.... Bost., [1968]. 2 vols. 4to & folio portfolio, cloth. Inscr. wa Apr 9 (240) $140

Leaf, Munro

— The Story of Ferdinand. NY, 1936. 1st Ed. In d/j. Inscr to Lena Barksdale. Manney copy. P Oct 11 (201) $850

Anr copy. In d/j. Epstein copy. sg Apr 30 (301) $1,600

Leake, William Martin, 1777-1860

— Journal of a Tour in Asia Minor. L, 1824. 8vo, early calf gilt; worn, edges scuffed. With folding map. Bottom margin of tp clipped; ink prize presentation, 1838, at reverse of front free endpaper. bbc Sept 23 (185) $130

Anr copy. Orig bds; worn, rebacked. With 3 maps & litho plate. Small flaw at c4 affecting letters; some browning. S Nov 15 (1177) £400 [Maggs]

— Researches in Greece. L, 1814. 4to, half calf; rubbed, upper joint split, hinges repaired, new endpapers. S June 30 (334) £900 [Chelsea]

— Travels in the Morea. L, 1830. 3 vols. 8vo, contemp calf gilt. With 17 maps & plans & 12 plates of inscriptions. Some spotting. S July 1 (632) £800 [Consolidated Real]

Anr copy. Contemp calf gilt; worn. With half-titles in Vols I & III only; with 17 maps & plans & 12 lithos of inscriptions. Some staining & spotting; minor tears & repairs. Blackmer copy. S July 1 (633) £650 [Axia]

Lean, Vincent Stuckey

— Lean's Collectanea: Collections of Proverbs, Folklore and Superstitions. Bristol, 1902-4. 4 vols in 5. pnE Oct 1 (218) £90

Leandro di Santa Cecilia

— Palestina ovvero primo viaggio. Rome, 1753. 4to, contemp vellum bds; stained, new endpapers. With folding map (torn & repaired), frontis & 4 plates. Stained & spotted throughout; wormed at lower margin. S July 1 (841) £300

Lear, Edward, 1812-88

See also: Sowerby & Lear

— A Book of Nonsense. L, 1846. 1st Ed. Part 1 (of 2). Oblong 8vo, orig bds; rebacked, corners retouched, worn. With litho title & 36 plates. Foxed & thumbed; some margins restored without loss; 4 leaves bound out of order & 2 leaves reversed. Manney copy. P Oct 11 (202) $3,250

Anr Ed. L, 1855. Oblong 8vo, contemp half vellum. 73 leaves, each with litho illust & accompanying limerick. A few bottom lines shaved or cropped; 6 illusts hand-colored by a former owner. SM Oct 11 (492) FF8,000

2d Ed. Oblong 8vo, contemp cloth; front joint cracked. With 73 plates. 2 plates with last line of text shaved. cb Sept 26 (141) $3,000

— Illustrations of the Family of Psittacidae, or Parrots. L, 1830-32. 1st Ed. Folio, 19th-cent cloth; discolored, rebacked. With 42 hand-colored plates. Marginal tears repaired; tp creased. S June 25 (65) £25,000 [Marshall]

— Journal of a Landscape Painter in Corsica.... L, 1870. 1st Ed. 8vo, orig cloth; worn, spine split. With map & 40 plates. bba Jan 16 (415) £110 [Goddard]

Anr copy. Orig cloth; worn & marked. bba Apr 30 (32) £130 [R. Clark]

Anr copy. Orig cloth; rubbed, endpapers foxed. bba June 25 (227) £180 [Scott]

Anr copy. Orig cloth; rebacked preserving orig spine, rubbed. bba July 23 (462) £150 [Sanderson]

Anr copy. With map & 40 plates. Institutional bookplate. sg Sept 6 (175) $120

— Journals of a Landscape Painter in Albania. L, 1851. 1st Ed. 8vo, orig cloth; rubbed & soiled. With map & 20 plates. bba June 25 (226) £320 [Thorp]

Anr copy. Orig cloth; spine worn. cb Dec 5 (73) $550

— Journals of a Landscape Painter in Southern Calabria.... L, 1852. 1st Ed. 8vo, half lea; worn. With 2 maps & 20 plates. SI June 9 (516) LIt2,000,000

— Nonsense Songs, Stories, Botany and Alphabets.* More Nonsense, Pictures, Rhymes.... L, 1871-72. 1st Ed. 8vo, orig bds, in d/j. Epstein copy. sg Apr 30 (302) $750

— Nonsense Songs, Stories, Botany and Alphabets. L, 1875. 5th thousand. 4to, orig cloth; worn. Some leaves foxed or soiled; 2 leaves torn. bba July 23 (463) £55 [Wise]

— Views in Rome and its Environs. L, 1841. Folio, contemp half lea; worn. With engraved title & 25 tinted plates. SI June 9 (517) LIt6,500,000

— Views in the Seven Ionian Islands. L, 1863. Folio, orig cloth; loose. With litho title & 20 plates. Some spotting. S June 25 (108) £1,300 [Tulip]

Anr copy. Orig cloth; spine discolored. With engraved title & 20 plates. S July 1 (635) £4,200 [Karavassilis]

Anr copy. Orig cloth; def, upper cover dampstained, loose. Some spotting; some edges frayed. S July 1 (636) £2,800 [Consolidated Real]

Anr Ed. Oldham, 1979. One of 1,000. Folio, cloth. Facsimile reprint. bba July 23 (469) £130 [Bailey]

Learmonth, Noel F.

— The Portland Bay Settlement. Being the History of Portland, Victoria.... Melbourne, 1934. Orig bdg; small section cut form head of front free endpaper. kh Nov 11 (285) A$50

Leavitt, Richard F. See: Williams & Leavitt

Leavitt, T. W. H.

— The Jubilee History of Victoria and Melbourne. Melbourne, 1888. 2 vols. 4to, bdg not described but worn & with amateur repairs. kh Nov 11 (541) A$160

Lebel, Robert

— Marcel Duchamp. NY, [1959]. Folio, cloth, in d/j. Claudio Arrau's copy. sg Feb 6 (72) $150

One of 17 hors commerce. Orig ptd wraps; small stain on rear cover. With folding case initialed in white paint; self-port, sgd, mtd to velvet-covered inner flap of case with stencil used for book's frontis mtd on verso of flap; photographic reproduction of the Larg Glass, hand-colored & inscr by Duchamp, mtd in a plastic window & affixed by a hinge to the case. P June 17 (188) $20,000

Lebesque, Octave. See: Montorgueil, Georges

Lebrun, Frederico

— Drawings for Dante's Inferno.... [N.p.]: Kanthos Press, 1963. Folio, orig cloth, in torn d/j. With 36 plates & 4 loose lithos. bbc June 29 (414) $95

Anr copy. Loose as issued. With 36 plates & 4 orig lithos, sgd in the plate. wa Mar 5 (111) $100

One of 100. Loose as issued. With 36 plates & 7 orig lithos, sgd by Lebrun in pencil. sg Feb 6 (159) $275

Lecky, William Edward Hartpole, 1838-1903. See: Clemens's copy, Samuel Langhorne

Leclerc Library, Charles

— Bibliotheca Americana: Histoire, geographie, voyages, archeologie et linguistique des deux ameriques et des Iles Philippines. Paris, Rouen [ptd], 1878. 8vo, new cloth. With 1st & 2d Supplements (1881 & 1887) bound in. sg Oct 31 (177) $275

Leclerc, Nicolas Gabriel

— Histoire physique, morale, civile et politique de la Russie moderne. Paris, 1783-[94]. 6 vols. 4to, half calf; needs rebdg. With 71 maps & plates. Some chipping and tearing. Lacking text. Sold w.a.f. sg Jan 9 (109) $130

Lecluse, Charles de, 1526-1609

— Rariorum plantarum historia. Antwerp, 1601. Folio, modern vellum. Lacking port & the Altera Appendix; some outer margins wormed; library stamps removed; engraved title trimmed. S June 25 (9) £1,100 [Bolognese]

Leconte de Lisle, Charles

— Les Erinnyes, tragedie antique.... Paris, [1873]. One of 100 with illusts in 3 states. 12mo, lev gilt by Charles Meunier, 1909. sg Nov 7 (130) $1,900

Lecuyer, Raymond

— Histoire de la photographie. Paris, 1945. 1st Ed. 4to, half cloth; extremities worn, joints starting. With 3-dimensional glasses in endpocket. sg Apr 13 (60) $425

Ledoux, Louis Vernon. See: Henderson & Ledoux

Leduc, Violette

— La Batarde. Paris, 1964. One of 35 on velin pur fil Lafuma-Navarre. Mor extra by Maylander, orig wraps bound in. S May 28 (374) £500 [Beres]

Ledwich, Edward, 1738-1823

— Antiquities of Ireland. Dublin, 1790. 1st Ed. 4to, contemp half russia; worn, bds detached, spine def. With engraved title vignette & 39 plates, 1 partly hand-colored. A few plates with smaller margins; some browning; stamp on tp. pn Sept 12 (317) £60 [Freeman]

Ledyard, John, 1751-89. See: Cook, Capt. James

Lee, Albert

— The Knave of Hearts. A Fourth of July Comedietta. NY, 1897. Cover illus by Maxfield Parrish. Pictorial wraps; spine head chipped, splits along backstrip. sg Jan 10 (121) $900

Lee, Amy Freeman. See: Derrydale Press

Lee, Guy Carleton —& Thorpe, Francis Newton

— The History of North America. Phila., [1903-7]. University Ed. 20 vols. Orig half mor; corners scuffed. cb Nov 14 (107) $300

Lee, Henry, 1756-1818

— Memoirs of the War in the Southern Department of the United States.... NY, 1869. Ed by Robert E. Lee. 8vo, cloth. Sgd by R. E. Lee at reverse of half-title. bbc June 29 (321) $4,100

Lee, Ida

— Early Explorers in Australia.... L, 1925. kh Nov 11 (543) A$80

Lee, James Melvin, 1878-1929

— Operation Lifeline: History and Development of the Naval Air Transport Service. Chicago, [1947]. One of 1,000, sgd by Admirals Forrestal, Nimitz, Radford & Reeves. 4to, cloth. bbc June 29 (295) $120

Lee Man-Fong

— Paintings and Statues from the Collection of President Sukarno of the Republic of Indonesia. Djakarta, 1964. 5 jols. Folio, cloth, in d/js. sg Sept 6 (272) $250

Lee, Norman N. See: Edmonds & Lee

Lee, Sir Sydney, 1859-1926

— The Dictionary of National Biography. See: Dictionary...

Leech, John, 1817-64

— Follies of the Year.... [L, 1866]. Oblong 4to, orig half mor gilt; rubbed. bba July 23 (335) £130 [Sotheran]

Anr copy. Half lea; rubbed. O Jan 14 (105) $90

— Mr. Briggs & his Doings: Fishing. L, 1860. Oblong folio, contemp half mor, orig wraps bound in. With 12 hand-colored plates. bba Nov 28 (45) £440 [Marlborough]

— Portraits of Children of the Nobility. L, 1841. 4to, orig cloth; rebacked. With frontis & 7 plates. DW Jan 29 (252) £50

Leeuwen, Simon van

— Batavia illustrata, ofte verhandelinge vanden oorspronk...van oud Batavien. The Hague, 1685. Folio, contemp half vellum; worn, endpaper chipped. Extra title trimmed at fore-edge; some old dampstaining to fore-edge margin. bbc Sept 23 (229) $70

Leeuwenhoek, Anthony van, 1632-1723

— Arcana naturae. Delft, 1695. Bound with the 1697 continuation. 4to, contemp vellum. pnE Oct 2 (364) £800

— [Werken]. Leiden & Delft, 1684-1718. 15 parts in 4 vols. 4to, vellum. With 2 (of 3) engraved titles & 98 plates. Lacking letters 37, 40 & 41; small stamp on 1st titles; some foxing; waterstains. B Nov 1 (498) HF7,500

Lefebure, Charlemagne Theophile, 1811-60 —& Others

— Voyage en Abyssinie execute pendant les Annees 1839-43. Paris, 1845-49. 6 vols of text & 3 vols of Atlas. 8vo & folio, contemp half mor. Text vols with 9 plates; Atlas vols with map & 202 lithos, many colored. Folding map with short tear at fold. S Nov

21 (349) £5,000 [Ant. Junk]

Leffingwell, William Bruce

— Shooting on Upland, Marsh, and Stream. Chicago, 1890. 8vo, cloth; worn. Koopman copy. O Oct 29 (197) $70

LeGear, Clara E. See: Phillips & LeGear

Leger, Fernand, 1881-1955

— Mes Voyages.... Paris, 1960. One of 5 with extra suite of plates in colors & black. Folio, unbound as issued in orig ptd folder. With 27 lithos in colors & black. P June 17 (263) $800

Legge, William Vincent

— A History of the Birds of Ceylon. L, [1878]-80. In 1 vol. 4to, contemp half mor gilt; joints & corners worn. With frontis diagram of feathers, 33 hand-colored plates, colored map & plate of eggs. C May 20 (191) £1,400 [Shapero]

Legh, Gerard, d.1563

— The Accedens of Armory. L, 1568. 8vo, later calf. Hall-Heber-Eaton copy. STC 15389. C June 24 (164) £250 [Heraldry Today]

Anr Ed. L: Henry Ballard, 1597. 4to, later half calf. Early Ms annotations in margins. S July 1 (1289) £190 [Laywood]

Legh, Thomas

— Narrative of a Journey in Egypt and the Country beyond the Cataracts. L, 1816. 4to, later mor; rubbed. With 2 plates. Some foxing. bba June 25 (73) £140 [Fetzer]

Legrand, Emile

— Bibliographie Hellenique ou description raisonee des ouvrages.... Paris, 1963. 4 vols. 8vo, orig cloth. Reprint of the 1885 Ed. Ck Nov 11 (436) £420

Leguina, Enrique de

— Bibliografia e historia de la esgrima Espanola. Madrid, 1904. Wraps. sg Mar 26 (167) $200

One of 150. Modern half calf, orig wraps bound in. sg Mar 26 (166) $250

— La Espada espanola. Madrid, 1914. 4to, modern cloth, orig wraps bound in. sg Mar 26 (168) $110

Lehmann-Hartleben, Karl. See: Kluge & Lehmann-Hartleben

Lehmann-Haupt, Hellmut —& Others

— Bookbinding in America: Three Essays. Portland ME, 1941. 1st Ed. Half cloth, unopened; worn. O Jan 14 (106) $50

Lehrs, Max

— Geschichte und kritischer Katalog des deutschen, niederlaendischen und franzoesischen Kupferstichs im XV Jahrhundert. NY, [n.d.]. 10 vols. 8vo & folio, cloth; joints cracked. Foxed. Facsimile reprint of the Vienna 1908 Ed. sg Feb 6 (163) $250

Leiber, Fritz

— Night's Black Agents. Sauk City: Arkham House, 1947. In d/j with a few tears at top edge. wa Sept 26 (346) $55

— Two Sought Adventure: Exploits of Fafhrd and the Gray Mouser. NY: Gnome Press, [1957]. In d/j. Browned. Label sgd by Leiber affixed to front free endpaper. pba July 9 (174) $70

Anr copy. In tape-reinforced d/j. Some browning. Inscr. sg June 11 (195) $90

Leibnitz, Gottfried Wilhelm von, 1646-1716 —& Bernoulli, Jean, 1667-1748

— Commercium philosophicum et mathematicum ab anno 1694 ad annum 1716. Lausanne & Geneva, 1745. 2 vols. 4to, contemp half calf; joints cracked. With port & 23 folding plates. Some browning. Ck Nov 29 (209) £650

Leichardt, Ludwig, 1813-48

— Journal of an Overland Expedition in Australia.... L, 1847. 8vo, orig cloth; corners bumped, repaired. With 7 plates. Lacking folder of separate maps; small stamp on tp offsetting onto frontis. S Feb 26 (760) £280 [Baring]

Anr copy. Contemp mor. Lacking ads. S June 25 (146) £900 [Quaritch]

Anr copy. Orig cloth. With 7 plates, 1 folding and with separately pbd map by Arrowsmith in orig matching folder. S June 25 (233) £10,500 [Brooke-Hitching]

Anr copy. Secondary cloth bdg. With 7 plates. Lacking separately pbd map. S June 25 (234) £1,700 [Arnold]

Leidinger, Georg

— Albrecht Duerer's und Lukas Cranachs Randzeichnungen zum Gebetsbuche Kaiser Maximilians I.... Munich, 1922. One of 150. Folio, vellum; bowed. With 58 color plates. sg Sept 26 (104) $275

— Meisterwerke der Buchmalerei aus Handschriften der Bayerischen Staatsbibliothek, Muenchen. Munich: Hugo Schmidt Verlag, [1920]. One of 1,000. Folio, unbound plates & text booklet loose in cloth portfoliio. sg May 21 (274) $200

Leigh, Charles, 1662-1701?

— The Natural History of Lancashire, Chesire and the Peak in Derbyshire. Oxford, 1700. 1st Ed. 3 parts in 1 vol. Folio, contemp calf gilt; upper cover detached. Frontis & tp trimmed & relaid. DW May 13 (293) £140

Anr copy. Contemp calf; worn. With port & 24 plates. Lacking the map. L Feb 27 (151) £50

Leigh, Edward, 1602-71

— Select and Choyce Ovservations Containing all the Romane Emperours.... L: J. Williams, 1670. 8vo, contemp sheep; joints worn, free endpapers loose. sg Oct 24 (188) $70

Leigh, Henry S., 1837-83

— Carols of Cockayne. L, 1869 [1868]. Illus by Alfred Concanen & John Leech. 8vo, mor gilt, orig covers & spine bound in. sg Oct 17 (307) $50

Leigh, Percival

— Portraits of Children of the Nobility. L, 1841. Illus by John Leech. Folio, half sheep; loose. With 8 lithos. sg Oct 17 (305) $90

Leigh, Richard

See also: Cecil, William

— The Copie of a Letter Sent Out of England to Don Bernardin Mendoza. L, 1588. Part 2 only, in the 1st setting: Certaine Advertisements out of Ireland.... Mor by Riviere; front cover detached. Small stain on tp; fore-margin of last leaf trimmed. DuPont copy. CNY Oct 8 (238) $1,100

Anr Ed. L: I. Vautrollier for R. Field, 1588. 4to, syn gilt by Lloyd. Tp of Part 1 soiled; marginal repairs to penultimate leaf of Part 2 & marginal repairs to last leaf; a few leaves of Part 2 with light marginal staining. STC 15412. CNY Oct 8 (237) $2,500

Leigh, W. H.

— Reconnoitering Voyages and Travels, with Adventures in...South Australia. L, 1839. 8vo, cloth; needs rebdg. sg Jan 9 (110) $200

Leighly, John. See: Grabhorn Printing

Leighton, Clare

— The Farmer's Year. L, 1933. Oblong folio, orig cloth, in worn d/j. wa Mar 5 (605) $50

Leighton, John M.

— The Lakes of Scotland. Glasgow, 1834. Folio, half mor. pnE May 13 (60) £100

— Select Views of Glasgow and its Environs. Glasgow, 1828. 4to, mor gilt. pnE Mar 11 (123) £100

Leinster, Murray

— Sidewise in Time and Other Scientific Adventures. Chicago, 1950. In d/j. Sgd. sg June 11 (196) $90

Leipnik, F. L.

— A History of French Etching.... L, 1924. 4to, half cloth; edges foxed. kh Nov 11 (151) A$90

Leiris, Michel

See also: Miro, Joan

— Picasso and the Human Comedy. NY, [1954]. Folio, orig bds; short tear at foot of spine, institutional handstamp on endpaper. wa Apr 9 (262) $300

Leisenring, James E.

— The Art of Tying the Wet Fly. NY, 1941. 8vo, cloth, in torn d/j. Koopman copy. O Oct 29 (198) $120

Leitner, Quirin de

— Die Waffensammlung des Oesterreichischen Kaiserhauses im K. K. Artillerie-Arsenal-Museum. Vienna, 1866-70. One of 250. Folio, half mor; rubbed. With frontis & 68 plates, some chromolithographs. Some foxing. bba Apr 9 (263) £1,000 [Forum]

Leland, Thomas, 1722-85

— The History of Ireland. L, 1773. 1st Ed. 3 vols. 4to, contemp calf gilt. bba Apr 9 (91) £160 [Tholstrup]

LeMassena, Robert A.

— Rio Grande...to the Pacific! Denver: Sundance, 1974. Ltd Ed. In d/j. cb Feb 13 (211) $55

Lemberger, Ernst

— Die Bildnis-Miniatur in Skandinavien. Berlin, 1912. One of 500. 2 vols. Folio, orig cloth. With 100 mtd colored plates. Some dampstaining. F Mar 26 (749) $90

Anr copy. Cloth, in d/j. sg Feb 6 (164) $200

Lemercier, Louis Jean Nepomucene

— Chants heroiques des montagnards et mateolts grecs. Paris, 1824-25. 2 vols. 8vo, modern half calf, orig wraps for Vol I bound in. Vol II half-title frayed & with tear repaired. S June 25 (335) £150 [Chelsea]

Lemery, Nicolas, 1645-1715

— Traite universel des drogues simples mises en ordre alphabetique. Paris, 1699. 4to, contemp half calf; spine restored. SI June 9 (529) LIt700,000

— Woordenboek of algemeene verhandeling def enkele droogeryen. Rotterdam, 1743. 4to, contemp half lea; upper joint splitting, rubbed. With engraved title & 25 folding plates. 1 plate torn at fold with loss of paper; some stains in inner margin. B Nov 1 (436) HF1,200

Lemoine, Henry

— Typographical Antiquities: History, Origin, and Progress of the Art of Printing. L, 1797. 12mo, modern mor. bba May 28 (615) £140 [Laywood]

Lemoisne, Paul Andre

— Degas et son oeuvre. Paris, [1946-49]. One of 980. 4 vols. 4to, orig cloth. bba Feb 13 (72) £1,400 [T. Hull]

Anr copy. Orig wraps. S Feb 11 (260) £1,500 [Martin]

Anr copy. Cloth. sg Sept 6 (86) $1,500

Anr Ed. NY: Garland, 1984. 4 vols. 4to, orig cloth. Reprint of Paris, [1946-49] Ed. DW Mar 11 (524) £280

Lenglet du Fresnoy, Pierre Nicolas, 1674-1755

— Geographia antiqua et nova...translated from the French. L, 1742. 4to, later calf. With 31 (of 33) maps; lacking maps 1 & 32. sg Feb 13 (120) $425

Lenin, Vladimir Il'ich, 1870-1924

— Sotsialdamokratija i vybory v dumu. St. Petersburg, 1907. Wraps; loose. Institional stamp on front wrap & in text. Epstein copy. sg Apr 29 (304) $500

Lennon, John

— Spaniard in the Works. L, 1965. Advance proof. Wraps. cb Sept 19 (122) $190

Lenotre, G.

— The Dauphin (Louis XVII). The Riddle of the Temple. L, 1921. In Cosway bdg of mor extra, set with 3 large miniatures by C. B. Currie. CNY Dec 5 (429) $900

Lentz, Harold B.

— The "Pop-Up" Pinocchio. NY: Blue Ribbon, [1932]. Pictorial bds; rubbed, lacking backstrip. wa Mar 5 (615) $70

Lenygon, Francis. See: Jourdain & Lenygon

Leo I, Pope

— Sermones. [Cologne: Bartholomaeus de Unkel, 1475]. Bound with: Gregory I. Homeliae in Evangeliis. [Cologne: Bartholomaeus de Unckel], 9 Dec 1475. Folio, contemp blind-stamped calf over wooden bds, with 2 brass fore-edge clasps, formerly chained; rebacked, renewed flyleaves but preserving orig vellum pastedowns. 1st work: 124 of 126 leave; lacking blanks. Goff L-133. 2d work: 134 leaves. Goff G-419. Schoyen copy. S Dec 12 (29) $8,000

Leo, Johannes

— A Geographical Historie of Africa. L, 1600. 1st Ed in English. Folio, contemp vellum; rear inner hinge split. With folding map of Africa. Tp & 1st few leaves creased; some soiling or dampstaining. STC 15481. C Oct 30 (110) £2,000 [Burdon]

Leon, Modena

— The History of the Rites, Customes, and Manner of Life, of the Present Jews.... L, 1650. 12mo, calf. pnE May 13 (4) £60

Leonard, Daniel

— Massachusettensis: or a Series of Letters.... L, 1776. 8vo, half lea. Some stains; library markings; lacking half-title. Sold w.a.f. O July 14 (119) $60

Leonard, John William

— History of the City of New York, 1609-1909. NY, 1910. 1st Ed. 8vo, cloth; bumped, shaken. Met Apr 28 (475) $60

Leonard, William

— A Discourse on the Order and Propriety of Divine Inspiration.... Harvard MA, 1853. 12mo, ptd wraps. Some pencil marginalia. Z Oct 26 (247) $80

Leonardi, Domenico Felice

— Le Delizie della Villa di Castellazzo. Milan, 1743. Illus by Marc-Antonio Dal Re. Folio, modern bds. With double-page port & 23 double-page plates, all hand-colored. bba Apr 30 (340) £5,500 [L'Acquaforte]

Leonardo da Vinci, 1452-1519

[-] Leonardo da Vinci. NY, 1956. Ed by Emil Vollmer. Folio, cloth, in d/j. sg Apr 2 (166) $110

— Traitte de la peinture. Paris, 1651. Folio, calf; rebacked. pnE Dec 4 (19) £150

— Trattato della pittura. Naples, 1733. Folio, contemp vellum; soiled & worn. DW Oct 9 (908) £340

Anr Ed. Florence, 1792. Folio, recent cloth. sg Sept 6 (176) $600

Leonardo y Argensola, Bartolome, 1562-1631. See: Argensola, Bartolome Leonardo y

Leone, Evasio

— Le Virtu del trono. Parma: Bodoni, 1796. Folio, modern half calf using contemp bds; rubbed. S May 13 (808) £200 [Casa D'Arte]

Leris, Antoine de, 1723-95

— Dictionnaire portatif des theatres.... Paris, 1754. 8vo, contemp sheep; broken, worn. Some foxing. sg Oct 17 (67) $100

Leroux, Gaston, 1868-1927
— Le Fantome de l'Opera. Paris, [1910]. 1st Ed. Half mor, orig wraps bound in; edge wear. Kaye-Epstein copy. sg Apr 29 (305) $1,700

Leroy d'Etiolles, J. J., 1798-1860
— Expose de divers procedes employes jusqu'a ce jour pour de la pierre.... Paris, 1825. 8vo, contemp half lea gilt. With 5 folding lithos. Foxed. sg Nov 14 (69) $375

Leslie, Alexander, of Aberdeen
— The Arctic Voyages of Adolf Erik Nordenskjoeld.... L, 1879. 8vo, orig cloth. Oates copy. W July 8 (254) £75

Leslie, Eliza, 1787-1858
— Domestic French Cookery. Phila., 1832. 12mo, orig cloth; worn. Some spotting. bbc Apr 27 (236) $190

Leslie, John, 1527-96
— De origine, moribus & rebus gestis Scotorum, libri decem. Rome, 1578. 4to, 17th-cent mor gilt; worn, spine repaired. Minor repairs in margins of 1st few leaves; flaw in R3 with slight loss of letters. S May 13 (809) £400 [Riex]

Lessing, Gotthold Ephraim, 1729-81
— Laokoon: oder ueber die Grenzen der Mahlerey und Poesie...Erster Theil [all pbd]. Berlin, 1766. 8vo, contemp half calf. Some browning. Ck Oct 31 (148) £650
— Nathan der Weise. [Berlin: Voss], 1779. 8vo, contemp half sheep. Ck Oct 31 (149) £400

Lessing, Julius
— Alt Orientalisch Teppichmuster. Berlin, 1877. Folio, orig bds; lacking spine. With 30 colored plates. Marginal soiling. Ck July 10 (139) £450

Lessius, Leonard, 1554-1623
— The Temperate Man, or the Right Ways of Preserving Life and Health.... L, 1678. 8vo, contemp calf; joints split, rubbed. Some browning; Ms notes on tp & endpapers; short tear in tp; blank corner torn from G6. S May 13 (893) £110 [Laywood]

Lesson, Rene Primevere, 1794-1849
— Histoire naturelle des oiseaux-mouches. Paris, [1829-30]. 8vo, recent half mor by Bayntun. With 86 hand-colored plates. Some plates spotted. DW Mar 4 (115) £520

L'Estrange, Sir Roger, 1616-1704
— The Observator in Dialogue. L, 1684-87. 3 vols in 2. Folio, contemp calf; covers detached & worn. Lacking final number in Vol III; text with minor wear from old folds; some browning & spotting. Milne copy. Ck June 12 (128) £800

Letainturier-Fradin, Gabriel. See: Fradin, Gabriel

Letarouilly, Paul, 1795-1855
— Edifices de Rome moderne. Liege, 1853. 3 vols. Contemp half mor; rubbed, worn. With port, map & 354 plates. DW Apr 8 (357) £150
— Editices de Rome moderne.... Paris, 1840-57. 3 vols (without text vol). Folio, later cloth; rubbed & stained. With 321 plates only & double-page map. Lacking frontis. Sold w.a.f. NH May 30 (17) $260
— Le Vatican et la Basilique de Saint-Pierre de Rome. Paris, 1882. Vol I only. Half lea. With 119 plates, 3 colored. NH May 30 (18) $75

Letchworth, Thomas. See: Franklin Printing, Benjamin

Letter...
— A Letter to a Member of Parliament concerning the Four Regiments commonly called Mariners. L, 1699. 4to disbound. bba Oct 24 (198) £90 [Musto]

Lettera...
— Lettera apologetica dell' esercitato accademico della crusca.... Naples, 1750. Folio, contemp vellum. SI June 9 (348) LIt5,000,000

Letters...
— Letters Written during the late Voyage of Discovery in the Western Arctic Sea. L, 1821. 8vo, modern half calf. With chart & 3 plates. W July 8 (236) £75

Lettres...
— Lettres edifiantes et curieuses, ecrites des missions etrangeres. Paris, 1780-83. 26 vols. 12mo, contemp half lea; rubbed. Possibly lacking 1 or 2 plates. O May 26 (115) $120

Letts, John M.
— A Pictorial View of California, including a Description of the Panama and Nicaragua Routes. NY, 1853. 8vo, modern half calf. With 48 plates. Some foxing. sg June 18 (95) $110

Lettsom, John Coakley
— The Natural History of the Tea-Tree.... L, 1772. 1st Ed. 4to, orig wraps; repaired & rebacked. Hand-colored frontis damaged & repaired in lower left corner with some loss to image & legend; wormhole affecting front wrap, frontis & 1st half of text. wd June 12 (399) $450

Anr Ed. L, 1799. Bound with: Ellis, John. An Historical Account of Coffee. L, 1774. And: Wissett, Robert. A Treatise on

Hemp....L, 1808. 4to, 20th-cent half mor. Some spotting & marginal dampstaining. Ck Oct 18 (17) £1,900

Anr copy. Bound with: Ellis, John. An Historical Account of Coffee. L, 1774. And: Wissett, Robert. A Treatise on Hemp.... L, 1808. Some dampstaining throughout. Ck Dec 11 (231) £680

Leupold, Jacob

— Theatrum machinarum generale, Schau-Platz des Grundes mechanischer Wissenschafften. Leipzig, 1724-25. 2 vols. Folio, contemp calf gilt. With 105 plates. FD Dec 2 (156) DM3,900

Anr copy. 9 (of 10) parts; lacking Vol II, Part 2. Contemp half calf; worn. With 412 (of 467) plates. Vol I tp heavily soiled; Vol V with several plates cut round & mtd; some plates waterstained or creased. Sold w.a.f. S Nov 21 (87) £2,200 [Shapero]

Anr copy. 2 vols in 1. Folio, contemp half calf; rubbed, spine worn at foot. With 107 (on 105) plates. Some browning of text. S Dec 5 (407) £800 [Salvador]

Leutmann, Johann Georg

— Vollstaendige Nachricht von den Uhren nebenst...Sonnen-Uhren. Halle, 1732-22. 2 parts in 1 vol. 8vo, contemp calf; worn & loose. With 2 frontises & 43 (of 45) plates & tables. Some dampstaining; 2 plates def. Sgd by Henry Voight. F Mar 26 (437) $200

Levaillant, Francois, 1753-1824

— Historie naturelle des oiseaux d'Afrique. Paris, 1805-2-8. Vol III only. 4to, bdg not stated. With 46 (of 53) plates. Lacking last 22 pp of text. bba Feb 13 (376) £320 [Quan-Yan Chui]

Levasseur, Victor

— Atlas national illustre des 86 departments et des possessions de la France. Paris, 1854. Folio, orig half sheep. With engraved title & 98 hand-colored maps. cb Oct 10 (119) $425

— Atlas national illustre.... Paris, 1869. Folio, orig half sheep; worn, broken, loose. With engraved title & c.101 maps. cb Jan 30 (149) $325

— Lafayette in America, in 1824 and 1825.... Phila., 1829. 1st Ed in English. 2 vols. 12mo, orig half cloth. NH Aug 23 (238) $200

Lever, Charles James, 1806-72

— Charles O'Malley, the Irish Dragoon. NY, 1897. Illus by Arthur Rackham. 8vo, orig cloth; spine head chipped. With 16 plates. cb Jan 16 (131) $160

— Works. L, [1897-99]. One of 1,000. 37 vols. 8vo, half mor gilt; worn. K July 12 (312) $90

Levertoff, Denise. See: Levertov, Denise

Levertov, Denise

— The Double Image. L, 1946. 1st Ed. In d/j. Sgd, with both spellings. sg Dec 12 (229) $200

Levi, Giorgio Enrico

— Catalogo della biblioteca del duello. Florence, 1929. One of 150. Inscr to Angelo Bruschi. sg Mar 26 (172) $275

Levi, Giorgio Enrico —& Gelli, Jacopo

— Bibliografia del duello. Milan, 1903. One of 400. Wraps; needs rebdg. sg Mar 26 (174) $375

Levinson, Andre, 1887-1933

— Bakst: The Story of the Artist's Life. L, 1923. One of 315. Folio, half calf. S Feb 11 (272) £300 [Sutherland]

— La Danse d'aujourd'hui.... Paris, 1929. 4to, orig wraps. b Mar 11 (84) £65

Anr copy. Bdg not described; shaken, soiled, inner hinge starting. K Sept 29 (231) $50

Anr copy. Cloth. sg Oct 17 (68) $130

— The Designs of Leon Bakst for The Sleeping Princess. L, 1923. One of 1,000. Folio, half vellum; bowed. With port by Picasso & 55 colored plates by Bakst. sg Apr 2 (19) $800

— Histoire de Leon Bakst. Paris, [1924]. One of 160. 4to, orig wraps. S Nov 14 (231) £600 [Toilet-Harman]

— Leon Bakst: The Story of his Life. NY, 1922. One of 250. Folio, orig vellum; soiled & stained. wd Dec 12 (414) $750

— Serge Lifar: Destin d'un danseur. [Paris], 1934. Ltd Ed. Folio, half mor, orig wraps bound in. With frontis by Picasso & 60 plates. Card of Serge Lifar inscr by him to Clement Crisp bound in. S Nov 14 (231) £600 [Toilet-Harman]

Levis, Howard C.

— A Descriptive Bibliography of the most Important Books in the English Language Relating to...Engraving. L, 1912-13. 1st Ed, one of 350. Without Supplement. 4to, half cloth; worn, inner joints broken. O Sept 24 (146) $90

Levy, Julien

— Surrealism. NY: Black Sun Press, 1936. Orig bds, in chipped d/j. sg Apr 2 (86) $325

Lewin, John William

— A Natural History of the Birds of New South Wales. Sydney, 1813. ("Birds of New South Wales.") 4to, orig Sydney lea bdg; rubbed & marked, spine a little wormed. With 18 hand-colored plates.

Unique copy on special wove paper, presented to Lewin's patron, Lachlan Macquarie. S June 25 (1170) £150,000 [Marshall]

Anr Ed. Melbourne: Queensbury Hill Press, [1978]. One of 500. 4to, orig mor. kh Nov 11 (545) A$140

— Prodromus Entomology. Natural History of Lepidopterous Insects of New South Wales. L, 1805. 1st Ed. 4to, 19th-cent cloth; worn, lower cover stained. With 18 plates, colored by the author. S June 25 (158) £15,000 [Maggs]

Lewin, William

— The Birds of Great Britain. L, 1795-1801. 2d Ed. 8 vols in 4. 4to, contemp russia gilt; rebacked, rubbed. With 278 hand-colored plates of birds & 58 of eggs. Plate 114 stained. S Nov 21 (29) £1,200 [Wheldon & Wesley]

— The Insects of Great Britain. L, 1795. 1st Ed. Vol I (all pbd). 4to, contemp mor gilt, armorial bdg. With 46 hand-colored plates. Stamps on verso of English title, head of 1st leaf & foot of final leaf of text. pn Mar 19 (302) £1,400 [Shapero]

Lewis, Angelo John

— Modern Magic, a Practical Treatise on the Art of Conjuring. NY, [c.1890]. 8vo, orig cloth. Sgd by Orson Welles. pba Aug 20 (231) $160

Lewis, C. S., 1898-1963

— The Lion, the Witch and the Wardrobe. L: Geoffrey Bles, [1950]. In d/j with tears & soiling at spine ends. P June 17 (253) $1,900

Lewis, Charles Thomas Courtney

— The Story of Picture Printing in England during the Nineteenth-Century. L, [1928]. 4to, orig cloth; marked & rubbed. bba Dec 19 (289) £89 [Ginnan]

Anr copy. Cloth, in chipped d/j. Some foxing. kh Nov 11 (153) A$280

Lewis, Frederick Christian

— Scenery of the River Exe. L, 1827. Folio, orig bds; rebacked with cloth, some wear. With engraved title & 29 views on 27 plates, all on india paper, mtd. Tp & a few plates spotted. L Nov 14 (133) £160

Lewis, George, Artist

— A Series of Groups Illustrating...the People of France and Germany. L, 1823. 4to, contemp mor gilt; rubbed. With dedication & 52 plates on india paper. bba Sept 19 (143) £280 [Erlini]

Lewis, James. See: Masson, Charles

Lewis, James, Architect

— Original Designs in Architecture.... L, 1797. 2d Ed. 2 vols in 1. Folio, contemp bds; rebacked & recornered with calf. With 63 plates. C Oct 30 (48) £2,400 [Buckingham Books]

Lewis, James O., 1799-1858

— The Aboriginal Port-folio. Phila., 1835. Part 6. Folio, orig wraps; worn. With 6 colored plates. 1 plate trimmed. O Nov 26 (104) $800

Lewis, John Frederick, 1805-76

— Illustrations of Constantinople made during a Residence in that City.... L, [1838]. Folio, orig half lea gilt; stained. With litho dedication & 27 tinted litho subjects on 25 plates. Some margins waterstained or frayed; a few plates becomming detached. S Nov 21 (261) £2,600 [Egel]

Anr copy. Orig half mor; worn. With litho title, dedication & 25 plates. S June 30 (336) £1,600 [Consolidated Real]

Anr copy. Orig half cloth; rebacked. With tinted litho title, litho dedication & 25 tinted litho plates. Title & a few plates spotted; short tear near lower fore-corner of 1st plate. S July 1 (641) £4,000 [Kog]

— Sketches and Drawings of the Alhambra.... L, [1835]. Folio, 19th-cent half lea. With 26 tinted litho. Lacking litho title, dedication & list of drawings; some foxing. Schlosser copy. P June 17 (564) $2,500

— Sketches of Spain and Spanish Character. L, [1836]. 1st Ed. Folio, loose in contemp lea-backed cloth; spine torn. With 22 (of 25) plates, 3 hand-colored, plus 2 duplicates. Some tears; 1 plate with margins trimmed; foxed. pn May 14 (153) £660 [Shapero]

Lewis, Lloyd —&
Pargellis, Stanley E.

— Granger Country: A Pictorial Social History of the Burlington Railroad. Bost., 1949. In d/j. cb Feb 13 (213) $55

Lewis, Matthew Gregory, 1775-1818

— Journal of a West India Proprietor.... L, 1834. 8vo, half calf. 1 margin torn. bba Sept 19 (28) £140 [Shapero]

Anr copy. Cloth; worn. rs Oct 17 (53) $200

— The Monk: a Romance. L, 1796. 1st Ed, 1st Issue. 3 vols. 12mo, 19th-cent bds; some staining & rubbing. Upper blank corners of E7 & 8 torn away in Vol I & lower outer corner on L2 of Vol II; glue marks along inner margins of titles. Martin-Manney copy. P Oct 11 (205) $4,000

— Romantic Tales. L, 1808. 1st Ed. 4 vols. 12mo, orig bds; wear at fore-corners.

Senhouse copy. CNY June 9 (110) $700

Lewis, Meriwether, 1774-1809. See: Limited Editions Club

Lewis, Meriwether, 1774-1809 —& Clark, William, 1770-1838

— History of the Expedition.... L, 1814. ("Travels to the Source of the Missouri River and across the American Continent to the Pacific Ocean....") 1st English Ed. 4to, contemp half calf; rebacked. With folding map & 5 maps on 3 plates. Lacking half-title; folding map foxed. S Nov 21 (324) £1,200 [Maggs]

1st Ed. Phila., 1814. 2 vols. 8vo, contemp sheep; worn. With 5 maps & plans. Lacking folding map. sg Dec 5 (133) $950

Anr copy. Calf gilt by Morrell; joints worn. With folding map frontis & 5 maps & plans. Epstein copy. With ALs from Nicholas Biddle tipped in Vol I. sg Apr 30 (3006) $16,000

— Message from the President of the United States, Communicating Discoveries Made in Exploring the Missouri, Red River, and Washita. Wash., 1806. House Issue. 8vo, modern calf. With folding map & folding table. sg June 18 (326) $6,500

— Original Journals of the Lewis and Clark Expedition.... NY, 1969. 8 vols. NH May 30 (329) $150

Lewis, Oscar. See: Byington & Lewis; Grabhorn Printing

Lewis, Samuel, d.1862

— A Topographical Dictionary of England. L, 1831. 6 vols. 4to, half mor; rubbed. b June 22 (254) £190

Anr copy. Atlas vol only. Cloth; worn. With 45 maps, some folding. Maps at end waterstained; 2 maps linen-backed. bba July 9 (48) £130 [Burden]

Anr copy. 4 vols. 4to, contemp half lea; worn. With 44 (of 45) maps. Some browning & spotting. pn May 14 (201) £130 [Magna]

Anr copy. Contemp half calf; rubbed. With 44 maps. S Nov 15 (952) £210 [Graham]

3d Ed. L, 1835-36. 5 vols, including Atlas. 4to, later cloth; rubbed & scuffed. With 45 maps, including 15 folding. Some scuffing. DW Mar 4 (81) £190

Anr Ed. L, 1842. 7 vols, including Atlas. 4to, orig cloth; worn & faded. bba Jan 30 (117) £160 [Kentish]

Lewis, Sinclair, 1885-1951

See also: Limited Editions Club

— Arrowsmith. NY, [1925]. 1st Ed, one of 500 L.p. copies, sgd. sg June 11 (198) $225

— Babbitt. NY, [1922]. 1st Ed. Cloth; front hinge starting. Inscr to Oman Kelleher; also sgd by the pbr, Alfred Harcourt. sg June 11 (199) $450

— Cheap and Contented Labor: The Picture of a Southern Mill Town in 1929. NY, 1929. Pictorial wraps. sg Dec 12 (232) $100

— Dodsworth. NY: Harcourt, Brace, [1929]. In chipped d/j. Inscr. sg June 11 (200) $1,000

— Elmer Gantry. NY, [1927]. 1st Ed, 1st Bdg. In chipped d/j. cb Dec 10 (92) $100

Anr copy. In d/j. sg Dec 12 (233) $450

Anr copy. In chipped d/j. sp Apr 16 (404) $90

— Hike and the Aeroplane. By Tom Graham. NY, [1912]. 1st Ed. Orig cloth, in d/j. Epstein copy. sg Apr 30 (307) $17,500

— The Innocents. NY, [1917]. 1st Ed. Orig cloth; mark on spine. K Dec 1 (262) $50

— John Dos Passos' Manhattan Transfer. NY, 1926. One of 975. Inscr. sg Dec 12 (234) $375

— Our Mr. Wrenn. NY, 1914. 1st Ed. sg June 11 (201) $110

— The Trail of the Hawk. NY, [1915]. Orig cloth. wa Sept 26 (200) $50

Lewis, Thomas, 1689-1749?

— Origines Hebraeae: the Antiquities of the Hebrew Republick. Dublin, 1725. 4 vols in 3. 8vo, calf; shaken. Some leaves loose. sg Dec 19 (54) $500

Lewis, William S. —& Phillips, Paul C.

— The Journal of John Work. Cleveland, 1923. cb Nov 14 (240) $140

Lewis, Wyndham, 1884-1957

— The Apes of God. L, 1930. One of 750. 4to, cloth. sg Dec 12 (237) $130

— Timon of Athens. [L: Cube Press, 1913]. Folio, unbound in orig pictorial wraps; spine rubbed & darkened. Lacking blank. CNY Dec 5 (273) $3,200

Leymarie, Jean

— French Painting, the Nineteenth Century. Geneva, 1962. Folio, cloth, in d/j. Met Apr 28 (96W) $60

— The Jerusalem Windows. NY, [1962]. 4to, orig cloth, in d/j. P Dec 12 (22) $900

Anr copy. Orig cloth; spine & corners worn. sg Sept 6 (64) $850

Anr copy. Orig cloth, in d/j. sg Feb 6 (52) $150; sg Apr 2 (51) $750; wa Dec 9 (406) $900

L'Hospital, Guillaume Francois Antoine, Marquis de, 1661-1704

— Analyse des infiniment petits.... Paris: francois Montalant, 1715. 4to, contemp calf; upper joints cracked. With 11 folding plates. Ck Nov 29 (206) £60

— An Analytick Treatise of Conick Sections.... L, 1723. 1st Ed in English. 4to, contemp sheep; spine reinforced with cloth tape, front cover detached. With 33 plates. 1st plate repaired on verso. sg May 14 (291) $175

Lhuyd, Edward, 1660-1709

— Archaeologia Britannica.... Oxford, 1707. 1st Ed. Vol I: Glossography [all pbd]. Folio, old sheep; rebacked. Prelims soiled & stained. sg Mar 12 (68) $350

Liancour, Wernesson de

— Le Maistre d'armes oul'exercise de l'epee seule. Paris, 1686. Oblong 4to, 18th-cent calf. With port & 14 plates, including engraved title. Marginal worming in title & additional title; port possibly from anr copy. sg Mar 26 (175) $1,600

Libavius, Andreas

— Alchymia.... Frankfurt, 1606. Bound with: Syntagma selectorum undiquaque et persipicue traditorum Alchymiae arcanorum. Frankfurt, 1611. 3 parts in 1 vol. Folio, contemp blindstamped pigskin, sgd MMBW & dated 1617. FD Dec 2 (221) DM4,000

Liber...

— Liber librorum 1955. [V.p., 1955]. One of 500. Folio, loose as issued, in half cloth folder; With 42 sample leaves. cb Oct 17 (542) $55; pba July 23 (131) $170

— Liber Librorum. Stockholm, 1956. One of 1,500. 4to, loose as issued in folder. sg Oct 31 (179) $140

— Liber Scriptorum: The Second Book of the Author's Club. NY, 1921. Out-of-series copy. Folio, orig mor; rubbed. With each article sgd by the contributor. O Nov 26 (105) $275

Liberi da Premariacco, Fiore dei

— Il Fior di Battaglia. Bergamo, 1902. 4to, cloth; front hinge cracked. sg Mar 26 (176) $250

Liberman, Alexander

— The Art and Technique of Color Photography. NY, 1951. Folio, cloth, in d/j. With 195 plates. sg Apr 13 (33) $250

Library...

— The Library. L, 1961-90. 5th Series, Vol 16 - 6th Series, Vol 12. Together, 30 vols. Orig wraps, preserved in orig half-cloth folders. 1 vol lacking 2 parts. bba Apr 30 (381) £70 [Dodgson]

Library Company of Philadelphia. See: Franklin Printing, Benjamin

Library of Congress—Washington, D.C.

— Children's Books in the Rare Book Division of the Library.... Totowa, N.J., 1975. 2 vols. 4to, orig cloth. bbc Sept 23 (106) $80

Lichtenberg, Georg Christoph

— Vermischte Schriften. Goettingen, 1800-6. 9 vols. 8vo, contemp half calf gilt; worn & def. HH May 12 (1486) DM2,700

Lichtenberge, Johann

— Dise Practica unnd Prenostication.... [N.p.], 1526. Bound after: Pirstinger, B. Theologia germanica. Augsburg: A. Weissenhorn, 1531. And: Onus ecclesiae temporibus.... Augsburg, 1531. Folio, 16th-cent blind-stamped pigskin over wooden bds. Some worming marginal dampstaining; Pirstinger lacking B6, a2-3 & de. S Dec 5 (162) £1,600 [Goldschmidt]

Lichtenberger, Johannes

— Prognosticatio in Latino. Venice: [Nicolo & Domenico deal Jesu de Sandro], 23 Aug [1511]. 4to, vellum; soiled. sg Mar 12 (220) $2,800

Liebault, Jean, d.1596. See: Estienne & Liebault

Life...

See also: Shirley, John

— Life Magazine. NY, 1936-37. Vol I, No 1-Vol II, No 20. 27 issues. Folio, orig wraps, inserted into cloth binders. Some rippling of paper. bbc Feb 17 (230) $75

— The Life of Mother Gin. L, 1736. 8vo, 19th-cent half calf; rubbed. Some browning, affecting text; some holes in last leaf. S May 14 (1009) £220 [Rainford]

Light, William, 1785?-1839 —& De Wint, Peter, 1784-1849

— Sicilian Scenery. L, 1823. 4to, 19th-cent cloth. With engraved title & 61 plates. S Nov 15 (1098) £320 [Erlini]

Ligon, Richard

— A True & Exact History of the Island of Barbados.... L, 1657. 1st Ed. Folio, contemp calf; spine ends repaired, joints splitting, loss of lea in some spots, front flyleaf torn. With folding map, 6 plates, 3 folding plans & folding table. Flame-damage to margins of a few leaves; inner edge of folding map repaired; 2 folding plans with long repaired tears; some soiling, foxing & staining. CNY Oct 8 (147) $2,500

Anr Ed. L, 1673. Folio, contemp calf with arms of George Monck, Duke of Albemarle; rebacked, endpapers renewed. With folding map, 6 plates & 3 folding tables;l Index leaf to the Ingenio folding plan bound in at end Map with marginal tears & 4 folds reinforced; 2 small burn-holes to Q1 & R1, affecting 9 letters; Y2 with 2 small marginal holes; tear to corner of penultimate leaf. CNY Oct 8 (148) $1,600

Lilford, Thomas L. Powys, 4th Baron

— Coloured Figures of the Birds of the British Islands. L, 1885-97. 7 vols. 8vo, contemp half mor gilt; rubbed. With port & 421 colored plates, some hand-finished. Some foxing. pn Mar 19 (230) £1,400 [Shapero]

Anr copy. Mor by Riviere. pnE Oct 1 (282) £1,200

Anr Ed. L, 1891-97. 7 vols. 4to, contemp mor gilt by Riviere. With port & 421 hand-finished color plates. C May 20 (193) £1,900 [Radclyffe]

— Notes on the Birds of Northamptonshire.... L, 1895. 2 vols. 8vo, orig cloth; rubbed & soiled. wa Mar 5 (483) $110

Liliuokalani, Queen of Hawaii

— Hawaii's Story. Bost., 1898. Cloth. cb Jan 30 (76) $90

Limited Editions Club—New York

— All Men are Brothers. 1948. Trans by Pearl Buck. 2 vols. K July 12 (270) $80; wa Dec 9 (58) $70

— The Arabian Nights. 1934. Burton's trans. cb Dec 19 (125) $180

Anr Ed. 1954. 4 vols. sg Jan 30 (195) $175

— Book of Job. 1946. One of 1,950. cb Oct 25 (115) $225; F Sept 26 (323) $70; sg Jan 30 (199) $175; wa Apr 9 (244) $90

One of 1,950. Hinges cracked. sg Sept 26 (162) $100; sp Feb 6 (525) $80

— The Book of Proverbs. 1963. K July 12 (272) $50

— The Book of Psalms. 1960. cb Feb 27 (115) $80; sg Jan 30 (20) $120

— The Book of Ruth. 1947. One of 1,950. Met Apr 28 (79) $50

One of 1,950. cb Oct 225 (116) $225; sg Jan 30 (202) $150

— The Book of the Prophet Isaiah. 1979. sg Jan 30 (200) $120; wa Sept 26 (80) $65

— The Dead Sea Scrolls. 1966. sg Jan 30 (217) $150

— Evergreen Tales. 1949-52. Series I-V (Nos 1-15). 15 vols. sg Jan 30 (225) $400

Anr Ed. 1952. 3 vols. cb Oct 31 (98) $60

— The Four Gospels. 1932. S Nov 14 (63) £260

— Journals and Other Documents on...Christopher Columbus. 1963. Morison, Samuel Eliot. sg Jan 30 (239) $100

— The Koran; Selected Sutras. 1958. cb Oct 25 (68) $75; cb Feb 27 (160) $55

— The Living Talmud. 1960. K July 12 (297) $90; sg Jan 30 (2446pUS140)

— Quarto-Millenary: the First 250 Publications.... 1959. K July 12 (314) $200; sg May 21 (261) $140

One of 2,250. bbc Sept 23 (444) $130; sg Sept 26 (189) $175

— The Romance of Tristan and Iseult. 1960. cb Oct 31 (150) $55

— The Song of Roland. 1938. cb Feb 27 (191) $65

— AESOP. - Fables. 1933. cb Oct 31 (1) $110; sg Sept 26 (157) $150

— ANDERSEN, HANS CHRISTIAN. - The Complete Andersen.... 1949. 6 vols. sg Jan 30 (192) $90; wa Dec 9 (48) $110

— ANDERSEN, HANS CHRISTIAN. - Fairy Tales. 1942. 2 vols. sg Jan 30 (193) $80

— APULEIUS, LUCIUS. - The Golden Ass. 1932. Mor extra by Curtis Walters. cb Feb 27 (104) $55

— APULEIUS, LUCIUS. - The Marriage of Cupid & Psyche. 1951. sg Jan 30 (194) $175; wa Dec 9 (49) $110; wa Apr 9 (241) $65

— ARISTOPHANES. - Lysistrata. 1934. Illus by Picasso and sgd by him. Head of spine worn, joints rubbed. sg Sept 26 (161) $4,200; sg Jan 30 (196) $3,200

One of 1,500, sgd by Picasso. Illus by Picasso. cb Dec 19 (133) $3,000; P June 17 (293) $2,500; P June 17 (294) $3,000; wa Mar 5 (119) $2,800; wd June 12 (401) $2,200; wd June 12 (402) $2,200

— ARISTOTLE. - Politics & Poetics. 1964. wa Dec 9 (51) $65

— AUGUSTINE. - The Confessions. 1962. cb Oct 31 (68) $60

— BALZAC, HONORE DE. - Droll Stories. 1932. 3 vols. K July12 (164) $60

— BECKFORD, WILLIAM. - Vathek. 1945. cb Feb 27 (109) $65

— BELLAMY, EDWARD. - Looking Backward. 1941. wa Sept 26 (84) $60

— BENNETT, ARNOLD. - The Old Wives' Tale. 1941. 2 vols. cb Feb 27 (112) $50; DW Dec 11 (401) £70

— BERNANOS, GEORGES. - The Diary of a Country Priest. NY, 1986. One of 1,000. sg Jan 10 (197) $175

— BIERCE, AMBROSE. - Tales of Soldiers and Civilians. 1943. cb Oct 31 (73) $75

— BOCCACCIO, GIOVANNI. - Decameron. 1930. 2 vols. bba Apr 9 (298) £50 [Ulysses]; sg Jan 30 (198) $100

— BORGES, JORGE LUIS. - Ficciones. 1984. sg Jan 10 (203) $400

— BRADBURY, RAY. - Fahrenheit 451. 1982. sg Jan 30 (204) $130
— BRADBURY, RAY. - The Martian Chronicles. 1974. sg Jan 30 (205) $110
— BRILLAT-SAVARIN, JEAN ANTHELME. - The Physiology of Taste. 1949. cb Oct 31 (75) $55
— BROWNING, ELIZABETH BARRETT. - Sonnets from the Portuguese. 1948. cb Dec 19 (211) $70; wa Mar 5 (120) $50
— BULFINCH, THOMAS. - The Age of Fable. 1958. cb Oct 31 (78) $50
— BUNYAN, JOHN. - The Pilgrim's Progress. 1941. sg Jan 30 (206) $80
— BUTLER, SAMUEL. - Erewhon. 1934. cb Dec 19 (26) $90; sg Jan 30 (207) $60
— CAESAR, CAIUS JULIUS. - The Gallic Wars. 1954. cb Oct 25 (12) $70
— CARSON, RACHEL. - The Sea Around Us. 1980. sg Jan 10 (210) $200
— CASANOVA DE SEINGALT, GIACOMO GIROLAMO. - Memoirs. 1940. 8 vols. sp Sept 22 (164) $50
— CELLINI, BENVENUTO. - The Life of Benvenuto Cellini Written by Himself. 1937. bba July 9 (282) £130 [Cox]; O Mar 31 (114) $100
— CERVANTES SAAVEDRA, MIGUEL DE. - Don Quixote. 1933. 2 vols. bba July 9 (280) £80 [Bookworks]

Anr Ed. 1950. 2 vols. K July 12 (200) $95; wa Dec 9 (56) $55
— CHAUCER, GEOFFREY. - The Canterbury Tales. 1934. 2 vols. sg Sept 26 (167) $110

Anr Ed. 1946. K July 12 (273) $60; sg Jan 30 (211) $250
— CLEMENS, SAMUEL LANGHORNE. - Huckleberry Finn. 1933. sg Sept 26 (199) $110

Anr Ed. 1942. sg Sept 26 (200) $150; sg Jan 30 (270) $250
— CLEMENS, SAMUEL LANGHORNE. - Life on the Mississippi. 1944. sg Jan 30 (272) $275
— CLEMENS, SAMUEL LANGHORNE. - Tom Sawyer. 1939. sg Jan 30 (271) $275
— COLLIER, JOHN PAYNE. - Punch and Judy. 1937. wa Dec 9 (63) $65
— CONFUCIUS. - The Analects. 1933. sg Jan 30 (212) $200
— CONRAD, JOSEPH. - The Secret Sharer. 1985. sg Jan 10 (213) $70
— COOK, CAPT. JAMES. - The Explorations in the Pacific. 1957. cb Oct 10 (20) $55; cb Dec 19 (38) $160; wa Dec 9 (68) $65
— COOPER, JAMES FENIMORE. - The Last of the Mohicans. 1932. K July 12 (4) $80; sg Sept 26 (168) $70
— CREASY, SIR EDWARD SHEPHERD. - The Fifteen Decisive Battles of the World. 1969. cb Dec 19 (40) $70
— DANA, RICHARD HENRY, JR. - Two Years Before the Mast. 1947. sg June 18 (59) $50
— DANTE ALIGHIERI. - The Divine Comedy. 1932. bba July 9 (279) £120 [Bookworks]; sg Jan 30 (214) $150
— DARWIN, CHARLES. - Journal of Researches...during the Voyage of the HMS Beagle. 1956. sg Jan 30 (215) $80; wa Dec 9 (71) $55
— DARWIN, CHARLES. - On The Origin of Species. 1963. sg Nov 14 (170) $100; sg Jan 30 (216) $130; wa Dec 9 (72) $120
— DE QUINCEY, THOMAS. - Confessions of an English Opium-Eater. 1930. bba July 9 (274) £60 [Bookworks]
— DEFOE, DANIEL. - Moll Flanders. 1954. cb Oct 31 (88) $50; sg Jan 30 (218) $175
— DIAZ DEL CASTILLO, BERNAL. - The Discovery and Conquest of Mexico. 1942. cb Oct 10 (13) $160; cb Dec 19 (39) $65
— DICKENS, CHARLES. - The Chimes. 1931. K July 12 (167) $325; O Mar 31 (116) $130; sg Sept 26 (263) $200; sg Jan 30 (219) $350; sp Apr 16 (447) $180
— DICKENS, CHARLES. - A Christmas Carol. 1934. cb Oct 31 (89) $50; K July 12 (169) $80; sg Sept 26 (170) $50
— DICKENS, CHARLES. - The Cricket on the Hearth. 1933. K July 12 (168) $60
— DODGSON, CHARLES LUTWIDGE. - Alice's Adventures in Wonderland. 1932. One of 500 sgd by Alice Hargreaves. Mor. sg Jan 30 (208) $750
— DODGSON, CHARLES LUTWIDGE. - Through the Looking-Glass. 1935. Sgd by Alice Hargreaves. sg Jan 30 (209) $700

One of 500 sgd by Alice Hargreaves. Ck Dec 11 (147) £400
— DOSTOEVSKY, FYODOR. - The Brothers Karamazov. 1949. 3 vols. cb Dec 19 (48) $55

Anr copy. 2 vols. cb Feb 27 (123) $65; sg Sept 26 (172) $130; wa Dec 9 (76) $65
— DOSTOEVSKY, FYODOR. - Crime and Punishment. 1948. 2 vols. wa Dec 9 (75) $60
— DOSTOEVSKY, FYODOR. - The Idiot. 1956. K July 12 (274) $65
— DOYLE, ARTHUR CONAN. - The Adventures of Sherlock Holmes. 1950. 3 vols. sg Jan 30 (220) $425; wa Dec 9 (144) $240
— DREISER, THEODORE. - An American Tragedy. 1954. cb Dec 19 (49) $55; sg Jan 30 (222) $110; wa Dec 9 (80) $70
— DREISER, THEODORE. - Sister Carrie. 1939. O Mar 31 (117) $70; sg Jan 30 (221) $150
— DUMAS, ALEXANDRE. - Camille. 1937. cb Oct 31 (95) $250; sg Jan 30 (223) $550
— DWIGGINS, WILLIAM ADDISON. - Towards a Reform of the Paper Currency.... 1932. One of 452. sg Jan 30 (224) $275; wa Sept 26 (83) $180
— EMERSON, RALPH WALDO. - Essays, First and Second Series. 1934. b&b Feb 19 (227) $150
— EPICURUS. - [Works]. 1947. sp Sept 22 (173) $65

— FAULKNER, WILLIAM. - Hunting Stories. 1988. sg Jan 10 (226) $175
— FIELDING, HENRY. - The History of Tom Jones. 1952. 2 vols. cb Oct 31 (101) $55; wa Mar 5 (123) $50
— FRANCIS OF ASSISI. - The Little Flowers. 1930. bba July 9 (275) £160 [Goddard]; cb Oct 31 (126) $60; K July 12 (204) $80; sg Sept 26 (191) $60; sg Jan 30 (260) $60
— FRANKLIN, BENJAMIN. - Autobiography. 1931. K July 12 (3) $60
Unnumbered ptr's copy. b&b Feb 19 (226) $60
— FRANKLIN, BENJAMIN. - Poor Richard's Almanacs.... 1964. sg Jan 30 (227) $225
— FROST, ROBERT. - Complete Poems. 1950. 2 vols. cb Oct 31 (106) $325; sg Jan 30 (228) $375; wa Dec 9 (104) $280; wa June 25 (338) $350
— GILBERT, SIR WILLIAM SCHWENCK & SULLIVAN, SIR ARTHUR. - The First Night Gilbert and Sullivan. 1958. 2 vols. wa Dec 9 (107) $65
— GRASS, GUNTER. - The Flounder. 1985. One of 1,000. 3 vols. cb Feb 12 (51) $350; sg Sept 26 (175) $275; sg Jan 30 (229) $200; wa Dec 9 (108) $210
— GRIMM BROTHERS. - Fairy Tales. 1962. 4 vols. cb Oct 31 (110) $70
— HARDY, THOMAS. - Far from the Madding Crowd. 1958.. cb Oct 31 (111) $55; wa Dec 9 (114) $50
— HARDY, THOMAS. - The Mayor of Casterbridge. 1964. K July 12 (193) $70
— HAWTHORNE, NATHANIEL. - The House of the Seven Gables. 1935. cb Oct 31 (114) $50; sg Sept 26 (176) $50; sg Jan 30 (231) $80; wa Dec 9 (115) $50
— HEANEY, SEAMUS. - Poems and a Memoir. 1982. sg Jan 10 (232) $175
— HEARN, LAFCADIO. - Kwaidan. 1932. K July 12 (52) $110; sg Jan 30 (233) $140
— HEMINGWAY, ERNEST. - For Whom the Bell Tolls. 1942. sg Jan 30 (234) $175
— HERODOTUS. - The History. 1958. cb Oct 31 (117) $50
— HERSEY, JOHN. - Hiroshima. 1983. sg Jan 10 (236) $450
— HOFFMANN, ERNST THEODOR WILHELM. - The Tales of Hoffmann. 1943. cb Feb 27 (147) $50
— HOMER. - The Iliad. 1931. S Nov 14 (72) £230 [Fuller]
— HUDSON, WILLIAM HENRY. - Far Away and Long Ago. 1943. K July 12 (53) $80; sg Jan 30 (237) $60
— HUGHES, RICHARD. - The Innocent Voyage. 1944. O Mar 31 (121) $50
— HUGO, VICTOR. - Notre-Dame de Paris. 1930. 2 vols. K July 12 (275) $160
— HUGO, VICTOR. - Toilers of the Sea. 1960. K July 12 (202) $50
— HUXLEY, ALDOUS. - Brave New World. 1974. cb Feb 27 (152) $55
— IONESCO, EUGENE. - Journeys Among the Dead. 1987. One of 1,000. sg Jan 30 (238) $150; wa Apr 9 (246) $65
— JEFFERSON, THOMAS. - Writings. 1967. wa Dec 9 (119) $55
— JOYCE, JAMES. - Dubliners. 1986. One of 1,000. sg Jan 10 (240) $275
— JOYCE, JAMES. - Ulysses. 1935. sg May 7 (128) $1,500
One of 250 sgd by Joyce & Matisse. wd June 12 (405) $4,000
Anr copy. Illus by H. Matisse. Sgd by Joyce & Matisse. sg Nov 7 (119) $4,600
Anr copy. Sgd by Matisse. sg Jan 30 (241) $4,400
— KAFKA, FRANZ. - In the Penal Colony. 1987. One of 800. sg Jan 10 (242) $120
— KAFKA, FRANZ. - Metamorphoses. 1984. sg Jan 10 (243) $140
— LANDOR, WALTER SAVAGE. - Imaginary Conversations. 1936. sg Sept 26 (180) $50
— LEWIS, MERIWETHER & CLARK, WILLIAM. - The Journals of the Expedition. 1962. 2 vols. cb Oct 10 (64) $80; wa Dec 9 (122) $110
— LEWIS, SINCLAIR. - Main Street. 1937. cb Oct 31 (125) $275; K July 12 (5) $160; sg Sept 26 (181) $300; sg Dec 12 (1237) $130; sg Jan 30 (244) $300
— LINCOLN, ABRAHAM. - The Literary Works. 1942. cb Feb 27 (163) $75
— LONDON, JACK. - The Call of the Wild. 1960. sg Jan 30 (247) $120
— LYTTON, EDWARD GEORGE EARLE BULWER. - The Last Days of Pompeii. 1956. cb Oct 31 (79) $65
— MALORY, SIR THOMAS. - Le Morte Darthur. 1936. 3 vols. sg Jan 30 (248) $120
— MANN, THOMAS. - The Magic Mountain. 1962. 2 vols. cb Oct 31 (129) $50; K July 12 (206) $120
— MARAN, RENE. - Batouala. 1932. K July 12 (271) $95
— MASTERS, EDGAR LEE. - Spoon River Anthology. 1942. cb Oct 31 (130) $90
— MAUGHAM, W. SOMERSET. - Of Human Bondage. 1938. 2 vols. cb Oct 31 (131) $250; sg Sept 26 (184) $275; sg Jan 30 (249) $400; wa Mar 5 (124) $400
— MELVILLE, HERMAN. - Moby Dick. 1943. 2 vols. sg Jan 30 (250) $175
— MELVILLE, HERMAN. - Typee. 1935. cb Jan 30 (85) $80; K July 12 (276) $60; sg Sept 26 (185) $110; sg Jan 30 (251) $110
— MILLER, ARTHUR. - Death of a Salesman. 1984. sg Jan 10 (252) $300
— MILTON, JOHN. - The Masque of Comus. 1954. wa Dec 9 (127) $55
— MILTON, JOHN. - Paradise Lost and Paradise Regain'd. 1936. Zellerbach copy. b&b Feb 19 (229) $150; cb Dec 19 (115) $80

— MITCHELL, MARGARET. - Gone With the Wind. 1968. 2 vols. K July 12 (6) $90; sg Sept 26 (186) $150; sg Jan 30 (253) $150; wa Dec 9 (130) $80
— MOLIERE, JEAN BAPTISTE POQUELIN DE. - Tartuffe, or The Hypocrite. 1930. K July 12 (209) $50
— MORE, SIR THOMAS. - Utopia. 1934. cb Oct 25 (98) $80; sg Sept 26 (187) $175
— MORISON, SAMUEL ELIOT. - Journals and Other Documents on...Christopher Columbus. 1963. wa Dec 9 (65) $75
— OVID (PUBLIUS OVIDIUS NASO). - Metamorphoses. 1958. cb Oct 31 (136) $75; O Mar 31 (125) $50; sg Jan 30 (254) $175; wa Dec 9 (131) $140
— PAINE, THOMAS. - Rights of Man. 1961. cb Oct 31 (137) $70
— PARKMAN, FRANCIS. - The Oregon Trail. 1943. cb Oct 31 (138) $85; cb Jan 16 (40) $50; cb Feb 12 (19) $90
— PAZ, OCTAVIO. - Three Poems. 1987. One of 750. Illus by Robert Motherwell. wa Apr 9 (243) $2,500

Anr Ed. 1988. sg May 7 (166) $3,200

— PETRARCA, FRANCESCO. - The Sonnets. 1965. cb Oct 31 (140) $60
— PLATO. - The Republic. 1944. 2 vols. cb Oct 31 (142) $85
— PLATO. - The Trial and Death of Socrates. 1962. K July 12 (130) $80; wa Dec 9 (133) $95
— PLUTARCH. - The Lives of the Noble Grecians and Romans. 1941. 8 vols. sg Jan 30 (255) $110
— POE, EDGAR ALLAN. - The Fall of the House of Usher. 1985. sg Jan 30 (256) $650; wa Dec 9 (134) $240
— PORTER, WILLIAM SYDNEY. - The Voice of the City and Other Stories. 1935. sg Sept 26 (177) $175; sg Jan 30 (235) $175
— PRESCOTT, WILLIAM HICKLING. - History of the Conquest of Peru. 1957. cb Oct 10 (89) $50; wa Dec 9 (135) $60
— PRESCOTT, WILLIAM HICKLING. - The History of the Reign of Ferdinand and Isabella the Catholic. 1967. cb Feb 27 (177) $55
— PUSHKIN, ALEKSANDR SERGYEEVICH. - The Golden Cockerel. [1949]. bbc Apr 27 (358) $75; cb Oct 25 (38) $100; cb Feb 27 (178) $90; Met Apr 28 (443) $80; O Jan 14 (108) $70

Anr Ed. 1950. Illus by Edmund Dulac. DW Dec 11 (417) £55

— READE, CHARLES. - The Cloister and the Hearth. 1932. 2 vols. K Dec 1 (268) $75
— RIGGS, LYNN. - Green Grow the Lilacs. 1954. bbc Apr 27 (359) $200; cb Oct 31 (149) $190; sg Sept 26 (190) $225; sg Jan 30 (258) $275; wa June 25 (383) $200
— RIMBAUD, ARTHUR. - A Season in Hell. 1986. One of 1,000. Illus by Robert Mapplethorpe. sg Jan 30 (259) $1,300; sg Apr 13 (65) $850; wa Sept 26 (88) $1,100
— ROBERT, MAURICE & WARDE, FREDERIC. - A Code for the Collector of Beautiful Books. 1936. sg Sept 26 (276) $50
— SCHREINER, OLIVE. - The Story of an African Farm. 1961. cb Feb 27 (184) $60
— SHAKESPEARE, WILLIAM. - Hamlet. 1933. sg Sept 26 (192) $110; sg Jan 30 (262) $120; wa Sept 26 (82) $160
— SHAKESPEARE, WILLIAM. - Works. 1939-41. 37 vols plus The Poems, in 2 vols. sg Jan 30 (261) $950
— SHAW, GEORGE BERNARD. - Back to Methuselah. 1939. bba July 9 (285) £85 [Goddard]; cb Feb 27 (188) $50
— SHELLEY, MARY WOLLSTONECRAFT. - Frankenstein, or the Modern Prometheus. 1934. bbc Dec 9 (527) $100; cb Dec 19 (158) $65; cb Jan 16 (172) $60
— SIENKIEWICZ, HENRYK. - Quo Vadis? 1959. K July 12 (208) $50
— SINCLAIR, UPTON. - The Jungle. 1965. cb Oct 31 (157) $70; K July 12 (7) $65; O Aug 25 (121) $60; wa Dec 9 (146) $65
— SINGER, ISAAC BASHEVIS. - The Gentleman from Cracow. 1979. bbc Dec 9 (502) $55; sg Jan 30 (263) $100; wa Sept 26 (89) $260
— SINGER, ISAAC BASHEVIS. - The Magician of Lublin. 1984. sg Jan 10 (264) $500
— SPENSER, EDMUND. - The Faerie Queene. 1953. 2 vols. wa Dec 9 (147) $110
— STEINBECK, JOHN. - The Grapes of Wrath. 1940. 2 vols. sg Jan 30 (265) $450
— STERNE, LAURENCE. - A Sentimental Journey.... 1936. bbc Apr 27 (362) $55; sg Sept 26 (193) $150
— STEVENSON, ROBERT LOUIS. - The Beach of Falsea. 1956. cb Feb 27 (193) $60
— STEVENSON, ROBERT LOUIS. - Strange Case of Dr. Jekyll and Mr. Hyde. 1952. cb Oct 31 (162) $55; K July 12 (195) $55; sp Sept 22 (169) $50
— STEVENSON, ROBERT LOUIS. - Treasure Island. 1941. cb Oct 31 (163) $60
— STEVENSON, ROBERT LOUIS. - Two Mediaeval Tales. 1930. cb Sept 19 (199) $55
— STOWE, HARRIET BEECHER. - Uncle Tom's Cabin. 1938. cb Oct 25 (114) $140; sg Sept 26 (194) $130; sg Jan 30 (266) $175
— SUETONIUS TRANQUILLUS, CAIUS. - The Lives of the Twelve Caesars. 1963. cb Oct 31 (164) $70
— SWIFT, JONATHAN. - Gulliver's Travels. 1929. sg Jan 30 (267) $175
— SWIFT, JONATHAN. - Voyage to Lilliput; Voyage to Brobdingnag. 1950. 2 vols. cb Oct 31 (165) $160; sg Sept 26 (196) $175; wa Dec 9 (151) $65
— TENNYSON, ALFRED. - Idylls of the King. 1952. cb Feb 27 (193) $60
— THOREAU, HENRY DAVID. - Cape Cod. 1968. K July 12 (8) $50
— THOREAU, HENRY DAVID. - Walden. 1936.

Illus by Edward Steichen. sg Sept 26 (197) $650; sg Oct 8 (64) $275; sg Jan 30 (268) $900
— TOLSTOY, LEO. - Anna Karenina. 1951. 2 vols. cb Oct 31 (167) $55
— TOLSTOY, LEO. - War and Peace. 1938. 6 vols. sg Sept 26 (198) $425; sg Jan 30 (269) $200
— UNTERMEYER, LOUIS. - The Wonderful Adventures of Paul Bunyan. 1945. cb Feb 27 (222) $55
— VASARI, GIORGIO. - Lives of the Most Eminent Painters. 1966. 2 vols. K July 12 (210) $100; wa Dec 9 (158) $50; wa Mar 5 (125) $70
— VERGILIUS MARO, PUBLIUS. - Georgics. 1952. wa Dec 9 (162) $65
— VERNE, JULES. - From the Earth to the Moon.... 1970. 2 vols. cb Feb 27 (207) $55
— VERNE, JULES. - The Mysterious Island. 1959. cb Feb 27 (208) $60; K July 12 (211) $65; sp Sept 22 (166) $55; wa Dec 9 (160) $50
— WALTON, IZAAK & COTTON, CHARLES. - The Compleat Angler. 1948. cb Oct 31 (174) $100; sg Jan 30 (273) $150
— WHITMAN, WALT. - Leaves of Grass. 1942. 2 vols. sg Jan 330 (275) $600
— WILDE, OSCAR. - Salome: Drame en un acte. *Salome: A Tragedy. 1938. Trans by Lord Alfred Douglas. 2 vols. cb Oct 31 (180) $130; sp Apr 16 (464) $110
— WILDER, THORNTON. - The Bridge of San Luis Rey. 1962. wa Dec 9 (165) $85

Anr Ed. NY, 1962. cb Dec 19 (184) $50
— WILDER, THORNTON. - Our Town. 1974. cb Feb 27 (219) $55
— WILLIAMS, TENNESSEE. - A Streetcar Named Desire. 1982. sg Sept 26 (202) $130; sg Jan 30 (276) $175
— WISTER, OWEN. - The Virginian. 1951. One of 15 for presentation. wa Sept 26 (90) $70
— WROTH, LAWRENCE C. - A History of the Printed Book. 1938. cb Oct 17 (1018) $95; cb Oct 31 (183) $65

Lincoln, Abraham, 1809-65

See also: Limited Editions Club
— Emancipation Proclamation. Wash.: Government Printing Office, [1863]. ("By the President of the United States of America. A Proclamation....") Single sheet, 332mm by 208mm. Eberstadt 10. CNY May 14 (3) $8,000
— General Orders, No. 1. War Department, Adjutant General's Office. Wash., 2 Jan 1863. 8vo, disbound. sg Dec 5 (134) $120
— Political Debates between Hon. Abraham Lincoln and Hon. Stephen A. Douglas.... Columbus, 1860. 1st Ed, 1st Issue. 8vo, orig cloth; extremities worn, spine torn & artlessly repaired with minor loss, rear free endpaper excised. Inscr in pencil by Lincoln to Hon. Jesse K. Dubois. P June 16 (248) $24,000

2d Issue. Orig cloth; spine ends frayed. bbc June 29 (220) $110

3d Issue. Orig cloth; worn. bbc June 29 (221) $110

4th Issue. Orig cloth; spine ends worn. bbc June 29 (222) $90

Later Issue. Orig cloth. sg Dec 5 (137) $175
[-] [Proclamation of Lincoln as victor in the Presidential race] Canandaigua, 1860. In: Ontario Republic Ties. Vol 9, No 29, for Friday, 9 Nov 1860. Folio. Some fold tears & browning. sg Dec 5 (135) $400
[-] Trial of the Assassins and Conspirators for the Murder of Abraham Lincoln.... Phila., [1865]. 8vo, new cloth. sp Apr 16 (102) $100
— Works. NY, [1905]. Gettysburg Ed, one of 700. 12 vols. Cloth. bbc June 29 (215) $300

Federal Ed. NY, [1905-6]. Ed by A. B. Lapsley; intro by Theodore Roosevelt. 8 vols. Half mor. b&b Feb 19 (58) $250

Anr copy. Half sheep. Some foxing. bbc Sept 23 (52) $170
— EVERETT, EDWARD. - Address at the Consecration of the National Cemetery at Gettysburg, 19th November, 1863. With the Dedicatory Speech of President Lincoln.... Bost., 1864. 8vo, orig ptd wraps; chipped, spine partly perished, front wrap soiled & dampstained in upper corner. Ls of Everett laid in. wd Dec 12 (415) $175
— EVERETT, EDWARD. - Lincoln's Gettysburg Address. NY, 1863. ("An Oration Delivered on the Battlefield of Gettysburg....") 8vo, orig ptd wraps; spine chipped. Epstein copy. sg Apr 30 (308) $2,600

Lind, John

— Remarks on the Rescript of the Court of Madrid.... L, 1779. 8vo, calf. P June 16 (141) $1,400

Lindahl, E. —& Ohrling, J.

— Lexicon Lapponicum. Stockholm: J. G. Lange, 1780. 4to, orig wraps, unopened; soiled. Dampstained at lower corner. S Feb 11 (559) £280 [Hannas]

Lindberg, Pehr

— Architectura mechanica of moole-boek. Amst., 1727. Folio, half vellum. With 32 plates. B Nov 1 (500) HF1,200

Anr copy. Modern half calf. Lower right corner of tp & 1st 5 leaves dampstained with some loss. wd June 12 (407) $650

Lindbergh, Charles A.

— Of Flight and Life. NY, 1948. Inscr to Irene Herrnstadt. wa Oct 19 (66) $400

— The Spirit of St. Louis. NY, 1953. In d/j. Inscr to Irene Herrnstadt. wa Oct 19 (67) $600

— "We." NY, 1927. One of 1,000, sgd. Half vellum. cb Nov 7 (54) $800

One of 1,000. Half vellum; worn. F Sept 26 (247) $525

Anr copy. Bds; spine soiled. sg Sept 12 (145) $750

Linden, Jean Jules, 1817-98

— Lindenia: Iconographie des Orchidees. Ghent, 1885-1901. 16 vols & Livraisons 1-8 (of 12) of Vol 17. Folio, contemp half mor gilt, Vol 17 parts in orig wraps; extremities worn. With 800 chromolithographed plates. McCarty-Cooper copy. CNY Jan 25 (92) $19,000

Anr copy. 17 vols (without livraisons 9-12 of Vol 17 ptd in 1906). Folio, half cloth, orig wraps for Vol 17 preserved. With 786 chromolithos numbered 1-800. Plate 550-51 with 2 tiny perforations at fold; 4 plates misbound; Plate 532 detached; minor marginal dampstaining to 8 plates in Vol X. CNY June 9 (148) $13,000

— Lindenia: Iconography of Orchids. Ghent, 1891-94. 13 parts in 7 vols. Folio, half mor by Zaehnsdorf; some wear to spines & extremities. With 304 chromolithos & 1 uncolored plates; plates numbered 265-576. Marginal tear to Plate 409; some foxing. CNY June 9 (149) $4,800

— Pescatorea. Iconographie des orchidees. Brussels, 1860. Vol I (all issued). Folio, contemp half mor gilt; inner joints strengthened. With 48 colored plates. Fore-edges at front slightly dampstained affecting 1st 7 plates; some foxing. McCarty-Cooper copy. CNY Jan 25 (91) $7,000

Lindley, John, 1799-1865
See also: Bauer, Franz Andreas

— Rosarum Monographia; or, a Botanical History of Roses. L, 1820. 4to, bds. With 1 plain & 18 hand-colored plates. S June 25 (39) £600 [Chimera]

— Sertum Orchidaceum: a Wreath of the Most Beautiful Orchidaceous Flowers. L, 1838. Folio, contemp mor gilt by J. Law of Liverpool; rejointed & spine ends renewed. With colored litho half-title & 49 hand-colored plates. Light, mostly marginal, foxing to about half of the plates; 1 text leaf with wrinkling & marginal tear. Derby copy. CNY June 9 (150) $12,000

Lindley, John, 1799-1865 —& Paxton, Sir Joseph, 1801-65

— Paxton's Flower Garden. L, 1882-84. 3 vols. Orig cloth. With 108 colored plates. A few plates brittle, 1 def. bba Sept 5 (90) £420 [Finney]

Lindsay, David, 1856-1922

— The Royal Geographical Society of Australasia...Explorations in the northern Territory of South Australia. Adelaide, 1888. With: Map of Exploration of Arnheims Land Northern Territory. Adelaide, 1883. Text is 4to, modern cloth. Map has rivers with color; size of map not given. Text is inscr by W. J.Sowden. C June 25 (270) £850 [Renard]

Lindsay, Sir David, fl.1490-1535

— A True Narration of All the Passages of the Proceedings in the Generall Assembly of the Church of Scotland...against a Seditious Pamphlet.... L, 1621. 4to, old vellum. pnE Mar 11 (136) £120

Lindsay, Jack

— A Homage to Sappho. L, 1928. One of 70. Illus by Norman Lindsay. 4to, vellum gilt; soiled. This copy unsgd. S Dec 12 (190) £1,300 [B. Marks]

Lindsay, Sir Lionel Arthur

— Conrad Martens. Sydney, 1920. 4to, half cloth; stained & marked. kh Nov 11 (167) A$90

Lindsay, Vachel, 1879-1931

— Collected Poems. NY, 1923. One of 400 L.p. copies. Half cloth. sg Dec 12 (239) $150

Anr Ed. NY, 1925. Cloth; extremities worn. Marginal dampstaining bleeding into extreme lower corner of text. Inscr & with 2 A Ls s from Lindsay & 1 ALs from his wife to C. C. Certain. wa Sept 26 (202) $140

— The Golden Book of Springfield. NY, 1920. With drawing of a flower sgd by au. cb Feb 12 (773) $50

Linguet, Simon Nicolas Henri, 1736-94

— Canaux navigables, ou developpement des avantages qui resulteraient de l'execution de plusierus projets en ce genre.... Amst., 1769. 12mo, contemp calf gilt. Gathering C browned. pn June 11 (122) £130

Linhart, Lubomir

— Josef Sudek. Prague, 1956. 4to, cloth, in d/j with small tear on spine. With 232 photogravures. sg Apr 13 (96) $650

Linn, John J.

— Reminiscences of Fifty Years in Texas. NY, 1883. 12mo, orig cloth; worn. NH May 30 (520) $260

Linnaeus, Carolus, 1707-78

— Hortus Cliffortianus. Amst., 1737. Folio, modern calf; rubbed, upper hinge tender, white pressmark on spine. With engraved title & 36 plates. Text leaves foxed; 1st plate soiled in margins; single wormhole in inner margin, occasionally costing a letter; a few plates shaved to plate-marks; accession-number & date on dedication. U of Wisconsin at Madison copy. P June 17 (254) $3,000

Anr copy. Contemp calf. Some prelim leaves stained in lower margins; erased stamp on tp; 2 plates trimmed to plate line at outer margin. S July 25 (40) £1,500 [Watson]

— Lachesis Lapponica, or a Tour in Lapland.... L, 1811. 1st Ed in English. Vol I only. Contemp calf; def. Sold w.a.f. sg Sept 19 (214) $300

Anr copy. 2 vols. 8vo, contemp sheep gilt; covers detached. sg Nov 14 (189) $175

— Philosophia botanica.... Stockholm, 1751. 1st Ed. 8vo, 19th-cent cloth. With 9 plates. Lacking port. bba Sept 5 (74) £240 [Hobbes]

— Vollstaendiges Pflanzensystem. Nuremberg, 1777-78. 14 vols in 15. 8vo, contemp half calf; rubbed. S May 14 (1043) £350 [Nielsen]

Linperch, Pieter. See: Lindberg, Pehr

Linschoten, Jan Huygen van, 1563-1611

— His Discours of Voyages unto ye Easte & West Indies.... L: John Wolfe, [1598]. 1st Ed in English. Folio, late 18th-cent mor gilt, with gilt device of Sir Stephen Fox, Baron Holland; spine repaired, joints cracked, extremities worn, rubbed. With engraved title, 10 maps on 12 sheets & 4 folding plates, including duplicate copies of double-sheet map, plus 29 double-page or folding plates inserted from orig Dutch Ed & 1 smaller folding plate from an unidentified English work. STC 15692. CNY Oct 8 (150) $24,000

— Histoire de la navigation.... Amst., 1619. Folio, half calf. With 2 engraved titles, 6 folding maps & 36 plates. B Nov 1 (575) HF22,000

— Itinerario, Voyage ofte Schipvaert naer Oost ofte Portugaels Indien.... Amst.: C. Claesz, 1595-96. 3 parts in 1 vol. Folio, 17th-cent calf; joints split, old repairs, abraded with some loss of lea. Gothic & roman type in double column; with 4 titles with engraved vignettes, port, 36 double-page or folding plates (bound out of order), 5 folding maps plus folding map of the world by Vrient. Lacking conjugate leaf Cc2.5 & with duplicate of Cc1.6 bound in its place; B3 of Part 3 wwith corner torn affecting pagination. Some fold tears & repairs; Africa map def & probably supplied from a later Ed. DuPont copy. CNY Oct 8J (149) $15,000

Linton, William, 1791-1876

— The Scenery of Greece and its Islands.... L, 1856. 4to, later cloth; rubbed. With map & 50 plates. DW Nov 6 (61) £105

Anr Ed. L, [1869]. 4to, contemp cloth; shaken, rebacked retaining portion of orig backstrip, new endpapers. With 49 (of 50) plates. Lacking map; some staining. bba July 23 (354) £200 [Nolan]

Linton, William James, 1812-97

— The History of Wood-Engraving in America. Bost., 1882. One of 1,000. Folio, orig half cloth. cb Oct 17 (547) $90

— The Masters of Wood-Engraving. L, 1889. One of 600. 4to, orig cloth; rubbed, front hinge shaken. bba June 11 (313) £130 [Ginnan]

Lion-Goldschmidt, Daisy —& Moreau-Gobard, Jean Claude

— Chinese Art. NY, [1962]. Folio, cloth, in d/j. sp Sept 22 (222) $100

Liot, W. B.

— Panama, Nicaragua, and Tehunatepec.... L, 1849. 1st Ed. 8vo, orig cloth. With 2 folding plates. Inscr & with related material. S June 25 (453) £900 [Holman]

Lippard, George, 1822-54

— Washington and his Generals, or Legends of the Revolution.... Phila., 1847. 1st Ed. 8vo, half mor; extremities rubbed. Inscr. sg June 18 (543) $450

Lipperheide Library, Franz Joseph von

— Katalog der Freiherrlich von Lipperheide'schen Kostuembibliothek. Berlin, 1965. ("Katalog der Kostuembibliothek.") 2 vols. 4to, cloth; worn. O Sept 24 (148) $260

Lipscomb, George, 1773-1846

— The History and Antiquities of the County of Buckingham. L, 1847. 4 vols. 4to, contemp calf; rubbed. With 68 plates. Some foxing. F Mar 26 (765) $150

Lipsius, Justus, 1547-1606

— De constantia libri duo. Antwerp: Christopher Plantin, 1585. 4to, contemp vellum. Inscr to Robert Dudley, Earl of Leicester. C June 24 (329) £7,500 [Kraus]

— De Militia Romana Libri Quinque. Antwerp: Plantin, 1596. 4to, 18th-cent calf gilt with arms of the Collegium Grassinaeum; small portion at head of spine missing, corners worn. Some browning. C Dec 16 (54) £400 [Mediolanum]

— Poliorcetion sive de machinis, tormentis, telis, libri quinque. Antwerp: Plantin, 1599. Folio, old vellum. Browned throughout. S July 1 (1290) £2,000 [Poole]

Lisiansky, Urey, 1773-1837

— A Voyage Round the World.... L, 1814. 4to, modern half calf. With 2 hand-colored folding maps & 11 (of 12) plates. sg Jan 9 (111) $950

Lister, Joseph Lister, 1st Baron, 1827-1912

— Contributions to Physiology and Pathology. L, 1859. 4to, wraps; spine replaced. Marginal annotations in anr hand on several leaves. Inscr to Dr. Bulloch. Offprint from Philosophical Transactions, Part II for 1858, pp 607-702, 549-557. wd June 12 (408) $475

Litke, Fedor Petrovich

— Chetyrekratnoe puteshestvie v severnyi ledovityi okean. St. Petersburg: Naval Press, 1828. 2 vols in 1. 4to, contemp half calf; rubbed, recased. With 20 maps (12 folding) & 14 plates of coastal profiles. Some browning; 2 leaves with outer margin strengthened. C May 20 (326) £2,800 [Quaritch]

Litta, Pompeo, Conte

— Celebri famiglie italianae. Milan, 1819-1902. 8 vols. Folio, contemp half lea; worn. SI Dec 5 (349) LIt7,500,000

Anr Ed. Milan, 1819. 20 vols & portfolio of plates. Folio, contemp half lea & contemp half mor. SI Dec 5 (917) LIt22,500,000

Littauer, Vladimir S. See: Derrydale Press

Little, Thomas. See: Moore, Thomas

Littlejohn, David. See: Grabhorn Printing

Littleton, Sir Thomas

— Les Tenures.... L, 1617. 12mo, disbound with each leaf mtd in a contemp 4to book bound in vellum. Annotated in an old hand. STC 15757. K July 12 (311) $325

Liturgy

— Index sive directorium horarum usum ritum chori Curien. Augsburg, 1520. 4to, contemp blind-stamped pigskin over wooden bds; spine damaged, lacking 1 clasp. Sussex copy. S Dec 5 (163) £600 [Schumann]

— Tupicon. Venice: fratelli dei Nicolini da Sabbio for Andreas Kounadis, 4 Jan 1545. Folio, contemp vellum; spine def. S Dec 5 (165) £7,500 [Franks]

Liudprandus, Bishop of Cremona, c.920-72

— Liutprandi...rerum gestarum per Europam ipsius praesertim temporibus libri sex. Paris: Badius Ascensius & Jean Petit, 1514. Bound with: Gregory, Saint & Adon, Saint. B. Gregorii...historiarum praecipue gallicarum.... Paris, 18 Oct & 13 Nov 1512 (2d part with misprint 1522). Folio, contemp blind-stamped pigskin over bevelled wooden bds. Roman types with Gothic-type headlines & some words of titles.. Marginal notes & corrections in the hand of Johann Thurmair, Aventinus. C June 24 (330) £1,000 [Kraus]

Livingston, Edward, 1764-1836

— Report Made to the General Assembly of the State of Louisiana.... New Orleans, 1822. 8vo, modern mor. Inscr, but with portion of signature excised in rebdg. sg June 18 (330) $1,100

Livingston, Luther Samuel, 1864-1914. See: Grolier Club

Livingstone, David, 1813-73

— The Last Journals of David Livingstone. L, 1874. 1st Ed. 2 vols. 8vo, half mor gilt, orig front covers & spines bound in. With 2 folding maps. sg Jan 9 (112) $175

— Missionary Travels and Researches in South Africa. L, 1857. 1st Ed. 8vo, calf gilt by C. Murton. bba June 25 (241) £240 [Bonham]

Anr copy. Contemp half cloth; rubbed. With frontis, port & 2 folding maps. bba Aug 13 (409) £50 [White]

Anr copy. Orig cloth; loose. With frontis & with 2 maps in end pocket. W July 8 (225) £60

Issue not stated. Orig cloth; hinges cracked. Sgd. Epstein copy. sg Apr 30 (3309) $1,600

Livingstone, David & Charles

— Narrative of an Expedition to the Zambesi and its Tributaries.... L, 1865. 1st Ed. 8vo, orig cloth; spine faded. bba Oct 10 (251) £70 [Remington]

Anr Ed. NY, 1866. 8vo, cloth. With folding map. Library markings. cb Oct 10 (65) $55

Anr copy. Orig cloth; rubbed & soiled, bds scratched, hinges tender. With folding map, double-page frontis & 35 other illusts, mostly full-page. wa Apr 9 (105) $80

Livius, Titus, 59 B.C.-17 A.D.

Decades

— Historiae Romanae decades. Milan: Uldericus Scinzenzeler for Alexander Minutianus, 25 May 1495. Folio, old vellum; spine repaired, upper joint strengthened. Type 3:110R, 52 lines. Unrubricated. Repaired tears within text of Q7-8; marginal worming to M2-b7. 311 (of 312) leaves; lacking final blank. Goff L-246. C Dec 16 (137) £1,800 [Sokol]

Anr Ed. Venice, 1506. ("Decades.") Folio, 19th-cent calf; hinges cracked, corners bumped, edges blackened. Marginal tears repaired, not affecting text; worming in quire A with small text loss; library stamp on tp; marginal notes; lacking final blank. P Dec 12 (65) $800

Anr Ed. Venice: Aldus, 1555. ("Historiarum ab urbe condita.") Folio, vellum. Some spotting. SI June 9 (544) LIt500,000

— Historiarum ab urbe condita. Leiden & Amst., 1738-46. 7 vols. 4to, calf gilt with arms of Zwolle. With frontis, port 7 3 plates. Some foxing & browning. B May 12 (1656) HF850

— Romische historie. Strassburg: Rihel, 1593. ("Von Ankunfft und Ursprung dess roemischen Reichs....") Bound with: Hegesippus. Fuenff Buecher.... [N.p., n.d.]. Folio, contemp pigskin over wooden bds with panel stamps of Emperor Charles V & of the arms of the Holy Roman Empire; worn, lacking clasps. sg Oct 24 (192) $700

— 1520. - Historiarum ab Urbe Condita.... Venice: Aldus. 8vo, contemp mor gilt. Some soiling. cb Dec 5 (74) $1,100

Livre...

— Le Livre des Rois. Lausanne, 1930. One of 195. Illus by F. L. Schmied. 4to, loose in orig folder as issued; some discoloration. With 26 colored initials, 15 colored wood-engravings in text, 5 full-page colored wood-engravings (1 in 3 states, 1 in 2 states), a suite of 20 sheets on japon showing progressive states for 1 of the illusts in the text; anr suite of 12 sheets on japon showing stages for 1 of the full-page wood-engravings. Some soiling. P June 17 (323) $1,100

— Le Livre et ses amis. Paris, 1945-1947. Nos 1-18 (all pbd). 4to, loose in pictorial wrap portfolios, unopened. O Sept 24 (151) $300

Lizars, William Home, 1788-1859. See: Ewbank & Lizars

Lloyd, Hannibal Evans

See also: Turner, Joseph M. W.

— Picturesque Views in England and Wales. L, [1827]. 2 vols. Folio, 19th-cent half mor gilt; extremities rubbed. With engraved titles & 96 plates. Ck May 15 (169) £1,100

Lloyd, Henri

— Introduction a l'histoire de la guerre en Allemagne.... L & Brussels, 1784. 4to, modern half mor gilt. With 5 folding plates & 6 folding maps. Some dampstaining in upper margins. sg Oct 24 (193) $200

Lloyd, Llewellyn, 1792-1876

— The Game Birds and Wild Fowl of Sweden and Norway. L, 1867. 1st Ed. 8vo, cloth; lacking front free endpaper. sg Jan 9 (280) $140

2d Ed. 8vo, modern half mor gilt; rubbed. With folding colored map & 48 color plates. bba Jan 30 (95) £380 [Bowers]

Lobchevsky, Nikolai Ivanovich

— Voobrazhaemaia geometriia. Kazan: University Press, 1835. Bound with: Primenenie voobrazhaemoi geometrii k nekotorym integralam. Kazan, 1836. 8vo, later wraps; torn, lacking spine. Some leaves browned; later marginalia. C Dec 16 (55) £2,500 [Watson]

Lobo, Jerome, 1593-1678

— A Voyage to Abyssinia. L, 1735. 1st Ed. Trans by Samuel Johnson. 8vo, contemp calf; spine restored. Some soiling & browning. Milne copy. Ck June 12 (94) £240

Anr copy. Modern half mor gilt. sg Nov 7 (103) $650

Anr copy. Old sheep; joints cracked. sg Mar 12 (148) $425

Anr Ed. L, 1789. 8vo, contemp calf; spine restored. Some soiling & browning. Milne copy. Ck June 12 (94) £240

Lobstein, Jean Frederic, 1777-1835

— Essai sur la nutrition du foetus. Strasbourg, 1802. 4to, later 19th-cent half cloth. With 2 plates. stain in upper outer corner of opening leaves. sg Nov 14 (71) $450

Locke, John, 1632-1704

— A Collection of Several Pieces, Never Before Printed.... L, 1720. 8vo, contemp calf; joints split, rubbed. With 1 plate. Some browning. S May 14 (953) £320 [Clark]

Anr copy. Contemp calf; worn. Some browning & soiling. S July 1 (954) £250 [Quaritch]

— Du Gouvernement Civil.... Amst.: Abraham Wolfgang, 1691. 12mo, contemp sheep; top of backstrip chipped, lower portion partly detached. sg Oct 24 (194) $700

— An Essay concerning Humane Understanding. L, 1690. 1st Ed, 1st Issue. Folio, later calf; joints cracked, some gouges. P Oct 11 (207) $14,000

Anr copy. Contemp calf; rubbed & stained,

foot of spine chipped. XX2-3 loosely inserted from anr copy & with margins soiled; sections torn from margins of L1-2 just shaving 3 letters; small hole in M2 affecting 3 or 4 letters; dampstain affecting headings of Rr-Tt; some dampstaining; some ink stains & other minor marginal faults; lacking free endpapers; later front pastedown. S Mar 19 (180) £3,000 [Pickering]

2d Ed. L, 1694. Folio, modern half mor. Piece torn from upper corner of U1; some waterstaining. bba Aug 13 (93) £180 [Gammon]

Anr copy. Orig bds; rubbed, front cover detached. Port & title detached; 1 leaf torn with loss of text; some dampstaining. F Sept 26 (614) $150

3d Ed. L, 1695. Folio, contemp calf; joints cracked. LH May 17 (711a) $90

Anr Ed. L, 1706. Folio, contemp calf; bds detached. LH Dec 11 (143) $250

Anr copy. Early 19th-cent sheep gilt. sg Oct 24 (195) $275

— Posthumous Works. L, 1706. 1st Ed. 8vo, contemp calf; rebacked. bba Nov 28 (253) £300 [Hannas]

Anr copy. Contemp calf; worn, lacking free endpapers. Blank portion cut from head of tp; some spots & stains. S July 1 (956) £200 [Quaritch]

— Several Papers Relating to Money, Interest and Trade. L, 1696. 8vo, contemp vellum; worn. S July 21 (316) £50 [Lawson]

— Some Familiar Letters between Mr. Locke, and Several of his Friends. L, 1708. 8vo, contemp calf; joints split. pnE May 13 (150) £100

Anr copy. 19th-cent half calf; rubbed. J.M. Robertson's copy. S July 1 (957) £180 [Hannas]

— Works. L, 1722. 3 vols. Folio, contemp calf gilt; covers wormed, spine ends chipped. Frontis torn, repaired & mtd; b1 in Vol I torn & repaired. C Dec 16 (215) £280 [Pickering & Chatto]

Anr copy. Contemp vellum; rebacked. SI June 9 (545) LIt1,000,000

Anr Ed. L, 1794. 9 vols. 8vo, contemp lea; worn. Staining & soiling. O Feb 25 (127) $170

Anr Ed. L, 1824. 9 vols. 8vo, contemp mor; rubbed. bba Aug 13 (94) £150 [Shapero]

Lockhart, John Gibson, 1794-1858

Lockhart, John Gibson, 1794-1854

— Ancient Spanish Ballads. L, 1841. Illus by Owen Jones. 4to, orig cloth; faded. cb Jan 9 (125) $100

— The Life of Robert Burns. Liverpool, 1914. Ltd Ed. 2 vols. Orig half vellum. bba Oct 10 (389) £85 [B. Turner]

Lockhart, John Gibson, 1794-1858

— Memoirs of the Life of Sir Walter Scott. L, 1900. 5 vols. 8vo, half mor gilt. Extra-illus with c.100 engravings, many inlaid to size. cb Jan 16 (136) $250

— Memoirs of the Life of Sir Walter Scott. Edin., 1902-3. ("The Life of Sir Walter Scott.") One of 1,040. 10 vols. 8vo, cloth. pnE Oct 2 (367) £60

Lockhart, Sir Robert Hamilton Bruce, 1887-1970

— My Rod my Comfort. L, 1949. One of 500. Illus by J. Gaastra. 8vo, orig half vellum gilt. Inscr to Mrs. Hardy. L Nov 14 (182) £50

Lockwood, Alice G. B.

— Gardens of Colony and State. Gardens of the American Colonies.... [NY]: Garden Club of America, 1931-34. 2 vols. Folio, cloth. F Sept 26 (292) $70

Anr copy. Orig cloth; joint worn. F Mar 26 (45) $350

Lockwood, Luke Vincent

— Colonial Furniture in America. NY, 1913. 2 vols. 4to, cloth. sg Apr 2 (118) $90

3d Ed. NY, 1926. 2 vols. Folio, cloth; worn. NH Oct 6 (133) $55

Loddiges, Conrad & Sons

— The Botanical Cabinet. L, [1817]-33. Vol V only. Later half lea. With 100 hand-colored plates, a few trimmed to plate margin. pn Apr 23 (228) £380

Anr copy. 20 vols. 4to, contemp calf gilt; spines rubbed, some joints renewed. With engraved titles, 200 hand-colored plates & 1 uncolored plats. Some spotting. Sold w.a.f. S June 25 (41) £5,000 [Junk]

Lodge, Edmund, 1756-1839

— Illustrations of British History, Biography and Manners. L, 1791. 3 vols. 4to, contemp calf over bds. LH Dec 11 (144) $130

— Portraits of Illustrious Personages of Great Britain. L, 1823-34. 12 vols in 6. 4to, contemp mor gilt. With 240 plates. W July 8 (9) £125

Anr Ed. L, 1835. 12 vols. 8vo, contemp half mor; rubbed. Library markings. bba May 14 (366) £60 [Corbett]

Anr copy. 12 vols in 6. 8vo, contemp half mor gilt; backstrips scuffed. Some foxing. bbc Dec 9 (233) $230

Anr copy. 12 vols in 4. 8vo, contemp half mor gilt; scuffed. With 240 ports. L Nov 14 (67) £70

Anr Ed. L, [c.1880]. Vols I-VII & X. Cloth. sg Feb 13 (194) $150

Lodge, George E. See: Bannerman & Lodge

Loehneyss, Georg Engelhart

— Gruendtlicher Bericht des Zeumens und ordentlicher Austheilung der Muendstueck und Stangen. L, 1588. Folio, later half calf; worn. Lacking f.36; repair at head of f.88 with slight loss; some other repairs; wormed at beginning, affecting text. S Feb 11 (495) £260 [Clarke]

Loening, Grover C.

— Military Aeroplanes. Bost., 1918. cb Nov 7 (58) $60

Lofting, Hugh, 1886-1947

— The Story of Dr. Doolittle. NY, 1920. 1st Ed. In d/j. Epstein copy. sg Apr 30 (310) $950

Logan, James, 1794?-1872 —& McIan, Robert Ronald, d.1856

— The Clans of the Scottish Highlands. L, 1845-47. Vol II only. Cloth; def. With 27 hand-colored plates. sg Feb 13 (180) $600

Anr copy. 2 vols. Folio, cloth; rubbed. With 2 colored armorial frontises & 72 hand-colored plates. Some wear along inner margins of several plates in Vol II affecting images; short tear & stamp to armorial frontis of Vol II; library markings. sg Apr 2 (74) $1,700

Anr Ed. L: Ackermann, 1857. 2 vols. Folio, orig mor gilt; loose. Not collated. Sold w.a.f. O Nov 26 (107) $1,600

Loggan, David, 1635-1700?

— Oxonia illustrata. Oxford, 1675. 2 vols in 1. Folio, contemp calf gilt; rebacked with orig spine laid down, 1 corner restored. With 70 plates & maps. Marginal dampstaining to title-leaf; Plate 6 with repair to edge of platemark; 2 sheets of folding plate 27 misaligned, obscuring image & caption; folding plate 25 in Vol II washed & resized with a 2-inch internal fold tear & several repaired tears; a few short marginal tears & fold breaks; some discoloration. McCarty-Cooper copy. CNY Jan 25 (43) $4,200

Anr copy. Folio, contemp calf; worn, rebacked. With pictorial engraved title & 40 double-page plates. A few thumb-marks; dust-soiling. S Nov 21 (119) £1,600 [Kentish]

Anr copy. Contemp calf; rebacked, worn. With engraved title & 40 double-page plates & a plan of Oxford. Minor repairs along plate-marks; some soiling; 3 leaves from a shorter copy. S June 25 (278) £1,800 [kentish]

Lohenstein, Daniel Casper von

— Werke. Breslau: Fellgiebel, 1685-89. 12 parts in 1 vol. 8vo, contemp vellum gilt, 1692. With 5 engraved titles & 24 plates. Ck Oct 31 (164) £650

Lolli, Giovanni Battista

— Osservazioni teorico-pratiche sopra il giuoco degli scacchi. Bologna, 1763. Folio, contemp sheep; rebacked with old spine preserved, new front free endpaper. Ck May 8 (126) £400

Anr copy. Contemp bds. SI June 9 (546) LIt1,300,000

Loncin von Gominn, Alberto Josepho. See: Conlin, Albert Joseph

London...

— The London and Country Brewer.... L, 1744. 5th Ed. 8vo, calf; rebacked. bba Nov 28 (126) £120 [Hughes]

— London and its Environs Described. L, 1761. 6 vols. 8vo, contemp calf; worn. With 78 plates. Lacking map & plan of London; ink stamp on some prelims. bba May 28 (381) £65 [Sanderson]

— London Interiors: A Grand National Exhibition. L, [1841]. 2 vols in 1. 4to, orig cloth; rebacked, orig backstrip laid down. Engraved title & frontis stained; lacking tp to Vol II. L Nov 14 (106) £90

— The Several Plans and Drawings Referred to in the Second Report from the Select Committee upon the Improvement of the Port of London. L, 1799. Folio, contemp wraps; extremities chipped. With 14 folding plates, some highlighted in color; 1 cropped. bba July 9 (50) £220 [Axe]

— The Several Plans and Drawings Referred to in the Third Report from the Select Committee upon the Improvement of the Port of London. L, 1800. Bound in 1 vol. Folio, 19th-cent half calf. With 21 double-page & folding plates, 7 of them hand-colored. S May 14 (1134) £300 [Glaister]

London, Charmian

— The Book of Jack London. NY, 1921. 1st Ed. 2 vols. Inscr in both vols and with check sgd by Jack London attached to front pastedown of Vol II. cb Dec 12 (104) $300

London, Jack, 1876-1916
See also: Limited Editions Club
— The Abysmal Brute. NY, 1913. 1st Issue. Rubbed. Orig cloth Minor foxing. wa Sept 26 (206) $85
3d Issue. In d/j. cb Feb 12 (75) $800
— The Acorn-Planter: A California Forest Play.... L: Mills & Boon, [1916]. 1st English Ed. Orig cloth; rubbed & spotted. Prelims foxed. wa Apr 9 (46) $110
— Adventure. NY, 1911. 1st Ed. Spine faded & rubbed. cb Sept 19 (124) $50
— Before Adam. L, 1907. Macmillan's Colonial Library Ed. K Mar 22 (235) $80
1st Trade Ed. NY, 1907. Rubbed. cb Sept 17 (125) $80
— Burning Daylight. NY, 1910. 2d Issue. pba July 9 (179) $110
— The Call of the Wild. NY, 1903. In d/j with short tears at edges. sg Dec 12 (240) $2,200
1st Ed. Cloth. K Sept 29 (241) $275
Anr copy. Orig cloth, in d/j. sg Dec 12 (240) $2,200
— Children of the Frost. NY, 1902. 1st Ed. Illus by Raphael M. Reay. sg Dec 12 (241) $425
— The Cruise of the Dazzler. NY, 1902. 1st Ed. Spine faded. cb Feb 12 (76) $1,400
1st Ed in Book form. Epstein copy. sg Apr 30 (311) $1,600
— The Cruise of the Snark. NY, 1911. bbc Apr 27 (363) $210; bbc June 29 (418) $120; sg Dec 12 (242) $175
— Dutch Courage and Other Stories. NY, 1922. Cloth. bbc Apr 27 (364) $225
— The Faith of Men and Other Stories. NY, 1904. Cloth; rubbed, spine soiled, ink name to front free endpaper. cb Sept 19 (130) $65
— The Game. NY, 1905. 1st Ed, 1st Issue, without magazine rubberstamp. K Mar 22 (237) $60
— The God of His Fathers. NY, 1901. 1st Ed. Cloth; rubbed, soiled & worn. cb Sept 19 (132) $110
— The House of Pride. NY, 1912. Cloth; rubbed, front hinge cracked. bbc Apr 27 (365) $200
— The Human Drift. NY, 1917. 1st Ed. Cloth; cocked & soiled. Frontis foxed. wa Apr 9 (47) $120
— The Iron Heel. Girard KS: Appeal to Reason, 1908. Cloth; rubbed & soiled. wa Sept 26 (207) $100
Anr Ed. NY: Macmillan, 1908. Bdg rubbed. cb Sept 19 (133) $60; cb Dec 12 (96) $85
Anr copy. Cloth; rubbed & soiled. wa Sept 26 (208) $75
— Jerry of the Islands. NY, 1917. 1st Ed. Cloth; corner bumped. cb Sept 19 (134) $80
Anr copy. Cloth; front cover spotted. sg June 11 (203) $100
— John Barleycorn. NY, 1913. 1st Ed. Orig cloth; spine bumped. pba July 9 (180) $70
1st ptg. K Mar 22 (236) $70
— The Kempton-Wace Letters. NY, 1903. 1st Ed. Cloth; spine ends worn; front hinge starting. Inscr. Epstein copy. sg Apr 30 (3313) $3,400
— A Klondike Trilogy: Three Uncollected Stories. Santa Barbara, 1983. One of 26 with mtd holograph check. 4to, lea gilt. sg Dec 12 (243) $425
One of 26 with a check, sgd. sg June 11 (204) $350
— The Little Lady of the Big House. NY, 1916. Orig cloth. cb Dec 12 (97) $130
— Lost Face. NY, 1910. 1st Ed. Cloth; joints rubbed. With frontis & 5 plates. cb Sept 19 (136) $85
1st English Ed. L: Mills & Boon, [n.d.]. Cloth; spine faded. cb Dec 12 (98) $110
— Love of Life and Other Stories. NY, 1907. Bdg rubbed. cb Sept 19 (137) $55
— Martin Eden. NY, 1909. 1st Pbd Ed. sg Dec 12 (245) $225
Anr copy. Cloth; spine soiled, edges rubbed. wa Sept 26 (205) $120
— Moon-Face. NY, 1906. Variant bdg with initials in light green; rear hinge cracked & glued. In: Argonaut Stories. cb June 19 (139) $50
— Moon-Face and Other Stories. NY, 1906. 1st Ed. Rear hinge cracked & glued. cb Sept 19 (139) $50
— The Mutiny of the Elsinore. NY, 1914. 1st Ed. cb Dec 12 (99) $150
Anr copy. Cloth; spine faded. cb Feb 12 (78) $120; K Mar 22 (238) $50
Anr copy. Orig cloth; spine decoration mostly rubbed off. pba July 9 (181) $70
— The Night Born. NY, 1913. 1st Ed, 1st Ptg. wa Apr 9 (48) $120
— On the Makaloa Mat. NY, 1919. 1st Ed. Sgd on paper affixed to front pastedown. cb Sept 19 (142) $350
— The People of the Abyss. NY, 1903. 1st Ed. Bdg rubbed. cb Sept 19 (144) $150; sg Dec 12 (246) $150
— The Red One. NY, 1918. 1st Ed. Orig bds, in pictorial d/j; front endpaper stained. CNY June 9 (111) $1,700
— The Road. NY, 1907. Cloth; edge-wear. sg June 11 (206) $175
1st Issue. Cover ptd in gilt & black. With 48 plates. Some foxing. wa Apr 9 (49) $230
— The Scarlet Plague. NY, 1915. 1st Ed. cb

Sept 19 (146) $110; K Dec 1 (281) $180; sg Dec 12 (247) $400

— The Sea-Wolf. NY, 1904. Pictorial cloth; spine faded, extremities rubbed. cb Dec 12 (101) $70

Anr copy. Orig cloth, B bdg. K Mar 22 (239) $65

Anr copy. Pictorial cloth; front hinge cracked. sg Dec 12 (249) $70; sg June 11 (207) $175

— Smoke Bellew. NY, 1912. 1st Ed. sg Dec 12 (248) $110

— A Son of the Sun. Garden City, 1912. 1st Ed. cb Dec 12 (102) $130

— The Son of the Wolf. Tales of the Far North. Bost. & NY, 1900. 1st Ed, 1st Ptg. 8vo, cloth; lacking front free endpaper. pba July 9 (182) $300

One of 19 of the 1st Ptg. Wraps; rubbed, separating from spine, shaken. Manney copy. P Oct 11 (208) $8,500

3d Issue. Cloth. sg Dec 12 (250) $275

— The Star Rover. NY, 1915. 1st American Ed. K Mar 22 (240) $55; sg Dec 12 (251) $70

— The Strength of the Strong. NY, 1914. 1st Ed. sg Dec 12 (252) $70

— The Valley of the Moon. NY, 1913. 1st Ed. Cloth; worn. sg Dec 12 (253) $150

— When God Laughs. NY, 1911. 1st Ed. K Mar 22 (241) $160

Londonderry, Frederick William Robert Stewart, Viscount Castlereagh, Marquess of. See: Stewart, Frederick William Robert

Long, Edward, 1734-1813

— The History of Jamaica. L, 1774. 3 vols. 4to, contemp calf; rebacked, loose. With 5 folding maps & plates & with several maps inserted from other copies. Browned & wormed. Sold w.a.f. wd June 12 (411) $150

Long, John, Indian Trader

— Voyages and Travels of an Indian Interpreter and Trader.... L, 1791. 1st Ed. 4to, old bds; disbound. With folding map. Some soiling & staining. O Mar 31 (130) $825

Anr copy. 19th-cent calf. Stain affecting tp & prelims. S Nov 21 (325) £650 [Beeleigh]

Long, Roger, 1680-1770

— Astronomy, in Five Books. Cambr., 1742-84. Vol I only. Contemp calf gilt; rubbed. With frontis & 68 folding plates (1 detached). b June 22 (187) £90

Longfellow, Henry Wadsworth, 1807-82

— The Belfry of Bruges and other Poems. Cambr., 1846. 12mo, orig wraps. Epstein copy. sg Apr 30 (314) $1,000

— Christus: A Mystery. Bost.: James R. Osgood, 1872. 1st Issue. 8vo, orig cloth; spines faded, ends worn. cb Dec 5 (76) $250

— The Courtship of Miles Standish and Other Poems. Bost., 1858. 1st American Ed. 12mo, orig cloth. Inscr to Mrs. Thies. Kern-Currie-Manney copy. P Oct 11 (211) $2,750

1st Issue. Orig cloth; worn. Inscr to Mrs. Rutherford. O May 26 (118) $2,600

— Hyperion. L, 1865. 4to, orig cloth; spine worn, torn, crudely reglued. With 24 mtd photos by Francis Frith. Marginal fading. cb Sept 26 (90) $110

Anr copy. Contemp mor gilt. W July 8 (325) £120

— The Poetical Works. Bost.: Houghton Mifflin, [1880]. 2 vols. 4to, orig mor gilt; spines scuffed, short strip of pigment lift from 1 front cover. wa Sept 26 (23) $120

— The Song of Hiawatha. Bost., 1855. 1st American Ed, 1st Ptg. 8vo, orig cloth. NH May 30 (335) $60

Anr copy. Orig cloth. Manney copy. P Oct 11 (210) $1,000

Mixed Issue. Orig cloth; spine ends & corners frayed & chipped. bbc Dec 9 (506) $95

Anr Ed. Bost., 1891. Ltd Ed. Illus by Frederic Remington. 4to, orig lea; rebacked, new endpapers. bbc June 29 (431) $85

Anr copy. Vellum. cb Feb 12 (79) $100

— Voices of the Night. Cambr. MA: John Owen, 1839. 12mo, orig bds. sg Oct 17 (308) $200

— Works. Bost., [1904]. One of 750. 11 vols. 8vo, mor extra; loose. sg Mar 5 (174) $450

Longolius, Christophorus

— Orationes duae pro defensione sua in crimen lesae majestatis.... Florence: haeredes Philippi Juntae, Dec 1524. 4to, 18th-cent calf. Lacking last blank. SI June 9 (547) LIt220,000

Longstreet, James, 1821-1904

— From Manassas to Appomattox.... Phila., 1896. 1st Ed. 8vo, orig cloth; spine chipped. With Cs mtd on pastedown. bbc Feb 17 (88) $390

Longueville, Peter

— The Hermit, or the Unparalleled Sufferings...of Mr. Philip Quarll.... Westminster, 1720. 1st Ed, Issue with author's initials at end of preface. 8vo, contemp sheep; rubbed, joints weak. With frontis, map & 1 folding plate. Minor discoloration; frontis cut close to neatline at foremargin. S Feb 26 (764) £220 [Sotheran]

Longus

See also: Ashendene Press; Golden Cockerel Press

— Daphnis and Chloe L, 1890. 4to, mor extra by Bonleu. L.p. copy. wd June 12 (367) $150

Anr Ed. L: Vale Press, 1893. One of 210. Illus by Charles Ricketts & Charles Shannon. Orig cloth. b June 22 (65A) £120; bba July 9 (304) £360 [Royal Academy Library]

Anr Ed. NY, [1977]. Illus by Marc Chagall. 4to, cloth, in d/j. Sgd on tp by Chagall. sg Sept 26 (73) $325

— Daphnis et Chloe. Paris, 1754. 4to, 18th-cent mor gilt. With frontis & 22 (of 29) plates. Some repairs; a few margins soiled. S Feb 11 (557) £240 [Shapero]

Anr Ed. Paris: Ambroise Vollard, 1902. ("Les Pastorales, ou Daphnis et Chloe.") One of 200. Trans by J. A. Amyot; illus by Pierre Bonnard. 4to, mor gilt by Creuzevault, orig wraps bound in. With 151 lithos. P June 18 (518) $6,500

Anr Ed. Paris, 1937. Hors commerce copy on chine, with a suite of the woodcuts in bistre & a suite of the "epreuves rares". Illus by Aristide Maillol. Loose in wraps, as issued. sg Nov 7 (132) $1,600

One of 250. Orig half vellum. HH May 12 (2396) DM4,000

Anr copy. Vellum; spotted & soiled. Lacking the extra suite of illusts. sg Sept 26 (223) $400

One of 25 hors commerce on chine, with additional suite on different papers, 7 of the illusts with a further impression in a different state. Unsewn as issued in orig wraps. S Dec 5 (310) £850 [Liechti]

Longworth, John Augustus

— A Year Among the Circassians. L, 1840. 1st Ed. 2 vols. 12mo, orig cloth; recased, orig spines preserved. O Jan 14 (110) $90

Lonicer, Adam, 1528-86

— Naturalis Historiae opus novum. Frankfurt, 1551. Vol I only. Bound with: Loritus, Henricus, Glareanus. Liber de asse, & partibus eius. Basel: M. Isingrin, 1550. Folio, contemp pigskin-backed wooden bds with later paper covering, with clasps; worn. 1st work with 2 leaves torn & several shorter tears affecting text; 2d work lacking final blank E6; both with some staining, 1st work browned. S Nov 21 (30) £1,000 [Reiss & Auvermann]

Lonicerus, Philippus

— Chronicorum turcicorum. Frankfurt, 1578. Bound with: Guagninus, Alexander. Sarmatiae Europeae descriptio.... Speier, 1581. 4 vols in 1. Folio, bdg described as blind-stamped wooden bds. Some stains & discoloration. S Nov 21 (262) £2,000 [Reiss & Auvermann]

Anr copy. 3 vols in 1. Folio, contemp blind-tooled deerskin over pastebd; joints cracked, lacking front free endpaper. Tear in 1st G4 affecting text. Harvard duplicate. sg Oct 24 (197) $500

Lonnberg, Einar. See: Wright, Magnus & Wilhelm & Ferdinand von

Lonsdale, John, Viscount Lonsdale

— Memoir of the Reign of James II. York, 1808. 4to, calf. Inscr. pnE May 13 (130) £50

Loomis, Alfred F. See: Derrydale Press

Lopes de Castanheda, Fernan, c.1501-59

— The First Booke of the Historie of the Discoverie and Conquest of the East Indias.... L: T. East, 1582. 4to, 19th-cent calf gilt, with crest of arms of George Wilbraham; extremities worn. Black letter. Marginal worming. STC 16806. CNY Oct 8 (152) $23,000

Lopez de Gomara, Francisco, 1510-60?

— Historia de Mexico, con el Descubrimiento dela nueva Espana. . . . Antwerp: I. Steelsio, 1554. 1st Ed. 8vo, 19th-cent mor; rubbed. Lacking leaves 201 & 208. Sold w.a.f. O Nov 26 (109) $1,200

— Historia di Don Ferdinando Cortez.... Venice: Francesco Lorenzini, 1560. 8vo, early vellum. Line reading Seconda parte rubbed from title. sg Dec 5 (138) $500

— The Pleasant Historie of the Conquest of the Weast India.... L; Thomas Creede, 1596. 4to, 18th-cent calf. Black letter.. STC 16808. CNY Oct 8 (153) $3,200

Anr copy. Mor gilt; extremities rubbed. Marginal repair in M3; tp & last few leaves foxed. STC 16808. CNY Oct 8 (154) $2,400

Lopez de Sigura, Ruy

— Il giuoco de gli scacchi. Venice, 1584. 4to, contemp vellum. Some dampstaining; Blass library stamp on tp. Ck May 8 (45) £900

Anr copy. Some dampstaining. Ck May 8 (46) £650

Anr copy. Vellum wraps from a 15th-cent book. Some foxing. SI June 9 (549) LIt220,000

— Libro de la invencion liberal y arte del juego del Axedrez.... Alcala: Andres de Angula, 1561. 4to, 19th-cent half mor. Dampstain to tp & prelims; tp torn at lower outer corner, affecting woodcut decorations; several prelim leaves repaired. Ck May 8 (44) £1,400

Lopez, Tomas

— Atlas geografico de Espana. Madrid, [1774, or later]. Oblong folio, modern half mor. With general map in 4 sheets & 98 numbered sectional maps, 1 folding. Annotated with campaign notes; tp repaired & with margins strengthened, contents on verso cropped; some dampstaining & soiling; first 2 & last 2 maps def; a few margins strengthened; 1 map from anr copy. Picked up in the field of battle of Vittoria by a Lieut. Thoreau, who saw to its repair & later presented it to the United Service Museum, so inscr on tp. pn Nov 14 (380) £1,100

Lord, Elizabeth

— Reminiscences of Eastern Oregon. Portland, 1903. Inscr. sg June 18 (445) $225

Lord, Henry

— A Discoverie of the Sect of the Banians.... L, 1630. 2 parts in 1 vol. 4to, modern bds. Lacking engraved general title; some staining. STC 16825. bba July 9 (83) £50 [Wilbraham]

Lord John Press

— Etchison, Dennis. - Lord John Ten: A Celebration. Northridge, 1988. One of 250, sgd by all the contribs. Half cloth. cb Sept 19 (113) $190

Lorenzini, Carlo. See: Collodi, Carlo

Lorini, Buonaiuto

— Le Fortificationi. Venice, 1609. 2 parts in 1 vol. Folio, contemp vellum; restored. Some spotting & soiling. SI June 9 (550) LIt4,000,000

L'Orme, Philibert de

— Le Premier Tome de l'architecture [all pbd]. Paris: F. Morel, 1568. 1st Ed, 2d Issue. Folio, 18th-cent half calf; rebacked with old backstrip laid down, corners worn. Tp def at upper right corner & with 2 old patches on verso; progressively dampstained at upper right corner from front to center of book; a1 with patch to blank portion; lacking blank e6; without the 2 additional unsgd leaves. McCarty-Cooper copy. CNY Jan 25 (44) $800

Lorrain, Jean

— La Maison Philibert. Paris, 1904. One of 25 on verge a la forme reimposed in 4to format. Illus by George Bottini. Half mor orig wraps bound in. With 2 holograph poems by the author & an ink drawing inscr by Bottini. Kochno copy. SM Oct 12 (493) FF16,000

Lory, Gabriel, The Younger

— Picturesque Tour Through the Oberland in the Canton of Berne, in Switzerland. L: Ackermann, 1823. 8vo, modern half mor gilt by Sangorski & Sutcliffe. With engraved map & 17 hand-colored plates. Small tear to upper blank margin of tp; some spotting. C May 20 (81) £1,900 [Chelsea]

Anr copy. Modern half calf. With hand-colored engraved map & 17 colored plates. Tp & a few leaves & plate margins soiled. S June 25 (319) £1,100 [American]

— Souvenirs de la Suisse. Geneva: Briquet et fils, [c.1860]. Oblong 8vo, orig cloth; shaken. With 49 colored views, 12 double-page. bba Sept 19 (152) £850 [Faber]

Loskiel, George Henry, 1740-1814

— Geschichte der mission der evangelischen Brueder unter den Indianern.... Barby, 1789. 8vo, contemp calf; rubbed. O Nov 26 (110) $225

Anr copy. Early calf. sg June 18 (332) $225

2d State, with full page of errata. Old lea; worn & rubbed. K July 12 (324) $300

Lossing, Benson John, 1813-91

— A History of the Civil War. NY, [1912]. 1st Ed, 1st Issue, in orig 16 parts. 4to, orig wraps; chipped. K Mar 22 (78) $75

— The Hudson; from the Wilderness to the Sea. NY, [1866]. 4to, lea; edges rubbed. Met Apr 28 (477) $50

— Our Country; a Household History of the United States. NY, 1877-78. 3 vols. 4to, orig half mor gilt. NH May 30 (83) $70

— Pictorial Field-Book of the Revolution. NY, 1859. 2 vols. Orig half lea; rubbed. K July 12 (15) $60

Anr Ed. NY, 1860. 2 vols. 4to, orig cloth; spines chipped, 1 def. K Sept 29 (243) $50

Lothrop, Amy. See: Wetherell & Lothrop

Loti, Pierre, 1850-1923

— Madame Chrysantheme. Paris, 1926. One of 65 on Holland. Illus by Foujita. 4to, mor with panel inlays by Foujita; spine worn, hinges starting. sg Sept 26 (113) $300

— La Troisieme jeunesse de Madame Prune. Paris, 1926. One of 325. Illus by Foujita. 4to, half mor gilt, orig wraps bound in;

rubbed. With 17 colored plates. P June 17 (211) $1,700

Lotter, Tobias Conrad

— Atlas geographicus portabilis.... [Augsburg, c.1760]. 32mo, old mor; rebacked, worn, covers detached. With double-page title & frontis & 29 double-page maps in contemp body color. S Nov 15 (1051) £400 [Benjamin]

— Atlas novus sive tabulae geographicae totius orbis. Augsburg, [c.1772]. Folio, old bds. With engraved title, engraved ad & 25 double-page maps with contemp body color. Some sheets with added or strengthened outer margins; a few stains. S June 25 (301) £2,200 [Map House]

Lottini, Giovanni Angelo

— Scelta d'alcuni miracoli e gravie.... Florence: Pietro Cecconcelli, 1619. Bound with: caglieri, Liborio. Compendio delle vite de santi orefici ed argentieri. Rome: Bernabo, 1727. 4to, 18th-cent mor gilt; spine wormed. With engraved title & 40 plates in 1st work & frontis & 14 plates in 2d work. Lower margins in 2d work all extended slightly. S Dec 5 (234) £900 [Mediolanum]

Lotz, Arthur

— Bibliographie der Modelbuecher. Leipzig, 1963. Ck Nov 1 (445) £80

Louandre, Charles, 1812-82

— Les Arts somptuaires. Paris, 1857-58. 3 vols. 4to, contemp mor; rubbed, def. With 318 plates. F Mar 26 (761) $340

Anr copy. 4 vols in 3. 4to, contemp half mor gilt. With 324 chromolitho plates. S July 1 (1291) £250 [Arnold]

Loudon, Jane Webb

— Annuals. L, 1840. ("The Ladies' Flower-Garden of Ornamental Annuals.") 4to, contemp half mor; extremities rubbed. With 48 hand-colored plates. Some foxing throughout. bba June 25 (230) £900 [Lloyd's of Kew]

Anr copy. Contemp half mor gilt; upper cover rubbed. With 48 colored plates. Some imprints shaved; Plate 25 with marginal tear repaired. pn June 11 (253A) £250

2d Ed. L, [c.1842]. 4to, half mor; spine browned; front cover loose. With 50 hand-colored plates. sg May 7 (141) $1,500

— British Wild Flowers. L, 1846. 1st Ed. 4to, contemp half mor; rubbed. With 60 hand-colored plates. Some spotting & browning. S May 14 (1044) £650 [Neale]

Anr copy. Orig cloth; spine worn. S June 25 (42) £750 [Shoten]

3d Ed. L, 1859. 4to, contemp half lea. Extra-illus with 51 plates. SI June 9 (552) LIt4,000,000

— Bulbous Plants. L, 1841. ("The Ladies' Flower-Garden of Ornamental Bulbous Plants.") 1st Ed. 4to, 19th-cent half mor gilt. With 58 hand-colored plates. b Nov 18 (371) £1,900

Anr copy. Contemp calf gilt; rebcked, new endpapers. Some spotting. S June 25 (44) £2,400 [Lack]

Anr Ed. L, 1844. 4to, contemp half mor; joints repaired. With 58 hand-colored plates. Some marginal staining. bba June 25 (229) £1,800 [Lloyd's of Kew]

2d Ed. L, [c.1845]. 4to, half mor; spine browned. With 58 hand-colored plates. sg May 7 (142) $2,400

— Greenhouse Plants. L, 1860. ("The Ladies' Flower-Garden of Ornamental Greenhouse Plants.") 3d Ed. 4to, half mor; spine browned, extremities rubbed. With 42 hand-colored plates. sg May 7 (143) $2,600

— Ornamental Perennials. L, 1843-44. ("The Ladies' Flower Garden of Ornamental Perennials.") 1st Ed. 2 vols. 4to, half mor; rubbed. With 45 hand-colored plates. b Nov 18 (372) £2,000

Loudon, John Claudius, 1783-1843

— Arboretum et Fruticetum Britannicum. L, [1835]-38. 1st Ed. 8 vols. 8vo, contemp calf gilt; rubbbed. bba June 11 (262) £240 [Lloyd's of Key]

— An Encyclopaedia of Cottage, Farm, and Villa Architecture... L, 1833. 1st Ed. 2 vols. 8vo, contemp half lea; worn. S Feb 11 (316) £340 [Lennox Money]

Anr copy. Contemp half calf; bds scratched, corners worn, inside rear hinge repaired. wa Apr 9 (184) $80

Anr Ed. L, 1835. 8vo, calf. Some foxing. kh Nov 11 (160) A$380

Lougheed, Victor

— Aeroplane Designing for Amateurs. Chicago: Reilly & Britton, [1912]. Orig cloth. cb Nov 7 (59) $50

Louis, Antoine

— Recueil de pieces sur differentes matieres chirurgicales. Paris, 1752. 6 parts in 1 vol. 12mo, contemp sheep gilt; spine ends chipped. Foxed at ends. sg Nov 14 (72) $200

Louis XIV, King of France

— Edit du Roy contre les duels.... Aix: Chez Charles David, 1679. 4to, modern half cloth. sg Mar 26 (181) $100

Louisiana

— Official Journal of the Proceedings of the Convention of the State of Louisiana. New Orleans, 1861. 8vo, wraps. sg Dec 5 (80) $250

— The Rules and Orders for Conducting Business in the House of Representatives of the State of Louisiana. New Orleans, 1833. 8vo, modern mor. Lower margin of title excised without loss. sg Dec 5 (174) $200

Louisiana Territory

— The Laws of the Territory of Louisiana Comprising all those which are not actually in Force.... St. Louis: Joseph Charless, 1808 [but not before 29 Apr 1809]. 218mm by 134mm, buckram over bds with sheep spine; loose, spine fragmentary. Tp & a few other leaves frayed. P June 16 (251) $9,000

Loutherbourg, Philippe Jacques de, 1740-1812

— The Romantic and Picturesque Scenery of England and Wales. L, 1805. Early Issue without frontis. Folio, later mor gilt by de Coverly; rebacked in mor, bds worn. With 18 hand-colored plates. In French & English. C May 20 (82) £2,800 [Arader]

Late Issue. Contemp half mor. With 18 hand-colored plates. In French & English. C Oct 30 (49) £600 [Bifolco]

Louvet de Couvray, Jean Baptiste, 1760-97

— Les Amours du chevalier de Faublas. Paris, 1798. 4 vols. 8vo, contemp half calf gilt. With port & 27 plates. S May 13 (847) £250 [Caribersa]

— Love and Patriotism! or, the Extraordinary Adventures of M. Duportail. Phila., 1797. 12mo, contemp sheep. sg Dec 5 (140) $325

Louys, Pierre, 1870-1925

— Aphrodite.... Paris: Ferroud, 1909. One of 497. Illus by Raphael Collin. 4to, mor gilt, orig wraps bound in; spine rubbed. With frontis & 4 colored plates. S Nov 14 (10) £150 [Greenwood]

Anr Ed. Paris, 1931. One of 200. 4to, mor extra with onlays by Leclerc, orig wraps bound in. sg May 7 (144) $1,000

— Astarte. Paris, 1891. One of 75 on hollande. 4to, half mor by R. Aussourd, orig wraps bound in. Annotated by Louys throughout. S May 28 (375) £950 [Beres]

— Les Aventures du Roi Pausole. Paris, 1901. One of 50 on hollande. 12mo, mor extra by Huser, orig wraps bound in. S May 28 (376) £800 [Beres]

Anr Ed. Paris: Artheme Fayard, [1941]. Illus by Foujita. Orig wraps. With 28 woodcuts. Some browning. wa Sept 26 (591) $60

— Les Chansons de Bilitis. L, 1925. One of 100 on japon ancien with an additional suite in black only. 4to, mor extra by G. Levitzky; silk on lower endpaper torn. With colored etched frontis & 11 illusts, all but 1 full-page. S Dec 5 (306) £1,200 [Rassamnn]

— The Songs of Bilitis. L & NY, 1904. One of 971. Illus by James Fagan. Half cloth; hinges cracked. sg Sept 26 (216) $80

Anr Ed. L: Fortune Press, [c.1928]. One of 923. b Nov 18 (28) £80

— Woman and Puppet. [N.p.: Pvtly Ptd, 1927]. One of 35 with 5 hand-colored drypoints. Mor gilt; corners worn, front hinge cracked. sg Jan 10 (176) $425

Lovecraft, Howard Phillips

— Beyond the Wall of Sleep. Sauk City: Arkham House, 1943. 1st Ed. In d/j. Epstein copy. sg Apr 30 (316) $1,600

Anr copy. In chipped d/j. sg June 11 (211) $400

— Dagon and Other Macabre Tales. Sauk City: Arkham House, 1965. In d/j. wa Mar 5 (222) $60

— Marginalia. Sauk City: Arkham House, 1944. 1st Ed. In d/j. Donald Wandrei's copy. pba July 9 (184) $250

Anr copy. In d/j with darkened spine panel. wa Sept 26 (349) $95

— The Outsider and Others. Sauk City: Arkham House, 1939. 1st Ed. In d/j. Epstein copy. sg Apr 30 (317) $1,600

— Selected Letters. Sauk City: Arkham House, 1965-75. 2d ptg of Vols I & II plus 1980 Index (Warwick RI: Necronomicon Press). 5 vols. In d/js. wa Mar 5 (223) $100

— The Shadow Over Innsmouth. Everett PA, 1936. Illus by Frank Utpatel. In d/j with some wear & soiling. Manney copy. P Oct 11 (214) $17,000

— The Shunned House. Athol MA: Pbd by W. Paul Cook/ The Recluse Press, 1928. 1st Ed. Orig half cloth; soiled, front cover blistered. Manney copy. P Oct 11 (213) $8,500

Arkham House Remainder Issue. Epstein copy. sg Apr 30 (318) $2,200

One of c.50 sets of unbound sheets. Inscr to Samuel Loveman. Manney copy. P Oct 11 (212) $13,000

— Something About Cats and Other Pieces. Sauk City: Arkham House, 1949. 1st Ed. In d/j; short paper lift affecting front panel titling. wa Sept 26 (350) $65

— Supernatural Horror in Literature. NY, 1945. Advance Review Copy. In d/j with tears along folds. bbc Dec 9 (581) $80

— Unusual Stories. N.p., 1934. Advance Issue of Vol I, No 1. Orig ptd wraps. Some browning. sg Dec 12 (258) $90

Lovejoy, Joseph C. & Owen

— Memoir of the Rev. Elijah P. Lovejoy; who was murdered in Defence of the Liberty of the Press, at Alton, Illinois, Nov. 7, 1837.... NY, 1838. 12mo, orig cloth; worn. Some foxing. sg June 18 (334) $100

Lover, Pseud.

— Au moins soyez discret. Paris, 1919. One of 500. Illus by Robert Bonfils. 4to, lea with lea inlaid design portraying a woman with her finger to her lips in a hushinig gesture. sg May 7 (65) $700

Lover, Samuel, 1797-1868

— Works. NY, 1900. 6 vols. 8vo, half mor gilt. sg Mar 5 (175) $250

Low, Charles Rathbone, 1837-1918

— Her Majesty's Navy. L, 1890-93. 3 vols. 4to, half calf; worn. S Nov 15 (867) £300 [Nichols]

Low, Frances H.

— Queen Victoria's Dolls. L, 1894. 4to, orig cloth; worn. bbc Dec 9 (269) $110

Lowe, Edward Joseph, 1825-1900

— Ferns: British and Exotic. L, 1872. 8 vols. 8vo, contemp half mor; worn & faded. With 479 plates. wa Dec 9 (540) $350

Lowe, Edward Joseph, 1825-1900 —& Howard, W.

— Beautiful Leaved Plants. L, 1872. 8vo, contemp half mor; worn. With 60 colored plates. Some foxing. wa Dec 9 (533) $210

Lowe, Sir Hudson, 1769-1844

— History of the Captivity of Napoleon at St. Helena.... L, 1853. 1st Ed. 3 vols. 8vo, contemp calf gilt; scuffed. With folding map & 2 plates. Tear in folding map; some spotting. pnL Nov 20 (136) £50 [Duncan]

Lowell, Guy

— Smaller Italian Villas & Farmhouses. NY, 1922. Folio, cloth. sg Apr 2 (168) $175

Lowell, James Russell, 1819-91

— Class Poem. [Cambr. MA: Metcalf, Torry & Ballou], 1838. 8vo, stitched in orig wraps, as issued. Epstein copy. sg Apr 30 (319) $900

— Works. Bost., 1904. 16 vols. Half mor; rubbed. O Jan 14 (111) $160

Lowell, Percival

— Mars and its Canals.... NY, 1906. Cloth; spine ends & corners rubbed, endpapers foxed. wa Mar 5 (474) $220

Lowell, Robert, 1917-77

— Land of Unlikeness. [Cummington MA], 1944. 1st Ed, one of 250. CNY Dec 5 (276) $1,800

— The Voyage, and other Versions of Poems by Baudelaire. L, 1968. One of 200. Illus by Sidney Nolan. 4to, orig cloth. With 8 colored plates. Sgd by author & artist. sg Dec 12 (260) $225

Lowndes, William Thomas, d.1843

— The Bibliographer's Manual of English Literature. L, 1834. 1st Ed. 4 vols. 8vo, cloth; spines worn. bba May 28 (585) £70 [Cox]

Anr copy. Half calf. LH Dec 11 (146) $150

Anr Ed. L, 1857-65. 11 parts in 4 vols. 8vo, half lea; rubbed. br May 29 (314) $140

Anr copy. 5 vols. 8vo, bdg not described. cb Oct 17 (553) $150

Anr Ed. L, 1890. 6 vols. 8vo, orig cloth; rubbed. DW Jan 29 (329) £100

Anr Ed. Detroit, 1967. 8 vols. Facsimile of the 1864 Ed. O Dec 17 (121) $90

Lowry, Malcolm

— Ultramarine: a Novel. L, [1933]. 1st Ed. In def & soiled d/j. S Dec 12 (119) £600 [Quaritch]

Lowther, John, Viscount Lonsdale. See: Lonsdale, John

Lozano, Pedro, 1697-1759

— A True and Particular Relation of the Dreadful Earthquake...at Lima. L, 1748. 8vo, contemp calf gilt. With 9 folding maps & plates. Ck May 15 (124) £260

Lubbock, Basil

— Sail. The Romance of the Clipper Ships. L, [1927-36]. Illus by J. Spurling. Vol I only. Orig cloth. With frontis, 30 colored plates & 1 folding map. pn May 14 (115) £60

Lubbock, Joseph Guy

— Art and the Spiritual Life. Leicester: Twelve by Eight Press, 1967. One of 150. Folio, bds. sg Sept 26 (217) $50

— Light and the Mind's Eye. Cambr., [1974]. One of 70. 4to, orig mor gilt by George Percival. b Mar 11 (155) £170

Lucanus, Marcus Annaeus, 39-65 A.D.

— Pharsalia. Venice: Nicolaus Battibovis, 13 May 1486. Folio, half lea. Some browning; some leaves repaired. 186 leaves. Goff L-302. SI Dec 5 (352) LIt1,200,000

Anr Ed. Venice: Aldus, Apr 1502. ("Civilis belli.") 8vo, 18th-cent vellum. Marginal spotting; 1st 2 leaves fingersoiled. SI Dec 5 (353) LIt1,300,000

Anr Ed. Milan: Scinzenzeler, 1525. Folio, 19th-cent half lea; worn. Some worming &

spotting. SI Dec 5 (354) LIt600,000

Anr Ed. Strawberry Hill, 1760. 4to, contemp mor gilt. C Dec 16 (216) £450 [Finch]

Anr copy. Contemp calf gilt; joints cracking. pn Apr 23 (85) £200 [Poole]

Lucas, Edward Verrall, 1868-1938
See also: Fore-Edge Paintings

— Edwin Austin Abbey: the Record of his Life and Work. NY, 1921. 2 vols. 4to, orig half cloth; hinges cracked. Some foxing at endpapers. bbc Apr 27 (425) $65

Lucas, Fielding, 1781-1854

— A General Atlas.... Balt., [1823]. Folio, contemp mor gilt; worn, spine repaired with loss, shaken at end. With engraved titl, 98 hand-colored maps & 3 engraved schematic charts, 2 hand-colored. P Dec 12 (129) $2,000

Lucas, Thomas J.

— Pen and Pencil Reminiscences of a Campaign in South Africa. L, [1861]. 8vo, orig cloth. With hand-colored litho title & 20 plates. S July 1 (1498) £380 [Maggs]

Lucas, Walter A.

— 100 Years of Railroad Cars. NY, 1958. In d/j. Sgd. cb Feb 13 (218) $55

Lucian of Samosata
See also: Golden Cockerel Press

— The Dialogues. L: Navarre Society, [1930]. One of 225 on Japon. Illus by L. S. Blanch. 4to, half mor by Sangorski & Sutcliffe. With 6 plates, each in 2 states, 1 being hand-colored. pba Aug 20 (139) $250

— Die Hetaerengespraeche des Lukian. Leipzig, 1907. One of 450. Illus by Gustav Klimt. Orig lea by Wiener Werkstaette; corners rubbed. With 15 plates. DW Oct 9 (585) £1,500

— I dilettevoli dialogi: le vere narrationi: le facete epistole. Venice: Zoppino, 1525. 8vo, contemp goatskin; repaired & recased. Lacking blank at end; tp border wormed; some marginal soiling; prelims & colophon leaf restored. Ck Oct 31 (166) £230

— Lucian's True History. L, 1894. One of 54 on japan vellum. 4to, cloth; rubbed. DW Mar 11 (467) £320

One of 251. Cloth. With 16 plates. sg Septt 26 (21) $110

— Opuscula. Basel: Froben, 1521. ("Saturnalia, Cronosolon....") Folio, contemp blind-stamped calf. Some worming in title & next few leaves, with loss, & in some leaves at end without loss; some dampstaining; old marginalia. S Feb 11 (509) £600 [Zioni]

Lucien-Graux. See: Graux, Lucien

Luckombe, Philip

— The History and Art of Printing. L, 1771. 1st Ed. 8vo, contemp calf; rubbed, covers detached. Minor worming. F Mar 26 (366) $200

Lucretius Carus, Titus, 96?-55 B.C.

— De la nature des choses. Paris: Bleuet, 1768. 2 vols. 8vo, 19th-cent mor gilt; joints broken. With engraved title & 6 plates. SI Dec 5 (919J) LIt500,000

— De rerum natura. Verona: Paulus Fridenperger, 28 Sept 1486. Folio, old bds back with modern lea; broken. Roman type; initial spaces, the 1st with guide letter. Thumbed; minor dampstains throughout. Goff L-333. C Dec 16 (139) £2,500 [Fletcher]

Anr Ed. Bologna: H. B. de Benedictis Platonicis, 1511. ("In Carus Lucretius poeta commentarii a Joanne Baptista Pio editi....") Folio, contemp vellum; rebacked. Lacking frontis & A1-2. SI June 9 (556) LIt250,000

Anr Ed. Paris & Lyons: G. Rouille, 1563. Ed by Denys Lambin. 4to, contemp pigskin. Some browning. Ck Oct 18 (159) £200

Anr Ed. Paris: J. Benenatus, 1570. 4to, old half vellum. Last leaf mtd; 1st half of vol wormed; tp repaired; lacking index. Sold w.a.f. sg Mar 12 (174) $90

Anr Ed. Leiden, 1725. One of 820. Ed by S. Havercamp. 2 vols. 4to, contemp mor gilt; rubbed. With engraved title & 6 plates. pn Apr 23 (86) £200 [Shapero]

Anr Ed. Amst., 1754. ("Della natura delle cose, libri sei.") 2 parts in 1 vol. 8vo, contemp mor gilt. Some browning & foxing. SI June 9 (555) LIt950,000

Anr Ed. Amst. [but Paris], 1754. 2 parts in 2 vols. 8vo, contemp mor. With engraved titles & 6 plates & 2 frontises. Some browning. SI Dec 5 (920) LIt550,000

Anr Ed. Birm: Baskerville, 1772. 4to, 19th-cent mor gilt; spine scuffed. sg Oct 24 (198) $175

Ludolf, Hiob, 1624-1704

— Ad suam historiam aethiopicam commentarius. Frankfurt, 1691. Folio, contemp vellum. Some browning. SI Dec 5 (357) LIt1,800,000

— Historia Aethiopica. Frankfurt, 1681. 2 parts in 1 vol. Folio, contemp vellum; soiled, spine def. With 2 ports, folding map, 16 plates (12 folding) & 2 folding tables. Lacking dedication; 3 plates torn; some cropping; bound without the 2 appendices. pn July 16 (16) £120

Ludolphus de Saxonia

— Dit es dleven ons liefs heren Jhesu christi.... Antwerp: H. E. van Homberch, 1521. Folio, 19th-cent calf. Some worming at begining; some soiling in margins of 1st few leaves; short tear in Z2 repaired. S Dec 5 (168) £5,800 [Forum]

— Vita Christi. Venice: Jacopo Sansovino the Younger, 1570. ("Vita di Giesu Christo nostro redentore.") Folio, old vellum; front cover partly detached. Some browning; old scored writing on tp. sg Oct 24 (199) $200

Ludwig, Christian Gottlieb

— Ectypa vegetabilium. Leipzig, 1760-[64]. Vol II only. Folio, contemp half calf. With 200 hand-colored nature-ptd plates. Schlosser copy. P June 18 (478) $5,500

Ludwig Salvator, Archduke of Austria

— Levkosia, die Hauptstadt von Cypern. Prague: Heinrich Mercy, 1873. 4to, orig cloth. With 12 plates. S June 30 (270) £300 [Bank of Cyprus]

— Sommertage auf Ithaka. Prague, 1903. 4to, vellum gilt by F. Bakala. With 102 plates. S July 1 (643) £650 [Spink]

Luff, John Nicholas

— The Postage Stamps of the United States. NY, 1902. 4to, cloth; worn & shaken. O Jan 14 (113) $50

Lugar, Robert

— Plans and Views of Buildings Executed in England and Scotland in the Castellated and Other Styles. L, 1811. 4to, modern half mor. With 32 plates. Ck Oct 18 (286) £180

Anr Ed. L, 1823. 4to, disbound. With 32 plates & plans. Sold w.a.f. O Feb 25 (128) $150

— Plans and Views of Ornamental Domestic Buildings.... L, 1836. 2d Ed. Folio, orig cloth; rebacked with orig backstrip laid down. With 32 plates, some colored. A few text leaves dampstained at foremargins; marginal tear to Plate 8; institutional stamps. CNY Jan 25 (45) $2,200

Lugard, Frederick John Dealtry, Baron, 1858-1945

— The Rise of our East African Empire. L, 1893. 2 vols. 8vo, orig cloth; rubbed. bba May 28 (339) £70 [Bookroom]

Lugt, Frits

— Les Marques de collections de dessins & d'estampes. The Hague, 1956. 2 vols, including supplement. 4to, orig cloth. DW Oct 9 (915) £180

Anr copy. Orig cloth; soiled. S Feb 11 (134) £280 [Artemide]

— Repertoire des catalogues de ventes publiques interessant l'art ou la curiosite. The Hague, 1938-64. 3 vols. 4to, orig cloth. S Feb 11 (135) £900 [Mudson]

Anr Ed. The Hague, 1982-85-88. 3 vols. Folio cloth. sg May 7 (31) $275

Lugt, Frits —& Vallery-Radot, J.

— Inventaire general des dessins des ecoles du nord. Paris, 1936. 10 vols. 4to, cloth & half cloth. S Feb 11 (133) £650 [Buer]

Luigi Amedeo of Savoy, Duke of the Abruzzi

— On the "Polar Star" in the Arctic Sea. L, 1903. 1st English Ed. Trans by William Le Queux. 2 vols. bba Sept 19 (41) £60 [B. Bailey]; DW Jan 29 (2) £95

Anr Ed. NY, 1903. 2 vols. cb Jan 30 (77) $85; DW Nov 6 (2) £85; sg Jan 9 (16) $300

Lumholtz, Karl Sofus, 1851-1922

— Among Cannibals: An Account of Four Years' Travels in Australia.... L, 1889. 4to, cloth. cb Jan 30 (79) $85

Anr Ed. NY, 1889. 8vo, cloth; soiled, rear endpaper partially glued down. Insect damage along lower edge of margin at end. wa Mar 5 (475) $65

Luna, Miguel de

— The History of the Conquest of Spain by the Moors. L, 1687. 8vo, contemp sheep; covers detached. sg Mar 12 (175) $300

Lunardi, Vincent, 1759-1806

— An Account of the First Aerial Voyage in England. L, 1784. 8vo, contemp lea; worn, covers detached. With port & 2 folding plates. Half-title cut; some spotting. bba June 25 (169) £600 [Dennistoun]

Anr copy. Disbound. With port & 2 folding plates (1 cropped). Some spotting. pn May 14 (90) £250 [Elliott]

Lund, Johannes, 1638-86

— Die alten judeschen Heiligthuemer.... Hamburg, 1738. Folio, contemp vellum. sg June 25 (140) $400

Lundborg, Jeinar

— The Arctic Rescue: How Nobile was Saved. NY, 1929. In d/j. Sgd on frontis & with related material laid in. cb Nov 7 (60) $55

Lupoldus Bambergensis

— Germanorum veterum principum zelus et fervor in christianam religionem Deique ministros. Basel: Johann Bergmann de Olpe, 15 May 1497. Folio, disbound, preserved in modern cloth slipcase. 1st 2 leaves def & repaired with loss of text; last 2 leaves with lower corner repaired. 28 leaves. Goff L-399. bba Oct 24 (1) £200 [Bernard]

Anr copy. 18th-cent half sheep; extremities

scuffed, spine chipped. 41 lines; types 4:22G (title & headings); 1:109aR (title & text); 3:77R (marginalia). Some worming, with single hole running from a1-b2; old dampstaining. 28 leaves. Goff L-399. C Dec 16 (140) £450 [Schilt]

Lupton, Donald, d.1676

— The Glory of their Times: or, the Lives of ye Primitive Fathers.... L, 1640. Illus by George Glover. 4to, 19th-cent sheep; extremities worn, needs rebacking. Some stains & tears in gutter of opening leaves. STC 16943. sg Oct 24 (200) $150

Lusignano, Steffano di

— Les Genealogies de soixante et sept tres-nobles et tres-illustres maisons.... Paris, 1586. 4to, old vellum; rebacked, soiled. Some staining. S Nov 21 (264) £1,400 [Christodoulou]

— Histoire contenant une sommaire description des genealogies.... Paris: G. Chaudiere, 1579. 4to, vellum; soiled. Minor stains. S June 30 (49) £1,200 [Christodoulou]

Luther, Martin, 1483-1546

— Der achte Teil und letzte aller Buecher.... Jena: Thomas Rebart, 1562. Folio, contemp blind-tooled pigskin dated 1562; backstrip partly cracked, last few gatherings loose. Marginal dampstaining & repairs at end, causing loss. May lack some leaves. Sold w.a.f. sg Oct 24 (202) $200

— Appellatio ad concilium a Leone Decimo.... Wittemberg: Melchior Lotter, [1520]. 4to, modern bds. S Dec 5 (169) £800 [Schumann]

— Colloquia Mensalia: or, Dr. Martin Luther's Divine Discourses. L, 1652. 1st Ed in English. Folio, 19th-cent russia; front joint restored. Worming in blank corner of last few leaves repaired; last leaf remargined. sg Oct 24 (205) $300

— Huss Postilla auer de Evangelia der Sondage unde vornemesten Feste.... Wittenberg: Samuel Selfisch, 1563. Folio, contemp blind-stamped pigskin over wooden bds, with brass fittings; lacking 1 cornerpiece & clasps. Some underscoring. sg Oct 24 (203) $900

— Der sechste Teil der Buecher. Wittenberg: Hans Lufft, 1553. Folio, contemp pigskin over wooden bds with 6 (of 8) cornerpieces; catches & clasps def, crack in spine. Lacking tp. Sold w.a.f. sg Oct 24 (201) $300

Lutke, Fedor Petrovich, Count

— Voyage autour du monde.... Paris, [1835]. Atlas vol only. Folio, loose in half-cloth portfolio; worn. With engraved title, 3 maps & 51 plates. FD Dec 2 (232) DM7,000

Luyken, Jan

— Afbeelding der Menschelyke Bezigheden bestaende in Hondert onderscheiden Printverbeeldingen. Amst.: R. & J. Ottens, [c.1730]. 4to, later half vellum. With frontis & 100 plates. Bottom half of 1 leaf torn off & repaired with last 2 lines of verse replaced in Ms; a few small tears in margins repaired. B Nov 1 (335) HF3,800

— Het Leerzaam Huisraad. Amst., 1711. 8vo, half lea; front joint splitting. With engraved title & 50 emblematical illusts. B Nov 1 (336) HF450

— Histoire les plus remarquables de l'Ancien et du Nouveau Testament. Amst., 1732. Folio, modern half calf. With 5 double-page maps & 61 double-page plates. Title torn & repaired; some plates torn at fold. bba Jan 16 (212) £550 [Erlini]

Lydekker, Richard, 1849-1915

— Animal Portraiture. L, [1912]. 1st Ed. Folio, orig cloth; soiled. With 50 colored plates. Stamp on verso of tp & final leaf of text; some soiling. pn Mar 19 (306) £70 [Titles of Oxford]

Anr copy. Orig cloth; spine faded, ends frayed. sg Nov 14 (191) $200

— The Great and Small Game of India, Burma, & Tibet. L, 1900. One of 250. Folio, orig cloth gilt; soiled. With 9 colored plates. S July 1 (1510) £550 [Cherrington]

— The Great and Small Game of Europe, Western & Northern Asia, and America. L, 1901. 1st Ed, one of 250. 4to, later cloth; worn. With 8 colored plates. Tp stamped. sg May 21 (64) $700

— The Royal Natural History. L, 1893-96. 6 vols. 8vo, modern cloth; spines faded. With 72 color plates. DW Jan 29 (123) £52

— Wild Oxen, Sheep & Goats of all Lands. L, 1898. 1st Ed, One of 500. Illus by J. Smit. 4to, orig cloth; shaken. Library markings. sg May 14 (225) $950

Lydis, Mariette

— Le Coran: Quarante Deux Miniatures. Paris, [1927]. One of 100. 12mo, calf gilt wallet bdg, in d/j. With 42 mtd color plates. sg May 7 (145) $425

Lydius, Jacobus

— Syntagma de re militari.... Dordrecht, 1698. 4to, contemp calf; spine worn, short split to head of joint. With engraved title & 12 plates. Rust hole in Q4 & 3a2 affecting a few letters. b June 22 (188) £90

Lyell, Sir Charles, 1797-1875

— The Geological Evidences of the Antiquity of Man. L, 1863. 1st Ed. 8vo, orig cloth; hinges cracked. Half-title browned. sg May 14 (99) $325

Lyell, Denis D.

— The Hunting & Spoor of Central African Game. L, 1929. sg Jan 9 (281) $250

Lyell, James P. R.

— Early Book Illustration in Spain. L, 1926. One of 500. 4to, orig cloth; shaken. Library markings. sg Oct 31 (180) $110

Lyly, John, 1554?-1606

— Sixe Court Comedies. L, 1632. 12mo, 19th-cent half calf; recased. Lacking half-title; tp torn at upper part of inner margin; inner margin of tp adhering to later front blank, obscuring several characters; library stamps; some browning. STC 17088. Milne copy. Ck June 12 (130) £400

Lyman, Albert

— Journal of a Voyage to California.... Hartford, 1852. 12mo, cloth; spine ends frayed. sg June 18 (97) $425

Lynch, Bohun

— The Prize Ring. L, 1925. One of 1,000. 4to, orig half vellum; worn & soiled. F Mar 26 (446) $60

Anr copy. Half lea; needs rebacking. sg May 21 (9) $50

Lynch, William F., 1801-65

— Narrative of the United States Expedition to the River Jordan and the Dead Sea. Phila., 1849. 1 vol in 2. 8vo, 19th-cent half calf. sg Jan 9 (113) $200

Lyndewood, William, 1375?-1446

— Provinciale seu constitutiones Anglie.... Paris & L, 1505-6. 2 parts in 1 vol. Folio, near-contemp calf; rebacked, rubbed & repaired. Some spotting & staining. STC 17109. pn May 14 (4) £800 [P & P]

Lyon, Danny

— Pictures from the New World. NY, 1981. Oblong 4to, cloth. sg Apr 13 (63) $110

Lyon, George Francis, 1795-1832

— A Brief Narrative of an Unsuccessful Attempt to Reach Repulse Bay. L, 1825. 8vo, half calf. With folding frontis map & 6 plates. sg Jan 9 (114) $175

Anr copy. Modern half calf. W July 8 (256) £110

— A Narrative of Travels in Northern Africa. L, 1821. 4to, modern half mor. With folding map & 17 colored plates. Inscr. bba Sept 19 (64) £420 [Chaffe]

Anr copy. Later half mor; worn & rubbed. Map creased. cb Jan 30 (80) $800

Anr copy. Half calf; worn. Some foxing & staining. O Feb 25 (129) $500

Anr copy. Modern half mor. Map repaired. S Nov 15 (1269) £190 [Shapero]

— The Private Journal.... Bost., 1824. 8vo, contemp half calf; rebacked. With frontis, folding map & 6 plates. DW Nov 6 (64) £75

Anr copy. Contemp half calf; rebacked with orig spine. With frontis, 6 plates & folding map. Some foxing. W July 8 (255) £110

Lyon, John, 1734-1817

— The History of the Town and Port of Dover.... Dover, 1813-14. 2 vols. 4to, orig bds, unopened; rubbed, rebacked. With 18 plates, 8 folding. bba Sept 19 (215) £80 [Blake]

Lysons, Daniel, 1762-1834

— The Environs of London. L, 1796 [but 1791]-95-95-96. 4 vols. 4to, contemp mor gilt; scuffed. With engraved titles, 3 maps & 60 plates (3 of them hand-colored) & 2 folding genealogical tables. Extra-illus with alternative states of 2 of the plates (1 hand-colored) & a larger alternative version of anr plate. C Oct 30 (110) £2,000 [Burdon]

Lysons, Daniel & Samuel

— Magna Britannia, being a Concise Topographical Account.... L, 1806-17. 6 vols in 8. 4to, contemp pigskin; rubbed. Sold w.a.f. Extra-illus with plates. pn May 14 (202) £650 [Burden]

Anr Ed. L, 1814. Vol III: Cornwall. 4to, later calf; rebacked, rubbed. With folding map & 37 plates. bba Jan 30 (23) £240 [Blake]

Lysons, Samuel, 1763-1819

— An Account of Roman Antiquities Discovered at Woodchester.... L, 1797. Folio, orig mor; rubbed. With hand-colored title & dedication & 40 hand-colored plates. Text foxed; some plates spotted. bba Sept 19 (216) £800 [Beard]

Anr copy. 19th-cent half mor; rubbed. With hand-colored title & dedication & 40 plates, including 39 hand-colored in full or part. Text spotted. C May 20 (275) £800 [Arader]

Anr copy. Contemp calf, upper cover with paper label from orig bds painted, marbled & laid down; rubbed. With hand-colored tp, hand-colored dedication page & 40 plates. Marginal stain on Plate XIV; foxed. McCarty-Cooper copy. CNY Jan 25 (46) $2,000

— A Collection of Gloucestershire Antiquities. L, 1803. Folio, contemp calf gilt; re-backed, orig spine preserved. With 110 plates, some hand-colored. DW Nov 6 (128) £155

Anr Ed. L, 1804. Folio, contemp half mor gilt; spine rubbed & upper hinge cracked. With 110 plates, 11 hand-colored & 5 orig working drawings by Lysons. DW Dec 11 (115) £240

Lytle, Horace. See: Derrydale Press

Lytton, Edward George Earle Bulwer, 1st Baron Lytton, 1803-73
See also: Limited Editions Club

— Eugene Aram. L, 1832. 3 vols. 8vo, contemp half calf; rubbed. Without half-titles. O July 14 (124) $50

— The Last Days of Pompeii. L, 1834. 1st Ed. 3 vols. 8vo, later half mor. With ALs bound in. cb Sept 5 (62) $375

Anr copy. Orig half cloth. Epstein copy. sg Apr 29 (47) $425

M

M., H. See: Mackworth, Sir Humphrey

M., J.K. See: Munro, J. K.

M., W.

— The Queens Closet Opened. L, 1656. Bound with: A Queens Delight: or, the Art of Preserving. And: The Compleat Cook, Expertly Prescribing.... 12mo, modern calf. Port torn, cropped & backed; some spotting & soiling. S May 14 (1010) £550 [Cooks]

Anr Ed. L: J. G. for Nath. Brook, 1663. Bound with: The Compleat Cook, Expertly Prescribing.... L, 1671. And: A Queen's Delight. L, 1671. 12mo, modern mor gilt with cipher of Lord Westbury on spine. wd June 12 (376) $700

Maak, Richard Karlovich

— Puteshestvie na Amur. St. Petersburg, 1859. 2 vols. 4to & folio, orig cloth & orig bd portfolio. With litho title & 38 plates. Lacking port; some dampstaining to Atlas. C May 20 (327) £900 [Shapero]

Maaskamp, Evert

— Afbeeldingen van de kleeding.... Amst., [1803]. In 4 orig parts. 4to, half cloth. With 20 hand-colored plates. Lacking frontis. B Nov 1 (590) HF1,400

— Costumes, moeurs et habillemens dans les Pays-Bas Unis. Amst., [c.1820]. 8vo, orig bds. With 20 hand-colored plates. Lacking preface. bba Apr 30 (341) £150 [B. Bailey]

Maberly, Joseph

— The Print Collector. NY, 1880. Unique copy ptd on vellum. 4to, mor gilt extra by Francis Bedford. With 8 plates. Robert Hoe copy, sgd by him and with his note about the ptg on vellum. CNY Dec 5 (358) $8,000

Mabillon, Jean, 1632-1707

— De re diplomatica. Paris, 1681. 1st Ed. Folio, mor by Sangorski & Sutcliffe. With engraved title & 68 plates. Wormholes affecting additional title, tp & text up to B1, also later leaves, affecting text; ownership stamp of Jastrzehski on tp & verso of final leaf. Ck Nov 29 (113) £550

Mac Orlan, Pierre, 1882-1970

— Germaine Krull. Paris, 1931. Wraps with mtd photographic reproduction. sg Oct 8 (44) $140

— Vlaminck. Monte Carlo & NY, 1958. Trans by J. B. Sidgwick. Folio, wraps over bds. With 5 lithos & 35 mtd color plates. sg Feb 6 (297) $120

McAlmon, Robert

— A Companion Volume. [Paris, 1923]. 1st Ed. Wraps. cb Sept 19 (158) $275

Macaroni and Theatrical Magazine

— The Maraconi and Theatrical Magazine; or, Monthly Register of the Fashions and Diversions of the Times. L, 1773. For Jan-Mar & May. 4 vols. 8vo, orig wraps; frayed, May issue lacking rear wrap. sg Oct 17 (69) $325

McArthur, John, 1755-1840
See also: Clarke & McArthur; Fore-Edge Paintings

— The Army and Navy Gentleman's Companion; or a New and Complete Treatise on the Theory and Practice of Fencing. L, [1780]. 1st Ed. 4to, contemp mor gilt. With frontis & 19 plates. sg Mar 26 (182) $1,200

Anr copy. Orig bds. Some staining & browning. sg Mar 26 (184) $475

2d Ed. L, 1784. 4to, contemp bds; re-backed. Lacking the plates. sg Mar 26 (186) $60

Macaulay, Thomas Babington, 1st Baron Macaulay, 1800-59

— The History of England. L, 1849-61. 5 vols. 8vo, later half calf. bba Oct 10 (359) £190 [Cumming]

— Works. L, 1844-76. 15 vols. 8vo, calf gilt; extremities rubbed. sg Mar 5 (177) $350

Anr Ed. L, 1875-76. 10 vols. 8vo, calf gilt; spine heads chipped, front joint of Vol I split, many joints rubbed. ALs from Charles Choate to Bishop William Lawrence laid in. wa Sept 26 (24) $230

Albany Ed. L, 1898. one of 250. 12 vols. 8vo, half mor gilt by Sotheran; some wear. wa Mar 5 (52) $280

Anr Ed. NY: F. De Fau, [1898?]. one of 225. 12 vols. 8vo, half mor. cb Dec 5 (81) $550

McCammon, Robert R.

— Swan Song. Arlington Heights IL: Dark Harvest, 1989. In d/j. Inscr. cb Dec 12 (235) $50

M'Carthy, Justin

— A History of Our Own Times.... L, 1879-80. 5 vols. 8vo, calf by Zaehnsdorf; rubbed, joints worn. O Feb 25 (131) $90

Anr Ed. L, 1881. 4 vols. 8vo, calf gilt by Bicker. cb Oct 31 (50) $225

McCarthy, Justin —& Praed, Mrs. Campbell

— The Grey River. L, 1889. One of 230. Illus by Mortimer Menpes. Folio, orig cloth; worn. With 12 plates. W July 8 (226) £180

MacCarthy Reagh Library, Justin de

— [Sale Catalogue] Catalogue des livres rares et precieux.... Paris, 1815-17. 2 vols. 8vo, contemp half calf; joints split, worn. bba May 28 (559) £220 [Dawson]

McCauley, Lois B.

— Maryland Historical Prints, 1752-1889. Balt.: Maryland Historical Society, [1975]. 4to, cloth, in d/j. bbc Dec 9 (394) $100; bbc June 29 (490) $90

McCausland, Elizabeth. See: Abbott & McCausland

Macchiavelli, Niccolo. See: Machiavelli, Niccolo

Macchiavelli, Niccolo, 1469-1527. See: Machiavelli, Niccolo

McClellan, Elisabeth

— History of American Costume, 1607-1870. NY, 1937. 4to, cloth; spine faded. sp Feb 6 (362) $110

McClellan, George Brinton, 1865-1940

— Manual of Bayonet Exercise.... Phila., 1862. 12mo, orig cloth; worn & soiled. With 24 plates. F mar 26 (518) $70

Anr copy. Cloth; spine ends frayed. Scattered foxing on plates. sg Mar 26 (187) $50

McClelland, Nancy

— Duncan Phyfe and the English Regency, 1795-1830. NY, [1939]. 1st Ed, One of 1,000. Folio, cloth. Sgd on half-title. wa Mar 5 (589) $140

M'Clintock, Sir Francis Leopold, 1819-1907

— The Voyage of the "Fox" in the Arctic Seas. L, 1859. 1st Ed. 8vo, orig cloth; upper cover stained. With 3 folding maps. bba Sept 19 (48) £50 [Boring]

Anr copy. Contemp half calf; rubbed & scuffed. With frontis, 4 maps (1 in facsimile). Inscr by Wilkie Collins. cb Oct 10 (67) $400

Anr copy. Modern half calf, part of orig cloth bound in at end. With 18 plates & maps, 1 loose in end pocket. W July 8 (258) £70

McClure, Alexander K.

— Three Thousand Miles through the Rocky Mountains. Phila., 1869. 12mo, cloth; spine repaired. Sgd on front flyleaf. sg Dec 5 (141) $175

MacColl, Donald Sutherland. See: Harrison & MacColl

McCorison, Marcus A.

— Vermont Imprints, 1778-1820: a Check List. Worcester, 1963. wa Apr 9 (1) $55

McCormick, Richard C., 1832-1901

— Arizona, its Resources and Prospects. NY, 1865. 1st Ed. 8vo, orig ptd front wrap; detached & hinged to folding map. With folding map. Library markings. bbc June 29 (299) $80

M'Cormick, Robert, 1800-90

— Voyages of Discovery in the Arctic and Antarctic Seas. L, 1884. 2 vols. 8vo, contemp calf, prize bdg. W July 8 (259) £350

McCoy, Isaac, 1784-1846

— History of the Baptist Indian Missions.... Wash., 1840. 8vo, rebound in old cloth; inner hinges reinforced. Foxed; library markings. K July 12 (331) $120

McCreery, John

— The Press, a Poem, Published as a Specimen of Typography. Liverpool, 1803-27. 1st Ed. 2 vols in 1. 4to, modern half calf. Ck July 10 (175) £150

McCullers, Carson

— The Ballad of the Sad Cafe. Bost., [1951]. Inscr to Joshua Logan. wd Dec 12 (416) $100

— The Heart is a Lonely Hunter. Bost., 1940. 1st Ed. In d/j. sg Dec 12 (263) $275

Anr copy. In chipped d/j. sg June 11 (220) $200

— The Member of the Wedding. Bost., 1946. In d/j. cb Dec 12 (107) $80

Macculloch, John, 1773-1835

— Remarks on the Art of Making Wine. L, 1817. 2d Ed. 12mo, half calf. sg Mar 5 (334) $60

McCulloch, John Ramsey, 1789-1864

— Treatises and Essays on Economical Policy. Edin., 1853. 8vo, contemp half calf; worn. Title stuck to Notice leaf. Library markings. DW Nov 6 (305) £240

McDade, Thomas M.

— The Annals of Murder: A Bibliography of Books and Pamphlets on American Murders.... Norman, 1961. 4to, cloth, in d/j. sg Oct 31 (182) $60

McDonald, Edward David

— A Bibliography of the Writings of Theodore Dreiser. Phila., 1928. One of 35. O Dec 17 (122) $55

MacDonald, George, 1824-1905

— At the Back of the North Wind. NY, 1871. 1st Ed. 8vo, orig cloth; worn & shaken. O Jan 14 (116) $80

Anr Ed. L, 1911. 8vo, orig cloth. With 12 color plates. sp June 18 (124) $65

Anr Ed. Phila., 1919. Illus by Jessie Willcox Smith. 4to, cloth; worn. With pictorial title & 8 color plates. F June 25 (117) $60

Anr copy. Orig cloth; inner joints just starting. K Mar 22 (245) $90

— Dealings with the Fairies. L, 1867. Illus by Arthur Hughes. 16mo, orig cloth; rubbed & worn, poorly rebacked. DW Jan29 (256) £90

— Phantastes. A Faerie Romance for Men and Women. L, 1858. 1st Ed. 8vo, orig cloth; faded, covers stained. bba Oct 24 (111) £140 [Baring]

Macdonald, James David. See: Cave & Macdonald

MacDonald, John D.

— Wine of the Dreamers. NY, [1951]. In d/j. Bookplate sgd by MacDonald affixed to front free endpaper. pba July 9 (188) $90

Macdonald, John Graham

— Journal of...an Expedition from Port Denison to the Gulf of Carpentaria.... Brisbane: T. P. Pugh, 1865. 12mo, presentation bdg of half calf over cloth. With port, folding map & errata slip. C June 25 (255) £4,000 [Quaritch/Hordern]

Anr copy. Presentation bdg of half calf over purple cloth. With port & folding map. Flyleaf inscr "With the Authors Compts". S June 25 (147) £4,200 [Quaritch]

MacDonald, John Ross

— The Art of Charles Wheeler. Melbourne, 1952. 4to, cloth, in frayed d/j. kh Nov 11 (246) A$90

Macdonald, Reginald James

— The History of the Dress of the Royal Regiment of Artillery. L, 1899. 4to, orig half cloth; covers soiled. O May 26 (120) $70

MacDonald, Ross, Pseud.

— The Barbarous Coast. NY, 1956. Review copy. In d/j with def spine & stain on rear panel. LC deaccession stamp. wa Mar 5 (225) $55

— The Ferguson Affair. NY, 1960. In d/j. pba July 9 (190) $65

M'Dougall, Capt George Frederick

— The Eventful Voyage of H. M. Discovery Ship "Resolute".... L, 1857. 8vo, later cloth; spine faded, rubbed. With 8 colored plates & folding map Some spotting. bba Oct 24 (325) £190 [Lewcock]

Mace, Thomas

— Musick's Monument. L, 1676. Folio, contemp calf gilt; rebacked, rubbed, lower bd chipped at foot. Minor marginal dampstaining to last few leaves. Sir John Reresby's copy, from the author. pn Oct 24 (409) £1,400

Macewen, Sir William, 1848-1924

— Pyogenic Infective Diseases of the Brain and Spinal Cord. Glasgow, 1893. 8vo, orig cloth. Library markings. bba Apr 30 (308) £160 [Phelps]

Macfall, Haldane, 1860-1928

— A History of Painting. Bost., [1916?]. One of 1,000. 8 vols. orig cloth. With 200 tipped-in color plates. pba Aug 20 (141) $50

M'Farlan, John

— Inquiries concerning the Poor. Edin., 1782. 8vo, contemp calf; lower cover stained. b June 22 (191) £400

MacFarlane, Charles, 1799-1858

— Constantinople in 1828. L, 1829. 1st Ed. 4to, 19th-cent half calf; upper cover detached. With 1 plain, 1 tinted & 3 hand-colored plates. Tinted plate shaved. S June 30 (158) £450 [Kutluoglu]

Anr copy. 2 vols. 8vo, contemp calf gilt. With hand-colored frontis & 2 folding plates. Lacking half-titles; 1 plate loose. S June 30 (340) £700 [Kutluoglu]

McFee, William, 1881-1966

— Casuals of the Sea. L, 1916. 1st Ed. Inscr. sg June 11 (222) $110

Macfie, Matthew

— Vancouver Island and British Columbia.... L, 1865. 8vo, contemp calf gilt; extremities worn. Defect to 1 map. sg Dec 5 (42) $200

MacGibbon, David —& Ross, Thomas

— The Castellated and Domestic Architecture of Scotland. Edin., 1887-92. 5 vols. 8vo, orig cloth; worn. S July 1 (1292) £180 [Sotheran]

Macgillivray, John

— Narrative of the Voyage of H.M.S. Rattlesnake.... L, 1852. 2 vols. 8vo, later half calf. pnE Dec 4 (245) £200

Anr copy. Orig cloth; spines faded. With folding map & 13 plates. Inscr. S June 25 (207) £7,200 [McCormick]

Macgillivray, William, 1796-1852. See: Edinburgh...

McGlashan, Charles F., 1847-1931

— History of the Donner Party. Truckee CA, [1879]. 1st Ed. 8vo, orig cloth; spine torn, front hinge cracked. sg June 18 (98) $400

2d Ed. San Francisco: A.L. Bancroft, 1880. 8vo, orig cloth; rubbed, worn & soiled; several hinges starting. cb Sept 12 (114) $60

Anr Ed. San Francisco, 1881. 8vo, cloth. Inscr. sg June 18 (99) $175

McGrandle, Leith

— Europe, the Quest for Unity. Verona: Officina Bodoni, 1975. One of 475 with sgd etched frontis. Illus by Pietro Annigoni. Folio, half mor. b Mar 11 (121) £85

Anr copy. Orig mor gilt. b Mar 11 (122) £120; b June 22 (27) £75

McGrath, Daniel F.

— Bookman's Price Index. Detroit, [1964-86]. Vols 1-32, lacking 4-11. Together, 26 vols. Orig cloth. cb Nov 21 (150) $750

Vols 25-28. Detroit, 1983-84. 2 vols. K Dec 1 (381) $200

M'Gregor, John, 1797-1857

— British America. L, 1833. 2d Ed. 2 vols. 8vo, orig cloth; worn. With 13 maps & 2 folding plans. bba Apr 30 (52) £50 [Charles]

MacGregor, Miriam

— Country Chaos. Andoversford: Whittington Press, 1980. One of 30 hand-colored. Pictorial bds, spiral-bound. sg Jan 30 (180) $110

Mach, Ernst, 1838-1916

— Die Mechanik in ihrer Engwicklung historisch-kritisch dargestellt. Leipzig, 1883. 8vo, orig cloth. Yakovenko copy. sg Nov 14 (261) $225

Machen, Arthur Llewelyn Jones, 1863-1947

— The Bowmen and Other Legends of the War. L, 1915. Orig wraps. cb Sept 19 (154) $55

— Works. L, 1923. One of 1,000. 9 vols. sg Dec 12 (261) $250

Machiavelli, Niccolo, 1469-1527

— Discourses, upon the First Decade of T. Livius. L, 1636. 1st Ed in English. 12mo, old calf; damaged, spine partly perished, loose. Text soiled & foxed throughout; tp repaired, affecting 1 word. STC 17160. wd June 12 (412) $200

— The Florentine Historie.... L, 1595. 1st Ed in English. Trans by Thomas Bedingfeld. Folio, modern bds. Title mtd; pp cropped. bba Mar 26 (221) £160 [Land]

Anr copy. Contemp calf; rubbed, spine repaired. Wormed at end with some loss. STC 17162. Ck Oct 18 (159A) £300

— Historie Fiorentine. Geneva, 1550 [but c.1640]. 5 parts in 2 vols. 4to, 18th-cent mor gilt by John Brindley; rebacked retaining orig spines, rubbed. S July 9 (1086) £450 [Quaritch]

— Opere. [Rome?], 1550. 5 parts in 1 vol. 4to, modern vellum. Some browning. SI June 10 (560) LIt550,000

Anr copy. 17th-cent vellum. Some browning; marginal repairs to 3 leaves. SI June 10 (561) LIt750,000

Anr Ed. [Geneva], 1650 [c.1610]. 5 parts in 1 vol. 18th-cent sheep; joints cracked & varnished. sg Mar 12 (176) $225

1st "Testina" Ed. [Geneva], 1550 [c.1610]. 5 parts in 1 vol. 4to, 18th-cent calf. Browned & spotted. SI June 10 (562) LIt400,000

— Il Principe.... Venice: Zanetti, 1537. 8vo, 19th-cent mor by Wood. Italic types; roman initials. Wormhole partly damaging the headline & 1st line of 1st 9 leaves. Manney copy. P Oct 11 (1216) $1,200

— Works. L, 1675. 1st Ed in English. 4 parts in 1 vol. Folio, later calf; rebacked, worn. Final leaf holed. bba Oct 10 (301) £100 [Jacob]

Anr copy. Contemp calf; covers detached. bba May 14 (63) £190 [R. Clark]

Anr Ed. L, 1680. Folio, contemp calf; spine rubbed. Lacking 1st leaf. C Dec 16 (217) £450 [Brooke-Hitching]

Anr Ed. L, 1762. 2 vols. 4to, contemp calf; rubbed, Vol II upper cover detached. bba July 9 (112) £70 [Hobbes]

McIan, Robert Ronald, d.1856. See: Logan & McIan

M'Ilvaine, William, Jr. See: Grabhorn Printing

McIntosh, Charles, 1794-1864

— The Practical Gardener, and Modern Horticulturist.... L, 1828-29. 2 vols. 8vo, contemp half calf gilt; rubbed. With engraved title, frontis & 31 plates, 16 hand-colored. Tear to 1 plate; some foxing. bba June 11 (264) £120 [Freddie]

Anr copy. Half calf; worn. With frontis & 13 colored plates only. pnE Oct 2 (414) £80

Anr Ed. L, 1835-40. 2 vols. 8vo, half calf; rubbed. With engraved title & 28 plates, 14 hand-colored. b Nov 18 (374) £80

Mackail, John William, 1859-1945. See: Kelmscott Press

Mackaness, George

— The Art of Book Collecting in Australia. Sydney, 1956. One of 500. In d/j. kh Nov 11 (163) A$120

Mackay, George

— The History of Bendigo. Melbourne, 1891. 8vo, orig bdg; front free endpaper excised. kh Nov 11 (293) A$220

McKay, George Leslie

— American Book Auction Catalogues, 1713-1934: A Union List. NY, 1937. 8vo, wraps; worn, head of spine torn. O Sept 24 (153) $50

— A Stevenson Library. Catalogue of a Collection...Formed by Edwin J. Beinecke. New Haven, 1951-64. One of 500. 6 vols. Inscr by Edwin Beinecke. sg May 21 (310) $375

Mackay, Malcolm S.

— Cow Range and Hunting Trail. NY, 1925. 1st Ed. In d/j. Koopman copy. O Oct 29 (200) $200

McKelvey, Susan Delano

— The Lilac. NY, 1928. 1st Ed. 4to, cloth; worn. O Aug 25 (130) $120

McKenna, Paul. See: Wolfe & McKenna

McKenney, Thomas L., 1785-1859 —& Hall, James, 1793-1868

— History of the Indian Tribes of North America. Phila.: Biddle, 1837, Rice & Clark, 1842-44. State B of Vols I & II, State A of Vol III. 3 vols. Folio, modern cloth. With 120 hand-finished colored plates. Map not mentioned; 1 plate repaired on verso; some foxing & browning. sg Dec 5 (142) $16,500

Anr Ed. Phila.: D. Rice, [c.1870]. Vol III only. Orig cloth; def. sg Feb 13 (195) $800

Anr Ed. Edin., 1933-34. ("The Indian Tribes of North America.") 3 vols. 4to, orig cloth. Ck Feb 14 (24) £95

Anr copy. Orig cloth; Vol I frayed along rear joint, hinges tender. wa Dec 9 (301) $180

Anr copy. Cloth. wd June 12 (414) $200

Mackenzie, Sir Alexander, 1764-1820

— Voyages from Montreal, on the River St. Laurence.... L, 1801. 1st Ed. 4to, modern half calf incorporating old bds; rubbed. With port & 3 folding maps. Some foxing; minor stains & soiling; maps with a few tears repaired on versos. O Aug 25 (126) $1,400

Anr copy. Half calf. With port & 3 folding maps, 1 colored in outline. S Nov 21 (327) £850 [Beeleigh]

Anr copy. Later half mor gilt. With port & 3 folding maps. 1 map torn from gutter. sg Jan 9 (115) $1,700

Mackenzie, Frederick, 1788?-1854

— Specimens of Gothic Architecture.... L, [1825?]. 4to, orig cloth; worn & chipped, partial tear along upper joint. With pictorial title & 60 plates. With Nattali ad leaf but with orig price on spine. bbc Apr 27 (426) $150

Mackenzie, James C. See: Derrydale Press

McKerrow, Ronald B., 1872-1940

— An Introduction to Bibliography for Literary Students. Oxford, 1928. Cloth, in d/j. cb Oct 17 (595) $50

— Printers' & Publishers' Devices in England & Scotland.... L, 1949. 4to, orig half cloth. bba Apr 9 (5) £75 [Adrian]

Mackintosh, Alexander

— The Driffield Angler. Gainsborough: Pvtly ptd, 1806. 8vo, modern lea. Koopman copy. O Oct 29 (201) $350

Mackintosh, George

— A Whaling Cruise in the Arctic Regions. L, 1884. 8vo, cloth. sg June 18 (562) $175

Mackley, George

— Engraved in the Wood. L: Two Horse Press, 1968. One of 300. With 68 wood-engraved illusts, each on separate sheets, illusts in the accompanying book. S Nov 14 (121) £160 [Nelson]

Anr copy. Loose as issued in orig wraps. sg Sept 26 (219) $175

Mackworth, Sir Humphrey, 1657-1727

— England's Glory, or the Great Improvement of Trade in General.... L, 1694. 8vo, contemp calf. b June 22 (18) £750

Maclean, Donald

— Typographia Scoto-Gadelica. Edin., 1915. One of 250. pnE May 13 (171) £70

MacLeish, Archibald

— Land of the Free. NY, [1938]. In chipped & repaired d/j. bbc Feb 17 (233) $85

M'Leod, John, 1777?-1820

— Voyage of his Majesty's Ship Alceste.... L, 1817. ("Narrative of a Voyage in His Majesty's late ship Alceste to the Yellow Sea.") 1st Ed. 8vo, orig bds; front joint cracked. With port & 4 colored plates. cb Feb 12 (82) $400

2d Ed. L, 1818. 8vo, modern half calf by Lewis & Harris. With 5 hand-colored plates. Lacking port. Browned & foxed; some smudging; dampstain bleeds into text & plates from upper gutter. wa Apr 9 (150) $55

3d Ed. L, 1819. 8vo, contemp half lea gilt; worn. With folding chart & 5 colored plates. sg May 21 (66) $250

Maclure, Robert

— The Discovery of the North-West Passage. L, 1856. 8vo, orig cloth. With folding colored map & 3 lithos. Some foxing. W July 8 (266) £270

Maclure, William, 1763-1840

— Observations on the Geology of the United States of North America. Phila., 1818. 4to, orig bds, unopened; lacking rear cover, worn. With 2 folding hand-colored plates. In: Transactions of the American Philosophical Society, New Series Vol I. Accompanied by a copy of the Transactions for 1804 & 1809, in 1 vol, containing the 1st version of Maclure's paper. Lacking the mmap. O Nov 26 (112) $550

MacMahon, Bernard, 1775?-1816

— The American Gardener's Calendar; Adapted to the Climates and Seasons of the United States.... Phila., 1806. 8vo, contemp sheep; front cover loose, spine ends chipped. Leaf G4 lacking lower fore-edge corner, affecting a few words of text. sg Dec 5 (143) $110

MacMahon, T. W.

— Cause and Contrast: An Essay on the American Crisis. Richmond, Va., 1862. 8vo, orig wraps; front wraps browned. sg Dec 5 (79) $80

McMaster, S. W.

— 60 Years on the Upper Mississippi.... Rock Island, 1893. 12mo, wraps. sg June 18 (337) $150

MacMichael, William, 1784-1839

— Journey from Moscow to Constantinople.... L, 1819. 4to, modern half mor. With 6 plates. Some browning & soiling. S Nov 15 (1124) £170 [Ozbek]

Anr copy. Modern half mor by Sangorski & Sutcliffe. With 6 uncolored plates. S June 30 (341) £280 [Gonul]

McMullan, Joseph V.

— Islamic Carpets. NY, 1965. 4to, orig cloth; hinges repaired. sg Apr 2 (216) $325

Anr copy. Orig cloth, in d/j. Inscr. sp June 18 (277) $750

McMurtrie, Douglas Crawford

— Early Printing in New Orleans. New Orleans, 1929. One of 410. 4to, orig half cloth; rubbed. Dedication copy, inscr to Wilberforce Eames & with Ls to Eames tipped in. K Sept 29 (244) $130

— Early Printing in Tennessee... Chicago, 1933. One of 900. cb Oct 17 (601) $60

— A History of Printing in the United States. NY, 1936. Vol II (all pbd). F Mar 26 (369) $50

McMurtrie, Douglas Crawford —& Allen, Albert H.

— Colorado Imprints not listed in the Bibliography on Early Printing in Colorado. Evanson: Pvtly ptd, 1943. cb Oct 17 (620) $65

— Early Printing in Colorado. Denver, 1935. One of 250. cb Oct 17 (621) $110; sg Oct 31 (183) $350

— Jotham Meeker, Pioneer Printer of Kansas.... Chicago, 1930. One of 650. Inscr by McMurtrie to his mother. K Sept 29 (219) $65

McMurtry, Larry

— Cadillac Jack. NY, [1982]. One of 250. wa Sept 26 (215) $85

— The Last Picture Show. NY, 1966. In soiled d/j; new endpapers. Inscr. cb Sept 19 (161) $160

Anr copy. In d/j. wa Sept 26 (216) $170

— Lonesome Dove. NY, [1985]. In d/j. cb Sept 19 (162) $120

MacNeice, Louis, 1907-63

— Autumn Journal. L, 1939. In d/j. sg Dec 12 (264) $50

McNicol, Donald, 1735-1802

— Remarks on Dr. Samuel Johnson's Journey to the Hebrides. L, 1779. 8vo, modern half calf; some margins wormed. sg Mar 12 (157) $175

MacNish, Robert, 1802-37

— The Philosophy of Sleep. Glasgow, 1830. 12mo, contemp half calf gilt. DW Nov 6 (381) £52

Macomb, John N.

— Report of the Exploring Expedition from Santa Fe.... Wash., 1876. 4to, cloth; rebacked. With folding map & 22 plates, some tinted. Library markings. sg June 18 (338) $400

MacOrlan, Pierre, 1882-1970

— La Glace a 2 Faces. [N.p., 1957]. Illus by Michel Cot. 4to, cloth, in d/j after design by Cocteau, worn along edges. With 40 mtd plates. sg Sept 26 (220) $50

Macpherson, David, 1746-1816

— Annals of Commerce, Manufactures.... L, 1805. 4 vols. 4to, cloth. With 1 folding plate. Library stamps. bba June 11 (100) £140 [Quaritch]

MacPherson, H. A.

— A History of Fowling. Edin., 1897. 4to, orig cloth; rubbed. DW Jan 29 (125) £60

Anr copy. Cloth. sg Jan 9 (282) $90

MacPherson, John, 1710-65

— Critical Dissertations on the Origin, Antiquities, Language...of the Ancient Caledonians.... L, 1768. 4to, contemp calf; worn. bba July 9 (116) £50 [Land]

Macquarie, Lachlan, 1761-1824

— A Letter to...Viscount Sidmouth in Refutation of Statements.... L, 1821. 8vo, disbound. First & last leaves soiled. S June 25 (178) £1,400 [Simpson]

Macquarie's copy, Lachlan

— Burn, Richard. - The Justice of the Peace, and Parish Officer. L, 1772. Vol IV only. 8vo, modern calf. Some staining. Sgd twice & dated 10 May 1809. Inscr by him to H. C. Antill in 1822. C June 25 (165) £2,200 [McCormick]

Macquart, Louis Charles Rene

— Manuel sur les proprietes de l'eau.... Paris, 1783. 8vo, contemp half sheep gilt. sg Nov 14 (733) $350

Macquoid, Percy

— A History of English Furniture. L, 1904-8. 4 vols in orig 20 parts. Folio, cloth; worn. bba Jan 30 (343) £110 [Lobo]

Anr copy. 4 vols. Folio, orig cloth. Ck Oct 18 (287) £180

Anr copy. Cloth; rubbed, spines faded. DW Mar 11 (732) £120

Anr copy. Contemp half mor gilt; rubbed. pn May 14 (146) £160 [Elliott]

Anr copy. Orig cloth. W Mar 6 (8) £150

Anr copy. Orig cloth; soiled & rubbed. wa Mar 5 (588) $230

Anr Ed. L, 1919. 4 vols. Folio, cloth. pnE Oct 2 (556) £160

Anr Ed. L, 1923-28. 4 vols. Folio, orig cloth; shaken, covers discolored. sg Feb 6 (171) $140

Anr Ed. L, 1925-28. 4 vols. Folio, orig cloth. pn July 16 (114) £110

Anr Ed. L, 1938. 4 vols. Folio, orig cloth; soiled & marked. S May 13 (533) £140 [Cox]

Anr copy. Orig cloth; dampstain to some covers. W July 8 (125) £105

Macquoid, Percy —& Edwards, Ralph

— The Dictionary of English Furniture. L, 1924-27. Vol III (of 3) only. Folio, orig cloth, in d/js. Some foxing. kh Nov 11 (166) A$70

Anr copy. 3 vols. Folio, orig cloth; rubbed. pn Dec 12 (158) £95 [Elliott]

Anr copy. Orig cloth, in d/j. pn July 16 (113) £360

Anr copy. Vols I-II. Orig cloth. rs Oct 17 (30) $225

Anr copy. 3 vols. Folio, orig cloth; rubbed & soiled. With 51 colored plates. S May 13 (532) £150 [Angeline]

Anr copy. Vols I-II only. Orig cloth; Vol II abraded. sg Apr 2 (169) $130

Anr copy. 3 vols. Folio, orig cloth; soiled, Vol III in chipped d/j. W July 8 (126) £150

2d Ed. L, 1954. 3 vols. Folio, orig cloth, in d/js. Ck Sept 6 (181) £550

Anr copy. Cloth; rubbed. pn Dec 12 (159) £290 [White]

Anr copy. Orig cloth. S Feb 11 (319) £380 [Heneage]

Anr copy. Orig cloth, in def d/js; bdgs rubbed & stained. With 43 color plates. S Feb 11 (320) £380 [Heneage]

Macrobius, Ambrosius Theodosius

— In Somnium Scipionis expositio.... Brescia: Boninus de Boninis, 6 June 1483. Folio, 19th-cent mor gilt; extremities rubbed. 37 lines & headline; types 3:111R (text), 85 R, Haebler 12:58G (diagrams & map), 111G. First leaf, last leaf & some inner margins stained; n1-6 & C8 repaired at inner margin. 191 (of 192) leaves; lacking front blank. Goff M-9. C Dec 16 (141) £2,500

[Sawyer]

MacTaggart, Maxwell Fielding

— From Colonel to Subaltern.... L, 1928. One of 150, sgd. Orig vellum gilt. b Mar 11 (162) £100

McWilliam, Robert

— An Essay on the Origin and Operation of the Dry Rot. L, 1818. 4to, orig bds, unopened; spine rubbed, joints split. With 3 plates. bba Sept 5 (228) £55 [Town]

Madan, Falconer, 1851-1935

— Books in Manuscript.... L, 1893. One of 150. cb Oct 17 (562) $70

— Oxford Books. A Bibliography.... Oxford, 1895-1931. 3 vols. 8vo, orig cloth. O Sept 24 (154) $160; O Dec 17 (124) $250

Madan, Patrick, Thief

— Authentic Memoirs of the Life, Numerous Adventures, and Remarkable Escapes.... L: A. Milne, [1782?]. 8vo, 19th-cent half calf. Foxed at ends; lacking half-title or initial blank. sg Mar 12 (178) $200

Madariaga, Salvador de. See: Gregynog Press

Madden, Sir Frederic, 1801-73

— Illuminated Ornaments Selected from Manuscripts and Early Printed Books.... L: Pickering, 1833. 4to, contemp half mor; rebacked. bba Jan 30 (399) £120 [Pearson]

Anr copy. Contemp mor gilt; extremities rubbed. With engraved title & 59 plates, hand-finished & illuminated in gold & colors, by Henry Shaw. DW May 13 (294) £500

Anr copy. Folio, half mor. pnE Oct 2 (531) £130

Madden, Frederic William

— Coins of the Jews. L, 1881. Folio, cloth. sg June 25 (159) $175

Madden, Richard Robert, 1798-1886

— Travels in Turkey, Egypt, Nubia, and Palestine.... L, 1829. 2 vols. 8vo, contemp half calf; lower joint of Vol I partly split, extremities rubbed. Ck May 15 (127) £240

Anr copy. Contemp half calf; rubbed, upper joint of Vol I split, spine with small hole. Lacking half-title; some spotting. S June 30 (342) £420 [Gonul]

Maddock, James

— The Florist's Directory; or a Treatise on the Culture of Flowers. L, 1792. 8vo, contemp half calf; rubbed. With 6 plates, 4 hand-colored. 1 plate loose. bba May 14 (490) £65 [Selzer & Selzer]

Maddox, Willes

— Views of Lansdown Tower, Bath. L & Bath, 1844. Folio, orig half mor. With chromolitho title ptd in gold with hand-colored vignette (laid down) & 13 hand-colored plates mtd on card. Lacking tp; blank margins of 2 plates with wormholes repaired. C Oct 30 (50) £70 [Buckingham Books]

Madox, John

— Excursions in the Holy Land, Egypt, Nubia.... L: Richard Bentley, 1834. 2 vols. 8vo, later half calf; rubbed. With ports & 25 plates. Some plates shaved, 1 torn with loss. S July 1 (775) £260 [Sofer]

Madox, Thomas, 1666-1727

— Baronia Anglia. L, 1736. Folio, contemp calf; rubbed, covers detached. bba Jan 16 (19) £110 [Fetzer]

— Firma Burgi, or an Historical Essay Concerning the Cities, Towns and Boroughs of England. L, 1726. 1st Ed. Folio, contemp calf; rubbed. bba Jan 16 (18) £75 [Vine]

Maeterlinck, Maurice, 1862-1949

— The Blue Bird. NY, 1911. 1st American Ed. Illus by F. Cayley Robinson. 4to, orig cloth. With 25 mtd color plates. sg Jan 300 (160) $90

— La Vie des abeilles. Paris, 1918. One of 100 with additional suite in black onloy. 8vo, mor extra by G. Levitzky, orig wraps bound in. With colored frontis & 21 illusts. S Dec 5 (308) £700 [Way]

— Works. NY, 1911-16. 18 vols. 8vo, half mor gilt; spines rubbed. Sold w.a.f. sg Mar 5 (178) $200

Maffei, Francesco Scipione, 1675-1755

— Della scienza chiamata cavalleresca. Rome, 1710. 4to, contemp vellum. sg Mar 26 (188) $200

— Istoria diplomatica che serve d'introduzione all'arte critica in tal materia. Mantua, 1727. 4to, contemp calf; worn. SI Dec 5 (409) LIt180,000

— Museum Veronense.... Verona, 1749. Folio, contemp calf; worn, partly rebacked. bba Feb 27 (332) £240 [Etching]

Anr copy. Contemp vellum. SI June 10 (566) LIt1,000,000

— Verona illustrata. Verona, 1732-31. 4 parts. Folio, contemp vellum. With 54 plates. Ck May 15 (128) £550

Anr copy. 4 parts in 2 vols. Folio, 19th-cent calf; joints weak, upper cover of Vol I scuffed. With 18 plates on 4 leaves. Ink spot slightly affecting plate of town houses. Ck May 15 (129) £550

Anr copy. 4 parts in 2 vol. Folio, modern lea. SI June 10 (367) LIt1,400,000

Maffei, Paolo Alessandro
— Gemme antiche figurate. Rome, 1707-9. 4 vols. 4to, later mor. Library markings. F Dec 18 (301) $250
Anr Ed. Rome, 1727-29. 4 vols. 4to, contemp calf gilt. With 112 plates. Marginal foxing. F Mar 26 (750) $325

Maffei, Raffaello, 1451-1522
— Commentariorum urbanorum.... Basel: Froben, 1530. Folio, contemp pigskin with metal clasps; soiled. Margins dampstained; some Ms annotations in faded ink; occasional ink stains. Ck Nov 29 (327) £260

Magalotti, Lorenzo, 1637-1712
— Travels of Cosmo the Third, Grand Duke of Tuscany, through England.... L, 1821. 4to, contemp half calf; rebacked & recornered. With port & 39 plates. bba June 25 (231) £300 [Bifolco]

Magee, David
See also: Grabhorn Printing
— Victoria R. I.: A Collection.... San Francisco, [1969-70]. One of 625. 3 vols. Bds. K July 12 (326) $80; sg May 21 (266) $120

Magee, Dorothy & David. See: Grabhorn Printing

Maggs Brothers
— Bibliotheca Americana et Philippina. L, 1922-28. ("Bibliotheca Americana.") Parts 1-9 in 7 vols. 8vo, cloth, orig wraps bound in; wraps worn & soiled. O Sept 24 (155) $225

Magini, Giovanni Antonio. See: Wytfliet & Magini

Magnus, Joannes, 1488-1544
— Gothorum Sueonumque historia. Rome, 1554. 1st Ed. Folio, 19th-cent russia gilt; joints split. Lacking final blank; old dampstaining. C June 24 (331) £850 [Sagen]
Anr Ed. Basel: Isengrinius, 1558. 8vo, contemp calf; rubbed & wormed. bba Nov 28 (174) £420 [Stanley]

Magnus, Olaus, 1490-1558
— Historia de gentibus septentrionalibus. Rome, 1555. 1st Ed. Folio, modern vellum. Rusthole at R2 affecting letters; tear at 2Y6 affecting letters & repaired; some waterstains & discoloration. Jeanson 1080. S June 25 (328) £2,200 [Franks]
Anr Ed. Antwerp: Christopher Plantin, 1558. 8vo, later bds; rebacked. Last leaf lined. B May 12 (25) HF1,300
Anr Ed. Basel, 1567. Bount with: Pantaleon, Henricus. Militaris Ordinis Johannitarum, Rhodiorum, at Melitensium Equitum, rerum memorabilium..historia nova. Basel: Thomas Guarinus, 1581. Folio, contemp blind-stamped pigskin over wooden bds, metal clasps. Tear in fold of map in 1st work. C June 24 (332) £1,700 [Cooper]

Magra, James. See: Cook, Capt. James

Mahony, Bertha Everett —& Others
— Illustrators of Children's Books, 1744-1945 Bost.: The Horn Book, 1947. 1st Ed. 4to, half cloth. bbc Dec 9 (186) $85
Anr copy. Bdg not described. K Sept 29 (248) $60

Maier, Michael, 1568?-1622
— Scrutinium Chymicum. Frankfurt: Georg Heinrich Oehring, 1708. ("Chymisches Cabinet. Derer grossen Geheimnussen der Natur....") 4to, half lea. With 50 plates. B Nov 1 (646) HF10,000
— Viridarium chymicum, das ist Chymisches Lust-Gaertlein. Frankfurt: H. von Sand, 1688. 8vo, old vellum. With frontis & 52 plates. Some headlines shaved. S Dec 5 (408) £3,200 [Quaritch]

Mailer, Norman
— Death for the Ladies and Other Disasters. NY, [1962]. Orig wraps. Inscr to Dwight Macdonald. CNY June 9 (118) $240
— Marilyn. NY, 1973. Ltd Ed, sgd. In d/j. cb Sept 19 (155) $85
— The Naked and the Dead. NY, [1948]. Advance copy. Orig wraps; worn, front cover detached. sg June 11 (215) $100
1st Ed. In d/j. F Dec 18 (233) $90
Anr copy. In soiled d/j. pba July 9 (195) $55
Anr copy. In d/j; edges worn. sg Dec 12 (265) $120

Maillard de Tournon, Carlo Tommaso
— Considerazioni su la scrittura intitolata Riflessioni sopra la causa della Cina.... Rome, 1709. 4to, contemp vellum. S July 9 (1511) £350 [Ad Orientem]

Maillard, Leon
— Les Menus et programmes illustres. Paris, 1898. One of 1,025. 4to, modern cloth, orig front wrap bound in. sg Apr 2 (237) $900

Mails, Thomas E.
— The Mystic Warriors of the Plains. Garden City, 1972. 4to, cloth, in chipped d/j. NH Oct 6 (170) $85
— The People Called Apache. Englewood Cliffs, [1974]. Folio, orig cloth, in d/j. F Mar 26 (206) $90

Maimbourg, Louis, 1620?-86
— The History of the League.... L, 1684. 1st Ed in English. Trans by John Dryden. 8vo, old calf; worn, cover detached. O Dec 17 (127) $80
— The History of the Crusade.... L, 1685. Trans by John Nalson. Folio, later half mor; extremities rubbed. Marginal staining; tp torn. bba July 9 (92) £70 [Land]

Maindron, Ernest, 1838-1908
— Les Affiches illustrees. Paris, 1886. One of 525. 4to, half mor, orig wraps bound in; spine ends worn. With 20 plates. Epstein copy. sg Apr 30 (3384) $1,000
— Les Affiches illustrees 1886-1895. Paris, 1896. One of 1,000. 4to, half mor, orig wraps bound in. Inscr. Epstein copy. With article on Maindron by H. B. Coudray bound in. sg Apr 30 (385) $2,600
— Les Programmes illustres, des theatres et des cafes-concerts. Paris, [n.d.]. Vol I only. Folio, cloth; hinges cracked, orig front cover bound in. With 49 plates. sg Apr 2 (238) $300

Mainwaring, John
— Memoirs of the Life of the late George Frederic Handel. L, 1760. 1st Ed. 8vo, contemp half calf; joints cracked, spine rubbed. Some foxing. pn Oct 24 (410) £190 [Macnutt]

Mairui, Amedeo
— La Villa dei Misteri. Rome 1947. 2d Ed. 2 vols. 4to, orig cloth, plates loose in matching portfolio. With plan & 18 mtd color plates. sg Apr 2 (173) $275

Maitland, William, 1693?-1757
— The History of London. L, 1756. ("The History and Survey of London.") 3 vols, including 1772 Supplement. Folio, contemp calf; hinges worn. With 113 plates & maps only. b June 22 (257) £520

Anr copy. Vol II only. Cloth with library markings. With 121 (of 122) plates & maps. Plates stamped; some plates cropped; folding map laid down; 1 folding plate torn; last leaf of Vol II strengthened with a layer of gauze. pn Apr 23 (270) £300 [Russell]

Anr Ed. L, 1772. 2 vols. Folio, contemp calf; joints split, worn. With 129 (of 131) plates 7 maps. Some cropping, browning & soiling; marginal tears & repairs; partly misbound; lacking list of subscribers. pn June 11 (278) £460 [Russell]

Maitres...
— Les Maitres de l'affiche. Paris, 1896-1900. 1st Ed in orig 60 parts. Folio, loose in orig pictorial wraps as issued; 18 wraps repaired along folds. With 16 lithos & 240 colored reproductions of posters. Epstein set. sg Apr 29 (386) $16,000

Major, Howard
— The Domestic Architecture of the Early American Republic.... Phila. & L, 1926. 4to, cloth; shaken. sg Feb 6 (173) $140

Major, Joannes, 1470-1550
— Historia maioris Britanniae. [Paris]: Jodocus Badius Ascensius, 1521. 1st Ed. 4to, 18th-cent calf. Tp soiled; some Ms annotations. Ck Nov 29 (115) £500
— In premum sententiarum. Paris: H. Estienne, 29 Apr 1510. Bound with: In secundum sententiarum. Paris, 24 Dec 1510. And: Quartus sententiarum. Paris, 1512. 3 works in 2 vols. Folio, 16th-cent blind-stamped pigskin over wooden bds. S Dec 5 (171) £450 [Pickering]

Major, Richard Henry
— The Discovery of Australia by the Portuguese in 1601.... L: J. B. Nichols, 1861. 4to, contemp lea gilt. Some spotting. Inscr to Sir David Dundas. C June 25 (79) £550 [Arnold]
— Early Voyages to Terra Australis.... L, 1859. 8vo, contemp mor gilt; joints rubbed. Inscr to the Earl of Winchelsea. S June 25 (78) £700 [Arnold]

Major, Thomas
— Die Ruinen von Paestum oder Posidonia.... Wuerzburg: Johann Jakob Stahel, 1781. Folio, contemp half sheep, armorial bdg; spine ends chipped. With 25 plates. sg May 7 (147) $1,000
— The Ruins of Paestum, otherwise Posidonia.... L, 1768. Folio, contemp half calf; worn. With 25 plates on thick paper. Some waterstaining & browning. S July 1 (645) £1,000 [Consolidated Real]

Malamud, Bernard
— Life—From Behind a Counter. NY, [1932]. In: Saplings. Seventh Series, 1932. Sgd on p.114. sg June 11 (217) $110
— The Natural. NY, [1952]. Advance copy. In d/j. Inscr. sg June 11 (216) $850

Malaspina, Alejandro. See: Viana, Francisco Xavier de

Malcolm, Sir Howard
— Travels in South-Eastern Asia.... L, 1839. 2 vols. 12mo, orig cloth; backstrips damaged, some gatherings loose in Vol II. With folding map in Vol I. sg May 21 (67) $150

Malcolm, James Peller
— Anecdotes of the Manners and Customs of London during the Eighteenth Century. L, 1810. 2d Ed. 2 vols. 8vo, contemp calf; rebacked. sg Oct 17 (310) $60

Malcolm, Sir John, 1769-1833

— The History of Persia. L, 1815. 2 vols. 4to, contemp calf gilt; rubbed. With folding map & 21 plates. Some spotting. S June 25 (109) £700 [Grant]

Anr copy. Later half mor on contemp bds. With folding map & 22 plates. Map torn & repaired; some leaves with margins soiled & torn. S July 1 (845) £700 [Ghani]

Malcolm X

— The Autobiography of Malcolm X. L, [1966]. 1st English Ed, Advance Proof. Wraps. cb Sept 19 (80) $65

Maldonado, Lorenzo Ferrer

— Voyage de la mer atlantique a l'ocean pacifique.... Piacenza, 1812. 4to, contemp wraps. SI Dec 5 (704) LIt250,000

Malebranche, Nicolas, 1638-1715

— Intrigues du serail, histoire turque.... The Hague: au depens de la Compagnie, 1739. 8vo, contemp calf. Tp & anr leaf holed with loss of letters. S June 30 (160) £250 [Kutluoglu]

Malham, John, 1747-1821

— The Naval Gazeteer: or Seaman's Complete Guide. L, 1795. 2 vols. 8vo, contemp calf; rubbed. Some foxing & soiling; piece clipped from blank margin of tp. O Aug 25 (127) $270

Malinowski, Bronislaw

— Coral Gardens and Their Magic. NY, [1935]. 2 vols. sg Jan 9 (116) $120

Malkin, Benjamin Heath

— The Scenery, Antiquities, and Biography of South Wales. L, 1804. 1st Ed. 4to, half calf; rubbed, hinges weak. With folding map & 12 plates with pale wash heightened with white. bba Jan 16 (338) £110 [Scott]

Mallarme, Stephane, 1842-98

— L'Apres-midi d'un faune. Paris, 1876. 1st Ed, one of 170 on Hollande. Illus by Edouard Manet. 4to, loose in orig wraps, unopened. S May 28 (227) £2,000 [Sims Reed]

Anr copy. Half mor, orig wraps bound in. S May 28 (381) £2,300 [Rosenthal]

— Un Coup de Des jamais n'abolira le hasard. Paris, 1914. 1st Pbd Ed, one of 90 on velin d'Arches. 4to, half mor by Maylander, orig wraps bound in. S May 28 (382) £700 [Beres]

— Pages. Brussels, 1891. One of 50 on japon. Frontis by Renoir. 4to, half mor gilt by Canape, orig wraps bound in. S May 28 (383) £4,200 [Lardanchet]

One of 325. Bds. S July 1 (1193) £850 [Sims Reed]

— Poesies. Lausanne, 1932. One of 95 on velin d'Arches, sgd by Henri Matisse. Illus by Matisse. 4to, loose as issued in orig wraps. With separate suite on japon. CNY May 11 (416) $22,000

Mallet, Allain Manesson

— Beschreibung des ganzen Welt-Kreises. Frankfurt, 1719. 5 parts in 4 vols. 4to, contemp calf gilt; worn. With 5 engraved titles & 613 mostly full-page plates & maps. Lacking Plate 16 in Vol I; repairs to upper corner in Vol II; Z4 & Plate L in Vol V damaged & repaired with loss; stamps on titles. S Nov 21 (135) £3,900 [Map House]

— Les Travaux de Mars, ou l'art de la guerre. Paris, 1684-85. Vol I only. contemp calf; upper cover detached, spine torn. With 155 plates. Lacking engraved title; 1 plate torn without loss; pp. 209-18 misbound after p. 224. Sold w.a.f. pn Nov 14 (381) £50

Anr copy. 3 vols. 8vo, conemp calf; chipped & rubbed. With engraved titles, port & 300 illusts. Some browning. S July 1 (1295) £360 [Erlini]

Mallet, David, 1705-65

— The Life of Francis Bacon. L, 1740. 1st Ed. 8vo, contemp calf; hinges strengthened, endpapers spotted. bba May 28 (30) £50 [Land]

Mallowan, M. E. L.

— Nimrud and its Remains. L, 1966. 3 vols, including Atlas. Folio, orig cloth, text vols in d/js. bba May 14 (306) £140 [Museum Bookshop]; pn Sept 12 (102) £120 [Heneage]

Malo, Charles, 1790-1871

— Guirlande de flore. Paris, [1815]. 12mo, bds; worn & soiled. With hand-colored engraved title & 15 hand-colored plates. O Mar 31 (134) $140

— Voyage pittoresque de Paris au Havre sur les rives de la Seine. Paris, [1828]. 18mo, contemp calf. With engraved title & 5 plates. sg Jan 9 (66) $140

Malory, Sir Thomas, fl.1470

See also: Limited Editions Club

Le Morte Darthur

— 1578. - The Storye of the most noble and worthy Kynge Arthur.... L: Thomas East. Folio, contemp blind-stamped calf over wooden bds; spine ends repaired, extremities rubbed, upper joint split, clasps lacking. 44 lines, double column, black letter. With large woodcut of St. George slaying the dragon on the tp & 23 smaller woodcuts in the text. Wormed from title to Q1 with occasional loss of characters; repairs to 3L3 with a few characters supplied in Ms facsimile & to H3; some marginal tears. STC 805. C Dec 16 (218)

£22,000 [Quaritch]

— 1634. - The Most Ancient and Famous History of the Renowned Prince Arthur.... L: William Stansby. 4to, later calf; worn, broken, spine def. Black letter. Lacking frontises to Parts 1 & 3; tp cropped at lower margin; browned throughout. Sold w.a.f. bba May 28 (15) £160 [Krown & Spellman]

— 1893-94. - L. One of 300 on Dutch handmade paper. Illus by Aubrey Beardsley. 3 vols. 4to, half mor gilt by Worsfold, orig wraps bound in; joints starting. P June 17 (108) $1,100

One of 1,500. Vellum gilt. b&b Feb 19 (245) $1,400

— 1910-11. - L: Riccardi Press One of 500. Illus by W. Russell Flint. 4 vols. 4to, orig half cloth. Ck July 10 (237) £380

— 1917. - L. One of 500. Abridged by A. W. Pollard; illus by Arthur Rackham. 4to, orig vellum; rubbed. bba Jan 16 (398) £80 [Frew Mackenzie]

— 1917. - The Romance of King Arthur. L. Illus by Arthur Rackham. 4to, orig cloth, in d/j. With 16 colored plates. bba Apr 9 (335) £220 [W. White]

Anr copy. Orig cloth. With 16 colored plates & 7 uncolored plates. K Mar 22 (390) $95

One of 500. Orig vellum gilt. With 16 color plates. sg Nov 7 (172) $1,100

— 1917. - NY 4to, orig cloth; worn. With 16 color plates. F Mar 26 (110) $100

Anr copy. Orig cloth; back cover scratched. With 16 color plates & 7 uncolored plates. K Dec 1 (376) $150

— 1923. - L: Medici Society. 2 vols. bba Apr 9 (315) £65 [Dawson]

— 1927. - L. Illus by Aubrey Beardsley. 4to, orig cloth; rebacked, orig spine retained. sg Sept 26 (23) $80

— 1927. - NY One of 1,600. Illus by Aubrey Beardsley. 4to, orig cloth; lower covers bumped; front hinge cracking. cb Dec 5 (10) $650; pnL Nov 20 (196) £85 [Williams]

— 1976. - L. One of 50 on Barcham Green handmade paper. 4to, mor. Facsimile of 1485 Ed. sg May 21 (248) $275

Malpighi, Marcello, 1628-94

— Opera. L: Robert Scott & George Wells, 1686. 2 vols in 1. Folio, contemp vellum. With 116 plates. SI Dec 5 (417) LIt1,700,000

Anr Ed. Leiden, 1687. 2 vols in 1. 4to, contemp vellum; soiled & worn. With frontis & 117 plates, 10 folding. Some plates trimmed close; minor marginal dampspots or tears; some foxing or browning to text; a few gatherings at end sprung. wa Sept 26 (455) $650

— Opera posthuma.... Amst., 1698. 4to, contemp sheep gilt; spine ends & front joint chipped. With 19 folding plates. Prelims browned; lacking frontis; tp loose. sg May 14 (101) $450

Malraux, Andre

— La Condition humaine. Paris: Gallimard, [1933]. One of 30. Mor extra by Maylander, orig wraps bound in. S May 28 (385) £1,700 [Beres]

One of 150. Orig wraps. Epstein copy. sg Apr 30 (320) $800

— L'Espoir. Paris, 1937. One of 3 hors commerce on hollande. Mor extra by Maylander, orig wraps bound in. Inscr. S May 28 (386) £2,400 [Beres]

— Lunes en Papier. Paris: Editions de la Galerie Simon, 1921. One of 112. Illus by Fernand Leger. Folio, orig wraps; worn & discolored. With 7 woodcuts (including cover), 3 on separate sheets, 3 in text. bba Mar 26 (198A) £2,400 [Sims Reed]

— Psychologie de l' Art. [Geneva & Paris, 1949-50]. 3 vols. 4to, wraps. sg Feb 6 (174) $130

— The Psychology of Art. [NY, 1949-50]. 3 vols. 4to, cloth, in d/js. sg Apr 2 (176) $80

— La Tentation de l'occident. Paris, 1926. One of 8 on japon. Mor gilt by Maylander, orig wraps bound in. Inscr. S May 28 (384) £1,200 [Sims Reed]

Malte-Brun, Conrad

— Atlas de la Geographie Universelle.... Paris: Garnier Freres, [1837]. Folio, modern half vellum. With 72 maps, hand-colored in outline First 2 pages loose. S Feb 11 (710) £450 [Vilsuet]

— Universal Geography.... Bost., 1834. ("A System of Universal Geography: or, a Description of all the Parts of the World....") 3 vols. 4to, contemp mor; worn. sg Feb 13 (131) $150

Malthe, Francois de

— Pratique de la guerre. Paris: la veuve Gervais Clousier, 1681. 8vo, contemp calf; rubbed. With 28 folding plates. Some browning. S July 9 (297) £280 [American Museum]

— Traite des feux artificiels pour la guerre, et pour la recreation. Paris, 1640. 8vo, old vellum; rubbed & soiled. Lacking last leaf; some browning & soiling. S July 1 (1296) £210 [American Mus.]

Malthus, Thomas Robert, 1766-1834

— An Essay on the Principle of Population.... L, 1803. 4to, contemp calf; rubbed, spine darkened. Some spotting & soiling; tp creased; tear repaired on F3; short tear in upper margin of 4B3; lacking final blank. P Dec 12 (70) $3,000

1st American Ed. George Town, 1809. 2 vols. 8vo, contemp sheep; extremities worn. sg Nov 7 (133) $500

— Principles of Political Economy.... L, 1836. 2d Ed. 8vo, contemp calf gilt. Hadzor Library stamp in blank margin of tp. b Nov 18 (279) £400

Malton, Thomas, 1748-1804

— A Picturesque Tour through the Cities of London and Westminster. L, 1792. 2 vols in 1. Folio, contemp russia gilt. With 100 uncolored plates. A few plate imprints shaved; some plate numerals cropped; some spotting. C Oct 30 (133) £6,500 [Marlborough]

Malvasio, Carlo Cesare, 1616-93

— Felsina pittrice: vite de pittore Bolognesi. Bologna, 1678. 2 vols. 4to, contemp half vellum; rubbed. Lower corner of Vol I waterstained. bba Sept 19 (340) £380 [Erlini]

Anr copy. Vol I (of 2) only. 4to, calf; rebacked. bba Feb 27 (256) £100 [Hetherington]

Anr copy. 2 vols. 4to, old vellum bds; soiled. With p.471 in Vol I with 1st reading in line 14. S Feb 11 (137) £700 [Ursus]

Malvaux, —, Abbe. See: Smith's copy, Adam

Malvezzi, Virgilio, 1599-1654

— Discourses upon Cornelius Tacitus. L, 1642. 1st Ed in English. Folio, modern sheep. Title & last page soiled. cb Dec 5 (82) $160

Man, John, of Reading

— The History and Antiquities of the Borough of Reading.... L & Reading, 1816. 4to, contemp cloth; extremities worn, joints starting. With 20 plates & maps. Some browning. bba July 23 (364) £130 [Fetzer]

Manchester Anglers' Association

— Anglers' Evenings: Papers by Members. Manchester & L, 1880-94. Series 1-3 (all pbd). 8vo, cloth. Koopman copy. O Oct 29 (203) $90

Manchester, Herbert. See: Derrydale Press

Mander, Carel van

— Het Leven der Doorluchtige Nederlandsche en eenige Hoogduitsche Schilders.... Amst., 1764. 2 vols. 8vo, contemp calf; rubbed. With frontis, port of author & 51 plates. S Feb 11 (140) £240 [Debennin]

— Het schilder Boeck.... Amst., 1618. 4to, calf; def. With engraved title & port. Some stains. B Nov 1 (357) HF2,800

Anr Ed. Haarlem, 1604. 2 parts in 1 vol. 4to, vellum; dust-soiled. With port & 2 engraved titles. B Nov 1 (356) HF6,000

Mandeville, Bernard de, 1670?-1733

— The Fable of the Bees. L, 1724. 8vo, contemp calf; rebacked, worn. Wormed. cb Feb 12 (83) $70

Mandeville, Sir John, d.1372
See also: Grabhorn Printing

— The Foreign Travels and Dangerous Voyages of.... L: ptd for M. Hotham at the Black Boy on London-bridge, [c.1704-28]. 4to, half mor. Inner margin of tp strengthened; headlines of 4 pp cropped or shaved; tp & final page stained. Collier-duPont copy. CNY Oct 8 (156) $280

Mandeville, Mildred S.

— The Used Book Price Guide. Kenmore WA, 1977-83. 5 vols, including Supplements. Reprint of the 5-year guide plus the 5-year supplement, covering 1968-83. cb Nov 21 (131) $150

Mandey, Venterus —& Moxon, James

— Mechanick Powers.... L, 1702. ("Mechanick Powers: or the Mystery of Nature and Art Unvail'd....") 4to, modern half sheep; spine rubbed. With 16 folding plates; 1 turn & laid down. bba Sept 5 (229) £170 [Rogers Turner]

Manec, J. P.

— Traite theorique et pratique de la ligature des arteres.... Paris, 1836. Folio, orig half cloth; shaken. With 14 partly hand-colored plates. Text foxed. sg Nov 14 (74) $275

Manget, Jean Jacques, 1652-1742
See also: Le Clerc & Manget

— Bibliotheca Pharmaceutico-Medica, seu rerum ad pharmaciam.... Geneva, 1704. 2 vols. Folio, old half vellum. sg Nov 14 (75) $400

— Theatrum anatomicum. Geneva, 1717. 2 vols, including the Tabulae anatomicae. Folio, old half vellum. With port and 131 (of 136) plates. Foxed throughout; some plates cropped. sg Nov 14 (76) $425

Manly, William Lewis

— Death Valley in '49: Important Chapter of California Pioneer History. San Jose, 1894. 1st Ed. 8vo, cloth; lacking free endpapers, hinges cracked. sg June 18 (100) $200

Mann, Daniel Dickenson

— The Present Picture of New South Wales.... L, 1811. 4to, 19th-cent half lea. With folding colored map. Lacking the 4 plates. S June 25 (168) £1,200 [Baring]

Mann, John F.

— Eight Months with Dr. Leichhardt in the Years 1846-47. Sydney, 1888. 8vo, modern half cloth, orig wraps (spotted) bound in. With the Appendix. Inscr. S June 25 (239) £1,300 [Arnold]

Mann, Thomas, 1875-1955

See also: Limited Editions Club

— Death in Venice. Balt. & NY: Aquarius Press, 1971. One of 25. Illus by Warrington Colescott. Folio, loose in wraps as issued. With 2 suites of the etchings. sg Jan 30 (99) $400

— The Magic Mountain. NY, 1927. One of 200, sgd. 2 vols. Half vellum. Epstein copy. sg Apr 30 (321) $800

— Nocturnes. NY, 1934. One of 1,000, sgd. cb Jan 16 (90) $160

— Waelsungenblut. Munich: Phantasus Verlag, [1921]. One of 530. 4to, orig half cloth. C Dec 16 (56) £1,000 [Schumann]

Anr copy. Orig mor gilt. HH May 12 (2405) DM3,800

— Der Zauberberg. Berlin, 1924. 2 vols. Bds. sg Dec 12 (266) $175

Manners, Lady Victoria

— John Zoffany, R.A., his Life and Works. L & NY, 1920. One of 500. 4to, orig half cloth, in d/j; soiled & stained. DW Mar 11 (836) £190

Manni, Dominico Maria

— Vita de Aldo Pio Manuzio. Venice, 1759. 8vo, old bds. Some foxing. SI June 10 (580) LIt220,000

Manning, Owen, 1721-1801 —& Bray, William

— The History and Antiquities of the County of Surrey. L, 1804-14. 1st Ed. 3 vols. Folio, contemp half mor; worn, some covers detached, lacking some pieces of spines. Some dampstaining. S Feb 26 (767) £160 [Thorp]

Manning, Samuel

— American Pictures Drawn with Pen and Pencil. L: Religious Tract Society, [1876]. 8vo, orig cloth; extremities worn, lacking flyleaf. NH May 30 (58) $60

Manningham, Henry

— A Complete Treatise on Mines. L, 1756. 8vo, contemp calf; chipped. With 19 folding plates. S July 9 (298) £200 [Middleton]

Mansfield, Howard. See: Caxton Club

Mansfield, Katherine, 1888-1923

— The Garden Party and Other Stories. L, 1922. 1st Ed, 1st Issue. In d/j. sg Apr 30 (322) $850

Anr Ed. L: Verona Press, 1939 [1947]. One of 1,200. Illus by Marie Laurencin. 4to, orig cloth, in soiled d/j. Ck Dec 11 (133) £1,400

Anr copy. Orig cloth, in frayed d/j. Without tipped-in pbr's note. pn Dec 12 (200) £1,200 [Marlborough]

Mantecon, Jose Ignacio. See: Millares & Mantecon

Mantell, Gideon Algernon, 1790-1852

— The Fossils of the South Downs. L, 1822. 1st Ed. 4to, calf gilt. With 41 (of 42) plates; lacking Plate 6. pnE Oct 2 (353) £75

Anr copy. Half cloth. pnE Dec 4 (225) £100

Manuel II, King of Portugal

— Livros Antigos Portuguezes 1489-1600. L: Maggs, 1929-35. One of 650. 3 vols. 4to, orig cloth. Ck Nov 1 (447) £1,000

Anr copy. Orig cloth in repaired d/js. sg Oct 31 (185) $1,200

Manutius, Paulus, 1512-74

— Commentarius...in epistolas M. T. Ciceronis.... Frankfurt: Andreas Wechel, 1580. 8vo, old vellum. Some underscoring & marginalia; blank corner off title. sg Mar 12 (179) $90

— Epistolarum. Venice: Aldus, 1580. 8vo, contemp blind-tooled pigskin over wooden bds with brass clasps & catches. Some dampstaining. sg Oct 24 (209) $175

— Lettere volgari di diversi nobilissimi huomini.... Venice: [Aldus], 1543-45. 2 vols. 8vo, later calf; not uniform. bba Feb 27 (225) £400 [Sokol]

Manwood, John, d.1610

— A Treatise and Discourse of the Lawes of the Forrest. L, 1598. 4to, 18th-cent calf gilt; rubbed, rebacked. Later port tipped in & cropped. STC 17291. pn May 14 (5) £580 [Way]

Manzoni, Alessandro, 1785-1873

— I Promessi Sposi.... Livorno: G. P. Pozzolini. 3 vols. 8vo, contemp calf gilt by John Mackenzie. Currer copy. C June 24 (173) £1,000 [Lyon]

Map...

— Map Collectors' Circle. L, 1963-75. Ed by R. V. Tooley. Nos 1-110 [all pbd]. Cloth, orig wraps preserved. DW Nov 20 (64) £620

Mapei, Camillo

— Italy: Classical, Historical, and Picturesque. Glasgow, 1847. 4to, contemp mor gilt. With engraved title & 60 plates. Some corners waterstained. b Nov 18 (342) £650

Anr copy. Disbound. With engraved title & 59 (of 60) plates. Title soiled; early leaves dampstained; lacking frontis. DW Jan 29 (40) £530

Anr Ed. Glasgow, 1856. 4to, contemp mor gilt; worn. With engraved title & 62 plates. S May 14 (1202) £850 [Bifolco]

Maps & Charts

Africa

— Blaeu, Willem & Jan. - Africae nova descriptio. [Amst., c.1650]. 41cm by 55cm, hand-colored, framed. b June 22 (2) £450

Anr Ed. [Amst., c.1663]. 560mm by 415mm. Old surface soiled; tear at bottom of central crease. wa Apr 9 (159) $180

— De Wit, Frederick. - Totius Africae Accuratissima Tabula. Amst., [17th cent]. 490mm by 578mm, Hand-colored in outline. cb Oct 10 (158) $350

— Hondius, Jodocus. - Africa nova tabula. [Amst., 1632]. 405mm by 552mm. cb Oct 10 (178) $500

— Jaillot, Charles Hubert Alexis. - L'Afrique. Paris, 1690. 570mm by 888mm, hand-colored in outline. Repairs along vertical fold on verso; minor marginal tears. sg Sept 19 (61) $375

— Janssonius, Joannes. - Guinea. Amst., [c.1650]. 390mm by 530mm, hand-colored in outline. Browned; cellotape repair on verso. sg Feb 13 (46) $325

— Mercator, Gerard. - Tab. I Africae, in qua Mauritania Tingitana et Caesariensis. Amst., [c.1600]. 330mm by 460mm. sg Feb 13 (54) $200

— Mercator, Gerard. - Tab. II Africae, Complectens Africam Proprie dictum. Amst., [c.1600]. 345mm by 460mm. sg Feb 13 (55) $300

— Mercator, Gerard. - Taurica Chersones. Amst., [c.1630]. 320mm by 405mm, hand-colored in outline. Margins trimmed. sg Feb 13 (56) $200

— Mortier, Pieter. - In Notitiam Ecclesiasticam Africae. Amst., 1705. 395mm by 545mm, hand-colored. sg Feb 13 (68) $200

— Ortelius, Abraham. - Africae tabula nova.... Antwerp, 1570. 380mm by 500mm, hand-colored. Latin text on verso. Ck Oct 31 (182) £350

Anr copy. 370mm by 500mm, Two small worm holes repaired. Ck Oct 31 (184) £1,200

— Ortelius, Abraham. - Fessae, et Marocchi regna Africae celeberr. Antwerp, 1595. 38.6cm by 50.4cm cb Oct 10 (200) $150

— Ortelius, Abraham. - Presbiteri Johannis, sive Abissinorum imperii descriptio. Antwerp, [1572 or later]. 370mm by 430mm, hand-colored in outline, framed. Ck Oct 18 (76) £110

— Robert de Vaugondy, Gilles & Didier. - L'Afrique. Paris, 1756. 490mm by 630mm, hand-colored in outline. sg Sept 19 (107) $200

— Seutter, Matthaeus. - Africa. [Augsburg, c.1740]. 510mm by 590mm, handcolored, cartouche uncolored. cb Jan 30 (262) $200

— Speed, John. - Africae. L, 1626. 15 inches by 20 inches Soiled. English text on verso. DW Dec 11 (211) £260

Anr Ed. L, 1626 [but 1627]. 390mm by 510mm, hand-colored in outline, framed Foot of fold repaired. Ck May 15 (192) £420

Americas

— A Plan of the Battle on Bunkers Hill.... L: Sayer & Bennett, 27 Nov 1775. 600mm by 475mm, partly colored by a contemp hand. Some creasing & dust-staining. pn Mar 19 (429) £1,500 [Burgess]

— Allard, Karel. - Recentissima novi orbis, sive Americae septentrionalis et meridionalis tabula. [Amst., 1696, or later]. 500mm by 580mm, framed. Margins cropped; defs to lower border. pnL Nov 20 (29A) £240 [Spring]

— Bellin, Jacques Nicolas. - Carte de la Louisiane et des pays voisins. [Paris, 1750 but 1755]. 530mm by 935mm. Margins trimmed; lower margin cut close; corner mtd on verso to larger sheet. sg Feb 13 (4) $700

— Berry, William. - South America Divided into its Principal Parts.... L, 1680. 35 by 22.25 inches, hand-colored. wd June 12 (340) $350

— Blaeu, Willem & Jan. - Americae nova tabula. [Amst., c.1650]. 410mm by 550mm, hand-colored. No text on verso. Marginal repairs. S Nov 21 (313) £1,900 [Potter]

Anr Ed. [Amst., 1662]. 410mmm by 550mm, contemp hand-coloring. Fold worn & strengthened. S Nov 21 (314) £1,300 [Potter]

— Blaeu, Willem & Jan. - Mappa aestivarum insularum, alias Barmudas.... Amst., [c.1640 or later]. 400mm by 530mm, hand-colored in outline. Latin text on verso. Ck Oct 18 (42) £650

— Blaeu, Willem. - Nova Hispania et Nova

Gallica. [Amst., c.1663]. 380mm by 500mm, hand-colored. Browned; split at centerfold. pn Sept 12 (400) £150 [Orssich]

— BONNE, RIGOBERT. - Le Nouveau Mexique avec la Partie Septentrionale de l'Ancien ou de la Nouvelle Espagne. [Paris, c.1780]. 210mm by 320mm, later hand-coloring. cb Jan 30 (169) $200

— BRY, THEODOR DE. - America sive Novus Orbis.... [Frankfurt, 1596]. 330m by 395mm. Top margin cut to plate mark & remargined; 3 small holes at lower corners; browned. S June 25 (426) £1,800 [Map]

— BRY, THEODOR DE. - Chorographia nobilis & opulentae Peruanae Provinciae, atque Brasiliae, quas a decimo ad quintum & quinquagesimum ferre gradum ultra aequatorem in longitudinem patere.... Frankfurt, 1592. 360mm by 440mm. Repair at left side & at fold; some browning. S June 25 (443) £1,300 [Map]

— CHATELAIN, HENRI ABRAHAM. - Carte du Gouvernement de l'Amerique. [Amst., c.1708]. 131mm by 920mm, framed. cb Jan 30 (178) $400

— CHATELAIN, HENRI ABRAHAM. - Carte tres curieuse de la Mer du Sud. [Amst., c.1719]. 810mm by 1,400mm, in 4 sheets joined. With 2 small tears at folds. S Nov 21 (134) £4,000 [Ferguson]

— COVENS, JOHANNES & MORTIER, CORNELIS. - Archipelague du Mexique.... Amst., [after 1750]. 590mm by 990mm, hand-colored in outline. sg Sept 19 (34) $325

— COVENS, JOHANNES & MORTIER, CORNELIS. - Carte de la Louisiane, Maryland, Virginie.... Amst., 1758. 420mm by 590mm, hand-colored in outline. sg Sept 19 (35) $400

— COVENS, JOHANNES & MORTIER, CORNELIS. - Nouvelle Carte particuliere de l'Amerique.... Amst., [after 1757]. 605mm by 532mm, hand-colored in outline. Right margin trimmed to platemark. sg Sept 19 (36) $300

— DANET,GUILLAUME. - L'Amerique Meridionale et Septentrionale.... Paris, 1750. 482mm by 695mm, hand-colored in outline. Some foxing & soiling. cb Jan 30 (188) $1,600

— DELISLE, GUILLAUME. - L'Amerique Septentrionale. Paris, 1700. 452mm by 600mm, hand-colored in outline.. Some dampstaining & wrinkling; weak impression. sg Sept 19 (38) $500

— DUDLEY, SIR ROBERT. - Carta particolare della costa del Peru.... [Florence, 1661]. 14.4 by 18.75 inches. wd June 12 (346) $500

— DUDLEY, SIR ROBERT. - Carta particolare della Brasilia australe.... [Florence, 1661]. 14.7 by 18.5 inches. wd June 12 (347) $300

— EVANS, LEWIS & POWNALL, T. - A Map of the Middle British Colonies in North America. L, 1776. 510mm by 860mm, colony boundaries colored in green. Tear along 1 fold, mtd on cloth. C Oct 30 (150) £1,100 [Nat. Library of Wales]

— HOMANN HEIRS. - Domina Anglorum America Septentrionali. Nuremberg, [1760 or later]. 510mm by 560mm, hand-colored. Extraneous fold through portion of map; marginal tears; browning. sg Sept 19 (60) $275

— HOMANN, JOHANN BAPTIST. - Regni Mexicani seu Novae Hispaniae, Floridae, Novae Angliae.... Nuremberg, [c.1725]. 475mm by 565mm, contemp body color. Small hole in fold; staining to top & lower center. S Nov 15 (1214) £380 [Cousteau]

Anr copy. 495mm by 590mm, hand-colored in outline. Closed tear along vertical fold; mtd to stiff bd. sg Sept 19 (57) $650

— HOMANN, JOHANN BAPTIST. - Totius Americae Septentrionalis et Meridionalis. Nuremberg, [c.1700]. 484mm by 567mm, hand-colored. Repaired tears at lower central crease. cb Oct 10 (171) $900

Anr Ed. Nuremberg, [c.1720]. 19 by 22 inches, hand-colored. Reinforced at bottom; lower corner margin supplied. wa Nov 21 (5) $475

— HOMANN, JOHANN BAPTIST. - Virginia, Marylandia et Carolina in America Septentrionali. Nuremberg, [1714]. 20.7 by 24.5 inches, hand-colored. wd June 12 (349) $950

— JANSSONIUS, JOANNES. - America septentrionalis. Amst., [c.1645]. 465mm by 550mm, hand-colored in outline. Crease in center of map strengthened. S Nov 21 (316) £950 [Twaalfhoven]

— JANSSONIUS, JOANNES. - Nova Anglia Novum Belgium et Virginia. Amst., [c.1636]. 385mm by 500mm, contemp hand coloring. Slight cracking of green; repairs to upper & lower fold. S Feb 26 (668) £420 [Map House]

Anr Ed. Amst., [1650 or later]. 15 by 19.75 inches, contemp outline color & both cartouches with wash color. Framed. Some worm holes in margin. wa Nov 21 (115) $550

— JANSSONIUS, JOANNES. - Terra Firma et Novum Regnum Granatense et Popayan. Amst., [1660s]. 375mm by 480mm, hand-colored. pn Sept 12 (401) £240 [Rota]

— JANVIER, JEAN. - L'Amerique divisee en ses principaux etates.... Paris, 1762. 12 by 17.5 inches, orig wash color. Mtd. wa Nov 21 (6) $180

— LOTTER, CONRAD. - Recens Edita totius Novi Belgii.... Augsburg, [c.1730]. 500mm by 582mm, hand-colored. Some soiling to extremities; tear at bottom edge, just extending into image; some tears expertly closed on verso. sg Apr 2 (68) $1,600

— LOTTER, TOBIAS CONRAD. - Recens edita totius Novi Belgii in America Septentrionali. [Augsburg, c.1765]. 527mm by 615mm, partly hand-colored, framed. A few closed tears. P June 16 (250) $3,250

— MERCATOR, GERARD. - America sive India nova. Amst., [c.1620]. 375mm by 465mm, partly colored. French text on verso. sg Sept 19 (69) $1,900

— MOLL, HERMANN. - A Map of the West-Indies. L, [c.1720]. 590mm by 1,020mm, hand-colored in outline. Some repairs on verso; foxed & browned. sg Feb 13 (63) $650

— MORDEN, R. & MOLL, HERMANN. - The Seat of War in the West Indies. [L, c.1700]. 590mm by 990mm, laid down on card. Some soiling. Ck Oct 18 (111) £350

— MORTIER, PIETER. - L'Amerique septentrionale. Amst., [1708]. 17.5 by 22.7 inches, colored. Some fraying. wa Nov 21 (82) $550

— MOUNT & PAGE. - New and Correct Chart of the Sea Coast of New-England.... L, [1767?]. 18.7 by 45.7 inches. Some reinforcing on verso; soiled. wa Nov 21 (99) $425

— MUENSTER, SEBASTIAN. - Nie Neuwen Inseln so hinder Hispanien gegen Orient. Basel, [c.1540]. 255mm by 335mm. German text on verso. Some foxing. sg Sept 19 (86) $1,500

— MUNSTER, SEBASTIAN. - Americae sive orbis nova descriptio. [Basel, 1588]. 310mm by 360mm, hand-colored. Some staining & spotting. German text. S Nov 15 (1206) £400 [Achenbach]

— ORTELIUS, ABRAHAM. - Americae sive novi orbis, nova descriptio. [Antwerp, 1570 or later]. 360mm by 500mm, hand-colored, mtd. Ck May 15 (188) £1,300

Anr Ed. [Antwerp, 1587 or later]. State 3. 355mm by 485mm, Contemp hand-coloring. Slight worming at lower fold. S Feb 26 (614) £1,000 [Broecke]

— ORTELIUS, ABRAHAM. - Americiae sive Novi Orbis... Antwerp, [1570 or later]. 370mm by 510mm, hand-colored. Latin text on verso. Some repairs; soiled. Ck Oct 18 (75) £850

— ORTELIUS, ABRAHAM. - Culiacanae, Americae regionis, descriptio; Hispaniolae, Cubae.... [Antwerp, c.1570]. 355mm by 500mm, hand-colored. Latin text on verso. Some browning. pn Nov 14 (537) £190 [Map House]

— ORTELIUS, ABRAHAM. - Peruuiae Auriferae Regionis Typus La Florida Guastecan. Antwerp, 1584 or later. 330mm by 462mm, hand-colored. Latin text on verso. sg Sept 19 (95) $950

— OTTENS, REGNER & JOSUE. - Nieuwe Kaart van het Eyland St. Eustatius. Amst., 1775. 390mm by 500mm, hand-colored in outline. sg Sept 19 (98) $950

— RENARD, LOUIS. - Pascaert van Westindien end Caribisch Eylanden.... Amst., [1715]. 483mm by 560mm, contemp body color. S June 25 (442) £1,600 [Arader]

— ROBERT DE VAUGONDY. - Carte de la Californie et des Pays Nord Ouest. Paris, [c.1780]. 293mm by 367mm. cb Jan 30 (195) $475

Anr copy. 323mm by 400mm. Left margin trimmed to platemark; browned; marginal tears. sg Sept 19 (18) $150

— SANSON D'ABBEVILLE, NICOLAS. - Amerique septentrionale.... L, 1692. 570mm by 840mm, hand-colored in outline. Some tears along folds with occasional loss. Ck Oct 31 (185) £450

— SAYER, ROBERT. - Couse of the River Mississippi.... L, 1 June 1775. 2 sheets joined, 1145mm by 368mm, partly hand-colored in outline; framed. P June 16 (283) $600

— SENEX, JOHN. - North America, Corrected from the Observations Communicated to the Royal Society at London.... L, 1710. 95cm by 66.5cm. Left margin scorched with small tears, split starting at central creases. cb Oct 10 (217) $425

— SEUTTER, MATTHIAS. - Recens Edita totius Novi Belgii.... Augsburg, [c.1730]. 500mm by 580mm, hand-colored. State 2. S June 25 (429) £2,000 [Franks]

— SMITH, CAPT. JOHN. - New England. L, [1631]. State 7. 355mm by 830mm. Some stains & browning; tear at fold barely affecting surface. S Nov 21 (315) £4,600 [Tooley Adams]

— SPEED, JOHN. - A Map of Jamaica and Barbados. [L, 1676]. Size not given, hand-colored. Fold repair. wd June 12 (359) $600

— THORNTON, J. - Virginia, Maryland, Pennsilvania, East and West New Jarsey. L, 1689. 2 sheets joined, 510mm by 805mm, hand-colored. Small tears at folds. S Nov 21 (317) £1,800 [Voorhees]

— VAN LANGEREN, A. - Delineatio omnium orarum totius australis partis Americae. [Amst., c.1600]. 385mm by 545mm. Some fold-strengthening; margins trimmed. S Nov 15 (1001) £1,100 [Map House]

— VISSCHER, NIKOLAUS JANSSON. - Jamaica, Americae Septentrionalis ampla insula. Amst., [1680?]. 515mm by 595mm, hand-colored in outline. Minor browning overall. sg Sept 19 (147) $200

— VISSCHER, NIKOLAUS JANSSON. - Nova Tabula Geographica complectens Borealiorem AMericae partem.... Amst.: Schenk, [1718 or later]. 590mm by 470mm, hand-colored in outline. Some repairs along horizontal fold with loss. Ck Oct 31 (186) £300

— WIT, FREDERICK DE. - Septentrionaliora Americae a Groenlandia.... [Amst., 1675 or later]. 498mm by 576mm. Chip in upper margin extends into image. sg Sept 19 (153) $110

— ZATTA, ANTONIO. - Messico ovvero Nuova Spagna. Venice, 1785. 325mm by 415mm, hand-colored in outline. Some browning along fold. sg Sept 19 (154) $110

— ZUERNER, A. F. - Americae tam septentrionalis quam meridionalis...delineatio. Amst.: P. Schenk, [1700 or later]. 498mm by 575mm, contemp body color; repair to fold. S June 25 (427) £800 [Arader]

Asia

— BAGAY, NICOLAS DE LA CRUZ. - Iaponia. [Manila, c.1735?]. 217mm by 277mm, on native paper. Repaired tears. S Nov 21 (353) £3,000 [Walter]

— BELLIN, JACQUES NICOLAS. - Plan du port et de la ville Nangasaki. [Paris, 1750]. 230mm by 365mm, hand-colored. sg Feb 13 (47) $200

— BLAEU, WILLEM & JAN. - Cyprus insula. [Amst., 1663]. 380mm by 495mm. S June 30 (3) £520 [Map House]

— BLAEU, WILLEM & JAN. - Natolia quae olim Asia Minor. [Amst., 1635]. 390mm by 505mm, hand-colored in outline. German text on verso. Some browning. sg Feb 13 (5) $225

— BOWLES, CARINGTON. - New and Accurate Map of Asia. L, [1789]. 4 sheets joined as 2, 995mm by 1,140mm, contemp outline color. S Feb 26 (616) £250 [R. S. Books]

— CASSINI, G. M. - Le Isole del Giappone e La Corea. Rome, [1797]. 345mm by 475mm, contemp hand-coloring. S Feb 11 (655) £500 [Tooley Adams]

— CORONELLI, V. M. - Royaume de Siam.... Paris, 1742. 615mm by 450mm, hand-colored. pn Nov 14 (561) £460 [Potter]

— CORONELLI, VICENZO MARIA. - Isole dell'Indie, divise in Filippine, Molucche, e della Sonda. Venice, [1696]. 475mm by 615mm. Margins trimmed; hole in image; minor browning & offsetting along vertical fold. sg Feb 13 (12) $550

— DE LISLE, GUILLAUME. - Carte de Perse. Amst.: Covens & Mortier, [before 1759]. 510mm by 615mm, colored in outline. Minor soiling & browning, mainly to margins. sg Apr 2 (44) $130

— DE WIT, FREDERICK. - Noordoost Cust van Asia van Iapan tot Nova Zemla. [Amst., c.1670 or later]. 445mm by 545mm cb Jan 30 (199) $700

— DUDLEY, SIR ROBERT. - Carta particolare della Grande Isola del'Giapone e di Iezo.... [Florence, c.1647]. 485mm by 745mm. Small centerfold repair. pn Nov 14 (557) £300

Anr copy. 480mm by 745mm. Browned at fold; marginal spotting. S Nov 15 (1280) £170 [R. S. Books]

— HARENBURG, J. C. - Palestina. Nuremberg, 1750. 505mm by 570mm, hand-colored. Some soiling. sg Apr 2 (55) $225

— HOMANN, JOHANN BAPTIST. - Judaea seu Palaestina.... Nuremberg, [c.1720]. 485mm by 561mm, hand-colored cb Oct 10 (169) $225

Anr copy. 490mm by 565mm, hand-colored. Some dampstaining in lower margin, just entering platemark. sg Feb 13 (41) $400

— HONDIUS, HENRICUS & JANSSON, J. - Asia, recens summa cura delineata. Amst., [1633]. 370mm by 590mm, hand-colored. French text on verso. Ck May 15 (218) £260

— HONDIUS, JODOCUS. - Asiae nova descriptio. [Amst., c.1610]. 373mm by 500mm, colored by a contemp hand. Centerfold repaired. pn Nov 14 (550) £320

— JANSSONIUS JOANNES. - Tartaria, sive Magni Chami Imperium. Antwerp, [1570 or later]. 352mm by 472mm., hand-colored & heightened with gold. Repaired along vertical fold in lower part of image. sg Sept 19 (97) $400

— KAEMPFER, ENGELBERT. - The Empire of Japan. L, 1794. 480mm by 635mm, hand-colored in outline. S Feb 26 (656) £380 [Map House]

— LOWITZ, G. M. - Carte Hydrographique & Chorographique des Isles Philippines. Nuremberg: Homann's Heirs, 1760 [or later]. 950mm by 540mm, hand-colored. Margins trimmed; some use of pen facsimile. pn Nov 14 (562) £170 [Map House]

— MUENSTER, SEBASTIAN. - Secunda Asie Tabula. Basel, 1540. 420mm by 540mm. Washed; closed tears & paper-loss repairs in upper margin, affecting legend. sg Feb 13 (76) $225

— MUENSTER, SEBASTIAN. - Tabula I Asiae. [Basel, 1540]. 375mm by 535mm. Browned; marginal tape repairs on verso. sg Feb 13 (78) $550

— MUENSTER, SEBASTIAN. - Undecima Asiae Tabula. Basel, 1540. 443mm by 580mm. Washed. sg Feb 13 (79) $275

— NOLIN, JEAN BAPTISTE. - La Terre Sainte.... Paris, 17700. 975mm by 1,220mm, 4 sheets joined, laid down & backed on linen. S July 1 (817) £3,000

— ORTELIUS, ABRAHAM. - Asiae nova descriptio. [Antwerp, 1570 or later]. 370mm by 500mm, hand-colored. Latin text on verso. Some repairs; soiled. Ck Oct 18 (74) £400

Anr Ed. [Antwerp, c.1570]. 370mm by

500mm, hand-colored. Latin text on verso. Ck Oct 31 (183) £650

Anr Ed. [Antwerp, 1570 or later]. 370mm by 500mm, hand-colored. Small stain in bottom of image; tear closed on verso. Latin text on verso. sg Feb 13 (85) $650

— ORTELIUS, ABRAHAM. - Cypri Insulae nova descriptio. Antwerp, [c.1575]. 380mm by 495mm, hand-colored. Latin text on verso. S June 30 (4) £350 [Severis]

Anr Ed. [Antwerp, 1598]. 350mm by 495mm. Dutch text on verso. Small crease at fold. S June 30 (1) £320 [Jeveris]

— OTTENS, REGNER & JOSUE. - Partie de la nouvelle grande carte des Indes Orientales. Amst., [c.1735]. 4 sheets joined, 955mm by 1,185mm, contemp hand-coloring. S June 25 (457) £1,600 [Barberini]

— PTOLEMAEUS, CLAUDIUS. - Sexta Asie tabula. [Venice: J. Pentius de Leucho, 1511]. 335mm by 520mm. S July 1 (814) £380 [Folios]

— ROBERT DE VAUGONDY, GILLES & DIDIER. - Carte de l'Asie. Paris, 1750. 495mm by 543mm, hand-colored in outline. sg Feb 13 (91) $300

— ROBERT DE VAUGONDY, G. & D. - L'Empire du Japon. [Paris], 1750. Size not given,. colored in outline. Framed. L Nov 14 (358) $600

Anr copy. 490mm by 557mm, hand-colored in outline. sg Sept 19 (111) $500

— SENEX, JOHN. - A New Map of Asia. L, [1719]. 540mm by 640mm, hand-colored. Ck May 15 (227) £220

— SEUTTER, MATTHEW. - Prospectus Sanctae olim et celeberrimae Urbis Hierosolynae. Augsburg, [c.1734]. 490mm by 570mm, contemp hand-coloring. S Feb 11 (657) £480 [Tooley Adams]

— SPEED, JOHN. - The Kingdom of Persia.... L: Bassett & Chiswell, [1676]. 400mm by 515mm, hand-colored in outline, with border vignettes fully colored. Some staining to margin remnants; minor tears closed; mtd to stiff cardbd. sg Sept 19 (130) $200

— SPEED, JOHN. - Oxfordshire.... L: G. Humble, 1626 [but 1627, or later]. 380mm by 510mm, hand-colored in outline, framed. Ck May 15 (193) £340

Anr Ed. L: G. Humble, 1610 [but 1646]. 384mm by 522mm, partly colored. Some dampstaining & soiling. pn Apr 23 (341) £330 [Map House]

Anr Ed. L: Bassett & Chiswell, [1676]. 380mm by 510mm, hand-colored in outline, framed. Ck May 15 (201) £180

— VAN LANGREN, A. F. - Exacta & accurata delineatio cum orarum maritimorum tum etiam locorum terrestrium...China, Cauchinchina.... [Amst., 1595 or later]. 385mm by 530mm, hand-colored. Framed. Cut close with some loss of surface at top & bottom. S Nov 15 (995) £1,200 [Potter]

Australasia

— Laurie and Whittle's New Chart of the Indian and Pacific Oceans between the cape of Good Hope, New Holland and Japan. L, 2 Jan 1797. 735mm by 1,080mm, hand-colored, framed. Repairs at folds & margins. C June 25 (142) £1,000 [Hassan]

— BOWEN, THOMAS. - A New & Accurate Chart of the Discoveries Made by the Late Capt. James Cook...Exhibiting Botany Bay with the Whole Coast of New South Wales.... L, [c.1780]. 440mm by 380mm. Repaired at central crease. cb Oct 10 (131) $160

— CORONELLI, VINCENZO MARIA. - [Australia and Southeast Asia]. [Venice, c.1691]. 610mm by 450mm, framed. C June 25 (22) £700 [Notaros]

— DE WIT, FREDERICK. - Orientalior Indiarum Orientalium cum Insulis Adjacentibus.... [Amst., 1675 or later]. 440mm by 540mm, contemp hand coloring, framed. S June 25 (20) £1,300 [Doelman]

— LESEUR, C. A. - Plan de la Ville de Sydney.... [Paris, 1812]. 340mm by 480mm, coastline outlined in color, framed. C June 25 (176) £450 [Graham]

— THEVENOT, MELCHISEDEC. - Hollandia Nova detecta 1644.... [N.p., 1663-72]. 370mm by 510mm, framed. Repaired tear at left. C June 25 (19) £1,700 [Stokes]

— ZATTA, ANTONIO,. - La Nuova Zelanda.... Venice, 1778. 12.5 by 16.75 inches, hand-colored in outline. Some worming to lower margin. wa Nov 21 (122) $140

Canada

— JEFFERYS, THOMAS. - An Exact Chart of the River St. Laurence.... L, 1775. 24 by 38 inches, colored in outline. Some browning in fold; marginal tears repaired. wa Nov 21 (79) $210

Celestial

— BACKER, REMMET THEUNISSE. - Sterre Kaert of Hemels Pleyn. Amst., [c.1720]. 475mm by 585mm, hand-colored. Marginal repairs. S June 25 (343) £500 [Arader]

— SCHENK, PIETER. - Planisphaerium Coeleste. Amst., [1690]. 485mm by 555mm, hand-colored. Lower margins close-cut. S Feb 11 (629) £480 [L. C. Lih]

Europe

— BEAULIEU, SEBASTIAN DE PONTAULT. - Plan de l'isle de Candie jadis crete. Paris, [1674]. 442mm by 530mm, framed. S July 1 (476) £440 [Spink]

— BERTELLI, FERANDO. - Malta. [Rome,

c.1560]. 255mm by 188mm, hand-colored. Cut to platemark. S July 1 (494) £420 [Ganado]

— BERTELLI, FERDINAND. - Totius Graeciae Descriptio.... Venice, [1564]. 390mm by 620mm, 2 sheets joined. Stained. S Nov 21 (230) £1,500 [Lepanto]

— BLAEU, WILLEM & JAN. - Brandenburgum Marchionatus, cum Ducatibus Pomeraniae et Mekelenburgi. Amst., [1640]. 15.5 by 20.7 inches, contemp hand coloring. wa Mar 5 (445) $375

— BLAEU, WILLEM & JAN. - Lacus Lemanni locorumque circumiacentium. [Amst., c.1635]. 40.7 by 51.7cm, hand-colored.. French text on verso. cb Oct 10 (122) $250

Anr copy. 407mm by 517mm. cb Jan 30 (163) $225

— BLAEU, WILLEM & JAN. - Magnus Ducatus Finlandiae. [Amst., 1663]. 434mm by 530mm, hand-colored. Spanish text on verso. pn Nov 14 (517) £260 [Tooley Adams]

— BLAEU, WILLEM & JAN. - Tabula Islandiae. [Amst., 1631]. 375mm by 490mm, hand-colored. French text on verso. Tears & repairs. pn Apr 23 (348) £180

— BOWLES, JOHN. - Map of the Kingdom of Poland and the Grand Dutchy of Lithuania. L, [c.1760]. 485mm by 555mm, hand-colored in outline. sg Sept 19 (14) $200

— BRAUN, GEORG & HOGENBERG, FRANZ. - Barcelona; Ectia. [Cologne, c.1590]. 325mm by 470mm, contemp hand-coloring. Some cracking of green; slight wear to fold. S May 14 (1174) £150 [Delstres]

— BRAUN, GEORG & HOGENBERG, FRANZ. - Sevilla. [Cologne, c.1590]. 355mm by 480mm, contemp hand-coloring. Some wear & discoloration at fold; marginal soiling. S May 14 (1187) £220 [Pulido]

— CORONELLI, VINCENZO MARIA. - Golfo della Prevesa. Venice, [1696]. 450mm by 605mm. S July 1 (503) £240 [Spink]

— CORONELLI, VINCENZO MARIA. - Isola di Corfu. Venice, [c.1690]. 460mm by 610mm. Small tear to upper fold. S July 1 (473) £580 [Map House]

— CORONELLI,VINCENZO MARIA. - Isola e Regno di Candia. Venice, [1690]. 2 double-page mapsheets, 450mm by 1,200mm. Crack in plate of left-hand sheet. S July 1 (478) £1,300 [Dimakarakas]

— CRISPI, GIAMBATTISTA & AELST, NICOLAS VAN. - Afedelis sima citta di Gallipoli. Rome, [1591]. 380mm by 520mm. Margins cut close, just affecting surface; 1 small hole. S July 1 (506) £1,000 [Franks]

— DE JODE, CORNELIS. - Videbus totius Graeciae limites divisos per montes.... [Antwerp, 1593]. 385mmby 510mm, framed. S July 1 (488) £2,200 [Franks]

— DE JODE, GERARD & CORNELIS. - Helvetia seu Suiciae quae Multis Confoederatorum Terra.... [Antwerp, c.1593]. 385mm by 517mm. Lower margin trimmed to just inside neatline; some chips & tears; a few old repairs on verso. cb Jan 30 (189) $600

— DE JODE, GERARD. - Saxonum regionis... delineatio. [Antwerp,, 1578]. 330mm by 445mm. S May 14 (1186) £220 [Nolan]

— DE WIT, FREDERICK. - Insula sive Regnum Siciliae. Amst., [c.1680]. 495mm by 585mm, hand-colored in outline. Margins trimmed close. sg Feb 13 (16) $450

— DE WIT, FREDERICK. - Regnum Neapolis. Amst.: Covens & Mortier, [c.1725]. 590mm by 490mm, partially hand-colored, framed. sg Feb 13 (17) $120

— DELAPOINTE, F. - Aspect ou profil oriental de la grande et petite citte de Basle.... Paris, [c.1750]. 255mm by 770mm. Some worming at fold. S May 14 (1176) £200 [Tooley Adams]

— DELAPOINTE, F. - Nouvelle description de la fameuse ville de Barcelone. Paris, [c.1750]. 280mm by 720mm, browned & frayed. Tear to fold with loss. S May 14 (1175) £260 [Delstres]

— DELISLE, GUILLAUME. - L'Italie. Amst.: Covens & Mortier, [after 1757]. 505mm by 600mm, hand-colored in outline. sg Sept 19 (48) $275

— DU VAL, PIERRE. - Candie; Isle de Candie. Paris, [1667]. 510mm by 390mm. Marginal tear. S July 1 (480) £350 [Caramondanis]

— DU VAL, PIERRE. - Romanum Imperium. [Amst., c.1689]. 450mm by 535mm, hand-colored in outline, framed. S July 9 (1429) £240 [Potter]

— ELWE, JAN BAREND. - La Pologne. Amst., [c.1790]. 500mm by 610mm, hand-colored. sg Feb 13 (21) $225

— FINCKH, GEORG PHILIPP. - S. Rom. Imperii Circuli et Electoratus Bavariae Tabula Chorographia.... Munich, 1671. 1,211mm by 910mm, dissected into 28 sections, hand-colored to show boundaries, folded into contemp calf slipcase. S Nov 21 (149) £750 [Kiefer]

— HOELTZL, ABRAHAM. - Tabula Geographica Ducatus Wuertembergensis. [Before 1628]. 4 sheets jointed, 610mm by 630mm. Extensive loss to lower left corner; lesser damage elsewhere. S Nov 21 (147) £750 [Kiefer]

— HOMANN HEIRS. - Bosphorus Thraciscus. Nuremberg, [1764]. 790mm by 500mm, contemp hand-coloring. S July 1 (453) £300 [Map House]

— HOMANN, JOHANN BAPTIST. - Belgii pars septentrionalis communi nomine vulgo Hollandia. Nuremberg, [c.1720]. 495mm by 575mm, hand-colored, mtd to bd. Some browning along vertical fold. sg Feb 13 (40) $300

— HOMANN, JOHANN BAPTIST. - Insularum Maltae et Gozae. Nuremberg, [c.1730, or later]. 19 by 23 inches, contemp part-coloring. Small worm-hole at head; browned along centerfold. DW May 13 (170) £380

— HOMANN, JOHANN BAPTIST. - Prospect und Grund-riss der Kayserl. Residenz-Stadt Wien. Nuremberg, [1712-30]. 485mm by 575mm, contemp hand-coloring. Small tear & browning & fold; staining to top & lower center. S Nov 15 (1068) £480 [Quaritch]

— HOMANN, JOHANN BAPTIST. - Regni Hungariae. Nuremberg, [c.1730]. 495mm by 580mm, hand-colored. Margins trimmed to platemark. sg Feb 13 (42) $100

— HONDIUS, JODOCUS, THE YOUNGER. - Nova Helvetiae tabula. Amst.: [J. Janssonius, 1621, but 1630]. 406mm by 524mm. Some wear, tears & chipping to edges; old paper reinforcements. cb Oct 10 (175) $325

— HURTER, JOHANN CHRISTOPH. - Geographica provinciarum Sveviae descriptio. Augsburg, [c.1670?]. Index map & 28 map sections, if joined c.1,080mm by 900mm, folded into contemp vellum slipcase. S Nov 21 (148) £1,150 [Kiefer]

— JANSONNIUS, JOANNES. - Pascaart vande Noort-Zee. Amst., [1650] or later. 432mm by 546mm, hand-colored. Latin text on verso. Small portion of top right sea area supplied in pen facsimile. pn Nov 14 (520) £200

— JODE, GERARD DE. - Natoliam modern dicunt. [Antwerp, 1593]. 385mm by 510mm. Some marginal staining. Latin text on verso. S July 1 (452) £850 [Franks]

— JOLIVET, JEAN. - Galliae regni. Antwerp: Ortelius, [c.1570]. 350mm by 500mm. sg Feb 13 (48) $250

— LAURENBERG, J. - Peloponneso, hoggidi Morea. [Paris, 1656]. 445mm by 605mm. Stained at lower corners. S July 1 (498) £280 [Map House]

— LAURO, JACOMO. - Citta vechia di Malta. [Rome, 1635]. 575mm by 235mm. S July 1 (493) £420

— LOSI, CARLO. - Nuova Pianta di Roma.... Rome, 1773. 9 sheets, mtd on linen, dissected & folding, over-all size 130cm by 110cm. Some discoloration; stained on lower left corner; several small tears repaired on verso. C May 20 (273) £900 [Bifolco]

— MALLET, S. H. - Carte de la Suisse Romande.... [N.p.], 1781. 1,360mm by 1,060mm, on 4 sheets. Partially hand-colored. Some soiling. cb Jan 30 (234) $375

— MERCATOR, GERARD. - Bohemia. Amst., [c.1630]. 350mm by 495mm, hand-colored in outline. Some soiling. sg Feb 13 (52) $200

— MERCATOR, GERARD. - Helvetia cum finitimis regionibus confederatis. [Amst., c.1610]. 350mm by 467mm. Torn and chipped. cb Jan 30 (238) $250

— MORTIER, PIETER. - Germano-Sarmatia. Amst., 1705. 400mm by 550mm, hand-colored. sg Feb 13 (66) $200

— MORTIER, PIETER. - Illyricum Occidentis. Amst., 1705. 420mm by 525mm, hand-colored. sg Feb 13 (67) $150

— MOUNT, WILLIAM & PAGE, THOMAS. - A Correct Chart of the Mediterranean Sea form the Coast of Portugal to the Levant. [N.p., c.1740]. 470mm by 1,150mm, 2 sheets joined. Folds strengthened. S July 1 (497) £250 [Orssich]

— NOLIN, JEAN BAPTISTE. - Le Canal Royal de Languedoc.... Paris, [1697]. 3 sheets joined, 585mm by 1,420mm, hand-colored. Cut close at upper left; small repaired tear; some browning at fold. S June 25 (307) £720 [San Lorenzo]

— ORTELIUS, ABRAHAM. - Europae. [Antwerp, 1570 or later]. 340mm by 570mm. Latin text on verso. Some repairs on verso. Ck Oct 18 (73) £140

— ORTELIUS, ABRAHAM. - Graeciae Universae secundum hodiernum.... [Antwerp, 1598]. 360mm by 510mm. Dutch text. Minor worming. S July 1 (485) £350 [Caramondanis]

— ORTELIUS, ABRAHAM. - Islandia. [Antwerp, 1589 or later]. 335mm by 490mm, hand-colored. Some browning. Latin text on verso. S June 25 (477) £2,000 [Map]

— ORTELIUS, ABRAHAM. - Italiae novissima descriptio.... Amst., [1570 or later]. 360mm by 510mm, hand-colored. Latin text on verso. Small stain on image. sg Feb 13 (86) $650

— ORTELIUS, ABRAHAM. - Regni Neapolitani. Amst., [1570 or later]. 365mm by 500mm, hand-colored. Latin text on verso. sg Feb 13 (87) $275

— ORTELIUS, ABRAHAM. - Romani Imperii, imago. Antwerp, [1580 or later]. 353mm by 508mm. sg Sept 19 (96) $275

— ORTELIUS, ABRAHAM. - Turonensis ducatus. Amst., 1592. 360mm by 460mm, hand-colored. Tear in image; browned. sg Feb 13 (88) $110

— ORTELIUS, ABRAHAM. - Valentiae regni. Amst., 1584. 345mm by 490mm, hand-colored. Latin text on verso. sg Feb 13 (89) $250

— PALMA, GAETANO. - Carte de la plus grande partie de la Turquie d'Europe. Trieste, 1811. 2 sheets joined, dissected & backed on linen, 735mm, by 1,060mm, hand-colored in outline, folding into contemp slipcase with Napoleonic crest at center & bees at corners. S June 30 (370) £480 [Atabey]

— PTOLEMAEUS, CLAUDIUS. - Tabula Neoterica Crete sive Candie insule. Strassburg: Jacob Eszler & Georgius Ubelin, 1513. 15 by 21 inches, hand-colored. Strengthened along fold; pin holes throughout. wd June 12 (360) $950

— RENARD, LOUIS. - Totius Europae littora novissime edita. Amst., [1715]. 705mm by 875mm, contemp hand-color. Fold repaired. S June 25 (305) £2,000 [Rieden]

— ROBERT DE VAUGONDY, GILLES & DIDIER. - Graecia Vetus. Paris, [after 1750]. 490mm by 555mm, hand-colored in outline. Some small stains. sg Sept 19 (103) $200

— ROBERT DE VAUGONDY, GILLES & DIDIER. - Le Royaume de Pologne. Paris, 1752. 485mm by 545mm, hand-colored in outline. Some browning along vertical fold. sg Feb 13 (92) $130

— ROSSI, G. G. - La Morea. Rome, [1686]. 420mm by 550mm, framed. Some repairs. S July 1 (499) £300 [Apostolakis]

— SAMBUCUS, JOANNES. - Transilvania. Vienna, 1566. 325mm by 450mm. Latin text on verso Small stains on image; minor wrinkling & soiling. sg Feb 13 (93) $200

— SANSON D'ABBEVILLE, NICOLAS. - Isle et Royaume de Sicile. Paris, 1663. 395mm by 575mm, hand-colored in outline. sg Feb 13 (95) $150

— SANSON D'ABBEVILLE, NICOLAS. - Romani Imperii qua oriens est descriptio geographica. Padua, 1696. 410mm by 550mm, hand-colored in outline. Repair in lower margin at fold. sg Feb 13 (97) $100

— SENEX, JOHN. - A New Map of Europe. L, [c1720]. 500mm by 598mm, hand-colored in outline. Some browning; mtd to stiff bd; closed tear along vertical fold. sg Sept 19 (124) $275

— SEUTTER, MATTHEW. - Barcino. Augsburg, [c.1730]. 490mm by 570mm, contemp coloring. S May 14 (1173) £480 [Delstres]

— SPEED, JOHN. - Greece. L: Bassett & Chiswell, 1676. 385mm by 495mm. Some worming & discoloration at fold. S July 1 (489) £150 [Dimakarakos]

— VISSCHER, NICOLAUS. - Novissima et Accuratissima Totius Americae Descriptio. [Amst., 1680 or later]. 480mm by 580mm, hand-colored, framed. Some browning. Ck Oct 18 (104) £650

— WAGHENAER, LUCAS JANSZ. - Beschrijvinge vande vermaerde stromen Tvlie ende t'Maersdiep.... [Leiden], 1583 [but 1586]. 355mm by 515mm. Margins cropped; some soiling. S Nov 15 (923) £150 [Potter]

Great Britain

— A Balloon View of London as seen from Hampstead. L, 1851. 680mm by 1,110mm, hand-colored, linen-backed. Some short tears to linen between several sections; folded into def contemp cloth folder. sg Feb 13 (50) $550

— BERRY, WILLIAM & HOLLAR, WENZEL. - A New Mapp of the Kingdome of England and Principalitie of Wales. L, [1673]. 3 sections joined, 616mm by 790mm, place names underlined in color. Trimmed to plate mark & remargined. Some fold strengthening. S June 25 (259) £3,000 [Burden]

— BICKHAM, G. - A Map of Surrey. West from London. L, [1751]. 255mm by 140mm, hand-colored. S Nov 15 (992) £160 [R. W. Lewis]

— BLAEU, WILLEM & JAN. - Cestria Comitatus Palatinus. [Amst., 1663]. 382mm by 500mm, hand-colored. pn Nov 14 (467) £150 [Vanbrugh]

— BLAEU, WILLEM & JAN. - Darbiensis comitatus, vernacule Darbie Shire. [Amst., 1663]. 382mm by 502mm, hand colored. French text on verso. Hole to left margin touching surface. pn Nov 14 (468) £130 [Potter]

— BLAEU, WILLEM & JAN. - Devonia, vulgo Devon-Shire. [Amst., 1648]. 405mm by 512mm, hand-colored in outline, decorations fully colored. Framed & mtd, glazed on both sides. L Nov 14 (172) £190

— BLAEU, WILLEM & JAN. - Gloucestria Ducatus, vulgo Glocester Shire. [Amst., 1663]. 500mm by 410mm, hand-colored title & decorations. DW Oct 2 (179) £195

— BLAEU, WILLEM. - Hertfordia comitatus. [Amst., 1663]. 380mm by 500mm, hand-colored. French text on verso. Marginal dampstaining & spotting. pn Nov 14 (472) £160 [Map House]

— BLAEU, WILLEM & JAN. - Magnae Britanniae et Hiberniae Tabula. Amst., [1630]. 385mm by 500mm, Hand-colored. Marginal dampstains. pn Nov 14 (453) £150 [Vanbrugh]

— BLAEU, WILLEM & JAN. - Middle-sexia. [Amst., 1648]. 380mm by 403mm. Hand-colored arms & cartouche. Marginal dampstains. cb Oct 10 (128) $300

Anr Ed. [Amst., 1663]. 390mm by 405mm, hand-colored. French text on verso. pn Nov 14 (482) £120 [Vanbrugh]

— BLAEU, WILLEM & JAN. - Oxonium comitatus, vulgo Oxfordshyre. [L, c.1607]. 270mm by 287mm. Matted, framed & glazed.. Dampstains to lower margin just intruding on image. cb Jan 30 (253) $130

— BLAEU, WILLEM & JAN. - Oxonium comitatus, vulgo Oxford Shire. [Amst., 1645]. 15 by 20 inches, hand-colored. French text on verso. DW May 13 (145) £190

Anr copy. Contemp hand-coloring.. Marginal browning. S Nov 15 (946) £300 [Marlborough]

— BLAEU, WILLEM & JAN. - Staffordiensis comitatus; vulgo Stafford Shire. [Amst., 1663]. 410mm by 500mm, hand-colored. French text on verso. pn Nov 14 (497) £100 [Vanburgh]

— BLAEU, WILLEM & JAN. - Wigorniensis comitatus et comitatus Warwicensis... Worcester, Warwik Shire.... [Amst., 1645]. 410mm by 500mm, hand-colored. French text on verso. pn Nov 14 (508) £120 [Vanburgh]

— BLAEU, WILLEM. - Wiltonia, sive comitatus Wiltoniensis.... [Amst., 1648]. 413mm by 500mm, hand-colored. French text on verso. pn Nov 14 (506) £220

— BOWEN, EMANUEL. - An Accurate Map of the County of Essex. L, [c.1760]. 530mm by 710mm, hand-colored in outline. Some browning. pn Dec 12 (410) £140 [Potter]

Anr copy. 515mm by 695mm, hand-colored in outline. pn Dec 12 (412) £140 [Potter]

— BOWLES, THOMAS. - A Mapp containing the Townes, Villages, Gentlemens Houses...for 20 miles round London. L, 1730. 510mm by 545mm, hand-colored in outline. S May 14 (1110) £200 [Tooley Adams]

— BRAUN, GEORG & HOGENBERG, FRANZ. - Brightstowe. Cologne, [1581 or later]. 340mm by 440mm, fully hand-colored. Centerfold tape-strengthened. Latin text on verso. DW Oct 2 (183) £200

— BRAUN, GEORG & HOGENBERG, FRANZ. - Londinum feracissimi Angliae Regni metropolis. [Cologne, 1572, but 1574 or later]. 325mm by 480mm, hand-colored.. Some repairs to centerfold & margins supplied in pen facsimile. pn Dec 12 (411) £150

Anr Ed. Cologne, 1572 [but 1575 or later]. 330mm by 480mm, hand-colored. French text on verso. Ck Oct 18 (107) £800

— BRYANT, A. - Map of the County of Surrey... L, 1823. 4 sheets joined, 1,290mm by 1,570mm, hand-colored & backed with fine tissue. Some repaired tears, affecting surface. S Feb 26 (689) £200 [Al Fieri]

— BRYANT, A. - Map of the County of Norfolk. L, 1826. 6 sheets joined as 2, dissected in 72 sections & backed on linen, totalling 2,275mm by 1,495mm, folding into 4to calf case; rubbed. Contemp hand-coloring. S Nov 15 (985) £220 [Woodruff]

— BRYANT, A. - Map of the County of Lincoln.... L, 1828. 8 sheets joined as 2, dissected & mtd on linen, each sheet 1,050mm by 1,605mm, folding into orig calf case Hand-colored. S Nov 15 (979) £150 [Oldfield]

— DE JODE, G. - Angliae, Scotiae, et Hiberniae.... [Antwerp, 1593]. 345mm by 495mm, contemp hand-coloring. Some surface soiling. S May 14 (1093) £800 [Lundy]

— FADEN, W. - Hampshire, or the County of Southampton.... L, 1791-96. 6 sheets dissected into 36 sections, 1,480mm by 1,405mm, folding into contemp calf case; worn. With contemp hand-coloring. Some browning. S Nov 15 (974) £190 [Tooley Adams]

— GREENWOOD, C. & J. - Map of the County of Dorset. L, 1826. 1,200mm by 1,570mm. Hand-colored in outline. Ck July 10 (341) £180

Anr copy. 1,150mm by 1,555mm. Dissected into 48 sections & backed on linen & folded into 4to, contemp mor case. With contemp hand-coloring. S Nov 15 (970) £150 [Blackwell]

— GREENWOOD, CHRISTOPHER & JOHN. - Map of London. L, 1830. 1,280mm by 1,980mm, hand-colored, mtd on cloth, folded into mor slipcase C Oct 30 (103) £650 [Marlborough]

— GREENWOOD, CHARLES. - Map of the County of York. L, [1817]. 3 parts, each part c.182cm by 72cm, mtd on linen & folded into contemp calf book box pnL Nov 20 (35) £200 [Bates]

— HOMANN, JOHANN BAPTIST. - Regionis circa London. L, 1741. 20 by 23 inches contemp coloring.. Closely trimmed. DW May 13 (167) £105

— HOMANN'S HEIRS. - Urbium Londini et West-Monasterii nec non suburbii Southwark.... Nuremberg, 1736. 3 sheets joined, extending to 510mm by 1,680mm, hand-colored by a contemp hand.. Some soiling & creasing; a few marginal tears & repairs. pn Apr 23 (337) £320 [Saville]

— JANSSONIUS, JOANNES. - Comitatis Cantabrigiensis.... Amst., [c.1650]. 413mm by 514mm, hand-colored. pn Nov 14 (465) £180

— JANSSONIUS, JOANNES. - Comitatus Darbiensis. Amst., [1646]. 382mm by 492mm. Some rubbing & creasing at centerfold. pn Apr 23 (333) £120

— JANSSONIUS, JOANNES. - Oxonium comitatus.... Amst, [c.1646]. 380mm by 485mm, hand-colored. pn July 16 (258) £180 [Thorpe]

— MERCATOR, GERARD. - Irlandiae Regnum. [Amst.: Hondius, 17th cent]. 34 cm by 46.9cm. 2 sheets. Central hinges repaired. cb Oct 10 (191) $375

Anr Ed. [Amst.: Hondius, 1609]. 625mm by 465mm, hand-colored. 2 small repairs at fold. S Nov 15 (939) £200 [Warbritton]

Anr Ed. [Amst.: Hondius, c.1630]. 338mm by 465mm. Creased. cb Jan 30 (237) $150

— MERCATOR, GERARD. - Scotia Regnum. [Amst.: Hondius, 1609]. 545mm by 455mm, contemp hand-color. Small repair to lower fold; some marginal spotting. S

Nov 15 (949) £160 [Warbritton]

— MORRIS, W. - Chart of St. George's Channel.... L, [1800]. 2 sheets jointed, 890mm by 890mm. 1st sheet, glazed & framed; 2d sheet, unframed. DW Nov 20 (175) £110

— MUENSTER, SEBASTIAN. - Londen oder Lunden. [Basle, 1598]. 285mm by 360mm, hand-colored. Marginal repairs & stains. S May 14 (1112) £260 [Saville]

— ORTELIUS, ABRAHAM. - Angliae Regni florentissimi nova descriptio.... Antwerp, 1573. 377mm by 465mm, French text on verso Lower portion of centerfold repaired; a few wormholes. DW Nov 20 (178) £190

— ORTELIUS, ABRAHAM. - Angliae, Scotiae, et Hiberniae.... [Antwerp, 1573, or later]. 340mm by 495mm, hand-colored, framed. Ck May 15 (189) £380

Anr Ed. [Antwerp, 1595]. 350mm by 500mm, contemp hand-coloring. Latin text. S Feb 26 (623) £200 [V. A. Kidd]

— ORTELIUS, ABRAHAM. - Insularum Britannicarum acurata delineatio.... Amst., [c.1651]. 393mm by 512mm, hand-colored. Centerfold repaired. pn Nov 14 (456) £220

— OVERTON, J. - Somerset Shire Described... L, [c.1670]. 370mm by 490mm, hand-colored. Small stain. S May 14 (1120) £200 [Tooley Adams]

— PTOLEMAEUS, CLAUDIUS. - Prima Europae Tabula. Ulm, 1486. 410mm by 570mm, colored in a contemp hand. C Oct 30 (158) £1,300 [Jonathan Potter]

— ROCQUE, JOHN. - An Exact Survey of the City's of London, Westminster, ye Borough of Southwark.... L, [1746]. 24 sheets joined, 1961mm by 2602 mm, hand-colored, framed. Some small stains. P Dec 12 (79) $3,500

— ROCQUE, JOHN. - A Map of the Kingdom of Ireland. L; R. Sayer, [1765]. 4 sheets joined, 1,225mm by 970mm, hand-colored in outline. Backed on linen; repairs to joins & folds with slight loss of surface; some discoloration & fraying. S June 25 (261) £500 [Arader]

Anr Ed. L, 1794. 1,235mm by 970mm, 4 sheets joined as 2, hand-colored in outline. Some foxing & browning; marginal tears. sg Sept 19 (116) $375

— ROCQUE, JOHN. - Plan of the Cities of Westminster and the Borough of Southwark. L, 1746 [but c.1749]. 2 vols, including An Alphabetical Index, 1747. Folio & 4to, contemp half calf; rebacked. C Oct 30 (136) £2,400 [Marlborough]

— ROCQUE, JOHN. - A Plan of the city of Dublin.... L, [c.1750]. 515mm by 725mm. Margins trimmed close; tears & marginal chips; tears repaired on verso; remargined. sg Sept 19 (117) $375

— ROCQUE, JOHN. - A Topographical Map of the County of Surrey. L, [c.1760]. 9 sheets, 3ach dissected in 4 sections & mtd on linen, each sheet c.535mm by 680mm.. Contemp hand-coloring. Some browning; edges strengthened & frayed. S Nov 15 (993) £280 [Alfieri]

— SAXTON, CHARLES. - Salopiae Comitatus. L, [1579]. 390mm by 505mm, in contemp hand color. Small hole at top left; cracking of green in places. S Nov 15 (990) £300 [Nichols]

— SAXTON, CHRISTOPHER & LEA, PHILIP. - The County of Hereford...1665. L: P. Lea, [1693]. 375mm by 505mm, hand-colored in outline. Some marginal soiling. S Nov 15 (973) £200 [Brigantian]

— SAXTON, CHRISTOPHER. - Norfolciae Comitatus.... L, [1579]. 390mm by 460mm, hand-colored, framed. Browned at bottom fold. b Mar 11 (23) £340

Anr copy. 335mm by 495mm, contemp hand-coloring. S Nov 15 (986) £800 [J. Sands]

Anr copy. 380mm by 455mm, contemp hand color. Some fraying; cut close at lower margin; some browning. S July 1 (1391) £250 [Cartographia]

— SAXTON, CHRISTOPHER. - Norfolk Described by C. Saxton.... L, [c.1732]. 335mm by 495mm, hand-colored in outline. S Nov 15 (988) £200 [Brigantian]

— SAXTON, CHRISTOPHER. - Oxonii, Buckinghamiae et Berceriae comitatuum.... L, 1574. 390mm by 445mm, colored by a contemp hand. Some soiling & creasing; 1 repaired tear. pn Apr 23 (340) £880 [Sotheran]

— SAXTON, CHRISTOPHER. - Suffolciae comitatus.... L, [c.1610]. 280cm by 380cm, hand-colored, framed. b Mar 11 (25) £190

— SAXTON, CHRISTOPHER. - Worcestershire. L, [1577 but 1689 or later]. 370mm by 490mm, hand-colored in outline. Margins repaired; some soiling. Ck Dec 11 (254) £160

— SEALE, R. W. - England and Ireland. L, [1747]. 1,480mm by 1520mm, contemp hand color; folding into 4to slipcase. Some staining & wear at folds. S July 9 (1386) £320

— SENEX, JOHN. - A New Map of England. L, [c.1720]. 515mm by 610mm, hand-colored in outline. Some browning; mtd to stiff bd; closed tear along vertical fold. sg Sept 19 (123) $225

— SENEX, JOHN. - A New Map of Ireland. L, 1720. 580mm by 490mm, hand-colored in outline. Small abrasion to surface; some wrinkling & browning. sg Sept 19 (125) $250

— SPEED, JOHN. - Anglesey. Antiently Called Mona. L: J. Sudbury & G. Humble, 1610 [1612]. 385mm by 513mm, hand-colored. Marginal tear at centerfold. pn Nov 14

(460) £160 [Russell]

— SPEED, JOHN. - Anno Darbieshire described 1610. L: Sudbury & Humble, [1614-16]. 390mm by 510mm, contemp hand-coloring. Wear & repair to fold; some marginal spotting. S May 14 (1100) £280 [Map House]

— SPEED, JOHN. - Bedfordshire. L: George Humble, [1627-31]. 383mm by 505mm, hand-colored. Repair in centerfold; marginal browning. pn Nov 14 (462) £160 [Russell]

— SPEED, JOHN. - Berkshire. L: Sudbury & Humble, [1611]. ("Barkshire.") 380mm by 503mm, hand-colored. Small holes causing loss to plate surface. pn July 16 (247) £220 [Map House]

— SPEED, JOHN. - Britain as it was Devided in the Tyme of the Englishe-Saxons. L: T. Bassett & R. Chiswell, [1676, or later]. 385mm by 510mm, hand-colored, framed. b June 22 (22) £750

— SPEED, JOHN. - Buckingham, both Shyre and Shiretowne Described. L, 1610 [1611]. 375mm by 502mm, hand-colored.. Latin text on verso.. pn July 16 (248) £160 [Thorpe]

Anr Ed. L, 1610 [but 1646]. 376mm by 505mm, English text on verso Centerfold repaired with loss; some soiling. pn July 16 (249) £160

— SPEED, JOHN. - Caermarden.... L, 1610 [but later]. 15 inches by 20 inches. Centerfold strengthened. DW NOv 20 (200) £120

— SPEED, JOHN. - Cambridgeshire. L: Bassett & Chiswell, 1610 [but 1676]. 380mm by 520mm, hand-colored, framed. Ck May 15 (202) £380

— SPEED, JOHN. - Cornwall. L: Sudbury & Humble, [1611, or later]. 380mm by 510mm, hand-colored, framed. English text on verso. pn Sept 12 (389) £400 [Tooley Adams]

— SPEED, JOHN. - The Countie and Cities of Lyncolne Described. L, 1610. 380mm by 510mm, hand-colored in outline. Framed. b Nov 18 (235) £320

— SPEED, JOHN. - The Countie of Leinster. L: Sudbury & Humble, [1616]. 385mm by 510mm. Top margin trimmed close; tear repaired along vertical fold. sg Sept 19 (127) $275

— SPEED, JOHN. - The Countie of Nottingham Described.... L: Sudbury & Humble, 1610. 16 by 21.25 inches. Later hand-coloring. Repaired along fold. rs Oct 17 (99) $100

Anr Ed. L, [c.1676]. 380mm by 495mm, hand-colored, framed. b Mar 11 (31) £190

— SPEED, JOHN. - The Countie of Warwick.... L, 1610 [but 1611-12, or later]. 15 inches by 20 inches. English text on verso. DW Jan 29 (168) £180

Anr Ed. L, 1610 [but 1627 or later]. 385mm by 510mm, framed. b Mar 11 (32) £190

Anr Ed. L, 1610 [but c.1627]. 384mm by 512mm, hand-colored. Margins & centerfold repaired. pn Nov 14 (503) £160 [Russell]

— SPEED, JOHN. - The County Palatine of Chester.... L: Roger Rea, [1662]. 365mm by 485mm, hand-colored. pn Apr 23 (344) £160

— SPEED, JOHN. - The Countye of Monmouth.... L, 1610 [1614 or later]. 15 inches by 20 inches, hand-colored. English text on verso. Centerfold & lower margin strengthened. DW Nov 20 (206) £190

Anr Ed. L: J. Sudbury & G. Humble, 1610 [but 1614 or later]. 380mm by 512mm, colored by hand English text on verso. sg Sept 19 (128) $475

— SPEED, JOHN. - Cumberland. L: Sudbury & Humble, [1627]. 380mm by 510mm, hand-colored, framed. Ck May 15 (194) £180

— SPEED, JOHN. - Denbighshire. L, [1611]. c. 15 inches by 20 inches. English text on verso. DW Nov 20 (199) £105

Anr Ed. L, [1676 or later]. 15 inches by 20 inches, hand-colored. English text on verso. DW Nov 20 (201) £100

— SPEED, JOHN. - Devonshire with Exceter Described. L: J. Sudbury & G. Humble, [1611]. 385mm by 510mm, hand-colored, framed. b June 22 (23) £380

— SPEED, JOHN. - Dorsetshyre.... L: Sudbury & Humble, 1610 [1611-12]. 385mm by 510mm, hand-colored. Short tears in blank margins. bba Nov 7 (340) £240 [Elliott]

Anr Ed. L, [1676]. 39cm by 51cm, hand-colored, framed. b Mar 11 (33) £210

Anr copy. 382mm by 510mm, hand-colored. Repairs to top & lower fold. S Nov 15 (969) £260

— SPEED, JOHN. - Essex.... L: Bassett & Chiswell, [1676]. 384mm by 507mm, hand-colored, framed. Some creasing to centerfold. pn Sept 12 (391) £150 [Bailey]

Anr copy. 385mm by 510mm. Fold tear repaired. S May 14 (1104) £130 [Saville]

— SPEED, JOHN. - Glamorganshire. L, [1614 or later]. 15 inches by 20 inches. English text on verso. DW Nov 20 (201) £250

— SPEED, JOHN. - Hantshire. L, [1614-16]. 375mm by 505mm, hand-colored, framed. Folds & margins repaired. S July 1 (1388) £340 [Map House]

Anr Ed. L, [1627]. 380mm by 510mm, hand-colored in outline. Small repair to margin at foot of fold. Ck Dec 11 (255) £220

Anr Ed. L, [1713 or 1743]. 375mm by

505mm, hand-colored. Browned; a few marginal tears. S Feb 26 (648) £220 [Huntley]

— SPEED, JOHN. - The Invasions of England and Ireland...since the Conquest. L: G. Humble, [1646]. 380mm by 510mm, hand-colored, framed. Ck May 15 (200) £420

— SPEED, JOHN. - Kent.... L, [1611]. 15 inches by 20 inches. Soiled & creased. DW Jan 29 (170) £125

Anr Ed. L, [1676]. 380mm by 500mm, hand-colored in outline, framed. Some fold repairs. Ck Dec 11 (256) £280

Anr copy. 380mm by 505mm, hand-colored, framed. English text on verso. Marginal tears & repairs. pn Sept 12 (397) £280 [Tooley Adams]

Anr Ed. L, [after 1700]. 380mm by 500mm, framed. Some repairs at foot of fold. Ck Dec 11 (260) £260

— SPEED, JOHN. - The Kingdome of England. L, 1632. 390mm by 520mm, hand-colored in outline. Browned. Ck Oct 18 (96) £280

— SPEED, JOHN. - The Kingdome of Great Britaine and Ireland. L, 1610 [but 1614, or later]. 390mm by 520mm, hand-colored. English text on verso. DW Nov 20 (196) £380

— SPEED, JOHN. - The Kingdome of Irland.... L, 1610 [but 1614, or later]. 385mm by 510mm. English text on verso. sg Sept 19 (129) $425

Anr Ed. L, 1610 [1627]. 375mm by 493mm, hand-colored. English text on verso. Some soiling; a few tears; crude repairs to verso; small holes causing loss to plate surface. pn Mar 19 (450) £260 [Map House]

— SPEED, JOHN. - The Kingdome of Scotland. L, 1652. 385mm by 510mm. Hand-colored. Margins extensively glue-damaged; laid down on heavy bd. wa Apr 9 (176) $230

— SPEED, JOHN. - Midle-sex Described.... L: G. Humble, 1610 [but 1627, or later]. 380mm by 380mm, hand-colored, framed. Ck May 15 (199) £340

Anr Ed. L: G. Humble, 1610. 390mm by 515mm, hand-colored. Repair to foot of centerfold; laid down. bba Nov 7 (341) £320 [Potter]

Anr Ed. L: G. Humble, [1627]. 380mm by 505mm. Some creasing. pn Apr 23 (350) £280 [Map House]

— SPEED, JOHN. - Norfolk. L: T. Bassett & R. Chiswell, [1676, or later]. 380mm by 500mm. Small repair at lower fold; mtd. S May 14 (1113) £160 [Wayman]

Anr Ed. L: Sudbury & Humble, [1631]. About 15 by 20 inches, hand-colored, framed. English text on verso. pn Sept 12 (398) £220 [Map House]

— SPEED, JOHN. - The North and East Riding of Yorkshire. L, [1611]. 39cm by 52cm, hand-colored, framed. Small portion torn away from upper margin; some staining. pn Nov 20 (36) £120

— SPEED, JOHN. - Northamptonshire. L, [1611]. 15 inches by 20 inches. English text on verso. DW Dec 11 (210) £100

— SPEED, JOHN. - The Province of Connaugh. L: Sudbury & Humble, [1612]. 380mm by 515mm, hand-colored. Wear & repair to fold. S May 14 (1098) £120 [Catach]

— SPEED, JOHN. - Shropshyre Described. L: George Humble, [1614]. 380mm by 510mm, hand-colored. Repaired. pn Apr 23 (351) £150

— SPEED, JOHN. - Somerset-Shire Described.... L: Bassett & Chiswell, [1676]. 380mm by 510mm, hand-colored, framed. b June 22 (24) £250

— SPEED, JOHN. - Stafford Countie and Towne.... L, [1713]. 387mm by 515mm, in contemp hand-color. Repaired centerfold. S May 14 (1125) £160 [Saville]

— SPEED, JOHN. - Suffolke described. L: J. Sudbury & G. Humble, 1610 [1627]. 378mm by 511mm, hand-colored. pn Apr 23 (352) £200 [Map House]

— SPEED, JOHN. - Surrey Described.... L: J. Sudbury & G. Humble, [1646 or later]. 410mm by 540mm, framed. Ck July 10 (346) £320

— SPEED, JOHN. - Sussex. L: Bassett & Chiswell, [1676]. 385mm by 510mm. Small repair to lower fold. S May 14 (1127) £280 [Tooley Adams]

— SPEED, JOHN. - Sussex Described. L: Bassett & Chiswell, [1676]. 385mm by 510mm, hand-colored. Framed. b Mar 11 (37) £260

— SPEED, JOHN. - Wales. L, 1610 [but 1611-12]. 380mm by 507mm, hand-colored. English text on verso. pn July 16 (262) £340

Anr Ed.

— SPEED, JOHNL: Sudbury & Humble, [1616]. 385mm by 500mm. Tear at fold; narrow top margin. S May 14 (1128) £360 [Map House]

— SPEED, JOHN. - Wight Island. L, 1676. 383mm by 505mm, hand-colored, framed. pn Sept 12 (396) £160 [Map House]

— SPEED, JOHN. - Wiltshire. L: George Humble, [1614 or later]. 390mm by 510mm, hand-colored in outline; framed. Ck May 15 (191) £280

— SPEED, JOHN. - Worcestershire Described. L: J. Sudbury & G. Humble, 1610 [but 1614, or later]. 375mm by 498mm, hand-colored in outline. pn Apr 23 (354) £200 [Map House]

Anr Ed. L: J. Sudbury & G. Humble, [1627]. 380mm by 510mm, partially hand-

colored, framed. Ck May 15 (194) £180
— STOBIE, JAMES. - The Counties of Perth and Clackmannan. L, 26 May 1783. 9 sheets, totalling 1,665mm by 1,800mm, hand-colored in outline, backed with linen. Some dust-soiling. S Feb 11 (678) £480 [Kyd]
— STRYPE, JOHN. - A New Plan of the City of London, Westminster and Southwark. L, [c.1720]. 490mm by 670mm, hand-colored. Some browning. Ck Oct 18 (114) £180

Anr copy. 484mm by 660mm, pn July 16 (254) £280
— SYMONSON, PHILIP. - A New Description of Kent. L, 1659. 785mm by 530mm, uncolored. Small holes & tears with loss of ptd area. C Oct 30 (165) £300 [Jonathan Potter]
— VERTUE, GEORGE. - Civitas Londinum circiter Ano Domini M D L X. L, 1737. 8 sheets joined, 700mm by 1,894mm. pn Apr 23 (349) £850
— WAGHENAER, LUCAS JANSZ. - Beschrijvinghe van een deel vann Schottlandt van Bainbourg tot Aberdein.... Amst., [1590]. 350mm by 525mm, hand-colored, framed. S July 1 (1395) £300 [Young]
— WILLDEY, GEORGE. - A New & Correct Map of Thirty Miles round London. L, [1755]. 2 sheets joined, 650mm by 980mm, hand-colored in outline. Small tear at center; marginal repairs. S May 14 (1108) £260 [Tooley Adams]

Pacific Ocean

— ARROWSMITH, AARON. - Chart of the Pacific Ocean.... L, 1798-[1820]. 9 sheets, each c.625mm by 790mm. Small tear to title-sheet; 3 sheets frayed, just affecting engraved surface. S June 25 (480) £2,800 [Quaritch]
— COOK, CAPT. JAMES. - Chart of the Sandwich Islands. [L, c.1784]. 280mm by 460mm, framed. cb Jan 30 (181) $550
— CORONELLI, VINCENZO MARIA. - Mare del Sud, detto altrimenti Mare Pacifico. [Venice, c.1690]. 450mm by 600mm. Small repair to top edge & lower fold. S June 25 (482) £50 [Map]

Anr Ed. [Venice, 1691]. 450mm by 600mm. Framed. S June 25 (23) £650 [George]
— DE WIT, FREDERICK. - Magnum Mare del Zur cum Insula California. Amst., [c.1670]. 19.5 by 22.5 inches, hand-colored, framed. With 7-inch tear repaired on verso. wa Mar 5 (449) $700
— ORTELIUS, ABRAHAM. - Maris Pacifici.... [Antwerp], 1589 [but 1603]. 340mm by 490mm, framed & glazed. S June 25 (2) £1,1700 [Stokes]
— RENARD, LOUIS. - Magnum Mare del Zur.... Amst., [1715]. 495mm by 564mm, contemp body color. S June 25 (483) £1,500 [Arader]

Polar Regions

— BLAEU, WILLEM & JAN. - Regiones sub polo arctico. [Amst., 1650]. 410mm by 530mm, early hand-coloring. S May 14 (1307) £200 [Lundy]
— TIRION, ISAAK. - Nuova carta del polo Artico. [N.p., c.1755]. 295mm by 350mm, hand-colored in outline. Some browning along fold. sg Feb 13 (104) $375

Southern Hemisphere

— JANSSONIUS, JOANNES. - [Untitled map including South Pole, Australia, South America & South Africa] Amst.: Gerard Valk & Pieter Schenk, [c.1700]. 430mm by 485mm, hand-colored. S June 25 (478) £500 [Arader]

United States

— Asbury Park, Ocean Grove and Vicinity. NY, 1897. 12 sections, 865mm by 1,125mm, contemp linen backing, torn along several folds. sg Sept 19 (88) $200
— Johnson's California.... [NY, c.1860]. 405mm by 600mm plus border, sealed in mylar. Marginal stains & tears. cb Feb 12 (48) $110
— Map of Gold Hill Front Lodes on the Comstock Range.... Bost., [c.1864]. 324mm by 556mm. cb Sept 12 (197) $130
— Plan of the City of Washington.... NY: Reid, Wayland & Smith, 1795. 415mm by 535mm. Margins trimmed to platemark; some stains & closed tears; linen backed. Sold w.a.f. sg Sept 19 (149) $275
— Topographical Sketch of the Gold & Quicksilver District of California. Phila.: P. S. Duval, [c.1848]. 550mm by 385mm, hand-colored. Some staining & foxing; remargined at left edge. cb Sept 12 (201) $650
— BLAEU, WILLEM & JAN. - Virginiae partis australis, et Floridae, partis orientalis.... [Amst., 1650]. 385mm by 505mm, contemp hand-coloring. Dutch text on verso. Some wear at fold. S Feb 26 (691) £380 [Lin Ching Lih]
— BOWEN, EMMANUEL. - A New and Accurate Map of Louisiana, with Parts of Florida and Canada, and the Adjacent Countries.... [L, 1747]. 343mm by 415mm, hand-colored. pn Nov 14 (530) £220
— COLTON, J. H. - Colton's Map of the State of Indiana. NY, 1859. 960mm by 730mm, hand-colored, folding into orig 12mo mor case. Small ink stamp on verso. sg June 18 (185) $375
— COLTON, J. H. - Township Map of the State of Iowa. NY, 1855. 630mm by 750mm, hand-colored, folding into orig 12mo cloth case. Some fold breaks; inked stamp on verso. sg June 18 (186) $550
— DE L'ISLE, GUILLAUME. - America

Septentrionalis. Nuremberg: T. C. Lotter, [c.1760]. 480mm by 580mm, hand-colored. Fold breaks. sg Feb 13 (13) $750

— FADEN, WILLIAM. - Plan of the Operations of General Washington, against the Kings Troops in New Jersey from the 26th of December 1776 to the 3d January 1777. L, 15 Apr 1777. 311mm by 412mm, partly handcolored to show movement of troops. Framed. P June 16 (215) $3,750

— FADEN, WILLIAM. - The United States of North America. L, 1796. 21 by 25 inches, outline & wash color.. Some edge tears, repaired. wa Nov 21 (137) $650

— FRENCH, J. H. - The State of New York. Syracuse: Robert Pearsall, 1860. 1,720mm by 1,880mm, hand-colored, wooden rods. Some dampstaining along top edge; linen-backed. sg Dec 5 (177) $110

— FRY, JOSHUA & JEFFERSON, PETER. - Carte de la Virginie et du Maryland.... [Paris], 1755. 19 by 25 inches, contemp outline color. Some waterstains in margins. wa Nov 21 (129) $350

— GUSSEFELD, F. L. - Charte ueber die XIII vereinigte Staaten von Nord-America. [N.p.], 1784. 465mm by 590mm, hand-colored. sg Feb 13 (43) $550

— HOLLAND, SAMUEL. - The Provinces of New York and New Jersey.... [L, 1776]. 52.5 by 20.4 inches, NY counties in contemp hand-coloring, as are outlines for remainder of map.. Margins chipped. bbc Dec 9 (59) $1,250

— HOMANN, JOHANN BAPTIST. - Amplissimae regionis Mississippi seu Provinciae Ludovicianae.... Nuremberg, [c.1687]. 19 by 22.5 inches, hand-colored. wa Nov 21 (138) $850

— HOMANN, JOHANN BAPTIST. - Nova Anglia. Nuremberg, [c.1730]. 485mm by 575mm, contemp body color. Small tears to upper & lower fold; some browning & soiling. S Nov 15 (1210) £280 [Cousteau]

Anr copy. 485mm by 570mm, Some staining at top & lower centerfold. S Nov 15 (1211) £190 [Cousteau]

— HOMANN, JOHANN BAPTIST. - Virginia, Marylandia et Carolina. Nuremberg, [c.1730]. 485mm by 570mm, contemp body color. Some staining at top & lower center; some browning at fold. S Nov 15 (1217) pS420 [Cousteau]

— JEKYLL, THOMAS. - Map of the United States.... Wash.: Selmar Siebert, [c.1858]. 515mm by 580mm, sealed in mylar. cb Feb 12 (47) $250

— JOHNSON & WARD. - Johnson's California, Territories of New Mexico, Arizona, Colorado, Nevada and Utah. NY, [c.1865]. 400mm by 590mm, hand-colored. cb Sept 12 (196) $140

— JOLLAIN, GERARD OR FRANCOIS. - Nowel Amsterdam en l'Amerique 1672. Paris, [c.1672]. 350mm by 505mm. Marginal tears & tear at bottom of vertical fold; date altered to 1662 by a previous owner. Entirely fictitious view of New York; the city actually portrayed is Lisbon. sg Sept 19 (92) $1,600

— LAY, AMOS. - Map of the State of New-York. Map of the State of New-York.. NY, 1820 40-section map, 1,300mmm by 1,300mm, hand-colored in outline, linen-backed & folding into contemp 8vo half sheep folder. Some foxing & dampstaining. sg Dec 5 (178) $225

— ORD, EDWARD OTHO CRESAP. - Topographical Sketch of the Gold & Quicksilver District of California. Phila.: P. S. Duval, [c.1848]. 545mm by 385mm. Margin chipped. cb Feb 12 (30) $375

— PREUSS, CHARLES. - Map of Oregon and Upper California from the Surveys of John Charles Fremont and Other Authorities. Wash., 1858. 840mm by 675mm, sealed in mylar. Tears repaired. cb Feb 12 (51) $350

— RATZER, BERNARD. - To His Excellency Sr. Henry Moore...This Plan of the City of New York...Survey'd in 1767.... L: Jefferys & Faden, 12 Jan 1776. 1,005mm by 895mm, segmented & mtd on cloth with green silk-edged margins. Lacking lower panoramic of the New Jersey shore & the Parish of Brookland on Long Island. C Oct 30 (160) £2,800 [Quaritch]

— ROBERT DE VAUGONDY, GILLES & DIDIER. - Carte de la Virginie et du Maryland. Paris, 1755. 490mm by 660mm, hand-colored in outline, cartouche possibly colored later. sg Sept 19 (110) $425

— ROBERT DE VAUGONDY. - Partie de l'Amerique septentrionale.... [Paris, c.1750]. 475mm by 600mm, hand-colored. S Nov 15 (1208) £280 [Map House]

Anr Ed. Paris, [1755]. 490mm by 625mm, hand-colored in outline, coloring on cartouche probably later. sg Sept 19 (115) $225

— ROSS, J. - Course of the River Mississippi, from the Balise to Fort Chartres.... L: R. Sayer, 1 June 1775. 2d State. 44.5 by 13.5 inches, left edge uneven, with outline color. wa Nov 21 (120) $750

— SENEX, JOHN. - A Map of Louisiana and of the River Mississippi. L, [1721 or later]. 480mm by 570mm, orig outline color. With 4 small wormholes, 2 just affecting surface. S Nov 21 (318) £550 [Map House]

— SENEX, JOHN. - A New Map of Virginia, Mary-Land and the Improved Parts of Pennsylvania & New Jersey. L, [1721 or later]. 480mm by 550mm, hand-colored in outline. S Nov 21 (319) £850 [Map House]

— SPEED, JOHN. - A Map of Virginia and

Maryland. L: Bassett & Chiswell, [1676]. 15 by 19 inches. bbc Dec 9 (55) $1,400
— TANNER, H.S. - City of New-York. Phila., 1835. 390mm by 315mm, partly hand-colored. Small stain in outer portion of image. sg Feb 13 (84) $150
— TIRION, ISAAK. - Kaart van het Nieuw Mexico en van California. Amst., 1765. 327mm by 352mm. Hand-colored (possibly later) in outline. cb Jan 30 (268) $475
— VISSCHER, NICOLAS. - Novi Belgii Novaeque Angliae nec non partis Virginiae tabula.... [Amst., c.1690]. 470mm by 554mm, hand-colored in outline, the view fully so.. Cut to plate mark & remargined; restoration at edges in 3 places in pen & ink. S June 25 (431) £2,500 [Map]
— WHITNEY, J. D. - Map of California. NY, 1874. 20-part sectional map, 1,050mm by 895mm, hand-colored in outline, linen-backed, folding into orig 8vo cloth cover. Some tears between sections. sg June 18 (148) $400

World

— Ignem vent mittere in terram. Dillingen, 1664. 910mm by 635mm, hand-colored;. Some restoration at folds; margins close cut & backed. S June 25 (356) £3,000 [Map]
— AA, PETER VAN DER. - Nova delineatio totius orbis terrarum. Leiden, [c.1728]. 252mm by 342mm, hand-colored. S June 25 (338) £950 [Arader]
— ARIAS MONTANUS, BENEDICTUS. - Sacrae Geographiae Tabulam.... Antwerp: Christopher Plantin, 1571. 310mm by 525mm. S June 25 (1) £2,500 [Stokes]
— BERRY, WILLIAM. - A Mapp of all the World in two Hemispheres.... L, 1680. 35 by 22 inches, hand-colored. Repaired along folds & in margins. wd June 12 (341) $1,800
— BLAEU, WILLEM. - Nova totius terrarum orbis.... [Amst., c.1668]. 480mm by 550mm, contemp hand-color. Repair to lower fold. S June 25 (349) £2,800 [George]
— BOWEN, EMANUEL. - A New and Accurate Map of the World. L, [c.1750]. 28.6cm by 54.3cm. Modern hand-coloring. Verso repaired. cb Oct 10 (130) $225
— BOWEN, THOMAS. - The World including the Discoveries made by Captain Cook. [L, c.1782]. 280mm by 450mm, recent hand-coloring. cb Jan 30 (171) $275
— CHATELAIN, HENRI. - Mappe-Monde. Paris, [c.1760]. 336mm by 460mm, hand-colored. sg Sept 19 (30) $1,500
— CHATELAIN, HENRI ABRAHAM. - Mappe-Monde pour connoitre les progres & les conquestes les plus Remarquables des Provinces-Unis.... [Amst., c.1708]. 335mm by 460mm. cb Jan 30 (176) $350
— CLOUET, JEAN BAPTISTE LOUIS. - Carte general de la terre.... Paris: Mondhare, [1788]. 4 sheets joined, 965mm by 1,220mm, hand-colored. Some fold repairs with slight loss in 2 places. S June 25 (344) £7,000 [Map House]
— CORONELLI, VINCENZO MARIA & TILLEMONT, JEAN NICOLAS DE TRALAGE DE. - Le Globe Terrestre. Paris: Jean-Baptiste Nolin, [1690]. State 1. 452mm by 600mm, hand-colored. Repaired at margins & fold. S June 25 (348) £1,200 [Map House]
— DE FER, NICOLAS. - Mappe-Monde, ou carte generale de la terre. Paris: J. F. Benard, 1718. 440mm by 700mm, hand-colored in outline; small tear to lower fold. S Feb 26 (694) £750 [Map House]
— DE WIT, FREDERICK. - Nova totius terrarum orbis tabula. Amst.: R. & J. Ottens, [1685]. 500mm by 565mm, contemp body color, framed. Small tear at top left. S Nov 21 (229) £2,000 [Warbratton]
— DELEMARCHE, CHARLES FRANCOIS. - Mappe Monde. Paris, [1786]. 4 sheets joined, 985mm by 1,145mm, hand-colored in outline. Some annotations; tear repaired with slight loss; mtd on linen but linen torn in places; some staining. S June 25 (350) £500 [Burden]
— DU VAL, PIERRE. - La Carte generale du monde. Paris: H. Jaillot, 1682. 410mm by 532mm, hand-colored. Restored along top margin. S June 25 (351) £1,200 [Map]
— DU VAL, PIERRE. - Planisphere, ou Carte Generale du Monde. Paris, 1676. 332mm by 588mm, cb Jan 30 (204) $550
— FER, NICOLAS DE. - Mappe-Monde, ou carte generale de la terre.... Paris, 1718. 2 sheets joined, 440mm by 700mm, hand-colored. Trimmed to plate mark & remargined. S June 25 (346) £1,200 [George]
— JANSSONIUS, JOANNES. - Orbis Terrarum Veteribus Cogniti Typus Geographicus. [Amst., c.1650]. 405mm by 505mm, hand-colored. pn Nov 14 (566) £240

Anr copy. 400mm by 510mm, hand-colored in outline. Margins stained, with slight soiling to map surface; mtd to cardbd. sg Sept 19 (65) $350
— JODE, GERARD DE. - Totius Orbis cogniti universalis descriptio. Antwerp: C. de Jode, 1593. 350mm by 505mm. Some restoration at fold & lower edge. S June 25 (347) £4,200 [Map House]
— LOCHOM, MICHAEL VAN. - Hoc est Puctum quod inter tot gentes ferro et igne dividitur. Paris, [c.1640]. 160mm by 225mm, hand-colored in outline. Some foxing & browning. sg Feb 13 (49) $400
— LOTTER, TOBIAS CONRAD. - Mappa totius mundi.... [Augsburg?, c.1760]. 440mm by 650mm, hand-colored. Some dampstaining in bottom margin; portion of bottom margin lacking, not affecting surface. sg

Feb 13 (15) $900

— MERCATOR, RUMOLD. - Orbis terrae compendiosa descriptio.... [Amst., 1628]. 285mm by 520mm, early hand-color. Repair to fold & 2 marginal tears; browned. S June 25 (358) £1,800 [Kasim]

— MOLL, HERMANN. - New and Correct Map of the World. L, 1709. 22.5 by 39 inches, outline color. Some browning; side folds split & reattached with tape on reverse; 2 repaired tears. wa Nov 21 (153) $800

— MUENSTER, SEBASTIAN. - Das Erst General. Basel, [c.1540]. 263mm by 380mm. German text on verso. Side margins trimmed close. sg Sept 19 (85) $600

— ORTELIUS, ABRAHAM. - Typus orbis terrarum. [Antwerp, 1570 or later]. 340mm by 490mm, hand-colored. Text in Latin. Repair to central fold. Ck Oct 31 (180) £1,200

State 1. 337mm by 495mm. Hand-colored. Some wear at fold; plate cracked at lower left corner; tear at bottom fold. S Feb 26 (697) £1,100 [Faupel]

Anr Ed. [Paris, 1575]. 335mm by 495mm, hand-colored. Thinning at fold & 2 small wormholes infilled. French text. S June 25 (340) £1,600 [Arader]

Anr Ed. [Antwerp, 1587]. 330mm by 485mm, contemp hand-coloring. French text. Marginal soiling. S Nov 21 (222) £1,500 [Arader]

— OVERTON, HENRY. - A New Mapp of the Whole World. L, 1738. 4 sheets joined & mtd on linen, 1,210mm by 1,330mm, hand-colored. Some restoration, mainly at borders. S June 25 (361) £11,500 [Arader]

— PITT, MOSES. - Nova totius terrarum orbis geographica ac hydrographica tabula. Oxford, [1680]. 400mm by 535mm, hand-colored in outline. S Nov 21 (228) £3,200 [Map House]

— PLANCIUS, PETRUS. - Orbis terrarum typhus de integro multis in locis emendatus. [Amst., 1594, or later]. 283mm by 510mm, hand-colored. Dutch text. Browned. S Nov 21 (223) £1,200 [Arader]

Anr Ed. [Amst., c1599]. 405mm by 575mm, hand-colored. Shaved, just affecting engraved surface; small fold holes. S Nov 21 (224) £2,500 [Potter]

— PTOLEMAEUS, CLAUDIUS. - Typus Orbis Universalis. Basel: H. Petri, [1540]. 275mm by 380mm, hand-colored. Fold strengthened. S May 14 (1231) £480 [Casa d'Arte]

— REISCH, GREGOR. - Typus universalis terrae. [Strassburg, 1513]. 180mm by 285mm. Small hole at edge not affecting map. S June 25 (368) £2,200 [Casten]

— SANSON D'ABBEVILLE, NICOLAS. - Orbis vetus, et orbis veteris utraque continens. Amst.: Mortier, [c.1705]. 400mm by 545mm, hand-colored in outline. Some soiling & browning, mainly to margins. sg Sept 19 (120) $425

— SPEED, JOHN. - A New and Accurat Map of the World. L: G. Humble, [1627]. 390mm by 510mm, hand-colored, framed. Repaired tear at top left corner; small wormhole at top center. S Nov 21 (225) £2,400 [Map House]

Anr Ed. L: Bassett & Chiswell, [1676]. 395mm by 525mm, hand-colored, the continents in outline. S Nov 21 (227) £2,400 [Map House]

— VALCK, GERARD. - Orbis Terrarum Nova et Accurata Tabula. Amst., [c.1700]. 485mm by 580mm, hand-colored. Mtd to stiff bd. sg Sept 19 (145) $1,600

— VISSCHER, N. - Orbis Terrarum Tabula. [Amst., c.1663]. 305mm by 467mm, hand-colored. Marginal soiling. S May 14 (1230) £800 [Kafka]

— VISSCHER, N. - Werelt Caert. [Amst., c.1680]. 310mm by 460mm, hand-colored. S May 14 (1232) £850 [Map House]

— VISSCHER, NICOLAUS JANSSOON. - Orbis Terrarum typus de integro in plurimis emendatus.... [Amst., c.1657]. 305mm by 475mm, hand-colored. Repairs to small splits at upper & lower folds. S Nov 21 (226) £1,600 [Dal Mondo]

— VISSCHER, NICOLAUS JANSSOON. - Orbis terrarum tabula recens emendata.... [Dordrecht, 1682]. 355mm by 460mm, hand-colored. S June 25 (366) £1,300 [George]

— WALDSEEMUELLER, MARTIN. - [Untitled world map]. [Lyon, 1535]. 300mm by 455mm, hand-colored. Repaired. S June 25 (369) £1,500 [Kasim]

— WELLS, EDWARD. - A New Map of the Terraqueous Globe. Oxford, [c.1720]. 370mm by 515mm, hand-colored. Laid at edges on bd; some wear to old centerfold. bba Nov 7 (297) £200 [Sanders of Oxford]

Mara, Sally. See: Queneau, Raymond

Maran, Rene, 1887-1960. See: Limited Editions Club

Marat, Jean Paul

— Recherches physiques sur le feu. Paris, 1780. 8vo, contemp half sheep; spine ends chipped, lacking front free endpaper. sg May 14 (292) $450

Marbury, Mary Orvis

— Favorite Flies and their Histories. Bost., 1892. 4to, orig cloth; worn, spine wrinkled. O Oct 29 (204) $200

Marc, Franz, 1880-1916. See: Kandinsky & Marc

Marcel, Jean Jacques

— Fables de Loqman, surnomme Le Sage. Cairo, 1799. 4to, contemp wraps. S July 1 (846) £750 [Marlborough]

Marcelli, Francesco Antonio

— Regole della scherma insegnate da Lelio e Titta Marcelli. Rome: D. A. Ercole, 1686. 4to, early vellum. sg Mar 26 (192) $2,400

Marcellinus, Ammianus

— Delle guerre de' Romani. Venice: Gabriel Giolito de' Ferrari, 1550. 8vo, old vellum. Dampstaining at ends; small wormhole through 1st few leaves. sg Mar 12 (180) $120

— The Roman Historie.... L, 1609. Trans by Philemon Holland. Folio, contemp calf; rebacked. W July 8 (91) £130

Marchand, Prosper, d.1756

— Histoire de l'origine et des premiers progres de l'imprimerie. The Hague, 1740. 2 parts in 1 vol. 4to, contemp half calf; rubbed & soiled. cb Dec 5 (83) $170

Marchant, W. T.

— In Praise of Ale.... L, 1888. 8vo, cloth. sg Mar 5 (179) $225

Marchesinus, Joannes

— Mammotrectus super Bibliam. Venice: Franciscus Renner de Heilbronn & Nicolaus de Frankfordia, 1476. 4to, 19th-cent bdg of early Ms vellum over bds. 39 lines & headline; types 2:75G (text) & 3:150G (headlines); double column. With 7-line initial in blue with red infill; 8-line initial in red with green infill; rubricated. Short copy; some worming & marginal repair; dampstaining in lower inner corner throughout. 226 (of 228) leaves; lacking 1st & last blanks. Goff M-236. Doheny copy. sg Oct 24 (210) S1,300

Anr Ed. Strassburg: [Martin Flach], 1494. 4to, contemp half pigskin; front cover cracked, lacking catch & clasp. Dampstained at beginning & end; 1st few leaves wormed. 315 (of 316) leaves. Goff M-253. sg Mar 12 (124) $1,100

Marchionni, Alberto

— Trattato di scherma sopra un nuovo sistema di Giuoco Misto.... Florence, 1847. 8vo, half vellum. sg Mar 26 (193) $225

Marchmont, Frederick

— The Three Cruikshanks: a Bibliographical Catalogue.... L, 1897. One of 500. 8vo, bdg not stated. cb Oct 17 (574) $150

Marcy, Randolph Barnes, 1812-87

— Exploration of the Red River of Louisiana.... Wash., 1853. Without the Atlas of 2 maps 8vo, orig cloth; worn & frayed. Some browning & foxing. bbc Sept 23 (333) $80

Anr copy. Without the Atlas vol. 8vo, cloth. sg June 18 (340) $50

Anr Ed. Wash., 1854. 2 vols, including folding maps in separate folder. 8vo, orig cloth. With 65 plates & 2 folding maps. Maps wrinkled. NH May 30 (576) $220

Anr copy. Cloth. sp Apr 16 (32) $80

— Message of the President...the Report and Maps of Captain Marcy of his Explorations of the Big Wichita.... Wash., 1856. 8vo, disbound. Folding map in end pocket. NH May 30 (522) $110

— The Prairie Traveller: a Hand-Book for Overland Expeditions. NY, 1859. 1st Ed. 8vo, orig cloth. Map repaired. cb Sept 12 (110) $325

Anr copy. Half mor; extremities worn. NH Aug 23 (443) $410

Anr Ed. L, 1863. Ed by Sir Richard F. Burton. 8vo, lea gilt. b&b Feb 19 (3) $225

Anr copy. Cloth; rebacked. bba Jan 16 (290) £85 [Trophy Room]

Anr copy. Orig cloth; spine worn. bba Apr 30 (53) £85 [J. Bonhom]

Anr copy. Contemp half calf. With folding map. cb Nov 14 (115) $250

Anr copy. Orig cloth; spine worn. With frontis & folding map. With 26 pp only of ads at end. S June 225 (381) £1,200 [Quaritch]

Mardersteig, Giovanni

— Die Officina Bodoni. Das Werk einer Handpresse 1923-1977. Hamburg: Maximilian Gesellschaft, [1979]. One of 1,500. 4to, cloth. K July 12 (328) $65

— The Officina Bodoni. Verona, 1980. One of 1,500. 4to, orig cloth. b Mar 11 (157) £60; b Mar 11 (158) £350

Anr copy. Orig half mor. bba Mar 26 (185) £400 [Forster]

Mardersteig, Hans. See: Mardersteig, Giovanni

Marey, Etienne Jules

— Animal Mechanism: A Treatise on Terrestrial and Aerial Locomotion. NY, 1874. 8vo, orig cloth; spine faded. Appleton's International Scientific Series, Vol XI. sg Jan 14 (81) $200

— La Machine animale, locomotion terrestre et arienne. Paris, 1873. 8vo, orig cloth; spine faded. sg Nov 14 (79) $250

Margarita...

— Margarita Poetarum. Oratorum omnium poetarum hystoricorum.... [N.p., 1502]. Folio, contemp half pigskin over wooden bds; lacking clasps. Ck Nov 29 (249) £420

Marguerite d'Angouleme, 1492-1549

— L'Heptameron. Berne: la Nouvelle Societe Typographique, 1792. ("Les Nouvelles de Marguerite, reine de Navarre.") 3 vols. 8vo, mor by Bozerian jeune; stain on lower cover of Vol I. With 3 engraved calligraphic titles, frontis in Vol I & 73 plates. Some foxing & browning. S Dec 5 (281) £2,400 [Sourget]

— Les Memoires de la Roine Marguerite. Paris, 1628. 1st Ed, Issue not specified. 8vo, vellum. sg Mar 12 (181) $120

Mariana, Juan de, 1536-1623?

— Historiae de rebus Hispaniae libri XX. Toledo, 1592. 1st Ed. Folio, 19th-cent half vellum. Some marginal staining & browning. SI Dec 5 (931) LIt750,000

Mariani, Giovanni

— Tariffa perpetua con la ragion fatte per secontro de qualunque mercadante. Venice: F. Rampazetto, 1564. 12mo, contemp vellum. Some browning & marginal spotting. SI Dec 5 (436) LIt2,000,000

Mariano, Vincent C.

— In the Ring of the Rise. NY, [1976]. One of 175. 4to, half lea. Koopman copy. O Oct 29 (205) $225

Marichal, Robert. See: Samaran & Marichal

Marie de Medicis, Queen of France

— The Remonstrance made by the Queene-mother of France, to the King her Sonne.... L: T. S. for Nathanaell Newbery, 1619. 4to, modern cloth. Margins trimmed; hole through last 2 leaves costing a few letters. STC 17555. sg Oct 24 (211) $350

Marie Therese Charlotte de France

[-] Relation de l'inauguration solemnelle de sa sacree majeste Marie Therese...comme comtesse de Flandres.... Ghent, 1744. Folio, contemp calf, upper cover with gilt Imperial arms & lower cover with city arms. With frontis & large folding plate. Fraying affecting 1 edge of folding plate. C Oct 30 (53) £350 [Taro-Zagnoli]

Mariette, Pierre Jean

— Description des travaux qui ont accompagne, precede et suivi la fonte en bronze d'un seul jet de la statue equestre de Louis XV. Paris, 1768. Folio, orib bds, unpressed copy; worn. With 59 plates. S Feb 11 (321) £750 [Mathais Mill]

Mariette Library, Pierre Jean

— Catalogue raisonne des differens objets de curiosites dans les sciences et arts.... Paris, 1775. One of 12 on Hollande. Compiled by Francois Basan. 8vo, contemp vellum; corners bumped. Interleaved throughout with blanks; prices and buyers inked in. bba Mar 26 (36) £420 [Quaritch]

Marillier, Henry Currie

— Dante Gabriel Rossetti. L, 1899. 4to, cloth, in d/j. sg Feb 6 (175) $200

Marin, John

— Drawings and Water Colors. NY, [1950]. One of 125 with sgd etching. 4to, loose as issued in half-lea portfolio; joints rubbed. sg Sept 6 (182) $400

Marinaro, Vincent

— A Modern Dry-Fly Code. NY: Crown, [1970]. One of 350. Lea. Koopman copy. O Oct 29 (206) $170

Marinelli, Giovanni, Physician

— Gli Ornamenti delle donne.... Venice, 1562. 8vo, 19th-cent half lea. SI June 10 (392) LIt850,000

Marini, Giovanni Battista, 1569-1625

— Il Libro del perche. [L, 1784]. One of 200. 12mo, contemp mor gilt. SI Dec 5 (844) LIt2,200,000

Marini, Giovanni Filippo de

— Delle missioni de' padri della compagnia di Giesu nella Provincia del Giappone.... Rome, 1663. 4to, 18th-cent vellum. With folding frontis (repaired) & 3 folding plates. Some worming at beginning; some discoloration. S Nov 21 (362) £2,000 [Forum]

Marinis, Tammaro de. See: De Marinis, Tammaro

Marinoni, Giovanni Jacopo de

— De astronomia specula domestica et organico apparatus astronomico.... Vienna, 1745. Folio, contemp calf; restored. With engraved title & 43 folding plates. SI June 10 (394) LIt6,500,000

Mariti, Giovanni, 1736-1806

— Travels through Cyprus, Syria, and Palestine. Dublin, 1792. 2 vols. 8vo, contemp calf; repaired. Fore-edge of 2F3-end in Vol II wormed. S Nov 21 (265) £1,800 [Shapero]; S June 30 (52) £1,200 [Atabey]

— Voyages dans l'Isle de Chypre, la Syrie et la

Palestine.... Neuwied, 1791. 2 vols. 8vo, 19th-cent half mor; some wear, library label. Lacking A2-3 in Vol I. S June 30 (346) £750 [Atabey]

Anr Ed. Paris, 1791. 2 vols in 1. 8vo, contemp half calf; lower cover rubbed. S June 30 (51) £900 [Quaritch]

Markham, Edwin, 1852-1940

— Lincoln: The Man of the People. NY: Bernhardt Wall, 1922. Illus by Bernhardt Wall. Folio, wraps, one of a few hand-bound by Wall. With 16 plates. Etching of Lincoln, dated 1944, bound in. cb Dec 5 (137) $250

Markham, Francis, 1565-1627

— Five Decades of Epistles of Warre. L, 1622. 1st Ed. Folio, contemp calf; rebacked. Title torn at edges. bba Oct 24 (199) £160 [Beeleigh Abbey]

Anr copy. Modern calf. Some leaves shaved; some soiling. bba Jan 30 (130) £130 [Land]

Markham, Gervase, 1568?-1637

— The English House-Wife.... L, 1631. 4to, modern half calf. Lacking initial blank; corner of c.10 leaves cut away; some waterstaining; lacking initial blank. bba June 25 (173) £380 [Bernard]

— A Way to Get Wealth.... L, 1683. 14th Ed. 6 parts in 1 vol. 12mo, later half calf; rubbed. Title & some leaves frayed. bba Jan 30 (143) £240 [Hughes]

Marle, Raimond van. See: Van Marle, Raimond

Marlowe, Christopher, 1564-93

— Doctor Faustus. L: Vale Press, 1903. One of 310. Ed by John Masefield; Illus by Charles Ricketts. bba July 9 (319) £150 [Blackwell]

Marlowe, Christopher, 1564-93 —& Chapman, George, 1559?-1634

— Hero and Leander. L: Vale Press, 1894. One of 220. 8vo, vellum gilt; soiled. bba July 9 (305) £320 [Rota]

Marmaduke...

— Marmaduke Multiply's Merry Method of Making Minor Mathematicians. L: J. Harris, 1827 [but imprints dated 1816-17]. Issue not specified. 16mo, modern half calf. With title & 61 (of 69) hand-colored plates. cb Sept 26 (155) $130

Marmion, Shackerley, 1603-39

— The Antiquary. L, 1641. 4to, late 19th-cent half mor by Riviere. Tp repaired. Ck Oct 31 (188) £380

Marmontel, Jean Francois, 1723-99

— Les Contes moraux. Paris, 1765. 3 vols. 12mo, contemp calf gilt. SI June 10 (596) LIt900,000

— Les Incas, ou la destruction de l'empire. Paris, 1777. 2 vols. 12mo, contemp calf gilt. S July 1 (1125) £180 [Scheffen]

Marmora, Andrea

— Della Historia di Corfu.... Venice: Curti, 1672. 4to, 19th-cent vellum. With engraved title, port & 3 double-page maps & town plans & 5 plates of coins. Sold w.a.f. b Nov 18 (342A) £380

Anr copy. Uncut, in paper-covered bds; rubbed. With engraved title, port, 3 double-page maps & plans & 5 plates of coins. Ink corrections to text; some browning & waterstaining. S Nov 21 (266) £900 [Christodoulou]

Maroldus, Marcus

— Sententia veritatis humanae redemptionis. [Rome: Stephen Plannck, after Mar 1481]. 4to, modern half vellum. Gothic type. 6 leaves. Goff M-280. sg Mar 12 (125) $700

Marolles, Michel de, 1600-81

— Tableaux du Temple des Muses.... Paris, 1655. Folio, modern cloth. With engraved title, port & 57 plates. Some soiling & browning. P June 17 (265) $900

Anr Ed. Amst., 1676. Folio, half mor; rubbed. With folding frontis & 56 (of 58) plates. 1 scuffed, 1 torn. bba Mar 26 (172) £75 [Wilbraham]

Marozzo, Achille

— Arte dell'armi. Venice: Antonio Pinargenti, 1568. Bound with: Agrippa, Camillo. Trattato di scienza d'arme. Venice: Antonio Pinargenti, 1568. 4to, contemp vellum. With 26 plates in 1st work & 17 plates in 2d work; both works with engraved titles. Short tear in F1 repaired. S Dec 5 (173) £2,000 [Mediolanum]

Anr Ed. Venice: Antonio Pinargenti, 1568 [colophon dated 1569]. 4to, modern mor. With engraved title & 26 plates. sg Mar 26 (196) $1,900

— Opera nova. Venice, 1568. 4to, old vellum. With 76 plates. sg Mar 26 (197) $1,500

Marra, John

— Journal of the Resolution's Voyage.... L, 1775. Recent calf. Some repairs to leaves along the hinge. kh Nov 11 (563) A$3,000

Anr Ed. L: for F. Newbery, 1775. 8vo, contemp calf; rebacked, new inner hinges. With folding chart & 5 plates plus folding map of the New Hebrides & New Caledonia. Marginal chip in P1. CNY Oct 8 (74) $3,500

Anr copy. Contemp calf gilt; rebacked. With folding chart & 5 plates. S June 25 (51) £1,800 [Quaritch/Hordern]

Marriott, Ida Lee. See: Lee, Ida

Marroni, Salvatore

— Raccolta dei principali costumi religiosi e militari della corte Pontificia. Rome: Tommaso Cuccioni, [c.1830]. 4to, orig cloth; spine worn. With hand-colored engraved title & 162 costume vignettes on 9 double-page sheets. Torn along 1 join. Ck Nov 29 (296) £750

Marrot, Harold Vincent

— A Bibliography of the Works of John Galsworthy. L, 1928. One of 210, sgd by Galsworthy. DW Apr 8 (509) £50

Marrow, James H.

— Passion Iconography in Northern European Art.... Kortrijk, 1979. Folio, cloth, in d/j. sg Oct 31 (233) $225

Marryat, Capt. Frederick, 1792-1848

— A Diary of America, with Remarks on its Institutions. L, 1839. 1st Ed. 3 vols. 8vo, orig half cloth. sg June 18 (355) $90

— Jacob Faithful. L, 1837. 3 vols. 8vo, contemp cloth; soiled. With 12 hand-colored plates. Lacking half-titles & ad leaf. CNY Oct 8 (158) $600

— The Novels. NY & Bost & L, 1895-96. One of 750 for America. Ed by R. Brinley Johnson. 24 vols. 8vo, orig cloth; some covers dampstained at edges. wa Sept 26 (212) $160

— Peter Simple. L, 1834. 3 vols. 12mo, contemp half calf; extremities rubbed. Tp & inserted frontis in Vol I loose; 2 ad leaves at end of Vol III not preserved. Inserted in Vol I are port & proofs of 3 plates (foxed) by R. W. Buss for the 1837 Ed. Ink corrections on 2 leaves. Inscr by E. D. Ingraham. ALs to Ingraham tipped in; Marryat's calling card pasted to inside front cover. CNY Oct 8 (157) $420

— The Phantom Ship. L, 1839. 1st English Ed. 3 vols. 8vo, orig bds; rubbed. Tipped in Vol I is holograph Ms of ptd dedication for the 1st Ed. With related material. DuPont copy. CNY Oct 8 (159) $850

Marsh, E. A.

— The Evolution of Automatic Machinery as Applied to the Manufacture of Watches... by the American Waltham Watch Company. Chicago, 1896. Orig cloth. cb Feb 27 (45) $50

Marsh, Othniel Charles, 1831-99

— Dinocerata. A Monograph of an extinct Order of Gigantic Mammals. Wash., 1884. 4to,7bd syn With 56 lithos. Inscr to Daniel Cady Eaton & his wife. sg Nov 14 (194) $325

— Odontornithes...Extinct Toothed Birds of North America. Wash., 1880. 4to, syn. sg Nov 14 (193) $200

Marsh, W. Lockwood

— Aeronautical Prints and Drawings. L, 1924. One of 1,000. 4to, orig cloth; rubbed. pn May 14 (92) £110 [Browning]

Anr copy. Cloth; shaken. sg Nov 14 (263) $100

Marshall, Alfred

— Principles of Economics. L, 1891. Vol I (all pbd). 8vo, orig cloth; rubbed. DW Nov 6 (304) £1,350

Marshall, John, 1755-1835

— The Life of George Washington. L, 1804-7. 5 vols. 4to, orig bds; worn, a few covers detached. F Sept 26 (456) $95

Anr copy. 5 vols plus Atlas. 4to, old calf; rubbed, spines worn. Atlas vol with 10 maps. K Sept 29 (250) $250

Anr copy. 5 vols. 8vo, lea. Foxed. Met Apr 28 (479) $150

Anr copy. Half calf, not uniform. With port & 14 plates & maps. Several maps in Vol V trimmed close costing imprint; some foxing. Manney copy. P Oct 11 (217) $2,000

Anr copy. 5 vols. 4to, mor extra by Sangorski & Sutcliffe. Extra-illus with ports, views, maps & facsimiles. P Dec 12 (182) $6,500

Anr Ed. Phila., 1804-7. 5 vols. 8vo, calf gilt. Extremities worn Minor worm damage to first few leaves of Vol III. NH Oct 6 (38) $225

Anr Ed. Phila., 1805-7. 2d Issue. 5 vols. Without Atlas. Contemp sheep; worn. sg June 18 (544) $175

Anr Ed. Phila.: C. P. Wayne, 1807. Atlas only. Old half lea; dry & rubbed. With 10 double-page or folding maps. Fold break to 1 map. O May 26 (123) $250

Marshall, John, 1784?-1837

— Royal Naval Biography. L, 1823-35. 12 vols, including Supplement. 8vo, orig cloth. Library markings. bba Mar 26 (240) £85 [The Bookroom]

Marshall, William, 1745-1818

— The Rural Economy of Norfolk.... L, 1787. 1st Ed. 2 vols. 8vo, contemp calf; joints split. bba Oct 10 (2779) £100 [Land]

Marsigli, Luigi Ferdinando, Count, 1658-1730

— L'Etat militaire de l'Empire Ottoman.... The Hague, 1732. 2 vols in 1. Folio, contemp calf; worn. With 2 hand-colored folding maps (1 torn) & 34 plates & maps & 3 folding tables. Some spotting & browning. Stephen Riou's copy. S June 30 (348) £750 [Keskiner]

Marsy, Francois Marie de —& Richer, Adrien

— Histoire moderne des Chinois, des Japonnois.... Paris, 1755-78. 30 vols, 18th-cent calf Rubbed, 1 bdg chipped. Some browning; dampstains in 3 vols. S Feb 11 (561) £750 [Booth]

Martelli, Ugolino

— La Chiave del calendaro gregoriano. Lyons: [F. Conrard], 1583. 8vo, 19th-cent half sheep gilt; spine chipped, front joint cracked. sg May 14 (293) $175

Martena, G. B.

— Flagello militare overo il terror de conflitti. Naples: C. Troise, 1687. 4to, modern vellum. With engraved title, port & 18 plates. Some staining. S July 9 (302) £300 [Middleton]

Martens, Robert W. See: Sisson & Martens

Marthens, John F.

— Typographical Bibliography. Pittsburgh, 1875. Annotated & with articles & reviews pasted on pack pages & back cover. cb Oct 17 (578) $110

Marti, Emmanuel

— Discours sur la musique zephyrienne adresse aux venerables crepitophiles.... Paris, 1873. One of 20 on Whatman. 8vo, contemp half mor gilt by Allo. sg Mar 5 (181) $325

Martial...

— The Martial Achievements of Great Britain.... L: James Jenkins, [plates watermarked 1812]. 4to, contemp mor gilt by Hering; covers detached, rubbed. With engraved title, dedication & 52 colored plates. Some soiling. P June 17 (243) $1,000

Martialis, Marcus Valerius

— Epigrammata. Venice: Baptista de Tortis, 17 July 1485. Folio, later vellum; soiled. 63 lines of commentary surrounding text; types 1:114R (text), 2:78R. Wormed throughout, with some loss to text; a1 laid down. 172 leaves. Goff M-308. C Dec 16 (143) £850 [Bifolco]

Anr Ed. Venice: Aldus, Dec 1501. 8vo, 19th-cent vellum. Lacking final blank. SI June 10 (597) LIt700,000

Anr Ed. Paris, 1783. ("Epigrammatum libri XV.") 6 vols. 8vo, 19th-cent calf gilt; extremities rubbed, spine ends of Vol III chipped. C June 24 (334) £200 [Maggs]

— Epigrammaton libri XIV. Paris: S. Colinaeum, 1540. 16mo, early calf gilt; worn, wormed. cb Dec 5 (84) $100

Martin, B. L. Henri

— Histoire de France.... Paris, 1852-54. 19 vols. 8vo, contemp calf gilt. Ck July 10 (350) £450

Martin, Benjamin, 1704-82

— Philosophia Britannica; or, a New and Comprehensive System of the Newtonian Philosophy. L, 1788. 4th Ed. 3 vols. 8vo, contemp calf; joints cracked. Foxed, affecting some plates. Titles & some text leaves stamped. sg Nov 14 (264) $200

Martin, Charles & Leopold

— The Civil Costume of England from the Conquest to the Present Period. L, 1842. 4to, orig cloth. With hand-colored title & 49 (of 60) hand-colored plates. Library stamp on front pastedown; upper margins soiled. pn Sept 12 (274) £80 [Fleming]

Martin, Corneille

— Les genealogies et ancinnes descentes des forestiers.... Antwerp: Jean Baptist Vrients, [1598]. Foli, 19th-cent calf. With engraved title & 43 plates. Q2-4 torn with loss & restored; marginal soiling. Ck Oct 31 (189) £240

Martin du Gard, Roger

— Les Thibault. Paris, 1922-40. 11 vols. Half mor by Devauchelle, orig wraps bound in. Vol XI is one of 30 author's copies. With 2 A Ls s. S May 28 (389) £1,300 [Beres]

Martin, Fredrik Robert

— The Miniature Painting and Painters of Persia.... L, 1912. 2 vols. Folio, orig cloth; Vol I marked & stained. S Feb 11 (357) £450 [Lygo]

Anr Ed. L, 1968. Folio, orig cloth, in d/j. DW Mar 11 (839) £105

Martin, Henry, 1858-1927

— Le Terence des Ducs. Paris, 1907. One of 255. Folio, orig wraps; spine ends torn. With color frontis & 36 heliogravure plates. sg May 21 (276) $50

Martin Library, Henry Bradley

— [Sale Catalogue] The Library of H. Bradley Martin. NY, 1989-90. 9 vols. Folio, cloth; some wear. O Sept 24 (159) $170

Anr copy. 9 vols. 4to, With price lists. wa Mar 5 (100) $260

Martin, John, 1789-1869

— An Account of the Natives of the Tonga Islands. Bost., 1820. 1st American Ed. 8vo, rebound. K Sept 29 (317) $90

Martin Le Roy Collection, Victor

— Catalogue raisonne de la Collection.... Paris, 1905-9. One of 360. Ed by Jean Joseph Marquet de Vasselot. 5 vols. Folio, loose as issued in cloth portfolios; rebacked. sg Sept 6 (184) $700

Martin, Louis Claude St. See: Saint-Martin, Louis Claude de

Martin, Martin, d.1719

— A Description of the Western Islands of Scotland. L, 1716. 2d Ed. 8vo, calf; rebacked. With folding map & 1 plate. pnE Oct 2 (378) £170

Martin, Robert Montgomery, 1803?-68

— The British Colonies, their History, Extent.... L, [1855]. 5 vols. 4to, half lea; worn. Some internal staining. Sold w.a.f. O Feb 25 (133) $300

— The Indian Empire; History, Topography, Geology. L, [1858-61]. 3 vols in 4. 4to, contemp mor. DW Nov 6 (68) £155

— Statistics of the Colonies of the British Empire.... L, 1839. 8vo, later cloth. Library markings; tear in folding colored map. kh Nov 11 (567) A$50

— Tallis's Illustrated Atlas.... L, [c.1857]. Folio, contemp half calf; worn. With engraved title & 78 maps only, hand-colored in outline. Lacking 2 plates & 3 maps; tp frayed & loose; some spotting & staining. S July 1 (1421) £1,650 [Map House]

Martin, Sarah Catherine

— The New Experienced English-Housekeeper for the Use and Ease of Ladies.... Doncaster, 1795. 8vo, contemp sheep; spine ends worn, joints cracked. Some foxing & brown smudging; half-title with def upper margin. wa Sept 26 (488) $150

Martindale, Frances

— Words of Hope & Comfort for the Sorrowful. [L: Mitchell, 1867]. Folio, orig cloth; worn. Ptd throughout in chromolithography in imitation of a medieval illuminated Ms. cb Sept 26 (117) $60

Martineau, Harriet, 1802-76

— Retrospect of Western Travel. NY: Charles Lohman, 1838. 12mo, orig half cloth; worn, hole in front free endpaper of Vol I. Some foxing & browning. bbc Dec 9 (390) $100

Martinez de Araujo, Juan

— Manual de los santos sacramentos en el idioma de Michuacan. Mexico: por Dona Maria de Benavides; Viuda de Juan de Ribera, 1690. 4to, old vellum; soiled, pastedowns damaged. Dampstained; a few small wormholes; fore-margins of last 2 leaves torn away not affecting letters. S Nov 21 (335) £1,500 [Maggs]

Martini, Giambatista

— Storia della musica. Bologna, 1757-81. 3 vols. 4to, modern bds. With 6 plates & 8 folding plates of musical notation. Some tears at folds; 1 leaf torn; some dampstaining & browning. pn Oct 24 (413) £380 [Bifolco]

Martini, Martinus, 1614-61

— Regni Sinensis a Tartaris Tyrannice evastati.... Amst.: Jansson Valkenier, 1661. 12mo, contemp vellum. With engraved title, double-page map & 12 double-page plates. C May 20 (278) £150 [Maggs]

Martius, Karl Friedrich Philipp von

— Flora Brasiliensis, seu enumeratio Plantarum in Brasilia. Munich & Leipzig, 1840-1906. Vol III: Parts 4-6 only: Alfred Cogniaux's Orchidaceae I-III. 3 vols. Folio, contemp half cloth; backstrips chipped, inner joints weak. With 472 uncolored plates. Stamps of the Lindley Library, Royal Horticultural Society on spines. McCarty-Cooper copy. CNY Jan 25 (87) $750

Martyn, Thomas, 1735-1825

— Flora Rustica exhibiting Accurate Figures of...Plants.... L, 1792-94. 4 vols in 2. 8vo, contemp calf; joints split, spines worn. With 144 hand-colored plates. S Nov 15 (748) £400 [Erlini]

Anr copy. Some spotting. S Feb 26 (932) £480 [Vilsoet]

— Thirty-Eight Plates with Explanations: Intended to Illustrate Linnaeus's System of Vegetables. L, 1817. 8vo, contemp bds; broken. With 38 hand-colored plates. Some foxing on text leaves. sg Feb 13 (196) $250

Martyn, Thomas, fl.1760-1816

— Aranei, or a Natural History of Spiders.... L, 1793. 2 parts in 1 vol. 4to, contemp mor gilt by Hering; rubbed. With 2 engraved titles, hand-colored frontis, 28 hand-colored plates & 2 plates of medals. Ink stain on 1st title; stamps on pastedowns, verso of title & head of Preface. pn Mar 19 (307) £1,300 [Baring]

— Entomologist Anglois ouvrage ou l'on a rassemble tous les Insectes Coleopteres.... L, 1792. 4to, contemp mor; extremities rubbed. With 2 plain & 42 hand-colored plates. Marginal browning. C May 20 (196) £360 [Shapero]

Martyn, William Frederick

— A New Dictionary of Natural History. L, 1785. 2 vols. Folio, contemp calf gilt; rubbed, joints worn. With 100 hand-colored plates. Some browning & spotting. O Nov 26 (115) $950

Martyr, Peter, d.1525

— The Decades of the Newe Worlde or West India.... L, 1555. 1st Ed in English, 3d Issue. Trans by Rycharde Eden. 4to, 18th-cent mor gilt; 2 small gouges to lower cover, extremities & raised bands worn. Minor marginal soiling; some mostly marginal dampstains; 2 small stains to fol. 3B1; 3D1 with burn-hole affecting 4 letters; headlines of c.15 leaves shaved. STC 647. CNY Oct 8 (163) $42,000

— Extraict ou recueil des isles nouvellement trouvees en la grand mer Oceane.... Paris: Simon de Colines, 1532. 4to, late 18th-cent mor gilt; rubbed & scuffed. 1st & last 2 leaves soiled; marginal dampstains; some spotting & browning; 1 leaf holed in margin; tear to A7; A8 repaired. DuPont copy. CNY Oct 8 (162) $44,000

— The History of Travayle in the West and East Indies.... L: Richard Jugge, 1577. 4to, contemp calf; rebacked in 17th-cent, lea of upper cover cracking, 2 small holes to lower cover, spine & joints rubbed, some restorations. Black letter Some soiling; some spotting from mold, occasionally affecting letters; dampstains entering text of last 100 leaves; a few sidenotes shaved; 1 marginal repair. STC 649. CNY Oct 8 (164) $24,000

Anr copy. Mor. Tp remargined; some leaves soiled; hole in margin of D6 affecting 1 letter in sidenote; repair to margin of 3E4 with loss of page numeral. STC 649. S Nov 21 (218) £6,000 [Quaritch]

Marullus, Michael

— Hymni et epigrammata. Florence: Societas Colubris (Compagnia del Drago), 26 Nov 1497. 4to, 19th-cent mor gilt. Type 1:110R, 25 lines. Unrubricated. Some staining in gathering f; some other margins foxed. 96 leaves. Goff M-342. S Dec 5 (22) £2,000 [Mediolanum]

Marvell, Andrew, Pseud. See: Broadsides

Marvell, Andrew, 1621-78

— Miscellaneous Poems. L, 1681. 1st Ed. Folio, contemp calf; upper cover stained, upper hinge split, early pen-trials on lower free endpapers. Lacking the usually omitted 16 leaves occasioned by the excision of 3 poems on Cromwell. Hogan-Manney copy. P Oct 11 (218) $10,000

Anr copy. Mor; rubbed, upper joint cracking. With the port.. With Ms copies of Marvell's poem on Col. Blood's attempt to steal the crown jewels. Kern-Martin copy. P June 17 (266) $3,000

Anr copy. Mor gilt by Zaehnsdorf. John Lehmann's copy. S Nov 14 (589) £500 [Conrad]

Marx, Karl, 1818-83

— Das Kapital. Hamburg, 1867-94. 1st Ed. Vol I only. Contemp half calf; rubbed. C June 24 (175) £6,500 [Hannas]

2d Ed. Hamburg, 1872. Vol I (all pbd). 8vo, contemp cloth; worn; spine gouged. O Nov 26 (116) $90

Anr copy. 3 vols in 4. 8vo, contemp half lea; top of spines chipped, joints rubbed or starting, Vol II backstrip partly detached. sg Mar 5 (182) $2,000

— Kapital. Kritika Poleticeskoj Ekonomii. St. Petersburg: N. P. Poliakov, 1872-96. 3 vols. 8vo, contemp half mor & half lea. Lacking half-title in Vol I; some spotting & browning; some crayon gloss & scoring on a few leaves. C June 24 (176) £2,800 [Goldhar]

Anr Ed. St. Petersburg: N. P. Poliakov, 1872. 8vo, contemp half calf; rubbed & def. Some browning & fingersoiling. HH May 12 (1078) DM6,000

— Gellert, Hugo. - Karl Marx Capital in Pictures. White Plains, 1933. One of 133. Folio, loose in cloth portfolio as issued. With 61 sgd lithos. sg Jan 10 (100) $2,600

Mary, Queen of Scotland. See: Buchanan, George

Maryland

See also: Atlas

— The City Hall, Baltimore; History of Construction and Dedication. Balt., 1877. 4to, orig cloth; worn. bbc June 29 (461) $50

— Laws of Maryland, Made Since M,DCC,LXXIII...and Acts of Assembly since the Revolution. Annapolis, 1787. Folio, recent calf; no orig blanks retained. Tp & last leaf repaired. bbc Apr 27 (595) $190

Marzagaglia, Gaetano

— Del calcolo balistico o sia del metodo di calcolare con la medesima facilita'i tiri delle bombe orizzontali e gli obliqui libro unico. Verona, [1748]. 4to, contemp bds. SI June 10 (600) LIt300,000

Anr copy. Bds. SI June 10 (601) LIt350,000

Mas Latrie, Rene de

— Chronique d'Ernoul et de Bernard le Tresorier. Paris, 1871. 8vo, half mor, orig ptd wrap bound in. S June 30 (54) £200 [Bank of Cyprus]

— Chroniques d'Amadi et de Strambaldi. Paris, 1891-93. 2 vols. 4to, orig ptd wraps. S June 30 (55) £450 [Bank of Cyprus]

Anr copy. Moderne loth. S June 30 (56) £600 [Christodoulou]

Masal, Francois —& Wittek, Martin

— Manuscrits dates conserves en Belgique. Brussels, 1968-82. Vols I-IV. 4to, cloth. sg Oct 31 (234) $300

Mascagni, Paolo, 1752-1815

— Anatomia universale.... Florence, 1833. Folio, half cloth; rubbed. With 75 colored plates, each accompanied by outline plate. SI Dec 5 (447) LIt2,400,000

— Prodromo della grande anotomia. Florence, 1819. Folio, modern cloth. Some soiling. SI Dec 5 (446) LIt1,800,000

Masclet, Daniel

— Nus, La Beaute de la Femme. Paris, 1933. Folio, embossed-wraps, laced; some soiling. sg Oct 8 (53) $400

Masefield, John, 1878-1967

— The Country Scene. L, [1937]. 1st Ed. 4to, orig cloth, in def d/j. With 42 colored plates by Edward Seago. b Mar 11 (160) £70

— Salt-Water Ballads. L, 1902. 1st Ed, 1st Issue. Orig cloth. O July 14 (126) $275

Anr Ed. L: Grant Richards, 1902. Orig royal blue cloth. bba Apr 9 (49) £190 [Dawson]; sg Dec 12 (268) $225

— Sard Harker. L, 1925. One of 380. Half vellum, in worn & repaired d/j; endpapers foxed. Inscr to his son, 27 Oct 1924. sg Dec 12 (267) $225

Masereel, Frans

— Danse Macabre. Bern, [1941]. One of 950. Folio, bds; foot of spine chipped. Minor browning. sg Sept 26 (225) $60

— Die Idee, einleitung von Hermann Hesse. Munich: Kurt Wolff, 1927. 1st Ed. Orig bds. With 83 plates. Met Apr 28 (228) $80

— Mein Stundenbuch. Munich, 1920. 8vo, bds. Met Apr 28 (230) $80

— Die Passion eines Menschen. Munich: Kurt Wolff, 1921. 4to, bds. With 25 illusts. Met Apr 28 (229) $80

Mask...

— The Mask: A Monthly Journal of the Art of the Theatre. L, 1908-29. Vols 1-4 only. Vellum, orig wraps bound in. sg Mar 5 (215) $600

Anr copy. Vols 1-11 plus bound vol containing orig wraps for Vols 4-7 (other wraps bound in appropriate vols). 8vo & 4to, half vellum. Eva Le Gallienne's copy. sg Mar 5 (216) $1,600

Maskell, Alfred

— Wood Sculpture. L, 1911. 8vo, bdg not described. Stamp erased from tp. kh Nov 11 (168) A$50

Mason, A. E. W.

— The Four Feathers. L, 1902. Inscr to Dennis Wheatley. Manney copy. P Oct 11 (1219) $600

Mason, G. Finch

— Tit Bits of the Turf. L, 1887. Oblong folio, orig pictorial bds; worn. With 16 hand-colored plates. S May 14 (1017) £320 [Grigoropoulos]

Mason, George, 1735-1806

— A Supplement to Johnson's English Dictionary.... L, 1801. 4to, contemp calf; front cover detached. sg Nov 7 (114) $200

Mason, George Henry

— The Costume of China. L, 1800. Folio, contemp half russia gilt; rebacked, orig backstrip retained. With 60 hand-colored plates. sg May 7 (148) $650

— The Punishments of China. L, 1801. Folio, contemp half calf; rubbed & worn, covers detached. With 22 hand-colored plates. Lacking English title. bba Feb 27 (342) £150 [Blumenkron & Ramirez]

Anr copy. Contemp mor gilt; rubbed. With 22 colored plates. DW Oct 2 (83) £90

Anr copy. Old mor; scuffed, upper joint week. With 22 hand-colored plates. DW Apr 8 (46) £185

Anr copy. Disbound. With 21 (of 22) hand-colored plates. Sold w.a.f. DW May 13 (41) £100

Anr Ed. L, 1808. Folio, later half mor gilt; extremities rubbed. With 22 hand-colored plates. sg Jan 9 (117) $450

Mason, Monck, 1803-89?

— Aeronautica: or, Sketches Illustrative of the Theory and Practice of Aerostation.... L, 1838. 8vo, orig cloth; rubbed. With frontis on india paper mtd & 5 plates. Piece torn from margin of B6; some browning &

foxing. pn May 14 (93) £300

Mason, Stuart. See: Millard, Christopher Sclater

Massachusetts

— Acts and Laws, of Her Majesties Province.... Bost, 1714. 2 parts in 1 vol. Folio, contemp calf; some wear. Some rippling & foxing. bbc Dec 9 (396) $1,200

— The Boston Directory. Bost., 1798. 12mo, disbound. With folding map. sg June 18 (356) $700

— A Constitution or Frame of Government.... Bost., 1780. 8vo, modern cloth. sg June 18 (358) $800

— County Atlas of Hampshire, Massachusetts. NY: F. W. Beers, 1873. Folio, cloth; worn. Some foxing & soiling. O July 14 (26) $250

— Official Topographical Atlas of Massachusetts. Bost., 1871. Compiled by H. F. Walling & O. W. Gray. Folio, orig cloth. With maps hand-colored, but some foxing. NH Oct 30 (399) $95

Masse, Gertrude C. E.

— A Bibliography of...Books Illustrated by Walter Crane. L, 1923. 1st Ed. Half cloth, in d/j. Pencil marginalia. sg Oct 31 (269) $175

Masson, Charles, Pseud.

— Narrative of Various Journeys in Balochistan, Afghanistan, and Punjab.... L, 1844. 8vo, orig cloth; worn. O Nov 16 (118) $1,200

Masson, Frederic, 1847-1923

— L'Imperatrice Marie-Louise. Paris, 1902. One of 1,000. Folio, lea gilt; cover reattached. sp Nov 24 (252) $200

— Josephine: Imperatrice et reine. Paris, 1899. Folio, contemp mor gilt with Napoleonic-style stamping, orig wraps bound in; some wear. bbc Sept 23 (56) $100

Masters, Edgar Lee, 1869-1950

See also: Limited Editions Club

— A Book of Verses. Chicago, 1898. 1st Ed. 8vo, orig bds; cover spotted. sg Dec 12 (269) $225

— Spoon River Anthology. NY, 1915. 1st Ed, 1st Issue. Inscr. Epstein copy. sg Apr 30 (323) $2,200

Mather, Cotton, 1663-1728

— Magnalia Christi Americana; or, the Ecclesiastical History of New England.... L, 1702. 1st Ed. 7 parts in 1 vol. Folio, contemp calf; rebacked. With the folding map , 2 ad leaves & blank 6M2. Without the errata leaves. C May 20 (277) £1,100 [Arader]

Anr copy. Old calf; rebacked, rubbed. With the folding map, ad leaves & errata leaves. Library acquisition mark in gutter margin of 1st text leaf. L.p. copy. O Nov 26 (119) $3,700

— The Wonders of the Invisible World. L: John Dunton, 1693. 8vo, contemp sheep; rubbed. Marginal stains. pn May 14 (39) £1,400

Mathers, E. Powys, 1892-1939. See: Eastern...; Golden Cockerel Press

Mathes, W. Michael

— Mexico on Stone: Lithography in Mexico, 1826-1900. San Francisco: Book Club of California, 1984. One of 550. cb Sept 12 (113) $60; pba July 23 (137) $100

Mathews, Alfred E.

— Gems of Rocky Mountain Scenery. NY, 1869. Folio, orig cloth; rebacked. With 20 plates. Dampstained in gutters and upper inner corner throughout. sg Nov 7 (136) $1,300

Mathews, Anne

— Memoirs of Charles Mathews, Comedian. L, 1838-39. 4 vols in 5. 8vo, later mor by W. Pratt; spines rubbed & chipped at ends. Extra-illus with c.350 ports, views & orig letters. S May 14 (954) £200 [Sutherland]

Mathews, Gregory Macalister

— Birds and Books. The Story of the Mathews Ornithological Library. Canberra, 1942. One of 200. 8vo, orig wraps. kh Nov 11 (569) A$80

— The Birds of Norfolk & Lord Howe Islands.... L, 1928. One of 225. 4to, orig wraps; some wear. Marginal foxing. kh Nov 11 (570) A$900

Mathison, Gilbert Farquhar

— Narrative of a Visit To Brazil, Chile, Peru, and the Sandwich Islands. L, 1825. 8vo, early half calf; worn. Some foxing. kh Nov 11 (365) A$260

Matho. See: Baxter, Andrew

Matisse, Henri, 1869-1954

— Cinquante dessins. Paris, 1920. Ltd Ed. Folio, orig wraps. With orig frontis etching, sgd, & 50 plates. CGen Nov 18 (417) SF4,500

Anr copy. Orig wraps; needs rebacking; tape remnants on covers. sg Nov 7 (137) $2,200

— Dernieres oeuvres.... Paris, 1958. Folio, bds; spine chipped at head, joints cracked. Mtd decoupage reproductions crudely outlined in pencil. Verve, No 35/36. sg Sept 6 (186) $350

Anr copy. Verve, No 35/36. Folio, orig bds; bowed, soiled, bumped. Damp-rippled at fore-edge with waterstaining visible

principally on text leaves. wa June 25 (505) $600
— Jazz. NY: Braziller, [1983]. Folio, loose as issued in cloth. sg Sept 26 (226) $110
— Portraits. Monte Carlo, 1954. Ltd Ed in French. 4to, wraps. F Sept 26 (132) $300; sg Sept 6 (188) $500; sg May 7 (149) $350

Anr Ed. Monte Carlo, 1955. One of 500 in English. 4to, orig wraps. With 33 mtd color & 60 plain plates. sg Apr 2 (179) $300
— Vence, 1944-48. Paris, [1948]. Wraps. Verve, Nos 21 & 22. Inscr by Matisse to Maria. F June 25 (312) $1,150

Matra, James. See: Cook, Capt. James

Matrix
— Matrix. L: Whittington Press, 1981-90. Ltd Ed. 10 vols plus Vols 7-10 with additional folder in each box. Half mor; rubbed. Sold w.a.f. P June 18 (624) $3,750

Matta, Sebastian
— Come detta dentro vo significando. Lausanne, 1962. One of 5 hors commerce on japon nacre with extra suite of 16 of the etchings. Folio, unsewn as issued in orig wraps. P June 17 (271) $6,500

Matthew of Westminster
— Flores historiarum...praecipue de rebus Britannicis. Frankfurt: Wechel, 1601. ("Flores historiarum per Matthaeum Westmonasteriensem collecti....") Folio, later bds; rubbed. Some browning & marginal waterstaining; first & last leaves ink-stamped. bba Apr 9 (20) £65 [Ash]

Anr copy. 19th-cent calf gilt. Some spotting & browning. FD Dec 2 (28) DM500

Matthews, Brander, 1852-1929
— Bookbindings, Old and New.... NY, 1895. 8vo, cloth. cb Oct 17 (585) $50

Matthews, Sallie R.
— Interwoven: A Pioneer Chronicle.... El Paso: Hertzog, 1958. One of 1,500. Illus by E. M. Schiwetz. Inscr by author's son. bbc Apr 27 (616) $100

Matthieu, Pierre, e1563-1621
— The Heroyk Life and deploable Death of...Henry the Fourth. L: George Eld, 1612. 4to, early 19th-cent half sheep; needs rebacking. Some soiling & dampstaining. STC 17661. sg Oct 24 (214) $400

Mattioli, Pietro Andrea, 1500-77
— Commentarii in libros sex Pedacii Dioscoridis de medica materia. Venice: Valgrisi, 1560. ("Commentarii secundo aucti, in libros sex Pedacii Dioscoridis de medica materia.") 2 parts in one vol. Folio, contemp blind-stamped pigskin; worn, lacking clasps. Minor staining; extensive annotations in an early hand. S Nov 21 (31) £2,000 [Rizzo]

Anr Ed. Venice: Valgrisi, 1583. ("Commentarii in VI. libros....") Folio, modern vellum. Lacking frontis in Vol I; repairs & defs. Sold w.a.f. SI June 10 (605) LIt6,800,000
— I Discorsi.... Venice: Valgrisi, 1568. ("I Discorsi nelli sei libri de Pedacio Dioscoride Anazarbeo della materia medicinale.") Folio, later half vellum. Crude repairs & defs, mainly to prelims, EE1-FF1 & last 4 leaves; some tears; tp & a few other leaves very def; tp laid down. Sold w.a.f. S Feb 25 (599) £2,250 [Erlini]

Anr Ed. Venice: Valgrisi, 1573. ("I Discorsi di M. Pietro Andrea Matthioli ne i sei libri di Pedacio Dioscoride...della materia medicinale.") Folio, half vellum. Marginal repairs; lacking several leaves. Sold w.a.f. SI June 10 (606) LIt2,000,000
— Opera. Frankfurt: Nicolaus Bassaeus, 1598. Folio, old buckskin; worn, lacking front flyleaf. B Nov 1 (472) HF3,200

Anr Ed. Basel: Koenig, 1674. Folio, calf; def. Lacking port of Bauhinus; foxing & browning. B Nov 1 (473) HF1,800

Mattsperger, Melchior
— Geistliche Hertzens-Einbildungen...in Biblischen Figur-Spruechen. Augsburg, [c.1728]. 2 vols in 1. Oblong 4to, later half calf; rebacked & rubbed. Vol I lacking title & prelims; anr title to Vol II loosely inserted. bba Feb 27 (330) £170 [Elliott]

Mauclair, Camille, 1872-1945
— Louis Legrand, peintre et graveur. Paris, [1910]. 4to, half mor gilt, orig front wrap bound in. Tp & a few leaves rehinged; 2 leaves of index detached. sg Feb 6 (162) $400

Maugham, W. Somerset, 1874-1965
See also: Limited Editions Club
— Cakes and Ale.... L, 1930. 1st Ed. In d/j. cb Sept 19 (157) $80

Anr copy. In d/j. Inscr. sg Dec 12 (270) $300

1st American Ed. NY, 1930. Cloth; spine faded. With tipped-in leaf, sgd, as issued. wa Sept 26 (214) $80

Anr Ed. L, [1954]. One of 1,000. Illus by Graham Sutherland. Orig calf. bba Apr 9 (140) £170 [Dawson]
— The Casuarina Tree. L, 1926. In d/j. sg Dec 12 (271) $375
— Don Fernando. NY, 1935. 1st American Ed. cb Dec 12 (111) $110
— Liza of Lambeth. L, 1897. 1st Ed. 8vo, orig cloth. W Mar 6 (71) £170

1st Issue. Orig cloth, sgd H. B. within gilt

rule. Manney copy. P Oct 11 (220) $1,000

Anr copy. Orig cloth. Epstein copy. sg Apr 30 (324) $600

— The Moon and Sixpence. L, [1919]. 1st Ed, 1st Issue. Orig cloth, in frayed d/j. Browned. Inscr to Earle J. Bernheimer. CNY June 9 (122) $1,200

Anr Ed. NY, [1919]. Inscr to A. Krock. sg Sept 12 (161) $175

— Of Human Bondage. NY, [1915]. 1st American Ed. Orig cloth; hinges tender, upper endpaper split. Inscr to Frank Hogan. P Dec 12 (183) $1,600

1st Ed, 1st Issue. Cloth; hinge repaired. sg June 11 (219) $475

Anr Ed. Garden City, 1936. One of 751. bbc Dec 9 (508) $95

Anr copy. Illusts by Randolf Schwabe. In frayed d/j. LH May 17 (634) $170

— Strictly Personal. Garden City, 1941. 1st Ed, One of 515. With photo frontis by G.P. Lynes. wa Mar 5 (226) $110; wa Mar 5 (238) $75

— A Writer's Notebook. L, 1949. One of 1,000. DW Oct 2 (374) £75

Ltd Ed. Orig half vellum. bba Dec 19 (145) £90 [Whiteson]

1st American Ed. NY, 1949. One of 1,000. wa Sept 26 (213) $75

Maund, Benjamin, 1790-1863. See: Botanic...

Maundrell, Henry

— A Journey from Aleppo to Jerusalem.... Oxford, 1707. 2d Ed. 8vo, contemp calf. With 9 plates. cb Oct 10 (71) $100

7th Ed. Oxford, 1749. 8vo, contemp calf gilt; rubbed. With 15 plates. b June 22 (190) £90

Anr copy. Contemp calf. Some spotting & browning. S June 30 (340) £150 [Sofer]

Maupassant, Guy de, 1850-93

— Bel-ami. Paris, 1885. 12mo, half mor, orig wraps bound in. Epstein copy. sg Apr 30 (326) $350

— Works. L & NY, [1903]. Autograph Ed. 17 vols. Half mor gilt. sg Mar 5 (183) $1,000

Alliance Francaise Ed. L & NY: M. W. Dunne, 1903. 17 vols. Half mor gilt; upper joint of Vol VIII cracked. P June 17 (344) $1,100

Bourget Ed, one of 750. 17 vols. Half lea; rubbed. O May 26 (124) $175

Cambridge Ed. 17 vols. Contemp half mor gilt; scuffed & soiled; minor stains to Vols I-II. wa Mar 5 (53) $450

Mauriac, Francois

— Genitrix. Paris, 1923. One of 4 hors commerce copies on chine, with port on japon & on velin. Mor gilt, orig wraps bound in. With ALs. S May 28 (392) £1,500 [Beres]

— Therese Desqueyroux. Paris, 1927. One of 55 on Annam de Rives. Mor gilt by Maylander, orig wraps bound in. Inscr to Paul Petit, 1951. S May 28 (394) £1,900 [Beres]

Maurois, Andre, 1885-1967

— Ariel ou la vie de Shelley. Paris, 1923. 1st Ed. Inscr to Arnold Bennett. Epstein copy. sg apr 30 (325) $300

Maury, Matthew Fountaine, 1806-73

— The Physical Geography of the Sea. NY, 1855. 8vo, orig cloth; spine faded. With 8 folding plates. sg Nov 14 (265) $130

Mavor, William Fordyce, 1758-1837

— The Juvenile Olio, or Mental Medley. L, 1796. 12mo, contemp sheep; joints cracked, rubbed. ESTC t003346. bba July 23 (256) £280 [Marlborough]

Maw, George, 1832-1912

— A Monograph of the Genus Crocus.... L, 1886. 4to, orig cloth; rubbed & soiled. With 81 hand-colored plates, 1 colored double-page map & 2 double-page ptd tables. Stamps on tp verso, last leaf of text & both pastedowns. pn Mar 19 (310) £1,200 [Wheldon & Wesley]

Mawe, John, 1764-1829

— Familiar Lessons on Mineralogy and Geology. L, 1821. 3d Ed. 8vo, orig cloth; broken & loose. With 4 hand-colored plates. bba Sept 5 (232) £80 [Worthing]

— Travels in the Interior of Brazil.... L, 1821. 2d Ed. 8vo, orig bds; worn. With map & 5 colored plates. O Feb 25 (137) $350

— A Treatise on Diamonds and Precious Stones.... L, 1813. 1st Ed. 8vo, contemp half calf; rubbed, head of spine torn. With 3 hand-colored plates. pn July 16 (45) £380 [Thorpe]

Mawman, Joseph

— An Excursion to the Highlands of Scotland.... L, 1805. 8vo, half calf. pnE May 13 (57) £80

Mawson, Sir Douglas, 1882-1958

— The Home of the Blizzard. L, 1914. 2 vols DW Nov 6 (69) £200

Anr Ed. L, [1915]. 2 vols. bba Mar 26 (333) £240 [Simper]

Anr copy. With 3 folding maps. cb Oct 10 (72) $225

Anr copy. Orig cloth; loose. Library markings. sg May 21 (71) $140

Maximilian zu Wied-Neuwied, Prince

— Abbildungen zur Naturgeschichte Brasiliens. Weimar, 1822-31. Folio, orig wraps; worn. With 1 plain & 89 hand-colored plates. FD Dec 2 (450) DM19,500

— Reise in das Innere Nord-America.... Coblenz: J. Hoelscher, 1839-41. Illus by Karl Bodmer. 4 vols including Atlas. 4to & oblong folio, contemp half mor (rebacked with orig spines preserved), plates loose in 4 orig ptd wraps. With 81 hand-colored plates, some heightened with gum arabic, & with plan, litho key-plate & litho table. Plate 35 with closed marginal tear into imprint; other marginal repairs; map laid down on linen. Manney copy. P Oct 11 (221) $160,000

Maximus Tyrius

— Sermones.... Rome: Jacobus Mazochius, 1517. Folio, modern calf. Waterstains at margins; P1 torn at lower margin. Ck Oct 31 (318) £420

Maxwell, Sir Herbert Eustace

— Memories of the Months. L, 1907-22. Half mor gilt. pnE Oct 2 (375) £90

— Salmon and Sea Trout. L, 1898. One of 130 L.p. copies. 8vo, orig calf. Annotated by J. A. Harvie-Brown in pencil. S Feb 11 (875) £260 [Montague]

Maxwell, James Clerk, 1831-79

— A Treatise on Electricity and Magnetism. Oxford, 1873. 1st Ed. 2 vols. 8vo, modern calf. Ck Oct 18 (18A) £650

Maxwell, Marius

— Stalking Big Game with a Camera. L, 1925. 4to, cloth; fore-edges soiled. cb Feb 12 (88) $120

Maxwell, Robert

— The Practical Husbandman: being a Collection.... Edin., 1757. 8vo, orig calf; rubbed. Some leaves cut in outer margins. Sgd. pnE Dec 4 (84) £80

Maxwell, William Hamilton, 1792-1850

— History of the Irish Rebellion in 1798. L, 1845. 1st Ed in orig 15 parts in 12. Illus by George Cruikshank. 8vo, orig wraps; 1 supplied from anr copy. pn Apr 23 (38) £140

May, Thomas, 1595-1650

— The History of the Parliament of England.... L, 1647. 3 parts in 1 vol. Folio, contemp calf; rubbed. W July 8 (63) £210

Mayakovsky, Vladimir

— 13 Let Raboty. Moscow, 1922. 2 vols. 8vo, orig wraps; backstrip of Vol II repaired. Inscr to Boris Kochno. SM Oct 12 (497) FF15,000

— Dlya Golosa. Berlin, 1923. Illus by El Lissitzky. 8vo, orig wraps; worn. S May 28 (250) £600 [Arenthon]

Anr copy. Illus by El Lissitsky. Orig wraps; spine & edges of upper cover discolored. Inscr to Boris Kochno. SM Oct 11 (500) FF22,000

— Izbranny. Berlin, 1923. Orig wraps. Inscr to Boris Kochno. SM Oct 12 (499) FF8,500

— Lirika. Moscow, 1923. Orig wraps. Inscr to Sergei Diaghilev. Kochno copy. SM Oct 12 (498) FF8,500

— Tuda i obratno. Moscow, 1930. Orig wraps; spine ends worn. sg Nov 7 (214) $275

Mayer, August Liebmann

— Velasquez. L, 1936. 4to, orig cloth; marked. S Feb 11 (143) £150 [Heneage]

Mayer, Brantz

— Baltimore Past and Present. Balt., 1871. 8vo, orig mor gilt; upper cover detached, spine def. With 45 albumen ports & 16 other albumen prints. bbc Dec 9 (359) $250

Anr copy. Orig mor gilt; worn, hinge repaired. With engraved title & 61 albumen photo ports. Tear to 1 port. bbc June 29 (489) $70

— Mexico, Aztec, Spanish and Republican.... Hartford, 1852. 2 vols. 8vo, contemp sheep; worn. Foxed throughout. sg June 18 (361) $90

Anr Ed. Hartford, 1853. 2 vols in 1. 8vo, orig mor gilt. sg June 18 (362) $175

Mayer, E.

— International Auction Records. Paris, 1973-81. For 1973-81. 9 vols. Cloth; shaken, some wear. O Sept 24 (162) $140

Mayer, Joseph

— On the Art of Pottery. Liverpool, 1873. 8vo, orig wraps; spine strengthened with tape, soiled. sg Sept 6 (56) $60

Mayer, Luigi

— Interesting Views in Turkey. L, 1819. 8vo, orig bds; worn. With 16 hand-colored plates. S July 1 (650) £190 [Sossidis]

— A Selection of the most interesting of Sir Robert Ainslie's Collection of views in Turkey.... L, 1812. 3 parts in 1 vol. Folio, later half calf over contemp bds; worn. With 56 hand-colored plates. Some marks. S Nov 21 (296) £1,000 [Lepanto]

Anr copy. 2 parts in 1 vol. Folio, later

19th-cent cloth. With 48 hand-colored plates. Crease at folding plate. S July 1 (651) £1,300 [Storey]

— A Selection of the Most Interesting of Sir Robert Ainslies's Celebrated Collection of Views in Egypt, Asia Minor.... L, 1812. Folio, contemp half sheep; front cover loose. With 23 hand-colored plates. Some foxing, mainly marginal. sg Jan 9 (118) $850

— Views in Egypt. L, 1801. Folio, contemp russia gilt; joints weak. With hand-colored dedication in Part I, hand-colored additional titles in Parts I & II & 59 (of 60) hand-colored plates. S June 25 (110) £1,000 [Toscani]

Anr copy. With 48 colored plates. Bound with: Mayer, Views in Palestine.... L, 1804. With 24 colored plates. And: Mayer. Views in the Ottoman Empire....L, 1803. With port & 24 colored plates. contemp mor gilt. De Mille copy. S June 30 (60) £1,900 [Dennistoun]

Anr copy. Contemp mor gilt by Bozerian with border of Egyptian motifs; joints rubbed. With 48 hand-colored plates. Lacking port. sg Nov 7 (138) $1,500

Anr copy. Contemp half lea; rubbed. SI Dec 5 (933) LIt2,800,000

Anr Ed. L, 1804. With 39 colored plates dated 1801-4. Bound with: Mayer. Views in Palestine.... L, 1804. With 24 colored plates dated 1803-4. And: Mayer. Views in the Ottoman Empire.... L, 1803. With 21 colored plates dated 1803. Folio, contemp half mor; rubbed. W July 8 (227) £2,500

— Views in Palestine. L, 1804. Bound with: Mayer, Luigi. Views in the Ottoman Empire. L, 1803. Folio, contemp half mor; worn & dampstained. With 24 colored plates in each work. Some marginal dampstaining; occasional foxing. F Mar 26 (763) $3,600

— Views in the Ottoman Dominions. L, 1801 [plates dated 1780-1806]. ("Views in Turkey in Europe and Asia...Selected from the Collection of Sir Robert Ainslie.") 3 parts in 1 vol. Folio, contemp bds; rebacked & recornered with calf. With 2 engraved titles & 60 hand-colored plates, all within ruled & gray wash borders. L.p. copy. C May 20 (83) £6,000 [Simon Finch]

— Views in the Ottoman Empire. L, 1803. Bound with: Views in Palestine.... Folio, modern half mor. With frontis & 48 hand-colored plates. Repair to tp of 1st work & perforated library stamp on last leaf of 2d work. W July 8 (99) £1,500

— Views in the Ottoman Dominions... L, 1810. 2 parts. Folio, orig bds; rebacked, corners repaired. With 71 hand-colored plates, including large folding view of Constantinople. Some text leaves spotted. C May 20 (85) £2,600 [Sedgwick]

Anr copy. Part 1 only. Folio, half mor; upper cover detached. With 31 hand-colored plates. rs Oct 17 (31A) $900

Mayer, Tobias, 1723-62

— Mathematischer Atlas in welchem auf 60 Tabellen.... Augsburg, 1745. Folio, contemp half vellum; soiled, spine def. With engraved title & 68 plates, including Supplement, several hand-colored. S Nov 21 (89) £700 [Massold]

Mayes, Charles

— The Australian Builders' Price-Book.... Melbourne, 1883. 4th Ed. 8vo, orig bdg. Some inked notes; several leaves from an earlier Ed tipped-in; folding table tipped to inside of rear cover. kh Nov 11 (571) A$70

Maygrier, Jacques Pierre

— Nouveau Elemens de la science et de l'art des accouchemens. Paris, 1814. 8vo, contemp half sheep. Blank corner off last index leaf. Inscr. sg Nov 14 (82) $500

Mayhew, Augustus, 1826-75

— Paved with Gold, or the Romance and Reality of the London Streets. L, 1858. Illus by Hablot K. Browne. 8vo, old half calf; worn & rubbed. With 1 tinted & 3 hand-colored plates & folding chart. Some foxing. kh Nov 11 (365) A$260

Mayhew, Henry, 1812-87

— 1851: or the Adventures of Mr. and Mrs. Sandboys.... L, [1851]. Illus by George Cruikshank. 8vo, orig cloth; soiled, spine ends worn, spine had frayed. Plates foxed. wa Dec 9 (421) $70

— The Upper Rhine.... L, 1858. 8vo, orig cloth. With engraved title & 19 plates. DW Nov 6 (70) £90

Mayhew, Horace

— The Tooth-Ache. L, [1849]. Illus by George Cruikshank. 12mo, orig bds; soiled, spine worn, soiled. With 43 plates on folding sheet. sg Oct 17 (173) $550

Maynard, Charles Johnson, 1845-1929

— The Butterflies of New England. Bost., 1886. Folio, cloth; worn & soiled. With 10 hand-colored lithos. O May 26 (121) $170

Mayo, Robert, 1784-1864

— Political Sketches of Eight Years in Washington. Balt., 1839. 1st Ed. Part 1 (all pbd). 8vo, orig cloth; worn & soiled. Foxed. NH May 30 (523) $120

Mazer, Sonia
— Yossele's Holiday. Garden City, 1934. Half cloth. Inscr. sg Jan 10 (102) $80

Mazuchelli, Nina Elizabeth
— The Indian Alps and How We Crossed Them. L, 1876. 4to, orig cloth. Some discoloration. bba May 14 (307) £120 [Scott]

Mazze, Clemens
— Vita di San Zenobio. Florence: [Bartolommeo di Libri], 8 Dec 1487. 4to, early 16th-cent mor gilt with central medallion of the Sacred Monogram & S. Lorenza lettered on either side of the medallion; rebacked & all corners renewed. 28 lines; roman letter. Some foxing. 46 leaves. Goff M-417. S Dec 5 (23) £2,200 [Pampaloni]

Mazzinelli, Alessandro
— Uffizio della settimana santa. Rome, 1758. 8vo, contemp mor gilt. Some browning. Sold w.a.f. Harmsworth-Abbey copy. S May 28 (140) £850 [Lib. Panini]

Mead, Braddock
— Remarks, in Support of the New Chart of North and South America.... L, 1753. 4to, later wraps. With: A Chart of North America. L, 1753. 6 sheets, Atlas folio, each sheet with vertical central fold, hand-colored in outline. DuPont copy. CNY Oct 8 (166) $12,000

Mead, Peter B.
— An Elementary Treatise on American Grape Culture and Wine Making. NY, 1867. 8vo, orig cloth; worn. Library markings. O Mar 31 (135) $80

Mead, Richard, 1673-1754
— A Mechanical Account of Poisons.... L, 1745. 3d Ed. 8vo, contemp calf gilt; rubbed. With 4 plates. b June 22 (193) £70

Meadows, Lindon. See: Greatrex, Charles Butler

Meadows, Thomas Taylor
— Desultory Notes on the Government and People of China. L, 1847. 8vo, orig cloth; rebacked with part of old spine laid down. With folding hand-colored map, 2 folding tables & 4 hand-colored plates. DW Dec 11 (51) £110

Meares, John, 1756?-1809
— Voyages de la Chine a la cote nord-ouest d'Amerique.... Paris: Buuisson, 1794. 4 vols, including Atlas. 8vo & 4to, contmep half calf; upper cover scraped. With port, 10 charts & 17 plates, most folding. Some staining. S May 14 (1219) £550 [Quaritch]
— Voyages Made in the Years 1788 and 1789.... L, 1790. 4to, contemp calf; rebacked, upper cover detached, backstrip def. With port, 10 maps & 17 plates. Fold tear in 2 maps; Ii2 with long repaired tear; some plates spotted. CNY Oct 8 (167) $1,300

Anr copy. Contemp half calf gilt; upper joint cracked, spine worn. First folding chart torn, repaired & stained; 2d folding chart with smaller repair; some browning. CNY Oct 8 (168) $1,400

Anr Ed. L, 1791. 4to, contemp calf; joints weak. With port & 14 maps & plates. Port shaved; some plates shaved at fore-margins. S Feb 26 (770) £600 [Swigert]

Mease, James, 1771-1846
— The Picture of Philadelphia.... Phila., 1811. 1st Ed. 12mo, contemp sheep; rubbed, front cover detached. With folding panorama (minor wrinkling & foxing). Some browning. F Mar 26 (139) $60

Anr copy. Contemp sheep; worn. sg Dec 5 (201) $60

Mecham, Clifford Henry
— Sketches & Incidents of the Siege of Lucknow.... L, 1858. Folio, orig cloth; soiled & worn, spine damaged. With litho title & 26 plates on 17 sheets. Plates foxed. W July 8 (229) £105

Mede, Joseph, 1586-1638
— The Key of the Revelation.... L, 1650. 4to, disbound. Tp soiled. sg Mar 12 (183) $120

Meder, Joseph
— Albrecht Duerer Handzeichnungen als Ergaenzung.... Vienna, 1927. Folio, text booklet & plates laid in half vellum folder. With 20 mtd reproductions. sg Feb 6 (181) $275
— Handzeichnungen deutscher Meister des XV. und XVI. Jahrhunderts. Vienna, 1922. Folio, loose in half-vellum folding case; def. With 33 mtd facsimile plates only. Sold w.a.f. sg Sept 19 (198) $50

One of 500. Bds. sg Feb 6 (177) $150
— Handzeichnungen franzoesischer Meister des XVI.-XVIII. Jahrhunderts. Vienna, 1922. One of 500. Folio, bds. With 40 mtd reproductions. sg Feb 6 (178) $225
— Handzeichnungen italienischer Meister des XV.-XVIII Jahrhunderts. Vienna, 1923. 4to, loose in half vellum portfolio as issued; 1 flap def. With 40 mtd plates & text booklet. sg Apr 2 (180) $200

One of 500. Text booklet & plates laid in vellum-backed bd folder. sg Feb 6 (179) $225
— Handzeichnungen vlaemischer und hollaendischer Meister des XV-XVII Jahrhunderts. Vienna, 1923. One of 500. Folio, text booklet & plates laid in half vellum folder.

sg Feb 6 (180) $110

Medici...

— Medici antiqui omnes.... Venice: Aldus, 1547. Folio, contemp vellum. Some browning; piece torn from margin of final leaf. SI Dec 5 (453) LIt650,000

Anr copy. Contemp vellum; 3 ties lacking. Some browning & waterstaining. SI Dec 5 (934) LIt1,000,000

Anr copy. Modern vellum. Some water-spotting & browning. SI June 10 (613) LIt1,400,000

Medina, Pedro de, 1493-1567

— L'Art de Naviguer de Maistre Pierre de Medine.... Lyon: Guillaume Rouille, 1561. Bound with: Thevet, Andre. Les Singularitez de la France Antarctique.... Paris, 1558. 2 vols in 1. 4to, contemp calf gilt; joints restored but cracking, repaired. DuPont copy. CNY Oct 8 (169) $54,000

Mee, Margaret

— Flowers of the Brazilian Forest.... L, [1968]. One of 100 with orig sgd watercolor bound in. Folio, orig vellum gilt, in d/j. With 31 colored plates. L Nov 14 (222) £1,500

Meehan, Thomas, 1826-1901

— The Native Flowers and Ferns of the United States. Bost., 1878-[80]. Series I only. 4to, half lea; rubbed & shaken, covers detached. With 96 plates. K Sept 29 (257) $300

Anr Ed. Bost.: L. Prang, 1879. Second Series, Parts 1-21 & 23 (of 24). Orig wraps; chipped. Sold w.a.f. bbc June 29 (135) $180

Anr Ed. Bost.: L. Prang, 1879 & Phila., 1880. First & Second Series. 4 vols. 4to, orig half mor; rubbed, def. With 192 color plates. F Sept 26 (258) $210

Meeker, Ezra, 1830-1928

— Pioneer Reminiscences of Puget Sound.... Seattle, 1905. 8vo, cloth; covers stained. Sgd on front free endpaper. sg June 18 (363) $60

Meeker, Nathan Cook, 1814-79

— First Annual Report of the Union Colony of Colorado.... NY, 1871. 8vo, yellow wraps; front wrap chipped. sg June 18 (181) $110

Meibom, Johann Heinrich

— De flagrorum usu in re veneria. L, 1770. 16mo, modern half mor. bba Sept 5 (287) £140 [Poolee]

Meibom, Marcus, d.1711

— Antiquae musicae.... Amst.: Elzevir, 1652. 1st Ed. 2 vols in 1. 4to, contemp vellum. S May 13 (729) £200 [Tosi]

Meiffren Laugier de Chartrouse, G.M.J., Baron. See: Temminck & Meiffren Laugier de Chartrouse

Meikle, James. See: Shields & Meikle

Meinertzhagen, Richard

See also: Nicoll & Meinertzhagen

— Birds of Arabia. L, 1954. 4to, orig cloth, in d/j. O Apr 28 (36) $350

— Nicoll's Birds of Egypt. L, 1930. 2 vols. 4to, half mor by Period binders. With port, folding map & unspecified number of colored plates. C May 20 (198) £400 [Travers]

Meinhold, William. See: Kelmscott Press

Meiss, Millard

— French Painting in the Time of Jean de Berry. L, 1967. 2 vols. 4to, cloth, in d/js. sg Oct 31 (236) $60

Anr Ed. NY, 1974. 3 vols. 4to, orig cloth in d/js. sg Oct 31 (237) $110

[-] Studies in Late Medieval and Renaissance Painting in Honor of.... NY, 1977. Ed by Irving Lavin & John Plummer. 2 vols. Folio, cloth. sg Oct 31 (238) $60

Mela, Pomponius

— Cosmographia. Paris: Christian Wechel, 1540. ("De orbis situ libri tres.") Bound with: Cicero, Marcus Tullius. Tuscularum quaestiones libri quinque. Paris, 1533. Folio, 16th-cent calf gilted pigskin; lower compartment of spine chipped away. With the woodcut world map (Shirley's state 4) with minor repairs without loss. R6 torn & repaired without loss. S Nov 21 (217) £7,200 [Quaritch]

Anr Ed. L, 1739. ("De situ orbis libri tres.") 4to, contemp calf; rubbed, rebacked, new endpapers. With 27 double-page maps. Lacking 1st & last blanks. pn Nov 14 (436) £190

Melanchthon, Philipp, 1497-1560

— Erotemata.... Wittenberg: Johann Lufft, 1547. 8vo, 19th-cent half mor. Italic letter; woodcut title border colored by an early hand. Annotated; minor stains; Ms index added at back. Doheny-Salloch copy. Ck Oct 31 (192) £250

— Grammatica Graeca.... Leipzig, [n.d.]. Bound with: Syntaxis...nunc locupletata. Leipzig: Ernst Voegelin, 1568 8vo, contemp blind-tooled pigskin over wooden bds, dated 1578. Some marginalia; large ink stain on last leaf of 1st work. sg Oct 24 (219) $400

— Loci communes theologici. Basel: Joannes Oporinus, 1550. 8vo, contemp blind-tooled pigskin over wooden bds; lacking catches & clasps, rear bd partly cracked, rear endpapers missing. Stamp & old scored writing on tp; some underscoring; incision through several text leaves; small hole in 1 index leaf. sg Oct 24 (217) $300

— Loci praecipui theologici. Leipzig: Valentin Papst, 1552. 8vo, contemp blind-tooled pigskin over wooden bds; lacking clasps & catches. Some stains & soiling; scattered contemp marginalia; small wormhole through last several index leaves. sg Oct 24 (218) $250

Melber, Johannes

— Vocabularius Praedicantium sive Variloquus. [Strassburg: Georg Husner, c.1500]. 4to, 16th-cent pigskin-backed bds; lacking 1 clasp. 36 lines & headline; gothic letter. Some dampstaining, mainly in margins. 172 leaves. Goff M-472. S Dec 5 (24) £1,050 [Thompson]

Melbourne...

— Melbourne International Exhibition, 1880-1881. Official Record.... Melbourne, 1880. 8vo, mor for Sir George Verdon; broken & def. With 61 photographic prints mtd on stiff card. Lacking Plate 13; 1st print silverfished at 1 corner. kh Nov 11 (574A) A$800

Meline, James F.

— Two Thousand Miles on Horseback, Santa Fe and Back. NY, 1867. 1st Ed. 8vo, orig cloth; worn. Folding map torn & detached. NH May 30 (578) $60

Mellerio, Andre

— La Lithographie Originale en Couleurs. Paris, 1898. One of 200 on holland. 4to, orig wraps; detached. With litho frontis on chine & cover in color by Pierre Bonnard. Schlosser copy. P June 18 (516) $1,600

— Odilon Redon, peintre, dessinateur et graveur. Paris, 1923. 4to, orig wraps; worn. sg Feb 6 (239) $70

Melling, Antoine Ignace

— Voyage pittoresque de Constantinople.... Paris, 1819. 2 vols. Folio, contemp half mor gilt, Atlas in contemp mor gilt. With port, 3 double-page maps, engraved title to plates & 48 double-page plates. Some discoloration & spotting. S June 30 (163) £1,500 [Consolidated Real]

Anr copy. Half lea gilt; worn. With frontis, 3 maps & 40 (of 48) plates Some repairs & spotting. SI June 10 (616) LIt10,000,000

Mellon Collection, Paul & Mary

— Alchemy and the Occult; a Catalogue of Books.... New Haven, 1968. One of 500. Compiled by Ian Macphail & others. 2 vols. 4to, orig cloth. O Sept 24 (168) $475

Anr Ed. New Haven, 1968-77. One of 500 sets. 4 vols. 4to, orig cloth. sg Oct 31 (270) $600

Melville, George John Whyte, 1821-78

— The Arab's Ride to Cairo. L, [1857?]. 4to, contemp mor by Seton & Mackenzie. pnE Oct 1 (327) £400

Melville, Henry

— Van Diemen's Land...Statistical and Other Information.... Hobart Town: Henry Melville, 1833. 8vo, orig cloth; worn, 1 gathering detached. cb Jn 30 (84) $375

Melville, Herman, 1819-91

See also: Limited Editions Club

— Battle-Pieces and Aspects of the War. NY, 1866. 1st Ed. 12mo, recent calf. Browned throughout; no orig blanks retained. bbc Dec 9 (509) $250

Anr copy. Orig green cloth. Inscr to Major Edwin Y. Lansing. Sold with letter-book containing pressed copies of Lansing's letters & an account of his military career. Manney copy. P Oct 11 (226) $57,500

Anr copy. Cloth; spine faded, ends chipped, hinges tender. sg Oct 17 (311) $450

— The Encantadas. Northampton: Gehenna Press, 1963. One of 150. Illus by Rico Lebrun. Old dampstain affecting text. bbc Sept 23 (421) $150

— Mardi: and a Voyage Thither. NY, 1849. 1st American Ed. 2 vols. 12mo, contemp half calf; worn. Some foxing. sg Oct 17 (312) $300

Anr copy. Orig cloth; spine ends chipped. sg Nov 7 (139) $700

— Moby Dick. L, 1851. ("The Whale") 1st Ed. 3 vols. 8vo, mor gilt by Brentano; spine ends of 2 vols worn, outer joints rubbed. Charles Reade's copy. CNY Oct 8 (171) $17,000

Anr copy. Orig cloth; spine ends & extremities frayed. Wiggin-Manney copy. P Oct 11 (224) $42,500

Anr copy. Modern mor gilt. Prelims in Vol I & tp of Vol II extended along inner margins; marginal tears repaired; some spotting & browning. P Dec 12 (72) $7,500

1st American Ed. NY, 1851. ("Moby Dick; or, the Whale.") 12mo, orig cloth, 2d bdg; spine ends & 3 fore-corners worn, upper third of spine filled in with black ink to imitate a label, shaken. Some foxing. CNY Oct 8 (172) $4,800

Anr copy. Orig cloth, 1st bdg; spine & extremities repaired, spine ends frayed. Minor dampstaining; tp foxed. P Oct 11 (225) $17,000

Anr copy. Orig cloth laid down over cloth bds. Marginal tears, mostly in 1st gatherings. P June 17 (273) $3,250

Anr copy. Orig cloth; rebacked retaining most of orig backstrip. Some dampstaining, especially at beginning; browned & foxed. sg Mar 5 (184) $3,800

Anr copy. 8vo, orig black cloth, 1st bdg. Epstein copy. sg Apr 29 (327) $8,000

Anr copy. ("Moby Dick; or, the Whale.") 12mo, orig cloth; fore-corners worn; some rubbing. sg May 7 (152) $15,000

Anr Ed. Chicago, 1930. One of 1,000. Illus by Rockwell Kent. 4to, cloth, in aluminum slipcase. P June 18 (622) $1,800

Anr copy. 3 vols. 4to, orig cloth, in aluminum slipcase. sg Sept 26 (148) $900

Anr copy. Cloth. sg Jan 30 (93) $2,800

Anr copy. 4to, cloth, in aluminum slipcase. sg May 7 (132) $1,500

Anr Ed. NY, 1930. 4to, cloth. cb Dec 19 (84) $90

Anr copy. Cloth, in d/j. sp Feb 6 (408) $80

Anr Ed. Mt. Vernon, 1975. One of 1,500. Preface by Jacques Cousteau; illus by LeRoy Neiman. Folio, mor. With 12 double-page plates. cb Nov 21 (152) $750; sg Sept 26 (231) $475

Anr Ed. San Francisco: Arion Press, 1979. ("Moby-Dick, or the Whale.") One of 265. 4to, mor. cb Sept 5 (64) $2,000

One of 265. Illus by Barry Moser. Mor. cb Feb 12 (89) $1,600

Anr copy. Folio, mor gilt. With pen-and-ink study for head-piece for Chapter 1, sgd in pencil by Moser & with other related material. sg Sept 26 (229) $2,200

California Deluxe Ed. Berkeley, [1981]. One of 750. sg Sept 26 (230) $175

— Omoo: A Narrative of Adventures in the South Seas. L, 1847. 1st Ed. 12mo, bds. cb Dec 5 (85) $425

Anr copy. Cloth; tear in spine, bumped, rubbed. Library markings; lacking 1 double flyleaf at front. K Sept 29 (259) $55

1st American Ed. NY, 1847. 12mo, orig ptd wraps; stained, spines & extremities worn, portion of text rubbed away on rear cover of Vol II. Some dampstaining & foxing; lower right corner clipped from front free endpaper in Vol II. Martin-Manney copy. P Oct 11 (223) $4,250

Anr Ed. NY, 1947. 12mo, orig cloth; small tear at head of spine. sg Mar 5 (186) $600

— The Piazza Tales. L & NY, 1856. 1st Ed, American Issue. 12mo, orig cloth; rubbed & worn. Dampstained. sg Oct 17 (313) $450

— Redburn. NY, 1849. 1st American Ed. 8vo, orig cloth; some wear. B May 12 (725a) HF600

1st ptg. Orig cloth; extremities worn, rear joint split. Foxed; some smudging. wa Mar 5 (228) $400

— Typee. L, 1846. ("Narrative of a Four Months' Residence among the Natives....") 8vo, later half calf. kh Nov 11 (576) A$70

Anr copy. Half mor gilt. NH Aug 23 (267) $1,100

Anr copy. Cloth, bdg variant B; joints starting. sg Mar 5 (185) $475

1st American Ed. NY, 1846. ("Typee: A Peep at Polynesian Life....") 2 parts in 1 vol. 12mo, orig wraps; corners restored, some soiling. With frontis map in Vol I. Foxed. Doheny-Manney copy. P Oct 11 (222) $7,500

Anr Ed. NY, 1847. 4th ptg. 8vo, orig cloth; worn, spine ends frayed, lacking front free endpaper. bbc June 29 (420) $50

Revised Ed. 8vo, orig cloth; upper rear joint split, rubbed. Browned & foxed; 1 gathering sprung. wa Mar 5 (227) $130

— White-Jacket; or the World in a Man-of-War. NY, 1850. 1st American Ed. 12mo, orig cloth; rebacked. cb Dec 5 (86) $200

— Works. L, 1922-24. Standard Ed, one of 750. 16 vols. Calf gilt, unopened. CNY Oct 8 (173) $4,200

Melzi, Giovanni Battista

— Dizionario di opere anonime e pseudonime di scrittori Italiani.... NY: Burt Franklin, [n.d.]. Facsimile of 1848 Ed. O Sept 24 (169) $130

Memoirs...

— Memoirs of the Secret Societies of the South of Italy, particularly the Carbonari. L, 1821. 8vo, later mor gilt by Cambridge Binding Guild. With 7 folding & 5 full-page plates. S Feb 11 (717) £380 [Baring]

— Memoirs of the History of France during the Reign of Napoleon.... L, 1823. 7 vols. 8vo, old half calf; worn, some spines missing. K Sept 29 (264) $55

Memorial...

— A Memorial and Biographical History of the Counties of Merced, Stanislaus, Calaveras, Tuolumne and Mariposa, California. Chicago, 1891. 1st Ed. 4to, orig mor gilt; scuffed, joints rubbed & cracking. cb Nov 14 (68) $170

Menavino, Giovanni Antonio

— I Costumi, et la vita de Turchi.... Florence: Lorenzo Torrentino, 1551. 8vo, contemp vellum; soiled. Some discoloration. S Nov 21 (268) £1,000 [Kutluoglu]

— Tuerckische Historien.... Frankfurt, 1570. Folio, contemp vellum. Some browning; stamp on tp; 1 leaf torn affecting letters. S Nov 21 (269) £1,100 [Reiss & Auvermann]

Menavino, Giovanni Antonio —& Others

— Tuerckische Historien.... Frankfurt, 1572. Bound with: Geuffroy, Antoine. Hoffhaltung des Tuerckhischen Keisers.... Basel: S. Henricpetri, [1573] Folio, contemp vellum over wooden bds; soiled, lacking 1 clasp. S Nov 21 (267) £2,200 [Bank of Cyprus]

Mencken, Henry Louis, 1880-1956

— The American Language. NY, 1919. 1st Ed, On eof 25 L.p. copies. In d/j. Epstein copy. sg Apr 30 (328) $1,700

Anr Ed. NY, 1945-48. Supplements I & II. 4to, cloth. Both inscr to B. Lorraine Yerkes. sg June 11 (223) $325

— Newspaper Days. NY, 1941. 1st Ed. Sgd & dated, 1941. bbc Apr 27 (367) $65

— Prejudices: Fifth Series. NY, [1926]. In worn & chipped d/j. With related material laid in. bbc Apr 27 (368) $125

— Prejudices: Fourth Series. NY, [1924]. In d/j. bbc Sept 23 (451) $110

Mencken, Henry Louis, 1880-1956 —& Others

— The Sunpapers of Baltimore, 1837-1937. NY, 1937. 4to, cloth, in chipped d/j. bbc June 29 (491) $60

Mendelsohn, Erich

— Amerika: Bilderbuch eines Architekten. Berlin, 1926. 4to, half cloth; soiled, head of spine frayed. sg Sept 6 (189) $300

Mendelssohn, Sidney

— South African Bibliography. L, 1968. One of 500. 2 vols. 4to, orig cloth, in d/js. DW Dec 11 (373) £220

Mendes Pinto, Fernando, 1509?-83

— Peregrinacao correcta e acrecentada com o itinerario de A. Tenreyro.... Lisbon, 1725. Folio, modern calf. Tp repaired & stains; next few leaves stained; some worming. S Nov 21 (363) £550

Mendibil, Pablo de

— Descripcion abreviada del mundo. Inglaterra, Escocia e Irlanda. L: Ackermann, 1828. 2 vols. 12mo, contemp calf gilt; spines rubbed. With 81 hand-colored plates. b June 22 (145) £110

Mennie, Donald

— The Grandeur of the Gorges. Shanghai, 1926. One of 1,000. 4to, orig silk; rubbed. bba Oct 24 (326) £50 [Fine Bks Oriental]

— The Pageant of Peking. Shanghai, 1920. One of 1,000. Folio, silk. Some wear & soiling. pn Apr 23 (242) £80

3d Ed. Shanghai, 1922. 4to, orig cloth; corners bumped, worn. With 66 Vandyke photogravures. sg Oct 8 (29) $275

Menpes, Dorothy & Mortimer

— The Durbar. L, 1903. Ltd Ed, sgd. 4to, orig cloth; soiled. L Nov 14 (70) £100

— World Pictures. L, 1902. Orig cloth; spine scuffed. L Nov 14 (69) £50

Menpes, Mortimer, 1859-1938

— Whistler as I Knew Him. L, 1904. One of 500. 4to, half mor gilt. Frontis etching not mentioned. sg Sept 6 (308) $140

Menzel, Adolph

— Fuenfzig Zeichnungen, Pastelle und Aquarelle aus dem Besitz der Nationalgalerie. Berlin, 1921. Out-of-series copy. Folio, cloth, orig wraps bound in; worn. With 50 mtd reproductions. Sgd by Georg Grosz, 1942. sg Feb 6 (183) $300

Menzies, William

— Forest Trees and Woodland Scenery. L, 18175. Folio, orig cloth; rubbed. bba Jan 30 (96) £1770 [Thorp]

Merbitz, Johann Valentin

— De Varietate Faciei Humanae, Discursus Physicus. Dresden: Mart. Gabriel Hubner, 1676. 4to, contemp half vellum. With frontis & 1 plate. cb Feb 12 (90) $350

Mercator, Gerard, 1512-94. See: Ptolemaeus, Claudius

Mercator, Gerard, 1512-94 —& Hondius, Jodocus, 1563-1611

— Atlas Minor. Amst., [1609]. Oblong 8vo, contemp blind-stamped vellum; rebacked, preserving orig backstrip, stained & worn. With allegorial plate & 152 maps, all in contemp hand-coloring. Lacking ptd German title & 3 pages of text; some soiling & staining, mainly in margins; engraved title torn & repaired with loss; allegorical plate & 1st 7 maps with marginal tears & defs repaired. C May 20 (279) £5,500 [Arader]

Anr Ed. Amst. [1610?]. Oblong 8vo, orig vellum gilt; masking tape across spine, upper inner hinge broken, 1st 2 quires coming unsewn. With engraved title, allegorical engraving & 153 maps, fully colored in a contemp hand, the title heightened in gold. Engraved title abraded & with marginal repair incurring slight loss to border; marginal worming to 1st 4 leaves;

2-inch tear to F1 affecting 8 letters; Lithuania & Germania inferior with tears just entering borders; c.14 leaves with marginal tears or repairs; some browning throughout; minor marginal dampstaining. CNY June 9 (138) $14,500

Anr Ed. Amst., [c.1630]. Oblong 4to, 18th-cent half vellum; worn & soiled, front hinge open. With engraved title (with cancel slips over title & imprint) & 143 full-page maps. Some worming at end. P June 17 (274) $4,800

Anr Ed. Amst.: Johannes Jansson, 1651. 2 vols in 1. Oblong 4to, half calf. With 1 (of 2) ptd titles within engraved borders & 215 full-page maps. HH May 12 (648) DM8,000

— Atlas minor, ou briefve & vive description de tout le monde.... Amst.: Joannes Jansson, 1628. 4th French text Ed. Oblong 8vo, contemp vellum; soiled. With 142 maps, the first few partly colored in an early hand. Small rust-hole with slight loss in Turcici Imperii at 4D4; some browning & dust-soiling. S Nov 21 (126) £4,500 [Map House]

— Atlas sive cosmographicae meditationes.... Dusseldorf: Bernardus Busius, 1602. Folio, contemp calf; spine ends & corners restored, rubbed, scratched & wormed. Boulogne with outer border shaved & half-inch tear; a few short marginal tears & repairs; some staining & soiling to margins. CNY Oct 8 (176) $32,000

— Historia mundi: or Mercator's Atlas. L, 1635. 1st English Ed. Trans by William Saltonstall. Folio, old calf; hinges broken, spine perishing. Foxed & dampstained in margins. wd Dec 12 (418) $5,750

Mercer, Asa Shinn

See also: Grabhorn Printing

— The Banditti of the Plains.... [Cheyenne, Wyoming], 1894. 8vo, orig cloth; rubbed, shaken. Manney copy. P Oct 11 (228) $1,300

Mercier, D. F. F. J., Cardinal, Archbishop of Malines

— Patriotism & Endurance. Pastoral Letter.... Turnhout, 1921. One of 1,250. 4to, unbound. With 34 color plates. sg Jan 10 (103) $175

Mercurialis, Hieronymus, 1530-1606

— De arte gymnastica, libri sex. Venice: Juntas, 1573. 2d Ed. 4to, half vellum. Marginal soiling. SI June 10 (623) LIt1,500,000

Anr Ed. Amst., 1672. 4to, contemp vellum; rubbed & spotted. Some waterspotting. HH May 12 (1083) DM1,100

Anr copy. Contemp vellum gilt, armorial bdg. With engraved title & 6 plates. Some worming in inner margin, occasionally affecting illusts; 1 plate torn. S Feb 26 (879) £170 [Grant & Shaw]

Meredith, Louisa Anne Twamley

— Our Wild Flowers.... L, 1839. 12mo, orig mor gilt. Some foxing. kh Nov 11 (394) A$50

Anr copy. Orig mor gilt; worn. With 12 hand-colored plates. kh Nov 11 (396) A$300

— Over the Straits. L, 1861. 8vo, bdg not described; sprung, small flaw to head of backstrip. kh Nov 11 (578) A$90

— The Romance of Nature. L, 1836. 1st Ed. 8vo, contemp mor gilt; rubbed. With 27 handcolored plates, including engraved title. L Nov 14 (465) £220

Meredith, William George

— A Tour to the Rhine with Antiquarian and other Notices. L, 1825. One of 25. 8vo, orig bds; upper joint split, rubbed. Inscr & with ALs tipped in. bba Sept 19 (144) £320 [Shapero]

Merian, Maria Sibylla, 1647-1717

— De Europische insecten. Amst., 1730. Folio, contemp calf gilt; repaired. With 184 plates on 47 leaves. Some waterstaining in upper margin of a few leaves; some foxing. B Nov 1 (481) HF55,000

— Over de Voortteeling en Wonderbaerlyke veranderingen der Surinaamsch Insecten. Amst., 1730. Folio, calf gilt by Middleton. With hand-colored frontis & 72 hand-colored plates. C May 20 (197) £16,000 [Arader]

Merian, Matthaeus, 1593-1650

— Topographia Alsatiae. Frankfurt: Merian, 1663. Text by Martin Zeiler; plates by Merian. Folio, contemp vellum. With 36 mostly double-page plates. Some splits or tears without loss; some browning & thumb-marks; tp stamped. S Nov 21 (186) £1,300 [Kiefer]

— Topographia Bohemiae Moraviae et Silesiae. Frankfurt, 1650. Folio, 19th-cent bds. With engraved title & 34 (of 37) double-page maps & views. HH May 12 (689) DM3,200

Anr copy. Bds. Waterstaining & browning. HH May 12 (690) DM2,200

— Topographia Franconiae, das ist Beschreibung und eygentliche Contrafactur der vornebsten Staette und Plaetze des Franckenlandes.... Frankfurt, [1648]. Text by Martin Zeiler; engravings by Merian. Folio, contemp half vellum. With engraved title, double-page map & 42 plates. HH May 12 (568) DM10,000

— Topographia Germaniae inferioris.... Frankfurt, [1659]. Text by Martin Zeiler; engravings by Merian. Folio, contemp pigskin-backed wooden bds. With engraved title, 12 double-page maps & 105 (of 108) plates. HH May 12 (682) DM3,600

— Topographia Italia, das ist: Warhaffte und curioese Beschreibung von gantz Italier. Frankfurt, 1688. 1st Ed. 2 parts in 1 vol. Folio, 19th-cent half vellum. With 57 maps & views. SI June 10 (624) LIt14,000,000

— Topographia provinciarum Austriacarum, Austriae, Styriae, Carinthiae...das ist Beschreibung und Abbildung der fuernebsten Staat und Plaetz in den Oesterreichischen Landen.... Frankfurt, 1649. Text by Martin Zeiler; engravings by Merian. Folio, contemp vellum. Lacking views numbered 14, 90 & 96; some repairs & browning. SI June 10 (625) LIt6,500,000

— Topographia Sueviae. Frankfurt, 1655-56. ("Topographia Sueviae, das ist Beschreib: und aigentliche Abcontrafeitung fuer nembste Staett und Plaetz in Ober und Nider Schwaben....") Text by Martin Zeiler; plates by Merian. Folio, half vellum. With 4 double-page maps & 59 double-page plates. FD Dec 2 (297) DM17,000

— Topographia urbis Romae. Das ist: Eigentliche Beschreibung der Stadt Rom. Frankfurt, 1681 [but c.1700]. Folio, 19th-cent half lea. Some browning. SI June 9 (161) 1,100,000

Merignac, Emile

— Histoire de l'escrime. Paris, 1883-86. One of 650. 2 vols. 8vo, modern syn. sg Mar 26 (204) $150

Merigot, James

— Promenades ou Itineraire des Jardins de Chantilly.... Paris, 1791. 8vo, contemp bds; rebacked in mor, modern endpapers. With folding plan & 20 hand-colored plates. Some spotting. C May 20 (87) £230 [Denniston]

Anr copy. Bdg not described. With folding view & 20 plates. Extra-illus with c.34 plates. K July 12 (341) $190

— A Select Collection of Views and Ruins in Rome.... L, 1797-99. 2 parts in 1 vol. Folio, disbound. With 41 (of 61) plates on india paper mtd. Sold w.a.f. b June 22 (259) £180

Anr copy. Contemp mor gilt; extremities rubbed. With 61 plates, most tinted by hand Some spotting. C Oct 30 (112) £500 [Hoolin]

Anr copy. Modern mor. With 47 mtd plates only, washed in red by hand. sg Sept 19 (199) $375

Anr copy. Half lea gilt. With 61 plates. Marginal repairs. SI June 10 (626) LIt2,200,000

Anr Ed. L, [c.1819]. 2 parts in 1 vol. Folio, 19th-cent lea over bds; worn. With 30 hand-colored plates. McCarty-Cooper copy. CNY Jan 25 (47) $3,500

Anr Ed. L, [plates watermarked 1827-28]. Folio, orig half lea; abrasions to label & upper cover. With frontis & 61 hand-colored plates plus additional plate, The Cascatelle and Stables of Mecoenas. L.p. colored copy. C May 20 (86) £1,300 [Spelman]

Merimee, Prosper, 1803-70

— Mateo Falcone. Paris, 1906. One of 250 on velin blanc. Illus by Alexandre Lunios. 8vo, lev extra janseniste with border of strawberry plants on doublures, by Marius Michel. Marlborough copy. CNY Dec 5 (415) $1,000

Merino de Jesu-Christo, Andres

— Escuela Paleographica o de leer letras cursivas antiguas y modernas. Madrid, 1780. 1st Ed. Folio, half calf. With engraved title & 59 plates. HH May 12 (1071) DM1,200

Merken, Johann

— Liber artificiosus alphabeti maioris. Mulheim, 1782-85. 2 vols. Oblong folio, contemp half calf; restored. With 56 plates. HH May 12 (1071a) DM2,200

Anr copy. 2 parts in 1 vol. Oblong folio, disbound. With 52 (of 56) plates. General title def; next leaf frayed. sg Sept 19 (200) $500

Merriam, John Campbell —& Stock, Chester

— The Felidae of Rancho La Brea. Wash., 1932. 4to, cloth; worn. With 43 heliotype plates. sg Nov 14 (195) $475

Merrick, George Byron

— Old Times on the Upper Mississippi. Cleveland, 1909. sg June 18 (364) $120

Merry Milkmaid...

— The Merry Milkmaid of Islington.... L: Dan. Browne et al, 1680. 4to, modern half mor. Leaves trimmed & inlaid to size; lacking a general title. Sold w.a.f. John Philip Kemble's copy; Chatsworth copy. sg May 7 (154) $325

Merryweather, F. Somner

— Bibliomania in the Middle Ages. L, 1849. 1st Ed. 16mo, orig cloth. cb Oct 17 (628) $90

Mersenne, Marin, 1588-1648

— Cogitata physico-mathematica.... Paris, 1644. 4to, contemp calf gilt with later arms of Pierre Seguier; spines restored, upper joints cracked. Clean tear to 2H2 of Vol I; 2M3 in same vol holed at upper margin; some browning. Sold w.a.f. Ck Nov 29 (221) £2,000

Mery, Francois Joseph Pierre Andre, 1797-1865

— Constantinople et la Mer Noire. Paris, 1855. 8vo, contemp mor. With frontis & 20 plates, 6 hand-colored. Some discoloration chiefly in text. S June 30 (164) £200

Meryman, Richard

— Andrew Wyeth. Bost., 1968. Oblong 4to, orig cloth, in chipped d/j. bbc Sept 23 (169) $95

Anr copy. Orig cloth, in d/j. With 121 plates. K Mar 22 (455) $170

Anr copy. Orig cloth, in worn d/j. K July 12 (535) $80

Mestrovic, Ivan

— Mestrovic. Zagreb, 1935. 4to, orig cloth, in worn d/j. kh Nov 11 (171) A$50

Mesue, Joannes

— De re medica. Lyons: Apud Ioan. Tornaesium & Gulielmum Gazeium, 1548. 8vo, later calf gilt; rebacked, rubbed. Lacking 2 final blanks; some waterstaining. bba Sept 5 (319) £240 [Poole]

Metalious, Grace

— Peyton Place. NY, [1956]. In d/j with 1 tear tape-mended on rear panel. Inscr to Herbert F. West. sg Dec 12 (273) $60

Metastasio, Pietro, 1698-1782

— Opere. Paris: Vedova Herissant, 1780-82. 12 vols. 8vo, lea. br May 29 (75) $170

Meteyard, Eliza, 1816-79

— Choice Examples of Wedgwood Art.... L, 1879. Folio, orig cloth; worn, hinges & endpapers renewed. With 28 mtd plates. sg Sept 6 (297) $60

— The Life of Josiah Wedgwood.... L, 1865-66. 2 vols. 8vo, half mor gilt; extremities worn. sg Apr 2 (297) $100

Metterleiter, Franz X., 1791-1873

— Grundzuege der Lithographie. Mainz: Theodor von Zabern, 1818. 8vo, sewn as issued in wraps, uncut. Schlosser copy. P June 17 (571) $1,800

Metzdorf, Robert F. See: Tinker Library, Chauncey Brewster

Metzinger, Jean, 1883-1956. See: Gleizes & Metzinger

Meurer, Noe

— Von Forstlicher Oberherrligkeit und gerechtigkeit. Frankfurt: Weygand Han & Georg Raben, 1561. 3 parts in 1 vol. Folio, vellum bds. Tp & last leaf rebacked with loss of text on tp; some stains. S Dec 5 (118) £900 [Schwing]

— Wasser Recht und gerechtigkait fuernemlich des Weitberuehmbten und Goltreichen Rheinstrams. Frankfurt: Nicolaus Basse for Siegmnudt Feyeerabendt, 1570. Folio, 18th-cent bds; worn. Tp shaved along fore-margin. S Nov 21 (188) £900 [Hellwig]

Meursius, Joannes, 1579-1639

— Exercitationum criticarum partes II. Leiden: Elzevir, 1599. 2 parts in 1 vol. 8vo, contemp vellum. Inscr to Lambert van der Burch. S May 28 (53) £500 [Edwards]

Mexia, Pedro, 1496-1552

— The Historie of all the Romane Emperors.... L, 1604. 1st Ed in English. Folio, old sheep; needs rebdg. Margins trimmed; 3 leaves holed with slight loss. sg Mar 12 (185) $250

Mexico

— Bases organicas de la republica Nexicana.... Mexico, 1843. 12mo, orig wraps; chipped. Foxed. sg June 18 (366) $300

Meyer, Adolphe de

— L'Apres-midi d'un Faune: Nijinsky 1912. NY: Eakins Press Foundation, [n.d.]. One of 250. Folio, orig cloth. With 33 palladium prints. Kochno copy. SM Oct 12 (531) FF8,500

Meyer, Erna

— How to Cook in Palestine. Tel Aviv: for the Palestine Federation of WIZO, [c.1925]. Orig pictorial wraps; 1st 4 leaves detached. Text in English, German & Hebrew. sg June 25 (65) $650

Meyer, Franz

— Marc Chagall: Life and Works. NY: H. N. Abrams, [1964]. 4to, cloth, in pictorial d/j. With 53 tipped-in colored plates. bbc Apr 27 (443) $80

Anr copy. Some soiling. F June 25 (521) $120; sg Feb 6 (53) $300

Meyer, Henry Leonard

— Illustrations of British Birds. L, [1835-41] & [1838-44]. Combination of 1st & 2d Issues. 4 vols in 2. Folio, contemp half mor gilt; rubbed, front inner hinges split. With 325 hand-colored plates. Tear to lower blank margin of Red-necked Phalarope. Extra-illus with 11 orig watercolors of eggs. C Oct 20 (212) £4,000 [Wheldon & Wesley]

Meyer, Jacob, of Bailleul

— Commentarii sive annales rerum Flandricarum. Antwerp, 1561. Folio, 19th-cent half vellum. SI Dec 5 (941) LIt300,000

Meyer, Johann Jakob

— Voyage pittoresque sur la nouvelle route depuis Glurns en Tyrol...jusqu'a Milan. Innsbruch: Fr. Unterberger, [1833]. 6 orig parts. Folio, orig portfolio with engraved labels on upper cover preserving orig wraps. With engraved title & 36 uncolored plates. Lacking map. S Nov 21 (189) £4,500 [Bifolco]

Meyers, William H. See: Grabhorn Printing

Meyrick, Sir Samuel Rush
See also: Shaw & Meyrick

— A Critical Inquiry into Antient Armour. L, 1824. 3 vols. 4to, contemp calf gilt; rubbed. O May 26 (125) $1,300

— Heraldic Visitations of Wales and Part of the Marches. Llandovery, 1846. 2 vols. 4to, orig cloth. L Feb 27 (175) £180

Michael de Hungaria

— Sermones praedicabiles. Strassburg: [Printer of the 1483 Jordanus de Quedlinburg (Georg Husner)], 24 Mar 1487. 4to, modern calf. Leaf h8 holed with slight loss; p1 marginally repaired. 127 (of 128) leaves. Goff M-541. bba Apr 9 (15) £1,500 [Bernard]

Michaud, Joseph Francois, 1767-1839

— Histoire des croisades. Paris, 1819-22. 7 vols. 8vo, contemp half calf. With 7 folding maps & plans. S June 30 (168) £550 [Popular Bank]

Michaux, Francois Andre, 1770-1855

— Histoire des arbres forestiers de l'Amerique septentrionale.... Paris, 1810-13. Vols I-II only. 8vo, contemp half mor; extremities rubbed. With 75 hand-colored plates. Some soiling & browning. Ck Nov 29 (26) £500

Michaux, Henri

— Au pays de la Magie. Paris: Gallimard, [1941]. Orig wraps. Review copy. Epstein copy. sg Apr 29 (330) $600

— Voyage en grande Garabagne. Paris: Gallimard, [1936]. One of 1,200. Orig wraps. Epstein copy. sg Apr 29 (329) $275

Michel, Jean —& Benoist, Rene

— L'Anatomie du corps politique.... Douai: Jean Bogard, 1581. 8vo, 18th-cent sheep gilt; joints rubbed, corners worn. Some stains. sg Oct 24 (222) $325

Michel, Marius

— La Reliure francaise. Paris, 1880. 1st Ed. 4to, mor gilt by Michel, orig wraps bound in. Inscr by Michel. CNY Dec 5 (414) $800

Michelangelo Buonarotti, 1475-1564

— Poesie. Montagnola: Officina Bodoni, 1923. One of 175. Orig vellum, unopened; worn. O Jan 14 (139) $225

— Rime.... Florence: Giunti, 1623. 1st Ed. 4to, old bds; recased, spine worn. Erased ownership inscrs on tp. Ck Nov 29 (62) £800

Michener, James A.

— Facing East. NY, 1970. Illus by Jack Levine. 2 parts in 1 vol. Folio, loose in satin folding-case. sg Sept 26 (233) $250

Anr copy. With 4 orig colored lithos. sg Jan 30 (104) $200; sg Feb 6 (188) $250

Anr copy. 2 parts in 1 vol plus Sketchbook portfolio. Folio, wa Dec 9 (437) $200

— Tales of the South Pacific. NY, 1947. 1st Ed, 3d impression. Inscr to John Mason Brown by Michener, Richard Rogers & Joshua Logan. Met Apr 28 (718) $700

Michigan

— Report of the Committee of the House of Representatives...Transmitting a Report from the Governor and Presiding Judge of the Territory of Michigan.... Wash., 1806. 8vo, disbound. sg June 18 (369) $100

Middiman, Samuel

— Select Views in Great Britain. L, [1813]. Oblong 8vo, contemp mor gilt. With 53 plates. Text & plates foxed. sg Jan 9 (120) $225

Middleton, Charles Theodore

— A New and Complete System of Geography. L, 1778-79. 2 vols. Folio, contemp calf; hinges cracked. With 21 maps & 100 plates. Minor spotting. DW Nov 6 (71) £660

Middleton, Erasmus, 1739-1805

— The New Complete Dictionary of Arts and Sciences. L, 1778. 2 vols. Folio, contemp calf; rebacked. With 80 plates. W July 8 (10) £150

Middleton, J. J.

— Grecian Remains in Italy. L, 1812. Folio, contemp mor gilt; some wear. With 2 plain & 23 colored plates. SI Dec 5 (463) LIt3,800,000

Miers, John, 1789-1879

— Travels in Chile and La Plata. L, 1826. 2 vols. 8vo, contemp calf gilt; Vol I broken. DW Apr 8 (47) £155

Mies van der Rohe, Ludwig. See: Museum of Modern Art

Mihaly, Nemes

— A Magyar Viseletek Tortenete. Budapest, 1900. 4to, pictorial cloth; extremities rubbed. With 71 uncolored & 39 chromolitho plates. Library markings. sg Jan 9 (95) $140

Milam. See: Thompson, Henry

Milasius, Oskaras Vladislovas. See: Milosz, Oscar Vladislas de Luricz

Miles, Edmund

— An Epitome, Historical and Statistical of the Royal Naval Service of England. L: Ackermann, 1841. 1st Ed. 8vo, later mor gilt by A. Taffin; rebacked with old spine laid down. With 8 hand-colored plates. Some browning. C May 20 (88) £180 [Way]

Anr Ed. L, 1844. 8vo, half mor gilt. With 8 hand-colored plates. Foxed throughout. wd June 12 (415) $450

Miles, Henry Downes, 1806-89

— The Book of Field Sports. L: Henry Lea, [1860-63]. 2 vols. 4to, contemp half calf; worn. With 71 (of 74) plates, 7 hand-colored. Some plates shaved or with marginal tears; some leaves torn, affecting text, several def or lacking; Vol II lacking tp. Sold w.a.f. pn May 14 (181) £340 [Swan]

— British Field Sports. L: Wm. Mackenzie, [n.d.].. 7 orig parts only. Orig wraps; rubbed & soiled. Sold w.a.f. bba Sept 5 (169C) £95 [Hildebrandt]

Anr copy. 4to, contemp half calf; worn. With 50 plates, 16 in color. S July 1 (923) £350 [Nicholson]

Miles, Nelson Appleton

— Personal Recollections and Observations...Civil War.... Chicago, 1896. 1st Ed, 1st Issue, with "General" at frontis port. Illus by Frederic Remington. 4to, orig cloth; lower hinge cracked. Inscr to John Hays Hammond. bbc Dec 9 (397) $85

Miles, William J.

— Modern Practical Farriery.... L, [1873-74]. 5 parts. 4to, orig half cloth. L Nov 14 (196) £50

Military...

— The Military Costume of Turkey. L, 1818. Folio, contemp mor gilt; spine faded, rubbed. With frontis & 29 hand-colored plates. bba Sept 19 (123) £340 [Butcher]

Anr copy. With engraved title, hand-colored port & 30 hand-colored plates. S July 1 (593) £450 [Kutluoglu]

Anr Ed. L, 1818 [text watermarked 1819, plates 1820]. Folio, loose. With engraved title & 11 colored plates. DW Dec 11 (198) £230

— The Military Costume of Europe. L, 1822. 2 vols. Folio, modern half mor gilt. With 97 hand-colored plates, some heightened with varnish. C May 20 (64) £1,150 [Traylen]

Mill, James, 1773-1836

— History of British India. L, 1848. 9 vols. 8vo, calf; rubbed. Some stains. O Feb 25 (139) $250

Mill, John Stuart, 1806-73

— Considerations on Representative Government. L, 1861. 1st Ed. 8vo, orig cloth. bba Jan 16 (21) £50 [Goddard]

— On Liberty. L, 1859. 1st Ed. 8vo, orig cloth; rubbed & faded. bba Feb 27 (144) £80 [Holland]

Anr copy. Orig cloth; short tear to upper joint, extremities rubbed. Some soiling; 1 leaf of pbr's cat torn. pn Sept 12 (215) £200 [Spaderman]

— Principles of Political Economy. L, 1848. 1st Ed. 2 vols. 8vo, orig cloth; spine labels discolored & chipped. C Dec 16 (260) £1,300 [Quaritch]

4th Ed. L, 1857. 2 vols. 8vo, orig cloth; hinges weak. bba Jan 16 (20) £65 [Sotheran]

Millais, John Guille, 1865-1931

— A Breath from the Veldt. L, 1895. 4to, modern cloth, orig cover preserved. bba Sept 19 (66) £160 [Loppert]

— British Deer and their Horns. L, 1897. Folio, orig cloth; soiled & rubbed. DW Apr 8 (169) £165

— British Diving Ducks. L, 1913. One of 450. 2 vols. Folio, orig cloth. With 74 plates, 39 in color. C May 20 (200) £600 [Grahame]

Anr copy. Orig cloth; discolored. S June 25 (46) £1,100 [Vitale]

— Far Away Up the Nile. L, 1924. 1st Ed. Cloth; front cover spotted. cb Oct 10 (74) $50; sg Jan 9 (153) $110

— The Mammals of Great Britain and Ireland. L, 1904-6. One of 1,025. 3 vols. 4to, orig cloth; edges worn. Some soiling; stamps on verso of tp, 1st & final leaf & Plate 41 in Vol II. pn Mar 19 (312) £95 [Toscani]

Anr copy. Orig cloth; rubbed. S Feb 26

(931) £150 [Russell]

— The Natural History of the British Surface-Feeding Ducks. L, 1902. One of 600 L.p. copies. 4to, half cloth. pnE May 13 (96) £360

— The Natural History of British Game Birds. L, 1909. One of 550. Folio, orig cloth. With 37 plates, 18 of them colored. C Oct 30 (215) £450 [Traylen]

Anr copy. Orig cloth; rubbed. With 37 plates, including 18 in color. Some soiling. Ck Sept 6 (52) £300

Anr copy. Orig pigskin; upper cover soiled & rubbed, rebacked. S May 14 (1048) £220 [Way]

— Newfoundland and its Untrodden Ways. L, 1907. Orig cloth; worn & soiled. Library markings. F Dec 18 (447) $60

Anr copy. 8vo, orig cloth; worn. O Oct 29 (208) $80

Millar, George Henry

— The New and Universal System of Geography. L, 1782. Folio, contemp calf; rebacked. With 92 plates & 28 maps. Ck Dec 11 (238) £750

— A New Complete and Universal Natural History. L: Alexander Hogg, [1785]. ("A New, Complete and Universal Body, or System of Natural History.") Folio, orig lea; repaired with wide lea straps. With 84 plates. Chunk of text missing on p. 254. NH Oct 6 (218) $475

Millar, Kenneth. See: MacDonald, Ross

Millard, Christopher Sclater

— Bibliography of Oscar Wilde. L, [1914]. bba May 28 (592) £75 [Symonds]; sg Oct 17 (582) $50

One of 100. 2 vols. Bdg worn. O Sept 24 (160) $60

Millares, Carlo —& Mantecon, Jose Ignacio

— Album de Paleografia Hispanoamericana de los Siglos XVI y XVII. Barcelona, 1975. 3 parts in 2 vols. Folio, syn, in d/js. sg Oct 31 (239) $175

Millay, Edna St. Vincent, 1892-1950

— Baccalaureate Hymn. [Poughkeepsie, NY, 1917]. Broadside, 227mm by 140mm. sg Dec 12 (2774) $450

— The Ballad of the Harp-Weaver. NY, 1922. 1st Ed. Orig red wraps. sg Dec 12 (275) $100

[-] A Book of Vassar Verse. Poughkeepsie, 1916. Half cloth. Contains Millay's "Interim," "Why Did I Ever Come to This Place," & "The Suicide". sg Dec 12 (285) $200

— Conversations at Midnight. NY, 1937. One of 600. 4to, half cloth; minor wear. O Aug 25 (132) $80

— Fatal Interview. NY, 1931. One of 36 on Japan vellum, sgd. Half vellum. sg Dec 12 (276) $225

— Make Bright the Arrows. NY, 1940. Unbound signatures, unopened. sg Dec 12 (280) $120

— Renascence and Other Poems. NY, 1917. 1st Ed. Orig cloth, in repaired d/j; cloth rippled. sg June 11 (224) $600

Anr copy. Bds. wd Dec 12 (419) $75

Issue on watermarked Glaslan paper. Sgd. Epstein copy. sg Apr 30 (331) $700

— Second April. NY, 1921. 1st Ed, 1st State. sg Dec 12 (281) $70

Millay, Edna St. Vincent, 1892-1950 —& Taylor, Deems

— The King's Henchman [opera adaptation]. NY, 1927. Artist's Ed, One of 500. Unopened. With 3 proof etchings of Joseph Urban's sets for the opera version & a facsimile page of Deems Taylor's Ms, sgd by him. sg Dec 12 (279) $140

Miller & Richard

— Specimens of Modern, Old Style and Ornamental Type Cast on Point Bodies. Edin., [c.107]. cb Sept 5 (116) $120

Miller, Alfred W.

— Fishless Days, by Sparse Grey Hackle. NY, 1954. One of 591. Inscr. Koopman copy. O Oct 29 (209) $375

Miller, Arthur

See also: Limited Editions Club

— Death of a Salesman. NY: Viking, 1949. 1st Ed. In d/j. F June 25 (496) $100

Anr copy. Inscr to John Mason Brown. Met Apr 28 (721) $325

Miller, C. William

— Franklin's Philadelphia Printing, 1728-1766: a Descriptive Bibliography. Phila., 1974. 4to, cloth, in d/j. NH Aug 23 (99) $70

Anr copy. Cloth. pba Aug 20 (146) $75

Miller, Chuck. See: Underwood & Miller

Miller, Edmund Morris

— Australian Literature from its Beginnings to 1935. Melbourne, 1940. 2 vols. Cloth, in d/js with silverfish damage. kh Nov 11 (580) A$160

Miller, Francis Trevelyan

See also: Photographic...

— Lindbergh: His Story in Pictures. NY, 1929. One of 250. Affixed to front pastedown is envelope carried by Lindbergh on his 1st international air mail flight from Miami. cb Nov 7 (57) $375

Anr copy. With mtd First Flight Cover carried by Lindbergh on his 1st international mail flight from Miami to the Canal Zone. sg May 21 (62) $110

— The World in the Air.... NY, 1930. 2 vols. 4to, cloth, in d/js. sg Nov 14 (267) $70

Miller, Henry

See also: Grabhorn Printing

— The Air-Conditioned Nightmare. NY: New Directions, [1945]. 1st Ed, 1st Ptg. In chipped & repaired d/j. Inscr to Bill Targ, 1972 & with ALs to Dick, 1963, laid in. Epstein copy. sg Apr 29 (332) $475

— Aller Retour New York. Paris, 1935. 1st Ed, One of 150, sgd. Orig wraps. Inscr. sg Dec 12 (286) $1,200

— Black Spring. Paris: Obelisk Press, [1936]. 1st Ed. Orig wraps; spine rubbed. K July 12 (347) $375

Anr copy. Orig wraps; front joint torn. Inscr. sg Dec 12 (287) $1,300

— The Colossus of Maroussi. L, 1942. 1st English Ed. In d/j. cb Sept 19 (163) $55

— Into the Night Life. [Berkeley, 1947]. One of 800. sg Sept 26 (234) $650

— Miscellanea. [N.p.]: Bern Porter, 1945. One of 500. Inscr to Edna, 1948. pba July 9 (204) $225

— The Nightmare Notebook. New Directions, [1975]. Ltd Ed, sgd. Facsimile Ed. pba July 9 (205) $160

— Order and Chaos chez Hans Reichel. [Tucson, Arizona]: Loujon Press of New Orleans, [1966]. One of 26, sgd & with ALs. In d/j. Inscr to dedicatee. sg Dec 12 (289) $800

Anr Ed. [Tucson, Arizona]: Loujon Press, [1966]. One of 1,399. Orig bdg incorporating cork, card, gauze, a mtd photo & pictorial d/j. sg Dec 12 (290) $150

— Plexus. Paris: Olympia Press, [1953]. 2 vols. Orig wraps; rubbed & soiled. cb Sept 19 (164) $80; pba July 9 (206) $160

— Quiet Days in Clichy. Paris, 1956. 2d ptg. 16mo, wraps; hinges starting, edges worn. sg Apr 13 (17) $450

— Scenario. Paris: Obelisk Press, 1937. One of 200, sgd. Wraps. sg Dec 12 (291) $475

— Tropic of Cancer. Paris: Obelisk Press, [1934]. 1st Ed. Orig wraps. Manney copy. P Oct 11 (229) $8,000

Anr copy. Orig wraps; edges worn, backstrip chipped. Epstein copy. sg Apr 30 (333) $3,800

— Tropic of Capricorn. Paris: Obelisk Press, [1939]. 1st Ed. Orig wraps; soiled & worn. cb Sept 19 (165) $275

Anr copy. Orig wraps, unopened; rear cover dust-soiled. Errata slip tipped on to title. CNY June 9 (126) $450

Anr copy. Orig wraps; worn. Inscr to George & Elanor. Manney copy. P Oct 11 (230) $6,000

Anr copy. Orig wraps. With errata slip tipped in. Epstein copy. sg Apr 30 (3334) $2,400

— What Are You Going to Do About Alf? L, [1971]. One of 100 specially bound. Wraps. Inscr. sg Dec 12 (293) $850

Miller, Joe

— Joe Miller's Jests: or, the Wits Vade-mecum. See: Mottley, John

Miller, P. Schuyler

— The Titan. Reading: Fantasy Press, 1952. One of 350. In d/j. sg June 11 (226) $50

Miller, Patrick. See: Golden Cockerel Press

Miller, Philip, 1691-1771

— Figures of Plants.... L, 1771. ("Figures of the Most Beautiful, Useful...Plants Described in the Gardeners Dictionary.") 2d Ed. 2 vols. Contemp calf gilt; rebacked, orig spine preserved. With 300 hand-colored plates. Some soiling. bba Jan 30 (97) £5,200 [Bifolco]

— The Gardener's Dictionary.... L, 1731. Folio, contemp calf; repaired, rebacked. With 4 plates. Flaw in 1 leaf, affecting text; waterstained. Sold w.a.f. bba Jan 16 (352) £100 [Burkhardt]

Anr Ed. Dublin, 1732. Folio, old calf; rebacked. Some soiling & spotting; frontis & tp soiled & creased; frontis laid down with marginal loss; some inking to letters on title. wa Sept 26 (468) $425

2d Ed. L, 1733. Folio, contemp calf; lacking sections of lower cover & head & foot of spine, stamps on front free endpaper. With frontis & 4 plates.. pn June 11 (255) £50

Anr Ed. L, 1737-39. 2 vols. Folio, contemp calf; Vol I worn, joints cracked. With frontis & 11 plates. L Nov 14 (223) £60

Anr Ed. L, 1737. Folio, half calf. LH Dec 11 (152) $200

7th Ed. L, 1759. 2 vols. Folio, later half mor. With frontis & 19 plates. Some soiling & minor repairs. pn June 11 (256) £260 [Cumming]

Miller, Thomas, 1807-74

— Turner and Girtin's Picturesque Views of English, Scotch & Welsh Scenery. L, 1854. 4to, orig cloth; extremities worn. With port, folding facsimile & 30 plates. Some spotting. DW Nov 20 (18) £120

Milles de Souvigny, Jean
— Praxis criminis persequendi, elegantibus aliquot figuris illustrata. Paris: Simon de Colines & Arnould & Charles L'Angelier, 1541. Folio, 18th-cent calf gilt. With 13 full-page woodcuts. Waterstains in upper margins of last few leaves. S Dec 5 (174) £6,000 [Pirages]

Milles, Thomas, 1550-1627
— The Treasurie of Auncient and Moderne Times.... L, 1613-19. 1st Ed. Vol I only. Folio, contemp calf; spine ends chipped. Paper fault in N2, affecting a few letters. STC 17936. sg Oct 24 (223) $450

Milliken, Henry Oothovt. See: Goodwin & Milliken

Millingen, James V., 1774-1845
— Ancient Unedited Monuments. L, 1822-26. 2 vols in 1. 4to, modern cloth. With 40 colored plates in Vol I & 22 plates in Vol II. Some foxing, mainly to text leaves. sg Apr 2 (182) $800

Millingen, John Gideon, 1782-1862
— The History of Duelling. L, 1841. 2 vols. 8vo, orig cloth; spine ends frayed, joints rubbed with minor loss. sg Mar 26 (206) $70

Anr copy. Half calfs; worn, front hinge cracked in Vol I. sg Mar 26 (207) $60

Milne, Alan Alexander, 1882-1956
— A Gallery of Children. L, [1925]. Illus by H. W. Le Mair. 4to, cloth. sg Ocg 17 (317) $120

One of 500. Cloth. Epstein copy. sg Apr 30 (335) $450

— The House at Pooh Corner. L, 1928. 1st Ed. Illus by E. H. Shepard. In d/j. Ck July 10 (359) £280

Anr copy. Some margins nicked. K Sept 29 (266) $60

Anr copy. In d/j. pn Sept 12 (164) £100

One of 250. Orig bds, unopened. Sgd by author & artist. Epstein copy. sg Apr 30 (336) $1,400

One of 350. bba Apr 9 (141) £70 [Heuer]

Anr copy. In soiled d/j. Ck Dec 11 (170) £220

Anr copy. In d/j with short tears. Pforzheimer copy. P June 17 (279) $2,000

— The King's Breakfast. L: Methuen, [1925]. One of 100. Music by H. Fraser-Simson, decorations by E. H. Shepard. Folio, orig half cloth, in d/j. bba July 23 (260) £50 [Sotheran]

— Now We Are Six. L, 1927. 1st Ed. Illus by E. H. Shepard. In torn d/j. sg Oct 17 (318) $130

One of 200. In d/j. Sgd by author & artist. Epstein copy. sg Apr 30 (337) $1,200

— Toad of Toad Hall.... L, [1929]. In d/j. cb Dec 12 (114) $70

Anr copy. In d/j. Hersholt copy. sg June 11 (227) $120

One of 200, sgd by author & Kenneth Grahame. Half cloth, in d/j. Unopened copy. b Nov 18 (77) £420

Anr copy. Half cloth, in soiled d/j. Manney copy. P Oct 11 (232) $1,300

Anr copy. 4to, orig half cloth, unopened, in d/j. Epstein copy. sg Apr 30 (340) $1,300

— When I Was Very Young. NY, 1930. 1st Ed, One of 842, sgd by Milne. Illus by E. H. Shepard. K July 12 (349) $300

— When We Were Very Young. L, 1924. 1st Ed. Illus by E. H. Shepard. S Nov 14 (184) £360 [Sotheran]

1st Ptg of 25 of the poems. L, Jan-June 1924. In: Punch, Vol 166. Epstein copy. sg Apr 29 (338) $150

Later ptg. [NY, 1925]. Illus by E. H. Shepard. Lea by Sangorski & Sutcliffe; rubbed. With ALs of Daphne Milne. K July 12 (348) $55

— Winnie-the-Pooh. L, 1926. 1st Ed. Illus by E. H. Shepard. In soiled d/j. Ck July 10 (356) £280; DW Oct 2 (376) £65

Anr copy. In d/j. S Nov 14 (181) £300 [Georges]

One of 20 on japan, sgd by author & illustrator. Orig vellum. Manney copy. P Oct 11 (231) $7,500

One of 350, sgd by author & artist. 4to, orig half cloth. S Nov 14 (187) £600 [Sotheran]; S Apr 28 (77) £380 [Haverhand]

Milosz, Oscar Vladislas de Luricz
— Fourteen Poems.... San Francisco: Peregrine Press, 1952. One of 129. Trans by Kenneth Rexroth; illus by Edward Hagedorn; designed & ptd by Henry Herman Evans. cb Oct 17 (636) $150

Milton, John, 1608-74
See also: Cresset Press; Doves Press; Fore-Edge Paintings; Gregynog Press; Limited Editions Club; Nonesuch Press

— Areopagitica. L, 1738. 2d Ed. 4to, newer half calf; rubbed, upper joint worn. O May 26 (128) $350

Anr Ed. L: Rampant Lions Press, [1973]. One of 100. Folio, mor gilt by Gray. wa Mar 5 (134) $120

— Comus. L & NY, [1921]. One of 550. Illus by Arthur Rackham. 4to, bds; very stained & soiled. Met Apr 28 (436) $150

Anr copy. Cloth. sg Sept 26 (268) $120

— The History of Britain. L, 1670. 1st Ed, 1st Issue. 4to, contemp calf; rubbed. Port cut to image, remtd & rebacked; marginal staining; AA1 with marginal tear repaired; some rust stains. pn May 14 (8) £280 [Thorp]

— Letters of State.... L, 1694. Trans by Edward Phillips. 12mo, contemp calf; worn. L Nov 14 (425) £220

— On the Morning of Christ's Nativity. Andoversford: Whittington Press, [1981]. One of 325. 4to, half vellum. sg Sept 26 (55) $250

— Paradise Lost. L, [1667?]. 1st Ed, Amory's 1b subissue (traditional 1st title). 4to, orig bdg of contemp sheep; early repairs. With the initial blank.. Chew-Benz-Manney copy. P Oct 11 (234) $90,000

Amory's No 2 Issue (traditional 4th title). L, 1668. 4to, 19th-cent sheep; extremities rubbed, needs rebacking. Tp gutter reinforced; 1 leaf with bottom edge shaved. sg Oct 24 (224) $3,400

Amory's No 3 Issue. L, 1669. 4to, contemp sheep; upper cover detached, spine & corners repaired. Small piece torn from 2F1 with loss of catchword on recto & line reference on verso; some browning & rust spots. Milne copy. Ck June 12 (145) £3,600

Anr Ed. L, 1674. 8vo, 18th-cent calf; corners repaired, spine repaired but worn. Some headlines shaved; small rusthole in Y4; Y7 with repaired hole in blank area beneath text. C Dec 16 (261) £450 [Chung Saw Lin]

3d Ed. L, 1678. 8vo, 19th-cent calf gilt; extremities scuffed, joints tender. F Dec 18 (633) $210

4th Ed. L, 1688. Folio, contemp calf; covers detached, spine chipped. With port & 12 plates. Leaf entitled The Verse lacking. Very large copy. C Dec 16 (220) £800 [Franklin]

Anr copy. Modern half calf incorporating contemp bds. W July 8 (32) £220

Anr Ed. L, 1732. Ed by Richard Bentley. 4to, old calf; covers detached. K Mar 22 (271) $110

Anr Ed. L, 1770. 12mo, contemp calf; hinges weak. With port & 12 plates. LH Dec 11 (152) $200

Anr Ed. L, 1827. Illus by John Martin. 2 vols. Folio, mor gilt; worn. With 24 plates. Some foxing. P June 17 (282) $2,750

Anr copy. Contemp mor gilt; rubbed. L.p. copy. pn Apr 23 (88) £1,500

Anr copy. Contemp calf gilt; spines worn. Spotted. pn Apr 23 (211) £320

Anr copy. 19th-cent calf gilt; rubbed. Spotted throughout. S Dec 12 (191) £520 [Dawson]

Anr copy. Half calf; rubbed & worn, upper cover of Vol I loose, lacking foot of spine, joints of Vol II split. Some leaves spotted & soiled. S Dec 12 (192) £500 [Sellars]

Anr copy. Contemp mor; worn, upper cover of Vol I detached. S July 1 (994) £400 [Tsuboi]

Anr Ed. L: Charles Whittingham, 1846. 4to, contemp half mor; rubbed. Library markings. F Dec 18 (697) $600

Anr Ed. L, 1882. Illus by Gustave Dore. Folio, orig cloth; soiled, corners worn. cb Sept 26 (79) $55

Anr copy. Mor gilt. pnE Dec 4 (176) £120

— Paradise Regain'd. L, 1671. 1st Ed. 8vo, contemp calf; rebacked, extremities rubbed. C Dec 16 (222) £950 [Finch]

1st Issue, with misprint "loah" on page 67. Calf; rubbed. bba Dec 19 (350) £350 [Maggs]

Early Issue. Contemp calf; rebacked. Lacking license leaf (supplied in facsimile); tp with tear at inner margin & with date partly in Ms; some soiling. Milne copy. Ck June 12 (148) £220

Anr Ed. L, 1721. 16mo, early half calf; worn. Browned; some foxing; some pencil notes & underlining. bbc Apr 27 (370) $90

— Poemata. L: Ruth Raworth for Humphrey Moseley, 1645. Separate issue of the Latin section of Poems. 8vo, contemp sheep; spine scuffed & chipped at head. Marginal browning. C Dec 16 (219) £150 [Quaritch]

— Poems.... L, 1673. 2d Ed, 1st state with "White Lion" in imprint. 2 parts in 1 vol. 8vo, contemp calf; worn, rebacked, new endpapers. Some spotting & soiling; a few minor tears; tp restored at inner margin a few annotations; upper margin cropped, touching a few words & page numerals. S May 13 (782) £300 [Clark]

— Poetical Works. Oxford, 1824. 4 vols. 8vo, contemp mor; rubbed. O Aug 25 (133) $130

Anr Ed. Bost., [1909]. One of 550. 4 vols. 8vo, pigskin; spine heads chipped. Ptd at the Merrymount Press. wa Mar 5 (59) $65

— Pro populo Anglicano defensio contra Claudii Anonymi, alias Salmasii, defensionem regiam. L: Typis du Gardianis, 1651. 4to, old calf; rubbed. Some early underscoring & marginalia. Madan 1: 1st Ed, 3d Issue. O May 26 (129) $200

— Prose Works. Amst. [but L], 1698. ("A Complete Collection of the Historical, Political, and Miscellaneous Works.") 3 vols. Folio, contemp calf; worn. bba Oct 24 (55) £180 [R. Clark]

Anr copy. Old sheep gilt; Vol I front cover detached, Vol III taller & with bdg not

uniform & front joint cracked. Some foxing. sg Oct 24 (226) $325
— The Shorter Poems. L, 1889. One of 135. Illus by Samuel Palmer. Folio, orig cloth; rubbed. With 12 plates. bba Dec 19 (56) £80 [Maggs]
— Works. L, 1867. 8 vols. 8vo, calf gilt; spines rubbed. cb Jan 16 (97) $100

Paradise Lost bound with or accompanied by Paradise Regain'd

— 1688. - L. Folio, contemp calf; rubbed. Tp & prelims of PL repaired & several leaves lacking & supplied in Ms. F Sept 26 (423) $90
— 1691-88. - L. Folio, contemp mor gilt; spine ends repaired. William Morris copy. C Dec 16 (221) £3,500 [Jarndyce]
— 1758. - Birm.: Baskerville. 2 vols. 4to, mor gilt by Hayday. Irregular pagination though apparently complete. Sold w.a.f. L Nov 14 (299) £400

Anr copy. Modern half calf. Some foxing & soiling. O Aug 25 (25) $325

Anr copy. Contemp calf; rebacked. With fore-edge paintings of Milton's cottage at Chalfont St. Giles and of Westminster Abbey and St. James's Palace. sg Nov 7 (17) $750

Anr copy. Later mor. Inside PR are pasted leaves from a tree planted by Milton. wd Dec 12 (421) $275

Milton, Thomas —& Others

— The Chimney-Piece-Maker's Daily Assistant. L, 1766. 8vo, contemp calf; rebacked, repaired. With frontis & 54 plates. Some stains. bba May 14 (369) £580 [Shell]

Minadoi, Giovanni Tommaso

— Historia della guerra fra Turchi et Persiani. Venice: Andrea Muschio & Barezzo Barezzi, 1588. 4to, contemp vellum; soiled. Small wormhole at fore-margin of flyleaf & title-A3 without loss. Lascarides copy. S July 1 (657) £350 [Kutluoglu]

Anr Ed. Venice, 1594. 4to, contemp vellum. With folding map. S June 30 (353) £1,100 [Reiss & Auvermann]

Mind, Geoffroi

— Oeuvre de Geofroi Minde de Berne. Berne: Lamy, [c.1818]. Oblong folio, half mor. With engraved title & 18 colored plates. Some discoloration to backgrounds. S June 25 (324) £4,000 [Rondeau]

Minelli, Deodato

— Solenne Processione vaticana del Corpus Domini Diretta da uno de cerimonieri di sua Santita Gregorio XVI. Rome, [n.d.]. Oblong folio, contemp mor gilt with arms of Gregory XVI; rebacked & recornered. With hand-colored engraved title & folding hand-colored panorama on 33 sheets, heightened in gilt. Ck Nov 29 (297) £3,800

Miner, Dorothy E.

[-] Gatherings in Honor of Dorothy E. Miner. Balt., 1974. 4to, cloth. sg Oct 31 (240) $50

Miniature Books

— Bijou Picture of London.... L: Rock Brothers & Payne, [n.d.]. 40mm by 25mm, orig mor gilt. With engraved title & 30 views. Ck July 10 (370) £95
— The Book of Nouns, or Things which may be Seen. L, 1800. 55mm by 42mm, orig half lea; worn & creased, upper cover chipped. With 62 plates. Some soiling. S Nov 14 (221) £480 [B. Stone]
— English Bijou Almanac for 1837. L, [1836]. 40mm by 25mm, orig bds. Ck July 10 (369) £75
— English Bijou Almanac for 1838. L: Schloss [1837]. 19mm by 15mm, orig wraps. bbc Apr 27 (72) $80
— English Bijou Almanac for 1840. L, [1839]. 3/4 x 1/2 inches, orig wraps with mor gilt onlay; in orig velvet case, with magnifying glass. bbc Sept 23 (53) $80
— Petite Excursion en France. Paris, [c.1850]. 3 by 2.2 inches. Orig bds. With engraved title & 11 plates. O May 26 (130) $160
— Youthful Recreations. Phila., [1802]. 1st American Ed. 3.5 by 2.5 inches orig wraps, sewn as issued. With engraved title & 15 plates. bba Oct 10 (139) £80 [Rosenthal]
— ANACREON. - Odai. Glasgow: Foulis, 1751. 80mm by 47mm, modern lev. sg Nov 7 (143) $225
— CROSBY, HARRY. - The Sun. Paris: Black Sun Press, 1929. 1st Ed, One of 100 on japan. 1 by 3/4 inches orig lea gilt. sg Jan 30 (10) $1,900
— GALILEI, G. - Galileo a Madama Cristina di Lorcua. Padua: Salmin, 1897. 16mm by 10mm, mor gilt, orig wraps bound in, with magnifying glass in matching fitted case. S Apr 28 (90) £850 [Bondy]
— HORACE. - Opera. L, 1824. 3 5/8 by 2 inches vellum. pnE May 13 (120) £50
— MILLS, ALFRED. - Pictures of English History in Miniature. L, 1811. 2d Ed. 2 vols. 62mm by 57mm, orig bds; Vol II lacking backstrip. With 96 plates. bba Oct 10 (98) £140 [Bickersteth]

Minotaure...

— Minotaure: Revue artistique et litteraire. Paris, 1935 [but 1934]. No 6. 4to, orig wraps; rear wraps soiled. cb Sept 5 (68) $550

Minucius Felix, Marcus

— Octavius et Caecilli Cypriani De Vanitate Idolorum.... Paris: Vidua Mathurini du Puis, 1643. Bound with: Commodianus. Instructiones adversus Gentium Deos. 8vo, contemp calf; spine repaired, rebacked, orig backstrip preserved. bba Apr 30 (260) £140 [C.L. Edwards]

Mirabeau, Honore Gabriel Riquetti, Comte de, 1749-91

— Erotika Biblion. Rome: l'Imprimerie du Vatican, 1783. 8vo, 19th-cent mor gilt. b June 22 (84) £190

Mirabeau, Victor de Riquetti, Marquis de

— L'Ami des hommes, ou traite de la population. Avignon, 1756. 6 parts in 3 vols. 4to, 18th-cent calf; joints worn & split. Lacking port; lower outer corner of Aa2 torn away; 1 leaf with small hole from paper flaw. With "Ex dono authoris" on 1st title. S Dec 5 (338) £2,000 [Kinocoulya]

Anr Ed. [N.p.], 1758. 4 vols in 2. 4to, contemp sheep gilt; spine ends & corners worn. Lacking frontis. sg Oct 24 (230) $225

Anr Ed. Avignon, 1762-64-61. 6 parts in 3 vols. 4to, 18th-cent half calf; joints damaged. With frontis. S May 13 (848) £220 [Maggs]

Mirchond, Mohammede

— Historia priorum Regum Persarum post firmatum in regno Islamismum. Vienna, 1782. 4to, contemp calf gilt. SI Dec 5 (945) LIt650,000

Mireur, Hippolyte, 1841-1914

— Dictionnaire des ventes d'art.... Paris, 1901-12. 7 vols. Contemp half mor, orig wraps preserved. CG Oct 7 (444) £110

Mirliton

— Le Mirliton. Paris, 1885-93. Ed by Aristide Bruant. 194 issues bound in 3 vols (complete set). 8vo & folio, half mor. SM Oct 12 (425) FF7,000

Miro, Joan

— Les Essencies de la terra.... Barcelona, [1968]. One of 1,120. Folio, unsewn in orig wraps. sg Sept 26 (235) $800

— Homage. NY, [1976]. 4to, cloth, in d/j. sg Apr 2 (184) $300

— Lithographs. NY: Tudor Publishing, [1972]-75. Ed by Michel Leiris & Fernand Mourlot. Vols I-II (of 3). Folio, orig cloth, in d/js. bbc Apr 27 (469) $425

Anr Ed. NY: Tudor Publishing, [1972]-81. Vol I only. Folio, cloth, in d/j. sg Sept 26 (236) $275

Anr copy. 4 vols. Folio, sg May 7 (52) $1,200

Vol I only. In d/j. sg Apr 2 (185) $200

— Litografo. Barcelona, 1972-77. 3 vols. With 32 colored lithos. S Feb 11 (284) £450 [Bauer]

— L'Oiseau solaire, L'Oiseau lunaire, etincelles. Paris: Maeght, 1967. Text by Patrick Waldberg. Folio, pictorial wraps, unbound. Special No 164/165 of Derriere le Miroir. Met Apr 28 (24) $110

— Peintures Murales. Paris: Maeght, 1961. Folio, wraps. Derrier le miroir, No. 128. Met Apr 28 (25) $130

— Trace sur l'eau. Paris, 1963. One of 20 on grand velin de Rives, this copy unnumbered but sgd. Oblong 4to, Unsewn in orig wraps. CGen Nov 18 (418) SF3,800

Miscellanea...

— Miscellanea Curiosa. Containing a Collection of some of the Principal Phaenomena in Nature.... L, 1708. 2d Ed. 3 vols. 8vo, contemp calf; Vol III rejointed. bba Apr 9 (185) £520 [Bickersteth]

Miscellaneous...

— Miscellaneous Poems, by Several Hands. L, 1726. Ed by D. Lewis. 8vo, modern half calf. T4 detached. bba Oct 10 (312) £60 [Oatley]

Mislin, Jacob

— Les saints lieux, pelerinage a Jerusalem. Paris, 1858. 3 vols. 8vo, contemp half mor. With 12 maps. Some spotting & dampstaining in Vol I. S July 1 (850) £400 [O'Neill]

Missal

— c.1483-84. - Missale Hafniense. Mainz: Peter Schoeffer. 2 leaves. Folio, in linen folder. 36 lines; double column; type 7A:149G; rubricated. First leaf with a few glue marks, a crease & a small tear; 2d leaf soiled on the verso & with heavier glue marks on the recto. Schoyen copy. P Dec 12 (39) $9,000

— 1506, 18 Apr. - [Use of Monte Cassino]. Venice: L. Giunta. Folio, contemp blindstamped pigskin over wooden bds with brass clasps & catches; rebacked with later vellum, brass center- & corner-pieces missing. With c.300 woodcut illusts & historiated initials, including the Crucifixion & the Consecration cuts in the canon colored by a contemp hand; with 13 woodcut pictorial borders. Marginal repairs to O2-5; minor worming at beginning & end; small hole in final leaf; some staining in the Canon. C Nov 27 (43) £5,200 [Turner]

— 1563. - Missale Romanum. Venice: heirs of Luc'Antonio Giunta. Folio, 19th-cent lea; joints cracked with brass catches & clasps. Lacking 4 leaves, including tp. Sold w.a.f. sg Oct 24 (231) $300

— 1674. - Missale Romanum ex decreto sacrosancti Councilii Tridenti restitutum.... Venice: Cieras. Folio, contemp Italian embroidered bdg highlighted with ruby chips, with arms of the Della Rovere family on lower cover & unidentified arms on upper cover. C June 24 (180) £1,300 [Delucia]

— 1725. - Canon missale ad usum episcoporum, ac prelatorum...sub auspiciis Innocentii XIII. Rome Folio, 18th-cent mor gilt with arms of an Italian cardinal; upper joint split at foot. Some soiling & browning. S May 28 (132) £1,600 [Panini]

— 1765. - Missale Romanum. Antwerp 4to, contemp mor gilt with emblems of the Society of Jesus; upper cover def, repaired. bba June 25 (79) £110 [Dawes]

Mississippi

— Statutes of the Mississippi Territory. Natchez, 1816. 8vo, contemp sheep; head of spine lacking, rubbed. sg Dec 5 (154) $350

Missouri

— Hand-Book of Missouri...Issued by the Missouri Immigration Society. St. Louis, 1880. 2d Ed. 8vo, wraps; front wrap loose. With folding map. sg June 18 (384) $120

Mitchell, Margaret, 1900-49

See also: Limited Editions Club

— Gone With the Wind. NY, 1936. Advance Review Copy. Cloth, in glassine wrap. cb Oct 25 (997) $1,700

1st Ed, 1st Issue, with May 1936 date. bbc Dec 9 (52) $350

Anr copy. In d/j. Sgd. sg Dec 12 (301) $5,400

Anr copy. In d/j. Sgd. Epstein copy. sg Apr 30 (343) $3,800

Anr copy. Cloth; worn, "backstrip gone with the wind". Sgd. sg June 11 (228) $400

Issue not indicated. Bdg worn & shaken. cb Sept 19 (166) $800

Anr copy. In frayed & worn d/j. P June 17 (283) $900

Later ptg. In chipped & worn d/j. cb Dec 12 (115) $55

Printer's proof. Hole-punched & secured with twine. Dampstained; a few pencil markings. Manney copy. P Oct 11 (234) $3,750

Mitchell, Samuel Augustus, 1792-1868

See also: Atlas

— Mitchell's New Traveler's Guide through the United States. Phila., 1852. 16mo, mor gilt; rubbed. With folding map, hand-colored in outline. Fold tears. sg June 18 (385) $300

— Mitchell's Traveller's Guide Through the United States. Phila.: T. Cowperthwait, [1844]. 16mo, orig lea. With colored folding map (with ink outline of previous traveler's itinerary). sp Feb 6 (109) $270

— New General Atlas.... Phila., 1860. Folio, orig half lea; rubbed, 1 joint open. With 76 hand-colored maps on 43 sheets. K Sept 29 (42) $600

— A New Map of Texas, Oregon and California.... Phila., 1846. 16mo, orig cloth & stamped lea folder; some minor splits at folds. With accompanying text pamphlet. O Nov 26 (125) $1,400

— A New Universal Atlas. Phila., 1850. Folio, half mor; extremities rubbed. With engraved title & 73 colored maps. Several maps browned. sg Sept 19 (89) $1,600

— New Universal Atlas. Phila., 1854. Folio, half sheep; needs rebdg. With colored title & 129 maps on 75 sheets. sg Sept 19 (90) $1,500

Mitchell, Sir Thomas Livingstone, 1792-1855

— 1846. New South Wales. Despatches and Map relating to...Exploration to the North. Sydney, 1846. 4to, modern mor folder. With folding litho map, hand-colored & laid down on Japanese tissue. Tears to map repaired; title wrap torn & laid down. C June 25 (236) £5,400 [Quaritch/Hordern]

— Journal of an Expedition into the Interior of Tropical Australia. L, 1848. 8vo, orig cloth; badly rebacked. kh Nov 11 (583) A$500

Anr copy. Contemp calf; rubbed. With frontis, 11 tinted plates & 7 maps. Last map shaved at foot; lacking ads. S June 25 (148) £500 [Arnold]

— Three Expeditions into the Interior of Eastern Australia. L, 1839. 2d Ed. 2 vols. 8vo, orig cloth; rubbed. With folding map & 51 plates, some hand-colored. Some foxing & soiling; corner of Q1 in Vol II def just touching text. bba June 11 (345) £350 [Woodstock]

Anr copy. With 51 plates and maps, a few colored, a few folding & with colored folding map in pocket of Vol I. S June 25 (223) £700 [Arnold]

Mitchill, Samuel Latham, 1764-1831

— The Picture of New-York, or Traveller's Guide.... NY, 1807. 1st Ed. 16mo, half lea; rubbed. Folding map at front. K Sept 29 (270) $225

Mitford, Edward Ledwich

— A Land March from England to Ceylon.... L, 1884. 2 vols. 8vo, orig cloth. With port, 20 plates & 3 folding maps. bba June 11 (364) £150 [Scott]

Mitford, John, 1781-1859

— My Cousin in the Army: or, Johnny Newcome on the Peace Establishment. L, [c.1825]. 2d Ed. 8vo, half calf; rubbed. With 16 hand-colored plates. Foxed & stained. O Feb 25 (140) $180

Mitford, Mary Russell, 1787-1855

— Recollections of a Literary Life. L, 1852. 1st Ed. 3 vols. 12mo, calf by Tout; rubbed. Extra-illus with "numerous" ports & other material. O Feb 25 (141) $80

Mivart, St. George Jackson, 1827-1900

— Dogs, Jackals, Wolves, and Foxes.... L, 1890. 1st Ed. 4to, contemp half mor; rubbed. With 45 hand-colored plates. C May 20 (203) £1,300 [Travers]

Anr copy. Orig cloth. DW Nov 6 (178) £600

— A Monograph of the Lories, or Brush-Tongued Parrots.... L, 1896. 4to, orig cloth. With 3 (of 4) colored maps & 61 hand-colored plates. C Oct 30 (287) £2,100 [Grahame]

Anr copy. Orig cloth, with Quaritch lettered at foot of spine; corners rubbed. With 4 maps & 61 hand-colored plates. C May 20 (202) £2,600 [Petretti]

Anr copy. Cloth. S Nov 21 (35) £2,400 [Sims, Reed]

— On the Genesis of Species. L, 1871. 8vo, orig cloth; spine ends worn. bbc Dec 9 (341) $110

Mizner, Addison

— Florida Architecture. NY, [1928]. Folio, recent cloth; bound from orig sheets but trimmed. With port & 184 plates. sg Sept 6 (192) $425

Anr copy. Half cloth; extremities worn. sg Feb 6 (193) $650

Mocquet de Meaux, Jean

— Travels and Voyages into Africa, Asia, and America.... L, 1696. 8vo, half mor by Club Bindery; joints & corners rubbed. Borders of 3 woodcuts shaved, 1 with loss;l 4 leaves of quire S cropped, affecting catchwords & 1 last line; marginal repair to H4 with loss to catchword on verso; repair to U2 with loss repaired in pen facsimile; large repair to Z2r with ink touch-up; washed. Sargent-Andrews-duPont copy. CNY Oct 8 (177) $2,400

Modern...

See also: Shepherd, Thomas Hosmer

— Modern Book Production. L: The Studio, 1928. Ed by Charles Holme. 4to, orig half vellum. cb Jan 16 (98) $50

— The Modern Traveller. A Popular Description...of the Various Countries of the Globe. L, 1825-27. 13 vols. 12mo, orig half lea gilt. Milne copy. Ck June 12 (55) £180

Modigliani, Amedeo, 1884-1920

— Forty-Five Drawings by Modigliani. NY, 1959. One of 250 with text in English. Text by Lamberto Vitali. Folio, unsewn in orig case; worn. sg Feb 6 (197) $175

Modius, Franciscus

— Pandectae triumphales, sive pomparum et festorum ac solennium apparatuum conviviorum.... Frankfurt: Sigismund Feyerabend, 1586. 2 parts in 1 vol. Folio, 16th-cent blind-stamped pigskin. Worming at ends. S Dec 5 (176) £850 [Goldschmidt]

Moe, Jorgen I, 1813-82. See: Asbjornsen & Moe

Moellhausen, Balduin, 1825-1905

— Diary of a Journey from the Mississippi to the Coasts of the Pacific. L, 1858. 2 vols. 8vo, contemp calf gilt; joints weak. With folding map & 11 colored or tinted lithos & 12 wood-engraved illusts. S Nov 15 (1228) £320 [Ginsberg]

Moeser, Justus

— Harlequin; or, a Defence of Grotesque Comic Performances. L, 1766. 8vo, 19th-cent half sheep. Stain on title; marginal foxing; lacking half-title. sg Mar 5 (246) $350

Moffatt, Elizabeth Whitney. See: Gardilanne & Moffatt

Moffett, Thomas, 1553-1604

— Insectorum sive minimorum animalium theatrum.... L, 1634. Folio, contemp vellum; stained. Tp soiled & with old inscr at head. STC 17993. S June 25 (47) £850 [Dillon]

Moholy-Nagy, Laszlo

— The New Vision: Fundamentals of Design, Painting.... NY, 1938. Cloth; endpapers foxed. sg Feb 6 (198) $225

Molesworth, Robert, Viscount, 1656-1725

— An Account of Denmark.... L, 1694. 1st Ed. 8vo, contemp calf; spine nicked. b June 22 (194) £220

Moleville, Antoine Francois Bertrand de

— The Costume of the Hereditary States of the House of Austria.... L, 1804. 4to, contemp mor gilt. With 50 hand-colored plates. Some plates spotted. Colas 2112. bba Oct 10 (185) £450 [Kiefer]; HH May 12 (962) DM6,000

Anr Ed. L, 1804 [but some plates watermarked 1819]. Folio, contemp half mor; rubbed. With 50 colored plates. Soiled. bba Sept 19 (145) £420 [Bifolco]

Moliere, Jean Baptiste Poquelin de, 1622-73
See also: Limited Editions Club

— Oeuvres. Paris, 1773. 6 vols. 8vo, contemp calf gilt; rubbed. With frontis & 33 plates. S May 13 (851) £400 [Casa D'Arte]

Anr Ed. Paris, 1788. 6 vols. 8vo, contemp calf; edges rubbed. With 34 plates. Some gatherings browned. bba Oct 10 (515) £240 [Robertshaw]

Anr copy. Orig bds. pnE Mar 11 (162) £70

Anr copy. Mor gilt by de Coverly; marked. With port & 33 plates. Some browning & dampstaining; Vol VI with fore-margin of C3 repaired. S July 1 (997) £230 [Shapero]

Anr Ed. Paris, 1873-89. One of 200. 10 vols. 8vo, mor gilt by Marius Michel; scuffed. bbc Sept 23 (54) $625

— [Works] The Dramatic Works. Edin, 1875-76. 6 vols. 8vo, mor gilt, unopened, by Grieve; rubbed; covers of 2 vols water-stained. Sold w.a.f. O Feb 25 (142) $350

Molina, Alonso de, d.1535

— Vocabulario en lengua castellana y mexicana.... Mexico: Antonio de Spinoza, 1571. 2d Ed. 2 parts in 1 vol. Folio, modern vellum. The following in facsimile: first title-A2, 2d title & following leaf, T8-end; several other leaves damaged with loss & repaired without restoration of text. S Nov 21 (337) £1,500 [Maggs]

Moll, Herman, d.1732

— A Set of Fifty New and Correct Maps of England and Wales.... L, 1724. Oblong folio, contemp half calf; spine repaired with tape, some wear. With 2 colored folding maps & 48 double-page county maps. Some marginal vignettes with later coloring. b Nov 18 (227) £1,400

Anr Ed. L, 1739. Bound with: A Set of Thirty Six New and Correct Maps of Scotland. L, 1725. And: A Set of Twenty New and Correct Maps of Ireland. L, 1728. Oblong folio, modern half calf. Lacking 9 maps in 1st work; some spotting; 2 maps cut close at lower margins. S June 25 (262) £3,000 [Baskes]

— A Set of Thirty-Two New and Correct Maps of the Principal Parts of Europe. L, [c.1727]. 4to, old calf; worn. With 32 hand-colored double-page maps. Minor soiling & dampstaining. O Nov 26 (126) $1,400

Mollien, Gaspard Theodore, Comte de

— Travels in the Interior of Africa.... L, 1820. 4to, contemp half calf; rubbed, rebacked. With folding map & 6 plates. bba Sept 19 (67) £300 [Graves-Johnston]

Molloy, Charles, 1646-90

— De jure maritimo et navali. L, 1676. 1st Ed. 8vo, contemp calf; needs rebacking. Lower portion dampstained with traces of mold. Sold w.a.f. sg May 21 (73) $60

Moloko...

— Moloko Kobylits. Moscow, 1914. 1st Ed, One of 100. Orig wraps; re-attached. sg Nov 7 (217) $500

Monacazione

— Monacazione di Orsola e Cecilia Santonini: La Perfezione religiosa canti IX. Padua, 1763. Folio, modern vellum. Lacking 1 plate. SI Dec 5 (533) LIt200,000

Monardes, Nicholas, 1498-1588
See also: Orta, Garcia da; Orta & Monardes

— Joyful Newes Out of the New-Found Worlde.... L: assign of Bonham Norton, 1596. 3d Ed in English. Trans by John Frampton. 4to, 19th-cent mor gilt by Bedford; front joint cracked. Washed; lacking initial leaf. STC 18007. sg May 14 (110) $1,900

Moncada, Francisco de, Marques de Aytona, 1586-1635

— Expedicion de los Catalanes y Aragoneses contra Turcos y Griegos.... Madrid: Antonio de Sancha, 1777. 8vo, contemp vellum; soiled, hinges starting. cb Feb 12 (91) $275

Monconys, Balthasar de

— Voyages. Paris, 1695. 3 (of 5) parts in 3 vols. Contemp calf. With engraved title & 40 plates. Short tear to final leaf of Vol II; 1 plate inverted; worming to a few blank margins in Vol II; some waterstains. b June 22 (195) £90

Mongez, Antoine, 1747-1835

— Tableaux, Statues, Bas-Reliefs et Camees, de la Galerie de Florence et du Palais Pitti. Paris, 1789-1821. 2 vols. Folio, contemp half mor gilt; rubbed. With 152 plates on 78 leaves. HH May 12 (893) DM1,700

Anr copy. 4 vols. Folio, contemp mor gilt; rubbed. Waterspotting to lower margins throughout. SI Dec 5 (243) LIt2,000,000

Anr copy. Vols I-II. Folio, contemp bds; worn. SI June 9 (374) LIt1,100,000

Monk, Maria, 1817?-50

— Awful Disclosures of Maria Monk. NY, 1836. 12mo, cloth; rubbed. sg June 18 (386) $60

Monkhouse, William Cosmo, 1840-1901

— The Turner Gallery.... L, [1878]. 3 vols. Folio, orig cloth; rubbed. With port, engraved title & 119 plates. pn June 11 (213) £720 [Bailey]

— The Works of Sir Edwin Landseer.... L, [1879-80]. Folio, mor gilt; rubbed. Some browning. b Mar 11 (55) £160

Monro, Robert, d.1680?

— Monro, his Expedition with the Worthy Scots Regiment.... L, 1637. 2 parts in 1 vol. Folio, contemp calf; rebacked. Title frayed & soiled. bba Oct 24 (201) £200 [Trotman]

Monro, Vere

— A Summer Ramble in Syria.... L, 1835. 2 vols. 8vo, orig cloth. With litho frontises. S Nov 15 (1178) £300 [Lazard]

Monroe, John

— The American Botanist, and Family Physician.... Wheelock VT, 1824. 1st Ed. 2 vols in 1. 12mo, calf; worn. Inkstamp on front flyleaf. NH May 30 (351) $140

Monstrelet, Enguerrand de, 1390?-1453

— The Chronicles.... Hafod, 1809. 5 vols, including plate vol & index. 4to, contemp calf gilt; rebacked. bba Apr 9 (95) £65 [Abdullah]

Montagu, Lady Barbara —& Scott, Sarah

— A Description of Millenium Hall.... L, 1762. 12mo, later half calf. Corner of D8 torn away with loss of pagination; some foxing. ESTC 124052. bba July 23 (265) £50 [Carr-Ellison]

Montagu, George, 1751-1815

— Testacea Britannica; or, Natural History of British Shells. Romsey & L, 1803. 1st Ed. 2 vols in 1. 4to, later cloth; bowed. With 2 engraved titles & 16 hand-colored plates. Library markings. bba Sept 5 (83) £150 [M. Phelps]

Anr copy. 2 vols plus 1808 Supplement. 4to, old bds with modern calf backs & tips; worn. With 2 engraved titles & 30 hand-colored plates. O Jan 14 (128) $375

Montagu, Lady Mary Wortley, 1689-1762

— Verses Address'd to the Imitator of the First Satire of the Second Book of Horace. L, [1733]. 1st Ed. Folio, disbound. Tp soiled & creased where folded. Ck June 12 (150) £85

— Works. L, 1803. 1st Ed. 5 vols. 8vo, old calf. O Jan 14 (129) $80

Montaigne, Michel Eyquem de, 1533-92
See also: Nonesuch Press

— Les Essais. Paris: Abel Angelier, 1595. 1st Issue. Folio, contemp mor gilt with small mor onlays with gilt squirrel tool. Lower margins dampstained throughout; first few leaves seriously affected & repaired with occasional minor loss of signature; Aaa1 with small tear in blank foremargin repaired. C Dec 16 (145) £3,800 [Chaponniere]

Anr Ed. Paris: Michel Sonnius, 1595. Folio, mor extra by Hardy-Menil, gilt by Marius Michel. Small rusthole with minimal loss at head of H4. S May 28 (404) £10,000 [Bonna]

Anr Ed. Paris, 1935-36. One of 30 on japon. Illus by Louis Jou. 3 vols. 4to, mor extra by Madeleine Gras, 1955. CGen Nov 18 (420) SF9,000

— The Essayes.... L, 1603. 1st Ed in English. Trans by John Florio. 3 parts in 1 vol. Folio, calf gilt. Tp & some other leaves remargin; worming at top of a number of leaves in the middle; early annotations at beginning. NH Aug 23 (162) $2,200

Anr copy. Contemp calf; front joint and head of spine restored. Dampstaining at beginning and end. sg Nov 7 (146) $6,000

Anr Ed. L, 1923. ("Essays.") One of 150. Cotton's trans. 5 vols. Mor gilt by Riviere. wa Mar 5 (62) $250

Montanus, Arnoldus, 1625?-83

— Atlas Chinensis.... L, 1671. 1st Ed in English. Folio, contemp calf. With map & 38 plates. Some fraying & browning. SI June 10 (657) LIt1,800,000

— Gedenkwaerdige Gesantschappen der Oost-Indische Maetschappy in't Vereenigde Nederland.... Amst., 1669. Folio, contemp calf; rebacked, corners restored. With engraved title & 22 (of 24) plates. Lacking folding map & 15 leaves of text. DW Nov 6 (73) £400

Monte, Guidobaldo del

— La Mechaniche.... Venice, 1581. 4to, contemp vellum; soiled. Inkstain on M2; some waterstaining to upper margins. Ck Nov 29 (246) £800

Monten, D. See: Eckert & Monten

Montes de Oca, Rafael

— Hummingbirds and Orchids of Mexico. Mexico, [1963]. One of 1,500. Folio, cloth, in frayed d/j. With 60 color plates. sg May 14 (234) $150

Anr copy. Cloth, in tape-reinforced d/j. wa Dec 9 (571) $80

Montesquieu, Charles de Secondat, Baron de, 1689-1755

— Lettres persanes. Paris, 1926. One of 200. Illus by Charles Martin. 4to, mor gilt with 4 floral corner onlays by Flammarion. With frontis & 19 plates in 2 states, 1 hand-colored. sg Sept 26 (238) $450

— Le Temple de Gnide. Paris, 1772. 8vo, 18th-cent calf gilt with arms of the comte d'Alby; spine damaged & repaired at head & foot of spine. With engraved title & 10 plates. WIth Ls of the comte d'Alby, 1779, loosely inserted. S May 13 (852) £400 [Shapero]

Montfaucon, Bernard de, 1665-1741

— L'Antiquite expliquee et representee en figures. Paris, 1719. 5 vols in 10. Folio, contemp calf; worn. With port & 967 plates only. Some dampstains; some browning of margins; some leaves in Vol I detached. Sold w.a.f. Ck Nov 29 (298) £920

Anr copy. 5 vols in 10. With: Supplement. Paris, 1724. Vols I-III (of 5). Together, 13 vols. Folio, half russia; worn, some hinges cracked. sg Sept 6 (1965) $1,800

— The Antiquities of Italy.... L, 1725. 2d Ed. Folio, modern cloth. Some foxing & soiling. sg Sept 6 (195) $300

Anr copy. 19th-cent half lea; worn. SI June 10 (659) LIt650,000

— Diarium Italicum. Paris, 1702. 1st Ed. 4to, contemp mor gilt, armorial bdg; rubbed, upper cover holed. Lacking final blank; outer blank margin of leaves to E1 holed. C Dec 16 (198) £1,100 [Quaritch]

Anr copy. Contemp sheep; worn, covers detached. sg Oct 31 (243) $225

Montgomery, Bernard Law, 1st Viscount Montgomery of Alamein

— El Alamein to the River Sangro.... L, 1971. One of 265, sgd & specially bound. Orig mor. bba Apr 30 (151) £160 [FouFou]

— A History of Warfare. L: Arcadia Press, 1969. One of 265, sgd. Orig mor gilt. bba Apr 30 (150) £200 [Bernard]

Anr copy. Orig mor with inlays, by Zaehnsdorf. sg Jan 9 (137) $500

Montgomery, James, 1771-1854

— The Sacred Annual, being The Messiah, a Poem. L, 1834. 4th Ed. 8vo, orig cloth; rebacked preserving spine. With illuminated tp & 11 plates colored by hand. S July 21 (425) £650 [Sellars]

Montgomery, Rutherford G. See: Derrydale Press

Montherlant, Henry de

— Les Celibataires. Paris, 1934. One of 19 on japon. Mor extra by Crette, orig wraps bound in. S May 28 (405) £1,200 [Beres]

— Les Jeunes filles. Paris, 1938. One of 382. Illus by Mariette Lydis. 4to, orig wraps; loose as issued. With 12 colored plates. F June 25 (339) $120

Montor, Artaud de

— The Lives and Times of the Popes. NY: Catholic Publication Society of America, [1911]. One of 1,000. 10 vols. Contemp mor gilt. Each vol with an ALs or Ls from a Pope or Cardinal tipped-in. Ck Nov 29 (299) £1,100

Montorgueil, Georges

— Bonaparte. Paris, [1910]. Illus by Job. 4to, orig cloth; worn & shaken. sg Oct 17 (282) $275

Montucla, Jean Etienne, 1725-99

— Histoire des mathematiques. Paris, 1799-1802 [An VII-X]. 4 vols. 4to, later 19th-cent half mor; joints rubbed. With 2 ports & 45 folding plates. With 2 plates repaired at outer margins. Ck Nov 29 (224) £350

Monumenta Boica

— Monumenta Boica. Munich, 1763-87. Vols I-XV. 4to, contemp half vellum. With 170 mostly folding plates. Some browning. S Nov 21 (190) £1,500 [Reinhold]

Moody, Eleazer

— The School of Good Manners, composed for the Help of Parents.... Bost., 1775. 16mo, orig bds with paper covering perished & lea backing deteriorating; front cover def. Prelims gone. NH may 30 (224) $290

Moorcroft, W. —& Trebeck, George

— Travels in the Himalayan Provinces of Hindustan and the Panjab. L, 1841. 2 vols. 8vo, contemp calf gilt; spines rubbed. With frontises & folding map. S June 25 (464) £1,100 [Hosains]

Moore, Sir Alan Hilary

— Sailing Ships of War.... L & NY, 1926. One of 1,500. 4to, orig cloth. wa Sept 26 (509) $90

Moore, Charles, Rector of Custon

— A Full Inquiry in to the Subject of Suicide. L, 1790. 2 vols. 8vo, early 19th-cent russia; rebacked, worn. Some foxing. sg May 14 (111) $600

Moore, Charles, b.1855

— Daniel H. Burnham, Architect, Planner of Cities. Bost., 1921. 2 vols. Library markings. bbc Sept 23 (133) $90; sg Apr 2 (7) $175

Moore, Clement Clarke, 1779-1863

— The Night before Christmas. NY, 1837. ("A Visit from St. Nicolas.") 8vo, orig mor gilt. In: The New York Book of Poetry. sg Mar 5 (199) $425

— Night Before Christmas L, 1931. One of 550, sgd by artist. Illus by Arthur Rackham. Orig vellum. With 4 colored plates. br May 29 (8) $575

Anr Ed. Phila., [1931]. With 4 color plates. sp Feb 6 (343) $80

Moore, Dennis Times

— A Manual of Pyrotechny. Written by Practicus.... L, 1872. 8vo, orig cloth; rear joint cracked. Some stains & pencil marginalia. sg Nov 14 (298) $225

— Pyrotechny; or, The Art of Making Fireworks.... L, [1873?]. 8vo, orig cloth; hinges cracked. With 11 plates. sg Nov 14 (299) $225

Moore, Edward, 1712-57

— Poems, Fables, and Plays. L, 1756. 4to, contemp sheep; joints cracked, front hinge reinforced. sg Oct 24 (234) $50

Moore, Edward, 1712-57 —& Brooke, Henry, 1703?-83

— Fables for the Female Sex. L, 1749. 3d Ed. 8vo, lea; repaired, rear joint weak. sp Apr 16 (328) $65

Moore, Francis

— A Voyage to Georgia.... L, 1744. 8vo, calf gilt by Sangorski & Sutcliffe; spine def. Lacking half-title. DuPont copy. CNY Oct 8 (178) $3,200

Moore, Frank, 1828-1904

— The Rebellion Record: a Diary of American Events. NY, 1861-68. Vols I-V half mor by Andrus McChain of Ithaca; worn. Some stamps. bbc Feb 17 (98) $55

Moore, George, 1852-1933

— The Brook Kerith. NY, 1929. One of 500, sgd by author & artist. Illus by Stephen Gooden. Half vellum. With 12 plates. DW Mar 4 (354) £50; sg Sept 26 (125) $90

Anr copy. Vellum, unopened. sg Jan 30 (63) $50

— Memoirs of my Dead Life. L, 1906. 1st Ed. Orig cloth; worn. sg Dec 12 (302) $90

— Peronnik the Fool. L, 1933. One of 525, sgd by author & artist. Illus by Stephen Gooden. Orig vellum. bbc Apr 27 (376) $80

Moore, Henry Spencer

— Heads, Figures, and Ideas. L & Greenwich CT, 1958. Folio, orig bds, in torn d/j. DW Oct 9 (601) £115

Anr Ed. L & Greenwich, Conn., 1958. Folio, half cloth, in d/j. With an autolitho. Plate loose. sg Feb 6 (199) $175

— Shelter Sketch Book. [L, 1940?]. Oblong 8vo, cloth; worn, hinges cracked. Sgd & dated Oct 1940. cb Sept 5 (773) $50

Moore, Henry Spencer —& Auden, Wystan Hugh, 1907-73

— Auden Poems: Moore Lithographs. L, 1974. one of 150. Folio, cloth; hinges sprung. With additonal portfolio of 4 loose lithos. sg Jan 10 (105) $1,000

Moore, John, Apothecary

— A Treatise on Domestic Pigeons. L, 1765. 8vo, calf; worn, front hinge weak. K Mar 22 (350) $500

Anr copy. Half calf; worn. With frontis & 13 plates plus 1 duplicate plate which is cropped. K July 12 (408) $450

Moore, John C. See: Sheringham & Moore

Moore, John Hamilton

— A New and Complete Collection of Voyages and Travels. L, 1778-[80]. Vol I only. Contemp calf; rebacked, with old spine laid down. With frontises & 98 plates & maps. Ck Dec 11 (239) £500

— The Seaman's Complete Daily Assistant.... L, 1796. 8vo, old calf with added cloth d/j; worn. Some browning, foxing & soiling; annotated. O July 14 (134) $160

Moore, Lieut. Joseph

— Eighteen Views Taken at and near Rangoon. L, [1825-26]. Bound with: Views in the Birman Empire. Oblong folio, modern calf, text for Series I & II & the folding map are disbound & attached to card insert at beginning in wraps. With 24 hand-colored plates, Plate 16 of 1st work in 1st State with the spelling "ajacent". Some soiling; minor marginal tears. C May 20 (91) £4,500

Moore, Marianne

— Poems. L: Egoist Press, 1921. 1st Ed. Orig wraps. Epstein copy. sg Apr 30 (344) $500

— Tell Me, Tell Me. NY, [1966]. 1st Ed. Half cloth, in d/j. Inscr, 4 Nov 1966. wa Dec 9 (210) $50

Moore, N. Hudson

— The Lace Book. NY, 1904. 4to, later half mor. With 70 plates. bba June 25 (232) £100 [Thorp]

Moore, Thomas

— The History of Devonshire. L, [plates dated 1829-36]. 3 vols. 8vo, contemp half calf; rubbed. With engraved titles, 2 folding maps & 102 plates (1 def). Sold w.a.f. W July 8 (230) £190

Moore, Thomas, 1779-1852

See also: Fore-Edge Paintings

— Lalla Rookh. L, 1817. 4to, contemp mor extra by D. Davies of London; joints & corners repaired, joints rubbed. Extra-illus with a Ms poem & mtd ALs to James Perry, presenting the book. C Dec 16 (263) £700 [Maggs]

Anr Ed. L, 1846. 8vo, in Cosway bdg of mor extra with 8 miniatures by C. B. Currie. CNY Dec 5 (430) $8,000

Anr Ed. L, 1861. Illus by the Brothers Dalziel. 8vo, contemp mor gilt by Riviere. Inscr by Davison Dalziel to his wife. cb Sept 26 (67) $400

Anr Ed. Bost., 1885. One of 500 on Japan vellum. Folio, mor extra by Bruhn. sg Mar 5 (195) $425

Moore, Thomas, 1821-87

See also: Floral...; Gardeners'...

— The Ferns of Great Britain and Ireland. L, 1855. Folio, contemp half mor gilt. With 51 colored nature-ptd plates. C Oct 30 (217) £1,600 [Hayley]

Anr copy. Contemp half mor; spine restored. C May 20 (204) £1,800 [Arader]

Anr copy. Modern half calf. With 78 nature-ptd plates. Tp & last leaf restored in margins without loss; some foxing. Schlosser copy. P June 18 (483) $2,500

Moorehead, Alan

— Darwin and the Beagle. L: Arcadia Press, 1970. One of 265. 4to, orig mor gilt by Zaehnsdorf. b Mar 11 (127) £110

Moran, James

— Printing Presses. Berkeley, 1973. In d/j. cb Oct 17 (648) $60

Morant, Philip, 1700-70

— The History and Antiquities of the County of Essex. L, 1768. 1st Ed. 2 vols. Folio, contemp calf gilt; rebacked. With folding map & 32 plates & maps. 2 torn or repaired. Extra-illus with 2 plates, 1 hand-colored. bba Apr 30 (6) £750 [Baxter]

Morante

— Libro del Gigante Morante. Venice: G. A. Vavassore, 12 May 1531. 8vo, modern vellum. Some spotting; lower margins of early leaves shaved with loss of a few signature marks; small repair to inner margin of last leaf. C Dec 16 (64) £2,600 [Montaro]

Morazzoni, Giuseppe

— Il Libro illustrato veneziano del settecento. Milan, 1943. 4to, orig bds; worn, backstrip loose. bba Feb 27 (435) £150 [Montero]

Anr copy. Orig bds; rubbed. With 154 plates. bbc Sept 23 (115) $80

Morden, Robert

— Geography Rectified. L, 1680. 4to, contemp half calf; def. With 60 (of 62) miniature maps. Brazil damaged; some shaving & browning. S July 9 (1422) £1,100 [Franks]

More, Cresacre, 1572-1649

— The Life and Death of Sir Thomas Moore. [Douai: B. Bellore, 1631?]. 1st Ed. 4to, 18th-cent calf; covers detached. Tp detached & soiled. STC 18066. Ck Nov 29 (266) £220

More, Hannah, 1745-1833

— Hints Towards Forming the Character of a Young Princess. L, 1819. 2 vols. 8vo, contemp calf; rubbed. Inscr to Master Thornhill, 20 Mar 1821. Milne copy. Ck June 12 (152) £120

— Strictures on the Modern System of Female Education.... L, 1799. 2d Ed. 2 vols. 8vo, contemp half calf; rubbed. DW Mar 4 (238) £55

— Works. Phila., 1818. 8 vols. 8vo, lea gilt; Vol I front joint weak; spines chipped. sp Apr 16 (488) $200

More, Henry, 1586-1661

— An Explanation of the Grand Mystery of Godliness. L, 1660. Folio, contemp calf; rebacked. bba June 25 (80) £150 [Howes]

More, Henry, 1614-87

— A Collection of Several Philosophical Writings. L: J. Flesher, 1662. 2d Ed. Folio, contemp calf; spine ends chipped. General title soiled & spotted. sg Mar 12 (189) $250

More, Thomas

— The Life of Sir Thomas More...by his Great Grandson. L, 1726. 8vo, contemp calf; hinges weak. With port. bba Oct 24 (65) £70 [R. Clark]

More, Sir Thomas, 1478-1535

See also: Ashendene Press; Limited Editions Club

— De optimo reip. statu deque nova insula Utopia libellus vere aureus.... Cologne, 1555. 3 parts in 1 vol. 4to, 18th-cent calf; joints cracked. Tp ink-stained at foot from library number stamped on verso; some browning. Ck Nov 29 (254) £55

— A Dialogue of Cumfort against Tribulation.... Antwerp: John Fowler, 1573. 2d Ed. 8vo, 19th-cent calf, armorial bdg. Tp repaired at inner margin; A3 torn with loss of marginalia; G7 torn with slight loss & restored; H7 holed with loss. STC 18083. Ck Nov 29 (251) £260

— A Dyaloge of Syr Thomas More Knyghte... wheryn be Treated...the Veneracyon & Worshyp of Ymagys.... L: John Rastell, June 1529. 1st Ed. Folio, old vellum; soiled, spine cracked. Lacking errata leaf & final blank; some restoration & repairs; minor worming, occasionally affecting text; repairs to C1, H5, N4, R2, R5, S1, T6, U1 & small hole in H2 affecting text. STC 18084. S Dec 12 (5) £2,500 [Rota]

— Epigrammata. Basel: Froben, Dec 1520. 4to, contemp blind-stamped calf; extremities worn, upper cover detached. Roman type. Tp soiled & stained with blindstamp & accession number on verso; d2 stamped; Sig. C waterstained at upper margin. Ck Nov 29 (252) £850

Anr copy. Contemp vellum. 2 leaves misbound in inverted order. George Milne copy. CNY Dec 5 (281) $1,700

Anr Ed. L, 1638. 8vo, 19th-cent calf; covers detached. With engraved title. Upper margins shaved affecting running titles; some lower margins cropped. STC 18086. Ck Nov 29 (253) £50

Anr copy. Later sheep; worn. Margins stained throughout, affecting text in some cases; some leaves soiled. STC 18086. pn Dec 12 (13) £80 [Rix]

— Lucubrationes. Basel, 1563. 8vo, contemp vellum with yapp edges. With full-page woodcut plan on d3. Tp soiled & stained; some phrases or lines crossed through in green ink. Ck Nov 29 (255) £1,600

— Utopia. L, 1624. ("Sir Thomas Moore's Utopia....") 4th Ed in English. Trans by Ralph Robinson. 4to, 19th-cent half calf; rubbed. Tp soiled with section excised at upper margin; R3 & S1 soiled. STC 18097. Ck Nov 29 (256) £320

Anr Ed. Amst., 1629. 16mo, 19th-cent mor gilt. Ck Nov 29 (257) £200

Anr Ed. L, 1903. One of 210. Folio, half cloth. pnE Mar 11 (188) £60

— Works. L, 1557. 1st Ed. Folio, modern mor. Black letter; double-column; with the inserted leaf between CC5 & CC6. Lacking final blank & that after the table; Ms notes at margins in various hands; some worming affecting text at beginning & end; 1 wormhole affecting most leaves. STC 18076. S July 21 (6) £2,300 [Franklin]

Anr copy. 19th-cent mor gilt by Riviere. First & last leaves repaired. STC 18076. W July 8 (33) £880

Morea...

— La Morea combattuata dall'armi venete.... Venice, 1686. 8vo, old vellum. Some browning. S July 1 (673) £500 [Maggs]

Moreau, Brigitte. See: Renouard & Moreau

Moreau-Gobard, Jean Claude. See: Lion-Goldschmidt & Moreau-Gobard

Moreri, Louis, 1643-80

— Le Grand Dictionaire Historique.... Lyons, 1743-49. 16 vols. Folio, contemp vellum. SI June 10 (668) LIt500,000

Moresby, John, 1830-1922

— New Guinea and Polynesia. L, 1876. 8vo, modern cloth with panel from orig cloth set to upper bd. kh Nov 11 (585) A$300

Moret, Philippe —&
Chapuy, Nicolas Marie Joseph, 1790-1858

— Moyen-age pittoresque, monumens d'architecture, meubles et decors.... Paris, 1837-38. Folio, later cloth. With 180 plates. Library markings; some foxing. F Dec 18 (686) $675

Morey, Charles Rufus. See: Jones & Morey

Morga, Antonio de

— Sucesos de las islas Philipinas. Mexico: Cornelio Adriano Cesar for Geronimo Balli, 1609. 4to, mor gilt by V. Arias. With both an engraved title & a ptd title. Marginal wormholes at beginning & end repaired with only minimal loss in A1. From the library of the Spanish Discalced Hermits of St. Augustine. C June 25 (3) £36,000 [Quaritch/Hordern]

Morgagni, Giovanni Battista, 1682-1771

— De sedibus, et causis morborum.... Venice, 1761. 1st Ed. 2 vols. Folio, contemp half vellum; rubbed. With port. Occasional spotting. C June 24 (182) £1,500 [Thomas Scheler]

2d Ed. Padua, 1765. 2 vols. Folio, contemp bds. SI Dec 5 (489) LIt1,700,000

Anr Ed. Yverdun, 1779. ("Dissectiones et animadversiones....") 3 vols. 4to, contemp sheep; joints & spine ends restored. sg May 14 (114) $325

— The Seats and Causes of Diseases.... L, 1769. 1st Ed in English. 3 vols. 4to, modern half mor. Titles dusty, with institutional stamps; lower half of last leaf in Vol II torn away with text loss on recto. sg May 14 (113) $2,400

Morgan, Abel, 1673-1722. See: Franklin Printing, Benjamin

Morgan, Barbara
— Martha Graham. NY, 1941. 4to, cloth. sg Oct 17 (40) $50

Morgan, Dale Lowell
— Overland in 1846: The California-Oregon Trail. Georgetown CA, 1963. One of 1,000. Ed by Morgan. 2 vols. Half cloth, in d/js. NH May 30 (406) $120
— The West of William H. Ashley. Denver, 1964. 1st Trade Ed. Ed by Morgan. cb Nov 14 (7) $90
One of 250. Cloth. NH May 30 (231) $100

Morgan, Dale Lowell —& Wheat, Carl I.
— Jedediah Smith and His Maps of the American West. San Francisco, 1954. One of 530. With 7 folding maps, 3 in pocket. cb Sept 12 (126) $500
Anr copy. Orig cloth; soiled & stained, inner hinges cracked. Inscr by both & with accompanying broadside Apologia sgd by both. wa Nov 21 (130) $230

Morgan, Emanuel. See: Knish & Morgan

Morgan, John Hill —& Fielding, Mantle
— The Life Portraits of Washington and their Replicas. Phila., [1931]. One of 1,000. 4to, cloth, in d/j. sg Dec 5 (267) $375

Morgan, Joseph, Miscellaneous Writer
— A Complete History of Algiers.... L, 1728-29. 1st Ed. 2 vols. 4to, contemp calf; joints split, rubbed. bba June 25 (241) £240 [Bonham]

Morgan, W. T. & C. S.
— A Bibliography of British History (1700-1715). Bloomington, 1934-42. 5 vols. 4to, cloth; worn. sg May 21 (284) $100

Morghen, Filippo
— Raccolta delle cose piu notabili vedute da Cavaliere Wild Scull.... [Naples, c.1766]. Oblong folio, half mor by Riviere. With engraved title & 9 plates. Some spotting & soiling; dampstain in upper outer corner. C Dec 16 (65) £15,000 [Jackson]

Morier, Sir James Justinian, 1780?-1849
— A Journey through Persia, Armenia and Asia Minor.... Phila. & Bost., 1816. 8vo, orig half sheep; worn, spine stained. With 5 plates. Some foxing; index dampstained. sg May 21 (74) $80

Morin de la Masserie, Jacques
— Les Armes & blasons des chevaliers de l'Ordre du Sainct Esprit.... Paris: Pierre Firens, [1619]. 4to, old vellum. With engraved title & 78 coats-of-arms, all hand-colored & heightened in gold or silver. Fore-margin of tp repaired; 1st 2 leaves frayed at fore-edge. S May 13 (783) £360 [Casa d'Arte]

Morin, Lazare
— Dialogue d'entre le Maheustre et le Manant.... [N.p.], 1594. 8vo, 19th-cent sheep gilt by Koehler, with arms of J. A. M. du Plessis; rubbed. sg Oct 24 (91) $500

Morison, Robert, 1620-83
— Plantarum historiae universalis Oxoniensis. Oxford, 1680-99. Vols II & III (all pbd). Folio, contemp calf; rebacked & recornered, shelf marks on spines. With port & 292 plates. Some browning; dampstain to lower edge of last 20 plates in Vol II; some rust-marks or very small holes; minor marginal tears, just touching plate image in 1 case; stamps on versos of titles, 1st pages of text & foot of last plate in each vol. pn Mar 19 (316) £1,350 [Toscani]

Morison, Samuel Eliot
See also: Limited Editions Club
— History of United States Naval Operations in World War II. Bost., 1960-62. 15 vols. In d/js. F June 25 (27) $110
— The Maritime History of Massachusetts. Bost. & NY, 1921. Orig cloth; rubbed. Some pencil markings in margin; a few leaves roughly opened. Inscr to Anya Seton, 1962. bbc Apr 27 (547) $60

Morison, Stanley
See also: Grolier Club
— Four Centuries of Fine Printing. NY, 1949. In d/j. cb Oct 17 (652) $55
— Modern Fine Printing. L, 1925. One of 650 with English text. Folio, cloth; rubbed. bbc Apr 27 (160) $185
— The Typographic Book, 1450-1935. Chicago, [1963]. 1st American Ed. 4to, In d/j. pba July 23 (144) $90
Anr Ed. L, 1963. 4to, orig cloth, in d/j. cb Oct 17 (657) $130
Anr Ed. Chicago, [1964]. 4to, orig cloth, in d/j. bbc Apr 27 (159) $65
— Typographic Design in Relation to Photographic Composition. San Francisco: Book Club of California, 1959. 1st Ed, One of 400. Orig half vellum. cb Oct 17 (656) $55; O Sept 24 (172) $70

Morison, Stanley —& Carter, Harry
— John Fell.... Oxford, 1967. One of 1,000. Folio, orig cloth, in d/j. b Mar 11 (166) £75

Morley, C. D. See: Morley, Christopher

Morley, Christopher

— Blythe Mountain Vermont. Brattleboro VT, [1931]. 4to, half cloth; stain on front cover. Inscr to his daughter. sg June 11 (244) $700

— The Bookseller's Blue Book. NY, 1914. Inscr to Alfred P. Lee, 1937. sg June 11 (235) $2,600

— The Eighth Sin. Oxford, 1912. One of 250. Orig wraps; damaged by smoke, scorched. Last leaf def in margin. With ALs, sgd with initials, 20 Nov 1910. Ink correction on p.40. bbc Sept 23 (462) $300

— Friends, Romans.... Minneapolis: Ampersand Club, 1940. In chipped d/j. Inscr. sg June 11 (249) $130

— The Haunted Bookshop. Garden City, 1919. 1st Ed. Inscr to George Matthew Adams. sg June 11 (239) $475

— Hide and Seek. NY, 1920. In chipped d/j. Inscr. sg June 11 (240) $300

— I Know a Secret. NY, 1927. In d/j. Inscr to Vernon Hanson with an orig sketch. sg June 11 (242) $225

— Letters of Askance. Phila., [1939]. In d/j. Inscr. sg June 11 (248) $120

— Mandarin in Manhattan. NY, 1933. In worn d/j. Inscr to W. A. Kittredge, 1937. sg June 11 (246) $100

— Mince Pie. NY, [1919]. In torn d/j. Inscr to Thomas L. Masson, 1919. sg June 11 (238) $325

— Notes on Bermuda. NY, 1931. Inscr. sg June 11 (245) $375

— Parnassus on Wheels. Garden City, 1917. 1st Ed, 1st State. K Mar 22 (275) $80

— The Powder of Sympathy. NY, 1923. In chipped d/j. Inscr to Harold Earl, 1923. sg June 11 (241) $70

— Shandygaff. NY, 1918. In d/j. Inscr, 1951. sg June 11 (237) $300

— The Trojan Horse. Phila., 1937. In d/j. Inscr to Vincent Starrett & sgd by Starrett. sg June 11 (247) $225

— Where the Blue Begins. L & NY, [1925]. Illus by Arthur Rackham. With 4 colored plates. bba Jan 16 (394) £120 [Richardson]

Anr copy. Cloth. br May 29 (9) $60

One of 175. Half cloth. sg Jan 30 (152) $350

**Morley, Christopher —&
Daly, T. A.**

— The House of Dooner, the Last of Friendly Inns. Phila., 1928. One of 1,000. Sgd by both. sg June 11 (243) $110

Morley, John, Viscount Morley, 1838-1923

— The Life of Richard Cobden. L, 1881. 2 vols. 8vo, orig cloth; labels chipped. Inscr to S. L. Clemens by Jane Cobden Unwin. P June 17 (161) $2,500

Morley, Thomas, 1557-1604?

— A Plaine and Easie Introduction to Practicall Musicke.... L, 1608. Folio, 18th-cent lea gilt; rebacked, rubbed. Minor marginal tears & wormholes; tp, F2 & F3 trimmed, affecting illust on last 2. STC 18134. pn Oct 24 (417) £2,300 [Maggs]

Anr Ed. L, 1771. ("A Plain and Easy Introduction to Practical Music.") 4to, later half calf gilt. Some foxing. pn Oct 24 (418) £120 [Tosi]

Mormons

— The Book of Doctrine & Covenants. Liverpool, 1849. 12mo, modern cloth. Foxed. sg June 18 (389) $275

— The Times and Seasons. Nauvoo, 1844-46. Vols 5-6. 2 vols. 8vo, Vol 5 disbound, Vol 6 in half calf. sg June 18 (410) $500

— Udgorn Seion, neu seren y saint. Abertawy, 1856-57. Vols 9-10. 2 vols in 1. 8vo, contemp mor; front cover loose. sg June 18 (411) $350

Mornay, ——

— A Picture of St. Petersburgh, represented in a Collection of Twenty Interesting Views of the City.... L, [1815; plates watermarked 1820; some guards watermarked 1829]. Folio, contemp half mor gilt; spine worn & soiled. With engraved title & 20 hand-colored plates. CNY Jan 25 (48) $3,500

Moroni, Gaetano, 1802-83

— Dizionario de erudizione storico-ecclesiastica. Venice, 1840-61. 103 vols in 56. 8vo, half vellum. Library markings. O May 26 (133) $400

Morrell, Benjamin, 1795-1839

— A Narrative of Four Voyages.... NY, 1832. 8vo, old bds. Foxed. O Jan 14 (132) $375

Morris, Beverley Robinson

— British Game Birds and Wildfowl. L, 1855. 4to, disbound. With 60 hand-colored plates. Some marginal staining. b June 22 (367) £840

Anr copy. Later half mor; rubbed. With 58 (of 60) hand-colored plates. bba Sept 5 (153) £700 [Elliott]

Anr copy. Modern half mor, section of orig cloth from upper cover mtd on front pastedown. With 60 hand-colored plates. C Oct 30 (218) £1,200 [Galleria Etching]

Anr copy. Later half cloth; cancelled library slips on front endpapers. Stamp on tp verso; some soiling. C Oct 30 (219) £900

[Bifolco]

Anr copy. Contemp half mor gilt. C Oct 30 (245) £1,200 [Kresto]

Anr copy. Contemp half calf; extremities scuffed. With 60 hand-finished color plates. C May 20 (205) £1,800 [Orti]

Anr copy. Orig cloth; joints rubbed. With 60 hand-colored plates. Ck Sept 6 (35) £1,100

Anr copy. Contemp half mor; def, worn, joints crudely repaired with tape. pn Sept 12 (301) £1,100

Anr copy. Contemp half mor gilt; worn. S June 25 (48) £1,300 [Bifolco]

Anr Ed. L, [1889]. 4to, orig cloth. With 60 hand-colored plates. bba Jan 30 (99) £1,200 [Thorp]

Anr Ed. L, 1891. 4to, orig cloth; extremities rubbed. With 60 hand-colored plates. Ck Dec 11 (240) £1,900

Anr copy. Cloth. Some captions cropped; some soiling; library markings, not affecting plates. S June 25 (49) £900 [Bifolco]

Anr Ed. L, 1895. 2 vols. 8vo, orig cloth. With 60 hand-colored plates. LH Dec 11 (204) $750

Morris, Drake

— The Travels of Mr. Drake Morris, Merchant in London.... L, 1755. 12mo, contemp calf; rebacked, worn, rear inner hinge broken. DuPont copy. CNY Oct 8 (207) $800

Morris, Francis Orpen, 1810-93

— Butterflies. L, 1853. ("A History of British Butterflies.") 8vo, mor gilt. With 71 hand-colored plates. Plate 57 frayed & laid down; Plate 56 strengthened at edge. pn June 11 (236) £180

Anr Ed. L, 1890. 8vo, orig cloth; extremities rubbed. With 72 hand-colored plates. bba Aug 13 (372) £75 [Clarke]

6th Ed. L, 1891. 8vo, orig cloth; head of spine torn. With 74 plates, 72 hand-colored. bba Oct 10 (212) £65 [Dover]

— A History of British Birds. L, 1851-57. 1st Ed. 6 vols. 8vo, recent half mor. With 358 colored plates. C Oct 30 (246) £400 [Gerits]

Anr copy. Half calf gilt by Arthur & Colley. Tp of Vol I crudely repaired & loose; some spotting. Inscr "from the author". pn Sept 12 (301A) £320 [Morrison]

Anr copy. Mor gilt; worn. Some browning to last few leaves in Vol VI. pn June 11 (235) £520 [Sotheran]

Anr copy. Orig cloth; rubbed. With 354 (of 358) hand-finished plates. Some foxing. pn June 11 (257) £290 [Russell]

Mixed Ed. L, 1851-64. 6 vols. 8vo, contemp half mor gilt; rubbed. With 357 colored plates. pn Mar 19 (235) £340 [Map House]

"2d" Ed. L, 1870. 6 vols. 8vo, orig cloth. With 365 hand-colored plates. Tear to outer blank margin of 2 leaves; 3 leaves almost detached at beginning of Vol V. C Oct 30 (220) £450 [Raimi]

Anr copy. 6 vols. Cloth; rubbed & soiled. DW Dec 11 (152) £350

Anr copy. Cloth; rubbed & soiled; inner hinges of Vol II broken. DW Mar 4 (118) £380

Anr copy. 5 (of 6) vols only; lacking Vol I. Cloth; worn. O Apr 28 (39) $375

Anr copy. 6 vols. 8vo, contemp calf gilt; Vol I rebacked with old spine laid down, Vol IV with lower cover detached. With 365 hand-colored plates. S July 1 (924) £350 [Bailey]

Anr copy. Half mor gilt; several vols def. With 328 (of 354) plates. About 12 plates def. sg Feb 13 (154) $1,100

Anr copy. Orig cloth. Some spotting. SI Dec 5 (950) LIt950,000

Anr Ed. L, 1880. 8 vols. 8vo, orig cloth. With 358 hand-colored plates. DW Oct 2 (157) £260

Anr Ed. L, [1888]. 8 vols. 8vo, orig cloth; rubbed. Some plates loose in 5 vols. bba Aug 13 (371) £240 [Books & Prints]

Anr copy. Orig cloth; some hinges loose. With 358 hand-colored plates. Some foxing. pn June 11 (258) £300

"3d" Ed. L, 1891. 6 vols. 8vo, orig cloth. With 394 hand-colored plates. Ck May 15 (39) £400

"4th" Ed. L, 1895-97. 6 vols. 8vo, contemp half mor gilt; hinges rubbed. With 394 hand-colored plates. DW Oct 2 (158) £330

Anr copy. Orig cloth; rubbed. With 314 (of 394) hand-colored plates. DW Jan 29 (128) £155

Anr copy. With 394 hand-colored plates. S Feb 26 (933) £550 [Pampaloni]

"5th" Ed. L, 1903. 6 vols. Orig cloth. With 400 hand-colored plates. Ck May 15 (40) £350

— A Natural History of British Moths. L, 1871. 4 vols. 8vo, orig cloth. With 132 colored plates. bba Sept 5 (85) £140 [Freddie]; pnE Dec 4 (33) £60

5th Ed. L, 1896. ("A History of British Moths.") 4 vols. 8vo, orig cloth; rubbed & shaken. With 132 hand-colored plates. bba Aug 13 (373) £75 [Ginnan]

— Nests & Eggs. L, 1864. ("A Natural History of the Nests and Eggs of British

Birds.") 3 vols. 8vo, orig cloth. With 225 colored plates. pnE Oct 1 (281) £80

Anr Ed. L, 1866-67. 3 vols. 8vo, orig cloth; some joints split, worn. With 225 plates, 72 in color, the remainder tinted. K Sept 29 (276) £180

"2d" Ed. L, 1875. 3 vols. 8vo, orig cloth; worn. O Apr 28 (40) $375

"4th" Ed. L, 1896. 3 vols. 4to, cloth. With 248 colored plates. cb Feb 12 (94) $100

— A Series of Picturesque Views of Seats of the Noblemen and Gentlemen of Great Britain and Ireland. L, [c.1880]. 7 vols, including vol of facsimile autographs. 4to, orig cloth; rubbed. bba Sept 19 (218) £110 [Bowers]

Anr copy. 6 vols. 4to, bba Dec 19 (91) £190 [Fetzer]

Anr copy. Cloth; joints weak. bba Jan 30 (400) £150 [Finbar McDonnell]

Anr copy. Vols I-IV only. Orig mor gilt; spines rubbed & chipped, Vol I with section lacking at foot. With vignette titles & 156 plates, colored from woodblocks. Ck Sept 6 (136) £55

Anr copy. 6 vols. 4to, cloth. kh Nov 11 (174) A$380

Anr copy. 6 vols plus vol of facsimile autographs. 4to, contemp mor gilt; Vol VI cracked between frontis & additional title. With 240 colored plates, including titles. L Nov 14 (428) £220

Anr copy. 6 vols. 4to, mor gilt. LH Dec 11 (205) $900

Anr copy. Orig cloth; rubbed, shelf mark on spines. With 6 colored lithos frontises, 6 additional pictorial titles & 228 chromo-litho plates. Some spotting. pn Mar 19 (398) £130 [Bifolco]

Morris, Henry
See also: Taylor & Morris

— Bird & Bull Pepper Pot.... [North Hills, Pa.]: Bird & Bull Press, 1977. One of 250. Half mor by Gray Parrot. cb Sept 19 (9) $120

— Japonica: The Study and Appreciation of...Japanese Paper. North Hills PA: Bird & Bull Press, 1981. One of 250. Half mor. With 44 paper specimens. NH Aug 23 (54) $225

— A Visit to Hayle Mill.... North Hills PA, 1970. One of 210. Orig half mor. pba July 23 (31) $150

Morris, Richard, F.L.S.

— Essays on Landscape Gardening.... L, 1825. 1st Ed. 4to, orig half cloth; rebacked with orig spine laid down, extremities worn. With 6 plates, 2 with overslips. CNY Jan 25 (49) $2,000

Anr copy. Orig bds; rebacked, bd edges & corners worn. Marginal tear to B4. CNY Jan 25 (50) $1,100

Morris, William, 1834-96
See also: Kelmscott Press

— An Address Delivered by William Morris at the Distribution of Prizes to Students of the Birmingham Municipal School of Art on Feb. 21. 1894. L, 1898. 8vo, orig half cloth; worn. sg Apr 2 (193) $50

Anr Ed. L: Chiswick Press, 1898. 8vo, orig half cloth. bba July 9 (336) £50 [Goddard]

— Architecture and History, and Westminster Abbey. L, 1900. 8vo, orig half cloth, unopened. cb Oct 17 (658) $70

— The Hollow Land: A Romance.... [Hingham, Mass: Village Press, 1905]. One of 200. sp Apr 16 (457) $85

— Love is Enough. L, 1873 [1872]. 8vo, mor gilt extra by Sangorski & Sutcliffe with mor onlays & inset with 35 stones & with heart & leaf design. CNY Dec 5 (437) $19,000

[-] [Sale Catalogue] Catalogue of a Portion of the Valuable Collection of Manuscripts.... L: Sotheby, Wilkinson & Hodge, 1898. 8vo, half cloth, orig wraps bound in. Priced in ink. sg May 21 (285) $150

— Some Hints on Pattern Designing. L: Chiswick Press, 1899. 8vo, orig half cloth, unopened. cb Oct 17 (660) $50

— A Tale of the House of the Wolfings.... L, 1889. 8vo, orig cloth. Inscr to A. C. Swinburne, 21 Dec 1888. Ck Oct 18 (210) £1,700

Morris, Wright

— The Inhabitants. NY, 1946. 4to, cloth, in worn. sg Apr 13 (68) $110

Morrison, Arthur, 1863-1945

— The Painters of Japan. NY, 1911. 2 vols. Folio, cloth. cb Feb 12 (95) $190

Morrison, John H.

— History of American Steam Navigation. NY, 1903. Inscr. sg June 18 (416) $120

Morrison, John Robert

— Proceedings relative to the formation of a Society for the Diffusion of Useful Knowledge in China. Canton, 1835. 8vo, 19th-cent cloth, preserving orig wraps. Ptd on pith paper. S July 9 (1513) £480 [Quaritch]

Morrison, Robert

— A Grammar of the Chinese Language. Serampore, 1815. 4to, modern cloth. Some browning. S May 14 (1299) £400 [Short]

Morritt, John Bacon Sawrey

— A Vindication of Homer.... York, 1798. Bound with: Additional Remarks on the Topography of Troy. L, 1800. 4to, contemp calf; rubbed, rebacked, new endpapers. With folding map & 5 folding plates. Tear to map. S July 1 (661) £200 [Hantzis]

Morse, Albert Reynolds

— The Works of M. P. Shiel. Los Angeles, 1948. One of 1,000. In d/j. Ls laid in. cb Oct 17 (661) $55

Morse, Edward S., 1838-1925. See: Hobson & Morse

Morse, Jedidiah, 1761-1826

— The American Gazetteer.... Bost., 1797. 1st Ed. 8vo, contemp sheep; worn. sg June 18 (417) $300

— Annals of the American Revolution.... Hartford, 1824. 1st Ed. 8vo, contemp calf; rubbed. Some foxing. O Jan 14 (133) $110

Morse, Willard S. —& Brinckle, Gertrude

— Howard Pyle: A Record of his Illustrations and Writings. Wilmington DE, 1921. One of 500. cb Oct 17 (663) $100

Mortier, Pieter

See also: Sanson d'Abbeville & Mortier

— Atlas nouveau.... Amst., [c.1694-1711]. 2 vols. Folio, contemp calf gilt; rubbed. With 2 engraved titles (hand-colored & heightened with gum-arabic) & 223 mapsheets & 23 double-page tables. Most maps hand-colored in outline. Stamps on ptd titles; some creases; browning. S Nov 21 (129) £15,000 [Haas]

— Les Delices de la France. Amst., 1699. 2 vols. 12mo, contemp mor gilt; damaged by fire. With 49 double-page or folding city maps of views. Dampstaining & browning throughout. Sold w.a.f. sg Feb 13 (133) $225

— Les Forces d'Europe. Amst., [1702]. 14 parts in 1 vol, including supplement. Folio, contemp calf gilt. With 5 engraved titles & 303 plates. Stamp on Part 1 title; a few soft creases. S Nov 21 (132) £2,500 [Baskes]

Mortimer, G. W.

— A Manual of Pyrotechny. L, [after 1824?]. 1st Ed, Remainder Issue, with cancel title. 8vo, orig cloth. With 2 folding plates. sg Nov 14 (300) $450

Anr Ed. L: J. S. Hodson, [1856]. 12mo, later bds; rear joint cracked. sg Nov 14 (301) $100

— The Pyrotechnist's Companion.... Phila., 1852. 12mo, orig cloth. Some foxing. sg Nov 14 (302) $225

Mortimer, George

— Observations and Remarks made during a Voyage to the Islands of Teneriffe, Amsterdam, Maria's Islands near Van Diemen's Land.... Dublin, 1791. 1st Dublin Ed. 4to, contemp calf; front cover loosening, ends of spine & corners worn. CNY Oct 8 (179) $6,000

Mortimer, Roger. See: Seth-Smith & Mortimer

Mortimer, Ruth

— French 16th Century Books. Cambr. MA, 1964. 2 vols. 4to, cloth. DW Apr 8 (364) £125; O Sept 24 (273) $200; sg Oct 31 (272) $225

— Italian 16th Century Books. Cambr., 1974. 2 vols. 4to, cloth. O Sept 24 (174) $190; sg Oct 31 (273) $225

Mortimer, W. Golden

— Peru. History of Coca "The Divine Plant" of the Incas. NY, 1901. sg May 14 (115) $130

Morton, John, Rector of Oxenden

— The Natural History of Northamptonshire. L, 1712. Folio, 19th-cent half mor; recased, rubbed. With folding map & 14 plates. W July 8 (231) £200

Morton, John Chalmers

— A Cyclopaedia of Agriculture.... Glasgow, 1855. 2 vols. 8vo, contemp half mor gilt; rubbed & worn. DW Oct 2 (159) £50

Morton, Nathaniel, 1613-85

— New-Englands Memoriall.... Cambr. MA, 1669. Bound following: L., S. A Letter from a Gentleman of the Lord Ambassador Howard's Retinue.... L, 1670. 4to, 18th-cent calf gilt; rubbed, upper joint cracked. Some lower outer portions with old dampstain; some leaves browned. CNY Oct 8 (180) $22,000

Morvan de Bellegarde, Jean Baptiste

— Allgemeine historische Einleitung, zu allen bissher ans Licht getretenen Reisen zu Wasser und Land.... Hamburg: heirs of Thomas von Wiering, 1708. 8vo, contemp sheep; spine rubbed & chipped at bottom. sg June 18 (418) $175

Moryson, Fynes, 1566-1630

— An Itinerary.... L, 1617. 1st Ed. Folio, calf; rebacked. First 2 leaves & last leaf restored in margin; 3A6 & 3T2 with minor repairs; lacking blanks at beginning & end; no pp.151-54 but apparently complete. Inscr as from the author. S June 30 (357) £600 [Gonul]

Anr copy. Contemp calf; spine ends & corners worn, front cover detached. Half-title adhered to initial blank; tp with stains & soil; lacking 2 blanks at end. STC

18205. sg Oct 24 (235) $550

Mosely, Martin E.

— The Dry-Fly Fisherman's Entomology. L, 1921. With 16 hand-colored plates of insects. Koopman copy. O Oct 29 (212) $160

Anr copy. Bound in at end is Mosely's 6-page The March Brown. A Correction. 1932. O Oct 29 (213) $160

Moses, Henry. See: Englefield Collection, Sir Henry Charles

Moskowitz, Ira

— Great Drawings of All Time. NY, 1962. 4 vols. 4to, cloth. sg Apr 2 (104) $110; wa Apr 9 (225) $70

Moskowitz, Saul

— Five Years of Historical Technology. Marblehead: Historical Technology Press, 1978-83-87. 30 parts in 3 vols. 4to, cloth preserving orig wraps. Ck June 18 (29) £240; Ck June 18 (30) £240; Ck June 18 (31) £200; Ck June 18 (32) £190; Ck June 18 (33) £200

Mosley, Seth Lister

— A History of British Birds.... Huddersfield, 1884-87-92. 3 vols, with Vol III in 15 orig parts. 8vo, contemp half calf gilt, Vol III in orig 15 ptd wraps. With 177 hand-colored plates. C Oct 30 (247) £2,600 [Grahame]

Moss, Hugh

— By Imperial Command. Hong Kong, [1976]. One of 1,000. 2 vols. Folio, orig cloth. cb Nov 21 (158) $90

Mother Goose. See: Smith, Jessie Wilcox

Motif...

— Motif: A Journal of the Visual Arts.... L, 1958-64. Ed by Ruari Mclean. Nos 1-11. Folio, orig bdgs. DW Oct 9 (602) £125

Motley, John Lothrop, 1814-77

— The Rise of the Dutch Republic. NY, 1863. 3 vols. 8vo, half calf; rubbed. cb Jan 16 (101) $110

Motograph...

— The Motograph Moving Picture Book. L, 1898. 4to, orig half cloth with cover design by Henri de Toulouse-Lautrec. With title & 22 plates, each of which appears to more or change when accompanying transparency placed on top & moved. Transparency cracked, front endpaper browned. S Apr 28 (78) £190 [Nekes]

Moton, Robert Russa

— What the Negro Thinks. Garden City, 1929. In d/j. cb Feb 27 (69) $60

Mott, Frank Luther

— A History of American Magazines, 1741-1905. Cambr. MA, 1957-68. 5 vols. Cloth, 4 vols in d/j. O Sept 24 (175) $190

Mottelay, Paul Fleury

— Bibliographical History of Electricity & Magnetism. L, 1922. bba June 25 (156) £120 [Baldwin]

Anr copy. Cloth; worn. O Sept 24 (176) $250

Mottley, John

— Joe Miller's Jests: or, the Wits Vade-mecum. L: J. Barker, [n.d.]. 8vo, mor gilt. Owner's stamp on tp. Rosebery copy. bba Aug 13 (106) £100 [Page]

Moule, Horace Frederick. See: Darlow & Moule

Moule, Thomas

See also: Westall & Moule

— Bibliotheca heraldica Magnae Britanniae. L, 1822. 4to, half mor; bds soiled & worn, new spine & endpapers. Tp & frontis foxed & browned. wa Sept 26 (76) $90

— The English Counties in the Nineteenth Century. L, 1836. 4to, 19th-cent half calf; worn, upper hinge loose, spine def. With 2 additional titles, 50 maps, 5 town plans, 1 view & 1 folding map. Some cropping; folding map torn. S July 9 (1400) £800 [Map House]

— The English Counties Delineated.... L, 1839. 2 vols in 1. 8vo, contemp half calf. With engraved frontis & title to Vol I only & 61 plates & maps. Some spotting. Sold w.a.f. bba Apr 30 (14) £850 [Ash]

— An Essay on the Roman Villas of the Augustan Age.... L, 1833. 8vo, cloth. bba Jan 16 (278) £55 [Graves-Johnston]

— Great Britain Illustrated. L, 1830. Illus by William Westall. 4to, contemp half calf; head of spine torn away, joints cracked. With engraved title & 118 (on 59) plates. b June 22 (286) £110

Anr copy. Later half mor; rubbed. Some foxing. bba July 23 (375) £180 [Books & Prints]

Anr copy. Contemp half mor; worn. Upper margins waterstained. DW Nov 20 (26) £200

Anr copy. Disbound. Some foxing & soiling. Sold w.a.f. O Aug 25 (136) $200

Anr copy. Later half calf; rubbed. With engraved title & 118 (on 59) plates. Some spotting & browning. pn Apr 23 (284) £200

— Winkles's Architectural and Picturesque Illustrations of the Cathedral Churches of England and Wales. L, 1836-42. 3 vols. 8vo, orig cloth; joints splitting. bba Jan 16 (341) £75 [Hark]

Anr copy. Later half mor. With 30 maps. Each map with crease & slight repairs on verso at ends of creases; foxed; cut close; tp loose. Sold w.a.f. sg Feb 13 (134) $450

Mouradja d'Ohsson, Ignace de

— Tableau general de l'empire Othoman. Paris, 1787-1820. 1st Ed. 2 (of 3) vols. Folio, calf gilt; joints weak. With 135 plates on 35 plates only. Some creases, tears & repairs; Plate 25 in Vol I cut close; Vol I has Ms trans into Turkish Arabic in 1st 140 pp; some discoloration. S June 30 (166) £3,200 [Sedgwick]

Mourlot, Fernand

See also: Buffet, Bernard; Chagall, Marc; Miro, Joan

— Souvenirs et portraits d'artistes. Paris, [1972]. One of 800 on velin d'Arches. Folio, loose as issued in wraps. sg Nov 7 (1477) $1,000

Moxon, James. See: Mandey & Moxon

Moxon, Joseph, 1627-1700

— A Brief Discourse of a Passage by the North-Pole to Japan.... L, 1674. 4to, orig vellum. Map shaved at top; stained. DuPont copy. CNY Oct 8 (182) $4,800

— Mechanick Exercises on the Whole Art of Printing. L, 1958. In d/j. cb Oct 17 (665) $55; sp Sept 22 (435) $60

— A Tutor to Astronomy and Geography. L: J. Moxon, 1659. 1st Ed. 4to, contemp calf; upper cover stained, spine restored, endpapers renewed. With engraved title in Latin. Upper corner of A4 torn with loss to a border rule; 2 other minor tears to corners; ink deletion of a line & part of anr on E2r & 2 words on I3v; minor stains. CNY Oct 8 (181) $1,000

3d Ed. L, 1674. 4to, old bds; worn. bba Apr 30 (1309) £75 [Raiklen]

Anr copy. Modern mor gilt. Sold w.a.f. Ck June 18 (34) £240

Mozart, Leopold, 1719-87

— Gruendliche Violinschule. Augsburg, 1770. 2d Ed. 4to, old calf; worn & chipped. Frontis, tp & 1st 3 leaves of text clumsily repaired in margins. wd Dec 12 (423) $250

Mucha, Alphonse, 1860-1939

[-] Alphonse Mucha et son Oeuvre. Paris, 1897. 8vo, orig wraps; fragile, corners chipped. With cover & 127 text illusts. Special No of La Plume. sg Feb 6 (201) $130

— Le Pater. Paris: H. Piazza, [1899]. One of 510. 4to, orig wraps; def. Lacking general title, 2 sectional titles, 1 text leaf & 1 collotype. sg Feb 13 (199) $800

— The Point of View. L, 1905. One of 250. 4to, half mor gilt; extremities rubbed, shaken. With mtd india-proof etching by Mucha. sg Apr 2 (194) $300

Mudford, William, 1782-1848

— A Critical Enquiry into the Writings of Dr. Samuel Johnson. L, 1803. 2d Ed. 8vo, contemp bds; broken. Library Company of Philadelphia duplicate. sg Mar 5 (197) $90

— An Historical Account of the Campaign in the Netherlands.... L, 1817. 4to, contemp cloth; rebacked. With hand-colored additonal title & 27 plates & 2 folding map, 1 aquatinted in green & black. Lacking Abbey's Plate 23; marginal spotting. C May 20 (92) £950 [Old Hall]

Mudge, William —& Dalby, Isaac

— An Account of the Operations carried on for accomplishing a Trigonometrical Survey of England and Wales.... L, 1799-1811. 3 vols. 4to, contemp mor. With engraved dedication, 2 folding tables & 50 maps & plates. A few neatlines cropped; text in Vol I discolored. S Nov 15 (916) £650 [Georges]

Mudie, Robert, 1777-1842

— Gilbert's Modern Atlas of the Earth. L, [1840?]. 4to, half mor gilt; contents loose in bdg. With 56 maps outlined in color. World map tape-marked. DW Oct 23 (51) £80

— Gleanings of Nature. L, 1838. 4to, orig cloth; rubbed. With 43 plain & 14 hand-colored plates. bba Oct 10 (213) £70 [Elliott]

— The Picture of Australia.... L, 1829. 1st Ed. 12mo, recased in orig bds with new backstrip. kh Nov 11 (567) A$100

Mueller, Gerhard Friedrich

— Voyages from Asia to America for Completing the Discoveries of the North West Coast of America.... L, 1761. 1st Ed in English. 4to, contemp calf gilt; upper joint with split at top, corners worn. With 2 folding hand-colored maps & 2 small maps. Some worming to extreme lower blank margins; small tear to each folding map. CNY Oct 8 (183) $3,600

Anr copy. Contemp calf; crudely rebacked. With 4 folding maps on 3 sheets. DW Nov 6 (56) £1,100

Anr copy. Contemp half calf; rubbed. With 3 folding hand-colored maps (2 colored in outline) & 2 small maps Minor marginal dampstaining. O Nov 26 (130) $3,300

Anr copy. Modern half calf. With 4 folding maps on 3 sheets. One map separated from book & laid down on bd; folding map separated into 3 pieces; separate map damaged along fold; prelims dampstained; browned. wd June 12 (416) $300

Anr Ed. L, 1764. 4to, modern half mor. With 4 maps, 2 hand-colored in outline & folding. C Oct 30 (56) £550 [Remington]

Mueller, Hans Alexander

— Woodcuts and Wood Engravings: How I Make Them. NY, 1939. one of 250. Folio, loose as issued, in cloth box. O Mar 31 (137) $60; sg Feb 6 (202) $60

Mueller, Johann Ulrich

— Neu-Ausgefertigter Kleiner Atlas. Ulm: George Wilhelm Kuehnen, 1702. 2 parts in 1 vol. 8vo, contemp vellum; soiled. With double-page engraved title & 163 miniature maps. Double-page map split without loss. S June 25 (295) £3,000 [Map House]

Muenster, Sebastian, 1489-1552

— A Briefe Collection and Compendious Extract of Straunge and Memorable Thinges.... L: Thomas Marshe, 1574. 8vo, contemp vellum wraps from an early Ms; rubbed & soiled, spine torn. Upper corners of 1st & last 3 leaves torn with loss to foliation of 3 leaves; marginal tear to F8 entering headline; small hole in H3 affecting 1 letter; small stain on C2v & C3r obscuring a few letters of 5 words. STC 18243. DuPont copy. CNY Oct 8 (184) $6,000

— Cosmographey: das ist beschreibung aller Laender.... Basel: Sebastian Henricpetri, 1598. Folio, contemp wooden bds; worn. Defs to 1st 9 leaves; some browning & spotting. HH May 12 (745) DM7,500

Anr Ed. Basel: Henricpetri, 1614. Folio, contemp blindstamped pigskin; lower forecorner of upper cover damaged. With 26 double-page woodcut maps after Ortelius & 67 other double-page maps & plans, including the folding panoramas of Heidelberg & Vienna. Lower forecorner of tp restored. S June 25 (286) £6,000 [Marshall]

— Dictionarium Chaldaicum non tam ad Chaldaicos interpretes.... Basel: Froben, 1527. 4to, contemp vellum; rear hinge split. With 2 folding woodcut plates. sg Dec 19 (183) $4,200

Muhammad, of Baghdad

— Libro del modo di dividere le superficie.... Pesaro: G. Concordia, 1570. Bound with: Danti Pellegrino. La Prospettiva di Euclid.... Florence: Giunta, 1573. 4to, old bds; rebacked in calf. Some browning; final leaf of 2d part of 2d work repaired. Ck Nov 29 (166) £1,150

Muhsin Fani

— The Dabistan; or, School of Manners. Paris, 1843. 3 vols. 8vo, orig cloth. sg May 7 (157) $400

Muir, John, 1838-1914

— The Cruise of the Corwin. Bost. & NY, 1917. One of 550 L.p. copies. 8vo, half cloth. sg Jan 9 (155) $175

— The Mountains of California. NY, 1894. 1st Ed. 8vo, cloth. Some foxing. sg June 18 (106) $150

1st Issue. Pictorial cloth. Small stain on tp; library stamps. sg Dec 5 (168) $175

— Picturesque California and the Region West of the Rocky Mountains, from Alaska to Mexico. NY & San Francisco: J. Dewing, [1887-88]. One of 750. 4 (of 10) parts. Folio, wraps. cb Nov 14 (131) $275

India-proof Ed. 10 vols. Folio, orig wraps & portfolios. Accompanied by the 14 etchings on silk in orig mats. sg June 18 (108) $600

Anr Ed. NY, [1888]. Vols I & II (of 3) only. Folio, half mor; extremities worn. sg June 18 (109) $500

— Stickeen. Bost. & NY, 1909. 1st Ed. Front cover stained. Sgd. cb Nov 14 (133) $120

Anr Ed. Bost., 1910. 8th Impression. Sgd. cb Nov 14 (132) $275

— Travels in Alaska. Bost. & NY, 1915. bbc Sept 23 (189) $75

Anr copy. Cloth. sg June 18 (420) $50

Muir, Percy H. See: Carter & Muir

Mullaly, John

— A Trip to Newfoundland; Its Scenery and Fisheries.... NY, 1855. 4to, cloth; worn, hinges cracked. sg Dec 5 (43) $200

Mullen, Stanley

— Kinsmen of the Dragon. Chicago: Shasta Publishers, [1951]. In d/j with edges worn & reinforced on verso. sg June 11 (253) $50

Muller, Alexandre

— Theorie sur l'escrime a cheval. Paris, 1816. 4to, later vellum. With 51 plates. Dampstaining along fore-edges. Sgd. sg Mar 26 (209) $175

Muller, Andreas

— Des verwirreten Europae Continuation.... Amst.: widow of J. von Sommer et al, 1680. Folio, contemp sheep gilt; rubbed, spine ends chipped. With 13 (of 19) double-page views & battle scenes & 16 ports. Small hole in 2Z6. sg May 21 (74A) $275

Muller, Frederik

— Catalogue of Books, Maps, Plates on America.... Amst., 1872-75. 5 parts in 1 vol. 8vo, modern cloth, orig wraps bound in. bba June 25 (16) £90 [Montero]

Mulsant, Martial Etienne —& Vereaux, J. B. E.

— Histoire naturelle des oiseaux-mouches ou colibris. Lyon, 1874-77. 4 vols, without the Supplement. 4to, contemp half mor; rubbed. With 119 hand-colored plates only. Some soiling; waterstain in upper margin of Vol I; partly erased library stamp on titles. C Oct 30 (288) £2,200 [Junk]

Multatuli, Pseud.

— Max Havelaar, of de koffij-veilingen der Nederlandsche Handel-Maatschappij. Amst., 1860. 2 vols. Half vellum, orig covers preserved. B Nov 1 (1046) HF1,100

Anr copy. 2 parts in 1 vol. Contemp half mor. B May 12 (871) HF1,000

Mumey, Nolie

— John Williams Gunnison.... Denver, 1955. One of 500. 4to, half cloth. sg June 18 (422) $80

— The Life of Jim Baker, 1818-1898.... Denver, 1931. One of 250. Half cloth. sg June 18 (423) $200

— March of the First Dragoons to the Rocky Mountains.... Denver, 1957. One of 350. 4to, half cloth. sg June 18 (424) $130

— Old Forts and Trading Posts of the West. Denver, 1956. One of 500. In d/j. Inscr to Peter Decker. sg June 18 (425) $150

— Rocky Mountain Dick. Denver, 1953. One of 500. sg June 18 (426) $80

— A Study of Rare Books.... Denver, 1930. One of 1,000. 4to, half cloth; bumped, ink spots on spine. K Sept 29 (279) $80; O Mar 31 (138) $70

— The Teton Mountains. Denver, 1947. One of 700. sg June 18 (427) $120

Munby, Alan Noel Latimer

— Phillipps Studies. Cambr., 1951-60. 1st Ed. 5 vols. In d/js. sg Oct 31 (274) $275; wa Apr 9 (11) $150

Munchausen, Baron. See: Raspe, Rudolph Erich

Munckerus, Thomas, d.1652

— Mythographi Latini. Amst., 1681. 2 vols. 8vo, 18th-cent mor. With engraved title, port & 43 vignettes. cb Feb 12 (96) $350

Mundy, Godfrey Charles

— Our Antipodes: or, Residence and Rambles in the Australian Colonies. L, 1852. 2d Ed. 3 vols. 8vo, orig cloth; rubbed & soiled; Vols I & III broken. With 15 plates. bba Oct 24 (311) £150 [Scott]

Munnings, Sir Alfred James, 1878-1959

— Pictures of Horses and English Life. L, 1927. One of 250. 4to, orig vellum gilt; soiled & bowed. Marginal dampstaining. pn Mar 19 (370) £400 [Dawson]

Anr copy. Orig vellum. With 28 mtd color plates. With ALs laid in. sg May 7 (158) $1,900

Anr copy. Orig vellum; bowed & soiled. Ck May 15 (41) £380

Munro, J. K.

— The Mary Ira. Being the Narrative Journal of a Yachting Expedition from Auckland to the South Sea Islands.... L, 1867. 8vo, orig cloth; worn & shaken, spine detached. With 5 lithos. Some stains & soiling. O Aug 25 (129) $80

Munro, Thomas. See: Guillaume & Munro

Munsell, J.

— A Chronology of Paper and Paper-making. Albany, 1864. 3d Ed. cb Oct 17 (672) $120

Mural...

— Mural Painting of the Mexican Revolution, 1921-1960. [Mexico, 1960]. Folio, cloth. sg Feb 6 (204) $120

Muratori, Lodovico, 1672-1750

— Annali d'Italia dal principio dell'era volgare sino all'anno MDCLXIX. Milan, 1753-56. 18 vols. 8vo, half calf. S July 1 (662) £500 [Spink]

Murchison, Sir Roderick Impey, 1792-1871

— Siluria, the History of the Oldest Known Rocks. L, 1854. 1st Ed. Illus by J. D. C. Sowerby. 8vo, orig cloth; spine soiled, tail repaired. Ink writing on tp. bba May 14 (443) £80 [Henly]

Murison, David D. See: Grant & Murison

Murphy, Bailey Scott

— English and Scottish Wrought Ironwork. L, 1904. Folio, cloth; rebacked retaining orig backstrip. With 80 plates. sg Sept 6 (160) $225

Murphy, Charles J. V.
— Parachute. NY, 1930. In d/j. cb Nov 7 (80) $55

Murphy, James Cavanah
— The Arabian Antiquities of Spain. L, 1815. Folio, half mor by J. Wright. Met Apr 28 (65) $3,300

Murray, Alexander Sutherland
— Twelve Hundred Miles on the River Murray. L, 1898. Oblong 4to, orig cloth. With 15 colored plates. pn Apr 23 (243) £130 [Baring]

Murray, Sir Charles Augustus
— Travels in North America. L, 1839. 1st Ed. 2 vols. 8vo, early half mor gilt; worn & scuffed. bbc Dec 9 (399) $325

Anr copy. Orig cloth; spines faded; rear hinge of Vol I split. cb Nov 14 (136) $160

1st American Ed. NY, 1839. 2 vols. 12mo, cloth. O Mar 31 (140) $120

Murray Collection, Charles Fairfax
— Catalogue of a Collection of Early French Books.... L, 1910. One of 100. 2 vols. Orig half cloth; soiled. sg Oct 31 (275) $2,600
— Catalogue of a Collection of Early German Books.... L, 1913. One of 100. Compiled by Hugh W. Davies. 2 vols. 4to, orig half cloth; Vol II spine holed. sg Oct 31 (276) $1,400

Anr Ed. L, 1962. One of 250. 2 vols. 4to, orig cloth, in d/js; worn. O Sept 24 (177) $150

Anr copy. Orig bds. SI Dec 5 (229) LIt380,000

Murray, Hugh, 1779-1846
— Historical Account of Discoveries and Travels in North America.... L, 1829. 2 vols. 8vo, modern calf. With folding map. Small tear at gutter. sg Dec 5 (169) $250

Murray, John
— Practical Remarks on Modern Paper. North Hills PA: Bird & Bull Press, 1981. One of 300. Half mor. NH Aug 23 (56) $100

Murray, Robert Dunbar
— A Summer at Port Phillip. L, 1843. 8vo, half calf; rubbed. Margin of frontis with stain; bound without the ads. kh Nov 11 (589) A$100

Musaeus
— Opusculum de Herone & Leandro. Venice: Aldus, [1517]. 8vo, 19th-cent half russia gilt. Tp & last leaf foxed. B Nov 1 (258) HF2,600

Anr copy. 18th-cent mor; rebacked. SI June 10 (677) LIt2,000,000

Musee...
— Musee Francais: Recueil des plus beaux tableaux, statues, et bas-reliefs qui existaient au Louvre.... Paris: Galignani, [1829-30]. 3 (of 4) vols. Folio, calf gilt; scuffed, extremities worn, tears in spines on 2 vols, most hinges cracked. With engraved titles, vignettes & 210 plates. sg Sept 6 (200) $3,600

Musee de Cluny—Paris
— Etoffes Anciennes.... Paris, [early 1900s]. Folio, loose as issued in half-cloth portfolio; worn. With 52 plates, some in color Library markings, including stamps on tp & plate rectos; marginal dampstaining. sg Sept 6 (199) $225

Museum...
— A Museum for Young Gentlemen and Ladies.... L, 1778. 9th Ed. 12mo, orig bds; rebacked. ESTC n035238. bba July 23 (268) £85 [Demetzy]

Museum of Modern Art
— Ludwig Mies van der Rohe. Drawings in the Collection of.... NY, 1969. Notes by Ludwig Glaeser. Oblong folio, bds; rubbed, front cover with surface imperfection. With 31 plates. Some stains on tp. sg Sept 6 (190) $130

Anr copy. Spiral-bound bds. sg Apr 2 (182) $800

Mussard, Pierre
— Historia deorum fatidicorum, vatum, sibyllarum.... Cologne: Pierre Chouet, 1675. 4to, old half vellum. Some foxing; small piece excised from blank margin of tp & restored. sg Mar 12 (226) $200

Musset, Alfred de, 1810-57
— La Nuit venetienne. Paris, [1913]. One of 500 on japon. Illus by U. Brunelleschi. 4to, orig wraps. sg Jan 30 (15) $120
— Works. NY, 1905. One of 58 on japon, with plates in 2 states. 10 vols. Orig mor extra. CNY June 9 (132) $900

Musset-Pathay, Victor Donatien de
— Bibliographie Agronomique; ou, dictionairre raisonne.... Paris, 1810. 1 vol interleaved & bound in 2. 8vo, new cloth. With extensive additions & notes in a contemp hand. sg Oct 31 (277) $800

Mustafa I, Sultan of the Turks
— La grande cruaute et tyrannie exercee par Mustapha.... Lyon: Francois Yurad, 1618. 8vo, modern vellum bds. S Feb 11 (513) £320 [Quaritch]

Mutio, Girolamo
- Le Combat de Mutio Justinopolitain.... Lyon, 1561. 4to, old vellum. sg Mar 26 (210) $175
- Il duello de Mutio Justinopolitano. Venice, 1554. 8vo, old vellum. sg Mar 26 (211) $175

  Anr Ed. Venice, 1564. 8vo, old sheep. sg Mar 26 (212) $175

Muybridge, Eadweard, 1830-1904
- Animal Locomotion. An Electro-Photographic Investigation of Consecutive Phases of Animal Movements. Phila., 1887. Group of 102 photogravures only, with ptd tp. sg Apr 13 (69) $28,000
- Animals in Motion. L, 1907. Oblong 4to, cloth; stained, frayed, some tears along joints & spine ends, hinges cracked; old dampstain along bottom margin edge of some leaves. bbc Feb 17 (242) $75
- The Human Figure in Motion. L, 1907. Oblong folio, orig cloth; soiled & rubbed. First few leaves stained at edges. pn Sept 12 (109) £70 [Walford]

Muzio, Girolamo, 1496-1576. See: Gamucci, Bernardo

Myer, Isaac
- Oldest Books in the World. L, 1900. One of 500. cb Oct 17 (672) $85

Myers, Capt. John
- The Life, Voyages and Travels.... L, 1817. 8vo, contemp half calf; spine ends repaired. Tear in blank area of tp mended. DuPont copy. CNY Oct 8 (185) $5,500

Mynors, Roger Aubrey Baskerville
- Durham Cathedral Manuscripts.... Oxford, 1939. One of 250. 4to, orig cloth. With frontis & 56 plates. S July 1 (1170) £380 [Dawson]

Myrick, David F.
- New Mexico's Railroads: An Historical Survey. Golden: Colorado Railroad Museum, 1970. In d/j. cb Feb 13 (236) $50
- Railroads of Nevada and Eastern California. Berkeley, 1962-63. 2 vols. In d/js. cb Feb 13 (237) $140

N

N., G. See: Nichol, George

Nabokov, Vladimir
- Lolita. Paris, 1955. 1st Ed. 2 vols. Wraps. Epstein copy. sg Apr 30 (345) $2,400

  1st Issue. Wraps; ends chipped, short tear on front cover of Vol II. sg June 11 (255) $500

Nadel, Arno
- Rot und gluehend is das Auge des Juden. Berlin: Verlag fuer Juedische Kunst und Kultur, 1920. Illus by Jakob Steinhardt. Folio, pictorial bds; worn. With 8 lithos. K Mar 22 (207) $50

Nadir, William. See: Douglas, William

Naef, Weston. See: Grolier Club

Nagler, Georg Kaspar, 1801-66
- Die Monogrammisten und diejenigen bekannten und unbekannten Kuenstler aller Schulen. Munich, 1858-79. 5 vols. 8vo, orig half cloth. S Feb 11 (150) £150 [Gilgemann]

Nalson, John, 1638?-86
- A True Copy of the Journal of the High Court of Justice for the Tryal of K. Charles I. L, 1684. Folio, deteriorating lea bdg. rs Oct 17 (85A) $200

  Anr copy. Old half sheep; worn, covers detched. sg Mar 12 (192) $250

  Anr copy. Calf; rebacked. W July 8 (65) £105

Nance, Ernest Morton
- The Pottery and Porcelain of Swansea and Nantgarw. L, 1942. 4to, orig cloth, in d/j. S July 1 (1156) £150 [Nelson]

Nance, Robert Morton
- Sailing Ship Models. L, 1924. 4to, orig cloth; extremities rubbed. DW May 13 (386) £50

Nannini, Remigio
- Orationi militari. Venice: Gabriel Giolito, 1560. 4to, old vellum; occasional soiling & staining. sg Mar 12 (193) $175

Nansen, Fridtjof, 1861-1930
- Farthest North. L, 1897. 2 vols. 8vo, orig cloth. With 16 colored plates. DW Nov 6 (77) £55

  Anr Ed. NY, 1897. 2 vols. 8vo, orig cloth. With 16 colored plates & with maps in pockets. NH May 30 (67) $130

  Anr Ed. NY, 1898. 2 vols in 20 orig parts. 8vo, orig pictorial wraps; frayed. Manney copy. P Oct 11 (235) $1,200

  Anr copy. 2 vols. 8vo, orig cloth; scuffed & worn, prelims loose; Vol I front hinge cracked. sg Oct 17 (18) $50

  Anr copy. Orig cloth; worn. sg Jan 9 (17) $90

  1st American Ed. 2 vols. 8vo, orig cloth. With 16 colored plates & 4 folding maps.. sg May 21 (75) $70
- The First Crossing of Greenland.... L, 1890. 2 vols. 8vo, orig cloth. DW Nov 6 (79) £125
- In Northern Mists. L, 1911. 2 vols. 4to,

cloth; spines faded & rubbed. DW Nov 6 (78) £60

Anr copy. Orig cloth; worn. sg May 21 (76) $120

Napier, Francis

— Notes of a Voyage from New South Wales to the North Coast of Australia. [Glasgow?, 1876]. 8vo, orig cloth. With 8 plates & 4 folding maps. S June 25 (257) £520 [Arnold]

Naples

— Real Museo Borbonico. Naples, 1825-43. Vols II-XIV (of 16). 4to, contemp half calf; upper bd of Vol XIV detached, rubbed. With frontises & 852 plates. Some spotting. pn Dec 12 (77) £100 [Bifolco]

Narbrough, Sir John, 1640-88 —& Others

— An Account of Several Late Voyages & Discoveries to the South and North.... L, 1694. 8vo, contemp calf; spine ends & 2d compartment restored, joints split, a few small gouges to covers & spine. With 2 folding maps, folding weather table & 19 plates, 7 folding Perforation to fol. E1 affecting 3 letters; small stain to K4v obscuring 2 letters; fold break to 1st folding map; folding weather table with outer border cropped with loss to a letter & numeral of the Latitude column & 1 small repaired tear; short tear at inner edge of folding plate Q; some foxing & dampstaining to margins. CNY Oct 8 (186) $2,400

Anr copy. 18th-cent calf; rebacked. Gutter of tp renewed; tear to upper left corner of 1st folding map; 2d folding map with fold breaks; 3 small marginal repairs & 1 short tear at inner edge; marginal tear to fol. F8 just entering text; some foxing & marginal dampstaining. CNY Oct 8 (187) $1,800

Anr copy. Contemp calf; rebacked. With 19 plates & 1 folding table. S June 25 (24) £1,700 [Arnold]

— An Account of Several Late Voyages & Discoveries.... L, 1711. 8vo, contemp calf; rebacked, covers & 1st gathering detached. Repaired tears to each map; a few plates creased. White Kennett's copy. CNY Oct 8 (188) $1,400

Anr copy. Contemp calf; joints repaired. With 3 folding maps & 19 plates. S June 25 (25) £900 [Renard]

Nardi, Jacopo

— Le Historie della citta di Firenze. Florence: Sermartelli, 1584. ("Le Storie della citta di Firenze.") 4to, 18th-cent half lea. Some foxing. SI Dec 5 (499) LIt450,000

Nardini, Famiano

— Roma Antica. Rome, 1704. 2d Ed. 4to, contemp vellum. Some foxing. SI June 10 (684) LIt850,000

Anr Ed. Rome, 1771. 2 parts in 1 vol. 4to, contemp vellum. Corner of title excised. sg Jan 9 (156) $100

Nares, Sir George Strong, 1831-1915

— Narrative of a Voyage to the Polar Sea.... L, 1878. 4th Ed. 2 vols. 8vo, orig cloth. sg Jan 9 (19) $650

Narodni a Universitni Knihovna, Prague

— TRULHAR, JOSEPH. - Catalogus codicum man scriptorum Latinorum qui in C. R. Bibliotheca Publica atque Universitatis Pragensis asservantur. Prague, 1905-6. 2 vols in 1. 8vo, new cloth. sg Oct 31 (247) $900

Narvaez, Luis Pacheco de

— Adicion a la filosofia de las armas. [N.p.], 1660. 8vo, modern bds. Browned. sg Mar 26 (213) $250

— Compendio de la filosofia y destreza de las armas de Geronimo de Carranca. Madrid, 1612. 8vo, early vellum. 17th-cent inked notations on tp verso & dedication leaf. sg Mar 26 (214) $350

— Modo facil y nuevo parra examinarse los maestros en la destreza de las armas. Madrid, 1659. 8vo, modern half calf. sg Mar 26 (215) $375

Nash, Frederick

— A Series of Views Interior and Exterior of the Collegiate Chapel of St. George at Windsor. L, 1805. Folio, contemp half mor; scuffed. With engraved title, 9 plates ptd in black, mostly proofs. Marginal soiling. C May 20 (281) £500 [Marlborough]

Nash, John, 1752-1835 —& Brayley, Edward Wedlake, 1773-1854

— Illustrations of her Majesty's Palace at Brighton. L, 1838. Folio, modern half mor & half mor portfolio. With 31 plates & portfolio containing engraved title & 31 hand-colored plates on 28 sheets. Plate 11 bound upside down. McCarty-Cooper copy. CNY Jan 25 (51) $15,000

Nash, Joseph, 1809-78

— The Mansions of England in the Olden Time. L, 1839-49. Series 1-4. Folio, orig half mor gilt; worn. With tinted litho titles & 100 plates. Scattered spotting. DW Apr 8 (1105) £380

Anr copy. Series 1-3 (of 4). Folio, half lea; worn & shaken. O Feb 25 (145) $350

Anr copy. Series 1-4 in 2 vols. Folio, modern calf. With litho titles, dedications to each part & 100 tinted litho plates. Some scuffing & short tears to margins. S Nov 15 (897) £480 [Yamanaka]

Anr Ed. L, 1869-72. 4 vols. Folio, orig cloth. With 104 tinted plates. DW May 13 (92) £170

Anr copy. Vols I-III. Orig cloth; spine ends frayed. With litho titles & 78 plates. Plates stamped on versos. sg Feb 6 (206) $225

— Views of the Interior and Exterior of Windsor Castle. L, 1848. Folio, orig half mor & velvet; worn & gutta-percha perished. With colored title & 25 colored plates. Plates finished by hand, cut round & mtd on thick card, no imprints & with some spotting mainly to borders. C Oct 30 (57) £1,900 [Shapero]

Nash, Treadway Russell

— Collections for the History of Worcestershire. L, 1781-82. 2 vols. Folio, 19th-cent half mor gilt; rubbed. With engraved titles, 1 (of 2) dedication leaves, folding map & 87 (of 89) plates. With additional port in Vol I. Some spotting & browning. pn May 14 (204) £600 [Burgess Browning]

2d Ed. L, 1799. 2 vols. Folio, later half mor gilt; rubbed. With frontis to Vol I, folding map & plates as listed. DW Dec 11 (118) £860

National Library of Medicine. See: Durling, Richard J.

National Maritime Museum

— Catalogue of the Library. L, 1968-76. Vols I-III (of 5) in 5 vols. In d/js. S Apr 28 (569) £200 [Tantonlos]

Natrus, Leendert van —& Others

— Groot volkomen moolenboek; of naauwkeurig Ontwerp, van allerhande tot nog toe bekende soorten van moolens. Amst., 1734-36. 2 vols. Folio, half vellum. With 54 plates. B Nov 1 (501) HF2,000

Natta d'Alifiano, Giacomo

— Riflessioni sopra il libro intitolato della scienza chiamata cavalleresca. Madrid, 1659. 8vo, old vellum. sg Mar 26 (215) $375

Natta, Marcus Antonius

— De Dei locutione oratio. Venice, 1558. 4to, old vellum; bowed. Ck Nov 29 (9) £420

Nattes, John Claude

— Bath, Illustrated by a Series of Views. L, 1806. Folio, mor gilt by Bayntun. With title & final text leaf with hand-colored aquatint vignettes & with 28 hand-colored plates. C May 20 (93) £3,200 [Traylen]

— Scotia Depicta, or the Antiquities, Castles, etc. of Scotland. L, 1804. Oblong 4to, contemp half mor; extremities rubbed. With engraved title & 48 plates. L.p. copy. Ck Dec 11 (220) £220

Natural...

— Natural History of Quadrupeds and Cetaceous Animals. Bungay, 1811. 2 vols. 8vo, contemp calf; rubbed. Some foxing. bba Sept 5 (88) £360 [C. Mason]

— The Natural History of Birds, from the Works of the Best Authors.... Bungay, 1815. 2 vols. 8vo, contemp calf; spine of Vol II torn at foot, rubbed. With 151 (of 152) hand-colored plates only. Ck Sept 6 (8) £350

Anr copy. Contemp calf; rubbed. With 152 hand-colored plates. Marginal worming at end of Vol II; 1 leaf in Vol I lacking small section; some spotting & browning. pn May 14 (168) £140

Nature-Printing

— [Feathers]. England, [not before 1807]. 4to, contemp half sheep; later flyleaves, interleaved with glassine throughout, worn, shaken. With 52 hand-colored nature-ptd plates. Schlosser copy. P June 17 (479) $6,000

— Impressions of Leaves. England, [c.1840]. Folio, orig cloth; spine worn at top. With 127 leaves with nature-ptd leaves arranged 1-8 per page. Schlosser copy. P June 17 (480) $600

— Naturselbstdruck: Album der k. k. Hof- und Staatsdruckerei in Wien. [Vienna, 1853]. Folio, loose in orig half mor folding case. With letterpress bastard titles & 59 (of 61) nature-ptd plates, many ptd in colors. Some foxing. Schlosser copy. P June 17 (481) $7,000

Naumann, Johann Andreas, 1747-1826

— Naturgeschichte der Voegel Mitteleuropas. Gera-Untermhaus: Koehler, [1895]-97-1905. 12 vols. Folio, contemp half lea. With 448 (of 449) plates, 439 colored. HH May 12 (502) DM3,800

Anr copy. Cloth; worn & marked. With 10 plain & 439 colored lithos. A few leaves of text in Vol X damaged by adhesion to plates. S June 25 (54) £950 [Russell]

Anr copy. Orig half lea. SI June 10 (685) LIt3,200,000

Nausea, Fridericus, d.1552

— Libri mirabilium septem. Cologne, 1532. 4to, 19th-cent half calf. S May 28 (9) £1,000 [Fletcher]

Naval...

See also: Aspin, Jehoshaphat

— The Naval Achievements of Great Britain.... L: James Jenkins, 1817 [plates watermarked 1811]. 4to, half calf gilt over bds; rubbed. With uncolored engraved title &

55 colored plates on Whatman or Whatman Turkey Mills paper. Without the ports & the plan of the Bombardment of Algiers. CNY Oct 8 (138) $4,000

Anr Ed. L, [plates watermarked 1825]. 4to, contemp mor gilt; lower cover detached, worn. With engraved title & 54 (of 55) hand-colored plates. Lacking the View of Gibraltar. Also lacking 2 ports & list of subscribers; Plate 3 marginally torn affecting image; stained & soiled. Loosely inserted are 3 plates & some text leaves from the Martial Achievements..... pn Sept 12 (272) £2,600 [Kafka]

Anr Ed. L, [1827]. 4to, contemp half mor gilt; rubbed. With engraved title, plan & 55 colored plates. Lacking the 2 ports; some staining & soiling. pn Nov 14 (365) £3,000

— Naval Documents related to the Quasi-War between the United States and France.... Wash., 1935-38. 7 vols. Orig half vellum; spines rubbed. Library markings. bbc Dec 9 (431) $170

Naylor, Gloria

— The Women of Brewster Place. NY, [1982]. In d/j. Sgd. wa Sept 26 (222) $220

Neale, John Preston

— Views of the Seats of Noblemen and Gentlemen. L, 1818-29. 1st Series: 6 vols. 2d Series: 5 vols. Together, 11 vols. 8vo, contemp half lea gilt; some inner hinges broken. S June 25 (280) £950 [Maggs]

Neander, Michael, 1525-95

— Graecae linguae erotemata.... Basel: Joannes Oporinus, 1565. 8vo, contemp blind-tooled pigskin over wooden bds with brass catches & clasps. sg Oct 24 (238) $475

Neckclothitania...

— Neckclothitania; or, Tietania: Being an Essay on Starchers. By One of the Cloth. L, 1818. Illus by George Cruikshank. 16mo, mor. With frontis. Salomons sale. sg Oct 17 (174) $200

Necker de Saussure, Louis Albert

— Voyage en Ecosse et aux Iles Hebrides. Geneva, 1821. 3 vols. 8vo, contemp half calf; rubbed. bba Sept 19 (243) £110 [Robertshaw]

Necker, Jacques, 1732-1804

— De l'administration des finances de la France. [Paris], 1784. 1st Ed. 3 vols. 8vo, contemp calf; worn. Lacking half-title in Vol II. S May 13 (855) £240 [Benedetti]

Anr copy. Early 19th-cent half sheep gilt. sg Mar 12 (194) $450

Needham, Joseph

— Science and Civilization in China. Cambr., 1954-88. Vols I-IV, Part 2 in 5 vols. 4to, orig half cloth, in d/js. sg Nov 14 (270) $175

Anr copy. Vols I-III, IV (Parts 1-3), V (Parts 1-5, 7, 9) & VI (Parts 1-2). 4to, wa Sept 26 (530) $475

Anr Ed. Cambr., 1965-88. Vols I-IV, Part 2 in 5 vols. 4to, cloth, in d/js. O Sept 24 (181) $160

Nehru, Jawaharlal

— The Discovery of India. Calcutta, 1948. Orig cloth. Marginal spotting. bba May 28 (354) £80 [Mandl]

Neild, James, 1744-1814

— State of the Prisons in England, Scotland and Wales. L, 1812. 4to, half calf, backstrip def, covers detached. bba Nov 28 (320) £85 [Drury]

Neill, John R.

— Lucky Bucky in Oz. Chicago: Reilly & Lee, [1942]. In d/j. sg Oct 17 (339) $250

— The Scalawagons of Oz. Chicago: Reilly & Lee, [1941]. Orig cloth; lower cover discolored & spotted. bbc Dec 9 (136) $80

Nelson, Henry Loomis, 1846-1908

— The Army of the United States. Wash., [1888]. Folio, loose as issed in cloth folder. DW Oct 2 (225) £460

Nereis. See: Stackhouse, John

Neri, Antonio

— Art de la verrerie. Paris, 1752. 4to, half lea; worn. With 17 plates. B Nov 1 (496) HF1,700

— The Art of Glass. L, 1662. 8vo, contemp calf; rubbed. Title frayed; some water-staining. bba Jan 30 (137) £260 [Thomas Plume's Library]

Nerses IV, Glayetsi, Patriarch of Armenia

— Preces sancti Nersetis clajensis...viginti quatuor linguis editae. Venice, 1837. 12mo, half lea; worn. With engraved title & port. Extracts in 24 languages. sp Apr 16 (327) $80

Neruda, Pablo

— Toros. Paris, 1960. One of 50 with orig litho, sgd by Picasso. Illus by Pablo Picasso. Folio, loose as issued in cloth portfolio. With 15 plates. P June 17 (295) $1,800

— Twenty Poems. Madison MN: The Sixties Press, 1967. In d/j. Inscr. sg Dec 12 (304) $90

Nerval, Gerard de, 1808-55

— Aurelia. Monaco, 1960. One of 20 in Auvergne. Illus by Leonor Fini. 4to, loose in orig wraps. With a watercolor by Fini and an extra suite of selected illusts and 1 plate. sg Sept 26 (242) $600

One of 20 on auvergne. Loose in orig wraps. sg Jan 30 (109) $450

Neue...

— Neue Bilder Gallerie fuer junge Soehne und Toechter. Berlin, 1805-23. Mixed Ed. Vols II-IV & VI-XV (of 15). Bds; joints broken. With 13 colored titles & 250 (of 255) colored plates. HH May 12 (1786) DM3,800

Neufforge, Jean Francois de

— Recueil elementaire d'architecture contenant plusiers etudes.... Paris, 1757-80. 10 vols in 6, including the 2 Supplement vols. Folio, contemp half calf; rubbed. With 8 engraved titles & 900 plates. Index leaf at end of Supplement & anr leaf loosely inserted; 1 or 2 plates creased. S Nov 21 (88) £3,600 [Bifolco]

Nevill, Ralph

— Old English Sporting Prints and their History. L, 1923. One of 1,500. 4to, orig cloth. K Mar 22 (284) $90

— Old English Sporting Books. L, 1924. One of 1,500. 4to, orig cloth. Koopman copy. O Oct 29 (215) $110

— Old French Line Engravings. L, 1924. One of 1,250. 4to, cloth; rubbed. O Aug 25 (139) $50

Nevill, Samuel. See: New Jersey

New...

— New Display of the Beauties of England. L, 1776. 2 vols. 8vo, contemp calf; rubbed. With engraved titles & 179 plates (of 177 listed), a few colored by a former owner. Some leaves in Vol II frayed & repaired at edge. S Nov 15 (919) £360 [Burden]

— A New Display of the Beauties of England.... L, 1787. Vol II (of 2) only. 8vo, contemp calf; worn. With 81 plates. Sold w.a.f. DW Dec 11 (120) £120

— The New Flora and Sylva. L, 1929-40. 11 vols. Orig cloth. bba Aug 13 (359) £110 [Lloyd's of Kew]

— A New Geographical Dictionary. L, 1759-60. 2 vols in 1. Folio, contemp calf. DW Nov 6 (80) £540

— The New Naturalist: A Survey of British Natural History L, 1945-79. Nos 1-63. All but Vol 6 in d/js. S Feb 26 (934) £700 [Thorp]

New England...

— The New England Historical and Genealogical Register. Bost., 1847-1987. Vols 1-141 & 4 vols of Indexes. 145 vols. 8vo, various bdgs. Some vols with library stamps. Sold w.a.f. O Mar 31 (135) $1,300

New Hampshire

— Walling, H. F. & Hitchcock, Charles H. - Atlas of the State of New Hampshire. NY: Comstock & Cline, [1877]. Folio, half sheep; extremities worn, spine def, hinges cracked. With 86 maps, partially hand-colored. Some soiling. sg Feb 13 (136) $200

New Jersey

— Acts of the General Assembly of the Province of New Jersey, 17 April 1702 to 14 January 1776. Burlington, 1776. Compiled by Samuel Allinson. Folio, calf; worn. Library markings. NH May 30 (395) $205

— The Petitions and Memorials of the Proprietors of West and East-Jersey.... NY, [1784]. 8vo, unbound, sewn, part of plain rear wrap present. With folding map; comprises 72 pages & errata leaf, as in Evans 18640. O May 26 (135) $1,600

— Nevill, Samuel. - The Acts of the General Assembly the Province of New Jersey. [Phila.] & Woodbridge, 1752. Folio, old calf; worn. Blank piece torn from corner of tp; lacking front blanks; tears to first 2 leaves; some browning. K July 12 (361) $400

New Numbers

— New Numbers. Ryton Dymock, 1914. Vol I, Nos 1-4 [all pbd]. 4to, wraps. Includes works of W. W. Gibson, Rupert Brooke, Lascelles Abercrombie & John Drinkwater. sg Dec 12 (31) $150

New South Wales Agricultural Society. See: Australia

New York...

— The New-York Historical Society's Dictionary of Artists in America, 1564-1860. New Haven, 1957. Ed by George C. Groce & David H. Wallace. F Mar 26 (425) $50

— The New-York Revised Prices for Manufacturing Cabinet and Chair Work. June, 1810. NY, 1810. Bound with: Revised Constitution and Rules of Order of the New-York Society of Cabinet-Makers.... 8vo, contemp half sheep; worn, 1 gathering loose. Dampstaining to 1st gathering. sg Dec 5 (104) $2,000

New York (City)

— NEW-YORK HISTORICAL SOCIETY. - Catalogue of American Portraits.... New Haven, 1974. Vols I-II sp June 18 (170) $60

— WORLD'S FAIR—1939. - Futurama. [NY, 1939]. One of 1,000. 4to, pictorial bds. Ptd on the occasion of Paul Garrett's Party at the University Club. sg Apr 2 (302) $300

New York (Colony & State)

— Journal of the Senate of the State.... Poughkeepsie, 1788. Folio, unbound as issued. Stamp on reverse of title. bbc Dec 9 (401) $375

— Laws of New-York, from the 11th Nov. 1752 to 22d May, 1762.... NY, 1762. Vol II (of 2) only. Folio, contemp calf; worn. Some foxing. bbc Dec 9 (402) $125

Newbold, T.J.

— Political and Statistical Account of the British Settlements in the Straits of Malacca.... L, 1839. 2 vols. 8vo, half calf. With 8 maps & plates. Library stamps; 2 plates shaved at fore-edges. S July 1 (1514) £380 [Maggs]

Newcastle, William Cavendish, Duke of

— A General System of Horsemanship. L, 1743. 2 vols. Folio, contemp calf. With double-page engraved title & 61 (of 62) plates, 42 double-page & 1 folding. bba Sept 5 (181) £4,200 [Burdeen]

Anr copy. Contemp calf; rubbed, spines blackened & worn. With double-page engraved title & 33 (of 42) double-page plates, 19 engraved anatomical plates of horses, 12 ptd in sepia or red. Guarded. Sold w.a.f. C June 24 (184) £2,800 [Armero]

Anr copy. Contemp mor gilt by John Brindley, presentation bdg. With double-page engraved title & 62 plates, 44 double-page. Some foxing. S June 25 (87) £4,400 [Maggs]

Anr Ed. L, 1748. 2 vols. Folio, 19th-cemt mor gilt. With double-page engraved title & 42 double-page plates in Vol I & 20 plates in Vol II, 2 double-page. HH May 12 (1029) DM12,000

— Methode et invention nouvelle de dresser les chevaux.... Antwerp, 1658. Folio, modern half mor retaining old marbled bds. With engraved title & 42 plates. Tp with long tear repaired; several plates with short tears repaired, mostly marginal; some soiling; lacking text. S Dec 5 (240) £3,500 [Russell]

— A New Method and Extraordinary Invention, to Dress Horses.... L, 1667. 1st Ed in English. Folio, contemp calf; rubbed & rebacked. With 8 additional leaves inserted. Some marginal waterstaining. bba Sept 5 (180) £320 [Hoffer]

Newdigate, Bernard

— The Art of the Book. L: The Studio, 1938. 4to, cloth; soiled. wa Apr 9 (9) $60

Newell Collection, Edward T.

— Ancient Oriental Seals in the Collection.... Chicago, [1934]. 4to, cloth. With 41 photographic plates. sg Feb 6 (208) $175

Newell, Peter, 1862-1924

— The Hole Book. NY, 1908. 4to, cloth. K Mar 22 (290) $55

Anr copy. Orig cloth in def d/j. Epstein copy. sg Apr 30 (347) $1,200

— The Rocket Book. NY, 1912. 4to, orig cloth. With 22 colored plates. K Mar 22 (291) $150

— Topsys & Turvys. NY, 1893. 1st Ed. Oblong 8vo, orig bds; backstrip chipped, edges worn. With 31 colored illusts. F June 25 (195) $50

New-England Lasses

— New-England Lasses. [N.p., c.1800]. Single sheet, 350mm by 111mm, irregular. Framed. Roman types (93R).. P June 16 (258) $800

Newgate Calendar

— The Newgate Calendar. L: Navarre Society, 1926. ("The Complete Newgate Calendar.") Ed by G. T. Crook. 5 vols. Z Apr 18 (103) $120

— WILKINSON, GEORGE THEODORE. - The Newgate Calendar Improved. L, [c.1840]. 6 vols. 8vo, calf gilt; rebacked. sg Oct 17 (400) $300

Newhall, Nancy

— Time in New England. NY, 1950. 1st Ed. Illus by Paul Strand. 4to, orig cloth, in d/j. bbc Feb 17 (269) $70

Anr copy. Cloth, in chipped d/j. sg Apr 13 (95) $120

Newman, John Henry, Cardinal, 1801-90

— Apologia pro vita sua. L, 1864. 1st Ed in Book form. 8vo, half calf; rubbed. cb Dec 5 (88) $120

Newte, Thomas

— Prospects and Observations on a Tour in England and Scotland.... L, 1791. 4to, later calf gilt; rebacked. With folding map & 23 plates. Extra-illus with 16 tinted aquatints. bba Jan 30 (118) £130 [The Bookroom]

Anr copy. Contemp calf gilt; soiled. bba Feb 27 (96) £220 [Grant & Shaw]

Anr copy. Half calf. pnE May 13 (63) £140

Newton, Alfred Edward, 1863-1940

— The Amenities of Book-Collecting.... Bost., 1918. 1st Ed, 1st Issue. Sgd. With caricature sent by author. cb Oct 17 (1676) $110

— Doctor Johnson. A Play. Bost., 1923. 1st Ed. Sgd. With 3 letters from Newton.. cb Oct 17 (679) $70

— The Format of the English Novel. Cleveland, 1928. One of 289. 4to, cloth. cb Oct 17 (681) $95

— The Greatest Book in the World. Bost., [1925]. One of 470. cb Oct 17 (683) $55

— Mr. Strahan's Dinner Party. San Francisco: Book Club of California, 1930. One of 350. Half cloth. pba Aug 20 (151) $80

— This Book-Collecting Game. Bost., 1928. 1st Trade Ed. cb Feb 27 (73) $60

One of 990, sgd. cb Oct 17 (687) $50; cb Feb 27 (72) $120; K Sept 29 (292) $55

— A Tourist in Spite of Himself. [Bost., 1930]. One of 525. Half cloth. cb Feb 27 (74) $80

Newton Library, Alfred Edward

— [Sale Catalogue] Rare Books.... NY, 1941. 4 vols. 4to, bds; spine end bds of 2 vols pulling away. pba Aug 20 (152) $60

Newton, Sir Isaac, 1642-1727

— Arithmetica universalis.... Leiden, 1732. 4to, contemp vellum; rubbed. With 13 folding plates. bba Sept 5 (236) £125 [Raiklen]

Anr Ed. Cambr., 1979. 8vo, contemp calf gilt; joints renewed. Newton's own library copy with his holograph corrections & emendations. S July 21 (291) £27,000 [Quaritch]

— The Correspondence. L, 1959-[77]. 7 vols. 4to, orig cloth, in d/js. pn June 11 (126) £160 [Cumming]

— Lectiones opticae. L, 1729. 4to, contemp sheep; worn & stained, rebacked & repaired. With 23 folding plates. Some spotting. Library markings. bba Sept 5 (235) £140 [M. Phelps]

— The Mathematical Principles of Natural Philosophy. L, 1729. 1st Ed in English. Trans by Andrew Motte. 2 vols. 8vo, contemp calf gilt; rubbed, rebacked in calf gilt. With 52 folding plates & 2 folding letterpress tables. Manney copy. P Oct 11 (240) $6,000

— Optice.... L, 1706. 1st Ed in Latin. 4to, contemp vellum. With 19 folding plates. Plates dampstained. Ck Nov 29 (225) £1,000

Anr Ed. Lausanne & Geneva, 1740. 4to, contemp calf. Some browning. SI June 10 (687) LIt500,000

— Opticks.... L, 1704. 1st Ed. 4to, contemp calf; rebacked. With 19 folding plates. S May 28 (10) £4,500 [Haver]

— Philosophiae naturalis principia mathematica. L, 1687. 1st Ed, 1st Issue. 4to, contemp calf; extremities restored. With P4 present in both states. Unpressed copy. Manney copy. P Oct 11 (239) $105,000

1st "Jesuits" Ed. Geneva, 1739-42. 3 vols in 4. 4to, contemp calf; some joints cracked. Ck Nov 29 (229) £200

[-] TELESCOPE, TOM. - The Newtonian System of Philosophy. L, 1787. 12mo, contemp half vellum; soiled. With 9 plates. Some spotting. bba July 23 (111) £160 [Excell]

Newton, James, 1639-1718

— A Compleat Herbal. L, 1805. ("A Complete Herbal.") 8vo, orig bds. With frontis & 175 plates. pnE Oct 2 (418) £90

Newton, John, 1725-1807. See: Cowper & Newton

New-York Historical Society. See: New York (City)

Nibby, Antonio, 1792-1839

— Raccolta delle vedute pittoresche di Roma e de'suoi contorni. Rome, 1825. Vol I, Part 1 only. Folio, contemp half vellum; worn. With 20 plates. Some foxing. sg Sept 19 (203) $400

Nibby, Antonio, 1792-1839 —& Gell, Sir William, 1777-1836

— Le Mura di Roma disegnate da Sir William Gell.... Rome, 1820. With: Suite of plates to the Mura di Roma, comprising engraved title, 31 views & map, all facing the orig ink drawings by Gell, each inlaid to size, together with 2 sgd rejected drawings of the Walls of Servius. 2 vols. 4to & folio, contemp mor. S Nov 21 (173) £3,800 [Sotheran]

Nicaise, Claude

— Les Sirenes; ou, Discours sur leur forme et figure. Paris: Jean Anisson, 1691. 4to, old bds with sheep back & vellum tips. sg Oct 24 (239) $325

Niceron, Jean Pierre, 1685-1738

— Memoires pour servir a l'histoire des hommes illustres dans la republique des lettres. Paris, 1729-45. 42 vols only, bound in 14. 8vo, contemp vellum; soiled. Some browning; 1 prelim leaf lacking from Vol I. Ck Nov 1 (461) £190

Nichol, George

— The Story of the Three Bears. L, 1837. 1st Ed. Oblong 8vo, orig bds; rebacked, worn & soiled. Epstein copy. sg Apr 30 (350) $2,800

Nicholas, John Liddiard

— Narrative of a Voyage to New Zealand. L, 1817. 2 vols. 8vo, contemp half calf; rubbed. With frontises, folding map & 3 plates. Lacking half-titles & ad leaves. bba June 11 (348) £300 [Bonham]

Nicholas, Thomas

— Annals and Antiquities of the Counties and Country Families of Wales. L, 1872. 2 vols. 8vo, contemp half mor; rubbed. DW Apr 8 (123) £64

Nicholls, William Henry

— Orchids of Australia.... Melbourne, 1969. 4to, orig bdg, in d/j. kh Nov 11 (593) A$240

Nichols, Beverley

— A Book of Old Ballads. L, 1934. Ltd Ed. Illus by H. M. Brock. 4to, bds; worn. O Jan 14 (136) $80

Nichols, John

— Literary Anecdotes of the Eighteenth Century. L, 1812-16. Vols I-IX. 8vo, bdg not stated. cb Oct 17 (689) $160

Nicholson, Ben. See: Russell, John

Nicholson, Benedict

— Joseph Wright of Derby. L & NY, 1968. 2 vols. 4to, orig cloth, in d/js. Ck Feb 14 (31) £50

Nicholson, Francis, 1753-1844

— The Practise of Drawing and Painting Landscape from Nature.... L, 1823. 2d Ed. 4to, orig bds; rebacked. pnE Dec 4 (227) £65

Nicholson, James Bartram, 1820-91

— A Manual of the Art of Bookbinding. Phila., 1856. 8vo, orig cloth; spine ends & upper joint split. bbc Dec 9 (1889) $850

Anr Ed. Phila., 1887. 8vo, orig cloth; rebacked preserving orig spine, new endpapers, rubbed. Waterstaining in upper margin. bba May 28 (495) £170 [Laywood]

Nicholson, Samuel & George

— Twenty-Six Lithographic Drawings in the Vicinity of Liverpool. Liverpool, 1821. Folio, 19th-cent half mor gilt. With frontis & 26 plates. Some spotting. S Nov 21 (121) £500 [Pagan]

Nicholson, William, 1665-1727

— The English Historical Library. L, 1696-97. 2 vols. 8vo, calf; broken. b&b Feb 19 (111) $60

Nicholson, William, 1785-1845

— The History of the Wars Occasioned by the French Revolution. L, 1816. Folio, contemp calf; rebacked, covers laid down. With 22 hand-colored plates. F Mar 26 (768) $350

Anr Ed. L, 1817. Folio, later half pigskin; rubbed. With 21 hand-colored plates only; lacking frontis. Some dampstaining. S May 14 (1069) £190 [Pulido]

Nicholson, William, 1872-1949

— An Alphabet. L, 1898. 4to, orig half cloth; rubbed & chipped. With litho title & 26 chromolitho plates, title & 24 of the plates sgd, the other 2 marked with initials (some signatures smudged). Some spotting & soiling. Manney copy. P Oct 11 (241) $3,000

Library Ed, Deluxe issue on handmade paper. Folio, orig cloth; soiled, lacking most of spine. With 26 colored plates mtd on brown paper. S July 22 (427) £500 [Liechti]

Anr Ed. L, 1899. 2d Impression. 4to, orig half cloth; soiled & worn, inner hinges broken. DW Dec 11 (445) £220

— London Types, Quatorzains by W. E. Henley. L, 1898. 4to, orig half cloth; inner hinges split. With 11 colored plates & front cover by Nicholson. Ck July 10 (388) £140

Anr Ed. NY, 1898. 4to, orig half cloth; worn & soiled. With 11 colored plates & front cover by Nicholson. DW Dec 11 (442) £165

Anr copy. Orig half vellum; soiled. DW Mar 4 (372) £400

Anr copy. Orig half cloth; extremities rubbed, front hinge starting. F Sept 26 (568) $125

Anr copy. Orig half cloth; hinge broken, soiled, spine torn. pn May 14 (118) £120 [Walford]; pnE Dec 4 (254) £130

Anr copy. Orig half cloth; soiled & worn. wa Sept 26 (633) $200

— Twelve Portraits. L, 1899. Ltd Ed. Folio, cloth; loose. Foxed & stained; prelims lacking. sg Feb 13 (200) $650

Nickson, Geoffrey

— A Portrait of Salmon Fishing. Rugby: Anthony Atha, [1976]. One of 200. Oblong 4to, lea. Koopman copy. O Oct 29 (218) $475

Nicolaus de Lyra, 1270?-1340?

— Moralia super totam Bibliam. Cologne: Johann Koelhoff the Elder, 1478. Folio, contemp blindstamped deerskin over wooden bds with metal fitting; added shelf mark. 50 lines; double column; type 6:107G; rubricated. Marginal tears on e4 & s1; some stains. 284 leaves. Goff N-111. Schoyen copy. P Dec 12 (30) $12,000

— Postilla super totam Bibliam. Venice: [B. Locatellus] for O. Scotus, 9 Aug 1488. Vol III only. Folio, modern half sheep. Some marginal staining throughout; lacking initial & final blanks. 326 (of 328) leaves; lacking initial & final blanks. Goff N-132. sg Mar 12 (126) $1,400

Nicolay, Charles G.

— The Oregon Territory. L, 1846. 8vo, orig wraps; spine worn. With frontis, folding map & full-page map. cb Feb 12 (64) $250

Nicolay, John George, 1832-1901 —& Hay, John Milton, 1838-1905

— Abraham Lincoln: a History. NY, 1890. 10 vols. 8vo, orig cloth. K Sept 29 (235) $110

Nicolay, Nicolas de, 1517-83

— Le navigationi et viaggi nella Turchia.... Antwerp: W. Silvius, 1576. 4to, contemp vellum. With 60 full-page illusts. Lacking final blank; tp stamped. S July 1 (665) £700 [Hantzis]

Anr Ed. Venice: Francesco Ziletti, 1580. ("Le Navigationi et viaggi fatti nella Turchia....") Folio, recased in old vellum. With 67 plates. With a cut round engraving showing a reversible port of Mohammed versus Satan pasted onto p.185; L8 repaired affecting text & image surface; M4 repaired at foot touching image; some stains & fraying & worming. S July 1 (663) £2,500 [Quaritch]

— Les Navigations, peregrinations, et voyages, faicts en la Turquie. Antwerp, 1576. 4to, 18th-cent sheep gilt. With 60 plates. sg May 7 (160) $1,200

Nicoll, Allardyce

— A History of English Drama 1660-1990. Cambr., 1965. 4th Ed. 6 vols. O Sept 24 (185) $70

Nicoll, Michael J. —& Meinertzhagen, Richard

— Birds of Egypt. L, 1930. 2 vols. 4to, orig cloth; rubbed, new endpapers. With 3 folding colored maps, 8 uncolored & 30 colored plates. S May 14 (1046) £150 [Hannas]

Nicols, Arthur

— Wild Life and Adventure in the Australian Bush. L, 1887. 2 vols. 8vo, later calf extra; spines faded. cb Dec 5 (89) $120

Nicolson, Benedict

— Hendrik Terbrugghen. L, 1958. In torn d/j. S Feb 11 (152) £240 [Schmidt]

— Joseph Wright of Derby. L & NY, 1968. 2 vols. 4to, orig cloth, in d/js. DW Oct 9 (929) £50; DW Mar 11 (841) £50

Niedieck, Paul

— With Rifle in Five Continents. L: Rowland Ward, 1908. Front joint torn. sg Jan 9 (295) $175

Nieuhoff, Jan

— L'Ambassade de la Compagnie Orientale des Provinces Unies vers l'empereur de la Chine.... Leiden, 1665. 1st Ed in French. 2 parts in 1 vol. Folio, half lea; needs rebdg. Stained; fold splits in plates; repairs; margins with loss. Sold w.a.f. wa Sept 26 (483) $280

— Gedenkweerdige Brasiliaense Zee-en Lant-Reise door de voornaemste Landschappen van West en Oostindien. Amst., 1682. 2 parts in 1 vol. Folio, contemp vellum. With 4 folding maps & 45 plates. General title frayed & marked. bba Sept 19 (11) £1,900 [Butcher]

Anr copy. Folio, disbound. Lacking 13 plates; engraved title frayed & loose; lacking 4 text leaves. sg May 21 (77) $500

Night Visions

See also: Winter, Douglas E.

— Night Visions 4. Arlington Heights IL: Dark Harvest, 1987. One of 500, sgd by all contribs. In d/j. cb Sept 19 (168) $85

Nightingale, Florence, 1820-1910

— Notes on Nursing.... L, [1859]. 1st Ed. 8vo, Library cloth. bba Nov 28 (166) £55 [Pickering & Chatto]

Anr Ed. Bost., 1860. 12mo, orig cloth. sg May 14 (117) $400

Nijhoff, Wouter

— Nederlandsche Bibliographie van 1500 tot 1540. The Hague, 1923-71. 3 vols in 6 plus 2 supplements. B May 12 (124) HF900

Anr Ed. The Hague, 1923-40. 3 vols. Half syn. sg Oct 31 (278) $110

Nijhoff, Wouter —& Kronenberg, M. E.

— Nederlandsche bibliographie van 1500 tot 1540. The Hague, 1965. 6 parts in 3 vols. Contemp half mor. Ck Nov 1 (462) £110

Nimrod. See: Apperley, Charles J.

Nin, Anais

— D. H. Lawrence: an Unprofessional Study. Paris: Black Manikin Press, 1932. 1st Ed, one of 500. In d/j. sg Dec 12 (305) $400

— This Hunger. NY: Gemor Press, [1945]. One of 1,000. Illus by Ian Hugo. Pictorial bds. pba July 9 (211) $55

— Under a Glass Bell. [NY, 1944]. One of 300. Illus by Ian Hugo. Sticker of the Institute for Sex Research to lower front free endpaper. pba July 9 (212) $70

Nisbet, Alexander, 1657-1725

— An Essay on the Ancient and Modern Use of Armories. Edin., 1748. 8vo, contemp calf; split. With 7 plates. pnE May 13 (156) £60

— A System of Heraldry.... Edin., 1722-42. 1st Ed. 2 vols. Folio, contemp calf; joints cracked. DW Mar 4 (242) £85

Nissen, Claus

— Die illustrierten Vogelbuecher. Stuttgart, 1953. 4to, cloth, in d/j. O Sept 24 (186) $250

— Die Zoologische Buchillustration. Stuttgart, 1969-78. 2 vols. Folio, cloth. O Sept 24 (187) $450

Niven, Larry

— Ringworld. L, 1972. 1st English Ed, Advance Proof. Wraps. cb Sept 19 (170) $300

Nixon, Francis Russell

— The Cruise of the Beacon.... L, 1857. 8vo, cloth; def. With engraved title, frontis & 8 plates. kh Nov 11 (595) A$380

Nixon, Richard M.

— The Real War. [NY, 1980]. Cloth, in d/j. Inscr to Michael Cohen. wa Oct 19 (326) $80

— Six Crises. NY, 1962. In d/j. Inscr. sp Apr 16 (408) $70

Noble, Thomas —& Rose, Thomas

— The Counties of Chester, Derby, Leicester, Lincoln, and Rutland. L, 1836-[37]. 4to, contemp calf gilt; extremities rubbed, front cover soiled. With engraved title & 72 (on 36) plates. Some spotting & staining. bba July 23 (365) £150 [Adamson]

Anr copy. Cloth. With engraved title & 73 (on 37) plates. Some waterstaining & foxing. bba July 23 (366) £260 [Adamson]

Nodier, Charles, 1780-1844 —& Others

— Voyages pittoresques et romantiques dans l'ancienne France. Paris, 1820-25. 2 vols in 3. Folio, half mor; worn. Some foxing. O May 26 (137) $2,100

Anr copy. 2 vols. Folio, contemp half calf gilt; rebacked with crude repairs, rubbed. With litho frontis & 242 lithos numbered 1-232 with 6 in 2 states. Lacking Croquis pl. XVII in Vol I; some spotting & foxing. Schlosser copy. P June 18 (595) $1,200

Noel, E. B. —& Clark, J. O. M.

— A History of Tennis. Oxford, 1924. 2 vols. 4to, orig cloth. Stamps on versos of titles & pastedowns. pn Mar 19 (361) £200 [Way]

Noel, Theophilus, b.1804

— Autobiography and Reminiscences.... Chicago, 1904. Orig cloth; worn & soiled. NH May 30 (173) $135

Nogaret, Francois Felix

— L'Aretin francois, par un membre de l'Academie des Dames.... L [Paris], 1787. 2 parts in 1 vol. 18mo, early 20th-cent mor gilt. Lacking 1 leaf. HH May 12 (1074) DM2,500

Nolhac, Pierre de, 1859-1936

— Histoire du Chateau de Versailles. Paris, 1911. One of 350 on velin d'Arches. 2 vols in 1. 4to, mor extra with onlays by Marius Michel. Marlborough copy. CNY Dec 5 (416) $6,500

Nollet, Jean Antoine, 1700-70

— Lecons de physique experimentale. Paris, 1775. Vol III only. Lea; worn. sp June 18 (240) $70

— Recherches sur les causes particulieres de phenomenes electriques.... Paris, 1754. 12mo, contemp calf gilt. With 8 folding plates. sg Nov 14 (273) $200

Nonesuch Press—London

— Bible, The Holy. 1924-27. One of 1,000 & 1,250. 5 vols, including Apocrypha O May 26 (138) $650; pnE Mar 11 (187) £60

— ANACREON. - Poems. 1923. One of 725. O Mar 31 (143) $60

— BECKFORD, WILLIAM THOMAS. - Vathek. 1929. One of 1,050. bba May 14 (320) £60 [Dawson]

— BLAKE, WILLIAM. - The Note-Book...Called the Rossetti Manuscript. 1935. One of 650. bba Dec 19 (40) £70 [Kitazawa]

— BLAKE, WILLIAM. - Pencil Drawings. 1927. One of 1,550. sg Feb 6 (21) $50

— BLAKE, WILLIAM. - The Writings. 1925. One of 1,500. 3 vols. bba Dec 19 (12) £150 [Books & Prints]

Anr Ed. 1927. 3 vols. sg Feb 6 (22) $250

— BUNYAN, JOHN. - The Pilgrim's Progress. 1928. One of 195. cb Dec 19 (23) $50

— BURTON, ROBERT. - The Anatomy of Melancholy. 1925. One of 750. 2 vols. Bdg soiled. pn July 16 (81) £80 [Bookroom]; pnE Mar 11 (229) £100; sg Jan 30 (112) $140

Out-of-series copy. DW Nov 6 (558) £100

— CERVANTES SAAVEDRA, MIGUEL DE. - Don Quixote. 1930. One of 1,475. 2 vols. b Nov 18 (33) £80

— COLLIER, JOHN. - The Devil and All. 1934.

One of 1,000. bba Apr 30 (165) £50 [Kurita]

— CONGREVE, WILLIAM. - The Complete Works. 1923. One of 900. 4 vols. Half cloth. pnE Oct 1 (241) £150

— DANTE ALIGHIERI. - La Divina Commedia. 1928. One of 1,475. pnE Oct 1 (248) £140; S Nov 14 (69) £320 [Marks]

Anr copy. With 42 plates, 8 full-page, the remainder double-page. S Nov 14 (70) £170 [Riex]; sg Jan 30 (113) $140

— DICKENS, CHARLES. - Works. 1937-38. One of 877. 23 vols, including 1 orig metal plate. With Retrospectus & Prospectus & with a copy of the Limited Editions Club's Ed of Great Expectations. P June 17 (336) $6,000

Anr copy. 23 vols; lacking Our Mutual Friend, plus the Nonesuch Dickensiana. Orig cloth; some spines soiled & rubbed, 1 corner frayed. pn July 16 (82) £850

Anr copy. 24 vols, including the engraved plate Monmouth Street by George Cruikshank S Dec 12 (170) £5,200 [Lehrer]

— DRYDEN, JOHN. - The Dramatic Works. 1931-32. One of 750. 6 vols. pnE Oct 1 (245) £110; pnE Mar 11 (231) £120

— FONTENELLE, BERNARD LE BOVIER DE. - A Plurality of Worlds. 1929. One of 1,600. b&b Feb 19 (240) $60

— HERODOTUS. - The History. 1935. One of 675. pnE Mar 11 (235) £70; S Nov 14 (71) £280 [Fuller]

— HOMER. - The Iliad & The Odyssey. 1931. One of 1450 & 1400. Trans by Pope. 2 vols. bba June 11 (179) £150 [Sotheran]; pn Apr 23 (92) £320 [Mackenzie]

— KEYNES, SIR GEOFFREY. - Jane Austen: A Bibliography. 1929. One of 875. In d/j. cb Oct 17 (496) $95; sp Sept 22 (455) $80

— KEYNES, SIR GEOFFREY. - William Hazlitt: A Bibliography. 1931. One of 750. O Sept 24 (137) $90

— MILTON, JOHN. - The Mask of Comus. 1937. One of 950. wa Dec 9 (31) $130

— MONTAIGNE, MICHEL EYQUEM DE. - Essays. 1931. One of 1,375. b Mar 11 (176) £55

— OTWAY, THOMAS. - Works. 1926. Out-of-series copy. 3 vols. Inscr to Lady Cunard by Montague Summers. pn Apr 23 (93) £60 [Clark]

— PLUTARCH. - The Lives of the Noble Grecians and Romans. 1929-30. One of 1,550. 5 vols. b Nov 18 (36) £90; bba June 11 (180) £150 [Deighton Bell]; K Sept 29 (295) $80; wa Dec 9 (32) $60

— RICKETTS, CHARLES DE SOUSY. - Some Recollections of Oscar Wilde. 1932. One of 800. bba Jan 16 (371) £120 [Whetman]; sg Jan 30 (114) $200

— SHAKESPEARE, WILLIAM. - Works. 1929-33. One of 1,600. 7 vols. S Dec 12 (9) £520 [Frew Mackenzie]

Coronation Ed. 1953. 4 vols. O Mar 31 (144) $70; wd Dec 12 (425) $75

— TOLLER, ERNST. - Brokenbow. [1926]. Half cloth. bba Dec 19 (147) £50 [Bowers]

— VANBRUGH, SIR JOHN. - Collected Works. 1927. One of 1,300. 4 vols. bba June 11 (182) £75 [Clark]; pnE Oct 1 (243) £80

— WALTON, IZAAK. - Works. 1929. One of 1,600. pnE Oct 1 (247) £60

— WHITE, GILBERT. - The Writings. 1938. One of 850. 2 vols. pnE Mar 11 (232) £220; S Dec 12 (183) £600 [Wall]

— WILSON, MONA. - The Life of William Blake. 1927. One of 1,480. bba Dec 19 (49) £85 [Whetman]; bba Dec 19 (149) £60 [Dawson]; sg Sept 26 (56) $70; sg Feb 6 (29) $120

— WYCHERLEY, WILLIAM. - Works. 1924. One of 900. 4 vols. pnE Oct 1 (242) £160

Nonnenmacher, Marcus

— Der Architectonische Tischler oder Architectur-Kunst und Seaulen-Buch. Frankfurt, 1751. Folio, contemp bds; worn. With 42 plates. HH May 12 (825) DM3,400

Noorthouck, John, 1746?-1816

— A New History of London. L, 1773. 4to, 19th-cent calf gilt; broken. With 38 plates (6 folding) & 4 folding maps, 2 hand-colored. Repair to 1 map; 1 plate with hole affecting image. pn May 14 (205) Ps180 [Walford]

Norden, Charles. See: Durrell, Lawrence

Norden, Friderik Ludwig

— Travels in Egypt and Nubia.... L, 1757. 1st Ed in English. 2 vols in 1. Folio, contemp calf; def. With frontis, port & 162 plates. Some foxing; a few edges frayed & stained. pn Dec 12 (363) £200

Anr copy. Vol II only. Contemp bds; worn. With 85 plates on 84 leaves only. Lacking title & port; some dampstaining. Sold w.a.f. pn June 11 (289) £170

Anr copy. 2 vols. Folio, contemp calf. With port, frontis & 159 (on 157) plates. SI Dec 5 (957) LIt2,400,000

— Voyage d'Egypte et de Nubie. Copenhagen, 1755. 2 vols. Folio, contemp calf; worn. With port, frontis & 159 maps & plates. 1 folding plate torn. CNY Dec 5 (303) $2,000

Norden, John, 1548-1625?

— Speculi Britanniae Pars. A Topographicall and Historicall Description of Cornwall. L, 1728. 4to, modern half calf. With engraved title, dedication, table of distances, 10 double-page maps on guards & plate. bba Jan 30 (25) £650 [Potter]

Anr copy. Old calf gilt; rebacked. Engraved title & map shaved. C May 20 (283) £400 [Arader]

Nordenskiold, Gustav

— The Cliff Dwellers of the Mesaverde, Southwestern Colorado.... Chicago & Stockholm [ptd], 1893. One plate loose. sg Dec 5 (189) $1,100

Nordenskiold, Nils Adolf Erik, 1832-1901

— Facsimile-Atlas to the Early History of Cartography. Stockholm, 1889. Folio, orig half lea gilt; shaken, extremities worn. H. W. Poor copy. sg May 21 (288) $350

— The Voyage of the Vega round Asia and Europe. L, 1881. 2 vols. 8vo, contemp calf gilt; spines rubbed. DW Nov 6 (82) £115

Nordhoff, Charles, 1830-1901

— Northern California, Oregon, and the Sandwich Islands. NY, 1874. 8vo, orig cloth; front joint cracking. sp Apr 16 (36) $55

Nordhoff, Charles Bernard, 1887-1947 —& Hall, James Norman, 1887-1951

— The Lafayette Flying Corps. Bost., 1920. 2 vols. 4to, cloth. sg May 21 (43) $550

— Mutiny on the Bounty, Bost., 1932. 1st Ed, 1st Issue. In d/j. sg Dec 12 (306) $100

Normand, Charles Pierre Joseph

— Vergleichende darstellung der architectonischen Ordnungen der griechen und roemer und der neueren Baumeister. Potsdam: Ferdinand Riegel, 1830. Foliio, orig cloth; spine worn. With engraved title, key plate & 63 plates. Some foxing. S June 25 (212) £450 [Ungers]

Normyx. See: Douglas, Norman

Noronha Freyre, Joao. See: Giovanni Giuseppe di Santa Teresa

Norris, Frank, 1870-1902

— McTeague: a Story of San Francisco. NY, 1899. 1st Ed, 1st Issue. 12mo, orig cloth; rubbed. Epstein copy. sg Apr 30 (351) $400

Anr Ed. San Francisco: Colt Press, 1941. One of 500. Half cloth. cb Sept 12 (128) $50

— The Pit. A Story of Chicago. NY, 1903. 1st Ed, 1st Ptg. Bds; head of spine split. sg Dec 12 (307) $80

Norris, Thaddeus

— The American Angler's Book.... Phila., 1864. 1st Ed. 8vo, orig cloth; rebacked, orig spine preserved. Koopman copy. O Oct 29 (221) $190

Anr Ed. Phila., 1865. 8vo, orig cloth; extremities worn, hinges tender. F Sept 26 (449) $60

Norroena...

— Norroena: Anglo-Saxon Classics, Embracing the History and Romance of Northern Europe. L, [1905]-11. One of 450. 15 vols. Lea gilt; 3 vols with breaks in lea on spine, some spine ends chipped. wa Sept 26 (1) $140

North...

— The North Georgia Gazette and Winter Chronicle. L, 1821. 1st Ed. 4to, orig bds; spine chipped. Some browning. S Feb 26 (826) £220 [Sotheran]

North American...

— North American Big Game. A Book of the Boone and Crockett Club.... NY & L, 1939. Koopman copy. O Oct 29 (78) $425

Anr copy. Worn, spine torn. Koopman copy. O Oct 29 (222) $140

North, Roger, 1653-1743

— A Discourse of Fish and Fish-Ponds.... L, 1794. ("The History of the Esculent Fish....") 4to, contemp lea gilt; rubbed. With 17 (of 18) hand-colored plates. Some cropping, affecting platemarks & captions; stamps on tp verso & verso of final leaf. pn Mar 19 (317) £900 [Shapero]

Anr Ed. L, [1832-35]. ("A Treatise on Fish and Fish-Ponds.") Illus by Elizabeth Eleazar & Fortin Albin. 4to, contemp half mor; worn, rebcked, old spine laid down. With 18 hand-colored plates. Tp soiled. S June 25 (52) £1,350 [Marshall]

North, Sterling —& Kroch, Carl

— So Red the Nose; or Breath in the Afternoon. NY, [1935]. 12mo, cloth, in d/j. Recipes include Hemingway's Death in the Afternoon Cocktail. sg Dec 12 (154) $60

North-American Pilot...

— The North-American Pilot, for Newfoundland, Coast of Labradore, and Gulf and River St. Laurence. L: Sayer & Bennett, 1784-83 [but some charts pbd 1786]. 2 vols. Folio, contemp russia gilt; a remboitage. With dedication leaf, index & 35 charts. Some fold tears & repairs; tp of Vol II has some letters strengthened in 3d line; minor soiling. CNY Oct 8 (190) $18,000

Northcote, James, 1746-1831

— One Hundred Fables, Original and Selected.... L, 1828-33. 2 vols. 8vo, contemp half mor by Webb & Hunt. b Mar 11 (108) £70

Norton, Alice Mary
— The Beast Master. NY: Harcourt, [1959]. In d/j. Bookplate inscr by Norton affixed to front free endpaper. pba July 9 (213) $80; sg June 11 (257) $110
— Ride, Proud Rebel! Cleveland: World, [1961]. In d/j. cb Sept 19 (172) $75

Norton, Andre, Pseud. See: Norton, Alice Mary

Nostits und Jaenckendorf, G. A. E. von
— Beschreibung der koenigl. saechsischen Heil-und Verpflegungsanstalt Sonnenstein. Dresden, 1829. 2 vols in 3. 8vo, contemp half sheep. Old stamp on titles. sg Nov 14 (92) $375

Nostradamus, Michel de, 1503-66
— Les Merveilleuses Centuries et prophetes. Geneva: Alliance des Bibliophiles, 1961. One of 880. Illus by Jean Gradassi. 4to, mor with metal cartouchesis. b&b Feb 19 (94) $225
— The True Prophecies or Prognostications. L, 1672. Folio, contemp calf; spine ends chipped, covers detached. sg Oct 24 (240) $900
— Les Veritables Propheties.... Turin: Reycends & Guibert, 1720. 12mo, contemp calf; rebacked, front cover detached. sg Oct 24 (241) $200

Notes...
— Notes and Queries. 1849-79. 49 vols. 4to, contemp half calf. L Nov 14 (430) £420

Notitia...
— Notitia Dignitatum: Notitia utraque cum Orientis tum Occidentis ultra Arcadii Honoriique Caesarum tempora.... Basel: Froben, 1552. Folio, contemp vellum; spine ends worn, soiled. Ck Nov 29 (300) £750
— Notitia utraque cum orientis tum occidentis ultra Arcadii Honoriique Caesarum tempora.... Basel: Froben, 1552. Folio, modern vellum. Some browning. FD Dec 2 (33) DM1,500

Nott, John
— The Cook's and Confectioner's Dictionary.... L, 1723. 8vo, modern calf gilt. With frontis. Lacking C4, E2, E6, F1, Q7 & Bb8; some browning & spotting. S May 14 (998) £400 [Lerner]
3d Ed. L, 1726. 8vo, modern cloth. Library markings. Sold w.a.f. O Mar 31 (145) $160

Nott, Stanley Charles
— A Catalogue of Rare Chinese Jade Carvings. St. Augustine, 1940. 4to, cloth. Library markings. sp June 18 (374) $55
— Chinese Jade Throughout the Ages. NY, 1937. Cloth. With 148 plates, 39 in color. sg Sept 6 (204) $80

Novak, William. See: Reagan & Novak

Novena...
— Novena al Sacratisimo Corazon de Jesus. Buenos Aires: Ninos Espositos, 1785. 16mo, later vellum. sg Dec 5 (190) $90
— Novena del Santo de los Santos Nuestro Senor Jesu-Christo Sacramentado. Buenos Aires: Ninos Espositos, 1784. 16mo, later vellum. sg Dec 5 (191) $90

Noverre, Jean Georges, 1727-1810
— Lettres sur la danse et sur les ballets.... Paris, [1927]. One of 550. 4to, orig wraps. Inscr by Andre Levinson to John Mason Brown. Met Apr 28 (740) $70

Nozeman, Cornelis —& Others
— Nederlandsche vogelen, volgens hunne Huishouding, Aert, en Eigenschappen Beschreeven. Amst., 1770-1829. Vols I-IV only, in 1 vol. Folio, modern blind-stamped calf gilt. With 1 engraved title only, ptd title to Vol I only (torn & repaired & 155 hand-colored plates only. Sold w.a.f. C Oct 30 (289) £8,000 [Arader]
Anr copy. 5 vols. Folio, unbound & uncut in 5 19th-cent calf boxes; spines & joints restored. With 5 engraved titles & 249 (of 250) hand-colored plates. S June 25 (55) £16,000 [Shapero]

Nugent, Thomas, 1700?-72
— Travels through Germany.... L, 1768. 2 vols. 8vo, contemp sheep. With folding map & 10 folding plates. Small piece missing from 3 plates. sg May 21 (78) $80

Numerals...
— The Numerals and the Pence Table Fancifully Depicted. L: J. Harris, [watermarked 1818]. 16mo, orig half lea; rubbed & marked. 32 engraved leaves, each with hand-colored illusts. Some soiling. Moon 584a. S Apr 28 (79) £250 [Quaritch]

Nunez de Avandano, Pedro
— De exequendis mandatis regum Hispaniae. Madrid, 1593. Bound with: Aviso de Cacadores, y Caca....Madrid, 1593. 4th Ed of 1st work; 2d Ed of 2d work. Folio, old vellum; soiled. First work with small wormhole at upper foremargin from 2h5 onwards; some shaving; 2 leaves torn along vertical crease without loss. S June 25 (320) £5,000 [Quaritch]

Nuova...
— Nuova Raccolta di cento principali vedute...dell'alma Citta' di Roma.... Rome, 1796. Oblong 4to, old mor over contemp bds; soiled & worn. With 99 (of 100) plates & 2 partly-folding plates bound in. Interleaved with blanks. Sold w.a.f. DW Mar 4

(41) £400

Nuovo...

— Nuovo Portolano non piu stampato molto particolare de'l levante e de'l Ponente. Venice: Paulo Gerardo [per Comin da Trino di Monferrato], 1544. 4to, modern half mor. Some underlinings & annotations; a few leaves browned or stained; a few headlines shaved. S June 30 (365) £800 [Bank of Cyprus]

Nuremberg

— Vollstaendiges Nuernbergisches Koch-Buch. Nuermberg: W.M. Endter 1691. 4to, contemp calf gilt armorial bdg; spine def, lower joint weak. With 15 folding tables & 2 folding plates (1 with tears & repairs). S Dec 5 (228) £3,400 [Segal]

Nuremberg Chronicle

— SCHEDEL, HARTMANN. - Das Buch der Croniken.... Nuremberg: Anton Koberger, 23 Dec 1493. Folio, contemp Nuremberg blind-stamped calf over wooden bds; lea abraded in places & joints worn & repaired. Complete copy with full contemp coloring of woodcuts & with 3 illuminated armorial endleaves dated 1508. Tp bound with recto facing 2r & pasted to front flyleaf; tp soiled; some repaired tears. 297 leaves. Goff S-309. Blum copy. P June 25 (322) $240,000

— SCHEDEL, HARTMANN. - Liber chronicarum. Nuremberg: Anton Koberger, 12 July 1493. Folio, 17th-cent calf over oak bds, tooled in blind; corners, worn, rebacked, orig spine laid down. 64 lines & headline; types 16:110Gb (text) & 9:165G (headings);l 2- & 3-line pearled lombard initials. 645 woodblooks repeated to a total of 1,809 impressions. Folios CCLXVIIII & CCLX supplied from anr copy with upper margins extended; several other leaves supplied; lower margin of tp extended without touching text; other stains; some repaired margins & corners. 324 (of 326) leaves; lacking 2 blanks. Goff S-30. Manney copy. P Oct 11 (271) $39,000

Anr copy. 1 leaf only. Double-page world map. S Feb 26 (698) £2,300 [Rizzo]

Anr copy. Folio, mor gilt by Riviere; joints worn. Some headlines shaved; some margins stained or extended; tears & repairs in World Map; some worming at end. 326 leaves. Goff S-307. S May 28 (29) £16,000

Anr copy. 18th-cent calf. 64 lines & headlines; double column; gothic letter; with 1809 woodcuts, including 1164 repeats & large double-page map of Europe at end colored by hand (just shaved at fore-margins); text rubricated throughout; large capitals in red & blue; coats of arms on ff. 203-5 colored by hand. Lower margins of f.21 restored; other marginal repairs. 326 leaves. Goff S-307. S June 25 (284) £23,000 [George]

Nuttall, Thomas, 1786-1859

— A Journal of Travels into the Arkansa Territory, During the Year 1819.... Phila., 1821. 1st Ed. 8vo, orig bds; worn, spine gone. With folding map & 5 aquatints. F Mar 26 (705) $1,450

Anr copy. Later half mor. Map backed & torn at folds, with some pieces gone; 1 plate stamped on verso; tp tape-stained & with a few small tears; library stamp on tp & 1 other page. K Sept 29 (296) $225

— Manual of Ornithology of the United States and Canada. Cambr., 1832-34. 2 vols. 12mo, orig cloth; repaired. bbc June 29 (140) $250

Nutter, M. E.

— Carlisle in the Olden Time. Carlisle, 1835. Folio, orig half lea. With frontis, litho title & 16 plates on india paper. C Oct 30 (60) £200 [Spelman]

Anr copy. Orig cloth with lea spine. With litho title with hand-colored vignette & with 17 hand-colored plates. C May 20 (94) £1,250 [Quaritch]

Nutting, Wallace, 1861-1941

Nutting, Wallace, 1861-1914

Nutting, Wallace, 1861-1941

— Furniture Treasury. NY, 1948-49. Vols I-II. Cloth. LH May 17 (686) $80

Nutting, Wallace, 1861-1914

— Old New England Pictures. Framingham, 1913. One of 200. Folio, orig mor; worn. With 35 tinted plates. rs Oct 17 (69A) $1,300

Nylandt, Petrus. See: Van der Groen & Nylandt

O

O Cathasaigh, P. See: O'Casey, Sean

Oakleaf, Joseph Benjamin

— Lincoln Bibliography. Cedar Rapids, Iowa, 1925. One of 100, sgd. Half mor. bbc June 29 (232) $280

Oates, Joyce Carol

— By the North Gate. NY, [1963]. In d/j. Sgd. sg Dec 12 (308) $250

O'Brien, Capt. C.

— A Series of Fifteen Views in Ceylon. L, 1864. Folio, orig cloth. With tinted litho title, litho dedication & 7 (of 15) tinted plates. S June 25 (111) £400 [Remington]

Obsequens, Julius

— Prodigiorum liber. Lyons: J. Tornaesius, 1589. 16mo, contemp vellum. Some browning. SI June 10 (694) LIt300,000

Observations. See: Whately, Thomas

O'Callaghan, Edmund Bailey, 1797-1880

— The Documentary History of the State of New York. Albany, 1849-51. 4 vols. 4to, orig cloth; spine ends frayed, joints torn. Old dampstains at margins; library markings. bbc Sept 23 (342) $90

Anr copy. 4 vols. 8vo, cloth; worn. O Dec 17 (137) $90

O'Casey, Sean, 1880-1964

— The Flying Wasp. L, 1937. 1st Ed. In d/j. Inscr. sg Dec 12 (309) $110

— The Plough and the Stars. L, 1926. Half cloth. Half-title browned. Inscr to Tom Kealy. sg Dec 12 (311) $375

— The Silver Tassie. L, 1928. Inscr. sg Dec 12 (312) $100

— Songs of the Wren. Dublin, [1918]. New Series, No 1. Single sheet, 8vo, unopened. sg Dec 12 (313) $110

— The Story of the Irish Citizen Army. Dublin, 1919. 1st Issue. Ptd wraps. sg Dec 12 (315) $325

Anr copy. Ptd wraps; spine chipped & split. Creasing to lower corner of contents. wa Dec 9 (216) $160

— Windfalls. L, 1934. In d/j with 1 short closed tear. Inscr to Katharine Gregory. sg Dec 12 (317) $175

— Within the Gates. L, 1933. Half cloth Corners bumped. Inscr to Lady Astor. sg Dec 12 (319) $90

Occoni, A.

— Imperatorum Romanorum numismata. Milan, 1730. Folio, contemp calf; worn. SI June 10 (696) LIt700,000

Ockley, Simon, 1678-1720

— The Conquest of Syria, Persia, and Aegypt, by the Saracens. L, 1708. 8vo, later calf. sg Jan 9 (147) $225

O'Connell, James F.

— A Residence of Eleven Years in New Holland and the Caroline Islands.... Bost., 1841. 12mo, orig cloth; stained, repaired. With 2 wood-engraved plates. Minor repairs touching text; some soiling. S Nov 15 (1323) £200 [Lewis]

O'Conner, Jack

— The Big Game Animals of North America. NY, [1961]. Folio, cloth. sg May 21 (79) $150

See also: Derrydale Press

— Hunting in the Rockies. NY, 1947. Cloth; some wear. Koopman copy. O Oct 29 (225) $80

— Sheep and Sheep Hunting. NY: Winchester, [1974]. In d/j. Koopman copy. O Oct 29 (227) $110

O'Connor, Roger

— Chronicles of Eri; being the History of...the Irish People. L, 1822. 2 vols. 8vo, half russia. Some pencilled underlinings. bba Jan 16 (158) £65 [Freddie]

O'Day, Nell

— A Catalogue of Books Printed by John Henry Nash. San Francisco: John Henry Nash, 1937. One of 500. b&b Feb 19 (239) $90; cb Jan 16 (105) $90; sg Oct 31 (280) $80

Odell, George Clinton Densmore

— Annals of the New York Stage. NY, 1927-49. 15 vols. Worn & shaken. O Dec 17 (139) $260

Anr copy. Library markings. sg Oct 17 (76) $1,000

O'Donoghue, Freeman. See: British Museum

O'Donovan, Edmond

— The Merv Oasis. L, 1882. 2 vols. 8vo, orig cloth; upper cover of Vol II marked. With port, 15 plates & facsimiles & folding map in pocket at end of Vol II. Map repaired. S Nov 15 (1297) £240 [Maggs]

Anr copy. Cloth. sg Jan 9 (159) $175

Oeconomische...

— Oeconomische Nachrichten. Leipzig, 1750-63. Vols 1-15 [all pbd]. 8vo, half vellum; some spines def. S Dec 5 (340) £500 [Quaritch]

Oeconomy...

— The Oeconomy of Human Life. L, 1751. 1st Ed. 8vo, modern half mor; new endpapers. With frontis. bba June 25 (43) £50 [Land]

Oeder, Georg Christian von

— Flora Danica. Copenhagen, 1761-70. ("Icones plantarum sponte nascentium in Regnis Daniae et Norvegiae....") Vols 1, 3 & 9 only. half calf & russia gilt; worn, 1 cover detached. With 540 plate, 360 hand-colored. Sold w.a.f. S May 14 (1049) £1,500 [Hermans]

Oenslager, Donald

— Stage Design: Four Centuries of Scenic Invention. NY, 1975. In d/j. Inscr to Mr & Mrs John Mason Brown. Met Apr 28 (758) $110

Oersted, Hans Christian

— Recherches sur l'identite des forces chimiques et electriques. Paris, 1813. 8vo, contemp half calf. sg Nov 14 (274) $1,900

Oesterricher, Johann Heinrich, 1805-43

— Anatomischer Atlas oder bildliche Darstellung des Menschlichen Koerpers. Munich, 1845. 2 vols. 8vo & folio, half lea; not uniform, worn. With 180 plates. S Feb 11 (603) £700 [American Book Store]

— Atlas of Human Anatomy. Cincinnati, [1879]. Text by John A. Jeancon. Atlas only. contemp half lea; needs rebacking. With 197 plates. sg Feb 13 (193) $200

Official...

See also: United States of America

— Official Records of the Union and Confederate Navies in the War of the Rebellion. Wash., 1894-1922. Series I, in 30 vols, plus 1961 Index. sg Dec 5 (66) $425

Officina Bodoni

— The Officina Bodoni: The Operation of a Hand-Press during the First Six Years of its Work. Paris & NY, 1929. One of 500. Folio, cloth, in d/j. cb Oct 17 (697) $425

Officium

— 1545. - Officium Beate Marie Virginis. Venice: Marcolini. 8vo, contemp blind-tooled goatskin; worn, clasps removed. 22 lines & headline; type 95G; ptd in red & black throughout; with full-page emblematicc title-cut & arabesque border, 4 cuts of Evangelists & 12 full-page blocks repeated to 22 impressions. Marginal worming at beginning & end; some stains; upper border strips shaved in a few cases. C Dec 16 (68) £6,000 [Panini]

— 1585. - Officium Defunctorum ad usum Maronitarum S.D.N. Gregorii XII Pont. Max. impensa Chalaicis characteribus impressum. Rome: Doninicus Basa. 4to, 19th-cent half calf. Syriac text. Old dampstaining. C June 24 (169) £500 [Mediolanum]

— 1646. - L'Office de la Semaine Saincte.... Paris 8vo, contemp mor gilt; rubbed, clasps missing. bba May 14 (18) £130 [Wilkinson]

— 1716. - Office de la semaine sainte, latin et francois. Paris: Nicolas Pepie. 12mo, contemp mor gilt with arms of the duchesse d'Orleans [Olivier 2564]. S Feb 11 (567) £240 [Voltaire]

— 1732. - Office de la Semaine Sainte. Paris: Jacques Colombat. 8vo, contemp mor gilt to a post-fanfare design, with arms of Louis XV. S May 28 (138) £50 [Zioni]

— 1763. - The Divine Office for the use of Laity. [N.p.] 4 vols. 12mo, 18th-cent mor gilt. Sold w.a.f. S Feb 11 (564) £500 [Saave Fianinetta]

— 1777. - Officium beatae Mariae Virginis. Venice: ex typographia Balleoniana. 8vo, contemp mor over woodent bds gilt, with silver gilt plaquettes with the Virgin holding a rosary with the Child on the upper cover & St. Anne teaching the Virgin to read on the lower cover; minute insect damage at the foot of the upper cover. S May 28 (103) £1,100 [Franklin]

— 1787. - Office de l'Eglise en latin et en francois. Rouen: P. Seyer. 4 vols. 12mo, contemp mor gilt. Sold w.a.f. S May 28 (142) £1,300 [Shapero]

Offner, Richard

— A Critical and Historical Corpus of Florentine Painting. NY, 1931-[84]. Section 3, Vols 1-9 & Section 4, Vols 1-6 & Supplement. S Feb 11 (156) £2,800 [Doll]

O'Flaherty, Liam

— The Informer. L, 1925. 1st Ed. In d/j. sg Apr 30 (352) $750

1st American Ed. NY: Knopf, 1925. Mor with mor onlay. Inscr. cb Sept 19 (176) $375

— Joseph Conrad, an Appreciation. L: E. Lahr, [1930]. One of 100. String-tied paper wrap. cb Dec 12 (39) $75

Ogden, James, Angler

— Ogden on Fly Tying, etc. Cheltenham, 1897. 8vo, cloth; worn, inner joints broken. Koopman copy. O Oct 29 (228) $160

Ogden, John Cosens, 1751-1800

— A Tour through Upper and Lower Canada.... Litchfield, 1799. 1st Ed. 16mo, contemp calf; rubbed. Foxed & soiled. O Nov 26 (135) $425

Ogilby, John, 1600-76

— Asia, the First Part.... L, 1673. 1st Ed. Vol I (all pbd). Folio, contemp calf gilt; broken & repaired. Lacking 1 plate. FD Dec 2 (436) DM2,500

Anr copy. Bound with: Montanus. Atlas Japanensis...English'd by John Ogilby. L, 1670. old calf; worn & broken, spine gone. Lacking some plates from both vols. Sold w.a.f. O Feb 25 (148) $2,500

— Britannia.... L, 1675. 1st Ed. Vol I (all pbd). Folio, contemp calf; worn, rebacked, upper cover detached, frontis detached. With frontis, general map & 100 road maps. Many maps with later annotations in pencil. Later ink annotations by Thomas Langton. C Oct 30 (155) £4,500 [Vanbrugh]

Anr copy. Contemp calf; hinges split & worn. First road-map with contemp repair. John Evelyn's copy. S June 25 (268) £6,200 [Arader]

Ogilby, John, 1600-76 —& Senex, John, d.1740

— The Roads through England Delineated. L, 1759. Oblong 4to, orig calf; worn. With general map & 101 strip road-maps on 51 leaves. Some tears & fraying; general map trimmed; final 3 leaves stained. pn Apr 23 (303) £260

Ogilvie, Katharine Nairn —& Ogilvie, Patrick

[-] The Trial of Katharine Narin and Patrick Ogilvie for the Crimes of Incest and Murder. Edin., 1765. 8vo, half calf. K July 12 (505) $100

Ogilvie, Patrick. See: Ogilvie & Ogilvie

Ogle, George, 1704-46

— Antiquities Explained. Being a Collection of Figured Gems. L, 1737. Vol I (all pbd). 4to, contemp calf gilt; worn. With frontis & 50 plates. Some foxing. bba May 28 (28) £75 [Graves-Johnston]

O'Hara, Frank

— In Memory of my Feelings: a Selection of Poems. NY, [1967]. Folio, loose as issued in half cloth. K Sept 29 (297) $90; sg Jan 30 (116) $300

Anr copy. Half cloth; loose as issued. sg June 11 (259) $200

O'Hara, John, 1905-70

— Appointment in Samarra. NY, [1934]. 1st Ed. In edge-repaired d/j. Ns laid in. P June 17 (289) $800

1st Issue. In pictorial d/j. Epstein copy. sg Apr 30 (353) $3,000

— Butterfield 8. NY: Harcourt Brace, [1935]. In d/j with short tears on rear panel. sg June 11 (260) $200

— The Doctor's Son. NY, [1935]. In chipped d/j. sg Dec 12 (324) $350

Ohnefalsch-Richter, Max

— Kypros die Bibel und Homer. Berlin, 1893. 2 vols. 4to, orig half calf; joints cracked. With frontis & 208 plates & maps. Tp of text vol stained. S June 30 (64) £750 [Christodoulou]

Ohrling, J. See: Lindahl & Ohrling

Old...

— Old Master Drawings: A Quarterly Magazine for Students and Collectors. L, 1926-40. Vols I-XIV (complete set) in 7 vols. 4to, cloth; 1 spine marked. S Feb 11 (155) £100 [Creed]

— The Old Water-Colour Society.... L, 1924-27. Vols 1-4. 4to, orig half cloth. DW Mar 11 (842) £75

Old Bookseller. See: West, William

Oldfield, Otis. See: Grabhorn Printing

Oldham, James Basil

— Blind Panels of English Binders. Cambr., 1958. 1st Ed. Folio, orig cloth, in soiled d/j. bba May 28 (496) £75 [Laywood]

Anr copy. Orig cloth. bba May 28 (497) £75 [Cox]

Anr copy. Orig cloth, in d/j. O Sept 24 (189) $100

— English Blind-Stamped Bindings. Cambr., 1952. 1st Ed, one of 750. Folio, orig cloth. bba June 25 (157) £70 [Forster]

Oliphant, Laurence, 1829-88

— Minnesota and the Far West. Edin. & L, 1855. 8vo, early half calf; backstrip scuffed, covers soiled. Some foxing. bbc Sept 23 (340) $110

— Narrative of the Earl of Elgin's Mission to China and Japan.... L, 1860. 2d Ed. 2 vols. 8vo, later half mor. bba Sept 19 (110) £90 [Hildebrandt]

Oliver, John

— A Present to be given to Teeming Women.... Bost., 1694. 1st American Ed. 12mo, 18th-cent sheep; covers detached. Small tear to inner margin of tp affecting 1 letter; tear to D1 with loss to catchword & 1 word of text; D2 torn with loss of c.8 words; 2 tears to M2 affecting 3 or 4 words; some tears; dampstaining. CNY June 9 (160) $2,500

Oliver, Peter

— A New Chronicle of the Compleat Angler. NY, 1936. cb Oct 17 (703) $55; O Dec 17 (140) $60

Olivier, Eugene —& Others

— Manuel de l'amateur de reliures armoriees francaises. Paris, 1924-38. One of 1,000 on velin. 30 vols, including Index. 4to, loose in orig wraps. DW Jan 29 (336) £420

Anr copy. Cloth, orig wraps bound in. sg Oct 31 (41) $1,200

Anr copy. Vols 1-24 (of 30). 4to, Orig wraps; worn & soiled. wa Mar 5 (599) $375

Olivier, Guillaume Antoine

— Voyage dans L'Empire Othoman, L'Egypte et la Perse. Paris, [1801-7]. 3 vols; without Atlas. 4to, contemp half calf. With 50 plates Library stamps on titles. S June 30 (173) £600 [Maggs]

Olivier, J., Fencing Master

— Fencing Familiarized.... L & York, 1771. 1st Ed. 8vo, later cloth. With folding frontis & 8 plates. Minor marginal worming on several leaves. sg Mar 26 (219) $225

Anr Ed. L, 1780. 8vo, contemp calf. With 14 plates. sg Jan 9 (296) $200

Anr copy. Half mor gilt. sg Mar 26 (220) $400

Anr copy. Modern half calf gilt. sg Mar 26 (221) $225

Anr copy. Contemp sheep; rebacked. sg Mar 26 (222) $425

Olmstead, Frederick Law, 1822-1903

— A Journey through Texas.... NY, 1857. 1st Ed. 12mo, orig cloth; spine with inexpert repairs. With frontis & folding map. sg June 18 (524) $70

Olschki, Leo Samuel

— Choix de livres anciens rares et curieux.... Florence, 1907-40. 12 vols. SI June 10 (702) LIt2,800,000

Olympic Games

— Die Olympischen Spiele 1936 in Berlin und Garmisch-Partenkirchen. Berlin, 1936. 2 vols. 4to, cloth. sg Jan 9 (297) $300

Oman, Sir Charles, 1860-1946

— A History of the Peninsular War. Oxford, 1902-30. 7 vols. Orig cloth; rubbed, some joints cracked. Stamps on titles of Vols I & II. pn July 16 (49) £400 [Maggs]

Omar Khayyam, d.c.1123

The Rubaiyat

— 1879. - L. 8vo, half lea; worn, corners bumped. wa Mar 5 (73) $65

— 1884. - Bost. Illus by Elihu Vedder & with script-text by him. Folio, cloth. cb Jan 9 (218) $110

Anr copy. Orig cloth; spine & tips frayed. Some rubbing & soiling. wa Mar 5 (622) $110

— 1901. - L. One of 500. Illus by B. McManus. Orig half cloth. bba July 9 (316) £190 [Collinge & Clark]

— L: Hodder & Stoughton [1909]. - Illus by Edmund Dulac. 4to, orig cloth. With 20 colored plates. sg Jan 30 (45) $150

— 1909. - L. Illus by Gilbert James. 4to, cloth, in d/j. With 16 colored plates. kh Nov 11 (181) A$200

Anr copy. Illus by Willy Pogany. Folio, bds, in d/j. sg Jan 30 (130) $100

— [1909]. - L: Hodder & Stoughton One of 750. Illus by Edmund Dulac. 4to, orig vellum gilt; soiled. With 20 mtd colored plates. Ck Dec 11 (152) £420

— [1910]. - Paris Illus by Edmund Dulac. 4to, orig cloth; spine glazed & ends frayed. With 10 tipped-on color plates & 19 mtd color text plates. Marginal soiling. wa Apr 9 (272) $100

— [1911]. - L. One of 550. Reproduced from a calligraphic Ms written & illuminated by Sangorski & Sutcliffe. 4to, cloth; worn. O Jan 14 (140) $90

— 1913. - L. One of 250. Illus by Rene Bull. 4to, orig cloth. DW Dec 11 (404) £135

— [c.1915]. - L. One of 200. Illus by Edmund Dulac. 4to, cloth. O Mar 31 (147) $100

Anr copy. Cloth; spine faded. With 12 tipped-in color plates. sp Nov 24 (212) $110

— 1919. - L & Edin. Illus by Frank Brangwyn. 4to, cloth. With 15 mtd colored plates. kh Nov 11 (180) A$60

— 1920. - L. Illus by Frank Brangwyn. 4to, cloth. wd Dec 12 (426) $100

— [1924]. - L. Trans by Frederic Baron Corvo; illus by Hamzeh Carr. 4to, cloth; worn. With 16 colored plates. O Jan 14 (51) $80; O Jan 14 (167) $100

— 1930. - L. Illus by Willy Pogany. 4to, orig cloth, in d/j. With 12 colored plates. bba Apr 9 (321) £120 [Ulysses]

Anr copy. Orig cloth, in chipped d/j. bbc Apr 27 (388) $50

Anr copy. Orig cloth, in d/j. K July 12 (416) $160

One of 750. Mor extra with oval panel containing Eve in the Garden of Eden, by Riviere. CNY Dec 5 (431) $1,700

One of 1,250. Orig mor gilt with colored mor onlays on upper cover; upper cover & spine scuffed. Some leaves soiled or browned. S Apr 28 (42) £170 [Riex]

Onassis, Jacqueline Bouvier Kennedy —& Radziwill, Lee Bouvier

— One Special Summer. NY, 1974. One of 500. Sgd. cb Sept 19 (11) $90; wa Oct 19 (308) $290; wa Dec 9 (252) $240; wa Apr 9 (288) $210

One of the Cloth. See: Neckclothitania...

One who Thinks for Himself. See: Cruikshank, George

O'Neill, Eugene, 1888-1953

— Ah, Wilderness! NY, [1933]. Inscr. sg Dec 12 (325) $150

— Before Breakfast. NY, 1916. 1st Ed. Wraps; spine worn. In: The Provincetown Plays. Third Series. Met Apr 28 (744) $200

— Desire Under the Elms. NY, 1925. In chipped d/j. sg Dec 12 (327) $90

— The Emperor Jones. NY, 1928. One of 775 L.p. copies. Illus by Alexander King. 4to, half cloth, in d/j. With 8 colored plates. sg

Dec 12 (328) $200

One of 775 L.p. copies, sgd. Half cloth; corners worn. With 8 colored plates. sg June 11 (261) $130

— The Great God Brown. The Fountain. The Moon of the Caribbbees and other Plays. NY, 1926. In d/j. sg Dec 12 (329) $100

— The Hairy Ape. NY, 1929. One of 775 L.p. copies. Illus by Alexander King. 4to, half-cloth, in d/j. sg Dec 12 (331) $225

— The Iceman Cometh. NY, 1982. Illus by Leonard Baskin. sg Sept 26 (188) $100

— Lazarus Laughed. NY, 1927. One of 775. bba Feb 19 (134) $125; K July 12 (366) $70; sg Dec 12 (332) $70

— Mourning Becomes Electra. NY, [1931]. Cloth. With ALs to John Mason Brown, 2 Apr 1932, laid in. Met Apr 28 (751) $1,300

One of 550. sg Dec 12 (334) $225

— The Provincetown Plays. NY, 1916. 1st Series. Orig wraps, in remnant of d/j. sg Dec 12 (337) $300

3d Series. Orig wraps, in remnants of d/j. sg Dec 12 (338) $200

— Strange Interlude. NY, 1928. One of 775, sgd. Orig vellum over bds; soiled. Gertrude Lawrence's copy. K July 12 (365) $90

One of 775. Orig vellum over bds. sg Dec 12 (335) $250

— Thirst. Bost., [1914]. 1st Ed. In d/j. CNY Dec 5 (305) $800

Anr copy. Orig bds. Met Apr 28 (874A) $60

— Works. NY, 1924. One of 1,200. 2 vols. Half cloth; bumped. Sgd. Met Apr 28 (752) $70

Ongania, Ferdinando, 1842-1911

— L'Art de l'imprimerie a Venise. Venice, 1895. Folio, vellum, orig wraps bound in. O July 14 (144) $160

— La Basilica di San Marco in Venezia. Venice, [1877-92]. 13 livraisons of plates & 11 vols of text. 4to & folio, half cloth folders, orig wraps or vellum. With 847 plates, some colored. Sold w.a.f. S Feb 11 (326) £1,500 [Halwas]

— Early Venetian Printing Illustrated. Venice, 1895. cb Oct 17 (705) $50

Onomatologica...

— Onomatologica curiosa, artificiosa et magica oder ganz natuerliches Zauber-Lexicon. Frankfurt, 1759. 8vo, vellum; spine def. S Dec 5 (280) £500 [Schumann]

Oppe, Adolf Paul

— Thomas Rowlandson: His Drawings and Water-Colours. L: The Studio, 1923. Folio, half vellum; soiled. kh Nov 11 (182) A$60

One of 200. Vellum gilt; soiled, spine bumped. With 96 plates. sp Feb 6 (209) $70

Oppen, Edward A.

— A Description of the Northern Territory of South Australia.... Hertford, 1864. 8vo, cloth, orig maps bound in. With folding map. S June 25 (254) £950 [Arnold]

Oppert, Ernest

— A Forbidden Land: Voyages to the Corea. NY, 1880. 8vo, cloth. Maps with repairable tears. sg Jan 9 (160) $175

Oppianus

— De venatione libri IIII. Leiden: Plantin, 1597. 8vo, 17th-cent vellum gilt. S July 1 (532) £400 [Poole]

Oracles...

— The Oracles, Containing some Particulars of the History of Billy and Kitty Wilson.... L: J. Harris, [c.1803]. 32mo, orig bds. Contemp scribbling to frontis, tp & endpapers. Attributed to Stephen Jones. bba July 23 (112) £360 [Laywood]

Orange, James. See: Chater Collection, Sir Catchick P.

Orationes...

— Orationes clarorum hominum, vel honoris officiique causa ad principes.... Venice, 1559. 4to, 20th-cent mor gilt by Gozzi. Ck Nov 29 (12) £450

Orbigny, Alcide Dessalines d', 1802-57

— Voyage pittoresque dans les deux Ameriques.... Paris, 1836. 4to, contemp half lea. SI June 10 (704) LIt350,000

Orcutt, William Dana

— The Book in Italy during the Fifteenth and Sixteenth Centuries. L, [1928]. One of 750. 4to, half cloth. cb Oct 17 (1707) $95

Anr copy. Half cloth; worn. O May 26 (140) $80; sp Sept 22 (465) $60

— The Kingdom of Books. Bost., 1927. One of 475. cb Oct 17 (711) $60

— The Magic of the Book. Bost., 1930. One of 375. 8vo, half vellum. cb Feb 27 (80) $70

Ordeman, John T.

— Frank W. Benson. Master of the Sporting Print. Brooklandville: Pvtly ptd, [1983]. One of 50. 4to, cloth, in d/j. O Apr 28 (182) $110

Ordonnances. See: Golden Fleece

O'Reilly, Edward

— An Irish-English Dictionary. Dublin, 1817. 4to, contemp calf gilt; rebacked. Some foxing. bba Feb 27 (310) £50 [Elliott]

Orfila, Mathieu Joseph Bonaventure

— Secours a donner aux personnees empoisonees ou asphyxiees. Paris, 1818. 12mo, contemp sheep gilt. Some foxing. sg Nov 14 (93) $300

Orgel, Stephen —& Strong, Roy

— The Theatre of the Stuart Court.... Berkeley & Los Angeles, 1973. 2 vols. Folio, orig cloth, in d/js. b Mar 11 (60) £110

Anr copy. Cloth, in d/js. bba Jan 16 (279) £160 [Kyle]

Origen

— Works. Paris: J. B. Ascensianis, [1512-19]. ("Primus-[quartus] tomus operum.") 4 parts in 2 vols. Folio, 18th-cent sheep; extremities bumped, joints weak. Marginal staining; Vol II lacking final blank. C June 24 (335) £150 [Rix]

Anr copy. Vol II (of 2). Folio, contemp pigskin over wooden bds with brass catches & clasps; front cover wormed. Opening leaves wormed. sg Mar 12 (242) $225

Orleans, Charles d', 1394-1465

— Poemes. Paris: Teriade, 1950. One of 1,230. Illus by Henri Matisse. Folio, unsewn in orig wraps. Inscr by Matisse on a prelim leaf & on tp verso. S Dec 5 (312) £1,600 [Tannenbaum]

Orleans Collection, Louis Philip Joseph, Duc d'

— Description des principales pierres gravees du cabinet de.... Paris, 1780-84. 2 vols. Folio, 19th-cent vellum. Repaired tears; waterspotting. SI Dec 5 (327) LIt480,000

Orleans Collection, Louis Philip Joseph, Duc de

— [Sale Catalogue] A Catalogue of the Orleans' Italian Pictures.... L, [1798]. 2 parts in 1 vol. 8vo, contemp lea; rubbed, spine def. Copy belonging to the son of the collector & then to W. Buchanan. S Feb 11 (154) £1,000 [Doll]

Orleans Collection, Louis Philip Joseph, Duc d'

— Description des principales pierres gravees du cabinet de M. le Duc d'Orleans de.... Paris, 1780-84. 2 vols. Folio, mor gilt by Derome le jeune, with his ticket, dated 1785. C Dec 16 (130) £6,500 [Breslauer]

Orme, Edward

— An Essay on Transparent Prints, and on Transparencies in General. L, 1807. 1st Ed. 4to, orig bds; worn & soiled. With frontis & 14 (of 15) plates, 9 hand-colored. Lacking final leaf. S Nov 14 (193) £420 [Quadrille]

— Historic, Military, and Naval Anecdotes.... L, [1819]. 4to, contemp mor gilt. With 40 hand-colored plates Minor spotting to a few leaves. C Oct 30 (113) £1,100 [Marlborough]

Early Issue with title dated & pre-publication watermarks. Modern half mor gilt. With 40 hand-colored plates. One text leaf with tear repaired. L.p. copy. C May 20 (95) £2,300 [Traylen]

Anr Ed. L, [plates watermarked 1831-34]. 4to, orig mor gilt; head of spine repaired. With 40 hand-colored plates. One plate mtd on a guard; some browning or spotting at beginning & end. C May 20 (96) £700 [Page]

— An Historical Memento, Representing the Different Scenes of Public Rejoicing.... L, 1814. Folio, later half mor gilt. With 6 hand-colored plates. Ck Dec 11 (199) £320

Orme, Robert, 1728-1801

— A History of the Military Transactions of the British Nation in Indostan. L, 1773-78. 2 vols in 3. 4to, contemp mor gilt; spine scuffed. With 36 plates & maps, 29 folding. Minor tears to 2 plates; some waterstain in upper margin; some spotting. C Dec 16 (223) £2,000 [Skiathos]

Ormsby, Waterman Lilly, 1809-88

— A Description of the Present System of Bank Note Engraving.... NY, 1852. Folio, orig cloth; rubbed. With 13 plates, including color frontis. Some foxing. sg May 7 (162) $2,200

Orozco, Jose Clement

— Jose Clement Orozco. NY, 1932. 4to, cloth; front inner hinge cracked & repaired. wa Mar 5 (610) $90

Orrery, Roger Boyle, 1st Earl of. See: Boyle, Roger

Orsini, I.

— Storia delle monete de Granduchi di Toscana. Florence, 1760. Folio, contemp calf. SI Dec 5 (961) LIt2,200,000

Orta, Garcia da

— Aromatum et simplicium aliquot medicamentorum apud Indos nascentium historia. Antwerp: Plantin, 1567. 8vo, later vellum; stained. With woodcut initials & 16 illusts, all hand-colored. C May 20 (208) £1,600 [Phelps]

— Aromatum, et simplicum aliquot medicamentorum apud Indos nascentium historia. Antwerp: Plantin, 1593. Bound with: Monardes, Nicholas. Simplicium medicamentorum ex novo orbe delatorum. Antwerp: Plantin, 1593. 8vo, contemp wallet-edged vellum. Ck Oct 31 (135) £800

Orta, Garcia da —& Monardes, Nicholas, 1498-1588

— Dell'historia de i semplici aromati... dall'Indie. Venice, 1589. 2 parts in 1 vol. 8vo, contemp vellum,; soiled. Tp shaved at lower margin; several running titles shaved; some dampstaining to I1-8 of Vol II; some browning & soiling. Ck May 15 (38) £420

Ortelius, Abraham, 1527-98

— Deorum dearumque capita.... Antwerp, 1573. 4to, 19th-cent vellum. With engraved title & 54 plates. Colonna family library stamp on tp. sg Oct 24 (242) $900

Anr Ed. Antwerp, 1573 [but 1582]. 4to, old sheep gilt; some wear. With 60 plates, including title. Lacking colophon leaf dated 1582. sg Sept 6 (208) $300

— Theatre de l'univers, contenant les cartes de tout le monde. Antwerp: Plantin, [1587]. Folio, contemp vellum; endpapers renewed, covers stained, extremities rubbed. With port & 112 engraved mapsheets, the title, port, initials & maps fully colored in a contemp hand. Repairs to mapsheets 3, 6, 11 & 48 with loss to text on recto; a few other repaired tears; maps 12 & 42 each with an abrasion or stain partially effacing several place names; a few fold breaks, some repaired with slight loss; headline of mapsheet 12 cropped; marginal repairs; a few small surface abrasions, 1 affecting 2 letters of text on mapsheet 7; small rusthole to mapsheet 83, affecting 3 letters of text on recto & a place name of the map; some marginal dampstaining. CNY Oct 8 (193) $26,000

— Il Theatro del mondo.... Brescia, 1598. 8vo, contemp vellum; portion missing from spine, worn. With 109 maps. Tp with 2 holes; some manuscripting & library stamp; 2 pages with edges torn; index wormed at edge. S Nov 21 (124) £1,100 [Franks]

— Theatrum oder Schawbuech des Erdtkreys. Antwerp: Plantin, 1580. Folio, old calf; rubbed. With colored title, port & 93 double-page colored plates, a few heightened with gold. Some surface dirt; a few minor repairs without loss; some discoloration of green-painted areas. Koeman III, Ort 16 A. S June 25 (289) £13,000 [Baskes]

— Theatrum orbis terrarum. Antwerp: Aegid. Coppenium Diesth, 20 May 1570. 1st Ed. Folio, modern half vellum. With engraved title & 53 double-page maps. Lower corner of tp repaired not affecting surface; some staining; old repair to inner corner of Piedmont. C Dec 16 (67) £8,000 [Sawyer]

1st Issue. Contemp vellum, with armorial shield; extremities rubbed, covers soiled, upper inner hinge broken. With 53 mapsheets. Engraved title soiiled & margins repaired; 2 small holes to C2 affecting 10 letters; repaired tears to center folds of maps 1, 20 & 36 with slight loss to captions or image; clean fold break to Map 33; marginal repairs & tears; some creases; browning to last text section. CNY Oct 8 (192) $38,000

Anr Ed. Antwerp: Plantin, 1579. 3 parts in 1 vol. Folio, remboitage in later vellum gilt. With port & 90 mapsheets & 3 in the Parergon, all hand-colored. A few maps repaired without loss; foremargins of Map 7 repaired. S June 25 (288) £22,000 [George]

— Theatrum orbis terrarum, dit tonneel des aert-bodems. Antwerp, 1598. Folio, half lea. With engraved title, port & 91 plates, all colored. B Nov 1 (273) HF55,000

— Theatrum orbis terrarum. Antwerp: Plantin, 1612-7. 3 parts in 1 vol. Folio, contemp vellum; stained, inner hinges cracked. With engraved title, port & 166 double-page mapsheets, including the 2 plates of arms & the 3 views. Slightly discolored throughout; some staining to outer margins; tp detached; 9 maps torn along centerfold; outer margins of 11 leaves of the Nomenclator affected by worm. Koeman III Ort 41. C Oct 30 (157) £20,000 [Reiss & Auvermann]

Orthodox...

— The Orthodox Communicant, by Way of Meditation on the Order for the Administration of the Lord's Supper.... L, 1721. 8vo, contemp mor. Engraved throughout. bba May 28 (25) £150 [Cox]

Orville, Jacobus Philippus d'

— Sicula quibus Siciliae veteris rudera.... Amst., 1764. 2 parts in 2 vols. Folio, contemp calf gilt; rubbed. SI June 10 (711) LIt900,000

Orwell, George

— Animal Farm. L, 1945. 1st Ed. In chipped d/j. DW Apr 8 (540) £110

1st American Ed. NY: Harcourt, Brace, [1946]. Advance proof copy. Wraps; some wear. bbc Apr 27 (382) $190

— Keep the Aspidistra Flying. L, 1936. 1st Ed. In stained d/j, chipped at head & foot. Some spotting at beginning. S Dec 12 (128) £600 [Pearson]

— Nineteen Eighty Four. L, 1949. 1st Ed. Orig green d/j; tape repairs. bba Feb 27 (185) £110 [Heuer]

Anr copy. Orig green cloth with orig Evening Standard wrap-around band; spine ends & extremities worn. Manney copy. P Oct 11 (246) $3,500

1st American Ed. NY, [1949]. In worn d/j; front endpaper browned. Stamp on endpaper & half-title. sg June 11 (262) $60

Osbaldiston, William Augustus

— The British Sportsman. L, [1792]. 4to, calf; rubbed. With 42 hand-colored plates. Lacking engraved title; a few leaves torn; some soiling; ink stamp on endpaper; index leaf repaired. Sold w.a.f. pn Mar 19 (371) £190

Osbeck, Pehr

— A Voyage to China and the East Indies. L, 1771. Trans by John Reinhold Forster. 2 vols. 8vo, calf; rubbed; Vol I dampsttained. Sold w.a.f. O Feb 25 (1511) $425

Osborn, Sherard, 1822-75

— Japanese Fragments, with Facsimiles of Illustrations by Artists of Yedo. L, 1861. Orig cloth. With 6 hand-colored plates. cb Sept 26 (167) $225

— Stray Leaves from an Arctic Journal. L, 1852. 8vo, calf gilt. sg Jan 9 (20) $350

Anr copy. With folding map & 4 colored plates, including frontis. sg May 21 (80) $375

Anr copy. Modern half calf. Some foxing. W July 8 (265) £200

Osborne Collection, Edgar

— The Osborne Collection of Early Children's Books. Toronto, 1958-75. Compiled by Judith St. John. 2 vols. 4to, orig cloth. sg Oct 17 (326) $110

Anr copy. Orig cloth; worn. sg Oct 31 (281) $120

Anr Ed. Toronto, 1975. 2 vols. 4to, orig cloth. O Sept 24 (190) $90

Osborne, Francis, 1593-1659

— Advice to a Son. Oxford, 1656. 1st Ed. 8vo, modern bds. S May 13 (784) £260 [Mosley]

Osborne, Thomas, d.1767

— A Collection of Voyages and Travels.... L, 1745. 2 vols. Folio, contemp calf; worn. With 37 maps & charts & 14 plates. 2 leaves holed. George Milne copy. CNY Dec 5 (306) $700

Anr copy. Contemp calf; rebacked, worn, stamped Home Office on covers, new endpapers. With frontis, 15 plates & 36 maps. Browned; 1 map repaired; 2 tears in text. S Feb 26 (775) £620 [Burden]

— Geographia Magane Britanniae. or, Correct Maps of...England, Scotland and Wales. L, 1748. Oblong 4to, old sheep; cover detached. With engraved title, folding map & 60 double-page maps. DW Apr 8 (1107) £780

Osbourne, Lloyd. See: Stevenson & Osbourne

Osgood, Ernest Staples

— The Day of the Cattleman. Minneapolis, 1929. 8vo, In d/j; rubbed. cb Sept 12 (130) $120

Osler, Sir William, 1849-1919

— The Principles and Practice of Medicine. NY, 1892. 1st Ed. 8vo, modern lea; Occasional underscoring. sg Jan 14 (94) $750

Osley, A. S.

— Luminario. An Introduction to the Italian Writing-Books.... Nieuwkoop, 1972. Folio, cloth, in d/j. sg Oct 31 (244) $70

Anr Ed. Nieuwkoop: Miland Publishers, 1972. One of 800. In d/j. cb Oct 17 (715) $110

Osorio y Gomez, Pedro

— Tractado de esgrima a pe' e a cavallo.... Lisbon, 1842. 8vo, later calf gilt, orig wraps bound in. With 24 litho plates. sg Mar 26 (225) $425

Anr copy. Mor gilt. With 24 plates. sg Mar 26 (226) $200

Ostayen, Paul van, 1896-1928

— Bezette stad. Antwerp: Het Sienjaal, 1921. One of 540. 4to, wraps; minor defs. B Nov 1 (1025) HF1,400

Otis, James. See: Kaler, James Otis

Ott, Josef

— Figuren zur Fechtkunst a la contrepointe. [N.p.], c.1850. Oblong 4to, cloth; front cover loose. With 59 plates. Lacking prelims & text. sg Mar 26 (227) $200

— Lithografirte Abbildungen zem ersten Buche des System der Fechtkunst.... Olmuetz: Franz Slawik, 1852-53. 2 parts in 1 vol. Oblong 4to, cloth, orig wraps bound in. With 89 plates. sg Mar 26 (228) $425

Ottley, William Young, 1771-1836

— A Collection of 129 Fac-Similes.... L, 1828. Folio, later half vellum. With 129 plates. F Mar 26 (751) $300

Anr copy. Contemp half vellum; rubbed & soiled. With 129 mtd engravings on india paper & 13 duplicate silver-ptd plates. Some spotting. pn Apr 23 (155) £200 [Harrington]

— An Inquiry into the Origin and Early History of Engraving upon Copper and in

Wood. L, 1816. 2 vols. 4to, contemp half mor; joints & extremities rubbed. With 22 plates. F Mar 26 (354) $175

Anr copy. Early half mor; new calf spines, orig bds worn. Some plates dampstained in margins. wa Apr 9 (227) $350

One of 60 L.p. copies. Contemp half vellum. sp May 7 (163) $275

— The Italian School of Design. L, 1823. Folio, bds; front cover detached. With 84 plates. bba Feb 13 (189) £360 [Corbett]

Ottley, William Young, 1771-1836 —& Tomkins, Peltro William

— Engravings of the most Noble Marquis of Stafford's Collection of Pictures. L, 1818. 4 vols in 2. Folio, contemp mor gilt; rubbed. With 13 plans & 126 sheets of engravings. bba Feb 13 (236) £300 [Nolan]

Anr copy. Contemp half mor; soiled & worn, upper covers of both vols detached. Foxed. W Mar 6 (9) £200

Otto, Adolph Willhelm

— Monstrorum sexcentorum descriptio anatomica.... Vratislava, 1841. Folio, contemp half sheep; spine damaged, loose in bdg. With 30 plates. Spotted; library stamp on tp. sg Nov 14 (95) $800

Otway, Thomas, 1652-85. See: Nonesuch Press

Ouless, Philip John

— Jersey Illustrated. [L, 1864]. Oblong 8vo, orig cloth; lower cover soiled. With 37 plates, including title. L Nov 14 (111) £160

Outcault, Richard Felton

— Tige—His Story. NY: Frederick A. Stokes, [1905]. In d/j. Epstein copy. sg Apr 29 (356) $225

Outerbridge, Paul

— Photographing in Color. [NY, 1940]. 1st Ed. 4to, cloth; extremities stained, edges worn. With 15 color plates. sg Apr 13 (78) $100

Anr copy. Cloth, in soiled d/j. wa Sept 26 (644) $120

Outhier, Reginald

— Journal d'un voyage au nord en 1736 & 1737. Amst., 1746. 12mo, modern calf. With 16 (of 18) folding maps & plans. S Nov 15 (1100) £150 [Rinne]

Ovalle, Alonso de, 1601-51

— Historica relacion del Reyno di Chile.... Rome, 1646. 4to, half vellum. With folding map & 14 plates Some browning & soiling. SI June 10 (712) LIt2,800,000

Over, Charles

— Ornamental Architecture in the Gothic, Chinese and Modern Taste. L, 1758. 8vo, contemp calf gilt; rubbed. With 54 plates. Library markings. bba June 25 (234) £650 [Temple]

Overbeke, Bonaventura ab

— Les Restes de L'ancienne Rome. Amst., 1709. Ed by Michael ab Overbeke. 3 vols. Folio, 19th-cent half lea; worn. SI June 10 (713) LIt2,400,000

— Stampe degli avanzi dell' antica Roma. L, 1739. Folio, contemp half calf; worn. SI Dec 5 (514) LIt300,000

Overfield, T. Donald. See: Skues & Overfield

Ovid (Publius Ovidius Naso), 43B.C.-17?A.D.
See also: Cresset Press; Limited Editions Club

— L'Art d'aimer. [Lausanne: Philippe Gonin, 1935]. One of 225. Illus by Aristide Maillol. Folio, loose as issued in orig wraps; spine foxed. With 12 lithos & 15 woodcuts. Some light discoloration. With 2 extra suites of woodcuts, 1 in sanguine, the other in black. P Dec 12 (66) $2,000

— Epistolae Heroides. Parma, 1517. Folio, later vellum. Roman type. Top restored at inner margin; worming affecting some text throughout; some marginal staining & soiling. Ck Oct 31 (205) £750

— Epistolae Heriodes. Venice: Hieronymus Scotum, 1543. ("Heroides epistolae cum omnibus commentariis....") Bound with: Metamorphoseon Pub. Ovidii Nasonis Libri XV. Venice, 1545. Folio, late 18th-cent mor gilt; rebacked. Some leaves browned. Ck Oct 31 (212) £700

— Excellente Figueren ghesneden vuyten uppersten Poete Ovidius.... Lyon: Ian van Tournes, 1557. 8vo, 18th-cent calf; spine rubbed. With 178 woodcut illusts by Bernard Salomon. Tp soiled; b2 with tear at lower margin into border. Ck Oct 31 (217) £850

— Fastorum libri vi.... Toscolano: Alexandrus Paganinus, 1527. 4to, modern vellum. Minor def to 1st leaf; some browning & waterstaining. SI Dec 5 (515) LIt350,000

Anr Ed. Lyon: Seb. Gryphium, 1554. 8vo, contemp vellum, with arms & monogram of Denis de Sallo. Italic type. Some staining; slit in last leaf. Ck Oct 31 (216) £850

— Le Grand Olympe des Histoires Poetiques.... Paris: J. Real for Vivant Gaultherot, 1539. 3 vols in 1. 8vo, modern mor gilt. Lettres batardes; with 155 woodcut illusts. Prelims & final leaves affected by damp. Broxbourne-Salloch copy. Ck Oct 31 (210) £2,500

— Opera. [Venice]: Jacobus Rubeus, [before

Dec] 1474. Folio, later vellum. First & last few leaves heavily statined; last leaf wormed. Sold w.a.f. 198 (of 412) leaves. O-128. bba Jan 16 (213A) £650 [Bernard]

Anr Ed. Parma: Stephanus Corallus, 1 July 1477. Vols I-II (of 3). Folio, Vol I in 19th-cent lea & Vol II in contemp goatskin. 326 (of 328) leaves; lacking aa2 in Vol II & final blank in Vol I. Goff O-129.. SI June 10 (718) LIt3,800,000

Anr Ed. Vicenza: Hermannus Liechtenstein, 10 May & 12 Aug 1480. Part 2 (of 2) only. 18th-cent half sheep. Fingersoiled & heavily annotated in 1st 15 pages in a contemp hand; A7 with clean tear from margin into last 4 lines of text; B1, E6 & G8 also torn at margin; H8 with some old ink marks; some dampstaining & worming. 167 (of 168) leaves; lacking final blank. Goff O-131. Ck Oct 31 (201) £1,800

Anr Ed. Venice: Christophorus de Pensis, 1498. 2 vols in 1. Folio, late 18th-cent lea gilt; scuffed. 61 lines & headline; type 3:82R. Tp with 3 repaired holes; lower outer corner of EE5-8 torn away but replaced; old dampstaining to 1st few leaves. 308 leaves. Goff O-183 & O-137. C Dec 16 (147) £2,200 [Tenschert]

Anr Ed. Venice: Aldus, 1501-2. Vol I only. Contemp mor gilt. Abbey-Salloch copy. Ck Oct 31 (203) £2,400

Anr Ed. Toscolano: Alexandri de Paganinis, 1521. Vol I only. 32mo, 19th-cent mor gilt. Ink marks to tp; some prelims & final leaves stained. Ck Oct 31 (207) £120

Anr Ed. Basel, Mar 1549. Folio, later lea; worn & soiled. Text wormed & not collated. Sold w.a.f. O Dec 17 (141) $130

Anr Ed. Leiden: Elzevir, 1629. 3 vols. 16mo, 19th-cent mor gilt. Ck Oct 31 (235) £220

— Les XXI Epistres.... Paris: Galliot du Pre, 1528. 12mo, 19th-cent mor gilt. Roman type. Some browning & dampstaining. Ck Oct 31 (209) £800

English Versions of Metamorphoses

— 1612. - The Fifteene Bookes entituled Metamorphoses. L: Thomas Purfoot. 4to, contemp calf; rebacked. Black letter. Lacking leaf before title; some leaves laminated; some stains; burn to P7 affecting characters on recto; some worming at end. STC 18962. Ck Oct 31 (230) £200

— 1632. - Ovid's Metamorphosis Englished.... Oxford Trans by George Sandys. Folio, contemp calf; spine restored. With frontis, additional title & 15 plates. Tp soiled; additional title browned; some staining & soiling; wormhole at lower margins of last leaves. STC 18966. Ck Oct 31 (237) £190

Anr copy. Calf. With 16 plates. Some marginal worming repaired; 1 plate repaired in fore-margin; short tear in lower margin of Z3; 3A3 bound before 3A2; hole in 3G4 affecting text. STC 18966. S Feb 25 (516) £260 [Rix]

— 1640. - Metamorphoses. L. Trans by George Sandys. Folio, early 19th-cent calf. With engraved title, port & 15 plates. Extra-illus with 2 duplicate ports & 15 duplicate plates (the duplicate plates cut down & mtd). STC 18968. Ck Oct 31 (238) £240

— 1717. - L. Folio, contemp calf; rebacked, rubbed. With engraved title, port & 15 plates. Ck Oct 31 (249) £120

— 1732. - Metamorphosis. Amst. 2 vols in 1. Folio, contemp calf; rebacked. SI June 10 (717) LIt1,400,000

French Versions of Metamorphoses

— La Metamorphose...figuree. Lyons: Jean de Tournes, 1564. 2d Ed. 8vo, mor gilt by Trautz-Bauzonnet. sg May 7 (164) $950

— 1557. - Lyons: Jean de Tournes. 8vo, 18th-cent calf; spine rubbed. With 178 illusts by Bernard Salomon. Tp soiled; b2 with tear at lower margin into woodcut border; occasional stains. Ck Oct 31 (217) £850

— [1557 or 1583]. - Lyons: Jean de Tournes. 8vo, contemp vellum. Tp holed with loss of date; dampstained; lacking D3 & M4; interleaved with Ms poems in Latin. Ck Oct 31 (225) £80

— 1650. - Les Metamorphoses. Paris 4 parts in 1 vol. 8vo, old vellum. With 52 plates. Plate 41 dampstained at margin. Ck Oct 31 (240) £750

— 1676. - Metamorphoses en rondeaux. Paris 4to, modern half calf; spine dampstained at foot. Tp holed with loss; tp & some other leaves soiled; some dampstains. Ck Oct 31 (244) £100

— 1770. - Les Metamorphoses, gravees sur les dessins.... Paris 4to, 19th-cent mor gilt by Lloyd; upper joint cracked. With 140 plates. Ck Oct 31 (253) £300

— 1801. - Metamorphoses ornees de 138 gravures.... Paris 2 vols in 1. 4to, old cloth. Ck Oct 31 (254) £160

— 1931. - Les Metamorphoses. Lausanne One of 95. Illus by Pablo Picasso. 4to, half mor gilt by Hourades; corners worn. With 30 orig etchings in remarque state, mtd on guards. P Dec 12 (75) $2,250

German & Latin Versions

— 1563. - Tetrasticha in Ovidii Metamorphoses.... Frankfurt Oblong 4to, 19th-cent calf. With 178 woodcuts by Virgil Solis. Tp soiled at margins. Ck Oct 31 (219) £1,600

German Versions of Metamorphoses

— 1551. - Metamorphosis. Das ist von der wunderbarlichen Verenderung der Gestalten der Menschen.... Mainz: J. Schoeffer Illus by Georg Wickram. Folio, contemp blind-stamped half pigskin; joints cracked. With 47 woodcut illusts. Tp restored; verso of N1 repaired with adhesive tape at lower margin; other repairs; dampstained. Ck Oct 31 (214) £1,400

— 1571. - Dess Sinnreychen und Hochverstendigen Poeten Metamorphoses.... Augsburg 8vo, modern calf. Lacking final leaf; tp restored at outer margin. Ck Oct 31 (221) £260

— 1631. - Metamorphosis oder Wuenderbarliche und seltzame Beschreibung.... Frankfurt 4to, 19th-cent mor gilt by Canape. Ck Oct 31 (236) £280

— [1715]. - Funffzehen Verwandlungs-Buecher.... Nuremberg: Monath. Oblong folio, modern half calf. With frontis & 150 plates. Some dampstaining. Ck Oct 31 (248) £400

Italian Versions of Metamorphoses

— 1559. - La Vita et metamorfoseo.... Lyons: G. de Tournes. 8vo, contemp vellum; worn. Text soiled. cb Feb 12 (101) $750

— 1584. - Le Metamorfosi.... Venice 4to, 18th-cent calf. Some browning. SI June 10 (716) LIt850,000

— 1584. - Venice: Giunta. 4to, modern half mor. Dampstains throughout; DD6 badly stained, with small hole in blank area. Ck Oct 31 (225) £450

Latin & French Versions

— 1732. - Les Metamorphoses. Amst. 2 vols. Folio, contemp calf; scuffed, spines worn. Some browning. Ck Nov 29 (273) £850

— 1767-71. - Paris 4 vols. 4to, lea gilt; spine bumped, joints starting. With 140 plates. sp June 18 (295) $2,100

Latin Versions of Metamorphoses

— 1502, Oct. - Metamorphoseon libri quindecim. Venice: Aldus. 2 parts in 1 vol. 8vo, Renaissance bdg of mor gilt. Tp & a2-3 browned; b5-d4 with repaired wormhole at lower margins; some waterstains, mainly to lower margins. Abbey copy. Ck Oct 31 (203) £2,400

— 1505. - Metamorphoses, cum Raphaelis Regii Commentariis.... Parma Folio, 18th-cent vellum. Roman type. Tp & prelims dampstained & soiled at margins; 4 leaves browned; worming at end. Ck Oct 31 (204) £6,200

— 1518. - Metamorphoseos. Lyons: Jacobo Huguetan. 4to, modern bds. Roman type. Tp holed with slight loss on verso; blindstamp; some worming to margins; e7 stained on verso; some soiling. Ck Oct 31 (206) £190

— 1526. - Metamorphoses. Toscolano: A. Paganini. 4to, modern bds. Some leaves yellowed by damp. Ck Oct 31 (208) £450

Anr copy. Contemp vellum. Some waterstaining. SI June 19 (714) LIt800,000

— 1540. - Metamorphosin. Venice: B. Bindoni. Folio, old vellum. Dampstained; 1st gathering pulled; G6 with tear at upper margin. Ck Oct 31 (211) £350

— 1545. - Metamorphoseon libri XV. Venice: Hieronymum Scotum. Folio, modern half calf. Lacking final leaf; some browning. Ck Oct 31 (213) £250

— 1565. - Venice: Joan. Gryphium. Folio, 19th-cent half lea; worn. SI Dec 5 (516) LIt200,000

— 1583. - Metamorphoses Ovidii. Paris 16mo, contemp vellum. With 178 woodcut illusts. Ck Oct 31 (224) £170

— 1591. - Metamorphoses. [Antwerp] Oblong 8vo, calf; minor defs. With engraved title, port & 178 plates. B May 12 (43) HF6,500

Anr copy. Contemp vellum; spine soiled. Some marginal browning & soiling; plate on N4 with fault in impression; plate on T1 with small stain. Ck Oct 31 (227) £1,500

— c.1607]. - XV Metamorphoseon Librorum.... [N.p. Illus by Crispin Van der Passe. 4to, old calf with arms of Jean-Baptiste Colbert. With engraved title & 120 (of 134) plates only. Tp restored at outer margin; 2 plates torn with loss. Colbert's copy, with the uncancelled Plate 92. Ck Oct 31 (228) £420

Owen, David Dale

— Report of a Geological Exploration of Part of Iowa, Wisconsin, and Illinois. Phila., 1852. 4to, orig cloth; worn. O Jan 14 (141) $110

Owen, Hugh, 1761-1827 —& Blakeway, John Brickdale, 1765-1826

— History of Shrewsbury. L, 1825. 2 vols. 4to, contemp calf gilt by Eddowes, 1825; soiled, spines torn. L NOv 14 (431) £130

Owen, John. See: Watts's copy, Isaac

Owen, John, of the Middle Temple —& Bowen, Emanuel, d.1767

— Britannia Depicta or Ogilby Improv'd. L, 1720. 4to, modern calf. With engraved title, 2 leaves of "Table" & 273 road maps. Some marginal browning & spotting. S Nov 15 (960) £600 [Burden]

Anr copy. Contemp calf; worn & repaired. A few maps cut close; some discoloration. S July 1 (1401) £400 [Burden]

Anr Ed. L, 1751. 4to, old calf; worn. With engraved title & 273 road maps. Some spotting; 6 (of 8) pp of tables present. bba Aug 13 (394) £600 [Faupel]

Owen, Major John, 1818-89

— The Journals and Letters of.... NY, 1927. One of 50 L.p. sets. 2 vols. With 2 folding maps & 30 plates. O Jan 14 (142) $250

Owen, Robert, 1771-1858

— A New View of Society.... L, 1813-14. 1st Ed. Part 1 (of 4) only. 8vo, later half cloth. Epstein copy. sg Apr 30 (357) $900

Owen, Samuel. See: Westall & Owen

Owen, Wilfred, 1893-1918

— Poems. L, 1920. 1st Ed. Epstein copy. sg Apr 30 (358) $275

— Thirteen Poems, with Drawings by Ben Shahn. Northampton MA: Gehenna Press, 1956. One of 400, sgd by Leonard Baskin. Folio, half lea. sg Sept 26 (247) $200

Owens, Harry J. See: Caxton Club

Oxford English Dictionary

— A New English Dictionary on Historical Principles. Oxford, 1888-1933. 10 vols in 16. Folio, half cloth. Milne copy. Ck June 12 (153) £80

Anr copy. 10 vols in 20; without Supplement. Folio, contemp half mor gilt; rubbed & worn. Library markings; some soiling & marginal fraying. DW May 13 (314) £90

Anr copy. Half mor gilt; some spine ends chipped. sg Mar 5 (201) $650

Anr Ed. Oxford, 1933. 13 vols, including Supplement. Orig cloth. pn May 14 (58) £220

Compact Microprint Ed. Oxford, 1971. 2 vols. Folio, cloth. With magnifying glass & slipcase. bba Apr 9 (124) £65 [Goddard]

Anr copy. Cloth, in box with magnifying glass. F Sept 26 (516) $50

Anr copy. Cloth. Lacking magnifying glass & slipcase. wa Apr 9 (18) $55

Anr Ed. Oxford, 1978-86. 17 vols, including Supplements. Orig cloth, most in d/js. Library markings. bba Oct 24 (165) £220 [Jaffe]

Anr copy. Orig cloth, Supplements in d/js. pn Apr 23 (43) £260

Oxford University

— The Judgment and Decree of the University...Against Certain Pernicious Books and Damnable Doctrines. [Oxford], 1683. Folio, disbound. Washed & repaired. bba May 28 (530) £140 [Blackwood]

Oxley, John, 1781-1828

— Journals of Two Expeditions into the Interior of New South Wales.... L, 1820. 4to, contemp calf gilt; worn, spine def. With 2 dedications, 3 folding maps (discolored), 2 folding tbles, folding plate (spotted) & 5 aquatints, 2 hand-colored. S June 25 (149) £2,000 [Maggs]

Anr copy. Contemp half calf. With 3 folding maps, 2 folding tables & 6 plates (2 colored, 1 folding). S June 25 (212) £3,000 [Maggs]

Oyved, Moysheh. See: Good, Edward

Ozanam, J. A. F.

— Histoire medicale generale et particuliere des maladies epidemiques.... Paris, 1817. 5 vols. 8vo, contemp half calf. sg Nov 14 (96) $300

Ozanam, Jacques, 1640-1717

— Recreations mathematiques et physiques. Paris, 1750. 4 vols. 8vo, contemp calf; some stains. With 136 plates. S July 1 (1312) £250 [Booth]

P

P., G. See: Peignot, Gabriel

P., M. See: Kilner, Dorothy

Pachymeres, Georgius

— Michael Palaeologus sive Historia rerum a Michael Palaeologo ante imperium.... Rome, 1666. 2 vols in 1. Folio, contemp vellum; spine def. Some thumbing. S June 30 (177) £400 [Dallegio]

Packard, Alpheus Spring, 1839-1905

— Monograph of the Bombycine Moths of America.... Wash., 1895-1905-1914. Vol I only. Later cloth. With 49 plates (30 in color) & 10 maps. sg May 14 (235) $200

Padgett, Lewis, Pseud.

— Mutant. NY: Gnome Press, [1953]. In d/j; ink spots to bottom edges of covers. pba July 9 (218) $50

— Robots Have No Tails. NY: Gnome Press, [1952]. In d/j. sp Nov 24 (473) $60

Page

— The Page. Carshalton, Surrey: Edward Gordon Craig, 1900. Christmas No. One of 300 for America. cb Oct 17 (719) $95

Page, Thomas Nelson, 1853-1922

— Works. NY, 1906-12. One of 230. 18 vols. 8vo, mor extra. CNY Dec 5 (421) $850

Paget, Guy

— The Melton Mobray of John Ferneley. Leicester, 1931. One of 220. 4to, orig half mor, in d/j. Ck Sept 6 (40) £110

Paget, John, 1811-98

— The New "Examen". [Halifax]: Haworth Press, 1934. Ltd Ed, sgd by Winston Churchill. Intro by Churchill. Orig mor by Sangorski & Sutcliffe. Inscr to George Trevelyan & with Ls to Trevelyan, 10 Mar 1934. S Dec 12 (282) £1,500 [Fine Art Society]

Paine, Albert Bigelow

— The Hollow Tree. NY, 1898. 1st Ed. Illus by J. M. Conde. 4to, orig half cloth; worn. Inscr to Orson Lowell. Epstein copy. sg Apr 29 (359) $1,900

Paine, Thomas, 1737-1809
See also: Limited Editions Club

— Rights of Man.... L: Jourdan, 1791. 8vo, contemp half lea; crudely tape-repaired, worn. Lacking half-title. bba Oct 10 (466) £80 [Rosenthal]

— Works. Albany, [1792]. 8vo, orig sheep; spine ends reinforced with cloth tape. sg June 18 (450) $175

Painter, William, 1540?-94. See: Cresset Press

Palardy, Jean

— The Early Furniture of French Canada.... Toronto, 1965. 4to, orig cloth, in d/j. F Mar 26 (27) $80

Palatino, Giovanni Battista

— Libro...nel qual s'insegna a scrivere ogni sorte lettera.... Rome, 1545. 19th-cent calf. Cockerell copy. C June 24 (236) £3,200 [Jackson]

Anr Ed. Rome: Antonio Blado, [1553]. 4to, old bds. Some soiling. sg May 7 (165) $3,400

Anr Ed. Rome: Valerio Dorico for Giovanni della Gatta, 1561. 8vo, modern vellum. Lacking final blank; tp spotted. C June 24 (237) £850 [Wilsey]

Palau y Dulcet, Antonio

— Manual del librero hispano-americano. Barcelona, 1923-27. 1st Ed. 7 vols in 4. 4to, contemp half vellum; spines soiled. Ck Nov 1 (473) £190

Vols 1-28. Barcelona, 1948-77. 4to, later half vellum; 1 spine stained. Ck Nov 1 (474) £1,700

Anr copy. New cloth. O Sept 24 (192) $1,800

Palazzi, Giovanni

— Aquila Romana. Venice, 1679. Folio, contemp vellum; worn. Some marginal defs. SI Dec 5 (518) LIt550,000

Palgrave, Francis Turner, 1824-97

— The Golden Treasury. L, 1904. 2 vols. 8vo, orig cloth, in d/j. kh Nov 11 (183) A$50

— A Golden Treasury of Songs and Lyrics. NY, 1911. Illus by Maxfield Parrish. Orig cloth. With 8 color plates. sg Jan 30 (123) $80

Palladio, Andrea, 1518-80

— The Architecture.... L, 1715. ("The Architecture of A. Palladio.") 3 (of 4) vols. Folio, contemp calf; worn, covers detached. With frontis, port & 262 plates (some in text). Some soiling to titles; other light staining to lower margins; library margins. Ck May 15 (138) £1,000

Anr Ed. L, 1721. Vol I only. Folio, modern half mor. With title, 6 folding plates & 63 illusts. Lacking 2 leaves; 1 misbound. bba Oct 10 (187) £90 [Mason]

Anr Ed. L, 1738. ("The Four Books of....") 4 parts in 1 vol. Folio, half calf; worn. With 4 engraved titles & 219 plates. First engraved title laid down; some discoloration & waterstaining; lacking subscribers list. S June 25 (214) £400 [Gorini]

Anr Ed. L, 1742. 2 vols in 1. 4to, contemp half calf; rubbed. With port & 28 plates only. Lacking frontis; some browning; occasional staining; 1st title & some prelims repaired at inner margins. Sold w.a.f. Ck Nov 29 (274) £700

Anr copy. Contemp calf; rebacked with old backstrip laid down, corners restored. With frontis, port & 230 plates on 208 sheets. Minor wormholes; 9 plates with old ink writing. CNY Jan 25 (54) $3,500

— Architettura. Venice, 1570. ("I Quattro Libri dell'architettura.") 4 parts in 1 vol. Folio, contemp vellum; soiled & worn. Main title repaired with some loss; several other marginal repairs & small loss of text at H2; dampstained throughout. DW Ocgt 9 (935) £750

Anr copy. Contemp vellum bds. S May 28 (144) £950 [Uceta]

Anr Ed. Venice: Bartolomeo Carampello, 1581. ("I Quattro Libri dell architettura.") Folio, old half sheep; backstrip worn & loose. Some stains. sg Feb 6 (210) $2,000

Anr copy. Modern half lea. Some repairs & browning. SI June 10 (727) LIt2,300,000

— Le Fabbriche e i desegni.... Vicenza, 1786. Vols III & IV only, bound in 1 vol. Contemp half vellum; worn. With 104 plates on 106 sheets. Some soiling. pn Sept 12 (276) £550 [Talanti]

— Le Fabbriche e i disegni.... Vicenza, 1786. Vol I only (of 4). Contemp half calf; spine worn. With port & 53 folding plates. Faint waterstain towards end; small stamp on tp. S Nov 21 (90) £650
— The First Book of Architecture.... L, 1663. 1st Ed in English. 4to, 19th-cent calf; rubbed. With 58 (of 65) plates. Lacking engraved title. bba July 9 (86) £110 [Wilbraham]
— The Four Books of Architecture. L: R. Ware, [c.1750]. Folio, later bds; rubbed & worn, front cover detached. With 212 plates. Tp soiled; ink stain to leaf A; marginal dampstaining; minor soiling to several plates; a few plates repaired; engraved title for Book 3 only. F Mar 26 (762) $900
— Les Quatre Livres de L'Architecture.... Paris, 1650. Folio, old calf; corners repaired but worn, joints splitting, later endpapers. Some old dampstaining; 7 leaves with repaired tears or paper faults. C May 20 (284) £580 [Marlborough]

Anr copy. 18th-cent calf gilt; repaired, upper cover becoming detached. 2A3-4 supplied in pen-facsimile. S June 25 (213) £400 [Gorini]

Pallas, Peter Simon, 1741-1811
— Miscellanea Zoologica.... The Hague: Petrus van Cleef, 1766. 4to, early half mor. Some spotting; fore-edge margin of half-title supplied. wa Sept 26 (476) $400
— Travels through the Southern Provinces of the Russian Empire.... L, 1802-3. 2 vols. 4to, contemp calf gilt; Vol I rebacked with old spine laid down. With 51 plates, most hand-colored, & 4 maps. C May 20 (286) £400 [Valentine]

Anr copy. Contemp half russia; worn. With 51 plates (43 hand-colored) & 4 double-page maps. Most vignettes hand-colored. S May 14 (1206) £320 [Bolognese]

Anr Ed. L, [plates watermarked 1805-9]. 2 vols. 4to, later half cloth. With 4 folding maps & 29 plates, most colored by hand. C Oct 30 (134) £550 [Marlborough]

Anr Ed. L, 1812. 2 vols. 4to, later half lea. With 53 (of 54) plans & maps, 41 plates & 2 plans hand-colored. Lacking Plate 23 in Vol I; Plate 5 in Vol I supplied from a smaller copy. C Oct 30 (61) £200 [Arader]
— Voyages dans les gouvernemens meridionaux de l'Empire de Russie. Paris, 1805. 3 vols. 4to & folio, contemp half russia gilt & contemp russia gilt; text vols rebacked. With 52 plates, 3 maps & 28 vignette plates. Blank portion cut from foot of leaf with pp. 305-6 in Vol I. Francis Mary Richardson Currer's copy. S Nov 15 (1128) £320 [Greenwood]

Palliser, Fanny Bury
— History of Lace. L, 1902. Later mor gilt, orig wraps bound in. bba June 25 (233) £170 [Thorp]; sg Apr 2 (159) $110

Pallucchini, Rodolfo
— Guardia Zeichnungen im Museum Correr zu Venedig. Venice, [1943]. Folio, bds, in frayed d/j. Endpapers & prelims foxed. sg Feb 6 (212) $50

Palma Cayet, Pierre Victor. See: Cayet, Pierre Victor Palma

Palmedo, Roland. See: Derrydale Press

Palmer, Alfred Herbert
— The Life and Letters of Samuel Palmer. L, 1892. 4to, orig cloth; rebacked preserving orig spine, rubbed. Plates include an orig etching by Palmer. Some foxing to prelims. bba July 23 (473) £170 [Hashimoto]

Palmer, Elihu
— Principles of Nature, or a Development of the Moral Causes of Happiness and Misery.... NY, 1801. Bound with: Palmer. Posthumous Pieces. L, 1824. 12mo, later half calf. Library stamp on tp; foxed. bba May 14 (130) £65 [Thorp]

Palmer, George
— Kidnapping in the South Seas. Edin., 1871. 8vo, orig cloth; backstrip repaired. kh Nov 11 (604) A$160

Palmer, Samuel, 1805-81
— Sketchbook 1824. Clairvaux & L: Trianon Press for the William Blake Trust, 1962. One of 50. Ed by Martin Butlin & Sir Geoffrey Keynes. 2 vols. Oblong 8vo, orig cloth. bba Dec 19 (26) £160 [Godderd]

Palmer, Thomas, of Wingham
— An Essay of the Meanes how to make our Travailes into Forraine Countries.... L, 1606. 4to, 19th-cent mor; joints & spine ends rubbed. Tp soiled; single wormhole through all leaves; folding tables with half-inch tears at mount; some repairs. STC 19156. CNY Oct 8 (195) $2,600

Palmer, Thomas Fyshe
— A Narrative of the Sufferings of.... Cambr., 1797. 2d Ed. 8vo, later half calf; upper joint split. Title soiled & spotted. S June 25 (132) £550 [Quaritch/Hordern]

Palmer, William J., 1836-1909
— Report of Surveys across the Continent in 1867-68.... Phila., 1869. 8vo, orig wraps; chipped and detached; lacking rear wrap. cb Nov 14 (152) $130

Anr copy. Half calf, orig wraps bound in. Lacking 1 map (of 3). sg June 18 (451) $200

Palmer, William Thomas

— The English Lakes. L, 1905. Illus by A. Heaton Cooper. 4to, orig cloth; rebacked. DW Dec 11 (95) £135

Palmerin

— Palmerin de Oliva & sus grandes fechos. Venice: Gregorio de Gregoriis, 23 Nov 1526. Folio, 19th-cent mor gilt by Riviere. Huth copy. C Dec 16 (69) £5,000 [Quaritch]

Paltock, Robert, 1697-1767

— The Life and Adventures of Peter Wilkins.... L, 1751. 1st Ed. 2 vols. 12mo, contemp calf gilt; rubbed. With 2 frontises & 4 plates. Ck Oct 18 (78) £700

Panciroli, Guido

— Notitia utraque, dignitatum, cum orientis, tum occidentis. Lyons, 1608. 3 parts in 1 vol. Folio, contemp lea; worn, front cover detached. Lacking title; marginal dampstaining toward end. sg Mar 12 (195) $90

Pancoucke, Charles Louis Fleurie

— L'Ile de Staffa et sa grotte basaltique. Paris, 1831. Folio, orig bds; spine worn, rubbed. With aquatint pictorial title & 11 plates, all hand-colored, engraved double-page map & 1 engraved plate. Some dampstaining. S Feb 26 (776) £170 [Elliott]

Panofsky, Erwin

— Albrecht Duerer. L, 1945. 2d Ed. 2 vols. Orig cloth; soiled. Some spotting & soiling. F June 25 (306) $70

Panormitanus de Tedeschis, Nicolaus

— Lectura super V libris decretalium. Venice: Johannes de Colonia & Johannnes Manthen, 1476. Vols I & IV only (of 6). Folio, pigskin-backed bds covered at a later date with paper & calf spines; upper bd of Vol I split. 58 lines; double column; gothic letter; initials & paragraph-marks in blue & red. Wormed at beginning & end of both vols & in some other margins; some margins stained or spotted. 306 & 180 leaves. Goff P-44. S Dec 5 (29) £6,500 [Stewart]

Pantling, Robert. See: King & Pantling

Pantzer, Katharine F. See: Short-Title Catalogue

Panvinio, Onofrio, 1529-68

— De ludis circensibus libri II. Padua, 1642. Bound with: Antiquitatum Veronensium libri VIII. Padua, 1648. Folio, old sheep; worn, covers detached. With 32 plates in each vol. sg Sept 6 (209) $1,200

Anr copy. Modern lea. With frontis, port & 33 plates. SI June 10 (733) LIt1,400,000

— De ludis circensibus, libri II.... Venice, 1600. 2 parts in 1 vol. Folio, contemp vellum; worn. With frontis & 31 plates. Some foxing. S June 10 (732) LIt1,300,000

Anr Ed. Padua, 1681. Folio, old vellum; spine darkened. With engraved title & 33 plates only. Several plates remargined. sg Oct 24 (245) $800

Panzer, Georg Wolfgang

— Annales typographici...ad annum MD-[MDXXXVI]. Hildesheim, 1963-64. 11 vols. 4to, orig cloth. Reprint of the Nuremberg 1793-1803 Ed. Ck Nov 1 (465) £160

Papageorgiou, Athanasius

— Icons of Cyprus.... L: Arcadia Press, 1971. One of 265. Folio, mor gilt by Zaehnsdorf. W Mar 6 (10) £90

Papillon, Jean Baptiste Michel

— Traite historique et pratique de la gravure en bois. Paris, 1766. 3 vols in 2. 8vo, contemp half vellum; rubbed & chipped. With woodcut port & 6 chiaroscuro plates. 2B2 with small tear. Abbey-Schlosser copy. P June 18 (488) $2,250

Pappafave, Giacomo. See: Monacazione

Paprocki, Bartlomeij

— Diadochos; id est, Successio: Ginak Pslaupnost knijzat a kraluw Czeskych.... Prague, 1602. 5 parts in 2 vols. Folio, old vellum. Some browning; repairs & marginalia; c.15-20 leaves supplied in Ms in each part except the 2d. Sold w.a.f. sg Oct 24 (246) $300

Papworth, John Buonarotti

— Hints on Ornamental Gardening. L: Ackermann, 1823. 8vo, later half mor. With 27 hand-colored plates & 1 uncolored plate with a flap. Plate II without the overslip giving the title in English. C May 20 (100) £850 [Heywood Hill]

Anr copy. Orig bds, unopened; recovered with brown paper, orig ptd spine laid down, backstrip split. With 1 plain & 27 hand-colored plates. C Oc 30 (63) £800 [Bradley]

Anr copy. Modern half mor gilt by Sangorski & Sutcliffe. Half-title soiled. S Nov 21 (91) £1,000 [Bonch]

— Rural Residences... L: Ackermann, 1818. 1st Ed. 8vo, orig bds, unopened. With 27 hand-colored plates. C May 20 (98) £975 [Heywood Hill]

2d Ed. L, 1832. 8vo, orig cloth by Remnant & Edmonds; upper free endpaper renewed. With 27 colored plates. Minor foxing to a few plates. McCarty-Cooper copy. CNY Jan 25 (56) $1,800

— Select Views of London. L: Ackermann, 1816. 1st Ed in Book form. 8vo, modern calf gilt; lower hinge weak. With 76 hand-colored plates. pn Sept 12 (320) £1,500 [Sotheran]

Anr copy. Contemp calf; rebacked preserving orig backstrip, worn. With 76 hand-colored plates, 5 folding. A few plates trimmed affecting platemark. pn Apr 23 (271) £950

Issue without Papworth's name on title. Contemp half mor gilt. With 76 hand-colored plates, 5 folding. C May 20 (97) £2,400 [Drizen]

Papworth, John Buonarotti —& Others

— Poetical Sketches of Scarborough. L, 1813. Illus by Thomas Rowlandson. 8vo, contemp calf; rebacked, old spine preserved & recornered. With 21 hand-colored plates. Some soiling & offsetting. bba Sept 19 (221) £110 [Traylen]

Anr copy. Contemp half calf; rebacked, spine worn; hinges repaired. cb Sept 26 (183) $300

Anr copy. Contemp russia gilt; rubbed, rebacked. pn Apr 23 (213) £130

Anr copy. Calf gilt; worn, rear cover detached. Some soiling & foxing. wa Mar 5 (621) $210

Paracelsus, 1493?-1541

— Opera. Strassburg: Lazarus Zetzner, 1603. 2 vols. Folio, modern pigskin. With 2 leaves in photocopy; browned. B Nov 1 (676) HF8,500

Paradin, Claude —& Simeoni, Gabriele

— Symbola Heroica. Antwerp: Plantin, 1567. 12mo, 17th-cent sheep. Tp dusty with corner torn. sg Mar 12 (77) $1,000

Paramore, Edward E., Jr.

— The Ballad of Yukon Jake. NY, 1928. sg Jan 30 (94) $60

Anr copy. Illus by Rockwell Kent as Hogarth, Jr. Orig bds, in d/j. bbc Apr 27 (346) $75

Pardoe, Julia, 1806-62

See also: Beattie, William

— Les Beautes du Bosphore. L & Paris, 1838. 4to, half mor; worn. With engraved title, port, map & 78 plates. Tp & port discolored. S June 30 (179) £300 [Merriou]

— The Beauties of the Bosphorus. L, 1838. Illus by W. H. Bartlett. 4to, orig lea gilt; lower joint weak. With engraved title, port, map & 78 plates. Waterstained towards end; foxed. S July 1 (670) £300 [Merthurkmen]

Anr copy. Contemp half calf gilt. Minor foxing. S July 1 (671) £450 [Dalleggio]

Anr Ed. L, 1839. 4to, contemp half mor gilt. With engraved title, port, map & 78 plates. bba June 11 (354) £280 [Dupont]

Anr copy. Orig mor. wa Apr 9 (277) $450

Anr Ed. L, [c.1840]. 4to, contemp half lea. With port, frontis & 84 plates.. Some dampstains affecting frontis & additional title; 1 plate with dried flower adhering to plate surface. pn May 14 (216) £360 [Ozbek]

Anr copy. Orig cloth. With port, engraved title, 85 plates & 1 map. Some spotting. pn June 11 (290) £280

Anr copy. Contemp half mor; upper hinge broken, joints rubbed. With engraved title (stamped), port, map & 85 plates. Library stamps on plate versos. S Nov 15 (823) £240 [Alpha Gallery]

Anr copy. 19th-cent half calf; worn. With map, vignette title, port & 85 plates. S Nov 15 (1180) £340 [Map House]

Anr copy. Orig cloth; rubbed & soiled, upper joint torn. With port, additional title, map & 79 plates.. Some leaves stained at upper outer corner. S May 14 (1237) £320 [Alpha Gall]

— The City of the Sultan; and Domestic Manners of the Turks in 1836. L, 1837. 2 vols in 1. 8vo, modern half calf. With 9 plates. S Nov 15 (1179) £220 [Beeleigh Abbey]

— Lady Arabella; or the Adventures of a Doll. L: Kerby & Son, [1856]. Illus by G. Cruikshank. 4to, calf gilt, orig cover bound in; worn. With frontis & 3 plates. sg Oct 17 (175) $120

Pare, Ambroise, 1510?-90

— Works. L, 1678. Folio, later calf; rebacked, rubbed. Lacking final leaf; Dd1 def & repaired; Ee2 holed with slight loss of text. Some soiling & waterstaining. bba Sept 5 (291) £1,300 [M. Phelps]

Pargellis, Stanley E. See: Lewis & Pargellis

Paris...

— Paris Guide par les principaux ecrivains et artistes de la France. Paris, [c.1870]. 8vo, cloth; worn, hinges cracked. sg Jan 9 (162) $140

— Paris moderne: grand album representant les vues et les monuments les plus curieux de Paris.... Paris, [c.1860]. Oblong 4to, orig cloth; rubed, covers & backstrip detached. With vignette title & 23 plates. bba Sept 19 (147) £80 [Rainer]

Paris, Edmond, 1806-93

— Le Musee de marine du Louvre. Histoire, description...des navires a rames et a voiles. Paris, 1883. One of 300. Folio, half cloth; needs rebdg. sg Jan 9 (161) $300

Paris, Matthaeus, 1200?-59

— Historia major.... L, 1640-39. ("Matthaei Paris Monachi Albanensis Angli Historia major....") 2 parts in 1 vol. Folio, calf; rebacked. Small holes in tp & following leaf, affecting 1 letter. STC 19210. S June 30 (65) £250 [Kay]

Anr copy. 17th-cent blind-stamped vellum; rebacked retaining most of orig backstrip. With port. Some foxing. STC 19210. sg Oct 24 (248) $150

Park, John James

— The Topography and Natural History of Hampstead. L, 1814. 8vo, contemp half calf; rubbed, spine loose at top. With 9 (of 10) plates (1 colored) & 1 folding map. pn Nov 14 (404) £70 [Marlborough]

Park, Mungo, 1771-1806

— The Journal of a Mission to the Interior of Africa.... L, 1815. 1st Ed. 4to, calf gilt; rebacked, rubbed. With folding map with hand-colored routes. bba Sept 19 (70) £160 [Sotheran]

Anr copy. Contemp half calf; worn. With folding map. Stained. bba July 9 (42) £85 [Kay Books]

2d Ed. 4to, contemp half calf; rebacked. With folding map. bba July 9 (43) £110 [Hobbes]

— Travels in the Interior Districts of Africa. L, 1799. 1st Ed. 4to, contemp mor gilt. With port, 5 plates & 3 folding maps, 1 with routes indicated in colors. Lower margin of 1 map shaved; small clean tear to anr. C Oct 30 (114) £420 [Grabin]

Anr copy. Modern cloth. With 6 plates, 2 engraved sheets of music & 3 folding maps. cb Oct 10 (84) $50

Anr copy. Contemp calf; joints cracked, backstrip def. With 3 folding maps & 5 plates. DW Apr 8 (53) £95

Anr copy. Contemp bds; worn, spine chipped. With 2 plates. O Apr 28 (131) $85

Anr Ed. L, 1817-16. 2 vols. 4to, later half calf; worn & rubbed. cb Oct 10 (85) $130

Parker, Dorothy, 1893-1967

— After Such Pleasures. NY, 1933. One of 250. sg June 11 (264) $200

— Death and Taxes. NY, 1931. One of 250. sg Dec 12 (341) $150

— Not so Deep as a Well: the Collected Poems of.... NY 1936. One of 485. Illus by Valenti Angelo. Half cloth. sg Dec 12 (342) $225

— Sunset Gun. L, 1928. One of 250, this copy with limitation crossed out & Presentation written in anr hand alongside. bbc Sept 23 (464) $100

Parker, E. H.

— Up the Yang-Tse. Shanghai, 1899. 8vo, contemp half lea; worn. With 8 litho maps. Library stamps. sg May 21 (83) $130

Parker, John Henry

— A Glossary of Terms Used in Grecian, Roman, Italian and Gothic Architecture. Oxford, 1850. 2 vols in 3. 8vo, half mor; backs & joints worn, some covers detached. wa Dec 9 (399) $90

Parker, Mary Ann

— A Voyage Round the World in the Gorgon Man of War.... L, 1795. 8vo, later half sheep; head of spine torn. Dedication leaf & K7 holed in margin. S June 25 (139) £1,100 [McCormick]

Parker, Nathan Howe

— The Minnesota Handbook, for 1856-7. Bost., 1857. 12mo, orig cloth; scuffed, spine worn at ends. With folding hand-colored map. wa Apr 9 (88) $75

Parker, Robert B.

— The Godwulf Manuscript Bost., 1974. In d/j. F Dec 18 (200) $80

Parker, Samuel, 1779-1866

— Journal of an Exploring Tour Beyond the Rocky Mountains. Ithaca, NY, 1838. 1st Ed. 12mo, early half calf; worn & scuffed. Map with repaired tear & mtd on stub. bbc Dec 9 (406) $190

Anr Ed. Ithaca, NY, 1842. 12mo, orig cloth. Spine rubbed. cb Nov 14 (154) $110

Anr copy. Cloth; worn. With folding map. Some dampstaining. sg June 18 (452) $100

Parker, William B.

— Notes Taken during the Expedition Commanded by Capt. R. B. Marcy, through Unexplored Texas.... Phila., 1867. 12mo, orig cloth. Sgd on front free endpaper. sg Dec 5 (197) $475

Parkinson, John, 1567-1650

— Paradisi in sole paradisus terrestris.... L, 1629. 1st Ed. Folio, 18th-cent calf, armorial bdg; worn. With woodcut title, port & 110 full-page woodcuts. Some worming, mostly marginal; tp shaved at outer edge; L1 torn; some dampstaining at beginning & end. STC 19300. S June 25 (59) £1,300 [Lan]

2d Ed. L, 1656. Folio, contemp calf; rebacked & restored, lacking free endpapers. Lacking last 2 leaves; tp soiled & with short tear at head; C2 torn; ptg flaw on

2F2v; several leaves of index frayed; some browning. S July 1 (926) £800 [Marshall]

Anr Ed. L, 1904. Folio, bds. Reprint of the 1629 Ed. pnE Oct 2 (533) £100

— Theatrum botanicum.... L, 1640. Bound in 2 vols. Folio, 18th-cent russia gilt; rrebacked preserving old spines. Some browning; 22 leaves inlaid to size & probably supplied from a smaller copy; tears repaired in 2G2 & 2I6; some marginal browning. L.p. copy. John Townley's copy. STC 19302. S June 25 (58) £1,800 [Watson]

Parkinson, Sydney. See: Cook, Capt. James

Parkman, Francis, 1823-93
See also: Limited Editions Club

— The California and Oregon Trail. NY, 1849. 1st Ed, 1st Ptg. 12mo, modern half mor, orig cloth at rear. cb Nov 14 (155) $1,100

Anr copy. Cloth; rebound very skillfully with covers and spine laid down. With 1 leaf of ads at front & 4 leaves at end. Epstein copy. sg Apr 30 (361) $2,600

Anr Ed. Bost., 1892. ("The Oregon Trail.") Illus by Frederic Remington. 8vo, pictorial cloth. sg Dec 5 (214) $375

Anr copy. Orig cloth; extremities rubbed. wa Apr 9 (94) $150

Anr Ed. Garden City, 1945. One of 1,000 sgd by artist. Illus by Thomas Hart Benton. sg Jan 30 (7) $350; wa Mar 5 (563) $150

— Works. Bost., 1897-98. Champlain Ed. 20 vols. 8vo, half mor gilt; extremities worn. sg Mar 5 (202) $150

One of 300. Mor extra. cb Dec 5 (93) $425

Ed Deluxe. 21 vols. 8vo, half calf; spines rubbed. cb Jan 16 (116) $140

Anr Ed. Bost., 1898. 12 vols. 8vo, cloth; rubbed. With 24 plates. wa Feb 20 (37) $75

Parkyns, George Isham

— Monastic and Baronial Remains. L, 1816. 2 vols. 8vo, contemp mor gilt. With 98 (of 99) plates. bba Sept 19 (222) £100 [Martinez]

Parkyns, Sir Thomas, 1664-1741

— Progymnasmata. The Inn-play: or Cornish-Hugg Wrestler. Nottingham, 1714. 2d Ed. 4to, contemp calf gilt; rebacked. bba Jan 30 (28) £220 [Brewer]

Parley, Peter. See: Goodrich, Samuel Griswold

Parmelin, Helene

— Picasso: The Artist and his Model. NY: Abrams, [c.1965]. Endpapers soiled. sp Sept 22 (322) $70

Anr Ed. NY: Harry N. Abrams, [n.d.]. 4to, cloth, in d/j. sg Feb 6 (227) $120

Parnell, Thomas, 1679-1718. See: Goldsmith & Parnell

Paroles...

— Paroles peintes IV. Paris, 1970. One of 150. 4to, loose as issued. CGen Nov 18 (426) SF1,000

Parr, Richard

— The Life of...James Usher.... L, 1686. Folio, contemp calf; rebacked, worn. Port remtd. LH Dec 11 (209) $70

Parras, Pedro Joseph

— Gobierno de los regulares de la America. Madrid, 1783. Vol II only. Orig vellum; worn & with piece torn from center of front cover. bbc June 29 (304) $50

Parrott, William

— London from the Thames.... Novato CA: Newton K. Gregg, [1973]. One of 100. Ed by Hermione Hobhouse. Folio, wraps. With 13 hand-colored plates & a suite of uncolored plates. C Oct 30 (42) £300 [Ramsay Antiques]

Parry, Sir Edward Abbott. See: Cervantes Saavedra, Miguel de

Parry, William

— The Last Days of Lord Byron.... L, 1825. 8vo, orig cloth; spine worn. With 3 hand-colored plates. Lacking half-title. DW Mar 4 (243) £95

Parry, Sir William Edward, 1790-1855

— Journal of a Voyage for the Discovery of a North-West Passage.... L, 1821. 1st Ed. 4to, orig bds; worn, lower joint partly split. Marginal stains; browned. Manney copy. P Oct 11 (247) $1,200

1st American Ed. Phila., 1821. 4to, modern half calf; rubbed. With 26 maps & plates, 4 folding. 1 map torn. cb Oct 10 (86) $475

Anr copy. Wit 20 plates & maps. Tp & frontis browned; plates foxed. W July 8 (267) £280

— Journal of a Second Voyage for the Discovery of a North-West Passage.... L, 1824. 4to, modern half calf. With 25 (of 26) plates & 13 maps, charts & profiles, 8 folding. cb Oct 10 (87) $425

— Journal of a Third Voyage.... L, 1826. 4to, modern half calf. With 11 plates & charts, the folding charts at end mtd on linen. Some foxing. W July 8 (270) £370

— Journal of the First, Second and Third Voyages for the Discovery of a North-West Passage. L, 1828. 5 vols. 16mo, contemp calf. W July 8 (272) £80

— Narrative of an Attempt to Reach the North Pole. L, 1828. 1st Ed. 4to, modern half calf. With 4 plates & 3 maps. Some foxing. W July 8 (271) £340

Parsifal. See: Wagner, Richard

Parsons, George F. See: Grabhorn Printing

Partington, Charles Frederick

— The National History and Views of London. L, [n.d.]. 2 vols. 8vo, cloth; lacking front free endpapers. Some spotting. bba July 23 (362) £130 [Marlborough]

Partington, James Riddick

— A History of Chemistry. L, 1970. 4 vols. O Sept 24 (193) $600

— A History of Greek Fire and Gunpowder. Cambr., [1960]. In d/j. sg Nov 14 (303) $325

Pascal, Blaise, 1623-62

— Pensees.... Paris, 1761. 12mo, contemp calf; upper joint weak, lower joint cracked. Inscr & annotated by Hannah More. Milne copy. Ck June 12 (155) £850

Pascoli, Lione

— Vite de' pittori, scultori ed architetti Perugini. Genoa, 1768-69. 2 vols. 4to, contemp vellum bds; soiled, short tear to spine of Vol II. S Feb 11 (208) £420 [Erlini]

Pashley, Robert, 1805-59

— Travels in Crete. L, 1837. 8vo, calf gilt by Bedford. With folding map, 10 lithos & 4 wood-engraved plates. S June 30 (372) £1,400 [Consolidated Real]

Anr copy. 2 vols. 8vo, orig cloth; worn. With frontises, 8 plates, folding map & folding plate of inscriptions. Staniforth Library labels. S July 1 (672) £700 [Consolidated Real]

Pasquali, Giovanni Battista. See: Smith Library, Joseph

Pasquin, Peter. See: Pyne, William Henry

Pasrenti, Marino

— Dizionario dei Luoghi di Stampa Falsi.... Florence, 1951. One of 666. In d/j. sg Oct 31 (281A) $100

Pass, Crispin van de

— Les Abus du mariage, ou sont clairement representez..... [Amst.?], 1641. Oblong 4to, later half vellum. With engraved title, 50 ports, 1 other plate & 1 page of music. Some waterstains. B Nov 1 (372) HF13,000

— Hortus floridus. Utrecht & Arnheim, 1614-[16]. 4to, old vellum; loose. With engraved title (loose & frayed), 2 allegorical plates, 2 garden views & 172 botanical plates. Stain in blank upper outer corner through most of work. sg Feb 13 (201) $14,500

Passeri, Giovanni Battista, 1610?-79

— Lucernae fictiles musei Passerii. Pesaro, 1739-51. 3 vols in 2. Folio, modern cloth. With port & 320 plates only. Frontis rehinged; lacking plates 24 & 25 in Vol II. sg Sept 6 (211) $200

Passsavanti, Jacopo

— Specchio de vera Penientia. [Florence, 12 Mar 1495]. 4to, old vellum over bds. Some foxing a1 with worm hole & laid down on old backing sheet. cb Dec 5 (94) $1,400

Pasternak, Boris Leonidovich

— Dr. Zhivago. L, 1958. 1st Ed in English. In d/j. bbc Sept 23 (466) $80

Pasteur, Louis, 1822-95

— Etudes sur le vin.... Paris, 1866. 1st Ed. 8vo, orig wraps, rear cover loose. With 32 plates, most colored. sg May 14 (120) $750

— Examen critique d'un ecrit posthume de Claude Bernard sur la fermentation. Paris, 1879. 8vo, orig wraps; soiled, spine worn & broken. Inscr. pn June 11 (127) £220 [Rivlin]

Pastissier...

— Le Pastissier Francois. Ou est enseigne la maniere de faire toute sorte de Pastisserie.... Amst.: Elzevier, 1655. Bound with: Le Cuisinier francois. The Hague: Vlacq, 1656. 12mo, contemp vellum. Some waterspotting. HH May 12 (900) DM56,000

Patchen, Kenneth

— Cloth of the Tempest. NY & L, [1943]. In d/j, which has tape residue on reverse & some browning. Sgd. wa Sept 26 (227) $70

— Sleepers Awake. [NY, 1946]. One of 148. In d/j with tape stains on reverse. Sgd. wa Sept 26 (228) $70

— A Surprise for the Bagpipe Player. Palo Alto, 1956. One of 200. Suite of poems ptd in Ms facsimile. wa Dec 19 (217) $180

Pater, Walter, 1839-94

— Marius the Epicurean. L, 1929. One of 325. Illus by Thomas Mackenzie. 2 vols. 4to, half vellum gilt; some wear. O Aug 25 (142) $50

— Sebastian Van Storck. L & NY, 1927. One of 1,050, with 1 plate sgd. Illus by Alastair. 4to, orig cloth; soiled. With 8 colored illusts. K Sept 29 (2) $65; sg Sept 26 (2) $150

Anr copy. Library stamps. sg Jan 30 (2) $110

— Works. L, 1910-14. Library Ed. 10 vols. wa Feb 20 (100) $200; wa Apr 9 (51) $75

Paterson, Daniel, 1739-1825

— British Itinerary, being a New and Accurate Delineation.... L, 1785. 2 vols. 8vo, contemp calf; worn, 1 cover detached. b Nov 18 (229) £100

Paterson, Robert F.

— The America and the Defenders of the America's Cup.... NY, 1934-[35]. One of 250. Folio, loose as issued in lea folding case. With uncolored engraved title with colored flag & 16 colored plates, each sgd & numbered; extra plate at end showing 1934 Match. Sold w.a.f. DuPont copy. CNY Oct 8 (196) $4,500

Paterson, William, 1755-1810

— A Narrative of Four Journeys into the Country of the Hottentots and Caffraria.... L, 1789. Folio, orig bds. S June 25 (114) £620 [Lawson]

Patterson, James Laird

— Journal of a Tour in Egypt.... L, 1852. 8vo, later half calf; joints cracked. With folding frontis & 5 plates. S July 1 (784) £150 [Sofer]

Pattison, Mark, 1813-84. See: Grabhorn Printing

Paul, Elliot. See: Quintanilla, Luis

Paul, Sir James Balfour

— The Scots Peerage. Edin., 1904-14. 9 vols, including Index. Orig cloth. pnE Oct 1 (309) £420

Paul, William, 1822-1905

— The Rose Garden. L, 1848. 1st Ed. 8vo, contemp half calf; rubbed. With 15 hand-colored plates. Tp browned. Ck May 15 (44) £350

10th Ed. L, 1903. 4to, orig cloth. Inscr to his daughter. pnE Oct 2 (425) £140

Paulhan, Jean

— Les Hain-Teny. [Paris, 1956]. One of 116 on Auvergne. Illus by Andre Masson. Folio, half mor, orig covers bound in. P June 17 (269) $2,500

Pauli, Frederick G.

— A Record of a Trip Through Canada's Wilderness.... NY: Pvtly ptd, 1907. Half cloth. With folding map laid in. Koopman copy. O Oct 29 (229) $1,000

Pauli, Johannes

— Schimpff und Ernst, das ist ein nuetzliches Buch.... Frankfurt: Nicolaum Basse, 1570. 8vo, contemp calf over wooden bds with metal clasps; worn. Some foxing & browning. O May 26 (141) $675

Paulini, I.

— Alfabeto di iniziali animate da figure mitologiche su fondo di paesaggio e incorniciate da rettangoli ornate di figure e groteschi. [Italy, c.1560]. Oblong 4to, modern vellum bds. With 20 plates. First 3 plates soiled. C June 24 (240) £1,800 [Franks]

Paulmier, Julien de. See: Le Paulmier de Grentemesnil, Jacques

Pauly, Theodore de

— Description Ethnographique des peuples de la Russie. St. Petersburg, 1862. Folio, orig mor; worn. With 62 color costume plates, tinted litho of skulls, double-page ethnographic table & doublepage colored ethnographic map. Foxed, mostly in margins. sg Jan 9 (163) $1,200

Pauquet, Hippolyte & Polidor

— Modes et costumes historiques. Paris, [1864]. 4to, orig cloth; front joint cracked, rubbed at corners. With engraved title & 96 colored plates. bba May 28 (472) £320 [Brown]

Anr copy. Contemp mor gilt; rubbed, spine ends chipped, gutta-percha perished. With 96 hand-colored plates. Some marginal browning. C Oct 30 (64) £350 [Roseigno]

Pausanias

— Opera. Venice: Aldus, July 1516. Folio, 18th-cent mor gilt. C Nov 27 (20) £7,500 [Turner]

Pauw, Corneille de, 1739-99

— Recherches philosophiques sur les Egyptiens et les Chinois. Berlin, 1773. 2 vols. 12mo, contemp calf gilt. SI June 10 (835) LIt220,000

Pavlov, Ivan Petrovich, 1849-1936

— Lectures on Conditioned Reflexes.... NY: International Publishers, [1928]. 1st Ed in English. bbc Apr 27 (554) $75

— Lektsii o rabotie glavnykh pishchevaritelnykh zhelyoz. St. Petersburg, 1897. 8vo, contemp half calf; spine worn. C June 24 (186) £5,000 [Rota]

— The Work of the Digestive Glands. L, 1902. 1st Ed in English. sg May 14 (122) $375

Paxton, Sir Joseph, 1801-65
See also: Lindley & Paxton

— The Magazine of Botany, and Register of Flowering Plants. L, 1834-49. Vol 14 only. Contemp half mor; 1 signature partially detached. With 48 hand-colored plates. b June 22 (370) £360

Anr copy. Vols I & II only. 8vo, contemp half mor gilt; rubbed. With 86 hand-colored plates. DW Mar 4 (119) £740

Anr copy. Vol I only. Half mor. With 42 hand-colored plates. Minor foxing. Sold w.a.f. sg Sept 19 (205) $800

Reissue of Vol I. L, 1841-36-49. Vols I-XIII. contemp half mor; worn, most joints & some inner hinges lacking. With 419 haand-colored plates only. Various defs. Sold w.a.f. CNY June 9 (152) $4,000

Anr Ed. L, 1841-49. 16 vols. 8vo, contemp half mor gilt; Vol XVI not quite uniform. With 716 (of 717) hand-colored plates of flowers & 1 (of 6) plates of garden designs. Some plates trimmed affecting captions; lacking half-titles. Sold w.a.f. S June 25 (60) £6,000 [Toscani]

Payer, Julius von

— New Lands within the Arctic Circle. L, 1876. 1st English Ed. 2 vols. 8vo, orig cloth; rubbed, extremities worn. DW Jan 29 (47) £120

Payne, Albert Henry

— The Royal Dresden Gallery. Dresden, [1845?-50]. 2 vols. 4to, later calf gilt; worn, half-inch tear at top of Vol II spine. Some spotting. bbc Apr 27 (452) $160

Payne, William

— Picturesque Views in Devonshire, Cornwall &c. L, 1826. Oblong 4to, modern half mor by Zaehnsdorf. With 16 colored plates. C May 20 (102) £1,300 [Harley-Mason]

Payne-Gallwey, Sir Ralph

— The Book of Duck Decoys. L, 1886. 4to, orig cloth; stained. With hand-colored litho frontis & 13 plates, 4 tinted. Library stamps, not affecting plates; a few leaves carelessly cut. pn Mar 19 (362) £180

— The Crossbow. L, 1903. 4to, orig cloth; worn. S July 1 (1316) £150 [Trotman]

Paz, Octavio
See also: Limited Editions Club

— Petrificada petrificante. Paris, 1978. One of 175. Illus by Antoni Tapies. Folio, loose as issued. CGen Nov 18 (428) SF11,000

Peacham, Henry, 1576?-1643?

— The Compleat Gentleman. L, 1661. 4to, contemp vellum. Tp stained. sg Oct 24 (249) $325

— The Worth of a Penny.... L, 1669. 4th Ed. 4to, later mor. Title cut down & mtd; some leaves repaired. bba Oct 24 (52) £70 [Ash Rare Books]

Peacock, Thomas Love, 1785-1866
See also: Gregynog Press

— Crochet Castle. L, 1831. 1st Ed. 8vo, half mor; rubbed. Lacking leaf of ads. bba Jan 30 (180) £440 [Bickersteth]

Anr copy. Orig bds. O July 14 (146) $275

— The Genius of the Thames.... L, 1810. 1st Ed. 8vo, orig bds; worn, rebacked. A4 holed in margin. bba Jan 30 (171) £220 [Holleyman & Treacher]

Anr copy. Modern half calf. bba Jan 30 (172) £110 [Bickersteth]

— Headlong Hall. L, 1816. 1st Ed. 12mo, contemp half calf. bba Jan 30 (174) £400 [Jarndyce]

Anr copy. 19th-cent half calf; rubbed. Some browning & soiling. S July 1 (999) £400 [Marlborough]

— The Misfortunes of Elphin. L, 1829. 1st Ed. 12mo, orig bds; rubbed. bba Jan 30 (178) £220 [Thorp]

Anr copy. Modern half mor. bba Jan 30 (179) £100 [Laywood]

— Nightmare Abbey. L, 1818. 12mo, contemp half calf; backstrip def. bba Jan 30 (175) £400 [Jarndyce]

Anr copy. Calf. rs Oct 17 (78A) $150

— Palmyra and Other Poems. L, 1806. 1st Ed. 12mo, contemp half calf. bba Jan 30 (170) £298 [S. Clarke]

— The Philosophy of Melancholy. L, 1812. 1st Ed. 4to, orig bds; rubbed & discolored. bba Jan 30 (173) £230 [Holleyman & Treacher]

— Rhododaphne: or the Thessalian Spell.... L, 1818. 12mo, orig bds; rubbed, lower cover detached. bba Jan 30 (176) £160 [Grant & Shaw]

— Works. L, 1891. One of 100 L.p. copies. 10 vols. 8vo, cloth. pnE Dec 4 (149) £160

Peacocke, Stephen Ponsonby

— Views in the Neilgherry & Koondah ranges.... L, 1847. Folio, orig half mor gilt; worn. With tinted litho title & 15 tinted litho views. Some spotting & staining, touching images; most plates detached. S May 14 (1300) £600 [Shapero]

Peake, Mervyn

— The Gormenghast Trilogy. L, 1946-59. ("Titus Groan; Gormenghast; Titus Alone.") In d/js. S Feb 11 (413) £280 [Sotheran]

Pearce, Thomas, fl.1722-56

— The Laws and Customs of the Stannaries in...Cornwall and Devon. L, 1725. Folio, contemp calf; rebacked, orig spine preserved. bba Jan 30 (29) £280 [Ambra]

Pearson, William, of Shrewsbury

— A Selection of Antiquities in the County of Salop. L, 1824. 4to, contemp bds with later backstrip; worn. With engraved title, map & 40 plates. Some spotting & offsetting. DW Dec 11 (122) £150

Peary, Robert Edwin, 1856-1920

— The North Pole. L, 1910. One of 500. 4to, orig vellum gilt; soiled. Manney copy. P Oct 11 (248) $2,250

General Hubbard Ed. In d/j. Manney copy. P Oct 11 (1249) $300

Peck, George Wilbur, 1840-1916

— Peck's Bad Boy and his Pa. Chicago, 1883. 1st Ed, 1st State. 12mo, orig wraps. Epstein copy. sg Apr 30 (362) $200

Peck's...

— Peck's New Pocket Base Ball Score Book. NY, 1866. 8vo, orig cloth over flexible bds. About a quarter of the vol with pencil notations from games played. sg Jan 9 (214) $225

Peets, Elbert. See: Hegemann & Peets

Peignot, Gabriel, 1767-1849

— Essai historique sur la lithographie...par G. P. Paris: Renouard, 1819. 8vo, early wraps, uncut. With litho frontis. Schlosser copy. P June 17 (574) $1,900

Peirce, John

— The New American Spelling-Book, Improved. Phila., 1795. 8vo, calf; worn. Text browned; some stains. bbc Sept 23 (347) $350

Pelekanidis, S. M. —& Others

— The Treasures of Mount Athos: Illuminated Manuscripts. Athens, 1974-75. Vols I & II. Folio, syn, in d/js. sg Oct 31 (246) $325

Pelham, Camden, Pseud.

— Chronicles of Crime, or the New Newgate Calendar. L, 1841. 2 vols. 8vo, half mor; rubbed. O May 26 (142) $70

Anr Ed. L, 1887. 2 vols. 8vo, half mor gilt, orig cloth covers bound in. With 52 plates. sg Oct 17 (350) $90

Pelham, Cavendish

— The World, or the Present State of the Universe. Liverpool & L, 1808. 2 vols. 4to, contemp half calf. bba Sept 19 (12) £140 [B. Bailey]

Peltier, Louis

— Voyage de Louis Peltier par terre et par mer.... Quebec, 1862. 8vo, orig wraps. sg June 18 (577) $800

Pemberton, Henry, 1694-1771

— A View of Sir Isaac Newton's Philosophy. L, 1728. 4to, contep calf gilt; rubbed. With 12 folding plates. S July 1 (1317) £280 [Phillips]

Pemberton, Israel —& Others

— An Address to the Inhabitants of Pennsylvania, by those Freemen of the City of Philadelphia.... L, 1777. 12mo, disbound. bbc Dec 9 (408) $350

Pembroke, Henry Herbert, 10th Earl of, 1734-94

— A Method of Breaking Horses and Teaching Soldiers to Ride.... L, 1761. 1st Ed. 8vo, early calf; some wear. With 2 folding plates. bbc Apr 27 (533) $130

Pendennis, Arthur. See: Thackeray, William Makepeace

Penfield, Edward. See: Pollard, Percival

Penn, Irving

— Moments Preserved. NY, 1960. 4to, cloth, in d/j. bbc Feb 17 (252) $300

Anr copy. Cloth. cb Dec 5 (95) $140

Anr copy. Orig cloth; spine scuffed, foot of spine bumped, extremities worn. sg Oct 8 (54) $425

Anr copy. Cloth, in d/j. sg Apr 13 (80) $500

Penn, William, 1644-1718

— Primitive Christianity Revived in the Faith and Practice of the People called Quakers. L: T. Sowle, 1696. 8vo, contemp calf; spine chipped. S Feb 11 (518) £300 [Rizzo]

Pennant, Thomas, 1726-98

— The Antiquities of London.... L, 1818. 8vo, orig bds; front cover detached, spine browned. With 50 plates. sg Apr 2 (220) $200

— Arctic Zoology. L, 1784-85. 1st Ed. 2 vols plus 1787 Supplement. Also bound in is the 1786 Ed of Histoire naturelle des oiseaux.... 4to, contemp mor gilt; extremities rubbed. P June 17 (290) $2,000

— British Zoology. L, 1766. Folio, contemp calf gilt; worn, rebacked & recornered. With 107 hand-colored plates. Without the Supplement. C Oct 30 (221) £7,000

[Arader]

Anr copy. Contemp bds; rebacked & recornered with mor. With 133 hand-colored plates. Roebuck with tear just affecting surface; 2 text leaves with long tears. C May 20 (191A) £9,500 [Marshall]

Anr Ed. L, 1776-77. 4 vols. 8vo, contemp calf; rebacked, worn at edges. With 4 engraved titles (2 numbered as plates) & 280 (of 284) plates. Some spotting. pn June 11 (261) £180

— The History of the Parishes of Whiteford and Holywell. L, 1796. 4to, recent half mor gilt. Library markings. DW May 13 (94) £55

— The Journey from Chester to London. L, 1782. 4to, old calf gilt; rebacked, rubbed. With engraved title & 22 plates. L Nov 14 (114) £50

— Of London. L, 1793. ("Some Account of London.") "3d" Ed. Bound in 3 vols. 4to, contemp half lea; rubbed. Sold w.a.f. Extra-illus with c.330 maps, ports & plates. C Oct 30 (135) £300 [Burden]

Anr copy. 4to, contemp russia gilt; rubbed, rebacked with old spines laid down, covers of Vol V detached. Extra-illus to a total of 764 plates & 5 watercolors, all mtd. Ck Nov 29 (277) £6,000

Anr copy. 5 vols. 4to inlaid to folio, contemp russia gilt; rubbed, some corners detached. Library markings; lacking some plates. Sold w.a.f. Extra-illus with 254 plates. pn Apr 23 (274) £120 [Jeffrey]

Anr Ed. L, 1805. Folio, calf gilt; worn & rebacked. With engraved title (stained), folding map & 15 plates. Marginal staining towards end of vol. L Nov 14 (115) £50

Anr Ed. L, [c.1820]. 2 vols. 4to, contemp calf gilt; rebacked, def. A few plates mtd & cut down, 1 repaired; 2 leaves of text in Vol I loose. Extra-illus with c.163 plates & ports.. pn Dec 12 (314) £130

— A Tour in Wales. L, 1784. 2 vols. 4to, contemp half mor; rubbed. With 63 plates, 11 folding. Title waterstained. bba Sept 19 (262) £110 [Hay Cinema]

Anr copy. Contemp calf gilt; upper cover of Vol I detached; Vol II rebacked, orig spine preserved. With 3 engraved titles & 63 plates, including the 10 supplemental plates. Some plates folded. DW Nov 20 (48) £105

Pennell, Elizabeth Robins & Joseph

— The Glory of New York. NY, 1926. One of 355. Folio, orig cloth; corners frayed, endpapers & prelims foxed. With 24 colored plates. sg Feb 6 (217) $150

— The Life of James McNeill Whistler. L: Heinemann, 1908. One of 150. 2 vols. 4to, orig half lea; some wear & soiling. wa Apr 9 (285) $90

— Lithography and Lithographers: Some Chapters in the History of the Art. L, 1898. Folio, orig cloth; rubbed & soiled. With 7 orig lithos. DW Mar 11 (543) £110

Pennell, Joseph, 1857-1926

— Etchers and Etching: Chapters in the History of Art. NY, 1919. Folio, cloth, in torn d/j; front free endpaper with silverfish damage. kh Nov 11 (184) A$70

Pennsylvania

See also: Franklin Printing, Benjamin

— New Topographical Atlas of the State of Pennsylvania. Phila., 1872. Folio, orig half sheep. With 27 hand-colored maps. Tp chewed & soiled; 1 map with tape repair on reverse. bbc Dec 9 (11) $130

Pennsylvania Gazette

— Pennsylvania Gazette. Phila.: Franklin & Hall, 13 Feb 1740. No 503. 2 leaves. Folio, disbound. Margins repaired; loss to lower fore-edge corners costing c.30 letters. P June 16 (13) $1,500

Anr Ed. Phila.: Franklin & Hall, 1764. No 1848. 2 leaves. Folio, disbound. Small holes costing several letters; some staining. P June 16 (100) $500

No 1901. [Phila., 1765]. Folio, disbound. Small gouge costing a few letters; some staining. P June 16 (110) $1,500

No 1923. Folio, disbound. Restored at central fold; trimmed close at bottom shaving a few words on p.3; some staining. P June 16 (114) $8,500

No 1924. Folio, disbound. Some soiling. Issued without an imprint so as to avoid violation of the Stamp Act. P June 16 (115) $8,500

No 1925. Folio, disbound. Small gouge costing a few letters. Issued without an imprint so as to avoid violation of the Stamp Act. P June 16 (116) $4,000

Nos 1918-22. 5 issues, each 2 leaves. Folio, disbound. Gouge costing a few letters. P June 16 (113) $4,750

Nos 1926-31. 6 Nos, each 2 leaves. Folio, disbound. Some staining & browning. P June 16 (117) $3,250

Anr Ed. Phila.: Hall & Sellers, 10 July 1776. 2 leaves. Folio, disbound. Lower left corner lost, costing portion of text; abraded in spots; some browning; a few stains. Contains early ptg of the Declaration of Independence.. P June 16 (210) $14,500

Pennsylvania Hospital. See: Franklin Printing, Benjamin

Pennsylvania Magazine...

— Pennsylvania Magazine: Or American Monthly Museum. Phila., 1776. For 1776. Disbound. Some browning. Contains 1st publication in magazine form of the Declaration of Independence. sg Dec 5 (199) $2,200

— Pennsylvania Magazine of History and Biography. Phila.: Historical Society of Pennsylvania, 1906-17. Vols 30-41. 12 vols. K Sept 29 (346) $325

Penther, Johann Friedrich

— Gnomonica fundamentalis & mechanica. Ausgburg, 1752. Folio, contemp bds. With frontis & 15 folding plates. Some marginal staining. S Dec 5 (418) £500 [Pirages]

Penzer, Norman M.

— An Annotated Bibliography of Sir Richard Francis Burton. L, 1923. Ltd Ed, sgd. 4to, cloth; upper hinges weak. Frontis loose. bba Feb 27 (436) £110 [Baring]

Pepys, Samuel, 1633-1703

— Memoires relating to the State of the Royal Navy of England.... [L], 1690. 1st Ed. 8vo, contemp calf; rebacked, most of old spine laid down. C Dec 16 (224) £850 [McCann]

Anr copy. Contemp calf; spine ends worn, extremities rubbed. L.p. copy. CNY Oct 8 (197) $3,800

— Memoirs.... L, 1825. 2 vols. 4to, orig bds; spines repaired, some rubbing & chipping. Tear into text on 2P2 of Vol II. P June 17 (291) $1,800

Anr copy. Calf; covers detached. Browning, foxing & offsetting. sg Oct 17 (351) $175

One of 12 for presentation. Contemp mor gilt; joints split. 2C4 in Vol II repaired. Inscr by the Master of Magdalene College. Epstein copy. sg Apr 30 (363) $3,000

Anr Ed. L, 1875-79. ("Diary and Correspondence....") 6 vols in 12. 8vo, mor gilt by Riviere; some joints broken. Extra-illus with plates & an autograph endorsement, sgd. P June 17 (345) $2,500

Anr Ed. L, 1897-99. ("The Diary.") 10 vols, including Index & Pepysiana. 8vo, contemp half mor gilt. bba Oct 24 (135) £180 [Beeleigh Abbey]

Anr Ed. L, 1927. ("Everybody's Pepys.") Ed by O. F. Morshead; illus by E. H. Shepard. Mor gilt with mor onlays by Riviere. b Nov 18 (284) £190

Anr copy. Mor with colored lea inlay of a yawning Pepys holding a candlestick, by Riviere. K Sept 29 (64) $375

Perceval le Gallois

— The High Holy Graal.... L, 1903. Illus by Jessie M. King. 8vo, orig cloth; rubbed, soiled. DW Apr 8 (526) £190

Percier, Charles, 1764-1838 —& Fontaine, Pierre Francois Leonard, 1762-1853

— Choix des plus celebres maisons de plaisance de Rome.... Paris, 1809. Folio, modern half vellum; endpapers renewed, edges rubbed. With 77 plates, including titles & Plate 39 bis. Marginal tears; Plate 75 creased; Plates 28-35 misbound between Plates 3 & 4 & Plate 39 bis between 42 & 43; small dampstains to Plates 46 & 52; some foxing. McCarty-Cooper copy. CNY Jan 25 (57) $3,800

— Description des ceremonies et des fetes qui ont eu lieu pour le mariage se S.M. l'Empereur Napoleon avec S.A.I. Madame l'Archiduchesse Marie-Louise d'Autriche. Paris: Didot l'aine, 1810. Folio, contemp bds; edges & corners rubbed & scuffed. With 13 plates. C Oct 30 (66) £320 [Bifolco]

— Palais, maisons et autre edifices modernes dessines a Rome. Paris, 1798. Folio, contemp bds. Some browning. SI June 10 (749) LIt800,000

Percival, Robert, 1765-1826

— An Account of the Island of Ceylon. L, 1803. 4to, contemp half calf; rubbed. With folding map & 3 folding charts. bba Sept 19 (91) £900 [Baring]

Percival, Thomas, 1740-1804

— Medical Ethics; or a Code of Institutes.... Manchester, 1803. 8vo, early 19th-cent half lea; joints rubbed. Lacking half-title. sg Nov 14 (99) $950

Percy, Henry Algernon, 5th Earl of Northumberland

— The Regulations and Establishment of the Household of Henry Algernon Percy.... L: [Pvtly ptd], 1770. 8vo, contemp calf; upper cover detached, rubbed. bba May 14 (91) £180 [Alec-Smith]

Percy, Thomas, 1729-1811

— Reliques of Ancient English Poetry. L, 1767. 2d Ed. 3 vols. 8vo, contemp calf. wa Dec 9 (484) $50

Perdriel-Vaissieres, J.

— Rupert Brooke's Death and Burial. New Haven, 1917. One of 300. Trans by Vincent O'Sullivan. Wraps. sg Dec 12 (32) $100

Peret, Benjamin. See: Breton & Peret

Peret, Benjamin —& Aragon, Louis
— 1929 Brussels: Editions de la Revue Varietes, 1929. One of 160. Illus by Man Ray. 4to, wraps. CGen Nov 18 (412) SF9,000

Perez de Luxan, Diego
— Expedition into New Mexico Made by Antonio de Espejo, 1582-1583.... Los Angeles: Quivira Society, 1929. One of 500. Orig bds; worn, spine detached. NH May 30 (396) $50

Perez de Mendoza y Quizada, Miguel
— Resumen de la verdadera destreza de las armas.... Madrid, 1675. 4to, modern syn; needs rebdg. Later caption mtd over orig on plate. sg Mar 26 (203) $250

Perez de Villa-Amil, Genaro
— Espana artistica y monumental. Paris, 1842-50. Vol I. Folio, contemp half mor; worn. With 48 plates. Text dampstained. Ck Dec 11 (245) £450

Perez, Isaac Loeb
— Gleichnisse. Berlin, 1920. Illus by Jakob Steinhardt. 4to, pictorial wraps; worn. K Mar 22 (209) $120

Pergaud, Louis
— La Guerre des boutons. Paris, 1912. One of 19 on hollande Van Gelder. Mor extra by P. L. Martin, orig wraps bound in. S May 28 (417) £1,600 [Lardanchet]

Perilla, F.
— Il Monte Athos. Salonica, 1927. One of 525. 4to, half mor preserving pictorial wraps. With 12 colored plates & 18 photographic plates. Softening near lower inner margin of 1st few leaves. S July 1 (674) £500 [Consolidated Real]

Perkins, John
— A Profitable Booke...Treating of the Lawes of Englande. L: Richard Totell, [1559?]. 8vo, disbound. Black letter. Interleaved, with early marginalia; prelims frayed with loss. STC 19634; Beale T427. sg Mar 12 (246) $700

Perkins, Justin
— A Residence of Eight Years in Persia. Andover & NY, 1843. 8vo, orig cloth; worn. With frontis, folding map & 26 lithos, some hand-colored. S Nov 15 (1182) £200 [Ozbek]

Pernau, F. A.
— Gruendliche Anweisung alle Arten voegel zu fangen. Nuremberg, 1796. 8vo, 19th-cent bds; rubbed. With frontis & 44 (of 45) plates. HH May 12 (927) DM2,000

Perneder, Andreas
— Een Tractaet van criminele saken.... Antwerp: H. de Laet, 1550. 8vo, bdg not described. B May 12 (20) HF750

Pernety, Antoine Joseph
— The History of a Voyage to the Malouine.... L, 1771. 1st Ed in English. 4to, contemp calf; rebacked, rubbed. With 16 plates. A few tears. bba Apr 9 (150) £400 [Dawson]

Pernot, Francois Alexandre —& Pichot, Joseph
— Vues pittoresques de l'Escosse. Paris, 1826. 4to, contemp half mor; With 60 lithos & 12 litho vignettes.. With 72 plates Interleaved; some foxing. P June 18 (57) $400

Anr copy. 12 parts. 4to, orig wraps as issued; some soiling. With 60 lithos, mtd proofs on chine & with 12 litho vignettes, also mtd proofs on chine. P June 18 (576) $500

Pernot, Hubert
— En paysturc. L'ile de Chio. Paris, 1903. Inscr. S June 30 (369) £380 [Lemos]

Peron, Francois —& Others
— Voyage de decouvertes aux Terres Australes. Paris, 1824. 2d Ed. 4 vols; lacking Atlas. 8vo, modern cloth. SI Dec 5 (912) LIt350,000

Perottus, Nicolaus, 1430-80
— Cornucopiae.... Venice: Joannes de Tridino alias Tacuinum, 1504. ("Cornucopie nuper emendatum a dno Benedicto Brugnolo....") Folio, contemp pigskin over wooden bds with brass catches; lacking clasps; bottotm of spine damaged. sg Mar 12 (69) $850

Anr Ed. Venice: Aldus, Nov 1513. ("In hoc volumine habentur haec Cornucopiae sive linguae latinae commentarii.") Folio, contemp vellum; tears at head & foot of hinges, small wormholes in spine. Lacking 1 blank; some leaves browned & waterstained; some marginalia. C Dec 16 (150) £750 [Soave]

Perrault, Charles, 1628-1703
— La Belle au bois dormant.... Paris, 1910. One of 400. Illus by Edmund Dulac. 4to, half mor extra, orig wraps bound in. cb Oct 25 (37) $150
— Les Contes. Paris, 1883. 8vo, mor gilt. Foxed. bba Oct 10 (54) £160 [Thorp]

Anr Ed. Paris, [1922]. One of 283. Folio, wraps; partly disbound. sg Jan 30 (35) $50
— Festiva ad capita annulumque decursio, a rege Ludovico XIV principibus.... Paris, 1670. Folio, half vellum; rubbed. HH May 12 (887) DM4,800
— Old-Time Stories. L, 1921. Illus by W. Heath Robinson. 4to, orig cloth; tears

along lower inner hinge. With 6 colored plates. P Oct 11 (268) $400

Perrault, Claude, 1613-88

— Memoirs for a Natural History of Animals. L: J. Streater, 1688. Folio, contemp mor gilt; worn. With frontis & 35 plates. Some Ms corrections in text. Honeyman copy. S May 28 (12) £1,200 [Phelps]

Anr copy. Contemp calf; worn, rebacked. sg May 7 (167) $650

Perrault, Claude & Pierre

— Oeuvres diverses de physique et de mechanique. Leiden, 1721. 4to, contemp calf; joints cracked, rubbed. With port, 3 folding plates & 8 other plates. bba Sept 5 (241) £80 [Winterdawn Books]

Perret, Steven

— XXV. fables des animaux. Delft: Adrien Gerards, 1621. Folio, old bds; worn. With 25 full-page illusts. Upper half of vol dampstained throughout. sg Oct 24 (251) $450

Perrier, Francois, 1590-1656

— Icones et Segmenta Illustrium e Marmore Tabularum quae Romae adhuc Extant. Rome, 1645. Bound with: Icones et segmenta illustrium e marmore tabularum quae Romae adhuc extant. Oblong folio, old vellum bds; loose. With engraved title & 100 plates in 1st work & 50 plates in 2d work. Tp spotted & soiled in 1st work; tp of 2d work torn; some fraying & staining. S Feb 11 (163) £450 [Barker]

— Segmenta nobilium signorum et statuarum.... Rome & Paris, 1638. Folio, modern vellum. With engraved title & 100 plates. Some browning & staining. SI June 10 (753) LIt1,000,000

Perrinet D'Orval, Jean Charles

— Essay sur les feux d'artifice pour le spectacle et pour la guerre. Paris, 1745. 1st Ed. 8vo, modern half mor. With 13 folding plates. S July 1 (1318) £250 [Middleton]

Perrot, Georges, 1832-1914 —& Others

— Exploration archeologique de la Galatie et de la Bithynie.... Paris, 1872. 2 vols. Folio, orig bds; soiled, backstrips repaired. With 80 plates & 7 maps. S June 30 (180) £500 [Pagan]

Perrott, Leslie M.

— Concrete Homes. Melbourne, [n.d.]. Half cloth. kh Nov 11 (609) A$80

Perry, Charles, 1698-1780

— A View of the Levant: Particularly of Constantinople.... L, 1743. 1st Ed. Folio, contemp half calf; rubbed. With 33 plates on 20 leaves. Ck Dec 11 (246) £900

Anr copy. Contemp calf; rebacked preserving spine, rebacked. With 33 on 20 plates. Some discoloration to text. S Nov 21 (297) £1,300 [Quaritch]

Perry, George, Conchologist

— Conchology, or the Natural History of Shells. L, [watermarked 1822-28]. Folio, contemp mor gilt; upper cover stained, corners scuffed. With 61 hand-colored plates. C Oct 30 (222) £1,800 [Schuster]

Perry, John, 1670-1732

— An Account of the Stopping of Daggenham Breach. L, 1721. 8vo, modern half calf. bba Apr 9 (189) £170 [Cline]

Perry, Matthew Calbraith, 1794-1858

— Narrative of the Expedition of an American Squadron to the China Seas and Japan.... Wash., 1856. 1st Ed. Vol I only. Orig cloth; worn & soiled. F Mar 26 (635) $300

Anr copy. Orig cloth; worn, spine torn. With 89 plates & 6 maps Some foxing. NH May 30 (305) $275

Perse, St. John

— Anabasis. L, 1930. One of 350, sgd by T. S. Eliot. Trans by Eliot. bba Oct 10 (439) £60 [Ball]

Anr copy. Epstein copy. sg Apr 29 (145) $250

Pershing, John J., 1860-1948

— My Experiences in the World War. NY, 1931. 2 vols. In d/js. cb Dec 5 (96) $120

Anr copy. In chipped d/js, 1 with spine def. Inscr. wa Oct 19 (241) $75

Persius Flaccus, Aulus, 34-62 A.D. See: Juvenalis & Persius Flaccus

Personne. See: DeFontaine, Felix G.

Pertusier, Charles

— Promenades pittoresques dans Constantinople et sur les rives du Bosphore.... Paris, 1815-17. 4 vols. 8vo & folio, contemp half mor gilt. With 25 plates, 4 folding. Some spotting; 1 short tear; 3 of the double-page plates detached from guards; stamp of Sibirskago Universiteta on titles of text vols. S June 30 (183) £3,400 [Consolidated Real]

Peruschi, Giovanni Battista

— Informatione del regno, e stato del gran re di Mogor. Brescia: P. M. Marchetti, 1597. 8vo, modern vellum. Some spotting. S May 14 (1297) £320 [Sokol]

Peter I, Emperor of Russia

— Pis'ma Petra Velikako k Grafu Borisu Petrovichu Sheremetevu. Moscow, 1774. Folio, needs rebdg. Some foxing; writing on tp inked over. sg Oct 24 (252) $250

Peters, DeWitt Clinton

— The Life and Adventures of Kit Carson. NY, 1858. 1st Ed. 8vo, cloth; extremities rubbed. sg Dec 5 (200) $140

Peters, Fred J.

— Sporting Prints by N. Currier and Currier & Ives. NY, 1930. One of 750. 4to, cloth; worn. O Jan 14 (144) $70

Peters, Harry Twyford

— America on Stone.... Garden City, 1931. One of 751. 4to, cloth. sg Nov 7 (152) $200

— California on Stone. Garden City, 1935. Out-of-series copy. 4to, orig cloth. bbc Apr 27 (610) $175

Anr Ed. NY, [1976]. 4to, cloth; soiled. Facsimile reprint of the 1935 Ed. sg Oct 31 (283) $50

— Currier & Ives, Printmaker to the American People. NY, [1976]. 4to, cloth; soiled. Facsimile reprint of the 1929-31 Ed. sg Oct 31 (284) $50

Peters, Samuel A.

— A General History of Connecticut. L, 1781. 8vo, modern half mor; worn. O Nov 26 (142) $275

Petis de la Croix, Francois, 1653-1713

— Memoires du sieur de la Croix.... Paris, 1684. 2 vols. 8vo, contemp calf; worn. Fore-edge of Vol I tp cut into; some browning. S June 30 (181) £2,400 [Kutluoglu]

Peto, Sir Samuel Morton

— The Resources and Prospects of America. L & NY, 1866. 8vo, cloth, unopened; worn. With 2 plates. O Jan 14 (145) $90

Petrarca, Francesco, 1304-74

See also: Fore-Edge Paintings; Limited Editions Club

— De rebus memorandis...vergleichen auch in Teutscher. Frankfurt: Egenolph, 1566. Bound with: Vives, J. L. Von gebuerlichem Thun und Lassen eines Christlichen Ehemanns. frankfurt: Egenolff, 1566. Folio, contemp calf with date 1569 stamped on upper cover; head of spine chipped. Small hole in 1 title. S Dec 5 (180) £6,800 [Das Bucher Kabinett]

Anr copy. Bound with: Vives, J. L. Von gebuerlichem Thun und Lassen eines Christlichen Ehemanns. Frankfurt, 1566. contemp blindstamped calf dated 1569; spine head chipped. Lacking 2 prelim leaves of Part 2 of 2d work; small hole in 2d title. S May 28 (57) £800 [Maggs]

— Opera. Basel: Johann Amerbach, 1496. 1st Collected Ed. Folio, 19th-cent half lea. 55 lines, roman letter. Some repairs; water-stains & other defs. Sold w.a.f. 381 (of 389) leaves. Goff P-365. SI June 10 (762) LIt450,000

Anr Ed. Venice: per Simon Papiensem dictum Bivilaquam, 1503. Folio, 17th-cent vellum. Small piece of Z1 repaired with loss of a few letters (restored in pen facsimile); some staining. S May 28 (55) £1,200 [Zioni]

Anr Ed. Basel, 1554. 2 vols. Folio, contemp vellum. Frontis repaired at inner margin; some browning & spotting; stain on BBB7-8; some worming at end of Vol II. SI Dec 5 (971) LIt400,000

— Trostspiegel in glueck und Unglueck. Frankfurt, 1572. Bound with: De rebus memorandis in Teutscher spraach. Frankfurt, 1566. Folio, old vellum; worn, spine def. With 260 woodcut illusts in 1st work & 5 in 2d work, all after Burgkmair. Some soiling & browning; a few tears; library markings. Ck Nov 29 (279) £1,800

— Le Vite degli huomini illustri. Venice: Gregorio de Gregorii, Jan 1527. 8vo, contemp mor with name on front cover, Sebastian Horabon; spine restored. SI June 10 (761) LIt2,500,000

Canzonieri

— 1548. - Sonetti, canzoni, et triomphi. Venice: Alessandro Brucioli. 8vo, 16th-cent mor gilt; corners & edges worn, hole in spine. Some spotting or soiling; 1st few leaves stained; a few lines crossed out in ink on L3v, L4r, O2v & in index. S May 13 (786) £580 [Maggs]

— 1553. - Il Petrarcha.... Venice: D. Giglio. 2 parts in 1 vol. 4to, 18th-cent calf gilt; extremities worn. Lower margins water-stained. DW Mar 4 (245) £200

— 1574. - Venice: I. Vidali. 4to, contemp vellum. With woodcut map & with 6 woodcut illusts to the Trionfi. Old scored writing on tp; modern owner's stamp in text. sg Oct 24 (253) $275

— 1581. - Venice: Alessandro Griffio. 4to, old vellum; loose. Some browning; lacking last leaf. sg Mar 12 (247) $200

— 1902. - Sonnets. New Rochelle: George D. Sproul One of 18 ptd on vellum. 4to, mor extra. sg May 7 (168) $4,600

Petrasanta, Silvester

— De symbolis heroicis, libri IX. Amst., 1682. ("Symbola Heroica.") 4to, contemp calf; worn. Some browning & spotting. SI June 10 (783) LIt850,000

Petrizky, Anatol

— Anatol Petrizky: Teatral'ni Stroy. Kiev, 1929. Text by V. Khmurogo. Folio, wraps; rebacked. sg Apr 2 (70) $650

Petronius Arbiter

— Le Satyricon. Paris, 1910. One of 150. Illus by Rochegrosse. 4to, contemp lev gilt by Ourvand. With 4 hand-colored plates. bbc Sept 23 (57) $600

Anr Ed. Paris, 1949. One of 218. Illus by E. Othon Friesz. Folio, unsewn in orig wraps. With 40 colored lithos, including upper cover. sg Sept 26 (115) $325; sp Sept 22 (316) $375

Petrucci, Gioseffo

— Prodomo apologetico alli studi Chicheriani. Amst., 1677. 4to, contemp vellum. With frontis & 8 plates. Some foxing. SI Dec 5 (538) LIt1,800,000

Petrus Comestor

See also: Rolewinck, Werner

— Scolastica historica sacre scripture. [Strasbourg: Ptr of the 1483 Jordanus de Quedlinburg (Georg Husner)], 1485. Folio, contemp blind-stamped pigskin over wooden bds, with brass clasp plates. 47 lines & headlines; double column; types 3:91G (text), 2:91G (secondary headings) & 1:160G (title, headlines, chapter incipits); rubricated; 1st initial in pale pink-brown with leafwork within a green frame. Heavily annotated in several inks. 231 (of 232) leaves; lacking the blank. Goff P-462. Schoyen copy. P Dec 12 (33) $17,000

Petrus Lombardus, 1100?-c.1160

— Sententiarum. Basel: Nicolaus Kesler, 22 Sept 1488. ("Sententiarum libri IV.") Folio, contemp half deerskin; lacking catches & clasps; needs rebacking. 280 (of 281) leaves. Goff P-491. sg Mar 12 (127) $1,500

Anr Ed. [Nuremberg]: Anton Koberger, [after 2 Mar 1491]. ("Quaestiones super IV libros Sententiarum Petri Lombardi cum textu eiusdam.") Part 2 only. Folio, modern bds. 64 lines & headline; gothic letter; large initials on A2r in red & blue; other initials in red. Hole through 3&3-6 repaired with some loss; lacking initial blank. 218 leaves. Goff P-486. sg Mar 12 (128) $600

Anr Ed. Venice: Lazarum Soardum, 1507. ("Quattuor sententiarum volumina....") 4to, contemp blind-stamped calf over wooden bds with remains of lea clasps; wormed & worn. Dampstained; wormed. bba May 14 (1) £280 [Gray]

Pett, Sir Peter

— The Happy Future State of England.... L, 1688. Folio, contemp calf; rebacked preserving most of spine, rubbed. Variant with "As to the Candour of the English Nation" at beginning of discourse. Dedicastions to the Marquesses of Halifax & Powys misbound; some browning; lacking final blank. pn May 14 (10) £110 [Clarke]

Pettigrew, Thomas Joseph

— A History of Egyptian Mummies. L, 1834. 4to, modern half mor; worn. With 13 plates, several hand-colored. O Nov 26 (143) $250

— Medical Portrait Gallery. L, [1838-40]. 4 vols. 4to, contemp half calf; worn. S May 13 (901) £320 [Rizzo]

Petzendorfer, Ludwig

— Schriften Atlas: eine Sammlung der Wichtigsten Schreib- und Druckschriften aus alter und neuer Zeit.... Stuttgart, [early 1900s]. Folio, loose in cloth folder. With 144 color plates. sp Feb 6 (538) $220

Petzholdt, Julius

— Bibliotheca Bibliographica. Nieuwkoop, 1972. 8vo, cloth. sg Oct 31 (285) $80

Peucer, Caspar

— Les Devins, ou commentaire des principales sortes de devinations. Lyon: Honorati, 1584. 4to, vellum. SI June 10 (768) LIt1,700,000

Peurbach, Georg

— Tabulae eclypsium.... Vienna: J. Winterburger for L. & L. Alantsee, 1514. Folio, modern vellum. Has the 2-leaf Tabella manualis. S Dec 5 (419) £3,500 [Lib. Scheler]

Peyre, Marie Joseph

— Oeuvres d'architecture. Paris, 1765. Folio, 19th-cent half lea; joints rubbed. With 19 plates. sg May 7 (169) $900

Peysonnel, Claude Charles de

— Observations historiques et geographiques, sur les peuples barbares qui ont habite les bords du Danube.... Paris, 1765. 4to, contemp calf; rubbed, upper joint split. With frontis, 4 folding maps & 9 plates. bba Sept 19 (146) £180 [Greenwood]

Pfannstiel, Arthur

— Modigliani. Paris, [1929]. 4to, orig wraps; chipped & browned. sg apr 2 (192) $140

Pfeiffer, Ida

— Visit to Iceland and the Scandinavian North. L, 1852. 8vo, cloth. With chromolitho title & 7 chromolitho plates. sg Jan 9 (164) $175

Pfeiffer, Ludwig G. C.

— Abbildung und Beschreibung bluehender Cacteen.... Cassel, [1838]-43-50. 2 vols. 4to, disbound. With 60 hand-colored plates. Some browning & discoloration; a few plates trimmed; lacking tp to Vol I. S June 25 (62) £1,400 [Koch]

Pfintzing, Melchior

— Der Aller-Durchleuchtigste Ritter.... Ulm, [1679]. Folio, vellum dated 1682. Browned. FD Dec 2 (39) DM4,300

— Theur-Danck. Ulm: Matthaes Schultes, 1679. Folio, bds covered in a vellum Ms leaf. With frontis & 123 woodcuts in the text. Some leaves browned. S Dec 5 (241) £1,400 [Schumann]

Pfister, Rudolf. See: Sedlmaier & Pfister

Pfnor, Rudolph. See: Champollion-Figeac, Jacques Joseph

Pforzheimer Library, Carl Howard

— The Carl H. Pforzheimer Library: English Literature, 1475-1700. NY, 1940. 1st Ed, one of 150. 3 vols. Folio, orig cloth. Houghton-Manney copy. P Oct 11 (250) $4,500

Phaedrus. See: Aesop

Phair, Charles. See: Derrydale Press

Pharmacopoea...

— Pharmacopoea Wirtenbergica. Stuttgart, 1785. 2 parts in 1 vol. 4to, contemp half lea. B Nov 1 (451) HF2,600

Phelps'...

— Phelps' Travelers' Guide through the United States. NY: Horace Thayer, 1852. 16mo, mor gilt. With folding map, hand-colored in outline. sg June 18 (453) $350

Phelps, William D.

— Fore and Aft. Bost., 1871. 8vo, cloth; lacking front free endpaper. sg June 18 (113) $130

Philadelphia Centennial Exhibition

— The Masterpieces of the Centennial International Exhibition Illustrated. Phila: Gebbie & Barrie, [1876?]. 3 vols 4to, orig half sheep gilt; extremities worn. sg Feb 6 (218) $325

Philanthropos. See: Ladd, William

Philby, Harry St. John Bridges, 1885-1960

— The Heart of Arabia. L, 1922. 2 vols. sg Jan 9 (165) $300

Philelphus, Franciscus, 1398-1481

— Epistolae. Venice: Bernardinus Benalius, 1493-94. Bound with: Orationes et opuscula. Venice: Philippus Pincius, 1 June 1496. Folio, 18th-cent calf; rebacked, lower cover scraped, extremities rubbed, 1st & last quires disbound. Roman & Greek types. Some worming at beginning; some staining; a few leaves browned. 94 leaves; Goff P-594. 80 leaves; Goff P-611. Milne copy. CNY Dec 5 (307) $1,300

Philephus, Franciscus, 1378-1481

— Epistolae. [Basel, c.1496]. 8vo, contemp pigskin over oak bds with orig brass fittings; clasp broken. Lacking tp & last 3 leaves; 2 leaves def affecting text; early Ms notes in some margins. Sold w.a.f. b Mar 11 (109) £120

— Orationes cum quibusdam aliis eiusdam operibus. [Milan: Leonardus Pachel & Uldericus Scinzenzeler, 1483-84]. 1st Ed. 4to, 18th-cent vellum. 38 lines; roman letter. Browned. 224 leaves. Goff P-607. SI June 10 (772) LIt2,500,000

Philidor, Francois Andre Danican, 1726-95

— Analysis of the Game of Chess. L, 1790. 2 vols in 1. 8vo, contemp calf; spine rubbed, joints cracked. Ck May 8 (140) £100

— L'Analyze des echecs. L, 1749. 8vo, modern half mor. Tp & A2 repaired at inner margin; tp dampstained & with Blass library stamp at foot; gatherings A-C dampstained. Ck May 8 (133) £700

Anr Ed. L, 1752. 8vo, contemp calf. Ck May 8 (135) £220

— Chess Analysed. L, 1750. 8vo, contemp half sheep; upper joints cracked. T2 & T3 torn. Ck May 8 (138) £240

Anr Ed. L, 1773. 8vo, contemp sheep; joints cracked. Ck May 8 (139) £100

— Studies of Chess. L, 1803. 2 vols. 8vo, orig bds; rubbed. Library markings. bba Apr 9 (52) £110 [Grigoropoules]

Philip, Duke of Edinburgh —& Fisher, James

— Wildlife Crisis. L, 1971. One of 265, specially bound & with an added title, sgd by Prince Philip. 4to, orig mor. bba Apr 30 (319) £110 [Mandl]

Philip, Arthur, 1738-1814

— Extracts of Letters from Arthur Phillip...to Lord Sydney... L, 1791. 4to, modern half mor. C June 25 (125) £4,800 [Baring]

Philip II, King of Spain

— Ordinantie ende nieuwe declaratie onssheeren des Couincx op de onderhoudenisse vande pacificatie van Ghendt.... Antwerp: Plantin, 1578. 4to, bdg not described. B Nov 1 (291) HF220

Philip, John

— Researches in South Africa. L, 1828. 2 vols. 8vo, orig bds; rubbed & spotted, spines def. With 2 maps. bba Sept 19 (71) £160 [Mitchell]

Philips, Katherine, 1631-64

— Poems. L, 1669. Folio, mor extra; rubbed. With frontis. Cropped. W July 8 (34) £140

Phillip, Arthur, 1738-1814

— The Voyage of Governor Phillip to Botany Bay. L, 1789. 1st Ed. 4to, contemp calf; rebacked, modern endpapers, orig spine label mtd on rear pastedown. With engraved title, port & 53 plates. Some marginal browning to plates; tears to dedication leaf, pp. 271-72 & 7 plates or charts. C Oct 30 (67) £1,800 [Riverreds]

Anr copy. Contemp calf; rubbed. With engraved title, port & 53 plates & maps. Kangeroo Rat torn along lower plate mark; some spotting. Ck Oct 18 (79) £1,500

Anr copy. Contemp calf; rebacked, rubbed, corners chipped. With engraved title, port & 53 plates. Vulpine plate in later state; with the errata leaf. Small holes to centerfolds of 3 charts with slight loss to 2; caption to No 11 shaved; small hole to 2P2, affecting signature & 1 word on verso; foremargins of Plates 1 & 3 def; frontis & engraved title foxed. CNY Oct 8 (19) $1,300

Anr copy. Later half mor; worn, upper cover detached. With engraved title, 7 folding maps & charts & 46 plates. Lacking port. DW Mar 4 (36) £660

Anr copy. Contemp calf; rejointed, preserving orig backstrip. Plate at p.150 partly perforated along the plate-mark. kh Nov 11 (707) A$3,500

Anr copy. Contemp calf; rebacked, orig spine largely preserved. With engraved title, port & 53 plates, 32 with contemp hand-coloring and on laid paper. Some spotting & repairs. S June 25 (100) £6,500 [Quaritch/Hordern]

Phillipps, Evelyn March. See: Latham, Charles

Phillipps-Wolley, Sir Clive, 1854-1918

— Big Game Shooting. L, 1894. One of 250 L.p. copies. 2 vols. 4to, half mor. sg Jan 9 (299) $250

Phillips, Catherine Coffin
See also: Grabhorn Printing

— Portsmouth Plaza.... San Francisco: John Henry Nash, 1932. 4to, half vellum. b&b Feb 19 (223) $150

Anr copy. Half vellum; worn. cb Sept 12 (139) $130

Anr copy. 4to, sg June 18 (114) $80

Phillips, Henry, 1801-76

— The True Enjoyment of Angling. L, 1843. One of 100. 8vo, orig cloth; spine worn & repaired. bba Nov 28 (58) £100 [Sanders of Oxford]

Phillips, John, 1800-74

— Illustrations of the Geology of Yorkshire. L, 1835-36. 2d Ed. 2 vols in 1. 4to, contemp half calf gilt. With 47 plates & plans, 2 folding, 7 hand-colored. pnE Dec 4 (156) £150

Phillips, John Charles

— A Natural History of the Ducks. Cambr. MA, 1922-26. 4 vols. 4to, orig half cloth. CNY Dec 5 (296) $1,300

Phillips, John Charles —& Hill, Lewis Webb

— Classics of the American Shooting Field. Bost. & NY, 1930. sg May 21 (84) $140

Phillips, Le Roy

— A Bibliography of the Writings of Henry James. Bost., 1906. One of 250. cb Oct 17 (7740) $95

Phillips, Paul C. See: Lewis & Phillips

Phillips, Philip A. S.

— Paul de Lamerie, Citizen and Goldsmith of London. L, 1968. Folio, cloth, in d/j with lower cover torn. bba Aug 13 (40) £130 [Robertshaw]

Anr copy. Cloth, in d/j. bba Aug 13 (41) £120 [Heneage]

Phillips, Philip Lee

— A List of Geographical Atlases in the Library of Congress.... Wash., 1909-20. 4 vols. 4to, orig cloth; frayed, Vol IV with upper joint split. Some leaves chipped. bbc Sept 23 (68) $140

Anr copy. Vols I and III loose in bdg. sg Oct 31 (75) $275

— A List of the Maps of America in the Library of Congress. Wash., 1901. 4to, cloth; worn, shaken. O Sept 24 (194) $80

Anr Ed. Amst., [1967]. 4to, cloth. Reprint of 1901 Ed. sg Oct 31 (76) $100

Phillips, Philip Lee —& LeGear, Clara E.

— A List of Geographical Atlases in the Library of Congress.... Wash., 1909-20 & 1958-74. 8 vols. 4to, cloth; 1st few vols worn & shaken. O Sept 24 (195) $350

Phillips, Sir Richard, 1767-1840

— A Collection of Modern and Contemporary Voyages and Travels. L, 1805-9. Vol III only. Contemp calf; joints worn, 1 starting. Foxed. wa Mar 5 (551) $95

— Modern London: Being the History and the Present State of the British Metropolis. L, 1805. 4to, half calf. With folding frontis & map & 22 plates. Map cropped at top. Sold w.a.f. Extra-illus with 17 plates from a different series. bba Sept 19 (211) £70 [Cline]

— The Natural and Artificial Wonders of the United Kingdom. L, 1825. 3 vols. 12mo, contemp half mor. DW Nov 20 (48) £105

Phillpotts, Eden, 1862-1960

— Adventure in the Flying Scotsman. L, 1888. 1st Ed. Orig cloth; rubbed & soiled. With autograph postcard, sgd, tipped in. Epstein copy. sg Apr 30 (378) $750

— A Dish of Apples. L & NY, [1921]. One of 500. Illus by Arthur Rackham. 4to, orig cloth; soiled. Met Apr 28 (440) $300

Anr copy. Orig cloth. With 3 colored plates. Manney copy. P Oct 11 (262) $900

Anr copy. Orig cloth; soiled. sg Sept 26 (269) $500

Anr copy. With 3 color plates. sg Nov 7 (173) $750

Anr copy. Orig cloth; blistered. With 3 colored plates. sg Jan 30 (153) $475

— The Girl and the Faun. L, 1916. Ltd Ed. Illus by Frank Brangwyn. 4to, orig half vellum; stained. With colored frontis & 3 plates. b Nov 18 (52) £70

Philo of Byzantium

— De septem orbis spectaculis. Rome: Mascardus, 1640. 8vo, 18th-cent calf gilt; joints rubbed. C June 24 (279) £420 [Franks]

Philosophe inconnu. See: Saint-Martin, Louis Claude de

Philostratus, Flavius

— De la vie d'Apollonius Thyaneen.... Paris, 1611. 2 vols in 1. 4to, later vellum. Lightly stained. bba Oct 24 (17) £250 [Poole]

— De vita Apollonii Tyanei.... Bologna: Benedictus Hectoris, 1501. Folio, 18th-cent vellum. Some waterstaining & browning. SI Dec 5 (542) LIt850,000

Anr Ed. [Lyons: Balthasar de Gabiano, c.1506]. Folio, old bds; needs rebacking. Early underscoring & marginalia; title soiled. sg Mar 12 (249) $375

— Les Images ou tableaux de platte peinture des deux Philostrates.... Paris, 1637. Folio, contemp half calf; rebacked. Tp laid down & repaired; some margins repaired, with loss to text of p. 9. W July 8 (12) £210

Phipps, Constantine John, Baron Mulgrave, 1744-92

— A Voyage towards the North Pole. L, 1774. 1st Ed. 4to, modern calf. With 3 folding charts, 12 folding plates & 11 folding ptd tables. W July 8 (273) £450

Phiz. See: Browne, Hablot K.

Phoclydes. See: Pythagoras & Phoclydes

Photographic...

— The Photographic History of the Civil War. NY, 1911-12. Ed by Francis Trevelyan Miller. 10 vols. 4to, cloth; some hinges cracked. sg Dec 5 (64) $200

Piacenza, Francesco

— L'Egeo redivivo, o'sia chorographia dell'Archipelago, Modena, 1688. 4to, 19th-cent half calf. With engraved title & 63 maps. Lacking the port; some dampstaining at lower fore-corners. S Nov 21 (272) £1,400 [Tantoulos]

Picart, Bernard

— Ceremonies et coutumes religieuses de tous les peuples du monde. Amst., 1723-43. Vols I-V only. Contemp calf gilt; joints split. With 182 plates; lacking 2 plates. S May 13 (856) £440 [Shapero]

Anr Ed. Amst.: Laporte, 1783. 4 vols. Folio, contemp half calf; rubbed. With 264 plates. Sold w.a.f. Ck Nov 29 (280) £500

Anr Ed. Paris, 1807-10. 12 vols in 6. Folio, half vellum; worn. Dampstained; bound without plates. wa Mar 5 (539) $260

— Histoire generale des ceremonies.... Paris, 1741. Vols I-VII (of 9). Folio, contemp calf gilt; spine ends and corners worn. With 228 plates. sg May 7 (171) $1,900

— Impostures innocentes.... Amst., 1734. Folio, contemp vellum; wormed, soiled & rubbed. With 78 plates. bba Mar 26 (173) £320 [Barker]

— The Religious Ceremonies and Customs of the...World. L, 1733-39. ("The Ceremonies and Religious Customs of the...World....") 7 vols in 6. Folio, lea; 1 bdg damaged. br May 29 (37) $450

— Tafereel, of beschryving van den practigen Tempel der zang-goginnen. Amst., 1733. Folio, contemp calf gilt. With engraved title & 60 plates. Text browned. B Nov 1 (373) HF2,600

Anr copy. Contemp half calf gilt. Marginal

stains. B Nov 1 (374) HF1,800

— Le Temple des muses. Amst., 1749. Folio, half sheep gilt; joints & corners chafed. With 62 plates, several possibly from anr Ed or work. sg Sept 19 (206) $400

— The Temple of the Muses. Amst., 1733. Folio, contemp mor gilt with crown & fleur-de-lys tools. With engraved title & 60 plates. Chalfont House copy. C June 24 (218) £650 [Cumming]

Anr copy. Modern cloth. With 60 plates. Text leaves toned. sg Oct 24 (256) $550

Picasso, Pablo
See also: Sabartes, Jaime

— Couleur de Picasso. Paris, [1948]. Folio, bds, in pictorial d/j. Verve No 19/20. sg Feb 6 (220) $150

— Le Desir attrape par la Queue. [N.p., n.d.]. Folio, orig wraps. Inscr to Boris Kochno. SM Oct 12 (503) FF25,000

— Picasso 347. NY, [1970]. 2 vols. Oblong 4to, orig half cloth. bbc Apr 27 (479) $110; K Mar 22 (343) $150; O Jan 14 (148) $110

Anr copy. Orig half cloth; some wear. O Aug 25 (143) $110

Anr copy. Half syn. sg Sept 6 (219) $200

Anr copy. Orig half syn. sg Feb 6 (224) $100

— Picasso lithographe. Monte Carlo, 1949-50-56-64. Text by Fernand Mourlot. 4 vols. Folio, orig wraps. bba Oct 24 (351) £180 [Elliott]

Anr copy. Vols I-II (of 4). Orig wraps; spines def. Ck Sept 6 (180) £320

Anr Ed. Monte Carlo, 1949-50. Vol II (of 4). Folio, orig wraps; edges worn, shaken. sg Sept 6 (218) $200

— Picasso Lithographs. Bost.: Boston Book & Art Pbrs, [1970]. Notes by Fernand Mourlot; trans by Jean Didry. 4to, cloth, in d/j. bbc Dec 9 (284) $70

— Picasso, the Blue and Rose Period: a Catalogue Raisonne, 1900-1906. L & NY, 1967. Ed by Pierre Daix & Georges Boudaille. Folio, cloth, in d/j. With 61 tipped-on color plates. wa Apr 9 (261) $95

— Les Quatres Petites Filles. Paris, 1968. One of 60. Orig wraps. Inscr with a drawing to Boris Kochno, 1969. SM Oct 12 (504) FF80,000

— Sueno y mentira de Franco. [Paris, 1937]. One of 150 on japon. Oblong folio, unsewn in orig wraps. Facsimile of the Ms text, with English trans. S May 28 (232) £6,500 [Sandstrom]

— A Suite of 180 Drawings, 1953-54. NY, [1954]. Folio, orig bds, in d/j. Verve Nos 29/30. sg Feb 6 (221) $300

Piccolomini, Alessandro, 1508-78

— De la sfera del mondo.... Venice, 1540. 1st Ed. 2 vols in 1. 4to, contemp vellum; worn. A few star maps shaved at outer margin. bba Oct 24 (4) £200 [Bernard]

Anr Ed. Venice: G. Varisco, 1561. 2 parts in 1 vol. 4to, contemp vellum; soiled, split along backstrip. Slight loss to 1 leaf. bba July 9 (35) £160 [Shapero]

Piccolpasso, Cipriano

— The Three Books of the Potter's Art. L, 1934. Ltd Ed. Folio, orig cloth, in d/j. DW Mar 11 (770) £80

Pichon, Jerome, Baron. See: Grolier Club

Pichon, Thomas Jean —& Gobet, Nicolas

— Le Sacre et couronnement de Louis XVI.... Paris, 1775. 4to, contemp mor gilt with later arms of Ralph Sneyd. With engraved title, 10 double-page plates (small tear to margin of 1), 39 costume plates & folding map of Rheims (small tear to margin). L.p. copy on hollande. C Dec 16 (153) £700 [Paradise]

Pichot, Joseph. See: Pernot & Pichot

Pickering, Harold G. See: Derrydale Press

Pico della Mirandola, Giovanni, 1463-94

— Opera. Strassburg: Knobloch, 1506-7. Folio, contemp calf. sg May 7 (173) $1,900

Pictorial...

— A Pictorial Encyclopedia of the Oriental Arts. NY: Crown, [c.1969]. Ed by Kadokawa Shoten. 4 vols Japan; 2 vols China; 1 vol Korea. Together, 7 vols. 4to, orig cloth. F June 25 (262) $130

Anr copy. 2 vols. sp Sept 22 (238) $50

— Pictorial Photography in America. NY, 1926. Vol 4 of 2d Ed, one of 1,500. Folio, half cloth; shelf number on backstrip, some wear. bbc Feb 17 (255) $75

Picture. See: Latrobe, John H. B.

Picturesque...

— Picturesque America.... NY, [1872-74]. Ed by William Cullen Bryant. 2 vols. 4to, orig mor gilt; scuffed. cb Oct 25 (9) $190

Anr copy. 4 vols. 4to, contemp half mor; worn. With 43 views. DW Nov 20 (5) $145

Anr copy. 2 vols. 4to, half mor gilt; rubbed. With 49 plates, including frontises & titles. K July 12 (403) $250

Anr copy. Orig lea; spine def, rubbed. K July 12 (404) $200

Anr copy. Half lea; worn. Met Apr 28 (482) $130

Anr copy. Half lea; bumped. Some foxing.

Met Apr 28 (483) $140

Anr copy. Orig mor gilt; rubbed. Some foxing & soiling. O Jan 14 (149) $150

Anr copy. Half lea & lea. O Apr 28 (186) $125

Anr copy. Orig mor gilt; rubbed. Owners' names on titles. pn Nov 14 (414) £110 [Bailey]

Anr copy. 2 vols in 48 parts. 4to, orig wraps; worn. sg Nov 7 (154) $800

Anr copy. 2 vols. 4to, orig lea gilt; scuffed. sp Nov 24 (15) $450

Anr copy. Orig mor gilt; worn. wa Dec 9 (454) $280

Anr Ed. L, 1894 [1893]-97. 4 vols. 4to, cloth; loose & musty. Some foxing. sp June 18 (8) $80

— Picturesque Europe: A Delineation by Pen and Pencil.. NY, [1875-79]. Ed by Bayard Taylor. 3 vols. Folio, orig mor gilt; rubbed. With 63 plates. F Sept 26 (476) $160

Anr copy. Half mor; rubbed. With 60 full-page plates & 3 engraved titles. K Mar 22 (344) $200

— Picturesque Representations of the Dress and Manners of the English. L, 1814. 8vo, contemp half mor; rubbed. With 50 hand-colored plates. Some spotting and soiling. Ck July 10 (79) £160

Picus de Mirandula, Johannes, 1463-94

— Opera. Bologna: Benedictus Hectoris, 1496 [but Lyons: Jacobinus Suigus & Nicolaud de Benedctis, 1498-1500]. Folio, modern mor. Some early marginalia & scoring; some browning & staining; 2B7 holed. Reprint of Bologna 1496 Ed. bba Jan 16 (214) £1,800 [Kyle]

Anr Ed. Paris: Jean Petit, 9 June 1517. Folio, contemp calf; worn & restored, rebacked in mor. Some staining; last leaf repaired; small burn hole to outer margin of c3-6 affecting a few characters. C Dec 16 (154) £1,100 [Cooper]

Pidou de Saint-Olon, Francois. See: Saint Olon, Francois Pidou de

Pierce, Robert Morris

— Dictionary of Aviation. NY, [1914]. cb Nov 7 (89) $60

Pietrasancta, Silvestro

— Symbola Heroica. Amst., 1682. 4to, 19th-cent mor gilt; extremities rubbed. With engraved title & 268 engraved illusts. Ck Nov 29 (88) £650

Pietro da Lucca

— Arte del ben pensare e contemplare la Passione.... Venice: Niccolo Zoppino, Apr 1527. 8vo, old lea gilt. sg Oct 24 (257) $2,400

Pigage, Nicolas de

— La Galerie electorale de Dusseldorff.... Basel, 1778. Oblong 4to, 19th-cent mor gilt; rubbed & stained. With engraved title & 30 plates. Some browning; waterstained at lower edge. S July 1 (1158) £150

Pigna, Giovanni Battista —& Others

— Carminum lib. quatuor.... Venice: ex officina Erasmiana, 1553. 8vo, old vellum. Some browning & soiling at margins. Ck Oct 31 (262) £140

Pignoria, Lorenzo, 1571-1631

— Mensa isiaca, qua, sacrorum apud aegyptios ratio & simulacra subjectis tabulis aeneis simul exhibentur & explicantur. Amst: Andreas Fries, 1669. Bound with: Magnae deum matris idaeae & attidis initia. Amst.: Andreas Fries, 1669. 4to, vellum. Blank lower margin of last leaf renewed. B Nov 1 (679) HF750

Anr copy. Disbound. With 8 folding plates & 9 full-page engravings. General title soiled. sg Mar 12 (227) $400

— Vetustissimae tabulae Aeneae... Venice, 1605. 1st Ed. 4to, bds. SI June 10 (785) LIt450,000

Pigot & Co., James

— Royal National and Commercial Directory...of the Counties of Bedford, Cambridge.... L, 1844. 8vo, modern calf. With 10 folding maps. Sold w.a.f. bba Apr 30 (16) £350 [Tyger Press]

Pike, Samuel, 1717?-73

— A Compendious Hebrew Lexicon. Adapted to the English Language.... Cambr. MA, 1811. 8vo, contemp calf; worn. Margins cropped to form Hebrew alphabet tabs. O July 14 (150) $110

Pike, Warburton M.

— Through the Subarctic Forest.... L, 1896. 8vo, orig cloth. sg Jan 9 (21) $175

Pike, Zebulon Montgomery, 1779-1813

— An Account of Expeditions to the Sources of the Mississippi.... Phila., 1810. 1st Ed. 8vo, lea; shabby. Lacking the 3 folding tables. NH Oct 6 (308) $255

Piles, Roger de. See: Tortebat, Francois

Pilleau, Henry

— Sketches in Egypt. L, 1845. Folio, contemp half calf; extremities rubbed. With 12 colored plates. Some marginal spotting. Ck Nov 29 (281) £500

Pilotelle, Georges

— Avant, pendant et apres la commune. L: Delatre, [1873]. Folio, contemp lea gilt. With etched title & 19 plates, all mtd. S July 9 (320) £450 [Robertshaw]

Pina, Domingo de

— Memorial de suplica e informe que hazen.... Sevilla, 1675. 4to, modern wraps. sg Mar 26 (235) $175

Pinchard, Mrs.

— The Blind Child, or Anecdotes of the Wyndham Family. L, 1791. 1st Ed. 12mo, contemp calf; spine splitting. bba July 23 (121) £170 [Bickersteth]

Pinckney, Charles, 1758-1824

— Three Letters.... Phila., 1799. 8vo, later wraps; chipped & soiled. Foxed; prelims browned. wa Mar 5 (338) $75

Pindar, 522?-443 B.C.

Odes

— 1513. - Venice: Aldus. 8vo, 18th-cent mor gilt; rubbed. Greek type. Lacking final blank; a few stains. C June 24 (280) £2,500 [Kraus]

Pine, John

— The Tapestry Hangings of the House of Lords. L, 1753. 3 parts in 1 vol. Folio, contemp half lea; worn. With engraved title & 19 double-page plates & charts, 1 partly hand-colored & heightened in gilt. Most plates with tears to margins & folds, 1 repaired; some dampstaining to lower margins, not affecting images. Sold w.a.f. Ck Dec 11 (248) £3,000

Pinelli, Bartolomeo

— Istoria Romana. Rome, 1818-19. Oblong folio, half mor; worn, upper cover detached. With 101 plates. Title detached. bba Mar 26 (217) £550 [B.Bailey]

Anr copy. Contemp mor; worn & broken. With frontis & 100 plates. Frontis laid down. Sold w.a.f. S July 1 (936) £400 [Shapero]

— Nuova Raccolta di cinquanta costumi pittoreschi. Rome, 1816. Oblong folio, contemp half mor; worn, covers detached. With engraved title & 50 plates. Some spotting, mostly marginal; tp & 1st plates creased. bba Nov 7 (31) £900 [L'Acquaforte]

Anr copy. 19th-cent half calf. HH May 12 (967) DM2,000

Anr copy. Bound with: Nuova Raccolta di cinquanta costumi de' contorni di Roma. Rome, 1823. later half mor; rubbed, 1 corner def. With 44 plates only in each work (of 50 in each). pn June 11 (212) £1,400

Anr Ed. Rome, 1817. Oblong 8vo, wraps; broken. With engraved title & 50 hand-colored plates. Some waterstains & browning. SI June 10 (789) LIt1,900,000

— Nuova raccolta di cinquanta costumi de' contorni di Roma. Rome, 1823. 4to, contemp half calf; broken, loose. With 50 plates. HH May 12 (965) DM2,200

Anr copy. Contemp wraps. Some spotting; tp wormed. HH May 12 (966) DM2,400

— Raccolta di cinquanta costumi pittoreschi. Rome, 1809. Oblong 4to, early 19th-cent half calf; joints cracked, foot of spine chipped. With 50 hand-colored plates & engraved title. C May 20 (287) £2,000 [Toscani]

Anr copy. Contemp half vellum; rubbed. With etched title & 50 plates.. Extra-illus with 23 plates, most of bandits, all by Pinelli. Ck Sept 6 (140) £1,000

Anr copy. Contemp wraps. With additional title & 50 plates. HH May 12 (964) DM2,800

— Tasso figurato. Rome, 1826-27. Oblong folio, modern half lea. With frontis & 72 plates. SI June 10 (788) LIt2,700,000

— Twenty-Seven Etchings Illustrative of Italian Manners and Costume. Rome, 1844. Folio, loose in orig half mor; worn. DW Dec 11 (62) £380

Pinelli, Bartolomeo —& Hullmandel, C.

— Roman Costumes Drawn from Nature.... L: Rodwell & Martin, [1820]. Oblong 4to, cloth; rubbed, front joints openeing. With litho title & 24 plates. 2 plates foxed. K July 12 (411) $950

Anr copy. Contemp half lea; worn. With litho title & 20 (of 24) plates. Tp & several plates reinforced at inner margi: s; some soiling. pn July 16 (206) £280 [Elliott]

Pinkerton, John, 1758-1826

— An Essay on Medals.... L, 1789. 2 vols. 8vo, calf; broken. b&b Feb 19 (115) $60

— A General Collection of the Best and Most Interesting Voyages.... L, 1808-14. 17 vols. 4to, contemp calf gilt; rebacked, corners renewed, joints cracked, a few spines chipped. With 195 plates on 192 sheets, 2 folding. Some wear & foxing. CNY Oct 8 (200) $2,600

Anr copy. Bdg not stated; affected by varying degrees of water damage, stains, or mustiness. Sold w.a.f. O Feb 25 (155)

$650

— The Medallic History of England. L, 1802. 4to, modern cloth; edges frayed. With frontis & 39 plates. Some plates stained. pn Dec 12 (73) £50

— A Modern Atlas. L, 1815. Folio, contemp half russia; rubbed & worn. With 62 hand-colored maps. Maps at end with vertical crease. C May 20 (288) £1,700 [Cherrington]

— Modern Geography. L, 1807. 2 vols. 4to, contemp calf gilt. With 51 maps, 3 folding. DW Oct 2 (60) £85

Pinsker, Leo

— "Autoemancipation!" Mahnruf an seine Stammesgenossen von einem russischen Juden. Berlin, 1882. 8vo, modern half cloth. Some stains & pencil markings; a few wormholes in margins. Isaac Leib Goldberg copy. sg June 25 (160A) $800

Pinter, Harold

— The Homecoming. L, 1968. Ltd Ed. Illus by Harold Cohen. Folio, orig cloth. With 9 lithos. b June 22 (64) £70

— Poems. L: Enitharmon Press, 1968. One of 200. Half mor. Sgd. O Dec 17 (143) $100

Anr Ed. L: Enitharmon Press, 1971. One of 100. Half mor. Inscr. O Dec 17 (142) $80

Pinter von der Au, Johann Christoph

— Vollkommener Pferd-Schatz. Frankfurt, 1688. ("Neuer, vollkommener, verbesserter und ergaentzer Pferd-Schatz.") Folio, contemp calf gilt; rubbed. With engraved title & 25 plates. Folding plate at p. 241 repaired; some shaving; library stamp on tp. S Nov 21 (37) £850 [Shapero]

Piozzi, Hester Lynch Thrale, 1741-1821

— Anecdotes of the late Samuel Johnson. L, 1786. 1st Ed. 8vo, contemp calf; rebacked. Lacking half-title. sg Nov 7 (115) $350

Anr copy. Contemp calf; rebacked, orig backstrip retained. sg Mar 12 (158) $110

— Autobiography, Letters, and Literary Remains.... L, 1861. 2 vols. 8vo, modern calf. cb Oct 25 (104) $160

— British Synonymy.... L, 1794. 1st Ed. 2 vols. 8vo, orig bds. sg Nov 7 (117) $475

— Letters to and from the late Samuel Johnson. L, 1788. 1st Ed. 2 vols. 8vo, later half calf; rebacked using orig backstrips. Lacking errata leaf; some spotting. bba July 9 (122) £55 [Archdale]

Anr copy. Modern half calf. Vol I with initial blank but lacking errata-slip; some dampstaining. S May 13 (623) £180 [Scott]

— Observations and Reflections made in the Course of a Journey through France.... L, 1789. 1st Ed. 2 vols. 8vo, later 19th-cent mor. sg Nov 7 (116) $275

— Retrospection.... L, 1801. 2 vols. 4to, later half lea. Port stained in margin; some foxing; library stamps. bba Aug 13 (141) £80 [Mrs. Carr-Ellison]

Piper, Peter, Pseud.

— Peter Piper's Practical Principles of Plain and Perfect Pronunciation. L, 1813. 1st Ed. 16mo, orig wraps; worn. Manney copy. P Oct 11 (165) $1,600

Piranesi, Giovanni Battista, 1720-78

— Antichita Romane de' Tempi della Repubblica, e de' primi imperatori. Rome, 1748. 2 parts in 1 vol. Folio, contemp half calf; worn, spine renewed, inner hinge cracked with last plate & rear free endpaper detached. With 30 plates, including title, dedication plate & 2 plates of inscrs. Some foxing, not affecting plates. P June 17 (299) $5,500

Anr copy. Old bds. With 29 plates. S June 25 (220) £3,500 [Cucchio]

Anr copy. 19th-cent half lea. Some browning. SI June 10 (790) LIt12,000,000

— Le Antichita Romane. Rome, 1756. 4 vols. Folio, contemp half calf; spines renewed. With port & 217 (of 218?) plates. Some foxing. P June 17 (298) $23,000

— Campus Martius antique urbis. Rome, 1762. Folio, modern calf. With 2 engraved titles & 42 (of 48?) plates, 2 folding & 1 double-page; large folding plan in pocket on rear pastedown & foxed. P June 17 (300) $5,500

Anr copy. Modern half mor gilt. With 48 full-page or folding plates (the large folding plan of Rome on plates V-IX joined & housed in pocket at end). S June 25 (217) £5,200 [Bifolco]

— Carceri d'invenzione. [Rome, not before 1778]. Folio, half calf. With 16 double-page plates. Tear in margin of Plate 6 repaired. S June 25 (321) £19,000 [Bifolco]

— Diverse maniere d'adornare i cammini.... Rome, 1769. 1st Ed. Folio, 19th-cent half mor gilt; worn. With double-page dedication & 72 plates bound in irregular order. Plate 36 repaired without loss; dedication with split at lower fold repaired. S Nov 21 (94) £3,800 [Gorini]

Anr copy. Modern half mor gilt. With double-page engraved title, 4 unnumbered & 66 numbered plates. Minor spotting to text. S June 25 (219) £5,200 [Batassa]

— Vasi, candelabri, cippi... [Rome], 1778. 2 vols. Folio, modern half mor; spines gilt. With folding title, double-page dedication & 19 full-page or folding plates. Plate 15 just shaved at upper right; Plate 22 shaved at right affecting letters; torn & repaired at

1 fold; plates 51 & 60 discolored. S June 25 (218) £6,000 [Bifolco]

Piringer, Benedict, 1780-1826

— Garten-Verschoenerungen.... Vienna: Heinrich Friedrich Muller, [1823?]. Folio, orig bds; stained. With 14 plates. C June 24 (190) £700 [Lehar]

Piroli, Tomasso

— Le Antichita de Ercolano.... Rome, 1789-90. Vols I-III (of 6). Modern half lea. With 162 plates. Some foxing. sg Sept 6 (142) $90

Piron, Alexis, 1689-1773

— Oeuvres. Paris, 1758. 3 vols. 12mo, contemp calf; repaired. With frontis & 6 plates. Half-title in Vol II only. S July 1 (1128) £200 [Robertshaw]

Pisanelli, Baldassare

— Trattato della natura de'cibi et del bere. Turin: Antonio de' Bianchi, 1587. 8vo, contemp vellum; cockled. S Dec 5 (370) £750 [Lib. Scheler]

Pissaro, Ludovic-Rodo —& Venturi, Lionello

— Camille Pissaro. Paris, 1939. Ltd Ed. 2 vols. 4to, contemp cloth; worn. bba Feb 13 (73) £340 [Sims Reed]

Anr copy. Orig wraps. S July 1 (1159) £600

Pistofilo, Bonaventura

— Oplomachia.... Siena: Hercole Gori, 1621. Oblong 4to, contemp paper bds. With engraved title, 2 ports & 54 full-page illusts. Short tear in A3; 3 small wormholes in title; some soiling. S Dec 5 (243) £1,800 [Mediolanum]

Anr copy. Old vellum. Tp backed & rehinged. sg Mar 26 (237) $1,500

— Il Torneo. Bologna: Clemente Ferroni, 1626. 4to, contemp vellum; spine def. With engraved title (shaved), port & 117 plates. Short tear at head of Z1; some dampstaining. S Dec 5 (242) £1,400 [Knill]

Pistolese, Erasmo

— Il Vaticano. Rome, 1829-38. 8 vols. Folio, contemp calf, elaborately ruled & tooled; extremities scuffed & bumped, several joints cracked. With engraved titles & 850 plates & plans. Some spotting & browning. Ck Nov 29 (302) £600

Anr copy. Half mor. Library stamps on all titles & plates. S Nov 15 (889) £190 [Erlini]

Anr Ed. Rome, 1829. 8 vols. Folio, contemp mor gilt; some joints broken. SI June 10 (794) LIt1,000,000

Anr copy. Contemp half mor; rubbed. W Mar 6 (11) £360

Piton, Camille

— Le Costume civil en France du XIIIe au XIXe siecle. Paris, [1926]. 4to, pictorial bds. sp June 18 (306) $85

Pitt-Rivers, Augustus Henry Lane Fox, 1827-1900

— Excavations in Cranborne Chase near Rushmore. L, 1887-1905. 6 vols, including Index Orig cloth; rubbed, Vol I rebacked with spine preserved. bba Sept 19 (225) £260 [Vine]

Pius V, Pope, 1504-72

— Bulla lecta in die Coenae Domin. [Rome, 1566]. Single sheet, 630mm by 460mm. S May 28 (60) £2,000 [Franklin]

Pivati, Giovanni Francesco

— Della elettricita medica lettera.... Lucca, 1747. 8vo, contemp wraps; shaken, minor stains on front cover. sg Nov 14 (103) $450

Plakat...

— Das fruhe Plakat in Europa und den USA. Berlin, [1973-80]. 3 vols in 4. 4to, orig cloth, in d/js. sg Apr 2 (230) $550

— Das Plakat: Mitteilungen des Vereins der Plakatfreunde. Berlin, 1916. Vol 7. 6 Nos in 7 vols. 4to, loose in half cloth portfolio. HH May 12 (1051) DM750

Vol 8. Berlin, 1917. 6 Nos. 4to, loose in orig half-cloth portfolio. HH May 12 (1052) DM1,400

Vol 9. Berlin, 1918. 4 Nos. 4to, loose in orig half cloth portfolio. HH May 12 (1053) DM1,100

Vol 10. Berlin, 1919. 6 Nos. 4to, loose in orig half cloth portfolio. HH May 12 (1054) DM1,100

Vol 11. Berlin, 1920. 12 nos in 1 vol. 4to, orig half cloth. HH May 12 (1055) $1,300

Vol 12. Berlin, 1921. 12 nos in 1 vol. 4to, orig cloth. Some waterspotting. HH May 12 (1057) DM1,400

Anr copy. 12 Nos in 10 vols. Orig wraps; worn. HH May 12 (1058) DM1,400

Plan, Pierre Paul

— Jacques Callot: maitre graveur.... Brussels & Paris, 1914 [1913]. Orig cloth; rubbed. bba Feb 13 (265) £180 [Barkham]

Planche, James Robinson, 1796-1880

See also: Tomkins & Planche

— A Cyclopedia of Costume. L, 1876-79. 1st Ed. 2 vols. 4to, cloth. Library markings. bba June 11 (198) £80 [Besley]

Planiscig, Leo

— Andrea Riccio. Vienna, 1927. 4to, contemp half mor; upper joint broken. S Feb 11 (1711pPS700) [Henneage]

— Piccoli bronzi italiani de rinascimento.

Milan, 1930. 4to, orig cloth. S Feb 11 (170) £280 [Angelini]

— Venezianische Bildhauer der Renaissance. Vienna, 1921. Folio, orig cloth; soiled. S Feb 11 (169) £320 [Scaglia]

Planta, Joseph. See: British Museum

Platea, Franciscus

— Opus restitutionum, usurarum, et excommunicationum. Venice: Johannes de Colonis & Johannes Manthem, 25 Mar 1474 & 22 Jan 1477. Bound with: Robertus Caracciolus. Sermones de Timore Divinorum Iudicorum. Venice, 1475. 4to, contemp blind-stamped calf over oak bds, with brass clasps; worn, bosses removed, front joint broken, endpapers renewed. 40 lines; double column; type 2:78G; rubricated uniformly.. 150 (of 152) leaves; lacking 2 final blanks;l Goff P-755. 94 leaves; Goff C-184. Kloss-Bruce-Grolier Club copy. C June 24 (191) £2,000 [Mediolanum]

Plath, Sylvia

— Crystal Gazer and Other Poems. L: Rainbow Press, 1971. One of 400. Folio, orig half cloth. cb Feb 12 (1003) $140

Platina, Bartholomaeus Sacchi de, 1421-81

— De honesta voluptate. Venice, 1516. 8vo, modern lea. SI June 10 (796) LIt3,600,000

— Vitae pontificum. [Venice]: Johannes de Colonia Agripiensi & Johannes Manthen de Gheretzem, 11 June 1479. 1st Ed. Folio, later vellum. Some margins repaired; K5 with tear repaired; some worming & soiling. 238 (of 240) leaves. Goff P-768. bba Apr 30 (252) £945 [Bernard]

Anr copy. Modern half lea. 228 (of 240) leaves; the 1st 10 leaves replaced by 6 leaves from the Treviso 1485 Ed, leaves c2 & conjugate c7 supplied in Ms. Goff P-768. SI June 10 (798) LIt1,500,000

Plato, 427?-347 B.C.

See also: Limited Editions Club

— Dialogues. L, 1757-67. Trans by Floyer Sydenham. 2 vols. 4to, later sheep; rebacked. sg Oct 24 (258) $225

Anr Ed. L, 1892. 5 vols. 8vo, contemp calf gilt with arms of Wellington College. Ls inserted. bba July 9 (19) £260 [D & D Galleries]

— Opera. Venice: Aldus, Sept 1513. Folio, 19th-cent russia gilt; joints & corners worn. Greek type. Minor stains. Birkenhead copy. C June 23 (281) £23,000 [Pregliasco]

Anr Ed. Basel, 1534. Folio, later calf; worn, rebacked. Some soiling. S July 1 (522) £360 [Dimakarakos]

— Septem selecti dialogi.... Dublin, 1738. 8vo, contemp calf with arms of Trinity College, Dublin, prize bdg. bba Aug 13 (64) £60 [Ogino]

Platt, Charles Adams

[-] Monograph of the Work of Charles A. Platt. NY, 1913. Folio, orig cloth; worn, front blank loose. sg Feb 6 (228) $130

Platt, Sir Hugh

— The Jewel House of Art and Nature.... L, 1653. 4to, modern mor gilt by Lewis & Harris, with stamp of Brent Gration-Maxfield. 4 leaves of preface tipped-in; B4 of preface with hole affecting a few words & repaired; some cropping, occasionally affecting catchwords & signatures; some early Ms annotations in margins. S May 14 (1000) £800 [Petta]

Plautus, Titus Maccius, 254?-184 B.C.

See also: Shelley's copy, Percy Bysshe; Swift's copy, Jonathan

— Comoediae. Venice: Matteo Capcasa (di Codeca), 23 Nov 1495. 4to, later half lea. Lacking blank part of title; 1st 12 leaves & some others stained; marginal repairs. 250 leaves; but C5 in Ms. Goff P-782. B May 12 (1660) HF4,200

Anr Ed. Milan: Uldericus Scinzenzeler, 18 Jan 1500. Folio, 18th-cent mor gilt; extremities scuffed, upper joint split. 59 lines of commentary surrounding text & headline; types 4:145G (title, leaded to 165), 3:110R (text), 10:80R (commentary, with occasional quote in Greek). First & last leaf soiled. 422 leaves. Goff P-785. C Dec 16 (155) £2,200 [Mediolanum]

Anr Ed. Venice: Aldus, July 1522. 8vo, old vellum. Tp soiled; 1 leaf torn & repaired; a8 soiled on verso; some browning & staining. Ck Oct 31 (3) £250

Anr Ed. Amst.: Typographia Blaviana, 1684. 2 vols. 8vo, 18th-cent calf; worn. SI June 10 (800) LIt320,000

Plaw, John

— Ferme Ornee; or Rural Improvements. L, 1796. 4to, 19th-cent half calf; extremities rubbed, lower cover scuffed. With 38 plates. B2 torn at outer margin. Ck May 15 (142) £260

— Rural Architecture; or Designs from the Simple Cottage to the Decorated Villa. L, 1802. 4to, contemp bds. With frontis & 61 plates. Plate 5 damaged. DW Oct 9 (938) £55

Playfair, James, 1738-1814

— A New General Atlas. L, 1814. Folio, later half calf; split. With 44 double-page maps. Some foxing. pnE Oct 2 (493) £110

Playford, John

— A Brief Introduction to the Skill of Musick. L, 1666. 8vo, 19th-cent half calf gilt. Contemp Ms corrections; lacking port; some repairs & marginal worming. Wing P-2452. William Cummings's copy. pn Oct 24 (431) £160 [Macnutt]

11th Ed. L, 1687. 8vo, contemp sheep; spine worn. Port shaved at fore-edge; wormholes in upper margin just touching text. pn Oct 24 (435) £280

Pleasant...

— The Pleasant and Delightful History of Jack and the Giants. Nottingham: ptd for the Running Stationers, [c.1780]. 12mo, 20th-cent half mor; lower joint split. Ck Dec 11 (160) £240

Pleasants, Jacob Hall —& Sill, Howard

— Maryland Silversmiths, 1715-1830. Balt., 1930. One of 300. 4to, half cloth; extremities worn, hinges tender. With 67 plates. sg Sept 6 (259) $375

Anr copy. Half cloth; worn & shaken. With frontis & 67 plates. sg Feb 6 (263) $150; sp June 18 (381) $170

Anr Ed. Harrison, NY, 1972. One of 1,000. 4to, cloth, in chipped d/j. With frontis & 67 plates. Facsimile of the 1930 Ed. sp Feb 6 (290) $75

Plesch Library, Arpad

— Mille et un Livres botaniques.... Brussels, 1973. One of 60. 3 parts in 1 vol. 4to, cloth. wd June 12 (424) $700

— [Sale Catalogue] The Magnificent Botanical Library.... L, 1975-76. Parts 1-3 (complete set) in 3 vols. 4to, bds. With price lists. sg May 21 (293) $50

Anr copy. Price list laid in. sp Sept 22 (428) $85

Plimpton, George Arthur. See: Smith, David Eugene

Plimsoll, Samuel

— Cattle Ships.... L, 1890. 8vo, orig cloth. pnE May 13 (171a) £55

Plinius Secundus, Gaius, 23-79

— Buecher und schrifften von der Natur.... Frankfurt: Peter Schmidt for S. Feyerabend & S. Hueter, 1565. Folio, 18th-cent bds. Tp stamped; some browning & staining. S Nov 21 (38) £950 [Burden]

— Historia naturalis. Venice: Nicolaus Jenson, 1476. Folio, early 18th-cent calf; joints worn. 50 lines; type 1:115(111)R with ranging Greek. Finely illuminated with fully painted frontis, 3/24, & book initials historiated in camaieu gris with skies of red, blue & green, the initial of the frontis page with additional gold filigree on the colored ground. Marginal wormhole in 1st few leaves; last leaf roughtly repaired with patch of paper below colophon; frontis leaf with several marginal chips & tears; other marginal tears. 413 (of 415) leaves; lacking first & final blanks. Goff P-801. Bolani-Pembroke-de Marnis-Vollbehr-Williams copy. P Dec 12 (186) $370,000

Anr Ed. Venice: Marinus Saracenus, 14 June 1487. ("Naturalis hystoriae....") Folio, 19th-cent half vellum. 56 lines & headline; type 1:82R. Worming at the beginning affecting text; some marginal worming; occasional dampstaining. 270 (of 272) leaves; lacking initial & final blank. Goff P-795. C Nov 27 (21) £1,500 [Mediolanum]

Anr Ed. Venice: Bartholomaeus de Zanis, 12 Sept 1489. ("Historia naturale.") Trans into Italian by Cristoforo Landino. Folio, contemp vellum. Some worming & spotting. 260 leaves. Goff P-803. SI June 10 (803) LIt1,400,000

Anr Ed. Venice: Barnardinus Benalius, 1497 [but not before 13 Feb 1498]. Folio, old wooden bds with brass fore-edge clasps; spine replaced with recent half pigskin. 55 lines & headling; types 108R & 105Gk; rubricated. Marginal worming in 1st few leaves. 268 leaves. Goff P-799. Schoyen copy. P Dec 12 (34) $15,000

Anr Ed. Basel: Froben, 1525. ("Historia mundi.") Folio, contemp Cambridge bdg of calf over wooden bds from the bindery of Nicholas Spierinck; wormed, covers detached, lacking catches & clasps, early vellum Ms pastedown inside front cover but absent inside rear cover. Marginal repairs; some worming at beginning & end, sometimes affecting text; outer margin of 2 leaves excised. sg Oct 24 (259) $700

Anr Ed. Venice, 1525. ("Prima [Secunda] Pars Plyniana....") Folio, old vellum. Roman type. some worming; Part 2 bound before Part 1. Ck Nov 29 (282) £1,200

Anr Ed. Basel, 1539. ("Historia mundi, libri XXXVII....") Folio, modern vellum. Old marginal annotations; some soiling, worming & browning. SI Dec 5 (555) LIt400,000

Anr Ed. Venice: Aldus, 1559-58. ("Naturalis historiae....") Folio, later sheep; worn. A few notes shaved. bba Sept 5 (93) £480 [P & P Books]

Anr Ed. Lyons: Joannes Frellonius, 1563. ("Historiae mundi libri XXXVII.") Folio, contemp vellum; front cover chipped. sg May 7 (174) $750

Anr Ed. Leiden: Elzevir, 1635. ("Historiae naturalis libri XXXVII.") 3 vols. 12mo, 19th-cent mor gilt. Marginal tears. Hoe copy. Ck Nov 29 (83) £320

Anr copy. 18th-cent mor gilt with arms of Emmanuel-Felicite de Durfot, duc de Duras. S May 28 (86) £600 [Zioni]

Anr Ed. Leiden & Rotterdam, 1669-68. ("Naturalis historiae.") 3 vols. 8vo, later mor gilt; Vol I spine cracked; rubbed. bba Sept 5 (94) £180 [Subun-So]

— The Historie of the World.... L: G.B., 1601. 1st Ed in English. Trans by Philemon Holland. 2 vols. Folio, contemp calf; rebacked, rubbed. Vol I lacking Nn2 & Nn5 but with errata leaf. bba Nov 28 (217) £300 [Gammon]

Anr Ed. L, 1634. 2 vols in 1. Folio, later calf; rebacked, worn. Lacking title; some leaves repaired; some waterstaining. Sold w.a.f. bba Jan 30 (133) £130 [J. Bailey]

Plinius Secundus, Gaius Caecilius, 62-113

— Epistolae. Basel: And. Cratandrum, 1521. ("Epistolarum libri decem.") 8vo, early 19th-cent bds; extremities worn. sg Mar 12 (251) $90

Anr Ed. Venice, 1548. ("Epistole di G. Plinio, di M. Franc. Petrarca, del S. Pico della Mirandola....") 8vo, modern vellum. Some waterstaining. SI June 10 (806) LIt450,000

Plinval de Guillebon, Regine de

— Porcelain of Paris 1770-1850. NY, [1972]. Trans by Robin R. Charleston. 4to, orig cloth. F Mar 26 (38) $70

Plomer, Henry Robert

— Wynkyn de Worde & his Contemporaries.... L, 1925. 4to, half cloth. cb Oct 17 (748) $60

Plomer, William

— Address Given at the Memorial Service for Ian Fleming. September 15th 1964. [N.p.: Pvtly ptd at the Westerham Press, 1964]. One of 350. cb Sept 19 (67) $140

Ploos van Amstel, Cornelis

— Collection d'imitations de dessins d'apres les principaux maitres hollandais et flamands. L, 1821-28. One of 100. 2 vols. Folio, contemp half mor; hinges weak, corners bumped, rubbed. With port & 105 mtd plates on 101 sheets, some in color aquatint, with color highlights added by hand. Plates with Van Amstel's stamp on verso; lacking engraved title; Plate 104 foxed. Schlosser copy. P June 18 (490) $8,000

Plotzek, Joachim M. See: Euw & Plotzek

Plutarch, 46?-120?

See also: Limited Editions Club; Nonesuch Press

— Apostemi. Venice, 1566. 4to, contemp vellum. sg Mar 12 (254) $275

— Lives. Florence: Giunta, 1517. ("Vitae parallelae Romanorum & Graecorum quadraginta novem.") Folio, 19th-cent mor gilt; rubbed. Greek type. Sheet G3.6 inserted from anr copy; tp creased; some staining at beginning & end. Sykes-Todd copy. C June 24 (282) £1,600 [Pregliasco]

Anr Ed. L: T. Vautrollier, 1579. ("The Lives of the Noble Grecians and Romanes....") Trans by Thomas North. Folio, contemp calf; joints repaired but upper joint cracking. Some stains; lower outer corner of tp, Nnn4 & final leaf restored, affecting text at Nnn4 & colophon (supplied in Ms facsimile); some worming affecting text towards end; minor tears. STC 20065. Brownlowe-Goyder copy. S July 21 (7) £6,000 [Knohl]

Anr Ed. L, 1595. Folio, old lea gilt; worn, rebacked in the 19th-cent,new endpapers. Hole in margin of 1 leaf affecting several words of a rubric; partly erased signature on last leaf. STC 20067. K Mar 22 (353) $650

Anr Ed. L: R. Field, 1603. Folio, old half calf; later spine. STC 20068. W July 8 (35) £280

Anr Ed. L, 1727. 8 vols. 8vo, modern half calf; Vol VI marginally wormed & repaired. bba Jan 30 (44) £140 [Harrington]

Anr Ed. L, 1729-23-24. ("Vitae Parallelae.") 5 vols. 4to, contemp red mor gilt bound for Chretien Guillaume de Lamoignon de Malesherbes. Some old dampstaining, particularly to Vol III; some spotting. C Dec 16 (156) £900 [Smith]

Anr Ed. L, 1813. 6 vols. 8vo, mor-backed calf; rubbed. O May 26 (147) $300

Anr Ed. L, 1823. 6 vols. 8vo, contemp calf. sg Mar 5 (277) $200

Anr Ed. Oxford: Shakespeare Head Press, 1928. ("The Lives of the Noble Grecians and Romanes.") One of 500. Illus by Thomas Lowinsky. 8 vols. cb Dec 5 (97) $250; pnE Oct 1 (259) £130

— Moralia. Basel, 1572. 2 parts in 1 vol. 8vo, early half pigskin. Beginning & end dampstained. sg Mar 12 (255) $70

Anr Ed. Paris, 1581. ("Les Oeuvres morales & philosophiques.") Bound in 2 vols. Folio, 18th-cent calf gilt; rubbed, joints split. Some browning. pn June 11 (154) £110 [Bailey]

Anr Ed. Venice: Fioravante Prati, 1598.

("Opuscoli Morali....") 2 vols. 4to, old vellum. Some browning & marginal worming. sg Oct 24 (260) $225

Anr Ed. L, 1657. ("The Philosophy, commonly called the Morals.") Folio, 18th-cent calf; spine chipped at ends. William Sacheverell's copy. C Dec 16 (225) £150 [Shapero]

— Les Oeuvres morales et meslees. Paris: Michel de Vascovan, 1574. Trans by Jacques Amyot. 7 vols. 8vo, 18th-cent vellum gilt. Lacking frontis in Vol VII; some browning. SI Dec 5 (980) LIt200,000

Pocket...

— Pocket Signal Book. Semaphoric Telegraph. New Bedford: Benjamin Lindsey, 1856. 8th Ed. 16mo, orig wraps; chipped. sg June 18 (350) $275

Pococke, Richard, 1704-65

— A Description of the East. L, 1743-45. 3 parts in 2 vols. Folio, contemp mor gilt; worn. With engraved titles, dedication & 178 maps, plans & plates. Lacking final blank in Vol I; tears in tp & 4K1 of Vol I & in tp of Vol II; 1 plate bound upside down, anr torn with loss of inner blank corner. S Nov 15 (1301) £400

Anr copy. Contemp calf; worn. With engraved title, dedication & 178 plates & maps. sg Jan 9 (166) $1,200

Anr copy. Contemp calf gilt; joints broken. SI Dec 5 (981) LIt2,000,000

Poe, Edgar Allan, 1809-49

See also: American...; Burton's...; Grabhorn Printing; Graham's...; Limited Editions Club

— The Atlantic Crossed in Three Days. NY, 1844. Minor portion lacking. In: New York Sunday Times & Noah's Weekly Messenger, Vol 3, No 42. sg Mar 5 (271) $275

— The Bells, and other Poems. L, [1912]. Illus by Edmund Dulac. 4to, orig cloth. b Nov 18 (58) £70

Anr copy. Cloth; rubbed. NH Aug 23 (139) $60

Anr copy. Orig cloth; soiled. With 28 colored plates. sg Sept 26 (97) $250; sg Jan 30 (46) $150

One of 1,000. Orig vellum gilt; some soiling. With 28 tipped-in colored plates. pn July 16 (76) £220 [Pordes]

Anr copy. Vellum; covers bowed. sg Nov 7 (73) $450

— Le Corbeau. Paris, 1875. One of 240. Trans by Stephane Mallarme; illus by Edouard Manet. Folio, bdg not described. br May 29 (150) $9,300

— Eureka. Paris, 1923. One of 30 with extra suite of illusts & vignettes bound at rear. Trans by Charles Baudelaire; intro by Paul Valery. Calf gilt with onlays by Legrain, orig wraps bound in; rebacked with spine laid down. ALs of Valery bound in. sg Sept 26 (254) $650

— Eureka: a Prose Poem. NY, 1848. 1st Ed. 8vo, orig cloth; rebacked, orig spine laid down, worn. Very spotted. Tupper-Evelyn copy. P June 17 (304) $500

Anr copy. Orig cloth; spotted. wd Dec 12 (431) $850

— The Fall of the House of Usher. Paris, 1928. One of 300. Illus by Alastair. 4to, orig wraps. With 5 plates, mtd on silver paper. cb Nov 21 (189) $140

— The Masque of the Red Death. Balt.: Aquarius Press, 1969. ("The Mask of the Red Death.") One of 25 with an extra suite of 22 lithos, each sgd. Illus by Federico Castellon. 2 vols. Folio, half lea. With 16 lithos. sg Sept 26 (255) $500

— The Murders in the Rue Morgue. Antibes, France: Allen Press, 1958. One of 150. cb Oct 31 (7) $150

— The Narrative of Arthur Gordon Pym. NY, 1838. 1st Ed. Orig cloth; marked & soiled, ends of spine & corners worn. Some foxing. CNY Oct 8 (209) $1,600

Anr copy. Orig cloth; soiled. Scribbling on 1 margin. K Dec 1 (368) $1,200

— Poems. L, 1900. Illus by W. Heath Robinson. Ptd on japan vellum. sg Mar 5 (265) $300

— The Raven. L, 1883. Illus by Gustave Dore. Folio, cloth; rubbed. cb Sept 26 (80) $160

— The Raven and Other Poems. NY, 1845. 1st Ed in Book form, 1st Issue. 8vo, orig ptd wraps; worn & soiled, lower joints split at tail, spine chipped & restored without loss. Prescott-Manney copy. P Oct 11 (254) $32,500

— Tales. NY, 1845. 1st Ed, 1st Issue. 8vo, contemp half calf. Lacking ads at end. Bound after C. M. Kirkland's Western Clearings. NY, 1845. P Dec 12 (76A) $2,000

— Tales of Mystery and Imagination. L, 1852. ("Tales of Mystery, Imagination & Humour....") 8vo, orig half cloth; rubbed & worn, hinges cracked & tape-reinforced. Some foxing & soiling. Readable Books No. 1. cb Sept 19 (180) $225

Anr Ed. L, 1919. Illus by Harry Clarke. 4to, cloth. bba Dec 19 (121) £140 [Ginnan]; DW Apr 8 (487) £60

Anr Ed. NY, [c.1920]. 4to, cloth, in d/j. sp Sept 22 (262) $90

Anr Ed. L & NY, [1923]. 4to, orig cloth; discolored. With 32 plates. cb Jan 16 (120) $55

Anr Ed. L, 1935. Illus by Arthur Rackham. 4to, orig cloth, in d/j. bba Jan 16 (397) £180 [Ulysses]; bba Apr 9 (337) £260 [Fox]

One of 460. Orig vellum bds, unopened. CNY June 9 (168) $1,000

Anr copy. Orig vellum gilt. With 12 mtd color plates. sg Sept 26 (270) $1,500; sg Nov 7 (174) $1,200

— Tales of the Grotesque and Arabesque.... Phila., 1840. 1st Ed, One of 750. 2 vols. 12mo, orig cloth. Inscr to Nicholas Biddle. Manney copy. P Oct 11 (252) $31,000

Anr copy. Vol I only. Orig cloth; stained. sg Mar 5 (266) $500

— Tamerlane and Other Poems. Bost.: Calvin F. S. Thomas, 1827. 12mo, orig ptd wraps; stained & frayed. This copy measures 160mm by 110mm. Stained & browned. Manney copy. P Oct 11 (251) $130,000

— William Wilson. Phila., [1839]. 8vo, orig mor gilt; extremities rubbed. In: The Gift: A Christmas and New Year's Present for 1840. sg Mar 5 (270) $150

— Works. L, [c.1900]. 6 vols. 8vo, half mor gilt by Bayntun. sg Mar 5 (268) $450

Poesie...

— Poesie de mots inconnus. Paris, 1949. One of 158. Folio, In 5 ptd folders with orig vellum wraps. With 25 prints in various media. P June 17 (239) $13,000

Poetical...

— The Poetical Magazine. L: Ackermann, 1809-11. 4 vols. 8vo, old bds; rebacked in lea. With engraved titles, 1 uncolored, 1 tinted & 50 hand-colored. One plate in Vol I loosely inserted; others suppied from a smaller copy; some browning. Extra-illus with 50 ports & plates, some mtd. C May 20 (122) £260 [Franklin]

Anr Ed. L: R. Ackermann, 1809-11. Vols I-IV. 8vo, contemp half calf; rebacked, some covers detached. With engraved title & 51 plates, 49 hand-colored. bba Oct 10 (161) £160 [S. Heneage]

Anr copy. Later calf gilt; 3 joints broken. With 50 (of 52) plates & 4 engraved titles. A few plates cropped; browned & foxed; bound without supplement titles & to Readers leaves as usual. pn Apr 23 (46) £140

Poets. See: British Poets

Poet's Magazine

— The Poet's Magazine, a Repository of Original and Selected American Poetry. Albany, [1842]. Vol I, Nos 1-2. 2 issues. 8vo, orig wraps. sg Mar 5 (272) $110

Poggendorff, Johann Christian

— Biographisch-literarisches Handwoerterbuch zur Geschichte der exacten Wissenschaften.... Amst., 1965. 4 vols in 6. Reprint of 1863 Ed. O Sept 24 (196) $275

Poggi, Mauro

— Alfabeto di lettere iniziali inventate.... Florence, [c.1730]. Oblong folio, old vellum; soiled. Engraved throughout; with 24 plates, all hand-colored in a contemp hand. Tp cut to just outside plate mark & mtd to size; some marginal tears; final leaf with light crease & lower margin reinforced on verso. C June 24 (242) £1,700 [Quaritch]

Pohl, Johann Baptist Emanuel

— Plantarum Brasiliae icones et descriptiones.... Vienna, 1827-31. Vol II only. Contemp half calf. With 100 hand-colored plates, numbered 101-200. Some oxidizing of color pigment; 2 plates with discoloration. Sold w.a.f. C May 20 (210) £2,000 [Sims Reed]

Poirson, J. B.

— Statistique generale et particuliere de la France.... Paris, 1804. One vol only (of 7). 4to, contemp sheep; rubbed. With 9 folding maps, hand-colored in outline. sg Feb 13 (137) $650

Poiteau, Pierre Antoine. See: Risso & Poiteau

Poivre, Pierre, 1719-86

— The Travels of a Philosopher.... L, 1769. 12mo, contemp sheep; extremities worn, covers detached. sg Nov 14 (195) $475

Polain, Marie-Louis

— Marques des imprimeurs et libraires en France au XVe Siecle. Paris, 1926. One of 900. 4to, new cloth. sg Oct 31 (165) $250

Polano, Pietro Soave

— The Historie of the Council of Trent. See: Sarpi, Paolo

Poldo d'Albenas, Jean

— Discours historial de l'antique et illustre cite de Nismes. Lyons, 1560. Folio, later calf gilt; rubbed. bba Apr 9 (205) £1,400 [Dawson]

Pole, Reginald, Cardinal, 1500-58

— De concilio liber. Rome: Aldus, 1562. 4to, 19th-cent half lea. Some foxing. SI Dec 5 (562) LIt220,000

Poleni, Giovanni

— Exercitationes Vitruvianae. Padua & Venice, 1739. 3 parts in 1 vol. Folio, contemp half lea. Dampstained. DW Oct 9 (939) £240

Polidori, John William

— The Vampyre. L, 1819. 8vo, orig wraps; spine lacking, stains. Some foxing; lacking ads. bbc Dec 9 (587) $420

2d Issue. Orig wraps; rebacked & repaired. Some soiling & staining; marginal tears. Manney copy. P Oct 11 (256) $3,000

Political...

— A Political and Satyrical History of the Years 1756 to 1757. L: E. Morris, [c.1757]. 2 parts in 1 vol. 4to, contemp calf gilt; rebacked, rubbed. With 75 plates. bba Oct 10 (58) £360 [Korn]

Politician's...

— The Politician's Dictionary, or a Summary of Political Knowledge. L, 1775-76. 2d Ed of Vol II, 1st Ed of Vol I. 2 vols. 8vo, contemp sheep; repaired, joints cracking. Ms note in text. C June 25 (89) £1,100 [Quaritch/Hordern]

Politzer, Adam

— Zehn Wandtafeln zur Anatomie des Gehoerorgans.... Vienna: Wilhelm Braumueller, 1874. Folio, looas as issued in half cloth folder; worn, front cover stained. With 10 litho plates, 714mm by 556mm.. sg Nov 14 (104) $375

Pollard, Alfred William

See also: Bartlett & Pollard; Caxton Club; Short-Title Catalogue

— Books about Books. L, 1893-94. 6 vols. 8vo, uniform half mor gilt. DW Oct 2 (296) £105

— Cobden-Sanderson and the Doves Press. San Francisco: John Henry Nash, 1929. One of 339. Folio, vellum gilt. b&b Feb 19 (237) $150

— Early Illustrated Books. L, 1893. cb Oct 17 (751) $65

— Fine Books. NY & L: Connoisseur's Library, 1912. 1st Ed. In d/j, unopened. With 40 plates. cb Oct 17 (764) $75

Pollard, Graham. See: Carter & Pollard

Pollard, Hugh Bertie Campbell

— Wildfowl & Waders; Nature & Sport in the Coastlands. L, 1928. One of 950. Illus by Frank Southgate. 4to, orig half vellum; extremities rubbed. sg Jan 9 (300) $90

Pollard, Percival, 1869-1911

— Posters in Miniature. NY, 1896. Intro by Edward Penfield. 4to, cloth; smudged. Some finger-soiling. bbc June 29 (181) $50

Anr copy. Orig cloth; soiled. K July 12 (420) $75

Anr Ed. NY, 1897. 4to, cloth. sg Apr 2 (240) $130

Pollok, Robert. See: Fore-Edge Paintings

Polly...

— Polly Put the Kettle On We'll All Make Jell-O. N.p., [1924]. Cover illus by Maxfield Parrish. Oblong 12mo, pictorial wraps. sg Jan 10 (124) $70

Polwhele, Richard

— Biographical Sketches in Cornwall. Truro, 1831. 3 vols. 12mo, orig bds; rubbed, lacking free endpaper in Vol III. With 6 ports & plates. bba Sept 19 (226) £140 [Brewer]

— The History of Cornwall. L, 1816. 7 vols in 2, including Whitaker's Supplement. 4to, modern calf gilt. Some browning. bba Sept 19 (227) £460 [Beeleigh Abbey]

— The History of Devonshire. Exeter, 1797-93-1806. 3 vols in 1. Folio, contemp mor gilt. bba Jan 30 (119) £360 [Blake]

Polybius, 205?-125? B.C.

See also: Aelian (Aelianus Tacticus) & Polybius

— Historiarum.... Hagenau: Johann Secer, 1530. Folio, later vellum. Lacking A2-4; title repaired. bba Nov 28 (173) £170 [Stamatoyannopoulos]

Pomerania

— Kirchen-Ordnung im Lande zu Pommern.... Stralsund & Grieffswald: Jacob Loefler, 1731. Folio, old bds; spine worn. With 2 related items bound at end. sg Oct 24 (264) $300

Pomet, Pierre

— A Compleat History of Druggs.... L, 1712. 2 vols in 1. 4to, contemp calf; rubbed. bba June 11 (225) £200 [Smith]

— Histoire generale des drogues.... Paris, 1694. 1st Ed. 4 parts in 1 vol. Folio, contemp calf; worn. Some browning. SI June 10 (810) LIt2,450,000

Pomodoro, Giovanni

— Geometria prattica tratta dagl'elementi d'Euclide et altri auttori.... Rome, 1624. Folio, contemp vellum; stained. With engraved title & 51 plates. bba Apr 9 (191) £420 [Erlini]

Pompei, Alberto

— Essame dell'honore cavalleresco. Venice, 1625. 8vo, contemp vellum. sg Mar 26 (240) $110

Poncelin de la Roche-Tilhac, Jean Charles, 1746-1828

— Chef-d'Oeuvres de l'Antiquite sur les Beaux-Arts.... Paris, 1784. Illus by Bernard Picart. 2 vols in 1. Folio, contemp sheep gilt; extremities worn, front joint cracked. With 80 plates numbered 1-81. sg Oct 24 (265) $275

Pontanus, Johannes Jovianus, 1426-1503

— Opera. Venice: Aldus, 1505. 8vo, old vellum. Tp stamped. sg Mar 12 (256) $500

Anr Ed. Venice: heirs of Aldus, 1533. 8vo, 19th-cent vellum gilt. Stains on tp & last few leaves. sg Oct 24 (266) $225

Pontifical

— Pontificale Romanum ad omnes ceremonias...accomodatum. Venice: Giunta, 1572. Folio, old calf with arms of a cardinal in center. SI June 10 (816) LIt900,000

— Pontificale Romanum. Paris: Rolin Thierry & Eustach Foucault, 1615. Folio, 18th-cent mor gilt. Rust hole in lower blank margin of 2 leaves. C Dec 16 (157) £600 [Maggs]

Ponting, Herbert George

— The Great White South. Being an Account.... L, 1921. 8vo, orig cloth; rubbed. bba Sept 19 (44) £140 [Simper]

Anr copy. Orig cloth; extremities worn. DW Nov 6 (85) £85

Ponziani, Domenico Lorenzo

— Il Giuoco incomparabile degli Scacchi. Modena, 1769. 3 parts in 1 vol. 8vo, contemp vellum; small tear to head of spine. Some browning at end. Inscr "Ex dono Auctoris". Ck May 8 (147) £450

Anr Ed. Venice, 1773. 3 parts in 1 vol. 8vo, modern cloth. R5-S2 dampstained; final leaves repaired at inner margins. Ck May 8 (148) £160

Anr Ed. Modena, 1782. 4to, contemp half sheep; bottom section of spine lacking. Gathering S browned. Ck May 8 (149) £300

Pool, Robert —& Cash, John

— Views of the Most Remarkable Public Buildings...in the City of Dublin.... Dublin, 1780. 4to, contemp calf; rubbed, joints weak. With engraved title, 2 folding maps (1 repaired) & 29 plates. Some margins trimmed; some spotting & soiling. pn Apr 23 (276) £230 [Elliott]

Poor, M. C.

— Denver South Park & Pacific. Denver: Rocky Mountain Railroad Club, 1949. One of 15 unnumbered & bound in red Fabrikoid. In d/j. cb Feb 13 (256) $275

Poortenaar, Jan

— The Art of the Book and its Illustration. L, [1935]. 4to, orig cloth; rubbed & soiled. wa Mar 5 (95) $95

Pope, Alexander, 1688-1744

— The Dunciad. L, 1729. ("The Dunciad Variorum. With the Prolegomena of Scriblerus.") Bound with: Edward Young. Love of Fame. L, 1728. 4to, contemp calf; worn. bba Oct 10 (313) £60 [Ball]

1st Complete Ed of 1st 3 books. 4to, contemp calf; joints weakened, rubbed. With engraved title. Some browning. bba May 14 (78) £60 [Crozier]

— An Epistle to the Right Honourable Richard Lord Visct. Cobham. L, 1733. 1st Ed. Folio, disbound, top edges gilt, others untrimmed. Leaf E1 frayed & E2 trimmed; some stains. J. B. Clemens copy. P Dec 12 (187) $400

— An Epistle...Dr. Arbuthnot. L, 1734. Folio, modern bds. Tp & verso of final leaf soiled. Milne copy. Ck June 12 (164) £180

— An Essay on Man. L, [1733-34]. 1st Eds. 4 vols in 1. Folio, modern calf. Tp of Vol I with crease; some spotting or soiling. C Dec 16 (226) £1,300 [Finch]

— Letters of Mr. Alexander Pope, and Several of his Friends. L, 1737. 4to, half calf; rubbed, hinges weak. bba Nov 28 (268) £50 [Oatley]

— Of the Characters of Women.... L, 1735. 1st Ed. Folio, modern bds. Milne copy. Ck June 12 (166) £95

— Of the Use of Riches, an Epistle to the Right Honourable Allen Lord Bathhurst. L, 1732. 1st Ed, 1st Issue. Folio, modern half calf. Text previously folded leaving crease in center throughout. W July 8 (36) £55

— The Rape of the Lock. L, 1896. Illus by Aubrey Beardsley. 4to, orig cloth. bba July 23 (339) £85 [Frew Mackenzie]; S Nov 14 (86) £150 [Riex]

— Works. L, 1717-35. 2 vols. Folio, calf. With folding port. pnE May 13 (70) £50

Anr Ed. L, 1751. 9 vols. 8vo, contemp calf gilt. L Nov 14 (439) £50

Anr copy. Contemp calf. L Nov 14 (440) £50

Anr copy. Contemp calf gilt; rubbed. S July 1 (1000) £420 [Baring]

Anr Ed. L, 1824. 10 vols. 8vo, contemp calf. Rubbed. O Jan 14 (151) $250

Pope, Alexander, 1688-1744 —& Others
— Miscellanea in Two Volumes. Never before published.... L: E. Curll, 1727 [1726]. 2 vols. 8vo, contemp calf; rubbed. Variant with Laus Ululae in Vol II. pn Apr 23 (122) £320

Pope, Arthur Upham —& Ackerman, Phyllis
— A Survey of Persian Art. L & NY, 1938-39. 6 vols. Folio, orig cloth, in d/js. Stamp on titles. bba July 9 (23) £900 [Hosains]

Anr copy. Vols I-IV (of 6). Folio, orig cloth; worn. Ck July 10 (145) £600

Anr Ed. L & NY, 1938-58. 7 vols, including Index. Folio, orig cloth; rubbed. DW Mar 11 (845) £1,050

Anr Ed. L & NY, 1938-39. 6 vols. Folio, orig cloth. Some soiling. pn Mar 19 (169) £1,000 [Han Shan Tang]; S July 1 (1160) £900

Anr copy. Cloth; minor rubbing & wear to extremities, hinges reinforced, endpapers foxed. With 1482 plates, 201 in color. sg Sept 6 (226) $1,900

Pope, John Alexander
— Chinese Porcelains from the Ardebil Shrine. Wash., 1956. 4to, cloth, in d/j. sg Sept 6 (72) $110

Anr copy. Cloth, in chipped d/j. sp June 18 (383) $75

Popham, Arthur Ewart
See also: British Museum
— Catalogue of Drawings in the Collection Formed by Sir Thomas Phillipps. L, 1935. One of 150. 4to, orig cloth. S Feb 11 (173) £180 [Dawson]
— Catalogue of the Drawings of Parmigianino. New Haven, 1971. 3 vols. 4to, orig cloth. Ck Feb 14 (82) £850

Poppel, Johann
— Malerische Ansichten aus Nuernberg. Nuremberg: J. L. Schrag, [c.1840]. 8vo, cloth; worn. With engraved title & 21 plates. O Nov 26 (145) $400

Porroni, Annibale
— Trattato universale militare moderno. Venice: Francesco Nicolini, 1676. Folio, old vellum. With engraved title & 40 plates. Half-title with lower margin restored; 1 other repair; lower outer corner stained throughout. S July 9 (322) £200 [Elliott]

Porta, Giovanni Battista della, 1538-1615
— De furtiuis literarum notis vulgo de Ziferis libri III. Naples, 1602. 4to, modern half cloth. Some browning. SI June 10 (821) LIt1,400,000
— Elementorum curvilineorum libri tres.... Rome: Bartholomaeus Zanettus, 1610. 4to, contemp vellum; soiled. Tp hole affecting vignette, date & port on verso; port repaired at corner with loss to margin of image; D1-4 holed at inner margin; K1-2 repaired at inner margins; N2 inkstained on recto; some staining & browning. Ck Oct 18 (22) £240
— La Fisonomia dell' huomo.... Venice, 1652. 8vo, 18th-cent bds. Some staining & browning; some leaves short. SI Dec 5 (984) LIt600,000
— Magiae naturalis, sive de miraculis rerum naturalium libri IIII. Cologne: Birckmann & Richvuinis, 1562. 16mo, later calf. B Nov 1 (680) HF750

Anr Ed. Naples: H. Salviani, 1589. ("Magiae naturalis libri XX.") Folio, contemp vellum. Some browning & foxing. SI June 10 (825) LIt6,800,000

Anr Ed. Frankfurt, 1597. ("Magiae naturalis libri viginti.") 8vo, 18th-cent half vellum. SI June 10 (826) LIt420,000

Anr Ed. Rouen, 1650. 8vo, 19th-cent half sheep gilt; worn. sg Mar 12 (228) $200

Anr Ed. Amst.: Elizeum Weyerstraten, 1664. 12mo, contemp calf; spine ends chipped. sg Mar 12 (229) $325
— Phytognomonica. Naples: O. Salviani, 1588. Folio, calf. SI June 10 (827) LIt3,200,000

Portalis, Roger
— Les Dessinateurs d'illustrations au dix-huitieme siecle. Paris, 1877. One of 500 on hollande. 2 vols. 8vo, calf gilt by Yseux, orig wraps bound in. Extra-illus with c.280 plates & drawings. S Feb 11 (325) £160 [Klein]

Porter, Bruce —& Others
— Art in California: a Survey of American Art.... San Francisco, 1916. Folio, half cloth; spine discolored. cb NOv 21 (13) $300

Porter, Cole
— Red Hot and Blue; A Musical Comedy. NY, 1936. One of 300. Folio, orig silk over bds; spine worn. Epstein copy. sg Apr 29 (382) $1,600

Porter, Sir James, 1710-86
— Observations on the Religion, Law, Government and Manners, of the Turks. L, 1771. 2d Ed. 8vo, modern calf. Library markings. bba Jan 16 (322) £120 [Shapero]

Porter, Jane, 1776-1850
— The Scottish Chiefs, a Romance. L, [c.1840]. 2 vols. 12mo, half calf by Root; rubbed. O July 14 (152) $80

Porter, Katherine Anne

— Flowering Judas, and Other Stories. NY, [1935]. 1st Complete Ed. In def d/j. Inscr, 1962. sg June 11 (266) $110

— Hacienda. [NY]: Harrison of Paris, [1934]. One of 895. Inscr. sg Dec 12 (347) $200; sg June 11 (267) $50

— Pale Horse, Pale Rider. NY, [1939]. 1st Ed. In d/j. sg June 11 (268) $110

Porter, Sir Robert Ker, 1777-1842

— Travelling Sketches in Russia and Sweden.... L, 1809. 2 vols. 4to, contemp calf; rebacked, portions of orig spines laid down. With 41 plates, many hand-colored. cb Feb 12 (105) $425

Anr copy. Contemp half calf; worn. With 41 plates, 28 hand-colored. Some browning & soiling; 1 folding plate torn & repaired, the other with short tear at 1 fold; tear in tp of Vol I; leaf of prelims in Vol II torn & repaired; lacking half-title in Vol II. S Nov 15 (1130) £300 [Rinne]

Anr Ed. L, 1813. 2 vols in 1. 4to, half calf over marbled bds; later cloth spine with orig backstrip laid down. With 41 plates. wa Dec 9 (417) $425

Porter, William Sydney, 1862-1910
See also: Limited Editions Club

— Works. Garden City, 1917. One of 1,075. Illus by Gordon Grant. 14 vols. Mor gilt; some spines chipped. With some plates in 2 states. P June 17 (346) $2,250

Portland Museum

— [Sale Catalogue] A Catalogue of the Portland Museum...Property of the Duchess Dowager of Portland. L, [1786]. 4to, contemp half calf. Some browning & staining. S June 25 (53) £1,900 [Renard]

Anr copy. 19th-cent half sheep. sg Nov 7 (157) $500

Portlock, Nathaniel

— A Voyage Round the World. L, 1789. 1st Ed. 4to, orig bds; rebacked, inner hinges reinforced with linen tape, some plates detached. With port, 5 hand-colored & 8 plain plates & with 6 folding maps. CNY Oct 8 (210) $2,500

Anr copy. Contemp calf; lower cover detached. S Nov 21 (328) £950 [Remington]

Anr copy. Contemp mor; spine soiled. With port, 6 folding maps & charts & 13 plates. S June 25 (119) £3,000 [Quaritch]

Portolano. See: Nuovo...

Portraits...

— Portraits and Characters of the Kings of England. L: John Harris, [n.d.-1825]. 2 vols. 12mo, orig wraps; soiled. With 2 titles & 33 ports. DW Apr 8 (429) £90

Posner, Donald

— Annibale Carracci, a Study.... L, 1971. 2 vols. Folio, orig cloth, in d/js. bba Feb 13 (159) £440 [Zwemmer]

Posselius, Johannes

— Calligraphia oratoria linguae Graecae. Frankfurt: apud heredes Andreae Wecheli, 1594. 8vo, contemp vellum, arms in gilt on fore-edge with Hebrew lettering. S May 13 (812) £200 [Maggs]

Possevino, Giovanni Battista

— Dialogo dell'honore.... Venice, 1556. 4to, old vellum. Dampstained throughout. sg Mar 26 (243) $200

Possevinus, Antonius

— Moscovia. Antwerp: Christopher Plantin, 1587. 8vo, calf. Minor stains. B May 12 (41) HF700

Post, Augustus. See: Curtiss & Post

Post, Wiley —&
Gatty, Harold

— Around the World in Eight Days. NY: Rand McNally, [1931]. Intro by Will Rogers. In d/j. cb Nov 7 (90) $55

Postel, Guillaume

— De Etruriae regionis, quae prima in orbe europaeo habitata est.... Florence: Lorenzo Torrentino, 1551. 4to, 16th-cent pigskin over pastebds; tear at head of spine. S Dec 5 (184) £2,200 [Goldschmidt]

— De orbis terrae concordia libri quatuor. [Basel: J. Oporinus, 1544]. Folio, late 18th-cent mor gilt; rubbed. Some annotations & underlining. Ck Oct 31 (270) £2,000

Poster...

— The Poster: An Illustrated Monthly Chronicle. L, 1898-1900. Vols I-III (of 5). 4to, orig cloth with orig wraps bound in; some hinges cracked, minor wear. John Hassall's set, with note by him in Vol III. sg Apr 2 (241) $650

Postlethwayt, Malachy

— Great-Britain's True System.... L, 1757. 8vo, contemp calf gilt; short split to head of joints. b June 22 (200) £400

Potain, —

— Details des ouvrages de menuiserie pour les batimens. Paris, 1759. 8vo, contemp calf gilt; front joint with piece missing. sg Feb 6 (50) $500

Pote, Joseph, 1703?-87

— The History and Antiquities of Windsor Castle.... L, 1749. 4to, contemp calf. Lower margin wormed throughout; 1 plate stained. bba May 14 (279) £100 [Thorp]

Pott, Percival, 1714-88

— The Chirurgical Works. L, 1808. 3 vols. 8vo, modern bds. With port & 22 plates. Old institutional stamps, not affecting plates; some foxing. sg May 14 (132) $250

Potter, Ambrose George

— A Bibliography of the Rubaiyat of Omar Khayyam. L, 1929. One of 300. Orig half cloth, in d/j, unopened. cb Oct 17 (755) $180

Anr copy. Orig half cloth. K Sept 29 (301) $75

Potter, Beatrix

— Appley Dapply's Nursery Rhymes. L, 1917. 16mo, orig bds. pn Apr 23 (169) £220

— Cecily Parsley's Nursery Rhymers. L, [1922]. 16mo, orig bds. pn Apr 23 (170) £380

— Cecily Parsley's Nursery Rhymes. L, [1922]. 16mo, orig bds; edges worn. pn Apr 23 (171) £190 [Sotheran]

— Changing Pictures, a Book of Transformation Pictures. L: Nister, [c.1894]. 4to, orig half cloth; broken & loose. bba Oct 10 (35) £100 [Miles]

— The Fairy Caravan. Phila., 1929. 4to, orig bdg. With 6 color plates. K Mar 22 (356) $160

— Ginger and Pickles. L, [1909]. 1st Ed. 4to, orig bds. b Nov 18 (80) £80; pn Apr 23 (172) £150 [Sotheran]

Anr copy. Some leaves soiled. pn Apr 23 (173) £120 [Sotheran]

3d Issue. Orig cloth. b Nov 18 (81) £60

— The Pie and the Patty-Pan. L, 1905. 1st Ed. 4to, orig cloth; rubbed. Some leaves soiled. pn Apr 23 (176) £120 [Sotheran]

Anr copy. Orig bds. pn Apr 23 (177) £150 [Joseph]

Anr copy. Pictorial bds. pnE May 13 (88) £60

— The Roly-Poly Pudding. L, 1908. 1st Ed. 4to, orig cloth; rubbed & soiled. DW Jan 29 (448) £50

Anr copy. A few leaves with soil. pn Apr 23 (178) £180 [Sotheran]

— The Story of a Fierce Bad Rabbit. L, 1906. 1st Ed. 16mo, orig cloth wallet-type bdg; rubbed, soiled & lacking tongue. bba July 23 (279) £110 [Schuster]

Anr copy. Orig cloth wallet-type bdg; upper cover with soil. pn Apr 23 (179) £320 [Weber]

— The Story of Miss Moppet. L, 1906. 1st Ed. 16mo, orig cloth wallet-type bdg; upper cover soiled. One leaf soiled. pn Apr 23 (180) £320 [Weber]

— The Tailor of Gloucester. L, 1902. 1st Ed, one of 500. 16mo, orig bds. With colored frontis & 15 plates. b Nov 18 (83A) £1,700

Anr copy. Orig pictorial bds. S Apr 28 (80) £1,700 [Schuster]

1st Pbd Ed. L & NY, 1903. 16mo, orig cloth. bba July 23 (278) £900 [Bennett]

Anr copy. Orig bds; rubbed & darkened. DW Dec 11 (447) £110

Anr copy. Cloth. pnE Oct 2 (438) £140

— The Tale of Jemima Puddle-Duck. L, 1908. 1st Ed. 16mo, orig bds. pn Apr 23 (181) £380

Anr copy. Orig bds; small piece torn from head of spine. pn Apr 23 (182) £150

— The Tale of Johnny Town-Mouse. L & NY, [1918]. 1st Ed. 4to, orig bds; spine head chipped. cb Feb 12 (107) $50; pn Apr 23 (183) £190

— The Tale of Mr. Jeremy Fisher. L, 1906. 1st Ed. 16mo, orig bds. Some soiling to a few leaves. pn Apr 23 (185) £180 [Sotheran]

— The Tale of Mr. Tod. L & NY, 1912. 1st Ed. 16mo, orig bds; corners knocked. Some leaves soiled. pn Apr 23 (188) £120 [Sotheran]

— The Tale of Mrs. Tiggy-Winkle. L, 1905. 1st Ed. 16mo, orig bds. pn Apr 23 (186) £200; pn Apr 23 (186) £200

— The Tale of Mrs. Tittlemouse. L & NY, 1910. 1st Ed. 16mo, orig bds; spine rubbed. pn Apr 23 (187) £170

— The Tale of Peter Rabbit. L, [Dec 1901]. 1st Pbd Ed, 1st Issue. One of 250. 16mo, orig bds. "A fine copy." Epstein copy. sg Apr 30 (387) $50,000

1st Pbd Ed. [L], Feb 1902. 2d Issue. 16mo, orig bds; bowed. With frontis & 41 plates plus extra copy of the frontis. S Nov 14 (194) £11,000 [Ross]

Anr copy. Orig cloth. "A fine copy". Epstein copy. sg Apr 30 (388) $19,000

1st Pbd Ed. L, Oct 1902. later issue. 16mo, orig bds; small tear to lower cover. Glue-staining to tp; 2 pages with minor adhesion marks. pn Apr 23 (189) £310 [Sotheran]

— The Tale of Pigling Bland. L, [1913]. 1st Ed. 16mo, bds. pn Apr 23 (191) £150

— The Tale of Squirrel Nutkin. L, 1903. 1st Ed. 16mo, orig bds; piece torn from head of spine. pn Apr 23 (192) £100 [Schuster]

— The Tale of the Flopsy Bunnies. L, 1909. 1st Ed. 16mo, orig bds; stained. pn Apr 23 (194) £160 [Sotheran]

— The Tale of Timmy Tiptoes. L, 1911. 1st

Ed. 16mo, orig bds. cb Feb 12 (108) $55

Anr copy. Orig bds. Manney copy. P Oct 11 (258) $1,300; pn Apr 23 (193) £170 [Joseph]

— The Tale of Tom Kitten. L, 1907. 1st Ed. 16mo, orig bds; marked. bba Aug 13 (312) £55 [Harlow]

— The Tale of Two Bad Mice. L, 1904. 1st Ed. 16mo, orig bds; recased with repair along inner hinges, stamp on verso of front free endpaper. Half-title inserted & frayed. Manney copy. P Oct 11 (257) $1,100

Pouncey, Philip. See: British Museum

Pound, Ezra

— A Draft of XXX Cantos. Paris: Hours Press, 1930. 1st Ed, One of 200. Orig half cloth. Epstein copy. sg Apr 30 (389) $2,600

— Drafts & Fragments of Cantos CX-CXVII. NY: New Directions, [1968]. 1st Ed, one of 310. Folio, orig cloth. bba May 14 (245) £110 [Blumenkron]

— Hugh Selwyn Mauberley. L, 1920. 1st Ed, One of 200. Orig cloth; upper joint split. With signatures of Robin Holloway & Dorothy Wellesley on front pastedown. S Nov 14 (661) £440 [Shepherd]

Anr copy. Orig half cloth. Epstein copy. sg Apr 30 (390) $2,400

— Imaginary Letters. Paris: Black Sun Press, 1930. 1st Ed, one of 300. Orig wraps. CNY Dec 5 (309) $2,400

— Indiscretions. Paris: Three Mountains Press, 1923. Out-of-series copy. 4 bi-folio ptd sheets unfolded & unbound sg June 11 (270) $200

— Lustra. NY, 1917. One of 200. Orig cloth. Epstein copy. sg Apr 30 (391) $1,200

— Mr. Housman's Message. [Palo Alto: Harvest Press, 1931]. One of 25. Broadside, 4to. In cloth folder. S July 21 (168) £500 [Macklin]

— The Pisan Cantos. [NY]: New Directions, [1948]. 1st Ed. In chipped d/j. F Dec 18 (245) $50

— Redondillas, or Something of that Sort. [NY]: New Directions, [1967]. 1st Ed, one of 110. 4to, orig half cloth, in d/j. CNY Dec 5 (312) $800

— The Seafarer. From the Anglo-Saxon. Frankfurt, [1965]. One of 195. Illus by Oskar Kokoschka. Folio, unbound as issued in bd portfolio. CNY Dec 5 (310) $2,400

Pountney, William Joseph

— Old Bristol Potteries. Bristol, 1920. sg Sept 6 (57) $150

Pouqueville, Francois Charles Hugues Laurent

— Voyage dans la Grece. Paris, 1826-27. 2d Ed. 6 vols. 8vo, contemp half calf; rebacked. With 36 plates & maps; without the 2 maps at the end of Vol VI. Ck Dec 11 (249) £240

Poussin, Nicolas

— The Drawings of Nicolas Poussin. Catalogue Raisonne. L, [1939]-53. Ed by Walter Friedlaender. 3 vols. 4to, orig cloth. S Feb 11 (71) £700 [Ars]

Powell, H. M. T.

— The Santa Fe Trail to California. NY: Sol Lewis, 1981. One of 350. cb Sept 12 (142) $160; O Mar 31 (7) $60

Anr copy. Folio, lea. Facsimile of 1931 Ed. O Mar 31 (151) $70; O Mar 31 (163) $70; O July 14 (157) $110; O July 14 (158) $80; O Aug 25 (145) $110; sg June 18 (461) $90; sg June 18 (462) $100

Powell, Lawrence Clark

— Heart of the Southwest: A Selective Bibliography of Novels. . . laid in Arizona and New Mexico.... Los Angeles, 1955. In d/j. cb Sept 12 (143) $110

— A Southwestern Century: A Bibliography of One Hundred Books of Non-Fiction About the Southwest. Van Nuys, CA, [1958]. One of 500. Half cloth, in d/j. cb Oct 17 (761) $190

Anr copy. Bds. Inscr to Ben Grauer. H. P. Kraus's copy. K Sept 29 (359) $140

— Southwestern Book Trails. Albuquerque, [1963]. 1st Ed. In d/j. cb Oct 17 (1762) $55

Powell, Robert

— Depopulation Arraigned, Convicted and Condemned.... L, 1636. 8vo, 18th-cent blind-stamped calf; def. Some worming in upper & inner margins, occasionally just affecting rule border or running title; lacking final leaf. STC 20160. S May 13 (790) £180 [Johnson]

Power, Henry

— Experimental Philosophy, in Three Books. L, 1664. 1st Ed. 4to, later half calf; joints cracked. Folding plate replaced in facsimile. Sold w.a.f. Ck June 18 (40) £300

Power, Tyrone, 1797-1841

— Impressions of America During the Years 1833, 1834 and 1835. L, 1836. 1st Ed. 2 vols. 8vo, half lea. sp Nov 24 (52) $55

Powers, Stephen
— Afoot and Alone: a Walk from Sea to Sea by the Southern Route. Hartford, 1872. 1st Ed. 8vo, cloth; extremities worn. sg June 18 (463) $100

Pownall, Henry
— Some Particulars Relating to the History of Epsom. Epsom, 1825. 8vo, contemp half calf. With 6 colored plates. bba Sept 19 (228) £95 [Scott]

Pownall, Thomas, 1722-1805
— The Administration of the Colonies. L, 1765. 2d Ed. 8vo, modern bds. sg June 18 (464) $375
— Hydraulic and Nautical Observations on the Currents in the Atlantic Ocean.... L, 1787. 4to, orig wraps. With folding chart. P June 16 (266) $2,750
— A Memorial...to the Sovereigns of Europe on the Present State of Affairs between the Old and New World. L, 1780. 8vo, half mor. Some foxing. P June 16 (265) $800

Powys, Llewelyn, 1884-1939. See: Golden Cockerel Press

Poynting, Frank
— Eggs of British Birds with an Account of their Breeding-Habits, Limicolae. L, 1895-96. 4to, contemp half mor; worn & scuffed. With 54 colored plates. With mtd Ls, 8 Mar 1897. wa Mar 5 (484) $220

Anr copy. Contemp half mor; soiled & scuffed. wa Mar 5 (487) $120

Pozzo, Andrea, 1642-1709
— Perspectiva pictorum et architectorum. Rome, 1693-1700. 1st Ed. 2 parts in 2 vols. Folio, contemp vellum; upper cover of Part II renewed at an early date. With 2 engraved architectural dedication plates, 2 frontises, plate of Palladio & Scamozzi's comparative architectural orders in Part 1 & 218 plates. Small corner tear in Plate 95 of Part 1; Plate 106/7 in Part 2 detached; some discoloration at end. b June 22 (202) £1,700

Anr copy. Contemp vellum; soiled, Vol I worn, hinges broken, lacking front pastedown & flyleaf. With engraved titles & 218 numbered & 4 unnumbered plates (of 223). Plate 28 in Vol II torn with loss; dampstaining in Vol I affecting titles, text & 1 or 2 plates; some browning. S June 25 (221) £1,100 [Chimera]

Anr Ed. Rome, 1741-37. 2 parts in 2 vols. Folio, contemp vellum; soiled & worn. Some spotting & soiling. DW Oct 9 (941) £1,000
— Rules and Examples of Perspective Proper for Painters and Architects. L, 1707. Folio, old half calf; worn. With 2 engraved titles, dedication, frontis & 101 plates. Some discoloration & surface dirt. S July 1 (1380) £500 [Sotheran]

Practicus. See: Moore, Dennis Times

Praed, Mrs Campbell. See: McCarthy & Praed

Praet, Joseph Basile Bernard van, 1754-1837
— Catalogue de livres imprimes sur velin.... Paris, 1824-28. One of 200. 4 vols. 8vo, orig cloth. bba Apr 30 (387) £120 [Montero]

Pratt, Anne, 1806-93
— The Flowering Plants, Grasses, Sedges, and Ferns of Great Britain. L, [c.1873]. 6 vols. 8vo, contemp half calf; spines faded, rubbed. With 317 (of 319) plates. bba Sept 5 (95) £260 [Town]

Anr copy. Orig cloth; spine ends worn. DW May 13 (126) £300

Anr copy. Half mor gilt. With 315 (of 316) color plates & 1 uncolored plate. pn June 11 (237) £220 [Bailey]

Anr Ed. L & NY, 1889. 4 vols. 8vo, orig cloth; spine ends bumped, lower cover of Vol II dampstained. With 317 (of 319) colored plates & 1 uncolored plate. Dampstaining to end of Vol II affecting a few plates. pn May 14 (185) £190 [Bifolco]

Anr Ed. L, 1899-1900. 4 vols. 8vo, contemp half mor. With 314 chromolitho plates & 1 uncolored plate. Ck May 15 (45A) £420

Anr Ed. L, [n.d.]. 3 vols. 8vo, orig cloth. With 229 color plates only. Some plates loose or repaired in margin; some soiling. pn Dec 12 (292) £100 [Map House]
— Wild Flowers. L, 1852. 2 vols. 16mo, orig cloth; rubbed. bba Sept 5 (96) £50 [Manasek]

Pratt, Fletcher. See: De Camp & Pratt

Pratt, Parley Parker
— A Voice of Warning. NY, 1839. 12mo, orig cloth; front cover loose, worn, hole along gutter on spine. sg June 18 (394) $2,400

Pratt, Peter, fl.1810
— The Theory of Chess. L, 1799. Contemp half calf over bds; extremities rubbed. Ck May 8 (152) £180

Pratt, Peter Parley
— A Voice of Warning and Instruction.... NY, 1837. 18mo, orig bds. Some dampstaining. NH Oct 6 (209) $2,300

Pratt, Samuel Jackson

— Pity's Gift: a Collection of Interesting Tales.... L, 1801. 3d Ed. 12mo, contemp calf. Some browning. bba July 23 (123) £70 [Excell]

Prayer Books

— Ein new Christliches nuetzes und schones Betbuechlein. Magdeburg: Ambrosius Kirchner, 1595. 12mo, contemp German embroidered bdg, edges gilt & gauffered. Sold w.a.f. S May 28 (41) £1,800 [Jackson]

Praz, Mario

— Studies in Seventeenth Century Imagery. Rome, 1964. In d/j. O Sept 24 (199) $70

Preece, Louisa. See: Symonds & Preece

Prescott, William Hickling, 1796-1859
See also: Limited Editions Club

— History of the Reign of Ferdinand and Isabella. Bost., 1838. 3 vols. 8vo, orig plum cloth with star & medallion pattern, variant bdg; edges worn. bbc June 29 (287) $90

— History of the Conquest of Mexico. L, 1843. 3 vols. 8vo, orig cloth. sg Dec 5 (206) $200

Anr Ed. Phila., 1892. 2 vols. 8vo, cloth. sg June 18 (456) $110

— History of the Conquest of Peru. NY, 1847. 1st Ed. 2 vols. 8vo, contemp half lea; rubbed. With 2 ports & a map. NH Oct 6 (312) $120

Anr copy. Cloth. With 2 ports & a facsimile. Epstein copy. sg Apr 30 (392) $300

1st English Ed. L, 1847. 2 vols. 8vo, orig cloth; hinges cracked. sg June 18 (467) $200

Present...

— The Present State of Ireland.... L, 1673. 8vo, calf by Bayntun; worn, cover detached. O May 26 (149) $225

Prestel, Johann G.

— Dessins des meilleurs peintres d'Italie, d'Allemagne et des Pays-Bas.... Frankfurt, [1779-81]. Folio, modern half calf; bookplate removed from upper pastedown. With engraved title, 37 plates mtd within wash borders on 34 leaves, plate 24 heightened with gold. Some foxing. Schlosser copy. P June 17 (491) $7,500

Preston, William

— Illustrations of Masonry.... L, 1812. 12th Ed. 12mo, contemp sheep; lower joint cracked. bba Mar 26 (237) £55 [Sotheran]

Prevert, Jacques

— Adonides. Paris, 1975. One of 200. Illus by Joan Miro. Folio, loose as issued. CGen Nov 18 (438) SF17,000

Prevost d'Exiles, Antoine Francois, 1697-1763

— Histoire generale des voyages. The Hague, 1747-63. Atlas only. Contemp calf. With 59 maps. sg Feb 13 (138) $950

— Manon Lescaut. Paris, 1797 [An V]. ("Histoire de Manon Lescaut....") 2 vols. 12mo, contemp mor gilt. Copy on velin with plates before letters. S May 28 (420) £900 [Beres]

Anr Ed. L, 1928. One of 1,850. Illus by John Austen. 4to, cloth, in d/j. In English. sg Jan 30 (3) $175

Anr Ed. Stamford: Overbrook Press, 1958. One of 200. Illus by T. M. Cleland. br May 29 (42B) $170

Preziosi, Amadeo

— Stamboul. Paris, 1858. Oblong folio, loose in orig cloth; worn. With litho title & 12 (of 29) chromolithos. Some dampstaining to margins. Sold w.a.f. bba Nov 7 (199) £800 [Dupont]

Anr copy. Folio, With litho title & 12 chromolitho plates only (of 29). Sold w.a.f. bba Nov 7 (199) £800 [Dupont]

Anr copy. Oblong folio, contemp half mor; worn. With tinted litho title & 29 chromolithos. S July 1 (678A) £800 [Musca]

Price, Charles Matlack

— Poster Design: A Critical Study.... NY, [1922]. 4to, cloth, in d/j. With 215 mtd plates, 65 in color. sg Sept 6 (238) $275

Price, Con

— Trails I Rode. Pasadena: H. E. Britzman, 1947. One of 350. Orig lea, in frayed d/j; spine ends rubbed. Inscr to Justice William O. Douglas. wa Mar 5 (425) $100

Price, Frederic Newlin

— The Etchings & Lithographs of Arthur B. Davies. NY, 1929. 4to, cloth; stained, front joint cracked. sg Feb 26 (66) $140

One of 200 with orig etching by Davies. Half mor. Some soiling. sg Sept 6 (83) $225

Anr copy. Orig cloth; rubbed & marked. wa Apr 9 (205) $90

Price, George

— A Treatise on Fire & Thief-Proof Depositories and Locks and Keys. L, 1856. 8vo, contemp half calf; worn. Lacking ads. K Dec 1 (279) $225

Price, Harry

— Short-Title Catalogue of Works on Psychical Research.... L, 1929-35. 2 vols in 1, including Supplement. 8vo, half lea; worn. O Dec 17 (147) $160

Price, J. —& Haley, C. S.

— The Buyer's Manual and Business Guide.... San Francisco, 1872. sg June 18 (115) $200

Price, Lake

— Tauromachia, or the Bull-Fights of Spain.... L, 1852. Folio, modern half mor gilt preserving gilt decoration of orig upper cover. With engraved title & 25 plates. Marginal nicks repaired. S June 25 (322) £3,800 [Franks]

Price, Capt. R. K.

— Astbury, Whieldon and Ralph Wood Figures and Toby Jugs. L, 1922. Ltd Ed. 4to, orig cloth; rubbed & soiled. DW Mar 11 (770) £80

Price, Richard, 1723-91

— Observations on the Nature of Civil Liberty.... L, 1776. 7th Ed. 8vo, disbound. Half-title lacking top right corner & bottom right corner with some loss to bottom tp corner & ensuring few leaves; lacking leaves after 1st 8 pages in appendix. bbc Sept 23 (348) $60

Price, Sarah

— Illustrations of the Fungi of our Fields and Woods. L, 1864-65. 2 vols in 1. 4to, contemp cloth; soiled & worn. With 20 colored plates. Some wear & soiling. Ck Dec 11 (222) £280

Price, William, d.1666

— Ars concionandi. Amst.: Lodewijk & Elzevier, 1657. 8vo, contemp vellum. sg Mar 12 (257) $300

Price-Tannatt, T. E. See: Tannatt, Thomas Edwin Pryce

Prichard, Hesketh Vernon

— Through the Heart of Patagonia. L, 1902. Cloth; repaired. bba Jan 16 (303) £55 [Brewer]

Anr copy. Modern cloth. sg Dec 5 (207) $50

Prichard, James Cowles, 1786-1848

— The Natural History of Man. L, 1843. 8vo, later sheep; worn. With 40 plates, most hand-colored. sg Feb 13 (204) $225

4th Ed. L, 1855. 2 vols. 8vo, half mor; extremities worn. sg Feb 13 (205) $350

Prideaux, Sara T.

— Aquatint Engraving. L, 1909. 1st Ed. Major J. R. Abbey's copy, with his ink marginalia. C May 20 (103) £270 [Maggs]

— Bookbinders and their Craft. NY, 1903. One of 500. cb Oct 17 (768) $140

— A Catalogue of Books Bound by S. T. Prideaux.... L, [1900]. Ltd Ed. 8vo, bds. cb Oct 17 (769) $180

— Modern Bookbindings: Their Design and Decoration. NY, 1906. cb Oct 17 (770) $90

Priest, Cecil Damer

— The Birds of Southern Rhodesia. L, 1933-36. 4 vols. 4to, orig cloth. bba Feb 13 (361) £160 [Baring]

Anr copy. Orig cloth; covers blistered. With 40 color plates. sg May 14 (237) $200

Priestley, Sir Raymond E.

— Antarctic Adventure, Scott's Northern Party.... L, 1914. 1st Ed. Orig cloth; spine faded. bba Sept 19 (45) £240 [Simper]

Primaleon

— Los tres libros de muy efforcado cavallero Primaleon.... Venice: Giovanni Antonio dei Nicolini da Sabbio for Giovanni Baptista Pederzano, 1534. Folio, later 19th-cent mor gilt. Some spotting. C Dec 16 (72) £7,500 [Smith]

Prime, William Cowper, 1825-1905

— Pottery and Porcelain of All Times and Nations. NY, 1878. 8vo, contemp half calf; spine scuffed, corners worn. wa Sept 26 (557) $85

Primer...

— The Primer set Foorth by the Kynges Maiestie.... L, [c.1710]. 8vo, modern calf. Reprint of the 1546 Ed. bba Jan 30 (43) £100 [Bickersteth]

Prin, Alice. See: Hemingway, Ernest

Prince, John, 1643-1723

— Danmonii Orientales Illustres: or, The Worthies of Devon. Exeter, 1701. 1st Ed. Folio, contemp calf extra; covers detached. cb Dec 5 (99) $140

Anr Ed. L, 1810. 4to, contemp vellum; soiled & added. DW Dec 11 (319) £55

Anr copy. Cloth. With 6 ports & 5 plates of arms. sp Feb 6 (433) $75

Prince, Thomas, 1687-1758

— A Chronological History of New-England in the Form of Annals. Bost.: Kneeland & Green for Gerrish, 1736. 1st Ed. 8vo, modern calf. O Jan 14 (154) $650

Principall. See: Hakluyt, Richard

Printer's...

— Printer's Choice: A Selection of American Press Books, 1968-1978. Austin: W. Thomas Taylor, 1983. One of 325. Folio, cloth. With 8 specimens of printing tipped in. sg May 21 (217) $225

Printing History

— Printing History: The Journal of the American History Association. NY, 1979-89. Vol I, No 1 to Vol XI, No 2. 22 issues in 21. 4to, pictorial wraps; worn. O Sept 24 (201) $90

Prior, Matthew, 1664-1721

— Poems on Several Occasions. L, 1718. Folio, contemp calf; rebacked, joints split. bba Jan 16 (100) £65 [Wilkinson]

Pritchard, James Avery, 1816-62

— The Overland Diary.... [Denver], 1959. In d/j. With port, 2 folding maps & 1 folding chart in pocket. cb Nov 14 (163) $80

Anr copy. In worn d/j. With 3 maps & folding chart. NH May 30 (407) $60

Anr copy. With port, 2 folding maps & 1 folding chart in pocket. NH Aug 23 (445) $65

Pritchett, R. T.

— Smokiana, ye Pipes of all Nations. L, 1890. 8vo, orig half mor. bbc Apr 27 (202) $225

Pritt, Thomas Evan

— North-Country Flies. L, 1886. 8vo, cloth; worn. With 12 plates, including 11 hand-colored. Koopman copy. O Oct 29 (233) $210

Anr copy. Orig cloth. W Mar 6 (110) £110

— Yorkshire Trout Flies. Leeds, 1885. One of 50 hand-colored by the author. 8vo, orig cloth; extremities rubbed. With 11 hand-colored plates & 1 plain plate. With ALs. Ck May 15 (46) $750

One of 200. Half calf; rubbed. With 11 hand-colored plates & 1 plain plate Library markings. Koopman copy. O Oct 29 (234) $225

Anr copy. Contemp half mor gilt. With 1 plain & 11 hand-colored plates. pn Mar 19 (382) £680

Pritzel, Georg August

— Thesaurus literaturae botanicae, omnium gentium. Milan, [1950]. 4to, orig cloth; worn. Facsimile of the 1871 Ed. O Sept 24 (202) $120

Procede...

— Procede actuel de la lithographie, mise a la portee de l'artiste et de l'amateur. Paris: Delaunay & Le Normant, 1818. 8vo, orig wraps. With 2 folding litho plates. Schlosser copy. P June 17 (528) $1,400

Proceedings...

— Proceedings of the Committee appointed to manage the Contributions begun at London Dec. XVIII MDCCLVIIII for Cloathing French Prisoners of War. L, 1760. Folio, contemp mor gilt; front hinge split, extremities rubbed. Milne copy. Ck June 12 (170) £1,700

Processional

— 1526, 29 Dec. - Liber processionarius secundumconsuetudinem ordinis sancti patris nostri Hieronymi.... Alcala de Henares: Miguel de Eguia. 8vo, contemp calf over wooden bds, with brass clasps; some repairs. This copy ptd on vellum. C Nov 27 (44) £12,000 [Sawyer]

Proclus, Diadochus, 410?-85

— De sphaera.... Basel, 1547. 8vo, modern wraps. In Greek & Latin. sg May 14 (302) $325

Procter, Adelaide Anne

— Legends and Lyrics. L, 1863. 7th Ed. 8vo, mor gilt. sg May 7 (84) $250

Pronti, Domenico

— Nuova Raccolta di 100 vedutine antiche [moderne] della citta di Roma... Rome [1795]. 2 vols. 4to, contemp half vellum by Riviere. With 2 engraved titles & 170 views on 85 plates. Ck May 15 (143) £260

Propert, Walter Archibald

— The Russian Ballet in Western Europe, 1909-1920.... NY, 1921. One of 450. 4to, new cloth. Library markings. O Mar 31 (152) $140

Anr copy. Orig half cloth. Inscr to Lydia Lopkova. S Nov 14 (235) £300 [Schimmel]

Propertius, Sextus

— Elegiae. Bologna: Franciscus Plato de Benedictis for Benedictus Hectoria, 1487. Folio, 18th-cent vellum. Types 1:112R (text) & 2:80R (commentary). Minor worming towards end. 104 leaves. Goff P-1017. C Nov 27 (22) £2,400 [Panini]

Prose...

— Prose and Poetry of the Live Stock Industry of the United States. NY: Antiquarian Press, 1959. One of 550. 4to, half lea. Reprint of 1905 Ed. NH May 30 (148) $120

Proskouriakoff, Tatiana Avenirovna

— An Album of Maya Architecture.... Wash., 1946. Oblong folio, orig half cloth; corners worn. wa Mar 5 (558) $140

Proust, Marcel

See also: Atget, Eugene

— Du cote de chez Swann. Paris, 1914 [wraps dated 1913]. 1st Ed, 1st Issue. Mor gilt, orig wraps bound in. Epstein copy. sg Apr 30 (393) $5,000

Anr Ed. Paris, 1914. 2d Issue. Modern half mor, orig wraps bound in. bba Jan 30 (322) £55 [Spademan]

— Les Plaisirs et les jours. Paris, 1896. One of 20 on japon, with 1 orig watercolor. Illus by Madeleine Lemaire. 4to, mor extra by Huser, orig wraps bound in; rubbed. S May 28 (421) £1,500 [Lardanchet]

— A la recherche du temps perdu. Paris: Bernard Grasset & Editions de la Nouvelle Revue Francaise, [1913]-27. 1st Ed. 13 vols. Mor extra by Devauchelle, orig wraps bound in. S May 28 (422) £8,000 [Friedman]

Prout, Samuel, 1783-1852

— Rudiments of Landscape. L: Ackermann, 1813. Oblong 4to, later half mor. With 64 plates, 16 hand-colored. C May 20 (104) £1,100 [Spelman]

Anr copy. Contemp half mor; covers detached; lacking spine. With 63 (of 64) plates, 15 hand-colored. Lacking title; lightly soiled throughout. Sold w.a.f. Ck July 10 (105) £350

Anr copy. Modern half mor gilt. With 64 plates, 16 hand-colored. Tp dampstained; soiling to some plates. Schlosser copy. P June 18 (492) $900

Prudentius Clemens, Aurelius, 348-410?

— Opera. Amst.: Elzevir, 1667. 12mo, contemp vellum; lower joint split. cb Dec 5 (114) $60

Pruetz, Gustav

— Illustrirtes Mustertauben-Buch. Hamburg, [c.1884]. 4to, half mor; front hinge cracked. With 81 full-page chromolithos. K July 12 (409) $900

Pryce, William, 1725?-90

— Archaeologia Cornu-Britannica.... Sherborne, 1790. 4to, contemp half calf; rubbed, backstrip def, upper hinge weak. bba Nov 28 (310) £140 [Land]

— Mineralogia Cornubiensis; a Treatise on...Mining. L, 1778. 1st Ed. Folio, modern half calf; upper cover sunned. With port, 7 plates & 2 folding tables. Title repaired. bba Jan 30 (31) £680 [Thorp]

Psalmanazar, George, 1679-1763

— An Historical and Geographical Description of Formosa. L, 1705. 2d Ed. 8vo, contemp calf; covers detached. With folding engraved map, 16 plates (1 folding) & folding engraved table of the Formosan alphabet. Map with small, clean tear; table margins browned. Milne copy. Ck June 12 (171) £200

— Memoirs of ***, a Reputed Native of Formosa. L, 1764. 1st Ed. 8vo, contemp calf gilt. With port. b June 22 (203) £270

Psalms & Psalters

Arabic & Latin Versions

— 1614. - Liber psalmorum Davidis regis et prophetae. Rome: Stephanus Paulinus for the Typographia Savariana. 4to, contemp vellum. Some dampstaining. D & M 1641. S Dec 5 (225) £950 [Scheler]

Anr copy. Modern mor. Some stains. D & M 1641. S May 28 (70) £750 [Panini]

English Versions

— 1607. - L. 4to, old vellum. sg Mar 12 (28) $70

— 1624. - The Whole Booke of Psalmes.... L. 32mo in 8s, contemp embroidered bdg; soiled, extremities rubbed, some loss of applied thread. STC 2588. C June 24 (108) £1,600 [Edison]

— 1634. - The Whole Booke of Psalmes...in English Meeter.... L. 32mo, contemp needlework bdg; very worn. Some cropping. STC 2653. S Apr 28 (93) £380 [Fletcher]

— 1636. - L: for the Company of Stationers. 32mo, 19th-cent mor gilt, the orig woven covers preserved as doublures. S Apr 28 (94) £2,800 [Fletcher]

— 1754. - L. Trans by Stephen Wheatland & Tipping Sylvester. 8vo, 18th-cent mor gilt. S July 1 (940) £260 [Chelsea]

— 1786. - The Psalms of David, Imitated in the Language of the New Testament.... Worcester MA: Isaiah Thomas. Bound with: Watts. Hymns. Worcester, 1786. Ed by Isaac Watts. 8vo, lea. sp Apr 16 (57) $55

— 1902. - The Psalter or Psalms of David from the Bible of Archbishop Cranmer. L. One of 250. 4to, orig vellum; warped. bba Aug 13 (304) £150 [Wand]

— 1903. - The Bay Psalm Book. NY: The New England Society Facsimile Reprint. cb Oct 17 (64) $50

French Versions

— 1549. - Cinquante pseaumes de David. Paris: Gilles Corrozet. 16mo, 16th-cent calf. S Dec 5 (58) £600 [Pickering & Chatto]

German versions

— Das kleine Davidische Psalterspiel der Kinder Zions.... Germantown: Micahel Billmeyer, 1797. 8vo, contemp sheep over bds, hinges & clasps present. Evans 31816. sg Dec 5 (12) $150

— 1569. - Der gantze Psalter des koeniglichen propheten Davids.... Nuremberg: Christoph Heussler. Folio, contemp blind-tooled pigskin over wooden bds, with brass fittings. Some browning. sg Oct 24 (36) $475

— 1760. - Das kleine Davidische Psalterspiel der Kinder Zions.... Germantown: Sauer. 12mo, modern half mor. Tp backed with paper & def; lacking some text; marginal repairs. sg Dec 5 (224) $100

— 1911. - Die Psalmen. Darmstadt One of 500. Trans by Martin Luther. Folio, vellum gilt. HH May 12 (2231) DM1,100

Greek Versions

— 1543. - Psalterion. Paris: Francois Estienne. 16mo, old sheep gilt; needs rebacking. Some headlines cropped; dampstain in upper outer corner throughout. sg Mar 12 (22) $3,200

Hawaiian Versions

— 1869. - Ka Buke o Na Halelu. NY 8vo, orig mor; joint cracked, spine frayed at head. sg June 18 (279) $130

Hebrew & Latin Versions

— 1632. - Psalmi Davidis, proverbia a Salomonis.... Paris: Cramoisy. 8vo, calf gilt. Title holed. bba Feb 27 (319) £160 [Malagadi]

Latin Versions

— 1459, 29 Aug. - Psalterium Benedictinum (Congregationis Bursfeldensis). Mainz: Johann Fust & Peter Schoeffer. Folio. With several slits; some worming, affecting text; torn; stained. A single leaf (Folio 40), ptd on vellum; used previously as a bdg. Goff P-1062. Schoyen copy. P Dec 12 (35) $20,000

— 1494. - Psalterium. [Nuremberg]: Anton Koberger. 4to, contemp pigskin over wooden bds; rebacked, metal fittings removed. 54 lines; double column of gloss surrounding single column of text; types 14:130G (title, headlines), 15:91G (text), 21:74G (preliminaries) & 20:63G (gloss); rubricated. Marginal dampstaining at the beginning. 173 leaves; lacking final blank. Goff P-1050. C Nov 27 (23) £2,200 [Aspin]

Ptolemaeus, Claudius

— Armonikon. Harmonicorum libri tres. Oxford, 1682. 4to, contemp calf; rubbed, joints split. Some staining. pn Oct 24 (274) £550

— Liber de analemmate. Rome: Aldus, 1562. 4to, contemp vellum; front inner hinges split. Dampstained; 1st gathering loose; recto of A1 & verso of A2 soiled; Q3 torn & repaired. Ck Nov 29 (233) £700

— Liber diversarum rerum. Venice: Petrus Liechtenstein, 1509. 4to, later wraps. Some stains & early marginalia. Formerly attributed to Ptolemaeus. sg May 7 (176) $1,600

Geographia

— 1511, 20 Mar. - Liber geographiae cum tabulis et universali figura. Venice: J. Pentius de Leucho. Folio, 19th-cent vellum. With 28 double-page maps. Lacking initial blank; 3 repaired tears to tp, 1 affecting the last 3 lines of the poem on verso; marginal repairs; corners of most of the maps repaired; woodcut cloud at fore-margin of world map shaved; some discoloration to margins. Barlow copy. CNY Oct 8 (213) $34,000

— 1513, 12 Mar. - Geographiae opus novissima.... Strassburg: Johannes Schott. Folio, contemp calf over wooden bds with remains of orig metal clasps & metal cornerpieces; rebacked, endpapers renewed, rubbed, covers wormed. With 45 woodcut mapsheets & 2 single-page maps, this copy with variant map of Switzerland. First few leaves wormed, mainly in margins; worm track through quires F-H affecting up to 3 letters; other worming, affecting last 7 or 8 maps; repaired tears to edges of 2 maps entering images; world map of Part 2 with tear to fore-margin affecting border; small repaired tear to map 17 with loss to 4 letters of a place name; map 18 of Part 2 creased & with 2 large repaired tears; a few fold breaks; lacking final blank; some browning & stains; conjugate leaves G3.4 & G2.5 misbound in inverted order; map 18 bound in upside down; contemp marginalia in 2 contemp hands. CNY Oct 8 (214) $70,000

— 1535. - Geographicae enarrationis libri octo. Lyons: Melchior & Gaspar Trechsel. Folio, 16th-cent blind-tooled calf; rebound preserving sides. With 50 maps. Several leaves recornered; Tabula Moderna Galliae torn & repaired across ptd surface; Tabula Nova Helvetiae torn at lower margin & neatly repaired without loss; a few text borders just shaved at extremities; a few stains. S Nov 21 (125) £9,000 [Rizzo]

— 1561. - Venice: Vincenzo Valgrisi. 3 vols in

1. 4to, contemp vellum. With 64 double-page maps. A few holes affecting outer margins; upper margins shaved. C May 20 (291) £2,500 [Chan]

Anr copy. Vellum gilt with crest of the Earl of Leicester; soiled, spine cracked. Ms marginalia; 1 or 2 maps misbound. S June 25 (287) £2,800 [Franks]

— 1584. - Geographiae libri octo.... Cologne: Gerard Mercator. Folio, contemp vellum. With 28 maps, all hand-colored; Ms table of maps bound in at front. sg Feb 13 (132) $9,000

— 1597-98. - Geografia, coie descrittione universale della terra. Venice: Galignani. 4to, old vellum; upper joint split, spine ends def. With 64 maps, mostly inset in the text. Small wormholes in upper blank margins of 1st 7 leaves. C Oct 30 (159) £1,800 [Sifton Praed]

Anr copy. Old vellum; soiled. With engraved world map & 63 half-page maps. Last quarter of vol dampstained; some stains & soiling elsewhere; 2 small burn holes in 2d3; general title mtd, with tears in blank margins restored. sg Sept 19 (101) $2,800

— 1597. - Geographiae universiae. Cologne: Petrus Keschedt. 2 parts in 1 vol. 4to, 18th-cent half calf; rubbed. With 2 engraved titles, folding map (trimmed) & 64 maps. Some annotations; minor dampstaining; 2 blank corners of leaves torn away. pn May 14 (11) £1,400 [Elliott]

— 1605. - Geographiae libri octo Graeco-Latini. Frankfurt: J. Hondius. Folio, 19th-cent calf with contemp calf gilt covers laid down; worn. With engraved title, port & 28 double-page maps. Some 18th-cent Ms corrections & annotations. C Oct 30 (116) £1,700 [Bank of Cyprus]

— 1620-21. - Geografia, coie descrittione universale della terra. Venice: Galignani. 2 parts in 1 vols. Folio, later pigskin; worn, spine repaired, lacking clasps. With 2 engraved titles, 63 half-page maps & 1 full-page map. Tp & inner margins of several leaves repaired; marginal stains; some leaves browned; a few leaves trimmed, affecting heading in 2 cases; some underlining & pen marginalia. pn June 11 (303) £1,900 [Map House]

— 1704. - Tabulae geographicae Orbis Terrarum veteribus cogniti. Amst. & Utrecht Folio, contemp half mor; rubbed & marked. With engraved title & 28 double-page maps. Margins of title soiled. bba Sept 19 (18) £900 [Erlini]

— 1966. - Geographia. Amst. Folio, cloth, in d/j. Facsimile of the Strassburg 1513 Ed. sg Feb 13 (139) $350

Puaux, Rene

— Grece terre aimee des dieux. Paris, 1932. One of 400. 4to, pictorial wraps. With port & 41 plates, 8 in color. S July 1 (680) £380 [Consolidated Real]

Publicius, Jacobus

— Artes orandi, epistolandi, memorandi. Venice: Erhard Ratdolt, 31 Jan 1485. ("Oratoriae artis epitoma.") 4to, contemp lea-backed wooden bds, with brass clasps; wormed, spine repaired, later endpapers. Some worming, affecting text; stain at end. 66 leaves. Goff P-1097. Ck May 18 (14) £5,000

Puckle, James

— The Club, or a Dialogue between Father and Son. L, 1711. 1st Ed. 12mo, early 19th-cent calf gilt; joints tender. C Dec 16 (265) £200 [Burmester]

Pufendorf, Samuel, Baron von, 1632-94

— De jure naturae et gentium libri octo.... L, 1672. 1st Ed. 4to, contemp half calf gilt. SI Dec 5 (985) LIt250,000

Puget de la Serre, Jean

— The Mirrour which Flatters Not. L, 1639. 8vo, modern mor gilt. Engraved title & explanation leaf supplied from anr copy; some browning & staining; inner margins cut close. STC 20490. pn May 14 (12) £180 [Vanbrugh]

Pugh, Edward, d.1813

— Cambria Depicta: a Tour through North Wales. L, 1816. 4to, 19th-cent mor gilt; spine restored. With 71 hand-colored plates. Marginal repairs to B1 & 2G2. S June 25 (282) £550 [Nicholson]

Pugin, Augustus Charles, 1762-1832 —& Others

— Examples of Gothic Architecture. L, 1850. 3 vols. Folio, orig cloth; rubbed. Library markings, some leaves loose. bba June 11 (297) £65 [Fetzer]

Pugin, Augustus Charles, 1762-1832 —& Heath, Charles, 1785-1848

— Paris and its Environs. L, 1829-31. 2 vols in 1. 4to, contemp half calf; upper joint broken. With 2 engraved titles & 202 plates on 101 leaves, on india paper mtd. pn June 11 (291) £95

Anr copy. 2 vols. 4to, mor; rebacked. With engraved titles & 204 views on 103 plates. pnE May 13 (22) £100

Anr Ed. L, 1831. 2 vols in 1. 4to, contemp cloth; rubbed. With 2 engraved titles & 202 views on 101 plates. Small waterstain on upper margin throughout; lacking 1 title. bba July 23 (356) £90 [Books & Prints]

Anr copy. Vol II only. Contemp calf.

Lacking 1 plate. pnE Oct 2 (484) £50

Pugin, Augustus Welby, 1812-52

— Floriated Ornament: A Series of Thirty-One Designs. L, 1849. 4to, contemp half mor; rubbed, foot of spine chipped. With chromolitho title & 30 chromolitho plates. b Mar 11 (63) £420

Pulci, Luigi, 1432-84

— Morgante maggiore. Florence [but Naples], 1732. 4to, contemp French red mor gilt by Padeloup; corners repaired. Possibly lacking final blank. C June 24 (339) £480 [Pirages]

Pulman, George Philiip Rigney

— The Vade Mecum of Fly-Fishing for Trout. L, 1846. Bound with 2 fragmentary works: The Compleat Angler, Part II, L, 1772 & Part the Second, The Complete Fly-Fisher (Title & pp 73-124). 2d Ed. 12mo, calf; rubbed. Koopman copy. O Oct 29 (236) $250

Punch...

— Punch: Or the London Charivari. L, 1841-1939. 98 vols in 83. 4to, half lea gilt. sg May 7 (177) $1,300

Vols 1-219. L, 1841-1950. Bound in 134 vols. 4to, half mor gilt. pnE Oct 1 (337) £1,800

Punshon, Morley. See: McFee, William

Purcell, Henry, 1659-95

— Orpheus Britannicus. L, 1721. 2 vols. Folio, 19th-cent calf; rubbed, spine & corners worn. Library markings. 3 leaves torn, 1 repaired. bba Mar 26 (312) £140 [Tosi]

Purchas, Samuel, 1575?-1626

— Purchas his Pilgrimage.... L, 1614. 2d Ed. Folio, contemp calf gilt; spine worn. Slight dampstaining; 1 leaf holed. STC 20506. George Milne copy. CNY Dec 5 (313) $400

— Purchas his Pilgrimes. L, 1625. 1st Ed. 4 vols. With: Purchas. Purchas his Pilgrimage. L, 1626. 2d Ed, 2d Issue. Together, 5 vols. Folio, contemp calf; rubbed, spine ends chipped,3 vols with old paper shelf-mark label; some repairs. Lacking 2 blanks; 5M4 & 7K4 in Vol II each with 4-inch partly repaired tear affecting text; adhesive stains costing letters on 2 leaves; D6 with rusthole costing 4 letters; staining to T3v-T4r; marginal tear to 3Z3; folding map of Greenland foxed, that of Virginia in Vol IV washed & backed & possibly supplied; some foxing; 7R4 with 3-inch tear affecting text & sidenote; first & last few leaves of Vol V foxed; fore-edge of world map on E2r shaved; marginal wormhole grazing map border on I4r; some marginal tears throughout; some foxing. 5 text engravings in Vol II not ptd in this copy & cut-out copies from anr copy are tipped in over the appropriate blank spaces. STC 2059 & 2058.5. From the Ducal Library of Gotha. CNY Oct 8 (215) $10,000

Anr copy. 1st Ed. 4 vols. With: Purchas. Purchas his Pilgrimage. L, 1626. 2d Ed, 2d Issue. Together, 5 vols. contemp calf; rebacked, rubbed. Engraved title in Vol I laid down & restored in Ms at lower inner margin; Virginia map in Vol IV from anr copy & shaved at neatlines; some leaves supplied from a shorter copy; some leaves lacking lower forecorners; leaves O3-V6, 2A-2G6 in Vol V damaged at head occasionally affecting letters; engraved title & Vol IV title creased & scuffed at lower fore-margin. STC 20508 & 20509. S Nov 21 (219) £9,000 [Graton & Graton]

Anr Ed. Glasgow, 1905-7. ("Hakluytus Posthumus or Purchas His Pilgrimes.") One of 1,000. 20 vols. Orig cloth; spines frayed. Library markings. DW Jan 29 (50) £140

Anr copy. Orig cloth; backstrip repaired at head. kh Nov 11 (381) A$300

Anr copy. Orig half vellum; 1 spine with tear. S May 14 (1221) £220 [Quaritch]

— A Theatre of Political Flying-Insects. L: R. I. for Thomas Parkhurst, 1657. 4to, modern calf by Bayntun. Some browning & staining. pn Dec 12 (107) £210

Purdy, Richard Little

— Thomas Hardy: a Bibliographical Study. L, 1954. cb Oct 17 (775) $65

Purton, Thomas

— A Midland Flora; or a Botanical Description of British Plants in the Midland Counties.... Stratford, 1817-21. 4 vols. 8vo, library cloth. With 38 hand-colored plates. Library stamps. bba Oct 10 (216) £120 [Shifrin]

Pushkin, Aleksandr Sergyeevich, 1799-1837
See also: Limited Editions Club

— Eugene Onegin.... [NY, 1964]. Trans by Vladimir Nabokov. 4 vols. In d/js. bbc Apr 27 (378) $130

— Four Stories. Greenbrae CA: Allen Press, 1987. One of 145. Mor with reproduction of the author's signature in onlaid mor, by Denise Lubett. CNY June 9 (115) $900

— Gabriel: a Poem in One Song. NY, 1929. One of 750. Trans by Max Eastman; illus by Rockwell Kent. Vellum; upper cover stained, worn. sg Sept 26 (149) $50; sg Jan 30 (95) $60

Anr copy. Vellum; wrinkled. Z Oct 23 (121) $60

— The Golden Cockerel. L, 1950. Illus by Edmund Dulac. Folio, cloth. sg Jan 30 (257) $175

Anr copy. Cloth; scratched. wa Dec 9 (137) $90

Putnam, George Granville

— Salem Vessels and their Voyages.... Salem: Essex Institute, 1924-30. 4 vols. Half cloth. NH Oct 6 (226) $100

Putnam, George Haven, 1844-1930

— Books and their Makers During the Middle Ages.... NY, 1896-97. 2 vols. 8vo, bdg not given. cb Oct 17 (776) $60

Anr Ed. NY, 1962. 2 vols. Cloth; worn. Reprint of the 1896-97 Ed. NH Oct 6 (51) $60

Puydt, Paul Emile de

— Les Orchidees. Paris, 1880. 8vo, contemp half mor gilt; corners worn. McCarty-Cooper copy. CNY Jan 25 (93) $380

Anr copy. Contemp half mor; joints & spine rubbed. With 50 hand-finished chromolithos. CNY June 9 (153) $500

Puyo, C. See: Demachy & Puyo

Puysegur, Jacques Francois de Chastenet de

— Art de la guerre, par principes et par regles. Paris, 1748. Vol I only. Contemp calf gilt. pnE Oct 1 (324) £50

Anr Ed. Paris, 1749. 2 parts in 1 vol. Folio, contemp calf; joints split at head of Vol I. With 51 maps & plates. wa Sept 26 (518) $250

Pyle, Howard, 1853-1911

— Book of Pirates. NY, [1921]. Compiled by Merle Johnson. Orig half cloth; extremities worn. NH Oct 6 (153) $85

One of 50 on vellum stock, sgd. In d/j. Inscr by Merle Johnson. sg Jan 30 (135) $2,600

— The Garden Behind the Moon. NY, 1895. 8vo, cloth; spine ends worn. K Sept 29 (363) $55

— Howard Pyle's Book of the American Spirit. NY, 1923. 1st Ed. Compiled by Merle Johnson. 4to, orig half cloth; worn. K Mar 22 (370) $65

Anr copy. Half cloth, in d/j. sg Jan 30 (133) $250

— Pepper & Salt, or Seasoning for Young folk. NY, 1886. 1st Ed. 4to, orig cloth; worn. F Mar 26 (106) $70

— The Ruby of Kishmoor. NY, 1908. Orig cloth; rubbed. With 10 color plates. K Mar 22 (371) $70

— The Story of King Arthur and his Knights. NY, 1903. 1st Ed. Front hinge cracked. sg Sept 26 (260) $150

Pynchon, Thomas

— Gravity's Rainbow. NY, [1973]. In d/j. F Dec 18 (225) $300

Pyne, James Baker

— The Lake Scenery of England. L, 1859. 4to, orig cloth; rebacked, orig spine preserved. With engraved title & 24 plates. DW Oct 2 (117) £90

Anr copy. Contemp mor. With color litho title & 25 color lithos. Interleaved; marginal dampstain to a few plates; some browning. P June 18 (581) $300

Anr Ed. L, 1870. Folio, orig cloth; rubbed, gutta-percha perished. With 25 colored plates, including title. bba May 28 (385) £50 [Elliott]

Pyne, William Henry

— The Costume of Great Britain. L, 1808. Folio, contemp russia gilt; rebacked in calf. With hand-colored vignette on title & 60 hand-colored plates with most backgrounds fully colored. Some surface dirt. S June 25 (160) £550 [Temperley]

— Etchings of Rustic Figures.... L, [c.1840]. 4to, later cloth; worn. With 60 plates. O July 14 (159) $120

— The History of the Royal Residences.... L, 1819. 3 vols. Folio, contemp mor with gothic window design on covers; rebacked, old spines preserved. With 100 hand-colored plates. Colored copy. bba Sept 19 (230) £4,200 [Chamberlain]

Anr copy. Contemp mor gilt with large cathedral screen stamp; joints & corners rubbed, upper joint of Vol III split. Lacking sub-titles & list of plates. Colored copy. C May 20 (292) £3,000 [Kafka]

Anr copy. Contemp mor; spine extremities repaired. Colored copy. McCarty-Cooper copy. CNY Jan 25 (59) $6,500

Anr copy. Modern half mor gilt; rubbed. With 100 hand-colored plates, many heightened with gum-arabic. Colored copy. S Nov 21 (96) £3,000 [Cherrington]

Anr Ed. L, [plates watermarked to 1835]. 3 vols. Folio, modern mor gilt. With 100 hand-colored plates. Advertisement leaf misbound at start of Vol III; 3 section titles misbound as half-titles, the others lacking. Colored copy. C Oct 30 (70) £4,800 [Arader]

— Microcosm, or a Picturesque delineation.... L, 1806-8. 2d Ed. 2 vols. Oblong folio, contemp bds. With frontis & 120 sepia aquatint plates. C Oct 30 (69) £800 [Kidd]

Anr Ed. L: Ackermann, [1822-24]. 2 vols. Oblong folio, modern half calf. With frontis & 120 plates. Text browned. pn Dec 12 (261) £780

Pyrnelle, Louise Clarke

— Diddie, Dumps and Tot, or Plantation Child-Life. NY, 1882. 1st Ed. 12mo, orig cloth. Epstein copy. sg Apr 30 (394) $500

Pythagoras —& Phoclydes

— Poemata. [Strassburg: Crato Mylius, 1545]. 8vo, old vellum. Dampstained throughout; lacking colophon leaf; interlinear Latin trans of Phoclydes in an early hand. sg Mar 12 (258) $140

Q

Quadri, Antonio

— Il Canal Grande di Venezia. Venice, 1828. Bound with: Quadri. La Piazza di San Marco in Venezia. Venice, 1831. Folio. 19th-cent half mor; rebacked with old backstrip laid down, corners renewed. With map & 47 hand-colored plates & 8 uncolored plates in 2d work. Some dampstaining, mostly to lower margins; some foxing; Plates 1 & 2 stained; some browning. McCarty-Cooper copy. CNY Jan 25 (59) $6,500

Quadrum...

— Quadrum. Revue internationale d'art moderne. Brussels, 1956-66. Nos 1-20 (all pbd). 4to, orig wraps; some frayed. bba Oct 24 (344) £340 [Quaritch]

Quain, Jones, 1796-1865 —& Wilson, Sir William James Erasmus

— A Series of Anatomical Plates. Phila., 1842. 5 vols in 1. Folio, orig sheep. With 200 (of 201) plates. Frontis creased; scattered foxing. sg Nov 14 (106) $600

Quarenghi, Giacomo

— Fabriche e disegni. Mantua: presso i fratelli Negretti, 1834-44. Folio, 19th-cent bds; worn. With frontis, port & 124 plates. Some spotting. S Nov 21 (97) £1,100 [Pagan]

Quaritch, Bernard, 1819-99

— A Catalogue of English and Foreign Bookbindings. L, 1921. 4to, sheepskin with design of interwoven circles, by Irene Kaye. With 80 plates, some colored. pn June 11 (173) £110

Quarles, Francis, 1592-1644

— Emblemes.... L, 1736. ("Emblems, Divine and Moral.") 12mo, calf by Bayntun; worn. O May 26 (150) $250

Quarll, Philip. See: Longueville, Peter

Quarterly...

— The Quarterly Review. L, 1809-32. Vol I, 2d Ed; others 1st Ed. Vols 1-48. Contemp half calf; worn, some backstrips def. DW Mar 4 (247) £75

Quatrefages de Breau, J. L. A. de —& Hamy, E. T. J.

— Crania Ethnica: Les Cranes des races humaines. Paris, 1872-82. 2 vols. 4to, modern syn. With 100 plates. sg May 12 (135) $325

Quayle, Eric

— The Collector's Book of Detective Fiction. [L, 1972]. Folio, cloth, in d/j. Munby copy. K Mar 22 (373) $60

Queard, P.

— Apercu d'un Plan d'Education Publique. Paris, 1796. One of 12. 12mo, contemp mor gilt. bba June 25 (170) £950 [Braunschweig]

Queen, Ellery, Pseud.

— The French Powder Mystery: A Problem in Deduction. NY, 1930. Minor foxing to fore-edge. K July 12 (432) $90

Queeny, Edgar M.

— Prairie Wings: Pen and Camera Flight Studies. NY, 1946. 1st Ed. Illus by Richard E. Bishop. 4to, orig cloth; worn. F Mar 26 (64) $100

One of 225. Orig cloth; worn. Inscr. F Sept 26 (10) $130; F Sept 26 (446) $55

Anr copy. Cloth; worn. O Jan 14 (155) $60; wa Mar 5 (549) $80

Anr Ed. NY, 1947. 4to, orig cloth, in chipped d/j. Text with smudge on p. 36; short tear to rear free endpaper. wa Feb 20 (225) $50

Queiros, Pedro Fernandez de. See: Fernandez de Queiros, Pedro

Queneau, Raymond

— Journal intime. Paris, 1950. One of 120 on alpha. Calf gilt by Leroux, orig wraps bound in. S May 28 (425) £650 [Beres]

— Zazie dans le Metro. Paris, 1959. One of 5 hors commerce on hollande van Gelder. Mor with large pictorial panels depicting graffiti on wooden bds, photographed by Robert Morian, by Micheline de Bellefroid, orig wraps bound in. S May 28 (426) £1,500 [Beres]

Quenioux, Gaston

— Les Arts decoratifs modernes.... Paris, [1925]. 4to, cloth; front hinge cracked. sg Apr 2 (97) $200

Querelles,——, Chevalier de

— Hero et Leandre, poeme nouveau.... Paris: Didot l'aine, 1801. 4to, contemp mor gilt, sgd P. R. Raparlier. With frontis & 8 color aquatint. Inscr. Schlosser copy. P June 18 (455) $5,500

Quiller-Couch, Sir Arthur, 1863-1944

— In Powder and Crinoline: Old Fairy Tales.... L, [1913]. Illus by Kay Nielsen. 4to, bds; worn, spine scuffed. O Jan 14 (156) $300

Anr copy. Orig half cloth; worn, inner joints tape-strengthened. With 24 colored plates. O Jan 14 (157) $170

Anr copy. Orig half cloth; worn. pnE May 13 (220) £90

— The Sleeping Beauty and Other Fairy Tales.... L, [1910]. Illus by Edmund Dulac. 4to, cloth. b Nov 18 (59) £50

Anr copy. Cloth; rubbed. DW Mar 4 (347) £110

One of 1,000. Orig cloth; rubbed. Manney copy. P Oct 11 (123) $1,300

Anr copy. Orig lea. With 30 tipped-in colored plates. Some spotting to margin. pn Sept 12 (133) £60

Anr copy. Orig cloth. pnE Dec 4 (143) £55

Anr copy. Mor gilt; covers detached; backstrip lacking. sg Jan 30 (50) $550

— The Twelve Dancing Princesses, and other Tales. Garden City, 1930. Illus by Kay Nielsen. In chipped d/j. cb Jan 16 (112) $85

Quintanilla, Luis

— All the Brave. NY, [1939]. One of 440. Text by Elliot Paul & Jay Allen; preface by Ernest Hemingway. 4to, orig half mor; spine scuffed. F Dec 18 (48) $140

Anr copy. Half sheep. With extra color litho laid in. sg Dec 12 (153) $200

Quintilianus, Marcus Fabius

— Institutiones oratoriae. Venice: Peregrinus de Pasqualibus, 18 Aug 1494. Folio, old vellum. Roman type. Lower margin of a2 excised & restored. 246 (of 248) leaves; lacking tp (supplied in facsimile) & final blank. Goff Q-30. sg Mar 12 (129) $800

Anr Ed. Paris: P. Vidoue, 1527. ("Oratoriarum institutionum lib. XII.") Folio, old vellum. sg Mar 12 (260) $275

Quintino, Antonio

— Gioiello di Sapienza nel quale si contengono gl'Avuisi d'arme. Florence: alle scale di Badia, 1625. 8vo, mor gilt by Maillard. C Dec 16 (73) £1,500 [Jackson]

Quintus, Icilius. See: Guischardt, Charles

Quinze Joyes...

— Les Quinze Joyes de Mariage. Paris: Editions du Rameau d'Or, [n.d.]. One of 750. Illus by Henry Lemarie. 8vo, mor extra by Gruel. Illusts hand-colored. With a suite of the illusts in outline, 3 ink drawings for the upper cover & 2 large illusts & the watercolor design from anr illust. S May 28 (428) £450 [White]

Quirini, Angelo Maria, Bishop of Brescia

— Primordia Corcyrae post editionem lyciensem.... Brescia, 1738. 2 (of 3) parts in 1 vol. 4to, contemp calf. Some waterstaining. S July 1 (581) £420 [Spink]

Quiz. See: Caswall, Edward

R

Rabaut, Jean Pierre

— Precis de la revolution francaise.... Paris: Didot, 1792. 3 parts in 1 vol. 18mo, later 18th-cent mor gilt. With 6 plates before letters. S May 13 (859) £240 [Shapero]

Rabelais, Francois, 1494?-1553

— Gargantua. Valence: Claude La Ville, 1547 [but Geneva, c.1600]. 3 parts in 1 vol. 16mo, mor gilt by Trautz-Bauzonnet. Defs to H2-3, affecting text; washed. C June 24 (192) £4,500 [Wood]

Anr Ed. Paris, 1955. One of 200. Illus by Antoni Clave. 4to, unsewn in orig wraps. With 61 colored lithos. CGen Nov 18 (440) SF7,000

— Les Horribles et espovantables faictz et prouesses du tres renomme Pantagruel. Paris, [1943]. One of 275. Illus by Andre Derain. 4to, unsewn in orig wraps. CGen Nov 18 (441) SF18,000

Anr Ed. Paris: Skira, 1943. One of 275 on velin d'Arches. 4to, unbound as issued in orig wraps. With 180 colored woodcuts, including 39 large illusts. Schlosser copy. P June 18 (420) $13,000

— Oeuvres. Amst., 1741. Ed by Le Duchat. 3 vols. 4to, contemp calf gilt; spines rubbed. With frontis, 2 engraved titles, port, 12 plates, 3 folding views, 1 folding map & 1 plate of a bottle. C Dec 16 (159) £550 [Maggs]

— Les Songes drolatiques de Pantagruel. Paris, 1869. One of 15 on chine fort. 8vo, contemp half mor by David. Schlosser copy. P June 17 (582) $800

— Works. L & NY, [1927]. Trans by Urquhart & Motteux. 2 vols. 8vo, half mor by Stikeman. K Sept 29 (76) $150

Anr Ed. NY, 1929. One of 200. Illus by Jean de Bosschere. 3 vols. 4to, orig half cloth; rubbed & bumped. wa Mar 5 (617)

$80

One of 1,300. Half cloth; faded & soiled. sp Sept 22 (3060) $275

Raccolta...

— Raccolta di quadri dipinti dai piu' famosi pennelli e posseduti da...Pietro Leopoldo Arciduca d'Austria.... Florence, 1778. 2 vols. Folio, half mor; worn. With engraved title & 148 plates. Library stamp on tp. S Nov 15 (830) £4,800 [Toscani]

Racine, Jean, 1639-99

— Oeuvres. Paris, 1768. 7 vols. 8vo, contemp calf; 1 backstrip def. bba Oct 10 (509) £380 [Maggs]

Anr copy. Contemp calf gilt; joints split. With 12 plates. Some stains. S July 1 (1131) £250 [Booth]

Anr Ed. Paris: Didot l'Aine, 1783. One of 200. 3 vols. 4to, contemp mor gilt extra. sg May 7 (178) $3,800

Racinet, Auguste

— Le Costume historique. Paris, [1876-88]. Parts 1-11. Folio, loose in portfolios, as issued; worn, a few ties lacking. With 259 (of 500) plates. Some dampstaining, mostly to text. 1 plate torn. Sold w.a.f. cb Dec 19 (139) $600

Anr copy. 21 orig parts. 4to, orig wraps, plate vols unbound as issued in orig half-cloth; some spines worn. With 200 plates "en camaieu" & 298 (of 300) in colors, gold & silver. Ck Sept 5 (142) £350

Anr copy. 10 (of 11) vols; lacking Vol IX. Half cloth; worn. With c.450 chromolithos. Eva Le Gallienne's copy. sg Feb 13 (182) $275

Anr copy. Livraisons 1-20 in 19 vols. Orig cloth portfolios; lacking those for the 1st 2 parts. Plate count not given. Sold w.a.f. sg Apr 2 (252) $600

Anr Ed. Paris, 1888. 6 vols. 4to, modern cloth. With 200 plates "en camaieu" & 300 in colorrs, gold & silver. Ck Nov 29 (286) £520

Anr copy. Contemp half calf. Lacking 17 plates; stamps on plate & title versos; some creases; a few leaves creased. pnL Nov 20 (185) £400

Anr copy. Half mor; joints & extremities worn, 1st vol with front flyleaf detached. With 200 plates "en camaieu" & 300 in colors, gold & silver. Some foxing, mostly to text. sg Sept 6 (76) $850

Anr copy. Contemp half mor gilt; joints & extremities worn, tear along joint of Vol VI. Stamps at bottom edges of titles & blanks at beginning & end. sg Feb 6 (234) $1,400

Anr copy. Half mor giltmor. sg Feb 13 (183) $325

— L'Ornement polychrome. Paris, [c.1873]. Parts 1-10 in 10 vols. Folio, orig mor gilt; rubbed. With 100 color plates. Some spotting. bba Oct 24 (254) £260 [Baring]

— Polychromatic Ornament. L, 1877. Folio, orig cloth. With 100 color plates. 1 text leaf torn. bba Feb 27 (360) £300 [Marsden]

Rackham, Arthur, 1867-1939

— Arthur Rackham's Book of Pictures. L, 1913. 4to, orig cloth. bba Jan 16 (379) £110 [Harrington]

Anr copy. Orig cloth, in d/j. bba Apr 9 (326) £280 [Ulysses]

— The Arthur Rackham Fairy Book. L, 1933. 4to, cloth, in d/j. With 8 colored plates. bba Apr 9 (338) £200 [Fox]

One of 460. Vellum gilt, unopened. With 8 color plates. sg Jan 10 (142) $1,400

— The Peter Pan Portfolio. L, [1912]. One of 500. 4to, orig half vellum; stitching broken, stained by damp. With 12 colored plates. Corners of prelims with a few small holes. pn Dec 12 (204) £1,250

Anr copy. Orig half vellum; worn. Endpaper & limitation leaf torn. S Dec 12 (193) £850 [M.P.L.]

— Some British Ballads. L, [1919]. 4to, orig cloth. bba Jan 16 (401) £85 [Ulysses]

Anr copy. Orig cloth, in d/j. bba Apr 9 (341) £200 [W. White]

One of 575. Half vellum; worn & stained. O Feb 25 (160) $260

Anr copy. Mor gilt by Zaehnsdorf with Rackham design on front cover. sg Nov 7 (178) $850

Rackham, Bernard

See also: Schreiber Collection, Lady Charlotte

— The Ancient Glass of Canterbury Cathedral. L, 1949. 4to, orig cloth. sg Sept 6 (266) $100

— Catalogue of the Glaisher Collection of Pottery and Porcelain. Cambr., 1935. 2 vols. 4to, orig half cloth; rubbed & soiled. DWD Mar 11 (774) £230

Rackham, Bernard —& Read, Herbert, 1893-1968

— English Pottery. Its Development from Early Times.... L, 1924. 4to, cloth, in def d/j. With 115 plates. kh Nov 11 (191) A$100

Anr copy. Cloth. kh Nov 11 (192) A$100

One of 75. Orig pigskin gilt. DW Mar 11 (775) £130

Anr copy. Cloth. sg Sept 6 (58) $200; sg Feb 6 (235) $100

Rada, Francisco Lorenz de

— Nobleza de la espada.... Madrid, 1705. 3 vols in 2. 4to, contemp vellum. Marginal dampstaining on several leaves in Vol I. sg Mar 26 (257) $1,600

Anr copy. 3 vols. 4to, later calf. sg Mar 26 (258) $850

Radaelli, Giuseppe

— Istruzione per la scherma di sciabola.... Milan, 1876. 8vo, half calf; lacking front free endpaper. With 10 folding lithos. Short tears along folds. sg Mar 26 (260) $375

Radcliffe, Ann, 1764-1823

— The Mysteries of Udolpho. L, 1794. 1st Ed. 4 vols. 12mo, mor with sides inset with portions of orig bds. A few leaves stained; half-titles & final blank lacking; small hole in blank area of tp. CNY June 9 (169) $650

Radcliffe, Frederick Peter Delme

— The Noble Science: a Few General Ideas on Fox-Hunting.... L, 1911. 2 vols in 1. 8vo, cloth. 1 plate loose. sg Jan 9 (258) $60

Radclyffe, Charles

— Memorials of Rugby. Rugby, 1843. Folio, later mor gilt with arms of Rugby. With 24 hand-finished tinted lithos, mtd on guards throughout. C May 20 (106) £1,000 [Maggs]

Raden, Woldemar

— Switzerland. L, 1878. 4to, contemp mor gilt; rubbed at extremities. DW May 13 (51) £220

Rader, Jesse Lee

— South of Forty; from the Mississippi to the Rio Grande.... Norman, 1947. 1st Ed. 4to, cloth. K Sept 29 (367) $75

Radiguet, Raymond

— Le Bal du comte d'Orgel. Paris, 1924. One of 150 on hollande Van Gelder. Mor gilt by Alix, orig wraps bound in. Inscr by Jean Cocteau to Henri Bernard, 1927. S May 28 (436) £1,400 [Beres]

— Devil in the Flesh. Wash., 1948. Trans by Kay Boyle; intro by Aldous Huxley. Ptd wraps; soiled. sg Dec 12 (26) $175

— Devoirs de vacances. Paris, 1921. One of 3 on japon. Illus by Irene Lagut. Mor extra by Micheline de Bellefroid, orig wraps bound in. Inserted is ALs (with initials) to Irene Lagut, written around the proof of a poem, the initial letters of the five lines spelling Irene. S May 28 (437) £1,900 [Beres]

— Le Diable au corps. Paris 1923. One of 165. Orig wraps. Epstein copy. sg apr 30 (395) $500

— Les Joues en feu. Paris, 1925. One of 50 on japon with 2 copies of the port. Illus by Pablo Picasso. 12mo, vellum. CGen Nov 18 (442) SF38,000

Radziwill, Lee Bouvier. See: Onassis & Radziwill

Radziwill, Mikolaj Krzysztof, Prince

— Hierosolymitana peregrinatio. Antwerp, 1614. Folio, later half calf. With engraved title & 5 full-page engravings in text. Library stamp on tp. S July 1 (785) £500 [Handler-Wayntraub]

Raemaekers, Louis

— The Great War. L, 1917-19. One of 1,050 or 1,030. Vols I-II. Orig half cloth; rubbed. O Aug 25 (149) $80

Raemond, Florimond de

— Erreur populaire de la Papesse Jane.... Lyons: Benoist Rigaud, 1595. 8vo, old calf; rear joint cracked. sg Mar 12 (263) $300

Raffald, Elizabeth

— The Experienced English Housekeeper. L, 1801. 8vo, contemp calf; rebacked, new endpapers. With frontis & 3 folding plates. bba Aug 13 (142) £100 [Houle]

Raffles, Sir Thomas Stamford, 1781-1826

— The History of Java. L, 1817. 1st Ed. 2 vols. 4to, later half mor; rubbed. With folding map hand-colored in outline, 54 uncolored & 10 hand-colored plates & 2 extra plates. Lacking half-titles; inscr cut from foot of titles; Vol I with lower outside corner of 2Z3 torn away & 3A1 repaired in lower outside corner; some dampstaining. S Nov 15 (1302) £600

Anr copy. Contemp calf gilt. With folding map colored in outline, 10 hand-colored plates & 56 plates including 2 pages of engraved music. S June 25 (472) £2,400 [Owlet]

2d Ed. L, 1830-44. Text vol only. Orig cloth; worn. DW Mar 4 (39) £58

Rafinesque-Schmaltz, Constantine Samuel, 1783-1840

— Medical Flora, or Manual of the Medical Botany of the United States.... Phila., 1828-30. Vol II only. Orig cloth; joints cracked. Dampstaining & foxing throughout. sg May 14 (136) $550

Ragguaglio...

— Ragguaglio della vittoria navale conseguita a' Dardanelli dall'armata della...Venetia. Venice, 1656. 4to, bds. Stain at foot of each leaf. S July 1 (681) £280 [Maggs]

— Ragguaglio delle nozze delle Maesta di Filippo Quinto e di Elisabetta Farnese. Parma, 1717. Folio, contemp vellum;

soiled. With frontis & 5 folding plates. Some plates torn & repaired. bba Sept 19 (307) £700 [Erlini]

Raimondo di Sangro

— Pratica piu agevole, e piu utile di esercizi militari per l'infanteria. Naples: Giovanni di Simone, 1747. Folio, contemp calf gilt; rubbed. O May 26 (151) $600

Raine, James

— The History and Antiquities of North-Durham. L, 1852. Folio, contemp calf gilt. With port, map & 10 plates. Some browning. L Feb 27 (153) £110

Anr copy. Contemp half lea; worn. With port, 10 plates, 1 map & 1 double-page pedigree. Some spotting & soiling. pn Apr 23 (277) £90

Rainerus de Pisis, d.1351

— Pantheologia. [Augsburg: Guenther Zainer], 1474. 2 vols. Folio, contemp blind-stamped pigskin over wooden bds, Bavarian bdg, Kyriss shop 62; clasps & bosses removed, hinges cracking. 60 lines; type 4:95R; partially rubricated Some staining to lower corners in Vol II. 990 leaves. Goff R-6. Doheny-Schoyen copy. P Dec 12 (37) $19,000

Rainolds, John, 1549-1607

— De Romanae Ecclesiae idolatria in cultu sanctorum. Oxford: J. Barnesium, 1596. 4to, modern half calf. STC 20606. bba May 14 (56) £55 [Rix]

Rainsford, Marcus

— An Historical Account of the Black Empire of Hayti.... L, 1805. 4to, contemp bds; worn, cover detached. With 11 plates or maps, some folding. O Nov 26 (146) $375

Raleigh, Sir Walter, 1552?-1618

[-] A Declaration of the Demeanor and Cariage of Sir Walter Raleigh.... L, 1618. STC 20653. 4to, old half lea; joints broken. Dampstaining from C4 to D4 & on last 2 leaves. CNY Oct 8 (219) $850

— Discoverie of...Guiana. L: R. Robinson, [1596]. ("The Discoverie of the Large, Rich, and Bewtiful Empire of Guiana....") 1st Ed, 2d Issue. 4to, 19th-cent mor; joints cracked, spine & corners worn. Tp dust-soiled & with repair at upper margin; final leaf repaired at upper margin; some browning. STC 20635. CNY Oct 8 (217) $5,500

Anr Ed. L: Argonaut Press, 1928. ("The Discoverie of the Large and Bewtiful Empire of Guiana.") One of 975 on Japan vellum. 4to, half vellum gilt; some wear. O May 26 (152) $100

— The History of the World. L, 1614. Folio, 18th-cent half calf; rebacked, corners restored, joints broken, backstrip def. With engraved title & 8 maps & plates, 1 colored by hand. The Minde of the Front & title leaves restored & with some facsimile; a few inner margins renewed at front; 3 plates cropped affecting surface; 2 others inserted; some staining. STC 20637. CNY Oct 8 (218) $4,000

Anr copy. 19th-cent half calf; rubbed. With engraved title & 8 double-page maps. Some dampstaining; tears & holes in a few leaves with some loss of text; fore-margins of the tables & of 6 maps shaved; tp & The Minde of the Frontispiece cut down & mtd; colophon leaf def & repaired; lacking 2 blanks. STC 20637. S July 1 (1099) £380 [Rosenbush]

Anr Ed. L, 1677. Folio, needs rebdg. With extra engraved title, port & 8 double-page maps. sg Mar 12 (264) $250

Anr Ed. L, 1687. Folio, contemp calf; joints split. With 8 double-page maps. Lacking frontis & port. pnE Mar 11 (114) £220

Anr Ed. L, 1736. 2 vols. Folio, contemp calf; worn. With 10 maps & plates, 8 folding. DW Dec 11 (322) £145

— Judicious and Select Essayes and Observations upon the First Invention of Shipping.... L, 1650. 4 parts in 1 vol. 8vo, mor gilt by Root. With port. Lacking ads; marginal repairs. pn May 14 (13) £360

Ralfe, James

— The Naval Chronology of Great Britain. L, 1820. 3 vols. 8vo, modern half mor gilt by Bayntun-Riviere. With 2 frontises, colored port & 60 hand-colored plates. C May 20 (107) £3,200 [Traylen]

Anr copy. Lev extra, Vol I with lev doublure set withan oval port miniature of Nelson, by Bayntun. With 60 plates with later coloring. DuPont copy. CNY Oct 8 (11) $2,800

Ramal, Walter. See: De la Mare, Walter

Rameau, Jean Philippe, 1683-1764

— Generation harmonique.... Paris, 1737. 1st Ed. 8vo, contemp calf gilt. With 12 folding plates. Ck Oct 31 (297) £350

— Traite de l'Harmonie reduite a ses Principes naturels.... Paris, 1742. 4to, modern calf gilt. Some holes & tears, affecting text; lower margins of 2 leaves torn away. bba June 25 (167) £300 [Braunschweig]

— A Treatise of Musick.... L, 1752. Bound with: Lampe, John Frederick. A Plain and Compendious Method of teaching through, Bass.... L, 1737. 4to, contemp calf; worn at edges. Some spotting & browning. pn Oct 24 (439) £280 [Baron]

Ramelli, Agostino

— Le diverse et artificiose machine. Paris, 1588. Folio, contemp calf gilt; worn. With engraved title with port of author on verso, 195 (of 194) plates. Some staining & discoloration; Plate CII ptd upside down; stamp at foot of tp; some ink drawings of machinery inserted at end. S Dec 5 (423) £5,800 [Erlini]

Anr copy. 17th-cent calf. With engraved title, port & 195 plates. SI June 10 (845) LIt16,500,000

Ramie, Suzanne & Georges

— Ceramiques de Picasso. Geneva, 1948. 4to, orig wraps. With port & 18 colored plates. b Nov 18 (258) £90

Anr copy. Outer margins soiied. bba May 14 (568) £55 [K. Y. Books & Art]

Anr copy. Loose in orig wraps; rubbed & soiled. With port & 18 colored plates. DW Oct 9 (620) £50

Ramsay, Andrew Michael Chevalier, 1686-1743

— The Travels of Cyrus. L, 1727-28. 8vo, contemp calf; rebacked, hinges reinforced. sg Oct 17 (355) $60

Ramsay, David, of Scotland

— Military Memoirs of Great Britain.... Edin., 1779. 8vo, contemp calf; rebacked. With 12 ports. bbc Dec 9 (409) $525

Ramus, Petrus, 1515-72

— Arithmeticae libri duo: Geometriae septem et viginti. Basel: Eusebius Episcopius & Nicolae fratris haeredes, 1580. 2d Ed. 2 parts. 4to, contemp vellum; rubbed. Wormed throughout. bba Sept 5 (242) £480 [Quaritch]

Rand, Ayn

— Anthem. L, 1938. Orig cloth, in 1st d/j. P June 17 (312) $4,000

— Atlas Shrugged. NY: Random House, [1957]. Orig cloth, in d/j. bbc Apr 27 (393) $280

Anr copy. In chipped d/j. pba July 9 (227) $80; sp June 18 (449) $60

Anniversary Ed. NY: Random House, [1967]. Sgd. Manney copy. P Oct 11 (1266) $1,600; P June 17 (315) $1,100

— The Fountainhead. Indianapolis, [1943]. 1st bdg. bbc Sept 23 (472) $65

Anr copy. In 1st d/j with chipping & a repair. bbc Apr 27 (393) $280

Anr copy. Inscr to Isabel Patterson. Manney copy. P Oct 11 (265) $4,000

Anr copy. In edge-worn d/j. Epstein copy. sg Apr 30 (395A) $650

Randall, David A. See: Van Winkle & Randall

Randolph, Bernard, 1643-90?

— The Present State of the Morea.... L, 1689. 3d Ed. With folding map & 2 double-page plates. Bound with: Randolph. The Present State of the Islands in the Archipelago.... Oxford, 1687. 1st Ed. With folding map & 3 plates. 4to, modern cloth. 1st work with minor tears along fold of map & some browning; 2d work with map trimmed to platemark & with fold tears & view of Negroponte with tear. Milne copy. Ck June 12 (174) £420

Anr copy. 3d Ed. With folding map & 2 double-page plates. Bound with: Randolph. The Present State of the Islands in the Archipelago.... Oxford, 1687. 1st Ed. With folding map & 3 plates & folding panorama of Constantinople by David Loggan after H. Cuttance. contemp calf; worn, rebacked. S Nov 21 (274) £1,000 [Knohl]

Random de Berenger, Charles, Baron de Beaufain

— Helps and Hints how to Protect Life and Property. L, 1835. 8vo, contemp calf; joints worn. Inscr. sg Oct 17 (186) $100

Rangachari, K. See: Thurston & Rangachari

Ranis, Heinrich Christoph

— Anweisung zur Fechtkunst. Berlin, 1771. 8vo, contemp bds. With 4 folding plates. Library stamps at bottom of each plate. sg Mar 26 (261) $225

Ranke, Leopold von, 1795-1886

— The Ecclesiastical and Political History of the Popes of Rome during the 16th and 17th Centuries. L, 1841. Trans by S. Austin. 3 vols. 8vo, bdg not described. LH Dec 11 (225) $70

Rankine, William John Macquorn, 1820-72

— Shipbuilding, Theoretical and Practical. L, 1866. Folio, contemp calf; rubbed, small piece torn at spine, head of spine frayed. With 44 mostly double-page folding plates. b June 22 (267) £170

Ranks, Harold E. See: Kratville & Ranks

Ransom, Will

— Kelmscott, Doves and Ashendene: The Private Press Credos. San Francisco: Book Club of Calif., 1952. One of 300. cb Oct 17 (491) $120

Ransonnet-Villez, Eugene de, Baron

— Sketches of the Inhabitants, Animal Life and Vegetation in...Ceylon. Vienna, 1867. Folio, orig cloth; worn, covers detached, spine lacking. With 26 plates, 4 colored, some tinted Some dampstains. pn Dec 12 (262) £270

Rantzau, Henricus, 1526-98

— Traite astrologique des jugemens des themes genetliaques.... Paris, 1657. 8vo, vellum. Some stains & foxing; tables repaired with tape. sg Mar 12 (232) $175

Rapin de Thoyras, Paul, 1661-1725

— The History of England. L, 1732-47. "2d" Ed. 4 vols in 5. Folio, calf gilt. Extra-illus with c.700 plates. Sold with the Acta Regia, [1733]. W July 8 (67) £1,100

3d Ed. L, 1743-47. 4 vols in 5. Folio, later half mor; 1 vol with covers detached. With 4 frontises, 22 folding maps, 9 genealogical tables & 184 plates. 1 map def; 1 folding plate torn. bba Jan 16 (113) £900 [B. Bailey]

Rapp, Heinrich

— Das Geheimniss des Steindrucks in seinem ganzen Umfange.... Schweinfurt: Georg Jacob Giegler, 1810. 2d Ed. 4to, wraps. With 7 folding litho plates. Schlosser copy. P June 18 (583) $4,750

Rashleigh, Philip

— Specimens of British Minerals. L, 1797-1802. 2 parts in 1 vol. 4to, later half calf; spine faded. With 54 plates, most hand-colored. bba Jan 30 (33) £2,600 [Watson]

Raspe, Rudolph Erich, 1737-94

— Gulliver Revived, containing Singular Travels...by Baron Munchausen. L, 1789. 6th Ed. 12mo, contemp calf. With folding frontis & 13 plates. Some staining. bba July 23 (284) £550 [Ribose]

Anr Ed. Hamburg: B. G. Hoffman, 1790. ("Gulliver Revived; or, the Vice of Lying Properly Exposed....") 8vo, contemp half sheep; worn. With 7 plates, including frontis. Dampstain in corner of a few plates. sg Oct 24 (270) $225

Anr Ed. L, 1811. ("The Surprising Adventures of the Renowned Baron Munchausen....") Illus by Thomas Rowlandson. 12mo, orig wraps. sg Mar 5 (286) $200

Anr Ed. L, 1859. ("The Travels and Surprising Adventures of Baron Munchausen.") Illus by Alfred Crowquill. 8vo, orig cloth; worn. cb Sept 26 (175) $70

Anr Ed. L, 1868. 8vo, Orig cloth. With 23 hand-colored plates; some double-page. sg Oct 17 (177) $300

— Specimen historiae naturalis globi terraquei. Amst. & Leipzig, 1763. 8vo, contemp calf; worn. SI June 10 (847) LIt450,000

Rastell, John, d.1536

— A New Boke of Purgatory whiche is a Dyaloge.... [L]: John Rastell, 1530. Folio, modern lea. Upper half & lower outer corner of tp torn away & repaired with loss; some headlines cropped; small wormhole running through text repaired with some loss; accounts ina 16th-cent hand on front flyleaves. STC 20719.5. S July 1 (1097) £800 [Quaritch]

Rastell, William

— A Collection of All the Statutes.... L: Richard Tottel, 1566. 4to, old sheep. Black letter. Wormed; last 6 leaves holed with loss; lacking final blank. Sold w.a.f. STC 9308.5. C Dec 16 (228) £320 [Taussig]

Ratcliff, Carter

— Red Grooms. NY, [1984]. 4to, cloth, in d/j. Sgd by Grooms. sg Apr 2 (132) $150

Rathbone, Frederick

— Old Wedgwood. L, 1898. 8 parts in 1 vol. Folio, mor by Zaehnsdorf, orig wraps bound in. With 65 color & 2 plain plates. O Nov 26 (147) $1,600

Rathbun, Jonathan

— The Narrative of Jonathan Rathbun of the Capture of Groton Fort.... [New London?, 1840]. 12mo, cloth. sp Apr 16 (45) $60

Rathenau, Ernest. See: Westheim & Rathenau

Ratta, Cesare

— Gli adornatori del libro in Italia.... Bologna, 1923-27. One of 850. 9 vols. Folio, orig wraps. F Dec 18 (704) $270

Rau, Charles

— Prehistoric Fishing in Europe and North America. Wash., 1884. 4to, mor; needs rebdg. sg Jan 9 (302) $120

Raulinus, Johannes

— Itinerarium paradisi. Paris: Berthold Rembolt for Jean Petit, 14 Oct 1514. 4to, contemp calf; rebacked retaining only part of orig spine & sides laid down on modern calf. Tp with repair touching edge of text & with hole; anr leaf with hole; some dampstains. S Feb 25 (525) £350 [Voltaire]

Ravenscroft, Edward James

— The Pinetum Britannicum. L, [1863]-84. 3 vols. Folio, half mor gilt by Sangorski & Sutcliffe, orig wraps to 3 parts bound in. With 48 hand-colored lithos, 1 leaf with 3 maps & 4 mtd albumen prints. Sucscriber's copy of Henry G. Bohn. C Oct 30 (271) £3,500 [Spot]

Anr copy. Contemp mor gilt; worn. With 48 hand-colored plates, 4 mtd albumen prints & 1 plate of maps. Some foxing & soiling. S June 25 (63) £1,000 [Arader]

Rawlings, Marjorie Kinnan

— The Yearling. NY, 1939. One of 770 L.p. copies. Illus by N. C. Wyeth. sg Jan 30 (191) $800

Rawstorne, Lawrence

— Gamonia: or, the Art of Preserving Game. L: Ackermann, 1837. 8vo, orig mor gilt; stitching loose. With 15 hand-colored plates. C May 20 (108) £1,200 [Joseph]

Anr copy. Orig mor gilt; rebacked with old spine laid down. Ck Sept 6 (42) £650

Anr copy. Orig mor gilt; rubbed. Lacking errata slip; some contemp annotations in pencil; some leaves loose. Inscr. S Nov 15 (750) £700 [S. P. Nichols]

Anr Ed. L, 1929. One of 125. 4to, half calf gilt by Sangorski & Sutcliffe; some soiling. With 15 color plates. wa Mar 5 (80) $65

Ray, Gordon N.

— The Illustrator and the Book in England from 1790 to 1914. NY, 1976. 4to, cloth; worn. O Dec 17 (151) $130; sg May 21 (295) $50

Ray, John, 1628-1705

— L'Histoire naturelle eclaircie dans une de ses parties principales l'ornithologie.... Paris, 1767. 4to, later bds; rubbed, joint broken. With frontis & 29 (of 30) plates; lacking Plate 6. First 3 leaves loose; some spotting. bba May 14 (494) £130 [Lib. Naturalistica Bolognese]

Anr copy. Contemp calf gilt. With color frontis & 30 colored plates. FD Dec 2 (267) DM2,800

— Methodus plantarum nova. L & Amst., 1703. ("Methodus plantarum, emendata et aucta.") 8vo, contemp sheep; covers detached. With port & 2 folding tables (the 1st cropped). Dampstaining at ends. sg May 14 (239) $175

— Observations Topographical, Moral, & Physiological, Made in a Journey through Part of the Low-Countries, Germany, Italy and France.... L, 1673. 1st Ed. 2 parts in 1 vol. 8vo, contemp calf; spine restored. With port & 3 folding plates. Some inner margins wormed at foot, occasionally affecting letters. b June 22 (205) £90

— Philosophical Letters.... L, 1718. 8vo, contemp calf; front cover detached. sg May 14 (240) $225

Ray, Man

— La Photographie n'est pas l'art. [Paris], 1937. Foreword by Andre Breton. Unsewn in orig wraps. sg Oct 8 (49) $1,000

— Self-Portrait. Bost., 1963. In d/j. Inscr to Virginia Townsend. sg Apr 2 (88) $225

Raye, Charles

— A Picturesque Tour through the Isle of Wight. L, 1825. Oblong 4to, contemp half lea gilt; spine chipped at head & foot, joints split. With 24 colored plates. C May 20 (109) £450 [Traylen]

Rayer, Pierre Francois Olive

— A Theoretical and Practical Treatise on the Diseases of the Skin. Paris, 1835. 4 vols. 8vo & folio, contemp half calf (rebacked), Atlas in orig bds rebacked in cloth. Atlas with 26 hand-colored plates. sg May 14 (137) $325

Raymond, Eleanor

— Early Domestic Architecture of Pennsylvania. NY, 1931. One of 1,100. 4to, orig cloth; worn & soiled. F Mar 26 (26) $100

Anr copy. Cloth. With frontis & 158 plates. K Sept 29 (370) $85

Raymond, Jean Paul. See: Ricketts, Charles de Sousy

Raynal, Guillaume Thomas Francois, 1713-96

— Histoire philosophique des etablissemens & du commerce des Europeens dans les deux Indes. The Hague, 1776. 7 vols. 12mo, contemp calf; worn. With 8 plates & 6 folding maps. Some browning; 1 map torn. S Feb 11 (779) £150 [Stokeley Holland]

— Histoire philosophique et politique des etablissemens et du commerce des Europeens dans les deux Indes. Geneva, 1780. 11 vols, including Atlas. 4to, contemp sheep (text) and contemp bds (Atlas). sg Jan 9 (167) $550

— A Philosophical and Political History of the Settlements...in the East and West Indies. L, 1776. 4 (of 5) vols. 8vo, contemp calf gilt; head & foot of spines chipped. DW Mar 4 (248) £80

Anr Ed. L, 1783. 8 vols. 8vo, calf; scuffed, some hinges weak. With frontis & 7 plates. wd June 12 (430) $225

— Revolution de l'Amerique. L: Lockier Davis, 1781. 12mo, lea. sp Apr 16 (47) $55

Raynal, Maurice —& Others

— The History of Modern Painting. Geneva, [1949-45-50]. 3 vols. Folio, cloth, in worn d/js. kh Nov 11 (193) A$70

Raynolds, William F.

— Report on the Exploration of the Yellowstone River. Wash., 1868. 8vo, cloth. With folding map. Minor tears along some folds. 40th Congress, 1st Session, Sen. Exec. Doc. 77. sg June 18 (477) $250

Reach, Angus B.
— Clement Lorimer; or, the Book with the Iron Clasps. L, 1849. Illus by George Cruikshank. 8vo, later calf. With frontis & 11 plates. cb Dec 5 (53) $150

Read, Alexander
— Somatographia Anthropine, or a Description of the Body of Man by Artificial Figures Representing the Members. L, 1616. 8vo, contemp calf with metal clasps; def. Lacking A1, S1, S8, V1 & V8; some staining; many leaves loose. Sold w.a.f. STC 20782. pn Nov 14 (288) £160

Read, Herbert, 1893-1968
See also: Rackham & Read
— Unit 1. L, 1934. 4to, orig cloth, in d/j with stain. pn Sept 12 (113) £140

Reade, Charles, 1814-84
See also: Limited Editions Club
— The Course of True Love Never Did Run Smooth. L, 1857. 8vo, orig bds; spine lacking. sg Mar 5 (279) $60
— Peg Woffington. L, 1899. One of 200 L.p. copies. Illus by Hugh Thomson. 8vo, cloth; rubbed. kh Nov 11 (194) A$60

Reagan, Nancy Davis —& Novak, William
— My Turn. NY, [1989]. One of 300. pba July 9 (229) $70

Reasons...
— Reasons to Shew, that there is a Great Probability of a Navigable Passage to the Western American Ocean.... L, 1749. 8vo, half mor by Sangorski & Sutcliffe. CNY Oct 8 (90) $2,000

Reaumur, Rene Antoine Ferchault, 1683-1757
— The Art of Hatching and Bringing Up Domestick Fowls.... L, 1750. 8vo, old calf; rebacked, rubbed. With 15 folding plates. O Apr 28 (53) $300

Rechberg, Charles de —& Depping, George Bernhard
— Les Peuples de la Russie.... Paris, 1812-13. 2 vols. Folio, contemp half calf; worn. With 96 plates, 93 hand-colored & 3 plain sepia aquatints. A few margins discolored. S June 25 (162) £3,500 [Arader]

Recollections. See: Beckford, William Thomas

Record, Robert
— The Ground of Arts. L: Henry Binneman & John Harison, 1575. ("The Grounde of Artes: teaching the Work and practise of Arithmetike.") 8vo, 19th-cent calf; rubbed, joints cracked. Tp spotted & reinserted. Inscr twice by John Heales. STC 20801. C Dec 16 (266) £1,900 [Halwas]

Anr Ed. L: John Beale for Roger Jackson, 1623. 8vo, contemp vellum; soiled. Partly ptd in black letter. Later leaves dampstained. STC 20808. Ck Nov 29 (234) £460

Anr Ed. L: J. H., 1699. ("Arithmetick, or the Ground of Arts.") 2 parts in 1 vol. 4to, contemp calf; rubbed. bba Feb 13 (401) £320 [Laywood]

Records...
— Records of North American Big Game.... NY: Boone & Crockett Club, 1932. One of 500. Koopman copy. O Oct 29 (80) $1,100

Anr Ed. NY: Boone & Crockett Club, 1964. In frayed d/j. Koopman copy. O Oct 29 (237) $80

Recueil...
— Recueil des loix constitutives des colonies angloises, confederees sous la demoniation d'Etats-Unis. Phila. & Paris, 1778. 12mo, half calf; rubbed. P12 with marginal tear repaired with transparent tape; dampstaining to lower margin of 1st few leaves. P June 16 (137) $1,000
— Recueil d'estampes representant les differents evenemens de la guerre qui a procure l'independence aux Etats de l'Amerique. Paris, [1784?]. 4to, orig bds. With 14 plates (including title) & 2 maps. Some spotting. S July 1 (1475) £340 [Browning]

Redding, Cyrus
— A History and Description of Modern Wines. L, 1836. 2d Ed. 8vo, orig cloth; spine frayed. K July 12 (519) $140

Redgrave, Gilbert Richard. See: Short-Title Catalogue

Redi, Francesco, 1626?-97
— Esperienze intorno alla generazione degl'insetti. Florence, 1674. 8vo, later half mor. With 38 plates, 2 folding. Some waterstaining. bba Sept 5 (99) £420 [The Bookroom]
— Experimenta circa generationem insectorum. Amst., 1671. 12mo, contemp vellum; stained, small tear at joint, 1 corner worn. With engraved title & 39 plates, 10 folding. One plate torn at fold; corner of G1 torn away affecting a few letters; some waterstaining. b June 22 (88) £150
— Opere. Milan, 1809-11. 9 vols. 8vo, modern half lea. SI Dec 5 (577) LIt200,000

Redon, Odilon, 1840-1916
— Oeuvre graphique complet. The Hague, [1913]. 2 vols. Folio, loose as issued i cloth folders; stains on Vol I front cover, repairs on inside of Vol II folder. sg Feb 6 (238) $400

Redoute, Pierre Joseph, 1759-1840

— Album de Redoute. L, 1954. Folio, half mor. br May 29 (317) $400

— Les Liliacees. Paris, 1802-[16]. Plates only. Folio, disbound. With 63 (of 486) hand-finished plates only. S June 25 (51) £12,000 [Tamura]

Redoute, Pierre Joseph, 1759-1840 —& Thory, Claude Antoine

— Les Roses. Paris: Didot, 1817-21-24. 1st Ed. Vols II & III only. Contemp half lea; joints & corners repaired. With 113 hand-finished color plates. Some spotting, mainly to titles & text. C Oct 30 (223) £34,000 [Arader]

Reece, Robert, of Cheltenham

— Hints to Young Barbados-Planters. Barbados, [1857]. 8vo, orig cloth, unopened; spine chipped. S July 1 (1487) £180 [Remington]

Reed, Henry M.

— The A. B. Frost Book. Rutland VT, [1967]. 4to, orig cloth, in pictorial dj. Inscr, 1970, to Leon Kroll. bbc Apr 27 (557) $180

Reed, John, 1887-1920

— Ten Days that Shook the World. NY, 1919. 1st Ed. Orig cloth, in d/j. sg Apr 30 (396) $2,800

Reed, Ronald

— The Nature and Making of Parchment. [Leeds, 1975]. Ltd Ed. 4to, half vellum. NH Aug 23 (311) $130

Rees, Abraham

— The Cyclopaedia.... Phila, 1805-25. ("The Cyclopaedia; or Universal Dictionary of Arts, Sciences, and Literature.") Vol I, Part 1 - Vol XLI, Part 2 plus 4 Atlas vols & final unnumbered vol. Together, 87 vols. 4to, orig bds; worn, lacking a few covers. Foxed & torn. Not collated. Sold w.a.f. O Nov 26 (150) $1,400

Anr Ed. L, 1819-20. 44 (of 45) vols. Contemp half calf; soiled & worn. Sold w.a.f. W Mar 6 (131) £400

Reeve, Emma

— Character and Costume in Turkey and Italy. L: Fisher, Son, [1845]. Illus by Thomas Allom. Folio, contemp mor gilt; rubbed. With 21 plates. Additional title with marginal soiling; last plate with staining at lower corner not affecting image. S July 1 (682) £900 [Gonul]

Regimen...

— Regimen sanitatis.... Frankfurt: C. Egenolph, [1553]. ("De conservanda bona valetudine, opusculum Scholae Salernitanae....") Bound with: Seb. Austrius. De infantium sive puerorum....Basel, 1540. 16mo, vellum. 1st work lacking leaf 9. B Nov 1 (401) HF1,500

Anr Ed. Frankfurt: heirs of C. Egenolph, [1557]. ("De conservanda bona valetudine, opusculum Shcolae Salernitanae....") 8vo, later vellum; hinges wormed. Marginal dampstaining. sg May 14 (139) $450

Anr Ed. Antwerp: I. Bellerus, 1562. ("De conservanda bona valetudine, opusculum Scholae Salernitanae....") 16mo, later calf. Some stains. B Nov 1 (402) HF400

Anr Ed. [Geneva]: J. Stoer, 1591. ("Medicina Salernitana, id est conservandae bonae valetudinis praecepta....") 32mo, 18th-cent half calf. A few stains. B Nov 1 (403) HF200

Registrum...

— Registrum omnium brevium tam originalium quam iudicialium. L, 1595. Folio, contemp calf; 2 corners worn, upper cover soiled. Old signature torn from top edge of tp, anr crossed out. STC 20838. L Nov 14 (444) £530

Regius, Henricus. See: Le Roy, Henri

Regley, ——, Abbe

— Atlas chorographique, historique, et portatif des elections du royaume.... Paris, 1763. 4to, contemp calf gilt. With engraved title, folding plate & 25 partially colored maps. sg Feb 13 (118) $800

Regnier, Henri Francois Joseph de, 1864-1936

— Monsieur d'Amercoeur. Paris, 1910. 4to, mor extra by Crette. Ptd on vellum & with orig watercolor, ink & pencil drawings & sketches by Maurice Ray. Manney copy. P Oct 11 (1267) $3,500

Regoor, M.

— De Schermkunst. The Hague, 1866. 8vo, orig cloth. With frontis & 2 plates. sg Mar 26 (265) $175

Reichard, Gladys A.

— Navajo Shepherd and Weaver. NY: J. J. Augustin, [1936]. Orig burlap over bds. cb Sept 12 (146) $160

Reichenbach, Heinrich Gottlieb Ludwig, 1793-1879

— Handbuch der Speciellen Ornithologie... Alcedineae. Dresden & Leipzig, 1851. 8vo, contemp half calf; spine rubbed. With 44 hand-colored plates. S Feb 11 (936) £600 [Vilsoet]

Reichenow, Anton, 1847-1941

— Vogelbilder aus fernen zonen.... Cassel, 1878-83. 4to, orig bds; rebacked & recornered. With 33 color plates. Repair to leaf of text to Plate VI; some spotting or soiling. S Nov 21 (39) £700 [Tooley Adams]

Reichenthal, Ulrich von

— Costnitzer concilium. Frankfurt: Paul Reffeler, 1575. Folio, later vellum; upper cover stained, spine def. Small tears & repairs in margins, that to Y2 with small loss; some browning. S Dec 5 (186) £550 [Schwing]

Reichhelm, Gustavus Charles

— Chess in Philadelphia. Phila., 1898. Half mor; joints & extremities scuffed. Library markings. F Mar 26 (121) $70

Reid, James D.

— The Telegraph in America.... NY, 1879. 4to, orig cloth. Title stamped. sg Nov 14 (311) $250

Reid, John, 1808-41

— Turkey and the Turks. L, 1840. 8vo, orig cloth. With 5 (of 6) plates, 4 of them colored & 2 maps. S June 30 (185) £220 [O'Neill]

Reid, John C.

— Reid's Tramp; or, a Journal of the Incidents of Ten Months Travel Through Texas, New Mexico, Arizona, Sonora, and California. Selma, 1858. 8vo, orig cloth. NH Oct 6 (353) $65

Reidi, Adrian von, 1746-1809

— Reise Atlas von Bajern oder Geographisch-geometrische Darstellung aller bajrischen Haupt- und Landstrassen.... Munich, 1796-1803-[n.d.]. Parts 1-4 (of 5). 4to, orig wraps; backstrips worn, lower cover & last leaf of Part 1 holed. With engraved title & 51 general & strip road maps, 49 hand-colored. S Nov 21 (156) £2,300 [Garwood & Voigt]

Reigart, J. Franklin

— The Life of Robert Fulton. Phila., 1856. 8vo, orig cloth; spine ends nicked & chipped, joints cracked. With port & 25 plates, some in color. Some leaves chipped. bbc June 29 (312) $60

Anr copy. Orig cloth; worn. Some foxing & soiling. Ambrose Swasey's copy. O July 14 (165) $275

Reilly, Franz Johann Josef von

— Grosser deutscher Atlas. Vienna, [1796]. Folio, contemp half calf; worn. With engraved title, double-page index, double-page table & 27 double-page maps, hand-colored in wash & outline. Some water-staining in upper margins; fold breaks. S Nov 21 (143) £1,200 [Map House]

Reinagle, George Philip

— Illustrations of the Battle of Navarin. L, 1828. Folio, 19th-cent half calf; worn. With litho title, plan & 12 plates. Litho title cut round & mtd on upper cover & very soiled; plan torn; some spotting. S July 1 (685) £3,600 [Constantalopoulos]

— Illustrations of the Occurrences at the Entrance of the Bay of Patras.... L: Colnaghi, [1828]. Folio, modern calf gilt, orig wraps bound in. With map & 6 hand-colored lithos. Dedication soiled & frayed; map spotted at edges. S July 1 (687) £3,600 [Chelsea]

— Particolari della Battaglia di Navarino.... Naples, 1828. Folio, modern half calf. With colored vignette on tp, uncolored plan & 12 hand-colored lithos. Leaf of descriptions torn & repaired. S July 1 (686) £4,000 [Constantalopoulos]

Reinhard, Count of Solms-Lich

— Beschreibung von Ursprung, Anfang und Herkomen des Adels. Frankfurt: M. Lechler for S. Feyerabend & S. Hueter, 1564. Bound with: Befassung. Ein kurtzer Bericht wie Statt, Schloesser oder Flecken mit Kriegs Volck sollen besetzt sein. Frankfurt, 1564. And: Thournier, Kampff unnd Ritterspiel inn Eroberunge aines Gefaehrlichenn Thuerns unnd Zauberer Schloss.... Frankfurt: C. Egenolff, 1550. Folio, later bds, spine damaged. Repair in fore-margin of C4 of 3d work; some stains. S Dec 5 (187) £1,100 [Goldschmidt]

Reisch, Gregorius, d.1525

— Margarita philosophica. Freiburg: J. Schott, [before 13 July] 1503. 4to, later half vellum. With woodcut title, 19 full-page woodcuts, 2 folding woodcuts including world map & 8 pp of musical scores. Waterstains; world map lined. B Nov 1 (625) HF15,000

8th Ed. Basel, 1517. 8vo, old half vellum; worn, loose. Lacking 20 leaves of text, folding world map & 2 folding diagrams. Some worming. Final leaf torn & repaired. Sold w.a.f. DW Jan 29 (270) £60

Reiss, Heinrich

— Sammlung der schoensten Miniaturen des Mittelalters aus dem 14. & 15. Jahrhunderts.... Vienna: Ludwig Lott, [c.1870]. Parts 1-7 in 1 vol. 8vo, half cloth. With 70 chromolitho plates with gold & silver, partly hand-finished. sg Oct 31 (248) $400

Reland, Adrian

— Palaestina ex monumentis veteribus illustrata. Utrecht, 1714. 2 vols. 4to, contemp blind-stamped vellum; joints cracked, Vol II rebacked preserving orig spine. With engraved title, folding port (with tear), 9 maps & 4 folding plates. S July 1 (790) £280 [Milkain]

Relation...

See also: Grelot, Guillaume Joseph

— Relation de l'audience publique donnee par le Grand-Seigneur, a l'envoye extraordinaire de la Republique Francaise pres la Porte Ottomane.... Constantinople, [1796]. 4to, half cloth; worn. S July 1 (690) £380 [Atabey]

— A Relation of the Invasion and Conquest of Florida by the Spaniards.... L, 1686. 8vo, contemp calf; rubbed. DuPont copy. CNY Oct 8 (31) $4,200

Relations...

— Relations veritables et curieuses de l'Isle de Madagascar et du Bresil. Paris, 1651. 4to, old vellum bds; repaired, modern endpapers. With 2 folding maps. Worming affecting text; repaired; library stamp on tp. S Feb 26 (771) £380 [Voltaire]

Remak, Robert, 1815-65

— Galvanotherapie der Nerven—und Muskel-krankheiten. Berlin, 1858. 1st Ed. 8vo, contemp bds; joints rubbed. Pencil underscoring. sg Nov 14 (109) $350

Remarque, Erich Maria, 1898-1970

— All Quiet on the Western Front. L, 1929. In frayed d/j. bba Dec 19 (212) £75 [Blodget]

1st Ed in Yiddish. Warsaw, 1929. Trans by Isaac Bashevis Singer. bba Dec 19 (213) £120 [Rassam]

Rembrandt van Rijn, 1606-69

— Complete Etchings. NY: Weyhe, [1921]. Ed by Hans Wolfgang Singer. 3 vols. Folio, loose as issued in bd portfolios. Plate count not given. Sold w.a.f. sg Apr 2 (253) $90

Remembrancer...

— The Remembrancer; or, Impartial Repository of Public Events. L: Ptd for J. Almon, 1776. 3 vols. 8vo, contemp bds; rebacked in calf, extremities rubbed. Some soiling; tp of Vol I with short marginal tear. Includes early British ptg of the Declaration of Independence. P June 16 (212) $2,500

Remington, Frederic, 1861-1909

— Crooked Trails. NY, 1898. 1st Ed. 8vo, orig cloth, in d/j. With ALs, 21 July [1902], laid in. Epstein copy. sg Apr 30 (397) $1,700

— Frontier Sketches. Chicago, [1898]. Oblong 4to, pictorial bds; hinges cracked, soiled. sp June 18 (44) $80

— Men with the Bark On. NY & L, 1900. 1st Ed, 1st Issue. bbc Sept 23 (474) $80

— Pony Tracks. NY, 1895. 1st Ed. 8vo, pictorial cloth. sg Dec 5 (211) $325

Anr copy. Pictorial cloth; repair in lower front corner. sg Dec 5 (212) $100

Anr copy. Cloth; corners bumped. wd Dec 12 (439) $150

— Sundown Leflare. NY & L, 1899. 8vo, orig cloth; rubbed. With frontis & 11 plates. wa Mar 5 (399) $60

— The Way of an Indian. NY, 1906. 1st Ed, 1st Issue. 8vo, orig cloth. sg Dec 5 (213) $275

Remise, Jac —&
Fondin, Jean

— The Golden Age of Toys. Lausanne, [1967]. 4to, orig cloth, in d/j with 3 small tears. K Mar 22 (440) $120

Remy, Jules —&
Brenchley, Julius L., 1816-73

— A Journey to Great-Salt-Lake City. L, 1861. 2 vols. 8vo, modern half mor. With frontises, folding map & 8 plates (3 in facsimile).. cb Feb 12 (73) $225

Anr copy. Orig cloth; extremities worn. With frontises, folding map & 8 plates. DW Oct 2 (63) £130

Renard, Jules

— Coquecigrues. Paris, 1893. 12mo, half mor by Huser, orig wraps bound in. Inscr to his wife. S May 28 (431) £450 [Beres]

— Histoire naturelles. [Paris,] 1899. One of 100. Illus by Henri de Toulouse-Lautrec. Folio, orig wraps. With 23 lithos, including cover design & with an etching of Toulouse-Lautrec by Maurin. S May 28 (235) £8,000 [Sims Reed]

— Histoires naturelles. Paris, 1896. One of 10 on hollande. 16mo, mor extra by P. L. Martin, orig wraps bound in. S May 28 (430) £2,400 [Beres]

— La Lanterne sourde. Paris, 18893. One of 10 on hollande. 16mo, mor extra by P. L. Martin, orig wraps bound in. S May 28 (429) £800 [Lardanchet]

Renard, Maurice

— New Bodies for Old. NY, [1923]. In d/j. sg June 11 (272) $100

Renault, Jules

— La Legion d'Honneur et les anciens ordres francais. Paris, 1924. One of 500. 4to, half mor; rubbed. O May 26 (156) $70

Renger-Patzsch, Albert

— Baeume. Mit einer essay von Ernst Juenger. Ingelheim am Rhein, 1962. Folio, cloth. With 65 plates. sg Oct 8 (58) $450

— Lob des Rheingaus. Ingelheim, 1953. 4to, orig cloth; front cover dampstained. sg Oct 8 (60) $175

— Die Welt ist Schoen. Munich: Wolff, [1928]. 4to, cloth. With 100 plates. sg Oct 8 (59) $500

Rennell, James, 1742-1830

— Memoir of a Map of Hindoostan. L, 1788. 4to, contemp calf; rebacked. DW Nov 6 (88) £80

— Observations on the Topography of the Plain of Troy.... L, 1814. 4to, half calf. With folding map. Blackmer copy. S July 1 (698) £100 [Frew Mackenzie]

Rennell, James Rodd, Baron. See: Rodd, James Rennell

Renner, Victor von

— Wien im Jahre 1683. Vienna, 1883. 4to, orig cloth. S June 30 (381) £320 [Kutluoglu]

Rennie, James

— Alphabet of Scientific Angling.... L, 1833. 12mo, cloth. Koopman copy. O Oct 29 (238) $50

Renny, Robert

— A History of Jamaica. L: J. Cawthorn, 1807. 4to, modern half calf. Folding map in facsimile; tp & 1st few pages stained; some browning. S May 14 (1263) £140 [Walcot]

Renoir, Auguste, 1841-1919

— Seize aquarelles et sanguines. Paris, [1948]. One of 500. Folio, loose as issued in folder. sg Feb 6 (241) $50

Renouard, Antoine Augustin

— Annales de l'Imprimerie des Alde.... Paris, 1825. 2d Ed. 3 vols. 8vo, contemp cloth. Ck Nov 1 (489) £300

3d Ed. Paris, 1934. 8vo, half mor; rubbed. O Sept 24 (205) $180

Anr Ed. Bologna, 1953. 8vo, cloth. sg Oct 31 (291) $400

Renouard de Bussierre, M. T.

— Lettres sur l'Orient, ecrites pendant les annees 1827 et 1828. [N.p.], 1829. 2 vols plus Atlas. 8vo & folio, text in contemp half calf, plates unbound in plain wraps. With 3 folding maps & 32 plates on india paper. Some spotting, mostly in margins. S June 30 (188) £1,400 [Consolidated Real]

Renouard, Philippe

— Bibliographie des impressions et des oeuvres de Josse Badius Ascensius.... NY, [1967]. 3 vols. 4to, orig cloth. Reprint of 1908 Ed. bba July 9 (23) £85 [Bedford]

Renouard, Philippe —& Moreau, Brigitte

— Inventaire chronologique des editions parisiennes du XVIe Siecle. Paris, 1972-77. Vols I-II only. Cloth, orig wraps bound in. sg Oct 31 (292) $110

Renseignemens...

— Renseignemens sur la Grece et sur l'administration du comte Capodistrias. Paris, 1833. 8vo, contemp mor gilt. S June 30 (382) £300 [Spink]

Renversement...

— Renversement de la morale chretienne par les desordres du monachisme. Holland, [c.1690]. 2 parts in 1 vol. 4to, 19th-cent mor gilt; worn. With 50 grotesque plates of degenerate clerics. Lacking frontis; small copy. wa Mar 5 (544) $300

Report...

— Report of the Commission to Locate the Sites of the Frontier Forts of Pennsylvania. [Harrisburg], 1896. 1st Ed. 2 vols. 8vo, half calf; extremities rubbed. Inked presentation stamp on 1st title. sg Dec 5 (198) $110

Anr copy. Cloth; recased. wa Dec 9 (287) $85

Reports...

— Reports of Explorations and Surveys...for a Railroad from the Mississippi River to the Pacific Ocean.... Wash., 1855-61. 12 vols in 13 (complete set). 4to, orig cloth; some spines faded; Vol XI joints cracked. Vol XI with 36 (of 38) maps. Senate Issue. cb Feb 12 (65) $1,500

Anr copy. Modern cloth; 1 spine vertically cracked. Map vol worn with some maps torn along creases; some staining. Mixed House & Senate set. sg Dec 5 (209) $1,600

Vol I. Cloth. 33rd Congress, 2d Session, Sen. Exec. Doc. 78. sp Nov 24 (78) $60

Vol II. Orig half calf; scuffed. 33rd Congress, 2d Session, Sen. Exec. Doc. 78. cb Sept 12 (132) $190

Anr copy. Orig half calf; scuffed & worn. With 13 color plates. 33rd Congress, 2d Session, Sen. Exec. Doc. 78. cb Nov 14 (148) $90

Anr copy. Cloth. 33rd Congress, 2d Session, Sen. Exec. Doc. 78. sp Nov 24 (79) $120

Anr copy. Orig cloth; worn. Plates dampstained at edges. wa Feb 20 (41) $70

Vol III. Modern cloth. Title & pp 3-4

lacking but supplied in facsimile. cb Feb 12 (110) $130

Anr copy. Cloth; spine chipped, frayed. Some foxing & soiling. Sold w.a.f. O Aug 25 (152) $70

Vol IV. Orig half calf; rubbed, joints cracked. cb Sept 12 (133) $150

Anr copy. Orig half calf; rubbed, joints cracking. cb Nov 14 (149) $110

Anr copy. Cloth. With 59 plates. 33rd Congress, 2d Session, Sen. Exec. Doc. 78. sp Nov 24 (80) $60

Vol V. Orig half calf; rubbed & worn; front cover detached. cb Nov 14 (150) $225

Anr copy. Cloth. With foldout maps & charts. 33rd Congress, 2d Session, Sen. Exec. Doc. 78. sp Nov 24 (81) $200

Vol VI. 8vo, half calf; worn. sg June 18 (473) $50

Vol VII. Cloth. 33rd Congress, 2d Session, Sen. Exec. Doc. 78. sp Nov 24 (82) $60

Vol XI. Cloth. 33rd Congress, 2d Session, Sen. Exec. Doc. 78. sp Nov 24 (82) $60; sp Nov 24 (83) $425

Vol XII. Cloth. With 70 plates & folding maps & charts. 33rd Congress, 2d Session, Sen. Exec. Doc. 78. sp Nov 24 (84) $280

— Reports on the Collections made by the British Ornithologists' Union Expedition and the Wollaston Expedition in Dutch New Guinea. L, 1916. 2 vols. 4to, contemp cloth; worn. C May 20 (209) £700 [Gramm]

Repton, Humphry

— Observations on the Theory and Practice of Landscape Gardening. L, 1803. 4to, contemp calf; rebacked with old spine laid down, scuffed. With 27 plates (3 tinted, 12 hand-colored), 12 with overslips & 2 overslips to text illusts. C Oct 30 (73) £3,500 [Goodwin]

Anr copy. Modern mor by Maltby of Oxford. With 26 plates (3 tinted, 11 hand-colored), 11 with overslips plus 2 overslips to text illusts. G2 with lower half torn away but repaired with text in Ms facsimile & illust on verso copied in grisaille; lacking port & Burley, Rutlandshire plate; some soiling. C Oct 30 (74) £800 [McCann]

Anr copy. Contemp bds; rebacked. With port & 27 plates (12 colored by hand, 4 tinted), 12 with overslips; also 2 other overslips to illusts. C May 20 (112) £3,800 [Heywood Hill]

Anr copy. Mor gilt by Stikeman. With port & 28 plates, with all the overslips. Folding plate General View of Bayham torn affecting image; some foxing throughout. P Dec 12 (77) $3,250

Anr copy. 19th-cent mor gilt. With port & 27 plates, with all the overslips. Library stamps, not affecting plates; outer margins of frontis port & last plate affected by damp & with minor deterioration of the paper. pn Mar 19 (354) £2,000 [Shapero]

Anr copy. Contemp calf gilt; rebacked preserving spine, rubbed. With port, dedication leaf & 27 plates (9 hand-colored aquatints with overlays, 3 plain with overlays). Large folding plate with short tears touching border; port & 1 plate spotted. Pymme's Library copy. S June 25 (222) £2,000 [Marlborough]

2d Ed. L, 1805. 4to, early 20th-cent half mor by Zaehnsdorf; rubbed. With port & 27 plates, including 1 folding, 12 with overlays, 12 hand-colored or tinted. Port torn at upper margin & repaired; slight tear at folds of folding plate; some spotting. Ck Sept 6 (43) £1,700

— The Red Books of Humphry Repton. L: Basilisk Press, 1976. One of 515. 4 vols. 4to, half mor. C May 20 (113) £800 [Finch]

— Sketches and Hints on Landscape Gardening. L, [1794]. Oblong folio, modern half mor. With 16 plates, 11 colored, 4 double-page, all but 2 with overslips. Small stain on 1st 2 prelims. bba June 25 (235) £3,000 [Heywood Hill]

Anr copy. Orig bds with contemp paper backstrip; soiled, backstrip def, lower cover detached. With 6 plain & 10 hand-colored plates & a total of 13 overslips. Some overslips creased; 11th plate with small section torn away from upper blank margin; 1 word scratched out from 1st line of note on p.51. Subscriber's copy. C Oct 30 (75) £3,500 [Pagan]

Anr copy. Contemp half mor; rebacked, old spine laid down. With 6 plain & 10 hand-colored plates & a total of 13 overlays. Some overslips creased; small tears in 1 double-page plate; 1 word scratched out from 1st line of note on p. 51. C May 20 (111) £4,800 [Simon Finch]

Anr copy. Contemp bds; rebacked with new paper. With 16 plates, 10 hand-colored (all with overslips). Dampstained at front affecting prelims; some browning in folds. McCarty-Cooper copy. CNY Jan 25 (61) $7,000

Anr copy. Half mor gilt; upper joint cracked. With 6 plain & 10 hand-colored plates & a total of 8 overlays. Martin —McCarty-Cooper copy. CNY Jan 25 (62) $3,200

One of 250. Recent calf gilt; restored. With 16 aquatints after drawings by Repton, 14 with aquatint overslips, 10 hand-colored. Some foxing & marginal waterstaining; marginal tears; Plate 2 browned; Plate 14 with marginal waterstain & torn overslip. P June 18 (493) $3,750

Repton, Humphry —& Others

— Designs for the Pavillon at Brighton. L, 1808. Folio, modern half mor gilt by Sangorski & Sutcliffe. With 20 plates, including hand-colored General ground Plan & 9 hand-colored aquatints; 6 plates with overslips, 1 with overpage. Small tear to inner margin of final folding plate. C May 20 (114) £4,600 [Quaritch]

Anr Ed. L, [watermarked 1821]. Folio, modern half calf. 1 plate torn & repaired; margin of 1 plate stained. CNY Dec 7 (316) $3,200

Anr Ed. L, [c.1822]. Folio, later half mor over bds; rubbed & chipped. With 20 illusts, some full-page, some colored; 1 plate with overlay, anr with overpage & 1 with 2 images, 1 of which has an overlay & 2 double-page or folding plates with 2 overlays. Some repairs; marginal tears; 1 of the double-page plates backed. P June 17 (318) $2,000

Repton, Humphry & John Adey

— Fragments on the Theory and Practice of Landscape Gardening.... L, 1816. 4to, contemp bds; rebacked. With 43 colored or tinted plates & plans, complete with required overslips. C May 20 (115) £4,000 [Heywood Hill]

Anr copy. Old bds; rebacked with paper, edges & corners worn. With 24 hand-colored plates (10 with overslips), 5 tinted plates (1 with overslip) & 14 uncolored plates (3 with overslips). CNY Jan 25 (63) $6,000

Resende, Lucius Andrea

— Libri quatuor de antiquitatibus Lusitaniae. Evora, 1593. 1st Ed. Folio, modern calf. First few leaves stained & repaired in lower corner. bba Apr 9 (209) £250 [Hesketh & Ward]

Resident, A. See: Alexander, Sir James Edward

Rest, Quirinus

— Rosengarten; das ist, Fuenff unnd viertzig catholische Predigen auff die fuernemeste Fest und Feyertaeg dess gantzen Jars. Ingolstadt: David Sartorius, 1585. 4to, contemp blind-tooled pigskin over wooden bds, dated 1560 with monogram NF; lacking front free endpaper. Some foxing & dampstaining. sg Oct 24 (272) $200

Resta, Sebastiano

— The True Effigies of the most Eminent Painters.... L [Antwerp], 1694. Folio, contemp calf; rubbed. With 3 engraved titles & 119 (of 122) plates. Tear to head of tp, not affecting text; cut down. F Mar 26 (755) $170

Restif de la Bretonne, Nicholas Edme, 1734-1806

— Monsieur Nicholas, or the Human Heart Unveiled. L, 1930-31. One of 825. 6 vols. Half cloth. sg Mar 5 (280) $70

— Monsieur Nicolas, ou le coeur humain devoile.... Paris, 1924. Illus by Sylvain Sauvage. 4 vols. 8vo, half mor; rubbed. O Aug 25 (152) $70

— Tableaux de la bonne compagnie.... Paris, 1787. 2 vols. 12mo, mor gilt by Bedford. With 16 plates. Washed. Hoe-Bishop copy. C June 24 (193) £1,500 [Shapero]

Restle, Marcell

— Byzantine Wall Painting in Asia Minor. Shannon, 1969. 3 vols. 4to, orig cloth, in d/js. DW Dec 11 (381) £160

Retza, Franciscus de

— De Generatione Christi, sive defensorium inviolatae castitatis B.V.M. [Basel: Lienhart Ysenhut, c.1490]. 4to, bds. 32 lines; types 2:162G, 3:79G & 1:94G (text); rubricated; with 2 full-page woodcuts & 52 woodcuts in the text. 30 leaves. Goff R-153. Morris-Brunschwig copy. C Nov 27 (37) £15,000 [Hellmutt Schumann]

Reuchlin, Johannes, 1455-1522

— De arte cabalistica, libri tres. Hagenau: T. Anshelmum, 1517. Folio, old vellum; lower cover slit. Tp soiled & restored at margins; final leaf damaged at margins & laid down; marginal dampstains, affecting text. Ck Nov 29 (287) £2,800

Reusner, Nicolaus

— Icones sive imagines virorum literis illustrium.... Strassburg, 1587. 8vo, contemp vellum. With 100 ports. Tp frail at upper margin. Ck Nov 29 (288) £750

Anr Ed. Basel, 1589. ("Icones sive imagines vivae....") 8vo, old half sheep gilt; corners worn, front joint cracked. Some headlines shaved; dampstains at end; lacking last leaf. sg May 7 (180) $1,100

Reverdy, Pierre

— Cravates de chanvre. Paris, 1922. One of 15 on Hollande, with 3 orig etchings. Illus by Pablo Picasso. Orig bdg. With 3 plates. CGen Nov 18 (445) SF62,000

Reverdy, Pierre —& Duthuit, Georges

— The Last Works of Henri Matisse. NY, [1958]. Orig bds; backstrip detached. wa Apr 9 (250) $400

Revere, Joseph Warren

— A Tour of Duty in California.... NY, 1849. 1st Ed. 12mo, orig cloth; fore-edges ink-stained. Map loose & with a short repaired tear. cb Feb 12 (74) $250

Anr copy. Cloth. With folding map & 6 plates. sg June 18 (116) $550

Anr copy. Foxed. sg June 18 (117) $250

Revett, Nicholas, 1720-1804. See: Stuart & Revett

Revue...

— Revue de l'Orient Latin. Paris, 1893-1911. 12 vols (all pbd). 8vo, cloth. S June 30 (70) £2,500 [Bank of Cyprus]

Rewald, John. See: Dorra & Rewald

Rexroth, Kenneth

— In What Hour. NY, 1940. In chipped d/j. Inscr to Kenneth Patchen. CNY June 9 (170) $480

Rey de Planazu, Francois Joseph

— Oeuvres d'agriculture et d'economie rurale.... Paris, 1801. 4to, contemp calf. With frontis, 1 uncolored & 28 colored plates. C June 24 (194) £1,000 [Quaritch]

Rey, Emmanuel Guillaume

— Etude sur les monuments de l'architecture militaire des Croises en Syrie.... Paris, 1871. 4to, orig bds; spine soiled. With 24 plates, some in color. S Nov 21 (275) £4,200 [Bank of Cyprus]

Rey, Etienne —& Others

— Voyage pittoresque en Grece et dans le Levant. Lyons, 1867. 2 vols in 1. Folio, 19th-cent half mor; rubbed. With 3 maps & 52 plates on india paper mtd. Some spotting. S June 30 (190) £1,800 [Consolidated Real]

Anr copy. Mor gilt. With 2 litho maps & a plan of Athens & 52 plates, 32 hand-colored. One plate spotted. Presentation letter from Rey's son-in-law pasted in at beginning. S July 1 (699) £4,200 [Chelsea]

Reybaud, Louis —& Others

— Histoire scientifique et militaire de l'expedition francaise en Egypte. Paris, 1830-34. 2 Atlas vols only. Oblong 4to, half sheep; def. With 309 (of 310) plates. sg Jan 9 (129) $550

Reynard the Fox

— Reynard the Fox, a Poem in Twelve Cantos. Dresden & Leipzig & L, [1852]. Illus by H. Leuteman. 4to, mor extra by Kelliegram, orig cloth preserved. With 40 plates on 37 leaves. CNY Dec 5 (410) $950

Reynolds, John, 1788-1865

— The Pioneer History of Illinois. Belleville IL, 1852. 1st Ed. 12mo, orig cloth; restored with orig spine laid down. bbc Dec 9 (410) $275

Reynolds, Sir Joshua, 1723-92

— A Discourse, Delivered...the Royal Academy.... L, 1769-90. 1st Eds of Discourses. 7 (of 15) discourses. 4to, 19th-cent half mor; joints rubbed. Sold w.a.f. Inscr on 1 title & 1 half-title. Milne copy. Ck June 12 (175) £150

— Engravings from the Works. L, [1833-39]. 3 vols. Folio, half mor gilt; rubbed. With engraved titles & 300 plates. b Mar 11 (64) £480

— [Sale Catalogue] A Catalogue of the First Part of the Cabinet of Ancient Drawings.... L: A. C. de Poggi, [1794]. 8vo, orig wraps. S Feb 11 (179) £360 [Quaritch]

— Seven Discourses Delivered in the Royal Academy.... L, 1778. 1st Ed. Dedication by Samuel Johnson. 8vo, later half calf; worn. Prelims & latter leaves darkened. cb Oct 25 (105) $65

Reynolds Historical Library, Lawrence

— Rare Books and Collections. A Bibliography. Birmingham, Alabama, [1968]. 4to, cloth. cb Oct 17 (790) $85

Rezanov, Count Nicolae P.

— The Rezanov Voyage to Nueva California.... San Francisco, 1926. One of 260. Half cloth. sg June 18 (478) $200

Rhazes, 850-923

— Liber Rasis ad Almansorem.... Venice: Johannes Hamman, 19 Feb 1500. Folio, modern vellum. Gothic type. Contemp annotations to margins; several outer margins restored not affecting letters. 112 leaves. Goff R-177. C Dec 16 (74) £3,000 [Mediolanum]

Rhead, George Woolliscroft

— History of the Fan. L, 1910. One of 450. Folio, orig cloth; rubbed & soiled. DW Mar 11 (738) £280

Anr copy. Orig cloth; worn. S Feb 11 (328) £220 [Davis]

Out-of-series copy. Orig cloth; joints worn with a few splits, hinges starting. With 100 uncolored & 27 color plates. Library markings. sg Apr 2 (255) $275

Rhead, Louis John

— American Trout-Stream Insects: a Guide.... NY, [1916]. In chipped d/j. Koopman copy. O Oct 29 (239) $90

— The Basses Fresh-Water and Marine. NY, [1905]. Simulated bass-skin bds, in d/j. Koopman copy. O Oct 29 (240) $140

Rheims, Maurice

— The Flowering of Art Nouveau. NY: Abrams, [n.d.]. With 12 tipped-in plates. sp Sept 22 (375) $75

Rhode Island

— The Public Laws of the State of Rhode-Island and Providence Plantations. Providence, 1798. 8vo, contemp sheep; worn. sg Dec 5 (215) $100

Rhodes, Ebenezer

— Peak Scenery.... L, 1818-23. 4 parts in 2 vols. Folio, contemp mor gilt, armorial bdg. With 29 plates on india paper. bba Sept 19 (231) £260 [Dawson]

Rhodes, Eugene Manlove

— The Desire of the Moth. NY, 1916. Inscr. O Jan 14 (161) $100

Rhodes, John

— The Surprising Adventures and Sufferings of John Rhodes, a Seaman of Workington. NY: Forman for Cotton, 1798. 8vo, disbound. Some leaves heavily stained. Sold w.a.f. O Nov 26 (90) $100

Rhodiginus, Ludovicus Coelius. See: Richerius, Ludovicus Coelius

Rhodiginus, Richerius. See: Richerius, Ludovicus Coelius

Ribelles Comin, Jose

— Bibliografia de la Langua Valenciana.... Madrid, 1915-31. 3 vols. 4to, half sheep. sg Oct 31 (293) $130

Ribeyro, Joao

— Histoire de l'Isle de Ceylan.... Amst., 1701. 8vo, contemp sheep; rubbed. Title stamped. sg Jan 9 (168) $300

Ricardo, David, 1772-1823

— On the Principles of Political Economy and Taxation. L, 1817. 1st Ed. 8vo, contemp half calf gilt; rubbed, corners knocked. Lacking pbr's ads; some underlining or marginal marking on several leaves; some spotting. P June 17 (319) $9,500

Anr copy. Contemp calf gilt; rubbed. sg Nov 7 (180) $11,000

Riccardi, Pietro

— Biblioteca matematica Italiana. Modena, 1873-93. 4 parts in 1 vol. Folio, half lea; scuffed. sg Oct 31 (294) $375

Anr Ed. Milan, 1952. 2 vols. bbc Sept 23 (113) $65; O Sept 24 (208) $130

Anr Ed. Sala Bolognese, 1985. 2 vols. sg Nov 14 (312) $225

Riccati, Vincenzo

— De seriebus recipientibus summam generalem algebraicam aut exponentialem commentarius. Bologna, 1756. 4to, old bds. SI Dec 5 (581) LIt500,000

Ricci, Elisa

— Antiche trine italiane. Bergamo, 1908. 2 vols. Folio, cloth. sg Feb 6 (156) $275

— Old Italian Lace. L & Phila., 1913. One of 300. 2 vols. Folio, orig cloth; rubbed. sg Feb 6 (243) $400

Riccius, Bartholomaeus

— Triumphus Jesu Christi crucifixi. Antwerp: Plantin, 1608. 8vo, later mor gilt; front cover damaged. With 70 full-page plates, including engraved title Some dampstaining; lacking 1 index leaf. sg Oct 24 (273) $300

Riccoboni, Luigi

— An Historical and Critical Account of the Theatres in Europe. L, 1741. 8vo, later half sheep. Eva Le Gallienne's copy. sg Mar 5 (250) $175

Rice, Anne

— Interview with the Vampire. NY, 1976. Half cloth, in d/j. bbc Apr 27 (395) $180

Anr copy. In d/j. F Dec 18 (195) $220

Anr Ed. NY, 1990. Boxed with: The Vampire Lestat. And: The Queen of the Damned. 3 vols. Sgd. cb Dec 12 (250) $120

Rice Library, John A.

— [Sale Catalogue]. NY, 1870. 8vo, half lea; rubbed. O Feb 25 (166) $110

Rice, Maj. Gen. William

— "Indian Game" (from Quail to Tiger). L, 1884. 8vo, orig cloth; hinges starting. sg Jan 9 (304) $130

Richards, J. M.

— High Street. L, 1938. Illus by Eric Ravilious. Orig bds; head of backstrip chipped. With 24 colored lithos. bba Dec 19 (122A) £350 [Marlborough]

Richards, Thomas Addison, 1820-1900

— American Scenery Illustrated. NY: Leavitt & Allen, [1854]. 4to, mor; rubbed. With 32 plates. K Sept 29 (17) $150

Anr copy. Lea; worn. Some foxing. NH Oct 6 (118) $85

Anr copy. Lea gilt. NH May 30 (216) $150

Anr copy. Orig mor; rubbed, inner joint repaired. Title stamped. O Nov 29 (151) $110

Anr copy. Orig cloth. With 32 plates. Titles pencilled under images; some foxing. wa Apr 9 (279) $170

Richardson, Albert Deane

— Beyond the Mississippi.... Hartford, 1867. 1st Ed. 8vo, cloth; scuffed. sg June 18 (479) $60

Richardson, Albert Edward —& Eberlein, Harold Donaldson

— The Smaller English House of the Later Renaissance, 1660-1830. NY, [1925]. 4to, cloth; stained. sp Feb 6 (174) $80

Richardson, Charles, Sportsman —& Others

— Racing at Home and Abroad. L, 1923-31. 3 vols. 4to, orig mor; rubbed, spines faded. bba Sept 5 (183) £550 [Shapero]

Richardson, Charles James, 1806-71

— Studies from Old English Mansions.... L, 1841-48. Series 1-4. 4 vols in 3. Folio, contemp mor; loose, worn. With litho titles & 133 plates, some tinted, a few hand-finished. Sold w.a.f. S July 1 (1325) £200 [Rostron]

Richardson, Gabriel

— On the State of Europe. Oxford, 1627. 4to, 18th-cent half calf. W July 8 (92) £55

Richardson, George, 1736?-1817?

— Iconology or a Collection of Emblematical Figures. L, 1779. 2 vols. Folio, half mor. With 109 plates, some with later coloring. pnE Dec 4 (206) £600

Richardson, John, 1667-1753. See: Bownas & Richardson

Richardson, Sir John, 1787-1865
See also: Swainson & Richardson

— Arctic Searching Expedition: A Journal of a Boat Voyage...in Search of...Sir John Franklin. L, 1851. 2 vols. 8vo, orig cloth. With 9 (of 10) lithos. DW Oct 2 (65) £110

Richardson, Samuel, 1689-1761

— Clarisse Harlowe. Traduction nouvelle.... Geneva, 1785-86. 10 vols. 8vo, contemp calf gilt. With port & 21 plates. HH May 12 (1869) DM600

— The History of Sir Charles Grandison. L, 1754. 1st Ed. 7 vols. 8vo, contem calf; joints cracked, rubbed. Lacking final leaf in Vol VII. bba Jan 16 (122) £120 [Martin]

Anr copy. Contemp calf gilt; rebacked, rubbed. Lacking U6 in Vol VII. bba Apr 9 (87) £70 [Harlow]

— Works. L, 1883. One of 750. 12 vols. 8vo, contemp calf gilt; some chipping & rubbing. P June 17 (348) $800

Anr Ed. L, 1884. One of 250. 12 vols. 8vo, half mor gilt. sg Mar 5 (281) $550

Edition de Bibliophile. NY, [1901-2]. ("Novels.") one of 20 on handmade japan paper, this the Lord Macaulay copy, with most plates in 3 states. 20 vols. 8vo, mor extra by Stikeman. Inscr by William Lyon Phelps. P June 17 (347) $2,250

Richardson, William, Architect —& Churton, Edward, 1800-74

— The Monastic Ruins of Yorkshire. York, 1843. 2 vols. Folio, contemp half mor; worn. With 2 tinted litho plates, dedication, 30 views including 3 mtd & hand-colored, 26 tinted litho vignettes, 29 ground plates & hand-colored map. pnL Nov 20 (100) £640 [Moorly]

Richer, Adrien. See: Marsy & Richer

Richerius, Christopher. See: Richier, Christophe

Richerius, Ludovicus Coelius

— Lectionum antiquarum libri xvi. Basel: Johann Froben, 1517. Folio, contemp half pigskin over wooden bds with brass catches & clasps; spine painted gray at early date with shelfmark added, paint rubbed & chipped. Some contemp marginalia. sg Oct 24 (275) $800

— Lectionum antiquarium libri triginta. Frankfurt, 1599. Folio, 18th-cent vellum. Some waterstaining & foxing. SI June 10 (858) LIt250,000

Richier, Christophe

— De rebus Turcaru libri quinque. Paris: R. Estienne, 1540. 4to, contemp calf; worn, spine def. S Nov 21 (277) £1,400 [Kutluoglu]

Richter, Jean Paul

— Saemmtliche Werke. Berlin, 1826-28. 60 vols in 27. 8vo, contemp bds. HH May 12 (1370) DM1,400

Richter, Jean Paul —& Taylor, A. Cameron

— The Golden Age of Classic Christian Art. L, 1904. 4to, cloth. DW Mar 11 (851) £80

Richthofen, Walter, Baron von
— Cattle-Raising on the Plains.... NY, 1885. 12mo, orig cloth; worn & soiled. NH Oct 6 (369) $260

Rickett, Harold William
— Wild Flowers of the United States. NY, 1966-73. 6 vols in 14 parts plus Index. Library markings. bbc Apr 27 (558) $550
Anr Ed. NY, 1966-71. Vol III, Parts 1 & 2 only. Orig cloth. bbc June 29 (149) $110
Anr copy. Vol III only: Texas, in 2 parts. wa Dec 9 (511) $190
Anr copy. Vols I-VI in 14 parts. wa Mar 5 (519) $550

Ricketts, Charles de Sousy
See also: Nonesuch Press
— Beyond the Threshold. L: Curwen Press, 1929. One of 150. 4to, mor gilt. Ck Oct 18 (257) £700
Anr copy. Orig mor gilt. With 5 plates & cover design by the author. Inscr to Gordon Bottomly & with separate impressions of the 5 plates ptd in blue, each with autograph caption. S July 21 (433) £800 [Marks]
— A Bibliogrpahy of the Books Issued by Hacon & Ricketts. L, 1904. One of 250. 4to, orig bds. Siegfried Sassoon's copy. bba July 9 (321) £230 [Bookworks]
Anr copy. Bds; warped. sp Apr 16 (509) $90
— A Defence of the Revival of Printing. L: Vale Press, 1899. One of 10 on vellum. 8vo, mor gilt sgd HR. Charles Ricketts' copy. S July 22 (392) £2,800 [Maggs]
One of 250. Orig bds, unopened. bba July 9 (297) £190 [Cox]

Rickman, John. See: Cook, Capt. James

Rickman, Philip
— A Selection of Bird Paintings and Sketches.... L, 1979. One of 500. Folio, half mor gilt. Foreword sgd by the Duke of Edinburgh. pnE May 13 (98) £300

Ricord, Philippe, 1800-89
— Letters on Syphilis. Phila., 1852. 8vo, orig sheep. Dampstained throughout. sg Nov 14 (110) $225

Riddle, Jeff C.
— The Indian History of the Modoc War.... [N.p.]: Pvtly Ptd, [1914]. Orig cloth; extremities rubbed. cb Sept 12 (149) $65

Rider, William
— Views in Stratford-upon-Avon, illustrative of the Biography of Shakspeare.... L, 1828. Folio, orig bds; rebacked. With 5 mtd india-proof plates. Dampstain in lower margins; plates foxed. L.p. copy. sg Oct 17 (356) $110

Ridgway, Robert
— The Birds of North and Middle America. Wash., 1901-50. 11 vols (all pbd) in 10. Half lea, cloth or wraps. Library markings. O Apr 28 (54) $50

Riding, Laura
— The Life of the Dead. L, 1933. One of 200. Illus by John Aldridge. Orig bds; marked & rubbed. bba Dec 19 (215) £140 [Whiteson]
Anr copy. Wraps. DW Apr 8 (550) £135
— Twenty Poems Less. Paris: Hours Press, 1930. One of 200, sgd. Half lea; extremities worn. sg Dec 12 (349) $175

Ridley, Nicholas, 1500?-55
— De coena Dominica assertio. Geneva, 1556. 8vo, mor gilt by Riviere. C June 24 (195) £420 [Wood]; C June 24 (195) £420 [Wood]

Riedinger, Johann Elias
— Vorstellueng und Beschreibueng dere Schuel und Campagne Pferden nach inhren Lecionen.... Augsburg, 1760-61. Part 1 only. Bds; soiled. With engraved title & 46 plates. Library stamp on tp. S Nov 21 (40) £3,000 [Maggs]

Riegel, Christoph
— Der neuste Staat von Lothringen, Savojen.... Frankfurt, 1713. 12mo, contemp calf. With port double-page frontis & 109 miniature town views. S Nov 21 (193) £2,200 [Stopp]

Riemer, Jacob de, 1678?-1762
— Beschryving van 's Graven-Hage, behelzende deszelfs Oorsprong Benaming.... Delft & The Hague, 1730-39. 3 vols. Folio, vellum; tears to backstrip of last vol. Some foxing; fold repairs to plates. B Nov 1 (308) HF2,600

Rienits, Rex & Thea
— Early Artists of Australia. Sydney, 1963. In plasticized d/j. kh Nov 11 (196) A$50
Anr copy. In d/j. kh Nov 11 (197) A$90

Riesenthal, Otto von
— Gefiederte freunde. Bilder zur Naturgeschichte angenehmer und nuetzlicher Voegel Mitteleuropas. Leipzig, [1880-83]. Atlas only. Folio, contemp half lea; joints & extremities worn. With 60 mtd chromolitho plates. sg May 7 (181) $500

Rigaud, Jacques, 1681-1754
— Recueil choisi des plus belles vues des palais, chateaux et maisons royales de Paris et des environs.... Paris: Treuttel & Wurtz, [c.1820]. Folio, 19th-cent half mor; rubbed. With 121 plates. Without title; Plate 28 damaged affecting image; some

spotting. S June 25 (329) £3,000 [American]

Rigby, Edward —& Stewart, Duncan

— Nouveau Traite sur les hemorrhages de l'uterus.... Paris, 1818. Trans by Marie Anne Victoire Boivin. 8vo, contemp half sheep; spine rubbed. Sgd by the translator. sg Nov 14 (112) $425

Riggs, Lynn. See: Limited Editions Club

Riggs, Stephen R.

— Mary and I. Forty Years with the Sioux. Chicago: W. G. Holmes, [1880]. 12mo, orig cloth; spine ends & bd tips worn & frayed, shaken. Some marks in blue pencil. wa Mar 5 (359) $50

Rijn, H. van. See: Heussen & Rijn

Riley, James, 1777-1840

— Loss of the American Brig Commerce.... Hartford, 1817. ("An Authentic Narrative of the Loss of the American Brig Commerce....") 8vo, orig calf; early, crude rebacking in lea. Lacking 1 plate. NH Oct 6 (317) $90

Riley, James Whitcomb, 1849-1916

— Works. New Castle PA, [c.1913]. Elizabeth Marine Riley Ed. 6 vols. 4to, mor extra. With several mtd watercolors sgd by S. J. Beebee. CNY Dec 5 (424) $1,300

Riling, Ray

— Guns and Shooting: a Selected Chronological Bibliography. NY, [1951]. One of 1,500. O Sept (208) $70

Anr copy. In chipped d/j. sg May 21 (88) $80

Rilke, Rainer Maria, 1875-1926

— Gesammelte Gedichte. Leipzig, 1930-34. One of 200. 4 vols. 4to, orig half vellum. HH May 12 (2473) DM2,200

Rimbaud, Arthur, 1854-91

See also: Limited Editions Club

— Une Saison en enfer. Brussels, 1873. 1st Ed, one of 250. 12mo, orig wraps. S May 28 (432) £3,200 [Sims Reed]

Rimbault, Edward Francis

— The Pianoforte: its Origin, Progress, and Construction.... L, 1860. 1st Ed. 4to, contemp half cloth; worn at edges. Library markings; frontis torn. pn Oct 24 (441) £75

Rimmel, Eugene

— The Book of Perfumes. L, 1865. 4to, orig cloth; nicked at corners & ends. Some foxing. wa Mar 5 (538) $70

Rimmer, Alfred

— Ancient Streets and Homesteads of England. L, 1877. 8vo, lev gilt by Bayntun. O May 26 (6) $225

Rimon

— Rimon. A Hebrew Illustrated Magazine of Art and Letters. Berlin, 1922-24. Ed by M. Vishnitzer & B. Krupnik. Nos 1-6 [all pbd]. 4to, contemp syn, orig wraps bound in. Stamps effaced. sg June 25 (164) $225

Rinder, Frank

— D. Y. Cameron: An Illustrated Catalogue.... Glasgow, 1912. One of 500. 4to, lea gilt; spine & front bd detached. Met Apr 28 (14) $100

Rinehart, Frank

— Rinehart's Indians. Omaha, 1899. 8vo, pictorial wraps; spine chipped. sg Oct 8 (61) $225

Ringgold, Cadwalader, 1802-67

— A Series of Charts, with Sailing Directions. Embracing Surveys of the...Bay of San Francisco.... Wash., 1851. 4to, orig cloth; rubbed. With 11 tinted plates & 6 folding charts. Some browning & foxing; 1 chart with closed tear, the others with short fold separations. Inscr to Gouverneur Kemble. P June 16 (267) $2,000

Ringhieri, Innocentio

— Cento giuochi liberali, et d'ingegno. Bologna: A. Giaccarelli, 1551. 4to, contemp vellum; waterstained, hole in lower cover. Tp dampstained & with repair at top of page affecting 2 characters; contents leaf torn & repaired. Ck May 8 (54) £400

Anr copy. 18th-cent calf. Some marginal soiling. SI June 10 (868) LIt950,000

Ringmann, Mathias, 1482?-1511

— Passio Domini Nostri Jesu Christi.... Strassburg: Matthias Hupfuff, 1513. Folio, mor gilt by Roger de Coverly; upper joint split. With 25 full-page woodcuts by Urs Graf. Corners restored; wormholes repaired, with small loss; tear in D3 repaired; some waterstaining. S Dec 5 (181) £5,800 [Klein]

Ringold, T. See: Franklin Printing, Benjamin

Ringrose, Basil. See: Exquemelin, Alexandre Olivier

Ringwalt, John Luther

— American Encyclopaedia of Printing. Phila., 1871. 4to, cloth. cb Oct 17 (795) $140

Rio, Ercole del

— Sopra il giuoco degli scacchi.... Modena, 1750. 4to, modern vellum. Ck May 8 (154) £2,200

Rio Grande Western Railway

— A Few Facts about the Climate and Resources of the New State of Utah.... Salt Lake City, 1896. cb Feb 13 (127) $70

Riolan, Jean, 1577-1657

— Opera. Paris: Plantin, 1610. Folio, contemp sheep; worn, front cover detached. With 2 plates. Minor marginal worming. sg Nov 14 (113) $250

Ripa, Cesare

— Della novissima iconologia. Padua, 1625-24. 3 parts in 1 vol. 4to, old vellum bds; soiled. Some dampstaining; hole in K6 with loss. S Feb 11 (183) £280 [Barrans]

— Iconologia overo descrittione di diverse imagini cavate dall'antichita. Padua: Pietro Paolo Tozzi, 1611. 4to, contemp vellum; front hinge split. Tear in R1. sg Mar 12 (78) $650

— Iconologie ou nouvelle explication de plusieurs images.... Paris, 1677. 4to, contemp sheep; worn, joints cracked. Minor worming in gutters at end. sg Oct 24 (276) $375

Risso, J. Antoine —& Poiteau, Pierre Antoine

— Histoire naturelle des orangers. Paris, 1818-[20]. Folio, contemp half mor. With 109 hand-finished color plates. Some spotting & staining; plates 3-8 smaller. L.p. copy. C Oct 30 (224) £5,100 [Riepera]

Ritchie, Leitch, 1800-65

— Travelling Sketches in the North of Italy.... L, 1832. Illus by Clarkson Stanfield. 8vo, orig lea gilt; joints worn. With 26 plates. Foxed. sg Jan 9 (169) $70

Ritson, Joseph, 1752-1803

— Robin Hood. A Collection of All the Ancient Poems, Songs and Ballads. L, 1885. One of 100 L.p. copies. 4to, calf gilt; worn, covers detached. sg Oct 17 (115) $100

Rittenhouse, Jack D.

— The Santa Fe Trail: A Historical Bibliography. Albuquerque, [1971]. In d/j. cb Oct 17 (797) $65

Rivera, Diego

— Frescoes. NY: Museum of Modern Art, [1933]. Folio, loose in orig portfolio. With 19 mtd color plates. Sgd twice. sg Sept 6 (247) $450

— Portrait of America. NY, [1934]. In d/j. Sgd. cb Dec 19 (141) $180

Rivero, Mariano Eduardo de —& Tschudi, Juan Diego de

— Antiguedades Peruanas. Vienna, 1851. Atlas vol only. Oblong folio, orig bds; soiled. With chromolitho title & 58 chromolitho plates (of 59). Some stains. S May 14 (1264) £350 [Burton-Garbett]

Rivers, Larry

— Drawings and Digressions. NY, [1979]. Foreword by John Ashbery. 4to, cloth. sg Apr 2 (256) $175

Riviere, Georges

— Renoir et ses amis. Paris, 1921. 4to, later cloth. sg Apr 2 (254) $650

Riviere, Lazare, 1589-1665

— The Practice of Physick.... L, 1655. Bound with: Four Books of Lazarus Riverius. L, 1658. 1st Ed in English. Folio, later vellum; worn. Lacking title & frontis. Some browning, soiling, & worming. DW Jan 29 (273) £120

Riviere, Robert & Son

— Examples of Bookbinding...Exhibited at the Leipzig Exhibition in 1914.... L, 1920. 4to, contemp cloth by Henry Young & Sons. bba Oct 10 (544) £140 [Maggs]

Robb, E. M.

— Early Toorak and District. Melbourne, 1934. 4to, cloth; spotted. kh Nov 11 (304) A$200

Robberds, J. W. See: Stark & Robberds

Robert de Vaugondy, Gilles & Didier

— Atlas universel. Paris, 1757-[58]. Folio, contemp russia; def. With engraved title & 108 maps, hand-colored in outline & mtd on guards. Some edges soiled & frayed; tp soiled & torn at edges; Britannicas Insulae repaired; some blank corners in central portion dampstained; last map soiled. pn Nov 14 (438) £2,700

Robert, Maurice. See: Limited Editions Club

Roberts, David, 1796-1864

Egypt and Nubia

— Egypt and Nubia, from Drawings Made on the Spot.... L, 1846-49-49. 3 vols. Folio, contemp half mor gilt; joints & corners rubbed. With 3 litho titles with hand-colored views & 121 plates hand-colored & mtd on card. Minor spotting affecting Vol I title & a few plates only; map & 2 text leaves dampstained. Copy with plates hand-colored & mtd on card. C May 20 (298) £46,000 [Tulbot]

Anr copy. 19th-cent half mor gilt; upper cover of Vol II detached. With 5 litho titles, 2 maps & 121 tinted litho views, of which 61 are full-page. Some spotting affecting image of several plates. S Nov 21 (301) £6,500 [Map House]

Sets of Both Works

— The Holy Land, Syria, Idumea, Arabia, Egypt and Nubia. With: Egypt and Nubia. L, 1842-49. 6 vols in 4. Folio, half lea by J. Wright. With engraved titles, 2 maps, 1 port & 241 tinted plates. Met Apr 28 (76) $15,000

Anr copy. 6 vols. Folio, contemp half mor gilt; worn. With 247 plates, including titles, 2 maps & port. Lacking subscribers' list; marginal foxing & dampstaining; some edges in vol VI frayed; marginal tears affecting half-page plate in Vol V. pn Mar 19 (401) £8,000 [Schuster]

Anr Ed. L, 1855-56. 6 vols in 3. 4to, contemp half mor; scuffed. With 6 tinted litho titles, port, 2 maps & 240 plates; lacking Plate 127. Ck Oct 18 (86) £1,100

Anr copy. Contemp half mor gilt, armorial bdg. With 250 plates. Some leaves loose; a few leaves dampstained. S Nov 15 (1184) £1,200 [Baum]

Anr copy. Contemp half mor; needs rebdg. sg Feb 13 (207) $1,900

Anr Ed. NY: Appleton, [c.1855-56]. 6 vols. 4to, contemp half mor gilt; scuffed. With 250 plates, 2 hand-colored. wa Sept 26 (659) $2,500

The Holy Land

— The Holy Land, Syria, Idumea, Arabia, Egypt and Nubia. L, 1842-49. 3 vols. Folio, orig half mor; rubbed, recased. With uncolored port (holed with minor loss), tinted litho titles, map & 112 tinted lithos (61 full-page, 61 half-page). Lacking list of subscribers; some soiling; small tears to margins of 2 plates; minor damage to surface of 1 plate in Vol II; repair to inner margin of 1 plate in Vol III. C Oct 30 (76) £4,000 [Shapero]

Anr copy. 3 vols in 4. Folio, contemp half mor; joints & corners rubbed. With uncolored port on india paper mtd, 4 litho titles with hand-colored vignette views, map & 120 plates hand-colored & mtd on card. Title vignettes & 2 small plates in Vol I slightly cockled; lacking the 2 text leaves Bethlehem & Idumea. Copy with plates hand-colored & mtd on card. C May 20 (297) £46,000 [Tulbot]

Anr copy. 3 vols in 2. Folio, cloth; rubbed. With 3 litho titles, port, map & 120 plates colored & mtd on card. Some foxing; tp to Vol I cockled & split; a few plates cockled; mtd card of title to Vol II with marginal loss. Colored copy. P Dec 12 (78) $27,000

Anr copy. 3 vols. Folio, contemp half mor gilt; hinges reinforced. With tinted litho titles, port, 120 tinted lithos (60 full-page) & map, all with hand-coloring. Foxed throughout; some creasing; 1 plate & tp to Vol III repaired in margin. pn Mar 19 (402) £3,200 [Baring]

Anr copy. 3 vols in 2. Folio, contemp half calf; rubbed, upper joint splitting. With port, 2 (of 3) pictorial title & 60 plates. Lacking map from Vol III & leaf of description of tp vignettes from Vol I. S Nov 15 (839) £3,400 [Russell]

Anr copy. 19th-cent half mor; worn. With 2 litho titles, port, map & 120 plates. Some spotting; 6 plates with worming affacting image. S June 25 (112) £4,600 [Tulip]

Anr copy. Vols I-II only. Contemp half mor gilt. With tinted litho titles & 84 tinted plates & port. S July 1 (854) £2,500 [Pollak]

Anr copy. 3 vols in 2. Folio, contemp half mor gilt; def. With 3 litho titles, port & 120 plates. Some waterstaining; a few plates becoming loose. S July 1 (855) £3,000 [Sofer]

Anr copy. With 3 litho titles, port, map & 120 plates. Several leaves dampstained at edges. sg May 7 (182) $5,000

Anr Ed. L, [1879-84]. 3 vols in 1. 4to, orig cloth; broken. With 120 plates. Last 2 plates with red mark in margin. L Nov 14 (171) £450

Anr copy. 3 vols. 4to, orig cloth; stained. With 120 tinted litho lates, 3 tipped-in from anr Ed. pn Dec 12 (365) £380 [Franks]

Roberts, Capt. George

— The Four Years of Voyages. L, 1726. 8vo, contemp sheep; worn, joints & spine cracked. With folding map & 4 plates. Some browning. sg May 21 (89) $400

Roberts, John S., of Newcastle —& Others

— The Life and Explorations of David Livingstone, LL.D.... L, [1874-77]. 4to, orig cloth. bba Sept 19 (63) £55 [Sanderson]

Roberts, Kenneth, 1885-1957

— Lydia Bailey. Garden City, 1947. One of 1,050. With page from orig typescript inserted. O Mar 31 (156) $50

— Oliver Wiswell. One of 1,050. In chipped d/j Tapestain at gutter of tp. O Aug 25 (154) $80

— Trending Into Maine. Bost., 1938. One of 1,075, but this copy lacking extra suite of plates. Illus by N. C. Wyeth. O Aug 25 (155) $60

Roberts, Lewes, 1596-1640
— The Merchants Mappe of Commerce. L, 1700. ("The Merchants Map of Commerce.") Folio, old calf; worn & scuffed, joints tender. bbc Sept 23 (252) $200

Roberts, Thomas Sadler
— The Birds of Minnesota. Minneapolis, 1932. One of 300. 2 vols. 4to, bdg not described. With 92 color plates. K Sept 29 (80) $120
Anr copy. Orig half mor by Kittredge; spine ends scuffed, half-inch tear at head of Vol I. wa Mar 5 (485) $140

Roberts, Warren
— Bibliography of D. H. Lawrence. L, 1963. In d/j. O Dec 17 (153) $60

Roberts, William. See: Ward & Roberts

Roberts, William, 1862-1940
— The Book-Hunter in London. L, 1895. cb Oct 17 (803) $80

Robertson, Archibald, of Charles St.
— A Topographical Survey of the Great Road from London to Bath.... L, 1792. 2 vols. 8vo, contemp calf; upper cover of Vol II detached. With 65 plates. Lacking map. DW Jan 29 (97) £155

Robertson, David, fl.1794
— A Tour through the Isle of Man. L, 1794. 8vo, contemp calf gilt; rubbed, rebacked with orig backstrip laid down. With map & 8 plates. L Nov 14 (117) £60

Robertson, Edward Graeme
— Early Buildings of Southern Tasmania. Melbourne, 1970. 2 vols. 4to, bds, in d/js. kh Nov 11 (624) A$160
— Sydney Lace. Ornamental Cast Iron in Architecture.... Melbourne, 1962. 4to, syn, in d/j. kh Nov 11 (625) A$50
— Victorian Heritage. Ornamental Cast Iron in Architecture. Melbourne, 1960. 4to, cloth, in d/j coated with plastic & repaired. kh Nov 11 (626) A$50

Robertson, Edward Graeme —& Craig, Edith N.
— Early Houses of Northern Tasmania.... Melbourne, 1964. One of 1,000. 2 vols. 4to, cloth, in d/js. kh Nov 11 (628) A$440

Robertson, John Wooster. See: Grabhorn Printing

Robertson, William, 1721-93
— L'Histoire de l'Amerique. Paris, 1778. 2 vols. 4to, 19th-cent half calf. With 4 folding maps & folding plate. Some browning. SI June 10 (872) LIt400,000
— The History of the Reign of the Emperor Charles V.... Phila., 1812. 2d American Ed. 3 vols. 4to, lea. sp Feb 6 (151) $85

Robins, Benjamin, 1707-51
— New Principles of Gunnery.... L, 1742. 1st Ed. 8vo, 18th-cent calf gilt; worn, joints split, front free endpaper with portion torn away. With folding plate. Tp stained. S July 1 (1326) £280 [Middleton]

Robins, William Palmer
— Etching Craft. L, 1922. One of 65 with sgd drypoint by Robins. Half cloth; soiled. sg Feb 6 (244) $80

Robinson, Alan James
— A Fowl Alphabet. Twenty-six Wood Engravings.... Easthampton MA: Cheloniidae Press, 1986. One of 50 with suite of engravings. Lettering by Suzanne Moore. Orig bdg. Schlosser copy. P June 17 (612) $600

Robinson, Alfred, 1806-95
— Life in California during a Residence of Several Years.... NY, 1846. 2 parts in 1 vol. 12mo, cloth; spine ends frayed. With 9 plates. Inkstains on a few leaves, chiefly marginal. sg June 18 (118) $350
— Life in California before the Conquest. Oakland, 1947. One of 750. cb Nov 14 (181) $50

Robinson, Charles N.
— Old Naval Prints, their Artists and Engravers. L: The Studio, 1924. One of 1,500. 4to, orig cloth, in d/j. Some foxing. kh Nov 11 (199) A$250
Anr copy. Orig cloth. O Sept 23 (209) $80

Robinson, Edwin Arlington, 1869-1935
— The Torrent and the Night Before. Gardiner ME: Ptd for the Author, 1896. 1st Ed. 12mo, ptd wraps; frayed & split along spine. Inscr but with name of recipient erased. O May 26 (157) $900

Robinson, Stanford F. H.
— Celtic Illuminative Art.... Dublin, 1908. 4to. DW Apr 8 (372) £65

Robinson, William, 1838-1935
— Flora and Sylva. L, 1903-5. 3 vols. 4to, orig half vellum; dampstained. S Feb 26 (937) £280 [Montevecchi]
Anr copy. Orig cloth. W July 8 (365) £260

Robinson, William Davis
— Memoirs of the Mexican Revolution. L, 1821. 2 vols. 8vo, lea gilt; rubbed. Some foxing. NH May 30 (359) $225

Robinson, William Heath, 1872-1944

— The Adventures of Uncle Lubin. L, 1902. 4to, orig cloth; spine ends & corners scuffed. With colored frontis. Some grubby marks. L Feb 27 (129) £220

Anr Ed. NY, 1902. Orig cloth; hinges cracked. With colored frontis & 49 plates. Prelims spotted. S Nov 14 (135) £280 [Ross]

— Bill the Minder. L, 1912. One of 380. 4to, orig pictorial bds; soiled. With 16 color plates. Inscr in 1944 by "Granny Heath Robinson". S Apr 28 (45) £260 [Proctor]

— Railway Ribaldry. L, 1935. 4to, orig wraps; minor soiling. O July 14 (166) $60

— The Saintly Hun, a Book of German Virtues. L: Duckworth, [1917]. Folio, orig wraps. bba Feb 27 (377) £90 [Frew]

Roboaut, Alfred

— L'Oeuvre complet de Eugene Delacroix. Paris, 1885. 4to, half lea gilt; spine chipped, bumped. Met Apr 27 (77) $350

Roborovskii, Vsevolod Ivanovich

— Trudy ekspeditsii...po Tsentral'noi Azii. St. Petersburg, 1899-1902. Parts 1-2 (of 3) in 5 vols. 8vo, orig wraps; torn, 2 lacking. With 36 plates & 5 folding maps. C May 20 (333) £700 [Randall]

Robson, George Fennell

See also: Britton & Robson

— Scenery of the Grampian Mountains. L, 1819. Oblong folio, contemp half mor; rebacked preserving orig backstrip. With hand-colored folding map & 41 hand-colored plates. C May 20 (117) £1,050 [Simon Finch]

Robson, Joseph

— An Account of Six Years Residence in Hudson's Bay.... L, 1752. 1st Ed. 8vo, contemp calf; rebacked, forecorners worn. With folding plan & 2 folding maps. Edge of each closely trimmed; some soiling to text. CNY Oct 8 (222) $900

Rochambeau, Rene Lacrois de Vimeux, Comte de

— Bibliographie des oeuvres de La Fontaine. Paris, 1911. One of 300. Bound in 1 vol. Modern bds, orig front wrap bound in. Ck Nov 1 (494) £50

Roche, Odilon

— Les Meubles de la Chine. Paris: Calavas, [c.1925]. 1st & 1d Series. 4to, loose as issued, in half cloth folders; rubbed. With 54 plates in each folder. DW Mar 11 (740) £90

Rochefort, Charles de, b.1605

— Histoire naturelle et morale des Iles Antilles de l'Amerique. Rotterdam, 1658. Issue with Dedication sgd C. de Rochefort, but this copy with Preface in 8 pages. 4to, contemp vellum. With engraved title, port of Amproux, 30 half-page & 13 full-page plates. Lower portion of many leaves dampstained; small piece torn from blank corner of XI. pn May 14 (17) £920 [Phelps]

— The History of the Carriby-Islands, viz., Barbados, St. Christophers.... L, 1666. 1st Ed in English. Folio, contemp calf; rebacked, old spine preserved. With 6 (of 9) plates. Missing plates supplied in facsimle. bba Mar 26 (335) £190 [Poel]

Anr copy. Contemp calf; rebacked, worn. With 9 plates. Tp cut down & mtd; lacking final blank; some browning. C Oct 30 (77) £420 [Sotheran]

Rock, Marion T.

— Illustrated History of Oklahoma. Topeka, 1890. 8vo, orig cloth; worn, front inner hinge broken, front flyleaf & frontis detached. NH May 30 (399) $250

Rocque, John

— A New and Accurate Survey of the Cities of London and Westminster.... L, 1747. Folio, contemp bds; worn. With 16 double-page sheets. Sheet 1 strengthened & repaired along plate-mark; Sheet 15 split without loss; some browning. S Nov 21 (111) £650 [Marlborough]

Anr Ed. L, 1751 [but 1769]. Folio, later half mor. With map on 16 double-page sheets, mtd on guards throughout, plus an additional double-page hand-colored map, A New Survey of the Environs of London, 1817. Occasional minor marginal tears repaired. C Oct 30 (137) £1,200 [Woodruff]

— A Plan of the Cities of London and Westminster.... L, 1746. 2 vols, including 1747 Index. 4to, modern half calf & contemp bds (rebacked). With double-page index map & 24 double-page mapsheets. Some browning. S Nov 21 (110) £1,400 [Marlborough]

Rodd, James Rennell, Baron Rennell

— Rose Leaf and Apple Leaf. Phila., 1882. Intro by Oscar Wilde. 8vo, orig vellum; bowed. sg Mar 5 (331) $130

Rodenbach, Georges

— Le Carillonneur. Paris, 1926. One of 280, with an extra suite of etchings avec remarques, some in 2 states. Illus by Louis Titz. Mor gilt, orig wraps bound in. S Apr 28 (12) £250 [Weston]

Rodenberg, Julius. See: Simon & Rodenberg

Rodin, August

— Les Cathedrales de France. Paris, 1914. 4to, orig wraps; worn. bba Apr 9 (251) £55 [Weston]

Rodin, Auguste

— L'Art. Paris, 1911. Lea, orig wraps bound in; front cover detached, spine def. Inscr, June 1913. Epstein copy. sg Apr 30 (398) $275

Rodler, Hieronymus

— Perspectiva. Eyn schoen nuetzlich Buechlin und Unterweisung der Kunst des Messens. Frankfurt: Cyriacus Jacob, 1546. Folio, modern bds; spine def. Lacking final blank. S May 28 (13) £2,100 [Halwas]

Rodrigues, Joao Barbosa

— Sertum palmarum Brasiliensium ou Relation des palmiers nouveaux du Bresil. Brussels, 1903. 2 vols. Folio, half mor; worn, hinges splitting. Lacking 1 port; repaired tears to some plates & leaves; some images with adhesive loss from cellotape; some soiling. CNY June 9 (158) $3,500

Roe, Fred

— Ancient Coffers and Cupboards: their History and Description.... L, 1902. 4to, orig cloth; stained, rebacked with new endpapers, orig spine retained. Frontis waterstained. K July 12 (154) $55

Roeloffs, Roeloff

— Cyclus von Schiffen aller seefahrenden Nationen. Hamburg: Charles fuchs, 1839. Oblong 4to, orig half cloth; soiled. With 50 hand-colored plates, some heightened with gum-arabic. Tp stamped; some thumbmarks in fore-corners. S Nov 21 (221) £4,500 [Maggs]

Roesel von Rosenhof, August Johann

— De natuurlyke historie der insecten. Haarlem & Amst., [1765-88]. 4 vols in 8 (without Supplement). 4to, contemp half calf; scuffed, small tears in a few hinges. With hand-colored frontis to Vols I-III, port & 356 hand-colored plates on 288 leaves. C Oct 30 (290) £3,200 [Junk]

Roethel, Hans Konrad

— Kandinsky: Das graphische Werk. Cologne, [1970]. 4to, orig cloth. HH May 12 (2352) DM3,200

Roger-Marx, Claude

— Bonnard: Lithographe. Monte Carlo, 1952. 4to, orig wraps. bba Oct 24 (353) £60 [Collinge & Clark]

— L'Oeuvre grave de Vuillard. Monte Carlo, [1948]. 4to, cloth, in d/j. bba Feb 13 (66) £160 [Holstein]; bba Mar 26 (10) £120 [Sims Reed]

Anr copy. Orig wraps over bds; chipped. bbc Apr 27 (491) $210

Rogers, Bruce, 1870-1957

— Paragraphs on Printing Elicited from Bruce Rogers in Talks with James Hendrickson.... NY, 1943. 4to, cloth. pba Aug 20 (181) $60

— The Work of Bruce Rogers: Catalogue of an Exhibition Arranged by the A.I.G.A. NY, 1939. wa Mar 5 (135) $55

Rogers, Fairman

— A Manual of Coaching. L, 1900. 8vo, orig cloth; rubbed, spine worn. bba Dec 19 (153) £160 [Binns]; pnE Aug 12 (43) £120

Rogers Locomotive & Machine Works

— A Reproduction of Rogers Locomotive & Machine Works Illustrated Catalogue. Berkeley, 1963. One of 1,250. cb Feb 13 (266) $60

Rogers, Meyric Reynold

— Carl Milles: An Interpretation of his Work. New Haven, 1940. Folio, cloth. sg Feb 6 (189) $80

Rogers, Robert, 1731-95

— A Concise Account of North America.... L, 1765. 8vo, contemp sheep; rubbed. Soiled. bba Jan 30 (121) £500 [Felcone]

— Journals of Major Robert Rogers.... L, 1765. 1st Ed. 8vo, contemp half calf; rubbed. bba Jan 30 (122) £500 [Felcone]

Rogers, Samuel, 1763-1855

See also: Fore-Edge Paintings

— An Epistle to a Friend.... L, 1798. 1st Ed. 4to, calf. Author's copy, with his holograph revisions. L Nov 14 (312) £450

— Poems. L, 1834. 8vo, mor gilt by F. Bedford. With 72 proof vignettes. Inscr to Arthur Burgess by John Ruskin & with ALs by William Pickering. Ck Oct 18 (221) £380

[-] [Sale Catalogue] Catalogue of the Celebrated Collection of Works of Art.... L: Christie & Manson, 1856. Bdg broken. cb Oct 17 (813) $55

Rogers, Will

— Ether and Me or "Just Relax." NY, 1929. In d/j. Inscr to Tiny Johnston. sg Oct 17 (85) $275

Rogers, Capt. Woodes, d.1732

— A Cruising Voyage Round the World.... L, 1712. 1st Ed. 2 parts in 1 vol. 8vo, contemp calf; rebacked. With 5 folding maps. Some discoloration. Phillipps copy. S Feb 26 (782) £700 [Ramblers]

Anr Ed. L, 1718. 8vo, contemp calf;

rebacked, spine worn. With 5 folding maps. S Nov 15 (1144) £400 [Potter]

Anr copy. Contemp calf; rebacked, spine worn, joints cracked. S June 25 (31) £600 [Notoras]

Rogissard, ——, Sieur de

— Les Delices de l'Italie. Leiden, 1706. 3 vols. 12mo, contemp calf. Some browning. SI June 10 (874) LIt1,800,000

Roh, Franz —& Tschichold, Jan

— Photo-eye. Stuttgart, 1929. 4to, orig wraps. B May 12 (564) HF650

Rohault, Jacques

— Tractatus physicus. Amst.: Joannes Wouters, 1708. 8vo, old bds. With 19 folding plates. sg Nov 14 (314) $225

Rohlfs, Anna Katharine Green. See: Green, Anna Katharine

Rohrbach, Carl —& Kretschmer, Albert

— The Costumes of all Nations.... L, 1882. Folio, modern mor gilt, orig cloth bound in. With additional chromolitho title & 104 chromolitho plates. pn Apr 23 (208) £150

Roland, George

— A Treatise on the Theory and Practice of the Art of Fencing. Edin., 1823. 8vo, 19th-cent half sheep; worn. With 12 litho plates. sg Mar 26 (272) $120

Rolando, Guzman

— The Modern Art of Fencing.... L, 1822. 24mo, later vellum gilt. With 22 hand-colored plates. sg Mar 26 (274) $350

Rolewinck, Werner, 1425-1502

— Fasciculus temporum. Venice: Erhard Ratdolt, 24 Nov 1480. Folio, later vellum; soiled. Index misbound at end; 2 small wormholes in 10 leaves. 75 (of 76) leaves; lacking 1st blank. Goff R-261. C Dec 16 (162) £1,500 [Licini]

Anr Ed. [Cologne: Ludwig von Renchen?, c.1483]. Folio, recent paper bds with vellum spine having painted monograms in roundels. Types 90G (text), 180G (headings); 53 lines; rubricated; roundels & cuts hand-colored in green, brown & russet; last leaf mtd on recent paper; some worming, mostly marginal. 74 leaves. Goff R-269. P Dec 12 (80) $3,000

Anr Ed. [Strassburg: Johann Pruess, not before 1490]. 4to, contemp lea-backed wooden bds. Some worming & spotting. 96 leaves. Goff R-276. FD Dec 2 (37) DM4,400

Rolfe, Frederick William

— Chronicles of the House of Borgia. L, 1901. 1st Ed. Orig cloth; rubbed. With 10 plates. DW Oct 2 (389) £75

Rolland, Romain

— Jean-Christophe. Paris: Cahiers de la Quinzaine, 1904-12. 1st Ed. 17 vols. 8vo, half mor gilt by Stroobants, orig wraps bound in. Bound in are 6 A Ls s. S May 28 (433) £2,300 [Beres]

Rolland, Victor

— Armouries des familles contenues dans l'Armorial General.... Paris & The Hague, 1903-26. 6 vols. 4to, contemp half mor; rubbed. S July 9 (327) £250 [Milkain]

Rolleston, Samuel

— Oinos Krithinos. A Dissertation concerning the Origin and Antiquity of Barley Wine. Oxford, 1750. Bound with: A Philosophical Dialogue concerning Decency. L, 1751. 4to, contemp half calf; rebacked & rubbed. bba Apr 9 (86) £170 [Bickersteth]

Rollin, Charles

— The Ancient History of the Egyptians.... L, 1734-39. 13 vols in 14. 12mo, contemp calf; worn, 1 or 2 covers detached. O Mar 31 (158) $130

Roma...

— Roma antica e moderna, o sia nuova descrizione di tutti gl'edifici antichi & moderni sacri.... Rome, 1765. 3 vols. 8vo, contemp mor. HH May 12 (732) DM1,300

Romaine, Lawrence B.

— A Guide to American Trade Catalogs, 1744-1900. NY, 1960. O Mar 31 (159) $70

Roman, Alfred

— The Military Operations of General Beauregard in the War Between the States. NY, 1884. 1st Ed. 2 vols. 8vo, orig cloth; spine ends & corners frayed. bbc Feb 17 (114) $60

Romance. See: Malory, Sir Thomas

Romano, Giacomo

— Il primo Libro de Scrivere.... Rome, 1589. Oblong 4to, modern lea. Lacking at least 2 leaves; browned; repairs to outer margin of tp & a few other leaves; final leaf torn with loss; port leaf, A4 & I1 holed; tear in decorative margin of K1. C June 24 (244) £300 [Gherucci]

Romer, Isabella F.

— A Pilgrimage to the Temples and Tombs of Egypt.... L, 1846. 2 vols. 8vo, later half calf; rubbed. With tinted litho frontises & 3 plates, 1 hand-colored. Lacking half-titles; some spotting. S July 1 (792) £200 [Sotheran]

Ronalds, Alfred

— The Fly-Fisher's Entomology. L, 1836. 1st Ed. 8vo, orig cloth; rebacked. With 19 hand-colored plates. Some foxing. bba Sept 5 (170) £420 [J. Mason]

Anr copy. Modern mor; worn, rear cover gouged. Koopman copy. O Oct 29 (243) $1,000

3d Ed. L, 1844. 8vo, cloth; stained. With 20 plates. DW Oct 2 (163) £60

Ronalds, Hugh, 1759-1833

— Pyrus Malus Brentfordiensis: or, a Concise Description of Selected Apples. L, 1831. Folio, contemp half mor gilt; upper joint split. With 42 hand-colored plates. Some foxing. S June 25 (66) £1,200 [Heuer]

Ronphile,——

— La Chyromantie naturelle de Ronphyle. Paris, 1665. 8vo, old half vellum. Some browning & soiling. sg Mar 12 (235) $175

Anr Ed. Paris, 1671. 8vo, old vellum. Tp stamped. sg Mar 12 (236) $175

Ronsard, Pierre de, 1524-85

See also: Eragny Press

— Les Amours. Paris: Ambroise Vollard, 1915. One of 250. Illus by Emile Bernard. 4to, unsewn in orig wraps. With 16 plates hors texte. Schlosser copy. P June 18 (418) $700

— Livret de folastries. Paris, 1838-40. One of 25 on verge de Montval, hors commerce. Illus by Aristide Maillol. 4to, unsewn in orig wraps. P Dec 12 (67) $1,200

Roo, Gerard von

— Annales rerum belli domique ab Austriacis Habspurgicae gentis principibus a Rudolpho primo, usque ad Carolum V. Gestarum.... Innsbruck: Joannes Agricola, 1592. 1st Ed. Folio, contemp blind-tooled pigskin & corners over pastebd, stained vellum sides with blind fillets; rubbed, corners worn. Minor staining. C June 24 (343) £850 [Rosenthal]

Anr copy. 19th-cent half lea. SI Dec 5 (999) LIt700,000

Rooses, Max, 1839-1914

— L'Oeuvre de P. P. Rubens. Antwerp, 1886-92. 5 vols. 4to, contemp half mor; joints rubbed. S Feb 11 (187) £600 [Artemide]

Roosevelt, Eleanor, 1884-1962

— This I Remember. NY, [1949]. One of 1,000 L.p. copies. bbc Dec 9 (412) $125

Roosevelt, Franklin D., 1882-1945

[-] The Democratic Book 1936. [N.p., c.1936]. Ltd Ed. Orig lea; ends worn, spine ends def. wa Mar 5 (297) $450

— The Happy Warrior, Alfred E. Smith.... Bost., 1928. 8vo, In d/j. Inscr to M.A.L., 5 Oct 1928. P June 16 (272) $2,500

— On Our Way. NY, 1934. Inscr to Babe (Missy Le Hand). P June 16 (273) $1,600

Anr copy. 8vo, cloth. Inscr to Louis Howe. wd Dec 12 (441) $1,400

— Public Papers and Addresses. NY, 1938-[50]. 13 vols. Cloth, in d/js. bbc Dec 9 (415) $75

Anr copy. Vols I-IX. sg Dec 5 (218) $50

— State of New York. Public Papers of Franklin D. Roosevelt, Forty-Eighth Governor of the State of New York, 1929. Albany, 1930. Inscr to Ernest M. Lindley. wa Oct 19 (338) $260

— Whither Bound? Bost., 1926. In d/j. Inscr to M.A.L., 19 June 1926. P June 16 (271) $2,500

Anr copy. Inscr to Mamie Low. sg Sept 12 (207) $750

Roosevelt, Theodore, 1858-1919

— African Game Trails. NY, 1910. One of 500. 2 vols. 8vo, orig cloth. bba Jan 16 (365) £60 [Harrington]

— Big Game Hunting in the Rockies and on the Great Plains. NY & L, 1899. One of 1,000 L.p. copies, sgd. sg Jan 9 (305) $425

One of 1,000 L.p. copies. Epstein copy. sg Apr 30 (400) $475

— Hunting Trips of a Ranchman. NY, 1885. Medora Ed, one of 500. 4to, orig cloth; rubbed. Sgd on a loosely inserted piece of cloth. pn Sept 12 (303) £130 [Head]

Anr copy. Orig cloth; front joint starting. sg Jan 9 (306) $375

— The Naval War of 1812. NY, 1882. 1st Ed. 8vo, orig cloth; extremities worn. NH May 30 (472) $230

— Outdoor Pastimes of an American Hunter. NY, 1905. 4to, orig cloth; spine ends worn. sg May 21 (91) $60

— The Wilderness Hunter: An Account of the Big Game of the United States.... NY, [1893]. 8vo, orig cloth. sg May 21 (90) $120

— The Winning of the West. NY, 1900. One of 200 L.p. sets, with leaf of Ms. 4 vols. 4to, half mor; needs rebdg. Sold w.a.f. sg Dec 5 (219) $750

Anr Ed. NY, 1906. 6 vols. Half lea; spines faded. sp Sept 22 (19) $65

— Works. NY, 1900. 15 vols. 12mo, half calf; extremities worn. sg Mar 5 (282) $175

Anr Ed. Phila., 1903. One of 26. 15 (of 22) vols only. Mor gilt. With plates in 2 states. cb Dec 5 (118) $1,700

Uniform Ed, Ltd Ed. 22 vols. Mor extra with Theodore Roosevelt's gilt monogram. With 88 plates, each in 3 states. Presentation copy, inscr, to Louis of Bergdolle; this copy with c.350 orig marginal ink drawings by Daniel Garber & with fragment of a holograph Ms of Roosevelt bound into Vol I of The Winning of the West. CNY June 9 (171) $4,000

National Ed. NY, [1926]. 20 vols. In d/js. K Sept 29 (384) $130

Roosevelt, Theodore, 1858-1919 —& Grinnell, George Bird, 1849-1938

— American Big-Game Hunting. NY, 1893. 8vo, cloth; worn. Koopman copy. O Oct 29 (245) $110

Root, Frank A. —& Connelley, William Elsey, 1855-1930

— The Overland Stage to California. Topeka, 1901. Inked stamp to front free endpaper. sg June 18 (120) $120

Root, Riley

— Journal of the Travels...St. Josephs to Oregon.... Galesburg, Ill., 1850. 1st Ed. 8vo, cloth; spine tarnished. cb Nov 14 (182) $80

Roper, J. See: Cole & Roper

Rops, Felicien

— Dix eaux-fortes pour illustrer Les Diaboliques de J. Barbey-d'Aurevilly. Paris, 1886. 12mo, orig bds. With 10 etchings on loose sheets. S May 28 (434) £450 [Sims Reed]

Roques, Joseph

— Plantes usuelles, indigenes et exotiques. Paris, 1809. 2d Ed. 2 vols. 4to, half lea gilt. With colored engraved title & 132 colored plates. SI June 10 (883) LIt2,200,000

Roquet, Antoine Ernest. See: Thoinan, Ernest

Rosaccio, Giuseppe

— Teatro del cielo, e della terra. Venice: Domenico Lovisa, [c.1660]. 4 parts in 1 vol. 8vo, modern half calf. bba Sept 5 (244) £200 [J. Franks]

— Viaggio da Venetia a Constantinopoli per mare, e per terra.... Venice, 1606. Oblong 4to, modern half mor. With 77 plates & maps. Tp in facsimile; some thumb-marks. S Nov 21 (234) £3,000 [Lepanto]

Rosborough, E. H. ("Polly")

— Tying and Fishing the Fuzzy Nymphs. Harrisburg: Stackpole, [1978]. One of 300, with artificial fly in sunken mount on front cover. Syn gilt. Sgd. Koopman copy. O Oct 29 (246) $180

Roscoe, Margaret Lace

— Floral Illustrations of the Seasons. L: T. Richardson & Son, [watermarked 1834-36]. 4to, contemp half lea; spine missing, covers detached. With 55 hand-colored plates. Some plates trimmed within plate-mark; some discoloration. S June 25 (67) £2,000 [Lack]

Roscoe, Sydney

— Thomas Bewick: A Bibliography Raisonne. L, 1953. O Sept 24 (212) $80

Roscoe, Thomas, 1791-1871

— The Tourist in Spain. L, 1835-38. 4 vols. 8vo, orig mor gilt. Each vol with engraved title & 20 plates on india paper; Vols I-II with wood-engraved headpieces, each with a 2d state on india paper. S Feb 26 (751) £550 [Russell]

Roscoe, William, 1753-1831

— The Butterfly's Ball and the Grasshopper's Feast. L, 1808. 16mo, orig wraps; rubbed. With engraved title & 7 plates. bba Oct 10 (114) £110 [Moon]

— Monandrian Plants of the Order Scitamineae.... Liverpool, [1824]-28. One of 150. Folio, contemp half mor; rubbed, spine ends worn. With 112 hand-colored plates. Some spotting. pn Mar 19 (323) £6,000 [Burden]

Roscoe Library, William

— [Sale Catalogue] Catalogue of the...Library. Liverpool, 1816. 8vo, modern half cloth. Waterstained in upper margin; priced in ink & pencil. bba May 28 (563) £90 [Maggs]

Rose, John Holland

— The Life of Napoleon. L, 1912. 2 vols. School bdg of calf gilt. wa Mar 5 (64) $85

Rose, Thomas. See: Noble & Rose

Rose, Thomas, Topographer

— Westmoreland, Cumberland, Durham and Northumberland L, 1832-[35]. 3 vols. 4to, contemp cloth; spine worn. With 213 views on 108 plates. DW May 13 (97) £180

— Westmorland, Cumberland, Durham and Northumberland L, 1832-[35]. 3 vols. 4to, contemp half lea; edges rubbed. With engraved title, 2 frontises & 191 views on 124 leaves only. pn Dec 12 (324A) £60 [Magnagal]

Anr Ed. L, 1833-[35]. Illus by Thomas Allom. 4to, contemp half calf; covers detached; backstrip def. With engraved title & 214 views. Some spotting. DW Nov 20 (22) £155

Anr copy. Half lea gilt; rubbed. With engraved title & 124 views on 62 plates, many hand-colored. L Nov 14 (119) £220

Anr Ed. L, 1838. 4to, contem half calf gilt; rubbed, worn. With title & 215 views on 108 leaves. Spotted & soiled. DW Jan 29 (98) £180

Rosenbach, A. S. W., 1876-1952
See also: Widener Library, Harry Elkins

— An American Jewish Bibliography.... [Phila.], 1926. Bdg with inner joints cracked. K Sept 29 (387) $65

— A Book Hunter's Holiday. Bost., 1936. One of 760. Inscr. K Sept 29 (386) $80

— Books and Bidders: the Adventures of a Bibliophile. Bost., 1927. One of 785. Half cloth; covers stained. sg May 21 (296) $90

— Early American Children's Books. Portland, 1933. One of 88 on Zerkall Halle. 4to, half mor. sg Oct 31 (295) $200

Anr copy. Pigskin. Epstein copy. sg Apr 30 (401) $1,200

One of 585. Bds; rubbed. bbc Dec 9 (193) $340

Anr copy. Bdg not stated, unopened. Sgd. cb Oct 17 (816) $275

Anr Ed. NY, 1966. O Sept 24 (213) $50

Rosenberg, Isaac

— Youth. L, 1915. 1st Ed. Orig wraps. S July 1 (1041) £150 [Sarner]

Rosenberg, J. See: Bock & Rosenberg

Rosenberg, Jakob

— Jacob van Ruisdael. Berlin, 1928. One of 360. Folio, orig cloth; rebacked retaining orig spine, new endpapers. S Feb 11 (189) £650 [Schmidt & Gunther]

Rosenberg, Mary Elizabeth

— The Museum of Flowers. L, 1856. 8vo, orig cloth. With 37 hand-colored plates. bba Apr 30 (318) £450 [Neale]

Rosenthal, Leonard

— The Kingdom of the Pearl. L, [1920]. One of 675. Illus by Edmund Dulac. In d/j. sg Sept 26 (101) $400

Anr copy. Mor gilt by Bayntun with gilt crown inlaid with 25 pearls on front cover. sg Nov 7 (74) $1,300

Anr copy. Half cloth; front joint torn. sg Jan 30 (47) $250

Rosieres, Francois de

— Stemmatum Lotharingiae ac Barri ducum tomi septem. Paris: Guillaume Chaudiere, 1580. Folio, contemp blind-tooled pigskin over wooden bds; lacking front free endpaper. sg Oct 24 (278) $700

Rosiglia, Marco

— Rispetti d'amore. Siena: Symione di Nicolo & Giovanni di Alexandro, 1512. 8vo, modern mor gilt. Tp & margins of early lives spotted. C Dec 16 (75) £1,800 [Jackson]

Ross, Alexander, 1783-1856

— The Fur Hunters of the Far West. L, 1855. 2 vols. 8vo, modern half mor gilt. sg June 18 (481) $400

Ross, Andrew, S.S.C.

— Old Scottish Regimental Colours. Edin., 1885. Folio, cloth; marked, front hinge weak. kh Nov 11 (384) A$160

Ross, Frederick

— The Ruined Abbeys of Britain. L: Wm. Mackenzie, [1882]. 2 vols. 4to, orig cloth. With 12 colored plates. L Nov 14 (120) £70; SI Dec 5 (590) LIt350,000

Ross, James, of Van Dieman's Land

— South Australia. Mr. J. Ross's Explorations, 1874. [Adelaide, 1875]. Folio, unbound as issued. R. J. Maria copy. C June 25 (266) £320 [Arnold]

Ross, Sir James Clark, 1800-62

— A Voyage of Discovery and Research in the Southern and Antarctic Regions... L, 1847. 1st Ed. 2 vols. 8vo, modern mor, orig cloth bound in. With 8 tinted lithos & 8 maps & charts, 2 folding. W July 8 (274) £800

Ross, John —& Gunn, Hugh

— The Book of the Red Deer and Empire Big Game. L, 1925. One of 500. 4to, orig cloth; soiled. sg Jan 9 (307) $130

Ross, Sir John, 1777-1856

— Narrative of a Second Voyage in Search of a North-West Passage.... L, 1835. 2 vols, including Appendix. 4to, contemp cloth; rebacked, Vol I spine preserved. With hand-colored folding chart & 49 views & charts, including 21 colored lithos. Frontis & tp frayed; folding chart with corner tear; some spotting; tp & 2 other leaves stamped. b June 22 (269) £140

Anr copy. 2 vols, including Appendix. 8vo, library cloth; upper cover detached. With 20 plates & 5 maps. Vol I lacking frontis & folding map. Library markings. bba Oct 10 (255) £50 [B. Bailey]

Anr copy. 8vo, contemp calf; rubbed. With 25 plates (9 colored) & 6 maps. Some spotting. bba May 14 (313) £120 [Hildebrandt]

Anr copy. Modern mor gilt. With 30 plates, 9 hand-colored & 5 maps (large folding map, colored in outline, at end). 1 leaf torn & repaired. DW Apr 8 (61) £170

Anr copy. 2 vols (including Appendix). 8vo, early half lea gilt; minor defs. With folding map & 50 plates & maps, 21 in color. kh Nov 11 (385) A$380

Anr copy. With: Appendix to the Narrative.... L, 1835. 8vo, modern half calf. With 2 frontises, 42 plates (some hand-colored) & 6 maps. Frontis to Narrative cut round & mtd; most plates foxed. W July 8 (278) £180

Vol I only. Calf gilt. Plates & maps partly colored. Folding map torn & repaired. Ms map of the arctic laid in. Manney copy. P Oct 11 (269) $1,900

— A Voyage of Discovery, Made under the Orders of the Admiralty...for the Purpose of Exploring Baffin's Bay.... L, 1819. 2d Ed. 4to, later half calf gilt. With 2 folding frontises. W July 8 (277) £220

Ross, Thomas. See: MacGibbon & Ross

Rosset, Francois de

— Le romant des chevaliers de la gloire.... Paris: Pierre Bertaud, 1612. 3 parts in 1 vol. 4to, 18th-cent calf with arms of the Bernstorff family; rubbed, joints split. S July 9 (1098) £200 [Booth]

Rossetti, Christina Georgina, 1830-94

— Goblin Market. L, 1893. Illus by Laurence Housman. 8vo, orig cloth; spine dulled. DW Apr 8 (522) £90

Anr Ed. L, 1933. Illus by Arthur Rackham. Orig wraps, in d/j. With 4 colored plates. kh Nov 11 (200) A$50

One of 410. Orig vellum. With 4 colored plates Last leaf of text spotted. Manney copy. P Oct 11 (264) $900; sg Nov 7 (175) $550

Anr Ed. Phila., 1933. Orig cloth, in chipped d/j. With 4 colored plates. K Mar 22 (392) $80

— Poems. L, 1910. One of 350. Illus by Florence Harrison. 4to, orig vellum; soiled. With 36 colored plates. bba Apr 9 (312) £340 [Ulysses]

Anr copy. Orig cloth; rubbed & marked. DW Apr 8 (517) £75

— Speaking Likenesses. L, 1874. 1st Ed. Illus by Arthur Hughes. 8vo, orig cloth; uper cover bumped. bba Nov 28 (373) £100 [Marsden]; cb Jan 9 (192) $95

Rossetti, Dante Gabriel, 1828-82
See also: Kelmscott Press

— The House of Life. New Rochelle: Elston Press, 1901. One of 310 on handmade paper. 4to, half cloth; worn. sg Sept 26 (106) $80

— Sir Hugh the Heron. A Legendary Tale. L, 1843. 1st Ed. 4to, half mor by Riviere, orig wraps bound in. Front free endpaper sgd by Charles Brumwell. C June 24 (196) £1,200 [Quaritch]

Rossetti, William Michael, 1829-1919

— Ruskin: Rossetti: Pre-Raphaelitism. L, 1899. One of 250. 4to, orig cloth; spine ends frayed, spine rubbed, hinges cracked. bbc June 29 (182) $65

Rossi, Domenico

— Raccolta di statue antiche e moderne. Rome, 1704. Folio, 19th-cent calf. Lacking Plate 55; Plate 2 cut round, mtd & from anr copy; dedication bound at end before the text. Sold w.a.f. b June 22 (209) £750

Anr Ed. Rome, 1704 [but 1742]. Folio, old half calf. With frontis, title & 162 (of 163) plates. One plate cut down; some staining at edges. S Feb 11 (139) £600 [Erlini]

Rossi, Filippo, fl.1645

— Ritratto di Roma moderna. Rome, 1688. 8vo, modern vellum. Some foxing. SI June 10 (880) LIt550,000

Rossi, Giovanni Bernardo de

— Dizionario storico degli autori ebrei.... Parma: Bodoni, 1802. 2 vols in 1. 8vo, contemp half calf; spine torn at head, rubbed. Some spotting. sg June 25 (35) $250

Rossi, Giovanni Gherardo de

— Scherzi poetici e pittorici. Parma: Bodoni, 1804. 4to, half mor. SI June 9 (157) LIt1,100,000

Rossi, Giovanni Giacomo de

— Insignium Romae templorum prospectus.... Rome, [1684]. Bound with: Disegni vari altari ete capelle nelle chise di Roma. Rome, [1684]. And: Raphael de Sanzio Urbino. Imagines veteris ac Novi Testamenti. Rome, [c.1675]. Folio, contemp calf. Library stamp; some stains & repairs. b June 22 (210) £1,400

Anr copy. Contemp half calf; worn. With 72 plates including title. Some brownstains & waterspots. SI June 10 (887) LIt1,600,000

Rossi, Giovanni Giacomo de —& Falda, Giovanni Battista

— Il Nuovo Teatro delle fabriche et edificii, in prospettiva di Roma moderna. Rome, 1665-99. Parts 1-4 (of 5) in 1 vol. contemp mor gilt; rubbed. With 4 engraved titles, 4 dedications & 134 plates. Minor spotting. S June 25 (197) £4,000 [Pregliasco]

Rossini, Luigi

— Le Antichita dei contorni di Roma. Rome, 1819-23. Folio, 19th-cent half russia gilt by Colnaghi; upper cover detached. With 101 plates. Lacking tp; a few soft creases; some dust-soiling. S June 25 (102) £7,900 [DiCastro]

Anr Ed. Rome, 1824-26. 2 vols. Folio, contemp half vellum gilt; corners bumped, spine abraded. With engraved title & 72 plates. Fore-edge of Plate 69 cropped; marginal soiling to half-title & Plate 50. McCarty-Cooper copy. CNY Jan 25 (65) $12,000

— Le Antichita Romane. Rome, 1829. Folio, contemp half vellum gilt; extremities rubbed, spine chipped. With 101 plates. Folding fore-edge of Plate 86 split through the caption & repaired with cloth; marginal soiling to tp; Plate 101 foxed & dampstained; other minor defs. McCarty-Cooper copy. CNY Jan 25 (66) $17,000

Anr copy. Oblong folio, 19th-cent half mor. Frontis & plates 15 & 86 shaved along right margins; Plate 81 touching upper right neatline; lower edge of Plate 86 dust-soiled & frayed without loss. S June 25 (103) £7,700 [Toscani]

— Gli Archi Trionfali, Onorarii e Funebri degli Antichi Romani.... Rome, [1836]. Folio, contemp half vellum gilt; spine & extremities rubbed. With 73 plates. Last plate cropped; long tear in margin of Plate 58; some foxing; marginal soiling to tp & 3 plates. McCarty-Cooper copy. CNY Jan 25 (67) $8,000

Rossmaessler, E. A.

— Die vier Jahreszeiten. Gotha, 1855. 4to, orig cloth; rebacked. With 4 wood-engraved plates & 17 nature-ptd text illusts of leaves. Some foxing. Schlosser copy. P June 17 (484) $200

Rostand, Edmond, 1868-1918

— Cyrano de Bergerac. Paris, 1898. One of 50 on japon. 8vo, mor extra by Marius Michel, orig wraps bound in. S May 28 (439) £3,200 [Beres]

— La Princesse Lointaine. Paris, 1920. One of 100 for the members of the Societe du Livre. 4to, mor by Meunier, 1928. W July 8 (335) £60

Roth, Henry Ling

— Oriental Silverwork. L, 1910. Orig cloth; rubbed. F Mar 26 (291) $120

Roth, J. See: Schubert & Roth

Roth, Philip

— Goodbye, Columbus.... Bost.: Houghton Mifflin, 1959. In chipped d/j. F Dec 18 (232) $140

Rothenstein, Sir John K. M.

— The Portrait Drawings of William Rothenstein, 1889-1925. L, 1926. One of 520. 4to, orig cloth; worn. sg Feb 6 (246) $130

Rothenstein, Sir William, 1872-1945

— English Portraits. L, 1898. One of 750. 12 orig parts. Folio, orig wraps & portfolio. With 24 ports. O July 14 (168) $100

Rothschild, Lionel Walter, Baron, 1868-1937

— Extinct Birds. L, 1907. One of 300. Folio, half mor. With 45 colored plates & 4 outline plates. Text marginally soiled. CNY Dec 5 (297) $1,800

Rothschild Library, Nathan James Edouard

— Catalogue des livres composant la bibliotheque.... NY: Burt Franklin, [1965]. Ed by Emile Picot. 5 vols. Reprint of the 1884-1920 Ed. O Sept 24 (214) $70; SI June 9 (224) LIt280,000

Rothschild Library, Victor Nathan Meyer

— Rothschild Library: a Catalogue of the Eighteenth-Century Printed Books and Manuscripts. Cambr.: Pvtly ptd, 1954. 1st Ed. 2 vols. 4to, cloth. O Sept 24 (215) $350

Anr Ed. L, 1969. 2 vols. 4to, orig cloth. Ck Nov 1 (496) £140

Anr copy. Cloth. sg May 21 (298) $275

Rottiers, Bernard Eugene Antoine, 1771-1858

— Itineraire de Tiflis a Constantinople. Brussels, 1829. 8vo, 19th-cent half mor gilt, lower wrap preserved. With 7 plates & 3 folding maps & port inserted. Tp repaired. S June 30 (189) £320 [Thor]

Rotz, John. See: Roxburghe Club

Rouault, Georges, 1871-1958

— Divertissement. Paris: Teriade, 1943. One of 1,270. Folio, unbound; text & plates loose in wraps as issued. With 15 mtd color plates. sg Feb 6 (247) $200

— Stella Vespertina. Paris, 1947. Folio, loose as issued in orig wraps. With 12 mtd colored plates. sg Jan 30 (161) $90; sg Apr 2 (260) $90

Roubo, Andre Jacob

— L'Art de Menuisier. Paris, 1769-75. 6 parts in 3 vols. Folio, modern half calf. With 383 plates. Some browning. From: Academie des Sciences. Descriptions des Arts et Metiers. CNY Dec 5 (319) $5,500

— L'Art du menuisier. [Paris], 1769-75. 6 parts. Folio, modern mor by Lesort; rubbed. With 6 divisional titles & 383 plates. Vol VI tp & Plate 337 laid down on heavy paper; Plate 208 creased; some foxing or discoloration; marginal dampstaining to Vol V & last 10 plates of Vol VI. CNY June 9 (172) $2,500

Anr Ed. Paris, 1823. 2 vols. 12mo, orig bds; scuffed. With frontis & 66 plates. Some spotting. Ck Oct 18 (188) £220

Roupell, Arabella E.

— Specimens of the Flora of South Africa. L, 1849. Folio, orig mor gilt; spine repaired, loose. With litho title & 8 plates, all hand-colored. S June 25 (68) £2,000 [Shapero]

Rousseau, Jean Jacques, 1712-78

— La Botanique. Paris, 1822. Illus by Redoute. Folio, 19th-cent half mor gilt; rubbed. With 65 hand-finished color plates. Extra-illus with 2 ports & several watercolor drawings, most soiled & mtd. S June 25 (69) £2,500 [Beaux Arts]

— Du contrat social ou principes du droit politique. Amst., 1762. 8vo, contemp bds; worn. DW Nov 6 (313) £50

— The Miscellaneous Works. L, 1767. 5 vols. 12mo, contemp sheep; worn, several covers loose. sg Oct 17 (358) $200

— La nouvelle Heloise, ou lettres de deux amans. Paris: Cazin, 1781. 7 vols. 8vo, contemp calf gilt. With frontis & 12 plates. Some leaves browned. L.p. copy. S May 13 (861) £280 [Shapero]

— Oeuvres. Geneva, 1782-89. 17 vols. 8vo, contemp calf gilt; some joints splitting, some wear. With port, frontis, 33 plates, 10 plates of music & 13 folding tables. Some browning. bbc Dec 9 (251) $575

Anr copy. 33 vols, including Supplements. 8vo, contemp calf; rubbed, a few joints split. Lacking general title & half-title; some browning; lacking some blanks. pn Apr 23 (97) £260 [Harrington]

Anr Ed. [Paris], 1788-93. 37 (of 39) vols (lacking Vols 37 & 38). 4to, contemp calf. With 44 hand-colored plates. 2 vols badly water-damaged; a few gatherings browned. Sold w.a.f. bba Oct 10 (516) £160 [Elliott]

Rousselet, Louis

— India and its Native Princes.... NY, 1876. 4to, modern cloth incorporating orig cloth; new endpapers. bba May 28 (355) £50 [Mandl]

Anr copy. Half mor; rubbed. O Feb 25 (168) $250

Anr Ed. L, 1878. 4to, contemp mor gilt; rubbed. bba Apr 9 (180) £110 [Remington]

Rousselot de Surgy, Jacques Philibert

— Memoires geographiques, physiques et historiques sur l'Asie, l'Afrique & l'Amerique. Paris: Durand, 1767. 4 vols. 12mo, contemp half sheep gilt; spines worn at top. sg May 21 (92) $250

Rouveyre, Andre

— Apollinaire. Paris, [1952]. One of 30 with an extra suite of the lithos. Illus by Henri Matisse. 4to, unsewn in orig wraps. With 8 orig lithos. S May 28 (230) £1,500

One of 300. Unsewn in orig wraps. With 8 orig lithos. CGen Nov 18 (451) SF2,200

Rouveyre, Edouard. See: Beauchamp & Rouveyre

Roux, Joseph

— Recueil de 163 des principaux Plans des Portes et Rades de la Mediterranee.... Genes: Yves Gravier, 1804. Oblong 4to, contemp sheep; joints & corners rubbed. With engraved title & 163 plans. Tp stained; a few upper margins affected by damp. C May 20 (299) £700 [Bifolco]

Roux, Ludwig Caesar

— L'Escrime dans les Universites allemandes. Paris, 1895. 8vo, later cloth. sg Mar 26 (275) $150

Roux, Marcel. See: Courboin & Roux

Rovinsky, Dmitri Alexandrovich

— Russkya Nardodniya Kartinki. St. Petersburg, 1881. Vols I-II bound in 1 vol only. Contemp half lea; rear joint starting. Plate count not given. sg Feb 6 (250) $70

Rowfant Club. See: Clark, Arthur Henry

Rowlands, Richard, fl.1565-1620

— A Restitution of Decayed Intelligence. L, 1628. 4to, 18th-cent sheep gilt; joints cracked. Some dampstaining at beginning & end. STC 21361. sg Oct 24 (281) $110

— Theatrum crudelitatum haereticorum nostri temporis. Antwerp: Adrien Hubert, 1592. 1st Ed. 4to, later blind-tooled vellum. With large engraving on title & 29 half-page engravings. Thumbed; some stains. B May 12 (15) HF2,600

Rowlandson, Thomas, 1756-1827
See also: Grabhorn Printing

— The Comforts of Bath. L, [1798]. Oblong folio, modern half mor album. With 12 hand-colored plates mtd on card; In this copy only plates 8, 9 & 11 are without Rowlandson's signature & these also have no plate numerals. C May 20 (118) £12,000 [Marlborough]

— Hungarian & Highland Broad Sword. L, 1799. Oblong folio, contemp mor gilt. With colored aquatint title & 23 colored plates & with additional hand-colored plate of The Guards of the Highland Broadsword as taught at Mr. H. Angelo's Academy. C May 20 (120) £2,600 [Maggs]

— Loyal Volunteers of London & Environs.... L: Ackermann, 1798-99. 4to, mor gilt with arms of George III, by Hering, with his ticket. With engraved hand-colored title & 86 hand-colored plates, heightened with gold & silver plus 2 folding plates of Sadlers Flying Artillery & Expedition or Military Fly bound at end. C May 20 (119) £6,500 [Maggs]

Anr copy. Mor gilt for C. J. Sawyer. With hand-colored title & 86 hand-colored plates, most heightened with gold or silver. S June 25 (165) £4,500 [George]

— Miseries of Human Life. L: Ackermann, 1808. Oblong 4to, later half mor. With 49 (of 50) hand-colored plates, including title. Lacking last plate. bba Jan 16 (417) £420 [W. Fleming]

Anr Ed. L: Ackermann, 1808 [watermarked 1811-14]. Oblong 4to, later mor gilt. With 50 hand-colored plates, including title. Small repaired tear to 1 plate margin; dampstaining to margins of 2 others; anr plate with repair to plate mark. C May 20 (121) £1,200 [Maggs]

Rowley, George

— Ambrogio Lorenzetti. Princeton, 1958. 4to, orig cloth, in torn d/j. S Feb 11 (192) £340 [Doll]

Rowley, George Dawson

— Ornithological Miscellany. L, 1875-78. 3 vols. 4to, contemp half mor, orig front wraps to the 14 parts bound in. With litho frontises, 3 distribution maps & 132 plates, including 78 hand-colored. sold w.a.f. C May 20 (212) £1,400 [Greyfriars]

Roworth, C.

— The Art of Defence on Foot with the Broad Sword and Sabre. L, 1798. 8vo, orig bds; extremities worn. With 9 plates. sg Mar 26 (276) $225

Rowson, Susanna Haswell

— Charlotte. A Tale of Truth. Phila., 1794. 1st American Ed, 1st state. 2 vols in 1. 12mo, old calf. Tp & next leaf torn; tear in gutter at pp. 14-15; damage to lower margin of pp.21-22 with loss of 2 or 3 letters; tear in p.27-28 sewn; other marginal tears; Vol Ii with 2d title torn through middle; ink underlining on p.7; repair to 1 leaf; marginal tears. K July 12 (450) $3,300

Roxburghe Club—London

— A Picture Book of the Life of St. Anthony the Abbot.... 1937. bba June 25 (86) £190 [Bennett & Kerr]

— Rotz, John. - The Maps and Text of the Boke of Idrography.... 1981. bba June 25 (87) £400 [Laws]; S June 25 (87) £450 [McCormick]

Roxburghe Library, John Ker, Duke of

— [Sale Catalogue] A Catalogue of the Library.... L, 1812. Bound with: A Supplement to the Catalogue of the Library. L, 1812. Contemp calf; rebacked; detached. Annotated with prices and buyers. cb Oct 17 (821) $425

Roy, Claude

— La France de profil. Lausanne, [1952]. Ltd Ed. 4to, bds, in chipped d/j. sg Oct 8 (65) $700

Royal Academy of Arts—London

— Royal Academy Pictures. L, 1892-1909. 18 vols. 4to, contemp half mor; worn. DW Oct 9 (953) £150

Royal Geographical Society of London

— Journal. L, 1841. Vol 10. Early half calf; rubbed & scuffed. kh Nov 11 (386) A$90

Royal Horticultural Society. See: Horticultural Society of London

Royal Society of Edinburgh

— Transactions. Edin., 1788-1806. Vols I-VI, Part 1. 4to, contemp calf; joints cracked. With 55 folding plates. Vol II lacking half-title; some browning. Ck Nov 29 (236) £320

Royal Society of London

— Philosophical Transactions....Abridged. L, 1809. Vols I-XVIII. Contemp calf gilt. bba Sept 5 (247) £160 [Weiner]

Royaumont, Sieur de. See: Fontaine, Nicolas

Royce, C. C.

— John Bidwell, Pioneer, Statesman, Philanthropist.... Chico, 1906-7. 2 parts in 1 vol. 8vo, half mor. cb Feb 12 (5) $325

Rubeis, Domici de

— Romanae magnitudinis monumenta. Rome, 1699. Oblong folio, contemp vellum; stitching weak. With engraved title, dedication & 135 plates only; lacking plate 106. Marginal dampstaining; inner margins wormed. Ck Sept 6 (62) £480

Ruben, Paul

— Die Reklame: Ihre Kunst und Wissenschaft. Berlin, 1914. 2 vols. 4to, cloth; worn, hinges cracked, rubber stamps on endpapers. sg Apr 2 (242) $600

Rubens, Peter Paul, 1577-1640

— La Gallerie du Palais de Luxembourg. Paris, 1710. Folio, 19th-cent half lea; worn. With engraved title, port & 25 plates. Some spotting & browning. HH May 12 (896) DM3,400

Anr copy. Later bds. With engraved title & 21 plates. pnE Oct 1 (275) £700

Anr copy. Contemp calf; worn & loose. With engraved title, port & 24 plates. Plate margins soiled; lacking dedication leaf. sg Sept 6 (252) $1,100

— Palazzi antichi di Genova. Palazzi moderni di Genova. [Antwerp], 1622. Vol II only. Folio, contemp vellum; rubbed. With 57 (of 67) plates, 13 folding. Some cropped. bba Sept 19 (293) £240 [Kunkler]

Anr copy. Contemp calf; extremities rubbed, joints split. With 67 plates, 17 double-page, 3 folding. Half-title soiled & creased; 8 plates shaved, with loss to image in 6 of them; 1 folding plate with outer margin creased & with small tears; 2 plates with rustholes. C May 20 (300) £550 [Etching]

Anr copy. Vol I only. Old half calf by Priestley & Weale. With 72 plates. Plate 4 stained; Plate 38 repaired; Plate 65 creased; some dust-soiling. S Nov 15 (890) £500 [San Lorenzo]

Rueff, Jacob, 1500-58

— De conceptu et generatione hominis. Zurich: C. Froschauer, 1554. 4to, half vellum. Some stains & soiling; c4, d1-2 & 31 in facsimile. S Feb 11 (605) £700 [Voltaire]

Anr Ed. Frankfurt: [G. Corvinus], 1580. 4to, old vellum; stained, new endpapers. Lacking b2; b1 repaired affecting a few letters. S May 13 (903) £2,400 [Phelps]

Ruelens, Charles

— Correspondence de Rubens et documents epistolaires concernant sa vie et ses oeuvres. Antwerp, 1887-1909. 6 vols. 4to, contemp half mor; spines rubbed. Some spotting; Vol I pp 225-32 bound upside down. S Feb 11 (194) £700 [Jaffe]

Ruellius, Johannes

— De Natura stirpium libri tres. Basel: Froben & Episcopius, Aug 1543. Folio, old paper-covered calf bds. Marginal dampstaining. S Nov 21 (41) £500 [Bifolco]

Rueppell, Eduard, 1794-1884

— Neue Wirbelthiere, zu der Fauna von Abyssinien gehoerig.... Frankfurt, 1835-40. 4 parts in 1 vol. Folio, contemp half mor; rubbed. With 83 (of 95) plates, most colored. Some spotting to text;letterpress to 12 missing bird plates lacking. S Nov 21 (351) £1,350 [Maggs]

Ruhraeh, John

— Pediatrics of the Past: an Anthology. NY, 1925. Inscr. bbc June 29 (150) $90

Ruinetti, Tomaso

— Idea del buon Scrittore.... Rome: Christof. Blanco, 1619. Oblong folio, later sheep; spine chipped, corners rubbed. With 39 (of 44) engraved leaves only; lacking tp, dedication & plates numbered 10, 14 & 31. Old staining; port torn with loss & laid down; other leaves with repairs. C June 24 (247) £50 [Franks]

Anr Ed. Rome: Intagliata da Christoforo Blanco, 1619. Oblong folio, late 19th-cent calf. With engraved title & 43 plates, including port & dedication. Dedication & Plate 31 trimmed to platemarks & mtd; some inner margins strengthened; waterstain towards upper margin. C June 24 (246) £1,100 [Franks]

Rules...

— Rules and Regulations for the Sword Exercise of the Cavalry.... L, 1796. 8vo, modern half calf gilt. With 29 folding plates. Some spotting; a few plates torn & repaired. pn Nov 14 (375) £65

Anr copy. Contemp bds; needs rebdg. With 27 (of 29) plates. sg Mar 26 (280) $110

Rumpf, Georg Eberhard

— Thesaurus imaginum piscium testaceorum...cochlearum.... The Hague, 1739. 2d Ed. Folio, contemp calf gilt; worn. With frontis, engraved title, port & 60 plates. FD Dec 2 (268) DM2,200

Runge, Heinrich, 1817-86

— Die Schweiz in Original-Ansichten.... Darmstadt, 1866-70. 2 vols. 4to, later half cloth; rubbed. With engraved title & 119 plates. bba Apr 30 (34) £1,350 [Gorwood & Voigt]

Runge, Philipp Otto

— Von dem Fischer un syner Fru. Berlin, 1914. One of 180. Illus by Marcus Behmer. 4to, mor. Foxed throughout. sg Sept 26 (26) $300

Runyon, Damon, 1884-1946

— Guys and Dolls. NY, 1931. In d/j. sg Dec 12 (350) $275

Ruscelli, Girolamo

— Le Imprese illustri. Venice, 1572. 4to, vellum. Soiled & stained; lacking 3 pp. sg Mar 12 (79) $700

Anr Ed. Venice, 1584-83. 4to, old vellum. sg May 7 (184) $1,500

— Tre Discorsi a M. Lodovico Dolce. Venice:

Plinio Pietrasanta, 1553. 4to, later half calf. R1 & 2 misbound; some waterstains. bba Feb 27 (234) £95 [W. Poole]

Rush, Benjamin, 1745-1813

— An Account of the Bilious Remitting Yellow Fever.... Phila., 1794. 1st Ed. 8vo, contemp sheep; spine ends chipped, front cover detached. sg Nov 14 (119) $275

2d Ed. 8vo, old calf; upper cover & front blank detached. bbc June 29 (151) $140

— An Account of the Life...of Christopher Ludwick.... Phila., 1831. 12mo, bdg not described but rubbed. Ad leaf clipped along bottom edge. Z Apr 18 (125) $75

— An Eulogium, Intended to Perpetuate the Memory of David Rittenhouse.... Phila., [1796]. 1st Ed. 8vo, 19th-cent mor gilt, orig wrap bound in. F Dec 18 (483) $110

— Medical Inquiries and Observations. Phila.: Prichard & Hall, 1789-1809. 4 vols. 8vo, contemp sheep (not uniform); worn, some covers detached. Opening leaves of Vol I gnawed in corner; marginal dampstaining throughout Vol II. sg Nov 14 (119) $275

— Sixteen Introductory Lectures, to Courses of Lectures upon the Institutes and Practice of Medicine.... Phila., 1811. 8vo, modern cloth. sg Nov 14 (121) $275

Rushworth, John, 1612?-90

— Historical Collections. L, 1659. Vol I. Folio, contemp mor gilt; chipped. With 2 ports & double-page map. Lower edges dampstained. DW Apr 8 (274) £125

Ruskin, John, 1819-1900

See also: Doves Press

— Catalogue of the Educational Series. [L, 1871]. 8vo, mor gilt by the Doves Bindery, 1915. CNY Dec 5 (381) $400

— Fors Clavigera. Letters to the Workmen and Labourers of Great Britain. Orpington & L, 1896. 4 vols. 8vo, orig cloth. bba Feb 13 (321) £60 [Deardon]

— The Harbours of England. L, 1856. Illus by J. M. W. Turner. Folio, rebound in cloth. Library markings. K Sept 29 (423) $120

— Hortus Inclusus. Orpington, 1887. 8vo, orig cloth. bba Feb 13 (311) £110 [Dearden]

— The King of the Golden River. L, 1932. Illus by Arthur Rackham. Wraps, in d/j. With 4 colored plates. sg Oct 17 (354) $140

One of 570. Orig vellum gilt. With 4 colored plates. Manney copy. P Oct 11 (263) $1,600

Anr copy. Half mor. sg Sept 26 (271) $200

— Lectures on Landscape. Orpington & L, 1897. One of 150. Folio, orig cloth; rubbed. cb Sept 26 (184) $50

— Modern Painters. L, 1846-600. Vol I, 3d Ed; others, 1st Ed. 5 vols. 8vo, orig cloth; faded, some spines def. bba Oct 10 (558) £130 [Maggs]

Anr Ed. L, 1873. 5 vols. 4to, contemp mor gilt; rubbed, spines discolored. Extra-illus with 4 proofs of plates for the 1888 Ed & 1 plate or the orig etching for 1 plate. bba Feb 13 (270) £140 [Dearden]

One of 1,000. Contemp mor gilt; rubbed. pn June 11 (176) £130 [Book Room]

Anr Ed. Orpington, 1888. 6 vols, including Index. 8vo, orig cloth. bba Feb 13 (271) £300 [Kurita]

— Notes...on his Collection of Drawings by...J. M. W. Turner.... L, 1878. 4to, orig half mor; rubbed. bba Feb 13 (298) £80 [Ginnan]

— Poems. Orpington & L, 1891. 2 vols. 4to, orig half vellum; soiled. bba Feb 13 (315) £80 [Boyes-Watson]

— The Political Economy of Art. L, 1857. 1st Ed. 8vo, orig cloth; rubbed, discolored & bowed. bba Feb 13 (281) £85 [Lucas]

— Sesame and Lilies. L, 1865. 1st Ed. 8vo, orig cloth; rubbed. bba Feb 13 (283) £60 [Ginnan]

— The Seven Lamps of Architecture. L, 1849. 1st Ed. 8vo, contemp half mor gilt by W. J. Mansell; rubbed. With 14 plates. bba Feb 13 (276) £170 [Baxter]

Anr copy. Orig cloth. sg Sept 6 (254) $175

Anr copy. Half calf. sg Apr 2 (263) $225

2d Ed. L, 1855. 8vo, orig cloth; lacking backstrip. bba Feb 13 (274) £65 [Ginnan]

— St. Mark's Rest. The History of Venice. Orpington, 1884. 12mo, contemp mor gilt; rubbed. bba Feb 13 (296) £120 [Pagan]

— The Stones of Venice. L, 1873-74. Autograph Ed [but Vol I a "remainder" from 2d Ed with new title page]. 3 vols. 8vo, orig cloth; spine torn & rubbed. bba Feb 13 (292) £85 [Ginnan]

4th Ed. Orpington, 1886. One of 220 on Dutch hand-made paper. 3 vols. 8vo, cloth. bba Feb 13 (293) £189 [Baxter]

— Two Letters Concerning "Notes on the Construction of Sheepfolds." L: Pvtly ptd, 1890. One of 40. 8vo, orig bds; soiled. Forman-Wise piracy. Todd 207p. bba Feb 13 (324) £240 [Pagan]

— The Two Paths: Being Lectures on Art.... L, 1859. 8vo, orig cloth; spine faded. bba Feb 13 (282) £65 [Scott]

Russ, Karl F. Otto

— The Speaking Parrots, a Scientific Manual. L, [1884]. Trans by Leonora Schultze. 8vo, orig cloth; faded & rubbed. With 8 colored plates. bba Sept 5 (156) £50 [Rainer]

Russell, Archibald George Blomefield

— The Engravings of William Blake. L, 1912. One of 500. 4to, cloth. With 32 plates. bba Dec 19 (45) £60 [Kurita]

Russell, Bertrand, 1872-1970

See also: Whitehead & Russell

— An Essay on the Foundations of Geometry. Cambr., 1897. Orig cloth; rebacked, new endpapers. bba June 25 (88) £75 [Rota]

Russell, Charles E.

— English Mezzotint Portraits.... L, 1926. 2 vols. 4to, orig half mor, in d/js. bba June 11 (314) £120 [Sims Reed]; bba June 11 (315) £120 [Sims Reed]

Anr copy. Orig half mor gilt. DW Nov 6 (525) £160

One of 625. Half pigskin gilt. With 64 plates. pn Dec 12 (166) £60

Russell, Charles Marion

— More Rawhides. Great Falls, 1925. 1st Ed. 4to, orig wraps; short tears along edges. sg June 18 (482) $120

— Pen and Ink Drawings. Pasadena, [1946]. Books 1 & 2. Half cloth. Foxed. bbc Dec 9 (285) $150

Russell, Henry Stuart

— Exploring Excursions in Australia. Extracted from the London Geographical Journal Vol XV. L, [1845]. 8vo, orig lea gilt; spine def. With folding map. R. J. Maria copy. C June 25 (232) £850 [Williams]

Russell, John, Writer on Art

— Ben Nicholson: Drawings, Paintings and Reliefs, 1911-1968. L, 1969. 4to, orig cloth, in d/j. bba Feb 13 (45) £340 [Pearl]

Ltd Ed. Orig cloth, in frayed d/j. pn Sept 12 (114) £240 [Sims & Reed]

Russell, John Scott, 1808-82

— The Modern System of Naval Architecture. L, 1865. 3 vols. Folio, contemp half mor; worn. With frontis & 167 plates, most folding. Upper margins of Vols II-III dampstained; some soiling to outer margins. Sold w.a.f. Ck Oct 18 (88) £600

Russell, Kenneth Fitzpatrick

— British Anatomy, 1525-1800. Melbourne, [1963]. One of 750, sgd. O Sept 24 (216) $80

Russell, Osborne

— Journal of a Trapper, or Nine Years in the Rocky Mountains.... [Boise], 1921. sg June 18 (483) $110

Russell, Thomas Herbert. See: Jackman & Russell

Russell, Sir William Howard

— The Atlantic Telegraph. L: Day & Son, [1865]. 4to, orig cloth; lower joint split. With litho title & 22 plates & 1 plan. Tp tipped in with tape & slightly affected by adhesive; some spotting. Ck May 15 (151) £110

Anr copy. Orig cloth; rubbed, hinges cracked. With tinted litho title, 24 plates & chart. Library stamp on prelims. DW May 13 (52) £115

Russell, Sir William Howard —& Dudley, Robert

— A Memorial of the Marriage of Albert Edward Prince of Wales and Alexandra Princess of Denmark. L, 1863. Folio, orig cloth; broken. Sold w.a.f. kh Nov 11 (79) A$280

Anr Ed. L: Day & Son, [1864]. Folio, disbound. With chromolitho title & 42 tinted litho plates finished by hand (1 uncolored) & mtd. Sold w.a.f. b Mar 11 (112) £190

Russoil, Franco. See: Berenson Collection, Bernard

Russoli, Franco

— Picasso: Venti Pochoirs Originali. Milan: Silvana, [1955]. Folio, orig half cloth; spine frayed, remains of adhesive tape to front & rear inside covers. DW May 13 (398) £60

Ruth, George Herman

— The Babe Ruth Story. NY, 1948. 1st Ed. Inscr to Tommy. bbc June 29 (68) $1,450

Rutherford, Ernest, 1871-1937

— Radio-Activity. Cambr., 1904. 1st Ed. Orig cloth. Institutional stamps. sg May 14 (305) $450

Rutilius Namatianus, Claudius

— Itinerarium.... Amst.: J. Wolters, 1687. 12mo, contemp calf; front joint starting. With folding map. sg Mar 12 (267) $150

Rutter, John

— Delineations of Fonthill and its Abbey. L, 1823. 4to, contemp half mor; extremities rubbed. With hand-colored title, folding map (colored in outline) & 11 plates, including 2 hand-colored. Ck Oct 18 (90) £180

Rutter, Owen, 1889-1944. See: Golden Cockerel Press

Ruttledge, Hugh

— Everest 1933. L, 1934. 4to, cloth. sg Jan 9 (293) $100

Rutty, John. See: Franklin Printing, Benjamin

Ruxton, George Frederick

— Adventures in Mexico and the Rocky Mountains. L, 1847. 1st Ed. 8vo, cloth. Library stamp on tp. sg June 18 (484) $80

— Life in the Far West. NY, 1849. 1st American Ed. 8vo, cloth. Foxed. sg June 18 (485) $70

1st Ed. 8vo, orig cloth; rubbed. Some soiling. cb Nov 14 (183) $110

Ruylopez de Sigura. See: Lopez de Sigura, Ruy

Ruysch, Frederik, 1638-1731

— Opera omnia anatomico-medico-chirurgica. Amst., 1737. 4to, old bds; backed with cloth, front cover detached. Old institutional stamp on tp & blank recto of additional title. sg May 14 (146) $2,600

Ruzicka, Rudolph. See: Grolier Club

Ryan, Marah Ellis

— The Flute of the Gods.... NY, 1909. Cloth; hinges cracked. bbc Feb 17 (198) $50

Ryan, Richard

— Dramatick Table Talk. L, 1825. 3 vols. 12mo, 19th-cent calf; rebacked. Extra-illus with c.90 plates & related ephemera, including an ALs of Macready. sg Mar 5 (220) $400

Rycaut, Sir Paul, 1628-1700

— Histoire de l'etat present de l'Empire Ottoman.... Amst., 1670. 1st Ed in French. Trans by M. Briot. 12mo, contemp calf; worn. With engraved title & 21 illusts in the text. Worming at head of L4-Z1 affecting some headlines; 2Y1 torn 7 repaired affecting illust & letterpress. S June 30 (192) £550 [Sedgwick]

— The History of the Turkish Empire. L, 1680-79. 2 parts in 1 vol. Folio, contemp calf; rebacked. Some stains. S May 14 (1239) £380 [Theocharak]

Anr copy. Contemp calf; worn. With 4 ports & 1 plate. Some dust-soiling; plate shaved at neatline. S July 1 (705) £350 [Sossidis]

— The History of the Turks. Beginning with the year 1679. L, 1700. Folio, modern cloth. With frontis & 6 ports. Marginal worming. bba Jan 30 (151) £300 [Shapero]

— The Present State of the Greek and Armenian Churches. L, 1680. 8vo, contemp half calf; joints split. With frontis & 19 plates. Some soiling. Ck May 15 (152) £260

Ryd, Valerius Anselmus

— Catalogus annorum et principum geminus ab homine condito.... Berne, 1550. Folio, old vellum. Final blank present; some foxing & browning. bba June 25 (165) £500 [Braunschweig]

Rye, Edgar

— The Quir and the Spur. Chicago, [1909]. 1st Ed. Cloth. NH May 30 (528) $160

Ryff, Walther Hermann

— Newe Aussgerueste Deutsche Apoteck.... Strassburg: L. Zetzner, 1602. Folio, contemp blind-stamped pigskin; stain on lower cover, worn. Some text woodcuts colored by hand. Some browning. S Dec 5 (425) £3,000 [Bucher Kabinett]

Ryley, Arthur Beresford

— Old Paste. L, 1913. 4to, orig cloth; worn & soiled. F Mar 26 (314G) $190

S

Saavedra Fajardo, Diego de, 1584-1648

— Idea de un principe politico Christiano. Amst.: Jansson, 1659. 16mo, contemp blind-panelled calf; rebacked. Engraved title with 2 small holes repaired; small waterstain to a few corners; marginal worming & repairs, affecting a few catchwords; marginal tear in 1 leaf just touching illust; rust hole in 4T4 touching a few letters. b June 22 (89) £250

Anr copy. Contemp vellum bds. With engraved title & 102 engraved emblems. Dampstain in lower half of text in final leaves. S Dec 5 (246) £2,000 [Rota]

— The Royal Politician.... L, 1700. 2 vols. 8vo, contemp sheep; rebacked, covers detached. sg Mar 12 (79A) $300

Sabartes, Jaime

— Les Menines et la Vie. Paris, [1958]. One of 20 hors commerce. Illus by Pablo Picasso. 4to, vellum imprinted in colors after a Picasso drawing. With an orig drawing, sgd. CGen Nov 18 (452) SF3,700

— Picasso: Toreros. L & Monte Carlo, 1961. Oblong 4to, orig cloth, in d/j. With 103 reproductions & 4 lithos, 1 in color. sg Sept 6 (223) $475

Anr copy. With 4 lithos, 1 colored & with 103 illusts. Some fixing to 2 uncolored lithos. sg Apr 2 (226) $325

Anr copy. Orig cloth. With 4 lithos, 1 colored. wa June 25 (525) $500

Anr Ed. NY, 1961. Oblong 4to, orig cloth, in d/j. With 4 lithos, 1 colored. cb Feb 1 (102) $300

Anr copy. Trans by Patrick Gregory. Orig

cloth; spine soiled. wa Apr 9 (260) $100

Sabbattini, Nicola

— Practica di fabricar scene e machine ne' Teatri.... Pesaro: Flaminio Concordia, 1637. Folio, contemp bds. Some staining; 2 small marginal tears. C June 24 (200) £15,000 [Kraus]

Sabellicus, Marcus Antonius Coccius

— Rerum Venetarum decades. Venice: Andreas Torresanus, 21 May 1487. 1st Ed. Folio, old vellum; soiled. 48 lines & headline; types 5:111R (text), 93Gb (errata). Some soiling to 1st 2 leaves. 240 leaves. Goff S-5. C Dec 16 (163) £4,500 [Shapero]

Sabin, Joseph, 1821-81

— A Dictionary of Books Relating to America. Amst., 1961-62. ("Bibliotheca Americana: A Dictionary of Books....") 29 vols in 15. bbc Dec 9 (195) $525; Ck Nov 1 (497) £200

Mini-Print Ed. NY, [1967]. 29 vols in 2. Oblong 4to, orig cloth. cb Nov 21 (201) $350; O Dec 17 (160) $225; sg Oct 31 (2296) $475; sg Dec 5 (220) $475

Sabine, Lorenzo, 1803-77

— Biographical Sketches of Loyalists in the American Revolution. Bost., 1864. 2 vols. 8vo, cloth; extremities worn. NH May 30 (468) $180

Sabretache. See: Barrow, Albert Stewart

Sacchi, Antonio

— Il Primo Libro di Mostre Cancellaresche.... [Ravenna, 1602]. Oblong 4to, old vellum; rebacked, modern endpapers. 42 leaves all ptd recto only. With 73 plates numbered to 42. Some repairs; old staining. C June 24 (248) £1,100 [Abrams]

Sacerdotale...

— Sacerdotale ad consuetudinem Sacro Sacte Romane ecclesie.... Venice: Guerra, 1576. 4to, vellum; lower cover shaved at head. Top corner of tp worn away; early annotations to tp & flyleaves. S Nov 14 (486) £135 [Bass]

Anr Ed. Venice: Domenico Nicolini, 1579. 4to, blind-stamped vellum with brass & lea fittings, from the Jesuit College at Landsberga. S Nov 15 (692) £420 [Maggs]

Sacheverell, Henry

[-] The Tryal of Dr. Henry Sacheverell.... L, 1710. Folio, contemp mor gilt; spine worn. DW May 13 (325) £80

Sachs, Hans

— Eygentliche Beschreibung aller Staende auff Erden.... [Frankfurt: Sigmund Feyerabend, 1568]. 4to, contemp pigskin with Justitia & Fortuna plaques. Q3 from anr copy; some browning & spotting; tape repair on V2; single wormhole through all leaves; lacking final blank. Schlosser copy. P June 18 (415) $14,000

Sackville-West, Victoria, 1892-1962

— Constantinople: Eight Poems. L: Pvtly ptd, 1915. 1st Ed. Inscr. DW Oct 2 (391) £220

— The Heir. L, [1922]. 1st Ed, one of 100. Orig half cloth; rubbed & soiled. Inscr by the author's mother. DW Oct 2 (390) £155

— Invitation to Cast Out Care. L, 1931. One of 200 L.p. copies. Bds. Ariel Poems 37. sg Dec 12 (352) $90

Sacramento...

— Sacramento Illustrated: A Reprint of the Original Edition Issued by Barber & Baker in 1855. Sacramento: Sacramento Book Collectors Club, 1950. One of 300. cb Sept 12 (152) $130

Sacrarum. See: Ceremonials

Sacrobosco, Johannes

— Annotationi sopra la lettione della Spera del Sacro Bosto.... Florence, 1550. 4to, contemp vellum; worn. Dampstained; minor wormholes at beginning & end. S May 13 (904) £280 [Casa D'Arte]

— Sphaera mundi. Venice: Heredem Hieronymus Scoti, 1574. ("La Sfera....") 12mo, later half vellum gilt. Sold w.a.f. Ck June 18 (45) £160

Sadeler, Marco

— Vestigi delle antichita di Roma... Rome, 1660. Oblong folio, contemp lea; worn. With engraved title & dedication & 49 plates. Some browning & marginal spotting. SI June 10 (900) LIt2,000,000

Sadleir, John

— Recollections of a Victorian Police Officer. Melbourne, 1913. One plate strengthened at fore-edge. kh Nov 11 (635) A$50

Sadleir, Michael, 1888-1957

— Daumier, the Man and the Artist. L, 1924. One of 700. 4to, bdg not described. kh Nov 11 (203) A$80

— XIX Century Fiction. A Bibliographical Record. L, 1951. One of 1,025. 2 vols. 4to, cloth, in d/js. S May 13 (575) £220 [Yablon]; sg Oct 31 (298) $200

Anr copy. Cloth, in smudged d/js. wa Apr 9 (5) $210

Anr Ed. NY, 1969. 2 vols. 4to, orig cloth. bba July 23 (474) £170 [Marlborough]; DW Jan 29 (340) £210

Anr copy. Orig cloth; worn. O Sept 24 (217) $350; S May 13 (576) £180 [Seibu]; sg Oct 31 (299) $225

Anr copy. Cloth. sg May 21 (299) $325

Anr copy. Orig cloth. sp Feb 6 (543) $180

Saga-bon

— Ise monogatari. [N.p., postface dated 1608]. Ed by Nakanoin Michikatsu. 2 vols. Folio, orig covers; soiled & damaged. Ptd in ink with movable type, with 49 block illusts on prepared & sometimes tinted paper; with brush drawn kakihan Some sheets with stains; minor tears on a few leaves. CNY Nov 111 (114) $28,000

Sagard-Theodat, Gabriel

— Le Grand Voyage du pays des Hurons.... Paris, 1865. 2 vols. 8vo, orig wraps, unopened; spines chipped. Z Nov 23 (186) $75

— Histoire du Canada. Paris, 1866. 4 vols. 8vo, wraps, unopened. Z Nov 23 (187) $90

Sage, Dean

— The Ristigouche and its Salmon Fishing.... Goshen, CT, 1973. One of 205. 4to, lea; worn. Koopman copy. O Oct 29 (247) $425

— A Visit to Badminton England 1888. Santa Fe: Rydal Press, 1934. One of 50. Bds. wd Dec 12 (442) $400

Saggi...

— Saggi di naturali esperienze.... Florence, 1691. 2d Ed. Folio, contemp calf; worn. With 75 plates. SI Dec 5 (410) LIt3,20,000

Anr Ed. Naples, 1714. Folio, modern vellum. Waterspotting & foxing. SI Dec 5 (411) LIt600,000

Sagra, Ramon de la

— Historia fisica, politica y natural de la isla de Cuba. Paris: Libreria de Arthus Bertrand, 1855. Atlas de Zoologia only. Folio, modern half mor. With 143 plates, 125 of them hand-colored. Some spotting. C Oct 30 (291) £2,200 [Junk]

St. Aubin, Gabriel de —& Others

— Abrege de l'Histoire Romaine.... Paris, 1789. 4to, sheep; spine repaired at head & foot, later endpapers. With frontis & 48 plates, 3 folding. C June 24 (344) £300 [Meister]

St. Clair, Philip R.

— Frederic Remington: The American West. Kent, 1978. Oblong 4to, cloth. K July 12 (443) $55

Saint German, Christopher

— The Dialogue in English.... L: Richard Tottel, 1580. ("The Dialogues in Englishe....") 8vo, contemp calf; rubbed. Black letter. Some Ms sidenotes; browning; wormholes in lower margins from L2 to end; T1 with paper marker pasted to lower margin. STC 21574. pn May 14 (18) £320 [Vanburgh]

— The Dialogue in English, betweene a Doctor of Divinitie, and a Student in the Lawes of England. [L: Richard Tottell, 1580]. 8vo, old half sheep; worn, needs rebacking. Upper margins wormed. sg Mar 12 (269) $550

St. John, J. Hector. See: Crevecoeur, Michel Guillaume St. Jean de

St. John, Spenser, 1825-1910

— Life in the Forests of the Far East. L, 1862. 2 vols. 8vo, half calf; rubbed. O Feb 25 (171) $325

Saint Olon, Francois Pidou de

— Relation de l'empire de Maroc. Paris, 1695. 12mo, contemp calf; worn. With frontis, folding map & 8 plates. b June 22 (197) £260

St. Paul, Henry

— Our Home and Foreign Policy. Mobile, 1863. 8vo, wraps. sg Dec 5 (82) $200

Saint-Amant, Pierre C. F. de

— Voyages en Californie et dans l'Oregon. Paris, 1854. 8vo, contemp half mor. cb Nov 14 (185) $160

Anr copy. Orig wraps; frayed, soiled, spine split. Some foxing; 1 leaf torn. NH May 30 (141) $115

Saint-Exupery, Antoine de

— Flight to Arras. NY, 1942. 1st American Ed. Illus by Bernard Lamotte. Orig cloth, in d/j. bbc Apr 27 (399) $70

One of 500, sgd by author & artist. Orig half cloth; spotted. F June 25 (498) $110

Anr copy. Half calf. Epstein copy. sg Apr 30 (401) $475

Anr copy. Half pigskin; some wear. wa Mar 5 (236) $170

— The Little Prince. NY, 1943. In advance proof of 1st Ed wraps; rubbed & soiled. Manney copy. P Oct 11 (270) $1,800

Anr Ed. L, 1944. Orig cloth, in worn d/j. bba Dec 19 (216) £75 [Ulysses]

— Vol de Nuit. Paris: Gallimard, [1931]. 12mo, orig ptd wraps. Inscr. sg Apr 30 (403) $3,000

Saint-Julien, Francois. See: Bovis & Saint-Julien

Saint-Martin, J. de

— L'Art de faire des armes reduit a ses vrais principes. Vienna, 1804. 4to, old wraps; spine reinforced with tape. With frontis & 72 plates. sg Mar 26 (285) $500

Saint-Martin, Louis Claude de

— Des Erreurs et de la Verite...par un philosophe inconnu. "Edimbourg" [but Lyons], 1782. 2 parts in 1 vol. 8vo, contemp sheep gilt; spine ends chipped; corners worn. sg Mar 13 (237) $175

Saint-Non, Jean Claude Richard de

— Fragment choisis dans les peintures et les tableaux les plus interessans des palais et des eglises de l'Italie. Rome, 1770-73. 3 suites in 1 vol. 4to, contemp calf; rubbed, expertly rebacked. With 100 plates. Premiere suite with engraved aquatint title & 39 plates in bistre; Seconde suite with engraved title & 19 plates in bistre; Troisieme suite with engraved title & 39 plates in sepia. Title plate of Part 1 soiled; some spotting. Sir Joshua Reynolds's copy. Schlosser copy. P June 18 (495) $6,500

Anr Ed. Rome, [c.1780]. 3d & 4th suites only. 4to, later mor gilt; rubbed. With 77 mtd plates. Some flaws and adhesion damage. DW Mar 11 (855) £780

— Voyage pittoresque ou description des royaumes de Naples et de Sicile. Paris, 1781-86. Vols I-II. Orig bdg; worn. SI June 10 (905) LIt3,800,000

Saint-Pierre, Bernardin de, 1713-1814

— Paul et Virginie. Paris, 1838. 8vo, half mor gilt by Corfmat. With 29 wood-engraved & 7 steel-engraved plates including frontis & additional title.. Schlosser copy. P June 18 (437) $300

Saintsbury, George

— Notes on a Cellar-Book. L, 1921. Ed de Luxe, One of 500 L.p. copies. 4to, half cloth; soiled, spine faded. cb Dec 5 (120) $225

St.-Simon, Louis de Rouvroy, Duc de, 1675-1755

— Memoires. Paris, 1856-57-58. One of 100 L.p. copies. 20 vols. Mor extra by Chambolle-Duru. Extra-illus with 448 ports. wd June 12 (431) $1,700

Sakisian, Armenag B.

— La Miniature persane du XIIe au XVIIe siecle. Paris & Brussels, 1929. Folio, orig wraps; faded. DW Mar 11 (856) £50

Sala, Giovanni Domenico

— De alimentis et eorum recta administratione. Padua, 1628. 2 parts in 1 vol. 4to, contemp half vellum. SI Dec 5 (599) LIt650,000

Salaberry, Charles Marie d'Irumberry, Comte de

— Voyage a Constantinople, en Italie, et aux iles de l'archipel, par l'Allemagne et la Hongrie. Paris, 1799. 8vo, modern half calf. S Nov 15 (1186) £250 [Shapero]

Salaman, Malcolm Charles

— The Etchings of Sir Francis Seymour Haden. L, 1923. Folio, cloth. kh Nov 11 (204) A$60

One of 200 with additional suite of 16 etched plates, ptd on japon. Half lea; spine ends worn. sg Feb 6 (121) $90

— French Colour-Prints of the XVIII Century. L, 1913. 4to, cloth; spine ends chipped. With 50 colored plates. sg Feb 6 (254) $100

— Modern Woodcuts and Lithographs by British and French Artists. L: The Studio, 1919. 4to, half cloth; extremities worn. sg Sept 6 (243) $70

Salayman, al Tajir. See: Hasan ibn Yazid, Abu Zaid

Sale, Sir Robert Henry

— The Defence of Jellalabad. L, [c.1845]. Illus by W. L. Walton. Folio, loose in orig half mor portfolio. With pictorial title, double-page plan & 22 hand-colored plates mtd as watercolors on 11 sheets of card & captioned in pencil. Lacking port; minor surface abrasions, mostly to margins; minor marginal staining; plan frayed. pn Nov 14 (369) £400

Salinger, J. D.

— The Catcher in the Rye. L, [1951]. In d/j with small tear on tail of spine; ink writing on front endpapers. bba May 14 (246) £100 [Martin]

Anr copy. In d/j. cb Feb 12 (114) $1,500

Anr copy. In chipped d/j. sg Dec 12 (3553) $950

Anr copy. In d/j. Epstein copy. sg Apr 30 (404) $850

— Nine Stories. Bost., [1953]. In worn d/j. sg Dec 12 (354) $325

— The Hang of It. Chicago, 1943. In: The Kit Book for Soldiers, Sailors and Marines, pp.332-36. cb Dec 12 (120) $90

Sallengre, Albert Henri de

— Novus Thesaurus Antiquitatum Romanarum. The Hague, 1716-19. Vols I & II (of 3) only. Folio, modern cloth. bba Oct 10 (505) £50 [Tosi]

Anr copy. 3 vols. Folio, 19th-cent half vellum. SI Dec 5 (1002) LIt900,000

Salmasius, Claudius

— De Re Militari Romanorum Liber. Leiden: Elsevir, 1657. 12mo, modern bds. bba Oct 10 (501) £80 [Poole]

Salmon, Richard

— Trout Flies. NY, 1975. One of 29. 4to, lea; worn. With mtd samples of fly-tying materials & with an orig pencil drawing by Salmon. Koopman copy, inscr to him. O Oct 29 (257) $600

Salmon, Thomas, 1679-1767

— The Universal Traveller; or, a Compleat Description of the Several Nations of the World.... L, 1752. 2 vols. Folio, contemp calf; rubbed & worn. With frontis & 224 plates. Lacking 2 plates; Vol I index pages loose & 3 plates def;Vol II with tears to some plates & maps torn, 2 plates with corners missing; some spotting & browning. S May 14 (1223) £850 [Hildebrandt]

Salmon, William, Carpenter-Builder

— Palladio Londinensis: or the London Art of Building. L, 1755. 4to, contemp calf; stitching cracked. With 54 plates, some folding. Some gutters dampstained just touching plates. CNY Jan 25 (69) $550

Anr Ed. L, 1773. 4to, old calf; rebacked rubbed. Some browning; minor soiling. O May 26 (160) $275

Salmon, William, 1644-1713

— The Family Dictionary: or Houshold Companion.... L, 1696. 8vo, contemp calf; spine & corners worn. Recipe for pickling mangos on verso of final blank; anr recipe pasted to inside lower cover. L Nov 14 (253) £220

Salo, Ippolito

— Tbulae gnomonicae una cum earum dilucidatione. Brescia: G. P. Bizardi, 1617. 4to, contemp vellum. Dampstain in lower margin of 1st few leaves. S Dec 5 (426) £850 [Franks]

Salt, Sir Henry

— Twenty-Four Views Taken in St. Helena, the Cape.... L, 1809. 2 vols. Folio, contemp bds; rebacked & recornered with calf. With uncolored title & 24 hand-colored plates on thick paper. Some plates smaller; lacking text; larger plates with marginal dust-soiling & occasional small tears. C May 20 (301) £12,000 [McNaughton]

— A Voyage to Abyssinia. L, 1814. 4to, later half calf; upper hinge worn. With 27 plates & 7 (of 8) maps & charts. bba Apr 9 (181) £420 [Remington]

Anr copy. Contemp half calf; corners bumped, rebacked. With folding map, hand-colored & 7 other folding maps & charts on 6 sheets & 27 plates. Lacking half-title; some tears & repairs to maps. S Nov 15 (1274) £450 [Sotheran]

Salter, Robert

— The Modern Angler. Oswestry, 1811. 12mo, orig bds; rebacked in vellum. bba Nov 28 (39) £130 [Hereward Bks]

Salter, Thomas Frederick

— The Angler's Guide, or Complete London Angler.... L, 1815. ("The Angler's Guide, Being a Complete Practical Treatise....") L.p. copy. 8vo, new half calf; rubbed. Koopman copy. O Oct 29 (257) $600

3th Ed. L, 1833. 8vo, contemp calf; worn, upper cover detached. Koopman copy. O Oct 29 (259) $70

Salucci, L.

— Vedute della Grecia. [Italy, c.1830]. Oblong folio, silk-covered bds; worn. With litho title & 9 litho plates, cut round, mtd on gray leaves & captioned in ink in English. S Nov 21 (279) £550 [Maggs]

Salusbury, Thomas

— Mathematical Collections and Translations in Two Parts. L, 1661-65. Vol I, Parts 1 & 2 & Vol II, Part 1 only. Folio, contemp bds; rebacked & recornered in calf, covers restored. Vol I lacking the contents leaf & the errata leaf; tp & prelims to Vol I restored & 2 of the plates laid down; some leaves affected by damp; Vol II with occasional browning. Ck Nov 29 (237) £7,500

Saluste du Bartas, Guillaume de, 1544-90. See: Du Bartas, Guillaume de Saluste

Salva y Mallen, Pedro

— Catalogo de la Biblioteca de Salva. Barcelona, 1963. 2 vols. Cloth, orig wraps bound in. Facsimile of 1872 Ed. O Sept 24 (218) $70

Salvator, Ludwig L.

— Eine Blume aus dem Goldenen Lande oder Los Angeles. Prague, 1878. 12mo, pictorial cloth; dampstained, foot of spine ragged. sg Dec 5 (38) $300

Salver, Johann Octavian

— Proben des hohen deutschen Reichs Adels. Wuerzburg, 1775. Folio, vellum bds. With frontis & 29 plates. 4C2-3 supplied from a shorter copy. S Dec 5 (288) £750 [Halwas]

Salvio, Alessandro

— Il Giuoco degli scacchi. Naples, 1723. 4to, contemp vellum; stained & bowed. Affected by damp. Ck May 8 (57) £160

— Il Puttino altramente detto, Il Cavaliero Errante del Salvio, sopra il gioco di Scacchi. Naples, 1634. Bound with: Trattato dell'Inventione et Arte Liberale del Gioco di Scacchi...Libro quarto, 2d impression. 2 parts in 1 vol. 4to, contemp vellum. With woodcut arms on titles. Some browning & dampstaining. Ck May 8 (56) £600

— Trattato dell' inventione et arte liberale del gioco di scacchi. Naples, 1604. 4to, contemp vellum. E4 torn & repaired; some soiling; final leaves waterstained at outer margins; minor emendations to text in a contemp hand; some marginalia in pencil. Ck May 8 (55) £950

Salwechter, Jacob. See: Perneder, Andreas

Samaran, Charles —& Marichal, Robert

— Catalogues des manuscrits en ecriture latine.... Paris, 1959-84. Vols I-III & V-VII in 12. 4to, cloth. sg Oct 31 (250) $850

Sambucus, Joannes, 1531-84

— Emblemata, cum aliquot nummis antiqui operis. Antwerp: Plantin, 1564. 8vo, later vellum; worn & bowed. bba Sept 19 (282) £550 [Goldschmidt]

Anr copy. 18th-cent calf gilt; spine ends chipped. 1 leaf repaired. sg Mar 12 (80) $2,000

Sammes, Aylett

— Britannia Antiqua Illustrata: or, the Antiquities of Ancient Britain. L, 1676. 1st Ed. Vol I (all pbd). Folio, later calf; rubbed. Some headlines cropped; browned; name cut from lower margin of tp. bba Aug 13 (87) £70 [Bennett & Kerr]

Anr copy. Contemp calf gilt; needs rebacking. Some dampstaining in upper inner corner at end. sg Oct 24 (284) $225

Sampson, Henry

— A History of Advertising.... L, 1875. 8vo, orig cloth; worn. With folding chromolitho frontis & other plates. sg Apr 2 (1) $110

Sampson, John. See: Gregynog Press

Sams, William

— A Tour through Paris. L, [c. 1825-28]. Folio, modern mor gilt by Bayntun-Riviere. With 21 hand-colored plates. C May 20 (126) £2,000 [Litup]

San Francisco

— Future Development of the San Francisco Bay Area, 1960-2020. Wash., 1959. Wraps. With 21 plates of folding maps, some in color. cb Sept 12 (153) $120

— A Map and Street Directory of San Francisco.... San Francisco: Henry G. Langley, 1870. 8vo, orig cloth; recased. With folding map (tear affecting ocean). cb Feb 12 (75) $300

— San Francisco Vigilance Committee of '56. San Francisco, 1883. Ed by Frank Meriweather Smith. Orig wraps. sg June 18 (130) $120

San Roman, Antonio de

— Historia general de la Yndia oriental. Valladolid: L. Sanchez, 1603. Folio, contemp vellum. Some stains & discoloration. S June 25 (337) £4,500 [Quaritch]

Sancta Ella, Rodericus de

— Oratio in die Parasceve anno 1477. [Rome: Stephen Plannck, 1481-87]. 4to, disbound. Some foxing. 8 leaves. Goff S-124. sg Mar 12 (131) $550

Sand, Maurice, Pseud., 1823-89

— Masques et bouffons. L, 1860. 2 vols. 8vo, orig cloth. Some foxing. SI Dec 5 (1003) LIt1,200,000

Sandburg, Carl, 1878-1967

— Abraham Lincoln: The War Years. NY, [1939]. 1st Trade Ed. 4 vols. cb Dec 19 (148) $55

One of 525. Inscr. cb Sept 5 (147) $110; F Dec 18 (49) $425

— Abraham Lincoln: The Prairie Years and The War Years. NY, [1954]. In d/j. Inscr. bbc Feb 17 (115) $65

— The American Songbag. NY, [1927]. Cloth, in chipped & repaired d/j. Inscr to John Storrs. sg Dec 12 (355) $275

— Chicago Poems. NY, 1916. 1st Ed. In d/j. sg Dec 12 (356) $950

Anr copy. Cloth (front cover bumped) in d/j with a few tears. sg June 11 (275) $225

— Cornhuskers. NY, 1918. 1st Ed, 1st Issue. sg Dec 12 (357) $200

Later Issue. Orig bds; extremities worn. Inscr, 1922. F Sept 26 (268) $80

— Good Morning America. NY, 1928. Sgd. sg Dec 12 (358) $150

— Lincoln Collector: the Story of Oliver R. Barrett's Great Private Collection. NY. [1949]. 1st Ed. cb Sept 5 (148) $120

— The People, Yes. NY, 1940. 5th ptg. Inscr. br May 2 (4) $70

— Remembrance Rock. NY, [1948]. 1st Ed, One of 1,000. 2 vols. sg Dec 12 (360) $60

— Smoke and Steel. NY, 1920. Bds. Sgd, & with later inscr. sg Dec 12 (361) $500

Anr copy. Cover spotted. sp Apr 16 (412) $55

Anr copy. Bds. Inscr, 12 Feb 1926. wa Oct 19 (54) $75

— Steichen the Photographer. NY, [1929]. One of 925. 4to, orig cloth; rubbed. Endpapers foxed. bbc Feb 17 (263) $525

Anr copy. Orig cloth. Epstein copy. sg Apr 30 (406) $750

— Wind Song. NY, [1960]. Inscr to Ernie Kovacs & with Ls inserted. sg Dec 12 (362) $275

Sandby, Paul, 1725-1809

— A Collection of One Hundred and Fifty Select Views in England, Wales, Scotland and Ireland. L, 1783-82. 2 vols in 1. Folio, contemp mor gilt; joints & corners worn. With 150 plates. Derby copy. C June 24 (220) £1,000 [Bifolco]

— XII Views in Aquatint from Drawings Taken on the Spot in South-Wales.... L, 1775-77. Parts 1 & 3 in 1 vol. Folio, contemp bds; rebacked & recornered. With 25 sepia aquatints & with 3 separate plates from Part 1 on half-sheets of large paper. Schlosser copy. P June 18 (496) $9,500

Sandeman, Fraser

— Angling Travels in Norway. L, 1895. 4to, orig half vellum, unopened; spine soiled. Koopman copy. O Oct 29 (262) $160

Sander, August

— Deutschenspiegel. Hamburg, 1962. 4to, cloth, in d/j. wa Apr 9 (259) $140

— Menschen ohne Maske. Lucerne & Frankfurt, [1971]. 4to, bds, in worn d/j. sg Oct 8 (62) $750

Sander, Henry Frederick Conrad

— Reichenbachia. Orchids Illustrated and Described. L & St. Albans, [1886-95]. 1st & 2d Series. 4 vols. Folio, orig cloth; worn, Vol I head of spine torn, most outer joints & inner hinges to Vols II & IV splitting. With 180 (of 192) chromolithos. About 10 plates cracking along inner margins; marginal tears; repaired tear just grazing 2 leatters of caption of Plate II:48; 2 plates with abraded areas; 1 plate cropped. Sold w.a.f. CNY June 9 (154) $2,500

Anr copy. Second Series Vol I & part of Vol II, in 2 vols. Folio, contemp half mor; broken. With 76 color plates only. Sold w.a.f. S May 14 (1053) £1,000 [Walford]

Anr Ed. L & St. Albans, 1888-94. 1st & 2d Series in 4 vols. Folio, contemp mor gilt; joints & edges rather worn. With 192 chromolitho plates, some finished by hand. Some tissue-guards adhered to plates; some minor marginal tears or repairs; a few corners creased; Plate 57 of 2d Series trimmed; some library stamps, not affecting plates; 1 leaf of text repaired. pn Mar 19 (324) £3,200 [Shapero]

One of 100. 1st & 2d Series. 4 vols. Folio, contemp mor gilt by Zaehnsdorf, with John Rylands monogram. With 192 color plates, mtd, some finished by hand. Spencer-Rylands—McCarty-Cooper copy. CNY Jan 25 (94) $32,000

Anr copy. 1st Series, Vols I & II & 2d Series, Vol I. Contemp half mor gilt; rubbed. With 144 color plates, some finished by hand. Some tissue-guards adhering. S June 25 (85) £2,000 [Shuster]

Anr copy. 1st & 2d Series. 2 vols in 4 parts in 4 vols. Orig half lea gilt. With 192 color plates. Some light foxing. sg May 7 (186) $8,000

Sander, Max

— Le Livre a figures italiens depuis 1467 jusque a 1530. Milan, 1942. 7 vols in 6. 4to, orig cloth; spines soiled at foot. Ck Nov 1 (499) £1,300

Anr copy. 7 vols in 5 plus Supplement. 4to, O Sept 24 (219) $850

Anr copy. 6 vols. 4to, sg Oct 31 (300) $475

Sanders, Nicholas

— De visibili monarchia ecclesiae libri octo. Louvain: J. Fowler, 1571. Folio, contemp vellum. Tp stamped. S Feb 11 (526) £240 [Voltaire]

Sanderson, Arthur

— A Catalogue of a Collection of Plaques, Medallions, Vases...produced by Josia Wedgwood...exhibited at the Museum of Science and Art.... Edin., 1901. One of 100. 4to, orig cloth; shaken. Inscr. sg Feb 6 (305) $275

Sanderson Collection, Arthur

— A Catalogue of a Collection of Plaques, Medallions...Produced by Josiah Wedgwood. L, 1903. L.p. Ed. Ed by F. Rathbone. 4to, cloth. With 3 ports & 22 mtd photographic plates. sg Sept 6 (295) $250

Sanderson, George P.

— Thirteen Years among the Wild Beasts of India.... L, 1879. 2d Ed. 4to, orig cloth; upper joint torn. bba Feb 13 (379) £65 [Corbett]

Anr copy. Cloth; worn. Some stains. O Feb 25 (172) $170

Sanderson, Sir William, 1586-1676

— Aulicus Coquinariae: or a Vindication in Answer to a Pamphlet.... L, 1650. 1st Ed. 8vo, later mor gilt; spine rubbed. Contents browned. DW Mar 4 (250) £100

— A Compleat History of the Life and Raigne of King Charles from his Cradle to his Grave. L, 1658. 1st Ed. Folio, contemp calf; rebacked. With port. W July 8 (72) £90

Sanderus, Antonius, 1586-1664

— Chorographia sacra Brabantiae. The Hague, 1726-27. Vol III (of 3) only. Folio, contemp calf gilt; worn. With 27 plates. bba Jan 30 (403) £360 [Thorp]

Sandford, Francis, 1630-94

— A Genealogical History of the Kings and Queens of England.... L, 1677. ("A Genealogical History of the Kings of England.") Folio, modern half calf. bba Jan 30 (40) £280 [Thorp]

Anr Ed. L, 1707. Folio, later mor gilt by T. Aitken. DW Oct 2 (304) £170

Sandi, Vettor

— Principi di storia civile della republica di Venezia.... Venice, 1755-56. 6 vols. 4to, contemp vellum. SI June 10 (912) LIt800,000

Sandifort, Eduard

— Observationes anatomico-pathologicae. Leiden, 1777-81. 4 parts in 2 vols. 4to, half calf. With 36 folding plates. Stamps removed from 2 titles; some marginal soiling. B Nov 1 (382) HF3,000

Sandrart, Joachim von, 1606-88

— Teutsche Academie der Bau-Bildhauer- und Maler-Kinst. Nuremberg: Johann Andreas Endter, 1768-75. 8 vols. Folio, contemp calf; rubbed. With 14 frontis, engraved titles, 3 ports & 787 plates. Folding plan of Ancient Rome in Vol II torn & repaired with loss; Vol VII with lower fore-corner showing worm traces. S Nov 21 (100) £5,800 [Reiss & Auvermann]

Sands & Kenny

— Landscape Scenery Illustrating Sydney, Paramatta.... Sydney etc., 1855. Oblong 4to, orig cloth; edges rubbed. With engraved title & 37 plates. Some foxing, affecting a few plates. Inscr by Sir Alfred Stephen. kh Nov 11 (205) A$1,500

— Sands & Kenny's Commercial and General Melbourne Directory for 1857. Melbourne, 1857. 8vo, bdg with external wear. Section cut from head of tp. kh Nov 11 (298) A$160

Sands, Frank

— A Pastoral Prince: the History and Reminiscences of J. W. Cooper. Santa Barbara, 1893. 1st Ed. 12mo, cloth. Inscr by Cooper. sg June 18 (121) $60

Sandwich, John Montagu, 4th Earl of

— A Voyage Round the Mediterranean in 1738 and 1739. L, 1799. 4to, contemp calf; joints split, rubbed. With port, 25 plates & hand-colored folding map. bba June 25 (264) £280 [Dennistoun]

Anr copy. Early 19th-cent calf gilt. With port, 21 plates, 1 folding hand-colored map & 4 plates of Greek inscriptions. pn Apr 23 (247) £200

Sandys, George, 1578-1644

— A Relation of a Journey.... L, 1615. ("A Relation of a Journey begun An. Dom 1610...Description of the Turkish Empire.") 1st Ed. Folio, modern lea. Engraved title trimmed & remounted; lacking double-page map. Some dampstaining & soiling. Sold w.a.f. O Mar 31 (162) $160

Anr copy. Calf; worn. Sold w.a.f. pnE Oct 1 (313) £95

Anr copy. Contemp calf; rebacked, worn. With engraved title, double-page map & folding panoram. Map & engraved title with margins chipped & laid down; later leaves with margins stained. S July 1 (857) £250 [Lewin]

4th Ed. L, 1637. Folio, later calf; rebacked preserving remains of orig spine. With engraved title & folding map. Lacking folding panorama; rusthole in I6, affecting image; some waterstaining. STC 21730. S July 1 (793) £150 [Kyriacou]

Anr copy. Later calf; upper joint cracked. With engraved title, folding map & folding panorama. Contemp Ms annotations in ink throughout. STC 21730. S July 1 (794) £220 [Kalafat]

Anr Ed. L, 1658. ("Sandys Travailes....") Folio, contemp calf; spine def. With engraved title (with tear), folding map & 1 plate. Some soiling & staining. S June 30 (389) £550 [Consolidated Real]

Sansom, William

— The Equilibriad. L: Hogarth Press, 1948. One of 750. Illus by Lucien Freud. Half cloth. b Nov 18 (39) £65

Sanson d'Abbeville, Nicolas

— Atlas portatif et nouveau du voyageur. Amst.: Pieter Mortier, [1708?]. 6 vols in 2. 8vo, contemp calf; worn. With engraved titles & 127 double-page or folding maps (of 128), all but 1 hand-colored in outline. A few maps shaved at neatlines. S Nov 21 (130) £2,000 [Baskes]

— Voyage ou relation de l'etat present du Royaume de Perse. Paris, 1695. 12mo, contemp calf; joint split. With folding map, frontis & 5 plates. Marginal worming; some waterstains. b June 22 (213) £240

Sanson d'Abbeville, Nicolas —& Mortier, Pieter

— Atlas nouveau contenant toutes les parties du monde.... Amst., [1692-96]. Folio, later half calf; worn & split. With engraved title & 97 mostly double-page hand-colored maps. pnE Oct 1 (317) £6,000

Sansovino, Francesco

— Della origine de' cavalieri. Venice, 1570. 8vo, old wraps. Inked owner's stamp on tp. sg Mar 26 (290) $250

— Della origine, et de fatti delle famiglie illustri d'Italia...libro primo. Venice, 1609. 8vo, later calf; joints cracked, rubbed. Worming in last few leaves affecting text. S Feb 11 (527) £150 [American Book Store]

— Historia universale dell' origine guerre, et imperio de turchi. Venice: F. Rampazetto, 1564. 4to, contemp vellum. S Nov 21 (280) £850 [Kutluoglu]

— Venetia, citta nobilissima, et singolare. Venice, 1604. 2 parts in 1 vol. 4to, contemp vellum; worn. bba Feb 27 (245) £170 [Bifolco]

Santa Maria, Agostinho de

— Historia da fundacao do Real Convento de Santa Monica da Cidade de Goa.... Lisbon: Antonio Pegrozo Galram, 1699. 8vo, early 19th-cent calf; rubbed, joints split. S Feb 11 (528) £360 [Ad Orientem]

Santa Teresa, Joao Jose de. See: Giovanni Giuseppe di Santa Teresa

Santayana, George

— Poems. L, [1922]. One of 100. Sgd. Epstein copy. sg Apr 30 (407) $600

— Sonnets and Other Verses. NY, 1906. Inscr with holograph dedicatory poem. sg Dec 12 (364) $150

Santee, Ross

— Men and Horses. NY & L: Century, [1926]. Pictorial cloth. Library stamp on tp. sg Dec 5 (221) $50

Anr copy. In soiled d/j. Z Nov 23 (33) $85

Santini, Piero. See: Derrydale Press

Santorini, Giovanni Domenico, 1681-1737?

— Observationes anatomicae. Venice, 1724. 1st Ed. 4to, contemp calf; rebacked. With 3 folding plates. SI June 10 (918) LIt800,000

Sanuto, Livio

— Geografia.... Venice: Damiano Zenaro, 1588. Folio, modern vellum gilt. With 12 double-page maps, the first 2 oversewn. Lower margins affected by damp; some leaves restored, affecting imprint on tp; lower margins of maps often shaved with loss. C Dec 16 (76) £3,000 [Sacher]

Anr copy. Late 17th-cent vellum gilt & with gilt coronet corner ornaments; rebacked in calf preserving spine, soiled. With 12 double-page maps. Map III just shaved within neatlines at lower corners; Map VII with short tears repaired at lower right margin; X4 with small rust-hole affecting letters. S Nov 21 (345) £5,000 [Panini]

Sappho

— Fragments. Paris, 1933. One of 45. Illus by Mariette Lydis. 4to, contemp half vellum; soiled. With 15 plates. pn July 16 (85) £200 [Thorpe]

Sarazin, Jean

— Horographicum catholicum seu universale...horologia sciotherica. Paris: Sebastian Cramoisy, 1630. 4to, contemp vellum. With 2 plates. Waterstained in upper margins. S Dec 5 (427) £850 [Martayan Lan]

Sardi, Pietro

— L'artiglieria. Venice: Giovanni Guerrigli, 1621. Folio, vellum; joints wormed. With engraved title (shaved at head) & 9 plates. Margins of 1 plate wormed; a few plates & headlines shaved; some dampstaining. S July 9 (330) £450 [Liccini]

Sargent, Charles Sprague, 1841-1927

— Forest Flora of Japan. Bost., 1894. Folio, orig bds; worn. Library markings. Sold w.a.f. O Mar 31 (164) $50

— Trees and Shrubs: Illustrations of New or Little Known Ligneous Plants.... Bost., [1902]-5-13. 2 vols. Folio, contemp half mor gilt. With 200 plates. C Oct 30 (272) £250 [Heuer]

Sargent, John Singer, 1856-1925

— Work. L, 1903. Folio, cloth; worn, hinges cracked. Library markings. sg Apr 2 (266) $120

Saroyan, William

See also: Grabhorn Printing

— Harlem as Seen by Hirschfeld. NY, [1941]. One of 1,000. Illus by Al Hirschfeld. Folio, cloth. sg Jan 30 (83) $950

— My Heart's in the Highlands. NY, 1939. In torn d/j. Inscr. Met Apr 27 (780) $70

— My Name is Aram. NY, [1940]. In chipped d/j. bbc Apr 27 (400) $100

Anr copy. Inscr. F Dec 18 (113) $100

Anr copy. Cloth; backstrip def. Inscr to Burns Mantle. sg June 11 (277) $60

— The Time of Your Life. NY, 1939. Inscr to John Mason Brown. Met Apr 27 (781) $120

Sarpi, Paolo, 1552-1623

— The Historie of the Council of Trent. L, 1620. 1st Ed in English. Folio, old calf; rebacked. Tp defaced. W July 8 (66) £185

— The Historie of the Councel of Trent. L, 1620. 1st Ed in English. Trans by N. Brent. Folio, modern half calf; broken & loose. Tp & 1st leaf repaired; text soiled & foxed. STC 21761. wd June 12 (425) $125

Anr Ed. L, 1676. ("The History of the Council of Trent.") Folio, contemp calf; rubbed, spine & corners damaged. bba June 11 (70) £60 [Scardocchia]

— The History of the Quarrels of Pope Paul V. with the State of Venice. L, 1626. 1st Ed in English. 4to, contemp calf; front cover detached, portion of free endpapers torn out. 2N2 torn & repaired. STC 21766. sg Oct 24 (285) $400

Sarratt, J. H.

— The Works of Gianutio and Gustavus Selenus.... L, 18117. 2 vols in 1. Contemp half mor; rubbed. Ck May 8 (159) £70

Sarre, Friedrich, 1865-1945 —& Trenkwald, Hermann

— Alt-Orientalische Teppiche. Vienna & Leipzig, 1926-28. 2 vols. Folio, orig cloth; extremities worn. With 119 (of 120) plates, some colored. Ck July 10 (146) £600

— Old Oriental Carpets.... Vienna & Leipzig, 1926-29. 2 vols. Folio, contemp half mor; rubbed. With 67 colored & 53 plain plates. S May 13 (539) £1,000 [Randall]

Sarton, George, 1884-1956

— Introduction to the History of Science. Baltimore, 1927-47. 3 vols in 5 parts. 4to, cloth, 3 vols rebound. Library markings. sg Nov 14 (315) $275

Anr Ed. Wash., 1927-48. 3 vols in 5 parts. 4to, cloth; worn. O Sept 24 (220) $250

Sartorius, Carl Christian Wilhelm, 1796-1872

— Mexico: Landskapsbilder och Skizzer ur Folklifet.... Stockholm, 1862. 4to, contemp half lea; spine repaired at head. With engraved title & 17 plates. Some browning. pn Mar 19 (404) £160 [Mackenzie]

Sartre, Jean Paul

— Huis clos. Paris, 1945. One of 20 on Madagascar. Mor extra by Tchekeroul, orig wraps bound in. S May 28 (444) £1,500 [Beres]

— Le Mur. Paris, 1939. 1st Ed, One of 40 on velin pur fil Lafuma-Navarre. Mor extra by Devauchelle, orig wraps bound in. S May 28 (443) £1,200 [Saxhoff]

— La Nausee. Paris: Gallimard, [1938]. 1st Ed. Orig wraps. Epstein copy. sg Apr 30 (408) $425

Sassi, Panfilio, c.1455-1527

— Epigrammata.... Brescia: Bernardinus de Misintis for Angelus Britannicus, 6 July 1499. 2 parts in 1 vol. 4to, 19th-cent russia gilt. 29 lines & headline; roman letter. Small wormhole running through the 1st half of text. 192 leaves. Goff P-24. S Dec 5 (26) £3,400 [Burgess-Browning]

Sassoon, David Solomon

— Ohel Dawid. Descriptive Catalogue of the Hebrew and Samaritan Manuscripts in the Sassoon Library. L, 1932. 2 vols. 4to, orig cloth. With 73 plates.. sg Dec 19 (41) $650

Sassoon, Siegfried, 1886-1967

— The Heart's Journey. NY & L, 1927. 1st Ed, One of 599, sgd. 4to, bds, in d/j. bba July 9 (298) £160 [Sarner]

— In Sicily. L, 1930. 1st Ed, One of 400. DW Oct 2 (392) £60

One of 750. bba Dec 19 (218) £70 [Palladour]

— Memoirs of a Fox-Hunting Man. L, 1928. 1st Ed, One of 260, sgd. DW Oct 2 (394) £90

— Memoirs of an Infantry Officer. L, 1930. 1st Ed, One of 750, sgd. Cloth; spine faded. b Nov 18 (311) £50

Anr Ed. L, 1931. One of 320. Vellum over pictorial designs; bowed. Epstein copy. sg Apr 30 (409) $500

— Nativity. NY: Rudge, Dec 1927. 1st American Ed, One of 27 ptd to secure copyright. Orig wraps. sg June 11 (278) $130

— Recreations. [L: Pvtly ptd, 1923]. One of 75. Orig half vellum; some wear. Inscr to Henry Harris. S July 21 (174) £400 [Blackwell]

— Sherston's Progress. L, 1936. 1st Ed, One of 300 on homemade paper. W Mar 6 (81) £140

— To the Red Nose. L, 1931. One of 400 L.p. copies. Ariel Poems 34. sg Dec 12 (366) $80

— Vigils. [Bristol] 1934. One of 272. Illus by Stephen Gooden. Orig mor. Engraved throughout. b Mar 11 (180) £140

Satchell, Thomas. See: Westwood & Satchell

Satchwell, Richard

— Scripture Costume Exhibited in a Series of Engravings. L, 1819. 4to, old half lea; broken & repaired. One plate bound out of order & anr as frontis. kh Nov 11 (206)

A$180

Satie, Erik

— Sports & Divertissements. Paris, 1914. Out-of-series copy. Illus by Charles Martin. Loose in pictorial folder with printed cover label; 1 flap detached. With 20 motifs each consisting of a pochoir plate & a sheet of music. pn Sept 12 (140) £110 [Hildebrandt]

Sato Shozo

— The Art of Arranging Flowers. NY: Abrams, [1966]. sp Sept 22 (213) $50

Saturday Review...

— Saturday Review of Literature. NY, 1924-45. Vol 1, No 1 to Vol 28. Folio & 4to, loose issues in slipcases. sg June 11 (251) $3,400

Satyre...

— Satyre Menippee de la vertue du Catholicon d'Espagne.... [N.p.], 1624. 12mo, half calf. Some stains. bba Feb 27 (249) £60 [Greenwood]

Saude, Jean

— Traite d'enluminure d'art au pochoir. Paris, 1925. One of 25 lettered copies hors commerce. 4to, loose as issued. Related material inserted. S July 1 (1198) £1,900 [Sims Reed]

One of 500. Unbound as issued in orig half cloth with mtd illusts on front & rear cover & pochoir pastedowns. With 20 pochoir plates. Schlosser copy. P June 18 (585) $3,500

Sauer, Martin

— An Account of a Geographical and Astronomical Expedition to the Northern Parts of Russia.... L, 1802. 1st Ed. 2 parts in 1 vol. 4to, contemp calf gilt; spine worn, joints cracked. With 14 plates & 1 folding map. S Nov 15 (1101) £320 [Walcot]

Saul, Arthur

— The Famous Game of Chesse-Play.... L: T. Paine for John Jackson, 1640. 8vo, later half calf; extremities rubbed. Lacking A1; tp cropped at lower margin with partial loss of imprint; lacking table at end. Ck May 8 (58) £650

Anr Ed. L, [1672]. 8vo, old calf; spine restored. Lacking A1; tp cropped at lower margin affecting imprint; lacking table at end. Ck May 8 (59) £550

Saulo convertito...

— Saulo convertito, e santificato. Rome, 1796. 8vo, contemp mor gilt with arms of Cardinal Giulo Maria Cavazzi della Somaglia. Dedication copy; Abbey copy. C Dec 16 (77) £500 [Gurr Johns & Angier Bird]

Saunders, Ann

— Narrative of the Shipwreck and Sufferings. Providence, 1827. 8vo, remains of contemp front wrap. sg June 18 (488) $175

Saunders, James, of Newton Awbery

— The Compleat Fisherman. L, 1724. 12mo, early 19th-cent mor gilt. Some spotting. S Feb 26 (885) £380 [Montague]

Saunders, Louise

— The Knave of Hearts. NY, 1925. Illus by Maxfield Parrish. Folio, orig pictorial wraps; front wrap detaching, worn. K Sept 29 (325) $350

Anr copy. Cloth. sg Sept 26 (250) $600; sg Jan 30 (125) $1,600

Anr copy. Orig pictorial wraps; soiled & worn, tears at ends of spiral binder. wa Mar 5 (611) $450

Saunders, Margaret Marshall

— Beautiful Joe. Phila., 1894. 1st Ed, 2d Issue. With 4-page inscr by Saunders on front flyleaves. Epstein copy. sg Apr 30 (410) $1,100

Saunderson, Nicholas, 1682-1737

— The Elements of Algebra. Cambr., 1740. 2 vols. 4to, lea; hinges starting. sp Feb 6 (506) $95

Sauvage, Marcel

— Vlaminck.... Geneva, 1956. bba May 14 (573) £50 [Sims & Reed]

Sauvan, Jean Baptiste Balthazar

— Picturesque Tour of the Seine.... L: Ackermann, 1821. 4to, modern mor. With 24 hand-colored plates & colored folding map. C Oct 30 (138) £1,500 [Harley-Mason]

Anr copy. Mor gilt by Zaehnsdorf. With map, title vignette & 24 plates, all hand-colored. Date erased from title. C May 20 (303) £3,200 [Arader]

Savage, George

— The American Birds of Dorothy Doughty. Worcester MA, [1962]. One of 1,500. Folio, lea gilt. With 70 mtd color plates. sg Sept 6 (231) $225

Savary des Bruslons, Jacques

— The Universal Dictionary of Trade and Commerce. L, 1751-55. 1st Ed in English. 2 vols. Folio, contemp calf gilt; spines rubbed. With frontis, maps on 26 folding sheets & 26 folding tables. Some waterstain, mainly in tail margin of text & on map of Coast of Africa; some discoloration; small hole in foot of 10 leaves at front of Vol I affecting a few letters. b June 22 (201) £650

Anr copy. Contemp calf; worn, 1 cover

detached. With frontis, 24 double-page or folding maps & 25 folding tables. Some dampstaining & foxing; prelims misbound. pn June 11 (304) £420

Saverien, Alexandre

— Histoire des philosophes modernes. Paris, 1760-69. Vols I-VI (of 8). 4to, early calf; worn, a few hinges cracked. With 79 plates in sanguine in maniere de crayon. Vol I frontis shaved; Vol II with frontis in black; some spotting. Schlosser copy. P June 18 (497) $500

Savile, Sir Henry, 1549-1622

— A Libell of Spanish Lies. L: John Windet, 1596. 4to, mor gilt by Zaehnsdorf; scuffed, extremities rubbed. Lacking blank A1; washed; 1 numeral shaved. STC 6511. Ives-Church-duPont copy. CNY Oct 8 (224) $26,000

— Rerum Anglicarum scriptores post Bedam praecipui.... L: G. Bishop, R. Newberie & R. Barker, 1596. 1st Ed. Folio, contemp calf gilt, bound for Henry Frederick, Prince of Wales, with his arms & large badge of a Tudor Rose; rebacked in mor, corners repaired. STC 21783. British Museum duplicate. C June 24 (202) £2,600 [Quaritch]

Anr copy. Contemp calf gilt; joints weak. Some dampstaining. Evelyn copy. STC 21783. S June 30 (72) £900 [Christodoulou]

Saville-Kent, William. See: Kent, William Saville

Savonarola, Giovanni Michele

— Canonica de febribus. Venice: Bernardinus Vercellensis, 28 Sept 1503. Bound with: Practica. Venice: Bernardinus Vercellensis, 27 Feb 1502. Folio, late 18th-cent bds. Some dampstaining; 1st lack lacking ff. 1 & 2; last few leaves of 2d work wormed, affecting text, ff.203-5 damaged & repaired at head. S May 13 (907) £500 [Van Hee]

Savonarola, Girolamo, 1452-98

— Prediche qquadragesimale dell'anno 1495. Florence: [Bartolommeo di Libri], 8 Feb 1496/97. 4to, old vellum. With illuminated initial with profile port in colors & gold on a1r. 214 (of 220) leaves. Goff S-243. sg Mar 12 (132) $550

— Prediche utilissime per la quadragesima.... Venice: Bernardino Benalio, 12 Dec 1517. Caracciolus, Robertus. Prediche vulgare novamente hystoriate.... Venice: Giovanni Rosso da Vercelle, 11 Aug 1509. 4to, 18th-cent vellum bds. S Dec 5 (191) £1,200 [Goldschmidt]

Savoy...

— The Savoy: an Illustrated Quarterly. L, 1896. Ed by Arthur Symons; illus by Aubrey Beardsley. Nos 1-8 (all pbd). 4to, wraps & orig bds; soiled & worn, backstrips chipped. With suppressed prospectus & final notice for the periodical. With Christmas card inserted in No 1. S Nov 14 (87) £420 [Shapero]

Sawyer, Charles J. —& Darton, F. J. Harvey

— English Books, 1475-1900. L, 1927. 2 vols. In d/js. cb Oct 17 (839) $90

Sawyer, Eugene T. See: Grabhorn Printing

Sawyer, Eugene Taylor

— The Life and Career of Tiburcio Vasquez, the California Bandit and Murderer. [San Jose, 1875]. 8vo, orig wraps; foxed. sg June 18 (122) $1,400

Sawyer, Lorenzo

— Way Sketches containing Incidents of Travel Across the Plains. NY, 1926. One of 35. Half vellum. Inscr by Edward Eberstadt, 1926. sg June 18 (489) $170

Saxo Grammaticus, 1150?-1220?

— Danorum regum heroumque historie.... Soroe, 1644-45. ("Historiae Danicae libri XVI.") 2 vols in 1. Folio, later bds; rubbed. Some woodcuts loose. bba Apr 30 (261) £240 [Poole]

Saxton, Christopher

— An Atlas of England and Wales. L, [1579]. Folio, contemp calf gilt with Tudor Rose & 1 brass catch. With frontis, 35 double-page or folding maps, double-page plate showing 84 escutcheons & table of towns. Small wormhole touching surface at foot of some map, 1 or 2 shaved at neatlines; minor marginal tears or stains. S June 25 (266) £40,000 [Burden]

Anr Ed. L, 1936. Folio, half mor gilt; rubbed. With color port & 35 double-page & folding maps. Facsimile of 1574-79 Ed. pn Dec 12 (395) £450

Anr Ed. L, 1979. One of 500. Folio, orig half calf; soiled. Facsimile of 1579 Ed. bba Oct 24 (290) £100 [Sabin]

Saxus, Pamphilus. See: Sassi, Panfilio

Saybrook Platform

— A Confession of Faith Owned and Consented to by the Elders and Messengers of the Churches in the Colony of Connecticut. New London: Timothy Green, 1760. 8vo, old calf; worn. Some stains. O July 14 (170) $100

Sayer, Robert

— The Emperor of China's Palace at Pekin.... L, 1753. Oblong folio, half mor by Sangorski & Sutcliffe. bba June 25 (236) £4,000 [Pagan]

— Ruins of Athens, with Remains and Other Valuable Antiquities.... L, 1759. Folio, early 19th-cent half mor gilt; spine rubbed. With frontis & 26 plates. Frontis & last 3 plates browned. CNY Dec 5 (320) $1,500

Sayers, Dorothy Leigh

— Catholic Tales and Christian Songs. Oxford, 1918. 1st Ed. Wraps; soiled & rubbed. cb Sept 19 (185) $130

Sayers, Dorothy Leigh —& Byrne, Muriel Saint Clare

— Busman's Honeymoon. L, 1937. Wraps; soiled & rubbed. cb Sept 19 (184) $120

Sayger, C. —& Desarnod, A.

— Relation d'un voyage en Romelie. Paris, 1830-34. 2 vols. 8vo & folio, contemp half calf, Atlas in contemp half mor. With 51 plates, including 2 double-page (1 with overlays) & 4 hand-colored. Spotted & stained; 1 leaf torn & repaired. S June 30 (391) £1,200 [Consolidated Real]

Sazerac, Hilaire Leon de —& Engelmann, Gustav

— Lettres sur la Suisse. Paris, 1823-24. Parts 1-3 (of 5) in 1 vol. Contemp calf gilt; rebacked & repaired. Tp to Part 2 spotted; Plate 7 in Part 2 with small tear into view; some edges just touched by damp. pn Mar 19 (414) £1,000

Scali, Pietro Paolo

— Introduzione alla practica del commercio ovvero notizie necessarie per l'esercizio della mercatura. Livorno, 1751. Folio, contemp calf; somewhat worn. Some marginal spotting. SI Dec 5 (312) LIt420,000

Scaliger, Joseph Justus, 1540-1609

— Cyclometrica elementa duo. Leiden: Plantin, 1594. 3 parts in 1 vol. Folio, 17th-cent calf; rubbed. Some ink underlining & notes. bba Sept 5 (249) £340 [Quaritch]

Scalzi, Paolo de

— La scuola della spada. Genoa, 1852-53. Fascicules 2-9. 8vo, half cloth, orig wraps bound in. sg Mar 26 (294) $110

Scammon, Charles M.

— The Marine Mammals of the North-Western Coast of North America.... San Francisco & NY, 1874. 4to, orig cloth; rebacked worn. Library markings. O May 26 (163) $325

Scammon, L. N. See: Grabhorn Printing

Scamozzi, Vincenzo, 1552-1616

— De Vijf Colom-Orden, met derzelver Deuren en Poorten.... Amst., 1784. Folio, half lea. With engraved title, 6 plates & 48 full-page engravings (1 double-page). B Nov 1 (364) HF1,000

— L'Idea della architettura universale. Venice, 1615. 1st Ed. 2 parts in 1 vol. Folio, contemp vellum; worn. SI June 10 (921) LIt3,500,000

Anr copy. 19th-cent half vellum. Some waterstaining. SI June 10 (922) LIt1,850,000

— The Mirror of Architecture.... L, 1676. 3d Ed. 4to, modern calf by Lloyd. With engraved title & 52 plates, 6 folding. Some soiling; marginal repairs. pn July 16 (19) £280 [Thorpe]

Scarlattini, Ottavio

— Homo et ejus partes figuratus & symbolicus.... Augsburg & Dillingen, 1695. 2 parts in 1 vol. Folio, contemp vellum gilt. Browned. SI June 10 (923) LIt1,800,000

Scarpa, Antonio, 1747-1832

— Reflexions et observations anatomico-chirurgicales sur l'aneurisme.... Paris, 1813. Plate vol only. Folio, contemp half sheep gilt, orig backstrip retained. With 18 plates, including 5 duplicates in outline. sg Nov 14 (128) $450

— Sull' ernie memorie anatomico-chirurgiche. Pavia, 1819. 2d Ed. Folio, contemp half calf. With 11 double-page plates, each accompanied by an outline plate. SI Dec 5 (611) LIt900,000

Scarpatetti, Beat Matthias von

— Katalog der datierten Handschriften in der Schweiz.... Zurich, 1977-83. Vols I-II in 4. 4to, cloth, in d/js. sg Oct 31 (251) $325

Scenery. See: Haseler, H.

Scenes...

— Scenes from the Winter's Tale. L: Day & Son, [1866]. Illus by Owen Jones & Henry Warren. Folio, orig cloth gilt; worn. WIth 24 chromolitho leaves in gold & colors. cb Sept 26 (132) $140

Schaefer Library, Otto

— Katalog der Bibliothek...Teil I: Drucke, Manuskripte, und Einbaende des 15 Jahrhunderts. Stuttgart, [1984]. One of 800. 2 vols. Folio, cloth. sg Oct 31 (166) $50

Schaeffer, Jacob Christian

— Fungorum, qui in Bavaria et Palatinatu circa Ratisbonam nascuntur icones nativis coloribus expressae. Regensburg, 1762-[74]. Vols I-II only. Old calf; not uniform, rubbed. With engraved titles & 200 hand-colored plates. Some soiling; library stamps. Ck Oct 31 (104) £1,000

Schaeffer, Johann Gottlieb

— Die Kraft und Wirkung der Electricitet in dem menschlichen Koerper und dessen Krankheiten. Regensburg: E. F. Bader, 1752. 8vo, contemp bds; spine def. Some foxing. S May 13 (908) £300 [Phillips]

Schaeffer, Luther M.

— Sketches of Travels in South America, Mexico and California. NY, 1860. 1st Ed. 12mo, orig cloth. bbc Apr 27 (612) $65

Schaikevitch, Andre

— Serge Lifar et le Destin du Ballet de l'Opera. Paris, 1971. One of 200 hors commerce. Orig wraps, unopened. Inscr by Lifar to Boris Kochno, with colored ink drawing by lifar, sgd with initials. SM Oct 12 (533) FF12,000

Schaldach, William J.

— Carl Rungius, Big Game Painter. West Hartford VT, [1945]. One of 1,250. 4to, cloth; worn. Koopman copy. O Oct 29 (265) $600; O May 26 (164) $475

— Coverts and Casts: Field Sports and Angling.... NY, [1943]. One of 160, sgd. 4to, half cloth; spine darkened. sg Jan 9 (309) $60

— Fish by Schaldach. Phila., 1937. One of 1,500. Folio, cloth; worn. Koopman copy. O Oct 29 (264) $130

Schalletar, Joseph

— Divus Leopoldus Austria Marchio Pius felix. Vienna, 1692. 8vo, old calf; rubbed. With 15 emblems. Ck Oct 31 (87) £700

Scharf, Alfred

— Filippino Lippi. Vienna, 1935. 4to, orig half cloth. With frontis & 129 plates. S Feb 11 (200) £350 [Seidinger]

Scharf, John Thomas, 1843-98

— The Chronicles of Baltimore. Balt., 1874. 1st Ed. 8vo, orig cloth; worn. bbc June 29 (494) $70

— History of Baltimore City and County.... Phila., 1881. 1st Ed. 4to, orig half sheep; worn & repaired. Text soiled. bbc Apr 27 (599) $55

Anr copy. Orig half sheep; worn & frayed, short tear at top of upper joint, loose. bbc June 29 (496) $80

— History of the Confederate States Navy.... NY, 1887. 8vo, orig bds; worn & chipped. bbc Feb 17 (118) $200

— History of Westchester County.... Phila., 1886. 2 vols. 4to, orig half lea; worn & loose. bbc Dec 9 (403) $85

Anr copy. Bdg not described. In generally poor condition. Met Apr 28 (488) $50

Scharmann, Hermann B.

— Overland Journey to California.... NY, 1918. One of 50. Cloth. sg June 18 (124) $275

Schedel, Hartmann. See: Nuremberg Chronicle

Schefferus, Joannes, 1624-77

— The History of Lapland.... Oxford, 1674. Folio, contemp calf; rebacked. With engraved title & folding map (laid down on linen). Later leaves with waterstaining in upper margin. S July 1 (1456) £300 [Hagelstam]

Scheiner, Christoph, 1579?-1650

— Oculus, hoc est: fundamentum opticum in quo ex accurata oculi anatome.... Innsbruck, 1619. 4to, contemp vellum. S Dec 5 (429) £3,000 [Lib. Scheler]

Schenck von Grafenberg, Johannes, 1530-98

— Monstrorum historia mirabilis, monstrosa humanorum partuum miracula.... Frankfurt: M. Becker, 1609. 4to, contemp calf; covers detached and backstrip def. With 56 plates. DW Mar 4 (251) £230

Schenk, Charles

— Draperies in Action. NY, 1902. Folio, cloth; front cover detached. With 32 (of 36) albertype plates. Soiled, plates loose as issued. sg Apr 13 (86) $425

Schenk, Pieter

— Neuer Saechsicher Atlas. [Amst., 1710-59]. Folio, modern half cloth. With Ms index & 42 double-page mapsheets (of 50), most hand-colored in outline, a few in contemp body color. Some waterstaining at upper & lower edges; Leipzig with some abrasion at center affecting surface. S June 25 (310) £2,200 [Hass]

Anr Ed. [Amst., 1752-59]. Folio, contemp calf; worn. With index leaf inlaid to folio & 40 double-page mapsheets only, most hand-colored in outline. Some browning & fraying; most mapsheets becoming detached from guards. S June 25 (315) £1,300 [Haas]

— Roma aeterna. [Amst., c.1700]. Oblong 4to, contemp wraps with cardbd spine. With 36 color-ptd plates. Small tear to Plate I, repaired; the last 3 plates mtd; last 2 plates lacking captions; some spotting & browning throughout. Schlosser copy. P June 18 (498) $17,000

Scheuchzer, Johann Jacob, 1672-1733

— Geestelyte Natuurkunde. Amst., 1735-38. 15 parts in 8 vols. Folio, half lea; some defs. With frontis, port & 758 (of 760) plates. Lacking port of author. B Nov 1 (480) HF4,000

Anr copy. Contemp half calf; rubbed, some wear at extremities, a few leaves loose. With engraved frontis, 2 ports & 760 plates. C Oct 30 (292) £3,200 [Vanhaverbeke]

— Ouresiphoites Helveticus, sive itinera Alpina tria.... L, 1708. 3 parts in 1 vol. 4to, disbound. With port, 3 frontises & 41 plates. Blank corner of last few plates gnawed. sg May 14 (308) $650

Schewitzer, Christoph. See: Frick & Schewitzer

Schiele, Egon

— Das Egon Schiele Buch. Vienna & Leipzig, 1921. One of 1,000. 8vo, orig wraps; frayed. DW Oct 9 (626) £65

Anr copy. Orig bds; chipped. DW Oct 9 (627) £150

Anr copy. Bds; reproduction mtd on front pastedown. With mtd port & 62 plates. sg Apr 2 (268) $500

Schiff, Gert

— Johann Heinrich Fuessli. Zurich & Munich, 1973. 2 vols. 4to, orig cloth, in d/js. bba Feb 13 (133) £420 [Lane Fine Art]

Schiff Collection, Mortimer L.

— [Sale Catalogue] Catalogue of a Selected Portion of the Famous Library.... L, 1938. 3 vols. 4to, wraps; worn, shaken. O Sept 24 (221) $100

Schiller, Friedrich von, 1759-1805

— Die Horen, eine Monatsschrift. Tuebingen, 1795-97. Ed by Schiller. 36 parts in 10 vols. 8vo, contemp half calf; worn. HH May 12 (1602) DM3,500

— Rheinische Thalia. Manheim, 1785. Bound with: Thalia. Leipzig, 1786. Contemp half lea, orig wraps bound in. NH Oct 6 (331) $750

— Theater von Schiller. Tuebingen, 1805-7. 5 vols. 8vo, contemp calf gilt. HH May 12 (1612) DM1,200

— Werke. Stuttgart & Tuebingen, 1812-15. 12 vols. 8vo, calf. Some spotting. B May 12 (700) HF1,000

Anr copy. Contemp half calf gilt. Without list of subscribers; some browning. HH May 12 (1595) DM1,300

Anr Ed. Stuttgart & Tuebingen, 1835-36. 12 vols. 8vo, contemp half calf. HH May 12 (1596) DM520

Schimmelpennick, Mary Anne

— Theory on the Classification of Beauty and Deformity.... L, 1815. 1st Ed. 4to, modern half mor. With 2 folding tables & 38 colored plates. pn Dec 12 (167) £120 [Biltcliffe]

Schinkel, Karl Friedrich

— Sammlung architektonischer entwuerfe enthaltend theils Werke.... Berlin, 1858. 2 vols. Folio, half cloth. With 172 (of 174) plates. Some waterspotting & worming. HH May 12 (834) DM7,000

Schioppalalba, Joan Baptista

— In perantiquam sacram tabulam graecam... dissertatio. [Venice], 1767. Folio, contemp wraps; spine lacking. With engraved title & 4 plates, 3 folding. S June 30 (392) £210 [Consolidated Real]

Schlegel, Hermann, 1804-84 —& Westerman, Gerardus Friedrich

— De Toerako's afgebeeld en beschreven. Amst., 1860. Folio, modern half mor, orig upper wrap preserved. With 17 plates in uncolored & hand-colored states. C Oct 30 (293) £2,600 [Marshall]

Schlichtegroll, Nathanael

— Talhofer, ein Beitrag zur Literatur der gerichtlichen zweykaempfe im Mittelalter. Munich, 1817. Oblong folio, orig wraps; edges chipped & torn. With 6 plates. sg Mar 26 (298) $100

Schliemann, Heinrich, 1822-90

— Mycenae.... L, 1878-[77]. 8vo, orig cloth; worn, spine ends torn. Some foxing & soiling; top corner dampstained at beginning. bbc June 29 (153) $80

Anr Ed. NY, 1878. 8vo, orig cloth; spine soiled. wa Mar 5 (470) $95

Anr Ed. L, 1880. 8vo, orig cloth; corners & extremities frayed. With 25 plates (4 colored) & 8 plans. F Mar 26 (131) $100

— Troja. L, 1884 [1883]. 8vo, cloth. With color frontis map & 3 colored folding maps & plans at rear Marginal markings in pencil; ink notation at bottom margin of last leaf & reverse of rear free endpaper. bbc June 20 (154) $125

Schloss, Albert. See: Miniature Books

Schmid, Hermann —& Stieler, Karl

— The Bavarian Highlands and the Salzkammergut. L, 1874. Folio, orig cloth; rubbed. bba Sept 19 (149) £85 [Maliya]

Schmidt, Johann Andreas

— Gruendlich lehrende Fecht-Schule. Nuremberg, 1749. Oblong 12mo, half vellum. sg Mar 26 (300) $1,900

Schmied, F. L. See: Livre...

Schmitt, Joseph

— L'Ile d'Anticosti, whose Wild and Barbaris Charm.... Hartford: Pvtly ptd, 1940. One of 50 on Rives liampre. Wraps. With 9 mtd photographs & folding map in rear cover pocket. Koopman copy. O Oct 29 (267) $350

Schmoller, Hans

— Mr. Gladstone's Washi: A Survey of Reports.... Newton PA, 1984. One of 500. 4to, half mor. With extra set of prints in portfolio. bbc Apr 27 (101) $110; NH Aug 23 (57) $200; pba July 23 (33) $160

Schmutzler, Emil

— Altorientalische Teppiche in Siebenburgen. Leipzig, 1933. 4to, orig half cloth; worn at extremities. Ck July 10 (148) £550

Schneider, Antoine. See: Bory de Saint Vincent & Schneider

Schnitzler, Arthur, 1862-1931

— Die Hirtenfloete. Vienna, 1912. One of 400. Orig bdg. HH May 12 (2559) DM900

Schoberl, Frederick

— Picturesque Tour from Geneva to Milan.... L: Ackermann, 1820. 8vo, modern half mor gilt for C. J. Sawyer. With plan & 36 colored plates. C May 20 (127) £1,900 [Litup]

— Voyage pittoresque de Geneve a Milan par le Simplon. Basel, 1819. Illus by Gabriel Lory, the younger. Folio, 19th-cent mor gilt. With 35 hand-colored plates. Bound at end are 14 pp comprising ptd title & text & an engraved map from Bridel & Birmann's Voyage pittoresque de Basle a Bienne, 1802. C Oct 30 (132) £12,000 [Salmanowitz]

— The World in Miniature: Japan. L: Ackermann, [1823]. Ed by Schoberl. 12mo, contemp calf gilt. With 20 hand-colored plates. Lacking some text leaves; foxed & soiled. Soiled w.a.f. bba Apr 9 (182) £70 [B. Bailey]

Schoene, Albrecht. See: Henkel & Schoene

Schola Italica...

— Schola Italica Artis Pictoriae sive Tabulae insigniores in Romanis Pinacothecis Adservatae. Rome, 1806 [but some plates later]. Folio, half lea; worn, spine cracked & tape-reinforced, hinges broken. Some foxing & browning. sg Sept 6 (161) $500

Schomburgk, Sir Robert Hermann

— Twelve Views in the Interior of Guiana. L, 1841. Folio, orig wraps; soiled. With hand-colored litho title, map & 12 hand-colored lithos. Minor nicks repaired. S June 25 (455) £2,800 [Arader]

Schongauer, Martin

— Oeuvre. Paris: Armand-Durand, 1881. Text by Georges Duplessis. Folio, loose in cloth folder. With 104 (of 117) mtd reproductions. Sold w.a.f. bba Feb 27 (368) £160 [Bifolco]

Schoolcraft, Henry Rowe, 1793-1864

— Archives of Aboriginal Knowledge.... Phila., 1860. Vol VI (of 6) only. 8vo, orig cloth; broken, spine torn. Contents in 2 parts. Sold w.a.f. cb Nov 14 (197) $150

— Historical and Statistical Information Respecting...the Indian Tribes of the United States. Phila., 1855. ("Information Respecting the History...of the Indian Tribes of the United States....") Vol V (of 6) only. 8vo, orig cloth; spine and margins faded. cb Nov 14 (196) $325

— Narrative Journal of Travels, through the Northwestern Regions...to the Sources of the Mississippi River. Albany, 1821. 1st Ed. 8vo, contemp half calf; rubbed. With 8 plates & folding map. Lacking errata slip. cb Feb 12 (78) $325

Anr copy. Old calf. With engraved title, folding map & 7 plates. wd Dec 12 (443) $325

— Notes on the Iroquois.... NY, 1846. 8vo, cloth. sg June 18 (490) $175

Anr Ed. Albany, 1847. 8vo, cloth. sg June 18 (491) $175

Anr copy. Orig cloth; rubbed & soiled. Foxing at beginning & end; lacking the 2 color ports. wa Apr 9 (76) $85

— A View of the Lead Mines of Missouri. NY, 1819. 8vo, contemp calf; rubbed, covers detached. With 3 plates. F June 25 (673A) $300

Schoonhovius, Florentius

— Emblemata. Leiden: Elzevir, 1626. 2d Ed. 4to, modern half lea. With engraved title, port & 74 illusts. Lacking some prelims. SI June 10 (927) LIt300,000

Schopenhauer, Arthur

— Die Welt als Wille un Verstellung. Leipzig, 1819. 8vo, 19th-cent half calf. Some spotting at beginning & end. S May 28 (191) £2,000 [Schumann]

Schopper, Hartmann

— Panoplia omnium illiberalium mechanicarum.... Frankfurt: Georgius Corvinus for Sigismund Feyerabend, 1568. Illus by Jost Amman. 8vo, mor gilt by Riviere. With 132 woodcut illusts. C Dec 16 (79) £6,000 [Laube]

Schott, Frans

— Italy in Its Original Glory, Ruine and Revival. L, 1660. 1st Ed in English. Trans by Edmund Warcup. Folio, contemp sheep; head of spine worn & foot restored. With engraved title & double-page map, both detached. b June 22 (224) £700

Schott, Gaspar

— Technica curiosa, sive mirabilia artis, libris XII. Nuremberg, 1664. Vol I only. Old vellum. With 42 plates, including additional title. Foxing & marginal stains; Plate 3 backed & partly separated at fold; tear in Plate 32. sg Nov 14 (316) $550

Schottmueller, Frida

— Furniture and Interior Decoration of the Italian Renaissance. NY, 1921. 4to, half cloth. sg Feb 6 (257) $130

Schouten, Willem Corneliszoon

— Journal ou Relation exacte du Voyage.... Paris: Govert & Tavernier, 1619. 2d Issue, with date on tp changed & most of pagination errors corrected. 12mo, mor gilt by W. Pratt. With 4 folding maps & 4 folding plates. Spotting to Mer du Sud; marginal wormholes. DuPont copy. CNY Oct 8 (225) $8,000

— The Relation of a Wonderful Voiage...South from the Straights of Magelan.... L: T. D. for Nathanaell Newbery, 1619. 4to, early 19th-cent calf. Light stains affecting title & a few leaves at end. S June 25 (17) £12,500 [Quaritch/Hordern]

Schow, David J.

— Silver Scream. Arlington Heights IL: Dark Harvest, 1988. One of 500, sgd by all contribs. In d/j. cb Dec 12 (252) $80

Schramm, Albert

— Der Bilderschmuck der Fruehdrucke. Leipzig, 1922-30 & Stuttgart, 1981-86. Vols 1-23. Folio, wraps or cloth. sg Oct 31 (167) $3,600

Schreber, Johann Christian Daniel

— Die Saugthiere in Abbildungen nach der Natur mit Beschreibungen. Erlangen & Leipzig, 1755-1855. Part 4 only. Contemp half sheep. With 300 plates. Sold w.a.f. sg Sept 19 (209) $3,400

Schreiber, Lady Charlotte, 1812-95

— Journals.... L, 1911. 2 vols. Orig cloth. sg Sept 6 (256) $275

Anr copy. Orig cloth; extremities rubbed. Some foxing. sg Feb 6 (258) $130

Schreiber Collection, Lady Charlotte

— Catalogue of English Porcelain, Earthenware, Enamels, and Glass.... L, 1928-24-30. Compiled by Bernard Rackham. 3 vols. Orig wraps; spine ends & joints chipped. sg Sept 6 (257) $100

Schreiber, Wilhelm Ludwig

— Der Buchholzschnitt im 15. Jahrhundert. Munich, 1929. One of 100. Folio, loose in orig cloth box. With 43 (of 55) leaves of 15th-cent ptg, each separately mtd. S May 13 (796) £430 [Byrne]

— Un Catalogue des incunables a figures imprimes en Allemagne.... Stuttgart, 1969. 2 vols. 4to, cloth. sg Oct 31 (168) $425

Schreiner, Olive, 1855-1920. See: Limited Editions Club

Schrenck von Nozing, Jacob, d.1612

— Der aller durchleuchtigisten und grossmaechtigen Kayser.... Innsbruck, [1603]. Folio, contemp calf; worn. With frontis & 125 ports, some hand-colored.Some stains; tears repaired to 2 leaves at end. S June 30 (74) £1,00 [Sophoclides]

— Augustissimorum imperatorum, serenissimorum Regum, atque Archiducum... verissimae imagines. Innsbruck, 1601. Folio, early 20th-cent mor gilt, with recent cardinal's arms; corners rubbed, joints cracked. With dedicatory port & 125 other ports. C Dec 16 (80) £2,800 [Bifolco]

Schreyvogel, Charles

— My Bunkie and Others. NY, 1909. Oblong folio, modern cloth. With 36 plates. Inscr. sp Feb 6 (325) $550

Schroeder, Johann

— Vollstaendige und Nutzreich Apotheke.... Frankfurt & Leipzig, 1709. Folio, contemp calf; worn, backed with old paper. With frontis & 49 plates. Some browning & staining; frontis, tp & 2 plates just shaved. S Dec 5 (431) £800 [Shapero]

Schubert, Gotthilf Heinrich von —& Roth, J.

— Album des heiligen Landes. Stuttgart: J. F. Steinkopf, 1858. Oblong 8vo, orig cloth; edges rubbed. With wood-engraved frontis, folding litho map & 50 tinted litho plates. Some spotting to text & margins. S Nov 21 (306) £550 [Baum]

Schubert, Gotthilf Heinrich von, 1780-1860 —& Bernatz, Johann Martin

— Bilder aus dem heiligen Lande. Stuttgart, [c.1842]. Oblong 8vo, contemp half calf; rubbed. With 38 plates numbered 1-40, on india paper mtd. Marginal dampstaining. pn Sept 12 (339) £160 [Elliott]

Schubert, Walter F.

— Die Deutsche Werbe-Graphik. Berlin, 1927. Folio, orig cloth; joints frayed. cb Feb 12 (115) $425

Schubring, Paul

— Cassoni. Truhen und Truhenbilder der Italienischen Fruehrenaissance. Leipzig, 1923. 2d Ed. 2 vols. 4to, half cloth; corners knocked. bba Feb 13 (191) £850 [Angelini]

Anr copy. 3 vols (including Supplement). 4to & folio, cloth. Tp of plate vol torn. S Feb 11 (198) £800 [Heneage]

Schullery, Paul

— American Fly Fishing. A History.... [Manchester, 1987]. One of 100. 4to, half mor by Gray Parrot. Koopman copy. O Oct 29 (268) $600

Schulz, Aurel —& Hammar, August

— The New Africa, a Journey.... L, 1897. 8vo, orig cloth. sg Jan 9 (176) $325

Schunke, Ilse

— Die Einbaende der Palatine in der Vatikanischen Bibliothek. Vatican City, 1962. 3 vols. Wraps. sg Oct 31 (42) $140

Schurig, Martin

— Spermatologia historico-medica. Frankfurt, 1720. 1st Ed. 4to, contemp half vellum. Some browning. SI June 10 (928) LIt350,000

Schurmann, Ulrich

— Caucasian Rugs. Braunschweig, [n.d.]. sp June 18 (279) $250

Schurz, Carl

— Abraham Lincoln.... Bost., 1907. 1st Ed, One of 1,040. Half cloth, with inset medallion of Lincoln. With 19 ports. cb Sept 5 (149) $55

Schuyler, Montgomery

— American Architecture. NY, 1892. 8vo, orig blindstamped lea; rubbed, recased. sg Feb 6 (259) $225

Schwarz, Arturo

— The Complete Works of Marcel Duchamp. NY, [1969]. 4to, orig cloth; hinges repaired. Some annotations & underlining. wa Sept 26 (586) $550

— The Large Glass and Related Works. Milan, [1967-68]. One of 150. Illus by Marcel Duchamp. 2 vols. Folio, loose as issued in folder. With 18 orig etchings. CNY May 11 (376) $7,000

Schwarz, Heinrich

— David Octavius Hill: Der Meister der Photographie. Leipzig, 1931. 4to, cloth; scuffed & worn. sg Apr 13 (51) $80

— David Octavius Hill: Master of Photography. NY, 1931. 1st American Ed. 4to, cloth. sg Oct 8 (42) $300

Anr Ed. L, 1932. 4to, orig cloth, in d/j. Some foxing. kh Nov 11 (208) A$80

Schweiger, F. L. A.

— Handbuch der classischen Bibliographie. Leipzig, 1830-34. 2 vols in 3. 8vo, 19th-cent half cloth; joints frayed, corners chipped. sg Oct 31 (303) $375

Schwerdt, C. F. G. R.

— Hunting, Hawking, Shooting.... L, 1928-37. Vols I-III only. Half mor by Kelly; rubbed & soiled. With 266 plates, 84 of which are in color. S Nov 15 (751) £700 [Maggs]

Out-of-series copy. Vol IV only. Lea; rubbed, worn. K Mar 22 (408) $160

Anr Ed. Hildesheim, 1985. 4 vols. 4to, orig cloth. bba June 25 (160) £150 [Mazzo]

Schwob, Marcel, 1867-1905

— Vies Imaginaires. Paris, 1896. Half mor, orig wraps bound in. This copy illus by Jean Hugo with 3 gouache ports. Kochno copy. SM Oct 12 (509) Ff11,000

Anr Ed. Paris, 1929. One of 120. Illus by Georges Barbier. 4to, unsewn as issued in orig wraps. S May 28 (219) £2,600 [Fox]

Sclater, Philip Lutley

— A Monograph of the Birds Forming the Tanagrine Genus Calliste. L, 1857. 8vo, modern half mor. With map & 45 hand-colored lithos; several stained. S Nov 21 (44) £700 [Marshall]

— A Monograph of the Jacamars and Puff-Birds. L, [1879-82]. 4to, contemp half mor gilt; worn, hinges weak. With 55 hand-colored plates. Some foxing, mainly to text leaves. C Oct 30 (294) £3,000 [Grahame]

— On the Curassows Now or Lately Living in the Society's Gardens. L, 1873-78. 4to, cloth. With 21 color lithos. 2 extracts from Transactions of the Zoological Society. S Feb 26 (939) £350 [Shapero]

Sclater Collection, Philip Lutley

— Catalogue of a Collection of American Birds. L, 1862. 8vo, orig cloth; worn. With 20 hand-colored plates. Some plates dust-soiled. S May 14 (1054) £350 [Maggs]

Sclater, Philip Lutley —& Hudson, William Henry, 1841-1922

— Argentine Ornithology. L, 1888-89. One of 200. 2 vols. 8vo, orig half mor; rubbed. With 20 hand-colored plates. Inscr to W. R. Ogilvie-Grant. S June 25 (70) £1,600 [Quaritch]

Sclater, Philip Lutley —& Thomas, Michael R. Oldfield

— The Book of Antelopes. L, 1894-1900. 4 vols. 4to, orig cloth; extremities worn, free endpapers browned & nearby text leaves foxed. With 100 hand-colored lithos. Plate 29 badly torn; some leaves lose; marginal browning. P Dec 12 (82) $4,000

Anr copy. With 100 colored plates. Several prelims in Vol I carelessly opened causing tears in lower margins. S June 25 (72) £4,200 [Al-Thani]

Sclater, William Lutley. See: Shelley & Sclater

Scoresby, William, 1789-1857

— An Account of the Arctic Regions.... Edin., 1820. 1st Ed. 2 vols. 8vo, later cloth. With 24 plates & maps. Some fold tears; a few edges shaved; some spotting. pn Mar 19 (405) £440 [Remington]

— Journal of a Voyage to the Northern Whale-Fishery.... Edin., 1823. 8vo, later calf; joints rubbed. With 2 folding maps & 6 plates. S May 14 (1311) £220 [Remington]

Anr copy. 19th-cent half calf; worn. With folding map & 7 plates. Library markings; some foxing. sg June 18 (578) $275

Anr copy. Old calf; modern spine. With 2 folding maps & 6 plates. Both maps torn & repaired; 1 map laid on linen; 1 plate creased & torn on the folds. W July 8 (282) £185

— Journal of a Voyage to Australia and Round the World.... L, 1859. 8vo, recent half calf gilt; rubbed. With frontis & folding map. Frontis pencil-marked. DW Apr 8 (64) £95

Scorza, Rosaroll —& Grisetti, Pietro

— La Scienza della scherma. Milan, 1803. 8vo, later half cloth. With 9 (of 10) folding plates. Sgd by both. sg Mar 26 (302) $110

Anr Ed. Naples, 1811. 8vo, 19th-cent half sheep. With 10 folding plates. sg Mar 26 (303) $130

Scot, Reginald, 1538-99

— The Discoverie of Witchcraft. L, 1651. ("The Discovery of Witchcraft.") 2d Ed. 4to, modern calf. Some shaving & browning; annotations at end. pn May 14 (19) £750

Reprint of 1584 Ed. [L]: John Rodker, 1930. One of 1,275. Folio, orig half mor; stained. bba Oct 10 (496A) £100 [Andersson]

— A Perfite Platforme of a Hoppe Garden.... L: Henrie Denham, 1574. 1st Ed. 4to, bds; worn, rebacked & tipped in calf. Some dampstaining & soiling. STC 21865. wa Mar 5 (525) $750

2d Ed. L: Henrie Denham, 1576. 4to, disbound. K3 supplied in photostat facsimile; lacking final blank; corner of tp cut away; some staining towards end. Sold w.a.f. bba June 25 (172) £220 [Kunkler]

Scotcher, George

— The Fly Fisher's Legacy. L: Honey Dun Press, 1974. One of 55 L.p. copies. Mor gilt. With hand-colored frontis & 30 flies on 4 sunken mounts. Koopman copy. O Oct 29 (269) $1,100

One of 400. Half mor. Koopman copy. O Oct 29 (270) $70

Scotland

— Court of Session Cases. Edin., 1839-1980. 142 vols. Calf or cloth; some bdgs worn. pnE Mar 11 (87) £3,000

— Scottish Current Law Statutes. Edin., 1947-88. 61 vols. pnE Mar 11 (89) £130

— A True Representation of the Proceedings of the Kingdom of Scotland.... Edin.: R. Bryson, 1640. 4to, modern half lea. Some dampstaining; 1st & last leaves soiled; some leaves damaged in margins without loss. NH May 30 (486) $80

Scots...

— Scots Law Times. Edin., 1948-85. 39 vols. pnE Mar 11 (90) £440

Scots Musical Museum. See: Johnson, James

Scott, Sir Ernest

— The Life of Captain Matthew Flinders. Sydney, 1914. Foxed. kh Nov 11 (639) A$120

Scott, Genio C.

— Fishing in American Waters. NY, 1869. 8vo, half mor; rubbed. Koopman copy. O Oct 29 (272) $60

Scott, Hew

— Fasti ecclesiae scoticanae. Edin., 1915-50. Vols I-VII. pnE Oct 1 (301) £220

Scott, John

— British Field Sports. See: Lawrence, John

Scott, John, 1783-1821

— Picturesque Views of the City of Paris.... L, 1820-23. 2 vols in 1. 4to, contemp mor gilt. With 50 india proofs & 7 etched plates. Some foxing. Ck May 15 (143) £280

Scott, Peter
— Morning Flight. L, 1935. One of 750. 4to, orig cloth. b Mar 11 (238) £150
— Wild Chorus. L, 1938. One of 1,250. 4to, orig cloth. b Mar 11 (237) £140
Anr copy. Later mor gilt by Bayntun Riviere. DW Dec 11 (159) £270
Anr copy. Orig cloth, in d/j. pn May 14 (187) £220 [Elliott]
Anr copy. Cloth, in torn d/j. With 24 mtd color plates. sg May 21 (95) $600

Scott, Capt. Robert Falcon
— Scott's Last Expedition. L, 1913. 2 vols. bba Dec 19 (394) £85 [L. Kerr]
Anr copy. Orig cloth. Inscr by Kathleen Scott to Mrs. Bowers, mother of Lieut. H. R. Bowers, who froze to death with Scott. C Oct 30 (78A) £850 [Waterhouse]; sg Jan 9 (7) $80
2d Ed. 2 vols. Orig cloth. bba Apr 9 (69) £65 [Kent]
— The Voyage of the "Discovery." L, 1905. 2 vols. Orig cloth. Inscr to Sir Allen Young, Sept 1907. C Oct 30 (78A) £850 [Waterhouse]
Anr copy. Orig cloth; extremities rubbed. sg Jan 9 (8) $250

Scott, Sarah. See: Montagu & Scott

Scott, Temple
— Oliver Goldsmith, Bibliogrpahically & Biographically Considered. Ny, 1928. One of 1,000. 4to, cloth. Inscr. pba Aug 20 (153) $110

Scott, Sir Walter, 1771-1832
See also: Fore-Edge Paintings
— The Border Antiquities.... L, 1814-17. 2 vols. 4to, modern half calf. With extra titles & 92 plates. bba Sept 19 (245) £150 [Great NW Bookstore]
Anr copy. Contemp half mor gilt. With titles, frontises & 91 plates on india paper, mtd. bba Oct 10 (335) £100 [Axe]
Anr copy. Contemp mor gilt; joints rubbed, corners bumped. With frontises, additional titles & 91 plates. Some spotting & browning. Milne copy. Ck June 12 (181) £95
Anr copy. Half calf; worn. pnE Mar 11 (129) £75
Anr copy. Calf gilt. pnE May 13 (49) £200
Anr copy. 19th-cent half vellum; soiled. Most plates in Vol II and a few in Vol I dampstained. sg Oct 17 (363) $90
— The Field of Waterloo. Edin., 1815. 1st Ed. 8vo, modern half calf gilt. cb Nov 21 (209) $65
Anr copy. Half mor gilt, orig wraps bound in. sg Mar 5 (291) $100
— Ivanhoe. Edin., 1820. 1st Ed. 3 vols. 12mo, later half calf. bba Nov 28 (331) £95 [Ogino]
Anr copy. Orig bds; spines chipped, joints cracking, some soiling. Manney copy. P Oct 11 (273) $2,500
Anr copy. Orig bds; needs rebacking. sg Oct 17 (364) $375
— The Journal.... Edin., 1890. 1st Ed. 2 vols. 8vo, mor gilt by Henry Young & Sons. Extra-illus with c.55 engraved ports & plates & 13 signatures or A Ls s. CNY Dec 5 (390) $300
— The Lady of the Lake. L, 1810. 1st Ed. 4to, later half mor; extremities worn. sg Oct 17 (365) $70
Anr Ed. Edin., 1871. 8vo, orig bds. With 6 mtd photos. cb Sept 26 (185) $55
— Letters on Demonology and Witchcraft.... L, 1830. 1st Ed. 12mo, later lev gilt for C. J. Sawyer. With 12 plates in 2 states. bbc Sept 23 (40) $260
Anr Ed. NY, 1830. 12mo, orig cloth. Harper's Family Library, No XI. cb Sept 5 (95) $50
2d Ed. L, 1831. 12mo, contemp mor, rebacked with modern mor; worn. With 12 plates. cb Jan 9 (195) $55
— The Life of Napoleon. Edinburgh, 1827. 9 vols. 8vo, half mor; rubbed. bba Jan 16 (160) £130 [Harrington]
— Marmion: A Tale of Flodden Field. Edin., 1808. 1st Ed. Illus by Richard Westall. 4to, contemp calf; rubbed. With engraved title & 6 plates. bba Jan 30 (183) £60 [Kohler]
Anr copy. Modern half mor; rubbed. Minor foxing & soiling. O July 14 (173) $80
— Memoirs of John Dryden. Paris, 1826. 2 vols in 1. 12mo, contemp calf; extremities rubbed, corners bumped. Inscr to Mrs Hughes. Ck June 12 (185) £280
— Peveril of the Peak. Edin., 1822. 1st Ed. 8vo, contemp half mor gilt; worn. sg Oct 17 (366) $80
— The Poetical Works. Edin., 1821. 10 vols. 8vo, contemp russia gilt; rubbed. Some foxing. bba July 9 (204) £180 [Shapero]
Anr copy. Mor gilt. pnE Mar 11 (115) £150
— The Private Letter-Books. L, 1930. One of 40, sgd by Hugh Walpole & W. Partington. Mor gilt by Wallis with Scott's port in gilt on upper cover. bba Nov 28 (336) £75 [Axe]
— Redgauntlet.... Edin., 1824. 1st Ed. 3 vols. 8vo, orig bds; Covers of Vols I & III detached or starting. sg Oct 17 (367) $130
— Rokeby. Edin., 1813. 1st Ed. 4to, contemp half calf; rubbed. bba Jan 30 (184) £50

[Jacob]

— Tales of My Landlord, Third Series. Edin., 1819. 1st Ed. 4 vols. 12mo, contemp half calf gilt; worn. sg Oct 17 (368) $110

— Waverley.... Edin., 1814. 1st Ed, 1st Issue. 3 vols. 12mo, orig bds; washed & recased, rebacked preserving orig labels, front outer joint of Vol I cracked. Hogan-Doheny-Manney copy. P Oct 11 (272) $2,250

— Works. Edin., 1822-33. 48 vols. 8vo, contemp half calf. pn Apr 23 (132) £260 [Harrington]

Anr Ed. Edin., 1829-33. ("Waverley Novels.") 48 vols. 12mo, contemp mor; a few spines torn. b Nov 18 (312) £180

Anr copy. Later half mor gilt; rubbed. bba Feb 27 (112) £950 [Classic Bindings]

Anr copy. Half calf. pn Oct 1 (221) £260

Anr copy. Half calf gilt. Some ink stains; repair to frontis in Vol XVIII. pnL Nov 20 (140) £420 [Woodage]

Abbotsford Ed. Edin. & L, 1842-47. 12 vols. 8vo, later half mor; rubbed. DW Dec 11 (324) £125

Anr copy. Mor gilt. Some spotting. P June 17 (349) $3,000

Anr copy. Contemp lea gilt. pnE Oct 2 (528) £130

Anr copy. Calf gilt. pnE Mar 11 (42) £200

Library Ed. Edin., 1857. 25 vols. 8vo, calf gilt; rubbed, spines scuffed. O Feb 25 (174) $325

Anr Ed. Edin., 1860. 48 vols. 8vo, half mor gilt; spines faded. bba Oct 24 (114) £300 [Classic Bindings]

Anr copy. Contemp half mor; rubbed. Some spotting. pn June 11 (132) £350 [McKenzie]

Anr Ed. L, 1865-69. 98 (of 100)) vols. 8vo, contemp half calf gilt. cb Dec 5 (125) $2,250

Anr Ed. Edin, 1871. ("Waverley Novels.") 25 vols. 8vo, later half calf. bba Oct 10 (337) £280 [Thorp]

Border Ed. L, 1892-94. 48 vols. 8vo, half mor. pnE Aug 12 (275) £570

One of 365. Contemp half mor gilt by Blunson. S July 21 (71) £1,250 [Baring]

Dryburgh Ed. 16 (of 25) vols. 8vo, later half mor. cb Dec 5 (124) $110

Beaux-Arts Ed. Bost., 1893-94. one of 500. 30 vols. 8vo, half mor gilt. NH May 30 (85) $400

Illustrated Cabinet Ed. Bost., 1893. 48 vols. 8vo, half mor gilt; spines browned. bbc Dec 9 (252) $500

Anr Ed. NY: George D. Sproul, 1900. One of 1,000. 24 (of 26) vols. 4to, orig half mor gilt. Ls of George D. Sproul laid in. wa Sept 26 (31) $280

Anr Ed. NY: The Chaucer Company, [n.d.]. ("The Waverly Novels.") One of 1,200, each vol with 3 frontises. 51 vols. 4to, mor extra; some headcaps chipped, some scuffing to lower bd edges. CNY Dec 5 (441) $4,000

Scott, William Henry. See: Lawrence, John

Scoutetten, Raoul Henri Joseph, 1799-1871

— A Medical and Topographical History of the Cholera Morbus.... Bost., 1832. 8vo, orig half cloth; front joint & top of spine chipped. Foxed; map partly separated at folds. sg May 14 (150) $100

Scripps, John Locke

— Life of Abraham Lincoln. Chicago, 1860. 1st Ed, 2d Issue. 8vo, sewn. Small holes at gutter of last leaf. bbc June 29 (245) $400

Anr Ed. NY, 1860. East Coast Issue. 8vo, disbound. bbc June 29 (246) $200

Anr Ed. [Detroit], 1900. ("The First Published Life of Abraham Lincoln.") One of 245. 8vo, half vellum. cb Sept 5 (150) $190

Scrope, George Poulet, 1797-1876

— History of the Manor and Ancient Barony of Castle Combe. L: Pvtly ptd, 1852. 4to, orig cloth; spine faded. With 4 plates. Bound without map. DW Apr 8 (136) £165

Scrope, William

— The Art of Deer Stalking. L, 1838. 1st Ed. 8vo, mor gilt. With engraved title, frontis & 10 tinted plates. sg Jan 9 (311) $350

Anr Ed. L, 1839. 8vo, orig cloth gilt. Appendix leaf repaired; library markings. pnE May 13 (38) £60

— Days and Nights of Salmon Fishing in the Tweed. L, 1843. 1st Ed. 8vo, cloth; worn & shaken. With frontis & 12 plates. Koopman copy. O Oct 29 (274) $275

Anr copy. With 13 colored plates. Some plates frayed or torn at edge. O Oct 29 (274) $275

Anr copy. Orig cloth. pnE Mar 11 (215) £145

Anr copy. Later half mor; mor gilt by Morrell. orig cloth bound in. With frontis & 12 plates. sg Jan 9 (312) $700

Scudder, Samuel Hubbard, 1837-1911

— The Butterflies of the Eastern United States and Canada. Cambr. MA, 1888-89. 1st Ed in orig 12 parts. 12 vols. 4to, cloth. With 89 lithos, some in color. Titles & most prelims lacking; library markings. sg Feb 13 (208) $140

Scudery, George de

— Curia Politae: or the Apologies of Several Princes.... L, 1654. 1st Ed in English. Folio, contemp sheep; head of spine damaged, loose. sg Oct 24 (290) $200

Scultetus, Joannes, 1595-1645

— L'Arcenal de chirurgie. Lyons, 1675. 4to, contemp calf; rubbed. Lacking 5 leaves; k3 holed. Sold w.a.f. bba Sept 5 (301) £170 [Medical Museum]

Seabury, George J.

— An Ode to the Lake Bass. NY, 1890. 8vo, pictorial cloth; worn & soiled. Koopman copy. O Oct 29 (276) $130

Sealy, T. H.

— The Little Old Man of the Wood. L, [1839]. Illus by George Cruikshank. 8vo, calf gilt, front wrap bound in. Wormhole affecting bottom margin throughout; marginal repair on last leaf of text. Salomons copy. sg Oct 17 (178) $375

Search-Light

— The Search-Light. A Monthly Journal. Melbourne, June-Dec 1896. Vol I, Nos 1-7 (all pbd), bound in 1 vol. 8vo, contemp lea; worn, spine ends chipped. sg May 21 (5) $150

Seaver, James E.

— A Narrative of the Life of Mrs. Mary Jemison.... Howden, 1826. 1st English Ed. 16mo, orig bds; spine def, front cover loose. sg June 18 (492) $150

Sebastianus a Matre Dei

— Firmamentum Symbolicum, in quo deiparae elogia.... Lublin, 1652. 4to, modern calf. With 50 engraved emblems. Tp wormed at outer margin & with library stamps on verso. Ck Oct 31 (88) pS700

Seckendorf, Vitus Lodewyk von

— Commentarius historicus et apologeticus de Lutheranismo.... Leipzig, 1694. Folio, old vellum. sg Mar 12 (276) $60

Second...

— The Second Chapter of Accidents and Remarkable Events.... L, 1801. 16mo, resewn into later wraps; joints split. With 15 engraved illusts. bba July 23 (42) £55 [James]

Sedlmaier, Richard —& Pfister, Rudolf

— Die Fuerstbischoefliche Residenz zu Wuerzburg. Munich, 1923. 2 vols. 4to, cloth. Met Apr 28 (288) $70

Seebohm, Henry, 1832-95

— Coloured Figures of the Eggs of British Birds. Sheffield, 1896. 8vo, later half mor gilt. With port & 60 colored plates. bba Jan 30 (101) £60 [Incisioni]

— The Geographical Distribution of the Family Charadriidae, or the Plovers, Sandpipers.... L, [1887-88]. 4to, orig cloth, unopened. With 21 hand-colored plates. b Mar 11 (240) £300

Anr copy. Orig cloth; joints & spine ends rubbed, endpapers spotted. C May 20 (214) £450 [Travers]

Anr copy. Half lea. HH May 12 (519) DM1,100

— A History of British Birds. L, 1883-85. 1st Ed. 4 vols. 8vo, orig cloth. With 68 colored plates. bba Jan 30 (426) £80 [Bonner]

Anr copy. Contemp half mor, orig wraps bound in; rubbed. Mtd on guards throughout; some spotting. pn Mar 19 (242) £60 [Incisioni]

Seebohm, Henry, 1832-95 —& Sharpe, Richard Bowdler, 1847-1909

— A Monograph of the Turdidae or Family of Thrushes. L, [1898]-1902. Vol I only. Contemp half mor; rubbed. With port & 78 colored plates. bba Nov 7 (111) £180 [Elliott]

Anr copy. 2 vols. 4to, contemp half mor gilt; rubbed. With port & 149 colored plates. Some spotting & dustsoiling, mostly marginal. C Oct 30 (295) £3,500 [Grahame]

Anr copy. Contemp half mor, orig wraps to the 12 parts bound in. C May 20 (213) £4,200 [Travers]

Seeger, Alan

— Poems. NY, 1916. In repaired d/j. Epstein copy. sg Apr 30 (411) $275

Seeman, Berthold Carl

— Viti: an Account of a Government Mission to the Vitian or Fijian Islands.... L, 1862. 8vo, contemp calf; rubbed. bba May 14 (314) £160 [Axe]

Anr copy. Cloth; lower joint split, stained. kh Nov 11 (640) A$50

Sefi, Alexander Joseph

— An Introduction to Advanced Philately. L, 1926. One of 250. 4to, cloth. With 26 mtd plates. K Sept 29 (351) $140

Segalen, Victor —& Others

— Mission Archeologique en Chine.... Paris, 1923. Atlas, Tome I: La Sculpture et les Monuments Funeraires (Provinces du Chan-si et du Sseu-tch'ouan). Folio, loose as issued in folder. With 68 photographic plates. Bahr copy. sg Feb 6 (260) $250

Segard, W. —& Testard, Francois Martin

— Picturesque Views of the Public Edifices in Paris. L, 1814 [watermarked 1811-18]. 4to, modern mor gilt. With 20 circular hand-colored plates. Blank margins of 1 text leaf repaired. C May 20 (128) £350 [Frew Mackenzie]

Segaro, Giuseppe

— Dell' Idea dello scrivere. Genoa: Giuseppe Pavoni, 1624. Oblong folio, modern calf. With 47 plates including title. Engraved title & final leaf stained; marginal tears repaired & laid down; marginal waterstain on ff. 2 & 3. C June 24 (253) £850 [Franks]

Segni, Bernardo

— Storie fiorentine.... Augusta: Mertz & Majer, 1723. 2 parts in 1 vol. Folio, contemp vellum. Lacking 1 port; some browning. SI June 10 (930) LIt450,000

Seguin, Lisbeth Gooch

— A Picturesque Tour in Picturesque Lands. L, [1881]. One of 300. 4to, orig half vellum gilt; worn. With c.300 mtd proof plates. bbc Sept 23 (191) $65

— Rural England. L, [1881]. One of 600. Folio, contemp vellum-backed pigskin; rubbed & soiled. S May 14 (1155) £50 [Beaumont]

Segur, Sophie, Comtesse de, 1799-1874

— Old French Fairy Tales. Phila.: Penn Publishing Co., [1920]. Illus by Virginia Frances Sterrett. Cloth; worn, hinges starting. sg Jan 30 (169) $80

Seguy, E. A.

— Papillons. Paris, [1925]. Folio, unbound as issued in orig half cloth portfolio. With 20 colored plates. Ck Oct 18 (26) £750

— Samarkande. Paris, [c.1925]. Folio, half cloth portfolio; worn. With 19 (of 20) color pochoir plates. sg Sept 19 (210) $325

Seignobesc, Francoise. See: Francoise

Seitz, Adalbert

— The Macrolepidoptera of the World. Stuttgart, 1909-38. Parts 1-645 in 16 vols. 4to, various bdgs; some orig wraps worn or lacking. Sold w.a.f. Ck May 15 (47) £2,800

Anr copy. Vols I-XVI in 27, including Supplements to Vols I-IV. 4to, orig cloth; 1 spine damaged. With 89 colored plates. Some spotting & marginal browning. S May 14 (1055) £160 [Bookroom]

Selby, Prideaux John

— Illustrations of British Ornithology. Edin., 1833-34. 4 vols. 8vo & folio, half calf & half mor. With 2 engraved titles & 221 (of 222) plates. A few large plates folded at edges & torn; some soiling. S Nov 21 (45) £7,000 [Marshall]

Anr Ed. Edin., 1841. 2 plate vols (without the 2 text vols). Folio, modern half calf. With 4 plain & 218 hand-finished colored plates. Titles & 1st plate in Vol I with vertical crease. C Oct 30 (228) £17,000 [L'Acquaforte]

— Parrots. Edin., 1836. 8vo, contemp half calf; rubbed. With port, hand-colored vignette title & 30 hand-colored plates. The Naturalist's Library, Vol XV (Ornithology Vol VI). bba July 23 (320) £135 [Ginnan]

— Pigeons. Edin., 1835. ("The Natural History of Pigeons.") Illus by Edward Lear. 8vo, contemp half lea gilt; rubbed. With engraved title & 30 hand-colored plates. Margins browned. The Naturalist's Library, Ornithology, Vol V, Part 3. bba July 23 (319) £80 [Ginnan]

Selden, John, 1584-1654

— The Duello, or, Single Combat.... L, [c.1711]. 8vo, early sheep; rebacked. sg Mar 26 (307) $175

— The Historie of Tithes. L, 1618. 4to, contemp calf; joints rubbed. Title dust-soiled. DW Nov 6 (314) £135

— Titles of Honour. L, 1631. 2d Ed. 4to, contemp calf; rubbed, rebacked, orig spine preserved. 1 leaf crudely tape-repaired. bba Jan 16 (25) £65 [B. Bailey]

3d Ed. L, 1672. 4to, contemp calf; worn, front cover loose. sg Oct 17 (370) $70

Select. See: Smith, John

Selection. See: Mayer, Luigi

Selenus, Gustavus, Pseud.

— Das Schach oder Koenig-Spiel.... Leipzig, 1616. 1st Ed. Folio, contemp vellum; soiled. Some diagrams cropped at foot. Inscr by August II to Otto von Omptede. Ck May 8 (17) £2,200

Selfridge, Thomas O.

[-] Trial of Thomas O. Selfridge, Attorney at Law...for Killing Charles Austin. Bost., 1806. Bound with: Selfridge, Thomas. A Correct Statemen of the Whole Preliminary Controversy between Tho. O. Selfridge and Benj. Austin. Charlestown, 1807 2 vols in 1. 8vo, 19th-cent sheep. sg June 18 (192) $150

Selous, Frederick Courteney, 1851-1917

— Travel and Adventure in South-East Africa. L, 1893. 8vo, orig cloth. bba Sept 19 (72) £200 [Sharp]

Semedo, F. Alvarez. See: Semmedo, Alvaro

Semmedo, Alvaro

— The History of that Great and Renowned Monarchy of China.... L, 1655. Folio, contemp calf. LH Dec 11 (229) $750

Semmes, Raphael, 1809-77

— The Cruise of the Alabama and the Sumter. L, 1864. 2d Ed. 2 vols. 8vo, cloth; worn & shaking. Lacking frontis in Vol I. Inscr to Capt. Maury in both vols. O July 14 (174) $300

— My Adventures Afloat.... Balt., 1887. ("Service Afloat....") 8vo, pictorial cloth. sg Dec 5 (67) $250

Semple Lisle, James George

— The Life of Major J. G. Semple Lisle.... L, 1799. 8vo, contemp calf; lower cover marked. With port & errata leaf. Some foxing. C June 25 (146) £220 [Jessup]

Semple, Robert Baylor, 1769-1831

— A History of the Rise and Progress of the Baptists in Virginia. Richmond: John O'Lynch, 1810. 8vo, early sheep; scuffed & worn, bds bowed. Browned; some dampstaining at ends. wa Mar 5 (417) $100

Senac, Jean Baptiste

— Traite de la structure du coeur.... Paris, 1749. 1st Ed. 2 vols. 4to, contemp calf; some wear. With 17 folding plates. Some browning. SI Dec 5 (619) LIt1,800,000

Anr Ed. Paris, 1777. 2 vols. 4to, contemp calf. With engraved port & 23 folding plates. Title of Vol I torn. bba Sept 5 (302) £350 [M. Phelps]

Sendak, Maurice

— Pictures by Maurice Sendak. NY, 1971. One of 500, with a reproduction sgd by Sendak. Folio, orig bdg. cb Sept 5 (96) $225

Seneca, Lucius Annaeus, 54?B.C.-39A.D.

— Flores. Antwerp: Christopher Plantin, 1555. 8vo, contemp vellum. S May 28 (62) £700 [Maggs]

— Opera omnia. Leiden: Elzevir, 1649. 4 vols. 12mo, 18th-cent mor gilt. S May 28 (89) £500 [Zioni]

— Opera philosophicae. Venice: B. de Choris & S. de Luere, 5 Oct 1490. Folio, 18th-cent half sheep; spine ends & joints repaired, upper joint split. 62 lines & headline; types 3:107R, 7, 13:80R, 80Gk. Tp holed & repaired with some characters on verso supplied in Ms facsimile; small hole in k1; B8 stained. 215 (of 216) leaves; lacking final blank. Goff S-370. C Dec 16 (165) £1,000 [Bossi]

Anr copy. Old vellum; top of spine damaged. 62 lines & headline; roman letter; initials in red or blue. Some old underscoring & marginalia. 216 leaves. Goff S-370. sg Mar 12 (133) $1,400

Anr Ed. Leiden: Elzevir, 1640-39. 3 vols. 12mo, contemp vellum. b&b Feb 19 (10) $70

Anr copy. Mor gilt. Vol III lacking final 2 blanks. bba Oct 24 (21) £160 [Pickering & Chatto]

Anr Ed. Antwerp: Plantin, 1652. Folio, 18th-cent half mor; rubbed, def. With engraved title, port & 2 plates. Some browning. B Nov 1 (264) HF500

— Proverbios. Seville: for Jacobo Cromberguer Aleman, 1512. Folio, modern bds. Roman type. Margins stained; final leaf soiled on verso & damaged at lower margin; last 3 leaves with wormhole at outer margin. Ck Nov 29 (311) £500

— Seneca's Morals by Way of Abstract.... L, 1817. 2d Ed of Sir Roger L'Estrange's trans. 3 parts in 1 vol. 8vo, contemp sheep gilt; spine chipped & restored. Inscr by all 4 Harper Brothers for William Cowper Prime. Manney copy. P Oct 11 (162) $5,500

— Tragoediae. Venice: Aldus, Oct 1517. 8vo, contemp vellum; upper joint split. Ownership inscription erased on tp affecting a few letters on verso; first few leaves rehinged; small hole in last leaf touching a few letters; 2 leaves partly detached; a few headlines cropped. b June 22 (85) £60

Anr copy. 19th-cent vellum; worn. Frontis repaired in upper margin. SI June 10 (931) LIt250,000

— Works. L, 1614. 1st Complete Ed in English. Folio, 18th-cent sheep gilt; rebacked retaining orig backstrip, worn. Port, engraved title & [-]6 mtd. STC 22213. sg Oct 24 (294) $375

Anr copy. Later calf. With engraved title. STC 22213. W July 8 (39) £290

Senefelder, Alois, 1771-1834

— Albrecht Duerer's Christlich-Mythologische Handzeichnungen. [Munich, 1808]. Folio, loose in contemp portfolio. With litho title in black & violet, 2 litho ports & Duerer, 2 pages litho text in Senefelder's hand & 43 lithos by Strixner after Duerer ptd in single colors. Some foxing. Schlosser copy. P June 17 (535) $4,250

— L'Art de la lithographie. Munich, 1819. 8v, contemp calf. With folding litho plate. Schlosser copy. P June 17 (588) $900

Anr Ed. Paris, 1819. 4to, orig calf; rebacked, covers laid down. With port & 20 plates. Bedford-Schlosser copy. P June 17 (587) $7,000

— A Complete Course of Lithography.... L:

Ackermann, 1819. 4to, recent half mor. With port & 13 plates, 3 ptd in colors. Port spotted around the face; double-page plate cut & remtd as 2 single plates with some loss of image; anr plate trimmed with loss; several closed tears in letterpress. Schlosser copy. P June 18 (589) $700

Anr copy. Later half cloth; extremities rubbed. sg Feb 6 (261) $600

— Lithography. Stone Paper, (A Cheap and Advantageous Substitute for the Lithographic Stones).... L, 1821. 8vo, unsewn in wrap. Schlosser copy. P June 17 (590) $1,000

— Vollstaendiges Lehrbuch der Steindruckery.... Munich, 1818. 2 vols, including 1818 Supplement: Sammlung von mehreren Musterblaettern in verschiedenen lithographischen Kunstmanieren. 4to, bds. With 20 litho plates, 1 ptd additionally in silver & gold & hand-colored. Schlosser copy. P June 17 (586) $13,000

Senesius, Alexander

— Il Vero Maneggio di Spada. Bologna, 1660. Folio, early vellum. With engraved title & 10 plates. sg Mar 26 (309) $950

Senex, John, d.1740
See also: Ogilby & Senex

— A New General Atlas. L, 1721. Folio, contemp calf; extremities rubbed, spine ends split & chipped. With 3 double-page plans & 31 double-page maps ahnd-colored in outline. Some browning; blank margin of tp & 1st few leaves with damp or worm damage; 12 maps & 1 plan with clean tears mostly to the folds; map of England shaved with a little loss. C Oct 30 (162) £3,000 [Burden]

Anr copy. Contemp calf gilt; rebacked, worn. With 34 double-page maps, hand-colored in outline & 13 plates ptd recto & verso showing arms of subscribers. Europe split at fold without loss; some browning. S June 25 (299) £4,000 [Map House]

Senior, William

— Travel and Trout in the Antipodes. Melbourne, etc., 1880. 8vo, orig cloth; rubbed. bba Nov 28 (62) £55 [Hereward Bks]

Sepp, Christiaan

— Beschouwing der wonderen Gods in de minstgeachte Schepzelen of Nederlandsche Insecten. Amst., 1762-1860. Vols I-IV (of 8) only. 4to, contemp half calf; scuffed. With hand-colored engraved titles & 200 hand-colored folding plates. Some leaves misbound. C Oct 30 (296) £1,600 [Brittain]

Serafini, Camillo

— Le Monete e le bolle plumbee pontificie del medagliere Vaticano.... Milan, 1910-28. 4 vols. 4to, contemp half lea. SI June 10 (932) LIt400,000

Sereno, Bartholomeo

— Commentari della guerra di Cipro. Monte Cassino, 1845. 8vo, half calf. S June 30 (76) £900 [Sophoclides]

Serie...

— Serie de' Senatori Fiorentini. Florence: Giuseppe Manni, 1722. 4to, contemp wraps. sg Mar 12 (91) $500

Serlio, Sebastiano, 1475-1554

— The First [-Fift] Booke of Architecture.... L, 1611. 1st Ed in English from the Dutch trans of Peter Cocke. 5 parts in 1 vol. Folio, 19th-cent calf gilt; rebacked with orig spine laid down, corners restored, endpapers renewed. Fore-margins of all leaves reinforced due to water damage; 1st title-leaf creased & with 2 short internal tears without loss; cropping to woodcuts 4 leaves; minor marginal tears. McCarty-Cooper copy. CNY Jan 25 (70) $4,800

— Il Terzo Libro d'Architettura.... Venice: Corneli & Pietro de Nicolini for Marchio Sessa, 1551. Bound with: Regole Generali di Architettura. And: Il Secundo Libro d'Architettura. Folio, later half calf. Some staining; H4 of 1st work torn with loss, affecting illust & lacking N & N4; 3d work lacking tp & browned. S May 14 (1086) £240 [Kunkler]

— Tutte l'opere d'architettura.... Venice, 1619. 7 parts in 1 vol. 4to, 18th-cent calf; worn. Library stamp on tp. S June 25 (225) £1,800 [Bury]

Serranius, Joannes

— Comentarius, in Solomonis Ecclesiasten. Geneva: Petrus Santandreanus, 1579. 8vo, early calf. sg Oct 24 (295) $225

Serres, Olivier de, Seigneur du Pradel, 1539-1619

— Le Theatre d'agriculture et mesnage des champs. Paris: Jamet Metayer, 1600. Folio, contemp calf gilt; rebacked. HH May 12 (920) DM5,200

Sesti, Emanuela

— La Miniatura Italiana tra Gotico e Rinascimento. Florence, 1985. 2 vols. 4to, cloth. sg May 21 (279) $100

— La Miniature Italiana tra Gotico e Rinascimento. Florence, 1985. 2 vols. 4to, cloth. sg Oct 31 (252) $140

Sesti, Giovanni Battista

— Piante delle citta, piazze e castelli fortificati in questo stato di Milano. Milan, 1707. 4to, contemp calf gilt. With hand-colored folding map & 23 plans, 1 folding, with water hand-colored with green wash. Waterstain at bottom margins extending into foot of a few plates & keys. b June 22 (215) £1,700

Anr copy. 19th-cent half lea. With 24 maps hand-colored in outline. SI June 10 (934) LIt4,500,000

Seth-Smith, David

— Parrakeets, a Handbook to the Imported Species. L, [1902]-3. Half calf by Lewis & Harris, orig wraps bound in at end. With 18 hand-colored lithos & 2 other color plates. S Feb 26 (941) £350 [Shapero]

Anr Ed. L, 1926. 6 orig parts bound in 1 vol. Orig cloth. With 20 colored plates. DW Nov 6 (193) £220

Anr copy. With 18 hand-colored plates & 2 color plates. S Feb 26 (940) £250 [Cumming]

Seth-Smith, Michael —& Mortimer, Roger

— The Official Story of the Blue Riband of Turf. Derby 200.... L, [1979]. One of 10 with a fore-edge painting. 4to, orig mor gilt, with painting of a horse race. S May 14 (1018) £220 [Way]

Seton, Ernest Thompson, 1860-1946

— The Arctic Prairies. A Canoe-Journey.... NY, 1911. Library markings. NH Oct 6 (333) $50

— Life-Histories of Northern Animals. NY, 1909. 2 vols. 4to, later cloth. sg May 14 (243) $110

— Wild Animals I Have Known. NY, 1898. 1st Ed, 1st Issue. 8vo, cloth. Inscr. Epstein copy. sg Apr 30 (412) $1,100

Seuss, Dr.

— The Seven Lady Godivas. NY, [1939]. 1st Ed, 1st Ptg. 4to, cloth, in chipped d/j. F June 25 (534) $270

Anr copy. Cloth. wd Dec 12 (445) $200

Seutter, Matthaeus

— Atlas novus indicibus instructus oder neur mit Wort-Registern versehener Atlas. Augsburg & Vienna, 1730-[38]. Folio, contemp calf; worn. With engraved additional titles (fully hand-colored), double-page engraved dedication & 53 double-page mapsheets, hand-colored in wash & outline. Tp & several maps torn at margins or split along folds. S Nov 21 (136) £4,000 [Hassold]

Severino, Marco Aurelio

— La Filosofia overo il perche degli scacchi.... Naples, 1690. Bound with: Dell' Antica Pettia.... 4to, contemp vellum. Some browning; final leaves wormed at lower margain. Ck May 8 (60) £260

Sevigne, Marie de Rabutin-Chantal, Marquise de, 1626-96

— Lettres.... Paris, 1882-1925. ("Lettres de Madame de Sevigne de sa famille et de ses amis.") 14 vols. 8vo, later half mor. W July 8 (40) £110

Seward, William Wenman

— Topographia Hibernica; or the Topography of Ireland. L, 1795. 4to, contemp calf. pnE Aug 12 (295) £140

Sewel, William, 1653-1720

— The History of the Rise, Increase, and Progress of the Christian People Called Quakers. Phila.: Samuel Keimer, 1728. Folio, orig calf by William Davies (Miller stamp a, fillet B); worn, restored, rebacked with new endpapers. Tp with extensive marginal restoration & 2 closed tears costing a bit of border rule; marginal repairs; browned & stained; lacking final 3 leaves of index. P June 16 (4) $1,300

3d Ed. Burlington NJ: Collins, 1774. Folio, recent cloth. Browned. bbc June 29 (337) $130

Sexton, J. J. O'Brien. See: Binyon & Sexton

Seymour, Robert

— Sketches. L, [c.1840]. 5 vols in 2. 8vo, half calf; worn, lacking backstrips. With 5 engraved titles & 180 plates on various colored papers. Some browning; 2 titles torn at inner edge & 2 plates loose. L Nov 14 (83) £50

Sgrilli, Bernardo Sansone

— Descrizione della regia villa, fontane, e fabbriche di Pratolino. Florence, 1742. Illus by Stefano della Bella. 4to, orig bds; spine rubbed. With 12 double-page plans & views; Plate 1 has engraved text (the title), added. C Dec 16 (81) £3,800 [Jackson]

Shackleton, Sir Ernest Henry, 1874-1922

See also: Aurora...

— The Antarctic Book. L, 1909. One of 300, sgd by the members of the shore party. 4to, orig half vellum. With 6 plates & 4 mtd colored ports. sg May 21 (3) $3,000

— The Heart of the Antarctic. L, 1909. 2 vols. 4to, orig cloth. b June 22 (273) £140

Anr copy. Cloth; rubbed, 1 joint cracked. bba Mar 26 (337) £90 [Harrington]

Anr copy. Orig cloth; faded, spines rubbed. DW Apr 8 (65) £140

One of 300. 3 vols, including The Antarctic Book. 4to, orig vellum gilt. Sold with The Antarctic Book, Winter Quarters, one of 300. Manney set. P Oct 11 (1275) $4,500

One of 300, sgd by all members of the Shore Party. Vellum & half vellum. With 3 folding maps & folding panorama in pocket at end of Vol II. Inscr to Sir James Charles. W July 8 (283) £2,300

Anr Ed. Phila., 1909. 2 vols. 4to, cloth. 1 plate loose. bba Oct 10 (256) £170 [Remington]

Anr copy. Orig cloth; rubbed. pn Dec 12 (366) £75 [Proctor]

Anr copy. Cloth; extremities worn, hinges cracked. sg Jan 9 (10) $150

Anr copy. Half mor gilt. Library markings. sg Jan 9 (11) $120

— South.... L, 1919. 1st Ed. Orig cloth, in d/j. C Oct 30 (81) £900 [Lascaux]

Shaffer, Ellen Kate

— The Nuremberg Chronicle: A Pictorial World History.... Los Angeles, 1950. One of 300. 4to, cloth. With orig leaf from the 1497 Augsberg Latin Ed laid in. cb Oct 31 (55) $225

Shaftesbury, Anthony Ashley Cooper, 3d Earl of, 1671-1713

— Characteristicks of Men, Manners, Opinions, Times. Birm.: Baskerville, 1773. "5th Ed". 3 vols. 8vo, Vol I & III, mor by J. Wright; Vol II, modern calf; rubbed. O Feb 25 (175) $110

Anr copy. Early calf; worn, rebacked. sg Oct 17 (114) $110

Shakers

— A Declaration of the Society of People.... Albany, 1815. 8vo, disbound. Some foxing. sg June 18 (494) $250

Shakespeare, William, 1564-1616

See also: Cranach Press; Doves Press; Fletcher & Shakespeare; Fore-Edge Paintings; Golden Cockerel Press; Grabhorn Printing; Kelmscott Press; Limited Editions Club; Nonesuch Press

— As You Like It. L: Hodder & Stoughton, [1909]. Illus by Hugh Thomson. 4to, orig vellum gilt. W July 8 (338) £210

— Hamlet. L: Selwyn & Blount, [1922]. ("Hamlet, Prince of Denmark.") Illus by John Austen. 4to, orig half cloth. b Nov 18 (313) £70

— The Merry Wives of Windsor. L: De Vinne, 1903. One of 7 on vellum. 4to, mor extra, inlaid & gilt. Illuminated throughout by John H. Tearle, with watercolor & gilt floral borders on every page & with watercolor drawings. CNY Dec 5 (379) $4,500

Anr Ed. L, 1910. Illus by Hugh Thomson. 4to, cloth; spine stained. With 40 colored plates. sp Nov 24 (213) $65

Anr copy. Orig cloth; worn. wa Sept 26 (673) $70

— A Midsummer-Night's Dream. L, 1908. Illus by Arthur Rackham. 4to, cloth. bba Jan 16 (399) £160 [Ulysses]

Anr copy. Orig cloth; backstrip repaired. bba Apr 9 (283) £85 [Axe]

Anr copy. Mor gilt. K Mar 22 (393) $180

Anr copy. Orig cloth; front hinge cracked. sg Jan 30 (154) $250

One of 1,000. Orig vellum gilt; spine mottled. Ck Dec 11 (178) £420

One of 1,000, sgd by Rackham. Orig vellum. CNY June 9 (166) $900

One of 1,000. Orig vellum gilt; soiled. S Apr 28 (43) £150 [Droller]

1st American Ed. NY, 1908. 4to, half cloth, in d/j. sg Sept 26 (272) $450

Anr copy. Half cloth. sg Jan 30 (155) $300

Anr Ed. L, 1914. Illus by W. Heath Robinson. 4to, orig cloth. bba Apr 9 (344) £220 [Ulysses]

Anr copy. Orig cloth; worn. With 12 tipped-in color plates. K Sept 29 (393) $80

Anr Ed. L, 1919. Illus by Arthur Rackham. 4to, orig cloth, in d/j with small tears. Some spotting. bba May 14 (342) £85 [Axe]

Anr Ed. L, 1925. 4to, orig cloth, in d/j. With 40 colored plates. bba Apr 9 (339) £240 [W. White]

— The Tempest. L, [1908]. Illus by Edmund Dulac. 4to, orig cloth. O Mar 31 (165) $100

Anr copy. Orig cloth; worn. With 40 colored plates. Some text pages foxed. sg Jan 30 (48) $150

One of 500. Orig vellum gilt; unopened. With 21 mtd color plates. sg Nov 7 (177) $1,200

Anr Ed. L, [1926]. Illus by Arthur Rackham. Lacking d/j. bba Jan 16 (400) £120 [Pordes]

Anr copy. Orig cloth, in d/j. bba Apr 9 (340) £280 [Ulysses]

— The Tragedie of Julius Caesar. L: Shakespeare Head Press, 1925. Out-of-series copy. 4to, half mor. sg Jan 10 (164) $130

1st Folio

— As You Like It; The Taming of the Shrew: All's Well that Ends Well.... L, 1623. Modern bds. Waterstained at inner & bottom margin; corner of 1st leaf restored. Manney copy. P Oct 11 (277) $3,250

— Comedies, Histories, & Tragedies. L: Isaac Jaggard & Ed. Blount, 1623. Mor. Lacking

29 leaves, supplied in facsimile. 7 or 8 leaves with repairs or tears affecting up to 10 words; marginal repairs to c.28 leaves. George Milne copy. CNY Dec 5 (324) $90,000

— Coriolanus; Titus Andronicus.... L, 1623. Mor gilt by Sangorski & Sutcliffe. Manney copy. P Oct 11 (278) $6,000

2d Folio

— Comedies, Histories, and Tragedies. L, 1632. 17th-cent calf; rebacked, corners and edges renewed. 1st 2 leaves and last leaf lacking and supplied in facsimile; D1 and quires i and ii "probably" supplied from anr copy. Scattered staining throughout. George Milne copy. CNY Dec 5 (325) $4,500

Anr copy. Mor gilt by Hayday. Tp imprint is Todd's state Ia; page with Milton's verse is his state Ib, corrected. To the Reader inlaid; marginal repair on Aa6 touching a letter; marginal repairs & a few small holes. Manney copy. P Oct 11 (279) $36,000

— Richard the Second. First [and Second] Part of Henry the Fourth. L, 1632. Modern cloth. With a single leaf (from Henry IV, Part I) from the 1st Folio Ed. George Milne copy. CNY Dec 5 (326) $320

4th Folio

— Comedies, Histories, and Tragedies. L, 1685. 1st state of imprint without Chiswell's name. Contemp calf; repaired. Worming to upper margins to N5 occasionally affecting headline; lower margins of 3B5-3E6 wormed; rusthole or paper fault to A3, E6, T1, 2X4; small tears to N3, 3D3, 3F1, 4Z5;l upper margin of final leaf strengthened. C Dec 16 (230) £8,000 [Finch]

Anr copy. Contemp calf; rebacked, covers detached. With 1807 facsimile port crudely mtd on front free endpaper; section of tp & dedication torn with loss & restored in 18th-cent ink facsimile; tp to A4 of preface with loss to lower margin; H2 lacking section of outer margin; 2G4 repaired at lower margin; 2I2 & 2R6 torn at margins; 4C2 laid down; some soiling. Sold w.a.f. Milne copy. Ck June 12 (186) £2,400

Anr copy. Mor gilt by Bedford. Last leaf remargined; corner of Aaaa3-4 restored; some tears repaired. Manney copy. P Oct 11 (280) $30,000

Collected Works

— 1709-10. - L: Jacob Tonson L.p. Issue. Ed by N. Rowe. 7 vols. 8vo, contemp calf, Vol VII bound to match. Last few leaves of Vol I dampstained; Vol VI with worming of margins to Dd5 & lacking front blank A1; Vol VII with rusthole in lower margin of H7 & Dd5 & without final blank. C Dec 16 (231) £2,800 [Franklin]

— 1723-25. - Works. L: Jacob Tonson Ed by Alexander Pope. 6 vols in 10. 4to, 19th-cent sheep gilt; spines rubbed. Some gatherings browned; Vol V lacking tp; other titles trimmed & rehinged, the 1st mtd. sg Oct 24 (296) $500

— 1725-23-25. - L. 7 vols. 4to, contemp calf, Vol VII bound to match; joints rubbed & with splits, spines chipped. Some browning & spotting. C Dec 16 (232) £1,100 [Maggs]

Anr copy. Vols I-VI (of 7). 4to, contemp calf gilt; rebacked in the 19th-cent. S July 1 (1043) £500 [Arnold]

— 1733. - L. Ed by Lewis Theobald. 7 vols. 8vo, calf; rebacked. pnE Oct 1 (219) £80

— 1762. - L. 8 vols. 8vo, later half calf. bba Jan 30 (49) £220 [Fletcher]

— 1765. - L. 8 vols. 8vo, contemp calf; spines worn. With port. L Nov 14 (447) £140

Anr copy. Modern half mor. sg May 7 (188) $1,200

— 1768. - The Plays. L. Ed by Samuel Johnson. 8 vols. 8vo, contemp calf; joints worn, rubbed. bba Feb 27 (86) £150 [Harrington]

— 1770-71. - The Works of Shakespear... Adorned with Sculptures. Oxford 6 vols. 4to, contemp mor gilt; spin & extremities scuffed. Some browning; prelim blank in Vol I detached; 4A4-4H2 in Vol III wormed in lower blank margin. C Dec 16 (233) £800 [Brooke-Hitching]

— 1773. - L. Ed by Samuel Johnson & George Steevens. 10 vols. 8vo, contemp calf; rubbed. S July 1 (1042) £150

— 1793. - L. Notes by Samuel Johnson & George Steevens. 15 vols. 8vo, 19th-cent half calf; spines worn. Some foxing. bbc Dec 9 (253) $625

Anr copy. Contemp mor gilt; rubbed & discolored, some spines worn. S May 13 (632) £220 [Edwards]

— 1796. - The Plays. L. 8 vols. 8vo, contemp calf gilt; spine & corners repaired, rubbed. With 2 engraved titles & 89 plates. Some foxing; 1 plate with tear. pn Apr 23 (133) £150 [Harrington]

— 1802. - L. Ed by George Steevens. Folio, contemp mor gilt; rubbed, some restoration. Some spotting & soiling. P June 17 (351) $3,500

— 1803. - L. Notes by Johnson & Steevens; Ed by Isaac Reed. 21 vols. 8vo, 19th-cent mor gilt by J. Bohn; spines rubbed. S July 21 (15) £900 [Joseph]

— 1825. - L: Pickering. Wreath Ed. 11 vols. 8vo, contemp half mor; rubbed. Ck Dec 11 (140) £220

— 1853-65. - L. One of 150. Ed by James O. Halliwell. 16 vols bound in 32. Folio, mor extra by Barrie. With ALs by Halliwell bound in. CNY Dec 5 (442) $7,500
— 1858. - L. Ed by J. Payne Collier. 6 vols. 8vo, contemp calf gilt. pn June 11 (133) £95 [Sotheran]
— 1863-66. - Cambr. & L. Ed by W. G. Clark & others. 9 vols. 8vo, half mor gilt by Pratt; some soiling. S Nov 14 (597) £190 [Joseph]
— 1866. - L. 9 vols. 8vo, half mor gilt by Ramage. pnE Aug 12 (277) £300
— 1868. - Bost.Author's Ed, one of 1,000. 12 vols. 8vo, contemp half mor gilt. wa Dec 9 (14) $70
— 1875-76. - L. Ed by Alexander Dyce. 9 vols. 8vo, orig cloth; rubbed. cb Jan 9 (197) $160

Anr copy. Ed by Charles Knight. 2 vols. 8vo, later mor gilt; spines scuffed. Extra-illus with plates of scenes & players and settings. cb Oct 25 (110) $300

— 1875-76. - NY: Virtue & Vorston. Imperial Ed. Ed by Charles Knight. 2 vols. 4to, contemp mor gilt; extremities worn, front hinge of Vol I cracked. sg Oct 17 (373) $110
— 1891. - L. 10 vols. 8vo, half mor by Riviere. S Feb 11 (417) £380 [Sotheran]
— 1891-93. - L.Cambr. Ed. 9 vols. Contemp half calf by Henry Young & Sons; lower cover of 3 vols stained. bba Oct 10 (376) £170 [Barker]
— 1900-03. - L: Vale Press One of 310. 37 (of 39) vols; lacking Poems & Sonnets. Orig cloth; spines soiled. bba July 9 (314) £320 [Shapero]
— 1904-7. - Stratford: Shakespeare Head Press One of 1,000. 10 vols. 4to, cloth. LH May 17 (628) $100
— [1906]. - NY: Harper. Cambridge Ed. 20 vols. Cloth. wa Feb 20 (105) $95
— 1936. - Garden City One of 750. Illus by Rockwell Kent. 2 vols. 4to, cloth. wd Dec 12 (447) $250

Facsimile Editions

— 1866. - L. Folio, contemp calf gilt; rebcked, rubbed, orig backstrip laid down. Photo-lithographed from the Ellesmere & British Museum copies by R. W. Preston, under the supervision of Howard Staunton. L Feb 27 (224) £140
— 1968. - NY Folio, orig half mor. The Norton Facsimile. bba Jan 16 (182) £60 [Vaughan]
— [n.d.]. - The National Shakespeare. L: W. Mackenzie Illus by J. Noel Paton. Folio, orig cloth. Facsimile of 1st Folio. bba Apr 9 (109) £95 [Kerpel]

Anr copy. 3 vols. Folio, orig mor gilt. Facsimile of 1st Folio. LH Dec 11 (243) $425

Poems, Sonnets, etc.

— A Collection of Poems, viz. I. Venus and Adonis. II. The Rape of Lucrece.... L: Bernard Lintott, [c.1709-10]. 4 parts in 1 vol. 8vo, contemp calf gilt; joints cracked, rubbed. Some headlines shaved; some foxing & browning. bba June 25 (182) £650 [Selzer & Selzer]

Anr copy. 2 parts in 1 vol. 8vo, later mor. Some browning; hole in port. C Dec 16 (229) £380 [Frew Mackenzie]

— Poems. L, 1640. 8vo, calf gilt; wormhole in bottom compartment of spine. With both dated & undated titles. Benz-Manney copy. P Oct 11 (282) $50,000
— Songs from the Plays. L, 1899. One of 100. 4to, mor extra by the Guild of Women Binders. With hand-colored tp & 12 hand-colored plates. S Apr 28 (48) £450 [Temperley]
— Sonnets. Stratford: Shakespeare Head Press, 1905. One of 520. Contemp mor with intricate border by Zaehnsdorf. cb Sept 5 (98) $600
— The Sonnets. L, 1928. Mor gilt with miniature bust port painting on ivory of Shakespeare. sg Mar 5 (293) $450
— The Sonnets of Shakespeare. L: Vale Press, 1899. One of 210. 4to, orig cloth; soiled. bba July 9 (309) £100 [Deighton Bell]; bba July 9 (310) £160 [Bernard]; bba July 9 (311) £130 [Blackwell]
— Venus and Adonis. Rochester: Printing House of Leo Hart, 1931. One of 1,250. Illus by Rockwell Kent. sg Sept 26 (150) $70

Shannon, Joseph

— Manual of the Corporation of the City of New York. NY, 1869. 8vo, orig cloth. Tears to folds of folding map. K Dec 1 (320) $150

Shapiro, Elliott. See: Dichter & Shapiro

Sharp, Henry

— Modern Sporting Gunnery. L, 1906. Koopman copy. O Oct 29 (278) $120

Sharp, Samuel, 1700?-78

— A Treatise on the Operations of Surgery. L, 1739. 1st Ed. 8vo, contemp calf; worn & loose. With 14 plates. Lacking last leaf; some browning. S July 1 (111) £180

Sharpe, Philip B.

— The Rifle in America. NY, 1938. 1st Ed. 4to, cloth. Inscr. sp Apr 16 (320) $70

Sharpe, Richard Bowdler, 1847-1909
See also: Seebohm & Sharpe

— A Monograph of the Alcedinidae: or, Family of Kingfishers. L, 1868-71. 4to, contemp half mor; repaired, scuffed. With map, 1 plain & 120 hand-colored plates. Repaired tear to 1 colored plate affecting image. C Oct 30 (298) £4,600 [Marshall]

Anr copy. Contemp half mor; corners rubbed. George Dawson Rowley's subscriber's copy. C May 20 (215) £5,800 [Grahame]

— Scientific Results of the Second Yarkand Mission...Aves. Calcutta, 1891. Oblong folio, modern calf, orig wraps bound in. With 24 hand-colored plates. C May 20 (216) £1,000 [Soffer]

Sharpe, Richard Bowdler, 1847-1909 —& Wyatt, Claude Wilmott

— A Monograph of the Hirundinidae or Family of Swallows. L, 1885-94. 2 vols. 4to, orig cloth; rubbed & soiled, short tear in 1 spine. With 103 hand-colored plates, 26 maps (most partly hand-colored) & 15 double-page tables. Some leaves & plates loose. pn Mar 19 (328) £2,300 [Shapero]

Shaw, George Bernard, 1856-1950
See also: Gregynog Press; Limited Editions Club

— The Adventures of the Black Girl in her Search for God. L, 1932. 1st Ed. Inscr. sg Dec 12 (367) $425

— The Apple Cart. L, 1930. Inscr. sg Dec 12 (368) $425

1st Ed. LH Dec 11 (245) $65

— The Doctor's Dilemma, Getting Married, & The Shewing-up of Blanco Posnet. L, 1911. 1st Ed. Orig cloth. Thomas Hardy's copy. K Mar 22 (175) $170

— The Intelligent Woman's Guide to Socialism and Capitalism. L, 1928. In d/j. Inscr to Lucy Clifford. sg Dec 12 (370) $400

— Press Cuttings.... L, 1913. Wraps. Sgd. sg June 11 (280) $275

— Saint Joan. L, 1924. In d/j. Inscr twice by Shaw. Epstein copy. sg Apr 30 (416) $1,800

— Works. L, 1930-38. One of 1,025. F Dec 18 (54) $150

Anr copy. In frayed d/js. pn Dec 12 (252) £110 [Shapiro]

Shaw, Henry, 1800-73

— Dresses and Decorations of the Middle Ages. L, 1843. 2 vols. 4to, later half mor gilt. With additional title & 93 plates, hand-colored & tinted & heightened in gilt & silver. Some spotting. Ck Nov 29 (312) £220

Anr copy. Contemp half mor; extremities rubbed, endpapers perished at inner margins & detached. With 94 plates, many hand-colored, several heightened in gilt & silver. L.p. copy. Ck Nov 29 (313) £180

Anr copy. Bdg not described but broken. Some foxing. F Mar 26 (760) $350

Anr copy. Half mor. pnE Oct 2 (529) £420

Anr Ed. L, 1858. 2 vols. 4to, contemp mor gilt. With hand-colored additional title & 94 plates, mostly colored or tinted, the majority finished by hand. S July 1 (1334) £200 [Shapero]

Anr copy. Half sheep. Plate count not specified. sg Sept 19 (213) $175

— The Encyclopedia of Ornament. L, 1842. Folio, half mor gilt by Bedford. With color title & 59 color plates. wd June 12 (533) $550

— The Hand Book of Mediaeval Alphabets and Devices. L, 1853. 4to, new cloth. With 36 plates Title & versos of plates stamped. sg Oct 31 (253) $225

— Illuminated Ornaments Selected from Manuscripts and Early Printed Books.... See: Madden, Sir Frederic

Shaw, Henry, 1800-73 —& Meyrick, Sir Samuel Rush

— Specimens of Ancient Furniture. L: Pickering, 1836. Folio, half mor. With 74 colored plates, including engraved title. pnE Oct 2 (530) £180

Shaw, Lachlan

— The History of the Province of Moray.... Edin., 1775. 4to, orig bds. pnE Oct 1 (300) £75

Shaw, Norton

— The Royal Illustrated Atlas. L & Edin., [1862]. Folio, contemp calf gilt; rubbed, front hinge broken. With engraved title & 76 colored maps. Some small tears; 1 map shaved; 1 text leaf loose. pn May 14 (246) £580

Shaw, Reuben C.

— Across the Plains in Forty-Nine. Farmland IN, 1896. 1st Ed. 12mo, orig cloth. sg June 18 (126) $110

Shaw, Stebbing

— The History and Antiquities of Staffordshire. L, 1798-1801. Vols I & II, Part 1 (all pbd). Folio, contemp half lea; worn, upper cover detached. With 2 folding maps mtd on linen, 1 with shaved & repaired margins & with 82 plates. Lacking half-title & half-sheet table; some tears & repairs; minor dampstaining. pn May 14 (206) £480

— A Tour to the West of England in 1788. L, 1789. 8vo, old bds; rebacked with calf, corners worn. L Nov 14 (134) £100

Shaw, Thomas, 1694-1757

— Travels or Observations relating to Several Parts of Barbary and the Levant. Oxford, 1738-46. Without Supplement. Folio, modern half calf. With 21 plates & 12 maps & plans. Marginal worming to first few leaves & at inner margin of 4N2-4Q2. Extra-illus with 5 plates. Ck Dec 12 (262) £350

Anr copy. 2 vols, including Supplement, in 1. Folio, contemp calf; joints broken. With 9 folding or double-page maps & 25 maps & plates. Some soiling. S May 14 (1241) £480 [Theocharak]

Anr copy. Without Supplement. Folio, contemp calf gilt; rebacked, worn. With 32 folding maps & plates. Some dustsoiling. S July 1 (859) £450 [Severis]

Shaw, Vero Kemball

— The Illustrated Book of the Dog. L, [1881]. 4to, contemp half mor gilt; rubbed, upper cover almost detached. With 28 color plates. bba Sept 5 (103) £260 [Shockney]

Anr copy. Contemp half mor; covers detached, lacking backstrip. Lacking last leaf of index; 1 plate stained. pn July 16 (163) £380 [Map House]

Shaw, William, Late Midshipman, R.N.

— Golden Dreams and Waking Realities. L, 1851. 12mo, cloth. sg June 18 (127) $110

Shawn, Ted

— Ruth St. Denis: Pioneer & Prophet. San Francisco, 1920. One of 350. 2 vols. 4to, half cloth; extremities damaged by insects. sg Oct 17 (93) $90

Shcherbatov, Prince M. M.

— Letopis o mnogikh myatezhakh i o razorenii Moskovskago Gosudarstva.... St. Petersburg, 1771. 8vo, contemp calf; shellacked, hinges reinforced. Dampstained. From the library of Prince Golitsin at Petrovskoe. sg Oct 24 (190) $175

Sheckley, Robert

— Untouched by Human Hands. NY: Ballantine, [1954]. In d/j with a few tears & chips. Some foxing. wa Sept 26 (360) $50

Sheffield, John, Duke of Buckingham, 1648-1721

— Works. L, 1723. 1st Ed. 2 vols. 4to, contemp calf; joints cracked, rubbed. bba Apr 30 (77) £100 [Oatley]

Sheldon, Charles

— The Wilderness of the Upper Yukon.... NY, 1911. Cloth; worn. Koopman copy. O Oct 29 (279) $150

— The Wilderness of the North Pacific Coast Islands. NY, 1912. Cloth; spine ends rubbed. sg May 21 (98) $90; sp Sept 22 (26) $75

Sheldon, Harold P. See: Derrydale Press

Shelley, George Ernest

— A Monograph of the Nectariniidae, or Family of Sun-Birds. L, 1876-80. 4to, contemp mor gilt; scuffed. With 121 hand-colored plates. C Oct 30 (297) £4,800 [Grahame]

Anr copy. Contemp half mor gilt; joints & corners rubbed. C May 20 (217) £4,000 [Travers]

Shelley, George Ernest —& Sclater, William Lutley

— The Birds of Africa, Comprising all the Species...in the Ethiopian Region. L, 1896-1912. 5 vols in 7. 8vo, orig cloth. With 57 hand-colored plates. C May 20 (218) £2,700 [Grahame]

Shelley, Mary Wollstonecraft

See also: Limited Editions Club

— Frankenstein. L, 1818. 1st Ed. 3 vols. 12mo, orig bds, uncut; some wear to spines, joints starting on Vols I & II. Oval stamp deleted from verso of each tp. P Oct 11 (283) $85,000

Anr copy. 3 vols in 1. 12mo, contemp calf; front joint renewed, rear joint splitting. Epstein copy. sg Apr 30 (417) $28,000

— The Last Man. L, 1826. 3 vols. 12mo, old lea; worn, rebacked. Library stamp on titles; attempts to obliterate stamps affecting text in Vol II. S July 1 (1006) £600 [Hannas]

— Lodore. L, 1835. 1st Ed, late issue. 3 vols in 1. 8vo, orig cloth; hinges & joints split, lower cover loose. S Feb 11 (416) £480 [Valentine]

— Mounseer Nontongpaw: a New Version. L: The Juvenile Library, 1811. 3d Ed. Illus by William Mulready. 16mo, orig ptd wraps; stained. With frontis & 11 plates, hand-colored. Some stains. S July 21 (73) £700

[Bindman]

Shelley, Percy Bysshe, 1792-1822
See also: Golden Cockerel Press; Kelmscott Press

— The Cenci. Italy [Leghorn]: Ptd for C. & J. Ollier of London, 1819. 1st Ed. 8vo, mor extra; joints cracked. Some leaves soiled. CNY Dec 5 (329) $2,400

Anr copy. Mor gilt by Riviere; spine darkened. CNY Dec 5 (330) $1,800

— The Masque of Anarchy.... L, 1832. 1st Ed. 12mo, orig bds; soiled, spine lacking. Milne copy. Ck June 12 (188) £170

— The Poetical Works. L, 1839. Ed by Mary Shelley. 4 vols. 8vo, contemp half mor; extremities scuffed, some corners worn. Inscr to John George Perry by Mary Shelley. C. L. Dodgson's copy with his ink monogram. CNY June 9 (177) $6,000

Anr copy. Half mor; rubbed. K Sept 29 (395) $180

Anr Ed. L: Vale Press, 1901-2. One of 310. 3 vols. bba July 9 (317) £160 [Deighton Bell]

Anr copy. Half mor; rubbed. O Aug 25 (181) $180

— Prometheus Unbound. L, 1820. 1st Ed, 2d Issue. 8vo, later mor; discolored. Some leaves dampstained; lacking ads at end. S Nov 14 (260) £260 [Finch]

Anr Ed. L: Essex House Press, 1904. One of 200. Orig bds. bba July 9 (260) £65 [Wand]

— Queen Mab. L, 1813. 1st Ed. 8vo, contemp half lea; spine scuffed. C Dec 16 (268) £5,000 [Finch]

1st Pbd Ed. L, 1821. Half mor by Bradstreet; rubbed. Ms note on verso of last leaf; some foxing & soiling. O July 14 (176) $300

1st American Ed. NY, 1821. Half lea. br May 29 (55) $475

— Rosalind and Helen. L, 1819. 1st Ed. 8vo, modern mor. Lacking ads. bba July 9 (143) £300 [Hannas]

Shelley's copy, Percy Bysshe

— Plautus, Titus Maccius. - Comoediae viginti. Lyons: Seb. Gryphinium, 1537. 8vo, 18th-cent calf; rebacked, rubbed. Tp & k4 repaired; marginal staining & tears; small blank section of a5 cut away; worming in upper margin of last few gatherings, some of it repaired with text loss; lacking final blank. Sgd by Shelley on title. P June 17 (362) $2,000

Shelvocke, Capt. George

— A Voyage Round the World.... L, 1726. 8vo, contemp calf; rebacked, corners renewed. With folding map & 5 plates. Folding map with minor repaired tears; tp grubby & with a corner renewed. CNY Oct 8 (227) $700

Anr copy. Contemp calf; rebacked, upper cover detached. With folding map & 4 plates. Map creased, torn & repaired; small repairs to each folding plate & to several text leaves. CNY Oct 8 (228) $700

Anr copy. Contemp calf; rubbed, joints split. With 4 plates & 1 folding map. Some spotting & staining; corner torn from H7, just affecting page numeral. S May 14 (1224) £400 [Cumming]

Anr copy. Contemp calf gilt; worn, rebacked & recornered. With folding map & 4 plates. K7 and N7 repaired. S June 25 (32) £550 [Renard]

2d Ed. L, 1757. 8vo, modern half mor gilt. Some discoloration. S Nov 15 (1327) £280 [Hayes]

Shenstone, William, 1714-63

— The Judgement of Hercules, a Poem. L, 1741. 8vo, modern calf gilt by Riviere. C Dec 16 (269) £280 [Quaritch]

Shepherd, John Chiene —& Jellicoe, Geoffrey Alan

— Italian Gardens of the Renaissance. L, 1925. Folio, bdg not described; worn. With 92 plates. K Sept 29 (225) $70

Shepherd, Thomas Hosmer

— Modern Athens: Displayed.... L, 1829. 4to, contemp half lea; rubbed. With engraved title & 192 plates on 80 leaves, many on india paper mtd. pn Sept 12 (323) £120 [Goodez]

Anr Ed. L, 1831. 4to, contemp half mor gilt; rubbed. With extra title & 88 plates. DW Apr 8 (113) £140

Anr copy. Bds. With engraved title, 101 views & 48 plates. pnE Oct 2 (485) £120

Shepherd, Thomas Hosmer —& Elmes, James, 1782-1862

— London and its Environs in the Nineteenth Century. L, 1829. 4to, disbound. With engraved title, 190 views on 82 sheets. DW Apr 8 (112) £140

Anr copy. Bdg not described but rubbed. Some foxing. LH May 17 (696) $80

— Metropolitan Improvements; or London in the Nineteenth Century. L, 1827. 4to, contemp half mor; rubbed. bba Jan 30 (370) £810 [Fisher & Sperr]

Anr copy. Bound with: London and its Environs in the Nineteenth Century. L,

1829. contemp half calf; rebacked. 1st work with engraved title, plan & 160 plates on 80 sheets (3 with tears); 2d work with engraved title & 96 plates on 42 sheets only. Sold w.a.f. bba July 23 (363) £220 [Marsden]

Anr copy. Contemp half calf; rubbed. With engraved title & 160 views on 80 plates. One plate torn along platemark. Ck Oct 18 (94) £200

Anr copy. Contemp half mor; covers partly detached. With engraved title & 81 leaves of plates. DW Oct 2 (121) £125

Anr copy. Bound with: London and its Environs in the Nineteenth Century, Illustrated by a Series of Views.... L, 1829. With engraved title & 64 views on 32 leaves. contemp half calf gilt; worn & spotted. With engraved title & 158 views on 79 leaves. DW Nov 20 (9) £230

Anr copy. Bound with: Shephaerd. London and its Environs in the Nineteenth Century. recent half calf gilt. With engraved title & 232 engravings on 109 leaves. Spotted & soiled. DW Mar 4 (70) £200

Anr copy. Contemp half calf; spine def, upper cover detached. With engraved title & 81 leaves of plates. DW Apr 8 (111) £145

Anr copy. 19th-cent mor; joints & spines worn, lower cover of Vol I detached, hinges repaired with tape. With 2 engraved titles & 341 viewss on 157 leaves only (of 160). Ownership stamp on verso of 1 plate; some spotting. pn Mar 19 (406) £280 [Tilleke]

Anr copy. Contemp calf; def. With 2 engraved titles & 347 plates on 158 leaves only (of 160). pn May 14 (207) £220

Anr copy. Bound with: London and Its Environs. L, 1829. contemp half mor; edges worn, joints cracked, cover of Vol II detached. Some browning & offsetting. Sold w.a.f. Extra-illus with plates. pn July 16 (190) £100 [Jeffrey]

Anr Ed. L, 1828. 2 vols. 4to, orig bds; worn. With engraved title & 163 views on 81 plates. bba Dec 8 (89) £220 [Cline]

Anr Ed. L, [1847]. 8vo, orig cloth. With engraved title & 44 plates only. bba Apr 9 (156) £80 [Cline]

Anr copy. Orig cloth; def. With 44 plates. Tp foxed. kh Nov 11 (388) A$100

Sheppard, William, d.1675?

— An Epitome of all the Common & Statute Laws. L, 1656. Folio, contemp calf; rubbed & worn, spine def, joints split. bba Jan 16 (27) £180 [Land]

Anr copy. Contemp calf; joints split, rubbed. Some browning & soiling; some worming at foot of inner margins, not affecting text; rust-hole in 6P6, with slight loss. S July 1 (1080) £150 [Knohl]

Sheraton, Thomas, 1751-1806

— The Cabinet Dictionary. L, 1803. 8vo, modern mor gilt. With 86 (of 87) plates. Some soiling or discoloration. S July 1 (938) £300 [Lerner]

— The Cabinet-Maker and Upholsterer's Drawing-Book.... L, 1794-96. 2 vols. 4to, modern half mor gilt. With frontis & 121 plates. Washed copy with old stains & minor repairs; Plate LXI detached. McCarty-Cooper copy. CNY Jan 25 (71) $800

Sherburne, John Henry

— Life and Character of Chevalier John Paul Jones. Wash., 1825. 1st Ed. 8vo, orig bds; spine split, rear cover nearly detached, endpapers foxed. pba Aug 20 (190) $50

Sherementev, Boris Petrovich

— Zapiska puteshestviya Grafa Borisa Petrovicha Sheremeteva. Moscow, 1773. Folio, modern cloth, orig wraps bound in. Lacking port. Library markings. sg Jan 9 (178) $275

Sherer, John

— Europe Illustrated: its Picturesque Scenes and Places of Note. 1st Series. L & NY, [1876-79]. 70 parts. Orig wraps; some covers chipped or stained. sg Jan 9 (75) $325

Anr copy. 2 vols. 4to, contemp half mor; worn. With 2 engraved titles & 118 plates. Minor foxing to plates; 1 plate folded along edges of image. wa Apr 9 (280) $230

— Rural Life Described and Illustrated. L, [1868-69]. 2 vols. 4to, contemp half calf; spines rubbed & worn. DW Oct 2 (167) £1100

Sheridan, Richard Brinsley, 1751-1816

— The Critic.... L, 1781 [i.e., 1795]. 8vo, mor gilt by Riviere; joints rubbed. Lacking half-title. sg Oct 24 (297) $130

Sheridan, Thomas, 1719-88

— British Education: or, the Source of the Disorders of Great Britain. L, 1756. 1st Ed. 8vo, contemp calf. Some spotting to lower forecorners; some discoloration. b June 22 (216) £100

Sheringham, Hugh Tempest —& Moore, John C.

— The Book of the Fly-Rod. L, 1931. One of 195. Half mor by Bayntun; worn. Koopman copy. O Oct 29 (281) $140

Sherman, John

— Recollections of Forty Years in the House, Senate and Cabinet. Chicago, 1895. 8vo, half lea. O Feb 25 (177) $120

Sherwood, Robert E.

— The Petrified Forest. NY, 1935. In d/j. ALs to John Mason Brown laid in. Met Apr 27 (798) $325

— Waterloo Bridge. NY, 1930. With 2 A Ls s to John Mason Brown laid in. Met Apr 27 (799) $300

Shields, Henry —& Meikle, James

— Famous Clyde Yachts 1880-87. Glasgow, 1888. Folio, orig cloth; spine ends & corners worn. With frontis & 31 mtd chromolitho plates. Marginal spotting. C Oct 30 (82) £1,500 [Shapero]

Shillinglaw, John J.

— Historical Records of Port Phillip: the First Annals of the Colony of Victoria. Melbourne, 1879. 8vo, bdg not described. Tp stamped; signs of use. kh Nov 11 (644) A$80

Shipley, M. A.

— Artificial Flies and How to Make Them. Phila., 1888. 12mo, cloth; worn & spotted. Koopman copy. O Oct 29 (283) $200

— A Dictionary of Trout and Bass Flies. Phila., 1898. Oblong 8vo, pictorial wraps; worn. Koopman copy. O Oct 29 (284) $325

Shirley, James, 1596-1666

— Dramatic Works and Poems.... L, 1833. 6 vols. 8vo, contemp calf; worn. Foxed. Met Apr 28 (801) $50

Shirley, John, 1648-79

— The Life of the Valiant and Learned Sir Walter Raleigh.... L, 1677. 1st Ed. 8vo, contemp calf; rebacked, rubbed. Some browning & rust spots. pn May 14 (20) £90

Shirley, Rodney W.

— The Mapping of the World.... L: Holland Press, [1983]. In d/j. pn Apr 23 (160) £90; sg Oct 31 (77) $140

Anr Ed. L: Holland Press, [1987]. In d/j. wa Mar 5 (456) $75

Shoberl, Frederick. See: Schoberl, Frederick

Shoemaker, Richard H.

— A Checklist of American Imprints for 1820-1829. NY & L, 1964-73. Vols I-V only. bbc Apr 27 (91) $65

Short, Frank Hamilton. See: Grabhorn Printing

Short, Thomas, 1690?-1772

See also: Franklin Printing, Benjamin

— The Natural, Experimental, and Medicinal History of the Mineral Waters of Derbyshire, Lincolnshire.... L, 1734-40. 2 vols in 1. 4to, contemp calf; spine chipped at head. With 5 plates, 4 folding. Vol II with 4 leaves browned. b June 22 (217) £140

Shortt, Angela

— The Hunting If. NY: Derrydale Press, 1932. One of 100. 16mo, orig lea. O Mar 31 (51) $450

Short-Title Catalogue

— A Short-Title Catalogue of Books Printed in England, Scotland & Ireland...1475-1640. L, 1926. Ed by A. W. Pollard & G. R. Redgrave. 4to, bdg not stated. cb Oct 17 (7750) $110

Anr copy. Half cloth; worn & soiled. NH May 30 (451) $70

2d Ed. L, 1976-86-91. Ed by W. A. Jackson, F. S. Ferguson & Katharine F. Pantzer. 3 vols. 4to, cloth, in d/js. bba Apr 30 (383) £130 [Forrest]

Anr Ed. L, 1976-86. 2 vols. 4to, cloth, in d/js. bba May 28 (601) £80 [Symonds]

Anr copy. Vols I & II (of 3). sg Oct 31 (287) $225

Shuck, Oscar T.

— Bench and Bar in California.... San Francisco, 1887-89. 3 vols. 8vo, orig cloth (each vol in different color); rubbed. cb Feb 12 (79) $190

— History of the Bench and Bar of California.... Los Angeles, 1901. cb Nov 14 (200) $50

Sibyllina...

— Sibyllina oracula ex vett. codd. aucta, renovata, et notis illustrata.... Paris, 1607. 8vo, early 19th-cent russia gilt; front joint partly cracked. sg Mar 12 (238) $425

Sibyllinorum...

— Sibyllinorum oraculorum libri octo. Basel: J. Oporinus, 1545. 4to, calf; rubbed, upper hinge weak. In Greek & Latin. bba Feb 27 (229) £240 [W. Poole]

Sichem, Christoffel von

— Die Dryzehn Ort, der loblichen Eydgnosschaft, des alten bundts hoher Teutscher Nation.... Basel, 1573. Folio, later half vellum bds; soiled. With 13 woodcut town views with verses. Stamp on tp; some annotations. S Nov 21 (195) £2,500 [Reiss & Auvermann]

Sidney, Sir Philip, 1554-86

— The Countesse of Pembrokes Arcadia. L: [R. Field] for Wm. Ponsonbie, 1598. 3d Ed. Folio, late 18th-cent calf gilt; extremities rubbed. Old dampstaining; lower margins of A1-P2 wormed; some rustholes. STC 22541. C Dec 16 (234) £1,800 [Maggs]

10th Ed. L, 1638. Folio, later half calf; rubbed. Lacking 1 blank; title laid down; several leaves wormed or waterstained. bba Jan 16 (57A) £100 [Martin]

"9th" Ed. Folio, contemp calf. STC 22550. L Nov 14 (449) £160

— The Defense of Poesie. L: Caradoc Press, 1906. One of 350. 4to, orig half calf; spine rubbed. bba July 9 (299) £65 [Deighton Bell]

— The Sonnets. L: Vale Press, 1898. One of 210. Illus by Charles Ricketts. 8vo, orig bds; spine soiled. bba July 9 (307) £140 [Deighton Bell]

Sidney, Samuel

— The Book of the Horse. L, [1884-86]. 3d Ed. 4to, later mor. With 25 color plates. 1 loose & frayed. bba Dec 19 (92) £360 [Map House]

Anr copy. Contemp half calf; edges rubbed & soiled. pn July 16 (164) £280 [Map House]

Anr Ed. L, 1892-[93]. 8vo, half calf. LH Dec 11 (247) $110

— The Three Colonies of Australia. L, 1853. 2d Ed. 8vo, contemp half mor; rubbed. With folding map & 9 plates. bba Oct 24 (313) £70 [Pordes]

Siebmacher, Johann

— Das grosse und vollstaendige anfangs Siebmacherische, hernacher Fuerstische und Helmerische, nun aber Weigelische Wappen-Buch.... Nuremberg, 1734. 11 parts in 4 vols, including Supplements to 1765. Folio, contemp calf gilt; rubbed. With frontis & c.778 plates only. Lacking tp & 3 plates in 4th Supplement; small hole in 1st tp. Sold w.a.f. S July 1 (1335) £250 [Toscani]

Siebold, Philipp Franz von, 1796-1866

— Fauna japonica sive descriptio anaimalium. Leiden, [1844]-50. 6 parts in 4 vols. Folio, half mor gilt by Arthur E. Colley, orig wraps bound in at end of each vol; soiled & rubbed, shelf marks on spines. With 402 plates, many hand-colored & with additional folding map at end of Vol II. A few plates of Crustacea stained, 1 or 2 trimmed; some spotting & soiling in other vols; stamps on front pastedowns. pn Mar 19 (327) £12,000 [Junk]

— Nippon: Archiv zur Beschreibung von Japan. Berlin, 1930. 2 text & plate vols. Folio, half mor; Vol II spine torn. Facsimile of 1852 Ed. sg Jan 9 (179) $1,000

Siegel, Gustav A.

— Deutschlands Heer und Flotte in Wort und Bild. Akron OH, 1900. Folio, orig cloth; rubbed, upper joint torn, corners worn. With 41 colored plates (2 torn). pn June 11 (134) £320 [Cumming]

Siegel, Henry A. —& Others

— The Derrydale Press: A Bibliography. Goshen CT: The Angler's & Shooter's Press, 1981. One of 1,250. Koopman copy. O Oct 29 (285) $110; sg Oct 31 (304) $175; sg May 21 (303) $140

Siemenowicz, Casimir

— Artis magnae artillieriae pars prima. Amst.: J. Jansson, 1650. Folio, vellum; spine wormed. With engraved title & 17 plates. Marginal worming; some browning. S July 9 (338) £450 [American Museum]

— Auessfuehrliche Beschreibung der grossen Feuerwercks- oder Artiillerie-Kunst. Frankfurt: Johann David Zuennern, 1676. Folio, contemp calf; rebacked, preserving old spine. With engraved title with German text; remainder of work with French text. With 22 plates. Folding plate torn at foot; some worming, affecting line border of 1 plate; blank corner torn from Z4. S July 9 (1340) £450 [American Museum]

— Grand art d'artillerie.... Amst., 1651. Folio, 18th-cent calf; joints splits, rubbed. With engraved title & 21 (of 22) plates. Some dampstaining. S July 9 (336) £350 [American Museum]

Siemens, Werner von

— Lebenserinnerungen. Berlin, 1892. 8vo, contemp half lea gilt. sg Nov 14 (317) $150

Siemienowicz, Casimir

— The Great Art of Artillery.... L, 1729. 1st Ed in English. Folio, later half calf; joints & corners rubbed. With frontis & 22 folding plates. With Ms notes at end. Inscr as being the gift of the translator, George Shelvocke. S July 1 (1337) £620 [American Mus.]

Sienkiewicz, Henryk, 1846-1916. See: Limited Editions Club

Sifridus de Arina

— Expositiones sive declarationes titulorum utriusque juris. Cologne: Johann Koellhoff, 3 Dec 1491. Folio, later bds. 45 lines & headline; double column; gothic letter. some worming at ends; F6r soiled; annotations. 274 leaves. Goff S-496. S Dec 5 (27) £2,400 [Ramos Arroyo]

Sigel, Gustav A.

— Germany's Army and Navy by Pen and Picture. Akron, 1900. Folio, cloth. With 41 color plates. sg Nov 7 (233) $500

Anr copy. Cloth; worn. With 41 color plates, 1 with marginal tear. Some marginal soil; 1 leaf torn. wa Mar 5 (567) $210

Sigonius, Carolus

— Fasti consulares, ac Triumphi acti a Romulo Rege.... Basel: Episcopius, 1559. Folio, later vellum. Marginal staining. bba Oct 10 (9) £130 [Erlini]

Silius Italicus, Caius, 25-101 A.D.

— De Bello Punico. Venice: Bonetus Locatellus for Octavianus Scotus, 18 May 1492. ("Punica cum Commentariis Petri Marsi.") Folio, old half sheep; extremities worn, spine wormed. Badly dammpstained at beginning & end. 156 leaves. Goff S-508. sg Mar 12 (134) $400

Sill, Howard. See: Pleasants & Sill

Silva. See: Evelyn, John

Silver...

— The Silver Mines of Nevada. Ny, 1865. 8vo, wraps. Library markings. sg June 18 (379) $200

Silvestre, Joseph Balthazar

— Alphabet-Album. Paris, 1843. 8vo, half cloth; spine torn. With engraved title & 59 plates, 1 double-page. Short tear to title without loss; Plate 30 repaired; some foxing. pn Dec 12 (82) £70 [Bifolco]

Silvestre, M. L. C.

— Marques Typographiques.... Amst., 1971. Reprint of the 1867 Ed. cb Oct 17 (862) $55

Simak, Clifford D.

— City. NY: Gnome Press, [1952]. In chipped d/j. sg June 11 (282) $200

Anr copy. In foxed d/j; cloth bdg stained. Stamp on tp & front free endpaper. wa Mar 5 (239) $120

Simeoni, Gabriele

See also: Paradin & Simeoni

— Commentarii sopra alla tetrarchia di Vinegia, di Milano.... Venice: Comin da Trino di Monferrato, 1548. 8vo, contemp vellum. sg Oct 24 (307) $350

Simms, P. Marion

— The Bible in America. NY, 1936. In d/j. cb Oct 17 (864) $55

Simon, Andre Louis

— Bibliotheca Bacchica. L, 1927-32. One of 250 & 275. 2 vols. 4to, half cloth. bbc Sept 23 (122) $225

Anr Ed. L: Holland Press, [1972]. 2 vols in 1. In d/j. Facsimile of 1927 Ed. O Sept 24 (225) $60

Simon, Henri, Engraver

— Armorial general de l'Empire Francais. Paris, 1812. 2 vols. Folio, contemp bds; worn. With 2 engraved titles & 140 plates. Some dampstaining. S July 1 (1339) £180 [Milkain]

Simon, James, F.R.S.

— An Essay on Irish Coins. Dublin, 1810. 4to, contemp half calf; rubbed. bba Jan 16 (155) £50 [Apsley]

Simon, Oliver —& Rodenberg, Julius

— Printing of To-day.... L, 1928. One of 300. 4to, Cloth; soiled, spine ends frayed, endpapers foxed. pba July 23 (200) $50

Simond, Louis

— Switzerland: or, a Journal of a Tour.... L, 1822. 2 vols. 8vo, contemp half calf; worn. DW Mar 4 (45) £55

Simplicissimus...

— Simplicissimus: Illustrierte Wochenschrift.... Munich, 1896-1920. Vols 1-18 & 20-24. 26 vols. Folio, various bdgs. HH May 12 (2501) DM8,000

Simplicius of Cilicia

— Commentarii in quatuor Aristotelis libros de coelo. Venice: Aldus, 1526. Folio, 18th-cent calf gilt, armorial bdg; worn, upper cover detached. Tp stained & torn; some spotting. pn Nov 14 (289) £420

Simpson, Alexander

— The Life and Travels of Thomas Simpson.... L, 1845. 8vo, cloth, unopened. O Feb 25 (179) $160

Simpson, Christopher

— A Compendium of Practical Musick. L, 1678. 3d Ed. 8vo, modern half mor. pn Oct 24 (453) £170 [Macnutt]

Anr copy. Contemp calf; spine worn, joints broken. pn Oct 24 (454) £220 [Macnutt]

Simpson, Sir George, 1792-1860

— Narrative of a Journey Round the World. L, 1847. 1st Ed. 2 vols. 8vo, orig cloth; spines faded. With port & hand-colored folding map. bba Apr 9 (151) £150 [Laywood]

Anr copy. With port & folding map. cb Feb 12 (121) $325

1st American Ed. Phila., 1847. ("An

Overland Journey Round the World....") 2 vols in 1. 8vo, crudely rebound in cloth. cb Nov 14 (201) $55

Simpson, James H., 1813-83

— Report and Map of Wagon Road Routes in Utah Territory. Wash., 1859. 8vo, recent cloth. Marginal tear to folding map. 35th Congress, 2d Session, Senate Ex. Doc 40. cb Feb 12 (80) $170

— The Shortest Route to California. Phila., 1869. 8vo, cloth. Folding map wrinkled at edges. Inscr by "The Author" on tp. sg June 18 (128) $250

Simpson, John, Cook

— A Complete System of Cookery, on a Plan entirely New. L, 1822. 8vo, library half mor. Library markings. bba Oct 24 (85) £60 [Demetzy]

Simpson, William, 1823-99

— The Seat of the War in the East. First and Second Series. L, 1855-56. 1st Series only. Folio, contemp half mor; worn, broken & loose. With hand-colored title & 39 plates. bba Oct 24 (256) £440 [Russell]

Anr copy. Folio, contemp half mor; worn. With 2 litho titles & 78 (of 79) plates. Some frayed, soiled and loose. Sold w.a.f. bba Apr 30 (363) £350 [Corbett]

Anr copy. 2 vols. Folio, contemp half mor gilt; worn. Lacking tp to Vol II & initial text leaves crumpled & torn. DW May 13 (58) £390

Anr copy. Folio, contemp half mor; joints repaired, foot of spine worn, additional cloth cover. With 2 litho titles & 79 plates. Lacking plate lists; some numerals shaved; tp & margins spotted. pn Nov 14 (385) £340

Anr copy. Half mor gilt; extremities rubbed. Foxed. sg Jan 9 (151) $600

Anr copy. 2 vols in 1. Folio, contemp half mor; rubbed. With colored litho title & 79 plates. Some foxing. W July 8 (292) £1,700

Second Series only. L, 1856. Folio, disbound. With litho title & 39 plates. Some foxing & dampstaining; a few tears. pn July 16 (233) £160

Simson, Frank B.

— Letters on Sport in Eastern Bengal. L, 1886. Folio, orig cloth; dampstained. With 10 tinted lithos. Some foxing. pn Apr 23 (220) £100 [R & S Books]

Sinclair de Rochemont, H. A.

— Keuze. The Hague, 1939. One of 100. Illus by John Buckland Wright. Folio, half cloth. Library stamp. With additional example of the engraving. S Apr 28 (19) £420

Sinclair, George, 1786-1834

— Hortus gramineus Woburnensis.... L, 1816. 1st Ed. Folio, disbound. With 122 mtd botanical specimens & mtd specimens of 35 seed varieties. Tp loose, frayed & soiled. sg May 14 (245) $950

— Hortus Gramineus Woburnensis: Or, an Account of the Results on the Produce and Nutritive Qualities of Different Grasses.... L, 1825. 8vo, later half calf. With 60 hand-colored plates. A few leaves waterstained. bba Apr 9 (203) £100 [Wise]

Sinclair, Upton, 1878-1968

See also: Limited Editions Club

— The Jungle. NY, 1906. 1st Ed, 1st Issue. Orig cloth. Witih TLs attached to front endpaper. cb Dec 12 (123) $225

— Springtime and Harvest. NY, [1901]. Inscr to Al Buig. sg Dec 12 (371) $200

Sinel, Joseph

— A Book of American Trade-Marks and Devices. NY, 1924. One of 20 ptd on double leaves of handmade paper. 4to, half mor, in d/j. Inscr. With several proofs of engravings by Sinel laid in. cb Nov 21 (213) $190

Singer, Charles Joseph —& Others

— A History of Technology. Oxford, 1954-58. 5 vols. 4to, cloth, in d/js except for Vol V. bba June 25 (211) £110 [Camden]

Anr copy. Cloth, in d/js. sg Nov 14 (318) $175

Vols 1-7. Oxford, 1954-78. 4to, cloth. O Sept 24 (226) $180

Singer, Dorothea Walet

— Catalogue of Latin and Vernacular Alchemical Manuscripts in Great Britain and Ireland.... Brussels, 1928-31. 3 vols. Cloth, orig wraps bound in. sg Oct 31 (254) $600

Singer, Hans Wolfgang. See: Rembrandt van Rijn

Singer, Isaac Bashevis

See also: Limited Editions Club

— The Family Moskat. NY, 1950. In d/j. sg Dec 12 (374) $175

— A Young Man in Search of Love. Garden City, 1978. One of 300. Illus by Raphael Soyer. With numbered color print sgd by Soyer laid in loose. sg Jan 30 (165) $150

— Zlateh the Goat and Other Stories. NY, [1966]. One of 500. Illus by Maurice Sendak. sg Jan 30 (166) $400; sg June 25 (57) $350

Singer, Samuel Weller

— Researches into the History of Playing Cards.... L, 1816. One of 250. 4to, contemp calf gilt by Root; joints cracked, rubbed. bba May 28 (623) £400 [Forster]

Singh, Madanjeet

— Himalayan Art: Wall-Painting and Sculpture in Ladakh, Lahaul and Spiti.... Greenwich CT: NY Graphic Society, [1968]. In d/j. pba Aug 20 (192) $50

Sinitsyn, P. V.

— Preobrazhenskoe i okruzhaiushchiia ego mesta.... Moscow: I. N. Kushnerev, 1895. 4to, contemp calf gilt with lea onlays. With chromolitho additional title & 34 plates & 1 map. From the library of Alexander III of Russia. sg Nov 7 (222) $550

Sirat, Colette. See: Beit-Arie & Sirat

Siren, Osvald, 1879-1966

— China and Gardens of Europe of the Eighteenth Century. NY, [1950]. 4to, cloth. With 16 color plates, some double-page. K July 12 (467) $140

— Early Chinese Painting from the A. W. Bahr Collection. L, 1938. Out-of-series copy. Cloth; rubbed. sp Sept 22 (216) $170

— Gardens of China. NY, [1949]. 4to, orig cloth. cb Dec 19 (160) $110; sg Feb 6 (267) $275

Anr copy. Cloth. With 11 color plates. sp Sept 22 (230) $225

— A History of Early Chinese Art. L, 1929-30. 4 vols. Orig cloth, in frayed d/js. DW Oct 9 (959) £400

— Les Palais Imperiaux de Pekin. Paris, 1926. 3 vols. 4to, cloth, orig front wraps bound in. With 274 plates & 14 plans. Library markings. sg Feb 6 (264) $275

— La Sculpture Chinoise du Ve au XIVe siecle. Paris & Brussels, 1925-26. 5 vols. 4to, orig wraps. b&b Feb 19 (267) $500

Siringo, Charles A., 1855-1928

— Riata and Spurs: The Story of a Lifetime Spent in the Saddle.... Bost., 1927. sp Feb 6 (72) $120; sp June 18 (50) $140

Siskind, Aaron

— Photographs. NY, 1959. Intro by Harold Rosenberg. Folio, cloth, in d/j; worn. sg Oct 8 (63) $130

Anr copy. Cloth; worn. sg Apr 13 (87) $130

Sisson, James E., III —& Martens, Robert W.

— Jack London First Editions. Oakland: Star Rover House, 1979. One of 1,000. cb Nov 21 (128) $60

Sitgreaves, Lorenzo

— Report of an Expedition Down the Zuni and Colorado Rivers. Wash., 1853. 1st Ed, 1st Issue. 8vo, modern half calf, orig cloth bound in. With folding map & 78 plates. Some foxing. sg June 18 (498) $250

Anr Ed. Wash., 1854. 2d Issue. 8vo, orig cloth. Lacking the map. sg June 18 (499) $80

Sitwell, Dame Edith

— Green Song & Other Poems. L, 1944. Orig cloth, in d/j. Geoffrey Grigson's annotated copy. L Feb 27 (90) £620

Sitwell, Dame Edith —& Walton, Sir William

— Facade. L, 1972. One of 250. Orig half mor, with 45 rpm record in pocket. sg Oct 17 (104) $90

Sitwell, Hervey Degge Wilmot

— The Crown Jewels and other Regalia in the Tower of London. L: Dropmore Press, [1953]. One of 99. Ed by Clarence Winchester. Folio, orig cloth, in d/j. F Mar 26 (310) $70

Sitwell, Sacheverell

See also: Beaumont & Sitwell

— A Book of Towers and Other Buildings of Southern Europe.... L, 1928. One of 350. Illus by Richard Wyndham. 4to, orig half vellum; soiled. With additional title & 24 plates. bba July 9 (300) £95 [Bookworks]

Anr copy. Orig half vellum; rubbed, some smudges to covers. bbc Apr 27 (495) $95

Sitwell, Sacheverell —& Others

— Fine Bird Books. L, 1953. Folio, orig half cloth, in d/j. bba Apr 30 (385) £200 [Corbett]

Anr copy. Orig half cloth. bba Aug 13 (14) £110 [Symonds]

Anr copy. Orig half cloth, in d/js. bba Aug 13 (15) £140 [Ginnan]

Anr copy. Orig half cloth, in repaired d/j. O Aug 25 (162) $225

Anr copy. Orig half cloth, in d/j. S Nov 15 (752) £120 [Agazzi]

Anr copy. Half lea. Sgd. SI Dec 5 (624) LIt1,000,000

One of 295. Orig half mor. Martin copy, with extensive annotations by him. With Martin's autograph Want List. Fine Bird Books laid in. bba Sept 5 (159) £290 [Forster]

— Old Garden Roses. L, 1955-57. One of 160. 2 vols. Folio, orig cloth, in d/j. b Nov 18 (381) £60

Anr copy. Orig half vellum. bba Feb 13 (381) £320 [Gramm]

Skarsten, M. O.

— George Drouillard: Hunter and Interpreter for Lewis and Clark.... Glendale, 1964. In d/j. With map tipped in. cb Nov 14 (205) $65

Skeat, Walter William, 1866-1912 —& Blagden, Charles Otto

— Pagan Races of the Malay Peninsula. L, 1906. 1st Ed. 2 vols. pnE May 13 (8) £130

Skelton, Sir John, 1831-97

— Charles I. L, 1898. One of 500. 4to, half mor gilt; extremities worn, front joint starting. sg Mar 5 (297) $90

— Mary Stuart. L, 1893. 4to, mor gilt by Hopkins of Glasgow, orig wraps bound in. Some soiling & staining. wa Mar 5 (70) $50

Anr Ed. L, 1898. One of 500. Lev extra by Sangorski & Sutcliffe, with paintings on ivory in doublures of Mary Queen of Scots & Elizabeth I. P June 17 (128) $4,500

Skelton, Joseph

— Engraved Illustrations of the Principal Antiquities of Oxfordshire.... Oxford, 1823. 4to, contemp half mor; joints split, spine def. bba Jan 16 (28) £120 [Townsend]

Anr copy. Orig cloth; soiled & rebacked. With frontis, 1 map & 49 plates. Some spotting; dampstained at beginning; tp browned. pn Apr 23 (280) £180

— Oxonia antiqua restaurata. Oxford, 1823. 4to, contemp half calf; worn, extremities rubbed. With 133 plates, 1 folding plan & 4 full-page illusts. Some marginal spotting. Ck May 15 (155) £480

Skelton, Raleigh Ashlin

— Decorative Printed Maps of the 15th to 18th Centuries. L & NY, [1952]. 4to, cloth; worn. bbc June 29 (79) $65; O Sept 24 (227) $60

Skene, Alexander

— Memorialls for the Government of the Royall-Burghs in Scotland.... Aberdeen, 1685. 1st Ed. 8vo, contemp sheep; rubbed, upper joint wormed. Q4 lacking corner. bba Sept 19 (246) £80 [Grant & Shaw]

Skene, James Henry

— The Danubian Principalities, the Frontier Lands of the Christian and the Turk. L, 1854. 2 vols. 8vo, contemp half calf gilt. With plate & folding map. Lacking half-title. S July 1 (710) £200 [O'Neill]

Skinner, Andrew. See: Taylor & Skinner

Skinner, John

— The Present State of Peru.... L, 1805. 1st Ed. 4to, contemp half calf; worn. With 20 hand-colored plates. Some foxing. S July 1 (1488) £200 [Toscani]

Skogman, Carl Johan Alfred

— Fregatten Eugenies Resa Omkring Jorden aren 1851-1853.... Stockholm: Adolf Bonnier, [1854-55]. 1st Ed. 2 vols in 1. 8vo, half mor gilt; worn, inner hinges strengthened. With 20 lithos, 18 colored, & 3 folding colored maps. Dampstains to 2 plates. DW Jan 29 (54) £55

Skowronski, Carl A. See: Sloan & Skowronski

Skrine, Henry

— A General Account of All the Rivers of Note in Great Britain. L, 1801. 1st Ed. 8vo, modern half mor. With folding frontis & 17 maps. Cropped note "From the Author" on half-title. bba Aug 13 (398) £50 [Howell Williams]

Skues, G. E. M.

— Nymph Fishing for Chalk Stream Trout. L, 1939. Koopman copy. O Oct 29 (286) $100

— Side-Lines, Side-Lights & Reflections. L, 1932. Bdg worn. O Oct 29 (287) $100

— Silk, Fur and Feather; the Trout-Fly Dresser's Year Kent, [1950]. Koopman copy. O Oct 29 (288) $70

— The Way of a Trout with a Fly.... L, 1921. Orig cloth; rubbed & soiled. With 3 plates. Marginal dampstaining to endpapers. pn July 16 (178) £70

Skues, G. E. M. —& Overfield, T. Donald

— The Way of a Man with a Trout. L, [1977]. One of 150. 2 vols. Vol I, mor; Vol II, half mor. With 20 nymphs on 4 sunken mounts. Koopman copy. O Oct 29 (290) $600

Slade, Sir Adolphus

— Records of Travels in Turkey, Greece.... L, 1833. 2 vols. 8vo, contemp mor gilt. With 2 hand-colored frontises, folding map & facsimile plate. Some discoloration; no half-titles; some stains. S July 1 (713) £280 [Gonul]

Anr copy. 2 vols in 1. 8vo, half lea. sp Feb 6 (413) $110

Slange, Niels —& Gram, Hans

— Den Stormaegtigste Konges Christian den Fierdes, Konges til Danmark og Norge, Histoire. Copenhagen: Royal Press, 1749. Folio, mor gilt examination bdg by an apprentice in the workshop of Niels Anthon. C June 24 (203) £1,800 [Franklin]

Slave...

— Slave Songs of the United States. NY, 1867. 1st Ed. 8vo, orig half mor; scuffed. Inscr by a compiler, Wm. Francis Allen, to his father. bbc Dec 9 (420) $475

Sleeman, Sir William Henry

— Rambles and Recollections of an Indian Official. L, 1844. 2 vols. 8vo, orig cloth; worn. With 30 colored plates & 2 colored frontises. bba Oct 24 (329) £140 [Dewar]

Anr copy. Orig cloth; recased, rubbed & soiled. bba Jan 16 (299) £220 [Shapero]

Sleidanus, Johannes, 1506?-56

— De statu religionis et reipublicae.... Strassburg: heirs of Wendelin Rihel, 1555. Folio, contemp blind-tooled pigskin over wooden bds; lacking catches & clasps. Some foxing; a few marginalia. sg Oct 24 (298) $500

— Der erste Theyl ordentlicher Beschreibunge unnd Verzeychnisse.... Strassburg: Theodosius Rihel, 1571. 2 parts in 1 vol. Folio, contemp blindstamped pigskin over wooden bds, sgd SR. Marginal foxing throughout; some minor worming & dampstaining in lower margins. sg Oct 24 (299) $2,200

— Histoire de l'estat de la religion.... Strassburg, 1558. 8vo, contemp vellum; head of spine chipped. Tp loose. sg Mar 12 (279) $225

Sloan, Robert E. —& Skowronski, Carl A.

— The Rainbow Route. Denver, 1975. Sgd. cb Feb 13 (280) $70

Sloane, Sir Hans, 1660-1753

— A Voyage to the Islands Madera, Barbados, Nieves, S. Christophers and Jamaica.... L, 1707-25. 1st Ed. 2 vols. Folio, contemp calf gilt; worn, corners repaired. With folding map & 283 (of 284) double-page & folding plates. Some cropping. Isaac Newton's copy. S July 1 (1341) £3,100 [Traylen]

Sloane, William Milligan, 1850-1928

— Life of Napoleon Bonaparte. NY, 1896. 4 vols. 4to, half mor; worn. O May 26 (166) $150

Anr Ed. NY, 1906. 4 vols. 4to, cloth. b Mar 11 (183) £50

Slocum, John J. —& Cahoon, Herbert

— A Bibliography of James Joyce.... New Haven, 1953. In d/j. K July 12 (296) $70; O Dec 17 (166) $800

Slover, John. See: Knight & Slover

Small, Henry Beaumont

— The Canadian Handbook and Tourist's Guide.... Montreal, 1866. 8vo, orig cloth; worn. Koopman copy. O Oct 29 (291) $375

Small, John William

— Scottish Woodwork of the Sixteenth and Seventeenth Centuries. Stirling & L: Mackay & Quaritch, [1878]. One of 500. Folio, cloth; worn & soiled, hinges tender. With 100 plates. sg Sept 6 (310) $150

Smalley, Eugene Virgil, 1841-99

— History of the Northern Pacific Railroad. NY, 1883. Advance Issue. Orig cloth; worn. With 6 maps, including folding map in rear pocket. cb Feb 12 (81) $130

Smart, Christopher, 1722-71

— A Translation of the Psalms of David. L, 1765. 4to, contemp calf; upper cover detached. Margins cut close; lacking final blank. Milne copy. Ck June 12 (190) £260

Smeaton, John, 1724-92

— A Narrative of the Building...of the Edystone Lighthouse. L, 1813. Folio, half calf; worn. With engraved title & 23 plates. Some dampstaining. Sold w.a.f. Ck June 18 (47) £240

Anr copy. Modern half mor; scuffed. Library markings. DW Mar 4 (94) £110

Smet, Pierre Jean de, 1804-73. See: De Smet, Pierre Jean

Smids, Ludolph

— Pictura loquens, sive heroicarum tabularum Hadriani Schoonebeeck enarratio et explicatio. Amst., 1695. 8vo, contemp vellum. With frontis, port & 60 plates. Ck Oct 31 (91) £350

Smith, Capt. ——

— Asiatic Costumes. L: Ackermann, 1828. 8vo, orig wraps; lacking backstrip. With 44 plates. Some foxing. bba May 14 (350) £75 [C. Smith]

Smith, Adam, 1723-90

— An Inquiry into the Nature and Causes of the Wealth of Nations. L, 1776. 1st Ed. 2 vols. 4to, modern half calf; rubbed. Leaves M3, Q1, U3, 2Z3, 3A4, 3O4 in Vol I & leaves D1 & 3Z4 in Vol II cancelled; marginal tear on D1; corner cut away on blank preceding title; lacking final blank in Vol I; hole in D1 in Vol II affecting 1 word. P Dec 12 (83) $10,000

Anr copy. Cloth; soiled, rubbed. Leaves M3, Q1, U3, 2Z3, 3A4, 3O4 in Vol I & D1 & 3Z4 in Vol II cancelled; lacking final blank in Vol I & half-title in Vol II; small hole in M2 of Vol I affecting pagination; marginal tears; gatherings 2X & 3F in Vol I repaired in margins; some soiling. P Dec 12 (84) $12,000

Anr copy. Contemp calf; rebacked & recornered. Some spotting. S July 21 (321) £7,000 [Joseph]

Anr copy. Contemp calf; joints tender, front cover scraped. 1 leaf in Vol II torn. sg Nov 7 (234) $27,000

Anr copy. Modern calf. Inner margin repair on E & corner renewed on Yy1 in Vol I. Epstein copy. sg Apr 30 (418) $24,000

Anr Ed. L, 1789. 3 vols. 8vo, contemp calf; spines worn, joints split. pn July 16 (20) £140 [Scott]

1st American Ed. Phila., 1789. 3 vols. 8vo, later half mor; rubbed & soiled. Ck Oct 18 (132) £150

Anr Ed. L, 1793. 3 vols. 8vo, contemp calf; rubbed. b June 22 (86) £160

Anr copy. 2 vols. 8vo, LH Dec 11 (249) uS350

Anr Ed. Hartford, 1804. 2 vols. 8vo, contemp sheep; 1 cover loose. Library markings. sg June 18 (511) $250

Anr Ed. L, 1811. 3 vols. 8vo, contemp calf; rebacked. bba Jan 16 (52) £130 [Pordes]

Anr copy. Contemp calf; worn, some covers detached, 1 lacking. bba May 14 (124) £55 [Bitterman]

Anr Ed. Edin., 1817. 4 vols. 8vo, calf; rebacked, extremities scuffed. F Mar 26 (18) $190

Smith's copy, Adam

— Malvaux, —. - Les Moyens de detruire la mendicite en France. Calons-sur-Marne, 1780. 8vo, contemp half calf; rubbed. With Smith's bookplate. S Dec 12 (320) £2,000 [Quaritch]

Smith, Albert Richard, 1816-60

— The Struggles and Adventures of Christopher Tadpole. L, 1850. Illus by John Leech. 8vo, half mor gilt. sg Oct 17 (306) $130

Smith, Charles, Bookseller

— New English Atlas being a Complete Set of County Maps. L, 1804. Folio, recent half mor gilt. With hand-colored double-page general map & 45 county maps. General map torn at fold. DW Nov 6 (134) £820

Anr copy. Half calf. With 20 hand-colored maps. DW Mar 4 (144) £150

Smith, Charles, Topographer

— The Ancient and Present State of the County of Kerry. Dublin, 1774. 8vo, modern calf. CG Oct 7 (500) £280

— The Antient and Present State of the County and City of Cork. Dublin, 1750. 1st Ed. 2 vols. 8vo, modern calf. CG Oct 7 (499) £380

Anr copy. Contemp calf; rubbed. With 2 folding maps & 11 plates, all but 1 folding. Some browning. S July 1 (1342) £280 [Gamble]

— Waterford. Dublin, 1746. ("The Antient and Present State of...Waterford.") 8vo, modern calf. CG Oct 7 (503) £170

2d Ed. Dublin, 1774. ("The History, Topography and Antiquities...of Waterford.") 8vo, early 20th-cent half mor; rubbed. With port, 6 folding plates & 1 folding map. Ck May 15 (158) £95

Smith, Charles Hamilton

— The Natural History of the Human Species.... Edin., 1848. 16mo, orig cloth; worn. With vignette title, engraved port & 34 plates, some hand-colored. cb Jan 9 (201) $55

— Selections of the Ancient Costume of Great Britain and Ireland.... L, 1814. Bound with: Meyrick & Smith. The Costume of the Original Inhabitants of the British Islands. L, 1815. Folio, calf; rebacked, rubbed. With frontis & 60 colored plates in 1st work & frontis, half-title & 24 plates in 2d work. Some soiling. P June 17 (363) $700

Anr copy. Contemp russia gilt; rubbed, hinges splitting, spine torn. With engraved dedication & 61 hand-colored plates. pn Sept 12 (283) £220 [J. C. Books]

Anr copy. Contemp mor gilt; hinges & spine repaired, rubbed. With engraved dedication, 61 hand-colored plates; ink stamp on tp partially erased. pn Apr 23 (56) £190

Smith, Christopher Webb —& D'Oyly, Sir Charles, 1781-1845

— Oriental Ornithology. Patna: Behar Amateur Lithographic Press, 1828-29. 2 vols in 1. Oblong folio, orig half mor; worn. With hand-colored litho title (in Part 2) & 24 litho plates, all heightened with varnish. Some amateur additional hand-coloring to surround of title; 6 plates detached; 12 mounts torn or lacking; several plates soiled. Sold w.a.f. Ck Sept 6 (47A) £1,000

Smith, Clark Ashton

— Genius Loci and Other Tales. Sauk City: Arkham House, 1948. In d/j. sg June 11 (285) $120

— The Star Treader and Other Poems. San Francisco, 1912. In d/j. sg June 11 (286) $120

Smith, Clark Ashton, 1893-1961

— The Double Shadow and Other Fantasies. Auburn CA: Auburn Journal Print, 1933. Folio, ptd wraps. Inscr & with ink corrections by Smith. bbc Dec 9 (589) $450

— Out of Space and Time. Sauk City: Arkham House, 1942. In d/j. Epstein copy. sg Apr 30 (420) $550

Smith, David Eugene, 1860-1944

— Rara Arithmetica: a Catalogue of the Arithmetics written before the Year 1601...in the Library of G. A. Plimpton. Bost. & L, 1908. bba June 25 (20) £130 [Casella]

Anr copy. Unopened. cb Oct 17 (869) $100

One of 151. 2 vols. Vellum. sg Oct 31 (305) $275

Smith, David Murray

— Arctic Expeditions from British and Foreign Shores. Edin., 1875. 3 vols. Folio, orig cloth. W July 8 (261) £140

Anr Ed. Edin., 1877. 4to, orig bds; rebacked in calf, lower bd replaced in cloth. With 2 folding maps, 22 tinted plates & 2 chromolithos. Frontis margins chipped. kh Nov 11 (389) A$140

Smith, David Seth. See: Seth-Smith, David

Smith, Edmund Ware
See also: Derrydale Press

— The Further Adventures of the One-Eyed Poacher. NY, [1947]. Ltd Ed, sgd. Cloth; rubbed. K Sept 29 (407) $75

Smith, Edward E., 1890-1965

— Galactic Patrol. Reading: Fantasy Press, 1950. One of 500. In d/j. sg June 11 (287) $150

— Gray Lensman. Reading: Fantasy Press, 1951. One of 500. In d/j. Inscr. sg June 11 (288) $150

Smith, Edwin, The Edwin Smith Surgical Papyrus, Published in Facsimile....

— The Edwin Smith Surgical Papyrus.... See: Breasted, James Henry

Smith, Frank Meriweather. See: San Francisco

Smith, Garden G. See: Hilton & Smith

Smith, George, M.D.

— History of Delaware County.... Phila., 1862. 1st Ed. 8vo, half lea; rubbed, inner joints repaired. With 2 folding maps having amateur paper repairs. Inscr. K Sept 29 (343) $50

Smith, George, Upholsterer

— Cabinet-Maker and Upholsterer's Guide. L, 1826. 4to, old half mor; extremities worn. With engraved title & 170 plates, 55 of them hand-colored. Some plates cropped; a few plates dampstained. McCarty-Cooper copy. CNY Jan 25 (72) $4,800

Smith, George, 1815-71

— A Narrative of an Exploratory Visit to Each of the Consular Cities of China.... L, 1847. 8vo, cloth. sp Sept 22 (233) $50

Smith, Gertrude

— The Arabella and Araminta Stories.... Bost., 1895. One of 15 on Japan vellum. Illus by Ethel Reed. Folio, half mor; corners worn, hinges reinforced. With 15 plates, each ptd on 6 different kinds of paper. Epstein copy. sg Apr 30 (421) $24,000

Smith, Sir Grafton Elliot —& Dawson, Warren Royal

— Egyptian Mummies. L, 1924. 4to, orig cloth. O Dec 17 (167) $120

Smith, H. D. —& Horner, William Edmonds, 1793-1853

— Anatomical Atlas, illustrative of the Structure of the Human Body. Phila., 1845. 8vo, orig cloth with skeletons stamped in gold & blind; worn. K July 12 (20) $160

Anr copy. Orig cloth; worn. With frontis, title vignette & 634 illusts on 184 leaves. Minor dampstains. O Aug 25 (163) $100

Smith, Harry B., 1860-1936

— A Sentimental Library.... [N.p.]: Pvtly ptd, 1914. Half vellum, in repaired d/j. With 56 plates. sg May 21 (304) $140

Anr copy. Half vellum; spine soiled & stained. wa Mar 5 (137) $80

Smith, Harry Worcester. See: Derrydale Press

Smith, Sir James Edward, 1759-1828
See also: Sowerby & Smith

— Exotic Botany.... L, 1804-5-[8]. 2 vols. 4to, later half mor; rubbed. With 120 hand-colored plates. Some spotting. L.p. copy. pn Mar 19 (329) £1,400 [Junk]

— A Specimen of the Botany of New Holland. L, 1793-[95]. Vol I (all pbd). 4to, contemp bds; worn. With 16 hand-colored plates. Plate 5 stained & with short tear. S June 25 (127) £6,500 [Maggs]

Smith, Jerome V. C.

— Natural History of the Fishes of Massachusetts. Bost., 1833. 8vo, modern cloth. Koopman copy. O Oct 29 (292) $160

Smith, Jessie Wilcox

— Mother Goose: A Careful and Full Selection.... NY: Dodd Mead, [1914]. Folio, cloth. cb Jan 16 (140) $325

Smith, John, LL.B.

— Chronicon Rusticum-Commerciale; or, Memoirs of Wool.... L, 1747. 2 vols. 8vo, contemp calf; rebacked. Tear in 2N1 of Vol II. b June 22 (219) £240

Anr copy. Contemp calf; rubbed. Ck Oct 18 (134) £550

Smith, John, Picture Dealer

— A Catalogue Raisonne of the Works of the Most Eminent Dutch, Flemish and French Painters. L, 1829-42. 8 vols plus Supplement. 8vo, orig cloth; extremities worn, 1 spine repaired. Ck Feb 14 (121) £110

Anr Ed. L, 1908. One of 1,250. 9 vols, including Supplement Facsimile reprint of the 1829-42 Ed. DW May 13 (402) £50

Smith, John, 1749-1831

— Select Views in Italy.... L, 1792-96. 2 vols in 1. Oblong folio, contemp mor gilt; upper joint restored, extremities rubbed. With engraved dedication, engraved map & 72 plates. Marginal foxing to plates in Vol II. Holland House—Kissner—McCarty Cooper copy. CNY Jan 25 (73) $1,800

Anr copy. Contemp calf gilt; scuffed & rubbed. With engraved dediction & 72 plates. W July 8 (294) £660

Smith, Capt. John, 1580-1631

— Advertisements for the unexperienced Planters of New-England.... L: John Haviland for Robert Milbourne, 1631. 8th state. 4to, mor jenseniste by Sangorski & Sutcliffe. With folding map. lower & fore-margins cropped, affecting catchwords & signatures of 9 leaves, 3 words of poem on A3v & a few sidenotes; washed with loss on F14; repair to E1; map backed. STC 22787. DuPont copy. CNY Oct 8 (234) $19,000

— The Generall Historie of Virginia, New-England, and the Summer Isles.... [Cleveland, 1966]. Folio, vellum gilt. Facsimile of the 1624 Ed. bba Dec 19 (399) £50 [Willcocks]

— The True Travels, Adventures and Observations.... L, 1630. Folio, lev gilt by W. Pratt; joints & lower corners & edges rubbed, front free endpaper torn at gutter. Plate torn & linen-backed with some minor losses at edges; washed. CNY Oct 8 (233) $5,500

Anr Ed. Richmond, 1819. 2 vols. 8vo, contemp calf; repaired. LH Dec 11 (250) $140

Smith, John Jay, 1798-1881. See: Walter & Smith

Smith, John Russell, 1810-94

— A Bibliographical Catalogue of English Writers on Angling and Ichthyology. L, 1856. 12mo, old half mor by Riviere; rubbed. Interleaved. A.N.L. Munby's copy. K Sept 29 (166) $110

Smith, John Thomas, 1766-1833

— Antiquities of Westminster. L, 1807-9. Atlas vol only. Half mor. With 133 subjects (14 hand-colored) on 100 plates. L.p. copy. S Feb 26 (784) £250 [Shapero]

— The Cries of London. L, 1839. 4to, orig half cloth; rubbed. With port & 30 plates. Some spotting & staining. pn Nov 14 (397) £90 [Marlborough]

Anr copy. Orig cloth; spine ends chipped. A few leaves loose. sg Nov 7 (235) $375

— Nollekens and His Time. L, 1829. 2d Ed. 2 vols. 8vo, contemp calf; rebacked, orig spines preserved. Margin of port & leaves at start of Vol I ink-stained. bba Dec 19 (57) £s65 [Cline]

Smith Library, Joseph

— Bibliotheca Smithiana, seu catalogus librorum D. Josephi Smithii. Venice, 1755. Compiled by Giovanni Battista Pasquali. 4to, contemp wraps; front hinge cracked. sg May 7 (192) $425

Smith, Joseph, 1805-44

— The Book of Mormon. Palmyra, NY, 1830. 1st Ed. 8vo, orig sheep; extremities worn, covers bowed. Some foxing & browning; ink marginalia. sg June 18 (396A) $8,500

Anr copy. Contemp calf; rebacked, cracked & damaged, spine perished. wd June 12 (434) $4,000

2d Ed. Kirtland OH, 1837. 12mo, contemp sheep; worn. First gathering in facsimile; some foxing. sg June 18 (397) $1,700

3d Ed. Nauvoo IL, 1840. 16mo, orig sheep; worn, front cover loose. With testimonies on facing pages & without the index. Some foxing. sg June 18 (398) $3,200

Anr Ed. Liverpool, 1849. 8vo, cloth. Inscr to William Cullen Bryant by Samuel Henry Dickson. sg June 18 (399) $1,300

Anr copy. Orig sheep; loose. Lacking half-title; some foxing. sg June 18 (400) $800

Anr Ed. Liverpool, 1854. Flake 602. 12mo, orig sheep; rebacked. sg June 18

(402) $140

Flake 603. Contemp sheep; rebacked. sg June 18 (403) $120

Anr Ed. NY, [1858]. Brooks Issue. 8vo, contemp half mor; needs rebdg. Some foxing & pencil notations. sg June 18 (404) $300

1st Ed in Deseret. NY, 1869. 8vo, orig cloth; spine ends chipped, extremities rubbed. Library markings. sg June 18 (405) $800

Anr Ed. Salt Lake City, 1871. 18mo, orig sheep gilt; loose. sg June 18 (406) $350

— Doctrine and Covenants of the Church of the Latter Day Saints.... Nauvoo, 1845. 12mo, contemp sheep; worn & loose. sg June 18 (390) $3,200

— General Smith's Views of the Powers and Policy of the Government. NY: E. J. Bevin, 1844. 8vo, sewn as issued. Some foxing; 1 leaf creased. P June 16 (286) $1,000

— Mormons Bog. Copenhagen, 1851. 16mo, orig blindstamped sheep; extremities worn. Some foxing. sg June 18 (393) $800

— Mormons Bok. En Berattelse Skrifven med Mormons Hand Pa Platar Efter Nephi Platar. Copenhagen: Utgifven af N. C. Flygare, 1878. 1st Ed in Swedish. Orig sheep; edges rubbed. cb Feb 12 (60) $200

— O Le Tusi a Mamona. Salt Lake City: Deseret News, 1903. 1st Ed in Samoan. Orig cloth, secondary bdg. cb Feb 12 (61) $190

Smith, Julian

— Fifty Masterpieces of Photography.... Melbourne, 1948. Folio, text brochure & plates in orig card portfolio. With 50 plates. kh Nov 11 (648) A$90

Smith, Michael, of Philadelphia

— A Geographical View of the Province of Upper Canada.... Hartford, 1813. 12mo, orig half calf; worn & stained. Some foxing & browning; edge tear to frontis. bbc Dec 9 (432) $110

Smith, Pamela Colman

— Widdicombe Fair. L & NY, 1899. One of 500. 4to, unsewn as issued in orig portfolio. pba Aug 20 (194) $275

Smith, Richard Somers, 1813-77

— A Manual of Topographical Drawing. NY, 1854. 8vo, orig cloth; rubbed. With 14 folding or double-page plates. bba Apr 9 (254) £50 [Bernard]

Smith, Robert, 1689-1768

— Harmonics, or the Philosophy of Musical Sounds. Cambr., 1749. 8vo, contemp calf; spine & edges rubbed. With 25 folding plates. pn Oct 24 (456) £220 [Finch]

Anr Ed. L, 1759. 8vo, orig bds; upper cover detached, lacking backstrip. With 29 folding plates. Some soiling. pn Oct 24 (457) £60 [Elliott]

— Vollstaendiger Lehrbegriff der Optik. Altenburg, 1755. 4to, modern cloth. With engraved title & 22 folding plates Some pencil marginalia. wa Mar 5 (536) $475

Smith, Samuel, 1720-76

— The History of the Colony of Nova-Caesaria, or New-Jersey. Burlington, 1765. One of 600. 8vo, modern lea; soiled. Browned & stained. O May 26 (169) $120

1st Ed, 2d Issue. 8vo, contemp calf; hinges reinforced. sg June 18 (512) $550

Anr copy. Old calf; front cover detached. Browned & foxed throughout. wd June 12 (435) $250

Smith, Scottie Fitzgerald

— The Romantic Egoists. See: Fitzgerald, "Scottie"

Smith, Stevie

— A Good Time Was Had by All. NY, 1937. In d/j. DW Oct 2 (397) £75

Smith, Sydney Ure —& Stevens, Bertram

— The Art of J. J. Hilder. Sydney, 1918. 4to, half cloth, in d/j. kh Nov 11 (121) A$120

Smith, Thomas, 1638-1710

— Remarks upon the Manners, Religion and Government of the Turks. L, 1678. 8vo, contemp calf; repaired. Lacking imprimatur leaf; tp frayed; some soiling; last ad leaf torn. S Nov 21 (282) £550 [O'Neill]

Smith, Thorne

— Topper. NY, 1926. In d/j with edge wear. sg June 11 (290) $800

Smith, W. Eugene

— Japan. A Chapter of Image. NY, 1963. 4to, bds; extremities worn. sg Apr 13 (88) $400

Smith, Walter E.

— Charles Dickens in the Original Cloth.... Los Angeles, 1982-83. 2 vols. 4to, cloth, in d/js. bbc Apr 27 (21) $65; cb Nov 21 (80) $65; sg May 21 (305) $100

Smith, William

— Journal of a Voyage in the Missionary Ship Duff.... NY, 1813. 8vo, modern half calf. cb Jan 30 (111) $250

Smith, William, 1727-1803, Provost

— Relation historique de l'expedition contre les Indiens de l'Ohio.... Amst., 1769. 8vo, old bds; spine corroded, covers detached. With 6 maps & plates. O Nov 26 (159) $475

Smithwick, Noah

— The Evolution of a State or Recollections of Old Texas Days. Austin, [1900]. 12mo, cloth. With 5 plates. sg Dec 5 (252) $80

Smollett, Tobias, 1721-71

— The Adventures of Peregrine Pickle. L, 1751. 1st Ed. 4 vols. 12mo, later calf gilt; worn, some spines def. bba Jan 16 (120) £220 [Scott]

— The Expedition of Humphry Clinker. L, MDCLXXI [sic, but 1771]. 1st Ed, Rothschild's Variant A4 but with 147 correctly numbered & page vi so labeled. 3 vols. 8vo, contemp calf; Vol I joints worn & split. F8 torn. bba Nov 28 (286) £200 [Hannas]

— The Regicide: or, James the First, of Scotland.... L, 1749. 8vo, old calf; back cover detached. Some foxing & water-stains. rs Oct 17 (83) $200

— Works. L, 1895. One of 150. 12 vols. 8vo, half calf by Root; worn. O May 26 (170) $450

Anr Ed. Oxford: Shakespeare Head Press, 1925-26. ("Novels.") 11 vols. Orig cloth. bba Feb 27 (381) £70 [Dawson]

Smythe, F. S.

— The Valley of Flowers. L, 1938. One of 250. With 16 mtd color plates & 2 maps. Packet of seeds from Bhyundar Valley laid in. sg May 21 (99) $300

Smythies, Bertram Evelyn

— The Birds of Borneo. Edin. & L, 1960. sg May 14 (246) $130

Smythies, E. A.

— Big Game Shooting in Nepal.... Calcutta, 1942. With 40 plates & 2 folding maps. sg May 21 (100pUS130)

Snape, Andrew, Farrier

— The Anatomy of an Horse.... L, 1683. 1st Ed. 2 parts in 1 vol. Folio, later half calf; rubbed. Lacking 1 plate; some staining & soiling. O Jan 14 (175) $650

Snellius, Willebrord, 1591-1626

— Appolonius Batavus, seu Exsuscitata Apollonii Pergaei. Leiden: Johannes a Dorp, 1608. Bound with: Tiphys Batavus, sive Histiodromice, de navium cursibus.... Leiden: Elzevir, 1624. 4to, contemp ellum; bowed. Ck Nov 29 (240) £350

— Cyclometricus de circuli dimensione secundum logistarum abacos.... Leiden: Elzevir, 1621. 1st Ed. 4to, old calf; worn. Ck Nov 29 (241) £150

Snodgrass, John James

— Narrative of the Burmese War. L, 1827. 8vo, orig half cloth; worn & soiled, spine split. With folding map (tear at bdg edge) & 2 plates. wa Apr 9 (139) $110

Snow, Jack

— The Magical Mimics in Oz. Chicago: Reilly & Lee, [1946]. Cloth, in chipped d/j. K Mar 22 (320) $100

Snowden, William John

— The Northern Territory As It Is. Adelaide, 1882. 8vo, orig cloth. S June 25 (268) £950 [Quaritch/Hordern]

Snowman, Abraham Kenneth

— The Art of Carl Faberge. L, 1953. 4to, orig cloth; worn. F Mar 26 (316) $50

— Eighteenth Century Gold Boxes of Europe. Bost., 1966. In d/j. sp June 18 (391) $140

Soave, Pietro. See: Sarpi, Paolo

Soby, James Thrall

— The Prints of Paul Klee. NY, 1945. One of 1,000. 4to, loose as issued in pbr's case. With 40 plates. sg Feb 6 (148) $80

Social Club...

— The Social Club: consisting of a Series of Stories; and accompanied by Humorous Prints of each Subject. L, 1822. Illus by William Henry Pyne. Parts 1-4 (all pbd). Folio, lev gilt by Morrell, orig wraps bound in (lower wrap of Part 4 lacking). With 12 colored plates. Some foxing; 1 plate torn, backed & repaired. DuPont copy. CNY Oct 8 (216) $2,800

Society for the Diffusion of Useful Knowledge

— The Family Atlas.... L, 1865. 4to, contemp half mor gilt; rubbed. With 80 hand-colored maps, star maps & plans. Maps 3 & 4 with marginal repair; 1st map loose. L Nov 14 (451) £190

— Maps. L, 1844. 2 vols. 4to, orig cloth; worn. With 218 mapsheets, including 51 town plans & 6 star charts, 1 hand-colored. b Mar 11 (30) £820

Anr copy. Early 20th-cent half mor gilt; rubbed. With port, 6 folding plates & 1 folding map. Ck May 15 (158) £95

Anr copy. 2 vols in 1. 4to, contemp half mor; worn. DW Nov 6 (97) £720

Anr copy. Contemp half mor; worn. With 168 (of 212) maps & plans colored in outline. Sold w.a.f. DW Dec 11 (70) £250

Anr copy. 2 vols. 4to, contemp half calf; worn. With 205 maps, all colored in outline. Bound without gnomonic maps & geological map of England in Vol I & star maps in Vol II. DW May 13 (59) £760

Anr copy. 2 vols in 1. 4to, contemp half lea; worn. With 212 maps & plans, hand-colored in outline, with the 6 star maps similar. Additional map of The Netherlands bound in. L Nov 14 (159) £680

Anr copy. 2 vols. 4to, contemp half russia gilt; worn. With 218 mapsheets (the 7 double-page subjects counted as 2), most hand-colored in outline. Some dust-soiling; several sheets becoming detached. S Nov 21 (145) £800 [Map House]

Anr copy. 2 vols in 1. 4to, modern cloth. With 151 maps only, hand-colored in outline. S Feb 26 (711) £450 [Mead Cain]

Anr Ed. L, 1848. 2 vols. Folio, contemp calf; def. With 163 maps hand-colored in outline. Some tears at fold; 8 tears repaired; some edges browned & soiled; lacking tp & contents. Sold w.a.f. pnL Nov 20 (27) £660

Anr copy. Contemp half calf; worn. With 206 maps & plans only, hand-colored in outline, & 6 hand-colored star charts. Paris soiled; Parma, St. Petersburg & Philadelphia badly torn. S Nov 15 (768) £1,000 [Orssich]

Society of Artists

— A Catalogue of the Pictures, Sculptures...at the Great Room in Spring-Garden, Charing-Cross, May the 9th, 1761.... L, [n.d.]. 4to, disbound. With frontis & 1 plate (dampstained). Ck June 12 (192) £480

Soderini, Giovanni Vettorio —& Others

— Trattato della coltivazione delle viti.... Florence: Manni, 1734. 3 parts in 1 vol. 4to, half calf. Some leaves finger-soiled. SI Dec 5 (626) LIt450,000

Soemmerring, Samuel Thomas von, 1755-1830

— Icones Embryonum Humanorum. Frankfurt, 1799. Folio, orig bds. With 2 plates. Foxed. sg Nov 14 (134) $1,000

Solander, Dr Daniel. See: Banks & Solander

Soliday, George W. See: Decker, Peter

Soliday Library, George W.

— A Descriptive Check List...describing...Western Americana...Compiled by Peter Decker. NY, 1940-45. 5 parts in 1 vol. sg Oct 31 (99) $175

Solinus, Caius Julius

— Polyhistor.... Basel, 1538. ("Rerum toto orbe memorabilium thesaurus locupletissimus....") Bound with: Chronicon opus felicissime renatum infinitis membris emendatis. Basel: Heinrich Petri, 1536. Folio, 2 parts in 1 vol. Folio,; contemp calf over wooden bds. rebacked, lacking clasps Some soiling to 2d work. S June 30 (78) £700 [Dallegio]

Solis y Ribadeneyra, Antonio de, 1610-86

— Historia de la conquista de Mexico.... Madrid, 1684. 1st Ed. Folio, contemp mor gilt; joints weak, head of spine chipped. Waterstain at foot in 1st half. S Nov 21 (341) £800 [Skiathos]

— The History of the Conquest of Mexico.... L, 1724. 1st Ed in English. Folio, orig calf; rebacked. With 7 plates, 6 folding & 2 maps, 1 folding. cb Oct 10 (96) $700

Anr Ed. L, 1738. 2 vols. 8vo, contemp calf; rubbed. With folding port frontis, 2 folding maps & 6 folding plates. Some browning. S July 1 (1489) £200 [Toscani]

— Istoria della conquista del Messico.... Venice, 1715. 4to, contemp vellum. With 3 ports & 5 plates. sg Dec 5 (237) $350

Solon, Louis Marie Emmanuel

— The Art of the Old English Potter. L, 1883. One of 250. Folio, cloth. Library markings. bba Feb 27 (451) £90 [Rose]

Anr copy. Orig cloth, in def d/j. With 50 plates Metropolitan Museum of Art duplicate. sg Sept 6 (240) $100

Soltau, G. W.

— Trout Flies of Devon and Cornwall.... L & Plymouth, 1847. 8vo, half mor; rubbed. With 2 color plates Plates stained. Koopman copy. O Oct 29 (293) $130

Solvyns, Frans Baltasar

— The Costume of Hindostan. L, 1804. 4to, contemp mor. With 60 hand-colored plates. Rodent damage affecting outer margins throughout; some soiling & staining to text; English title torn at inner margin & soiled. Ck Dec 11 (263) £180

Some...

— Some Account of the Conduct of the Religious Society of Friends towards the Indian Tribes.... L, 1844. 8vo, orig cloth; spine ends worn, joints repaired. With 2 colored maps. Some foxing. wa Mar 5 (360) $170

Some Considerations...

— Some Considerations on the Establishment of the French Strolers.... L: R. Freeman, [1749]. 8vo, early 19th-cent half lea; spine imperf. sg Mar 5 (230) $300

Somers, John, Baron Somers, 1651-1716

— A Collection of Scarce and Valuable Tracts. L, 1809-15. 13 vols. 4to, half cloth; rubbed. Library markings. bba Feb 27 (101) £130 [Makrocki]

Anr copy. Contemp calf; rubbed, spines worn. Vol I with 8 double-page plates; Vol II with 1 full-page plate; Vol XIII with folding table. Lacking half-titles; some spotting. S Feb 25 (465) £190 [Mackrocki]

Somervile, William, 1675-1742. See: Fore-Edge Paintings

Somner, William, 1598-1669

— A Treatise of the Roman Ports and Forts in Kent. Oxford, 1693. 1st Ed. 8vo, 19th-cent calf gilt; rubbed. Ck May 15 (160) £80

Sonn, Albert H.

— Early American Wrought Iron. NY, 1928. 3 vols. 4to, orig cloth. With 320 plates. Library markings, with text & plates unmarked. sg Feb 6 (139) $325

Sonnerat, Pierre

— Voyage a la Nouvelle Guinee.... Paris, 1776. 4to, contemp half calf. With 118 (of 120) plates. HH May 12 (657) DM2,000

— Voyage aux Indes Orientales et a la Chine.... Paris, 1782. 1st Ed. 2 vols. 4to, contemp calf gilt; spines & extremities worn, joints cracked. With 139 (of 140) plates; wash copy of missing Plate 76 supplied. Plate 47 in Vol I dampstained; small hole to Ff3 in Vol II affecting 4 letters; marginal tear to Gg2; some foxing & browning; dampstaining to gutters of 1st & last few quires of Vol II. CNY Oct 8 (236) $350

Anr copy. 2 vols. 8vo, recent mor gilt. Some worming throughout. DW Oct 2 (68) £80

Sonnet, Thomas, Sieur de Courval

— Satyre contre les charlatans.... Paris, 1610. 8vo, mor by Trautz-Bauzonnet; rubbed. With 2 ports. O May 26 (171) $750

Sophocles, 496?-406 B.C.

— Ediop Re. Verona: Officina Bodoni, 1968. Illus by Giacomo Manzo. 4to, unsewn in vellum bds. With 7 etchings. SI Dec 5 (433) LIt6,500,000

— King Oedipus. NY, [1968]. One of 105, sgd by artist. Illus by Giacomo Manzu. 4to, loose in wraps as issued. With 7 etchings. sg Jan 30 (167) $1,200

— Tragoediae septem. Venice: Aldus, 1502. 1st Ed. 8vo, 19th-cent calf with gilt arms of the 1st Duke of Sutherland; joints worn. Greek type. Minor stains. C June 24 (283) £2,800 [Kraus]

Soranzo, Lazaro

— L'Ottomanno...doue si da pieno ragguaglio non solamente della potenza del presente signor de' turchi Mehemeto III.... Ferrara: Vittorio Baldini, 1598. 4to, later half vellum. Lacking 2 leaves of prelims before A1, errata leaf & colophon leaf; C1 lacking blank corner. S July 1 (714) £800 [Kutluoglu]

Sorel, Charles, Sieur de Souvigny

— The Comical History of Francion. L, 1655. Folio, modern calf. Tp rehinged. W July 8 (25) £115

Sorlier, Charles

— The Ceramics and Sculptures of Chagall. Monaco, 1972. 4to, orig cloth, in d/j. bbc Apr 27 (440) $140; wa June 25 (452) $210

Sossius, Gulielmus

— De vita Henrici magni libri IV. Paris: Pierre Chevalier, 1522. 8vo, early vellum. sg Mar 12 (281) $250

Sotheby, William, 1757-1838

— A Tour through Parts of Wales.... L, 1794. 4to, contemp calf; rebacked, orig spine laid on. cb Sept 5 (101) $55

Soule, Frank —& Others

— The Annals of San Francisco. NY, 1855. 1st Ed. 8vo, orig mor gilt. With 6 plates. Lacking folding map. cb Nov 14 (208) $75

Anr copy. Lea gilt. NH Aug 23 (117) $110

Anr copy. Orig sheep gilt; extremities rubbed. With 2 maps, 1 folding with small tear; 6 plates. sg June 18 (131) $120

Anr Ed. Palo Alto, 1966. Cloth by Joseph Donato. With folding map. Map detached. Facsimile reprint. cb Dec 19 (161) $120

Soules, Francois, 1748-1809

— Histoire des troubles de l'Amerique anglaise.... Paris, 1787. 4 vols. 8vo, contemp calf gilt; spine ends chipped, joints dry, lacking 1 front free endpaper. With 3 folding maps with outline color. Lower binding edge margins trimmed to borders. wa Dec 9 (338) $425

Sourget, Patrick & Elisabeth

— Manuscrits enlumines et livres precieux.... [Chartres: Sourget, n.d.]. Catalogue VI. Folio, cloth, in d/j. cb Jan 16 (141) $50

Sousa, John Philip

— Marching Along. Bost., 1928. Orig cloth; shaken. Inscr. F Sept 26 (558) $90

South...

— South Polar Times. L, 1907-14. One of 250. Ed by E. H. Shackleton & L. C. Bernacchi. 3 vols. 4to, orig cloth. b Nov 18 (355) £2,400

Anr copy. Pictorial cloth; several gatherings loose in Vol II. sg Jan 9 (12) $6,000

Anr copy. Orig cloth, Vol III disbound. W July 8 (284) £1,700

South Sea Company

See also: True...

— The Proceedings of the Directors.... L, 1721. 8vo, modern cloth. Portion of fore-edge margin lacking on tp & 2d leaf, not affecting text; upper fore-edge corners lacking on several other leaves. sg Jan 9 (183) $130

Southard, Charles Z.

— The Evolution of Trout and Trout Fishing in America. NY, 1928. One of 100. 4to, mor gilt; worn. With 9 colored plates. Inscr & with Ls to Philip Hale. O May 26 (172) $650

Southey, Robert, 1774-1843

— Joan of Arc. Bristol, 1796. 4to, contemp half lea; rubbed. Lacking half-title; some browning; marginal worming. pn July 16 (55) £150 [Edwards]

— Poetical Works. L, 1837-38. 10 vols. 8vo, orig cloth. bba Jan 30 (772) £120 [Kitzawa]

Southgate, Horatio

— Narrative of a Tour through Armenia, Kurdistan, Persia and Mesopotamia. L, 1840. 2 vols. 8vo, orig cloth; worn & foxed, 1 spine loose. O Aug 25 (164) $160

Souvenir...

— Souvenir de la Suisse. Lucerne: Schuermann, [c.1850]. 4to, orig cloth; loose. With engraved title & 24 plates.. HH May 12 (778) DM2,000

— Souvenir of Scotland. L, 1891. 4to, orig cloth. With 120 (on 30) colored plates. pnE Dec 4 (80) £110

Sowerby, Arthur de C.

See also: Clark & Sowerby

— Sport and Science on the Sino-Mongolian Frontier. L, 1918. sg May 21 (103) $175

— A Sportsman's Miscellany. Tientsin, 1917. 4to, cloth; front joint cracked. Library markings. sg May 21 (102) $150

Sowerby, E. Millicent. See: Jefferson Library, Thomas

Sowerby, George Brettingham, 1812-84

— A Conchological Manual. L, 1846. 8vo, orig cloth; rubbed, hinges splitting. Plates colored. Some spotting & staining. bba May 14 (497) £100 [Lib. Naturalistica Bolognese]

— Illustrated Index of British Shells. L, 1859. 1st Ed. 4to, later cloth. With 24 hand-colored plates. Library markings. bba Sept 5 (107) £120 [Kafka]

Anr copy. Orig cloth; rubbed. Ink signature on tp. bba May 14 (498) £90 [Ginnan]

Anr copy. Cloth; soiled. Tp stamped. pn Mar 19 (332) £65

— Popular British Conchology.... L, 1854. 8vo, cloth; spine ends repaired. With 19 hand-colored plates. sg Feb 13 (209) $120

Sowerby, James, 1757-1822

— Coloured Figures of English Fungi. L, [1795]-1797-1803. 3 vols. Folio, 19th-cent half mor gilt. With 400 (of 440) hand-colored plates. Some spotting; 2 plates supplied from anr copy. Ck Oct 31 (105) £3,000

Anr copy. Vol III only. Contemp half lea; rubbed, front cover detaching, spine worn. With 160 hand-colored plates. Lacking 1 plate but with 1 plate from anr vol. K Mar 22 (428) $1,100

Anr copy. 4 vols in 3, including 1815 Supplement. Folio, later calf gilt; rubbed & soiled. With 440 hand-colored or color-ptd plates on 436 leaves. Plates bound as Vols II & III; 2 plates with minor stains; stamps on tp, 1st & last pages of text & versos of last plate in each vol. pn Mar 19 (331) £1,300 [Toscani]

Sowerby, James, 1757-1822 —& Smith, Sir James Edward, 1759-1828

— English Botany. L, 1790-1814. Vols I-V only. Contemp half calf; rubbed. With 366 hand-colored plates. Ck Oct 18 (28) £350

Anr copy. 36 vols in 12. 8vo, contemp half calf; rubbed, several covers detached. Ck May 15 (48) £1,500

Anr Ed. L, [1832]-46. 12 vols. 8vo, contemp calf; rebacked preserving orig spines, Vols VI & XII rebound to match. With c.2,580 hand-colored or partly colored plates. Library stamp on titles & 1st text leaves; lacking 4 leaves of text in Vol I. C Oct 30 (229) £1,200 [Graves]

Anr copy. Vols I-XIII but lacking Vol XII. Contemp half calf; rubbed. W Mar 6 (113) £420

Mixed Ed. L, [1832]-54. 12 vols. 8vo, contemp half mor gilt; rubbed. With 2,752 colored plates. A few plates repaired in Vol II; some spotting. Sold w.a.f. S Nov 21 (46) £700 [kiefer]

3d Ed. L, 1863-86. 12 vols. Library cloth. bba Oct 24 (269) £700 [Princeton Rare books]

Anr copy. 13 vols, including 1902 Supplement. Contemp mor gilt; rubbed, last 4 vols faded. Library markings. bba Feb 277 (411) £620 [Elliott]

Anr copy. Vols I-XI (of 12). Contemp half

mor gilt; rubbed. With 1,824 hand-colored plates. DW Nov 6 (194) £440

Anr copy. 11 vols. Modern cloth. Library stamps on versos of 1st & last plate in 8 vols & on verso of each plate in 3 vols.; some marginal tears & repairs. Sold w.a.f. pnL Nov 20 (164) £270 [Almar]

Anr Ed. L, 1877-76-86. 12 vols. 8vo, later cloth. Library markings. bba Sept 5 (105) £650 [Gyldenlak]

Anr Ed. L, 1899. 13 vols, including Supplement. Orig cloth. Sold w.a.f. DW Apr 8 (177) £400

Anr copy. 13 vols, including Supplement. 8vo, modern cloth; stamps on edges, shelf marks on spines. With 1,951 hand-colored plates. Blindstamps on most leaves & plates; stamps on endpapers, verso of tp & verso of each plate. Sold w.a.f. pn Mar 19 (334) £150

Sowerby, James, 1757-1822 —& Sowerby, James de Carle, 1787-1871

— The Mineral Conchology of Great Britain. L, 1812-29. 5 vols only. Contemp russia; edges worn, spines def. Sold w.a.f. With 615 hand-colored plates. Stamps on front pastedowns, verso of tp, 1st & final leaf of text. Sold w.a.f. pn Mar 19j (333) £1,300 [Junk]

Sowerby, James de Carle, 1787-1871. See: Sowerby & Sowerby

Sowerby, James de Carle, 1787-1871 —& Lear, Edward, 1812-88

— Tortoises, Terrapins and Turtles. L, 1872. Folio, contemp half mor; worn. With 60 plates, 57 hand-colored. bba Apr 30 (321) £1,900 [Baring]

Anr copy. Orig cloth; rubbed & soiled. With 61 litho plates. Stamps on pastedowns & verso of tp; some browning. pn Mar 19 (335) £1,200

Anr copy. Orig cloth; upper joint torn. With 61 plates. Text spotted. S June 25 (34) £1,600 [Beaux Arts]

Anr copy. Later cloth. With 60 plates. Text leaves browned. Library stamps on endpapers & title. sg Nov 7 (236) $2,600

Sowerby, John E., 1825-70. See: Johnson & Sowerby

Spalding, Albert Goodwill, 1850-1915

— America's National Game; Historic Facts Concerning...Baseball. NY, 1911. Bdg rubbed, hinges cracked. Last several signatures with rippling; 1 plate with scratched; lacking 2 tipped-in double-page groups of photographs of stadiums at rear. bbc Sept 23 (192) $180

Spallanzani, Lazzaro

— Opuscules de physique animale et vegetale. Paris & Padua, 1787. 2 vols. 8vo, 19th-cent half mor gilt. With 6 folding plates. sg May 14 (157) $300

— Tracts on the Natural History of Animals and Vegetables.... Edin., 1803. 2 vols. 8vo, contemp half calf; Vol II spine chipped. With 11 folding plates. sg May 14 (159) $325

— Travels in the Two Sicilies.... L, 1798. 4 vols. 8vo, contemp calf. With 11 folding plates. Minor defs. SI June 10 (948) LIt900,000

Spangenberg, Cyriacus

— Adels-Spiegel. Schmalkalden: Michael Schmueck, 1591. 2 vols. Folio, vellum. Repair to upper margin of last few leaves of Vol I with minimal loss; 2d title cut down & mtd; some staining. S May 13 (797) £260 [Milkain]

Spanish. See: Celestina...

Spargo, John, 1876-1966

— The Potters and Potteries of Bennington. Bost., 1926. One of 800. 4to, half cloth, in d/j. With 44 plates. F Mar 26 (273) $50

Sparke, Michael

— The Narrative History of King James.... L, 1651. 4to, old calf; worn, spine chipped. O Dec 17 (170) $140

Anr copy. Later calf; joints & edges rubbed. With engraved title, port & folding port (with small tear & repair). I4 cropped affecting text; small hole in Q2; lacking V4; marginal tears; some browning & soiling. pn Dec 12 (16) £90 [Rix]

Sparks, Jared, 1789-1866

— The Life of John Ledyard, the American Traveller. Cambr. MA, 1828. 1st Ed. 8vo, 19th-cent half lea; rubbed. Phillipps copy. S Feb 26 (787) £160 [Quaritch]

Anr Ed. Cambr. MA, 1829. 8vo, orig half cloth; scuffed. Some foxing & browning. bbc Dec 9 (424) $75

Sparks, Timothy. See: Dickens, Charles

Sparling, Henry Halliday

— The Kelmscott Press and William Morris.... L, 1924. Half cloth. bba Oct 10 (546) £50 [Elstree Bks]

Anr copy. Unopened. cb Oct 17 (880) $55

Sparrow

— Sparrow. Los Angeles: Black Sparrow Press, 1973-78. Nos 13-72, each, one of 50. Bound in 5 vols. 8vo, cloth. sg June 11 (291) $225

Sparrow, Anthony

— A Collection of Articles, Injunctions, Canons.... L, 1675. 3d Ed. 4to, old calf; rebacked, worn. O Dec 17 (41) $60

Sparrow, Walter Shaw

— Angling in British Art. L, 1923. 4to, orig cloth. Some foxing. kh Nov 11 (217) A$120; L Feb 27 (115) £80

— Ben Alken. L & NY, 1927. 4to, cloth, in def d/j. sg Jan 9 (205) $80

Spatharakis, Joannis

— Corpus of Dated Illuminated Greek Manuscripts to the Year 1453. Leiden, 1981. 2 vols. Folio, cloth. sg Oct 31 (257) $300

Spaulding, E. G.

— History of the Legal Tender Paper Money issued during the Great Rebellion. Buffalo, 1869. 8vo, cloth. Inscr to Millard Fillmore. sg Dec 5 (238) $200

Spear, Dorothea N.

— Bibliography of American Directories through 1860. Worcester, 1961. 8vo, orig cloth. K Sept 29 (404) $50

Specimens...

— Specimens of Printing Types, and Ornaments, from the Letter-Foundry of E. White, No. 11 Thames-Street, New-York. NY, 185. 8vo, orig cloth; worn, crudely repaired. Some soiling. F Mar 26 (202) $500

— Specimens of Polyautography. L, 1803-7. Oblong folio, in cloth retaining cover & spine of early album bdg, sgd by J. Kelly. With litho title, 25 lithos & 9 additional early lithos on mounts with watercolor borders. One of the extra lithos badly damaged & imperf; some browning & waterstaining. Schlosser copy. P June 17 (593) $36,000

Spectator

— The Spectator [By Addison, Steele & others]. L, 1712-15. 1st Collected Ed. 8 vols. 8vo, contemp calf gilt; not uniform, scuffed, 2 spines chipped. C Dec 16 (175) £600 [Quaritch]

Anr Ed. L, 1753. 8 vols. 16mo, contemp calf. LH Dec 11 (51) $90

Speed, John, 1552-1629

Abridgement of Theatre

— England, Wales, Scotland and Ireland Described.... L, 1627. 2 parts in 1 vol. Oblong 8vo, modern cloth. Vol I with 16 (of 20) maps; lacking all before B2 except title. Vol II with 62 (of 63) maps. Soiled, some maps def. Sold w.a.f. DW Nov 6 (99) £1,150

Anr copy. Old calf; rebacked, worn. Staining & soiled. O Nov 26 (160) $1,300

Anr copy. 1 part only; without Prospect. Oblong 8vo, calf; rubbed & wormed. With 62 maps. Lacking Worcester & Gloucester but repeating Glamorgan & Radnor; tp cropped along lower edge; stained & worn; a few pages wormed at lower edge; some staining; 2 maps cropped. S Nov 15 (959) £850 [Kidd]

Continuation of Theatre

— The Historie of Great Britaine under the Conquests.... L, 1614. Folio, contemp calf; rubbed, rebacked. Engraved title cut down & mtd; some cropping at top. STC 23046. bba July 9 (80) £180 [Land]

Anr Ed. L, 1623. Folio, calf; worn, front cover detached. Tp detached. NH Aug 23 (173) $250

Theatre

— The Theatre of the Empire of Great Britaine. L, 1676. ("The Theatre of the Empire of Great Britain.") 2 parts in 1 vol. Folio, contemp calf; worn, 1 hinge split. With engraved title, frontis with arms of Charles II, 96 double-page maps & 5 double-page tables. Text & maps mtd on guards; 5 maps torn or split at fold, anr flawed & repaired. Evelyn copy. S June 25 (296) £26,000 [Map House]

Speed, Samuel, d.1681

— Fragmenta carceris.... L, 1675. 2d Ed. 4to, 19th-cent mor gilt by Matthews; rebacked. Tp cut down & mtd, affecting date & vignette; some worming with occasional loss. Ck Sept 6 (87) £110

Speke, John Hanning, 1827-64

— Journal of the Discovery of the Source of the Nile. Edin & L, 1863. 8vo, contemp half calf; rubbed. With 2 ports & 24 plates & maps. Lacking map in end pocket. bba Sept 19 (74) £160 [Maggs]

Anr copy. Half calf; rubbed. With 2 maps & 1 folding plate. bba Apr 30 (47) £170 [Woodstock]

2d Ed. Edin. & L, 1864. 8vo, orig cloth; rubbed. Short tear in pocket holding folding map at end. L Nov 14 (455) £130

1st American Ed. NY, 1864. 8vo, orig cloth; rebacked; hinges tape-reinforced. cb Oct 10 (97) $90

Spelen...

— Spelen van Sinne, vol scoone moralisacien wtleggingen ende Bediedenissen op all loeflijcke Consten. Antwerp: W. Silvius, 1562. 2 parts in 1 vol. 4to, calf; def. With folding plate & 37 woodcuts, 15 full-page. Some thumbing & stains. Bibl Belg. S224a & b. B Nov 1 (325) HF5,500

Spelman, Sir Henry, 1564-1641
— Archaeologus. In modum glossarii... L, 1664. ("Glossarium archaiologicum: continens Latino-Barbara...Vocabula.") Folio, contemp calf with Colbert's arms on sides; very worn. Some browning. Bibliotheca Colbertina copy. S May 13 (752) £150 [Claridge]
— The English Works.... L, 1723. Folio, contemp calf; rebacked, orig spine preserved. bba Jan 16 (30) £100 [Hay Cinema]
Anr copy. Later half calf gilt; worn, front cover detached. cb Dec 5 (127) $190

Spelman, Sir John, 1594-1643
— Aelfredi Magni Anglorum Regis invictissimi vita. Oxford, 1678. 1st Ed. Folio, 18th-cent half sheep; worn, needs rebacking. With 7 plates. Title loose; plates lightly stained. sg Mar 12 (285) $80

Spence, Joseph, 1699-1768
— A Parallel in the Manner of Plutarch.... Strawberry Hill, 1758. 1st Ed. 8vo, mor gilt. bba June 25 (92) £170 [Kunkler]
— Polymetis.... L, 1747. 1st Ed. Folio, old calf; worn, covers nearly detached. With port & 41 plates. Some browning & foxing; marginal repairs. sg Sept 6 (261) $110
Anr copy. Modern cloth with old gilt russia backstrip laid down. sg Feb 6 (269) $140
2d Ed. L, 1755. Folio, modern half calf gilt. With port & 41 plates.. W July 14 (41) £125

Spencer, Sir Baldwin —& Gillen, Francis J.
— The Arunta. A Study of a Stone Age People. L, 1927. 2 vols. Cloth, in d/js. kh Nov 11 (650) A$550

Spencer, John, 1630-93
— Kaina kai palaia. Things New and Old.... L, 1658. Folio, early 19th-cent half calf gilt; extremities worn. Some stains. sg Mar 12 (286) $325

Spender, Stephen
— Poems. L, [1933]. In d/j. Inscr. sg Dec 12 (376) $175
1st Ed. Orig cloth; soiled. Inscr to John Lehmann, 1 Feb 1933. S Nov 14 (606) £200 [Mytze]
— Twenty Poems. Oxford, [1930]. Orig wraps; soiled. Sgd. bba July 9 (234) £65 [Poetry Bookshop]

Spender, Stephen —& Hockney, David
— China Diary. L, 1982. One of 1,000. With orig litho, Red Square and the Forbidden City, sgd, loosely inserted. Ck Dec 11 (282) £180

Spenser, Edmund, 1552?-99
See also: Cresset Press; Limited Editions Club
— Colin Clouts Come Home Againe. L: William Ponsonbie, 1595. 1st Ed. 4to, mor gilt by Riviere. Washed; rust-hole in inner margin of tp. Marchbank-Robinson copy. P Dec 12 (190) $2,000
— Complaints. L, 1591. 1st Ed. 3 parts in 1 vol. 8vo, 17th-cent calf gilt; rebacked, extremities rubbed, top forecorners restored. Early marginalia; quire E dampstained. Stanley-Wray-Charterhouse-Robinson copy. P Dec 12 (189) $4,500
— Epithalamion. L: Essex House Press, 1901. One of 150, ptd on vellum. Vellum; soiled & bowed with pastedowns starting to lift. wa Sept 26 (69) $300
— The Faerie Queene. L: William Ponsonby, 1590-96. 1st Ed, Part 1 Issue with leaves Pp6, 7 & 8 before cancellation. Part 1 only. Contemp calf gilt with single plain flyleaves & single waste-paper flyleaves from Camden's Britannia, 1594. On blank [590] is only known early Ms copy of the 1st sonnet of Spenser's Amoretti. Hogan-Hartz-Manney copy. P Oct 11 (285) $42,500
1st Folio Ed. L, 1609. 2 parts in 1 vol. Folio, later calf; upper cover detached. Tp spotted & frayed at lower margins; some marginal soiling. STC 23083. Ck Nov 29 (314) £450
Anr Ed. L, 1751. 3 vols. 4to, contemp calf gilt; extremities rubbed. With 31 (of 32) double-page plates. Prelims of Vol I wormed at upper margins; 2Y4 holed with loss of 4 letters; K2 of Vol II torn with loss of 2 letters; some spotting. Ck Sept 6 (88) £50
Anr copy. Contemp calf; worn. LH Dec 11 (254) $325
Anr copy. Contemp calf gilt; 2 vols with covers detached, 1 spine lacking, rubbed. With 32 folding plates. NH May 30 (495) $250
Anr copy. Later calf gilt; rubbed. With 32 double-page plates. CC4 torn without loss. pn Apr 23 (103) £200
Anr Ed. L, 1894-97. One of 1,000. Illus by Walter Crane. 6 vols. 4to, cloth, orig wraps bound in. sp Apr 16 (171) $3252
Anr Ed. Cambr., 1909. One of 350. 2 vols. 4to, orig half cloth; rubbed. DW Dec 11 (500) £50
— The Shepheard's Calendar. L & NY, 1898. Illus by Walter Crane. 4to, cloth; soiled. cb Oct 25 (54) $60
— Works. L, 1611-12. ("The Faerie Queene: The Shepheards Calendar: Together with Other Works of England's Arch-Poet.") 1st

Collected Ed, STC 23083.7. Folio, early 18th-cent calf; spine repaired but chipped. Lacking final blank; conjugate pair transposed, anr duplicated. C Dec 16 (235) £1,000 [Maggs]

Anr Ed. L, 1617. STC 23085. Folio, modern calf; hinges weak. Tp remtd. LH Dec 11 (255) $200

Sphere...

— Sphere: An Illustrated Newspaper for the Home. L, 1914-1919. Nos 758-1,014 in 14 vols. Folio, cloth; spines rubbed. DW Apr 8 (219) £210

Spieghel, Adriaan van der. See: Spigelius, Adrianus

Spielmann, Marion Harry —& Layard, George Somes, 1857-1925

— Kate Greenaway. NY & L, 1905. Orig cloth; worn, head of spine chipped. F Dec 18 (279) $50; kh Nov 11 (220) A$60

Anr copy. Bdg rubbed. sg Jan 30 (81) $120

One of 500, sgd by John Greenaway & with pencil sketch by Kate laid in. 4to, lev gilt by Sangorski & Sutcliffe. With orig drawing of a young woman with basket & parasol. Ck Oct 18 (244) £500

Anr copy. Orig cloth. Epstein copy. sg Apr 29 (195) $950

Spielmann Library, Percy Edwin

— Catalogue of the...Library of Miniature Books. L, 1961. One of 500, sgd by John Greenaway & with pencil sketch by Kate laid in. Orig half cloth, in d/j. K Mar 22 (272) $120

Anr copy. Orig half cloth. O Sept 24 (231) $160

Spiera, Ambrosius de

— Quadragesimale de floribus sapientiae. Venice: Bonetus Locatellus for Octavianus Scotus, 20 Feb 1488/9. 4to, early lea over wooden bds, with brass fittings, the vellum quire guards are the remains of a Carolingian codex. 60 lines & headlines; double column; types 3:62G & 2:130G. Some staining at beginning & end. 314 leaves. Goff S-681. Schoyen copy. P Dec 12 (41) $2,250

Spigelius, Adrianus, 1578-1625

— De formatu foetu.... Padua: J. B. Martinis & L. Pasquatum, [1626]. Folio, modern half vellum. With 8 (of 9) plates. sg Nov 14 (135) $650

Spilberghen, Joris van, 1568-1620

— Speculum orientalis occidentalisque indiae navigationum. Leiden: Nicolaum a Geelkercken, sumptibus Judoci Hondii, 1619. 1st Ed in Latin. Oblong 4to, contemp vellum; rebacked. With folding world map & 20 plates. Worming near foot of some leaves touching engraved surface; a few leaves creased. S June 25 (498) £17,000 [Quaritch]

Spiller, Burton L. See: Derrydale Press

Spiller, Robert E.

— The Philobiblon Club of Philadelphia. [North Hills PA]: Bird & Bull Press, 1973. One of 100. Half vellum. pba July 23 (34) $55

Spilsbury, Francis B.

— Picturesque Scenery in the Holy Land and Syria. L, 1803. 1st Ed. Folio, contemp half mor; worn & rebacked preserving spine. With port & 19 hand-colored plates. S Nov 21 (308) £2,500 [Talhouni]

Anr copy. Contemp mor gilt by C. Frost; stained, rubbed. Tp dust-soiled. S Nov 21 (309) £1,000 [Egee Art]

Anr Ed. L, 1823. 4to, modern half mor. With 19 hand-colored plates. bba Sept 19 (125) £380 [Hooper]

Spilsbury, John

— A Collection of Fifty Prints from Antique Engraved Gems.... L, 1785. 4to, half cloth; hinges starting. With 50 plates. sg Sept 6 (118) $150

Anr copy. Mor gilt; front cover detached. Some foxing. sg Feb 6 (102) $175

Spinniker, Adriaan

— Leerzaame zinnebeelden. Haarlem, 1714-58. 2 vols. 4to, contemp half calf; joints tender. C June 24 (348) £850 [Ursus]

— Vervolg der Leerzaame Zinnebeelden. Haarlem: Jan Bosch, 1758. 4to, mor gilt by the Club Bindery; corners worn. Some browning at end. Hoe copy. CNY Dec 5 (335) $300

Spinoza, Baruch, 1632-77

— Renati Des Cartes principiorum philosophiae.... Amst., 1663. Bound with: Opera posthuma. Amst., 1677. 1st Eds. 4to, contemp calf; worn & wormed. O May 26 (175) $6,000

— Tractatus theologico-politicus.... Hamburg, 1670. 1st Ed, 1st Issue. 4to, half calf. Some stains & foxing. O May 26 (176) $3,600

Land B Ed; Bamberger's 2d Ed, 2d Issue. Hamburg, 1670 [but Amst., 1672]. 4to, blind-stamped pigskin by Zaehnsdorf. C Dec 16 (82) £650 [Quaritch]

Spirito, Lorenzo, c.1430-90

— El Libro dala Ventura overo il Libro da le Sorte. Milan: Guillaume le Signerre for Gottardo da Ponte, 28 Oct 1501. Folio, mor janseniste by Riviere. 56 lines & headline; 2 white-on-black woodcut full borders repeated to 6 impressions; 2 woodcut quarter borders repeated to 20 impressions; 15 woodcut ports of kings repeated to 20 impressions; full-page wheel of fortune cut; 20 woodcuts illus as many pp of 6-column combinations of thrown dice, the same 20 signs from different blocks within an arabesque frame; 20 woodcut ports of prophets & other Biblical figures. washed & pressed. Dyson Perrins copy. C Nov 27 (46) £28,000 [Turner]

Spitzer Collection, Frederic

— La Collection.... Paris & L, 1890-92. 6 vols. Folio, loose as issued in orig cloth portfolios. b June 22 (48) £350

Spon, Jacob, 1647-85 —& Wheler, Sir George

— Voyage d'Italie, de Dalmatie, de Grece et du Levant. Amst., 1679. 2 vols. 8vo, contemp calf. With engraved titles, 2 folding maps & 30 plates. Waterstain in Vol I affecting titles & a few plates & leaves at the front. Sold w.a.f. b June 22 (220) £190

Sponsel, Jean Louis

— Das Moderne Plakat. Dresden, 1897. Folio, orig wraps; spine repaired, recased with covers reinforced. Some wear to edges of prelims. sg Apr 2 (243) $850

Spontone, Ciro

— Historia della Transilvania. Venice: Giacomo Sarzina, 1638. 4to, modern vellum. Some discoloration. S July 1 (715) £250 [Longworth]

Spooner, Shearjashub

— A Biographical and Criticl Dictionary of Painters, Engravers.... NY, 1853. 8vo, orig cloth; spine chipped. sg Feb 6 (270) $225

Sporting...

— Sporting Magazine: Or, Monthly Calendar.... L, 1831. Vol IV, Second Series, Nos XIX & XX bound with the Racing Calendar for 1831 contemp half calf; worn. cb Sept 5 (103) $80

— The Sporting Repository. L, 1822. Vol I, Nos 1-6 (all pbd). 8vo, modern mor gilt by Morrell. With 19 hand-colored plates. C May 20 (12) £2,400 [Grahame]

Spottiswoode, John

— The History of the Church of Scotland. L, 1655. 1st Ed. Folio, modern half calf. bba Jan 16 (64) £85 [Cameron]

Sprague, Isaac. See: Goodale & Sprague

Sprange, J.

— The Tunbridge Wells Guide. Tunbridge Wells, 1786. 12mo, contemp calf; rebacked, rubbed. With engraved title with vignette, dedication & 8 plates. bba Sept 19 (251) £60 [E. Hill]

Sprat, Thomas, 1635-1713

— The History of the Royal Society of London. L, 1667. 1st Ed. 4to, contemp mor gilt with cipher of King Charles II, probably by Samuel Mearne; extremities rubbed. With frontis & 2 folding plates. Dedication copy. P Dec 12 (150) $6,500

3d Ed. L, 1722. 4to, contemp calf; joints split, scuffed. With frontis & 2 folding plates. Ck May 15 (49) £100

Spratt, Thomas Abel Bremage

— Travels and Researches in Crete. L, 1865. 2 vols. 8vo, orig cloth; rubbed. With 14 tinted litho plates (1 folding & torn), 3 plates of inscriptions & coins & 2 hand-colored folding maps. Some spotting or soiling. S June 30 (403) £650 [Martinos]

Spreat, W.

— Picturesque Sketches of the Churches of Devon. Exeter, 1842. Oblong folio, half lea; hinges repaired, rubbed. With title & 70 plates only. Library markings with stamps on plate versos. pn Dec 12 (319) £110

Sprigge, Joshua

— Anglia Rediviva: England's Recovery.... L, 1647. Folio, contemp calf; worn. With folding port, folding table & large plate of the Battle of Naseby. Some soiling; 1st section detached. Library markings. bba Nov 28 (238) £280 [Land]

Spring, Agnes Wright

— The Cheyenne and Black Hills Stage and Express Routes. Glendale, Calif., 1949. Spine faded. cb Nov 14 (211) $120

Sprunt, Alexander

— Florida Bird Life. NY, [1954]. 4to, cloth. sg May 14 (247) $140

Spry, W. J. J.

— The Cruise of Her Majesty's Ship Challenger. L, 1877. 2d Ed. 8vo, cloth; rubbed. kh Nov 11 (652) A$80

Spuhler, Friedrich

— Islamic Carpets and Textiles in the Keir Collection. L, 1978. 4to, cloth, in d/j. S Nov 15 (1202) £240 [Folios]

Spurzheim, Johann Gaspar, 1776-1832

— Phrenology, in Connexion with the Study of Physiognomy. Part I. Characters. L, 1826. 8vo, orig half cloth; worn. With 34 plates. Foxed & dampstained. sg May 14 (161) $175

Spyri, Johanna

— Heidi's Lehr- und Wanderjahre. Gotha: Friedrich Andreas Perthes, 1880-81. 2 parts in 2 vols. 8vo, orig cloth; minor defs. Manney copy. P Oct 11 (286) $4,750

Squires, Frederick

— Architec-Tonics: The Tales of Tom Thumtack, Architect. NY, 1914. 1st Ed. Illus by Rockwell Kent. Inscr. sg Jan 30 (96) $600

Stackhouse, John

— Nereis Britannica.... Bath, 1795-1801. Folio, contemp mor gilt extra; rubbed. With engraved titles & 24 plates, including the plates to the appendix; cropped, affecting 2 plate numbers. bba Sept 5 (108) £950 [Maggs]

Stadler, Franz

— Hans von Kulmbach. Vienna, 1936. 4to, orig cloth. S Feb 11 (210) £220 [Madonna]

Stafford, Elizabeth, Marchioness of

— Views in Orkney and on the North-Eastern Coast of Scotland. L, [1807]. One of 120. Folio, mor gilt; rubbed. With 28 plates & with small map on tp. pnE Dec 4 (180) £60

Stafford, Thomas, fl.1633

— Pacata Hibernia, Ireland Appeased and Reduced. L, 1633. Folio, 19th-cent calf gilt; upper cover detached. With 2 ports & 18 maps & plans, including folding Speed map of Munster dated 1610 (mtd on linen) & with the additional plate of Carigfoyle Castle at p.666. Repair to 1 plate. STC 23132. b June 22 (275) £280

Anr copy. Contemp calf; rebacked, spine repaired. With 2 ports & 16 (of 17) maps & plates, most double-page. Some maps with small repaired tears; Aa3 with rust-hole affecting text. S May 14 (1156) £230 [Cathach]

Stafford, William Cooke —& Ball, Charles

— Italy Illustrated. L, [1860-61]. 2 vols. 4to, contemp half calf. With engraved title, 1 port, 2 folding maps hand-colored in outline & 66 plates. Lacking 1 port & 1 plate with extra plate; some spotting. Sold w.a.f. S May 14 (1208) £420 [Ex Libris]

Stage...

— The Stage Acquitted. Being a Full Answer to Mr. Collier.... L, 1699. 8vo, vellum; soiled, front flyleaf loose. Met Apr 28 (833) $50

— The Stage and its Stars. Phila., [c.1890]. One of 400. Ed by H. P. & G. Gebbie. 3 vols. Folio, mor gilt. sg Mar 5 (255) $425

Stahl, Georg Ernst, 1660-1734

— Opusculum chymico-physico-medicum. Halle, 1715. 4to, later calf gilt with arms of the 3d Earl of Bute; front joint cracked. Some browning. sg May 14 (162) $600

Stamma, Philip

— Essai sur le jeu des echecs.... Paris, 1737. 12mo, modern half cloth. Ck May 8 (61) £600

Anr Ed. The Hague, 1741. 12mo, contemp half sheep; some wear to spine. Ck May 8 (62) £160

— The Noble Game of Chess. L, 1745. 8vo, modern half vellum. Folding diagram torn & lacking half; some damage to inner margin of final leaf. Ck May 8 (63) £280

Stanfield, Clarkson, 1793-1867

— Sketches on the Moselle, the Rhine and the Meuse. L, 1838. Folio, contemp half lea with gilt royal cypher. With tinted litho title, litho dedication & 25 tinted litho views. Margins spotted. C Oct 30 (85) £1,200 [Hildebrandt]

Anr copy. Contemp half mor; section of spine lacking, rubbed. With litho title & 29 views on 25 sheets. Lower inner margin dampstained. Ck Dec 12 (264) £1,200

Anr copy. Folio, orig half mor gilt. With tinted litho title, dedication & 29 tinted litho views on 25 plates. Tp & some plates spotted. S June 25 (104) £1,300 [Haas]

— Stanfield's Coast Scenery: a Series of Views in the British Channel. L, 1836. 4to, orig mor gilt; some wear. With frontis, engraved title & 38 plates. Browned; plates foxed. bbc Apr 27 (531) $120

Stanfield, Clarkson, 1793-1867 —& Others

— Ansichten in Tyrol, der Schweiz und Italien. L & Berlin: A. Asher, [plates dated 1829-32]. 4to, contemp half lea gilt. With 110 plates, 1 detached. Tp stamped. C Oct 30 (84) £500 [Galleria Etching]

Stanford, Sir William

— An Exposition of the Kings Prerogative... L, 1607. Bound in 1 vol with Les Plees del Coron. 8vo, old sheep; worn & broken. Black letter. Minor stains & soiling. O Aug 25 (167) $275

Stanger, Frank M.
— South from San Francisco. San Mateo County, 1963. cb Sept 12 (166) $120

Stanhope, Leicester Fitzgerald Charles, 5th Earl of Harrington
— Greece in 1823 and 1824.... L, 1824. 8vo, half calf. With 6 folding or double-page facsimiles. S June 30 (406) £300 [Spink]

Anr Ed. Phila., 1825. 8vo, orig bds. Marginal worming; some discoloration. S June 30 (405) £150 [Spink]

Stanihurst, Richard
— De rebus in Hibernia gestis. Antwerp: Plantin, 1584. 4to, later calf. CG Oct 7 (547) £350

Stanley, Edward, Bishop
— Address Delivered on board H.M.S. Rattlesnake. L, 1850. 8vo, unbound, unopened. R. J. Maria copy. C June 25 (206) £480 [Quaritch/Hordern]

Stanley, Edward, 1793-1862
— An Account of the Mode of Performing the Lateral Operation of Lithotomy. L, 1829. 4to, orig bds; rebacked, spine chipped at foot. With 7 plates, a few partly hand-colored. Institutional stamp on half-title & tp. sg Nov 14 (137) $150

Stanley, Sir Henry Morton, 1841-1904
— The Congo and the Founding of its Free State.... L, 1885. 1st Ed. 2 vols. 8vo, orig cloth; rubbed. bba Oct 10 (253) £150 [Remington]; DW Oct 2 (69) £100

1st American Ed. NY, 1885. 2 vols. 8vo, orig cloth. wd Dec 12 (451) $225

— How I Found Livingstone. NY, 1872. 1st American Ed. 8vo, orig cloth; front joint torn. cb Oct 10 (98) $190

— In Darkest Africa. L, 1890. 1st Ed. 2 vols. 8vo, orig cloth. Some spotting. L Nov 14 (162) £120

Anr copy. Orig cloth; worn. With 3 folding maps inside rear-cover pockets. O July 14 (182) $55

One of 250. Orig half mor; rubbed. bba Mar 26 (338) £550 [Sanderson]

Anr copy. 2 vols. 4to, contemp half lev gilt; extremities rubbed. Manney copy. P Oct 11 (288) $1,600

Anr copy. 2 vols. 8vo, orig half mor gilt; spines & corners worn. Epstein copy. sg Apr 30 (423) $1,600

1st American Ed. NY, 1890. 2 vols. 8vo, cloth. sg Jan 9 (184) $110

Anr copy. Orig cloth; some wear. sg May 21 (104) $100

Anr Ed. NY, 1891. 2 vols. 8vo, orig cloth. With 3 folding maps in rear pockets. Small splits in map folds. cb Oct 10 (99) $120

Anr copy. Orig cloth; spines soiled. K Sept 29 (409) $50

— Through the Dark Continent. NY, 1878. 1st American Ed. 2 vols. 8vo, orig half mor; worn. cb Oct 10 (100) $275

Stansbury, Howard
— Exploration and Survey of the Valley of the Great Salt Lake.... Phila., 1852. 1st Ed. 8vo, contemp mor gilt, seal of U.S. in center of both covers. With 2 large folding maps. O Nov 26 (161) $275

Anr Ed. Wash., 1853. Senate Issue. 8vo, cloth; Lacking the vol with the 2 maps. sg June 18 (515) $110

Stanzoni, Tomaso. See: Vanbrugh, Sir John

Stapleton, Olaf, 1886-1950
— Last and First Men. NY, [1931]. In chipped & split d/j. sg June 11 (292) $100

— Star Maker. L, [1937]. In chipped d/j. sg June 11 (293) $225

Stapley, Mildred. See: Byne & Stapley

Stark, James —&
Robberds, J. W.
— Scenery of the Rivers of Norfolk. Norwich & L, 1834. 4to, contemp mor gilt; rubbed. With engraved title & 35 plates on india paper mtd. Spotted, some waterstaining. bba Sept 19 (252) £160 [Vine]

Starratt, William
— The Doctrine of Projectiles.... Dublin, 1733. 8vo, modern mor backed bds. With 4 folding plates. Hole in tp & following leaf, not affecting text; some dampstaining. S July 9 (1344) £280 [Middleton]

Starrett, Vincent
— Buried Caesars: Essays in Literary Appreciation. Chicago, 1923. cb Oct 17 (889) $55

— Murder on "B" Deck. NY, 1929. In d/j, unopened. cb Oct17 (886) $100

— Seaports in the Moon. Garden City, 1928. In d/j. Inscr to Karl Yost, 6 Mar 1934. sg June 11 (294) $150

Starte, Ottomar
— Schippeliana: Ein Burgerliches Bilderbuch. Leipzig, 1917. Met Apr 27 (290) $230

Starye Gody
— Starye Gody. St. Petersburg, 1907-16. 76 Issues only; lacking July-Sept 1910 & Jan 1913. 8vo, orig wraps; torn or loose. Ck Dec 12 (290) £700

Stasov, Vladimir

— L'Ornement slave et oriental d'apres les manuscrits anciens et modernes. St. Petersburg, 1887. Folio, contemp half mor gilt; front joint cracked, hinges reinforced with cloth tape. With 147 chromolitho plates. sg Nov 7 (227) $475

Statius, Publius Papinius, 45?-96? A.D.

— Opera. Venice: Aldus, Aug-Nov 1502. ("Sylvarum, libri quinque; Thebaidos libri duodecim; Achilleidos duo.") 8vo, vellum. Lacking Orthographia. SI June 10 (960) LIt500,000

Anr Ed. Venice: Aldus, 1519. ("Sylvarum libri V. Achilleidos libri XII. Thebaidos libri II.") 8vo, 19th-cent vellum gilt. Lacking colophon leaf; title stamped. sg Mar 12 (287) $375

Staunton, George Leonard, 1737-1801

— An Authentic Account of an Embassy from the King of Great Britain to the Emperor of China. L, 1797. Atlas only. Folio, loose in portfolio made up from contemp half calf bds; worn. bba June 25 (238) £1,600 [Cumming]

Anr copy. 2 vols plus Atlas, 4to & folio, contemp half mor gilt; corners rubbed. Text with frontis ports of Mccartney & Tchien Lung; Atlas with 44 views & charts, 7 double-page or folding. Inscr to Sir James Edward Smith, 1797. C May 20 (305) £3,000 [Gurr Johns & Angier Bird]

Anr copy. 2 vols, without Atlas. 4to, contemp calf gilt; extremities refurbished. DW May 13 (62) £50

Abridged Ed. ("An Historical Account of the Embassy to the Emperor of China.") 8vo, modern half calf. With 25 plates. Some foxing. cb Oct 10 (102) $225

Anr copy. 2 vols. 4to, contemp russia gilt; rebacked, corners restored. With 3 plates. Lacking the Atlas. sg Jan 9 (185) $425

Anr Ed. L, 1798. 3 vols. 8vo, contemp half calf; upper cover of Vol I detached. With frontis, engraved title, 21 plates & 5 folding maps. Some tears to folds; 1 plate shaved. pn June 11 (293) £240

Staunton, Howard

— The Chess Tournament. L, 1851. 8vo, orig cloth; rebacked in mor. Ck May 8 (170) £70

Stearn, William T.

— The Australian Flower Paintings of Ferdinand Bauer. L: Basilisk Press, 1976. One of 550. Folio, orig half lea. With 25 mtd color plates. bba Sept 5 (109) £300 [Burgess Browning]

Anr copy. Half mor. kh Nov 11 (433) A$1,200

Stearns, Charles

— The Ladies' Philosophy of Love.... Leominster MA, 1797. 1st Ed. 4to, sewn as issued, unopened. bba Aug 13 (138) £75 [Fort]

Stebbing, Henry, 1799-1883

— The Christian in Palestine. L, [1847]. Illus by W. H. Bartlett. 4to, early calf gilt. With 80 plates. Some foxing. kh Nov 11 (221) A$200

Stechow, Wolfgang

— Salomon van Ruysdael. Berlin, 1938. 4to, orig cloth. S Feb 11 (211) £200 [Weidinger]

Stedman, John Gabriel

— Narrative of a Five Years' Expedition against the Revolted Negroes of Surinam.... L, 1796. 2 vols. 4to, contemp calf; rebacked, rubbed. With engraved titles, frontis, 3 folding maps & 72 plates. bba Dec 19 (8) £2,000 [Ginnan]

Anr copy. Contemp russia; Vol I bds detached, Vol II hinges weak, rubbed. With 83 hand-colored plates , including titles, 16 engraved by William Blake; plates 8 & 32 enhanced with gold. Plate 62 misbound; some foxing & marginal browning. L.p. copy. Schlosser copy. P June 18 (440) $2,750

Steel, David

— The Elements and Practise of Rigging and Seamanship. L, 1794. 2 vols in 1. 4to, contemp calf; joints cracked, worn. With frontis & 93 plates. Frontis stained; 2 volvelles detached; a few plates torn & with imprint shaved; lacking half-titles & 1 leaf in Vol II. S May 14 (1074) £600 [Lewcock]

Steel, Flora Annie, 1847-1929

— English Fairy Tales. NY, 1918. One of 250. Illus by Arthur Rackham. 4to, orig vellum gilt; soiled. S Nov 14 (133) £620 [Sotheran]

Steele, John. See: Caxton Club

Steele, Sir Richard, 1672-1729. See: Spectator...

Steffens, Franz

— Lateinische Palaeographie.... Berlin, 1929. Folio, text booklet & unbound plates loose in half cloth portfolio as issued. sg Oct 31 (258) $80

Steffens, Lincoln

— John Reed: Under the Kremlin. Chicago: Walden Book Shop, [1922]. One of 235. Orig wraps. sg Jan 10 (168) $200

Stegmueller, Friedrich
— Repertorium biblicum medii aevi. Madrid, 1940-80. 11 vols. 8vo, later cloth. sg Oct 31 (259) $700

Stein, Gertrude, 1874-1946
— Four Saints in Three Acts. NY, 1934. 1st Ed. Inscr to Julian Sawyer by Stein & by Virgil Thomson. sg June 11 (295) $600
— The Making of Americans, being a History of a Family's Progress. Paris, [1925]. 1st Ed. Half lea, orig wraps bound in. sg Dec 12 (379) $425

Anr copy. Half mor, orig wraps bound in; front joint starting. sg June 11 (296) $425
— Portraits and Prayers. NY, [1934]. 1st Ed. Inscr to Thomas L. Stix. bbc June 29J (440) $250

Anr copy. Inscr. K Mar 22 (432) $325

Anr copy. In d/j. Inscr. sg Dec 12 (380) $450
— A Village Are You Ready Yet Not Yet. Paris, [1928]. 1st Ed, one of 10 on Japon ancien vellum. Illus by Elie Lascaux. Orig wraps, in glassine d/j. Minor stain on half-title. P June 17 (372) $1,500
— The World is Round. NY, [1939]. 1st Ed, one of 350. Illus by Clement Hurd. 4to, bds; backstrip browned. sg June 11 (297) $250

Stein, Sir Marc Aurel, 1862-1943
— On Alexander's Track to the Indus. L, 1929. In worn d/j. kh Nov 11 (392) A$425
— On Ancient Central-Asian Tracks. L, 1933. Library markings. O Apr 28 (197) $80
— Ruins of Desert Cathay. L, 1912. 2 vols. Recent cloth. Library markings. DW Oct 2 (70) $70

Anr copy. Orig cloth; rubbed & soiled. DW Dec 11 (75) £280
— The Thousand Buddhas: Ancient Buddhist Paintings from the Cave-Temples of Tun-Huang. L, 1921. 2 vols. 4to & folio, wraps & loose in half cloth portfolio. With 48 plates, some in color. sg Apr 2 (271) $1,500

Steinbeck, John, 1902-68
See also: Limited Editions Club
— Bombs Away: The Story of a Bomber Team. NY, 1942. Cloth, in pictorial d/j. sg Dec 12 (382) $2,000
— Burning Bright. NY, 1950. In d/j. cb Dec 12 (126) $85

Anr copy. In d/j. Sgd by Orson Welles. pba Aug 20 (197) $90
— Cannery Row. NY, 1945. 1st Ed. In chipped d/j. Sgd by Orson Welles. pba Aug 20 (198) $120
— Cup of Gold: a Life of Henry Morgan.... NY, 1929. 1st Ed, 1st Issue. In frayed d/j with portion of front inner flap cut away with loss of a word in title. CNY June 9 (179) $4,000; sg Dec 12 (3833) $200

Anr Ed. NY, [1936]. In chipped d/j. pba July 9 (262) $80
— East of Eden. NY, 1952. 1st Ed. In d/j. bbc Dec 9 (530) $100

Anr copy. In chipped d/j. cb Sept 19 (195) $55

Anr copy. In rubbed d/j. pba July 9 (263) $90

Anr copy. In frayed d/j. wa Sept 26 (248) $50

One of 750. In def clear plastic d/j. bbc Dec 9 (531) $675

One of 1,500. bbc Sept 23 (477) $500

Anr copy. Sgd. Epstein copy. sg Apr 30 (424) $750
— The Grapes of Wrath. NY, [1939]. 1st Ed. In d/j. bbc Dec 9 (532) $210; CNY June 9 (182) $700

Anr copy. In d/j; upper cover detached. Minor soiling. Inscr to Frances Schumacher, 1939 & with postcard, sgd, 13 Mar 1964, to Mrs. Leo Kogan. P Dec 12 (87) $1,000

Anr copy. In d/j. Inscr. Epstein copy. sg Apr 30 (425) $4,200; sg June 11 (298) $1,200
— How Edith McGillcuddy Met RLS. Cleveland: Rowfant Club, 1943. 1st Ed, one of 152, ptd at the Grabhorn Press. 4to, orig half cloth, in d/j. CNY Dec 5 (337) $1,000
— In Dubious Battle. NY, [1936]. 1st Ed. In d/j. wd Dec 12 (453) $325
[-] John Steinbeck: his Language. Aptos, 1970. One of 150. Wraps. cb Dec 12 (127) $70
— Letters to Elizabeth: A Selection.... San Francisco: Book Club of California, 1978. One of 500. Half cloth, in d/j. Book Club of California No 157. pba July 23 (170) $120
— The Log from the Sea of Cortez. NY, 1951. 2d Ed. In d/j. bbc Dec 9 (534) $170

Anr copy. Orig cloth, in d/j. NH May 30 (278) $130

Anr copy. Cloth, in repaired d/j; rubbed. pba July 9 (264) $100
— The Long Valley. NY, 1938. 1st Ed. In d/j with tears at head of spine. bbc Dec 9 (535) $170

Anr copy. In chipped d/j; endpapers with glue show-through. K July 12 (486) $140
— The Moon is Down. NY, 1942. 1st Ed. In d/j. Sgd by Orson Welles. pba Aug 20 (236) $90

1st Issue. In rubbed d/j. pba Aug 20 (199) $70

One of 700. Orig wraps; extremities rubbed. sg June 11 (299) $450

Uncorrect galley proofs. Wraps. CNY Dec 5 (336) $2,000

— Of Mice and Men. NY, [1937]. 1st Ed, 1st Issue. In chipped d/j. bbc Dec 9 (537) $340

Anr copy. In d/j. cb Feb 12 (124) $350

Anr copy. In d/j with small stain on rear panel. Inscr to Harold Ross. CNY June 9 (180) $2,200

Anr copy. In d/j. Inscr. Epstein copy. sg Apr 30 (426) $1,600

— The Pearl. NY, 1947. In 1st d/j. pba Aug 20 (200) $65

— The Red Pony. NY, 1937. 1st Ed. pba Aug 20 (201) $50

One of 699. bbc Dec 9 (538) $550; CNY June 9 (181) $550

Anr copy. Epstein copy. sg Apr 30 (427) $800

— Saint Katy the Virgin. [NY: Covici-Friede, 1936]. 1st Ed, one of 199. Half cloth; rubbed. Lacking the Christmas greeting. sg Dec 12 (386) $550

Anr copy. Orig bds. With the "Merry Christmas" slip laid in. Epstein copy. sg Apr 30 (428) $1,000

Anr copy. Orig bds, in d/j; rubbed. Lacking the Christmas slip. wa Dec 9 (223) $550

— To a God Unknown. NY, [1933]. 1st Ed. In d/j. Spine creased. Epstein copy. sg Apr 30 (429) $800

1st Issue. In d/j. sg Dec 12 (387) $800

— Tortilla Flat. NY, [1935]. 1st Ed. Orig cloth, in chipped d/j. bba Feb 27 (187) £110 [Blumenkron & Ramirez]

Advance copy. Orig wraps; spine chipped. bbc Apr 27 (409) $475

Steinberg, Saul

[-] Steinberg. Paris, 1966. Folio, bds & wraps. Derriere le miroir No 157. Met Apr 28 (29) $50

Steinilber-Oberlin, Emile, b.1878

— Chansons de Geishas.... Paris, 1926. One of 87 on japon imperial. Illus by Leonard Foujita. Mor gilt, janseniste. CGen Nov 18 (378) SF2,000

Steinlen, Theophile Alexandre, 1859-1923

— Des Chats: images sans paroles. Paris, [1898]. Folio, orig half cloth. CGen Nov 18 (457) SF1,000; pnE Mar 11 (255) £150

Steinmetz, Andrew

— The Gaming Table: Its Votaries and Victims.... L, 1870. 2 vols. 8vo, contemp half mor gilt; extremities worn. sg Oct 17 (255) $200

— The Romance of Duelling in all Times and Countries. L, 1868. 2 vols. 8vo, orig cloth; spine tear in Vol I. sg Mar 26 (314) $60

Stella, Jacques, 1596-1657

— Les Jeux et plaisris de l'enfance. Paris, 1657. Oblong 4to, mor gilt. With engraved title, frontis & 50 plates. B Nov 1 (378) HF10,000

Step, Edward

— Favourite Flowers of Garden and Greenhouse. L, [1896-97]. 4 vols. 8vo, orig cloth. With 308 (of 312) color plates. Some browning of text. Ck Sept 6 (49) £650

Stephanopoli, Dimo & Nicolo

— Voyage...en Grece. Paris, 1800. 2 vols. 8vo, contemp calf. With 8 plates, some folding. Some repairs. S June 30 (407) £650 [Constantalopoulos]

Stephen I, Saint, Pope

— Statuti dell' ordine de' cavalieri di Sto. Stephano. Florence, 1665. 4to, contemp vellum. SI Dec 5 (628) LIt600,000

Stephen, Sir Leslie. See: Dictionary...

Stephens, James, 1882-1950

— Irish Fairy Tales. NY, 1920. Illus by Arthur Rackham. 4to, orig cloth. With 16 colored plates. F Dec 18 (67) $130

— The Outcast. L, 1929. One of 500 on English handmade paper, sgd. Bds; rubbed. sg Dec 12 (3389) $60

Stephens, James Francis, 1792-1852

— Illustrations of British Entymology; or a Synopsis of Indigenous Insects... Mandibulata [Haustellata]. With: Supplement. L, 1827-46. 12 vols. 8vo, contemp half lea; edges worn, shelf marks on spines. With 95 colored plates. Plate 40 cropped; stamps on endpapers, verso of tp, 1st & final leaves of text; many plates in Mandibulata misbound. pn Mar 19 (336) £420

Stephens, John Lloyd, 1805-52

— Incidents of Travel in Central America, Chiapas, and Yucatan. L, 1841. 1st English Ed. 2 vols. 8vo, contemp half mor; joints & extremities rubbed. With folding map & 69 plates & plans. Library markings; some foxing. F Dec 18 (470) $150

1st American Ed. NY, 1841. 2 vols. 8vo, later cloth. Some foxing. sg June 18 (517) $225

Anr Ed. NY, 1848-50. 2 vols. 8vo, half lea; rubbed. Some foxing. O May 26 (178) $100

Anr Ed. L, 1854. 8vo, contemp half mor; worn, front joint cracked. cb Oct 10 (103) $110

— Yucatan. NY, 1843. ("Incidents of Travel in Yucatan.") Illus by F. Catherwood. 2

vols. 8vo, contemp half mor. With 2 maps, 2 plans & 64 plates. Some foxing; library markings. F Dec 18 (471) $160

Anr copy. Orig cloth; worn. Foxed & soiled; a few plates loose. O Dec 17 (172) $125

Anr copy. Cloth; needs rebdg. Some foxing. sg June 18 (518) $250

Stephens, Lorenzo Dow

— Life Sketches of a Jayhawker.... [San Jose], 1916. One of 300. Orig wraps. sg June 18 (133) $120

Stephenson, George

— A Description of the Safety Lamp.... L, 1817. 2d Ed. 8vo, recent half calf. With 4 plates. Part 1 soiled & browned. DW Nov 6 (407) £75

Stephenson, John, 1790-1864 —& Churchill, James Morss

— Medical Botany. L, [1828]-31. 4 vols. 8vo, contemp half calf; rubbed. With 186 colored plates. bba Nov 28 (139) £1,000 [Lloyd's of Kew]

Anr Ed. L, 1834-36. 3 vols. 8vo, half calf; joints splitting. With 187 hand-colored plates. No half-titles; some foxing. P June 17 (374) $1,600

Anr copy. Contemp half calf; edges worn, shelf labels on spines. Plate 99 shaved; some spotting, mainly to endpapers. pn Mar 19 (337) £850

Anr copy. Vol II only. Half mor; def. With 61 hand-colored plates. Sold w.a.f. sg Sept 19 (216) $425

Sterling, George, 1869-1926 —& Others

— Continent's End: an Anthology of Contemporary California Poets. San Francisco: Book Club of California, 1925. One of 600. Ed by Sterling, G. Taggard & J. Rorty. Half vellum. cb Jan 16 (142) $120

Sterne, Laurence, 1713-68

See also: Golden Cockerel Press; Limited Editions Club

— The Life and Opinions of Tristram Shandy. [York] & L, 1760-67. 1st Ed. 9 vols. 8vo, contemp calf; joints rubbed. Sgd, as usual, in Vols V, VII & IX. C Dec 16 (270) £550 [Gurr Johns & Angier Bird]

Anr copy. Modern half calf. Some spotting & browning. Sgd, as usual, in Vols V, VII & IX. Bradley Martin copy. Ck Oct 18 (169) £850

Anr copy. Contemp calf; rebacked, orig spines laid down. A few leaves in Vol IV trimmed close, affecting last letters; inner margin tear on L1 in Vol VIII; lacking front blank in Vol V. Sgd, as usual, in Vols V, VII & IX. Epstein copy. sg Apr 30 (431) $3,400

Mixed Ed. [York] & L, 1760-69. 9 vols. 8vo, contemp calf. Sgd, as usual, in Vols V, VII & IX. pnE May 13 (125) £340

8th Ed of Vols I & II; 1st Ed of others. [York] & L, 1770 & 1761-67. 9 vols. 8vo, contemp calf; rebacked. Sgd, as usual, in Vols V, VII & IX. sg Mar 12 (289) $325

— A Sentimental Journey.... L, 1809. 12mo, modern sheep; needs rebacking. With 2 hand-colored plates. sg Mar 5 (287) $140

Anr Ed. Paris, 1929. One of 333. Ptd wraps. sg Jan 30 (11) $60

Anr Ed. Paris: Black Sun Press, 1929. Ptd wraps. sg Sept 26 (31) $80

— Works. L, 1873. 4 vols. 8vo, calf gilt. O Feb 25 (182) $110

Anr Ed. NY, [1904]. ("Life and Works.") One of 150 on Japan. 12 vols. Half mor gilt. b&b Feb 19 (19) $500

York Ed, one of 250 of Coxwold Issue. 12 vols. Contemp half mor gilt; bd tips worn, front joint of Vol I starting. wa Dec 9 (16) $260

Anr Ed. L: Shakespeare Head Press, 1926-27. One of 500. 7 vols. Half mor gilt. sg Mar 5 (300) $275

Steuart, John

— Bogota in 1836-37. NY, 1838. 1st Ed. 12mo, modern cloth. Scattered foxing. sg Dec 5 (240) $50

Stevens, Bertram. See: Smith & Stevens

Stevens, Charles Augustus, b.1835

— Berdan's United States Sharpshooters in the Army of the Potomac 1861-1865. St. Paul, 1892. 8vo, orig cloth. K July 12 (120) $275

Stevens, Charles W.

— Fly-Fishing in Maine Lakes.... Bost., 1881. 8vo, cloth. Koopman copy. O Oct 29 (295) $85

Stevens, Francis

— Views of Cottages and Farm-houses in England and Wales. L, 1815. 4to, modern half calf. With etched title & 53 plates. L Nov 14 (125) £90

Stevens, Henry, 1819-86

— An Account of the Proceedings at the Dinner Given by Mr. George Peabody to the Americans Connected with the Great Exhibition. L, 1851. 4to, mor gilt. rs Oct 17 (71) $75

— The Bibles in the Caxton Exhibition, 1877. L, 1878. 4to, orig half mor. L.p. copy. cb Oct 17 (897) $140

— Recollections of Mr. James Lenox of New York.... L, 1886. 8vo, orig half cloth; spine soiled, scuffed. With ports ptd on india paper. L.p. copy. wa Apr 9 (24) $50

Stevens, Henry, Son, and Stiles, London

— Rare Americana: a Catalogue of Historical and Geographical Books.... L, [1926]. Wraps. O Sept 24 (232) $60

Stevens, Isaac Ingalls

— Reports of Explorations and Surveys...from the Mississippi River to the Pacific Ocean. Wash, 1855. Vol I only. 8vo, orig half calf; rubbed. cb Sept 12 (131) $130

Stevens, Capt. John, d.1726

— A New Collection of Voyages and Travels.... L, 1708-10. 7 parts in 2 vols. 4to, late 18th-cent calf; gutters perforated from former sewing, joints cracking, spines chipped. Rust-hole in B2 of Part 2, affecting 6 letters; Part 3 lacking initial blank; short tear to mount of folding map of Part 4; Part 5 without quire A; ink stain to map of Part 7, obscuring part of headline & border, hole to G1 affecting 10 letters. King George II's copy; duPont copy. CNY Oct 8 (239) $17,000

Stevens, Wallace

— Esthetique du Mal. A Poem. Cummington MA, 1945. One of 40. Illus by Wightman Williams. Orig half calf; some rubbing & discoloration. With illusts hand-colored. P Dec 12 (88) $3,000

— Harmonium. NY, 1923. In chipped d/j with tear at folds. S July 21 (181) £600 [Arunder]

Anr copy. In 3d bdg, in def d/j. sg June 11 (301) $90

— Poems. San Francisco: Arion Press, 1985. One of 300. Frontis by Jasper Johns. Half mor. Schlosser copy. P June 17 (605) $1,900

Stevens-Nelson Paper Corporation

— Specimens: a Stevens-Nelson Paper Catalogue. [NY, 1953]. Text designed or ptd by Bruce Rogers, Mardersteig, Dropmore, Golden Cockerel, etc.. 4to, half mor. With over 100 specimen sheets of handmade & mouldmade paper. sg May 21 (309) $130

Anr copy. Orig half mor. wa Sept 26 (116) $140

Stevenson, Alan, 1807-65

— Account of the Skerryvore Lighthouse. Edin., 1848. 4to, contemp half calf; rubbed & scuffed. DW Apr 8 (311) £90

Stevenson, John. See: Franklin Printing, Benjamin

Stevenson, John Robert Horne

— Heraldry in Scotland. Glasgow, 1914. One of 210. 2 vols. 4to, orig half vellum, in torn d/js. DW Mar 4 (319) £115

Stevenson, Robert, 1772-1850

— An Account of the Bell Rock Light-House. Edin., 1824. 4to, contemp calf; worn, covers detached, lacking spine. With 23 plates. Dampstained & spotted; 2 marginal wormholes at end. S Feb 26 (788) £220 [Elton Engineering]

Stevenson, Robert Louis & Fanny

— More New Arabian Nights: The Dynamiter. L, 1885. 1st Ed. 8vo, half mor, orig wraps bound in; rubbed. O Aug 25 (169) $90

Stevenson, Robert Louis, 1850-94

See also: Grabhorn Printing; Limited Editions Club

— Acoss the Plains. L, 1892. One of 100 L.p. copies. 4to, orig cloth; soiled & worn. NH Oct 6 (348) $75

— Across the Plains. Hillsborough: Allen, 1950. One of 200. Illus by Mallette Dean. cb Jan 16 (7) $300

— The Body Snatcher. NY, 1884. 4to, orig cloth; front hinge cracked; frontis detached. Epstein copy. sg Apr 30 (433) $275

— A Child's Garden of Verses. L, 1885. 1st Ed. 8vo, orig cloth; rubbed, endpapers browned. Some soiling; offsetting from an inserted fern; leaf with poem has mark scratched out in lower margin. Inscr to & with a poem on the death of his godson, J. L. M. Robertson. Manney copy. P Oct 11 (290) $9,500

Anr copy. Orig cloth. Epstein copy. sg Apr 30 (434) $900

Anr Ed. L, 1896. Illus by Charles Robinson. 8vo, orig cloth. cb Jan 9 (188) $90

Anr Ed. NY, 1902. 8vo, lea gilt with concentric ring design, by binder whose stamp is a tortoise. K Sept 29 (79) $150

Anr Ed. NY, 1905. cb Nov 21 (214) $55

— David Balfour. NY, 1886. 12mo, wraps; worn. With Eugene Field II forgery of the signatures of the author & of Eugene Field. sg Oct 17 (241) $200

1st American Ed. NY, 1893. 8vo, orig cloth, in restored d/j. Manney copy. P Oct 11 (1291) $1,000

— Edinburgh: Picturesque Notes... L, 1954. In d/j. bbc Feb 17 (194) $110

— Father Damien: An Open Letter to the Reverend Dr. Hyde of Honolulu.... Sydney: Pvtly ptd, 1890. 1st Ed. 8vo, stapled. CNY Dec 5 (338) $1,200

— Kidnapped. Being Memoirs of the Adventures of David Balfour. L, 1886. 1st Ed. 8vo, orig cloth; worn & waterstained. Some foxing; half-title & tp soiled. NH Oct 6 (349) $80

1st Issue. Orig cloth; front hinge tender. Epstein copy. sg Apr 30 (435) $900

— The Master of Ballantrae. A Winter's Tale. L, 1889. 1st English Ed. 8vo, orig cloth. Some spotting. bba June 11 (131) £65 [Jacob]

— Memoirs of Himself. Phila.: Pvtly ptd, 1912. 1st Ed, One of 45 on Whatman. 4to, bds; backstrip worn. sg Apr 30 (437) $2,000

— The Strange Case of Dr. Jekyll and Mr. Hyde. L, 1886. 1st English Ed. 8vo, wraps. Lacking final blank. Sgd as R. L. Stevenson and Eugene Field by Eugene Field II. sg Oct 17 (242) $450

Anr copy. Orig wraps; backstrip def. Epstein copy. sg Apr 30 (438) $1,500

1st Ed. NY, 1886. 8vo, orig cloth. kh Nov 11 (393) A$750

Anr copy. Orig wraps; spine chipped. Epstein copy. sg Apr 30 (437) $2,000

— Treasure Island. L, 1883. 1st Ed, early Issue. 8vo, orig cloth; extremities rubbed. bba Feb 27 (151) £2,000 [C. H. Edwards]

Anr copy. Later mor gilt by Bayntun, orig cloth bound in. bba June 11 (130) £700 [Boz]

Anr copy. Orig cloth; extremities rubbed, inner hinges tender. CNY Oct 8 (240) $4,500

Anr copy. Orig red cloth; restored. Some fraying. Manney copy. P Oct 11 (289) $2,250

Anr copy. Orig cloth; rubbed. Epstein copy. sg Apr 30 (439) $2,400

Later Issue. Orig cloth; extremities rubbed, stains on back endpapers. CNY June 9 (184) $1,000

Anr Ed. L: Humphrey Milford, [1929]. Orig cloth, in d/j. With 12 mtd color plates. sg Jan 30 (170) $60

— Works. Edin., 1894-1901. 32 vols. 8vo, half mor; 1 cover detached. O Nov 26 (164) $500

Anr Ed. Edin., 1894. One of 1035. 33 vols. 8vo, half mor; rubbed. With check, sgd tipped in. Accompanied by Balfour's Life, 1901. Extra-illus by the insertion of plates & ALs to Morris, sgd with initials. P June 17 (352) $1,600

Anr Ed. Edin., 1895. 34 vols. 8vo, mor gilt; rubbed. Some staining; marginal worming in Miscellanea vol. P June 17 (353) $3,250

Anr Ed. NY, 1905. 25 (of 27) vols. Half mor; faded & scuffed. cb Jan 16 (143) $425

Thistle Ed. NY, 1909-12. 27 vols. cb Oct 31 (58) $275

Swanston Ed. L, 1911-12. 25 vols. Half mor. K Sept 29 (77) $750; pnE Aug 12 (250) £140

Stevenson, Robert Louis, 1850-94 —& Henley, William Ernest, 1849-1903

— Deacon Brodie or the Double Life. Edin., 1888. 8vo, orig wraps; foot of spine chipped. Epstein copy. sg Apr 30 (442) $400

Stevenson, Robert Louis, 1850-94 —& Osbourne, Lloyd

— The Wrecker. L, 1892. 1st Ed. 8vo, orig cloth; hinges cracked. Inscr by Stevenson. Epstein copy. sg Apr 30 (443) $1,500

— The Wrong Box. NY, 1889. 1st American Ed. 8vo, orig cloth; rubbed. sg Oct 17 (243) $300

Stevenson, Thomas George

— Edinburgh in the Olden Time Displayed.... Edin., 1880. One of 350. Folio, half mor. With 63 plates. Library stamps. b June 22 (276) £50

Stevenson, William Bennett

— A Historical and Descriptive Narrative of Twenty Years' Residence in South America. L, 1825. 1st Ed. 3 vols. 8vo, contemp calf gilt; spines rubbed. With 3 frontises & 4 plates. Library markings. DW Apr 8 (69) £145

Stewart, Basil

— Japanese Colour-Prints. L, 1920. One of 125. kh Nov 11 (222) £180

— Subjects Portrayed in Japanese Colour-Prints. L, 1922. Folio, half cloth. Some foxing. kh Nov 11 (223) A$380

Stewart, Donald William

— Old and Rare Scottish Tartans. Edin., 1893. One of 50 on handmade paper. 4to, orig cloth; rubbed & soiled. With 45 tartan specimens mtd. bba Aug 13 (50) £120 [Barry]

Stewart, Dugald, 1753-1828

— Philosophical Essays. Edin., 1810. 1st Ed. 4to, later half calf. Foxed; new endpapers. bba May 14 (121) £180 [Clark]

Stewart, Duncan. See: Rigby & Stewart

Stewart, Frederick William Robert, Viscount Castlereach, Marquess of Londonderry

— A Journey to Damascus through Egypt, Nubia.... L, 1847. 2 vols. 8vo, orig cloth. With frontis & 8 plates. S July 1 (803) £450 [Kossow]

Stewart, Oliver

— Aeolus, or the Future of the Flying Machine. NY, [1928]. In d/j. cb Nov 7 (93) $50

Stewart, Philemon

— A Holy, Sacred and Divine Roll and Book. Canterbury NH, 1843. 8vo, contemp sheep; rubbed, joints worn. O Nov 26 (165) $100

Stickley, Gustav

— Craftsman Homes. NY, [1909]. 4to, cloth. LH Dec 11 (259) $160

Stieglitz, Alfred

[-] Stieglitz Memorial Portfolio, 1864-1946. NY, [1947]. One of 1,500. Folio, loose as issued. cb Feb 12 (125) $250; sg Apr 13 (92) $275

Stieglitz, Christian Ludwig

— Plans et dessins tires de la belle architecture. Paris, 1801. Folio, modern half mor. With allegorical order plate & 113 plates on 103 sheets. First few leaves softened at foremargin. S June 25 (227) £900 [Shapero]

Stieler, Adolph, 1775-1836

— Hand Atlas ueber alle Theile deer Erde. Gotha: Justus Perthes, [c.1837]. Folio, half sheep; worn, 1 plate detached. cb Jan 30 (151) $325

Stieler, Karl

See also: Schmid & Stieler

— Italia. Viaggio pittoresco dall' Alpi all' Etna. Milan, 1885. 4to, contemp half lea; worn. Some foxing. SI Dec 5 (632) LIt450,000

— Italy from the Alps to Mount Etna. L, 1877 [1876]. Trans by Frances Eleanor Trollope. 4to, orig cloth; worn. SI Dec 5 (673) LIt300,000

Stifter, Adalbert

— Witiko. Pesth, 1865-67. 1st Ed. 3 vols. 8vo, contemp cloth. With 3 engraved titles. HH May 12 (1667) DM1,300

Stiles, Ezra, 1727-95

— A History of the Judges of King Charles I.... Hartford: E. Babcock, 1794. 1st Ed, 1st Issue. 12mo, contemp calf; joints & edges worn, spine chipped. With port & 8 maps. Some foxing & browning. bbc Dec 9 (425) $60

Still, William, 1821-1902

— The Underground Rail Road: a Record of Facts.... Phila., [1872]. 8vo, orig cloth; inner hinge starting. Lacking port of C. Cleveland; marginal tears, some affecting text. K Sept 29 (26) $85

Anr copy. Cloth; extremities rubbed, front hinge cracked. sg June 18 (510) $60

Stillman, Jacob D. B., 1819-88

— The Horse in Motion.... Bost., 1882. Illus by Eadweard Muybridge. 4to, orig cloth; spine lacking, corners worn. With 5 heliotypes, 9 chromolithos & 93 other plates. Handstamps to prelims. wa Sept 26 (645) $160

Stillman, Samuel

— Two Sermons...Delivered the Lords-Day before the Execution of Levi Ames. Bost., 1773. 8vo, later half mor; worn. Some browning. sg Dec 5 (84) $175

Stillman, William James

— Poetic Localities of Cambridge. Bost., 1876. 4to, orig cloth; shaken. With 12 plates. NH May 30 (431) $70

Stimson, Thomas Douglas

— The Log of the Good Ship Waco.... Seattle: Pvtly ptd, 1928. One of 50. cb Nov 7 (94) $225

Stindt, Fred A. —& Dunscomb, Guy L.

— Locomotives of the Western Pacific. San Francisco: Western Pacific Railroad Company, 1954. Sgd by both on p. 34. cb Feb 13 (289) $80

Stirrup, Thomas

— Horometria: or the Compleat Diallist. L, 1659. 2d Ed. 4to, later half vellum. Lacking frontis; margins frayed. bba Jan 16 (67) £80 [Rogers Turner]

Stobaeus, Johannes

— The Sayings of the Seven Sages of Greece.... Verona: Officina Bodoni, 1976. One of 160. 8vo, orig half vellum. pba July 23 (156) $750

Stochove, Vincent de

— Voyage de Sieur de Stochove.... Brussels, 1643. 4to, contemp calf gilt; spine frayed, inner hinge def. With engraved title, 2 maps, plan & 26 plates. Small wormhole to inner margin, affecting a few plates; some waterstain to plates & leaves; some plates detached. Sold w.a.f. b June 22 (222) £130

Stock...

— Stock Jobbing Extraordinary!!! Brookman v. Rothschild. L, [n.d.]. 8vo, half calf, orig wraps bound in. Frontis torn & holed; marginal worming throughout. Sgd by George Cruikshank in pencil on frontis. Salomons copy. sg Oct 17 (155) $130

Stock, Chester. See: Merriam & Stock

Stockdale, Frederick Wilton Litchfield

— Excursions in the County of Cornwall. L, 1824. 8vo, later calf gilt; rubbed. With engraved title & 48 plates. bba Jan 30 (35) £90 [Blake]

Stockton, Frank R., 1834-1902

— Ting-a-Ling. NY, 1870. 1st Ed. 8vo, orig cloth, A bdg; edges & corners worn. K Dec 1 (403) $55

Anr copy. Orig cloth; ends & corners frayed, joints rubbed & starting. Some spotting & staining. wa Mar 5 (244) $110

Stoddard, Charles Warren. See: Grabhorn Printing

Stoddard, Herbert L.

— The Bobwhite Quail. NY, 1931. One of 250. 4to, half vellum. With 69 plates. K Mar 22 (434) $550

Stoddart, Sir John, 1773-1856

— Remarks on Local Scenery & Manners in Scotland. L, 1801. 2 vols. 4to, contemp calf; rubbed. With folding map & 32 plates. bba Sept 19 (249) £85 [Hay Cinema]

Anr copy. Contemp mor gilt. With 2 engraved titles, folding map & 32 hand-colored plates. Spotting affecting half-titles, titles & text at beginning; a few plate imprints cropped. C Oct 30 (88) £250 [Baskett]

Stoeffler, Johann

— Elucidatio fabricae ususque astrolabii. Paris, 1553. Bound with: Koebel, Jakob. Astrolabii. Paris, 1551. 8vo, contemp vellum; worn. bba June 25 (166) £850 [Quaritch]

Stoerck, Anton

— Libellus, quo demonstratur, cicutam non solum usu interno rutissime exhiberi.... Vienna, 1762. 12mo, contemp sheep; rubbed. With 3 folding plates. bba Sept 5 (111) £190 [D. White]

Stoke, Melis

— Hollandse Jaar-boeken of Rijm-Kronkjk.... Leyden: Johannes de Vivie en Isaak Severinus, 1699. Folio, contemp mor gilt. With 35 plates, 1 double-page. C Dec 16 (166) £450 [Forum]

Stoker, Bram, 1847-1912

— Dracula. L, 1897. 1st Ed. 8vo, orig cloth; soiled. bba Apr 30 (202) £350 [Blumenkron & Ramirez]

Anr copy. Orig cloth. Inscr on the day of publication, 2 June 1897, to Sir James Dewar. Manney copy. P Oct 11 (292) $40,000

Anr copy. Orig cloth; rubbed & soiled, inner hinges split. S May 13 (672) £440 [Fox]

Anr copy. Orig cloth; rubbed & soiled, endpapers marked. S July 1 (1047) £380 [Spademan]

Later Issue. Orig cloth; soiled, inner hinges cracked. Some marginal tears, not affecting text; some leaves roughly opened; some soiling & browning. P June 17 (376) $2,000

Later Issue, with later ads. Orig cloth. Epstein copy. sg Apr 30 (444) $10,000

Stokes, Isaac Newton Phelps

— The Iconography of Manhattan Island.... NY, 1915-28. One of 360. 6 vols. 4to, half vellum, 5 vols in d/js; some spines soiled & foxed. Stamp of Law Library, New York City Railroad Company. P Dec 12 (140) $3,250

Anr copy. Orig half vellum, in orig cloth d/js. P June 16 (288) $3,000

Anr copy. Orig sheep gilt; some covers detached or starting. sg May 7 (196) $4,600

Stokes, Isaac Newton Phelps —& Haskell, Daniel Carl

— American Historical Prints.... NY, 1932. 4to, cloth; worn. O Nov 26 (166) $190

Anr Ed. NY, 1933. 4to, cloth; rubbed. With 118 plates. bbc Dec 9 (427) $65

Anr copy. Index booklet laid in. sg Oct 31 (307) $110; sp June 18 (395) $140

Stokes, John Lort

— Discoveries in Australia. L, 1846. 2 vols. 8vo, half calf. With litho frontises & 24 plates, 8 folding maps (6 in pockets at end of vols, several of these soiled or cropped). S Nov 21 (382) £850 [Quaritch]

Anr copy. Orig cloth; spines faded. With 8 folding maps & 26 plates. With 2 A Ns s in case with maps. Inscr. S June 25 (208) £7,000 [Maggs]

Anr Ed. [Adelaide, 1969]. 2 vols. Australiana Facsimile Editions, No. 33. kh Nov 11 (654) A$100

Stokes's copy, John Lort

— COOK, CAPT. JAMES. - Narrative of Captain James Cook's Voyages round the World.... L, 1836. 12mo, orig cloth. Inscr by Stokes on tp. C June 25 (209) £140 [McCormick]

Stoll, Caspar, d.1795

— Representation exactement...des spectres, des mantes, des sauterelles.... Amst., 1787-88. 3 vols. 4to, contemp mor gilt. With 2 hand-colored titles & 100 hand-colored plates. Lacking half-title in Vol I; 1 plate numeral cropped. C May 20 (219) £4,000 [Marshall]

Stone, Herbert L. See: Derrydale Press

Stone, Irving

— Lust for Life. NY, 1936. Inscr but not sgd by Franklin D. Roosevelt & with ANs, 12 Feb 1942, of Roosevelt to Missy Le Hand. P June 16 (277) $6,000

Stone, Olivia M.

— Tenerife and its Six Satellites.... L, 1887. 1st Ed. 2 vols. 8vo, orig cloth; rubbed & soiled. With 9 tinted maps. DW Oct 2 (72) £55

Stone, Reynolds

— Engravings. L, 1977. Ltd Ed. 4to, cloth. Sgd wood-engraving loosely inserted. DW Apr 8 (559) £190

Stone, William Leete, 1792-1844

— Life of Joseph Brant—Thayendanegea, including the Border Wars.... NY, 1838. 1st Ed. 2 vols. 8vo, orig cloth; spine & joint ends chipped. Library markings. bbc Dec 9 (428) $110

Anr copy. Cloth. sg June 18 (519) $50

Anr Ed. Albany, 1864. One of 50 L.p. copies. 2 vols. 4to, orig mor. With 7 plates & plans. bbc Sept 23 (358) $260

Stone, Witmer, 1866-1939

— Bird Studies at Old Cape May. Phila., 1937. One of 1,400. 2 vols. 4to, orig cloth. Some soiling & spotting. F June 25 (452) $110

Stoneback, H. R.

— Cartographers of the Deus Loci: The Mill House. North Hills PA: Bird & Bull Press, 1982. One of 240. Half vellum, in d/j. NH Aug 23 (58) $145; pba July 23 (35) $70

Stonehenge. See: Walsh, John Henry

Stonehill, Charles A. —& Others

— Anonyma and Pseudonyma. NY, 1927. 2d Ed. 4 vols. 12mo, cloth. cb Oct 17 (902) $60

Anr copy. Cloth; worn & spotted. O Sept 24 (235) $90

Stoneman, Vernon C.

— John and Thomas Seymour: Cabinetmakers in Boston, 1794-1816. Bost., 1959. 2 vols, including 1965 Supplement. 4to, cloth. O Mar 31 (169) $175

Anr copy. Cloth; front hinge of Vol I cracked. sp Feb 6 (296) $120

Stones, Margaret —&
Curtis, Winifred

— The Endemic Flora of Tasmania. L, 1967-78. 6 vols. Folio, cloth, in d/js. kh Nov 11 (473) A$700

Anr copy. Orig bds, in soiled d/js. wa Mar 5 (576) $70

Stoney, Henry Butler

— A Residence in Tasmania, with a Descriptive Tour.... L, 1856. 8vo, contemp calf gilt; rubbed. With frontis & 7 plates. bba Sept 19 (98) £100 [Dewar]

Anr copy. Old calf, prize bdg; rubbed. Bound without final book ads; caption of 1 plate shaved. Robert Carl Sticht's copy. kh Nov 11 (655) A$200

Anr copy. Bdg not described; backstrip repaired at head. kh Nov 11 (656) A$200

Stonham, Charles

— The Birds of the British Islands. L, 1906-11. 20 orig parts. 4to, orig wraps; some soiled & frayed. With 118 hand-colored plates. DW Apr 8 (178) £300

Stops, Mr.

— Punctuation Personified, or Pointing Made Easy. L, 1824. 8vo, orig bds; spine rubbed. Manney copy. P Oct 11 (166) $3,250

Storer, James S. —&
Greig, John

— Antiquarian and Topical Cabinet. L, 1807-11. 10 vols. 8vo, contemp mor gilt. With engraved title in each vol & 490 plates. sg May 7 (197) $750

— Cowper, Illustrated by a Series of Views.... L, 1803. 4to, orig bds; spine worn. With engraved title & 12 plates. bba Apr 30 (99) £55 [K. Graham]

Storer, James S. & Henry S.

— Delineations Graphical and Descriptive of Fountains' Abbey. L & Cambr., [c.1820]. 4to, contemp cloth; rubbed. With frontis & 15 plates. Some foxing. pnL Nov 20 (75) £60 [Miles]

Storer, Tracy. See: Grinnell & Storer

Stork, William

— A Description of East Florida, with a Journal kept by John Bartram of Philadelphia.... L, 1769. 3d Ed. 4to, half sheep. With folding map & 2 folding plans. Map stained, backed & with tears, affecting lower longitude scale; 2d plan rebacked; part-title for Bartram's journal stained & frayed & possibly supplied. P June 16 (289) $1,000

Story...

— The Story of the Jubilee Singers. L, 1877. 8vo, cloth; spine ends bumped. With albumen frontis. Minor staining. sg Apr 13 (9) $150

Story, Joseph, 1779-1845

— Commentaries on the Constitution of the United States. Bost., 1833. 1st Ed. 3 vols. 8vo, half cloth; needs rebdg. sg Dec 5 (243) $850

Stott, Raymond Toole

— A Bibliography of English Conjuring.... Derby, 1976-78. One of 900. 2 vols. In d/js. O Dec 17 (173) $160; O Mar 31 (170) $125

Anr copy. In d/js. Vol I sgd. sg Oct 31 (308) $100

— Circus and Allied Arts, a World Bibliography.... Derby, 1958-71. One of 1,200. 4 vols. 4to, orig cloth, in slightly torn d/js. O Dec 17 (174) $155

Stout, Capt. Benjamin

— Narrative of the Loss of the Ship Hercules.... NY: for James Chevalier, [1798?]. 8vo, orig wraps; spine lacking. Top edge of tp slightly chipped. DuPont copy. CNY Oct 8 (242) $42

Stout, Rex, 1886-1975

— Some Buried Caesar. NY, 1939. In d/j with short tear. NH Oct 6 (98) $850

Stow, John, 1525?-1605

— The Annales. L: Thomas Marshe, 1565. ("A Summarie of Englyshe Chronicles.") 1st Ed. 8vo, later calf. Title supplied in Ms; some headlines cropped or shaved. bba Jan 30 (126) £60 [Bernard]

Anr Ed. L, [1580]. ("The Chronicles of England, from Brute....") 4to, modern half calf. Trimmed on all sides with sporadic effect on running heads & to right & bottom edges of title border; minor stains & tears. STC 23333. bbc Dec 9 (305) $320

Anr Ed. L, 1615. ("The Annales, or a Generall Chronicle of England.") Folio, later bds; front cover detached, rubbed. Lacking tp; tears with some losses at beginning & end. Sold w.a.f. STC 23338. bba July 9 (81) £55 [Gammon]

— A Survay of London. L, 1633. ("The Survey of London.") Folio, later half sheep; needs rebdg. A few leaves torn without loss; some others, torn. STC 23345. sg Oct 17 (376) $110

Anr Ed. L, 1754-55. ("A Survey of the Cities of London and Westminster....") 2 vols. Folio, contemp russia; rebacked, rubbed, spines chipped. With 132 maps & plates. Folding frontis & port of Stow repaired; some browning; stains on 6M2 of Vol I & 5D1 of Vol II; some tears, mostly marginal; some pencil markings. P June 17 (377) $2,500

Anr copy. Modern mor gilt. With folding plan & 131 plates & maps. Some browning. S Nov 21 (122) £2,800 [Marlborough]

Stowe...

— Stowe: A Description of the Magnificent House and Gardens. L, 1817. 8vo, orig bds; spine torn. With frontis, 23 plates (2 double-page) & 7 plans (2 folding). Plates dated 1797. Marginal spotting; 1 imprint shaved. b June 22 (214) £160

Stowe, Harriet Beecher, 1811-96

See also: Limited Editions Club

— A Key to Uncle Tom's Cabin. Bost., 1853. 1st Ed. 8vo, orig cloth; hole in front joint, endpapers foxed, owner's name stamped across front endpapers. wa Sept 26 (434) $55

2d ptg. Orig cloth, bdg C; worn. K Mar 22 (435) $50

Anr copy. Orig cloth; spine ends chipped. NH Oct 6 (339) $50

— Uncle Tom's Cabin.... Bost., 1852. 15th thousand. 2 vols. 12mo, orig cloth; extremities worn, spine ends chipped. NH Oct 6 (340) $110

1st Ed. 8vo, orig cloth; worn, chipped & torn. O Apr 28 (198) $500

Anr copy. Orig cloth; spine ends torn. With port & 27 plates. Stain along upper margin on pp. 96-97. P June 17 (378) $2,750

Anr copy. 2 vols. 8vo, sg Apr 30 (445) $4,800

Anr copy. Orig cloth, 1st bdg; repaired. Some spotting. wa Mar 5 (247) $1,800

1st Ptg. Orig cloth; spine extremities worn, corners bumped. Inscr to Mrs. Luther Dana. Arthur Swann—Sang—Manney copy. P Oct 11 (293) $32,000

3d Ptg. Orig cloth; spine ends chipped. Some foxing; a few signatures sprung; old library ink notation at front pastedown. bbc Apr 27 (413) $130

Later ptg. 8vo, orig wraps; spines reglued; some chipping & soiling. Vol II lacking 2 front flyleaves. With 6 plates. Hannibal Hamlin's copy. With several ephemeral items from Hamlin's library. cb Feb 12 (126) $2,750

Stoy, Johann Siegmund

— Manuel pour l'Instruction de la Jeunesse. Breslauer, 1817. Oblong 4to, contemp half lea; rubbed. With engraved title & 52 plates. 1 torn & repaired. bba Oct 10 (121) £280 [Binnan]

Strabo, 63 B.C.-24 A.D.

— Geographia. Venice: Aldus, Nov 1516. ("De situ orbis.") 1st Ed in Greek. Folio, contemp blind-tooled calf over pastebd; restored. Greek type. Upper blank margin of tp & last few leaves repaired; dampstaining towards end. C June 24 (285) £14,000 [Maggs]

Anr copy. Bound with: Hesychius. Dictionarium. Venice: Aldus, Aug 1514. 16th-cent blind-stamped pigskin over wooden bds, with 2 clasps & catches; upper cover wormed. S Dec 5 (197) £24,000 [Jackson]

Anr Ed. Basel: ex officina Henricpetrina, [1571]. ("Rerum geographicarum libri septemdecim....") Folio, contemp vellum; worn. With 27 double-page woodcut maps & 6 smaller maps in text. Tp restored; some worming, not affecting maps. Ck Nov 29 (317) £1,000

Anr Ed. [Geneva], 1587. ("Rerum Geographicarum libri XVII.") Folio, 18th-cent half vellum. Some browning. SI June 10 (965) LIt400,000

Strada, Famiano, 1572-1649

— De bello Belgico. Rome, 1632-47. 2 vols. Folio, contemp vellum; worn. HH May 12 (684) DM3,600

Anr Ed. Rome, 1700-1. 2 vols. 12mo, contemp calf gilt. With 26 plates & folding map. sg Mar 12 (290) $325

Strahlenberg, Philip Johann von

— An Histori-geographical Description of the North and Eastern Part of Europe and Asia.... L, 1736. 4to, 19th-cent half calf; rubbed, rebacked with orig spine laid down. With folding woodcut map, 2 folding tables & 10 plates. Some staining. S May 14 (1209) £110 [Graves Johnson]

Strahorn, Carrie A.

— Fifteen Thousand Miles by Stage.... NY, 1911. NH May 30 (484) $230

2d Ed. NY, 1915. cb Nov 14 (214) $90

Strand...

— Strand Magazine: An Illustrated Monthly. L, 1891. Vol II. Cloth; rubbed. sp Nov 24 (300) $225

Strand, Paul

— Living Egypt. L, [1969]. Text by James Aldridge. 4to, cloth, in d/j. sg Oct 8 (66) $250

— Paul Strand: A Retrospective Monograph.... Phila.: Phila. Museum of Art, [1971]. 2 vols in 1. 4to, pictorial bds; extremities worn. sg Apr 13 (93) $140

— Photographs of Mexico. NY, 1940. One of 250. Folio, orig wraps. With 20 plates. Some foxing on intro & mounts, plates not affected. sg Oct 8 (67) $5,400

2d Ed. NY: Da Capo Press, 1967. ("The Mexican Portfolio.") one of 1,000. Loose as issued in portfolio. sg Oct 8 (68) $1,500; sg Apr 13 (94) $1,600

— Tir a'Mhurain: Outer Hebrides. L, [1962]. 4to, cloth, in chipped d/j. sg Oct 8 (69) $225

Strange, Edward F.

— Chinese Lacquer. L, 1926. One of 500. Orig bdg; tear to front hinge, spine bumped. sp June 18 (397) $100

— The Colour-Prints of Hiroshige. L, 1925. 4to, orig cloth, in d/j. kh Nov 11 (225) A$240

Anr copy. Orig cloth; worn & smudged, some stains to front cover, 2 short splits at head. wa Apr 9 (237) $90

Out-of-series copy. Orig vellum; rubbed, upper cover somewhat warped, edge tear at front free endpaper. With 52 plates, including 16 in color. bbc Dec 9 (287) $220

Straparola, Giovanni Francesco, d.c.1557

— The Most Delectable Nights. Paris, 1906. One of 1,000. 2 vols. 8vo, half mor. O July 14 (184) $110

Stratton, Arthur. See: Garner & Stratton

Stratton, Royal B. See: Grabhorn Printing

Straub, Peter. See: King & Straub

Strauss, David Friedrich, 1808-74

— The Life of Jesus.... L, 1846. Trans by George Eliot. 3 vols. 8vo, orig cloth; joints & spines restored, come color renewed at extremities. Manney copy. P Oct 11 (127) $2,500

Anr copy. Orig cloth; worn. Library markings. S Feb 25 (401) £340 [Spademan]

Stravinsky, Igor

— Ragtime. Paris, 1919. One of 1,000. Folio, unsewn as issued in wraps; small tears to upper cover. Full score. Ck Nov 1 (508) £220

Streeter Library, Thomas Winthrop

— [Sale Catalogue] The Celebrated Collection of Americana. NY, 1966-70. 8 vols, including Index. 4to, bds. cb Feb 12 (83) $475; O Sept 24 (236) $425; O Dec 17 (175) $425; sg Oct 31 (310) $650

Streett, William B. See: Derrydale Press

Strelakov, S.

— Russkija istoricheskija odezhdy ot X do XII veka. Moscow: Grossman i Knebel, [c.1900]. Folio, syn. With 30 litho plates, 28 in color. Foxed. sg Sept 6 (267) $300

Streletz...

— Streletz. Petrograd, 1915. Ed by A. Belenson. No 1. 4to, orig wraps; spine renewed, upper cover repaired. DW May 13 (349) £320

Strickland, Agnes, 1796-1874

— Lives of the Queens of England. L, 1842-48. 12 vols. 8vo, half mor. b&b Feb 19 (44) $350

Strojnowski, Hieronim

— Nauka Prawa Przyrodzonego, Politycznego, Ekonomiki Polityczney, i Prawa Narodow. Vilnius: w Drukarni Krolewskiey przy Akademie, 1785. 8vo, contemp half calf; rubbed. Some spotting. C Dec 16 (83) £450 [Bjorck & Borjesson]

Strong, George Templeton

— Diary, 1835-1875. NY, 1952. Ed by Allan Nevins & Milton H. Thomas. 4 vols. 8vo, cloth. sg Dec 5 (244) $90

Strong, Roy. See: Orgel & Strong

Strozzi, Giulio

— La Venetia edificata, poema eroico.... Venice: Antonio Pinelli, [1624]. Folio, old calf; worn, rebacked. With engraved title, 3 ports & 24 full-page illusts in text. Some shaving; library stamp on recto of I2; some browning. S July 9 (1101) £300 [Vine]

Struck, Hermann

— Die Kunst des Radierens. Berlin, 1908. 4to, orig bds; head of spine chipped, soiled & rubbed. With 5 plates. Ck July 10 (109) £260

Anr copy. Orig cloth; extremities worn, lacking front free endpaper. F Sept 26 (264) $175

Anr Ed. Berlin, 1919. 4to, orig bds. With 5 etched plates & 1 litho. S Feb 11 (266) £200 [Klein]

Anr Ed. Berlin, 1920. 4to, orig bds gilt; joints cracked, loose at beginning. sg Feb 6 (272) $175

Strutt, Jacob George

— Deliciae Sylvarum; or Grand and Romantic Forest Scenery in England and Scotland. L, 1828-[33?]. Folio, contemp half mor; joints & corners rubbed. With etched dedication & 12 plates on india paper mtd. C Oct 30 (274) £200 [Arader]

— Sylva Britannica. L, 1822-26. Folio, contemp half mor gilt by J. Wright; joints & corners rubbed & scuffed. With etched frontis, dedication & 48 etched plates, all on india paper mtd. Spotting in some margins. C Oct 30 (273) £420 [Schuster]

Anr Ed. L, 1826. Folio, contemp mor gilt; soiled & worn. With 50 plates, including engraved title. Stamps on tp verso & rear free endpaper. pn Mar 19 (338) £380

Strutt, Joseph, 1749-1802

— Biographical Dictionary...of all the Engravers.... L, 1785-86. 2 parts in 2 vols. 4to, contemp half calf; joints & edges worn. With 20 plates; 4 extra cuts from Nuremberg Chronicle on mounts or pasted in 2d vol. Some foxing & offsetting; some browning at edges. sg Sept 6 (268) $300

— Glig-Gamena Angel-Deod.... L, 1801. 1st Ed. 4to, contemp calf; worn. With hand-colored frontis & 38 plates. Tp spotted, stained & stamped; frontis affected by Ms on verso; some spotting & dampstaining to text. Ck Nov 15 (50) £150

Anr copy. Old calf; rebacked. With 40 plates. W July 8 (77) £55

Anr Ed. L, 1876. ("The Sports and Pastimes of the People of England.") 4to, orig cloth; hinges splitting. L.p. copy. bba Apr 9 (266) £55 [Cline]

— Horda Angel-Cynnan.... L, 1775-76. 3 vols. 4to, contemp half calf; worn, spines chipped. Sold w.a.f. O Feb 25 (184) $350

— The Regal and Ecclesiastical Antiquities of England. L, 1842. 4to, modern half mor, using old bds. With frontis & 72 hand-colored plates by Planche. Library stamp on tp. W July 8 (76) £110

Struys, Jan Janszoon

— Voyages...en Moscovie, en Tartarie, en Perse.... Amst., 1681. 1st Ed in French. 2 parts in 1 vol. 4to, contemp vellum, armorial bdg; repaired. With engraved title, folding map & 19 folding plates. Some discoloration. S July 1 (861) £800 [Dennistoun]

Anr Ed. Amst., 1724. 3 vols. 8vo, contemp calf. With 29 plates & 1 folding map. Tear & repair to 1 plate. S June 30 (409) £240 [Tant]

Stryker, Roy Emerson —& Wood, Nancy

— In This Proud Land. Greenwich, [1973]. 4to, cloth, in d/j. sg Apr 13 (43) $150

Strzelecki, Sir Paul Edmund de

— Physical Description of New South Wales and Van Diemen's Land. L, 1845. 8vo, orig cloth; chipped. kh Nov 11 (658) A$200

Anr copy. Old half calf; worn, hinges opening. Map strengthened at folds on verso; library stamp on tp. kh Nov 11 (659) A$200

Anr copy. Orig cloth; spine restored at head. With 21 plates, 1 folding. S June 25 (231) £1,100 [Rutherford]

Stuart, Charles Beebe

— The Naval Dry Docks of the United States. NY, 1852. 1st Ed. 4to, mor gilt; loose. With 24 plates. sg June 18 (351) $225

Stuart, Charles Edward. See: Stuart & Stuart

Stuart, Granville

— Forty Years on the Frontier.... Cleveland, 1925. 2 vols in 1. cb Nov 14 (215) $60

Stuart, James, 1713-88 —& Revett, Nicholas, 1720-1804

— The Antiquities of Athens. L, 1762-1830. 4 vols. Folio, 19th-cent half mor gilt by Upham & Beet. With 316 views and charts. George Milne copy. CNY Dec 5 (339) $4,800

Anr copy. Vols I-III. contemp russia presentation bdg with large gilt medallion onlay of Athena & her emblems within a wreath, this neo-classical bdg designed by James Stuart; minor wear & restoration, a few gouges or scrapes to lower covers, upper cover of Vol II dampstained. With port & 288 plates & charts. Vol I lacking subscribers' list; 10-inch repaired tear to 2d folding plate in Vol I; c.8 other plates shaved or cropped; port & tp of Vol II marginally dampstained; some other damp-staining & marginal foxing. McCarty-Cooper copy. CNY Jan 25 (75) $7,500

Anr copy. Vols I only. Folio, half calf; worn, spine def, front cover detached, lacking final blank & rear free endpaper. Some browning, foxing & marginal soiling. sg Sept 6 (269) $650

Anr Ed. L, 1825-30. 4 vols. Folio, modern half calf. With 2 ports & 191 plates & maps. 1 ptd upside down; some spotted. bba sept 19 (153) £420 [Stamatoyannopoulos]

Anr copy. Half calf; worn, 4 covers detached. With 193 plates. Some foxing. sg Sept 6 (270) $550

Anr Ed. L, 1830. Vol V only. Contemp half mor; worn. With engraved ports & 50 plates. Ck May 15 (164) £800

Stuart, John McDouall, 1815-66

— Across the Continent.... Melbourne, 1863. ("Explorations Across the Continent of Australia.") 8vo, recased with wraps mtd. With folding map. Some foxing & discoloring; map with tape repairs. kh Nov 11 (660) A$340

Anr copy. Orig wraps. Short tear in map repaired. S June 25 (250) £450 [Maggs]

— Stuart's Journey into the Interior of Australia. Adelaide & Melbourne, 1860. 12mo, modern half calf. R. J. Maria copy. C June 25 (249) £7,200 [Quaritch/Hordern]

Stuart, John Sobieski Stolberg —& Stuart, Charles Edward

— The Costume of the Clans. Edin., 1892. One of 500. Folio, orig half mor gilt. pnE Oct 2 (523) £75

— Lays of the Deer Forest. L, 1848. 2 vols. 8vo, orig cloth; rubbed, heads of spines chipped. bba Feb 27 (132) £70 [MacCormack]

Stuart-Stubbs, Basil. See: Verner & Stuart-Stubbs

Stuart-Wortley, James Archibald, Lord Wharncliffe. See: Wharncliffe, John Stuart-Wortley

Stubbs, Harry Clement. See: Clement, Hal

Studer, Jacob Henry

— The Birds of North America. NY, 1888. Folio, half lea; front cover nearly detched. With 119 colored plates. sp Apr 16 (306) $650

— Studer's Popular Ornithology: The Birds of North America. Columbus OH & NY, 1881. Folio, orig sheep; very worn. With litho title & 119 colored plates. Prelims def & bound out of order. Sold w.a.f. sg Sept 19 (218) $350

Anr copy. Orig lea gilt; rebacked. With 119 colored plates. Sold w.a.f. sg Nov 14 (200) $6500

Anr copy. Orig half mor gilt; worn, front cover loose. With litho title & 119 colored plates. sg Feb 13 (155) $325

1st Canadian Ed. Montreal, 1881. Folio, cloth with most of calf bdg laid down; worn. With litho title & 119 colored plates. bbc Sept 23 (276) $275

Stumpf, Johann, 1500-77?

— Gemeiner loblicher Eydgnoschafft stetten landen und voelckeren Chronick.... Zurich: C. Froschauer, 1548. 13 parts in 1 vol. Folio, 19th-cent calf. With 13 woodcut maps by Stumpff & 10 smaller woodcut maps by Johann Honter in the text. Lacking final blank 3M6; some repairs, occasionally touching letters as at foot of tp, which is laid down, affecting imprint. A few headlines shaved. S June 25 (326) £4,000 [Sagen]

Sturgis, William B. See: Derrydale Press

Sturm, Johann Christoph

— Collegium experimentale sive curiosum.... Nuremberg, 1676-1715. 2 parts in 1 vol. 4to, contemp vellum. With 4 folding plates. Some shaving. S Dec 5 (438) £1,000 [Gaskell]

Sturmy, Samuel

— The Mariners Magazine: or Sturmey's Mathematical and Practical Arts. L, 1684. 3d Ed. Folio, contemp calf; worn, rebacked & recornered. With engraved title (cut close), frontis & 10 plates, 3 with volvelles. Lacking a leaf but without obvious interruption to text; 1 plate repaired; O3 holed with loss; some spotting. S July 1 (1348) £350

Sturt, Capt. Charles, 1795-1869

— Two Expeditions into the Interior of Southern Australia.... L, 1833. 1st Ed. 2 vols. 8vo, orig cloth. With 4 hand-colored & 9 plain plates & folding map. S June 25 (219) £1,300 [Arnold]

Styl

— Styl. Blaetter fuer mode und die Angenehmen Dinge des Lebens. Berlin, 1922. Nos 1-10 in 7 vols. 4to, contemp vellum gilt, orig wraps bound in. S Feb 11 (288) £850 [Sims Reed]

Styron, William

— Lie Down in Darkness. Indianapolis & NY, [1951]. 1st Ed. In d/j. Inscr. sg Dec 12 (393) $110; sg Dec 12 (394) $100

Suares, Andre, Pseud.

— Paris. Paris, 1950. One of 50 with a suite in Auvergne. Illus by Albert Decaris. 4to, mor gilt with designs of monuments of Paris, by Mercher. CGen Nov 18 (458) SF6,000

Suares, Joseph Marie

— Praenestes antiquae. Rome, 1655. 4to, contemp vellum. Some browning & spotting. SI Dec 5 (636) LIt600,000

Suarez de Figueroa, Cristobal

— Hechos de Don Garcia Hurtado de Mendoza, Quarto Marques de Canete. Madrid, 1613. 1st Ed. 4to, old vellum. Lacking 4 (of 8) prelim leaves, a few repairs to title with some damage; A4 holed, 1 wormhole in last few leaves; A1 and 4 soiled. S June 25 (8) £1,800 [Klee]

Suarez de Figueroa, Diego

— Camino de el Cielo. [N.p., 1738]. Vols I-II (of 3). 8vo, contemp vellum; loose. With engraved titles & 106 emblems. sg Mar 12 (81) $275

Suckling, Sir John, 1609-42

— The Poems. L: Vale Press, 1896. One of 310. Illus by Charles Ricketts. Mor, orig wraps bound in. wd Dec 12 (456) $150

Sudek, Josef

— Praha panoramatika. Prague, 1959. Oblong 4to, cloth, in soiled & torn d/j. With 284 plates. Dampstaining on several pages, plates unaffected. sg Apr 13 (97) $700

Sue, Eugene, 1804-57

— The Mysteries of Paris. L, 1845-46. 3 vols. 8vo, half mor; worn. O May 26 (180) $100

Anr copy. 3 vols. 4to, half calf; spine faded & rubbed. sg Oct 17 (379) $60

— Works. Bost.: Francis A. Nicolls, [1900]. One of 1,000. 20 vols. 8vo, mor gilt; some joints chipped, a few inner hinges splitting. Vol I of Pride marginally dampstained. CNY Dec 5 (443) $1,000

Suetonius Tranquillus, Caius
See also: Limited Editions Club

— Commentationes conditiae a Philippo Beroaldo in Suetonium Tranquillum. Venice: Phillip Pincius, 1510. Folio, 19th-cent half vellum; rubbed. Some leaves wormed, affecting text at beginning & end; contemp marginalia; some marginal dampstains. C Dec 16 (167) £600 [Hesketh & Ward]

— De vitae XII Caesarum. Venice: Simon Bevilaqua, 1496. ("Vitae Caesarum.") Folio, 18th-cent calf. 62 lines & headline for commentary, varying number of lines of text; types 18:80R (commentary), Haebler 19:105R (text; 80Gkb (quotations). Small wormhole at the beginning affecting a few letters; a few minor stains. 353 (of 354) leaves; lacking final blank. Goff S-827. C Nov 27 (25) £1,900 [Panini]

Anr Ed. Venice: Aldus, Aug 1516. ("XII Caesares.") 8vo, contemp mor gilt with author's name in center of upper cover; some rubbing, hinges broken. Last leaf detached; upper margin of 1st few leaves stained. S Dec 5 (200) £1,600

— Opera. Utrecht, 1690. 2 vols. 8vo, contemp vellum. sg Oct 24 (305) $110

Anr Ed. The Hague, 1691. 4to, contemp vellum; worn, piece missing from foot of spine. With 11 (of 12) ports.12 plates Lacking engraved title & O2-3; tear in 2 folding leaves; adhesion between 4E3 & 4E4 with loss; tear to 4F1 with loss; some staining to 1 outer corner. Thomas Hardy's copy, sgd, with Max Gate bookplate, Sir Sydney Cockerell having purchased the book at the Hardy sale & then inscr it to Siegfried Sassoon. With autograph postcard, sgd, by Cockerell to Sassoon. S July 21 (129) £500 [Quaritch]

Suffolk, Henry Charles Howard, 18th Earl of

— The Encyclopaedia of Sport. L, 1897-98. 2 vols. 8vo, half calf; rubbed. bba Jan 16 (367) £65 [Mason]

Sugden, Alan Victor —& Edmondson, John Ludlam

— A History of English Wallpaper. L, [1925]. 4to, orig cloth; spine faded. DW Mar 11 (742) £190

Suidas

— To men paron biblion, suida. Basel: Froben & Episcopius, 1544. Folio, contemp blind-tooled pigskin over wooden bds; worn, lacking clasps & front free endpaper. sg Oct 24 (306) $850

Sulaiman. See: Hasan ibn Yazid, Abu Zaid

Suliman Ben Ibrahaim Baemer. See: Dinet & Suliman Ben Ibrahaim Baemer

Sullivan, Alan

— Aviation in Canada, 1917-1918.... Toronto, [1919]. cb Nov 7 (95) $85

Sullivan, Sir Arthur, 1842-1900. See: Limited Editions Club

Sullivan, Dennis

— A Picturesque Tour Through Ireland. L, 1824. Oblong 4to, contemp half lea gilt; rebacked & recornered, orig spine laid down. With 25 hand-colored plates. C May 20 (129) £2,000 [Finch]

Sullivan, Louis Henry

— Kindergarten Chats. [N.p.]: Scarab Fraternity Press, 1934. In worn d/j. sg Feb 6 (274) $200

Sullivan, Maurice S.

— The Travels of Jedidiah Smith.... Santa Ana CA, 1934. With frontis & 11 plates. Folding map in facsimile. cb Feb 12 (84) $275

Sullivant, William S.

— Icones muscorum; or, Figures and Descriptions of...Mosses.... Cambr. MA, 1864-74. 2 vols, including Supplement. 8vo, 19th-cent cloth; rebacked retaining orig backstrips, endpapers renewed. With 129 plates plus 81 plates in Supplement. sg Nov 14 (201) $550

Sully, Maximilien de Bethune, Duc de

— Memoires des sages et royales oeconomies d'estat, domestiques, politiques...de Henry le Grand. Londres [Paris], 1763. 8 vols. 12mo, contemp calf; some spine ends chipped, some joints tender, a few leaves sprung or detached. wa Sept 26 (33) $130

Sunday's...

— A Sunday's Walk round London. L, 1883. 8vo inlaid to folio, 19th-cent half mor. Extra-illus with 49 plates. S Nov 21 (120) £1,700 [Dinan & Chighine]

Surius, Bernardin

— Le Pieux pelerin ou voyage de Jerusalem. Brussels, 1666. 4to, contemp vellum; soiled. With engraved title, port & folding map. S Nov 21 (310) £1,300 [Bank of Cyprus]

Surrealism...

— Le Surrealisme, meme. [Paris, 1956-59]. Ed by Andre Breton. Nos 1-5 (all pbd). 8vo, pictorial wraps. sg Apr 2 (90) $300

Surtees, Robert, 1779-1834

— The History and Antiquities of...Durham. L, 1816-40. 6 parts in 4 vols, including Taylor's Memoir. Folio, bdg not described but def. F Mar 26 (766) $250

Surtees, Robert Smith, 1803-64

— The Analysis of the Hunting Field. L: Ackermann, 1846. 1st Ed, 2d Issue. 8vo, mor gilt; crudely rebacked. With engraved title & 6 hand-finished color plates. Text & plates soiled. sg Jan 9 (314) $250

Anr Ed. L, 1903. One of 50. With 13 colored plates. L Feb 27 (190) £120

— "Ask Mama...." L, 1858. 1st Ed in Book form. Illus by John Leech. 8vo, orig cloth; worn & damp-wrinkled; hinges startting. sg Jan 9 (315) $50

— Jorrocks's Jaunts and Jollities. L: Ackermann, 1843. 2d Ed. Illus by Henry Alken. 8vo, modern mor gilt by Zaehnsdorf, orig cloth covers & spine bound in at back. With 15 hand-colored plates, including additional title. C May 20 (123) £1,400 [Portno]

— Mr. Facey Romford's Hounds. L, 1865. 1st Ed in orig 112 monthly parts. 8vo, orig ptd wraps; some backstrips repaired. With 24 hand-colored plates. C May 20 (124) £650 [Marlborough]

— [Sporting Novels]. L, 1899-1900. M.F.H. Ed. 11 vols. 8vo, calf by Riviere with gilt-tooled sporting motifs. sg Oct 17 (382) $750

Anr copy. Contemp half mor gilt in Art Nouveau style. With 87 hand-colored plates. wa Dec 9 (17) $850

Survivor. See: Fernyhough, Thomas

Susio, Giovanni Battista

— I Tre Libri della ingiustitia del duello.... Venice: Giolito de Ferrari, 1558. 4to, contemp vellum. sg Mar 26 (316) $250

Sutcliff, Robert

— Travels in Some Parts of North America.... Phila., 1812. 12mo, disbound. Some browning. bbc June 29 (341) $90

Sutherland, Alexander

— Victoria and its Metropolis, Past and Present.... Melbourne, 1888. 2 vols. 4to, orig mor; worn. Some foxing. kh Nov 11 (307) A$300

Sutherland, Capt. David

— A Tour up the Straits from Gibraltar to Constantinople. L, 1790. 8vo, contemp mor gilt. Some browning. S Nov 15 (1190) £380 [Kutluoglu]

Sutherland, Elizabeth, Duchess of. See: Stafford, Elizabeth

Sutherland, James, Hunter

— The Adventures of an Elephant Hunter. L, 1912. Bdg waterstained. bba Feb 13 (363) £100 [Sotheran]; O Apr 28 (199) $250

Sutor, Petrus

— De tralatione Bibliae, et novarum reprobatione interpretationum. Paris: J. Petit, Mar 1525. Folio, 18th-cent calf; joints split, rubbed. Some worming & soiling, just affecting text; tp shaved at foot. S Feb 11 (530) £350 [Edwards]

Sutter, John A. See: Grabhorn Printing

Svenskt...

— Svenskt Silversmide, 1520-1850. Stockholm, [1941-45, 1963]. Vols I-II (of 4). Vellum. sg Feb 6 (262) $500

Sverdrup, Otto

— New Land. Four Years in the Arctic Regions. L, 1904. 2 vols. 8vo, cloth. DW Jan 29 (57) £145

Svetlov, Valerian. See: Ivchenko, Valerian

Svin'in, Pavel Petrovich

— Picturesque United States of America.... NY: Rudge, 1930. One of 1,000. Ed by Avram Yarmolinsky. Folio, cloth; rubbed. With 52 plates. bbc June 29 (342) $50

— Sketches of Russia. L, [some plates watermarked 1827]. 8vo, modern lea gilt. With 2 ports & 13 plates, all hand-colored, & leaf of engraved music. sg Jan 9 (186) $450

Swadesh, Frances Leon

— 20,000 Years of History.... Santa Fe: Sunstone Press, 1973. Sgd. cb Oct 17 (908) $80

Swainson, William, 1789-1855

— Exotic Conchology. L, 1841. 4to, contemp half mor gilt; spine & edges worn, upper hinge weak. With 48 hand-colored plates. Tp, 1st leaf of text & rear endpaper stamped. pn Mar 19 (339) £720 [Shapero]

2d Ed. 4to, later cloth. With 48 hand-colored plates. bba Sept 5 (112) £450 [Travers]

— Zoological Illustrations. L, 1820-23. 3 vols. 8vo, contemp russia gilt; rebacked & repaired at corners. With 182 hand-colored plates. S June 25 (73) £2,000 [Tamura]

Swainson, William, 1789-1855—& Richardson, Sir John, 1787-1865

— Fauna Boreali-Americana, or the Zoology...Part Second, The Birds. L, 1831. 4to, contemp half mor gilt; rubbed. With 55 hand-colored plates. DW Nov 6 (198) £600

Swammerdam, Jan, 1637-80

— The Book of Nature; or, the History of Insects.... L, 1758. Folio, modern cloth. Dampstained throughout. sg May 14 (248) $400

— Bybel der natuure, of historie der insecten.... Leiden, 1737-38. 2 vols in 3. Folio, contemp calf; some wear. With 53 plates. Most outer margins in Vol II & Atlas dampstained. C Oct 30 (299) £700 [Maggs]

— Tractatus physico-anatomico-medicus, de respiratione usuque pulmonum.... Leiden, 1679. Bound with: Thruston, Malachi. De respirationis usu primario, diatriba. L, 1670. And: Mayow, John. Tractatus duo...Leiden, 1671. 3 parts in 1 vol. 16mo, calf. Institutional stamp on tp; some worming in lower margin of prelims. sg May 14 (165) $900

Swan, Charles

— Journal of a Voyage up the Mediterranean.... L, 1826. 2 vols. 8vo, orig cloth; rubbed, spines worn & torn. Tp spotted. S June 30 (412) £260 [Eser]

Swan, James

— The Northwest Coast; or, Three Years' Residence in Washington Territory. NY, 1857. 8vo, orig cloth; spine torn, front hinge cracked. Some foxing. sg June 18 (520) $225

Swan, John

— Speculum Mundi or, a Glass Representing the Face of the World. L, 1635. 4to, contemp calf; rubbed, upper joint cracking at head. Rust hole in Nn affecting headline; a few leaves loose. STC 23516. pn May 14 (22) £240

Swarbreck, Samuel D.

— Sketches in Scotland. L, 1839. Folio, orig half mor gilt; worn. With 25 (of 26) plates. DW Oct 2 (122) £540

Anr copy. Orig half mor; spine repaired. With litho title & 14 plates on 13 leaves only. Some tape-repairs. pn Apr 23 (281) £220

Swayne, George

— Gramina pascua.... Bristol, 1790. Folio, orig bds; rebacked, rubbed, waterstained. With 6 plates containing actual specimens of dried grass. bba Sept 5 (113) £170 [Elliott]

Swayne, Harold George Carlos

— Seventeen Trips through Somaliland.... L, 1895. 8vo, orig cloth; shaken, spine chipped at head. sg May 21 (105) $100

— Through the Highlands of Siberia. L, 1904. sg Jan 9 (187) $225

Swaysland, Walter

— Familiar Wild Birds. L, 1883-[88?]. Series 1-4. 8vo, contemp half mor gilt; rubbed. With 160 colored plates. Some browning. L Nov 14 (227) £60

Anr copy. Contemp half lea; discolored. With 160 color plates. Verso of 1 plate in 1st series stained; 1 marginal Ms note & 1 plate partly shaken in 2d series; some spotting. pnL Nov 20 (153) £75 [Waplington]

Swedberg, Jesper

— America illuminata. Skara, [1732]. 8vo, modern calf gilt by g. Hedberg. With 4 leaves at end unrecorded in any bibliography & not present in the Royal Library Stockholm copy, comprising verses by Germund Folkiern. Tp & following leaf restored at fore-margins with slight loss of letters on verso of title; some browning. S June 25 (437) £1,900 [Arader]

Swediaur, Francois Xavier

— Traite complet sur les symptomes...des maladies syphilitiques. Paris, 1798. 2 vols. 8vo, early 19th-cent bds. Sgd. sg Nov 14 (139) $325

Sweeney, James Johnson

— Paul Klee. NY, [1941]. Folio, orig ptd wraps, spiral bound. With 2 orig tipped-in color serigraphs & 65 collotype plates. cb Sept 5 (55) $140

Sweert, Emanuel

— Florilegium, tractans de variis floribus.... Frankfurt, 1612-14. 2d Ed of Part 2; 1st Ed of Part 1. 2 parts in 1 vol. Folio, late 17th-cent vellum gilt; rebacked with mor preserving orig spine, endpapers renewed. With engraved title, port & 110 plates, all in contemp hand-coloring, the title heightened with gold. Tp, port & 1st text leaf with marginal tears reparied. C May 20 (220) £24,000 [Litup]

Sweet, Robert, 1783-1835

— The British Flower Garden. L, 1823-35. Series I-II. 7 vols. 8vo, contemp half calf; 2 vols rebacked, 1 with old spine laid down. With 712 hand-colored plates. Some plates trimmed to within plate-mark at outer edge occasionally shaving image. S June 25 (75) £5,500 [Kafka]

— The British Warblers. L, 1823-[29]. 8vo, old bds; some wear to spine, tear in free endpapers. With 16 hand-colored plates. Some spotting & staining. S Nov 15 (757) £520 [Maggs]

— Cistineae: The Natural Order of Cistus.... L, 1825-30. 8vo, contemp mor gilt; rubbed. With 110 (of 112) hand-colored plates. bba Sept 5 (114) £750 [Shapero]

Anr copy. Modern half calf. With 112 hand-colored plates. Tp & a few text leaves spotted. C May 20 (221) £1,000 [Beeleigh Abbey]

Anr copy. Later cloth. Library stamps, not affecting text; accession number showing through to title. pn Mar 19 (340) £900 [Russell]

— Geraniaceae. L, 1820-30. 5 vols. 8vo, 4 vols in 19th-cent half mor, last vol in contemp half calf; rubbed. With 500 hand-colored plates. Plate 340 spotted; library stamps, not affecting plates. pn Mar 19 (341) £4,000

Anr copy. Contemp calf gilt; rebacked, old spines laid down. Sir Richard Colt Hoare's copy. S June 25 (74) £5,000 [Thorold]

Sweetser, Moses Forster, 1848-97

— Views in the White Mountains. Portland: Chisholm Brothers, 1879. Folio, orig cloth; extremities worn. With 10 plates. NH Oct 6 (381) $55

Swem, Earl G.

— A Bibliography of Virginia. Richmond, 1916-32. Parts 1-4 in 2 vols. Cloth. K Sept 29 (429) $75

Swieten, Geerard L. B. van

— Commentaria in Hermanni Boerhaave aphorismos de cognoscendis, et curandis morbis. Venice, 1759-64. 7 vols. 4to, old bds; spines faded. Prelims of some vols wormed; titles stamped. sg Nov 14 (140) $225

3d Ed of Vol I, other Vols unspecified. Paris, 1769-73. 5 vols. 4to, contemp calf; marginal worming. bba Sept 5 (307) £190 [Quaritch]

Swift, Jonathan, 1667-1745
See also: Cresset Press; Limited Editions Club
— A Discourse on the Contests and Dissensions between the Nobles and the Commons in Athens and Rome. L: John Nutt, 1701. 1st Ed, 2d Issue. 4to, half mor. Lacking final blank; small stain on E3; marginal discoloration. S Feb 11 (419) £700 [St. Patricks]
— Gulliver's Travels L, 1726. ("Travels into Several Remote Nations of the World.") Teerink's "A" Ed (1st 8vo Ed). 4 parts in 1 vol. 18th-cent calf; rebacked. Some leaves loose. L.p. copy. Sion College copy. Manney copy. P Oct 11 (294) $45,000
Anr copy. 2 vols. Mor gilt by Matthews. With port in 2d state & 6 plates. Some worming. P June 17 (380) $3,250
Anr copy. Contemp calf; rubbed. With port in 1st state & 6 plates. pnE Oct 2 (492) £7,300
Anr copy. Contemp calf; joints wworn, spine ends repaired. With port in 2d state & 6 plates. With the spurious Vol III. Stockhausen-Epstein copy. sg apr 30 (446) $32,0000
Teerink's AA (2d 8vo) Ed. 2 vols. contemp calf; upper cover of Vol I bumped, upper joints to Vol II cracked, extremities rubbed. With port & 6 plates. Ck Sept 6 (89) £320
Teerink's B Ed (3d 8vo Ed). 2 vols in 1. Contemp calf; joints cracked, upper joint strengthened, rubbed. With port & 6 plates. Port in 2d state, bound verso to title & with outer edge frayed; 1st gathering crudely bound in; library markings; foxing & soiling; some tears. bba May 14 (75) £120 [Krown & Spellman]
Anr copy. 2 vols. contemp calf gilt; joints & spine ends repaired. With port (in 2d state) & 6 plates. C Dec 16 (238) £400 [Shapero]
Teerink's B Ed. 2 vols. contemp calf; rebacked preserving old spines. With frontis, 4 maps & 2 plates. Ck Oct 31 (310) £280
Teerink's B Ed; 2d state of the port. 2 vols. contemp calf; rebacked, orig backstrips retained. With port & 5 maps. sg Nov 7 (239) $1,100
Anr Ed. L & NY, 1909. Illus by Arthur Rackham. 4to, orig cloth. With 12 colored plates. bba Jan 16 (403) £90 [Ulysses]
Anr copy. Some pencilling. K Mar 22 (394) $70
Anr copy. Orig cloth; endpapers foxed. K Mar 22 (395) $95
— The History of the Four Last Years of the Queen. L, 1758. 1st Ed. 8vo, contemp calf; rebacked, recornered. bba Jan 16 (93) £65 [Sanderson]
— The Prose Works. Oxford, 1939-68. 14 vols, including Index vol. bba Apr 30 (362) £280 [Makrocki]
— The Publick Spirit of the Whigs. L, 1714. 1st Ed. 4to, modern half mor. bba Jan 16 (91) £160 [Jarndyce]
— A Tale of a Tub. L, 1705. 4th Ed. 8vo, old calf; covers detached. cb Dec 19 (167) $55
Anr Ed. [N.p.], 1711. Bound with: Swift. A Complete Key to the Tale of a Tub. L, 1714. 12mo, contemp calf. Worn, upper joint weak. DW Apr 8 (278) £65
— Works. L, 1784. 17 vols. 8vo, early calf; rebacked, spines scuffed. Some foxing & browning. wa Mar 5 (82) $230

Swift's copy, Jonathan
— Plautus, Titus Maccius. - Comoediae XX. Paris: Robertus Stephanus, 1530. Folio, calf; rebacked & recornered. Inscr by Swift saying that the book was given him by Matthew Prior. S July 21 (29) £4,500 [Swales]

Swinburne, Algernon Charles, 1837-1909
See also: Fore-Edge Paintings; Golden Cockerel Press; Kelmscott Press
— Atalanta in Calydon. L, 1865. 1st Ed, One of 100. 8vo, orig cloth; worn. Soiled & darkened. O Jan 14 (182) $60
— Essays and Studies. L, 1875. 1st Ed. 8vo, mor gilt with double fore-edge views; front bd & free endpaper detached. LH May 17 (610) $600
— The Poems. L, 1904. 6 vols. half mor by the Cragg Bindery; rubbed. O Aug 25 (171) $160
Anr copy. Contemp half mor gilt; bd tips worn, some wear. wa Dec 9 (18) $140
— The Springtide of Life. L, 1918. Illus by Arthur Rackham. 4to, orig cloth. With 8 colored plates. bba Jan 16 (404) £55 [Sotheran]
— William Blake: A Critical Essay. L, 1868. 2d Ed. 8vo, orig cloth; rebacked, orig spine preserved. bba Dec 19 (47) £85 [Kurita]
— Works. L, 1925-27. Bonchurch Ed, One of 780. Ed by Sir Edmund Gosse & T. J. Wise. 20 vols. pn Apr 23 (104) £240 [Holleyman & Treacher]

Swinburne, Henry, 1743-1803
— Picturesque Tour through Spain. L, 1806. Oblong folio, disbound. With map (creased) & 15 plates. W July 8 (297) £340
— Travels in the Two Sicilies. L, 1783-85. 1st Ed. 2 vols. 4to, modern half calf. With folding map, 22 plates & folding table. Some tears; small pieces cut from upper fore-corners of titles; some discoloration throughout. S Nov 15 (1104) £500

[Casella]

Anr copy. Modern lea. With folding map & table & 21 (of 22) plates & plans. SI June 10 (969) LIt1,250,000

Anr copy. Early calf gilt; spines worn, joints split. With folding map, folding table & 17 (of 22) plates. Small handstamp to tp of Vol I. wa Apr 9 (131) $140

— Travels through Spain. L, 1779. 4to, contemp half russia; split to head of upper joint, lower joint rubbed. With folding map & 18 plates & views, including 5 plates not in the list. A few top margins waterstained. b June 22 (221) £650

Sydenham, Thomas, 1624-89

— Opera medica. Venice, 1735. 2 vols. Folio, old bds; 1 spine split. Waterstaining & browning. SI Dec 5 (641) LIt320,000

— Opuscula quotquot hactenus separatim prodiere omnia.... Amst., 1683. 8vo, contemp calf; worn. Some foxing & soiling. O Aug 25 (172) $200

— Works. L, 1696. 1st Ed in English. 8vo, modern half calf. bba Jan 16 (82) £200 [Bickersteth]

2d Issue. Contemp calf. Some browning; bound without quire a. S May 13 (910) £260 [Rizzo]

9th Ed. L, 1729. Trans by John Pechey. 8vo, contemp calf; rubbed. bba Sept 5 (308) £120 [Quaritch]

Sydney...

— Sydney Gazette and New South Wales Advertiser. Sydney, 1818. Vol XVI, Nos 737-788 (Jan 3 to Dec 26, 1818) half calf. Some pp torn & repaired; some browning. S June 25 (175) £2,400 [Maggs]

Sykes Library, Sir Mark Masterman

— [Sale Catalogue] Catalogue of the Highly Valuable Collection of Prints.... [L, 1824]. 5 parts in 1 vol. 4to, contemp half calf. bba Mar 26 (15) £170 [Sims Reed]

— [Sale Catalogue] Catalogue of the Splendid, Curious, and Extensive Library.... [L, 1824]. 3 parts in 1 vol. 4to, modern bds. Priced in ink; some foxing. bba May 28 (569) £300 [Wilfred]

Sylva. See: Bacon, Sir Francis; Evelyn, John

Sylvius, Franciscus de la Boe. See: Le Boe, Sylvius Franciscus de

Symbolum...

— Symbolum Apostolicum. A Facsimile...of the Earliest Known Block-Book Printed in Colours. Paris: Pegasus Press, 1927. One of 150. 2 vols. 8vo, facsimile in vellum, explanatory text vol in wraps. sg May 21 (250) $150

Syme, Patrick

— Werner's Nomenclature of Colours. Edin., 1814. 8vo, later half calf; worn & broken. Library markings. bbc June 29 (184) $70

Symes, Michael

— An Account of an Embassy to the Kingdom of Ava.... L, 1800. Plate vol only. 4to, contemp half calf; worn. With 28 plates. Spotted & soiled. DW Mar 4 (46) £80

Symonds, Mary —& Preece, Louisa

— Needlework through the Ages. L, 1928. 4to, orig half vellum; rubbed & soiled. DW Oct 9 (973) £170

Anr copy. Orig wraps; soiled. DW Dec 11 (385) £180

Symonds, Robert Wemyss

— English Furniture from Charles II to George II. L, 1929. One of 1,000. 4to, orig cloth; 1 corner bumped. pn May 14 (149) £50 [Nelson]; W July 8 (134) £150

Symons, Arthur, 1865-1945

— A Study of Thomas Hardy. L, 1927. One of 100. 4to, orig cloth. With frontis port of Hardy by Alvin Langdon Coburn, sgd by Coburn in pencil in the margin. cb Dec 19 (32) $160

Symons, George James

— The Eruption of Krakatoa.... L, 1888. Ed by Symons. 4to, orig cloth; badly dampstained. With 2 frontises & 43 plates. DW Dec 11 (76) £90

Szarkowski, John —& Hambourg, Maria Morris

— The Work of Atget. NY: Museum of Modern Art, [1981-82]. Vols I-III (of 4). 4to,. cloth, in d/j. sp Feb 6 (356) $75

Szyk, Arthur

— Ink & Blood: a Book of Drawings. NY, 1946. One of 1,000, sgd. Folio, orig lea; worn & scuffed. With 74 plates. Discard stamp on tp margin. Sold w.a.f. K July 12 (496) $160

Anr copy. Mor; spine worn. sg Jan 30 (171) $550

— The New Order. NY, [1941]. 4to, cloth, in d/j. sg Dec 19 (216) $120; sg Jan 30 (172) $275; sp Nov 24 (211) $73

Anr copy. Cloth, in soiled d/j. Z Oct 26 (269) $100

T

Taber, Thomas T. —& Casler, Walter

— Climax: An Unusual Steam Locomotive. Rahway NJ, 1960. cb Feb 13 (311) $80

Tableaux....

— Tableaux de Paris. Paris, 1927. 1st Ed, one of 25 on japon but lacking the additional suite. 4to, orig wraps. S Dec 5 (309) £1,500 [Marks]

Tachard, Gui

— Voyage de Siam de Peres Jesuites. Paris, 1686. 4to, contemp calf. With 30 folding plates. Minor worming to 2d part, not affecting plates. b June 22 (223) £320

Tacitus, Publius Cornelius
See also: Doves Press

— Aminta. Parma: Bodoni, 1789. 8vo, contemp mor; worn. SI June 10 (977) LIt750,000

— The Annales...the Description of Germanie. L, 1598. Bound with: Tacitus. The Ende of Nero and Beginning of Galba.... L, 1598. 2d Ed. 1st Ed in English. Folio, half cloth; loose in bdg. Marginal soiling & dampstaining; old scrawls on 1st title; last few leaves of 2d work def. STC 23644 & 23643. sg Oct 24 (310) $300

Anr Ed. L, 1604-5. 2 parts in 1 vol. Folio, later calf gilt; joints & edges rubbed. Lacking initial & final blanks; some browning & staining; minor flaws & teaars; ownership stamp on front endpaper & tp. STC 23645. pn Apr 23 (105) £130 [Cumming]

— Annalium, libri sedecim.... Lyons, 1542. 8vo, 19th-cent half sheep gilt; spine ends & raised bands worn. Contemp underscoring & marginalia (cropped); some paper cracks; old stamp on tp. sg Oct 24 (308) $275

— Obras. Madrid: widow of Alonso Martin, 1614. 4to, contemp vellum. Some sidenotes shaved; wormhole in upper margins affecting some headlines; lacking last leaf. sg Mar 12 (292) $400

— Opera. Venice: Aldus, 1534. 8vo, 19th-cent half lea; worn. Some dampstaining. SI June 10 (974) LIt550,000

Anr Ed. Venice: Aldus, Nov 1534. 8vo, 19th-cent vellum. Ink annotations. LH Dec 11 (260) $375

Anr Ed. Antwerp: C. Plantin, 1585. 8vo, 18th-cent calf gilt with Sorbonne monogram, prize bdg with prize leaf inserted before tp. Some worming. C Dec 16 (168) £400 [Maggs]

Anr Ed. Antwerp, 1607. Folio, contemp vellum; front hinge cracked. sg Oct 24 (309) $150

Tacquet, Andreas

— Opera Mathematica. Antwerp, 1669. 3 parts in 1 vol. Folio, old calf; worn & rebacked. With engraved title & port. Some spotting & staining. S July 1 (1113) £170 [Lucas]

Taft, Robert

— Photography and the American Scene. NY, 1938. Cloth; extremities worn. sg Apr 13 (98) $50

Tagart, Edward

— A Memoir of the late Captain Peter Haywood. L, 1832. 8vo, contemp half calf. Lacking half-title. S June 25 (63) £150 [Lascaux]

Tagg, Tommy. See: Collection...

Tagliente, Giovanantonio

— Lo presente libro Insegna la vera arte de lo excellente scrivere. Venice: Giovannantonio & Pietro da Sabio, 1542. 4to, modern vellum. All inner & some outer margins repaired; some soiling; repaired tear to final leaf. C June 24 (255) £800 [Gnerucci]

Anr Ed. Venice: Francesco Rampazetto, 1561. 4to, 17th-cent vellum gilt. Outer margin of D shaved with slight loss to flourish of 1st initial on verso. C June 24 (256) £850 [Abrams]

Taillandier, Yvon

— The Indelible Miro.... NY, 1972. Folio, cloth, in d/j with repair to spine. bbc Apr 27 (470) $90

Anr copy. Cloth, in d/j. With 2 color lithos & unspecified number of plates, some in color. sg Apr 2 (187) $225

— Wifredo Lam. [Paris, 1970]. One of 100 with a sgd etching by Lam. Folio, unbound as issued. sg Apr 2 (161) $500

Tait, Arthur Fitzwilliam. See: Butterworth & Tait

Talbot, Frederick A.

— Aeroplanes and Dirigibles of War. Phila., 1915. cb Nov 7 (97) $50

Tanaka, Ichimatsu

— Wall Paintings in the Kondo Horyuji Monastery. Tokyo, 1951. Folio, loose as issued in portfolio. With 36 plates. sg Apr 2 (214) $90

Tancoigne, J. M.

— Voyage a Smyrne, ddans l'Archipel.... Paris, 1817. 2 vols. 12mo, modern half calf. With 2 hand-colored folding plates. Vol II spotted. S June 30 (414) £480 [Consolidated Real]

Tancred, George

— Historical Record of Medals and Honorary Distinctions.... L, 1891. 4to, half mor. bba Mar 26 (39) £75 [The Bookroom]

Tanglewood. See: Hawthorne, Nathaniel

Tannatt, Thomas Edwin Pryce

— How to Dress Salmon Flies. L, 1914. With 4 plain & 8 colored plates. Koopman copy. O Oct 29 (235) $180

Tanner, Henry

— English Interior Woodwork of the XVI, XVII & XVIIIth Centuries.... L, 1902. Folio, cloth; extremities worn. With 50 plates. 9 plates loose. sg Sept 6 (274) $70

Tanner, Thomas, 1674-1735

— Notitia Monastica; or a Short History of the Religious Houses in England and Wales. Cambr., 1787. 8vo, contemp calf; rubbed, spine rebacked. bba Jan 16 (32) £100 [Fetzzer]

Tansillo, Luigi, 1510-68

— Stanze di cultura sopra gli horti de le donne. Venice: Niccolo Zoppino, 1537. Bound with: Stanze in lode della menta. [Venice, c.1538]. 8vo, recent mor gilt. C Dec 16 (84) £950 [Franks]

Tapie, Michel

— Mirobolus, Macadam et Cie, Hautes Pates de Jean Dubuffet. Paris, 1946. One of 30 with orig litho. 4to, wraps. CGen Nov 18 (465) SF9,000

Taplin, William

— The Sporting Dictionary. L, 1803. 2 vols. 8vo, modern cloth; soiled. Minor tears to titles. F June 25 (96) $90

Anr copy. Old calf; covers detached. Some stains & soiling. Sold w.a.f. O Aug 25 (173) $80

— The Sportsman's Cabinet.... L, 1803-4. 2 vols. 4to, contemp calf; worn. Some marginal dampstaining. Ck May 15 (52) £280

Anr copy. Later half mor. With engraved titles & 26 plates. Some browning. S Feb 26 (890) £480 [Montague]

Tarbell, Ida. See: Mizner, Addison

Tarbell, Ida Minerva, 1857-1914

— The History of the Standard Oil Company. NY, 1904. 1st Ed. 2 vols. 8vo, cloth. cb Jan 16 (113) $50; sg Dec 5 (247) $80

Tarkington, Booth, 1869-1946

— The Gentleman from Indiana. NY, 1899. 1st Ed, 1st State. 8vo, orig cloth. cb Sept 18 (203) $50; sg Dec 12 (395) $150

Anr copy. Orig cloth. Inscr, 1946. sg June 11 (302) $550

— Monsieur Beaucaire. NY, 1900. 1st Ed. Orig cloth; soiled & rubbed. Inscr. wa Mar 5 (248) $55

— Penrod. Garden City, 1914. 1st Ed. Orig cloth; worn, partly detached. Inscr. rs Oct 17 (33) $55

— Works. NY, 1918-32. Autograph Ed, one of 565. Vols 1-14 only. Half mor gilt. sg Mar 5 (303) $300

Seawood Ed. Garden City, 1922-24. one of 1,075. Vols I-XVI (of 27). Half cloth. O Aug 25 (174) $70

Tarleton, Sir Banastre, 1754-1833

— A History of the Campaigns of 1780 and 1781 in the Southern Provinces of North America. L, 1787. 4to, contemp calf; rubbed. With 4 maps only. F Mar 26 (489) $475

Tartu University, Estonia

— Die kaiserliche Universitaet zu Dorpat. Dorpat: Johann Christian Schuenmann, 1827. Folio, contemp half calf; worn. With engraved title & 19 plates. Some stains. S June 25 (229) £1,800 [Marlborough]

Tasman, Abel Janszoon, 1603-59

— Journal of his Discovery of Van Diemens Land and New Zealand.... Amst., 1898. Folio, vellum. With 5 folding maps. S June 25 (82) £750 [Quaritch/Hordern]

Tassie, James, 1735-99

— A Descriptive Catalogue of a General Collection of Ancient and Modern Engraved Gems.... L, 1791. 2 vols. 4to, contemp calf; edges & spines worn, covers detached. With frontis & 58 plates. Some foxing. sg Sept 6 (122) $900

Tassin, Nicolas

— Les Plans et profils de toutes les principales villes et lieux considerables de France. [Paris: Tavernier, 1636]. 2 vols. Oblong 4to, contemp sheep; worn, spine ends chipped, front joints cracked. With 449 plates only. Dampstaining in upper margins of prelims in Vol I & in outer margins throughout Vol II. sg Feb 13 (140) $3,400

Tasso, Torquato, 1544-95

— Aminta.... Crisopoli [Parma], 1789. 4to, contemp half mor; rubbed. Marginal waterstaining. bba May 28 (463) £150 [Cox]

Anr Ed. Crisopoli [Parma], 1793. 4to, orig bdg; spine worn. SI June 10 (978) LIt1,000,000

— La Gerusalemme liberata. Mantua: Osanna, 1584. ("La Gierusalemme liberata....") 3 parts in 1 vol. 4to, vellum. First 2 leaves repaired; some spotting. SI June 10 (981) LIt250,000

Anr Ed. Genoa: Girolamo Bartoli, 1590. 3 parts in 1 vol. 4to, 19th-cent half vellum. With engraved title & 20 full-page illusts. Marginal soiling & staining; tp trimmed & mtd. sg Oct 24 (312) $325

Anr copy. Contemp lea. Some repairs & stains. SI June 10 (982) LIt280,000

Anr copy. 18th-cent mor gilt; worn. Some foxing & browning. SI June 10 (983) LIt1,300,000

Anr Ed. Pavia: Viano, 1594. ("Gerusalemme conquista....") 4to, modern vellum. Some foxing. SI June 10 (980) LIt350,000

Anr Ed. Padua: Bolzetta, 1616. ("Il Goffredo....") 2 parts in 1 vol. 4to, contemp vellum. Marginal repairs. SI June 10 (984) LIt300,000

Anr Ed. Venice: Sarzina, 1625. Illus by G. B. Piazzetta. Folio, modern lea. Some browning & spotting. SI June 10 (986) LIt300,000

Anr Ed. Venice, 1673. 4to, 19th-cent half lea. Some waterstaining & browning. SI June 10 (988) LIt280,000

Anr Ed. Urbino, 1735. Folio, contemp calf; 1 joint broken. Some browning. SI June 10 (989) LIt900,000

Anr Ed. Venice, 1745. Illus by G. B. Piazzetta. Folio, contemp mor gilt; spine rubbed at top. Lacking 6 plates. SI June 10 (991) LIt5,000,000

Anr Ed. Venice: Albrizzi, 1745. 1st Issue, with the engraved dedications & arms on each plate. Folio, contemp mor gilt. Frontis atamped. SI Dec 5 (649) LIt7,500,000

Anr Ed. Venice: A. Groppo, 1760-61. ("Il Goffredo....") 2 vols. 4to, contemp vellum. With frontis, port & 20 plates. Saks copy. S Dec 5 (291) £1,500 [Pollock]

Anr Ed. Paris: Didot l'aine, 1784-86. 2 vols. 4to, mor by Bozerian. With engraved frontis & 40 plates. Some spotting. S May 28 (149) £1,400 [Maggs]

Anr Ed. Paris: Didot, [1785-86]. 2 vols. 4to, contemp calf; 1 spine restored. Some browning. SI June 10 (994) LIt1,500,000

Anr Ed. Parma: Bodoni, 1794. 3 vols. Folio, orig wraps. SI Dec 5 (650) LIt5,500,000

Anr Ed. Parma, 1807. 2 vols. 4to, contemp bds. SI Dec 5 (651) LIt800,000

Anr Ed. Florence: Marenigh, 1820. 2 vols. Folio, contemp half lea. SI June 10 (995) LIt500,000

Anr Ed. Florence: Giovanni Marenigh, 1840. 2 vols. 4to, contemp calf. Some spotting. SI Dec 5 (652) LIt900,000

Anr Ed. Brussels, 1844. 8vo, mor gilt. Some browning. SI June 10 (996) LIt600,000

— Godfrey of Bulloigne.... L, 1600. Trans by Edward Halifax. Folio, early 18th-cent calf with gilt monogram in spine compartments. STC 23698. C Dec 16 (239) £380 [Grant & Shaw]

Anr Ed. L, 1803. ("Jerusalem Delivered.") Trans by John Hoole. 4to, contemp calf; rebacked. O Jan 14 (183) $60

— Jerusalem Delivree.... Paris, 1774. 2 vols. 8vo, contemp mor gilt. Some browning. SI June 10 (993) LIt650,000

Anr Ed. Paris: Bossange & Masson, 1811. Folio, contemp calf. SI June 10 (992) LIt750,000

Tassoni, Alessandro, 1565-1635

— La Secchia rapita.... Modena, 1744. 4to, contemp bds. With port, frontis, 2 folding maps, 12 plates, folding facsimile & folding genealogical table. SI Dec 5 (654) LIt450,000

Tate, Allen

— The Mediterranean and Other Poems. NY: Alcestis Press, 1936. 1st Ed, one of 12. Orig wraps. Inscr, 1966. sg June 11 (303) $700

Out-of-series copy. sg Dec 12 (397) $250

Tate, Nahum, 1652-1715

— The Island-Princess. L: R. H. for W. Canning, 1687. 4to, later half lea; broken. Some soiling & browning; minor stains. O May 26 (185) $170

Tattersall, Creassey Edward Cecil. See: Kendrick & Tattersall

Taubert, Sigfried

— Bibliopola. Hamburg, L & NY, 1966. 2 vols. Folio, orig cloth. bba July 9 (25) £70 [Hay Cinema]

Anr copy. Cloth; worn. O Sept 27 (238) $70; pba July 23 (207) $80

Taunton, Thomas Henry
— Portraits of Celebrated Racehorses of the Past and Present.... L, 1887-88. 4 vols. 4to, half mor gilt. Some spotting. S Nov 15 (759) £720 [Erlini]

Taverner, Eric —& Others
— Salmon Fishing. L, 1931. One of 275. Orig mor. With 7 orig flies mtd at end. Koopman copy. O Oct 29 (301) $700
— Trout Fishing from all Angles. L, 1929. Out-of-series copy. With 30 flies in sunken mounts. Koopman copy. O Oct 29 (302) $550

Taverner, Richard
— The Garden of Wysdome Conteyning Pleasaunte Floures.... L, 1539. 2 parts in 1 vol. 8vo, later calf. Black letter. Marginal worming affecting last few leaves; some soiling. STC 23711A. pn Nov 14 (291) £2,100 [Quaritch]

Tavernier, Jean Baptiste, 1605-89
— A Collection of Several Relations & Treatises.... L, 1680. 1st Ed in English. 2 parts in 1 vol. Folio, contemp calf; joints cracked. With folding map & 7 folding plates. Small wormholes near lower margin without loss. Panos Gratsos copy. S Nov 21 £1,800 [Asian Collector]
— Nouvelle Relation de l'interieur de Serrail du Grand Seigneur.... Paris, 1675. 1st Ed. 4to, late 19th-cent half mor gilt. S June 30 (416) £600 [Quaritch]
— The Six Voyages.... L, 1678. 3 parts in 1 vol. Folio, later calf; rebacked, worn. With 24 plates. bba Sept 19 (126) £600 [Rainer]

Anr copy. Folio, conemp calf; worn, rebacked & repaired. With 22 (of 24) plates. Tp laid down. Sold w.a.f. S June 30 (415) £420
— Les Six Voyages en Turquie, en Perse et aux Indes.... Paris, 1677. 2 vols. 4to, contemp calf; worn. With 33 (of 34) plates. Some browning; Vol I without frontis & front flyleaf. S June 30 (202) £450 [Consolidated Real]

Mixed Ed. Paris: Gervai Clouzier, 1682-81. 3 vols, including the suites de Voyage. 12mo, 18th-cent calf gilt. With 2 ports, 2 folding maps & 42 plates, 17 folding. Some shaving; 5 folding plates torn with loss; 1 leaf holed; map of Japan with repaired tears. C Oct 30 (119) £950 [Gebt Haas]

Taylor, A. Cameron. See: Richter & Taylor

Taylor, Bayard, 1825-78
See also: Picturesque...
— Eldorado, or Adventures in the Path of Empire. NY, 1850. 2d Ed. 2 vols. 12mo, orig cloth; spines faded. With 8 plates. With carte-de-visite of Taylor and with portion of Ds. cb Nov 14 (217) $12[illegible]

7th Ed. NY, 1855. 12mo, orig half m[illegible] Lacking 1 plate. NH Oct 6 (369) $260

Taylor, Deems
See also: Millay & Taylor
— Fantasia. NY, 1940. 4to, cloth, in worn & chipped d/j. bbc Dec 9 (458) $150

Taylor, Frederick Winslow
— The Principles of Scientific Management. NY & L, 1911. Epstein copy. sg Apr 30 (449) $250

Taylor, G.
— A Voyge to North America.... Nottingham, 1771. 8vo, modern half calf by Sangorski & Sutcliffe. Tp in facsimle; marginal repairs to 1st contents leaf & last 2 leaves; last page soiled. DuPont copy. CNY Oct 8 (243) $1,300

Taylor, George —& Skinner, Andrew
— Survey and Maps of the Roads of North Britain or Scotland. L, 1776. Oblong folio, orig calf wraps; worn. Stained. pnE Oct 2 (432) £200

Taylor, Isaac, 1759-1829
— Scenes in Asia.... L, 1821. 2d Ed. 12mo, orig half lea; worn. With folding map & 84 hand-colored engravings on 28 plates. bba Jan 16 (420) £75 [Hashimoto]
— Scenes in Europe.... L, 1818. 1st Ed. 12mo, contemp half calf; backstrip repaired, bds worn. With folding map & 28 plates, hand-colored. bba July 23 (134) £130 [James]

Taylor, Jane & Ann
— Little Ann and Other Poems. L: Routledge [1883]. 1st Ed. Illus by Kate Greenaway. 8vo, orig half cloth; heavily soiled. bba Feb 27 (367) £50 [Ginnan]

Taylor, Jeremy, 1613-67
— Ductor Dubitantium, or the Rule of Conscience.... L, 1660. 1st Ed. 2 parts in 1 vol. Folio, later bds. With extra engraved title. Last few leaves dampstained & def. bba Dec 19 (347) £50 [Hilton]

Taylor, John, The Water Poet, 1580-1653
— The Water-Cormorant his Complaint. [L: George Eld, 1622]. 1st Ed. 4to, modern half mor. Tp & 2 following leaves cropped & extended affecting image & text; Br repaired; some staining & worming at blank margins; a few catchwords & signatures cropped. STC 23813. S Dec 12 (14) £1,000 [Cameron]

ndian Life.... l. 8vo, modern , $225

odus: A Record of Human , [1939]. Illus by Dorothea loth, in worn & chipped d/j. bbc (227) $200

ylor, Capt. Philip Meadows, 1808-76

— Sketches in the Deccan. L, 1837. Folio, orig half cloth; stained. With litho title & 19 plates. Some spotting. Ck Oct 18 (101) £600

Taylor, Robert William, 1842-1906

— A Clinical Atlas of Venereal Skin Diseases.... Phila., 1888-89. 1 vol in 2. Folio, contemp half sheep; joints & corners worn. With 58 colored plates. sg Nov 14 (141) $225

Taylor, Samuel, Angler

— Angler in all its Branches.... L, 1800. 1st Ed. 8vo, later calf gilt; spine ends frayed. sg Jan 9 (317) $90

Taylor, Tom

— Birket Foster's Pictures of English Landscape. L, 1881. One of 1,000. Folio, orig vellum; soiled. cb Jan 9 (61) $130

Taylor, W. Thomas —& Morris, Henry

— Twenty-One Years of Bird & Bull. [North Hills PA]: Bird & Bull Press, 1980. One of 350. Half mor. KH Aug 23 (59) $175; NH Aug 23 (52) $90

Tchemerzine, Stephane & Avenir

— Bibliographie d'editions originales et rares d'auteurs francais des XVe, XVIe, XVIIe et XVIIIe siecles. Paris, 1927-33. One of 88. 10 vols in 30. Later cloth. Ck Nov 1 (510) £320

One of 800 on papier surglace. 10 vols. 8vo, cloth. O Sept 24 (240) $375

Anr Ed. Teaneck, 1973. 10 vols in 1. sg Oct 31 (312) $80

Tchernykhov, Jacob

— Architectural Fictions. Leningrad, 1933. 4to, orig cloth; spine torn. Title in English, Russian, German & French; text in Russian. P June 17 (381) $1,600

Teasdale-Buckell, George Teasdale

— Experts on Guns and Shooting. L, 1900. 8vo, cloth; shaken. Library markings. sp Apr 16 (321) $100

Teerink, Herman

— A Bibliography of the Writings of Jonathan Swift. Phila.. [1963]. 2d Ed. In d/j. bba July 9 (28) £130 [Forster]; sg Oct 31 (313) $250

Teesdale, Henry

— New British Atlas. L, [c.1830]. 4to, contemp half lea; worn, covers detached. With 47 (of 48) hand-colored linen-backed maps. Lacking title & map of England & Wales; some soiling & repairs; 7 of the maps with portions torn away. pn Apr 23 (306) £130 [Hunter]

Teffi, N. A., Pseud.

— Baba-Yaga. Paris: YMCA Press, 1932. 4to, wraps. sg Jan 10 (173) $100

Tegetmeier, William B.

— Pheasants.... L, 1881. 2d Ed. Illus by T. W. Wood. 4to, orig cloth; worn. With 13 plates. K July 12 (391) $50

— Pigeons.... L, 1868. 8vo, contemp half calf gilt; rubbed. DW Oct 2 (172) £80

Anr copy. Orig half lea; worn. With 16 color plates. K Mar 22 (349) $190

Anr copy. Orig cloth; worn, corners bumped. K July 12 (410) $95

— The Poultry Book. L, 1867. 8vo, orig cloth; worn & rubbed, joints cracked. With 30 plates. Soiled; last leaves dampstained. cb Sept 26 (209) $450

Anr copy. Half lea; worn & rubbed. With frontis, additional title & 28 color plates. K July 12 (424) $350

Anr copy. Orig cloth; upper hinge broken, worn, foot of spine repaired with tape, library labels on front endpapers. With chromolitho title, 29 chromolitho plates & 14 uncolored plates. Library stamp & accession number at foot of additional title. pn Mar 19 (246) £200 [Sotheran]

Teixera, Jose

— The Strangest Adventure that ever Happened.... L: for Frances Henson, 1601. 4to, 19th-cent half mor; rubbed. First line of text cropped on several leaves. bba Nov 28 (218) £180 [Rix]

Telescope, Tom. See: Newton, Sir Isaac

Temminck, Coenraad Jacob —& Meiffren Laugier de Chartrouse, G.M.J., Baron

— Nouveau Recueil de planches coloriees d'oiseaux. Paris, [1820]-38-[39]. 5 vols in 6. 4to, modern half mor; rubbed. With 600 hand-colored plates bound in systematic order; Cuvier Prospectus in Vol I. Some browning & spotting. S Nov 21 (47) £5,000 [Shapero]

Tempsky, G. F. von

— Mitla. A Narrative of Incidents...a Journey in Mexico, Guatemala.... L, 1858. 8vo, contemp calf gilt,prize bdg; rubbed & soiled. With 14 plates, 5 colored & with folding map hand-colored in outline. S Feb 11 (794) £240 [Stokeley Holland]

Ten...

— Ten Lithographic Coloured Flowers with Botanical Descriptions drawn and coloured by a Lady. Edin.: David Brown, 1826. Parts 1-3 (of 4) in 1 vol. Folio, 19th-cent half mor gilt; rubbed. With 2 litho titles & 30 hand-colored plates only. Lacking subscribers list & title to 2d part; some spotting & soiling. pn Mar 19 (247) £900 [Toscani]

Tench, Capt. Watkin

— A Complete Account of the Settlement at Port Jackson in New South Wales. L, 1793. 4to, orig bds, uncut; backstrip worn, stain on upper bd. With folding map. Some duststaining. S June 25 (121) £5,500 [Brooke-Hitching]

— Letters written in France to a Friend in London.... L: J. Johnson, 17968vo,. Orig bds. C June 25 (141) £3,000 [Quaritch/Hordern]

— A Narrative of the Expedition to Botany Bay. L, 1789. 1st Ed. 8vo, later half calf; rubbed. Some soiling & spotting; lacking final ads. pn June 11 (294) £2,300 [Quaritch]

Teniers, David, 1610-92

— Theatrum pictorium.... Antwerp: H. & C. Verdussen, [1684]. Folio, 18th-cent calf; spine ends def. With frontis, vignette on title, port & 245 plates. S Feb 11 (215) £2,600 [Marlborough]

Tennant, Stephen

— The Story of Felix Littlejohn.... L, 1929. In d/j. Inscr to Boris Kochno. SM Oct 12 (514) FF5,500

Tennyson, Alfred, Lord, 1809-92

See also: Limited Editions Club

— Idylls of the King. L, 1868. Illus by Gustave Dore. Folio, orig mor gilt by Bainamage. With 36 plates. bbc Sept 23 (61) $170

— In Memoriam. L, 1850. 1st Ed. 12mo, modern mor gilt by Zaehnsdorf; front cover detached. sg Oct 17 (383) $60

Anr Ed. L, 1900. One of 320. Illus by Charles Ricketts. 8vo, orig cloth; rubbed & soiled. bba July 9 (312) £110 [Wand]

— Locksley Hall Sixty Years After.... L, 1886. 8vo, orig cloth. Tp soiled at fore-margin. Inscr to Mary Brotherton, 1886. S Apr 28 (634) £360 [Swales]

— Poems, 1833. L, 1833. 1st Ed. 12mo, mor gilt by Wallis; rubbed. S July 1 (1011) £350 [Jarndyce]

— Tiresias, and other Poems. L, 1885. 1st Ed. 8vo, orig cloth. Inscr to his niece, Cecelia Lushington. S July 1 (1050) £350 [Quaritch]

— Works. Bost., 1893. 6 vols. 8vo, contemp half calf; extremities rubbed. F Mar 26 (161) $210

Anr Ed. L, 1893. 10 vols. 8vo, mor gilt. cb Jan 16 (149) $400

Anr Ed. Bost.: Estes & Lauriat, 1895-98. One of 1,000. 12 vols. 8vo, contemp half mor gilt; rubbed, 1 spine def at top. K July 12 (497) $325

Anr Ed. L, 1898-99. One of 1,050. 12 vols. 8vo, each vol with different Art Nouveau cuir-cisele bdg after designs by Alice Shepherd, by Chivers of Bath; Vol IV with small stain on upper cover, some rubbing. pn Sept 12 (18) £300 [Elliott]

Centenary Ed. L, 1909. one of 1,000. 8 vols. 8vo, half calf. LH May 17 (624) $225

Tennyson, Alfred & Charles

— Poems by Two Brothers. L, 1827. 1st Ed. 8vo, orig remainder wraps; worn, joints & backstrip rubbed & with pieces missing. S Dec 12 (36) £1,400 [Rota]

Tensini, Agostino

— La Vera regola dello scrivere.... Bassano, [c.1680?]. Oblong 4to, modern vellum bds. With engraved title & 16 plates. Last 3 leaves; some soiling. Engraved throughout. C June 24 (257) £1,200 [Franks]

Terentius Afer, Publius, 185-159 B.C.

— Comoediae. Paris, 1545. 4to, recent antique mor. Some spotting & soiling. DW Dec 11 (329) £420

Anr Ed. Venice: Aldus, 1575. 3 parts in 1 vol. 8vo, later half vellum. Lacking blanks; some worming. bba June 11 (29) £95 [Kent]

Anr Ed. Paris, 1753. 2 vols. 12mo, 18th-cent mor gilt. With 6 plates. S May 13 (865) £200 [Shapero]

Anr Ed. Rome, 1767. 2 vols. Folio, contemp half sheep; worn. Half-title in Vol I only; N3 in Vol I torn without loss; some marginal dampstaining; some soiling. pn Mar 19 (184) £120 [Bifolco]

Anr copy. 2 vols in 1. Folio, modern cloth. sg Mar 12 (293) $275

Anr copy. 2 vols. Folio, 19th-cent half lea. SI June 10 (1001) LIt550,000

Terrace, Claude, 1867-1923
— Petit Solfege illustre. Paris: Libraires reunis, [1893]. Illus by Pierre Bonnard. 4to, orig bds; spine stained. With 30 lithos. Tp & endleaves with small stains. Schlosser copy. P June 18 (515) $2,000

Tertullianus, Quintus Septimus Florens, 160?-230?
— Scripta. Basel: Froben & Episcopius, 1562. Folio, contemp blind-tooled pigskin over wooden bds; lacking clasps. sg Oct 24 (316) $250

Tesauro, Emmanuele, Conte
— De Regno d'Italia sotto i barbari epitome.... Turin, 1664. Folio, later vellum. With engraved title, 3 folding maps & 66 plates. bba Apr 9 (215) £600 [Erlini]

Anr Ed. Venice, 1672. 12mo, modern vellum. Some foxing & browning. SI Dec 5 (656) LIt150,000

Testard, Francois Martin. See: Segard & Testard

Texas
— The Constitution, as Amended, and Ordinances of the Convention of 1866.... Austin, 1866. 8vo, disbound. sg June 18 (523) $150

Texier, Charles Felix Marie
— Description de l'Asie Mineure faite par ordre du Gouvernement Francais de 1833 a 1837. Paris, 1839-49. 3 vols. Folio, 19th-cent half calf; rubbed. With map in 4 separate sheets & 249 plates, 5 in color. Some spotting & waterstaining. S June 30 (204) £4,200 [Consolidated Real]

Thacher, Amos Bateman
— Turkoman Rugs: An Illustrative Monograph.... NY, 1940. 4to, cloth. With 55 plates. Some waterstaining. sp June 18 (279) $250

Thacher, James, 1754-1844
— A Military Journal during the American Revolutionary War.... Bost., 1823. 8vo, contemp half sheep; joints & extremities worn. Some browning & marginal stains; clean tear in 1 leaf; lacking rear free endpaper. sg Dec 5 (256) $90

Thacher, John Boyd, 1847-1909
— Christopher Columbus. NY, 1903-4. 3 vols. 4to, cloth. Library markings. K Dec 1 (128) $55

Thackeray, William Makepeace, 1811-63
— The Adventures of Philip on his Way through the World. L, 1862. 1st Ed. 3 vols. 8vo, orig cloth, Sadleir's B bdg; extremities rubbed. O May 26 (186) $130
— Ballads. L, 1855. 1st Ed, 1st Issue. 3 vols. 8vo, later half mor, orig wraps bound in. cb Feb 12 (129) $85
— Etchings...while at Cambridge.... L, 1878. 8vo, orig bds; soiled & darkened. With engraved titles & 8 hand-colored plates. Marginal dampstaining. cb Jan 9 (208) $50
— Henry Esmond. L, 1852. ("The History of Henry Esmond.") 1st Ed. 3 vols. 8vo, later half calf by Henry Young and Sons. bba Oct 10 (356) £120 [Jarndyce]

Anr copy. Orig cloth; extremities worn. O July 14 (185) $70
— The Loving Ballad of Lord Bateman. L, 1839. 1st Ed, 1st Issue. Preface & notes by Charles Dickens; illus by George Cruikshank. 16mo, orig wraps; worn. O May 26 (187) $275

Anr copy. Cloth. sg Oct 17 (180) $600
— Mrs. Perkins's Ball. [L, 1847]. 1st Ed. 4to, orig bds; rebacked, head of spine chipped. With 22 colored plates. Charles Dickens's copy, with ALs of Dickens to Sir J. F. Pollack, 15 Mar 1864. P Dec 12 (167) $2,500
— The Newcomes. L, 1853-55. 1st Ed. Orig 24/23 parts. 8vo, orig wraps; soiled. With 2 engraved titles & 46 plates; ad leaves present in each part. Some soiling; 1 plate marginally repaired. pn Dec 12 (253) £95

1st Ed in Book form. L, 1854-55. 2 vols. 8vo, contemp calf; rubbed. Some foxing. O July 14 (187) $250

Anr copy. Half calf. pnE Mar 11 (134) £70

Anr copy. Contemp half mor gilt. Plates foxed. sg Oct 17 (384) $80
— Notes of a Journey from Cornhill to Grand Cairo. L, 1846. 1st Ed. 12mo, half mor; rubbed. With hand-colored frontis. Soiled & foxed. O Mar 31 (174) $60
— "Our Street." L, 1848. 2d Ed. 4to, contemp half calf; extremities worn. cb Sept 26 (197) $50
— Pendennis. L, 1848-50. ("The History of Pendennis.") 1st Ed in 24/23 parts, 1st Issue. 8vo, orig wraps. bba Oct 10 (353) £170 [Spademan]
— Vanity Fair. L, 1848. 1st Ed in Book form, 1st Issue. 2 vols. 8vo, modern mor extra. cb Dec 5 (133) $375

Anr copy. 8vo, orig cloth; outer joints split; hinges cracked. With 40 plates & illusts. With portion of Ms leaf containing 24 lines in Thackeray's hand. Epstein copy. sg Apr 30 (450) $2,000

Early Issue. Orig cloth; spine split at lower joint. Lacking half-title. L Nov 14 (462) £80

Anr copy. Orig cloth; frayed, small repair at head of spine. Minor defs. Manney copy. P Oct 11 (295) $2,750

Anr copy. Lev extra with oval port miniature of the author, by Sangorski & Sutcliffe. Penultimate plate shaved at fore-edge, costing part of 1 letter. Marks copy. P Dec 12 (13) $1,000

Anr Ed. L, 1849. 8vo, modern half mor gilt. Sgd W. M. Thackeray and Eugene Field by Eugene Field II. sg Oct 17 (244) $350

Anr Ed. L, [c.1913]. One of 350. Illus by Lewis Baumer. 4to, orig vellum gilt. With 20 colored plates. Ck Dec 11 (187) £140

— The Virginians. L, 1857-59. 1st Ed. Orig 24 parts. 8vo, orig wraps; worn, 1 rear wrap with closed tear. Two leaves in Part 3 with top blank corner torn off; lacking Grace Aguilar's Works ad in Part 24 & rear ads or slips in parts 8, 9, 12, 17 & 18. bbc Dec 9 (539) $130

Anr copy. Orig wraps; tear on upper cover of Part 23 repaired, spines repaired, some soiling. Lacking ads at back of Parts 2, 4 & 8, the slip for Byron's Complete Works in Part 14, the slips of the New Serial Work and The Daily News in Part 20 and for Grace Aguilar's Works in Part 24; some soiling. With 1 holograph leaf of the Ms for this work, 20 lines. P Dec 12 (195) $1,100

1st Ed in Book form. L, 1858-59. 2 vols. 8vo, later half calf by Henry Young & Sons. bba Oct 10 (357) £50 [Freddie]

Anr copy. Orig cloth. Part of an envelope in author's hand tipped in to Vol I. bba Apr 9 (62) £65 [Camac]

— Works. L, 1869. 22 vols. 8vo, contemp half calf. pn Sept 12 (225) £420 [Stone]

Anr Ed. L, 1869-86. 24 vols. 8vo, half mor gilt; joints rubbed. sg Mar 5 (303) $300

Anr Ed. L, 1878-86. One of 1,000. 52 vols. 4to, half mor gilt. Illusts on india paper. Some spotting. Autograph Ms verse tipped in. P June 17 (355) $2,750

Standard Ed. L, 1883-86. 26 vols. 8vo, half calf. pn Sept 12 (226) £340 [Stone]

Thane, John

— British Autography. L, [1788-1839]. 3 vols in 1, without Supplement. 4to, contemp half russia gilt. With engraved frontises & titles, 2 plates & 181 ports. bba Aug 13 (329) £160 [Page]

Anr copy. 3 vols, without Supplement. 4to, contemp mor gilt. Repair to 1 plate verso; a few leaves in Vol III with damage to lower blank margin. C Dec 16 (241) £550 [Brooke-Hitching]

Thayer, Emma Homan

— Wild Flowers of the Pacific Coast.... [Rocky Mountains]. NY, [1887-89]. Together, 2 vols. Folio, pictorial cloth; rubbed & soiled. Each work, 24 color plates. sg Nov 14 (202) $200

Thayer, Ernest L.

— Casey at the Bat. NY: Amsterdam Book Co., [1901]. 8vo, orig wraps; covers detached. P June 17 (384) $2,250

Thayer, Scofield

— Living Art. NY: Dial, [1923]. One of 500. Folio, text booklet & plates in vellum-backed bd folder; worn. With 29 (of 30) plates. sg Feb 6 (167) $200

Theakston, Michael

— British Angling Flies. L, 1862. 8vo, cloth; worn. Koopman copy. O Oct 29 (303) $110

Theatrum...

— Theatrum diabolorum, das ist, warhaffte eigentliche kurze Beschreibung allerley grewlicher schrecklicher und abschewlicher Laster. Frankfurt: Peter Schmid for Sigmund Feyeraben, 1575. Folio, 16th-cent blind-stamped pigskin over wooden bds, with 2 clasps & catches. Minor spotting. S Dec 5 (204) £3,000 [Reiss & Auvermann]

Anr Ed. Frankfurt: Peter Schmid for Sigmund Feyerabend, 1587-88. 2 parts in 1 vol. Folio, contemp blind-tooled pigskin over wooden bds with brass catches; lacking clasps. Dampstaining in upper inner corners throughout. sg Oct 24 (117) $1,100

— Theatrum sympatheticum auctum, exhibens varios authores de pulvere sympathetico.... Nuremburg, 1662. Ed by Sylvester Rattray. 4to, contemp vellum. Some waterstaining. SI June 10 (1006) LIt900,000

Theocritus, Bion & Moschus

Idylls

— Jan 1516. - Rome: Zacharias Callierges. 8vo, mor gilt. Greek type. Some staining. C June 24 (262) £950 [Kraus]

— 1604. - [Heidelberg]: ex Bibliopolo commeliniano. 4to, vellum. Some browning & foxing. bba June 11 (30) £150 [Poole]

— 1699. - Oxford 2 parts in 1 vol. 8vo, contemp calf; rubbed, rebacked. Frontis shaved. bba Apr 30 (70) £65 [Gammon]

— 1780. - Parma: Bodoni. 5 parts in 1 vol. 4to, 19th-cent half vellum. SI Dec 5 (1033) LIt350,000

— 1921. - Idyllen des Klassischen Altertums. Vienna One of 1,400. Illus by W. Russell

Flint. Folio, bds. With 20 mtd colored plates. sg Jan 30 (53) $90

— 1971. - Sixe Idyllia. NY One of 417. Illus by Anthony Gross. Folio, orig half cloth. bba Dec 19 (155) £55 [Thorp]

Theophrastus, d.c.287 B.C.

— De suffruticibus, herbisque, ac frugibus libri quattuor. Strassburg: Heinrich Seybold, Aug 1529. 8vo, orig wraps; upper joint partly split, upper cover with dampstains. 28 lines plus direction-line; roman types with greek; 2 9-line woodcut historiated initials. Tp soiled; some dampstaining. P June 17 (129) $1,700

Theotoky, Emmanuel, Baron

— Details sur Corfou. Corfu, 1826. 4to, cloth. L.p. copy. Phillipps copy. S June 30 (419) £1,700 [Spink]

Thespian...

— Thespian Dictionary: or Dramatic Biography of the Eighteenth Century.... L, 1805. 12mo, later half lea; front bd detached. With 7 engraved ports (foxed). Met Apr 28 (837) $70

Anr copy. Mor gilt. Extra-illus with 96 plates. Eva Le Gallienne's copy. sg Mar 5 (257) $600

Thetard, Henri

— La Merveilleuse Histoire du Cirque. [Paris], 1947. 2 vols. 4to, cloth, in torn d/js. sg Oct 17 (100) $150

Thevenot, Jean de

— Gedenkwaardige en zeer naauwkeurige Reizen. Amst., 1682-88. 3 parts in 2 vols. 4to, later half vellum; spine wormed. With 3 extra titles & 41 plates, 2 folding. cb Jan 30 (121) $550

— Relation d'un voyage fait au Levant. Paris, 1663 [but 1664]. 4to, contemp calf; worn. Some spotting & discoloration. S June 30 (205) £750 [Consolidated Real]

Thevenot, Melchisedec

— Relations de divers voyages curieux.... Paris, 1663-72. Part 1. Folio, contemp calf; joints weak, spine chipped at head and foot. With 5 maps and 4 plates. Small wormhole in a few inner margins affecting 1 map; library stamp on title. S June 25 (18) £5,000 [Quaritch Hordern]

Thevet, Andre

— Historia dell'India America detta altramente Francia antartica. Venice, 1561. 8vo, modern vellum. First 8 leaves repaired in margins, not affecting text. SI June 10 (1004) LIt350,000

Thieme, Ulrich —& Becker, Felix

— Allgemeines Lexikon der Bildenden Kuenstler von der Antike bis zur Gegenwart. Leipzig, 1907-50. 37 vols. 4to, half calf & half mor; some joints rubbed or broken. S Feb 11 (216) £1,200 [Eimers]

Anr Ed. Leipzig, 1954-57. 37 vols. 4to, orig half mor. bba Feb 13 (126) £1,250 [Blum]

Thiers, Louis Adolphe, 1797-1877

— Historie du Consulat et de l'Empire.... Paris, 1845-62. 20 vols. 8vo, half calf; rubbed. bbc Dec 9 (258) $525

— History of the Consulate and the Empire of France under Napoleon. L, 1845-62. 20 vols in 10 plus Atlas vol from the French Ed. 8vo & 4to, half calf, Atlas in half lea. With 6 ports in text vols & 24 maps in Atlas, some hand-colored in outline. Some marginal foxing; waterstain on 1 prelim leaf. K Sept 29 (413) $275

Anr Ed. L, 1893-94. 12 vols. 8vo, half mor gilt. b&b Feb 19 (60) $350

Thimm, Carl Albert

— A Complete Bibliography of Fencing and Duelling. L, 1891. 8vo, half vellum; soiled. Inscr to A. P. Dunlop. sg Mar 26 (318) $225

Anr Ed. L, 1896. 8vo, orig cloth; worn & shaken. O Dec 17 (179) $100

Anr copy. Half cloth; extremities worn. sg Mar 26 (319) $325

Anr copy. Half cloth; worn, hinges reinforced, lettered plastic tabs added at fore-edges. sg Mar 26 (320) $120

Anr Ed. [NY, 1968]. sg Mar 26 (321) $225; sg Mar 26 (322) $225

This Quarter...

— This Quarter.... Paris, Sept 1932. Ed by Andre Breton. Vol V, No 1: Surrealist No. Orig wraps. With 6 illusts. sg Apr 2 (91) $175

Thistle...

— The Thistle, by Sir John de Grahame Knight. Edin., 1734. Nos 21-40. 4to, 19th-cent half calf; upper cover detached. Mtd on guards; No 26 cropped at head with partial loss of 1st line. Milne copy. Ck June 12 (199) £220

Thode, Jackson C.

— A Century of Passenger Trains. Denver, 1972. Bound upside down & backwards. cb Feb 13 (312) $150

Thoinan, Ernest, Pseud.

— Les Relieurs francais (1500-1800). Paris, 1893. One of 20 on Japon. 4to, mor extra by Petrus Ruban. Benz copy. CNY Dec 5 (434) $2,500

Thomas a Becket, Saint, 1118?-70

— Vita & processus...super libertate ecclesiastica. Paris: Johannes Philippus, 27 Mar 1495. Without the Bertrandi. 4to, modern mor gilt. 98 leaves. Goff T-159. C Dec 16 (169) £1,100 [Paradise]

— Vita et processus sancti Thome.... Paris: Johann Philippi, 27 Mar 1495. 4to, half sheep. 45 lines & headline; double column; type 8:83G (text), 12:108G (title page, chapter incipits). First & last leaves stained; some minor waterstaining. 116 leaves. Goff T-159 & B-516. Schoyen copy. P Dec 12 (45) $7,000

Thomas a Kempis, Saint, 1380-1471

See also: Fore-Edge Paintings

— The Christian Pattern, or the Imitation of Jesus Christ. Germantown, 1749. 8vo, contemp sheep. Final text leaf adhering to rear cover; small tear on tp; library markings. sg June 18 (487) $200

— De imitatione Christi. Augsburg: Anton Sorg, 20 Nov 1486. ("Ein ware nachvolgung Cristi....") 4to, contemp blindstamped calf over wooden bds; sides laid down & rebacked, 1 catch & clasp. 23 lines & headline; types 3:140G (title, headlines, headings, colophon), 4:109G (text), with Maiblumen-style initials in red & green. Some worming to first few leaves & a few other inner margins. 191 (of 198) leaves; lacking 6 leaves of index & final blank. Goff I-40. S Dec 5 (28) £3,200 [Mauss]

Anr Ed. Venice: Rossi, 22 Mar 1488. 4to, modern bds. 35 lines & headline; roman letter; initials in red. Some marginal repairs, not affecting text; k5 & k6 repaired, affecting text; some browning. 78 leaves. Goff I-45. SI June 10 (1013) LIt650,000

Anr Ed. Parma: Bodoni, 1793. Folio, contemp calf gilt. SI June 10 (1012) LIt4,000,000

Anr Ed. L, 1828. ("Of the Imitation of Jesus Christ.") Trans by Thomas Frognall Dibdin. 8vo, contemp cloth; upper cover & spine detached. bba Jan 30 (195) £60 [Harrington]

Anr Ed. Paris, 1856-58. ("L'imitation de Jesus-Christ.") 2 vols, including Appendix. 4to, mor extra. With chromolitho tp, frontis, dedication, 4 full-page plates & many chromolitho borders, totalling more that 400 pp of chromolithos; Appendix has uncolored wood engravings. Some browning & discoloration, mostly of Appendix. Reprint of the 1626 Nicolas Gasse Ed. P June 18 (525) $900

Anr Ed. Paris, 1903. One of 280 on velin du Marais. Illus by Maurice Denis. 4to, unsewn in orig wraps. sg Jan 30 (183) $600

Anr Ed. L: Essex House Press, 1904. ("Of the Imitation of Christ.") One of 10 on vellum. 4to, mor extra by F. S. Tolson, 1925. With 1 wood-engraved illust repeated twice with different hand-coloring. S Dec 12 (180) £1,500 [maggs]

Anr Ed. L, 1908. Illus by W. Russell Flint. Mor extra, orig cloth bound in. sg Mar 5 (305) $275

— De l'imitation de Jesus-Christ. Paris: L. Curmer, [1856-58]. 2 vols. 4to, mor gilt extra by A. Bertrand; inner joint of Vol I cracked. CNY Dec 5 (378) $1,000

— Of the Following of Christ.... Paris: Mistris Blageart, 1636. 16mo, contemp mosaic bdg of mor with mor inlays, elaborately gilt, edges painted, gilt & gauffered. Wormed affecting a few leaves; lacking 1 prelim leaf; frontis & 1 prelim leaf from a different Ed inserted at the beginning. Sold w.a.f. STC 23992. S Dec 5 (249) £2,400 [Jackson]

— Opera. Nuremberg: Caspar Hochfeder, 29 Nov 1494. Folio, 18th-cent mor gilt; scarred. 53 lines & headline; double column; types 2:168aG (title, headlines) & 1:83G (text). Hole in final leaf; a few stains. 182 (of 184) leaves. Goff T-352. C Nov 27 (26) £3,000 [Quaritch]

Thomas Aquinas, Saint, 1225?-74

— Catena aurea super quattuor evangelistas. Lyons: G. Huyon for Guinta, 1520. ("Catena aurea in quatuor evangelia.") 4 vols in 2. 8vo, 19th-cent calf. Some browning; marginal dampstains; old writing washed out of titles; 1 leaf backed with loss; 4 blanks lacking. sg Oct 24 (317) $225

— Opuscula. Venice: Hermannus Leichtenstein, 7 Sept 1490. 4to, old vellum; pastedowns and lst few leaves wormed. Tear in a2 with some loss. 434 (of 436) leaves. Goff T-258. sg Mar 12 (136) $475

— Summa contra gentiles. [Strassburg: Printer of Henricus Ariminensis type 1, not after 1474]. Folio, contemp calf over wooden bds, with brass fittings; rebacked, remains of orig spine laid down. 49 lines; type 1:120G; double column; rubricated. 248 leaves. Goff T-190. Schoyen copy. P Dec 12 (42) $14,000

Anr Ed. Venice: Alex. Calcedonii, 7 Nov 1501. Folio, later half calf; rubbed. bba Sept 19 (272) £520 [Maggs]

— Summa theologicae. [Strassburg: Johann Mentelin, before Advent 1463]. ("Summa theologiae, secunda pars, secundus liber.") Folio, contemp blind-stamped calf over wooden bds with 2 brass clasp plates, from the monastic shop of St. Peter of Erfurt; worn & cracked, bosses removed, corners restored. 59 lines; type 3:92G; double column; rubricated. 244 (of 247) leaves; lacking 16/4.5 & blank 22/10. Goff T-208. Schoyen copy. P Dec 12 (43) $18,000

Anr Ed. Venice: Antonius de Strata, Dec 1484. Bound with: Philelpus, Franciscus. Epistolae. Venice: Philippus Pinzius, 5 Sept 1492. And: Orationes Philelphi cum aliis opusculis. Venice: Philippus Pinzius, 14 Oct 1492. Folio, later vellum. 1st work: 56 lines & headline, double column, gothic letter. 2d work: 60 lines, roman letter. 3d work: 59 lines, roman letter. Some staining & worming; lower margins of last few leaves frayed. 215 (of 216) leaves, lacking final blank; Goff T-200; 91 (of 92) leaves, lacking a1; Goff P-591; 79 (of 80) leaves, lacking final blank; Goff P-610. S Dec 5 (30) £1,800 [Soave]

Anr Ed. Basel: Michael Wenssler, 16 Aug 1485. 4 vols in 1. Folio, contemp calf over wooden bds; front cover detached; lea over spine missing. Scattered staining. 174 (of 176), 163 (of 164), 240 (of 242) & 157 (of 160) leaves. Goff T-194. sg Mar 12 (135) $4,000

— Tractatus resolvens dubia circa septem sacramenta de scriptis S. Thomae de Aquino et aliorum doctorum. Strassburg: Johann Reinhard Grueninger, 9 Feb 1496. 4to, 19th-cent half sheep; worn. Early marginalia; old stamp on tp verso. 52 (of 54) leaves; lacking blank & d1. Goff T-334. sg Oct 24 (318) $1,200

Thomas, Corbinianus

— Mercurii philosophici firmamentum firmianum.... Frankfurt & Leipzig, 1730. Oblong 4to, contemp calf; worn. With frontis & 84 plates. Minor dampstaining. S Dec 5 (439) £2,800 [Watson]

Thomas, Dylan, 1914-53

— Deaths and Entrances. L, 1946. 1st Ed. Cloth, in d/j. sg Dec 12 (398) $110

— Eighteen Poems. L: Fortune Press, 1934. 1st Ed, 1st Issue. Inscr to Norman & Elfriede Cameron & by Norman Cameron to Joyce Gott. pn July 16 (66) £650

Anr copy. In d/j. Epstein copy. sg Apr 30 (451) $2,200

3d Issue. In d/j. K July 12 (500) $50

— A Portrait of the Artist as a Young Dog. Norfolk CT: New Directions, [1940]. 1st American Ed. In torn d/j. sg Dec 12 (399) $130

— Twenty-Five Poems. L, 1936. 1st Ed. In d/j. bba Feb 27 (188) £140 [Aspin]

Anr copy. In d/j. Epstein copy. sg Apr 30 (452) $1,000

— Under Milk Wood. L, 1954. In d/j. sg Dec 12 (400) $70

2d impression. In torn & soiled d/j. Review slip laid in. Sgd by the readers at the Old Vic on 7 Mar 1954: Emlyn Williams, Diana Maddox, Richard Burton & Sibyl Thorndike. S Nov 14 (669) £150 [Freize]

Thomas, Edward, 1878-1917

See also: Gregynog Press

— The Woodland Life. L, 1897. 1st Ed. 8vo, orig cloth. pn Dec 12 (221) £70

Thomas, Capt. George Powell

— Views of Simla. L, 1846. Folio, orig bds; rebacked & recornered. With litho title, map & 23 plates. Tp with vertical crease; colored title with small tear in blank foremargin repaired; 3 other plates with small tears in blank margins. C Oct 30 (92) £600 [Rahim]

Thomas, Isaiah, 1750-1831

— The History of Printing in America.... Barre, Mass., 1970. cb Jan 16 (152) $70

Thomas, Lowell

— The First World Flight. Bost., 1925. One of 575, sgd. Half vellum, unopened. cb Oct 10 (104) $250

Anr copy. Half vellum. sg Jan 9 (188) $175

Thomas, Michael R. Oldfield. See: Sclater & Thomas

Thomas, William, d.1554

— The Historie of Italie. L: Thos. Berthelet, 1549. 1st Ed. 4to, old sheep; needs rebacking, tp & next few leaves attached to loose front cover. 2G1 torn & repaired; lacking 2T4 & 3I4. STC 24018. sg Oct 24 (319) $550

Thomase, Eudaldo

— Tratado de esgrima a pie y a caballo. Barcelona, 1823. 8vo, later wraps. With 16 plates. sg Mar 26 (323) $150

Thomassin, Simon

— Recueil des figures, groupes, thermes, fontaines...de Versailles. Amst., 1695. 4to, contemp sheep; rebacked. With frontis, folding plan & 218 plates. sg Oct 24 (320) $300

Thomas-Stanford, Charles

— Early Editions of Euclid's Elements. San Francisco, 1977. 4to, cloth. Reprint of 1926 Ed. bbc Dec 9 (183) $110

Thome, Otto Wilhelm

— Flora von Deutschland, Oesterreich und der Schweiz.... Gera-Untermhaus, 1886 [1885]-89. Vols I-IV. 8vo, contemp half lea; rubbed. With 613 colored plates only. Library stamps, not affecting plates. pn Mar 19 (342) £200

Thompson, Charles, Traveler

— The Travels.... Reading, 1744. 3 vols. 8vo, contemp calf; rubbed, rebacked. With 7 hand-colored maps & 13 other plates. Some plates torn along folds; 1 map torn & repaired. S June 30 (423) £380 [Gonul]

Thompson, Daniel Pierce

— The Green Mountain Boys. Montpelier VT, 1839. 1st Ed. 2 vols. 12mo, orig bds; worn, recased. Some foxing & staining; a few margins chipped. Epstein copy. sg Apr 30 (453) $700

Thompson, David, 1770-1857. See: Henry & Thompson

Thompson, Sir Edward Maunde, 1840-1929

— An Introduction to Greek and Latin Palaeography. Oxford, 1912. sg Oct 31 (260) $150

Thompson, George, fl.1794

— Slavery and Famine, Punishments for Sedition.... L, 1794. 8vo, modern calf; joints rubbed. S June 25 (130) £1,800 [Quaritch/Hordern]

Thompson, George Alexander

— Narrative of an Official Visit to Guatemala from Mexico. L, 1829. 8vo, cloth; spine repaired. sg June 18 (527) $325

Thompson, Henry

— Texas. Sketches of Character. By Milam. Phila., 1839. 16mo, cloth. sg Dec 5 (255) $1,100

Thompson, Sir Henry, 1820-1904

— A Catalogue of Blue and White Nankin Porcelain.... L, 1878. One of—120. 4to, orig cloth; spine ends chipped. With 26 plates. Some foxing. sg Feb 6 (279) $400

Thompson Library, Henry Yates

— Illustrations from One Hundred Manuscripts in the Library.... L, 1914. Vol IV (of 7). Folio, cloth; needs rebdg. Inscr to George D. Smith. sg Oct 31 (261) $400

Thompson, Jim

— The Killer Inside Me. Los Angeles: Blood & Guts Press, 1989. One of 350, sgd by Stephen King. In d/j. cb Sept 19 (114) $60

Thompson, Pishey

— The History and Antiquities of Boston. Bost., 1856. Folio, cloth. bba Dec 19 (425) £70 [Staniland]

Thompson, Robert A.

— Conquest of California.... Santa Rosa CA, 1896. 8vo, orig wraps; lower edges chippedd & worn. cb Feb 12 (85) $60

Thompson, Ruth Plumly

— Handy Mandy in Oz. Chicago: Reilly & Lee, [1937]. Illus by John R. Neill. Orig cloth; minor wear. bbc Dec 9 (151) $110

— The Hungry Tiger of Oz. Chicago, [1926]. 1st Ed, later state. Orig cloth; spine ends worn. With 12 color plates. Soiling & 2 small tears to 1 plate. K Mar 22 (321) $120

— Jack Pumpkinhead of Oz. Chicago, [1929]. 1st Ed. Orig cloth; worn & frayed, hinges cracked, endpapers browned. bbc Dec 9 (152) $70

— Kabumpo in Oz. Chicago, [1922]. 1st Ed, 1st State. Orig cloth; rubbed, endpapers browned. bbc Dec 9 (153) $100; K Mar 22 (322) $130

— The Lost King of Oz. Chicago, [1925]. 1st Ed. sg Oct 17 (341) $225

1st Issue. In d/j. sg Oct 17 (341) $225
Early State, plates coated on 1 sides. Cloth; front joint opening. K Mar 22 (323) $150

— Ozoplaning with the Wizard of Oz. Chicago: Reilly & Lee, [1938]. 1st Ed. Illus by John R. Neill. Orig cloth; rubbed. bbc Dec 9 (154) $90

Anr copy. Orig cloth; front joint open. K Mar 22 (324) $130

— The Purple Prince of Oz. Chicago, [1932]. 1st Ed. Orig cloth; worn, hinges cracked, some plates loose. bbc Dec 9 (156) $80

— Speedy in Oz. Chicago, [1934]. 1st Ed. Orig cloth; spine ends frayed, gouge to top edge of lower cover, hinges cracked. bbc Dec 9 (257) $80

— The Yellow Knight of Oz. Chicago, [1930]. 1st Ed. In d/j. sg Oct 17 (342) $275

Thoms, William J.

— Early English Prose Romances. Edin., 1904. One of 500. 3 vols. 4to, half cloth. kh Nov 11 (344) A$50

Thomson, Sir Charles Wyville

— The Voyage of the "Challenger." L, 1877. 1st Ed. 2 vols. 8vo, half calf; rubbed. bba Jan 16 (305) £60 [Hay Cinema]

Thomson, James, Naturalist

— Arcana naturae ou recueil d'histoire naturelle. Paris, 1859. Vol I (all pbd). Folio, modern half mor, orig wraps bound in. With frontis & 13 plates. Ck Oct 18 (29) £190

Thomson, James, 1700-48

— The Seasons. L, 1730. 4to, contemp calf; joints cracked, extremities rubbed. With engraved title vignette & 5 plates. Milne copy. Ck June 12 (200) £100

Anr copy. Bound with: A Poem Sacred to the Memory of Sir Isaac Newton. contemp calf; rebacked. pn Sept 12 (12) £65 [Cox]

Anr Ed. L, 1793. Ed by Percival Stockdale. 8vo, contemp calf gilt; rubbed, joints cracking. L Nov 14 (464) £100

Anr Ed. L, 1797. Illus by F. Bartolozzi & P. W. Tomkins after W. Hamilton. Folio, bds; rebacked in mor. LH May 17 (590) $100

Anr copy. Early 19th-cent mor gilt; hinges cracked. With frontis & 7 color-ptd plates. Some foxing. Colored copy. Schlosser copy. P June 18 (501) $9,500

Anr copy. Half mor; bds worn & shabby, lacking spine, shaken. With 6 plates. wa Mar 5 (574) $270

Anr Ed. L: James Wallis, 1805. Illus by Bewick after Thurston. 8vo, contemp calf; worn, joints cracked. cb Sept 26 (18) $90

Thomson, James, 1800-83

— A Letter to the Vice-President of the Board of Trade, on Protection to Original Designs and Patterns.... Clitheroe: H. Whalley, [c.1840]. Bound with: A Letter to the Right Honourable Sir Robert Peel, Bart. on Copyright....[N.d.] And: Notes on the Present State of Calico Printing in Belgium. [N.d.]. 3 parts in 1 vol. 8vo, orig cloth; rubbed. bba May 28 (70) £260 [Quaritch]

— Retreats: a Series of Designs.... L, 1827. 4to, modern half mor. With 10 uncolored plans & 31 hand-colored plates. Some plates smaller. C May 20 (130) £700 [Harcourt-Williams]

Thomson, John, Cartographer

— A New General Atlas. Edin., 1827. Folio, contemp half lea; rubbed, hinges worn. With 2 double-page plates, engraved dedication & 75 hand-colored map sheets within wash borders. Short tear to 1 map. b June 22 (26) £1,700

Thomson, John, F.R.G.S.

— Illustrations of China and its People. L, 1873-74. 1st Ed of Vols II, III & IV; 2d Ed of Vol I. 4 vols. Folio, orig cloth; spines lacking. With 96 plates. b June 22 (277) £2,000

— The Straits of Malacca, Indo-China, and China.... NY, 1875. 8vo, cloth; worn & spotted. O Feb 25 (189) $125

Thomson, Mortimer

— The Witches of New York. By Q. K. Philander Doesticks, P.B. NY, 1859. 12mo, cloth. sg Oct 17 (101) $110

Thomson, S. Harrison

— Latin Bookhands of the Later Middle Ages. Cambr., 1969. Folio, cloth, in d/j. sg Oct 31 (262) $275

Thomson, Thomas, 1773-1852

— Travels in Sweden during the Autumn of 1812. L, 1813. 1st Ed. 4to, early half mor. With 13 maps & plates. Frontis loose. sg Jan 9 (189) $175

Thomson, William, fl.1725-53

— Orpheus Caledonius: or, a Collection of Scots Songs. L, 1733. 2d Ed. 2 vols in 1. 8vo, later half mor gilt; rubbed. bba Feb 27 (63) £100 [R. Clark]

Thomson, William George

— A History of Tapestry. L, 1906. 4to, cloth. sg Feb 6 (277) $120

Thorburn, Archibald

— Birds of Prey. L, 1919. One of 150. Folio, text loose as issued, plates all framed. With 12 colored proof plates. Repair to 1 plate with loss to edge of image & slight damage to surface; 3 plates with dampstains. With envelope with ALs from A. Baird Carter indicating his intention to publish the set, the orig prospectus & a sgd receipt. pn June 11 (269) £500

— British Birds. L, 1915-18. 4 vols, without Supplement. 4to, orig cloth. With 80 colored plates. Marginal staining. b Nov 18 (382) £250

Anr copy. 5 vols, including Supplement. 4to, orig cloth, in d/js with some loss. With 81 (of 82) colored plates; lacking Plate 52. Ck May 15 (53) £360

Anr copy. 4 vols. 4to, orig cloth. With 80 colored plates. L Nov 14 (234) £320

Anr copy. Orig cloth; dampstained. With 80 color plates. Text browned. S Feb 26 (945) £280 [Montevecchio]

Anr copy. Orig cloth; rubbed. With 80 colored plates. Some browning. S May 14 (1062) £200 [Way]

2d Ed. 1916-18. 5 vols, including Supplement. 4to, orig cloth, Supplement in orig wraps; rubbed, spines stained. With 82 colored plates. Some foxing. pn June 11 (270) £300

Anr Ed. L, 1916-18. 4 vols. 4to, orig cloth; rubbed, Vol I soiled with spine torn. With 80 colored plates. Text with foxing. pn Sept 12 (307) £240 [Graham]

Anr copy. Orig cloth; worn. pnE Mar 11 (190) £210

3d Ed of Vols I & II; 2d Ed of Vols II & IV. L, 1917-18. 4 vols. 4to, orig cloth, in torn d/js. pnE May 13 (147) £420; pnE Aug 12 (247) £230

Anr Ed. L, 1918. 4 vols. 4to, contemp half mor. With 80 colored plates. Ck May 15 (53A) £400

Anr Ed. L, 1925-26. One of 205. 4 vols. 4to, orig cloth; spines stained. With 192 colored plates mtd on gray card. C Oct 30 (250) £400 [Grahame]

— British Mammals. L, 1920-21. 2 vols. 4to, cloth; soiled & worn. With 50 colored plates. Scattered spotting. DW Dec 11 (165) £250; O Apr 28 (140) $350

Anr copy. Orig cloth; spines rubbed. Some spotting & soiling. pn June 11 (271) £140 [Russell]

Anr copy. Orig half mor. S May 14 (1061) £220 [Graham]

— Game Birds and Wild-Fowl of Great Britain and Ireland. L, 1923. Folio, orig cloth; rubbed. With 30 colored plates. C Oct 30 (249) £600 [Kresto]

One of 155 L.p. copies. Orig cloth, in cloth wrap. With 30 colored plates. pn June 11 (272) £720

Anr copy. Orig cloth; worn. pnE Mar 11 (189) £210

Anr copy. Modern half mor gilt. pnE May 13 (97) £440

— A Naturalist's Sketch Book. L, 1919. 4to, orig cloth; spine rubbed. DW Dec 11 (166) £390

Anr copy. Orig cloth; worn. With 36 plain & 24 colored plates. O Apr 28 (141) $200

Anr copy. Orig cloth; rubbed & stained. Some soiling to text. pn Dec 12 (295) £120

Anr copy. Orig cloth; rubbed. pn June 11 (273) £170

One of 105. Orig cloth; spine faded, rear cover discolored. With 36 plain & 24 colored plates. sg Nov 14 (203) $175

Thoreau, Henry David, 1817-62

See also: Limited Editions Club

— Autumn. Bost & NY, 1892. 1st Ed. 8vo, cloth. NH May 30 (282) $220

— Cape Cod. Bost., 1865. 1st Ed. 12mo, cloth, Bdg A; spine ends worn & chipped. NH May 30 (283) $175

Anr copy. Orig cloth; spines worn. NH May 30 (284) $80

Anr Ed. Bost., 1896. 2 vols. 12mo, cloth; spine bumped. sp June 18 (161) $80

— In the Maine Woods. Bost., 1864. 8vo, orig cloth. Lacking ads. Epstein copy. sg Apr 30 (455) $425

— Letters to Various Persons. Bost., 1865. 1st Ed. 12mo, orig cloth; spine ends worn. NH May 30 (285) $100

— The Maine Woods. Bost., 1864. 1st Ed. 12mo, orig cloth; spine bumped. sp June 18 (455) $450

— Walden. Bost., 1854. 1st Ed. 8vo, orig cloth; spine ends repaired. With map & ads dated May 1854. bba June 25 (201) £1,300 [Dailey]

Anr copy. Orig cloth; rubbed. With map & ads dated Sept 1854. NH May 30 (288) $600

Anr copy. Orig cloth. With ads dated May 1854. Manney copy. P Oct 11 (296) $11,000

Anr copy. Orig cloth; rubbed, spine ends frayed. With ads dated Sept 1855 Tp browned; fore-edge of leaf 5-1 roughly opened; blank corner loss on 6-6. P June 17 (389) $4,750

Anr copy. Orig cloth; spine ends repaired. With ads dated June 1854. Epstein copy. sg Apr 30 (457) $5,000

— A Week on the Concord and Merrimack Rivers. Bost. & Cambr., 1849. 1st Ed. 8vo, orig cloth; rubbed. Epstein copy. sg Apr 30 (456) $3,200

1st Issue. Orig cloth; rebacked, new endpapers. NH May 30 (289) $1,600

— Works. Cambr., Mass, [1894]. Riverside Ed, One of 150. 11 vols. 8vo, orig half mor; worn. bbc June 29 (98) $350

Manuscript Ed. Bost., 1906. one of 600, with leaf of autograph Ms in Vol I. 20 vols. 8vo, half mor gilt; spines darkened. sg May 7 (200A) $4,600

Thoresby, Ralph, 1658-1725

— Ducatus Leodiensis: or, The Topography of...Leedes. Leeds, 1715. Folio, contemp calf with armorial bearings of Henry J. B. Clements; rebacked. With port, 12 plates & armorial bearings in text. pnL Nov 20 (57) £180 [Bates]

2d Ed. Leeds, 1816. 2 vols. Folio, modern half cloth. With 64 (of 65) plates. Some spotting; 1 plate loose. pnL Nov 20 (58) £180 [Almar]

Thorley, John

— Melissologia, or the Female Monarchy...of Bees. L, 1744. 8vo, contemp calf; rubbed, joints split. With 5 plates. Folding plate torn & repaired & with corner torn away, affecting plate surface; others cropped at inner margins; frontis with portion of margin torn away; some browning. pn Dec 12 (112) £160

Thornbury, Walter —& Walford, Edward

— Old and New London. L, [c.1880]. 6 vols. 4to, contemp half calf gilt; scratched. DW Dec 11 (127) £60

Thorndike, Lynn, 1882-1965

— A History of Magic and Experimental Science. NY, 1947-58. 8 vols. O Sept 24 (242) $250

Anr Ed. NY, 1959-66. 8 vols. Vols II-IV dampwrinkled. sg Oct 31 (315) $300

Thorndike, Lynn, 1882-1965 —& Kibre, Pearl

— A Catalogue of Incipits of Mediaeval Scientific Writings in Latin. L, 1963. 4to, orig cloth. sg Oct 31 (263) $275

Thornhill, Richard Badham

— The Shooting Directory. L, 1804. 1st Ed, 2d Issue. 4to, contemp half mor; spine def, joints cracked. With aquatint port, 6 aquatint plates, 2 engraved plates & 3 folding charts. S Feb 26 (892) £500 [Royal Armouries]

Thornton, Alfred, fl.1820

— The Adventures of a Post Captain.... L, [1817]. 8vo, orig bds; rebacked, lower joint splitting. With engraved title & 24 hand-colored plates. bba Dec 19 (95) £140 [Thorp]

Anr copy. Calf gilt; hinges worn. K Mar 22 (438) $225

Thornton, Jessy Quinn

— Oregon and California in 1848.... NY, 1849. 1st Ed. 2 vols. 12mo, cloth; damage along several joints. With folding map & 12 plates. Ad leaf def; ink owner's stamp. sg June 18 (138) $350

Thornton, Robert John

— A New Family Herbal. L, 1810. 1st Ed. 8vo, contemp half russia gilt; rubbed. Marginal spotting & foxing. pn July 16 (168) £90

— New Illustration of the Sexual System of...Linnaeus. Comprehending...The Temple of Flora.... L, [1799]-1807-[10].. Folio, lea; rubbed, joints worn. With 5 plates. All color botanical plates removed. Sold w.a.f. O Nov 26 (180) $600

— The Temple of Flora, or Garden of the Botanist. L, 1812. 4to, 19th-cent mor gilt. With frontis, double-page engraved title & 28 hand-colored plates. FD Dec 2 (213) DM10,000

Anr copy. Cloth. With engraved title with vignette on 2 leaves, colored allegorical frontis, 2 plain plates & 28 colored plates of flowers. Persian Cyclamen with short tear in margin; some staining & soiling; lacking ptd title & engraved dedication. S Nov 21 (48) £1,400 [Schuster]

Anr copy. With engraved title with vignette on 2 leaves, 2 uncolored plates & 27 (of 28) colored plates of flowers. Lacking frontis & Blue Egyptian Water Lily; also lacking ptd title & engraved dedication. S Nov 21 (49) £2,200 [Burden]

Anr copy. Contemp mor; spine def, upper cover detached. With engraved title with vignette on 2 leaves, colored frontis, 2 plain & 28 colored plates. Engraved title & uncolored plates stained; Queen Flower detached & frayed; American Aloe oxidized; Indian Reed with imprint cropped; lacking ptd title & engraved dedication. S June 25 (77) £3,000 [Tamura]

Anr copy. Contemp mor gilt; worn. Some imprints trimmed; some browning; lacking ptd title & engraved dedication. Plesch copy. S June 25 (78) £3,000 [Sheehy]

Thornton, Thomas, d.1814

— The Present State of Turkey. L, 1807. 1st Ed. 4to, contemp calf; rubbed, upper joint split. S June 30 (417) £180 [Shapero]

Thornton, Col. Thomas, 1757-1823

— Sporting Tour through the Northern Parts of England.... L, 1804. 4to, contemp calf gilt; rebacked, orig backstrip laid down. With 15 plates. L Nov 14 (202) £70

— A Sporting Tour through Various Parts of France. L, 1806. 2 vols in 1. 4to, modern mor by De Samblancx, armorial bdg. With engraved titles, port, 5 plates & 59 views on 47 sheets. bba Sept 19 (154) £750 [Baring]

Anr copy. 2 vols. 4to, half mor; rubbed. O May 26 (188) $250

Thoroton, Robert, 1623-78

— The Antiquities of Nottinghamshire. L, 1677. 1st Ed. Folio, calf; misbound. With title, folding map 15 plates, 13 double-page or folding & 4 plates of arms. Misbound, K2 holed. bba Sept 19 (255) £s480 [Wand]

Anr copy. Later calf; worn, upper cover detached. With folding map & 16 plates & 4 sheets with 8 plates of coats of arms. A few rust-holes; some ink annotations; lacking imprimatur leaf. bba July 23 (373) £240 [Adamson]

2d Ed. L, 1790. ("Thoroton's History of Nottinghamshire.") Vol I (of 3) only. 4to, later cloth; worn. With frontis & 33 plates. Library markings. DW Jan 29 (106) £60

Thorpe, Francis Newton. See: Lee & Thorpe

Thorpe, Thomas Bangs

— The Hive of "The Bee-Hunter".... NY, 1854. 12mo, orig cloth; spine stained, worn. Some foxing & browning; some leaves chipped or stained. wa Mar 5 (411) $65

Thory, Claude Antoine. See: Redoute & Thory

Three...

— Three Hundred Masterpieces of Chinese Painting in the Palace Museum. Taipei, 1959. Vols I-VI. bba Dec 19 (125) £80 [Ivens]

Threlkeld, Lancelot Edward

— An Australian Language as Spoken by the Awabakal, the People of Awaba or Lake Macquarie. Sydney, 1892. 8vo, orig mor, stamped Presentation Copy; rubbed. With folding map (some edge-fraying) & heliotype plate of an Awabaklin. O May 26 (189) $120

Thruston, Gates Phillips

— The Antiquities of Tennessee and the Adjacent States.... Cincinnati, 1890. 8vo, cloth; rubbed. Stamp on tp. wa Mar 5 (356) $110

Thucydides, 471?-400? B.C.

See also: Ashendene Press

— De bello Peloponnesiaco, libri octo. Venice: Aldus, May 1502. Bound with the Thucydides scholia from the Aldine Xenophon of 1503. Folio, 18th-cent mor gilt. Lacking a prelim blank. Porso-Sebright-Powis copy. C June 24 (286) £9,000 [Kraus]

Anr Ed. [Geneva]: Henricus Stephanus, 1588. 2 parts in 1 vol. Folio, contemp calf with arms of William Cecil, Lord Burghley; spine damaged at foot. Chatsworth copy. S July 1 (536) £4,000 [Quaritch]

Anr copy. Oldd half vellum; worn. sg Mar 12 (297) $475

Anr Ed. Frankfurt: heirs of Andreas Wechel, 1589. 8vo, vellum; browned. sg Mar 12 (295) $90

Anr Ed. Frankfurt: Andraes Wechel, 1594. Folio, 19th-cent calf gilt; worn. Chatsworth copy. S July 1 (537) £260 [Dimakarakos]

Anr Ed. Oxford, 1696. Folio, contemp blind-stamped vellum; rebacked, new endpapers. With 2 double-page maps. Some leaves with contemp ink annotations in margins. S Feb 25 (533) £150 [Delbridge]

Anr Ed. Amst., 1731. Folio, contemp calf with gilt arms of Dublin College; rebacked preserving part of orig spine, corners repaired, rubbed. With frontis & 2 folding maps, hand-colored in outline. Marginal worming & waterstaining; 1 leaf repaired. bba May 28 (453) £140 [Nicolas]

— The History of the Peloponnesian War. L, 1676. ("The History of the Grecian War....") Trans by Thomas Hobbes. Folio, contemp calf; rebacked, rubbed. LH Dec 11 (262) $150

Anr Ed. L, 1753. 2 vols. 4to, contemp sheep; joints worn through. Wormed at end. sg Mar 12 (296) $200

Thumtack, Tom. See: Squires, Frederick

Thunberg, Carl Peter, 1743-1828

— Voyages au Japon. Paris, An IV [1796]. 4 vols. 4to, 19th-cent half mor. With port & 28 plates. Some browning. Ck Oct 31 (315) £350

Thurah, Lauritz de

— Den Danske Vitruvius.... Copenhagen, 1746-49. 1st Ed. 2 vols. Folio, contemp calf gilt; joints & extremities worn, a few scrapes to sides. With frontis & 281 plates. Dampstaining to upper margins & tops of plates of both vols; borders of 3 plates shaved; 2 plates with discoloration. McCarty-Cooper copy. CNY Jan 25 (76) $6,500

Thurber, James

— The Last Flower: a Parable in Pictures. NY & L, 1939. Oblong 4to, pictorial bds (warped), in soiled d/j. F June 25 (174) $70

Anr copy. Pictorial bds, in torn d/j. Inscr Dec 1939, & with 3 pencil drawings of dog chasing a rabbit or a rabbit chasing a dog. sg Dec 12 (401) $1,500

Thurmair, Johann, Aventinus. See: Aventinus, Joannes

Thurston, Edgar —& Rangachari, K.

— Castes and Tribes of Southern India. Madras, 1909. 7 vols. Some underlining & notes in Vol I. K July 12 (287) $225

Anr copy. Cloth; worn. Foxed. wa Apr 9 (130) $250

Tibaldeo, Antonio, 1463-1537

— Opere. [Venice, c.1500]. 4to, mor gilt by Bedford. 30 lines; roman letter. Some worming at end. 132 leaves. Goff T-363. Huth copy. S Dec 5 (31) £2,300 [Burgess Browning]

Tice, Henry Allen

— Early Railroad Days in New Mexico. Santa Fe, 1965. One of 700. In d/j. cb Feb 13 (314) $60

Ticozzi, Stefano

— Dizionario dei pittori dal rinnovamento.... Milan, 1818. 2 vols. 8vo, half lea; worn. With 2 plates. SI Dec 5 (662) LIt400,000

Tiedemann, Friedrich

— Tabulae arteriarum corporis humani.... Carlsruhe, 1822. 2 vols, including Atlas. 4to & folio, contemp bds (text) & contemp half lea (Atlas); Atlas needs rebacking. With 38 hand-colored plates, each with outline plate. sg Nov 14 (144) $3,000

— Von der Verengung und Schliessung der Pulsadern in Krankheiten. Heidelberg, 1843. 4to, orig bds; extremities worn. With 3 folding hand-colored plates. Text browned; plates foxed. sg Nov 14 (146) $500

Tiemann & Company, George

— The American Armamentarium Chirurgicum. NY, [1879]. 8vo, modern cloth; worn. O Sept 24 (243) $250

Tietkens, William H.

— Journal of the Central Australian Exploring Expedition, 1889. Adelaide, 1891. 8vo, orig wraps. With folding map & colored geographical chart (hole in blank margin). C June 25 (271) £850 [Arnold]

— The Nullabor Plains and the West Boundary of the Province. Adelaide, 1889. 8vo, modern cloth. With litho folding map, which is loose. C June 25 (272) £450 [Baring]

— Paper Read before the Geographical Section of the British Association, Plymouth 1877. An Account of the Latest Exploring Expedition across Australia. L, [1877 or 1878]. 8vo, modern wraps. R. J. Maria copy. C June 25 (263) £2,000 [Quaritch/Hordern]

Tiffany Studios

— Tiffany Studios Collection of Antique Chinese Rugs. NY, [1908]. One of 1,000. 8vo, cloth. With colored frontis & 32 plates. sp Feb 6 (297) $57

Tilke, Max, 1869-1942

— Le Costume de l'Europe orientale. Berlin: Ernst Wasmuth, [1926]. 4to, cloth; worn, hinges cracked. With 96 color plates. Library markings but plates unmarked. sg Apr 2 (75) $325

Tilley, Frank

— Teapots and Tea. Newport, England, 1957. One of 1,000. 4to, orig cloth. sg Sept 6 (59) $375; sp June 18 (402) $135

Tillotson, John

— Picturesque Scenery in Wales. L, [1860]. 4to, orig cloth; worn & broken. With 38 plates. Some spotting. bba July 23 (374) £80 [Davies]

Timberlake, Henry

— Two Journeys to Jerusalem. L, 1730. 12mo, later half calf; rubbed. With frontis & 2 plates. Some leaves with minor tears & other defs. S July 1 (805) £220 [Sofer]

Timlin, William M.

— The Ship that Sailed to Mars. L, [1923]. 4to, orig half vellum. Lacking 4 plates. b Nov 18 (114) £100

Anr copy. Orig half vellum, in repaired d/j. With calligraphic text & 48 colored plates. cb Dec 5 (134) $1,400

Anr copy. Orig half vellum. sg Jan 30 (177) $600

Anr copy. Orig half vellum. Epstein copy. sg Apr 30 (458) $850

Timms, W. H.

— Twelve Coloured Views of Reading.... Reading, 1823. Oblong 4to, modern half mor. With 12 colored views. Caption to Plate 9 partly erased. bba Sept 19 (256) £1,500 [Traylen]

Timoni, Alexndre

— Nouvelles promenades dans le Bosphore.... Pera de Constantinople, 1844. 2 vols. 8vo, half mor; Vol II lower cover dampstained. With port. Vol II lacking & supplied in facsimile; library stamps erased; some discoloration. S June 30 (206) £380 [Ther]

Timperlake, J.

— Illustrated Toronto: Past and Present. Toronto, 1877. 8vo, cloth. sp Feb 6 (439) $85

Timperley, C. H.

— Encyclopaedia of Literary and Typographical Anecdote.... L, 1842. 2d Ed. cb Oct 17 (923) $100

Ting, Wallasse

— Hot and Sour Soup. [N.p.: Sam Francis Foundation, 1969]. One of 1,050. Folio, unbound as issued in wraps. With 22 color lithos. DW Mar 11 (561) £170

— One-Cent Life. Berne, 1964. Folio, unsewn in orig cloth folder & d/j; head of spine torn. P June 25 (634) $1,200

Tinker, Chauncey Brewster, 1876-1963

— The Wedgwood Medallion of Samuel Johnson.... Cambr., Mass., 1926. One of 385. Designed by Bruce Rogers. 4to, half cloth. With 8 plates. sg Jan 30 (178) $150

Tinker Library, Chauncey Brewster

— The Tinker Library; Bibliographical Catalogue. New Haven, [1959]. Compiled by

Robert Metzdorf. sp Sept 22 (457) $95

Tinkham, George H.

— A History of Stockton.... San Francisco, 1880. 8vo, cloth; front hinge cracked, shaken. With 2 mtd photographic plates, 4 ports & 3 leaves of woodcut views. NH Aug 23 (118) $180

Tipping, Henry Avray

— English Gardens. L, 1925. Folio, half cloth. cb Nov 21 (221) $50

— English Homes. L, 1920-34. 7 (of 9) vols. Orig cloth. S Feb 11 (338) £550 [Richardson]

Anr Ed. L, 1921-37. 8 (of 9) vols. Folio, orig cloth. Some waterstains. Sold w.a.f. b Mar 11 (66) £75

Anr copy. 8 (of 9) vols. CNY Jan 25 (77) $600

Anr copy. 9 vols. Folio, orig cloth, 5 vols in worn d/js. S May 13 (546) £600 [Sims Reed]

— Grinling Gibbons and the Woodwork of his Age. L, 1914. Folio, orig half cloth; worn. Library markings. sg Feb 6 (281) $120

Tipping, Marjorie

— Eugene von Guerard's Australian Landscapes. Melbourne, 1975. One of 1,000, sgd. Folio, cloth. kh Nov 11 (236) A$100

Tiraboschi, Girolamo, 1731-94

— Storia della letteratura italiana. Modena, 1787-94. 8 vols in 9. 4to, contemp half vellum; worn. Ck Nov 1 (512) £230

Titmarsh, M. A. See: Thackeray, William Makepeace

Toaldo, Giuseppe

— Della vera influenze degli astri.... Padua, 1770. 4to, bds. With folding plate & 5 folding tables. Minor defs. SI Dec 5 (663) LIt1,500,000

Tod, George

— Plans, Elevations and Sections, of Hot-Houses, Green-houses.... L, 1807. Folio, later half calf; def. With 27 hand-colored plate, watermarked 1802. C May 20 (132) £1,100 [Spelman]

Todd, Frank Morton

— The Story of the Exposition. NY, 1921. 5 vols. 4to, cloth. cb Sept 12 (169) $90

Todd, Henry John, 1763-1845

— The History of the College of Bonhommes, at Ashridge.... L, 1823. Folio, contemp half mor gilt; joints starting, front hinge cracked. sg May 7 (201) $500

Todd, Ruthven Todd

— Fifteen Poems, A Collaboration using the Printing Methods of William Blake. NY: Atelier 17, 1951. Folio, loose as issued. With tp, 11 etchings & 7 surface prints (from the projected set of 30).. CNY May 12 (484) $3,800

Toesca, Pietro

— La pittura e la miniatura nella Lombardia. Milan, 1912. 4to, orig cloth; spine torn at head. S Feb 11 (219) £150 [Creed]

Toland, John, 1670-1722

— Anglia Libera. l, 1701. 8vo, contemp sheep; front cover detached. Some foxing. sg Mar 12 (297) $200

Tolfrey, Frederic

— Jones' Guide to Norway, and Salmon-Fisher's Pocket Companion. L, 1848. 16mo, cloth; worn & shaken. With frontis, pictorial title & 8 hand-colored plates. Koopman copy. O Oct 29 (305) $3,400

— The Sportsman in Canada. L, 1845. 2 vols. 8vo, modern half mor gilt. cb Dec 5 (136) $375

Tolkien, John Ronald Reuel

— Farmer Giles of Ham. Bost, 1950. 1st American Ed. In chipped d/j. pba July 9 (275) $50

— The Hobbit. L, 1937. 1st Ed. In d/j with chip at top edge of lower cover. Inscr to members of the Jennings family & sgd with initials, Oct 1937. Manney copy. P Oct 11 (297) $18,000

— The Lord of the Rings. Bost., 1954-56. 1st American Ed. 3 vols. In d/js. sg June 11 (305) $900

1st Ed. L, 1954-55. 3 vols. Orig cloth, in d/js. Inscr in Feanorian script. Manney copy. P Oct 11 (298) $20,000

Anr copy. In d/js. P Oct 11 (299) $8,500

India paper Ed. L, 1969. 3 vols. S May 13 (674) £330 [Joliffe]

— The Return of the King. L, 1955. In d/j. With folding map at end. DW Apr 8 (563) £65

Toller, Ernst, 1893-1939. See: Nonesuch Press

Tollius, Jacobus

— Epistolae itinerariae. Amst., 1700. 1st Ed. 4to, contemp lea. With engraved title & 16 plates. HH May 12 (786) DM1,000

Tolson, Francis

— Hermathenae or Moral Emblems and the Ethnick Tales. L, [c.1740]. Vol I [all pbd]. 8vo, contemp calf; rebacked. Lacking 1 prelim leaf. SI Dec 5 (664) LIt250,000

Tolstoy, Leo, 1828-1910
See also: Limited Editions Club
— Rasskasy o Zhivotnykh. Moscow: Academia, 1932. Half cloth; front joint cracked. sg Jan 10 (179) $100
— What Men Live By. Belvedere CA: Allen Press, 1951. One of 150. wa Mar 5 (90) $160

Tomasini, Jacopo Filippo
— Petrarcha redivivus. Padua, 1635. 4to, contemp vellum. With engraved title, 9 engraved & 9 woodcut ports & illusts. With 6 pages of annotations at end in a contemp hand. Thick paper copy. S July 9 (1458) £320 [Maggs]

Tomb...
— The Tomb of Ramses VI. [NY, 1954]. 2 vols. Folio, cloth. Bollingen Series XL. wa Feb 20 (167) $55

Tombeau...
— Le Tombeau de Theophile Gautier. Paris: Alphonse Lemerre, 1873. 4to, mor extra by Tallibart. With 16 A Ls s or A Ns s by the contributors tipped in onto inserted leaves of heavy paper. CNY Dec 5 (444) $500

Tombleson, William —&
Fearnside, William Gray
— Eighty Picturesque Views on the Thames and Medway. L, [1834]. 4to, orig cloth; upper joint restored, lower joint split. With engraved title & dedication, folding panoramic map & 79 plates. Engraved title frayed; some browning; lacking tp. b June 22 (278) £360

Anr copy. Contemp mor; spine faded. With engraved title, dedication & 79 plates. bba Jan 30 (372) £400 [Burden]

Anr copy. Disbound. With engraved title, engraved dedication leaf, folding panorama & 79 plates. K Sept 29 (414) $600

Anr copy. Orig cloth; rubbed, edges worn, spine torn. With engraved title & 79 plates. Lacking folding panorama; marginal soiling & dampstaining. pn Dec 12 (320) £380

Anr copy. Later half lea gilt; edges rubbed. Lacking folding panorama; some browning & marginal soiling. pn Dec 12 (321) £420 [Ventnor]

Anr copy. Contemp cloth; rubbed, spine repaired with tape. With engraved title, dedication & 79 plates. Lacking panorama; engraved title spotted. pn Apr 23 (283) £400 [Walford]

Anr copy. Contemp half calf gilt. With engraved title, dedication, folding panorama & 79 plates. Panorama with pieces torn from margin; 2 plates marginally torn, 1 with loss of large section. pn June 1 (281) £340 [Russell]

Anr copy. Orig lea; rebacked & repaired. With engraved title, dedication & 78 (of 79) plates. Lacking panorama; some soiling. pn June 11 (282) £300 [Map House]

Anr Ed. L, [c.1845]. 4to, orig cloth. With 80 plates, including folding panorama. Ck May 15 (167) £480

Anr copy. Orig mor gilt; spine def, rubbed, lacking front free endpaper. With half-title & 80 plates. Ink stains on frontis verso; dampstain to corner of a few plates; marginal foxing or to tissue guards. pnL Nov 20 (121) £400

— The Upper Rhine. L, [1834]. 8vo, later cloth; covers stained. With engraved title, folding map & 60 plates. bba May 14 (295) £210 [Davies]
— Views of the Rhine. L, 1832. 8vo, contemp half calf; rubbed. With engraved title, folding panorama & 68 plates. Lacking title & contents leaf. Sold w.a.f. bba Oct 24 (308) £80 [B. Bailey]

Anr copy. Contemp half mor gilt; rubbed. With engraved title & 68 plates. Some spotting & waterstaining. DW Dec 11 (77) £105

Anr copy. Contemp half calf; edges rubbed. With engraved title & 68 plates only. Lacking folding panorama; some spotting. pn Sept 12 (342) £110

Anr copy. Contemp calf gilt; rubbed, head of spine worn. With engraved title, 68 plates & folding panorama. Some spotting & browning. pn Dec 12 (370) £110

Anr copy. Contemp half calf; worn. With engraved title & 132 (of 137) plates, panorama & map. pnE Dec 4 (253) £280

Anr Ed. L, 1832-[34]. 2 vols, including The Upper Rhine. 8vo, orig cloth; spine def. With engraved titles, 137 plates, folding map & large folding panorama. Some soiling. pn Dec 12 (369) £240

Tomes, Robert, 1817-82
— Battles of America by Sea and Land.... NY, [1878]. 5 parts in 3 vols. 4to, orig half mor. Some dampstaining to top margins. bbc Apr 27 (83) $100
— The War with the South.... NY, [1862]. 4to, half mor gilt. sg Dec 5 (257) $325

Tomkins, C. F. —&
Planche, James Robinson, 1796-1880
— Twelve Designs for the Costume of Shakespeare's Richard the Third. L, 1830. 4to, orig bds; rebacked. With litho title & 13 plates, 5 hand-colored. sg Oct 17 (82) $600

Tomkins, Peltro William. See: Ottley & Tomkins

Tomlinson, Charles, 1808-97

— Cyclopaedia of Useful Arts.... L & NY, 1854. 2 vols. 8vo, orig cloth; text of Vol I disbound. Lacking about half the plates. bbc Sept 23 (278) $50

Tomlinson, Henry Major, 1873-1958

— The Sea and the Jungle. NY, 1930. cb Sept 19 (207) $50

Anr copy. Calf extra by Riviere. pba Aug 20 (214) $200

Anr copy. In chipped d/j. sp Apr 16 (193) $60

— War Books: A Lecture Given at Manchester University.... Cleveland: The Rowfant Club, 1930. One of 215. cb Oct 17 (926) $50

Toms, William Henry. See: Badeslade & Toms

Tonti, Henri de, 1650-1704
See also: Caxton Club

— An Account of Monsieur de la Salle's Last Expedition...in North America.... L, 1698. 1st Ed in English. 8vo, contemp calf; rebacked, corners renewed. Some browning; stamp of Windsor Castle, Chapter Library. CNY Oct 8 (244) $3,500

Tooke, John Horne, 1736-1812

— Epea Ptereonta. Or, the Diversions of Purley. L, 1798-1805. 2d Ed of Vol I, 1st Ed of Vol II. 2 vols. 4to, later half lea; extremities worn. O July 14 (188) $150

Tooley, Ronald Vere

— Some English Books with Coloured Plates.... L, [1954]. ("English Books with Coloured Plates....") In d/j. cb Oct 17 (927) $60

Anr copy. In chipped d/j. sg Oct 31 (316) $90

Torio de la Riva, Torquato

— Arte de escriber por reglas y con muestras.... Madrid, 1798. 1st Ed. Folio, contemp sheep; rubbed. With port & 58 plates. bba May 28 (295) £250 [Poel]

Torreilles, Pierre

— Errantes Graminees. Paris, 1971. One of 103 with a colored litho. Illus by Joan Miro. Mor mosaic bdg with star wheels of different colors. CGen Nov 18 (468) SF8,000

Torrens, Robert

— Colonisation of South Australia. L, 1835. 8vo, contemp half calf. With folding map hand-colored in outline. Some spotting at beginning & end. S June 25 (154) £300 [Quaritch]

Torrentinus, Hermannus

— Elucidarius carminum & historiarum.... [Paris: Denis Roce, 1510 or later]. 4to, modern lea. Tear in K3; wormed throughout, affecting text; marginal stains to last leaf. pn June 11 (157) £140

Torres, Bartolome, Bishop of the Canary Islands

— Commentaria in decem et septem quaestiones primae partis Sancti Thomae de ineffabili trinitatis mysterio. Alcala de Henares: Quirinus Gerardus for Juan Gutierrez, 1583. Folio, contemp vellum. sg Oct 24 (322) $275

Torriano, Hugh Arthur. See: Marchmont, Frederick

Torricelli, Evangelista, 1608-47

— Opera geometrica. Florence, 1644. ("De sphaera et solidis sphaeralibus; De motu gravium; De dimensione parabolae....") 1st Ed. 2 parts in 1 vol. 4to, 18th-cent calf; worn. Some worming with small affect on text; half-title laid down; prelims to Part 2 soiled. Ck Nov 29 (245) £1,500

Tortebat, Francois

— Abrege d'anatomie accommode aux arts de peinture et de sculpture. Paris, 1760. Folio, loose in old wraps. With engraved title & 10 plates. Marginal spotting & soiling. bba Sept 5 (310) £400 [M. Phelps]

Tory, Geofroy, 1480?-1533?
See also: Grolier Club

— Itinerarium Provinciarum omnium Antonini Augusti. Paris: Henri Estienne, [not before 19 Aug 1512]. 16mo, 18th-cent calf gilt; worn. With folding woodcut map. Extreme upper blank margin of tp repaired; short split in map, which is inserted on a stub; some staining. C Dec 16 (86) £5,000 [Fletcher]

Totten, George Oakley

— Maya Architecture. Wash., [1926]. Folio, cloth; frontis loose. Library markings but plates unmarked. sg Apr 2 (276) $110

Touchstone, Geoffrey, Pseud.

— Race Horses. L, 1890. Oblong folio, orig cloth; rubbed & stained. With colored title & 60 colored plates. bba Sept 5 (184) £500 [Corbett]

Toulouse-Lautrec, Henri de, 1864-1901

— Douze Lithographies. Paris, [1948]. Folio, loose as issued in half cloth portfolio. sg Feb 6 (284) $275

— Elles. Monte Carlo: Andre Sauret, [1952]. Pictorial wraps. With 11 color lithos. wa Mar 5 (624) $60

Tournefort, Joseph Pitton de

— Institutiones rei herbariae. Paris, 1700-[3]. 3 vols. 4to, contemp calf; worn. With engraved titles to Vols II & III & 476 plates. S July 1 (928) £250 [Chelsea]

— Relation d'une voyage du Levant.... Amst., 1718. 2 vols in 1. 4to, contemp calf; worn. With 87 mostly full-page plates & 46 engraved illusts in the text. Tear at foremargin of Plate 29 in Vol I; I2 in Vol I torn at foot affecting footnote; some browning. S June 30 (208) £1,700 [Consolidated Real]

— A Voyage into the Levant. L, 1741. Vols I & II (of 3). 8vo, calf; worn & stained. Sold w.a.f. O Feb 25 (190) $160

Anr copy. 3 vols. 8vo, contemp half calf; rubbed, 1 vol rebacked with mor. With 151 (of 152) plates & maps. Tear to 1 plate; Vol III title soiled; last leaf in Vol II torn & with fore-margins cut down. S June 30 (422) £2,000 [Gonul]

Toussaint, Franz. See: Golden Cockerel Press

Tower, Charlemagne

— The Charlemagne Tower Collection of American Colonial Laws. Phila., 1890. 4to, cloth; worn, spine frayed. O Sept 24 (246) $50

Townshend, Samuel Nugent

— Colorado: Its Agriculture, Stock-feeding, Scenery, and Shooting. L, 1879. 8vo, orig cloth; front cover & 1st few leaves with minor dampstaining. sg June 18 (529) $110

Tradescant, John

— Musaeum Tradescantianum.... L: John Grismond for Nathanael Brooke, 1656. 8vo, calf gilt by Mackenzie; rebacked. Lacking frontis & 2 ports. K July 12 (502) $350

Traite...

— Traite des batiments propres a loger les animaux, qui sont necessaires a l'economie rurale. Leipzig, 1802. Folio, early bds; rebacked. With 50 plates. C June 24 (140) £700 [Marlborough]

— Traite theoretique et pratique du jeu des echecs.... Paris, 1786. 12mo, modern half mor. Half-title soiled; A1 repaired at inner margin. Ck May 8 (86) £60

— Traite Theorique et Practique du Jeu des Echecs par une Societe d'Amateurs. Paris, 1775. 8vo, contemp calf gilt; extremities rubbed. Ck May 8 (85) £190

Traits. See: Grabhorn Printing

Trakl, Georg, 1887-1914

— Der Herbst des Einsamen. Munich, 1920. One of 350. Mor gilt. B May 12 (242) HF850

Trapnell, Alfred

— A Catalogue of Bristol and Plymouth Porcelain. L, 1912. One of 250. 4to, orig wraps. DW Mar 11 (7784) £75

Trapwit, Tommy. See: Be Merry...

Travels...

— The Travels of Tom Thumb over England and Wales. L, 1746. 12mo, later calf; extremities rubbed. Lacking map. bba July 23 (137) £100 [Quaritch]

Traven, B.

— The Treasure of the Sierra Madre. NY, 1935. 1st American Ed. In d/j with spine panel chipped. sg June 11 (306) $325

Travers, William T. L., 1819-1903. See: Barraud & Travers

Treaties

— A Treaty of Amity and of Commerce between the United States of America, and his Majesty, the King of Prussia. L, 1786. 8vo, disbound, restitched into old wraps. P June 16 (150) $12,000

Trebeck, George. See: Moorcroft & Trebeck

Tredgold, Thomas

— Elementary Principles of Carpentry. L, 1870. 4to, cloth; worn & shaken. O Jan 14 (186) $70

Trelawny, Edward John, 1792-1881

— Recollections of the Last Days of Shelley and Byron. L, 1878. ("Records of Shelley, Byron, and the Author.") 2 vols. 8vo, cloth. cb Oct 17 (930) $120

Trembley, Abraham, 1700-84

— Memoires pour servir a l'histoire d'un genre de polypes d'eau douce.... Leiden, 1744. 8vo, contemp half vellum; rubbed. Many text leaves waterstained. bba Sept 5 (311) £95 [Bifolco]

Trenkwald, Hermann. See: Sarre & Trenkwald

Trent, Council of

— Canones et decreta sacrosancti oecumenici, et generalis Concilii Tridentini. Antwerp: Christopher Plantin, 1586. 8vo, contemp vellum; soiled. bba May 28 (435) £55 [Maggs]

Tresham, Henry —& Others

— The British Gallery of Pictures.... L, [c.1808]. Folio, contemp mor gilt; rubbed. With 20 plates. bba Feb 13 (243) £220 [Vitale]

Trevelyan, Sir George Otto. See: Clemens's copy, Samuel Langhorne

Trevers, Joseph

— An Essay to the Restoring of our Decayed Trade. L, 1675. 1st Ed. 4to, disbound. sg Mar 12 (299) $275

Trew, Christoph Jakob

— Hortus nitidissimis. Nuremberg, 1750-86. 3 vols in 2. Folio, 18th-cent half calf; worn. With 58 hand-colored plates only. Plate 50 shaved at sides; short marginal tear & small stain on Plate 58. P Dec 12 (92) $20,000

Trier

— Undergerichts Ordnung der Ertzstiffts Thrier. Mainz: Ivo Schoeffer, 1537. 4to, disbound. Lower outer corner of D2 torn away & missing text supplied in Ms facsimile; tear in text of E3; some browning. S Dec 5 (208) £450 [Reiss & Auvermann]

Triggs, Henry Inigo

— Formal Gardens in England and Scotland. L, 1902. 2 vols. Folio modern half mor. With 122 plates. Some spotting. pn Dec 12 (171) £190

Anr copy. 3 parts. Folio, loose in half cloth portfolios as issued. sg Apr 2 (279) $250

Anr copy. Loose as issued in orig portfolios. sp Feb 6 (176) $170

Trimmer, Mary. See: Fore-Edge Paintings

Trimmer, Sarah

— Fabulous Histories, or History of the Robins. L: N. Hailes, 1821. 12mo, later half calf; joints repaired. Some spotting. bba July 23 (139) £55 [Ginnan]

Trinum Marinum...

— Trinum Marinum: oder, die an einander hangende drey Meer. Pontus Euxinus, Propontis, cum Archipelago.... Augsburg: Anthonius Nepperschmid for Jacob Enderlin, 1693. Bound with: Arca temporum mundi reserata.... Augsburg, 1693. Folio, contemp calf; worn. First work with 24 maps & views on 17 plates; 2d work with 5 views & natural-history subjects on 3 plates. S Nov 21 (252) £2,000 [Atabey]

Tripp, C.E. See: Grabhorn Printing

Tripp, F. E.

— British Mosses, their Homes, Aspects, Structure and Uses.... L, 1888. 2 vols. 4to, orig cloth; 1 hinge worn. bba Sept 5 (116) £50 [Town]

Trissino, Giovanni Giorgio, 1478-1550

— La Italia liberata da Gotthi. Rome & Venice, 1547-48. 1st Ed. 3 vols. 8vo, contemp vellum. Some stains. S Dec 5 (209) £2,200 [Goldschmidt]

Tristram, Ernest William —& Bardswell, Monica

— English Medieval Wall Painting: The Twelfth Century. L, 1944. Folio, cloth. With 106 plates. Library markings, but plates unmarked. sg Feb 6 (286) $325

Tristram, Ernest William —& Bardswell, Minoca

— English Medieval Wall Painting.... L, 1944-50. Vol I only. Cloth. sg Apr 2 (280) $300

Tristram, W. Outram

— Coaching Days and Coaching Ways. L, 1893. One of 250. 4to, later half mor; faded & rubbed; joints cracking. cb Sept 26 (200) $50

Anr copy. Modern calf gilt; upper cover scuffed. Ck Sept 6 (53) £60

Trithemius, Joannes, 1462-1516

— Polygraphie et universelle escriture cabalistique.... Paris: Kerver, 1561. Bound at end is G. de Collange. Tables et figures planispheriques, extensives & dilatives des recte & averse, servantes a l'universelle intelligence de toutes escritures. 4to, half mor. B Nov 1 (662) HF3,600

1st Ed in French. 3 parts in 1 vol. 4to, moder half calf; head of spine repaired. With 13 woodcuts with movable parts. Library stamps on verso. bba Jan 16 (222) £2,200 [J. Franks]

— Steganographia: hoc est: ars per occultam scripturam animi voluntatem absentibus.... Darmstadt, 1621. 2 parts in 1 vol. 4to, vellum. Annotations; browning. SI June 10 (1026) LIt850,000

Trittenheim, Johannes. See: Trithemius, Joannes

Troil, Uno von, 1746-1803

— Letters on Iceland. L, 1780. 8vo, contemp sheep; lacking front free endpaper. Tp with tear repaired & top edge excised. sg May 21 (106) $80

Trollope, Anthony, 1815-82

— The Claverings. L, 1867. 1st English Ed in Book form. 2 vols. 8vo, orig cloth; worn, 1 hinge split. Some stains. S July 21 (76) £500 [Cox]

— Doctor Thorne. NY, 1858. 1st American Ed. 8vo, orig cloth. K Dec 1 (409) $160

Anr copy. Orig cloth; tips & corners worn. Foxed. wa Mar 5 (250) $65

— The Duke's Children. L, 1880. 1st Ed. 3

vols. 8vo, later half calf; rubbed. bba Jan 30 (214) £50 [Johnson]

— The Fixed Period. Leipzig: Tauchnitz, 1882. 2 vols. 8vo, orig cloth. L Feb 27 (229) £100

— The Golden Lion of Granpere. NY, 1872. 1st American Ed. 8vo, orig cloth; soiled, head of spine rubbed. With frontis & 7 plates. pn Dec 12 (254) £50

— How the "Mastiffs" Went to Iceland. L, 1878. 1st Ed. 4to, orig cloth; joints cracked. With colored frontis map, 2 mtd photographs & 14 lithos. Some spotting. S Feb 25 (420) £320 [Hannas]

— Is he Popenjoy. L, 1878. 1st Ed in Book form. 3 vols. 8vo, orig cloth; recased with new endpapers, rubbed, spines frayed. Shaken, some leaves starting. wd Dec 12 (460) $350

— Lady Anna. L, 1874. 1st English Ed in Book form. 2 vols. 8vo, orig cloth; rebacked, orig spines preserved, rubbed. bba Apr 30 (129) £200 [Swales]

— The Last Chronicle of Barset. L, [1866-67]. 1st Ed, in orig 32 parts. 8vo, orig wraps; soiled. Epstein copy. sg Apr 30 (459) $3,000

1st English Ed in Book form. L, 1867. 2 vols. 8vo, orig cloth, rebacked. bba Oct 24 (116) £50 [Culley]

Anr copy. Orig cloth. L Feb 27 (228) £190

Anr copy. Orig cloth; worn & soiled. NH Aug 23 (412) $200

Anr copy. Contemp half mor by W. J. Scopes. With 32 plates. Some foxing; margin to tp clipped at top. wa Mar 5 (86) $130

— Miss Mackenzie. L, 1865. 1st Ed. 2 vols. 8vo, orig cloth; rubbed. bba Apr 30 (124) £350 [Blackwell]

— Mr. Scarborough's Family. L, 1883. 1st Ed in Book form. 3 vols. 8vo, orig cloth; recased & repaired. bba July 9 (167) £220 [Sotheran]

— Orley Farm. L, 1862. 1st Ed in Book form, Issue not specified. 2 vols. 8vo, contemp half calf; worn & rubbed, rebacked. cb Dec 19 (171) $110

Vol I, 4th Issue; Vol II, 3d Issue. Orig cloth; worn. bba Apr 30 (122) £50 [Culley]

— Phineas Finn. L, 1869. 1st English Ed in Book form. 2 vols. 8vo, orig cloth; rubbed & soiled. bba Apr 30 (126) £130 [Yablon]

— Phineas Redux. L, 1874. 1st Ed in Book form. 2 vols. 8vo, orig cloth; rebacked, orig spine preserved. With 24 plates. Vol II lacking final blank. bba Apr 30 (128) £140 [Ash]

— The Prime Minister. L, 1876. 1st English Ed in Book form. 4 vols. 8vo, orig cloth; head and foot of each spine repaired. bba Apr 30 (130) £400 [Culley]

— The Small House at Allington. L, 1864. 1st Ed in Book form. 2 vols. 8vo, orig cloth; rebacked, orig spines preserved. bba Apr 30 (123) £150 [Ash]

— The Struggles of Brown, Jones, and Robinson. L, 1870. 1st English Ed in Book form. 8vo, orig cloth; rebacked, orig spine preserved. bba Apr 30 (127) £170 [Collinge & Clark]

— Travelling Sketches. L, 1866. 1st Ed in Book form. 8vo, orig cloth. Lacking pbr's cat; some spotting. bba July 9 (166) £50 [Sotheran]

— Works. Phila., 1900-2. Royal Ed, one of 1,250. 30 vols. 8vo, mor gilt; rubbed & stained. Some plates in several states. Water damage causing rippling & staining; some soiling. P June 17 (356) $1,600

Anr Ed. L, 1948-54. 15 vols. Orig cloth; a few covers stained. S July 1 (1013) £180 [Sotheran]

Trombelli, Giovanni Cristostomo, 1697-1784

— Arte di conoscere l'Eta de Codici Latini e Italiani. Bologna, 1756. 4to, half cloth. With 2 plates repaired. SI June 10 (1027) LIt400,000

Trotsky, Leon, 1877-1940

— The Revolution Betrayed. Garden City, 1937. 1st American Ed. Cloth; hinges starting, front pastedown worn. sg Mar 5 (307) $300

1st Ed. Front hinge cracked. Inscr. Epstein copy. sg Apr 30 (460) $2,400

Trotter, William Edward

— Select Illustrated Topography of Thirty Miles Round London. L, 1839. 8vo, orig cloth; spine & extremities worn. With frontis & 32 (of 33) plates. Lacking map. DW May 13 (101) £50

Trucchi, Lorenza

— Francis Bacon. NY: Abrams, [1975]. In d/j. DW Mar 11 (562) £75

True...

— A True Account of the Design and Advantages of the South-Sea Trade. L, 1711. 8vo, disbound, new stitching. Lacking final blank. CNY Oct 8 (86) $900

Truesdell, Winfred Porter

— Engraved and Lithographed Portraits of Abraham Lincoln. Champlain: Pvtly ptd at Troutsdale Press, 1933. One of 200 on "suede laid" paper. Vol II [all pbd]. 4to, bds. This copy with 26 prelim leaves. bbc June 29 (252) $400

Trulhar, Joseph. See: Narodni a Universitni Knihovna, Prague

Truman, Harry S.

— Memoirs. Garden City, NY, [1955-56]. 2 vols. In d/js. Both vols inscr. cb Feb 12 (130) $300

Anr Ed. Garden City, [1955-56]. 2 vols. In d/js. Sgd. wa Mar 5 (306) $130

Trumbull, John, 1750-1820

— M'Fingal: A Modern Epic Poem.... NY, 1795. 8vo, contemp half calf; worn, spine split. wa Sept 26 (405) $450

Trusler, John, 1735-1820

— A Descriptive Account of the Islands lately Discovered in the South-Seas.... L, 1778. 8vo, contemp calf; outer joints cracked, worn. CNY Oct 8 (246) $4,200

— The Progress of Man and Society. L, 1791. Illus by John Bewick. 12mo, modern half calf incorporating old bds; front hinges strengthened. bba July 23 (397) £65 [Abbey]

Tschichold, Jan

See also: Roh & Tschichold

— Designing Books. NY, [n.d.]. In d/j. cb Oct 17 (934) $110

Tschudi, Juan Diego de. See: Rivero & Tschudi

Tuer, Andrew White, 1838-1900

— Bartolozzi and his Works.... L, 1885. 8vo, orig vellum; ties lacking. sg Feb 6 (287) $60

— The Book of Delightful and Strange Designs of the Art of the Japanese Stencil-Cutter. L: Leadenhall Press, [1893]. Oblong 8vo, later cloth; rubbed. Ltd Ed. bba July 9 (380) £65 [Kay Books]

— History of the Horn-Book. L, 1896. 2 vols. 4to, vellum gilt; worn & soiled. With 5 (of 7) facsimile horn-books & battledores. O Sept 24 (248) $75

Anr Ed. L, 1897. 2 vols. 4to, cloth; soiled, front joint split, 1 ad leaf detached. Pocket at end contains 3 facsimile horn books on oak, on card & on ivory. wa Mar 5 (109) $130

— London Cries. L, 1883. 4to, orig half cloth. Some spotting at beginning and end. bba Oct 10 (130) £150 [Finney]; bba Jan 30 (408) £150 [Kitazawa]

— Luxurious Bathing. L, 1879. 8vo, vellum; soiled. DW Mar 4 (95) £80

Tull, Jethro, 1671-1741

— The New Horse-Houghing Husbandry.... Dublin, 1723. ("The Horse-Hoing Husbandry....") 8vo, contemp bds; rebacked, rubbed. bba Sept 5 (117) £130 [Town]

Anr Ed. L, 1829. 8vo, orig cloth. bba June 11 (91) £85 [Henly]

Tully, Richard

— Narrative of a Ten Years' Residence at Tripoli in Africa. L, 1817. 2d Ed. 4to, contemp calf; repaired at fold. With hand-colored frontis, 6 plates & folding map. Some spotting; folding plate repaired at fold. Ck May 15 (168) £380

Tulpius, Nicolaus

— Observationum medicarum, libri tres.... Amst., 1672. ("Observationes medicae.") 3d Ed. 8vo, contemp vellum; rear cover warped. sg Nov 14 (148) $650

Turnbull, David

— Travels in the West. L, 1840. 8vo, cloth. Library markings. sg June 18 (531) $90

Turnbull, George

— A Treatise on Ancient Painting. L, 1740. 1st Ed. Folio, disbound. With 54 plates. Tp torn & repaired. bba May 14 (81) £280 [Selzer & Selzer]

Turnbull, John, fl.1800-13

— A Voyage Round the World.... L, 1813. 2d Ed. 4to, later half lea; backstrip rubbed. Lacking half-title; lower margin of 1 leaf lost; general discoloration; last 30 leaves with ink stain in outer blank margin. Hobill Cole copy. kh Nov 11 (676) A$340

Anr copy. Contemp mor gilt; corners restored. Lacking half-title. S June 25 (163) £1,000 [McCormick]

Turnbull, Robert J.

— Bibliography of South Carolina. Charlottesville, Va., [1956-60]. 5 vols, without Index. K Sept 29 (402) $275

Turner, A. A.

— Villas on the Hudson. NY, 1860. Oblong folio, orig cloth; rebacked. With 31 tinted photographic plates & 20 measured diagram plates. Paper of floor plans browned; some boxing. Schlosser copy. P June 18 (596) $2,750

Turner, Charles C.

— Aerial Navigation of To-Day. Phila., 1910. cb Nov 7 (99) $130

Turner, Dawson

— Fuci; or, Coloured Figures and Descriptions.... L, 1808-19. 4 vols. 4to, contemp half calf; joints split, some covers loose. With 261 hand-colored plates, including 3 not called for. Library stamps, not affecting plates; many plates shaved. pn Mar 19 (343) £1,300 [Junk]

Turner, Joseph M. W., 1775-1851

— Liber Fluviorum, or River Scenery of France. L, 1853. 8vo, cloth; worn & rubbed. cb Sept 26 (201) $130

— Picturesque Views on the Southern Coast of England. L, 1814-26. 2 vols in 1. 4to, contemp calf gilt; some scuffing. With 48 plates.. C Oct 30 (120) £500 [Marlborough]

Anr Ed. L, 1826. 2 vols in 1. 4to, contemp half mor; rubbed, upper joints splitting. With 48 plates. Sold w.a.f. bba Apr 30 (20) £350 [Burden]

Anr copy. 2 vols. 4to, orig mor gilt; rubbed. cb Sept 26 (202) $8950

Anr copy. 2 vols in 1. 4to, contemp half mor; hinges weak. With 80 plates. P June 18 (502) $900

— Picturesque Views in England and Wales. L, 1838. 2 vols. 4to, contemp half mor gilt. With 96 plates. Some plates browned or with light stain in lower outer corner. L Nov 14 (128) £1,200

— The Rivers of France. L, 1837. 4to, half mor; rubbed. With 60 plates. pnE Dec 4 (78) £80

— The Turner Gallery: a Series of Sixty Engravings.... L, 1875. Folio, contemp half mor; rubbed. With port & 60 plates on india paper mtd. Some marginal spotting. Ck Nov 29 (320) £400

Anr Ed. NY, [c.1880]. Bound in 2 vols. Folio, half mor; worn. With engraved title & 120 plates. Library markings. sg Apr 2 (281) $850

Turner, Samuel, 1749?-1802

— An Account of an Embassy to the Court of the Teshoo Lama, in Tibet. L, 1800. 1st Ed. 4to, old bds with recent lea backstrip. With folding map & 13 plates. Some spotting; old library stamps. DW Oct 2 (77) £280

Anr copy. Contemp calf; upper cover detached, lower joint broken, covers marked with sticky tape, spine worn. Some dampstaining. S Nov 15 (1304) £400 [Blackwell]

2d Ed. L, 1806. 4to, later mor by the Rose Bindery; rubbed & dampstained. With 13 plates & folding map. Some leaves repaired, with loss; musty. Sold w.a.f. O Feb 25 (193) $600

— Ambasceria au Thibet e al Butan. Paris, 1800. 12mo, contemp half lea; rubbed. With folding map & 14 plates. SI Dec 5 (674) LIt250,000

Turner, William, d.1568

— A New Herball, wherein are Contained the Names of Herbes.... L: Steven Mierdman, 1551. ("A New Herball, wherin are Conteyned the Names of Herbes....") Bound with: Turner. The Seconde Parte....Cologne: Arnold Birckman, 1562. And: The Thirde Parte.... Cologne: Arnold Birckman, 1568. Folio, 19th-cent lea with metal fittings. Black letter. First work with tp lacking & tp from Cologne 1568 Ed supplied in its stead & wormed, repaired tears to J2 & O6; 2d work partly misbound after 3d work, lacking blank A4 & final blank D6, small hole in 2 leaves; 2 leaves repaired; 3d work has 3d part only but lacking final blank & errata leaf; some leaves repaired. STC 24365, 24366 & 24367. C May 20 (225) £1,350 [Marshall]

Turner, William, 1651-1740

— Sound Anatomiz'd, in a Philosophical Essay on Musick. L, 1724. 1st Ed. 4to, 19th-cent calf. Tp soiled & repaired at corners with 2 letters suppied in pen facsimile; last leaf cut down & repaired. pn Oct 24 (465) £120 [Maggs]

Turner, William, 1792-1867

— Journal of a Tour in the Levant. L, 1820. 3 vols. 8vo, half calf. With 2 folding maps & 22 plates. S June 30 (80) £3,400 [Consolidated Real]

Anr copy. 19th-cent calf. With 2 folding maps (1 damaged) & 22 plates, 6 hand-colored. S July 1 (722) £1,700 [Consolidated Real]

Turnor, Christopher Hatton, 1840-1914

— Astra castra. Experiments and Adventures in the Atmosphere.... L, 1865. Folio, orig cloth; worn & frayed, hinges broken. With 39 plates. pn May 14 (101) £90

Turpin de Crisse, Lancelot

— Essai sur l'art de la guerre. Paris, 1754. 2 vols. 4to, contemp calf; rebacked. With 25 folding plans. W July 8 (106) £105

Turrecremata, Johannes de, 1388-1468

— Expositio psalterii. Venice, 1513. 8vo, modern half vellum. SI June 10 (1030) LIt280,000

— Expositio super toto psalterio. Mainz: Peter Schoeffer, 11 Sept 1474. Folio, contemp blind-stamped calf over wooden bds with remains of 2 brass clasps & brass corner fittings, an Erfurt bdg; joints cracked but firm, lea lost from top & bottom compartments of spine. 35 lines; types 5:118G (text), 1:234G (Psalm incipits); rubricated in red & blue; with 2 large initials of red & blue interlock with filigree & foliate extensions. Some soiling & marginal waterstaining; worming in 1st leaves touching some letters. 173 leaves. Goff T-520. Phillipps copy. P Dec 12 (197) $30,000

— Meditationes. Rome: Stephan Plannck, 21 Aug 1498. 4to, 19th-cent mor. 32 lines; type 8:95G; 33 woodcuts. Tp with stains. 29 leaves; lacking final blank. Goff T-541. Huth-Brunschwig copy. C Nov 27 (48) £20,000 [Librairie Thomas-Scheler]

Turton, John

— The Angler's Manual; or, Fly-Fisher's Oracle. L, 1836. 8vo, cloth. bba Nov 28 (70) £130 [Hereward Bks]

Tussac, F. Richard de

— Flore des Antilles, ou Histoire generale botanique.... Paris, 1808-27. One of 150. 4 vols in 2. Folio, half mor; rubbed. With 140 hand-finished colored plates. Some staining; some tears in plates repaired; Plate 27 in Vol IV with a loss in image; Plate 4 in Vol II smaller; tears & holes in text leaves, mostly without loss except on p. 74 in Vol IV. L.p. copy. P June 17 (394) $10,000

Tusser, Thomas, 1524?-80

— Five Hundred Points of Good Husbandry.... L, 1672. 4to, modern mor gilt by Bedford. P2 repaired with loss of a few letters; marginal repairs. wd June 12 (438) $200

Tuttle, Capt. Francis

— Report of the Cruise of the U. S. Revenue Cutter Bear.... Wash., 1899. 8vo, orig cloth. bbc Apr 27 (548) $80

Twain, Mark. See: Clemens, Samuel Langhorne

Twamley, Louisa Anne. See: Meredith, Louisa Anne Twamley

Twice a Year...

— Twice a Year: A Semi-Annual Journal of Literature, the Arts, and Civil Liberties. NY, 1938-47. 2d Ptg of Vol I, 1st Ptg of remaining issues. Nos 1-15 in 9 vols Orig wraps (No 1 issued without d/j). bbc Feb 17 (247) $350

Twining, Edward Francis, Baron Twining

— A History of the Crown Jewels of Europe. L, 1960. 4to, cloth, in d/j. bba May 14 (621) £400 [Pearl]

Twiss, Richard

— Chess. L, 1787-89. 2 vols. 8vo, contemp half calf; Vol II rebacked with old spine preserved. Ck May 8 (161) £200

— Travels through Portugal and Spain. L, 1775. 4to, contemp half mor; spine broken, covers becoming detached. With folding map & 6 plates. wd Dec 12 (464) $75

Twitchell, Ralph Emerson

— The Leading Facts of New Mexican History. Cedar Rapids, 1911-12. One of 1,500. 2 vols. sp Nov 24 (69) $160

Twyne, Brian

— Antiquitatis academiae Oxoniensis apologia. Oxford: J. Barnes, 1608. 4to, old calf; rebacked, worn. STC 24405. wd June 12 (440) $50

Tyler, Anne

— If Morning Ever Comes. NY, 1964. In d/j with gouge to spine panel. wa Mar 5 (254) $475

— The Tin Can Tree. NY, 1965. In torn d/j. wa Dec 19 (226) $220

Tymms, William Robert —& Wyatt, Sir Matthew Digby, 1820-77

— The Art of Illuminating as Practised in Europe.... L, [1859] 1860. Folio, later half mor gilt. With colored decorative half-title, title, tail-piece & 99 tinted or colored lithos. bba Dec 19 (97) £120 [Fetzer]

Anr copy. Orig cloth; rebacked. With title & 99 plates. Soiled. DW Nov 6 (488) £130

Anr copy. Contemp half mor gilt; worn, upper cover detached. With colored decorative half-title, title, tail-piece & 99 tinted or colored lithos. DW Apr 8 (378) £120

Tyndale, Walter

— An Artist in Egypt. L, [1912]. One of 150. 4to, orig vellum gilt. bba Dec 19 (127) £270 [M. Edwards]

Tyndall, John, 1820-93

— The Glaciers of the Alps. L, 1860. Bound in 2 vols. 12mo, later half mor. Some marginal stains. bba July 9 (44) £110 [Berg]

Tyndall, William

— The Whole Workes of W. Tyndall, John Frith and Doct. Barnes. L: J. Daye, 1572. 3 parts in 1 vol. Folio, contemp calf over wooden bds; rubbed, rebacked, lacking clasps. Black letter. Tp border torn & soiled; date on tp altered in ink to 1573; tear in CC5 without loss; lacking B4, HH1 & AAa1; some soiling. Sold w.a.f. STC 24436. S Feb 11 (531) £550 [Seibu]

Typotius, Jacobus

— Symbola varia diversorum principum.... Amst.: Ysbrand Haring, 1686. 12mo, 19th-cent calf; scuffed. sg Oct 24 (326) $350

Tyrrell, Henry

— The History of the War with Russia.... L, [c.1856]. 3 vols. 4to, half calf. bba Oct 10 (361) £50 [E. Nolan]

Anr copy. Half lea; worn & soiled. Some foxing. NH Oct 6 (95) $85

Tyson, Philip T.

— Report of the Secretary of War Communicating Information in Relation to the Geology and Topography of California. Wash., 1850. 8vo, disbound. With 13 folding maps. 31st Congress, 1st Session, Sen. Exec. Doc. 47. sg June 18 (140) $100

Tzara, Tristan, 1896-1963

— Dada 3. Zurich, 1918. 4to, orig wraps. bba Aug 13 (303) £500 [Kiefer]

— Le Fruit permis. Paris, 1956. One of 60. Illus by Sonia Delaunay. 4to, loose as issued. CGen Nov 18 (470) SF8,000

— La Main Passe. Paris, 1935. One of 20 sgd by author & containing the frontis. Illus By Wassily Kandinsky. 4to, orig wraps. Frontis sgd by Kandinsky. CGen Nov 18 (469) SF31,000

— Midis gagnes. Paris, [1939]. One of 50 hors commerce with a holograph dedication by Tzara, in this instance, the name of the dedicatee cut out. Illus by Henri Matisse. 4to, half mor. CGen Nov 18 (471) SF400

— Le Signe de vie. Paris, 1946. One of 500. Illus by Henri Matisse. 4to, orig wraps; worn. Has the orig sgd litho by Matisse. CNY May 11 (417) $19,500

U

Ufano, Diego

— Artillerie, c'est a dire, vraye instruction de l'artillerie et de toutes ses appartenances.... Zutfen, 1621. Folio, vellum; new endpapers. With 49 plates. Lacking R2 & apparently an index; washed copy. S July 1 (1355) £350 [American Mus.]

— Artillerie ou vraye instruction de l'artillerie. Rouen, 1628. Folio, 18th-cent calf; rubbed. With 30 plates. Some browning. S July 1 (1354) £400 [Dennistoun]

Uffenbach, Zacharias Conrad von

— Merkwuerdige Reisen durch Niedersachsen Holland und Engelland. Ulm: Johann Friederich Baum, 1753-54. 3 vols. 8vo, orig bds; worn. With frontis & 51 folding plates. S Nov 21 (201) £600 [Bifolco]

Ukhtomskij, Esper Esperovitch, Prince

— Puteshestvie na vostok ego imperatoriskago bysochestva gosudarya naslednika tsarevicha 1890-1891. St. Petersburg, 1893. 3 vols. Folio, modern cloth, orig front covers laid down; bdg sticky. Port loose & foxed. sg Jan 9 (191) $500

Ulloa, Alfonso de

— La Historia dell' impressa di Tripoli di Barbaria.... [Venice, 1566]. 4to, contemp vellum. With folding map. Some damage to head of spine & inner margins. S Nov 21 (284) £600 [Atabey]

Ulloa, Antonio de, 1716-95

— Memoires...concernant la decouverte de l'Amerique.... Paris, 1787. 2 vols. 8vo, old half calf; worn & panels coming loose. bbc June 29 (343) $80

Underhill, Francis T.

— Driving for Pleasure; or, the Harness Stable. NY, 1897. 8vo, orig half calf; spine scuffed. cb Dec 19 (174) $60

Underwood, Tim —& Miller, Chuck

— Bare Bones: Conversations on Terror with Stephen King. Los Angeles, 1988. One of 52 specially bound in half lea. cb Dec 12 (1228) $150

One of 1,100. cb Dec 12 (1229) $55

Unger, Franz Xaver —& Kotschy, T.

— Die Insel Cypern ihrer physischen und organischen Natur. Vienna, 1865. 8vo, orig cloth; spine head stained. With frontis (stained) & folding litho map. S June 30 (425) £580 [Lepanto]

Union Theological Seminary

— Catalogue of the McAlpin Collection of British History and Theology.... L, 1927-30. 5 vols. Ck Nov 1 (405) £110; O Sept 24 (99) $130; O Nov 26 (73) $200

United States of America

See also: Constitution of the United States of America; Jay's copy, John

— Acts Passed at the First Session of the Congress.... Phila., 1793. Vol I. 8vo, contemp sheep; lacking front free endpaper. sg June 18 (532) $150

— A Bill Establishing Offices for the Sale of Lands in the Territory North-West of the River Ohio. [Phila., 1796]. Folio, unbound. Laid paper with Delaware & spread-wing eagle with shield watermarks. bbc Dec 9 (404) $2,500

— Laws of the United States of America.... NY, [1791]. 8vo, contemp sheep; worn, front free endpaper lacking. Tp browned & stained. sg Dec 5 (258) $250

— The Laws of the United States of America. Phila., 1796. Vols I-II (of 3). Contemp calf; worn & scuffed, Vol II taller & with covers coming loose. bbc Apr 27 (592) $85

— Official Army Register of the Volunteer Force...1861...1865.... Gaithersburg: Olde

Soldier Books, 1987. 8 vols. wa Sept 26 (386) $80

— Official Records of the Union and Confederate Armies in the War of the Rebellion. Wash., 1880-1901. 128 vols. 8vo, various bdgs; some joints splitting, some wear. bbc Feb 17 (105) $1,125

— Reglement concernant les Prises que des Corsaires Francois conduiront dans les Ports des Etats-Unis de l'Amerique, & celles que les Corsaires Americains ameneront dans les Ports de France. Paris, 19 Oct 1778. Single leaf, 240mm by 174mm, in modern bds. Supplement to la Gazette du Lundi. P June 16 (136) $900

— Report of the Commissioner of Patents for 1849. Part I: Arts and Manufactures. Wash., 1850. 8vo, orig half sheep; worn & scuffed. Some foxing; pencil scribbling on a few leaves at rear. With statement by Abraham Lincoln on p 262. bbc Feb 17 (83) $95

Anr copy. Orig half sheep; worn. Library markings; some foxing. With statement by Abraham Lincoln on p 262. bbc June 29 (233) $55

— Report of the Superintendent of the Coast Survey, showing the Progress of the Survey during the Year 1854. Wash., 1855. 4to, orig cloth; spine broken. Incomplete copy but doesn't mention whether Whistler engraving present. rs Oct 17 (46) $175

— Report of the Superintendent of the Coast Survey...during the Year 1859. Wash., 1860. 4to, cloth. Some dampstaining. sg June 18 (177) $250

— Reports upon Geographical & Geological Explorations and Surveys West of the One Hundredth Meridian. Wash., 1875-89. 7 vols in 9 plus 2 Atlas vols bound in 1. 4to & folio, half mor gilt (needs rebdg) & half mor. sg June 18 (581) $2,600

Anr Ed. Wash., 1889. Vol I. 4to, orig half mor; rubbed. With 3 folding maps & 24 plates. 2 plates detached. cb Sept 12 (189) $375

Universal...

— An Universal History, from the Earliest Account of Time.... L: T. Osborne, 1747-54. 20 (of 21) vols. Contemp calf gilt; rubbed. Sold w.a.f. bba May 14 (83) £240 [Elliott]

Untermeyer, Louis. See: Limited Editions Club

Updike, Daniel Berkeley

— Printing Types. Cambr. MA, 1922. 2 vols. cb Oct 17 (943) $60

2d Ed. Cambr. MA, 1937. 2 vols. In def d/js. wa Apr 9 (41) $55

Updike, John

— The Carpentered Hen.... NY, [1958]. In 1st d/j. sg June 11 (307) $275

— Midpoint and Other Poems. NY, 1969. 1st Ed, one of 250 L.p. copies. In d/j. wa Dec 9 (227) $55

Upham, Charles Wentworth

— Salem Witchcraft: with an Account of Salem Village. Bost., 1867. 3 parts in 2 vols. 8vo, cloth; extremities worn, several hinges weak. sg Dec 5 (259) $90

Upton, Bertha & Florence K.

— The Adventures of Two Dutch Dolls.... L & NY, [1895]. 1st Ed. Oblong 4to, half cloth. With 32 colored plates. Epstein copy. sg Apr 30 (473) $375

Upton, William

— The School-Boy. L: Wm. Darton, 1820. 16mo, orig wraps; spine repaired. With 6 hand-colored illusts on 6 leaves. bba July 23 (141) £400 [Moon]

Urban, Joseph

— Theatres. NY, 1929. One of 200. 4to, bds; spine rubbed. sg Mar 5 (258) $200

Urbanus Bellunensis

— Institutiones Graecae grammatices. Venice: Aldus, Jan 1497. 1st Ed. 4to, 19th-cent half mor. 27 lines; greek & roman letter; with the 1st issue of the errata leaves. Some dampstains at beginning & end; tear in lower margin of g6; corners of the errata leaves repaired; some worming in inner margin of errata leaves; hole in text of final leaf. 214 leaves. Goff U-66. Richard Copley Christie—John Rylands copy. S May 28 (32) £6,000 [Fletcher]

Urbanus Bolzanius. See: Urbanus Bellunensis

Urfe, Honore d', 1568-1625

— L'Astree. Paris: Antoine de Sommaville, 1633-47. 5 vols. 8vo, 18th-cent mor extra. With 9 ports & 60 plates. some shaving; Vol I lacking p. 876 to end; Vol IV lacking 1 prelim leaf; small portion of pp.845-46 in Vol II torn away with minimal loss. S Dec 5 (250) £11,500 [Scheler]

Uring, Capt. Nathaniel

— A History of the Voyages and Travels of.... L, 1726-25. 2 parts in 1 vol. 8vo, contemp calf gilt; worn, rebacked. With 4 folding charts, the 1st torn. S Feb 11 (796) £580 [Barron]

Urquhart, Beryl Leslie

— The Camellia. Sharpthorne, [1956-60]. 2 vols. Folio, orig bds, in soiled & torn d/js. With 36 colored plates. wa Mar 5 (577) $130

Ursula, Saint
— The Legend of Saint Ursula and Her Companions. L, 1869. 4to, orig purple silk bdg with modern mor spine; worn. cb Sept 26 (118) $100

Utamaro, Kitagawa, 1754?-1806. See: Grabhorn Printing

Uthman ibn Umar, called Ibnu'l-Hajib
— Grammatica arabica. [Rome: Typographia Medicaea, 1592]. 8vo, contemp vellum. In Arabic throughout. Some browning; stamps. S Nov 21 (311) £1,100 [Brill]

Uttenhofer, Caspar
— Circinus geometricus, zu teutsch Mess-Circkel.... Nuremberg, 1626. Bound with: Pes mechanicus, oder Werckschuch....Nuremberg, [n.d.]. 4to, contemp vellum; spine ends damaged. Some worming at beginning & end of 1st work, affecting text. sg May 14 (316) $650

Uzanne, Octave, 1852-1931
See also: Caxton Club
— La Chronique scandaleuse. Paris, 1879. Bound with: Anecdotes sur la Comtesse Du Barry. Paris, 1880. Each, one of 50 on papier de Chine. 8vo, half mor by Petit. O May 26 (192) $100
— La Reliure moderne. Paris, 1887. One of 1,500. 8vo, wraps; loose in casing. O Feb 25 (194) $80

V

Vachon, Marius
— W. Bouguereau. Paris, 1900. Folio, mor, orig front wrap bound in. sg Nov 7 (26) $300

Vaenius, Otto
— Amorum emblemata. Antwerp, 1608. 1st Ed. Oblong 4to, calf; rebacked, 3 corners repaired. With plate & 124 emblems within oval frames. Some browning; stamp on verso of tp & last leaf; small hole in 1 leaf. B Nov 1 (341) HF3,200; B Nov 1 (342) HF3,200
— Emblemata Horatiana. Amst., 1684. Bound with: Bygedichten op Otto Vaenius Zinnebeelden uit Horatius. 8vo, contemp calf gilt. With engraved title & 103 illusts. B May 12 (866) HF600
— Emblemata sive symbola a principibus.... Brussels: Hubert Antoine, 1624. 4to, old vellum; rear turn-in sprung. With 23 engravings showing 207 emblems. sg Mar 12 (83) $175
— Emblemes de l'amour divin. Paris: P. Landry, [c.1660]. 12mo, 19th-cent mor gilt; needs rebacking. With engraved title & 56 emblems with Latin mottoes & French text. sg Mar 12 (82) $325

Vaillant, Sebastien
— Botanicon parisiense. Leiden & Amst., 1727. Folio, 19th-cent half sheep; spine faded & rubbed. With port map & 33 plates. sg May 7 (205) $850

Valencia, Gregorio de
— Analysis fidei catholicae. Ingolstadt: David Sartorius, 1585. 4to, contemp blind-tooled pigskin over wooden bds. sg Oct 24 (329) $275

Valentia, George, Viscount. See: Annesley, George

Valentia, George Annesley, Viscount. See: Annesley, George

Valentini, Michael Bernard
— Viridarium reformatum, seu regnum vegetabile.... Frankfurt, 1719. Part 1 (of 2) only. Folio, contemp calf; rebacked. Lacking all but 2 of the plates. Sold w.a.f. bba Oct 24 (272) £260 [Erlini]

Valentino's copy, Rudolph
— Great Operas. L, 1899. 5 vols. Folio, half mor with silk floral bds. With the William Menzies-designed bookplate in each vol. b&b Feb 19 (149) $1,000

Valeriano Bolzano, Giovanni Pietro
— Hieroglyphica, sive de sacris aegyptiorum literis commentarii. Basel: T. Guerin, 1567. Folio, contemp pigskin with clasps. Tp holed with loss of borders; g6 wormed affecting some letters & illust; ink blotches to emblems on S6, 3C1-3. Ck Oct 31 (83) £550

Anr Ed. Leiden: Pauli Frellon, 1610. Bound with: Pro Sacredotum Barbis. Leiden, 1610. And: Hieroglyphcorum Collectanea. Leiden, 1610. Folio, old bds; lower cover detached. Last leaf & some margins dampstained. Ck Oct 31 (84) £400

Valerio, Theodore
— Costume de la Hongrie et les provinces Danubiennes.... Paris, [1885]. 5 parts in 1 vol. Folio, loose in orig folder. With 78 plates. HH May 12 (971) DM1,500

Valerius Maximus, Gaius
— Dictorum et factorum memorabilium.... Venice: Aldus, Oct 1502. 1st Aldine Ed, 2d Issue. 8vo, mor gilt. wa Dec 9 (478) $270

Anr Ed. Paris, 1535. Folio, old sheep; worn, covers detached. sg Oct 24 (330) $275
— Exempla quatuor et viginti nuper inuenta ante caput de omnibus. Venice: Aldus, Oct 1514. 8vo, 18th-cent calf; worn. Some soiling; 2 leaves short. SI Dec 5 (679) LIt550,000

Valery, Paul, 1871-1945

— Charmes ou poemes. Paris, 1922. 1st Ed, one of 325. 4to, mor gilt extra. Epstein copy. sg Apr 30 (474) $900

— Dialogue de l'Arbe. [Paris, n.d.]. One of 100 with additional suite of wood engravings & supplementary etching on japon; this copy also with suite of plates in colors on Arches. Illus by Edouard Pignon. Folio, loose as issued in wraps. sg Sept 26 (253) $225

— The Graveyard by the Sea. L [Verona: Bodoni ptd], 1946. One of 500, sgd by trans. Trans by C. Day Lewis. Orig wraps. In English & French. DW May 13 (458) £75

— Poesies. Paris, 1929. One of 235. Folio, mor. B May 12 (244) HF600

— Le Serpent. Paris, 1922. One of 30 on hollande verge. Calf extra by Semet & Plumelle, orig wraps bound in. Inscr to Henri Barthlemy. S May 28 (458) £600 [Beres]

Valle, Pietro della, 1586-1652

— De volkome beschryving der voortreffelyke Reizen.... Amst., 1664-66. 6 parts in 2 vols. 4to, old calf gilt; head of spine chipped, front joint cracked. With 35 plates. Dampstained. sg Jan 9 (192) $250

— Les Fameux Voyages.... Paris, 1662-64. 4 vols. 4to, contemp calf; last vol not uniform. With 4 ports, 1 folding map & 2 plates. Hand-colored woodcut illust tipped in at beginning of each vol. Tp repaired with letters supplied in ink; Vol II dampstained; Vol III with frontis torn & tp cropped & lacking a leaf after title; Vol IV title torn without loss. S June 30 (428) £1,000 [Kutluoglu]

Anr Ed. Paris, 1663-65. 4 vols. Folio, contemp calf; last vol not uniform & with upper joint split. With 4 ports, 1 folding map & 2 plates. Tp repaired with letters supplied in ink; Vol II dampstained; Vol III with frontis torn tp cropped & possibly lacking a leaf after tp; tp of Vol IV torn without loss; hand-colored woodcut illust tipped in at the beginning of each vol. S June 30 (428) £1,000 [Kutluoglu]

Anr Ed. Paris: G. Clousier, 1670-64. 4 vols. Folio, contemp calf; repaired. With 2 ports & 2 frontises. Irregular pagination in Vol II from pp. 160-201, without loss of text; some worming occasionally touching letters; some discoloration. S Nov 21 (285) £2,000 [Bank of Cyprus]

— The Travels...into East-India and Arabia Deserta. L, 1665. 1st Ed in English. Folio, contemp calf; worn, rebacked. Corner dampstatined. Lacking folding map.. Wing V-47. DW Mar 4 (48) £100

Vallee, Leon

— Courtiers and Favourites of Royalty. L: Merrill & Banker, [n.d.]. One of 50 specially bound copies. 20 vols. 8vo, mor, elaborately gilt; rubbed. O Nov 26 (47) $600

Vallery-Radot, J. See: Lugt & Vallery-Radot

Vallet, Louis

— Travers l'Europe: Croquis de cavalrie. Paris, 1893. Folio, half lea gilt. SI June 10 (1043) LIt800,000

Vallotton, Felix

— Crimes et chatiments. Paris, 1902. Folio, pictorial wraps. With 23 color lithos. Special issue of L'Assiette au Beurre. Epstein copy. sg Apr 30 (476) $1,500

Valmarana, Giulio Cesare, Count

— Modo del far pace in via cavaleresca e christiana. Padua, 1648. 8vo, sheep; rebacked. sg Mar 26 (325) $110

Valturius, Robertus

— De re militari. Verona: Boninus de Boninis, 13 Feb 1483. Folio, vellum gilt, dated 1922. 37 lines & headline; type 2:114R. With 96 woodcut illusts, some full-page, all hand-colored (the coloring is old but not contemp); initials in red, green & yellow; red & green paragraph marks; yellow capital strokes. Hand-colored coat-of-arms on 1st page of text, flanked by the initials T.L. Some soiling; outer margin of 1 leaf repaired; some inner margins strengthened; dampstaining; initials smudged. 252 (of 254) leaves; lacking 2 blanks. Goff V-89. C Dec 16 (89) £10,000 [Tenschert]

Valverde de Hamusco, Juan

— Anatomia del corpo humano.... Rome, 1560. 1st Ed, 2d Issue of the Italian trans. Folio, 18th-cent vellum; inner hinges split. With engraved title & 42 plates. Some dampstaining at head, with plates in final 2 gatherings most severely affected; some other soiling; tp loosening at inner margin. P Dec 12 (93) $3,000

Anr copy. Vellum; worn. With engraved title & 40 (of 42) plates. Some browning & soiling. SI Dec 5 (684) LIt700,000

Vambery, Armin, 1832?-1913

— Travels in Central Asia. NY, 1865. Orig cloth; worn & soiled, shaken. Library markings. F Dec 18 (434) $60

Anr copy. With folding map in rear pocket. sg Jan 9 (193) $120

Van de Velde, C. W. M.
— Narrative of a Journey through Syria and Palestine. L, 1854. 2 vols. 8vo, orig cloth; spines chipped. With folding map, plan & plate of inscriptions; margins browned. S July 1 (07) £320 [Kanaan]

Van der Groen, Jan —& Nylandt, Petrus
— Het Vermakelijck Landt-leven.... Amst: Michiel de Groot, 1679. 6 parts in 3 in 1 vol. 4to, contemp vellum; soiled. With 2 engraved titles, 15 plates & 56 full-page woodcuts. I2 with small rust-hole; H2 in Part 3 holed with loss. S July 9 (1093) £380 [Marlborough]

Van Dine, S. S.
— The Kennel Murder Case. NY, 1933. In chipped d/j. cb Dec 12 (156) $65

Van Duzer Library, Henry Sayre
— Thackeray Library: First Editions and First Publications. NY, 1919. One of 175. Compiled by Edward Turnbull. O Dec 17 (187) $70; sg Oct 31 (319) $120

Van Gogh, Vincent, 1853-90
— The Complete Letters.... Greenwich CT: New York Graphic Society, [1958]. 3 vols. 4to, cloth; reinforced with tape. sg Feb 6 (290) $150; sg Apr 2 (284) $80

2d Ed. Greenwich CT: New York Graphic Society, [1959]. 3 vols. Bdg stained. sp Feb 6 (217) $80

Van Gulik, Robert, 1910-67
— The Chinese Maze Murders. The Hague, 1956. 1st Ed. In d/j. O Aug 25 (183) $200

Anr Ed. L: Michael Joseph, [1962]. Advance proof. Wraps. cb Sept 19 (214) $130
— The Lacquer Screen: A Chinese Detective Story. L: Heinemann, [1964]. 1st Ed, Advance Uncorrected Proof. Ptd wraps. cb Sept 19 (215) $75
— The Red Pavilion. Kuala Lumpur, 1961. Orig wraps; some wear. O Aug 25 (184) $200

Van Laar, G.
— Magazijn van tuin-sieraaden. Amst., 1802. 4to, later half mor gilt; crack to lower joint, corners bumped. With engraved title & 190 hand-colored plates. CNY Jan 25 (78) $1,500

Van Loon, Gerard
— Aloude Hollandsche histori der keyzeren, koningen, hertogen en Graaven.... The Hague, 1734. 2 vols. Folio, contemp vellum; soiled. With engraved dedication, 13 folding maps (a few margins cut close), 10 plates (3 folding) & 21 ptd genealogical tables (20 folding). Some browning; marginal dampstains. pn June 11 (158) £220

Van Marle, Raimond
— The Development of the Italian Schools of Painting. The Hague, 1923-38. 19 vols. Orig cloth; spines soiled. S Feb 11 (220) £600 [Messagerie]

Anr Ed. NY, 1970. 19 vols. sg Feb 6 (176) $400
— Iconographie de l'art profane au Moyen-age et a la Renaissance.... The Hague, 1931. 4to, orig cloth, in d/j; hinges weakened. bba Feb 13 (233) £170 [Bernett]

Van Nostrand, Jeanne
— The First Hundred Years of Painting in California.... San Francisco, 1980. In d/j. With 43 colored plates. cb Oct 25 (118) $65; K Sept 29 (427) $50

Anr copy. In d/j. pba July 23 (218) $120
— San Francisco, 1806-1906 in Contemporary Paintings, Drawings.... San Francisco: Book Club of California, 1975. One of 500. Book Club of California No 150. cb Sept 12 (173) $130; cb Nov 21 (228) $95

Van Praet, Joseph, 1754-1837. See: Praet, Joseph Basile Bernard van

Van Vogt, Alfred Elton
— Slan. Sauk City, 1946. 1st Ed. pba July 9 (284) $55

Van Winkle, C. S.
— The Printer's Guide. NY, 1970. Bds. Reprint of 1818 Ed. sg Oct 31 (320) $110

Van Winkle, William Mitchell —& Randall, David A.
— Henry W. Herbert: a Bibliography.... Portland ME, 1936. Unopened. H. P. Kraus's copy. K Sept 29 (198) $90

Vanbrugh, Sir John, 1664-1726
See also: Nonesuch Press
— The Mistake. A Comedy. L, 1706. 8vo, modern half calf. Lacking half-title; browned; wormed. bba July 9 (96) £85 [Hannas]

Vance, Jack
— Big Planet. NY: Avalon, [1957]. In d/j. Sgd. sg June 11 (311) $120

Vancouver, George, 1757-98
— Voyage de decouvertes, a l'ocean Pacifique du Nord.... Paris, 1799-1800 [An VIII]. 3 vols; lacking Atlas. 4to, orig bds. With 18 plates. Vol III dampstained as far as p.170 & affecting 2 plates; small burnhole in 1 leaf. DuPont copy. CNY Oct 8 (249) $800
— A Voyage of Discovery to the North Pacific Ocean and Round the World. L, 1798. 1st Ed. 4 vols, including Atlas. 4to & folio, old half calf; not uniform, joints breaking, 2 backstrips def, upper cover of Atlas de-

tached. With 18 plates in text vols & 16 maps in Atlas; plus 1 inserted map at end from 1801 Ed. Vol III dampstained to p.170; burnhole in Vv3 of Vol II. CNY Oct 8 (248) $4,500

Anr copy. Contemp calf, Atlas bound to match in modern half calf. With 34 plates & charts. pnE Oct 2 (491) £4,800

Anr copy. 3 vols; without Atlas. 4to, contemp mor; spines soiled. With 18 maps & charts. Some discoloration. S June 25 (117) £5,000 [Arader]

Vandam, Albert Dresden

— An Englishman in Paris. L, 1892. 2 vols. 8vo, mor gilt by Bayntun; joints rubbed. Letterpress titles supplied. Extra-illus with c.100 plates. sg Jan 9 (194) $500

Vanderbilt, Lucille Parsons

— Safari. Sands Point, 1936. One of 50. Half vellum. sg Jan 9 (318) $1,500

Vandermaelen, P. M. G.

— Atlas universel de geographie physique, statistique et mineralogique.... Brussels, 1827. 6 vols. Folio, contemp half lea; rubbed. With hand-colored litho table of mountains & 387 double-page maps & plates, hand-colored in outline throughout. C Oct 30 (166) £7,000 [Hanssens]

Anr copy. Part 2. Folio, contemp half calf; rubbed, lower joint split. With general map & 111 maps, hand-colored in outline. Sold w.a.f. C May 20 (307) £800 [Chan]

Vane, Sir Henry, 1613-62

— The Retired Mans Meditations.... L: Robert White, 1655. Wing V75A - variant imprint. 4to, 19th-cent calf gilt. Some foxing; blank corner of 3E2 restored; 3C2.3 & 3S2 supplied. sg Oct 24 (331) $475

Vaniere, Jacques

— Praedium rusticum.... Paris, 1774. 8vo, contemp mor gilt, with fore-edge painting of a pastoral scene in a Romantic landscape. P Dec 12 (153) $1,500

Vanini, Giulio Cesare, 1585-1619

— Amphitheatrum aeternae providentiae divino-magicum.... Lyons, 1615. 8vo, contemp mor gilt. SI June 10 (1045) LIt1,300,000

Vanity...

— The Vanity Fair Album. L, 1877-78. Vols 9-10. Folio, orig cloth; rubbed. pn Sept 12 (368) £480 [MacDonnell]

Thirteenth Series. L, 1881. Folio, orig cloth; upper cover stained, some leaves loose at beginning. With 55 ports. L Nov 14 (88) £460

Vansittart, Robert. See: Gregynog Press

Vanvitelli, Luigi, 1700-73

— Dichiarazione dei disegni del reale palazzo di Caserta. Naples, 1756. Folio, contemp mor gilt. With engraved title & 14 double-page plates. Some discoloration; small dampstain at lower forecorner of last plate. S June 25 (231) £2,800 [Pregliasco]

Varchi, Benedetto, 1503-65

— Due Lezzione. Florence, 1549. 4to, 19th-cent half vellum. SI Dec 5 (1043) LIt850,000

Varignon, Pierre

— Projet d'un nouvelle mechanique. Paris, 1687. 1st Ed. 4to, contemp calf; worn. With 13 plates. Some browning. SI Dec 5 (688) LIt900,000

Varin, A. & E.

— L'Architecture pittoresque en Suisse. Paris, 1861. Folio, orig bds; rebacked with new endpapers. With 48 plates, hinges throughout. b June 22 (281) £220

Anr copy. Contemp half mor; rubbed. With 48 plates. O Nov 26 (187) $250

Anr copy. Contemp half mor; rebacked with old spine preserved, rubbed. S May 14 (1210) £350 [Bookroom]

Varnum, Charles

— I, Varnum: The Autobiographical Reminiscences of Custer's Chief of Scouts.... Glendale, 1982. One of 350. cb Feb 12 (86) $95

Varthema, Ludovico di

— The Itinerary of Ludovico de Varthema of Bologna.... L: Argonaut Press, 1928. One of 975. 4to, half vellum gilt. sg Jan 9 (195) $110

Vasaeus, Joannes

— Chronici rerum memorabilium Hispaniae. Tomus prior [all pbd]. Salamanca: Joannes de Giunta, 1552. Folio, contemp vellum. Small hole in text of I8. S Dec 5 (212) £600 [Martin]

Vasari, Giorgio, 1511-74

See also: Limited Editions Club

— Lives of the most Eminent Painters, Sculptors, and Architects. L, 1876. 5 vols. 12mo, early half calf; joints & edges worn. bbc Sept 23 (63) $120

— Ragionamenti. Florence: F. Giunti, 1588. ("Ragionamenti del Sig. Cavaliere Giorgio Vasari...inventioni da lui dipinte in Firenze nel Palazzo di loro Altezze Serenissime.") 4to, 18th-cent calf; rubbed. Lacking E2-E6. bba Sept 19 (284) £220 [Kunkler]

Anr Ed. Arezzo, 1762. 4to, 19th-cent half lea; worn. SI June 10 (1049) LIt320,000

— Le Vite de piu eccellenti architetti, pittori, et scultori Italiani.... Florence, 1550. 4to, 19th-cent mor gilt; joints worn. Marginal wormhole in last few leaves; 1 sheet misfolded. Kettaneh-Manney copy. P Oct 11 (301) $9,000

Anr copy. 3 parts in 2 vols. 4to, 19th-cent vellum. First title shaved at fore-edge; some staining, mainly in margins; marginal worming at end of Vol II. Lowe copy. S Dec 5 (213) £4,200 [Chellini]

Anr copy. ("Le Vite de' piu eccellenti pittori, scultori, e architettori.") 19th-cent vellum bds; soiled. Some dampstaining, with slight loss to border of 1st title & a few page numerals; repairs at head & upper corners of some leaves at ends of Vol I; marginal scribbles to some leaves in Vol II; H3 misbound before H2 in Vol I; Vol II lacking 3 leaves at end. S Feb 11 (225) £1,300 [Lorenzo]

Anr Ed. Florence: Lorenzo Torrentino, 1550. Part 3 only. Later vellum; rubbed, upper cover & spine loose. Marginal repairs; some soiling & browning; lacking YY1-4 (supplied in Ms) & final blank. pn July 16 (22) £150

Anr Ed. Florence, 1568. Variant issue with allegorical woodcut on title. 3 parts in 3 vols. 4to, old vellum bds; soiled, new endpapers. With titles, port & medallion ports. Vol III with ptd cancel-label pasted on recto of 3R4 & Ms correction on recto of 5Y3; some browning & soiling; some headlines in Vol I shaved; titles cut down, that of Vol I mtd; Vol I with first A2-3 misbound & with last leaf lacking most of lower half, repaired & with missing text supplied in pen facsimile; Vol II with z4 supplied from anr copy & inlaid; Vol III lacking 6H3 & 6H4. S Feb 11 (226) £1,400 [Messagerie]

Anr Ed. Florence: Giunta, 1568. ("Le Vite de' piu eccellenti pittori, scultori, e architettori.") Vols I & III (of 3). Contemp vellum. Some worming at beginning of each vol; a few stains in margins. S Dec 5 (214) £1,800 [Goldschmidt]

Anr Ed. Bologna, 1647. 3 vols. 4to, 18th-cent half lea. Margin of frontis repaired; some spotting. SI June 10 (1048) LIt1,500,000

— Le Vite de piu eccelenti architetti, pittori, et scultori Italiani.... Livorno & Florence, 1767-72. ("Le Vite de' piu eccellenti pittori, scultori, e architettori.") 7 vols. 8vo, old mor gilt; spines soiled & scuffed. Hole in 2Z3 of Vol VII, with loss; stain in bottom margin of 3A1-3 of Vol IV. C June 24 (350) £1,050 [Parikian]

Vasi, Giuseppe Agostino

— Delle magnificenze di Roma antica e moderna.... Rome, 1766-68. Vols VII & VIII only, in 1 vol. Oblong folio, contemp vellum bds; soiled. With 51 plates. S Nov 21 (202) £700 [Forum]

Vastey, Pompee Valentine de

— Reflexions politiques sur quelques ouvrages et journaux francais, concernant Hayti. Sans-Soucci [i.e., Port au Prince], 1817. 8vo, contemp half vellum; soiled. Presentation by the Count de Limmade. S May 14 (1269) £650 [Fletcher]

Vattel, Emerich von

— Le Droit des gens. Neuchatel, 1773. 2 vols. 4to, contemp calf; rebacked. bba Apr 30 (278) £75 [Frognal]

Vaucaire, Michel

— Barres Paralleles. Paris: Francois Bernouard, [1927]. One of 301. Illus by Foujita. 4to, orig wraps. With 5 plates. Some foxing. sg Sept 26 (114) $950

Vaudoncourt, Gen. Frederic Guillaume de

— Memoirs on the Ionian Islands.... L, 1816. 8vo, contemp calf gilt; covers detached. With folding map. S June 30 (431) £380 [Metaxas]

Vaughan, Henry, 1622-95. See: Gregynog Press

Vaux, Calvert, 1824-95

— Villas and Cottages. NY, 1857. 8vo, orig cloth; rubbed. Some foxing. sg Feb 6 (291) $130

Vaux, Charles Maurice, Baron de

— Les Tireurs au pistolet. Paris, 1883. One of 600. 8vo, half mor, orig wraps bound in; extremities rubbed. sg Mar 26 (328) $110

Anr copy. Half cloth, orig wraps bound in. sg Mar 26 (329) $80

Vavra, Jaroslav Raimund

— 5000 Years of Glass-Making.... Prague, [1954]. Folio, cloth, in torn d/j. sg Feb 6 (292) $90

Veblen, Thorstein

— The Theory of the Leisure Class. NY, 1899. 1st Ed. 8vo, orig cloth; spine frayed. bbc Sept 23 (280) $90

Vecellio, Cesare, 1530-1600

— Corona delle nobili et virtuose donne.... Venice: Vecellio, 1592-1608. Counterfeit Ed. 4 parts in 1 vol. 8vo, contemp vellum. SI Dec 5 (691) LIt3,000,000

— Costumes anciens et modernes. Paris, 1860. 2 vols. 8vo, contemp half lea; 1 spine loose, edges rubbed. With 513 plates. pn Dec 12 (264) £80

— Degli habiti antichi, et moderni di diverse

parti del mondo. Venice: Sessa, [1598]. ("Habiti antichi et moderni di tutto il mondo.") 2d Ed. 8vo, mor gilt by Chambolle-Duru. With 501 costume plates & 5 views. C June 24 (210) £2,600 [Mediolanum]

Veed-Fald, Joergen

— Belysning af nogle af vore Dages ulholdbare Troesbekjendelser. Aalborg, 1855-57. 3 vols in 1. 12mo, later half cloth, orig wraps of Vols II & III bound in; library markings on spine. Library stamps. sg Dec 5 (165) $250

Veen, Jan van der

— Zinne-beelden oft adams appel. Amst., 1659. 4to, vellum; new endpapers. With engraved title & 50 emblematical plates. Some staining. B Nov 1 (344) HF550

Veen, Otto van. See: Vaenius, Otto

Veer, Gerrit de

— Diarium nauticum seu vera descriptio trium navigationum admirandum.... Amst., 1598. Folio, recent pigskin. Tp soiled; marginal repairs; L3 restored at upper inner margin with some loss of letters; pen trials at L3v. S Nov 21 (369) £2,100 [Arader]

Vega Carpio, Lope Felix de, 1562-1635
See also: Gregynog Press

— La Dorotea. Madrid, 1632. 8vo, contemp vellum; soiled. V2 with tear into text; hole in inner margin of 1st 60 leaves, occasionally touching text; some other minor tears. C May 28 (259) £4,200

Vegetius Renatus, Flavius

— De re militari. Paris: Christian Wechel, 1553. ("De re militari libri quatuor. Sexti Iulii Frontini....") Folio, 18th-cent calf gilt; both covers scraped, joints repaired, new endpapers. With 121 full-page woodcuts, 3 half-page woodcuts. Small portion of inner margin of D3-6 torn away with minimal loss; a few small wormholes in margins. S July 1 (1331) £400 [Morris]

Anr Ed. Antwerp: Plantin, 1585. 4to, contemp calf; upper joint cracked at foot. Some waterstaining; folding table torn. bba Apr 9 (18) £400 [Erlini]

Anr Ed. Leiden, 1592. 2 parts in 1 vol. 8vo, contemp vellum. SI June 10 (1051) LIt400,000

Anr Ed. Wesel: Andrea ab Hoogenhuysen, 1670. ("Veteres de re militari scriptores") 2 parts in 1 vol. 8vo, contemp calf; rubbed. Appendixes misbound. DW Nov 6 (477) £70

Vehling, Joseph Dommers

— Platina and the Rebirth of Man. Chicago: Walter M. Hill, 1941. One of 500. In d/j. cb Oct 17 (947) $55

Veitch, James Herbert

— A Manual of Orchidaceous Plants Cultivated under Glass in Great Britain. L, 1887-94. L.p. Ed. 10 parts in 2 vols. 8vo, later half mor. wa Dec 9 (633) $400

Venables, Robert, 1612-87

— The Experienc'd Angler. L, 1827. ("The Experienced Angler.") 12mo, contemp half mor; rubbed. bba Nov 28 (71) £85 [Hereward Bks]

Venegas, Miguel

— A Natural and Civil History of California.... L, 1759. 1st Ed in English. 2 vols. 8vo, contemp calf; worn, most covers detached. With folding map & 4 plates. cb Sept 12 (175) $400

— Noticia de la California, y de su conquista....hasta el tiempo presente.... Madrid, 1757. 3 vols. 4to, orig vellum; rippled & wrinkled. With 4 folding maps. Fold break to 1 map. bbc June 29 (344) $600

Veniard, John

— Fly-Dressing Materials. L, [1977]. One of 100. 4to, half lea. Koopman copy. O Oct 29 (317) $80

Venice. See: Italy

Venner, Tobias

— Via recta ad vitam longam: or, a plaine Philosophicall Demonstration.... L: Felix Kyngston for Richard Moore, 1628. 2 parts in 1 vol. 4to, contemp vellum; worn. First 2 & last 2 leaves repaired; new endpapers at end. STC 24645. S May 13 (913) £190 [Quaritch]

Venture...

— Venture: an Annual of Art and Literature. L, 1903. First No. only. 4to, half cloth. Loose plate laid in. cb Oct 17 (948) $50

Venturi, Adolfo, 1856-1941

— Storia dell'arte italiana. Milan, 1901-40. 11 vols. Contemp vellum. SI Dec 5 (1047) LIt1,200,000

Venturi, Lionello
See also: Pissaro & Venturi

— Les Archives de l'Impressionisme: Lettres de Renoir, Monet.... Paris & NY, 1939. One of 1,000. 2 vols. Orig wraps. Met Apr 28 (88) $100

— Cezanne, son art, son oeuvre. Paris, 1936. One of 1,000. 2 vols. 4to, contemp cloth. bba Feb 13 (75) £1,100 [tulkens]

Anr copy. Orig cloth. S July 1 (1163) £750

Venuswagen...

— Der Venuswagen: Eine Sammlung erotischer Privatsdrucke mit Original-Graphik. Berlin, 1919-20. One of 700. 9 vols. 4to, orig half vellum; rubbed. DW Oct 9 (562) £260

Anr Ed. Berlin, 1919. Vols I-IX. 4to, orig half vellum. Lacking 1 plate. HH May 12 (2540) DM2,000

Venuti, Ridolfino

— Accurata e succincta descrizione topografica e istorica di Roma moderne. Rome, 1766. 2 vols in 4. 8vo, contemp half vellum; worn & scuffed. With 58 plates. A few torn in margin. bba Feb 27 (333) £950 [Etching]

— Accurata e succincta descrizione topografica delle antichita di Roma. Rome, 1803. 2 vols. 4to, contemp vellum. With engraved title vignettes, 96 plates & folding map of Rome. Some browning. Ck Nov 29 (305) £400

Ver, Moi

— Ein Ghetto im Osten-Vilna. Zurich, 1931. Intro by Salman Chneour. Pictorial bds; some wear. sg Oct 8 (74) $500

Ver Sacrum

— Ver Sacrum. Vienna: Gerlach & Schebk, 1898-99. Vol I, No 1-Vol II, No 12 & 1 special issue (complete set). 4to, orig wraps; some loose, those of 1 issue def. S May 28 (238) £1,500 [Quaritch]

Verdizotti, Giovanni Mario

— Cento Favole morali. Venice: Ziletti, 1570. 1st Ed. 4to, mor gilt by Rivieref; joints rubbed. With full-page woodcut of an astrologer & 101 full-page woodcuts of fables. Tear at inner corner of A8 repaired. C Dec 16 (91) £3,800 [Quaritch]

Anr copy. 18th-cent calf; rebacked. Some browning. SI June 10 (1056) LIt1,300,000

— Cento favole belissime dei piu illustri e moderni autori Greci e Latini. Venice: F. Ginammi, 1661. 8vo, old vellum. With 100 full-page woodcuts by Verdizotti within single line frame. Some outer margins shaved affecting woodcut borders; L8 to end wormed at inner margins; later leaves quite heavily dampstained. Ck Nov 29 (322) £260

Vereaux, J. B. E. See: Mulsant & Vereaux

Vergennes, Charles G. de

— Memoire historique et politique sur la Louisiane.... Paris, 1802. 8vo, half calf gilt; corners rubbed. Prelims foxed; some gatherings browned. wa Mar 5 (369) $130

Vergerio, Pietro Paolo

— De Republica Veneta. Toscolano: Alessandro dei Paganini, 1526. 4to, 19th-cent calf. Lower margins of several leaves stained. C Dec 16 (92) £2,700 [Jackson]

Vergil, Polydore, 1470?-1555?

— Adagiorum liber. Basel: Johann Frober, July 1521. Folio, contemp calf; foot of spine def. S Dec 5 (215) £2,000 [Halwas]

— De rerum inventoribus. Amst.: Elzevir, 1671. ("De inventoribus rerum libri VIII....") 12mo, 19th-cent mor gilt; rubbed. 20 lines & headline; Arringhi's last cursive type. Marginal staining; lacking final blank. Ck May 8 (66) £950

Anr Ed. Nijmegen: Reiner Smets, 1671. 12mo, contemp calf; spine wormed at foot. Ck May 8 (65) £70

Vergilius Maro, Publius, 70-19 B.C.

See also: Cranach Press; Limited Editions Club

— Opera. Nuremberg: Anton Koberger, 1492. Foliio, contemp bds; rebacked in lea. 62 lines of commentary surrounding text & headline; types 22:108R (text), 23:75R (commentary). Ms initials in blue & red; on a1r a six-line initial T illuminated in gold & colors. Sheet a4.5 sprung; f6 with upper outer corner torn away with loss to 1 numeral of foliation; b7 with tear to lower margin; l1 with tear at inner margin; red ink spilled but wiped off o7v; some old dampstaining. 353 (of 354) leaves; lacking final blank. Goff V-188. C Dec 16 (172) £1,800 [Tenschert]

Anr Ed. Lyons: Jacobo Sachon, 1517. 2 parts in 1 vol. Folio, old vellum. First title repaired & heavily soiled; dampstains at inner margins, most severe from N3 to N7; a1-2 browned; z4 holed with loss; small section torn from lower margin of V4; lacking 2d colophon leaf. Ck Nov 29 (324) £2,600

Anr Ed. Venice: Luc'Antonio Giunta, 1533. Folio, old vellum; rebacked, front hinge cracked. Marginal repairs at beginning & end; tp soiled & creased; lacking 2F1.8. sg Oct 24 (333) $300

Anr Ed. Leeuwarden, 1717. 2 vols. 4to, contemp calf; rubbed, rebacked, cover loose. With extra engraved title. bba Apr 30 (270) £60 [Tosi]

Anr Ed. Amst., 1746. 4 vols. 4to, vellum. B May 12 (1668) HF600

Anr Ed. Birm: Baskerville, 1757. ("Bucolica, Georgica, et Aeneis....") 4to, contemp calf. B Nov 1 (267) HF700

Anr copy. Contemp pigskin gilt; stab-hole extending through back cover through most margins. pn Apr 23 (68) £230

Anr Ed. Rome, 1763-65. 3 vols. Folio, contemp calf; extremities worn. L.p. copy. Ck Oct 31 (322) £400

Anr copy. Contemp half lea. SI June 10 (1078) LIt850,000

Anr Ed. Birm: Baskerville, 1766. 8vo, later calf gilt; upper cover detached. bba Jan 30 (52) £60 [Vine]

Anr Ed. L: T. Payne, 1793. 2 vols. Folio, mor gilt; spines rubbed & soiled, some tips bumped or worn. wa Sept 26 (38) $400

Anr Ed. L, 1800. ("Bucolica, Georgica et Aenis.") 2 vols. 8vo, contemp mor gilt. bba Jan 16 (152) £300 [Gammon]

Anr copy. ("Bucolica, Georgica et Aeneis.") Contemp mor gilt; spines repaired. Some browning. SI June 10 (1079) LIt680,000

— Works. L, 1697. 1st Ed of Dryden's trans. Folio, modern calf, old calf covers preserved. With frontis & 101 plates. 1 plate holed & 1 repaired. bba Jan 30 (42) £230 [Page]

2d Ed of Dryden's trans. L, 1698. Folio, contemp calf; joints weakened, scuffed, front cover detached. With frontis & 101 plates, 2 hand-colored. Frontis & tp loose, cut & repaired; 1 plate torn along margin. bba Aug 13 (96) £170 [Bailey]

Aeneid in English

— The Aeneids. L, 1876. Trans by William Morris. 8vo, orig cloth. Inscr by William Morris to Theodore Watts-Dunton. George Milne copy. CNY Dec 5 (282) $1,200

Aeneid in German

— Vergilii Maronis dreyzehen Buecher von dem tewren Helden Enea.... Frankfurt: David Zoepffeln, 1559. 8vo, contemp blind-stamped pigskin; worn, spine & corners damaged, wormed. With 13 woodcuts. One leaf torn. bba July 23 (378) £250 [Hesketh & Ward]

Anr copy. Contemp blind-stamped vellum; extremities worn & soiled, lower cover wormed. Some dampstains & soiling. Ck Oct 31 (321) £240

Aeneid in Italian

— Dell'Eneide di Virgilio.... Paris, 1760. 2 vols. 8vo, contemp calf; rebacked. SI June 10 (1077) LIt650,000

— L'Eneide di Virgilio. Venice: B. Giunta, 1581. 1st Ed of Annibale Caro's trans. 4to, old vellum. sg Mar 12 (303) $250

— Virgilio volgare qual narra le aspre battaglie & li fatti de Enea.... Venice: Nicolo Zoppino, 1528. 8vo, 19th-cent half vellum. Lacking final blank. S Dec 5 (216) £1,400 [Pickering & Chatto]

Aeneid in Scots

— Virgil's Aeneid, translated into Scottish Verse.... Edin., 1710. Trans by Gawin Douglas. Folio, calf. pnE Aug 12 (35) £220

Bucolica in Latin & English

— Bucolica. L, 1749. Trans by J. Martyn. 4to, orig calf; rubbed, covers detached. With port & 16 plates, 12 hand-colored. Front matter loose; some foxing. F Mar 26 (182) $130

Georgica in French

— Les Georgiques.... Paris: C. Bleuet, 1770. 8vo, contemp mor gilt; joints wormed. With frontis & 4 plates. S May 13 (869) £360 [Shapero]

Anr Ed. Paris, 1937-43-[50]. One of 750. Illus by Aristide Maillol. 2 vols. 4to, loose as issued in orig wraps. CNY Dec 5 (278) $900

Verheiden, Jacobus

— Imagines et elogia praestantium aliquot theologorum.... The Hague, 1725. Folio, bdg not described but worn & rubbed. K Sept 29 (377) $190

Verlaine, Paul, 1844-96

— Chansons pour elle. Paris, 1939. One of 175. Illus by Aristide Maillol. Mor gilt, orig wraps bound in. Schlosser copy. P June 18 (435) $1,500

— Dedicaces. Paris, 1890. 1st Ed, One of 50 on hollande. 16mo, orig wraps. Inscr to Francois Coppee & with ANs to Coppee. S May 28 (452) £1,300 [Shapero]

— Femmes/Hombres. L, 1972. One of 100. Illus by Michael Ayrton. Oblong folio, orig half mor. With 15 etchings. S Nov 14 (79) £280 [Nelson]

One of 15 with a separate folder of 17 proofs including 2 planches refusees, a suite on hand-made paper & an orig drawing, this being copy B, for Robert Eddison. Half mor & half mor folder, both by Sangorski & Sutcliffe. b June 22 (51) £1,400

— Fetes Galantes. Paris, 1928. One of 175 for America. Illus by Georges Barbier. 4to, wraps; spine torn. sg Sept 26 (14) $800

One of 25 on japon with an orig watercolor laid in & with 2 extra suites of plates, 1 in color. Orig wraps; spine worn. P June 25 (509) $3,500

Anr Ed. Paris, 1971. Illus by Marie Laurencin. Loose as issued. sg Jan 30 (97) $200

— Liturgies intimes. Mars 1892. Paris, 1892. 1st Ed, one of 50 L.p. copies. Orig wraps, unopened. S May 28 (453) £450 [Beres]

— Parallelement. Paris, 1900. Suppressed Ed,

one of 170 on hollande. Illus by Bonnard. 4to, mor gilt. With 108 lithos in rose-sanguine & 9 wood-engravings in black. Schlosser copy. P June 18 (517) $14,500

Anr copy. Mor by Creuzevault, orig wraps bound in. S May 28 (220) £15,500 [Panini]

— Poemes Saturniens. Paris, 1866. 12mo, mor extra by Mercier, orig wraps bound in. Inscr to Leopold Gravier. S May 28 (450) £1,500 [Shapero]

Verne, Jules, 1828-1905

— Twenty Thousand Leagues Under the Sea. L, 1873. 8vo, pictorial cloth; spine ends & corners worn, spine cocked. Some foxing. sg June 11 (313) $325

— Works. NY, [1911]. Prince Edward of Wales Ed, one of 500. 15 vols. Half mor gilt. ANs tipped in. P June 17 (357) $1,700

Verner, Collie —& Stuart-Stubbs, Basil

— The Northpart of America. Toronto, 1979. Oblong folio, cloth; rear endpapers torn out. sg Oct 31 (78) $130

Verner, William Willoughby Cole

— Sketches in the Soudan. L, 1885. Oblong folio, orig bds; upper cover stained & soiled. With litho title, map & 37 plates. b Nov 18 (358) £170

Vernet, Antoine Charles Horace. See: Vernet, Carle

Vernet, Carle, 1758-1835

— Campagnes des Francais sous le Consulat & l'Empire.... Paris, [c.1840]. Folio, orig cloth. With port & 57 plates. Last 15 plates with staining at lower corner; some marginal soiling. S Nov 15 (857) £550 [Erlini]

— Tableaux historiques des compagnes d'Italie depuis l'An IV jusqu'a la bataille de Marengo. Paris, 1806. Folio, modern sheep. With port, 24 plates & double-page map & 2 plates to the precis historique de la campagne d'Allemagne. C June 24 (221) £850 [Bifolco]

Anr copy. Contemp mor; corners worn. With frontis, double-page map, 1 double-page plate of the battle of Austerlitz & 28 plates. Some spotting & browning. S Dec 5 (298) £3,800 [Kaiser]

Anr copy. Contemp mor gilt; worn & def. With port, 28 plates & double-page map & engraved title to coronation supplement with medallion ports. Port & tp stained; staining mainly at lower margins. S Feb 26 (797) £1,400 [Gal D'Arte]

Anr copy. Half lea; joint broken. With 25 plates & 1 folding map, colored in outline. S June 10 (1058) LIt2,500,000

Vernet, Carle, 1758-1835 & Horace —& Lami, Eugene

— Collection des uniformes des Armees Francaises de 1791 a 1814 [de 1814 a 1824]. Paris, 1822-25. 2 parts in 2 vols. 4to, contemp half mor. With 149 hand-colored plates mtd on guards. Edges discolored & brittle. C May 20 (308) £550 [Etching]

Verneuil, Maurice Pillard

— L'Animal dans la decoration. Paris, 1897. Copy with 3 orig drawings. Folio, half mor. CGen Nov 18 (475) SF6,000

Verral, William

— A Complete System of Cookery. L, 1759. 1st Ed. 8vo, modern cloth; browned & stained. Library markings. O Apr 28 (200) $160

Anr copy. Cloth. sp Apr 16 (341) $500

Verstegen, Richard. See: Rowlands, Richard

Vertot, Rene Aubert de, 1655-1735

— Histoire des Chevaliers Hospitaliers de S. Jean de Jerusalem.... Paris, 1726. 4 vols. 4to, contemp calf; rubbed. With 6 maps & 71 ports. S June 22 (83) £1,200 [Grnado]

— The History of the Knights of Malta. L, 1728. 2 vols. Folio, contemp half mor; rubbed. With port, 69 plates & 5 maps. Some foxing throughout; Vol I with stain throughout; some leaves repaired at foot. bba Aug 13 (100) £100 [Shapero]

Anr copy. Contemp calf; rebacked. With 71 engraved ports & 4 maps and plans. sg Nov 7 (243) $425

Vertue, George, 1684-1756

— A Catalogue and Description of King Charles the First's Capital Collection of Pictures.... L, 1753. With: A Catalogue of the Collection of Pictures...James the Second.... And: A Catalogue of the Curious Collection...George Villiers, Duke of Buckingham.... 4to, mor gilt by Clarke & Bedford; becoming disbound. With 160 holograph annotations by Thomas Gray in the text & 8 pages of Ms at end of 3d work. Rosebery copy. C Dec 16 (254) £1,800 [Quaritch]

Anr Ed. L, 1757. 4to, contemp calf; rubbed. bba Feb 13 (245) £240 [Spellman]

— A Description of the Works of...Wenceslaus Hollar. L, 1745. 1st Ed. 4to, recent half calf; rubbed. Old ink annotations. DW Mar 11 (867) £360

Verve...

[For Issues on individuals, See Bonnard, Braque, Chagall, etc.] .

— Verve: An Artistic and Literary Quarterly. Paris, [1938]. Vol I, No 3. 4to, orig wraps. cb Sept 5 (119) $180

— Verve. Revue artistique et litteraire. Paris, 1937-60. Nos 1-37/38. 4to, orig bdgs. Epstein copy. sg Apr 30 (477) $13,000

No 1. Paris, 1937. Wraps; worn. One leaf loose & wrinkled at edges. bbc June 29 (186) $105

Anr copy. Wraps. French text. sg Sept 6 (281) $225

Vol I, Nos 2-6. Bound in 1 vol.. 4to, cloth or disbound. Sold w.a.f. O July 14 (190) $160

No 3. Paris, 1938. 4to, orig wraps. Light stain on prelims. sg Sept 6 (282) $200

Nos 2-4 in 1 vol. Paris, 1938-39. wa June 25 (457) $300

Vervliet, Hendrik D. L.

— The Book through 5,000 Years. L & NY, [1972]. 4to, orig cloth, in repaired d/j. bbc Sept 23 (125) $125

Anr copy. Orig cloth, in d/j. cb Oct 17 (950) $160

Vesalius, Andreas, 1514-64

See also: Bremer Press

— Opera. Leiden, 1725. 2 vols. Folio, newer half lea; worn & broken. With port & 76 (of 82) plates. Some foxing & soiling. O May 26 (195) $1,100

Vespucci, Amerigo, 1454-1512

See also: Grabhorn Printing

— Von der new gefunnden Region die wol ein welt genennt mag werden, durch die Christenlichen Kuenig von Portugall, wunnderbarlich erfunden. Nuremberg: Wolffganng Hueber, 1506 [but Paris: Adam Pilinski, 1861]. 4to, bdg not described. bbc Sept 23 (193) $80

Vesy

— Vesy. Nauchno-Literaturiy i Kritiko-Bibliograficheskii Ekhemesyanik'. Moscow, 1904-9. Vols I-VI (complete set). 72 issues bound in 24 vols. 4to, modern half calf, orig wraps bound in (lacking covers of Vol 4, No 4). Lacking 6 plates. S Dec 5 (326) £600 [Lewinson]

Vetterling, Herman

— The Illuminate of Goerlitz, or Jakob Boehme's...Life and Philosophy. Leipzig, 1922. One of 50. B Nov 1 (672) HF375

Vettori, Pietro

— Variarum lectionum libri XXV. Florence: Laurentius Torrentinus, 1553. Folio, contemp vellum. sg Mar 12 (301) $425

Vever, Henri

— La Bijouterie francaise au XIXe siecle. Paris, 1906. One of 1,000. 2 vols. 4to, later cloth, orig covers bound in. Some dampstaining & soiling. F Mar 26 (308) $100

Vey, Horst

— Die Zeichnungen Anton van Dycks. Brussels, 1962. 2 vols. In d/js. S Feb 11 (231) £180 [Bernett]

Viaggi...

— Viaggi fatti da Vinetia, alla Tana, in Persia.... Venice: Aldus, 1543. 8vo, 19th-cent half mor. Some soiling; M1-2 torn with loss & repaired; library stamp on tp. S June 30 (344) £280 [Dallegio]

Viana, Francisco Xavier de

— Diario del viage explorador de las corbetas espanolas 'Descubierta' y 'Atrevida'.... Cerrito de la Victoria [Montevideo], 1849. 8vo, modern calf, old wraps bound in. S June 25 (61) £5,000 [Quaritch/Hordern]

Viaud, Julian. See: Loti, Pierre

Vicaire, Georges

— Bibliographie gastronomique. L, 1954. In d/j. bbc Apr 27 (258) $60

— Manuel de l'amateur de livres du XIXe Siecle.... Paris, 1894. One of 1,000. 8 vols. 8vo, contemp half mor; rubbed. bba Dec 19 (305) £260 [Kiefer]

Vicentio, Ludovico degli Arrighi

— La Operina da imparare di scrivere littera Cancellarescha. Rome, 1522. 4to, modern vellum; early flyleaf bound in. Lacking final leaf; some soiling; stamp removed from title, the resultant hole repaired. C June 24 (224) £8,000 [Jackson]

— Regola da imparare scrivere varii caratteri de Littere.... Venice: Nicolo d'Aristottle detto Zoppino, 1533. 4to, later 19th-cent mor gilt. Tp & last leaf in facsimile; upper margins restored with occasional losses. C June 24 (225) £300 [Gherucci]

Victor, Benjamin

— The History of the Theatres of London and Dublin. L, 1761. 2 vols. 8vo, contemp calf. sg Mar 5 (259) $175

Victor, Frances Fuller

— The River of the West. Hartford, 1870. 8vo, orig cloth; spine chipped. cb Sept 12 (177) $160

Anr copy. Cloth; spine repaired, extremities rubbed. sg June 18 (535) $80

Victoria History of the Counties of England

— Bedfordshire. L, 1904-72. Mixed Ed. 4 vols, including Index. Folio, orig cloth. bba May 28 (390) £85 [Traylen]

— Berkshire. L, 1906-72. Mixed Ed. 5 vols, including Index. Folio, orig cloth. bba May 28 (391) £110 [Townsend]

— Buckinghamshire. L, 1905-28. 5 vols. Folio, orig cloth, Vol V in half mor. Some leaves in Index brittle or torn. bba May 28

(392) £240 [Quaritch]
— Hampshire and the Isle of Wight. L, 1900-14. 6 vols. Folio, orig cloth. L Nov 14 (129) £110
— Yorkshire East Riding L, 1969-79. 4 vols. Folio, orig cloth. pnL Nov 20 (93) £120 [Miles]

Vida, Marcus Hieronymus, 1480?-1566
— Christidos libri sex. Cremona: Lodovico Britannico, Oct 1535. 4to, contemp mor; rubbed. Italic letters. S Dec 5 (218) £1,500 [Martin]
— De arte poetica lib. III.... [Venice: Melchior Sessa, 1538]. 8vo, contemp vellum. Italic type. Lacking final blank; some marginal dampstains. Ck May 8 (69) £180

Vidal, Emeric Essex
— Picturesque Illustrations of Buenos Ayres and Monte Video.... L: Ackermann, 1820. 4to, modern mor gilt. With 24 hand-colored plates. Crease to double-page plate; some marginal soiling to text. C May 20 (309) £3,000 [Traylen]

Vidal, Gore
— Williwaw: A Novel. NY, 1946. In d/j. cb Sept 19 (217) $100; cb Dec 12 (158) $60

Vidocq, Francois Eugene, 1775-1857
— Memoirs of Vidocq: Principal Agent of the French Police. L, 1828-30. 4 vols. Modern calf. Epstein copy. sg Apr 30 (478) $1,300
Anr Ed. L, 1829. 4 vols bound in 2. 8vo, contemp half calf gilt; rubbed. cb Feb 12 (144) $200

Vieillot, Louis Jean Pierre
— La Galerie des oiseaux. Paris, 1834. 2 vols in 4. 4to, contemp half calf; rubbed. With 325 lithos, all but 5 hand-colored & with 33 uncolored plates of bills. Some spotting & discoloration; a few plate numerals cropped; a few leaves of text inserted from a shorter copy; library stamp, not affecting plates. S Nov 21 (50) £2,000 [Maggs]

Vieussens, Raymond de, 1641-1715
— Oeuvres francoises. Toulouse, 1715. 2 vols in 1. 4to, modern mor. With port & 20 plates. 1 plate torn; some spotting & soiling. bba Sept 5 (313) £580 [N. Phillips]

Views...
— Views in America, Great Britain, Switzerland, Turkey, Italy, the Holy Land.... NY, 1853. 4to, orig mor gilt; front joint repaired. With 135 plates. Some foxing; ad leaf torn. wa Dec 19 (455) $400
— Views of Paris. [Paris: Ledot & Aubrun, c.1860]. Oblong 4to, contemp half mor; rubbed & worn. With 45 (of 46) plates. First plate soiled; some foxing throughout. wd Dec 12 (428) $425
— Views of the Adirondack Mountain Region. NY: Bufford's Lithography, [1838]. 4to, orig wraps; chipped & with edge tears. With 15 full-page & folding maps & views. Some dampstain, affecting images at corner. bbc Sept 23 (343) $600
— Views of Valencia Harbour.... L: Day & Son, [1849]. Folio, contemp half calf gilt; worn. With litho map & 6 tinted litho views. S Nov 21 (123) £950 [H. D. Lyon]

Vigeant, Arsene
— L'Almanach de l'escrime. Paris, 1889. One of 525. Orig wraps; 1st gathering loose. Inscr to Mme Sylvain. sg Mar 26 (333) $200

Viggiani, Angelo
— Lo Schermo. Venice, 1575. 8vo, old vellum. sg Mar 26 (336) $1,900

Vigne, Godfrey Thomas
— Travels in Mexico, South America.... L, 1863. 2 vols. 8vo, contemp calf gilt; rubbed. With folding map & 10 plates. bba Feb 27 (20) £180 [Sotheran]

Vigneron, Pierre-Roch
— Costumes suisses. Paris, [1822]. 4to, orig cloth; rubbed. With 22 chromolitho plates in a continuous folding panorama, all finished by hand. Scuffing to 2 plates. Ck Oct 18 (55) £140

Vignola, Giacomo Barozzi da. See: Barozzi, Giacomo

Vigny, Alfred de, 1797-1863
— Chatterton. Paris, 1835. 1st Ed. 8vo, half calf by Maylander. ALs laid in. S May 28 (457) £600 [Beres]

Vigo, Joannes de
— Prattica utilissima et necessaria di cirugia. Venice: Valgrisi & Costantini, 1558. 4to, old bds; worn. S Dec 5 (445) £1,800 [Phelps]

Vigo, Johannes de
— Practi. Jo. de Vigo copiosa in arte chirugica.... [Venice: heredum O. Scoti, 1520]. Margin of t.p. cut away. Bound with: Vigo. Practica compendioso.... [Venice: heredum O. Scoti, 1520]. Folio, 18th-cent vellum; spine worn. Marginal repairs at beginning & end; Ms note at end. SI June 10 (1071) LIt3,200,000
— Works. L: T. East, 1586. 1 (of 3) parts in 1 vol. 4to, 19th-cent calf; joints rubbed. Black letter. STC 24723. sg May 14 (174) $2,600

Villamena, Francesco

— Columnae traiani imperatoris quae adhuc Romae.... Rome, [early 17th-cent]. Oblong folio, old vellum bds; soiled. With 130 plates. Repairs to inner margins; a few plates stained; some marginal soiling & fraying. S Feb 11 (232) £520 [Shapero]

Villani, Giovanni, 1280?-1348

— Croniche...nelle quali si tratta dell'origine di Firenze.... Venice, 1537. 1st Ed. Folio, 18th-cent vellum. With uncancelled leaves Q2 & 7. C June 24 (352) £550 [Mediolanum]

Villani, Matteo, d.1363

— Istorie. Florence, 1581-77. 2 parts in 1 vol. 4to, 18th-cent lea. SI June 10 (1073) LIt320,000

— La Prima Parte della Cronica universale de suoi tempi. Florence: Lorenzo Torrentino, 1554. 8vo, old calf gilt; head of spine chipped. Marginal dampstaining. sg Mar 12 (302) $450

Ville, Antoine de

— Les Fortifications...contenans la maniere de fortifier toute sorte de places.... Lyons, 1640. Folio, old bds. With engraved title, port & 53 plates. Waterstain at lower fore-corner throughout; minor worming, not affecting text or plates. S Nov 21 (104) £500 [Marioni]

Villena, Enrique de Aragon

— Arte Cisoria, o Tratado del Arte del Cortar del Cuchillo.... Madrid: A. Marin, 1766. 4to, modern vellum bds. S Dec 5 (290) £1,100 [Smith]

Villeneuve, Eugene de

— Journal fait en Grece.... Brussels, 1827. 8vo, orig wraps; spine broken, lower cover soiled, upper cover torn with loss. With port & 4 facsimiles. Inscr. S June 30 (432) £400 [Maggs]

Villermaules, Michel, 1672-1757

— Anecdotes sur l'etat de la religion dans la Chine. Paris, 1733-35. 7 vols. 12mo, contemp calf; Vol VII not uniform. bba Jan 16 (294) £130 [Robertshaw]

Villiers de l'Isle Adam, Auguste de, Comte

— Contes cruels. Paris, 1883. 12mo, orig wraps. Epstein copy. sg Apr 30 (479) $600

Villon, Francois, b.1431

See also: Eragny Press

— Oeuvres. Paris: Ambroise Vollard, 1918. One of 25 on papier japon. 4to, loose in orig wraps. sg Jan 30 (184) $400

Villotte, Jacques

— Voyages en Turquie, en Perse, en Armenie.... Paris, [1730]. 12mo, contemp calf; rebacked, worn. S July 1 (867) £320 [Maggs]

Vinciolo, Federico di

— Les Singuliers et nouveaux Pourtraicts.... Paris: Jean le Clerc, 1601. 8vo, contemp vellum; soiled. Tp & some leaves lacking. Sold w.a.f. b June 22 (92) £200

Anr Ed. Lyon, 1603. 4to, mor gilt by Trautz-Bauzonnet. CNY Dec 5 (342) $7,000

Vindel, Francisco

— El Arte tipografico en Espana durante el siglo XV. Madrid, 1945-51. 9 vols. Bound with: Vindel. El Arte tipografico en Cataluna durante el siglo XV. Madrid, 1954. Folio. One of 500. Orig wraps; several covers detached. DW Jan 29 (347) £480

— Manual grafico-descriptivo del bibliofilo Hispano-Americano. Madrid, 1930-34. 12 vols. Folio, Vol XII, wraps, unopened; others, sheep; extremities rubbed; last 2 vols dampstained. sg Oct 31 (321) $1,300

— Mapas de America en los libros espanoles de los siglos XVI al XVIII. Madrid, 1955-59. One of 520. 2 vols, including Supplement. Folio, Earlier vol newly bound in cloth; Supplement in half sheep. Both with orig wraps bound in. sg Oct 31 (79) $850

Vineyard...

— The Vineyard: Being a Treatise shewing I. The Nature and Method of Planting... Vines. II. Proper Directions for Drawing, Pressing...Wine. III. An Easy and Familiar Method of Planting and Raising Vines.... L, 1732. 2d Ed. 8vo, contemp half calf; spine def. Cropped. bba Oct 10 (219) £160 [Roberts]

Vingtieme Siecle

— XXe Siecle: Cahiers d'art. Paris, 1929-39. Ire Annee, No 1 - IInd Annee, No 1. 7 issues in 6, as issued Orig wraps; scuffed & rubbed. bba Feb 13 (79) £1,200 [Sims Reed]

Anr Ed. Paris, 1963. New Series, No 22 Bds. bba May 14 (349) £110 [Koos]

Vinycomb, John

— On the Processes for the Production of Ex Libris (Book-Plates). L, 1894. cb Oct 17 (955) $50

Viollet-le-Duc, Eugene Emmanuel, 1814-79

— Dictionnaire raisonne de l'architecture francais du XIe au XVIe siecle. Paris, 1858-68. 10 vols. 8vo, half mor; edges worn, scuff marks retouched on spines. sg Sept 6 (286) $1,900

— Dictionnaire raisonne du mobilier francais.... Paris, 1872-75. 6 vols. 8vo, contemp half mor. S July 1 (1364) £180 [Hetherington]

— Dictionnaire raisonne de l'architecture francais du XIe au XVIe siecle. Paris, 1875. 10 vols. Half cloth. B May 12 (419) HF1,000

Viollis, Jean

— Bonne-Fille. Paris: Editions Mornay, 1926. One of 18 on japon with 2 large ink & watercolor drawings & 2 smaller designs, each sgd by the artist. 8vo, mor gilt, orig wraps bound in. S Nov 14 (12) £200 [Deitch]

Virchow, Rudolf, 1821-1902

— Cellular Pathology.... NY, [c.1861]. 1st American Ed. 8vo, orig cloth; spine ends & rear joint chipped, corners worn. sg May 14 (175) $500

Virginians. See: Thackeray, William Makepeace

Vishniac, Roman

— Polish Jews: A Pictorial Record. NY, 1947. 4to, cloth, in chipped d/j; bdg corners bumped. sg Apr 13 (100) $130

Visit...

— A Visit to the Bazaar. L, 1818. 1st Ed. 16mo, orig half calf; rubbed. With frontis & 31 plates, some partly colored. Some spotting. bba July 23 (145) £180 [James]

Visscher, Nikolaus Jansson

— Atlas Minor. Amst. [c.1695]. 3 vols. Folio, modern vellum gilt. With 3 engraved titles, hand-colored & heightened with gold, & 199 mostly double-page maps hand-colored throughout. Some repairs without loss; 2 engraved titles inlaid to size. S June 25 (294) £80,000 [Arader]

— Brabantiae Ducatus cum adjacentibus provinciis. [Amst.], 1650. 585mm by 498mm. A few repairs on verso. cb Jan 30 (270) $100

Vitali, Lamberto

— Quarantacinque disegni di Alberto Giacometti. Turin, 1963. One of 1,250. Folio, unsewn in orig box. With 45 mtd reproductions. SI Dec 5 (719) LIt1,600,000

Vitruvius Pollio, Marcus

In French

— Les Dix Livres d'architecture. Paris, 1684. 2d Ed of Perrault's trans. Folio, contemp calf; worn. With frontis & 68 plates. Dedication leaf repaired with adhesive tape, affecting some letters; a few short tears touching text. S Nov 21 (106) £650 [Gorini]

In German

— Zehen Buecher von der Architectur.... Basel, 1614. Bound with: Ryff, Walter H. Bawkunst. Basel, 1582. Folio, 19th-cent bds; stitching split at beginning. Woodcut on O2 verso of 2d work just shaved at fore-margin; some stains, browning & marginal tears. S June 25 (181) £1,600 [Koch]

Anr copy. Contemp vellum; rebacked. Marginal dampstains; some contemp marginalia; browned. sg Sept 6 (287) $1,300

In Italian

— De Architectura.... Venice: Francesco Marcolini, 1556. ("I Dieci libri dell' architettura.") Folio, recent calf; rubbed. With 131 woodcut illusts & diagrams, 6 with overslips or extensions. Pasted-on cancel illusts at E8v & F7r; lacking 6 leaves at end; some waterstaining. S June 25 (180) £800 [Gorini]

Anr Ed. Venice, 1567. ("I Dieci Libri del architettura.") 4to, 18th-cent half lea. Frontis damaged, not affecting surface; some browning & marginal soiling. SI June 10 (1081) LIt1,350,000

Anr Ed. Naples, 1758. ("L'Architettura.") Folio, contemp vellum; spine rubbed. With frontis & 25 plates. Marginal worming; some browning. SI Dec 5 (720) LIt1,000,000

Anr Ed. Naples: Fratelli Terres, 1790. Folio, 19th-cent half vellum. With frontis & 25 plates. SI Dec 5 (1052) LIt750,000

In Latin

— De Architectura, libri decem.... Amst.: Elzevir, 1649. 8vo, 18th-cent mor gilt. Engraved title with small repaired tear with loss. C Dec 16 (173) £1,400 [Mediolanum]

Vittadini, Carlo

— Descrizione dei Funghi Mangerecci piu Communi dell'Italia. Milan: Felice Rusconi, 1835. 2 vols. Folio, presentation bdg of contemp mor gilt. Ck Oct 31 (107) $2,800

Vivian, Sir Arthur Pendarves

— Wanderings in the Western Land. L, 1879. 8vo, half calf. sg June 18 (536) $140

Viviani, Vincenzo

— De maximis, et minimis geometrica divinatio.... Florence, 1659. 1st Ed. Folio, early 19th-cent half calf; spine detached. First dedication leaf & T4 of Part 1 repaired at lower margin; N1 of Part 1 creased & torn at inner margin; N2-3 of Part 2 soiled at outer margin. Ck Nov 29 (247) £480

Vizetelly, Ernest Alfred

— The True Story of the Chevalier d'Eon. L, 1895. One of 600. 8vo, cloth; extremities worn. sg Mar 26 (337) $200

Vlaminck, Maurice, 1876-1958

— A la Sante du corps. Paris: Imprimerie Francois Bernourard, 1919. One of 104. Illus by Andre Derain. Orig wraps; minor foxing. With 4 lithos. With 2 small wormholes. Schlosser copy. P June 18 (532) $1,400

Vocabulary...

— A Vocabulary, or Pocket Dictionary. Birm. & L: Baskerville, 1765. 12mo, contemp bds; rebacked, rubbed, new endpapers. bba June 11 (62) £400 [Thomson]

Voit, Johann Peter

— Unterhaltungen fuer junge Leute aus der Naturgeschichte.... Nuremberg; Schneider & Wiegel, 1794-90. 3d Ed of Vol I, 2d Ed of Vol II, 1st Ed of Vol III. 3 vols. Orig half calf; rubbed & worn. With port & 145 hand-colored plates. S Dec 5 (259) £4,000 [Schiller]

Volboudt, Pierre

— Les Assemblages de Jean Dubuffet: signes, sols, sorts. Paris, 1958. One of 208. Illus by Jean Dubuffet. 4to, unsewn in orig wraps. sg Jan 30 (38) $650

Vollard, Ambroise

— Sainte Monique. Paris, 1930. One of 257, with 2 extra suites of illusts. Illus by Pierre Bonnard. 4to, half mor. CGen Nov 18 (478) SF7,000

— La Vie et l'oeuvre de Pierre-Auguste Renoir. Paris, 1919. One of 525. Folio, half vellum, orig wraps bound in. With 3 extra prints loosely inserted. S Feb 11 (267) £1,300 [Sims Reed]

Vollkommen...

— Vollkommen ergaentzter Pferdt-Schatz auss der Theoria und Praxi. Frankfurt: T. M. Goetz, 1664. 2 parts in 1 vol. Folio, vellum; upper cover stained. With engraved title & 19 (of 25) plates. Lacking 2d ptd title & final 10 leaves of text. S Feb 11 (519) £380 [Shapero]

Vollmer, Hans

— Allgemeines Lexicon der Bildenden Kuenstler des XX. Jahrhunderts. Leipzig, 1953-62. 6 vols. Orig half mor. S Feb 11 (268) £320 [Eimers]

Volney, Constantin Francois, Comte de

— Considerations sur la guerre actuelle des Turcs. [N.p.], 1788. 8vo, modern bds. With engraved title & folding map. Tp & edges dust-soiled. S Nov 15 (1191) £200 [Kutluoglu]

— Tableau du climat et du sol des Etats-Unis d'Amerique. Paris, 1803 [An XII]. 1st Ed. 2 vols in 1. 4to, modern half calf. With 2 maps & 2 plates. sg Dec 5 (260) $275

Voltaire, Francois Marie Arouet de

— Candide. NY, 1928. One of 95 hand-colored copies. Illus by Rockwell Kent. 4to, orig half mor. Epstein copy. sg Apr 30 (480) $1,000

One of 1,470. Cloth. K Mar 22 (217) $65

— Candide, ou l'optimisme. [France], 1759. 12mo, orig wraps. Wade 11. C Dec 16 (174) £250 [Ximenes]

Anr Ed. [L: for Jean Nourse], 1759. 12mo, bdg not described. br May 29 (18) $475

Anr Ed. [Paris, probably Ballard for Michel Lambert], 1759. 12mo, contemp calf; worn. Ck Sept 6 (93) £140

Anr Ed. Paris: Jean Porson, [1948]. One of 250. Illus by Antoni Clave. Folio, loose in wraps as issued. sg May 7 (60) $1,300

— Elementi della Filosofia del Neuton. Venice, 1741. 8vo, orig vellum. F Sept 26 (313) $160

— La Henriade. L, 1728. 4to, later half sheep. With frontis & 10 plates. bba Feb 27 (267) £60 [Howell]

— L'Ingenu. Paris: Rene Kieffer, [1922]. One of 40 on japon, with an additional suite of the illusts on chine. Illus by Sylvain Sauvage. Half mor. Inscr by Sauvage & with 3 watercolors. sg Apr 30 (481) $900

— Letters Concerning the English Nation. L, 1733. 1st Ed. 8vo, contemp calf; rubbed, joints repaired. Minor soiling. pn June 11 (159) £220 [Pickering & Chatto]

Anr copy. Contemp calf; rubbed, joints split. S May 14 (966) £200 [Marlborough Rare Books]

— Oeuvres. Kehl, 1785-89. 70 vols. 8vo, 19th-cent half mor gilt; spine ends worn. Some foxing & browning, generally not affecting plates; stain on 2 text leaves in Vol I; Vol 47 lacking port. sg Mar 5 (315A) $900

— Poem upon the Lisbon Disaster. Lincoln MA: Penmaen Press, 1977. One of 200.

Illus by Lynd Ward. 4to, half cloth. pba July 23 (167) $80

— Works. L & NY, [1901]. Edition de la Pacification, Ltd Ed. 43 vols, including Index. Half lea; some spines chipped. wa Sept 26 (541) $230

— Zadig, ou la destine. L: J. Brindley, 1749. 12mo, bdg not described. Met Apr 28 (857) $70

Von Hagen, Victor Wolfgang

— The Aztec and Maya Papermakers. NY, [1943]. Intro by Dard Hunter. 4to, cloth. b&b Feb 19 (264) $175

Anr copy. Cloth, in d/j. cb Oct 17 (956) $50

Von Wieser, F. R. See: Fischer & Von Wieser

Vonnegut, Kurt, Jr.

— God Bless You, Mr. Rosewater.... NY, [1965]. In d/j. Bookplate sgd by Vonnegut affixed to front free endpaper. pba July 9 (288) $50

— Player Piano. NY, 1952. In chipped d/j. Ralph Vonnegut's copy. sg June 11 (314) $250

— Slaughterhouse-Five or the Children's Crusade. NY, 1969. In d/j. sp Apr 16 (425) $60

Voragine, Jacobus de, 1230?-98?

— Legenda aurea. [Augsburg: Johann Baemler, 1477?]. ("Leben der Heiligen. Winterteil.") Folio, 16thk-cent German blind-stamped calf over wooden bds; rebacked, lacking clasps. 29 lines; gothic letter; maiblumen initial at beginning; woodcut initials; woodcut of St. Michael with woodcut floral borderpiece in margin at beginning of text; woodcuts & initials all hand-colored Upper margin of 2d leaf cut away & repaired; 7 leaves repaired with loss; tears in 4 other leaves repaired at least in part; some staining & soiling throughout, heavier at beginning. 509 leaves only; lacking woodcut frontis, all after f.513 & at least 12 other leaves. Goff Supplement J-157a. S Dec 5 (20) £11,000

Anr Ed. Feb Strassburg: Ptr of the 1483 Jordanus de Quedlinburg 1489. Folio, 18th-cent mor gilt. 46 lines & headline, double column, types 1:160G & 2:91aG. Sheets M2-5 & M3.4 reversed; inner margin of title strengthened; minor worming at beginning & end; some initials smudged. 263 (of 264) leaves; lacking final blank. C Nov 27 (18) £1,800 [Aspin]

— La Legende doree en francoys nouvellement imprimee. Lyons: Jean de la Place for Etienne Gueynard, 1518. 4to, 17th-cent vellum. Croxteth Library copy. S May 28 (49) £2,600 [Halwas]

— Passionael efte Dat levent der hyllinghen to duede. Basel: Adam Petri, 1517. Folio, contemp pigskin over wooden bds; rubbed, lacking clasps. With 282 woodcut illusts, 6 full-page; Pp1 in Part 2 with lower outer corner torn diagonally away with loss of text to 14 lines of 1 column; some tears & repairs; tp & last gathering reinserted with margins trimmed; browned & soiled; lacking 2 leaves. C Nov 27 (42) £4,000 [Schulz]

Vorobeichic, M. See: Ver, Moi

Vorschriften...

— Neue Vorschriften zum gebrauch der Schulen in den anstalten des Waisenhauses.... Halle, 1751. Oblong 8vo, self-wraps. Some soiling & staining. wa Mar 5 (528) $750

Vossius, Gerardus Joannes

— Ars historica. Sive, de historiae & historices natura.... Leiden, 1653. Bound with: De Historicis Graecis LibriIv. Amst., 1650. And: De Historicis Latinis Libri III. Amst., 1651 4to, contemp vellum; soiled. bba Mar 26 (127) £130 [Maurice]

Votes. See: Franklin Printing, Benjamin

Voyage...

See also: Daniel, Gabriel; Fracker, George

— Voyage pittoresque de la France, avec la description de toutes ses provinces. Paris: Lamy, 1789-87-86-[92]. 3 vols. Folio, contemp half calf; rubbed. With engraved title & 347 plates on 217 sheets & 4 maps & plans. Sold w.a.f. S June 25 (327) £5,500 [Museion]

Voyages. See: Acuna, Christoval

Vries, Jan Vredemann, b.1527

— Variae architecturae formae.... Antwerp: Theodorus Gallaeus, 1601. Oblong 4to, modern vellum. With engraved title & 49 plates (of 50). Minor stains; some thumbing at corners. S June 25 (233) £1,400 [Bifolco]

Vues...

— Vues de la Grece moderne.... Paris, 1824. Illus by A. Joly. Oblong folio, modern half mor. With 10 plates. S June 30 (325) £1,100 [Chelsea]

— Vues des villes, edifices & autre choses remarquables de l'Ecosse & d'Irlande. Leiden: Pieter van der Aa, [c.1720]. Vol V only. half calf; worn. With 2 maps & 33 plates of Scotland only. bba May 14 (281) £100 [Elliott]

Vuillier, Gaston

— A History of Dancing. L, 1898. 4to, orig cloth. With 20 plates. pn Oct 24 (466) £240

VVV

— VVV Almanac for 1943. NY, 1943. Number 2/3 Wraps, with lower cover of Duchamp chicken-wire cover. cb Sept 5 (32) $1,600

Vyse, Howard

— Operations Carried on at the Pyramids of Gizeh in 1837. L, 1840. 2 vols. 4to, cloth; worn. SI June 10 (1088) LIt1,200,000

W

Wachenhusen, Hans —& Others

— The Rhine from its Source to the Sea. L, 1878. 4to, orig cloth; worn. With 60 plates. pn July 16 (210) £65

Anr copy. Half mor gilt by Fazakerley. sg May 21 (86) $175

Wade, Allan

— A Bibliography of the Writings of W. B. Yeats. L, 1968. 3d Ed. In d/j. O Dec 17 (189) $110

Wade, Henling Thomas

— With Boat and Gun in the Yangtze Valley. Shanghai, 1910. 4to, cloth. sg May 21 (111) $275

Wade, Henry

— Halcyon; or, Rod-Fishing with Fly, Minnow, and Worm. L, 1861. 8vo, orig cloth; worn. Koopman copy. O Oct 29 (319) $140

Wafer, Lionel, 1660?-1705?

— A New Voyage and Description of the Isthmus of America.... L, 1699. 1st Ed. 8vo, half calf; extremities worn. With folding map & 3 folding plates. Margins on all 3 plates renewed, but not affecting captions. CNY Oct 8 (250) $700

Anr copy. Old calf; rebacked, worn. Some stains & marginal fraying. O May 26 (196) $375

Wafhafftige...

— Warhafftige Erbaermliche und Klaegliche Zeitung un Bericht einer fuernemen Personen von der grewlichen Tyranney des Muscowiters aus Riga.... Rostock: Jakob Lutz, 1578. 4to, calf. Some soiling & spotting. S July 1 (729) £600 [Reiss & Auvermann]

Wagenaar, Jan

— Vaderlandsche Historie, vervattende de Geschiedenissen der Vereenigde Nederlanden.... Amst., 1782. 21 vols plus Munniks' 1781-87 continuation in 17 vols. Together, 38 vols. Half calf; minor defs. B May 12 (1527) HF1,300

Wagenseil, Johann Christof

— Tel ignea Satanae.... Altdorf, 1681. 4to, contemp vellum. Some browning. SI June 10 (1890) LIt1,200,000

Waghenaer, Lucas Janssen

— The Mariners Mirrour.... Amst.: Theatrum Orbis Terrarum, 1966. Folio, cloth, in d/j. Facsimile of the 1588 Ed. sg Feb 13 (141) $225

— Miroir de la Navigation.... Antwerp: Jean Bellere, 1590. 2 parts in 1 vol Folio, contemp vellum gilt; soiled & worn, vellum cracked at joints, repaired, gouge to upper cover. With 2 engraved titles & 47 double-page charts, all in Koeman's state d except for Plate 40, which is unnumbered & apparently from his b state. With 2 engraved diagrams, 1 with volvelle, & 2 full-page woodcut diagrams. Some soiling, dampstaining & discoloring; 2 small holes to Compas tournant engraving with loss of 1 ornament & 3 letters on verso & partial loss of anr ornament & 4 other letters; 1st chart cropped at lower border; small hole through charts 3 & 4 deleting 3 letters of letterpress description; small wormhole to charts 7-14. DuPont copy. CNY Oct 8 (251) $37,000

— Spieghel der Zeevaerdt. Amst., 1964. Folio, orig cloth. Facsimile of the Utrecht copy. S Nov 15 (1052) £150 [Hagstrom]

Wagner, Arthur L. —& Kelley, J. D. Jerrold, 1847-1922

— The United States Army and Navy. Akron, 1899. Folio, orig cloth; worn & shaken. Some plates torn. O Mar 31 (188) $300

Anr copy. Syn. sg Dec 5 (152) $110

Wagner, Henry Raup

See also: Grabhorn Printing

— California Imprints, August 1846-June 1851. Berkeley, 1922. One of 25. 4to, orig wraps; spine darkened; cover stained. Facsimile plates tipped in. sg Oct 31 (323) $100

— The Cartography of the Northwest Coast of America to the Year 1800. Berkeley, 1937. 2 vols. 4to, cloth. O Sept 24 (251) $350

— Juan Rodriguez Cabrillo: Discoverer of the Coast of California. San Francisco, 1941. One of 750. sg June 18 (141) $90

— Nueva Bibliografia mexicana del siglo XVI. Mexico, 1940 [1946]. One of 1,000. Folio, new cloth, orig wraps bound in. sg Oct 31 (324) $300

— The Plains and the Rockies.... Columbus, 1953. Revised by Charles L. Camp. Worn, front hinge cracked. cb Nov 14 (228) $55

4th Ed. San Francisco, 1982. Revised by Charles L. Camp & then by Robert H. Becker. sg Dec 5 (263) $60; wa Mar 5 (91) $65

— Sir Francis Drake's Voyage around the World.... San Francisco, 1926. 1st Ed. sp Apr 16 (246) $95

Wagner, Ludwig

— Der Szeniker Ludwig Sievert. Berlin, 1926. 4to, orig bds; worn. DW Mar 11 (565) £60

Wagner, Richard, 1813-83

— Parsifal. L, 1912. Folio, modern cloth; orig cover retained. With 16 colored plates. sg Sept 26 (258) $110

Anr copy. Illus by Willy Pogany. Orig cloth. bba Apr 9 (323) £85 [Ulysses]

One of 525. Vellum gilt. sg Jan 30 (131) $375

— The Rhinegold & the Valkyrie. NY, 1910. Illus by Arthur Rackham. 4to, lea. br May 29 (34) $190

Anr copy. Cloth. br May 29 (34) $190

One of 1,150. Orig vellum gilt. b Nov 18 (107) £140

Anr copy. Half vellum; soiled. b Nov 18 (108) £130

Anr copy. Orig cloth; spines rubbed & faded. DW Nov 6 (568) £75

Anr copy. Orig vellum gilt; worn. O Jan 14 (159) $110

Anr copy. Orig vellum gilt; soiled. S July 1 (1003) £200 [Chandor]

Anr Ed. L, [1914]. 2d impression. 4to, orig cloth; extremities worn. F Sept 26 (82) $70

— Siegfried & The Twilight of the Gods. L, 1911. Illus by Arthur Rackham. 4to, orig cloth; spotted. With 30 mtd plates. bba Apr 9 (285) £65 [Sotheran]; br May 29 (35B) $105

One of 1,150. Illus by Arthur Rackham. Bds; spine soiled. b Nov 18 (106) £140

— The Tale of Lohengrin, Knight of the Swan.... L, [1913]. Illus by Willy Pogany. 4to, orig cloth. With 8 colored plates. bba Apr 9 (324) £85 [Ulysses]

— Tannhauser. L, 1911. Illus by Willy Pogany. 4to, orig cloth, in d/j. bba Apr 9 (322) £85 [Ulysses]

Anr copy. Orig cloth. br May 29 (35C) $95

Anr copy. Orig cloth; soiled. sg Sept 26 (258) $110

Anr copy. Cloth. sg Jan 30 (132) $275

Wait, Walter Ernest

— Coloured Plates of the Birds of Ceylon. L, 1927-35. Illus by G. M. Henry. Parts 2 & 4 (of 4). Orig wraps. With 32 color plates. sg Sept 19 (190) $110

Wakefield, John Allen. See: Caxton Club

Wakeman, Capt. Edgar

— The Log of an Ancient Mariner. San Francisco, 1878. 8vo, cloth. sg June 18 (142) $120

Walch, Johann Ernst Immanuel. See: Knorr & Walch

Walcott, John

— Synopsis of British Birds. L, 1789. 2 vols. 4to, contemp calf gilt; rebacked, orig spines preserved, corners repaired. With 255 plates & with the errata leaf. C Oct 30 (251) £1,000 [Cockell]

Walcott, Mary Vaux, 1860-1940

— North American Wild Flowers. Wash., 1925-29. 5 vols. In portfolios. With 200 color plates only. sg Sept 19 (221) $130

Anr copy. In stained portfolios. With 400 plates.. wa Dec 9 (532) $270

Reprint of Vol I. Wash., 1950-29. 5 vols. In portfolios. With 400 color plates. L Nov 14 (228) £220

Walden, Howard T. See: Derrydale Press

Waley, Arthur, 1889-1966

— An Introduction to the Study of Chinese Painting. L, 1923. 4to, cloth, in d/j. kh Nov 11 (241) A$100

Walford, Edward. See: Thornbury & Walford

Walford, J. F. —&
Hunt, P. F.

— A Book of Orchid Paintings. L, 1972. One of 490. Folio, orig half vellum. With 24 colored plates by Walford. bba Feb 13 (383) £80 [Page]

Walker, Charles Edward

— Old Flies in New Dresses. L, 1898. 8vo, cloth; worn & shaken. Koopman copy. O Oct 29 (320) $50

Walker, Edward

— The Art of Book-Binding, its Rise and Progress. NY, 1850. 8vo, orig cloth; minor wear. Handstamp at bottom margin corner of 1 leaf. bbc Dec 9 (198) $1,300

Walker, Franklin

— The Seacoast of Bohemia: an Account of Early Carmel. San Francisco: Book Club of California, 1966. One of 500. Bds. cb Sept 12 (181) $80

Walker, George

— New Directions for Sailing along the Coast of North America.... L, 1799. 8vo, contemp wraps; stained, chipped. Library release stamp on tp & inside rear wrap; soiled, a few corners turned. P June 16 (299) $2,000

Walker, George, 1781-1856
See also: Costume...

— The Costume of Yorkshire. L, 1814. Folio, contemp mor gilt; rebacked preserving orig backstrip. With frontis & 40 plates, each in 2 states: 1 hand-colored aquatint before titles with gray wash borders, the other outline etching (except Plate 5 which is in uncolored aquatint in place of outline etching). C Oct 30 (93) £6,200 [Marlborough]

Anr copy. Modern half calf gilt. With 39 (of 41) hand-colored plates. Lacking J3; outer margin of M4 dampstained. Ck Dec 11 (267) £1,200

Anr copy. Contemp half calf; rubbed & soiled. With 41 hand-colored plates. Some spotting; minor dampstains affecting 1 leaf of description & verso of 1 plate; anr plate with marginal repairs. pn Mar 19 (149) £1,700 [Toscani]

Anr copy. Orig bds, uncut; modern mor spine. With hand-colored frontis & 40 plates. S June 25 (161) £1,500 [Arader]

Walker, James, 1781-1861

— An Accurate Description of the Liverpool and Manchester Rail-way.... Liverpool, 1832. 3d Ed. 8vo, wraps; spines gone. With folding frontis & 1 plate. Frontis split & soiled. O Jan 14 (189) $90

— Liverpool and Manchester Railroad: Report to the Directors...on the Comparative Merits of Locomotive and Fixed Engines.... Phila.: Carey & Lea, 1831. 8vo, orig bds; soiled. With frontis, map, plate & 2 folding charts. Text foxed & browned. wd Dec 12 (467) $50

Walker, Joseph Cooper

— Historical Memoirs of the Irish Bards.... Dublin, 1786. 4to, contemp calf; lower cover worn. Small piece cut from upper margin of tp; some soiling. pn Oct 24 (471) £140

— Historical Memoir on Italian Tragedy. L, 1799. 4to, contemp calf; broken, worn. Met Apr 28 (663) $160

Anr copy. Contemp half sheep; rebacked. Frontis & title foxed. sg Oct 17 (103) $225

Wall, Bernhardt, 1872-1953

— Following Abraham Lincoln, 1809-1865. Lime Rock CT, [1944]. 4 vols. Orig half cloth, in d/js. With 535 copperplate etchings, each sgd below plate in pencil. Inscr. cb Sept 5 (155) $15,000

— A Lincoln Reprimand. [N.p.]: Bernhardt Wall, 1950. One of 100. Half cloth, in wraps, hand-bound by Wall. Inscr. cb Sept 5 (157) $800

Wall, Oscar Garrett

— Recollections of the Sioux Massacre. Lake City, MN, 1909. 12mo, orig cloth; rebacked preserving orig spine, old clippings mtd to inside front bd. wa Dec 9 (312) $95

Wallace, Alfred R.

— Contributions to the Theory of Natural Selection. L, 1870. 8vo, cloth; worn. sg Nov 14 (205) $275

— Darwinism: an Exposition of the Theory of Natural Selection. L, 1889. 8vo, orig cloth; rubbed. bbc June 29 (161) $100

1st Ed. 8vo, orig cloth; hinges weak. bba Feb 13 (417) £85 [Shapero]

— The Geographical Distribution of Animals.... L, 1876. 1st Ed. 2 vols. 8vo, orig cloth. bba Feb 13 (384) £85 [Henly]

Anr copy. Orig cloth; hinges weak. With 20 maps & plates. bba Feb 13 (415) £260 [Shapero]

Anr copy. 19th-cent half mor; scuffed. Some foxing; owner's stamp on half-titles. sg May 14 (251) $275

— Island Life: or, The Phenomena and Causes of Insular Faunas and Floras. L, 1880. 1st Ed. 8vo, orig cloth; front cover blistered. Title browned & stamped. sg Nov 14 (206) $250

Anr copy. Orig cloth; recased, spine ends rubbed. sg May 14 (252) $175

— The Malay Archipelago. L, 1869. 2 vols. 8vo, contemp half calf; rubbed. bba Feb 13 (414) £240 [Axe]

Anr Ed. NY, 1869. 8vo, orig cloth; front joint starting. Endpapers stained. sg Nov 14 (204) $120

— Palm Trees of the Amazon.... L, 1853. 1st Ed. 12mo, orig cloth. With frontis & 47 plates. W July 8 (366) £300

Wallace, David H. See: New York...

Wallace, Harold Frank. See: Edwards & Wallace

Wallace, Philip B.

— Colonial Ironwork in Old Philadelphia. NY: Architectural Book Publishing Co., [1930]. 4to, cloth; worn. K Sept 29 (134) $65

Waller, Edmund, 1606-87

— Poems, &c. Written upon Several Occasions.... L: By I. N. for Hu. Mosley, 1645. 8vo, mor by Riviere. S Nov 14 (496) £150 [Knohl]

Waller, Erik, 1875-1955

— Bibliotheca Walleriana. Stockholm, 1955. Compiled by Hans Sallander. 2 vols. O Sept 24 (252) $325; sg Oct 31 (325) $350; sg Nov 14 (154) $250

Wallhausen, Johann Jacobi von

— L'Art militaire pour l'infanterie.... Franeker, [1638]. Folio, vellum. With 34 plates. Some short tears & browning. S July 1 (1368) £2,000 [Maggs]

— La Milice Romaine.... Frankfurt: P. Jacob, 1616. 2 parts in 1 vol. Folio, 18th-cent calf gilt; joints & edges rubbed. With 21 double-page plates. Library stamp on 1st plate. S July 9 (1367) £350 [Shapero]

Wallich, Nathaniel

— Plantae Asiaticae Rariores; or, Descriptions and Figures of a Select Number of Unpublished East Indian Plants. L, 1829-31-[32]. Parts 1-6 (of 12) in 1 vol. Folio, modern half mor. With 144 hand-colored lithos. Lacking Plates 22-24, 42, 80 & 138; some text leaves damaged & repaired in outer margins. Sold w.a.f. S Nov 21 (51) £4,000 [Burden]

Walling, H. F. See: New Hampshire

Wallis, James

— New Pocket Edition of the English Counties or Travellers Companion.... L, [1810]. 12mo, contemp half mor; upper cover detached. With 42 hand-colored maps plus Isle of Wight at rear. Lacking folding map of England & Wales. DW May 13 (102) £145

Wallis, John, 1616-1703

— Operum mathematicorum. Oxford, 1657-56. 2 vols. 4to, contemp calf & 19th-cent half mor. Hole to 2O3 in Vol I, affecting several characters. Ck Nov 29 (248) £850

— A Treatise of Algebra, both Historical and Practical. L: J. Playford, 1685. 3 parts in 1 vol. Bound with: Cassel, John. A Brief (but full) Account of the Doctrine of Trigonometry. L, 1685. Folio, contemp calf; rubbed. With port & 10 folding plates. L Nov 14 (466) £540

Walpole, Horace, 4th Earl of Orford

— Aedes Walpolianae: or, a Description of the Collection of Pictures at Houghton-Hall in Norfolk.... L, 1752. 2d Ed. 4to, half calf. With 6 plates. bba June 25 (99) £130 [Spelman]

Anr copy. Contemp half calf; spine rubbed. With 2 ports & 4 folding plates & plans. L Nov 14 (467) £110

— Anecdotes of Painting in England. Strawberry Hill, 1762-71. 4 vols. 4to, old calf; broken & worn. Sold w.a.f. O Aug 25 (188) $70

2d Ed of Vols I-III; 1st Ed of Vol IV. Strawberry Hill, 1765. 4 vols plus the Catalogue of Engravers. 4to, contemp sheep; rebacked at an early date, some covers detached or starting. With 104 plates plus 9 plates in the Catalogue. sg Feb 6 (299) $250

Anr Ed. L, 1828. 5 vols. 8vo, later mor gilt. With frontises & 75 plates. Some spotting. bba Oct 10 (281) £260 [Thorp]

— The Castle of Otranto. Parma: Bodoni, 1791. 6th Ed. 4to, contemp mor gilt. With frontis, port & 6 plates in 2 states, both on india paper. Lacking pp. 59-62. Sold w.a.f. pn Sept 12 (229) £50 [Solomon]

Anr Ed. L, 1796. 8vo, contemp mor gilt; rubbed. With frontis & 6 color plates in gilt borders.. Schlosser copy. P June 25 (504) $1,400

— A Catalogue of the Royal and Noble Authors of England.... L, 1759. 2d Ed. 2 vols. 8vo, mor gilt by Kalthoeber; spines rubbed. Vol I H1 torn & repaired with loss to upper blank margin. Inscr by Samuel Whitbread to the effect that he bought the work at Dr. Johnson's sale in 1785. C Dec 16 (207) £3,000 [Maggs]

Anr copy. Later mor gilt by Kalthoeber; spines rubbed. Lacking frontis to Vol I, H1 in Vol I torn & repaired with loss to upper margin. Titles inscr by Samuel Whitbread as having been bought at Dr. Johnson's sale, 18 Feb 1795. C June 24 (152) £800 [Edwards]

Anr Ed. L, 1806. 5 vols. 8vo, orig calf; 1 joint splitting. bba Oct 24 (76) £90 [Beeleigh Abbey]

— Correspondence. New Haven & L, 1937-83. Ed by W. S. Lewis.. Vols 1-42 in 41 vols. Some bdgs affected by damp, all but 7 vols in d/js. S Feb 25 (421) £440 [Axe]

— Historic Doubts on the Life and Reign of King Richard the Third. L, 1768. 4to, contemp calf gilt; rubbed. bba Jan 16 (131) £85 [Murray Hill]

Anr copy. Bound with: Gresset, J. B. Louis. Ver-Vert: or, the Nunnery Parrot. L, 1759. And: Woty, William. The Female Advocate. A Poem. L, 1770. half calf; worn. K July 12 (510) $110

— Letters. L, 1877. Ed by Peter Cunningham. 9 vols. 8vo, half calf gilt; rubbed. pnE Oct 1 (202) £100

— The Letters of Horace Walpole.... Oxford, 1903-25. One of 260. Ed by Mrs. Paget

Toynbee. 19 vols, including 3 Supplements. pnE Mar 11 (242) £100

— Works. L, 1798. 9 vols. 4to, contemp calf; joints weakened, scuffed. bba Mar 26 (142) £400 [Heath]

Walpole Library, Horace

— [Sale Catalogue] A Catalogue of the Classic Contents of Strawberry Hill. L, [1842]. 4to, half calf; rubbed. bba Mar 26 (65) £90 [Whetman]

Anr copy. Half mor. cb Oct 17 (960) $180

Anr copy. Orig cloth; upper joint splitting. With typescript price list laid in. L Feb 27 (118) £180

Walpole, Hugh, 1884-1941. See: Golden Cockerel Press

Walpole, Robert, 1781-1856

— Memoirs Relating to European and Asiatic Turkey. L, 1818. 2d Ed. 4to, later half mor; rubbed. With 4 maps & plans & 10 plates. Some foxing and dampstaining. Sold w.a.af. O Feb 25 (196) $250

Walpole-Bond, John

— A History of Sussex Birds. L, 1938. 3 vols. In frayed d/js. With 53 colored plates. DW May 13 (134) £100

Anr copy. Cloth, in d/js. L Nov 14 (229) £120

Anr copy. In torn & frayed d/js. With 53 colored plates. ALs inserted. pn July 16 (169) £150

Walpoole, George Augustus

— The New British Traveller. L, [1782]. Folio, half calf; split. Frontis map torn & def. pnE Aug 12 (242) £200

Anr Ed. L, [maps dated 1784]. Folio, old bds; worn & broken. Some stains & soiling; margins frayed. Sold w.a.f. O Aug 25 (189) $425

Walsh, John Henry, 1810-88

— Dogs of the British Islands. L, 1878. 8vo, orig cloth. b Mar 11 (214) £200

Walsh, Robert, 1772-1852

— Constantinople and the Scenery of the Seven Churches of Asia Minor. L, [c.1839]. 2 vols in 1. 4to, contemp half calf; corners rubbed. With 94 plates, 2 engraved titles & 2 maps. b June 22 (282) £280

Anr copy. 2 vols. 4to, orig lea gilt; rubbed. With 2 frontises, 2 engraed titles, 92 plates & 2 maps, 1 double-page. Some spotting. pn Sept 12 (343) £260 [Frew Mackenzie]

— Voyage en Turquie et a Constantinople. Paris, 1828. 8vo, orig wraps; worn. With 3 folding maps, 5 plates & folding facsimile. S June 30 (218) £480 [Kutlouglu]

Walsh, Capt. Thomas

— Journal of the Late Campaign in Egypt. L, 1803. 4to, orig bds; rebacked with cloth. pnE Aug 12 (28) £120

Anr copy. Contemp calf; worn, front cover detached. With 7 folding & 9 full-page maps & 20 views. A few tears. wa Apr 9 (155) $170

Walter, Johann Ernst Christian

— Nordisk Ornithologie eller trovaerdige efter naturen egenhaendig tegnede, stukne og colorerede Afbildninger af Danske, Faeroiske, Gronlandske og Islandske Fugle. Copenhagen, 1828-[41]. Second Series only. Folio, contemp half lea; rebacked preserving orig spine. With 60 hand-colored plates. Some staining to upper margins. C May 20 (228) £800 [Shapero]

Walter, S. See: Bromley & Walter

Walter, Thomas U., 1804-87 —& Smith, John Jay, 1798-1881

— Two Hundred Designs for Cottages and Villas. Phila., 1846. Part 4 only. Folio, pictorial bds. With 30 plates. Clean tear in last plate & rear free endpaper; some foxing. sg Apr 2 (292) $300

Walters Art Gallery

— The History of Bookbinding, 525-1950 A.D.: An Exhibition. Balt., 1957. 4to, pictorial cloth; rubbed. bbc Apr 27 (106) $95

Walters Library, Henry

— Incunabula Typographica: a Descriptive Catalogue to the Books...in the Library.... Balt., 1906. 4to, orig calf. bba Jan 30 (336) £65 [Kurita]

Anr copy. Lea. O Dec 17 (190) $100

Anr copy. Sheep. sg Oct 31 (169) $50

Anr copy. Orig calf gilt. wa Mar 5 (110) $110

Walters, Henry Beauchamp

— History of Ancient Pottery. L, 1905. 2 vols. 8vo, cloth; worn & soiled. cb Sept 12 (21) $50

Walters, Lettice d'Oyley

— The Year's at the Spring. L, 1920. Illus by Harry Clarke. 4to, cloth; worn, old stain at bottom left corner of front cover, small hole in backstrip. Some foxing. bbc Dec 9 (449) $60

Walton, Augustus Q.

— A History of the Detection, Conviction, Life...of John A. Murel, the Great Western Land Pirate. Athens TN: Geo. White, 1835. 12mo, sewn, spine reinforced with linen. Tp & many succeeding leaves with tears in inner margin; hole in tp; last leaf with heavily darkened area. K Sept 29 (430) $85

Walton, Izaak, 1593-1683

See also: Limited Editions Club; Nonesuch Press

— The Lives of Doctor John Donne, Sir Henry Wotton.... York, 1796. 4to, modern half calf; rubbed. cb Oct 25 (120) $120

— The Lives of Dr. John Donne, Sir Henry Wotton.... L, 1838. 8vo, mor gilt by Dudley & Hodge. O July 14 (193) $275

Anr Ed. L, 1904. One of 210. 4to, mor gilt. b&b Feb 19 (25) $225

Walton, Izaak, 1593-1683 —& Cotton, Charles, 1630-87

Compleat Angler

— 1760. - L.1st Hawkins Ed. 2 parts in 1 vol. 8vo, contemp half mor; rubbed, upper joint split. bba Nov 28 (73) £80 [Hereward]

Anr copy. Mor gilt, the sides with medallion ports of Walton & Cotton, by Hering using Gosden's tools. pn Mar 19 (375) £1,600

— 1808. - L. 8vo, contemp calf gilt; rebacked. bba Nov 28 (774) £80 [Kurita]

Anr copy. Contemp calf gilt. Extra-illus with 6 hand-colored plates. LH May 17 (587) $550

— 1810. - L. 16mo, old calf, rebacked with modern calf. Joseph Haslewood's copy. cb Oct 25 (119) $275

— 1815. - L: Samuel Bagster. 2 parts in 1 vol. 8vo, mor gilt. With 2 ports & 12 plates. pn Mar 19 (384) £190

— 1823. - L. Intro by John Major. 16mo, contemp mor gilt; rubbed. bba Nov 28 (78) £70 [Hereward Bks]

— 1824. - L. 8vo, mor gilt by Thomas Gosden, sgd on turn-in. Bound with Zouch's Life of Isaac Walton, 1825. pn Mar 19 (380) £1,100

— 1825. - L. 8vo, mor gilt. Frontis abraded in lower left margin. O Aug 25 (10) $130

Anr copy. Orig lea; joints rubbed. sg May 21 (113) $350

— 1836. - L. Ed by Sir Harris Nicolas. 2 vols. 4to, mor extra, front & back covers with inset medallions of Walton & Cotton. With 61 proof inmpressions of engravings, most in 2 states, 1 in 3 states. William Randolph Hearst's copy. cb Feb 12 (145) $1,000

Anr copy. Mor gilt; rubbed. Some dampstaining in Vol I; some foxing. NH May 30 (86) $180

Anr copy. 3 vols. 4to, modern lea. With engraved titles & 13 plates. Koopman copy. O Oct 29 (321) $550

Anr copy. 2 vols. 4to, calf gilt; rubbed. O Jan 14 (190) $375

Anr copy. Mor gilt by Hayday; rubbed. With engraved titles & 13 plates. pn Mar 19 (385) £300

Unbound signatures. Folded sheets in mor case. sg Nov 7 (247) $750

— 1856. - L. 12mo, calf gilt by Morrell. sg Oct 17 (394) $200

— 1885. - His Wallet Booke. L. One of 100. 8vo, vellum gilt. pba July 23 (129) $190

— 1888. - L. One of 500. 2 vols. 4to, contemp mor gilt with combined mongram of Cotton & Walton. C May 20 (134) £700 [Maggs]

Anr copy. Orig mor gilt; rubbed. pnE Dec 4 (196) £140

Anr copy. Half vellum; soiled. wd June 12 (442) $150

— 1889. - L. One of 500. 8vo, contemp half mor. cb Dec 19 (178) $80

— 1897. - L & NY Ed by Richard Le Gallienne. 8vo, half mor gilt. With a full-page watercolor of a cowboy on a bucking bronco sgd as Frederic Remington and as Julia S. Field by Eugene Field II. Also with a (genuine) ALs from Richard Le Galliene, 15 July 1889. sg Oct 17 (250) $1,100

— 1902. - L.Winchester Ed, one of 150, sgd by the artists William Strang & D. Y. Cameron, & with plates in 2 states. 2 vols. 4to, contemp half mor; shelf mark on spine. Library stamps, not affecting plates. pn Mar 19 (364) £50

— 1925. - L: Navarre SocietyOrig half cloth, in d/j. bba Apr 9 (350) £55 [Ulysses]

— 1930. - L. One of 450. Illus by Frank Adams. 4to, half vellum. LH May 17 (639) $160; pnE Oct 1 (239) £95; sg Jan 30 (185) $300

— 1931. - L. Illus by Arthur Rackham. 4to, cloth, in d/j. With 12 colored plates. bba Jan 16 (406) £110 [Sotheran]

Anr copy. Orig cloth, in d/j. bba Apr 9 (343) £220 [Hughes-Games]

Anr copy. Orig mor gilt; rubbed at extremities. DW May 13 (468) £140

Anr copy. Orig cloth. LH Dec 11 (267) $70

One of 775. Orig vellum gilt. With 12 colored plates. b Nov 18 (109) £340

Anr copy. Orig vellum gilt; discolored. cb Dec 5 (117) $375; sg Nov 7 (179) $750; sg Jan 30 (156) $425

— [1931]. - Phila.: McKay Illus by Arthur Rackham. Orig cloth. With 12 color plates. K Mar 22 (397) $65

Walton, J. See: Fielding & Walton

Walton, William, 1843-1915

— Paris Known and Unknown. Phila.: G. Barrie, [1898-1901]. 3 vols. Folio, half mor gilt; extremities rubbed. sg Jan 9 (196) $550

— World's Columbian Exposition...Official Illustrated Publication: Art and Architecture. Phila., [1893]. 2 vols. Folio, calf gilt. LH Dec 11 (271) $80

Walton, William, fl.1890

— The Army and Navy of the United States, from the Period of the Revolution to the Present Day. Phila., [1889-95]. 12 orig parts. Folio, cloth portfolios, the text in orig wraps but without portfolio. With 44 colored plates & 210 mtd india-proof text illusts. Some foxing & edge wear. wa Mar 5 (627) $300

Walton, Sir William. See: Sitwell & Walton

Wansey, Henry

— The Journal of an Excursion to the United States of North America.... Salisbury & L, 1796. 8vo, mor gilt by Canape. With frontis & folding plate. sg June 18 (537) $325

Wappenbuch

— Das erneuerte und vermehrte Teutsche Wappenbuch. Nuremberg, 1657-56-[67]. 5 vols. Oblong 4to, contemp vellum; worn, spines crudely reinforced with cloth. With 1,246 plates. Small piece excised from margin of extra title in 2 vols. sg Mar 12 (278) $1,400

War...

— The War of the Rebellion: a Compilation of the Official Records of the Union and Confederate Armies. Wash., 1880-1902. 127 vols. 8vo, orig cloth; worn. O Mar 31 (189) $850

Warburton, John, 1682-1759

— Vallum Romanum: or, the History and Antiquities of the Roman Wall.... L, 1753. 4to, contemp calf. pnE Oct 2 (551) £100

Warburton, Peter Egerton, 1813-89

— Journey Across the Western Interior of Australia. L, 1875. 8vo, orig cloth; recased, rubbed. With port, 8 wood-engraved plates & folding map (laid down). Some foxing & marginal soiling. bba June 11 (346) £320 [Woodstock]

Anr copy. Orig cloth; rubbed. Folding map taped on verso; stamp removed from title. kh Nov 11 (685) A$240

Anr copy. With folding map, port & 8 plates. S June 25 (261) £1,500 [Brooke-Hitching]

Warburton, Roland E. Egerton

— Hunting Songs, Ballads, &c. Chester, 1834. 8vo, half mor; spine rubbed. cb Dec 5 (138) $150

Ward, Henry George

— Mexico in 1827. L, 1829. ("Mexico.") 2d Ed. 2 vols. 8vo, 19th-cent calf; Vol II def. With 2 folding maps & 13 plates, 1 colored. S Feb 26 (799) £260 [Holland]

Ward, Humphry —& Roberts, William

— Romney: a Biographical and Critical Essay. L, 1904. 4to, orig cloth; spines frayed. DW Mar 11 (868) £90

Ward, Mrs Humphry. See: Ward, Mary Augusta

Ward, James

— A Series of Lithographic Drawings of Celebrated Horses. L: Ackermann, 1823-25. 1st Ed. Oblong folio, bdg not described. With 15 lithos, india proofs before letters. Some dampstaining; Plate 8 hinged to interleaf. Schlosser copy. P June 17 (597) $8,000

Ward, Lynd

— Gods' Man, a Novel in Woodcuts. NY, [1929]. Half cloth; soiled. cb Jan 16 (164) $70

— Madman's Drum. NY, [1930]. cb Jan 16 (165) $130

— Prelude to a Million Years. NY, 1933. One of 920. Unopened. cb Jan 16 (163) $160; O Jan 20 (191) $185

— Song without Words. NY, 1936. Bds; spine darkened. cb Jan 16 (166) $200

One of 1,250. Orig bds; spine darkened. cb Jan 16 (166) $200

— Vertigo, a Novel in Woodcuts. NY, 1937. Orig cloth; rubbed & soiled. cb Jan 16 (167) $80

Ward, Mary Augusta, 1851-1920

— Robert Elsmere. L, 1883. 3 vols. 8vo, orig cloth. bba Nov 28 (380) £65 [Pickering & Chatto]

— Works. Bost. & NY, 1909-12. ("The Writings of Mrs. Humphry Ward.") Autograph Ed, sgd, with 2-1/2 page Ms. 16 vols. Mor extra with mor onlays in floral design. CNY Dec (447) $1,400

Anr copy. Half mor gilt by Yseux. S Feb 25 (422) £300 [Holland]

Ward, Robert, Gentleman

— Animadversions of Warre; or a Militarie Magazine.... L, 1639. 1st Ed. 2 parts in 1 vol. Folio, contemp calf gilt; foot of spine worn. With extra title, 2 folding plates. Bottom of final leaf torn & def; waterstained throughout. bba Nov 28 (226) £300 [Trotman]

Ward, Rowland

— Records of Big Game.... L, 1896. 2d Ed. 8vo, contemp half mor; extremities rubbed. Library markings. F Dec 18 (407) $100

Ward, Samuel, d.1643

— The Wonders of the Loadstone.... L, 1640. 12mo, contemp sheep; joints starting. Tear in D3 repaired. STC 25030. sg Nov 14 (323) $650

Warde, Frederic

See also: Limited Editions Club

— Printers Ornaments. L, 1928. 4to, orig cloth. cb Jan 16 (175) $85

Warder, Joseph

— The True Amazons: or the Monarchy of Bees. L, 1713. 8vo, modern calf; rebacked. With port. Marginal wormholes; some browning. pn Dec 12 (113) £180

Ware, Eugene F., 1841-1911

— The Indian War of 1864.... Topeka, 1911. 1st Ed. 12mo, orig cloth; bottom corner of lower cover stained & discolored. Small dampstain in bottom margin throughout. bbc Feb 17 (130) $60

Ware, Isaac, d.1766

— A Complete Body of Architecture.... L, 1756. 1st Ed. Folio, contemp calf; joints cracked, corners restored. With frontis & 114 plates. Some creasing at front & back; tt2-3 with small tears; some staining. CNY Jan 25 (79) $950

Anr copy. Contemp calf; worn. With frontis & 113 (of 114) plates. Frontis torn; frontis, title & 1st few leaves dampstained. DW Oct 9 (985) £380

Anr copy. Disbound. Tp soiled & def; frontis soiled, torn & loose; lacking 9F onwards. Sold w.a.f. S May 14 (1088) £270 [Kafka]

Anr Ed. L, 1767. Folio, contemp calf; worn. With frontis & 122 plates, 15 folding. Some discoloration; small wormhole towards end without loss. S June 25 (93) £700 [Nicholson]

Anr Ed. L, 1768. Folio, old calf; worn, corners repaired. With frontis & 114 plates. Some worming at front & back; some browning; dampstained at end. McCarty-Cooper copy. CNY Jan 25 (80) $550

— The Plans, Elevations, and Sections; Chimney-Pieces, and Ceilings of Houghton in Norfolk.... L, 1760. Folio, modern half calf gilt. With engraved title, engraved dedication, double-page engraved plan & 35 numbered engraved plates on 27 sheets. Washed & with old stains; some tears repaired. CNY Jan 25 (81) $600

Ware, Sir James, 1594-1666

— The Antiquities and History of Ireland. Dublin, 1705. 8vo, contemp half calf; spine def. With port (frayed), map of Ireland & 4 plates. Some browning. L Nov 14 (468) £55

— Works. Dublin, 1764. 3 vols in 2. Folio, contemp calf; corners rubbed. With frontis & 39 plates. b June 22 (284) £100

Ware, William Rotch

— The Georgian Period: Being Photographs and Measured Drawings of Colonial Work.... NY, 1923. 6 vols in 3. With 454 plates. K Sept 29 (8) $150

Wargentin, I. E.

— Gruppen des Lebens, mit Arabesken von E. Lamoral. Stuttgart, 1825. 4to, orig bds; spine damaged. With litho title & 6 litho plates. Ptd entirely in gold ink. Schlosser copy. P June 17 (598) $1,000

Warhol, Andy

— Andy Warhol's Index Book. NY, 1967. 4to, pictorial foil wraps. F Sept 26 (285) $180

Anr copy. Orig cloth. F Sept 26 (286) $300

Anr copy. Half cloth with 3-D pictorial laminated sheet on front cover. With 2 facing pages adhered with glue used to mount balloon; some tears. sg Sept 6 (291) $600

Anr copy. Pictorial foil wraps. sg Feb 6 (300) $300

Anr copy. With 7 pop-ups, Velvet Underground record & rubber balloon. 2 facing pages adhered with glue used to mount balloon; 1 pop-up not popping-up. sg Apr 2 (294) $400

— Andy Warhol's Children's Book. [Zurich, 1983]. Pictorial bds. Sgd 8 times throughout & inscr to Bobby. sg Sept 6 (290) $2,200

— A Gold Book. NY, 1957. Out-of-series copy, but sgd. Folio. CGen Nov 18 (480) SF7,000

— The Philosophy of Andy Warhol (from A to B & Back Again). NY: Harcourt Brace Jovanovich, [1975]. Half cloth, in d/j. Inscr & with inevitable sketch of a soup can on half-title. S Dec 12 (195) £450 [Scriptorium]

2d Ptg. Half cloth, in d/j. Sgd with initials on half-title. pba July 9 (289) $50

Waring, F.

— Twelve Views of Scotland, Delineated by a Lady.... L: Ackermann, 1803. Folio, loose. With 12 lithos. Tp lacking. Schlosser copy. P June 17 (599) $1,750

Waring, John Burnley

— Masterpieces of Industrial Art and Sculpture.... L, 1863. 3 vols. Folio, contemp half mor; rubbed. Slight spotting to plates. bba Dec 19 (98) £200 [Cherrington]

Anr copy. 3 vols. Mor; rubbed; contents loose. A few plates chipped or dust-soiled. DW Dec 11 (390) £420

Anr copy. 3 vols. Folio, orig cloth; rebacked retaining orig spines. With 3 chromolitho titles & 301 plates. Library stamps on versos. S Nov 15 (848) £420

Anr copy. Lea gilt; broken. Some foxing. sg Sept 6 (292) $550

Warner, Charles Dudley, 1829-1900

See also: Clemens & Warner

— Works. Hartford, 1904. One of 612. 15 vols. Contemp half mor extra with mor onlays of art nouveau floral design; extremities worn. Leaf of autograph Ms & ALs tipped in. cb Dec 5 (139) $425

Anr copy. Mor extra. With AMs of short story, "The Education of Sam." 25 pp. CNY Dec 5 (448) $1,100

Anr copy. Orig cloth. Leaf of autograph Ms & ALs tipped in. sg Oct 17 (395) $150

Warner, Sir George Frederic. See: British Museum

Warner, Richard, 1763-1857

— Antiquitates Culinariae, or Curious Tracts relating to the Culinary Affairs of the Old English. L, 1791. 1st Ed. 4to, half mor; worn & soiled, front joint repaired. With the suppressed Peacock Feast plate. wa Sept 26 (489) $290

Warner, Robert

— Select Orchidaceous Plants. L, 1862-75-[77]. 2 vols. Folio, orig cloth; rebacked with orig backstrip laid down, corners strengthened. With 79 hand-colored plates. Some foxing. McCarty-Cooper copy. CNY Jan 25 (95) $9,000

Anr copy. First & Second Series & Parts 1-9 of Third Series, bound in 3 vols. Folio, contemp half mor gilt, Vol III in orig cloth with torn spine. With 106 hand-colored plates only. Spots on Plates 38 & 39 in Vol II. Sold w.a.f. Doheny copy. CNY June 9 (155) $9,000

— Select Orchidaceous Plants. First series: Fort Caroline Orchids. Jacksonville, 1975. Folio, orig lea gilt; soiled. With 40 color plates. wa Dec 9 (634) $70

Warner, Robert —& Others

— The Orchid Album. L, 1882-97. 11 vols. 4to, orig cloth; extremities worn, new endpapers. With 528 partly hand-colored, partly color-ptd lithos & uncolored port. McCarty-Cooper copy. CNY Jan 25 (96) $12,000

Anr copy. Orig cloth; joints & extremities rubbed, a few inner hinges splitting. With 528 plates, partly hand-colored, partly color-ptd plus duplicate copy of Plate 184 & its text. Plate 340 detached; fore-edge of Plate 482 frayed. Sold w.a.f. CNY June 9 (156) $11,000

Anr copy. Vols I-III only. Disbound. With 144 colored plates. Plate 99 frayed & soiled. Sold w.a.f. S June 25 (79) £3,500 [Vitale]

Warner Collection, Worcester Reed

— Selections from Oriental Objects of Art Collected by.... Tarrytown NY, 1921. 4to, half cloth. LH May 17 (682) $50

Warnery, Charles Emmanuel de

— Remarks on Cavalry. L, 1798. 4to, contemp bds; detached, lacking backstrip. Lacking half-title. bba July 9 (129) £70 [Spelman]

Warr, George C.

— Echoes of Hellas.... L: Marcus Ward, [c.1887]. Illus by Walter Crane. Folio, cloth; soiled. Prelim & final leaves foxed. cb Sept 26 (43) $225

Warre, Sir Henry James

— Sketches in North America and the Oregon Territory. L: Dickinson & Co., [1848]. Folio, contemp half mor gilt; rubbed & soiled. With 20 hand-colored lithos on 16 sheets & 1 map with outline color. Some outer blank corners stained. Inscr to Lady Musgrave, 9 June 1848. S June 25 (438) £12,000 [Arader]

Anr copy. Unbound. With 19 (of 20) hand-colored lithos on 15 (of 16) sheets & 1 map with outline color. Some stains touching images; text creased & torn. Colored copy. S June 25 (439) £6,000 [Arader]

Warren, Arthur. See: Grolier Club

Warren, Benjamin Harry

— Report on the Birds of Pennsylvania. Harrisburg, 1888. 1st Ed. 8vo, cloth; spotted. K Sept 29 (431) $55

Anr copy. Cloth; worn. With 50 color plates. Library markings. O Apr 28 (60) $60

2d Ed. Harrisburg, 1890. 8vo, cloth; broken. With 100 colored plates. F Mar 26 (454) $50

Anr copy. Contemp half mor; rubbed.

With 1 uncolored & 99 colored plates. F June 25 (600) $80

Anr copy. Cloth. K Sept 29 (432) $65

Anr copy. Half lea; worn & broken. O Apr 28 (61) $110

Anr copy. Later half cloth; rubbed & soiled, front free endpaper detached. With 99 color plates. wa Mar 5 (488) $95

Warren, John Collins, 1778-1856

— Remarks on some Fossil Impressions in the Sandstone Rocks of Connecticut River. Bost., 1854. 4to, orig cloth; worn. Inscr. O Nov 26 (190) $400

Anr copy. Cloth. O Dec 17 (191) $1170

Warrington, William, Glass Stainer

— The History of Stained Glass. L, 1848. Folio, contemp half mor; scuffed. With color title & 22 chromolithos, 4 double-page. Some browning; 1 plate repaired. bba June 11 (339) £180 [Fetzer]

Warton, Thomas, 1728-90

— The History of English Poetry.... L, 1824. 4 vols. 8vo, contemp calf. Some foxing. O Aug 25 (192) $50

Waseurtz af Sandels, G. M.

— A Soujourn in California by the King's Orphan. San Francisco: Book Club of California, 1945. Special copy for Ted Lilienthal from Ed Grabhorn. Half calf. cb Feb 12 (88) $275

Washington, Booker T., 1856-1915

— The Story of the Negro. NY, 1909. 2 vols. sp Apr 16 (119) $95

Anr copy. Cloth; worn. wa Dec 9 (278) $85

Washington, George, 1732-99
See also: Grabhorn Printing

— Diary, from 1 October 1789 to 10 March 1790. NY, 1858. One of 100. 4to, modern half mor gilt by Sangorski & Sutcliffe, orig front wrap bound in. Marginal tears repaired. sg June 18 (539) $50

— Letters from His Excellency George Washington, to Arthur Young. L, 1801. 8vo, contemp calf gilt; joints & spine ends worn. With folding map. Josiah Parkes's copy. b June 22 (285) £200

— Writings.... Wash., 1931-44. Ed by John C. Fitzpatrick. 39 vols, including 2-vol Index. K Sept 29 (433) $450

Wassebourg, Richard de

— Premier (Second) Volume des antiquitez de la Gaule Belgicque, Royaulme de France.... Paris, 1549. 2 vols in 1. Folio, calf. S Dec 5 (220) £500 [Greenwood]

Wasson, Robert Gordon —& Others

— Maria Sabina and her Mazatec Mushroom Velada. NY, [1974]. One of 50. 4to, half mor. With separate box containing the 4 records & the musical score. sg May 7 (209) $200

Waterhouse, Charles Owen

— Aid to the Identification of Insects. L, 1880-90. 2 vols. 4to, contemp half lea; rubbed. With 189 hand-colored plates. Library stamps, not affecting plates. pn Mar 19 (344) £420

Waterman, Thomas Tileston —& Barrows, John A.

— Domestic Colonial Architecture of Tidewater Virginia. NY, 1932. Folio, cloth. sp June 18 (219) $110

Wathen, James

— Journal of a Voyage, in 1811 and 1812, to Madras and China.... L, 1814. 1st Ed. 4to, orig cloth; rebacked. With 24 hand-colored plates. First 3 leaves reattached. cb Oct 10 (107) $1,100

— A Series of Views, Illustrative of the Island of St. Helena. L, 1821. 4to, modern half mor. With engraved title with hand-colored vignette, uncolored port & 9 hand-colored views, including folding panorama (torn). C May 20 (134) £700 [Maggs]

Watkins, Thomas

— Travels Through Switzerland, Italy...to Constantinople. L, 1792. 2 vols. 8vo, contemp half calf. Lacking half-title in Vol II. S June 30 (437) £240 [Consolidated Real]

Watson, A. E. T. See: Beaufort & Watson

Watson, Douglas S.
See also: Grabhorn Printing

— California in the Fifties. San Francisco, 1936. One of 850. Oblong 4to, cloth; spotted. bbc June 29 (347) $200; cb Sept 12 (184) $150

Anr copy. Cloth. Orig ephemera inserted. K Dec 1 (57) $225

— West Wind, the Life Story of Joseph Reddeford Walker.... Los Angeles, 1934. 1st Ed, one of 100. 4to, mor. Presentation copy, sgd by pbr. cb Feb 12 (89) $400

Watson, Elkanah

— History of the Rise...of the Western Canals in...New York.... Albany, 1820. 8vo, later half cloth. With port, 2 maps & 3 double-page plates. O Mar 31 (190) $350

Watson, Frank John Bagolt
— The Wrightson Collection. NY, 1966-73. Vols I-II only. In d/js. bba May 14 (592) £350 [Archivia]
Anr copy. 5 vols. 4to, orig cloth, in d/js. sg Feb 6 (301) $850

Watson, Frederick, 1885-1935. See: Derrydale Press

Watson, John, 1725-83
— The History and Antiquities of the Parish of Halifax. L, 1775. 1st Ed. 4to, contemp calf; front cover detached. Frontis cropped & repaired. bba June 11 (383) £55 [Townsend]

Watson, Peter William, 1761-1830
— Dendrologia Britannica.... L, 1825. 2 vol. 4to, later half calf. With 172 hand-colored plates. Some plate captions & numerals cropped. C Oct 30 (275) £600 [Heuer]

Watson, Richard, 1737-1816
— Chemical Essays. Dublin, 1786. 2 vols in 1. 8vo, contemp calf; worn. DW Oct 2 (315) £60

Watson, Steven
— Artifacts at the End of a Decade. [N.p., 1981]. One of 100. Folio, loose as issued in folding case; extremities worn. sg Sept 26 (297) $200

Watt, Robert, 1774-1819
— Bibliotheca Britannica. Edin., 1824. 4 vols. 4to, contemp mor gilt; rubbed. DW Mar 4 (322) £100
Anr copy. 4 vols in 2. 4to, later cloth; worn. O Sept 24 (253) $110

Watts, Isaac, 1674-1748
See also: Psalms & Psalters
— Divine Songs Attempted in Easy Language for the Use of Children. L, 1778. 16mo, orig Dutch floral bds; rebacked. Lacking frontis; some browning & soiling. pn Nov 14 (357) £140 [Quaritch]
— Horae Lyricae. Poems chiefly of the Lyric kind.... L: W. Wilkins for S. Cliff, 1715. 12mo, contemp sheep; rubbed. F Mar 26 (505) $200
— The Knowledge of the Heavens and the Earth made Easy.... L, 1765. 7th Ed. 8vo, contemp calf; rebacked; worn. With 6 folding plates. Soiled & foxed. cb Jan 30 (130) $110

Watts's copy, Isaac
— OWEN, JOHN. - A Practical Exposition on the CXXX. Psalm. L, 1669. Contemp calf; rebacked & repaired. A few outer leaves frayed; a few pages with blank sections or margins excised affecting text. Sold w.a.f. Inscr by Watts on a half-leaf & with about 80 pages. S July 21 (307) £1,800 [Quaritch]

Watts, William, 1752-1851
— The Seats of the Nobility and Gentry.... L, [1779-86]. Oblong 4to, mor gilt; lower cover detached. With engraved title & 84 plates. bba June 25 (239) £400 [Thorp]
Anr copy. Contemp mor gilt, bound for John Smyth with his crest & monogram. C Oct 30 (121) £900 [Sotheran]
Anr copy. Contemp mor gilt; covers detached. C May 20 (311) £450 [Thornhill]
Anr copy. Contemp or gilt; rubbed. With 83 plates. Lacking tp & 1st view; final 8 plates with 1 corner stained; final 2 plates & text detached. L Nov 14 (130) £320
Anr copy. Contemp mor. Name in ink on tp; some foxing. wd Dec 12 (468) $125

Waugh, Arthur, 1866-1943
— The Square Book of Animals. L, 1900 [1899]. Illus by William Nicholson. 4to, orig half cloth; worn, contents loose. With 12 colored plates. Sold w.a.f. sg Oct 17 (325) $110

Waugh, Evelyn, 1903-66
See also: Greene's copy, Graham
— Basil Seal Rides Again. L, 1963. 1st Ed, one of 750. Inscr to Graham Greene. S Dec 12 (95) £1,800 [Rassam]
— Black Mischief. L, [1932]. One of 210. Orig cloth; rubbed. Inscr to Kaye Ball, May 1943. pn Sept 12 (173) £280 [Ulysses]
1st Ed. In d/j. bba Dec 19 (227) £120 [Thorp]
Anr copy. In slightly torn d/j. W Mar 6 (87) £120
— Brideshead Revisited. L, 1945. 1st Ed. In d/j. b Mar 11 (187) £50
Anr copy. In soiled d/j. Inscr to his wife. S Dec 12 (66) £6,000 [Rassam]
One of 600. In d/j. bba Dec 19 (228) £85 [Thorp]
— Decline and Fall. L, 1928. 1st Ed. Orig cloth, in d/j. Epstein copy. sg Apr 30 (484) $2,800
— A Handful of Dust. L, 1934. 1st Ed. DW Apr 8 (568) £65
— Helena. L, 1950. 1st Ed, One of 50 L.p. copies. Orig cloth. Inscr to Anne Ford, with related material. CNY June 9 (191) $1,400
— The Holy Places. L, 1952. 1st Ed, One of 50. Illus by Reynolds Stone. In d/j with a few small holes in spine. C June 9 (192) $350
One of 950. In d/j. b June 22 (66) £60
Anr copy. In d/j. Inscr to Graham Greene. S Dec 12 (96) £1,800 [Rota]
— Love Among the Ruins. L, 1953. 1st Ed, one of 350. In d/j. sg Dec 12 (402) $450
— Men at Arms. L, 1952. 1st English Ed.

Orig cloth, in frayed d/j. b Nov 18 (319) £50

— Scoop. L, 1938. 1st Ed. In chipped d/j. W Mar 6 (86) £200

Wawra, Heinrich

— Botanische Ergebnisse der Reise seiner Majestaet des Kaisers von Mexico Maximilian I nach Brasilien. Vienna, 1866. Folio, original bds. With 104 plates. HH May 112 (537) DM1,800

Way, Thomas R.

— The Lithographs by Whistler. NY, 1914. One of 400. 4to, cloth; rubbed. LH May 17 (676) $800

Wayne, Henry C.

— The Sword Exercise. Wash., 1850. 8vo, orig cloth; spine ends frayed. With 23 folding plates. sg Mar 26 (339) $130

Weale, John

— Divers Works of Early Masters in Christian Decoration. L, 1846. 2 vols. Folio, contemp half mor gilt; rebacked. DW Mar 4 (323) £90

Anr copy. Contemp half mor gilt; rubbed. With 30 hand-colored plates. DW Mar 11 (871) £120

— Quarterly Papers on Architecture. L, 1844-45. 2 vols. 4to, half mor gilt. With 230 plates & 1 map only, many colored. pnE Dec 4 (207) £260

Anr Ed. L, 1845. Vol III only. 4to, disbound. Stained. Sold w.a.f. O Feb 25 (197) $50

Weatherly, George

— The Little Folks Painting Book. L: Cassell, Petter & Galpin, [1879]. Illus by Kate Greenaway. 4to, orig cloth; worn, joints weak. One leaf torn & repaired. cb Sept 26 (98) $50

Weaver, Sir Lawrence

See also: Jekyll & Weaver

— Houses and Gardens by E. L. Lutyens. L, 1913. Folio, modern calf. Marginal tear repaired. sg Apr 2 (295) $200

Anr Ed. L, 1914. Folio, half cloth. bba Jan 16 (285) £60 [Lamb]

Anr copy. Orig half cloth; rubbed & soiled, bowed. pn June 11 (178) £85

Anr Ed. L, 1925. ("Houses and Gardens by Sir Edwin Lutyens....") Folio, cloth; shaken, spine ends worn. sg Feb 6 (169) $225

Weaver, William D.

[-] Catalogue of the Wheeler Gift of Books, Pamphlets and Periodicals in the Library of the American Institute of Electrical Engineers. NY, 1909. 2 vols. O Sept 24 (254) $180

Webb, Peter

— The Erotic Arts. L, 1975. Ltd Ed. With colored screenprint by Allen Jones & etching by David Hockney, each sgd & numbered. sg Nov 7 (90) $1,100

Webb, Walter Prescott

— The Texas Rangers.... Bost., 1935. In d/j. cb Nov 14 (233) $95

Webber, James, 1750?-93

— Views in the South Seas.... L, 1808 [plates watermarked 1819]. Folio, old half mor gilt over orig bds; worn. With 16 hand-colored plates. Some soiling; ink stain to margin of Plate 16 & preceding blank margin of a text leaf. CNY Oct 8 (252) $13,000

Weber, Carl Jefferson

— Fore-Edge Painting. Irvington, NY, 1966. Orig cloth, in d/j. cb Oct 17 (967) $225; O Sept 24 (255) $120; pba July 23 (222) $120; sg Oct 31 (326) $130

Anr copy. Orig cloth, in chipped d/j. sg May 21 (314) $80

Weber, Johann Carl

— Die Alpen-Pflanzen Deutschlands und der Schweiz.... Munich, 1872. 3d Ed. Vols I-III (of 4). Orig cloth. b Nov 18 (383) £150

Anr Ed. Munich, 1880. 4 vols. 12mo, orig cloth. With 400 hand-colored plates. Spotted. DW Jan 29 (136) £160

Anr copy. Orig cloth; Vol III not uniform. L Nov 14 (230) £190; SI June 10 (1092) LIt1,400,000

Weber, Max, 1881-1961

— Woodcuts and Linoleum Blocks. NY, [1956]. One of 225. sg Feb 6 (302) $600

Webster, Daniel, 1782-1852

— Works. Bost., [1903]. ("Writings and Speeches.") National Ed, one of 1,050. 18 vols. Orig cloth; some soiling. O July 14 (194) $200

Webster, John

— The Displaying of Supposed Witchcraft. L, 1677. Folio, contemp calf; rubbed. Rust hole in B just affecting text; hole in S3 affecting text. S Feb 25 (536) £400 [Symonds]

Webster, John, 1580?-1625?

— Vittoria Corombona, or The White Devil, a Tragedy. L, 1672. 4to, old bds. Tp & final leaf restored; inner margins strengthened; K1 holed with some loss of text on verso. Ck June 12 (209) £65

Webster, John White, 1793-1850

— A Description of the Island of St. Michael.... Bost., 1821. 8vo, 19th-cent half lea; spine ends chipped, corners worn. sg Nov 14 (324) $50

Webster, Malcolm R. See: Cescinsky & Webster

Webster, Noah, 1758-1843

— An American Dictionary of the English Language. NY, 1828. 2 vols. 4to, later cloth; cloth. O Nov 26 (192) $1,000

Anr copy. Orig bds. Epstein copy. sg Apr 30 (485) $8,000

— Dissertations on the English Language.... Bost., 1789. 8vo, disbound. sg June 18 (547) $600

— A Philosophical and Practical Grammar of the English Language. New Haven, 1807. 12mo, contemp sheep; rebacked. Library stamp on tp. sg June 18 (548) $80

— The Prompter; or a Commentary on Common Sayings. Bost., 1794. 12mo, contemp half calf; worn. Stained & browned. With clipped signature of Webster tipped to front pastedown. O Nov 26 (193) $175

Wechsler, Herman Joel

— Portfolio of Twenty-four Reproductions of Masterpieces of Graphic Art. NY: Triton Press—Far Gallery, [1961]. One of 250. Folio, unbound as issued in folder. With 24 mtd plates. sg Feb 13 (214) $150

Weddell, Alexander W.

— A Memorial Volume of Virginia Historical Portraiture.... Richmond, 1930. One of 1,000. Folio, pigskin gilt; spine worn, repaired. Ck Feb 14 (19) £100

Weddell, James, 1784-1834

— A Voyage towards the South Pole. L, 1825. 1st Ed. 8vo, orig bds; grafitti inside front cover. With hand-colored frontis, 6 uncolored plates & 8 maps & charts. Some foxing. W July 8 (285) £900

Wedekind, Frank, 1864-1914

— Die Buechse der Pandora. Munich: Mueller, [1920]. One of 500 sets. Illus by Alastair. 2 vols. 4to, bds; worn. sg Sept 26 (3) $350

Wedel, Johann Georg

— An Introduction to the Whole Practice of Physick.... L, 1685. 8vo, contemp calf; worn. Some worming, afffecting text; a few page-numerals shaved; some browning & soiling. S July 9 (1114) £300 [Knohl]

Wedmore, Sir Frederick

— Turner & Ruskin. An Exposition of the Work of Turner from the Writings of Ruskin. L, 1900. 2 vols. 4to, orig cloth; rubbed & soiled. DW Dec 11 (391) £50

Weedon, Lucy L.

— The Land of Long Ago. L: E. Nister, [1898]. Oblong 4to, orig half cloth; rubbed & soiled. With 6 colored plates folding down to form 3-dimensional views. cb Nov 21 (190) $475

Weegee

— Naked City. NY, [1945]. 1st Ed. Cloth; hinges starting, minor staining. sg Oct 8 (76) $70

Anr copy. Cloth; soiled. sg Apr 13 (101) $110

Weeks, Edward

— The Moisie Salmon Club. Barre, 1971. One of 1,500. 4to, cloth. Koopman copy. O Oct 29 (322) $130

Wegelin, Oscar

— Early American Fiction 1774-1830. NY, 1929. 3d Ed. cb Oct 17 (968) $55

— Early American Poetry. NY, 1930. One of 500. 2 vols in 1, plus 1969 supplement by R. E. Stoddard. Together, 2 vols. sg Oct 31 (327) $50

— Early American Poetry. A Compilation.... NY, 1930. 2d Ed, one of 500. 2 vols in 1. cb Oct 17 (969) $75

Weickhmann, Christoph

— New-erfundenes grosse Koenigs-Spihl. Ulm, 1664. Folio, modern bds. With frontis & 8 plates. Frontis wormed with loss & repaired at outer margin; tp with wormhole affecting 2 characters; some browning; marginal annotations in a contemp hand. Ck May 8 (79) £900

Weidenmann, Jacob

— Beautifying Country Homes: A Handbook.... NY: O. Judd, [1870]. Folio, cloth; hinges cracked. With 24 color plates. Library markings; some dampstaining to a few plates. sg Apr 2 (162) $550

Weigel, Christoph, 1654-1725

— Historiae Celebriores Veteris [Novi] Testamenti.... Nuremberg, [1712]. ("Historiae celebriores Veteris Testamenti iconibus repraesentatae.") 2 vols in 1. Folio, half calf; spine & joints torn. With engraved titles & 259 plates. Last 80 plates affected by stain at upper marginal corner; Plate 69 with small hole in image. wa June 25 (469) $600

Weik, Jesse W. See: Herndon & Weik

Weinbaum, Stanley Graumann, 1900-35
— Dawn of Flame and Other Stories. [Milwaukee: American Fiction Guild, 1936]. Syn. Epstein copy. sg Apr 30 (486) $750
— A Martian Odyssey. Reading: Fantasy Press, 1949. sp Nov 24 (505) $50

Weinmann, Johann Wilhelm
— Phytanthoza iconographia. Amst., 1736-48. ("Duidelyke Verstoning Eeniger Duizend in alle Vier Waerelds Deelen wassende Bomen, Stammen, Kuriden, Bloemen, Vrugten....") In 5 vols. Half lea. With 829 (of 1025) hand-finished color plates. Lacking text. B Nov 1 (479) HF53,000

Weir, Harrison
— Our Poultry and All About Them. L, 1903. 2 vols. 4to, cloth. DW Apr 8 (182) £120

Weird...
— Weird Tales: The Unique Magazine. Popular Fiction Co., Feb 1928. Vol 11, No 2. Wraps. Inscr by Tennessee Williams, whose first appearance in print is a short story titled The Vengeance of Nitocris. P June 17 (408) $3,000

Weis, J. M.
— Representation des Fetes donnees par la Ville de Strasbourg pour la Convalescence du Roi. Paris, [1745]. Folio, orig red mor gilt by Padeloup, with his ticket; worn. With 11 double-page plates. Engraved throughout. Tp stamped. S Nov 21 (203) £1,100 [Schmidt]

Weismann, August, 1834-1914
— Das Keimplasma. Eine Theorie der Vererbung. Jena, 1892. 8vo, orig wraps. sg Nov 14 (155) $400

Weisse, Franz
— The Art of Marbling. [North Hills PA]: Bird & Bull Press, 1980. One of 300. Half lev. With 14 mtd colored samples. NH Aug 23 (60) $215

Weissenborn, Hellmuth
— Hellmuth Weissenborn: Painter and Graphic Artist. L: Bachman & Turner, [1976]. One of 200. pba July 23 (224) $100; wa Apr 9 (282) $70

Weitenkampf, Frank
— The Illustrated Book. Cambr. MA, 1938. One of 210 L.p. copies. bbc Apr 27 (177) $55

Weizaecker, Heinrich
— Adam Elsheimer der Maler von Frankfurt. Berlin, 1936-52. 2 vols in 3. 4to, orig cloth; 2 spines rubbed & soiled. S Feb 11 (238) £700 [Sims Reed]

Welch, d'Alte A.
— Bibliography of American Children's Books Printed prior to 1821. [Worcester, Mass.], 1972. Ed by Marcus A. McCorison. cb Oct 17 (970) $60; O Sept 24 (265) $70; O Dec 17 (192) $60

Welch, Stuart Cary. See: Firdausi

Welch, William Henry, 1850-1934
— Papers and Addresses. Balt., 1920. 3 vols. 4to, orig cloth. Library markings. bbc Dec 9 (354) $75

Weld, Isaac, 1774-1856
— Illustrations of the Scenery of Killarney. L, 1807. 4to, orig cloth; soiled. With 2 maps & 17 plates. Some browning. bba June 25 (103) £75 [Howes]

Anr Ed. L, 1812. 4to, contemp calf gilt; worn, upper cover detached. With 2 maps (1 folding), 1 vignette and 18 engraved plates (1 folding). Waterstained at beginning and end; some worming. bba Apr 30 (22) £60 [Davidson]

Anr copy. Contemp calf; worn, joints cracked, spine ends chipped. With engraved title & 20 plates & maps. bbc Sept 23 (194) $55

— Travels through the States of North America.... L, 1799. 1st Ed. 4to, contemp calf gilt; spine ends & corners scuffed, front free endpaper detached. With 15 plates & folding map hand-colored in outline. Erratum slip pasted at foot of plate list; piece torn from lower outer corner of last leaf without loss. C Oct 30 (94) £340 [Toscani]

Anr copy. Contemp half calf. Some staining. DW Nov 6 (1108) £220

4th Ed. L, 1807. 2 vols. 8vo, modern half calf. With 16 maps & plates. sg June 18 (549) $250

Wellcome Historical Medical Library
— Catalogue of Printed Books.... L, 1962-76. 3 vols. bba June 25 (161) £260 [Forster]

Weller, Emil
— Die falschen und fingierten Druckorte. Hildesheim, 1960-61. 3 vols, including the Nachtraege. Cloth; worn & soiled. Facsimile of 1864 Ed. O Sept 24 (258) $110

Welling, Georg von
— Opus mago-cabbalisticum et theosophicum.... Frankfurt & Leipzig, 1784. 4to, lea. With 15 folding plates. B Nov 1 (651) HF1,200

Wellington, Arthur Wellesley, 1st Duke of
— The Dispatches of Field Marshal the Duke of Wellington.... L, 1837-39. 13 vols. 8vo, contemp calf gilt. b Nov 18 (320) £160

Anr copy. Contemp calf gilt; 1 spine def, 2

torn. pn Nov 14 (387) £150

— Obsequies of His Grace the Late Illustrious Field Marshal the Duke of Wellington, 18th November, 1852. L, [n.d.]. Folio, contemp half mor; covers detached. With litho title, port & 6 tinted litho plates. bba Nov 7 (27) £240 [Grosvenor Prints]

[-] A Series of Drawings of the Orders of Knighthood...conferred upon the Duke of Wellington. L, [1852]. Oblong folio, contemp mor gilt. With 34 chromolitho plates, heightened with gold & silver. S July 1 (1381) £250 [Hooper]

— Supplementary Despatches and Memoranda of Field Marshal Arthur Duke of Wellington. L, 1858-72. 15 vols. 8vo, orig cloth; joints & edges worn. Vol I lacking map. pn Nov 14 (388) £180 [Maggs]

Wellman, Walter

— The Aerial Age. NY, 1911. cb Nov 7 (101) $60

Wells, Carolyn —& Goldsmith, Alfred F.

— A Concise Bibliography of Walt Whitman. Bost., 1922. One of 550. Contemp lev gilt. bbc Sept 23 (127) $85

Wells, Charles K.

— The Life and Adventures of Polk Wells: the Notorious Outlaw. [Halls, Missouri, 1907]. 1st Ed. Orig cloth; spine soiled & spotted. Minor edge tear to prelims. wa Dec 9 (327) $90

Wells, H. G., 1866-1946

See also: Golden Cockerel Press

— Anticipations, of the Reaction of Mechanical and Scientific Progress upon Human Life and Thought. L, 1902. Orig ptd wraps; split along front joint. Some foxing. Inscr to Arthur Conan Doyle. Epstein copy. sg Apr 30 (487) $1,900

— The Door in the Wall and Other Stories. NY & L, 1911. One of 600. Folio, orig half cloth; soiled & faded. With frontis & 9 plates after A. L. Coburn. cb Dec 5 (51) $550

— The First Men in the Moon. L, 1901. 1st Ed. bba Jan 30 (258) £80 [Thorp]

Anr copy. 2d bdg, in def d/j. sg June 11 (318) $700

1st Ed in Book form. Sgd. Epstein copy. sg Apr 30 (490) $1,700

— Floor Games. L, 1911. Orig cloth; extremities rubbed. Inscr to A. B. Darle, Christmas 1911. Manney copy. P Oct 11 (309) $500

— The Invisible Man: A Grotesque Romance. L, 1897. 1st Ed in Book form. 8vo, orig cloth; endpapers cracked along hinges. Inscr to Dennis Wheatley. Manney copy. P Oct 11 (307) $6,500

Anr copy. Orig cloth; some wear. sg June 11 (319) $650

— The Island of Doctor Moreau. L, 1896. 1st Ed. 8vo, orig cloth. Sgd on half-title. Manney copy. P Oct 11 (306) $1,500

Anr copy. Orig cloth; soiled & rubbed. pn Sept 12 (177) £85 [Scott]; pn Sept 12 (178) £70 [Oakes]

— Love and Mr. Lewisham. L & NY, 1900. 8vo, orig cloth; stain on lower cover. ALs inserted. S July 1 (1016) £180 [Sarner]

— The Outline of History. L: Newnes, [1919-20]. 24 orig parts in 1 vol. 4to, orig wraps. Epstein copy. sg Apr 30 (491) $600

— Tales of Space and Time. L & NY, 1900 [1899]. 8vo, cloth. sg June 11 (321) $150

— The Time Machine. An Invention. L, 1895. 1st English Ed. 8vo, orig wraps; worn & restored. Zimbalist-Manney copy. P Oct 11 (304) $900

Anr copy. Orig cloth; soiled. Inscr to Cosmo Rowe & with ALs laid in. Manney copy. P Oct 11 (305) $7,500

Anr copy. Orig cloth; hinges tender. Inscr. Epstein copy. sg Apr 30 (492) $2,800

1st Ed. NY, 1895. 1st Ptg, with author's name as H. S. Wells. 8vo, orig cloth. Manney copy. P Oct 11 (302) $1,800

Anr Ed. NY: Holt, [1895]. 2d Ptg. 8vo, cloth. Manney copy. P Oct 11 (303) $550

— Tono-Bungay. L, 1909. 1st Ed, 1st Issue. Manney copy. P Oct 11 (308) $100

— The War of the Worlds. NY, 1897. In: The Cosmopolitan Iillustrated Monthly Magazine, Apr-Dec 1897. 1st American Ed. 9 vols. 4to, orig wraps; worn. sg June 11 (322) $350

— Works. L, 1924-27. Atlantic Ed, One of 620. Half mor gilt; rubbed. P June 17 (358) $2,000

Anr copy. Some soiling to edges of text blocks. Unopened. wa Dec 9 (229) $650

Wells, Harry Laurenz

— History of Nevada County, California.... Oakland, 1880. Oblong folio, orig half mor; worn; rear cover dampstained. Prelims marginally dampstained. cb Nov 14 (138) $550

Wells, Lawrence Allen

— Abstract of Journal of Explorations in Western Australia, 1896-97. Adelaide: J. L. Bonython, [1899]. 8vo, orig wraps. C June 25 (275) £750 [Brooke-Hitching]

— Western Australia.Journal of the Calvert Scientific Exploring Expedition, 1896-7. Perth, [1902]. Folio, cloth. With 2 folding maps. C June 25 (274) £900 [Quaritch/ Hordern]

Wells, Polk. See: Wells, Charles K.

Wells, Seth Y. See: Green & Wells

Welty, Eudora

— Acrobats in a Park. Northridge CA: Lord John Press, 1980. One of 300. Half cloth. wa Sept 26 (274) $75

— The Bride of the Innisfallen and other Stories. NY, [1955]. In d/j. Sgd. cb Feb 12 (147) $110

— A Curtain of Green. Garden City, [1943]. In def d/j. sg June 11 (324) $225

— Delta Wedding. NY, [1946]. In frayed & chipped d/j. Sgd on tp. wa Sept 26 (275) $150

— The Golden Apples. NY: Harcourt Brace, [1949]. In d/j. Inscr. wa Sept 26 (681) $140

— Ida M'Toy. Urbana: University of Illinois, [1979]. One of 350. 4to, cloth; spine bumped. wa Sept 26 (276) $65

— Losing Battles. NY, [1970]. 1st Ed, one of 300. sg June 11 (325) $200

— Music from Spain. Greenville MS, 1948. 1st Ed, one of 750. Bds. sg June 11 (326) $350

— The Optimist's Daughter. NY, [1972]. One of 300. sg June 11 (327) $225

— A Pageant of Birds. NY: Albondocani Press, 1974. One of 300. Wraps. wa Sept 26 (267) $75

— Place in Fiction. NY: House of Books, 1957. One of 300. wa Sept 26 (277) $325

— The Ponder Heart. NY, [1954]. In soiled d/j. Inscr. wa Sept 26 (682) $110

— The Robber Bridegroom. Garden City, 1942. In chipped d/j. sg June 11 (328) $175

Anr copy. In d/j with tape reinforcement to spine ends on reverse. wa Sept 26 (281) $110

— The Shoe Bird. NY, [1964]. In d/j. Corner of 1 text leaf poorly trimmed by binder. wa Sept 26 (282) $75

— The Wide Net and Other Stories. NY: Harcourt Brace, [1943]. In chipped d/j. sg June 11 (329) $175

Anr copy. In soiled & chipped d/j. wa Sept 26 (683) $170

Wende...

— Wende der buchkunst. Literarisch-kuenstlerische Zeitschriften aus den Jahren 1895 bis 1900. Stuttgart: Hoehere facschule fuer das Graphische Gewerbe, 1962. 4to, bds; worn, spine edge torn. O Sept 24 (260) $50

Wentworth, Lady Judith Anne

— Thoroughbred Racing Stock. L, 1960. 2d Ed. 4to, orig cloth, in d/j. bba May 14 (515) £60 [Allen]

— Thoroughbred Racing Stock and its Ancestors. NY, 1962. One of 300 with the American imprint. 4to, orig cloth. With 24 colored & 368 plain plates. bba June 11 (285) £75 [Franks]

Wentworth, William Charles, 1793-1872

— New South Wales. L, 1819. ("A Statistical, Historical, and Political Description of the Colony of New South Wales....") 1st Ed. 8vo, early half calf; most of backstrip lost, upper joint cracking. Lacking half-title; small inkstain on tp. kh Nov 11 (686) A$240

Anr copy. Orig bds; worn, rebacked. Lacking final blank. James Macarthur's copy, sgd, with his markings and annotations. S June 25 (181) £1,400 [Williams]

Wentz, Roby

— The Grabhorn Press: A Biography. San Francisco: Book Club of California, 1981. One of 750. Half cloth. Book Club of California No 168. pba July 23 (87) $55

Anr copy. Half cloth, in d/j. Book Club of California No 168. sg May 21 (315) $110

Werbemittel...

— Die Werbemittel der Schwerindustrie. [N.p., c.1920]. 4to, wraps; spine & joints def. sg Sept 6 (239) $350

Werkman, Hendrik Nicolaas, 1882-1945

[-] Hommage a Werkman. Stuttgart, 1958. 4to, half cloth. sg Apr 2 (299) $325

Werner, Johann Adolph Ludwig

— Versuch einer theoretischen Anweisung zur Fechtkunst im Hiebe. Leipzig, 1824. Oblong 4to, cloth. Owner's stamp on tp. sg Mar 26 (340) $275

Werner, Karl

— Nilbilder. Wandsbeck: Seitz, 1881. Folio, orig cloth; spine torn, corners rubbed. With 24 color plates mtd on card & frontis location map. pn July 16 (211) £260

Wescher, Herta

— Collage. NY: Abrams, [1968]. Trans by Robert E. Wolf. In d/j. sg Apr 2 (66) $150

Wesley, Samuel, 1662-1735

— Poems on Several Occasions. L, 1736. 4to, old calf; worn, hinges cracking. K July 12 (513) $85

West, Anthony

— John Piper. L, [1979]. One of 126. 4to, orig mor. bba Oct 10 (159) £130 [The Bookroom]

West Library, James

— [Sale Catalogue] Catalogue of the Large and Justly Admired Museum of Curiosities. Langford, 1773. 8vo, disbound. bba Apr 30 (388) £260 [Quaritch]

— [Sale Catalogue] Bibliotheca Westiana.... Langford, 1773. 8vo, contemp calf. Interleaved & priced by hand. cb Oct 17 (979) $500

West, Leonard

— The Natural Trout Fly and its Imitations. St. Helens, [1912]. 1st Ed, Deluxe Issue. 8vo, orig mor gilt. With 16 plates, 13 in color & with 108 flies in 9 mounts. pn Nov 14 (432) £1,100 [Laywood]

West, Michael Philip

— Claire de Lune and Other Troubadour Romances. [L: Harrap, 1913]. Illus by Evelyn Paul. 4to, orig pictorial cloth, in d/j. bba Apr 9 (352) £55 [Weston]

West, Nathanael

— The Day of the Locust. NY, [1939]. 1st Ed. In d/j. Manney copy. P Oct 11 (310) $3,250

Anr copy. In worn d/j. Inscr. Epstein copy. sg Apr 30 (493) $3,000

— Miss Lonelyhearts. NY, [1933]. 2d Ed. Inscr to Lou Breslau. sg Dec 12 (406) $650

West, William, 1770-1854

— Fifty Years' Recollections of an Old Bookseller. L, 1837. Bound with: Three Hundred and Fifty Years Retrospection of an Old Bookseller. L, 1835. 8vo, later cloth. bba May 28 (628) £100 [Grigoropoulos]

Anr copy. Bound with: Three Hundred and Fifty Years Retrospection of an Old Bookseller. L, 1835. cloth; worn, backstrip detached & loosely inserted. Some leaves foxed. bba May 28 (629) £75 [Maggs]

— Picturesque Views and Descriptions of Cities, Towns, Castles...in Staffordshire and Shropshire. Birm., 1830-31. 2 parts in 1 vol. 4to, half calf. pnE Dec 4 (210) £200

Anr copy. Part 1 only. 4to, half mor; worn. With engraved title & 38 plates. Some foxing & browning. sg Sept 6 (263) $150

Westall, Richard

— Victories of the Duke of Wellington. L, 1819. Folio, contemp half mor; rebacked, old spine laid down, covers recovered, modern endpapers. With 12 hand-colored plates. L.p. copy. C May 20 (138) £240 [Old Hall]

Westall, William

— Drawings. L, 1962. Ed by T. M. Perry & D. H. Simpson. Folio, cloth; marked. kh Nov 11 (245) A$60

— Great Britain Illustrated. L, 1830.. 4to, recent mor gilt. With 118 views on 59 leaves. Spotted & browned. DW Mar 4 (96) £200

— Views of Australian Scenery. L: G. & W. Nicol, [1814]. Oblong folio, orig wraps. With 9 plates. Spotted. L.p. copy. C June 25 (201) £700 [Quaritch/Hordern]

Westall, William —& Others

— The Mansions of England. L: M. A. Nattali [watermarked 1828-43]. 2 vols. 8vo, contemp half mor gilt. With 146 colored plates. C May 20 (137) £2,700 [Simon Finch]

Westall, William —& Moule, Thomas

— Great Britain Illustrated, a Series of Original Views.... L, 1830. 4to, contemp half calf; rubbed. With engraved title & 59 plates. S May 14 (1160) £210 [Walford]

Westall, William —& Owen, Samuel

— Picturesque Tour of the River Thames. L: Ackermann, 1828. 4to, mor gilt by Bayntun Riviere, with initials of H. L. Bradfer-Lawrence on spine. With folding map & 24 hand-colored plates. L.p. copy. C May 20 (135) £5,000 [Joseph]

Anr copy. Orig cloth. C May 20 (136) £3,000 [Simon Finch]

Anr copy. Modern half mor. Washed, with occasional smudging of text; pp. 39-40 torn in 2 places & repaired. pn Nov 14 (408) £950 [Elliott]

Anr copy. Later 19th-cent half mor gilt; rubbed. Oxidation flaw at Plate 12; Plate 19 & following leaf of letterpress repaired at inner margin without loss; tp & 2 plate margins marked. S June 25 (283) £2,600 [George]

Westcott, Thompson, 1820-88

— Centennial Portfolio: A Souvenir of the International Exhibition at Philadelphia. Phila., 1876. Oblong folio, orig cloth; spine worn. With map & 52 colored lithos. K Dec 1 (65) $160

Anr copy. Cloth. sg June 18 (454) $60

Westerman, Gerardus Friedrich. See: Schlegel & Westerman

Westgarth, William, 1815-89

— Victoria and the Australian Gold Mines.... L, 1857. 8vo, old half calf; rubbed & soiled. Lacking final ads. kh Nov 11 (690) A$120

Westheim, Paul —& Rathenau, Ernest

— Kokoschka Drawings. L, [1962]. One of 50 with orig colored litho, sgd. 4to, orig cloth. DW Oct 9 (586) £230; DW Dec 11 (369) £300

Westmacott, Charles Molloy

— The English Spy. L, 1825-26. 2 vols. 8vo, contemp half lea; worn. Some plates repaired in margins; may lack a few plates. Sold w.a.f. O Aug 25 (194) $160

Anr copy. Illus by Cruikshank. Modern mor gilt by Riviere. With hand-colored frontis & 71 plates. C May 20 (139J) £750 [Mandalay Interiors]

Anr copy. Modern mor extra by Riviere. With 71 hand-colored plates. cb Dec 5 (140) $1,400

Anr copy. Later half mor gilt; rubbed. With frontis & 71 plates, all but 1 hand-colored. pn Sept 12 (287) £580 [Frew Mackenzie]

Anr copy. Mor gilt by Riviere. With 71 colored plates & with The Five Pillars of Society. Small stain in text in Vol II. S Nov 15 (727) £480 [Baring]

Weston, Edward

— Edward Weston: Fifty Years. NY, [1973]. Oblong folio, half syn; corners bumped. sg Apr 13 (102) $225

— My Camera on Point Lobos. Yosemite National Park & Bost., 1950. Folio, spiral bdg; worn, corners chipped. With 30 plates. bbc Feb 17 (274) $120

Anr copy. Dampstain on edges. NH May 30 (432) $170

Anr copy. Spiral bdg, in d/j; rubbed & scuffed. With 30 plates. sg Oct 8 (77) $250

Weston, Edward —& Others

— Fifty Photographs. NY, [1947]. One of 1,500. 4to, half cloth, in worn d/j. sg Apr 13 (103) $500

Weston, Edward & Charis W.

— The Cats of Wildcat Hill. NY, [1947]. 1st Ed. Oblong 4to, cloth; extremities worn. sg Oct 8 (78) $70

Westreen van Tiellandt, W. H. J. van, Baron

— Rapport sur les recherches, relatives a l'invention premiere et a l'usage le plus ancient de l'imprimerie stereotype. The Hague, 1833. 8vo, contemp mor gilt. With 4 plates. Some foxing; head of Dutch title cut away; 1 plate with small tear. bba May 28 (620) £100 [Maggs]

Westwood, John Obadiah, 1805-93

See also: Humphreys & Westwood

— Fac-Similes of the Miniatures and Ornaments of Anglo-Saxon and Irish Manuscripts. L, 1868. Folio, half mor by Bedford; rubbed & soiled. With 53 colored plates, 9 tinted. Library stamps on verso of tp, head of 1st text leaf & verso of final plate. pn Apr 23 (166) £140

— Palaeographia Sacra Pictoria... L, 1843-45. 4to, later half mor gilt. With 50 hand-finished color plates. Marginal spotting. DW May 13 (410) £95

Westwood, Thomas

— The Chronicle of the Compleat Angler.... L, 1864. 4to, mor gilt extra with elaborated floral design. Westwood's copy, with his bookplate and stencilled monogram. Extra-illus with 5 photographs and 100 ports and plates. CNY Dec 5 (449) $500

Westwood, Thomas —& Satchell, Thomas

— Bibliotheca Piscatoria: a Catalogue of Books on Angling.... L, 1883. 8vo, half mor; joints worn. O Oct 29 (325) $180

Wetherell, Elizabeth —& Lothrop, Amy

— Mr. Rutherford's Children. L, 1865. 1st Series. Illus by John Dawson Watson. 8vo, orig cloth. With 3 orig watercolors by Watson, sgd with initials. cb Sept 26 (208) $425

Wethey, Harold

— El Greco and his School. Princeton, 1962. 2 vols. 4to, cloth, in d/js. S Feb 11 (242) £320 [Higbee]

Wettergren, Erik

— The Modern Decorative Arts of Sweden. Malmo, 1926. 4to, half cloth; worn. sg Sept 6 (273) $60

Wetzel, Charles M.

— American Fishing Books: A Bibliography.... Newark DE, 1950. One of 200. 4to, lea; some wear. Koopman copy. O Oct 29 (326) $1,100

Anr copy. Half mor; rubbed. Inscr. O Nov 26 (194) $1,150

— Practical Fly Fishing. Bost.: Christopher, [1943]. In worn d/j. Koopman copy. O Oct 29 (327) $80

Wharncliffe, John Stuart-Wortley, Lord

— Sketches in Egypt and in the Holy Land.... L: Day & Son, [1855]. Folio, orig half mor gilt; corners worn. With litho title with hand-colored vignette & 18 views on 17 tinted & hand-colored lithos. S Feb 26 (789) £360 [Sotheran]

Wharton, Edith, 1862-1937
See also: Book, Booke•for Boke

— Ethan Frome. NY, 1911. 1st Ed, 1st Issue. In d/j. Epstein copy. sg Apr 30 (494) $3,600

— The House of Mirth. NY, 1905. Inscr. sg Dec 12 (407) $3,200

— Italian Villas and their Gardens. NY, 1907. Illus by Maxfield Parrish. Cloth; rubbed. bbc Dec 9 (334) $80

Whately, Thomas, d.1772

— Observations on Modern Gardening. L, 1770. 8vo, contemp calf gilt; spine chipped. DW Jan 29 (137) £310

Whately, William, 1583-1639

— Prototypes...out of...Genesis. L, 1647. Folio, contemp sheep; worn, needs re-backing. Lacking initial blank or license leaf. sg Oct 24 (338) $400

Whatley, Stephen

— England's Gazetteer; or, an Accurate Description.... L, 1751. 3 vols. 12mo, contemp calf; worn. sg Mar 12 (307) $375

Wheat, Carl I.
See also: Grabhorn Printing; Morgan & Wheat

— Books of the California Gold Rush. San Francisco: Colt Press, 1949. One of 500. Half cloth; worn. O Sept 24 (262) $140

Anr copy. Front endpapers browned. sg Oct 31 (319) $150

Wheat, Marvin

— Travels on the Western Slopes of the Mexican Cordillera. San Francisco, 1857. 12mo, cloth. sg June 18 (580) $110

Wheatley, Henry Benjamin, 1838-1917

— Bookbinding Considered as a Fine Art.... L, 1882. cb Oct 17 (983) $80

Wheatley, Hewett

— The Rod and Line: or, Practical Hints and Dainty Devices.... L, 1849. 12mo, half mor; rubbed, joints worn. With 9 hand-colored plates. Koopman copy. O Oct 29 (328) $250

Anr copy. Orig cloth; rubbed. pn Mar 19 (387) £140

Wheeler, Daniel

— Extracts from the Letters and Journals.... Phila., 1840. 8vo, orig cloth; extremities worn & frayed. Some foxing. F Sept 26 (421) $50

Anr copy. Orig cloth; some signatures sprung. O July 14 (196) $60

Wheeler, George M. See: United States of America

Wheler, Sir George
See also: Spon & Wheler

— A Journey into Greece, in Company of Dr. Spon. L, 1682. 1st Ed. Folio, contemp mor gilt. With folding map (with repaired tear), 3 plates on 1 folding leaf & 4 plates of coins. Final coin plate pasted onto back free endpaper; small hole in 1 leaf costing a few characters. C Oct 30 (122) £900 [Spelman]

Anr copy. Contemp calf gilt; rubbed, upper cover detached. With folding map (small hole at junction of folds) & 5 plates. First plate just shaved at foot; tp torn at inner margin without loss. S July 1 (730) £1,700 [Consolidated Real]

— Voyage de Dalmatie, de Grece, et du Levant. Amst., 1689. 2 vols. 12mo, contemp vellum. With engraved title, folding map & 88 plates & plans. Tear in B2 of Vol I. S June 30 (441) £300 [Lepanto]

Whistler, James Abbott McNeill, 1834-1903.
See: Dodgson, Campbell

— The Gentle Art of Making Enemies. L, 1890. 4to, orig half cloth; soiled. Inscr & sgd with butterfly. Epstein copy. sg Apr 30 (495) $600

Whistler, Laurence —& Fuller, Ronald

— The Work of Rex Whistler. L, 1960. 4to, orig cloth in d/j. DW Dec 11 (392) £200

Whistler, Rex, 1905-44

— The Koenigsmark Drawings. L, 1952. One of 1,000. Intro by Laurence Whistler. 4to, orig cloth. Some soiling. sg Sept 26 (298) $150

Whitaker, Charles H.

— Bertram Grosvenor Goodhue: Architect and Master of Many Arts. NY, 1925. Folio, orig cloth; soiled. With 5 color & 273 plates. F Sept 26 (186D) $70

Whitaker, Thomas Dunham

— The History and Antiquities of the Deanery of Craven. L, 1805. 4to, contemp half calf gilt; rebacked preserving orig spine, corners repaired. With port & 35 (of 36) plates. Some foxing. bba June 11 (384) £130

[Harley]

Anr copy. Contemp half calf. With 17 aquatint plates, 13 engraved plates & folding tables.. pnE Dec 4 (214) £75

Anr copy. With 17 aquatint plates & 13 engraved plates & folding tables. pnE Mar 11 (70) $60

Anr Ed. Leeds, 1878. Folio, contemp calf gilt; rebacked. Plates including hand-colored half-title & geological map. pnL Nov 20 (65) £170 [Tuston]

3d Ed. 4to, contemp half mor; rubbed, rear bd stained. With hand-colored half-title & 62 plates, some tinted or colored. Inner margin of 1 prelim leaf torn; some soiling. pnL Nov 20 (105) £120 [Miles]

— An History of Richmondshire.... L, 1823. 2 vols. Folio, contemp calf gilt; rebacked. With 45 plates, 4 hand-colored. Some spotting; dampstains to a few plates. pnL Nov 20 (74) £350 [Taylor]

— An History of the Original Parish of Whalley and Honor of Clitheroe. L, 1818. Folio, contemp half mor; edges scuffed. pnL Nov 20 (81) £80 [Irgol]

Anr Ed. L, 1872-76. 2 vols. 4to, orig cloth. pnL Nov 20 (104) £85 [Miles]

— Loidis and Elmete: or an Attempt to Illustrate the Districts.... Leeds, 1816. 1st Ed. Folio, half mor; rubbed. bba Feb 27 (36) £85 [Stanley]

2d Ed. Folio, later half mor gilt by Frank Murray; hinges rubbed. Sold w.a.f. DW Dec 11 (131) £220

White...

— The White House Gallery of Official Portraits of the Presidents. NY, 1901. Folio, half mor; def. Some foxing. sg Feb 13 (202) $110

Anr Ed. [N.p., 1903]. Folio, half mor gilt; joints cracked. sg Feb 13 (203) $140

— The White House Library: A Short-Title List. Wash., 1967. One of 300, sgd by Lady Bird Johnson. Half mor. sg May 21 (317) $130

— The White House Porcelain Service; Designs by an American Artist, Illustrating Exclusively American Fauna and Flora. [N.p.], 1879. 8vo, orig ptd wraps; chipped. sg Sept 6 (232) $225

White, Adam

— Notes on some Insects from King George's Sound. L, [1841]. 8vo, wraps. Offprint from George Grey's Journals of Two Expeditions of Discovery in North-west and Western Australia, 1841, Vol II, pp. 450-8, with specially ptd tp. Inscr to Milne Edwards. R. J. Maria copy. C June 25 (225) £1,000 [Stokes]

— A Popular History of Birds. L, 1855. 8vo, cloth. With 20 hand-colored plates. sg Feb 13 (156) $200

White, Alain Campbell —& Others

— The Succulent Euphorbieae. Pasadena, 1941. 2 vols. 4to, cloth; worn. Library markings. O Apr 28 (143) $300

White, Charles, 1728-1813

— A Treatise on the Management of Pregnant and Lying-In Women.... L, 1773. 8vo, contemp calf; worn, upper cover detached. With Ms notes on fever on plate versos & 2 blank leaves. b Nov 18 (281) £400

White, Elwyn Brooks

— Stuart Little. NY, [1945]. Illus by Garth Williams. sg June 11 (332) $50

White, Frederick. See: Derrydale Press

White, George Francis

— Views in India, Chiefly Among the Himalaya Mountains. L, 1838. 4to, recent mor gilt. With engraved title & 37 plates. DW Jan 29 (59) £85

White, Gilbert, 1720-93

See also: Nonesuch Press

— The Natural History and Antiquities of Selborne. L, 1789. 1st Ed. 4to, contemp calf; broken. With 2 engraved titles & 7 plates. Piece torn away at end of advertisement. Sold w.a.f. b Nov 18 (383A) £160

Anr copy. Contemp mor gilt; spine scuffed. With folding frontis & 6 plates. Frontis with repaired tears; folding plate & tp with marginal tears repaired. C Oct 30 (239) £500 [Maggs]

Anr copy. Modern half calf. With folding frontis & 6 plates, 1 folding. B1 torn with serious loss. Sold w.a.f. Ck Dec 11 (268) £160

Anr copy. Contemp half calf; rebacked, rubbed. With folding frontis & 6 plates. Some spotting & staining. Ck May 15 (55) £500

Anr copy. Contemp half sheep; joints cracking, spine rubbed. Browning from insert on pp. 92-93; some spotting at front & back. Bemis copy. P Dec 12 (198) $800

Anr Ed. L, 1900. 2 vols. 4to, bdg not described. LH May 17 (693) $100

— The Works in Natural History.... L, 1802. 2 vols. 8vo, contemp calf. With 2 plain & 2 colored plates. LH Dec 11 (269) $225

White, James, Esq.

— The Adventures of Sir Frizzle Pumpkin.... Edin. & L, 1836. Illus by George Cruikshank. 8vo, half mor; edges worn. With 8 plates, including that to face p 157. sg Oct 17 (181) $175

White, John, fl.1788-96
— Journal of a Voyage to New South Wales. L, 1790. Bound with: Gilbert, Thomas. Voyage from New South Wales to Canton in the Year 1788. L, 1789. With 4 folding plates 4to, contemp calf; rebacked. With engraved title & 65 hand-colored plates. S June 25 (103) £8,500 [Quaritch/Hordern]

White, Minor
— Mirrors, Messages, Manifestations. [NY, 1969]. 4to, cloth, in chipped d/j. With pamphlet of comments laid into rear pocket. sg Oct 8 (79) $200

White, Patrick
— Happy Valley, a Novel. L, 1939. 8vo, cloth; worn, front free endpaper set down. kh Nov 11 (694) A$280

White, Stanford, 1853-1906
— Sketches and Designs; with an Outline of his Career.... NY, 1920. Folio, cloth, in d/j; worn. O Jan 14 (192) $250

Anr copy. Cloth; spine worn. With 56 plates. wd June 12 (443) $275

— Sketches and Designs by Stanford White. NY, 1920. 1st Ed. With color frontis & 56 plates. wa Sept 26 (552) $300

White, Terence Hanford
— The Sword in the Stone. L, 1938. In chipped d/j. sg June 11 (333) $200

White, William F.
— A Picture of Pioneer Times in California. San Francisco, 1881. 8vo, cloth. sg June 18 (147) $60

White, William Smith
— The Professional: Lyndon B. Johnson. Bost., 1964. In d/j. Inscr by Johnson. sp Nov 24 (1) $130

Whitecar, William B.
— Four Years aboard the Whaleship, embracing Cruises.... Phila., 1860. 12mo, cloth; faded. cb Jan 30 (133) $85

Whitefield, George. See: Franklin Printing, Benjamin

Whitehead, Alfred North —& Russell, Bertrand, 1872-1970
— Principia mathematica. Cambr., 1950. 2d Ed. 3 vols. bba Apr 9 (193) £220 [Abdullah]

Whitehead, P. J. P. —& Edward, P. I.
— Chinese Natural History Drawings. L, 1974. One of 400. Folio, half mor; rubbed & stained. bba Sept 5 (121) £55 [C. White]

Anr copy. Orig half calf. bba Mar 26 (203) £75 [Ad Orientem]

Whitehead, Peter James Palmer
— Forty Drawings of Fishes made by the Artists who Accompanied Captain James Cook. L, 1968. Folio, orig cloth, in d/j. With frontis & 36 plates. bba Dec 19 (100) £90 [Ginnan]; DW Mar 4 (104) £50

Whitelocke, Sir Bulstrode, 1605-75
— Memorials of the English Affairs.... L, 1709. Folio, contemp calf; rebacked. W July 8 (78) £70

Whitelocke, Lieut.-Gen. John
— An Authentic Narrative of the Proceedings of the Expedition under the command of Brigadier-General Craufurd, until its Arrival at Monte Video, with an Account of the Operations against Buenos Ayres under the Command of Lieut.-Gen. Whitelocke, by an Officer of the Expedition. L, 1808. 8vo, contemp calf gilt. With 3 (of 4) folding maps. Errata slip pasted to tp verso; some foxing. bba June 25 (265) £120 [Sanderson]

Whitfield, Christopher. See: Golden Cockerel Press

Whitman, Sarah Helen, 1803-78
— Edgar Poe and his Critics. NY, 1860. 1st Ed. 12mo, cloth; embossed stamps on tp & front free endpaper. sg Mar 5 (276) $60

2d Ed. Providence, 1885. 12mo, orig cloth. sp Apr 16 (428) $55

Whitman, Walt, 1819-92
See also: Grabhorn Printing; Limited Editions Club

— After All, Not to Create Only. Bost., 1871. 1st Pbd Ed. 8vo, orig cloth; spine ends worn. wa Sept 26 (283) $260

— Leaves of Grass. Brooklyn, 1855. 1st Ed, 1st State. 4to, orig cloth; spine repaired, minor wear to extremities, minor soiling on front cover. Doheny-Manney copy. P Oct 11 (312) $29,000

Anr copy. Orig cloth; rehinges, extremities restored. Frontis & prelims partly dampstained. P Dec 12 (94A) $8,000

Anr copy. Orig cloth; rebacked to match orig spine. Title reinforced along inner hinge on verso. Epstein copy. sg Apr 30 (500) $28,000

2d Ed. Brooklyn, NY, 1856. 12mo, orig cloth; spine dulled, ends worn. sg Nov 7 (248) $1,500

4th Ed. NY, 1867. 8vo, half mor; needs rebdg. sg Mar 5 (319) $130

Author's Ed. Camden NJ, 1876. One of 100, sgd on tp. 8vo, orig half mor; front cover detached, backstrip missing. Inscr to H. R. Haweis. P June 16 (312) $1,000

Anr copy. Orig half calf; rebacked, orig

backstrip laid down. Ad leaf tipped in at rear. Epstein copy. sg Apr 30 (498) $1,100

Anr Ed. [Phila., 1888-89]. ("Complete Poems & Prose, 1855-1888.") 8vo, bds; shaken & loose, soiled. wd Dec 12 (470) $1,000

One of 600, sgd. Orig half cloth; edges worn. With 4 ports. Inscr by Horace Traubel. Epstein copy. sg Apr 30 (497) $1,300

"Death-Bed Edition". Phila., 1891-92. 2d Issue. 8vo, green cloth; front free endpaper lacking. Split in title leaf along gutter. wa Dec 9 (230) $75

Anr Ed. NY, 1940. Intro by Christopher Morley. 4to, lea. Sgd by Morley & by Danielto Harry Scherman. sg June 11 (250) $250

Anr Ed. Mount Vernon NY: Peter Pauper Press, [1943]. One of 1,100. Folio, half mor; corners worn. sg Sept 26 (251) $140

— Memoranda During the War. Camden, N.J., 1875-76. 1st Ed, Issue with ports & "Remembrance Copy" leaf. 8vo, orig cloth; rubbed, inner hinges cracked. Some leaves becoming loose; some soiling or browning. Inscr to Jackson Prestwitch. P June 16 (311) $1,200

Anr copy. Orig cloth; worn. Inscr to J. Q. A. Ward. S July 21 (77) £2,500 [Chappel Hill]

— November Boughs. Phila., 1888. 1st Ed. 8vo, orig cloth; spine & corners worn. bbc Sept 23 (486) $200

— Two Rivulets. Camden, 1876. 1st Ed. 8vo, orig half mor; front cover detached, backstrip missing. Some glue stains on frontis. Frontis sgd. P June 16 (314) $1,500

2d Ptg. Mor gilt. Tearing along the inner margin of the mount for the port; some browning. Frontis sgd. P June 16 (313) $1,500

[-] Walt Whitman in Camden. Camden, 1938. One of 1,100. Preface by Christopher Morley; illus by Arnold Genthe. 4to, cloth. F Dec 18 (46) $90

Whitney, Henry C.

— Life on the Circuit with Lincoln. Bost: Estes & Lauriat, [1892]. 8vo, orig cloth; edges worn, rubbed, hinges reinforced. bbc June 29 (257) $110

Whitney, Joel P.

— Silver Mining Regions of Colorado. NY, 1865. 16mo, front wrap only with minor damage. sg June 18 (184) $200

Whitney, Josiah D., 1819-96

— The Yosemite Book.... NY, 1868. 4to, orig half mor; rubbed, endpapers chipped, loose in bdg. With 28 mtd photos. Library bookplate; Yosemite map torn; Sierra Nevada map torn; some spotting & soiling. P Dec 12 (94) $2,000

— The Yosemite Guide-Book. NY, 1869. 8vo, orig cloth; front bd nearly detached, with free endpaper torn, fore-edge stained. With 8 wood-engraved plates & 2 folding pocket maps (1 split along folds & tape-repaired). wa Sept 26 (454) $230

Whitney, Peter

— The History of the County of Worcester. Worcester: Isaiah Thomas, 1793. 8vo, contemp sheep; extremities worn. With folding map (repaired). sg June 18 (360) $175

Whittier, John Greenleaf, 1807-92

— Leaves from Margaret Smith's Journal.... Bost., 1849. 1st Ed. 8vo, half mor; corners worn. sg Oct 17 (397) $60

— Snowbound.... Bost., 1866. 1st Ed, 1st State. 8vo, orig cloth; corners & spine ends worn, flyleaves foxed. Some foxing. pba Aug 20 (243) $60

— The Stranger in Lowell. Bost., 1845. 12mo, modern half mor, orig wraps bound in. O Dec 17 (195) $60

— Works. Bost. & NY: Houghton, Mifflin, 1892. Amesbury Ed. 7 vols. 8vo, half mor; spines rubbed. O Jan 14 (193) $100

Whittle, James. See: Laurie & Whittle

Whittock, Nathaniel

— The Decorative Painters' and Glaziers' Guide. L, 1827. 4to, contemp half calf; worn. With 63 hand-colored plates. Title & first few leaves creased; some foxing & soiling. Sold w.a.f. bba Apr 30 (339) £60 [Biltcliffe]

Whole...

— The Whole Art of Hocus Pocus.... L: Thomas Tegg, 1812. 12mo, orig wraps. With hand-colored frontis by George Cruikshank. Lower portion of last few leaves stained. S Apr 28 (165) £3,050 [Huber]

— The Whole Art of Making Fireworks...by an Experienced Artist. L, [1820s?]. 8vo, later wraps. Marginal soiling & spotting. sg Nov 14 (310) $850

Whymper, Edward, 1840-1911

— Scrambles Amongst the Alps in the years 1860-69. L, 1893. 4th Ed. 8vo, contemp cloth by Zaehnsdorf. bba Sept 19 (156) £110 [Grigor-Taylor]

— Travels amongst the Great Andes. L,

1891-92. 2 vols, including supplementary Index. 8vo, orig cloth. b Nov 18 (358A) £160

— Travels Amongst the Great Andes of the Equator. NY, 1892. 8vo, cloth; worn. O July 14 (198) $80

Whyte, Samuel

— The Shamrock: or, Hibernian Cresses.... Dublin, 1772. 4to, contemp calf. CG Oct 7 (545) £150

Whyte-Melville, George John, 1821-78

— Works. L, 1898-1902. Ed by Sir Herbert Maxwell. 24 vols. 8vo, half lea. br May 29 (31) $380

Wichmann, Siegfried

— Posters 1900. [N.p., n.d.]. Folio, cloth, in d/j. With 38 mtd color plates. sg Apr 2 (244) $200

Wickersham, James

— A Bibliography of Alaskan Literature. Cordova, 1927. sg Oct 31 (330) $100

Wickes, Charles

— Illustrations of the Spires and Towers of the Mediaeval Churches of England. L, 1853-59. 2 vols, including Supplement. Folio, orig half mor; rubbed. With 52 plates. DW Mar 11 (873) £220

Widener Library, Harry Elkins

— A Catalogue of the Books and Manuscripts of Robert Louis Stevenson in the Library.... Phila.: Pvtly ptd, 1913. One of 150. With a Memoir by A. S. W. Rosenbach. 4to, half mor; rubbed. K Sept 29 (445) $250

— A Catalogue of the Works Illustrated by George Cruikshank, and Isaac and Robert Cruikshank, in the Library of.... Phila.: Pvtly ptd, 1918. Compiled by A. S. W. Rosenbach. 4to, orig cloth. K Sept 29 (144) $80

Widmann, George Rudolf

— Erster [-dritte] Theil der Warhafftigen Historien von...D. Johannes Faustus. Hamburg: Hermann Moeller, 1599. 3 parts in 1 vol. 4to, 18th-cent vellum; soiled. Browned; a few leaves torn & repaired; final leaf with tear affecting 7 lines of text. C Dec 16 (95) £2,200 [Preissler-Kahan]

Wiegleb, Johann Christian

— Historisch-Kritische Untersuchung der Alchemie.... Wiemar: Carl Ludolf Hoffmann, 1777. 8vo, contemp bds; rubbed. Blank corner off title & next leaf. sg Nov 14 (325) $250

Wiener Werkstaette

— Mode 1914/15. Vienna: Eduard Kosmack, 1915. One of 50. Ed by Josef Hoffmann. 12 parts. Folio, in folders. With Ms tp & 144 plates, each sgd, the macjority colored by hand, each on separate mount, the ptd contents listing in each of the 12 parts pasted inside covers. S May 28 (239) £17,000 [Beres]

— Wiener Werkstaette, 1903-1928. Modernes Kunstgewerbe und Sein Weg. Vienna, 1929. 4to, orig bds with figural designs in relief by Vally Wieseltheir & Gudrun Baudisch; extremities rubbed. sg Apr 2 (301) $1,200

Wier, Johannes

— Histoires, disputes et discours, des illusions et impostures des diables.... Geneva: Jacques Chouet, 1579. 8vo, old calf gilt; front joint cracked. sg Mar 12 (241) $1,400

Wierzbicki, Felix Paul, 1815-60. See: Grabhorn Printing

Wiggin, Kate Douglas, 1856-1923

— The Birds' Christmas Carol. San Francisco, 1887. 1st Ed. 12mo, rebound in stiff paper with orig pictorial front & rear covers laid down. Epstein copy. sg Apr 30 (502) $1,600

Wikgren, Allen P.

— The Coverdale Bible. San Francisco: Book Club of California, 1974. One of 425. With facsimile reproductions & an orig leaf. b&b Feb 19 (282) $150

Wilbour Library, Charles Edwin

— Catalogue of the Egyptological Library and other Books.... NY, 1924. Compiled by W. B. Cook, Jr. cb Oct 17 (992) $60

Wilbur, Richard

— A Bestiary. NY, [1955]. One of 50. Illus by Alexander Calder. Folio, cloth. sg Jan 30 (20) $350

One of 750. Cloth; worn. sg Sept 26 (69) $250

Wilcox, R. N.

— Reminiscences of California Life.... Avery, Ohio, 1897. 1st Ed. 12mo, cloth. sg June 18 (150) $110

Wilcox, Virginia Lee

— Colorado: A Selected Bibliography.... Denver, 1954. In d/j. cb Oct 17 (993) $110

Wild Flowers...

— Wild Flowers of America. NY: G. H. Buek, [1894]. Oblong 4to, later cloth, orig wraps bound in. With 288 colored illusts, 2 per plate. K Mar 22 (450) $75

Anr copy. 18 parts. 4to, orig wraps; some wraps def. With c.144 plates only. sg Feb

13 (165) $175

Wild, Frank

— Shackleton's Last Voyage. The Story of the Quest. L, 1923. 1st Ed. Some text leaves spotted. bba Sept 19 (46) £220 [Simper]

Anr copy. Orig cloth. Inscr by John Quiller Rowett to A. V. Lansley. C Oct 30 (94A) £1,200 [Grigor-Taylor]

Wild, J. C.

— Panorama and Views of Philadelphia, and its Vicinity. Phila., 1838. 1st Ed. Folio, modern half cloth. With 20 plates. Some foxing. F Sept 26 (293) $1,450

Wilde, Oscar, 1854-1900

See also: Limited Editions Club

— The Ballad of Reading Gaol. L, 1898. 1st Ed, one of 800. 8vo, orig buckram-backed cloth; some soiling. pn Sept 12 (183) £280 [Joseph]

Anr copy. Orig cloth; soiled. S Feb 25 (432) £170 [Lewis]

Anr copy. Orig cloth; spine darkened. With a clipped signature of Wilde tipped in. Epstein copy. sg Apr 30 (503) $1,200

Anr Ed. L, 1899 [i.e., 1904]. 8vo, cloth; spine darkened. sg Oct 17 (398) $70

Anr Ed. Munich, 1923. One of 250. Illus by Frans Masereel. 4to, calf; rubbed. sg Jan 30 (186) $250

Anr Ed. L, 1924. One of 50. Contemp half mor; rubbed. bba Jan 30 (259) £170 [Thorp]

Anr Ed. NY, 1928. Illus by Lynd Ward. Bds; rear spine hinge splitting. cb Jan 16 (174) $50

— Ballade de la geole de Reading. Paris, 1918. One of 30 on japon with 2 extra suites of the woodcuts on japon & chine, each sgd, & a drawing for 1 of the illusts. Illus by Daragnes. Mor extra by Ch. Lanoe, orig wraps bound in. S May 28 (460) £1,200 [Beres]

— De Profundis. L, [1905]. cb Sept 19 (221) $85; sg Dec 12 (413) $90

— The Happy Prince and Other Tales. L, 1888. One of 75 with illusts in mtd India-proof state & plates in 2 states. Illus by Walter Crane & Jacomb Hood. 4to, vellum bds; spine ends worn; hinges cracked. Epstein copy. sg Apr 30 (504) $8,500

1st Ed. 4to, orig bds. cb Sept 19 (222) $650

Anr copy. Orig half Japan vellum; soiled. sg Dec 12 (410) $1,200

— A House of Pomegranates. L, 1891. 1st Ed. 4to, orig half cloth. bba July 9 (325) £130 [Royal Academy Library]

Anr copy. Orig cloth; worn, front free endpaper loose. Dedication leaf excised. Inscr to Lord Alfred Douglas. S Dec 12 (37) £2,500 [Rocklin]

Anr copy. Orig cloth; darkened. S May 13 (676) £280 [Hawthorne]

Anr Ed. L, 1915. Illus by Jessie M. King. 4to, orig cloth. b Nov 18 (118) £170

Anr copy. Orig cloth; soiled & stained. With color title & 16 tipped-on color plates Some foxing. wa Mar 5 (604) $90

— An Ideal Husband. L, 1899. 1st Ed, one of 1,000. 4to, cloth; soiled & rubbed. cb Sept 19 (223) $190

Anr copy. Orig cloth. Eva Le Gallienne's copy. sg Mar 5 (323) $225

— The Importance of Being Earnest. L, 1899. One of 1,000. 8vo, orig cloth. Epstein copy. sg Apr 30 (505) $450

1st Ed. 4to, orig cloth; spine darkened. cb Sept 19 (224) $400

Anr copy. 8vo, orig cloth. Eva Le Gallienne's copy. sg Mar 5 (324) $400

Out-of-series copy. 4to, orig cloth; rubbed & soiled. pn Sept 12 (184) £140

— Impressions of America. Sunderland, 1906. One of 500. Wraps. bba July 9 (184) £140 [Quaritch]

Anr copy. Wraps, unopened. sg Dec 12 (411) $60

— Irish Poets and Poetry of the Nineteenth Century: A Lecture.... San Francisco: Book Club of California, 1972. One of 500. cb Sept 19 (225) $50

— Lady Windermere's Fan. L, 1893. 1st Ed. 4to, orig cloth. bba July 9 (181) £80 [Rota]

Anr copy. Cloth; spine stained. cb Sept 19 (226) $140

Anr copy. Cloth; edges worn. sg Dec 12 (412) $80

Pirated Ed. Paris [Ptd in England], 1903. one of 250. sg Mar 5 (325) $70

— Lord Arthur Savile's Crime and other Stories. L, 1891. 1st Ed. 8vo, orig bds; soiled & rubbed. sg Mar 5 (326) $110

Anr copy. Bds; worn. Epstein copy. sg Apr 30 (506) $350

— Oscariana. L, 1910. 8vo, orig wraps, unopened; covers detached. bba July 9 (182) £100 [Rota]

— The Picture of Dorian Gray. Phila., 1890. 8vo, half cloth. sg Mar 5 (327) $90

1st Ed. L, [1891]. 1st Issue. 8vo, orig bds, in soiled d/j with tears at spine ends. Inscr to Arthur Clifton. Manney copy. P Oct 11 (314) $12,000

1st Ed in Book form, One of 250 L.p. copies. 4to, orig half vellum bds; upper joint split. Ck Dec 11 (193) £1,400

Anr Ed. L: Ward, Lock & Bowen, [1891].

8vo, half cloth. Epstein copy. sg Apr 30 (507) $550

Ed B. L, [1968]. one of 225 with 4 sgd etchings in separate folder. Illus by Jim Dine. Folio, orig velvet-covered bds by Rudolph Rieser. With 12 color plates. P June 18 (613) $2,500

— Poems. Bost., 1881. 1st American Ed. 12mo, orig cloth; edge wear, spine ends frayed. bbc Apr 27 (420) $75

Anr Ed. L, 1881. One of 250. 12mo, orig vellum gilt. bba June 25 (107) £320 [Fou Fou]

2d Ed. 8vo, orig vellum; soiled. S May 13 (678) £340 [Rota]

Anr Ed. L, 1892. One of 220. 8vo, orig cloth; spine ends rubbed away, upper joint partly split. S Dec 12 (40) £500 [Rocklin]

— Ravenna. Oxford, 1878. 1st Ed. 8vo, orig wraps; front cover detached. Epstein copy. sg Apr 30 (508) $600

— Salome. A Tragedy in One Act. L & Bost., 1894. One of 100 L.p. copies on Japanese vellum. Trans by Lord Alfred Douglas; illus by Aubrey Beardsley. 4to, modern mor gilt. Lacking 1 plate. bba Aug 13 (330) £100 [Marks]

Anr copy. Orig cloth. With wood-engraved frontis & 10 plates. Ck Oct 18 (224) £280

Anr copy. Orig cloth; joints split, spine ends chipped. With 10 plates. This copy with additional suppressed plate of the Toilette of Salome. S Nov 14 (81) £1,100 [Marks]

— Salome, drame en un acte. Paris & L, 1893. 1st Ed, one of 600. 8vo, half calf. S Feb 25 (43) £150 [Freenwood]

— Some Letters from Oscar Wilde to Alfred Douglas.... San Francisco, 1924. One of 225. 4to, orig half vellum bds. Browning on frontis from offset. b&b Feb 19 (225) $100

— The Sphinx. L, 1920. One of 1,000. Illus by Alastair. 4to, orig cloth; rubbed & soiled. bba Oct 10 (160) £80 [Mytze]; sg Sept 26 (4) $200

Anr copy. Marginal tear in last page of text. sg Jan 30 (4) $300

[-] Wilde v. Whistler: Being an Acrimonious Correspondence on Art... L: Pvtly ptd, 1906. Pirated Ed, One of 400. Wraps; spine repaired. sg Dec 12 (414) $300

— A Woman of No Importance. L, 1894. 1st Ed, One of 500. 4to, orig cloth; soiled. cb Sept 19 (227) $500

Anr copy. Orig cloth. Eva Le Gallienne's copy. sg Mar 5 (328) $200

— Works. L & NY, 1907. University Ed, one of 800. 15 vols. sg Mar 5 (330) $350

Anr Ed. L: Methuen, [1910-12]. 13 vols. 8vo, half mor gilt; some wear. sg Mar 5 (329) $950

Anr Ed. Garden City, 1923. 12 vols. Half calf. LH May 17 (623) $350

Wilde, Sir William Robert Wills, 1815-76

— Narrative of a Voyage to Madeira.... Dublin, 1840. 2 vols. Orig cloth; recased, orig spine preserved. With 2 frontises. O Jan 14 (195) $120

Wilder, Thornton

— The Angel that Troubled the Waters.... NY, 1928. One of 775 L.p. copies. Bds, in d/j. sg Dec 12 (415) $120

— The Bridge of San Luis Rey. L, 1927. In d/j. sg June 11 (334) $120

Anr Ed. NY, 1927. In chipped d/j. Inscr on front free endpaper. sg June 11 (335) $275

Anr Ed. NY, 1929. One of 1,100. Illus by Rockwell Kent. 4to, cloth. O Jan 14 (196) $120; sg Sept 26 (151) $100

— The Cabala. NY, 1926. 1st Ed, 1st Issue. Inscr. K Mar 22 (451) $275

— Our Town. NY, [1938]. In d/j. NH May 30 (281) $80

— The Woman of Andros. NY, 1920. With 2 A Ls s glued in. rs Oct 17 (20) $275

Wildman, Thomas

— A Treatise on the Management of Bees. L, 1768. 1st Ed. 4to, contemp half calf; rebacked. With 3 folding plates. Some spotting & browning. pn Dec 12 (115) £290

Anr copy. Contemp calf; worn, upper cover detached. Some browning. pn Dec 12 (116) £250 [Burgess]

Wilhelm, Gottlieb Tobias

— Unterhaltungen aus der Naturgeschichte. Die Pflanzenreich. Augsburg, 1810-20. Vols I-VI (of 10) bound in 12. Contemp half vellum. With 6 engraved titles, 5 half-titles & 384 hand-colored plates. Lacking port; Plate XLI in Vol V marked. Sold w.a.f. S Dec 5 (447) £850 [Maggs]

Anr copy. 10 vols. 8vo, contemp half sheep gilt. With port, 9 (of 10) titles & 607 (of 608) hand-colored plates. sg May 7 (211) $3,000

Wilkes, Benjamin

— The English Moths and Butterflies. L, 1773. ("One Hundred and Twenty Copper-Plates of English Moths and Butterflies.") 4to, contemp mor gilt; rubbed. With 120 hand-colored plates, each with Ms caption. Library stamps on tp verso, head of dedication, foot of index & verso of last plate. pn Mar 19 (346) £2,600

Wilkes, Charles, 1798-1877

— Narrative of the United States Exploring Expedition, during the Years 1838-42.... Phila., 1845. 5 vols, lacking Atlas. 4to, cloth. With 10 folding maps. cb Jan 30 (134) $400

Anr copy. 6 vols, including Atlas. 4to, cloth; worn, spines gone, Atlas loose. Some tears or splits to maps. Sold w.a.f. O May 26 (199) $450

Anr copy. 5 vols, lacking Atlas. 4to, orig cloth. sg June 18 (582) $300

Wilkes, George, 1820-85

— Project of a National Railroad from the Atlantic to the Pacific Ocean.... NY, 1845. 8vo, modern half mor. With folding map. sg Dec 5 (273) $1,600

Wilkes's copy, John

— Les Muses en belle humeur.... Ville Franche, 1742. 8vo, contemp calf gilt; worn. With port of Wilkes tipped in. Some spotting & staining. Sgd on tp & with 4 obscene poems in his hand on tp verso & front endpapers. S Dec 12 (276) £1,700 [Quaritch]

— The Political Register and Impartial Review of New Books. L, for J. Almon, [1767-72]. 11 vols. 8vo, calf gilt by Morrell; rubbed. Sgd & annotated by Wilkes & with contemp news cuttings pasted in & annotated by him. Rosebery copy. S Dec 12 (277) £1,900 [May]

Wilkie, Sir David, 1785-1841

— Sketches Spanish and Oriental.... L, 1846. 4to, orig half mor; worn. With tinted litho title & 25 plates. Final plate torn; some marginal tears; some spotting. Ck Oct 18 (102) £300

Wilkins, Ernest Hatch. See: Caxton Club

Wilkins, George H.

— Flying the Arctic. NY, 1928. In d/j. cb Nov 7 (104) $80

Wilkins, John, 1614-72

— A Discovery of a New World.... [Oxford]: E. Griffin for Michael Sparke and Edward Forrest, 1638. ("The Discovery of a World in the Moone.") 8vo, modern calf. First leaf of title shorter & possibly supplied; short tear in upper margin of tp affecting rule & a star in the diagram; some checkmarks & underlining; some soiling & staining. STC 25640. Sang-Manney copy. P Oct 11 (315) $600

Anr copy. Old half calf; worn, upper cover detached. Some browning; 1st title leaf def & detached. STC 25640. S July 1 (1103) £1,050 [Youngs]

— An Essay towards a Real Character.... L, 1668. 1st Ed. Folio, contemp calf; rubbed. With 2 folding plates & 3 folding tables, 2 on 1 page. Some soiling to tp & damp-staining to margins; 2F1 with small hole to blank margin. Milne copy. Ck June 12 (211) £280

Wilkins, William, 1778-1839

— The Antiquities of Magna Graecia. Cambr., 1807. Folio, contemp calf; worn, covers detached. With engraved title vignette & 73 plates, 21 hand-colored. Tp torn at outer margin; some spotting & browning. Ck May 15 (173) £700

Anr copy. Modern half calf gilt over contemp bds. Occasional stains; small tear to Plate 12. Kissner—McCarty-Cooper copy. CNY Jan 25 (82) $2,600

Wilkinson, George Theodore. See: Newgate Calendar

Wilkinson, Henry

— Sketches of Scenery in the Basque Provinces of Spain.... L, 1838. 4to, orig cloth; front hinge broken, spine split. With 12 hand-colored plates. Marginal chip to frontis. wa Dec 9 (418) $700

Wilkinson, Sir John Gardner, 1797-1875

— Dalmatia and Montenegro.... L, 1848. 2 vols. 8vo, orig cloth; worn. With 7 lithos, 7 wood-engraved plates & folding engraved map. S June 30 (442) £200 [Frew Mackenzie]

— The Manners and Customs of the Ancient Egyptians. L, 1837. 1st Series only. 3 vols. 8vo, calf by Tout; rubbed; Vol I stained. O Feb 25 (198) $180

Wilkinson, Joseph, Rector of Wretham

— Select Views in Cumberland, Westmorland, and Lancashire. L, 1810. Folio, contemp half calf; worn. With 44 (of 48) plates. S May 14 (1161) £200 [Jaye]

Anr Ed. L, 1817. Folio, unbound. With 48 plates. S May 14 (1162) £320 [Jaye]

Anr Ed. L, 1821-[25]. Folio, recent half calf. With 48 hand-colored plates, Plate 12 torn without loss; some marginal stains. S July 1 (1411) £350 [Edwards]

Wilkinson, Nevile Redwell

— Wilton House Pictures. L, 1907. One of 300. 2 vols. Folio, orig cloth; rubbed, spines chipped. Ck Feb 14 (38) £60

Wilkinson, Robert, Publisher

— A General Atlas. L, 1809. 4to, contemp half calf; worn. With engraved title, plate-list & 48 colored maps. Both double-page maps torn, 1 def; some other maps with marginal defs or tears; some spotting. bba July 23 (342) £240 [Marsden]

Wilkinson, Tate, 1739-1803

— Memoirs of his own Life. York, 1790. 1st Ed. 4 vols. 12mo, contemp calf; Vol I with spine def. b&b Feb 19 (45) $90

Wilkomm, Heinrich Moritz

— Naturgeschichte Pflanzenreichs nach dem Linneschen System.... Elkingen & Munich, [c.1890]. 4to, half cloth; needs rebdg. With 54 double-page plates. sg Feb 13 (166) $275

Willard, John Ware

— A History of Simon Willard, Inventor and Clockmaker. [Bost.], 1911. One of 500. 4to, orig cloth; worn, 1st signature loose. bbc Dec 9 (293) $65

Willems, Alphonse

— Les Elzevier. Histoire et annales typographiques. Brussels, Paris & The Hague, 1880. 8vo, half lea; rubbed, cover detached. O Sept 24 (264) $500

William, Abbot of Tyre

— Historia Belli Sacri verrissima.... Basel: Nicolaus Brylingerus, 1564. 2 vols in 1. Folio, modern half calf gilt; extremities rubbed. Roman & italic type. Tp altered & laid down; some underlining; ownership stamp on tp partially excised; some dampstaining. Ck Oct 31 (323) £400

Williams, Aaron

— The Harmony Society, at Economy, Penn'a. Pittsburgh, 1866. 12mo, cloth. sg Dec 5 (275) $475

Williams, Anna

— Miscellanies in Prose and Verse. L, 1766. 1st Ed. 4to, contemp half sheep; rubbed, joints cracked. sg Mar 12 (159) $1,200

Williams, Arthur Bryan

— Game Trails in British Columbia. L, 1925. Library markings. sg Jan 9 (320) $130

Williams, Ben Ames. See: Derrydale Press

Williams, Carl M.

— Silversmiths of New Jersey, 1700-1825.... Phila.: MacManus, 1949. 4to, orig cloth. F Mar 26 (298) $150

Williams, Charles

— Heroes & Kings. L: Sylvan Press, [1930]. One of 250. 4to, cloth. sg Jan 10 (187) $70

Williams, Gardner F., 1842-1922

— The Diamond Mines of South Africa. NY, 1902. One of 100. Silk over bds; worn. bbc Feb 17 (235) $125

Anr Ed. NY, 1905. 2 vols. 8vo, orig sheep gilt; extremities worn, covers detached. sg Jan 9 (198) $140

Williams, Sir Harold Herbert

— Book Clubs & Printing Societies of Great Britain and Ireland. L, 1929. One of 750. cb Oct 17 (998) $60

Williams, Henry Smith

— The Historian's History of the World. L, 1907. 25 vols. Orig mor. bba Jan 30 (84) £220 [Harrington]

Williams, Henry T.

— The Pacific Tourist. Williams' Illustrated Trans-Continental Guide.... NY, 1876. 4to, orig cloth; spine faded, extremities worn. Prelims marginally dampstained. cb Nov 14 (239) $60

Williams, Hugh Noel

— Five Fair Sisters. L, 1906. 1 vol extended to 4. 8vo extended to 4to, mor gilt by Riviere. Extra-illus with c.200 ports & views. bbc Dec 9 (260) $525

— Queen Margot, Wife of Henry of Navarre. L, 1907. 1 vol extended to 4. 4to, contemp mor gilt by Riviere. Extra-illus with 220 ports & views. bbc Dec 9 (261) $525

Williams, Hugh W., 1773-1829

— Select Views in Greece. L, 1829. 2 vols. 4to, contemp half mor gilt; rubbed. With 64 plates on india paper mtd, some before letters. Some spotting. b June 22 (226) £480

Anr copy. 2 vols in 1. 4to, later cloth. With 60 (of 64) plates. Sold w.a.f. bba Apr 30 (42) £210 [Barker]

Anr copy. Contemp mor gilt, armorial bdg. With 64 plates. Marginal browning. S July 1 (728) £750 [Dalleggio]

Williams, Iolo A.

— Points in Eighteenth-Century Verse. L, 1934. One of 500. Orig vellum bds; worn. O Sept 24 (266) $60

Williams, John, 1796-1839

— A Narrative of Missionary Enterprises in the South Sea Islands. L, 1837. 8vo later cloth. sg June 18 (286) $90

13th thousand. L, 1840. 8vo, orig sheep. With frontis, port & map. cb Jan 30 (135) $65

Williams, John Lee

— The Territory of Florida. NY, 1837. 8vo, contemp cloth. With folding map & 3 litho plates. Some foxing. sg June 18 (584) $1,000

Williams, Margery

— The Velveteen Rabbit or How Toys become Real. L, 1922. 1st Ed. Illus by William Nicholson. In d/j with marginal chipping. Inscr by William Nicholson. Manney copy. P Oct 11 (1316) $3,000

Anr copy. In d/j with marginal chipping. Manney copy. P Oct 11 (1317) $1,400

Williams, Mary Floyd

— History of the San Francisco Committee of Vigilance of 1851. Berkeley, 1921. Inscr. sg June 18 (151) $80

Williams, Tennessee
See also: Limited Editions Club

— Battle of Angels. Murray, Utah: Pharos No 1/2, 1945. Orig front wrap only. sg June 11 (336) $175

— Cat on a Hot Tin Roof. NY, 1955. In chipped d/j. pba July 9 (295) $70

Anr copy. In d/j. sg Dec 12 (418) $275

— The Glass Menagerie. NY, [1945]. In repaired d/j. sg June 11 (337) $150

— A Streetcar Named Desire. New Directions, [1947]. In chipped d/j. bbc June 29 (445) $350

Anr copy. In d/j. Sgd. CNY June 9 (197) $2,600

Anr copy. In d/j; bdg split along rear joint, bumped. sg June 11 (338) $400

Williams, Tennessee —& Leavitt, Richard F.

— The World of Tennessee Williams. NY, [1978]. One of 250. In d/j. sg Dec 12 (420) $250

Williams, William Carlos, 1883-1963

— A Book of Poems: Al Que Quiera! Bost., 1917. 1st Ed, 1st Issue. Orig bds; corners worn. Inscr. Epstein copy. sg Apr 30 (510) $650

— The Cod Head. San Francisco: Harvest Press, 1932. Trial proof with variants. bbc Dec 9 (545) $75

— The Desert Music and other Poems. NY, [1954]. 1st Ed. In chipped & tape-repaired d/j. pba Aug 20 (247) $55

Anr copy. In chipped d/j. Cut signature tipped in. sg June 11 (340) $70

— In the American Grain. NY, 1925. cb Dec 12 (161) $50

— The Knife of the Times and Other Stories. Ithaca: The Dragon Press, [1932]. One of 500. Orig cloth, in d/j with 2 small pieces missing. K July 12 (518) $140

— Manikin Number Two. Go Go. NY: Monroe Wheeler, [1923]. 1st Ed, One of 150. Orig ptd wraps; minor wear. sg June 11 (341) $225

— Paterson. NY, 1946-59. Books 1-5. 3 vols with d/js. Epstein copysr. sg Apr 30 (509) $1,600

Williamson, George Charles, 1858-1942

— Andrew & Nathaniel Plimer. L, 1903. One of 365. 4to, lev gilt extra by Riviere & Son; each cover set with 5 oval port miniatures of women after the Plimers. CNY Dec 5 (432) $5,000

— The Book of Famille Rose. L, 1927 [1926]. One of 750. In chipped d/j. F Mar 26 (247) $150

Anr copy. In d/j. kh Nov 11 (248) A$300

Anr Ed. L, 1927. 4to, orig cloth, in worn d/j. kh Nov 11 (248) A$300

— Daniel Gardner, Painter. L & NY, 1921. One of 500. 4to, orig half cloth. Some foxing. kh Nov 11 (249) A$70

— The History of Portrait Miniatures. L, 1904. One of 50. 2 vols. Folio, lev gilt extra by Sangorski & Sutcliffe; upper covers each set with an oval port miniature by Alyn Williams. With 35 hand-colored plates. CNY Dec 5 (439) $5,500

One of 520. Orig cloth, in d/js. L Nov 14 (42) £80

Anr copy. Cloth; worn. With 107 plates. sg Sept 6 (309) $120

— The Imperial Russian Dinner Service. L, 1909. One of 300. 4to, orig half vellum; corners worn, front hinge cracked. sg Sept 6 (302) $650

Anr copy. Orig half vellum; hinges cracked. Some dampstaining at end. sg Feb 6 (306) $325

Anr copy. Orig half vellum; worn, backstrip darkened, hinges cracked. sg Apr 2 (298) $300

Williamson, George M.

[-] Catalogue of a Collection of the Books of Robert Louis Stevenson in the Library of.... Jamaica: Marion Press, 1901. One of 150. O Sept 24 (233) $50

Williamson, Henry

— The Patriot's Progress.... L, 1930. 1st Ed, one of 350 L.p. copies. Half vellum. b Nov 18 (45) £55

One of 350. Orig half mor. bba May 28 (266) £120 [Kay]

— Tarka the Otter.... L & NY, 1927. 1st Ed, One of 1,100. K Sept 29 (446) $85; sg June 11 (342) $50

Williamson, Jack

— The Cometeers. Reading: Fantasy Press, 1950. In d/j. Inscr. bbc Dec 9 (592) $70

One of 500. In chipped d/j. sg June 11 (343) $80

— Darker Than You Think. Reading PA: Fantasy Press, 1948. Advance Review Copy. Illus by Edd Cartier. Orig wraps. bbc Dec 9 (593) $65

— The Legion of Time. Reading: Fantasy Press, 1952. One of 350. In d/j. bbc Dec 9 (594) $65

Williamson, Joseph

— A Bibliography of the State of Maine.... Portland, 1896. 2 vols. 8vo, cloth; worn, shaken. Library markings. O Sept 24 (268) $70

Williamson, Capt. Thomas —& Howitt, Samuel, 1765?-1822

— Oriental Field Sports. L, 1807. Oblong folio, contemp mor gilt; rubbed, lower hinge split. With colored engraved title & 40 colored plates. Lacking half-title; some leaves soiled. C Oct 30 (240) £550 [Bradley]

Anr copy. Contemp calf with animal tools by Staagemeier & Welcher; rebacked, rubbed. Additional title duplicated on inside of upper cover. Some spotting. Ck May 15 (56) £6,500

Anr copy. Half mor; worn. First few leaves creased; some foxing. P June 17 (409) $13,000

Anr Ed. L, 1808. 2 vols. 4to, contemp calf; covers detached. With 2 frontises & 40 plates. Title to Vol I torn & repaired. DW Oct 2 (78) £110

Anr copy. Contemp russia gilt. With etched additional titles & 40 tinted plates. Vol II dampstained affecting title & first few plates; tp damaged. S July 1 (1522) £220 [Shapero]

Anr Ed. L, 1807 [plates watermarked 1816-18]. Oblong folio, later russia with ptd upper wraps from 2 orig parts laid down on covers; extremities worn. With colored engraved title & 41 colored plates. Repairs to 5 plates, 2 of these laid down with tears into image area; all but 5 plates with imprints removed, some with surface damage; engraved title repaired at inner margin. C May 20J (227) £4,200 [Arader]

Anr Ed. L, 1819. 2 vols. Oblong folio, mor gilt; upper joint cracked, rubbed. With 40 hand-colored plates. Repaired marginal tears on text leaves; engraved title creased; marginal tears on several plates, affecting text below the image on Plate 35; Page 25/26 extended along inner margin & soiled & creased. P Dec 12 (95) $8,500

Anr copy. Contemp mor gilt; rubbed & soiled, small tears to upper cover of Vol II. With 42 hand-colored plates. Library stamps, not affecting plates; some browning & soiling. pn Mar 19 (365) £550

Willink, Daniel

— Amsterdamsche Buitensingel. Amst., 1738. 2d Ed. 8vo, half lea. With engraved title, 4 folding views, 22 views on 11 plates & 1 other plate. Bound with 11 plates from A. Rademaker's Nederlandsche Oudheeden en Gesigten. B Nov 1 (301) HF300

Willis, Nathaniel Parker, 1806-67

— American Scenery. L, 1840. Vol I only. Orig cloth; rubbed, backstrip split. With 66 plates. bba May 28 (348) £120 [Kafka]

Anr copy. 2 vols. 4to, contemp sheep; broken, lacking 1 backstrip. With 2 engraved titles, port & 117 plates. Lacking map; 2 additional plates bound in. Stains in Vol I extending to plates. Sold w.a.f. bbc Apr 27 (625) $400

Anr copy. Orig cloth. With 2 engraved titles, port, map & 117 plates. Some plates foxed, generally along outer margins. K Sept 29 (18) $700

Anr copy. Mor gilt; rebcked, new endpapers. Marginal staining; some foxing; 1 plate in Vol I torn; 1 text leaf torn. K Sept 29 (19) $550

Anr copy. Vol II only. Contemp half mor gilt; rubbed. With engraved title & 51 (of 52) plates. Foxing affecting some plates; many leaves loose. pn July 16 (212) £90 [Kafka]

Anr copy. Illus by W. H. Bartlett. 2 vols in 1. 4to, later half mor; worn, covers detached. With map, 2 engraved titles & 117 plates. Some waterstaining, mostly marginal; some foxing. bba July 23 (350) £200 [Davies]

Anr copy. Vol II (of 2) only. 4to, contemp half mor gilt; worn. With engraved title & 47 (of 52) plates. Spotting throughout. DW Jan 29 (60) £85

Anr copy. 6 orig parts. 4to, orig lea-backed pictorial bds; rubbed. With port, additional titles, map & 117 views. Browned; some spotting. L Nov 14 (168) £200

Anr copy. 2 vols. 4to, orig lea gilt; rubbed. With port, 2 engraved titles, map & 117 plates. Some spotting & marginal dampstaining. pn Sept 12 (345) £300

Anr copy. Orig mor gilt. With engraved titles, frontis, map & 117 plates. Occasional foxing. pn Nov 14 (423) £320 [Map House]

Anr Ed. L, [1842]. 2 vols. 4to, orig cloth. With 2 engraved title, 118 plates & 1 map. pn Apr 23 (251) £480

— Canadian Scenery. L, 1842. Illus by W. H. Bartlett. 2 vols in 1. 4to, contemp half lea; rubbed. With engraved titles, map & 117 plates.lates Lacking port & 8 plates in the list but with 8 unlisted plates; some marginal spotting & waterstaining. b June 22

(288) £260

Anr copy. 2 vols. 4to, contemp mor gilt. With engraved titles, port & 117 plates. Some spotting. Ck May 15 (174) £550

— Picturesque American Scenery. Bost., 1883. 4to, orig cloth. With 25 plates. F Dec 18 (701) $60

Willis, Nathaniel Parker, 1806-67 —& Coyne, Joseph Stirling, 1803-68

— The Scenery and Antiquities of Ireland. L: Virtue, [1841]. 2 vols. 4to, contemp half mor. With engraved titles, map & 117 plates. Some spotting. S May 14 (1163) £220 [Map House]

Willis, Thomas, 1621-75

— Opera. Venice: Joh. Malachinus for J. de Mapheis, 1720. 2 vols in 1. Folio, contemp vellum. Some marginal spotting. SI Dec 5 (728) LIt550,000

Willmott, Ellen Ann

— The Genus Rosa. L, 1910-14. 2 vols. Folio, half mor, orig wraps bound in. With 126 (of 132) color plates. Some leaves frayed because of def stitching; lacking tp to Vol II. Sold w.a.f. S Nov 21 (55) £1,100 [Map House]

Anr copy. Half calf. With 132 color plates. S June 25 (82) £1,300 [Garisenda]

Anr Ed. L, 1914. 2 vols. Folio, contemp half calf. With 132 colored plates. C Oct 30 (233) £1,400 [Samuels]

Anr copy. Orig half mor, orig wraps & portfolio in accompanying box. C May 20 (229) £1,400 [Gramm]

Anr copy. Vol II only (Parts 17-25). Orig wrap. With 71 plates. Ck May 15 (57) £700

Anr copy. 2 vols. Folio, orig half mor, orig wraps bound in; rubbed, corners knocked. With 130 colored plates & 81 uncolored plates. A few tissues adhered to plates. P June 17 (410) $1,700

Anr copy. 25 orig parts. Folio, wraps. With 132 colored plates. sg May 7 (212) $3,400

Wills, Sir Alfred

— The Eagle's Nest in the Valley of Sixt.... L, 1860. 8vo, orig cloth; rubbed. With 12 plates & 2 maps. pn May 14 (218) £150

Willsford, Thomas

— Natures Secrets, of the Admirable and Wonderfull History of the Generation of Meteors. L, 1658. 8vo, contemp calf; worn. pnE Dec 4 (28) £65

Willughby, Francis

— Ornithologiae libri tres. L, 1676. Folio, contemp calf; corners rubbed. With 2 tables & 77 plates. Lacking imprimatur leaf. C Oct 30 (234) £900 [Wheldon & Wesley]

Anr copy. Contemp vellum. Some browning; some repairs. SI Dec 5 (725) LIt3,400

— The Ornithology.... L, 1678. Folio, contemp calf; rebacked. With 2 tables & 80 plates. Waterstained throughout. bba Sept 5 (163) £320 [Bickersteth]

Willyams, Cooper, 1762-1816

— A Selection of Views in Egypt, Palestine, Rhodes.... L, 1822. Folio, modern half mor; scuffed. With 36 hand-colored plates. Tp stained; inner margins of 1st few leaves repaired & strengthened. Ck Nov 29 (331) £620

Anr copy. Modern half calf. S July 1 (868) £550 [Atabey]

Wilmont, Sir John Eardley Eardley, 2d Baronet, 1810-2

— Our Journal of the Pacific. L, 1873. 8vo, modern mor gilt. Some foxing. cb Oct 10 (39) $200

Wilmott, Ellen Ann

— The Genus Rosa.... L: John Murray, 1914. Illus by Alfred Parsons. 25 parts. Folio, orig wraps, in 2 contemp cloth portfolios; some covers mildly browned. With 132 color plates. wa Sept 26 (462) $2,600

Wilson, Adrian

— Printing for the Theater. San Francisco, 1957. One of 250. Cloth. b&b Feb 19 (295) $700; cb Oct 17 (1004) $750

Wilson, Alexander, 1766-1813

— American Ornithology. Phila., 1808-14. 1st Ed. Vol V only. orig half calf; rebacked in sheep, later endpapers. With 9 hand-colored plates Some text leaves with later tape repairs to margin tears; first few leaves with partial splits at bottom end of gutters; other defs. bbc Sept 23 (369) $450

Anr Ed. NY & Phila., 1828-29. 4 vols, including Atlas vol. 4to & folio, Text, modern cloth; Atlas, half mor; Atlas very worn. With 76 hand-colored plates. 2 plates with horizontal crease; last 2 plates dampstained. CNY Dec 5 (300) $1,000

L.p. copy. Text, half russia; Atlas, half mor; Atlas very worn; upper cover of Vol I & both covers of Vol III and Atlas, detached. With 76 hand-colored plates. Scattered foxing throughout text. CNY Dec 5 (301) $1,200

Anr copy. Contemp half lea gilt; spine ends chipped, joints rubbed. Plate 24 repaired. sg May 7 (213) $5,600

Wilson, Alexander, 1766-1813 —& Bonaparte, Charles Lucien, 1803-57

— The American Ornithology. L, 1832. 3 vols. 8vo, contemp half lea gilt; scuffed; Vol III lacking rear cover. With port & 97 hand-colored plates. cb Oct 25 (122) $900

Anr Ed. L, 1876. 3 vols. 4to, contemp half mor. Some spotting. S May 14 (1065) £350 [Rose]

Anr copy. Half lea; rebacked, covers stained. wd Dec 12 (471) $125

Wilson, Arthur, 1595-1652

— The History of Great Britain, being the Life of King James the First. L, 1653. 1st Ed. Folio, modern half calf. Some leaves holed. bba Oct 10 (295) £55 [Thomas Plume's Library]

Wilson, Carroll Atwood

— Thirteen Author Collections of the Nineteenth Century.... NY, 1950. One of 375. 2 vols. Pencil marginalia. bbc Sept 23 (129) $50

Wilson, Sir Charles William

— Picturesque Palestine. L, [1880-84]. 4 vols. 4to, orig cloth. pnE Mar 11 (71) £100

Wilson, Edmund

— The Boys in the Back Room. San Francisco: Colt Press, 1941. Ltd Ed, sgd. Met Apr 28 (866) $50

Wilson, Ernest Henry

— A Naturalist in Western China with Vasculum, Camera and Gun.... NY, 1913. 2 vols. Vol I dampstained. sg Jan 9 (321) $300

Wilson, Harriette

— Memoirs of Harriette Wilson, Written by Herself. L, 1909. 2 vols. 8vo, half mor. b&b Feb 14 (67) $125

Wilson, Harry

— Fugitive Sketches in Rome, Venice.... L, 1838. Folio, contemp half mor; worn. With litho title & 12 plates, 1 torn. bba Apr 9 (164) £320 [Finney]

Wilson, Horace Hayman, 1786-1860. See: Moorcroft & Trebeck

Wilson, J. S., bookseller at Meppel

— Autotypie: De Natuur zich zelveafbeeldende Meppel: J. S. Wilson, 1857. 8vo, orig ptd bds; spine perished. With 17 nature-ptd plates. 1 marginal tear without loss. Schlosser copy. P June 17 (485) $1,500

Wilson, Capt James. See: Wilson, William

Wilson, Sir John Mitchell H.

— The Royal Philatelic Collection.... L, 1952. Ed by Clarence Winchester. Folio, mor with Royal Arms on upper cover & Tudor Rose on lower cover. W July 8 (15) £55

Wilson, Mona. See: Nonesuch Press

Wilson, Richard, 1714-82

— Etchings.... L, 1825. 4to, later half calf; worn, joints starting. With 40 plates. cb Sept 26 (210) $75

Wilson, Samuel Sheridan

— A Narrative of the Greek Mission.... L, 1839. 8vo, contemp calf gilt, with Signet arms; joints weak. With Baxter-print oleographed frontis. S July 1 (731) £180 [Granado]

Wilson, Thomas, Solicitor

— A Catalogue Raisonne of the Select Collection of Engravings of an Amateur. L: [Pvtly ptd], 1828. One of 100 L.p. copies. 4to, orig cloth; faded. Inscr. bba Oct 10 (194) £220 [Scott]

Wilson, W. J. See: De Ricci & Wilson

Wilson, William, Chief Mate of the Ship Duff

— A Missionary Voyage to the Southern Pacific Ocean.... L, 1799. 1st Ed. 4to, modern half mor. With folding map & 12 plates & maps. Ck Oct 18 (103) £300

Anr copy. Contemp calf; corners rubbed or repaired, rebacked. Some plates foxed. kh Nov 11 (699) A$380

Wilson, Sir William James Erasmus. See: Quain & Wilson

Wilson, William Rae

— Travels in Russia. L, 1828. 2 vols. 8vo, contemp half calf; worn. Lacking folding map. DW Mar 4 (49) £100

Anr copy. Contemp mor gilt. With 6 plates. S Nov 15 (1133) £250 [Beeleigh]

Wilson, Woodrow, 1856-1924

— A History of the American People. NY, [1918]. Autographed Documentary Ed, one of 400. 10 vols. Half mor. Library stamps. cb Sept 5 (122) $900

Wiltsee, Ernest A. See: Grabhorn Printing

Winchelsea, Heneage Finch, 2d Earl of

[-] A Narrative of the Success of the Voyage of.... L, 1661. 4to, 19th-cent mor gilt; rubbed. Lacking final blank; tp laid down. With 6 Ms pages at end, possibly in the hand of Julia Pardoe. S June 30 (362) £2,400 [Kut]

Windham, Donald

— As if...A Personal View of Tennessee Williams. Verona, 1985. One of 50. Pictorial wraps. sg June 11 (339) $110

Windsor...

— The Windsor Magazine. L, 1895-1900. 12 vols (all pbd). 8vo, orig cloth. bba Aug 13 (331) £170 [Ginnan]

Windsor, Edward, Duke of

— A King's Story. L, 1951. 1st Ed, one of 250. 8vo, orig mor gilt by Sangorski & Sutcliffe. sg Sept 12 (66) $175

Windus, John

— A Journey to Mequinez. L, 1725. 8vo, contemp clf; extremities rubbed. With 6 folding plates. One plate holed without loss. Milne copy. Ck June 12 (213) £170

Winfield, Charles H.

— History of the County of Hudson, N.J.,.... NY, 1874. 8vo, orig half mor; extremities worn. NH Oct 6 (238) $65

Wing, Donald

— Short-Title Catalogue of Books Printed in England...1641-1700. NY, 1945-51. 3 vols. 4to, orig cloth. DW Jan 29 (352) £200

Anr copy. Orig cloth; worn & shaken. O Dec 17 (196) $300

2d Ed. NY, 1972. Vol I only. Cloth. NH May 30 (452) $110

Wingler, Hans Maria

— Das Bauhaus. Bramsche, 1962. 4to, cloth, in chipped d/j. sg Feb 6 (312) $110

— The Bauhaus. Cambr., Mass., 1969. Folio, cloth; rubbed & soiled. DW Mar 11 (5770) £100

— Graphic Work from the Bauhaus. L, 1969. 4to, cloth, in d/j. Met Apr 28 (92) $50

— Oskar Kokoschka. Salsburg, 1951. 4to, orig wraps; minor wear with small hole on front cover. Sgd by Kokoschka. sg Sept 26 (153) $300

Winkler, Ernest W.

— Check List of Texas Imprints, 1846-1860....[1862-76]. Austin, 1949-63. 2 vols. Cloth, in d/js. O Dec 17 (197) $90

Winkler, Friedrich

— Die Zeichnungen Albrecht Duerers. Berlin, 1936-39. 4 vols. 4to, orig cloth. Met Apr 28 (315) $90

Anr copy. Vols I-II. sg Apr 2 (108) $50

Winlove, Samuel

— Moral Lectures on the Following Subjects: Pride, Envy, Avarice.... L, 1769. 1st Ed. 12mo, orig Dutch floral bds; worn. Final leaf holed. DW Apr 8 (447) £680

Winnecke, Charles

— South Australia. Mr. Winnecke's Explorations during 1883. [Adelaide, 1884]. Folio, stapled as issued. With folding plan. Lower margins of last 3 leaves restored. R. J. Maria copy. C June 25 (269) £320 [Baring]

Winship, George Parker

See also: Doves Press

— William Caxton and the First English Press. NY, 1928. 4to, orig cloth. With orig leaf of the Polycronicon mtd at end. Milne copy. Ck June 12 (30) £380

Winsor, Justin, 1831-97

— The Memorial History of Boston 1630-1880. Bost., 1880-81. 4 vols. 4to, orig cloth; rubbed. K July 12 (68) $50

Anr Ed. Bost., 1882. 4 vols. 4to, half calf; rubbed & stained. rs Oct 17 (32) $100

Winston, Charles

— An Inquiry into the difference of Style...in Ancient Glass Paintings.... L, 1867. 2d Ed. 2 vols. 8vo, orig cloth. With 75 plates. bba Oct 10 (571) £55 [Axe]

— Memoirs Illustrative of the Art of Glass Painting. L, 1865. 8vo, orig bdg; upper joint split. kh Nov 11 (251) A$70

Winter, Douglas E.

— Night Visions 5. Arlington Heights IL: Dark Harvest, 1988. One of 850, sgd by all the contribs. In d/j. cb Sept 19 (169) $90; cb Dec 12 (230) $50

— Prime Evil. West Kingston RI: Donald M. Grant, [1988]. One of 1,000. Ed by Winter. Syn gilt. Sgd by all the contributors. cb Sept 19 (117) $325

Winter, George Simon

— Bellerophon, sive eques peritus.... Nuremberg: Endter, 1678. Bound with: Hippiater Expertus, seu medicina equorum absolutissima.... Nuremberg, 1678. Folio, contemp blind-stamped pigskin. With engraved title & 170 plates in 1st work & 1 double-page plates in 2d work. Library stamp on half-title of 1st work. S Nov 21 (56) £4,000 [Marshall]

— Tractatio nova de re equaria. Nuremberg, 1672. Folio, contemp vellum. With 14 plates & double-page table. Marginal tears & wormholes; corner off K4 with loss. sg Jan 9 (322) $175

Winterbotham, William

— The American Atlas. NY, 1796. 4 vols. 8vo, old calf; worn, some covers detached. Lacking separate Atlas vol. Sold w.a.f. O Mar 31 (198) $120

Winterthur Museum

— Collection of Printed Books and Periodicals. General Catalog. Wilmington, [1974]. 9 vols. Folio, cloth; worn. O Sept 24 (270) $150

Wintzleben, Jonas Thomsen von

— Den Adelige Fegte-Kunst i et kort Begreb. Copenhagen, 1756. 12mo, later half mor. With 24 plates, including frontis. sg Mar 26 (344) $275

Wirtsung, Christoph

— Artzney Buch.... Heidelberg: J. Mayer, 1568. Folio, contemp blind-stamped pigskin; lacking clasps. With extra leaf containing woodcut port of Hippocrates & on verso a port of Galen, both colored by a contemp hand. Some browning; a few tears affecting text. S Dec 5 (450) £2,200 [Bucher Kabinett]

Wisconsin

— Directory of the City of Milwaukee, for the Years 1848-49...Second Year. Milwaukee, 1848. 12mo, orig half sheep. Some browning. sg Dec 5 (276) $300

Anr copy. Some browning; lacking the map. sg June 18 (589) $200

— Journal of the Covnention to Form a Constitution for the State of Wisconsin.... Madison, 1847. 8vo, contemp half sheep; front cover loose. sg June 18 (590) $140

Wisden, John

— Cricketers' Almanack. L, 1889. Orig wraps; soiled. DW Apr 15 (85) £200

Anr Ed. L, 1895-96. 2 vols. Orig ptd wraps; spines worn. DW Apr 15 (93) £150

Anr Ed. L, 1896-1900. 5 vols. Orig ptd wraps; 3 vols lacking rear wrap, worn. DW Apr 15 (102) £300

Anr Ed. L, 1898-1902. 4 vols. Orig wraps; tape-repaired. DW Apr 15 (94) £210

Anr Ed. L, 1900-1. 2 vols. Orig wraps, 101 in recent cloth retaining orig rear wrap. DW Apr 15 (92) £155

Anr Ed. L, 1901-10. 10 vols. Orig ptd wraps; spines worn, 1902 lacking rear cover. DW Apr 15 (101) £510

Anr Ed. L, 1911-12. 2 vols. Orig cloth; soiled. DW Apr 15 (95) £220

Anr Ed. L, 1911-15. 5 vols. Orig ptd wraps; spines worn. DW Apr 15 (100) £230

Anr Ed. L, 1936. Orig cloth; rubbed. DW Apr 15 (90) £115

Anr Ed. L, 1937. Orig wraps; soiled. DW Apr 15 (98) £55

Anr Ed. L, 1946. Orig cloth. DW Apr 15 (89) £80

Vols 84-121. L, 1947-84. Library markings. bba June 11 (286) £260 [Franks]

Anr Ed. L, 1948-70. 23 vols. Orig cloth; rubbed, last 6 vols in d/js. DW Apr 15 (96) £360

Wise, George, d.1923

— History of the Seventeenth Virginia Infantry, C.S.A. Balt., 1870. 1st Ed. 12mo, bdg not described. Inscr. K Mar 22 (101) $180

Anr copy. Cloth; spine ends frayed, some wear at extremities. sg Dec 5 (69) $200

Wise, Henry Augustus

— Los Gringos: or, An Inside View of Mexico and California.... NY, 1849. 1st Ed. 12mo, orig cloth; rebacked. cb Jan 30 (137) $55

Anr copy. Orig cloth; extremities worn. Some foxing. NH May 30 (147) $140

Wise, John, 1808-79

— A System of Aeronautics, Comprehending its Earliest Investigations.... Phila., 1850. 1st Ed. 8vo, contemp half calf; rubbed, spine torn, upper cover detached. With port & 12 plates. Minor foxing. pn May 14 (102) £260

— Through the Air: A Narrative of Forty Years' Experience.... L, 1873. 1st English Ed. 8vo, orig cloth; lower cover detached. Some soiling. pn May 14 (103) £280

Wise, Thomas James, 1859-1937

— The Ashley Library: A Catalogue.... Folkestone, 1971. 11 vols. 4to, cloth. bba Feb 27 (440) £280 [Freddie]

— A Bibliography of the Writings of Joseph Conrad. L, 1921. 2d Ed, One of 170. 4to, bds; rubbed. DW Jan 29 (354) £70

— A Bibliography of the Writings in Verse and Prose of...Byron. L, 1932-33. One of 180. 2 vols. 4to, orig cloth in d/js. DW Jan 29 (353) £70

— A Byron Library. L: Privately ptd, 1928. One of 200. 4to, orig cloth. bba May 28 (632) £110 [Dawson]

Anr copy. Cloth. K Sept 29 (448) $110

Anr Ed. L: Pvtly ptd, 1928. 4to, cloth. cb Oct 17 (1011) $120

— A Complete Bibliography of the Writings in Prose and Verse of John Ruskin. L, 1893. One of 250. 2 vols. 4to, contemp half mor gilt, orig wraps bound in. With E. T. Cook's extensive annotations & additions. bba Feb 13 (337) £620 [Quaritch]

Anr copy. Contemp half calf; rubbed. O Dec 17 (198) $110

— A Conrad Library. L: Privately ptd, 1928. One of 25. 4to, orig cloth. John Howell's copy. K Sept 29 (449) $170

— A Swinburne Library. L, 1925. One of 30. cb Oct 17 (1012) $275

Wiseman, Richard, 1622?-76

— Eight Chirurgical Treatises.... L, 1697. Folio, contemp calf; joints split. Some staining. S Feb 11 (609) £420 [Joffe]

— Several Chirurgicall Treatises. L: R. Norton & J. Macock, 1686. 2d Ed. Folio, old calf; worn & broken. Some stains, fraying & soiling. Sold w.a.f. O Aug 25 (199) $300

Wislizenus, Frederick

— Memoir of a Tour to Northern Mexico...with Col. Doniphan's Expedition. Wash., 1848. 8vo, disbound. With 3 folding maps. Minor worming to text and maps. cb Feb 12 (90) $100

Wister, Owen, 1860-1938

See also: Limited Editions Club

— The Virginian. NY, 1902. 1st Ed. Orig cloth; rubbed & soiled. Some leaves soiled. Manney copy. P Oct 11 (318) $450

Anr copy. With ALs, 14 Dec 1906, tipped in. Epstein copy. sg Apr 30 (511) $500

Wit, Frederick de. See: De Wit, Frederick

— Atlas. See: De Wit, Frederick

Witherby, H. F. —& Others

— The Handbook of British Birds. L, 1938-41. 5 vols. In d/js. pnE Dec 4 (14) £55

Withering, William, 1741-99

— A Botanical Arrangement of all the Vegetables Naturally Growing in Great Britain. L, 1776. 2 vols. 8vo, disbound. With 12 folding plates. Marginal dampstaining with traces of mold. Sold w.a.f. sg May 14 (255) $350

Withers, Alexander S.

— Chronicles of Border Warfare, or a History.... Clarksburg, Va., 1831. 12mo, orig calf; worn & scuffed. Foxed & browned; annotated. bbc Apr 27 (628) $75

Anr copy. Contemp sheep; worn. Foxed & stained throughout. wa Dec 9 (298) $160

Withers, Robert

— Description of the Grand Signour's Seraglio.... L: for John Ridley, 1653. Ed by John Greaves. 8vo, contemp calf. A8 with small hole resulting in loss of page numeral; some small wormholes at lower inner corner. S June 30 (445) £850 [Atabey]

Witsen, Nicolaas

— Aeloude en Hedendaegsche Scheeps-Bouw en Bestier. Amst., 1671. 1st Ed. Folio, blind-stamped vellum; front joint split. With engraved title & 114 plates. Some stains; hole in 1 leaf; tear repaired in 1 leaf. B Nov 1 (562) HF8,400

Wittek, Martin. See: Masal & Wittek

Wittkower, Rudolf. See: Brauer & Wittkower

Wittman, William

— Travels in Turkey, Asia-Minor, Syria.... L, 1803. 1st Ed. 4to, contemp calf; rebacked with old spine laid down. With folding frontis, folding plate of firman, folding map & 21 plates, 16 hand-colored. Ck Oct 18 (105) £700

Wodehouse, Pelham Grenville

— Bill the Conqueror.... NY, [1924]. 1st American Ed. In chipped d/j. bba July 9 (238) £180 [Hopkins]

— The Inimitable Jeeves. L, 1923. 1st Ed, 1st Ptg. In chipped d/j. Epstein copy. sg Apr 30 (513) $1,100

— Joy in the Morning. Garden City, 1946. In d/j. cb Dec 12 (164) $55

— The Little Nugget. NY: W. J. Watt, [c.1914]. Orig cloth; lacking front free endpaper. bbc Sept 23 (487) $95

— My Man Jeeves. L, [1919]. 1st Ed. Orig cloth; faded. bba Jan 16 (197) £450 [C. H. Edwards]

— The Pothunters. L, 1902. 1st Issue. Illus by R. Noel Pocock. bba Feb 27 (193) £400 [Grant & Shaw]

Wolf, Edwin, 2d

— American Song Sheets, Slip Ballads, and Poetical Broadsides, 1850-1870. Phila., [1963]. 4to, cloth. K Sept 29 (52) $65; K July 12 (45) $65

Wolf, Edwin, 2nd. See: Grolier Club

Wolfe, Richard J.

— Jacob Bigelow's American Medical Botany..... [North Hills, Pa.]: Bird & Bull Press, 1979. Half lev. With 1 colored & 1 plain plate. bbc Apr 27 (102) $120

Anr copy. Half mor; worn. O Sept 24 (271) $180

— On Improvements in Marbling the Edges of Books and Papers. Newtown: Bird & Bull Press, 1983. One of 350. Half mor by Grey Parrot. With 14 mtd samples. NH Aug 23 (63) $100

— Three Early French Essays on Paper Marbling 1642-1765. Newtown: Bird & Bull Press, [1986]. One of 310. Ed by Wolfe. Half mor. bbc Apr 27 (104) $120; pba July 23 (37) $225

Wolfe, Richard J. —& McKenna, Paul

— Louis Herman Kinder and Fine Bookbinding in America. Newtown: Bird & Bull Press, 1985. One of 325. Half mor. bbc Apr 27 (103) $150; NH Aug 23 (62) $140

Anr copy. Half mor; worn. O Sept 24

(272) $120; pba July 23 (36) $190

Wolfe, Thomas, 1900-38

— From Death to Morning. NY, 1935. 1st Ed. In d/j. cb Sept 19 (230) $75; cb Dec 12 (165) $80

— Look Homeward Angel. NY, 1929. 1st Ed. In d/j, restored, color on front cover renewed. Inscr to Waldo Buckham. Manney copy. P Oct 11 (319) $2,750

Anr copy. In chipped & torn d/j. Manney copy. P Oct 11 (320) $2,750; sg Dec 12 (423) $700

Anr copy. In chipped & worn d/j. Epstein copy. sg Apr 30 (514) $900

— A Note on Experts: Dexter Vespasian Joyner. NY, 1939. 1st Ed, one of 300. bbc Dec 9 (547) $100; sg June 11 (344) $100

— Of Time and the River. NY, 1935. 1st Ed. In worn d/j. sg Dec 12 (424) $70

— The Web and the Rock. NY, 1939. 1st Ed. In d/j. sg Dec 12 (415) $150

Wolff, Joseph, 1795-1863

— Journal of the Rev. Joseph Wolff...in a series of Letters to Sir Thomas Baring.... L, 1839. 8vo, contemp cloth; spine torn & def. Tp soiled. S June 30 (446) £320 [Severis]

Wollaston, William

— The Religion of Nature Delineated. L, 1725. 4to, calf; rebacked, worn. Some dampstain at lower corner; tear in 1 leaf repaired. wa Mar 5 (556) $55

Wolley, Sir Clive Phillipps, 1854-1918. See: Phillipps-Wolley, Sir Clive

Wollstonecraft, Mary, 1759-97

— Letters Written during a Short Residence in Sweden, Norway and Denmark. L, 1796. 1st Ed. 8vo, orig bds; rebacked, worn. Soiled & spotted. bba Dec 19 (58) £220 [Ginnan]

Anr copy. Contemp calf; joints weak. Milne copy. Ck June 12 (214) £320

— Original Stories from Real Life. L, 1791. 12mo, contemp calf; rebacked & recornered. With frontis & 5 plates. Some browning. bba July 23 (152) £1,500 [Pickering]

Anr copy. Later mor; rubbed & worn; spine chipped. O Nov 26 (195) $1,500

— A Vindication of the Rights of Woman.... L, 1792. 8vo, contemp calf; rebacked. Epstein copy. sg Apr 30 (515) $2,200

Woman...

— Woman: In All Ages and in All Countries. Phila.: George Barrie, [1907-8]. One of 1,000 on japan vellum, this set bound for Herbert Katz. Orig half mor. cb Dec 19 (186) $325

Wonders...

— The Wonders of the Telescope.... L: Richard Phillips 1805. 8vo, modern half mor. With 12 plates, some folding. Some foxing; a few plates repaired. bba July 23 (310) £75 [Ginnan]

Wood, Anthony a, 1632-95

— Athenae oxoniensis. L, 1691-92. 2 vols in 1. Folio, calf; rebacked. W July 8 (80) £140

Anr Ed. L, 1721. 2 vols in 1. Folio, half cloth. Some leaves with old stain at top margin; tp & a few other leaves with minor edge tears; old library stamp at tp. bbc Apr 27 (180) $160

Anr copy. 2 vols. Folio, contemp calf; joints & covers worn. DW Jan 29 (289) £125

Anr copy. 4 parts in 2 vols. Folio, later cloth. LH May 17 (591) $50

2d Ed. 2 vols. Folio, contemp calf gilt; spines frayed. DW Oct 2 (320) £90

Wood, Casey Albert

— An Introduction to the Literature of Vertebrate Zoology. L, 1931. 4to, orig cloth; edges worn. McGill University Publications. Series XI (Zoology). No 24. bbc Apr 27 (181) $70

Anr copy. Orig cloth; shelf mark on spine, stamp on edges. pn May 14 (192) £55 [Maggs]

Anr Ed. Oxford, 1931. 4to, cloth. O Sept 24 (273) $250

Wood, John

— [Town Atlas of Scotland.] Edin., 1818-27. Folio, later half calf; worn. With 47 double-page plans on 48 leaves, the streets on most with pale yellow wash. All maps mtd on guards; Hamilton repaired; some foxing. pnE Mar 11 (275) £2,500

Wood, John George, 1827-89

— Animate Creation. NY, [1885]. Ed by Joseph B. Holder. 3 vols. Folio, cloth; spine ends chipped. bbc June 29 (447) $120

Anr copy. Half mor. With 30 mtd color plates. K Mar 22 (454) $55

Anr copy. 3 vols in 6. Folio, bdg not described. With 30 color plates & 60 wood-engravings. K July 12 (522) $120

Anr copy. 3 vols. Folio, half lea; rubbed & shaken. Met Apr 28 (500) $50

— Our Living World. NY, [1885]. 3 vols. Folio, orig cloth; spine ends & joints worn. With 42 chromolithos & 84 wood-engraved plates. sg Sept 19 (223) $60

Wood, John Turtle

— Discoveries at Ephesus, including the Site and Remains of the Great Temple of Diana. L, 1877. 8vo, orig cloth. With 35 plates. sg May 21 (118) $80

Wood, Nancy. See: Stryker & Wood

Wood, Robert, 1717?-71

— The Ruins of Balbec. L, 1757. 1st Ed. Folio, contemp half calf; worn. With 46 plates. Title detached. George Milne copy. CNY Dec 5 (354) $2,400

— Ruins of Palmyra, otherwise Tedmor, in the Desert. L, 1753. Folio, half russia gilt; worn. George Milne copy. CNY Dec 5 (355) $1,900

1st Ed. Folio, 18th-cent calf; rebacked with old backstrip laid down, corners restored, covers abraded. With 47 plates on 59 sheets. Plate I shaved past plate mark at left & with some abrasions; additional plate at front cropped past lower plate mark; some browning & spotting. McCarty-Cooper copy. CNY Jan 25 (83) $1,900

— The Ruins of Palmyra, Otherwise Tedmor, in the Desert. L, 1827. ("The Ruins of Palmyra and Balbec.") Folio, later half mor. With 57 plates in sequential order but not noted in plate list & 38 non-sequential plates, some of which are listed. Sold w.a.f. sg Jan 9 (199) $250

Wood, Stanley

— The White City (As It Was). Chicago, 1894. Vol I, Series 1-20. Oblong 4to, wraps; some brittle & chipped. With 80 plates. cb Feb 12 (150) $100

Wood, William, 1609-91

— Zoography; or, the Beauties of Nature Displayed. L, 1807. 3 vols. 8vo, contemp half mor; rubbed. With 60 uncolored plates by Wm. Daniell. Ck Nov 29 (334) £140

Wood, William, 1774-1857

— Index Entomologicus, or a Complete Illustrated Catalogue.... L, 1854. 8vo, contemp half mor gilt. With 59 hand-colored plates. L Nov 14 (471) £210

Anr copy. Contemp half lea gilt. Tp stamped. pn Mar 19 (347) £120

— Index Testaceologicus, or a Catalogue of Shells, British and Foreign.... L, [1824]-1825. 2 vols in 11, including 1828 Supplement. 8vo, later cloth. With 46 plates in 2 states, 1 set hand-colored. Library markings. bba Sept 5 (123) £100 [Lib. Naturalista Bolognese]

2d Ed of Vol I, 1st Ed of Supplement. L, 1828. 2 vols. 8vo, modern bds. With 46 hand-colored plates. C May 20 (230) £250 [Maggs]

— Index Testaceologicus, an Illustrated Catalogue of British and Foreign Shells. L, 1856. 8vo, contemp half lea gilt; rubbed. With 46 color plates. Stamps on verso of tp & verso of final leaf. pn Mar 19 (348) £130

Woodard, Capt. David

— The Narrative of Captain Woodard and four Seamen who Lost their Ship.... L, 1805. 2d Ed. 8vo, later half mor; joints worn. With 4 plates. Some spotting & dampstaining. DW Oct 2 (321) £65

Woodcut...

— The Woodcut, an Annual. L: The Fleuron, 1927-30. Vols 1-4 (all pbd). 4to, cloth. DW Oct 9 (989) £230

Woods, Daniel B.

— Sixteen Months at the Gold Diggings. NY, 1851. 12mo, modern cloth. Dampstaining to 1st 3 gatherings; foxed throughout. sg Dec 5 (280) $225

Anr copy. Cloth; spine ends frayed, back cover stained. Some foxing. Inscr by "the Author". sg June 18 (154) $175

Woods, Frederick

— Bibliography of the Works of Sir Winston Churchill.... Toronto, [1969]. In d/j. cb Dec 5 (46) $60

Woodville, William, 1752-1805

— Medical Botany. L, 1790-94. 4 vols. 4to, contemp half calf; extremities rubbed. With 210 hand-colored plates. Some spotting & soiling. Ck Oct 18 (35) £220

Anr copy. 19th-cent half calf; rubbed & stained, joints split. With 273 (of 274) hand-colored plates; lacking No. 99. Some browning :& spotting; tp of Vol II cut down. S Feb 26 (947) £950 [Vilsoet]

3d Ed. L, 1832. 5 vols. 4to, half mor by Bayntun. With 274 hand-colored engraved plates & 36 hand-colored lithos. No plate numbered 112, but 2 plates numbered 181. C May 20 (231) £2,100 [Heuer]

Anr copy. Contemp half lea; spine edges worn, hinge of Vol I broken. With 301 hand-colored plates. Plate 81 browned; titles light-stained. pn Mar 19 (349) £1,500

Woodward, John, 1665-1728

— The Natural History of the Earth.... L, 1726. 8vo, contemp calf; rubbed. Title waterstained. bba Sept 5 (124) £300 [Quaritch]

Woolf, Leonard, 1880-1969

— Stories of the East. Richmond: Hogarth Press, 1921. 8vo, orig wraps, unopened. Some browning at edges with a few small chips. sg June 11 (346) $120

Woolf, Virginia, 1882-1941

— Beau Brummell. NY, 1930. 1st Ed, one of 550. Folio, orig half cloth. CNY June 9 (202) $400

Anr copy. Orig half cloth; worn. O Mar 31 (200) $225

— The Common Reader. L: Hogarth Press, 1925. 1st Ed. Orig half cloth. bba Apr 30 (206) £90 [Blackwell]

— Flush: A Biography. Bost., 1933. 4to, ptd wraps. In: The Atlantic Monthly, July-Oct 1933 [Vol 152, Nos 1-4]. sg Dec 12 (429) $90

— Kew Gardens. Richmond: Hogarth Press, 1927. One of 500. Illus by Vanessa Bell. 4to, orig bds; spine lacking, bds creased & cracked, tape stains to rear joint. Tp foxed. Sgd by both Woolf & Bell. wa Dec 9 (234) $300

— Monday or Tuesday. L, 1921. 1st Ed. bba Dec 19 (234) £260

— Orlando. NY: Crosby Gaige, 1928. ("Orlando, a Biography.") 1st American Ed, One of 861. Unopened copy. CNY June 9 (200) $650; wa Dec 9 (235) $280

— A Room of One's Own. L & NY, 1929. 1st English Ed, One of 492. In d/j. pba July 9 (300) $120

— Street Haunting. San Francisco, 1930. one of 500. Orig half mor. Ck July 10 (451) £220

— To the Lighthouse. L: Hogarth Press, 1927. 1st Ed. In torn & slightly def d/j. S Feb 25 (440) £240 [Maggs]; sg Dec 12 (426) $175

— The Voyage Out. L, 1915. 1st Ed. bba Dec 19 (233) £85 [Mayou]

Anr copy. Calf gilt by Ramage. ALs (with initials) to Desmond MacCarthy inserted. S July 1 (1022) £350 [Shapero]

— The Waves. L, 1931. 1st Ed. In d/j. bba Apr 30 (207) £260 [Axe]

Anr copy. In d/j with a few small tears. bba May 28 (141) £90 [Robinson]

Anr copy. In d/j. sg Dec 12 (427) $850

Woolf, Virginia & Leonard

— Two Stories. Richmond, 1917. 1st Ed, one of 150. Orig wraps. Lacking blanks. S May 13 (681) £360 [Rota]

Woolman, John, 1720-72

See also: Franklin Printing, Benjamin

— A Journal of the Life and Travels of John Woolman.... L: Essex House Press, 1901. One of 250. 16mo, vellum. wd June 12 (446) $100

Woolnough, C. W.

— The Whole Art of Marbling as Applied to Paper Book-Edges. L, 1881. 8vo, orig cloth; loose in bdg. With 54 examples of marbled paper. sg May 21 (320) $1,300

Woolward, Florence H.

— The Genus Masdevallia. L, [1890]-96. 9 parts (all pbd). Folio, contemp calf; extremities rubbed. With double-page map & 87 hand-colored plates. Some spotting. Ck May 15 (60) £3,200

Anr copy. 9 parts (all pbd) in 1 vol. Folio, contemp half mor gilt; rebacked with orig backstrip laid down, inner joints cracked. Some foxing. CNY Jan 25 (97) $9,500

Wooster, David

— Alpine Plants. L, 1872. 1st Series only. 2 vols. 8vo, orig cloth; spine worn. With 54 plates. Spotted. DW Mar 4 (125) £120

Anr Ed. L, 1874. 8vo, orig cloth; spine def, edges rubbed. With 54 colored plates. pn Dec 12 (299) £75

2d Ed. 2 vols. 8vo, orig cloth; spines rubbed. With 108 colored plates. DW Nov 6 (201) £135

Wordsworth, Christopher, 1807-85

— Athens and Attica: Journal of a Residence.... L, 1836. 8vo, contemp calf gilt. With 3 litho plates, 2 folding maps & folding leaf of inscriptions. No half-title. S July 1 (732) £180 [Sossidis]

— Greece. L, 1859. 8vo, mor gilt extra. bba Sept 19 (158) £180 [Stamatoyannopoulos]

Anr Ed. L, 1868. 4to, contemp calf; rehinged with extremities rubbed. Some stains. bba July 23 (357) £110 [Frew Mackenzie]

Anr Ed. L, 1871. 8vo, calf gilt. LH Dec 11 (271) $80

Anr Ed. L, 1882. 8vo, orig cloth; spine rubbed. With engraved title, 5 maps & 15 plates. DW Jan 29 (62) £110

Anr copy. Orig cloth; spine frayed & rubbed. DW Mar 4 (50) £100

Wordsworth, William, 1770-1850

See also: Darwin's copy, Charles; Fore-Edge Paintings

— A Letter to a Friend of Robert Burns. L, 1816. 1st Ed. 8vo, disbound. Tp & last several leaves detached & chipped; tp lacking strip at gutter; browned; library stamp. bbc Sept 23 (492) $80

— Poems. L, 1807. 1st Ed. 2 vols. 12mo, mor gilt by Bedford. Minor foxing. Inscr. bba June 25 (194) £2,200 [Jarndyce]

Anr copy. Contemp calf; scuffed. With errata slip in Vol I & with sectional title B1 in Vol II. C Dec 16 (242) £1,600 [Ximenes]

Anr copy. Contemp calf. Some soiling, chiefly at margins; tp & prelims to Vol II browned. Milne copy. Ck June 12 (217) £550

Anr copy. Contemp half calf tooled with lyre motif; rubbed. With errata slip in Vol I. Ck July 10 (452) £750

Anr copy. Mor extra by S. David. S Dec 12 (42) £1,600 [Lewis]

Anr copy. Contemp calf; rebacked. Epstein copy. sg Apr 30 (516) $1,600

— Poetical Works. L, 1892-93. 7 vols. 8vo, mor extra. cb Jan 16 (178) $170

— The River Duddon, a Series of Sonnets.... L, 1820. 1st Ed. 8vo, orig bds; spine worn. Ck June 12 (218) £320

Wordsworth, William, 1770-1850 —& Coleridge, Samuel Taylor, 1772-1834

— Lyrical Ballads. L, 1798-1800. 1st Ed, 2d Issue of Vol I. 2 vols. 8vo, contemp calf; rebacked with mor, rubbed & worn. Milne copy. Ck June 12 (215) £900

2d Ed of Vol I, 1st Ed, 1st Issue of Vol II. L, 1800. 2 vols. 8vo, contemp calf; spine head of Vol I worn, rubbed, lacking rear free endpaper. A2 torn; some soiling. bba June 25 (193) £2,200 [Marlborough]

2d Ed of Vol I, 1st Ed of Vol II. 2 vols. 8vo, contemp calf; rebacked retaining orig spines, corners strengthened, worn. Milne copy. Ck June 12 (216) £1,500

Workman, William Hunter & Fanny Bullock

— The Call of the Snowy Hispar. NY, 1911. sg Jan 9 (294) $450

World...

— The World Displayed; or, a Curious Collection of Voyages and Travels... L, 1759-61. Intro by Samuel Johnson. Vols I-X. 18mo, contemp half calf; extremities rubbed, corners bumped. Some maps hand-colored in outline. Milne copy. Ck June 12 (220) £480

World's Fair—1939. See: New York (City)

Worlidge, John, fl.1669-98

— Systema Agriculturae, the Mystery of Husbandry Discovered. L, 1669. 1st Ed. Folio, contemp calf; rebacked & repaired. Engraved title from anr copy & restored; some browning; 3d part title with marginal tears. pn May 14 (26) £240 [Ventinor]

— Vinetum Britannicum: or a Treatise of Cider.... L, 1691. 3d Ed. 2 parts in 1 vol. 8vo, contemp calf; repaired. With 6 plates. Some browning. S May 14 (1006) £400 [Rainford]

Worlidge, Thomas
See also: Fore-Edge Paintings

— A Select Collection of Drawings from Curious Antique Gems.... L, 1768. 4to, modern cloth. Foxed. F Dec 18 (300) $180

Anr copy. Contemp mor gilt. With port & 180 (of 181) plates plus additional plate at end. Some soiling; library stamp on verso of tp & last plate. pn July 16 (125) £140 [Edwards]

Anr copy. Mor gilt; some wear, rear hinge splitting at top. With frontis & 182 plates. Some foxing, mostly to margins. sg Sept 6 (120) $550

Anr copy. Half lea; some wear along edges. Some foxing & browning. sg Feb 6 (101) $225

Anr copy. Vols II & III (of 3) 4to, contemp sheep; def. With 120 plates, some hand-colored. sg Feb 13 (190) $375

Wormald, francis —& Giles, Phyllis M.

— A Descriptive Catalogue of the Additional Illuminated Manuscripts in the Fitzwilliam Museum.... Cambr., 1982. 2 vols. 4to, cloth, in d/js. sg Oct 31 (266) $150

Worthington, Greville

— A Bibliography of the Waverley Novels. L, 1931. 1st Ed, one of 500. Orig half vellum; spine soiled. bbc Sept 23 (121) $50

Wotton, Sir Henry, 1568-1639

— The Elements of Architecture. L, 1624. 1st Ed. 4to, modern calf gilt. With B4 in cancelled state. Some soiling; dampstaining to inner corners of last 3 leaves; blank verso of last leaf soiled & with ink stain; lacking initial blank. STC 26011. pn June 11 (160) £420 [Clark]

Wraxall, Sir Nathaniel William

— A Short Review of the Political State of Great-Britain.... L, 1787. 6th Ed. 8vo, half calf. Half-title & verso of final blank dust-soiled. C June 25 (93) £180 [Quaritch/Hordern]

Wren, Christopher, 1675-1747

[-] Christopher Wren, 1632-1723. L, 1923. Folio, orig cloth; worn, inner joints broken. O Jan 14 (198) $60

— The Life and Works of Sir Christopher Wren. L: Essex House Press, 1903. One of 250. 4to, orig cloth; soiled. bba July 9 (259) £65 [Wand]

Wright, Andrew

— Court Hand Restored, or the Student's Assistant.... L, 1879. 9th Ed. 4to, modern cloth. With 23 plates. pba July 23 (228) $60

Wright, Edward

— Certain Errors in Navigation Detected and Corrected.... L, 1610. 3 parts in 1 vol. 4to, old vellum. Last 6 leaves gnawed & def at lower outer corners, affecting catchwords & a few other letters & numerals; tp worn & rubbed, with partial loss of fore-edge border. CNY Oct 8 (253) $4,800

Anr Ed. L, 1657. 3 parts in 1 vol. 4to, modern calf gilt. With engraved title, 4 inserted woodcut diagrams, 6 metal engravings (2 full page) & 2 folding maps. Some upper portions darkened throughout from old damp; some old stains at lower 7 inner portions at end; upper border of tp cropped; small hole catching 2 words on Pp2; 2 ink blots on world map which is also worn at center of 2 central folds. CNY Oct 8 (254) $16,000

Wright, Frank Lloyd, 1869-1959

— American System-Build Houses Designed by Frank Lloyd Wright. Milwaukee: The Richards Company, [c.1916]. A collection of 39 pieces of descriptive material for Wright's prefabricated housing project, including 14 illusts of building facades, 11 sheets of elevations & plans, 10 sheets of plans, additional plan & view & dealer agreement. Folio size, in orig envelope. LH May 17 (272) $1,100

— An Autobiography. L & NY, 1932. 1st Ed. 4to, orig cloth. Sgd. Epstein copy. sg Apr 30 (517) $1,300

— Buildings, Plans and designs. NY: Horizon Press, [1963]. Text by W. W. Peters. Folio, loose as issued in portfolio. With 100 plates & with text booklet laid in paper sleeve. sg Apr 2 (303) $1,200

Anr copy. With 100 plates. sg May 7 (215) $500

— Drawings for a Living Architecture. NY, 1959. 1st Ed. In d/j. cb Feb 12 (152) $700; sg Sept 6 (311) $600

— The Future of Architecture. NY, 1953. 4to, cloth, in d/j. sp Apr 16 (252) $60

— Genius and the Mobocracy. NY, [1949]. 1st Ed. 4to, orig cloth; soiled. K Sept 29 (31) $60

— The Japanese Print: An Interpretation. Chicago, 1912. One of 50. Orig bds; spine ends worn. sg Sept 6 (314) $1,700

Anr Ed. NY: Horizon Press, [1967]. Folio, cloth; smudged. bbc Sept 23 (1167) $85

Anr copy. Cloth; rear cover dampstained. sg Sept 6 (315) $70

— Modern Architecture. Princeton, 1931. sg apr 2 (304) $250

— The Natural House. NY: Horizon Press, 1954. In chipped d/j. bbc Sept 23 (168) $110

Anr copy. In def d/j. wa Sept 26 (678) $60

— On Architecture: Selected Writings 1894-1940. NY, 1941. In soiled & frayed d/j. wa Sept 26 (677) $160

Wright, George Newenham

— Belgium, The Rhine, Italy, Greece, and the Shores and Islands of the Mediterranean. L, [1851]. Orig cloth; back cover detached, spine split. bba Feb 27 (26) £280 [Menikov]

Anr copy. 2 vols. 4to, contemp calf; worn. With 2 frontises & 149 plates. Some plates at end foxed; dampstaining to earliest plates in Vol I. wa Apr 9 (281) $600

— China in a Series of Views. L, [1843]. 4 vols in 2. 4to, half mor; rubbed, lacking upper cover of 1 vol. With engraved titles & 124 plates. bba Mar 26 (321) £320 [Finney]

Anr copy. 4 vols in 2. Contemp mor; rubbed, extemities frayed. With extra title for each vol. DW Oct 2 (80) £360

Anr copy. 4 vols. 4to, contemp calf gilt; def. With 4 engraved titles & 124 plates. pn Sept 12 (346) £340 [Black]

Anr copy. 4 vols in 2. 4to, modern half syn. With 3 (of 4) engraved titles & 124 plates. A few plates with smaller margins. pn Mar 19 (411) £380 [Russell]

Anr copy. Contemp mor gilt; rubbed & stained. With 4 engraved titles & 124 plates. Some foxing. pn July 16 (213) £400

Anr copy. 4 parts in 1 vol. 4to, contemp half lea. Some foxing. Sold w.a.f. SI June 9 (21) LIt700,000

— The Chinese Empire Illustrated. L, [c.1860]. 2 vols. 4to, cotnemp half mor; worn & scuffed. With 4 engraved titles, 3 hand-colored folding maps & 159 plates. Some foxing; 1 text leaf missing portion of bottom & side margins; 1 plate with diagonal crease. bbc apr 27 (498) $500

Anr copy. Contemp half mor; rubbed. With 4 engraved titles, 3 hand-colored folding maps & 157 plates. S Nov 15 (1306) £440 [Ant. of Orient]

— France Illustrated. L, [1845-47]. 4 vols in 2. 4to, contemp calf gilt by J. Clarke; extremities rubbed. With engraved titles & 128 plates. Some spotting. Ck May 15 (176) £220

Anr copy. Half mor. With engraved titles & 127 plates. pnE Aug 12 (270) £240

— The Gallery of Engravings. L: Fisher, Son

& Co., [1844]. 2 vols. 4to, orig mor; worn, joints starting. With 40 plates. cb Sept 26 (211) $120

— Ireland Illustrated from Original Drawings.... L, 1831. 4to, half mor; rubbed. With engraved title & 40 sheets of views. bba Dec 19 (102) £140 [Scott]

— Lancashire its History, Legends and Manufactures. L, [1843]. 4 vols in 2. 4to, mor gilt; ends & corners worn, 1 joint starting. With 128 plates. Some browning & foxing. wa Sept 26 (564) $500

— The Shores and Islands of the Mediterranean. L, [1840]. 4to, modern cloth. With folding map & 63 plates. Some spotting. bba July 9 (46) £260 [Finbar McDonnell]

Anr copy. Contemp half mor gilt; hinges rubbed. With engraved title, folding map & 56 (of 63) plates. DW Oct 2 (79) £120

Wright, John, Horticulturist

— The Flower Growers' Guide. L: Virtue, [1891-94]. 3 vols. 4to, contemp half lea gilt; rubbed. With 46 color plates. Spotting, affecting a few plates. pn Dec 12 (300) £240

— The Fruit Growers' Guide. L: Virtue, [1891-94]. 3 vols in 6 orig divisions. 4to, orig cloth. b Mar 11 (244) £650

Anr copy. 3 vols. 4to, orig cloth; rubbed, extremities worn. With 3 pictorial titles & 43 plates, all colored. DW Apr 8 (185) £600

Anr copy. Orig cloth; spines worn, lower inner joints cracked. With 3 colored titles & 43 plates. Frontises spotted. L Nov 14 (235) £560

Anr copy. Contemp half lea; rubbed. With 3 colored titles & 43 colored plates. Some foxing. pn Dec 12 (301) £780 [Map House]

Anr copy. Divisions 1-4 & 6 only. Orig cloth; rubbed, lower covers of 2 vols dampstained at top. With 3 colored pictorial titles & 36 colored plates. pn Apr 23 (232) £550 [Talanti]

Wright, John, 1836-1919

— Early Bibles of America. NY, 1892. 8vo, cloth. cb Oct 17 (1014) $90

Anr Ed. L, 1893. One of 50 L.p. copies. cb Oct 17 (1015) $70

Wright, John Michael

— An Account of His Excellence Roger, Earl of Castlemaine's Embassy, from...James the IId.... L, 1688. Folio, contemp calf; rebacked. With port, frontis & 15 plates. Folding plate repaired & on new guards; some foxing & browning; blank verso of Q2 soiled. pn May 14 (27) £180 [Thorp]

Anr copy. Folding plate just shaved; some surface dirt. S June 25 (232) £600 [Quaritch]

Wright, Lewis

— The Illustrated Book of Poultry. L, 1880. 4to, contemp half calf; rubbed. With 50 colored plates. b Nov 18 (384) £550

Anr copy. Contemp half calf; backstrip def. With color frontis & 49 plates. Some marginal dampstains. Sold w.a.f. DW Nov 6 (202) £580

Anr Ed. L, [1886]. 4to, contemp half mor; worn, upper cover detached. With 50 colored plates. Some marginal tears & stains. bba Sept 5 (165) £550

Anr copy. With 48 (of 50) plates only. Lacking text; loose. Sold w.a.f. bba Apr 9 (204) £400 [Erlini]

Anr copy. Half mor; rubbed. With 50 colored plates. K Mar 22 (357) $1,200

Anr copy. Half mor; rubbed, spine def. With 50 chromolithos. K July 12 (425) $1,000

Anr copy. Modern half mor. With 49 (of 50) chromolithos. Some short tears; library stamps in blind in margins. S Nov 15 (853) £400 [Cherrington]

Anr copy. Orig cloth; chipped & worn. With 50 colored plates. S July 1 (930) £650 [Hagelstam]

Anr Ed. L, 1890. 4to, modern cloth. With color frontis & 49 plates. A few plates & text leaves misbound. bba Sept 5 (164) £500 [Burden]

Anr copy. Orig cloth; rubbed, hinges weak. bba May 14 (504) £550 [Nolan]

Anr copy. Half calf; worn & broken, spine lacking. With color frontis & 48 (of 49) plates. S Nov 15 (762) £450 [Kafka]

Anr Ed. L, [1910-11]. ("Wright's Book of Poultry.") Ed by Sidney H. Lewer. 4to, contemp half mor; rubbed. bba Nov 28 (143) £460 [Kafka]

Anr copy. Contemp half mor; worn, lower hinge broken, upper hinge repaired. With 30 colored plates. pn Apr 23 (233) £130

Wright, Lyle Henry, 1903-

— American Fiction, 1774-1850...1851-1875... 1876-1900. San Marino: Huntington Library, 1965-69. 3 vols. In d/js. sg May 21 (321) $70

Wright, Magnus & Wilhelm & Ferdinand von

— Svenska faglar efter naturen och pa sten ritade. Stockholm, [1917]-29. 3 vols. 4to, contemp half calf gilt. With 364 color plates. FD Dec 2 (277A) DM2,550

Anr copy. Text by Einar Lonnberg. Contemp half calf. With 364 colored lithos. Ck May 14 (62) £1,200

Anr copy. Contemp calf gilt. Ck May 15

(61) £1,200

Anr Ed. Stockholm, 1924-29. 3 vols. Oblong folio, contemp half calf; scuffed. With 162 (of 184) hand-colored plates. C Oct 30 (300) £1,300 [Rose]

Wright, Richard, 1908-60

— Native Son. NY & L, 1940. In d/j. sg Dec 12 (430) $250; sg June 11 (347) $150

Wright, Robert M.

— Dodge City. The Cowboy Capital.... [Wichita: Wichita Eagle Press, 1913]. 1st Ed. Cloth. wa Dec 9 (286) $210

Wright, Stephen —&
Jager, Otto

— Ethopia Illuminated Manuscripts. Bost.: New York Graphic Society, [1961]. Folio, cloth, in d/j. cb Jan 16 (49) $65

Wright, Thomas, 1810-77

— The History and Topography of the County of Essex. L, [1831]-36. 2 vols. 4to, later half calf; rubbed. With folding hand-colored map & 97 (of 98) plates. Folding map & 2 others torn. bba Apr 30 (7) £260 [Ash]

— Universal Pronouncing Dictionary and General Expositor of the English Language. L, [1852-56]. 5 vols. 8vo, half mor gilt; rubbed & scuffed. With 25 double-page maps, colored in outline. DW Mar 4 (52) £460

— The Works of James Gillray the Caricaturist. L, [1873]. 4to, contemp half mor; rebcked preserving section of orig spine. With port & 81 plates, 1 double-page. ALs from the publishers tipped in. pn Dec 12 (86) £80

Wright, Thomas, 1859-1936

— The Life of William Blake. Olney, 1929. 2 vols. 4to, cloth. bba Dec 19 (50) £140 [London Library]; sg Feb 6 (30) $130

Wright, William, of Nevada

— History of the Big Bonanza.... Hartford, 1877. 8vo, orig cloth; rubbed, inner hinges splitting. On front free endpaper is inquiry as to whether Mark Twain had "planned this book for the author before you knew he had written it?" with Twain's sgd answer "Yes, it is true." Manney copy. P Oct 11 (52) $3,000

2d Ptg. Orig cloth; spine ends frayed, hinges cracked. wa Apr 9 (60) $100

Wroth, Lawrence C.

See also: Grolier Club; Limited Editions Club

— The Colonial Printer. Portland, Me., 1938. One of 1,500. sg May 21 (322) $130

— The Early Cartography of the Pacific. [NY, 1944]. Some pencil marginalia. Papers of the Bibliographical Society of America, Vol. 38, No. 2. sg Oct 31 (81) $150

— A History of Printing in Colonial Maryland.... Balt., 1922. One of 500. O Sept 24 (274) $70

— Some Reflections on the Book Arts in Early Mexico. Cambr., 1945. One of 165. Folio, wraps. sg Oct 31 (333) $90

Wuerth, Louis A.

— Catalogue of the Lithographs of Joseph Pennell. Bost., 1931. One of 425. 4to, orig half calf. Met Apr 28 (94) $200

Wulff, Lee

— The Atlantic Salmon. NY, 1958. One of 200. 4to, half mor. Koopman copy. O Oct 29 (331) $300

— Leaping Silver: Words and Pictures on the Atlantic Salmon. NY, [1940]. sg May 21 (121) $110

Wyatt, Claude Wilmott. See: Sharpe & Wyatt

Wyatt, Sir Matthew Digby, 1820-77

See also: Tymms & Wyatt

— The Industrial Arts of the Nineteenth Century. L, 1851-53. 2 vols. Folio, contemp half mor gilt; shelfmark to spine, rubbed. Wit colored litho title & 78 plates. Stamp to margin of each plate. DW May 13 (43) £125

Anr copy. Orig mor gilt; rubbed, hinges weak. With 2 additional titles & 158 color plates.. Schlosser copy. P June 18 (601) $2,750

Wyatt, Thomas

— A Manual of Conchology, according to the System laid down by lamarck. NY, 1838. 8vo, new cloth. With 35 (of 36) plates. Title stamped. sg Nov 14 (207) $300

Wyatville, Jeffry

— Illustrations of Windsor Castle. L, 1841. 2 vols. 4to, modern half mor. With 39 plates. Some spotting, 8 plates with repairs to margins or plate-marks. C May 20 (314) £700 [Thornhill]

Wycherley, William, 1640?-1716. See: Nonesuch Press

Wyeth, Andrew

— The Four Seasons. NY: Art in America, [1963]. Folio, loose as issued in cloth portfolio, in box. sp Feb 6 (218) $65

Wyld, James, 1812-87

— A General Atlas. Edin., 1819. Folio, contemp half calf; spine repaired, corners worn. With engraved title, 2 charts & 41 colored maps. b Nov 18 (237) £320

Wyman, Charles William Henry. See: Bigmore & Wyman

Wynne, Ellis. See: Gregynog Press

Wynne, James, 1814-71

— Private Libraries of New York. NY, 1860. One of 100. 8vo, 19th-cent mor gilt. sg Oct 31 (334) $120

Wynne, John Huddlestone

— Choice Emblems.... L, 1772. 1st Ed. 12mo, contemp calf; joints weakened, corners rubbed. bba July 23 (154) £50 [James]

Anr Ed. L, 1784. 12mo, contemp sheep; rebacked. With frontis & 64 emblems. Some soiling; outer margins creased; owner's stamp on half-title. Ck Oct 31 (85) £160

Wyse, Sir Thomas

— An Excursion in the Peloponnesus.... L, 1865. 2 vols. 8vo, contemp cloth. With 1 folding map, frontises & 22 plates. HH May 12 (711) DM1,000

Wyss, Johann David, 1743-1818

— Le Robinson Suisse.... Paris, 1845. 8vo, orig cloth. bba July 23 (146) £55 [Travers]

— Swiss Family Robinson L, 1814. ("The Family Robinson Crusoe....") 1st Ed in English. 12mo, orig bds; spines cracked, chipped, rubbed. With frontises & 2 text plates. Manney copy. P Oct 11 (321) $5,500

2d Ed in English of Vol I; 1st Ed in English of Vol II. L, 1814-16. 2 vols. 8vo, contemp calf. One leaf in Vol II chipped with loss. CNY Oct 8 (255) $1,000

Wytfliet, Cornelius —& Magini, Giovanni Antonio

— Histoire universelle des indes occidentales et orientales. Douai: Francois Fabri, 1607. 3 parts in 1 vol. Folio, 19th-cent half calf; worn. B Nov 1 (287) HF700

Wytsman, Philogene Auguste Galilee

— Genera avium. Brussels, 1905-14. 26 parts (all pbd). 4to, orig wraps. bba Sept 5 (166) £240 [Shapaero]

X

Xavier, Hieronymus

— Historia Christa Persice conscripta.... Leiden: Elzevir, 1639. 3 parts in 1 vol. 4to, 19th-cent calf; rebacked. S May 28 (96) £600 [Marlborough]

Xenophon, c.430-c.355 B.C.

— Opera. Florence: P. Giunta, June 1516. Folio, 18th-cent English mor gilt; corners rubbed. Stamp & ownership inscr (erased) on tp. In Greek. Chatsworth copy. C Nov 27 (27) £800 [O'Keefe]

XXe Siecle. See: Vingtieme Siecle

Y

Yarrell, William, 1784-1856

— Fishes. L, 1841. ("A History of British Fishes.") 2d Ed. 2 vols. 8vo, contemp half calf; rubbed. bba Sept 5 (125) £65 [Freddie]

— A History of British Birds. L, 1843. 3 vols. 8vo, mor, armorial bdg; rubbed. O Dec 17 (200) $120

— On the Growth of the Salmon in Fresh Water. L, 1839. Oblong folio, orig cloth; bdg detached. With 3 hand-colored plates. Tp browned; some soiling; stamps on pastedowns, verso of tp & head of 1st page. pn Mar 19 (350) £380

Yates, William Holt

— The Modern History and Condition of Egypt. L, 1843. 2 vols. 8vo, orig cloth. With port & 12 plates. bba Dec 19 (406) £320 [Ulysses]

Yeats, William Butler, 1865-1939
See also: Cuala Press

— Later Poems. L, 1922. 1st Ed. sg Dec 12 (431) $70

— Plays and Controversies. NY, 1924. One of 250. Half cloth. sg June 11 (348) $425

— Poems. L & Bost., 1895. 8vo, cloth; rubbed & soiled. DW Oct 2 (406) £80

— Responsibilities and Other Poems. L, 1916. 1st Ed. Unopened. sg Dec 12 (432) $60

— Three Things. L, 1929. 1st Ed, one of 500 L.p. copies. sg Dec 12 (433) $300

— The Tower. L, 1928. 1st Ed. In d/j. sg Dec 12 (434) $375

— The Trembling of the Veil. L, 1922. 1st Ed, one of 1,000, sgd. pnE Aug 12 (41) £175

One of 1,000. Orig half vellum, in d/j. S Nov 14 (677) £170 [Louise Ross]; sg Dec 12 (435) $350

— A Vision. L, 1925. 1st Ed, One of 600, sgd. Orig bds, in d/j. S Nov 14 (675) £240 [Libris Antikuariat]

Anr copy. Half vellum, in torn d/j. sg Dec 12 (436) $300

Anr copy. Orig bds, in worn & stained d/j. wa June 25 (88) $200

— The Winding Stair and Other Poems. NY: Fountain Press, 1929. ("The Winding Stair.") One of 642, sgd. Epstein copy. sg Apr 30 (518) $375

— Works. Stratford-on-Avon: Shakespeare Head Press, 1908. 8 vols. Orig half vellum; front hinge of Vol I cracked. Library markings. bba Mar 26 (191) £200 [Nolan]

Yellow...

— The Yellow Book: an Illustrated Quarterly. L, 1894-97. Vols 1-13 (all pbd). 8vo, orig cloth; rubbed. bba Dec 19 (242) £180 [Ginnan]

Anr copy. Orig cloth; soiled. bba Mar 26 (152) £140 [Cox]; Ck Sept 6 (156) £480

Anr copy. Orig cloth; soiled & worn. Some spines darkened. O Jan 14 (199) $180

Anr copy. Orig cloth; minor wear. Manney set. P Oct 11 (322) $1,800

Anr copy. Orig cloth; soiled, spines frayed. pn May 14 (124) £300 [Bifolco]; pnE Oct 1 (205) £260

Yemeniz, Nicolas

— Catalogue de mes livres. Lyons: Louis Perrin, 1865-66. One of 100. 4to, orig wraps, frayed, broken. Inscr to Paul Lacroix. sg Oct 31 (335) $375

Yerushalmi, Yosef Hayim

— Haggadah and History. Phila., 1975. 4to, cloth, in d/j. sg Dec 19 (100) $60

Yonge, Charlotte Mary, 1823-1901

— The Instructive Picture Book.... Edin., 1867. Folio, half lea; lower cover detached, rubbed. With 29 (of 31) double-page hand-colored plates. Some spotting & soiling. pn Sept 12 (308) £190 [Sotheran]

Yorke, James, fl.1640

— The Union of Honour. L, 1640. 1st Ed. 3 parts in 1 vol. Folio, later calf; worn, Ms notes on free endpaper. STC 26103. W July 8 (94) £140

Yosemite...

— Yosemite Illustrated in Color. San Francisco: Crocker, 1890. Folio, cloth; rubbed, bottom edge of back cover soiled. With 13 colored plates. Some marginal soiling & some foxing on the ptd tissues. K July 12 (538) $250

Anr copy. Soiling to 1 plate. sp June 18 (10) $250

Young...

— Young Albert, the Roscius. L, 1811. 1st Ed. 12mo, orig wraps. With 7 cut-out aquatint figure & 1 (of 3) heads, colored by hand. Lacking 2 hats. S Nov 14 (219) £220 [Anstee]

— Young Child's ABC, or First Book. NY: Samuel Wood & Sons, [c.1820]. 12mo, orig wraps. wd June 12 (447) $100

Young, Arthur, 1741-1820

— A Six Weeks Tour through the Southern Counties of England and Wales. L, 1772. 3d Ed. 8vo, contemp calf; rubbed, upper joint split. bba Sept 5 (126) £80 [Town]

— Travels during the Years 1787, 1788, and 1789 in the Kingdom of France. Bury St. Edmunds, 1792-94. 1st Ed on Vol I; 2d Ed of Vol II. 4to, later half mor. With 3 folding maps. 1 map torn. sg Jan 9 (201) $90

2d Ed. Bury St. Edmunds, 1794. 2 vols. 4to, orig bds; soiled & rubbed. With 4 folding maps, 1 hand-colored. Gathering I2 & I3 loose; some spotting & browning; marginal soiling. Ck May 15 (177) £140

Young, Edward, 1683-1765

— The Complaint, and the Consolation; or Night Thoughts. L, 1797. Bound with: Blake, William. The Grave. L, 1808. 2d Ed. Text by Robert Blair Illus by William Blake. Folio, early 19th-cent half mor gilt; spine & corners worn. With 43 plates. Some offsetting & staining. George Milne copy. CNY Dec 5 (167) $4,500

Young, G. O.

— Alaskan Yukon Trophies Won and Lost. Huntington WV: Standard, 1947. 4to, cloth, in worn d/j. Koopman copy. O Oct 29 (332) $110; O Oct 29 (333) $120; O Oct 29 (334) $155

Young, Sir George

— Facsimile of a Proposal for a Settlement on the Coast of New South Wales. Sydney, 1888. 4to, modern half calf, orig wraps bound in. S June 25 (90) £100 [Quaritch/ Hordern]

Young, Jess

— Recent Journey of Exploration across the Continent of Australia.... NY, 1878. 8vo, orig wraps. In: Bulletin of the American Geographical Society, 1878, Vol 10, No 2, pp.116-41. C June 25 (264) £250 [Arnold]

Young, John, 1755-1825

— A Catalogue of the Collection of Pictures of the Marquess of Stafford at Cleveland House.... L, 1825. 2 vols. Folio, contemp half mor; rubbed. With frontis port & 102 plates. Some waterstaining; spotted. bba June 11 (310) £80 [Hildebrandt]

— A Catalogue of the Collection of Pictures...at Cleveland House. L, 1825. 2 vols. 4to, contemp mor gilt; rubbed. With port & 282 subjects on 103 plates. Some spotting. S Feb 11 (247) £200 [Artemide]

— A Series of Portraits of the Emperors of Turkey from the Foundation of the Monarchy to the Year 1815. L, [1815]. 1st Ed. Folio, 19th-cent mor gilt; joints repaired.

With mezzotint title & 30 hand-finished color plates. Lacking the leaf of letterpress for Mahmud II; some spotting. S July 1 (734) £29,000 [Kutluoglu]

Issue with title as above. Contemp mor gilt. With mezzotint title & 28 hand-finished color plates. Some spotting, mainly to plate margins. Finely colored copy. S Nov 21 (62) £23,000 [Sims Reed]

Young, John Russell

— Around the World with General Grant. NY, [1879]. 2 vols. 4to, orig mor gilt. Library markings. bbc Apr 27 (85) $80

Young, Thomas, 1773-1829

— A Course of Lectures on Natural Philosophy and the Mechanical Arts. L, 1845. 2 vols. later calf gilt. DW Nov 6 (426) £210

Anr copy. 8vo, contemp half calf. With 41 double-page plates (2 colored), 2 double-page maps & 2 folding tables. sg May 14 (318) $225

Younghusband, Sir Francis Edward

— The Heart of a Continent: A Narrative of travels in Manchuria.... L, 1896. 8vo, cloth. sg Jan 9 (203) $175

Z

Zaehnsdorf, Joseph, 1816-86

— The Art of Bookbinding. L, 1880. 8vo, half mor; rubbed. O Jan 14 (200) $130

Anr Ed. L, 1890. 8vo, contemp mor gilt by Zaehnsdorf; rebacked preserving orig spine. Inscr. bba May 28 (499) £240 [Mandl]

8th Ed. L, 1914. 8vo, half calf by Zaehnsdorf. cb Oct 17 (1023) $75

Zaglada...

— Zaglada Zydostwa Polskiego: Album Zdjec. [Lodz, 1945]. Oblong 4to, wraps; worn. sg Dec 19 (111) $425

Zallonis, Markos Philippos

— Traite sur les princes de la Valachie et de la Moldavie.... Paris, 1830. 8vo, half mor. S June 30 (220) £700 [Dallegio]

Zamorano...

— The Zamorano 80: a Selection of Distinguished California Books... Los Angeles: Zamorano Club, 1945. One of 500. sg June 18 (155) $110

Anr Ed. NY: Kraus, 1969. Reprint of 1945 Ed. cb Dec 19 (189) $85

Zampetti, Pietro

— A Dictionary of Venetian Painters.... Leigh-on-Sea, 1969-79. 5 vols. 4to, cloth, in d/js. CG Oct 7 (447) £100

Zanetti, Antonio Maria, the Elder & the Younger

— Delle antiche statue greche e romane che nell'antisala della libreria di San Marco.... Venice, 1740-43. 2 parts in 1 vol. Folio, contemp calf; rubbed. SI June 10 (1106) LIt1,600,000

Anr copy. Part 1 only. Folio, contemp calf, armorial bdg. With 50 plates. SI June 10 (1107) LIt800,000

— Varie pitture a fresco de' principali maestri Veneziani. Venice, 1760. Folio, modern half vellum. With engraved title, port & 24 plates. SI June 10 (1108) LIt1,500,000

Zanotto, Francesco

— Storia Veneta. Venice: Giuseppe Grimaldo, 1863. 2 vols. Oblong folio, orig bds; spines worn. With frontis & 150 plates. S June 30 (82) £720 [Christodoulou]

— Venezia prospettica, monumentale, sotrica, et artistica.... Venice: Giovanni Brizeghel, [c.1860]. Oblong folio, orig half lea; rubbed. With 60 (of 61) hand-colored plates. Some foxing. sg Nov 7 (250) $3,600

Zapata y Sandoval, Juan

— De justitia distributiva. Valladolid, 1609. 8vo, old vellum. Tp & A4 with marginal repairs; minor marginal dampstaining. sg June 18 (592) $850

Zapf, Hermann

— Manuale Typographicum. Frankfurt, 1954. One of 1,000. In d/j. cb Jan 16 (179) $300

Zarate, Augustin de, b.1514

— Historia del descubrimiento y conquista del Peru. Antwerp: Martin Nucio, 1555. 1st Ed. 8vo, mor gilt by Riviere; rubbed. O Nov 26 (198) $3,500

— Le Historie del Sig. Agostino di Zarate contatore et consigliero dell' Imperatore Carlo V. Venice: Giolito, 1563. 8vo, 18th-cent vellum. Some browning. SI Dec 5 (1055) LIt1,700,000

Zatta, Antonio

— Atlante novissimo [Atlas novissimo]. Venice, 1779-85. 4 vols in 1. Folio, contemp half vellum; rubbed. With 4 engraved titles & 218 double-page maps, all colored in outline. Lacking 1 map of Venice. SI June 10 (1113) LIt19,500,000

Zaunmueller, Wolfram

— Bibliographisches Handbuch der Sprachwoerter-buecher. NY etc., 1958. 4to, cloth, in d/j. sg Oct 31 (337) $120

Zavattini, Cesare

— Un Paese. [Turin, 1955]. Illus by Paul Strand. 4to, cloth, in d/j. sg Oct 8 (70) $375

Zbinevich, Y. O. —& Grishanin, V. C.

— Ot 16 k 17. C'ezdy VKP(b). Moscow, 1934. 4to, unbound as issued in orig cloth folder. S Dec 5 (327) £800 [Foto Folio]

Zeeusche Nachtegael...

— Zeeusche Nachtegael ende des selfs dryderley gesang.... Middelburgh: Jan Peterss vande Venne, 1623. 4 parts in 1 vol. 4to, recent half vellum. With allegorical plate & 15 half-page engravings. Margins of 22 leaves repaired; some defs. B Nov 1 (324) HF2,000

Zeiler, Martin, 1589-1661. See: Merian, Matthaeus

Zeisberger, Daniel

— Grammar of the Language of the Lenni Lenape or Delaware Indians. Phila., 1827. 4to, later half mor; worn. sg June 18 (593) $200

Zeisberger, David, 1721-1808

— Zeisberger's Indian Dictionary.... Cambr. MA, 1887. 4to, orig cloth; worn. O Nov 226 (199) $100

Zeitlin, Jake. See: Grabhorn Printing

Ziegler, Jacobus

— Quae intus continentur. Syria, Palestina, Arabia.... Strassburg: P. Opilio, 1532. Bound with: Vadianus, Joachim. Epitome trium terrae partium.... Zurich: Christoph Froschauer, 1534. Folio, 19th-cent calf gilt; spine repaired. With 8 maps in 1st work 2d work lacking world map; library stamp. S July 1 (870) £3,200 [Franks]

Zimmer, Heinrich Robert, 1890-1943

— The Art of Indian Asia. NY, [1955]. Ed by Joseph Campbell. 2 vols. Folio, orig cloth. F June 25 (263) $60

Zinner, Ernst

— Deutsche und Niederlaendische Astronomische Instrumente des 11-18 Jahrhunderts. Munich, 1956. Cloth; worn. O Sept 24 (275) $100

Zinzendorff, Nikolaus Ludwig, Graf von, 1700-60. See: Franklin Printing, Benjamin

Zocchi, Giuseppe

— Scelta di XXIV vedute delle principali contrade, piazze, chiese, e palazzi della citta di Firenze. Florence, 1754 [plan dated 1755]. Folio, 19th-cent half lea; worn. With double-page engraved title, plan of Florence & 24 double-page views after Zocchi. Faint stains touching title & plates XXIII-XXIV. S Nov 21 (107) £12,000 [Gorini]

Zola, Emile, 1840-1902

— L'Argent. Paris, 1891. One of 250 on hollande. 12mo, half mor gilt by Durvand-Thivet, orig wraps bound in. S May 28 (462) £700 [Holinger]

— Nana. Paris: Charpentier, 1880. 1st Ed. 12mo, later half mor. Bds, orig wraps bound in. Epstein copy. sg Apr 30 (519) $425

One of 325. Half mor by Aussour, orig wraps bound in. S May 13 (872) £220 [Grigorlopohlas]

Zorgdrager, Cornelius Gijsbertsz

— Bloeijende opkomst der aloude en hedendaagische Groenlandsche Visschery.... Amst., 1720. 4to, contemp half lea; rubbed. With engraved title, 7 plates & 6 folding maps. B Nov 1 (552) HF3,200

Zorn, Johannes

— Icones plantarum medicinalium; Abbildungen von Arzneygewaechsen. Nuremberg, 1779-90. 6 vols of plates. 8vo, contemp half calf. With port & 600 plates. HH May 12 (542) DM2,200

Zorzi, Giangiorgio

— Le Opere Pubbliche e i Palazzi Privati di Andrea Palladio. Venice, 1965. Folio, cloth. sg Feb 6 (211) $225

Zrecin, J.

— Beschreibung der Kaiserstadt Constantinopel. Darmstadt, 1828. 8vo, contemp wraps. With 2 litho folding maps, port & facsimile. S June 30 (447) pS200 [Atabey]

Zuallardo, Giovanni. See: Zuallart, Jean

Zuallart, Jean

— Il Devotissimo viaggio di Gerusalemme. Rome, 1595. 4to, contemp vellum; spine soiled & torn. Some worming at inner corner of pp.243-66; some stains; C8 torn with significant loss. S June 30 (448) £700 [Bank of Cyprus]

Zuccaro, Taddeo, Federico & Ottaviano
— Illustri Fatti Farnesiani coloriti nel Real Palazzo di Caprarola. Rome, 1748. Illus by Georg Casper von Prenner. Folio, contemp calf with arms of Charles Stanhope, 3d Earl of Harrington. With port & 24 (of 36) plates. Lacking tp. sg Sept 19 (225) $300

Zurbriggen, Mattias
— From the Alps to the Andes.... L, 1899. 8vo, cloth; soiled. Some marginal foxing. cb Jan 30 (140) $425

Zuzarte Cortesao, Armando
— The Nautical Chart of 1424 and the Early Discovery and Cartographical Representation of America. Coimbra: University Press, 1954. Folio, orig wraps. DW Oct 2 (25) £85
One of an unspecified number, sgd. Cloth. bbc Dec 9 (312) $70

Zweig, Stefan. See: Caxton Club

Zwinner, Electus
— Blumen-Buch dess heiligen Lands Palestinae. Munich, 1661. 4to, contemp calf; worn, later endpapers. With engraved title, double-page map & 17 plates & plans. Some cropping & staining; a few wormholes affecting letters. S Nov 21 (312) £500 [Lazard]

A book auction at Sotheby's, circa 180